1972 census OF Transportation

VOLUME III

Commodity Transportation Survey

Part 1.

Commodity and Special Statistics

Issued June 1976

U.S. DEPARTMENT OF COMMERCE
Elliot L. Richardson, Secretary

BUREAU OF THE CENSUS
Vincent P. Barabba, Director
Robert L. Hagan, Deputy Director
Shirley Kallek, Associate Director for Economic Fields
Melvin A. Hendry, Assistant Director for Economic and
Agriculture Censuses

TRANSPORTATION DIVISION
Dayton P. Jorgenson, Chief

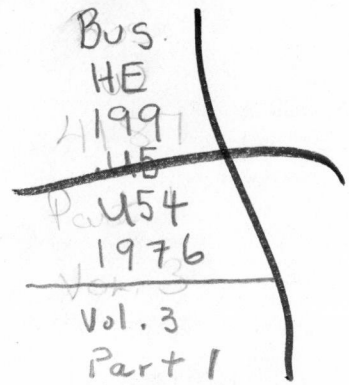

ACKNOWLEDGMENTS—Many persons participated in the various activities of the 1972 Census of Transportation. Primary direction of the program was performed by **Shirley Kallek,** Associate Director for Economic Fields, and **Melvin A. Hendry,** Assistant Director for Economic Censuses.

This report was prepared in the Transportation Division under the general direction of **Dayton P. Jorgenson,** Chief, and **Walter F. Buhl,** Assistant Chief. Within this division responsibility was shared by the following individuals who contributed significantly to the entire program: **Jerome Litzky,** Chief, Survey Programs Branch; **Donald G. Wright,** Chief, Research Programs Branch; **Evelyn S. Davis,** publications specialist; and **Helen L. Buckley,** clerical supervisor. **Sylvia Leaver,** Data User Services Division, was responsible for the computer planning and programing. **Dorcus Dupree** coordinated the activities among Transportation Division, Data Preparation Division, and Computer Services Division.

Responsibility for data collection was in the Field Division under the direction of **Richard C. Burt,** Chief; **George T. Reiner,** Chief, Economic Coordination Branch; and **Dwight P. Dean** and **Thomas J. Manning,** Survey Statisticians.

The mailing, collecting of data, and processing of administrative record information were conducted by the Economic Surveys Division under the direction of **Roger Bugenhagen,** Chief. Assistance was provided by **Samuel Schweid, Andrew Grieco, Charles Venters, Shirley Roberts, Robert Viehman, Jerry McDonald, Joel Richardson,** and **Sandra Katis.**

Forms design was performed in the Administrative Services Division, **Henry J. Husmann,** Chief. **Gladys Potts, Joyce Teague, Helen Hindt,** and **Margaret Swinton** made significant contributions.

Within the Publications Services Division, many individuals made significant contributions in the areas of publication planning and design, editorial review, composition, and printing procurement.

Clerical and data keying operations were performed in the Data Preparation Division at Jeffersonville, Indiana, under the direction of **O. Bryant Benton,** Chief, who was assisted by **Don L. Adams** and **Robert L. Allen.**

The geographic coding procedures were developed in the Geography Division under the direction of **Jacob Silver,** Chief, assisted by **Zigmund Decker, Terence McDowell, Silla Tomasi, Robert Hamill, David Christy, Kurt LeGait,** and **John Hawkins.** Computer processing was directed by **James R. Pepal,** Chief, Computer Services Division. **C. Thomas DiNenna, Jesse Verdeja,** and **Willie E. Clark** provided staff assistance.

Donald Young of the Economic Census Staff participated in the overall planning and review of the census operations.

Special acknowledgment is also due the many businesses whose cooperation has contributed to the publication of these data.

The statistics presented in this volume incorporate the commodity, special, and area report series TC72C1, TC72C3, and TC72C2.

Library of Congress Card No. 73-600337

SUGGESTED CITATION

U.S. Bureau of the Census, Census of Transportation, 1972

VOLUME III. COMMODITY TRANSPORTATION SURVEY
PART 1. COMMODITY AND SPECIAL STATISTICS

U.S. Government Printing Office, Washington, D.C., 1976

Commodity Transportation Survey

CONTENTS

Part 1 Commodity and Special Statistics

CONTENTS—Continued

COMMODITY STATISTICS—Continued

CONTENTS—Continued

COMMODITY STATISTICS—Continued

Regions and Geographic Divisions of the United States

NORTHEAST

New England

MAINE

VT. N.H.

MASS.

CONN. R.I.

N.Y.

Middle Atlantic

N.J.

PA.

DEL.

D.C.

MD.

NORTH CENTRAL

East North Central

OHIO

MICH.

IND.

ILL.

WIS.

West North Central

MINN.

IOWA

MO.

N. DAK.

S. DAK.

NEBR.

KANS.

SOUTH

South Atlantic

W. VA.

VA.

N.C.

S.C.

GA.

FLA.

East South Central

TENN.

KY.

ALA.

MISS.

West South Central

ARK.

LA.

OKLA.

TEXAS

WEST

Mountain

MONT.

WYO.

COLO.

N. MEX.

IDAHO

UTAH

NEV.

ARIZ.

WASH.

OREG.

CALIF.

Pacific

HAWAII

ALASKA

MILES
0 200 400

MILES
0 100 200

MILES
0 200 400

BUREAU OF THE CENSUS

U.S. DEPARTMENT OF COMMERCE

Commodity Statistics

INTRODUCTION

DESCRIPTION OF THE COMMODITY TRANSPORTATION SURVEY

General

The Commodity Transportation Survey is one of the three components of the Census of Transportation, one of the Economic Censuses conducted every 5 years ending in "2" and "7". Two previous Commodity Transportation Surveys have been conducted—the first in 1963 and the second in 1967. The prime objective of this survey is to measure the transportation and geographic distribution of commodities[1] shipped by manufacturing establishments in the United States beyond the local area. The Commodity Transportation Survey, as it now exists, consists of two independent surveys: A mail summary-data survey and a main shipper survey.

Mail Survey

The first and smaller component of the survey consists of data collection by mail on a simplified 1-page summary questionnaire. About 2,000 plants are sampled which have 10 to 19 employees, and about 1,000 plants are sampled in the Printing and Publishing Industry. In this mail survey, information relating to individual shipments is not collected. The respondent replies only to questions in terms of annual-percent-of-total-value shipped. Value is used as a unit of measure rather than tons since it was felt that the small manufacturers would not have summary data available on tons shipped. Data collected for the census year as a whole include value of product and services, major product shipped, distance shipped (six categories), type of transport used (six modes), and the geographic divisions of destination. Also included is the percent shipped for export to foreign countries. The sample designs used for this survey are simple one-stage systematic random samples of plants from the respective universes. These designs are described in published reports relating to these surveys and are not discussed further in this report.

Shipper Survey

The major part of the Commodity Transportation Survey is commonly referred to as the Shipper Survey. Traffic flow data is gathered, processed, and disseminated relating to the volume of commodities shipped by means of transport, length of haul, size of shipment, and areas of origin and destination in tons and ton-miles. The data sources are bills of lading or other shipping documents pertaining to individual shipments from a sample of about 13,000 plants selected from the census of manufactures universe of manufacturing establishments with 20 employees or more. The sample design is multistaged, utilizing a stratified probability sampling to obtain approximately 13,000 plants at the first stage and a systematic random sample of 1.6 million shipping documents (100 to 200 from each sampled plant) at the second stage. Although the source of the shipping information pertaining to each individual shipment is the shipping document, the primary sampling unit (PSU) may be either a plant or the shipping document itself. The primary sampling unit is the plant for all but the "certainty plants," those with a probability of "1" or greater at the first stage. For certainty plants, the PSU is usually the shipping document (bill of lading) drawn systematically from a random start.

SCOPE OF THE SHIPPER SURVEY

Sample of Plants

The source list.—The universe of manufacturing plants used as the first-stage sampling frame for the Commodity Transportation Survey is the mail file of the census of manufactures as of January 1, 1972. This file consists of all manufacturing plants in the Standard Industrial Classification 20 through 39 (except as noted below) with 20 employees or more. Plants with 10 to 19 employees are surveyed independently as described above. (See Mail Survey.)

Industry universe.—The sampling frame for the Shipper Survey includes the entire industrial universe of manufacturing establishments with 20 employees or more except the following exclusions for the reasons indicated.[2]

SIC 19, Ordnance and
accessories . . . . Excluded for security reasons

---

[1] See appendix B for a description of changes between the 1967 and 1972 versions of the Transportation Commodity Code (TCC) used for shipment commodity classifications.

[2] The CTS sample was drawn from the 1972 Census of Manufactures based upon the 1967 Standard Industrial Classification (SIC) code. The 1967 code classification was the most recent available at the time of sampling. Some realinements have been effected to the SIC as defined by the Office of Management and Budget in the Standard Industrial Classification Manual: 1972.

SIC 2026, Fluid milk . . .
SIC 2051, Bread and
other bakery products,
except cookies
and crackers . . . .
SIC 2097, Manufactured
ice . . . .
SIC 241, Primary forest
products . . . .

} Excluded because they serve local markets and the survey is intended to measure nonlocal commodity flows.

SIC 27, Printing,
publishing, and allied
industries .

Excluded because they are covered by the Mail Summary-Data Survey with the 10-to-19-employees size establishments.

Plant size.—The 1963 Commodity Transportation Survey found that the primary distributions of products by plants with less than 20 employees tended to be local and that this segment of the industry generated only about 4 percent of the total nonlocal tons shipped by all manufacturing plants. However, these small plants constitute about two-thirds of the total number of establishments in the industrial universe. These findings led to the conclusion that the survey costs and reporting effort could be significantly reduced by independently sampling and surveying the 10-to-19-employees size class plants by mail on the general characteristics of their shipping patterns. Data for plants with less than 10 employees are obtained from administrative records and therefore are not included in the census of manufactures universe mail file. Consequently, they are not included in any phase of the Commodity Transportation Survey. It is also felt that the omission of plants with fewer than 10 employees allows increased emphasis on quality of data compiled from larger establishments.

Geographic scope.—Plants located in the 48 contiguous States are eligible for inclusion in the Shipper Survey. Shipments *to* Alaska and Hawaii from these 48 origin States are also identified as are the domestic movement of exports. (See "Shipments for export," below.)

Sample of Shipments

Local shipments.—Generally, the survey is designed to exclude "local shipments." Plants shipping 90 percent or more of their volume less than 25 miles are excluded from the survey. However, if shipments from the plant are to a "local" warehouse or other temporary storage or consolidation facility, the subsequent shipments from this facility are in scope to the survey if 10 percent or more of these shipments move over 25 miles.

Local shipments from plants that are in scope to the survey are excluded in the sampling process at the plant or subsequently by computer edit.

Method of transport.—The following modes of transport are in scope to the survey:

Rail, including combinations such as piggyback in which the major distance was by rail (railway express is included under other);

Motor carrier, including combinations in which the major distance was by motor carrier (This includes all highway transport, except by private truck.);

Private truck, trucks operated by the shipper or the customer;

Air, including air freight and air express and combinations in which the major distance was by air;

Water, including combinations in which the major distance was by water;

Other, including railway express, united parcel service, bus, freight forwarder when major means of transport (such as rail and air) is not known, messenger service etc.; and

Unknown, used when the principle type of transport is not shown on shipping documents and cannot be readily determined by the respondent.

Excluded from the survey are the following:

Own power or towed "shipments", including motorized vehicles, aircraft, or vessels which are sometimes moved from the manufacturer under their own power, and other commodities (such as prefabricated buildings) which are towed away;

Pipeline, primarily affecting shipments of petroleum products from refineries; and

Parcel post, shipments through the U.S. postal service.

Shipments for export.—Shipments for export are included in the survey with destination of the U.S. port of export. Distances and other characteristics of these shipments relate only to the domestic movement from the shipping plant to the U.S. port of export.

Classified shipments.—Shipments of manufactured commodities from an in-scope plant which would otherwise have been

included in the survey are excluded if they are classified or relate to the movement of classified materials.

Mixed shipments.—When a bill of lading or other shipping document that contains more than one commodity line is selected, the total weight is taken and ascribed to the commodity that contributed the greatest proportion to the total weight.

SAMPLE DESIGN

As mentioned earlier (see Shipper Survey), a two-stage probability sample design was used. The first stage involved the drawing of a probability sample of about 13,000 plants from the universe. The second involved the selection of a probability sample of about 100 to 200 bills of lading or other shipping documents on file at each of the sampled plants.

The term "probability sample," as used here, means that the chance for selecting each document from the millions of such documents in the universe is known and is not equal to zero. The information from a probability sample can be expanded to approximate the total that would have been obtained by a complete count, and the sampling variability can be estimated from the sample itself.

The sample design is rather complex.[3] In general, the first stage involved the classification of manufacturing plants into 85 shipper classes based upon the plant's Standard Industrial Classification (SIC). These classes were then regrouped into nine "tonnage divisions," based on the total tons shipped by each shipper class in the 1963 and 1967 surveys. Each manufacturing plant also was identified by its location and classified into two geographic strata: (1) Located in a "selected industrial State" or (2) located in any other State. The selected industrial States are those in which the major production areas are located and include the following:

California	Minnesota
Colorado	Missouri
Connecticut	New Jersey
Delaware	New York
Georgia	Ohio
Indiana	Pennsylvania
Illinois	Rhode Island
Maryland	Texas
Massachusetts	Washington
Michigan	Wisconsin

---

[3] A detailed technical description may be obtained from the Transportation Division, Bureau of the Census, Washington, D.C. 20233.

Within each of the nine tonnage divisions and two geographic strata, the probability of selecting any given plant in the universe was proportionate to the "intercity tonnage rating" of the plant. The rating for each plant was based on the intercity tons shipped by the average plant of the same shipper class and employee size group in the 1963 and 1967 surveys.

With respect to the allocation of plants within the sample, it was decided that the relative degree of precision and detail should be somewhat greater for the shipper classes in the large tonnage divisions than for those in the small tonnage divisions. An average of 205 plants per shipper class was obtained in each of the 4 largest tonnage divisions, 176 in the 5th division, and an average of 132 per shipper class in the 4 smallest tonnage divisions. It also was decided that greater precision was needed for data on traffic flows from production areas than from the balance of the country. The probability of selecting a specific plant located in a selected industrial State was set at 1.5 times the probability of selecting an otherwise comparable plant in any other State.

After selecting the plants, the next stage involved the selection of a probability sample of bills of lading or other shipping papers at the company headquarters or individual plants. Several alternative standard plans were used, depending largely on the filing system used by the company. For example, in files organized by serial number, the procedure involved drawing every "nth" record, after taking a random-number start. In large chronological files, a two-stage design was used—a sample of dates and a sample of shipping papers within those dates. Special designs were made for recordkeeping situations that could not be sampled readily by one of the standard plans.

METHODS FOR ESTIMATING

The basic source document for obtaining size of shipment (in pounds) and origin/destination information is the sampled individual shipping paper—bill of lading, sales invoice, summary shipping record, etc.

Estimates of Tons

Estimates of total tons are shown in the first column of tables involving tons shipped. These figures represent the approximate total that would have been obtained by a complete enumeration of all shipments. These estimates are subject to sampling variability, response variations, and other nonsampling errors. The estimates of tons were made by multiplying the actual weight shown on the record for each shipment by the reciprocal of the sampling fraction for that ship-

ment,[4] aggregating the expanded value, and converting to tons. For example, if a manufacturing establishment was selected at the rate of 1 in 5, and shipments within that plant were drawn at the rate of 1 in 20, the weight in pounds of that shipment would be multiplied by 100 (that is, 5 times 20) and divided by 2,000 for purposes of estimating total tons shipped.

Estimates of Ton-Miles

Estimates of total ton-miles are shown in the first column of tables involving ton-miles. These figures are the product of weight times distance. For example, a 10-ton shipment that moved between places that were 1,000 miles apart is equivalent to a 50-ton shipment that moved 200 miles. Both represent 10,000 ton-miles, although they differ in terms of both weight and distance.

Estimates of Distance

The distance component is calculated by a computer program known as PICADAD.[5] Distance is the straight-line miles between the plant as origin and the destination shown on the shipping paper, without allowance for circuity in actual route used by the carrier. The actual route-mile distance is somewhat longer. On the average, railroad "short-line" and highway "direct-route" distances exceed the calculated straight-line miles by about 24 percent and 21 percent, respectively.

Estimates of Size

Observations based on summary reports and other types of records generally show weights that are aggregates of several shipments. While both classes of records were used for estimating total tons, the latter was excluded from the analyses by size of shipment. Therefore, tabulations showing the distribution of shipments by weight class were estimated from shipment data that were based on bills of lading and sales invoices.

The size of shipment in this report is the weight shown on the bill of lading or sales invoice, and is not necessarily the weight actually shipped in one freight car, truck, or other vehicle. Doubtless many of the smaller shipments shown in this survey were consolidated by the shipper into carload or truck lots, while some large shipments were moved in more than one freight car or truck.

RELIABILITY OF DATA

Estimates of total tons (and ton-miles) and percentage distributions have been presented for each commodity or commodity class, provided (1) the estimate contained shipments from at least three companies and five plants, (2) the estimate did not disclose the shipments of an individual company or plant, and (3) one relative standard error did not exceed 50 percent of the estimate with which it was associated.

SAMPLING VARIABILITY

General Description

The statistics presented in this book are estimates from a sample. The particular sample that was selected is one of the large number of all possible samples of the same size that could have been selected using the same sample design. Estimates derived from the different samples would differ from each other and from the results of a complete census using the same procedures. This variation among the possible estimates is called sampling variability. For example, hypothesize that shipments of Transportation Commodity Code (TCC) 201 (Meat; fresh, chilled, or frozen) were estimated to have been 26,800,000 tons during 1972 and the "sampling variability" was estimated to be about 10.6 percent. In that instance, the sampling variability was expressed in relative terms which is technically called the relative standard error. Variability may also be expressed in absolute terms (such as tons), which in this illustration was 2,840,800 tons or the equivalent of 10.6 percent of 26,800,000 tons. When expressed in absolute (rather than percentage) terms, the variability is known technically as one standard error.[6]

Interpretation of Sampling Variability

General guide.—The following general guide is given for the interpretation of sampling variability: Had all elements of the universe been canvassed, the value for a given item would be included in the range—

From 1.0 standard error below to 1.0 standard error above the estimate obtained for about two-thirds of all possible samples;

---

[4] Adjusted for nonresponse. The response rate for the survey was above 99 percent.
[5] A program developed by the Bureau of the Census specifically for processing transportation data.

[6] In fact, from a computational standpoint, a standard error is estimated from the observed values, and the relative error is the standard error divided by the estimated total to which it applies.

From 1.6 standard errors below to 1.6 standard errors above the estimate obtained for about 90 percent of all possible samples;

From 2.0 standard errors below to 2.0 standard errors above the estimate obtained for about 95 percent of all possible samples; and

From 3.0 standard errors below to 3.0 standard errors above the estimate obtained, almost always.

These values may be interpreted, therefore, as defining approximate probabilities that the estimate shown would not differ by more than 1.0, 1.6, 2.0, or 3.0 of its standard errors, respectively, from the result for a complete census.

Illustration (variability).—For example, hypothesized total shipments of TCC 201 (as noted above) were estimated to have been 26.80 million tons, plus or minus 2.84 million tons. Using the probability guide above, those figures may be interpreted as follows:

1. The chances are about 2 out of 3 that a complete enumeration would have shown between 23.96 and 29.64 million tons (that is, plus or minus 1.0 standard error);

2. The chances are about 9 out of 10 that a complete enumeration would have shown between 22.26 and 31.34 tons (that is, plus or minus 1.6 times the standard error); and

3. There is almost no chance that a complete enumeration would have shown less than 18.28 or more than 35.32 tons (that is, plus or minus 3 times the standard error).

Illustration (relative variability).—The interpretation of relative variability corresponds to the interpretation for absolutes. Again using the same illustration, the relative variability was estimated to be 10.6 percent. The chances are about 2 out of 3 that the estimate is not more than 10.6 percent above or below the figure that would have been obtained by a complete enumeration. The chances are about 9 out of 10 that the estimate is within 17 percent of the actual (that is, plus or minus 1.6 times the relative standard error), and almost no chance that the estimate is more than 31.8 percent above or below the total that would have been obtained from a complete enumeration.

Standard error of a percent.—The standard error of a percent in published percent distributions that are based upon an estimate from the survey cannot be determined directly from the relative standard errors published with the data tables. In general, the order of magnitude of the standard error of a percent depends upon the size of the percent and the size of the base from which it was derived.

Differences between two estimates.—Sometimes the question arises as to what is the sampling variability of the difference between two items. For example, say for illustration purposes, the total tonnage of TCC 263 (Paperboard, pulpboard, and fiberboard) is shown as 20.6 million tons as compared with 14.4 million tons of TCC 265 (Containers and boxes, paperboard). The estimates indicate that TCC 263 tonnage is approximately 6.2 million tons greater than the volume of TCC 265.

Was the tonnage of TCC 263 actually larger than TCC 265? What is the variability of that 6.2 million ton difference? A rough, conservative estimate can be made readily on the basis of the standard errors shown for the two items. For example, say the relative errors are 11.4 percent for TCC 263 and 9.8 percent for TCC 265. Translating those into absolutes[7], the standard errors are 2.3 million and 1.4 million tons for TCC 263 and TCC 265, respectively. To obtain a rough estimate of the standard error of the difference, multiply the larger of the two standard errors by a factor of 1.4[8] which in this instance is 1.4 times 2.3 million tons or about 3.2 million tons. The chances are about 2 out of 3 that the difference attributable to sampling would not be more than 3.2 million tons and about 9 out of 10 that it would not be greater than 5.1 million tons (that is, 1.6 times 3.2 million tons).

However, at the highest level of confidence (3 standard errors or near certainty), the difference attributable to sampling may be as high as 9.6 million tons (3 times 3.2 million tons) and, since the difference between statistics was 6.2 million tons, we cannot say with absolute confidence that a difference exists. As mentioned above, this is a rough but conservative estimate of variability of the difference between two items.

Ton-Miles

The sampling variability shown in this report relates to estimates of tons shipped. No variances were estimated for ton-miles. The sampling variability for ton-miles for any given item probably is similar to, but somewhat higher than, the sampling variability for tons on the same item.

---

[7] 11.4 percent of 20,597 and 9.8 percent of 14,410.

[8] The standard error of a difference is actually

$$\sigma_{A-B} = \sqrt{\sigma^2{}_A + \sigma^2{}_B - 2\sigma_{AB}}$$

where

$\sigma^2{}_A$ is the variance of A, $\sigma^2{}_B$ is the variance of B, and σ_{AB} is the covariance of A and B.

Non-Sampling Errors

In addition to sampling variability, the data are subject to "response errors" at the second stage of sampling that may have arisen from misinterpretation of questions, failure to find and sample some files, or other similar sources of error. This type of error probably is generally minor in this survey; however no statistical measure of the impact of these errors has been made. For certain industries (specifically, refined petroleum products), this error may be substantial due to ambiguities concerning the exclusion of local shipments and pipeline shipments or the greater use of a date sample procedure which is believed to be subject to greater error than other methods employed. The sampling procedures at each plant were relatively clear, and the precise facts were transcribed directly from individual shipping documents by company personnel in most instances. In the processing of data, careful efforts were made at each step to reduce the effects of errors. Errors occurred through failure to obtain complete and consistant information, incorrect recording of information on the schedules, incorrect transcriptions, and the like. Computer edits and review were used to identify and correct large errors.

Textile Mill Products Including Apparel

CONTENTS

[Page numbers listed here omit the State prefix number that appears as part of the number for each page]

TABLES   (The tables listed below are shown for each of the Transportation Commodity Classification groups in this report)

Comparisons of Tons and Ton-Miles of Shipments for Geographic Divisions of Origin and for Sampling Variability: 1972 and 1967

1. Percent Distribution of Geographic Division of Origin and Distance Shipped, by Means of Transport: 1972

2. Percent Distribution of Geographic Division of Origin and Means of Transport, by Geographic Division of Destination: 1972

3. Percent Distribution of Geographic Division of Destination and Means of Transport, by Geographic Division of Origin: 1972

4. Percent Distribution of Distance Shipped and Weight of Shipment, by Means of Transport: 1972

TCC 222. Manmade Fiber and Silk Broadwoven Fabrics

Comparisons of Tons and Ton-Miles of Shipments for
Geographic Divisions of Origin and for Sampling Variability: 1972 and 1967

Geographic division of origin	Estimates				Relative sampling variability in tons (percent)	
	1972		1967		1972	1967
	Tons (thousands)	Ton-miles (millions)	Tons (thousands)	Ton-miles (millions)		
U.S. total	1,486	570	1,025	495	11.0	20.6
New England	168	82	124	53	37.2	(*)
Middle Atlantic	(D)	(D)	114	39	(*)	(*)
East North Central	(D)	(D)	1	—	(*)	(*)
West North Central	(D)	(D)	—	—	(*)	(*)
South Atlantic	1,121	442	625	319	15.8	(*)
East South Central	(D)	(D)	159	83	(*)	(*)
West South Central	(D)	(D)	—	—	(*)	(*)
Mountain	(D)	(D)	—	—	(*)	(*)
Pacific	(D)	(D)	2	1	(*)	(*)

— Represents or rounds to zero.   (D) Withheld to avoid disclosing figures for individual companies.   (*) Data not published.

TABLE 1. **TCC GROUP 222**—Percent Distribution of Geographic Division of Origin and Distance Shipped, by Means of Transport: 1972

Geographic division of origin[1] and distance shipped[2]	Number	Percent distribution by means of transport							
		All means of transport	Rail	Motor carrier	Private truck	Air	Water	Other	Unknown
TONS OF SHIPMENTS	(thousands of tons)								
U.S. TOTAL..........	1 486	100.0	5.0	76.7	18.2	.1	-	.1	-
NEW ENGLAND............	168	100.0	3.1	87.7	8.5	.4	-	.2	-
UNDER 100 MILES.......	51	100.0	-	96.6	3.4	-	-	-	-
100 TO 199 MILES......	38	100.0	-	98.5	.7	.1	-	.7	-
200 TO 299 MILES......	1	100.0	-	99.3	.7	-	-	-	-
300 TO 499 MILES......	1	100.0	-	99.9	-	.1	-	-	-
500 TO 999 MILES......	58	100.0	.2	78.0	21.1	.6	-	-	.1
1000 TO 1499 MILES....	9	100.0	2.9	96.9	-	.1	-	.1	-
1500 MILES OR OVER....	7	100.0	67.0	29.0	-	3.9	-	-	-
SOUTH ATLANTIC..........	1 121	100.0	4.7	77.4	17.8	-	-	.1	-
UNDER 100 MILES.......	260	100.0	2.1	78.7	19.2	-	-	-	-
100 TO 199 MILES......	243	100.0	-	78.4	21.6	-	-	-	-
200 TO 299 MILES......	123	100.0	-	65.1	34.9	-	-	-	-
300 TO 499 MILES......	144	100.0	2.1	78.9	19.0	-	-	-	-
500 TO 999 MILES......	298	100.0	9.7	82.6	7.6	-	-	-	-
1000 TO 1499 MILES....	14	100.0	-	89.2	10.8	-	-	-	-
1500 MILES OR OVER....	37	100.0	39.6	50.6	7.7	-	-	2.1	-
TON-MILES OF SHIPMENTS	(millions of ton-miles)								
U.S. TOTAL..........	570	100.0	12.9	73.6	12.9	.2	-	.3	-
NEW ENGLAND............	82	100.0	15.9	72.5	10.3	1.2	-	.1	.1
UNDER 100 MILES.......	2	100.0	-	97.9	2.1	-	-	-	-
100 TO 199 MILES......	5	100.0	-	98.5	.7	.1	-	.7	-
200 TO 299 MILES......	-	100.0	-	99.4	.6	-	-	-	-
300 TO 499 MILES......	-	100.0	-	99.9	-	.1	-	-	-
500 TO 999 MILES......	42	100.0	.2	79.2	19.8	.7	-	-	.1
1000 TO 1499 MILES....	12	100.0	3.2	96.7	-	.1	-	.1	-
1500 MILES OR OVER....	18	100.0	67.4	29.2	-	3.4	-	-	-
SOUTH ATLANTIC..........	442	100.0	12.1	75.0	12.5	-	-	.4	-
UNDER 100 MILES.......	12	100.0	2.2	73.5	24.2	-	-	-	-
100 TO 199 MILES......	36	100.0	-	80.2	19.8	-	-	-	-
200 TO 299 MILES......	29	100.0	-	64.1	35.9	-	-	-	-
300 TO 499 MILES......	57	100.0	2.6	81.1	16.2	-	-	-	-
500 TO 999 MILES......	207	100.0	9.5	82.4	8.0	-	-	-	-
1000 TO 1499 MILES....	18	100.0	-	87.9	12.1	-	-	-	-
1500 MILES OR OVER....	79	100.0	39.8	50.2	7.7	-	-	2.2	-

See footnotes at end of table 4.

TABLE 2. **TCC GROUP 222**—Percent Distribution of Geographic Division of Origin and Means of Transport, by Geographic Division of Destination: 1972

Geographic division of origin[1] and means of transport	Number	Percent distribution by division of destination									
		U.S. total	New England	Middle Atlantic	East North Central	West North Central	South Atlantic	East South Central	West South Central	Mountain	Pacific
TONS OF SHIPMENTS	(thousands of tons)										
U.S. TOTAL..............	1 486	100.0	10.7	16.3	3.8	1.6	53.8	7.2	3.2	.4	3.1
RAIL..................	73	100.0	28.1	17.5	-	5.9	16.3	.1	5.3	-	26.8
MOTOR CARRIER.........	1 140	100.0	11.6	17.6	4.2	1.5	52.1	7.7	2.9	.5	1.9
PRIVATE TRUCK.........	269	100.0	2.3	10.9	3.1	.7	71.5	6.9	3.4	-	1.1
AIR...................	-	100.0	1.6	6.3	7.9	29.0	10.4	.8	14.3	-	29.7
WATER.................	-	100.0	-	-	-	-	-	-	-	-	-
OTHER.................	1	100.0	.2	23.7	2.9	.6	3.7	.1	-	4.7	64.1
UNKNOWN...............	-	100.0	-	-	-	100.0	-	-	-	-	-
NEW ENGLAND............	168	100.0	22.6	32.0	3.3	1.7	31.1	2.3	2.7	.1	4.1
RAIL..................	5	100.0	-	-	.7	.7	1.4	.8	3.8	-	92.6
MOTOR CARRIER.........	148	100.0	24.5	36.2	2.0	1.7	28.9	2.5	2.9	.1	1.3
PRIVATE TRUCK.........	14	100.0	13.9	.2	17.5	-	67.1	1.3	-	-	-
AIR...................	-	100.0	-	4.5	1.6	37.7	10.6	.9	15.3	-	29.5
WATER.................	-	100.0	-	-	-	-	-	-	-	-	-
OTHER.................	-	100.0	1.0	95.3	-	2.4	1.2	-	-	-	-
UNKNOWN...............	-	100.0	-	-	100.0	-	-	-	-	-	-
SOUTH ATLANTIC..........	1 121	100.0	10.1	13.2	2.5	1.7	57.9	7.7	3.3	.2	3.3
RAIL..................	52	100.0	28.5	22.1	-	8.3	10.8	-	2.1	-	28.3
MOTOR CARRIER.........	868	100.0	10.9	14.7	2.5	1.5	56.8	7.9	3.2	.3	2.1
PRIVATE TRUCK.........	200	100.0	2.0	4.7	2.8	1.0	75.2	8.8	4.1	-	1.4
AIR...................	-	100.0	3.0	27.3	36.9	-	1.9	-	24.5	.4	5.9
WATER.................	-	100.0	-	-	-	-	-	-	-	-	-
OTHER.................	-	100.0	-	1.8	3.9	-	4.7	.1	-	-	89.5
UNKNOWN...............	-	100.0	-	-	-	-	-	-	-	-	-

See footnotes at end of table 4.

TABLE 2. **TCC GROUP 222—Percent Distribution of Geographic Division of Origin and Means of Transport, by Geographic Division of Destination: 1972**—Continued

Geographic division of origin[1] and means of transport	Number	Percent distribution by division of destination									
		U.S. total	New England	Middle Atlantic	East North Central	West North Central	South Atlantic	East South Central	West South Central	Mountain	Pacific
TON-MILES OF SHIPMENTS	(millions of ton-miles)										
U.S. TOTAL	570	100.0	15.8	16.6	3.9	3.3	27.2	6.6	8.1	.9	17.7
RAIL	73	100.0	19.0	10.8	-	4.4	1.8	.1	3.5	-	60.5
MOTOR CARRIER	420	100.0	17.5	18.9	4.2	3.2	27.4	8.0	8.2	1.2	11.5
PRIVATE TRUCK	73	100.0	4.0	10.0	6.2	2.3	52.1	5.2	11.9	-	8.3
AIR	1	100.0	.7	1.3	2.8	19.7	7.4	.5	14.5	.1	53.0
WATER	-	100.0	-	-	-	-	-	-	-	-	-
OTHER	1	100.0	-	2.6	.9	.4	.9	-	-	.5	94.6
UNKNOWN	-	100.0	-	-	100.0	-	-	-	-	-	-
NEW ENGLAND	82	100.0	2.1	8.5	4.7	4.0	46.1	4.5	8.0	.2	22.0
RAIL	13	100.0	-	-	.2	.3	.5	.3	2.3	-	96.4
MOTOR CARRIER	59	100.0	2.8	11.6	3.4	5.0	52.4	5.9	10.2	.3	8.4
PRIVATE TRUCK	8	100.0	1.0	-	20.7	-	76.5	1.7	-	-	-
AIR	-	100.0	-	.4	.9	24.1	6.3	.6	15.8	-	51.9
WATER	-	100.0	-	-	-	-	-	-	-	-	-
OTHER	-	100.0	.6	81.8	-	13.4	4.2	.1	-	-	-
UNKNOWN	-	100.0	-	-	100.0	-	-	-	-	-	-
SOUTH ATLANTIC	442	100.0	19.0	18.6	3.0	3.3	21.9	7.2	8.2	.9	17.9
RAIL	53	100.0	18.5	13.6	-	5.9	.6	-	1.8	-	59.5
MOTOR CARRIER	331	100.0	21.5	21.0	3.2	3.0	21.6	8.5	8.2	1.1	11.9
PRIVATE TRUCK	55	100.0	5.2	9.7	5.0	3.0	45.1	6.5	14.4	-	11.1
AIR	-	100.0	3.5	19.1	27.4	-	1.3	-	29.1	1.1	18.4
WATER	-	100.0	-	-	-	-	-	-	-	-	-
OTHER	1	100.0	-	.4	1.0	-	.8	-	-	-	97.8
UNKNOWN	-	100.0	-	-	-	-	-	-	-	-	-

See footnotes at end of table 4.

TABLE 3. TCC GROUP 222—Percent Distribution of Geographic Division of Destination and Means of Transport, by Geographic Division of Origin: 1972

Geographic division of destination and means of transport	Number	U.S. total	New England	Middle Atlantic	East North Central	West North Central	South Atlantic	East South Central	West South Central	Mountain	Pacific
					Percent distribution by division of origin[1]						
TONS OF SHIPMENTS	(thousands of tons)										
U.S. TOTAL..............	1 486	100.0	11.4	(D)	(D)	(D)	75.5	(D)	(D)	(D)	(D)
RAIL.................	73	100.0	7.2	(D)	(D)	(D)	71.1	(D)	(D)	(D)	(D)
MOTOR CARRIER.........	1 140	100.0	13.0	(D)	(D)	(D)	76.1	(D)	(D)	(D)	(D)
PRIVATE TRUCK.........	269	100.0	5.3	(D)	(D)	(D)	74.1	(D)	(D)	(D)	(D)
AIR.................	-	100.0	76.9	(D)	(D)	(D)	10.3	(D)	(D)	(D)	(D)
WATER.................	-	100.0	-	(D)	(D)	(D)	-	(D)	(D)	(D)	(D)
OTHER.................	1	100.0	23.5	(D)	(D)	(D)	71.7	(D)	(D)	(D)	(D)
UNKNOWN..............	-	100.0	100.0	(D)	(D)	(D)	-	(D)	(D)	(D)	(D)
NEW ENGLAND............	158	100.0	24.1	(D)	(D)	(D)	71.6	(D)	(D)	(D)	(D)
RAIL.................	20	100.0	-	(D)	(D)	(D)	72.0	(D)	(D)	(D)	(D)
MOTOR CARRIER.........	131	100.0	27.5	(D)	(D)	(D)	71.7	(D)	(D)	(D)	(D)
PRIVATE TRUCK.........	6	100.0	33.0	(D)	(D)	(D)	67.0	(D)	(D)	(D)	(D)
AIR.................	-	100.0	-	(D)	(D)	(D)	20.0	(D)	(D)	(D)	(D)
WATER.................	-	100.0	-	(D)	(D)	(D)	-	(D)	(D)	(D)	(D)
OTHER.................	-	100.0	99.3	(D)	(D)	(D)	-	(D)	(D)	(D)	(D)
UNKNOWN..............	-	100.0	-	(D)	(D)	(D)	-	(D)	(D)	(D)	(D)
MIDDLE ATLANTIC.........	243	100.0	22.2	(D)	(D)	(D)	61.1	(D)	(D)	(D)	(D)
RAIL.................	12	100.0	-	(D)	(D)	(D)	90.2	(D)	(D)	(D)	(D)
MOTOR CARRIER.........	200	100.0	26.8	(D)	(D)	(D)	63.7	(D)	(D)	(D)	(D)
PRIVATE TRUCK.........	29	100.0	.1	(D)	(D)	(D)	31.7	(D)	(D)	(D)	(D)
AIR.................	-	100.0	54.9	(D)	(D)	(D)	45.1	(D)	(D)	(D)	(D)
WATER.................	-	100.0	-	(D)	(D)	(D)	-	(D)	(D)	(D)	(D)
OTHER.................	-	100.0	94.3	(D)	(D)	(D)	5.5	(D)	(D)	(D)	(D)
UNKNOWN..............	-	100.0	-	(D)	(D)	(D)	-	(D)	(D)	(D)	(D)
EAST NORTH CENTRAL......	56	100.0	10.0	(D)	(D)	(D)	48.7	(D)	(D)	(D)	(D)
RAIL.................	-	100.0	100.0	(D)	(D)	(D)	-	(D)	(D)	(D)	(D)
MOTOR CARRIER.........	48	100.0	6.3	(D)	(D)	(D)	45.6	(D)	(D)	(D)	(D)
PRIVATE TRUCK.........	8	100.0	29.7	(D)	(D)	(D)	66.5	(D)	(D)	(D)	(D)
AIR.................	-	100.0	15.2	(D)	(D)	(D)	48.1	(D)	(D)	(D)	(D)
WATER.................	-	100.0	-	(D)	(D)	(D)	-	(D)	(D)	(D)	(D)
OTHER.................	-	100.0	-	(D)	(D)	(D)	98.3	(D)	(D)	(D)	(D)
UNKNOWN..............	-	100.0	100.0	(D)	(D)	(D)	-	(D)	(D)	(D)	(D)
WEST NORTH CENTRAL......	23	100.0	12.2	(D)	(D)	(D)	83.5	(D)	(D)	(D)	(D)
RAIL.................	4	100.0	.9	(D)	(D)	(D)	99.1	(D)	(D)	(D)	(D)
MOTOR CARRIER.........	16	100.0	15.2	(D)	(D)	(D)	78.7	(D)	(D)	(D)	(D)
PRIVATE TRUCK.........	1	100.0	-	(D)	(D)	(D)	100.0	(D)	(D)	(D)	(D)
AIR.................	-	100.0	100.0	(D)	(D)	(D)	-	(D)	(D)	(D)	(D)
WATER.................	-	100.0	-	(D)	(D)	(D)	-	(D)	(D)	(D)	(D)
OTHER.................	-	100.0	96.3	(D)	(D)	(D)	-	(D)	(D)	(D)	(D)
UNKNOWN..............	-	100.0	-	(D)	(D)	(D)	-	(D)	(D)	(D)	(D)
SOUTH ATLANTIC..........	799	100.0	6.6	(D)	(D)	(D)	81.2	(D)	(D)	(D)	(D)
RAIL.................	12	100.0	.6	(D)	(D)	(D)	47.2	(D)	(D)	(D)	(D)
MOTOR CARRIER.........	594	100.0	7.2	(D)	(D)	(D)	83.0	(D)	(D)	(D)	(D)
PRIVATE TRUCK.........	193	100.0	5.0	(D)	(D)	(D)	77.9	(D)	(D)	(D)	(D)
AIR.................	-	100.0	78.0	(D)	(D)	(D)	1.9	(D)	(D)	(D)	(D)
WATER.................	-	100.0	-	(D)	(D)	(D)	-	(D)	(D)	(D)	(D)
OTHER.................	-	100.0	7.9	(D)	(D)	(D)	92.1	(D)	(D)	(D)	(D)
UNKNOWN..............	-	100.0	-	(D)	(D)	(D)	-	(D)	(D)	(D)	(D)
EAST SOUTH CENTRAL......	106	100.0	3.7	(D)	(D)	(D)	80.9	(D)	(D)	(D)	(D)
RAIL.................	-	100.0	100.0	(D)	(D)	(D)	-	(D)	(D)	(D)	(D)
MOTOR CARRIER.........	87	100.0	4.2	(D)	(D)	(D)	78.2	(D)	(D)	(D)	(D)
PRIVATE TRUCK.........	18	100.0	1.0	(D)	(D)	(D)	94.0	(D)	(D)	(D)	(D)
AIR.................	-	100.0	91.4	(D)	(D)	(D)	-	(D)	(D)	(D)	(D)
WATER.................	-	100.0	-	(D)	(D)	(D)	-	(D)	(D)	(D)	(D)
OTHER.................	-	100.0	4.9	(D)	(D)	(D)	95.1	(D)	(D)	(D)	(D)
UNKNOWN..............	-	100.0	-	(D)	(D)	(D)	-	(D)	(D)	(D)	(D)
WEST SOUTH CENTRAL......	46	100.0	9.8	(D)	(D)	(D)	79.0	(D)	(D)	(D)	(D)
RAIL.................	3	100.0	5.1	(D)	(D)	(D)	27.7	(D)	(D)	(D)	(D)
MOTOR CARRIER.........	33	100.0	12.8	(D)	(D)	(D)	82.5	(D)	(D)	(D)	(D)
PRIVATE TRUCK.........	9	100.0	-	(D)	(D)	(D)	88.7	(D)	(D)	(D)	(D)
AIR.................	-	100.0	82.3	(D)	(D)	(D)	17.7	(D)	(D)	(D)	(D)
WATER.................	-	100.0	-	(D)	(D)	(D)	-	(D)	(D)	(D)	(D)
OTHER.................	-	100.0	-	(D)	(D)	(D)	-	(D)	(D)	(D)	(D)
UNKNOWN..............	-	100.0	-	(D)	(D)	(D)	-	(D)	(D)	(D)	(D)
MOUNTAIN................	5	100.0	1.6	(D)	(D)	(D)	46.3	(D)	(D)	(D)	(D)
RAIL.................	-	100.0	-	(D)	(D)	(D)	-	(D)	(D)	(D)	(D)
MOTOR CARRIER.........	5	100.0	1.6	(D)	(D)	(D)	46.6	(D)	(D)	(D)	(D)
PRIVATE TRUCK.........	-	100.0	-	(D)	(D)	(D)	100.0	(D)	(D)	(D)	(D)
AIR.................	-	100.0	-	(D)	(D)	(D)	100.0	(D)	(D)	(D)	(D)
WATER.................	-	100.0	-	(D)	(D)	(D)	-	(D)	(D)	(D)	(D)
OTHER.................	-	100.0	-	(D)	(D)	(D)	-	(D)	(D)	(D)	(D)
UNKNOWN..............	-	100.0	-	(D)	(D)	(D)	-	(D)	(D)	(D)	(D)
PACIFIC.................	45	100.0	15.3	(D)	(D)	(D)	80.9	(D)	(D)	(D)	(D)
RAIL.................	19	100.0	24.8	(D)	(D)	(D)	74.9	(D)	(D)	(D)	(D)
MOTOR CARRIER.........	21	100.0	8.5	(D)	(D)	(D)	84.2	(D)	(D)	(D)	(D)
PRIVATE TRUCK.........	2	100.0	-	(D)	(D)	(D)	100.0	(D)	(D)	(D)	(D)
AIR.................	-	100.0	76.3	(D)	(D)	(D)	2.1	(D)	(D)	(D)	(D)
WATER.................	-	100.0	-	(D)	(D)	(D)	-	(D)	(D)	(D)	(D)
OTHER.................	-	100.0	-	(D)	(D)	(D)	100.0	(D)	(D)	(D)	(D)
UNKNOWN..............	-	100.0	-	(D)	(D)	(D)	-	(D)	(D)	(D)	(D)

See footnotes at end of table 4.

TABLE 3. **TCC GROUP 222**—Percent Distribution of Geographic Division of Destination and Means of Transport, by Geographic Division of Origin: 1972—Continued

Geographic division of destination and means of transport	Number	Percent distribution by division of origin[1]									
		U.S. total	New England	Middle Atlantic	East North Central	West North Central	South Atlantic	East South Central	West South Central	Mountain	Pacific
TON-MILES OF SHIPMENTS	(millions of ton-miles)										
U.S. TOTAL.............	570	100.0	14.4	(D)	(D)	(D)	77.4	(D)	(D)	(D)	(D)
RAIL................	73	100.0	17.8	(D)	(D)	(D)	72.5	(D)	(D)	(D)	(D)
MOTOR CARRIER.......	420	100.0	14.2	(D)	(D)	(D)	78.9	(D)	(D)	(D)	(D)
PRIVATE TRUCK.......	73	100.0	11.5	(D)	(D)	(D)	74.9	(D)	(D)	(D)	(D)
AIR.................	1	100.0	82.1	(D)	(D)	(D)	5.2	(D)	(D)	(D)	(D)
WATER...............	-	100.0	-	(D)	(D)	(D)	-	(D)	(D)	(D)	(D)
OTHER...............	1	100.0	2.8	(D)	(D)	(D)	96.7	(D)	(D)	(D)	(D)
UNKNOWN.............	-	100.0	100.0	(D)	(D)	(D)	-	(D)	(D)	(D)	(D)
NEW ENGLAND.............	90	100.0	2.0	(D)	(D)	(D)	93.0	(D)	(D)	(D)	(D)
RAIL................	13	100.0	-	(D)	(D)	(D)	70.7	(D)	(D)	(D)	(D)
MOTOR CARRIER.......	73	100.0	2.3	(D)	(D)	(D)	97.1	(D)	(D)	(D)	(D)
PRIVATE TRUCK.......	2	100.0	3.0	(D)	(D)	(D)	97.0	(D)	(D)	(D)	(D)
AIR.................	-	100.0	-	(D)	(D)	(D)	28.0	(D)	(D)	(D)	(D)
WATER...............	-	100.0	-	(D)	(D)	(D)	-	(D)	(D)	(D)	(D)
OTHER...............	-	100.0	95.9	(D)	(D)	(D)	-	(D)	(D)	(D)	(D)
UNKNOWN.............	-	100.0	-	(D)	(D)	(D)	-	(D)	(D)	(D)	(D)
MIDDLE ATLANTIC.........	94	100.0	7.4	(D)	(D)	(D)	87.0	(D)	(D)	(D)	(D)
RAIL................	7	100.0	-	(D)	(D)	(D)	91.7	(D)	(D)	(D)	(D)
MOTOR CARRIER.......	79	100.0	8.7	(D)	(D)	(D)	87.8	(D)	(D)	(D)	(D)
PRIVATE TRUCK.......	7	100.0	-	(D)	(D)	(D)	72.9	(D)	(D)	(D)	(D)
AIR.................	-	100.0	25.3	(D)	(D)	(D)	74.6	(D)	(D)	(D)	(D)
WATER...............	-	100.0	-	(D)	(D)	(D)	-	(D)	(D)	(D)	(D)
OTHER...............	-	100.0	86.6	(D)	(D)	(D)	13.1	(D)	(D)	(D)	(D)
UNKNOWN.............	-	100.0	-	(D)	(D)	(D)	-	(D)	(D)	(D)	(D)
EAST NORTH CENTRAL......	22	100.0	17.5	(D)	(D)	(D)	59.5	(D)	(D)	(D)	(D)
RAIL................	-	100.0	100.0	(D)	(D)	(D)	-	(D)	(D)	(D)	(D)
MOTOR CARRIER.......	17	100.0	11.6	(D)	(D)	(D)	59.6	(D)	(D)	(D)	(D)
PRIVATE TRUCK.......	4	100.0	38.6	(D)	(D)	(D)	60.4	(D)	(D)	(D)	(D)
AIR.................	-	100.0	27.2	(D)	(D)	(D)	51.9	(D)	(D)	(D)	(D)
WATER...............	-	100.0	-	(D)	(D)	(D)	-	(D)	(D)	(D)	(D)
OTHER...............	-	100.0	-	(D)	(D)	(D)	99.1	(D)	(D)	(D)	(D)
UNKNOWN.............	-	100.0	100.0	(D)	(D)	(D)	-	(D)	(D)	(D)	(D)
WEST NORTH CENTRAL......	18	100.0	17.6	(D)	(D)	(D)	78.8	(D)	(D)	(D)	(D)
RAIL................	3	100.0	1.4	(D)	(D)	(D)	98.6	(D)	(D)	(D)	(D)
MOTOR CARRIER.......	13	100.0	22.1	(D)	(D)	(D)	72.9	(D)	(D)	(D)	(D)
PRIVATE TRUCK.......	1	100.0	-	(D)	(D)	(D)	100.0	(D)	(D)	(D)	(D)
AIR.................	-	100.0	100.0	(D)	(D)	(D)	-	(D)	(D)	(D)	(D)
WATER...............	-	100.0	-	(D)	(D)	(D)	-	(D)	(D)	(D)	(D)
OTHER...............	-	100.0	99.1	(D)	(D)	(D)	-	(D)	(D)	(D)	(D)
UNKNOWN.............	-	100.0	-	(D)	(D)	(D)	-	(D)	(D)	(D)	(D)
SOUTH ATLANTIC..........	155	100.0	24.5	(D)	(D)	(D)	62.4	(D)	(D)	(D)	(D)
RAIL................	1	100.0	4.6	(D)	(D)	(D)	25.3	(D)	(D)	(D)	(D)
MOTOR CARRIER.......	115	100.0	27.2	(D)	(D)	(D)	62.1	(D)	(D)	(D)	(D)
PRIVATE TRUCK.......	38	100.0	16.9	(D)	(D)	(D)	64.8	(D)	(D)	(D)	(D)
AIR.................	-	100.0	69.9	(D)	(D)	(D)	.9	(D)	(D)	(D)	(D)
WATER...............	-	100.0	-	(D)	(D)	(D)	-	(D)	(D)	(D)	(D)
OTHER...............	-	100.0	12.5	(D)	(D)	(D)	87.5	(D)	(D)	(D)	(D)
UNKNOWN.............	-	100.0	-	(D)	(D)	(D)	-	(D)	(D)	(D)	(D)
EAST SOUTH CENTRAL......	37	100.0	10.0	(D)	(D)	(D)	84.6	(D)	(D)	(D)	(D)
RAIL................	-	100.0	100.0	(D)	(D)	(D)	-	(D)	(D)	(D)	(D)
MOTOR CARRIER.......	33	100.0	10.5	(D)	(D)	(D)	83.7	(D)	(D)	(D)	(D)
PRIVATE TRUCK.......	3	100.0	3.8	(D)	(D)	(D)	93.6	(D)	(D)	(D)	(D)
AIR.................	-	100.0	99.1	(D)	(D)	(D)	-	(D)	(D)	(D)	(D)
WATER...............	-	100.0	-	(D)	(D)	(D)	-	(D)	(D)	(D)	(D)
OTHER...............	-	100.0	12.0	(D)	(D)	(D)	88.0	(D)	(D)	(D)	(D)
UNKNOWN.............	-	100.0	-	(D)	(D)	(D)	-	(D)	(D)	(D)	(D)
WEST SOUTH CENTRAL......	45	100.0	14.3	(D)	(D)	(D)	78.7	(D)	(D)	(D)	(D)
RAIL................	2	100.0	11.5	(D)	(D)	(D)	36.4	(D)	(D)	(D)	(D)
MOTOR CARRIER.......	34	100.0	17.8	(D)	(D)	(D)	79.3	(D)	(D)	(D)	(D)
PRIVATE TRUCK.......	8	100.0	-	(D)	(D)	(D)	90.0	(D)	(D)	(D)	(D)
AIR.................	-	100.0	89.5	(D)	(D)	(D)	10.5	(D)	(D)	(D)	(D)
WATER...............	-	100.0	-	(D)	(D)	(D)	-	(D)	(D)	(D)	(D)
OTHER...............	-	100.0	-	(D)	(D)	(D)	-	(D)	(D)	(D)	(D)
UNKNOWN.............	-	100.0	-	(D)	(D)	(D)	-	(D)	(D)	(D)	(D)
MOUNTAIN................	4	100.0	3.6	(D)	(D)	(D)	77.0	(D)	(D)	(D)	(D)
RAIL................	-	100.0	-	(D)	(D)	(D)	-	(D)	(D)	(D)	(D)
MOTOR CARRIER.......	4	100.0	3.6	(D)	(D)	(D)	77.0	(D)	(D)	(D)	(D)
PRIVATE TRUCK.......	-	100.0	-	(D)	(D)	(D)	100.0	(D)	(D)	(D)	(D)
AIR.................	-	100.0	-	(D)	(D)	(D)	100.0	(D)	(D)	(D)	(D)
WATER...............	-	100.0	-	(D)	(D)	(D)	-	(D)	(D)	(D)	(D)
OTHER...............	-	100.0	-	(D)	(D)	(D)	-	(D)	(D)	(D)	(D)
UNKNOWN.............	-	100.0	-	(D)	(D)	(D)	-	(D)	(D)	(D)	(D)
PACIFIC.................	101	100.0	17.9	(D)	(D)	(D)	78.0	(D)	(D)	(D)	(D)
RAIL................	44	100.0	28.4	(D)	(D)	(D)	71.4	(D)	(D)	(D)	(D)
MOTOR CARRIER.......	48	100.0	10.4	(D)	(D)	(D)	81.5	(D)	(D)	(D)	(D)
PRIVATE TRUCK.......	6	100.0	-	(D)	(D)	(D)	100.0	(D)	(D)	(D)	(D)
AIR.................	-	100.0	80.3	(D)	(D)	(D)	1.8	(D)	(D)	(D)	(D)
WATER...............	-	100.0	-	(D)	(D)	(D)	-	(D)	(D)	(D)	(D)
OTHER...............	1	100.0	-	(D)	(D)	(D)	100.0	(D)	(D)	(D)	(D)
UNKNOWN.............	-	100.0	-	(D)	(D)	(D)	-	(D)	(D)	(D)	(D)

See footnotes at end of table 4.

TABLE 4. TCC GROUP 222—Percent Distribution of Distance Shipped and Weight of Shipment, by Means of Transport: 1972

Distance shipped and weight of shipment[2][3]	Number	Percent distribution by means of transport							
		All means of transport	Rail	Motor carrier	Private truck	Air	Water	Other	Unknown
TONS OF SHIPMENTS	(thousands of tons)								
U.S. TOTAL..........	1 460	100.0	5.0	77.9	16.9	.1	-	.1	-
UNDER 100 MILES.........	366	100.0	1.5	84.6	13.9	-	-	-	-
UNDER 1000 POUNDS.....	14	100.0	-	97.8	2.2	-	-	-	-
1000 TO 9999 POUNDS...	87	100.0	-	89.0	11.0	-	-	-	-
10000 TO 29999 POUNDS.	112	100.0	4.0	72.9	23.1	-	-	-	-
30000 TO 59999 POUNDS.	134	100.0	.8	87.9	11.3	-	-	-	-
60000 TO 89999 POUNDS.	9	100.0	-	100.0	-	-	-	-	-
90000 POUNDS AND OVER.	8	100.0	-	100.0	-	-	-	-	-
100 TO 199 MILES........	312	100.0	.9	77.4	21.6	-	-	.1	-
UNDER 1000 POUNDS.....	23	100.0	-	90.7	7.7	.1	-	1.5	-
1000 TO 9999 POUNDS...	87	100.0	-	89.2	10.8	-	-	-	-
10000 TO 29999 POUNDS.	101	100.0	-	73.5	26.5	-	-	-	-
30000 TO 59999 POUNDS.	80	100.0	3.5	60.1	36.4	-	-	-	-
60000 TO 89999 POUNDS.	13	100.0	-	100.0	-	-	-	-	-
90000 POUNDS AND OVER.	6	100.0	-	100.0	-	-	-	-	-
200 TO 299 MILES........	162	100.0	1.8	66.8	31.4	-	-	-	-
UNDER 1000 POUNDS.....	11	100.0	-	94.3	5.5	.1	-	-	-
1000 TO 9999 POUNDS...	38	100.0	-	70.0	30.0	-	-	-	-
10000 TO 29999 POUNDS.	52	100.0	-	42.7	57.3	-	-	-	-
30000 TO 59999 POUNDS.	59	100.0	4.9	81.2	13.9	-	-	-	-
60000 TO 89999 POUNDS.	-	100.0	-	-	-	-	-	-	-
90000 POUNDS AND OVER.	-	100.0	-	-	100.0	-	-	-	-
300 TO 499 MILES........	169	100.0	1.8	76.5	21.6	-	-	-	-
UNDER 1000 POUNDS.....	13	100.0	-	83.9	15.5	.3	-	.3	-
1000 TO 9999 POUNDS...	53	100.0	-	80.3	19.7	-	-	-	-
10000 TO 29999 POUNDS.	39	100.0	-	70.3	29.7	-	-	-	-
30000 TO 59999 POUNDS.	57	100.0	5.3	73.7	20.9	-	-	-	-
60000 TO 89999 POUNDS.	-	100.0	-	100.0	-	-	-	-	-
90000 POUNDS AND OVER.	3	100.0	-	100.0	-	-	-	-	-
500 TO 999 MILES........	379	100.0	10.2	80.1	9.6	.1	-	-	.3
UNDER 1000 POUNDS.....	24	100.0	.8	94.1	3.9	.8	-	.2	-
1000 TO 9999 POUNDS...	111	100.0	1.0	85.5	13.3	.2	-	-	-
10000 TO 29999 POUNDS.	137	100.0	9.1	80.9	10.0	-	-	-	-
30000 TO 59999 POUNDS.	86	100.0	16.0	76.2	7.8	-	-	-	-
60000 TO 89999 POUNDS.	16	100.0	42.7	57.3	-	-	-	-	-
90000 POUNDS AND OVER.	4	100.0	100.0	-	-	-	-	-	-
1000 TO 1499 MILES......	24	100.0	1.1	92.1	6.6	.1	-	-	-
UNDER 1000 POUNDS.....	5	100.0	5.1	94.1	.2	.5	-	.1	-
1000 TO 9999 POUNDS...	9	100.0	-	100.0	-	-	-	-	-
10000 TO 29999 POUNDS.	2	100.0	-	100.0	-	-	-	-	-
30000 TO 59999 POUNDS.	2	100.0	-	32.7	67.3	-	-	-	-
60000 TO 89999 POUNDS.	-	100.0	-	-	-	-	-	-	-
90000 POUNDS AND OVER.	5	100.0	-	100.0	-	-	-	-	-
1500 MILES OR OVER......	46	100.0	42.6	48.8	6.2	.7	-	1.7	-
UNDER 1000 POUNDS.....	13	100.0	43.1	46.2	2.4	2.6	-	5.7	-
1000 TO 9999 POUNDS...	14	100.0	38.1	56.3	5.6	-	-	-	-
10000 TO 29999 POUNDS.	4	100.0	-	79.8	20.2	-	-	-	-
30000 TO 59999 POUNDS.	8	100.0	29.5	59.5	10.9	-	-	-	-
60000 TO 89999 POUNDS.	4	100.0	100.0	-	-	-	-	-	-
90000 POUNDS AND OVER.	1	100.0	100.0	-	-	-	-	-	-
TON-MILES OF SHIPMENTS	(millions of ton-miles)								
U.S. TOTAL..........	568	100.0	12.9	73.9	12.6	.2	-	.3	-
UNDER 100 MILES.........	18	100.0	1.6	81.7	16.7	-	-	-	-
UNDER 1000 POUNDS.....	-	100.0	-	97.5	2.4	-	-	-	-
1000 TO 9999 POUNDS...	4	100.0	-	87.4	12.6	-	-	-	-
10000 TO 29999 POUNDS.	.6	100.0	3.9	70.7	25.3	-	-	-	-
30000 TO 59999 POUNDS.	6	100.0	.7	84.4	14.9	-	-	-	-
60000 TO 89999 POUNDS.	-	100.0	-	100.0	-	-	-	-	-
90000 POUNDS AND OVER.	-	100.0	-	100.0	-	-	-	-	-
100 TO 199 MILES........	46	100.0	.6	79.3	20.0	-	-	.1	-
UNDER 1000 POUNDS.....	3	100.0	-	89.7	8.6	.1	-	1.6	-
1000 TO 9999 POUNDS...	12	100.0	-	88.9	11.1	-	-	-	-
10000 TO 29999 POUNDS.	14	100.0	-	75.8	24.2	-	-	-	-
30000 TO 59999 POUNDS.	11	100.0	2.5	64.4	33.1	-	-	-	-
60000 TO 89999 POUNDS.	2	100.0	-	100.0	-	-	-	-	-
90000 POUNDS AND OVER.	1	100.0	-	100.0	-	-	-	-	-

See footnotes at end of table 4.

TABLE 4. **TCC GROUP 222—Percent Distribution of Distance Shipped and Weight of Shipment, by Means of Transport: 1972**—Continued

Distance shipped and weight of shipment[2][3]	Number	Percent distribution by means of transport							
		All means of transport	Rail	Motor carrier	Private truck	Air	Water	Other	Unknown
TON-MILES OF SHIPMENTS	(millions of ton-miles)								
200 TO 299 MILES........	38	100.0	1.5	66.4	32.1	-	-	-	-
UNDER 1000 POUNDS.....	2	100.0	-	93.6	6.2	.1	-	-	-
1000 TO 9999 POUNDS...	9	100.0	-	70.4	29.6	-	-	-	-
10000 TO 29999 POUNDS.	12	100.0	-	41.9	58.1	-	-	-	-
30000 TO 59999 POUNDS.	13	100.0	4.2	81.9	13.9	-	-	-	-
60000 TO 89999 POUNDS.	-	100.0	-	-	-	-	-	-	-
90000 POUNDS AND OVER.	-	100.0	-	-	100.0	-	-	-	-
300 TO 499 MILES........	66	100.0	2.3	78.8	18.9	-	-	-	-
UNDER 1000 POUNDS.....	5	100.0	-	85.2	14.3	.3	-	.3	-
1000 TO 9999 POUNDS...	20	100.0	-	82.5	17.5	-	-	-	-
10000 TO 29999 POUNDS.	15	100.0	-	74.7	25.3	-	-	-	-
30000 TO 59999 POUNDS.	22	100.0	6.5	75.2	18.2	-	-	-	-
60000 TO 89999 POUNDS.	-	100.0	-	100.0	-	-	-	-	-
90000 POUNDS AND OVER.	1	100.0	-	100.0	-	-	-	-	-
500 TO 999 MILES........	264	100.0	9.8	80.2	9.8	.1	-	-	-
UNDER 1000 POUNDS.....	16	100.0	.9	94.1	3.7	.9	-	.1	.3
1000 TO 9999 POUNDS...	76	100.0	1.3	84.7	13.7	.3	-	-	-
10000 TO 29999 POUNDS.	94	100.0	8.0	81.0	11.0	-	-	-	-
30000 TO 59999 POUNDS.	61	100.0	15.1	77.8	7.1	-	-	-	-
60000 TO 89999 POUNDS.	11	100.0	42.3	57.7	-	-	-	-	-
90000 POUNDS AND OVER.	3	100.0	100.0	-	-	-	-	-	-
1000 TO 1499 MILES......	30	100.0	1.2	91.3	7.4	.1	-	-	-
UNDER 1000 POUNDS.....	6	100.0	5.8	93.3	.2	.6	-	.1	-
1000 TO 9999 POUNDS...	12	100.0	-	100.0	-	-	-	-	-
10000 TO 29999 POUNDS.	2	100.0	-	100.0	-	-	-	-	-
30000 TO 59999 POUNDS.	3	100.0	-	25.8	74.2	-	-	-	-
60000 TO 89999 POUNDS.	-	100.0	-	-	-	-	-	-	-
90000 POUNDS AND OVER.	6	100.0	-	100.0	-	-	-	-	-
1500 MILES OR OVER......	102	100.0	43.3	48.3	6.0	.7	-	1.7	-
UNDER 1000 POUNDS.....	31	100.0	44.1	45.5	2.2	2.4	-	5.7	-
1000 TO 9999 POUNDS...	34	100.0	40.1	54.6	5.3	-	-	-	-
10000 TO 29999 POUNDS.	8	100.0	-	78.7	21.3	-	-	-	-
30000 TO 59999 POUNDS.	16	100.0	29.7	59.5	10.8	-	-	-	-
60000 TO 89999 POUNDS.	8	100.0	100.0	-	-	-	-	-	-
90000 POUNDS AND OVER.	3	100.0	100.0	-	-	-	-	-	-

Note: Detail may not add to total due to rounding. The introductory table shows the estimates of sampling variability for tons; sampling variability for ton-miles has not been estimated. See the map in the Introduction for the States comprising the geographic divisions of the United States.

Shipments excluded from the survey are those moving by pipeline (primarily petroleum products from refineries), parcel post shipments, and commodities moved by own power (motorized vehicles, aircraft, etc.) or towed (prefabricated buildings, etc.). Local shipments (commodities shipped less than 25 miles from the plant) and shipments within the same city are also excluded. Shipments to Alaska and Hawaii from the 48 conterminous States and the District of Columbia are included; however, no data were obtained for shipments originating in Alaska and Hawaii.

- Represents zero or rounds to zero.   (D) Withheld to avoid disclosing figures for individual companies.

[1]Production of this commodity is concentrated in the geographic divisions shown; figures and distributions for geographic divisions not shown are included in the total.

[2]Distances of shipments to foreign destinations are calculated only to the U.S. port of exit.

[3]Includes only shipments represented by bills of lading and invoices. Summary records which did not show individual weights of shipments are not included.

TCC 225. Knit Fabrics

Comparisons of Tons and Ton-Miles of Shipments for
Geographic Divisions of Origin and for Sampling Variability: 1972 and 1967

Geographic division of origin	Estimates				Relative sampling variability in tons (percent)	
	1972		1967		1972	1967
	Tons (thousands)	Ton-miles (millions)	Tons (thousands)	Ton-miles (millions)	1972	1967
U.S. total	840	346	(*)	(*)	17.8	(*)
New England	(D)	(D)	(*)	(*)	(*)	(*)
Middle Atlantic	315	121	(*)	(*)	39.6	(*)
East North Central	(D)	(D)	(*)	(*)	(*)	(*)
West North Central	(D)	(D)	(*)	(*)	(*)	(*)
South Atlantic	408	153	.(*)	(*)	31.6	(*)
East South Central	(D)	(D)	(*)	(*)	(*)	(*)
West South Central	(D)	(D)	(*)	(*)	(*)	(*)
Mountain	(D)	(D)	(*)	(*)	(*)	(*)
Pacific	(D)	(D)	(*)	(*)	(*)	(*)

(D) Withheld to avoid disclosing figures for individual companies.   (*) Data not published.

TABLE 1. **TCC GROUP 225**—Percent Distribution of Geographic Division of Origin and Distance Shipped, by Means of Transport: 1972

Geographic division of origin[1] and distance shipped[2]	Number	Percent distribution by means of transport							
		All means of transport	Rail	Motor carrier	Private truck	Air	Water	Other	Unknown
TONS OF SHIPMENTS	(thousands of tons)								
U.S. TOTAL..........	840	100.0	.7	62.4	36.3	.2	-	.4	.1
MIDDLE ATLANTIC........	315	100.0	-	78.7	20.9	.1	-	.2	.1
UNDER 100 MILES......	139	100.0	-	79.1	20.8	-	-	-	-
100 TO 199 MILES......	59	100.0	-	97.3	1.8	-	-	.6	.3
200 TO 299 MILES......	38	100.0	-	10.3	89.6	-	-	.1	-
300 TO 499 MILES......	19	100.0	-	94.9	5.0	-	-	.2	-
500 TO 999 MILES......	26	100.0	-	97.0	1.9	.4	-	.7	-
1000 TO 1499 MILES....	4	100.0	-	97.1	-	2.7	-	.2	-
1500 MILES OR OVER....	28	100.0	.5	99.0	-	.2	-	.2	-
SOUTH ATLANTIC..........	408	100.0	-	49.7	49.4	.1	-	.7	-
UNDER 100 MILES......	83	100.0	-	25.4	74.4	-	-	.1	-
100 TO 199 MILES......	67	100.0	-	29.9	70.1	-	-	.1	-
200 TO 299 MILES......	48	100.0	-	58.7	41.2	-	-	.2	-
300 TO 499 MILES......	88	100.0	-	79.5	19.0	.3	-	1.2	-
500 TO 999 MILES......	103	100.0	-	53.6	45.6	.1	-	.7	-
1000 TO 1499 MILES....	11	100.0	-	25.4	73.8	-	-	.8	-
1500 MILES OR OVER....	5	100.0	1.9	80.7	.6	3.9	-	12.9	-
TON-MILES OF SHIPMENTS	(millions of ton-miles)								
U.S. TOTAL..........	346	100.0	2.0	68.7	27.8	.4	-	.8	.2
MIDDLE ATLANTIC........	121	100.0	.3	90.1	8.9	.3	-	.3	-
UNDER 100 MILES......	3	100.0	-	87.7	12.2	-	-	.1	-
100 TO 199 MILES......	8	100.0	-	97.5	1.4	-	-	.7	.3
200 TO 299 MILES......	10	100.0	-	9.8	90.1	-	-	.1	-
300 TO 499 MILES......	8	100.0	-	94.3	5.6	-	-	.2	-
500 TO 999 MILES......	18	100.0	-	97.2	1.6	.6	-	.7	-
1000 TO 1499 MILES....	4	100.0	-	97.2	-	2.6	-	.2	-
1500 MILES OR OVER....	67	100.0	.6	99.0	-	.3	-	.1	-
SOUTH ATLANTIC..........	153	100.0	.1	58.9	38.7	.4	-	1.8	-
UNDER 100 MILES......	4	100.0	-	36.9	62.9	-	-	.1	-
100 TO 199 MILES......	10	100.0	-	29.1	70.8	-	-	.1	-
200 TO 299 MILES......	13	100.0	-	58.2	41.7	-	-	.2	-
300 TO 499 MILES......	35	100.0	-	79.8	18.7	.3	-	1.1	-
500 TO 999 MILES......	65	100.0	-	55.8	43.3	.1	-	.7	-
1000 TO 1499 MILES....	12	100.0	-	25.8	73.2	.1	-	.9	-
1500 MILES OR OVER....	12	100.0	1.7	80.4	.6	3.9	-	13.4	-

See footnotes at end of table 4.

TABLE 2. **TCC GROUP 225**—Percent Distribution of Geographic Division of Origin and Means of Transport, by Geographic Division of Destination: 1972

Geographic division of origin[1] and means of transport	Number	Percent distribution by division of destination									
		U.S. total	New England	Middle Atlantic	East North Central	West North Central	South Atlantic	East South Central	West South Central	Mountain	Pacific
TONS OF SHIPMENTS	(thousands of tons)										
U.S. TOTAL................	840	100.0	5.6	43.1	4.1	1.2	34.5	4.7	2.3	.8	3.7
RAIL................	6	100.0	-	-	26.3	-	32.1	31.1	-	1.4	9.2
MOTOR CARRIER..........	578	100.0	8.2	53.4	3.6	1.9	18.6	5.6	1.7	1.2	5.7
PRIVATE TRUCK..........	336	100.0	1.2	26.7	4.3	-	62.1	2.3	3.3	-	-
AIR..................	1	100.0	.4	16.7	8.3	8.1	11.6	32.9	.4	1.8	19.8
WATER...............	-	100.0	-	-	-	-	-	-	-	-	-
OTHER...............	3	100.0	4.9	30.0	10.1	3.7	22.6	3.2	3.8	1.9	19.9
UNKNOWN..............	-	100.0	-	23.3	-	-	-	76.7	-	-	-
MIDDLE ATLANTIC..........	315	100.0	2.1	60.7	2.3	.8	22.5	1.9	.7	1.4	7.7
RAIL................	-	100.0	-	-	-	-	-	-	-	-	100.0
MOTOR CARRIER..........	248	100.0	2.6	64.8	2.9	1.0	14.2	2.2	.8	1.7	9.7
PRIVATE TRUCK..........	65	100.0	-	45.6	-	-	54.0	.4	-	-	-
AIR..................	-	100.0	-	4.7	1.3	30.9	41.2	-	-	-	22.0
WATER...............	-	100.0	-	-	-	-	-	-	-	-	-
OTHER...............	-	100.0	6.4	56.1	7.6	1.4	16.3	5.9	2.5	.7	3.2
UNKNOWN..............	-	100.0	-	100.0	-	-	-	-	-	-	-
SOUTH ATLANTIC..........	408	100.0	6.9	31.2	5.3	1.8	42.7	7.1	3.5	.2	1.3
RAIL................	-	100.0	-	-	-	-	-	-	-	78.7	21.3
MOTOR CARRIER..........	202	100.0	13.1	33.2	6.1	3.4	28.1	10.7	2.8	.3	2.2
PRIVATE TRUCK..........	201	100.0	.7	29.4	4.4	-	57.8	3.5	4.2	-	-
AIR..................	-	100.0	1.0	36.2	17.4	2.6	1.4	2.6	.3	4.2	34.3
WATER...............	-	100.0	-	-	-	-	-	-	-	-	-
OTHER...............	2	100.0	4.6	17.5	11.4	4.6	26.3	2.7	4.4	2.4	26.0
UNKNOWN..............	-	100.0	-	-	-	-	-	-	-	-	-

See footnotes at end of table 4.

TABLE 2. **TCC GROUP 225—Percent Distribution of Geographic Division of Origin and Means of Transport, by Geographic Division of Destination: 1972**—Continued

Geographic division of origin [1] and means of transport	Number	Percent distribution by division of destination									
		U.S. total	New England	Middle Atlantic	East North Central	West North Central	South Atlantic	East South Central	West South Central	Mountain	Pacific
TON-MILES OF SHIPMENTS	(millions of ton-miles)										
U.S. TOTAL..............	346	100.0	6.6	23.7	4.7	2.7	25.7	5.6	5.8	3.7	21.4
RAIL...................	7	100.0	-	-	19.3	-	24.9	34.2	-	2.1	19.6
MOTOR CARRIER.........	264	100.0	9.1	22.9	4.1	3.9	15.2	5.7	4.2	5.3	29.7
PRIVATE TRUCK.........	107	100.0	1.1	27.9	5.3	-	52.8	2.3	10.5	-	.1
AIR...................	1	100.0	.3	6.3	4.8	6.4	10.1	27.9	.4	3.1	40.8
WATER.................	-	100.0	-	-	-	-	-	-	-	-	-
OTHER.................	3	100.0	3.1	13.9	6.5	3.9	9.7	1.6	4.5	3.6	53.2
UNKNOWN...............	-	100.0	-	4.3	-	-	-	95.7	-	-	-
MIDDLE ATLANTIC.........	121	100.0	1.1	9.2	3.7	2.1	22.8	3.5	2.1	7.1	48.4
RAIL...................	-	100.0	-	-	-	-	-	-	-	-	100.0
MOTOR CARRIER.........	109	100.0	1.2	9.6	4.1	2.3	15.9	3.7	2.3	7.9	53.1
PRIVATE TRUCK.........	10	100.0	-	5.0	-	-	93.4	1.6	-	-	-
AIR...................	-	100.0	-	.1	.8	21.9	34.3	-	-	-	42.9
WATER.................	-	100.0	-	-	-	-	-	-	-	-	-
OTHER.................	-	100.0	2.9	20.1	10.7	3.4	23.8	7.8	9.0	3.7	18.6
UNKNOWN...............	-	100.0	-	100.0	-	-	-	-	-	-	-
SOUTH ATLANTIC..........	153	100.0	9.6	39.1	7.2	4.0	16.4	5.5	9.6	.9	7.6
RAIL...................	-	100.0	-	-	-	-	-	-	-	74.0	26.0
MOTOR CARRIER.........	90	100.0	15.1	33.6	6.1	6.6	13.7	7.2	6.2	1.1	10.4
PRIVATE TRUCK.........	59	100.0	1.5	49.4	9.1	.1	21.3	3.3	15.2	-	.1
AIR...................	-	100.0	.6	13.8	9.6	1.5	.4	1.4	.2	6.8	65.7
WATER.................	-	100.0	-	-	-	-	-	-	-	-	-
OTHER.................	2	100.0	3.1	8.4	6.4	4.2	8.6	.9	4.2	3.8	60.3
UNKNOWN...............	-	100.0	-	-	-	-	-	-	-	-	-

See footnotes at end of table 4.

TABLE 3. TCC GROUP 225—Percent Distribution of Geographic Division of Destination and Means of Transport, by Geographic Division of Origin: 1972

Geographic division of destination and means of transport	Number (thousands of tons)	Percent distribution by division of origin[1]									
		U.S. total	New England	Middle Atlantic	East North Central	West North Central	South Atlantic	East South Central	West South Central	Mountain	Pacific
TONS OF SHIPMENTS											
U.S. TOTAL	840	100.0	(D)	34.0	(D)	(D)	44.0	(D)	(D)	(D)	(D)
RAIL	6	100.0	(D)	2.4	(D)	(D)	1.7	(D)	(D)	(D)	(D)
MOTOR CARRIER	578	100.0	(D)	43.0	(D)	(D)	35.1	(D)	(D)	(D)	(D)
PRIVATE TRUCK	336	100.0	(D)	19.6	(D)	(D)	59.9	(D)	(D)	(D)	(D)
AIR	1	100.0	(D)	22.5	(D)	(D)	43.3	(D)	(D)	(D)	(D)
WATER	-	100.0	(D)	-	(D)	(D)	-	(D)	(D)	(D)	(D)
OTHER	3	100.0	(D)	19.8	(D)	(D)	73.7	(D)	(D)	(D)	(D)
UNKNOWN	-	100.0	(D)	20.8	(D)	(D)	-	(D)	(D)	(D)	(D)
NEW ENGLAND	51	100.0	(D)	12.6	(D)	(D)	54.3	(D)	(D)	(D)	(D)
RAIL	-	100.0	(D)	-	(D)	(D)	-	(D)	(D)	(D)	(D)
MOTOR CARRIER	47	100.0	(D)	13.7	(D)	(D)	56.0	(D)	(D)	(D)	(D)
PRIVATE TRUCK	4	100.0	(D)	-	(D)	(D)	34.1	(D)	(D)	(D)	(D)
AIR	-	100.0	(D)	-	(D)	(D)	100.0	(D)	(D)	(D)	(D)
WATER	-	100.0	(D)	-	(D)	(D)	-	(D)	(D)	(D)	(D)
OTHER	-	100.0	(D)	26.2	(D)	(D)	69.9	(D)	(D)	(D)	(D)
UNKNOWN	-	100.0	(D)	-	(D)	(D)	-	(D)	(D)	(D)	(D)
MIDDLE ATLANTIC	400	100.0	(D)	47.9	(D)	(D)	31.8	(D)	(D)	(D)	(D)
RAIL	-	100.0	(D)	-	(D)	(D)	-	(D)	(D)	(D)	(D)
MOTOR CARRIER	308	100.0	(D)	52.1	(D)	(D)	21.8	(D)	(D)	(D)	(D)
PRIVATE TRUCK	89	100.0	(D)	33.4	(D)	(D)	66.0	(D)	(D)	(D)	(D)
AIR	-	100.0	(D)	6.3	(D)	(D)	93.7	(D)	(D)	(D)	(D)
WATER	-	100.0	(D)	-	(D)	(D)	-	(D)	(D)	(D)	(D)
OTHER	1	100.0	(D)	37.1	(D)	(D)	43.0	(D)	(D)	(D)	(D)
UNKNOWN	-	100.0	(D)	89.1	(D)	(D)	-	(D)	(D)	(D)	(D)
EAST NORTH CENTRAL	37	100.0	(D)	19.6	(D)	(D)	57.4	(D)	(D)	(D)	(D)
RAIL	1	100.0	(D)	-	(D)	(D)	-	(D)	(D)	(D)	(D)
MOTOR CARRIER	20	100.0	(D)	35.1	(D)	(D)	59.2	(D)	(D)	(D)	(D)
PRIVATE TRUCK	14	100.0	(D)	-	(D)	(D)	60.6	(D)	(D)	(D)	(D)
AIR	-	100.0	(D)	3.5	(D)	(D)	90.6	(D)	(D)	(D)	(D)
WATER	-	100.0	(D)	-	(D)	(D)	-	(D)	(D)	(D)	(D)
OTHER	-	100.0	(D)	14.9	(D)	(D)	83.6	(D)	(D)	(D)	(D)
UNKNOWN	-	100.0	(D)	-	(D)	(D)	-	(D)	(D)	(D)	(D)
WEST NORTH CENTRAL	11	100.0	(D)	22.8	(D)	(D)	62.8	(D)	(D)	(D)	(D)
RAIL	-	100.0	(D)	-	(D)	(D)	-	(D)	(D)	(D)	(D)
MOTOR CARRIER	11	100.0	(D)	22.5	(D)	(D)	62.7	(D)	(D)	(D)	(D)
PRIVATE TRUCK	-	100.0	(D)	-	(D)	(D)	100.0	(D)	(D)	(D)	(D)
AIR	-	100.0	(D)	85.9	(D)	(D)	14.1	(D)	(D)	(D)	(D)
WATER	-	100.0	(D)	-	(D)	(D)	-	(D)	(D)	(D)	(D)
OTHER	-	100.0	(D)	7.2	(D)	(D)	91.4	(D)	(D)	(D)	(D)
UNKNOWN	-	100.0	(D)	-	(D)	(D)	-	(D)	(D)	(D)	(D)
SOUTH ATLANTIC	319	100.0	(D)	22.2	(D)	(D)	54.5	(D)	(D)	(D)	(D)
RAIL	2	100.0	(D)	-	(D)	(D)	-	(D)	(D)	(D)	(D)
MOTOR CARRIER	107	100.0	(D)	32.7	(D)	(D)	53.0	(D)	(D)	(D)	(D)
PRIVATE TRUCK	209	100.0	(D)	17.0	(D)	(D)	55.7	(D)	(D)	(D)	(D)
AIR	-	100.0	(D)	80.0	(D)	(D)	5.3	(D)	(D)	(D)	(D)
WATER	-	100.0	(D)	-	(D)	(D)	-	(D)	(D)	(D)	(D)
OTHER	-	100.0	(D)	14.3	(D)	(D)	85.7	(D)	(D)	(D)	(D)
UNKNOWN	-	100.0	(D)	-	(D)	(D)	-	(D)	(D)	(D)	(D)
EAST SOUTH CENTRAL	43	100.0	(D)	13.5	(D)	(D)	66.2	(D)	(D)	(D)	(D)
RAIL	2	100.0	(D)	-	(D)	(D)	-	(D)	(D)	(D)	(D)
MOTOR CARRIER	32	100.0	(D)	17.1	(D)	(D)	66.6	(D)	(D)	(D)	(D)
PRIVATE TRUCK	7	100.0	(D)	3.6	(D)	(D)	91.8	(D)	(D)	(D)	(D)
AIR	-	100.0	(D)	-	(D)	(D)	3.4	(D)	(D)	(D)	(D)
WATER	-	100.0	(D)	-	(D)	(D)	-	(D)	(D)	(D)	(D)
OTHER	-	100.0	(D)	36.7	(D)	(D)	63.2	(D)	(D)	(D)	(D)
UNKNOWN	-	100.0	(D)	-	(D)	(D)	-	(D)	(D)	(D)	(D)
WEST SOUTH CENTRAL	21	100.0	(D)	10.1	(D)	(D)	67.6	(D)	(D)	(D)	(D)
RAIL	-	100.0	(D)	-	(D)	(D)	-	(D)	(D)	(D)	(D)
MOTOR CARRIER	9	100.0	(D)	21.4	(D)	(D)	58.6	(D)	(D)	(D)	(D)
PRIVATE TRUCK	11	100.0	(D)	-	(D)	(D)	75.4	(D)	(D)	(D)	(D)
AIR	-	100.0	(D)	-	(D)	(D)	34.9	(D)	(D)	(D)	(D)
WATER	-	100.0	(D)	-	(D)	(D)	-	(D)	(D)	(D)	(D)
OTHER	-	100.0	(D)	13.0	(D)	(D)	87.0	(D)	(D)	(D)	(D)
UNKNOWN	-	100.0	(D)	-	(D)	(D)	-	(D)	(D)	(D)	(D)
MOUNTAIN	7	100.0	(D)	58.2	(D)	(D)	11.4	(D)	(D)	(D)	(D)
RAIL	-	100.0	(D)	-	(D)	(D)	100.0	(D)	(D)	(D)	(D)
MOTOR CARRIER	7	100.0	(D)	59.8	(D)	(D)	9.0	(D)	(D)	(D)	(D)
PRIVATE TRUCK	-	100.0	(D)	-	(D)	(D)	100.0	(D)	(D)	(D)	(D)
AIR	-	100.0	(D)	-	(D)	(D)	100.0	(D)	(D)	(D)	(D)
WATER	-	100.0	(D)	-	(D)	(D)	-	(D)	(D)	(D)	(D)
OTHER	-	100.0	(D)	7.7	(D)	(D)	92.3	(D)	(D)	(D)	(D)
UNKNOWN	-	100.0	(D)	-	(D)	(D)	-	(D)	(D)	(D)	(D)
PACIFIC	34	100.0	(D)	70.0	(D)	(D)	15.6	(D)	(D)	(D)	(D)
RAIL	-	100.0	(D)	26.4	(D)	(D)	4.0	(D)	(D)	(D)	(D)
MOTOR CARRIER	32	100.0	(D)	72.8	(D)	(D)	13.3	(D)	(D)	(D)	(D)
PRIVATE TRUCK	-	100.0	(D)	-	(D)	(D)	100.0	(D)	(D)	(D)	(D)
AIR	-	100.0	(D)	24.9	(D)	(D)	75.1	(D)	(D)	(D)	(D)
WATER	-	100.0	(D)	-	(D)	(D)	-	(D)	(D)	(D)	(D)
OTHER	-	100.0	(D)	3.2	(D)	(D)	96.6	(D)	(D)	(D)	(D)
UNKNOWN	-	100.0	(D)	-	(D)	(D)	-	(D)	(D)	(D)	(D)

See footnotes at end of table 4.

TABLE 3. **TCC GROUP 225**—Percent Distribution of Geographic Division of Destination and Means of Transport, by Geographic Division of Origin: 1972—Continued

Geographic division of destination and means of transport	Number	Percent distribution by division of origin[1]									
		U.S. total	New England	Middle Atlantic	East North Central	West North Central	South Atlantic	East South Central	West South Central	Mountain	Pacific
TON-MILES OF SHIPMENTS	(millions of ton-miles)										
U.S. TOTAL	346	100.0	(D)	31.5	(D)	(D)	39.7	(D)	(D)	(D)	(D)
RAIL	7	100.0	(D)	5.1	(D)	(D)	2.8	(D)	(D)	(D)	(D)
MOTOR CARRIER	264	100.0	(D)	41.3	(D)	(D)	34.1	(D)	(D)	(D)	(D)
PRIVATE TRUCK	107	100.0	(D)	10.1	(D)	(D)	55.2	(D)	(D)	(D)	(D)
AIR	1	100.0	(D)	26.0	(D)	(D)	45.1	(D)	(D)	(D)	(D)
WATER	-	100.0	(D)	-	(D)	(D)	-	(D)	(D)	(D)	(D)
OTHER	3	100.0	(D)	10.0	(D)	(D)	84.9	(D)	(D)	(D)	(D)
UNKNOWN	-	100.0	(D)	2.9	(D)	(D)	-	(D)	(D)	(D)	(D)
NEW ENGLAND	25	100.0	(D)	5.1	(D)	(D)	57.8	(D)	(D)	(D)	(D)
RAIL	-	100.0	(D)	-	(D)	(D)	-	(D)	(D)	(D)	(D)
MOTOR CARRIER	23	100.0	(D)	5.3	(D)	(D)	56.8	(D)	(D)	(D)	(D)
PRIVATE TRUCK	1	100.0	(D)	-	(D)	(D)	75.3	(D)	(D)	(D)	(D)
AIR	-	100.0	(D)	-	(D)	(D)	100.0	(D)	(D)	(D)	(D)
WATER	-	100.0	(D)	-	(D)	(D)	-	(D)	(D)	(D)	(D)
OTHER	-	100.0	(D)	9.2	(D)	(D)	84.5	(D)	(D)	(D)	(D)
UNKNOWN	-	100.0	(D)	-	(D)	(D)	-	(D)	(D)	(D)	(D)
MIDDLE ATLANTIC	91	100.0	(D)	12.2	(D)	(D)	65.6	(D)	(D)	(D)	(D)
RAIL	-	100.0	(D)	-	(D)	(D)	-	(D)	(D)	(D)	(D)
MOTOR CARRIER	60	100.0	(D)	17.2	(D)	(D)	50.0	(D)	(D)	(D)	(D)
PRIVATE TRUCK	29	100.0	(D)	1.8	(D)	(D)	97.5	(D)	(D)	(D)	(D)
AIR	-	100.0	(D)	.5	(D)	(D)	99.5	(D)	(D)	(D)	(D)
WATER	-	100.0	(D)	-	(D)	(D)	-	(D)	(D)	(D)	(D)
OTHER	-	100.0	(D)	14.4	(D)	(D)	51.2	(D)	(D)	(D)	(D)
UNKNOWN	-	100.0	(D)	67.2	(D)	(D)	-	(D)	(D)	(D)	(D)
EAST NORTH CENTRAL	18	100.0	(D)	24.7	(D)	(D)	60.7	(D)	(D)	(D)	(D)
RAIL	1	100.0	(D)	-	(D)	(D)	-	(D)	(D)	(D)	(D)
MOTOR CARRIER	10	100.0	(D)	41.1	(D)	(D)	50.4	(D)	(D)	(D)	(D)
PRIVATE TRUCK	5	100.0	(D)	-	(D)	(D)	95.3	(D)	(D)	(D)	(D)
AIR	-	100.0	(D)	4.1	(D)	(D)	89.5	(D)	(D)	(D)	(D)
WATER	-	100.0	(D)	-	(D)	(D)	-	(D)	(D)	(D)	(D)
OTHER	-	100.0	(D)	16.5	(D)	(D)	83.4	(D)	(D)	(D)	(D)
UNKNOWN	-	100.0	(D)	-	(D)	(D)	-	(D)	(D)	(D)	(D)
WEST NORTH CENTRAL	10	100.0	(D)	24.4	(D)	(D)	57.8	(D)	(D)	(D)	(D)
RAIL	-	100.0	(D)	-	(D)	(D)	-	(D)	(D)	(D)	(D)
MOTOR CARRIER	10	100.0	(D)	24.1	(D)	(D)	57.6	(D)	(D)	(D)	(D)
PRIVATE TRUCK	-	100.0	(D)	-	(D)	(D)	100.0	(D)	(D)	(D)	(D)
AIR	-	100.0	(D)	89.7	(D)	(D)	10.3	(D)	(D)	(D)	(D)
WATER	-	100.0	(D)	-	(D)	(D)	-	(D)	(D)	(D)	(D)
OTHER	-	100.0	(D)	8.7	(D)	(D)	90.8	(D)	(D)	(D)	(D)
UNKNOWN	-	100.0	(D)	-	(D)	(D)	-	(D)	(D)	(D)	(D)
SOUTH ATLANTIC	99	100.0	(D)	28.0	(D)	(D)	25.4	(D)	(D)	(D)	(D)
RAIL	1	100.0	(D)	-	(D)	(D)	-	(D)	(D)	(D)	(D)
MOTOR CARRIER	40	100.0	(D)	43.3	(D)	(D)	30.6	(D)	(D)	(D)	(D)
PRIVATE TRUCK	56	100.0	(D)	17.9	(D)	(D)	22.3	(D)	(D)	(D)	(D)
AIR	-	100.0	(D)	88.8	(D)	(D)	1.6	(D)	(D)	(D)	(D)
WATER	-	100.0	(D)	-	(D)	(D)	-	(D)	(D)	(D)	(D)
OTHER	-	100.0	(D)	24.5	(D)	(D)	75.5	(D)	(D)	(D)	(D)
UNKNOWN	-	100.0	(D)	-	(D)	(D)	-	(D)	(D)	(D)	(D)
EAST SOUTH CENTRAL	21	100.0	(D)	19.6	(D)	(D)	39.3	(D)	(D)	(D)	(D)
RAIL	2	100.0	(D)	-	(D)	(D)	-	(D)	(D)	(D)	(D)
MOTOR CARRIER	15	100.0	(D)	26.8	(D)	(D)	42.9	(D)	(D)	(D)	(D)
PRIVATE TRUCK	2	100.0	(D)	7.0	(D)	(D)	79.2	(D)	(D)	(D)	(D)
AIR	-	100.0	(D)	-	(D)	(D)	2.3	(D)	(D)	(D)	(D)
WATER	-	100.0	(D)	-	(D)	(D)	-	(D)	(D)	(D)	(D)
OTHER	-	100.0	(D)	49.2	(D)	(D)	50.8	(D)	(D)	(D)	(D)
UNKNOWN	-	100.0	(D)	-	(D)	(D)	-	(D)	(D)	(D)	(D)
WEST SOUTH CENTRAL	22	100.0	(D)	11.2	(D)	(D)	65.8	(D)	(D)	(D)	(D)
RAIL	-	100.0	(D)	-	(D)	(D)	-	(D)	(D)	(D)	(D)
MOTOR CARRIER	11	100.0	(D)	22.6	(D)	(D)	50.8	(D)	(D)	(D)	(D)
PRIVATE TRUCK	11	100.0	(D)	-	(D)	(D)	80.4	(D)	(D)	(D)	(D)
AIR	-	100.0	(D)	-	(D)	(D)	25.7	(D)	(D)	(D)	(D)
WATER	-	100.0	(D)	-	(D)	(D)	-	(D)	(D)	(D)	(D)
OTHER	-	100.0	(D)	20.0	(D)	(D)	80.0	(D)	(D)	(D)	(D)
UNKNOWN	-	100.0	(D)	-	(D)	(D)	-	(D)	(D)	(D)	(D)
MOUNTAIN	14	100.0	(D)	60.5	(D)	(D)	9.5	(D)	(D)	(D)	(D)
RAIL	-	100.0	(D)	-	(D)	(D)	100.0	(D)	(D)	(D)	(D)
MOTOR CARRIER	13	100.0	(D)	61.9	(D)	(D)	7.4	(D)	(D)	(D)	(D)
PRIVATE TRUCK	-	100.0	(D)	-	(D)	(D)	100.0	(D)	(D)	(D)	(D)
AIR	-	100.0	(D)	-	(D)	(D)	100.0	(D)	(D)	(D)	(D)
WATER	-	100.0	(D)	-	(D)	(D)	-	(D)	(D)	(D)	(D)
OTHER	-	100.0	(D)	10.1	(D)	(D)	89.9	(D)	(D)	(D)	(D)
UNKNOWN	-	100.0	(D)	-	(D)	(D)	-	(D)	(D)	(D)	(D)
PACIFIC	82	100.0	(D)	71.2	(D)	(D)	14.1	(D)	(D)	(D)	(D)
RAIL	1	100.0	(D)	26.1	(D)	(D)	3.7	(D)	(D)	(D)	(D)
MOTOR CARRIER	78	100.0	(D)	74.0	(D)	(D)	12.0	(D)	(D)	(D)	(D)
PRIVATE TRUCK	-	100.0	(D)	-	(D)	(D)	100.0	(D)	(D)	(D)	(D)
AIR	-	100.0	(D)	27.4	(D)	(D)	72.6	(D)	(D)	(D)	(D)
WATER	-	100.0	(D)	-	(D)	(D)	-	(D)	(D)	(D)	(D)
OTHER	1	100.0	(D)	3.5	(D)	(D)	96.4	(D)	(D)	(D)	(D)
UNKNOWN	-	100.0	(D)	-	(D)	(D)	-	(D)	(D)	(D)	(D)

See footnotes at end of table 4.

TABLE 4. TCC GROUP 225—Percent Distribution of Distance Shipped and Weight of Shipment, by Means of Transport: 1972

Distance shipped and weight of shipment [2] [3]	Number	Percent distribution by means of transport							
		All means of transport	Rail	Motor carrier	Private truck	Air	Water	Other	Unknown
TONS OF SHIPMENTS	(thousands of tons)								
U.S. TOTAL	832	100.0	.7	62.1	36.5	.2	-	.4	.1
UNDER 100 MILES	240	100.0	-	58.7	41.3	-	-	.1	-
UNDER 1000 POUNDS	36	100.0	-	93.0	6.6	-	-	.4	-
1000 TO 9999 POUNDS	144	100.0	-	68.6	31.2	-	-	-	-
10000 TO 29999 POUNDS	57	100.0	-	10.2	89.8	-	-	-	-
30000 TO 59999 POUNDS	1	100.0	-	100.0	-	-	-	-	-
60000 TO 89999 POUNDS	-	100.0	-	-	-	-	-	-	-
90000 POUNDS AND OVER	-	100.0	-	-	-	-	-	-	-
100 TO 199 MILES	185	100.0	-	73.4	26.3	-	-	.2	.1
UNDER 1000 POUNDS	24	100.0	-	90.4	7.0	-	-	1.8	.8
1000 TO 9999 POUNDS	125	100.0	-	76.3	23.7	-	-	-	-
10000 TO 29999 POUNDS	34	100.0	-	49.1	50.9	-	-	-	-
30000 TO 59999 POUNDS	2	100.0	-	100.0	-	-	-	-	-
60000 TO 89999 POUNDS	-	100.0	-	-	-	-	-	-	-
90000 POUNDS AND OVER	-	100.0	-	-	-	-	-	-	-
200 TO 299 MILES	94	100.0	-	42.4	57.5	-	-	.1	-
UNDER 1000 POUNDS	19	100.0	-	75.2	24.1	-	-	.7	-
1000 TO 9999 POUNDS	46	100.0	-	54.8	45.2	-	-	-	-
10000 TO 29999 POUNDS	28	100.0	-	-	100.0	-	-	-	-
30000 TO 59999 POUNDS	-	100.0	-	-	-	-	-	-	-
60000 TO 89999 POUNDS	-	100.0	-	-	-	-	-	-	-
90000 POUNDS AND OVER	-	100.0	-	-	-	-	-	-	-
300 TO 499 MILES	111	100.0	-	82.9	15.9	.2	-	1.0	-
UNDER 1000 POUNDS	15	100.0	-	79.4	15.0	1.6	-	3.9	-
1000 TO 9999 POUNDS	62	100.0	-	88.3	10.9	-	-	.8	-
10000 TO 29999 POUNDS	34	100.0	-	74.6	25.4	-	-	-	-
30000 TO 59999 POUNDS	-	100.0	-	-	-	-	-	-	-
60000 TO 89999 POUNDS	-	100.0	-	-	-	-	-	-	-
90000 POUNDS AND OVER	-	100.0	-	-	-	-	-	-	-
500 TO 999 MILES	216	100.0	1.7	47.8	49.6	.3	-	.5	-
UNDER 1000 POUNDS	27	100.0	-	73.2	21.3	1.4	-	4.1	-
1000 TO 9999 POUNDS	105	100.0	1.6	66.1	32.0	.3	-	-	-
10000 TO 29999 POUNDS	82	100.0	2.5	14.9	82.6	-	-	-	-
30000 TO 59999 POUNDS	1	100.0	-	100.0	-	-	-	-	-
60000 TO 89999 POUNDS	-	100.0	-	-	-	-	-	-	-
90000 POUNDS AND OVER	-	100.0	-	-	-	-	-	-	-
1000 TO 1499 MILES	22	100.0	8.8	49.1	37.8	.5	-	.4	3.3
UNDER 1000 POUNDS	3	100.0	-	94.0	.3	3.1	-	2.6	-
1000 TO 9999 POUNDS	13	100.0	15.0	56.0	23.4	-	-	-	5.6
10000 TO 29999 POUNDS	1	100.0	-	-	100.0	-	-	-	-
30000 TO 59999 POUNDS	4	100.0	-	-	100.0	-	-	-	-
60000 TO 89999 POUNDS	-	100.0	-	-	-	-	-	-	-
90000 POUNDS AND OVER	-	100.0	-	-	-	-	-	-	-
1500 MILES OR OVER	48	100.0	1.4	96.2	.1	.6	-	1.7	-
UNDER 1000 POUNDS	8	100.0	6.0	86.1	.4	2.8	-	4.7	-
1000 TO 9999 POUNDS	33	100.0	.5	98.2	-	.2	-	1.2	-
10000 TO 29999 POUNDS	6	100.0	-	100.0	-	-	-	-	-
30000 TO 59999 POUNDS	-	100.0	-	-	-	-	-	-	-
60000 TO 89999 POUNDS	-	100.0	-	-	-	-	-	-	-
90000 POUNDS AND OVER	-	100.0	-	-	-	-	-	-	-
TON-MILES OF SHIPMENTS	(millions of ton-miles)								
U.S. TOTAL	343	100.0	2.0	68.6	27.9	.4	-	.8	.2
UNDER 100 MILES	8	100.0	-	59.3	40.5	-	-	.1	-
UNDER 1000 POUNDS	1	100.0	-	90.6	8.6	-	-	.7	-
1000 TO 9999 POUNDS	4	100.0	-	71.2	28.7	-	-	-	-
10000 TO 29999 POUNDS	2	100.0	-	17.4	82.6	-	-	-	-
30000 TO 59999 POUNDS	-	100.0	-	100.0	-	-	-	-	-
60000 TO 89999 POUNDS	-	100.0	-	-	-	-	-	-	-
90000 POUNDS AND OVER	-	100.0	-	-	-	-	-	-	-
100 TO 199 MILES	29	100.0	-	74.4	25.3	-	-	.2	.1
UNDER 1000 POUNDS	3	100.0	-	91.0	6.4	-	-	1.9	.7
1000 TO 9999 POUNDS	19	100.0	-	78.3	21.7	-	-	-	-
10000 TO 29999 POUNDS	5	100.0	-	48.2	51.8	-	-	-	-
30000 TO 59999 POUNDS	-	100.0	-	100.0	-	-	-	-	-
60000 TO 89999 POUNDS	-	100.0	-	-	-	-	-	-	-
90000 POUNDS AND OVER	-	100.0	-	-	-	-	-	-	-

See footnotes at end of table 4.

TABLE 4. **TCC GROUP 225—Percent Distribution of Distance Shipped and Weight of Shipment, by Means of Transport: 1972**—Continued

Distance shipped and weight of shipment [2] [3]	Number	Percent distribution by means of transport							
		All means of transport	Rail	Motor carrier	Private truck	Air	Water	Other	Unknown
TON-MILES OF SHIPMENTS	(millions of ton-miles)								
200 TO 299 MILES.........	25	100.0	-	41.4	58.4	-	-	.1	-
UNDER 1000 POUNDS......	5	100.0	-	73.9	25.4	-	-	.7	-
1000 TO 9999 POUNDS...	12	100.0	-	54.1	45.9	-	-	-	-
10000 TO 29999 POUNDS.	7	100.0	-	-	100.0	-	-	-	-
30000 TO 59999 POUNDS.	-	100.0	-	-	-	-	-	-	-
60000 TO 89999 POUNDS.	-	100.0	-	-	-	-	-	-	-
90000 POUNDS AND OVER.	-	100.0	-	-	-	-	-	-	-
300 TO 499 MILES........	45	100.0	-	83.1	15.7	.2	-	.9	-
UNDER 1000 POUNDS.....	6	100.0	-	79.7	14.5	1.7	-	4.1	-
1000 TO 9999 POUNDS...	24	100.0	-	88.7	10.6	-	-	.7	-
10000 TO 29999 POUNDS.	14	100.0	-	75.0	25.0	-	-	-	-
30000 TO 59999 POUNDS.	-	100.0	-	-	-	-	-	-	-
60000 TO 89999 POUNDS.	-	100.0	-	-	-	-	-	-	-
90000 POUNDS AND OVER.	-	100.0	-	-	-	-	-	-	-
500 TO 999 MILES........	139	100.0	2.4	50.3	46.3	.4	-	.5	-
UNDER 1000 POUNDS.....	19	100.0	-	75.7	19.0	1.4	-	4.0	-
1000 TO 9999 POUNDS...	69	100.0	2.1	67.3	30.1	.5	-	-	-
10000 TO 29999 POUNDS.	49	100.0	3.8	15.8	80.4	-	-	-	-
30000 TO 59999 POUNDS.	1	100.0	-	100.0	-	-	-	-	-
60000 TO 89999 POUNDS.	-	100.0	-	-	-	-	-	-	-
90000 POUNDS AND OVER.	-	100.0	-	-	-	-	-	-	-
1000 TO 1499 MILES......	25	100.0	10.2	48.8	36.4	.5	-	.5	3.6
UNDER 1000 POUNDS.....	4	100.0	-	93.9	.3	3.1	-	2.8	-
1000 TO 9999 POUNDS...	15	100.0	17.2	54.4	22.3	-	-	-	6.0
10000 TO 29999 POUNDS.	1	100.0	-	-	100.0	-	-	-	-
30000 TO 59999 POUNDS.	4	100.0	-	-	100.0	-	-	-	-
60000 TO 89999 POUNDS.	-	100.0	-	-	-	-	-	-	-
90000 POUNDS AND OVER.	-	100.0	-	-	-	-	-	-	-
1500 MILES OR OVER......	108	100.0	1.5	96.2	.1	.6	-	1.6	-
UNDER 1000 POUNDS.....	20	100.0	6.3	86.1	.4	2.8	-	4.5	-
1000 TO 9999 POUNDS...	75	100.0	.5	98.2	-	.1	-	1.2	-
10000 TO 29999 POUNDS.	12	100.0	-	100.0	-	-	-	-	-
30000 TO 59999 POUNDS.	-	100.0	-	-	-	-	-	-	-
60000 TO 89999 POUNDS.	-	100.0	-	-	-	-	-	-	-
90000 POUNDS AND OVER.	-	100.0	-	-	-	-	-	-	-

Note: Detail may not add to total due to rounding. The introductory table shows the estimates of sampling variability for tons; sampling variability for ton-miles has not been estimated. See the map in the Introduction for the States comprising the geographic divisions of the United States.

Shipments excluded from the survey are those moving by pipeline (primarily petroleum products from refineries), parcel post shipments, and commodities moved by own power (motorized vehicles, aircraft, etc.) or towed (prefabricated buildings, etc.). Local shipments (commodities shipped less than 25 miles from the plant) and shipments within the same city are also excluded. Shipments to Alaska and Hawaii from the 48 conterminous States and the District of Columbia are included; however, no data were obtained for shipments originating in Alaska and Hawaii.

- Represents zero or rounds to zero.   (D) Withheld to avoid disclosing figures for individual companies.

[1] Production of this commodity is concentrated in the geographic divisions shown; figures and distributions for geographic divisions not shown are included in the total.

[2] Distances of shipments to foreign destinations are calculated only to the U.S. port of exit.

[3] Includes only shipments represented by bills of lading and invoices. Summary records which did not show individual weights of shipments are not included.

TCC 227. Floor Coverings

Comparisons of Tons and Ton-Miles of Shipments for
Geographic Divisions of Origin and for Sampling Variability: 1972 and 1967

Geographic division of origin	Estimates				Relative sampling variability in tons (percent)	
	1972		1967		1972	1967
	Tons (thousands)	Ton-miles (millions)	Tons (thousands)	Ton-miles (millions)		
U.S. total	3,670	2,312	1,426	1,056	27.9	20.4
New England	(D)	(D)	40	25	(*)	(*)
Middle Atlantic	(D)	(D)	267	220	(*)	(*)
East North Central	(D)	(D)	24	11	(*)	(*)
West North Central	(D)	(D)	—	—	(*)	(*)
South Atlantic	2,825	1,885	808	492	31.9	(*)
East South Central	(D)	(D)	3	2	(*)	(*)
West South Central	(D)	(D)	68	62	(*)	(*)
Mountain	(D)	(D)	—	—	(*)	(*)
Pacific	(D)	(D)	216	244	(*)	(*)

— Represents or rounds to zero.   (D) Withheld to avoid disclosing figures for individual companies.   (*) Data not published.

TABLE 1. **TCC GROUP 227—Percent Distribution of Geographic Division of Origin and Distance Shipped, by Means of Transport: 1972**

Geographic division of origin[1] and distance shipped[2]	Number	Percent distribution by means of transport							
		All means of transport	Rail	Motor carrier	Private truck	Air	Water	Other	Unknown
TONS OF SHIPMENTS	(thousands of tons)								
U.S. TOTAL	3 670	100.0	18.7	52.5	28.4	.1	-	.1	.1
SOUTH ATLANTIC	2 825	100.0	16.6	50.5	32.5	.1	-	.1	.1
UNDER 100 MILES	198	100.0	-	23.3	76.6	-	-	-	-
100 TO 199 MILES	106	100.0	39.0	20.9	40.1	-	-	-	-
200 TO 299 MILES	267	100.0	-	23.1	76.8	-	-	.1	-
300 TO 499 MILES	333	100.0	8.5	76.0	15.3	-	-	.1	-
500 TO 999 MILES	1 495	100.0	18.2	57.0	24.4	.2	-	.2	-
1000 TO 1499 MILES	168	100.0	-	80.2	19.7	-	-	.1	-
1500 MILES OR OVER	254	100.0	50.1	21.7	26.7	.1	-	-	1.5
TON-MILES OF SHIPMENTS	(millions of ton-miles)								
U.S. TOTAL	2 312	100.0	25.5	49.6	24.3	.2	-	.1	.3
SOUTH ATLANTIC	1 885	100.0	22.7	50.2	26.5	.1	-	.1	.4
UNDER 100 MILES	10	100.0	-	31.4	68.6	-	-	-	-
100 TO 199 MILES	14	100.0	40.1	22.1	37.7	-	-	.1	-
200 TO 299 MILES	62	100.0	-	26.4	73.5	-	-	.1	-
300 TO 499 MILES	134	100.0	8.3	76.2	15.3	-	-	.1	-
500 TO 999 MILES	945	100.0	15.9	57.7	26.1	.2	-	.2	-
1000 TO 1499 MILES	191	100.0	-	81.1	18.8	-	-	.1	-
1500 MILES OR OVER	525	100.0	49.8	22.8	26.0	.1	-	-	1.3

See footnotes at end of table 4.

TABLE 2. **TCC GROUP 227—Percent Distribution of Geographic Division of Origin and Means of Transport, by Geographic Division of Destination: 1972**

Geographic division of origin[1] and means of transport	Number	Percent distribution by division of destination									
		U.S. total	New England	Middle Atlantic	East North Central	West North Central	South Atlantic	East South Central	West South Central	Mountain	Pacific
TONS OF SHIPMENTS	(thousands of tons)										
U.S. TOTAL	3 670	100.0	2.1	12.8	26.5	7.6	24.7	4.4	8.9	6.0	7.0
RAIL	685	100.0	-	6.8	28.2	9.3	29.3	6.0	1.5	4.5	14.2
MOTOR CARRIER	1 928	100.0	2.3	14.8	34.2	8.3	14.0	3.3	9.5	7.8	5.9
PRIVATE TRUCK	1 041	100.0	3.2	13.0	10.9	5.3	41.8	5.3	12.6	3.9	4.0
AIR	5	100.0	2.3	.1	53.1	19.7	7.3	1.5	3.1	2.5	10.4
WATER	-	100.0	-	9.8	-	-	-	90.2	-	-	-
OTHER	4	100.0	2.1	4.6	64.5	10.0	7.2	3.8	1.9	1.9	4.1
UNKNOWN	3	100.0	-	.1	-	-	.1	-	.3	-	99.5
SOUTH ATLANTIC	2 825	100.0	2.3	9.2	27.4	8.3	24.1	3.8	11.0	7.3	6.6
RAIL	470	100.0	-	.9	38.3	9.2	22.2	-	2.1	6.5	20.6
MOTOR CARRIER	1 427	100.0	2.7	11.8	34.6	9.4	13.2	3.6	11.9	9.5	3.1
PRIVATE TRUCK	918	100.0	2.8	9.4	10.6	6.0	42.2	6.0	14.3	4.2	4.5
AIR	3	100.0	3.0	.1	69.5	19.8	-	-	1.1	1.7	4.9
WATER	-	100.0	-	-	-	-	-	-	-	-	-
OTHER	1	100.0	5.5	6.5	35.9	18.9	17.8	9.6	4.8	.8	.3
UNKNOWN	3	100.0	-	.1	-	-	-	-	-	-	99.9
TON-MILES OF SHIPMENTS	(millions of ton-miles)										
U.S. TOTAL	2 312	100.0	2.5	11.8	19.4	7.7	14.7	2.3	10.3	12.6	18.7
RAIL	590	100.0	-	5.2	16.3	5.5	23.1	4.2	1.2	8.9	35.6
MOTOR CARRIER	1 147	100.0	3.0	13.7	25.5	9.4	9.4	1.7	11.4	15.0	10.9
PRIVATE TRUCK	560	100.0	4.2	15.1	10.1	6.5	17.0	1.5	18.0	11.6	15.9
AIR	4	100.0	2.6	.1	35.0	16.1	8.8	.9	4.1	4.4	28.1
WATER	-	100.0	-	.7	-	-	-	99.3	-	-	-
OTHER	1	100.0	5.4	9.7	25.3	19.9	7.6	1.8	3.3	6.1	20.8
UNKNOWN	7	100.0	-	-	-	-	-	-	.2	-	99.7
SOUTH ATLANTIC	1 885	100.0	2.9	8.9	21.5	8.3	9.0	1.1	12.0	14.6	21.6
RAIL	428	100.0	-	.7	21.1	6.0	9.5	1.6	12.3	12.3	48.7
MOTOR CARRIER	946	100.0	3.5	11.2	27.2	9.9	6.4	1.3	12.5	17.1	10.8
PRIVATE TRUCK	499	100.0	4.2	11.5	11.1	7.3	13.8	1.7	20.2	12.3	17.9
AIR	2	100.0	4.1	.1	57.4	20.3	-	-	1.1	3.2	13.8
WATER	-	100.0	-	-	-	-	-	-	-	-	-
OTHER	1	100.0	9.0	9.1	30.7	28.2	11.8	2.9	5.5	1.7	1.0
UNKNOWN	7	100.0	-	-	-	-	-	-	-	-	100.0

See footnotes at end of table 4.

TABLE 3. **TCC GROUP 227**—Percent Distribution of Geographic Division of Destination and Means of Transport, by Geographic Division of Origin: 1972

Geographic division of destination and means of transport	Number	Percent distribution by division of origin[1]									
		U.S. total	New England	Middle Atlantic	East North Central	West North Central	South Atlantic	East South Central	West South Central	Mountain	Pacific
TONS OF SHIPMENTS	(thousands of tons)										
U.S. TOTAL..............	3 670	100.0	(D)	(D)	(D)	(D)	77.0	(D)	(D)	(D)	(D)
RAIL..............	685	100.0	(D)	(D)	(D)	(D)	68.6	(D)	(D)	(D)	(D)
MOTOR CARRIER........	1 928	100.0	(D)	(D)	(D)	(D)	74.0	(D)	(D)	(D)	(D)
PRIVATE TRUCK.........	1 041	100.0	(D)	(D)	(D)	(D)	88.2	(D)	(D)	(D)	(D)
AIR..............	5	100.0	(D)	(D)	(D)	(D)	72.4	(D)	(D)	(D)	(D)
WATER...............	-	100.0	(D)	(D)	(D)	(D)	-	(D)	(D)	(D)	(D)
OTHER..............	4	100.0	(D)	(D)	(D)	(D)	38.7	(D)	(D)	(D)	(D)
UNKNOWN..............	3	100.0	(D)	(D)	(D)	(D)	99.6	(D)	(D)	(D)	(D)
NEW ENGLAND..............	77	100.0	(D)	(D)	(D)	(D)	83.4	(D)	(D)	(D)	(D)
RAIL..............	-	100.0	(D)	(D)	(D)	(D)	96.9	(D)	(D)	(D)	(D)
MOTOR CARRIER........	43	100.0	(D)	(D)	(D)	(D)	89.7	(D)	(D)	(D)	(D)
PRIVATE TRUCK.........	33	100.0	(D)	(D)	(D)	(D)	75.2	(D)	(D)	(D)	(D)
AIR..............	-	100.0	(D)	(D)	(D)	(D)	94.9	(D)	(D)	(D)	(D)
WATER...............	-	100.0	(D)	(D)	(D)	(D)	-	(D)	(D)	(D)	(D)
OTHER..............	-	100.0	(D)	(D)	(D)	(D)	100.0	(D)	(D)	(D)	(D)
UNKNOWN..............	-	100.0	(D)	(D)	(D)	(D)	-	(D)	(D)	(D)	(D)
MIDDLE ATLANTIC.........	468	100.0	(D)	(D)	(D)	(D)	55.5	(D)	(D)	(D)	(D)
RAIL..............	46	100.0	(D)	(D)	(D)	(D)	9.5	(D)	(D)	(D)	(D)
MOTOR CARRIER........	285	100.0	(D)	(D)	(D)	(D)	59.1	(D)	(D)	(D)	(D)
PRIVATE TRUCK.........	135	100.0	(D)	(D)	(D)	(D)	63.8	(D)	(D)	(D)	(D)
AIR..............	-	100.0	(D)	(D)	(D)	(D)	50.7	(D)	(D)	(D)	(D)
WATER...............	-	100.0	(D)	(D)	(D)	(D)	-	(D)	(D)	(D)	(D)
OTHER..............	-	100.0	(D)	(D)	(D)	(D)	54.3	(D)	(D)	(D)	(D)
UNKNOWN..............	-	100.0	(D)	(D)	(D)	(D)	100.0	(D)	(D)	(D)	(D)
EAST NORTH CENTRAL......	971	100.0	(D)	(D)	(D)	(D)	79.8	(D)	(D)	(D)	(D)
RAIL..............	193	100.0	(D)	(D)	(D)	(D)	93.0	(D)	(D)	(D)	(D)
MOTOR CARRIER........	658	100.0	(D)	(D)	(D)	(D)	75.0	(D)	(D)	(D)	(D)
PRIVATE TRUCK.........	113	100.0	(D)	(D)	(D)	(D)	86.4	(D)	(D)	(D)	(D)
AIR..............	2	100.0	(D)	(D)	(D)	(D)	94.7	(D)	(D)	(D)	(D)
WATER...............	-	100.0	(D)	(D)	(D)	(D)	-	(D)	(D)	(D)	(D)
OTHER..............	3	100.0	(D)	(D)	(D)	(D)	21.5	(D)	(D)	(D)	(D)
UNKNOWN..............	-	100.0	(D)	(D)	(D)	(D)	-	(D)	(D)	(D)	(D)
WEST NORTH CENTRAL......	280	100.0	(D)	(D)	(D)	(D)	83.5	(D)	(D)	(D)	(D)
RAIL..............	64	100.0	(D)	(D)	(D)	(D)	67.7	(D)	(D)	(D)	(D)
MOTOR CARRIER........	159	100.0	(D)	(D)	(D)	(D)	84.2	(D)	(D)	(D)	(D)
PRIVATE TRUCK.........	54	100.0	(D)	(D)	(D)	(D)	100.0	(D)	(D)	(D)	(D)
AIR..............	1	100.0	(D)	(D)	(D)	(D)	72.9	(D)	(D)	(D)	(D)
WATER...............	-	100.0	(D)	(D)	(D)	(D)	-	(D)	(D)	(D)	(D)
OTHER..............	-	100.0	(D)	(D)	(D)	(D)	73.2	(D)	(D)	(D)	(D)
UNKNOWN..............	-	100.0	(D)	(D)	(D)	(D)	-	(D)	(D)	(D)	(D)
SOUTH ATLANTIC..........	907	100.0	(D)	(D)	(D)	(D)	75.1	(D)	(D)	(D)	(D)
RAIL..............	200	100.0	(D)	(D)	(D)	(D)	52.0	(D)	(D)	(D)	(D)
MOTOR CARRIER........	270	100.0	(D)	(D)	(D)	(D)	69.9	(D)	(D)	(D)	(D)
PRIVATE TRUCK.........	435	100.0	(D)	(D)	(D)	(D)	88.9	(D)	(D)	(D)	(D)
AIR..............	-	100.0	(D)	(D)	(D)	(D)	-	(D)	(D)	(D)	(D)
WATER...............	-	100.0	(D)	(D)	(D)	(D)	-	(D)	(D)	(D)	(D)
OTHER..............	-	100.0	(D)	(D)	(D)	(D)	96.0	(D)	(D)	(D)	(D)
UNKNOWN..............	-	100.0	(D)	(D)	(D)	(D)	-	(D)	(D)	(D)	(D)
EAST SOUTH CENTRAL......	160	100.0	(D)	(D)	(D)	(D)	66.3	(D)	(D)	(D)	(D)
RAIL..............	41	100.0	(D)	(D)	(D)	(D)	.1	(D)	(D)	(D)	(D)
MOTOR CARRIER........	63	100.0	(D)	(D)	(D)	(D)	80.5	(D)	(D)	(D)	(D)
PRIVATE TRUCK.........	55	100.0	(D)	(D)	(D)	(D)	100.0	(D)	(D)	(D)	(D)
AIR..............	-	100.0	(D)	(D)	(D)	(D)	-	(D)	(D)	(D)	(D)
WATER...............	-	100.0	(D)	(D)	(D)	(D)	-	(D)	(D)	(D)	(D)
OTHER..............	-	100.0	(D)	(D)	(D)	(D)	98.4	(D)	(D)	(D)	(D)
UNKNOWN..............	-	100.0	(D)	(D)	(D)	(D)	-	(D)	(D)	(D)	(D)
WEST SOUTH CENTRAL......	325	100.0	(D)	(D)	(D)	(D)	95.8	(D)	(D)	(D)	(D)
RAIL..............	10	100.0	(D)	(D)	(D)	(D)	100.0	(D)	(D)	(D)	(D)
MOTOR CARRIER........	183	100.0	(D)	(D)	(D)	(D)	92.7	(D)	(D)	(D)	(D)
PRIVATE TRUCK.........	131	100.0	(D)	(D)	(D)	(D)	100.0	(D)	(D)	(D)	(D)
AIR..............	-	100.0	(D)	(D)	(D)	(D)	25.8	(D)	(D)	(D)	(D)
WATER...............	-	100.0	(D)	(D)	(D)	(D)	-	(D)	(D)	(D)	(D)
OTHER..............	-	100.0	(D)	(D)	(D)	(D)	100.0	(D)	(D)	(D)	(D)
UNKNOWN..............	-	100.0	(D)	(D)	(D)	(D)	-	(D)	(D)	(D)	(D)
MOUNTAIN..............	221	100.0	(D)	(D)	(D)	(D)	92.7	(D)	(D)	(D)	(D)
RAIL..............	30	100.0	(D)	(D)	(D)	(D)	99.8	(D)	(D)	(D)	(D)
MOTOR CARRIER........	150	100.0	(D)	(D)	(D)	(D)	90.5	(D)	(D)	(D)	(D)
PRIVATE TRUCK.........	40	100.0	(D)	(D)	(D)	(D)	95.5	(D)	(D)	(D)	(D)
AIR..............	-	100.0	(D)	(D)	(D)	(D)	49.2	(D)	(D)	(D)	(D)
WATER...............	-	100.0	(D)	(D)	(D)	(D)	-	(D)	(D)	(D)	(D)
OTHER..............	-	100.0	(D)	(D)	(D)	(D)	16.4	(D)	(D)	(D)	(D)
UNKNOWN..............	-	100.0	(D)	(D)	(D)	(D)	-	(D)	(D)	(D)	(D)
PACIFIC..............	257	100.0	(D)	(D)	(D)	(D)	72.6	(D)	(D)	(D)	(D)
RAIL..............	97	100.0	(D)	(D)	(D)	(D)	99.3	(D)	(D)	(D)	(D)
MOTOR CARRIER........	114	100.0	(D)	(D)	(D)	(D)	39.3	(D)	(D)	(D)	(D)
PRIVATE TRUCK.........	41	100.0	(D)	(D)	(D)	(D)	99.9	(D)	(D)	(D)	(D)
AIR..............	-	100.0	(D)	(D)	(D)	(D)	33.8	(D)	(D)	(D)	(D)
WATER...............	-	100.0	(D)	(D)	(D)	(D)	-	(D)	(D)	(D)	(D)
OTHER..............	-	100.0	(D)	(D)	(D)	(D)	2.4	(D)	(D)	(D)	(D)
UNKNOWN..............	3	100.0	(D)	(D)	(D)	(D)	100.0	(D)	(D)	(D)	(D)

See footnotes at end of table 4.

TABLE 3. TCC GROUP 227—Percent Distribution of Geographic Division of Destination and Means of Transport, by Geographic Division of Origin: 1972—Continued

Geographic division of destination and means of transport	Number	Percent distribution by division of origin [1]									
		U.S. total	New England	Middle Atlantic	East North Central	West North Central	South Atlantic	East South Central	West South Central	Mountain	Pacific
TON-MILES OF SHIPMENTS	(millions of ton-miles)										
U.S. TOTAL................	2 312	100.0	(D)	(D)	(D)	(D)	81.5	(D)	(D)	(D)	(D)
RAIL..................	590	100.0	(D)	(D)	(D)	(D)	72.6	(D)	(D)	(D)	(D)
MOTOR CARRIER.........	1 147	100.0	(D)	(D)	(D)	(D)	82.5	(D)	(D)	(D)	(D)
PRIVATE TRUCK.........	560	100.0	(D)	(D)	(D)	(D)	89.0	(D)	(D)	(D)	(D)
AIR...................	4	100.0	(D)	(D)	(D)	(D)	58.6	(D)	(D)	(D)	(D)
WATER.................	-	100.0	(D)	(D)	(D)	(D)	-	(D)	(D)	(D)	(D)
OTHER.................	1	100.0	(D)	(D)	(D)	(D)	60.1	(D)	(D)	(D)	(D)
UNKNOWN...............	7	100.0	(D)	(D)	(D)	(D)	99.8	(D)	(D)	(D)	(D)
NEW ENGLAND..............	58	100.0	(D)	(D)	(D)	(D)	92.9	(D)	(D)	(D)	(D)
RAIL..................	-	100.0	(D)	(D)	(D)	(D)	95.8	(D)	(D)	(D)	(D)
MOTOR CARRIER.........	34	100.0	(D)	(D)	(D)	(D)	95.6	(D)	(D)	(D)	(D)
PRIVATE TRUCK.........	23	100.0	(D)	(D)	(D)	(D)	88.9	(D)	(D)	(D)	(D)
AIR...................	-	100.0	(D)	(D)	(D)	(D)	93.2	(D)	(D)	(D)	(D)
WATER.................	-	100.0	(D)	(D)	(D)	(D)	-	(D)	(D)	(D)	(D)
OTHER.................	-	100.0	(D)	(D)	(D)	(D)	100.0	(D)	(D)	(D)	(D)
UNKNOWN...............	-	100.0	(D)	(D)	(D)	(D)		(D)	(D)	(D)	(D)
MIDDLE ATLANTIC..........	273	100.0	(D)	(D)	(D)	(D)	61.1	(D)	(D)	(D)	(D)
RAIL..................	30	100.0	(D)	(D)	(D)	(D)	10.1	(D)	(D)	(D)	(D)
MOTOR CARRIER.........	157	100.0	(D)	(D)	(D)	(D)	67.4	(D)	(D)	(D)	(D)
PRIVATE TRUCK.........	84	100.0	(D)	(D)	(D)	(D)	67.8	(D)	(D)	(D)	(D)
AIR...................	-	100.0	(D)	(D)	(D)	(D)	94.2	(D)	(D)	(D)	(D)
WATER.................	-	100.0	(D)	(D)	(D)	(D)	-	(D)	(D)	(D)	(D)
OTHER.................	-	100.0	(D)	(D)	(D)	(D)	56.5	(D)	(D)	(D)	(D)
UNKNOWN...............	-	100.0	(D)	(D)	(D)	(D)	100.0	(D)	(D)	(D)	(D)
EAST NORTH CENTRAL......	448	100.0	(D)	(D)	(D)	(D)	90.5	(D)	(D)	(D)	(D)
RAIL..................	96	100.0	(D)	(D)	(D)	(D)	94.1	(D)	(D)	(D)	(D)
MOTOR CARRIER.........	292	100.0	(D)	(D)	(D)	(D)	87.9	(D)	(D)	(D)	(D)
PRIVATE TRUCK.........	56	100.0	(D)	(D)	(D)	(D)	97.8	(D)	(D)	(D)	(D)
AIR...................	1	100.0	(D)	(D)	(D)	(D)	96.0	(D)	(D)	(D)	(D)
WATER.................	-	100.0	(D)	(D)	(D)	(D)	-	(D)	(D)	(D)	(D)
OTHER.................	-	100.0	(D)	(D)	(D)	(D)	72.8	(D)	(D)	(D)	(D)
UNKNOWN...............	-	100.0	(D)	(D)	(D)	(D)		(D)	(D)	(D)	(D)
WEST NORTH CENTRAL......	177	100.0	(D)	(D)	(D)	(D)	88.5	(D)	(D)	(D)	(D)
RAIL..................	32	100.0	(D)	(D)	(D)	(D)	79.5	(D)	(D)	(D)	(D)
MOTOR CARRIER.........	107	100.0	(D)	(D)	(D)	(D)	87.5	(D)	(D)	(D)	(D)
PRIVATE TRUCK.........	36	100.0	(D)	(D)	(D)	(D)	100.0	(D)	(D)	(D)	(D)
AIR...................	-	100.0	(D)	(D)	(D)	(D)	73.8	(D)	(D)	(D)	(D)
WATER.................	-	100.0	(D)	(D)	(D)	(D)	-	(D)	(D)	(D)	(D)
OTHER.................	-	100.0	(D)	(D)	(D)	(D)	85.2	(D)	(D)	(D)	(D)
UNKNOWN...............	-	100.0	(D)	(D)	(D)	(D)		(D)	(D)	(D)	(D)
SOUTH ATLANTIC..........	339	100.0	(D)	(D)	(D)	(D)	50.2	(D)	(D)	(D)	(D)
RAIL..................	136	100.0	(D)	(D)	(D)	(D)	30.0	(D)	(D)	(D)	(D)
MOTOR CARRIER.........	107	100.0	(D)	(D)	(D)	(D)	56.5	(D)	(D)	(D)	(D)
PRIVATE TRUCK.........	95	100.0	(D)	(D)	(D)	(D)	72.1	(D)	(D)	(D)	(D)
AIR...................	-	100.0	(D)	(D)	(D)	(D)	-	(D)	(D)	(D)	(D)
WATER.................	-	100.0	(D)	(D)	(D)	(D)	-	(D)	(D)	(D)	(D)
OTHER.................	-	100.0	(D)	(D)	(D)	(D)	93.2	(D)	(D)	(D)	(D)
UNKNOWN...............	-	100.0	(D)	(D)	(D)	(D)		(D)	(D)	(D)	(D)
EAST SOUTH CENTRAL......	53	100.0	(D)	(D)	(D)	(D)	39.7	(D)	(D)	(D)	(D)
RAIL..................	24	100.0	(D)	(D)	(D)	(D)	-	(D)	(D)	(D)	(D)
MOTOR CARRIER.........	19	100.0	(D)	(D)	(D)	(D)	65.2	(D)	(D)	(D)	(D)
PRIVATE TRUCK.........	8	100.0	(D)	(D)	(D)	(D)	100.0	(D)	(D)	(D)	(D)
AIR...................	-	100.0	(D)	(D)	(D)	(D)	-	(D)	(D)	(D)	(D)
WATER.................	-	100.0	(D)	(D)	(D)	(D)	-	(D)	(D)	(D)	(D)
OTHER.................	-	100.0	(D)	(D)	(D)	(D)	95.6	(D)	(D)	(D)	(D)
UNKNOWN...............	-	100.0	(D)	(D)	(D)	(D)		(D)	(D)	(D)	(D)
WEST SOUTH CENTRAL......	239	100.0	(D)	(D)	(D)	(D)	94.4	(D)	(D)	(D)	(D)
RAIL..................	6	100.0	(D)	(D)	(D)	(D)	100.0	(D)	(D)	(D)	(D)
MOTOR CARRIER.........	131	100.0	(D)	(D)	(D)	(D)	90.0	(D)	(D)	(D)	(D)
PRIVATE TRUCK.........	100	100.0	(D)	(D)	(D)	(D)	100.0	(D)	(D)	(D)	(D)
AIR...................	-	100.0	(D)	(D)	(D)	(D)	16.0	(D)	(D)	(D)	(D)
WATER.................	-	100.0	(D)	(D)	(D)	(D)	-	(D)	(D)	(D)	(D)
OTHER.................	-	100.0	(D)	(D)	(D)	(D)	100.0	(D)	(D)	(D)	(D)
UNKNOWN...............	-	100.0	(D)	(D)	(D)	(D)		(D)	(D)	(D)	(D)
MOUNTAIN................	290	100.0	(D)	(D)	(D)	(D)	94.9	(D)	(D)	(D)	(D)
RAIL..................	52	100.0	(D)	(D)	(D)	(D)	99.8	(D)	(D)	(D)	(D)
MOTOR CARRIER.........	172	100.0	(D)	(D)	(D)	(D)	93.9	(D)	(D)	(D)	(D)
PRIVATE TRUCK.........	65	100.0	(D)	(D)	(D)	(D)	94.1	(D)	(D)	(D)	(D)
AIR...................	-	100.0	(D)	(D)	(D)	(D)	43.7	(D)	(D)	(D)	(D)
WATER.................	-	100.0	(D)	(D)	(D)	(D)	-	(D)	(D)	(D)	(D)
OTHER.................	-	100.0	(D)	(D)	(D)	(D)	17.3	(D)	(D)	(D)	(D)
UNKNOWN...............	-	100.0	(D)	(D)	(D)	(D)	-	(D)	(D)	(D)	(D)
PACIFIC.................	432	100.0	(D)	(D)	(D)	(D)	94.3	(D)	(D)	(D)	(D)
RAIL..................	210	100.0	(D)	(D)	(D)	(D)	99.3	(D)	(D)	(D)	(D)
MOTOR CARRIER.........	124	100.0	(D)	(D)	(D)	(D)	82.4	(D)	(D)	(D)	(D)
PRIVATE TRUCK.........	89	100.0	(D)	(D)	(D)	(D)	100.0	(D)	(D)	(D)	(D)
AIR...................	1	100.0	(D)	(D)	(D)	(D)	28.7	(D)	(D)	(D)	(D)
WATER.................	-	100.0	(D)	(D)	(D)	(D)	-	(D)	(D)	(D)	(D)
OTHER.................	-	100.0	(D)	(D)	(D)	(D)	3.0	(D)	(D)	(D)	(D)
UNKNOWN...............	7	100.0	(D)	(D)	(D)	(D)	100.0	(D)	(D)	(D)	(D)

See footnotes at end of table 4.

TABLE 4. **TCC GROUP 227—Percent Distribution of Distance Shipped and Weight of Shipment, by Means of Transport: 1972**

Distance shipped and weight of shipment[2] [3]	Number	Percent distribution by means of transport							
		All means of transport	Rail	Motor carrier	Private truck	Air	Water	Other	Unknown
TONS OF SHIPMENTS	(thousands of tons)								
U.S. TOTAL..........	3 589	100.0	19.1	51.7	28.8	.1	-	.1	.1
UNDER 100 MILES.........	342	100.0	1.2	49.2	48.9	-	-	.7	-
UNDER 1000 POUNDS.....	58	100.0	-	86.2	13.5	-	-	.3	-
1000 TO 9999 POUNDS...	160	100.0	-	52.7	45.9	-	-	1.4	-
10000 TO 29999 POUNDS.	74	100.0	5.6	41.8	52.6	-	-	-	-
30000 TO 59999 POUNDS.	48	100.0	-	4.7	95.3	-	-	-	-
60000 TO 89999 POUNDS.	-	100.0	-	-	-	-	-	-	-
90000 POUNDS AND OVER.	-	100.0	-	-	-	-	-	-	-
100 TO 199 MILES........	128	100.0	34.4	29.3	36.2	-	-	.1	-
UNDER 1000 POUNDS.....	24	100.0	-	83.1	16.4	-	-	.5	-
1000 TO 9999 POUNDS...	51	100.0	-	33.0	67.0	-	-	-	-
10000 TO 29999 POUNDS.	52	100.0	84.6	.6	14.8	-	-	-	-
30000 TO 59999 POUNDS.	-	100.0	-	-	-	-	-	-	-
60000 TO 89999 POUNDS.	-	100.0	-	-	-	-	-	-	-
90000 POUNDS AND OVER.	-	100.0	-	-	-	-	-	-	-
200 TO 299 MILES........	336	100.0	-	38.7	61.2	-	-	.1	-
UNDER 1000 POUNDS.....	30	100.0	-	83.3	16.0	-	-	.8	-
1000 TO 9999 POUNDS...	59	100.0	.1	72.7	27.2	-	-	-	-
10000 TO 29999 POUNDS.	171	100.0	-	28.5	71.5	-	-	-	-
30000 TO 59999 POUNDS.	75	100.0	-	17.3	82.7	-	-	-	-
60000 TO 89999 POUNDS.	-	100.0	-	-	-	-	-	-	-
90000 POUNDS AND OVER.	-	100.0	-	-	-	-	-	-	-
300 TO 499 MILES........	463	100.0	14.3	69.5	16.0	-	-	.2	-
UNDER 1000 POUNDS.....	97	100.0	.6	85.9	12.5	.2	-	.8	-
1000 TO 9999 POUNDS...	186	100.0	-	81.6	18.4	-	-	-	-
10000 TO 29999 POUNDS.	152	100.0	24.9	57.2	17.9	-	-	-	-
30000 TO 59999 POUNDS.	27	100.0	98.2	-	1.8	-	-	-	-
60000 TO 89999 POUNDS.	-	100.0	-	-	-	-	-	-	-
90000 POUNDS AND OVER.	-	100.0	-	-	-	-	-	-	-
500 TO 999 MILES........	1 793	100.0	20.0	55.4	24.3	.2	-	.1	-
UNDER 1000 POUNDS.....	227	100.0	.7	71.7	26.5	.6	-	.5	-
1000 TO 9999 POUNDS...	527	100.0	.2	60.8	38.4	.5	-	-	-
10000 TO 29999 POUNDS.	899	100.0	31.1	49.8	19.1	-	-	-	-
30000 TO 59999 POUNDS.	139	100.0	54.3	44.7	1.0	-	-	-	-
60000 TO 89999 POUNDS.	-	100.0	-	-	-	-	-	-	-
90000 POUNDS AND OVER.	-	100.0	-	-	-	-	-	-	-
1000 TO 1499 MILES......	259	100.0	32.5	54.6	12.8	.1	-	-	.1
UNDER 1000 POUNDS.....	18	100.0	.1	60.3	37.8	1.2	-	.5	.1
1000 TO 9999 POUNDS...	34	100.0	.2	52.3	47.4	.2	-	-	-
10000 TO 29999 POUNDS.	122	100.0	34.7	57.3	8.0	-	-	-	-
30000 TO 59999 POUNDS.	83	100.0	49.7	50.3	-	-	-	-	-
60000 TO 89999 POUNDS.	-	100.0	-	-	-	-	-	-	-
90000 POUNDS AND OVER.	-	100.0	-	-	-	-	-	-	-
1500 MILES OR OVER......	266	100.0	48.2	23.8	26.3	.2	-	.1	1.4
UNDER 1000 POUNDS.....	33	100.0	11.4	54.5	29.4	.6	-	.6	3.6
1000 TO 9999 POUNDS...	112	100.0	45.6	35.1	16.8	.3	-	-	2.2
10000 TO 29999 POUNDS.	103	100.0	67.4	5.4	27.2	-	-	-	-
30000 TO 59999 POUNDS.	16	100.0	21.3	-	78.7	-	-	-	-
60000 TO 89999 POUNDS.	-	100.0	-	-	-	-	-	-	-
90000 POUNDS AND OVER.	-	100.0	-	-	-	-	-	-	-
TON-MILES OF SHIPMENTS	(millions of ton-miles)								
U.S. TOTAL..........	2 275	100.0	25.9	49.0	24.5	.2	-	.1	.3
UNDER 100 MILES.........	16	100.0	2.0	50.5	46.9	-	-	.6	-
UNDER 1000 POUNDS.....	2	100.0	-	79.8	19.7	-	-	.4	-
1000 TO 9999 POUNDS...	8	100.0	-	58.0	40.9	-	-	1.0	-
10000 TO 29999 POUNDS.	4	100.0	8.4	39.1	52.5	-	-	-	-
30000 TO 59999 POUNDS.	2	100.0	-	9.1	90.9	-	-	-	-
60000 TO 89999 POUNDS.	-	100.0	-	-	-	-	-	-	-
90000 POUNDS AND OVER.	-	100.0	-	-	-	-	-	-	-
100 TO 199 MILES........	18	100.0	34.8	31.2	33.9	-	-	.1	-
UNDER 1000 POUNDS.....	3	100.0	-	82.4	17.1	-	-	.5	-
1000 TO 9999 POUNDS...	6	100.0	-	36.7	63.3	-	-	-	-
10000 TO 29999 POUNDS.	7	100.0	84.0	.6	15.4	-	-	-	-
30000 TO 59999 POUNDS.	-	100.0	-	-	-	-	-	-	-
60000 TO 89999 POUNDS.	-	100.0	-	-	-	-	-	-	-
90000 POUNDS AND OVER.	-	100.0	-	-	-	-	-	-	-

See footnotes at end of table 4.

TABLE 4. **TCC GROUP 227—Percent Distribution of Distance Shipped and Weight of Shipment, by Means of Transport: 1972**—Continued

Distance shipped and weight of shipment [2] [3]	Number	Percent distribution by means of transport							
		All means of transport	Rail	Motor carrier	Private truck	Air	Water	Other	Unknown
TON-MILES OF SHIPMENTS	(millions of ton-miles)								
200 TO 299 MILES........	80	100.0	-	42.6	57.3	-	-	.1	-
UNDER 1000 POUNDS.....	7	100.0	-	82.4	16.8	-	-	.8	-
1000 TO 9999 POUNDS...	15	100.0	.1	71.5	28.5	-	-	-	-
10000 TO 29999 POUNDS.	39	100.0	-	32.6	67.4	-	-	-	-
30000 TO 59999 POUNDS.	17	100.0	-	21.6	78.4	-	-	-	-
60000 TO 89999 POUNDS.	-	100.0	-	-	-	-	-	-	-
90000 POUNDS AND OVER.	-	100.0	-	-	-	-	-	-	-
300 TO 499 MILES........	186	100.0	13.0	70.6	16.3	-	-	.2	-
UNDER 1000 POUNDS.....	41	100.0	.6	85.6	12.9	.2	-	.7	-
1000 TO 9999 POUNDS...	73	100.0	-	81.8	18.2	-	-	-	-
10000 TO 29999 POUNDS.	60	100.0	21.8	59.4	18.9	-	-	-	-
30000 TO 59999 POUNDS.	10	100.0	97.9	-	2.1	-	-	-	-
60000 TO 89999 POUNDS.	-	100.0	-	-	-	-	-	-	-
90000 POUNDS AND OVER.	-	100.0	-	-	-	-	-	-	-
500 TO 999 MILES........	1 133	100.0	18.1	56.0	25.7	.2	-	.1	-
UNDER 1000 POUNDS.....	152	100.0	.7	71.5	26.8	.5	-	.5	-
1000 TO 9999 POUNDS...	357	100.0	.2	60.2	39.2	.4	-	-	-
10000 TO 29999 POUNDS.	538	100.0	30.0	49.7	20.3	-	-	-	-
30000 TO 59999 POUNDS.	84	100.0	49.1	49.8	1.1	-	-	-	-
60000 TO 89999 POUNDS.	-	100.0	-	-	-	-	-	-	-
90000 POUNDS AND OVER.	-	100.0	-	-	-	-	-	-	-
1000 TO 1499 MILES......	291	100.0	31.5	56.0	12.4	.1	-	-	-
UNDER 1000 POUNDS.....	20	100.0	.1	61.4	36.5	1.3	-	.5	.1
1000 TO 9999 POUNDS...	38	100.0	.2	55.8	43.9	.2	-	-	-
10000 TO 29999 POUNDS.	139	100.0	33.7	57.6	8.7	-	-	-	-
30000 TO 59999 POUNDS.	94	100.0	47.5	52.5	-	-	-	-	-
60000 TO 89999 POUNDS.	-	100.0	-	-	-	-	-	-	-
90000 POUNDS AND OVER.	-	100.0	-	-	-	-	-	-	-
1500 MILES OR OVER......	548	100.0	47.9	25.0	25.6	.2	-	.1	1.3
UNDER 1000 POUNDS.....	70	100.0	12.4	57.9	25.3	.6	-	.5	3.3
1000 TO 9999 POUNDS...	245	100.0	45.0	34.2	18.6	.3	-	-	1.9
10000 TO 29999 POUNDS.	201	100.0	68.0	6.1	25.9	-	-	-	-
30000 TO 59999 POUNDS.	31	100.0	21.4	-	78.6	-	-	-	-
60000 TO 89999 POUNDS.	-	100.0	-	-	-	-	-	-	-
90000 POUNDS AND OVER.	-	100.0	-	-	-	-	-	-	-

Note: Detail may not add to total due to rounding. The introductory table shows the estimates of sampling variability for tons; sampling variability for ton-miles has not been estimated. See the map in the Introduction for the States comprising the geographic divisions of the United States.

Shipments excluded from the survey are those moving by pipeline (primarily petroleum products from refineries), parcel post shipments, and commodities moved by own power (motorized vehicles, aircraft, etc.) or towed (prefabricated buildings, etc.). Local shipments (commodities shipped less than 25 miles from the plant) and shipments within the same city are also excluded. Shipments to Alaska and Hawaii from the 48 conterminous States and the District of Columbia are included; however, no data were obtained for shipments originating in Alaska and Hawaii.

- Represents zero or rounds to zero.   (D) Withheld to avoid disclosing figures for individual companies.

[1] Production of this commodity is concentrated in the geographic divisions shown; figures and distributions for geographic divisions not shown are included in the total.

[2] Distances of shipments to foreign destinations are calculated only to the U.S. port of exit.

[3] Includes only shipments represented by bills of lading and invoices. Summary records which did not show individual weights of shipments are not included.

TCC 228. Thread and Yarn

Comparisons of Tons and Ton-Miles of Shipments for
Geographic Divisions of Origin and for Sampling Variability: 1972 and 1967

Geographic division of origin	Estimates				Relative sampling variability in tons (percent)	
	1972		1967		1972	1967
	Tons (thousands)	Ton-miles (millions)	Tons (thousands)	Ton-miles (millions)		
U.S. total	3,338	1,112	3,849	1,030	9.4	34.2
New England	(D)	(D)	78	27	(*)	(*)
Middle Atlantic	89	27	128	43	28.7	(*)
East North Central	(D)	(D)	40	23	(*)	(*)
West North Central	(D)	(D)	—	—	(*)	(*)
South Atlantic	2,437	780	3,232	794	11.2	(*)
East South Central	562	215	370	142	21.0	(*)
West South Central	(D)	(D)	—	—	(*)	(*)
Mountain	(D)	(D)	1	1	(*)	(*)
Pacific	(D)	(D)	—	—	(*)	(*)

— Represents or rounds to zero.   (D) Withheld to avoid disclosing figures for individual companies.   (*) Data not published.

TABLE 1. **TCC GROUP 228**—Percent Distribution of Geographic Division of Origin and Distance Shipped, by Means of Transport: 1972

Geographic division of origin[1] and distance shipped[2]	Number	Percent distribution by means of transport							
		All means of transport	Rail	Motor carrier	Private truck	Air	Water	Other	Unknown
TONS OF SHIPMENTS	(thousands of tons)								
U.S. TOTAL...........	3 338	100.0	3.9	65.1	30.4	-	-	.4	.1
MIDDLE ATLANTIC.........	89	100.0	.1	67.1	32.7	-	-	-	-
UNDER 100 MILES.......	11	100.0	-	96.5	3.5	-	-	-	-
100 TO 199 MILES......	14	100.0	-	87.8	12.2	-	-	-	-
200 TO 299 MILES......	18	100.0	-	39.5	60.5	-	-	-	-
300 TO 499 MILES......	35	100.0	-	63.6	36.4	-	-	-	-
500 TO 999 MILES......	9	100.0	-	64.9	35.1	-	-	-	-
1000 TO 1499 MILES....	-	100.0	-	100.0	-	-	-	-	-
1500 MILES OR OVER....	-	100.0	74.3	25.7	-	-	-	-	-
SOUTH ATLANTIC..........	2 437	100.0	4.0	63.0	32.9	-	-	.1	.1
UNDER 100 MILES.......	594	100.0	.7	49.2	49.8	-	-	.1	.1
100 TO 199 MILES......	500	100.0	.1	59.8	40.0	-	-	.2	-
200 TO 299 MILES......	559	100.0	.3	77.0	22.7	-	-	-	.1
300 TO 499 MILES......	359	100.0	7.3	72.1	20.5	-	-	-	.1
500 TO 999 MILES......	326	100.0	3.8	65.9	30.2	-	-	-	-
1000 TO 1499 MILES....	20	100.0	42.9	47.6	9.3	-	-	-	-
1500 MILES OR OVER....	75	100.0	56.7	37.8	5.5	.2	-	-	-
EAST SOUTH CENTRAL......	562	100.0	5.6	67.6	26.7	-	-	-	-
UNDER 100 MILES.......	80	100.0	2.4	55.0	42.6	-	-	-	-
100 TO 199 MILES......	78	100.0	.6	90.1	9.1	-	-	-	-
200 TO 299 MILES......	150	100.0	1.3	87.1	11.6	-	-	-	.3
300 TO 499 MILES......	128	100.0	1.3	56.9	41.8	-	-	-	-
500 TO 999 MILES......	96	100.0	9.9	57.3	32.8	-	-	-	-
1000 TO 1499 MILES....	7	100.0	7.3	16.6	76.0	-	-	-	-
1500 MILES OR OVER....	20	100.0	76.8	22.6	.5	-	-	-	-
TON-MILES OF SHIPMENTS	(millions of ton-miles)								
U.S. TOTAL...........	1 112	100.0	14.2	61.5	23.6	-	-	.7	.1
MIDDLE ATLANTIC.........	27	100.0	.9	64.0	35.1	-	-	-	-
UNDER 100 MILES.......	-	100.0	-	98.2	1.8	-	-	-	-
100 TO 199 MILES......	1	100.0	-	85.2	14.8	-	-	-	-
200 TO 299 MILES......	4	100.0	-	39.6	60.4	-	-	-	-
300 TO 499 MILES......	14	100.0	-	64.8	35.2	-	-	-	-
500 TO 999 MILES......	5	100.0	-	68.1	31.9	-	-	-	-
1000 TO 1499 MILES....	-	100.0	-	100.0	-	-	-	-	-
1500 MILES OR OVER....	-	100.0	77.0	23.0	-	-	-	-	-
SOUTH ATLANTIC..........	780	100.0	15.1	61.1	23.7	-	-	-	-
UNDER 100 MILES.......	32	100.0	.5	53.7	45.5	-	-	.3	-
100 TO 199 MILES......	72	100.0	.1	61.8	38.0	-	-	.3	.1
200 TO 299 MILES......	135	100.0	.2	77.1	22.6	-	-	-	.1
300 TO 499 MILES......	142	100.0	8.7	72.6	18.6	-	-	-	.1
500 TO 999 MILES......	219	100.0	3.6	62.3	34.1	-	-	-	-
1000 TO 1499 MILES....	23	100.0	42.1	48.8	8.8	-	-	-	-
1500 MILES OR OVER....	154	100.0	56.5	38.0	5.5	.2	-	-	-
EAST SOUTH CENTRAL......	215	100.0	17.5	56.9	25.6	-	-	-	-
UNDER 100 MILES.......	4	100.0	3.8	49.7	46.5	-	-	-	-
100 TO 199 MILES......	12	100.0	.6	89.3	9.8	-	-	-	-
200 TO 299 MILES......	40	100.0	1.3	87.2	11.4	-	-	-	.3
300 TO 499 MILES......	46	100.0	1.3	55.7	42.9	-	-	-	-
500 TO 999 MILES......	65	100.0	11.1	58.1	30.8	-	-	-	-
1000 TO 1499 MILES....	8	100.0	8.7	15.5	75.8	-	-	-	-
1500 MILES OR OVER....	37	100.0	75.6	23.8	.5	-	-	-	-

See footnotes at end of table 4.

TABLE 2. **TCC GROUP 228**—Percent Distribution of Geographic Division of Origin and Means of Transport, by Geographic Division of Destination: 1972

Geographic division of origin[1] and means of transport	Number	Percent distribution by division of destination									
		U.S. total	New England	Middle Atlantic	East North Central	West North Central	South Atlantic	East South Central	West South Central	Mountain	Pacific
TONS OF SHIPMENTS	(thousands of tons)										
U.S. TOTAL.............	3 338	100.0	5.2	14.3	3.1	.6	63.8	7.3	2.6	.3	2.8
RAIL................	131	100.0	-	11.2	11.3	2.6	20.5	1.0	8.6	.8	43.9
MOTOR CARRIER.........	2 173	100.0	5.9	17.8	3.5	.5	59.2	9.8	1.6	.3	1.5
PRIVATE TRUCK.........	1 014	100.0	4.5	7.3	1.0	.5	79.5	2.4	4.2	.2	.4
AIR.................	-	100.0	1.2	12.2	-	.7	.1	53.0	16.6	15.7	-	.5
WATER...............	1	100.0	100.0	-	-	-	-	-	-	-	-
OTHER...............	14	100.0	-	.1	7.0	1.3	63.4	27.8	.1	-	.2
UNKNOWN.............	3	100.0	-	50.7	-	-	38.5	10.8	-	-	-

See footnotes at end of table 4.

TABLE 2. TCC GROUP 228—Percent Distribution of Geographic Division of Origin and Means of Transport, by Geographic Division of Destination: 1972—Continued

Geographic division of origin[1] and means of transport	Number	Percent distribution by division of destination									
		U.S. total	New England	Middle Atlantic	East North Central	West North Central	South Atlantic	East South Central	West South Central	Mountain	Pacific
TONS OF SHIPMENTS	(thousands of tons)										
MIDDLE ATLANTIC	89	100.0	6.1	47.4	6.5	.7	35.7	3.3	.1	-	.1
RAIL	-	100.0	-	-	-	-	-	-	-	-	100.0
MOTOR CARRIER	59	100.0	9.0	52.0	7.7	1.1	25.1	4.9	.2	-	-
PRIVATE TRUCK	29	100.0	-	38.1	4.2	-	57.6	.2	-	-	-
AIR	-	100.0	-	-	-	100.0	-	-	-	-	-
WATER	-	100.0	-	-	-	-	-	-	-	-	-
OTHER	-	100.0	-	-	-	-	-	-	-	-	-
UNKNOWN	-	100.0	-	-	-	-	-	-	-	-	-
SOUTH ATLANTIC	2 437	100.0	3.6	12.5	2.0	.4	70.7	5.6	2.0	.2	3.0
RAIL	96	100.0	-	6.5	14.8	3.5	21.6	-	9.4	-	44.1
MOTOR CARRIER	1 535	100.0	3.9	16.4	2.1	.3	67.5	7.3	.5	.4	1.6
PRIVATE TRUCK	801	100.0	3.4	5.8	.4	.4	82.6	2.8	4.1	-	.5
AIR	-	100.0	1.4	3.9	.1	-	59.1	17.7	17.6	-	.2
WATER	-	100.0	-	-	-	-	-	-	-	-	-
OTHER	1	100.0	.3	1.0	3.5	.6	86.7	4.9	1.1	-	1.9
UNKNOWN	1	100.0	-	-	-	-	74.6	25.4	-	-	-
EAST SOUTH CENTRAL	562	100.0	3.8	6.8	3.7	.7	58.7	16.9	5.3	.6	3.5
RAIL	31	100.0	-	26.7	1.6	-	9.4	4.2	7.1	3.5	47.5
MOTOR CARRIER	380	100.0	3.4	6.5	4.1	.4	53.5	24.2	6.5	-	1.2
PRIVATE TRUCK	150	100.0	5.5	3.2	2.9	1.4	82.2	1.3	2.0	1.4	.1
AIR	-	100.0	-	50.0	33.4	-	-	-	-	-	16.6
WATER	-	100.0	-	-	-	-	-	-	-	-	-
OTHER	-	100.0	2.5	3.9	-	13.0	31.2	46.8	1.2	-	1.3
UNKNOWN	-	100.0	-	-	-	-	100.0	-	-	-	-
TON-MILES OF SHIPMENTS	(millions of ton-miles)										
U.S. TOTAL	1 112	100.0	7.8	18.3	4.3	1.2	37.6	6.9	5.8	1.2	17.0
RAIL	157	100.0	-	6.4	4.7	1.7	5.9	.2	7.0	1.0	73.1
MOTOR CARRIER	684	100.0	8.3	23.6	4.9	1.0	39.1	9.7	2.5	1.4	9.5
PRIVATE TRUCK	262	100.0	11.2	12.3	2.2	1.6	51.9	2.9	13.6	.9	3.4
AIR	-	100.0	1.5	10.8	.9	.2	19.3	21.0	43.3	.1	2.9
WATER	-	100.0	100.0	-	-	-	-	-	-	-	.8
OTHER	7	100.0	.1	.1	10.4	1.3	62.2	24.9	.2	-	-
UNKNOWN	-	100.0	-	61.4	-	-	25.6	13.0	-	-	-
MIDDLE ATLANTIC	27	100.0	5.6	27.4	7.4	1.9	48.8	7.3	.5	.1	1.1
RAIL	-	100.0	-	-	-	-	-	-	-	-	100.0
MOTOR CARRIER	17	100.0	8.8	29.1	8.8	3.0	37.8	11.4	.8	.1	.2
PRIVATE TRUCK	9	100.0	-	24.8	5.0	-	69.9	.2	-	-	-
AIR	-	100.0	-	-	-	100.0	-	-	-	-	-
WATER	-	100.0	-	-	-	-	-	-	-	-	-
OTHER	-	100.0	-	-	-	-	-	-	-	-	-
UNKNOWN	-	100.0	-	-	-	-	-	-	-	-	-
SOUTH ATLANTIC	780	100.0	7.8	18.9	3.3	1.1	36.8	6.0	5.9	1.2	19.1
RAIL	117	100.0	-	2.9	6.1	2.3	6.2	-	8.5	-	74.1
MOTOR CARRIER	476	100.0	8.3	25.4	3.5	.6	39.6	8.2	1.3	1.9	11.1
PRIVATE TRUCK	184	100.0	11.4	12.4	.9	1.6	49.1	4.0	16.0	-	4.6
AIR	-	100.0	1.7	6.3	.1	-	21.1	21.4	48.1	.1	1.2
WATER	-	100.0	-	-	-	-	-	-	-	-	-
OTHER	-	100.0	1.5	3.4	13.0	2.2	48.7	5.0	5.1	-	21.0
UNKNOWN	-	100.0	-	-	-	-	61.2	38.8	-	-	-
EAST SOUTH CENTRAL	215	100.0	8.8	12.3	4.6	1.0	38.9	9.8	5.6	1.9	17.0
RAIL	37	100.0	-	17.5	.6	-	1.0	1.0	2.7	4.3	72.8
MOTOR CARRIER	122	100.0	9.2	13.7	5.8	.8	38.8	16.7	7.6	.1	7.3
PRIVATE TRUCK	55	100.0	14.1	5.7	4.4	2.2	65.0	.7	3.1	4.4	.4
AIR	-	100.0	-	49.3	16.3	-	-	-	-	-	34.5
WATER	-	100.0	-	-	-	-	-	-	-	-	-
OTHER	-	100.0	7.5	8.0	-	19.8	30.3	25.1	1.8	-	7.5
UNKNOWN	-	100.0	-	-	-	-	100.0	-	-	-	-

See footnotes at end of table 4.

TABLE 3. **TCC GROUP 228**—Percent Distribution of Geographic Division of Destination and Means of Transport, by Geographic Division of Origin: 1972

Geographic division of destination and means of transport	Number	Percent distribution by division of origin [1]									
		U.S. total	New England	Middle Atlantic	East North Central	West North Central	South Atlantic	East South Central	West South Central	Mountain	Pacific
TONS OF SHIPMENTS	(thousands of tons)										
U.S. TOTAL	3 338	100.0	(D)	2.7	(D)	(D)	73.0	16.9	(D)	(D)	(D)
RAIL	131	100.0	(D)	.1	(D)	(D)	73.6	24.0	(D)	(D)	(D)
MOTOR CARRIER	2 173	100.0	(D)	2.8	(D)	(D)	70.7	17.5	(D)	(D)	(D)
PRIVATE TRUCK	1 014	100.0	(D)	2.9	(D)	(D)	79.1	14.8	(D)	(D)	(D)
AIR	-	100.0	(D)	.1	(D)	(D)	89.4	1.4	(D)	(D)	(D)
WATER	1	100.0	(D)	-	(D)	(D)	-	-	(D)	(D)	(D)
OTHER	14	100.0	(D)	-	(D)	(D)	10.3	.5	(D)	(D)	(D)
UNKNOWN	3	100.0	(D)	-	(D)	(D)	42.5	6.8	(D)	(D)	(D)
NEW ENGLAND	173	100.0	(D)	3.1	(D)	(D)	50.5	12.2	(D)	(D)	(D)
RAIL	-	100.0	(D)	-	(D)	(D)	-	-	(D)	(D)	(D)
MOTOR CARRIER	127	100.0	(D)	4.2	(D)	(D)	47.6	10.2	(D)	(D)	(D)
PRIVATE TRUCK	45	100.0	(D)	-	(D)	(D)	59.7	18.1	(D)	(D)	(D)
AIR	-	100.0	(D)	-	(D)	(D)	100.0	-	(D)	(D)	(D)
WATER	1	100.0	(D)	-	(D)	(D)	-	-	(D)	(D)	(D)
OTHER	-	100.0	(D)	-	(D)	(D)	64.5	23.8	(D)	(D)	(D)
UNKNOWN	-	100.0	(D)	-	(D)	(D)	-	-	(D)	(D)	(D)
MIDDLE ATLANTIC	477	100.0	(D)	8.8	(D)	(D)	63.8	8.0	(D)	(D)	(D)
RAIL	14	100.0	(D)	-	(D)	(D)	42.8	57.2	(D)	(D)	(D)
MOTOR CARRIER	387	100.0	(D)	8.0	(D)	(D)	65.0	6.4	(D)	(D)	(D)
PRIVATE TRUCK	73	100.0	(D)	15.1	(D)	(D)	63.1	6.6	(D)	(D)	(D)
AIR	-	100.0	(D)	-	(D)	(D)	28.4	5.8	(D)	(D)	(D)
WATER	-	100.0	(D)	-	(D)	(D)	-	-	(D)	(D)	(D)
OTHER	-	100.0	(D)	-	(D)	(D)	82.6	13.7	(D)	(D)	(D)
UNKNOWN	1	100.0	(D)	-	(D)	(D)	-	-	(D)	(D)	(D)
EAST NORTH CENTRAL	102	100.0	(D)	5.7	(D)	(D)	48.4	20.2	(D)	(D)	(D)
RAIL	14	100.0	(D)	-	(D)	(D)	96.6	3.4	(D)	(D)	(D)
MOTOR CARRIER	76	100.0	(D)	6.0	(D)	(D)	41.6	20.7	(D)	(D)	(D)
PRIVATE TRUCK	10	100.0	(D)	12.1	(D)	(D)	32.7	43.5	(D)	(D)	(D)
AIR	-	100.0	(D)	-	(D)	(D)	16.2	72.4	(D)	(D)	(D)
WATER	-	100.0	(D)	-	(D)	(D)	-	-	(D)	(D)	(D)
OTHER	-	100.0	(D)	-	(D)	(D)	5.1	-	(D)	(D)	(D)
UNKNOWN	-	100.0	(D)	-	(D)	(D)	-	-	(D)	(D)	(D)
WEST NORTH CENTRAL	20	100.0	(D)	3.1	(D)	(D)	53.5	18.6	(D)	(D)	(D)
RAIL	3	100.0	(D)	-	(D)	(D)	100.0	-	(D)	(D)	(D)
MOTOR CARRIER	11	100.0	(D)	5.6	(D)	(D)	36.8	14.4	(D)	(D)	(D)
PRIVATE TRUCK	5	100.0	(D)	-	(D)	(D)	60.6	39.4	(D)	(D)	(D)
AIR	-	100.0	(D)	100.0	(D)	(D)	-	-	(D)	(D)	(D)
WATER	-	100.0	(D)	-	(D)	(D)	-	-	(D)	(D)	(D)
OTHER	-	100.0	(D)	-	(D)	(D)	4.8	4.6	(D)	(D)	(D)
UNKNOWN	-	100.0	(D)	-	(D)	(D)	-	-	(D)	(D)	(D)
SOUTH ATLANTIC	2 129	100.0	(D)	1.5	(D)	(D)	80.9	15.5	(D)	(D)	(D)
RAIL	26	100.0	(D)	-	(D)	(D)	77.7	11.0	(D)	(D)	(D)
MOTOR CARRIER	1 286	100.0	(D)	1.2	(D)	(D)	80.6	15.8	(D)	(D)	(D)
PRIVATE TRUCK	805	100.0	(D)	2.1	(D)	(D)	82.2	15.3	(D)	(D)	(D)
AIR	-	100.0	(D)	-	(D)	(D)	99.7	-	(D)	(D)	(D)
WATER	-	100.0	(D)	-	(D)	(D)	-	-	(D)	(D)	(D)
OTHER	8	100.0	(D)	-	(D)	(D)	14.1	.2	(D)	(D)	(D)
UNKNOWN	1	100.0	(D)	-	(D)	(D)	82.4	17.6	(D)	(D)	(D)
EAST SOUTH CENTRAL	242	100.0	(D)	1.2	(D)	(D)	55.7	39.2	(D)	(D)	(D)
RAIL	1	100.0	(D)	-	(D)	(D)	-	100.0	(D)	(D)	(D)
MOTOR CARRIER	212	100.0	(D)	1.4	(D)	(D)	52.8	43.3	(D)	(D)	(D)
PRIVATE TRUCK	24	100.0	(D)	.2	(D)	(D)	91.7	8.1	(D)	(D)	(D)
AIR	-	100.0	(D)	-	(D)	(D)	95.3	-	(D)	(D)	(D)
WATER	-	100.0	(D)	-	(D)	(D)	-	-	(D)	(D)	(D)
OTHER	3	100.0	(D)	-	(D)	(D)	1.8	.8	(D)	(D)	(D)
UNKNOWN	-	100.0	(D)	-	(D)	(D)	100.0	-	(D)	(D)	(D)
WEST SOUTH CENTRAL	88	100.0	(D)	.1	(D)	(D)	56.4	34.1	(D)	(D)	(D)
RAIL	11	100.0	(D)	-	(D)	(D)	80.1	19.9	(D)	(D)	(D)
MOTOR CARRIER	34	100.0	(D)	.3	(D)	(D)	22.6	72.8	(D)	(D)	(D)
PRIVATE TRUCK	42	100.0	(D)	-	(D)	(D)	77.1	7.0	(D)	(D)	(D)
AIR	-	100.0	(D)	-	(D)	(D)	100.0	-	(D)	(D)	(D)
WATER	-	100.0	(D)	-	(D)	(D)	-	-	(D)	(D)	(D)
OTHER	-	100.0	(D)	-	(D)	(D)	89.5	4.6	(D)	(D)	(D)
UNKNOWN	-	100.0	(D)	-	(D)	(D)	-	-	(D)	(D)	(D)
MOUNTAIN	9	100.0	(D)	.1	(D)	(D)	59.7	35.6	(D)	(D)	(D)
RAIL	1	100.0	(D)	-	(D)	(D)	-	100.0	(D)	(D)	(D)
MOTOR CARRIER	6	100.0	(D)	.1	(D)	(D)	91.0	1.9	(D)	(D)	(D)
PRIVATE TRUCK	2	100.0	(D)	-	(D)	(D)	-	100.0	(D)	(D)	(D)
AIR	-	100.0	(D)	-	(D)	(D)	100.0	-	(D)	(D)	(D)
WATER	-	100.0	(D)	-	(D)	(D)	-	-	(D)	(D)	(D)
OTHER	-	100.0	(D)	-	(D)	(D)	100.0	-	(D)	(D)	(D)
UNKNOWN	-	100.0	(D)	-	(D)	(D)	-	-	(D)	(D)	(D)
PACIFIC	94	100.0	(D)	.1	(D)	(D)	76.1	20.8	(D)	(D)	(D)
RAIL	57	100.0	(D)	.2	(D)	(D)	73.8	26.0	(D)	(D)	(D)
MOTOR CARRIER	32	100.0	(D)	.1	(D)	(D)	77.5	14.1	(D)	(D)	(D)
PRIVATE TRUCK	4	100.0	(D)	-	(D)	(D)	95.1	2.5	(D)	(D)	(D)
AIR	-	100.0	(D)	-	(D)	(D)	36.8	50.0	(D)	(D)	(D)
WATER	-	100.0	(D)	-	(D)	(D)	-	-	(D)	(D)	(D)
OTHER	-	100.0	(D)	-	(D)	(D)	89.9	2.8	(D)	(D)	(D)
UNKNOWN	-	100.0	(D)	-	(D)	(D)	-	-	(D)	(D)	(D)

See footnotes at end of table 4.

TABLE 3. **TCC GROUP 228—Percent Distribution of Geographic Division of Destination and Means of Transport, by Geographic Division of Origin: 1972**—Continued

Geographic division of destination and means of transport	Number	Percent distribution by division of origin[1]									
		U.S. total	New England	Middle Atlantic	East North Central	West North Central	South Atlantic	East South Central	West South Central	Mountain	Pacific
TON-MILES OF SHIPMENTS	(millions of ton-miles)										
U.S. TOTAL...............	1 112	100.0	(D)	2.5	(D)	(D)	70.1	19.4	(D)	(D)	(D)
RAIL....................	157	100.0	(D)	.2	(D)	(D)	74.8	24.0	(D)	(D)	(D)
MOTOR CARRIER..........	684	100.0	(D)	2.6	(D)	(D)	69.7	17.9	(D)	(D)	(D)
PRIVATE TRUCK..........	262	100.0	(D)	3.7	(D)	(D)	70.5	21.0	(D)	(D)	(D)
AIR....................	-	100.0	(D)	.2	(D)	(D)	90.0	3.9	(D)	(D)	(D)
WATER..................	-	100.0	(D)	-	(D)	(D)	-	-	(D)	(D)	(D)
OTHER..................	7	100.0	(D)	-	(D)	(D)	3.4	.3	(D)	(D)	(D)
UNKNOWN................	-	100.0	(D)	-	(D)	(D)	33.4	5.1	(D)	(D)	(D)
NEW ENGLAND............	86	100.0	(D)	1.8	(D)	(D)	70.3	22.1	(D)	(D)	(D)
RAIL....................	-	100.0	(D)	-	(D)	(D)	-	-	(D)	(D)	(D)
MOTOR CARRIER..........	56	100.0	(D)	2.7	(D)	(D)	69.7	19.8	(D)	(D)	(D)
PRIVATE TRUCK..........	29	100.0	(D)	-	(D)	(D)	71.5	26.6	(D)	(D)	(D)
AIR....................	-	100.0	(D)	-	(D)	(D)	100.0	-	(D)	(D)	(D)
WATER..................	-	100.0	(D)	-	(D)	(D)	-	-	(D)	(D)	(D)
OTHER..................	-	100.0	(D)	-	(D)	(D)	70.8	28.1	(D)	(D)	(D)
UNKNOWN................	-	100.0	(D)	-	(D)	(D)	-	-	(D)	(D)	(D)
MIDDLE ATLANTIC........	203	100.0	(D)	3.7	(D)	(D)	72.4	13.1	(D)	(D)	(D)
RAIL....................	10	100.0	(D)	-	(D)	(D)	33.8	66.2	(D)	(D)	(D)
MOTOR CARRIER..........	161	100.0	(D)	3.2	(D)	(D)	75.1	10.4	(D)	(D)	(D)
PRIVATE TRUCK..........	32	100.0	(D)	7.5	(D)	(D)	71.4	9.8	(D)	(D)	(D)
AIR....................	-	100.0	(D)	-	(D)	(D)	52.2	17.9	(D)	(D)	(D)
WATER..................	-	100.0	(D)	-	(D)	(D)	-	-	(D)	(D)	(D)
OTHER..................	-	100.0	(D)	-	(D)	(D)	83.4	15.4	(D)	(D)	(D)
UNKNOWN................	-	100.0	(D)	-	(D)	(D)	-	-	(D)	(D)	(D)
EAST NORTH CENTRAL......	47	100.0	(D)	4.3	(D)	(D)	53.5	20.7	(D)	(D)	(D)
RAIL....................	7	100.0	(D)	-	(D)	(D)	96.8	3.2	(D)	(D)	(D)
MOTOR CARRIER..........	33	100.0	(D)	4.6	(D)	(D)	48.8	21.3	(D)	(D)	(D)
PRIVATE TRUCK..........	5	100.0	(D)	8.5	(D)	(D)	30.9	42.6	(D)	(D)	(D)
AIR....................	-	100.0	(D)	-	(D)	(D)	12.1	73.3	(D)	(D)	(D)
WATER..................	-	100.0	(D)	-	(D)	(D)	-	-	(D)	(D)	(D)
OTHER..................	-	100.0	(D)	-	(D)	(D)	4.3	-	(D)	(D)	(D)
UNKNOWN................	-	100.0	(D)	-	(D)	(D)	-	-	(D)	(D)	(D)
WEST NORTH CENTRAL......	13	100.0	(D)	3.9	(D)	(D)	64.1	16.6	(D)	(D)	(D)
RAIL....................	2	100.0	(D)	-	(D)	(D)	100.0	-	(D)	(D)	(D)
MOTOR CARRIER..........	6	100.0	(D)	8.0	(D)	(D)	46.1	15.5	(D)	(D)	(D)
PRIVATE TRUCK..........	4	100.0	(D)	-	(D)	(D)	70.6	29.4	(D)	(D)	(D)
AIR....................	-	100.0	(D)	100.0	(D)	(D)	-	-	(D)	(D)	(D)
WATER..................	-	100.0	(D)	-	(D)	(D)	-	-	(D)	(D)	(D)
OTHER..................	-	100.0	(D)	-	(D)	(D)	6.0	4.2	(D)	(D)	(D)
UNKNOWN................	-	100.0	(D)	-	(D)	(D)	-	-	(D)	(D)	(D)
SOUTH ATLANTIC.........	417	100.0	(D)	3.2	(D)	(D)	68.7	20.1	(D)	(D)	(D)
RAIL....................	9	100.0	(D)	-	(D)	(D)	78.9	4.1	(D)	(D)	(D)
MOTOR CARRIER..........	267	100.0	(D)	2.5	(D)	(D)	70.6	17.8	(D)	(D)	(D)
PRIVATE TRUCK..........	136	100.0	(D)	5.0	(D)	(D)	66.7	26.3	(D)	(D)	(D)
AIR....................	-	100.0	(D)	-	(D)	(D)	98.1	-	(D)	(D)	(D)
WATER..................	-	100.0	(D)	-	(D)	(D)	-	-	(D)	(D)	(D)
OTHER..................	4	100.0	(D)	-	(D)	(D)	2.7	.1	(D)	(D)	(D)
UNKNOWN................	-	100.0	(D)	-	(D)	(D)	79.9	20.1	(D)	(D)	(D)
EAST SOUTH CENTRAL......	76	100.0	(D)	2.7	(D)	(D)	61.2	27.8	(D)	(D)	(D)
RAIL....................	-	100.0	(D)	-	(D)	(D)	-	100.0	(D)	(D)	(D)
MOTOR CARRIER..........	66	100.0	(D)	3.0	(D)	(D)	59.4	30.9	(D)	(D)	(D)
PRIVATE TRUCK..........	7	100.0	(D)	.3	(D)	(D)	94.5	5.2	(D)	(D)	(D)
AIR....................	-	100.0	(D)	-	(D)	(D)	91.8	-	(D)	(D)	(D)
WATER..................	-	100.0	(D)	-	(D)	(D)	-	-	(D)	(D)	(D)
OTHER..................	1	100.0	(D)	-	(D)	(D)	.7	.3	(D)	(D)	(D)
UNKNOWN................	-	100.0	(D)	-	(D)	(D)	100.0	-	(D)	(D)	(D)
WEST SOUTH CENTRAL......	63	100.0	(D)	.2	(D)	(D)	71.9	18.7	(D)	(D)	(D)
RAIL....................	11	100.0	(D)	-	(D)	(D)	90.7	9.3	(D)	(D)	(D)
MOTOR CARRIER..........	17	100.0	(D)	.8	(D)	(D)	37.3	53.9	(D)	(D)	(D)
PRIVATE TRUCK..........	35	100.0	(D)	-	(D)	(D)	82.8	4.7	(D)	(D)	(D)
AIR....................	-	100.0	(D)	-	(D)	(D)	100.0	-	(D)	(D)	(D)
WATER..................	-	100.0	(D)	-	(D)	(D)	-	-	(D)	(D)	(D)
OTHER..................	-	100.0	(D)	-	(D)	(D)	94.8	2.7	(D)	(D)	(D)
UNKNOWN................	-	100.0	(D)	-	(D)	(D)	-	-	(D)	(D)	(D)
MOUNTAIN...............	13	100.0	(D)	.1	(D)	(D)	66.1	30.7	(D)	(D)	(D)
RAIL....................	1	100.0	(D)	-	(D)	(D)	-	100.0	(D)	(D)	(D)
MOTOR CARRIER..........	9	100.0	(D)	.2	(D)	(D)	94.0	1.3	(D)	(D)	(D)
PRIVATE TRUCK..........	2	100.0	(D)	-	(D)	(D)	-	100.0	(D)	(D)	(D)
AIR....................	-	100.0	(D)	-	(D)	(D)	100.0	-	(D)	(D)	(D)
WATER..................	-	100.0	(D)	-	(D)	(D)	-	-	(D)	(D)	(D)
OTHER..................	-	100.0	(D)	-	(D)	(D)	100.0	-	(D)	(D)	(D)
UNKNOWN................	-	100.0	(D)	-	(D)	(D)	-	-	(D)	(D)	(D)
PACIFIC................	189	100.0	(D)	.2	(D)	(D)	78.6	19.4	(D)	(D)	(D)
RAIL....................	115	100.0	(D)	.2	(D)	(D)	75.8	23.9	(D)	(D)	(D)
MOTOR CARRIER..........	65	100.0	(D)	.1	(D)	(D)	81.2	13.8	(D)	(D)	(D)
PRIVATE TRUCK..........	8	100.0	(D)	-	(D)	(D)	94.7	2.3	(D)	(D)	(D)
AIR....................	-	100.0	(D)	-	(D)	(D)	38.1	46.9	(D)	(D)	(D)
WATER..................	-	100.0	(D)	-	(D)	(D)	-	-	(D)	(D)	(D)
OTHER..................	-	100.0	(D)	-	(D)	(D)	91.7	2.6	(D)	(D)	(D)
UNKNOWN................	-	100.0	(D)	-	(D)	(D)	-	-	(D)	(D)	(D)

See footnotes at end of table 4.

TABLE 4. TCC GROUP 228—Percent Distribution of Distance Shipped and Weight of Shipment, by Means of Transport: 1972

Distance shipped and weight of shipment[2][3]	Number	Percent distribution by means of transport							
		All means of transport	Rail	Motor carrier	Private truck	Air	Water	Other	Unknown
TONS OF SHIPMENTS	(thousands of tons)								
U.S. TOTAL.........	3 104	100.0	3.8	67.8	27.8	-	-	.4	.1
UNDER 100 MILES.........	666	100.0	.7	53.7	45.3	-	.2	.2	-
UNDER 1000 POUNDS.....	20	100.0	-	83.2	14.6	-	1.4	.2	.6
1000 TO 9999 POUNDS...	223	100.0	-	54.4	45.1	.1	.4	-	.1
10000 TO 29999 POUNDS.	263	100.0	-	53.9	45.7	.1	-	.4	-
30000 TO 59999 POUNDS.	139	100.0	-	53.4	46.6	-	-	-	-
60000 TO 89999 POUNDS.	20	100.0	21.6	15.4	63.0	-	-	-	-
90000 POUNDS AND OVER.	-	100.0	-	-	-	-	-	-	-
100 TO 199 MILES........	585	100.0	.1	74.2	25.5	-	-	-	.2
UNDER 1000 POUNDS.....	20	100.0	-	88.0	11.3	-	-	.5	.2
1000 TO 9999 POUNDS...	161	100.0	-	71.6	28.2	-	-	-	.2
10000 TO 29999 POUNDS.	178	100.0	-	79.7	20.1	-	-	-	.3
30000 TO 59999 POUNDS.	187	100.0	.3	66.1	33.5	-	-	-	.1
60000 TO 89999 POUNDS.	9	100.0	-	64.2	35.8	-	-	-	-
90000 POUNDS AND OVER.	29	100.0	-	100.0	-	-	-	-	-
200 TO 299 MILES........	741	100.0	.4	80.3	19.1	-	-	-	.3
UNDER 1000 POUNDS.....	11	100.0	-	93.6	6.1	.1	-	.2	-
1000 TO 9999 POUNDS...	135	100.0	-	82.7	17.3	-	-	-	-
10000 TO 29999 POUNDS.	280	100.0	-	77.5	21.9	-	-	-	.7
30000 TO 59999 POUNDS.	282	100.0	.6	79.7	19.8	-	-	-	-
60000 TO 89999 POUNDS.	17	100.0	7.6	92.4	-	-	-	-	-
90000 POUNDS AND OVER.	14	100.0	-	100.0	-	-	-	-	-
300 TO 499 MILES........	532	100.0	5.2	68.4	26.4	-	-	-	-
UNDER 1000 POUNDS.....	14	100.0	-	95.4	3.6	.6	-	.4	-
1000 TO 9999 POUNDS...	121	100.0	-	76.4	23.6	-	-	-	-
10000 TO 29999 POUNDS.	150	100.0	-	63.7	36.3	-	-	-	-
30000 TO 59999 POUNDS.	207	100.0	1.5	73.2	25.3	-	-	-	-
60000 TO 89999 POUNDS.	17	100.0	56.2	22.5	21.3	-	-	-	-
90000 POUNDS AND OVER.	19	100.0	76.1	23.9	-	-	-	-	-
500 TO 999 MILES........	462	100.0	5.3	66.7	25.3	-	-	2.7	-
UNDER 1000 POUNDS.....	14	100.0	-	84.2	13.7	.3	-	1.5	.2
1000 TO 9999 POUNDS...	135	100.0	-	76.1	21.1	-	-	2.8	-
10000 TO 29999 POUNDS.	169	100.0	2.4	63.2	29.9	-	-	4.5	-
30000 TO 59999 POUNDS.	108	100.0	8.6	67.6	23.0	-	-	.8	-
60000 TO 89999 POUNDS.	28	100.0	38.5	38.9	22.6	-	-	-	-
90000 POUNDS AND OVER.	6	100.0	-	28.6	71.4	-	-	-	-
1000 TO 1499 MILES......	30	100.0	31.1	39.8	29.0	.1	-	-	-
UNDER 1000 POUNDS.....	2	100.0	-	74.6	23.9	1.5	-	-	-
1000 TO 9999 POUNDS...	6	100.0	-	78.6	21.4	-	-	-	-
10000 TO 29999 POUNDS.	6	100.0	-	42.1	57.9	-	-	-	-
30000 TO 59999 POUNDS.	14	100.0	65.4	14.7	19.9	-	-	-	-
60000 TO 89999 POUNDS.	-	100.0	-	-	-	-	-	-	-
90000 POUNDS AND OVER.	-	100.0	-	-	-	-	-	-	-
1500 MILES OR OVER......	85	100.0	55.5	39.5	5.0	-	-	-	-
UNDER 1000 POUNDS.....	2	100.0	.7	96.7	1.5	-	-	1.1	-
1000 TO 9999 POUNDS...	6	100.0	7.4	87.8	4.8	-	-	-	-
10000 TO 29999 POUNDS.	22	100.0	44.9	42.8	12.3	-	-	-	-
30000 TO 59999 POUNDS.	49	100.0	66.6	31.0	2.4	-	-	-	-
60000 TO 89999 POUNDS.	4	100.0	84.7	15.3	-	-	-	-	-
90000 POUNDS AND OVER.	-	100.0	-	-	-	-	-	-	-
TON-MILES OF SHIPMENTS	(millions of ton-miles)								
U.S. TOTAL..........	1 029	100.0	13.2	64.2	21.8	-	-	.7	.1
UNDER 100 MILES.........	35	100.0	.4	57.2	41.9	-	.1	.3	.1
UNDER 1000 POUNDS.....	1	100.0	-	85.5	12.6	-	.7	.4	.7
1000 TO 9999 POUNDS...	11	100.0	-	59.2	40.5	.1	.2	-	.1
10000 TO 29999 POUNDS.	14	100.0	-	58.2	41.2	-	-	.7	-
30000 TO 59999 POUNDS.	8	100.0	-	53.1	46.9	-	-	-	-
60000 TO 89999 POUNDS.	-	100.0	20.0	20.4	59.7	-	-	-	-
90000 POUNDS AND OVER.	-	100.0	-	-	-	-	-	-	-
100 TO 199 MILES........	87	100.0	.1	75.3	24.4	-	-	-	.1
UNDER 1000 POUNDS.....	2	100.0	-	87.7	11.6	-	-	.5	.2
1000 TO 9999 POUNDS...	22	100.0	-	74.8	25.0	-	-	-	.2
10000 TO 29999 POUNDS.	27	100.0	-	79.1	20.6	-	-	-	.2
30000 TO 59999 POUNDS.	27	100.0	.4	67.0	32.6	-	-	-	.1
60000 TO 89999 POUNDS.	1	100.0	-	59.9	40.1	-	-	-	-
90000 POUNDS AND OVER.	4	100.0	-	100.0	-	-	-	-	-

See footnotes at end of table 4.

TABLE 4. TCC GROUP 228—Percent Distribution of Distance Shipped and Weight of Shipment, by Means of Transport: 1972—Continued

Distance shipped and weight of shipment [2] [3]	Number	Percent distribution by means of transport							
		All means of transport	Rail	Motor carrier	Private truck	Air	Water	Other	Unknown
TON-MILES OF SHIPMENTS	(millions of ton-miles)								
200 TO 299 MILES	182	100.0	.4	80.5	18.9	-	-	-	.2
UNDER 1000 POUNDS	2	100.0	-	93.8	5.8	.1	-	.2	-
1000 TO 9999 POUNDS	32	100.0	-	83.0	17.0	-	-	-	-
10000 TO 29999 POUNDS	67	100.0	-	77.4	21.9	-	-	-	.7
30000 TO 59999 POUNDS	71	100.0	.5	80.0	19.5	-	-	-	-
60000 TO 89999 POUNDS	4	100.0	8.7	91.3	-	-	-	-	-
90000 POUNDS AND OVER	3	100.0	-	100.0	-	-	-	-	-
300 TO 499 MILES	205	100.0	6.3	68.7	24.9	-	-	-	-
UNDER 1000 POUNDS	5	100.0	-	95.7	3.4	.6	-	.4	-
1000 TO 9999 POUNDS	48	100.0	-	77.8	22.2	-	-	-	-
10000 TO 29999 POUNDS	56	100.0	-	65.0	35.0	-	-	-	-
30000 TO 59999 POUNDS	79	100.0	1.7	74.0	24.4	-	-	-	-
60000 TO 89999 POUNDS	7	100.0	62.9	19.3	17.8	-	-	-	-
90000 POUNDS AND OVER	8	100.0	81.1	18.9	-	-	-	-	-
500 TO 999 MILES	312	100.0	5.2	65.5	26.9	-	-	2.4	-
UNDER 1000 POUNDS	9	100.0	-	82.9	15.1	.4	-	1.4	.1
1000 TO 9999 POUNDS	90	100.0	-	75.9	22.1	-	-	2.1	-
10000 TO 29999 POUNDS	115	100.0	1.9	62.0	32.1	-	-	4.0	-
30000 TO 59999 POUNDS	71	100.0	8.7	64.2	26.0	-	-	1.1	-
60000 TO 89999 POUNDS	19	100.0	39.8	40.7	19.5	-	-	-	-
90000 POUNDS AND OVER	4	100.0	-	39.1	60.9	-	-	-	-
1000 TO 1499 MILES	33	100.0	30.8	40.9	28.2	.1	-	-	-
UNDER 1000 POUNDS	2	100.0	-	77.6	21.0	1.4	-	-	-
1000 TO 9999 POUNDS	8	100.0	-	80.6	19.4	-	-	-	-
10000 TO 29999 POUNDS	7	100.0	-	41.6	58.4	-	-	-	-
30000 TO 59999 POUNDS	16	100.0	65.3	14.4	20.4	-	-	-	-
60000 TO 89999 POUNDS	-	100.0	-	-	-	-	-	-	-
90000 POUNDS AND OVER	-	100.0	-	-	-	-	-	-	-
1500 MILES OR OVER	172	100.0	55.2	39.7	5.1	-	-	-	-
UNDER 1000 POUNDS	3	100.0	.9	95.9	1.8	.1	-	1.2	-
1000 TO 9999 POUNDS	13	100.0	7.8	87.3	4.9	-	-	-	-
10000 TO 29999 POUNDS	44	100.0	43.8	43.5	12.7	-	-	-	-
30000 TO 59999 POUNDS	100	100.0	66.0	31.7	2.3	-	-	-	-
60000 TO 89999 POUNDS	9	100.0	84.4	15.6	-	-	-	-	-
90000 POUNDS AND OVER	-	100.0	-	-	-	-	-	-	-

Note: Detail may not add to total due to rounding. The introductory table shows the estimates of sampling variability for tons; sampling variability for ton-miles has not been estimated. See the map in the Introduction for the States comprising the geographic divisions of the United States.

Shipments excluded from the survey are those moving by pipeline (primarily petroleum products from refineries), parcel post shipments, and commodities moved by own power (motorized vehicles, aircraft, etc.) or towed (prefabricated buildings, etc.). Local shipments (commodities shipped less than 25 miles from the plant) and shipments within the same city are also excluded. Shipments to Alaska and Hawaii from the 48 conterminous States and the District of Columbia are included; however, no data were obtained for shipments originating in Alaska and Hawaii.

- Represents zero or rounds to zero.   (D) Withheld to avoid disclosing figures for individual companies.

[1] Production of this commodity is concentrated in the geographic divisions shown; figures and distributions for geographic divisions not shown are included in the total.

[2] Distances of shipments to foreign destinations are calculated only to the U.S. port of exit.

[3] Includes only shipments represented by bills of lading and invoices. Summary records which did not show individual weights of shipments are not included.

TCC 231. Men's, Youths', and Boys' Clothing

Comparisons of Tons and Ton-Miles of Shipments for
Geographic Divisions of Origin and for Sampling Variability: 1972 and 1967

Geographic division of origin	Estimates				Relative sampling variability in tons (percent)	
	1972		1967		1972	1967
	Tons (thousands)	Ton-miles (millions)	Tons (thousands)	Ton-miles (millions)	1972	1967
U.S. total	1,911	1,130	965	556	21.7	13.2
New England	(D)	(D)	13	5	(*)	(*)
Middle Atlantic	182	86	180	91	22.8	(*)
East North Central	59	30	111	67	24.6	(*)
West North Central	57	36	52	22	49.9	(*)
South Atlantic	553	395	240	137	27.7	(*)
East South Central	425	281	265	148	27.6	(*)
West South Central	175	154	98	83	26.0	(*)
Mountain	(D)	(D)	—	—	(*)	(*)
Pacific	43	39	6	3	46.0	(*)

— Represents or rounds to zero.   (D) Withheld to avoid disclosing figures for individual companies.   (*) Data not published.

TABLE 1. **TCC GROUP 231—Percent Distribution of Geographic Division of Origin and Distance Shipped, by Means of Transport: 1972**

Geographic division of origin[1] and distance shipped[2]	Number	Percent distribution by means of transport							
		All means of transport	Rail	Motor carrier	Private truck	Air	Water	Other	Unknown
TONS OF SHIPMENTS	(thousands of tons)								
U.S. TOTAL..........	1 911	100.0	2.7	77.4	12.1	1.8	-	5.9	.1
MIDDLE ATLANTIC.........	182	100.0	1.4	75.0	10.2	1.4	.1	11.8	-
UNDER 100 MILES.......	39	100.0	-	67.6	25.6	-	.1	6.7	-
100 TO 199 MILES......	23	100.0	-	71.1	18.5	.1	.3	10.0	-
200 TO 299 MILES......	22	100.0	.1	72.4	14.8	.5	-	12.2	-
300 TO 499 MILES......	43	100.0	-	90.5	-	.6	-	8.9	-
500 TO 999 MILES.....	31	100.0	.6	76.6	2.3	3.0	-	17.2	.2
1000 TO 1499 MILES....	12	100.0	.6	67.1	.4	6.9	-	25.0	-
1500 MILES OR OVER....	9	100.0	24.1	57.1	-	3.8	-	14.9	.1
EAST NORTH CENTRAL......	59	100.0	-	67.4	11.3	.7	-	20.3	.4
UNDER 100 MILES.......	12	100.0	-	66.1	22.2	-	-	11.7	-
100 TO 199 MILES......	8	100.0	-	45.9	37.6	-	-	16.4	.1
200 TO 299 MILES......	5	100.0	-	64.5	2.0	-	-	32.6	.7
300 TO 499 MILES......	9	100.0	-	72.5	2.3	.4	-	24.6	.2
500 TO 999 MILES.....	18	100.0	-	74.9	3.5	1.6	-	19.4	.5
1000 TO 1499 MILES....	2	100.0	-	71.4	-	1.8	-	23.8	3.1
1500 MILES OR OVER....	4	100.0	-	69.9	-	.5	-	29.3	.2
WEST NORTH CENTRAL......	57	100.0	-	88.5	1.2	2.3	-	7.9	-
UNDER 100 MILES.......	-	100.0	-	49.3	-	-	-	50.7	-
100 TO 199 MILES......	17	100.0	-	95.9	3.1	-	-	1.0	-
200 TO 299 MILES......	5	100.0	-	80.7	-	-	-	19.3	-
300 TO 499 MILES......	4	100.0	-	78.7	3.4	.1	-	17.8	-
500 TO 999 MILES.....	13	100.0	-	84.3	-	3.3	-	12.5	-
1000 TO 1499 MILES....	15	100.0	-	90.1	-	5.6	-	4.2	-
1500 MILES OR OVER....	-	100.0	-	93.3	-	2.4	-	4.3	-
SOUTH ATLANTIC..........	553	100.0	.3	85.3	5.9	1.3	-	7.1	.1
UNDER 100 MILES.......	29	100.0	-	72.0	24.8	-	-	3.2	.1
100 TO 199 MILES......	33	100.0	-	70.9	23.5	.1	-	5.4	.1
200 TO 299 MILES......	46	100.0	.1	84.2	10.4	.1	-	4.5	.7
300 TO 499 MILES......	115	100.0	.2	85.7	7.6	.2	-	5.9	.4
500 TO 999 MILES.....	237	100.0	.2	86.5	.9	2.5	-	9.9	-
1000 TO 1499 MILES....	30	100.0	-	92.9	.1	.9	-	6.1	-
1500 MILES OR OVER....	60	100.0	1.7	91.2	2.3	1.3	-	3.5	-
EAST SOUTH CENTRAL......	425	100.0	10.8	52.3	29.1	1.7	.1	6.0	.1
UNDER 100 MILES.......	61	100.0	-	15.1	79.7	1.6	-	3.5	-
100 TO 199 MILES......	24	100.0	.8	63.5	24.3	1.1	-	10.3	-
200 TO 299 MILES......	32	100.0	20.5	62.1	12.6	.2	.8	3.8	-
300 TO 499 MILES......	75	100.0	2.6	65.0	13.4	4.2	-	14.6	.1
500 TO 999 MILES.....	153	100.0	2.7	58.5	32.6	.9	-	5.3	-
1000 TO 1499 MILES....	10	100.0	47.2	45.0	3.9	1.7	-	2.3	-
1500 MILES OR OVER....	66	100.0	41.8	49.9	6.2	1.6	-	.2	.3
WEST SOUTH CENTRAL......	175	100.0	-	71.3	20.3	6.7	-	1.7	.1
UNDER 100 MILES.......	10	100.0	-	46.5	53.5	-	-	-	-
100 TO 199 MILES......	5	100.0	.3	82.8	14.9	-	-	.2	1.9
200 TO 299 MILES......	6	100.0	-	89.7	10.2	-	-	.1	-
300 TO 499 MILES......	31	100.0	-	45.9	54.0	-	-	.1	-
500 TO 999 MILES.....	52	100.0	-	82.0	12.9	3.4	-	1.7	-
1000 TO 1499 MILES....	43	100.0	-	71.6	7.5	17.8	-	3.2	-
1500 MILES OR OVER....	25	100.0	-	82.8	5.8	8.9	-	2.5	-
PACIFIC..................	43	100.0	2.8	69.8	13.8	6.1	-	7.3	.1
UNDER 100 MILES.......	6	100.0	-	86.9	5.9	.5	-	6.6	-
100 TO 199 MILES......	6	100.0	-	98.0	-	.1	-	1.9	-
200 TO 299 MILES......	3	100.0	-	91.5	-	1.2	-	7.2	-
300 TO 499 MILES......	3	100.0	-	91.4	2.0	-	-	5.5	1.0
500 TO 999 MILES.....	9	100.0	-	86.2	1.7	.1	-	12.0	-
1000 TO 1499 MILES....	3	100.0	-	57.1	29.7	9.3	-	3.9	-
1500 MILES OR OVER....	12	100.0	10.0	27.1	36.1	18.4	-	8.3	-
TON-MILES OF SHIPMENTS	(millions of ton-miles)								
U.S. TOTAL..........	1 130	100.0	6.4	75.6	8.5	3.3	-	6.1	.1
MIDDLE ATLANTIC.........	86	100.0	6.2	72.1	2.8	3.1	-	15.7	.1
UNDER 100 MILES.......	2	100.0	-	68.2	25.6	-	.1	6.1	-
100 TO 199 MILES......	3	100.0	-	71.2	18.1	.1	.2	10.4	-
200 TO 299 MILES......	5	100.0	.1	75.2	11.8	.5	-	12.4	-
300 TO 499 MILES......	15	100.0	-	89.7	-	.7	-	9.6	-
500 TO 999 MILES.....	22	100.0	.6	77.2	1.9	2.5	-	17.5	.2
1000 TO 1499 MILES....	14	100.0	.6	67.2	.5	6.8	-	24.9	-
1500 MILES OR OVER....	21	100.0	24.4	56.7	-	4.4	-	14.5	.1
EAST NORTH CENTRAL......	30	100.0	-	70.8	3.4	1.1	-	24.1	.5
UNDER 100 MILES.......	-	100.0	-	73.3	13.2	-	-	13.5	-
100 TO 199 MILES......	1	100.0	-	42.1	40.6	-	-	17.2	.1
200 TO 299 MILES......	1	100.0	-	64.1	2.3	-	-	32.9	.8
300 TO 499 MILES......	3	100.0	-	72.5	2.0	.4	-	24.9	.2
500 TO 999 MILES.....	12	100.0	-	76.8	3.0	1.9	-	17.8	.5
1000 TO 1499 MILES....	2	100.0	-	72.3	-	1.7	-	23.0	3.1
1500 MILES OR OVER....	8	100.0	-	65.7	-	.6	-	33.6	.1

See footnotes at end of table 4.

TABLE 1. **TCC GROUP 231**—Percent Distribution of Geographic Division of Origin and Distance Shipped, by Means of Transport: 1972—Continued

Geographic division of origin[1] and distance shipped[2]	Number	Percent distribution by means of transport							
		All means of transport	Rail	Motor carrier	Private truck	Air	Water	Other	Unknown
TON-MILES OF SHIPMENTS	(millions of ton-miles)								
WEST NORTH CENTRAL	36	100.0	-	88.6	.4	3.8	-	7.2	-
UNDER 100 MILES	-	100.0	-	74.5	-	-	-	25.5	-
100 TO 199 MILES	2	100.0	-	95.1	3.8	-	-	1.1	-
200 TO 299 MILES	1	100.0	-	83.8	-	-	-	16.2	-
300 TO 499 MILES	1	100.0	-	78.4	2.9	.1	-	18.6	-
500 TO 999 MILES	11	100.0	-	85.3	-	3.3	-	11.3	-
1000 TO 1499 MILES	18	100.0	-	91.0	-	5.1	-	3.9	-
1500 MILES OR OVER	-	100.0	-	90.1	-	5.8	-	4.1	-
SOUTH ATLANTIC	395	100.0	.6	88.6	2.6	1.6	-	6.5	.1
UNDER 100 MILES	1	100.0	-	77.7	18.1	-	-	4.1	-
100 TO 199 MILES	5	100.0	-	70.4	23.5	.1	-	6.0	.1
200 TO 299 MILES	11	100.0	.1	84.8	9.7	.1	-	4.7	.6
300 TO 499 MILES	46	100.0	.3	85.1	8.1	.2	-	6.1	.3
500 TO 999 MILES	165	100.0	.2	86.8	.9	2.5	-	9.5	-
1000 TO 1499 MILES	37	100.0	-	93.4	.1	.8	-	5.7	-
1500 MILES OR OVER	128	100.0	1.6	92.1	1.8	1.3	-	3.3	-
EAST SOUTH CENTRAL	281	100.0	22.0	54.2	18.0	1.6	-	4.0	.2
UNDER 100 MILES	2	100.0	-	19.5	75.0	2.0	-	3.5	-
100 TO 199 MILES	3	100.0	.8	63.5	24.1	1.2	-	10.4	-
200 TO 299 MILES	7	100.0	18.6	63.1	13.3	.2	.8	4.0	-
300 TO 499 MILES	30	100.0	3.2	65.2	12.2	4.0	-	15.3	.1
500 TO 999 MILES	104	100.0	2.9	57.7	33.6	.9	-	4.9	-
1000 TO 1499 MILES	11	100.0	44.9	47.0	4.0	1.7	-	2.4	-
1500 MILES OR OVER	120	100.0	42.6	49.0	5.9	1.8	-	.2	.4
WEST SOUTH CENTRAL	154	100.0	-	75.6	12.0	10.2	-	2.2	-
UNDER 100 MILES	-	100.0	-	67.6	32.4	-	-	-	-
100 TO 199 MILES	-	100.0	.4	86.3	11.7	-	-	.2	1.5
200 TO 299 MILES	1	100.0	-	87.8	12.1	-	-	.1	-
300 TO 499 MILES	13	100.0	-	45.2	54.7	-	-	.1	-
500 TO 999 MILES	38	100.0	-	84.1	10.0	4.2	-	1.7	-
1000 TO 1499 MILES	54	100.0	-	71.0	7.6	18.4	-	3.0	-
1500 MILES OR OVER	44	100.0	-	82.4	6.1	9.0	-	2.5	-
PACIFIC	39	100.0	5.4	44.8	28.2	12.5	-	9.0	-
UNDER 100 MILES	-	100.0	-	85.9	2.1	.3	-	11.8	-
100 TO 199 MILES	-	100.0	-	97.9	-	.1	-	2.1	-
200 TO 299 MILES	-	100.0	-	91.0	-	1.3	-	7.7	-
300 TO 499 MILES	1	100.0	-	91.6	1.8	-	-	5.4	1.2
500 TO 999 MILES	6	100.0	-	84.7	2.2	-	-	13.1	-
1000 TO 1499 MILES	4	100.0	-	56.6	29.4	10.0	-	4.0	-
1500 MILES OR OVER	25	100.0	8.5	26.1	38.4	17.8	-	9.2	-

See footnotes at end of table 4.

TABLE 2. **TCC GROUP 231**—Percent Distribution of Geographic Division of Origin and Means of Transport, by Geographic Division of Destination: 1972

Geographic division of origin[1] and means of transport	Number	Percent distribution by division of destination									
		U.S. total	New England	Middle Atlantic	East North Central	West North Central	South Atlantic	East South Central	West South Central	Mountain	Pacific
TONS OF SHIPMENTS	(thousands of tons)										
U.S. TOTAL	1 911	100.0	20.4	16.6	15.1	5.4	14.0	9.5	7.1	2.5	9.2
RAIL	51	100.0	.2	6.1	3.7	.1	4.0	13.2	13.1	.5	59.1
MOTOR CARRIER	1 479	100.0	25.6	15.7	15.9	5.5	13.4	5.6	7.0	2.8	8.5
PRIVATE TRUCK	231	100.0	1.6	24.3	5.2	4.1	18.4	33.9	7.5	1.2	3.7
AIR	34	100.0	8.7	18.9	37.4	2.5	7.6	4.5	3.9	.6	15.8
WATER	-	100.0	-	27.8	-	-	-	72.2	-	-	-
OTHER	112	100.0	4.5	18.2	23.5	10.0	20.2	9.4	6.6	2.5	5.2
UNKNOWN	1	100.0	-	15.2	8.4	.3	22.5	29.9	.3	4.3	19.2
MIDDLE ATLANTIC	182	100.0	6.6	47.8	18.1	5.5	9.6	3.0	4.7	1.0	3.7
RAIL	2	100.0	-	.7	5.8	2.1	1.6	.3	18.5	1.0	70.0
MOTOR CARRIER	137	100.0	7.4	47.8	18.4	5.0	10.5	3.2	4.2	.9	2.6
PRIVATE TRUCK	18	100.0	.9	86.4	8.2	-	4.2	-	.3	-	-
AIR	2	100.0	8.0	1.2	34.6	11.0	14.7	.6	15.6	1.0	13.4
WATER	-	100.0	-	100.0	-	-	-	-	-	-	-
OTHER	21	100.0	7.3	26.4	23.8	13.4	9.4	4.5	8.8	2.4	4.0
UNKNOWN	-	100.0	-	-	67.2	1.4	22.9	-	-	6.1	2.4
EAST NORTH CENTRAL	59	100.0	2.6	10.9	33.7	12.2	12.1	7.5	9.9	3.8	7.2
RAIL	-	100.0	-	-	-	-	-	-	-	-	-
MOTOR CARRIER	40	100.0	3.4	10.3	34.0	9.4	11.5	7.2	12.6	4.0	7.6
PRIVATE TRUCK	6	100.0	-	1.2	41.1	34.5	8.9	14.3	.1	-	-
AIR	-	100.0	.7	11.3	1.7	11.3	28.8	-	38.9	1.2	6.1
WATER	-	100.0	-	-	-	-	-	-	-	-	-
OTHER	12	100.0	1.6	17.8	30.1	9.6	15.3	5.3	5.7	4.6	10.1
UNKNOWN	-	100.0	-	36.9	14.8	1.7	9.5	3.8	2.2	31.1	-

See footnotes at end of table 4.

TABLE 2. TCC GROUP 231—Percent Distribution of Geographic Division of Origin and Means of Transport, by Geographic Division of Destination: 1972—Continued

Geographic division of origin[1] and means of transport	Number	Percent distribution by division of destination									
		U.S. total	New England	Middle Atlantic	East North Central	West North Central	South Atlantic	East South Central	West South Central	Mountain	Pacific
TONS OF SHIPMENTS	(thousands of tons)										
WEST NORTH CENTRAL......	57	100.0	7.1	15.2	8.6	36.9	9.7	6.2	2.1	1.5	12.6
RAIL...................	-	100.0	-	-	-	-	-	-	-	-	-
MOTOR CARRIER.........	50	100.0	6.2	14.7	8.0	38.7	10.0	5.2	1.8	1.6	13.8
PRIVATE TRUCK........	-	100.0	-	-	-	-	-	100.0	-	-	-
AIR...................	1	100.0	53.1	41.6	.5	-	-	-	-	-	4.8
WATER.................	-	100.0	-	-	-	-	-	-	-	-	-
OTHER.................	4	100.0	5.6	15.8	19.6	33.3	11.2	4.5	6.5	.5	3.0
UNKNOWN...............	-	100.0	-	-	-	-	-	-	-	-	-
SOUTH ATLANTIC.........	553	100.0	4.3	14.1	20.9	5.1	23.7	8.4	10.0	4.8	8.7
RAIL...................	1	100.0	3.0	11.1	10.4	-	10.0	8.0	2.5	2.2	52.9
MOTOR CARRIER.........	472	100.0	4.5	14.4	21.3	4.9	21.8	7.4	11.1	5.0	9.6
PRIVATE TRUCK........	32	100.0	-	4.0	.4	-	65.5	24.3	1.5	3.8	.5
AIR...................	7	100.0	8.5	9.1	61.6	.5	2.1	4.0	3.4	1.4	9.5
WATER.................	-	100.0	-	-	-	-	-	-	-	-	-
OTHER.................	39	100.0	4.4	20.5	26.7	12.0	16.6	7.1	6.0	3.3	3.5
UNKNOWN...............	-	100.0	-	-	-	-	46.4	53.5	.1	-	-
EAST SOUTH CENTRAL.....	425	100.0	1.2	16.7	17.3	5.0	16.7	21.9	5.2	.8	15.2
RAIL...................	45	100.0	.1	6.4	.7	-	4.0	14.5	13.5	.4	60.3
MOTOR CARRIER.........	222	100.0	1.8	12.9	26.9	6.4	18.8	11.9	5.6	1.0	14.6
PRIVATE TRUCK........	123	100.0	.4	29.5	4.6	5.1	13.0	43.0	1.2	.8	2.5
AIR...................	7	100.0	5.0	13.7	42.2	1.6	3.4	16.5	2.2	.7	14.7
WATER.................	-	100.0	-	-	-	-	-	100.0	-	-	-
OTHER.................	25	100.0	1.1	6.4	18.5	2.2	42.5	21.4	7.3	.6	.2
UNKNOWN...............	-	100.0	-	10.4	19.4	-	-	-	-	-	70.2
WEST SOUTH CENTRAL.....	175	100.0	2.6	10.0	18.9	7.2	12.6	16.1	22.4	4.4	5.7
RAIL...................	-	100.0	-	-	-	-	-	-	100.0	-	-
MOTOR CARRIER.........	124	100.0	2.4	10.2	23.4	9.9	13.6	9.6	19.1	6.1	5.7
PRIVATE TRUCK........	35	100.0	1.0	2.3	.7	.2	9.0	43.8	43.3	-	-
AIR...................	11	100.0	8.8	32.0	24.7	-	11.4	-	-	.2	22.6
WATER.................	-	100.0	-	-	-	-	-	-	-	-	-
OTHER.................	2	100.0	6.8	8.5	25.4	8.1	16.4	19.0	3.3	5.7	6.8
UNKNOWN...............	-	100.0	-	8.0	-	-	-	92.0	-	-	-
PACIFIC................	43	100.0	2.2	5.9	12.7	5.6	3.3	.8	4.2	6.3	59.0
RAIL...................	1	100.0	-	-	100.0	-	-	-	-	-	-
MOTOR CARRIER.........	30	100.0	-	2.2	4.0	3.7	1.2	.9	4.0	8.1	75.8
PRIVATE TRUCK........	6	100.0	11.5	20.5	29.8	15.2	11.0	-	.8	4.3	7.1
AIR...................	2	100.0	1.8	17.0	36.1	12.9	9.9	2.0	13.1	.1	7.2
WATER.................	-	100.0	-	-	-	-	-	-	-	-	-
OTHER.................	3	100.0	5.8	6.7	11.0	1.0	5.4	.1	6.0	1.4	62.7
UNKNOWN...............	-	100.0	-	-	-	-	-	-	-	-	100.0
TON-MILES OF SHIPMENTS	(millions of ton-miles)										
U.S. TOTAL.............	1 130	100.0	10.0	15.1	14.9	5.5	10.8	4.2	8.8	5.4	25.3
RAIL...................	72	100.0	.1	2.4	3.5	.1	2.2	2.1	9.3	.7	79.7
MOTOR CARRIER.........	854	100.0	12.0	13.7	15.7	5.8	10.7	3.3	9.2	6.1	23.5
PRIVATE TRUCK........	96	100.0	3.3	35.3	7.8	4.0	16.7	14.0	6.9	3.9	8.2
AIR...................	37	100.0	9.0	22.2	27.1	2.5	7.7	1.1	4.2	.9	25.3
WATER.................	-	100.0	-	14.1	-	-	-	85.9	-	-	-
OTHER.................	68	100.0	4.9	14.2	20.6	11.9	15.2	4.5	9.2	5.8	13.6
UNKNOWN...............	1	100.0	-	9.2	5.9	.2	8.0	12.7	.4	7.8	55.7
MIDDLE ATLANTIC........	86	100.0	3.7	17.8	17.7	11.0	10.1	4.6	13.1	3.8	18.3
RAIL...................	5	100.0	-	.1	2.0	1.0	.8	.1	13.7	.9	81.3
MOTOR CARRIER.........	62	100.0	4.3	20.6	19.1	10.5	11.0	5.2	12.1	3.6	13.6
PRIVATE TRUCK........	2	100.0	.3	68.5	10.1	-	18.0	-	3.1	-	-
AIR...................	2	100.0	4.1	.3	17.3	10.2	13.1	.5	19.8	1.8	32.8
WATER.................	-	100.0	-	100.0	-	-	-	-	-	-	-
OTHER.................	13	100.0	3.3	5.8	18.7	19.9	7.2	5.1	18.1	6.8	15.1
UNKNOWN...............	-	100.0	-	-	59.6	1.9	17.6	-	-	12.8	8.1
EAST NORTH CENTRAL.....	30	100.0	3.9	11.9	8.5	7.7	11.4	5.1	15.3	8.3	27.8
RAIL...................	-	100.0	-	-	-	-	-	-	-	-	-
MOTOR CARRIER.........	21	100.0	4.8	11.3	8.3	6.5	11.5	4.9	18.5	8.2	26.1
PRIVATE TRUCK........	1	100.0	-	5.5	16.5	34.7	8.5	33.9	.5	-	.2
AIR...................	-	100.0	.7	7.8	.6	7.0	30.0	-	37.3	1.6	15.0
WATER.................	-	100.0	-	-	-	-	-	-	-	-	-
OTHER.................	7	100.0	2.0	14.5	8.3	7.7	11.0	2.0	7.2	9.2	38.1
UNKNOWN...............	-	100.0	-	28.6	4.3	.7	10.0	1.4	2.8	52.2	-

See footnotes at end of table 4.

TABLE 2. **TCC GROUP 231—Percent Distribution of Geographic Division of Origin and Means of Transport, by Geographic Division of Destination: 1972**—Continued

Geographic division of origin[1] and means of transport	Number	Percent distribution by division of destination									
		U.S. total	New England	Middle Atlantic	East North Central	West North Central	South Atlantic	East South Central	West South Central	Mountain	Pacific
TON-MILES OF SHIPMENTS	(millions of ton-miles)										
WEST NORTH CENTRAL......	36	100.0	13.6	23.5	6.1	9.0	13.4	2.9	1.5	1.9	28.2
RAIL.................	-	100.0	-	-	-	-	-	-	-	-	-
MOTOR CARRIER........	32	100.0	12.1	22.8	5.5	9.1	13.8	2.5	1.3	2.0	30.9
PRIVATE TRUCK........	-	100.0	-	-	-	-	-	100.0	-	-	-
AIR.................	1	100.0	56.3	34.9	.2	-	-	-	-	-	8.6
WATER...............	-	100.0	-	-	-	-	-	-	-	-	-
OTHER...............	2	100.0	10.4	26.3	16.7	13.1	16.4	3.7	5.1	1.0	7.4
UNKNOWN.............	-	100.0	-	-	-	-	-	-	-	-	-
SOUTH ATLANTIC..........	395	100.0	4.7	10.9	16.3	5.8	8.5	3.8	12.7	10.7	26.7
RAIL.................	2	100.0	1.7	4.8	4.5	-	2.8	2.5	1.5	2.6	79.6
MOTOR CARRIER........	350	100.0	4.7	10.6	15.7	5.4	8.0	3.1	13.5	10.9	28.1
PRIVATE TRUCK........	10	100.0	.1	8.2	.6	.1	34.1	30.1	4.2	19.3	3.5
AIR.................	6	100.0	7.5	6.6	50.2	.6	1.1	2.7	4.0	2.6	24.7
WATER...............	-	100.0	-	-	-	-	-	-	-	-	-
OTHER...............	25	100.0	5.2	18.1	23.4	15.0	8.2	3.5	7.7	7.5	11.3
UNKNOWN.............	-	100.0	-	-	-	-	33.2	66.6	.2	-	-
EAST SOUTH CENTRAL......	281	100.0	1.8	17.9	13.5	4.0	10.3	3.7	5.4	1.8	41.6
RAIL.................	62	100.0	.1	2.6	.3	-	2.3	2.3	9.5	.6	82.3
MOTOR CARRIER........	152	100.0	2.6	13.3	20.1	5.7	10.7	3.0	4.9	1.9	37.9
PRIVATE TRUCK........	50	100.0	1.0	53.0	6.6	4.5	12.4	6.4	2.0	2.9	11.2
AIR.................	4	100.0	6.9	12.8	23.3	1.4	2.5	2.7	2.2	1.6	46.6
WATER...............	-	100.0	-	-	-	-	-	100.0	-	-	-
OTHER...............	11	100.0	2.4	10.6	23.0	2.7	44.0	7.3	7.5	1.7	.8
UNKNOWN.............	-	100.0	-	5.6	5.8	-	-	-	-	-	88.7
WEST SOUTH CENTRAL......	154	100.0	5.2	18.7	22.1	6.1	18.9	9.2	8.4	3.3	8.0
RAIL.................	-	100.0	-	-	-	-	-	-	100.0	-	-
MOTOR CARRIER........	116	100.0	4.6	18.1	25.4	7.9	19.5	6.1	6.8	4.2	7.5
PRIVATE TRUCK........	18	100.0	3.7	8.2	1.8	-	22.9	36.2	27.2	-	-
AIR.................	15	100.0	10.1	37.0	20.8	.1	10.4	-	-	.1	21.5
WATER...............	-	100.0	-	-	-	-	-	-	-	-	-
OTHER...............	3	100.0	11.1	11.0	26.0	6.3	18.2	13.6	2.0	5.1	6.7
UNKNOWN.............	-	100.0	-	58.5	-	-	-	41.5	-	-	-
PACIFIC................	39	100.0	6.1	15.4	25.4	8.4	8.5	1.6	6.0	4.1	24.5
RAIL.................	2	100.0	-	-	100.0	-	-	-	-	-	-
MOTOR CARRIER........	17	100.0	.2	8.5	12.3	8.8	4.7	3.0	8.3	7.5	46.7
PRIVATE TRUCK........	11	100.0	15.7	27.0	29.5	10.8	13.8	-	.6	2.4	.2
AIR.................	4	100.0	2.5	21.0	35.3	10.4	11.5	1.9	11.0	-	6.3
WATER...............	-	100.0	-	-	-	-	-	-	-	-	-
OTHER...............	3	100.0	13.9	14.9	19.3	1.3	12.1	.1	8.2	.8	29.4
UNKNOWN.............	-	100.0	-	-	-	-	-	-	-	-	100.0

See footnotes at end of table 4.

TABLE 3. **TCC GROUP 231—Percent Distribution of Geographic Division of Destination and Means of Transport, by Geographic Division of Origin: 1972**

Geographic division of destination and means of transport	Number	Percent distribution by division of origin[1]									
		U.S. total	New England	Middle Atlantic	East North Central	West North Central	South Atlantic	East South Central	West South Central	Mountain	Pacific
TONS OF SHIPMENTS	(thousands of tons)										
U.S. TOTAL...............	1 911	100.0	(D)	9.6	3.1	3.0	29.0	22.3	9.2	(D)	2.3
RAIL..................	51	100.0	(D)	5.1	-	-	3.6	88.6	-	(D)	2.4
MOTOR CARRIER.........	1 479	100.0	(D)	9.3	2.7	3.4	31.9	15.0	8.4	(D)	2.1
PRIVATE TRUCK.........	231	100.0	(D)	8.1	2.9	.3	14.0	53.6	15.4	(D)	2.6
AIR...................	34	100.0	(D)	7.6	1.1	3.8	21.4	21.0	34.2	(D)	7.8
WATER................	-	100.0	(D)	27.8	-	-	-	72.2	-	(D)	-
OTHER................	112	100.0	(D)	19.2	10.7	4.0	34.9	22.7	2.6	(D)	2.9
UNKNOWN..............	1	100.0	(D)	4.5	13.0	-	43.5	17.8	6.6	(D)	1.9
NEW ENGLAND.............	390	100.0	(D)	3.1	.4	1.0	6.1	1.3	1.2	(D)	.2
RAIL..................	-	100.0	(D)	-	-	-	58.0	42.0	-	(D)	-
MOTOR CARRIER.........	378	100.0	(D)	2.7	.4	.8	5.7	1.1	.8	(D)	-
PRIVATE TRUCK.........	3	100.0	(D)	4.2	-	.2	.2	12.0	9.0	(D)	18.5
AIR...................	2	100.0	(D)	7.0	.1	23.4	20.9	12.1	34.9	(D)	1.6
WATER................	-	100.0	(D)	-	-	-	-	-	-	(D)	-
OTHER................	5	100.0	(D)	31.3	3.8	5.0	34.2	5.4	3.9	(D)	3.7
UNKNOWN..............	-	100.0	(D)	-	-	-	-	-	-	(D)	
MIDDLE ATLANTIC.........	318	100.0	(D)	27.5	2.0	2.7	24.6	22.3	5.5	(D)	.8
RAIL..................	3	100.0	(D)	.5	-	-	6.6	92.9	-	(D)	-
MOTOR CARRIER.........	231	100.0	(D)	28.3	1.8	3.2	29.4	12.4	5.5	(D)	.3
PRIVATE TRUCK.........	56	100.0	(D)	28.8	.1	-	2.3	65.1	1.5	(D)	2.2
AIR...................	6	100.0	(D)	.5	.7	8.4	10.2	15.2	57.9	(D)	7.0
WATER................	-	100.0	(D)	100.0	-	-	-	-	-	(D)	-
OTHER................	20	100.0	(D)	27.9	10.5	3.5	39.4	8.0	1.2	(D)	1.1
UNKNOWN..............	-	100.0	(D)	-	31.7	-	-	12.2	3.5	(D)	-
EAST NORTH CENTRAL......	288	100.0	(D)	11.5	6.9	1.7	40.1	25.5	11.5	(D)	1.9
RAIL..................	1	100.0	(D)	8.0	-	-	10.2	17.3	-	(D)	64.5
MOTOR CARRIER.........	235	100.0	(D)	10.7	5.8	1.7	42.7	25.5	12.4	(D)	.5
PRIVATE TRUCK.........	12	100.0	(D)	12.6	22.7	-	1.0	46.8	1.9	(D)	14.9
AIR...................	12	100.0	(D)	7.0	.1	.1	35.1	23.6	22.5	(D)	7.5
WATER................	-	100.0	(D)	-	-	-	-	-	-	(D)	-
OTHER................	26	100.0	(D)	19.4	13.7	3.4	39.5	17.9	2.8	(D)	1.3
UNKNOWN..............	-	100.0	(D)	35.8	23.0	-	-	41.3	-	(D)	-
WEST NORTH CENTRAL......	103	100.0	(D)	9.7	7.0	20.4	27.2	20.6	12.2	(D)	2.4
RAIL..................	-	100.0	(D)	100.0	-	-	-	-	-	(D)	-
MOTOR CARRIER.........	81	100.0	(D)	8.4	4.6	24.0	28.6	17.5	15.1	(D)	1.4
PRIVATE TRUCK.........	9	100.0	(D)	-	24.2	-	.1	66.1	-	(D)	9.6
AIR...................	-	100.0	(D)	32.8	5.1	-	4.4	13.1	2.1	(D)	39.8
WATER................	-	100.0	(D)	-	-	-	-	-	-	(D)	-
OTHER................	11	100.0	(D)	25.8	10.3	13.5	42.0	4.9	2.1	(D)	.3
UNKNOWN..............	-	100.0	(D)	21.8	78.2	-	-	-	-	(D)	-
SOUTH ATLANTIC..........	268	100.0	(D)	6.6	2.7	2.1	49.1	26.4	8.2	(D)	.5
RAIL..................	2	100.0	(D)	2.0	-	-	9.0	89.0	-	(D)	-
MOTOR CARRIER.........	197	100.0	(D)	7.3	2.3	2.6	52.1	21.2	8.6	(D)	-
PRIVATE TRUCK.........	42	100.0	(D)	1.9	1.4	-	49.9	37.7	7.5	(D)	1.6
AIR...................	2	100.0	(D)	14.7	4.4	-	6.0	9.5	51.5	(D)	10.2
WATER................	-	100.0	(D)	-	-	-	-	-	-	(D)	-
OTHER................	22	100.0	(D)	9.0	8.1	2.2	28.8	47.9	2.1	(D)	.8
UNKNOWN..............	-	100.0	(D)	4.5	5.5	-	89.9	-	-	(D)	-
EAST SOUTH CENTRAL......	181	100.0	(D)	3.0	2.5	1.9	25.5	51.3	15.5	(D)	.2
RAIL..................	6	100.0	(D)	.1	-	-	2.2	97.7	-	(D)	-
MOTOR CARRIER.........	83	100.0	(D)	5.3	3.4	3.1	41.6	31.6	14.3	(D)	.3
PRIVATE TRUCK.........	78	100.0	(D)	-	1.2	.9	10.0	68.0	19.9	(D)	-
AIR...................	1	100.0	(D)	1.0	-	-	18.8	76.7	-	(D)	3.5
WATER................	-	100.0	(D)	-	-	-	-	100.0	-	(D)	-
OTHER................	10	100.0	(D)	9.1	6.0	1.9	26.3	51.5	5.2	(D)	-
UNKNOWN..............	-	100.0	(D)	-	1.6	-	77.9	-	20.4	(D)	-
WEST SOUTH CENTRAL......	136	100.0	(D)	6.3	4.3	.9	40.5	16.2	28.8	(D)	1.3
RAIL..................	6	100.0	(D)	7.2	-	-	.7	91.8	.2	(D)	-
MOTOR CARRIER.........	103	100.0	(D)	5.5	4.9	.9	50.4	12.0	22.9	(D)	1.2
PRIVATE TRUCK.........	17	100.0	(D)	.3	-	-	2.7	8.3	88.3	(D)	.3
AIR...................	1	100.0	(D)	30.4	11.5	-	18.4	11.6	.3	(D)	26.4
WATER................	-	100.0	(D)	-	-	-	-	-	-	(D)	-
OTHER................	7	100.0	(D)	25.8	9.2	4.0	31.6	25.3	1.3	(D)	2.6
UNKNOWN..............	-	100.0	(D)	-	89.3	-	10.7	-	-	(D)	-
MOUNTAIN................	47	100.0	(D)	3.8	4.7	1.8	55.7	7.3	16.3	(D)	5.9
RAIL..................	-	100.0	(D)	10.4	-	-	15.7	73.9	-	(D)	-
MOTOR CARRIER.........	41	100.0	(D)	2.9	3.9	2.0	57.4	5.1	18.2	(D)	6.0
PRIVATE TRUCK.........	2	100.0	(D)	-	-	-	45.2	35.4	-	(D)	9.6
AIR...................	-	100.0	(D)	11.8	2.2	-	47.0	24.6	9.5	(D)	.6
WATER................	-	100.0	(D)	-	-	-	-	-	-	(D)	-
OTHER................	2	100.0	(D)	18.9	19.7	.9	46.1	5.2	5.9	(D)	1.6
UNKNOWN..............	-	100.0	(D)	6.3	93.7	-	-	-	-	(D)	-
PACIFIC.................	176	100.0	(D)	3.8	2.4	4.1	27.4	36.6	5.6	(D)	14.7
RAIL..................	30	100.0	(D)	6.1	-	-	3.2	90.3	-	(D)	-
MOTOR CARRIER.........	125	100.0	(D)	2.9	2.4	5.6	35.9	25.8	5.6	(D)	18.5
PRIVATE TRUCK.........	8	100.0	(D)	-	-	-	1.8	37.0	-	(D)	5.1
AIR...................	5	100.0	(D)	6.4	.4	1.1	12.8	19.5	48.8	(D)	3.6
WATER................	-	100.0	(D)	-	-	-	-	-	-	(D)	-
OTHER................	5	100.0	(D)	14.9	20.9	2.3	23.2	.7	3.4	(D)	34.5
UNKNOWN..............	-	100.0	(D)	.6	-	-	-	65.4	-	(D)	9.9

See footnotes at end of table 4.

TABLE 3. **TCC GROUP 231—Percent Distribution of Geographic Division of Destination and Means of Transport, by Geographic Division of Origin: 1972**—Continued

Geographic division of destination and means of transport	Number	Percent distribution by division of origin[1]									
		U.S. total	New England	Middle Atlantic	East North Central	West North Central	South Atlantic	East South Central	West South Central	Mountain	Pacific
TON-MILES OF SHIPMENTS	(millions of ton-miles)										
U.S. TOTAL	1 130	100.0	(D)	7.6	2.7	3.2	35.0	24.9	13.6	(D)	3.5
RAIL	72	100.0	(D)	7.5	-	-	3.4	86.1	-	(D)	3.0
MOTOR CARRIER	854	100.0	(D)	7.3	2.6	3.8	41.0	17.9	13.6	(D)	2.1
PRIVATE TRUCK	96	100.0	(D)	2.6	1.1	.1	10.5	52.7	19.2	(D)	11.6
AIR	37	100.0	(D)	7.1	.9	3.7	16.8	12.3	41.7	(D)	13.1
WATER	-	100.0	(D)	14.1	-	-	-	85.9	-	(D)	-
OTHER	68	100.0	(D)	19.7	10.8	3.8	37.6	16.3	5.0	(D)	5.2
UNKNOWN	1	100.0	(D)	4.8	13.8	-	17.3	42.1	2.4	(D)	1.2
NEW ENGLAND	112	100.0	(D)	2.9	1.1	4.4	16.4	4.5	7.1	(D)	2.1
RAIL	-	100.0	(D)	-	-	-	49.0	51.0	-	(D)	-
MOTOR CARRIER	102	100.0	(D)	2.6	1.0	3.8	16.1	3.9	5.2	(D)	55.4
PRIVATE TRUCK	3	100.0	(D)	.3	-	-	.2	15.6	21.8	(D)	55.4
AIR	3	100.0	(D)	3.2	.1	22.9	13.9	9.5	46.8	(D)	3.6
WATER	-	100.0	(D)	-	-	-	-	-	-	(D)	-
OTHER	3	100.0	(D)	13.3	4.4	8.1	39.5	7.8	11.2	(D)	14.6
UNKNOWN	-	100.0	(D)	-	-	-	-	-	-	(D)	-
MIDDLE ATLANTIC	170	100.0	(D)	9.0	2.2	5.0	25.3	29.5	16.9	(D)	3.6
RAIL	1	100.0	(D)	.2	-	-	6.9	92.9	-	(D)	-
MOTOR CARRIER	117	100.0	(D)	11.0	2.1	6.3	31.8	17.3	18.1	(D)	1.3
PRIVATE TRUCK	33	100.0	(D)	5.0	.2	-	2.4	79.1	4.5	(D)	8.9
AIR	8	100.0	(D)	.1	.3	5.7	5.0	7.1	69.4	(D)	12.4
WATER	-	100.0	(D)	100.0	-	-	-	-	-	(D)	-
OTHER	9	100.0	(D)	8.1	11.0	7.1	48.1	12.1	3.9	(D)	5.4
UNKNOWN	-	100.0	(D)	-	42.7	-	-	25.4	14.9	(D)	-
EAST NORTH CENTRAL	168	100.0	(D)	9.1	1.6	1.3	38.2	22.5	20.2	(D)	5.9
RAIL	2	100.0	(D)	4.2	-	-	4.4	6.3	-	(D)	85.1
MOTOR CARRIER	134	100.0	(D)	8.9	1.4	1.3	41.0	22.9	22.0	(D)	1.6
PRIVATE TRUCK	7	100.0	(D)	3.3	2.4	-	.8	45.1	4.4	(D)	44.1
AIR	10	100.0	(D)	4.5	-	-	31.1	10.6	32.0	(D)	17.1
WATER	-	100.0	(D)	-	-	-	-	-	-	(D)	-
OTHER	14	100.0	(D)	17.8	4.3	3.1	42.7	18.1	6.3	(D)	4.9
UNKNOWN	-	100.0	(D)	48.7	10.1	-	-	41.2	-	(D)	-
WEST NORTH CENTRAL	62	100.0	(D)	15.3	3.8	5.2	36.5	18.1	15.2	(D)	5.3
RAIL	-	100.0	(D)	100.0	-	-	-	-	-	(D)	-
MOTOR CARRIER	49	100.0	(D)	13.2	2.9	5.9	38.1	17.5	18.7	(D)	3.2
PRIVATE TRUCK	3	100.0	(D)	-	9.6	-	.3	58.8	.1	(D)	31.3
AIR	-	100.0	(D)	28.2	2.5	-	3.9	6.9	2.2	(D)	53.6
WATER	-	100.0	(D)	-	-	-	-	-	-	(D)	-
OTHER	8	100.0	(D)	32.9	7.0	4.2	47.5	3.7	2.6	(D)	.6
UNKNOWN	-	100.0	(D)	48.2	51.8	-	-	-	-	(D)	-
SOUTH ATLANTIC	122	100.0	(D)	7.1	2.9	4.0	27.5	23.7	23.8	(D)	2.7
RAIL	1	100.0	(D)	2.8	-	-	4.3	92.8	-	(D)	-
MOTOR CARRIER	91	100.0	(D)	7.5	2.7	4.8	30.5	17.8	24.7	(D)	.9
PRIVATE TRUCK	16	100.0	(D)	2.8	.6	-	21.5	39.2	26.4	(D)	9.6
AIR	2	100.0	(D)	12.0	3.6	-	2.4	4.0	56.3	(D)	19.6
WATER	-	100.0	(D)	-	-	-	-	-	-	(D)	-
OTHER	10	100.0	(D)	9.3	7.8	4.1	20.4	47.1	6.0	(D)	4.1
UNKNOWN	-	100.0	(D)	10.6	17.3	-	72.1	-	-	(D)	-
EAST SOUTH CENTRAL	46	100.0	(D)	8.4	3.4	2.2	32.0	21.9	30.4	(D)	1.3
RAIL	1	100.0	(D)	.5	-	-	4.1	95.4	-	(D)	-
MOTOR CARRIER	28	100.0	(D)	11.4	3.8	2.9	37.9	16.4	25.1	(D)	1.9
PRIVATE TRUCK	13	100.0	(D)	-	2.7	1.0	22.6	24.1	49.6	(D)	-
AIR	-	100.0	(D)	3.2	-	-	42.5	30.7	-	(D)	23.6
WATER	-	100.0	(D)	-	-	3.1	-	100.0	-	(D)	-
OTHER	3	100.0	(D)	22.1	4.8	3.1	28.8	26.0	15.0	(D)	.1
UNKNOWN	-	100.0	(D)	-	1.5	-	90.8	-	7.7	(D)	-
WEST SOUTH CENTRAL	99	100.0	(D)	11.4	4.7	.6	50.4	15.4	13.1	(D)	2.4
RAIL	6	100.0	(D)	11.1	-	-	.5	88.4	-	(D)	-
MOTOR CARRIER	78	100.0	(D)	9.6	5.1	.5	60.6	9.5	10.1	(D)	1.9
PRIVATE TRUCK	6	100.0	(D)	1.1	.1	-	6.4	15.2	76.1	(D)	1.1
AIR	1	100.0	(D)	33.3	8.1	-	15.9	6.5	.1	(D)	34.3
WATER	-	100.0	(D)	-	-	-	-	-	-	(D)	-
OTHER	6	100.0	(D)	38.8	8.5	2.1	31.4	13.3	1.1	(D)	4.6
UNKNOWN	-	100.0	(D)	-	93.2	-	6.8	-	-	(D)	-
MOUNTAIN	61	100.0	(D)	5.4	4.2	1.1	69.1	8.2	8.2	(D)	2.7
RAIL	-	100.0	(D)	10.1	-	-	12.8	77.1	-	(D)	-
MOTOR CARRIER	52	100.0	(D)	4.3	3.4	1.2	72.6	5.5	9.2	(D)	2.5
PRIVATE TRUCK	3	100.0	(D)	-	-	-	52.2	40.0	-	(D)	7.0
AIR	-	100.0	(D)	14.7	1.6	-	50.1	22.6	4.3	(D)	.2
WATER	-	100.0	(D)	-	-	-	-	-	-	(D)	-
OTHER	3	100.0	(D)	22.9	17.2	.7	48.6	4.8	4.4	(D)	.7
UNKNOWN	-	100.0	(D)	7.9	92.1	-	-	-	-	(D)	-
PACIFIC	285	100.0	(D)	5.5	3.0	3.6	36.9	41.1	4.3	(D)	3.4
RAIL	57	100.0	(D)	7.6	-	-	3.4	88.9	-	(D)	-
MOTOR CARRIER	200	100.0	(D)	4.2	2.8	4.9	49.2	28.9	4.4	(D)	4.1
PRIVATE TRUCK	7	100.0	(D)	-	-	-	4.4	71.8	.1	(D)	.3
AIR	9	100.0	(D)	9.2	.5	1.3	16.4	22.7	35.6	(D)	3.3
WATER	-	100.0	(D)	-	-	-	-	-	-	(D)	-
OTHER	9	100.0	(D)	21.8	30.2	2.1	31.2	.9	2.5	(D)	11.2
UNKNOWN	-	100.0	(D)	.7	-	-	-	67.1	-	(D)	2.1

See footnotes at end of table 4.

TABLE 4. TCC GROUP 231—Percent Distribution of Distance Shipped and Weight of Shipment,
by Means of Transport: 1972

Distance shipped and weight of shipment [2] [3]	Number	Percent distribution by means of transport							
		All means of transport	Rail	Motor carrier	Private truck	Air	Water	Other	Unknown
TONS OF SHIPMENTS	(thousands of tons)								
U.S. TOTAL..........	1 633	100.0	3.1	79.2	9.9	2.0	-	5.6	.1
UNDER 100 MILES.........	138	100.0	-	55.5	39.6	.8	-	4.1	-
UNDER 1000 POUNDS.....	54	100.0	-	80.6	9.0	1.9	-	8.4	-
1000 TO 9999 POUNDS...	70	100.0	-	43.9	54.6	-	-	1.5	-
10000 TO 29999 POUNDS.	7	100.0	-	15.9	84.1	-	-	-	-
30000 TO 59999 POUNDS.	-	100.0	-	100.0	-	-	-	-	-
60000 TO 89999 POUNDS.	-	100.0	-	-	-	-	-	-	-
90000 POUNDS AND OVER.	5	100.0	-	-	100.0	-	-	-	-
100 TO 199 MILES........	291	100.0	.1	92.6	4.7	.1	-	2.3	.1
UNDER 1000 POUNDS.....	72	100.0	-	88.4	1.7	.2	-	9.4	.2
1000 TO 9999 POUNDS...	165	100.0	-	96.3	3.5	.1	-	-	-
10000 TO 29999 POUNDS.	52	100.0	-	87.2	12.6	-	-	-	.2
30000 TO 59999 POUNDS.	-	100.0	66.2	-	33.8	-	-	-	-
60000 TO 89999 POUNDS.	-	100.0	-	-	-	-	-	-	-
90000 POUNDS AND OVER.	-	100.0	-	-	-	-	-	-	-
200 TO 299 MILES........	250	100.0	2.7	90.1	3.3	.1	.1	3.7	-
UNDER 1000 POUNDS.....	69	100.0	.1	80.3	6.7	.2	.4	12.2	.1
1000 TO 9999 POUNDS...	166	100.0	-	98.7	1.3	-	-	-	-
10000 TO 29999 POUNDS.	6	100.0	-	78.7	21.3	-	-	-	-
30000 TO 59999 POUNDS.	7	100.0	85.3	2.9	1.2	-	-	10.6	-
60000 TO 89999 POUNDS.	-	100.0	100.0	-	-	-	-	-	-
90000 POUNDS AND OVER.	-	100.0	-	-	-	-	-	-	-
300 TO 499 MILES........	277	100.0	.9	79.7	12.0	1.3	-	5.9	.2
UNDER 1000 POUNDS.....	147	100.0	.3	87.0	1.3	.4	-	11.0	.1
1000 TO 9999 POUNDS...	77	100.0	-	88.8	7.2	4.0	-	-	-
10000 TO 29999 POUNDS.	35	100.0	.3	62.8	35.8	-	-	-	1.2
30000 TO 59999 POUNDS.	16	100.0	11.0	10.7	78.3	-	-	-	-
60000 TO 89999 POUNDS.	-	100.0	-	-	-	-	-	-	-
90000 POUNDS AND OVER.	-	100.0	-	-	-	-	-	-	-
500 TO 999 MILES........	422	100.0	1.1	78.5	8.5	2.5	-	9.3	-
UNDER 1000 POUNDS.....	288	100.0	.3	81.6	3.4	1.7	-	12.9	.1
1000 TO 9999 POUNDS...	87	100.0	-	75.4	15.5	6.7	-	2.5	-
10000 TO 29999 POUNDS.	39	100.0	5.9	75.1	19.0	-	-	-	-
30000 TO 59999 POUNDS.	7	100.0	23.5	4.8	71.7	-	-	-	-
60000 TO 89999 POUNDS.	-	100.0	-	-	-	-	-	-	-
90000 POUNDS AND OVER.	-	100.0	-	-	-	-	-	-	-
1000 TO 1499 MILES......	98	100.0	5.2	72.0	4.5	10.3	-	7.9	.1
UNDER 1000 POUNDS.....	60	100.0	.2	74.8	3.1	9.2	-	12.7	.1
1000 TO 9999 POUNDS...	30	100.0	-	76.1	8.5	15.0	-	.4	-
10000 TO 29999 POUNDS.	1	100.0	-	100.0	-	-	-	-	-
30000 TO 59999 POUNDS.	4	100.0	89.0	11.0	-	-	-	-	-
60000 TO 89999 POUNDS.	-	100.0	83.5	16.5	-	-	-	-	-
90000 POUNDS AND OVER.	-	100.0	-	-	-	-	-	-	-
1500 MILES OR OVER......	155	100.0	20.7	63.1	7.3	4.5	-	4.2	.2
UNDER 1000 POUNDS.....	69	100.0	2.5	74.5	7.5	6.1	-	9.3	.2
1000 TO 9999 POUNDS...	57	100.0	49.3	38.8	6.8	4.7	-	.1	.3
10000 TO 29999 POUNDS.	25	100.0	2.8	90.1	7.1	-	-	-	-
30000 TO 59999 POUNDS.	2	100.0	70.7	12.5	16.8	-	-	-	-
60000 TO 89999 POUNDS.	-	100.0	-	-	-	-	-	-	-
90000 POUNDS AND OVER.	-	100.0	-	-	-	-	-	-	-
TON-MILES OF SHIPMENTS	(millions of ton-miles)								
U.S. TOTAL..........	938	100.0	7.6	74.5	7.5	3.9	-	6.4	.1
UNDER 100 MILES.........	7	100.0	-	64.4	30.2	.8	-	4.6	-
UNDER 1000 POUNDS.....	3	100.0	-	82.3	7.5	1.7	.1	8.4	-
1000 TO 9999 POUNDS...	3	100.0	-	56.0	42.2	-	-	1.8	-
10000 TO 29999 POUNDS.	-	100.0	-	13.4	86.6	-	-	-	-
30000 TO 59999 POUNDS.	-	100.0	-	100.0	-	-	-	-	-
60000 TO 89999 POUNDS.	-	100.0	-	-	-	-	-	-	-
90000 POUNDS AND OVER.	-	100.0	-	-	100.0	-	-	-	-
100 TO 199 MILES........	43	100.0	.1	92.7	4.6	.1	-	2.4	.1
UNDER 1000 POUNDS.....	10	100.0	-	87.8	1.7	.2	-	10.0	.2
1000 TO 9999 POUNDS...	24	100.0	-	96.7	3.1	.1	-	-	-
10000 TO 29999 POUNDS.	8	100.0	-	87.2	12.6	-	-	-	.1
30000 TO 59999 POUNDS.	-	100.0	65.7	-	34.3	-	-	-	-
60000 TO 89999 POUNDS.	-	100.0	-	-	-	-	-	-	-
90000 POUNDS AND OVER.	-	100.0	-	-	-	-	-	-	-

See footnotes at end of table 4.

TABLE 4. TCC GROUP 231—Percent Distribution of Distance Shipped and Weight of Shipment, by Means of Transport: 1972—Continued

Distance shipped and weight of shipment[2][3]	Number	Percent distribution by means of transport							
		All means of transport	Rail	Motor carrier	Private truck	Air	Water	Other	Unknown
TON-MILES OF SHIPMENTS	(millions of ton-miles)								
200 TO 299 MILES........	66	100.0	2.2	91.3	2.9	.1	.1	3.5	-
UNDER 1000 POUNDS.....	17	100.0	.1	81.1	5.8	.2	.4	12.3	.1
1000 TO 9999 POUNDS...	45	100.0	-	98.8	1.2	-	-	-	-
10000 TO 29999 POUNDS.	1	100.0	-	79.7	20.3	-	-	-	-
30000 TO 59999 POUNDS.	1	100.0	85.2	2.9	1.6	-	-	10.3	-
60000 TO 89999 POUNDS.	-	100.0	100.0	-	-	-	-	-	-
90000 POUNDS AND OVER.	-	100.0	-	-	-	-	-	-	-
300 TO 499 MILES........	106	100.0	1.1	78.8	12.5	1.3	-	6.1	.2
UNDER 1000 POUNDS.....	57	100.0	.3	86.7	1.1	.4	-	11.4	.1
1000 TO 9999 POUNDS...	29	100.0	-	88.6	7.3	4.0	-	-	-
10000 TO 29999 POUNDS.	12	100.0	.4	61.2	37.3	-	-	-	1.1
30000 TO 59999 POUNDS.	7	100.0	12.2	10.2	77.6	-	-	-	-
60000 TO 89999 POUNDS.	-	100.0	-	-	-	-	-	-	-
90000 POUNDS AND OVER.	-	100.0	-	-	-	-	-	-	-
500 TO 999 MILES........	296	100.0	1.2	79.1	7.8	2.7	-	9.2	-
UNDER 1000 POUNDS.....	201	100.0	.3	81.7	3.4	1.8	-	12.7	.1
1000 TO 9999 POUNDS...	65	100.0	-	76.9	14.3	6.5	-	2.3	-
10000 TO 29999 POUNDS.	24	100.0	6.2	77.4	16.3	-	-	-	-
30000 TO 59999 POUNDS.	4	100.0	31.4	6.1	62.5	-	-	-	-
60000 TO 89999 POUNDS.	-	100.0	-	-	-	-	-	-	-
90000 POUNDS AND OVER.	-	100.0	-	-	-	-	-	-	-
1000 TO 1499 MILES......	119	100.0	4.3	72.5	4.7	10.8	-	7.6	.1
UNDER 1000 POUNDS.....	72	100.0	.2	74.4	3.2	9.6	-	12.4	.1
1000 TO 9999 POUNDS...	39	100.0	-	75.8	8.5	15.3	-	.4	-
10000 TO 29999 POUNDS.	2	100.0	-	100.0	-	-	-	-	-
30000 TO 59999 POUNDS.	5	100.0	85.9	14.1	-	-	-	-	-
60000 TO 89999 POUNDS.	-	100.0	83.5	16.5	-	-	-	-	-
90000 POUNDS AND OVER.	-	100.0	-	-	-	-	-	-	-
1500 MILES OR OVER......	298	100.0	20.2	63.2	7.2	4.7	-	4.5	.2
UNDER 1000 POUNDS.....	143	100.0	2.6	74.3	7.4	6.1	-	9.3	.2
1000 TO 9999 POUNDS...	106	100.0	49.1	38.8	6.8	4.9	-	-	.3
10000 TO 29999 POUNDS.	44	100.0	3.1	89.8	7.1	-	-	-	-
30000 TO 59999 POUNDS.	3	100.0	71.5	13.8	14.6	-	-	-	-
60000 TO 89999 POUNDS.	-	100.0	-	-	-	-	-	-	-
90000 POUNDS AND OVER.	-	100.0	-	-	-	-	-	-	-

Note: Detail may not add to total due to rounding. The introductory table shows the estimates of sampling variability for tons; sampling variability for ton-miles has not been estimated. See the map in the Introduction for the States comprising the geographic divisions of the United States.

Shipments excluded from the survey are those moving by pipeline (primarily petroleum products from refineries), parcel post shipments, and commodities moved by own power (motorized vehicles, aircraft, etc.) or towed (prefabricated building, etc.). Local shipments (commodities shipped less than 25 miles from the plant) and shipments within the same city are also excluded. Shipments to Alaska and Hawaii from the 48 conterminous States and the District of Columbia are included; however, no data were obtained for shipments originating in Alaska and Hawaii.

- Represents zero or rounds to zero.   (D) Withheld to avoid disclosing figures for individual companies.

[1]Production of this commodity is concentrated in the geographic divisions shown; figures and distributions for geographic divisions not shown are included in the total.

[2]Distances of shipments to foreign destinations are calculated only to the U.S. port of exit.

[3]Includes only shipments represented by bills of lading and invoices. Summary records which did not show individual weights of shipments are not included.

TCC 233. Women's, Misses', Children's, and Infants' Clothing

Comparisons of Tons and Ton-Miles of Shipments for
Geographic Divisions of Origin and for Sampling Variability: 1972 and 1967

Geographic division of origin	Estimates				Relative sampling variability in tons (percent)	
	1972		1967		1972	1967
	Tons (thousands)	Ton-miles (millions)	Tons (thousands)	Ton-miles (millions)		
U.S. total	1,542	751	993	631	32.2	15.0
New England	58	27	127	66	34.4	(*)
Middle Atlantic	(D)	(D)	305	211	(*)	(*)
East North Central	29	14	36	29	33.7	(*)
West North Central	19	9	7	5	41.6	(*)
South Atlantic	439	151	401	255	47.0	(*)
East South Central	129	84	69	27	26.9	(*)
West South Central	(D)	(D)	31	14	(*)	(*)
Mountain	(D)	(D)	—	—	(*)	(*)
Pacific	(D)	(D)	17	24	(*)	(*)

—Represents or rounds to zero.   (D) Withheld to avoid disclosing figures for individual companies.   (*) Data not published.

TABLE 1. TCC GROUP 233—Percent Distribution of Geographic Division of Origin and Distance Shipped, by Means of Transport: 1972

Geographic division of origin[1] and distance shipped[2]	Number	Percent distribution by means of transport							
		All means of transport	Rail	Motor carrier	Private truck	Air	Water	Other	Unknown
TONS OF SHIPMENTS	(thousands of tons)								
U.S. TOTAL..........	1 542	100.0	1.5	66.5	22.3	3.8	-	5.7	.1
NEW ENGLAND.............	58	100.0	7.3	61.8	20.3	3.7	-	6.5	.4
UNDER 100 MILES........	7	100.0	1.7	96.5	-	-	-	1.5	.4
100 TO 199 MILES......	28	100.0	.2	52.9	40.8	-	-	5.5	.6
200 TO 299 MILES......	4	100.0	.2	92.6	-	.3	-	6.4	.6
300 TO 499 MILES......	2	100.0	32.9	57.4	-	2.2	-	7.5	-
500 TO 999 MILES......	7	100.0	19.3	56.6	2.2	7.0	-	14.9	-
1000 TO 1499 MILES....	3	100.0	9.3	77.7	-	3.5	-	9.5	-
1500 MILES OR OVER....	4	100.0	31.7	27.4	3.0	32.7	-	5.0	.2
EAST NORTH CENTRAL......	29	100.0	23.9	50.6	6.8	.3	-	18.2	.1
UNDER 100 MILES........	2	100.0	-	8.1	81.1	-	-	10.5	.3
100 TO 199 MILES......	9	100.0	-	97.5	.5	-	-	2.0	.1
200 TO 299 MILES......	2	100.0	-	82.1	-	.5	-	17.4	-
300 TO 499 MILES......	2	100.0	.4	60.6	-	.9	-	38.1	-
500 TO 999 MILES......	11	100.0	62.5	14.4	-	.4	-	22.7	-
1000 TO 1499 MILES....	-	100.0	-	40.6	-	.1	-	59.2	-
1500 MILES OR OVER....	1	100.0	-	32.1	-	2.2	-	65.6	-
WEST NORTH CENTRAL......	19	100.0	-	61.8	.1	5.4	-	32.6	-
UNDER 100 MILES.......	-	100.0	-	80.9	-	-	-	19.1	-
100 TO 199 MILES......	7	100.0	-	90.6	.2	-	-	9.1	-
200 TO 299 MILES......	-	100.0	-	31.6	-	14.1	-	54.4	-
300 TO 499 MILES......	2	100.0	-	50.7	-	.2	-	49.1	-
500 TO 999 MILES......	4	100.0	-	26.6	-	11.8	-	61.4	.1
1000 TO 1499 MILES....	2	100.0	-	68.3	-	2.9	-	28.7	.1
1500 MILES OR OVER....	-	100.0	-	35.1	-	50.3	-	14.6	-
SOUTH ATLANTIC..........	439	100.0	.3	37.6	57.8	.6	-	3.5	.2
UNDER 100 MILES........	197	100.0	-	5.4	94.5	-	-	.1	-
100 TO 199 MILES......	25	100.0	-	43.1	53.2	-	-	3.8	-
200 TO 299 MILES......	39	100.0	.2	27.9	67.2	1.2	-	3.6	-
300 TO 499 MILES......	46	100.0	.1	80.0	13.9	.5	-	5.4	.1
500 TO 999 MILES......	102	100.0	.9	73.2	19.5	.9	-	4.8	.7
1000 TO 1499 MILES....	17	100.0	.1	73.9	.1	1.0	-	25.0	-
1500 MILES OR OVER....	10	100.0	4.1	71.4	8.9	6.7	-	8.0	1.0
EAST SOUTH CENTRAL......	129	100.0	7.0	56.6	30.6	.9	-	4.9	-
UNDER 100 MILES........	19	100.0	-	3.3	96.4	-	-	.4	-
100 TO 199 MILES......	7	100.0	-	45.4	49.4	.2	-	5.0	-
200 TO 299 MILES......	9	100.0	-	94.5	-	.8	-	4.7	-
300 TO 499 MILES......	24	100.0	.3	77.1	16.1	.1	-	6.4	-
500 TO 999 MILES......	49	100.0	.5	75.6	15.8	1.5	-	6.5	-
1000 TO 1499 MILES....	7	100.0	-	19.7	74.6	.4	-	5.3	-
1500 MILES OR OVER....	12	100.0	69.6	24.7	1.0	1.9	-	2.8	-
TON-MILES OF SHIPMENTS	(millions of ton-miles)								
U.S. TOTAL..........	751	100.0	4.1	65.6	8.3	13.1	-	8.6	.2
NEW ENGLAND.............	27	100.0	17.7	50.2	8.9	15.6	-	7.3	.2
UNDER 100 MILES........	-	100.0	.2	97.7	-	-	-	1.9	.2
100 TO 199 MILES......	4	100.0	.2	52.7	40.6	-	-	5.8	.7
200 TO 299 MILES......	1	100.0	.2	92.6	-	.3	-	6.4	.5
300 TO 499 MILES......	1	100.0	31.7	58.7	-	2.3	-	7.4	-
500 TO 999 MILES......	5	100.0	19.5	55.5	2.5	8.0	-	14.6	-
1000 TO 1499 MILES....	4	100.0	9.1	77.8	-	3.7	-	9.3	-
1500 MILES OR OVER....	10	100.0	29.6	28.1	3.3	35.2	-	3.7	.2
EAST NORTH CENTRAL......	14	100.0	36.8	32.9	1.2	.7	-	28.3	-
UNDER 100 MILES........	-	100.0	-	9.7	82.8	-	-	7.1	.4
100 TO 199 MILES......	1	100.0	-	97.8	.4	-	-	1.7	.1
200 TO 299 MILES......	-	100.0	-	81.7	-	.5	-	17.8	-
300 TO 499 MILES......	-	100.0	.4	58.3	-	.7	-	40.6	-
500 TO 999 MILES......	8	100.0	64.1	13.2	-	.4	-	22.2	-
1000 TO 1499 MILES....	-	100.0	-	40.5	-	.1	-	59.3	-
1500 MILES OR OVER....	2	100.0	-	33.8	-	2.3	-	64.0	-
WEST NORTH CENTRAL......	9	100.0	-	47.4	-	11.9	-	40.6	.1
UNDER 100 MILES........	-	100.0	-	74.7	-	-	-	25.3	-
100 TO 199 MILES......	-	100.0	-	86.6	.3	-	-	13.1	-
200 TO 299 MILES......	-	100.0	-	31.1	-	12.9	-	56.0	-
300 TO 499 MILES......	1	100.0	-	49.2	-	.1	-	50.7	-
500 TO 999 MILES......	3	100.0	-	26.2	-	10.9	-	62.8	.2
1000 TO 1499 MILES....	2	100.0	-	68.7	-	2.8	-	28.5	.1
1500 MILES OR OVER....	1	100.0	-	30.5	-	57.4	-	12.0	-
SOUTH ATLANTIC..........	151	100.0	1.0	68.2	20.8	1.7	-	7.8	.5
UNDER 100 MILES........	4	100.0	-	11.1	88.5	-	-	.3	-
100 TO 199 MILES......	4	100.0	-	43.4	53.4	-	-	3.2	-
200 TO 299 MILES......	10	100.0	.2	27.5	67.7	1.2	-	3.5	-
300 TO 499 MILES......	18	100.0	.1	79.4	14.5	.5	-	5.5	-
500 TO 999 MILES......	70	100.0	1.0	73.7	18.6	.8	-	5.1	.7
1000 TO 1499 MILES....	19	100.0	.1	74.2	.1	.9	-	24.7	-
1500 MILES OR OVER....	22	100.0	3.0	72.0	8.9	6.9	-	8.3	.9

See footnotes at end of table 4.

TABLE 1. **TCC GROUP 233—Percent Distribution of Geographic Division of Origin and Distance Shipped, by Means of Transport: 1972—Continued**

Geographic division of origin[1] and distance shipped[2]	Number	Percent distribution by means of transport							
		All means of transport	Rail	Motor carrier	Private truck	Air	Water	Other	Unknown
TON-MILES OF SHIPMENTS	(millions of ton-miles)								
EAST SOUTH CENTRAL......	84	100.0	20.8	52.5	20.5	1.2	-	5.0	-
UNDER 100 MILES.......	1	100.0	-	4.2	95.5	-	-	.4	-
100 TO 199 MILES......	1	100.0	-	40.1	55.2	.2	-	4.5	-
200 TO 299 MILES......	2	100.0	-	94.3	-	.7	-	5.0	-
300 TO 499 MILES......	10	100.0	.2	76.8	16.8	.1	-	6.1	-
500 TO 999 MILES......	34	100.0	.7	73.6	17.9	1.4	-	6.5	-
1000 TO 1499 MILES....	9	100.0	-	18.9	76.2	.4	-	4.5	-
1500 MILES OR OVER....	25	100.0	69.0	25.3	.8	1.8	-	3.0	-

See footnotes at end of table 4.

TABLE 2. **TCC GROUP 233—Percent Distribution of Geographic Division of Origin and Means of Transport, by Geographic Division of Destination: 1972**

Geographic division of origin[1] and means of transport	Number	Percent distribution by division of destination									
		U.S. total	New England	Middle Atlantic	East North Central	West North Central	South Atlantic	East South Central	West South Central	Mountain	Pacific
TONS OF SHIPMENTS	(thousands of tons)										
U.S. TOTAL...............	1 542	100.0	3.9	46.1	7.4	3.7	21.2	4.5	5.5	1.0	6.7
RAIL.................	23	100.0	.8	5.6	7.9	3.2	9.7	.6	27.6	3.5	41.1
MOTOR CARRIER........	1 025	100.0	3.1	64.9	8.3	2.8	7.7	2.1	4.5	1.1	5.4
PRIVATE TRUCK........	343	100.0	5.9	5.3	.9	.1	64.9	11.7	5.8	.3	5.1
AIR..................	58	100.0	3.2	14.0	11.4	35.9	8.8	1.0	5.9	1.5	18.3
WATER................	-	100.0	-	-	-	-	-	-	-	-	-
OTHER................	88	100.0	5.9	19.4	19.2	7.7	18.8	7.6	9.1	2.0	10.3
UNKNOWN..............	2	100.0	6.3	33.8	15.4	1.0	9.6	1.9	25.1	2.6	4.3
NEW ENGLAND..........	58	100.0	34.1	36.5	9.7	1.9	8.9	1.2	1.8	.8	5.3
RAIL.................	4	100.0	3.0	1.4	31.3	6.1	23.4	1.7	6.5	8.1	18.6
MOTOR CARRIER........	36	100.0	22.3	53.0	8.8	1.8	9.1	1.4	1.1	.2	2.4
PRIVATE TRUCK........	11	100.0	97.5	.1	.4	-	1.0	-	-	-	1.1
AIR..................	2	100.0	-	.5	17.2	1.9	12.9	.3	6.3	2.0	58.8
WATER................	-	100.0	-	-	-	-	-	-	-	-	-
OTHER................	3	100.0	3.1	50.3	19.3	3.8	13.7	2.9	6.0	.2	.6
UNKNOWN..............	-	100.0	23.7	73.6	-	-	-	-	-	2.7	-
EAST NORTH CENTRAL......	29	100.0	2.2	6.9	49.2	2.9	6.9	5.1	21.8	1.2	3.8
RAIL.................	7	100.0	-	15.4	-	.1	8.0	-	76.5	-	-
MOTOR CARRIER........	15	100.0	3.8	4.5	77.9	2.2	2.4	2.4	3.2	1.3	2.3
PRIVATE TRUCK........	2	100.0	-	-	100.0	-	-	-	-	-	-
AIR..................	-	100.0	-	.1	33.7	-	40.0	-	.2	.3	25.6
WATER................	-	100.0	-	-	-	-	-	-	-	-	-
OTHER................	5	100.0	1.5	5.2	14.9	9.7	20.0	21.4	10.5	2.6	14.2
UNKNOWN..............	-	100.0	-	23.8	76.2	-	-	-	-	-	-
WEST NORTH CENTRAL......	19	100.0	6.7	7.8	17.6	38.4	6.4	7.1	7.1	5.1	3.8
RAIL.................	-	100.0	-	-	-	-	-	-	-	-	-
MOTOR CARRIER........	11	100.0	7.7	6.5	19.3	50.5	.7	3.7	2.9	6.3	2.4
PRIVATE TRUCK........	-	100.0	-	-	-	30.1	-	69.9	-	-	-
AIR..................	1	100.0	-	18.5	1.2	49.0	1.8	-	-	-	29.6
WATER................	-	100.0	-	-	-	-	-	-	-	-	-
OTHER................	6	100.0	6.1	8.5	17.2	13.7	18.1	14.6	16.0	3.8	2.0
UNKNOWN..............	-	100.0	-	25.9	-	-	-	-	74.1	-	-
SOUTH ATLANTIC..........	439	100.0	3.4	16.3	6.8	1.6	58.6	7.0	3.7	.8	1.8
RAIL.................	1	100.0	-	2.6	4.6	-	34.9	-	27.9	29.2	.7
MOTOR CARRIER........	165	100.0	5.8	32.9	15.8	3.7	23.9	4.7	8.2	1.2	3.8
PRIVATE TRUCK........	254	100.0	1.5	4.9	.1	-	84.1	8.5	.4	.3	-
AIR..................	2	100.0	7.2	8.5	31.9	2.8	15.7	2.8	1.6	1.8	27.7
WATER................	-	100.0	-	-	-	-	-	-	-	-	-
OTHER................	15	100.0	8.7	27.0	17.9	5.6	21.4	7.6	6.1	.2	5.6
UNKNOWN..............	-	100.0	3.9	38.2	-	-	2.6	-	43.5	5.4	6.5
EAST SOUTH CENTRAL......	129	100.0	6.3	14.6	15.4	2.2	18.8	20.6	11.7	.8	9.6
RAIL.................	9	100.0	-	-	-	-	2.9	.8	-	.4	95.8
MOTOR CARRIER........	73	100.0	4.1	19.4	24.5	2.7	21.1	10.2	12.6	1.3	4.2
PRIVATE TRUCK........	39	100.0	11.7	8.2	.1	-	19.7	46.8	13.2	-	.3
AIR..................	1	100.0	1.1	33.4	23.8	3.0	13.7	.7	.9	2.5	21.0
WATER................	-	100.0	-	-	-	-	-	-	-	-	-
OTHER................	6	100.0	7.4	16.3	25.8	9.3	14.7	10.6	10.3	.4	5.3
UNKNOWN..............	-	100.0	-	-	-	-	-	-	-	-	-
TON-MILES OF SHIPMENTS	(millions of ton-miles)										
U.S. TOTAL...............	751	100.0	4.6	38.0	9.3	8.5	10.3	2.7	8.2	2.4	15.9
RAIL.................	31	100.0	-	2.7	4.3	2.5	3.6	.3	17.4	4.4	64.7
MOTOR CARRIER........	492	100.0	3.2	50.4	9.9	4.5	7.9	2.0	6.5	2.5	13.1
PRIVATE TRUCK........	62	100.0	18.7	15.8	1.1	.3	29.5	9.0	16.9	2.9	5.8
AIR..................	98	100.0	4.7	19.2	8.8	35.5	9.4	.6	5.1	.9	15.7
WATER...............	-	100.0	-	-	-	-	-	-	-	-	-
OTHER................	64	100.0	4.1	10.7	16.3	8.7	14.4	6.1	12.5	2.6	24.6
UNKNOWN..............	1	100.0	2.6	18.5	23.5	1.1	7.9	2.0	26.7	5.7	12.0

See footnotes at end of table 4.

TABLE 2. **TCC GROUP 233—Percent Distribution of Geographic Division of Origin and Means of Transport, by Geographic Division of Destination: 1972**—Continued

Geographic division of origin[1] and means of transport	Number	Percent distribution by division of destination									
		U.S. total	New England	Middle Atlantic	East North Central	West North Central	South Atlantic	East South Central	West South Central	Mountain	Pacific
TON-MILES OF SHIPMENTS	(millions of ton-miles)										
NEW ENGLAND..............	27	100.0	9.1	15.5	15.3	4.7	14.5	2.3	6.0	3.2	29.5
RAIL....................	4	100.0	-	.3	20.6	6.2	8.6	1.2	8.9	12.4	41.9
MOTOR CARRIER..........	13	100.0	3.6	27.7	16.7	5.7	20.7	3.4	4.5	1.1	16.6
PRIVATE TRUCK..........	2	100.0	80.5	.1	1.6	-	4.0	-	-	-	13.8
AIR....................	4	100.0	-	.1	7.4	1.1	5.8	.1	5.1	1.9	78.5
WATER..................	-	100.0	-	-	-	-	-	-	-	-	-
OTHER..................	2	100.0	.5	19.3	27.0	8.1	18.1	5.1	18.0	.8	3.1
UNKNOWN................	-	100.0	11.1	61.2	-	-	-	-	-	27.7	-
EAST NORTH CENTRAL......	14	100.0	3.5	8.7	18.6	2.9	9.6	4.7	34.2	3.0	14.8
RAIL....................	5	100.0	-	14.7	-	.1	6.4	-	78.8	-	-
MOTOR CARRIER..........	4	100.0	9.1	6.1	49.4	3.9	4.2	1.4	6.1	5.4	14.4
PRIVATE TRUCK..........	-	100.0	-	-	100.0	-	-	-	-	-	-
AIR....................	-	100.0	-	.1	10.7	-	36.0	-	.2	.4	52.6
WATER..................	-	100.0	-	-	-	-	-	-	-	-	-
OTHER..................	3	100.0	1.6	4.4	3.6	5.5	19.7	15.2	11.2	4.3	34.5
UNKNOWN................	-	100.0	-	62.2	37.8	-	-	-	-	-	-
WEST NORTH CENTRAL......	9	100.0	15.5	15.9	9.4	14.1	10.9	5.5	6.9	7.9	13.8
RAIL....................	-	100.0	-	-	-	-	-	-	-	-	-
MOTOR CARRIER..........	4	100.0	23.6	18.2	9.5	18.9	1.7	2.0	4.0	11.8	10.2
PRIVATE TRUCK..........	-	100.0	-	-	-	39.8	-	60.2	-	-	-
AIR....................	1	100.0	-	16.7	.6	22.3	1.6	-	-	-	58.8
WATER..................	-	100.0	-	-	-	-	-	-	-	-	-
OTHER..................	3	100.0	10.7	13.1	11.9	6.1	24.2	11.1	12.2	5.7	5.0
UNKNOWN................	-	100.0	-	29.0	-	-	-	-	71.0	-	-
SOUTH ATLANTIC..........	151	100.0	8.0	27.8	11.8	3.9	17.4	5.4	10.2	3.8	11.8
RAIL....................	1	100.0	-	1.2	2.8	-	19.8	-	28.2	46.6	1.4
MOTOR CARRIER..........	103	100.0	7.2	30.1	14.9	4.9	10.5	3.0	12.7	3.0	13.7
PRIVATE TRUCK..........	31	100.0	10.5	23.1	.3	.1	44.0	13.8	1.8	5.7	.8
AIR....................	2	100.0	5.1	5.5	18.3	2.4	4.2	1.1	1.5	2.9	58.9
WATER..................	-	100.0	-	-	-	-	-	-	-	-	-
OTHER..................	11	100.0	9.7	27.8	15.8	6.9	10.3	5.0	8.2	.3	16.0
UNKNOWN................	-	100.0	4.3	23.6	-	-	.9	-	43.4	10.6	17.2
EAST SOUTH CENTRAL......	84	100.0	11.2	17.1	11.2	2.1	11.8	3.5	11.9	1.6	29.7
RAIL....................	17	100.0	-	-	-	1.3	.2	-	-	.3	98.2
MOTOR CARRIER..........	44	100.0	6.2	24.4	19.0	2.6	15.7	3.3	11.8	2.7	14.3
PRIVATE TRUCK..........	17	100.0	36.2	14.4	.1	-	14.3	7.6	26.3	-	1.2
AIR....................	1	100.0	1.2	26.8	14.2	2.1	6.3	.1	.5	3.8	45.1
WATER..................	-	100.0	-	-	-	-	-	-	-	-	-
OTHER..................	4	100.0	11.0	20.2	20.8	8.5	10.5	3.8	6.9	1.0	17.4
UNKNOWN................	-	100.0	-	-	-	-	-	-	-	-	-

See footnotes at end of table 4.

TABLE 3. **TCC GROUP 233—Percent Distribution of Geographic Division of Destination and Means of Transport, by Geographic Division of Origin: 1972**

Geographic division of destination and means of transport	Number	Percent distribution by division of origin[1]									
		U.S. total	New England	Middle Atlantic	East North Central	West North Central	South Atlantic	East South Central	West South Central	Mountain	Pacific
TONS OF SHIPMENTS	(thousands of tons)										
U.S. TOTAL.............	1 542	100.0	3.8	(D)	1.9	1.2	28.5	8.4	(D)	(D)	(D)
RAIL...............	23	100.0	17.9	(D)	29.9	-	6.3	38.2	(D)	(D)	(D)
MOTOR CARRIER.........	1 025	100.0	3.5	(D)	1.5	1.2	16.1	7.1	(D)	(D)	(D)
PRIVATE TRUCK.........	343	100.0	3.4	(D)	.6	1.2	74.0	11.5	(D)	(D)	(D)
AIR.................	58	100.0	3.7	(D)	.2	1.8	4.3	2.0	(D)	(D)	(D)
WATER...............	-	100.0	-	(D)	-	-	-	-	(D)	(D)	(D)
OTHER...............	88	100.0	4.3	(D)	6.1	7.0	17.3	7.2	(D)	(D)	(D)
UNKNOWN.............	2	100.0	11.0	(D)	.8	.4	38.2	-	(D)	(D)	(D)
NEW ENGLAND.............	59	100.0	33.4	(D)	1.1	2.2	25.0	13.6	(D)	(D)	(D)
RAIL...............	-	100.0	67.5	(D)	-	-	-	-	(D)	(D)	(D)
MOTOR CARRIER.........	31	100.0	25.2	(D)	1.8	2.8	29.9	9.3	(D)	(D)	(D)
PRIVATE TRUCK.........	20	100.0	57.0	(D)	-	-	18.8	22.9	(D)	(D)	(D)
AIR.................	1	100.0	-	(D)	-	-	9.4	.7	(D)	(D)	(D)
WATER...............	-	100.0	-	(D)	-	-	-	-	(D)	(D)	(D)
OTHER...............	5	100.0	2.3	(D)	1.6	7.3	25.8	9.1	(D)	(D)	(D)
UNKNOWN.............	-	100.0	41.3	(D)	-	-	23.4	-	(D)	(D)	(D)
MIDDLE ATLANTIC.........	711	100.0	3.0	(D)	.3	.2	10.1	2.7	(D)	(D)	(D)
RAIL...............	1	100.0	4.5	(D)	81.8	-	3.0	-	(D)	(D)	(D)
MOTOR CARRIER.........	665	100.0	2.9	(D)	.1	.1	8.2	2.1	(D)	(D)	(D)
PRIVATE TRUCK.........	18	100.0	-	(D)	-	-	69.1	17.9	(D)	(D)	(D)
AIR.................	8	100.0	.1	(D)	-	2.3	2.6	4.7	(D)	(D)	(D)
WATER...............	-	100.0	-	(D)	-	-	-	-	(D)	(D)	(D)
OTHER...............	17	100.0	11.1	(D)	1.6	3.1	24.1	6.1	(D)	(D)	(D)
UNKNOWN.............	-	100.0	23.9	(D)	.6	.3	43.2	-	(D)	(D)	(D)
EAST NORTH CENTRAL......	114	100.0	4.9	(D)	12.8	2.9	26.2	17.4	(D)	(D)	(D)
RAIL...............	1	100.0	70.5	(D)	-	-	3.7	-	(D)	(D)	(D)
MOTOR CARRIER.........	85	100.0	3.7	(D)	13.8	2.7	30.5	21.1	(D)	(D)	(D)
PRIVATE TRUCK.........	2	100.0	1.6	(D)	67.9	-	8.6	.7	(D)	(D)	(D)
AIR.................	6	100.0	5.6	(D)	.5	.2	11.9	4.1	(D)	(D)	(D)
WATER...............	-	100.0	-	(D)	-	-	-	-	(D)	(D)	(D)
OTHER...............	17	100.0	4.3	(D)	4.8	6.3	16.1	9.7	(D)	(D)	(D)
UNKNOWN.............	-	100.0	-	(D)	4.1	-	-	-	(D)	(D)	(D)
WEST NORTH CENTRAL......	57	100.0	1.9	(D)	1.5	12.7	12.2	5.0	(D)	(D)	(D)
RAIL...............	-	100.0	33.4	(D)	1.3	-	-	34.5	(D)	(D)	(D)
MOTOR CARRIER.........	28	100.0	2.3	(D)	1.2	20.7	21.1	6.9	(D)	(D)	(D)
PRIVATE TRUCK.........	-	100.0	-	(D)	-	1.8	11.7	1.4	(D)	(D)	(D)
AIR.................	20	100.0	.2	(D)	-	2.4	.3	.2	(D)	(D)	(D)
WATER...............	-	100.0	-	(D)	-	-	-	-	(D)	(D)	(D)
OTHER...............	6	100.0	2.1	(D)	7.7	12.4	12.4	8.7	(D)	(D)	(D)
UNKNOWN.............	-	100.0	-	(D)	-	-	-	-	(D)	(D)	(D)
SOUTH ATLANTIC..........	326	100.0	1.6	(D)	.6	.4	78.8	7.5	(D)	(D)	(D)
RAIL...............	2	100.0	43.1	(D)	24.6	-	22.8	3.1	(D)	(D)	(D)
MOTOR CARRIER.........	79	100.0	4.1	(D)	.5	.1	49.8	19.5	(D)	(D)	(D)
PRIVATE TRUCK.........	223	100.0	.1	(D)	-	-	95.9	3.5	(D)	(D)	(D)
AIR.................	5	100.0	5.5	(D)	.8	.4	7.7	3.1	(D)	(D)	(D)
WATER...............	-	100.0	-	(D)	-	-	-	-	(D)	(D)	(D)
OTHER...............	16	100.0	3.1	(D)	6.5	6.8	19.7	5.6	(D)	(D)	(D)
UNKNOWN.............	-	100.0	-	(D)	-	-	10.2	-	(D)	(D)	(D)
EAST SOUTH CENTRAL......	69	100.0	1.0	(D)	2.2	1.9	44.1	38.2	(D)	(D)	(D)
RAIL...............	-	100.0	55.0	(D)	-	-	-	-	(D)	(D)	(D)
MOTOR CARRIER.........	22	100.0	2.2	(D)	1.6	2.0	35.7	33.9	(D)	(D)	(D)
PRIVATE TRUCK.........	40	100.0	-	(D)	-	-	53.9	46.0	(D)	(D)	(D)
AIR.................	-	100.0	1.3	(D)	-	-	11.6	1.3	(D)	(D)	(D)
WATER...............	-	100.0	-	(D)	-	-	-	-	(D)	(D)	(D)
OTHER...............	6	100.0	1.7	(D)	17.3	13.6	17.3	10.1	(D)	(D)	(D)
UNKNOWN.............	-	100.0	-	(D)	-	-	-	-	(D)	(D)	(D)
WEST SOUTH CENTRAL......	84	100.0	1.2	(D)	7.7	1.6	19.4	17.9	(D)	(D)	(D)
RAIL...............	6	100.0	4.2	(D)	83.0	-	6.4	-	(D)	(D)	(D)
MOTOR CARRIER.........	45	100.0	.8	(D)	1.0	.8	29.6	20.1	(D)	(D)	(D)
PRIVATE TRUCK.........	20	100.0	-	(D)	-	-	5.3	26.1	(D)	(D)	(D)
AIR.................	3	100.0	4.0	(D)	-	-	1.2	.3	(D)	(D)	(D)
WATER...............	-	100.0	-	(D)	-	-	-	-	(D)	(D)	(D)
OTHER...............	8	100.0	2.8	(D)	7.1	12.4	11.7	8.2	(D)	(D)	(D)
UNKNOWN.............	-	100.0	-	(D)	-	1.1	66.3	-	(D)	(D)	(D)
MOUNTAIN...............	15	100.0	3.0	(D)	2.2	6.3	21.4	6.8	(D)	(D)	(D)
RAIL...............	-	100.0	41.2	(D)	-	-	53.0	4.7	(D)	(D)	(D)
MOTOR CARRIER.........	11	100.0	.6	(D)	1.8	6.6	17.3	8.6	(D)	(D)	(D)
PRIVATE TRUCK.........	-	100.0	-	(D)	-	-	98.2	-	(D)	(D)	(D)
AIR.................	-	100.0	4.9	(D)	-	-	5.1	3.3	(D)	(D)	(D)
WATER...............	-	100.0	-	(D)	-	-	-	-	(D)	(D)	(D)
OTHER...............	1	100.0	.5	(D)	7.9	13.0	1.5	1.6	(D)	(D)	(D)
UNKNOWN.............	-	100.0	11.3	(D)	-	-	78.9	-	(D)	(D)	(D)
PACIFIC................	102	100.0	3.0	(D)	1.1	.7	7.9	12.1	(D)	(D)	(D)
RAIL...............	9	100.0	8.1	(D)	-	-	.1	89.1	(D)	(D)	(D)
MOTOR CARRIER.........	55	100.0	1.6	(D)	.6	.5	11.5	5.6	(D)	(D)	(D)
PRIVATE TRUCK.........	17	100.0	.8	(D)	-	-	.7	.7	(D)	(D)	(D)
AIR.................	10	100.0	11.9	(D)	.2	2.9	6.5	2.3	(D)	(D)	(D)
WATER...............	-	100.0	-	(D)	-	-	-	-	(D)	(D)	(D)
OTHER...............	9	100.0	.3	(D)	8.4	1.4	9.3	3.7	(D)	(D)	(D)
UNKNOWN.............	-	100.0	-	(D)	-	-	58.5	-	(D)	(D)	(D)

See footnotes at end of table 4.

TABLE 3. TCC GROUP 233—Percent Distribution of Geographic Division of Destination and Means of Transport, by Geographic Division of Origin: 1972—Continued

Geographic division of destination and means of transport	Number	Percent distribution by division of origin[1]									
		U.S. total	New England	Middle Atlantic	East North Central	West North Central	South Atlantic	East South Central	West South Central	Mountain	Pacific
TON-MILES OF SHIPMENTS	(millions of ton-miles)										
U.S. TOTAL	751	100.0	3.7	(D)	1.9	1.2	20.1	11.3	(D)	(D)	(D)
RAIL	31	100.0	15.8	(D)	16.6	-	4.7	57.0	(D)	(D)	(D)
MOTOR CARRIER	492	100.0	2.8	(D)	.9	.9	20.9	9.0	(D)	(D)	(D)
PRIVATE TRUCK	62	100.0	3.9	(D)	.3	-	50.2	27.7	(D)	(D)	(D)
AIR	98	100.0	4.4	(D)	.1	1.1	2.6	1.0	(D)	(D)	(D)
WATER	-	100.0	-	(D)	-	-	-	-	(D)	(D)	(D)
OTHER	64	100.0	3.1	(D)	6.2	5.7	18.3	6.6	(D)	(D)	(D)
UNKNOWN	1	100.0	3.2	(D)	.3	.4	40.8	-	(D)	(D)	(D)
NEW ENGLAND	34	100.0	7.3	(D)	1.4	4.1	34.7	27.5	(D)	(D)	(D)
RAIL	-	100.0	7.0	(D)	-	-	-	-	(D)	(D)	(D)
MOTOR CARRIER	15	100.0	3.2	(D)	2.7	6.6	47.8	17.8	(D)	(D)	(D)
PRIVATE TRUCK	11	100.0	16.9	(D)	-	-	28.0	53.4	(D)	(D)	(D)
AIR	4	100.0	-	(D)	-	-	2.8	.3	(D)	(D)	(D)
WATER	-	100.0	-	(D)	-	-	-	-	(D)	(D)	(D)
OTHER	2	100.0	.3	(D)	2.4	14.9	43.5	17.7	(D)	(D)	(D)
UNKNOWN	-	100.0	13.7	(D)	-	-	68.0	-	(D)	(D)	(D)
MIDDLE ATLANTIC	285	100.0	1.5	(D)	.4	.5	14.7	5.1	(D)	(D)	(D)
RAIL	-	100.0	1.5	(D)	91.3	-	2.1	-	(D)	(D)	(D)
MOTOR CARRIER	248	100.0	1.5	(D)	.1	.3	12.5	4.4	(D)	(D)	(D)
PRIVATE TRUCK	9	100.0	-	(D)	-	-	73.5	25.2	(D)	(D)	(D)
AIR	18	100.0	-	(D)	-	1.0	.7	1.4	(D)	(D)	(D)
WATER	-	100.0	-	(D)	-	-	-	-	(D)	(D)	(D)
OTHER	6	100.0	5.7	(D)	2.5	7.1	47.6	12.5	(D)	(D)	(D)
UNKNOWN	-	100.0	10.6	(D)	.9	.7	52.2	-	(D)	(D)	(D)
EAST NORTH CENTRAL	70	100.0	6.0	(D)	3.7	1.2	25.4	13.5	(D)	(D)	(D)
RAIL	1	100.0	75.3	(D)	-	-	3.0	-	(D)	(D)	(D)
MOTOR CARRIER	48	100.0	4.8	(D)	4.7	.8	31.6	17.4	(D)	(D)	(D)
PRIVATE TRUCK	-	100.0	5.6	(D)	24.5	-	14.5	1.9	(D)	(D)	(D)
AIR	8	100.0	3.7	(D)	.1	.1	5.4	1.7	(D)	(D)	(D)
WATER	-	100.0	-	(D)	-	-	-	-	(D)	(D)	(D)
OTHER	10	100.0	5.2	(D)	1.4	4.2	17.8	8.5	(D)	(D)	(D)
UNKNOWN	-	100.0	-	(D)	.5	-	-	-	(D)	(D)	(D)
WEST NORTH CENTRAL	63	100.0	2.0	(D)	.6	2.0	9.3	2.7	(D)	(D)	(D)
RAIL	-	100.0	38.7	(D)	.5	-	-	28.7	(D)	(D)	(D)
MOTOR CARRIER	22	100.0	3.5	(D)	.8	3.7	22.5	5.1	(D)	(D)	(D)
PRIVATE TRUCK	-	100.0	-	(D)	-	.5	15.5	1.2	(D)	(D)	(D)
AIR	35	100.0	.1	(D)	-	.7	.2	.1	(D)	(D)	(D)
WATER	-	100.0	-	(D)	-	-	-	-	(D)	(D)	(D)
OTHER	5	100.0	2.9	(D)	3.9	4.0	14.5	6.4	(D)	(D)	(D)
UNKNOWN	-	100.0	-	(D)	-	-	-	-	(D)	(D)	(D)
SOUTH ATLANTIC	77	100.0	5.2	(D)	1.7	1.3	33.8	12.9	(D)	(D)	(D)
RAIL	1	100.0	38.0	(D)	30.0	-	25.9	2.4	(D)	(D)	(D)
MOTOR CARRIER	39	100.0	7.4	(D)	.5	.2	27.5	17.8	(D)	(D)	(D)
PRIVATE TRUCK	18	100.0	.5	(D)	-	-	74.6	13.4	(D)	(D)	(D)
AIR	9	100.0	2.7	(D)	.4	.2	1.2	.7	(D)	(D)	(D)
WATER	-	100.0	-	(D)	-	-	-	-	(D)	(D)	(D)
OTHER	9	100.0	4.0	(D)	8.4	9.7	13.1	4.8	(D)	(D)	(D)
UNKNOWN	-	100.0	-	(D)	-	-	4.7	-	(D)	(D)	(D)
EAST SOUTH CENTRAL	20	100.0	3.2	(D)	3.3	2.5	40.3	14.7	(D)	(D)	(D)
RAIL	-	100.0	61.8	(D)	-	-	-	-	(D)	(D)	(D)
MOTOR CARRIER	9	100.0	4.8	(D)	.6	.9	32.0	15.2	(D)	(D)	(D)
PRIVATE TRUCK	5	100.0	-	(D)	-	-	76.8	23.2	(D)	(D)	(D)
AIR	-	100.0	1.1	(D)	-	-	4.9	.2	(D)	(D)	(D)
WATER	-	100.0	-	(D)	-	-	-	-	(D)	(D)	(D)
OTHER	3	100.0	2.6	(D)	15.2	10.4	14.8	4.1	(D)	(D)	(D)
UNKNOWN	-	100.0	-	(D)	-	-	-	-	(D)	(D)	(D)
WEST SOUTH CENTRAL	61	100.0	2.7	(D)	7.8	1.0	25.0	16.4	(D)	(D)	(D)
RAIL	5	100.0	8.1	(D)	75.3	-	7.6	-	(D)	(D)	(D)
MOTOR CARRIER	32	100.0	2.0	(D)	.9	.5	40.8	16.4	(D)	(D)	(D)
PRIVATE TRUCK	10	100.0	-	(D)	-	-	5.3	43.1	(D)	(D)	(D)
AIR	5	100.0	4.4	(D)	-	-	.8	.1	(D)	(D)	(D)
WATER	-	100.0	-	(D)	-	-	-	-	(D)	(D)	(D)
OTHER	8	100.0	4.5	(D)	5.5	5.6	12.0	3.6	(D)	(D)	(D)
UNKNOWN	-	100.0	-	(D)	-	1.2	66.3	-	(D)	(D)	(D)
MOUNTAIN	18	100.0	4.8	(D)	2.3	4.0	31.5	7.4	(D)	(D)	(D)
RAIL	1	100.0	44.7	(D)	-	-	49.5	4.4	(D)	(D)	(D)
MOTOR CARRIER	12	100.0	1.2	(D)	2.0	4.1	25.1	9.8	(D)	(D)	(D)
PRIVATE TRUCK	1	100.0	-	(D)	-	-	99.4	-	(D)	(D)	(D)
AIR	-	100.0	8.8	(D)	-	-	8.0	4.1	(D)	(D)	(D)
WATER	-	100.0	-	(D)	-	-	-	-	(D)	(D)	(D)
OTHER	1	100.0	.9	(D)	10.1	12.5	2.2	2.4	(D)	(D)	(D)
UNKNOWN	-	100.0	15.4	(D)	-	-	75.4	-	(D)	(D)	(D)
PACIFIC	119	100.0	6.8	(D)	1.7	1.1	14.9	21.0	(D)	(D)	(D)
RAIL	20	100.0	10.2	(D)	-	-	.1	86.4	(D)	(D)	(D)
MOTOR CARRIER	64	100.0	3.6	(D)	1.0	.7	21.8	9.9	(D)	(D)	(D)
PRIVATE TRUCK	3	100.0	9.4	(D)	-	-	7.0	5.9	(D)	(D)	(D)
AIR	15	100.0	21.9	(D)	.3	4.1	9.8	3.0	(D)	(D)	(D)
WATER	-	100.0	-	(D)	-	-	-	-	(D)	(D)	(D)
OTHER	15	100.0	.4	(D)	8.6	1.2	11.8	4.7	(D)	(D)	(D)
UNKNOWN	-	100.0	-	(D)	-	-	58.3	-	(D)	(D)	(D)

See footnotes at end of table 4.

TABLE 4. **TCC GROUP 233—Percent Distribution of Distance Shipped and Weight of Shipment, by Means of Transport: 1972**

Distance shipped and weight of shipment[2] [3]	Number	Percent distribution by means of transport							
		All means of transport	Rail	Motor carrier	Private truck	Air	Water	Other	Unknown
TONS OF SHIPMENTS	(thousands of tons)								
U.S. TOTAL.........	1 256	100.0	1.6	78.6	8.7	4.4	-	6.5	.2
UNDER 100 MILES........	102	100.0	-	57.0	35.5	-	-	7.4	.1
UNDER 1000 POUNDS.....	46	100.0	-	69.9	13.6	-	-	16.3	.2
1000 TO 9999 POUNDS...	45	100.0	-	56.3	43.7	-	-	-	-
10000 TO 29999 POUNDS.	9	100.0	-	-	100.0	-	-	-	-
30000 TO 59999 POUNDS.	-	100.0	-	-	100.0	-	-	-	-
60000 TO 89999 POUNDS.	-	100.0	-	-	-	-	-	-	-
90000 POUNDS AND OVER.	-	100.0	-	-	-	-	-	-	-
100 TO 199 MILES........	90	100.0	.2	77.7	13.9	-	-	7.8	.4
UNDER 1000 POUNDS.....	41	100.0	.4	82.9	1.1	-	-	14.7	.9
1000 TO 9999 POUNDS...	42	100.0	-	82.8	15.0	-	-	2.1	-
10000 TO 29999 POUNDS.	6	100.0	-	7.5	92.5	-	-	-	-
30000 TO 59999 POUNDS.	-	100.0	-	-	-	-	-	-	-
60000 TO 89999 POUNDS.	-	100.0	-	-	-	-	-	-	-
90000 POUNDS AND OVER.	-	100.0	-	-	-	-	-	-	-
200 TO 299 MILES........	66	100.0	.2	55.0	34.3	.7	-	9.7	.1
UNDER 1000 POUNDS.....	25	100.0	.5	70.6	1.5	1.9	-	25.3	.2
1000 TO 9999 POUNDS...	37	100.0	-	47.7	52.3	-	-	-	-
10000 TO 29999 POUNDS.	4	100.0	-	23.9	76.1	-	-	-	-
30000 TO 59999 POUNDS.	-	100.0	-	-	-	-	-	-	-
60000 TO 89999 POUNDS.	-	100.0	-	-	-	-	-	-	-
90000 POUNDS AND OVER.	-	100.0	-	-	-	-	-	-	-
300 TO 499 MILES........	612	100.0	.1	94.8	2.4	.9	-	1.8	-
UNDER 1000 POUNDS.....	63	100.0	.6	76.7	3.9	1.0	-	17.7	.2
1000 TO 9999 POUNDS...	62	100.0	-	78.0	14.3	7.7	-	-	-
10000 TO 29999 POUNDS.	8	100.0	-	60.8	39.2	-	-	-	-
30000 TO 59999 POUNDS.	-	100.0	-	-	-	-	-	-	-
60000 TO 89999 POUNDS.	-	100.0	-	-	-	-	-	-	-
90000 POUNDS AND OVER.	477	100.0	-	100.0	-	-	-	-	-
500 TO 999 MILES........	211	100.0	4.5	71.6	7.6	2.4	-	13.4	.5
UNDER 1000 POUNDS.....	125	100.0	1.1	69.9	2.0	3.7	-	22.5	.7
1000 TO 9999 POUNDS...	59	100.0	.1	88.1	10.6	.8	-	.1	.4
10000 TO 29999 POUNDS.	14	100.0	25.0	31.2	43.7	-	-	-	-
30000 TO 59999 POUNDS.	4	100.0	36.4	55.2	8.4	-	-	-	-
60000 TO 89999 POUNDS.	2	100.0	100.0	-	-	-	-	-	-
90000 POUNDS AND OVER.	3	100.0	-	93.8	6.2	-	-	-	-
1000 TO 1499 MILES......	60	100.0	1.1	59.9	9.1	7.3	-	22.2	.4
UNDER 1000 POUNDS.....	47	100.0	1.4	59.0	1.5	9.2	-	28.2	.6
1000 TO 9999 POUNDS...	8	100.0	-	89.1	10.6	.3	-	-	-
10000 TO 29999 POUNDS.	3	100.0	-	5.2	94.8	-	-	-	-
30000 TO 59999 POUNDS.	-	100.0	-	-	-	-	-	-	-
60000 TO 89999 POUNDS.	-	100.0	-	-	-	-	-	-	-
90000 POUNDS AND OVER.	-	100.0	-	-	-	-	-	-	-
1500 MILES OR OVER......	112	100.0	8.5	47.8	1.1	35.5	-	6.9	.3
UNDER 1000 POUNDS.....	65	100.0	3.1	48.6	.6	35.5	-	11.7	.5
1000 TO 9999 POUNDS...	40	100.0	6.3	53.1	-	40.6	-	-	-
10000 TO 29999 POUNDS.	4	100.0	77.8	5.1	17.1	-	-	-	-
30000 TO 59999 POUNDS.	1	100.0	100.0	-	-	-	-	-	-
60000 TO 89999 POUNDS.	-	100.0	-	-	-	-	-	-	-
90000 POUNDS AND OVER.	-	100.0	-	-	-	-	-	-	-
TON-MILES OF SHIPMENTS	(millions of ton-miles)								
U.S. TOTAL.........	694	100.0	3.9	68.4	5.3	13.5	-	8.7	.3
UNDER 100 MILES........	5	100.0	-	49.6	44.2	-	-	6.1	.1
UNDER 1000 POUNDS.....	2	100.0	-	64.0	20.5	-	-	15.3	.2
1000 TO 9999 POUNDS...	2	100.0	-	50.5	49.5	-	-	-	-
10000 TO 29999 POUNDS.	-	100.0	-	-	100.0	-	-	-	-
30000 TO 59999 POUNDS.	-	100.0	-	-	100.0	-	-	-	-
60000 TO 89999 POUNDS.	-	100.0	-	-	-	-	-	-	-
90000 POUNDS AND OVER.	-	100.0	-	-	-	-	-	-	-
100 TO 199 MILES........	14	100.0	.2	75.7	15.7	-	-	8.0	.4
UNDER 1000 POUNDS.....	6	100.0	.4	82.8	1.0	-	-	14.8	1.0
1000 TO 9999 POUNDS...	6	100.0	-	81.3	16.0	-	-	2.7	-
10000 TO 29999 POUNDS.	1	100.0	-	7.5	92.5	-	-	-	-
30000 TO 59999 POUNDS.	-	100.0	-	-	-	-	-	-	-
60000 TO 89999 POUNDS.	-	100.0	-	-	-	-	-	-	-
90000 POUNDS AND OVER.	-	100.0	-	-	-	-	-	-	-

See footnotes at end of table 4.

TABLE 4. TCC GROUP 233—Percent Distribution of Distance Shipped and Weight of Shipment, by Means of Transport: 1972—Continued

Distance shipped and weight of shipment[2] [3]	Number	Percent distribution by means of transport							
		All means of transport	Rail	Motor carrier	Private truck	Air	Water	Other	Unknown
TON-MILES OF SHIPMENTS	(millions of ton-miles)								
200 TO 299 MILES.........	16	100.0	.2	54.3	35.5	.8	-	9.2	.1
UNDER 1000 POUNDS.....	6	100.0	.6	71.6	1.5	2.0	-	24.3	.1
1000 TO 9999 POUNDS...	9	100.0	-	45.4	54.6	-	-	-	-
10000 TO 29999 POUNDS.	-	100.0	-	26.9	73.1	-	-	-	-
30000 TO 59999 POUNDS.	-	100.0	-	-	-	-	-	-	-
60000 TO 89999 POUNDS.	-	100.0	-	-	-	-	-	-	-
90000 POUNDS AND OVER.	-	100.0	-	-	-	-	-	-	-
300 TO 499 MILES.........	198	100.0	.1	93.5	3.1	1.0	-	2.3	-
UNDER 1000 POUNDS.....	25	100.0	.6	76.4	3.9	1.0	-	17.9	.2
1000 TO 9999 POUNDS...	25	100.0	-	78.3	15.0	6.7	-	-	-
10000 TO 29999 POUNDS.	3	100.0	-	58.3	41.7	-	-	-	-
30000 TO 59999 POUNDS.	-	100.0	-	-	-	-	-	-	-
60000 TO 89999 POUNDS.	-	100.0	-	-	-	-	-	-	-
90000 POUNDS AND OVER.	144	100.0	-	100.0	-	-	-	-	-
500 TO 999 MILES.........	147	100.0	4.6	71.7	6.9	2.4	-	13.9	.5
UNDER 1000 POUNDS.....	89	100.0	1.1	69.9	1.7	3.7	-	22.9	.7
1000 TO 9999 POUNDS...	40	100.0	.1	89.4	9.4	.8	-	.1	.3
10000 TO 29999 POUNDS.	10	100.0	25.1	34.1	40.8	-	-	-	-
30000 TO 59999 POUNDS.	2	100.0	40.2	51.5	8.3	-	-	-	-
60000 TO 89999 POUNDS.	1	100.0	100.0	-	-	-	-	-	-
90000 POUNDS AND OVER.	2	100.0	-	93.3	6.7	-	-	-	-
1000 TO 1499 MILES......	71	100.0	1.1	58.8	10.1	8.2	-	21.4	.4
UNDER 1000 POUNDS.....	56	100.0	1.4	59.0	1.5	10.4	-	27.3	.5
1000 TO 9999 POUNDS...	9	100.0	-	86.8	12.9	.3	-	-	-
10000 TO 29999 POUNDS.	5	100.0	-	5.2	94.8	-	-	-	-
30000 TO 59999 POUNDS.	-	100.0	-	-	-	-	-	-	-
60000 TO 89999 POUNDS.	-	100.0	-	-	-	-	-	-	-
90000 POUNDS AND OVER.	-	100.0	-	-	-	-	-	-	-
1500 MILES OR OVER......	240	100.0	7.9	49.6	1.1	34.0	-	7.0	.3
UNDER 1000 POUNDS.....	147	100.0	2.9	48.4	.6	36.1	-	11.5	.4
1000 TO 9999 POUNDS...	81	100.0	6.1	58.7	-	35.2	-	-	-
10000 TO 29999 POUNDS.	9	100.0	77.9	3.9	18.2	-	-	-	-
30000 TO 59999 POUNDS.	2	100.0	100.0	-	-	-	-	-	-
60000 TO 89999 POUNDS.	-	100.0	-	-	-	-	-	-	-
90000 POUNDS AND OVER.	-	100.0	-	-	-	-	-	-	-

Note: Detail may not add to total due to rounding. The introductory table shows the estimates of sampling variability for tons; sampling variability for ton-miles has not been estimated. See the map in the Introduction for the States comprising the geographic divisions of the United States.

Shipments excluded from the survey are those moving by pipeline (primarily petroleum products from refineries), parcel post shipments, and commodities moved by own power (motorized vehicles, aircraft, etc.) or towed (prefabricated buildings, etc.). Local shipments (commodities shipped less than 25 miles from the plant) and shipments within the same city are also excluded. Shipments to Alaska and Hawaii from the 48 conterminous States and the District of Columbia are included; however, no data were obtained for shipments originating in Alaska and Hawaii.

- Represents zero or rounds to zero.   (D) Withheld to avoid disclosing figures for individual companies.

[1] Production of this commodity is concentrated in the geographic divisions shown; figures and distributions for geographic divisions not shown are included in the total.

[2] Distances of shipments to foreign destinations are calculated only to the U.S. port of exit.

[3] Includes only shipments represented by bills of lading and invoices. Summary records which did not show individual weights of shipments are not included.

TCC 239. Miscellaneous Fabricated Textile Products

Comparisons of Tons and Ton-Miles of Shipments for
Geographic Divisions of Origin and for Sampling Variability: 1972 and 1967

Geographic division of origin	Estimates				Relative sampling variability in tons (percent)	
	1972		1967		1972	1967
	Tons (thousands)	Ton-miles (millions)	Tons (thousands)	Ton-miles (millions)		
U.S. total	1,713	943	1,862	924	13.6	19.6
New England	(D)	(D)	74	68	(*)	(*)
Middle Atlantic	112	89	409	184	36.4	(*)
East North Central	465	178	244	128	18.9	(*)
West North Central	(D)	(D)	34	18	(*)	(*)
South Atlantic	673	343	427	273	26.1	(*)
East South Central	(D)	(D)	402	157	(*)	(*)
West South Central	(D)	(D)	105	32	(*)	(*)
Mountain	(D)	(D)	—	—	(*)	(*)
Pacific	(D)	(D)	167	64	(*)	(*)

— Represents or rounds to zero.   (D) Withheld to avoid disclosing figures for individual companies.   (*) Data not published.

TABLE 1. TCC GROUP 239—Percent Distribution of Geographic Division of Origin and Distance Shipped, by Means of Transport: 1972

Geographic division of origin[1] and distance shipped[2]	Number	Percent distribution by means of transport							
		All means of transport	Rail	Motor carrier	Private truck	Air	Water	Other	Unknown
TONS OF SHIPMENTS	(thousands of tons)								
U.S. TOTAL..........	1 713	100.0	27.2	60.4	10.3	.3	–	1.6	.1
MIDDLE ATLANTIC.........	112	100.0	6.6	87.7	1.8	.4	.4	3.0	–
UNDER 100 MILES.......	13	100.0	–	83.4	12.0	–	–	4.5	–
100 TO 199 MILES......	11	100.0	–	93.3	2.4	.2	–	4.1	–
200 TO 299 MILES......	6	100.0	–	96.4	.2	.7	–	2.6	–
300 TO 499 MILES......	15	100.0	1.6	93.1	.5	.8	.5	3.5	–
500 TO 999 MILES.....	37	100.0	1.2	95.4	–	.5	–	2.9	–
1000 TO 1499 MILES....	11	100.0	2.8	94.0	–	.4	–	2.8	–
1500 MILES OR OVER....	17	100.0	37.3	59.2	–	–	2.3	1.3	–
EAST NORTH CENTRAL......	465	100.0	57.2	38.9	2.9	.6	–	.3	.1
UNDER 100 MILES.......	126	100.0	49.4	49.1	1.5	–	–	.1	–
100 TO 199 MILES......	59	100.0	16.6	81.1	2.1	–	–	.2	–
200 TO 299 MILES......	55	100.0	83.5	14.0	.7	.2	–	1.0	.6
300 TO 499 MILES......	92	100.0	51.1	40.6	7.6	.6	–	.1	–
500 TO 999 MILES......	105	100.0	76.9	20.6	1.7	.3	–	.6	–
1000 TO 1499 MILES....	2	100.0	–	27.2	71.0	–	–	1.8	–
1500 MILES OR OVER....	24	100.0	80.7	12.4	–	6.9	–	–	–
SOUTH ATLANTIC..........	673	100.0	15.9	67.8	14.3	.1	–	1.8	.2
UNDER 100 MILES.......	86	100.0	–	64.8	33.7	–	–	1.5	–
100 TO 199 MILES......	88	100.0	–	59.1	37.3	–	–	3.6	–
200 TO 299 MILES......	93	100.0	54.9	41.2	3.0	–	–	.7	.3
300 TO 499 MILES......	165	100.0	3.2	84.8	9.6	–	–	2.4	–
500 TO 999 MILES......	180	100.0	15.4	79.3	3.6	.1	–	1.1	.5
1000 TO 1499 MILES....	8	100.0	–	93.8	–	2.7	–	3.5	–
1500 MILES OR OVER....	52	100.0	43.0	37.6	18.2	.1	–	1.1	–
TON-MILES OF SHIPMENTS	(millions of ton-miles)								
U.S. TOTAL..........	943	100.0	34.7	54.9	7.6	.8	.3	1.5	.1
MIDDLE ATLANTIC.........	89	100.0	18.7	76.5	.2	.3	2.2	2.2	–
UNDER 100 MILES.......	–	100.0	–	82.4	10.8	–	–	6.8	–
100 TO 199 MILES......	1	100.0	–	93.1	2.5	.3	–	4.1	–
200 TO 299 MILES......	1	100.0	–	96.4	.2	.6	–	2.7	–
300 TO 499 MILES......	5	100.0	2.0	92.6	.5	.8	.5	3.6	–
500 TO 999 MILES......	26	100.0	1.3	95.4	–	.5	–	2.9	–
1000 TO 1499 MILES....	13	100.0	2.6	94.3	–	.4	–	2.7	–
1500 MILES OR OVER....	40	100.0	39.3	54.6	–	–	4.9	1.2	–
EAST NORTH CENTRAL......	178	100.0	69.0	25.1	3.5	2.0	–	.4	–
UNDER 100 MILES.......	4	100.0	45.6	52.5	1.8	–	–	.1	–
100 TO 199 MILES......	7	100.0	20.4	76.9	2.4	–	–	.2	–
200 TO 299 MILES......	13	100.0	83.0	14.4	.7	.2	–	1.0	.6
300 TO 499 MILES......	38	100.0	51.2	40.1	7.9	.6	–	.1	–
500 TO 999 MILES......	66	100.0	76.7	20.4	1.9	.2	–	.7	–
1000 TO 1499 MILES....	2	100.0	–	31.1	67.0	–	–	1.9	–
1500 MILES OR OVER....	46	100.0	81.9	11.2	–	6.9	–	–	–
SOUTH ATLANTIC..........	343	100.0	24.2	62.9	11.0	.1	–	1.5	.2
UNDER 100 MILES.......	4	100.0	–	63.7	34.4	–	–	1.9	–
100 TO 199 MILES......	13	100.0	–	61.0	35.1	–	–	3.8	–
200 TO 299 MILES......	22	100.0	56.7	39.0	3.2	–	–	.7	.3
300 TO 409 MILES......	59	100.0	3.1	84.7	10.0	–	–	2.2	–
500 TO 999 MILES......	116	100.0	13.7	80.7	3.6	.1	–	1.3	.6
1000 TO 1499 MILES....	9	100.0	–	93.7	–	2.7	–	3.5	–
1500 MILES OR OVER....	118	100.0	44.6	36.8	17.5	.1	–	.9	–

See footnotes at end of table 4.

TABLE 2. TCC GROUP 239—Percent Distribution of Geographic Division of Origin and Means of Transport, by Geographic Division of Destination: 1972

Geographic division of origin[1] and means of transport	Number	Percent distribution by division of destination									
		U.S. total	New England	Middle Atlantic	East North Central	West North Central	South Atlantic	East South Central	West South Central	Mountain	Pacific
TONS OF SHIPMENTS	(thousands of tons)										
U.S. TOTAL..............	1 713	100.0	4.5	13.7	26.0	8.4	24.6	4.8	7.7	1.3	8.9
RAIL....................	465	100.0	1.2	5.4	38.4	11.3	19.1	2.7	6.8	–	15.0
MOTOR CARRIER...........	1 035	100.0	6.4	18.4	23.1	6.7	23.3	5.3	8.7	1.8	6.3
PRIVATE TRUCK...........	175	100.0	2.2	7.7	13.7	11.3	45.7	5.1	3.7	2.0	8.4
AIR.....................	5	100.0	1.2	27.5	10.8	8.3	14.9	2.0	4.0	.1	31.1
WATER...................	–	100.0	12.4	–	–	–	–	–	–	–	87.6
OTHER...................	28	100.0	5.6	9.8	10.8	5.0	34.6	17.5	11.1	2.6	3.0
UNKNOWN.................	1	100.0	.1	48.0	2.5	17.8	10.8	14.5	–	–	6.4

See footnotes at end of table 4.

TABLE 2. TCC GROUP 239—Percent Distribution of Geographic Division of Origin and Means of Transport, by Geographic Division of Destination: 1972—Continued

Geographic division of origin[1] and means of transport	Number	Percent distribution by division of destination									
		U.S. total	New England	Middle Atlantic	East North Central	West North Central	South Atlantic	East South Central	West South Central	Mountain	Pacific
TONS OF SHIPMENTS	(thousands of tons)										
MIDDLE ATLANTIC	112	100.0	6.0	22.8	28.4	5.8	10.6	5.6	7.0	2.0	11.8
RAIL	7	100.0	-	-	8.4	3.3	.5	.6	1.1	1.1	84.9
MOTOR CARRIER	98	100.0	6.4	23.4	30.6	6.2	11.0	6.0	7.7	2.2	6.5
PRIVATE TRUCK	2	100.0	11.3	84.9	1.4	-	2.3	-	-	-	-
AIR	-	100.0	-	11.4	69.7	.4	6.3	2.4	9.7	-	-
WATER	-	100.0	17.3	-	-	-	-	-	-	-	82.7
OTHER	3	100.0	4.6	23.4	23.9	3.5	25.3	8.9	5.1	.9	4.4
UNKNOWN	-	100.0	-	-	-	-	100.0	-	-	-	-
EAST NORTH CENTRAL	465	100.0	1.5	7.7	55.8	13.4	11.4	2.8	1.6	.5	5.2
RAIL	266	100.0	1.9	8.4	45.0	19.2	11.8	4.4	2.0	-	7.3
MOTOR CARRIER	180	100.0	1.0	7.1	71.9	5.2	11.3	.3	1.1	.4	1.7
PRIVATE TRUCK	13	100.0	-	-	69.0	7.0	8.6	4.3	-	-	-
AIR	2	100.0	-	11.6	3.6	12.1	5.4	2.8	.7	11.2	63.7
WATER	-	100.0	-	-	-	-	-	-	-	-	-
OTHER	1	100.0	6.5	26.8	24.4	18.8	6.4	12.3	3.0	1.8	.1
UNKNOWN	-	100.0	-	-	-	100.0	-	-	-	-	-
SOUTH ATLANTIC	673	100.0	6.6	19.8	9.5	3.4	43.9	6.0	2.6	.4	7.6
RAIL	106	100.0	-	25.9	-	-	52.8	-	-	-	21.3
MOTOR CAPRIER	456	100.0	9.6	27.1	7.7	5.0	35.5	7.4	3.1	.5	4.1
PRIVATE TRUCK	96	100.0	.8	8.7	.8	.1	73.6	3.9	2.2	.1	9.9
AIR	-	100.0	1.7	7.9	8.6	15.7	12.6	.6	36.2	.6	16.3
WATER	-	100.0	-	-	-	-	-	-	-	-	-
OTHER	11	100.0	1.5	3.1	4.8	2.5	49.4	25.8	8.3	3.6	1.1
UNKNOWN	1	100.0	.1	71.7	3.8	-	2.7	21.7	-	-	-
TON-MILES OF SHIPMENTS	(millions of ton-miles)										
U.S. TOTAL	943	100.0	5.1	10.6	15.8	8.8	13.4	3.5	10.8	2.6	29.3
RAIL	327	100.0	1.5	4.1	16.3	8.5	10.4	1.3	12.9	-	44.9
MOTOR CARRIER	518	100.0	7.9	15.0	15.6	9.9	13.8	5.0	10.1	3.8	19.0
PRIVATE TRUCK	72	100.0	1.4	7.7	18.3	4.6	23.3	1.7	6.1	4.1	32.8
AIR	7	100.0	2.0	28.1	6.2	3.7	10.1	1.1	3.4	.1	45.3
WATER	2	100.0	1.1	-	-	-	-	-	-	-	98.9
OTHER	14	100.0	8.1	9.0	9.6	6.2	22.0	11.4	17.9	8.0	7.8
UNKNOWN	1	100.0	.1	48.0	2.0	6.3	3.4	5.2	-	-	35.1
MIDDLE ATLANTIC	89	100.0	1.3	3.9	20.4	7.4	7.4	5.5	11.9	4.8	37.3
RAIL	16	100.0	-	-	2.3	1.5	.2	.2	.7	.9	94.1
MOTOR CARRIER	68	100.0	1.5	4.8	25.2	9.2	9.2	6.8	15.0	6.0	22.3
PRIVATE TRUCK	-	100.0	25.4	51.7	7.3	-	15.7	-	-	-	-
AIR	-	100.0	-	4.2	69.2	.8	2.1	2.0	21.7	-	-
WATER	2	100.0	1.3	-	-	-	-	-	-	-	98.7
OTHER	1	100.0	1.4	5.4	23.9	6.0	17.3	12.6	11.9	2.6	19.0
UNKNOWN	-	100.0	-	-	-	-	100.0	-	-	-	-
EAST NORTH CENTRAL	178	100.0	3.1	10.7	18.7	17.4	16.7	2.5	3.5	1.4	25.9
RAIL	123	100.0	3.4	9.8	12.5	21.6	15.1	3.1	3.7	-	30.7
MOTOR CARRIER	44	100.0	3.1	14.9	33.0	8.6	22.7	.5	3.8	1.8	11.5
PRIVATE TRUCK	6	100.0	-	-	50.2	3.7	15.4	4.7	-	25.9	-
AIR	3	100.0	-	4.1	.6	3.9	2.2	.7	.5	-	88.0
WATER	-	100.0	-	-	-	-	-	-	-	-	-
OTHER	-	100.0	11.9	38.1	9.3	11.1	9.6	10.2	4.7	4.8	.4
UNKNOWN	-	100.0	-	-	-	100.0	-	-	-	-	-
SOUTH ATLANTIC	343	100.0	8.2	15.1	10.6	5.8	16.0	5.0	4.4	1.3	33.5
RAIL	83	100.0	-	19.1	-	-	17.6	-	-	-	63.3
MOTOR CARRIER	216	100.0	12.8	21.9	9.0	9.0	13.5	7.2	5.8	1.7	19.2
PRIVATE TRUCK	37	100.0	1.4	9.7	1.1	.2	26.8	1.6	4.4	.2	54.4
AIR	-	100.0	1.6	5.5	8.0	8.9	5.8	.4	35.8	1.1	32.9
WATER	-	100.0	-	-	-	-	-	-	-	-	-
OTHER	5	100.0	2.3	2.9	6.4	6.6	23.1	19.2	17.6	15.8	6.2
UNKNOWN	-	100.0	.2	84.6	3.4	-	2.7	9.1	-	-	-

See footnotes at end of table 4.

TABLE 3. TCC GROUP 239—Percent Distribution of Geographic Division of Destination and Means of Transport, by Geographic Division of Origin: 1972

Geographic division of destination and means of transport	Number	Percent distribution by division of origin[1]									
		U.S. total	New England	Middle Atlantic	East North Central	West North Central	South Atlantic	East South Central	West South Central	Mountain	Pacific
TONS OF SHIPMENTS	(thousands of tons)										
U.S. TOTAL..............	1 713	100.0	(D)	6.6	27.2	(D)	39.3	(D)	(D)	(D)	(D)
RAIL.................	465	100.0	(D)	1.6	57.2	(D)	22.9	(D)	(D)	(D)	(D)
MOTOR CARRIER........	1 035	100.0	(D)	9.5	17.5	(D)	44.1	(D)	(D)	(D)	(D)
PRIVATE TRUCK........	175	100.0	(D)	1.2	7.8	(D)	54.9	(D)	(D)	(D)	(D)
AIR.................	5	100.0	(D)	7.1	44.8	(D)	7.3	(D)	(D)	(D)	(D)
WATER...............	-	100.0	(D)	71.2	-	(D)	-	(D)	(D)	(D)	(D)
OTHER...............	28	100.0	(D)	12.0	5.2	(D)	42.3	(D)	(D)	(D)	(D)
UNKNOWN.............	1	100.0	(D)	.1	17.8	(D)	66.9	(D)	(D)	(D)	(D)
NEW ENGLAND.............	77	100.0	(D)	8.7	9.2	(D)	57.3	(D)	(D)	(D)	(D)
RAIL.................	5	100.0	(D)	-	90.0	(D)	-	(D)	(D)	(D)	(D)
MOTOR CARRIER........	66	100.0	(D)	9.5	2.8	(D)	65.7	(D)	(D)	(D)	(D)
PRIVATE TRUCK........	3	100.0	(D)	5.9	-	(D)	19.2	(D)	(D)	(D)	(D)
AIR.................	-	100.0	(D)	-	-	(D)	10.6	(D)	(D)	(D)	(D)
WATER...............	-	100.0	(D)	100.0	-	(D)	-	(D)	(D)	(D)	(D)
OTHER...............	1	100.0	(D)	9.9	6.0	(D)	11.5	(D)	(D)	(D)	(D)
UNKNOWN.............	-	100.0	(D)	-	-	(D)	100.0	(D)	(D)	(D)	(D)
MIDDLE ATLANTIC.........	234	100.0	(D)	10.9	15.4	(D)	56.9	(D)	(D)	(D)	(D)
RAIL.................	25	100.0	(D)	-	89.0	(D)	-	(D)	(D)	(D)	(D)
MOTOR CARRIER........	190	100.0	(D)	12.1	6.7	(D)	65.0	(D)	(D)	(D)	(D)
PRIVATE TRUCK........	13	100.0	(D)	12.8	-	(D)	62.0	(D)	(D)	(D)	(D)
AIR.................	1	100.0	(D)	2.9	18.9	(D)	2.1	(D)	(D)	(D)	(D)
WATER...............	-	100.0	(D)	-	-	(D)	-	(D)	(D)	(D)	(D)
OTHER...............	2	100.0	(D)	28.5	14.2	(D)	13.2	(D)	(D)	(D)	(D)
UNKNOWN.............	-	100.0	(D)	-	-	(D)	100.0	(D)	(D)	(D)	(D)
EAST NORTH CENTRAL......	446	100.0	(D)	7.1	58.2	(D)	14.4	(D)	(D)	(D)	(D)
RAIL.................	178	100.0	(D)	.3	67.0	(D)	15.5	(D)	(D)	(D)	(D)
MOTOR CARRIER........	239	100.0	(D)	12.6	54.3	(D)	14.6	(D)	(D)	(D)	(D)
PRIVATE TRUCK........	24	100.0	(D)	.1	39.2	(D)	3.1	(D)	(D)	(D)	(D)
AIR.................	-	100.0	(D)	45.8	15.1	(D)	5.9	(D)	(D)	(D)	(D)
WATER...............	-	100.0	(D)	-	-	(D)	-	(D)	(D)	(D)	(D)
OTHER...............	3	100.0	(D)	26.7	11.8	(D)	18.8	(D)	(D)	(D)	(D)
UNKNOWN.............	-	100.0	(D)	-	-	(D)	100.0	(D)	(D)	(D)	(D)
WEST NORTH CENTRAL......	143	100.0	(D)	4.5	43.2	(D)	16.1	(D)	(D)	(D)	(D)
RAIL.................	52	100.0	(D)	.5	96.8	(D)	-	(D)	(D)	(D)	(D)
MOTOR CARRIER........	69	100.0	(D)	8.8	13.5	(D)	32.8	(D)	(D)	(D)	(D)
PRIVATE TRUCK........	19	100.0	(D)	-	4.8	(D)	.7	(D)	(D)	(D)	(D)
AIR.................	-	100.0	(D)	.4	65.1	(D)	13.8	(D)	(D)	(D)	(D)
WATER...............	-	100.0	(D)	-	-	(D)	-	(D)	(D)	(D)	(D)
OTHER...............	1	100.0	(D)	8.5	19.6	(D)	21.1	(D)	(D)	(D)	(D)
UNKNOWN.............	-	100.0	(D)	-	100.0	(D)	-	(D)	(D)	(D)	(D)
SOUTH ATLANTIC..........	421	100.0	(D)	2.8	12.6	(D)	70.1	(D)	(D)	(D)	(D)
RAIL.................	88	100.0	(D)	-	35.3	(D)	63.4	(D)	(D)	(D)	(D)
MOTOR CARRIER........	241	100.0	(D)	4.5	8.4	(D)	67.1	(D)	(D)	(D)	(D)
PRIVATE TRUCK........	80	100.0	(D)	.1	1.5	(D)	88.5	(D)	(D)	(D)	(D)
AIR.................	-	100.0	(D)	3.0	16.2	(D)	6.2	(D)	(D)	(D)	(D)
WATER...............	-	100.0	(D)	-	-	(D)	-	(D)	(D)	(D)	(D)
OTHER...............	9	100.0	(D)	8.8	1.0	(D)	60.3	(D)	(D)	(D)	(D)
UNKNOWN.............	-	100.0	(D)	1.1	-	(D)	16.9	(D)	(D)	(D)	(D)
EAST SOUTH CENTRAL......	81	100.0	(D)	7.6	16.1	(D)	49.7	(D)	(D)	(D)	(D)
RAIL.................	12	100.0	(D)	.4	94.4	(D)	-	(D)	(D)	(D)	(D)
MOTOR CARRIER........	55	100.0	(D)	10.7	1.0	(D)	61.0	(D)	(D)	(D)	(D)
PRIVATE TRUCK........	8	100.0	(D)	-	6.6	(D)	41.8	(D)	(D)	(D)	(D)
AIR.................	-	100.0	(D)	8.6	63.2	(D)	2.0	(D)	(D)	(D)	(D)
WATER...............	-	100.0	(D)	-	-	(D)	-	(D)	(D)	(D)	(D)
OTHER...............	4	100.0	(D)	6.1	3.7	(D)	62.3	(D)	(D)	(D)	(D)
UNKNOWN.............	-	100.0	(D)	-	-	(D)	100.0	(D)	(D)	(D)	(D)
WEST SOUTH CENTRAL......	131	100.0	(D)	6.0	5.6	(D)	13.4	(D)	(D)	(D)	(D)
RAIL.................	31	100.0	(D)	.3	16.4	(D)	-	(D)	(D)	(D)	(D)
MOTOR CARRIER........	89	100.0	(D)	8.5	2.3	(D)	16.0	(D)	(D)	(D)	(D)
PRIVATE TRUCK........	6	100.0	(D)	-	-	(D)	32.3	(D)	(D)	(D)	(D)
AIR.................	-	100.0	(D)	17.1	8.2	(D)	65.6	(D)	(D)	(D)	(D)
WATER...............	-	100.0	(D)	-	-	(D)	-	(D)	(D)	(D)	(D)
OTHER...............	3	100.0	(D)	5.6	1.4	(D)	31.6	(D)	(D)	(D)	(D)
UNKNOWN.............	-	100.0	(D)	-	-	(D)	-	(D)	(D)	(D)	(D)
MOUNTAIN................	22	100.0	(D)	9.8	10.3	(D)	12.9	(D)	(D)	(D)	(D)
RAIL.................	-	100.0	(D)	100.0	-	(D)	-	(D)	(D)	(D)	(D)
MOTOR CARRIER........	18	100.0	(D)	11.6	4.2	(D)	13.4	(D)	(D)	(D)	(D)
PRIVATE TRUCK........	3	100.0	(D)	-	43.1	(D)	1.5	(D)	(D)	(D)	(D)
AIR.................	-	100.0	(D)	-	-	(D)	36.0	(D)	(D)	(D)	(D)
WATER...............	-	100.0	(D)	-	-	(D)	-	(D)	(D)	(D)	(D)
OTHER...............	-	100.0	(D)	4.0	3.7	(D)	59.2	(D)	(D)	(D)	(D)
UNKNOWN.............	-	100.0	(D)	-	-	(D)	-	(D)	(D)	(D)	(D)
PACIFIC.................	152	100.0	(D)	8.7	15.8	(D)	33.4	(D)	(D)	(D)	(D)
RAIL.................	69	100.0	(D)	9.0	27.9	(D)	32.5	(D)	(D)	(D)	(D)
MOTOR CARRIER........	64	100.0	(D)	9.9	4.6	(D)	28.8	(D)	(D)	(D)	(D)
PRIVATE TRUCK........	14	100.0	(D)	-	-	(D)	64.6	(D)	(D)	(D)	(D)
AIR.................	1	100.0	(D)	-	91.9	(D)	3.8	(D)	(D)	(D)	(D)
WATER...............	-	100.0	(D)	67.2	-	(D)	-	(D)	(D)	(D)	(D)
OTHER...............	-	100.0	(D)	17.5	.2	(D)	15.5	(D)	(D)	(D)	(D)
UNKNOWN.............	-	100.0	(D)	-	-	(D)	-	(D)	(D)	(D)	(D)

See footnotes at end of table 4.

TABLE 3. **TCC GROUP 239—Percent Distribution of Geographic Division of Destination and Means of Transport, by Geographic Division of Origin: 1972**—Continued

Geographic division of destination and means of transport	Number	Percent distribution by division of origin [1]									
		U.S. total	New England	Middle Atlantic	East North Central	West North Central	South Atlantic	East South Central	West South Central	Mountain	Pacific
TON-MILES OF SHIPMENTS	(millions of ton-miles)										
U.S. TOTAL..............	943	100.0	(D)	9.5	19.0	(D)	36.4	(D)	(D)	(D)	(D)
RAIL..............	327	100.0	(D)	5.1	37.7	(D)	25.4	(D)	(D)	(D)	(D)
MOTOR CARRIER.........	518	100.0	(D)	13.3	8.7	(D)	41.8	(D)	(D)	(D)	(D)
PRIVATE TRUCK.........	72	100.0	(D)	.2	8.7	(D)	52.6	(D)	(D)	(D)	(D)
AIR................	7	100.0	(D)	2.9	46.2	(D)	6.5	(D)	(D)	(D)	(D)
WATER..............	2	100.0	(D)	79.0	-	(D)	-	(D)	(D)	(D)	(D)
OTHER..............	14	100.0	(D)	14.0	4.7	(D)	35.8	(D)	(D)	(D)	(D)
UNKNOWN.............	1	100.0	(D)	-	6.3	(D)	56.8	(D)	(D)	(D)	(D)
NEW ENGLAND.............	48	100.0	(D)	2.4	11.6	(D)	58.7	(D)	(D)	(D)	(D)
RAIL..............	4	100.0	(D)	-	85.5	(D)	-	(D)	(D)	(D)	(D)
MOTOR CARRIER.........	41	100.0	(D)	2.6	3.4	(D)	67.4	(D)	(D)	(D)	(D)
PRIVATE TRUCK.........	1	100.0	(D)	3.5	-	(D)	51.8	(D)	(D)	(D)	(D)
AIR................	-	100.0	(D)	-	-	(D)	5.4	(D)	(D)	(D)	(D)
WATER..............	-	100.0	(D)	100.0	-	(D)	-	(D)	(D)	(D)	(D)
OTHER..............	1	100.0	(D)	2.3	6.9	(D)	10.0	(D)	(D)	(D)	(D)
UNKNOWN.............	-	100.0	(D)	-	-	(D)	100.0	(D)	(D)	(D)	(D)
MIDDLE ATLANTIC.........	100	100.0	(D)	3.5	19.1	(D)	51.6	(D)	(D)	(D)	(D)
RAIL..............	13	100.0	(D)	-	91.4	(D)	-	(D)	(D)	(D)	(D)
MOTOR CARRIER.........	77	100.0	(D)	4.2	8.6	(D)	61.0	(D)	(D)	(D)	(D)
PRIVATE TRUCK.........	5	100.0	(D)	1.3	-	(D)	66.6	(D)	(D)	(D)	(D)
AIR................	2	100.0	(D)	.4	6.7	(D)	1.3	(D)	(D)	(D)	(D)
WATER..............	-	100.0	(D)	-	-	(D)	-	(D)	(D)	(D)	(D)
OTHER..............	1	100.0	(D)	8.4	20.1	(D)	11.4	(D)	(D)	(D)	(D)
UNKNOWN.............	-	100.0	(D)	-	-	(D)	100.0	(D)	(D)	(D)	(D)
EAST NORTH CENTRAL......	149	100.0	(D)	12.3	22.5	(D)	24.3	(D)	(D)	(D)	(D)
RAIL..............	53	100.0	(D)	.7	29.0	(D)	29.8	(D)	(D)	(D)	(D)
MOTOR CARRIER.........	80	100.0	(D)	21.4	18.3	(D)	24.3	(D)	(D)	(D)	(D)
PRIVATE TRUCK.........	13	100.0	(D)	.1	24.0	(D)	3.2	(D)	(D)	(D)	(D)
AIR................	-	100.0	(D)	32.5	4.6	(D)	8.3	(D)	(D)	(D)	(D)
WATER..............	-	100.0	(D)	-	-	(D)	-	(D)	(D)	(D)	(D)
OTHER..............	1	100.0	(D)	35.0	4.6	(D)	23.9	(D)	(D)	(D)	(D)
UNKNOWN.............	-	100.0	(D)	-	-	(D)	100.0	(D)	(D)	(D)	(D)
WEST NORTH CENTRAL......	83	100.0	(D)	8.0	37.2	(D)	24.0	(D)	(D)	(D)	(D)
RAIL..............	27	100.0	(D)	.9	95.8	(D)	-	(D)	(D)	(D)	(D)
MOTOR CARRIER.........	51	100.0	(D)	12.4	7.6	(D)	38.3	(D)	(D)	(D)	(D)
PRIVATE TRUCK.........	3	100.0	(D)	-	7.1	(D)	2.6	(D)	(D)	(D)	(D)
AIR................	-	100.0	(D)	.6	49.1	(D)	15.7	(D)	(D)	(D)	(D)
WATER..............	-	100.0	(D)	-	-	(D)	-	(D)	(D)	(D)	(D)
OTHER..............	-	100.0	(D)	13.6	8.5	(D)	38.4	(D)	(D)	(D)	(D)
UNKNOWN.............	-	100.0	(D)	-	100.0	(D)	-	(D)	(D)	(D)	(D)
SOUTH ATLANTIC.........	126	100.0	(D)	5.3	23.6	(D)	43.6	(D)	(D)	(D)	(D)
RAIL..............	34	100.0	(D)	.1	54.4	(D)	42.8	(D)	(D)	(D)	(D)
MOTOR CARRIER.........	71	100.0	(D)	8.8	14.2	(D)	40.6	(D)	(D)	(D)	(D)
PRIVATE TRUCK.........	16	100.0	(D)	.1	5.8	(D)	60.8	(D)	(D)	(D)	(D)
AIR................	-	100.0	(D)	.6	9.9	(D)	3.7	(D)	(D)	(D)	(D)
WATER..............	-	100.0	(D)	-	-	(D)	-	(D)	(D)	(D)	(D)
OTHER..............	3	100.0	(D)	11.0	2.1	(D)	37.6	(D)	(D)	(D)	(D)
UNKNOWN.............	-	100.0	(D)	1.2	-	(D)	45.5	(D)	(D)	(D)	(D)
EAST SOUTH CENTRAL......	33	100.0	(D)	15.0	13.3	(D)	51.7	(D)	(D)	(D)	(D)
RAIL..............	4	100.0	(D)	.8	86.9	(D)	-	(D)	(D)	(D)	(D)
MOTOR CARRIER.........	25	100.0	(D)	18.2	.8	(D)	60.1	(D)	(D)	(D)	(D)
PRIVATE TRUCK.........	1	100.0	(D)	-	23.7	(D)	49.6	(D)	(D)	(D)	(D)
AIR................	-	100.0	(D)	5.3	29.1	(D)	2.5	(D)	(D)	(D)	(D)
WATER..............	-	100.0	(D)	-	-	(D)	-	(D)	(D)	(D)	(D)
OTHER..............	1	100.0	(D)	15.4	4.3	(D)	60.2	(D)	(D)	(D)	(D)
UNKNOWN.............	-	100.0	(D)	-	-	(D)	100.0	(D)	(D)	(D)	(D)
WEST SOUTH CENTRAL......	101	100.0	(D)	10.5	6.2	(D)	15.0	(D)	(D)	(D)	(D)
RAIL..............	42	100.0	(D)	.3	10.8	(D)	-	(D)	(D)	(D)	(D)
MOTOR CARRIER.........	52	100.0	(D)	19.8	3.3	(D)	23.9	(D)	(D)	(D)	(D)
PRIVATE TRUCK.........	4	100.0	(D)	-	-	(D)	38.1	(D)	(D)	(D)	(D)
AIR................	-	100.0	(D)	18.3	6.7	(D)	67.4	(D)	(D)	(D)	(D)
WATER..............	-	100.0	(D)	-	-	(D)	-	(D)	(D)	(D)	(D)
OTHER..............	2	100.0	(D)	9.3	1.2	(D)	35.1	(D)	(D)	(D)	(D)
UNKNOWN.............	-	100.0	(D)	-	-	(D)	-	(D)	(D)	(D)	(D)
MOUNTAIN...............	24	100.0	(D)	18.0	10.3	(D)	18.9	(D)	(D)	(D)	(D)
RAIL..............	-	100.0	(D)	100.0	-	(D)	-	(D)	(D)	(D)	(D)
MOTOR CARRIER.........	19	100.0	(D)	20.8	4.1	(D)	18.5	(D)	(D)	(D)	(D)
PRIVATE TRUCK.........	2	100.0	(D)	-	55.1	(D)	3.2	(D)	(D)	(D)	(D)
AIR................	-	100.0	(D)	-	-	(D)	68.3	(D)	(D)	(D)	(D)
WATER..............	-	100.0	(D)	-	-	(D)	-	(D)	(D)	(D)	(D)
OTHER..............	1	100.0	(D)	4.5	2.9	(D)	70.8	(D)	(D)	(D)	(D)
UNKNOWN.............	-	100.0	(D)	-	-	(D)	-	(D)	(D)	(D)	(D)
PACIFIC................	276	100.0	(D)	12.1	16.7	(D)	41.7	(D)	(D)	(D)	(D)
RAIL..............	147	100.0	(D)	10.7	25.8	(D)	35.9	(D)	(D)	(D)	(D)
MOTOR CARRIER.........	98	100.0	(D)	15.6	5.2	(D)	42.2	(D)	(D)	(D)	(D)
PRIVATE TRUCK.........	23	100.0	(D)	-	-	(D)	87.3	(D)	(D)	(D)	(D)
AIR................	3	100.0	(D)	-	89.8	(D)	4.7	(D)	(D)	(D)	(D)
WATER..............	2	100.0	(D)	78.7	-	(D)	-	(D)	(D)	(D)	(D)
OTHER..............	1	100.0	(D)	33.9	.2	(D)	28.3	(D)	(D)	(D)	(D)
UNKNOWN.............	-	100.0	(D)	-	-	(D)	-	(D)	(D)	(D)	(D)

See footnotes at end of table 4.

TABLE 4. TCC GROUP 239—Percent Distribution of Distance Shipped and Weight of Shipment, by Means of Transport: 1972

Distance shipped and weight of shipment [2] [3]	Number	Percent distribution by means of transport							
		All means of transport	Rail	Motor carrier	Private truck	Air	Water	Other	Unknown
TONS OF SHIPMENTS	(thousands of tons)								
U.S. TOTAL...........	1 630	100.0	26.2	62.0	9.7	.4	-	1.6	.1
UNDER 100 MILES.........	251	100.0	25.6	56.4	17.1	-	-	.9	-
UNDER 1000 POUNDS.....	68	100.0	-	88.8	7.8	-	-	3.4	-
1000 TO 9999 POUNDS...	44	100.0	4.1	61.7	34.1	-	-	-	-
10000 TO 29999 POUNDS.	52	100.0	-	71.8	28.2	-	-	-	-
30000 TO 59999 POUNDS.	27	100.0	26.3	45.3	28.4	-	-	-	-
60000 TO 89999 POUNDS.	54	100.0	93.2	6.8	-	-	-	-	-
90000 POUNDS AND OVER.	4	100.0	100.0	-	-	-	-	-	-
100 TO 199 MILES........	180	100.0	5.6	72.7	19.2	-	-	2.4	.1
UNDER 1000 POUNDS.....	53	100.0	-	81.0	10.8	.1	-	8.1	-
1000 TO 9999 POUNDS...	53	100.0	.4	80.3	19.3	-	-	-	-
10000 TO 29999 POUNDS.	64	100.0	7.5	65.7	26.5	-	-	-	.3
30000 TO 59999 POUNDS.	8	100.0	57.6	26.8	15.7	-	-	-	-
60000 TO 89999 POUNDS.	-	100.0	-	-	-	-	-	-	-
90000 POUNDS AND OVER.	-	100.0	-	-	-	-	-	-	-
200 TO 299 MILES........	190	100.0	46.9	47.9	3.5	.1	-	1.5	.1
UNDER 1000 POUNDS.....	50	100.0	-	91.6	1.8	.2	-	5.7	.5
1000 TO 9999 POUNDS...	43	100.0	2.3	86.1	11.4	.1	-	-	-
10000 TO 29999 POUNDS.	11	100.0	39.5	57.7	2.8	-	-	-	-
30000 TO 59999 POUNDS.	46	100.0	97.6	1.5	.9	-	-	-	-
60000 TO 89999 POUNDS.	31	100.0	100.0	-	-	-	-	-	-
90000 POUNDS AND OVER.	7	100.0	100.0	-	-	-	-	-	-
300 TO 499 MILES........	327	100.0	14.7	72.5	10.5	.2	-	2.0	-
UNDER 1000 POUNDS.....	77	100.0	-	88.5	2.3	.6	.1	8.4	-
1000 TO 9999 POUNDS...	79	100.0	1.4	81.6	16.6	.4	-	-	-
10000 TO 29999 POUNDS.	106	100.0	4.1	85.4	10.5	-	-	-	-
30000 TO 59999 POUNDS.	25	100.0	15.2	52.5	32.4	-	-	-	-
60000 TO 89999 POUNDS.	38	100.0	100.0	-	-	-	-	-	-
90000 POUNDS AND OVER.	-	100.0	-	-	-	-	-	-	-
500 TO 999 MILES........	474	100.0	26.1	66.6	4.9	.4	-	1.9	.2
UNDER 1000 POUNDS.....	147	100.0	.6	89.1	3.5	.7	-	6.0	.1
1000 TO 9999 POUNDS...	119	100.0	7.3	86.4	5.3	.3	-	-	.7
10000 TO 29999 POUNDS.	92	100.0	50.1	40.4	9.2	.3	-	-	-
30000 TO 59999 POUNDS.	74	100.0	38.0	57.8	4.2	-	-	-	-
60000 TO 89999 POUNDS.	39	100.0	100.0	-	-	-	-	-	-
90000 POUNDS AND OVER.	1	100.0	-	100.0	-	-	-	-	-
1000 TO 1499 MILES......	79	100.0	33.6	59.8	5.2	.3	-	1.1	-
UNDER 1000 POUNDS.....	29	100.0	.8	92.7	2.6	.9	-	2.9	-
1000 TO 9999 POUNDS...	17	100.0	2.5	87.0	10.5	-	-	-	-
10000 TO 29999 POUNDS.	31	100.0	83.2	16.8	-	-	-	-	-
30000 TO 59999 POUNDS.	1	100.0	-	-	100.0	-	-	-	-
60000 TO 89999 POUNDS.	-	100.0	-	-	-	-	-	-	-
90000 POUNDS AND OVER.	-	100.0	-	-	-	-	-	-	-
1500 MILES OR OVER......	126	100.0	50.8	36.3	9.3	2.2	.5	.8	.1
UNDER 1000 POUNDS.....	30	100.0	17.1	71.0	4.4	2.4	1.3	3.4	.4
1000 TO 9999 POUNDS...	47	100.0	43.0	50.6	2.4	3.6	.4	-	-
10000 TO 29999 POUNDS.	13	100.0	27.5	-	69.6	2.9	-	-	-
30000 TO 59999 POUNDS.	4	100.0	92.5	7.5	-	-	-	-	-
60000 TO 89999 POUNDS.	31	100.0	100.0	-	-	-	-	-	-
90000 POUNDS AND OVER.	-	100.0	-	-	-	-	-	-	-
TON-MILES OF SHIPMENTS	(millions of ton-miles)								
U.S. TOTAL...........	891	100.0	32.8	56.5	7.9	.9	.3	1.5	.1
UNDER 100 MILES.........	10	100.0	18.5	59.2	20.9	-	-	1.4	-
UNDER 1000 POUNDS.....	3	100.0	-	89.0	6.9	-	-	4.1	-
1000 TO 9999 POUNDS...	2	100.0	3.3	54.1	42.5	-	-	.1	-
10000 TO 29999 POUNDS.	2	100.0	-	63.0	37.0	-	-	-	-
30000 TO 59999 POUNDS.	1	100.0	26.7	47.3	26.0	-	-	-	-
60000 TO 89999 POUNDS.	1	100.0	95.7	4.3	-	-	-	-	-
90000 POUNDS AND OVER.	-	100.0	100.0	-	-	-	-	-	-
100 TO 199 MILES........	25	100.0	6.1	71.8	19.2	-	-	2.7	.1
UNDER 1000 POUNDS.....	8	100.0	-	83.2	8.6	.1	-	8.2	-
1000 TO 9999 POUNDS...	7	100.0	.4	83.0	16.5	-	-	-	-
10000 TO 29999 POUNDS.	8	100.0	9.2	57.8	32.8	-	-	-	.3
30000 TO 59999 POUNDS.	1	100.0	57.1	28.7	14.2	-	-	-	-
60000 TO 89999 POUNDS.	-	100.0	-	-	-	-	-	-	-
90000 POUNDS AND OVER.	-	100.0	-	-	-	-	-	-	-

See footnotes at end of table 4.

TABLE 4. **TCC GROUP 239—Percent Distribution of Distance Shipped and Weight of Shipment, by Means of Transport: 1972**—Continued

Distance shipped and weight of shipment [2] [3]	Number	Percent distribution by means of transport							
		All means of transport	Rail	Motor carrier	Private truck	Air	Water	Other	Unknown
TON-MILES OF SHIPMENTS	(millions of ton-miles)								
200 TO 299 MILES.........	46	100.0	47.9	46.7	3.5	.1	–	1.7	.2
UNDER 1000 POUNDS.....	11	100.0	–	90.6	2.0	.2	–	6.5	.6
1000 TO 9999 POUNDS...	10	100.0	2.3	86.0	11.5	.2	–	–	–
10000 TO 29999 POUNDS.	2	100.0	40.3	57.0	2.7	–	–	–	–
30000 TO 59999 POUNDS.	11	100.0	97.9	1.4	.7	–	–	–	–
60000 TO 89999 POUNDS.	7	100.0	100.0	–	–	–	–	–	–
90000 POUNDS AND OVER.	1	100.0	100.0	–	–	–	–	–	–
300 TO 499 MILES.........	125	100.0	15.8	70.8	11.2	.3	–	1.9	–
UNDER 1000 POUNDS.....	29	100.0	–	88.9	2.4	.7	.1	7.9	–
1000 TO 9999 POUNDS...	30	100.0	1.7	80.3	17.5	.5	–	–	–
10000 TO 29999 POUNDS.	39	100.0	4.4	82.7	12.9	–	–	–	–
30000 TO 59999 POUNDS.	10	100.0	14.6	56.3	29.1	–	–	–	–
60000 TO 89999 POUNDS.	16	100.0	100.0	–	–	–	–	–	–
90000 POUNDS AND OVER.	–	100.0	–	–	–	–	–	–	–
500 TO 999 MILES.........	314	100.0	24.1	67.7	5.6	.4	–	2.1	.2
UNDER 1000 POUNDS.....	105	100.0	.6	88.8	3.6	.8	–	6.1	.1
1000 TO 9999 POUNDS...	81	100.0	7.0	86.2	5.9	.3	–	–	.7
10000 TO 29999 POUNDS.	57	100.0	49.6	38.1	12.0	.3	–	–	–
30000 TO 59999 POUNDS.	45	100.0	38.9	56.7	4.4	–	–	–	–
60000 TO 89999 POUNDS.	23	100.0	100.0	–	–	–	–	–	–
90000 POUNDS AND OVER.	–	100.0	–	100.0	–	–	–	–	–
1000 TO 1499 MILES......	103	100.0	36.9	57.0	4.8	.3	–	1.0	–
UNDER 1000 POUNDS.....	35	100.0	.9	92.7	2.6	.9	–	2.9	–
1000 TO 9999 POUNDS...	22	100.0	2.0	87.2	10.7	–	–	–	–
10000 TO 29999 POUNDS.	44	100.0	84.8	15.2	–	–	–	–	–
30000 TO 59999 POUNDS.	1	100.0	–	–	100.0	–	–	–	–
60000 TO 89999 POUNDS.	–	100.0	–	–	–	–	–	–	–
90000 POUNDS AND OVER.	–	100.0	–	–	–	–	–	–	–
1500 MILES OR OVER......	265	100.0	50.2	36.3	9.4	2.2	.9	.8	.2
UNDER 1000 POUNDS.....	65	100.0	18.6	68.5	3.7	2.3	3.0	3.1	.7
1000 TO 9999 POUNDS...	103	100.0	44.7	48.8	2.3	3.6	.5	–	–
10000 TO 29999 POUNDS.	27	100.0	24.7	–	72.8	2.5	–	–	–
30000 TO 59999 POUNDS.	8	100.0	92.6	7.4	–	–	–	–	–
60000 TO 89999 POUNDS.	59	100.0	100.0	–	–	–	–	–	–
90000 POUNDS AND OVER.	–	100.0	–	–	–	–	–	–	–

Note: Detail may not add to total due to rounding. The introductory table shows the estimates of sampling variability for tons; sampling variability for ton-miles has not been estimated. See the map in the Introduction for the States comprising the geographic divisions of the United States.

Shipments excluded from the survey are those moving by pipeline (primarily petroleum products from refineries), parcel post shipments, and commodities moved by own power (motorized vehicles, aircraft, etc.) or towed (prefabricated buildings, etc.). Local shipments (commodities shipped less than 25 miles from the plant) and shipments within the same city are also excluded. Shipments to Alaska and Hawaii from the 48 conterminous States and the District of Columbia are included; however, no data were obtained for shipments originating in Alaska and Hawaii.

– Represents zero or rounds to zero.   (D) Withheld to avoid disclosing figures for individual companies.

[1] Production of this commodity is concentrated in the geographic divisions shown; figures and distributions for geographic divisions not shown are included in the total.

[2] Distances of shipments to foreign destinations are calculated only to the U.S. port of exit.

[3] Includes only shipments represented by bills of lading and invoices. Summary records which did not show individual weights of shipments are not included.

Lumber and Wood Products, Except Furniture; Furniture and Fixtures; Pulp, Paper, and Allied Products

CONTENTS

[Page numbers listed here omit the State prefix number that appears as part of the number for each page]

TABLES (The tables listed below are shown for each of the Transportation Commodity Classification groups in this report)

Comparisons of Tons and Ton-Miles of Shipments for Geographic Divisions of Origin and for Sampling Variability: 1972 and 1967

1. Percent Distribution of Geographic Division of Origin and Distance Shipped, by Means of Transport: 1972

2. Percent Distribution of Geographic Division of Origin and Means of Transport, by Geographic Division of Destination: 1972

3. Percent Distribution of Geographic Division of Destination and Means of Transport, by Geographic Division of Origin: 1972

4. Percent Distribution of Distance Shipped and Weight of Shipment, by Means of Transport: 1972

TCC 242. Sawmill and Planing Mill Products

Comparisons of Tons and Ton-Miles of Shipments for
Geographic Divisions of Origin and for Sampling Variability: 1972 and 1967

Geographic division of origin	Estimates				Relative sampling variability in tons (percent)	
	1972		1967		1972	1967
	Tons (thousands)	Ton-miles (millions)	Tons (thousands)	Ton-miles (millions)		
U.S. total	38,732	24,858	35,118	25,284	6.8	14.2
New England	(D)	(D)	230	34	(*)	(*)
Middle Atlantic	(D)	(D)	1,108	234	(*)	(*)
East North Central	1,270	252	1,067	221	27.4	(*)
West North Central	(D)	(D)	1,153	589	(*)	(*)
South Atlantic	5,311	1,057	3,106	433	28.7	(*)
East South Central	4,182	1,018	2,989	858	23.3	(*)
West South Central	4,229	1,275	2,592	773	29.2	(*)
Mountain	2,830	2,598	3,960	4,096	32.3	(*)
Pacific	18,824	17,229	18,913	18,046	11.7	(*)

(D) Withheld to avoid disclosing figures for individual companies.   (*) Data not published.

TABLE 1. **TCC GROUP 242—Percent Distribution of Geographic Division of Origin and Distance Shipped, by Means of Transport: 1972**

Geographic division of origin[1] and distance shipped[2]	Number	Percent distribution by means of transport							
		All means of transport	Rail	Motor carrier	Private truck	Air	Water	Other	Unknown
TONS OF SHIPMENTS	(thousands of tons)								
U.S. TOTAL..........	38 732	100.0	45.4	18.7	33.3	-	2.4	-	.2
EAST NORTH CENTRAL......	1 270	100.0	23.5	12.8	62.5	-	-	-	1.2
UNDER 100 MILES.......	476	100.0	10.9	9.9	75.9	-	-	.1	1.2
100 TO 199 MILES......	354	100.0	8.6	13.8	77.3	-	-	.1	3.1
200 TO 299 MILES......	246	100.0	42.0	7.4	50.7	-	-	.2	-
300 TO 499 MILES......	86	100.0	40.9	22.9	36.1	-	-	-	-
500 TO 999 MILES......	96	100.0	78.4	19.5	1.9	-	.2	-	.1
1000 TO 1499 MILES....	-	100.0	-	100.0	-	-	-	-	-
1500 MILES OR OVER....	10	100.0	12.5	87.5	-	-	-	-	-
SOUTH ATLANTIC..........	5 311	100.0	35.9	17.5	46.7	-	-	-	-
UNDER 100 MILES.......	1 621	100.0	30.8	16.1	53.1	-	-	-	-
100 TO 199 MILES......	1 609	100.0	26.4	17.7	55.9	-	-	-	-
200 TO 299 MILES......	1 133	100.0	42.9	13.6	43.5	-	-	-	-
300 TO 499 MILES......	776	100.0	52.1	21.0	26.9	-	-	-	-
500 TO 999 MILES......	138	100.0	42.2	45.8	12.0	-	-	-	-
1000 TO 1499 MILES....	1	100.0	-	100.0	-	-	-	-	-
1500 MILES OR OVER....	30	100.0	99.3	.7	-	-	-	-	-
EAST SOUTH CENTRAL......	4 182	100.0	25.0	14.2	60.5	-	.	-	.2
UNDER 100 MILES.......	1 558	100.0	11.5	13.8	74.7	-	-	-	.2
100 TO 199 MILES......	997	100.0	13.8	12.0	73.7	-	-	-	-
200 TO 299 MILES......	304	100.0	14.4	30.9	53.3	-	-	.1	.4
300 TO 499 MILES......	657	100.0	41.6	18.1	40.3	-	-	-	1.4
500 TO 999 MILES......	643	100.0	61.7	6.7	31.6	-	-	-	-
1000 TO 1499 MILES....	8	100.0	71.6	3.7	24.7	-	-	-	-
1500 MILES OR OVER....	12	100.0	77.5	21.3	1.2	-	-	-	-
WEST SOUTH CENTRAL......	4 229	100.0	27.5	20.9	51.5	-	-	-	.1
UNDER 100 MILES.......	1 093	100.0	12.2	13.5	74.2	-	-	-	-
100 TO 199 MILES......	1 026	100.0	18.3	22.4	59.3	-	-	-	-
200 TO 299 MILES......	752	100.0	17.4	27.2	55.3	-	-	-	-
300 TO 499 MILES......	766	100.0	26.3	32.6	40.7	-	-	-	.4
500 TO 999 MILES......	368	100.0	83.5	8.4	8.1	-	-	-	-
1000 TO 1499 MILES....	178	100.0	96.3	3.7	-	-	-	-	-
1500 MILES OR OVER....	42	100.0	70.5	29.5	-	-	-	-	-
MOUNTAIN................	2 830	100.0	54.1	24.3	20.6	-	-	-	1.0
UNDER 100 MILES.......	380	100.0	9.5	35.6	50.4	-	-	-	4.4
100 TO 199 MILES......	267	100.0	3.0	48.3	48.8	-	-	-	-
200 TO 299 MILES......	99	100.0	21.8	9.3	65.5	-	-	-	3.3
300 TO 499 MILES......	123	100.0	23.1	37.8	33.5	-	-	-	5.6
500 TO 999 MILES......	697	100.0	42.3	38.6	19.1	-	-	-	-
1000 TO 1499 MILES....	644	100.0	81.9	14.8	3.2	-	-	-	.1
1500 MILES OR OVER....	617	100.0	99.7	.2	.1	-	-	-	-
PACIFIC.................	18 824	100.0	57.8	19.6	17.6	-	4.8	-	.2
UNDER 100 MILES.......	4 197	100.0	7.4	49.1	43.0	-	.3	-	.2
100 TO 199 MILES......	1 472	100.0	20.7	33.3	46.0	-	-	-	-
200 TO 299 MILES......	751	100.0	34.9	31.8	33.2	-	-	-	.1
300 TO 499 MILES......	1 743	100.0	50.8	28.7	20.5	-	-	-	-
500 TO 999 MILES......	3 089	100.0	74.8	11.9	7.0	-	6.0	-	.3
1000 TO 1499 MILES....	2 299	100.0	98.8	.8	.2	-	-	-	.2
1500 MILES OR OVER....	5 271	100.0	85.9	.3	.1	-	13.5	-	.2
TON-MILES OF SHIPMENTS	(millions of ton-miles)								
U.S. TOTAL..........	24 858	100.0	74.3	7.1	10.7	-	7.8	-	.1
EAST NORTH CENTRAL......	252	100.0	39.6	20.4	39.6	-	-	.1	.3
UNDER 100 MILES.......	24	100.0	13.5	11.1	72.2	-	-	.1	3.2
100 TO 199 MILES......	50	100.0	8.8	13.5	77.5	-	-	.2	-
200 TO 299 MILES......	58	100.0	41.6	7.1	51.3	-	-	-	-
300 TO 499 MILES......	35	100.0	44.0	22.9	33.0	-	-	-	-
500 TO 999 MILES......	64	100.0	77.7	20.1	2.0	-	.1	-	.1
1000 TO 1499 MILES....	-	100.0	-	100.0	-	-	-	-	-
1500 MILES OR OVER....	18	100.0	11.8	88.2	-	-	-	-	-
SOUTH ATLANTIC..........	1 057	100.0	44.4	18.6	37.0	-	-	-	-
UNDER 100 MILES.......	94	100.0	37.8	13.3	48.9	-	-	-	-
100 TO 199 MILES......	247	100.0	26.1	17.6	56.3	-	-	-	-
200 TO 299 MILES......	278	100.0	44.8	13.3	41.9	-	-	-	-
300 TO 499 MILES......	284	100.0	49.7	22.5	27.8	-	-	-	-
500 TO 999 MILES......	86	100.0	45.5	43.6	11.0	-	-	-	-
1000 TO 1499 MILES....	1	100.0	-	100.0	-	-	-	-	-
1500 MILES OR OVER....	63	100.0	99.3	.7	-	-	-	-	-
EAST SOUTH CENTRAL......	1 018	100.0	43.8	12.8	43.2	-	-	-	.2
UNDER 100 MILES.......	91	100.0	10.3	15.0	74.7	-	-	-	-
100 TO 199 MILES......	130	100.0	15.2	12.7	71.6	-	-	-	.5
200 TO 299 MILES......	73	100.0	13.6	31.0	54.0	-	-	-	1.5
300 TO 499 MILES......	257	100.0	43.6	16.9	39.4	-	-	-	-
500 TO 999 MILES......	432	100.0	62.5	6.5	30.9	-	-	-	-
1000 TO 1499 MILES....	10	100.0	71.4	3.6	25.0	-	-	-	-
1500 MILES OR OVER....	22	100.0	76.3	22.4	1.2	-	-	-	-

See footnotes at end of table 4.

TABLE 1. **TCC GROUP 242—Percent Distribution of Geographic Division of Origin and Distance Shipped, by Means of Transport: 1972**—Continued

Geographic division of origin[1] and distance shipped[2]	Number	Percent distribution by means of transport							
		All means of transport	Rail	Motor carrier	Private truck	Air	Water	Other	Unknown
TON-MILES OF SHIPMENTS	(millions of ton-miles)								
WEST SOUTH CENTRAL......	1 275	100.0	51.2	20.4	28.4	-	-	-	.1
UNDER 100 MILES.......	60	100.0	13.9	13.8	72.3	-	-	-	-
100 TO 199 MILES......	151	100.0	19.7	22.7	57.7	-	-	-	-
200 TO 299 MILES......	186	100.0	17.6	27.4	55.1	-	-	-	-
300 TO 499 MILES......	275	100.0	27.9	32.3	39.5	-	-	-	.3
500 TO 999 MILES......	241	100.0	84.1	7.9	8.0	-	-	-	-
1000 TO 1499 MILES....	239	100.0	96.2	3.8	-	-	-	-	-
1500 MILES OR OVER....	120	100.0	59.6	40.4	-	-	-	-	-
MOUNTAIN.................	2 598	100.0	79.1	13.7	7.0	-	-	-	.2
UNDER 100 MILES.......	23	100.0	7.1	30.6	60.9	-	-	-	1.5
100 TO 199 MILES......	37	100.0	3.3	49.9	46.8	-	-	-	-
200 TO 299 MILES......	26	100.0	21.3	8.8	66.4	-	-	-	3.4
300 TO 499 MILES......	47	100.0	22.6	38.0	34.4	-	-	-	5.0
500 TO 999 MILES......	522	100.0	44.8	37.5	17.7	-	-	-	-
1000 TO 1499 MILES....	801	100.0	83.1	14.0	2.8	-	-	-	.1
1500 MILES OR OVER....	1 139	100.0	99.7	.2	.1	-	-	-	-
PACIFIC..................	17 229	100.0	81.4	4.1	3.2	-	11.2	-	.2
UNDER 100 MILES.......	207	100.0	10.8	43.2	45.4	-	.3	-	.2
100 TO 199 MILES......	209	100.0	20.9	33.0	46.1	-	-	-	-
200 TO 299 MILES......	182	100.0	34.3	32.0	33.6	-	-	-	.1
300 TO 499 MILES......	721	100.0	52.2	28.5	19.3	-	-	-	.3
500 TO 999 MILES......	2 173	100.0	76.6	10.4	6.0	-	6.7	-	.3
1000 TO 1499 MILES....	3 055	100.0	98.9	.7	.2	-	-	-	.2
1500 MILES OR OVER....	10 678	100.0	82.7	.3	.1	-	16.6	-	.2

See footnotes at end of table 4.

TABLE 2. **TCC GROUP 242—Percent Distribution of Geographic Division of Origin and Means of Transport, by Geographic Division of Destination: 1972**

Geographic division of origin[1] and means of transport	Number	Percent distribution by division of destination									
		U.S. total	New England	Middle Atlantic	East North Central	West North Central	South Atlantic	East South Central	West South Central	Mountain	Pacific
TONS OF SHIPMENTS	(thousands of tons)										
U.S. TOTAL..............	38 732	100.0	1.6	6.8	12.5	8.1	13.8	9.8	13.8	6.6	26.9
RAIL...................	17 583	100.0	1.3	6.4	17.4	15.1	13.9	7.6	11.1	7.8	19.5
MOTOR CARRIER..........	7 241	100.0	.7	5.1	6.4	3.0	9.8	8.3	10.9	7.9	48.1
PRIVATE TRUCK..........	12 901	100.0	2.7	4.0	10.0	2.2	16.8	14.5	20.2	4.5	25.2
AIR....................	-	100.0	2.0	.8	42.3	38.8	1.6	-	2.7	9.4	2.4
WATER..................	919	100.0	-	67.7	-	-	5.2	-	-	-	27.2
OTHER..................	2	100.0	.5	1.0	57.1	13.8	.1	27.2	.1	-	-
UNKNOWN................	83	100.0	-	-	26.2	4.6	.1	3.3	10.2	28.6	27.1
EAST NORTH CENTRAL......	1 270	100.0	1.6	4.5	76.5	3.4	8.6	3.7	.8	-	.8
RAIL...................	298	100.0	3.3	6.9	56.0	5.9	15.4	9.1	3.0	-	.4
MOTOR CARRIER..........	162	100.0	5.7	10.2	65.8	3.7	5.3	2.7	1.0	-	5.6
PRIVATE TRUCK..........	793	100.0	.1	2.5	86.0	2.5	6.8	2.0	-	-	-
AIR....................	-	100.0	100.0	-	-	-	-	-	-	-	-
WATER..................	-	100.0	-	100.0	-	-	-	-	-	-	-
OTHER..................	1	100.0	.8	1.4	95.2	1.4	.2	.7	.2	-	-
UNKNOWN................	15	100.0	-	-	99.6	-	.4	-	-	-	-
SOUTH ATLANTIC..........	5 311	100.0	.3	12.9	9.5	.2	69.9	6.5	.2	-	.6
RAIL...................	1 904	100.0	-	10.8	12.2	-	67.0	8.4	-	-	1.6
MOTOR CARRIER..........	928	100.0	1.7	14.4	8.9	1.1	67.4	6.2	.3	-	-
PRIVATE TRUCK..........	2 478	100.0	-	13.8	7.7	-	73.0	5.2	.3	-	-
AIR....................	-	100.0	-	-	-	-	100.0	-	-	-	-
WATER..................	-	100.0	-	-	-	-	-	-	-	-	-
OTHER..................	-	100.0	100.0	-	-	-	-	-	-	-	-
UNKNOWN................	-	100.0	-	-	-	-	-	-	-	-	-

See footnotes at end of table 4.

TABLE 2. TCC GROUP 242—Percent Distribution of Geographic Division of Origin and Means of Transport, by Geographic Division of Destination: 1972—Continued

Geographic division of origin[1] and means of transport	Number	Percent distribution by division of destination									
		U.S. total	New England	Middle Atlantic	East North Central	West North Central	South Atlantic	East South Central	West South Central	Mountain	Pacific
TONS OF SHIPMENTS	(thousands of tons)										
EAST SOUTH CENTRAL......	4 182	100.0	.2	.9	10.0	2.8	14.5	50.9	20.3	.1	.3
RAIL...................	1 047	100.0	.6	1.3	17.3	4.1	25.2	38.2	12.0	.4	.9
MOTOR CARRIER.........	593	100.0	.2	1.4	8.6	1.9	11.1	59.0	17.2	.2	.4
PRIVATE TRUCK.........	2 532	100.0	-	.6	7.3	2.4	10.9	54.4	24.2	-	-
AIR...................	-	100.0	-	1.5	59.3	31.7	2.9	-	-	-	4.6
WATER.................	-	100.0	-	-	-	-	-	-	-	-	-
OTHER.................	-	100.0	-	-	.1	-	-	99.7	-	.1	-
UNKNOWN...............	8	100.0	-	-	-	-	-	-	100.0	-	-
WEST SOUTH CENTRAL......	4 229	100.0	.1	1.0	8.4	6.6	.9	16.8	65.4	.1	.6
RAIL...................	1 164	100.0	.5	3.5	26.0	10.3	2.8	15.4	40.3	-	1.2
MOTOR CARRIER.........	883	100.0	-	-	3.8	6.2	.2	21.7	66.4	.2	1.4
PRIVATE TRUCK.........	2 179	100.0	-	-	.9	4.8	.1	15.5	78.5	.1	-
AIR...................	-	100.0	-	-	-	-	-	-	-	-	-
WATER.................	-	100.0	-	-	-	-	-	-	-	-	-
OTHER.................	-	100.0	-	-	-	-	-	-	-	-	-
UNKNOWN...............	2	100.0	-	-	-	-	-	100.0	-	-	-
MOUNTAIN...............	2 830	100.0	.6	5.2	20.6	18.8	5.8	2.4	15.0	27.8	3.9
RAIL...................	1 532	100.0	.9	9.5	29.5	26.6	10.8	4.4	4.4	10.0	3.8
MOTOR CARRIER.........	686	100.0	.2	-	18.1	15.7	-	-	13.5	50.0	2.4
PRIVATE TRUCK.........	583	100.0	-	-	.7	3.0	-	-	45.3	45.6	5.5
AIR...................	-	100.0	-	-	-	-	-	-	-	-	-
WATER.................	-	100.0	-	-	-	-	-	-	-	-	-
OTHER.................	-	100.0	-	-	-	-	-	-	-	-	-
UNKNOWN...............	27	100.0	-	-	2.5	.8	-	-	-	84.6	12.1
PACIFIC...............	18 824	100.0	.8	6.7	8.3	10.3	3.6	2.4	6.5	8.9	52.5
RAIL...................	10 874	100.0	1.3	5.8	14.3	17.7	5.7	4.2	11.2	10.6	29.2
MOTOR CARRIER.........	3 691	100.0	.1	.1	.1	.5	-	-	-	6.0	93.2
PRIVATE TRUCK.........	3 317	100.0	-	-	-	.1	-	-	.1	9.2	90.6
AIR...................	-	100.0	-	-	24.6	48.6	-	-	6.0	20.7	-
WATER.................	912	100.0	-	68.2	-	-	5.2	-	-	-	26.6
OTHER.................	-	100.0	-	-	-	-	-	-	-	-	-
UNKNOWN...............	29	100.0	-	-	20.9	12.3	-	-	-	1.7	65.1
TON-MILES OF SHIPMENTS	(millions of ton-miles)										
U.S. TOTAL.............	24 858	100.0	1.9	14.7	18.7	14.1	11.1	6.5	11.5	6.0	15.5
RAIL...................	18 474	100.0	2.3	10.4	22.0	17.7	12.0	6.7	12.1	6.2	10.8
MOTOR CARRIER.........	1 754	100.0	1.5	4.8	14.8	8.0	6.5	6.5	11.4	10.6	35.8
PRIVATE TRUCK.........	2 653	100.0	1.1	4.1	11.9	3.5	11.9	9.9	15.6	6.6	35.4
AIR...................	-	100.0	1.7	.5	35.4	41.9	1.3	-	4.3	9.4	5.5
WATER.................	1 939	100.0	-	79.6	-	-	5.9	-	-	-	14.5
OTHER.................	-	100.0	1.5	1.8	23.0	59.9	.3	12.9	.4	.2	-
UNKNOWN...............	37	100.0	-	-	35.1	14.5	.1	2.5	4.5	8.5	34.9
EAST NORTH CENTRAL......	252	100.0	5.3	8.1	47.3	4.6	18.1	6.3	2.7	-	7.5
RAIL...................	99	100.0	5.8	9.1	27.3	7.0	29.4	13.5	5.7	-	2.2
MOTOR CARRIER.........	51	100.0	13.2	11.9	27.0	3.3	8.4	1.4	2.4	-	32.4
PRIVATE TRUCK.........	99	100.0	.8	5.0	77.3	3.0	12.1	1.8	-	-	-
AIR...................	-	100.0	100.0	-	-	-	-	-	-	-	-
WATER.................	-	100.0	-	100.0	-	-	-	-	-	-	-
OTHER.................	-	100.0	5.1	6.2	79.5	5.5	.9	1.3	1.5	-	-
UNKNOWN...............	-	100.0	-	-	97.3	-	2.7	-	-	-	-
SOUTH ATLANTIC.........	1 057	100.0	.9	18.4	17.2	.5	48.4	8.2	.2	-	6.0
RAIL...................	469	100.0	-	14.7	19.2	-	43.8	8.8	-	-	13.5
MOTOR CARRIER.........	196	100.0	4.9	25.4	14.0	2.9	43.9	8.2	.4	-	.2
PRIVATE TRUCK.........	391	100.0	-	19.3	16.4	-	56.3	7.5	.4	-	-
AIR...................	-	100.0	-	-	-	-	100.0	-	-	-	-
WATER.................	-	100.0	-	-	-	-	-	-	-	-	-
OTHER.................	-	100.0	100.0	-	-	-	-	-	-	-	-
UNKNOWN...............	-	100.0	-	-	-	-	-	-	-	-	-

See footnotes at end of table 4.

TABLE 2. **TCC GROUP 242—Percent Distribution of Geographic Division of Origin and Means of Transport, by Geographic Division of Destination: 1972**—Continued

Geographic division of origin[1] and means of transport	Number	Percent distribution by division of destination									
		U.S. total	New England	Middle Atlantic	East North Central	West North Central	South Atlantic	East South Central	West South Central	Mountain	Pacific
TON-MILES OF SHIPMENTS	(millions of ton-miles)										
EAST SOUTH CENTRAL......	1 018	100.0	.9	2.8	23.6	5.8	23.3	27.1	13.6	.5	2.2
RAIL...................	446	100.0	1.7	2.6	27.7	5.9	32.2	17.5	7.9	.8	3.8
MOTOR CARRIER.........	130	100.0	.6	4.9	16.6	2.2	13.8	36.9	20.4	.8	3.8
PRIVATE TRUCK.........	440	100.0	.3	2.5	21.7	6.9	17.2	34.2	17.0	.2	.1
AIR...................	-	100.0	-	1.6	47.5	27.3	4.5	-	-	-	19.1
WATER.................	-	100.0	-	-	-	-	-	-	-	-	-
OTHER.................	-	100.0	-	-	.4	-	-	98.1	-	1.6	-
UNKNOWN...............	1	100.0	-	-	-	-	-	-	100.0	-	-
WEST SOUTH CENTRAL......	1 275	100.0	.6	4.6	26.8	8.7	2.3	15.5	34.2	.2	7.0
RAIL...................	653	100.0	1.2	9.0	47.0	8.4	4.0	11.0	13.0	-	6.3
MOTOR CARRIER.........	259	100.0	-	-	9.6	7.7	.4	18.9	44.3	.4	18.7
PRIVATE TRUCK.........	361	100.0	-	-	2.8	10.0	.5	21.1	65.1	.5	-
AIR...................	-	100.0	-	-	-	-	-	-	-	-	-
WATER.................	-	100.0	-	-	-	-	-	-	-	-	-
OTHER.................	-	100.0	-	-	-	-	-	-	-	-	-
UNKNOWN...............	-	100.0	-	-	-	-	-	100.0	-	-	-
MOUNTAIN...............	2 598	100.0	1.3	11.3	30.6	20.3	12.6	4.3	9.5	7.4	2.7
RAIL...................	2 055	100.0	1.5	14.2	31.8	20.9	15.9	5.4	4.7	3.4	2.1
MOTOR CARRIER.........	357	100.0	.7	-	38.2	24.1	-	.1	15.3	19.4	2.2
PRIVATE TRUCK.........	182	100.0	-	-	3.2	6.7	-	-	51.8	27.4	10.9
AIR...................	-	100.0	-	-	-	-	-	-	-	-	-
WATER.................	-	100.0	-	-	-	-	-.°	-	-	-	-
OTHER.................	-	100.0	-	-	-	-	-	-	-	-	-
UNKNOWN...............	4	100.0	-	-	17.6	1.5	-	-	-	60.6	20.4
PACIFIC................	17 229	100.0	2.1	17.5	16.3	15.8	9.1	5.1	11.4	6.8	16.0
RAIL...................	14 026	100.0	2.5	10.4	19.9	19.1	10.4	6.2	13.9	6.8	10.7
MOTOR CARRIER.........	707	100.0	.8	.6	1.1	3.3	.1	-	.2	16.2	77.7
PRIVATE TRUCK.........	543	100.0	-	-	.2	.8	-	-	1.4	19.2	78.5
AIR...................	-	100.0	-	-	31.2	49.1	-	-	6.2	13.5	-
WATER.................	1 922	100.0	-	80.3	-	-	5.9	-	-	-	13.7
OTHER.................	-	100.0	-	-	-	-	-	-	-	-	-
UNKNOWN...............	29	100.0	-	-	39.2	18.2	-	-	-	1.5	41.2

See footnotes at end of table 4.

TABLE 3. **TCC GROUP 242**—Percent Distribution of Geographic Division of Destination and Means of Transport, by Geographic Division of Origin: 1972

Geographic division of destination and means of transport	Number	Percent distribution by division of origin[1]									
		U.S. total	New England	Middle Atlantic	East North Central	West North Central	South Atlantic	East South Central	West South Central	Mountain	Pacific
TONS OF SHIPMENTS	(thousands of tons)										
U.S. TOTAL.............	38 732	100.0	(D)	(D)	3.3	(D)	13.7	10.8	10.9	7.3	48.6
RAIL.................	17 583	100.0	(D)	(D)	1.7	(D)	10.8	6.0	6.6	8.7	61.8
MOTOR CARRIER........	7 241	100.0	(D)	(D)	2.2	(D)	12.8	8.2	12.2	9.5	51.0
PRIVATE TRUCK........	12 901	100.0	(D)	(D)	6.2	(D)	19.2	19.6	16.9	4.5	25.7
AIR.................	-	100.0	(D)	(D)	2.0	(D)	.1	52.5	-	-	45.4
WATER...............	919	100.0	(D)	(D)	-	(D)	-	-	-	-	99.2
OTHER...............	2	100.0	(D)	(D)	59.9	(D)	-	26.9	-	-	-
UNKNOWN.............	83	100.0	(D)	(D)	18.0	(D)	-	10.2	3.3	33.1	35.4
NEW ENGLAND............	625	100.0	(D)	(D)	3.2	(D)	2.5	1.4	.9	2.5	22.7
RAIL.................	228	100.0	(D)	(D)	4.2	(D)	-	2.8	2.5	6.3	61.3
MOTOR CARRIER........	47	100.0	(D)	(D)	19.4	(D)	32.7	1.9	-	6.3	61.3
PRIVATE TRUCK........	349	100.0	(D)	(D)	.3	(D)	-	.3	-	2.6	4.6
AIR.................	-	100.0	(D)	(D)	100.0	(D)	-	-	-	-	-
WATER...............	-	100.0	(D)	(D)	-	(D)	-	-	-	-	-
OTHER...............	-	100.0	(D)	(D)	99.9	(D)	.1	-	-	-	-
UNKNOWN.............	-	100.0	(D)	(D)	-	(D)	-	-	-	-	-
MIDDLE ATLANTIC........	2 626	100.0	(D)	(D)	2.2	(D)	26.0	1.5	1.6	5.6	47.8
RAIL.................	1 122	100.0	(D)	(D)	1.8	(D)	18.4	1.2	3.7	13.0	56.3
MOTOR CARRIER........	367	100.0	(D)	(D)	4.5	(D)	36.3	2.3	-	-	.6
PRIVATE TRUCK........	514	100.0	(D)	(D)	3.9	(D)	66.7	3.2	-	-	.6
AIR.................	-	100.0	(D)	(D)	-	(D)	-	100.0	-	-	-
WATER...............	621	100.0	(D)	(D)	-	(D)	-	-	-	-	100.0
OTHER...............	-	100.0	(D)	(D)	84.0	(D)	-	-	-	-	-
UNKNOWN.............	-	100.0	(D)	(D)	-	(D)	-	-	-	-	-
EAST NORTH CENTRAL......	4 835	100.0	(D)	(D)	20.1	(D)	10.5	8.6	7.3	12.0	32.4
RAIL.................	3 053	100.0	(D)	(D)	5.5	(D)	7.6	5.9	9.9	14.8	50.9
MOTOR CARRIER........	462	100.0	(D)	(D)	23.1	(D)	17.9	11.1	7.3	26.9	1.1
PRIVATE TRUCK........	1 295	100.0	(D)	(D)	52.7	(D)	14.7	14.3	1.4	.3	-
AIR.................	-	100.0	(D)	(D)	-	(D)	-	73.6	-	-	26.4
WATER...............	-	100.0	(D)	(D)	-	(D)	-	-	-	-	-
OTHER...............	1	100.0	(D)	(D)	99.9	(D)	-	.1	-	-	-
UNKNOWN.............	21	100.0	(D)	(D)	68.5	(D)	-	-	-	3.2	28.3
WEST NORTH CENTRAL......	3 156	100.0	(D)	(D)	1.4	(D)	.3	3.7	8.9	16.9	61.6
RAIL.................	2 655	100.0	(D)	(D)	.7	(D)	-	1.6	4.5	15.4	72.3
MOTOR CARRIER........	214	100.0	(D)	(D)	2.8	(D)	4.7	5.3	25.6	50.2	8.5
PRIVATE TRUCK........	282	100.0	(D)	(D)	7.1	(D)	-	21.7	37.3	6.2	1.1
AIR.................	-	100.0	(D)	(D)	-	(D)	-	43.0	-	-	57.0
WATER...............	-	100.0	(D)	(D)	-	(D)	-	-	-	-	-
OTHER...............	-	100.0	(D)	(D)	6.1	(D)	-	-	-	-	-
UNKNOWN.............	3	100.0	(D)	(D)	-	(D)	-	-	-	5.7	94.3
SOUTH ATLANTIC.........	5 361	100.0	(D)	(D)	2.0	(D)	69.2	11.3	.7	3.1	12.5
RAIL.................	2 445	100.0	(D)	(D)	1.9	(D)	52.2	10.8	1.3	6.7	25.4
MOTOR CARRIER........	707	100.0	(D)	(D)	1.2	(D)	88.4	9.3	.3	-	-
PRIVATE TRUCK........	2 161	100.0	(D)	(D)	2.5	(D)	83.7	12.8	.1	-	-
AIR.................	-	100.0	(D)	(D)	-	(D)	3.2	96.8	-	-	-
WATER...............	47	100.0	(D)	(D)	-	(D)	-	-	-	-	100.0
OTHER...............	-	100.0	(D)	(D)	100.0	(D)	-	-	-	-	-
UNKNOWN.............	-	100.0	(D)	(D)	100.0	(D)	-	-	-	-	-
EAST SOUTH CENTRAL......	3 811	100.0	(D)	(D)	1.2	(D)	9.1	55.8	18.7	1.8	11.9
RAIL.................	1 335	100.0	(D)	(D)	2.0	(D)	11.9	29.9	13.4	5.0	34.0
MOTOR CARRIER........	604	100.0	(D)	(D)	.7	(D)	9.6	57.9	31.7	-	-
PRIVATE TRUCK........	1 868	100.0	(D)	(D)	.9	(D)	6.9	73.8	18.1	-	-
AIR.................	-	100.0	(D)	(D)	-	(D)	-	-	-	-	-
WATER...............	-	100.0	(D)	(D)	-	(D)	-	-	-	-	-
OTHER...............	-	100.0	(D)	(D)	1.6	(D)	-	98.4	-	-	-
UNKNOWN.............	2	100.0	(D)	(D)	-	(D)	-	-	100.0	-	-
WEST SOUTH CENTRAL......	5 343	100.0	(D)	(D)	.2	(D)	.2	15.9	51.8	7.9	22.9
RAIL.................	1 947	100.0	(D)	(D)	.5	(D)	-	6.4	24.1	3.5	62.7
MOTOR CARRIER........	787	100.0	(D)	(D)	.2	(D)	.4	13.0	74.5	11.8	.1
PRIVATE TRUCK........	2 599	100.0	(D)	(D)	-	(D)	.3	23.6	65.8	10.2	.2
AIR.................	-	100.0	(D)	(D)	-	(D)	-	-	-	-	100.0
WATER...............	-	100.0	(D)	(D)	-	(D)	-	-	-	-	-
OTHER...............	-	100.0	(D)	(D)	100.0	(D)	-	-	-	-	-
UNKNOWN.............	8	100.0	(D)	(D)	-	(D)	-	100.0	-	-	-
MOUNTAIN...............	2 545	100.0	(D)	(D)	-	(D)	-	.2	.2	30.9	66.1
RAIL.................	1 368	100.0	(D)	(D)	-	(D)	-	.3	-	11.2	84.3
MOTOR CARRIER........	569	100.0	(D)	(D)	-	(D)	-	.2	.2	60.4	39.2
PRIVATE TRUCK........	584	100.0	(D)	(D)	-	(D)	-	.1	.5	45.5	52.2
AIR.................	-	100.0	(D)	(D)	-	(D)	-	-	-	-	100.0
WATER...............	-	100.0	(D)	(D)	-	(D)	-	-	-	-	-
OTHER...............	-	100.0	(D)	(D)	-	(D)	-	100.0	-	-	-
UNKNOWN.............	23	100.0	(D)	(D)	-	(D)	-	-	-	97.9	2.1
PACIFIC................	10 426	100.0	(D)	(D)	.1	(D)	.3	.1	.3	1.1	94.8
RAIL.................	3 426	100.0	(D)	(D)	-	(D)	.9	.3	.4	1.7	92.7
MOTOR CARRIER........	3 480	100.0	(D)	(D)	.3	(D)	-	.1	.4	.5	98.8
PRIVATE TRUCK........	3 245	100.0	(D)	(D)	-	(D)	-	-	-	1.0	92.5
AIR.................	-	100.0	(D)	(D)	-	(D)	-	100.0	-	-	-
WATER...............	249	100.0	(D)	(D)	-	(D)	-	-	-	-	97.2
OTHER...............	-	100.0	(D)	(D)	-	(D)	-	-	-	-	-
UNKNOWN.............	22	100.0	(D)	(D)	-	(D)	-	-	-	14.8	85.2

See footnotes at end of table 4.

TABLE 3. TCC GROUP 242—Percent Distribution of Geographic Division of Destination and Means of Transport, by Geographic Division of Origin: 1972—Continued

Geographic division of destination and means of transport	Number	Percent distribution by division of origin[1]									
		U.S. total	New England	Middle Atlantic	East North Central	West North Central	South Atlantic	East South Central	West South Central	Mountain	Pacific
TON-MILES OF SHIPMENTS	(millions of ton-miles)										
U.S. TOTAL	24 858	100.0	(D)	(D)	1.0	(D)	4.3	4.1	5.1	10.5	69.3
RAIL	18 474	100.0	(D)	(D)	.5	(D)	2.5	2.4	3.5	11.1	75.9
MOTOR CARRIER	1 754	100.0	(D)	(D)	2.9	(D)	11.2	7.4	14.8	20.4	40.3
PRIVATE TRUCK	2 653	100.0	(D)	(D)	3.8	(D)	14.7	16.6	13.6	6.9	20.5
AIR	-	100.0	(D)	(D)	1.7	(D)	-	28.9	-	-	69.4
WATER	1 939	100.0	(D)	(D)	-	(D)	-	-	-	-	99.1
OTHER	-	100.0	(D)	(D)	28.9	(D)	-	12.8	-	-	-
UNKNOWN	37	100.0	(D)	(D)	2.2	(D)	-	4.5	2.5	12.0	78.7
NEW ENGLAND	476	100.0	(D)	(D)	2.8	(D)	2.0	2.0	1.6	7.2	74.3
RAIL	421	100.0	(D)	(D)	1.4	(D)	-	1.8	1.8	7.5	82.7
MOTOR CARRIER	26	100.0	(D)	(D)	25.8	(D)	36.7	2.8	-	9.5	20.8
PRIVATE TRUCK	28	100.0	(D)	(D)	2.6	(D)	-	4.8	-	-	-
AIR	-	100.0	(D)	(D)	100.0	(D)	-	-	-	-	-
WATER	-	100.0	(D)	(D)	-	(D)	-	-	-	-	-
OTHER	-	100.0	(D)	(D)	99.9	(D)	.1	-	-	-	-
UNKNOWN	-	100.0	(D)	(D)	-	(D)	-	-	-	-	-
MIDDLE ATLANTIC	3 657	100.0	(D)	(D)	.6	(D)	5.3	.8	1.6	8.0	82.4
RAIL	1 920	100.0	(D)	(D)	.5	(D)	3.6	.6	3.0	15.2	76.3
MOTOR CARRIER	84	100.0	(D)	(D)	7.2	(D)	58.9	7.5	-	-	5.3
PRIVATE TRUCK	108	100.0	(D)	(D)	4.6	(D)	69.8	10.3		-	-
AIR	-	100.0	(D)	(D)	-	(D)	-	100.0	-	-	-
WATER	1 544	100.0	(D)	(D)	-	(D)	-	-	-	-	100.0
OTHER	-	100.0	(D)	(D)	98.6	(D)	-	-	-	-	-
UNKNOWN	-	100.0	(D)	(D)	-	(D)	-	-	-	-	-
EAST NORTH CENTRAL	4 655	100.0	(D)	(D)	2.6	(D)	3.9	5.2	7.4	17.1	60.3
RAIL	4 066	100.0	(D)	(D)	.7	(D)	2.2	3.0	7.6	16.1	68.5
MOTOR CARRIER	259	100.0	(D)	(D)	5.4	(D)	10.7	8.4	9.6	52.6	2.9
PRIVATE TRUCK	316	100.0	(D)	(D)	24.3	(D)	20.2	30.1	3.2	1.8	.3
AIR	-	100.0	(D)	(D)	-	(D)	-	38.8	-	-	61.2
WATER	-	100.0	(D)	(D)	-	(D)	-	-	-	-	-
OTHER	-	100.0	(D)	(D)	99.7	(D)	-	.2	-	-	-
UNKNOWN	13	100.0	(D)	(D)	6.1	(D)	-	-	-	6.0	87.9
WEST NORTH CENTRAL	3 500	100.0	(D)	(D)	.3	(D)	.2	1.7	3.2	15.1	77.6
RAIL	3 260	100.0	(D)	(D)	.2	(D)	-	.8	1.7	13.2	82.2
MOTOR CARRIER	141	100.0	(D)	(D)	1.2	(D)	4.1	2.0	14.1	61.1	16.8
PRIVATE TRUCK	92	100.0	(D)	(D)	3.3	(D)	-	32.7	38.8	13.3	4.5
AIR	-	100.0	(D)	(D)	-	(D)	-	18.8	-	-	81.2
WATER	-	100.0	(D)	(D)	-	(D)	-	-	-	-	-
OTHER	-	100.0	(D)	(D)	2.6	(D)	-	-	-	-	-
UNKNOWN	5	100.0	(D)	(D)	-	(D)	-	-	-	1.2	98.8
SOUTH ATLANTIC	2 758	100.0	(D)	(D)	1.7	(D)	18.6	8.6	1.1	11.9	57.1
RAIL	2 215	100.0	(D)	(D)	1.3	(D)	9.3	6.5	1.2	14.8	65.9
MOTOR CARRIER	114	100.0	(D)	(D)	3.8	(D)	75.8	15.8	.9	-	.5
PRIVATE TRUCK	314	100.0	(D)	(D)	3.8	(D)	70.0	24.1	.6	-	-
AIR	-	100.0	(D)	(D)	-	(D)	2.2	97.8	-	-	-
WATER	114	100.0	(D)	(D)	-	(D)	-	-	-	-	100.0
OTHER	-	100.0	(D)	(D)	100.0	(D)	-	-	-	-	-
UNKNOWN	-	100.0	(D)	(D)	100.0	(D)	-	-	-	-	-
EAST SOUTH CENTRAL	1 609	100.0	(D)	(D)	1.0	(D)	5.4	17.2	12.3	6.9	54.4
RAIL	1 230	100.0	(D)	(D)	1.1	(D)	3.4	6.3	5.8	9.0	71.1
MOTOR CARRIER	114	100.0	(D)	(D)	.6	(D)	14.2	42.0	42.9	.3	-
PRIVATE TRUCK	263	100.0	(D)	(D)	.7	(D)	11.2	57.1	29.0	-	-
AIR	-	100.0	(D)	(D)	-	(D)	-	-	-	-	-
WATER	-	100.0	(D)	(D)	-	(D)	-	-	-	-	-
OTHER	-	100.0	(D)	(D)	3.0	(D)	-	97.0	-	-	-
UNKNOWN	-	100.0	(D)	(D)	-	(D)	-	-	100.0	-	-
WEST SOUTH CENTRAL	2 847	100.0	(D)	(D)	.2	(D)	.1	4.9	15.3	8.6	68.8
RAIL	2 232	100.0	(D)	(D)	.3	(D)	-	1.6	3.8	4.4	87.3
MOTOR CARRIER	199	100.0	(D)	(D)	.6	(D)	.4	13.3	57.7	27.3	.6
PRIVATE TRUCK	413	100.0	(D)	(D)	-	(D)	.4	18.1	56.9	22.8	1.8
AIR	-	100.0	(D)	(D)	-	(D)	-	-	-	-	100.0
WATER	-	100.0	(D)	(D)	-	(D)	-	-	-	-	-
OTHER	-	100.0	(D)	(D)	100.0	(D)	-	-	-	-	-
UNKNOWN	1	100.0	(D)	(D)	-	(D)	-	100.0	-	-	-
MOUNTAIN	1 502	100.0	(D)	(D)	-	(D)	-	.4	.2	12.8	78.4
RAIL	1 138	100.0	(D)	(D)	-	(D)	-	.3	-	6.2	84.2
MOTOR CARRIER	185	100.0	(D)	(D)	-	(D)	-	.6	.5	37.3	61.7
PRIVATE TRUCK	175	100.0	(D)	(D)	-	(D)	-	.4	1.1	28.5	59.4
AIR	-	100.0	(D)	(D)	-	(D)	-	-	-	-	100.0
WATER	-	100.0	(D)	(D)	-	(D)	-	-	-	-	-
OTHER	-	100.0	(D)	(D)	-	(D)	-	100.0	-	-	-
UNKNOWN	3	100.0	(D)	(D)	-	(D)	-	-	-	86.2	13.8
PACIFIC	3 850	100.0	(D)	(D)	.5	(D)	1.7	.6	2.3	1.8	71.5
RAIL	1 988	100.0	(D)	(D)	.1	(D)	3.2	.9	2.1	2.1	75.5
MOTOR CARRIER	628	100.0	(D)	(D)	2.7	(D)	.1	.8	7.7	1.2	87.5
PRIVATE TRUCK	939	100.0	(D)	(D)	-	(D)	-	-	-	2.1	45.4
AIR	-	100.0	(D)	(D)	-	(D)	-	100.0	-	-	-
WATER	280	100.0	(D)	(D)	-	(D)	-	-	-	-	94.1
OTHER	-	100.0	(D)	(D)	-	(D)	-	-	-	-	-
UNKNOWN	12	100.0	(D)	(D)	-	(D)	-	-	-	7.0	93.0

See footnotes at end of table 4.

TABLE 4. TCC GROUP 242—Percent Distribution of Distance Shipped and Weight of Shipment, by Means of Transport: 1972

Distance shipped and weight of shipment[2][3]	Number	Percent distribution by means of transport							
		All means of transport	Rail	Motor carrier	Private truck	Air	Water	Other	Unknown
TONS OF SHIPMENTS	(thousands of tons)								
U.S. TOTAL............	32 991	100.0	42.7	18.7	36.3	–	2.2	–	.2
UNDER 100 MILES.........	8 860	100.0	11.1	30.5	58.0	–	.2	–	.3
UNDER 1000 POUNDS.....	5	100.0	–	26.3	72.5	–	–	1.2	–
1000 TO 9999 POUNDS...	170	100.0	.3	23.7	75.7	–	–	.1	.2
10000 TO 29999 POUNDS.	939	100.0	.9	25.4	73.5	–	–	–	.2
30000 TO 59999 POUNDS.	5 726	100.0	2.4	32.7	64.7	–	–	–	.2
60000 TO 89999 POUNDS.	989	100.0	33.0	34.1	32.2	–	.7	–	–
90000 POUNDS AND OVER.	1 029	100.0	49.8	20.3	28.3	–	.6	–	1.1
100 TO 199 MILES........	4 807	100.0	11.6	21.9	66.4	–	–	–	.1
UNDER 1000 POUNDS.....	2	100.0	–	88.1	11.1	–	–	.8	–
1000 TO 9999 POUNDS...	32	100.0	8.0	39.8	50.3	–	–	1.7	.2
10000 TO 29999 POUNDS.	185	100.0	4.1	21.6	74.0	–	–	.3	–
30000 TO 59999 POUNDS.	3 490	100.0	2.0	23.9	73.9	–	–	–	.1
60000 TO 89999 POUNDS.	508	100.0	29.5	13.1	57.4	–	–	–	–
90000 POUNDS AND OVER.	588	100.0	55.2	16.7	28.0	–	–	–	–
200 TO 299 MILES........	2 785	100.0	24.1	21.7	54.0	–	–	–	.2
UNDER 1000 POUNDS.....	1	100.0	–	66.8	31.0	–	–	.4	1.8
1000 TO 9999 POUNDS...	17	100.0	1.1	44.8	54.1	–	–	–	–
10000 TO 29999 POUNDS.	77	100.0	7.1	9.6	83.3	–	–	–	–
30000 TO 59999 POUNDS.	1 964	100.0	2.7	29.3	67.7	–	–	–	.3
60000 TO 89999 POUNDS.	291	100.0	68.4	4.5	27.1	–	–	–	–
90000 POUNDS AND OVER.	433	100.0	95.1	–	4.9	–	–	–	–
300 TO 499 MILES........	3 502	100.0	35.9	26.8	37.2	–	–	–	.1
UNDER 1000 POUNDS.....	2	100.0	.3	76.9	20.5	1.2	–	1.2	–
1000 TO 9999 POUNDS...	21	100.0	3.0	48.2	48.5	–	–	–	.3
10000 TO 29999 POUNDS.	95	100.0	7.0	25.4	67.4	–	–	–	.2
30000 TO 59999 POUNDS.	1 939	100.0	3.1	41.6	55.2	–	–	–	.1
60000 TO 89999 POUNDS.	449	100.0	76.2	11.3	12.5	–	–	–	–
90000 POUNDS AND OVER.	994	100.0	85.3	4.5	10.2	–	–	–	–
500 TO 999 MILES........	4 356	100.0	70.0	16.4	13.3	–	–	–	.2
UNDER 1000 POUNDS.....	2	100.0	–	92.8	5.7	.4	–	1.1	–
1000 TO 9999 POUNDS...	20	100.0	5.2	69.3	24.8	–	.8	–	–
10000 TO 29999 POUNDS.	75	100.0	13.3	38.0	47.9	–	.1	–	.7
30000 TO 59999 POUNDS.	1 187	100.0	5.4	52.4	42.2	–	–	–	–
60000 TO 89999 POUNDS.	1 244	100.0	95.7	1.9	2.3	–	–	–	.1
90000 POUNDS AND OVER.	1 824	100.0	97.7	1.4	.6	–	–	–	.4
1000 TO 1499 MILES......	2 947	100.0	94.6	4.1	1.1	–	–	–	.1
UNDER 1000 POUNDS.....	–	100.0	–	94.9	–	5.1	–	–	–
1000 TO 9999 POUNDS...	1	100.0	10.9	25.5	47.8	–	–	15.8	–
10000 TO 29999 POUNDS.	6	100.0	39.3	41.9	18.8	–	–	–	–
30000 TO 59999 POUNDS.	410	100.0	64.3	28.6	6.9	–	–	–	.2
60000 TO 89999 POUNDS.	1 616	100.0	99.6	–	.2	–	–	–	.2
90000 POUNDS AND OVER.	911	100.0	100.0	–	–	–	–	–	–
1500 MILES OR OVER......	5 731	100.0	83.1	.7	3.9	–	12.1	–	.1
UNDER 1000 POUNDS.....	–	100.0	11.0	87.6	.5	.9	–	–	–
1000 TO 9999 POUNDS...	9	100.0	8.7	75.3	14.5	–	1.6	–	–
10000 TO 29999 POUNDS.	45	100.0	35.9	8.5	54.8	–	.8	–	–
30000 TO 59999 POUNDS.	495	100.0	70.8	5.0	20.8	–	3.2	–	.1
60000 TO 89999 POUNDS.	3 060	100.0	98.9	.1	1.0	–	–	–	–
90000 POUNDS AND OVER.	2 118	100.0	64.6	.1	2.9	–	32.0	–	.4
TON-MILES OF SHIPMENTS	(millions of ton-miles)								
U.S. TOTAL............	21 810	100.0	73.4	7.0	11.5	–	7.9	–	.2
UNDER 100 MILES.........	468	100.0	12.9	27.9	58.8	–	.1	–	.3
UNDER 1000 POUNDS.....	–	100.0	–	30.4	68.5	–	–	1.1	–
1000 TO 9999 POUNDS...	6	100.0	.5	20.8	78.4	–	.1	–	.3
10000 TO 29999 POUNDS.	39	100.0	1.3	21.8	76.5	–	–	–	.3
30000 TO 59999 POUNDS.	310	100.0	2.3	28.6	68.9	–	–	–	.2
60000 TO 89999 POUNDS.	61	100.0	38.2	33.8	27.5	–	.5	–	–
90000 POUNDS AND OVER.	50	100.0	57.8	21.9	18.7	–	.5	–	1.1
100 TO 199 MILES........	691	100.0	12.1	22.2	65.5	–	–	–	.1
UNDER 1000 POUNDS.....	–	100.0	–	88.7	10.5	–	–	.9	–
1000 TO 9999 POUNDS...	4	100.0	8.2	37.2	53.2	–	–	1.3	.1
10000 TO 29999 POUNDS.	26	100.0	4.3	20.6	74.8	–	–	.3	–
30000 TO 59999 POUNDS.	498	100.0	2.0	24.8	73.0	–	–	–	.1
60000 TO 89999 POUNDS.	73	100.0	30.4	11.0	58.6	–	–	–	–
90000 POUNDS AND OVER.	87	100.0	56.8	16.7	26.5	–	–	–	–

See footnotes at end of table 4.

TABLE 4. TCC GROUP 242—Percent Distribution of Distance Shipped and Weight of Shipment, by Means of Transport: 1972—Continued

Distance shipped and weight of shipment[2][3]	Number	Percent distribution by means of transport							
		All means of transport	Rail	Motor carrier	Private truck	Air	Water	Other	Unknown
TON-MILES OF SHIPMENTS	(millions of ton-miles)								
200 TO 299 MILES.........	680	100.0	24.1	21.8	53.9	-	-	-	.2
UNDER 1000 POUNDS.....	-	100.0	-	64.2	33.4	-	-	.4	2.0
1000 TO 9999 POUNDS...	4	100.0	1.0	42.8	56.2	-	-	-	-
10000 TO 29999 POUNDS.	19	100.0	7.6	9.3	83.1	-	-	-	-
30000 TO 59999 POUNDS.	478	100.0	2.8	29.5	67.4	-	-	-	.3
60000 TO 89999 POUNDS.	71	100.0	67.6	4.8	27.6	-	-	-	-
90000 POUNDS AND OVER.	106	100.0	94.6	-	5.4	-	-	-	-
300 TO 499 MILES.........	1 378	100.0	38.0	26.6	35.3	-	-	-	.1
UNDER 1000 POUNDS.....	-	100.0	.3	76.5	20.7	1.2	-	1.3	-
1000 TO 9999 POUNDS...	7	100.0	3.1	49.2	47.4	-	-	-	.3
10000 TO 29999 POUNDS.	34	100.0	7.2	26.2	66.4	-	-	-	.2
30000 TO 59999 POUNDS.	742	100.0	3.2	42.3	54.3	-	-	-	.1
60000 TO 89999 POUNDS.	186	100.0	77.1	11.5	11.4	-	-	-	-
90000 POUNDS AND OVER.	406	100.0	87.0	4.2	8.7	-	-	-	-
500 TO 999 MILES.........	3 038	100.0	71.9	15.4	12.5	-	-	-	.2
UNDER 1000 POUNDS.....	1	100.0	-	93.1	5.4	.5	-	1.1	-
1000 TO 9999 POUNDS...	14	100.0	5.7	70.2	23.4	-	.6	-	-
10000 TO 29999 POUNDS.	50	100.0	13.8	35.0	50.2	-	.1	-	.9
30000 TO 59999 POUNDS.	776	100.0	5.7	52.7	41.5	-	.1	-	-
60000 TO 89999 POUNDS.	926	100.0	96.2	1.5	2.2	-	-	-	.1
90000 POUNDS AND OVER.	1 268	100.0	97.9	1.2	.6	-	-	-	.4
1000 TO 1499 MILES......	3 854	100.0	95.0	3.8	1.0	-	-	-	.2
UNDER 1000 POUNDS.....	-	100.0	-	94.7	-	5.3	-	-	-
1000 TO 9999 POUNDS...	2	100.0	12.0	25.9	48.6	-	-	13.5	-
10000 TO 29999 POUNDS.	8	100.0	42.4	40.9	16.7	-	-	-	-
30000 TO 59999 POUNDS.	529	100.0	66.9	26.6	6.3	-	-	-	.1
60000 TO 89999 POUNDS.	2 130	100.0	99.6	-	.1	-	-	-	.2
90000 POUNDS AND OVER.	1 184	100.0	100.0	-	-	-	-	-	-
1500 MILES OR OVER......	11 699	100.0	79.8	.9	4.4	-	14.7	-	.1
UNDER 1000 POUNDS.....	1	100.0	10.6	88.2	.5	.8	-	-	-
1000 TO 9999 POUNDS...	18	100.0	7.9	72.6	17.9	-	1.6	-	-
10000 TO 29999 POUNDS.	100	100.0	33.9	7.7	57.4	-	1.0	-	-
30000 TO 59999 POUNDS.	1 062	100.0	67.1	7.1	22.3	-	3.4	-	.1
60000 TO 89999 POUNDS.	5 968	100.0	98.7	.1	1.2	-	-	-	-
90000 POUNDS AND OVER.	4 548	100.0	59.3	.1	3.2	-	37.0	-	.4

Note: Detail may not add to total due to rounding. The introductory table shows the estimates of sampling variability for tons; sampling variability for ton-miles has not been estimated. See the map in the Introduction for the States comprising the geographic divisions of the United States.

Shipments excluded from the survey are those moving by pipeline (primarily petroleum products from refineries), parcel post shipments, and commodities moved by own power (motorized vehicles, aircraft, etc.) or towed (prefabricated buildings, etc.). Local shipments (commodities shipped less than 25 miles from the plant) and shipments within the same city are also excluded. Shipments to Alaska and Hawaii from the 48 conterminous States and the District of Columbia are included; however, no data were obtained for shipments originating in Alaska and Hawaii.

- Represents zero or rounds to zero.   (D) Withheld to avoid disclosing figures for individual companies.

[1]Production of this commodity is concentrated in the geographic divisions shown; figures and distributions for geographic divisions not shown are included in the total.

[2]Distances of shipments to foreign destinations are calculated only to the U.S. port of exit.

[3]Includes only shipments represented by bills of lading and invoices. Summary records which did not show individual weights of shipments are not included.

TCC 243. Millwork, Plywood, and Prefabricated Wood Products

Comparisons of Tons and Ton-Miles of Shipments for
Geographic Divisions of Origin and for Sampling Variability: 1972 and 1967

Geographic division of origin	Estimates				Relative sampling variability in tons (percent)	
	1972		1967		1972	1967
	Tons (thousands)	Ton-miles (millions)	Tons (thousands)	Ton-miles (millions)		
U.S. total	19,082	12,954	11,768	13,693	9.9	11.6
New England	(D)	(D)	79	63	(*)	(*)
Middle Atlantic	402	70	131	68	30.0	(*)
East North Central	1,792	618	1,258	421	33.5	(*)
West North Central	(D)	(D)	97	51	(*)	(*)
South Atlantic	3,495	1,061	995	280	28.2	(*)
East South Central	800	368	757	375	34.8	(*)
West South Central	2,575	946	393	179	39.6	(*)
Mountain	798	908	572	802	48.7	(*)
Pacific	8,248	8,695	7,486	11,454	17.6	(*)

(D) Withheld to avoid disclosing figures for individual companies.   (*) Data not published.

TABLE 1. **TCC GROUP 243—Percent Distribution of Geographic Division of Origin and Distance Shipped, by Means of Transport: 1972**

Geographic division of origin[1] and distance shipped[2]	Number	Percent distribution by means of transport							
		All means of transport	Rail	Motor carrier	Private truck	Air	Water	Other	Unknown
TONS OF SHIPMENTS	(thousands of tons)								
U.S. TOTAL............	19 082	100.0	50.2	11.8	37.1	-	.5	-	.3
MIDDLE ATLANTIC.........	402	100.0	.3	10.1	87.3	-	-	-	2.3
UNDER 100 MILES.......	128	100.0	-	15.7	84.2	-	-	-	.1
100 TO 199 MILES......	155	100.0	-	8.5	91.5	-	-	-	-
200 TO 299 MILES......	71	100.0	-	2.6	84.8	-	-	-	12.6
300 TO 499 MILES......	31	100.0	2.4	5.5	92.0	-	-	-	-
500 TO 999 MILES......	13	100.0	3.8	13.4	82.7	-	-	.1	-
1000 TO 1499 MILES....	2	100.0	-	76.7	23.1	-	-	.2	-
1500 MILES OR OVER....	-	100.0	-	100.0	-	-	-	-	-
EAST NORTH CENTRAL......	1 792	100.0	12.9	41.7	45.1	-	.1	-	.2
UNDER 100 MILES.......	380	100.0	3.2	24.9	71.9	-	-	-	.1
100 TO 199 MILES......	344	100.0	9.9	41.5	48.7	-	-	-	-
200 TO 299 MILES......	169	100.0	4.7	45.1	50.2	-	-	-	-
300 TO 499 MILES......	507	100.0	15.2	45.3	39.1	-	-	-	.4
500 TO 999 MILES......	330	100.0	22.4	53.2	23.8	.1	.3	-	.2
1000 TO 1499 MILES....	43	100.0	32.3	56.5	11.2	-	-	-	-
1500 MILES OR OVER....	15	100.0	79.1	18.2	2.2	-	-	-	.4
SOUTH ATLANTIC.........	3 495	100.0	53.8	18.0	27.3	-	.4	.2	.4
UNDER 100 MILES.......	928	100.0	25.0	17.0	56.7	-	.9	.2	.2
100 TO 199 MILES......	697	100.0	42.0	22.8	34.2	-	.3	.1	.6
200 TO 299 MILES......	507	100.0	77.8	11.9	10.0	-	.4	-	-
300 TO 499 MILES......	641	100.0	66.2	17.1	15.3	-	-	-	1.3
500 TO 999 MILES......	607	100.0	72.0	22.9	4.6	-	-	.5	-
1000 TO 1499 MILES....	99	100.0	86.8	.6	12.6	-	-	-	-
1500 MILES OR OVER....	13	100.0	86.1	13.6	-	-	-	.3	-
EAST SOUTH CENTRAL......	800	100.0	55.5	11.5	25.0	-	7.9	.1	-
UNDER 100 MILES.......	140	100.0	9.2	5.1	40.3	-	45.2	.2	-
100 TO 199 MILES......	100	100.0	44.0	10.6	44.8	-	-	.6	-
200 TO 299 MILES......	78	100.0	46.2	12.8	41.0	-	-	-	-
300 TO 499 MILES......	157	100.0	55.9	20.2	23.9	-	-	-	-
500 TO 999 MILES......	277	100.0	80.3	10.0	9.7	-	-	-	-
1000 TO 1499 MILES....	40	100.0	87.2	9.1	3.7	-	-	-	-
1500 MILES OR OVER....	5	100.0	74.0	18.6	7.4	-	-	-	-
WEST SOUTH CENTRAL......	2 575	100.0	44.2	7.7	48.1	-	-	-	-
UNDER 100 MILES.......	624	100.0	3.9	8.8	87.3	-	-	-	-
100 TO 199 MILES......	737	100.0	11.5	6.3	82.1	-	-	-	-
200 TO 299 MILES......	139	100.0	31.3	25.0	43.7	-	-	-	-
300 TO 499 MILES......	309	100.0	77.3	16.1	6.6	-	-	-	-
500 TO 999 MILES......	630	100.0	98.2	1.2	.6	-	-	-	-
1000 TO 1499 MILES....	75	100.0	93.5	6.0	.5	-	-	-	-
1500 MILES OR OVER....	56	100.0	98.4	1.6	-	-	-	-	-
MOUNTAIN...............	798	100.0	64.9	12.3	20.6	-	-	-	2.3
UNDER 100 MILES.......	62	100.0	-	51.5	48.5	-	-	-	-
100 TO 199 MILES......	92	100.0	-	11.2	88.8	-	-	-	-
200 TO 299 MILES......	50	100.0	12.8	42.2	44.2	-	-	-	.8
300 TO 499 MILES......	43	100.0	38.7	35.5	25.8	-	-	-	-
500 TO 999 MILES......	87	100.0	53.8	18.1	13.6	-	-	-	14.6
1000 TO 1499 MILES....	150	100.0	90.4	1.7	4.4	-	-	-	3.5
1500 MILES OR OVER....	312	100.0	99.7	.2	-	-	.1	-	-
PACIFIC................	8 248	100.0	63.8	4.5	31.2	-	.2	-	.2
UNDER 100 MILES.......	2 241	100.0	5.1	5.3	89.3	-	-	-	.3
100 TO 199 MILES......	681	100.0	36.7	10.4	52.2	-	-	-	.7
200 TO 299 MILES......	265	100.0	58.6	15.4	25.6	-	.3	-	-
300 TO 499 MILES......	400	100.0	61.1	16.0	22.7	-	-	-	.2
500 TO 999 MILES......	862	100.0	89.1	5.6	5.1	-	-	-	.1
1000 TO 1499 MILES....	503	100.0	97.8	1.2	.9	-	-	-	-
1500 MILES OR OVER....	3 293	100.0	98.3	.7	.3	-	.6	-	.1
TON-MILES OF SHIPMENTS	(millions of ton-miles)								
U.S. TOTAL..........	12 954	100.0	85.0	6.2	8.1	-	.4	-	.3
MIDDLE ATLANTIC.........	70	100.0	1.2	11.9	83.9	-	-	-	3.0
UNDER 100 MILES.......	6	100.0	-	18.2	81.7	-	-	-	.1
100 TO 199 MILES......	22	100.0	-	7.6	92.4	-	-	-	-
200 TO 299 MILES......	17	100.0	-	2.8	85.2	-	-	-	12.1
300 TO 499 MILES......	11	100.0	3.1	6.7	90.1	-	-	-	-
500 TO 999 MILES......	8	100.0	5.5	15.5	79.0	-	-	.1	-
1000 TO 1499 MILES....	2	100.0	-	77.8	22.0	-	-	.2	-
1500 MILES OR OVER....	1	100.0	-	100.0	-	-	-	-	-

See footnotes at end of table 4.

TABLE 1. **TCC GROUP 243—Percent Distribution of Geographic Division of Origin and Distance Shipped, by Means of Transport: 1972**—Continued

Geographic division of origin[1] and distance shipped[2]	Number	Percent distribution by means of transport							
		All means of transport	Rail	Motor carrier	Private truck	Air	Water	Other	Unknown
TON-MILES OF SHIPMENTS	(millions of ton-miles)								
EAST NORTH CENTRAL......	618	100.0	20.3	48.2	31.1	-	.1	-	.2
UNDER 100 MILES.......	20	100.0	5.1	19.8	75.0	-	-	-	.1
100 TO 199 MILES......	48	100.0	9.2	39.9	50.9	-	-	-	-
200 TO 299 MILES......	41	100.0	4.7	46.0	49.3	-	-	-	-
300 TO 499 MILES......	190	100.0	13.2	48.7	37.6	-	-	-	.5
500 TO 999 MILES......	242	100.0	23.4	53.4	22.6	.1	.2	-	.2
1000 TO 1499 MILES....	49	100.0	32.9	56.8	10.3	-	-	-	-
1500 MILES OR OVER....	25	100.0	76.5	20.7	2.4	-	-	-	.4
SOUTH ATLANTIC.........	1 061	100.0	67.0	17.7	14.5	-	.1	.2	.5
UNDER 100 MILES.......	61	100.0	29.0	16.6	52.9	-	1.1	.2	.1
100 TO 199 MILES......	95	100.0	40.9	24.2	33.7	-	.4	.1	.8
200 TO 299 MILES......	121	100.0	77.9	12.0	9.8	-	.4	-	-
300 TO 499 MILES......	250	100.0	63.5	17.1	17.8	-	-	-	1.6
500 TO 999 MILES......	395	100.0	71.1	23.5	4.9	-	-	.4	-
1000 TO 1499 MILES....	110	100.0	87.4	.6	12.0	-	-	-	-
1500 MILES OR OVER....	27	100.0	86.1	13.6	-	-	-	.3	-
EAST SOUTH CENTRAL......	368	100.0	72.1	12.3	14.5	-	1.1	-	-
UNDER 100 MILES.......	8	100.0	12.9	4.9	37.8	-	44.3	.1	-
100 TO 199 MILES......	15	100.0	45.9	11.4	42.2	-	-	.4	-
200 TO 299 MILES......	18	100.0	48.4	12.6	39.1	-	-	-	-
300 TO 499 MILES......	63	100.0	54.7	20.8	24.5	-	-	-	-
500 TO 999 MILES......	204	100.0	80.7	10.4	8.9	-	-	-	-
1000 TO 1499 MILES....	46	100.0	87.7	8.7	3.5	-	-	-	-
1500 MILES OR OVER....	11	100.0	73.4	18.9	7.7	-	-	-	-
WEST SOUTH CENTRAL......	946	100.0	79.4	5.3	15.4	-	-	-	-
UNDER 100 MILES.......	28	100.0	6.2	12.4	81.5	-	-	-	-
100 TO 199 MILES......	118	100.0	12.1	6.2	81.7	-	-	-	-
200 TO 299 MILES......	34	100.0	32.7	24.7	42.6	-	-	-	-
300 TO 499 MILES......	121	100.0	78.6	15.6	5.8	-	-	-	-
500 TO 999 MILES......	450	100.0	98.4	1.0	.6	-	-	-	-
1000 TO 1499 MILES....	95	100.0	94.0	5.5	.5	-	-	-	-
1500 MILES OR OVER....	97	100.0	98.3	1.7	-	-	-	-	-
MOUNTAIN...............	908	100.0	90.6	3.3	4.1	-	.1	-	2.0
UNDER 100 MILES.......	2	100.0	-	49.8	50.2	-	-	-	-
100 TO 199 MILES......	12	100.0	-	11.8	88.2	-	-	-	-
200 TO 299 MILES......	11	100.0	14.8	42.6	41.9	-	-	-	.8
300 TO 499 MILES......	15	100.0	39.0	38.1	22.9	-	-	-	-
500 TO 999 MILES......	67	100.0	56.1	16.6	11.8	-	-	-	15.4
1000 TO 1499 MILES....	199	100.0	90.3	1.7	4.3	-	-	-	3.8
1500 MILES OR OVER....	599	100.0	99.7	.2	-	-	.1	-	-
PACIFIC................	8 695	100.0	95.0	1.7	2.7	-	.5	-	.1
UNDER 100 MILES.......	78	100.0	7.6	7.4	84.5	-	.1	-	.5
100 TO 199 MILES......	100	100.0	38.5	9.8	50.8	-	-	-	.8
200 TO 299 MILES......	64	100.0	57.8	16.3	25.6	-	.3	-	-
300 TO 499 MILES......	153	100.0	59.3	17.5	22.9	-	-	-	.3
500 TO 999 MILES......	639	100.0	90.3	5.0	4.5	-	-	-	.1
1000 TO 1499 MILES....	687	100.0	97.9	1.2	.9	-	-	-	-
1500 MILES OR OVER....	6 971	100.0	98.0	.8	.4	-	.7	-	.1

See footnotes at end of table 4.

TABLE 2. **TCC GROUP 243—Percent Distribution of Geographic Division of Origin and Means of Transport, by Geographic Division of Destination: 1972**

Geographic division of origin[1] and means of transport	Number	Percent distribution by division of destination									
		U.S. total	New England	Middle Atlantic	East North Central	West North Central	South Atlantic	East South Central	West South Central	Mountain	Pacific
TONS OF SHIPMENTS	(thousands of tons)										
U.S. TOTAL..............	19 082	100.0	4.8	9.4	15.7	5.6	21.7	5.6	11.2	4.7	21.3
RAIL.................	9 572	100.0	4.8	10.1	18.5	8.2	26.2	6.9	7.4	5.5	12.3
MOTOR CARRIER.........	2 255	100.0	2.4	13.0	17.6	4.7	27.2	5.8	8.7	6.2	14.4
PRIVATE TRUCK.........	7 089	100.0	5.5	7.2	11.4	2.7	14.0	3.0	17.2	3.2	35.7
AIR..................	-	100.0	-	4.0	7.7	1.3	23.0	.4	54.4	7.1	2.0
WATER................	97	100.0	-	1.1	-	-	13.5	65.1	-	-	20.3
OTHER................	7	100.0	.2	1.5	.8	.5	81.3	11.8	-	.5	3.5
UNKNOWN..............	60	100.0	.8	22.8	18.9	.5	13.2	.5	19.2	2.5	21.5

See footnotes at end of table 4.

TABLE 2. **TCC GROUP 243—Percent Distribution of Geographic Division of Origin and Means of Transport, by Geographic Division of Destination: 1972**—Continued

Geographic division of origin[1] and means of transport	Number	U.S. total	New England	Middle Atlantic	East North Central	West North Central	South Atlantic	East South Central	West South Central	Mountain	Pacific
TONS OF SHIPMENTS	(thousands of tons)										
MIDDLE ATLANTIC	402	100.0	16.0	63.2	6.0	.6	13.7	.1	.2	-	.1
RAIL	1	100.0	-	59.8	40.2	-	-	-	-	-	-
MOTOR CARRIER	40	100.0	5.8	71.6	2.7	1.9	14.8	.3	1.7	.4	.8
PRIVATE TRUCK	351	100.0	17.7	61.5	6.4	.3	14.0	.1	-	-	-
AIR	-	100.0	-	-	-	-	-	-	-	-	-
WATER	-	100.0	-	-	-	-	-	-	-	-	-
OTHER	-	100.0	23.0	26.5	32.8	9.2	7.5	-	-	1.0	-
UNKNOWN	9	100.0	-	100.0	-	-	-	-	-	-	-
EAST NORTH CENTRAL	1 792	100.0	1.6	12.0	54.5	6.9	14.2	5.1	4.4	.5	.9
RAIL	231	100.0	3.5	10.4	47.8	9.0	11.3	.6	9.1	2.7	5.7
MOTOR CARRIER	747	100.0	2.7	16.9	40.3	7.3	21.8	4.7	5.8	.3	.4
PRIVATE TRUCK	808	100.0	-	7.8	69.9	5.9	7.9	6.8	1.7	-	-
AIR	-	100.0	-	8.2	.2	.5	-	-	89.2	-	1.9
WATER	1	100.0	-	100.0	-	-	-	-	-	-	-
OTHER	-	100.0	12.6	6.3	65.9	-	.2	14.7	.3	-	-
UNKNOWN	3	100.0	-	11.5	20.4	8.8	50.0	7.7	-	-	1.8
SOUTH ATLANTIC	3 495	100.0	3.0	7.1	6.1	1.6	73.1	6.7	2.0	.2	.3
RAIL	1 879	100.0	3.8	8.0	4.2	2.4	69.5	8.4	3.1	.3	.5
MOTOR CARRIER	629	100.0	2.8	12.6	9.9	2.0	62.4	8.5	1.5	.2	.1
PRIVATE TRUCK	954	100.0	1.8	1.6	7.0	-	87.2	2.3	.1	-	-
AIR	-	100.0	-	-	-	-	-	-	82.9	17.1	-
WATER	12	100.0	-	-	-	-	100.0	-	-	-	-
OTHER	5	100.0	-	-	-	-	99.3	-	-	.1	.5
UNKNOWN	14	100.0	-	29.3	29.5	-	41.0	.1	-	-	-
EAST SOUTH CENTRAL	800	100.0	3.3	6.4	19.2	2.4	23.8	39.5	3.4	1.1	.7
RAIL	444	100.0	4.9	8.6	23.6	2.0	26.3	29.7	2.5	1.3	1.0
MOTOR CARRIER	92	100.0	3.7	9.0	14.6	4.2	34.5	20.5	8.8	3.4	1.2
PRIVATE TRUCK	200	100.0	.7	2.3	17.8	3.5	21.0	50.4	4.0	-	.2
AIR	-	100.0	-	55.6	-	-	44.4	-	-	-	-
WATER	63	100.0	-	-	-	-	-	100.0	-	-	-
OTHER	-	100.0	-	-	-	-	-	100.0	-	-	-
UNKNOWN	-	100.0	-	-	-	-	-	-	-	-	-
WEST SOUTH CENTRAL	2 575	100.0	.2	1.5	12.3	7.0	11.8	7.6	59.5	.2	-
RAIL	1 138	100.0	.3	3.3	27.2	13.1	25.6	12.4	18.1	.1	-
MOTOR CARRIER	199	100.0	-	.4	3.4	12.3	6.0	10.9	65.7	.7	.5
PRIVATE TRUCK	1 237	100.0	-	-	-	.6	-	2.6	96.6	.2	-
AIR	-	100.0	-	-	-	18.5	81.5	-	-	-	-
WATER	-	100.0	-	-	-	-	-	-	-	-	-
OTHER	-	100.0	-	-	-	-	100.0	-	-	-	-
UNKNOWN	-	100.0	-	-	-	-	-	-	-	-	-
MOUNTAIN	798	100.0	8.0	13.4	23.3	6.1	6.8	.9	3.9	34.3	3.1
RAIL	517	100.0	12.4	20.7	33.2	8.2	10.5	1.4	3.6	8.0	2.1
MOTOR CARRIER	97	100.0	-	-	2.0	3.9	-	.2	.2	87.2	6.4
PRIVATE TRUCK	164	100.0	-	-	4.1	1.8	-	-	.7	88.7	4.7
AIR	-	100.0	-	-	-	-	-	-	-	-	100.0
WATER	-	100.0	-	-	-	-	-	-	-	-	100.0
OTHER	-	100.0	-	-	-	-	-	-	-	-	-
UNKNOWN	18	100.0	-	-	28.6	-	-	-	63.2	8.2	-
PACIFIC	8 248	100.0	3.4	7.1	11.8	6.2	8.6	2.7	4.9	6.8	48.6
RAIL	5 262	100.0	5.3	11.1	18.4	9.6	13.4	4.2	7.5	8.9	21.6
MOTOR CARRIER	373	100.0	-	.1	1.6	.8	.1	.4	1.0	12.5	83.5
PRIVATE TRUCK	2 577	100.0	-	-	.1	.1	-	-	.1	1.9	97.9
AIR	-	100.0	.1	.5	13.6	1.4	38.0	.7	30.9	12.7	2.1
WATER	20	100.0	-	-	-	-	-	2.9	-	-	97.1
OTHER	-	100.0	-	-	-	.2	-	-	-	.1	99.8
UNKNOWN	15	100.0	3.2	-	8.3	.2	3.0	.4	-	-	85.0
TON-MILES OF SHIPMENTS	(millions of ton-miles)										
U.S. TOTAL	12 954	100.0	8.1	15.9	21.3	8.0	21.8	5.6	8.0	4.3	7.0
RAIL	11 009	100.0	8.7	16.5	22.2	8.5	22.5	5.6	7.2	3.8	4.9
MOTOR CARRIER	802	100.0	3.4	14.7	13.8	6.3	24.2	6.6	9.7	6.8	14.6
PRIVATE TRUCK	1 051	100.0	5.7	11.5	18.0	4.8	14.0	4.6	14.6	7.3	19.6
AIR	1	100.0	.1	2.2	10.7	.9	40.0	.5	39.9	3.3	2.4
WATER	53	100.0	-	1.0	-	-	5.5	7.5	-	-	86.0
OTHER	2	100.0	.3	.4	.9	.5	88.9	3.7	-	1.8	3.5
UNKNOWN	33	100.0	3.5	13.0	35.7	.7	7.7	.5	28.9	2.1	8.1

See footnotes at end of table 4.

TABLE 2. **TCC GROUP 243—Percent Distribution of Geographic Division of Origin and Means of Transport, by Geographic Division of Destination: 1972**—Continued

Geographic division of origin[1] and means of transport	Number	Percent distribution by division of destination									
		U.S. total	New England	Middle Atlantic	East North Central	West North Central	South Atlantic	East South Central	West South Central	Mountain	Pacific
TON-MILES OF SHIPMENTS	(millions of ton-miles)										
MIDDLE ATLANTIC.........	70	100.0	18.9	42.4	16.2	3.4	15.8	.6	1.4	.4	1.0
RAIL....................	-	100.0	-	-	-	43.1	56.9	-	-	-	-
MOTOR CARRIER..........	8	100.0	5.7	29.0	7.6	9.4	24.3	1.5	10.8	3.2	8.5
PRIVATE TRUCK..........	58	100.0	21.7	42.8	17.5	1.9	15.4	.5	.1	-	-
AIR....................	-	100.0	-	-	-	-	-	-	-	-	-
WATER..................	-	100.0	-	-	-	-	-	-	-	-	-
OTHER..................	-	100.0	18.6	9.0	40.3	25.3	3.2	-	-	3.7	-
UNKNOWN................	2	100.0	-	100.0	-	-	-	-	-	-	-
EAST NORTH CENTRAL......	618	100.0	3.2	17.4	24.8	8.3	24.3	4.8	11.3	1.4	4.5
RAIL....................	125	100.0	5.3	13.1	20.6	7.8	16.6	.7	13.5	5.1	17.1
MOTOR CARRIER..........	298	100.0	4.3	21.6	15.3	7.5	31.6	3.3	13.9	.7	1.8
PRIVATE TRUCK..........	192	100.0	-	13.4	42.4	10.0	18.0	9.8	6.0	.1	.3
AIR....................	-	100.0	-	6.0	.1	.3	-	-	89.7	-	3.9
WATER..................	-	100.0	-	100.0	-	-	-	-	-	-	-
OTHER..................	-	100.0	29.6	11.4	24.5	-	.8	32.9	.8	-	-
UNKNOWN................	1	100.0	-	19.4	15.1	11.7	45.2	2.3	-	-	6.2
SOUTH ATLANTIC..........	1 061	100.0	7.3	9.8	10.8	6.0	47.4	10.0	5.8	.9	2.0
RAIL....................	711	100.0	7.3	10.5	5.9	7.3	48.1	9.5	7.7	1.1	2.7
MOTOR CARRIER..........	187	100.0	4.7	11.5	20.8	5.9	36.2	15.5	3.3	.9	1.1
PRIVATE TRUCK..........	153	100.0	10.9	3.5	21.1	.3	57.8	6.2	.3	-	1.1
AIR....................	-	100.0	-	-	-	.3	-	-	80.9	19.1	-
WATER..................	1	100.0	-	-	-	-	100.0	-	-	-	-
OTHER..................	2	100.0	-	-	-	-	96.0	.1	-	.7	3.3
UNKNOWN................	4	100.0	-	41.2	41.9	-	16.9	-	-	-	-
EAST SOUTH CENTRAL......	368	100.0	8.4	12.6	27.0	2.2	27.4	15.0	2.3	2.2	3.0
RAIL....................	265	100.0	9.6	13.3	27.6	1.5	28.3	13.7	.8	2.0	3.1
MOTOR CARRIER..........	45	100.0	8.3	16.7	15.8	2.7	31.8	7.2	6.4	6.5	4.6
PRIVATE TRUCK..........	53	100.0	3.1	7.0	35.3	5.1	21.0	21.1	5.9	-	1.6
AIR....................	-	100.0	-	78.5	-	-	21.5	-	-	-	-
WATER..................	3	100.0	-	-	-	-	-	100.0	-	-	-
OTHER..................	-	100.0	-	-	-	-	-	100.0	-	-	-
UNKNOWN................	-	100.0	-	-	-	-	-	-	-	-	-
WEST SOUTH CENTRAL......	946	100.0	.7	6.0	24.2	8.6	29.1	8.4	22.3	.5	.2
RAIL....................	751	100.0	.9	7.4	30.0	9.5	35.7	8.7	7.6	.2	-
MOTOR CARRIER..........	49	100.0	-	2.3	5.7	15.0	15.0	13.9	41.3	3.2	3.5
PRIVATE TRUCK..........	145	100.0	-	-	-	1.6	.2	4.9	92.0	1.2	.1
AIR....................	-	100.0	-	-	-	8.8	91.2	-	-	-	-
WATER..................	-	100.0	-	-	-	-	-	-	-	-	-
OTHER..................	-	100.0	-	-	-	-	100.0	-	-	-	-
UNKNOWN................	-	100.0	-	-	-	-	-	-	-	-	-
MOUNTAIN................	908	100.0	15.6	24.0	30.3	5.7	10.7	1.2	3.1	7.5	1.7
RAIL....................	823	100.0	17.2	26.5	31.2	5.7	11.8	1.3	2.1	3.1	1.1
MOTOR CARRIER..........	29	100.0	.2	-	9.1	9.2	-	1.1	.7	63.5	16.1
PRIVATE TRUCK..........	37	100.0	-	-	22.9	5.6	-	-	2.6	64.2	4.6
AIR....................	-	100.0	-	-	-	-	-	-	-	-	100.0
WATER..................	-	100.0	-	-	-	-	-	-	-	-	100.0
OTHER..................	-	100.0	-	-	-	-	-	-	-	-	-
UNKNOWN................	17	100.0	-	-	41.7	-	-	-	54.4	3.9	-
PACIFIC.................	8 695	100.0	8.3	16.1	21.0	8.7	19.2	5.0	7.5	4.9	9.5
RAIL....................	8 256	100.0	8.7	16.9	21.9	9.0	20.2	5.2	7.8	4.5	5.8
MOTOR CARRIER..........	151	100.0	.2	.4	7.1	2.8	.8	1.8	3.4	17.8	65.8
PRIVATE TRUCK..........	232	100.0	-	.2	1.2	1.0	.1	-	1.6	10.2	85.7
AIR....................	-	100.0	.1	.7	14.5	.9	52.7	.7	24.2	4.4	1.8
WATER..................	46	100.0	-	-	-	-	3.1	-	-	-	96.9
OTHER..................	-	100.0	-	-	-	4.5	-	.1	-	1.5	93.9
UNKNOWN................	7	100.0	16.2	-	31.0	.6	14.6	1.7	-	-	35.8

See footnotes at end of table 4.

TABLE 3. TCC GROUP 243—Percent Distribution of Geographic Division of Destination and Means of Transport, by Geographic Division of Origin: 1972

Geographic division of destination and means of transport	Number	Percent distribution by division of origin[1]									
		U.S. total	New England	Middle Atlantic	East North Central	West North Central	South Atlantic	East South Central	West South Central	Mountain	Pacific
TONS OF SHIPMENTS	(thousands of tons)										
U.S. TOTAL	19 082	100.0	(D)	2.1	9.4	(D)	18.3	4.2	13.5	4.2	43.2
RAIL	9 572	100.0	(D)	-	2.4	(D)	19.6	4.6	11.9	5.4	55.0
MOTOR CARRIER	2 255	100.0	(D)	1.8	33.2	(D)	27.9	4.1	8.8	4.3	16.6
PRIVATE TRUCK	7 089	100.0	(D)	5.0	11.4	(D)	13.5	2.8	17.5	2.3	36.4
AIR	-	100.0	(D)	-	41.4	(D)	.1	.6	1.6	.1	56.2
WATER	97	100.0	(D)	-	1.1	(D)	12.9	65.1	-	.2	20.7
OTHER	7	100.0	(D)	.5	.4	(D)	81.8	11.7	-	-	3.1
UNKNOWN	60	100.0	(D)	15.2	5.4	(D)	23.8	-	-	30.5	25.2
NEW ENGLAND	907	100.0	(D)	7.1	3.1	(D)	11.7	2.9	.4	7.0	31.0
RAIL	461	100.0	(D)	-	1.7	(D)	15.4	4.7	.8	13.8	60.9
MOTOR CARRIER	53	100.0	(D)	4.4	37.3	(D)	32.9	6.4	-	-	.2
PRIVATE TRUCK	391	100.0	(D)	15.9	-	(D)	4.4	.4	-	-	-
AIR	-	100.0	(D)	-	-	(D)	-	-	-	-	100.0
WATER	-	100.0	(D)	-	-	(D)	-	-	-	-	-
OTHER	-	100.0	(D)	72.4	27.6	(D)	-	-	-	-	-
UNKNOWN	-	100.0	(D)	-	-	(D)	-	-	-	-	100.0
MIDDLE ATLANTIC	1 786	100.0	(D)	14.2	12.0	(D)	13.9	2.9	2.1	6.0	32.7
RAIL	966	100.0	(D)	-	2.5	(D)	15.5	4.0	3.8	11.1	60.3
MOTOR CARRIER	292	100.0	(D)	10.0	43.2	(D)	27.1	2.8	.3	-	.1
PRIVATE TRUCK	512	100.0	(D)	42.2	12.3	(D)	2.9	.9	-	-	-
AIR	-	100.0	(D)	-	84.1	(D)	-	8.6	-	-	7.4
WATER	1	100.0	(D)	-	100.0	(D)	-	-	-	-	-
OTHER	-	100.0	(D)	9.4	1.6	(D)	.3	-	-	-	-
UNKNOWN	13	100.0	(D)	66.7	2.7	(D)	30.6	-	-	-	-
EAST NORTH CENTRAL	2 986	100.0	(D)	.8	32.7	(D)	7.1	5.2	10.6	6.2	32.7
RAIL	1 770	100.0	(D)	-	6.3	(D)	4.5	5.9	17.5	9.7	54.6
MOTOR CARRIER	397	100.0	(D)	.3	75.7	(D)	15.6	3.4	1.7	.5	1.5
PRIVATE TRUCK	806	100.0	(D)	2.8	70.0	(D)	8.3	4.4	-	.8	.2
AIR	-	100.0	(D)	-	1.0	(D)	-	-	-	-	99.0
WATER	-	100.0	(D)	-	-	(D)	-	-	-	-	-
OTHER	-	100.0	(D)	21.3	29.8	(D)	-	-	-	-	-
UNKNOWN	11	100.0	(D)	-	5.8	(D)	37.1	-	-	46.1	11.0
WEST NORTH CENTRAL	1 076	100.0	(D)	.2	11.5	(D)	5.4	1.8	16.8	4.6	47.2
RAIL	781	100.0	(D)	.1	2.7	(D)	5.7	1.1	19.1	5.4	64.4
MOTOR CARRIER	106	100.0	(D)	.7	51.0	(D)	12.1	3.6	23.1	3.6	2.8
PRIVATE TRUCK	187	100.0	(D)	.6	25.5	(D)	.2	3.7	3.7	1.5	1.0
AIR	-	100.0	(D)	-	16.9	(D)	-	-	22.7	-	60.4
WATER	-	100.0	(D)	-	-	(D)	-	-	-	-	-
OTHER	-	100.0	(D)	10.6	-	(D)	-	-	-	-	1.1
UNKNOWN	-	100.0	(D)	-	91.4	(D)	-	-	-	-	8.6
SOUTH ATLANTIC	4 142	100.0	(D)	1.3	6.1	(D)	61.6	4.6	7.3	1.3	17.1
RAIL	2 512	100.0	(D)	-	1.0	(D)	52.0	4.7	11.6	2.2	28.1
MOTOR CARRIER	612	100.0	(D)	1.0	26.6	(D)	64.1	5.2	2.0	-	.1
PRIVATE TRUCK	990	100.0	(D)	5.0	6.4	(D)	83.9	4.2	-	-	-
AIR	-	100.0	(D)	-	-	(D)	-	1.2	5.8	-	93.0
WATER	13	100.0	(D)	-	-	(D)	95.6	-	-	-	4.4
OTHER	5	100.0	(D)	-	-	(D)	99.9	-	-	-	-
UNKNOWN	7	100.0	(D)	-	20.3	(D)	73.9	-	-	-	5.8
EAST SOUTH CENTRAL	1 071	100.0	(D)	.1	8.5	(D)	21.8	29.5	18.2	.7	20.5
RAIL	661	100.0	(D)	-	.2	(D)	23.9	20.0	21.3	1.1	33.0
MOTOR CARRIER	131	100.0	(D)	.1	26.6	(D)	40.9	14.4	16.5	.2	1.1
PRIVATE TRUCK	214	100.0	(D)	.2	25.6	(D)	10.4	47.0	15.0	-	-
AIR	-	100.0	(D)	-	-	(D)	-	-	-	-	100.0
WATER	63	100.0	(D)	-	-	(D)	-	100.0	-	-	-
OTHER	-	100.0	(D)	-	.5	(D)	.2	99.3	-	-	-
UNKNOWN	-	100.0	(D)	-	78.4	(D)	3.5	-	-	-	18.1
WEST SOUTH CENTRAL	2 141	100.0	(D)	-	3.7	(D)	3.2	1.3	71.6	1.5	18.8
RAIL	710	100.0	(D)	-	3.0	(D)	8.2	1.6	28.9	2.6	55.8
MOTOR CARRIER	196	100.0	(D)	.3	22.0	(D)	4.7	4.2	66.8	.1	1.9
PRIVATE TRUCK	1 221	100.0	(D)	-	1.1	(D)	.1	.7	97.8	.1	.2
AIR	-	100.0	(D)	-	67.9	(D)	.2	-	-	-	31.9
WATER	-	100.0	(D)	-	-	(D)	-	-	-	-	-
OTHER	-	100.0	(D)	-	11.2	(D)	88.8	-	-	-	-
UNKNOWN	11	100.0	(D)	-	-	(D)	-	-	-	100.0	-
MOUNTAIN	901	100.0	(D)	-	.9	(D)	.7	1.0	.5	30.4	62.4
RAIL	529	100.0	(D)	-	1.2	(D)	1.0	1.0	.2	7.8	88.1
MOTOR CARRIER	140	100.0	(D)	.1	1.4	(D)	.7	2.3	1.0	61.0	33.4
PRIVATE TRUCK	229	100.0	(D)	-	.1	(D)	-	-	1.0	63.5	21.0
AIR	-	100.0	(D)	-	-	(D)	.2	-	-	-	99.8
WATER	-	100.0	(D)	-	-	(D)	-	-	-	-	-
OTHER	-	100.0	(D)	1.2	-	(D)	21.6	-	-	-	.4
UNKNOWN	1	100.0	(D)	-	-	(D)	-	-	-	100.0	-
PACIFIC	4 069	100.0	(D)	-	.4	(D)	.2	.1	-	.6	98.5
RAIL	1 177	100.0	(D)	-	1.1	(D)	.7	.4	-	.9	96.7
MOTOR CARRIER	324	100.0	(D)	.1	.9	(D)	.3	-	.3	1.9	96.1
PRIVATE TRUCK	2 534	100.0	(D)	-	-	(D)	-	-	-	.3	99.5
AIR	-	100.0	(D)	-	38.7	(D)	-	-	-	3.3	58.0
WATER	19	100.0	(D)	-	-	(D)	-	-	-	.8	99.2
OTHER	-	100.0	(D)	-	-	(D)	11.8	-	-	-	88.2
UNKNOWN	12	100.0	(D)	-	.4	(D)	-	-	-	-	99.6

See footnotes at end of table 4.

TABLE 3. **TCC GROUP 243—Percent Distribution of Geographic Division of Destination and Means of Transport, by Geographic Division of Origin: 1972**—Continued

Geographic division of destination and means of transport	Number	Percent distribution by division of origin[1]									
		U.S. total	New England	Middle Atlantic	East North Central	West North Central	South Atlantic	East South Central	West South Central	Mountain	Pacific
TON-MILES OF SHIPMENTS	(millions of ton-miles)										
U.S. TOTAL	12 954	100.0	(D)	.5	4.8	(D)	8.2	2.8	7.3	7.0	67.1
RAIL	11 009	100.0	(D)	-	1.1	(D)	6.5	2.4	6.8	7.5	75.0
MOTOR CARRIER	802	100.0	(D)	1.0	37.2	(D)	23.4	5.6	6.2	3.7	18.8
PRIVATE TRUCK	1 051	100.0	(D)	5.6	18.3	(D)	14.6	5.1	13.8	3.5	22.1
AIR	1	100.0	(D)	-	24.5	(D)	.1	.3	1.2	.1	73.7
WATER	53	100.0	(D)	-	1.0	(D)	2.8	7.5	-	.9	87.8
OTHER	2	100.0	(D)	.7	.5	(D)	92.6	3.5	-	-	.5
UNKNOWN	33	100.0	(D)	6.1	4.5	(D)	14.4	-	-	53.2	21.7
NEW ENGLAND	1 048	100.0	(D)	1.3	1.9	(D)	7.4	2.9	.6	13.5	68.5
RAIL	960	100.0	(D)	-	.7	(D)	5.4	2.6	.7	14.7	74.6
MOTOR CARRIER	26	100.0	(D)	1.8	47.7	(D)	32.9	13.9	-	.2	1.0
PRIVATE TRUCK	59	100.0	(D)	21.4	-	(D)	28.0	2.7	-	-	-
AIR	-	100.0	(D)	-	-	(D)	-	-	-	-	100.0
WATER	-	100.0	(D)	-	-	(D)	-	-	-	-	-
OTHER	-	100.0	(D)	50.0	50.0	(D)	-	-	-	-	-
UNKNOWN	1	100.0	(D)	-	-	(D)	-	-	-	-	100.0
MIDDLE ATLANTIC	2 064	100.0	(D)	1.4	5.2	(D)	5.0	2.3	2.8	10.6	67.7
RAIL	1 820	100.0	(D)	-	.9	(D)	4.1	1.9	3.1	12.0	76.7
MOTOR CARRIER	118	100.0	(D)	2.0	54.5	(D)	18.3	6.4	1.0	-	.5
PRIVATE TRUCK	121	100.0	(D)	20.9	21.2	(D)	4.4	3.1	-	-	.5
AIR	-	100.0	(D)	-	66.2	(D)	-	10.6	-	-	23.2
WATER	-	100.0	(D)	-	100.0	(D)	-	-	-	-	-
OTHER	-	100.0	(D)	14.8	11.8	(D)	.7	-	-	-	-
UNKNOWN	4	100.0	(D)	47.4	6.8	(D)	45.8	-	-	-	-
EAST NORTH CENTRAL	2 757	100.0	(D)	.4	5.6	(D)	4.2	3.6	8.3	10.0	66.1
RAIL	2 446	100.0	(D)	-	1.1	(D)	1.7	3.0	9.2	10.5	73.8
MOTOR CARRIER	110	100.0	(D)	.6	41.4	(D)	35.3	6.5	2.6	2.5	9.6
PRIVATE TRUCK	188	100.0	(D)	5.5	43.2	(D)	17.2	10.0	-	4.5	1.4
AIR	-	100.0	(D)	-	.2	(D)	-	-	-	-	99.8
WATER	-	100.0	(D)	-	-	(D)	-	-	-	-	-
OTHER	-	100.0	(D)	34.2	13.1	(D)	-	-	-	-	-
UNKNOWN	12	100.0	(D)	-	1.9	(D)	16.9	-	-	62.2	18.9
WEST NORTH CENTRAL	1 038	100.0	(D)	.2	5.0	(D)	6.2	.8	7.8	5.0	72.5
RAIL	936	100.0	(D)	.1	1.0	(D)	5.6	.4	7.6	5.1	79.7
MOTOR CARRIER	50	100.0	(D)	1.5	44.0	(D)	21.9	2.4	14.7	5.4	8.3
PRIVATE TRUCK	50	100.0	(D)	2.2	38.1	(D)	.8	5.4	4.7	4.1	4.8
AIR	-	100.0	(D)	-	7.6	(D)	-	-	12.6	-	79.8
WATER	-	100.0	(D)	-	-	(D)	-	-	-	-	-
OTHER	-	100.0	(D)	39.2	-	(D)	-	-	-	-	4.9
UNKNOWN	-	100.0	(D)	-	79.6	(D)	-	-	-	-	20.4
SOUTH ATLANTIC	2 830	100.0	(D)	.4	5.3	(D)	17.8	3.6	9.7	3.4	59.1
RAIL	2 481	100.0	(D)	-	.8	(D)	13.8	3.0	10.8	3.9	67.2
MOTOR CARRIER	194	100.0	(D)	1.0	48.4	(D)	35.0	7.4	3.9	-	.6
PRIVATE TRUCK	146	100.0	(D)	6.2	23.6	(D)	60.4	7.7	.2	-	.1
AIR	-	100.0	(D)	-	-	(D)	-	.2	2.8	-	97.1
WATER	2	100.0	(D)	-	-	(D)	49.9	-	-	-	50.1
OTHER	1	100.0	(D)	-	-	(D)	100.0	-	-	-	-
UNKNOWN	2	100.0	(D)	-	26.8	(D)	31.7	-	-	-	41.5
EAST SOUTH CENTRAL	720	100.0	(D)	.1	4.1	(D)	14.7	7.6	11.0	1.6	60.3
RAIL	615	100.0	(D)	-	.1	(D)	10.9	5.9	10.6	1.8	70.2
MOTOR CARRIER	52	100.0	(D)	.2	18.7	(D)	55.3	6.2	13.1	.6	5.2
PRIVATE TRUCK	48	100.0	(D)	.6	39.2	(D)	19.7	23.4	14.7	-	-
AIR	-	100.0	(D)	-	-	(D)	-	-	-	-	100.0
WATER	3	100.0	(D)	-	-	(D)	-	100.0	-	-	-
OTHER	-	100.0	(D)	-	4.1	(D)	1.9	94.1	-	-	-
UNKNOWN	-	100.0	(D)	-	22.1	(D)	1.1	-	-	-	76.8
WEST SOUTH CENTRAL	1 033	100.0	(D)	.1	6.8	(D)	6.0	.8	20.4	2.7	63.1
RAIL	791	100.0	(D)	-	2.1	(D)	6.9	.3	7.2	2.2	81.3
MOTOR CARRIER	77	100.0	(D)	1.2	53.6	(D)	8.1	3.8	26.5	.3	6.6
PRIVATE TRUCK	153	100.0	(D)	.1	7.5	(D)	.3	2.0	87.0	.6	2.4
AIR	-	100.0	(D)	-	55.1	(D)	.3	-	-	-	44.7
WATER	-	100.0	(D)	-	-	(D)	-	-	-	-	-
OTHER	-	100.0	(D)	-	9.3	(D)	90.7	-	-	-	-
UNKNOWN	9	100.0	(D)	-	-	(D)	-	-	-	100.0	-
MOUNTAIN	552	100.0	(D)	-	1.6	(D)	1.7	1.5	.9	12.4	76.5
RAIL	420	100.0	(D)	-	1.5	(D)	1.8	1.3	.4	6.0	88.3
MOTOR CARRIER	54	100.0	(D)	.5	3.8	(D)	3.0	5.4	2.9	34.7	49.3
PRIVATE TRUCK	76	100.0	(D)	-	.1	(D)	-	-	2.3	31.1	31.1
AIR	-	100.0	(D)	-	-	(D)	.8	-	-	-	99.2
WATER	-	100.0	(D)	-	-	(D)	-	-	-	-	-
OTHER	-	100.0	(D)	1.5	-	(D)	34.6	-	-	-	.4
UNKNOWN	-	100.0	(D)	.1	-	(D)	-	-	-	99.9	-
PACIFIC	908	100.0	(D)	.1	3.0	(D)	2.3	1.2	.2	1.7	90.8
RAIL	536	100.0	(D)	-	4.0	(D)	3.5	1.5	-	1.6	89.0
MOTOR CARRIER	116	100.0	(D)	.6	4.6	(D)	1.8	1.8	1.5	4.1	85.2
PRIVATE TRUCK	206	100.0	(D)	-	.3	(D)	-	.4	.1	.8	96.6
AIR	-	100.0	(D)	-	39.7	(D)	-	-	-	5.7	54.6
WATER	45	100.0	(D)	-	-	(D)	-	-	-	1.1	98.9
OTHER	-	100.0	(D)	-	-	(D)	86.3	-	-	-	13.7
UNKNOWN	2	100.0	(D)	-	3.5	(D)	-	-	-	-	96.5

See footnotes at end of table 4.

TABLE 4. **TCC GROUP 243—Percent Distribution of Distance Shipped and Weight of Shipment, by Means of Transport: 1972**

Distance shipped and weight of shipment[2] [3]	Number	Percent distribution by means of transport							
		All means of transport	Rail	Motor carrier	Private truck	Air	Water	Other	Unknown
TONS OF SHIPMENTS	(thousands of tons)								
U.S. TOTAL..........	16 384	100.0	50.5	12.0	36.7	-	.5	-	.3
UNDER 100 MILES.........	4 220	100.0	9.3	9.5	79.5	-	1.5	.1	.2
UNDER 1000 POUNDS.....	61	100.0	.1	27.6	69.8	-	-	.2	2.3
1000 TO 9999 POUNDS...	427	100.0	.1	19.3	80.0	-	-	.6	.1
10000 TO 29999 POUNDS.	566	100.0	.1	12.3	87.5	-	-	-	.1
30000 TO 59999 POUNDS.	959	100.0	1.7	20.0	77.0	-	.9	-	.4
60000 TO 89999 POUNDS.	155	100.0	26.5	23.2	50.0	-	.2	-	-
90000 POUNDS AND OVER.	2 050	100.0	16.2	.2	80.9	-	2.7	-	-
100 TO 199 MILES........	2 416	100.0	19.1	14.2	66.5	-	-	-	.2
UNDER 1000 POUNDS.....	39	100.0	-	30.2	66.6	-	-	1.5	1.7
1000 TO 9999 POUNDS...	134	100.0	-	20.0	77.0	-	-	.4	2.7
10000 TO 29999 POUNDS.	385	100.0	1.4	10.0	88.6	-	-	-	-
30000 TO 59999 POUNDS.	640	100.0	2.9	38.0	59.1	-	-	-	-
60000 TO 89999 POUNDS.	114	100.0	55.3	17.8	26.8	-	-	-	-
90000 POUNDS AND OVER.	1 101	100.0	34.0	.2	65.8	-	-	-	-
200 TO 299 MILES........	1 296	100.0	45.9	17.2	36.2	-	.1	-	.7
UNDER 1000 POUNDS.....	22	100.0	-	50.1	49.9	-	-	-	-
1000 TO 9999 POUNDS...	76	100.0	.1	43.8	55.5	-	-	-	.6
10000 TO 29999 POUNDS.	124	100.0	2.3	33.2	64.5	-	-	-	-
30000 TO 59999 POUNDS.	462	100.0	1.4	27.7	70.9	-	-	-	-
60000 TO 89999 POUNDS.	61	100.0	92.7	.7	5.2	-	1.4	-	-
90000 POUNDS AND OVER.	549	100.0	96.1	1.5	.7	-	-	-	1.6
300 TO 499 MILES........	1 888	100.0	51.9	27.5	20.4	-	-	-	.2
UNDER 1000 POUNDS.....	18	100.0	.3	71.7	27.6	-	-	.3	.1
1000 TO 9999 POUNDS...	83	100.0	1.7	66.7	31.3	-	-	-	.3
10000 TO 29999 POUNDS.	135	100.0	17.2	51.2	30.7	-	-	-	.9
30000 TO 59999 POUNDS.	596	100.0	4.4	51.2	44.2	-	-	-	.3
60000 TO 89999 POUNDS.	240	100.0	62.9	31.9	5.2	-	-	-	-
90000 POUNDS AND OVER.	814	100.0	95.5	-	4.5	-	-	-	-
500 TO 999 MILES........	2 566	100.0	77.5	15.2	6.5	-	-	.1	.5
UNDER 1000 POUNDS.....	15	100.0	1.6	82.6	14.3	.5	-	.2	.7
1000 TO 9999 POUNDS...	69	100.0	3.4	61.3	28.4	.4	-	4.6	1.9
10000 TO 29999 POUNDS.	172	100.0	34.9	42.5	19.1	-	.6	-	2.9
30000 TO 59999 POUNDS.	399	100.0	25.6	47.1	25.8	-	-	-	1.5
60000 TO 89999 POUNDS.	355	100.0	89.7	7.5	2.4	-	-	-	.4
90000 POUNDS AND OVER.	1 554	100.0	96.9	3.1	-	-	-	-	-
1000 TO 1499 MILES......	823	100.0	90.8	6.0	2.5	-	-	-	.6
UNDER 1000 POUNDS.....	1	100.0	12.5	70.8	14.0	1.2	-	1.4	-
1000 TO 9999 POUNDS...	11	100.0	14.3	54.0	30.7	1.1	-	-	-
10000 TO 29999 POUNDS.	39	100.0	67.0	11.5	21.5	-	-	-	-
30000 TO 59999 POUNDS.	144	100.0	79.9	14.2	5.9	-	-	-	-
60000 TO 89999 POUNDS.	302	100.0	92.6	5.6	-	-	-	-	1.7
90000 POUNDS AND OVER.	324	100.0	100.0	-	-	-	-	-	-
1500 MILES OR OVER......	3 172	100.0	98.0	1.0	.4	-	.6	-	.1
UNDER 1000 POUNDS.....	2	100.0	6.2	70.3	10.9	1.9	9.9	.5	.4
1000 TO 9999 POUNDS...	16	100.0	26.7	62.8	3.7	1.0	5.4	.1	.3
10000 TO 29999 POUNDS.	34	100.0	76.7	3.8	2.6	-	16.7	-	.2
30000 TO 59999 POUNDS.	246	100.0	88.5	7.0	3.8	-	.8	-	.1
60000 TO 89999 POUNDS.	1 405	100.0	99.5	-	.1	-	.3	-	.1
90000 POUNDS AND OVER.	1 467	100.0	99.6	-	-	-	.3	-	.1
TON-MILES OF SHIPMENTS	(millions of ton-miles)								
U.S. TOTAL..........	11 119	100.0	85.3	6.6	7.3	-	.5	-	.3
UNDER 100 MILES.........	191	100.0	14.2	10.9	72.5	-	2.1	.1	.2
UNDER 1000 POUNDS.....	2	100.0	.1	29.3	67.0	-	-	.2	3.4
1000 TO 9999 POUNDS...	18	100.0	.1	21.9	77.1	-	-	.8	.1
10000 TO 29999 POUNDS.	28	100.0	-	12.6	87.3	-	-	-	.1
30000 TO 59999 POUNDS.	55	100.0	1.7	19.1	78.0	-	.7	-	.5
60000 TO 89999 POUNDS.	8	100.0	32.3	17.7	49.8	-	.2	-	-
90000 POUNDS AND OVER.	77	100.0	30.2	.3	64.9	-	4.7	-	-
100 TO 199 MILES........	356	100.0	18.1	14.0	67.7	-	-	-	.2
UNDER 1000 POUNDS.....	5	100.0	-	30.8	66.4	-	-	1.2	1.6
1000 TO 9999 POUNDS...	19	100.0	-	21.7	74.9	-	-	.3	3.0
10000 TO 29999 POUNDS.	55	100.0	1.4	10.0	88.5	-	-	-	-
30000 TO 59999 POUNDS.	91	100.0	2.8	38.3	59.0	-	-	-	-
60000 TO 89999 POUNDS.	16	100.0	53.3	18.3	28.4	-	-	-	-
90000 POUNDS AND OVER.	168	100.0	31.3	.2	68.5	-	-	-	-

See footnotes at end of table 4.

TABLE 4. **TCC GROUP 243—Percent Distribution of Distance Shipped and Weight of Shipment, by Means of Transport: 1972**—Continued

Distance shipped and weight of shipment [2] [3]	Number	Percent distribution by means of transport							
		All means of transport	Rail	Motor carrier	Private truck	Air	Water	Other	Unknown
TON-MILES OF SHIPMENTS	(millions of ton-miles)								
200 TO 299 MILES.........	317	100.0	45.0	17.3	36.9	-	.1	-	.7
UNDER 1000 POUNDS.....	5	100.0	-	50.6	49.4	-	-	-	-
1000 TO 9999 POUNDS...	18	100.0	.1	45.7	53.7	-	-	-	.5
10000 TO 29999 POUNDS.	29	100.0	2.4	34.8	62.8	-	-	-	-
30000 TO 59999 POUNDS.	117	100.0	1.4	26.8	71.8	-	-	-	-
60000 TO 89999 POUNDS.	15	100.0	93.4	.6	4.7	-	1.2	-	-
90000 POUNDS AND OVER.	131	100.0	96.1	1.5	.9	-	-	-	1.6
300 TO 499 MILES........	728	100.0	51.1	29.0	19.7	-	-	-	.2
UNDER 1000 POUNDS.....	7	100.0	.3	74.5	24.8	-	-	.3	.1
1000 TO 9999 POUNDS...	33	100.0	1.8	67.3	30.7	-	-	-	.3
10000 TO 29999 POUNDS.	52	100.0	18.0	50.5	30.5	-	-	-	1.0
30000 TO 59999 POUNDS.	235	100.0	4.4	54.2	41.1	-	-	-	.3
60000 TO 89999 POUNDS.	89	100.0	61.8	32.7	5.5	-	-	-	-
90000 POUNDS AND OVER.	310	100.0	95.5	-	4.5	-	-	-	-
500 TO 999 MILES........	1 822	100.0	77.9	15.0	6.3	-	-	.1	.6
UNDER 1000 POUNDS.....	10	100.0	1.7	82.5	14.2	.5	-	.2	.9
1000 TO 9999 POUNDS...	45	100.0	3.7	62.8	26.7	.5	-	3.8	2.5
10000 TO 29999 POUNDS.	119	100.0	37.5	40.4	18.1	-	.5	-	3.5
30000 TO 59999 POUNDS.	286	100.0	27.5	45.1	25.7	-	-	-	1.7
60000 TO 89999 POUNDS.	258	100.0	91.0	6.3	2.3	-	-	-	.5
90000 POUNDS AND OVER.	1 102	100.0	96.1	3.9	-	-	-	-	-
1000 TO 1499 MILES......	1 068	100.0	91.6	5.3	2.3	-	-	-	.7
UNDER 1000 POUNDS.....	1	100.0	14.6	69.2	13.6	1.2	-	1.3	-
1000 TO 9999 POUNDS...	14	100.0	14.0	53.3	31.5	1.2	-	-	-
10000 TO 29999 POUNDS.	49	100.0	67.3	11.3	21.4	-	-	-	-
30000 TO 59999 POUNDS.	186	100.0	82.8	12.2	5.0	-	-	-	-
60000 TO 89999 POUNDS.	405	100.0	93.3	4.8	-	-	-	-	1.8
90000 POUNDS AND OVER.	410	100.0	100.0	-	-	-	-	-	-
1500 MILES OR OVER......	6 633	100.0	97.7	1.1	.5	-	.7	-	.1
UNDER 1000 POUNDS.....	5	100.0	5.4	68.7	11.2	1.8	11.9	.5	.5
1000 TO 9999 POUNDS...	31	100.0	26.9	62.2	3.2	1.3	6.0	.2	.3
10000 TO 29999 POUNDS.	69	100.0	74.7	3.8	2.5	-	18.8	-	.2
30000 TO 59999 POUNDS.	501	100.0	85.2	8.7	5.1	-	1.0	-	-
60000 TO 89999 POUNDS.	2 931	100.0	99.4	-	.1	-	.4	-	.1
90000 POUNDS AND OVER.	3 093	100.0	99.5	-	-	-	.4	-	.1

Note: Detail may not add to total due to rounding. The introductory table shows the estimates of sampling variability for tons; sampling variability for ton-miles has not been estimated. See the map in the Introduction for the States comprising the geographic divisions of the United States.

Shipments excluded from the survey are those moving by pipeline (primarily petroleum products from refineries), parcel post shipments, and commodities moved by own power (motorized vehicles, aircraft, etc.) or towed (prefabricated buildings, etc.). Local shipments (commodities shipped less than 25 miles from the plant) and shipments within the same city are also excluded. Shipments to Alaska and Hawaii from the 48 conterminous States and the District of Columbia are included; however, no data were obtained for shipments originating in Alaska and Hawaii.

- Represents zero or rounds to zero.   (D) Withheld to avoid disclosing figures for individual companies.

[1]Production of this commodity is concentrated in the geographic divisions shown; figures and distributions for geographic divisions not shown are included in the total.

[2]Distances of shipments to foreign destinations are calculated only to the U.S. port of exit.

[3]Includes only shipments represented by bills of lading and invoices. Summary records which did not show individual weights of shipments are not included.

TCC 249. Miscellaneous Wood Products

Comparisons of Tons and Ton-Miles of Shipments for
Geographic Divisions of Origin and for Sampling Variability: 1972 and 1967

Geographic division of origin	Estimates				Relative sampling variability in tons (percent)	
	1972		1967		1972	1967
	Tons (thousands)	Ton-miles (millions)	Tons (thousands)	Ton-miles (millions)		
U.S. total	11,012	5,238	9,720	5,404	12.1	20.2
New England	160	123	324	94	42.3	(*)
Middle Atlantic	(D)	(D)	324	81	(*)	(*)
East North Central	1,530	414	1,417	473	32.9	(*)
West North Central	727	328	651	316	45.7	(*)
South Atlantic	1,230	314	2,454	391	42.7	(*)
East South Central	2,177	1,216	902	468	36.6	(*)
West South Central	1,193	355	1,293	366	41.4	(*)
Mountain	(D)	(D)	30	23	(*)	(*)
Pacific	3,247	2,419	2,325	3,192	23.9	(*)

(D) Withheld to avoid disclosing figures for individual companies.   (*) Data not published.

TABLE 1. TCC GROUP 249—Percent Distribution of Geographic Division of Origin and Distance Shipped, by Means of Transport: 1972

Geographic division of origin[1] and distance shipped[2]	Number	Percent distribution by means of transport							
		All means of transport	Rail	Motor carrier	Private truck	Air	Water	Other	Unknown
TONS OF SHIPMENTS	(thousands of tons)								
U.S. TOTAL..........	11 012	100.0	38.4	13.1	47.5	-	.2	.2	.6
NEW ENGLAND.............	160	100.0	29.5	59.6	7.6	-	-	3.1	.1
UNDER 100 MILES.......	11	100.0	-	78.2	14.6	-	-	7.2	-
100 TO 199 MILES......	23	100.0	-	68.6	26.5	-	-	5.0	-
200 TO 299 MILES......	13	100.0	38.9	54.7	-	-	-	5.2	-
300 TO 499 MILES......	26	100.0	-	82.8	16.0	-	-	1.2	1.2
500 TO 999 MILES......	43	100.0	45.0	53.3	-	.1	-	1.6	-
1000 TO 1499 MILES....	17	100.0	46.7	48.7	-	.1	-	4.6	-
1500 MILES OR OVER....	23	100.0	59.7	38.1	-	-	-	2.2	-
EAST NORTH CENTRAL......	1 530	100.0	23.7	11.8	64.1	-	-	.4	-
UNDER 100 MILES.......	905	100.0	12.0	2.5	85.0	-	-	.6	-
100 TO 199 MILES......	257	100.0	20.4	12.4	67.2	-	-	-	-
200 TO 299 MILES......	76	100.0	30.2	52.0	17.8	-	-	-	-
300 TO 499 MILES......	95	100.0	34.7	42.8	22.5	-	-	.1	-
500 TO 999 MILES......	85	100.0	51.4	44.7	3.4	.1	.2	.2	-
1000 TO 1499 MILES....	26	100.0	80.8	19.0	-	-	-	.3	-
1500 MILES OR OVER....	83	100.0	97.0	3.0	-	-	-	-	-
WEST NORTH CENTRAL......	727	100.0	53.4	2.6	44.0	-	-	-	-
UNDER 100 MILES.......	100	100.0	3.2	5.0	91.8	-	-	-	-
100 TO 199 MILES......	74	100.0	42.7	2.0	55.3	-	-	-	-
200 TO 299 MILES......	136	100.0	36.3	3.4	60.3	-	-	-	-
300 TO 499 MILES......	145	100.0	28.1	2.8	69.0	-	-	-	-
500 TO 999 MILES......	252	100.0	97.4	1.4	1.2	-	-	-	-
1000 TO 1499 MILES....	17	100.0	97.8	2.1	-	.1	-	-	-
1500 MILES OR OVER....	-	100.0	-	100.0	-	-	-	-	-
SOUTH ATLANTIC..........	1 230	100.0	15.5	12.5	71.8	-	-	.3	-
UNDER 100 MILES.......	245	100.0	-	10.7	88.4	-	.1	.9	-
100 TO 199 MILES......	212	100.0	2.7	21.7	75.6	-	-	-	-
200 TO 299 MILES......	447	100.0	12.8	7.1	80.1	-	-	-	-
300 TO 499 MILES......	265	100.0	40.9	12.2	46.5	-	-	.4	-
500 TO 999 MILES......	50	100.0	22.4	32.5	45.0	.2	-	-	-
1000 TO 1499 MILES....	1	100.0	65.2	34.8	-	-	-	-	-
1500 MILES OR OVER....	7	100.0	91.2	8.8	-	-	-	-	-
EAST SOUTH CENTRAL......	2 177	100.0	72.0	18.9	8.2	-	.1	-	.8
UNDER 100 MILES.......	207	100.0	20.8	20.5	58.6	-	-	-	-
100 TO 199 MILES......	120	100.0	46.6	29.6	21.3	-	-	-	2.6
200 TO 299 MILES......	156	100.0	51.3	40.8	7.8	-	-	-	-
300 TO 499 MILES......	463	100.0	62.5	34.6	1.5	-	.3	-	1.0
500 TO 999 MILES......	1 074	100.0	87.7	10.2	1.2	-	-	-	.9
1000 TO 1499 MILES....	124	100.0	99.9	.1	-	-	-	-	-
1500 MILES OR OVER....	32	100.0	99.4	.6	-	-	-	-	-
WEST SOUTH CENTRAL......	1 193	100.0	24.3	5.3	67.0	-	-	-	3.4
UNDER 100 MILES.......	318	100.0	1.8	5.9	84.0	-	.1	-	8.3
100 TO 199 MILES......	291	100.0	-	3.8	95.4	-	-	-	.8
200 TO 299 MILES......	166	100.0	24.0	3.7	70.8	-	-	-	1.4
300 TO 499 MILES......	194	100.0	29.8	4.5	61.2	-	-	-	4.6
500 TO 999 MILES......	186	100.0	82.4	8.9	8.7	-	-	-	-
1000 TO 1499 MILES....	35	100.0	92.7	5.1	2.2	-	-	-	-
1500 MILES OR OVER....	-	100.0	-	100.0	-	-	-	-	-
PACIFIC................	3 247	100.0	42.3	12.6	44.1	-	.8	.1	.1
UNDER 100 MILES.......	941	100.0	1.7	11.3	86.5	-	-	.1	.4
100 TO 199 MILES......	389	100.0	4.1	20.7	75.2	-	-	-	-
200 TO 299 MILES......	218	100.0	29.2	18.7	51.9	-	-	-	.3
300 TO 499 MILES......	182	100.0	46.4	19.0	34.5	-	-	-	-
500 TO 999 MILES......	564	100.0	68.1	8.1	23.8	-	-	-	-
1000 TO 1499 MILES....	139	100.0	82.9	11.2	3.1	-	-	2.8	-
1500 MILES OR OVER....	810	100.0	85.2	10.5	1.1	-	3.2	-	-
TON-MILES OF SHIPMENTS	(millions of ton-miles)								
U.S. TOTAL..........	5 238	100.0	70.7	12.4	15.2	-	1.3	.2	.3
NEW ENGLAND.............	123	100.0	48.6	47.0	1.8	-	-	2.6	-
UNDER 100 MILES.......	-	100.0	-	80.7	13.1	-	-	6.2	-
100 TO 199 MILES......	3	100.0	-	72.8	21.7	-	-	5.6	-
200 TO 299 MILES......	3	100.0	42.0	52.5	-	-	-	4.2	1.2
300 TO 499 MILES......	9	100.0	-	83.8	15.0	-	-	1.2	-
500 TO 999 MILES......	32	100.0	44.4	53.9	-	.1	-	1.5	-
1000 TO 1499 MILES....	20	100.0	47.2	47.7	-	.1	-	5.0	-
1500 MILES OR OVER....	52	100.0	64.3	33.5	-	-	-	2.2	-

See footnotes at end of table 4.

TABLE 1. **TCC GROUP 249**—Percent Distribution of Geographic Division of Origin and Distance Shipped, by Means of Transport: 1972—Continued

Geographic division of origin[1] and distance shipped[2]	Number	Percent distribution by means of transport							
		All means of transport	Rail	Motor carrier	Private truck	Air	Water	Other	Unknown
TON-MILES OF SHIPMENTS	(millions of ton-miles)								
EAST NORTH CENTRAL......	414	100.0	61.6	16.2	22.0	-	-	.1	-
UNDER 100 MILES.......	58	100.0	9.4	2.1	87.9	-	-	.5	-
100 TO 199 MILES......	37	100.0	20.4	11.3	68.3	-	-	-	-
200 TO 299 MILES......	18	100.0	30.9	53.0	16.0	-	-	-	-
300 TO 499 MILES......	40	100.0	37.9	39.9	22.1	-	-	.1	-
500 TO 999 MILES......	60	100.0	53.6	42.9	3.0	.1	.2	.2	-
1000 TO 1499 MILES....	31	100.0	82.7	17.1	-	-	.2	.2	-
1500 MILES OR OVER....	166	100.0	97.4	2.6	-	-	-	-	-
WEST NORTH CENTRAL......	328	100.0	76.7	1.8	21.4	-	-	-	-
UNDER 100 MILES.......	6	100.0	3.0	3.6	93.4	-	-	-	-
100 TO 199 MILES......	11	100.0	42.3	1.9	55.7	-	-	-	-
200 TO 299 MILES......	34	100.0	37.2	3.7	59.1	-	-	-	-
300 TO 499 MILES......	52	100.0	30.4	2.6	66.9	-	-	-	-
500 TO 999 MILES......	205	100.0	97.5	1.2	1.3	-	-	-	-
1000 TO 1499 MILES....;	18	100.0	97.6	2.2	-	.2	-	-	-
1500 MILES OR OVER....	-	100.0	-	100.0	-	-	-	-	-
SOUTH ATLANTIC..........	314	100.0	27.6	13.0	59.2	-	-	.2	-
UNDER 100 MILES.......	12	100.0	-	10.5	88.3	-	.1	1.1	-
100 TO 199 MILES......	34	100.0	2.4	21.0	76.6	-	-	-	-
200 TO 299 MILES......	112	100.0	14.3	6.9	78.7	-	-	-	-
300 TO 499 MILES......	106	100.0	44.5	11.3	43.9	-	-	.4	-
500 TO 999 MILES......	31	100.0	23.3	33.2	43.3	.2	-	-	-
1000 TO 1499 MILES....	1	100.0	65.1	34.9	-	-	-	-	-
1500 MILES OR OVER....	15	100.0	91.1	8.9	-	-	-	-	-
EAST SOUTH CENTRAL......	1 216	100.0	84.5	12.8	1.9	-	-	-	.8
UNDER 100 MILES.......	11	100.0	24.6	18.1	57.2	-	-	-	-
100 TO 199 MILES......	18	100.0	45.0	30.2	22.6	-	-	-	2.1
200 TO 299 MILES......	37	100.0	51.2	40.6	8.2	-	-	-	-
300 TO 499 MILES......	184	100.0	64.8	32.3	1.3	-	.3	-	1.3
500 TO 999 MILES......	770	100.0	88.9	9.4	.9	-	-	-	.8
1000 TO 1499 MILES....	137	100.0	99.9	.1	-	-	-	-	-
1500 MILES OR OVER....	56	100.0	99.4	.6	-	-	-	-	-
WEST SOUTH CENTRAL......	355	100.0	53.6	6.0	38.9	-	-	-	1.5
UNDER 100 MILES.......	18	100.0	2.3	4.2	86.9	-	.1	-	6.6
100 TO 199 MILES......	39	100.0	-	4.2	94.9	-	-	-	.9
200 TO 299 MILES......	38	100.0	25.0	3.9	69.5	-	-	-	1.5
300 TO 499 MILES......	77	100.0	31.4	5.2	59.6	-	-	-	3.8
500 TO 999 MILES......	136	100.0	85.2	7.7	7.1	-	-	-	-
1000 TO 1499 MILES....	42	100.0	92.9	4.7	2.4	-	-	-	-
1500 MILES OR OVER....	-	100.0	-	100.0	-	-	-	-	-
PACIFIC................	2 419	100.0	75.4	11.2	10.3	-	2.8	.2	-
UNDER 100 MILES.......	44	100.0	2.3	15.4	81.8	-	-	.2	.3
100 TO 199 MILES......	57	100.0	3.5	21.7	74.8	-	-	-	-
200 TO 299 MILES......	52	100.0	31.3	18.6	49.9	-	-	-	.3
300 TO 499 MILES......	71	100.0	45.7	17.5	36.8	-	-	-	-
500 TO 999 MILES......	426	100.0	69.2	8.2	22.6	-	-	-	-
1000 TO 1499 MILES....	187	100.0	82.3	11.5	3.2	-	-	3.0	-
1500 MILES OR OVER....	1 579	100.0	83.8	11.0	1.0	-	4.3	-	-

See footnotes at end of table 4.

TABLE 2. **TCC GROUP 249**—Percent Distribution of Geographic Division of Origin and Means of Transport, by Geographic Division of Destination: 1972

Geographic division of origin[1] and means of transport	Number	Percent distribution by division of destination									
		U.S. total	New England	Middle Atlantic	East North Central	West North Central	South Atlantic	East South Central	West South Central	Mountain	Pacific
TONS OF SHIPMENTS	(thousands of tons)										
U.S. TOTAL..............	11 012	100.0	1.7	14.4	25.5	8.4	11.4	5.5	10.8	3.5	19.0
RAIL...................	4 230	100.0	2.2	11.5	28.3	14.4	11.9	7.0	7.7	5.4	11.8
MOTOR CARRIER..........	1 440	100.0	3.9	13.1	22.0	7.0	13.1	9.1	9.7	4.4	17.8
PRIVATE TRUCK..........	5 236	100.0	.4	17.3	24.4	4.0	10.6	3.1	13.1	1.7	25.4
AIR....................	-	100.0	1.4	12.5	57.7	6.5	16.2	1.7	.2	.2	3.6
WATER.................	27	100.0	68.7	.5	-	-	.5	-	5.8	-	24.4
OTHER.................	18	100.0	5.4	16.8	32.2	2.5	14.2	-	22.8	.2	6.0
UNKNOWN..............	62	100.0	-	.2	11.4	8.0	3.9	16.1	53.3	.9	6.2

See footnotes at end of table 4.

TABLE 2. **TCC GROUP 249—Percent Distribution of Geographic Division of Origin and Means of Transport, by Geographic Division of Destination: 1972**—Continued

Geographic division of origin[1] and means of transport	Number	Percent distribution by division of destination									
		U.S. total	New England	Middle Atlantic	East North Central	West North Central	South Atlantic	East South Central	West South Central	Mountain	Pacific
TONS OF SHIPMENTS	(thousands of tons)										
NEW ENGLAND............	160	100.0	18.2	25.2	18.0	6.0	15.7	1.8	5.8	.9	8.5
RAIL....................	47	100.0	-	10.8	41.7	13.9	-	3.7	6.9	1.8	21.1
MOTOR CARRIER.........	95	100.0	23.6	32.4	8.8	2.8	21.4	1.1	5.9	.5	3.4
PRIVATE TRUCK.........	12	100.0	46.4	18.4	-	-	35.2	-	-	-	-
AIR....................	-	100.0	-	-	83.0	14.7	-	2.3	-	-	-
WATER.................	-	100.0	-	-	-	-	-	-	-	-	-
OTHER.................	5	100.0	19.9	37.9	12.6	7.7	8.5	-	6.9	.9	5.6
UNKNOWN...............	-	100.0	-	100.0	-	-	-	-	-	-	-
EAST NORTH CENTRAL......	1 530	100.0	1.4	4.9	77.5	1.7	4.9	1.5	1.6	1.0	5.4
RAIL....................	363	100.0	3.6	10.2	42.6	.5	12.7	-	4.5	3.7	22.2
MOTOR CARRIER.........	180	100.0	4.9	18.7	41.6	9.7	13.0	6.3	3.9	.6	1.3
PRIVATE TRUCK.........	980	100.0	-	.5	97.0	.6	.5	1.2	.2	-	-
AIR....................	-	100.0	4.2	7.5	68.7	14.6	4.4	-	-	-	.5
WATER.................	-	100.0	-	100.0	-	-	-	-	-	-	-
OTHER.................	5	100.0	.1	1.2	94.2	1.3	2.0	.1	1.1	-	-
UNKNOWN...............	-	100.0	-	-	-	-	-	100.0	-	-	-
WEST NORTH CENTRAL......	727	100.0	.4	15.0	33.6	28.3	12.2	2.7	7.6	.3	-
RAIL....................	388	100.0	.8	26.8	19.5	17.9	22.1	3.9	8.5	.4	-
MOTOR CARRIER.........	19	100.0	.1	12.7	38.4	40.4	3.1	1.0	3.1	1.0	.2
PRIVATE TRUCK.........	319	100.0	-	.8	50.5	40.2	.7	1.2	6.7	-	-
AIR....................	-	100.0	-	-	-	-	-	-	-	-	100.0
WATER.................	-	100.0	-	-	-	-	-	-	-	-	-
OTHER.................	-	100.0	-	6.7	42.8	42.4	-	-	8.1	-	-
UNKNOWN...............	-	100.0	-	-	-	-	-	-	-	-	-
SOUTH ATLANTIC..........	1 230	100.0	2.9	32.2	5.4	.2	57.5	1.0	.2	-	.6
RAIL....................	190	100.0	12.3	36.5	1.4	.6	44.1	1.4	.4	-	3.4
MOTOR CARRIER.........	153	100.0	1.8	29.3	2.4	.5	64.2	1.0	.3	.1	.4
PRIVATE TRUCK.........	882	100.0	1.1	31.8	6.8	-	59.2	.9	.2	-	-
AIR....................	-	100.0	-	-	-	-	100.0	-	-	-	-
WATER.................	-	100.0	-	-	-	-	100.0	-	-	-	-
OTHER.................	3	100.0	-	35.1	-	-	64.8	-	-	-	-
UNKNOWN...............	-	100.0	-	-	-	-	-	-	-	-	-
EAST SOUTH CENTRAL......	2 177	100.0	1.9	6.8	33.4	18.0	7.6	18.3	11.3	1.3	1.3
RAIL....................	1 567	100.0	2.7	9.1	34.3	21.9	7.2	11.8	9.5	1.8	1.8
MOTOR CARRIER.........	411	100.0	-	1.5	34.9	10.0	8.0	24.9	20.7	-	-
PRIVATE TRUCK.........	179	100.0	-	-	22.0	1.8	9.7	62.4	4.0	-	-
AIR....................	-	100.0	-	-	-	-	-	-	-	-	-
WATER.................	1	100.0	-	-	-	-	-	-	100.0	-	-
OTHER.................	-	100.0	-	-	21.2	-	78.8	-	-	-	-
UNKNOWN...............	17	100.0	-	-	40.4	28.3	13.8	-	17.5	-	-
WEST SOUTH CENTRAL......	1 193	100.0	-	2.0	8.7	7.9	7.6	7.8	65.8	-	.1
RAIL....................	289	100.0	-	8.1	15.6	7.1	30.4	15.9	22.9	-	-
MOTOR CARRIER.........	63	100.0	-	.2	3.1	16.9	3.7	17.2	57.6	.7	.6
PRIVATE TRUCK.........	799	100.0	-	-	7.1	7.9	-	3.3	81.5	-	-
AIR....................	-	100.0	-	-	-	85.1	-	-	14.9	-	-
WATER.................	-	100.0	-	-	-	-	-	-	100.0	-	-
OTHER.................	-	100.0	-	-	-	-	-	-	-	-	-
UNKNOWN...............	40	100.0	-	-	-	-	-	25.0	75.0	-	-
PACIFIC.................	3 247	100.0	1.3	3.2	13.0	5.8	2.7	1.5	1.9	10.3	60.3
RAIL....................	1 372	100.0	.7	7.4	25.8	12.0	6.2	3.4	4.0	13.3	27.3
MOTOR CARRIER.........	409	100.0	3.0	.9	15.7	3.9	.5	.3	.8	14.7	60.3
PRIVATE TRUCK.........	1 431	100.0	-	-	.3	.6	-	-	-	6.3	92.7
AIR....................	-	100.0	-	20.9	69.5	-	7.7	-	-	.4	1.5
WATER.................	25	100.0	73.8	-	-	-	-	-	-	-	26.2
OTHER.................	4	100.0	-	-	.5	-	-	-	82.3	-	17.2
UNKNOWN...............	4	100.0	-	-	-	-	-	-	-	12.3	87.7
TON-MILES OF SHIPMENTS	(millions of ton-miles)										
U.S. TOTAL.............	5 238	100.0	3.8	13.2	29.3	11.7	11.8	4.3	6.9	4.7	14.3
RAIL....................	3 704	100.0	2.7	14.1	30.3	13.4	12.2	4.5	5.4	4.6	12.8
MOTOR CARRIER.........	647	100.0	6.4	8.5	34.9	9.9	11.6	5.3	8.0	5.3	10.1
PRIVATE TRUCK.........	794	100.0	1.1	14.3	23.0	6.0	11.2	2.9	12.7	4.9	23.9
AIR....................	-	100.0	1.0	20.3	52.4	5.1	14.3	.8	.1	.1	5.8
WATER.................	68	100.0	73.8	.2	-	-	-	-	.8	-	25.2
OTHER.................	10	100.0	.7	8.1	8.3	5.0	6.5	-	61.7	.9	8.7
UNKNOWN...............	14	100.0	-	.3	33.7	18.2	8.1	22.3	15.4	1.0	1.0

See footnotes at end of table 4.

TABLE 2. **TCC GROUP 249—Percent Distribution of Geographic Division of Origin and Means of Transport, by Geographic Division of Destination: 1972**—Continued

Geographic division of origin[1] and means of transport	Number	Percent distribution by division of destination									
		U.S. total	New England	Middle Atlantic	East North Central	West North Central	South Atlantic	East South Central	West South Central	Mountain	Pacific
TON-MILES OF SHIPMENTS	(millions of ton-miles)										
NEW ENGLAND	123	100.0	2.6	9.9	17.5	8.8	14.9	2.7	12.3	2.4	28.8
RAIL	59	100.0	-	2.5	24.4	12.5	-	3.6	9.6	3.4	44.0
MOTOR CARRIER	57	100.0	4.6	17.2	11.2	5.1	28.5	2.0	15.5	1.5	14.6
PRIVATE TRUCK	2	100.0	21.5	14.5	-	-	64.1	-	-	-	-
AIR	-	100.0	-	-	72.6	23.9	-	3.5	-	-	-
WATER	-	100.0	-	-	-	-	-	-	-	-	-
OTHER	3	100.0	2.2	11.9	14.8	14.7	13.8	-	16.7	2.8	23.1
UNKNOWN	-	100.0	-	100.0	-	-	-	-	-	-	-
EAST NORTH CENTRAL	414	100.0	3.1	6.2	25.9	2.3	9.9	1.9	5.7	4.7	40.3
RAIL	254	100.0	2.8	4.0	4.8	.4	10.7	-	6.4	7.1	63.7
MOTOR CARRIER	67	100.0	8.4	20.5	19.0	10.8	17.2	6.2	9.5	2.0	6.3
PRIVATE TRUCK	91	100.0	-	1.3	89.9	1.5	2.3	4.1	1.0	2.0	6.3
AIR	-	100.0	12.7	18.9	18.4	42.4	4.6	-	-	-	3.0
WATER	-	100.0	-	100.0	-	-	-	-	-	-	-
OTHER	-	100.0	.7	6.7	59.6	6.6	14.4	.3	11.1	-	.7
UNKNOWN	-	100.0	-	-	-	-	-	100.0	-	-	-
WEST NORTH CENTRAL	328	100.0	1.0	30.5	23.5	12.3	23.0	3.6	5.5	.6	-
RAIL	252	100.0	1.3	38.1	11.9	8.7	29.5	4.2	5.6	.7	-
MOTOR CARRIER	6	100.0	.3	30.9	36.1	17.2	6.1	.6	3.9	-	1.2
PRIVATE TRUCK	70	100.0	-	3.3	63.7	24.7	1.3	1.7	5.2	3.8	-
AIR	-	100.0	-	-	-	-	-	-	-	-	100.0
WATER	-	100.0	-	-	-	-	-	-	-	-	-
OTHER	-	100.0	-	22.0	41.8	17.8	-	-	18.4	-	-
UNKNOWN	-	100.0	-	-	-	-	-	-	-	-	-
SOUTH ATLANTIC	314	100.0	5.3	39.2	6.0	.5	41.7	1.3	.8	.1	5.0
RAIL	86	100.0	11.9	33.5	1.8	1.0	33.6	.4	1.1	-	16.7
MOTOR CARRIER	40	100.0	2.4	26.6	4.3	1.9	58.0	1.6	1.3	.7	3.2
PRIVATE TRUCK	186	100.0	2.9	44.5	8.3	-	42.0	1.7	.6	-	-
AIR	-	100.0	-	-	-	-	100.0	-	-	-	-
WATER	-	100.0	-	-	-	-	100.0	-	-	-	-
OTHER	-	100.0	-	74.4	-	-	25.5	.1	-	-	-
UNKNOWN	-	100.0	-	-	-	-	-	-	-	-	-
EAST SOUTH CENTRAL	1 216	100.0	4.3	11.1	37.9	20.3	7.1	5.5	7.2	2.4	4.2
RAIL	1 027	100.0	5.1	12.7	36.8	21.7	6.3	3.9	5.7	2.9	4.9
MOTOR CARRIER	155	100.0	.1	3.1	45.4	13.3	9.2	12.3	16.3	-	.2
PRIVATE TRUCK	23	100.0	-	-	29.0	3.3	24.7	35.0	7.9	-	-
AIR	-	100.0	-	-	-	-	-	-	-	-	-
WATER	-	100.0	-	-	-	-	-	-	100.0	-	-
OTHER	-	100.0	-	-	30.0	-	70.0	-	-	-	-
UNKNOWN	9	100.0	-	-	53.7	29.0	13.0	-	4.4	-	-
WEST SOUTH CENTRAL	355	100.0	-	8.7	17.9	11.0	19.0	9.8	33.2	.1	.3
RAIL	190	100.0	-	15.9	20.1	9.0	34.4	10.8	9.9	-	-
MOTOR CARRIER	21	100.0	-	.8	6.4	32.0	9.1	26.2	20.3	2.0	3.2
PRIVATE TRUCK	138	100.0	-	.2	17.2	10.9	.2	4.0	67.1	-	.4
AIR	-	100.0	-	-	-	85.0	-	-	15.0	-	-
WATER	-	100.0	-	-	-	-	-	-	100.0	-	-
OTHER	-	100.0	-	-	-	-	-	-	-	-	-
UNKNOWN	5	100.0	-	-	-	-	-	63.7	36.3	-	-
PACIFIC	2 419	100.0	4.4	9.7	32.0	10.7	8.0	3.9	4.0	7.8	19.5
RAIL	1 824	100.0	1.4	12.4	35.2	12.3	10.4	5.0	4.7	6.6	12.0
MOTOR CARRIER	271	100.0	11.3	3.0	45.7	7.9	1.6	.9	1.7	10.9	17.0
PRIVATE TRUCK	249	100.0	.2	-	3.2	5.0	-	-	.1	15.5	75.9
AIR	-	100.0	-	24.9	62.8	-	10.3	-	-	.1	1.9
WATER	67	100.0	74.6	-	-	-	-	-	-	-	25.4
OTHER	5	100.0	-	-	.7	-	-	-	97.9	-	1.4
UNKNOWN	-	100.0	-	-	-	-	-	-	-	50.4	49.6

See footnotes at end of table 4.

TABLE 3. **TCC GROUP 249—Percent Distribution of Geographic Division of Destination and Means of Transport, by Geographic Division of Origin: 1972**

Geographic division of destination and means of transport	Number	Percent distribution by division of origin[1]									
		U.S. total	New England	Middle Atlantic	East North Central	West North Central	South Atlantic	East South Central	West South Central	Mountain	Pacific
TONS OF SHIPMENTS	(thousands of tons)										
U.S. TOTAL...............	11 012	100.0	1.5	(D)	13.9	6.6	11.2	19.8	10.8	(D)	29.5
RAIL.................	4 230	100.0	1.1	(D)	8.6	9.2	4.5	37.1	6.9	(D)	32.4
MOTOR CARRIER........	1 440	100.0	6.6	(D)	12.5	1.3	10.7	28.6	4.4	(D)	28.4
PRIVATE TRUCK........	5 236	100.0	.2	(D)	18.7	6.1	16.9	3.4	15.3	(D)	27.3
AIR.................	-	100.0	9.2	(D)	33.3	2.6	11.8	-	.4	(D)	39.0
WATER...............	27	100.0	-	(D)	.5	-	.5	5.1	.8	(D)	93.1
OTHER...............	18	100.0	26.6	(D)	30.4	.1	17.4	-	-	(D)	25.1
UNKNOWN.............	62	100.0	.2	(D)	-	-	-	28.1	64.5	(D)	7.1
NEW ENGLAND............	189	100.0	15.4	(D)	11.5	1.6	18.8	22.2	-	(D)	21.5
RAIL.................	91	100.0	-	(D)	14.3	3.3	25.7	46.0	-	(D)	10.6
MOTOR CARRIER........	55	100.0	40.4	(D)	15.7	-	5.0	.4	-	(D)	21.7
PRIVATE TRUCK........	22	100.0	25.0	(D)	-	-	41.2	-	-	(D)	.9
AIR.................	-	100.0	-	(D)	100.0	-	-	-	-	(D)	-
WATER...............	18	100.0	-	(D)	-	-	-	-	-	(D)	100.0
OTHER...............	1	100.0	98.4	(D)	.5	-	-	-	-	(D)	-
UNKNOWN.............	-	100.0	-	(D)	-	-	-	-	-	(D)	-
MIDDLE ATLANTIC.........	1 581	100.0	2.6	(D)	4.8	6.9	25.1	9.4	1.5	(D)	6.6
RAIL.................	484	100.0	1.1	(D)	7.6	21.5	14.3	29.3	4.8	(D)	20.9
MOTOR CARRIER........	188	100.0	16.4	(D)	17.9	1.3	23.9	3.2	.1	(D)	1.9
PRIVATE TRUCK........	905	100.0	.2	(D)	.5	.3	31.1	-	-	(D)	-
AIR.................	-	100.0	-	(D)	20.0	-	-	-	-	(D)	64.9
WATER...............	-	100.0	-	(D)	100.0	-	-	-	-	(D)	-
OTHER...............	3	100.0	60.1	(D)	2.1	-	36.4	-	-	(D)	-
UNKNOWN.............	-	100.0	100.0	(D)	-	-	-	-	-	(D)	-
EAST NORTH CENTRAL......	2 805	100.0	1.0	(D)	42.3	8.7	2.4	25.9	3.7	(D)	15.1
RAIL.................	1 196	100.0	1.6	(D)	12.9	6.3	.2	44.9	3.8	(D)	29.6
MOTOR CARRIER........	317	100.0	2.6	(D)	23.7	2.3	1.1	45.2	.6	(D)	20.2
PRIVATE TRUCK........	1 278	100.0	-	(D)	74.4	12.6	4.7	3.1	4.5	(D)	.3
AIR.................	-	100.0	13.3	(D)	39.7	-	-	-	-	(D)	47.0
WATER...............	-	100.0	-	(D)	-	-	-	-	-	(D)	-
OTHER...............	6	100.0	10.4	(D)	88.9	.1	-	-	-	(D)	.4
UNKNOWN.............	7	100.0	-	(D)	-	-	-	100.0	-	(D)	-
WEST NORTH CENTRAL......	923	100.0	1.0	(D)	2.8	22.3	.2	42.5	10.3	(D)	20.4
RAIL.................	607	100.0	1.1	(D)	.3	11.4	.2	56.5	3.4	(D)	27.0
MOTOR CARRIER........	100	100.0	2.7	(D)	17.4	7.8	.8	40.9	10.7	(D)	15.8
PRIVATE TRUCK........	209	100.0	-	(D)	3.0	61.1	-	1.5	30.3	(D)	3.9
AIR.................	-	100.0	20.7	(D)	74.3	-	-	-	4.9	(D)	-
WATER...............	-	100.0	-	(D)	-	-	-	-	-	(D)	-
OTHER...............	-	100.0	82.6	(D)	16.1	1.0	-	-	-	(D)	-
UNKNOWN.............	4	100.0	-	(D)	-	-	-	100.0	-	(D)	-
SOUTH ATLANTIC..........	1 250	100.0	2.0	(D)	5.9	7.1	56.6	13.2	7.3	(D)	7.0
RAIL.................	502	100.0	-	(D)	9.2	17.1	16.7	22.4	17.6	(D)	17.0
MOTOR CARRIER........	188	100.0	10.8	(D)	12.5	.3	52.4	17.4	1.2	(D)	1.1
PRIVATE TRUCK........	554	100.0	.8	(D)	.8	.4	94.2	3.1	.1	(D)	-
AIR.................	-	100.0	-	(D)	9.1	-	72.4	-	-	(D)	18.5
WATER...............	-	100.0	-	(D)	-	-	100.0	-	-	(D)	-
OTHER...............	2	100.0	15.9	(D)	4.4	-	79.4	.2	-	(D)	-
UNKNOWN.............	2	100.0	-	(D)	-	-	-	100.0	-	(D)	-
EAST SOUTH CENTRAL......	601	100.0	.5	(D)	3.9	3.2	2.0	66.4	15.6	(D)	7.9
RAIL.................	296	100.0	.6	(D)	-	5.2	.9	62.2	15.6	(D)	15.6
MOTOR CARRIER........	130	100.0	.8	(D)	8.7	.1	1.1	78.5	8.3	(D)	1.0
PRIVATE TRUCK........	163	100.0	-	(D)	7.4	2.4	4.9	68.2	16.1	(D)	-
AIR.................	-	100.0	12.7	(D)	-	-	-	-	-	(D)	-
WATER...............	-	100.0	-	(D)	-	-	-	-	-	(D)	-
OTHER...............	-	100.0	-	(D)	60.9	-	15.8	-	-	(D)	-
UNKNOWN.............	10	100.0	-	(D)	-	-	-	-	100.0	(D)	-
WEST SOUTH CENTRAL......	1 186	100.0	.8	(D)	2.1	4.6	.2	20.7	66.2	(D)	5.2
RAIL.................	323	100.0	1.0	(D)	5.1	10.2	.2	46.0	20.5	(D)	16.9
MOTOR CARRIER........	140	100.0	4.0	(D)	5.0	.4	.4	60.8	26.0	(D)	2.4
PRIVATE TRUCK........	683	100.0	-	(D)	.2	3.1	.2	1.1	95.3	(D)	-
AIR.................	-	100.0	-	(D)	-	-	-	-	32.0	(D)	-
WATER...............	1	100.0	-	(D)	-	-	-	86.7	13.3	(D)	-
OTHER...............	4	100.0	8.1	(D)	1.5	-	-	-	-	(D)	90.5
UNKNOWN.............	33	100.0	-	(D)	-	-	-	9.3	90.7	(D)	-
MOUNTAIN...............	382	100.0	.4	(D)	3.9	.5	.1	7.4	.1	(D)	87.4
RAIL.................	226	100.0	.4	(D)	6.0	.8	-	12.5	-	(D)	80.4
MOTOR CARRIER........	63	100.0	.7	(D)	1.8	.3	.3	-	.7	(D)	94.3
PRIVATE TRUCK........	90	100.0	-	(D)	-	-	-	-	-	(D)	100.0
AIR.................	-	100.0	-	(D)	-	-	-	-	-	(D)	100.0
WATER...............	-	100.0	-	(D)	-	-	-	-	-	(D)	-
OTHER...............	-	100.0	97.0	(D)	-	-	-	-	-	(D)	.7
UNKNOWN.............	-	100.0	-	(D)	-	-	-	-	-	(D)	100.0
PACIFIC................	2 095	100.0	.6	(D)	4.0	-	.3	1.4	-	(D)	93.5
RAIL.................	500	100.0	2.0	(D)	16.1	-	1.3	5.7	-	(D)	74.8
MOTOR CARRIER........	255	100.0	1.3	(D)	.9	-	.2	.1	.2	(D)	96.5
PRIVATE TRUCK........	1 327	100.0	-	(D)	-	-	-	-	-	(D)	100.0
AIR.................	-	100.0	-	(D)	4.5	71.3	-	-	-	(D)	16.0
WATER...............	6	100.0	-	(D)	-	-	-	-	-	(D)	100.0
OTHER...............	1	100.0	24.9	(D)	.2	-	-	-	-	(D)	72.4
UNKNOWN.............	3	100.0	-	(D)	-	-	-	-	-	(D)	100.0

See footnotes at end of table 4.

TABLE 3. TCC GROUP 249—Percent Distribution of Geographic Division of Destination and Means of Transport, by Geographic Division of Origin: 1972—Continued

Geographic division of destination and means of transport	Number	Percent distribution by division of origin[1]									
		U.S. total	New England	Middle Atlantic	East North Central	West North Central	South Atlantic	East South Central	West South Central	Mountain	Pacific
TON-MILES OF SHIPMENTS	(millions of ton-miles)										
U.S. TOTAL	5 238	100.0	2.3	(D)	7.9	6.3	6.0	23.2	6.8	(D)	46.2
RAIL	3 704	100.0	1.6	(D)	6.9	6.8	2.3	27.7	5.1	(D)	49.3
MOTOR CARRIER	647	100.0	8.9	(D)	10.4	.9	6.3	24.0	3.3	(D)	41.9
PRIVATE TRUCK	794	100.0	.3	(D)	11.5	8.9	23.4	3.0	17.4	(D)	31.4
AIR	-	100.0	6.5	(D)	8.0	3.6	6.4	-	.2	(D)	73.6
WATER	68	100.0	-	(D)	.2	-	-	.8	-	(D)	99.0
OTHER	10	100.0	31.1	(D)	5.4	-	5.4	-	-	(D)	57.1
UNKNOWN	14	100.0	.3	(D)	-	-	-	62.7	35.0	(D)	2.0
NEW ENGLAND	198	100.0	1.6	(D)	6.5	1.6	8.4	26.5	-	(D)	53.4
RAIL	98	100.0	-	(D)	7.3	3.3	10.5	53.5	-	(D)	25.4
MOTOR CARRIER	41	100.0	6.3	(D)	13.5	-	2.4	.4	-	(D)	73.3
PRIVATE TRUCK	8	100.0	5.5	(D)	-	-	61.9	-	-	(D)	6.2
AIR	-	100.0	-	(D)	100.0	-	-	-	-	(D)	-
WATER	50	100.0	-	(D)	-	-	-	-	-	(D)	100.0
OTHER	-	100.0	92.4	(D)	5.3	-	-	-	-	(D)	-
UNKNOWN	-	100.0	-	(D)	-	-	-	-	-	(D)	-
MIDDLE ATLANTIC	693	100.0	1.8	(D)	3.7	14.5	17.8	19.5	4.4	(D)	33.7
RAIL	523	100.0	.3	(D)	2.0	18.3	5.6	24.9	5.8	(D)	43.1
MOTOR CARRIER	55	100.0	18.0	(D)	25.0	3.4	19.6	8.8	.3	(D)	14.7
PRIVATE TRUCK	113	100.0	.3	(D)	1.0	2.1	72.9	-	.3	(D)	-
AIR	-	100.0	-	(D)	7.4	-	-	-	-	(D)	90.0
WATER	-	100.0	-	(D)	100.0	-	-	-	-	(D)	-
OTHER	-	100.0	45.6	(D)	4.5	.1	49.5	-	-	(D)	-
UNKNOWN	-	100.0	100.0	(D)	-	-	-	-	-	(D)	-
EAST NORTH CENTRAL	1 535	100.0	1.4	(D)	7.0	5.0	1.2	30.0	4.1	(D)	50.4
RAIL	1 120	100.0	1.3	(D)	1.1	2.7	.1	33.7	3.4	(D)	57.2
MOTOR CARRIER	225	100.0	2.9	(D)	5.7	1.0	.8	31.2	.6	(D)	54.9
PRIVATE TRUCK	182	100.0	-	(D)	44.8	24.6	8.5	3.7	13.0	(D)	4.4
AIR	-	100.0	9.0	(D)	2.8	-	-	-	-	(D)	88.2
WATER	-	100.0	-	(D)	-	-	-	-	-	(D)	-
OTHER	-	100.0	55.2	(D)	39.0	.2	-	.1	-	(D)	4.7
UNKNOWN	4	100.0	-	(D)	-	-	-	100.0	-	(D)	-
WEST NORTH CENTRAL	611	100.0	1.8	(D)	1.6	6.6	.3	40.4	6.4	(D)	42.3
RAIL	496	100.0	1.5	(D)	.2	4.4	.2	44.9	3.4	(D)	45.3
MOTOR CARRIER	63	100.0	4.6	(D)	11.4	1.6	1.2	32.3	10.7	(D)	33.5
PRIVATE TRUCK	47	100.0	-	(D)	2.8	36.8	-	1.7	31.9	(D)	26.4
AIR	-	100.0	30.7	(D)	66.8	-	-	-	2.6	(D)	-
WATER	-	100.0	-	(D)	-	-	-	-	-	(D)	-
OTHER	-	100.0	92.3	(D)	7.2	.1	-	-	-	(D)	-
UNKNOWN	2	100.0	-	(D)	-	-	-	100.0	-	(D)	-
SOUTH ATLANTIC	617	100.0	3.0	(D)	6.6	12.3	21.2	14.0	11.0	(D)	31.4
RAIL	450	100.0	-	(D)	6.0	16.5	6.5	14.4	14.5	(D)	42.1
MOTOR CARRIER	74	100.0	22.0	(D)	15.4	.5	31.5	19.0	2.6	(D)	5.7
PRIVATE TRUCK	89	100.0	1.6	(D)	2.3	1.0	87.5	6.5	.3	(D)	-
AIR	-	100.0	-	(D)	2.6	-	44.4	-	-	(D)	53.0
WATER	-	100.0	-	(D)	-	-	100.0	-	-	(D)	-
OTHER	-	100.0	66.1	(D)	12.1	-	21.4	.3	-	(D)	-
UNKNOWN	1	100.0	-	(D)	-	-	-	100.0	-	(D)	-
EAST SOUTH CENTRAL	226	100.0	1.4	(D)	3.5	5.3	1.8	29.6	15.4	(D)	41.8
RAIL	165	100.0	1.3	(D)	-	6.4	.2	24.0	12.5	(D)	55.6
MOTOR CARRIER	34	100.0	3.3	(D)	12.1	.1	1.9	55.3	16.2	(D)	7.3
PRIVATE TRUCK	23	100.0	-	(D)	16.0	5.3	13.5	35.6	23.7	(D)	.2
AIR	-	100.0	26.9	(D)	-	-	-	-	-	(D)	-
WATER	-	100.0	-	(D)	-	-	-	-	-	(D)	-
OTHER	-	100.0	-	(D)	49.7	-	9.6	-	-	(D)	-
UNKNOWN	3	100.0	-	(D)	-	-	-	-	100.0	(D)	-
WEST SOUTH CENTRAL	362	100.0	4.2	(D)	6.5	4.9	.7	24.0	32.5	(D)	26.7
RAIL	201	100.0	2.8	(D)	8.1	7.0	.5	29.4	9.3	(D)	42.9
MOTOR CARRIER	51	100.0	17.3	(D)	12.4	.5	1.0	48.9	8.3	(D)	8.9
PRIVATE TRUCK	100	100.0	-	(D)	.9	3.7	1.1	1.9	92.3	(D)	.2
AIR	-	100.0	-	(D)	-	-	-	-	16.3	(D)	-
WATER	-	100.0	-	(D)	-	-	-	97.6	2.4	(D)	-
OTHER	6	100.0	8.4	(D)	1.0	-	-	-	-	(D)	90.6
UNKNOWN	2	100.0	-	(D)	-	-	-	17.7	82.3	(D)	-
MOUNTAIN	245	100.0	1.2	(D)	7.9	.8	.1	12.1	.2	(D)	77.0
RAIL	171	100.0	1.2	(D)	10.5	1.0	-	17.3	-	(D)	70.0
MOTOR CARRIER	34	100.0	2.5	(D)	3.9	.7	.9	-	1.3	(D)	86.1
PRIVATE TRUCK	38	100.0	-	(D)	-	-	-	-	-	(D)	100.0
AIR	-	100.0	-	(D)	-	-	-	-	-	(D)	100.0
WATER	-	100.0	-	(D)	-	-	-	-	-	(D)	-
OTHER	-	100.0	97.9	(D)	-	-	-	-	-	(D)	.3
UNKNOWN	-	100.0	-	(D)	-	-	-	-	-	(D)	100.0
PACIFIC	749	100.0	4.7	(D)	22.3	-	2.1	6.8	.2	(D)	63.1
RAIL	475	100.0	5.5	(D)	34.2	-	3.0	10.7	-	(D)	46.2
MOTOR CARRIER	65	100.0	12.9	(D)	6.5	.1	2.0	.5	1.0	(D)	70.7
PRIVATE TRUCK	190	100.0	-	(D)	-	-	-	-	.3	(D)	99.7
AIR	-	100.0	-	(D)	4.1	61.4	-	-	-	(D)	24.3
WATER	17	100.0	-	(D)	-	-	-	-	-	(D)	100.0
OTHER	-	100.0	82.4	(D)	.4	-	-	-	-	(D)	9.0
UNKNOWN	-	100.0	-	(D)	-	-	-	-	-	(D)	100.0

See footnotes at end of table 4.

TABLE 4. **TCC GROUP 249**—Percent Distribution of Distance Shipped and Weight of Shipment, by Means of Transport: 1972

Distance shipped and weight of shipment [2] [3]	Number	Percent distribution by means of transport							
		All means of transport	Rail	Motor carrier	Private truck	Air	Water	Other	Unknown
TONS OF SHIPMENTS	(thousands of tons)								
U.S. TOTAL..........	9 885	100.0	37.5	13.5	47.9	-	.3	.2	.6
UNDER 100 MILES.........	2 814	100.0	6.2	9.2	83.4	-	-	.3	1.0
UNDER 1000 POUNDS.....	13	100.0	.1	41.0	53.0	-	-	5.9	-
1000 TO 9999 POUNDS...	234	100.0	-	9.9	88.3	-	.2	1.4	.3
10000 TO 29999 POUNDS.	634	100.0	.9	6.3	92.7	-	-	-	.1
30000 TO 59999 POUNDS.	1 295	100.0	.8	9.8	88.0	-	-	.4	1.1
60000 TO 89999 POUNDS.	204	100.0	55.8	25.7	18.5	-	-	-	-
90000 POUNDS AND OVER.	431	100.0	10.2	2.3	84.9	-	-	-	2.6
100 TO 199 MILES........	1 434	100.0	10.6	15.9	73.0	-	-	.1	.4
UNDER 1000 POUNDS.....	8	100.0	-	73.6	11.6	.2	-	14.5	-
1000 TO 9999 POUNDS...	59	100.0	-	47.3	52.7	-	-	-	-
10000 TO 29999 POUNDS.	270	100.0	1.8	19.5	78.3	-	-	-	.4
30000 TO 59999 POUNDS.	866	100.0	2.7	14.8	82.0	-	-	-	.5
60000 TO 89999 POUNDS.	102	100.0	86.1	-	13.9	-	-	-	-
90000 POUNDS AND OVER.	126	100.0	28.1	10.3	61.6	-	-	-	-
200 TO 299 MILES........	1 186	100.0	25.2	15.6	59.0	-	-	.1	.2
UNDER 1000 POUNDS.....	6	100.0	3.0	82.9	3.8	.2	-	10.0	-
1000 TO 9999 POUNDS...	26	100.0	.5	44.7	54.3	-	-	-	.6
10000 TO 29999 POUNDS.	84	100.0	2.5	34.5	61.7	-	-	-	1.3
30000 TO 59999 POUNDS.	727	100.0	4.4	16.9	78.5	-	-	-	.2
60000 TO 89999 POUNDS.	99	100.0	77.1	14.8	8.1	-	-	-	-
90000 POUNDS AND OVER.	241	100.0	77.7	-	22.3	-	-	-	-
300 TO 499 MILES........	1 296	100.0	43.0	21.9	33.9	-	.1	.1	1.1
UNDER 1000 POUNDS.....	5	100.0	-	88.0	5.0	.2	-	6.7	-
1000 TO 9999 POUNDS...	47	100.0	2.1	56.3	39.1	-	-	2.5	-
10000 TO 29999 POUNDS.	98	100.0	.7	48.6	50.7	-	-	-	-
30000 TO 59999 POUNDS.	634	100.0	11.2	32.1	54.6	-	-	-	2.2
60000 TO 89999 POUNDS.	166	100.0	88.9	-	11.1	-	-	-	-
90000 POUNDS AND OVER.	342	100.0	98.1	-	1.5	-	.4	-	-
500 TO 999 MILES........	1 984	100.0	77.3	12.4	9.7	-	-	-	.5
UNDER 1000 POUNDS.....	12	100.0	1.2	89.1	1.0	1.2	-	7.5	-
1000 TO 9999 POUNDS...	36	100.0	6.1	82.3	11.3	-	.4	-	-
10000 TO 29999 POUNDS.	53	100.0	6.9	63.5	29.7	-	-	-	-
30000 TO 59999 POUNDS.	493	100.0	33.9	34.2	31.3	-	-	-	.5
60000 TO 89999 POUNDS.	356	100.0	96.4	.7	2.8	-	-	-	-
90000 POUNDS AND OVER.	1 032	100.0	98.5	-	.8	-	-	-	.7
1000 TO 1499 MILES......	310	100.0	86.7	10.1	1.6	-	-	1.5	-
UNDER 1000 POUNDS.....	6	100.0	.1	85.3	.2	.3	-	14.0	-
1000 TO 9999 POUNDS...	8	100.0	3.4	86.8	9.8	-	-	-	-
10000 TO 29999 POUNDS.	7	100.0	31.8	61.9	6.2	-	-	-	-
30000 TO 59999 POUNDS.	55	100.0	60.3	25.9	6.8	-	-	7.0	-
60000 TO 89999 POUNDS.	74	100.0	100.0	-	-	-	-	-	-
90000 POUNDS AND OVER.	158	100.0	100.0	-	-	-	-	-	-
1500 MILES OR OVER......	862	100.0	84.4	11.5	1.0	-	3.0	.1	-
UNDER 1000 POUNDS.....	5	100.0	3.0	84.3	.3	1.5	1.8	9.3	-
1000 TO 9999 POUNDS...	17	100.0	14.4	83.2	1.2	1.1	-	-	-
10000 TO 29999 POUNDS.	39	100.0	71.3	20.6	-	-	8.1	-	-
30000 TO 59999 POUNDS.	154	100.0	48.9	43.5	5.4	-	2.2	-	-
60000 TO 89999 POUNDS.	168	100.0	100.0	-	-	-	-	-	-
90000 POUNDS AND OVER.	476	100.0	95.1	.9	-	-	4.0	-	-
TON-MILES OF SHIPMENTS	(millions of ton-miles)								
U.S. TOTAL..........	4 675	100.0	68.4	13.0	16.5	-	1.5	.2	.3
UNDER 100 MILES.........	158	100.0	6.2	9.0	83.6	-	-	.3	.8
UNDER 1000 POUNDS.....	-	100.0	.2	51.9	42.0	-	-	5.8	-
1000 TO 9999 POUNDS...	10	100.0	-	11.6	85.6	-	.2	2.2	.4
10000 TO 29999 POUNDS.	30	100.0	.1	8.2	91.4	-	-	-	.2
30000 TO 59999 POUNDS.	73	100.0	.5	8.5	89.7	-	-	.4	1.0
60000 TO 89999 POUNDS.	11	100.0	58.2	32.1	9.7	-	-	-	-
90000 POUNDS AND OVER.	31	100.0	8.0	.8	89.7	-	-	-	1.5
100 TO 199 MILES........	209	100.0	10.7	16.5	72.3	-	-	.1	.4
UNDER 1000 POUNDS.....	1	100.0	.1	73.8	9.9	.2	-	16.1	-
1000 TO 9999 POUNDS...	8	100.0	-	47.1	52.9	-	-	-	-
10000 TO 29999 POUNDS.	40	100.0	2.0	20.0	77.6	-	-	-	.4
30000 TO 59999 POUNDS.	122	100.0	2.6	15.8	81.1	-	-	-	.5
60000 TO 89999 POUNDS.	14	100.0	86.1	-	13.9	-	-	-	-
90000 POUNDS AND OVER.	21	100.0	26.2	10.1	63.6	-	-	-	-

See footnotes at end of table 4.

TABLE 4. **TCC GROUP 249—Percent Distribution of Distance Shipped and Weight of Shipment, by Means of Transport: 1972**—Continued

Distance shipped and weight of shipment[2][3]	Number	Percent distribution by means of transport							
		All means of transport	Rail	Motor carrier	Private truck	Air	Water	Other	Unknown
TON-MILES OF SHIPMENTS	(millions of ton-miles)								
200 TO 299 MILES.........	291	100.0	26.3	15.5	57.9	-	-	.1	.2
UNDER 1000 POUNDS.....	1	100.0	2.9	83.9	3.7	.2	-	9.2	-
1000 TO 9999 POUNDS...	6	100.0	.4	47.3	51.6	-	-	-	.7
10000 TO 29999 POUNDS.	21	100.0	2.7	35.4	60.4	-	-	-	1.4
30000 TO 59999 POUNDS.	175	100.0	4.6	16.9	78.4	-	-	-	.2
60000 TO 89999 POUNDS.	24	100.0	77.7	14.2	8.1	-	-	-	-
90000 POUNDS AND OVER.	61	100.0	79.9	-	20.1	-	-	-	-
300 TO 499 MILES.........	508	100.0	45.1	20.8	32.8	-	.1	.1	1.1
UNDER 1000 POUNDS.....	2	100.0	-	88.4	5.1	.3	-	6.2	-
1000 TO 9999 POUNDS...	18	100.0	2.6	54.7	40.4	-	-	2.3	-
10000 TO 29999 POUNDS.	37	100.0	.7	48.3	51.0	-	-	-	-
30000 TO 59999 POUNDS.	242	100.0	12.5	31.2	54.1	-	-	-	2.2
60000 TO 89999 POUNDS.	66	100.0	88.7	-	11.3	-	-	-	-
90000 POUNDS AND OVER.	141	100.0	98.4	-	1.2	-	.4	-	-
500 TO 999 MILES.........	1 446	100.0	78.6	11.7	9.2	-	-	-	.4
UNDER 1000 POUNDS.....	9	100.0	1.1	89.8	1.0	1.0	-	7.1	-
1000 TO 9999 POUNDS...	26	100.0	5.3	83.6	10.6	-	.5	-	-
10000 TO 29999 POUNDS.	35	100.0	6.9	64.3	28.9	-	-	-	-
30000 TO 59999 POUNDS.	347	100.0	35.7	33.0	30.8	-	-	-	.4
60000 TO 89999 POUNDS.	261	100.0	96.3	.8	2.9	-	-	-	-
90000 POUNDS AND OVER.	766	100.0	98.8	-	.6	-	-	-	.6
1000 TO 1499 MILES......	377	100.0	86.1	10.3	1.8	-	-	1.8	-
UNDER 1000 POUNDS.....	7	100.0	.1	84.3	.2	.4	-	15.0	-
1000 TO 9999 POUNDS...	9	100.0	3.8	85.1	11.1	-	-	-	-
10000 TO 29999 POUNDS.	8	100.0	29.9	62.9	7.1	-	-	-	-
30000 TO 59999 POUNDS.	69	100.0	57.3	27.1	7.5	-	-	8.2	-
60000 TO 89999 POUNDS.	90	100.0	100.0	-	-	-	-	-	-
90000 POUNDS AND OVER.	191	100.0	100.0	-	-	-	-	-	-
1500 MILES OR OVER......	1 685	100.0	83.0	11.9	.9	-	4.0	.1	-
UNDER 1000 POUNDS.....	12	100.0	2.7	83.8	.3	1.7	1.8	9.7	-
1000 TO 9999 POUNDS...	36	100.0	13.9	83.6	1.5	1.0	-	-	-
10000 TO 29999 POUNDS.	86	100.0	72.5	17.8	-	-	9.7	-	-
30000 TO 59999 POUNDS.	306	100.0	48.8	43.7	4.7	-	2.8	-	-
60000 TO 89999 POUNDS.	318	100.0	100.0	-	-	-	-	-	-
90000 POUNDS AND OVER.	924	100.0	93.4	1.2	-	-	5.4	-	-

Note: Detail may not add to total due to rounding. The introductory table shows the estimates of sampling variability for tons; sampling variability for ton-miles has not been estimated. See the map in the Introduction for the States comprising the geographic divisions of the United States.

Shipments excluded from the survey are those moving by pipeline (primarily petroleum products from refineries), parcel post shipments, and commodities moved by own power (motorized vehicles, aircraft, etc.) or towed (prefabricated buildings, etc.). Local shipments (commodities shipped less than 25 miles from the plant) and shipments within the same city are also excluded. Shipments to Alaska and Hawaii from the 48 conterminous States and the District of Columbia are included; however, no data were obtained for shipments originating in Alaska and Hawaii.

- Represents zero or rounds to zero.   (D) Withheld to avoid disclosing figures for individual companies.

[1]Production of this commodity is concentrated in the geographic divisions shown; figures and distributions for geographic divisions not shown are included in the total.

[2]Distances of shipments to foreign destinations are calculated only to the U.S. port of exit.

[3]Includes only shipments represented by bills of lading and invoices. Summary records which did not show individual weights of shipments are not included.

TCC 251. Household and Office Furniture

Comparisons of Tons and Ton-Miles of Shipments for
Geographic Divisions of Origin and for Sampling Variability: 1972 and 1967

Geographic division of origin	Estimates				Relative sampling variability in tons (percent)	
	1972		1967		1972	1967
	Tons (thousands)	Ton-miles (millions)	Tons (thousands)	Ton-miles (millions)	1972	1967
U.S. total	7,750	3,989	4,604	2,306	15.2	11.2
New England	(D)	(D)	155	71	(*)	(*)
Middle Atlantic	552	200	779	318	20.5	(*)
East North Central	1,185	536	976	423	15.9	(*)
West North Central	302	199	113	58	45.8	(*)
South Atlantic	2,986	1,707	1,190	643	34.3	(*)
East South Central	1,480	887	415	211	36.2	(*)
West South Central	284	173	348	207	30.0	(*)
Mountain	(D)	(D)	16	3	(*)	(*)
Pacific	439	196	612	372	13.2	(*)

(D) Withheld to avoid disclosing figures for individual companies.   (*) Data not published.

TABLE 1. TCC GROUP 251—Percent Distribution of Geographic Division of Origin and Distance Shipped, by Means of Transport: 1972

Geographic division of origin[1] and distance shipped[2]	Number	Percent distribution by means of transport							
		All means of transport	Rail	Motor carrier	Private truck	Air	Water	Other	Unknown
TONS OF SHIPMENTS	(thousands of tons)								
U.S. TOTAL..........	7 750	100.0	26.9	30.5	42.0	-	-	.4	.1
MIDDLE ATLANTIC.........	552	100.0	14.9	42.8	41.9	-	-	.3	.1
UNDER 100 MILES.......	184	100.0	.7	31.3	67.8	-	-	.1	.1
100 TO 199 MILES......	124	100.0	14.3	33.4	52.2	-	-	.1	-
200 TO 299 MILES......	59	100.0	18.6	50.1	31.1	-	-	.1	-
300 TO 499 MILES......	57	100.0	26.2	42.3	31.3	-	-	.2	-
500 TO 999 MILES......	67	100.0	42.8	55.1	1.9	-	-	.2	-
1000 TO 1499 MILES....	42	100.0	12.6	78.5	8.5	-	.2	.1	.1
1500 MILES OR OVER....	16	100.0	17.6	74.6	.5	.5	-	5.4	1.3
EAST NORTH CENTRAL......	1 185	100.0	24.4	38.0	37.0	-	-	.4	.2
UNDER 100 MILES.......	253	100.0	1.5	34.0	62.9	-	-	1.2	.4
100 TO 199 MILES......	127	100.0	19.2	27.8	52.5	-	-	.6	-
200 TO 299 MILES......	201	100.0	14.5	43.9	41.3	-	-	.1	.1
300 TO 499 MILES......	182	100.0	20.8	48.7	30.2	-	-	.2	-
500 TO 999 MILES......	300	100.0	39.3	36.9	23.5	-	-	.1	.1
1000 TO 1499 MILES....	54	100.0	43.8	54.8	1.4	.1	-	.1	-
1500 MILES OR OVER....	63	100.0	80.0	16.1	3.8	-	-	.1	-
WEST NORTH CENTRAL......	302	100.0	50.0	25.4	22.0	-	-	1.6	1.0
UNDER 100 MILES.......	21	100.0	-	37.6	55.7	-	-	.4	6.4
100 TO 199 MILES......	29	100.0	38.1	16.5	41.7	-	-	-	3.7
200 TO 299 MILES......	41	100.0	17.3	49.0	33.1	-	-	.1	.5
300 TO 499 MILES......	64	100.0	51.5	22.5	25.3	-	-	.2	.5
500 TO 999 MILES......	74	100.0	53.2	30.4	12.1	-	-	4.3	-
1000 TO 1499 MILES....	23	100.0	65.3	19.9	9.8	.1	-	4.9	-
1500 MILES OR OVER....	48	100.0	92.8	4.0	2.3	-	-	.9	-
SOUTH ATLANTIC..........	2 986	100.0	38.0	25.6	36.2	-	-	.2	-
UNDER 100 MILES.......	301	100.0	4.7	12.1	82.7	-	-	.3	.2
100 TO 199 MILES......	186	100.0	5.5	29.8	64.3	-	-	.3	.1
200 TO 299 MILES......	252	100.0	31.4	38.5	30.0	-	-	.1	-
300 TO 499 MILES......	973	100.0	41.4	34.5	24.0	-	-	.1	-
500 TO 999 MILES......	972	100.0	39.0	20.9	39.9	-	-	.1	-
1000 TO 1499 MILES....	64	100.0	76.2	5.7	16.5	.1	-	1.5	-
1500 MILES OR OVER....	235	100.0	84.7	13.5	1.5	-	-	.3	.1
EAST SOUTH CENTRAL......	1 480	100.0	19.0	37.0	43.9	-	-	.1	-
UNDER 100 MILES.......	101	100.0	2.5	30.1	67.4	-	-	-	-
100 TO 199 MILES......	103	100.0	13.5	29.3	57.2	-	-	-	-
200 TO 299 MILES......	228	100.0	3.2	66.8	29.9	-	-	-	-
300 TO 499 MILES......	355	100.0	11.8	36.1	52.0	-	-	.1	-
500 TO 999 MILES......	499	100.0	20.3	32.6	46.9	-	-	.2	-
1000 TO 1499 MILES....	75	100.0	37.9	17.7	44.4	-	-	-	-
1500 MILES OR OVER....	117	100.0	73.0	25.4	1.3	.2	-	-	-
WEST SOUTH CENTRAL......	284	100.0	14.9	16.8	64.4	-	-	3.8	.1
UNDER 100 MILES.......	17	100.0	4.9	10.9	81.2	-	-	3.0	-
100 TO 199 MILES......	32	100.0	-	16.5	73.5	-	-	9.8	.1
200 TO 299 MILES......	26	100.0	5.5	10.9	78.4	-	-	5.2	-
300 TO 499 MILES......	58	100.0	9.9	17.2	66.5	-	-	6.4	-
500 TO 999 MILES......	103	100.0	23.9	15.0	59.1	-	-	2.0	-
1000 TO 1499 MILES....	36	100.0	21.9	30.7	46.7	-	-	-	.7
1500 MILES OR OVER....	8	100.0	15.0	7.4	77.7	-	-	-	-
PACIFIC.................	439	100.0	20.5	30.2	47.8	-	.7	.3	.5
UNDER 100 MILES.......	180	100.0	.4	15.0	84.1	-	-	.4	.2
100 TO 199 MILES......	37	100.0	.1	38.8	60.1	-	-	.6	.4
200 TO 299 MILES......	17	100.0	-	58.7	35.0	-	-	.7	5.6
300 TO 499 MILES......	67	100.0	6.0	63.7	29.3	-	-	.2	.8
500 TO 999 MILES......	77	100.0	60.0	29.8	9.9	-	-	.2	-
1000 TO 1499 MILES....	29	100.0	80.3	16.3	3.2	-	-	-	.2
1500 MILES OR OVER....	29	100.0	52.9	34.0	1.7	.5	10.6	.3	-
TON-MILES OF SHIPMENTS	(millions of ton-miles)								
U.S. TOTAL..........	3 989	100.0	44.3	28.5	26.5	-	.2	.4	.1
MIDDLE ATLANTIC.........	200	100.0	24.0	58.5	16.0	.1	.1	1.1	.3
UNDER 100 MILES.......	9	100.0	1.1	34.3	64.5	-	-	.1	-
100 TO 199 MILES......	18	100.0	14.7	33.7	51.5	-	-	.1	-
200 TO 299 MILES......	14	100.0	18.8	50.9	30.1	-	-	.1	-
300 TO 499 MILES......	22	100.0	27.6	42.6	29.6	-	-	.2	-
500 TO 999 MILES......	50	100.0	45.8	52.3	1.8	-	-	.2	-
1000 TO 1499 MILES....	47	100.0	13.9	77.1	8.6	-	.3	.1	.1
1500 MILES OR OVER....	36	100.0	17.4	74.7	.4	.4	-	5.7	1.4

See footnotes at end of table 4.

TABLE 1. **TCC GROUP 251—Percent Distribution of Geographic Division of Origin and Distance Shipped, by Means of Transport: 1972**—Continued

Geographic division of origin[1] and distance shipped[2]	Number	Percent distribution by means of transport							
		All means of transport	Rail	Motor carrier	Private truck	Air	Water	Other	Unknown
TON-MILES OF SHIPMENTS	(millions of ton-miles)								
EAST NORTH CENTRAL......	536	100.0	43.0	36.0	20.7	-	-	.2	.1
UNDER 100 MILES.......	12	100.0	1.2	33.5	63.0	-	-	1.9	.4
100 TO 199 MILES......	18	100.0	17.3	28.0	54.0	-	-	.6	-
200 TO 299 MILES......	50	100.0	14.6	43.6	41.6	-	-	.1	.1
300 TO 499 MILES......	70	100.0	21.6	48.7	29.4	-	-	.2	-
500 TO 999 MILES......	203	100.0	41.1	35.9	22.8	-	-	.1	.1
1000 TO 1499 MILES....	65	100.0	43.6	55.1	1.2	.1	-	.1	-
1500 MILES OR OVER....	115	100.0	80.0	16.1	3.7	-	-	.2	-
WEST NORTH CENTRAL......	199	100.0	67.8	18.4	11.3	-	-	2.3	.2
UNDER 100 MILES.......	-	100.0	-	14.6	82.0	-	-	.7	2.7
100 TO 199 MILES......	4	100.0	40.2	16.4	39.3	-	-	-	4.1
200 TO 299 MILES......	10	100.0	17.1	48.8	33.6	-	-	.1	.5
300 TO 499 MILES......	27	100.0	53.4	22.5	23.5	-	-	.2	.5
500 TO 999 MILES......	49	100.0	49.9	32.9	12.1	-	-	5.0	.1
1000 TO 1499 MILES....	25	100.0	64.7	20.3	10.1	.1	-	4.8	-
1500 MILES OR OVER....	81	100.0	93.0	4.0	2.2	-	-	.9	-
SOUTH ATLANTIC..........	1 707	100.0	54.6	21.0	24.1	-	-	.2	-
UNDER 100 MILES.......	13	100.0	9.4	16.0	74.2	-	-	.2	.2
100 TO 199 MILES......	28	100.0	5.1	30.1	64.4	-	-	.3	.1
200 TO 299 MILES......	63	100.0	32.4	38.0	29.5	-	-	.1	-
300 TO 499 MILES......	408	100.0	44.8	32.1	23.0	-	-	.1	-
500 TO 999 MILES......	636	100.0	40.7	20.1	39.1	-	-	.1	-
1000 TO 1499 MILES....	74	100.0	75.7	5.7	16.8	.1	-	1.7	-
1500 MILES OR OVER....	481	100.0	85.4	12.6	1.6	-	-	.3	.1
EAST SOUTH CENTRAL......	887	100.0	31.6	34.3	33.9	.1	-	.1	-
UNDER 100 MILES.......	4	100.0	3.6	24.5	71.8	-	-	-	-
100 TO 199 MILES......	15	100.0	12.2	30.9	56.9	-	-	-	-
200 TO 299 MILES......	58	100.0	3.3	66.5	30.2	-	-	-	-
300 TO 499 MILES......	145	100.0	12.4	36.9	50.7	-	-	.1	-
500 TO 999 MILES......	346	100.0	20.8	33.4	45.7	-	-	.2	-
1000 TO 1499 MILES....	91	100.0	40.6	19.5	39.8	-	-	-	-
1500 MILES OR OVER....	225	100.0	66.2	32.2	1.4	.2	-	-	-
WEST SOUTH CENTRAL......	173	100.0	20.4	18.8	58.6	-	-	2.1	.2
UNDER 100 MILES.......	-	100.0	4.2	13.8	79.6	-	-	2.4	-
100 TO 199 MILES......	4	100.0	-	17.2	73.8	-	-	8.9	-
200 TO 299 MILES......	6	100.0	5.5	11.2	78.1	-	-	5.2	-
300 TO 499 MILES......	23	100.0	10.5	17.2	65.9	-	-	6.4	-
500 TO 999 MILES......	77	100.0	25.8	15.2	57.3	-	-	1.7	-
1000 TO 1499 MILES....	44	100.0	22.6	30.8	45.9	-	-	-	.7
1500 MILES OR OVER....	14	100.0	15.9	7.3	76.9	-	-	-	-
PACIFIC................	196	100.0	49.2	33.5	12.3	.2	4.3	.2	.3
UNDER 100 MILES.......	5	100.0	.9	17.3	81.4	-	-	.2	.2
100 TO 199 MILES......	4	100.0	.1	39.2	59.7	-	-	.6	.4
200 TO 299 MILES......	4	100.0	-	58.9	35.4	-	-	.6	5.2
300 TO 499 MILES......	24	100.0	6.0	63.2	29.9	-	-	.2	.8
500 TO 999 MILES......	56	100.0	58.7	31.4	9.6	-	-	.3	-
1000 TO 1499 MILES....	36	100.0	81.2	15.6	3.1	-	-	-	.2
1500 MILES OR OVER....	64	100.0	50.5	33.6	1.9	.6	13.2	.3	-

See footnotes at end of table 4.

TABLE 2. **TCC GROUP 251—Percent Distribution of Geographic Division of Origin and Means of Transport, by Geographic Division of Destination: 1972**

Geographic division of origin[1] and means of transport	Number	Percent distribution by division of destination									
		U.S. total	New England	Middle Atlantic	East North Central	West North Central	South Atlantic	East South Central	West South Central	Mountain	Pacific
TONS OF SHIPMENTS	(thousands of tons)										
U.S. TOTAL...............	7 750	100.0	8.1	19.5	21.6	6.6	17.6	6.7	7.1	2.8	9.9
RAIL...................	2 084	100.0	3.8	20.9	13.9	7.9	12.7	5.2	12.0	5.1	18.6
MOTOR CARRIER..........	2 366	100.0	6.4	19.6	28.3	6.4	19.3	5.1	4.7	3.5	6.7
PRIVATE TRUCK..........	3 256	100.0	12.2	18.6	21.8	5.8	19.6	8.8	5.6	.9	6.6
AIR....................	-	100.0	2.7	20.7	3.6	8.9	9.4	-	9.9	4.6	40.1
WATER.................	3	100.0	-	-	-	-	-	-	3.1	-	96.9
OTHER.................	30	100.0	3.3	8.2	16.3	14.5	14.6	3.0	25.7	3.3	11.1
UNKNOWN...............	8	100.0	-	7.3	14.5	34.0	9.1	.8	3.1	-	31.1
MIDDLE ATLANTIC.........	552	100.0	13.5	46.8	12.2	3.1	16.2	2.8	2.7	.7	2.1
RAIL...................	82	100.0	10.8	15.9	21.6	10.7	21.1	11.2	5.9	.7	2.1
MOTOR CARRIER..........	236	100.0	10.3	37.2	16.2	3.5	21.6	2.3	3.9	1.3	3.7
PRIVATE TRUCK..........	231	100.0	17.8	67.9	4.8	-	9.0	.2	.2	-	-
AIR....................	-	100.0	-	-	-	-	-	-	100.0	-	-
WATER.................	-	100.0	-	-	-	-	-	-	100.0	-	-
OTHER.................	1	100.0	2.8	15.9	4.3	2.6	9.9	1.4	.1	.5	62.6
UNKNOWN...............	-	100.0	-	36.2	-	-	.2	-	6.9	-	56.6

See footnotes at end of table 4.

TABLE 2. TCC GROUP 251—Percent Distribution of Geographic Division of Origin and Means of Transport, by Geographic Division of Destination: 1972—Continued

Geographic division of origin[1] and means of transport	Number	Percent distribution by division of destination									
		U.S. total	New England	Middle Atlantic	East North Central	West North Central	South Atlantic	East South Central	West South Central	Mountain	Pacific
TONS OF SHIPMENTS	(thousands of tons)										
EAST NORTH CENTRAL	1 185	100.0	2.4	12.4	45.9	11.4	12.0	2.4	5.7	2.7	5.3
RAIL	288	100.0	4.3	13.7	18.0	7.6	20.6	1.5	11.3	5.0	17.9
MOTOR CARRIER	450	100.0	3.0	15.2	45.5	9.8	12.2	3.5	5.1	3.9	1.8
PRIVATE TRUCK	438	100.0	.5	8.6	64.3	15.3	6.2	2.0	2.6	-	.6
AIR	-	100.0	10.5	17.2	18.5	20.7	32.0	-	-	1.1	-
WATER	-	100.0	-	-	-	-	-	-	-	-	-
OTHER	4	100.0	1.7	10.1	67.1	17.6	1.5	.1	.7	-	1.2
UNKNOWN	1	100.0	-	8.6	70.4	7.2	.1	.5	13.2	-	-
WEST NORTH CENTRAL	302	100.0	3.5	5.4	19.4	29.1	7.0	5.1	9.6	4.6	16.2
RAIL	151	100.0	5.2	6.5	8.4	23.4	7.1	4.8	11.9	3.1	29.6
MOTOR CARRIER	76	100.0	2.4	6.9	23.4	34.8	11.3	6.5	5.6	5.7	3.2
PRIVATE TRUCK	66	100.0	.1	.4	41.7	34.4	.6	4.5	9.4	6.8	2.0
AIR	-	100.0	-	68.4	12.9	-	-	-	-	18.7	-
WATER	-	100.0	-	-	-	-	-	-	-	-	-
OTHER	4	100.0	15.6	20.0	2.6	1.2	30.8	2.7	10.3	7.6	9.2
UNKNOWN	3	100.0	-	1.0	-	96.8	-	2.1	-	-	-
SOUTH ATLANTIC	2 986	100.0	4.1	23.4	16.3	5.0	29.1	7.6	6.2	1.9	6.4
RAIL	1 134	100.0	2.7	29.0	13.4	6.5	11.9	5.9	12.1	2.9	15.7
MOTOR CARRIER	764	100.0	2.6	26.7	21.6	2.3	33.4	5.9	3.4	2.9	1.3
PRIVATE TRUCK	1 080	100.0	6.7	15.4	15.8	5.3	43.9	10.6	2.0	-	.3
AIR	-	100.0	12.4	-	-	12.2	-	-	-	25.0	50.4
WATER	-	100.0	-	-	-	-	-	-	-	-	-
OTHER	5	100.0	.5	5.7	.9	2.3	44.2	11.1	17.7	6.1	11.6
UNKNOWN	1	100.0	-	26.6	-	-	64.0	-	-	-	9.3
EAST SOUTH CENTRAL	1 480	100.0	3.3	14.6	31.8	6.0	13.5	13.3	7.0	2.7	7.8
RAIL	281	100.0	2.6	11.9	14.5	7.2	11.3	6.4	7.8	8.0	30.2
MOTOR CARRIER	547	100.0	4.3	13.1	41.4	7.7	13.0	7.5	5.2	2.6	5.1
PRIVATE TRUCK	649	100.0	2.7	16.9	31.3	4.1	14.9	21.3	8.1	.5	.2
AIR	-	100.0	-	37.7	-	-	-	-	-	-	62.3
WATER	-	100.0	-	-	-	-	-	-	-	-	-
OTHER	1	100.0	2.8	32.1	11.2	11.3	16.4	7.5	14.0	-	4.6
UNKNOWN	-	100.0	-	-	-	-	-	-	-	-	-
WEST SOUTH CENTRAL	284	100.0	.2	4.2	9.6	9.7	13.0	10.8	41.6	6.0	4.8
RAIL	42	100.0	-	10.6	21.2	7.7	18.5	2.3	24.1	7.2	8.3
MOTOR CARRIER	47	100.0	1.2	7.8	6.8	10.3	23.9	16.3	30.3	1.8	1.6
PRIVATE TRUCK	183	100.0	-	2.1	7.5	8.9	9.7	11.9	47.8	7.1	5.0
AIR	-	100.0	-	-	100.0	-	-	-	-	-	-
WATER	-	100.0	-	-	-	-	-	-	-	-	-
OTHER	10	100.0	-	-	11.7	29.5	-	.3	56.1	2.3	-
UNKNOWN	-	100.0	-	-	9.5	-	-	-	5.9	-	84.6
PACIFIC	439	100.0	.5	2.4	1.5	.3	.6	.3	7.4	12.8	74.0
RAIL	89	100.0	2.1	6.3	4.8	.8	1.7	1.4	28.3	30.4	24.2
MOTOR CARRIER	132	100.0	.1	3.3	1.8	.5	1.0	.2	3.3	15.6	74.2
PRIVATE TRUCK	209	100.0	.1	.2	-	-	-	-	1.4	4.0	94.4
AIR	-	100.0	-	9.1	2.6	.2	27.2	-	-	4.5	56.6
WATER	3	100.0	-	-	-	-	-	-	-	-	100.0
OTHER	1	100.0	-	-	5.1	-	-	-	-	3.3	91.6
UNKNOWN	2	100.0	-	-	-	-	-	-	-	-	100.0
TON-MILES OF SHIPMENTS	(millions of ton-miles)										
U.S. TOTAL	3 989	100.0	5.3	17.2	14.7	6.9	12.3	3.7	9.8	6.3	23.8
RAIL	1 765	100.0	2.9	13.7	7.7	5.6	7.5	2.3	12.4	7.1	40.7
MOTOR CARRIER	1 138	100.0	4.9	18.2	18.8	6.6	16.4	3.9	7.4	2.1	14.8
PRIVATE TRUCK	1 055	100.0	9.8	22.2	22.0	9.5	16.0	5.9	7.9	3.7	4.6
AIR	1	100.0	1.6	12.0	1.3	6.0	9.8	-	-	1.6	98.4
WATER	8	100.0	-	-	-	-	-	-	-	-	-
OTHER	16	100.0	5.5	8.8	8.3	9.9	11.9	2.5	18.0	6.5	28.6
UNKNOWN	2	100.0	-	8.0	3.6	14.2	2.3	1.0	8.8	-	62.1
MIDDLE ATLANTIC	200	100.0	6.9	12.5	16.1	8.0	23.1	6.2	9.9	3.3	13.9
RAIL	48	100.0	4.3	5.9	16.9	16.5	15.0	16.8	13.5	2.4	8.8
MOTOR CARRIER	117	100.0	4.5	7.8	17.0	6.8	27.3	3.4	10.5	4.6	18.0
PRIVATE TRUCK	32	100.0	20.4	40.7	13.3	-	21.9	1.2	2.0	.4	.1
AIR	-	100.0	-	-	-	-	-	-	100.0	-	-
WATER	-	100.0	-	-	-	-	-	-	100.0	-	-
OTHER	2	100.0	.4	1.1	1.4	1.6	3.4	.4	.1	.5	91.2
UNKNOWN	-	100.0	-	.7	-	-	-	-	5.5	-	93.8

See footnotes at end of table 4.

TABLE 2. **TCC GROUP 251—Percent Distribution of Geographic Division of Origin and Means of Transport, by Geographic Division of Destination: 1972**—Continued

Geographic division of origin[1] and means of transport	Number	Percent distribution by division of destination									
		U.S. total	New England	Middle Atlantic	East North Central	West North Central	South Atlantic	East South Central	West South Central	Mountain	Pacific
TON-MILES OF SHIPMENTS	(millions of ton-miles)										
EAST NORTH CENTRAL......	536	100.0	3.7	14.5	15.2	8.9	16.1	2.0	10.9	7.6	21.1
RAIL.................	230	100.0	3.9	9.9	4.2	4.5	16.7	.5	12.3	7.5	40.6
MOTOR CARRIER........	193	100.0	4.9	18.0	16.4	9.3	17.0	3.5	10.8	12.1	8.0
PRIVATE TRUCK........	111	100.0	1.4	17.8	35.8	17.1	13.3	2.7	7.9	.2	3.8
AIR..................	-	100.0	11.3	8.3	7.2	15.3	55.7	-	-	2.1	-
WATER...............	-	100.0	-	-	-	-	-	-	-	-	-
OTHER...............	1	100.0	6.1	22.2	28.6	18.6	3.5	.1	3.9	-	17.0
UNKNOWN.............	-	100.0	-	18.8	20.2	8.6	.3	1.0	51.1	-	-
WEST NORTH CENTRAL......	199	100.0	5.8	7.9	10.6	10.2	7.5	3.3	7.7	5.5	41.4
RAIL.................	135	100.0	6.3	7.4	4.4	8.0	5.3	2.7	7.7	2.3	56.0
MOTOR CARRIER........	36	100.0	5.6	13.1	17.6	14.0	16.9	5.7	6.2	9.9	10.9
PRIVATE TRUCK........	22	100.0	.4	.9	38.9	17.8	1.4	3.7	10.6	17.0	9.3
AIR..................	-	100.0	-	73.8	5.0	-	-	-	-	21.2	-
WATER...............	-	100.0	-	-	-	-	-	-	-	-	-
OTHER...............	4	100.0	17.9	17.6	.7	.3	28.0	1.6	7.9	9.6	16.4
UNKNOWN.............	-	100.0	-	7.0	-	87.1	-	5.9	-	-	-
SOUTH ATLANTIC..........	1 707	100.0	4.8	20.1	13.1	7.0	12.3	4.1	9.3	5.4	23.8
RAIL.................	932	100.0	1.9	17.5	8.2	5.8	5.7	2.4	12.8	5.7	40.0
MOTOR CARRIER........	359	100.0	3.3	26.0	19.0	3.9	19.4	5.1	6.0	10.6	6.5
PRIVATE TRUCK........	410	100.0	12.8	21.2	19.2	12.6	21.2	6.9	4.2	.2	1.7
AIR..................	-	100.0	8.0	-	-	6.5	-	-	-	20.2	65.4
WATER...............	-	100.0	-	-	-	-	-	-	-	-	-
OTHER...............	4	100.0	.5	3.3	.7	2.0	12.9	7.4	26.4	12.0	34.8
UNKNOWN.............	-	100.0	-	18.6	-	-	10.4	-	-	-	71.0
EAST SOUTH CENTRAL......	887	100.0	5.2	17.3	21.0	5.6	10.2	3.4	6.4	6.0	24.9
RAIL.................	280	100.0	2.8	9.2	7.9	4.3	6.2	1.1	4.8	10.8	52.8
MOTOR CARRIER........	304	100.0	6.6	14.8	24.5	6.5	9.8	2.6	5.9	6.5	22.8
PRIVATE TRUCK........	301	100.0	6.0	27.3	29.7	5.8	14.2	6.5	8.4	1.2	1.0
AIR..................	-	100.0	-	20.7	-	-	-	-	-	-	79.3
WATER...............	-	100.0	-	-	-	-	-	-	-	-	-
OTHER...............	-	100.0	3.6	35.9	7.3	10.2	10.0	2.2	16.7	-	14.1
UNKNOWN.............	-	100.0	-	-	-	-	-	-	-	-	-
WEST SOUTH CENTRAL......	173	100.0	.5	7.4	11.7	7.9	20.4	8.6	22.5	8.6	12.3
RAIL.................	35	100.0	-	12.3	17.2	4.4	19.3	.3	21.1	10.6	14.9
MOTOR CARRIER........	32	100.0	2.9	14.9	8.1	9.1	35.2	13.6	10.8	2.1	3.3
PRIVATE TRUCK........	101	100.0	-	3.6	10.7	7.8	16.8	10.3	26.1	10.2	14.4
AIR..................	-	100.0	-	-	100.0	-	-	-	-	-	-
WATER...............	-	100.0	-	-	-	-	-	-	-	-	-
OTHER...............	3	100.0	-	-	21.8	34.5	-	.2	39.6	3.8	-
UNKNOWN.............	-	100.0	-	-	5.0	-	-	-	.7	-	94.3
PACIFIC.................	196	100.0	2.9	12.3	6.2	1.1	3.2	1.5	19.7	15.4	37.8
RAIL.................	96	100.0	5.0	13.5	7.9	1.2	3.3	2.5	32.5	17.7	16.5
MOTOR CARRIER........	65	100.0	.6	15.7	6.6	1.6	4.5	.8	7.2	15.1	47.9
PRIVATE TRUCK........	24	100.0	1.8	3.2	-	-	-	-	10.2	13.3	71.5
AIR..................	-	100.0	-	9.0	2.1	.1	23.2	-	-	1.6	64.0
WATER...............	8	100.0	-	-	-	-	-	-	-	-	100.0
OTHER...............	-	100.0	-	-	29.0	-	-	-	-	5.4	65.6
UNKNOWN.............	-	100.0	-	-	-	-	-	-	-	-	100.0

See footnotes at end of table 4.

TABLE 3. **TCC GROUP 251—Percent Distribution of Geographic Division of Destination and Means of Transport, by Geographic Division of Origin: 1972**

Geographic division of destination and means of transport	Number	Percent distribution by division of origin[1]									
		U.S. total	New England	Middle Atlantic	East North Central	West North Central	South Atlantic	East South Central	West South Central	Mountain	Pacific
TONS OF SHIPMENTS	(thousands of tons)										
U.S. TOTAL..............	7 750	100.0	(D)	7.1	15.3	3.9	38.5	19.1	3.7	(D)	5.7
RAIL.................	2 084	100.0	(D)	4.0	13.9	7.3	54.4	13.5	2.0	(D)	4.3
MOTOR CARRIER........	2 366	100.0	(D)	10.0	19.0	3.2	32.3	23.1	2.0	(D)	5.6
PRIVATE TRUCK........	3 256	100.0	(D)	7.1	13.5	2.0	33.2	20.0	5.6	(D)	6.4
AIR..................	-	100.0	(D)	9.9	11.3	3.4	12.5	39.7	-	(D)	16.1
WATER................	3	100.0	(D)	3.1	-	-	-	-	-	(D)	96.9
OTHER................	30	100.0	(D)	4.7	15.7	16.3	18.3	4.2	35.7	(D)	4.6
UNKNOWN..............	8	100.0	(D)	4.1	20.1	33.6	14.2	-	3.3	(D)	24.7
NEW ENGLAND..........	630	100.0	(D)	11.8	4.5	1.7	19.5	7.7	.1	(D)	.3
RAIL.................	78	100.0	(D)	11.4	15.7	10.0	38.8	9.5	-	(D)	2.4
MOTOR CARRIER........	152	100.0	(D)	15.9	9.0	1.2	12.9	15.5	.4	(D)	.1
PRIVATE TRUCK........	398	100.0	(D)	10.3	.6	-	18.2	4.3	-	(D)	-
AIR..................	-	100.0	(D)	-	43.3	-	56.7	-	-	(D)	-
WATER................	-	100.0	(D)	-	-	-	-	-	-	(D)	-
OTHER................	-	100.0	(D)	3.9	8.2	77.5	2.9	3.6	-	(D)	-
UNKNOWN..............	-	100.0	(D)	-	-	-	-	-	-	(D)	-
MIDDLE ATLANTIC.......	1 508	100.0	(D)	17.2	9.7	1.1	46.4	14.3	.8	(D)	.7
RAIL.................	434	100.0	(D)	3.0	9.1	2.3	75.5	7.7	1.0	(D)	1.3
MOTOR CARRIER........	464	100.0	(D)	18.9	14.7	1.1	43.9	15.5	.8	(D)	.9
PRIVATE TRUCK........	605	100.0	(D)	26.0	6.2	-	27.5	18.1	.6	(D)	.1
AIR..................	-	100.0	(D)	-	9.3	11.4	-	72.2	-	(D)	7.1
WATER................	-	100.0	(D)	-	-	-	-	-	-	(D)	-
OTHER................	2	100.0	(D)	9.0	19.3	39.7	12.7	16.3	-	(D)	-
UNKNOWN..............	-	100.0	(D)	20.1	23.6	4.8	51.6	-	-	(D)	-
EAST NORTH CENTRAL......	1 673	100.0	(D)	4.0	32.5	3.5	29.1	28.2	1.6	(D)	.4
RAIL.................	289	100.0	(D)	6.2	18.0	4.4	52.4	14.1	3.1	(D)	1.5
MOTOR CARRIER........	668	100.0	(D)	5.7	30.7	2.7	24.6	33.9	.5	(D)	.4
PRIVATE TRUCK........	709	100.0	(D)	1.6	39.7	3.9	24.1	28.7	1.9	(D)	-
AIR..................	-	100.0	(D)	-	58.6	12.4	-	-	.2	(D)	11.6
WATER................	-	100.0	(D)	-	-	-	-	-	-	(D)	-
OTHER................	4	100.0	(D)	1.2	64.6	2.6	1.0	2.9	25.7	(D)	1.4
UNKNOWN..............	1	100.0	(D)	-	97.8	-	-	-	2.2	(D)	-
WEST NORTH CENTRAL......	513	100.0	(D)	3.3	26.2	17.1	28.9	17.4	5.4	(D)	.3
RAIL.................	165	100.0	(D)	5.4	13.4	21.4	44.7	12.3	2.0	(D)	.5
MOTOR CARRIER........	150	100.0	(D)	5.4	29.2	17.7	11.8	27.9	3.3	(D)	.5
PRIVATE TRUCK........	190	100.0	(D)	-	35.4	12.1	30.0	14.0	8.6	(D)	-
AIR..................	-	100.0	(D)	-	26.2	-	17.1	-	-	(D)	.3
WATER................	-	100.0	(D)	-	-	-	-	-	-	(D)	-
OTHER................	4	100.0	(D)	.8	19.0	1.4	2.9	3.2	72.5	(D)	-
UNKNOWN..............	3	100.0	(D)	-	4.3	95.7	-	-	-	(D)	-
SOUTH ATLANTIC........	1 364	100.0	(D)	6.6	10.4	1.6	63.6	14.7	2.7	(D)	.2
RAIL.................	264	100.0	(D)	6.6	22.5	4.1	51.2	12.0	3.0	(D)	.6
MOTOR CARRIER........	457	100.0	(D)	11.2	12.0	1.9	55.8	15.6	2.5	(D)	.3
PRIVATE TRUCK........	637	100.0	(D)	3.3	4.3	.1	74.4	15.2	2.8	(D)	-
AIR..................	-	100.0	(D)	-	38.3	-	-	-	-	(D)	46.5
WATER................	-	100.0	(D)	-	-	-	-	-	-	(D)	-
OTHER................	4	100.0	(D)	3.2	1.6	34.4	55.5	4.7	-	(D)	-
UNKNOWN..............	-	100.0	(D)	.1	.2	-	99.7	-	-	(D)	-
EAST SOUTH CENTRAL......	515	100.0	(D)	3.0	5.5	3.0	43.9	38.2	5.9	(D)	.3
RAIL.................	107	100.0	(D)	8.6	4.0	6.7	62.0	16.7	.9	(D)	1.1
MOTOR CARRIER........	120	100.0	(D)	4.6	12.9	4.2	37.2	34.0	6.5	(D)	.2
PRIVATE TRUCK........	286	100.0	(D)	.2	3.0	1.1	39.9	48.2	7.6	(D)	-
AIR..................	-	100.0	(D)	-	-	-	-	-	-	(D)	-
WATER................	-	100.0	(D)	-	-	-	-	-	-	(D)	-
OTHER................	-	100.0	(D)	2.2	.3	14.9	68.0	10.5	3.6	(D)	-
UNKNOWN..............	-	100.0	(D)	-	13.2	86.8	-	-	-	(D)	-
WEST SOUTH CENTRAL......	553	100.0	(D)	2.7	12.1	5.3	33.6	18.8	21.4	(D)	5.9
RAIL.................	251	100.0	(D)	1.9	13.0	7.2	54.5	8.8	4.1	(D)	10.1
MOTOR CARRIER........	110	100.0	(D)	8.4	20.6	3.9	23.5	25.9	13.1	(D)	3.9
PRIVATE TRUCK........	183	100.0	(D)	.3	6.1	3.4	11.9	28.8	47.9	(D)	1.6
AIR..................	-	100.0	(D)	100.0	-	-	-	-	-	(D)	-
WATER................	-	100.0	(D)	100.0	-	-	-	-	-	(D)	-
OTHER................	7	100.0	(D)	-	.4	6.6	12.6	2.3	78.0	(D)	-
UNKNOWN..............	-	100.0	(D)	9.0	84.8	-	-	-	6.3	(D)	-
MOUNTAIN..............	220	100.0	(D)	1.7	14.7	6.3	25.4	18.3	7.8	(D)	25.5
RAIL.................	105	100.0	(D)	.6	13.7	4.4	31.4	21.3	2.9	(D)	25.8
MOTOR CARRIER........	83	100.0	(D)	3.8	21.2	5.3	26.4	17.1	1.0	(D)	24.7
PRIVATE TRUCK........	30	100.0	(D)	.2	.6	15.0	1.3	11.8	43.0	(D)	27.7
AIR..................	-	100.0	(D)	-	2.8	14.0	67.7	-	-	(D)	15.6
WATER................	-	100.0	(D)	-	-	-	-	-	-	(D)	-
OTHER................	1	100.0	(D)	.6	-	37.1	33.3	-	24.3	(D)	4.5
UNKNOWN..............	-	100.0	(D)	-	-	-	-	-	-	(D)	-
PACIFIC...............	770	100.0	(D)	1.5	8.1	6.4	24.9	14.9	1.8	(D)	42.1
RAIL.................	387	100.0	(D)	.4	13.4	11.6	45.9	22.0	.9	(D)	5.6
MOTOR CARRIER........	158	100.0	(D)	5.5	5.2	1.6	6.5	17.6	.5	(D)	62.2
PRIVATE TRUCK........	215	100.0	(D)	-	1.1	.6	1.5	.7	4.3	(D)	91.8
AIR..................	-	100.0	(D)	-	-	-	15.7	61.6	-	(D)	22.7
WATER................	3	100.0	(D)	-	-	-	-	-	-	(D)	100.0
OTHER................	3	100.0	(D)	26.2	1.8	13.4	19.1	1.7	-	(D)	37.8
UNKNOWN..............	2	100.0	(D)	7.4	-	-	4.3	-	9.0	(D)	79.3

See footnotes at end of table 4.

TABLE 3. **TCC GROUP 251—Percent Distribution of Geographic Division of Destination and Means of Transport, by Geographic Division of Origin: 1972**—Continued

Geographic division of destination and means of transport	Number	Percent distribution by division of origin[1]									
		U.S. total	New England	Middle Atlantic	East North Central	West North Central	South Atlantic	East South Central	West South Central	Mountain	Pacific
TON-MILES OF SHIPMENTS	(millions of ton-miles)										
U.S. TOTAL	3 989	100.0	(D)	5.0	13.4	5.0	42.8	22.2	4.3	(D)	4.9
RAIL	1 765	100.0	(D)	2.7	13.1	7.7	52.8	15.9	2.0	(D)	5.5
MOTOR CARRIER	1 138	100.0	(D)	10.3	17.0	3.2	31.6	26.7	2.9	(D)	5.8
PRIVATE TRUCK	1 055	100.0	(D)	3.0	10.5	2.1	38.9	28.5	9.6	(D)	2.3
AIR	1	100.0	(D)	11.1	4.9	2.3	13.3	36.7	-	(D)	26.0
WATER	8	100.0	(D)	1.6	-	-	-	-	-	(D)	98.4
OTHER	16	100.0	(D)	13.4	6.3	26.9	24.2	4.6	21.4	(D)	2.7
UNKNOWN	2	100.0	(D)	19.3	14.9	14.9	21.7	-	11.2	(D)	18.0
NEW ENGLAND	211	100.0	(D)	6.6	9.5	5.4	38.9	21.7	.4	(D)	2.7
RAIL	51	100.0	(D)	4.0	17.4	16.6	34.2	15.4	-	(D)	9.4
MOTOR CARRIER	56	100.0	(D)	9.4	16.8	3.7	21.4	35.6	1.6	(D)	.7
PRIVATE TRUCK	103	100.0	(D)	6.3	1.5	.1	51.2	17.4	-	(D)	.4
AIR	-	100.0	(D)	-	34.2	-	65.8	-	-	(D)	-
WATER	-	100.0	(D)	-	-	-	-	-	-	(D)	-
OTHER	-	100.0	(D)	.9	7.0	86.7	2.1	3.0	-	(D)	-
UNKNOWN	-	100.0	(D)	-	-	-	-	-	-	(D)	-
MIDDLE ATLANTIC	686	100.0	(D)	3.7	11.3	2.3	50.1	22.4	1.9	(D)	3.5
RAIL	242	100.0	(D)	1.2	9.4	4.1	67.4	10.7	1.8	(D)	5.4
MOTOR CARRIER	207	100.0	(D)	4.4	16.8	2.3	45.1	21.7	2.3	(D)	5.0
PRIVATE TRUCK	234	100.0	(D)	5.6	8.4	.1	37.0	35.0	1.5	(D)	.3
AIR	-	100.0	(D)	-	3.4	14.1	-	63.0	-	(D)	19.5
WATER	-	100.0	(D)	-	-	-	-	-	-	(D)	-
OTHER	1	100.0	(D)	1.6	15.9	53.5	9.0	18.8	-	(D)	-
UNKNOWN	-	100.0	(D)	1.6	35.0	13.0	50.4	-	-	(D)	-
EAST NORTH CENTRAL	584	100.0	(D)	5.5	14.0	3.6	38.3	31.9	3.5	(D)	2.1
RAIL	136	100.0	(D)	5.9	7.1	4.3	56.0	16.3	4.4	(D)	5.6
MOTOR CARRIER	214	100.0	(D)	9.3	14.8	3.0	31.9	34.9	1.2	(D)	2.0
PRIVATE TRUCK	232	100.0	(D)	1.8	17.1	3.8	34.0	38.5	4.7	(D)	-
AIR	-	100.0	(D)	-	27.9	9.1	-	-	.3	(D)	42.4
WATER	-	100.0	(D)	-	-	-	-	-	-	(D)	-
OTHER	1	100.0	(D)	2.2	21.9	2.2	2.1	4.1	56.2	(D)	9.6
UNKNOWN	-	100.0	(D)	-	84.3	-	-	-	15.7	(D)	-
WEST NORTH CENTRAL	276	100.0	(D)	5.8	17.2	7.4	43.4	17.9	5.0	(D)	.8
RAIL	99	100.0	(D)	8.0	10.5	10.9	54.7	12.3	1.6	(D)	1.2
MOTOR CARRIER	75	100.0	(D)	10.7	24.0	6.9	18.7	26.4	4.0	(D)	1.4
PRIVATE TRUCK	100	100.0	(D)	-	19.0	4.0	51.6	17.5	7.9	(D)	-
AIR	-	100.0	(D)	-	12.3	-	14.4	-	-	(D)	.4
WATER	-	100.0	(D)	-	-	-	-	-	-	(D)	-
OTHER	1	100.0	(D)	2.1	12.0	1.0	4.8	4.8	74.9	(D)	-
UNKNOWN	-	100.0	(D)	-	9.0	91.0	-	-	-	(D)	-
SOUTH ATLANTIC	491	100.0	(D)	9.4	17.5	3.0	42.7	18.3	7.2	(D)	1.3
RAIL	133	100.0	(D)	5.4	28.8	5.4	39.6	13.1	5.1	(D)	2.4
MOTOR CARRIER	187	100.0	(D)	17.1	17.6	3.3	37.2	16.0	6.1	(D)	1.6
PRIVATE TRUCK	168	100.0	(D)	4.1	8.8	.2	51.5	25.3	10.1	(D)	-
AIR	-	100.0	(D)	-	27.6	-	-	-	-	(D)	61.3
WATER	-	100.0	(D)	-	-	-	-	-	-	(D)	-
OTHER	1	100.0	(D)	3.9	1.9	63.3	26.3	3.9	-	(D)	-
UNKNOWN	-	100.0	(D)	.3	2.1	-	97.6	-	-	(D)	-
EAST SOUTH CENTRAL	148	100.0	(D)	8.3	7.3	4.4	47.0	20.6	10.0	(D)	2.0
RAIL	41	100.0	(D)	19.6	2.6	8.7	55.5	7.4	.3	(D)	5.9
MOTOR CARRIER	44	100.0	(D)	8.9	15.3	4.7	41.3	17.8	9.9	(D)	1.2
PRIVATE TRUCK	62	100.0	(D)	.6	4.8	1.3	45.4	31.3	16.6	(D)	-
AIR	-	100.0	(D)	-	-	-	-	-	-	(D)	-
WATER	-	100.0	(D)	-	-	-	-	-	-	(D)	-
OTHER	-	100.0	(D)	2.3	.2	17.7	72.5	4.0	2.0	(D)	-
UNKNOWN	-	100.0	(D)	-	14.2	85.8	-	-	-	(D)	-
WEST SOUTH CENTRAL	389	100.0	(D)	5.1	15.0	4.0	40.9	14.6	10.0	(D)	9.9
RAIL	218	100.0	(D)	3.0	13.0	4.8	54.6	6.2	3.4	(D)	14.4
MOTOR CARRIER	84	100.0	(D)	14.6	24.8	2.7	25.6	21.3	4.1	(D)	5.6
PRIVATE TRUCK	83	100.0	(D)	.8	10.5	2.9	20.9	30.2	31.8	(D)	3.0
AIR	-	100.0	(D)	100.0	-	-	-	-	-	(D)	-
WATER	-	100.0	(D)	100.0	-	-	-	-	-	(D)	-
OTHER	3	100.0	(D)	.1	1.4	11.8	35.3	4.3	47.0	(D)	-
UNKNOWN	-	100.0	(D)	12.1	87.0	-	-	-	.9	(D)	-
MOUNTAIN	250	100.0	(D)	2.7	16.3	4.4	37.0	21.4	6.0	(D)	12.1
RAIL	125	100.0	(D)	.9	13.7	2.4	42.3	24.1	3.0	(D)	13.6
MOTOR CARRIER	101	100.0	(D)	5.3	23.0	3.6	37.7	19.6	.7	(D)	9.8
PRIVATE TRUCK	22	100.0	(D)	.6	1.1	17.4	3.3	16.1	47.0	(D)	14.6
AIR	-	100.0	(D)	-	2.8	13.1	72.7	-	-	(D)	11.4
WATER	-	100.0	(D)	-	-	-	-	-	-	(D)	-
OTHER	1	100.0	(D)	.9	-	39.4	44.5	-	12.6	(D)	2.3
UNKNOWN	-	100.0	(D)	-	-	-	-	-	-	(D)	-
PACIFIC	950	100.0	(D)	2.9	11.9	8.7	42.7	23.3	2.2	(D)	7.8
RAIL	718	100.0	(D)	.6	13.0	10.5	52.0	20.6	.7	(D)	2.2
MOTOR CARRIER	168	100.0	(D)	12.6	9.1	2.4	14.0	41.2	.6	(D)	18.8
PRIVATE TRUCK	48	100.0	(D)	.1	8.8	4.3	14.5	6.3	30.3	(D)	35.8
AIR	-	100.0	(D)	-	-	-	16.0	53.4	-	(D)	30.5
WATER	8	100.0	(D)	-	-	-	-	-	-	(D)	100.0
OTHER	4	100.0	(D)	42.7	3.8	15.4	29.5	2.3	-	(D)	6.3
UNKNOWN	1	100.0	(D)	29.2	-	-	24.8	-	17.1	(D)	29.0

See footnotes at end of table 4.

TABLE 4. **TCC GROUP 251—Percent Distribution of Distance Shipped and Weight of Shipment, by Means of Transport: 1972**

Distance shipped and weight of shipment[2][3]	Number	Percent distribution by means of transport							
		All means of transport	Rail	Motor carrier	Private truck	Air	Water	Other	Unknown
TONS OF SHIPMENTS	(thousands of tons)								
U.S. TOTAL..........	6 659	100.0	27.8	33.5	38.2	-	-	.4	.1
UNDER 100 MILES.........	1 147	100.0	1.9	23.9	73.7	-	-	.2	.3
UNDER 1000 POUNDS.....	216	100.0	-	34.4	64.4	-	-	.9	.3
1000 TO 9999 POUNDS...	574	100.0	1.2	20.6	77.6	-	-	.1	.6
10000 TO 29999 POUNDS.	309	100.0	4.8	20.3	74.9	-	-	-	-
30000 TO 59999 POUNDS.	28	100.0	-	64.4	35.6	-	-	-	-
60000 TO 89999 POUNDS.	2	100.0	-	-	100.0	-	-	-	-
90000 POUNDS AND OVER.	16	100.0	-	-	100.0	-	-	-	-
100 TO 199 MILES........	735	100.0	10.8	28.8	59.7	-	-	.6	.2
UNDER 1000 POUNDS.....	183	100.0	.5	50.2	47.2	-	-	2.0	.2
1000 TO 9999 POUNDS...	351	100.0	5.7	23.5	70.3	-	-	.2	.3
10000 TO 29999 POUNDS.	198	100.0	29.1	18.5	52.4	-	-	-	-
30000 TO 59999 POUNDS.	2	100.0	28.2	-	71.8	-	-	-	-
60000 TO 89999 POUNDS.	-	100.0	-	-	-	-	-	-	-
90000 POUNDS AND OVER.	-	100.0	-	-	-	-	-	-	-
200 TO 299 MILES........	774	100.0	10.4	49.9	39.2	-	-	.3	.2
UNDER 1000 POUNDS.....	170	100.0	2.7	63.8	32.3	-	-	1.1	.1
1000 TO 9999 POUNDS...	407	100.0	9.4	49.7	40.6	-	-	.1	.3
10000 TO 29999 POUNDS.	194	100.0	18.6	38.5	42.9	-	-	-	-
30000 TO 59999 POUNDS.	2	100.0	56.4	43.6	-	-	-	-	-
60000 TO 89999 POUNDS.	-	100.0	-	-	-	-	-	-	-
90000 POUNDS AND OVER.	-	100.0	-	-	-	-	-	-	-
300 TO 499 MILES........	1 557	100.0	33.2	39.2	27.2	-	-	.4	.1
UNDER 1000 POUNDS.....	359	100.0	5.8	70.4	22.5	-	-	1.2	.1
1000 TO 9999 POUNDS...	720	100.0	36.2	39.7	23.8	-	-	.2	.1
10000 TO 29999 POUNDS.	475	100.0	49.5	14.8	35.7	-	-	-	-
30000 TO 59999 POUNDS.	2	100.0	-	74.5	25.5	-	-	-	-
60000 TO 89999 POUNDS.	-	100.0	-	-	-	-	-	-	-
90000 POUNDS AND OVER.	-	100.0	-	-	-	-	-	-	-
500 TO 999 MILES........	1 651	100.0	38.6	33.8	27.2	-	-	.4	-
UNDER 1000 POUNDS.....	377	100.0	21.5	62.0	14.7	-	-	1.7	.1
1000 TO 9999 POUNDS...	576	100.0	32.2	40.9	26.7	-	-	.1	-
10000 TO 29999 POUNDS.	661	100.0	54.0	12.7	33.3	-	-	-	-
30000 TO 59999 POUNDS.	35	100.0	35.6	11.7	52.8	-	-	-	-
60000 TO 89999 POUNDS.	-	100.0	-	-	-	-	-	-	-
90000 POUNDS AND OVER.	-	100.0	-	-	-	-	-	-	-
1000 TO 1499 MILES......	295	100.0	43.1	33.0	23.0	-	-	.7	.1
UNDER 1000 POUNDS.....	45	100.0	28.3	55.7	11.8	.3	.2	3.4	.2
1000 TO 9999 POUNDS...	97	100.0	41.6	32.8	25.0	-	-	.6	-
10000 TO 29999 POUNDS.	124	100.0	56.2	13.9	29.6	-	-	-	.2
30000 TO 59999 POUNDS.	27	100.0	13.4	82.0	4.7	-	-	-	-
60000 TO 89999 POUNDS.	-	100.0	-	-	-	-	-	-	-
90000 POUNDS AND OVER.	-	100.0	-	-	-	-	-	-	-
1500 MILES OR OVER......	498	100.0	77.6	18.1	3.2	.1	.5	.4	.1
UNDER 1000 POUNDS.....	63	100.0	51.9	38.3	6.5	.7	.3	1.9	.4
1000 TO 9999 POUNDS...	228	100.0	71.2	25.0	2.3	-	1.0	.4	-
10000 TO 29999 POUNDS.	196	100.0	95.4	1.7	2.8	-	-	-	-
30000 TO 59999 POUNDS.	8	100.0	32.5	57.7	9.9	-	-	-	-
60000 TO 89999 POUNDS.	-	100.0	-	-	-	-	-	-	-
90000 POUNDS AND OVER.	-	100.0	-	-	-	-	-	-	-
TON-MILES OF SHIPMENTS	(millions of ton-miles)								
U.S. TOTAL..........	3 443	100.0	46.5	31.0	21.8	-	.2	.5	.1
UNDER 100 MILES.........	53	100.0	3.3	24.7	71.6	-	-	.1	.2
UNDER 1000 POUNDS.....	9	100.0	-	38.3	60.8	-	-	.6	.2
1000 TO 9999 POUNDS...	29	100.0	1.8	18.3	79.5	-	-	-	.3
10000 TO 29999 POUNDS.	11	100.0	11.0	22.6	66.4	-	-	-	-
30000 TO 59999 POUNDS.	1	100.0	-	83.7	16.3	-	-	-	-
60000 TO 89999 POUNDS.	-	100.0	-	-	100.0	-	-	-	-
90000 POUNDS AND OVER.	1	100.0	-	-	100.0	-	-	-	-
100 TO 199 MILES........	109	100.0	10.6	28.9	59.7	-	-	.6	.2
UNDER 1000 POUNDS.....	27	100.0	.5	50.1	47.3	-	-	1.9	.2
1000 TO 9999 POUNDS...	51	100.0	5.9	24.9	68.7	-	-	.2	.4
10000 TO 29999 POUNDS.	29	100.0	27.8	16.4	55.8	-	-	-	-
30000 TO 59999 POUNDS.	-	100.0	33.5	-	66.5	-	-	-	-
60000 TO 89999 POUNDS.	-	100.0	-	-	-	-	-	-	-
90000 POUNDS AND OVER.	-	100.0	-	-	-	-	-	-	-

See footnotes at end of table 4.

TABLE 4. TCC GROUP 251—Percent Distribution of Distance Shipped and Weight of Shipment, by Means of Transport: 1972—Continued

Distance shipped and weight of shipment[2] [3]	Number	Percent distribution by means of transport							
		All means of transport	Rail	Motor carrier	Private truck	Air	Water	Other	Unknown
TON-MILES OF SHIPMENTS	(millions of ton-miles)								
200 TO 299 MILES.........	192	100.0	10.9	50.3	38.4	-	-	.3	.2
UNDER 1000 POUNDS.....	42	100.0	2.8	64.5	31.4	-	-	1.1	.2
1000 TO 9999 POUNDS...	100	100.0	10.2	50.3	39.2	-	-	.1	.3
10000 TO 29999 POUNDS.	48	100.0	18.8	37.9	43.2	-	-	-	-
30000 TO 59999 POUNDS.	-	100.0	58.4	41.6	-	-	-	-	-
60000 TO 89999 POUNDS.	-	100.0	-	-	-	-	-	-	-
90000 POUNDS AND OVER.	-	100.0	-	-	-	-	-	-	-
300 TO 499 MILES........	640	100.0	36.2	37.6	25.7	-	-	.4	.1
UNDER 1000 POUNDS.....	140	100.0	6.3	70.1	22.2	-	-	1.2	.1
1000 TO 9999 POUNDS...	296	100.0	39.8	38.0	21.9	-	-	.2	.1
10000 TO 29999 POUNDS.	202	100.0	52.0	14.3	33.8	-	-	-	-
30000 TO 59999 POUNDS.	-	100.0	-	71.2	28.8	-	-	-	-
60000 TO 89999 POUNDS.	-	100.0	-	-	-	-	-	-	-
90000 POUNDS AND OVER.	-	100.0	-	-	-	-	-	-	-
500 TO 999 MILES........	1 124	100.0	39.1	33.6	26.7	-	-	.5	-
UNDER 1000 POUNDS.....	249	100.0	21.2	61.8	15.0	-	-	1.9	.1
1000 TO 9999 POUNDS...	398	100.0	31.6	41.5	26.8	-	-	.1	-
10000 TO 29999 POUNDS.	448	100.0	55.6	12.4	31.9	-	-	-	-
30000 TO 59999 POUNDS.	27	100.0	41.1	11.2	47.7	-	-	-	-
60000 TO 89999 POUNDS.	-	100.0	-	-	-	-	-	-	-
90000 POUNDS AND OVER.	-	100.0	-	-	-	-	-	-	-
1000 TO 1499 MILES......	348	100.0	43.9	33.1	22.1	-	-	.7	.1
UNDER 1000 POUNDS.....	54	100.0	29.5	54.7	11.4	.3	.2	3.6	.2
1000 TO 9999 POUNDS...	115	100.0	41.6	33.5	24.4	-	-	.5	-
10000 TO 29999 POUNDS.	148	100.0	56.8	15.4	27.6	-	-	-	.2
30000 TO 59999 POUNDS.	30	100.0	15.2	79.7	5.2	-	-	-	-
60000 TO 89999 POUNDS.	-	100.0	-	-	-	-	-	-	-
90000 POUNDS AND OVER.	-	100.0	-	-	-	-	-	-	-
1500 MILES OR OVER......	974	100.0	76.1	19.6	3.0	.1	.7	.5	.1
UNDER 1000 POUNDS.....	130	100.0	52.8	37.7	6.0	.7	.5	1.9	.5
1000 TO 9999 POUNDS...	465	100.0	69.5	26.4	2.3	-	1.3	.5	.1
10000 TO 29999 POUNDS.	359	100.0	95.3	2.2	2.6	-	-	-	-
30000 TO 59999 POUNDS.	18	100.0	33.5	58.8	7.8	-	-	-	-
60000 TO 89999 POUNDS.	-	100.0	-	-	-	-	-	-	-
90000 POUNDS AND OVER.	-	100.0	-	-	-	-	-	-	-

Note: Detail may not add to total due to rounding. The introductory table shows the estimates of sampling variability for tons; sampling variability for ton-miles has not been estimated. See the map in the Introduction for the States comprising the geographic divisions of the United States.
Shipments excluded from the survey are those moving by pipeline (primarily petroleum products from refineries), parcel post shipments, and commodities moved by own power (motorized vehicles, aircraft, etc.) or towed (prefabricated buildings, etc.). Local shipments (commodities shipped less than 25 miles from the plant) and shipments within the same city are also excluded. Shipments to Alaska and Hawaii from the 48 conterminous States and the District of Columbia are included; however, no data were obtained for shipments originating in Alaska and Hawaii.

- Represents zero or rounds to zero.   (D) Withheld to avoid disclosing figures for individual companies.

[1]Production of this commodity is concentrated in the geographic divisions shown; figures and distributions for geographic divisions not shown are included in the total.
[2]Distances of shipments to foreign destinations are calculated only to the U.S. port of exit.
[3]Includes only shipments represented by bills of lading and invoices. Summary records which did not show individual weights of shipments are not included.

TCC 253. Public Building and Related Furniture

Comparisons of Tons and Ton-Miles of Shipments for
Geographic Divisions of Origin and for Sampling Variability: 1972 and 1967

Geographic division of origin	Estimates				Relative sampling variability in tons (percent)	
	1972		1967		1972	1967
	Tons (thousands)	Ton-miles (millions)	Tons (thousands)	Ton-miles (millions)		
U.S. total	344	247	430	271	19.2	(*)
New England	(D)	(D)	(*)	(*)	(*)	(*)
Middle Atlantic	(D)	(D)	(*)	(*)	(*)	(*)
East North Central	98	63	(*)	(*)	34.6	(*)
West North Central	(D)	(D)	(*)	(*)	(*)	(*)
South Atlantic	(D)	(D)	(*)	(*)	(*)	(*)
East South Central	(D)	(D)	(*)	(*)	(*)	(*)
West South Central	94	64	(*)	(*)	41.1	(*)
Mountain	—	—	(*)	(*)	—	(*)
Pacific	(D)	(D)	(*)	(*)	(*)	(*)

— Represents or rounds to zero.   (D) Withheld to avoid disclosing figures for individual companies.   (*) Data not published.

TABLE 1. TCC GROUP 253—Percent Distribution of Geographic Division of Origin and Distance Shipped, by Means of Transport: 1972

Geographic division of origin[1] and distance shipped[2]	Number	Percent distribution by means of transport							
		All means of transport	Rail	Motor carrier	Private truck	Air	Water	Other	Unknown
TONS OF SHIPMENTS	(thousands of tons)								
U.S. TOTAL..........	344	100.0	38.7	40.0	19.9	.1	.5	.4	.3
EAST NORTH CENTRAL......	98	100.0	24.4	54.0	21.3	.2	-	-	-
UNDER 100 MILES........	6	100.0	-	84.9	15.1	-	-	-	-
100 TO 199 MILES......	9	100.0	2.0	74.2	23.7	-	-	-	-
200 TO 299 MILES......	13	100.0	2.3	54.8	42.7	.1	-	-	-
300 TO 499 MILES......	11	100.0	-	57.6	42.0	.3	-	-	-
500 TO 999 MILES......	35	100.0	19.4	61.2	19.0	.3	-	.1	-
1000 TO 1499 MILES....	14	100.0	90.3	9.3	-	.3	-	-	-
1500 MILES OR OVER....	7	100.0	44.5	50.8	4.4	.2	-	.1	-
WEST SOUTH CENTRAL......	93	100.0	21.8	42.9	33.7	-	-	.5	1.1
UNDER 100 MILES........	6	100.0	-	18.4	78.9	-	-	2.7	-
100 TO 199 MILES......	5	100.0	2.9	24.4	70.4	-	-	-	2.4
200 TO 299 MILES......	6	100.0	8.8	52.6	38.6	-	-	-	-
300 TO 499 MILES......	11	100.0	1.7	62.6	32.0	-	-	2.0	1.8
500 TO 999 MILES......	47	100.0	25.3	43.5	30.1	-	-	-	1.0
1000 TO 1499 MILES....	15	100.0	45.3	38.0	15.3	-	-	.4	1.0
1500 MILES OR OVER....	-	100.0	50.5	49.2	-	.2	-	-	-
MOUNTAIN...............	-	100.0	-	-	-	-	-	-	-
UNDER 100 MILES........	-	100.0	-	-	-	-	-	-	-
100 TO 199 MILES......	-	100.0	-	-	-	-	-	-	-
200 TO 299 MILES......	-	100.0	-	-	-	-	-	-	-
300 TO 499 MILES......	-	100.0	-	-	-	-	-	-	-
500 TO 999 MILES......	-	100.0	-	-	-	-	-	-	-
1000 TO 1499 MILES....	-	100.0	-	-	-	-	-	-	-
1500 MILES OR OVER....	-	100.0	-	-	-	-	-	-	-
TON-MILES OF SHIPMENTS	(millions of ton-miles)								
U.S. TOTAL..........	247	100.0	47.6	37.5	11.5	.1	2.0	.9	.3
EAST NORTH CENTRAL......	63	100.0	39.1	47.0	13.6	.3	-	-	-
UNDER 100 MILES........	-	100.0	-	80.8	19.2	-	-	-	-
100 TO 199 MILES......	1	100.0	1.7	76.7	21.5	-	-	-	-
200 TO 299 MILES......	3	100.0	2.4	55.7	41.8	.1	-	-	-
300 TO 499 MILES......	4	100.0	-	57.8	41.8	.3	-	.1	-
500 TO 999 MILES......	24	100.0	19.6	61.7	18.4	.3	-	-	-
1000 TO 1499 MILES....	16	100.0	89.5	10.1	-	.4	-	-	-
1500 MILES OR OVER....	12	100.0	39.0	57.0	3.7	.2	-	.1	-
WEST SOUTH CENTRAL......	64	100.0	30.1	44.1	24.4	-	-	.3	1.1
UNDER 100 MILES........	-	100.0	-	18.6	80.2	-	-	1.2	-
100 TO 199 MILES......	-	100.0	3.3	25.6	68.9	-	-	-	2.2
200 TO 299 MILES......	1	100.0	7.7	54.4	37.9	-	-	-	-
300 TO 499 MILES......	4	100.0	1.8	63.0	31.8	-	-	2.0	1.5
500 TO 999 MILES......	38	100.0	28.0	43.9	27.0	-	-	-	1.0
1000 TO 1499 MILES....	17	100.0	44.6	39.2	14.5	-	-	.3	1.3
1500 MILES OR OVER....	1	100.0	50.3	49.5	-	.2	-	-	-
MOUNTAIN...............	-	100.0	-	-	-	-	-	-	-
UNDER 100 MILES........	-	100.0	-	-	-	-	-	-	-
100 TO 199 MILES......	-	100.0	-	-	-	-	-	-	-
200 TO 299 MILES......	-	100.0	-	-	-	-	-	-	-
300 TO 499 MILES......	-	100.0	-	-	-	-	-	-	-
500 TO 999 MILES......	-	100.0	-	-	-	-	-	-	-
1000 TO 1499 MILES....	-	100.0	-	-	-	-	-	-	-
1500 MILES OR OVER....	-	100.0	-	-	-	-	-	-	-

See footnotes at end of table 4.

TABLE 2. TCC GROUP 253—Percent Distribution of Geographic Division of Origin and Means of Transport, by Geographic Division of Destination: 1972

Geographic division of origin[1] and means of transport	Number	Percent distribution by division of destination									
		U.S. total	New England	Middle Atlantic	East North Central	West North Central	South Atlantic	East South Central	West South Central	Mountain	Pacific
TONS OF SHIPMENTS	(thousands of tons)										
U.S. TOTAL...............	344	100.0	3.1	12.2	17.5	7.3	14.5	4.8	16.3	10.2	14.3
RAIL...................	133	100.0	1.7	7.3	12.2	3.6	15.2	.2	19.9	15.1	24.8
MOTOR CARRIER..........	138	100.0	4.7	17.4	21.4	8.9	12.6	8.1	11.6	9.0	6.3
PRIVATE TRUCK..........	68	100.0	2.7	11.2	21.2	11.5	17.0	6.9	18.8	3.6	7.1
AIR....................	-	100.0	.6	17.3	13.0	18.3	19.4	4.3	7.4	7.0	12.6
WATER..................	1	100.0	-	-	-	-	-	-	-	-	100.0
OTHER..................	1	100.0	3.2	14.0	3.0	3.7	1.9	2.4	26.9	.7	44.3
UNKNOWN................	1	100.0	1.2	11.0	.6	-	37.4	23.2	10.5	-	16.2

See footnotes at end of table 4.

TABLE 2. **TCC GROUP 253—Percent Distribution of Geographic Division of Origin and Means of Transport, by Geographic Division of Destination: 1972**—Continued

Geographic division of origin[1] and means of transport	Number	Percent distribution by division of destination									
		U.S. total	New England	Middle Atlantic	East North Central	West North Central	South Atlantic	East South Central	West South Central	Mountain	Pacific
TONS OF SHIPMENTS	(thousands of tons)										
EAST NORTH CENTRAL	98	100.0	4.3	17.2	27.9	9.0	19.2	6.3	6.4	6.0	3.7
RAIL	24	100.0	-	9.6	.8	5.4	58.5	-	7.5	13.7	4.5
MOTOR CARRIER	53	100.0	4.7	19.4	34.0	8.7	8.3	8.4	8.0	3.7	4.8
PRIVATE TRUCK	21	100.0	8.3	20.3	43.9	13.7	1.8	8.0	.9	3.0	-
AIR	-	100.0	-	21.2	3.5	23.3	23.3	5.5	9.4	7.6	6.2
WATER	-	100.0	-	-	-	-	-	-	-	-	-
OTHER	-	100.0	3.1	17.5	26.9	11.3	11.3	1.1	5.6	.9	22.2
UNKNOWN	-	100.0	-	-	-	-	-	-	-	-	-
WEST SOUTH CENTRAL	93	100.0	.8	10.0	19.3	9.9	18.1	5.3	22.4	11.8	2.5
RAIL	20	100.0	.3	23.7	46.4	2.2	17.7	1.3	2.5	1.7	4.1
MOTOR CARRIER	40	100.0	1.4	8.8	11.4	9.4	15.6	9.8	18.7	22.2	2.7
PRIVATE TRUCK	31	100.0	.2	2.6	12.6	15.9	21.2	1.7	39.4	5.6	.8
AIR	-	100.0	-	-	-	-	25.3	-	-	39.8	34.9
WATER	-	100.0	-	-	-	-	-	-	-	-	-
OTHER	-	100.0	-	13.0	2.9	-	-	-	84.1	-	-
UNKNOWN	-	100.0	-	11.3	-	-	38.6	23.9	10.8	-	15.5
MOUNTAIN	-	100.0	-	-	-	-	-	-	-	-	-
RAIL	-	100.0	-	-	-	-	-	-	-	-	-
MOTOR CARRIER	-	100.0	-	-	-	-	-	-	-	-	-
PRIVATE TRUCK	-	100.0	-	-	-	-	-	-	-	-	-
AIR	-	100.0	-	-	-	-	-	-	-	-	-
WATER	-	100.0	-	-	-	-	-	-	-	-	-
OTHER	-	100.0	-	-	-	-	-	-	-	-	-
UNKNOWN	-	100.0	-	-	-	-	-	-	-	-	-
TON-MILES OF SHIPMENTS	(millions of ton-miles)										
U.S. TOTAL	247	100.0	3.7	12.3	11.4	5.5	16.2	2.6	16.0	10.1	22.0
RAIL	117	100.0	2.0	7.5	10.8	2.4	16.2	.1	22.5	9.0	29.6
MOTOR CARRIER	92	100.0	5.8	19.2	11.1	7.2	14.6	5.2	11.4	13.5	12.0
PRIVATE TRUCK	28	100.0	4.7	12.3	18.5	14.6	24.5	5.1	8.8	6.9	4.6
AIR	-	100.0	1.8	10.8	8.9	15.3	23.3	1.5	6.1	8.2	24.1
WATER	5	100.0	-	-	-	-	-	-	-	-	100.0
OTHER	2	100.0	2.2	7.5	.9	1.8	.4	.2	4.5	.7	81.8
UNKNOWN	-	100.0	4.0	12.8	.4	-	38.7	6.7	4.7	-	32.8
EAST NORTH CENTRAL	63	100.0	5.0	15.8	8.3	5.6	28.2	4.2	8.0	13.2	11.7
RAIL	24	100.0	-	5.6	.1	2.4	59.3	-	6.2	19.0	7.3
MOTOR CARRIER	29	100.0	6.5	21.2	10.9	5.9	9.9	6.0	11.2	9.7	18.7
PRIVATE TRUCK	8	100.0	14.5	26.2	23.0	13.4	2.6	9.7	1.7	8.9	-
AIR	-	100.0	-	14.3	1.3	20.9	30.4	2.1	8.4	9.0	13.6
WATER	-	100.0	-	-	-	-	-	-	-	-	-
OTHER	-	100.0	3.2	12.4	7.6	6.8	10.0	.5	6.2	1.1	52.2
UNKNOWN	-	100.0	-	-	-	-	-	-	-	-	-
WEST SOUTH CENTRAL	64	100.0	1.5	16.2	21.9	7.5	23.0	3.1	7.2	14.7	4.9
RAIL	19	100.0	.5	28.5	44.4	.9	17.7	.9	.5	1.3	5.3
MOTOR CARRIER	28	100.0	2.8	13.4	10.9	5.8	19.5	5.3	8.5	28.3	5.5
PRIVATE TRUCK	15	100.0	.5	5.8	15.2	18.9	35.4	1.6	12.9	7.5	2.2
AIR	-	100.0	-	-	-	-	21.6	-	-	37.1	41.3
WATER	-	100.0	-	-	-	-	-	-	-	-	-
OTHER	-	100.0	-	36.8	4.6	-	-	-	58.6	-	-
UNKNOWN	-	100.0	-	14.0	-	-	42.3	7.3	5.1	-	31.4
MOUNTAIN	-	100.0	-	-	-	-	-	-	-	-	-
RAIL	-	100.0	-	-	-	-	-	-	-	-	-
MOTOR CARRIER	-	100.0	-	-	-	-	-	-	-	-	-
PRIVATE TRUCK	-	100.0	-	-	-	-	-	-	-	-	-
AIR	-	100.0	-	-	-	-	-	-	-	-	-
WATER	-	100.0	-	-	-	-	-	-	-	-	-
OTHER	-	100.0	-	-	-	-	-	-	-	-	-
UNKNOWN	-	100.0	-	-	-	-	-	-	-	-	-

See footnotes at end of table 4.

TABLE 3. **TCC GROUP 253—Percent Distribution of Geographic Division of Destination and Means of Transport, by Geographic Division of Origin: 1972**

Geographic division of destination and means of transport	Number	Percent distribution by division of origin[1]									
		U.S. total	New England	Middle Atlantic	East North Central	West North Central	South Atlantic	East South Central	West South Central	Mountain	Pacific
TONS OF SHIPMENTS	(thousands of tons)										
U.S. TOTAL............	344	100.0	(D)	(D)	28.6	(D)	(D)	(D)	27.1	-	(D)
RAIL................	133	100.0	(D)	(D)	18.0	(D)	(D)	(D)	15.3	-	(D)
MOTOR CARRIER........	138	100.0	(D)	(D)	38.6	(D)	(D)	(D)	29.1	-	(D)
PRIVATE TRUCK........	68	100.0	(D)	(D)	30.6	(D)	(D)	(D)	45.9	-	(D)
AIR.................	-	100.0	(D)	(D)	78.3	(D)	(D)	(D)	2.7	-	(D)
WATER...............	1	100.0	(D)	(D)	-	(D)	(D)	(D)	-	-	(D)
OTHER...............	1	100.0	(D)	(D)	2.8	(D)	(D)	(D)	31.7	-	(D)
UNKNOWN.............	1	100.0	(D)	(D)	-	(D)	(D)	(D)	97.1	-	(D)
NEW ENGLAND..........	10	100.0	(D)	(D)	40.2	(D)	(D)	(D)	6.7	-	(D)
RAIL................	2	100.0	(D)	(D)	-	(D)	(D)	(D)	3.1	-	(D)
MOTOR CARRIER........	6	100.0	(D)	(D)	38.7	(D)	(D)	(D)	8.9	-	(D)
PRIVATE TRUCK........	1	100.0	(D)	(D)	95.1	(D)	(D)	(D)	3.2	-	(D)
AIR.................	-	100.0	(D)	(D)	-	(D)	(D)	(D)	-	-	(D)
WATER...............	-	100.0	(D)	(D)	-	(D)	(D)	(D)	-	-	(D)
OTHER...............	-	100.0	(D)	(D)	2.6	(D)	(D)	(D)	-	-	(D)
UNKNOWN.............	-	100.0	(D)	(D)	-	(D)	(D)	(D)	-	-	(D)
MIDDLE ATLANTIC......	41	100.0	(D)	(D)	40.5	(D)	(D)	(D)	22.3	-	(D)
RAIL................	9	100.0	(D)	(D)	23.6	(D)	(D)	(D)	49.3	-	(D)
MOTOR CARRIER........	24	100.0	(D)	(D)	42.9	(D)	(D)	(D)	14.6	-	(D)
PRIVATE TRUCK........	7	100.0	(D)	(D)	55.7	(D)	(D)	(D)	10.5	-	(D)
AIR.................	-	100.0	(D)	(D)	96.0	(D)	(D)	(D)	-	-	(D)
WATER...............	-	100.0	(D)	(D)	-	(D)	(D)	(D)	-	-	(D)
OTHER...............	-	100.0	(D)	(D)	3.4	(D)	(D)	(D)	29.5	-	(D)
UNKNOWN.............	-	100.0	(D)	(D)	-	(D)	(D)	(D)	100.0	-	(D)
EAST NORTH CENTRAL....	60	100.0	(D)	(D)	45.5	(D)	(D)	(D)	29.8	-	(D)
RAIL................	16	100.0	(D)	(D)	1.2	(D)	(D)	(D)	58.1	-	(D)
MOTOR CARRIER........	29	100.0	(D)	(D)	61.3	(D)	(D)	(D)	15.5	-	(D)
PRIVATE TRUCK........	14	100.0	(D)	(D)	63.2	(D)	(D)	(D)	27.3	-	(D)
AIR.................	-	100.0	(D)	(D)	21.3	(D)	(D)	(D)	-	-	(D)
WATER...............	-	100.0	(D)	(D)	-	(D)	(D)	(D)	-	-	(D)
OTHER...............	-	100.0	(D)	(D)	25.1	(D)	(D)	(D)	30.9	-	(D)
UNKNOWN.............	-	100.0	(D)	(D)	-	(D)	(D)	(D)	-	-	(D)
WEST NORTH CENTRAL....	25	100.0	(D)	(D)	35.4	(D)	(D)	(D)	36.7	-	(D)
RAIL................	4	100.0	(D)	(D)	27.2	(D)	(D)	(D)	9.4	-	(D)
MOTOR CARRIER........	12	100.0	(D)	(D)	37.7	(D)	(D)	(D)	30.5	-	(D)
PRIVATE TRUCK........	7	100.0	(D)	(D)	36.4	(D)	(D)	(D)	63.2	-	(D)
AIR.................	-	100.0	(D)	(D)	99.8	(D)	(D)	(D)	-	-	(D)
WATER...............	-	100.0	(D)	(D)	-	(D)	(D)	(D)	-	-	(D)
OTHER...............	-	100.0	(D)	(D)	8.5	(D)	(D)	(D)	-	-	(D)
UNKNOWN.............	-	100.0	(D)	(D)	-	(D)	(D)	(D)	-	-	(D)
SOUTH ATLANTIC.......	49	100.0	(D)	(D)	38.0	(D)	(D)	(D)	34.0	-	(D)
RAIL................	20	100.0	(D)	(D)	69.2	(D)	(D)	(D)	17.8	-	(D)
MOTOR CARRIER........	17	100.0	(D)	(D)	25.4	(D)	(D)	(D)	36.0	-	(D)
PRIVATE TRUCK........	11	100.0	(D)	(D)	3.3	(D)	(D)	(D)	57.3	-	(D)
AIR.................	-	100.0	(D)	(D)	93.9	(D)	(D)	(D)	3.6	-	(D)
WATER...............	-	100.0	(D)	(D)	-	(D)	(D)	(D)	-	-	(D)
OTHER...............	-	100.0	(D)	(D)	16.6	(D)	(D)	(D)	-	-	(D)
UNKNOWN.............	-	100.0	(D)	(D)	-	(D)	(D)	(D)	100.0	-	(D)
EAST SOUTH CENTRAL....	16	100.0	(D)	(D)	37.8	(D)	(D)	(D)	30.4	-	(D)
RAIL................	-	100.0	(D)	(D)	-	(D)	(D)	(D)	100.0	-	(D)
MOTOR CARRIER........	11	100.0	(D)	(D)	40.4	(D)	(D)	(D)	35.3	-	(D)
PRIVATE TRUCK........	4	100.0	(D)	(D)	35.8	(D)	(D)	(D)	11.5	-	(D)
AIR.................	-	100.0	(D)	(D)	100.0	(D)	(D)	(D)	-	-	(D)
WATER...............	-	100.0	(D)	(D)	-	(D)	(D)	(D)	-	-	(D)
OTHER...............	-	100.0	(D)	(D)	1.3	(D)	(D)	(D)	-	-	(D)
UNKNOWN.............	-	100.0	(D)	(D)	-	(D)	(D)	(D)	100.0	-	(D)
WEST SOUTH CENTRAL....	56	100.0	(D)	(D)	11.2	(D)	(D)	(D)	37.4	-	(D)
RAIL................	26	100.0	(D)	(D)	6.8	(D)	(D)	(D)	1.9	-	(D)
MOTOR CARRIER........	15	100.0	(D)	(D)	26.7	(D)	(D)	(D)	47.0	-	(D)
PRIVATE TRUCK........	12	100.0	(D)	(D)	1.5	(D)	(D)	(D)	96.0	-	(D)
AIR.................	-	100.0	(D)	(D)	100.0	(D)	(D)	(D)	-	-	(D)
WATER...............	-	100.0	(D)	(D)	-	(D)	(D)	(D)	-	-	(D)
OTHER...............	-	100.0	(D)	(D)	.6	(D)	(D)	(D)	99.3	-	(D)
UNKNOWN.............	-	100.0	(D)	(D)	-	(D)	(D)	(D)	100.0	-	(D)
MOUNTAIN.............	35	100.0	(D)	(D)	16.8	(D)	(D)	(D)	31.5	-	(D)
RAIL................	20	100.0	(D)	(D)	16.3	(D)	(D)	(D)	1.8	-	(D)
MOTOR CARRIER........	12	100.0	(D)	(D)	15.8	(D)	(D)	(D)	71.8	-	(D)
PRIVATE TRUCK........	2	100.0	(D)	(D)	26.0	(D)	(D)	(D)	71.7	-	(D)
AIR.................	-	100.0	(D)	(D)	84.1	(D)	(D)	(D)	15.5	-	(D)
WATER...............	-	100.0	(D)	(D)	-	(D)	(D)	(D)	-	-	(D)
OTHER...............	-	100.0	(D)	(D)	3.6	(D)	(D)	(D)	-	-	(D)
UNKNOWN.............	-	100.0	(D)	(D)	-	(D)	(D)	(D)	-	-	(D)
PACIFIC..............	49	100.0	(D)	(D)	7.4	(D)	(D)	(D)	4.8	-	(D)
RAIL................	33	100.0	(D)	(D)	3.3	(D)	(D)	(D)	2.5	-	(D)
MOTOR CARRIER........	8	100.0	(D)	(D)	29.1	(D)	(D)	(D)	12.6	-	(D)
PRIVATE TRUCK........	4	100.0	(D)	(D)	-	(D)	(D)	(D)	5.3	-	(D)
AIR.................	-	100.0	(D)	(D)	38.4	(D)	(D)	(D)	7.6	-	(D)
WATER...............	1	100.0	(D)	(D)	-	(D)	(D)	(D)	-	-	(D)
OTHER...............	-	100.0	(D)	(D)	1.4	(D)	(D)	(D)	-	-	(D)
UNKNOWN.............	-	100.0	(D)	(D)	-	(D)	(D)	(D)	93.0	-	(D)

See footnotes at end of table 4.

TABLE 3. TCC GROUP 253—Percent Distribution of Geographic Division of Destination and Means of Transport, by Geographic Division of Origin: 1972—Continued

Geographic division of destination and means of transport	Number	Percent distribution by division of origin[1]									
		U.S. total	New England	Middle Atlantic	East North Central	West North Central	South Atlantic	East South Central	West South Central	Mountain	Pacific
TON-MILES OF SHIPMENTS	(millions of ton-miles)										
U.S. TOTAL.............	247	100.0	(D)	(D)	25.7	(D)	(D)	(D)	26.2	-	(D)
RAIL..................	117	100.0	(D)	(D)	21.1	(D)	(D)	(D)	16.6	-	(D)
MOTOR CARRIER.........	92	100.0	(D)	(D)	32.3	(D)	(D)	(D)	30.8	-	(D)
PRIVATE TRUCK.........	28	100.0	(D)	(D)	30.4	(D)	(D)	(D)	55.6	-	(D)
AIR..................	-	100.0	(D)	(D)	73.0	(D)	(D)	(D)	4.2	-	(D)
WATER................	5	100.0	(D)	(D)	-	(D)	(D)	(D)	-	-	(D)
OTHER................	2	100.0	(D)	(D)	1.4	(D)	(D)	(D)	7.5	-	(D)
UNKNOWN..............	-	100.0	(D)	(D)	-	(D)	(D)	(D)	91.6	-	(D)
NEW ENGLAND...........	9	100.0	(D)	(D)	35.3	(D)	(D)	(D)	10.7	-	(D)
RAIL..................	2	100.0	(D)	(D)	-	(D)	(D)	(D)	3.8	-	(D)
MOTOR CARRIER.........	5	100.0	(D)	(D)	36.5	(D)	(D)	(D)	15.1	-	(D)
PRIVATE TRUCK.........	1	100.0	(D)	(D)	92.9	(D)	(D)	(D)	5.7	-	(D)
AIR..................	-	100.0	(D)	(D)	-	(D)	(D)	(D)	-	-	(D)
WATER................	-	100.0	(D)	(D)	-	(D)	(D)	(D)	-	-	(D)
OTHER................	-	100.0	(D)	(D)	2.0	(D)	(D)	(D)	-	-	(D)
UNKNOWN..............	-	100.0	(D)	(D)	-	(D)	(D)	(D)	-	-	(D)
MIDDLE ATLANTIC.......	30	100.0	(D)	(D)	32.9	(D)	(D)	(D)	34.4	-	(D)
RAIL..................	8	100.0	(D)	(D)	15.8	(D)	(D)	(D)	62.9	-	(D)
MOTOR CARRIER.........	17	100.0	(D)	(D)	35.6	(D)	(D)	(D)	21.5	-	(D)
PRIVATE TRUCK.........	3	100.0	(D)	(D)	64.8	(D)	(D)	(D)	26.3	-	(D)
AIR..................	-	100.0	(D)	(D)	96.5	(D)	(D)	(D)	-	-	(D)
WATER................	-	100.0	(D)	(D)	-	(D)	(D)	(D)	-	-	(D)
OTHER................	-	100.0	(D)	(D)	2.3	(D)	(D)	(D)	36.6	-	(D)
UNKNOWN..............	-	100.0	(D)	(D)	-	(D)	(D)	(D)	100.0	-	(D)
EAST NORTH CENTRAL....	28	100.0	(D)	(D)	18.7	(D)	(D)	(D)	50.3	-	(D)
RAIL..................	12	100.0	(D)	(D)	.2	(D)	(D)	(D)	68.5	-	(D)
MOTOR CARRIER.........	10	100.0	(D)	(D)	31.8	(D)	(D)	(D)	30.3	-	(D)
PRIVATE TRUCK.........	5	100.0	(D)	(D)	37.8	(D)	(D)	(D)	45.8	-	(D)
AIR..................	-	100.0	(D)	(D)	11.0	(D)	(D)	(D)	-	-	(D)
WATER................	-	100.0	(D)	(D)	-	(D)	(D)	(D)	-	-	(D)
OTHER................	-	100.0	(D)	(D)	12.1	(D)	(D)	(D)	39.0	-	(D)
UNKNOWN..............	-	100.0	(D)	(D)	-	(D)	(D)	(D)	-	-	(D)
WEST NORTH CENTRAL....	13	100.0	(D)	(D)	26.0	(D)	(D)	(D)	35.3	-	(D)
RAIL..................	2	100.0	(D)	(D)	21.8	(D)	(D)	(D)	6.1	-	(D)
MOTOR CARRIER.........	6	100.0	(D)	(D)	26.3	(D)	(D)	(D)	25.1	-	(D)
PRIVATE TRUCK.........	4	100.0	(D)	(D)	27.9	(D)	(D)	(D)	72.0	-	(D)
AIR..................	-	100.0	(D)	(D)	99.8	(D)	(D)	(D)	-	-	(D)
WATER................	-	100.0	(D)	(D)	-	(D)	(D)	(D)	-	-	(D)
OTHER................	-	100.0	(D)	(D)	5.4	(D)	(D)	(D)	-	-	(D)
UNKNOWN..............	-	100.0	(D)	(D)	-	(D)	(D)	(D)	-	-	(D)
SOUTH ATLANTIC........	40	100.0	(D)	(D)	44.9	(D)	(D)	(D)	37.4	-	(D)
RAIL..................	19	100.0	(D)	(D)	77.2	(D)	(D)	(D)	18.2	-	(D)
MOTOR CARRIER.........	13	100.0	(D)	(D)	21.8	(D)	(D)	(D)	41.0	-	(D)
PRIVATE TRUCK.........	6	100.0	(D)	(D)	3.2	(D)	(D)	(D)	80.3	-	(D)
AIR..................	-	100.0	(D)	(D)	95.3	(D)	(D)	(D)	3.9	-	(D)
WATER................	-	100.0	(D)	(D)	-	(D)	(D)	(D)	-	-	(D)
OTHER................	-	100.0	(D)	(D)	32.2	(D)	(D)	(D)	-	-	(D)
UNKNOWN..............	-	100.0	(D)	(D)	-	(D)	(D)	(D)	100.0	-	(D)
EAST SOUTH CENTRAL....	6	100.0	(D)	(D)	40.7	(D)	(D)	(D)	30.6	-	(D)
RAIL..................	-	100.0	(D)	(D)	-	(D)	(D)	(D)	100.0	-	(D)
MOTOR CARRIER.........	4	100.0	(D)	(D)	37.3	(D)	(D)	(D)	31.2	-	(D)
PRIVATE TRUCK.........	1	100.0	(D)	(D)	58.6	(D)	(D)	(D)	17.8	-	(D)
AIR..................	-	100.0	(D)	(D)	100.0	(D)	(D)	(D)	-	-	(D)
WATER................	-	100.0	(D)	(D)	-	(D)	(D)	(D)	-	-	(D)
OTHER................	-	100.0	(D)	(D)	3.6	(D)	(D)	(D)	-	-	(D)
UNKNOWN..............	-	100.0	(D)	(D)	-	(D)	(D)	(D)	100.0	-	(D)
WEST SOUTH CENTRAL....	39	100.0	(D)	(D)	12.8	(D)	(D)	(D)	11.9	-	(D)
RAIL..................	26	100.0	(D)	(D)	5.9	(D)	(D)	(D)	.4	-	(D)
MOTOR CARRIER.........	10	100.0	(D)	(D)	31.7	(D)	(D)	(D)	22.9	-	(D)
PRIVATE TRUCK.........	2	100.0	(D)	(D)	5.8	(D)	(D)	(D)	81.7	-	(D)
AIR..................	-	100.0	(D)	(D)	100.0	(D)	(D)	(D)	-	-	(D)
WATER................	-	100.0	(D)	(D)	-	(D)	(D)	(D)	-	-	(D)
OTHER................	-	100.0	(D)	(D)	1.9	(D)	(D)	(D)	97.4	-	(D)
UNKNOWN..............	-	100.0	(D)	(D)	-	(D)	(D)	(D)	100.0	-	(D)
MOUNTAIN..............	25	100.0	(D)	(D)	33.6	(D)	(D)	(D)	38.1	-	(D)
RAIL..................	10	100.0	(D)	(D)	44.9	(D)	(D)	(D)	2.5	-	(D)
MOTOR CARRIER.........	12	100.0	(D)	(D)	23.2	(D)	(D)	(D)	64.8	-	(D)
PRIVATE TRUCK.........	1	100.0	(D)	(D)	38.9	(D)	(D)	(D)	60.2	-	(D)
AIR..................	-	100.0	(D)	(D)	80.3	(D)	(D)	(D)	19.1	-	(D)
WATER................	-	100.0	(D)	(D)	-	(D)	(D)	(D)	-	-	(D)
OTHER................	-	100.0	(D)	(D)	2.3	(D)	(D)	(D)	-	-	(D)
UNKNOWN..............	-	100.0	(D)	(D)	-	(D)	(D)	(D)	-	-	(D)
PACIFIC...............	54	100.0	(D)	(D)	13.7	(D)	(D)	(D)	5.8	-	(D)
RAIL..................	34	100.0	(D)	(D)	5.2	(D)	(D)	(D)	3.0	-	(D)
MOTOR CARRIER.........	11	100.0	(D)	(D)	50.4	(D)	(D)	(D)	14.0	-	(D)
PRIVATE TRUCK.........	1	100.0	(D)	(D)	-	(D)	(D)	(D)	26.2	-	(D)
AIR..................	-	100.0	(D)	(D)	41.2	(D)	(D)	(D)	7.3	-	(D)
WATER................	5	100.0	(D)	(D)	-	(D)	(D)	(D)	-	-	(D)
OTHER................	1	100.0	(D)	(D)	.9	(D)	(D)	(D)	-	-	(D)
UNKNOWN..............	-	100.0	(D)	(D)	-	(D)	(D)	(D)	87.5	-	(D)

See footnotes at end of table 4.

TABLE 4. **TCC GROUP 253—Percent Distribution of Distance Shipped and Weight of Shipment, by Means of Transport: 1972**

Distance shipped and weight of shipment[2][3]	Number	Percent distribution by means of transport							
		All means of transport	Rail	Motor carrier	Private truck	Air	Water	Other	Unknown
TONS OF SHIPMENTS	(thousands of tons)								
U.S. TOTAL.........	333	100.0	39.6	38.5	20.6	.1	.6	.4	.3
UNDER 100 MILES.........	16	100.0	-	41.5	56.3	-	-	2.2	-
UNDER 1000 POUNDS.....	2	100.0	-	39.2	48.8	-	-	12.0	-
1000 TO 9999 POUNDS...	10	100.0	-	25.2	73.9	-	-	.9	-
10000 TO 29999 POUNDS.	3	100.0	-	87.8	12.2	-	-	-	-
30000 TO 59999 POUNDS.	-	100.0	-	100.0	-	-	-	-	-
60000 TO 89999 POUNDS.	-	100.0	-	100.0	-	-	-	-	-
90000 POUNDS AND OVER.	-	100.0	-	100.0	-	-	-	-	-
100 TO 199 MILES........	22	100.0	.7	45.8	52.8	-	-	.1	.6
UNDER 1000 POUNDS.....	3	100.0	5.0	92.1	2.0	-	-	.8	-
1000 TO 9999 POUNDS...	14	100.0	-	37.5	61.6	-	-	-	.9
10000 TO 29999 POUNDS.	3	100.0	-	27.9	72.1	-	-	-	-
30000 TO 59999 POUNDS.	-	100.0	-	48.6	51.4	-	-	-	-
60000 TO 89999 POUNDS.	-	100.0	-	100.0	-	-	-	-	-
90000 POUNDS AND OVER.	-	100.0	-	100.0	-	-	-	-	-
200 TO 299 MILES........	25	100.0	11.8	51.4	36.6	.1	-	.1	-
UNDER 1000 POUNDS.....	5	100.0	2.8	68.0	28.3	.3	-	.6	-
1000 TO 9999 POUNDS...	7	100.0	-	67.5	32.5	-	-	-	-
10000 TO 29999 POUNDS.	4	100.0	57.9	5.1	37.0	-	-	-	-
30000 TO 59999 POUNDS.	7	100.0	-	50.8	49.2	-	-	-	-
60000 TO 89999 POUNDS.	-	100.0	-	100.0	-	-	-	-	-
90000 POUNDS AND OVER.	-	100.0	-	100.0	-	-	-	-	-
300 TO 499 MILES........	52	100.0	32.8	41.8	24.4	.1	-	.5	.4
UNDER 1000 POUNDS.....	8	100.0	.3	89.8	7.8	.4	-	.3	1.4
1000 TO 9999 POUNDS...	14	100.0	1.4	63.3	32.9	-	-	1.6	.7
10000 TO 29999 POUNDS.	19	100.0	63.0	15.2	21.9	-	-	-	-
30000 TO 59999 POUNDS.	9	100.0	47.6	26.0	26.4	-	-	-	-
60000 TO 89999 POUNDS.	-	100.0	-	18.0	82.0	-	-	-	-
90000 POUNDS AND OVER.	-	100.0	-	-	-	-	-	-	-
500 TO 999 MILES........	156	100.0	50.7	34.3	14.5	.1	-	.1	.3
UNDER 1000 POUNDS.....	14	100.0	4.5	86.8	6.6	.6	-	1.5	-
1000 TO 9999 POUNDS...	37	100.0	7.3	59.0	32.3	.1	-	-	1.3
10000 TO 29999 POUNDS.	42	100.0	69.5	11.2	19.3	-	-	-	-
30000 TO 59999 POUNDS.	40	100.0	63.7	32.4	3.9	-	-	-	-
60000 TO 89999 POUNDS.	22	100.0	93.6	6.4	-	-	-	-	-
90000 POUNDS AND OVER.	-	100.0	68.7	31.3	-	-	-	-	-
1000 TO 1499 MILES......	44	100.0	58.3	35.3	5.7	.1	-	.2	.3
UNDER 1000 POUNDS.....	6	100.0	5.2	68.8	23.3	1.0	-	1.7	-
1000 TO 9999 POUNDS...	7	100.0	5.6	81.3	11.1	-	-	-	2.0
10000 TO 29999 POUNDS.	16	100.0	78.0	20.5	1.5	-	-	-	-
30000 TO 59999 POUNDS.	1	100.0	-	100.0	-	-	-	-	-
60000 TO 89999 POUNDS.	-	100.0	-	100.0	-	-	-	-	-
90000 POUNDS AND OVER.	13	100.0	97.8	2.2	-	-	-	-	-
1500 MILES OR OVER.....	15	100.0	38.3	44.0	2.1	.2	12.1	3.1	.2
UNDER 1000 POUNDS.....	1	100.0	4.9	90.7	.1	2.2	1.0	1.1	-
1000 TO 9999 POUNDS...	3	100.0	16.3	71.5	-	-	-	12.0	.3
10000 TO 29999 POUNDS.	8	100.0	52.4	21.4	3.8	-	-	-	.3
30000 TO 59999 POUNDS.	1	100.0	80.4	19.6	-	-	22.2	-	.1
60000 TO 89999 POUNDS.	-	100.0	-	100.0	-	-	-	-	-
90000 POUNDS AND OVER.	-	100.0	-	100.0	-	-	-	-	-
TON-MILES OF SHIPMENTS	(millions of ton-miles)								
U.S. TOTAL..........	240	100.0	48.7	36.1	11.8	.1	2.1	.9	.3
UNDER 100 MILES.........	-	100.0	-	45.1	54.1	-	-	.8	-
UNDER 1000 POUNDS.....	-	100.0	-	55.2	39.3	-	-	5.4	-
1000 TO 9999 POUNDS...	-	100.0	-	22.8	76.9	-	-	.3	-
10000 TO 29999 POUNDS.	-	100.0	-	92.4	7.6	-	-	-	-
30000 TO 59999 POUNDS.	-	100.0	-	100.0	-	-	-	-	-
60000 TO 89999 POUNDS.	-	100.0	-	100.0	-	-	-	-	-
90000 POUNDS AND OVER.	-	100.0	-	100.0	-	-	-	-	-
100 TO 199 MILES........	3	100.0	.9	48.2	50.2	-	-	.1	.6
UNDER 1000 POUNDS.....	-	100.0	5.9	91.5	1.9	-	-	.7	-
1000 TO 9999 POUNDS...	2	100.0	-	40.9	58.2	-	-	-	.9
10000 TO 29999 POUNDS.	-	100.0	-	28.7	71.3	-	-	-	-
30000 TO 59999 POUNDS.	-	100.0	-	46.8	53.2	-	-	-	-
60000 TO 89999 POUNDS.	-	100.0	-	100.0	-	-	-	-	-
90000 POUNDS AND OVER.	-	100.0	-	100.0	-	-	-	-	-

See footnotes at end of table 4.

TABLE 4. **TCC GROUP 253—Percent Distribution of Distance Shipped and Weight of Shipment, by Means of Transport: 1972**—Continued

Distance shipped and weight of shipment[2][3]	Number	Percent distribution by means of transport							
		All means of transport	Rail	Motor carrier	Private truck	Air	Water	Other	Unknown
TON-MILES OF SHIPMENTS	(millions of ton-miles)								
200 TO 299 MILES........	6	100.0	10.9	52.7	36.2	.1	-	.1	-
UNDER 1000 POUNDS.....	1	100.0	3.0	68.1	28.0	.3	-	.6	-
1000 TO 9999 POUNDS...	2	100.0	-	68.0	32.0	-	-	-	-
10000 TO 29999 POUNDS.	1	100.0	55.6	5.0	39.4	-	-	-	-
30000 TO 59999 POUNDS.	1	100.0	-	52.6	47.4	-	-	-	-
60000 TO 89999 POUNDS.	-	100.0	-	100.0	-	-	-	-	-
90000 POUNDS AND OVER.	-	100.0	-	100.0	-	-	-	-	-
300 TO 499 MILES........	19	100.0	30.4	44.0	24.6	.1	-	.5	.4
UNDER 1000 POUNDS.....	3	100.0	.2	90.1	7.7	.4	-	.3	1.2
1000 TO 9999 POUNDS...	5	100.0	1.5	63.6	32.5	-	-	1.7	.6
10000 TO 29999 POUNDS.	7	100.0	59.8	15.7	24.6	-	-	-	-
30000 TO 59999 POUNDS.	3	100.0	45.0	30.4	24.7	-	-	-	-
60000 TO 89999 POUNDS.	-	100.0	-	23.1	76.9	-	-	-	-
90000 POUNDS AND OVER.	-	100.0	-	-	-	-	-	-	-
500 TO 999 MILES........	127	100.0	55.0	32.1	12.4	.1	-	.1	.3
UNDER 1000 POUNDS.....	10	100.0	4.3	86.8	6.8	.5	-	1.6	-
1000 TO 9999 POUNDS...	27	100.0	7.1	60.0	31.3	.1	-	-	1.4
10000 TO 29999 POUNDS.	31	100.0	72.5	10.0	17.5	-	-	-	-
30000 TO 59999 POUNDS.	35	100.0	67.5	30.0	2.5	-	-	-	-
60000 TO 89999 POUNDS.	21	100.0	94.9	5.1	-	-	-	-	-
90000 POUNDS AND OVER.	-	100.0	64.4	35.6	-	-	-	-	-
1000 TO 1499 MILES......	52	100.0	57.7	36.1	5.4	.1	-	.2	.4
UNDER 1000 POUNDS.....	7	100.0	5.4	69.7	22.7	.9	-	1.4	-
1000 TO 9999 POUNDS...	8	100.0	4.8	83.2	9.5	-	-	-	2.5
10000 TO 29999 POUNDS.	19	100.0	78.9	19.6	1.5	-	-	-	-
30000 TO 59999 POUNDS.	1	100.0	-	100.0	-	-	-	-	-
60000 TO 89999 POUNDS.	-	100.0	-	100.0	-	-	-	-	-
90000 POUNDS AND OVER.	14	100.0	97.4	2.6	-	-	-	-	-
1500 MILES OR OVER......	30	100.0	33.0	42.7	1.6	.2	16.4	5.9	.2
UNDER 1000 POUNDS.....	2	100.0	5.6	89.4	.2	1.9	1.5	1.3	-
1000 TO 9999 POUNDS...	7	100.0	13.4	62.6	-	-	-	23.6	.4
10000 TO 29999 POUNDS.	17	100.0	44.4	23.7	2.8	-	28.9	-	.2
30000 TO 59999 POUNDS.	1	100.0	75.3	24.7	-	-	-	-	-
60000 TO 89999 POUNDS.	-	100.0	-	100.0	-	-	-	-	-
90000 POUNDS AND OVER.	-	100.0	-	100.0	-	-	-	-	-

Note: Detail may not add to total due to rounding. The introductory table shows the estimates of sampling variability for tons; sampling variability for ton-miles has not been estimated. See the map in the Introduction for the States comprising the geographic divisions of the United States.

Shipments excluded from the survey are those moving by pipeline (primarily petroleum products from refineries), parcel post shipments, and commodities moved by own power (motorized vehicles, aircraft, etc.) or towed (prefabricated buildings, etc.). Local shipments (commodities shipped less than 25 miles from the plant) and shipments within the same city are also excluded. Shipments to Alaska and Hawaii from the 48 conterminous States and the District of Columbia are included; however, no data were obtained for shipments originating in Alaska and Hawaii.

- Represents zero or rounds to zero.   (D) Withheld to avoid disclosing figures for individual companies.

[1]Production of this commodity is concentrated in the geographic divisions shown; figures and distributions for geographic divisions not shown are included in the total.

[2]Distances of shipments to foreign destinations are calculated only to the U.S. port of exit.

[3]Includes only shipments represented by bills of lading and invoices. Summary records which did not show individual weights of shipments are not included.

TCC 254. Partitions, Shelving, Lockers, Office and Store Fixtures

Comparisons of Tons and Ton-Miles of Shipments for
Geographic Divisions of Origin and for Sampling Variability: 1972 and 1967

Geographic division of origin	Estimates				Relative sampling variability in tons (percent)	
	1972		1967		1972	1967
	Tons (thousands)	Ton-miles (millions)	Tons (thousands)	Ton-miles (millions)		
U.S. total	1,120	572	2,170	1,162	11.6	(*)
New England	(D)	(D)	(*)	(*)	(*)	(*)
Middle Atlantic	146	61	(*)	(*)	16.8	(*)
East North Central	474	248	(*)	(*)	21.0	(*)
West North Central	78	61	(*)	(*)	23.6	(*)
South Atlantic	(D)	(D)	(*)	(*)	(*)	(*)
East South Central	(D)	(D)	(*)	(*)	(*)	(*)
West South Central	(D)	(D)	(*)	(*)	(*)	(*)
Mountain	(D)	(D)	(*)	(*)	(*)	(*)
Pacific	72	28	(*)	(*)	42.8	(*)

(D) Withheld to avoid disclosing figures for individual companies.   (*) Data not published.

TABLE 1. TCC GROUP 254—Percent Distribution of Geographic Division of Origin and Distance Shipped, by Means of Transport: 1972

Geographic division of origin[1] and distance shipped[2]	Number	Percent distribution by means of transport							
		All means of transport	Rail	Motor carrier	Private truck	Air	Water	Other	Unknown
TONS OF SHIPMENTS	(thousands of tons)								
U.S. TOTAL..........	1 120	100.0	8.7	52.4	38.0	.1	-	.8	.1
MIDDLE ATLANTIC........	146	100.0	17.0	50.9	29.0	-	-	2.9	.1
UNDER 100 MILES.......	39	100.0	.1	51.0	43.3	-	-	5.4	.3
100 TO 199 MILES......	18	100.0	-	39.1	60.3	-	-	.2	.4
200 TO 299 MILES......	22	100.0	13.8	52.7	25.2	-	-	8.4	-
300 TO 499 MILES......	29	100.0	43.9	47.6	8.4	-	-	.1	-
500 TO 999 MILES......	23	100.0	29.5	56.0	13.5	-	-	1.0	-
1000 TO 1499 MILES....	6	100.0	11.1	51.2	37.2	-	-	.3	-
1500 MILES OR OVER....	7	100.0	19.2	71.3	9.5	-	-	-	.2
EAST NORTH CENTRAL......	474	100.0	13.4	57.0	28.9	.2	-	.4	.1
UNDER 100 MILES.......	116	100.0	-	26.6	73.3	-	-	-	-
100 TO 199 MILES......	40	100.0	2.7	77.5	19.6	.1	-	.1	-
200 TO 299 MILES......	50	100.0	3.1	73.5	23.2	.1	-	.1	.1
300 TO 499 MILES......	100	100.0	15.1	69.0	14.6	-	-	1.2	.1
500 TO 999 MILES......	101	100.0	17.2	70.4	11.9	.3	-	.2	-
1000 TO 1499 MILES....	25	100.0	63.0	27.0	8.3	.1	-	1.6	-
1500 MILES OR OVER....	38	100.0	30.8	60.0	7.5	.7	-	.5	.5
WEST NORTH CENTRAL......	78	100.0	-	77.9	21.5	.3	-	.2	-
UNDER 100 MILES.......	1	100.0	-	51.8	47.8	-	-	.4	-
100 TO 199 MILES......	2	100.0	-	98.9	.8	-	-	.4	-
200 TO 299 MILES......	3	100.0	-	97.7	2.2	-	-	.1	-
300 TO 499 MILES......	12	100.0	-	83.0	16.7	.1	-	.2	-
500 TO 999 MILES......	33	100.0	-	80.7	18.5	.5	-	.3	-
1000 TO 1499 MILES....	21	100.0	-	64.3	35.3	.4	-	-	-
1500 MILES OR OVER....	2	100.0	-	99.0	.5	.4	.1	-	-
PACIFIC................	72	100.0	-	31.6	68.1	-	.2	-	.2
UNDER 100 MILES.......	26	100.0	-	11.1	88.9	-	-	-	-
100 TO 199 MILES......	14	100.0	-	10.0	89.9	-	-	-	.1
200 TO 299 MILES......	3	100.0	-	40.7	59.3	-	-	-	-
300 TO 499 MILES......	14	100.0	-	34.7	65.3	-	-	-	-
500 TO 999 MILES......	3	100.0	-	68.2	31.7	-	-	-	-
1000 TO 1499 MILES....	4	100.0	-	100.0	-	-	-	-	-
1500 MILES OR OVER....	5	100.0	-	95.4	-	.1	2.3	.2	1.9
TON-MILES OF SHIPMENTS	(millions of ton-miles)								
U.S. TOTAL..........	572	100.0	15.9	59.2	23.8	.2	.1	.7	.1
MIDDLE ATLANTIC........	61	100.0	24.6	56.8	17.5	-	-	1.1	.1
UNDER 100 MILES.......	1	100.0	.2	62.6	34.3	-	-	2.9	.1
100 TO 199 MILES......	2	100.0	-	39.9	59.5	-	-	.2	.5
200 TO 299 MILES......	5	100.0	14.8	52.5	25.3	-	-	7.4	-
300 TO 499 MILES......	10	100.0	46.9	44.4	8.6	-	-	.1	-
500 TO 999 MILES......	16	100.0	29.3	56.7	12.9	-	-	1.1	-
1000 TO 1499 MILES....	7	100.0	12.4	53.0	34.1	-	-	.2	.3
1500 MILES OR OVER....	17	100.0	20.8	69.7	9.5	-	-	-	-
EAST NORTH CENTRAL......	248	100.0	28.0	59.2	11.6	.3	-	.6	.2
UNDER 100 MILES.......	5	100.0	-	38.6	61.4	-	-	-	-
100 TO 199 MILES......	5	100.0	3.5	77.8	18.5	.1	-	.1	-
200 TO 299 MILES......	12	100.0	3.1	75.4	21.4	.1	-	.1	.1
300 TO 499 MILES......	40	100.0	14.9	68.4	15.5	-	-	1.1	-
500 TO 999 MILES......	68	100.0	18.2	69.8	11.5	.3	-	.2	-
1000 TO 1499 MILES....	30	100.0	62.9	27.6	7.5	.1	-	1.8	-
1500 MILES OR OVER....	84	100.0	36.6	55.3	6.5	.6	-	.5	.5
WEST NORTH CENTRAL......	61	100.0	-	76.2	23.3	.4	-	.1	-
UNDER 100 MILES.......	-	100.0	-	40.2	59.2	-	-	.6	-
100 TO 199 MILES......	-	100.0	-	99.0	.6	-	-	.3	-
200 TO 299 MILES......	-	100.0	-	98.1	1.8	-	-	.1	-
300 TO 499 MILES......	5	100.0	-	83.1	16.7	.1	-	.2	-
500 TO 999 MILES......	25	100.0	-	79.0	20.2	.5	-	.2	-
1000 TO 1499 MILES....	25	100.0	-	66.5	33.0	.4	-	-	-
1500 MILES OR OVER....	4	100.0	-	99.1	.4	.3	.3	-	-
PACIFIC................	28	100.0	-	71.1	27.2	.1	1.0	.1	.6
UNDER 100 MILES.......	1	100.0	-	7.9	92.1	-	-	-	-
100 TO 199 MILES......	2	100.0	-	7.8	92.1	-	-	-	.1
200 TO 299 MILES......	-	100.0	-	37.0	63.0	-	-	-	-
300 TO 499 MILES......	4	100.0	-	36.0	64.0	-	-	-	-
500 TO 999 MILES......	2	100.0	-	77.0	23.0	-	-	-	-
1000 TO 1499 MILES....	6	100.0	-	100.0	-	-	-	-	-
1500 MILES OR OVER....	10	100.0	-	95.1	-	.2	2.9	.2	1.6

See footnotes at end of table 4.

TABLE 2. TCC GROUP 254—Percent Distribution of Geographic Division of Origin and Means of Transport, by Geographic Division of Destination: 1972

Geographic division of origin[1] and means of transport	Number	Percent distribution by division of destination									
		U.S. total	New England	Middle Atlantic	East North Central	West North Central	South Atlantic	East South Central	West South Central	Mountain	Pacific
TONS OF SHIPMENTS	(thousands of tons)										
U.S. TOTAL	1 120	100.0	6.7	13.8	25.9	6.2	15.7	8.6	8.8	3.7	10.7
RAIL	97	100.0	10.8	11.5	18.1	5.8	15.3	1.9	19.7	2.3	14.6
MOTOR CARRIER	586	100.0	5.7	16.4	26.6	9.5	17.5	5.1	7.3	3.3	8.6
PRIVATE TRUCK	425	100.0	7.1	10.1	27.3	1.7	12.9	15.2	8.5	4.7	12.6
AIR	1	100.0	1.7	23.2	6.8	17.9	7.0	.1	15.5	1.6	26.1
WATER	-	100.0	-	-	-	-	-	-	-	-	100.0
OTHER	8	100.0	.5	36.8	4.6	6.5	33.8	1.4	1.0	5.0	10.4
UNKNOWN	-	100.0	37.1	18.9	-	-	8.4	1.8	11.6	-	22.3
MIDDLE ATLANTIC	146	100.0	7.9	34.2	15.3	1.5	30.5	3.2	2.3	1.0	4.1
RAIL	24	100.0	-	9.1	56.2	-	24.3	1.7	2.8	.7	5.1
MOTOR CARRIER	74	100.0	12.8	32.5	8.3	2.2	30.8	3.0	3.4	1.6	5.4
PRIVATE TRUCK	42	100.0	4.6	49.3	4.8	1.2	33.4	4.7	.4	.1	1.6
AIR	-	100.0	-	-	-	-	-	-	3.0	-	97.0
WATER	-	100.0	-	-	-	-	-	-	-	-	-
OTHER	4	100.0	.3	58.8	4.8	.1	34.7	1.2	.2	-	-
UNKNOWN	-	100.0	34.7	55.2	-	-	.5	1.9	7.8	-	-
EAST NORTH CENTRAL	474	100.0	4.9	12.4	43.2	8.4	9.0	4.1	8.2	1.9	7.8
RAIL	63	100.0	16.5	12.8	4.2	6.0	8.7	2.2	27.7	3.0	18.8
MOTOR CARRIER	270	100.0	4.6	15.7	35.5	11.8	12.5	3.3	6.5	2.0	8.2
PRIVATE TRUCK	137	100.0	.3	5.3	77.2	2.7	2.4	6.7	2.5	1.1	1.8
AIR	-	100.0	1.0	35.0	8.4	-	7.0	.2	10.7	.4	37.3
WATER	-	100.0	-	-	-	-	-	-	-	-	-
OTHER	2	100.0	.8	25.6	5.0	25.0	12.2	1.2	2.5	20.0	7.7
UNKNOWN	-	100.0	.3	16.2	-	-	5.0	-	-	-	78.4
WEST NORTH CENTRAL	78	100.0	2.4	15.6	24.4	10.3	11.9	7.7	9.5	4.4	13.8
RAIL	-	100.0	-	100.0	-	-	-	-	-	-	-
MOTOR CARRIER	61	100.0	1.9	6.0	27.5	11.1	11.2	9.9	11.3	4.8	16.4
PRIVATE TRUCK	16	100.0	4.2	50.6	13.3	7.5	14.5	-	2.7	3.0	4.2
AIR	-	100.0	3.1	5.0	7.5	-	4.0	-	50.0	6.3	24.2
WATER	-	100.0	-	-	-	-	-	-	-	-	100.0
OTHER	-	100.0	.3	8.8	50.6	17.9	13.2	2.0	5.0	.1	2.1
UNKNOWN	-	100.0	-	-	-	-	-	-	-	-	-
PACIFIC	72	100.0	-	1.6	2.5	2.1	.7	.1	6.8	8.4	77.8
RAIL	-	100.0	-	-	-	-	-	-	-	-	-
MOTOR CARRIER	22	100.0	.1	5.1	7.8	6.5	2.4	.4	21.0	17.8	38.9
PRIVATE TRUCK	49	100.0	-	-	-	-	-	-	-	4.1	95.9
AIR	-	100.0	-	-	-	-	9.0	-	-	-	91.0
WATER	-	100.0	-	-	-	-	-	-	-	-	100.0
OTHER	-	100.0	28.8	15.6	-	-	-	8.8	-	-	46.8
UNKNOWN	-	100.0	-	1.4	-	-	-	-	91.0	-	7.6
TON-MILES OF SHIPMENTS	(millions of ton-miles)										
U.S. TOTAL	572	100.0	5.1	10.6	11.1	5.9	16.8	6.8	12.6	7.1	24.0
RAIL	90	100.0	8.1	4.6	7.4	2.6	10.2	1.3	23.4	2.6	39.8
MOTOR CARRIER	338	100.0	5.5	11.7	13.2	8.2	16.9	4.3	9.7	6.4	24.0
PRIVATE TRUCK	136	100.0	2.3	12.0	8.5	2.1	21.1	17.1	13.0	11.6	12.4
AIR	1	100.0	1.1	15.7	2.3	9.8	6.1	.1	12.2	1.8	50.9
WATER	-	100.0	-	-	-	-	-	-	-	-	100.0
OTHER	3	100.0	.9	10.7	5.2	5.7	15.8	1.8	1.8	15.3	42.9
UNKNOWN	-	100.0	3.8	3.8	-	-	3.1	.4	25.8	-	63.0
MIDDLE ATLANTIC	61	100.0	5.0	8.3	16.1	3.1	28.4	4.5	7.0	4.2	23.4
RAIL	15	100.0	-	4.0	38.4	-	26.0	1.8	6.1	2.6	21.1
MOTOR CARRIER	35	100.0	7.2	7.6	9.3	4.3	24.2	4.4	9.1	6.1	27.7
PRIVATE TRUCK	10	100.0	4.8	16.0	6.8	3.6	44.2	8.2	1.4	.7	14.4
AIR	-	100.0	-	-	-	-	-	-	1.6	-	98.4
WATER	-	100.0	-	-	-	-	-	-	-	-	-
OTHER	-	100.0	.3	22.7	21.3	.4	46.0	7.3	1.6	.4	-
UNKNOWN	-	100.0	32.5	4.6	-	-	.1	6.7	56.1	-	-
EAST NORTH CENTRAL	248	100.0	6.5	11.1	10.1	7.0	9.6	4.0	14.0	4.5	33.2
RAIL	69	100.0	10.6	4.5	.9	2.4	4.3	1.3	28.7	2.5	44.7
MOTOR CARRIER	146	100.0	5.8	13.6	11.9	9.3	12.4	2.6	8.9	4.8	30.8
PRIVATE TRUCK	28	100.0	.9	14.5	24.3	6.0	8.6	17.6	5.4	6.5	16.2
AIR	-	100.0	.7	18.7	1.3	-	5.9	.1	8.3	.5	64.6
WATER	-	100.0	-	-	-	-	-	-	-	-	-
OTHER	1	100.0	.7	13.5	1.2	13.8	7.3	.8	3.4	38.1	21.3
UNKNOWN	-	100.0	.1	2.4	-	-	1.0	-	-	-	96.4
WEST NORTH CENTRAL	61	100.0	3.3	19.3	16.3	2.8	13.1	5.9	8.3	5.1	25.8
RAIL	-	100.0	-	100.0	-	-	-	-	-	-	-
MOTOR CARRIER	47	100.0	2.7	7.5	19.3	3.2	12.7	7.8	9.9	5.6	31.4
PRIVATE TRUCK	14	100.0	5.2	58.5	6.8	1.5	14.8	-	2.7	3.4	7.3
AIR	-	100.0	3.4	5.1	4.8	-	4.0	-	37.8	7.1	37.7
WATER	-	100.0	-	-	-	-	-	-	-	-	100.0
OTHER	-	100.0	.6	13.9	46.4	5.9	21.4	2.0	4.3	.1	5.4
UNKNOWN	-	100.0	-	-	-	-	-	-	-	-	-
PACIFIC	28	100.0	.3	10.1	11.2	7.7	3.9	.6	22.9	9.4	33.9
RAIL	-	100.0	-	-	-	-	-	-	-	-	-
MOTOR CARRIER	20	100.0	.4	14.2	15.7	10.8	5.5	.8	31.5	8.8	12.3
PRIVATE TRUCK	7	100.0	-	-	-	-	-	-	-	11.5	88.5
AIR	-	100.0	-	-	-	-	7.7	-	-	-	92.3
WATER	-	100.0	-	-	-	-	-	-	-	-	100.0
OTHER	-	100.0	54.9	28.5	-	-	-	12.8	-	-	3.8
UNKNOWN	-	100.0	-	2.3	-	-	-	-	96.9	-	.8

See footnotes at end of table 4.

TABLE 3. **TCC GROUP 254**—Percent Distribution of Geographic Division of Destination and Means of Transport, by Geographic Division of Origin: 1972

Geographic division of destination and means of transport	Number	Percent distribution by division of origin[1]									
		U.S. total	New England	Middle Atlantic	East North Central	West North Central	South Atlantic	East South Central	West South Central	Mountain	Pacific
TONS OF SHIPMENTS	(thousands of tons)										
U.S. TOTAL..............	1 120	100.0	(D)	13.1	42.3	7.0	(D)	(D)	(D)	(D)	6.5
RAIL.................	97	100.0	(D)	25.7	65.3	-	(D)	(D)	(D)	(D)	-
MOTOR CARRIER.........	586	100.0	(D)	12.7	46.1	10.4	(D)	(D)	(D)	(D)	3.9
PRIVATE TRUCK.........	425	100.0	(D)	10.0	32.3	4.0	(D)	(D)	(D)	(D)	11.6
AIR..................	1	100.0	(D)	.1	52.4	19.4	(D)	(D)	(D)	(D)	.6
WATER................	-	100.0	(D)	-	-	2.4	(D)	(D)	(D)	(D)	97.6
OTHER................	8	100.0	(D)	50.3	24.7	1.6	(D)	(D)	(D)	(D)	.2
UNKNOWN..............	-	100.0	(D)	20.2	27.3	-	(D)	(D)	(D)	(D)	11.1
NEW ENGLAND............	74	100.0	(D)	15.5	31.1	2.5	(D)	(D)	(D)	(D)	-
RAIL.................	10	100.0	(D)	-	100.0	-	(D)	(D)	(D)	(D)	-
MOTOR CARRIER.........	33	100.0	(D)	28.5	37.1	3.5	(D)	(D)	(D)	(D)	.1
PRIVATE TRUCK.........	30	100.0	(D)	6.4	1.2	2.4	(D)	(D)	(D)	(D)	-
AIR..................	-	100.0	(D)	-	30.2	34.3	(D)	(D)	(D)	(D)	-
WATER................	-	100.0	(D)	-	-	-	(D)	(D)	(D)	(D)	-
OTHER................	-	100.0	(D)	30.1	37.1	1.1	(D)	(D)	(D)	(D)	12.1
UNKNOWN..............	-	100.0	(D)	18.8	.2	-	(D)	(D)	(D)	(D)	-
MIDDLE ATLANTIC........	154	100.0	(D)	32.6	38.1	8.0	(D)	(D)	(D)	(D)	.8
RAIL.................	11	100.0	(D)	20.3	72.5	.1	(D)	(D)	(D)	(D)	-
MOTOR CARRIER.........	96	100.0	(D)	25.3	44.2	3.8	(D)	(D)	(D)	(D)	1.2
PRIVATE TRUCK.........	43	100.0	(D)	48.7	16.9	19.8	(D)	(D)	(D)	(D)	-
AIR..................	-	100.0	(D)	-	78.9	4.1	(D)	(D)	(D)	(D)	-
WATER................	-	100.0	(D)	-	-	-	(D)	(D)	(D)	(D)	-
OTHER................	3	100.0	(D)	80.3	17.2	.4	(D)	(D)	(D)	(D)	.1
UNKNOWN..............	-	100.0	(D)	59.0	23.5	-	(D)	(D)	(D)	(D)	.8
EAST NORTH CENTRAL.....	290	100.0	(D)	7.7	70.5	6.6	(D)	(D)	(D)	(D)	.6
RAIL.................	17	100.0	(D)	79.6	15.0	-	(D)	(D)	(D)	(D)	-
MOTOR CARRIER.........	156	100.0	(D)	4.0	61.5	10.8	(D)	(D)	(D)	(D)	1.2
PRIVATE TRUCK.........	116	100.0	(D)	1.8	91.2	1.9	(D)	(D)	(D)	(D)	-
AIR..................	-	100.0	(D)	-	64.4	21.2	(D)	(D)	(D)	(D)	-
WATER................	-	100.0	(D)	-	-	-	(D)	(D)	(D)	(D)	-
OTHER................	-	100.0	(D)	51.8	26.8	17.5	(D)	(D)	(D)	(D)	-
UNKNOWN..............	-	100.0	(D)	-	100.0	-	(D)	(D)	(D)	(D)	-
WEST NORTH CENTRAL.....	69	100.0	(D)	3.1	57.4	11.6	(D)	(D)	(D)	(D)	2.1
RAIL.................	5	100.0	(D)	-	67.5	-	(D)	(D)	(D)	(D)	-
MOTOR CARRIER.........	56	100.0	(D)	3.0	57.0	12.1	(D)	(D)	(D)	(D)	2.7
PRIVATE TRUCK.........	7	100.0	(D)	7.0	51.4	17.6	(D)	(D)	(D)	(D)	-
AIR..................	-	100.0	(D)	-	-	-	(D)	(D)	(D)	(D)	-
WATER................	-	100.0	(D)	-	-	-	(D)	(D)	(D)	(D)	-
OTHER................	-	100.0	(D)	.5	94.9	4.4	(D)	(D)	(D)	(D)	-
UNKNOWN..............	-	100.0	(D)	-	-	-	(D)	(D)	(D)	(D)	-
SOUTH ATLANTIC.........	175	100.0	(D)	25.5	24.5	5.3	(D)	(D)	(D)	(D)	.3
RAIL.................	14	100.0	(D)	40.7	37.2	-	(D)	(D)	(D)	(D)	-
MOTOR CARRIER.........	102	100.0	(D)	22.4	32.9	6.7	(D)	(D)	(D)	(D)	.5
PRIVATE TRUCK.........	54	100.0	(D)	26.0	6.1	4.5	(D)	(D)	(D)	(D)	-
AIR..................	-	100.0	(D)	-	52.6	11.0	(D)	(D)	(D)	(D)	.8
WATER................	-	100.0	(D)	-	-	-	(D)	(D)	(D)	(D)	-
OTHER................	2	100.0	(D)	51.5	8.9	.6	(D)	(D)	(D)	(D)	-
UNKNOWN..............	-	100.0	(D)	1.3	16.4	-	(D)	(D)	(D)	(D)	-
EAST SOUTH CENTRAL.....	96	100.0	(D)	4.9	20.4	6.3	(D)	(D)	(D)	(D)	.1
RAIL.................	1	100.0	(D)	23.1	76.9	-	(D)	(D)	(D)	(D)	-
MOTOR CARRIER.........	30	100.0	(D)	7.4	29.9	20.2	(D)	(D)	(D)	(D)	.3
PRIVATE TRUCK.........	64	100.0	(D)	3.1	14.4	-	(D)	(D)	(D)	(D)	-
AIR..................	-	100.0	(D)	-	87.0	-	(D)	(D)	(D)	(D)	-
WATER................	-	100.0	(D)	-	-	-	(D)	(D)	(D)	(D)	-
OTHER................	-	100.0	(D)	42.6	21.1	2.3	(D)	(D)	(D)	(D)	1.3
UNKNOWN..............	-	100.0	(D)	21.3	-	-	(D)	(D)	(D)	(D)	-
WEST SOUTH CENTRAL.....	98	100.0	(D)	3.5	39.4	7.6	(D)	(D)	(D)	(D)	5.0
RAIL.................	19	100.0	(D)	3.7	92.2	-	(D)	(D)	(D)	(D)	-
MOTOR CARRIER.........	42	100.0	(D)	5.9	41.0	16.1	(D)	(D)	(D)	(D)	11.2
PRIVATE TRUCK.........	36	100.0	(D)	.4	9.6	1.3	(D)	(D)	(D)	(D)	-
AIR..................	-	100.0	(D)	-	36.0	62.3	(D)	(D)	(D)	(D)	-
WATER................	-	100.0	(D)	-	-	-	(D)	(D)	(D)	(D)	-
OTHER................	-	100.0	(D)	11.0	64.2	8.3	(D)	(D)	(D)	(D)	-
UNKNOWN..............	-	100.0	(D)	13.4	-	-	(D)	(D)	(D)	(D)	86.6
MOUNTAIN...............	41	100.0	(D)	3.5	21.9	8.3	(D)	(D)	(D)	(D)	14.5
RAIL.................	2	100.0	(D)	7.6	87.3	-	(D)	(D)	(D)	(D)	-
MOTOR CARRIER.........	19	100.0	(D)	6.3	27.4	15.2	(D)	(D)	(D)	(D)	20.9
PRIVATE TRUCK.........	19	100.0	(D)	.2	7.6	2.6	(D)	(D)	(D)	(D)	10.1
AIR..................	-	100.0	(D)	-	12.6	76.9	(D)	(D)	(D)	(D)	-
WATER................	-	100.0	(D)	-	-	-	(D)	(D)	(D)	(D)	-
OTHER................	-	100.0	(D)	.4	99.6	-	(D)	(D)	(D)	(D)	-
UNKNOWN..............	-	100.0	(D)	-	-	-	(D)	(D)	(D)	(D)	-
PACIFIC................	119	100.0	(D)	5.0	31.1	9.1	(D)	(D)	(D)	(D)	47.2
RAIL.................	14	100.0	(D)	9.0	83.9	-	(D)	(D)	(D)	(D)	-
MOTOR CARRIER.........	50	100.0	(D)	8.0	44.2	20.0	- (D)	(D)	(D)	(D)	17.7
PRIVATE TRUCK.........	53	100.0	(D)	1.3	4.5	1.3	(D)	(D)	(D)	(D)	88.7
AIR..................	-	100.0	(D)	.2	75.0	18.0	(D)	(D)	(D)	(D)	2.2
WATER................	-	100.0	(D)	-	-	2.4	(D)	(D)	(D)	(D)	97.6
OTHER................	-	100.0	(D)	-	18.3	.3	(D)	(D)	(D)	(D)	.9
UNKNOWN..............	-	100.0	(D)	-	96.2	-	(D)	(D)	(D)	(D)	3.8

See footnotes at end of table 4.

TABLE 3. **TCC GROUP 254—Percent Distribution of Geographic Division of Destination and Means of Transport, by Geographic Division of Origin: 1972**—Continued

Geographic division of destination and means of transport	Number	Percent distribution by division of origin[1]									
		U.S. total	New England	Middle Atlantic	East North Central	West North Central	South Atlantic	East South Central	West South Central	Mountain	Pacific
TON-MILES OF SHIPMENTS	(millions of ton-miles)										
U.S. TOTAL............	572	100.0	(D)	10.8	43.4	10.8	(D)	(D)	(D)	(D)	5.0
RAIL...............	90	100.0	(D)	16.7	76.5	-	(D)	(D)	(D)	(D)	-
MOTOR CARRIER.........	338	100.0	(D)	10.4	43.4	13.9	(D)	(D)	(D)	(D)	6.0
PRIVATE TRUCK.........	136	100.0	(D)	8.0	21.1	10.6	(D)	(D)	(D)	(D)	5.7
AIR................	1	100.0	(D)	.1	60.0	19.1	(D)	(D)	(D)	(D)	1.6
WATER..............	-	100.0	(D)	-	-	4.1	(D)	(D)	(D)	(D)	95.9
OTHER..............	3	100.0	(D)	16.8	39.9	2.0	(D)	(D)	(D)	(D)	.6
UNKNOWN............	-	100.0	(D)	5.6	65.2	-	(D)	(D)	(D)	(D)	23.4
NEW ENGLAND...........	29	100.0	(D)	10.5	55.2	7.0	(D)	(D)	(D)	(D)	.3
RAIL...............	7	100.0	(D)	-	100.0	-	(D)	(D)	(D)	(D)	-
MOTOR CARRIER.........	18	100.0	(D)	13.6	45.7	6.9	(D)	(D)	(D)	(D)	.4
PRIVATE TRUCK.........	3	100.0	(D)	16.3	8.2	23.4	(D)	(D)	(D)	(D)	-
AIR................	-	100.0	(D)	-	40.1	58.8	(D)	(D)	(D)	(D)	-
WATER..............	-	100.0	(D)	-	-	-	(D)	(D)	(D)	(D)	-
OTHER..............	-	100.0	(D)	5.4	32.2	1.4	(D)	(D)	(D)	(D)	38.2
UNKNOWN............	-	100.0	(D)	48.7	2.5	-	(D)	(D)	(D)	(D)	-
MIDDLE ATLANTIC.........	60	100.0	(D)	8.5	45.6	19.7	(D)	(D)	(D)	(D)	4.7
RAIL...............	4	100.0	(D)	14.6	75.2	.2	(D)	(D)	(D)	(D)	-
MOTOR CARRIER.........	39	100.0	(D)	6.8	50.6	8.9	(D)	(D)	(D)	(D)	7.2
PRIVATE TRUCK.........	16	100.0	(D)	10.6	25.5	51.5	(D)	(D)	(D)	(D)	-
AIR................	-	100.0	(D)	-	71.3	6.2	(D)	(D)	(D)	(D)	-
WATER..............	-	100.0	(D)	-	-	-	(D)	(D)	(D)	(D)	-
OTHER..............	-	100.0	(D)	35.6	50.1	2.6	(D)	(D)	(D)	(D)	1.6
UNKNOWN............	-	100.0	(D)	6.7	41.7	-	(D)	(D)	(D)	(D)	13.9
EAST NORTH CENTRAL......	63	100.0	(D)	15.8	39.8	16.0	(D)	(D)	(D)	(D)	5.0
RAIL...............	6	100.0	(D)	87.1	9.8	-	(D)	(D)	(D)	(D)	-
MOTOR CARRIER.........	44	100.0	(D)	7.3	39.0	20.3	(D)	(D)	(D)	(D)	7.1
PRIVATE TRUCK.........	11	100.0	(D)	6.4	60.8	8.5	(D)	(D)	(D)	(D)	-
AIR................	-	100.0	(D)	-	33.9	40.7	(D)	(D)	(D)	(D)	-
WATER..............	-	100.0	(D)	-	-	-	(D)	(D)	(D)	(D)	-
OTHER..............	-	100.0	(D)	69.4	8.9	18.0	(D)	(D)	(D)	(D)	-
UNKNOWN............	-	100.0	(D)	-	100.0	-	(D)	(D)	(D)	(D)	-
WEST NORTH CENTRAL......	33	100.0	(D)	5.6	51.5	5.2	(D)	(D)	(D)	(D)	6.5
RAIL...............	2	100.0	(D)	-	70.6	-	(D)	(D)	(D)	(D)	-
MOTOR CARRIER.........	27	100.0	(D)	5.4	48.8	5.5	(D)	(D)	(D)	(D)	7.8
PRIVATE TRUCK.........	2	100.0	(D)	13.5	60.5	7.4	(D)	(D)	(D)	(D)	-
AIR................	-	100.0	(D)	-	-	-	(D)	(D)	(D)	(D)	-
WATER..............	-	100.0	(D)	-	-	-	(D)	(D)	(D)	(D)	-
OTHER..............	-	100.0	(D)	1.1	96.5	2.1	(D)	(D)	(D)	(D)	-
UNKNOWN............	-	100.0	(D)	-	-	-	(D)	(D)	(D)	(D)	-
SOUTH ATLANTIC.........	96	100.0	(D)	18.3	24.8	8.4	(D)	(D)	(D)	(D)	1.2
RAIL...............	9	100.0	(D)	42.5	32.5	-	(D)	(D)	(D)	(D)	-
MOTOR CARRIER.........	57	100.0	(D)	14.8	31.7	10.4	(D)	(D)	(D)	(D)	1.9
PRIVATE TRUCK.........	28	100.0	(D)	16.7	8.6	7.4	(D)	(D)	(D)	(D)	-
AIR................	-	100.0	(D)	-	57.7	12.3	(D)	(D)	(D)	(D)	2.0
WATER..............	-	100.0	(D)	-	-	-	(D)	(D)	(D)	(D)	-
OTHER..............	-	100.0	(D)	49.1	18.4	2.7	(D)	(D)	(D)	(D)	-
UNKNOWN............	-	100.0	(D)	.2	20.6	-	(D)	(D)	(D)	(D)	-
EAST SOUTH CENTRAL......	39	100.0	(D)	7.1	25.2	9.4	(D)	(D)	(D)	(D)	.4
RAIL...............	1	100.0	(D)	23.5	76.5	-	(D)	(D)	(D)	(D)	-
MOTOR CARRIER.........	14	100.0	(D)	10.8	26.6	25.2	(D)	(D)	(D)	(D)	1.2
PRIVATE TRUCK.........	23	100.0	(D)	3.8	21.7	-	(D)	(D)	(D)	(D)	-
AIR................	-	100.0	(D)	-	89.8	-	(D)	(D)	(D)	(D)	-
WATER..............	-	100.0	(D)	-	-	-	(D)	(D)	(D)	(D)	-
OTHER..............	-	100.0	(D)	68.3	18.1	2.3	(D)	(D)	(D)	(D)	4.3
UNKNOWN............	-	100.0	(D)	85.2	-	-	(D)	(D)	(D)	(D)	-
WEST SOUTH CENTRAL......	72	100.0	(D)	6.0	48.1	7.1	(D)	(D)	(D)	(D)	9.0
RAIL...............	21	100.0	(D)	4.4	93.9	-	(D)	(D)	(D)	(D)	-
MOTOR CARRIER.........	32	100.0	(D)	9.8	39.8	14.3	(D)	(D)	(D)	(D)	19.4
PRIVATE TRUCK.........	17	100.0	(D)	.8	8.8	2.2	(D)	(D)	(D)	(D)	-
AIR................	-	100.0	(D)	-	40.4	58.9	(D)	(D)	(D)	(D)	-
WATER..............	-	100.0	(D)	-	-	-	(D)	(D)	(D)	(D)	-
OTHER..............	-	100.0	(D)	15.1	74.1	4.7	(D)	(D)	(D)	(D)	-
UNKNOWN............	-	100.0	(D)	12.2	-	-	(D)	(D)	(D)	(D)	87.8
MOUNTAIN.............	40	100.0	(D)	6.5	27.7	7.8	(D)	(D)	(D)	(D)	6.6
RAIL...............	2	100.0	(D)	17.1	74.5	-	(D)	(D)	(D)	(D)	-
MOTOR CARRIER.........	21	100.0	(D)	9.9	32.4	12.3	(D)	(D)	(D)	(D)	8.3
PRIVATE TRUCK.........	15	100.0	(D)	.5	11.8	3.1	(D)	(D)	(D)	(D)	5.6
AIR................	-	100.0	(D)	-	15.2	76.6	(D)	(D)	(D)	(D)	-
WATER..............	-	100.0	(D)	-	-	-	(D)	(D)	(D)	(D)	-
OTHER..............	-	100.0	(D)	.4	99.5	-	(D)	(D)	(D)	(D)	-
UNKNOWN............	-	100.0	(D)	-	-	-	(D)	(D)	(D)	(D)	-
PACIFIC..............	137	100.0	(D)	10.5	59.9	11.6	(D)	(D)	(D)	(D)	7.0
RAIL...............	36	100.0	(D)	8.8	85.9	-	(D)	(D)	(D)	(D)	-
MOTOR CARRIER.........	81	100.0	(D)	12.0	55.7	18.2	(D)	(D)	(D)	(D)	3.0
PRIVATE TRUCK.........	16	100.0	(D)	9.3	27.7	6.2	(D)	(D)	(D)	(D)	40.5
AIR................	-	100.0	(D)	.3	76.2	14.1	(D)	(D)	(D)	(D)	2.8
WATER..............	-	100.0	(D)	-	-	4.1	(D)	(D)	(D)	(D)	95.9
OTHER..............	1	100.0	(D)	-	19.8	.3	(D)	(D)	(D)	(D)	.1
UNKNOWN............	-	100.0	(D)	-	99.7	-	(D)	(D)	(D)	(D)	.3

See footnotes at end of table 4.

TABLE 4. TCC GROUP 254—Percent Distribution of Distance Shipped and Weight of Shipment, by Means of Transport: 1972

Distance shipped and weight of shipment[2][3]	Number	Percent distribution by means of transport							
		All means of transport	Rail	Motor carrier	Private truck	Air	Water	Other	Unknown
TONS OF SHIPMENTS	(thousands of tons)								
U.S. TOTAL..........	952	100.0	7.3	53.2	38.4	.1	-	.8	.1
UNDER 100 MILES.........	226	100.0	-	29.5	69.3	-	-	1.0	.2
UNDER 1000 POUNDS.....	15	100.0	.2	40.1	57.2	.1	-	1.6	.8
1000 TO 9999 POUNDS...	157	100.0	-	15.2	83.4	-	-	1.2	.2
10000 TO 29999 POUNDS.	32	100.0	-	59.8	40.2	-	-	-	-
30000 TO 59999 POUNDS.	15	100.0	-	75.3	24.7	-	-	-	-
60000 TO 89999 POUNDS.	-	100.0	-	-	-	-	-	-	-
90000 POUNDS AND OVER.	5	100.0	-	100.0	-	-	-	-	-
100 TO 199 MILES........	82	100.0	1.3	47.9	49.2	-	-	1.3	.2
UNDER 1000 POUNDS.....	9	100.0	-	83.1	15.6	.2	-	.9	.2
1000 TO 9999 POUNDS...	35	100.0	-	45.3	51.5	-	-	2.9	.3
10000 TO 29999 POUNDS.	20	100.0	5.4	52.6	42.0	-	-	-	-
30000 TO 59999 POUNDS.	17	100.0	-	29.3	70.7	-	-	-	-
60000 TO 89999 POUNDS.	-	100.0	-	100.0	-	-	-	-	-
90000 POUNDS AND OVER.	-	100.0	-	-	-	-	-	-	-
200 TO 299 MILES........	116	100.0	3.4	64.7	30.1	-	-	1.7	-
UNDER 1000 POUNDS.....	11	100.0	.9	78.2	19.6	.3	-	1.0	-
1000 TO 9999 POUNDS...	32	100.0	-	61.1	38.7	-	-	-	.1
10000 TO 29999 POUNDS.	46	100.0	1.7	59.0	38.4	-	-	.8	-
30000 TO 59999 POUNDS.	13	100.0	16.6	55.8	16.8	-	-	10.8	-
60000 TO 89999 POUNDS.	1	100.0	51.1	48.9	-	-	-	-	-
90000 POUNDS AND OVER.	10	100.0	-	100.0	-	-	-	-	-
300 TO 499 MILES........	165	100.0	11.7	66.8	21.0	-	-	.5	-
UNDER 1000 POUNDS.....	14	100.0	.4	89.3	8.9	.3	-	1.1	.1
1000 TO 9999 POUNDS...	55	100.0	5.3	71.9	21.6	-	-	1.2	.1
10000 TO 29999 POUNDS.	52	100.0	8.7	75.6	15.7	-	-	-	-
30000 TO 59999 POUNDS.	39	100.0	22.9	43.7	33.4	-	-	-	-
60000 TO 89999 POUNDS.	3	100.0	71.6	28.4	-	-	-	-	-
90000 POUNDS AND OVER.	-	100.0	-	-	-	-	-	-	-
500 TO 999 MILES........	239	100.0	8.1	60.0	31.4	.3	-	.2	-
UNDER 1000 POUNDS.....	18	100.0	.9	92.7	2.6	1.7	-	1.9	-
1000 TO 9999 POUNDS...	55	100.0	2.5	79.2	17.4	.7	-	.2	-
10000 TO 29999 POUNDS.	62	100.0	3.7	80.4	15.9	-	-	-	-
30000 TO 59999 POUNDS.	49	100.0	24.1	62.2	13.7	-	-	-	-
60000 TO 89999 POUNDS.	1	100.0	79.3	20.7	-	-	-	-	-
90000 POUNDS AND OVER.	50	100.0	3.8	.2	96.0	-	-	-	-
1000 TO 1499 MILES......	68	100.0	24.2	46.6	28.4	.1	-	.6	-
UNDER 1000 POUNDS.....	5	100.0	-	79.1	17.8	1.8	-	1.3	-
1000 TO 9999 POUNDS...	12	100.0	2.8	64.3	29.8	-	-	3.0	.1
10000 TO 29999 POUNDS.	15	100.0	15.4	66.2	18.4	-	-	-	-
30000 TO 59999 POUNDS.	10	100.0	4.1	92.5	3.5	-	-	-	-
60000 TO 89999 POUNDS.	-	100.0	-	-	-	-	-	-	-
90000 POUNDS AND OVER.	25	100.0	53.4	-	46.6	-	-	-	-
1500 MILES OR OVER......	53	100.0	16.4	73.6	7.3	.5	.1	1.7	.4
UNDER 1000 POUNDS.....	6	100.0	5.1	79.4	2.2	4.3	.4	8.5	-
1000 TO 9999 POUNDS...	11	100.0	17.0	71.2	7.9	-	.4	3.5	-
10000 TO 29999 POUNDS.	16	100.0	6.6	75.6	16.5	-	-	-	1.3
30000 TO 59999 POUNDS.	13	100.0	12.5	87.0	.5	-	-	-	-
60000 TO 89999 POUNDS.	2	100.0	48.6	51.4	-	-	-	-	-
90000 POUNDS AND OVER.	2	100.0	100.0	-	-	-	-	-	-
TON-MILES OF SHIPMENTS	(millions of ton-miles)								
U.S. TOTAL..........	472	100.0	14.6	60.2	24.1	.2	-	.8	.1
UNDER 100 MILES........	10	100.0	-	37.7	61.6	-	-	.5	.1
UNDER 1000 POUNDS.....	-	100.0	.4	46.9	51.3	-	-	1.1	.3
1000 TO 9999 POUNDS...	6	100.0	-	20.5	78.6	-	-	.7	.2
10000 TO 29999 POUNDS.	1	100.0	-	66.2	33.8	-	-	-	-
30000 TO 59999 POUNDS.	-	100.0	-	79.8	20.2	-	-	-	-
60000 TO 89999 POUNDS.	-	100.0	-	-	-	-	-	-	-
90000 POUNDS AND OVER.	-	100.0	-	100.0	-	-	-	-	-
100 TO 199 MILES........	12	100.0	1.7	46.6	50.3	-	-	1.3	.2
UNDER 1000 POUNDS.....	1	100.0	-	83.2	15.5	.2	-	.9	.2
1000 TO 9999 POUNDS...	5	100.0	-	46.3	50.6	-	-	2.8	.3
10000 TO 29999 POUNDS.	3	100.0	7.0	51.8	41.2	-	-	-	-
30000 TO 59999 POUNDS.	2	100.0	-	24.6	75.4	-	-	-	-
60000 TO 89999 POUNDS.	-	100.0	-	100.0	-	-	-	-	-
90000 POUNDS AND OVER.	-	100.0	-	-	-	-	-	-	-

See footnotes at end of table 4.

TABLE 4. TCC GROUP 254—Percent Distribution of Distance Shipped and Weight of Shipment, by Means of Transport: 1972—Continued

Distance shipped and weight of shipment [2] [3]	Number	Percent distribution by means of transport							
		All means of transport	Rail	Motor carrier	Private truck	Air	Water	Other	Unknown
TON-MILES OF SHIPMENTS	(millions of ton-miles)								
200 TO 299 MILES........	27	100.0	3.3	66.2	28.9	-	-	1.5	-
UNDER 1000 POUNDS.....	2	100.0	.9	79.4	18.5	.2	-	1.0	-
1000 TO 9999 POUNDS...	8	100.0	-	62.9	37.0	-	-	-	.1
10000 TO 29999 POUNDS.	10	100.0	1.5	60.4	37.2	-	-	.9	-
30000 TO 59999 POUNDS.	3	100.0	17.1	59.3	14.3	-	-	9.2	-
60000 TO 89999 POUNDS.	-	100.0	49.5	50.5	-	-	-	-	-
90000 POUNDS AND OVER.	2	100.0	-	100.0	-	-	-	-	-
300 TO 499 MILES........	65	100.0	12.3	65.2	22.1	-	-	.4	-
UNDER 1000 POUNDS.....	5	100.0	.3	89.2	9.0	.3	-	1.2	.1
1000 TO 9999 POUNDS...	21	100.0	5.6	70.0	23.3	-	-	1.0	.1
10000 TO 29999 POUNDS.	20	100.0	9.2	74.4	16.4	-	-	-	-
30000 TO 59999 POUNDS.	16	100.0	22.9	42.9	34.2	-	-	-	-
60000 TO 89999 POUNDS.	1	100.0	71.9	28.1	-	-	-	-	-
90000 POUNDS AND OVER.	-	100.0	-	-	-	-	-	-	-
500 TO 999 MILES........	162	100.0	8.3	60.6	30.7	.3	-	.2	-
UNDER 1000 POUNDS.....	13	100.0	1.0	92.6	2.6	1.9	-	1.9	-
1000 TO 9999 POUNDS...	40	100.0	2.8	79.3	17.1	.5	-	.3	-
10000 TO 29999 POUNDS.	41	100.0	4.0	77.9	18.1	-	-	-	-
30000 TO 59999 POUNDS.	32	100.0	24.6	64.0	11.4	-	-	-	-
60000 TO 89999 POUNDS.	1	100.0	71.1	28.9	-	-	-	-	-
90000 POUNDS AND OVER.	32	100.0	4.7	.2	95.1	-	-	-	-
1000 TO 1499 MILES......	78	100.0	25.2	46.9	27.0	.1	-	.7	-
UNDER 1000 POUNDS.....	5	100.0	-	79.2	17.5	2.0	-	1.3	-
1000 TO 9999 POUNDS...	14	100.0	2.6	65.1	28.6	-	-	3.5	.2
10000 TO 29999 POUNDS.	18	100.0	16.9	66.0	17.1	-	-	-	-
30000 TO 59999 POUNDS.	11	100.0	5.0	91.7	3.3	-	-	-	-
60000 TO 89999 POUNDS.	-	100.0	-	-	-	-	-	-	-
90000 POUNDS AND OVER.	28	100.0	55.7	-	44.3	-	-	-	-
1500 MILES OR OVER......	115	100.0	22.9	67.9	6.7	.4	.1	1.5	.4
UNDER 1000 POUNDS.....	11	100.0	6.1	78.2	2.3	4.3	.5	8.6	-
1000 TO 9999 POUNDS...	22	100.0	19.7	67.5	9.0	-	.4	3.3	-
10000 TO 29999 POUNDS.	30	100.0	6.3	74.9	17.3	-	-	-	1.4
30000 TO 59999 POUNDS.	27	100.0	10.1	89.3	.6	-	-	-	-
60000 TO 89999 POUNDS.	13	100.0	48.6	51.4	-	-	-	-	-
90000 POUNDS AND OVER.	10	100.0	100.0	-	-	-	-	-	-

Note: Detail may not add to total due to rounding. The introductory table shows the estimates of sampling variability for tons; sampling variability for ton-miles has not been estimated. See the map in the Introduction for the States comprising the geographic divisions of the United States.

Shipments excluded from the survey are those moving by pipeline (primarily petroleum products from refineries), parcel post shipments, and commodities moved by own power (motorized vehicles, aircraft, etc.) or towed (prefabricated buildings, etc.). Local shipments (commodities shipped less than 25 miles from the plant) and shipments within the same city are also excluded. Shipments to Alaska and Hawaii from the 48 conterminous States and the District of Columbia are included; however, no data were obtained for shipments originating in Alaska and Hawaii.

- Represents zero or rounds to zero.   (D) Withheld to avoid disclosing figures for individual companies.

[1]Production of this commodity is concentrated in the geographic divisions shown; figures and distributions for geographic divisions not shown are included in the total.

[2]Distances of shipments to foreign destinations are calculated only to the U.S. port of exit.

[3]Includes only shipments represented by bills of lading and invoices. Summary records which did not show individual weights of shipments are not included.

TCC 261. Pulp and Pulp Mill Products

Comparisons of Tons and Ton-Miles of Shipments for
Geographic Divisions of Origin and for Sampling Variability: 1972 and 1967

Geographic division of origin	Estimates				Relative sampling variability in tons (percent)	
	1972		1967		1972	1967
	Tons (thousands)	Ton-miles (millions)	Tons (thousands)	Ton-miles (millions)		
U.S. total	6,994	4,772	5,841	5,696	18.0	(*)
New England	(D)	(D)	(*)	(*)	(*)	(*)
Middle Atlantic	(D)	(D)	(*)	(*)	(*)	(*)
East North Central	(D)	(D)	(*)	(*)	(*)	(*)
West North Central	(D)	(D)	(*)	(*)	(*)	(*)
South Atlantic	2,332	745	(*)	(*)	44.6	(*)
East South Central	(D)	(D)	(*)	(*)	(*)	(*)
West South Central	(D)	(D)	(*)	(*)	(*)	(*)
Mountain	(D)	(D)	(*)	(*)	(*)	(*)
Pacific	1,826	2,857	(*)	(*)	40.5	(*)

(D) Withheld to avoid disclosing figures for individual companies.　　(*) Data not published.

TABLE 1. **TCC GROUP 261—Percent Distribution of Geographic Division of Origin and Distance Shipped, by Means of Transport: 1972**

Geographic division of origin[1] and distance shipped[2]	Number	Percent distribution by means of transport							
		All means of transport	Rail	Motor carrier	Private truck	Air	Water	Other	Unknown
TONS OF SHIPMENTS	(thousands of tons)								
U.S. TOTAL	6 994	100.0	78.0	6.8	.9	-	14.2	-	.2
SOUTH ATLANTIC	2 332	100.0	65.0	5.9	1.0	-	28.1	-	-
UNDER 100 MILES	771	100.0	8.5	9.6	.7	-	81.1	-	-
100 TO 199 MILES	382	100.0	78.5	13.0	.7	-	7.8	-	-
200 TO 299 MILES	196	100.0	96.7	2.8	.5	-	-	-	-
300 TO 499 MILES	437	100.0	96.5	1.0	2.5	-	-	-	-
500 TO 999 MILES	502	100.0	98.8	.6	.6	-	-	-	-
1000 TO 1499 MILES	32	100.0	100.0	-	-	-	-	-	-
1500 MILES OR OVER	9	100.0	100.0	-	-	-	-	-	-
PACIFIC	1 826	100.0	83.8	5.5	1.6	-	8.5	-	.6
UNDER 100 MILES	249	100.0	1.1	35.3	1.4	-	62.2	-	-
100 TO 199 MILES	65	100.0	61.4	12.0	26.6	-	-	-	-
200 TO 299 MILES	34	100.0	89.6	-	10.4	-	-	-	-
300 TO 499 MILES	3	100.0	69.9	-	30.1	-	-	-	-
500 TO 999 MILES	233	100.0	98.9	.2	.8	-	-	-	-
1000 TO 1499 MILES	24	100.0	90.0	6.9	3.0	-	-	-	-
1500 MILES OR OVER	1 216	100.0	98.9	.2	-	-	-	-	1.0
TON-MILES OF SHIPMENTS	(millions of ton-miles)								
U.S. TOTAL	4 772	100.0	96.3	1.4	.4	-	1.3	-	.6
SOUTH ATLANTIC	745	100.0	92.4	2.7	1.2	-	3.7	-	-
UNDER 100 MILES	32	100.0	10.8	15.8	.9	-	72.6	-	-
100 TO 199 MILES	61	100.0	76.9	15.5	.5	-	7.1	-	-
200 TO 299 MILES	49	100.0	96.8	2.6	.6	-	-	-	-
300 TO 499 MILES	189	100.0	96.0	1.1	2.8	-	-	-	-
500 TO 999 MILES	359	100.0	98.6	.6	.8	-	-	-	-
1000 TO 1499 MILES	34	100.0	100.0	-	-	-	-	-	-
1500 MILES OR OVER	19	100.0	100.0	-	-	-	-	-	-
PACIFIC	2 857	100.0	98.0	.5	.2	-	.3	-	.9
UNDER 100 MILES	15	100.0	1.0	41.0	1.1	-	56.9	-	-
100 TO 199 MILES	10	100.0	64.5	14.6	20.9	-	-	-	-
200 TO 299 MILES	8	100.0	89.2	-	10.8	-	-	-	-
300 TO 499 MILES	1	100.0	62.2	-	37.8	-	-	-	-
500 TO 999 MILES	154	100.0	98.8	.3	.9	-	-	-	-
1000 TO 1499 MILES	31	100.0	92.1	5.4	2.4	-	-	-	-
1500 MILES OR OVER	2 635	100.0	98.8	.2	-	-	-	-	1.0

See footnotes at end of table 4.

TABLE 2. **TCC GROUP 261—Percent Distribution of Geographic Division of Origin and Means of Transport, by Geographic Division of Destination: 1972**

Geographic division of origin[1] and means of transport	Number	Percent distribution by division of destination									
		U.S. total	New England	Middle Atlantic	East North Central	West North Central	South Atlantic	East South Central	West South Central	Mountain	Pacific
TONS OF SHIPMENTS	(thousands of tons)										
U.S. TOTAL	6 994	100.0	9.8	12.8	24.6	3.5	24.4	6.5	7.6	.4	10.4
RAIL	5 456	100.0	12.2	16.3	30.8	4.4	16.5	7.2	3.9	.5	8.0
MOTOR CARRIER	473	100.0	1.5	1.3	3.3	.6	29.4	12.5	29.1	-	22.3
PRIVATE TRUCK	62	100.0	8.7	3.7	25.9	-	16.6	-	-	.7	44.4
AIR	-	100.0	-	10.4	-	-	-	-	-	89.6	-
WATER	991	100.0	-	-	-	-	66.2	-	18.1	-	15.7
OTHER	-	100.0	15.1	41.5	28.3	-	-	-	-	-	15.1
UNKNOWN	11	100.0	50.0	-	50.0	-	-	-	-	-	-
SOUTH ATLANTIC	2 332	100.0	6.1	11.1	17.4	1.7	58.9	3.5	.8	.2	.3
RAIL	1 516	100.0	9.3	17.0	25.6	2.6	38.3	5.3	1.3	.2	.4
MOTOR CARRIER	137	100.0	1.6	1.1	3.6	-	93.7	-	-	-	-
PRIVATE TRUCK	23	100.0	-	-	60.2	-	39.8	-	-	-	-
AIR	-	100.0	-	-	-	-	-	-	-	-	-
WATER	656	100.0	-	-	-	-	100.0	-	-	-	-
OTHER	-	100.0	-	-	-	-	-	-	-	-	-
UNKNOWN	-	100.0	-	-	-	-	-	-	-	-	-
PACIFIC	1 826	100.0	7.5	20.3	26.3	2.1	6.1	4.5	.6	.8	31.8
RAIL	1 531	100.0	8.6	24.0	31.0	2.5	7.2	5.4	.7	1.0	19.6
MOTOR CARRIER	100	100.0	-	1.6	.4	-	-	-	-	-	98.0
PRIVATE TRUCK	28	100.0	-	1.0	-	-	-	-	-	1.5	97.6
AIR	-	100.0	-	10.4	-	-	-	-	-	89.6	-
WATER	155	100.0	-	-	-	-	-	-	-	-	100.0
OTHER	-	100.0	15.1	41.5	28.3	-	-	-	-	-	15.1
UNKNOWN	11	100.0	50.0	-	50.0	-	-	-	-	-	-

See footnotes at end of table 4.

COMMODITY TRANSPORTATION SURVEY

PULP, PAPER, AND ALLIED PRODUCTS 2-53

TABLE 2. **TCC GROUP 261—Percent Distribution of Geographic Division of Origin and Means of Transport, by Geographic Division of Destination: 1972**—Continued

Geographic division of origin[1] and means of transport	Number	Percent distribution by division of destination									
		U.S. total	New England	Middle Atlantic	East North Central	West North Central	South Atlantic	East South Central	West South Central	Mountain	Pacific
TON-MILES OF SHIPMENTS	(millions of ton-miles)										
U.S. TOTAL................	4 772	100.0	11.4	24.8	33.2	2.2	11.8	5.6	2.7	.5	7.8
RAIL....................	4 596	100.0	11.4	25.6	34.0	2.3	11.2	5.7	2.0	.5	7.5
MOTOR CARRIER..........	68	100.0	3.3	7.6	7.8	1.1	31.9	7.0	21.2	-	20.0
PRIVATE TRUCK..........	19	100.0	4.5	5.3	50.2	-	9.1	-	-	2.0	28.8
AIR....................	-	100.0	-	20.7	-	-	-	-	-	79.3	-
WATER..................	60	100.0	-	-	-	-	45.5	-	39.9	-	14.6
OTHER..................	-	100.0	20.4	49.7	27.9	-	-	-	-	-	1.9
UNKNOWN................	26	100.0	59.5	-	40.5	-	-	-	-	-	-
SOUTH ATLANTIC..........	745	100.0	11.9	21.3	32.5	3.1	22.1	4.2	2.3	.8	1.7
RAIL....................	688	100.0	12.7	23.0	33.6	3.4	17.5	4.5	2.5	.9	1.9
MOTOR CARRIER..........	20	100.0	6.7	2.2	13.2	-	77.9	-	-	-	-
PRIVATE TRUCK..........	8	100.0	-	-	90.0	-	10.0	-	-	-	-
AIR....................	-	100.0	-	-	-	-	-	-	-	-	-
WATER..................	27	100.0	-	-	-	-	100.0	-	-	-	-
OTHER..................	-	100.0	-	-	-	-	-	-	-	-	-
UNKNOWN................	-	100.0	-	-	-	-	-	-	-	-	-
PACIFIC.................	2 857	100.0	12.1	31.4	31.3	2.1	9.0	6.2	.8	.4	6.7
RAIL....................	2 800	100.0	11.8	31.9	31.5	2.2	9.2	6.3	.8	.4	6.0
MOTOR CARRIER..........	14	100.0	-	26.9	4.8	-	-	-	-	-	68.3
PRIVATE TRUCK..........	6	100.0	-	9.9	-	-	-	-	-	5.7	84.4
AIR....................	-	100.0	-	20.7	-	-	-	-	-	79.3	-
WATER..................	8	100.0	-	-	-	-	-	-	-	-	100.0
OTHER..................	-	100.0	20.4	49.7	27.9	-	-	-	-	-	1.9
UNKNOWN................	26	100.0	59.5	-	40.5	-	-	-	-	-	-

See footnotes at end of table 4.

TABLE 3. **TCC GROUP 261**—Percent Distribution of Geographic Division of Destination and Means of Transport, by Geographic Division of Origin: 1972

Geographic division of destination and means of transport	Number	Percent distribution by division of origin[1]									
		U.S. total	New England	Middle Atlantic	East North Central	West North Central	South Atlantic	East South Central	West South Central	Mountain	Pacific
TONS OF SHIPMENTS	(thousands of tons)										
U.S. TOTAL	6 994	100.0	(D)	(D)	(D)	(D)	33.4	(D)	(D)	(D)	26.1
RAIL	5 456	100.0	(D)	(D)	(D)	(D)	27.8	(D)	(D)	(D)	28.1
MOTOR CARRIER	473	100.0	(D)	(D)	(D)	(D)	29.0	(D)	(D)	(D)	21.2
PRIVATE TRUCK	62	100.0	(D)	(D)	(D)	(D)	36.9	(D)	(D)	(D)	45.5
AIR	-	100.0	(D)	(D)	(D)	(D)	-	(D)	(D)	(D)	100.0
WATER	991	100.0	(D)	(D)	(D)	(D)	66.2	(D)	(D)	(D)	15.7
OTHER	-	100.0	(D)	(D)	(D)	(D)	-	(D)	(D)	(D)	100.0
UNKNOWN	11	100.0	(D)	(D)	(D)	(D)	-	(D)	(D)	(D)	100.0
NEW ENGLAND	684	100.0	(D)	(D)	(D)	(D)	20.9	(D)	(D)	(D)	20.0
RAIL	666	100.0	(D)	(D)	(D)	(D)	21.2	(D)	(D)	(D)	19.7
MOTOR CARRIER	7	100.0	(D)	(D)	(D)	(D)	29.3	(D)	(D)	(D)	-
PRIVATE TRUCK	5	100.0	(D)	(D)	(D)	(D)	-	(D)	(D)	(D)	-
AIR	-	100.0	(D)	(D)	(D)	(D)	-	(D)	(D)	(D)	-
WATER	-	100.0	(D)	(D)	(D)	(D)	-	(D)	(D)	(D)	-
OTHER	-	100.0	(D)	(D)	(D)	(D)	-	(D)	(D)	(D)	100.0
UNKNOWN	5	100.0	(D)	(D)	(D)	(D)	-	(D)	(D)	(D)	100.0
MIDDLE ATLANTIC	898	100.0	(D)	(D)	(D)	(D)	28.8	(D)	(D)	(D)	41.2
RAIL	890	100.0	(D)	(D)	(D)	(D)	29.0	(D)	(D)	(D)	41.3
MOTOR CARRIER	6	100.0	(D)	(D)	(D)	(D)	24.4	(D)	(D)	(D)	26.2
PRIVATE TRUCK	2	100.0	(D)	(D)	(D)	(D)	-	(D)	(D)	(D)	11.8
AIR	-	100.0	(D)	(D)	(D)	(D)	-	(D)	(D)	(D)	100.0
WATER	-	100.0	(D)	(D)	(D)	(D)	-	(D)	(D)	(D)	-
OTHER	-	100.0	(D)	(D)	(D)	(D)	-	(D)	(D)	(D)	100.0
UNKNOWN	-	100.0	(D)	(D)	(D)	(D)	-	(D)	(D)	(D)	-
EAST NORTH CENTRAL	1 719	100.0	(D)	(D)	(D)	(D)	23.7	(D)	(D)	(D)	27.9
RAIL	1 682	100.0	(D)	(D)	(D)	(D)	23.1	(D)	(D)	(D)	28.2
MOTOR CARRIER	15	100.0	(D)	(D)	(D)	(D)	32.1	(D)	(D)	(D)	2.6
PRIVATE TRUCK	16	100.0	(D)	(D)	(D)	(D)	85.6	(D)	(D)	(D)	-
AIR	-	100.0	(D)	(D)	(D)	(D)	-	(D)	(D)	(D)	-
WATER	-	100.0	(D)	(D)	(D)	(D)	-	(D)	(D)	(D)	-
OTHER	-	100.0	(D)	(D)	(D)	(D)	-	(D)	(D)	(D)	100.0
UNKNOWN	5	100.0	(D)	(D)	(D)	(D)	-	(D)	(D)	(D)	100.0
WEST NORTH CENTRAL	243	100.0	(D)	(D)	(D)	(D)	16.3	(D)	(D)	(D)	15.7
RAIL	240	100.0	(D)	(D)	(D)	(D)	16.5	(D)	(D)	(D)	15.9
MOTOR CARRIER	2	100.0	(D)	(D)	(D)	(D)	-	(D)	(D)	(D)	-
PRIVATE TRUCK	-	100.0	(D)	(D)	(D)	(D)	-	(D)	(D)	(D)	-
AIR	-	100.0	(D)	(D)	(D)	(D)	-	(D)	(D)	(D)	-
WATER	-	100.0	(D)	(D)	(D)	(D)	-	(D)	(D)	(D)	-
OTHER	-	100.0	(D)	(D)	(D)	(D)	-	(D)	(D)	(D)	-
UNKNOWN	-	100.0	(D)	(D)	(D)	(D)	-	(D)	(D)	(D)	-
SOUTH ATLANTIC	1 707	100.0	(D)	(D)	(D)	(D)	80.5	(D)	(D)	(D)	6.5
RAIL	902	100.0	(D)	(D)	(D)	(D)	64.3	(D)	(D)	(D)	12.3
MOTOR CARRIER	139	100.0	(D)	(D)	(D)	(D)	92.4	(D)	(D)	(D)	-
PRIVATE TRUCK	10	100.0	(D)	(D)	(D)	(D)	88.4	(D)	(D)	(D)	-
AIR	-	100.0	(D)	(D)	(D)	(D)	-	(D)	(D)	(D)	-
WATER	656	100.0	(D)	(D)	(D)	(D)	100.0	(D)	(D)	(D)	-
OTHER	-	100.0	(D)	(D)	(D)	(D)	-	(D)	(D)	(D)	-
UNKNOWN	-	100.0	(D)	(D)	(D)	(D)	-	(D)	(D)	(D)	-
EAST SOUTH CENTRAL	453	100.0	(D)	(D)	(D)	(D)	17.8	(D)	(D)	(D)	18.2
RAIL	394	100.0	(D)	(D)	(D)	(D)	20.5	(D)	(D)	(D)	20.9
MOTOR CARRIER	59	100.0	(D)	(D)	(D)	(D)	-	(D)	(D)	(D)	-
PRIVATE TRUCK	-	100.0	(D)	(D)	(D)	(D)	-	(D)	(D)	(D)	-
AIR	-	100.0	(D)	(D)	(D)	(D)	-	(D)	(D)	(D)	-
WATER	-	100.0	(D)	(D)	(D)	(D)	-	(D)	(D)	(D)	-
OTHER	-	100.0	(D)	(D)	(D)	(D)	-	(D)	(D)	(D)	-
UNKNOWN	-	100.0	(D)	(D)	(D)	(D)	-	(D)	(D)	(D)	-
WEST SOUTH CENTRAL	532	100.0	(D)	(D)	(D)	(D)	3.6	(D)	(D)	(D)	2.1
RAIL	215	100.0	(D)	(D)	(D)	(D)	9.0	(D)	(D)	(D)	5.3
MOTOR CARRIER	137	100.0	(D)	(D)	(D)	(D)	-	(D)	(D)	(D)	-
PRIVATE TRUCK	-	100.0	(D)	(D)	(D)	(D)	-	(D)	(D)	(D)	-
AIR	-	100.0	(D)	(D)	(D)	(D)	-	(D)	(D)	(D)	-
WATER	179	100.0	(D)	(D)	(D)	(D)	-	(D)	(D)	(D)	-
OTHER	-	100.0	(D)	(D)	(D)	(D)	-	(D)	(D)	(D)	-
UNKNOWN	-	100.0	(D)	(D)	(D)	(D)	-	(D)	(D)	(D)	-
MOUNTAIN	26	100.0	(D)	(D)	(D)	(D)	13.5	(D)	(D)	(D)	57.9
RAIL	26	100.0	(D)	(D)	(D)	(D)	13.8	(D)	(D)	(D)	57.3
MOTOR CARRIER	-	100.0	(D)	(D)	(D)	(D)	-	(D)	(D)	(D)	-
PRIVATE TRUCK	-	100.0	(D)	(D)	(D)	(D)	-	(D)	(D)	(D)	100.0
AIR	-	100.0	(D)	(D)	(D)	(D)	-	(D)	(D)	(D)	100.0
WATER	-	100.0	(D)	(D)	(D)	(D)	-	(D)	(D)	(D)	-
OTHER	-	100.0	(D)	(D)	(D)	(D)	-	(D)	(D)	(D)	-
UNKNOWN	-	100.0	(D)	(D)	(D)	(D)	-	(D)	(D)	(D)	-
PACIFIC	727	100.0	(D)	(D)	(D)	(D)	.8	(D)	(D)	(D)	79.9
RAIL	439	100.0	(D)	(D)	(D)	(D)	1.4	(D)	(D)	(D)	68.4
MOTOR CARRIER	105	100.0	(D)	(D)	(D)	(D)	-	(D)	(D)	(D)	93.1
PRIVATE TRUCK	27	100.0	(D)	(D)	(D)	(D)	-	(D)	(D)	(D)	100.0
AIR	-	100.0	(D)	(D)	(D)	(D)	-	(D)	(D)	(D)	-
WATER	155	100.0	(D)	(D)	(D)	(D)	-	(D)	(D)	(D)	100.0
OTHER	-	100.0	(D)	(D)	(D)	(D)	-	(D)	(D)	(D)	100.0
UNKNOWN	-	100.0	(D)	(D)	(D)	(D)	-	(D)	(D)	(D)	-

See footnotes at end of table 4.

TABLE 3. **TCC GROUP 261—Percent Distribution of Geographic Division of Destination and Means of Transport, by Geographic Division of Origin: 1972**—Continued

Geographic division of destination and means of transport	Number	Percent distribution by division of origin[1]									
		U.S. total	New England	Middle Atlantic	East North Central	West North Central	South Atlantic	East South Central	West South Central	Mountain	Pacific
TON-MILES OF SHIPMENTS	(millions of ton-miles)										
U.S. TOTAL...............	4 772	100.0	(D)	(D)	(D)	(D)	15.6	(D)	(D)	(D)	59.9
RAIL...................	4 596	100.0	(D)	(D)	(D)	(D)	15.0	(D)	(D)	(D)	60.9
MOTOR CARRIER.........	68	100.0	(D)	(D)	(D)	(D)	29.3	(D)	(D)	(D)	21.6
PRIVATE TRUCK.........	19	100.0	(D)	(D)	(D)	(D)	46.5	(D)	(D)	(D)	34.2
AIR...................	-	100.0	(D)	(D)	(D)	(D)	-	(D)	(D)	(D)	100.0
WATER.................	60	100.0	(D)	(D)	(D)	(D)	45.5	(D)	(D)	(D)	14.6
OTHER.................	-	100.0	(D)	(D)	(D)	(D)	-	(D)	(D)	(D)	100.0
UNKNOWN...............	26	100.0	(D)	(D)	(D)	(D)	-	(D)	(D)	(D)	100.0
NEW ENGLAND..............	542	100.0	(D)	(D)	(D)	(D)	16.4	(D)	(D)	(D)	63.8
RAIL...................	524	100.0	(D)	(D)	(D)	(D)	16.7	(D)	(D)	(D)	63.1
MOTOR CARRIER.........	2	100.0	(D)	(D)	(D)	(D)	59.8	(D)	(D)	(D)	-
PRIVATE TRUCK.........	-	100.0	(D)	(D)	(D)	(D)	-	(D)	(D)	(D)	-
AIR...................	-	100.0	(D)	(D)	(D)	(D)	-	(D)	(D)	(D)	-
WATER.................	-	100.0	(D)	(D)	(D)	(D)	-	(D)	(D)	(D)	-
OTHER.................	-	100.0	(D)	(D)	(D)	(D)	-	(D)	(D)	(D)	100.0
UNKNOWN...............	15	100.0	(D)	(D)	(D)	(D)	-	(D)	(D)	(D)	100.0
MIDDLE ATLANTIC.........	1 184	100.0	(D)	(D)	(D)	(D)	13.4	(D)	(D)	(D)	75.9
RAIL...................	1 178	100.0	(D)	(D)	(D)	(D)	13.4	(D)	(D)	(D)	75.9
MOTOR CARRIER.........	5	100.0	(D)	(D)	(D)	(D)	8.5	(D)	(D)	(D)	76.0
PRIVATE TRUCK.........	1	100.0	(D)	(D)	(D)	(D)	-	(D)	(D)	(D)	63.1
AIR...................	-	100.0	(D)	(D)	(D)	(D)	-	(D)	(D)	(D)	100.0
WATER.................	-	100.0	(D)	(D)	(D)	(D)	-	(D)	(D)	(D)	-
OTHER.................	-	100.0	(D)	(D)	(D)	(D)	-	(D)	(D)	(D)	100.0
UNKNOWN...............	-	100.0	(D)	(D)	(D)	(D)	-	(D)	(D)	(D)	-
EAST NORTH CENTRAL......	1 586	100.0	(D)	(D)	(D)	(D)	15.3	(D)	(D)	(D)	56.4
RAIL...................	1 560	100.0	(D)	(D)	(D)	(D)	14.8	(D)	(D)	(D)	56.6
MOTOR CARRIER.........	5	100.0	(D)	(D)	(D)	(D)	49.6	(D)	(D)	(D)	13.4
PRIVATE TRUCK.........	9	100.0	(D)	(D)	(D)	(D)	83.4	(D)	(D)	(D)	-
AIR...................	-	100.0	(D)	(D)	(D)	(D)	-	(D)	(D)	(D)	-
WATER.................	-	100.0	(D)	(D)	(D)	(D)	-	(D)	(D)	(D)	-
OTHER.................	-	100.0	(D)	(D)	(D)	(D)	-	(D)	(D)	(D)	100.0
UNKNOWN...............	10	100.0	(D)	(D)	(D)	(D)	-	(D)	(D)	(D)	100.0
WEST NORTH CENTRAL......	105	100.0	(D)	(D)	(D)	(D)	22.2	(D)	(D)	(D)	57.5
RAIL...................	104	100.0	(D)	(D)	(D)	(D)	22.4	(D)	(D)	(D)	57.9
MOTOR CARRIER.........	-	100.0	(D)	(D)	(D)	(D)	-	(D)	(D)	(D)	-
PRIVATE TRUCK.........	-	100.0	(D)	(D)	(D)	(D)	-	(D)	(D)	(D)	-
AIR...................	-	100.0	(D)	(D)	(D)	(D)	-	(D)	(D)	(D)	-
WATER.................	-	100.0	(D)	(D)	(D)	(D)	-	(D)	(D)	(D)	-
OTHER.................	-	100.0	(D)	(D)	(D)	(D)	-	(D)	(D)	(D)	-
UNKNOWN...............	-	100.0	(D)	(D)	(D)	(D)	-	(D)	(D)	(D)	-
SOUTH ATLANTIC..........	564	100.0	(D)	(D)	(D)	(D)	29.2	(D)	(D)	(D)	45.7
RAIL...................	512	100.0	(D)	(D)	(D)	(D)	23.5	(D)	(D)	(D)	50.3
MOTOR CARRIER.........	21	100.0	(D)	(D)	(D)	(D)	71.5	(D)	(D)	(D)	-
PRIVATE TRUCK.........	1	100.0	(D)	(D)	(D)	(D)	50.7	(D)	(D)	(D)	-
AIR...................	-	100.0	(D)	(D)	(D)	(D)	-	(D)	(D)	(D)	-
WATER.................	27	100.0	(D)	(D)	(D)	(D)	100.0	(D)	(D)	(D)	-
OTHER.................	-	100.0	(D)	(D)	(D)	(D)	-	(D)	(D)	(D)	-
UNKNOWN...............	-	100.0	(D)	(D)	(D)	(D)	-	(D)	(D)	(D)	-
EAST SOUTH CENTRAL......	266	100.0	(D)	(D)	(D)	(D)	11.6	(D)	(D)	(D)	66.0
RAIL...................	261	100.0	(D)	(D)	(D)	(D)	11.9	(D)	(D)	(D)	67.3
MOTOR CARRIER.........	4	100.0	(D)	(D)	(D)	(D)	-	(D)	(D)	(D)	-
PRIVATE TRUCK.........	-	100.0	(D)	(D)	(D)	(D)	-	(D)	(D)	(D)	-
AIR...................	-	100.0	(D)	(D)	(D)	(D)	-	(D)	(D)	(D)	-
WATER.................	-	100.0	(D)	(D)	(D)	(D)	-	(D)	(D)	(D)	-
OTHER.................	-	100.0	(D)	(D)	(D)	(D)	-	(D)	(D)	(D)	-
UNKNOWN...............	-	100.0	(D)	(D)	(D)	(D)	-	(D)	(D)	(D)	-
WEST SOUTH CENTRAL......	129	100.0	(D)	(D)	(D)	(D)	13.2	(D)	(D)	(D)	17.0
RAIL...................	90	100.0	(D)	(D)	(D)	(D)	18.9	(D)	(D)	(D)	24.3
MOTOR CARRIER.........	14	100.0	(D)	(D)	(D)	(D)	-	(D)	(D)	(D)	-
PRIVATE TRUCK.........	-	100.0	(D)	(D)	(D)	(D)	-	(D)	(D)	(D)	-
AIR...................	-	100.0	(D)	(D)	(D)	(D)	-	(D)	(D)	(D)	-
WATER.................	24	100.0	(D)	(D)	(D)	(D)	-	(D)	(D)	(D)	-
OTHER.................	-	100.0	(D)	(D)	(D)	(D)	-	(D)	(D)	(D)	-
UNKNOWN...............	-	100.0	(D)	(D)	(D)	(D)	-	(D)	(D)	(D)	-
MOUNTAIN................	21	100.0	(D)	(D)	(D)	(D)	28.9	(D)	(D)	(D)	47.5
RAIL...................	21	100.0	(D)	(D)	(D)	(D)	29.5	(D)	(D)	(D)	46.6
MOTOR CARRIER.........	-	100.0	(D)	(D)	(D)	(D)	-	(D)	(D)	(D)	-
PRIVATE TRUCK.........	-	100.0	(D)	(D)	(D)	(D)	-	(D)	(D)	(D)	100.0
AIR...................	-	100.0	(D)	(D)	(D)	(D)	-	(D)	(D)	(D)	100.0
WATER.................	-	100.0	(D)	(D)	(D)	(D)	-	(D)	(D)	(D)	-
OTHER.................	-	100.0	(D)	(D)	(D)	(D)	-	(D)	(D)	(D)	-
UNKNOWN...............	-	100.0	(D)	(D)	(D)	(D)	-	(D)	(D)	(D)	-
PACIFIC.................	371	100.0	(D)	(D)	(D)	(D)	3.5	(D)	(D)	(D)	51.5
RAIL...................	342	100.0	(D)	(D)	(D)	(D)	3.8	(D)	(D)	(D)	48.6
MOTOR CARRIER.........	13	100.0	(D)	(D)	(D)	(D)	-	(D)	(D)	(D)	73.6
PRIVATE TRUCK.........	5	100.0	(D)	(D)	(D)	(D)	-	(D)	(D)	(D)	100.0
AIR...................	-	100.0	(D)	(D)	(D)	(D)	-	(D)	(D)	(D)	-
WATER.................	8	100.0	(D)	(D)	(D)	(D)	-	(D)	(D)	(D)	100.0
OTHER.................	-	100.0	(D)	(D)	(D)	(D)	-	(D)	(D)	(D)	100.0
UNKNOWN...............	-	100.0	(D)	(D)	(D)	(D)	-	(D)	(D)	(D)	-

See footnotes at end of table 4.

TABLE 4. TCC GROUP 261—Percent Distribution of Distance Shipped and Weight of Shipment, by Means of Transport: 1972

Distance shipped and weight of shipment [2] [3]	Number	Percent distribution by means of transport							
		All means of transport	Rail	Motor carrier	Private truck	Air	Water	Other	Unknown
TONS OF SHIPMENTS	(thousands of tons)								
U.S. TOTAL..........	6 175	100.0	80.8	4.9	1.0	-	13.1	-	.2
UNDER 100 MILES.........	1 483	100.0	34.7	11.9	.8	-	52.7	-	-
UNDER 1000 POUNDS.....	-	100.0	-	100.0	-	-	-	-	-
1000 TO 9999 POUNDS...	-	100.0	-	59.2	32.9	-	7.9	-	-
10000 TO 29999 POUNDS.	4	100.0	-	37.5	24.7	-	37.8	-	-
30000 TO 59999 POUNDS.	31	100.0	3.8	48.5	31.5	-	16.2	-	-
60000 TO 89999 POUNDS.	19	100.0	30.9	4.5	-	-	64.6	-	-
90000 POUNDS AND OVER.	1 427	100.0	35.5	11.1	-	-	53.4	-	-
100 TO 199 MILES........	760	100.0	81.9	11.4	2.8	-	3.9	-	-
UNDER 1000 POUNDS.....	-	100.0	-	100.0	-	-	-	-	-
1000 TO 9999 POUNDS...	1	100.0	3.4	28.6	68.0	-	-	-	-
10000 TO 29999 POUNDS.	2	100.0	9.7	10.8	79.5	-	-	-	-
30000 TO 59999 POUNDS.	57	100.0	18.1	67.0	14.9	-	-	-	-
60000 TO 89999 POUNDS.	10	100.0	100.0	-	-	-	-	-	-
90000 POUNDS AND OVER.	689	100.0	87.3	6.9	1.5	-	4.3	-	-
200 TO 299 MILES........	470	100.0	94.5	4.0	1.5	-	-	-	-
UNDER 1000 POUNDS.....	-	100.0	-	-	-	-	-	100.0	-
1000 TO 9999 POUNDS...	-	100.0	-	42.1	57.9	-	-	-	-
10000 TO 29999 POUNDS.	5	100.0	42.7	14.5	42.8	-	-	-	-
30000 TO 59999 POUNDS.	23	100.0	16.9	74.1	9.0	-	-	-	-
60000 TO 89999 POUNDS.	2	100.0	100.0	-	-	-	-	-	-
90000 POUNDS AND OVER.	438	100.0	99.5	-	.5	-	-	-	-
300 TO 499 MILES........	790	100.0	97.4	.9	1.6	-	-	-	-
UNDER 1000 POUNDS.....	-	100.0	-	-	-	-	-	-	-
1000 TO 9999 POUNDS...	-	100.0	-	100.0	-	-	-	-	-
10000 TO 29999 POUNDS.	11	100.0	67.6	18.6	13.8	-	-	-	-
30000 TO 59999 POUNDS.	33	100.0	77.6	14.6	7.7	-	-	-	-
60000 TO 89999 POUNDS.	24	100.0	100.0	-	-	-	-	-	-
90000 POUNDS AND OVER.	721	100.0	98.8	-	1.2	-	-	-	-
500 TO 999 MILES........	1 236	100.0	98.7	.7	.7	-	-	-	-
UNDER 1000 POUNDS.....	-	100.0	100.0	-	-	-	-	-	-
1000 TO 9999 POUNDS...	-	100.0	22.5	52.8	24.7	-	-	-	-
10000 TO 29999 POUNDS.	9	100.0	84.9	12.3	2.9	-	-	-	-
30000 TO 59999 POUNDS.	28	100.0	51.4	24.0	24.6	-	-	-	-
60000 TO 89999 POUNDS.	16	100.0	95.1	-	4.9	-	-	-	-
90000 POUNDS AND OVER.	1 180	100.0	100.0	-	-	-	-	-	-
1000 TO 1499 MILES......	147	100.0	98.3	1.2	.5	-	-	-	-
UNDER 1000 POUNDS.....	-	100.0	-	-	-	100.0	-	-	-
1000 TO 9999 POUNDS...	-	100.0	100.0	-	-	-	-	-	-
10000 TO 29999 POUNDS.	1	100.0	60.9	-	39.1	-	-	-	-
30000 TO 59999 POUNDS.	2	100.0	37.7	62.3	-	-	-	-	-
60000 TO 89999 POUNDS.	2	100.0	100.0	-	-	-	-	-	-
90000 POUNDS AND OVER.	139	100.0	100.0	-	-	-	-	-	-
1500 MILES OR OVER......	1 286	100.0	98.9	.2	-	-	-	-	.9
UNDER 1000 POUNDS.....	-	100.0	36.5	62.4	-	-	-	1.1	-
1000 TO 9999 POUNDS...	-	100.0	48.0	52.0	-	-	-	-	-
10000 TO 29999 POUNDS.	1	100.0	37.8	39.1	23.1	-	-	-	-
30000 TO 59999 POUNDS.	7	100.0	95.1	4.9	-	-	-	-	-
60000 TO 89999 POUNDS.	18	100.0	100.0	-	-	-	-	-	-
90000 POUNDS AND OVER.	1 259	100.0	99.0	.1	-	-	-	-	.9
TON-MILES OF SHIPMENTS	(millions of ton-miles)								
U.S. TOTAL..........	4 468	100.0	97.1	1.1	.4	-	.8	-	.6
UNDER 100 MILES.........	75	100.0	40.5	16.3	.7	-	42.5	-	-
UNDER 1000 POUNDS.....	-	100.0	-	100.0	-	-	-	-	-
1000 TO 9999 POUNDS...	-	100.0	-	70.4	20.6	-	9.0	-	-
10000 TO 29999 POUNDS.	-	100.0	-	49.4	19.7	-	30.9	-	-
30000 TO 59999 POUNDS.	1	100.0	3.8	50.2	32.1	-	13.9	-	-
60000 TO 89999 POUNDS.	-	100.0	34.1	1.2	-	-	64.7	-	-
90000 POUNDS AND OVER.	73	100.0	41.5	15.6	-	-	42.9	-	-
100 TO 199 MILES........	117	100.0	81.3	12.7	2.2	-	3.7	-	-
UNDER 1000 POUNDS.....	-	100.0	-	100.0	-	-	-	-	-
1000 TO 9999 POUNDS...	-	100.0	3.1	30.2	66.6	-	-	-	-
10000 TO 29999 POUNDS.	-	100.0	13.5	9.8	76.7	-	-	-	-
30000 TO 59999 POUNDS.	8	100.0	18.0	67.5	14.5	-	-	-	-
60000 TO 89999 POUNDS.	1	100.0	100.0	-	-	-	-	-	-
90000 POUNDS AND OVER.	106	100.0	86.2	8.7	1.0	-	4.1	-	-

See footnotes at end of table 4.

TABLE 4. TCC GROUP 261—Percent Distribution of Distance Shipped and Weight of Shipment, by Means of Transport: 1972—Continued

Distance shipped and weight of shipment [2] [3]	Number	Percent distribution by means of transport							
		All means of transport	Rail	Motor carrier	Private truck	Air	Water	Other	Unknown
TON-MILES OF SHIPMENTS	(millions of ton-miles)								
200 TO 299 MILES.........	118	100.0	94.6	3.9	1.6	-	-	-	-
UNDER 1000 POUNDS.....	-	100.0	-	-	-	-	-	100.0	-
1000 TO 9999 POUNDS...	-	100.0	-	44.3	55.7	-	-	-	-
10000 TO 29999 POUNDS.	1	100.0	42.2	14.4	43.5	-	-	-	-
30000 TO 59999 POUNDS.	5	100.0	16.7	73.5	9.8	-	-	-	-
60000 TO 89999 POUNDS.	-	100.0	100.0	-	-	-	-	-	-
90000 POUNDS AND OVER.	110	100.0	99.4	-	.6	-	-	-	-
300 TO 499 MILES.........	327	100.0	97.1	1.0	1.9	-	-	-	-
UNDER 1000 POUNDS.....	-	100.0	-	-	-	-	-	-	-
1000 TO 9999 POUNDS...	-	100.0	-	100.0	-	-	-	-	-
10000 TO 29999 POUNDS.	4	100.0	68.6	17.6	13.7	-	-	-	-
30000 TO 59999 POUNDS.	13	100.0	73.2	17.5	9.4	-	-	-	-
60000 TO 89999 POUNDS.	9	100.0	100.0	-	-	-	-	-	-
90000 POUNDS AND OVER.	300	100.0	98.6	-	1.4	-	-	-	-
500 TO 999 MILES.........	900	100.0	98.6	.7	.7	-	-	-	-
UNDER 1000 POUNDS.....	-	100.0	100.0	-	-	-	-	-	-
1000 TO 9999 POUNDS...	-	100.0	23.7	48.7	27.5	-	-	-	-
10000 TO 29999 POUNDS.	6	100.0	83.7	13.3	2.9	-	-	-	-
30000 TO 59999 POUNDS.	21	100.0	49.2	23.7	27.0	-	-	-	-
60000 TO 89999 POUNDS.	11	100.0	95.1	-	4.9	-	-	-	-
90000 POUNDS AND OVER.	859	100.0	100.0	-	-	-	-	-	-
1000 TO 1499 MILES......	179	100.0	98.6	1.0	.4	-	-	-	-
UNDER 1000 POUNDS.....	-	100.0	-	-	-	100.0	-	-	-
1000 TO 9999 POUNDS...	-	100.0	100.0	-	-	-	-	-	-
10000 TO 29999 POUNDS.	2	100.0	64.4	-	35.6	-	-	-	-
30000 TO 59999 POUNDS.	2	100.0	42.5	57.5	-	-	-	-	-
60000 TO 89999 POUNDS.	3	100.0	100.0	-	-	-	-	-	-
90000 POUNDS AND OVER.	170	100.0	100.0	-	-	-	-	-	-
1500 MILES OR OVER......	2 749	100.0	98.8	.2	-	-	-	-	1.0
UNDER 1000 POUNDS.....	-	100.0	37.0	61.8	-	-	-	1.2	-
1000 TO 9999 POUNDS...	-	100.0	42.3	57.7	-	-	-	-	-
10000 TO 29999 POUNDS.	2	100.0	36.7	36.0	27.3	-	-	-	-
30000 TO 59999 POUNDS.	17	100.0	94.7	5.3	-	-	-	-	-
60000 TO 89999 POUNDS.	39	100.0	100.0	-	-	-	-	-	-
90000 POUNDS AND OVER.	2 689	100.0	98.9	.1	-	-	-	-	1.0

Note: Detail may not add to total due to rounding. The introductory table shows the estimates of sampling variability for tons; sampling variability for ton-miles has not been estimated. See the map in the Introduction for the States comprising the geographic divisions of the United States.

Shipments excluded from the survey are those moving by pipeline (primarily petroleum products from refineries), parcel post shipments, and commodities moved by own power (motorized vehicles, aircraft, etc.) or towed (prefabricated buildings, etc.). Local shipments (commodities shipped less than 25 miles from the plant) and shipments within the same city are also excluded. Shipments to Alaska and Hawaii from the 48 conterminous States and the District of Columbia are included; however, no data were obtained for shipments originating in Alaska and Hawaii.

- Represents zero or rounds to zero.   (D) Withheld to avoid disclosing figures for individual companies.

[1]Production of this commodity is concentrated in the geographic divisions shown; figures and distributions for geographic divisions not shown are included in the total.

[2]Distances of shipments to foreign destinations are calculated only to the U.S. port of exit.

[3]Includes only shipments represented by bills of lading and invoices. Summary records which did not show individual weights of shipments are not included.

TCC 262. Paper, Except Building Paper

Comparisons of Tons and Ton-Miles of Shipments for
Geographic Divisions of Origin and for Sampling Variability: 1972 and 1967

Geographic division of origin	Estimates				Relative sampling variability in tons (percent)	
	1972		1967		1972	1967
	Tons (thousands)	Ton-miles (millions)	Tons (thousands)	Ton-miles (millions)		
U.S. total	20,024	11,338	18,969	9,035	2.1	4.8
New England	3,652	2,243	3,390	1,710	7.1	(*)
Middle Atlantic	2,020	833	3,748	1,287	11.9	(*)
East North Central	4,138	2,009	4,159	1,774	5.0	(*)
West North Central	437	250	379	213	8.9	(*)
South Atlantic	2,362	1,052	1,436	655	3.6	(*)
East South Central	2,410	1,343	2,726	1,519	13.1	(*)
West South Central	2,543	1,563	1,594	785	13.2	(*)
Mountain	—	—	—	—	—	—
Pacific	2,459	2,042	1,537	1,092	7.0	(*)

— Represents or rounds to zero.   (D) Withheld to avoid disclosing figures for individual companies.   (*) Data not published.

TABLE 1. **TCC GROUP 262**—Percent Distribution of Geographic Division of Origin and Distance Shipped, by Means of Transport: 1972

Geographic division of origin [1] and distance shipped [2]	Number	Percent distribution by means of transport							
		All means of transport	Rail	Motor carrier	Private truck	Air	Water	Other	Unknown
TONS OF SHIPMENTS	(thousands of tons)								
U.S. TOTAL..........	20 024	100.0	58.7	32.7	7.6	-	.8	-	.2
NEW ENGLAND..............	3 652	100.0	63.5	31.4	3.7	-	1.3	.1	-
UNDER 100 MILES.......	286	100.0	35.8	40.3	13.2	-	10.6	-	-
100 TO 199 MILES......	422	100.0	21.5	67.0	10.2	-	1.2	-	-
200 TO 299 MILES......	379	100.0	38.1	53.4	7.0	-	1.5	-	-
300 TO 499 MILES......	700	100.0	65.0	33.6	1.3	-	-	-	-
500 TO 999 MILES......	1 294	100.0	77.8	21.0	1.1	-	-	-	-
1000 TO 1499 MILES....	446	100.0	94.7	5.1	-	-	-	.2	-
1500 MILES OR OVER....	121	100.0	79.5	12.3	2.3	.2	5.1	.6	-
MIDDLE ATLANTIC.........	2 020	100.0	45.1	42.1	12.5	-	.1	-	.2
UNDER 100 MILES.......	383	100.0	22.0	52.6	25.1	-	.2	-	-
100 TO 199 MILES......	269	100.0	19.7	63.1	16.9	-	-	-	.4
200 TO 299 MILES......	482	100.0	45.8	48.5	5.6	-	-	-	.1
300 TO 499 MILES......	299	100.0	44.6	40.9	14.5	-	-	-	.1
500 TO 999 MILES......	433	100.0	67.9	23.0	8.9	-	-	-	.3
1000 TO 1499 MILES....	92	100.0	87.4	11.4	1.3	-	-	-	-
1500 MILES OR OVER....	59	100.0	74.5	21.7	2.3	-	1.3	-	.1
EAST NORTH CENTRAL......	4 138	100.0	43.5	41.6	14.1	-	.4	-	.4
UNDER 100 MILES.......	309	100.0	9.0	38.0	52.7	-	-	-	.2
100 TO 199 MILES......	622	100.0	25.7	42.6	30.0	-	1.6	-	.1
200 TO 299 MILES......	857	100.0	42.8	45.1	12.1	-	-	-	-
300 TO 499 MILES......	862	100.0	44.9	46.1	8.8	-	-	-	.1
500 TO 999 MILES......	1 151	100.0	60.7	33.5	4.4	-	.4	-	.9
1000 TO 1499 MILES....	126	100.0	60.4	37.6	1.3	-	-	-	.6
1500 MILES OR OVER....	208	100.0	39.3	58.4	1.2	.1	-	-	1.0
WEST NORTH CENTRAL......	437	100.0	59.3	37.5	2.7	-	-	-	.4
UNDER 100 MILES.......	14	100.0	9.1	75.7	15.1	-	-	.1	-
100 TO 199 MILES......	22	100.0	26.0	71.1	-	-	-	-	2.9
200 TO 299 MILES......	22	100.0	19.5	80.4	-	-	-	-	-
300 TO 499 MILES......	132	100.0	59.1	34.9	5.3	-	-	-	.6
500 TO 999 MILES......	186	100.0	69.1	29.8	.9	-	-	-	.2
1000 TO 1499 MILES....	51	100.0	68.8	30.3	.9	-	-	-	-
1500 MILES OR OVER....	7	100.0	75.1	19.4	4.4	1.0	-	-	-
SOUTH ATLANTIC..........	2 362	100.0	68.3	26.6	4.8	-	-	-	.3
UNDER 100 MILES.......	292	100.0	58.5	23.4	18.1	-	-	-	-
100 TO 199 MILES......	214	100.0	42.9	50.2	6.9	-	-	-	-
200 TO 299 MILES......	331	100.0	62.6	31.0	5.6	-	-	-	.9
300 TO 499 MILES......	651	100.0	71.5	25.8	2.5	-	-	-	.2
500 TO 999 MILES......	781	100.0	77.1	21.6	1.2	-	-	-	.1
1000 TO 1499 MILES....	74	100.0	83.8	15.1	-	-	-	-	1.0
1500 MILES OR OVER....	16	100.0	80.6	7.4	12.0	-	-	-	-
EAST SOUTH CENTRAL......	2 410	100.0	62.7	31.0	4.7	-	1.4	-	.2
UNDER 100 MILES.......	97	100.0	27.6	28.1	44.4	-	-	-	-
100 TO 199 MILES......	248	100.0	48.4	47.5	4.1	-	-	-	-
200 TO 299 MILES......	206	100.0	33.8	59.6	6.6	-	-	-	-
300 TO 499 MILES......	505	100.0	59.8	35.8	4.0	-	-	-	.4
500 TO 999 MILES......	1 141	100.0	71.7	22.9	2.3	-	2.9	-	.1
1000 TO 1499 MILES....	168	100.0	83.0	15.7	-	-	-	-	1.3
1500 MILES OR OVER....	43	100.0	77.7	22.3	-	-	-	-	-
WEST SOUTH CENTRAL......	2 543	100.0	72.0	22.3	5.6	-	-	-	.1
UNDER 100 MILES.......	134	100.0	41.6	45.3	13.0	-	-	-	-
100 TO 199 MILES......	295	100.0	64.8	22.6	12.6	-	-	-	-
200 TO 299 MILES......	240	100.0	63.1	24.3	12.6	-	-	-	-
300 TO 499 MILES......	515	100.0	69.4	23.1	7.5	-	-	-	-
500 TO 999 MILES......	932	100.0	75.8	22.3	1.7	-	-	-	.2
1000 TO 1499 MILES....	319	100.0	83.8	14.8	1.2	-	-	-	.3
1500 MILES OR OVER....	105	100.0	93.8	6.2	-	-	-	-	-
MOUNTAIN................	-	100.0	-	-	-	-	-	-	-
UNDER 100 MILES.......	-	100.0	-	-	-	-	-	-	-
100 TO 199 MILES......	-	100.0	-	-	-	-	-	-	-
200 TO 299 MILES......	-	100.0	-	-	-	-	-	-	-
300 TO 499 MILES......	-	100.0	-	-	-	-	-	-	-
500 TO 999 MILES......	-	100.0	-	-	-	-	-	-	-
1000 TO 1499 MILES....	-	100.0	-	-	-	-	-	-	-
1500 MILES OR OVER....	-	100.0	-	-	-	-	-	-	-
PACIFIC.................	2 459	100.0	61.2	29.6	6.9	-	2.3	-	-
UNDER 100 MILES.......	204	100.0	10.5	46.2	36.9	-	6.4	-	-
100 TO 199 MILES......	209	100.0	27.5	39.8	18.8	-	13.9	-	-
200 TO 299 MILES......	14	100.0	-	81.9	18.1	-	-	-	-
300 TO 499 MILES......	109	100.0	50.9	32.6	16.5	-	-	-	-
500 TO 999 MILES......	1 393	100.0	64.5	33.3	2.3	-	-	-	-
1000 TO 1499 MILES....	226	100.0	86.1	12.7	1.2	-	-	-	-
1500 MILES OR OVER....	300	100.0	92.1	3.1	-	-	4.8	-	-

See footnotes at end of table 4.

TABLE 1. **TCC GROUP 262—Percent Distribution of Geographic Division of Origin and Distance Shipped, by Means of Transport: 1972**—Continued

Geographic division of origin[1] and distance shipped[2]	Number	Percent distribution by means of transport							
		All means of transport	Rail	Motor carrier	Private truck	Air	Water	Other	Unknown
TON-MILES OF SHIPMENTS	(millions of ton-miles)								
U.S. TOTAL..........	11 338	100.0	69.6	25.9	3.4	-	.9	-	.2
NEW ENGLAND.............	2 243	100.0	77.4	20.1	1.5	-	.8	.1	-
UNDER 100 MILES.......	16	100.0	41.5	42.1	7.6	-	8.6	.1	-
100 TO 199 MILES......	65	100.0	21.6	66.0	10.8	-	1.5	-	-
200 TO 299 MILES......	96	100.0	39.2	52.7	7.0	-	1.2	-	-
300 TO 499 MILES......	272	100.0	65.4	33.3	1.3	-	-	-	-
500 TO 999 MILES......	997	100.0	78.9	20.0	1.0	-	-	-	-
1000 TO 1499 MILES....	519	100.0	94.6	5.2	-	-	-	.2	-
1500 MILES OR OVER....	275	100.0	80.2	11.6	1.7	.2	5.6	.6	-
MIDDLE ATLANTIC.........	833	100.0	61.4	30.4	7.8	-	.2	-	.2
UNDER 100 MILES.......	19	100.0	15.2	54.0	30.6	-	.1	-	.1
100 TO 199 MILES......	41	100.0	19.7	62.2	17.7	-	-	-	.4
200 TO 299 MILES......	118	100.0	45.5	48.8	5.6	-	-	-	.1
300 TO 499 MILES......	113	100.0	44.2	42.2	13.4	-	-	-	.1
500 TO 999 MILES......	305	100.0	68.2	23.4	8.1	-	-	-	.3
1000 TO 1499 MILES....	108	100.0	87.5	11.2	1.3	-	-	-	-
1500 MILES OR OVER....	127	100.0	73.3	22.2	2.7	-	1.6	-	.1
EAST NORTH CENTRAL......	2 009	100.0	50.6	41.8	6.6	-	.3	-	.7
UNDER 100 MILES.......	19	100.0	10.1	38.2	51.5	-	-	-	.2
100 TO 199 MILES......	94	100.0	26.3	42.8	29.0	-	1.8	-	.1
200 TO 299 MILES......	204	100.0	41.8	45.8	12.4	-	-	-	-
300 TO 499 MILES......	346	100.0	46.3	44.9	8.6	-	-	-	.1
500 TO 999 MILES......	817	100.0	62.5	31.8	4.1	-	.4	-	1.0
1000 TO 1499 MILES....	146	100.0	58.9	39.0	1.4	-	-	-	.6
1500 MILES OR OVER....	379	100.0	38.6	59.2	1.1	.1	-	.1	1.0
WEST NORTH CENTRAL......	250	100.0	64.6	33.2	1.9	.1	-	-	.3
UNDER 100 MILES.......	-	100.0	14.2	68.0	17.8	-	-	-	-
100 TO 199 MILES......	2	100.0	25.7	72.0	-	-	-	-	2.3
200 TO 299 MILES......	5	100.0	20.7	79.3	-	-	-	-	-
300 TO 499 MILES......	51	100.0	58.5	36.1	4.7	-	-	-	.7
500 TO 999 MILES......	119	100.0	67.1	31.7	.9	-	-	-	.3
1000 TO 1499 MILES....	58	100.0	69.9	29.2	.9	-	-	-	-
1500 MILES OR OVER....	11	100.0	74.0	20.1	4.8	1.1	-	-	-
SOUTH ATLANTIC.........	1 052	100.0	74.0	23.2	2.6	-	-	-	.3
UNDER 100 MILES.......	19	100.0	65.1	22.2	12.7	-	-	-	-
100 TO 199 MILES......	32	100.0	42.9	50.8	6.4	-	-	-	-
200 TO 299 MILES......	85	100.0	61.6	31.6	5.8	-	-	-	1.0
300 TO 499 MILES......	259	100.0	71.1	26.3	2.4	-	-	-	.3
500 TO 999 MILES......	536	100.0	77.9	20.6	1.4	-	-	-	.1
1000 TO 1499 MILES....	86	100.0	82.6	16.5	-	-	-	-	.9
1500 MILES OR OVER....	31	100.0	79.8	8.2	12.0	-	-	-	-
EAST SOUTH CENTRAL......	1 343	100.0	69.7	25.7	2.4	-	1.8	-	.3
UNDER 100 MILES.......	5	100.0	32.1	27.9	40.0	-	-	-	-
100 TO 199 MILES......	34	100.0	47.7	47.7	4.6	-	-	-	-
200 TO 299 MILES......	51	100.0	33.9	60.0	6.1	-	-	-	-
300 TO 499 MILES......	197	100.0	59.5	36.2	3.9	-	-	-	.3
500 TO 999 MILES......	788	100.0	71.9	22.6	2.3	-	3.0	-	.2
1000 TO 1499 MILES....	184	100.0	82.9	16.0	-	-	-	-	1.2
1500 MILES OR OVER....	80	100.0	78.3	21.7	-	-	-	-	-
WEST SOUTH CENTRAL......	1 563	100.0	77.8	19.1	3.0	-	-	-	.2
UNDER 100 MILES.......	8	100.0	44.9	39.8	15.3	-	-	-	-
100 TO 199 MILES......	45	100.0	63.8	21.7	14.5	-	-	-	-
200 TO 299 MILES......	62	100.0	64.0	23.8	12.2	-	-	-	-
300 TO 499 MILES......	205	100.0	68.2	24.1	7.7	-	-	-	-
500 TO 999 MILES......	686	100.0	76.0	22.2	1.6	-	-	-	.2
1000 TO 1499 MILES....	381	100.0	83.3	15.3	1.1	-	-	-	.3
1500 MILES OR OVER....	172	100.0	94.3	5.7	-	-	-	-	-
MOUNTAIN................	-	100.0	-	-	-	-	-	-	-
UNDER 100 MILES.......	-	100.0	-	-	-	-	-	-	-
100 TO 199 MILES......	-	100.0	-	-	-	-	-	-	-
200 TO 299 MILES......	-	100.0	-	-	-	-	-	-	-
300 TO 499 MILES......	-	100.0	-	-	-	-	-	-	-
500 TO 999 MILES......	-	100.0	-	-	-	-	-	-	-
1000 TO 1499 MILES....	-	100.0	-	-	-	-	-	-	-
1500 MILES OR OVER....	-	100.0	-	-	-	-	-	-	-
PACIFIC.................	2 042	100.0	75.0	20.7	2.0	-	2.3	-	-
UNDER 100 MILES.......	8	100.0	12.9	43.0	38.5	-	5.6	-	-
100 TO 199 MILES......	34	100.0	28.5	37.4	19.1	-	15.0	-	-
200 TO 299 MILES......	3	100.0	-	82.3	17.7	-	-	-	-
300 TO 499 MILES......	44	100.0	52.8	31.3	15.9	-	-	-	-
500 TO 999 MILES......	1 078	100.0	66.5	31.5	2.0	-	-	-	-
1000 TO 1499 MILES....	254	100.0	86.7	12.1	1.1	-	-	-	-
1500 MILES OR OVER....	619	100.0	90.1	3.2	-	-	6.7	-	-

See footnotes at end of table 4.

TABLE 2. **TCC GROUP 262—Percent Distribution of Geographic Division of Origin and Means of Transport, by Geographic Division of Destination: 1972**

Geographic division of origin[1] and means of transport	Number	Percent distribution by division of destination									
		U.S. total	New England	Middle Atlantic	East North Central	West North Central	South Atlantic	East South Central	West South Central	Mountain	Pacific
TONS OF SHIPMENTS	(thousands of tons)										
U.S. TOTAL..............	20 024	100.0	7.1	19.0	24.5	7.1	13.6	6.3	8.7	2.0	11.8
RAIL................	11 751	100.0	5.9	16.1	24.8	7.9	14.5	7.1	10.2	2.2	11.3
MOTOR CARRIER........	6 553	100.0	9.1	23.9	23.0	6.3	13.1	4.5	6.0	1.8	12.3
PRIVATE TRUCK........	1 524	100.0	5.8	18.7	31.4	4.6	10.9	7.9	9.2	1.3	10.2
AIR.................	1	100.0	25.0	13.2	7.8	5.0	14.1	3.5	15.2	.6	15.6
WATER...............	154	100.0	19.7	32.4	6.5	-	-	-	-	-	41.4
OTHER...............	3	100.0	5.4	8.1	16.5	1.5	30.2	5.1	4.1	3.7	25.4
UNKNOWN.............	36	100.0	13.7	25.9	22.1	2.4	20.7	4.2	2.5	2.5	6.1
NEW ENGLAND............	3 652	100.0	22.1	31.3	24.6	2.7	8.9	6.6	1.7	.1	2.1
RAIL................	2 320	100.0	17.1	23.8	32.6	3.8	9.8	8.3	2.0	.1	2.6
MOTOR CARRIER........	1 146	100.0	28.1	45.6	11.8	.9	7.5	4.2	1.1	-	.7
PRIVATE TRUCK........	134	100.0	41.7	43.0	4.1	-	9.0	-	1.9	-	.2
AIR.................	-	100.0	16.1	9.9	19.4	-	12.4	-	35.2	.7	6.3
WATER...............	47	100.0	64.3	22.6	-	-	-	-	-	-	13.1
OTHER...............	2	100.0	7.3	2.6	11.1	-	43.9	1.6	.3	-	33.1
UNKNOWN.............	-	100.0	85.6	1.1	13.4	-	-	-	-	-	-
MIDDLE ATLANTIC........	2 020	100.0	11.4	44.3	18.1	5.8	12.4	3.3	1.9	.6	2.2
RAIL................	910	100.0	7.2	33.4	25.1	8.1	13.1	5.0	3.5	1.1	3.3
MOTOR CARRIER........	851	100.0	16.4	51.0	12.0	3.4	12.7	2.4	.6	.1	1.3
PRIVATE TRUCK........	253	100.0	10.2	60.7	13.3	5.7	9.0	-	.5	-	.5
AIR.................	-	100.0	.9	76.0	2.7	1.0	9.3	2.1	-	-	8.0
WATER...............	1	100.0	-	52.9	-	-	.5	-	-	-	46.6
OTHER...............	-	100.0	-	58.0	7.1	2.6	15.4	2.8	-	-	14.0
UNKNOWN.............	3	100.0	1.5	59.6	34.9	-	.3	2.4	.1	-	1.3
EAST NORTH CENTRAL......	4 138	100.0	3.1	15.0	45.0	10.4	7.8	5.8	6.5	1.5	5.0
RAIL................	1 799	100.0	4.4	13.7	36.0	10.3	10.4	8.1	11.2	1.5	4.4
MOTOR CARRIER........	1 722	100.0	2.5	17.9	45.9	12.0	6.5	3.2	3.0	2.0	7.1
PRIVATE TRUCK........	584	100.0	.7	9.7	70.5	6.3	3.9	6.0	2.4	-	.4
AIR.................	-	100.0	41.5	7.9	-	9.8	14.1	2.4	5.1	.9	18.2
WATER...............	14	100.0	-	31.8	68.2	-	-	-	-	-	-
OTHER...............	-	100.0	2.9	18.6	36.7	4.4	2.1	16.8	3.7	.6	14.3
UNKNOWN.............	16	100.0	19.5	24.8	8.8	1.2	-18.0	8.7	5.4	.6	13.0
WEST NORTH CENTRAL......	437	100.0	1.0	7.9	53.7	20.6	4.4	3.7	4.1	1.2	3.4
RAIL................	259	100.0	.4	5.8	62.4	15.3	2.4	4.5	4.6	.2	4.3
MOTOR CARRIER........	164	100.0	1.8	11.6	39.6	29.2	7.7	2.7	2.6	3.0	1.9
PRIVATE TRUCK........	11	100.0	4.0	.3	62.2	15.6	2.2	.5	12.3	.1	2.8
AIR.................	-	100.0	2.1	4.0	8.0	-	36.6	.2	4.1	-	44.9
WATER...............	-	100.0	-	-	-	-	-	-	-	-	-
OTHER...............	-	100.0	-	4.8	2.4	87.7	3.9	-	1.2	-	-
UNKNOWN.............	1	100.0	-	20.8	43.2	36.0	-	-	-	-	-
SOUTH ATLANTIC.........	2 362	100.0	3.8	22.0	21.1	5.2	36.3	4.4	6.0	.8	.4
RAIL................	1 614	100.0	3.0	21.5	22.7	6.8	33.6	4.1	6.8	.8	.6
MOTOR CARRIER........	627	100.0	6.2	25.5	20.5	2.0	37.0	4.8	3.4	.6	.1
PRIVATE TRUCK........	114	100.0	.6	10.0	.6	-	71.3	6.9	8.8	1.8	-
AIR.................	-	100.0	-	22.7	-	50.9	-	-	-	-	26.4
WATER...............	-	100.0	-	-	-	-	-	-	-	-	-
OTHER...............	-	100.0	-	-	96.0	-	2.7	-	1.3	-	-
UNKNOWN.............	5	100.0	25.7	13.2	13.3	-	47.8	-	-	-	-
EAST SOUTH CENTRAL......	2 410	100.0	3.2	14.3	18.6	9.1	24.7	12.4	15.6	.3	1.7
RAIL................	1 510	100.0	2.7	14.3	18.8	10.8	23.5	9.0	18.3	.4	2.1
MOTOR CARRIER........	746	100.0	4.9	12.0	19.9	6.4	30.0	14.5	10.9	-	1.3
PRIVATE TRUCK........	114	100.0	-	3.5	10.0	7.8	14.2	49.0	15.5	-	-
AIR.................	-	100.0	84.8	-	-	-	-	-	-	-	15.2
WATER...............	33	100.0	-	100.0	-	-	-	-	-	-	-
OTHER...............	-	100.0	-	-	100.0	-	-	-	-	-	-
UNKNOWN.............	5	100.0	-	36.3	63.7	-	-	-	-	-	-
WEST SOUTH CENTRAL......	2 543	100.0	2.4	7.7	20.3	11.0	12.7	9.6	30.9	.7	4.7
RAIL................	1 830	100.0	2.7	9.2	20.2	12.0	12.6	10.5	26.1	.6	6.1
MOTOR CARRIER........	567	100.0	2.0	4.3	24.4	9.6	14.1	5.3	37.8	.9	1.5
PRIVATE TRUCK........	143	100.0	.4	1.2	5.2	5.0	7.1	15.6	65.6	-	-
AIR.................	-	100.0	.3	28.9	13.3	-	.5	52.2	2.1	-	2.7
WATER...............	-	100.0	-	-	-	-	-	-	-	-	-
OTHER...............	-	100.0	-	2.6	9.5	2.0	4.2	3.6	35.8	42.2	-
UNKNOWN.............	2	100.0	-	-	-	-	67.3	-	-	32.7	-
MOUNTAIN...............	-	100.0	-	-	-	-	-	-	-	-	-
RAIL................	-	100.0	-	-	-	-	-	-	-	-	-
MOTOR CARRIER........	-	100.0	-	-	-	-	-	-	-	-	-
PRIVATE TRUCK........	-	100.0	-	-	-	-	-	-	-	-	-
AIR.................	-	100.0	-	-	-	-	-	-	-	-	-
WATER...............	-	100.0	-	-	-	-	-	-	-	-	-
OTHER...............	-	100.0	-	-	-	-	-	-	-	-	-
UNKNOWN.............	-	100.0	-	-	-	-	-	-	-	-	-
PACIFIC................	2 459	100.0	.7	1.9	3.7	2.3	1.3	1.8	1.9	11.5	75.0
RAIL................	1 505	100.0	1.1	2.7	6.1	3.6	2.1	3.0	2.8	12.9	65.7
MOTOR CARRIER........	727	100.0	-	.7	-	.1	-	-	.6	9.8	88.7
PRIVATE TRUCK........	169	100.0	-	-	-	.5	-	-	-	10.4	89.1
AIR.................	-	100.0	-	19.9	-	16.2	-	-	45.6	.3	18.1
WATER...............	56	100.0	-	-	-	-	-	-	-	-	100.0
OTHER...............	-	100.0	-	-	-	-	-	-	50.0	-	50.0
UNKNOWN.............	-	100.0	-	-	-	-	-	-	-	-	-

See footnotes at end of table 4.

TABLE 2. TCC GROUP 262—Percent Distribution of Geographic Division of Origin and Means of Transport, by Geographic Division of Destination: 1972—Continued

Geographic division of origin[1] and means of transport	Number	Percent distribution by division of destination									
		U.S. total	New England	Middle Atlantic	East North Central	West North Central	South Atlantic	East South Central	West South Central	Mountain	Pacific
TON-MILES OF SHIPMENTS	(millions of ton-miles)										
U.S. TOTAL...............	11 338	100.0	5.0	16.0	22.2	7.9	12.1	6.1	8.5	3.4	19.0
RAIL..................	7 888	100.0	4.5	14.3	23.3	8.6	12.4	6.9	9.1	3.3	17.6
MOTOR CARRIER.........	2 938	100.0	6.4	19.7	19.7	6.3	11.3	4.1	6.3	3.9	22.2
PRIVATE TRUCK.........	384	100.0	4.1	17.4	22.6	8.8	13.8	6.1	13.3	3.6	10.3
AIR...................	1	100.0	17.0	5.9	5.7	3.0	10.7	2.1	24.2	1.0	30.4
WATER.................	96	100.0	1.5	30.3	1.7	-	-	-	-	-	66.5
OTHER.................	3	100.0	.7	2.1	6.7	.6	30.2	2.1	1.5	2.8	53.3
UNKNOWN...............	24	100.0	13.9	26.5	16.2	.7	17.4	2.8	2.6	4.4	15.5
NEW ENGLAND..............	2 243	100.0	6.4	18.0	34.9	5.5	10.7	11.0	4.5	.2	8.8
RAIL..................	1 736	100.0	5.0	13.8	39.2	6.4	10.2	11.6	4.5	.2	9.1
MOTOR CARRIER.........	450	100.0	11.5	33.0	22.0	2.5	12.1	10.1	4.1	.1	4.7
PRIVATE TRUCK.........	33	100.0	15.4	36.4	12.3	-	21.5	.2	12.2	-	2.1
AIR...................	-	100.0	.5	2.0	13.3	-	12.9	-	55.3	1.1	14.9
WATER.................	18	100.0	7.4	11.1	-	-	-	-	-	-	81.4
OTHER.................	3	100.0	.4	.3	5.6	-	35.7	.7	.3	-	57.0
UNKNOWN...............	-	100.0	60.6	.4	39.0	-	-	-	-	-	-
MIDDLE ATLANTIC.........	833	100.0	5.8	17.2	23.6	12.8	14.3	5.7	6.1	2.4	12.1
RAIL..................	511	100.0	2.9	11.0	25.2	14.0	14.6	6.6	8.4	3.5	13.7
MOTOR CARRIER.........	253	100.0	11.0	25.9	20.3	9.9	14.2	5.3	2.5	.8	10.1
PRIVATE TRUCK.........	64	100.0	8.8	31.8	23.2	15.6	13.1	-	2.2	.1	5.3
AIR...................	-	100.0	.6	8.4	6.1	2.8	10.4	5.2	-	-	66.5
WATER.................	2	100.0	-	1.1	-	-	.2	-	-	-	98.7
OTHER.................	-	100.0	-	17.7	5.8	4.6	9.0	2.9	.1	.1	59.7
UNKNOWN...............	1	100.0	.3	25.4	62.1	-	.2	4.8	.2	-	7.1
EAST NORTH CENTRAL......	2 009	100.0	4.9	17.7	19.6	8.5	10.2	5.1	11.6	3.6	18.7
RAIL..................	1 016	100.0	6.1	15.6	16.1	7.9	12.4	7.1	17.6	3.0	14.1
MOTOR CARRIER.........	839	100.0	3.7	19.7	20.5	9.1	7.7	2.3	5.3	5.0	26.7
PRIVATE TRUCK.........	132	100.0	2.3	18.8	42.5	9.6	8.9	7.6	6.9	.2	3.2
AIR...................	-	100.0	36.5	5.1	-	5.5	7.5	1.6	6.0	1.4	36.4
WATER.................	5	100.0	-	68.1	31.9	-	-	-	-	-	-
OTHER.................	-	100.0	3.5	11.5	11.2	3.7	2.1	12.4	6.1	1.6	48.0
UNKNOWN...............	†3	100.0	20.7	22.1	1.5	.8	16.3	4.7	4.8	.8	28.3
WEST NORTH CENTRAL......	250	100.0	2.0	12.8	43.4	13.1	6.8	4.8	6.9	1.7	8.7
RAIL..................	161	100.0	.8	9.0	48.2	13.0	4.5	6.4	7.8	.2	10.1
MOTOR CARRIER.........	83	100.0	3.8	20.7	34.1	13.4	11.3	2.0	4.4	4.9	5.6
PRIVATE TRUCK.........	4	100.0	10.9	.5	42.5	10.7	4.1	.4	19.2	.1	11.6
AIR...................	-	100.0	1.9	3.4	2.3	-	25.2	.1	1.9	-	65.2
WATER.................	-	100.0	-	-	-	-	-	-	-	-	-
OTHER.................	-	100.0	-	31.1	7.7	25.2	28.9	-	7.1	-	-
UNKNOWN...............	-	100.0	-	42.0	48.0	10.0	-	-	-	-	-
SOUTH ATLANTIC..........	1 052	100.0	6.1	23.6	23.9	8.8	20.0	3.4	9.6	2.5	2.0
RAIL..................	778	100.0	5.1	21.5	24.9	10.7	19.7	3.3	10.0	2.3	2.5
MOTOR CARRIER.........	243	100.0	9.7	31.0	23.5	3.9	19.0	3.2	7.1	2.0	.6
PRIVATE TRUCK.........	26	100.0	2.3	16.0	.8	-	36.2	10.8	19.9	14.1	.6
AIR...................	-	100.0	-	6.8	-	36.4	-	-	-	-	56.8
WATER.................	-	100.0	-	-	-	-	-	-	-	-	-
OTHER.................	-	100.0	-	-	97.3	-	.7	-	2.0	-	-
UNKNOWN...............	2	100.0	23.5	27.6	21.1	-	27.8	-	-	-	-
EAST SOUTH CENTRAL......	1 343	100.0	5.7	21.5	17.7	9.5	19.6	4.5	15.1	.6	5.8
RAIL..................	936	100.0	4.4	21.1	17.4	10.5	19.6	3.6	16.0	.9	6.4
MOTOR CARRIER.........	345	100.0	10.2	18.3	20.1	6.4	20.5	6.0	13.5	.1	5.0
PRIVATE TRUCK.........	32	100.0	-	8.5	9.6	20.2	26.0	17.6	18.1	-	-
AIR...................	-	100.0	75.9	-	-	-	-	-	-	-	24.1
WATER.................	23	100.0	-	100.0	-	-	-	-	-	-	-
OTHER.................	-	100.0	-	-	100.0	-	-	-	-	-	-
UNKNOWN...............	4	100.0	-	52.9	47.1	-	-	-	-	-	-
WEST SOUTH CENTRAL......	1 563	100.0	5.3	14.4	24.2	10.1	15.3	6.0	11.4	1.1	12.2
RAIL..................	1 215	100.0	5.6	15.8	22.2	10.5	14.8	6.3	9.2	1.0	14.7
MOTOR CARRIER.........	298	100.0	4.9	10.5	34.1	9.4	17.2	4.3	13.8	1.5	4.3
PRIVATE TRUCK.........	46	100.0	1.4	4.3	12.4	5.9	14.6	10.2	51.2	-	4.3
AIR...................	-	100.0	.5	39.5	14.9	-	.7	38.4	1.0	-	4.9
WATER.................	-	100.0	-	-	-	-	-	-	-	-	-
OTHER.................	-	100.0	-	5.6	13.4	2.3	6.8	3.0	13.0	56.0	-
UNKNOWN...............	2	100.0	-	-	-	-	58.1	-	-	41.9	-
MOUNTAIN................	-	100.0	-	-	-	-	-	-	-	-	-
RAIL..................	-	100.0	-	-	-	-	-	-	-	-	-
MOTOR CARRIER.........	-	100.0	-	-	-	-	-	-	-	-	-
PRIVATE TRUCK.........	-	100.0	-	-	-	-	-	-	-	-	-
AIR...................	-	100.0	-	-	-	-	-	-	-	-	-
WATER.................	-	100.0	-	-	-	-	-	-	-	-	-
OTHER.................	-	100.0	-	-	-	-	-	-	-	-	-
UNKNOWN...............	-	100.0	-	-	-	-	-	-	-	-	-
PACIFIC.................	2 042	100.0	2.1	5.5	8.0	4.1	3.8	4.3	3.6	11.6	57.0
RAIL..................	1 530	100.0	2.8	6.5	10.6	5.3	5.0	5.8	4.4	11.2	48.4
MOTOR CARRIER.........	422	100.0	-	2.8	.1	.2	.2	-	1.7	13.2	81.8
PRIVATE TRUCK.........	41	100.0	-	-	-	2.7	-	-	-	23.4	73.9
AIR...................	-	100.0	-	29.0	-	11.8	.1	-	35.9	.1	23.1
WATER.................	46	100.0	-	-	-	-	-	-	-	-	100.0
OTHER.................	-	100.0	-	-	-	-	-	-	99.5	-	.5
UNKNOWN...............	-	100.0	-	-	-	-	-	-	-	-	.-

See footnotes at end of table 4.

TABLE 3. **TCC GROUP 262**—Percent Distribution of Geographic Division of Destination and Means of Transport, by Geographic Division of Origin: 1972

Geographic division of destination and means of transport	Number	Percent distribution by division of origin[1]									
		U.S. total	New England	Middle Atlantic	East North Central	West North Central	South Atlantic	East South Central	West South Central	Mountain	Pacific
TONS OF SHIPMENTS	(thousands of tons)										
U.S. TOTAL.............	20 024	100.0	18.2	10.1	20.7	2.2	11.8	12.0	12.7	-	12.3
RAIL...............	11 751	100.0	19.7	7.7	15.3	2.2	13.7	12.9	15.6	-	12.8
MOTOR CARRIER........	6 553	100.0	17.5	13.0	26.3	2.5	9.6	11.4	8.7	-	11.1
PRIVATE TRUCK........	1 524	100.0	8.8	16.6	38.3	.8	7.5	7.5	9.4	-	11.1
AIR.................	1	100.0	32.8	5.6	42.8	9.4	.8	2.0	4.4	-	2.3
WATER...............	154	100.0	30.7	1.1	9.5	-	-	21.8	-	-	36.9
OTHER...............	3	100.0	65.7	3.7	21.4	.4	.2	-	8.5	-	-
UNKNOWN.............	36	100.0	.5	8.9	45.8	5.2	16.3	16.4	6.8	-	-
NEW ENGLAND............	1 415	100.0	56.9	16.3	9.1	.3	6.3	5.5	4.4	-	1.2
RAIL...............	697	100.0	56.9	9.4	11.3	.2	6.9	5.8	7.2	-	2.4
MOTOR CARRIER........	594	100.0	54.2	23.4	7.2	.5	6.5	6.2	1.9	-	-
PRIVATE TRUCK........	87	100.0	63.9	29.4	4.7	.5	.8	-	.6	-	-
AIR.................	-	100.0	21.1	.2	71.1	.8	-	6.7	-	-	-
WATER...............	30	100.0	100.0	-	-	-	-	-	-	-	-
OTHER...............	-	100.0	88.6	-	11.4	-	-	-	-	-	-
UNKNOWN.............	4	100.0	3.2	1.0	65.2	-	30.6	-	-	-	-
MIDDLE ATLANTIC........	3 799	100.0	30.1	23.6	16.3	.9	13.7	9.1	5.1	-	1.2
RAIL...............	1 891	100.0	29.2	16.1	13.0	.8	18.4	11.4	8.9	-	2.2
MOTOR CARRIER........	1 563	100.0	33.5	27.8	19.7	1.2	10.2	5.7	1.6	-	.3
PRIVATE TRUCK........	285	100.0	20.3	53.9	19.8	-	4.0	1.4	.6	-	-
AIR.................	-	100.0	24.6	32.3	25.7	2.9	1.4	-	9.6	-	3.5
WATER...............	49	100.0	21.4	1.8	9.3	-	-	67.4	-	-	-
OTHER...............	-	100.0	21.3	26.6	49.1	.2	-	-	2.8	-	-
UNKNOWN.............	9	100.0	-	20.6	43.9	4.2	8.3	23.0	-	-	-
EAST NORTH CENTRAL......	4 914	100.0	18.3	7.4	37.9	4.8	10.1	9.1	10.5	-	1.9
RAIL...............	2 908	100.0	26.0	7.9	22.3	5.6	12.6	9.8	12.7	-	3.1
MOTOR CARRIER........	1 509	100.0	9.0	6.8	52.4	4.3	8.5	9.9	9.2	-	-
PRIVATE TRUCK........	478	100.0	1.2	7.0	86.2	1.5	.1	2.4	1.6	-	-
AIR.................	-	100.0	80.9	2.0	.1	9.6	-	-	7.4	-	-
WATER...............	10	100.0	-	-	100.0	-	-	-	-	-	-
OTHER...............	-	100.0	44.2	1.6	47.8	.1	1.3	.2	4.9	-	-
UNKNOWN.............	7	100.0	.3	14.1	18.2	10.3	9.8	47.3	-	-	-
WEST NORTH CENTRAL......	1 414	100.0	7.0	8.3	30.3	6.4	8.7	15.6	19.9	-	4.0
RAIL...............	933	100.0	9.4	7.9	19.8	4.3	11.8	17.5	23.5	-	5.8
MOTOR CARRIER........	409	100.0	2.6	7.0	50.4	11.7	3.1	11.7	13.3	-	.2
PRIVATE TRUCK........	70	100.0	-	20.7	52.7	2.6	-	12.7	10.1	-	1.3
AIR.................	-	100.0	-	1.1	83.4	-	8.0	-	-	-	7.4
WATER...............	-	100.0	-	-	-	-	-	-	-	-	-
OTHER...............	-	100.0	-	6.4	60.8	21.6	-	-	11.2	-	-
UNKNOWN.............	-	100.0	-	-	22.4	77.6	-	-	-	-	-
SOUTH ATLANTIC.........	2 728	100.0	11.9	9.2	11.9	.7	31.5	21.8	11.8	-	1.2
RAIL...............	1 698	100.0	13.3	7.0	11.0	.4	31.9	20.9	13.6	-	1.9
MOTOR CARRIER........	855	100.0	10.1	12.7	13.0	1.5	27.2	26.1	9.3	-	-
PRIVATE TRUCK........	165	100.0	7.3	13.7	13.9	.2	49.1	9.8	6.1	-	-
AIR.................	-	100.0	28.9	3.7	42.9	24.4	-	-	.2	-	-
WATER...............	-	100.0	-	100.0	-	-	-	-	-	-	-
OTHER...............	-	100.0	95.4	1.9	1.5	-	-	-	1.2	-	-
UNKNOWN.............	7	100.0	-	.1	39.9	-	37.8	-	22.1	-	-
EAST SOUTH CENTRAL......	1 254	100.0	19.1	5.3	19.0	1.3	8.3	23.9	19.5	-	3.6
RAIL...............	834	100.0	23.0	5.5	17.5	1.4	8.0	16.3	23.0	-	5.3
MOTOR CARRIER........	296	100.0	16.1	6.9	18.7	1.5	10.2	36.5	10.2	-	-
PRIVATE TRUCK........	121	100.0	-	-	28.8	-	6.5	46.1	18.5	-	-
AIR.................	-	100.0	-	3.4	30.1	.5	-	-	66.0	-	-
WATER...............	-	100.0	-	-	-	-	-	-	-	-	-
OTHER...............	-	100.0	21.1	2.1	70.8	-	-	-	6.0	-	-
UNKNOWN.............	1	100.0	-	5.0	95.0	-	-	-	-	-	-
WEST SOUTH CENTRAL......	1 736	100.0	3.6	2.2	15.4	1.0	8.2	21.6	45.3	-	2.7
RAIL...............	1 198	100.0	3.9	2.7	16.8	1.0	9.2	23.1	39.9	-	3.5
MOTOR CARRIER........	395	100.0	3.1	1.3	13.2	1.1	5.4	20.6	54.2	-	1.1
PRIVATE TRUCK........	140	100.0	1.8	.8	9.9	1.0	7.1	12.5	66.7	-	-
AIR.................	-	100.0	75.8	-	14.2	2.5	-	-	.6	-	6.9
WATER...............	-	100.0	-	-	-	-	-	-	-	-	-
OTHER...............	-	100.0	5.4	-	19.3	.1	.1	-	75.0	-	.1
UNKNOWN.............	-	100.0	-	.2	99.8	-	-	-	-	-	-
MOUNTAIN..............	405	100.0	.5	2.9	15.2	1.3	4.5	1.7	4.2	-	69.8
RAIL...............	263	100.0	.7	3.9	10.3	.1	4.8	2.5	4.0	-	73.5
MOTOR CARRIER........	120	100.0	.2	1.0	28.1	4.0	2.9	.2	4.5	-	59.1
PRIVATE TRUCK........	19	100.0	-	.1	1.4	.1	10.2	-	-	-	88.3
AIR.................	-	100.0	37.9	-	61.2	-	-	-	-	-	1.0
WATER...............	-	100.0	-	-	-	-	-	-	-	-	-
OTHER...............	-	100.0	-	-	3.3	-	-	-	96.6	-	-
UNKNOWN.............	-	100.0	-	-	11.0	-	-	-	89.0	-	-
PACIFIC...............	2 356	100.0	3.2	1.9	8.8	.6	.4	1.8	5.1	-	78.2
RAIL...............	1 325	100.0	4.5	2.3	6.0	.8	.7	2.4	8.5	-	74.7
MOTOR CARRIER........	808	100.0	1.0	1.4	15.0	.4	.1	1.2	1.1	-	79.8
PRIVATE TRUCK........	155	100.0	.2	.9	1.6	.2	-	-	-	-	97.2
AIR.................	-	100.0	13.3	2.9	50.0	27.0	1.3	1.9	.8	-	2.7
WATER...............	63	100.0	9.7	1.2	-	-	-	-	-	-	89.1
OTHER...............	-	100.0	85.9	2.1	12.1	-	-	-	-	-	-
UNKNOWN.............	2	100.0	-	1.9	98.1	-	-	-	-	-	-

See footnotes at end of table 4.

TABLE 3. **TCC GROUP 262—Percent Distribution of Geographic Division of Destination and Means of Transport, by Geographic Division of Origin: 1972**—Continued

Geographic division of destination and means of transport	Number	Percent distribution by division of origin[1]									
		U.S. total	New England	Middle Atlantic	East North Central	West North Central	South Atlantic	East South Central	West South Central	Mountain	Pacific
TON-MILES OF SHIPMENTS	(millions of ton-miles)										
U.S. TOTAL..............	11 338	100.0	19.8	7.4	17.7	2.2	9.3	11.8	13.8	-	18.0
RAIL................	7 888	100.0	22.0	6.5	12.9	2.1	9.9	11.9	15.4	-	19.4
MOTOR CARRIER........	2 938	100.0	15.3	8.6	28.6	2.8	8.3	11.8	10.2	-	14.4
PRIVATE TRUCK........	384	100.0	8.7	16.9	34.6	1.2	7.0	8.6	12.2	-	10.8
AIR.................	1	100.0	36.5	1.7	39.9	11.0	.7	2.7	3.6	-	3.9
WATER...............	96	100.0	19.6	2.1	5.4	-	-	24.4	-	-	48.5
OTHER...............	3	100.0	82.5	1.6	11.1	-	.1	-	4.6	-	-
UNKNOWN.............	24	100.0	.2	5.9	53.2	3.1	11.7	16.4	9.5	-	-
NEW ENGLAND............	563	100.0	25.6	8.6	17.6	.9	11.5	13.5	14.7	-	7.6
RAIL................	355	100.0	24.2	4.2	17.5	.4	11.2	11.6	19.0	-	12.0
MOTOR CARRIER........	187	100.0	27.6	14.8	16.6	1.7	12.6	18.7	7.8	-	.1
PRIVATE TRUCK........	15	100.0	32.7	36.0	19.7	3.3	4.0	-	4.3	-	-
AIR.................	-	100.0	1.1	.1	85.5	1.2	-	12.0	.1	-	-
WATER...............	1	100.0	100.0	-	-	-	-	-	-	-	-
OTHER...............	-	100.0	46.2	-	53.8	-	-	-	-	-	-
UNKNOWN.............	3	100.0	.9	.1	79.2	-	19.7	-	-	-	-
MIDDLE ATLANTIC........	1 809	100.0	22.3	7.9	19.7	1.8	13.7	16.0	12.5	-	6.2
RAIL................	1 127	100.0	21.3	5.0	14.1	1.3	14.9	17.5	17.0	-	8.9
MOTOR CARRIER........	578	100.0	25.7	11.3	28.6	3.0	13.0	10.9	5.4	-	2.0
PRIVATE TRUCK........	66	100.0	18.2	30.8	37.3	-	6.4	4.2	3.0	-	-
AIR.................	-	100.0	12.2	2.4	34.8	6.4	.9	-	24.1	-	19.2
WATER...............	29	100.0	7.2	.1	12.2	-	-	80.5	-	-	-
OTHER...............	-	100.0	12.6	13.3	61.2	.6	-	-	12.3	-	-
UNKNOWN.............	6	100.0	-	5.7	44.5	4.9	12.2	32.8	-	-	-
EAST NORTH CENTRAL......	2 512	100.0	31.2	7.8	15.7	4.3	10.0	9.5	15.0	-	6.5
RAIL................	1 839	100.0	37.0	7.0	8.9	4.2	10.5	8.9	14.7	-	8.8
MOTOR CARRIER........	580	100.0	17.1	8.9	29.7	4.9	9.9	12.0	17.5	-	.1
PRIVATE TRUCK........	86	100.0	4.7	17.3	65.0	2.3	.3	3.6	6.7	-	-
AIR.................	-	100.0	84.5	1.8	-	4.5	-	-	9.3	-	-
WATER...............	1	100.0	-	-	100.0	-	-	-	-	-	-
OTHER...............	-	100.0	68.6	1.4	18.6	-	1.9	.4	9.2	-	-
UNKNOWN.............	4	100.0	.5	22.8	4.8	9.1	15.2	47.6	-	-	-
WEST NORTH CENTRAL......	894	100.0	13.8	11.9	19.0	3.7	10.4	14.3	17.7	-	9.3
RAIL................	676	100.0	16.6	10.6	11.9	3.1	12.3	14.6	18.8	-	12.0
MOTOR CARRIER........	184	100.0	6.1	13.6	41.3	6.0	5.2	12.0	15.3	-	.5
PRIVATE TRUCK........	33	100.0	-	29.9	37.6	1.5	-	19.6	8.1	-	3.3
AIR.................	-	100.0	-	1.6	74.0	-	9.0	-	-	-	15.4
WATER...............	-	100.0	-	-	-	-	-	-	-	-	-
OTHER...............	-	100.0	-	12.0	69.1	1.6	-	-	17.3	-	-
UNKNOWN.............	-	100.0	-	-	57.2	42.8	-	-	-	-	-
SOUTH ATLANTIC.........	1 371	100.0	17.5	8.7	14.9	1.2	15.3	19.2	17.5	-	5.7
RAIL................	979	100.0	18.1	7.6	12.9	.8	15.7	18.8	18.4	-	7.9
MOTOR CARRIER........	333	100.0	16.3	10.8	19.3	2.8	13.9	21.2	15.4	-	.2
PRIVATE TRUCK........	52	100.0	13.7	16.1	22.3	.4	18.4	16.2	13.0	-	-
AIR.................	-	100.0	44.2	1.6	28.0	25.9	-	-	.2	-	-
WATER...............	-	100.0	-	100.0	-	-	-	-	-	-	-
OTHER...............	1	100.0	97.7	.5	.8	-	-	-	1.0	-	-
UNKNOWN.............	4	100.0	-	.1	49.7	-	18.6	-	31.6	-	-
EAST SOUTH CENTRAL......	688	100.0	35.9	6.9	14.9	1.7	5.2	8.8	13.6	-	12.9
RAIL................	542	100.0	37.1	6.3	13.4	1.9	4.7	6.2	14.1	-	16.4
MOTOR CARRIER........	121	100.0	37.4	11.1	16.1	1.3	6.4	17.1	10.6	-	-
PRIVATE TRUCK........	23	100.0	.3	-	42.6	.1	12.3	24.5	20.2	-	-
AIR.................	-	100.0	-	4.1	30.2	.3	-	-	65.4	-	-
WATER...............	-	100.0	-	-	-	-	-	-	-	-	-
OTHER...............	-	100.0	27.2	2.1	64.2	-	-	-	6.5	-	-
UNKNOWN.............	-	100.0	-	10.2	89.8	-	-	-	-	-	-
WEST SOUTH CENTRAL......	958	100.0	10.5	5.3	24.4	1.8	10.5	21.1	18.5	-	7.8
RAIL................	720	100.0	10.8	6.0	24.9	1.8	10.9	20.8	15.6	-	9.3
MOTOR CARRIER........	185	100.0	9.9	3.5	24.1	2.0	9.3	25.2	22.2	-	3.9
PRIVATE TRUCK........	50	100.0	8.0	2.8	18.1	1.8	10.5	11.7	47.1	-	-
AIR.................	-	100.0	83.3	-	9.9	.9	-	-	.1	-	5.8
WATER...............	-	100.0	-	-	-	-	-	-	-	-	-
OTHER...............	-	100.0	15.6	.1	44.4	.2	.2	-	39.2	-	.3
UNKNOWN.............	-	100.0	-	.4	99.6	-	-	-	-	-	-
MOUNTAIN...............	390	100.0	1.0	5.1	18.7	1.1	6.8	2.2	4.4	-	60.6
RAIL................	261	100.0	1.3	6.8	11.8	.1	6.8	3.2	4.5	-	65.5
MOTOR CARRIER........	113	100.0	.3	1.8	36.7	3.6	4.3	.3	3.9	-	49.0
PRIVATE TRUCK........	13	100.0	-	.3	2.3	-	27.3	-	-	-	70.0
AIR.................	-	100.0	42.4	-	57.1	-	-	-	-	-	.5
WATER...............	-	100.0	-	-	-	-	-	-	-	-	-
OTHER...............	-	100.0	-	.1	6.3	-	-	-	93.7	-	-
UNKNOWN.............	1	100.0	-	-	9.8	-	-	-	90.2	-	-
PACIFIC................	2 150	100.0	9.2	4.7	17.5	1.0	1.0	3.6	8.9	-	54.2
RAIL................	1 386	100.0	11.4	5.0	10.3	1.2	1.4	4.4	12.9	-	53.4
MOTOR CARRIER........	652	100.0	3.2	3.9	34.3	.7	.2	2.7	2.0	-	53.0
PRIVATE TRUCK........	39	100.0	1.8	8.6	10.7	1.4	-	-	-	-	77.5
AIR.................	-	100.0	17.9	3.6	47.9	23.5	1.4	2.1	.6	-	3.0
WATER...............	64	100.0	24.0	3.1	-	-	-	-	-	-	72.8
OTHER...............	1	100.0	88.3	1.8	10.0	-	-	-	-	-	-
UNKNOWN.............	3	100.0	-	2.7	97.3	-	-	-	-	-	-

See footnotes at end of table 4.

TABLE 4. **TCC GROUP 262—Percent Distribution of Distance Shipped and Weight of Shipment, by Means of Transport: 1972**

Distance shipped and weight of shipment[2][3]	Number	Percent distribution by means of transport							
		All means of transport	Rail	Motor carrier	Private truck	Air	Water	Other	Unknown
TONS OF SHIPMENTS	(thousands of tons)								
U.S. TOTAL	18 139	100.0	57.7	33.9	7.3	-	.8	-	.2
UNDER 100 MILES	1 432	100.0	31.8	38.4	26.6	-	3.1	-	.1
UNDER 1000 POUNDS	22	100.0	.2	74.1	23.6	.5	.5	.8	.3
1000 TO 9999 POUNDS	126	100.0	-	56.1	42.6	.1	.6	-	.6
10000 TO 29999 POUNDS	170	100.0	6.5	49.8	43.6	-	-	-	.1
30000 TO 59999 POUNDS	616	100.0	7.6	52.8	34.7	-	4.9	-	-
60000 TO 89999 POUNDS	161	100.0	69.6	19.3	11.0	-	-	-	-
90000 POUNDS AND OVER	334	100.0	85.4	6.1	4.6	-	3.9	-	-
100 TO 199 MILES	2 205	100.0	33.0	49.2	15.7	-	2.0	-	.1
UNDER 1000 POUNDS	26	100.0	1.6	93.8	3.7	-	-	.6	.3
1000 TO 9999 POUNDS	150	100.0	2.9	73.8	22.7	-	-	-	.5
10000 TO 29999 POUNDS	259	100.0	1.8	71.6	26.0	-	-	-	.6
30000 TO 59999 POUNDS	1 000	100.0	8.9	68.3	21.4	-	1.5	-	-
60000 TO 89999 POUNDS	189	100.0	59.4	25.2	15.4	-	-	-	-
90000 POUNDS AND OVER	579	100.0	89.2	5.8	-	-	5.0	-	-
200 TO 299 MILES	2 380	100.0	45.8	45.8	8.1	-	.2	-	.2
UNDER 1000 POUNDS	15	100.0	1.4	93.6	4.1	.4	-	.3	.2
1000 TO 9999 POUNDS	109	100.0	2.3	87.4	9.8	-	.2	-	.3
10000 TO 29999 POUNDS	216	100.0	1.5	73.2	25.1	-	-	-	.2
30000 TO 59999 POUNDS	1 023	100.0	15.7	72.0	11.8	-	.5	-	-
60000 TO 89999 POUNDS	314	100.0	77.8	21.1	1.1	-	-	-	-
90000 POUNDS AND OVER	700	100.0	97.0	2.5	.5	-	-	-	-
300 TO 499 MILES	3 500	100.0	57.8	35.7	6.2	-	-	-	.2
UNDER 1000 POUNDS	19	100.0	2.4	93.7	1.6	.7	-	1.0	.5
1000 TO 9999 POUNDS	146	100.0	7.4	82.5	9.3	-	-	.1	.8
10000 TO 29999 POUNDS	226	100.0	13.5	67.9	18.6	-	-	-	.1
30000 TO 59999 POUNDS	1 353	100.0	23.3	66.7	9.7	-	-	-	.3
60000 TO 89999 POUNDS	465	100.0	89.8	9.6	.6	-	-	-	-
90000 POUNDS AND OVER	1 289	100.0	97.0	.8	2.2	-	-	-	-
500 TO 999 MILES	6 599	100.0	68.9	27.6	2.6	-	.6	-	.2
UNDER 1000 POUNDS	36	100.0	5.3	90.8	1.9	.9	-	.5	.6
1000 TO 9999 POUNDS	250	100.0	10.9	83.9	4.1	.1	.1	.1	.8
10000 TO 29999 POUNDS	277	100.0	25.2	63.5	10.6	-	-	-	.7
30000 TO 59999 POUNDS	2 010	100.0	35.3	57.7	6.6	-	.2	-	.2
60000 TO 89999 POUNDS	1 205	100.0	85.0	11.6	-	-	2.8	-	.6
90000 POUNDS AND OVER	2 818	100.0	96.4	3.6	-	-	-	-	-
1000 TO 1499 MILES	1 249	100.0	83.5	15.4	.7	-	-	.1	.4
UNDER 1000 POUNDS	5	100.0	17.1	78.6	.9	2.4	-	.8	.3
1000 TO 9999 POUNDS	29	100.0	23.4	71.6	2.1	.3	-	-	2.6
10000 TO 29999 POUNDS	37	100.0	36.3	60.3	3.4	-	-	-	-
30000 TO 59999 POUNDS	296	100.0	54.7	41.6	2.1	-	-	.3	1.3
60000 TO 89999 POUNDS	246	100.0	98.1	1.9	-	-	-	-	-
90000 POUNDS AND OVER	633	100.0	97.5	2.5	-	-	-	-	-
1500 MILES OR OVER	770	100.0	74.4	21.4	1.0	-	2.8	.1	.3
UNDER 1000 POUNDS	7	100.0	15.7	75.4	1.5	3.9	-	3.0	.5
1000 TO 9999 POUNDS	30	100.0	29.5	59.9	2.4	.2	5.8	1.0	1.2
10000 TO 29999 POUNDS	40	100.0	25.7	60.4	4.4	-	8.8	.6	-
30000 TO 59999 POUNDS	238	100.0	44.3	47.9	2.0	-	5.0	-	.8
60000 TO 89999 POUNDS	180	100.0	98.9	1.1	-	-	-	-	-
90000 POUNDS AND OVER	272	100.0	98.5	-	-	-	1.5	-	-
TON-MILES OF SHIPMENTS	(millions of ton-miles)								
U.S. TOTAL	10 222	100.0	68.2	27.2	3.4	-	.9	-	.2
UNDER 100 MILES	81	100.0	35.1	38.3	24.1	-	2.3	-	.1
UNDER 1000 POUNDS	1	100.0	.3	83.4	14.2	.3	.5	1.0	.4
1000 TO 9999 POUNDS	6	100.0	.1	60.1	38.8	-	.3	-	.7
10000 TO 29999 POUNDS	9	100.0	5.9	50.0	43.9	-	-	-	.1
30000 TO 59999 POUNDS	34	100.0	8.8	54.9	32.2	-	4.1	-	-
60000 TO 89999 POUNDS	7	100.0	72.5	18.6	8.9	-	-	-	-
90000 POUNDS AND OVER	21	100.0	90.2	4.2	3.5	-	2.1	-	-
100 TO 199 MILES	336	100.0	33.0	48.7	15.9	-	2.3	-	.1
UNDER 1000 POUNDS	3	100.0	2.0	93.4	3.6	-	-	.6	.3
1000 TO 9999 POUNDS	22	100.0	3.1	73.9	22.5	-	-	-	.5
10000 TO 29999 POUNDS	39	100.0	1.6	70.9	26.9	-	-	-	.6
30000 TO 59999 POUNDS	151	100.0	8.8	68.1	21.4	-	1.8	-	-
60000 TO 89999 POUNDS	29	100.0	58.2	24.4	17.4	-	-	-	-
90000 POUNDS AND OVER	89	100.0	88.6	5.6	-	-	5.8	-	-

See footnotes at end of table 4.

TABLE 4. TCC GROUP 262—Percent Distribution of Distance Shipped and Weight of Shipment, by Means of Transport: 1972—Continued

Distance shipped and weight of shipment[2] [3]	Number	Percent distribution by means of transport							
		All means of transport	Rail	Motor carrier	Private truck	Air	Water	Other	Unknown
TON-MILES OF SHIPMENTS	(millions of ton-miles)								
200 TO 299 MILES.........	587	100.0	45.8	45.8	8.1	-	.2	-	-
UNDER 1000 POUNDS......	3	100.0	1.4	94.0	3.7	.4	-	.2	.2
1000 TO 9999 POUNDS...	26	100.0	2.3	87.4	9.7	-	.3	-	.3
10000 TO 29999 POUNDS.	52	100.0	1.7	72.9	25.2	-	-	-	.2
30000 TO 59999 POUNDS.	253	100.0	15.6	72.2	11.8	-	.4	-	-
60000 TO 89999 POUNDS.	78	100.0	77.7	21.1	1.2	-	-	-	-
90000 POUNDS AND OVER.	172	100.0	96.8	2.7	.5	-	-	-	-
300 TO 499 MILES.........	1 388	100.0	58.1	35.7	6.1	-	-	-	.2
UNDER 1000 POUNDS.....	7	100.0	2.6	93.8	1.6	.6	-	.9	.5
1000 TO 9999 POUNDS...	56	100.0	7.4	82.7	9.0	-	-	.1	.7
10000 TO 29999 POUNDS.	88	100.0	12.9	68.7	18.3	-	-	-	.1
30000 TO 59999 POUNDS.	535	100.0	23.7	66.7	9.3	-	-	-	.3
60000 TO 89999 POUNDS.	189	100.0	89.4	10.0	.6	-	-	-	-
90000 POUNDS AND OVER.	510	100.0	97.0	.7	2.3	-	-	-	-
500 TO 999 MILES.........	4 839	100.0	70.2	26.6	2.4	-	.6	-	.3
UNDER 1000 POUNDS.....	26	100.0	5.7	90.7	1.6	.9	-	.4	.7
1000 TO 9999 POUNDS...	186	100.0	11.0	84.2	3.5	.2	.1	.1	.8
10000 TO 29999 POUNDS.	202	100.0	26.9	62.2	10.3	-	-	-	.6
30000 TO 59999 POUNDS.	1 424	100.0	36.3	57.0	6.2	-	.3	-	.2
60000 TO 89999 POUNDS.	898	100.0	85.5	11.3	-	-	2.6	-	.6
90000 POUNDS AND OVER.	2 101	100.0	96.9	3.1	-	-	-	-	-
1000 TO 1499 MILES......	1 450	100.0	83.5	15.5	.6	-	-	.1	.3
UNDER 1000 POUNDS.....	6	100.0	16.8	78.9	.8	2.4	-	.8	.3
1000 TO 9999 POUNDS...	35	100.0	24.8	70.6	2.0	.3	-	-	2.3
10000 TO 29999 POUNDS.	46	100.0	36.2	60.4	3.4	-	-	-	-
30000 TO 59999 POUNDS.	339	100.0	55.6	40.8	2.1	-	-	.3	1.2
60000 TO 89999 POUNDS.	291	100.0	97.9	2.1	-	-	-	-	-
90000 POUNDS AND OVER.	730	100.0	97.1	2.9	-	-	-	-	-
1500 MILES OR OVER......	1 537	100.0	74.6	20.4	.8	-	3.8	.1	.3
UNDER 1000 POUNDS.....	16	100.0	17.0	74.1	1.2	3.6	-	3.4	.6
1000 TO 9999 POUNDS...	61	100.0	28.1	59.0	2.5	.1	7.9	1.3	1.0
10000 TO 29999 POUNDS.	76	100.0	25.2	57.6	4.2	-	12.2	.8	-
30000 TO 59999 POUNDS.	471	100.0	44.6	46.1	1.7	-	6.9	-	.7
60000 TO 89999 POUNDS.	368	100.0	99.2	.8	-	-	-	-	-
90000 POUNDS AND OVER.	543	100.0	97.8	-	-	-	2.2	-	-

Note: Detail may not add to total due to rounding. The introductory table shows the estimates of sampling variability for tons; sampling variability for ton-miles has not been estimated. See the map in the Introduction for the States comprising the geographic divisions of the Unites States.

Shipments excluded from the survey are those moving by pipeline (primarily petroleum products from refineries), parcel post shipments, and commodities moved by own power (motorized vehicles, aircraft, etc.) or towed (prefabricated buildings, etc.). Local shipments (commodities shipped less than 25 miles from the plant) and shipments within the same city are also excluded. Shipments to Alaska and Hawaii from the 48 conterminous States and the District of Columbia are included; however, no data were obtained for shipments originating in Alaska and Hawaii.

- Represents zero or rounds to zero.   (D) Withheld to avoid disclosing figures for individual companies.

[1]Production of this commodity is concentrated in the geographic divisions shown; figures and distributions for geographic divisions not shown are included in the total.

[2]Distances of shipments to foreign destinations are calculated only to the U.S. port of exit.

[3]Includes only shipments represented by bills of lading and invoices. Summary records which did not show individual weights of shipments are not included.

TCC 263. Paperboard, Pulpboard, and Fiberboard

Comparisons of Tons and Ton-Miles of Shipments for
Geographic Divisions of Origin and for Sampling Variability: 1972 and 1967

Geographic division of origin	Estimates				Relative sampling variability in tons (percent)	
	1972		1967		1972	1967
	Tons (thousands)	Ton-miles (millions)	Tons (thousands)	Ton-miles (millions)		
U.S. total	25,721	12,926	20,597	11,369	4.0	11.4
New England	587	98	1,889	901	28.4	(*)
Middle Atlantic	1,713	262	1,471	299	38.7	(*)
East North Central	3,780	1,085	1,766	381	17.5	(*)
West North Central	(D)	(D)	93	11	(*)	(*)
South Atlantic	9,716	5,045	6,801	3,268	4.3	(*)
East South Central	2,993	1,715	1,601	1,188	9.0	(*)
West South Central	3,020	2,125	2,107	1,464	5.7	(*)
Mountain	(D)	(D)	815	919	(*)	(*)
Pacific	2,916	1,823	4,054	2,938	16.8	(*)

(D) Withheld to avoid disclosing figures for individual companies.   (*) Data not published.

TABLE 1. TCC GROUP 263—Percent Distribution of Geographic Division of Origin and Distance Shipped, by Means of Transport: 1972

Geographic division of origin[1] and distance shipped[2]	Number	Percent distribution by means of transport							
		All means of transport	Rail	Motor carrier	Private truck	Air	Water	Other	Unknown
TONS OF SHIPMENTS	(thousands of tons)								
U.S. TOTAL..........	25 721	100.0	71.9	15.1	10.8	-	2.2	-	-
NEW ENGLAND.............	587	100.0	21.6	42.4	35.7	-	-	-	.3
UNDER 100 MILES.......	357	100.0	4.4	49.6	45.5	-	-	-	.5
100 TO 199 MILES......	125	100.0	38.2	29.2	32.6	-	-	-	-
200 TO 299 MILES......	32	100.0	36.2	51.9	11.3	-	-	-	.6
300 TO 499 MILES......	26	100.0	63.2	30.5	6.3	-	-	-	-
500 TO 999 MILES......	29	100.0	93.1	6.9	-	-	-	-	-
1000 TO 1499 MILES....	14	100.0	43.8	56.2	-	-	-	-	-
1500 MILES OR OVER....	1	100.0	-	26.5	73.5	-	-	-	-
MIDDLE ATLANTIC.........	1 713	100.0	15.8	50.5	33.6	-	-	-	.1
UNDER 100 MILES.......	1 007	100.0	6.9	56.9	36.1	-	.1	-	-
100 TO 199 MILES......	437	100.0	15.4	51.4	33.3	-	-	-	-
200 TO 299 MILES......	116	100.0	34.1	17.1	48.8	-	-	-	-
300 TO 499 MILES......	31	100.0	4.2	65.5	30.2	.1	-	-	-
500 TO 999 MILES......	86	100.0	76.9	22.2	-	-	-	-	.8
1000 TO 1499 MILES....	33	100.0	77.4	22.6	-	-	-	-	-
1500 MILES OR OVER....	1	100.0	80.5	19.4	-	.1	-	-	-
EAST NORTH CENTRAL......	3 780	100.0	43.3	34.6	22.0	-	-	-	-
UNDER 100 MILES.......	837	100.0	5.5	43.8	50.7	-	-	-	-
100 TO 199 MILES......	838	100.0	19.2	49.9	30.8	-	-	-	-
200 TO 299 MILES......	846	100.0	47.6	40.3	12.1	-	-	-	-
300 TO 499 MILES......	688	100.0	76.2	18.3	5.5	-	-	-	-
500 TO 999 MILES......	476	100.0	87.8	10.1	1.9	-	-	.1	.1
1000 TO 1499 MILES....	53	100.0	98.5	.3	1.2	-	-	-	-
1500 MILES OR OVER....	39	100.0	78.9	21.0	-	.1	-	-	-
SOUTH ATLANTIC.........	9 716	100.0	83.5	7.2	6.3	-	2.9	-	-
UNDER 100 MILES.......	504	100.0	29.1	22.7	31.7	-	16.6	-	-
100 TO 199 MILES......	1 085	100.0	66.2	17.8	15.9	-	-	-	-
200 TO 299 MILES......	1 151	100.0	76.2	9.1	14.1	-	.5	-	.2
300 TO 499 MILES......	2 018	100.0	86.8	8.4	4.5	-	.3	-	-
500 TO 999 MILES......	4 594	100.0	92.8	2.6	.6	-	4.1	-	-
1000 TO 1499 MILES....	306	100.0	99.8	.2	-	-	-	-	-
1500 MILES OR OVER....	55	100.0	96.8	3.2	-	-	-	-	-
EAST SOUTH CENTRAL......	2 993	100.0	81.0	3.4	8.8	-	6.8	-	-
UNDER 100 MILES.......	68	100.0	80.4	7.9	11.7	-	-	-	-
100 TO 199 MILES......	477	100.0	41.8	1.4	14.3	-	42.6	-	-
200 TO 299 MILES......	200	100.0	59.9	5.3	34.9	-	-	-	-
300 TO 499 MILES......	594	100.0	82.1	4.8	13.1	-	-	-	-
500 TO 999 MILES......	1 366	100.0	93.8	3.4	2.8	-	-	-	.1
1000 TO 1499 MILES....	241	100.0	98.3	1.7	-	-	-	-	-
1500 MILES OR OVER....	45	100.0	99.9	.1	-	-	-	-	-
WEST SOUTH CENTRAL......	3 020	100.0	89.1	8.5	1.5	-	.9	-	-
UNDER 100 MILES.......	151	100.0	44.8	43.2	12.0	-	-	-	-
100 TO 199 MILES......	132	100.0	95.2	3.5	1.3	-	-	-	-
200 TO 299 MILES......	376	100.0	59.8	28.3	4.6	-	7.4	-	-
300 TO 499 MILES......	351	100.0	97.8	1.8	.5	-	-	-	-
500 TO 999 MILES......	1 389	100.0	94.7	5.1	.3	-	-	-	-
1000 TO 1499 MILES....	509	100.0	99.1	.9	-	-	-	-	-
1500 MILES OR OVER....	111	100.0	98.0	-	1.9	-	-	.1	-
PACIFIC.................	2 916	100.0	83.2	8.2	7.1	-	1.4	.2	-
UNDER 100 MILES.......	372	100.0	53.7	15.5	21.1	-	9.7	-	-
100 TO 199 MILES......	233	100.0	67.4	5.4	27.2	-	-	-	-
200 TO 299 MILES......	182	100.0	75.7	8.8	15.5	-	-	-	-
300 TO 499 MILES......	629	100.0	76.3	20.3	2.6	-	-	.8	-
500 TO 999 MILES......	1 108	100.0	96.5	1.8	1.7	-	-	-	-
1000 TO 1499 MILES....	141	100.0	99.5	.5	-	-	-	-	-
1500 MILES OR OVER....	249	100.0	96.4	1.3	-	-	2.3	-	-
TON-MILES OF SHIPMENTS	(millions of ton-miles)								
U.S. TOTAL..........	12 926	100.0	88.4	6.5	3.4	-	1.7	-	-
NEW ENGLAND.............	98	100.0	48.9	32.8	18.1	-	-	-	.2
UNDER 100 MILES.......	19	100.0	6.1	48.0	45.0	-	-	-	.8
100 TO 199 MILES......	19	100.0	42.0	28.4	29.6	-	-	-	-
200 TO 299 MILES......	8	100.0	39.5	49.9	10.1	-	-	-	.5
300 TO 499 MILES......	9	100.0	63.3	30.3	6.4	-	-	-	-
500 TO 999 MILES......	24	100.0	94.5	5.5	-	-	-	-	-
1000 TO 1499 MILES....	15	100.0	42.9	57.1	-	-	-	-	-
1500 MILES OR OVER....	2	100.0	-	21.5	78.5	-	-	-	-
MIDDLE ATLANTIC.........	262	100.0	42.9	35.7	21.2	-	-	-	.2
UNDER 100 MILES.......	45	100.0	5.8	56.2	37.8	-	.1	-	-
100 TO 199 MILES......	65	100.0	15.5	51.8	32.6	-	-	-	-
200 TO 299 MILES......	28	100.0	33.6	17.0	49.4	-	-	-	-
300 TO 499 MILES......	10	100.0	4.2	67.8	27.9	.1	-	-	-
500 TO 999 MILES......	70	100.0	80.9	18.4	-	-	-	-	.6
1000 TO 1499 MILES....	40	100.0	78.1	21.9	-	-	-	-	-
1500 MILES OR OVER....	1	100.0	78.3	21.5	-	.1	-	-	-

See footnotes at end of table 4.

TABLE 1. **TCC GROUP 263—Percent Distribution of Geographic Division of Origin and Distance Shipped, by Means of Transport: 1972**—Continued

Geographic division of origin[1] and distance shipped[2]	Number	Percent distribution by means of transport							
		All means of transport	Rail	Motor carrier	Private truck	Air	Water	Other	Unknown
TON-MILES OF SHIPMENTS	(millions of ton-miles)								
EAST NORTH CENTRAL......	1 085	100.0	66.9	23.4	9.6	-	-	-	-
UNDER 100 MILES.......	42	100.0	6.0	51.3	42.8	-	-	-	-
100 TO 199 MILES......	125	100.0	19.8	47.1	33.1	-	-	-	-
200 TO 299 MILES......	205	100.0	48.8	39.5	11.7	-	-	-	-
300 TO 499 MILES......	261	100.0	76.6	18.1	5.4	-	-	-	-
500 TO 999 MILES......	319	100.0	88.9	9.2	1.7	-	-	.1	.1
1000 TO 1499 MILES....	59	100.0	98.3	.3	1.4	-	-	-	-
1500 MILES OR OVER....	70	100.0	78.7	21.1	-	.2	-	-	-
SOUTH ATLANTIC..........	5 045	100.0	90.1	4.2	2.5	-	3.2	-	-
UNDER 100 MILES.......	36	100.0	31.3	19.6	27.6	-	21.6	-	-
100 TO 199 MILES......	161	100.0	67.6	18.3	14.1	-	-	-	-
200 TO 299 MILES......	295	100.0	77.0	9.1	13.3	-	.4	-	.2
300 TO 499 MILES......	817	100.0	87.1	8.1	4.4	-	.3	-	-
500 TO 999 MILES......	3 278	100.0	92.6	2.4	.5	-	4.5	-	-
1000 TO 1499 MILES....	334	100.0	99.8	.2	-	-	-	-	-
1500 MILES OR OVER....	121	100.0	97.1	2.9	-	-	-	-	-
EAST SOUTH CENTRAL......	1 715	100.0	90.0	3.2	4.7	-	2.0	-	-
UNDER 100 MILES.......	4	100.0	81.3	7.3	11.4	-	-	-	-
100 TO 199 MILES......	75	100.0	40.8	1.2	11.8	-	46.2	-	-
200 TO 299 MILES......	49	100.0	59.9	5.0	35.0	-	-	-	-
300 TO 499 MILES......	237	100.0	81.8	4.8	13.4	-	-	-	-
500 TO 999 MILES......	995	100.0	94.1	3.5	2.2	-	-	-	.1
1000 TO 1499 MILES....	267	100.0	98.4	1.6	-	-	-	-	-
1500 MILES OR OVER....	84	100.0	99.9	.1	-	-	-	-	-
WEST SOUTH CENTRAL......	2 125	100.0	94.6	4.5	.6	-	.3	-	-
UNDER 100 MILES.......	11	100.0	43.9	49.0	7.1	-	-	-	-
100 TO 199 MILES......	19	100.0	95.0	3.6	1.4	-	-	-	-
200 TO 299 MILES......	99	100.0	59.5	29.8	4.5	-	6.2	-	-
300 TO 499 MILES......	144	100.0	97.7	1.8	.4	-	-	-	-
500 TO 999 MILES......	1 047	100.0	94.9	4.9	.3	-	-	-	-
1000 TO 1499 MILES....	627	100.0	99.2	.8	-	-	-	-	-
1500 MILES OR OVER....	176	100.0	97.8	-	2.1	-	-	.1	-
PACIFIC.................	1 823	100.0	92.8	4.0	2.1	-	1.0	.1	-
UNDER 100 MILES.......	19	100.0	58.5	11.2	18.0	-	12.2	-	-
100 TO 199 MILES......	33	100.0	66.5	5.1	28.4	-	-	-	-
200 TO 299 MILES......	43	100.0	73.6	9.5	16.9	-	-	-	-
300 TO 499 MILES......	246	100.0	79.9	17.2	2.1	-	-	.7	-
500 TO 999 MILES......	842	100.0	96.7	1.8	1.6	-	-	-	-
1000 TO 1499 MILES....	176	100.0	99.5	.5	-	-	-	-	-
1500 MILES OR OVER....	461	100.0	95.2	1.3	-	-	3.5	-	-

See footnotes at end of table 4.

TABLE 2. **TCC GROUP 263—Percent Distribution of Geographic Division of Origin and Means of Transport, by Geographic Division of Destination: 1972**

Geographic division of origin[1] and means of transport	Number	Percent distribution by division of destination									
		U.S. total	New England	Middle Atlantic	East North Central	West North Central	South Atlantic	East South Central	West South Central	Mountain	Pacific
TONS OF SHIPMENTS	(thousands of tons)										
U.S. TOTAL...............	25 721	100.0	6.5	18.9	27.0	6.9	15.4	5.4	7.8	1.4	10.8
RAIL....................	18 497	100.0	5.5	16.4	27.2	8.0	15.0	5.9	7.7	1.8	12.4
MOTOR CARRIER..........	3 884	100.0	8.2	30.5	30.8	5.3	10.5	2.4	5.4	.4	6.5
PRIVATE TRUCK..........	2 770	100.0	8.0	19.6	25.8	3.0	24.2	6.9	5.0	.3	7.3
AIR.....................	-	100.0	.9	-	69.5	-	-	-	.2	-	29.4
WATER..................	555	100.0	18.3	15.4	-	-	16.1	1.0	41.6	-	7.5
OTHER..................	5	100.0	5.7	-	.2	1.5	5.1	-	-	-	87.5
UNKNOWN................	6	100.0	38.5	17.9	1.9	-	31.5	10.1	-	-	-
NEW ENGLAND.............	587	100.0	73.9	18.3	5.8	1.7	.2	-	-	-	.1
RAIL....................	126	100.0	50.3	22.7	25.6	1.4	-	-	-	-	-
MOTOR CARRIER..........	249	100.0	81.8	14.0	.5	3.2	.3	-	-	.1	-
PRIVATE TRUCK..........	209	100.0	78.7	20.8	-	-	.2	-	-	-	.4
AIR.....................	-	100.0	-	-	-	-	-	-	-	-	-
WATER..................	-	100.0	-	-	-	-	-	-	-	-	-
OTHER..................	-	100.0	-	-	-	-	-	-	-	-	-
UNKNOWN................	2	100.0	90.0	10.0	-	-	-	-	-	-	-

See footnotes at end of table 4.

TABLE 2. TCC GROUP 263—Percent Distribution of Geographic Division of Origin and Means of Transport, by Geographic Division of Destination: 1972—Continued

Geographic division of origin[1] and means of transport	Number	Percent distribution by division of destination									
		U.S. total	New England	Middle Atlantic	East North Central	West North Central	South Atlantic	East South Central	West South Central	Mountain	Pacific
TONS OF SHIPMENTS	(thousands of tons)										
MIDDLE ATLANTIC	1 713	100.0	8.6	75.6	2.8	.4	9.7	1.1	1.7	.1	-
RAIL	270	100.0	10.0	52.9	7.7	2.4	13.5	3.6	9.7	.3	-
MOTOR CARRIER	865	100.0	8.0	83.9	1.2	.1	5.3	1.0	.4	-	-
PRIVATE TRUCK	575	100.0	8.9	73.7	3.0	-	14.4	-	.4	-	-
AIR	-	100.0	-	-	97.8	-	-	-	.4	-	1.8
WATER	-	100.0	-	100.0	-	-	-	-	-	-	-
OTHER	-	100.0	-	-	-	-	-	-	-	-	-
UNKNOWN	1	100.0	14.7	17.0	-	-	-	-	68.3	-	-
EAST NORTH CENTRAL	3 780	100.0	1.4	10.8	65.2	6.6	5.5	5.0	4.0	.6	1.0
RAIL	1 637	100.0	2.9	14.2	50.8	8.0	8.8	4.6	7.5	1.4	1.8
MOTOR CARRIER	1 308	100.0	.2	12.1	74.6	4.7	2.1	4.1	1.6	-	.6
PRIVATE TRUCK	833	100.0	.1	2.1	78.7	6.8	4.1	7.1	1.0	.1	-
AIR	-	100.0	-	-	-	-	-	-	-	-	100.0
WATER	-	100.0	-	-	-	-	-	-	-	-	-
OTHER	-	100.0	76.6	.2	2.2	20.9	-	-	-	-	-
UNKNOWN	-	100.0	100.0	-	-	-	-	-	-	-	-
SOUTH ATLANTIC	9 716	100.0	8.3	23.7	22.8	3.7	28.9	7.4	4.6	.1	.6
RAIL	8 117	100.0	8.1	23.7	25.9	4.2	23.8	8.1	5.5	.1	.6
MOTOR CARRIER	702	100.0	6.0	34.2	11.9	1.1	44.1	1.8	.6	.1	.7
PRIVATE TRUCK	612	100.0	1.0	9.1	4.4	.6	78.2	6.7	.6	.2	-
AIR	-	100.0	100.0	-	-	-	-	-	-	-	-
WATER	281	100.0	36.1	30.2	-	-	31.8	1.9	-	-	-
OTHER	-	100.0	-	.2	-	-	99.8	-	-	-	-
UNKNOWN	2	100.0	-	-	-	-	100.0	-	-	-	-
EAST SOUTH CENTRAL	2 993	100.0	3.9	14.1	32.8	4.5	17.2	8.6	17.5	.1	1.2
RAIL	2 425	100.0	4.8	16.5	38.7	5.4	17.4	6.4	9.1	.1	1.5
MOTOR CARRIER	101	100.0	-	20.7	34.4	3.7	21.1	14.4	5.8	-	.1
PRIVATE TRUCK	262	100.0	-	-	3.0	.3	27.0	33.6	36.1	-	-
AIR	-	100.0	-	-	-	-	-	-	-	-	-
WATER	203	100.0	-	-	-	-	-	-	100.0	-	-
OTHER	-	100.0	-	-	-	-	-	-	-	-	-
UNKNOWN	-	100.0	-	100.0	-	-	-	-	-	-	-
WEST SOUTH CENTRAL	3 020	100.0	3.3	10.2	29.2	10.7	8.1	6.3	22.4	4.5	5.4
RAIL	2 690	100.0	3.7	11.3	30.6	11.5	8.8	6.8	16.3	4.9	5.9
MOTOR CARRIER	257	100.0	-	1.0	21.7	5.3	1.5	1.8	67.6	1.0	-
PRIVATE TRUCK	44	100.0	-	.8	1.9	1.4	7.2	7.3	76.7	-	4.8
AIR	-	100.0	-	-	-	-	-	-	-	-	-
WATER	27	100.0	-	-	-	-	-	-	100.0	-	-
OTHER	-	100.0	-	-	-	-	-	-	-	-	-
UNKNOWN	-	100.0	-	-	100.0	-	-	-	-	-	100.0
PACIFIC	2 916	100.0	.1	.2	3.9	3.6	.2	.2	3.0	5.8	83.0
RAIL	2 426	100.0	.1	.2	4.7	4.4	.3	.2	3.5	6.6	80.1
MOTOR CARRIER	237	100.0	-	.4	-	-	-	-	1.2	1.2	97.2
PRIVATE TRUCK	205	100.0	-	-	-	-	-	-	.2	3.4	96.4
AIR	-	100.0	-	-	86.8	-	-	-	-	-	13.2
WATER	41	100.0	-	-	-	-	-	-	-	-	13.2
OTHER	4	100.0	-	-	-	-	-	-	-	-	100.0
UNKNOWN	-	100.0	-	-	-	-	-	-	-	-	100.0
TON-MILES OF SHIPMENTS	(millions of ton-miles)										
U.S. TOTAL	12 926	100.0	7.7	17.6	28.0	9.3	9.6	4.0	8.3	2.1	13.3
RAIL	11 423	100.0	7.3	17.1	28.6	9.9	9.0	3.9	8.1	2.3	13.8
MOTOR CARRIER	840	100.0	6.2	24.4	31.3	7.0	9.1	3.3	7.5	1.3	9.9
PRIVATE TRUCK	439	100.0	5.0	13.0	20.4	3.9	28.6	8.3	10.5	.9	9.4
AIR	-	100.0	.3	-	38.0	-	-	-	.2	-	61.6
WATER	218	100.0	41.2	26.3	-	-	4.9	.5	18.7	-	8.4
OTHER	2	100.0	11.9	-	-	1.0	2.4	-	-	-	84.6
UNKNOWN	2	100.0	24.4	31.4	4.2	-	21.2	18.7	-	-	-
NEW ENGLAND	98	100.0	33.1	23.8	29.4	10.6	.5	-	-	.6	2.0
RAIL	48	100.0	19.1	19.1	58.1	3.7	-	-	-	-	-
MOTOR CARRIER	32	100.0	40.3	26.9	3.0	26.9	1.2	-	-	1.7	-
PRIVATE TRUCK	17	100.0	57.1	31.0	-	-	.6	-	-	-	11.3
AIR	-	100.0	-	-	-	-	-	-	-	-	-
WATER	-	100.0	-	-	-	-	-	-	-	-	-
OTHER	-	100.0	-	-	-	-	-	-	-	-	-
UNKNOWN	-	100.0	79.6	20.4	-	-	-	-	-	-	-
MIDDLE ATLANTIC	262	100.0	11.0	38.4	9.8	2.7	18.2	5.6	13.6	.6	.1
RAIL	112	100.0	5.4	13.5	12.8	5.6	26.3	7.2	27.9	1.3	-
MOTOR CARRIER	93	100.0	15.4	54.8	6.6	.8	10.8	7.2	4.6	1.3	-
PRIVATE TRUCK	55	100.0	14.8	61.6	9.0	-	14.6	6.6	4.6	.2	.3
AIR	-	100.0	-	-	92.0	-	-	-	1.0	-	7.0
WATER	-	100.0	-	100.0	-	-	-	-	-	-	-
OTHER	-	100.0	-	-	-	-	-	-	-	-	-
UNKNOWN	-	100.0	.7	1.6	-	-	-	-	97.7	-	-

See footnotes at end of table 4.

TABLE 2. **TCC GROUP 263**—Percent Distribution of Geographic Division of Origin and Means of Transport, by Geographic Division of Destination: 1972—Continued

Geographic division of origin[1] and means of transport	Number	Percent distribution by division of destination									
		U.S. total	New England	Middle Atlantic	East North Central	West North Central	South Atlantic	East South Central	West South Central	Mountain	Pacific
TON-MILES OF SHIPMENTS	(millions of ton-miles)										
EAST NORTH CENTRAL......	1 085	100.0	3.4	13.9	40.7	8.0	9.5	5.4	10.7	2.3	6.2
RAIL..............	726	100.0	4.7	15.1	31.5	7.8	11.5	5.0	13.9	3.3	7.2
MOTOR CARRIER.........	253	100.0	.7	14.5	57.3	7.9	4.6	4.6	4.6	-	5.8
PRIVATE TRUCK.........	104	100.0	.4	3.4	64.9	9.8	7.3	10.1	3.2	.8	-
AIR..................	-	100.0	-	-	-	-	-	-	-	-	100.0
WATER...............	-	100.0	-	-	-	-	-	-	-	-	-
OTHER...............	-	100.0	92.1	.1	.1	7.7	-	-	-	-	-
UNKNOWN..............	-	100.0	100.0	-	-	-	-	-	-	-	-
SOUTH ATLANTIC..........	5 045	100.0	12.0	24.7	28.2	5.9	13.3	6.0	7.4	.2	2.3
RAIL..............	4 548	100.0	10.8	24.0	30.0	6.3	11.7	6.3	8.1	.2	2.6
MOTOR CARRIER.........	212	100.0	10.5	39.9	19.8	3.1	20.9	2.2	2.0	1.6	-
PRIVATE TRUCK.........	125	100.0	2.7	11.0	11.0	2.4	66.2	6.8	.1	-	-
AIR..................	-	100.0	100.0	-	-	-	-	-	-	-	-
WATER...............	159	100.0	56.5	36.0	-	-	6.7	.7	-	-	-
OTHER...............	-	100.0	-	1.2	-	-	98.8	-	-	-	-
UNKNOWN..............	-	100.0	-	-	-	-	100.0	-	-	-	-
EAST SOUTH CENTRAL......	1 715	100.0	8.1	22.3	35.5	5.7	11.4	3.4	9.4	.2	4.1
RAIL..............	1 544	100.0	8.9	23.5	38.1	6.1	10.6	2.4	5.6	.2	4.5
MOTOR CARRIER.........	55	100.0	-	34.5	36.5	5.2	12.3	7.0	4.3	-	.2
PRIVATE TRUCK.........	80	100.0	-	-	2.3	.9	30.0	20.4	46.5	-	-
AIR..................	-	100.0	-	-	-	-	-	-	-	-	-
WATER...............	34	100.0	-	-	-	-	-	-	100.0	-	-
OTHER...............	-	100.0	-	-	-	-	-	-	-	-	-
UNKNOWN..............	-	100.0	-	100.0	-	-	-	-	-	-	-
WEST SOUTH CENTRAL......	2 125	100.0	6.7	16.3	30.9	8.6	9.2	3.2	7.4	5.9	11.7
RAIL..............	2 011	100.0	7.1	17.1	30.7	8.6	9.5	3.3	5.5	6.1	12.1
MOTOR CARRIER.........	94	100.0	.2	2.9	42.5	9.7	3.0	1.4	37.7	2.8	-
PRIVATE TRUCK.........	12	100.0	-	2.6	1.8	1.5	19.3	7.1	38.1	-	29.6
AIR..................	-	100.0	-	-	-	-	-	-	-	-	-
WATER...............	6	100.0	-	-	-	-	-	-	100.0	-	-
OTHER...............	-	100.0	-	-	-	-	-	-	-	-	100.0
UNKNOWN..............	-	100.0	-	-	100.0	-	-	-	-	-	-
PACIFIC.................	1 823	100.0	.3	.7	11.4	8.8	.8	.7	7.4	5.5	64.4
RAIL..............	1 691	100.0	.4	.6	12.3	9.5	.9	.7	7.8	5.7	62.3
MOTOR CARRIER.........	72	100.0	-	2.9	-	.1	-	-	6.1	2.0	89.0
PRIVATE TRUCK.........	38	100.0	-	-	-	-	-	-	.6	7.8	91.6
AIR..................	-	100.0	-	-	82.0	-	-	-	-	-	18.0
WATER...............	18	100.0	-	-	-	-	-	-	-	-	100.0
OTHER...............	1	100.0	-	-	-	-	-	-	-	-	100.0
UNKNOWN..............	-	100.0	-	-	-	-	-	-	-	-	-

See footnotes at end of table 4.

TABLE 3. TCC GROUP 263—Percent Distribution of Geographic Division of Destination and Means of Transport, by Geographic Division of Origin: 1972

Geographic division of destination and means of transport	Number	Percent distribution by division of origin[1]									
		U.S. total	New England	Middle Atlantic	East North Central	West North Central	South Atlantic	East South Central	West South Central	Mountain	Pacific
TONS OF SHIPMENTS	(thousands of tons)										
U.S. TOTAL..............	25 721	100.0	2.3	6.7	14.7	(D)	37.8	11.6	11.7	(D)	11.3
RAIL................	18 497	100.0	.7	1.5	8.9	(D)	43.9	13.1	14.5	(D)	13.1
MOTOR CARRIER.........	3 884	100.0	6.4	22.3	33.7	(D)	18.1	2.6	6.6	(D)	6.1
PRIVATE TRUCK........	2 770	100.0	7.6	20.8	30.1	(D)	22.1	9.5	1.6	(D)	7.4
AIR.................	-	100.0	-	47.4	25.1	(D)	.9	-	-	(D)	26.6
WATER...............	555	100.0	-	.1	-	(D)	50.7	36.6	5.0	(D)	7.5
OTHER...............	5	100.0	-	-	7.4	(D)	5.1	1.7	(D)	85.8
UNKNOWN.............	6	100.0	29.5	14.8	9.8	(D)	31.5	12.4	1.9	(D)	
NEW ENGLAND............	1 662	100.0	26.1	8.9	3.1	(D)	48.4	7.0	6.0	(D)	.1
RAIL................	1 016	100.0	6.3	2.7	4.7	(D)	64.5	11.5	9.8	(D)	.2
MOTOR CARRIER.........	318	100.0	64.1	21.8	.8	(D)	13.3	-	-	(D)	-
PRIVATE TRUCK........	222	100.0	74.1	22.9	.4	(D)	2.7	-	-	(D)	-
AIR.................	-	100.0	-	-	-	(D)	100.0	-	-	(D)	-
WATER...............	101	100.0	-	-	-	(D)	100.0	-	-	(D)	-
OTHER...............	-	100.0	-	-	100.0	(D)	-	-	-	(D)	-
UNKNOWN.............	2	100.0	69.0	5.6	25.4	(D)	-	-	-	(D)	-
MIDDLE ATLANTIC........	4 854	100.0	2.2	26.7	8.4	(D)	47.4	8.7	6.3	(D)	.1
RAIL................	3 041	100.0	.9	4.7	7.6	(D)	63.2	13.2	10.0	(D)	.1
MOTOR CARRIER.........	1 183	100.0	3.0	61.3	13.4	(D)	20.3	1.8	.2	(D)	.1
PRIVATE TRUCK........	542	100.0	8.0	78.3	3.3	(D)	10.3	-	.1	(D)	-
AIR.................	-	100.0	-	-	-	(D)	-	-	-	(D)	-
WATER...............	85	100.0	-	.8	-	(D)	99.2	-	-	(D)	-
OTHER...............	-	100.0	-	-	60.6	(D)	39.4	-	-	(D)	-
UNKNOWN.............	1	100.0	16.5	14.1	-	(D)	-	69.4	-	(D)	-
EAST NORTH CENTRAL......	6 948	100.0	.5	.7	35.5	(D)	31.9	14.1	12.7	(D)	1.6
RAIL................	5 038	100.0	.6	.4	16.5	(D)	41.8	18.6	16.4	(D)	2.3
MOTOR CARRIER.........	1 195	100.0	.1	.9	81.7	(D)	7.0	2.9	4.7	(D)	-
PRIVATE TRUCK........	714	100.0	-	2.4	91.8	(D)	3.8	1.1	.1	(D)	-
AIR.................	-	100.0	-	66.8	-	(D)	-	-	-	(D)	33.2
WATER...............	-	100.0	-	-	-	(D)	-	-	-	(D)	-
OTHER...............	-	100.0	-	-	100.0	(D)	-	-	-	(D)	-
UNKNOWN.............	-	100.0	-	-	-	(D)	-	-	100.0	(D)	-
WEST NORTH CENTRAL......	1 773	100.0	.6	.4	14.0	(D)	20.0	7.6	18.3	(D)	6.0
RAIL................	1 486	100.0	.1	.4	8.8	(D)	23.1	8.8	20.9	(D)	7.1
MOTOR CARRIER.........	204	100.0	4.0	.4	29.9	(D)	3.8	1.8	6.7	(D)	-
PRIVATE TRUCK........	82	100.0	-	-	68.7	(D)	4.4	1.0	.7	(D)	-
AIR.................	-	100.0	-	-	-	(D)	-	-	-	(D)	-
WATER...............	-	100.0	-	-	-	(D)	-	-	-	(D)	-
OTHER...............	-	100.0	-	-	100.0	(D)	-	-	-	(D)	-
UNKNOWN.............	-	100.0	-	-	-	(D)	-	-	-	(D)	-
SOUTH ATLANTIC.........	3 955	100.0	-	4.2	5.2	(D)	71.1	13.0	6.2	(D)	.2
RAIL................	2 783	100.0	-	1.3	5.2	(D)	69.4	15.2	8.5	(D)	.2
MOTOR CARRIER.........	409	100.0	.2	11.3	6.8	(D)	75.6	5.2	.9	(D)	-
PRIVATE TRUCK........	670	100.0	.1	12.4	5.1	(D)	71.5	10.6	.5	(D)	-
AIR.................	-	100.0	-	-	-	(D)	-	-	-	(D)	-
WATER...............	89	100.0	-	-	-	(D)	100.0	-	-	(D)	-
OTHER...............	-	100.0	-	-	-	(D)	100.0	-	-	(D)	-
UNKNOWN.............	2	100.0	-	-	-	(D)	100.0	-	-	(D)	-
EAST SOUTH CENTRAL......	1 378	100.0	-	1.4	13.7	(D)	51.9	18.7	13.8	(D)	.4
RAIL................	1 086	100.0	-	.9	7.0	(D)	60.4	14.3	16.7	(D)	.5
MOTOR CARRIER.........	94	100.0	-	9.2	56.5	(D)	13.6	15.5	5.0	(D)	-
PRIVATE TRUCK........	191	100.0	-	-	31.0	(D)	21.4	45.9	1.7	(D)	-
AIR.................	-	100.0	-	-	-	(D)	-	-	-	(D)	-
WATER...............	5	100.0	-	-	-	(D)	100.0	-	-	(D)	-
OTHER...............	-	100.0	-	-	-	(D)	-	-	-	(D)	-
UNKNOWN.............	-	100.0	-	100.0	-	(D)	-	-	-	(D)	-
WEST SOUTH CENTRAL......	1 998	100.0	-	1.5	7.6	(D)	22.5	26.3	33.8	(D)	4.3
RAIL................	1 419	100.0	-	1.8	8.7	(D)	31.4	15.6	30.9	(D)	5.9
MOTOR CARRIER.........	211	100.0	-	1.6	9.7	(D)	2.1	2.8	82.5	(D)	1.3
PRIVATE TRUCK........	137	100.0	-	-	5.8	(D)	.1	68.9	24.9	(D)	.2
AIR.................	-	100.0	-	100.0	-	(D)	-	-	-	(D)	-
WATER...............	230	100.0	-	-	-	(D)	-	88.0	12.0	(D)	-
OTHER...............	-	100.0	-	-	-	(D)	-	-	-	(D)	-
UNKNOWN.............	-	100.0	-	-	-	(D)	-	-	-	(D)	-
MOUNTAIN...............	360	100.0	.1	.3	6.5	(D)	2.0	.9	37.4	(D)	47.2
RAIL................	338	100.0	-	.2	6.7	(D)	1.6	.9	39.0	(D)	47.2
MOTOR CARRIER.........	13	100.0	2.1	.7	.2	(D)	12.7	-	19.0	(D)	21.5
PRIVATE TRUCK........	7	100.0	-	-	8.2	(D)	-	-	-	(D)	91.8
AIR.................	-	100.0	-	-	-	(D)	-	-	-	(D)	-
WATER...............	-	100.0	-	-	-	(D)	-	-	-	(D)	-
OTHER...............	-	100.0	-	-	-	(D)	-	-	-	(D)	-
UNKNOWN.............	-	100.0	-	-	-	(D)	-	-	-	(D)	-
PACIFIC................	2 789	100.0	-	-	1.3	(D)	1.9	1.3	5.8	(D)	86.8
RAIL................	2 287	100.0	-	-	1.3	(D)	2.4	1.6	7.0	(D)	85.0
MOTOR CARRIER.........	253	100.0	-	-	3.3	(D)	-	-	-	(D)	91.2
PRIVATE TRUCK........	201	100.0	.4	-	-	(D)	-	-	1.1	(D)	98.5
AIR.................	-	100.0	-	2.8	85.2	(D)	-	-	-	(D)	12.0
WATER...............	41	100.0	-	-	-	(D)	-	-	-	(D)	100.0
OTHER...............	5	100.0	-	-	-	(D)	-	-	2.0	(D)	98.0
UNKNOWN.............	-	100.0	-	-	-	(D)	-	-	-	(D)	-

See footnotes at end of table 4.

TABLE 3. **TCC GROUP 263—Percent Distribution of Geographic Division of Destination and Means of Transport, by Geographic Division of Origin: 1972**—Continued

Geographic division of destination and means of transport	Number	Percent distribution by division of origin[1]									
		U.S. total	New England	Middle Atlantic	East North Central	West North Central	South Atlantic	East South Central	West South Central	Mountain	Pacific
TON-MILES OF SHIPMENTS	(millions of ton-miles)										
U.S. TOTAL............	12 926	100.0	.8	2.0	8.4	(D)	39.0	13.3	16.4	(D)	14.1
RAIL.............	11 423	100.0	.4	1.0	6.4	(D)	39.8	13.5	17.6	(D)	14.8
MOTOR CARRIER.........	840	100.0	3.8	11.1	30.2	(D)	25.2	6.5	11.3	(D)	8.6
PRIVATE TRUCK.........	439	100.0	4.0	12.6	23.7	(D)	28.5	18.4	2.9	(D)	8.8
AIR..............	-	100.0	-	16.4	55.4	(D)	.3	-	-	(D)	27.8
WATER.............	218	100.0	-	-	-	(D)	72.9	15.9	2.8	(D)	8.4
OTHER.............	2	100.0	-	-	12.9	(D)	2.5	-	7.5	(D)	77.1
UNKNOWN............	2	100.0	8.4	19.1	17.7	(D)	21.2	29.4	4.2	(D)	-
NEW ENGLAND..........	1 001	100.0	3.2	2.9	3.7	(D)	60.6	13.8	14.2	(D)	.6
RAIL.............	836	100.0	1.1	.7	4.1	(D)	58.8	16.5	17.0	(D)	.7
MOTOR CARRIER.........	51	100.0	25.0	27.9	3.6	(D)	43.1	-	.3	(D)	-
PRIVATE TRUCK.........	22	100.0	45.9	37.0	2.0	(D)	15.1	-	-	(D)	-
AIR..............	-	100.0	-	-	-	(D)	100.0	-	-	(D)	-
WATER.............	90	100.0	-	-	-	(D)	100.0	-	-	(D)	-
OTHER.............	-	100.0	-	-	100.0	(D)	-	-	-	(D)	-
UNKNOWN............	-	100.0	27.2	.5	72.2	(D)	-	-	-	(D)	-
MIDDLE ATLANTIC.........	2 274	100.0	1.0	4.4	6.6	(D)	54.9	16.8	15.3	(D)	.5
RAIL.............	1 953	100.0	.5	.8	5.6	(D)	55.9	18.6	17.6	(D)	.5
MOTOR CARRIER.........	205	100.0	4.2	25.0	18.0	(D)	41.2	9.2	1.3	(D)	1.0
PRIVATE TRUCK.........	57	100.0	9.6	59.7	6.1	(D)	24.0	-	.6	(D)	-
AIR..............	-	100.0	-	-	-	(D)	-	-	-	(D)	-
WATER.............	57	100.0	-	.1	-	(D)	99.9	-	-	(D)	-
OTHER.............	-	100.0	-	-	34.5	(D)	65.5	-	-	(D)	-
UNKNOWN............	-	100.0	5.4	.9	-	(D)	-	93.6	-	(D)	-
EAST NORTH CENTRAL......	3 613	100.0	.8	.7	12.2	(D)	39.4	16.9	18.2	(D)	5.7
RAIL.............	3 261	100.0	.9	.4	7.0	(D)	41.9	18.0	18.9	(D)	6.4
MOTOR CARRIER.........	262	100.0	.4	2.3	55.3	(D)	16.0	7.6	15.3	(D)	-
PRIVATE TRUCK.........	89	100.0	-	5.6	75.4	(D)	15.4	2.0	.3	(D)	-
AIR..............	-	100.0	-	39.9	-	(D)	-	-	-	(D)	60.1
WATER.............	-	100.0	-	-	-	(D)	-	-	-	(D)	-
OTHER.............	-	100.0	-	-	100.0	(D)	-	-	-	(D)	-
UNKNOWN............	-	100.0	-	-	-	(D)	-	-	100.0	(D)	-
WEST NORTH CENTRAL......	1 207	100.0	.9	.6	7.2	(D)	24.6	8.0	15.1	(D)	13.3
RAIL.............	1 131	100.0	.2	.6	5.0	(D)	25.4	8.3	15.3	(D)	14.1
MOTOR CARRIER.........	59	100.0	14.6	1.2	33.7	(D)	11.0	4.8	15.5	(D)	.1
PRIVATE TRUCK.........	17	100.0	-	-	59.7	(D)	17.6	4.1	1.1	(D)	-
AIR..............	-	100.0	-	-	-	(D)	-	-	-	(D)	-
WATER.............	-	100.0	-	-	-	(D)	-	-	-	(D)	-
OTHER.............	-	100.0	-	-	100.0	(D)	-	-	-	(D)	-
UNKNOWN............	-	100.0	-	-	-	(D)	-	-	-	(D)	-
SOUTH ATLANTIC..........	1 239	100.0	-	3.9	8.3	(D)	54.1	15.7	15.8	(D)	1.2
RAIL.............	1 026	100.0	-	2.9	8.2	(D)	51.9	15.9	18.6	(D)	1.5
MOTOR CARRIER.........	76	100.0	.5	13.3	15.3	(D)	58.1	8.9	3.7	(D)	-
PRIVATE TRUCK.........	125	100.0	.1	6.5	6.1	(D)	66.1	19.4	2.0	(D)	-
AIR..............	-	100.0	-	-	-	(D)	-	-	-	(D)	-
WATER.............	10	100.0	-	-	-	(D)	100.0	-	-	(D)	-
OTHER.............	-	100.0	-	-	-	(D)	100.0	-	-	(D)	-
UNKNOWN............	-	100.0	-	-	-	(D)	100.0	-	-	(D)	-
EAST SOUTH CENTRAL......	516	100.0	-	2.9	11.4	(D)	58.2	11.2	13.3	(D)	2.3
RAIL.............	450	100.0	-	1.8	8.1	(D)	63.5	8.3	14.7	(D)	2.7
MOTOR CARRIER.........	27	100.0	-	22.4	42.0	(D)	16.7	13.9	4.7	(D)	-
PRIVATE TRUCK.........	36	100.0	-	-	28.9	(D)	23.3	45.3	2.5	(D)	-
AIR..............	-	100.0	-	-	-	(D)	-	-	-	(D)	-
WATER.............	1	100.0	-	-	-	(D)	100.0	-	-	(D)	-
OTHER.............	-	100.0	-	-	-	(D)	-	-	-	(D)	-
UNKNOWN............	-	100.0	-	100.0	-	(D)	-	-	-	(D)	-
WEST SOUTH CENTRAL......	1 072	100.0	-	3.3	10.8	(D)	34.7	15.1	14.7	(D)	12.7
RAIL.............	922	100.0	-	3.4	10.9	(D)	39.8	9.5	12.1	(D)	14.2
MOTOR CARRIER.........	62	100.0	-	6.9	18.7	(D)	6.7	3.8	56.9	(D)	7.0
PRIVATE TRUCK.........	46	100.0	-	-	7.3	(D)	.2	81.5	10.6	(D)	.5
AIR..............	-	100.0	-	100.0	-	(D)	-	-	-	(D)	-
WATER.............	40	100.0	-	-	-	(D)	-	84.9	15.1	(D)	-
OTHER.............	-	100.0	-	-	-	(D)	-	-	-	(D)	-
UNKNOWN............	-	100.0	-	-	-	(D)	-	-	-	(D)	-
MOUNTAIN.............	276	100.0	.2	.6	8.9	(D)	4.1	1.2	45.4	(D)	36.4
RAIL.............	261	100.0	-	.6	9.1	(D)	3.0	1.2	47.0	(D)	36.8
MOTOR CARRIER.........	11	100.0	4.9	1.5	.3	(D)	30.7	-	23.6	(D)	13.1
PRIVATE TRUCK.........	3	100.0	-	-	21.3	(D)	-	-	-	(D)	78.7
AIR..............	-	100.0	-	-	-	(D)	-	-	-	(D)	-
WATER.............	-	100.0	-	-	-	(D)	-	-	-	(D)	-
OTHER.............	-	100.0	-	-	-	(D)	-	-	-	(D)	-
UNKNOWN............	-	100.0	-	-	-	(D)	-	-	-	(D)	-
PACIFIC.............	1 725	100.0	.1	-	3.9	(D)	6.8	4.1	14.4	(D)	68.0
RAIL.............	1 580	100.0	-	-	3.3	(D)	7.4	4.4	15.4	(D)	66.7
MOTOR CARRIER.........	83	100.0	-	.3	17.8	(D)	.1	.1	-	(D)	77.4
PRIVATE TRUCK.........	41	100.0	4.9	-	-	(D)	-	-	9.2	(D)	86.0
AIR..............	-	100.0	-	1.9	90.0	(D)	-	-	-	(D)	8.1
WATER.............	18	100.0	-	-	-	(D)	-	-	-	(D)	100.0
OTHER.............	1	100.0	-	-	-	(D)	-	-	8.9	(D)	91.1
UNKNOWN............	-	100.0	-	-	-	(D)	-	-	-	(D)	-

See footnotes at end of table 4.

TABLE 4. **TCC GROUP 263—Percent Distribution of Distance Shipped and Weight of Shipment, by Means of Transport: 1972**

Distance shipped and weight of shipment [2] [3]	Number	Percent distribution by means of transport							
		All means of transport	Rail	Motor carrier	Private truck	Air	Water	Other	Unknown
TONS OF SHIPMENTS	(thousands of tons)								
U.S. TOTAL..........	20 918	100.0	72.0	16.0	10.5	-	1.5	-	-
UNDER 100 MILES.........	2 885	100.0	19.8	43.1	32.9	-	4.2	-	.1
UNDER 1000 POUNDS.....	6	100.0	-	28.2	71.6	-	-	.1	.1
1000 TO 9999 POUNDS...	166	100.0	.1	67.8	32.1	-	-	-	-
10000 TO 29999 POUNDS.	489	100.0	1.2	50.7	48.1	-	-	-	-
30000 TO 59999 POUNDS.	1 326	100.0	1.6	53.0	45.3	-	-	-	.1
60000 TO 89999 POUNDS.	232	100.0	55.4	33.4	11.2	-	-	-	.1
90000 POUNDS AND OVER.	664	100.0	62.8	15.0	4.2	-	18.0	-	-
100 TO 199 MILES........	2 759	100.0	47.8	30.2	21.9	-	-	-	-
UNDER 1000 POUNDS.....	2	100.0	-	95.4	4.5	-	-	-	-
1000 TO 9999 POUNDS...	62	100.0	.6	76.6	22.7	-	-	-	-
10000 TO 29999 POUNDS.	293	100.0	2.8	53.6	43.6	-	-	-	-
30000 TO 59999 POUNDS.	1 084	100.0	8.1	51.1	40.7	-	-	-	-
60000 TO 89999 POUNDS.	442	100.0	93.0	5.2	1.8	-	-	-	-
90000 POUNDS AND OVER.	874	100.0	92.8	5.7	1.4	-	-	-	-
200 TO 299 MILES........	2 486	100.0	62.3	23.1	14.5	-	-	-	-
UNDER 1000 POUNDS.....	1	100.0	-	98.6	1.4	-	-	-	-
1000 TO 9999 POUNDS...	23	100.0	2.0	58.1	39.5	-	-	.4	-
10000 TO 29999 POUNDS.	193	100.0	.6	46.5	52.8	-	-	-	-
30000 TO 59999 POUNDS.	713	100.0	9.7	58.4	31.8	-	-	-	.1
60000 TO 89999 POUNDS.	457	100.0	95.9	4.1	-	-	-	-	-
90000 POUNDS AND OVER.	1 096	100.0	94.9	3.1	2.1	-	-	-	-
300 TO 499 MILES........	3 475	100.0	82.7	11.4	5.7	-	.2	-	-
UNDER 1000 POUNDS.....	1	100.0	5.7	93.6	.7	-	-	-	-
1000 TO 9999 POUNDS...	20	100.0	5.3	68.7	25.9	.1	-	-	-
10000 TO 29999 POUNDS.	93	100.0	9.0	47.4	43.6	-	-	-	-
30000 TO 59999 POUNDS.	531	100.0	21.7	49.5	28.9	-	-	-	-
60000 TO 89999 POUNDS.	706	100.0	95.4	4.6	-	-	-	-	-
90000 POUNDS AND OVER.	2 121	100.0	97.9	1.8	-	-	.3	-	-
500 TO 999 MILES........	7 469	100.0	92.9	3.4	1.2	-	2.5	-	-
UNDER 1000 POUNDS.....	1	100.0	6.4	91.6	1.9	.1	-	-	-
1000 TO 9999 POUNDS...	18	100.0	8.8	63.8	21.1	.2	4.3	1.7	-
10000 TO 29999 POUNDS.	79	100.0	16.7	44.5	38.8	-	-	-	-
30000 TO 59999 POUNDS.	373	100.0	41.1	45.7	12.8	-	-	-	.4
60000 TO 89999 POUNDS.	1 020	100.0	99.2	.5	-	-	.3	-	.1
90000 POUNDS AND OVER.	5 975	100.0	96.4	.5	.1	-	3.1	-	-
1000 TO 1499 MILES......	1 380	100.0	98.1	1.8	.1	-	-	-	-
UNDER 1000 POUNDS.....	-	100.0	-	99.9	-	.1	-	-	-
1000 TO 9999 POUNDS...	3	100.0	43.7	56.3	-	-	-	-	-
10000 TO 29999 POUNDS.	15	100.0	46.9	53.1	-	-	-	-	-
30000 TO 59999 POUNDS.	59	100.0	84.1	13.7	2.1	-	-	-	-
60000 TO 89999 POUNDS.	152	100.0	97.4	2.6	-	-	-	-	-
90000 POUNDS AND OVER.	1 148	100.0	99.8	.2	-	-	-	-	-
1500 MILES OR OVER......	460	100.0	95.6	3.0	.2	-	1.3	-	-
UNDER 1000 POUNDS.....	-	100.0	-	91.6	-	8.4	-	-	-
1000 TO 9999 POUNDS...	1	100.0	66.8	21.6	-	-	11.6	-	-
10000 TO 29999 POUNDS.	3	100.0	39.7	28.9	-	-	31.4	-	-
30000 TO 59999 POUNDS.	28	100.0	53.0	35.4	2.8	-	8.9	-	-
60000 TO 89999 POUNDS.	73	100.0	100.0	-	-	-	-	-	-
90000 POUNDS AND OVER.	353	100.0	98.9	.6	-	-	.5	-	-
TON-MILES OF SHIPMENTS	(millions of ton-miles)								
U.S. TOTAL..........	10 507	100.0	88.3	6.6	3.4	-	1.7	-	-
UNDER 100 MILES.........	154	100.0	22.5	39.3	31.4	-	6.7	-	.1
UNDER 1000 POUNDS.....	-	100.0	-	38.0	62.0	-	-	-	-
1000 TO 9999 POUNDS...	7	100.0	.1	66.6	33.3	-	-	-	-
10000 TO 29999 POUNDS.	22	100.0	1.1	43.2	55.6	-	-	-	.1
30000 TO 59999 POUNDS.	72	100.0	1.9	53.9	44.0	-	-	-	.2
60000 TO 89999 POUNDS.	10	100.0	58.9	32.9	8.2	-	-	-	-
90000 POUNDS AND OVER.	41	100.0	65.0	8.4	1.6	-	25.0	-	-
100 TO 199 MILES........	407	100.0	49.3	30.0	20.7	-	-	-	-
UNDER 1000 POUNDS.....	-	100.0	-	95.7	4.3	-	-	-	-
1000 TO 9999 POUNDS...	8	100.0	.5	77.3	22.2	-	-	-	-
10000 TO 29999 POUNDS.	40	100.0	3.1	54.6	42.3	-	-	-	-
30000 TO 59999 POUNDS.	157	100.0	8.4	51.8	39.8	-	-	-	-
60000 TO 89999 POUNDS.	66	100.0	92.9	5.5	1.7	-	-	-	-
90000 POUNDS AND OVER.	134	100.0	92.7	6.0	1.2	-	-	-	-

See footnotes at end of table 4.

TABLE 4. TCC GROUP 263—Percent Distribution of Distance Shipped and Weight of Shipment, by Means of Transport: 1972—Continued

Distance shipped and weight of shipment[2][3]	Number	Percent distribution by means of transport							
		All means of transport	Rail	Motor carrier	Private truck	Air	Water	Other	Unknown
TON-MILES OF SHIPMENTS	(millions of ton-miles)								
200 TO 299 MILES	624	100.0	63.0	22.8	14.2	-	-	-	-
UNDER 1000 POUNDS	-	100.0	-	98.9	1.1	-	-	-	-
1000 TO 9999 POUNDS	5	100.0	1.8	57.5	40.2	-	-	.4	-
10000 TO 29999 POUNDS	46	100.0	.6	45.1	54.3	-	-	-	.1
30000 TO 59999 POUNDS	176	100.0	9.8	59.1	31.1	-	-	-	-
60000 TO 89999 POUNDS	112	100.0	95.7	4.3	-	-	-	-	-
90000 POUNDS AND OVER	283	100.0	94.7	3.1	2.2	-	-	-	-
300 TO 499 MILES	1 386	100.0	83.6	10.5	5.6	-	.2	-	-
UNDER 1000 POUNDS	-	100.0	6.8	92.7	.5	-	-	-	-
1000 TO 9999 POUNDS	8	100.0	5.9	67.7	26.3	.2	-	-	-
10000 TO 29999 POUNDS	35	100.0	9.0	47.1	43.9	-	-	-	-
30000 TO 59999 POUNDS	202	100.0	22.3	48.0	29.8	-	-	-	-
60000 TO 89999 POUNDS	277	100.0	95.4	4.6	-	-	-	-	-
90000 POUNDS AND OVER	861	100.0	98.2	1.5	-	-	.3	-	-
500 TO 999 MILES	5 462	100.0	93.1	3.2	1.0	-	2.7	-	-
UNDER 1000 POUNDS	-	100.0	6.3	92.1	1.4	.1	-	-	-
1000 TO 9999 POUNDS	12	100.0	9.1	64.9	19.2	.2	4.5	2.1	-
10000 TO 29999 POUNDS	51	100.0	19.1	45.0	35.9	-	-	-	.5
30000 TO 59999 POUNDS	258	100.0	41.9	46.1	11.6	-	-	-	.5
60000 TO 89999 POUNDS	746	100.0	99.2	.4	-	-	.3	-	.1
90000 POUNDS AND OVER	4 392	100.0	96.2	.4	.1	-	3.3	-	-
1000 TO 1499 MILES	1 621	100.0	98.1	1.8	.1	-	-	-	-
UNDER 1000 POUNDS	-	100.0	-	99.9	-	.1	-	-	-
1000 TO 9999 POUNDS	4	100.0	43.5	56.5	-	-	-	-	-
10000 TO 29999 POUNDS	18	100.0	47.6	52.4	-	-	-	-	-
30000 TO 59999 POUNDS	70	100.0	84.6	13.2	2.2	-	-	-	-
60000 TO 89999 POUNDS	178	100.0	97.5	2.5	-	-	-	-	-
90000 POUNDS AND OVER	1 349	100.0	99.8	.2	-	-	-	-	-
1500 MILES OR OVER	849	100.0	94.9	3.0	.2	-	1.9	-	-
UNDER 1000 POUNDS	-	100.0	-	89.4	-	10.6	-	-	-
1000 TO 9999 POUNDS	3	100.0	60.1	24.9	-	-	15.1	-	-
10000 TO 29999 POUNDS	7	100.0	33.8	24.0	-	-	42.2	-	-
30000 TO 59999 POUNDS	54	100.0	49.2	34.5	3.7	-	12.6	-	-
60000 TO 89999 POUNDS	136	100.0	100.0	-	-	-	-	-	-
90000 POUNDS AND OVER	646	100.0	98.6	.5	-	-	.8	-	-

Note: Detail may not add to total due to rounding. The introductory table shows the estimates of sampling variability for tons; sampling variability for ton-miles has not been estimated. See the map in the Introduction for the States comprising the geographic divisions of the United States.

Shipments excluded from the survey are those moving by pipeline (primarily petroleum products from refineries), parcel post shipments, and commodities moved by own power (motorized vehicles, aircraft, etc.) or towed (prefabricated buildings, etc.). Local shipments (commodities shipped less than 25 miles from the plant) and shipments within the same city are also excluded. Shipments to Alaska and Hawaii from the 48 conterminous States and the District of Columbia are included; however, no data were obtained for shipments originating in Alaska and Hawaii.

- Represents zero or rounds to zero.   (D) Withheld to avoid disclosing figures for individual companies.

[1]Production of this commodity is concentrated in the geographic divisions shown; figures and distributions for geographic divisions not shown are included in the total.

[2]Distances of shipments to foreign destinations are calculated only to the U.S. port of exit.

[3]Includes only shipments represented by bills of lading and invoices. Summary records which did not show individual weights of shipments are not included.

TCC 264. Converted Paper and Paperboard Products, Except Containers

Comparisons of Tons and Ton-Miles of Shipments for
Geographic Divisions of Origin and for Sampling Variability: 1972 and 1967

Geographic division of origin	Estimates				Relative sampling variability in tons (percent)	
	1972		1967		1972	1967
	Tons (thousands)	Ton-miles (millions)	Tons (thousands)	Ton-miles (millions)	1972	1967
U.S. total	14,131	6,555	9,055	4,473	8.3	9.0
New England	1,050	434	601	251	24.3	(*)
Middle Atlantic	2,738	905	2,141	834	16.6	(*)
East North Central	3,573	1,499	2,222	1,019	18.8	(*)
West North Central	(D)	(D)	420	231	(*)	(*)
South Atlantic	2,313	1,163	1,056	557	40.5	(*)
East South Central	945	477	844	468	12.0	(*)
West South Central	1,218	640	470	287	22.2	(*)
Mountain	(D)	(D)	119	117	(*)	(*)
Pacific	1,614	1,141	1,182	709	17.9	(*)

(D) Withheld to avoid disclosing figures for individual companies.   (*) Data not published.

TABLE 1. **TCC GROUP 264**—Percent Distribution of Geographic Division of Origin and Distance Shipped, by Means of Transport: 1972

Geographic division of origin[1] and distance shipped[2]	Number	Percent distribution by means of transport							
		All means of transport	Rail	Motor carrier	Private truck	Air	Water	Other	Unknown
TONS OF SHIPMENTS	(thousands of tons)								
U.S. TOTAL..........	14 131	100.0	51.3	34.8	12.4	-	1.2	.1	.2
NEW ENGLAND..............	1 050	100.0	45.5	44.2	9.6	-	-	-	.6
UNDER 100 MILES.......	254	100.0	11.4	65.3	23.2	-	-	.1	-
100 TO 199 MILES......	236	100.0	40.1	46.9	12.9	-	-	.1	-
200 TO 299 MILES......	121	100.0	54.9	36.2	6.3	-	-	-	2.6
300 TO 499 MILES......	127	100.0	63.7	36.0	.3	-	-	-	-
500 TO 999 MILES......	191	100.0	65.1	33.1	1.7	-	-	-	-
1000 TO 1499 MILES....	83	100.0	69.8	25.8	-	.1	-	.1	4.2
1500 MILES OR OVER....	35	100.0	65.4	34.4	-	.2	-	-	-
MIDDLE ATLANTIC..........	2 738	100.0	38.3	46.7	13.6	-	.9	.1	.3
UNDER 100 MILES.......	862	100.0	11.4	63.7	24.0	-	.6	.2	.1
100 TO 199 MILES......	642	100.0	41.8	44.2	13.9	-	-	-	.1
200 TO 299 MILES......	402	100.0	56.1	38.5	5.4	-	-	-	-
300 TO 499 MILES......	252	100.0	48.7	39.6	11.6	-	-	-	-
500 TO 999 MILES......	384	100.0	55.1	33.4	5.4	-	5.0	.1	1.0
1000 TO 1499 MILES....	132	100.0	69.8	25.9	2.2	-	.3	.1	1.8
1500 MILES OR OVER....	62	100.0	45.7	47.7	.7	.2	2.4	-	3.4
EAST NORTH CENTRAL......	3 573	100.0	50.3	39.7	9.4	.1	-	.2	.2
UNDER 100 MILES.......	469	100.0	11.2	55.5	32.7	.1	-	.1	.3
100 TO 199 MILES......	748	100.0	40.8	49.8	8.7	.2	-	.1	.3
200 TO 299 MILES......	637	100.0	58.5	36.3	5.1	-	-	.1	-
300 TO 499 MILES......	603	100.0	60.3	35.5	3.5	-	-	.1	.5
500 TO 999 MILES.....	887	100.0	60.5	32.8	5.8	.3	-	.7	-
1000 TO 1499 MILES....	107	100.0	79.9	16.5	3.4	.1	-	.1	-
1500 MILES OR OVER....	119	100.0	66.6	25.7	7.4	-	-	.3	-
SOUTH ATLANTIC..........	2 313	100.0	62.7	24.0	13.0	-	-	.1	.1
UNDER 100 MILES.......	209	100.0	16.0	24.1	58.7	-	-	.1	1.1
100 TO 199 MILES......	296	100.0	35.0	31.8	33.1	-	-	.1	-
200 TO 299 MILES......	294	100.0	42.5	43.7	13.6	-	-	.1	-
300 TO 499 MILES......	584	100.0	88.2	9.1	2.5	-	-	.1	-
500 TO 999 MILES......	770	100.0	71.6	25.7	2.5	-	-	.1	-
1000 TO 1499 MILES....	90	100.0	71.1	25.1	3.6	-	-	.2	-
1500 MILES OR OVER....	66	100.0	83.1	12.0	4.6	-	-	.3	-
EAST SOUTH CENTRAL......	945	100.0	68.3	23.9	7.7	-	-	.1	-
UNDER 100 MILES........	87	100.0	48.5	42.3	9.1	-	-	-	-
100 TO 199 MILES......	70	100.0	37.7	49.1	13.2	-	-	-	-
200 TO 299 MILES......	101	100.0	64.5	28.2	7.3	-	-	-	-
300 TO 499 MILES......	247	100.0	63.8	23.5	12.3	-	-	.4	-
500 TO 999 MILES......	386	100.0	81.0	16.5	2.5	-	-	-	-
1000 TO 1499 MILES....	35	100.0	78.1	9.7	12.2	-	-	-	-
1500 MILES OR OVER....	16	100.0	73.5	3.6	22.9	-	-	-	-
WEST SOUTH CENTRAL......	1 218	100.0	57.4	15.1	21.0	-	6.5	-	-
UNDER 100 MILES.......	86	100.0	11.3	17.7	70.6	-	-	-	.4
100 TO 199 MILES......	117	100.0	44.2	11.6	44.3	-	-	-	-
200 TO 299 MILES......	174	100.0	57.9	15.7	21.9	-	4.4	-	-
300 TO 499 MILES......	276	100.0	31.7	19.1	23.3	-	25.9	-	-
500 TO 999 MILES......	438	100.0	74.5	16.2	9.3	-	-	-	-
1000 TO 1499 MILES....	104	100.0	96.4	3.6	-	-	-	-	-
1500 MILES OR OVER....	21	100.0	99.2	.8	-	-	-	-	-
PACIFIC.................	1 614	100.0	56.8	27.8	11.4	-	3.8	-	.1
UNDER 100 MILES.......	288	100.0	14.3	35.3	50.2	-	.2	-	-
100 TO 199 MILES......	157	100.0	15.7	42.4	10.8	-	31.1	-	-
200 TO 299 MILES......	52	100.0	39.7	45.8	14.3	-	.2	-	-
300 TO 499 MILES......	261	100.0	45.9	53.3	.6	-	-	-	.1
500 TO 999 MILES......	493	100.0	81.4	16.8	1.6	-	.1	-	.1
1000 TO 1499 MILES....	151	100.0	87.9	11.4	.7	-	-	-	-
1500 MILES OR OVER....	210	100.0	83.4	8.0	2.4	-	5.5	-	.7
TON-MILES OF SHIPMENTS	(millions of ton-miles)								
U.S. TOTAL..........	6 555	100.0	65.7	26.6	5.8	.1	1.4	.1	.3
NEW ENGLAND..............	434	100.0	60.8	35.1	2.8	.1	-	-	1.2
UNDER 100 MILES.......	16	100.0	12.2	67.3	20.4	-	-	.1	-
100 TO 199 MILES......	34	100.0	39.9	47.6	12.5	-	-	.1	-
200 TO 299 MILES......	30	100.0	56.3	34.5	6.2	-	-	-	3.0
300 TO 499 MILES......	45	100.0	63.7	35.9	.3	-	-	-	-
500 TO 999 MILES......	139	100.0	64.8	33.4	1.7	-	-	-	-
1000 TO 1499 MILES....	97	100.0	68.4	27.0	-	.1	-	.1	4.4
1500 MILES OR OVER....	70	100.0	64.3	35.5	-	.2	-	-	-
MIDDLE ATLANTIC..........	905	100.0	52.3	37.4	6.6	.1	2.5	.1	1.2
UNDER 100 MILES.......	41	100.0	11.2	63.9	24.1	.1	.5	.1	.1
100 TO 199 MILES......	90	100.0	40.9	44.5	14.4	-	-	-	.1
200 TO 299 MILES......	102	100.0	56.5	38.2	5.3	-	-	-	-
300 TO 499 MILES......	98	100.0	50.0	38.1	11.9	-	-	-	-
500 TO 999 MILES......	279	100.0	54.3	32.6	5.4	-	6.3	.1	1.2
1000 TO 1499 MILES....	156	100.0	70.7	25.4	2.0	-	.3	.1	1.6
1500 MILES OR OVER....	136	100.0	45.2	47.2	.7	.2	2.9	-	3.6

See footnotes at end of table 4.

TABLE 1. **TCC GROUP 264**—Percent Distribution of Geographic Division of Origin and Distance Shipped, by Means of Transport: 1972—Continued

Geographic division of origin[1] and distance shipped[2]	Number	Percent distribution by means of transport							
		All means of transport	Rail	Motor carrier	Private truck	Air	Water	Other	Unknown
TON-MILES OF SHIPMENTS	(millions of ton-miles)								
EAST NORTH CENTRAL......	1 499	100.0	61.0	32.2	6.2	.2	-	.3	.1
UNDER 100 MILES........	24	100.0	11.2	60.0	28.1	.1	-	.1	.5
100 TO 199 MILES......	112	100.0	43.5	47.8	8.0	.2	-	.1	.4
200 TO 299 MILES......	157	100.0	58.9	35.8	5.2	-	-	.1	-
300 TO 499 MILES......	234	100.0	60.4	35.7	3.3	-	-	.1	.5
500 TO 999 MILES......	632	100.0	61.5	31.2	6.3	.3	-	.6	-
1000 TO 1499 MILES....	126	100.0	80.0	16.5	3.3	.1	-	.1	-
1500 MILES OR OVER....	210	100.0	65.2	26.4	8.0	-	-	.3	-
SOUTH ATLANTIC.........	1 163	100.0	72.1	22.7	5.1	-	-	.1	-
UNDER 100 MILES........	12	100.0	12.1	25.7	61.3	-	-	.1	.9
100 TO 199 MILES......	40	100.0	36.5	32.9	30.5	-	-	.1	-
200 TO 299 MILES......	74	100.0	41.9	44.4	13.6	-	-	.1	-
300 TO 499 MILES......	231	100.0	88.5	8.9	2.5	-	-	.1	-
500 TO 999 MILES......	566	100.0	70.9	26.5	2.5	-	-	.1	-
1000 TO 1499 MILES....	102	100.0	71.3	25.1	3.4	-	-	.2	-
1500 MILES OR OVER....	134	100.0	82.9	12.8	3.9	-	-	.3	-
EAST SOUTH CENTRAL......	477	100.0	75.2	17.8	6.8	-	-	.1	-
UNDER 100 MILES........	6	100.0	58.6	34.2	7.1	-	-	-	-
100 TO 199 MILES......	10	100.0	40.4	48.2	11.4	-	-	-	-
200 TO 299 MILES......	26	100.0	66.8	25.7	7.5	-	-	-	-
300 TO 499 MILES......	100	100.0	64.7	23.0	11.9	-	-	.3	-
500 TO 999 MILES......	266	100.0	81.6	16.1	2.2	-	-	-	-
1000 TO 1499 MILES....	38	100.0	77.5	9.4	13.1	-	-	-	-
1500 MILES OR OVER....	27	100.0	74.8	3.8	21.4	-	-	-	-
WEST SOUTH CENTRAL......	640	100.0	71.9	13.2	11.0	-	3.8	-	-
UNDER 100 MILES........	4	100.0	15.2	14.9	69.5	-	-	-	.3
100 TO 199 MILES......	16	100.0	38.6	13.7	47.7	-	-	-	-
200 TO 299 MILES......	41	100.0	57.4	16.0	21.7	-	4.9	-	-
300 TO 499 MILES......	105	100.0	34.5	19.9	24.2	-	21.3	-	-
500 TO 999 MILES......	315	100.0	76.5	15.6	7.9	-	-	-	-
1000 TO 1499 MILES....	121	100.0	96.4	3.6	-	-	-	-	-
1500 MILES OR OVER....	34	100.0	99.2	.8	-	-	-	-	-
PACIFIC................	1 141	100.0	77.2	16.6	2.2	-	3.6	-	.3
UNDER 100 MILES........	11	100.0	15.2	50.6	33.9	-	.3	-	-
100 TO 199 MILES......	25	100.0	14.2	40.7	10.2	-	34.9	-	-
200 TO 299 MILES......	12	100.0	39.1	47.2	13.4	-	.2	-	-
300 TO 499 MILES......	102	100.0	46.4	52.8	.6	-	-	-	.2
500 TO 999 MILES......	389	100.0	84.5	14.1	1.4	-	-	-	.1
1000 TO 1499 MILES....	192	100.0	86.1	13.2	.6	-	-	-	-
1500 MILES OR OVER....	409	100.0	80.4	8.3	2.5	-	7.9	-	.8

See footnotes at end of table 4.

TABLE 2. **TCC GROUP 264**—Percent Distribution of Geographic Division of Origin and Means of Transport, by Geographic Division of Destination: 1972

Geographic division of origin[1] and means of transport	Number	Percent distribution by division of destination									
		U.S. total	New England	Middle Atlantic	East North Central	West North Central	South Atlantic	East South Central	West South Central	Mountain	Pacific
TONS OF SHIPMENTS	(thousands of tons)										
U.S. TOTAL..............	14 131	100.0	6.8	19.4	25.8	7.9	14.8	4.0	9.2	2.8	9.4
RAIL.................	7 249	100.0	6.8	13.2	26.3	8.3	17.7	4.3	10.4	3.9	9.0
MOTOR CARRIER........	4 918	100.0	7.0	26.6	28.1	7.0	11.7	3.7	5.2	1.8	8.8
PRIVATE TRUCK........	1 745	100.0	6.5	26.9	19.4	9.2	10.7	3.9	11.7	1.4	10.5
AIR..................	6	100.0	1.6	17.7	37.7	.9	9.9	1.0	1.7	26.6	2.8
WATER................	167	100.0	-	.4	-	-	14.6	-	47.3	.1	37.5
OTHER................	15	100.0	30.4	20.7	20.9	6.8	10.7	2.1	4.4	.5	3.4
UNKNOWN..............	28	100.0	4.6	17.5	22.7	8.0	34.0	-	2.9	-	10.2
NEW ENGLAND.............	1 050	100.0	23.9	40.4	12.2	2.6	15.0	1.4	3.4	.2	1.0
RAIL.................	478	100.0	11.1	35.9	16.1	3.2	26.2	1.6	4.6	.2	1.1
MOTOR CARRIER........	464	100.0	27.8	47.9	10.8	2.6	5.3	1.6	2.8	.2	1.1
PRIVATE TRUCK........	101	100.0	68.1	27.5	.5	-	3.9	-	-	-	-
AIR..................	-	100.0	-	18.8	20.0	1.1	-	28.2	-	28.1	3.9
WATER................	-	100.0	-	-	-	-	-	-	-	-	-
OTHER................	-	100.0	41.7	32.2	11.1	4.3	10.5	-	-	-	.1
UNKNOWN..............	6	100.0	-	47.5	-	.1	52.4	-	-	-	-
MIDDLE ATLANTIC.........	2 738	100.0	13.2	52.1	10.7	2.0	15.8	1.6	2.4	.6	1.6
RAIL.................	1 048	100.0	20.2	33.0	14.3	1.8	21.0	2.6	4.7	.7	1.7
MOTOR CARRIER........	1 279	100.0	10.0	63.1	8.9	2.2	10.9	1.3	1.3	.7	1.6
PRIVATE TRUCK........	371	100.0	5.3	72.9	8.0	1.3	11.8	.5	.2	-	.1
AIR..................	-	100.0	-	56.0	13.7	1.1	2.1	.1	8.4	.8	18.0
WATER................	25	100.0	-	-	-	-	94.3	-	-	-	5.7
OTHER................	2	100.0	7.1	67.3	7.2	1.0	15.1	.8	.5	.5	.5
UNKNOWN..............	9	100.0	1.5	10.6	2.3	23.7	39.4	-	-	-	22.5

See footnotes at end of table 4.

TABLE 2. **TCC GROUP 264—Percent Distribution of Geographic Division of Origin and Means of Transport, by Geographic Division of Destination: 1972**—Continued

Geographic division of origin[1] and means of transport	Number	Percent distribution by division of destination									
		U.S. total	New England	Middle Atlantic	East North Central	West North Central	South Atlantic	East South Central	West South Central	Mountain	Pacific
TONS OF SHIPMENTS	(thousands of tons)										
EAST NORTH CENTRAL	3 573	100.0	3.8	7.9	55.8	12.5	5.2	4.2	5.8	1.6	3.3
RAIL	1 797	100.0	3.3	7.8	49.7	14.6	5.4	5.6	7.2	2.1	4.4
MOTOR CARRIER	1 419	100.0	4.7	9.3	60.6	10.6	5.5	2.7	3.6	1.0	2.1
PRIVATE TRUCK	336	100.0	1.2	2.4	69.0	9.9	3.3	3.5	7.4	.6	2.6
AIR	4	100.0	2.0	6.0	42.7	1.0	10.6	.2	1.1	35.3	1.1
WATER	-	100.0	-	-	-	-	-	-	-	-	-
OTHER	8	100.0	48.1	10.3	16.9	7.8	4.0	2.7	5.7	.6	4.0
UNKNOWN	7	100.0	1.3	10.1	87.2	-	-	-	.9	-	.5
SOUTH ATLANTIC	2 313	100.0	7.0	17.9	19.2	4.3	37.5	5.0	6.4	.1	2.7
RAIL	1 449	100.0	8.4	9.6	24.5	4.9	35.1	5.8	8.0	-	3.8
MOTOR CARRIER	555	100.0	3.4	22.4	15.3	4.5	44.7	4.6	3.6	.3	1.3
PRIVATE TRUCK	301	100.0	6.6	49.9	1.2	.8	35.5	2.3	3.7	-	-
AIR	-	100.0	-	37.5	20.7	-	33.1	-	2.7	-	6.0
WATER	-	100.0	-	-	-	-	-	-	-	-	-
OTHER	2	100.0	8.2	20.1	19.7	9.3	28.5	2.0	5.9	.4	6.0
UNKNOWN	2	100.0	-	.6	-	-	99.4	-	-	-	-
EAST SOUTH CENTRAL	945	100.0	1.3	11.2	20.1	4.3	24.8	15.7	19.3	2.0	1.3
RAIL	645	100.0	1.5	13.7	19.7	5.0	25.9	7.0	23.7	1.7	1.8
MOTOR CARRIER	225	100.0	.7	6.4	16.8	2.3	26.1	37.6	9.7	.1	.2
PRIVATE TRUCK	72	100.0	.3	4.4	32.6	4.5	11.7	24.8	11.1	10.6	-
AIR	-	100.0	16.9	-	16.9	-	66.2	-	-	-	-
WATER	-	100.0	-	-	-	-	-	-	-	-	-
OTHER	1	100.0	-	-	89.2	-	8.5	2.2	-	-	-
UNKNOWN	-	100.0	-	-	-	-	-	-	-	-	-
WEST SOUTH CENTRAL	1 218	100.0	2.0	5.1	12.5	13.5	13.9	5.2	44.0	1.7	2.0
RAIL	699	100.0	3.4	8.4	12.9	16.4	22.1	4.4	27.0	1.9	3.5
MOTOR CARRIER	183	100.0	.2	1.1	17.9	8.9	7.8	2.0	60.0	2.1	.1
PRIVATE TRUCK	256	100.0	-	.8	11.2	13.1	.3	11.6	61.5	1.6	-
AIR	-	100.0	-	-	95.2	4.2	-	-	-	-	.6
WATER	79	100.0	-	-	-	-	-	-	100.0	-	-
OTHER	-	100.0	-	-	97.6	2.4	-	-	-	-	-
UNKNOWN	-	100.0	-	-	-	-	-	-	100.0	-	-
PACIFIC	1 614	100.0	1.1	.3	4.8	4.9	.7	.5	5.7	16.3	65.7
RAIL	917	100.0	1.8	.4	7.9	7.7	.4	.5	8.4	23.0	50.0
MOTOR CARRIER	449	100.0	.1	.4	1.2	2.0	.7	.7	3.0	10.5	81.4
PRIVATE TRUCK	184	100.0	-	-	-	-	2.7	-	.5	2.8	94.0
AIR	-	100.0	.2	24.4	4.6	.8	.3	3.0	7.0	56.9	2.7
WATER	61	100.0	-	-	-	-	-	-	-	.4	99.6
OTHER	-	100.0	-	-	-	-	-	-	-	12.0	88.0
UNKNOWN	2	100.0	49.3	-	-	-	-	-	17.2	-	33.5
TON-MILES OF SHIPMENTS	(millions of ton-miles)										
U.S. TOTAL	6 555	100.0	6.0	11.8	21.8	9.5	14.4	3.8	12.5	5.0	15.1
RAIL	4 303	100.0	6.2	10.2	21.3	9.5	14.9	3.8	12.9	5.6	15.4
MOTOR CARRIER	1 745	100.0	5.6	15.8	25.6	9.4	12.3	3.7	9.7	3.9	14.0
PRIVATE TRUCK	382	100.0	5.2	14.3	16.8	12.1	16.5	4.6	17.5	5.3	7.6
AIR	4	100.0	2.1	18.1	13.8	.8	8.6	1.6	3.4	42.0	9.6
WATER	68	100.0	-	.7	-	-	20.6	-	27.7	.2	50.9
OTHER	8	100.0	35.5	8.7	13.8	7.2	11.0	1.8	7.6	1.3	13.3
UNKNOWN	21	100.0	12.7	6.1	6.8	10.6	35.8	-	3.2	-	24.8
NEW ENGLAND	434	100.0	5.5	18.3	20.4	7.2	25.2	3.6	13.0	.7	6.1
RAIL	264	100.0	2.7	14.2	19.9	6.8	33.6	3.4	13.8	.6	5.0
MOTOR CARRIER	152	100.0	7.3	24.6	23.3	8.8	9.1	4.2	13.0	1.0	8.7
PRIVATE TRUCK	12	100.0	46.3	31.8	2.6	-	19.0	.1	-	-	-
AIR	-	100.0	-	6.1	13.4	1.0	-	26.0	-	44.6	9.0
WATER	-	100.0	-	-	-	-	-	-	-	-	-
OTHER	-	100.0	12.8	16.3	24.4	18.0	27.7	-	-	-	.8
UNKNOWN	5	100.0	-	17.1	-	.2	82.8	-	-	-	-

See footnotes at end of table 4.

TABLE 2. **TCC GROUP 264—Percent Distribution of Geographic Division of Origin and Means of Transport, by Geographic Division of Destination: 1972**—Continued

Geographic division of origin[1] and means of transport	Number	Percent distribution by division of destination								
		U.S. total	New England	Middle Atlantic	East North Central	West North Central	South Atlantic	East South Central	West South Central	Mountain	Pacific
TON-MILES OF SHIPMENTS	(millions of ton-miles)										
MIDDLE ATLANTIC.........	905	100.0	7.1	17.8	17.6	5.8	24.0	4.0	9.1	2.9	11.6
RAIL....................	472	100.0	8.1	12.9	17.6	3.6	27.9	4.9	13.0	2.6	9.4
MOTOR CARRIER..........	338	100.0	6.7	23.1	18.5	8.5	14.9	3.5	6.0	4.1	14.8
PRIVATE TRUCK..........	59	100.0	5.9	37.2	22.2	7.5	22.1	2.1	1.4	-	1.7
AIR....................	-	100.0	-	6.2	11.4	1.4	1.1	.1	15.8	1.8	62.3
WATER.................	22	100.0	-	-	-	-	82.2	-	-	-	17.8
OTHER.................	-	100.0	5.1	13.3	19.5	4.4	43.8	2.2	2.9	3.8	5.1
UNKNOWN...............	10	100.0	.2	.9	1.4	21.1	30.9	-	-	-	45.4
EAST NORTH CENTRAL......	1 499	100.0	6.8	11.6	24.1	12.8	8.6	5.8	12.1	4.3	13.9
RAIL....................	913	100.0	5.4	10.4	22.7	13.4	8.7	7.0	12.7	4.8	14.9
MOTOR CARRIER..........	482	100.0	9.5	15.4	27.4	11.8	8.8	3.3	9.1	3.5	11.2
PRIVATE TRUCK..........	92	100.0	3.4	4.6	21.2	12.7	7.1	6.9	23.5	2.5	18.2
AIR....................	2	100.0	2.9	6.8	10.0	.9	10.3	.2	2.3	63.3	3.3
WATER.................	-	100.0	-	-	-	-	-	-	-	-	-
OTHER.................	5	100.0	52.8	9.2	5.0	5.1	4.3	1.8	7.6	1.2	13.0
UNKNOWN...............	1	100.0	3.7	17.7	72.6	-	-	-	2.8	-	3.1
SOUTH ATLANTIC..........	1 163	100.0	9.6	15.2	24.1	7.1	19.0	3.8	10.1	.2	11.0
RAIL....................	838	100.0	10.6	11.3	26.0	7.1	17.1	3.9	10.8	-	13.3
MOTOR CARRIER..........	263	100.0	5.5	25.2	23.1	7.8	20.7	3.6	7.0	1.0	6.1
PRIVATE TRUCK..........	59	100.0	12.7	25.5	2.8	2.9	38.3	2.6	15.2	-	-
AIR....................	-	100.0	-	34.5	19.0	-	24.6	-	3.5	-	18.4
WATER.................	1	100.0	-	-	-	-	-	-	-	-	-
OTHER.................	1	100.0	4.9	7.4	19.7	14.4	18.3	1.7	10.6	1.0	22.0
UNKNOWN...............	-	100.0	-	2.1	-	-	97.9	-	-	-	-
EAST SOUTH CENTRAL......	477	100.0	2.7	18.2	23.5	4.3	19.0	5.8	17.6	4.4	4.6
RAIL....................	359	100.0	3.1	20.9	22.7	4.4	17.2	3.6	19.7	2.7	5.8
MOTOR CARRIER..........	85	100.0	1.9	12.4	24.7	3.1	31.2	14.3	10.9	.3	1.2
PRIVATE TRUCK..........	32	100.0	.5	4.0	28.5	6.9	6.9	8.4	11.8	33.1	-
AIR....................	-	100.0	34.6	-	11.3	-	54.1	-	-	-	-
WATER.................	-	100.0	-	-	-	-	-	-	-	-	-
OTHER.................	-	100.0	-	-	87.6	-	11.7	.7	-	-	-
UNKNOWN...............	-	100.0	-	-	-	-	-	-	-	-	-
WEST SOUTH CENTRAL......	640	100.0	5.2	10.3	16.4	14.7	20.3	2.6	21.6	2.7	6.2
RAIL....................	460	100.0	7.1	13.5	13.9	15.2	26.2	2.1	10.6	2.8	8.6
MOTOR CARRIER..........	84	100.0	.6	2.7	29.9	10.3	10.6	1.5	40.9	3.4	.2
PRIVATE TRUCK..........	70	100.0	-	2.7	21.7	21.8	.6	7.9	42.6	2.7	-
AIR....................	-	100.0	-	-	96.6	2.4	-	-	-	-	1.0
WATER.................	24	100.0	-	-	-	-	-	-	100.0	-	-
OTHER.................	-	100.0	-	-	96.5	3.5	-	-	-	-	-
UNKNOWN...............	-	100.0	-	-	-	-	-	-	100.0	-	-
PACIFIC.................	1 141	100.0	3.9	1.1	12.8	10.1	2.3	1.3	12.2	16.1	40.0
RAIL....................	881	100.0	4.6	.9	15.5	11.6	1.1	1.1	13.7	17.8	33.6
MOTOR CARRIER..........	189	100.0	.7	2.3	5.2	7.2	3.4	2.8	9.1	12.2	57.1
PRIVATE TRUCK..........	25	100.0	-	-	.2	-	40.3	-	4.8	11.1	43.6
AIR....................	-	100.0	.4	42.5	5.9	.8	.5	4.6	8.9	35.1	1.2
WATER.................	41	100.0	-	-	-	-	-	-	-	.4	99.6
OTHER.................	-	100.0	-	-	-	-	-	-	-	28.9	71.1
UNKNOWN...............	3	100.0	72.1	-	-	-	-	-	16.8	-	11.1

See footnotes at end of table 4.

TABLE 3. TCC GROUP 264—Percent Distribution of Geographic Division of Destination and Means of Transport, by Geographic Division of Origin: 1972

Geographic division of destination and means of transport	Number	Percent distribution by division of origin[1]									
		U.S. total	New England	Middle Atlantic	East North Central	West North Central	South Atlantic	East South Central	West South Central	Mountain	Pacific
TONS OF SHIPMENTS	(thousands of tons)										
U.S. TOTAL.............	14 131	100.0	7.4	19.4	25.3	(D)	16.4	6.7	8.6	(D)	11.4
RAIL.................	7 249	100.0	6.6	14.5	24.8	(D)	20.0	8.9	9.6	(D)	12.7
MOTOR CARRIER........	4 918	100.0	9.4	26.0	28.9	(D)	11.3	4.6	3.7	(D)	9.1
PRIVATE TRUCK........	1 745	100.0	5.8	21.3	19.3	(D)	17.3	4.2	14.7	(D)	10.6
AIR..................	6	100.0	3.0	9.2	70.9	(D)	3.2	.8	2.5	(D)	1.3
WATER................	167	100.0	-	15.5	-	(D)	-	-	47.3	(D)	36.8
OTHER................	15	100.0	3.0	15.6	55.3	(D)	18.0	7.0	-	(D)	.1
UNKNOWN..............	28	100.0	23.9	33.4	25.2	(D)	8.4	-	1.4	(D)	7.8
NEW ENGLAND.............	961	100.0	26.1	37.5	14.0	(D)	16.8	1.2	2.5	(D)	1.8
RAIL.................	496	100.0	10.7	42.7	12.0	(D)	24.6	2.0	4.8	(D)	3.2
MOTOR CARRIER........	345	100.0	37.3	37.1	19.3	(D)	5.5	.5	.1	(D)	.1
PRIVATE TRUCK........	112	100.0	61.0	17.5	3.7	(D)	17.6	.2	-	(D)	-
AIR..................	-	100.0	-	-	89.9	(D)	-	8.7	-	(D)	.2
WATER................	-	100.0	-	-	-	(D)	-	-	-	(D)	-
OTHER................	4	100.0	4.1	3.7	87.4	(D)	4.9	-	-	(D)	-
UNKNOWN..............	1	100.0	-	10.6	6.8	(D)	-	-	-	(D)	82.5
MIDDLE ATLANTIC.........	2 742	100.0	15.5	52.0	10.3	(D)	15.1	3.9	2.3	(D)	.2
RAIL.................	955	100.0	17.9	36.2	14.7	(D)	14.5	9.2	6.1	(D)	.3
MOTOR CARRIER........	1 307	100.0	17.0	61.8	10.0	(D)	9.5	1.1	.2	(D)	.1
PRIVATE TRUCK........	469	100.0	5.9	57.7	1.7	(D)	32.1	.7	.4	(D)	-
AIR..................	1	100.0	3.1	29.3	24.0	(D)	6.8	-	-	(D)	1.8
WATER................	-	100.0	-	-	-	(D)	-	-	-	(D)	-
OTHER................	3	100.0	4.6	50.5	27.4	(D)	17.4	-	-	(D)	-
UNKNOWN..............	4	100.0	65.0	20.2	14.6	(D)	.3	-	-	(D)	-
EAST NORTH CENTRAL......	3 639	100.0	3.5	8.1	54.8	(D)	12.2	5.2	4.2	(D)	2.1
RAIL.................	1 906	100.0	4.0	7.9	46.8	(D)	18.6	6.7	4.7	(D)	3.8
MOTOR CARRIER........	1 382	100.0	3.6	8.2	62.2	(D)	6.1	2.7	2.4	(D)	.4
PRIVATE TRUCK........	338	100.0	.2	8.8	68.6	(D)	1.1	7.0	8.5	(D)	-
AIR..................	2	100.0	1.6	3.3	80.3	(D)	1.8	.4	6.2	(D)	.2
WATER................	-	100.0	-	-	-	(D)	-	-	-	(D)	-
OTHER................	3	100.0	1.6	5.4	44.7	(D)	17.0	29.7	.2	(D)	-
UNKNOWN..............	6	100.0	-	3.4	96.6	(D)	-	-	-	(D)	-
WEST NORTH CENTRAL......	1 109	100.0	2.5	4.9	40.2	(D)	8.9	3.7	14.9	(D)	7.2
RAIL.................	601	100.0	2.6	3.1	43.6	(D)	11.8	5.4	19.1	(D)	11.7
MOTOR CARRIER........	344	100.0	3.5	8.3	43.6	(D)	7.2	1.5	4.8	(D)	2.7
PRIVATE TRUCK........	160	100.0	-	3.0	20.8	(D)	1.5	2.0	20.9	(D)	-
AIR..................	-	100.0	3.4	10.4	74.2	(D)	-	-	10.9	(D)	1.1
WATER................	-	100.0	-	-	-	(D)	-	-	-	(D)	-
OTHER................	1	100.0	1.9	2.4	63.1	(D)	24.6	-	-	(D)	-
UNKNOWN..............	2	100.0	.4	99.6	-	(D)	-	-	-	(D)	-
SOUTH ATLANTIC..........	2 086	100.0	7.5	20.7	9.0	(D)	41.6	11.2	8.1	(D)	.6
RAIL.................	1 286	100.0	9.8	17.2	7.5	(D)	39.5	13.0	12.0	(D)	.3
MOTOR CARRIER........	577	100.0	4.3	24.2	13.6	(D)	43.0	10.2	2.5	(D)	.5
PRIVATE TRUCK........	186	100.0	2.1	23.5	6.0	(D)	57.3	4.6	.4	(D)	2.6
AIR..................	-	100.0	-	1.9	76.1	(D)	10.8	5.5	-	(D)	-
WATER................	24	100.0	-	100.0	-	(D)	-	-	-	(D)	-
OTHER................	1	100.0	2.9	22.0	20.7	(D)	48.1	5.5	-	(D)	-
UNKNOWN..............	9	100.0	36.8	38.7	-	(D)	24.5	-	-	(D)	-
EAST SOUTH CENTRAL......	564	100.0	2.7	8.0	26.6	(D)	20.5	26.3	11.3	(D)	1.3
RAIL.................	313	100.0	2.4	8.6	31.9	(D)	26.8	14.5	9.8	(D)	1.5
MOTOR CARRIER........	182	100.0	4.1	9.0	20.9	(D)	13.8	46.5	2.0	(D)	1.6
PRIVATE TRUCK........	68	100.0	-	2.6	17.4	(D)	10.0	26.5	43.5	(D)	-
AIR..................	-	100.0	80.0	.6	15.7	(D)	-	-	-	(D)	3.7
WATER................	-	100.0	-	-	-	(D)	-	-	-	(D)	-
OTHER................	-	100.0	-	5.6	68.9	(D)	16.5	7.3	-	(D)	-
UNKNOWN..............	-	100.0	-	-	-	(D)	-	-	-	(D)	-
WEST SOUTH CENTRAL......	1 295	100.0	2.7	5.1	15.9	(D)	11.3	14.1	41.4	(D)	7.1
RAIL.................	751	100.0	2.9	6.5	17.2	(D)	15.4	20.3	25.1	(D)	10.2
MOTOR CARRIER........	258	100.0	5.1	6.2	19.8	(D)	7.6	8.5	42.8	(D)	5.2
PRIVATE TRUCK........	204	100.0	-	.3	12.2	(D)	5.5	4.0	77.1	(D)	.5
AIR..................	-	100.0	-	44.3	43.9	(D)	5.0	-	-	(D)	5.2
WATER................	79	100.0	-	-	-	(D)	-	-	100.0	(D)	-
OTHER................	-	100.0	-	1.7	70.9	(D)	24.0	-	-	(D)	-
UNKNOWN..............	-	100.0	-	-	7.7	(D)	-	-	46.5	(D)	45.8
MOUNTAIN................	397	100.0	.4	4.0	13.9	(D)	.4	4.7	5.3	(D)	66.4
RAIL.................	282	100.0	.3	2.6	13.4	(D)	-	3.8	4.7	(D)	74.9
MOTOR CARRIER........	89	100.0	.9	9.7	15.7	(D)	2.0	.2	4.2	(D)	52.6
PRIVATE TRUCK........	23	100.0	-	-	8.0	(D)	-	32.9	17.7	(D)	21.9
AIR..................	1	100.0	3.1	.3	93.9	(D)	-	-	-	(D)	2.7
WATER................	-	100.0	-	-	-	(D)	-	-	-	(D)	100.0
OTHER................	-	100.0	-	15.2	68.7	(D)	13.8	-	-	(D)	2.3
UNKNOWN..............	-	100.0	-	-	-	(D)	-	-	-	(D)	-
PACIFIC.................	1 334	100.0	.8	3.2	8.8	(D)	4.7	.9	1.9	(D)	79.5
RAIL.................	654	100.0	.8	2.8	12.0	(D)	8.4	1.8	3.8	(D)	70.1
MOTOR CARRIER........	430	100.0	1.2	4.9	6.9	(D)	1.7	.1	-	(D)	84.9
PRIVATE TRUCK........	182	100.0	-	.2	4.8	(D)	-	-	-	(D)	95.0
AIR..................	-	100.0	4.1	59.4	27.2	(D)	6.9	-	.6	(D)	1.2
WATER................	62	100.0	-	2.4	-	(D)	-	-	-	(D)	97.6
OTHER................	-	100.0	.1	2.2	64.0	(D)	31.3	-	-	(D)	2.4
UNKNOWN..............	2	100.0	-	73.4	1.2	(D)	-	-	-	(D)	25.4

See footnotes at end of table 4.

TABLE 3. TCC GROUP 264—Percent Distribution of Geographic Division of Destination and Means of Transport, by Geographic Division of Origin: 1972—Continued

Geographic division of destination and means of transport	Number	Percent distribution by division of origin[1]									
		U.S. total	New England	Middle Atlantic	East North Central	West North Central	South Atlantic	East South Central	West South Central	Mountain	Pacific
TON-MILES OF SHIPMENTS	(millions of ton-miles)										
U.S. TOTAL...............	6 555	100.0	6.6	13.8	22.9	(D)	17.7	7.3	9.8	(D)	17.4
RAIL..................	4 303	100.0	6.1	11.0	21.2	(D)	19.5	8.3	10.7	(D)	20.5
MOTOR CARRIER.........	1 745	100.0	8.7	19.4	27.6	(D)	15.1	4.9	4.8	(D)	10.9
PRIVATE TRUCK.........	382	100.0	3.2	15.5	24.3	(D)	15.4	8.5	18.4	(D)	6.6
AIR..................	4	100.0	5.1	10.1	61.1	(D)	3.9	.8	3.0	(D)	2.6
WATER................	88	100.0	-	25.0	-	(D)	-	-	27.7	(D)	46.6
OTHER................	8	100.0	1.8	7.2	64.1	(D)	20.7	5.0	-	(D)	.1
UNKNOWN..............	21	100.0	24.1	49.9	8.4	(D)	.5	-	.1	(D)	17.0
NEW ENGLAND..............	392	100.0	6.1	16.5	25.9	(D)	28.3	3.3	8.5	(D)	11.4
RAIL..................	268	100.0	2.6	14.3	18.4	(D)	33.1	4.1	12.2	(D)	15.2
MOTOR CARRIER.........	97	100.0	11.4	23.2	46.8	(D)	14.9	1.6	.5	(D)	1.3
PRIVATE TRUCK.........	19	100.0	28.1	17.5	16.0	(D)	37.6	.8	-	(D)	-
AIR..................	-	100.0	-	-	84.6	(D)	-	13.5	-	(D)	.5
WATER................	-	100.0	-	-	-	(D)	-	-	-	(D)	-
OTHER................	2	100.0	.7	1.0	95.4	(D)	2.9	-	-	(D)	-
UNKNOWN..............	2	100.0	-	1.0	2.5	(D)	-	-	-	(D)	96.6
MIDDLE ATLANTIC..........	774	100.0	10.3	20.8	22.5	(D)	22.8	11.2	8.5	(D)	1.6
RAIL..................	440	100.0	8.5	13.8	21.6	(D)	21.5	17.0	14.1	(D)	1.9
MOTOR CARRIER.........	276	100.0	13.5	28.3	26.8	(D)	24.0	3.8	.8	(D)	1.6
PRIVATE TRUCK.........	54	100.0	7.0	40.4	7.7	(D)	27.5	2.4	3.4	(D)	-
AIR..................	-	100.0	1.7	3.5	23.1	(D)	7.5	-	-	(D)	6.2
WATER................	-	100.0	-	-	-	(D)	-	-	-	(D)	-
OTHER................	-	100.0	3.4	11.0	67.7	(D)	17.6	-	-	(D)	-
UNKNOWN..............	1	100.0	67.5	7.7	24.6	(D)	.2	-	-	(D)	-
EAST NORTH CENTRAL......	1 431	100.0	6.2	11.1	25.2	(D)	19.6	7.8	7.3	(D)	10.2
RAIL..................	917	100.0	5.7	9.1	22.6	(D)	23.7	8.9	7.0	(D)	14.9
MOTOR CARRIER.........	446	100.0	8.0	14.0	29.6	(D)	13.7	4.7	5.7	(D)	2.2
PRIVATE TRUCK.........	64	100.0	.5	20.4	30.6	(D)	2.6	14.4	23.7	(D)	.1
AIR..................	-	100.0	4.9	8.3	44.4	(D)	5.4	.7	21.2	(D)	1.1
WATER................	-	100.0	-	-	-	(D)	-	-	-	(D)	-
OTHER................	1	100.0	3.2	10.2	23.5	(D)	29.7	31.6	.3	(D)	-
UNKNOWN..............	1	100.0	-	9.9	90.1	(D)	-	-	-	(D)	-
WEST NORTH CENTRAL......	622	100.0	5.1	8.5	30.8	(D)	13.2	3.3	15.1	(D)	18.6
RAIL..................	409	100.0	4.4	4.2	29.9	(D)	14.5	3.8	17.1	(D)	24.9
MOTOR CARRIER.........	163	100.0	8.2	17.6	35.0	(D)	12.6	1.6	5.3	(D)	8.4
PRIVATE TRUCK.........	46	100.0	-	9.6	25.4	(D)	3.7	4.9	33.2	(D)	-
AIR..................	-	100.0	6.1	17.0	65.1	(D)	-	-	9.2	(D)	2.7
WATER................	-	100.0	-	-	-	(D)	-	-	-	(D)	-
OTHER................	-	100.0	4.6	4.4	45.7	(D)	41.3	-	-	(D)	-
UNKNOWN..............	2	100.0	.4	99.6	-	(D)	-	-	-	(D)	-
SOUTH ATLANTIC...........	946	100.0	11.5	23.0	13.6	(D)	23.4	9.6	13.7	(D)	2.8
RAIL..................	641	100.0	13.8	20.6	12.4	(D)	22.4	9.6	18.8	(D)	1.6
MOTOR CARRIER.........	214	100.0	6.5	23.5	19.8	(D)	25.5	12.4	4.2	(D)	3.0
PRIVATE TRUCK.........	63	100.0	3.6	20.7	10.4	(D)	35.8	3.6	.7	(D)	16.1
AIR..................	-	100.0	-	1.2	73.1	(D)	11.3	5.1	-	(D)	.2
WATER................	18	100.0	-	100.0	-	(D)	-	-	-	(D)	-
OTHER................	-	100.0	4.6	28.8	24.9	(D)	34.6	5.3	-	(D)	-
UNKNOWN..............	7	100.0	55.5	43.0	-	(D)	1.5	-	-	(D)	-
EAST SOUTH CENTRAL......	247	100.0	6.3	14.7	35.0	(D)	17.7	11.3	6.6	(D)	6.0
RAIL..................	165	100.0	5.4	14.0	38.8	(D)	19.8	7.8	5.8	(D)	5.7
MOTOR CARRIER.........	64	100.0	10.0	18.4	24.7	(D)	14.7	18.9	1.9	(D)	8.3
PRIVATE TRUCK.........	17	100.0	.1	7.2	36.6	(D)	8.8	15.6	31.8	(D)	-
AIR..................	-	100.0	82.6	.5	9.4	(D)	-	-	-	(D)	7.6
WATER................	-	100.0	-	-	-	(D)	-	-	-	(D)	-
OTHER................	-	100.0	-	9.0	66.3	(D)	19.6	1.9	-	(D)	-
UNKNOWN..............	-	100.0	-	-	-	(D)	-	-	-	(D)	-
WEST SOUTH CENTRAL......	820	100.0	6.9	10.1	22.2	(D)	14.4	10.2	16.8	(D)	17.0
RAIL..................	556	100.0	6.6	11.1	20.8	(D)	16.2	12.7	8.8	(D)	21.6
MOTOR CARRIER.........	170	100.0	11.7	11.9	25.8	(D)	10.8	5.5	20.3	(D)	10.2
PRIVATE TRUCK.........	67	100.0	-	1.3	32.5	(D)	13.4	5.8	44.7	(D)	1.8
AIR..................	-	100.0	-	46.9	41.6	(D)	4.0	-	-	(D)	6.9
WATER................	24	100.0	-	-	-	(D)	-	-	100.0	(D)	-
OTHER................	-	100.0	-	2.8	64.6	(D)	29.0	-	-	(D)	-
UNKNOWN..............	-	100.0	-	-	7.4	(D)	-	-	2.3	(D)	90.3
MOUNTAIN.................	329	100.0	1.0	7.9	19.6	(D)	.8	6.3	5.3	(D)	55.6
RAIL..................	239	100.0	.7	5.1	18.4	(D)	-	4.1	5.3	(D)	65.7
MOTOR CARRIER.........	67	100.0	2.3	20.5	24.6	(D)	3.8	.4	4.2	(D)	34.2
PRIVATE TRUCK.........	20	100.0	-	.1	11.2	(D)	-	52.8	9.3	(D)	13.8
AIR..................	1	100.0	5.4	.4	92.0	(D)	-	-	-	(D)	2.2
WATER................	-	100.0	-	-	-	(D)	-	-	-	(D)	100.0
OTHER................	-	100.0	-	21.5	61.3	(D)	15.9	-	-	(D)	1.3
UNKNOWN..............	-	100.0	-	-	-	(D)	-	-	-	(D)	-
PACIFIC..................	990	100.0	2.7	10.6	21.0	(D)	12.9	2.2	4.0	(D)	46.1
RAIL..................	664	100.0	2.0	6.7	20.5	(D)	16.7	3.1	6.0	(D)	44.5
MOTOR CARRIER.........	244	100.0	5.4	20.5	22.1	(D)	6.5	.4	.1	(D)	44.3
PRIVATE TRUCK.........	28	100.0	-	3.4	58.4	(D)	-	-	-	(D)	38.1
AIR..................	-	100.0	4.8	65.5	21.2	(D)	7.6	-	.3	(D)	.3
WATER................	45	100.0	-	8.8	-	(D)	-	-	-	(D)	91.2
OTHER................	1	100.0	.1	2.8	62.6	(D)	34.2	-	-	(D)	.3
UNKNOWN..............	5	100.0	-	91.3	1.1	(D)	-	-	-	(D)	7.6

See footnotes at end of table 4.

TABLE 4. TCC GROUP 264—Percent Distribution of Distance Shipped and Weight of Shipment, by Means of Transport: 1972

Distance shipped and weight of shipment[2][3]	Number	Percent distribution by means of transport							
		All means of transport	Rail	Motor carrier	Private truck	Air	Water	Other	Unknown
TONS OF SHIPMENTS	(thousands of tons)								
U.S. TOTAL.........	12 820	100.0	54.9	32.1	11.5	-	1.3	.1	.1
UNDER 100 MILES.........	1 892	100.0	15.6	47.6	36.1	-	.3	.1	.2
UNDER 1000 POUNDS.....	143	100.0	.1	73.0	26.0	.1	-	.6	.1
1000 TO 9999 POUNDS...	661	100.0	.7	52.4	46.5	.1	.1	-	.2
10000 TO 29999 POUNDS.	664	100.0	12.2	51.7	36.0	-	.1	-	-
30000 TO 59999 POUNDS.	336	100.0	45.5	28.2	25.3	-	-	-	1.0
60000 TO 89999 POUNDS.	26	100.0	28.2	36.2	19.5	-	16.2	-	-
90000 POUNDS AND OVER.	60	100.0	81.1	3.1	15.8	-	-	-	-
100 TO 199 MILES........	2 137	100.0	40.7	40.9	15.9	-	2.3	.1	.1
UNDER 1000 POUNDS.....	79	100.0	1.6	88.7	6.6	1.3	-	1.6	-
1000 TO 9999 POUNDS...	384	100.0	1.1	74.5	24.3	-	-	-	.1
10000 TO 29999 POUNDS.	830	100.0	45.0	33.7	21.1	-	-	-	.3
30000 TO 59999 POUNDS.	583	100.0	63.4	26.6	10.0	-	-	-	-
60000 TO 89999 POUNDS.	76	100.0	68.0	21.7	10.3	-	-	-	-
90000 POUNDS AND OVER.	183	100.0	37.9	35.5	-	-	26.6	-	-
200 TO 299 MILES........	1 681	100.0	58.2	31.7	9.4	-	.5	.1	.2
UNDER 1000 POUNDS.....	52	100.0	3.6	91.3	2.9	.1	.2	1.9	-
1000 TO 9999 POUNDS...	228	100.0	6.8	71.2	22.0	-	-	-	-
10000 TO 29999 POUNDS.	625	100.0	64.2	23.5	12.3	-	-	-	-
30000 TO 59999 POUNDS.	608	100.0	72.6	22.1	4.7	-	-	-	.5
60000 TO 89999 POUNDS.	109	100.0	100.0	-	-	-	-	-	-
90000 POUNDS AND OVER.	57	100.0	15.2	71.5	-	-	13.3	-	-
300 TO 499 MILES........	2 253	100.0	63.4	28.2	5.1	-	3.2	.1	-
UNDER 1000 POUNDS.....	70	100.0	3.0	93.2	1.8	.2	-	1.8	-
1000 TO 9999 POUNDS...	250	100.0	5.2	83.0	11.4	-	-	.4	-
10000 TO 29999 POUNDS.	778	100.0	69.6	27.2	3.2	-	-	-	-
30000 TO 59999 POUNDS.	649	100.0	70.5	21.3	8.2	-	-	-	-
60000 TO 89999 POUNDS.	224	100.0	96.4	1.7	1.8	-	-	-	.2
90000 POUNDS AND OVER.	281	100.0	70.8	2.8	1.0	-	25.4	-	-
500 TO 999 MILES........	3 709	100.0	69.2	26.1	4.0	.1	.5	.1	-
UNDER 1000 POUNDS.....	80	100.0	2.7	92.9	1.2	.9	.2	2.1	.1
1000 TO 9999 POUNDS...	295	100.0	9.7	79.8	9.5	.8	.1	.1	.1
10000 TO 29999 POUNDS.	1 044	100.0	69.9	21.7	6.4	-	1.9	-	.1
30000 TO 59999 POUNDS.	1 460	100.0	68.3	28.1	3.5	-	-	-	-
60000 TO 89999 POUNDS.	536	100.0	96.1	3.8	-	-	-	-	.1
90000 POUNDS AND OVER.	292	100.0	100.0	-	-	-	-	-	-
1000 TO 1499 MILES......	662	100.0	78.6	18.9	1.5	.1	.1	-	.9
UNDER 1000 POUNDS.....	18	100.0	3.3	93.0	.5	1.5	-	1.6	.1
1000 TO 9999 POUNDS...	52	100.0	13.7	80.4	4.1	.7	.7	-	.4
10000 TO 29999 POUNDS.	174	100.0	76.0	20.8	3.2	-	-	-	-
30000 TO 59999 POUNDS.	280	100.0	88.7	8.6	.7	-	-	-	2.0
60000 TO 89999 POUNDS.	113	100.0	95.6	4.4	-	-	-	-	-
90000 POUNDS AND OVER.	23	100.0	100.0	-	-	-	-	-	-
1500 MILES OR OVER......	483	100.0	77.2	16.8	3.6	-	2.0	.1	.3
UNDER 1000 POUNDS.....	16	100.0	8.0	85.6	1.9	1.2	1.3	1.8	.2
1000 TO 9999 POUNDS...	44	100.0	13.9	78.8	2.3	-	4.7	.3	-
10000 TO 29999 POUNDS.	108	100.0	69.2	18.8	4.4	-	6.6	-	1.0
30000 TO 59999 POUNDS.	203	100.0	88.8	5.7	5.4	-	-	-	-
60000 TO 89999 POUNDS.	47	100.0	99.2	-	-	-	-	-	.8
90000 POUNDS AND OVER.	63	100.0	100.0	-	-	-	-	-	-
TON-MILES OF SHIPMENTS	(millions of ton-miles)								
U.S. TOTAL.........	6 079	100.0	68.1	25.1	5.1	.1	1.3	.1	.2
UNDER 100 MILES.........	99	100.0	16.8	49.6	33.0	-	.3	-	.3
UNDER 1000 POUNDS.....	6	100.0	.2	81.0	17.8	.1	-	.7	.1
1000 TO 9999 POUNDS...	30	100.0	.7	59.4	39.5	.1	.1	-	.2
10000 TO 29999 POUNDS.	37	100.0	11.5	53.4	34.9	-	.1	-	-
30000 TO 59999 POUNDS.	18	100.0	40.4	28.3	30.1	-	-	-	1.2
60000 TO 89999 POUNDS.	1	100.0	36.1	34.9	14.2	-	14.8	-	-
90000 POUNDS AND OVER.	4	100.0	88.3	.3	11.5	-	-	-	-
100 TO 199 MILES........	310	100.0	41.2	40.7	15.0	.1	2.8	.1	.2
UNDER 1000 POUNDS.....	11	100.0	1.8	89.2	5.8	1.5	-	1.7	-
1000 TO 9999 POUNDS...	56	100.0	1.1	75.9	22.9	-	-	-	.1
10000 TO 29999 POUNDS.	118	100.0	46.2	33.3	20.1	-	-	-	.4
30000 TO 59999 POUNDS.	87	100.0	64.4	26.4	9.1	-	-	-	-
60000 TO 89999 POUNDS.	10	100.0	69.9	20.3	9.8	-	-	-	-
90000 POUNDS AND OVER.	25	100.0	32.4	33.3	-	-	34.3	-	-

See footnotes at end of table 4.

TABLE 4. TCC GROUP 264—Percent Distribution of Distance Shipped and Weight of Shipment, by Means of Transport: 1972—Continued

Distance shipped and weight of shipment[2] [3]	Number	Percent distribution by means of transport							
		All means of transport	Rail	Motor carrier	Private truck	Air	Water	Other	Unknown
TON-MILES OF SHIPMENTS	(millions of ton-miles)								
200 TO 299 MILES.........	420	100.0	58.5	31.6	9.2	-	.5	.1	.2
UNDER 1000 POUNDS.....	12	100.0	3.6	91.3	2.8	.1	.2	2.0	-
1000 TO 9999 POUNDS...	56	100.0	7.0	71.0	22.0	-	-	-	-
10000 TO 29999 POUNDS.	156	100.0	64.9	23.3	11.8	-	-	-	-
30000 TO 59999 POUNDS.	152	100.0	72.5	22.1	4.8	-	-	-	.6
60000 TO 89999 POUNDS.	26	100.0	100.0	-	-	-	-	-	-
90000 POUNDS AND OVER.	14	100.0	13.9	72.2	-	-	13.9	-	-
300 TO 499 MILES........	879	100.0	64.4	27.9	5.0	-	2.6	.1	-
UNDER 1000 POUNDS.....	27	100.0	2.8	93.2	1.8	.3	-	1.9	-
1000 TO 9999 POUNDS...	97	100.0	5.3	82.9	11.4	-	-	.4	-
10000 TO 29999 POUNDS.	303	100.0	70.4	26.5	3.1	-	-	-	-
30000 TO 59999 POUNDS.	257	100.0	70.8	21.3	8.0	-	-	-	-
60000 TO 89999 POUNDS.	97	100.0	96.7	1.3	1.8	-	-	-	.2
90000 POUNDS AND OVER.	96	100.0	72.8	2.9	.9	-	23.4	-	-
500 TO 999 MILES........	2 659	100.0	70.3	24.9	4.0	.1	.7	.1	-
UNDER 1000 POUNDS.....	56	100.0	2.7	92.9	1.2	1.0	.1	2.1	.1
1000 TO 9999 POUNDS...	209	100.0	9.9	79.2	9.6	1.0	.1	.1	.1
10000 TO 29999 POUNDS.	757	100.0	70.4	20.8	6.4	-	2.4	-	-
30000 TO 59999 POUNDS.	1 032	100.0	70.5	26.1	3.5	-	-	-	-
60000 TO 89999 POUNDS.	390	100.0	95.8	4.2	-	-	-	-	.1
90000 POUNDS AND OVER.	212	100.0	100.0	-	-	-	-	-	-
1000 TO 1499 MILES......	783	100.0	78.3	19.3	1.4	.1	.1	-	.8
UNDER 1000 POUNDS.....	22	100.0	3.4	93.1	.4	1.5	-	1.5	.1
1000 TO 9999 POUNDS...	60	100.0	13.4	81.0	3.8	.7	.7	-	.4
10000 TO 29999 POUNDS.	208	100.0	75.1	21.9	3.0	-	-	-	-
30000 TO 59999 POUNDS.	332	100.0	89.1	8.4	.7	-	-	-	1.9
60000 TO 89999 POUNDS.	134	100.0	94.5	5.5	-	-	-	-	-
90000 POUNDS AND OVER.	24	100.0	100.0	-	-	-	-	-	-
1500 MILES OR OVER......	927	100.0	75.5	17.4	3.6	-	2.9	.1	.4
UNDER 1000 POUNDS.....	35	100.0	7.6	85.3	1.7	1.1	2.4	1.7	.2
1000 TO 9999 POUNDS...	91	100.0	12.4	78.0	2.4	-	6.8	.3	-
10000 TO 29999 POUNDS.	209	100.0	66.0	18.3	4.7	-	9.6	-	1.3
30000 TO 59999 POUNDS.	380	100.0	88.8	5.7	5.5	-	-	-	-
60000 TO 89999 POUNDS.	85	100.0	99.3	-	-	-	-	-	.7
90000 POUNDS AND OVER.	125	100.0	100.0	-	-	-	-	-	-

Note: Detail may not add to total due to rounding. The introductory table shows the estimates of sampling variability for tons; sampling variability for ton-miles has not been estimated. See the map in the Introduction for the States comprising the geographic divisions of the United States.

Shipments excluded from the survey are those moving by pipeline (primarily petroleum products from refineries), parcel post shipments, and commodities moved by own power (motorized vehicles, aircraft, etc.) or towed (prefabricated buildings, etc.). Local shipments (commodities shipped less than 25 miles from the plant) and shipments within the same city are also excluded. Shipments to Alaska and Hawaii from the 48 conterminous States and the District of Columbia are included; however, no data were obtained for shipments originating in Alaska and Hawaii.

- Represents zero or rounds to zero.   (D) Withheld to avoid disclosing figures for individual companies.

[1]Production of this commodity is concentrated in the geographic divisions shown; figures and distributions for geographic divisions not shown are included in the total.

[2]Distances of shipments to foreign destinations are calculated only to the U.S. port of exit.

[3]Includes only shipments represented by bills of lading and invoices. Summary records which did not show individual weights of shipments are not included.

TCC 265. Containers and Boxes, Paperboard

Comparisons of Tons and Ton-Miles of Shipments for
Geographic Divisions of Origin and for Sampling Variability: 1972 and 1967

Geographic division of origin	Estimates				Relative sampling variability in tons (percent)	
	1972		1967		1972	1967
	Tons (thousands)	Ton-miles (millions)	Tons (thousands)	Ton-miles (millions)	1972	1967
U.S. total	18,196	3,211	14,410	3,255	11.9	9.8
New England	1,120	255	1,164	420	31.2	(*)
Middle Atlantic	3,772	424	2,660	509	31.1	(*)
East North Central	5,371	843	4,158	702	22.1	(*)
West North Central	1,181	359	1,421	301	47.6	(*)
South Atlantic	2,531	529	1,527	436	22.7	(*)
East South Central	(D)	(D)	1,079	248	(*)	(*)
West South Central	1,579	396	551	102	44.7	(*)
Mountain	(D)	(D)	6	3	(*)	(*)
Pacific	1,847	317	1,844	534	38.8	(*)

(D) Withheld to avoid disclosing figures for individual companies.   (*) Data not published.

TABLE 1. **TCC GROUP 265**—Percent Distribution of Geographic Division of Origin and Distance Shipped, by Means of Transport: 1972

Geographic division of origin[1] and distance shipped[2]	Number	Percent distribution by means of transport							
		All means of transport	Rail	Motor carrier	Private truck	Air	Water	Other	Unknown
TONS OF SHIPMENTS	(thousands of tons)								
U.S. TOTAL	18 196	100.0	7.2	40.8	51.3	-	.2	.3	.2
NEW ENGLAND	1 120	100.0	1.2	33.9	64.7	-	.1	-	-
UNDER 100 MILES	705	100.0	-	27.8	72.0	-	.1	-	-
100 TO 199 MILES	133	100.0	5.0	50.8	44.2	-	-	-	-
200 TO 299 MILES	39	100.0	-	36.2	62.8	-	1.0	-	-
300 TO 499 MILES	29	100.0	9.0	29.9	61.1	-	-	-	-
500 TO 999 MILES	140	100.0	.5	22.5	76.9	.1	-	-	-
1000 TO 1499 MILES	66	100.0	1.1	87.2	11.7	-	-	-	-
1500 MILES OR OVER	6	100.0	43.6	56.3	-	-	-	-	-
MIDDLE ATLANTIC	3 772	100.0	5.1	28.5	65.8	-	-	.4	-
UNDER 100 MILES	2 736	100.0	1.8	18.5	79.1	-	-	.5	.1
100 TO 199 MILES	447	100.0	6.4	44.1	49.5	-	-	-	-
200 TO 299 MILES	338	100.0	9.4	65.0	25.2	-	-	.3	-
300 TO 499 MILES	99	100.0	40.5	52.9	6.5	.1	-	-	-
500 TO 999 MILES	105	100.0	20.6	73.5	4.8	.5	-	.5	-
1000 TO 1499 MILES	29	100.0	50.5	49.2	.2	.1	-	-	-
1500 MILES OR OVER	15	100.0	53.1	45.6	.5	.6	-	.2	-
EAST NORTH CENTRAL	5 371	100.0	7.7	53.3	38.5	-	-	.4	.1
UNDER 100 MILES	3 029	100.0	1.6	46.5	51.7	-	-	.1	.2
100 TO 199 MILES	1 075	100.0	8.2	64.1	27.2	-	-	.5	.1
200 TO 299 MILES	474	100.0	8.4	62.7	28.5	-	-	.3	-
300 TO 499 MILES	395	100.0	18.1	69.8	10.7	.2	-	1.1	.1
500 TO 999 MILES	359	100.0	39.8	50.3	8.5	.1	-	1.1	.1
1000 TO 1499 MILES	11	100.0	41.9	56.6	.8	.8	-	.7	-
1500 MILES OR OVER	24	100.0	62.8	23.8	-	.1	-	12.8	.5
WEST NORTH CENTRAL	1 181	100.0	16.2	69.6	13.8	-	-	.2	.3
UNDER 100 MILES	335	100.0	4.1	57.6	38.3	-	-	-	-
100 TO 199 MILES	255	100.0	15.3	75.0	9.4	-	-	-	.3
200 TO 299 MILES	177	100.0	29.7	67.0	2.4	-	-	.9	-
300 TO 499 MILES	214	100.0	27.4	71.6	.5	.1	-	-	.4
500 TO 999 MILES	116	100.0	10.7	88.0	-	.1	-	.3	.9
1000 TO 1499 MILES	70	100.0	20.0	72.8	6.1	-	-	-	1.1
1500 MILES OR OVER	11	100.0	2.2	96.1	-	-	-	1.7	-
SOUTH ATLANTIC	2 531	100.0	11.8	30.8	57.1	-	-	.3	-
UNDER 100 MILES	1 090	100.0	2.9	24.7	72.3	-	-	.1	-
100 TO 199 MILES	747	100.0	3.4	31.4	64.8	-	-	.4	-
200 TO 299 MILES	174	100.0	31.9	40.8	27.3	.1	-	-	-
300 TO 499 MILES	228	100.0	25.3	34.7	39.2	.1	-	.7	-
500 TO 999 MILES	245	100.0	40.1	46.7	13.1	-	-	-	-
1000 TO 1499 MILES	24	100.0	74.0	11.5	14.5	-	-	-	-
1500 MILES OR OVER	19	100.0	60.7	32.6	-	.1	-	6.6	-
WEST SOUTH CENTRAL	1 579	100.0	7.4	49.8	41.4	-	-	-	1.5
UNDER 100 MILES	409	100.0	.1	81.0	18.2	-	-	-	.7
100 TO 199 MILES	553	100.0	1.8	44.7	52.7	-	-	-	.7
200 TO 299 MILES	202	100.0	13.5	30.0	56.5	-	-	-	-
300 TO 499 MILES	276	100.0	11.1	30.4	54.2	-	-	.2	4.0
500 TO 999 MILES	90	100.0	28.2	45.0	21.7	-	-	-	5.0
1000 TO 1499 MILES	33	100.0	32.2	59.8	7.2	-	-	-	.9
1500 MILES OR OVER	12	100.0	93.9	6.1	-	-	-	-	-
PACIFIC	1 847	100.0	2.9	34.3	60.7	-	1.5	.4	-
UNDER 100 MILES	1 133	100.0	1.5	31.7	66.6	-	-	.2	.1
100 TO 199 MILES	405	100.0	.5	32.5	66.4	-	-	.6	-
200 TO 299 MILES	75	100.0	7.8	50.6	41.3	-	-	.3	-
300 TO 499 MILES	114	100.0	5.4	51.0	41.7	-	-	1.8	.1
500 TO 999 MILES	79	100.0	21.4	54.8	22.9	-	-	.9	-
1000 TO 1499 MILES	1	100.0	59.1	34.2	-	-	-	6.7	-
1500 MILES OR OVER	38	100.0	15.5	7.7	2.9	.2	73.5	.1	-
TON-MILES OF SHIPMENTS	(millions of ton-miles)								
U.S. TOTAL	3 211	100.0	18.6	48.7	29.5	.1	2.2	.6	.3
NEW ENGLAND	255	100.0	3.8	53.3	42.8	-	.1	-	-
UNDER 100 MILES	30	100.0	-	34.4	65.5	-	.1	-	-
100 TO 199 MILES	19	100.0	5.8	56.6	37.6	-	-	-	-
200 TO 299 MILES	8	100.0	-	36.1	62.6	-	1.3	-	-
300 TO 499 MILES	11	100.0	8.3	31.5	60.1	-	-	-	-
500 TO 999 MILES	85	100.0	.5	27.8	71.6	.1	-	-	-
1000 TO 1499 MILES	80	100.0	1.2	87.9	10.9	-	-	-	-
1500 MILES OR OVER	19	100.0	31.9	68.0	-	-	-	-	-
MIDDLE ATLANTIC	424	100.0	18.6	48.8	32.2	.1	-	.3	-
UNDER 100 MILES	106	100.0	1.1	19.5	79.0	-	-	.4	-
100 TO 199 MILES	60	100.0	6.7	46.7	46.6	-	-	-	-
200 TO 299 MILES	78	100.0	9.8	65.4	24.5	-	-	.4	-
300 TO 499 MILES	38	100.0	39.8	54.0	6.1	.1	-	-	-
500 TO 999 MILES	72	100.0	19.9	74.6	4.4	.5	-	.5	-
1000 TO 1499 MILES	34	100.0	49.5	50.2	.2	.1	-	-	-
1500 MILES OR OVER	35	100.0	54.9	44.0	.4	.6	-	.2	-

See footnotes at end of table 4.

TABLE 1. **TCC GROUP 265**—Percent Distribution of Geographic Division of Origin and Distance Shipped, by Means of Transport: 1972—Continued

Geographic division of origin[1] and distance shipped[2]	Number	Percent distribution by means of transport							
		All means of transport	Rail	Motor carrier	Private truck	Air	Water	Other	Unknown
TON-MILES OF SHIPMENTS	(millions of ton-miles)								
EAST NORTH CENTRAL......	843	100.0	21.1	56.5	20.8	.1	-	1.4	.1
UNDER 100 MILES.......	149	100.0	2.1	49.9	47.7	-	-	.1	.2
100 TO 199 MILES......	139	100.0	8.4	65.1	26.0	-	-	.5	.1
200 TO 299 MILES......	112	100.0	8.9	62.8	27.9	-	-	.3	-
300 TO 499 MILES......	148	100.0	17.3	70.7	10.4	.2	-	1.3	.1
500 TO 999 MILES......	234	100.0	40.1	49.6	8.8	.1	-	1.2	.2
1000 TO 1499 MILES....	13	100.0	41.1	57.5	.7	-	-	.7	-
1500 MILES OR OVER....	44	100.0	61.6	24.2	-	.1	-	13.6	.6
WEST NORTH CENTRAL......	359	100.0	18.7	76.7	3.9	-	-	.3	.5
UNDER 100 MILES.......	15	100.0	7.2	73.2	19.7	-	-	-	-
100 TO 199 MILES......	34	100.0	17.6	71.8	10.2	-	-	-	.3
200 TO 299 MILES......	43	100.0	29.4	67.4	2.4	-	-	.8	-
300 TO 499 MILES......	85	100.0	26.9	72.2	.4	.1	-	-	.3
500 TO 999 MILES.....	80	100.0	11.4	87.4	-	.1	-	.3	.8
1000 TO 1499 MILES....	83	100.0	17.6	74.1	7.3	-	-	-	1.0
1500 MILES OR OVER....	17	100.0	2.4	95.8	-	-	-	1.8	-
SOUTH ATLANTIC..........	529	100.0	28.9	36.9	33.5	-	-	.7	-
UNDER 100 MILES.......	55	100.0	1.1	24.0	74.7	-	-	.2	-
100 TO 199 MILES......	107	100.0	3.9	32.9	62.8	-	-	.4	-
200 TO 299 MILES......	43	100.0	34.1	39.8	26.0	.1	-	-	-
300 TO 499 MILES......	86	100.0	26.3	35.6	37.3	.1	-	.8	-
500 TO 999 MILES.....	168	100.0	40.6	47.2	12.2	-	-	-	-
1000 TO 1499 MILES....	29	100.0	74.8	10.4	14.8	-	-	-	-
1500 MILES OR OVER....	38	100.0	52.3	41.7	-	.1	-	5.9	-
WEST SOUTH CENTRAL......	396	100.0	18.6	40.2	39.1	-	-	-	1.9
UNDER 100 MILES.......	23	100.0	-	79.7	19.4	-	-	-	.9
100 TO 199 MILES......	87	100.0	1.6	44.0	53.7	-	-	-	.7
200 TO 299 MILES......	49	100.0	13.5	30.2	56.3	-	-	-	-
300 TO 499 MILES......	110	100.0	12.3	29.1	55.4	-	-	.1	3.1
500 TO 999 MILES.....	64	100.0	30.3	46.9	17.9	-	-	-	4.8
1000 TO 1499 MILES....	40	100.0	34.4	57.8	6.9	-	-	-	.9
1500 MILES OR OVER....	20	100.0	93.7	6.3	-	-	-	-	-
PACIFIC.................	317	100.0	9.8	31.9	35.9	-	21.7	.7	-
UNDER 100 MILES.......	51	100.0	2.0	27.3	70.5	-	-	.2	-
100 TO 199 MILES......	59	100.0	.4	33.2	65.6	-	-	.9	-
200 TO 299 MILES......	19	100.0	8.0	51.4	40.2	-	-	.3	-
300 TO 499 MILES......	42	100.0	5.9	50.0	42.5	-	-	1.5	.1
500 TO 999 MILES.....	53	100.0	25.9	53.1	20.0	-	-	1.0	-
1000 TO 1499 MILES....	1	100.0	53.5	38.0	-	-	-	8.5	-
1500 MILES OR OVER....	89	100.0	12.1	7.9	2.4	.1	77.3	.1	-

See footnotes at end of table 4.

TABLE 2. **TCC GROUP 265**—Percent Distribution of Geographic Division of Origin and Means of Transport, by Geographic Division of Destination: 1972

Geographic division of origin[1] and means of transport	Number	Percent distribution by division of destination									
		U.S. total	New England	Middle Atlantic	East North Central	West North Central	South Atlantic	East South Central	West South Central	Mountain	Pacific
TONS OF SHIPMENTS	(thousands of tons)										
U.S. TOTAL..............	18 196	100.0	5.6	22.0	27.8	7.7	12.6	6.3	6.9	.7	10.4
RAIL.................	1 306	100.0	5.8	16.1	25.7	11.1	14.7	6.7	11.0	2.5	6.5
MOTOR CARRIER.........	7 429	100.0	5.1	15.5	36.1	13.0	10.2	3.2	7.3	.9	8.8
PRIVATE TRUCK.........	9 336	100.0	6.0	28.0	21.7	2.9	14.3	8.8	5.9	.3	12.0
AIR..................	3	100.0	.5	8.6	23.7	8.4	21.3	30.3	3.1	.3	3.8
WATER...............	29	100.0	2.3	1.4	-	-	-	-	-	-	96.4
OTHER...............	55	100.0	1.9	32.8	18.4	6.5	12.3	3.6	1.6	2.9	20.0
UNKNOWN..............	35	100.0	2.0	8.1	32.7	34.6	.7	-	19.5	-	2.5
NEW ENGLAND.............	1 120	100.0	69.9	9.6	2.4	6.2	11.1	.1	.3	-	.5
RAIL.................	13	100.0	24.6	42.7	2.5	-	10.5	-	3.3	2.5	13.9
MOTOR CARRIER.........	379	100.0	63.1	11.1	5.4	16.8	2.5	.2	.2	-	.8
PRIVATE TRUCK.........	725	100.0	74.3	8.1	.9	.7	15.7	-	.3	-	-
AIR..................	-	100.0	-	-	38.2	-	57.6	2.2	2.0	-	-
WATER...............	1	100.0	62.3	37.7	-	-	-	-	-	-	-
OTHER...............	-	100.0	-	-	-	-	-	-	-	100.0	-
UNKNOWN..............	-	100.0	82.0	18.0	-	-	-	-	-	-	-

See footnotes at end of table 4.

TABLE 2. **TCC GROUP 265—Percent Distribution of Geographic Division of Origin and Means of Transport, by Geographic Division of Destination: 1972**—Continued

Geographic division of origin[1] and means of transport	Number	Percent distribution by division of destination									
		U.S. total	New England	Middle Atlantic	East North Central	West North Central	South Atlantic	East South Central	West South Central	Mountain	Pacific
TONS OF SHIPMENTS	(thousands of tons)										
MIDDLE ATLANTIC.........	3 772	100.0	3.2	80.2	6.1	.7	8.5	.4	.4	.1	.3
RAIL..................	194	100.0	13.5	37.6	4.2	4.7	31.2	.6	4.0	-	4.3
MOTOR CARRIER.........	1 075	100.0	8.1	66.1	12.3	1.6	9.1	1.3	.8	.2	.4
PRIVATE TRUCK.........	2 484	100.0	.3	89.6	3.5	-	6.5	-	-	-	.1
AIR..................	-	100.0	1.5	20.6	55.6	.5	9.7	1.9	.5	.5	9.0
WATER................	-	100.0	-	-	-	-	-	-	-	-	-
OTHER................	15	100.0	.1	91.2	8.1	-	.4	-	-	-	.2
UNKNOWN..............	1	100.0	.3	98.8	.2	-	.3	.3	-	-	-
EAST NORTH CENTRAL......	5 371	100.0	1.0	6.1	79.0	6.3	2.8	3.3	.9	.2	.5
RAIL..................	411	100.0	5.4	8.2	48.0	11.7	8.1	8.8	5.3	.9	3.7
MOTOR CARRIER.........	2 864	100.0	1.1	8.4	76.8	6.8	3.0	2.6	.8	.2	.2
PRIVATE TRUCK.........	2 066	100.0	-	2.4	88.5	4.5	1.5	3.0	-	-	.2
AIR..................	1	100.0	-	4.2	4.4	12.9	3.4	69.4	4.7	-	1.0
WATER................	-	100.0	-	-	-	-	100.0	-	-	-	-
OTHER................	20	100.0	5.1	19.8	42.3	10.2	6.2	.1	1.0	-	15.4
UNKNOWN..............	6	100.0	7.5	-	83.3	7.2	.1	-	-	-	1.9
WEST NORTH CENTRAL......	1 181	100.0	.7	4.1	29.7	51.3	3.2	2.7	4.4	1.0	3.0
RAIL..................	191	100.0	1.4	7.8	44.3	31.8	2.4	3.5	8.6	.1	.1
MOTOR CARRIER.........	821	100.0	.6	4.0	29.3	49.9	3.9	3.0	4.2	1.4	3.7
PRIVATE TRUCK.........	162	100.0	-	-	14.7	81.6	-	.5	.5	-	2.7
AIR..................	-	100.0	.1	7.4	11.3	20.7	42.7	8.0	9.3	-	.5
WATER................	-	100.0	-	-	-	-	-	-	-	-	-
OTHER................	2	100.0	-	-	17.4	72.1	-	.3	1.4	-	8.7
UNKNOWN..............	3	100.0	-	22.7	49.7	22.4	5.1	-	-	-	-
SOUTH ATLANTIC.........	2 531	100.0	1.6	18.7	4.4	.9	64.8	5.6	3.1	.6	.4
RAIL..................	299	100.0	4.8	27.2	11.9	4.2	30.1	3.4	13.0	4.4	1.1
MOTOR CARRIER.........	778	100.0	1.8	14.5	7.2	1.2	66.6	4.6	3.3	-	.8
PRIVATE TRUCK.........	1 445	100.0	.9	19.3	1.3	.1	71.0	6.6	.9	-	-
AIR..................	-	100.0	.3	-	1.0	3.1	90.0	-	-	1.5	4.2
WATER................	-	100.0	-	-	-	-	-	-	-	-	-
OTHER................	7	100.0	.1	.7	.1	-	74.1	7.5	-	17.4	-
UNKNOWN..............	-	100.0	-	-	-	-	100.0	-	-	-	-
WEST SOUTH CENTRAL......	1 579	100.0	.4	.9	2.1	21.1	.8	6.8	63.7	3.1	1.1
RAIL..................	116	100.0	5.6	1.6	7.7	12.3	1.3	2.3	49.1	7.8	12.4
MOTOR CARRIER.........	785	100.0	-	1.2	2.5	34.4	1.4	2.6	55.3	2.1	.4
PRIVATE TRUCK.........	653	100.0	-	.4	.1	5.6	-	12.9	77.6	3.5	-
AIR..................	-	100.0	2.6	.5	2.6	94.2	-	-	-	-	-
WATER................	-	100.0	-	-	-	-	-	-	-	-	-
OTHER................	-	100.0	-	-	-	-	7.7	-	92.3	-	-
UNKNOWN..............	23	100.0	-	1.2	19.9	48.5	-	-	30.4	-	-
PACIFIC................	1 847	100.0	-	-	.1	-	-	.3	.1	2.4	97.1
RAIL..................	54	100.0	-	-	1.8	-	-	9.1	1.5	12.0	75.5
MOTOR CARRIER.........	634	100.0	-	-	.1	-	-	-	.1	4.5	95.2
PRIVATE TRUCK.........	1 121	100.0	-	-	.1	-	-	-	-	.8	99.1
AIR..................	-	100.0	-	1.7	89.6	-	1.1	-	-	-	7.6
WATER................	28	100.0	-	-	-	-	-	-	-	-	100.0
OTHER................	8	100.0	-	-	-	-	.6	-	1.3	3.9	94.2
UNKNOWN..............	-	100.0	-	-	-	-	-	-	-	-	100.0
TON-MILES OF SHIPMENTS	(millions of ton-miles)										
U.S. TOTAL............	3 211	100.0	4.5	14.6	20.5	11.8	13.2	7.1	10.5	3.2	14.6
RAIL..................	597	100.0	6.7	12.5	15.2	10.4	12.0	6.6	14.8	6.2	15.6
MOTOR CARRIER.........	1 564	100.0	4.6	14.8	25.5	17.1	10.6	4.2	8.4	3.1	11.7
PRIVATE TRUCK.........	948	100.0	3.2	16.8	17.2	4.6	19.3	13.0	12.2	1.5	12.3
AIR..................	1	100.0	.4	3.8	27.7	8.4	18.4	20.6	4.6	1.1	14.9
WATER................	69	100.0	-	.2	-	-	-	-	-	-	99.8
OTHER................	19	100.0	3.7	14.4	8.7	6.5	10.0	.9	2.7	12.9	40.2
UNKNOWN..............	10	100.0	3.5	11.2	39.6	33.8	1.3	-	7.6	-	3.0
NEW ENGLAND............	255	100.0	17.4	7.4	7.9	31.7	26.0	.3	2.0	.3	7.1
RAIL..................	9	100.0	6.5	14.1	2.3	-	12.4	-	7.2	6.9	50.7
MOTOR CARRIER.........	135	100.0	13.9	5.4	10.8	55.6	3.4	.5	.8	-	9.6
PRIVATE TRUCK.........	109	100.0	22.7	9.2	4.7	5.0	55.4	-	3.0	-	-
AIR..................	-	100.0	-	-	46.9	-	45.4	3.6	4.1	-	-
WATER................	-	100.0	21.4	78.6	-	-	-	-	-	-	-
OTHER................	-	100.0	-	-	-	-	-	-	-	100.0	-
UNKNOWN..............	-	100.0	48.3	51.7	-	-	-	-	-	-	-

See footnotes at end of table 4.

TABLE 2. **TCC GROUP 265—Percent Distribution of Geographic Division of Origin and Means of Transport, by Geographic Division of Destination: 1972**—Continued

Geographic division of origin[1] and means of transport	Number	Percent distribution by division of destination									
		U.S. total	New England	Middle Atlantic	East North Central	West North Central	South Atlantic	East South Central	West South Central	Mountain	Pacific
TON-MILES OF SHIPMENTS	(millions of ton-miles)										
MIDDLE ATLANTIC	424	100.0	5.9	40.2	16.9	5.6	15.6	2.6	4.8	1.0	7.3
RAIL	78	100.0	6.3	8.3	5.5	11.6	30.0	1.3	12.1	-	24.9
MOTOR CARRIER	207	100.0	8.9	29.9	24.6	7.2	12.0	4.6	5.2	2.1	5.5
PRIVATE TRUCK	136	100.0	1.2	74.2	11.4	-	12.8	.2	.1	.1	-
AIR	-	100.0	.8	4.1	49.3	.9	8.8	1.9	1.0	1.4	31.8
WATER	-	100.0	-	-	-	-	-	-	-	-	-
OTHER	1	100.0	.1	58.6	31.4	-	4.3	-	-	-	5.5
UNKNOWN	-	100.0	3.3	69.8	8.6	-	6.9	11.3	-	-	-
EAST NORTH CENTRAL	843	100.0	4.4	14.5	43.2	13.6	7.3	6.1	4.3	1.3	5.2
RAIL	177	100.0	9.2	10.1	19.3	14.0	10.5	9.4	10.1	2.3	15.0
MOTOR CARRIER	476	100.0	4.1	17.9	44.2	14.7	7.0	4.5	3.8	1.5	2.2
PRIVATE TRUCK	175	100.0	.2	9.3	67.2	10.7	5.0	7.3	.2	-	-
AIR	-	100.0	-	4.2	2.1	18.1	5.4	57.3	8.8	-	4.1
WATER	-	100.0	-	-	-	-	100.0	-	-	-	-
OTHER	11	100.0	6.1	18.3	9.5	7.8	5.8	-	1.7	.1	50.7
UNKNOWN	1	100.0	32.0	-	32.2	12.7	.2	-	-	-	22.9
WEST NORTH CENTRAL	359	100.0	2.4	12.3	27.8	22.1	8.6	3.5	6.8	2.5	14.1
RAIL	67	100.0	4.2	21.0	36.4	17.4	5.9	3.7	10.6	.2	.6
MOTOR CARRIER	275	100.0	2.1	10.7	26.1	22.7	9.7	3.5	6.1	3.2	15.9
PRIVATE TRUCK	13	100.0	-	-	18.8	34.3	-	1.5	1.7	.1	43.6
AIR	-	100.0	.2	10.2	8.1	15.0	46.4	5.7	13.0	-	1.5
WATER	-	100.0	-	-	-	-	-	-	-	-	-
OTHER	-	100.0	-	-	23.5	39.4	-	.3	1.7	-	35.0
UNKNOWN	1	100.0	-	44.6	43.0	6.0	6.4	-	-	-	-
SOUTH ATLANTIC	529	100.0	3.3	18.2	10.7	3.5	35.3	8.0	12.5	4.2	4.3
RAIL	153	100.0	3.4	21.0	11.8	6.4	15.0	2.1	23.2	12.6	4.4
MOTOR CARRIER	195	100.0	4.3	18.3	15.0	4.0	34.7	5.6	9.6	.3	8.2
PRIVATE TRUCK	177	100.0	2.2	16.0	5.2	.5	53.5	15.8	6.7	-	-
AIR	-	100.0	.4	-	1.0	4.5	70.9	-	-	6.3	16.9
WATER	-	100.0	-	-	-	-	-	-	-	-	-
OTHER	3	100.0	.1	.3	.1	.1	31.6	2.7	-	65.1	-
UNKNOWN	-	100.0	-	-	-	-	100.0	-	-	-	-
WEST SOUTH CENTRAL	396	100.0	2.6	4.2	7.1	15.1	2.2	9.2	45.2	8.2	6.2
RAIL	73	100.0	13.9	3.1	10.1	9.0	1.4	1.7	22.9	10.8	27.2
MOTOR CARRIER	159	100.0	.1	7.2	10.9	22.8	4.8	4.2	39.8	7.5	2.7
PRIVATE TRUCK	155	100.0	-	1.8	.2	8.5	-	18.5	63.0	8.0	-
AIR	-	100.0	8.9	1.7	3.5	85.9	-	-	-	-	-
WATER	-	100.0	-	-	-	-	-	-	-	-	-
OTHER	-	100.0	-	-	-	-	15.3	-	84.7	-	-
UNKNOWN	7	100.0	-	4.8	40.5	44.0	-	-	10.6	-	-
PACIFIC	317	100.0	.1	.1	1.6	-	.1	2.9	.6	6.7	87.8
RAIL	31	100.0	-	-	5.7	-	-	29.1	2.8	15.4	47.0
MOTOR CARRIER	101	100.0	.3	.4	1.0	.1	.3	-	.8	14.7	82.3
PRIVATE TRUCK	114	100.0	-	-	1.9	-	-	-	-	1.3	96.8
AIR	-	100.0	-	2.5	88.0	-	1.2	-	-	-	8.3
WATER	68	100.0	-	-	-	-	-	-	-	-	100.0
OTHER	2	100.0	-	-	-	-	5.3	.1	7.5	14.1	72.9
UNKNOWN	-	100.0	-	-	-	-	-	-	-	-	100.0

See footnotes at end of table 4.

TABLE 3. TCC GROUP 265—Percent Distribution of Geographic Division of Destination and Means of Transport, by Geographic Division of Origin: 1972

Geographic division of destination and means of transport	Number	Percent distribution by division of origin[1]									
		U.S. total	New England	Middle Atlantic	East North Central	West North Central	South Atlantic	East South Central	West South Central	Mountain	Pacific
TONS OF SHIPMENTS	(thousands of tons)										
U.S. TOTAL..............	18 196	100.0	6.2	20.7	29.5	6.5	13.9	(D)	8.7	(D)	10.2
RAIL..............	1 306	100.0	1.0	14.9	31.5	14.6	22.9	(D)	8.9	(D)	4.2
MOTOR CARRIER........	7 429	100.0	5.1	14.5	38.6	11.1	10.5	(D)	10.6	(D)	8.5
PRIVATE TRUCK........	9 336	100.0	7.8	26.6	22.1	1.7	15.5	(D)	7.0	(D)	12.0
AIR..................	3	100.0	5.0	29.9	41.7	8.8	11.4	(D)	.8	(D)	2.4
WATER...............	29	100.0	3.6	-	-	-	-	(D)	-	(D)	96.4
OTHER...............	55	100.0	-	28.0	36.5	3.9	13.1	(D)	1.0	(D)	14.8
UNKNOWN.............	35	100.0	.8	5.1	18.3	9.3	.2	(D)	64.3	(D)	2.1
NEW ENGLAND.............	1 014	100.0	77.1	11.9	5.5	.8	4.1	(D)	.7	(D)	-
RAIL..............	75	100.0	4.4	34.9	29.3	3.6	19.0	(D)	8.7	(D)	-
MOTOR CARRIER........	377	100.0	63.4	23.1	8.3	1.4	3.7	(D)	-	(D)	-
PRIVATE TRUCK........	559	100.0	96.3	1.3	.1	-	2.3	(D)	-	(D)	-
AIR..................	-	100.0	-	88.3	-	-	2.1	(D)	4.0	(D)	-
WATER...............	-	100.0	100.0	-	-	-	-	(D)	-	(D)	-
OTHER...............	1	100.0	-	1.2	98.3	-	.4	(D)	-	(D)	-
UNKNOWN.............	-	100.0	30.8	.8	68.4	-	-	(D)	-	(D)	-
MIDDLE ATLANTIC........	3 996	100.0	2.7	75.7	8.2	1.2	11.8	(D)	.3	(D)	-
RAIL..............	210	100.0	2.8	34.7	16.1	7.1	38.6	(D)	.9	(D)	-
MOTOR CARRIER........	1 148	100.0	3.7	61.9	20.9	2.8	9.8	(D)	.8	(D)	-
PRIVATE TRUCK........	2 615	100.0	2.3	85.1	1.9	-	10.7	(D)	.1	(D)	-
AIR..................	-	100.0	-	71.4	20.5	7.6	-	(D)	-	(D)	.5
WATER...............	-	100.0	100.0	-	-	-	-	(D)	-	(D)	-
OTHER...............	18	100.0	-	77.7	22.0	-	.3	(D)	-	(D)	-
UNKNOWN.............	2	100.0	1.7	62.4	-	26.1	-	(D)	9.8	(D)	-
EAST NORTH CENTRAL......	5 063	100.0	.5	4.5	83.8	6.9	2.2	(D)	.7	(D)	.1
RAIL..............	336	100.0	.1	2.4	58.8	25.1	10.6	(D)	2.7	(D)	.3
MOTOR CARRIER........	2 679	100.0	.8	5.0	82.1	9.0	2.1	(D)	.7	(D)	-
PRIVATE TRUCK........	2 025	100.0	.3	4.3	90.3	1.2	.9	(D)	-	(D)	.1
AIR..................	-	100.0	8.1	70.2	7.7	4.2	.5	(D)	.1	(D)	9.2
WATER...............	-	100.0	-	-	-	-	-	(D)	-	(D)	-
OTHER...............	10	100.0	-	12.3	83.9	3.7	.1	(D)	-	(D)	-
UNKNOWN.............	11	100.0	-	-	46.7	14.1	-	(D)	39.1	(D)	-
WEST NORTH CENTRAL......	1 396	100.0	4.9	1.9	24.3	43.4	1.6	(D)	23.8	(D)	-
RAIL..............	145	100.0	-	6.2	33.3	41.9	8.7	(D)	9.8	(D)	-
MOTOR CARRIER........	966	100.0	6.6	1.7	20.2	42.5	.9	(D)	28.0	(D)	-
PRIVATE TRUCK........	268	100.0	2.0	-	34.8	49.4	.4	(D)	13.5	(D)	-
AIR..................	-	100.0	-	1.8	63.7	21.7	4.2	(D)	8.7	(D)	-
WATER...............	-	100.0	-	-	-	-	-	(D)	-	(D)	-
OTHER...............	3	100.0	-	-	56.7	43.2	.1	(D)	-	(D)	-
UNKNOWN.............	12	100.0	-	-	3.8	6.0	-	(D)	90.2	(D)	-
SOUTH ATLANTIC.........	2 295	100.0	5.4	14.0	6.7	1.6	71.5	(D)	.6	(D)	-
RAIL..............	191	100.0	.7	31.6	17.4	2.4	47.1	(D)	.8	(D)	-
MOTOR CARRIER........	757	100.0	1.2	13.0	11.5	4.3	68.5	(D)	1.5	(D)	-
PRIVATE TRUCK........	1 338	100.0	8.5	12.1	2.3	-	76.6	(D)	-	(D)	-
AIR..................	-	100.0	13.6	13.7	6.6	17.7	48.3	(D)	-	(D)	.1
WATER...............	-	100.0	-	-	100.0	-	-	(D)	-	(D)	-
OTHER...............	6	100.0	-	.9	18.3	-	79.4	(D)	.7	(D)	.7
UNKNOWN.............	-	100.0	-	2.5	2.0	71.8	23.7	(D)	-	(D)	-
EAST SOUTH CENTRAL......	1 152	100.0	.1	1.4	15.2	2.8	12.3	(D)	9.3	(D)	.4
RAIL..............	87	100.0	-	1.4	41.7	7.6	11.6	(D)	3.0	(D)	5.7
MOTOR CARRIER........	236	100.0	.3	5.8	31.7	10.3	15.1	(D)	8.7	(D)	-
PRIVATE TRUCK........	826	100.0	-	.1	7.6	.1	11.5	(D)	10.2	(D)	-
AIR..................	-	100.0	.4	1.9	95.4	2.3	-	(D)	-	(D)	-
WATER...............	-	100.0	-	-	-	-	-	(D)	-	(D)	-
OTHER...............	2	100.0	-	-	.7	.3	27.2	(D)	-	(D)	.1
UNKNOWN.............	-	100.0	-	100.0	-	-	-	(D)	-	(D)	-
WEST SOUTH CENTRAL......	1 248	100.0	.3	1.3	3.7	4.2	6.2	(D)	80.6	(D)	.1
RAIL..............	143	100.0	.3	5.4	15.1	11.5	27.2	(D)	39.9	(D)	.6
MOTOR CARRIER........	541	100.0	.1	1.6	4.3	6.4	4.7	(D)	80.2	(D)	.1
PRIVATE TRUCK........	555	100.0	.4	-	.1	.1	2.3	(D)	91.3	(D)	-
AIR..................	-	100.0	3.2	5.2	64.8	26.7	-	(D)	-	(D)	-
WATER...............	-	100.0	-	-	-	-	-	(D)	-	(D)	-
OTHER...............	-	100.0	-	-	23.2	3.6	.2	(D)	60.7	(D)	12.3
UNKNOWN.............	7	100.0	-	-	-	-	-	(D)	100.0	(D)	-
MOUNTAIN...............	131	100.0	.3	1.8	7.4	8.9	11.2	(D)	36.7	(D)	33.7
RAIL..............	32	100.0	1.0	-	11.0	.6	39.7	(D)	27.7	(D)	19.9
MOTOR CARRIER........	65	100.0	-	3.5	9.4	17.7	.6	(D)	24.8	(D)	44.1
PRIVATE TRUCK........	31	100.0	-	.2	-	.1	-	(D)	72.3	(D)	27.4
AIR..................	-	100.0	-	48.6	-	-	51.4	(D)	-	(D)	-
WATER...............	-	100.0	-	-	-	-	-	(D)	-	(D)	-
OTHER...............	1	100.0	.1	-	.3	-	79.4	(D)	-	(D)	20.2
UNKNOWN.............	-	100.0	-	-	-	-	-	(D)	-	(D)	-
PACIFIC................	1 897	100.0	.3	.7	1.3	1.8	.5	(D)	.9	(D)	94.5
RAIL..............	84	100.0	2.2	9.8	17.8	.3	3.9	(D)	17.1	(D)	48.8
MOTOR CARRIER........	657	100.0	.5	.7	.9	4.6	1.0	(D)	.5	(D)	91.9
PRIVATE TRUCK........	1 115	100.0	-	-	-	.4	-	(D)	-	(D)	99.6
AIR..................	-	100.0	-	70.6	11.0	1.1	12.4	(D)	-	(D)	4.8
WATER...............	28	100.0	-	-	-	-	-	(D)	-	(D)	100.0
OTHER...............	11	100.0	-	.2	28.1	1.7	-	(D)	-	(D)	69.9
UNKNOWN.............	-	100.0	-	-	14.4	-	-	(D)	-	(D)	85.6

See footnotes at end of table 4.

TABLE 3. **TCC GROUP 265**—Percent Distribution of Geographic Division of Destination and Means of Transport, by Geographic Division of Origin: 1972—Continued

Geographic division of destination and means of transport	Number	Percent distribution by division of origin[1]									
		U.S. total	New England	Middle Atlantic	East North Central	West North Central	South Atlantic	East South Central	West South Central	Mountain	Pacific
TON-MILES OF SHIPMENTS	(millions of ton-miles)										
U.S. TOTAL............	3 211	100.0	7.9	13.2	26.3	11.2	16.5	(D)	12.3	(D)	9.9
RAIL..............	597	100.0	1.6	13.2	29.8	11.3	25.7	(D)	12.4	(D)	5.2
MOTOR CARRIER.........	1 564	100.0	8.7	13.2	30.5	17.6	12.5	(D)	10.2	(D)	6.5
PRIVATE TRUCK.........	948	100.0	11.5	14.4	18.5	1.5	18.7	(D)	16.4	(D)	12.0
AIR................	1	100.0	5.9	34.8	33.7	7.8	10.1	(D)	.5	(D)	7.2
WATER..............	69	100.0	.2	-	-	-	-	(D)	-	(D)	99.8
OTHER..............	19	100.0	-	5.8	60.1	4.6	17.4	(D)	1.0	(D)	10.7
UNKNOWN............	10	100.0	.2	.3	10.6	16.9	.2	(D)	71.3	(D)	.5
NEW ENGLAND.............	144	100.0	30.8	17.5	26.1	5.9	12.2	(D)	7.3	(D)	.2
RAIL..............	40	100.0	1.6	12.4	40.8	6.9	12.9	(D)	25.4	(D)	-
MOTOR CARRIER.........	71	100.0	26.2	25.7	27.4	8.0	11.8	(D)	.3	(D)	.4
PRIVATE TRUCK.........	30	100.0	80.7	5.4	1.1	-	12.9	(D)	-	(D)	-
AIR................	-	100.0	-	74.7	-	4.7	9.9	(D)	10.6	(D)	-
WATER..............	-	100.0	100.0	-	-	-	-	(D)	-	(D)	-
OTHER..............	-	100.0	-	.2	99.4	-	.3	(D)	-	(D)	-
UNKNOWN............	-	100.0	2.4	.3	97.4	-	-	(D)	-	(D)	-
MIDDLE ATLANTIC.........	469	100.0	4.0	36.4	26.0	9.4	20.5	(D)	3.6	(D)	.1
RAIL..............	74	100.0	1.9	8.8	24.1	19.0	43.2	(D)	3.0	(D)	-
MOTOR CARRIER.........	231	100.0	3.2	26.7	36.8	12.7	15.4	(D)	4.9	(D)	.2
PRIVATE TRUCK.........	159	100.0	6.3	63.8	10.3	-	17.9	(D)	1.7	(D)	-
AIR................	-	100.0	-	37.5	36.8	20.9	-	(D)	.2	(D)	4.6
WATER..............	-	100.0	100.0	-	-	-	-	(D)	-	(D)	-
OTHER..............	2	100.0	-	23.4	76.3	-	.3	(D)	-	(D)	-
UNKNOWN............	1	100.0	.8	1.6	-	67.0	-	(D)	30.6	(D)	-
EAST NORTH CENTRAL......	658	100.0	3.0	10.9	55.4	15.2	8.6	(D)	4.3	(D)	.8
RAIL..............	90	100.0	.2	4.8	37.9	27.0	19.9	(D)	8.2	(D)	2.0
MOTOR CARRIER.........	398	100.0	3.7	12.8	52.9	18.0	7.3	(D)	4.4	(D)	.3
PRIVATE TRUCK.........	162	100.0	3.1	9.6	72.5	1.6	5.7	(D)	.2	(D)	1.3
AIR................	-	100.0	9.9	61.9	2.6	2.3	.4	(D)	.1	(D)	22.9
WATER..............	-	100.0	-	-	-	-	-	(D)	-	(D)	-
OTHER..............	1	100.0	-	20.9	66.4	12.5	.3	(D)	-	(D)	-
UNKNOWN............	4	100.0	-	.1	8.6	18.3	-	(D)	73.0	(D)	-
WEST NORTH CENTRAL......	377	100.0	21.4	6.3	30.4	21.0	4.9	(D)	15.8	(D)	-
RAIL..............	62	100.0	-	14.7	40.0	18.8	15.9	(D)	10.7	(D)	-
MOTOR CARRIER.........	267	100.0	28.2	5.6	26.2	23.4	2.9	(D)	13.6	(D)	-
PRIVATE TRUCK.........	43	100.0	12.7	-	43.6	11.1	2.0	(D)	30.5	(D)	-
AIR................	-	100.0	-	3.6	72.4	13.9	5.4	(D)	4.7	(D)	-
WATER..............	-	100.0	-	-	-	-	-	(D)	-	(D)	-
OTHER..............	1	100.0	-	-	71.9	27.9	.2	(D)	-	(D)	-
UNKNOWN............	3	100.0	-	-	4.0	3.0	-	(D)	93.0	(D)	-
SOUTH ATLANTIC..........	422	100.0	15.7	15.7	14.6	7.3	44.2	(D)	2.1	(D)	.1
RAIL..............	71	100.0	1.7	33.1	26.1	5.6	32.1	(D)	1.4	(D)	-
MOTOR CARRIER.........	165	100.0	2.8	15.0	20.2	16.1	40.9	(D)	4.6	(D)	.2
PRIVATE TRUCK.........	183	100.0	33.1	9.5	4.8	-	51.8	(D)	-	(D)	-
AIR................	-	100.0	14.4	16.6	9.8	19.7	39.0	(D)	-	(D)	.5
WATER..............	-	100.0	-	-	100.0	-	-	(D)	-	(D)	-
OTHER..............	1	100.0	-	2.5	35.0	-	55.3	(D)	1.5	(D)	5.7
UNKNOWN............	-	100.0	-	1.4	1.9	81.8	14.9	(D)	-	(D)	-
EAST SOUTH CENTRAL......	228	100.0	.3	4.8	22.3	5.4	18.5	(D)	16.0	(D)	4.0
RAIL..............	39	100.0	-	2.6	42.6	6.4	8.3	(D)	3.3	(D)	23.0
MOTOR CARRIER.........	66	100.0	.9	14.5	32.2	14.7	16.6	(D)	10.0	(D)	.1
PRIVATE TRUCK.........	122	100.0	-	.3	10.4	.2	22.8	(D)	23.4	(D)	-
AIR................	-	100.0	1.0	3.1	93.7	2.1	-	(D)	-	(D)	-
WATER..............	-	100.0	-	-	-	-	-	(D)	-	(D)	-
OTHER..............	-	100.0	-	.2	2.1	1.6	49.8	(D)	-	(D)	1.7
UNKNOWN............	-	100.0	-	100.0	-	-	-	(D)	-	(D)	-
WEST SOUTH CENTRAL......	338	100.0	1.5	6.1	10.8	7.2	19.6	(D)	53.0	(D)	.5
RAIL..............	88	100.0	.8	10.8	20.2	8.0	40.1	(D)	19.1	(D)	1.0
MOTOR CARRIER.........	131	100.0	.8	8.2	13.7	12.9	14.2	(D)	48.1	(D)	.6
PRIVATE TRUCK.........	116	100.0	2.8	.1	.4	.2	10.2	(D)	84.2	(D)	-
AIR................	-	100.0	5.2	7.7	65.0	22.1	-	(D)	-	(D)	-
WATER..............	-	100.0	-	-	-	-	-	(D)	-	(D)	-
OTHER..............	-	100.0	-	-	37.7	2.8	.2	(D)	30.1	(D)	29.2
UNKNOWN............	-	100.0	-	-	-	-	-	(D)	100.0	(D)	-
MOUNTAIN...............	101	100.0	.7	4.4	11.1	8.9	21.8	(D)	32.0	(D)	21.2
RAIL..............	36	100.0	1.8	-	11.0	.3	52.2	(D)	21.6	(D)	12.9
MOTOR CARRIER.........	47	100.0	-	8.9	15.0	18.6	1.0	(D)	25.1	(D)	31.2
PRIVATE TRUCK.........	13	100.0	-	1.0	-	.1	-	(D)	88.7	(D)	10.2
AIR................	-	100.0	-	43.3	-	-	56.7	(D)	-	(D)	-
WATER..............	-	100.0	-	-	-	-	-	(D)	-	(D)	-
OTHER..............	2	100.0	.2	-	.3	-	87.9	(D)	-	(D)	11.7
UNKNOWN............	-	100.0	-	-	-	-	-	(D)	-	(D)	-
PACIFIC................	469	100.0	3.8	6.6	9.3	10.8	4.8	(D)	5.2	(D)	59.4
RAIL..............	93	100.0	5.3	21.1	28.7	.4	7.2	(D)	21.6	(D)	15.7
MOTOR CARRIER.........	182	100.0	7.1	6.2	5.8	24.0	8.7	(D)	2.4	(D)	45.7
PRIVATE TRUCK.........	116	100.0	-	-	-	5.2	-	(D)	-	(D)	94.8
AIR................	-	100.0	-	74.4	9.4	.8	11.5	(D)	-	(D)	4.0
WATER..............	68	100.0	-	-	-	-	-	(D)	-	(D)	100.0
OTHER..............	7	100.0	-	.8	75.8	4.0	-	(D)	-	(D)	19.4
UNKNOWN............	-	100.0	-	-	81.6	-	-	(D)	-	(D)	18.4

See footnotes at end of table 4.

TABLE 4. TCC GROUP 265—Percent Distribution of Distance Shipped and Weight of Shipment, by Means of Transport: 1972

Distance shipped and weight of shipment[2][3]	Number	Percent distribution by means of transport							
		All means of transport	Rail	Motor carrier	Private truck	Air	Water	Other	Unknown
TONS OF SHIPMENTS	(thousands of tons)								
U.S. TOTAL..........	15 492	100.0	7.3	44.0	48.2	-	.2	.3	.1
UNDER 100 MILES.........	8 159	100.0	1.9	36.5	61.2	-	-	.3	.1
UNDER 1000 POUNDS.....	133	100.0	.1	29.8	69.3	-	-	.7	.1
1000 TO 9999 POUNDS...	2 096	100.0	.1	35.5	63.9	-	-	.2	.3
10000 TO 29999 POUNDS.	4 961	100.0	1.1	37.1	61.7	-	-	.1	-
30000 TO 59999 POUNDS.	879	100.0	9.5	39.4	49.7	-	-	1.4	-
60000 TO 89999 POUNDS.	17	100.0	51.5	48.5	-	-	-	-	-
90000 POUNDS AND OVER.	71	100.0	8.1	-	91.9	-	-	-	-
100 TO 199 MILES........	3 286	100.0	4.5	51.6	43.8	-	-	.2	-
UNDER 1000 POUNDS.....	30	100.0	.1	67.2	32.0	-	-	.6	-
1000 TO 9999 POUNDS...	631	100.0	1.2	48.2	50.3	-	-	.2	.2
10000 TO 29999 POUNDS.	1 856	100.0	1.0	53.7	45.3	-	-	-	-
30000 TO 59999 POUNDS.	731	100.0	14.6	50.7	34.5	-	-	.2	-
60000 TO 89999 POUNDS.	36	100.0	39.8	3.7	49.6	-	-	6.9	-
90000 POUNDS AND OVER.	-	100.0	-	-	-	-	-	-	-
200 TO 299 MILES........	1 465	100.0	14.6	53.3	31.7	-	-	.3	-
UNDER 1000 POUNDS.....	14	100.0	1.3	86.2	10.6	1.0	-	.8	-
1000 TO 9999 POUNDS...	250	100.0	3.3	67.0	29.6	-	-	.1	-
10000 TO 29999 POUNDS.	668	100.0	12.6	53.4	33.4	-	.1	.6	-
30000 TO 59999 POUNDS.	476	100.0	13.6	51.5	34.9	-	-	-	-
60000 TO 89999 POUNDS.	56	100.0	100.0	-	-	-	-	-	-
90000 POUNDS AND OVER.	-	100.0	-	-	-	-	-	-	-
300 TO 499 MILES........	1 242	100.0	19.6	52.5	27.3	.1	-	.4	.1
UNDER 1000 POUNDS.....	15	100.0	.4	85.9	6.7	3.0	-	4.0	-
1000 TO 9999 POUNDS...	164	100.0	3.7	74.8	21.3	-	-	.2	-
10000 TO 29999 POUNDS.	436	100.0	7.1	55.4	36.5	.2	-	.8	-
30000 TO 59999 POUNDS.	546	100.0	23.7	49.9	26.2	-	-	-	.2
60000 TO 89999 POUNDS.	72	100.0	97.9	2.1	-	-	-	-	-
90000 POUNDS AND OVER.	7	100.0	100.0	-	-	-	-	-	-
500 TO 999 MILES........	982	100.0	26.3	52.2	21.0	.1	-	.2	.1
UNDER 1000 POUNDS.....	14	100.0	2.2	89.8	2.1	4.1	-	1.6	.2
1000 TO 9999 POUNDS...	154	100.0	8.6	76.6	13.7	.4	-	.7	.1
10000 TO 29999 POUNDS.	245	100.0	10.2	65.7	23.8	-	-	.4	-
30000 TO 59999 POUNDS.	464	100.0	25.2	47.3	27.3	-	-	-	.2
60000 TO 89999 POUNDS.	77	100.0	98.1	1.9	-	-	-	-	-
90000 POUNDS AND OVER.	26	100.0	100.0	-	-	-	-	-	-
1000 TO 1499 MILES......	233	100.0	27.3	65.4	6.7	-	-	-	.4
UNDER 1000 POUNDS.....	2	100.0	-	91.5	7.6	.9	-	-	-
1000 TO 9999 POUNDS...	33	100.0	4.0	88.4	7.3	-	-	.3	-
10000 TO 29999 POUNDS.	52	100.0	6.5	84.9	8.0	-	-	-	.5
30000 TO 59999 POUNDS.	134	100.0	36.0	56.8	6.6	-	-	-	.6
60000 TO 89999 POUNDS.	10	100.0	100.0	-	-	-	-	-	-
90000 POUNDS AND OVER.	-	100.0	-	-	-	-	-	-	-
1500 MILES OR OVER......	122	100.0	45.5	28.6	1.0	.2	23.1	1.5	.1
UNDER 1000 POUNDS.....	2	100.0	9.0	83.9	-	5.7	-	1.4	-
1000 TO 9999 POUNDS...	14	100.0	6.1	55.2	.6	.5	32.8	4.0	.9
10000 TO 29999 POUNDS.	24	100.0	44.4	50.4	-	-	-	5.2	-
30000 TO 59999 POUNDS.	68	100.0	45.2	18.8	1.6	-	34.4	-	-
60000 TO 89999 POUNDS.	-	100.0	100.0	-	-	-	-	-	-
90000 POUNDS AND OVER.	11	100.0	100.0	-	-	-	-	-	-
TON-MILES OF SHIPMENTS	(millions of ton-miles)								
U.S. TOTAL..........	2 877	100.0	18.4	50.3	28.4	.1	2.4	.3	.1
UNDER 100 MILES.........	388	100.0	1.7	39.3	58.7	-	-	.2	.1
UNDER 1000 POUNDS.....	5	100.0	.1	33.9	65.5	-	-	.6	-
1000 TO 9999 POUNDS...	91	100.0	.1	38.9	60.5	-	-	.2	.3
10000 TO 29999 POUNDS.	230	100.0	.9	40.6	58.4	-	-	.1	-
30000 TO 59999 POUNDS.	53	100.0	6.9	39.0	53.4	-	-	.6	-
60000 TO 89999 POUNDS.	1	100.0	51.0	49.0	-	-	-	-	-
90000 POUNDS AND OVER.	5	100.0	5.4	-	94.6	-	-	-	-
100 TO 199 MILES........	468	100.0	4.6	51.1	44.1	-	-	.2	-
UNDER 1000 POUNDS.....	4	100.0	.1	68.2	30.9	-	-	.6	-
1000 TO 9999 POUNDS...	87	100.0	1.0	49.0	49.5	-	-	.2	.2
10000 TO 29999 POUNDS.	258	100.0	1.0	52.6	46.4	-	-	-	-
30000 TO 59999 POUNDS.	113	100.0	14.2	50.5	35.1	-	-	.2	-
60000 TO 89999 POUNDS.	4	100.0	45.2	3.8	40.1	-	-	10.9	-
90000 POUNDS AND OVER.	-	100.0	-	-	-	-	-	-	-

See footnotes at end of table 4.

TABLE 4. **TCC GROUP 265—Percent Distribution of Distance Shipped and Weight of Shipment, by Means of Transport: 1972**—Continued

Distance shipped and weight of shipment[2][3]	Number	Percent distribution by means of transport							
		All means of transport	Rail	Motor carrier	Private truck	Air	Water	Other	Unknown
TON-MILES OF SHIPMENTS	(millions of ton-miles)								
200 TO 299 MILES.........	348	100.0	15.2	53.4	31.1	-	-	.3	-
UNDER 1000 POUNDS......	3	100.0	1.3	86.6	10.2	1.0	-	.8	-
1000 TO 9999 POUNDS....	59	100.0	3.0	68.1	28.7	-	-	.2	-
10000 TO 29999 POUNDS.	158	100.0	13.3	53.9	32.1	-	.1	.5	-
30000 TO 59999 POUNDS.	113	100.0	14.2	50.6	35.3	-	-	-	-
60000 TO 89999 POUNDS.	13	100.0	100.0	-	-	-	-	-	-
90000 POUNDS AND OVER.	-	100.0	-	-	-	-	-	-	-
300 TO 499 MILES.........	480	100.0	19.4	52.8	27.2	.1	-	.4	.1
UNDER 1000 POUNDS......	6	100.0	.4	86.5	6.4	3.2	-	3.5	-
1000 TO 9999 POUNDS....	63	100.0	3.8	75.5	20.4	-	-	.2	-
10000 TO 29999 POUNDS.	169	100.0	6.7	57.1	35.2	.2	-	.8	-
30000 TO 59999 POUNDS.	210	100.0	23.4	49.0	27.4	-	-	-	.2
60000 TO 89999 POUNDS.	27	100.0	97.9	2.1	-	-	-	-	-
90000 POUNDS AND OVER.	2	100.0	100.0	-	-	-	-	-	-
500 TO 999 MILES.........	657	100.0	26.9	53.9	18.7	.1	-	.2	.1
UNDER 1000 POUNDS......	9	100.0	2.3	89.9	1.9	4.1	-	1.7	.2
1000 TO 9999 POUNDS....	106	100.0	8.9	77.1	12.9	.3	-	.7	.1
10000 TO 29999 POUNDS.	166	100.0	10.7	66.5	22.4	-	-	.4	-
30000 TO 59999 POUNDS.	302	100.0	25.9	50.1	23.8	-	-	-	.2
60000 TO 89999 POUNDS.	55	100.0	97.8	2.2	-	-	-	-	-
90000 POUNDS AND OVER.	16	100.0	100.0	-	-	-	-	-	-
1000 TO 1499 MILES......	278	100.0	26.8	65.8	6.9	-	-	.1	.4
UNDER 1000 POUNDS......	2	100.0	-	92.2	6.9	.9	-	-	-
1000 TO 9999 POUNDS....	40	100.0	3.8	87.4	8.4	-	-	.4	.6
10000 TO 29999 POUNDS.	63	100.0	6.3	85.1	8.0	-	-	-	.5
30000 TO 59999 POUNDS.	159	100.0	35.5	57.3	6.7	-	-	-	-
60000 TO 89999 POUNDS.	12	100.0	100.0	-	-	-	-	-	-
90000 POUNDS AND OVER.	-	100.0	-	-	-	-	-	-	-
1500 MILES OR OVER......	254	100.0	40.1	30.3	.9	.2	27.1	1.3	.1
UNDER 1000 POUNDS......	4	100.0	10.5	81.7	-	6.3	-	1.5	-
1000 TO 9999 POUNDS....	30	100.0	6.8	50.4	.4	.4	37.7	3.4	.9
10000 TO 29999 POUNDS.	52	100.0	40.0	55.7	-	.4	-	4.3	-
30000 TO 59999 POUNDS.	148	100.0	39.9	19.8	1.5	-	38.9	-	-
60000 TO 89999 POUNDS.	1	100.0	100.0	-	-	-	-	-	-
90000 POUNDS AND OVER.	18	100.0	100.0	-	-	-	-	-	-

Note: Detail may not add to total due to rounding. The introductory table shows the estimates of sampling variability for tons; sampling variability for ton-miles has not been estimated. See the map in the Introduction for the States comprising the geographic divisions of the United States.

Shipments excluded from the survey are those moving by pipeline (primarily petroleum products from refineries), parcel post shipments, and commodities moved by own power (motorized vehicles, aircraft, etc.) or towed (prefabricated buildings, etc.). Local shipments (commodities shipped less than 25 miles from the plant) and shipments within the same city are also excluded. Shipments to Alaska and Hawaii from the 48 conterminous States and the District of Columbia are included; however, no data were obtained for shipments originating in Alaska and Hawaii.

- Represents zero or rounds to zero.   (D) Withheld to avoid disclosing figures for individual companies.

[1]Production of this commodity is concentrated in the geographic divisions shown; figures and distributions for geographic divisions not shown are included in the total.

[2]Distances of shipments to foreign destinations are calculated only to the U.S. port of exit.

[3]Includes only shipments represented by bills of lading and invoices. Summary records which did not show individual weights of shipments are not included.

Rubber and Miscellaneous Plastics Products

CONTENTS

[Page numbers listed here omit the State prefix number that appears as part of the number for each page]

TABLES (The tables listed below are shown for each of the Transportation Commodity Classification groups in this report)

Comparisons of Tons and Ton-Miles of Shipments for Geographic Divisions of Origin and for Sampling Variability: 1972 and 1967

1. Percent Distribution of Geographic Division of Origin and Distance Shipped, by Means of Transport: 1972

2. Percent Distribution of Geographic Division of Origin and Means of Transport, by Geographic Division of Destination: 1972

3. Percent Distribution of Geographic Division of Destination and Means of Transport, by Geographic Division of Origin: 1972

4. Percent Distribution of Distance Shipped and Weight of Shipment, by Means of Transport: 1972

TCC 301. Tires and Inner Tubes

Comparisons of Tons and Ton-Miles of Shipments for
Geographic Divisions of Origin and for Sampling Variability: 1972 and 1967

Geographic division of origin	Estimates				Relative sampling variability in tons (percent)	
	1972		1967		1972	1967
	Tons (thousands)	Ton-miles (millions)	Tons (thousands)	Ton-miles (millions)		
U.S. total	5,646	3,057	3,889	2,042	7.1	10.6
New England	(D)	(D)	155	59	(*)	(*)
Middle Atlantic	706	319	336	140	28.1	(*)
East North Central	1,564	660	1,321	629	4.8	(*)
West North Central	439	209	356	196	13.0	(*)
South Atlantic	407	254	222	100	4.9	(*)
East South Central	1,266	719	711	380	14.7	(*)
West South Central	331	244	367	276	3.9	(*)
Mountain	(D)	(D)	57	45	(*)	(*)
Pacific	466	339	364	217	8.2	(*)

(D) Withheld to avoid disclosing figures for individual companies.   (*) Data not published.

TABLE 1. **TCC GROUP 301**—Percent Distribution of Geographic Division of Origin and Distance Shipped, by Means of Transport: 1972

Geographic division of origin[1] and distance shipped[2]	Number	Percent distribution by means of transport							
		All means of transport	Rail	Motor carrier	Private truck	Air	Water	Other	Unknown
TONS OF SHIPMENTS	(thousands of tons)								
U.S. TOTAL...........	5 646	100.0	40.9	49.9	7.6	1.1	.1	.1	.3
MIDDLE ATLANTIC.........	706	100.0	28.5	55.9	15.1	-	.4	-	-
UNDER 100 MILES.......	181	100.0	29.0	53.7	17.3	-	-	-	-
100 TO 199 MILES......	82	100.0	14.1	56.6	29.2	-	-	-	-
200 TO 299 MILES......	104	100.0	1.8	90.8	7.4	-	-	-	-
300 TO 499 MILES......	141	100.0	23.1	50.1	26.9	-	-	-	-
500 TO 999 MILES......	116	100.0	48.3	49.3	2.4	-	-	-	-
1000 TO 1499 MILES....	43	100.0	54.3	40.3	5.4	-	-	-	-
1500 MILES OR OVER....	36	100.0	62.1	28.2	1.4	-	8.3	-	-
EAST NORTH CENTRAL......	1 564	100.0	43.3	49.6	6.3	-	-	.1	.7
UNDER 100 MILES.......	402	100.0	59.6	33.7	6.5	-	-	.3	-
100 TO 199 MILES......	282	100.0	37.4	56.1	6.1	-	-	-	.4
200 TO 299 MILES......	134	100.0	20.5	69.5	9.9	-	-	.1	-
300 TO 499 MILES......	266	100.0	28.3	63.0	5.0	-	-	.2	3.4
500 TO 999 MILES......	331	100.0	47.5	45.0	7.4	-	-	-	-
1000 TO 1499 MILES....	48	100.0	47.3	48.4	4.0	.2	-	-	-
1500 MILES OR OVER....	96	100.0	49.1	48.5	2.4	-	-	-	-
WEST NORTH CENTRAL......	439	100.0	27.7	71.3	.8	-	-	.1	.1
UNDER 100 MILES.......	43	100.0	26.7	73.2	.1	-	-	-	-
100 TO 199 MILES......	37	100.0	-	99.4	.6	-	-	-	-
200 TO 299 MILES......	71	100.0	37.8	60.7	1.5	-	-	-	-
300 TO 499 MILES......	123	100.0	28.6	71.4	-	-	-	-	-
500 TO 999 MILES......	129	100.0	21.3	76.7	1.6	-	-	-	-
1000 TO 1499 MILES....	12	100.0	40.1	59.9	-	-	-	.4	-
1500 MILES OR OVER....	20	100.0	73.0	23.9	-	-	-	-	3.0
SOUTH ATLANTIC.........	407	100.0	59.6	30.4	9.7	-	-	-	.2
UNDER 100 MILES.......	4	100.0	-	63.0	37.0	-	-	-	-
100 TO 199 MILES......	43	100.0	48.9	41.0	10.1	-	-	-	-
200 TO 299 MILES......	26	100.0	23.8	50.0	26.2	-	-	-	-
300 TO 499 MILES......	142	100.0	63.4	27.3	9.2	-	-	-	-
500 TO 999 MILES......	135	100.0	60.7	30.9	7.8	-	-	-	.6
1000 TO 1499 MILES....	27	100.0	69.1	20.9	9.9	-	-	-	-
1500 MILES OR OVER....	27	100.0	88.1	11.9	-	-	-	-	-
EAST SOUTH CENTRAL......	1 266	100.0	53.1	41.5	5.4	-	-	.1	-
UNDER 100 MILES.......	50	100.0	42.2	37.2	20.6	-	-	-	-
100 TO 199 MILES......	106	100.0	57.0	27.0	16.1	-	-	-	-
200 TO 299 MILES......	105	100.0	56.9	35.5	7.6	-	-	-	-
300 TO 499 MILES......	340	100.0	41.6	50.2	8.0	-	-	-	-
500 TO 999 MILES......	570	100.0	57.6	42.2	.3	-	-	.2	-
1000 TO 1499 MILES....	37	100.0	56.8	34.1	9.1	-	-	-	-
1500 MILES OR OVER....	55	100.0	70.0	28.2	1.7	.1	-	-	-
WEST SOUTH CENTRAL......	331	100.0	50.4	43.0	6.2	-	-	-	.4
UNDER 100 MILES.......	16	100.0	64.8	34.9	.3	-	-	-	-
100 TO 199 MILES......	6	100.0	25.3	74.7	-	-	-	-	-
200 TO 299 MILES......	42	100.0	77.1	22.9	-	-	-	-	-
300 TO 499 MILES......	35	100.0	57.3	38.1	4.5	-	-	-	-
500 TO 999 MILES......	143	100.0	42.4	49.1	8.5	-	-	-	-
1000 TO 1499 MILES....	83	100.0	46.3	44.2	7.9	-	-	-	1.5
1500 MILES OR OVER....	4	100.0	59.1	40.9	-	-	-	-	-
PACIFIC.................	466	100.0	38.6	59.3	2.0	-	.1	-	-
UNDER 100 MILES.......	85	100.0	44.7	54.3	1.0	-	-	-	-
100 TO 199 MILES......	42	100.0	-	86.3	13.7	-	-	-	-
200 TO 299 MILES......	42	100.0	27.2	68.5	4.3	-	-	-	-
300 TO 499 MILES......	62	100.0	35.0	64.1	.9	-	-	-	-
500 TO 999 MILES......	114	100.0	23.1	76.7	.2	-	-	-	-
1000 TO 1499 MILES....	40	100.0	71.8	28.2	-	-	-	-	-
1500 MILES OR OVER....	78	100.0	67.7	31.8	.1	.1	.4	-	-
TON-MILES OF SHIPMENTS	(millions of ton-miles)								
U.S. TOTAL...........	3 057	100.0	46.5	46.3	4.9	1.7	.3	-	.3
MIDDLE ATLANTIC.........	319	100.0	44.9	44.5	8.4	-	2.2	-	-
UNDER 100 MILES.......	11	100.0	28.8	56.4	14.8	-	-	-	-
100 TO 199 MILES......	13	100.0	9.4	57.4	33.2	-	-	-	-
200 TO 299 MILES......	26	100.0	1.7	90.5	7.7	-	-	-	-
300 TO 499 MILES......	52	100.0	25.5	49.1	25.5	-	-	-	-
500 TO 999 MILES......	86	100.0	51.1	46.6	2.3	-	-	-	-
1000 TO 1499 MILES....	50	100.0	54.4	40.5	5.1	-	-	-	-
1500 MILES OR OVER....	78	100.0	68.1	21.9	1.0	-	9.0	-	-

See footnotes at end of table 4.

TABLE 1. TCC GROUP 301—Percent Distribution of Geographic Division of Origin and Distance Shipped, by Means of Transport: 1972—Continued

Geographic division of origin[1] and distance shipped[2]	Number	Percent distribution by means of transport							
		All means of transport	Rail	Motor carrier	Private truck	Air	Water	Other	Unknown
TON-MILES OF SHIPMENTS	(millions of ton-miles)								
EAST NORTH CENTRAL......	660	100.0	42.5	51.5	5.3	-	-	.1	.7
UNDER 100 MILES........	22	100.0	59.7	35.3	5.0	-	-	.1	-
100 TO 199 MILES......	39	100.0	37.5	56.7	5.4	-	-	-	.4
200 TO 299 MILES......	33	100.0	21.3	68.6	10.0	-	-	.1	-
300 TO 499 MILES......	105	100.0	30.5	61.0	4.3	-	-	.3	3.9
500 TO 999 MILES......	224	100.0	45.9	46.2	7.7	-	-	*	-
1000 TO 1499 MILES....	54	100.0	47.6	48.3	3.8	.2	-	-	-
1500 MILES OR OVER....	180	100.0	46.6	51.1	2.3	-	-	-	-
WEST NORTH CENTRAL......	209	100.0	31.7	66.7	.9	-	-	.2	.5
UNDER 100 MILES.......	2	100.0	22.2	77.8	-	-	-	-	-
100 TO 199 MILES......	5	100.0	-	99.5	.5	-	-	-	-
200 TO 299 MILES......	18	100.0	39.7	59.0	1.3	-	-	-	-
300 TO 499 MILES......	47	100.0	27.2	72.8	-	-	-	-	-
500 TO 999 MILES......	86	100.0	20.4	77.1	1.9	-	-	.6	-
1000 TO 1499 MILES....	14	100.0	35.9	64.1	-	-	-	-	2.9
1500 MILES OR OVER....	33	100.0	66.8	30.3	-	-	-	-	-
SOUTH ATLANTIC..........	254	100.0	68.6	24.8	6.3	-	-	-	.3
UNDER 100 MILES.......	-	100.0	-	62.0	38.0	-	-	-	-
100 TO 199 MILES......	7	100.0	47.8	41.3	10.9	-	-	-	-
200 TO 299 MILES......	6	100.0	23.2	50.2	26.6	-	-	-	-
300 TO 499 MILES......	56	100.0	65.2	26.2	8.5	-	-	-	-
500 TO 999 MILES......	95	100.0	62.3	31.1	5.8	-	-	-	.7
1000 TO 1499 MILES....	30	100.0	69.7	20.5	9.8	-	-	-	-
1500 MILES OR OVER....	58	100.0	89.4	10.6	-	-	-	-	-
EAST SOUTH CENTRAL......	719	100.0	57.0	39.9	3.0	-	-	-	-
UNDER 100 MILES.......	4	100.0	42.8	36.1	21.1	-	-	-	-
100 TO 199 MILES......	18	100.0	57.6	24.7	17.7	-	-	-	-
200 TO 299 MILES......	25	100.0	56.6	36.2	7.2	-	-	-	-
300 TO 499 MILES......	140	100.0	42.9	50.2	6.7	-	-	.2	-
500 TO 999 MILES......	388	100.0	58.7	41.1	.2	-	-	-	-
1000 TO 1499 MILES....	45	100.0	61.1	30.5	8.4	-	-	-	-
1500 MILES OR OVER....	96	100.0	69.5	28.4	1.9	.1	-	-	-
WEST SOUTH CENTRAL......	244	100.0	46.5	45.7	7.0	-	-	-	.7
UNDER 100 MILES.......	1	100.0	63.3	36.6	.2	-	-	-	-
100 TO 199 MILES......	1	100.0	28.2	71.8	-	-	-	-	-
200 TO 299 MILES......	11	100.0	79.3	20.7	-	-	-	-	-
300 TO 499 MILES......	14	100.0	57.0	39.0	4.0	-	-	-	-
500 TO 999 MILES......	107	100.0	40.6	50.7	8.6	-	-	-	1.6
1000 TO 1499 MILES....	101	100.0	46.7	44.4	7.3	-	-	-	-
1500 MILES OR OVER....	7	100.0	58.3	41.7	-	-	-	-	-
PACIFIC.................	339	100.0	52.1	47.1	.6	-	.2	-	-
UNDER 100 MILES.......	3	100.0	30.5	68.5	.9	-	-	-	-
100 TO 199 MILES......	6	100.0	-	84.4	15.6	-	-	-	-
200 TO 299 MILES......	10	100.0	27.1	69.2	3.6	-	-	-	-
300 TO 499 MILES......	21	100.0	32.6	66.6	.8	-	-	-	-
500 TO 999 MILES......	86	100.0	24.9	74.9	.2	-	-	-	-
1000 TO 1499 MILES....	54	100.0	71.0	29.0	-	-	-	-	-
1500 MILES OR OVER....	156	100.0	67.5	31.8	.1	.1	.5	-	-

See footnotes at end of table 4.

TABLE 2. TCC GROUP 301—Percent Distribution of Geographic Division of Origin and Means of Transport, by Geographic Division of Destination: 1972

Geographic division of origin[1] and means of transport	Number	Percent distribution by division of destination									
		U.S. total	New England	Middle Atlantic	East North Central	West North Central	South Atlantic	East South Central	West South Central	Mountain	Pacific
TONS OF SHIPMENTS	(thousands of tons)										
U.S. TOTAL.............	5 646	100.0	2.4	13.3	29.0	11.9	11.2	8.5	7.7	4.0	11.9
RAIL................	2 311	100.0	.7	12.8	29.2	14.2	8.4	11.6	8.5	3.2	11.4
MOTOR CARRIER........	2 818	100.0	4.1	13.5	30.1	10.2	12.7	5.8	7.4	6.2	2.4
PRIVATE TRUCK........	427	100.0	.8	15.8	23.8	12.9	19.4	11.1	-	.2	.1
AIR................	63	100.0	-	.1	-	.2	-	-	-	-	99.1
WATER..............	3	100.0	-	-	-	-	-	-	-	-	100.0
OTHER..............	3	100.0	5.0	18.5	34.2	33.7	3.6	2.0	1.2	.1	1.7
UNKNOWN.............	19	100.0	6.5	34.2	51.1	4.9	-	.1	-	-	3.1

See footnotes at end of table 4.

TABLE 2. **TCC GROUP 301—Percent Distribution of Geographic Division of Origin and Means of Transport, by Geographic Division of Destination: 1972**—Continued

Geographic division of origin[1] and means of transport	Number	Percent distribution by division of destination									
		U.S. total	New England	Middle Atlantic	East North Central	West North Central	South Atlantic	East South Central	West South Central	Mountain	Pacific
TONS OF SHIPMENTS	(thousands of tons)										
MIDDLE ATLANTIC	706	100.0	6.3	37.3	18.1	6.3	17.5	5.6	3.3	2.7	2.7
RAIL	201	100.0	-	26.0	16.5	14.4	12.2	13.2	5.7	4.1	7.9
MOTOR CARRIER	395	100.0	11.3	39.0	23.4	4.0	14.0	2.9	2.7	2.5	.1
PRIVATE TRUCK	106	100.0	-	53.6	2.3	-	40.9	1.3	1.4	.5	-
AIR	-	100.0	-	-	-	-	-	-	43.1	56.9	-
WATER	2	100.0	-	-	-	-	-	-	-	-	100.0
OTHER	-	100.0	-	45.5	54.5	-	-	-	-	-	-
UNKNOWN	-	100.0	-	-	-	-	-	-	-	-	-
EAST NORTH CENTRAL	1 564	100.0	1.4	8.7	53.3	10.4	8.2	6.2	3.8	2.1	5.9
RAIL	677	100.0	-	5.5	53.8	11.7	7.1	7.3	4.4	3.2	7.0
MOTOR CARRIER	775	100.0	2.9	12.5	51.9	8.9	8.8	5.4	3.0	.9	5.8
PRIVATE TRUCK	99	100.0	-	2.7	55.8	13.4	11.1	6.0	6.7	4.3	-
AIR	-	100.0	.9	21.1	6.8	21.7	13.9	2.3	24.6	4.4	4.2
WATER	-	100.0	-	-	-	-	-	-	-	-	-
OTHER	2	100.0	1.1	3.7	59.0	25.4	5.9	2.3	1.6	-	1.1
UNKNOWN	10	100.0	-	-	98.6	1.2	-	.1	.1	-	-
WEST NORTH CENTRAL	439	100.0	.5	5.1	29.3	41.6	3.3	3.9	7.2	3.6	5.5
RAIL	121	100.0	-	4.2	17.8	53.2	-	-	12.7	-	12.1
MOTOR CARRIER	313	100.0	.7	5.3	34.2	37.4	4.6	5.4	4.5	5.0	2.8
PRIVATE TRUCK	3	100.0	-	-	4.5	24.7	-	9.3	61.4	-	-
AIR	-	100.0	-	-	-	-	57.0	-	43.0	-	-
WATER	-	100.0	-	-	-	-	-	-	-	-	-
OTHER	-	100.0	-	99.3	.2	-	.1	-	.4	-	-
UNKNOWN	-	100.0	-	-	-	-	-	-	-	-	100.0
SOUTH ATLANTIC	407	100.0	1.3	17.3	26.2	6.4	21.2	11.6	8.9	1.4	5.8
RAIL	242	100.0	.8	15.2	25.5	7.1	15.9	14.3	10.3	1.6	9.3
MOTOR CARRIER	123	100.0	2.6	23.1	28.6	6.2	24.2	6.0	7.0	1.4	.9
PRIVATE TRUCK	39	100.0	-	12.2	23.1	.6	44.2	13.0	6.8	-	-
AIR	-	100.0	-	6.9	38.0	41.1	-	-	13.9	-	-
WATER	-	100.0	-	-	-	-	-	-	-	-	-
OTHER	-	100.0	-	1.9	1.4	-	96.7	-	-	-	-
UNKNOWN	-	100.0	-	-	-	100.0	-	-	-	-	-
EAST SOUTH CENTRAL	1 266	100.0	1.4	13.5	22.3	11.1	15.1	16.5	13.6	2.2	4.4
RAIL	671	100.0	.6	17.7	22.3	13.7	7.6	16.3	12.8	3.1	5.8
MOTOR CARRIER	525	100.0	2.0	9.8	21.5	8.7	26.0	12.6	15.1	1.4	3.0
PRIVATE TRUCK	68	100.0	5.0	1.3	27.8	2.4	4.9	48.0	9.3	-	1.4
AIR	-	100.0	-	-	21.2	.2	1.7	.5	-	-	76.5
WATER	-	100.0	-	-	-	-	-	-	-	-	-
OTHER	-	100.0	-	-	-	96.3	-	2.8	.9	-	-
UNKNOWN	-	100.0	-	-	-	-	-	-	-	-	-
WEST SOUTH CENTRAL	331	100.0	2.6	9.4	22.1	11.7	16.8	16.2	10.8	3.4	6.9
RAIL	167	100.0	-	7.9	17.3	13.0	15.6	22.8	8.7	4.0	10.6
MOTOR CARRIER	142	100.0	5.1	11.4	27.5	9.6	15.7	9.7	14.9	2.4	3.7
PRIVATE TRUCK	20	100.0	-	8.2	24.7	16.7	35.7	8.6	.3	5.8	-
AIR	-	100.0	-	-	-	-	-	-	-	-	-
WATER	-	100.0	-	-	-	-	-	-	-	-	-
OTHER	-	100.0	-	33.3	-	-	33.3	33.3	-	-	-
UNKNOWN	1	100.0	100.0	-	-	-	-	-	-	-	-
PACIFIC	466	100.0	.3	3.0	6.7	5.9	1.4	2.6	4.6	15.7	59.9
RAIL	180	100.0	.6	7.7	7.9	13.2	3.5	5.0	7.6	7.1	47.3
MOTOR CARRIER	276	100.0	-	-	6.1	1.4	-	1.2	2.8	21.8	66.8
PRIVATE TRUCK	9	100.0	-	-	-	-	-	.4	-	1.6	98.0
AIR	-	100.0	.9	.4	35.7	-	15.0	3.9	1.0	43.0	.1
WATER	-	100.0	-	-	-	-	-	-	-	-	100.0
OTHER	-	100.0	-	-	-	-	-	-	-	7.3	92.7
UNKNOWN	-	100.0	-	-	-	-	-	-	-	-	-
TON-MILES OF SHIPMENTS	(millions of ton-miles)										
U.S. TOTAL	3 057	100.0	2.5	11.6	19.2	10.5	10.4	6.5	10.0	6.1	23.2
RAIL	1 421	100.0	.7	13.4	16.1	12.7	7.2	8.1	10.3	6.0	25.6
MOTOR CARRIER	1 415	100.0	4.3	10.6	23.1	8.4	12.6	5.1	9.8	6.4	19.7
PRIVATE TRUCK	149	100.0	2.6	7.8	18.3	14.4	25.1	8.2	15.3	5.9	2.4
AIR	53	100.0	-	-	.2	.1	.1	-	.4	.1	98.9
WATER	7	100.0	-	-	-	-	-	-	-	-	100.0
OTHER	1	100.0	.9	40.3	4.3	42.3	3.6	2.6	2.5	.5	3.2
UNKNOWN	8	100.0	19.5	10.2	49.6	8.8	-	-	.2	-	11.7

See footnotes at end of table 4.

TABLE 2. **TCC GROUP 301—Percent Distribution of Geographic Division of Origin and Means of Transport, by Geographic Division of Destination: 1972**—Continued

Geographic division of origin[1] and means of transport	Number	Percent distribution by division of destination									
		U.S. total	New England	Middle Atlantic	East North Central	West North Central	South Atlantic	East South Central	West South Central	Mountain	Pacific
TON-MILES OF SHIPMENTS	(millions of ton-miles)										
MIDDLE ATLANTIC	319	100.0	3.9	9.5	16.2	13.4	14.3	8.1	9.1	9.9	15.5
RAIL	143	100.0	-	3.1	10.5	19.2	6.3	12.0	10.0	10.0	28.8
MOTOR CARRIER	142	100.0	8.9	13.4	25.2	10.8	14.7	5.6	9.2	11.5	.7
PRIVATE TRUCK	26	100.0	-	26.1	3.4	-	59.0	2.5	6.1	3.0	-
AIR	-	100.0	-	-	-	-	-	-	34.0	66.0	-
WATER	7	100.0	-	-	-	-	-	-	-	-	100.0
OTHER	-	100.0	-	6.9	93.1	-	-	-	-	-	-
UNKNOWN	-	100.0	-	-	-	-	-	-	-	-	-
EAST NORTH CENTRAL	660	100.0	2.9	9.8	18.7	10.1	11.1	7.7	7.8	5.9	26.1
RAIL	280	100.0	-	7.2	14.2	11.4	10.0	9.8	9.1	8.3	30.0
MOTOR CARRIER	340	100.0	5.7	12.7	21.4	8.5	11.2	6.0	5.9	2.7	26.0
PRIVATE TRUCK	34	100.0	-	2.8	19.2	14.6	21.2	8.0	16.5	17.7	-
AIR	-	100.0	.4	8.3	1.3	20.0	14.8	1.8	36.0	7.5	9.9
WATER	-	100.0	-	-	-	-	-	-	-	-	8.2
OTHER	-	100.0	2.2	5.0	11.1	53.7	9.1	5.1	5.7	-	-
UNKNOWN	4	100.0	-	-	98.0	1.6	-	.1	.3	-	-
WEST NORTH CENTRAL	209	100.0	1.2	9.5	25.5	21.2	5.0	4.2	9.2	5.6	18.6
RAIL	66	100.0	-	7.9	16.8	27.6	-	-	13.8	-	33.9
MOTOR CARRIER	140	100.0	1.7	10.2	30.3	18.5	7.6	6.3	6.0	8.4	11.0
PRIVATE TRUCK	1	100.0	-	-	.9	9.7	-	3.9	85.4	-	-
AIR	-	100.0	-	-	-	-	52.0	-	48.0	-	-
WATER	-	100.0	-	-	-	-	-	-	-	-	-
OTHER	-	100.0	-	99.3	.1	-	.1	-	.4	-	-
UNKNOWN	-	100.0	-	-	-	-	-	-	-	-	100.0
SOUTH ATLANTIC	254	100.0	1.7	9.6	21.8	8.8	10.5	8.9	14.5	3.5	20.6
RAIL	174	100.0	1.1	8.2	19.3	8.3	6.7	9.9	14.4	3.4	28.6
MOTOR CARRIER	63	100.0	3.7	14.4	30.0	11.1	13.0	5.2	13.9	4.7	3.8
PRIVATE TRUCK	15	100.0	-	6.7	17.6	1.3	42.8	13.1	18.5	-	-
AIR	-	100.0	-	3.7	25.4	46.3	-	-	24.6	-	-
WATER	-	100.0	-	-	-	-	-	-	-	-	-
OTHER	-	100.0	-	1.0	1.7	-	97.2	-	-	-	-
UNKNOWN	-	100.0	-	-	-	100.0	-	-	-	-	-
EAST SOUTH CENTRAL	719	100.0	2.6	18.8	19.5	9.5	12.2	6.8	12.4	4.7	13.5
RAIL	410	100.0	1.1	22.6	19.1	11.4	4.5	6.4	12.0	6.5	16.4
MOTOR CARRIER	287	100.0	3.7	14.8	19.3	7.2	23.9	5.8	13.1	2.6	9.6
PRIVATE TRUCK	21	100.0	17.7	2.4	30.0	2.5	4.7	25.0	9.1	-	8.5
AIR	-	100.0	-	-	7.9	-	.7	-	-	-	91.3
WATER	-	100.0	-	-	-	96.8	-	2.1	1.1	-	-
OTHER	-	100.0	-	-	-	-	-	-	-	-	-
UNKNOWN	-	100.0	-	-	-	-	-	-	-	-	-
WEST SOUTH CENTRAL	244	100.0	5.0	15.5	24.4	6.6	20.1	8.5	3.5	3.5	13.0
RAIL	113	100.0	-	14.2	19.4	6.9	20.0	10.7	3.0	4.2	21.5
MOTOR CARRIER	111	100.0	9.4	17.4	29.1	6.1	17.6	6.7	4.6	2.5	6.5
PRIVATE TRUCK	17	100.0	-	12.5	28.4	8.5	38.6	6.5	5.5	-	-
AIR	-	100.0	-	-	-	-	-	-	-	-	-
WATER	-	100.0	-	47.2	-	-	27.2	25.6	-	-	-
OTHER	-	100.0	-	-	-	-	-	-	-	-	-
UNKNOWN	1	100.0	100.0	-	-	-	-	-	-	-	-
PACIFIC	339	100.0	.9	9.9	17.5	11.4	3.8	6.0	8.5	13.2	28.8
RAIL	176	100.0	1.5	19.1	15.7	19.0	7.2	8.4	10.6	5.9	12.5
MOTOR CARRIER	160	100.0	.1	-	19.7	3.2	-	3.3	6.3	21.5	45.7
PRIVATE TRUCK	1	100.0	-	-	-	-	-	3.5	-	4.2	92.3
AIR	-	100.0	1.5	.7	51.0	-	24.7	5.0	.8	16.3	-
WATER	-	100.0	-	-	-	-	-	-	-	52.0	48.0
OTHER	-	100.0	-	-	-	-	-	-	-	-	100.0
UNKNOWN	-	100.0	-	-	-	-	-	-	-	-	-

See footnotes at end of table 4.

TABLE 3. **TCC GROUP 301**—Percent Distribution of Geographic Division of Destination and Means of Transport, by Geographic Division of Origin: 1972

Geographic division of destination and means of transport	Number (thousands of tons)	Percent distribution by division of origin[1]								
		U.S. total	New England	Middle Atlantic	East North Central	West North Central	South Atlantic	East South Central	West South Central	Mountain	Pacific
TONS OF SHIPMENTS											
U.S. TOTAL	5 646	100.0	(D)	12.5	27.7	7.8	7.2	22.4	5.9	(D)	8.3
RAIL	2 311	100.0	(D)	8.7	29.3	5.3	10.5	29.1	7.2	(D)	7.8
MOTOR CARRIER	2 818	100.0	(D)	14.0	27.5	11.1	4.4	18.6	5.1	(D)	9.8
PRIVATE TRUCK	427	100.0	(D)	25.0	23.2	.8	9.3	16.0	4.8	(D)	2.2
AIR	63	100.0	(D)	-	.4	.8	.1	.2	-	(D)	2.2
WATER	3	100.0	(D)	91.4	-	-	-	.1	.2	(D)	.2
OTHER	3	100.0	(D)	-	-	-	-	-	-	(D)	8.6
UNKNOWN	19	100.0	(D)	-	57.7	16.4	.1	19.7	.1	(D)	1.2
			(D)	-	51.9	3.1	4.3	-	6.5	(D)	-
NEW ENGLAND	137	100.0	(D)	32.5	16.1	1.6	3.8	12.9	6.2	(D)	-
RAIL	16	100.0	(D)	-	-	-	11.7	23.9	-	(D)	.9
MOTOR CARRIER	115	100.0	(D)	38.6	19.2	1.9	2.8	8.9	6.3	(D)	6.6
PRIVATE TRUCK	3	100.0	(D)	.4	-	-	.4	99.2	-	(D)	.1
AIR	-	100.0	(D)	-	74.0	-	-	-	-	(D)	-
WATER	-	100.0	(D)	-	-	-	-	-	-	(D)	26.0
OTHER	-	100.0	(D)	-	12.5	-	-	-	-	(D)	-
UNKNOWN	1	100.0	(D)	-	-	-	-	-	100.0	(D)	-
MIDDLE ATLANTIC	751	100.0	(D)	35.1	18.2	3.0	9.4	22.8	4.2	(D)	-
RAIL	296	100.0	(D)	17.6	12.5	1.7	12.4	40.2	4.5	(D)	1.9
MOTOR CARRIER	380	100.0	(D)	40.6	25.4	4.4	7.5	13.5	4.3	(D)	4.7
PRIVATE TRUCK	67	100.0	(D)	85.1	4.0	-	7.2	1.3	2.5	(D)	-
AIR	-	100.0	(D)	-	81.9	-	7.2	-	-	(D)	-
WATER	-	100.0	(D)	-	-	-	-	-	-	(D)	.6
OTHER	-	100.0	(D)	-	-	-	-	-	-	(D)	-
UNKNOWN	6	100.0	(D)	-	11.4	87.7	-	-	.3	(D)	-
EAST NORTH CENTRAL	1 635	100.0	(D)	7.8	50.9	7.9	6.5	17.2	4.5	(D)	1.9
RAIL	674	100.0	(D)	4.9	54.0	3.2	9.2	22.3	4.3	(D)	2.1
MOTOR CARRIER	848	100.0	(D)	10.9	47.4	12.6	4.2	13.3	4.6	(D)	2.0
PRIVATE TRUCK	101	100.0	(D)	2.4	54.5	.2	9.0	18.8	5.0	(D)	-
AIR	-	100.0	(D)	-	15.0	-	22.7	16.7	-	(D)	28.8
WATER	-	100.0	(D)	-	-	-	-	-	-	(D)	-
OTHER	1	100.0	(D)	-	99.6	.1	-	-	-	(D)	-
UNKNOWN	10	100.0	(D)	-	100.0	-	-	-	-	(D)	-
WEST NORTH CENTRAL	673	100.0	(D)	6.7	24.1	27.1	3.9	20.8	5.8	(D)	4.1
RAIL	328	100.0	(D)	8.8	24.2	19.7	5.2	28.1	6.6	(D)	4.1
MOTOR CARRIER	288	100.0	(D)	5.5	24.0	40.7	2.7	15.8	4.7	(D)	7.2
PRIVATE TRUCK	54	100.0	(D)	-	24.1	1.5	.4	3.0	6.2	(D)	1.3
AIR	-	100.0	(D)	-	66.1	-	33.7	.2	-	(D)	-
WATER	-	100.0	(D)	-	-	-	-	-	-	(D)	-
OTHER	1	100.0	(D)	-	43.5	-	-	56.3	-	(D)	-
UNKNOWN	-	100.0	(D)	-	12.6	-	87.4	-	-	(D)	-
SOUTH ATLANTIC	634	100.0	(D)	19.5	20.1	2.3	13.6	30.0	8.8	(D)	1.0
RAIL	194	100.0	(D)	12.7	24.6	-	19.9	26.2	13.4	(D)	3.3
MOTOR CARRIER	356	100.0	(D)	15.5	19.2	4.0	8.4	38.2	6.3	(D)	-
PRIVATE TRUCK	82	100.0	(D)	52.8	13.3	-	21.1	4.0	8.8	(D)	-
AIR	-	100.0	(D)	-	68.0	2.4	-	2.9	-	(D)	26.6
WATER	-	100.0	(D)	-	-	-	-	-	-	(D)	-
OTHER	-	100.0	(D)	-	94.6	.3	2.3	-	1.4	(D)	-
UNKNOWN	-	100.0	(D)	-	-	-	-	-	-	(D)	-
EAST SOUTH CENTRAL	477	100.0	(D)	8.3	20.4	3.6	9.9	43.7	11.3	(D)	2.6
RAIL	267	100.0	(D)	9.9	18.5	-	13.0	40.9	14.3	(D)	3.4
MOTOR CARRIER	162	100.0	(D)	7.1	25.8	10.4	4.5	40.8	8.5	(D)	2.0
PRIVATE TRUCK	47	100.0	(D)	2.9	12.5	.7	10.8	69.2	3.7	(D)	.1
AIR	-	100.0	(D)	-	28.8	-	-	2.0	-	(D)	18.2
WATER	-	100.0	(D)	-	-	-	-	-	-	(D)	-
OTHER	-	100.0	(D)	-	66.6	-	-	28.2	2.5	(D)	-
UNKNOWN	-	100.0	(D)	-	100.0	-	-	-	-	(D)	-
WEST SOUTH CENTRAL	437	100.0	(D)	5.4	13.6	7.2	8.3	39.3	8.2	(D)	4.9
RAIL	195	100.0	(D)	5.8	15.1	7.9	12.7	44.0	7.4	(D)	7.0
MOTOR CARRIER	208	100.0	(D)	5.1	11.1	6.7	4.2	38.0	10.2	(D)	3.7
PRIVATE TRUCK	32	100.0	(D)	4.7	20.4	6.4	8.3	19.5	.2	(D)	-
AIR	-	100.0	(D)	6.1	50.1	.8	7.7	-	-	(D)	.7
WATER	-	100.0	(D)	-	-	-	-	-	-	(D)	-
OTHER	-	100.0	(D)	-	78.9	5.4	-	15.7	-	(D)	-
UNKNOWN	-	100.0	(D)	-	100.0	-	-	-	-	(D)	-
MOUNTAIN	228	100.0	(D)	8.2	14.3	6.9	2.4	12.3	5.0	(D)	32.0
RAIL	74	100.0	(D)	11.2	29.3	-	5.3	28.1	9.0	(D)	17.2
MOTOR CARRIER	127	100.0	(D)	7.8	5.3	12.4	1.3	5.7	2.7	(D)	47.2
PRIVATE TRUCK	26	100.0	(D)	1.9	16.0	-	-	-	4.5	(D)	.5
AIR	-	100.0	(D)	16.5	18.4	-	-	-	-	(D)	65.1
WATER	-	100.0	(D)	-	-	-	-	-	-	(D)	-
OTHER	-	100.0	(D)	-	-	4.5	-	-	-	(D)	66.9
UNKNOWN	-	100.0	(D)	-	-	-	-	-	-	(D)	-
PACIFIC	670	100.0	(D)	2.9	13.8	3.6	3.5	8.3	3.4	(D)	41.7
RAIL	263	100.0	(D)	6.0	18.1	5.6	8.6	14.7	6.7	(D)	32.4
MOTOR CARRIER	330	100.0	(D)	.1	13.6	2.7	.3	4.7	1.6	(D)	56.0
PRIVATE TRUCK	10	100.0	(D)	-	-	-	-	9.2	-	(D)	90.7
AIR	62	100.0	(D)	-	-	-	-	.1	-	(D)	-
WATER	3	100.0	(D)	91.4	-	-	-	-	-	(D)	8.6
OTHER	-	100.0	(D)	-	37.7	-	-	-	-	(D)	62.3
UNKNOWN	-	100.0	(D)	-	-	100.0	-	-	-	(D)	-

See footnotes at end of table 4.

TABLE 3. **TCC GROUP 301—Percent Distribution of Geographic Division of Destination and Means of Transport, by Geographic Division of Origin: 1972**—Continued

Geographic division of destination and means of transport	Number	Percent distribution by division of origin[1]									
		U.S. total	New England	Middle Atlantic	East North Central	West North Central	South Atlantic	East South Central	West South Central	Mountain	Pacific
TON-MILES OF SHIPMENTS	(millions of ton-miles)										
U.S. TOTAL	3 057	100.0	(D)	10.5	21.6	6.9	8.3	23.5	8.0	(D)	11.1
RAIL	1 421	100.0	(D)	10.1	19.7	4.7	12.3	28.9	8.0	(D)	12.4
MOTOR CARRIER	1 415	100.0	(D)	10.0	24.0	9.9	4.5	20.3	7.9	(D)	11.3
PRIVATE TRUCK	149	100.0	(D)	17.9	23.2	1.3	10.6	14.6	11.5	(D)	1.3
AIR	53	100.0	(D)	.1	.5	-	.1	.3	-	(D)	.3
WATER	7	100.0	(D)	90.6	-	-	-	-	-	(D)	9.4
OTHER	1	100.0	(D)	-	36.7	38.5	.1	23.1	.3	(D)	.4
UNKNOWN	8	100.0	(D)	-	50.6	11.7	8.0	-	19.5	(D)	-
NEW ENGLAND	75	100.0	(D)	16.6	25.4	3.2	5.6	25.0	16.0	(D)	3.9
RAIL	9	100.0	(D)	-	-	-	20.0	49.2	-	(D)	29.5
MOTOR CARRIER	61	100.0	(D)	20.6	31.6	4.0	3.9	17.3	17.2	(D)	.4
PRIVATE TRUCK	3	100.0	(D)	-	-	-	.1	99.8	-	(D)	-
AIR	-	100.0	(D)	-	32.5	-	-	-	-	(D)	67.5
WATER	-	100.0	(D)	-	-	-	-	-	-	(D)	-
OTHER	-	100.0	(D)	-	93.2	-	-	-	-	(D)	-
UNKNOWN	1	100.0	(D)	-	-	-	-	-	100.0	(D)	-
MIDDLE ATLANTIC	353	100.0	(D)	8.6	18.2	5.7	6.9	38.4	10.7	(D)	9.5
RAIL	189	100.0	(D)	2.3	10.7	2.8	7.6	48.8	8.5	(D)	17.7
MOTOR CARRIER	150	100.0	(D)	12.7	28.7	9.5	6.1	28.2	12.9	(D)	-
PRIVATE TRUCK	11	100.0	(D)	59.7	8.4	-	9.1	4.5	18.4	(D)	-
AIR	-	100.0	(D)	-	82.5	-	8.4	-	-	(D)	4.2
WATER	-	100.0	(D)	-	-	-	-	-	-	(D)	-
OTHER	-	100.0	(D)	-	4.5	95.0	-	-	.3	(D)	-
UNKNOWN	-	100.0	(D)	-	-	-	-	-	-	(D)	-
EAST NORTH CENTRAL	586	100.0	(D)	8.8	21.0	9.1	9.5	23.9	10.1	(D)	10.1
RAIL	228	100.0	(D)	6.6	17.5	4.9	14.8	34.4	9.7	(D)	12.2
MOTOR CARRIER	326	100.0	(D)	10.9	22.2	13.0	5.8	17.0	9.9	(D)	9.7
PRIVATE TRUCK	27	100.0	(D)	3.3	24.3	.1	10.3	24.0	17.8	(D)	-
AIR	-	100.0	(D)	-	2.7	-	12.5	9.5	-	(D)	65.2
WATER	-	100.0	(D)	-	-	-	-	-	-	(D)	-
OTHER	-	100.0	(D)	.2	95.1	1.3	-	-	-	(D)	-
UNKNOWN	4	100.0	(D)	-	100.0	-	-	-	-	(D)	-
WEST NORTH CENTRAL	322	100.0	(D)	13.3	20.6	13.8	7.0	21.2	5.0	(D)	12.0
RAIL	180	100.0	(D)	15.3	17.7	10.2	8.1	25.9	4.3	(D)	18.6
MOTOR CARRIER	118	100.0	(D)	12.9	24.5	21.8	5.9	17.3	5.8	(D)	4.4
PRIVATE TRUCK	21	100.0	(D)	-	23.4	.9	.9	2.6	6.8	(D)	-
AIR	-	100.0	(D)	-	65.2	-	34.7	.1	-	(D)	-
WATER	-	100.0	(D)	-	-	-	-	-	-	(D)	-
OTHER	-	100.0	(D)	-	46.5	-	-	53.0	-	(D)	-
UNKNOWN	-	100.0	(D)	-	9.1	-	90.9	-	-	(D)	-
SOUTH ATLANTIC	319	100.0	(D)	14.4	23.0	3.3	8.4	27.6	15.4	(D)	4.0
RAIL	102	100.0	(D)	8.8	27.3	-	11.4	18.0	22.1	(D)	12.4
MOTOR CARRIER	178	100.0	(D)	11.7	21.3	5.9	4.6	38.5	11.0	(D)	-
PRIVATE TRUCK	37	100.0	(D)	42.0	19.5	-	18.1	2.7	17.6	(D)	-
AIR	-	100.0	(D)	-	48.9	.9	-	1.3	-	(D)	48.9
WATER	-	100.0	(D)	-	-	-	-	-	-	(D)	-
OTHER	-	100.0	(D)	-	92.8	.8	3.0	-	2.3	(D)	-
UNKNOWN	-	100.0	(D)	-	-	-	-	-	-	(D)	-
EAST SOUTH CENTRAL	199	100.0	(D)	13.0	25.3	4.4	11.3	24.4	10.4	(D)	10.2
RAIL	115	100.0	(D)	15.0	23.8	-	14.9	22.9	10.5	(D)	12.9
MOTOR CARRIER	71	100.0	(D)	11.2	28.2	12.2	4.6	23.3	10.4	(D)	7.4
PRIVATE TRUCK	12	100.0	(D)	5.5	22.6	.6	17.1	44.5	9.1	(D)	.6
AIR	-	100.0	(D)	-	19.1	-	-	.3	-	(D)	32.0
WATER	-	100.0	(D)	-	-	-	-	-	-	(D)	-
OTHER	-	100.0	(D)	-	73.3	-	-	18.7	3.0	(D)	-
UNKNOWN	-	100.0	(D)	-	100.0	-	-	-	-	(D)	-
WEST SOUTH CENTRAL	307	100.0	(D)	9.5	16.7	6.3	12.0	29.0	2.8	(D)	9.4
RAIL	145	100.0	(D)	9.9	17.5	6.3	17.3	33.8	2.4	(D)	12.9
MOTOR CARRIER	138	100.0	(D)	9.5	14.5	6.1	6.4	27.3	3.7	(D)	7.4
PRIVATE TRUCK	22	100.0	(D)	7.2	24.9	7.2	12.9	8.6	-	(D)	-
AIR	-	100.0	(D)	6.1	43.6	.3	6.9	-	-	(D)	.6
WATER	-	100.0	(D)	-	-	-	-	-	-	(D)	-
OTHER	-	100.0	(D)	-	83.5	6.3	-	10.2	-	(D)	-
UNKNOWN	-	100.0	(D)	-	100.0	-	-	-	-	(D)	-
MOUNTAIN	185	100.0	(D)	17.0	20.9	6.3	4.8	18.3	4.6	(D)	24.3
RAIL	85	100.0	(D)	16.8	27.3	-	7.0	31.1	5.6	(D)	12.3
MOTOR CARRIER	90	100.0	(D)	18.0	10.2	12.9	3.3	8.1	3.1	(D)	37.8
PRIVATE TRUCK	8	100.0	(D)	9.1	70.2	-	-	-	10.7	(D)	.9
AIR	-	100.0	(D)	36.4	27.6	-	-	-	-	(D)	36.0
WATER	-	100.0	(D)	-	-	-	-	-	-	(D)	-
OTHER	-	100.0	(D)	-	-	3.1	-	-	-	(D)	46.0
UNKNOWN	-	100.0	(D)	-	-	-	-	-	-	(D)	-
PACIFIC	707	100.0	(D)	7.0	24.4	5.5	7.4	13.7	4.5	(D)	13.8
RAIL	363	100.0	(D)	11.4	23.1	6.2	13.7	18.5	6.7	(D)	6.1
MOTOR CARRIER	279	100.0	(D)	.4	31.7	5.5	.9	9.9	2.6	(D)	26.2
PRIVATE TRUCK	3	100.0	(D)	-	.3	-	-	50.9	-	(D)	48.8
AIR	52	100.0	(D)	-	-	-	-	.2	-	(D)	-
WATER	7	100.0	(D)	90.6	-	-	-	-	-	(D)	9.4
OTHER	-	100.0	(D)	-	93.9	-	-	-	-	(D)	6.1
UNKNOWN	-	100.0	(D)	-	-	100.0	-	-	-	(D)	-

See footnotes at end of table 4.

TABLE 4. **TCC GROUP 301—Percent Distribution of Distance Shipped and Weight of Shipment, by Means of Transport: 1972**

Distance shipped and weight of shipment[2] [3]	Number	Percent distribution by means of transport							
		All means of transport	Rail	Motor carrier	Private truck	Air	Water	Other	Unknown
TONS OF SHIPMENTS	(thousands of tons)								
U.S. TOTAL..........	5 466	100.0	40.0	50.7	7.7	1.2	.1	.1	.4
UNDER 100 MILES.........	762	100.0	41.8	46.0	12.0	-	-	.2	-
UNDER 1000 POUNDS.....	17	100.0	-	87.1	9.2	-	-	3.7	-
1000 TO 9999 POUNDS...	139	100.0	-	75.6	24.0	-	-	.4	-
10000 TO 29999 POUNDS.	250	100.0	11.9	75.5	12.6	-	-	-	-
30000 TO 59999 POUNDS.	336	100.0	80.4	12.3	7.3	-	-	-	-
60000 TO 89999 POUNDS.	18	100.0	100.0	-	-	-	-	-	-
90000 POUNDS AND OVER.	-	100.0	-	-	-	-	-	-	-
100 TO 199 MILES........	592	100.0	31.9	55.6	11.2	-	-	-	1.3
UNDER 1000 POUNDS.....	17	100.0	-	97.2	2.0	.1	-	.6	.1
1000 TO 9999 POUNDS...	103	100.0	.4	92.5	7.1	-	-	-	-
10000 TO 29999 POUNDS.	206	100.0	4.3	75.4	16.5	-	-	-	3.8
30000 TO 59999 POUNDS.	262	100.0	67.2	23.4	9.4	-	-	-	-
60000 TO 89999 POUNDS.	3	100.0	100.0	-	-	-	-	-	-
90000 POUNDS AND OVER.	-	100.0	-	-	-	-	-	-	-
200 TO 299 MILES........	556	100.0	31.2	62.0	6.8	-	-	-	-
UNDER 1000 POUNDS.....	20	100.0	-	98.5	.9	-	-	.5	-
1000 TO 9999 POUNDS...	100	100.0	.1	94.6	5.3	-	-	-	-
10000 TO 29999 POUNDS.	207	100.0	3.8	82.5	13.6	-	-	-	-
30000 TO 59999 POUNDS.	216	100.0	76.3	21.8	1.9	-	-	-	-
60000 TO 89999 POUNDS.	3	100.0	-	100.0	-	-	-	-	-
90000 POUNDS AND OVER.	7	100.0	-	100.0	-	-	-	-	-
300 TO 499 MILES........	1 167	100.0	35.4	52.7	11.0	-	-	.1	.8
UNDER 1000 POUNDS.....	24	100.0	.1	98.3	.4	.3	-	.8	-
1000 TO 9999 POUNDS...	176	100.0	-	93.0	6.8	-	-	.2	-
10000 TO 29999 POUNDS.	452	100.0	13.0	64.3	22.6	-	-	.1	-
30000 TO 59999 POUNDS.	494	100.0	69.5	25.8	2.8	-	-	-	1.8
60000 TO 89999 POUNDS.	16	100.0	41.3	58.7	-	-	-	-	-
90000 POUNDS AND OVER.	4	100.0	100.0	-	-	-	-	-	-
500 TO 999 MILES........	1 752	100.0	40.3	51.6	4.4	3.6	-	-	.1
UNDER 1000 POUNDS.....	34	100.0	1.1	97.1	.6	.7	-	.5	-
1000 TO 9999 POUNDS...	207	100.0	1.6	91.2	7.2	-	-	-	-
10000 TO 29999 POUNDS.	553	100.0	8.7	84.0	7.3	-	-	-	-
30000 TO 59999 POUNDS.	941	100.0	67.8	23.0	2.3	6.7	-	-	-
60000 TO 89999 POUNDS.	13	100.0	98.6	1.4	-	-	-	-	.1
90000 POUNDS AND OVER.	2	100.0	100.0	-	-	-	-	-	-
1000 TO 1499 MILES......	299	100.0	53.4	40.5	5.7	-	-	-	.4
UNDER 1000 POUNDS.....	6	100.0	.1	96.9	.9	1.8	-	.2	.1
1000 TO 9999 POUNDS...	45	100.0	1.9	95.9	2.2	-	-	-	-
10000 TO 29999 POUNDS.	89	100.0	27.8	52.9	17.9	-	-	-	1.4
30000 TO 59999 POUNDS.	158	100.0	85.0	15.0	-	-	-	-	-
60000 TO 89999 POUNDS.	-	100.0	-	-	-	-	-	-	-
90000 POUNDS AND OVER.	-	100.0	-	-	-	-	-	-	-
1500 MILES OR OVER......	335	100.0	66.8	30.9	1.1	.1	1.0	-	.2
UNDER 1000 POUNDS.....	5	100.0	.3	95.1	1.6	2.7	-	.4	-
1000 TO 9999 POUNDS...	15	100.0	2.2	92.1	3.3	.5	1.9	-	-
10000 TO 29999 POUNDS.	52	100.0	29.4	57.6	6.2	-	5.7	-	1.2
30000 TO 59999 POUNDS.	215	100.0	79.3	20.7	-	-	-	-	-
60000 TO 89999 POUNDS.	46	100.0	80.1	19.9	-	-	-	-	-
90000 POUNDS AND OVER.	-	100.0	-	-	-	-	-	-	-
TON-MILES OF SHIPMENTS	(millions of ton-miles)								
U.S. TOTAL..........	3 004	100.0	46.3	46.3	4.9	1.8	.3	-	.3
UNDER 100 MILES.........	42	100.0	39.2	50.0	10.8	-	-	-	-
UNDER 1000 POUNDS.....	-	100.0	-	91.8	6.9	-	-	1.3	-
1000 TO 9999 POUNDS...	7	100.0	-	81.5	18.4	-	-	.1	-
10000 TO 29999 POUNDS.	15	100.0	11.4	77.4	11.3	-	-	-	-
30000 TO 59999 POUNDS.	18	100.0	76.4	15.4	8.2	-	-	-	-
60000 TO 89999 POUNDS.	1	100.0	100.0	-	-	-	-	-	-
90000 POUNDS AND OVER.	-	100.0	-	-	-	-	-	-	-
100 TO 199 MILES........	89	100.0	31.6	54.9	12.4	-	-	-	1.1
UNDER 1000 POUNDS.....	2	100.0	-	97.1	2.1	.1	-	.6	.1
1000 TO 9999 POUNDS...	15	100.0	.4	91.5	8.0	-	-	-	-
10000 TO 29999 POUNDS.	30	100.0	3.9	76.3	16.4	-	-	-	3.3
30000 TO 59999 POUNDS.	40	100.0	65.7	22.5	11.8	-	-	-	-
60000 TO 89999 POUNDS.	-	100.0	100.0	-	-	-	-	-	-
90000 POUNDS AND OVER.	-	100.0	-	-	-	-	-	-	-

See footnotes at end of table 4.

TABLE 4. **TCC GROUP 301—Percent Distribution of Distance Shipped and Weight of Shipment, by Means of Transport: 1972**—Continued

Distance shipped and weight of shipment [2] [3]	Number	Percent distribution by means of transport							
		All means of transport	Rail	Motor carrier	Private truck	Air	Water	Other	Unknown
TON-MILES OF SHIPMENTS	(millions of ton-miles)								
200 TO 299 MILES........	140	100.0	31.6	61.7	6.7	-	-	-	-
UNDER 1000 POUNDS.....	5	100.0	-	98.6	.9	-	-	.5	-
1000 TO 9999 POUNDS...	25	100.0	.1	94.4	5.5	-	-	-	-
10000 TO 29999 POUNDS.	52	100.0	4.3	82.5	13.3	-	-	-	-
30000 TO 59999 POUNDS.	54	100.0	77.1	21.2	1.7	-	-	-	-
60000 TO 89999 POUNDS.	-	100.0	-	100.0	-	-	-	-	-
90000 POUNDS AND OVER.	1	100.0	-	100.0	-	-	-	-	-
300 TO 499 MILES........	457	100.0	36.9	52.0	10.1	-	-	.1	.9
UNDER 1000 POUNDS.....	9	100.0	.1	98.3	.4	.3	-	.9	-
1000 TO 9999 POUNDS...	67	100.0	-	93.9	5.8	-	-	.3	-
10000 TO 29999 POUNDS.	178	100.0	13.5	65.5	20.8	-	-	.2	-
30000 TO 59999 POUNDS.	194	100.0	71.5	23.6	2.8	-	-	-	2.1
60000 TO 89999 POUNDS.	5	100.0	51.0	49.0	-	-	-	-	-
90000 POUNDS AND OVER.	2	100.0	100.0	-	-	-	-	-	-
500 TO 999 MILES........	1 259	100.0	39.6	52.0	4.1	4.2	-	-	.1
UNDER 1000 POUNDS.....	24	100.0	1.1	97.2	.6	.6	-	.5	-
1000 TO 9999 POUNDS...	146	100.0	2.1	91.1	6.8	-	-	-	-
10000 TO 29999 POUNDS.	397	100.0	8.2	84.8	6.9	-	-	-	-
30000 TO 59999 POUNDS.	679	100.0	66.4	23.7	2.0	7.7	-	.1	.1
60000 TO 89999 POUNDS.	10	100.0	98.2	1.8	-	-	-	-	-
90000 POUNDS AND OVER.	2	100.0	100.0	-	-	-	-	-	-
1000 TO 1499 MILES......	357	100.0	54.2	40.0	5.3	-	-	-	.5
UNDER 1000 POUNDS.....	7	100.0	.1	96.9	.8	1.9	-	.1	.2
1000 TO 9999 POUNDS...	53	100.0	1.8	96.0	2.2	-	-	-	-
10000 TO 29999 POUNDS.	104	100.0	28.1	53.4	16.9	-	-	-	1.6
30000 TO 59999 POUNDS.	191	100.0	85.2	14.8	-	-	-	-	-
60000 TO 89999 POUNDS.	-	100.0	-	-	-	-	-	-	-
90000 POUNDS AND OVER.	-	100.0	-	-	-	-	-	-	-
1500 MILES OR OVER......	656	100.0	67.3	30.2	1.1	.1	1.2	-	.2
UNDER 1000 POUNDS.....	10	100.0	.4	94.7	1.8	2.7	-	.4	-
1000 TO 9999 POUNDS...	30	100.0	2.3	92.3	2.6	.4	2.4	-	-
10000 TO 29999 POUNDS.	105	100.0	32.9	53.8	5.6	-	6.7	-	.9
30000 TO 59999 POUNDS.	420	100.0	79.8	20.2	-	-	-	-	-
60000 TO 89999 POUNDS.	90	100.0	78.9	21.1	-	-	-	-	-
90000 POUNDS AND OVER.	-	100.0	-	-	-	-	-	-	-

Note: Detail may not add to total due to rounding. The introductory table shows the estimates of sampling variability for tons; sampling variability for ton-miles has not been estimated. See the map in the Introduction for the States comprising the geographic divisions of the United States.

Shipments excluded from the survey are those moving by pipeline (primarily petroleum products from refineries), parcel post shipments, and commodities moved by own power (motorized vehicles, aircraft, etc.) or towed (prefabricated buildings, etc.). Local shipments (commodities shipped less than 25 miles from the plant) and shipments within the same city are also excluded. Shipments to Alaska and Hawaii from the 48 conterminous States and the District of Columbia are included; however, no data were obtained for shipments originating in Alaska and Hawaii.

- Represents zero or rounds to zero.   (D) Withheld to avoid disclosing figures for individual companies.

[1]Production of this commodity is concentrated in the geographic divisions shown; figures and distributions for geographic divisions not shown are included in the total.

[2]Distances of shipments to foreign destinations are calculated only to the U.S. port of exit.

[3]Includes only shipments represented by bills of lading and invoices. Summary records which did not show individual weights of shipments are not included.

TCC 306. Miscellaneous Fabricated Rubber Products

Comparisons of Tons and Ton-Miles of Shipments for
Geographic Divisions of Origin and for Sampling Variability: 1972 and 1967

Geographic division of origin	Estimates				Relative sampling variability in tons (percent)	
	1972		1967		1972	1967
	Tons (thousands)	Ton-miles (millions)	Tons (thousands)	Ton-miles (millions)		
U.S. total	1,866	894	2,207	1,103	13.0	11.8
New England	96	42	284	130	15.4	(*)
Middle Atlantic	171	106	386	211	43.9	(*)
East North Central	812	263	1,119	413	19.9	(*)
West North Central	(D)	(D)	30	21	(*)	(*)
South Atlantic	190	126	192	181	26.1	(*)
East South Central	(D)	(D)	23	21	(*)	(*)
West South Central	(D)	(D)	31	33	(*)	(*)
Mountain	(D)	(D)	44	42	(*)	(*)
Pacific	(D)	(D)	98	51	(*)	(*)

(D) Withheld to avoid disclosing figures for individual companies.   (*) Data not published.

TABLE 1. **TCC GROUP 306—Percent Distribution of Geographic Division of Origin and Distance Shipped, by Means of Transport: 1972**

Geographic division of origin[1] and distance shipped[2]	Number	Percent distribution by means of transport							
		All means of transport	Rail	Motor carrier	Private truck	Air	Water	Other	Unknown
TONS OF SHIPMENTS	(thousands of tons)								
U.S. TOTAL...........	1 866	100.0	11.9	62.9	23.7	.8	.2	.4	.1
NEW ENGLAND.............	96	100.0	12.5	78.1	9.0	.2	-	.1	-
UNDER 100 MILES.......	39	100.0	6.0	80.1	13.7	-	-	.1	-
100 TO 199 MILES......	11	100.0	7.2	66.9	25.8	.1	-	.1	-
200 TO 299 MILES......	.4	100.0	.1	99.0	.8	-	-	-	-
300 TO 499 MILES......	8	100.0	-	99.7	-	.2	-	.1	-
500 TO 999 MILES......	16	100.0	18.7	79.0	1.2	1.0	-	.2	-
1000 TO 1499 MILES....	10	100.0	47.9	52.0	-	-	-	.1	-
1500 MILES OR OVER....	3	100.0	11.9	87.4	-	.4	-	.2	-
MIDDLE ATLANTIC.........	171	100.0	8.7	74.4	15.6	.5	-	.8	-
UNDER 100 MILES.......	17	100.0	-	63.3	34.7	.1	-	1.9	-
100 TO 199 MILES......	12	100.0	-	76.8	19.2	-	-	4.0	-
200 TO 299 MILES......	38	100.0	-	94.9	4.6	.2	-	.3	-
300 TO 499 MILES......	21	100.0	-	43.2	55.3	.1	-	1.4	-
500 TO 999 MILES......	51	100.0	8.3	88.8	2.4	.5	-	.6	-
1000 TO 1499 MILES....	13	100.0	33.5	57.7	7.8	.4	-	.6	-
1500 MILES OR OVER....	16	100.0	37.8	47.4	11.8	3.0	-	-	-
EAST NORTH CENTRAL......	812	100.0	8.3	79.3	10.8	1.1	-	.5	-
UNDER 100 MILES.......	224	100.0	3.8	83.8	12.1	-	-	.2	-
100 TO 199 MILES......	186	100.0	4.2	86.2	6.9	2.5	-	.2	-
200 TO 299 MILES......	116	100.0	6.3	76.1	16.2	.6	-	.7	-
300 TO 499 MILES......	105	100.0	11.0	71.5	16.2	.6	-	.8	-
500 TO 999 MILES......	142	100.0	12.0	78.6	6.4	1.8	-	1.2	-
1000 TO 1499 MILES....	14	100.0	44.7	53.6	.9	.1	-	.3	.4
1500 MILES OR OVER....	23	100.0	35.0	51.2	10.9	2.5	-	.3	.1
SOUTH ATLANTIC..........	190	100.0	21.6	32.7	44.7	-	-	.8	.2
UNDER 100 MILES.......	59	100.0	.5	15.6	83.9	-	-	.1	.7
100 TO 199 MILES......	21	100.0	7.3	48.3	42.9	-	-	.8	-
200 TO 299 MILES......	4	100.0	8.6	89.8	1.0	.1	-	.4	-
300 TO 499 MILES......	37	100.0	3.8	37.0	58.7	.1	-	.4	-
500 TO 999 MILES......	23	100.0	12.6	66.6	16.9	.1	-	3.1	.7
1000 TO 1499 MILES....	7	100.0	1.5	98.2	-	.1	-	.2	-
1500 MILES OR OVER....	36	100.0	95.1	3.8	-	-	-	1.1	-
TON-MILES OF SHIPMENTS	(millions of ton-miles)								
U.S. TOTAL...........	894	100.0	23.9	57.1	16.6	1.2	.3	.5	.4
NEW ENGLAND.............	42	100.0	22.6	75.1	1.8	.4	-	.1	-
UNDER 100 MILES.......	2	100.0	8.6	84.2	7.2	-	-	.1	-
100 TO 199 MILES......	1	100.0	5.7	69.4	24.7	-	-	.1	-
200 TO 299 MILES......	1	100.0	.1	99.0	.8	-	-	.1	-
300 TO 499 MILES......	3	100.0	-	99.7	-	.2	-	.2	-
500 TO 999 MILES......	12	100.0	20.8	77.2	1.0	.8	-	.1	-
1000 TO 1499 MILES....	12	100.0	46.3	53.6	-	-	-	.2	-
1500 MILES OR OVER....	9	100.0	12.0	87.4	-	.4	-	-	-
MIDDLE ATLANTIC.........	106	100.0	19.9	67.3	11.1	1.4	-	.4	-
UNDER 100 MILES.......	-	100.0	-	61.6	37.0	.1	-	1.4	-
100 TO 199 MILES......	1	100.0	-	78.8	16.2	-	-	5.0	-
200 TO 299 MILES......	9	100.0	-	95.1	4.4	.1	-	.3	-
300 TO 499 MILES......	9	100.0	-	42.1	56.4	.2	-	1.3	-
500 TO 999 MILES......	32	100.0	8.9	87.7	2.7	.7	-	-	-
1000 TO 1499 MILES....	15	100.0	33.5	58.2	7.3	.4	-	.6	-
1500 MILES OR OVER....	36	100.0	35.3	52.1	9.4	3.1	-	-	-
EAST NORTH CENTRAL......	263	100.0	16.8	71.4	9.3	1.5	-	.9	.1
UNDER 100 MILES.......	8	100.0	7.8	78.0	13.9	-	-	.3	-
100 TO 199 MILES......	28	100.0	4.4	86.6	6.5	2.3	-	.2	-
200 TO 299 MILES......	28	100.0	6.3	77.0	15.3	.6	-	.7	-
300 TO 499 MILES......	41	100.0	11.4	70.7	16.6	.6	-	.8	-
500 TO 999 MILES......	93	100.0	12.3	78.2	6.1	1.8	-	1.6	-
1000 TO 1499 MILES....	18	100.0	50.3	48.0	.9	.1	-	.3	.4
1500 MILES OR OVER....	45	100.0	33.7	53.4	9.9	2.6	-	.4	.1
SOUTH ATLANTIC..........	126	100.0	63.4	24.5	10.9	.1	-	1.1	.1
UNDER 100 MILES.......	2	100.0	1.3	24.4	74.2	-	-	.2	-
100 TO 199 MILES......	3	100.0	5.8	49.2	43.6	-	-	.8	.7
200 TO 299 MILES......	1	100.0	8.8	89.7	1.0	.1	-	.5	-
300 TO 499 MILES......	14	100.0	4.1	38.3	57.1	.1	-	.4	-
500 TO 999 MILES......	15	100.0	13.5	66.8	16.3	.1	-	2.8	.6
1000 TO 1499 MILES....	8	100.0	1.4	98.3	-	.1	-	.2	-
1500 MILES OR OVER....	80	100.0	95.4	3.6	-	-	-	1.0	-

See footnotes at end of table 4.

TABLE 2. **TCC GROUP 306—Percent Distribution of Geographic Division of Origin and Means of Transport, by Geographic Division of Destination: 1972**

Geographic division of origin¹ and means of transport	Number	Percent distribution by division of destination									
		U.S. total	New England	Middle Atlantic	East North Central	West North Central	South Atlantic	East South Central	West South Central	Mountain	Pacific
TONS OF SHIPMENTS	(thousands of tons)										
U.S. TOTAL.............	1 866	100.0	4.4	12.4	39.1	5.9	10.4	3.6	5.1	1.8	17.2
RAIL................	222	100.0	.7	7.5	15.9	7.3	7.2	3.1	5.3	8.6	44.5
MOTOR CARRIER........	1 173	100.0	5.7	13.2	46.1	6.3	8.5	3.0	5.5	.8	11.0
PRIVATE TRUCK........	441	100.0	3.1	12.4	33.0	4.3	17.1	5.7	3.4	1.1	19.9
AIR.................	14	100.0	1.7	20.5	40.7	5.7	6.6	.6	12.8	1.5	9.8
WATER...............	3	100.0	-	-	-	-	-	-	-	-	100.0
OTHER...............	8	100.0	1.2	21.0	26.8	6.9	16.9	2.7	15.8	.4	8.3
UNKNOWN.............	1	100.0	-	65.2	21.0	.5	8.2	-	.3	3.2	1.6
NEW ENGLAND............	96	100.0	42.9	23.2	9.5	8.2	7.0	2.1	3.3	.3	3.6
RAIL................	12	100.0	7.0	20.0	2.4	45.1	17.2	-	4.5	.1	3.7
MOTOR CARRIER........	75	100.0	42.5	26.3	11.6	3.3	6.1	2.4	3.5	.4	3.9
PRIVATE TRUCK........	8	100.0	96.8	.7	-	-	.3	2.3	-	-	-
AIR.................	-	100.0	2.8	11.5	55.6	10.8	6.9	4.4	.6	.1	7.3
WATER...............	-	100.0	-	-	-	-	-	-	-	-	-
OTHER...............	-	100.0	29.9	16.9	30.5	.7	7.5	6.5	.1	3.6	4.3
UNKNOWN.............	-	100.0	-	-	-	-	-	-	-	-	-
MIDDLE ATLANTIC........	171	100.0	3.8	30.0	32.5	3.8	10.1	3.5	7.0	1.2	8.1
RAIL................	14	100.0	-	-	-	-	-	28.2	31.2	-	40.6
MOTOR CARRIER........	127	100.0	4.3	33.6	33.4	3.7	11.9	1.4	5.8	.1	5.8
PRIVATE TRUCK........	26	100.0	3.6	28.8	49.0	5.7	5.7	-	-	7.1	5.8
AIR.................	-	100.0	-	5.2	5.4	23.4	11.2	1.3	.9	2.4	50.2
WATER...............	-	100.0	-	-	-	-	-	-	-	-	-
OTHER...............	1	100.0	-	66.8	1.4	-	31.1	-	-	.1	.5
UNKNOWN.............	-	100.0	-	-	-	-	-	-	-	-	-
EAST NORTH CENTRAL......	812	100.0	2.6	11.9	62.3	7.2	6.3	2.1	3.8	.5	3.3
RAIL................	67	100.0	-	11.8	35.1	8.8	13.8	3.3	5.1	4.6	17.5
MOTOR CARRIER........	644	100.0	3.3	10.2	66.2	6.7	5.7	2.0	3.9	.2	1.8
PRIVATE TRUCK........	87	100.0	-	23.0	55.7	9.5	4.6	2.7	1.5	-	3.0
AIR.................	9	100.0	.6	26.7	56.2	5.0	4.5	-	.4	.2	6.3
WATER...............	-	100.0	-	-	-	-	-	-	-	-	-
OTHER...............	4	100.0	1.3	9.4	42.4	11.5	5.0	1.9	26.3	.4	1.7
UNKNOWN.............	-	100.0	-	-	51.0	5.1	-	-	1.9	29.6	12.5
SOUTH ATLANTIC.........	190	100.0	3.0	10.0	9.8	1.8	40.9	4.4	11.0	.5	18.6
RAIL................	41	100.0	1.8	.6	.7	1.0	10.0	.9	1.4	.5	83.1
MOTOR CARRIER........	62	100.0	5.8	14.2	20.3	4.6	32.8	3.8	16.0	1.1	1.4
PRIVATE TRUCK........	84	100.0	1.5	11.3	6.4	.2	62.0	6.5	12.2	-	1.4
AIR.................	-	100.0	-	20.4	11.0	-	3.0	34.5	15.1	6.8	9.2
WATER...............	-	100.0	-	-	-	-	-	-	-	-	-
OTHER...............	1	100.0	.4	15.8	9.2	.7	37.7	8.7	1.0	.7	25.9
UNKNOWN.............	-	100.0	-	-	51.5	-	48.5	-	-	-	-
TON-MILES OF SHIPMENTS	(millions of ton-miles)										
U.S. TOTAL.............	894	100.0	3.6	12.4	21.1	6.8	9.7	2.8	8.9	2.6	32.2
RAIL................	213	100.0	.4	4.4	4.6	5.2	3.7	2.2	5.0	5.1	69.4
MOTOR CARRIER........	511	100.0	5.0	13.8	24.5	8.2	12.4	2.9	11.3	1.4	20.4
PRIVATE TRUCK........	148	100.0	3.3	16.8	34.2	4.4	9.1	3.3	5.5	3.7	19.6
AIR.................	10	100.0	4.2	21.7	17.2	6.0	10.9	.8	12.7	1.8	24.7
WATER...............	2	100.0	-	-	-	-	-	-	-	-	100.0
OTHER...............	4	100.0	1.0	11.4	13.1	7.1	17.0	2.6	25.2	1.1	21.6
UNKNOWN.............	3	100.0	-	88.7	6.3	.2	.7	-	.1	2.1	1.9
NEW ENGLAND............	42	100.0	6.2	12.5	14.7	19.3	11.2	4.6	9.6	1.1	20.7
RAIL................	9	100.0	1.1	1.8	2.2	57.6	17.4	-	8.1	.1	11.7
MOTOR CARRIER........	32	100.0	6.0	16.1	18.7	8.3	9.6	5.7	10.4	1.5	23.9
PRIVATE TRUCK........	-	100.0	81.2	.8	-	-	.7	17.3	-	-	-
AIR.................	-	100.0	.4	4.7	42.7	13.8	7.5	4.5	1.1	.2	25.1
WATER...............	-	100.0	-	-	-	-	-	-	-	-	-
OTHER...............	-	100.0	2.6	4.6	31.8	1.9	9.7	13.7	.2	14.6	20.8
UNKNOWN.............	-	100.0	-	-	-	-	-	-	-	-	-
MIDDLE ATLANTIC........	106	100.0	.8	9.0	24.4	5.2	9.7	3.5	12.7	3.6	31.2
RAIL................	21	100.0	-	-	-	-	-	13.5	24.7	-	61.8
MOTOR CARRIER........	71	100.0	.9	12.3	28.3	5.4	13.4	1.2	11.6	.5	26.5
PRIVATE TRUCK........	11	100.0	1.9	4.8	47.8	12.7	3.4	-	-	29.4	-
AIR.................	1	100.0	-	.6	1.9	13.3	4.7	.5	.7	3.4	74.9
WATER...............	-	100.0	-	-	-	-	-	-	-	-	-
OTHER...............	-	100.0	-	33.4	2.3	-	59.0	-	.6	-	4.7
UNKNOWN.............	-	100.0	-	-	-	-	-	-	-	-	-
EAST NORTH CENTRAL......	263	100.0	5.5	15.8	24.2	10.9	10.5	2.5	9.8	2.2	18.6
RAIL................	44	100.0	-	9.5	8.3	6.0	10.7	3.8	6.9	8.9	45.9
MOTOR CARRIER........	187	100.0	7.6	14.5	28.5	12.0	11.2	2.2	10.9	.9	12.1
PRIVATE TRUCK........	24	100.0	.1	35.0	21.9	11.6	6.6	2.4	4.2	-	18.1
AIR.................	3	100.0	.8	37.0	19.7	6.9	4.2	-	.6	.8	29.8
WATER...............	-	100.0	-	-	-	-	-	-	-	-	-
OTHER...............	2	100.0	1.3	6.5	16.3	12.7	5.2	1.7	48.5	1.1	6.7
UNKNOWN.............	-	100.0	-	-	15.2	3.4	-	-	3.0	45.3	33.1
SOUTH ATLANTIC.........	126	100.0	2.6	4.3	6.2	2.2	6.4	1.8	12.4	1.1	62.9
RAIL................	80	100.0	.9	.2	.2	.4	1.5	.1	.6	.4	95.6
MOTOR CARRIER........	30	100.0	6.3	11.7	18.5	7.4	10.7	2.1	33.3	3.4	6.6
PRIVATE TRUCK........	13	100.0	5.1	12.1	12.7	1.0	23.5	10.2	35.3	-	-
AIR.................	-	100.0	-	14.7	5.7	-	1.8	17.0	16.2	11.5	33.1
WATER...............	-	100.0	-	-	-	-	-	-	-	-	-
OTHER...............	1	100.0	.2	3.2	4.9	.4	24.7	5.0	1.4	1.3	58.9
UNKNOWN.............	-	100.0	-	-	81.6	-	18.3	-	-	-	-

See footnotes at end of table 4.

TABLE 3. **TCC GROUP 306**—Percent Distribution of Geographic Division of Destination and Means of Transport, by Geographic Division of Origin: 1972

Geographic division of destination and means of transport	Number	Percent distribution by division of origin [1]									
		U.S. total	New England	Middle Atlantic	East North Central	West North Central	South Atlantic	East South Central	West South Central	Mountain	Pacific
TONS OF SHIPMENTS	(thousands of tons)										
U.S. TOTAL	1 866	100.0	5.2	9.2	43.5	(D)	10.2	(D)	(D)	(D)	(D)
RAIL	222	100.0	5.4	6.7	30.1	(D)	18.4	(D)	(D)	(D)	(D)
MOTOR CARRIER	1 173	100.0	6.4	10.9	54.9	(D)	5.3	(D)	(D)	(D)	(D)
PRIVATE TRUCK	441	100.0	2.0	6.1	19.8	(D)	19.2	(D)	(D)	(D)	(D)
AIR	14	100.0	1.4	6.1	61.2	(D)	.6	(D)	(D)	(D)	(D)
WATER	3	100.0	-	-	-	(D)	-	(D)	(D)	(D)	(D)
OTHER	8	100.0	1.2	16.6	53.3	(D)	18.2	(D)	(D)	(D)	(D)
UNKNOWN	1	100.0	-	-	10.7	(D)	16.8	(D)	(D)	(D)	(D)
NEW ENGLAND	82	100.0	50.5	7.9	25.7	(D)	6.8	(D)	(D)	(D)	(D)
RAIL	1	100.0	53.1	-	-	(D)	46.9	(D)	(D)	(D)	(D)
MOTOR CARRIER	66	100.0	48.3	8.3	31.5	(D)	5.4	(D)	(D)	(D)	(D)
PRIVATE TRUCK	13	100.0	61.6	7.1	.2	(D)	9.1	(D)	(D)	(D)	(D)
AIR	-	100.0	2.4	-	20.7	(D)	-	(D)	(D)	(D)	(D)
WATER	-	100.0	-	-	-	(D)	-	(D)	(D)	(D)	(D)
OTHER	-	100.0	30.6	-	58.3	(D)	5.8	(D)	(D)	(D)	(D)
UNKNOWN	-	100.0	-	-	-	(D)	-	(D)	(D)	(D)	(D)
MIDDLE ATLANTIC	232	100.0	9.7	22.3	41.6	(D)	8.2	(D)	(D)	(D)	(D)
RAIL	16	100.0	14.5	-	47.3	(D)	1.6	(D)	(D)	(D)	(D)
MOTOR CARRIER	154	100.0	12.9	27.8	42.5	(D)	5.7	(D)	(D)	(D)	(D)
PRIVATE TRUCK	54	100.0	.1	14.1	36.8	(D)	17.5	(D)	(D)	(D)	(D)
AIR	3	100.0	.8	1.5	79.6	(D)	.6	(D)	(D)	(D)	(D)
WATER	-	100.0	-	-	-	(D)	-	(D)	(D)	(D)	(D)
OTHER	1	100.0	1.0	52.9	23.9	(D)	13.7	(D)	(D)	(D)	(D)
UNKNOWN	1	100.0	-	-	-	(D)	-	(D)	(D)	(D)	(D)
EAST NORTH CENTRAL	730	100.0	1.3	7.7	69.3	(D)	2.6	(D)	(D)	(D)	(D)
RAIL	35	100.0	.8	-	66.6	(D)	.8	(D)	(D)	(D)	(D)
MOTOR CARRIER	540	100.0	1.6	7.9	78.9	(D)	2.3	(D)	(D)	(D)	(D)
PRIVATE TRUCK	145	100.0	-	9.0	33.5	(D)	3.7	(D)	(D)	(D)	(D)
AIR	6	100.0	2.0	.8	84.6	(D)	.2	(D)	(D)	(D)	(D)
WATER	-	100.0	-	-	-	(D)	-	(D)	(D)	(D)	(D)
OTHER	2	100.0	1.4	.9	84.3	(D)	6.2	(D)	(D)	(D)	(D)
UNKNOWN	-	100.0	-	-	25.9	(D)	41.4	(D)	(D)	(D)	(D)
WEST NORTH CENTRAL	110	100.0	7.2	5.8	53.0	(D)	3.1	(D)	(D)	(D)	(D)
RAIL	16	100.0	33.6	-	36.3	(D)	2.5	(D)	(D)	(D)	(D)
MOTOR CARRIER	73	100.0	3.4	6.4	58.6	(D)	3.9	(D)	(D)	(D)	(D)
PRIVATE TRUCK	18	100.0	-	8.2	44.3	(D)	.9	(D)	(D)	(D)	(D)
AIR	-	100.0	2.7	25.0	54.1	(D)	-	(D)	(D)	(D)	(D)
WATER	-	100.0	-	-	-	(D)	-	(D)	(D)	(D)	(D)
OTHER	-	100.0	.1	-	88.2	(D)	1.8	(D)	(D)	(D)	(D)
UNKNOWN	-	100.0	-	-	100.0	(D)	-	(D)	(D)	(D)	(D)
SOUTH ATLANTIC	194	100.0	3.5	8.9	26.2	(D)	40.1	(D)	(D)	(D)	(D)
RAIL	15	100.0	13.1	-	58.2	(D)	25.7	(D)	(D)	(D)	(D)
MOTOR CARRIER	100	100.0	4.6	15.2	37.0	(D)	20.3	(D)	(D)	(D)	(D)
PRIVATE TRUCK	75	100.0	-	2.0	5.3	(D)	69.5	(D)	(D)	(D)	(D)
AIR	-	100.0	1.5	10.3	42.0	(D)	.3	(D)	(D)	(D)	(D)
WATER	-	100.0	-	-	-	(D)	-	(D)	(D)	(D)	(D)
OTHER	1	100.0	.5	30.6	15.9	(D)	40.7	(D)	(D)	(D)	(D)
UNKNOWN	-	100.0	-	-	-	(D)	100.0	(D)	(D)	(D)	(D)
EAST SOUTH CENTRAL	67	100.0	3.0	8.8	25.7	(D)	12.5	(D)	(D)	(D)	(D)
RAIL	6	100.0	-	62.0	32.7	(D)	5.2	(D)	(D)	(D)	(D)
MOTOR CARRIER	35	100.0	5.2	4.9	36.1	(D)	6.8	(D)	(D)	(D)	(D)
PRIVATE TRUCK	25	100.0	.8	-	9.4	(D)	21.8	(D)	(D)	(D)	(D)
AIR	-	100.0	10.2	12.9	2.4	(D)	34.3	(D)	(D)	(D)	(D)
WATER	-	100.0	-	-	-	(D)	-	(D)	(D)	(D)	(D)
OTHER	-	100.0	2.9	-	36.9	(D)	58.8	(D)	(D)	(D)	(D)
UNKNOWN	-	100.0	-	-	-	(D)	-	(D)	(D)	(D)	(D)
WEST SOUTH CENTRAL	94	100.0	3.4	12.8	32.8	(D)	22.1	(D)	(D)	(D)	(D)
RAIL	11	100.0	4.6	39.6	28.8	(D)	4.9	(D)	(D)	(D)	(D)
MOTOR CARRIER	64	100.0	4.1	11.5	39.0	(D)	15.5	(D)	(D)	(D)	(D)
PRIVATE TRUCK	15	100.0	-	-	8.6	(D)	68.7	(D)	(D)	(D)	(D)
AIR	1	100.0	.1	.4	1.7	(D)	.7	(D)	(D)	(D)	(D)
WATER	-	100.0	-	-	-	(D)	-	(D)	(D)	(D)	(D)
OTHER	1	100.0	-	.1	88.6	(D)	1.1	(D)	(D)	(D)	(D)
UNKNOWN	-	100.0	-	-	65.8	(D)	.3	(D)	(D)	(D)	(D)
MOUNTAIN	33	100.0	.8	6.3	13.2	(D)	2.7	(D)	(D)	(D)	(D)
RAIL	19	100.0	-	-	16.1	(D)	1.0	(D)	(D)	(D)	(D)
MOTOR CARRIER	8	100.0	3.0	2.1	13.6	(D)	7.7	(D)	(D)	(D)	(D)
PRIVATE TRUCK	4	100.0	-	38.2	-	(D)	-	(D)	(D)	(D)	(D)
AIR	-	100.0	.1	9.8	10.1	(D)	2.9	(D)	(D)	(D)	(D)
WATER	-	100.0	-	-	-	(D)	-	(D)	(D)	(D)	(D)
OTHER	-	100.0	10.4	-	56.6	(D)	32.4	(D)	(D)	(D)	(D)
UNKNOWN	-	100.0	-	-	100.0	(D)	-	(D)	(D)	(D)	(D)
PACIFIC	321	100.0	1.1	4.3	8.2	(D)	11.0	(D)	(D)	(D)	(D)
RAIL	99	100.0	.5	6.1	11.9	(D)	34.4	(D)	(D)	(D)	(D)
MOTOR CARRIER	129	100.0	2.3	5.8	8.9	(D)	.7	(D)	(D)	(D)	(D)
PRIVATE TRUCK	87	100.0	-	-	3.0	(D)	-	(D)	(D)	(D)	(D)
AIR	1	100.0	1.1	31.0	39.3	(D)	.6	(D)	(D)	(D)	(D)
WATER	3	100.0	-	-	-	(D)	-	(D)	(D)	(D)	(D)
OTHER	-	100.0	.6	1.0	11.1	(D)	57.0	(D)	(D)	(D)	(D)
UNKNOWN	-	100.0	-	-	81.0	(D)	-	(D)	(D)	(D)	(D)

See footnotes at end of table 4.

TABLE 3. TCC GROUP 306—Percent Distribution of Geographic Division of Destination and Means of Transport, by Geographic Division of Origin: 1972—Continued

Geographic division of destination and means of transport	Number	Percent distribution by division of origin[1]									
		U.S. total	New England	Middle Atlantic	East North Central	West North Central	South Atlantic	East South Central	West South Central	Mountain	Pacific
TON-MILES OF SHIPMENTS	(millions of ton-miles)										
U.S. TOTAL...............	894	100.0	4.8	11.9	29.4	(D)	14.1	(D)	(D)	(D)	(D)
RAIL................	213	100.0	4.5	9.9	20.7	(D)	37.5	(D)	(D)	(D)	(D)
MOTOR CARRIER.........	511	100.0	6.3	14.0	36.8	(D)	6.1	(D)	(D)	(D)	(D)
PRIVATE TRUCK..........	148	100.0	.5	7.9	16.5	(D)	9.3	(D)	(D)	(D)	(D)
AIR...................	10	100.0	1.4	13.6	35.6	(D)	.6	(D)	(D)	(D)	(D)
WATER.................	2	100.0	-	-	-	(D)	-	(D)	(D)	(D)	(D)
OTHER.................	4	100.0	1.1	7.9	49.6	(D)	29.4	(D)	(D)	(D)	(D)
UNKNOWN...............	3	100.0	-	-	4.7	(D)	3.8	(D)	(D)	(D)	(D)
NEW ENGLAND............	31	100.0	8.3	2.6	45.1	(D)	10.5	(D)	(D)	(D)	(D)
RAIL................	-	100.0	13.6	-	-	(D)	86.4	(D)	(D)	(D)	(D)
MOTOR CARRIER.........	25	100.0	7.5	2.4	55.6	(D)	7.6	(D)	(D)	(D)	(D)
PRIVATE TRUCK..........	4	100.0	12.5	4.6	.5	(D)	14.4	(D)	(D)	(D)	(D)
AIR...................	-	100.0	.1	-	7.2	(D)	-	(D)	(D)	(D)	(D)
WATER.................	-	100.0	-	-	-	(D)	-	(D)	(D)	(D)	(D)
OTHER.................	-	100.0	3.0	-	66.6	(D)	7.4	(D)	(D)	(D)	(D)
UNKNOWN...............	-	100.0	-	-	-	(D)	-	(D)	(D)	(D)	(D)
MIDDLE ATLANTIC.........	110	100.0	4.8	8.6	37.5	(D)	4.9	(D)	(D)	(D)	(D)
RAIL................	9	100.0	1.8	-	44.2	(D)	1.4	(D)	(D)	(D)	(D)
MOTOR CARRIER.........	70	100.0	7.3	12.4	38.5	(D)	5.1	(D)	(D)	(D)	(D)
PRIVATE TRUCK..........	25	100.0	-	2.3	34.4	(D)	6.7	(D)	(D)	(D)	(D)
AIR...................	2	100.0	.3	.4	60.8	(D)	.4	(D)	(D)	(D)	(D)
WATER.................	-	100.0	-	-	-	(D)	-	(D)	(D)	(D)	(D)
OTHER.................	-	100.0	.5	23.3	28.6	(D)	8.2	(D)	(D)	(D)	(D)
UNKNOWN...............	2	100.0	-	-	-	(D)	-	(D)	(D)	(D)	(D)
EAST NORTH CENTRAL......	188	100.0	3.3	13.7	33.8	(D)	4.1	(D)	(D)	(D)	(D)
RAIL................	9	100.0	2.2	-	37.6	(D)	1.7	(D)	(D)	(D)	(D)
MOTOR CARRIER.........	125	100.0	4.8	16.1	42.7	(D)	4.6	(D)	(D)	(D)	(D)
PRIVATE TRUCK..........	50	100.0	-	11.0	10.6	(D)	3.4	(D)	(D)	(D)	(D)
AIR...................	1	100.0	3.5	1.5	40.7	(D)	.2	(D)	(D)	(D)	(D)
WATER.................	-	100.0	-	-	-	(D)	-	(D)	(D)	(D)	(D)
OTHER.................	-	100.0	2.8	1.4	61.9	(D)	11.1	(D)	(D)	(D)	(D)
UNKNOWN...............	-	100.0	-	-	11.3	(D)	49.6	(D)	(D)	(D)	(D)
WEST NORTH CENTRAL......	60	100.0	13.6	9.1	47.1	(D)	4.6	(D)	(D)	(D)	(D)
RAIL................	11	100.0	50.1	-	23.8	(D)	3.2	(D)	(D)	(D)	(D)
MOTOR CARRIER.........	41	100.0	6.3	9.1	53.6	(D)	5.5	(D)	(D)	(D)	(D)
PRIVATE TRUCK..........	6	100.0	-	22.7	43.6	(D)	2.2	(D)	(D)	(D)	(D)
AIR...................	-	100.0	3.3	30.3	41.2	(D)	-	(D)	(D)	(D)	(D)
WATER.................	-	100.0	-	-	-	(D)	-	(D)	(D)	(D)	(D)
OTHER.................	-	100.0	.3	-	88.9	(D)	1.8	(D)	(D)	(D)	(D)
UNKNOWN...............	-	100.0	-	-	100.0	(D)	-	(D)	(D)	(D)	(D)
SOUTH ATLANTIC..........	87	100.0	5.5	11.8	31.7	(D)	9.3	(D)	(D)	(D)	(D)
RAIL................	7	100.0	21.1	-	59.5	(D)	15.4	(D)	(D)	(D)	(D)
MOTOR CARRIER.........	63	100.0	4.9	15.0	33.1	(D)	5.2	(D)	(D)	(D)	(D)
PRIVATE TRUCK..........	13	100.0	-	3.0	11.9	(D)	23.9	(D)	(D)	(D)	(D)
AIR...................	1	100.0	1.0	5.8	13.8	(D)	.1	(D)	(D)	(D)	(D)
WATER.................	-	100.0	-	-	-	(D)	-	(D)	(D)	(D)	(D)
OTHER.................	-	100.0	.6	27.5	15.1	(D)	42.6	(D)	(D)	(D)	(D)
UNKNOWN...............	-	100.0	-	-	-	(D)	100.0	(D)	(D)	(D)	(D)
EAST SOUTH CENTRAL......	24	100.0	7.9	15.0	26.5	(D)	9.1	(D)	(D)	(D)	(D)
RAIL................	4	100.0	-	61.5	36.3	(D)	2.2	(D)	(D)	(D)	(D)
MOTOR CARRIER.........	14	100.0	12.2	5.6	28.5	(D)	4.4	(D)	(D)	(D)	(D)
PRIVATE TRUCK..........	4	100.0	2.6	-	12.0	(D)	28.2	(D)	(D)	(D)	(D)
AIR...................	-	100.0	7.8	9.0	1.4	(D)	13.0	(D)	(D)	(D)	(D)
WATER.................	-	100.0	-	-	-	(D)	-	(D)	(D)	(D)	(D)
OTHER.................	-	100.0	6.1	-	32.7	(D)	58.2	(D)	(D)	(D)	(D)
UNKNOWN...............	-	100.0	-	-	-	(D)	-	(D)	(D)	(D)	(D)
WEST SOUTH CENTRAL......	79	100.0	5.2	17.0	32.5	(D)	19.8	(D)	(D)	(D)	(D)
RAIL................	10	100.0	7.2	48.3	28.5	(D)	4.6	(D)	(D)	(D)	(D)
MOTOR CARRIER.........	57	100.0	5.7	14.3	35.5	(D)	17.8	(D)	(D)	(D)	(D)
PRIVATE TRUCK..........	8	100.0	-	-	12.7	(D)	59.6	(D)	(D)	(D)	(D)
AIR...................	1	100.0	.1	.8	1.8	(D)	.8	(D)	(D)	(D)	(D)
WATER.................	-	100.0	-	-	-	(D)	-	(D)	(D)	(D)	(D)
OTHER.................	1	100.0	-	.2	95.6	(D)	1.6	(D)	(D)	(D)	(D)
UNKNOWN...............	-	100.0	-	-	99.5	(D)	.2	(D)	(D)	(D)	(D)
MOUNTAIN................	23	100.0	2.0	16.3	24.6	(D)	6.0	(D)	(D)	(D)	(D)
RAIL................	10	100.0	.1	-	36.1	(D)	3.1	(D)	(D)	(D)	(D)
MOTOR CARRIER.........	7	100.0	6.6	5.2	25.1	(D)	15.0	(D)	(D)	(D)	(D)
PRIVATE TRUCK..........	5	100.0	-	63.5	-	(D)	-	(D)	(D)	(D)	(D)
AIR...................	-	100.0	.2	25.8	16.3	(D)	3.9	(D)	(D)	(D)	(D)
WATER.................	-	100.0	-	-	-	(D)	-	(D)	(D)	(D)	(D)
OTHER.................	-	100.0	14.8	-	50.4	(D)	34.6	(D)	(D)	(D)	(D)
UNKNOWN...............	-	100.0	-	-	100.0	(D)	-	(D)	(D)	(D)	(D)
PACIFIC.................	288	100.0	3.1	11.5	17.0	(D)	27.7	(D)	(D)	(D)	(D)
RAIL................	148	100.0	.8	8.8	13.7	(D)	51.7	(D)	(D)	(D)	(D)
MOTOR CARRIER.........	104	100.0	7.3	18.1	21.9	(D)	2.0	(D)	(D)	(D)	(D)
PRIVATE TRUCK..........	29	100.0	-	-	15.3	(D)	-	(D)	(D)	(D)	(D)
AIR...................	2	100.0	1.5	41.3	43.1	(D)	.8	(D)	(D)	(D)	(D)
WATER.................	2	100.0	-	-	-	(D)	-	(D)	(D)	(D)	(D)
OTHER.................	1	100.0	1.1	1.7	15.4	(D)	80.0	(D)	(D)	(D)	(D)
UNKNOWN...............	-	100.0	-	-	81.2	(D)	-	(D)	(D)	(D)	(D)

See footnotes at end of table 4.

TABLE 4. TCC GROUP 306—Percent Distribution of Distance Shipped and Weight of Shipment, by Means of Transport: 1972

Distance shipped and weight of shipment [2] [3]	Number	Percent distribution by means of transport							
		All means of transport	Rail	Motor carrier	Private truck	Air	Water	Other	Unknown
TONS OF SHIPMENTS	(thousands of tons)								
U.S. TOTAL..........	1 788	100.0	11.4	63.7	23.5	.7	.2	.5	.1
UNDER 100 MILES.........	443	100.0	2.5	58.7	37.9	-	.6	.2	-
UNDER 1000 POUNDS.....	38	100.0	-	49.0	48.2	.1	-	2.7	-
1000 TO 9999 POUNDS...	203	100.0	2.7	83.9	13.3	-	-	-	-
10000 TO 29999 POUNDS.	101	100.0	5.6	53.5	40.9	-	-	-	-
30000 TO 59999 POUNDS.	42	100.0	-	39.0	54.8	-	6.2	-	-
60000 TO 89999 POUNDS.	-	100.0	-	-	-	-	-	-	-
90000 POUNDS AND OVER.	58	100.0	-	-	100.0	-	-	-	-
100 TO 199 MILES........	263	100.0	6.9	78.1	12.7	1.8	-	.5	.1
UNDER 1000 POUNDS.....	25	100.0	-	80.7	14.8	1.3	-	3.2	-
1000 TO 9999 POUNDS...	79	100.0	5.0	80.9	13.0	.4	-	.6	-
10000 TO 29999 POUNDS.	100	100.0	5.9	73.8	16.2	4.0	-	-	.1
30000 TO 59999 POUNDS.	48	100.0	6.2	88.1	5.7	-	-	-	-
60000 TO 89999 POUNDS.	8	100.0	62.5	37.5	-	-	-	-	-
90000 POUNDS AND OVER.	-	100.0	-	-	-	-	-	-	-
200 TO 299 MILES........	184	100.0	5.3	79.2	14.6	.2	-	.6	-
UNDER 1000 POUNDS.....	16	100.0	.1	87.6	3.6	2.4	-	6.2	-
1000 TO 9999 POUNDS...	54	100.0	5.3	84.2	10.4	-	-	-	.1
10000 TO 29999 POUNDS.	68	100.0	2.9	76.9	20.2	-	-	-	-
30000 TO 59999 POUNDS.	43	100.0	11.3	72.8	15.9	-	-	-	-
60000 TO 89999 POUNDS.	1	100.0	-	100.0	-	-	-	-	-
90000 POUNDS AND OVER.	-	100.0	-	-	-	-	-	-	-
300 TO 499 MILES........	321	100.0	9.6	50.1	39.6	.3	-	.4	-
UNDER 1000 POUNDS.....	24	100.0	-	91.2	.9	3.1	-	4.7	-
1000 TO 9999 POUNDS...	92	100.0	1.8	71.0	26.8	.2	-	.2	-
10000 TO 29999 POUNDS.	121	100.0	8.0	42.2	49.7	-	-	-	-
30000 TO 59999 POUNDS.	83	100.0	23.4	26.4	50.2	-	-	-	-
60000 TO 89999 POUNDS.	-	100.0	-	-	-	-	-	-	-
90000 POUNDS AND OVER.	-	100.0	-	-	-	-	-	-	-
500 TO 999 MILES........	371	100.0	17.0	70.7	10.2	1.4	-	.7	.1
UNDER 1000 POUNDS.....	29	100.0	.5	88.5	3.0	3.3	-	4.6	-
1000 TO 9999 POUNDS...	111	100.0	5.1	84.6	8.1	1.9	-	.1	.1
10000 TO 29999 POUNDS.	86	100.0	13.9	66.5	15.9	2.3	-	1.3	-
30000 TO 59999 POUNDS.	127	100.0	22.4	66.4	11.1	-	-	-	.1
60000 TO 89999 POUNDS.	16	100.0	100.0	-	-	-	-	-	-
90000 POUNDS AND OVER.	-	100.0	-	-	-	-	-	-	-
1000 TO 1499 MILES......	73	100.0	22.6	67.1	9.4	.6	-	.3	.1
UNDER 1000 POUNDS.....	9	100.0	.6	87.5	5.1	4.5	-	2.2	-
1000 TO 9999 POUNDS...	21	100.0	3.1	94.0	2.5	.1	-	-	.3
10000 TO 29999 POUNDS.	23	100.0	13.3	61.6	25.1	-	-	-	-
30000 TO 59999 POUNDS.	19	100.0	65.0	35.0	-	-	-	-	-
60000 TO 89999 POUNDS.	-	100.0	-	-	-	-	-	-	-
90000 POUNDS AND OVER.	-	100.0	-	-	-	-	-	-	-
1500 MILES OR OVER......	130	100.0	40.9	41.4	14.5	1.1	.7	.4	.9
UNDER 1000 POUNDS.....	22	100.0	1.3	90.1	1.9	5.0	-	1.6	.1
1000 TO 9999 POUNDS...	24	100.0	5.1	83.1	1.1	1.4	3.6	.8	4.8
10000 TO 29999 POUNDS.	28	100.0	47.3	36.7	16.0	-	-	-	-
30000 TO 59999 POUNDS.	49	100.0	65.8	6.2	28.0	-	-	-	-
60000 TO 89999 POUNDS.	6	100.0	100.0	-	-	-	-	-	-
90000 POUNDS AND OVER.	-	100.0	-	-	-	-	-	-	-
TON-MILES OF SHIPMENTS	(millions of ton-miles)								
U.S. TOTAL..........	854	100.0	23.5	57.9	16.5	1.0	.3	.5	.4
UNDER 100 MILES.........	15	100.0	5.3	60.4	33.6	-	.4	.3	-
UNDER 1000 POUNDS.....	1	100.0	-	59.7	37.1	.2	-	3.0	-
1000 TO 9999 POUNDS...	6	100.0	6.0	81.8	12.2	-	-	-	-
10000 TO 29999 POUNDS.	4	100.0	9.3	55.1	35.5	-	-	-	-
30000 TO 59999 POUNDS.	2	100.0	-	36.6	60.4	-	3.0	-	-
60000 TO 89999 POUNDS.	-	100.0	-	-	-	-	-	-	-
90000 POUNDS AND OVER.	-	100.0	-	-	100.0	-	-	-	-
100 TO 199 MILES........	39	100.0	6.7	78.6	12.5	1.6	-	.5	.1
UNDER 1000 POUNDS.....	3	100.0	-	81.7	13.6	1.4	-	3.2	-
1000 TO 9999 POUNDS...	12	100.0	4.4	81.1	13.3	.4	-	.7	-
10000 TO 29999 POUNDS.	15	100.0	6.2	73.7	16.4	3.6	-	-	.1
30000 TO 59999 POUNDS.	7	100.0	6.1	88.9	5.1	-	-	-	-
60000 TO 89999 POUNDS.	1	100.0	54.8	45.2	-	-	-	-	-
90000 POUNDS AND OVER.	-	100.0	-	-	-	-	-	-	-

See footnotes at end of table 4.

TABLE 4. TCC GROUP 306—Percent Distribution of Distance Shipped and Weight of Shipment, by Means of Transport: 1972—Continued

Distance shipped and weight of shipment [2] [3]	Number	Percent distribution by means of transport							
		All means of transport	Rail	Motor carrier	Private truck	Air	Water	Other	Unknown
TON-MILES OF SHIPMENTS	(millions of ton-miles)								
200 TO 299 MILES	45	100.0	5.2	79.7	14.3	.2	-	.6	-
UNDER 1000 POUNDS	4	100.0	.1	87.5	3.8	2.5	-	6.1	-
1000 TO 9999 POUNDS	13	100.0	5.6	84.8	9.5	-	-	-	.1
10000 TO 29999 POUNDS	17	100.0	2.7	76.9	20.4	-	-	-	-
30000 TO 59999 POUNDS	10	100.0	11.1	73.7	15.3	-	-	-	-
60000 TO 89999 POUNDS	-	100.0	-	100.0	-	-	-	-	-
90000 POUNDS AND OVER	-	100.0	-	-	-	-	-	-	-
300 TO 499 MILES	130	100.0	9.9	47.8	41.6	.3	-	.4	-
UNDER 1000 POUNDS	9	100.0	-	90.9	.9	3.3	-	4.8	-
1000 TO 9999 POUNDS	36	100.0	2.2	69.9	27.6	.2	-	.2	-
10000 TO 29999 POUNDS	49	100.0	8.4	39.3	52.4	-	-	-	-
30000 TO 59999 POUNDS	35	100.0	22.6	25.5	51.9	-	-	-	-
60000 TO 89999 POUNDS	-	100.0	-	-	-	-	-	-	-
90000 POUNDS AND OVER	-	100.0	-	-	-	-	-	-	-
500 TO 999 MILES	262	100.0	18.4	69.2	10.2	1.3	-	.8	.1
UNDER 1000 POUNDS	21	100.0	.7	88.9	3.0	3.2	-	4.1	-
1000 TO 9999 POUNDS	76	100.0	5.5	84.7	7.8	1.9	-	.1	.1
10000 TO 29999 POUNDS	59	100.0	14.6	66.5	15.0	2.1	-	1.8	-
30000 TO 59999 POUNDS	91	100.0	24.1	63.5	12.3	-	-	-	.1
60000 TO 89999 POUNDS	13	100.0	100.0	-	-	-	-	-	-
90000 POUNDS AND OVER	-	100.0	-	-	-	-	-	-	-
1000 TO 1499 MILES	87	100.0	23.0	67.3	8.8	.6	-	.3	.1
UNDER 1000 POUNDS	11	100.0	.6	87.6	5.1	4.6	-	2.0	-
1000 TO 9999 POUNDS	25	100.0	3.6	93.5	2.5	.1	-	-	.3
10000 TO 29999 POUNDS	27	100.0	13.4	63.3	23.2	-	-	-	-
30000 TO 59999 POUNDS	22	100.0	66.9	33.1	-	-	-	-	-
60000 TO 89999 POUNDS	-	100.0	-	-	-	-	-	-	-
90000 POUNDS AND OVER	-	100.0	-	-	-	-	-	-	-
1500 MILES OR OVER	273	100.0	41.7	42.0	12.8	1.2	.9	.4	1.1
UNDER 1000 POUNDS	46	100.0	1.3	90.0	1.7	5.3	-	1.6	.1
1000 TO 9999 POUNDS	54	100.0	4.3	83.1	.9	1.3	4.5	.7	5.3
10000 TO 29999 POUNDS	57	100.0	48.6	36.4	15.0	-	-	-	-
30000 TO 59999 POUNDS	100	100.0	68.1	6.9	25.0	-	-	-	-
60000 TO 89999 POUNDS	14	100.0	100.0	-	-	-	-	-	-
90000 POUNDS AND OVER	-	100.0	-	-	-	-	-	-	-

Note: Detail may not add to total due to rounding. The introductory table shows the estimates of sampling variability for tons; sampling variability for ton-miles has not been estimated. See the map in the Introduction for the States comprising the geographic divisions of the United States.

Shipments excluded from the survey are those moving by pipeline (primarily petroleum products from refineries), parcel post shipments, and commodities moved by own power (motorized vehicles, aircraft, etc.) or towed (prefabricated buildings, etc.). Local shipments (commodities shipped less than 25 miles from the plant) and shipments within the same city are also excluded. Shipments to Alaska and Hawaii from the 48 conterminous States and the District of Columbia are included; however, no data were obtained for shipments originating in Alaska and Hawaii.

- Represents zero or rounds to zero.   (D) Withheld to avoid disclosing figures for individual companies.

[1] Production of this commodity is concentrated in the geographic divisions shown; figures and distributions for geographic divisions not shown are included in the total.

[2] Distances of shipments to foreign destinations are calculated only to the U.S. port of exit.

[3] Includes only shipments represented by bills of lading and invoices. Summary records which did not show individual weights of shipments are not included.

TCC 307. Miscellaneous Plastics Products

Comparisons of Tons and Ton-Miles of Shipments for
Geographic Divisions of Origin and for Sampling Variability: 1972 and 1967

Geographic division of origin	Estimates				Relative sampling variability in tons (percent)	
	1972		1967		1972	1967
	Tons (thousands)	Ton-miles (millions)	Tons (thousands)	Ton-miles (millions)		
U.S. total	8,248	4,258	4,297	2,331	7.7	8.8
New England	999	451	596	427	32.9	(*)
Middle Atlantic	1,853	936	992	563	22.5	(*)
East North Central	2,219	858	1,256	557	13.9	(*)
West North Central	673	360	347	133	42.6	(*)
South Atlantic	1,465	919	404	164	16.7	(*)
East South Central	309	185	227	166	34.8	(*)
West South Central	(D)	(D)	168	130	(*)	(*)
Mountain	(D)	(D)	27	8	(*)	(*)
Pacific	547	441	280	183	31.1	(*)

(D) Withheld to avoid disclosing figures for individual companies.   (*) Data not published.

TABLE 1. **TCC GROUP 307**—Percent Distribution of Geographic Division of Origin and Distance Shipped, by Means of Transport: 1972

Geographic division of origin[1] and distance shipped[2]	Number	Percent distribution by means of transport							
		All means of transport	Rail	Motor carrier	Private truck	Air	Water	Other	Unknown
TONS OF SHIPMENTS	(thousands of tons)								
U.S. TOTAL	8 248	100.0	16.0	64.0	18.9	.3	.1	.5	.2
NEW ENGLAND	999	100.0	23.3	70.7	5.4	.3	-	.1	.2
UNDER 100 MILES	301	100.0	9.8	75.3	13.4	.6	-	.2	.7
100 TO 199 MILES	172	100.0	24.3	72.3	3.1	.3	-	.1	-
200 TO 299 MILES	78	100.0	4.6	92.4	2.9	-	-	.1	-
300 TO 499 MILES	89	100.0	29.8	69.7	.3	-	-	.1	-
500 TO 999 MILES	245	100.0	41.5	56.9	1.2	.3	-	-	-
1000 TO 1499 MILES	77	100.0	16.3	80.4	3.1	-	-	.2	-
1500 MILES OR OVER	33	100.0	48.7	50.3	.4	.2	-	.4	-
MIDDLE ATLANTIC	1 853	100.0	11.4	75.8	11.4	.2	.4	.6	.2
UNDER 100 MILES	423	100.0	.5	81.4	17.1	-	.4	.4	.3
100 TO 199 MILES	334	100.0	2.3	76.4	21.1	.1	-	.1	-
200 TO 299 MILES	217	100.0	.8	87.3	11.7	.1	-	.2	-
300 TO 499 MILES	187	100.0	9.7	85.0	3.7	.3	-	1.3	-
500 TO 999 MILES	380	100.0	26.4	64.1	8.3	.2	-	.8	.1
1000 TO 1499 MILES	216	100.0	15.9	78.4	2.2	.2	1.8	1.0	.6
1500 MILES OR OVER	92	100.0	50.0	43.4	.4	2.8	1.8	1.7	-
EAST NORTH CENTRAL	2 219	100.0	17.9	62.9	17.8	.4	-	.9	.2
UNDER 100 MILES	438	100.0	1.9	67.0	30.6	-	-	.5	-
100 TO 199 MILES	386	100.0	14.3	58.1	24.3	.2	-	2.8	.2
200 TO 299 MILES	373	100.0	17.5	68.6	12.7	.5	-	.7	-
300 TO 499 MILES	509	100.0	26.6	56.9	15.3	.5	-	.2	.5
500 TO 999 MILES	371	100.0	26.2	63.1	9.5	.7	.1	.2	.2
1000 TO 1499 MILES	45	100.0	7.4	90.4	1.2	.3	-	.6	-
1500 MILES OR OVER	93	100.0	33.8	58.3	4.5	1.3	.2	1.9	-
WEST NORTH CENTRAL	673	100.0	6.2	50.9	42.1	.2	-	.1	.5
UNDER 100 MILES	70	100.0	.7	56.6	42.4	-	-	.2	-
100 TO 199 MILES	109	100.0	8.2	45.8	45.9	-	-	-	.1
200 TO 299 MILES	36	100.0	1.3	93.0	4.3	.3	-	.2	.8
300 TO 499 MILES	151	100.0	.7	58.3	40.5	.5	-	.1	-
500 TO 999 MILES	230	100.0	6.3	39.3	52.9	.1	-	.1	1.3
1000 TO 1499 MILES	44	100.0	14.7	43.6	40.4	1.1	-	.3	-
1500 MILES OR OVER	30	100.0	30.8	68.9	-	.1	-	.1	-
SOUTH ATLANTIC	1 465	100.0	14.8	61.9	22.6	.1	-	.5	-
UNDER 100 MILES	274	100.0	-	65.2	32.5	-	-	2.1	.2
100 TO 199 MILES	138	100.0	-	56.0	43.9	-	-	.2	-
200 TO 299 MILES	211	100.0	.1	73.4	26.4	-	-	.2	-
300 TO 499 MILES	241	100.0	13.8	72.7	13.0	.1	-	.3	-
500 TO 999 MILES	343	100.0	8.6	65.4	25.9	.1	-	-	-
1000 TO 1499 MILES	64	100.0	39.2	55.0	5.1	.7	-	.1	-
1500 MILES OR OVER	190	100.0	67.6	30.9	1.1	.2	-	.2	-
EAST SOUTH CENTRAL	309	100.0	20.1	48.4	29.5	1.1	-	.9	-
UNDER 100 MILES	15	100.0	20.2	11.9	65.6	-	-	2.3	-
100 TO 199 MILES	16	100.0	-	50.2	46.2	2.7	-	.8	-
200 TO 299 MILES	30	100.0	-	26.1	68.0	5.0	-	.9	-
300 TO 499 MILES	55	100.0	13.2	48.1	34.7	1.5	-	2.5	-
500 TO 999 MILES	170	100.0	24.7	56.9	17.7	.4	-	.4	-
1000 TO 1499 MILES	10	100.0	29.8	69.6	-	-	-	.6	-
1500 MILES OR OVER	10	100.0	60.4	8.5	30.3	.8	-	-	-
PACIFIC	547	100.0	25.8	47.5	26.0	.3	.1	.2	.2
UNDER 100 MILES	142	100.0	1.5	20.0	78.2	.1	.2	.1	-
100 TO 199 MILES	25	100.0	-	79.9	18.0	-	-	1.6	.6
200 TO 299 MILES	18	100.0	-	82.6	17.3	.1	-	-	-
300 TO 499 MILES	88	100.0	.9	88.3	9.5	.1	.1	.5	.7
500 TO 999 MILES	70	100.0	41.8	50.0	7.6	.5	-	-	-
1000 TO 1499 MILES	62	100.0	66.6	26.7	6.4	.2	-	-	-
1500 MILES OR OVER	140	100.0	48.0	47.4	3.8	.7	.2	-	-
TON-MILES OF SHIPMENTS	(millions of ton-miles)								
U.S. TOTAL	4 258	100.0	29.6	57.6	11.5	.5	.2	.4	.1
NEW ENGLAND	451	100.0	36.1	62.0	1.6	.2	-	.1	-
UNDER 100 MILES	17	100.0	15.2	75.9	7.3	.3	-	.1	1.1
100 TO 199 MILES	27	100.0	26.6	70.2	2.8	.3	-	.1	-
200 TO 299 MILES	18	100.0	5.2	91.5	3.3	-	-	.1	-
300 TO 499 MILES	33	100.0	30.0	69.5	.3	-	-	.1	-
500 TO 999 MILES	184	100.0	46.4	52.4	.9	.3	-	-	-
1000 TO 1499 MILES	91	100.0	15.8	81.3	2.7	-	-	.2	-
1500 MILES OR OVER	78	100.0	53.1	45.9	.4	.3	-	.3	-
MIDDLE ATLANTIC	936	100.0	25.0	66.5	5.7	.7	.9	1.0	.2
UNDER 100 MILES	18	100.0	.5	82.1	16.9	-	.1	.3	.1
100 TO 199 MILES	45	100.0	2.9	75.5	21.4	.1	-	.1	-
200 TO 299 MILES	54	100.0	.8	87.9	11.1	.1	-	.1	-
300 TO 499 MILES	74	100.0	8.9	85.6	3.7	.3	-	1.4	-
500 TO 999 MILES	275	100.0	25.7	63.9	9.2	.2	-	.9	.1
1000 TO 1499 MILES	257	100.0	17.7	76.6	2.1	.2	1.8	1.1	.6
1500 MILES OR OVER	209	100.0	52.3	41.6	.4	2.6	1.9	1.2	-

See footnotes at end of table 4.

TABLE 1. **TCC GROUP 307**—Percent Distribution of Geographic Division of Origin and Distance Shipped, by Means of Transport: 1972—Continued

Geographic division of origin[1] and distance shipped[2]	Number	Percent distribution by means of transport							
		All means of transport	Rail	Motor carrier	Private truck	Air	Water	Other	Unknown
TON-MILES OF SHIPMENTS	(millions of ton-miles)								
EAST NORTH CENTRAL......	858	100.0	24.0	63.0	11.3	.7	.1	.7	.2
UNDER 100 MILES.......	24	100.0	2.1	68.0	29.5	-	-	.5	-
100 TO 199 MILES......	56	100.0	17.0	58.2	22.1	.2	-	2.3	.1
200 TO 299 MILES......	93	100.0	16.3	69.2	13.4	.5	-	.6	-
300 TO 499 MILES......	201	100.0	26.1	57.3	15.5	.5	-	.2	.4
500 TO 999 MILES......	253	100.0	25.8	62.9	10.2	.7	.1	.2	.2
1000 TO 1499 MILES....	51	100.0	7.6	90.2	1.3	.3	-	.7	-
1500 MILES OR OVER....	177	100.0	33.0	59.4	4.2	1.3	.4	1.7	-
WEST NORTH CENTRAL......	360	100.0	10.3	49.0	39.7	.3	-	.1	.6
UNDER 100 MILES.......	3	100.0	.9	72.8	26.1	-	-	.2	-
100 TO 199 MILES......	18	100.0	8.4	43.8	47.8	-	-	-	.1
200 TO 299 MILES......	8	100.0	1.3	93.2	4.2	.3	-	.2	.7
300 TO 499 MILES......	60	100.0	.8	55.9	42.8	.5	-	.1	-
500 TO 999 MILES......	164	100.0	6.8	40.1	51.6	.1	-	.1	1.3
1000 TO 1499 MILES....	54	100.0	15.4	43.1	40.2	1.0	-	.3	-
1500 MILES OR OVER....	49	100.0	30.7	69.0	-	.1	-	.1	-
SOUTH ATLANTIC..........	919	100.0	39.1	49.6	11.0	.2	-	.1	-
UNDER 100 MILES.......	14	100.0	-	70.7	27.5	-	-	1.7	.1
100 TO 199 MILES......	20	100.0	-	58.8	41.1	-	-	-	-
200 TO 299 MILES......	54	100.0	.1	73.3	26.4	-	-	.2	-
300 TO 499 MILES......	97	100.0	16.1	71.0	12.5	.1	-	.3	-
500 TO 999 MILES......	224	100.0	9.3	66.4	24.3	.1	-	-	-
1000 TO 1499 MILES....	72	100.0	37.6	56.3	5.2	.7	-	-	-
1500 MILES OR OVER....	436	100.0	67.7	31.0	.9	.2	-	.2	-
EAST SOUTH CENTRAL......	185	100.0	25.5	50.8	22.3	.7	-	.6	-
UNDER 100 MILES.......	-	100.0	10.1	14.4	73.8	-	-	1.7	-
100 TO 199 MILES......	2	100.0	-	49.3	46.4	3.3	-	1.0	-
200 TO 299 MILES......	7	100.0	-	25.8	68.3	5.0	-	.9	-
300 TO 499 MILES......	22	100.0	13.4	47.8	34.7	1.7	-	2.5	-
500 TO 999 MILES......	122	100.0	24.1	57.7	17.6	.3	-	.3	-
1000 TO 1499 MILES....	12	100.0	31.3	68.2	-	-	-	.5	-
1500 MILES OR OVER....	18	100.0	60.1	9.5	29.7	.8	-	-	-
PACIFIC................	441	100.0	45.9	47.2	6.1	.5	.1	.1	.1
UNDER 100 MILES.......	4	100.0	1.4	33.4	64.9	.1	.1	.2	-
100 TO 199 MILES......	3	100.0	-	80.3	17.8	-	-	1.4	.6
200 TO 299 MILES......	4	100.0	-	84.6	15.3	.1	-	-	-
300 TO 499 MILES......	30	100.0	1.0	88.0	9.7	.1	.1	.4	.7
500 TO 999 MILES......	56	100.0	44.9	47.2	7.4	.5	-	-	-
1000 TO 1499 MILES....	80	100.0	67.5	26.0	6.2	.2	-	-	-
1500 MILES OR OVER....	261	100.0	46.9	48.0	4.2	.7	.2	-	-

See footnotes at end of table 4.

TABLE 2. **TCC GROUP 307**—Percent Distribution of Geographic Division of Origin and Means of Transport, by Geographic Division of Destination: 1972

Geographic division of origin[1] and means of transport	Number	Percent distribution by division of destination									
		U.S. total	New England	Middle Atlantic	East North Central	West North Central	South Atlantic	East South Central	West South Central	Mountain	Pacific
TONS OF SHIPMENTS	(thousands of tons)										
U.S. TOTAL..............	8 248	100.0	6.9	20.0	23.8	8.2	18.5	5.7	6.6	1.7	8.7
RAIL..................	1 317	100.0	5.9	10.7	18.8	10.3	18.2	4.7	10.2	1.2	20.2
MOTOR CARRIER.........	5 282	100.0	7.7	22.5	24.7	6.5	20.0	4.6	6.4	1.8	5.8
PRIVATE TRUCK.........	1 555	100.0	5.1	19.7	25.3	12.7	13.0	9.9	3.9	1.6	8.8
AIR...................	26	100.0	10.7	10.6	30.6	4.6	13.8	4.8	4.9	10.3	9.6
WATER.................	8	100.0	-	20.3	.2	-	34.8	-	16.4	-	28.3
OTHER.................	44	100.0	2.3	5.6	21.8	4.5	42.2	6.6	6.0	3.4	7.6
UNKNOWN...............	13	100.0	.1	23.3	9.6	2.0	21.9	25.7	11.4	.2	5.8
NEW ENGLAND............	999	100.0	27.8	30.5	6.1	1.7	24.4	4.1	2.4	.5	2.4
RAIL..................	232	100.0	13.0	23.8	4.5	1.0	46.9	3.9	-	-	7.0
MOTOR CARRIER.........	706	100.0	29.7	33.2	6.4	2.1	18.9	4.5	3.4	.7	1.1
PRIVATE TRUCK.........	53	100.0	66.3	23.4	8.4	-	1.7	-	-	-	.2
AIR...................	3	100.0	60.0	16.0	16.7	.1	3.6	1.4	.1	.3	1.9
WATER.................	-	100.0	-	100.0	-	-	-	-	-	-	-
OTHER.................	1	100.0	47.0	17.5	7.7	9.5	5.8	.9	8.1	2.5	1.0
UNKNOWN...............	2	100.0	-	100.0	-	-	-	-	-	-	-
MIDDLE ATLANTIC........	1 853	100.0	7.9	40.6	15.3	3.2	16.5	3.3	8.5	.5	4.1
RAIL..................	210	100.0	1.2	5.3	35.1	9.4	8.6	1.2	17.4	-	21.9
MOTOR CARRIER.........	1 403	100.0	7.3	43.7	13.8	2.4	19.5	2.7	8.3	.5	1.9
PRIVATE TRUCK.........	211	100.0	19.8	58.3	6.1	2.1	4.0	9.5	.1	-	.1
AIR...................	4	100.0	8.8	2.4	14.7	8.5	5.2	.9	3.7	46.8	8.9
WATER.................	7	100.0	-	23.0	.1	-	35.2	-	18.7	-	23.0
OTHER.................	11	100.0	2.0	15.7	20.5	4.3	19.5	7.7	17.3	11.0	2.1
UNKNOWN...............	2	100.0	-	37.4	6.0	2.9	.8	10.4	42.5	-	-

See footnotes at end of table 4.

TABLE 2. TCC GROUP 307—Percent Distribution of Geographic Division of Origin and Means of Transport, by Geographic Division of Destination: 1972—Continued

| Geographic division of origin[1] and means of transport | Number | Percent distribution by division of destination ||||||||||
		U.S. total	New England	Middle Atlantic	East North Central	West North Central	South Atlantic	East South Central	West South Central	Mountain	Pacific
TONS OF SHIPMENTS	(thousands of tons)										
EAST NORTH CENTRAL......	2 219	100.0	1.9	12.7	50.1	10.0	11.5	5.4	3.8	.6	4.0
RAIL..................	396	100.0	1.3	14.8	30.7	19.6	16.9	3.2	5.0	.6	7.9
MOTOR CARRIER.........	1 395	100.0	2.6	10.7	52.4	9.0	11.2	5.4	4.4	.7	3.7
PRIVATE TRUCK.........	394	100.0	.2	18.1	63.2	4.5	5.4	7.0	.5	.6	.5
AIR...................	9	100.0	3.1	17.4	31.1	5.5	16.8	4.5	7.3	1.6	12.8
WATER.................	-	100.0	-	1.9	1.9	-	65.4	-	-	-	30.8
OTHER.................	19	100.0	.6	1.1	28.1	4.9	50.4	4.4	.6	.7	9.3
UNKNOWN...............	4	100.0	.3	1.8	18.8	3.2	-	67.3	8.1	-	.6
WEST NORTH CENTRAL......	673	100.0	.6	7.1	26.0	38.2	7.1	5.0	6.5	2.8	6.6
RAIL..................	41	100.0	7.7	2.9	4.5	22.1	29.7	3.3	-	3.2	26.6
MOTOR CARRIER.........	343	100.0	.3	7.1	25.8	33.7	6.9	4.1	10.6	3.6	7.8
PRIVATE TRUCK.........	283	100.0	-	7.8	29.7	46.6	3.1	6.4	2.4	1.7	2.2
AIR...................	1	100.0	7.4	17.7	39.6	11.6	9.5	.4	9.2	4.0	.5
WATER.................	-	100.0	-	-	-	-	-	-	-	-	-
OTHER.................	-	100.0	1.5	8.0	21.4	36.1	9.1	.8	9.2	5.6	8.3
UNKNOWN...............	3	100.0	-	-	10.3	1.8	87.9	-	-	-	-
SOUTH ATLANTIC..........	1 465	100.0	4.5	14.1	13.3	3.0	39.8	7.4	4.7	.3	12.9
RAIL..................	216	100.0	15.7	4.8	2.2	2.4	3.9	1.0	10.8	-	59.2
MOTOR CARRIER.........	907	100.0	3.4	13.8	19.2	1.8	45.8	4.5	4.6	.5	6.4
PRIVATE TRUCK.........	331	100.0	-	21.3	4.6	6.8	46.2	19.2	1.3	.2	.4
AIR...................	1	100.0	1.1	2.5	30.3	.9	29.1	1.7	1.8	4.4	28.2
WATER.................	-	100.0	-	-	-	-	-	-	-	-	-
OTHER.................	7	100.0	1.0	.7	.5	.5	84.1	8.4	-	-	4.9
UNKNOWN...............	-	100.0	-	7.8	-	-	-	92.1	-	-	-
EAST SOUTH CENTRAL......	309	100.0	8.3	10.2	19.5	12.0	13.8	13.3	16.3	3.7	2.9
RAIL..................	62	100.0	-	3.1	18.7	9.3	7.6	6.9	35.3	11.3	7.7
MOTOR CARRIER.........	149	100.0	16.3	16.1	20.1	10.3	20.4	8.4	7.3	.5	.6
PRIVATE TRUCK.........	91	100.0	1.3	5.9	16.5	17.3	6.9	25.3	19.1	4.2	3.6
AIR...................	3	100.0	1.0	-	59.9	1.3	18.9	15.5	1.0	.1	2.3
WATER.................	-	100.0	-	-	-	-	100.0	-	-	-	-
OTHER.................	2	100.0	1.3	3.9	52.0	2.4	10.7	19.0	10.6	-	-
UNKNOWN...............	-	100.0	-	-	-	-	-	-	-	-	-
PACIFIC.................	547	100.0	.2	2.4	8.9	4.1	5.3	8.0	8.1	11.8	51.2
RAIL..................	141	100.0	.2	1.6	13.1	11.4	13.0	20.0	17.9	3.2	19.6
MOTOR CARRIER.........	260	100.0	.2	4.0	11.0	2.2	3.0	5.8	5.8	18.9	49.0
PRIVATE TRUCK.........	142	100.0	.1	.4	.9	.3	1.8	.4	2.5	7.5	86.2
AIR...................	1	100.0	.9	6.7	26.4	2.0	20.2	2.8	11.5	14.2	15.2
WATER.................	-	100.0	-	-	-	-	-	-	-	-	100.0
OTHER.................	-	100.0	.1	.9	.2	.5	.3	.1	.1	2.0	95.9
UNKNOWN...............	-	100.0	-	-	2.3	.1	-	-	-	3.1	94.5
TON-MILES OF SHIPMENTS	(millions of ton-miles)										
U.S. TOTAL..............	4 258	100.0	3.7	11.0	16.6	7.5	17.1	6.2	11.5	2.7	23.7
RAIL..................	1 259	100.0	2.7	4.9	10.1	6.6	14.7	5.0	10.8	1.2	43.9
MOTOR CARRIER.........	2 451	100.0	4.7	12.0	18.4	6.6	19.4	5.9	13.1	3.0	16.9
PRIVATE TRUCK.........	491	100.0	1.8	22.0	25.1	14.4	11.2	10.9	5.2	3.6	5.8
AIR...................	20	100.0	2.6	7.9	18.5	3.9	12.8	2.7	5.1	23.5	22.9
WATER.................	10	100.0	-	.3	-	-	28.2	-	19.0	-	52.6
OTHER.................	19	100.0	1.3	2.5	15.9	5.4	16.1	6.6	16.3	11.7	24.2
UNKNOWN...............	6	100.0	.1	4.5	4.5	2.4	36.1	20.8	27.0	.2	4.3
NEW ENGLAND.............	451	100.0	4.5	12.1	9.5	4.3	37.4	9.1	7.1	2.1	13.8
RAIL..................	162	100.0	1.7	7.6	4.4	1.6	52.9	6.1	-	-	25.6
MOTOR CARRIER.........	279	100.0	6.0	14.3	11.3	6.0	29.4	11.1	11.4	3.3	7.1
PRIVATE TRUCK.........	7	100.0	11.5	26.6	50.1	-	7.2	-	-	-	4.6
AIR...................	-	100.0	5.6	9.4	47.4	.3	11.3	4.3	.7	2.1	19.1
WATER.................	-	100.0	-	100.0	-	-	-	-	-	-	-
OTHER.................	-	100.0	5.7	8.5	13.4	20.6	7.2	1.8	27.9	9.9	5.1
UNKNOWN...............	-	100.0	-	100.0	-	-	-	-	-	-	-
MIDDLE ATLANTIC.........	936	100.0	3.1	8.8	16.8	5.8	17.7	5.4	21.1	1.9	19.4
RAIL..................	234	100.0	.3	1.0	20.0	7.3	3.5	.7	20.4	-	46.8
MOTOR CARRIER.........	622	100.0	3.6	10.7	16.3	5.0	24.1	4.9	23.0	1.8	10.5
PRIVATE TRUCK.........	53	100.0	11.2	24.3	13.0	9.5	7.0	33.3	.6	-	1.1
AIR...................	6	100.0	1.1	.4	4.9	5.9	3.4	.5	3.5	65.5	14.9
WATER.................	8	100.0	-	.2	-	-	30.2	-	22.4	-	47.2
OTHER.................	8	100.0	.5	1.1	16.0	4.8	12.6	7.4	29.3	21.7	6.6
UNKNOWN...............	1	100.0	-	.8	4.7	3.9	.3	9.1	81.2	-	-

See footnotes at end of table 4.

TABLE 2. **TCC GROUP 307—Percent Distribution of Geographic Division of Origin and Means of Transport, by Geographic Division of Destination: 1972**—Continued

Geographic division of origin[1] and means of transport	Number	Percent distribution by division of destination								
		U.S. total	New England	Middle Atlantic	East North Central	West North Central	South Atlantic	East South Central	West South Central	Mountain	Pacific
TON-MILES OF SHIPMENTS	(millions of ton-miles)										
EAST NORTH CENTRAL......	858	100.0	3.6	15.9	20.1	10.7	15.2	4.0	8.6	2.2	19.7
RAIL..................	205	100.0	1.8	15.8	12.6	14.9	15.9	1.6	8.1	1.3	28.0
MOTOR CARRIER.........	540	100.0	4.8	13.1	21.0	10.1	15.3	4.7	10.1	2.3	18.7
PRIVATE TRUCK........	97	100.0	.5	33.2	32.8	5.9	13.3	4.6	1.9	3.6	4.2
AIR..................	5	100.0	3.3	13.6	11.5	4.3	15.1	2.9	7.4	2.6	39.5
WATER................	-	100.0	-	.7	-	-	28.2	-	-	-	71.0
OTHER................	6	100.0	1.3	2.1	13.2	5.7	20.5	4.3	1.9	2.9	48.1
UNKNOWN..............	1	100.0	.5	3.2	5.1	4.2	-	71.7	12.7	-	2.7
WEST NORTH CENTRAL......	360	100.0	1.4	12.4	25.0	15.9	11.6	6.0	5.2	3.4	19.0
RAIL..................	37	100.0	9.7	2.7	1.7	4.1	29.0	2.1	-	2.5	48.2
MOTOR CARRIER.........	176	100.0	.7	12.0	19.8	12.2	12.4	4.3	9.4	5.2	24.1
PRIVATE TRUCK........	143	100.0	-	15.5	37.9	24.0	4.7	9.3	1.5	1.5	5.6
AIR..................	1	100.0	12.1	28.2	22.0	6.1	14.3	.3	8.8	7.0	1.1
WATER................	-	100.0	-	-	-	-	-	-	-	-	-
OTHER................	-	100.0	2.8	12.7	14.6	7.6	16.1	1.3	12.1	10.8	22.1
UNKNOWN..............	2	100.0	-	-	3.5	.5	96.0	-	-	-	-
SOUTH ATLANTIC..........	919	100.0	4.3	9.1	10.9	3.7	13.0	3.2	7.8	.8	47.2
RAIL..................	359	100.0	5.5	1.9	.7	1.1	1.2	.3	6.9	-	82.2
MOTOR CARRIER.........	455	100.0	4.3	9.6	19.6	2.9	20.4	3.2	9.3	1.3	29.4
PRIVATE TRUCK........	101	100.0	-	32.8	8.0	16.2	21.5	13.1	4.4	1.1	2.9
AIR..................	1	100.0	.8	1.8	26.3	.8	10.0	1.0	1.8	5.8	51.5
WATER................	-	100.0	-	-	-	-	-	-	-	-	-
OTHER................	1	100.0	2.3	1.0	1.0	2.2	25.4	17.2	-	-	51.0
UNKNOWN..............	-	100.0	-	38.7	-	-	-	60.4	-	-	.8
EAST SOUTH CENTRAL......	185	100.0	12.8	13.5	17.1	10.6	12.9	3.6	14.2	6.8	8.5
RAIL..................	47	100.0	-	3.7	16.1	9.7	6.0	1.2	27.5	17.9	17.9
MOTOR CARRIER.........	94	100.0	23.8	19.9	18.5	9.0	18.4	2.7	5.0	.8	1.8
PRIVATE TRUCK........	41	100.0	2.7	10.8	12.9	15.9	7.8	8.3	20.1	8.2	13.2
AIR..................	1	100.0	2.1	-	49.1	1.9	26.3	8.3	1.1	.2	11.0
WATER................	-	100.0	-	-	-	-	100.0	-	-	-	-
OTHER................	1	100.0	3.0	8.7	51.9	4.0	13.6	5.2	13.7	-	-
UNKNOWN..............	-	100.0	-	-	-	-	-	-	-	-	-
PACIFIC.................	441	100.0	.5	7.0	19.7	7.0	14.0	16.3	12.7	6.5	16.1
RAIL..................	202	100.0	.3	2.6	16.1	11.0	19.1	22.5	15.9	1.6	11.0
MOTOR CARRIER.........	208	100.0	.7	11.6	24.6	3.9	8.2	12.1	9.3	9.7	20.1
PRIVATE TRUCK........	27	100.0	1.2	5.2	8.8	2.4	20.1	3.8	16.7	20.0	21.8
AIR..................	2	100.0	1.5	11.4	33.7	1.9	28.1	3.6	9.9	5.7	4.3
WATER................	-	100.0	-	-	-	-	-	-	-	-	100.0
OTHER................	-	100.0	1.0	8.0	1.2	3.3	2.6	.7	.3	4.5	78.5
UNKNOWN..............	-	100.0	-	-	12.1	.4	-	-	-	5.1	82.3

See footnotes at end of table 4.

TABLE 3. **TCC GROUP 307—Percent Distribution of Geographic Division of Destination and Means of Transport, by Geographic Division of Origin: 1972**

Geographic division of destination and means of transport	Number	Percent distribution by division of origin[1]								
		U.S. total	New England	Middle Atlantic	East North Central	West North Central	South Atlantic	East South Central	West South Central	Mountain	Pacific
TONS OF SHIPMENTS	(thousands of tons)										
U.S. TOTAL..............	8 248	100.0	12.1	22.5	26.9	8.2	17.8	3.7	(D)	(D)	6.6
RAIL..................	1 317	100.0	17.7	16.0	30.1	3.1	16.4	4.7	(D)	(D)	10.7
MOTOR CARRIER.........	5 282	100.0	13.4	26.6	26.4	6.5	17.2	2.8	(D)	(D)	4.9
PRIVATE TRUCK.........	1 555	100.0	3.5	13.6	25.3	18.2	21.3	5.9	(D)	(D)	9.1
AIR...................	26	100.0	12.3	17.5	36.0	6.1	5.9	13.4	(D)	(D)	6.3
WATER.................	8	100.0	.1	87.5	5.9	-	-	.1	(D)	(D)	6.4
OTHER.................	44	100.0	2.7	26.3	43.8	1.6	16.5	6.4	(D)	(D)	2.1
UNKNOWN...............	13	100.0	14.6	21.1	30.1	24.7	3.5	-	(D)	(D)	6.0
NEW ENGLAND.............	568	100.0	48.9	25.9	7.4	.8	11.5	4.5	(D)	(D)	.2
RAIL..................	77	100.0	39.2	3.4	6.7	4.1	43.9	-	(D)	(D)	.3
MOTOR CARRIER.........	407	100.0	51.5	25.0	8.8	.3	7.6	6.0	(D)	(D)	.1
PRIVATE TRUCK.........	80	100.0	44.5	52.5	1.1	-	.1	1.5	(D)	(D)	.2
AIR...................	2	100.0	68.7	14.4	10.4	4.2	.6	1.2	(D)	(D)	.5
WATER.................	-	100.0	-	-	-	-	-	-	(D)	(D)	-
OTHER.................	1	100.0	54.7	22.3	10.8	1.0	6.9	3.7	(D)	(D)	.1
UNKNOWN...............	-	100.0	-	-	-	100.0	-	-	(D)	(D)	-
MIDDLE ATLANTIC.........	1 646	100.0	18.5	45.7	17.1	2.9	12.5	1.9	(D)	(D)	.8
RAIL..................	141	100.0	39.2	7.9	41.7	.8	7.4	1.4	(D)	(D)	1.6
MOTOR CARRIER.........	1 188	100.0	19.7	51.6	12.6	2.1	10.6	2.0	(D)	(D)	.9
PRIVATE TRUCK.........	306	100.0	4.1	40.4	23.3	7.2	23.0	1.8	(D)	(D)	.2
AIR...................	2	100.0	18.5	3.9	58.8	10.2	1.4	-	(D)	(D)	4.0
WATER.................	1	100.0	.3	99.1	.5	-	-	-	(D)	(D)	-
OTHER.................	2	100.0	8.4	73.4	8.8	2.3	1.9	4.5	(D)	(D)	.3
UNKNOWN...............	3	100.0	62.7	33.8	2.3	-	1.2	-	(D)	(D)	-
EAST NORTH CENTRAL......	1 966	100.0	3.1	14.4	56.5	8.9	9.9	3.1	(D)	(D)	2.5
RAIL..................	247	100.0	4.2	29.9	49.3	.8	1.9	4.7	(D)	(D)	7.5
MOTOR CARRIER.........	1 307	100.0	3.4	14.8	55.9	6.8	13.3	2.3	(D)	(D)	2.2
PRIVATE TRUCK.........	393	100.0	1.2	3.3	63.3	21.4	3.9	3.8	(D)	(D)	.3
AIR...................	8	100.0	6.7	8.4	36.5	7.9	5.8	26.3	(D)	(D)	5.4
WATER.................	-	100.0	-	33.8	66.2	-	-	-	(D)	(D)	-
OTHER.................	9	100.0	1.0	24.7	56.4	1.6	.4	15.4	(D)	(D)	-
UNKNOWN...............	1	100.0	-	13.3	58.7	26.5	-	-	(D)	(D)	1.4
WEST NORTH CENTRAL......	679	100.0	2.5	8.6	32.7	37.9	6.5	5.5	(D)	(D)	3.3
RAIL..................	136	100.0	1.6	14.5	57.1	6.7	3.8	4.2	(D)	(D)	11.8
MOTOR CARRIER.........	342	100.0	4.3	9.8	36.5	33.8	4.7	4.5	(D)	(D)	1.7
PRIVATE TRUCK.........	197	100.0	-	2.2	8.9	67.0	11.5	8.0	(D)	(D)	.2
AIR...................	1	100.0	.1	32.3	42.9	15.4	1.1	3.9	(D)	(D)	2.7
WATER.................	-	100.0	-	-	-	-	-	-	(D)	(D)	-
OTHER.................	1	100.0	5.7	25.0	48.3	13.2	1.7	3.4	(D)	(D)	.3
UNKNOWN...............	-	100.0	-	30.5	47.4	21.8	-	-	(D)	(D)	.3
SOUTH ATLANTIC..........	1 525	100.0	16.0	20.0	16.8	3.2	38.2	2.8	(D)	(D)	1.9
RAIL..................	239	100.0	45.6	7.5	28.0	5.1	3.5	2.0	(D)	(D)	7.7
MOTOR CARRIER.........	1 055	100.0	12.7	26.0	14.8	2.3	39.3	2.9	(D)	(D)	.7
PRIVATE TRUCK.........	202	100.0	.4	4.2	4.6	4.3	75.5	3.1	(D)	(D)	1.2
AIR...................	3	100.0	3.2	6.6	43.6	4.2	12.4	18.3	(D)	(D)	9.1
WATER.................	2	100.0	-	88.5	11.0	-	-	.4	(D)	(D)	-
OTHER.................	18	100.0	.4	12.2	52.3	.4	33.0	1.6	(D)	(D)	-
UNKNOWN...............	3	100.0	-	.7	-	99.3	-	-	(D)	(D)	-
EAST SOUTH CENTRAL......	466	100.0	8.7	13.1	25.6	7.2	23.2	8.8	(D)	(D)	9.4
RAIL..................	61	100.0	14.6	4.1	20.6	2.2	3.5	7.0	(D)	(D)	45.9
MOTOR CARRIER.........	243	100.0	13.0	15.3	30.9	5.8	16.9	5.2	(D)	(D)	6.2
PRIVATE TRUCK.........	153	100.0	-	13.1	17.9	11.8	41.5	15.0	(D)	(D)	.4
AIR...................	1	100.0	3.6	3.4	33.8	.5	2.0	43.3	(D)	(D)	3.6
WATER.................	-	100.0	-	-	-	-	-	-	(D)	(D)	-
OTHER.................	2	100.0	.4	30.6	28.9	.2	21.0	18.5	(D)	(D)	-
UNKNOWN...............	3	100.0	-	8.6	78.8	-	12.6	-	(D)	(D)	-
WEST SOUTH CENTRAL......	541	100.0	4.5	29.1	15.5	8.0	12.8	9.3	(D)	(D)	8.1
RAIL..................	134	100.0	-	27.3	14.7	-	17.5	16.3	(D)	(D)	18.8
MOTOR CARRIER.........	340	100.0	7.1	34.1	17.9	10.7	12.3	3.2	(D)	(D)	4.4
PRIVATE TRUCK.........	60	100.0	-	.3	3.5	11.4	7.2	28.8	(D)	(D)	5.9
AIR...................	1	100.0	.3	13.1	53.4	11.5	2.2	2.7	(D)	(D)	14.7
WATER.................	1	100.0	-	100.0	-	-	-	-	(D)	(D)	-
OTHER.................	2	100.0	3.7	76.2	4.2	2.5	-	11.5	(D)	(D)	-
UNKNOWN...............	1	100.0	-	78.6	21.2	-	-	-	(D)	(D)	-
MOUNTAIN................	137	100.0	3.6	7.2	10.3	13.5	3.6	8.4	(D)	(D)	47.0
RAIL..................	15	100.0	.1	.4	14.5	8.7	-	46.2	(D)	(D)	30.1
MOTOR CARRIER.........	92	100.0	5.3	7.0	10.2	13.3	4.5	.8	(D)	(D)	53.0
PRIVATE TRUCK.........	25	100.0	-	-	8.8	19.3	2.9	15.0	(D)	(D)	42.1
AIR...................	2	100.0	.4	79.8	5.6	2.4	2.5	.1	(D)	(D)	8.7
WATER.................	-	100.0	-	-	-	-	-	-	(D)	(D)	-
OTHER.................	1	100.0	2.0	85.6	8.5	2.7	-	-	(D)	(D)	1.2
UNKNOWN...............	-	100.0	-	-	-	-	-	-	(D)	(D)	100.0
PACIFIC.................	716	100.0	3.4	10.6	12.4	6.2	26.3	1.3	(D)	(D)	39.1
RAIL..................	265	100.0	6.1	17.4	11.8	4.2	48.3	1.8	(D)	(D)	10.4
MOTOR CARRIER.........	305	100.0	2.6	8.8	17.1	8.8	19.1	.3	(D)	(D)	41.8
PRIVATE TRUCK.........	136	100.0	.1	.2	1.6	4.6	.9	2.4	(D)	(D)	89.5
AIR...................	2	100.0	2.4	16.2	48.1	.3	17.3	3.2	(D)	(D)	10.0
WATER.................	2	100.0	-	71.1	6.4	-	-	-	(D)	(D)	22.5
OTHER.................	3	100.0	.3	7.2	53.2	1.8	10.6	-	(D)	(D)	27.0
UNKNOWN...............	-	100.0	-	-	3.0	-	-	-	(D)	(D)	97.0

See footnotes at end of table 4.

TABLE 3. **TCC GROUP 307—Percent Distribution of Geographic Division of Destination and Means of Transport, by Geographic Division of Origin: 1972**—Continued

Geographic division of destination and means of transport	Number	Percent distribution by division of origin[1]									
		U.S. total	New England	Middle Atlantic	East North Central	West North Central	South Atlantic	East South Central	West South Central	Mountain	Pacific
TON-MILES OF SHIPMENTS	(millions of ton-miles)										
U.S. TOTAL..............	4 258	100.0	10.6	22.0	20.1	8.5	21.6	4.4	(D)	(D)	10.4
RAIL...................	1 259	100.0	12.9	18.6	16.3	2.9	28.5	3.8	(D)	(D)	16.1
MOTOR CARRIER..........	2 451	100.0	11.4	25.4	22.1	7.2	18.6	3.8	(D)	(D)	8.5
PRIVATE TRUCK..........	491	100.0	1.4	10.9	19.7	29.1	20.5	8.4	(D)	(D)	5.5
AIR....................	20	100.0	4.4	32.3	28.4	5.2	8.8	6.2	(D)	(D)	11.3
WATER..................	10	100.0	–	84.8	9.0	–	–	.1	(D)	(D)	6.2
OTHER..................	19	100.0	3.1	46.9	32.8	2.1	7.2	5.8	(D)	(D)	1.3
UNKNOWN................	6	100.0	3.2	29.4	24.7	37.5	.7	–	(D)	(D)	4.5
NEW ENGLAND............	157	100.0	12.9	18.6	19.3	3.1	24.9	15.0	(D)	(D)	1.4
RAIL...................	34	100.0	8.2	2.2	10.6	10.5	58.2	–	(D)	(D)	1.6
MOTOR CARRIER..........	114	100.0	14.7	19.7	22.9	1.0	17.0	19.7	(D)	(D)	1.2
PRIVATE TRUCK..........	8	100.0	9.2	66.9	5.3	–	.5	12.7	(D)	(D)	3.6
AIR....................	–	100.0	9.6	14.3	36.6	24.6	2.8	5.2	(D)	(D)	6.8
WATER..................	–	100.0	–	–	–	–	–	–	(D)	(D)	–
OTHER..................	–	100.0	13.6	17.5	34.3	4.7	12.7	13.6	(D)	(D)	–
UNKNOWN................	–	100.0	–	–	100.0	–	–	–	(D)	(D)	1.0
MIDDLE ATLANTIC........	467	100.0	11.7	17.6	29.2	9.5	17.9	5.4	(D)	(D)	6.6
RAIL...................	62	100.0	20.0	3.9	52.2	1.6	11.0	2.8	(D)	(D)	8.5
MOTOR CARRIER..........	294	100.0	13.6	22.6	24.0	7.2	14.9	6.4	(D)	(D)	8.2
PRIVATE TRUCK..........	108	100.0	1.7	12.0	29.8	20.4	30.6	4.1	(D)	(D)	1.3
AIR....................	1	100.0	5.3	1.5	48.9	18.5	2.0	–	(D)	(D)	16.3
WATER..................	–	100.0	4.2	70.6	25.2	–	–	–	(D)	(D)	–
OTHER..................	–	100.0	10.5	21.0	27.6	11.0	3.0	20.5	(D)	(D)	4.3
UNKNOWN................	–	100.0	71.7	5.2	17.3	–	5.9	–	(D)	(D)	–
EAST NORTH CENTRAL.....	708	100.0	6.0	22.2	24.4	12.7	14.2	4.5	(D)	(D)	12.3
RAIL...................	127	100.0	5.7	36.8	20.3	.5	2.0	6.0	(D)	(D)	25.7
MOTOR CARRIER..........	450	100.0	7.0	22.5	25.2	7.8	19.8	3.9	(D)	(D)	11.4
PRIVATE TRUCK..........	123	100.0	2.9	5.6	25.8	43.9	6.6	4.3	(D)	(D)	1.9
AIR....................	3	100.0	11.2	8.5	17.7	6.1	12.5	16.5	(D)	(D)	20.6
WATER..................	–	100.0	–	89.3	10.7	–	–	–	(D)	(D)	–
OTHER..................	3	100.0	2.6	47.2	27.2	2.0	.4	19.0	(D)	(D)	.1
UNKNOWN................	–	100.0	–	30.9	27.8	29.3	–	–	(D)	(D)	12.0
WEST NORTH CENTRAL.....	318	100.0	6.2	17.1	28.8	18.1	10.6	6.2	(D)	(D)	9.8
RAIL...................	82	100.0	3.1	20.6	37.1	1.8	4.9	5.5	(D)	(D)	26.9
MOTOR CARRIER..........	162	100.0	10.4	19.2	33.5	13.2	8.3	5.2	(D)	(D)	5.0
PRIVATE TRUCK..........	70	100.0	–	7.2	8.1	48.6	23.2	9.3	(D)	(D)	.9
AIR....................	–	100.0	.3	48.7	31.2	8.1	1.9	3.1	(D)	(D)	5.4
WATER..................	–	100.0	–	–	–	–	–	–	(D)	(D)	–
OTHER..................	1	100.0	11.7	41.1	34.5	3.0	2.9	4.3	(D)	(D)	.8
UNKNOWN................	–	100.0	–	47.9	43.4	7.9	–	–	(D)	(D)	.8
SOUTH ATLANTIC.........	726	100.0	23.2	22.9	18.0	5.8	16.4	3.3	(D)	(D)	8.5
RAIL...................	184	100.0	46.6	4.5	17.8	5.8	2.3	1.5	(D)	(D)	20.9
MOTOR CARRIER..........	475	100.0	17.3	31.6	17.4	4.6	19.5	3.6	(D)	(D)	3.6
PRIVATE TRUCK..........	55	100.0	.9	6.7	23.4	12.2	39.3	5.9	(D)	(D)	9.9
AIR....................	2	100.0	3.9	8.7	33.4	5.8	6.8	12.8	(D)	(D)	24.7
WATER..................	2	100.0	–	90.8	9.0	–	–	.2	(D)	(D)	–
OTHER..................	3	100.0	1.4	36.8	42.0	2.1	11.4	4.9	(D)	(D)	.2
UNKNOWN................	2	100.0	–	.2	–	99.8	–	–	(D)	(D)	–
EAST SOUTH CENTRAL.....	265	100.0	15.5	19.1	13.0	8.2	11.0	2.5	(D)	(D)	27.0
RAIL...................	63	100.0	15.7	2.4	5.0	1.2	1.9	.9	(D)	(D)	71.7
MOTOR CARRIER..........	145	100.0	21.4	21.0	17.5	5.2	10.1	1.8	(D)	(D)	17.3
PRIVATE TRUCK..........	53	100.0	–	33.3	8.3	24.8	24.6	6.4	(D)	(D)	1.9
AIR....................	–	100.0	6.8	5.4	29.7	.6	3.3	18.8	(D)	(D)	14.7
WATER..................	–	100.0	–	–	–	–	–	–	(D)	(D)	–
OTHER..................	1	100.0	.9	53.0	21.6	.4	18.8	4.6	(D)	(D)	.1
UNKNOWN................	1	100.0	–	12.9	85.1	–	2.0	–	(D)	(D)	–
WEST SOUTH CENTRAL.....	490	100.0	6.5	40.3	15.1	3.9	14.6	5.4	(D)	(D)	11.5
RAIL...................	136	100.0	–	35.1	12.2	–	18.3	9.6	(D)	(D)	23.6
MOTOR CARRIER..........	320	100.0	9.9	44.7	17.1	5.2	13.2	1.5	(D)	(D)	6.0
PRIVATE TRUCK..........	25	100.0	–	1.2	7.1	8.6	17.4	32.7	(D)	(D)	17.8
AIR....................	1	100.0	.6	21.8	41.0	8.9	3.1	1.3	(D)	(D)	21.8
WATER..................	1	100.0	–	100.0	–	–	–	–	(D)	(D)	–
OTHER..................	3	100.0	5.2	84.1	3.7	1.6	–	4.9	(D)	(D)	–
UNKNOWN................	1	100.0	–	88.4	11.6	–	–	–	(D)	(D)	–
MOUNTAIN...............	114	100.0	8.3	15.4	16.4	10.9	6.5	11.1	(D)	(D)	25.4
RAIL...................	15	100.0	.1	.6	17.3	6.0	–	55.0	(D)	(D)	21.0
MOTOR CARRIER..........	73	100.0	12.7	15.2	16.5	12.5	8.3	1.0	(D)	(D)	27.2
PRIVATE TRUCK..........	17	100.0	–	–	19.7	12.0	6.6	19.3	(D)	(D)	30.7
AIR....................	4	100.0	.4	89.8	3.1	1.5	2.2	.1	(D)	(D)	2.7
WATER..................	–	100.0	–	–	–	–	–	–	(D)	(D)	–
OTHER..................	2	100.0	2.6	86.8	8.1	2.0	–	–	(D)	(D)	.5
UNKNOWN................	–	100.0	–	–	–	–	–	–	(D)	(D)	100.0
PACIFIC................	1 009	100.0	6.2	17.9	16.7	6.8	43.0	1.6	(D)	(D)	7.1
RAIL...................	552	100.0	7.5	19.8	10.4	3.2	53.4	1.5	(D)	(D)	4.0
MOTOR CARRIER..........	413	100.0	4.8	15.8	24.4	10.3	32.4	.4	(D)	(D)	10.1
PRIVATE TRUCK..........	28	100.0	1.2	2.1	14.5	27.9	10.2	19.2	(D)	(D)	20.7
AIR....................	4	100.0	3.7	21.0	49.0	.2	19.8	3.0	(D)	(D)	2.1
WATER..................	5	100.0	–	76.2	12.1	–	–	–	(D)	(D)	11.7
OTHER..................	4	100.0	.6	12.7	65.2	2.0	15.1	–	(D)	(D)	4.3
UNKNOWN................	–	100.0	–	–	15.2	–	.1	–	(D)	(D)	84.7

See footnotes at end of table 4.

TABLE 4. TCC GROUP 307—Percent Distribution of Distance Shipped and Weight of Shipment, by Means of Transport: 1972

Distance shipped and weight of shipment [2] [3]	Number	Percent distribution by means of transport							
		All means of transport	Rail	Motor carrier	Private truck	Air	Water	Other	Unknown
TONS OF SHIPMENTS	(thousands of tons)								
U.S. TOTAL..........	7 540	100.0	16.3	64.6	18.2	.3	.1	.4	.1
UNDER 100 MILES.........	1 571	100.0	2.8	68.6	27.9	-	.1	.2	.2
UNDER 1000 POUNDS.....	159	100.0	.2	70.8	27.5	.1	-	1.3	-
1000 TO 9999 POUNDS...	892	100.0	.1	68.8	30.5	-	.2	.2	.2
10000 TO 29999 POUNDS.	283	100.0	.8	67.3	31.2	-	.1	-	.5
30000 TO 59999 POUNDS.	176	100.0	4.6	78.8	16.7	-	-	-	-
60000 TO 89999 POUNDS.	45	100.0	71.5	17.6	10.9	-	-	-	-
90000 POUNDS AND OVER.	13	100.0	-	100.0	-	-	-	-	-
100 TO 199 MILES........	1 049	100.0	10.3	66.7	21.6	.2	-	1.1	.1
UNDER 1000 POUNDS.....	80	100.0	1.0	85.0	9.3	2.0	-	2.7	.1
1000 TO 9999 POUNDS...	473	100.0	2.2	72.4	25.1	-	-	.3	-
10000 TO 29999 POUNDS.	315	100.0	16.4	64.1	19.4	-	-	-	.2
30000 TO 59999 POUNDS.	139	100.0	12.1	53.7	28.4	-	-	5.9	-
60000 TO 89999 POUNDS.	39	100.0	72.1	27.9	-	-	-	-	-
90000 POUNDS AND OVER.	-	100.0	-	-	-	-	-	-	-
200 TO 299 MILES........	935	100.0	8.1	75.9	15.2	.4	-	.4	-
UNDER 1000 POUNDS.....	69	100.0	.6	89.9	4.0	3.7	-	1.8	.1
1000 TO 9999 POUNDS...	398	100.0	4.8	79.5	14.8	.3	-	.5	.1
10000 TO 29999 POUNDS.	252	100.0	14.7	66.2	19.2	-	-	-	-
30000 TO 59999 POUNDS.	176	100.0	6.5	75.5	18.0	-	-	-	-
60000 TO 89999 POUNDS.	11	100.0	69.9	30.1	-	-	-	-	-
90000 POUNDS AND OVER.	26	100.0	-	100.0	-	-	-	-	-
300 TO 499 MILES........	1 260	100.0	16.3	66.6	16.5	.3	-	.3	.1
UNDER 1000 POUNDS.....	98	100.0	.4	91.0	2.7	2.9	.1	2.9	.1
1000 TO 9999 POUNDS...	505	100.0	5.8	76.3	17.5	.2	-	.2	-
10000 TO 29999 POUNDS.	395	100.0	22.7	52.6	24.5	-	-	-	.1
30000 TO 59999 POUNDS.	206	100.0	16.7	73.9	9.4	-	-	-	-
60000 TO 89999 POUNDS.	26	100.0	88.9	11.1	-	-	-	-	-
90000 POUNDS AND OVER.	27	100.0	99.0	-	1.0	-	-	-	-
500 TO 999 MILES........	1 688	100.0	23.8	57.1	18.6	.3	-	.2	.1
UNDER 1000 POUNDS.....	123	100.0	.6	90.8	3.8	3.1	-	1.6	.1
1000 TO 9999 POUNDS...	454	100.0	6.0	76.1	17.2	.2	.1	.2	.2
10000 TO 29999 POUNDS.	486	100.0	22.1	53.5	24.4	-	-	-	-
30000 TO 59999 POUNDS.	412	100.0	23.0	50.8	26.1	-	-	-	-
60000 TO 89999 POUNDS.	112	100.0	72.0	24.1	3.9	-	-	-	-
90000 POUNDS AND OVER.	100	100.0	90.6	9.4	-	-	-	-	-
1000 TO 1499 MILES.....	486	100.0	21.9	69.8	6.5	.2	.8	.5	.2
UNDER 1000 POUNDS.....	38	100.0	1.1	89.2	5.5	2.7	-	1.5	-
1000 TO 9999 POUNDS...	102	100.0	3.5	90.0	6.2	.1	-	.1	-
10000 TO 29999 POUNDS.	147	100.0	10.2	79.0	8.9	-	-	1.2	.7
30000 TO 59999 POUNDS.	142	100.0	32.2	58.0	7.1	-	2.7	-	-
60000 TO 89999 POUNDS.	50	100.0	72.9	27.1	-	-	-	-	-
90000 POUNDS AND OVER.	4	100.0	100.0	-	-	-	-	-	-
1500 MILES OR OVER......	549	100.0	52.6	43.5	2.2	.9	.4	.5	-
UNDER 1000 POUNDS.....	36	100.0	2.8	76.9	13.4	4.9	-	1.9	.1
1000 TO 9999 POUNDS...	95	100.0	10.5	82.1	3.9	1.2	.4	1.9	-
10000 TO 29999 POUNDS.	75	100.0	45.3	50.1	4.5	-	-	-	-
30000 TO 59999 POUNDS.	225	100.0	57.3	42.0	-	-	-	.7	-
60000 TO 89999 POUNDS.	102	100.0	98.0	-	-	-	2.0	-	-
90000 POUNDS AND OVER.	13	100.0	100.0	-	-	-	-	-	-
TON-MILES OF SHIPMENTS	(millions of ton-miles)								
U.S. TOTAL..........	3 872	100.0	30.1	57.3	11.5	.5	.3	.3	.1
UNDER 100 MILES.........	77	100.0	4.3	73.6	21.5	-	-	.3	.3
UNDER 1000 POUNDS.....	6	100.0	.6	79.2	18.6	.1	-	1.5	-
1000 TO 9999 POUNDS...	41	100.0	.1	76.1	23.1	-	-	.2	.5
10000 TO 29999 POUNDS.	14	100.0	.9	69.5	29.3	-	-	-	.2
30000 TO 59999 POUNDS.	9	100.0	3.0	81.7	15.3	-	-	-	-
60000 TO 89999 POUNDS.	3	100.0	81.6	17.0	1.4	-	-	-	-
90000 POUNDS AND OVER.	1	100.0	-	100.0	-	-	-	-	-
100 TO 199 MILES........	154	100.0	12.0	65.6	21.2	.2	-	.9	.1
UNDER 1000 POUNDS.....	11	100.0	1.1	84.8	9.3	2.2	-	2.5	.1
1000 TO 9999 POUNDS...	69	100.0	2.3	72.8	24.5	-	-	.3	-
10000 TO 29999 POUNDS.	47	100.0	19.1	62.0	18.8	-	-	-	.1
30000 TO 59999 POUNDS.	19	100.0	15.4	50.2	29.7	-	-	4.7	-
60000 TO 89999 POUNDS.	6	100.0	71.8	28.2	-	-	-	-	-
90000 POUNDS AND OVER.	-	100.0	-	-	-	-	-	-	-

See footnotes at end of table 4.

TABLE 4. **TCC GROUP 307—Percent Distribution of Distance Shipped and Weight of Shipment, by Means of Transport: 1972**—Continued

Distance shipped and weight of shipment²³	Number	Percent distribution by means of transport							
		All means of transport	Rail	Motor carrier	Private truck	Air	Water	Other	Unknown
TON-MILES OF SHIPMENTS	(millions of ton-miles)								
200 TO 299 MILES	234	100.0	7.8	76.2	15.3	.4	-	.3	-
UNDER 1000 POUNDS	17	100.0	.5	90.0	4.1	3.5	-	1.8	-
1000 TO 9999 POUNDS	99	100.0	5.0	79.2	15.0	.3	-	.5	.1
10000 TO 29999 POUNDS	63	100.0	14.1	66.7	19.3	-	-	-	.1
30000 TO 59999 POUNDS	44	100.0	6.0	76.4	17.7	-	-	-	-
60000 TO 89999 POUNDS	2	100.0	68.6	31.4	-	-	-	-	-
90000 POUNDS AND OVER	6	100.0	-	100.0	-	-	-	-	-
300 TO 499 MILES	496	100.0	16.5	65.9	16.9	.3	-	.3	-
UNDER 1000 POUNDS	38	100.0	.4	90.9	2.8	2.9	.1	2.8	.1
1000 TO 9999 POUNDS	199	100.0	5.8	76.2	17.6	.2	-	.2	-
10000 TO 29999 POUNDS	154	100.0	23.3	50.6	26.0	-	-	-	-
30000 TO 59999 POUNDS	81	100.0	15.5	75.4	9.2	-	-	-	.1
60000 TO 89999 POUNDS	9	100.0	89.6	10.4	-	-	-	-	-
90000 POUNDS AND OVER	13	100.0	99.2	-	.8	-	-	-	-
500 TO 999 MILES	1 195	100.0	25.0	56.5	18.0	.3	-	.2	.1
UNDER 1000 POUNDS	87	100.0	.6	91.1	3.6	3.0	-	1.6	.1
1000 TO 9999 POUNDS	313	100.0	6.5	76.2	16.7	.2	.1	.2	.2
10000 TO 29999 POUNDS	336	100.0	22.3	53.2	24.6	-	-	-	-
30000 TO 59999 POUNDS	295	100.0	23.1	51.8	25.0	-	-	-	-
60000 TO 89999 POUNDS	82	100.0	73.3	22.3	4.4	-	-	-	-
90000 POUNDS AND OVER	80	100.0	92.4	7.6	-	-	-	-	-
1000 TO 1499 MILES	578	100.0	23.0	68.6	6.6	.2	.8	.5	.2
UNDER 1000 POUNDS	46	100.0	1.1	89.0	5.8	2.6	-	1.5	-
1000 TO 9999 POUNDS	120	100.0	3.7	89.9	6.2	.1	-	.1	-
10000 TO 29999 POUNDS	174	100.0	10.5	78.0	9.4	-	-	1.3	.7
30000 TO 59999 POUNDS	171	100.0	34.4	56.1	6.8	-	2.6	-	-
60000 TO 89999 POUNDS	59	100.0	74.9	25.1	-	-	-	-	-
90000 POUNDS AND OVER	6	100.0	100.0	-	-	-	-	-	-
1500 MILES OR OVER	1 135	100.0	53.9	42.3	2.1	.9	.5	.4	-
UNDER 1000 POUNDS	74	100.0	3.0	76.6	13.4	5.0	-	1.8	.1
1000 TO 9999 POUNDS	191	100.0	9.8	82.8	4.0	1.2	.6	1.7	-
10000 TO 29999 POUNDS	148	100.0	45.8	50.2	4.0	-	-	-	-
30000 TO 59999 POUNDS	456	100.0	57.4	41.7	-	-	-	-	-
60000 TO 89999 POUNDS	232	100.0	98.2	-	-	-	.9	-	-
90000 POUNDS AND OVER	32	100.0	100.0	-	-	1.8	-	-	-

Note: Detail may not add to total due to rounding. The introductory table shows the estimates of sampling variablility for tons; sampling varia-bility for ton-miles has not been estimated. See the map in the Introduction for the States comprising the geographic divisions of the United States.
   Shipments excluded from the survey are those moving by pipeline (primarily petroleum products from refineries), parcel post shipments, and com-modities moved by own power (motorized vehicles, aircraft, etc.) or towed (prefabricated buildings, etc.). Local shipments (commodities shipped less than 25 miles from the plant) and shipments within the same city are also excluded. Shipments to Alaska and Hawaii from the 48 conterminous States and the District of Columbia are included; however, no data were obtained for shipments originating in Alaska and Hawaii.

- Represents zero or rounds to zero.   (D) Withheld to avoid disclosing figures for individual companies.

[1]Production of this commodity is concentrated in the geographic divisions shown; figures and distributions for geographic divisions not shown are included in the total.

[2]Distances of shipments to foreign destinations are calculated only to the U.S. port of exit.

[3]Includes only shipments represented by bills of lading and invoices. Summary records which did not show individual weights of shipments are not included.

Stone, Clay, Glass, and Concrete Products

CONTENTS

[Page numbers listed here omit the State prefix number that appears as part of the number for each page]

TABLES   (The tables listed below are shown for each of the Transportation Commodity Classification groups in this report)

Comparisons of Tons and Ton-Miles of Shipments for Geographic Divisions of Origin and for Sampling Variability: 1972 and 1967

1. Percent Distribution of Geographic Division of Origin and Distance Shipped, by Means of Transport: 1972

2. Percent Distribution of Geographic Division of Origin and Means of Transport, by Geographic Division of Destination: 1972

3. Percent Distribution of Geographic Division of Destination and Means of Transport, by Geographic Division of Origin: 1972

4. Percent Distribution of Distance Shipped and Weight of Shipment, by Means of Transport: 1972

TCC 321. Flat Glass

Comparisons of Tons and Ton-Miles of Shipments for
Geographic Divisions of Origin and for Sampling Variability: 1972 and 1967

Geographic division of origin	Estimates				Relative sampling variability in tons (percent)	
	1972		1967		1972	1967
	Tons (thousands)	Ton-miles (millions)	Tons (thousands)	Ton-miles (millions)		
U.S. total	3,083	1,335	1,655	722	9.6	(*)
New England	(D)	(D)	(*)	(*)	(*)	(*)
Middle Atlantic	850	314	(*)	(*)	35.3	(*)
East North Central	750	278	(*)	(*)	10.6	(*)
West North Central	(D)	(D)	(*)	(*)	(*)	(*)
South Atlantic	564	224	(*)	(*)	4.8	(*)
East South Central	(D)	(D)	(*)	(*)	(*)	(*)
West South Central	210	105	(*)	(*)	3.6	(*)
Mountain	(D)	(D)	(*)	(*)	(*)	(*)
Pacific	(D)	(D)	(*)	(*)	(*)	(*)

(D) Withheld to avoid disclosing figures for individual companies.   (*) Data not published.

TABLE 1. TCC GROUP 321—Percent Distribution of Geographic Division of Origin and Distance Shipped, by Means of Transport: 1972

Geographic division of origin[1] and distance shipped[2]	Number	Percent distribution by means of transport							
		All means of transport	Rail	Motor carrier	Private truck	Air	Water	Other	Unknown
TONS OF SHIPMENTS	(thousands of tons)								
U.S. TOTAL..........	3 083	100.0	26.5	54.2	19.2	-	-	-	.1
MIDDLE ATLANTIC.........	850	100.0	28.1	49.1	22.8	-	-	-	-
UNDER 100 MILES.......	93	100.0	1.5	59.7	38.6	-	-	-	.1
100 TO 199 MILES......	267	100.0	19.1	54.9	26.0	-	-	-	-
200 TO 299 MILES......	186	100.0	34.6	39.2	26.2	-	-	-	-
300 TO 499 MILES......	107	100.0	39.6	51.6	8.8	-	-	-	-
500 TO 999 MILES......	115	100.0	16.3	63.7	19.9	.1	-	-	-
1000 TO 1499 MILES....	60	100.0	75.8	13.6	10.5	-	-	-	-
1500 MILES OR OVER....	18	100.0	78.6	21.3	-	.1	-	-	-
EAST NORTH CENTRAL......	750	100.0	30.0	53.5	16.2	-	-	-	.2
UNDER 100 MILES.......	175	100.0	31.5	49.9	18.3	-	-	-	.2
100 TO 199 MILES......	100	100.0	34.0	52.8	13.2	-	-	-	-
200 TO 299 MILES......	159	100.0	19.5	61.4	18.3	-	-	-	.8
300 TO 499 MILES......	153	100.0	38.8	45.6	15.4	.1	-	-	-
500 TO 999 MILES......	110	100.0	28.0	54.3	17.7	-	-	-	-
1000 TO 1499 MILES....	20	100.0	12.0	87.3	.7	-	-	.1	-
1500 MILES OR OVER....	31	100.0	37.8	49.6	12.4	.1	-	-	-
SOUTH ATLANTIC..........	564	100.0	7.4	65.3	27.3	-	-	-	-
UNDER 100 MILES.......	63	100.0	-	14.2	85.8	-	-	-	-
100 TO 199 MILES......	62	100.0	-	71.4	28.6	-	-	-	-
200 TO 299 MILES......	188	100.0	1.4	75.3	23.2	.1	-	-	-
300 TO 499 MILES......	141	100.0	4.2	83.3	12.5	-	-	-	-
500 TO 999 MILES......	87	100.0	34.4	46.0	19.6	-	-	-	-
1000 TO 1499 MILES....	9	100.0	29.2	52.3	15.9	-	-	-	2.6
1500 MILES OR OVER....	12	100.0	-	83.9	16.1	-	-	-	-
WEST SOUTH CENTRAL......	210	100.0	11.9	62.2	25.7	-	-	-	.3
UNDER 100 MILES.......	8	100.0	-	81.9	18.1	-	-	-	-
100 TO 199 MILES......	22	100.0	4.5	69.3	26.2	-	-	-	-
200 TO 299 MILES......	21	100.0	14.4	52.7	33.0	-	-	-	-
300 TO 499 MILES......	68	100.0	9.1	57.8	33.0	-	-	-	.2
500 TO 999 MILES......	71	100.0	8.7	70.7	20.6	-	-	-	-
1000 TO 1499 MILES....	11	100.0	43.2	36.2	17.0	-	-	-	3.6
1500 MILES OR OVER....	5	100.0	60.6	39.4	-	-	-	-	-
TON-MILES OF SHIPMENTS	(millions of ton-miles)								
U.S. TOTAL..........	1 335	100.0	33.7	51.4	14.7	-	-	-	.1
MIDDLE ATLANTIC.........	314	100.0	42.5	41.1	16.3	.1	-	-	-
UNDER 100 MILES.......	5	100.0	1.8	64.7	33.4	-	-	-	-
100 TO 199 MILES......	39	100.0	19.0	54.4	26.6	-	-	-	-
200 TO 299 MILES......	46	100.0	32.4	41.5	26.1	-	-	-	-
300 TO 499 MILES......	42	100.0	36.7	54.2	9.1	-	-	-	-
500 TO 999 MILES......	76	100.0	20.1	58.8	21.0	.1	-	-	-
1000 TO 1499 MILES....	64	100.0	75.0	14.1	10.8	-	-	-	-
1500 MILES OR OVER....	39	100.0	80.3	19.6	-	.2	-	-	-
EAST NORTH CENTRAL......	278	100.0	30.6	54.5	14.7	.1	-	-	.1
UNDER 100 MILES.......	10	100.0	39.2	50.0	10.5	-	-	-	.4
100 TO 199 MILES......	12	100.0	27.0	57.1	15.9	-	-	-	-
200 TO 299 MILES......	41	100.0	19.1	62.0	18.1	-	-	-	.7
300 TO 499 MILES......	62	100.0	39.7	44.8	15.3	.1	-	-	-
500 TO 999 MILES......	72	100.0	26.3	55.2	18.5	-	-	-	-
1000 TO 1499 MILES....	21	100.0	15.1	84.2	.7	-	-	-	-
1500 MILES OR OVER....	57	100.0	39.5	47.7	12.7	.1	-	.1	-
SOUTH ATLANTIC..........	224	100.0	13.6	66.7	19.5	-	-	-	.1
UNDER 100 MILES.......	4	100.0	-	14.0	86.0	-	-	-	-
100 TO 199 MILES......	10	100.0	-	70.6	29.4	-	-	-	-
200 TO 299 MILES......	48	100.0	1.6	77.2	21.2	.1	-	-	-
300 TO 499 MILES......	55	100.0	4.4	83.9	11.8	-	-	-	-
500 TO 999 MILES......	66	100.0	36.3	41.5	22.2	-	-	-	-
1000 TO 1499 MILES....	11	100.0	28.3	55.7	13.3	-	-	-	2.7
1500 MILES OR OVER....	27	100.0	-	87.5	12.5	-	-	-	-
WEST SOUTH CENTRAL......	105	100.0	18.3	58.8	22.3	-	-	-	.6
UNDER 100 MILES.......	-	100.0	-	80.9	19.1	-	-	-	-
100 TO 199 MILES......	3	100.0	3.5	69.1	27.4	-	-	-	-
200 TO 299 MILES......	5	100.0	16.4	53.9	29.7	-	-	-	-
300 TO 499 MILES......	27	100.0	8.9	58.4	32.5	-	-	-	.2
500 TO 999 MILES......	44	100.0	10.1	69.2	20.7	-	-	-	-
1000 TO 1499 MILES....	14	100.0	41.2	37.0	17.9	-	-	-	3.9
1500 MILES OR OVER....	8	100.0	58.7	41.3	-	-	-	-	-

See footnotes at end of table 4.

TABLE 2. TCC GROUP 321—Percent Distribution of Geographic Division of Origin and Means of Transport, by Geographic Division of Destination: 1972

Geographic division of origin[1] and means of transport	Number	Percent distribution by division of destination									
		U.S. total	New England	Middle Atlantic	East North Central	West North Central	South Atlantic	East South Central	West South Central	Mountain	Pacific
TONS OF SHIPMENTS	(thousands of tons)										
U.S. TOTAL	3 083	100.0	2.2	18.3	34.8	8.5	14.7	6.6	5.9	1.1	7.8
RAIL	816	100.0	2.2	11.4	32.3	14.1	15.3	6.5	7.0	1.4	9.9
MOTOR CARRIER	1 669	100.0	2.5	19.2	34.6	8.0	14.2	7.4	5.0	1.3	7.9
PRIVATE TRUCK	593	100.0	1.4	25.6	39.0	2.3	15.6	4.4	6.9	.3	4.5
AIR	-	100.0	1.2	37.7	21.0	16.3	3.7	.3	8.5	1.0	10.4
WATER	-	100.0	-	-	-	-	-	-	-	-	-
OTHER	-	100.0	3.9	54.5	25.6	2.3	2.0	3.4	.7	.3	7.2
UNKNOWN	2	100.0	-	3.7	39.8	24.9	-	1.1	5.6	9.0	15.8
MIDDLE ATLANTIC	850	100.0	3.5	33.9	31.9	3.6	17.7	4.1	3.1	.2	2.0
RAIL	239	100.0	6.9	23.8	16.6	2.1	36.6	1.5	6.2	-	6.2
MOTOR CARRIER	417	100.0	2.1	39.5	35.1	5.8	7.4	6.8	2.3	.3	.6
PRIVATE TRUCK	193	100.0	2.2	34.5	44.0	.8	16.4	1.2	.9	-	-
AIR	-	100.0	-	5.7	31.6	32.3	7.6	.1	7.9	-	14.9
WATER	-	100.0	-	-	-	-	-	-	-	-	-
OTHER	-	100.0	9.2	53.1	4.6	10.3	12.7	9.1	1.0	-	-
UNKNOWN	-	100.0	-	100.0	-	-	-	-	-	-	-
EAST NORTH CENTRAL	750	100.0	.7	8.5	54.5	9.7	9.4	8.1	4.9	.2	4.0
RAIL	225	100.0	.2	3.4	50.8	19.6	5.2	14.2	1.4	-	5.3
MOTOR CARRIER	401	100.0	.8	8.9	56.2	6.1	12.2	5.9	5.9	.2	3.7
PRIVATE TRUCK	121	100.0	1.6	17.1	55.4	2.7	7.9	4.2	7.9	.6	2.6
AIR	-	100.0	2.1	46.4	28.3	.4	1.3	.8	9.5	-	11.2
WATER	-	100.0	-	-	-	-	-	-	-	-	-
OTHER	-	100.0	-	5.5	22.1	2.3	3.0	20.2	-	-	46.9
UNKNOWN	1	100.0	-	-	61.5	38.5	-	-	-	-	-
SOUTH ATLANTIC	564	100.0	2.3	26.0	29.5	4.3	26.7	4.4	4.2	.6	1.9
RAIL	41	100.0	-	3.5	9.4	33.7	4.5	8.1	38.7	2.0	-
MOTOR CARRIER	368	100.0	3.0	23.4	29.7	2.5	31.4	5.5	1.5	.3	2.7
PRIVATE TRUCK	154	100.0	1.1	38.3	34.7	.7	21.8	.7	1.5	.7	.6
AIR	-	100.0	2.3	80.9	15.6	-	-	-	-	1.2	-
WATER	-	100.0	-	-	-	-	-	-	-	-	-
OTHER	-	100.0	-	19.0	77.1	-	2.6	1.3	-	-	-
UNKNOWN	-	100.0	-	-	-	-	-	11.2	-	88.8	-
WEST SOUTH CENTRAL	210	100.0	.1	-	15.7	34.5	2.3	14.4	22.1	4.0	6.9
RAIL	25	100.0	-	-	1.4	33.8	3.0	11.0	13.6	13.8	23.4
MOTOR CARRIER	130	100.0	-	-	19.0	43.8	.7	11.1	16.8	3.7	4.9
PRIVATE TRUCK	54	100.0	.4	-	14.5	12.8	6.0	24.1	38.7	.2	3.4
AIR	-	100.0	-	-	-	-	-	-	-	-	-
WATER	-	100.0	-	-	-	-	-	-	-	-	-
OTHER	-	100.0	-	-	-	100.0	-	-	-	-	-
UNKNOWN	-	100.0	-	-	-	-	-	-	26.1	-	73.9
TON-MILES OF SHIPMENTS	(millions of ton-miles)										
U.S. TOTAL	1 335	100.0	2.7	11.0	21.3	11.0	16.5	6.6	11.1	2.5	17.2
RAIL	449	100.0	1.6	8.1	17.4	14.8	13.9	5.1	12.8	2.8	23.3
MOTOR CARRIER	686	100.0	3.8	12.2	22.2	10.5	16.3	7.7	9.7	2.6	15.0
PRIVATE TRUCK	196	100.0	1.6	13.0	27.4	3.8	23.6	6.1	12.3	1.5	10.7
AIR	-	100.0	.9	22.7	12.2	21.4	5.9	.2	11.3	2.0	23.4
WATER	-	100.0	-	-	-	-	-	-	-	-	-
OTHER	-	100.0	.5	26.6	31.5	4.9	2.2	2.0	1.7	1.5	29.0
UNKNOWN	1	100.0	-	.2	15.7	10.6	-	1.4	4.6	23.6	43.8
MIDDLE ATLANTIC	314	100.0	3.5	16.9	20.1	7.2	24.0	6.3	9.3	.7	11.9
RAIL	133	100.0	4.9	10.8	8.4	2.6	34.1	2.7	12.5	-	23.9
MOTOR CARRIER	129	100.0	2.8	22.2	25.1	13.6	11.0	11.3	7.9	1.8	4.3
PRIVATE TRUCK	51	100.0	1.8	19.7	37.8	2.7	30.6	3.1	4.3	-	-
AIR	-	100.0	-	.8	18.7	29.0	5.8	.1	9.6	-	36.2
WATER	-	100.0	-	-	-	-	-	-	-	-	-
OTHER	-	100.0	4.3	18.2	6.6	36.4	12.9	17.4	4.2	-	-
UNKNOWN	-	100.0	-	100.0	-	-	-	-	-	-	-
EAST NORTH CENTRAL	278	100.0	1.2	7.9	22.5	12.3	14.1	9.0	12.3	.9	19.9
RAIL	85	100.0	.3	4.2	17.1	22.6	7.7	16.5	4.8	-	26.8
MOTOR CARRIER	152	100.0	1.2	7.5	24.6	8.7	18.6	6.1	15.0	.9	17.3
PRIVATE TRUCK	41	100.0	2.6	17.0	25.7	4.0	10.7	4.4	17.7	2.8	15.1
AIR	-	100.0	2.1	35.7	15.8	.4	1.3	.6	8.1	-	35.8
WATER	-	100.0	-	-	-	-	-	-	-	-	-
OTHER	-	100.0	-	2.6	3.8	.9	.6	4.0	-	-	88.0
UNKNOWN	-	100.0	-	-	59.6	40.4	-	-	-	-	-
SOUTH ATLANTIC	224	100.0	2.8	13.3	23.1	8.0	23.5	5.4	10.4	2.1	11.5
RAIL	30	100.0	-	2.1	4.1	30.8	2.1	6.5	50.8	3.5	-
MOTOR CARRIER	149	100.0	3.7	15.8	24.5	4.9	23.5	6.5	4.0	1.1	16.0
PRIVATE TRUCK	43	100.0	1.7	12.6	31.4	2.4	39.0	.7	4.3	3.7	4.3
AIR	-	100.0	3.6	69.1	21.2	-	-	-	-	6.2	-
WATER	-	100.0	-	-	-	-	-	-	-	-	-
OTHER	-	100.0	-	10.9	82.6	-	5.3	1.2	-	-	-
UNKNOWN	-	100.0	-	-	-	-	-	-	5.5	94.5	-
WEST SOUTH CENTRAL	105	100.0	.3	-	18.7	29.2	3.6	11.9	10.6	6.1	19.7
RAIL	19	100.0	-	-	1.4	22.8	3.3	5.0	4.7	17.7	45.1
MOTOR CARRIER	61	100.0	-	-	24.3	37.7	1.1	9.3	8.1	4.7	14.7
PRIVATE TRUCK	23	100.0	1.2	-	18.6	12.7	10.4	24.6	21.9	.5	10.0
AIR	-	100.0	-	-	-	-	-	-	-	-	-
WATER	-	100.0	-	-	-	-	-	-	-	-	-
OTHER	-	100.0	-	-	-	100.0	-	-	-	-	-
UNKNOWN	-	100.0	-	-	-	-	-	-	9.6	-	90.4

See footnotes at end of table 4.

TABLE 3. TCC GROUP 321—Percent Distribution of Geographic Division of Destination and Means of Transport, by Geographic Division of Origin: 1972

Geographic division of destination and means of transport	Number	Percent distribution by division of origin [1]									
		U.S. total	New England	Middle Atlantic	East North Central	West North Central	South Atlantic	East South Central	West South Central	Mountain	Pacific
TONS OF SHIPMENTS	(thousands of tons)										
U.S. TOTAL	3 083	100.0	(D)	27.6	24.3	(D)	18.3	(D)	6.8	(D)	(D)
RAIL	816	100.0	(D)	29.3	27.6	(D)	5.1	(D)	3.1	(D)	(D)
MOTOR CARRIER	1 669	100.0	(D)	25.0	24.0	(D)	22.1	(D)	7.8	(D)	(D)
PRIVATE TRUCK	593	100.0	(D)	32.6	20.5	(D)	26.0	(D)	9.1	(D)	(D)
AIR	-	100.0	(D)	25.4	33.2	(D)	22.7	(D)	-	(D)	(D)
WATER	-	100.0	(D)	-	-	(D)	-	(D)	-	(D)	(D)
OTHER	-	100.0	(D)	5.4	13.3	(D)	10.3	(D)	-	(D)	(D)
UNKNOWN	2	100.0	(D)	3.6	64.8	(D)	10.1	(D)	21.5	(D)	(D)
NEW ENGLAND	67	100.0	(D)	44.0	8.2	(D)	18.9	(D)	.3	(D)	(D)
RAIL	17	100.0	(D)	93.8	2.2	(D)	-	(D)	-	(D)	(D)
MOTOR CARRIER	41	100.0	(D)	21.5	7.7	(D)	26.6	(D)	-	(D)	(D)
PRIVATE TRUCK	8	100.0	(D)	51.6	23.1	(D)	20.5	(D)	2.6	(D)	(D)
AIR	-	100.0	(D)	-	57.3	(D)	42.7	(D)	-	(D)	(D)
WATER	-	100.0	(D)	-	-	(D)	-	(D)	-	(D)	(D)
OTHER	-	100.0	(D)	12.7	-	(D)	-	(D)	-	(D)	(D)
UNKNOWN	-	100.0	(D)	-	-	(D)	-	(D)	-	(D)	(D)
MIDDLE ATLANTIC	565	100.0	(D)	51.0	11.3	(D)	26.0	(D)	-	(D)	(D)
RAIL	92	100.0	(D)	61.5	8.1	(D)	1.6	(D)	-	(D)	(D)
MOTOR CARRIER	320	100.0	(D)	51.4	11.1	(D)	27.0	(D)	-	(D)	(D)
PRIVATE TRUCK	151	100.0	(D)	44.0	13.7	(D)	38.9	(D)	-	(D)	(D)
AIR	-	100.0	(D)	3.8	40.9	(D)	48.8	(D)	-	(D)	(D)
WATER	-	100.0	(D)	-	-	(D)	-	(D)	-	(D)	(D)
OTHER	-	100.0	(D)	5.2	1.3	(D)	3.6	(D)	-	(D)	(D)
UNKNOWN	-	100.0	(D)	99.6	-	(D)	-	(D)	-	(D)	(D)
EAST NORTH CENTRAL	1 073	100.0	(D)	25.3	38.1	(D)	15.5	(D)	3.1	(D)	(D)
RAIL	263	100.0	(D)	15.1	43.4	(D)	1.5	(D)	.1	(D)	(D)
MOTOR CARRIER	577	100.0	(D)	25.3	39.1	(D)	18.9	(D)	4.3	(D)	(D)
PRIVATE TRUCK	231	100.0	(D)	36.8	29.2	(D)	23.1	(D)	3.4	(D)	(D)
AIR	-	100.0	(D)	38.1	44.6	(D)	16.9	(D)	-	(D)	(D)
WATER	-	100.0	(D)	-	-	(D)	-	(D)	-	(D)	(D)
OTHER	-	100.0	(D)	1.0	11.5	(D)	31.2	(D)	-	(D)	(D)
UNKNOWN	1	100.0	(D)	-	100.0	(D)	-	(D)	-	(D)	(D)
WEST NORTH CENTRAL	262	100.0	(D)	11.7	27.6	(D)	9.2	(D)	27.7	(D)	(D)
RAIL	115	100.0	(D)	4.3	38.3	(D)	12.2	(D)	7.4	(D)	(D)
MOTOR CARRIER	133	100.0	(D)	18.1	18.4	(D)	6.8	(D)	43.1	(D)	(D)
PRIVATE TRUCK	13	100.0	(D)	11.7	24.2	(D)	7.6	(D)	49.9	(D)	(D)
AIR	-	100.0	(D)	50.4	.8	(D)	-	(D)	-	(D)	(D)
WATER	-	100.0	(D)	-	-	(D)	-	(D)	-	(D)	(D)
OTHER	-	100.0	(D)	23.5	12.8	(D)	-	(D)	.6	(D)	(D)
UNKNOWN	-	100.0	(D)	-	100.0	(D)	-	(D)	-	(D)	(D)
SOUTH ATLANTIC	454	100.0	(D)	33.1	15.5	(D)	33.3	(D)	1.1	(D)	(D)
RAIL	125	100.0	(D)	70.0	9.3	(D)	1.5	(D)	.6	(D)	(D)
MOTOR CARRIER	236	100.0	(D)	13.1	20.8	(D)	48.9	(D)	.4	(D)	(D)
PRIVATE TRUCK	92	100.0	(D)	34.3	10.4	(D)	36.3	(D)	3.5	(D)	(D)
AIR	-	100.0	(D)	51.8	11.3	(D)	-	(D)	-	(D)	(D)
WATER	-	100.0	(D)	-	-	(D)	-	(D)	-	(D)	(D)
OTHER	-	100.0	(D)	33.2	19.7	(D)	12.9	(D)	-	(D)	(D)
UNKNOWN	-	100.0	(D)	-	-	(D)	-	(D)	-	(D)	(D)
EAST SOUTH CENTRAL	202	100.0	(D)	17.1	30.1	(D)	12.3	(D)	15.0	(D)	(D)
RAIL	52	100.0	(D)	6.9	60.5	(D)	6.3	(D)	5.2	(D)	(D)
MOTOR CARRIER	123	100.0	(D)	23.2	19.3	(D)	16.6	(D)	11.8	(D)	(D)
PRIVATE TRUCK	26	100.0	(D)	9.0	19.4	(D)	4.0	(D)	49.7	(D)	(D)
AIR	-	100.0	(D)	8.0	92.0	(D)	-	(D)	-	(D)	(D)
WATER	-	100.0	(D)	-	-	(D)	-	(D)	-	(D)	(D)
OTHER	-	100.0	(D)	14.5	79.6	(D)	3.9	(D)	-	(D)	(D)
UNKNOWN	-	100.0	(D)	-	-	(D)	100.0	(D)	-	(D)	(D)
WEST SOUTH CENTRAL	182	100.0	(D)	14.2	20.1	(D)	13.1	(D)	25.4	(D)	(D)
RAIL	57	100.0	(D)	25.9	5.7	(D)	28.2	(D)	6.0	(D)	(D)
MOTOR CARRIER	84	100.0	(D)	11.3	28.2	(D)	6.6	(D)	26.0	(D)	(D)
PRIVATE TRUCK	41	100.0	(D)	4.1	23.3	(D)	5.5	(D)	51.0	(D)	(D)
AIR	-	100.0	(D)	23.6	37.1	(D)	-	(D)	-	(D)	(D)
WATER	-	100.0	(D)	-	-	(D)	-	(D)	-	(D)	(D)
OTHER	-	100.0	(D)	7.5	-	(D)	-	(D)	-	(D)	(D)
UNKNOWN	-	100.0	(D)	-	-	(D)	-	(D)	100.0	(D)	(D)
MOUNTAIN	34	100.0	(D)	4.1	4.6	(D)	9.4	(D)	24.0	(D)	(D)
RAIL	11	100.0	(D)	-	-	(D)	7.5	(D)	30.5	(D)	(D)
MOTOR CARRIER	21	100.0	(D)	6.7	4.2	(D)	5.4	(D)	22.4	(D)	(D)
PRIVATE TRUCK	1	100.0	(D)	-	38.0	(D)	55.5	(D)	6.5	(D)	(D)
AIR	-	100.0	(D)	-	-	(D)	28.0	(D)	-	(D)	(D)
WATER	-	100.0	(D)	-	-	(D)	-	(D)	-	(D)	(D)
OTHER	-	100.0	(D)	-	-	(D)	100.0	(D)	-	(D)	(D)
UNKNOWN	-	100.0	(D)	-	-	(D)	-	(D)	-	(D)	(D)
PACIFIC	239	100.0	(D)	7.3	12.5	(D)	4.5	(D)	6.1	(D)	(D)
RAIL	80	100.0	(D)	18.3	14.7	(D)	-	(D)	7.3	(D)	(D)
MOTOR CARRIER	131	100.0	(D)	2.0	11.3	(D)	7.6	(D)	4.9	(D)	(D)
PRIVATE TRUCK	26	100.0	(D)	-	12.1	(D)	3.4	(D)	6.9	(D)	(D)
AIR	-	100.0	(D)	36.2	35.8	(D)	-	(D)	-	(D)	(D)
WATER	-	100.0	(D)	-	-	(D)	-	(D)	-	(D)	(D)
OTHER	-	100.0	(D)	-	86.9	(D)	-	(D)	-	(D)	(D)
UNKNOWN	-	100.0	(D)	-	-	(D)	-	(D)	100.0	(D)	(D)

See footnotes at end of table 4.

TABLE 3. **TCC GROUP 321**—Percent Distribution of Geographic Division of Destination and Means of Transport, by Geographic Division of Origin: 1972—Continued

Geographic division of destination and means of transport	Number	Percent distribution by division of origin[1]									
		U.S. total	New England	Middle Atlantic	East North Central	West North Central	South Atlantic	East South Central	West South Central	Mountain	Pacific
TON-MILES OF SHIPMENTS	(millions of ton-miles)										
U.S. TOTAL	1 335	100.0	(D)	23.5	20.9	(D)	16.8	(D)	7.9	(D)	(D)
RAIL	449	100.0	(D)	29.7	19.0	(D)	6.8	(D)	4.3	(D)	(D)
MOTOR CARRIER	686	100.0	(D)	18.8	22.1	(D)	21.8	(D)	9.0	(D)	(D)
PRIVATE TRUCK	196	100.0	(D)	26.1	20.9	(D)	22.3	(D)	12.0	(D)	(D)
AIR	-	100.0	(D)	33.3	25.6	(D)	8.9	(D)	-	(D)	(D)
WATER	-	100.0	(D)	-	-	(D)	-	(D)	-	(D)	(D)
OTHER	-	100.0	(D)	3.8	29.9	(D)	10.1	(D)	-	(D)	(D)
UNKNOWN	1	100.0	(D)	.2	26.4	(D)	25.0	(D)	48.4	(D)	(D)
NEW ENGLAND	36	100.0	(D)	30.3	8.8	(D)	17.3	(D)	.8	(D)	(D)
RAIL	7	100.0	(D)	87.7	3.2	(D)	-	(D)	-	(D)	(D)
MOTOR CARRIER	26	100.0	(D)	14.0	7.2	(D)	21.4	(D)	-	(D)	(D)
PRIVATE TRUCK	3	100.0	(D)	30.8	35.2	(D)	24.2	(D)	9.5	(D)	(D)
AIR	-	100.0	(D)	-	63.5	(D)	36.5	(D)	-	(D)	(D)
WATER	-	100.0	(D)	-	-	(D)	-	(D)	-	(D)	(D)
OTHER	-	100.0	(D)	30.3	-	(D)	-	(D)	-	(D)	(D)
UNKNOWN	-	100.0	(D)	-	-	(D)	-	(D)	-	(D)	(D)
MIDDLE ATLANTIC	146	100.0	(D)	36.3	15.1	(D)	20.4	(D)	-	(D)	(D)
RAIL	36	100.0	(D)	39.4	9.8	(D)	1.8	(D)	-	(D)	(D)
MOTOR CARRIER	84	100.0	(D)	34.1	13.6	(D)	28.1	(D)	-	(D)	(D)
PRIVATE TRUCK	25	100.0	(D)	39.4	27.3	(D)	21.5	(D)	-	(D)	(D)
AIR	-	100.0	(D)	1.1	40.3	(D)	27.0	(D)	-	(D)	(D)
WATER	-	100.0	(D)	-	-	(D)	-	(D)	-	(D)	(D)
OTHER	-	100.0	(D)	2.6	2.9	(D)	4.2	(D)	-	(D)	(D)
UNKNOWN	-	100.0	(D)	95.7	-	(D)	-	(D)	-	(D)	(D)
EAST NORTH CENTRAL	284	100.0	(D)	22.1	22.0	(D)	18.2	(D)	6.9	(D)	(D)
RAIL	78	100.0	(D)	14.3	18.6	(D)	1.6	(D)	.4	(D)	(D)
MOTOR CARRIER	152	100.0	(D)	21.3	24.5	(D)	24.1	(D)	9.9	(D)	(D)
PRIVATE TRUCK	53	100.0	(D)	36.1	19.6	(D)	25.6	(D)	8.1	(D)	(D)
AIR	-	100.0	(D)	50.9	33.2	(D)	15.4	(D)	-	(D)	(D)
WATER	-	100.0	(D)	-	-	(D)	-	(D)	-	(D)	(D)
OTHER	-	100.0	(D)	.8	3.6	(D)	26.5	(D)	-	(D)	(D)
UNKNOWN	-	100.0	(D)	-	100.0	(D)	-	(D)	-	(D)	(D)
WEST NORTH CENTRAL	146	100.0	(D)	15.3	23.3	(D)	12.2	(D)	21.0	(D)	(D)
RAIL	66	100.0	(D)	5.3	28.8	(D)	14.1	(D)	6.6	(D)	(D)
MOTOR CARRIER	72	100.0	(D)	24.3	18.3	(D)	10.2	(D)	32.4	(D)	(D)
PRIVATE TRUCK	7	100.0	(D)	18.5	21.7	(D)	14.2	(D)	39.8	(D)	(D)
AIR	-	100.0	(D)	45.0	.4	(D)	-	(D)	-	(D)	(D)
WATER	-	100.0	(D)	-	-	(D)	-	(D)	-	(D)	(D)
OTHER	-	100.0	(D)	28.3	5.7	(D)	-	(D)	.1	(D)	(D)
UNKNOWN	-	100.0	(D)	-	100.0	(D)	-	(D)	-	(D)	(D)
SOUTH ATLANTIC	220	100.0	(D)	34.2	17.8	(D)	24.0	(D)	1.7	(D)	(D)
RAIL	62	100.0	(D)	72.7	10.5	(D)	1.0	(D)	1.0	(D)	(D)
MOTOR CARRIER	111	100.0	(D)	12.7	25.3	(D)	31.5	(D)	.6	(D)	(D)
PRIVATE TRUCK	46	100.0	(D)	33.8	9.5	(D)	36.8	(D)	5.3	(D)	(D)
AIR	-	100.0	(D)	32.4	5.8	(D)	-	(D)	-	(D)	(D)
WATER	-	100.0	(D)	-	-	(D)	-	(D)	-	(D)	(D)
OTHER	-	100.0	(D)	23.0	8.4	(D)	24.7	(D)	-	(D)	(D)
UNKNOWN	-	100.0	(D)	-	-	(D)	-	(D)	-	(D)	(D)
EAST SOUTH CENTRAL	87	100.0	(D)	22.6	28.6	(D)	13.8	(D)	14.3	(D)	(D)
RAIL	23	100.0	(D)	15.6	60.9	(D)	8.7	(D)	4.2	(D)	(D)
MOTOR CARRIER	52	100.0	(D)	27.8	17.6	(D)	18.5	(D)	11.0	(D)	(D)
PRIVATE TRUCK	11	100.0	(D)	13.4	14.9	(D)	2.7	(D)	48.3	(D)	(D)
AIR	-	100.0	(D)	11.6	88.4	(D)	-	(D)	-	(D)	(D)
WATER	-	100.0	(D)	-	-	(D)	-	(D)	-	(D)	(D)
OTHER	-	100.0	(D)	32.8	58.4	(D)	5.8	(D)	-	(D)	(D)
UNKNOWN	-	100.0	(D)	-	-	(D)	100.0	(D)	-	(D)	(D)
WEST SOUTH CENTRAL	148	100.0	(D)	19.6	23.0	(D)	15.7	(D)	7.5	(D)	(D)
RAIL	57	100.0	(D)	29.1	7.1	(D)	27.1	(D)	1.6	(D)	(D)
MOTOR CARRIER	66	100.0	(D)	15.2	34.1	(D)	8.9	(D)	7.5	(D)	(D)
PRIVATE TRUCK	24	100.0	(D)	9.1	30.0	(D)	7.7	(D)	21.3	(D)	(D)
AIR	-	100.0	(D)	28.5	18.6	(D)	-	(D)	-	(D)	(D)
WATER	-	100.0	(D)	-	-	(D)	-	(D)	-	(D)	(D)
OTHER	-	100.0	(D)	9.8	-	(D)	-	(D)	-	(D)	(D)
UNKNOWN	-	100.0	(D)	-	-	(D)	-	(D)	100.0	(D)	(D)
MOUNTAIN	33	100.0	(D)	6.8	7.7	(D)	13.8	(D)	19.3	(D)	(D)
RAIL	12	100.0	(D)	-	-	(D)	8.4	(D)	27.0	(D)	(D)
MOTOR CARRIER	17	100.0	(D)	12.9	8.1	(D)	9.2	(D)	16.7	(D)	(D)
PRIVATE TRUCK	2	100.0	(D)	-	40.1	(D)	55.9	(D)	4.0	(D)	(D)
AIR	-	100.0	(D)	-	-	(D)	27.0	(D)	-	(D)	(D)
WATER	-	100.0	(D)	-	-	(D)	-	(D)	-	(D)	(D)
OTHER	-	100.0	(D)	-	-	(D)	-	(D)	-	(D)	(D)
UNKNOWN	-	100.0	(D)	-	-	(D)	100.0	(D)	-	(D)	(D)
PACIFIC	229	100.0	(D)	16.3	24.1	(D)	11.3	(D)	9.0	(D)	(D)
RAIL	104	100.0	(D)	30.4	21.8	(D)	-	(D)	8.3	(D)	(D)
MOTOR CARRIER	103	100.0	(D)	5.4	25.5	(D)	23.3	(D)	8.8	(D)	(D)
PRIVATE TRUCK	21	100.0	(D)	-	29.4	(D)	8.9	(D)	11.2	(D)	(D)
AIR	-	100.0	(D)	51.4	39.2	(D)	-	(D)	-	(D)	(D)
WATER	-	100.0	(D)	-	-	(D)	-	(D)	-	(D)	(D)
OTHER	-	100.0	(D)	-	90.7	(D)	-	(D)	-	(D)	(D)
UNKNOWN	-	100.0	(D)	-	-	(D)	-	(D)	100.0	(D)	(D)

See footnotes at end of table 4.

TABLE 4. **TCC GROUP 321**—Percent Distribution of Distance Shipped and Weight of Shipment, by Means of Transport: 1972

Distance shipped and weight of shipment[2][3]	Number	Percent distribution by means of transport							
		All means of transport	Rail	Motor carrier	Private truck	Air	Water	Other	Unknown
TONS OF SHIPMENTS	(thousands of tons)								
U.S. TOTAL..........	1 526	100.0	30.9	52.4	16.6	-	-	-	.1
UNDER 100 MILES.........	119	100.0	16.1	46.2	37.6	-	-	-	.1
UNDER 1000 POUNDS.....	2	100.0	-	70.7	28.5	-	-	-	-
1000 TO 9999 POUNDS...	7	100.0	-	38.5	60.3	-	-	.9	-
10000 TO 29999 POUNDS.	16	100.0	-	42.1	57.9	-	-	-	1.2
30000 TO 59999 POUNDS.	55	100.0	1.9	75.5	22.6	-	-	-	-
60000 TO 89999 POUNDS.	15	100.0	63.7	-	36.3	-	-	-	-
90000 POUNDS AND OVER.	21	100.0	37.4	8.5	54.1	-	-	-	-
100 TO 199 MILES........	206	100.0	26.7	54.0	19.2	-	-	.1	-
UNDER 1000 POUNDS....	2	100.0	-	80.5	15.5	.4	-	3.6	-
1000 TO 9999 POUNDS...	8	100.0	-	78.7	21.3	-	-	-	-
10000 TO 29999 POUNDS.	13	100.0	-	55.8	44.2	-	-	-	-
30000 TO 59999 POUNDS.	100	100.0	1.7	78.2	20.1	-	-	-	-
60000 TO 89999 POUNDS.	22	100.0	13.9	62.6	23.4	-	-	-	-
90000 POUNDS AND OVER.	59	100.0	85.4	4.2	10.4	-	-	-	-
200 TO 299 MILES........	322	100.0	27.5	57.3	15.2	-	-	-	-
UNDER 1000 POUNDS.....	2	100.0	-	98.7	.1	.2	-	1.0	-
1000 TO 9999 POUNDS...	10	100.0	-	84.4	14.3	1.3	-	-	-
10000 TO 29999 POUNDS.	20	100.0	-	72.6	27.4	-	-	-	-
30000 TO 59999 POUNDS.	158	100.0	1.7	74.5	23.8	-	-	-	-
60000 TO 89999 POUNDS.	31	100.0	5.2	81.1	13.7	-	-	-	-
90000 POUNDS AND OVER.	99	100.0	85.1	14.9	-	-	-	-	-
300 TO 499 MILES........	455	100.0	39.1	50.6	10.1	-	-	-	-
UNDER 1000 POUNDS.....	3	100.0	.2	92.5	4.5	1.4	-	1.3	-
1000 TO 9999 POUNDS...	18	100.0	-	91.8	7.8	.4	-	-	-
10000 TO 29999 POUNDS.	30	100.0	8.7	84.4	6.9	-	-	-	-
30000 TO 59999 POUNDS.	201	100.0	4.1	76.8	19.0	-	-	-	.1
60000 TO 89999 POUNDS.	46	100.0	49.0	42.1	8.9	-	-	-	-
90000 POUNDS AND OVER.	154	100.0	93.7	6.3	-	-	-	-	-
500 TO 999 MILES........	299	100.0	30.3	49.5	20.2	.1	-	-	-
UNDER 1000 POUNDS.....	4	100.0	-	63.0	32.6	2.2	-	1.5	.6
1000 TO 9999 POUNDS...	16	100.0	.5	74.3	24.8	.4	-	-	-
10000 TO 29999 POUNDS.	24	100.0	23.3	22.1	54.5	-	-	-	-
30000 TO 59999 POUNDS.	173	100.0	14.4	68.3	17.3	-	-	-	-
60000 TO 89999 POUNDS.	26	100.0	56.9	7.3	35.8	-	-	-	-
90000 POUNDS AND OVER.	54	100.0	82.6	13.7	3.6	-	-	-	-
1000 TO 1499 MILES......	54	100.0	21.1	65.5	12.1	-	-	-	1.2
UNDER 1000 POUNDS.....	-	100.0	-	96.7	-	2.4	-	.9	-
1000 TO 9999 POUNDS...	1	100.0	-	57.8	29.7	-	-	-	12.5
10000 TO 29999 POUNDS.	2	100.0	25.4	39.7	34.9	-	-	-	-
30000 TO 59999 POUNDS.	35	100.0	9.2	76.1	14.7	-	-	-	-
60000 TO 89999 POUNDS.	11	100.0	44.2	52.0	-	-	-	-	3.8
90000 POUNDS AND OVER.	2	100.0	100.0	-	-	-	-	-	-
1500 MILES OR OVER......	67	100.0	40.8	49.1	10.0	.1	-	-	-
UNDER 1000 POUNDS.....	-	100.0	-	87.0	-	12.2	-	.8	-
1000 TO 9999 POUNDS...	3	100.0	-	67.7	32.3	-	-	-	-
10000 TO 29999 POUNDS.	10	100.0	4.7	76.8	18.6	-	-	-	-
30000 TO 59999 POUNDS.	19	100.0	25.2	56.9	17.9	-	-	-	-
60000 TO 89999 POUNDS.	7	100.0	100.0	-	-	-	-	-	-
90000 POUNDS AND OVER.	25	100.0	58.4	41.6	-	-	-	-	-
TON-MILES OF SHIPMENTS	(millions of ton-miles)								
U.S. TOTAL..........	706	100.0	33.5	51.7	14.6	-	-	-	.1
UNDER 100 MILES.........	5	100.0	18.7	51.6	29.6	-	-	-	-
UNDER 1000 POUNDS.....	-	100.0	-	72.3	27.0	-	-	-	-
1000 TO 9999 POUNDS...	-	100.0	-	50.7	48.8	-	-	.7	-
10000 TO 29999 POUNDS.	-	100.0	-	41.3	58.7	-	-	-	.5
30000 TO 59999 POUNDS.	2	100.0	.4	77.5	22.1	-	-	-	-
60000 TO 89999 POUNDS.	-	100.0	76.6	-	23.4	-	-	-	-
90000 POUNDS AND OVER.	-	100.0	53.4	15.6	31.1	-	-	-	-
100 TO 199 MILES........	32	100.0	25.1	54.7	20.1	-	-	-	-
UNDER 1000 POUNDS.....	-	100.0	-	82.3	13.7	.3	-	3.6	-
1000 TO 9999 POUNDS...	1	100.0	-	80.1	19.9	-	-	-	-
10000 TO 29999 POUNDS.	2	100.0	-	55.5	44.5	-	-	-	-
30000 TO 59999 POUNDS.	15	100.0	1.7	78.3	20.0	-	-	-	-
60000 TO 89999 POUNDS.	3	100.0	14.8	60.4	24.8	-	-	-	-
90000 POUNDS AND OVER.	8	100.0	83.0	4.0	13.0	-	-	-	-

See footnotes at end of table 4.

TABLE 4. **TCC GROUP 321—Percent Distribution of Distance Shipped and Weight of Shipment, by Means of Transport: 1972**—Continued

Distance shipped and weight of shipment [2] [3]	Number	Percent distribution by means of transport							
		All means of transport	Rail	Motor carrier	Private truck	Air	Water	Other	Unknown
TON-MILES OF SHIPMENTS	(millions of ton-miles)								
200 TO 299 MILES........	79	100.0	26.5	58.5	14.9	-	-	-	-
UNDER 1000 POUNDS.....	-	100.0	-	98.8	.1	.2	-	.9	-
1000 TO 9999 POUNDS...	2	100.0	-	85.3	13.4	1.4	-	-	-
10000 TO 29999 POUNDS.	5	100.0	-	74.9	25.1	-	-	-	-
30000 TO 59999 POUNDS.	39	100.0	1.7	75.1	23.1	-	-	-	-
60000 TO 89999 POUNDS.	7	100.0	5.5	81.5	13.1	-	-	-	-
90000 POUNDS AND OVER.	23	100.0	85.0	15.0	-	-	-	-	-
300 TO 499 MILES........	188	100.0	40.8	49.8	9.4	-	-	-	-
UNDER 1000 POUNDS.....	1	100.0	.3	92.4	4.7	1.6	-	1.1	-
1000 TO 9999 POUNDS...	7	100.0	-	92.1	7.6	.3	-	-	-
10000 TO 29999 POUNDS.	12	100.0	9.4	83.6	7.0	-	-	-	-
30000 TO 59999 POUNDS.	81	100.0	4.3	77.7	17.9	-	-	-	.1
60000 TO 89999 POUNDS.	19	100.0	50.8	41.1	8.1	-	-	-	-
90000 POUNDS AND OVER.	66	100.0	93.9	6.1	-	-	-	-	-
500 TO 999 MILES........	211	100.0	30.4	48.5	21.0	.1	-	-	-
UNDER 1000 POUNDS.....	3	100.0	-	63.1	32.7	2.1	-	1.5	.6
1000 TO 9999 POUNDS...	11	100.0	.4	72.6	26.5	.5	-	-	-
10000 TO 29999 POUNDS.	16	100.0	23.2	20.7	56.2	-	-	-	-
30000 TO 59999 POUNDS.	122	100.0	15.1	67.7	17.2	-	-	-	-
60000 TO 89999 POUNDS.	20	100.0	53.5	5.5	41.0	-	-	-	-
90000 POUNDS AND OVER.	37	100.0	82.0	14.0	4.0	-	-	-	-
1000 TO 1499 MILES......	62	100.0	20.6	64.7	13.3	-	-	-	1.4
UNDER 1000 POUNDS.....	-	100.0	-	96.6	-	2.6	-	.8	14.5
1000 TO 9999 POUNDS...	2	100.0	-	57.3	28.2	-	-	-	-
10000 TO 29999 POUNDS.	2	100.0	27.1	38.6	34.3	-	-	-	-
30000 TO 59999 POUNDS.	41	100.0	8.9	74.5	16.6	-	-	-	4.6
60000 TO 89999 POUNDS.	12	100.0	44.2	51.3	-	-	-	-	-
90000 POUNDS AND OVER.	2	100.0	100.0	-	-	-	-	-	-
1500 MILES OR OVER......	126	100.0	41.6	48.6	9.7	.1	-	-	-
UNDER 1000 POUNDS.....	1	100.0	-	87.6	-	11.6	-	.8	-
1000 TO 9999 POUNDS...	7	100.0	-	65.5	34.5	-	-	-	-
10000 TO 29999 POUNDS.	18	100.0	5.1	74.6	20.4	-	-	-	-
30000 TO 59999 POUNDS.	35	100.0	25.6	57.8	16.6	-	-	-	-
60000 TO 89999 POUNDS.	13	100.0	100.0	-	-	-	-	-	-
90000 POUNDS AND OVER.	50	100.0	58.5	41.5	-	-	-	-	-

Note: Detail may not add to total due to rounding. The introductory table shows the estimates of sampling variability for tons; sampling variability for ton-miles has not been estimated. See the map in the Introduction for the States comprising the geographic divisions of the United States.

Shipments excluded from the survey are those moving by pipeline (primarily petroleum products from refineries), parcel post shipments, and commodities moved by own power (motorized vehicles, aircraft, etc.) or towed (prefabricated buildings, etc.). Local shipments (commodities shipped less than 25 miles from the plant) and shipments within the same city are also excluded. Shipments to Alaska and Hawaii from the 48 conterminous States and the District of Columbia are included; however, no data were obtained for shipments originating in Alaska and Hawaii.

- Represents zero or rounds to zero.   (D) Withheld to avoid disclosing figures for individual companies.

[1]Production of this commodity is concentrated in the geographic divisions shown; figures and distributions for geographic divisions not shown are included in the total.

[2]Distances of shipments to foreign destinations are calculated only to the U.S. port of exit.

[3]Includes only shipments represented by bills of lading and invoices. Summary records which did not show individual weights of shipments are not included.

TCC 322. Glass and Glassware, Pressed and Blown

Comparisons of Tons and Ton-Miles of Shipments for
Geographic Divisions of Origin and for Sampling Variability: 1972 and 1967

Geographic division of origin	Estimates				Relative sampling variability in tons (percent)	
	1972		1967		1972	1967
	Tons (thousands)	Ton-miles (millions)	Tons (thousands)	Ton-miles (millions)	1972	1967
U.S. total	14,003	3,628	12,220	3,274	5.8	11.0
New England	378	64	236	34	34.6	(*)
Middle Atlantic	3,286	677	3,504	792	7.8	(*)
East North Central	4,179	1,090	3,992	1,142	12.9	(*)
West North Central	(D)	(D)	—	—	(*)	(*)
South Atlantic	2,123	698	1,692	570	10.8	(*)
East South Central	569	141	474	170	47.0	(*)
West South Central	1,277	395	1,276	353	40.8	(*)
Mountain	(D)	(D)	—	—	(*)	(*)
Pacific	1,811	479	1,046	213	30.5	(*)

— Represents or rounds to zero.   (D) Withheld to avoid disclosing figures for individual companies.   (*) Data not published.

TABLE 1. **TCC GROUP 322**—Percent Distribution of Geographic Division of Origin and Distance Shipped, by Means of Transport: 1972

Geographic division of origin[1] and distance shipped[2]	Number	Percent distribution by means of transport							
		All means of transport	Rail	Motor carrier	Private truck	Air	Water	Other	Unknown
TONS OF SHIPMENTS	(thousands of tons)								
U.S. TOTAL..........	14 003	100.0	10.8	64.0	24.9	-	.1	.1	.1
NEW ENGLAND.............	378	100.0	6.2	42.6	51.1	-	-	-	-
UNDER 100 MILES.......	225	100.0	1.8	37.6	60.5	-	-	-	-
100 TO 199 MILES......	89	100.0	.9	46.4	52.7	-	-	-	-
200 TO 299 MILES......	21	100.0	7.4	56.7	35.9	-	-	-	-
300 TO 499 MILES......	15	100.0	17.8	68.4	13.7	-	-	.1	-
500 TO 999 MILES......	17	100.0	69.1	30.9	-	-	-	-	-
1000 TO 1499 MILES....	5	100.0	38.1	61.9	-	-	-	-	-
1500 MILES OR OVER....	4	100.0	11.4	86.6	-	1.9	-	-	-
MIDDLE ATLANTIC.........	3 286	100.0	4.8	78.9	16.0	-	-	.1	.2
UNDER 100 MILES.......	965	100.0	1.6	70.3	28.0	-	.1	-	-
100 TO 199 MILES......	973	100.0	5.5	79.9	14.1	-	-	-	.4
200 TO 299 MILES......	879	100.0	2.3	91.4	6.0	-	-	.1	.2
300 TO 499 MILES......	317	100.0	5.2	83.4	11.4	-	-	.1	-
500 TO 999 MILES......	106	100.0	26.6	45.1	27.8	-	-	.2	.3
1000 TO 1499 MILES....	21	100.0	44.5	54.9	-	.1	-	.4	.1
1500 MILES OR OVER....	22	100.0	65.6	31.5	-	.4	-	2.5	-
EAST NORTH CENTRAL......	4 179	100.0	16.0	70.0	13.7	-	-	.1	.1
UNDER 100 MILES.......	1 185	100.0	1.2	81.4	17.4	-	-	-	-
100 TO 199 MILES......	1 123	100.0	1.3	84.2	14.2	-	-	-	.2
200 TO 299 MILES......	605	100.0	7.8	76.1	15.5	-	-	.4	.1
300 TO 499 MILES......	820	100.0	41.0	47.5	11.3	-	-	.1	.1
500 TO 999 MILES......	354	100.0	51.6	43.7	4.5	-	-	.3	-
1000 TO 1499 MILES....	20	100.0	53.8	27.8	16.9	-	-	1.5	-
1500 MILES OR OVER....	69	100.0	92.1	5.0	2.7	-	-	.2	-
SOUTH ATLANTIC..........	2 123	100.0	14.7	49.6	35.2	-	.1	.1	.2
UNDER 100 MILES.......	284	100.0	2.0	41.9	56.1	-	-	-	-
100 TO 199 MILES......	624	100.0	3.5	59.0	36.2	-	.5	.1	.7
200 TO 299 MILES......	387	100.0	8.3	55.9	35.7	-	-	-	-
300 TO 499 MILES......	537	100.0	31.3	45.5	23.1	-	-	-	-
500 TO 999 MILES......	223	100.0	16.1	43.3	40.5	-	-	.1	-
1000 TO 1499 MILES....	12	100.0	44.3	22.9	32.6	.2	-	-	-
1500 MILES OR OVER....	53	100.0	82.0	9.2	8.6	-	-	.1	-
EAST SOUTH CENTRAL......	569	100.0	5.8	30.0	64.2	-	-	-	-
UNDER 100 MILES.......	159	100.0	-	11.0	89.0	-	-	-	-
100 TO 199 MILES......	104	100.0	.6	42.1	57.3	-	-	-	-
200 TO 299 MILES......	112	100.0	7.2	36.6	56.2	-	-	-	-
300 TO 499 MILES......	147	100.0	2.7	41.0	56.3	-	-	-	-
500 TO 999 MILES......	42	100.0	41.0	17.2	41.8	-	-	-	-
1000 TO 1499 MILES....	-	100.0	-	-	-	-	-	-	-
1500 MILES OR OVER....	3	100.0	96.1	3.9	-	-	-	-	-
WEST SOUTH CENTRAL......	1 277	100.0	21.2	45.6	33.2	-	-	-	-
UNDER 100 MILES.......	202	100.0	3.5	48.9	47.7	-	-	-	-
100 TO 199 MILES......	298	100.0	16.3	38.7	44.9	-	-	-	-
200 TO 299 MILES......	353	100.0	40.9	26.0	33.0	-	-	-	-
300 TO 499 MILES......	236	100.0	12.7	62.6	24.7	-	-	-	-
500 TO 999 MILES......	100	100.0	26.0	55.5	18.5	-	-	-	-
1000 TO 1499 MILES....	86	100.0	17.4	82.6	-	-	-	-	-
1500 MILES OR OVER....	-	100.0	-	99.9	-	.1	-	-	-
PACIFIC.................	1 811	100.0	2.6	78.1	18.8	-	.4	-	-
UNDER 100 MILES.......	678	100.0	-	62.7	37.3	-	-	-	-
100 TO 199 MILES......	398	100.0	-	87.2	12.8	-	-	-	-
200 TO 299 MILES......	118	100.0	2.0	84.0	14.0	-	-	-	-
300 TO 499 MILES......	396	100.0	.2	96.3	3.5	-	-	-	-
500 TO 999 MILES......	165	100.0	20.5	75.5	4.0	-	-	-	-
1000 TO 1499 MILES....	22	100.0	11.1	86.8	2.0	.1	-	-	-
1500 MILES OR OVER....	31	100.0	26.0	52.0	-	.1	21.9	-	-
TON-MILES OF SHIPMENTS	(millions of ton-miles)								
U.S. TOTAL..........	3 628	100.0	24.1	57.1	18.1	-	.5	.1	.1
NEW ENGLAND.............	64	100.0	23.8	51.1	24.9	.3	-	-	-
UNDER 100 MILES.......	10	100.0	1.6	39.5	58.8	-	-	-	-
100 TO 199 MILES......	13	100.0	.9	46.7	52.4	-	-	-	-
200 TO 299 MILES......	5	100.0	7.0	56.0	37.0	-	-	-	-
300 TO 499 MILES......	5	100.0	18.9	69.7	11.4	-	-	.1	-
500 TO 999 MILES......	14	100.0	73.3	26.7	-	-	-	-	-
1000 TO 1499 MILES....	6	100.0	37.3	62.6	-	-	-	-	-
1500 MILES OR OVER....	8	100.0	10.0	87.7	-	2.3	-	-	-

See footnotes at end of table 4.

TABLE 1. **TCC GROUP 322—Percent Distribution of Geographic Division of Origin and Distance Shipped, by Means of Transport: 1972**—Continued

Geographic division of origin[1] and distance shipped[2]	Number	Percent distribution by means of transport							
		All means of transport	Rail	Motor carrier	Private truck	Air	Water	Other	Unknown
TON-MILES OF SHIPMENTS	(millions of ton-miles)								
MIDDLE ATLANTIC.........	677	100.0	12.6	75.2	11.6	.1	-	.3	.2
UNDER 100 MILES.......	52	100.0	1.8	71.2	27.0	-	.1	-	-
100 TO 199 MILES......	137	100.0	5.5	80.7	13.3	-	-	-	.5
200 TO 299 MILES......	216	100.0	2.3	91.5	5.9	-	-	.1	.2
300 TO 499 MILES......	121	100.0	5.6	83.5	10.9	-	-	.1	.2
500 TO 999 MILES......	73	100.0	27.5	44.6	27.4	-	-	.2	.3
1000 TO 1499 MILES....	26	100.0	45.6	53.8	-	.1	-	.4	.1
1500 MILES OR OVER....	50	100.0	66.1	30.7	-	.4	-	2.7	
EAST NORTH CENTRAL......	1 090	100.0	37.7	51.4	10.6	-	-	.2	.1
UNDER 100 MILES.......	63	100.0	1.3	77.9	20.8	-	-	-	-
100 TO 199 MILES......	166	100.0	1.3	84.2	14.2	-	-	-	.2
200 TO 299 MILES......	149	100.0	7.6	76.5	15.3	-	-	.4	.1
300 TO 499 MILES......	315	100.0	42.2	46.3	11.2	-	-	.1	.1
500 TO 999 MILES......	238	100.0	55.1	40.7	4.0	-	-	.2	-
1000 TO 1499 MILES....	24	100.0	52.8	29.8	15.8	-	-	1.6	-
1500 MILES OR OVER....	133	100.0	89.2	5.3	5.3	-	-	.2	-
SOUTH ATLANTIC..........	698	100.0	29.3	41.4	29.0	-	.1	.1	.1
UNDER 100 MILES.......	18	100.0	2.1	47.1	50.8	-	-	-	-
100 TO 199 MILES......	97	100.0	3.7	58.9	35.8	-	.6	-	-
200 TO 299 MILES......	95	100.0	9.1	55.7	35.2	-	-	.2	.8
300 TO 499 MILES......	205	100.0	31.3	45.0	23.6	-	-	-	-
500 TO 999 MILES......	153	100.0	17.5	42.0	40.4	-	-	.1	-
1000 TO 1499 MILES....	13	100.0	43.9	23.7	32.3	.2	-	-	-
1500 MILES OR OVER....	114	100.0	82.5	8.9	8.3	.1	-	.1	-
EAST SOUTH CENTRAL......	141	100.0	14.9	33.2	51.9	-	-	-	-
UNDER 100 MILES.......	7	100.0	-	17.4	82.6	-	-	-	-
100 TO 199 MILES......	16	100.0	.7	42.4	56.9	-	-	-	-
200 TO 299 MILES......	28	100.0	7.7	38.3	54.0	-	-	-	-
300 TO 499 MILES......	53	100.0	3.0	40.7	56.3	-	-	-	-
500 TO 999 MILES......	29	100.0	40.0	19.3	40.7	-	-	-	-
1000 TO 1499 MILES....	-	100.0	-	-	-	-	-	-	-
1500 MILES OR OVER....	5	100.0	95.8	4.2	-	-	-	-	-
WEST SOUTH CENTRAL......	395	100.0	23.5	54.3	22.2	-	-	-	-
UNDER 100 MILES.......	14	100.0	3.5	52.4	44.1	-	-	-	-
100 TO 199 MILES......	48	100.0	17.6	38.0	44.3	-	-	-	-
200 TO 299 MILES......	86	100.0	43.2	26.0	30.8	-	-	-	-
300 TO 499 MILES......	86	100.0	14.6	59.3	26.1	-	-	-	-
500 TO 999 MILES......	66	100.0	26.6	57.0	16.3	-	-	-	-
1000 TO 1499 MILES....	92	100.0	18.0	82.0	-	-	-	-	-
1500 MILES OR OVER....	1	100.0	-	100.0	-	-	-	-	-
PACIFIC.................	479	100.0	9.0	80.6	6.3	-	4.0	-	-
UNDER 100 MILES.......	26	100.0	-	68.0	32.0	-	-	-	-
100 TO 199 MILES......	52	100.0	-	87.1	12.9	-	-	-	-
200 TO 299 MILES......	28	100.0	2.1	84.1	13.9	-	-	-	-
300 TO 499 MILES......	138	100.0	.2	96.2	3.6	-	-	-	-
500 TO 999 MILES......	125	100.0	18.6	77.0	4.3	-	-	-	-
1000 TO 1499 MILES....	28	100.0	11.4	86.6	1.9	.1	-	-	-
1500 MILES OR OVER....	79	100.0	19.9	55.8	-	.1	24.2	-	-

See footnotes at end of table 4.

TABLE 2. **TCC GROUP 322—Percent Distribution of Geographic Division of Origin and Means of Transport, by Geographic Division of Destination: 1972**

Geographic division of origin[1] and means of transport	Number	Percent distribution by division of destination									
		U.S. total	New England	Middle Atlantic	East North Central	West North Central	South Atlantic	East South Central	West South Central	Mountain	Pacific
TONS OF SHIPMENTS	(thousands of tons)										
U.S. TOTAL..............	14 003	100.0	5.1	20.9	25.1	4.5	14.6	7.4	8.3	2.3	11.8
RAIL...................	1 518	100.0	3.3	21.1	15.9	7.2	12.7	7.0	20.7	3.3	8.7
MOTOR CARRIER..........	8 958	100.0	4.8	23.5	29.1	3.2	13.0	5.5	4.9	2.7	13.2
PRIVATE TRUCK..........	3 491	100.0	6.5	14.1	19.1	6.6	19.3	12.3	11.8	.7	9.5
AIR....................	1	100.0	8.5	45.0	16.1	4.1	1.4	1.3	4.2	1.0	18.3
WATER..................	10	100.0	-	7.1	-	-	29.1	-	-	-	63.8
OTHER..................	8	100.0	4.5	30.9	21.3	2.6	13.7	13.4	5.1	.3	8.3
UNKNOWN................	14	100.0	10.5	18.0	21.5	5.7	44.3	-	.1	-	-
NEW ENGLAND.............	378	100.0	73.1	17.9	2.6	.8	2.0	1.9	.8	.4	.5
RAIL...................	23	100.0	24.2	14.9	19.5	6.9	-	31.0	3.6	-	-
MOTOR CARRIER..........	161	100.0	62.8	24.9	3.3	.9	4.8	-	1.4	.9	1.0
PRIVATE TRUCK..........	193	100.0	87.6	12.4	-	-	-	-	-	-	-
AIR....................	-	100.0	-	.3	-	-	-	1.2	-	-	98.5
WATER..................	-	100.0	-	-	-	-	-	-	-	-	-
OTHER..................	-	100.0	.1	61.8	3.1	-	35.0	-	-	-	-
UNKNOWN................	-	100.0	-	-	-	-	-	-	-	-	-

See footnotes at end of table 4.

TABLE 2. TCC GROUP 322—Percent Distribution of Geographic Division of Origin and Means of Transport, by Geographic Division of Destination: 1972—Continued

Geographic division of origin[1] and means of transport	Number	Percent distribution by division of destination									
		U.S. total	New England	Middle Atlantic	East North Central	West North Central	South Atlantic	East South Central	West South Central	Mountain	Pacific
TONS OF SHIPMENTS	(thousands of tons)										
MIDDLE ATLANTIC.........	3 286	100.0	7.7	64.5	9.6	1.1	15.1	.8	.5	.1	.6
RAIL.................	158	100.0	6.2	51.9	7.3	3.9	13.6	1.8	6.1	-	9.3
MOTOR CARRIER.........	2 592	100.0	8.1	64.9	8.9	.5	16.3	.6	.3	.1	.2
PRIVATE TRUCK.........	525	100.0	6.0	66.4	13.9	2.8	9.5	1.4	-	-	-
AIR..................	-	100.0	5.0	40.0	17.0	2.8	3.1	3.2	5.2	2.4	21.3
WATER................	-	100.0	-	100.0	-	-	-	-	-	-	-
OTHER................	1	100.0	5.0	24.6	17.7	2.2	14.8	2.2	4.4	.6	28.4
UNKNOWN..............	6	100.0	25.2	42.8	4.1	-	27.7	-	.2	-	-
EAST NORTH CENTRAL......	4 179	100.0	2.1	8.7	64.5	8.7	4.0	8.0	2.0	.8	1.4
RAIL.................	670	100.0	4.2	19.1	26.1	13.5	8.2	9.0	8.6	3.6	7.6
MOTOR CARRIER.........	2 925	100.0	1.8	5.1	74.2	7.5	3.4	7.0	.9	.1	.1
PRIVATE TRUCK.........	574	100.0	1.3	14.3	60.0	9.2	2.2	12.1	-	.6	.3
AIR..................	-	100.0	-	54.3	25.4	18.5	-	-	.9	-	.9
WATER................	-	100.0	-	100.0	-	-	-	-	-	-	-
OTHER................	5	100.0	4.7	39.6	9.2	1.9	15.6	20.3	6.1	-	2.5
UNKNOWN..............	3	100.0	-	-	77.6	22.4	-	-	-	-	-
SOUTH ATLANTIC.........	2 123	100.0	4.1	16.3	13.0	.8	53.5	8.0	1.8	.1	2.4
RAIL.................	312	100.0	2.2	28.9	13.0	.9	33.9	2.7	4.4	-	13.9
MOTOR CARRIER.........	1 053	100.0	5.9	20.8	15.8	.7	46.1	9.2	.9	.1	.4
PRIVATE TRUCK.........	747	100.0	2.3	5.0	9.0	.8	71.7	8.4	2.1	.2	.4
AIR..................	-	100.0	15.4	60.0	16.5	-	.7	-	-	-	7.4
WATER................	3	100.0	-	-	-	-	100.0	-	-	-	-
OTHER................	1	100.0	3.6	7.3	73.6	4.5	3.8	1.7	1.4	.4	3.7
UNKNOWN..............	4	100.0	-	.1	-	-	99.9	-	-	-	-
EAST SOUTH CENTRAL......	569	100.0	.5	.1	3.2	.8	23.0	46.7	25.2	-	.6
RAIL.................	33	100.0	-	-	2.1	11.0	28.6	19.2	30.0	-	9.1
MOTOR CARRIER.........	170	100.0	1.4	.4	5.0	.1	26.7	30.8	35.7	-	.1
PRIVATE TRUCK.........	365	100.0	.2	.1	2.4	.2	20.7	56.5	19.8	-	-
AIR..................	-	100.0	-	49.3	-	-	-	-	-	-	50.7
WATER................	-	100.0	-	-	-	-	-	-	-	-	-
OTHER................	-	100.0	1.0	23.6	27.5	1.0	14.1	32.7	-	-	-
UNKNOWN..............	-	100.0	-	-	-	-	-	-	-	-	-
WEST SOUTH CENTRAL......	1 277	100.0	.2	1.7	1.3	4.5	6.8	17.2	66.2	1.9	.3
RAIL.................	271	100.0	-	4.8	3.4	1.3	.3	7.4	79.6	2.0	1.2
MOTOR CARRIER.........	582	100.0	.3	1.4	1.2	5.0	14.7	21.5	53.6	2.1	.2
PRIVATE TRUCK.........	424	100.0	-	-	-	5.8	-	17.7	75.0	1.6	-
AIR..................	-	100.0	-	2.0	49.3	30.6	.7	-	10.4	-	7.2
WATER................	-	100.0	-	-	-	-	-	-	-	-	-
OTHER................	-	100.0	-	-	-	-	100.0	-	-	-	-
UNKNOWN..............	-	100.0	-	-	-	-	-	-	-	-	-
PACIFIC...............	1 811	100.0	-	.2	-	.1	.1	-	1.5	14.1	84.0
RAIL.................	47	100.0	-	6.4	-	2.7	.1	-	13.2	42.7	34.9
MOTOR CARRIER.........	1 415	100.0	-	-	-	-	.1	.1	1.5	15.6	82.7
PRIVATE TRUCK.........	341	100.0	-	-	-	-	-	-	.1	3.8	96.1
AIR..................	-	100.0	-	53.3	4.7	-	-	-	38.2	2.0	1.8
WATER................	6	100.0	-	-	-	-	-	-	-	-	100.0
OTHER................	-	100.0	-	-	-	-	-	-	71.6	-	28.4
UNKNOWN..............	-	100.0	-	-	-	-	-	-	-	-	-
TON-MILES OF SHIPMENTS	(millions of ton-miles)										
U.S. TOTAL.............	3 628	100.0	5.2	16.0	17.6	5.4	16.8	7.1	10.4	4.8	16.8
RAIL.................	874	100.0	3.1	14.3	10.4	6.2	10.6	5.3	16.4	5.3	28.5
MOTOR CARRIER.........	2 070	100.0	6.1	18.7	20.7	4.3	17.7	6.1	6.5	5.4	14.5
PRIVATE TRUCK.........	655	100.0	5.3	10.3	18.0	7.6	22.8	12.8	15.0	2.3	6.0
AIR..................	1	100.0	5.6	25.6	6.7	3.0	.6	1.1	5.4	2.0	50.0
WATER................	19	100.0	-	.5	-	-	3.0	-	-	-	96.6
OTHER................	4	100.0	4.6	14.7	10.3	3.2	8.9	9.5	11.1	.7	37.0
UNKNOWN..............	2	100.0	15.3	13.0	20.8	11.9	38.6	-	.5	-	-

See footnotes at end of table 4.

TABLE 2. **TCC GROUP 322—Percent Distribution of Geographic Division of Origin and Means of Transport, by Geographic Division of Destination: 1972**—Continued

Geographic division of origin[1] and means of transport	Number	Percent distribution by division of destination									
		U.S. total	New England	Middle Atlantic	East North Central	West North Central	South Atlantic	East South Central	West South Central	Mountain	Pacific
TON-MILES OF SHIPMENTS	(millions of ton-miles)										
NEW ENGLAND............	64	100.0	31.9	18.3	11.3	5.5	4.8	10.3	7.0	4.2	6.8
RAIL..................	15	100.0	3.4	7.7	24.4	12.8	-	43.0	8.7	-	-
MOTOR CARRIER.........	33	100.0	23.3	21.1	10.8	4.7	9.3	.2	9.7	8.3	12.7
PRIVATE TRUCK.........	16	100.0	77.1	22.9	-	-	-	-	-	-	-
AIR...................	-	100.0	-	-	-	-	-	.5	-	-	99.5
WATER.................	-	100.0	-	-	-	-	-	-	-	-	-
OTHER.................	-	100.0	-	43.7	9.4	-	46.8	-	-	-	-
UNKNOWN...............	-	100.0	-	-	-	-	-	-	-	-	-
MIDDLE ATLANTIC........	677	100.0	9.4	42.5	15.0	4.2	16.6	1.8	3.2	.5	6.6
RAIL..................	85	100.0	3.3	14.1	6.6	5.3	16.4	2.1	13.7	-	38.5
MOTOR CARRIER.........	509	100.0	10.3	48.5	15.1	2.5	17.6	1.5	1.9	.7	2.1
PRIVATE TRUCK.........	78	100.0	10.4	36.2	24.3	14.6	11.0	3.6	-	-	-
AIR...................	-	100.0	2.5	11.7	6.8	1.9	1.2	2.9	7.1	5.8	59.9
WATER.................	-	100.0	-	100.0	-	-	-	-	-	-	-
OTHER.................	1	100.0	1.6	3.4	6.2	1.9	5.3	1.3	5.4	1.1	73.7
UNKNOWN...............	1	100.0	33.4	27.9	12.6	-	25.0	-	1.0	-	-
EAST NORTH CENTRAL......	1 090	100.0	4.8	13.2	36.5	10.3	7.9	7.5	5.9	3.6	10.4
RAIL..................	410	100.0	4.2	14.4	13.8	9.8	8.3	5.7	12.2	7.3	24.3
MOTOR CARRIER.........	560	100.0	5.5	10.7	53.1	10.2	8.1	7.8	2.4	1.0	1.2
PRIVATE TRUCK.........	115	100.0	3.7	20.8	36.5	12.2	4.9	12.4	-	3.3	6.1
AIR...................	-	100.0	-	54.7	14.2	25.8	-	-	1.6	-	3.6
WATER.................	-	100.0	-	100.0	-	-	-	-	-	-	-
OTHER.................	2	100.0	7.1	24.8	6.3	2.6	12.2	17.8	17.4	-	11.8
UNKNOWN...............	-	100.0	-	-	55.7	44.3	-	-	-	-	-
SOUTH ATLANTIC..........	698	100.0	6.2	15.2	11.2	1.9	38.4	5.7	4.9	.7	15.7
RAIL..................	204	100.0	2.9	15.7	8.6	1.2	18.2	1.3	5.7	.1	46.3
MOTOR CARRIER.........	289	100.0	9.7	21.7	13.2	1.9	39.5	7.5	2.9	.8	2.8
PRIVATE TRUCK.........	202	100.0	4.4	5.5	11.0	2.6	56.9	7.8	7.1	1.3	3.5
AIR...................	-	100.0	11.0	39.7	10.5	-	.5	-	-	-	38.3
WATER.................	-	100.0	-	-	-	-	100.0	-	-	-	-
OTHER.................	-	100.0	5.6	8.3	41.2	9.4	4.3	2.0	3.0	2.0	24.2
UNKNOWN...............	-	100.0	-	.8	-	-	99.2	-	-	-	-
EAST SOUTH CENTRAL......	141	100.0	1.9	.3	5.2	2.1	26.2	24.3	36.1	-	3.9
RAIL..................	21	100.0	-	-	1.3	12.7	29.0	8.5	23.2	-	25.3
MOTOR CARRIER.........	46	100.0	4.2	.7	6.9	.1	23.9	20.3	43.4	-	.5
PRIVATE TRUCK.........	73	100.0	1.0	.1	5.1	.4	26.8	31.3	35.2	-	-
AIR...................	-	100.0	-	26.1	-	-	-	-	-	-	73.9
WATER.................	-	100.0	-	-	-	-	-	-	-	-	-
OTHER.................	-	100.0	2.6	40.5	19.6	2.2	13.1	22.0	-	-	-
UNKNOWN...............	-	100.0	-	-	-	-	-	-	-	-	-
WEST SOUTH CENTRAL......	395	100.0	.7	5.6	2.8	4.0	20.8	19.5	41.1	3.9	1.6
RAIL..................	93	100.0	-	14.4	7.1	1.2	.9	10.9	57.0	4.1	4.4
MOTOR CARRIER.........	214	100.0	1.3	4.0	2.0	4.1	37.9	20.0	25.9	3.6	1.0
PRIVATE TRUCK.........	87	100.0	-	-	-	6.7	-	27.4	61.6	4.3	-
AIR...................	-	100.0	-	3.1	46.5	31.3	.9	-	5.0	-	13.2
WATER.................	-	100.0	-	-	-	-	-	-	-	-	-
OTHER.................	-	100.0	-	-	-	-	100.0	-	-	-	-
UNKNOWN...............	-	100.0	-	-	-	-	-	-	-	-	-
PACIFIC.................	479	100.0	.1	1.5	.1	.7	.5	-	7.4	22.3	67.5
RAIL..................	43	100.0	-	16.3	-	3.9	.2	-	23.6	28.2	27.9
MOTOR CARRIER.........	386	100.0	.1	-	.1	.5	.5	-	6.4	23.2	69.2
PRIVATE TRUCK.........	30	100.0	-	-	-	-	-	-	1.8	15.7	82.5
AIR...................	-	100.0	-	69.5	4.1	-	-	-	25.4	.4	.6
WATER.................	19	100.0	-	-	-	-	-	-	-	-	100.0
OTHER.................	-	100.0	-	-	-	-	-	-	98.2	-	1.8
UNKNOWN...............	-	100.0	-	-	-	-	-	-	-	-	-

See footnotes at end of table 4.

TABLE 3. **TCC GROUP 322—Percent Distribution of Geographic Division of Destination and Means of Transport, by Geographic Division of Origin: 1972**

Geographic division of destination and means of transport	Number	Percent distribution by division of origin[1]									
		U.S. total	New England	Middle Atlantic	East North Central	West North Central	South Atlantic	East South Central	West South Central	Mountain	Pacific
TONS OF SHIPMENTS	(thousands of tons)										
U.S. TOTAL	14 003	100.0	2.7	23.5	29.8	(D)	15.2	4.1	9.1	(D)	12.9
RAIL	1 518	100.0	1.6	10.5	44.1	(D)	20.6	2.2	17.9	(D)	3.2
MOTOR CARRIER	8 958	100.0	1.8	28.9	32.7	(D)	11.8	1.9	6.5	(D)	15.8
PRIVATE TRUCK	3 491	100.0	5.5	15.1	16.4	(D)	21.4	10.5	12.1	(D)	9.8
AIR	1	100.0	7.5	38.4	15.4	(D)	30.6	.2	.7	(D)	5.3
WATER	10	100.0	-	5.6	1.5	(D)	29.1	-	-	(D)	63.8
OTHER	8	100.0	.4	22.1	60.4	(D)	14.7	.1	-	(D)	-
UNKNOWN	14	100.0	-	41.9	25.4	(D)	32.7	-	-	(D)	-
NEW ENGLAND	711	100.0	38.8	35.5	12.4	(D)	12.2	.4	.3	(D)	-
RAIL	50	100.0	11.3	19.3	55.7	(D)	13.7	-	-	(D)	-
MOTOR CARRIER	432	100.0	23.4	48.5	12.0	(D)	14.5	.5	.5	(D)	-
PRIVATE TRUCK	226	100.0	74.8	13.9	3.4	(D)	7.6	.4	-	(D)	-
AIR	-	100.0	-	22.5	-	(D)	55.5	-	-	(D)	-
WATER	-	100.0	-	-	-	(D)	-	-	-	(D)	-
OTHER	-	100.0	-	24.6	63.5	(D)	11.9	-	-	(D)	-
UNKNOWN	1	100.0	-	100.0	-	(D)	-	-	-	(D)	-
MIDDLE ATLANTIC	2 921	100.0	2.3	72.5	12.4	(D)	11.9	-	.7	(D)	.1
RAIL	320	100.0	1.1	25.7	40.0	(D)	28.2	-	4.0	(D)	1.0
MOTOR CARRIER	2 102	100.0	1.9	80.1	7.1	(D)	10.4	-	.4	(D)	-
PRIVATE TRUCK	492	100.0	4.9	70.8	16.7	(D)	7.6	-	-	(D)	-
AIR	-	100.0	.1	34.0	18.6	(D)	40.8	.2	-	(D)	6.3
WATER	-	100.0	-	79.4	20.6	(D)	-	-	-	(D)	-
OTHER	2	100.0	.8	17.6	77.3	(D)	3.5	-	-	(D)	-
UNKNOWN	2	100.0	-	99.8	-	(D)	.2	-	-	(D)	-
EAST NORTH CENTRAL	3 518	100.0	.3	9.0	76.6	(D)	7.8	.5	.5	(D)	-
RAIL	241	100.0	1.9	4.8	72.4	(D)	16.8	.3	3.9	(D)	-
MOTOR CARRIER	2 605	100.0	.2	8.9	83.3	(D)	6.4	.3	.3	(D)	-
PRIVATE TRUCK	666	100.0	-	11.0	51.7	(D)	10.2	1.3	-	(D)	-
AIR	-	100.0	-	40.5	24.4	(D)	31.4	-	2.2	(D)	1.6
WATER	-	100.0	-	-	-	(D)	-	-	-	(D)	-
OTHER	1	100.0	.1	18.4	26.2	(D)	50.8	.1	-	(D)	-
UNKNOWN	3	100.0	-	8.1	91.9	(D)	-	-	-	(D)	-
WEST NORTH CENTRAL	631	100.0	.5	5.5	57.4	(D)	2.6	.7	9.0	(D)	.4
RAIL	109	100.0	1.5	5.6	82.7	(D)	2.6	3.3	3.2	(D)	1.2
MOTOR CARRIER	289	100.0	.5	4.8	75.3	(D)	2.6	-	10.0	(D)	.5
PRIVATE TRUCK	231	100.0	-	6.4	22.7	(D)	2.6	.4	10.6	(D)	-
AIR	-	100.0	-	25.5	69.2	(D)	-	-	5.2	(D)	-
WATER	-	100.0	-	-	-	(D)	-	-	-	(D)	-
OTHER	-	100.0	-	18.9	44.8	(D)	25.7	-	-	(D)	-
UNKNOWN	-	100.0	-	-	100.0	(D)	-	-	-	(D)	-
SOUTH ATLANTIC	2 045	100.0	.4	24.3	8.1	(D)	55.6	6.4	4.2	(D)	-
RAIL	193	100.0	-	11.2	28.4	(D)	55.0	4.9	.4	(D)	-
MOTOR CARRIER	1 166	100.0	.7	36.3	8.4	(D)	41.7	3.9	7.3	(D)	.1
PRIVATE TRUCK	674	100.0	-	7.4	1.9	(D)	79.5	11.2	-	(D)	-
AIR	-	100.0	-	84.0	-	(D)	15.3	-	.3	(D)	-
WATER	3	100.0	-	-	-	(D)	100.0	-	-	(D)	-
OTHER	1	100.0	1.0	23.9	68.7	(D)	4.0	.1	-	(D)	-
UNKNOWN	6	100.0	-	26.2	-	(D)	73.8	-	-	(D)	-
EAST SOUTH CENTRAL	1 034	100.0	.7	2.6	32.4	(D)	16.3	25.7	21.3	(D)	-
RAIL	105	100.0	6.9	2.7	57.4	(D)	8.1	6.0	18.9	(D)	-
MOTOR CARRIER	496	100.0	-	3.3	41.1	(D)	19.6	10.6	25.2	(D)	-
PRIVATE TRUCK	431	100.0	-	1.7	16.1	(D)	14.6	48.0	17.4	(D)	-
AIR	-	100.0	6.9	93.1	-	(D)	-	-	-	(D)	-
WATER	-	100.0	-	-	-	(D)	-	-	-	(D)	-
OTHER	1	100.0	-	3.7	91.4	(D)	1.8	.1	-	(D)	-
UNKNOWN	-	100.0	-	-	-	(D)	-	-	-	(D)	-
WEST SOUTH CENTRAL	1 165	100.0	.3	1.5	7.1	(D)	3.3	12.3	72.6	(D)	2.4
RAIL	314	100.0	.3	3.1	18.3	(D)	4.3	3.1	68.6	(D)	2.0
MOTOR CARRIER	438	100.0	.5	1.8	5.7	(D)	2.1	13.9	71.2	(D)	4.8
PRIVATE TRUCK	411	100.0	-	-	-	(D)	3.8	17.6	77.2	(D)	.1
AIR	-	100.0	-	47.3	3.2	(D)	-	-	1.7	(D)	47.8
WATER	-	100.0	-	-	-	(D)	-	-	-	(D)	-
OTHER	-	100.0	-	19.4	73.2	(D)	4.0	-	-	(D)	.1
UNKNOWN	-	100.0	-	100.0	-	(D)	-	-	-	(D)	-
MOUNTAIN	316	100.0	.4	.6	9.9	(D)	.9	-	7.6	(D)	80.6
RAIL	49	100.0	-	-	47.7	(D)	.3	-	11.0	(D)	41.0
MOTOR CARRIER	242	100.0	.6	.7	1.7	(D)	.5	-	5.0	(D)	91.5
PRIVATE TRUCK	24	100.0	-	-	14.0	(D)	5.8	-	27.2	(D)	53.1
AIR	-	100.0	-	89.7	-	(D)	-	-	-	(D)	10.3
WATER	-	100.0	-	-	-	(D)	-	-	-	(D)	-
OTHER	-	100.0	-	53.3	-	(D)	22.8	-	-	(D)	-
UNKNOWN	-	100.0	-	-	-	(D)	-	-	-	(D)	-
PACIFIC	1 658	100.0	.1	1.2	3.4	(D)	3.0	.2	.3	(D)	91.8
RAIL	132	100.0	-	11.1	38.7	(D)	32.9	2.3	2.5	(D)	12.6
MOTOR CARRIER	1 184	100.0	.1	.4	.3	(D)	.3	-	.1	(D)	98.8
PRIVATE TRUCK	332	100.0	-	-	.6	(D)	.9	-	-	(D)	98.5
AIR	-	100.0	40.7	44.8	.7	(D)	12.4	.6	.3	(D)	.5
WATER	6	100.0	-	-	-	(D)	-	-	-	(D)	100.0
OTHER	-	100.0	-	75.2	18.3	(D)	6.5	-	-	(D)	-
UNKNOWN	-	100.0	-	-	-	(D)	-	-	-	(D)	-

See footnotes at end of table 4.

TABLE 3. **TCC GROUP 322—Percent Distribution of Geographic Division of Destination and Means of Transport, by Geographic Division of Origin: 1972**—Continued

Geographic division of destination and means of transport	Number	Percent distribution by division of origin[1]									
		U.S. total	New England	Middle Atlantic	East North Central	West North Central	South Atlantic	East South Central	West South Central	Mountain	Pacific
TON-MILES OF SHIPMENTS	(millions of ton-miles)										
U.S. TOTAL..............	3 628	100.0	1.8	18.7	30.0	(D)	19.3	3.9	10.9	(D)	13.2
RAIL.................	874	100.0	1.8	9.8	47.0	(D)	23.4	2.4	10.7	(D)	4.9
MOTOR CARRIER.........	2 070	100.0	1.6	24.6	27.1	(D)	14.0	2.3	10.4	(D)	18.7
PRIVATE TRUCK.........	655	100.0	2.5	12.0	17.6	(D)	30.9	11.2	13.4	(D)	4.6
AIR..................	1	100.0	20.1	33.9	8.2	(D)	23.4	.3	.7	(D)	11.2
WATER................	19	100.0	-	.2	.3	(D)	3.0	-	-	(D)	96.6
OTHER................	4	100.0	.2	39.0	48.6	(D)	10.3	-	-	(D)	-
UNKNOWN..............	2	100.0	-	45.8	26.9	(D)	27.3	-	-	(D)	-
NEW ENGLAND............	188	100.0	11.0	33.9	27.9	(D)	22.9	1.4	1.4	(D)	.2
RAIL.................	26	100.0	2.0	10.7	65.0	(D)	22.3	-	-	(D)	-
MOTOR CARRIER.........	126	100.0	6.1	41.4	24.3	(D)	22.3	1.6	2.1	(D)	.2
PRIVATE TRUCK.........	34	100.0	35.9	23.7	12.4	(D)	25.8	2.2	-	(D)	-
AIR..................	-	100.0	-	15.1	-	(D)	45.6	-	-	(D)	-
WATER................	-	100.0	-	-	-	(D)	-	-	-	(D)	-
OTHER................	-	100.0	-	13.2	74.4	(D)	12.4	-	-	(D)	-
UNKNOWN..............	-	100.0	-	100.0	-	(D)	-	-	-	(D)	-
MIDDLE ATLANTIC........	580	100.0	2.0	49.6	24.7	(D)	18.3	.1	3.8	(D)	1.2
PAIL.................	124	100.0	1.0	9.7	47.2	(D)	25.7	-	10.8	(D)	5.6
MOTOR CARRIER.........	386	100.0	1.8	63.8	15.5	(D)	16.2	.1	2.2	(D)	-
PRIVATE TRUCK.........	67	100.0	5.5	42.3	35.7	(D)	16.5	.1	-	(D)	-
AIR..................	-	100.0	-	15.5	17.4	(D)	36.3	.3	.1	(D)	30.3
WATER................	-	100.0	-	37.0	63.0	(D)	-	-	-	(D)	-
OTHER................	-	100.0	.5	9.1	82.0	(D)	5.8	.1	-	(D)	-
UNKNOWN..............	-	100.0	-	98.4	-	(D)	1.6	-	-	(D)	-
EAST NORTH CENTRAL......	638	100.0	1.2	16.0	62.2	(D)	12.3	1.1	1.7	(D)	.1
RAIL.................	90	100.0	4.2	6.2	62.7	(D)	19.4	.3	7.3	(D)	-
MOTOR CARRIER.........	429	100.0	.8	17.9	69.4	(D)	8.9	.8	1.0	(D)	.1
PRIVATE TRUCK.........	117	100.0	-	16.2	35.8	(D)	18.8	3.2	-	(D)	-
AIR..................	-	100.0	-	34.3	17.4	(D)	36.8	-	4.6	(D)	6.9
WATER................	-	100.0	-	-	-	(D)	-	-	-	(D)	-
OTHER................	-	100.0	.1	23.3	29.9	(D)	41.4	.1	-	(D)	-
UNKNOWN..............	-	100.0	-	27.8	72.2	(D)	-	-	-	(D)	-
WEST NORTH CENTRAL......	194	100.0	1.8	14.7	57.5	(D)	6.7	1.6	8.1	(D)	1.8
RAIL.................	54	100.0	3.6	8.3	73.6	(D)	4.4	4.9	2.1	(D)	3.1
MOTOR CARRIER.........	89	100.0	1.7	14.2	64.0	(D)	6.0	-	9.7	(D)	2.1
PRIVATE TRUCK.........	49	100.0	-	22.9	28.1	(D)	10.5	.6	11.8	(D)	-
AIR..................	-	100.0	-	22.1	70.9	(D)	-	-	7.0	(D)	-
WATER................	-	100.0	-	-	-	(D)	-	-	-	(D)	-
OTHER................	-	100.0	-	23.9	39.4	(D)	30.8	-	-	(D)	-
UNKNOWN..............	-	100.0	-	-	100.0	(D)	-	-	-	(D)	-
SOUTH ATLANTIC.........	610	100.0	.5	18.5	14.0	(D)	44.0	6.0	13.5	(D)	.4
RAIL.................	92	100.0	-	15.2	36.9	(D)	40.4	6.6	.9	(D)	.1
MOTOR CARRIER.........	366	100.0	.8	24.4	12.5	(D)	31.2	3.1	22.2	(D)	.6
PRIVATE TRUCK.........	149	100.0	-	5.8	3.8	(D)	77.2	13.2	-	(D)	-
AIR..................	-	100.0	-	74.7	-	(D)	22.8	-	1.1	(D)	-
WATER................	-	100.0	-	-	-	(D)	100.0	-	-	(D)	-
OTHER................	-	100.0	.8	23.4	66.4	(D)	4.9	.1	-	(D)	-
UNKNOWN..............	1	100.0	-	29.7	-	(D)	70.3	-	-	(D)	-
EAST SOUTH CENTRAL......	256	100.0	2.6	4.8	31.9	(D)	15.6	13.3	30.1	(D)	-
RAIL.................	46	100.0	14.2	3.8	50.6	(D)	5.8	3.8	21.8	(D)	-
MOTOR CARRIER.........	125	100.0	-	6.2	34.6	(D)	17.2	7.6	34.2	(D)	-
PRIVATE TRUCK.........	83	100.0	-	3.3	17.1	(D)	18.8	27.3	28.6	(D)	-
AIR..................	-	100.0	8.9	91.1	-	(D)	-	-	-	(D)	-
WATER................	-	100.0	-	-	-	(D)	-	-	-	(D)	-
OTHER................	-	100.0	-	5.3	90.6	(D)	2.2	.1	-	(D)	-
UNKNOWN..............	-	100.0	-	-	-	(D)	-	-	-	(D)	-
WEST SOUTH CENTRAL.....	377	100.0	1.2	5.7	17.0	(D)	9.1	13.5	43.2	(D)	9.4
RAIL.................	143	100.0	.9	8.2	34.9	(D)	8.2	3.4	37.0	(D)	7.1
MOTOR CARRIER.........	135	100.0	2.4	7.0	10.0	(D)	6.2	15.0	41.3	(D)	18.2
PRIVATE TRUCK.........	98	100.0	-	-	-	(D)	14.6	26.3	55.1	(D)	.5
AIR..................	-	100.0	-	44.6	2.4	(D)	-	-	.6	(D)	52.4
WATER................	-	100.0	-	-	-	(D)	-	-	-	(D)	-
OTHER................	-	100.0	-	19.0	76.2	(D)	2.8	-	-	(D)	.1
UNKNOWN..............	-	100.0	-	100.0	-	(D)	-	-	-	(D)	-
MOUNTAIN...............	172	100.0	1.6	2.0	22.8	(D)	3.0	-	8.9	(D)	61.8
RAIL.................	46	100.0	-	-	65.0	(D)	.4	-	8.2	(D)	26.4
MOTOR CARRIER.........	111	100.0	2.5	3.0	5.0	(D)	2.1	-	7.0	(D)	80.4
PRIVATE TRUCK.........	14	100.0	-	-	25.7	(D)	17.0	-	25.3	(D)	32.0
AIR..................	-	100.0	-	97.9		(D)	-	-	-	(D)	2.1
WATER................	-	100.0	-	-	-	(D)	-	-	-	(D)	-
OTHER................	-	100.0	-	59.2	-	(D)	28.2	-	-	(D)	-
UNKNOWN..............	-	100.0	-	-	-	(D)	-	-	-	(D)	-
PACIFIC................	609	100.0	.7	7.4	18.7	(D)	18.1	.9	1.0	(D)	53.1
RAIL.................	248	100.0	-	13.2	40.0	(D)	38.1	2.1	1.7	(D)	4.8
MOTOR CARRIER.........	299	100.0	1.4	3.5	2.3	(D)	2.7	.1	.7	(D)	89.2
PRIVATE TRUCK.........	39	100.0	-	-	18.1	(D)	17.9	-	-	(D)	64.0
AIR..................	-	100.0	40.1	40.7	.6	(D)	17.9	.4	.2	(D)	.1
WATER................	19	100.0	-	-	-	(D)	-	-	-	(D)	100.0
OTHER................	1	100.0	-	77.7	15.5	(D)	6.8	-	-	(D)	-
UNKNOWN..............	-	100.0	-	-	-	(D)	-	-	-	(D)	-

See footnotes at end of table 4.

TABLE 4. TCC GROUP 322—Percent Distribution of Distance Shipped and Weight of Shipment, by Means of Transport: 1972

Distance shipped and weight of shipment[+] [2] [3]	Number	Percent distribution by means of transport							
		All means of transport	Rail	Motor carrier	Private truck	Air	Water	Other	Unknown
TONS OF SHIPMENTS	(thousands of tons)								
U.S. TOTAL..........	11 351	100.0	9.7	63.2	26.9	-	.1	-	.1
UNDER 100 MILES.........	3 345	100.0	1.3	61.2	37.5	-	-	-	-
UNDER 1000 POUNDS.....	67	100.0	-	74.4	25.3	-	.1	.2	-
1000 TO 9999 POUNDS...	123	100.0	.9	39.1	59.9	-	-	.1	-
10000 TO 29999 POUNDS.	1 739	100.0	.7	65.5	33.8	-	-	-	-
30000 TO 59999 POUNDS.	1 224	100.0	1.6	60.3	38.0	-	-	-	-
60000 TO 89999 POUNDS.	30	100.0	18.5	76.2	5.3	-	-	-	-
90000 POUNDS AND OVER.	159	100.0	2.9	29.1	68.0	-	-	-	-
100 TO 199 MILES........	2 972	100.0	3.7	71.0	25.0	-	.1	-	.2
UNDER 1000 POUNDS.....	24	100.0	-	86.9	11.7	.1	-	1.3	-
1000 TO 9999 POUNDS...	110	100.0	.6	84.3	14.4	-	-	.7	-
10000 TO 29999 POUNDS.	1 261	100.0	1.3	71.9	26.4	-	-	-	.4
30000 TO 59999 POUNDS.	1 387	100.0	4.7	67.4	27.6	-	.2	-	.1
60000 TO 89999 POUNDS.	70	100.0	35.0	58.6	6.4	-	-	-	-
90000 POUNDS AND OVER.	118	100.0	2.0	94.7	3.3	-	-	-	-
200 TO 299 MILES........	1 874	100.0	4.9	67.1	27.9	-	-	.1	.1
UNDER 1000 POUNDS.....	22	100.0	1.0	95.3	.6	.7	-	2.0	.4
1000 TO 9999 POUNDS...	82	100.0	1.6	83.7	14.2	-	-	.4	-
10000 TO 29999 POUNDS.	735	100.0	3.4	63.3	33.2	-	-	-	.2
30000 TO 59999 POUNDS.	929	100.0	4.4	66.8	28.7	-	-	.2	-
60000 TO 89999 POUNDS.	11	100.0	-	100.0	-	-	-	-	-
90000 POUNDS AND OVER.	91	100.0	26.2	73.8	-	-	-	-	-
300 TO 499 MILES........	2 093	100.0	23.2	59.8	16.9	-	-	.1	-
UNDER 1000 POUNDS.....	45	100.0	.7	96.1	2.0	.4	-	.8	-
1000 TO 9999 POUNDS...	153	100.0	3.9	86.5	9.4	.1	-	-	-
10000 TO 29999 POUNDS.	624	100.0	12.3	67.4	20.2	-	-	-	.1
30000 TO 59999 POUNDS.	993	100.0	16.5	62.6	20.9	-	-	-	-
60000 TO 89999 POUNDS.	131	100.0	83.3	12.5	4.2	-	-	-	-
90000 POUNDS AND OVER.	145	100.0	89.6	10.4	-	-	-	-	-
500 TO 999 MILES........	827	100.0	30.2	49.9	19.8	-	-	.1	.1
UNDER 1000 POUNDS.....	53	100.0	3.5	94.5	.9	.3	-	.8	-
1000 TO 9999 POUNDS...	93	100.0	9.1	85.8	4.8	-	-	-	.3
10000 TO 29999 POUNDS.	205	100.0	24.0	50.7	25.2	-	-	-	-
30000 TO 59999 POUNDS.	437	100.0	37.3	38.2	24.5	-	-	-	-
60000 TO 89999 POUNDS.	33	100.0	79.3	20.7	-	-	-	-	-
90000 POUNDS AND OVER.	4	100.0	-	100.0	-	-	-	-	-
1000 TO 1499 MILES......	114	100.0	33.4	60.3	6.1	.1	-	.1	-
UNDER 1000 POUNDS.....	22	100.0	.9	98.2	-	.4	-	.4	.1
1000 TO 9999 POUNDS...	18	100.0	2.6	97.4	-	-	-	-	-
10000 TO 29999 POUNDS.	38	100.0	31.0	67.0	2.0	-	-	-	-
30000 TO 59999 POUNDS.	33	100.0	69.6	11.6	18.8	-	-	-	-
60000 TO 89999 POUNDS.	2	100.0	100.0	-	-	-	-	-	-
90000 POUNDS AND OVER.	-	100.0	-	-	-	-	-	-	-
1500 MILES OR OVER......	123	100.0	63.9	26.7	3.6	.2	5.0	.6	-
UNDER 1000 POUNDS.....	8	100.0	25.2	70.8	-	1.6	.1	2.3	-
1000 TO 9999 POUNDS...	32	100.0	30.5	65.6	.1	.2	3.5	.1	-
10000 TO 29999 POUNDS.	25	100.0	60.8	16.8	-	-	20.3	2.2	-
30000 TO 59999 POUNDS.	47	100.0	86.7	4.1	9.2	-	-	-	-
60000 TO 89999 POUNDS.	8	100.0	100.0	-	-	-	-	-	-
90000 POUNDS AND OVER.	1	100.0	100.0	-	-	-	-	-	-
TON-MILES OF SHIPMENTS	(millions of ton-miles)								
U.S. TOTAL..........	2 843	100.0	21.9	57.5	19.8	-	.6	.1	.1
UNDER 100 MILES.........	176	100.0	1.5	61.6	36.9	-	-	-	-
UNDER 1000 POUNDS....	2	100.0	-	83.9	15.5	-	-	.5	-
1000 TO 9999 POUNDS...	5	100.0	1.5	53.2	45.2	-	-	.1	-
10000 TO 29999 POUNDS.	88	100.0	.9	64.6	34.5	-	-	-	-
30000 TO 59999 POUNDS.	72	100.0	2.0	60.0	38.1	-	-	-	-
60000 TO 89999 POUNDS.	1	100.0	18.1	78.4	3.6	-	-	-	-
90000 POUNDS AND OVER.	6	100.0	1.1	37.7	61.2	-	-	-	-
100 TO 199 MILES........	432	100.0	3.9	70.8	24.8	-	.1	-	.2
UNDER 1000 POUNDS.....	3	100.0	-	88.0	10.4	.1	-	1.5	-
1000 TO 9999 POUNDS...	14	100.0	.6	82.9	15.5	-	-	1.1	-
10000 TO 29999 POUNDS.	186	100.0	1.4	72.1	26.1	-	-	-	.4
30000 TO 59999 POUNDS.	203	100.0	5.0	67.5	27.1	-	.3	-	.1
60000 TO 89999 POUNDS.	11	100.0	34.0	59.1	6.9	-	-	-	-
90000 POUNDS AND OVER.	14	100.0	2.5	94.0	3.5	-	-	-	-

See footnotes at end of table 4.

TABLE 4. TCC GROUP 322—Percent Distribution of Distance Shipped and Weight of Shipment, by Means of Transport: 1972—Continued

Distance shipped and weight of shipment [2] [3]	Number	Percent distribution by means of transport							
		All means of transport	Rail	Motor carrier	Private truck	Air	Water	Other	Unknown
TON-MILES OF SHIPMENTS	(millions of ton-miles)								
200 TO 299 MILES	459	100.0	5.0	67.6	27.2	-	-	.1	.1
UNDER 1000 POUNDS	5	100.0	1.0	95.4	.6	.7	-	2.0	.3
1000 TO 9999 POUNDS	20	100.0	1.5	83.3	14.7	-	-	.4	-
10000 TO 29999 POUNDS	182	100.0	3.2	64.6	31.9	-	-	-	.2
30000 TO 59999 POUNDS	224	100.0	4.5	67.1	28.3	-	-	.2	-
60000 TO 89999 POUNDS	3	100.0	-	100.0	-	-	-	-	-
90000 POUNDS AND OVER	23	100.0	28.3	71.7	-	-	-	-	-
300 TO 499 MILES	786	100.0	24.5	58.3	17.1	-	-	-	-
UNDER 1000 POUNDS	16	100.0	.8	95.7	2.1	.5	-	.8	-
1000 TO 9999 POUNDS	57	100.0	4.2	85.7	9.9	.1	-	-	-
10000 TO 29999 POUNDS	232	100.0	13.0	66.5	20.4	-	-	-	.1
30000 TO 59999 POUNDS	372	100.0	17.4	61.3	21.2	-	-	-	-
60000 TO 89999 POUNDS	51	100.0	85.6	10.6	3.8	-	-	-	-
90000 POUNDS AND OVER	55	100.0	91.1	8.9	-	-	-	-	-
500 TO 999 MILES	579	100.0	31.0	50.1	18.9	-	-	.1	-
UNDER 1000 POUNDS	43	100.0	3.5	94.8	.7	.2	-	.7	.1
1000 TO 9999 POUNDS	74	100.0	9.6	84.5	5.7	-	-	-	.2
10000 TO 29999 POUNDS	134	100.0	25.1	50.8	24.1	-	-	-	-
30000 TO 59999 POUNDS	301	100.0	38.9	37.0	24.1	-	-	-	-
60000 TO 89999 POUNDS	24	100.0	82.5	17.5	-	-	-	-	-
90000 POUNDS AND OVER	2	100.0	-	100.0	-	-	-	-	-
1000 TO 1499 MILES	133	100.0	33.5	60.4	5.9	.1	-	.1	-
UNDER 1000 POUNDS	27	100.0	1.0	98.2	-	.4	-	.4	.1
1000 TO 9999 POUNDS	20	100.0	2.6	97.4	-	-	-	-	-
10000 TO 29999 POUNDS	43	100.0	31.9	66.2	1.9	-	-	-	-
30000 TO 59999 POUNDS	38	100.0	69.7	11.8	18.5	-	-	-	-
60000 TO 89999 POUNDS	3	100.0	100.0	-	-	-	-	-	-
90000 POUNDS AND OVER	-	100.0	-	-	-	-	-	-	-
1500 MILES OR OVER	275	100.0	59.4	28.9	4.6	.2	6.3	.6	-
UNDER 1000 POUNDS	19	100.0	30.0	66.1	-	1.7	.1	2.0	-
1000 TO 9999 POUNDS	79	100.0	27.3	68.7	.1	.2	3.6	.1	-
10000 TO 29999 POUNDS	56	100.0	58.1	14.1	-	-	25.4	2.3	-
30000 TO 59999 POUNDS	96	100.0	82.6	4.4	13.0	-	-	-	-
60000 TO 89999 POUNDS	18	100.0	100.0	-	-	-	-	-	-
90000 POUNDS AND OVER	4	100.0	100.0	-	-	-	-	-	-

Note: Detail may not add to total due to rounding. The introductory table shows the estimates of sampling variability for tons; sampling variability for ton-miles has not been estimated. See the map in the Introduction for the States comprising the geographic divisions of the United States.

Shipments excluded from the survey are those moving by pipeline (primarily petroleum products from refineries), parcel post shipments, and commodities moved by own power (motorized vehicles, aircraft, etc.) or towed (prefabricated buildings, etc.). Local shipments (commodities shipped less than 25 miles from the plant) and shipments within the same city are also excluded. Shipments to Alaska and Hawaii from the 48 conterminous States and the District of Columbia are included; however, no data were obtained for shipments originating in Alaska and Hawaii.

- Represents zero or rounds to zero.   (D) Withheld to avoid disclosing figures for individual companies.

[1] Production of this commodity is concentrated in the geographic divisions shown; figures and distributions for geographic divisions not shown are included in the total.

[2] Distances of shipments to foreign destinations are calculated only to the U.S. port of exit.

[3] Includes only shipments represented by bills of lading and invoices. Summary records which did not show individual weights of shipments are not included.

TCC 324. Hydraulic Cement

Comparisons of Tons and Ton-Miles of Shipments for
Geographic Divisions of Origin and for Sampling Variability: 1972 and 1967

Geographic division of origin	Estimates				Relative sampling variability in tons (percent)	
	1972		1967		1972	1967
	Tons (thousands)	Ton-miles (millions)	Tons (thousands)	Ton-miles (millions)		
U.S. total	59,056	6,809	48,051	6,264	18.9	16.2
New England	(D)	(D)	8	6	(*)	(*)
Middle Atlantic	6,668	705	9,627	864	34.4	(*)
East North Central	17,958	2,660	9,489	873	39.7	(*)
West North Central	6,486	726	5,024	711	45.1	(*)
South Atlantic	(D)	(D)	6,037	510	(*)	(*)
East South Central	(D)	(D)	2,826	391	(*)	(*)
West South Central	(D)	(D)	4,638	537	(*)	(*)
Mountain	(D)	(D)	2,390	320	(*)	(*)
Pacific	10,902	1,212	8,012	2,052	25.9	(*)

(D) Withheld to avoid disclosing figures for individual companies.   (*) Data not published.

TABLE 1. **TCC GROUP 324—Percent Distribution of Geographic Division of Origin and Distance Shipped, by Means of Transport: 1972**

Geographic division of origin[1] and distance shipped[2]	Number	Percent distribution by means of transport							
		All means of transport	Rail	Motor carrier	Private truck	Air	Water	Other	Unknown
TONS OF SHIPMENTS	(thousands of tons)								
U.S. TOTAL..........	59 056	100.0	15.1	49.4	17.6	-	15.9	-	2.0
MIDDLE ATLANTIC.........	6 668	100.0	21.4	57.1	11.0	-	10.5	-	-
UNDER 100 MILES.......	4 840	100.0	14.6	60.8	10.1	-	14.5	-	-
100 TO 199 MILES......	1 386	100.0	25.7	62.1	12.2	-	-	-	-
200 TO 299 MILES......	135	100.0	45.9	-	54.1	-	-	-	-
300 TO 499 MILES......	71	100.0	97.2	2.8	-	-	-	-	-
500 TO 999 MILES......	192	100.0	99.9	.1	-	-	-	-	-
1000 TO 1499 MILES....	41	100.0	100.0	-	-	-	-	-	-
1500 MILES OR OVER....	-	100.0	-	-	-	-	-	-	-
EAST NORTH CENTRAL......	17 958	100.0	2.1	40.3	11.8	-	45.5	-	.4
UNDER 100 MILES.......	6 538	100.0	3.2	73.0	23.3	-	-	-	.5
100 TO 199 MILES......	5 950	100.0	1.6	37.3	8.6	-	52.1	-	.6
200 TO 299 MILES......	4 824	100.0	.8	2.6	.1	-	96.5	-	-
300 TO 499 MILES......	442	100.0	3.7	1.8	-	-	94.5	-	-
500 TO 999 MILES......	201	100.0	8.3	53.2	38.4	-	-	-	-
1000 TO 1499 MILES....	-	100.0	-	100.0	-	-	-	-	-
1500 MILES OR OVER....	1	100.0	-	98.3	1.7	-	-	-	-
WEST NORTH CENTRAL......	6 486	100.0	27.7	47.4	-	-	7.6	-	17.3
UNDER 100 MILES.......	2 854	100.0	22.8	73.7	-	-	-	-	3.5
100 TO 199 MILES......	2 907	100.0	20.2	30.0	-	-	16.9	-	32.8
200 TO 299 MILES......	576	100.0	76.0	15.2	-	-	-	-	8.9
300 TO 499 MILES......	148	100.0	81.0	9.2	-	-	-	-	9.8
500 TO 999 MILES......	-	100.0	-	-	-	-	-	-	-
1000 TO 1499 MILES....	-	100.0	-	-	-	-	-	-	-
1500 MILES OR OVER....	-	100.0	-	-	-	-	-	-	-
PACIFIC.................	10 902	100.0	18.1	45.0	36.9	-	-	-	-
UNDER 100 MILES.......	7 747	100.0	5.2	52.6	42.2	-	-	-	-
100 TO 199 MILES......	1 545	100.0	9.5	45.9	44.6	-	-	-	-
200 TO 299 MILES......	272	100.0	43.0	32.2	24.8	-	-	-	-
300 TO 499 MILES......	1 138	100.0	97.1	2.9	-	-	-	-	-
500 TO 999 MILES......	194	100.0	100.0	-	-	-	-	-	-
1000 TO 1499 MILES....	4	100.0	-	100.0	-	-	-	-	-
1500 MILES OR OVER....	-	100.0	-	-	-	-	-	-	-
TON-MILES OF SHIPMENTS	(millions of ton-miles)								
U.S. TOTAL..........	6 809	100.0	26.2	34.0	10.8	-	26.8	-	2.2
MIDDLE ATLANTIC.........	705	100.0	44.3	38.6	9.0	-	8.1	-	-
UNDER 100 MILES.......	287	100.0	15.5	57.9	6.7	-	19.9	-	-
100 TO 199 MILES......	177	100.0	26.8	59.3	14.0	-	-	-	-
200 TO 299 MILES......	34	100.0	43.8	-	56.2	-	-	-	-
300 TO 499 MILES......	22	100.0	95.7	4.3	-	-	-	-	-
500 TO 999 MILES......	139	100.0	99.9	.1	-	-	-	-	-
1000 TO 1499 MILES....	44	100.0	100.0	-	-	-	-	-	-
1500 MILES OR OVER....	-	100.0	-	-	-	-	-	-	-
EAST NORTH CENTRAL......	2 660	100.0	2.0	25.9	8.1	-	63.7	-	.2
UNDER 100 MILES.......	371	100.0	3.7	71.4	24.6	-	-	-	.3
100 TO 199 MILES......	838	100.0	1.6	36.0	7.4	-	54.6	-	.5
200 TO 299 MILES......	1 100	100.0	.8	3.0	.2	-	96.0	-	-
300 TO 499 MILES......	190	100.0	3.3	1.4	-	-	95.3	-	-
500 TO 999 MILES......	157	100.0	7.0	54.1	39.0	-	-	-	-
1000 TO 1499 MILES....	-	100.0	-	100.0	-	-	-	-	-
1500 MILES OR OVER....	2	100.0	-	98.3	1.7	-	-	-	-
WEST NORTH CENTRAL......	726	100.0	34.6	35.8	-	-	10.1	-	19.5
UNDER 100 MILES.......	173	100.0	25.7	70.1	-	-	-	-	4.2
100 TO 199 MILES......	376	100.0	19.7	30.2	-	-	19.5	-	30.6
200 TO 299 MILES......	130	100.0	72.8	15.7	-	-	-	-	11.5
300 TO 499 MILES......	46	100.0	80.3	9.5	-	-	-	-	10.1
500 TO 999 MILES......	-	100.0	-	-	-	-	-	-	-
1000 TO 1499 MILES....	-	100.0	-	-	-	-	-	-	-
1500 MILES OR OVER....	-	100.0	-	-	-	-	-	-	-
PACIFIC.................	1 212	100.0	49.5	30.2	20.3	-	-	-	-
UNDER 100 MILES.......	380	100.0	7.3	59.9	32.9	-	-	-	-
100 TO 199 MILES......	226	100.0	9.3	45.1	45.7	-	-	-	-
200 TO 299 MILES......	66	100.0	42.0	32.0	26.0	-	-	-	-
300 TO 499 MILES......	409	100.0	97.4	2.6	-	-	-	-	-
500 TO 999 MILES......	125	100.0	100.0	-	-	-	-	-	-
1000 TO 1499 MILES....	5	100.0	-	100.0	-	-	-	-	-
1500 MILES OR OVER....	-	100.0	-	-	-	-	-	-	-

See footnotes at end of table 4.

TABLE 2. TCC GROUP 324—Percent Distribution of Geographic Division of Origin and Means of Transport, by Geographic Division of Destination: 1972

Geographic division of origin[1] and means of transport	Number	Percent distribution by division of destination									
		U.S. total	New England	Middle Atlantic	East North Central	West North Central	South Atlantic	East South Central	West South Central	Mountain	Pacific
TONS OF SHIPMENTS	(thousands of tons)										
U.S. TOTAL	59 056	100.0	2.7	9.2	29.4	9.0	8.5	11.3	6.8	7.1	15.9
RAIL	8 906	100.0	3.9	7.4	7.7	15.9	29.4	9.7	4.8	12.0	9.1
MOTOR CARRIER	29 168	100.0	2.6	11.3	24.7	8.8	6.9	18.0	2.8	8.2	16.6
PRIVATE TRUCK	10 416	100.0	4.6	5.8	16.1	-	3.7	.4	26.1	7.1	36.2
AIR	-	100.0	-	100.0	-	-	-	-	-	-	-
WATER	9 369	100.0	-	9.1	82.8	2.8	-	5.3	-	-	-
OTHER	-	100.0	-	-	-	-	-	-	-	-	-
UNKNOWN	1 195	100.0	-	-	5.5	88.0	.7	-	5.7	-	-
MIDDLE ATLANTIC	6 668	100.0	16.6	74.8	.4	-	6.7	1.5	-	-	-
RAIL	1 429	100.0	24.4	45.3	-	-	23.2	7.2	-	-	-
MOTOR CARRIER	3 804	100.0	17.5	80.2	.1	-	2.2	-	-	-	-
PRIVATE TRUCK	732	100.0	12.3	79.9	3.3	-	4.5	-	-	-	-
AIR	-	100.0	-	100.0	-	-	-	-	-	-	-
WATER	700	100.0	-	100.0	-	-	-	-	-	-	-
OTHER	-	100.0	-	-	-	-	-	-	-	-	-
UNKNOWN	-	100.0	-	-	-	-	-	-	-	-	-
EAST NORTH CENTRAL	17 958	100.0	1.0	1.0	91.6	1.7	3.1	1.6	.1	-	-
RAIL	374	100.0	.8	2.3	71.8	6.8	14.8	1.6	1.9	-	-
MOTOR CARRIER	7 228	100.0	1.4	.2	92.7	.1	2.2	3.3	.1	-	-
PRIVATE TRUCK	2 115	100.0	3.7	-	78.1	-	16.1	2.1	-	-	-
AIR	-	100.0	-	100.0	-	-	-	-	-	-	-
WATER	8 174	100.0	-	1.8	94.9	3.2	-	-	-	-	-
OTHER	-	100.0	-	-	-	-	-	-	-	-	-
UNKNOWN	66	100.0	-	-	100.0	-	-	-	-	-	-
WEST NORTH CENTRAL	6 486	100.0	-	-	11.5	77.0	-	8.3	3.2	-	-
RAIL	1 797	100.0	-	-	22.2	76.3	-	.7	.8	-	-
MOTOR CARRIER	3 077	100.0	-	-	11.3	83.5	-	1.1	4.0	-	-
PRIVATE TRUCK	-	100.0	-	-	-	-	-	-	-	-	-
AIR	-	100.0	-	-	-	-	-	-	-	-	-
WATER	492	100.0	-	-	-	-	-	100.0	-	-	-
OTHER	-	100.0	-	-	-	-	-	-	-	-	-
UNKNOWN	1 119	100.0	-	-	-	94.1	-	-	5.9	-	-
PACIFIC	10 902	100.0	-	-	-	-	-	-	1.8	11.8	86.3
RAIL	1 968	100.0	-	-	-	-	-	-	9.9	49.0	41.1
MOTOR CARRIER	4 906	100.0	-	-	-	-	-	-	.1	1.4	98.5
PRIVATE TRUCK	4 028	100.0	-	-	-	-	-	-	-	6.4	93.6
AIR	-	100.0	-	-	-	-	-	-	-	-	-
WATER	-	100.0	-	-	-	-	-	-	-	-	-
OTHER	-	100.0	-	-	-	-	-	-	-	-	-
UNKNOWN	-	100.0	-	-	-	-	-	-	-	-	-
TON-MILES OF SHIPMENTS	(millions of ton-miles)										
U.S. TOTAL	6 809	100.0	4.3	5.9	35.4	8.8	10.4	8.9	6.8	9.5	9.9
RAIL	1 784	100.0	2.5	2.5	7.2	9.6	29.2	9.5	11.3	20.8	7.2
MOTOR CARRIER	2 312	100.0	6.6	9.2	26.1	8.8	6.2	15.3	4.2	8.3	15.2
PRIVATE TRUCK	738	100.0	12.9	6.2	15.5	-	5.8	.7	20.9	11.3	26.7
AIR	-	100.0	-	100.0	-	-	-	-	-	-	-
WATER	1 825	100.0	-	5.4	85.5	5.1	-	4.0	-	-	-
OTHER	-	100.0	-	-	-	-	-	-	-	-	-
UNKNOWN	147	100.0	-	-	3.5	89.9	.4	-	6.2	-	-
MIDDLE ATLANTIC	705	100.0	18.3	47.3	.3	-	23.9	10.2	-	-	-
RAIL	312	100.0	13.7	13.3	-	-	50.1	23.0	-	-	-
MOTOR CARRIER	272	100.0	26.3	70.5	.2	-	3.1	-	-	-	-
PRIVATE TRUCK	63	100.0	23.6	67.9	3.2	-	5.4	-	-	-	-
AIR	-	100.0	-	100.0	-	-	-	-	-	-	-
WATER	57	100.0	-	100.0	-	-	-	-	-	-	-
OTHER	-	100.0	-	-	-	-	-	-	-	-	-
UNKNOWN	-	100.0	-	-	-	-	-	-	-	-	-
EAST NORTH CENTRAL	2 660	100.0	5.5	1.8	84.8	3.8	2.4	1.3	.3	-	.1
RAIL	53	100.0	4.7	7.2	42.9	14.0	18.0	4.2	8.9	-	-
MOTOR CARRIER	690	100.0	11.9	.4	80.3	.2	2.4	4.0	.4	-	.4
PRIVATE TRUCK	216	100.0	28.3	-	52.0	-	17.4	2.3	-	-	-
AIR	-	100.0	-	100.0	-	-	-	-	-	-	-
WATER	1 694	100.0	-	2.4	92.1	5.5	-	-	-	-	-
OTHER	-	100.0	-	-	-	-	-	-	-	-	-
UNKNOWN	5	100.0	-	-	100.0	-	-	-	-	-	-
WEST NORTH CENTRAL	726	100.0	-	-	17.0	68.3	-	10.8	3.9	-	-
RAIL	250	100.0	-	-	34.2	63.9	-	1.0	1.0	-	-
MOTOR CARRIER	260	100.0	-	-	14.4	77.9	-	1.1	6.6	-	-
PRIVATE TRUCK	-	100.0	-	-	-	-	-	-	-	-	-
AIR	-	100.0	-	-	-	-	-	-	-	-	-
WATER	73	100.0	-	-	-	-	-	100.0	-	-	-
OTHER	-	100.0	-	-	-	-	-	-	-	-	-
UNKNOWN	141	100.0	-	-	-	93.7	-	-	6.3	-	-
PACIFIC	1 212	100.0	-	-	-	-	-	-	10.8	33.7	55.5
RAIL	600	100.0	-	-	-	-	-	-	20.9	57.6	21.5
MOTOR CARRIER	366	100.0	-	-	-	-	-	-	1.4	4.0	94.6
PRIVATE TRUCK	245	100.0	-	-	-	-	-	-	-	19.6	80.4
AIR	-	100.0	-	-	-	-	-	-	-	-	-
WATER	-	100.0	-	-	-	-	-	-	-	-	-
OTHER	-	100.0	-	-	-	-	-	-	-	-	-
UNKNOWN	-	100.0	-	-	-	-	-	-	-	-	-

See footnotes at end of table 4.

TABLE 3. **TCC GROUP 324**—Percent Distribution of Geographic Division of Destination and Means of Transport, by Geographic Division of Origin: 1972

Geographic division of destination and means of transport	Number	Percent distribution by division of origin[1]									
		U.S. total	New England	Middle Atlantic	East North Central	West North Central	South Atlantic	East South Central	West South Central	Mountain	Pacific
TONS OF SHIPMENTS	(thousands of tons)										
U.S. TOTAL	59 056	100.0	(D)	11.3	30.4	11.0	(D)	(D)	(D)	(D)	18.5
RAIL	8 906	100.0	(D)	16.1	4.2	20.2	(D)	(D)	(D)	(D)	22.1
MOTOR CARRIER	29 168	100.0	(D)	13.0	24.8	10.6	(D)	(D)	(D)	(D)	16.8
PRIVATE TRUCK	10 416	100.0	(D)	7.0	20.3	-	(D)	(D)	(D)	(D)	38.7
AIR	-	100.0	(D)	60.0	40.0	-	(D)	(D)	(D)	(D)	-
WATER	9 369	100.0	(D)	7.5	87.2	5.3	(D)	(D)	(D)	(D)	-
OTHER	-	100.0	(D)	-	-	-	(D)	(D)	(D)	(D)	-
UNKNOWN	1 195	100.0	(D)	-	5.5	93.6	(D)	(D)	(D)	(D)	-
NEW ENGLAND	1 598	100.0	(D)	69.1	11.5	-	(D)	(D)	(D)	(D)	-
RAIL	351	100.0	(D)	99.1	.9	-	(D)	(D)	(D)	(D)	-
MOTOR CARRIER	769	100.0	(D)	86.6	13.4	-	(D)	(D)	(D)	(D)	-
PRIVATE TRUCK	477	100.0	(D)	18.9	16.2	-	(D)	(D)	(D)	(D)	-
AIR	-	100.0	(D)	-	-	-	(D)	(D)	(D)	(D)	-
WATER	-	100.0	(D)	-	-	-	(D)	(D)	(D)	(D)	-
OTHER	-	100.0	(D)	-	-	-	(D)	(D)	(D)	(D)	-
UNKNOWN	-	100.0	(D)	-	-	-	(D)	(D)	(D)	(D)	-
MIDDLE ATLANTIC	5 416	100.0	(D)	92.0	3.2	-	(D)	(D)	(D)	(D)	-
RAIL	656	100.0	(D)	98.6	1.3	-	(D)	(D)	(D)	(D)	-
MOTOR CARRIER	3 303	100.0	(D)	92.4	.5	-	(D)	(D)	(D)	(D)	-
PRIVATE TRUCK	605	100.0	(D)	96.7	-	-	(D)	(D)	(D)	(D)	-
AIR	-	100.0	(D)	60.0	40.0	-	(D)	(D)	(D)	(D)	-
WATER	851	100.0	(D)	82.3	17.7	-	(D)	(D)	(D)	(D)	-
OTHER	-	100.0	(D)	-	-	-	(D)	(D)	(D)	(D)	-
UNKNOWN	-	100.0	(D)	-	-	-	(D)	(D)	(D)	(D)	-
EAST NORTH CENTRAL	17 389	100.0	(D)	.2	94.6	4.3	(D)	(D)	(D)	(D)	-
RAIL	688	100.0	(D)	-	39.0	58.0	(D)	(D)	(D)	(D)	-
MOTOR CARRIER	7 199	100.0	(D)	-	93.1	4.8	(D)	(D)	(D)	(D)	-
PRIVATE TRUCK	1 677	100.0	(D)	1.4	98.6	-	(D)	(D)	(D)	(D)	-
AIR	-	100.0	(D)	-	-	-	(D)	(D)	(D)	(D)	-
WATER	7 758	100.0	(D)	-	100.0	-	(D)	(D)	(D)	(D)	-
OTHER	-	100.0	(D)	-	-	-	(D)	(D)	(D)	(D)	-
UNKNOWN	66	100.0	(D)	-	100.0	-	(D)	(D)	(D)	(D)	-
WEST NORTH CENTRAL	5 317	100.0	(D)	-	5.6	93.9	(D)	(D)	(D)	(D)	-
RAIL	1 419	100.0	(D)	-	1.8	96.6	(D)	(D)	(D)	(D)	-
MOTOR CARRIER	2 579	100.0	(D)	-	.3	99.7	(D)	(D)	(D)	(D)	-
PRIVATE TRUCK	-	100.0	(D)	-	-	-	(D)	(D)	(D)	(D)	-
AIR	-	100.0	(D)	-	-	-	(D)	(D)	(D)	(D)	-
WATER	265	100.0	(D)	-	100.0	-	(D)	(D)	(D)	(D)	-
OTHER	-	100.0	(D)	-	-	-	(D)	(D)	(D)	(D)	-
UNKNOWN	1 052	100.0	(D)	-	-	100.0	(D)	(D)	(D)	(D)	-
SOUTH ATLANTIC	5 025	100.0	(D)	8.9	11.0	-	(D)	(D)	(D)	(D)	-
RAIL	2 620	100.0	(D)	12.6	2.1	-	(D)	(D)	(D)	(D)	-
MOTOR CARRIER	2 014	100.0	(D)	4.1	7.8	-	(D)	(D)	(D)	(D)	-
PRIVATE TRUCK	382	100.0	(D)	8.7	88.9	-	(D)	(D)	(D)	(D)	-
AIR	-	100.0	(D)	-	-	-	(D)	(D)	(D)	(D)	-
WATER	-	100.0	(D)	-	-	-	(D)	(D)	(D)	(D)	-
OTHER	-	100.0	(D)	-	-	-	(D)	(D)	(D)	(D)	-
UNKNOWN	8	100.0	(D)	-	-	-	(D)	(D)	(D)	(D)	-
EAST SOUTH CENTRAL	6 661	100.0	(D)	1.5	4.3	8.1	(D)	(D)	(D)	(D)	-
RAIL	867	100.0	(D)	11.8	.7	1.5	(D)	(D)	(D)	(D)	-
MOTOR CARRIER	5 257	100.0	(D)	-	4.5	.7	(D)	(D)	(D)	(D)	-
PRIVATE TRUCK	44	100.0	(D)	-	100.0	-	(D)	(D)	(D)	(D)	-
AIR	-	100.0	(D)	-	-	-	(D)	(D)	(D)	(D)	-
WATER	492	100.0	(D)	-	-	100.0	(D)	(D)	(D)	(D)	-
OTHER	-	100.0	(D)	-	-	-	(D)	(D)	(D)	(D)	-
UNKNOWN	-	100.0	(D)	-	-	-	(D)	(D)	(D)	(D)	-
WEST SOUTH CENTRAL	4 021	100.0	(D)	-	.3	5.1	(D)	(D)	(D)	(D)	4.9
RAIL	423	100.0	(D)	-	1.7	3.2	(D)	(D)	(D)	(D)	45.9
MOTOR CARRIER	813	100.0	(D)	-	.5	15.3	(D)	(D)	(D)	(D)	.5
PRIVATE TRUCK	2 714	100.0	(D)	-	-	-	(D)	(D)	(D)	(D)	-
AIR	-	100.0	(D)	-	-	-	(D)	(D)	(D)	(D)	-
WATER	1	100.0	(D)	-	-	-	(D)	(D)	(D)	(D)	-
OTHER	-	100.0	(D)	-	-	-	(D)	(D)	(D)	(D)	-
UNKNOWN	68	100.0	(D)	-	-	97.8	(D)	(D)	(D)	(D)	-
MOUNTAIN	4 209	100.0	(D)	-	-	-	(D)	(D)	(D)	(D)	30.6
RAIL	1 070	100.0	(D)	-	-	-	(D)	(D)	(D)	(D)	90.2
MOTOR CARRIER	2 395	100.0	(D)	-	-	-	(D)	(D)	(D)	(D)	2.8
PRIVATE TRUCK	743	100.0	(D)	-	-	-	(D)	(D)	(D)	(D)	34.6
AIR	-	100.0	(D)	-	-	-	(D)	(D)	(D)	(D)	-
WATER	-	100.0	(D)	-	-	-	(D)	(D)	(D)	(D)	-
OTHER	-	100.0	(D)	-	-	-	(D)	(D)	(D)	(D)	-
UNKNOWN	-	100.0	(D)	-	-	-	(D)	(D)	(D)	(D)	-
PACIFIC	9 415	100.0	(D)	-	-	-	(D)	(D)	(D)	(D)	100.0
RAIL	808	100.0	(D)	-	-	-	(D)	(D)	(D)	(D)	100.0
MOTOR CARRIER	4 836	100.0	(D)	-	-	-	(D)	(D)	(D)	(D)	100.0
PRIVATE TRUCK	3 771	100.0	(D)	-	-	-	(D)	(D)	(D)	(D)	100.0
AIR	-	100.0	(D)	-	-	-	(D)	(D)	(D)	(D)	-
WATER	-	100.0	(D)	-	-	-	(D)	(D)	(D)	(D)	-
OTHER	-	100.0	(D)	-	-	-	(D)	(D)	(D)	(D)	-
UNKNOWN	-	100.0	(D)	-	-	-	(D)	(D)	(D)	(D)	-

See footnotes at end of table 4.

TABLE 3. **TCC GROUP 324—Percent Distribution of Geographic Division of Destination and Means of Transport, by Geographic Division of Origin: 1972**—Continued

Geographic division of destination and means of transport	Number	Percent distribution by division of origin[1]									
		U.S. total	New England	Middle Atlantic	East North Central	West North Central	South Atlantic	East South Central	West South Central	Mountain	Pacific
TON-MILES OF SHIPMENTS	(millions of ton-miles)										
U.S. TOTAL..............	6 809	100.0	(D)	10.4	39.1	10.7	(D)	(D)	(D)	(D)	17.8
RAIL...................	1 784	100.0	(D)	17.5	3.0	14.1	(D)	(D)	(D)	(D)	33.6
MOTOR CARRIER..........	2 312	100.0	(D)	11.8	29.8	11.2	(D)	(D)	(D)	(D)	15.9
PRIVATE TRUCK..........	738	100.0	(D)	8.6	29.3	-	(D)	(D)	(D)	(D)	33.3
AIR....................	-	100.0	(D)	37.8	62.2	-	(D)	(D)	(D)	(D)	-
WATER.................	1 825	100.0	(D)	3.1	92.8	4.0	(D)	(D)	(D)	(D)	-
OTHER.................	-	100.0	(D)	-	-	-	(D)	(D)	(D)	(D)	-
UNKNOWN...............	147	100.0	(D)	-	3.5	95.9	(D)	(D)	(D)	(D)	-
NEW ENGLAND............	293	100.0	(D)	44.0	49.6	-	(D)	(D)	(D)	(D)	-
RAIL...................	45	100.0	(D)	94.5	5.5	-	(D)	(D)	(D)	(D)	-
MOTOR CARRIER..........	153	100.0	(D)	46.7	53.3	-	(D)	(D)	(D)	(D)	-
PRIVATE TRUCK..........	94	100.0	(D)	15.8	64.5	-	(D)	(D)	(D)	(D)	-
AIR....................	-	100.0	(D)	-	-	-	(D)	(D)	(D)	(D)	-
WATER.................	-	100.0	(D)	-	-	-	(D)	(D)	(D)	(D)	-
OTHER.................	-	100.0	(D)	-	-	-	(D)	(D)	(D)	(D)	-
UNKNOWN...............	-	100.0	(D)	-	-	-	(D)	(D)	(D)	(D)	-
MIDDLE ATLANTIC........	401	100.0	(D)	83.3	11.9	-	(D)	(D)	(D)	(D)	-
RAIL...................	45	100.0	(D)	91.4	8.5	-	(D)	(D)	(D)	(D)	-
MOTOR CARRIER..........	212	100.0	(D)	90.6	1.4	-	(D)	(D)	(D)	(D)	-
PRIVATE TRUCK..........	45	100.0	(D)	94.9	-	-	(D)	(D)	(D)	(D)	-
AIR....................	-	100.0	(D)	37.8	62.2	-	(D)	(D)	(D)	(D)	-
WATER.................	98	100.0	(D)	58.3	41.7	-	(D)	(D)	(D)	(D)	-
OTHER.................	-	100.0	(D)	-	-	-	(D)	(D)	(D)	(D)	-
UNKNOWN...............	-	100.0	(D)	-	-	-	(D)	(D)	(D)	(D)	-
EAST NORTH CENTRAL.....	2 413	100.0	(D)	.1	93.4	5.1	(D)	(D)	(D)	(D)	-
RAIL...................	128	100.0	(D)	-	17.8	66.6	(D)	(D)	(D)	(D)	-
MOTOR CARRIER..........	604	100.0	(D)	.1	91.7	6.2	(D)	(D)	(D)	(D)	-
PRIVATE TRUCK..........	114	100.0	(D)	1.7	98.3	-	(D)	(D)	(D)	(D)	-
AIR....................	-	100.0	(D)	-	-	-	(D)	(D)	(D)	(D)	-
WATER.................	1 560	100.0	(D)	-	100.0	-	(D)	(D)	(D)	(D)	-
OTHER.................	-	100.0	(D)	-	-	-	(D)	(D)	(D)	(D)	-
UNKNOWN...............	5	100.0	(D)	-	100.0	-	(D)	(D)	(D)	(D)	-
WEST NORTH CENTRAL.....	602	100.0	(D)	-	17.0	82.4	(D)	(D)	(D)	(D)	-
RAIL...................	171	100.0	(D)	-	4.4	93.6	(D)	(D)	(D)	(D)	-
MOTOR CARRIER..........	204	100.0	(D)	-	.8	99.1	(D)	(D)	(D)	(D)	-
PRIVATE TRUCK..........	-	100.0	(D)	-	-	-	(D)	(D)	(D)	(D)	-
AIR....................	-	100.0	(D)	-	-	-	(D)	(D)	(D)	(D)	-
WATER.................	93	100.0	(D)	-	100.0	-	(D)	(D)	(D)	(D)	-
OTHER.................	-	100.0	(D)	-	-	-	(D)	(D)	(D)	(D)	-
UNKNOWN...............	133	100.0	(D)	-	-	100.0	(D)	(D)	(D)	(D)	-
SOUTH ATLANTIC.........	709	100.0	(D)	23.7	9.0	-	(D)	(D)	(D)	(D)	-
RAIL...................	521	100.0	(D)	30.0	1.8	-	(D)	(D)	(D)	(D)	-
MOTOR CARRIER..........	144	100.0	(D)	5.9	11.5	-	(D)	(D)	(D)	(D)	-
PRIVATE TRUCK..........	42	100.0	(D)	8.0	88.0	-	(D)	(D)	(D)	(D)	-
AIR....................	-	100.0	(D)	-	-	-	(D)	(D)	(D)	(D)	-
WATER.................	-	100.0	(D)	-	-	-	(D)	(D)	(D)	(D)	-
OTHER.................	-	100.0	(D)	-	-	-	(D)	(D)	(D)	(D)	-
UNKNOWN...............	-	100.0	(D)	-	-	-	(D)	(D)	(D)	(D)	-
EAST SOUTH CENTRAL.....	603	100.0	(D)	11.9	5.7	13.0	(D)	(D)	(D)	(D)	-
RAIL...................	170	100.0	(D)	42.1	1.3	1.4	(D)	(D)	(D)	(D)	-
MOTOR CARRIER..........	354	100.0	(D)	-	7.7	.8	(D)	(D)	(D)	(D)	-
PRIVATE TRUCK..........	4	100.0	(D)	-	100.0	-	(D)	(D)	(D)	(D)	-
AIR....................	-	100.0	(D)	-	-	-	(D)	(D)	(D)	(D)	-
WATER.................	73	100.0	(D)	-	-	100.0	(D)	(D)	(D)	(D)	-
OTHER.................	-	100.0	(D)	-	-	-	(D)	(D)	(D)	(D)	-
UNKNOWN...............	-	100.0	(D)	-	-	-	(D)	(D)	(D)	(D)	-
WEST SOUTH CENTRAL.....	461	100.0	(D)	-	1.7	6.2	(D)	(D)	(D)	(D)	28.3
RAIL...................	201	100.0	(D)	-	2.4	1.2	(D)	(D)	(D)	(D)	62.2
MOTOR CARRIER..........	96	100.0	(D)	-	3.2	17.8	(D)	(D)	(D)	(D)	5.4
PRIVATE TRUCK..........	154	100.0	(D)	-	-	-	(D)	(D)	(D)	(D)	-
AIR....................	-	100.0	(D)	-	-	-	(D)	(D)	(D)	(D)	-
WATER.................	-	100.0	(D)	-	-	-	(D)	(D)	(D)	(D)	-
OTHER.................	-	100.0	(D)	-	-	-	(D)	(D)	(D)	(D)	-
UNKNOWN...............	9	100.0	(D)	-	-	97.2	(D)	(D)	(D)	(D)	-
MOUNTAIN...............	646	100.0	(D)	-	-	-	(D)	(D)	(D)	(D)	63.3
RAIL...................	370	100.0	(D)	-	-	-	(D)	(D)	(D)	(D)	93.3
MOTOR CARRIER..........	191	100.0	(D)	-	-	-	(D)	(D)	(D)	(D)	7.7
PRIVATE TRUCK..........	83	100.0	(D)	-	-	-	(D)	(D)	(D)	(D)	57.7
AIR....................	-	100.0	(D)	-	-	-	(D)	(D)	(D)	(D)	-
WATER.................	-	100.0	(D)	-	-	-	(D)	(D)	(D)	(D)	-
OTHER.................	-	100.0	(D)	-	-	-	(D)	(D)	(D)	(D)	-
UNKNOWN...............	-	100.0	(D)	-	-	-	(D)	(D)	(D)	(D)	-
PACIFIC................	677	100.0	(D)	-	.4	-	(D)	(D)	(D)	(D)	99.4
RAIL...................	129	100.0	(D)	-	-	-	(D)	(D)	(D)	(D)	100.0
MOTOR CARRIER..........	350	100.0	(D)	-	.7	-	(D)	(D)	(D)	(D)	98.9
PRIVATE TRUCK..........	197	100.0	(D)	-	-	-	(D)	(D)	(D)	(D)	100.0
AIR....................	-	100.0	(D)	-	-	-	(D)	(D)	(D)	(D)	-
WATER.................	-	100.0	(D)	-	-	-	(D)	(D)	(D)	(D)	-
OTHER.................	-	100.0	(D)	-	-	-	(D)	(D)	(D)	(D)	-
UNKNOWN...............	-	100.0	(D)	-	-	-	(D)	(D)	(D)	(D)	-

See footnotes at end of table 4.

TABLE 4. **TCC GROUP 324—Percent Distribution of Distance Shipped and Weight of Shipment, by Means of Transport: 1972**

Distance shipped and weight of shipment [2] [3]	Number	Percent distribution by means of transport							
		All means of transport	Rail	Motor carrier	Private truck	Air	Water	Other	Unknown
TONS OF SHIPMENTS	(thousands of tons)								
U.S. TOTAL..........	38 545	100.0	18.3	51.4	25.4	-	1.8	-	3.1
UNDER 100 MILES.........	26 101	100.0	11.0	56.6	29.2	-	2.7	-	.5
UNDER 1000 POUNDS.....	-	100.0	-	85.0	15.0	-	-	-	-
1000 TO 9999 POUNDS...	24	100.0	-	14.6	85.4	-	-	-	-
10000 TO 29999 POUNDS.	347	100.0	-	10.6	89.4	-	-	-	-
30000 TO 59999 POUNDS.	18 321	100.0	-	71.6	28.1	-	-	-	.3
60000 TO 89999 POUNDS.	444	100.0	20.3	24.6	53.8	-	-	-	1.3
90000 POUNDS AND OVER.	6 963	100.0	39.9	21.4	27.4	-	10.1	-	1.3
100 TO 199 MILES........	8 508	100.0	15.3	53.0	20.1	-	-	-	11.6
UNDER 1000 POUNDS.....	-	100.0	-	-	-	-	-	-	-
1000 TO 9999 POUNDS...	3	100.0	-	30.7	69.3	-	-	-	-
10000 TO 29999 POUNDS.	60	100.0	-	28.6	71.4	-	-	-	-
30000 TO 59999 POUNDS.	5 112	100.0	.3	73.7	25.2	-	-	-	.8
60000 TO 89999 POUNDS.	244	100.0	21.9	24.1	34.7	-	-	-	19.4
90000 POUNDS AND OVER.	3 087	100.0	39.8	21.5	9.4	-	-	-	29.2
200 TO 299 MILES........	1 724	100.0	55.2	20.2	21.7	-	-	-	3.0
UNDER 1000 POUNDS.....	-	100.0	-	100.0	-	-	-	-	-
1000 TO 9999 POUNDS...	-	100.0	-	97.3	-	2.7	-	-	-
10000 TO 29999 POUNDS.	1	100.0	-	-	100.0	-	-	-	-
30000 TO 59999 POUNDS.	524	100.0	-	42.1	57.9	-	-	-	-
60000 TO 89999 POUNDS.	11	100.0	-	-	50.9	-	-	-	49.1
90000 POUNDS AND OVER.	1 186	100.0	80.2	10.7	5.3	-	-	-	3.8
300 TO 499 MILES........	1 457	100.0	94.4	4.6	-	-	-	-	1.0
UNDER 1000 POUNDS.....	-	100.0	-	100.0	-	-	-	-	-
1000 TO 9999 POUNDS...	1	100.0	-	100.0	-	-	-	-	-
10000 TO 29999 POUNDS.	-	100.0	-	51.4	48.6	-	-	-	-
30000 TO 59999 POUNDS.	64	100.0	-	100.0	-	-	-	-	-
60000 TO 89999 POUNDS.	12	100.0	100.0	-	-	-	-	-	-
90000 POUNDS AND OVER.	1 377	100.0	98.9	-	-	-	-	-	1.1
500 TO 999 MILES........	680	100.0	72.7	15.9	11.4	-	-	-	-
UNDER 1000 POUNDS.....	-	100.0	-	100.0	-	-	-	-	-
1000 TO 9999 POUNDS...	-	100.0	-	100.0	-	-	-	-	-
10000 TO 29999 POUNDS.	-	100.0	-	-	-	-	-	-	-
30000 TO 59999 POUNDS.	3	100.0	73.4	26.6	-	-	-	-	-
60000 TO 89999 POUNDS.	201	100.0	23.3	53.0	23.6	-	-	-	-
90000 POUNDS AND OVER.	474	100.0	93.7	-	6.3	-	-	-	-
1000 TO 1499 MILES......	69	100.0	93.9	6.1	-	-	-	-	-
UNDER 1000 POUNDS.....	-	100.0	-	100.0	-	-	-	-	-
1000 TO 9999 POUNDS...	-	100.0	-	100.0	-	-	-	-	-
10000 TO 29999 POUNDS.	-	100.0	-	-	-	-	-	-	-
30000 TO 59999 POUNDS.	2	100.0	-	100.0	-	-	-	-	-
60000 TO 89999 POUNDS.	5	100.0	100.0	-	-	-	-	-	-
90000 POUNDS AND OVER.	61	100.0	96.5	3.5	-	-	-	-	-
1500 MILES OR OVER......	4	100.0	58.5	40.9	.6	-	-	-	-
UNDER 1000 POUNDS.....	-	100.0	-	100.0	-	-	-	-	-
1000 TO 9999 POUNDS...	-	100.0	-	96.9	3.1	-	-	-	-
10000 TO 29999 POUNDS.	-	100.0	-	100.0	-	-	-	-	-
30000 TO 59999 POUNDS.	-	100.0	58.1	41.9	-	-	-	-	-
60000 TO 89999 POUNDS.	-	100.0	100.0	-	-	-	-	-	-
90000 POUNDS AND OVER.	1	100.0	100.0	-	-	-	-	-	-
TON-MILES OF SHIPMENTS	(millions of ton-miles)								
U.S. TOTAL..........	4 011	100.0	37.3	40.2	17.3	-	1.4	-	3.7
UNDER 100 MILES.........	1 390	100.0	13.6	58.7	22.9	-	4.1	-	.6
UNDER 1000 POUNDS.....	-	100.0	-	89.5	10.5	-	-	-	-
1000 TO 9999 POUNDS...	1	100.0	-	17.2	82.8	-	-	-	-
10000 TO 29999 POUNDS.	18	100.0	-	12.2	87.8	-	-	-	-
30000 TO 59999 POUNDS.	963	100.0	-	75.1	24.7	-	-	-	.2
60000 TO 89999 POUNDS.	24	100.0	21.8	26.7	50.5	-	-	-	1.0
90000 POUNDS AND OVER.	381	100.0	48.1	21.8	13.3	-	15.0	-	1.8
100 TO 199 MILES........	1 117	100.0	15.4	53.2	20.7	-	-	-	10.7
UNDER 1000 POUNDS.....	-	100.0	-	-	-	-	-	-	-
1000 TO 9999 POUNDS...	-	100.0	-	28.0	72.0	-	-	-	-
10000 TO 29999 POUNDS.	8	100.0	-	31.8	68.2	-	-	-	-
30000 TO 59999 POUNDS.	688	100.0	.4	73.4	25.5	-	-	-	.8
60000 TO 89999 POUNDS.	32	100.0	23.0	25.4	30.7	-	-	-	20.8
90000 POUNDS AND OVER.	388	100.0	41.9	20.2	10.2	-	-	-	27.6

See footnotes at end of table 4.

TABLE 4. **TCC GROUP 324—Percent Distribution of Distance Shipped and Weight of Shipment, by Means of Transport: 1972**—Continued

Distance shipped and weight of shipment [2] [3]	Number	Percent distribution by means of transport							
		All means of transport	Rail	Motor carrier	Private truck	Air	Water	Other	Unknown
TON-MILES OF SHIPMENTS	(millions of ton-miles)								
200 TO 299 MILES.........	402	100.0	54.2	21.1	21.0	-	-	-	3.7
UNDER 1000 POUNDS......	-	100.0	-	100.0	-	-	-	-	-
1000 TO 9999 POUNDS...	-	100.0	-	97.9	-	2.1	-	-	-
10000 TO 29999 POUNDS.	-	100.0	-	-	100.0	-	-	-	-
30000 TO 59999 POUNDS.	115	100.0	-	43.5	56.5	-	-	-	-
60000 TO 89999 POUNDS.	2	100.0	-	-	48.7	-	-	-	51.3
90000 POUNDS AND OVER.	283	100.0	77.0	12.2	6.0	-	-	-	4.8
300 TO 499 MILES.........	525	100.0	94.7	4.4	-	-	-	-	.9
UNDER 1000 POUNDS......	-	100.0	-	100.0	-	-	-	-	-
1000 TO 9999 POUNDS...	-	100.0	-	100.0	-	-	-	-	-
10000 TO 29999 POUNDS.	-	100.0	-	51.3	48.7	-	-	-	-
30000 TO 59999 POUNDS.	22	100.0	-	100.0	-	-	-	-	-
60000 TO 89999 POUNDS.	5	100.0	100.0	-	-	-	-	-	-
90000 POUNDS AND OVER.	496	100.0	99.0	-	-	-	-	-	1.0
500 TO 999 MILES.........	491	100.0	70.1	17.5	12.5	-	-	-	-
UNDER 1000 POUNDS......	-	100.0	-	100.0	-	-	-	-	-
1000 TO 9999 POUNDS...	-	100.0	-	100.0	-	-	-	-	-
10000 TO 29999 POUNDS.	-	100.0	-	-	-	-	-	-	-
30000 TO 59999 POUNDS.	2	100.0	73.6	26.4	-	-	-	-	-
60000 TO 89999 POUNDS.	158	100.0	22.9	53.4	23.7	-	-	-	-
90000 POUNDS AND OVER.	330	100.0	92.8	-	7.2	-	-	-	-
1000 TO 1499 MILES......	76	100.0	93.1	6.9	-	-	-	-	-
UNDER 1000 POUNDS......	-	100.0	-	100.0	-	-	-	-	-
1000 TO 9999 POUNDS...	-	100.0	-	100.0	-	-	-	-	-
10000 TO 29999 POUNDS.	-	100.0	-	-	-	-	-	-	-
30000 TO 59999 POUNDS.	2	100.0	-	100.0	-	-	-	-	-
60000 TO 89999 POUNDS.	5	100.0	100.0	-	-	-	-	-	-
90000 POUNDS AND OVER.	67	100.0	96.1	3.9	-	-	-	-	-
1500 MILES OR OVER......	8	100.0	52.9	46.6	.5	-	-	-	-
UNDER 1000 POUNDS......	-	100.0	-	100.0	-	-	-	-	-
1000 TO 9999 POUNDS...	1	100.0	-	96.9	3.1	-	-	-	-
10000 TO 29999 POUNDS.	1	100.0	-	100.0	-	-	-	-	-
30000 TO 59999 POUNDS.	2	100.0	35.9	64.1	-	-	-	-	-
60000 TO 89999 POUNDS.	1	100.0	100.0	-	-	-	-	-	-
90000 POUNDS AND OVER.	2	100.0	100.0	-	-	-	-	-	-

Note: Detail may not add to total due to rounding. The introductory table shows the estimates of sampling variability for tons; sampling variability for ton-miles has not been estimated. See the map in the Introduction for the States comprising the geographic divisions of the United States.

Shipments excluded from the survey are those moving by pipeline (primarily petroleum products from refineries), parcel post shipments, and commodities moved by own power (motorized vehicles, aircraft, etc.) or towed (prefabricated buildings, etc.). Local shipments (commodities shipped less than 25 miles from the plant) and shipments within the same city are also excluded. Shipments to Alaska and Hawaii from the 48 conterminous States and the District of Columbia are included; however, no data were obtained for shipments originating in Alaska and Hawaii.

- Represents zero or rounds to zero.   (D) Withheld to avoid disclosing figures for individual companies.

[1] Production of this commodity is concentrated in the geographic divisions shown; figures and distributions for geographic divisions not shown are included in the total.

[2] Distances of shipments to foreign destinations are calculated only to the U.S. port of exit.

[3] Includes only shipments represented by bills of lading and invoices. Summary records which did not show individual weights of shipments are not included.

TCC 325. Structural Clay Products

Comparisons of Tons and Ton-Miles of Shipments for
Geographic Divisions of Origin and for Sampling Variability: 1972 and 1967

Geographic division of origin	Estimates				Relative sampling variability in tons (percent)	
	1972		1967		1972	1967
	Tons (thousands)	Ton-miles (millions)	Tons (thousands)	Ton-miles (millions)		
U.S. total	19,787	4,294	23,734	5,171	10.6	12.0
New England	(D)	(D)	241	71	(*)	(*)
Middle Atlantic	2,597	590	3,269	770	22.9	(*)
East North Central	3,891	783	6,533	1,202	26.5	(*)
West North Central	3,557	1,275	2,417	918	47.3	(*)
South Atlantic	3,887	677	5,096	998	25.9	(*)
East South Central	1,224	211	3,320	617	35.5	(*)
West South Central	2,828	512	1,639	424	27.0	(*)
Mountain	(D)	(D)	78	6	(*)	(*)
Pacific	612	132	1,141	165	45.1	(*)

(D) Withheld to avoid disclosing figures for individual companies.   (*) Data not published.

TABLE 1. TCC GROUP 325—Percent Distribution of Geographic Division of Origin and Distance Shipped, by Means of Transport: 1972

Geographic division of origin [1] and distance shipped [2]	Number (thousands of tons)	Percent distribution by means of transport							
		All means of transport	Rail	Motor carrier	Private truck	Air	Water	Other	Unknown
TONS OF SHIPMENTS									
U.S. TOTAL..........	19 787	100.0	24.0	39.2	35.3	-	.9	.3	.3
MIDDLE ATLANTIC.........	2 597	100.0	20.5	50.4	21.9	-	6.8	-	.3
UNDER 100 MILES.......	1 086	100.0	1.4	40.2	41.5	-	16.4	-	.4
100 TO 199 MILES......	541	100.0	6.4	79.6	14.0	-	-	-	.1
200 TO 299 MILES......	357	100.0	27.1	66.5	6.3	-	-	-	.1
300 TO 499 MILES......	351	100.0	56.1	40.4	3.2	-	-	-	.3
500 TO 999 MILES......	207	100.0	74.0	21.2	4.7	-	-	-	-
1000 TO 1499 MILES....	30	100.0	54.7	42.7	-	-	-	-	2.5
1500 MILES OR OVER....	23	100.0	78.8	21.1	-	.1	-	-	-
EAST NORTH CENTRAL......	3 891	100.0	25.0	42.6	30.7	-	-	1.4	.2
UNDER 100 MILES.......	1 424	100.0	1.8	52.5	43.2	-	-	2.3	.1
100 TO 199 MILES......	1 025	100.0	19.1	43.8	34.8	-	-	2.3	-
200 TO 299 MILES......	560	100.0	26.9	49.9	23.1	-	-	-	-
300 TO 499 MILES......	658	100.0	64.5	21.8	12.6	.1	-	-	1.0
500 TO 999 MILES......	182	100.0	76.3	18.6	5.0	-	-	-	-
1000 TO 1499 MILES....	25	100.0	86.1	12.9	.6	.4	-	-	-
1500 MILES OR OVER....	13	100.0	91.2	7.5	-	1.2	-	.1	-
WEST NORTH CENTRAL......	3 557	100.0	33.7	56.0	10.3	-	-	-	-
UNDER 100 MILES.......	408	100.0	.5	27.7	71.9	-	-	-	-
100 TO 199 MILES......	369	100.0	55.4	26.7	17.9	-	-	-	-
200 TO 299 MILES......	186	100.0	50.1	48.1	1.8	-	-	-	-
300 TO 499 MILES......	1 950	100.0	16.9	83.0	.1	-	-	-	-
500 TO 999 MILES......	516	100.0	85.7	14.1	.2	-	-	-	-
1000 TO 1499 MILES....	85	100.0	99.3	.7	-	-	-	-	-
1500 MILES OR OVER....	40	100.0	98.9	1.1	-	-	-	-	-
SOUTH ATLANTIC..........	3 887	100.0	25.8	28.6	45.6	-	-	-	-
UNDER 100 MILES.......	2 102	100.0	1.2	36.6	62.1	-	-	-	-
100 TO 199 MILES......	591	100.0	10.3	26.7	63.0	-	-	-	-
200 TO 299 MILES......	506	100.0	70.7	15.8	13.5	-	-	-	-
300 TO 499 MILES......	420	100.0	81.0	16.0	3.0	-	-	-	-
500 TO 999 MILES......	241	100.0	80.2	14.5	5.2	-	-	-	-
1000 TO 1499 MILES....	11	100.0	99.7	.3	-	-	-	-	-
1500 MILES OR OVER....	13	100.0	99.7	.3	-	-	-	-	-
EAST SOUTH CENTRAL......	1 224	100.0	11.3	55.1	33.6	-	-	-	-
UNDER 100 MILES.......	581	100.0	2.1	54.2	43.7	-	-	-	-
100 TO 199 MILES......	358	100.0	16.6	60.6	22.9	-	-	-	-
200 TO 299 MILES......	106	100.0	8.9	66.3	24.8	-	-	-	-
300 TO 499 MILES......	110	100.0	27.0	51.6	21.4	-	-	-	-
500 TO 999 MILES......	49	100.0	31.7	25.7	42.6	-	-	-	-
1000 TO 1499 MILES....	8	100.0	46.3	17.7	36.0	-	-	-	-
1500 MILES OR OVER....	8	100.0	90.1	.4	9.6	-	-	-	-
WEST SOUTH CENTRAL......	2 828	100.0	28.4	14.9	56.5	-	-	-	.2
UNDER 100 MILES.......	1 195	100.0	.8	25.7	72.9	-	-	-	.6
100 TO 199 MILES......	658	100.0	19.5	13.5	67.0	-	-	-	-
200 TO 299 MILES......	501	100.0	66.4	4.0	29.6	-	-	-	-
300 TO 499 MILES......	356	100.0	74.2	.4	25.4	-	-	-	-
500 TO 999 MILES......	106	100.0	61.7	.7	37.6	-	-	-	-
1000 TO 1499 MILES....	8	100.0	5.9	45.5	48.7	-	-	-	-
1500 MILES OR OVER....	-	100.0	-	-	100.0	-	-	-	-
PACIFIC.................	612	100.0	6.5	40.2	48.3	-	-	-	5.1
UNDER 100 MILES.......	253	100.0	4.5	24.9	63.4	-	-	-	7.2
100 TO 199 MILES......	85	100.0	2.1	47.2	50.3	-	-	-	.4
200 TO 299 MILES......	42	100.0	6.8	66.1	27.1	-	-	-	-
300 TO 499 MILES......	188	100.0	-	52.9	40.6	-	-	-	6.5
500 TO 999 MILES......	39	100.0	59.7	30.8	9.5	-	-	-	-
1000 TO 1499 MILES....	1	100.0	-	83.9	16.1	-	-	-	-
1500 MILES OR OVER....	2	100.0	11.8	72.0	11.8	2.9	1.5	-	-

See footnotes at end of table 4.

TABLE 1. **TCC GROUP 325**—Percent Distribution of Geographic Division of Origin and Distance Shipped, by Means of Transport: 1972—Continued

Geographic division of origin[1] and distance shipped[2]	Number	Percent distribution by means of transport							
		All means of transport	Rail	Motor carrier	Private truck	Air	Water	Other	Unknown
TON-MILES OF SHIPMENTS	(millions of ton-miles)								
U.S. TOTAL..........	4 294	100.0	48.0	34.1	17.2	-	.3	.1	.2
MIDDLE ATLANTIC.........	590	100.0	46.1	43.4	8.2	-	1.9	-	.3
UNDER 100 MILES.......	59	100.0	1.6	40.4	38.0	-	19.5	-	.5
100 TO 199 MILES......	80	100.0	6.4	79.4	14.1	-	-	-	.1
200 TO 299 MILES......	90	100.0	28.6	65.3	6.0	-	-	-	.1
300 TO 499 MILES......	135	100.0	57.3	39.4	3.1	-	-	-	.3
500 TO 999 MILES......	137	100.0	74.8	21.2	3.9	-	-	-	-
1000 TO 1499 MILES....	38	100.0	54.5	43.0	-	-	-	-	2.4
1500 MILES OR OVER....	49	100.0	78.8	21.1	-	.1	-	-	-
EAST NORTH CENTRAL......	783	100.0	47.3	32.3	19.2	.1	-	.8	.3
UNDER 100 MILES.......	73	100.0	2.3	51.8	42.4	-	-	3.5	.1
100 TO 199 MILES......	153	100.0	20.5	42.6	34.6	-	-	2.2	-
200 TO 299 MILES......	137	100.0	27.1	50.4	22.4	-	-	-	-
300 TO 499 MILES......	246	100.0	65.4	21.5	12.1	.1	-	-	.9
500 TO 999 MILES......	118	100.0	77.3	18.1	4.6	-	-	-	-
1000 TO 1499 MILES....	29	100.0	85.9	13.2	.5	.4	-	-	-
1500 MILES OR OVER....	24	100.0	90.3	8.2	-	1.4	-	.1	-
WEST NORTH CENTRAL......	1 275	100.0	50.2	47.6	2.2	-	-	-	-
UNDER 100 MILES.......	23	100.0	.2	31.1	68.7	-	-	-	-
100 TO 199 MILES......	55	100.0	56.2	26.8	17.0	-	-	-	-
200 TO 299 MILES......	49	100.0	50.5	47.9	1.6	-	-	-	-
300 TO 499 MILES......	640	100.0	19.9	80.0	.1	-	-	-	-
500 TO 999 MILES......	335	100.0	85.8	13.9	.3	-	-	-	-
1000 TO 1499 MILES....	106	100.0	99.2	.8	-	-	-	-	-
1500 MILES OR OVER....	63	100.0	98.9	1.1	-	-	-	-	-
SOUTH ATLANTIC..........	677	100.0	61.0	19.0	20.0	-	-	-	-
UNDER 100 MILES.......	99	100.0	2.2	39.1	58.7	-	-	-	-
100 TO 199 MILES......	82	100.0	12.6	28.3	59.1	-	-	-	-
200 TO 299 MILES......	135	100.0	72.7	14.9	12.4	-	-	-	-
300 TO 499 MILES......	161	100.0	81.7	15.4	2.9	-	-	-	-
500 TO 999 MILES......	156	100.0	81.6	13.7	4.7	-	-	-	-
1000 TO 1499 MILES....	15	100.0	99.7	.3	-	-	-	-	-
1500 MILES OR OVER....	26	100.0	99.8	.2	-	-	-	-	-
EAST SOUTH CENTRAL......	211	100.0	25.5	45.3	29.2	-	-	-	-
UNDER 100 MILES.......	25	100.0	2.2	57.8	40.0	-	-	-	-
100 TO 199 MILES......	51	100.0	17.0	61.2	21.8	-	-	-	-
200 TO 299 MILES......	26	100.0	9.4	65.3	25.3	-	-	-	-
300 TO 499 MILES......	45	100.0	27.6	51.7	20.8	-	-	-	-
500 TO 999 MILES....	35	100.0	30.4	19.9	49.7	-	-	-	-
1000 TO 1499 MILES....	9	100.0	47.5	17.6	34.9	-	-	-	-
1500 MILES OR OVER....	17	100.0	81.3	.3	18.4	-	-	-	-
WEST SOUTH CENTRAL......	512	100.0	50.1	7.7	42.2	-	-	-	-
UNDER 100 MILES.......	64	100.0	.4	23.3	76.0	-	-	-	.4
100 TO 199 MILES......	97	100.0	21.5	12.9	65.6	-	-	-	-
200 TO 299 MILES......	122	100.0	67.8	4.2	28.0	-	-	-	-
300 TO 499 MILES......	139	100.0	75.4	.3	24.2	-	-	-	-
500 TO 999 MILES......	74	100.0	61.8	.7	37.5	-	-	-	-
1000 TO 1499 MILES....	11	100.0	5.3	47.9	46.8	-	-	-	-
1500 MILES OR OVER....	-	100.0	-	-	100.0	-	-	-	-
PACIFIC.................	132	100.0	12.4	48.3	35.2	.1	.1	-	3.9
UNDER 100 MILES.......	14	100.0	6.8	23.9	61.6	-	-	-	7.7
100 TO 199 MILES......	11	100.0	2.7	46.5	50.3	-	-	-	.4
200 TO 299 MILES......	9	100.0	6.6	67.6	25.8	-	-	-	-
300 TO 499 MILES......	65	100.0	-	53.2	40.7	-	-	-	6.1
500 TO 999 MILES......	23	100.0	59.6	31.4	9.0	-	-	-	-
1000 TO 1499 MILFS....	1	100.0	-	87.6	12.4	-	-	-	-
1500 MILES OR OVER....	6	100.0	7.8	78.9	8.6	2.8	1.8	-	-

See footnotes at end of table 4.

TABLE 2. TCC GROUP 325—Percent Distribution of Geographic Division of Origin and Means of Transport, by Geographic Division of Destination: 1972

Geographic division of origin[1] and means of transport	Number	Percent distribution by division of destination									
		U.S. total	New England	Middle Atlantic	East North Central	West North Central	South Atlantic	East South Central	West South Central	Mountain	Pacific
TONS OF SHIPMENTS	(thousands of tons)										
U.S. TOTAL.............	19 787	100.0	4.5	13.2	29.1	5.3	19.4	6.9	14.7	4.0	2.9
RAIL..................	4 753	100.0	3.7	9.0	26.4	9.0	16.9	9.2	19.4	3.4	3.1
MOTOR CARRIER.........	7 758	100.0	4.5	16.6	42.7	2.7	16.3	7.1	6.4	1.4	2.3
PRIVATE TRUCK.........	6 981	100.0	5.0	10.3	16.3	6.0	25.3	5.1	21.2	7.4	3.2
AIR..................	1	100.0	12.7	17.5	31.4	.1	10.6	2.4	1.2	2.2	22.0
WATER................	177	100.0	-	100.0	-	-	-	-	-	-	-
OTHER................	56	100.0	-	.1	84.4	-	6.4	8.7	.1	-	.2
UNKNOWN..............	58	100.0	9.3	8.7	4.8	-	.7	10.8	13.2	20.9	31.6
MIDDLE ATLANTIC.........	2 597	100.0	6.1	57.1	23.2	.6	8.2	2.8	.9	.6	.5
RAIL..................	532	100.0	13.8	11.4	50.5	.5	7.0	10.1	2.4	2.5	1.8
MOTOR CARRIER.........	1 309	100.0	4.8	64.6	19.0	.5	8.6	1.4	.8	.1	.2
PRIVATE TRUCK.........	570	100.0	3.8	68.9	14.7	1.3	11.2	-	-	-	-
AIR..................	-	100.0	3.6	-	73.1	1.8	-	-	-	-	21.5
WATER................	177	100.0	-	100.0	-	-	-	-	-	-	-
OTHER................	-	100.0	4.5	35.8	26.0	3.9	25.7	4.0	-	-	-
UNKNOWN..............	7	100.0	-	68.0	15.9	-	5.7	-	10.3	-	-
EAST NORTH CENTRAL......	3 891	100.0	.8	16.9	67.7	1.9	6.1	3.8	2.3	.1	.3
RAIL..................	971	100.0	1.2	19.6	42.3	5.7	10.0	10.8	8.6	.5	1.3
MOTOR CARRIER.........	1 659	100.0	1.0	15.7	74.8	.6	6.6	.9	.3	-	.1
PRIVATE TRUCK.........	1 195	100.0	.2	17.1	78.2	.8	2.4	1.3	-	-	-
AIR..................	-	100.0	18.0	15.9	36.4	-	9.3	.7	-	2.1	17.6
WATER................	-	100.0	-	-	-	-	-	-	-	-	-
OTHER................	56	100.0	-	.1	84.9	-	6.4	8.7	-	-	-
UNKNOWN..............	8	100.0	-	-	20.5	-	-	79.5	-	-	-
WEST NORTH CENTRAL......	3 557	100.0	.1	2.2	62.2	21.9	1.5	3.1	4.7	2.3	1.9
RAIL..................	1 197	100.0	.3	5.1	38.6	21.0	3.9	7.7	11.2	6.7	5.6
MOTOR CARRIER.........	1 993	100.0	-	.9	87.4	8.7	.2	1.0	1.7	.1	-
PRIVATE TRUCK.........	366	100.0	-	-	2.8	96.9	.3	-	-	-	-
AIR..................	-	100.0	-	89.3	10.7	-	-	-	-	-	-
WATER................	-	100.0	-	-	-	-	-	-	-	-	-
OTHER................	-	100.0	-	-	-	-	-	-	-	-	-
UNKNOWN..............	-	100.0	-	-	-	-	-	-	-	-	-
SOUTH ATLANTIC..........	3 887	100.0	2.4	7.8	5.1	.1	79.1	4.2	.9	.3	.1
RAIL..................	1 004	100.0	7.7	11.5	7.4	.4	56.0	12.0	3.2	1.3	.5
MOTOR CARRIER.........	1 110	100.0	.9	10.0	5.4	-	80.7	2.9	.1	-	-
PRIVATE TRUCK.........	1 772	100.0	.3	4.2	3.6	-	91.2	.7	-	-	-
AIR..................	-	100.0	-	17.6	6.9	-	26.1	31.5	18.0	-	-
WATER................	-	100.0	-	-	-	-	-	-	-	-	-
OTHER................	-	100.0	6.3	5.3	.4	-	61.5	22.5	4.0	-	-
UNKNOWN..............	-	100.0	-	100.0	-	-	-	-	-	-	-
EAST SOUTH CENTRAL......	1 224	100.0	-	.6	5.0	4.6	20.1	60.5	6.9	1.6	.7
RAIL..................	138	100.0	-	-	-	17.5	36.1	34.3	4.1	2.3	5.7
MOTOR CARRIER.........	673	100.0	-	-	2.8	2.2	21.4	69.4	3.9	.2	-
PRIVATE TRUCK.........	411	100.0	-	1.8	10.3	4.1	12.5	54.8	12.7	3.7	.2
AIR..................	-	100.0	-	-	-	-	-	-	-	-	-
WATER................	-	100.0	-	-	-	-	-	-	-	-	-
OTHER................	-	100.0	-	-	-	22.7	47.1	29.9	.3	-	-
UNKNOWN..............	-	100.0	-	-	-	-	-	-	-	-	-
WEST SOUTH CENTRAL......	2 828	100.0	-	-	1.3	4.3	.7	4.3	88.4	.8	.1
RAIL..................	801	100.0	-	-	3.4	11.1	1.5	2.1	80.8	1.1	-
MOTOR CARRIER.........	422	100.0	-	-	.9	-	.1	-	99.0	-	-
PRIVATE TRUCK.........	1 597	100.0	-	-	.4	2.0	.5	6.6	89.4	.9	.3
AIR..................	-	100.0	-	-	-	-	-	-	-	-	-
WATER................	-	100.0	-	-	-	-	-	-	-	-	-
OTHER................	-	100.0	-	-	-	-	-	-	100.0	-	-
UNKNOWN..............	6	100.0	-	-	-	-	-	-	100.0	-	-
PACIFIC................	612	100.0	-	-	.1	-	-	-	.2	26.6	73.1
RAIL..................	39	100.0	-	-	-	-	-	-	.8	7.2	92.0
MOTOR CARRIER.........	245	100.0	-	-	-	-	-	-	.4	29.4	70.1
PRIVATE TRUCK.........	295	100.0	-	-	.1	-	-	-	-	25.4	74.5
AIR..................	-	100.0	-	26.6	11.1	-	30.6	-	.4	8.4	22.9
WATER................	-	100.0	-	-	-	-	-	-	-	-	100.0
OTHER................	-	100.0	-	.9	-	.2	-	-	-	.3	98.6
UNKNOWN..............	30	100.0	-	-	-	-	-	-	-	39.9	60.1

See footnotes at end of table 4.

TABLE 2. TCC GROUP 325—Percent Distribution of Geographic Division of Origin and Means of Transport, by Geographic Division of Destination: 1972—Continued

Geographic division of origin[1] and means of transport	Number	Percent distribution by division of destination								
		U.S. total	New England	Middle Atlantic	East North Central	West North Central	South Atlantic	East South Central	West South Central	Mountain	Pacific
TON-MILES OF SHIPMENTS	(millions of ton-miles)										
U.S. TOTAL..............	4 294	100.0	3.5	11.1	33.2	4.7	13.7	6.4	15.0	6.2	6.2
RAIL.................	2 061	100.0	3.9	8.8	24.2	5.9	14.4	8.0	18.5	7.1	9.1
MOTOR CARRIER.........	1 466	100.0	3.2	14.1	53.3	2.4	10.9	4.8	5.8	2.3	3.3
PRIVATE TRUCK.........	738	100.0	3.2	10.3	18.8	6.1	17.7	5.2	23.7	11.0	3.9
AIR..................	1	100.0	6.7	14.6	9.4	.2	14.2	.9	1.1	2.5	50.4
WATER................	11	100.0	-	99.1	-	-	-	-	-	-	.9
OTHER................	6	100.0	.1	.4	74.4	.1	10.5	13.8	.2	-	.4
UNKNOWN..............	9	100.0	1.5	4.0	4.9	-	.5	23.4	11.9	41.6	12.1
MIDDLE ATLANTIC.........	590	100.0	7.5	25.9	35.1	2.2	6.9	8.0	5.2	4.1	5.1
RAIL.................	272	100.0	8.2	3.6	45.9	1.1	5.4	13.7	5.6	8.0	8.3
MOTOR CARRIER.........	256	100.0	7.1	41.9	27.8	2.3	7.8	3.7	5.6	1.0	2.9
PRIVATE TRUCK.........	48	100.0	7.7	49.2	21.6	8.4	12.8	.3	-	-	-
AIR..................	-	100.0	1.7	-	49.5	2.5	-	-	-	-	46.3
WATER................	11	100.0	-	100.0	-	-	-	-	-	-	-
OTHER................	-	100.0	2.0	14.2	29.0	8.8	39.0	7.0	-	-	-
UNKNOWN..............	1	100.0	-	21.1	22.8	-	2.8	-	53.3	-	-
EAST NORTH CENTRAL......	783	100.0	2.3	19.2	45.8	3.1	9.5	7.3	8.8	.8	3.1
RAIL.................	370	100.0	1.9	17.0	28.7	5.1	10.9	11.8	17.0	1.7	6.0
MOTOR CARRIER.........	253	100.0	3.8	23.0	56.0	1.4	10.9	1.7	2.3	.2	.8
PRIVATE TRUCK.........	150	100.0	.9	19.4	70.6	1.4	3.6	4.1	.1	-	.8
AIR..................	-	100.0	12.5	9.5	7.6	-	13.9	.4	-	3.8	52.2
WATER................	-	100.0	-	-	-	-	-	-	-	-	-
OTHER................	6	100.0	.1	.3	75.2	-	10.2	13.9	-	-	-
UNKNOWN..............	2	100.0	-	-	3.7	-	-	96.3	-	-	.4
WEST NORTH CENTRAL......	1 275	100.0	.4	4.9	57.4	8.3	3.4	3.4	8.0	6.0	8.1
RAIL.................	640	100.0	.7	8.0	29.6	9.1	6.2	5.6	13.2	11.7	15.9
MOTOR CARRIER.........	606	100.0	-	2.0	89.3	3.5	.5	1.3	2.9	.4	.2
PRIVATE TRUCK.........	28	100.0	-	-	4.0	92.8	3.2	-	-	-	-
AIR..................	-	100.0	-	93.7	6.3	-	-	-	-	-	-
WATER................	-	100.0	-	-	-	-	-	-	-	-	-
OTHER................	-	100.0	-	-	-	-	-	-	-	-	-
UNKNOWN..............	-	100.0	-	-	-	-	-	-	-	-	-
SOUTH ATLANTIC.........	677	100.0	7.9	14.3	9.5	.4	52.5	6.2	4.3	3.3	1.5
RAIL.................	413	100.0	10.9	13.9	9.4	.6	42.4	8.0	6.9	5.4	2.4
MOTOR CARRIER.........	128	100.0	4.3	18.0	11.2	.3	60.3	5.3	.5	-	-
PRIVATE TRUCK.........	135	100.0	2.0	12.1	8.3	-	75.9	1.7	-	-	-
AIR..................	-	100.0	-	23.1	7.7	-	20.3	19.3	29.6	-	-
WATER................	-	100.0	-	-	-	-	-	-	-	-	-
OTHER................	-	100.0	15.4	11.3	.7	-	41.0	22.0	9.6	-	-
UNKNOWN..............	-	100.0	-	100.0	-	-	-	-	-	-	-
EAST SOUTH CENTRAL......	211	100.0	-	1.2	4.6	6.7	28.1	29.9	11.6	9.4	8.5
RAIL.................	54	100.0	-	-	-	9.4	36.3	12.4	8.7	6.2	27.0
MOTOR CARRIER.........	95	100.0	-	-	6.3	4.6	32.4	42.8	12.2	1.7	.1
PRIVATE TRUCK.........	61	100.0	-	4.2	6.0	7.5	14.3	25.4	13.1	24.2	5.4
AIR..................	-	100.0	-	-	-	-	-	-	-	-	-
WATER................	-	100.0	-	-	-	-	-	-	-	-	-
OTHER................	-	100.0	-	-	-	-	23.6	64.3	11.9	.2	-
UNKNOWN..............	-	100.0	-	-	-	-	-	-	-	-	-
WEST SOUTH CENTRAL......	512	100.0	-	-	6.5	8.1	2.5	4.4	74.1	3.3	1.1
RAIL.................	256	100.0	-	-	8.7	12.9	2.5	3.3	69.8	2.8	-
MOTOR CARRIER.........	39	100.0	-	-	14.1	-	.6	.1	85.2	.1	-
PRIVATE TRUCK.........	215	100.0	-	-	2.5	3.9	2.9	6.5	77.1	4.6	2.5
AIR..................	-	100.0	-	-	-	-	-	-	-	-	-
WATER................	-	100.0	-	-	-	-	-	-	-	-	-
OTHER................	-	100.0	-	-	-	-	-	-	100.0	-	-
UNKNOWN..............	-	100.0	-	-	-	-	-	-	100.0	-	-
PACIFIC................	132	100.0	.1	.1	.6	-	.2	-	1.3	43.2	54.5
RAIL.................	16	100.0	-	-	-	-	-	-	2.9	11.6	85.5
MOTOR CARRIER.........	64	100.0	.2	.2	.3	.1	.2	-	2.0	39.4	57.6
PRIVATE TRUCK.........	46	100.0	-	-	1.1	-	-	-	-	55.8	43.0
AIR..................	-	100.0	-	38.0	11.4	-	41.8	-	.3	3.3	5.1
WATER................	-	100.0	-	-	-	-	-	-	-	-	100.0
OTHER................	-	100.0	-	32.0	-	4.3	-	-	-	2.4	61.4
UNKNOWN..............	5	100.0	-	-	-	-	-	-	-	77.5	22.5

See footnotes at end of table 4.

TABLE 3. **TCC GROUP 325—Percent Distribution of Geographic Division of Destination and Means of Transport, by Geographic Division of Origin: 1972**

Geographic division of destination and means of transport	Number (thousands of tons)	Percent distribution by division of origin[1]									
		U.S. total	New England	Middle Atlantic	East North Central	West North Central	South Atlantic	East South Central	West South Central	Mountain	Pacific
TONS OF SHIPMENTS			—								
U.S. TOTAL	19 787	100.0	(D)	13.1	19.7	18.0	19.6	6.2	14.3	(D)	3.1
RAIL	4 753	100.0	(D)	11.2	20.4	25.2	21.1	2.9	16.9	(D)	.8
MOTOR CARRIER	7 758	100.0	(D)	16.9	21.4	25.7	14.3	8.7	5.4	(D)	3.2
PRIVATE TRUCK	6 981	100.0	(D)	8.2	17.1	5.3	25.4	5.9	22.9	(D)	4.2
AIR	1	100.0	(D)	6.0	69.4	3.6	6.2	-	-	(D)	8.1
WATER	177	100.0	(D)	100.0	-	-	-	-	-	(D)	-
OTHER	56	100.0	(D)	.2	99.5	-	-	.1	.1	(D)	.1
UNKNOWN	58	100.0	(D)	12.7	13.6	-	.1	-	11.9	(D)	52.5
NEW ENGLAND	880	100.0	(D)	17.9	3.6	.5	10.5	-	-	(D)	-
RAIL	174	100.0	(D)	42.2	6.7	2.2	44.2	-	-	(D)	-
MOTOR CARRIER	348	100.0	(D)	17.9	4.8	.1	3.0	-	-	(D)	-
PRIVATE TRUCK	351	100.0	(D)	6.1	.8	-	1.4	-	-	(D)	-
AIR	-	100.0	(D)	1.7	98.3	-	-	-	-	(D)	-
WATER	-	100.0	(D)	-	-	-	-	-	-	(D)	-
OTHER	-	100.0	(D)	42.5	42.8	-	14.8	-	-	(D)	-
UNKNOWN	5	100.0	(D)	-	-	-	-	-	-	(D)	-
MIDDLE ATLANTIC	2 619	100.0	(D)	56.6	25.1	3.0	11.5	.3	-	(D)	-
RAIL	428	100.0	(D)	14.2	44.5	14.2	27.0	-	-	(D)	-
MOTOR CARRIER	1 287	100.0	(D)	65.7	20.3	1.3	8.7	-	-	(D)	-
PRIVATE TRUCK	720	100.0	(D)	54.5	28.4	-	10.4	1.0	-	(D)	-
AIR	-	100.0	(D)	-	62.9	18.6	6.2	-	-	(D)	12.3
WATER	177	100.0	(D)	100.0	-	-	-	-	-	(D)	-
OTHER	-	100.0	(D)	55.2	41.7	-	2.0	-	-	(D)	1.0
UNKNOWN	5	100.0	(D)	99.2	-	-	.8	-	-	(D)	-
EAST NORTH CENTRAL	5 759	100.0	(D)	10.5	45.8	38.4	3.4	1.1	.6	(D)	-
RAIL	1 254	100.0	(D)	21.4	32.8	36.8	5.9	-	2.1	(D)	-
MOTOR CARRIER	3 313	100.0	(D)	7.5	37.5	52.6	1.8	.6	.1	(D)	-
PRIVATE TRUCK	1 140	100.0	(D)	7.4	81.9	.9	5.6	3.7	.5	(D)	-
AIR	-	100.0	(D)	14.0	80.5	1.2	1.4	-	-	(D)	2.9
WATER	-	100.0	(D)	-	-	-	-	-	-	(D)	-
OTHER	47	100.0	(D)	.1	99.9	-	-	-	-	(D)	-
UNKNOWN	2	100.0	(D)	41.9	58.1	-	-	-	-	(D)	-
WEST NORTH CENTRAL	1 052	100.0	(D)	1.6	7.1	74.2	.4	5.3	11.5	(D)	-
RAIL	426	100.0	(D)	.7	13.0	58.9	.9	5.7	20.9	(D)	-
MOTOR CARRIER	205	100.0	(D)	3.1	4.7	84.7	.2	7.2	-	(D)	-
PRIVATE TRUCK	420	100.0	(D)	1.8	2.2	84.5	-	4.0	7.5	(D)	-
AIR	-	100.0	(D)	100.0	-	-	-	-	-	(D)	-
WATER	-	100.0	(D)	-	-	-	-	-	-	(D)	-
OTHER	-	100.0	(D)	25.1	27.6	-	-	46.4	-	(D)	.9
UNKNOWN	-	100.0	(D)	-	-	-	-	-	-	(D)	-
SOUTH ATLANTIC	3 844	100.0	(D)	5.6	6.2	1.4	80.0	6.4	.5	(D)	-
RAIL	805	100.0	(D)	4.6	12.0	5.8	69.9	6.2	1.5	(D)	-
MOTOR CARRIER	1 266	100.0	(D)	8.9	8.6	.3	70.8	11.4	-	(D)	-
PRIVATE TRUCK	1 768	100.0	(D)	3.6	1.6	.1	91.4	2.9	.4	(D)	-
AIR	-	100.0	(D)	-	61.3	-	15.2	-	-	(D)	23.5
WATER	-	100.0	(D)	-	-	-	-	-	-	(D)	-
OTHER	3	100.0	(D)	.7	98.4	-	.4	.4	-	(D)	-
UNKNOWN	-	100.0	(D)	100.0	-	-	-	-	-	(D)	-
EAST SOUTH CENTRAL	1 358	100.0	(D)	5.4	10.8	8.2	12.1	54.5	9.1	(D)	-
RAIL	435	100.0	(D)	12.4	24.1	21.1	27.6	10.9	3.9	(D)	-
MOTOR CARRIER	552	100.0	(D)	3.4	2.7	3.4	5.8	84.6	-	(D)	-
PRIVATE TRUCK	358	100.0	(D)	.1	4.4	-	3.3	62.8	29.5	(D)	-
AIR	-	100.0	(D)	-	20.1	-	79.9	-	-	(D)	-
WATER	-	100.0	(D)	-	-	-	-	-	-	(D)	-
OTHER	4	100.0	(D)	.1	99.6	-	.1	.2	-	(D)	-
UNKNOWN	6	100.0	(D)	-	100.0	-	-	-	-	(D)	-
WEST SOUTH CENTRAL	2 906	100.0	(D)	.8	3.1	5.8	1.1	2.9	86.0	(D)	-
RAIL	921	100.0	(D)	1.4	9.1	14.6	3.5	.6	70.3	(D)	-
MOTOR CARRIER	497	100.0	(D)	2.2	1.2	6.8	.2	5.3	84.1	(D)	.2
PRIVATE TRUCK	1 479	100.0	(D)	-	-	-	-	3.5	96.5	(D)	-
AIR	-	100.0	(D)	-	2.5	-	94.9	-	-	(D)	2.6
WATER	-	100.0	(D)	-	-	-	-	-	-	(D)	-
OTHER	-	100.0	(D)	-	1.9	-	1.5	.1	96.5	(D)	-
UNKNOWN	7	100.0	(D)	9.9	-	-	-	-	90.1	(D)	-
MOUNTAIN	796	100.0	(D)	1.9	.6	10.4	1.7	2.5	3.0	(D)	20.4
RAIL	161	100.0	(D)	8.2	2.9	49.6	8.3	2.0	5.4	(D)	1.8
MOTOR CARRIER	107	100.0	(D)	1.4	.3	2.2	-	1.5	.1	(D)	67.5
PRIVATE TRUCK	514	100.0	(D)	-	-	-	-	3.0	2.9	(D)	14.6
AIR	-	100.0	(D)	-	68.5	-	-	-	-	(D)	31.5
WATER	-	100.0	(D)	-	-	-	-	-	-	(D)	-
OTHER	-	100.0	(D)	-	19.4	-	-	-	-	(D)	80.6
UNKNOWN	12	100.0	(D)	-	-	-	-	-	-	(D)	100.0
PACIFIC	568	100.0	(D)	2.2	2.4	11.9	.8	1.5	.7	(D)	78.7
RAIL	145	100.0	(D)	6.6	8.5	45.9	3.2	5.4	-	(D)	25.1
MOTOR CARRIER	179	100.0	(D)	1.7	.6	.4	-	-	-	(D)	96.0
PRIVATE TRUCK	225	100.0	(D)	-	-	-	-	.4	1.8	(D)	97.8
AIR	-	100.0	(D)	5.9	55.6	-	-	-	-	(D)	8.4
WATER	-	100.0	(D)	-	-	-	-	-	-	(D)	100.0
OTHER	-	100.0	(D)	-	16.2	-	-	-	-	(D)	83.8
UNKNOWN	18	100.0	(D)	-	-	-	-	-	-	(D)	100.0

See footnotes at end of table 4.

TABLE 3. **TCC GROUP 325—Percent Distribution of Geographic Division of Destination and Means of Transport, by Geographic Division of Origin: 1972**—Continued

Geographic division of destination and means of transport	Number	Percent distribution by division of origin[1]									
		U.S. total	New England	Middle Atlantic	East North Central	West North Central	South Atlantic	East South Central	West South Central	Mountain	Pacific
TON-MILES OF SHIPMENTS	(millions of ton-miles)		—							—	
U.S. TOTAL...............	4 294	100.0	(D)	13.7	18.3	29.7	15.8	4.9	11.9	(D)	3.1
RAIL...................	2 061	100.0	(D)	13.2	18.0	31.1	20.0	2.6	12.4	(D)	.8
MOTOR CARRIER..........	1 466	100.0	(D)	17.5	17.3	41.4	8.8	6.5	2.7	(D)	4.4
PRIVATE TRUCK..........	738	100.0	(D)	6.6	20.4	3.8	18.4	8.4	29.2	(D)	6.3
AIR....................	1	100.0	(D)	6.6	52.3	3.4	3.4	-	-	(D)	15.0
WATER.................	11	100.0	(D)	99.1	-	-	-	-	-	(D)	.9
OTHER.................	6	100.0	(D)	.7	98.7	-	.1	.2	.2	(D)	.1
UNKNOWN...............	9	100.0	(D)	17.7	24.3	-	.3	-	2.4	(D)	53.7
NEW ENGLAND.............	151	100.0	(D)	29.1	11.9	3.2	35.2	-	-	(D)	.1
RAIL...................	80	100.0	(D)	27.7	8.6	5.7	56.3	-	-	(D)	-
MOTOR CARRIER..........	47	100.0	(D)	38.4	20.4	.4	11.7	-	-	(D)	.2
PRIVATE TRUCK..........	23	100.0	(D)	15.5	5.7	-	11.4	-	-	(D)	-
AIR....................	-	100.0	(D)	1.7	98.3	-	-	-	-	(D)	-
WATER.................	-	100.0	(D)	-	-	-	-	-	-	(D)	-
OTHER.................	-	100.0	(D)	14.5	66.1	-	19.3	-	-	(D)	-
UNKNOWN...............	-	100.0	(D)	-	-	-	-	-	-	(D)	-
MIDDLE ATLANTIC.........	476	100.0	(D)	32.1	31.6	13.2	20.4	.5	-	(D)	-
RAIL...................	181	100.0	(D)	5.5	34.7	28.2	31.6	-	-	(D)	-
MOTOR CARRIER..........	207	100.0	(D)	51.8	28.1	5.8	11.2	-	-	(D)	.1
PRIVATE TRUCK..........	76	100.0	(D)	31.4	38.3	-	21.6	3.4	-	(D)	-
AIR....................	-	100.0	(D)	-	34.0	21.6	5.4	-	-	(D)	39.0
WATER.................	11	100.0	(D)	100.0	-	-	-	-	-	(D)	-
OTHER.................	-	100.0	(D)	25.2	65.0	-	3.4	-	-	(D)	6.4
UNKNOWN...............	-	100.0	(D)	93.2	-	-	6.8	-	-	(D)	-
EAST NORTH CENTRAL......	1 424	100.0	(D)	14.6	25.2	51.4	4.5	.7	2.3	(D)	.1
RAIL...................	499	100.0	(D)	25.1	21.3	37.9	7.8	-	4.5	(D)	-
MOTOR CARRIER..........	780	100.0	(D)	9.1	18.2	69.4	1.8	.8	.7	(D)	-
PRIVATE TRUCK..........	138	100.0	(D)	7.6	76.6	.8	8.1	2.7	3.9	(D)	.4
AIR....................	-	100.0	(D)	34.5	42.3	2.3	2.8	-	-	(D)	18.2
WATER.................	-	100.0	(D)	-	-	-	-	-	-	(D)	-
OTHER.................	4	100.0	(D)	.3	99.7	-	-	-	-	(D)	-
UNKNOWN...............	-	100.0	(D)	81.7	18.3	-	-	-	-	(D)	-
WEST NORTH CENTRAL......	202	100.0	(D)	6.4	12.2	52.3	1.5	7.0	20.6	(D)	-
PAIL...................	120	100.0	(D)	2.5	15.6	48.0	2.2	4.2	27.4	(D)	-
MOTOR CARRIER..........	35	100.0	(D)	16.3	10.1	60.0	.9	12.4	-	(D)	.2
PRIVATE TRUCK..........	45	100.0	(D)	9.0	4.5	57.7	-	10.2	18.5	(D)	-
AIR....................	-	100.0	(D)	100.0	-	-	-	-	-	(D)	-
WATER.................	-	100.0	(D)	-	-	-	-	-	-	(D)	-
OTHER.................	-	100.0	(D)	45.6	21.3	-	-	30.6	-	(D)	2.5
UNKNOWN...............	-	100.0	(D)	-	-	-	-	-	-	(D)	-
SOUTH ATLANTIC..........	587	100.0	(D)	7.0	12.6	7.4	60.6	10.1	2.2	(D)	-
RAIL...................	296	100.0	(D)	5.0	13.6	13.5	59.1	6.6	2.2	(D)	-
MOTOR CARRIER..........	159	100.0	(D)	12.5	17.3	1.8	48.7	19.4	.1	(D)	.1
PRIVATE TRUCK..........	130	100.0	(D)	4.8	4.1	.7	78.9	6.7	4.8	(D)	-
AIR....................	-	100.0	(D)	-	50.9	-	4.9	-	-	(D)	44.2
WATER.................	-	100.0	(D)	-	-	-	-	-	-	(D)	-
OTHER.................	-	100.0	(D)	2.8	95.6	-	.5	1.2	-	(D)	-
UNKNOWN...............	-	100.0	(D)	100.0	-	-	-	-	-	(D)	-
EAST SOUTH CENTRAL......	276	100.0	(D)	17.0	20.7	15.8	15.3	22.9	8.1	(D)	-
RAIL...................	165	100.0	(D)	22.6	26.5	21.7	20.1	4.1	5.1	(D)	-
MOTOR CARRIER..........	69	100.0	(D)	13.7	6.1	11.1	9.8	58.8	-	(D)	-
PRIVATE TRUCK..........	38	100.0	(D)	.3	16.0	-	5.9	40.9	36.8	(D)	-
AIR....................	-	100.0	(D)	-	25.5	-	74.5	-	-	(D)	-
WATER.................	-	100.0	(D)	-	-	-	-	-	-	(D)	-
OTHER.................	-	100.0	(D)	.4	99.3	-	.2	.2	-	(D)	-
UNKNOWN...............	2	100.0	(D)	-	100.0	-	-	-	-	(D)	-
WEST SOUTH CENTRAL......	642	100.0	(D)	4.7	10.7	15.9	4.5	3.8	59.0	(D)	.3
RAIL...................	382	100.0	(D)	4.0	16.5	22.2	7.4	1.2	46.9	(D)	.1
MOTOR CARRIER..........	84	100.0	(D)	16.8	6.7	20.6	.8	13.8	39.6	(D)	1.5
PRIVATE TRUCK..........	174	100.0	(D)	-	.1	-	-	4.6	95.3	(D)	-
AIR....................	-	100.0	(D)	-	1.8	-	94.6	-	-	(D)	3.6
WATER.................	-	100.0	(D)	-	-	-	-	-	-	(D)	-
OTHER.................	-	100.0	(D)	-	9.8	-	6.2	.2	83.7	(D)	-
UNKNOWN...............	1	100.0	(D)	79.4	-	-	-	-	20.6	(D)	-
MOUNTAIN................	265	100.0	(D)	9.2	2.5	28.9	8.4	7.5	6.4	(D)	21.6
RAIL...................	147	100.0	(D)	14.9	4.2	50.7	15.1	2.3	4.9	(D)	1.3
MOTOR CARRIER..........	33	100.0	(D)	7.6	1.3	6.5	-	4.9	.1	(D)	76.3
PRIVATE TRUCK..........	81	100.0	(D)	-	-	-	-	18.4	12.1	(D)	32.1
AIR....................	-	100.0	(D)	-	79.8	-	-	-	-	(D)	20.2
WATER.................	-	100.0	(D)	-	-	-	-	-	-	(D)	-
OTHER.................	-	100.0	(D)	-	40.2	-	-	-	-	(D)	59.8
UNKNOWN...............	4	100.0	(D)	-	-	-	-	-	-	(D)	100.0
PACIFIC.................	267	100.0	(D)	11.2	9.2	38.5	3.7	6.7	2.1	(D)	27.0
RAIL...................	188	100.0	(D)	12.1	11.8	54.1	5.3	7.7	-	(D)	7.5
MOTOR CARRIER..........	48	100.0	(D)	15.2	4.1	2.5	-	.1	-	(D)	76.4
PRIVATE TRUCK..........	28	100.0	(D)	-	-	-	-	11.4	19.0	(D)	69.5
AIR....................	-	100.0	(D)	6.1	54.2	-	-	-	-	(D)	1.5
WATER.................	-	100.0	(D)	-	-	-	-	-	-	(D)	100.0
OTHER.................	-	100.0	(D)	-	88.3	-	-	-	-	(D)	11.7
UNKNOWN...............	1	100.0	(D)	-	-	-	-	-	-	(D)	100.0

See footnotes at end of table 4.

TABLE 4. TCC GROUP 325—Percent Distribution of Distance Shipped and Weight of Shipment, by Means of Transport: 1972

Distance shipped and weight of shipment [2] [3]	Number	Percent distribution by means of transport							
		All means of transport	Rail	Motor carrier	Private truck	Air	Water	Other	Unknown
TONS OF SHIPMENTS	(thousands of tons)								
U.S. TOTAL	18 753	100.0	24.9	38.8	35.5	-	.3	.3	.3
UNDER 100 MILES	7 423	100.0	1.4	37.6	59.4	-	.6	.4	.5
UNDER 1000 POUNDS	5	100.0	-	32.1	58.9	1.2	-	3.1	4.7
1000 TO 9999 POUNDS	269	100.0	-	22.1	75.9	-	-	.6	1.4
10000 TO 29999 POUNDS	1 933	100.0	.1	17.5	82.0	-	-	.1	.2
30000 TO 59999 POUNDS	4 693	100.0	.5	45.0	53.3	-	-	.6	.6
60000 TO 89999 POUNDS	253	100.0	1.6	66.4	32.0	-	-	-	-
90000 POUNDS AND OVER	266	100.0	27.6	42.5	12.0	-	18.0	-	-
100 TO 199 MILES	3 603	100.0	19.2	38.3	41.9	-	-	.6	-
UNDER 1000 POUNDS	2	100.0	.1	78.0	17.2	.3	-	2.9	1.5
1000 TO 9999 POUNDS	50	100.0	.1	46.2	53.0	-	-	-	.7
10000 TO 29999 POUNDS	334	100.0	.6	33.3	66.0	-	-	-	.1
30000 TO 59999 POUNDS	2 406	100.0	.8	47.4	50.8	-	-	1.0	-
60000 TO 89999 POUNDS	141	100.0	34.5	51.7	13.9	-	-	-	-
90000 POUNDS AND OVER	668	100.0	92.9	4.4	2.7	-	-	-	-
200 TO 299 MILES	2 255	100.0	46.5	35.0	18.5	-	-	-	-
UNDER 1000 POUNDS	2	100.0	-	87.0	6.9	4.1	-	2.0	-
1000 TO 9999 POUNDS	26	100.0	4.8	73.6	21.2	-	-	.4	-
10000 TO 29999 POUNDS	153	100.0	14.7	42.1	43.2	-	-	-	-
30000 TO 59999 POUNDS	1 006	100.0	5.3	62.6	32.1	-	-	-	-
60000 TO 89999 POUNDS	120	100.0	43.6	52.4	4.0	-	-	-	-
90000 POUNDS AND OVER	945	100.0	97.1	1.0	1.8	-	-	-	-
300 TO 499 MILES	3 918	100.0	39.8	53.4	6.5	-	-	-	.3
UNDER 1000 POUNDS	3	100.0	-	80.9	1.9	11.5	-	1.6	4.1
1000 TO 9999 POUNDS	36	100.0	8.1	75.0	9.8	-	-	-	7.1
10000 TO 29999 POUNDS	134	100.0	22.2	58.6	16.5	-	-	-	2.7
30000 TO 59999 POUNDS	909	100.0	25.5	49.1	24.7	-	-	-	.7
60000 TO 89999 POUNDS	134	100.0	89.4	8.4	2.2	-	-	-	-
90000 POUNDS AND OVER	2 700	100.0	43.6	56.4	-	-	-	-	-
500 TO 999 MILES	1 275	100.0	79.6	15.0	5.4	-	-	-	-
UNDER 1000 POUNDS	3	100.0	1.7	91.6	-	3.6	-	1.8	1.3
1000 TO 9999 POUNDS	22	100.0	16.6	82.2	.7	.2	-	-	.3
10000 TO 29999 POUNDS	41	100.0	35.2	52.1	12.7	-	-	-	-
30000 TO 59999 POUNDS	243	100.0	28.0	49.3	22.7	-	-	-	-
60000 TO 89999 POUNDS	122	100.0	94.2	5.8	-	-	-	-	-
90000 POUNDS AND OVER	841	100.0	96.6	2.5	.9	-	-	-	-
1000 TO 1499 MILES	171	100.0	87.0	10.6	2.4	.1	-	-	-
UNDER 1000 POUNDS	-	100.0	-	84.2	-	15.8	-	-	-
1000 TO 9999 POUNDS	2	100.0	-	87.5	12.5	-	-	-	-
10000 TO 29999 POUNDS	7	100.0	29.4	65.1	5.6	-	-	-	-
30000 TO 59999 POUNDS	23	100.0	49.7	35.4	14.8	-	-	-	-
60000 TO 89999 POUNDS	38	100.0	93.1	6.9	-	-	-	-	-
90000 POUNDS AND OVER	99	100.0	100.0	-	-	-	-	-	-
1500 MILES OR OVER	105	100.0	91.8	6.7	1.1	.3	-	-	-
UNDER 1000 POUNDS	-	100.0	7.7	63.5	-	27.3	.1	1.5	-
1000 TO 9999 POUNDS	1	100.0	16.8	76.6	-	4.3	2.3	-	-
10000 TO 29999 POUNDS	4	100.0	43.9	56.1	-	-	-	-	-
30000 TO 59999 POUNDS	13	100.0	86.3	5.0	8.7	-	-	-	-
60000 TO 89999 POUNDS	24	100.0	100.0	-	-	-	-	-	-
90000 POUNDS AND OVER	60	100.0	96.7	3.3	-	-	-	-	-
TON-MILES OF SHIPMENTS	(millions of ton-miles)								
U.S. TOTAL	4 095	100.0	49.4	33.9	16.4	-	-	.1	.1
UNDER 100 MILES	369	100.0	1.8	38.6	58.0	-	.4	.7	.5
UNDER 1000 POUNDS	-	100.0	-	44.8	47.3	.4	-	3.2	4.3
1000 TO 9999 POUNDS	11	100.0	-	28.4	70.0	-	-	.4	1.2
10000 TO 29999 POUNDS	81	100.0	.2	20.2	79.2	-	-	.2	.3
30000 TO 59999 POUNDS	249	100.0	.4	43.7	54.4	-	-	.9	.6
60000 TO 89999 POUNDS	13	100.0	2.2	67.2	30.6	-	-	-	-
90000 POUNDS AND OVER	13	100.0	38.5	36.1	15.3	-	10.1	-	-
100 TO 199 MILES	525	100.0	20.6	38.3	40.4	-	-	.6	-
UNDER 1000 POUNDS	-	100.0	.1	79.0	16.2	.3	-	3.2	1.2
1000 TO 9999 POUNDS	6	100.0	.1	45.6	53.5	-	-	-	.7
10000 TO 29999 POUNDS	48	100.0	.8	33.1	66.0	-	-	-	.1
30000 TO 59999 POUNDS	344	100.0	.9	48.3	49.8	-	-	1.0	-
60000 TO 89999 POUNDS	20	100.0	32.6	54.7	12.7	-	-	-	-
90000 POUNDS AND OVER	104	100.0	94.1	3.7	2.2	-	-	-	-

See footnotes at end of table 4.

TABLE 4. **TCC GROUP 325—Percent Distribution of Distance Shipped and Weight of Shipment, by Means of Transport: 1972**—Continued

Distance shipped and weight of shipment [2] [3]	Number	Percent distribution by means of transport							
		All means of transport	Rail	Motor carrier	Private truck	Air	Water	Other	Unknown
TON-MILES OF SHIPMENTS	(millions of ton-miles)								
200 TO 299 MILES........	569	100.0	48.0	34.5	17.4	-	-	-	-
UNDER 1000 POUNDS.....	-	100.0	-	87.2	6.9	4.0	-	1.8	-
1000 TO 9999 POUNDS...	6	100.0	5.1	74.3	20.2	-	-	.4	-
10000 TO 29999 POUNDS.	37	100.0	15.5	42.8	41.7	-	-	-	-
30000 TO 59999 POUNDS.	248	100.0	5.4	63.4	31.2	-	-	-	-
60000 TO 89999 POUNDS.	30	100.0	46.0	50.5	3.6	-	-	-	-
90000 POUNDS AND OVER.	246	100.0	97.5	1.0	1.5	-	-	-	-
300 TO 499 MILES........	1 392	100.0	43.7	49.4	6.6	-	-	-	.3
UNDER 1000 POUNDS.....	1	100.0	-	81.5	1.7	12.0	-	1.5	3.3
1000 TO 9999 POUNDS...	14	100.0	7.2	77.7	9.2	-	-	-	5.8
10000 TO 29999 POUNDS.	51	100.0	22.1	59.8	15.8	-	-	-	2.3
30000 TO 59999 POUNDS.	335	100.0	27.1	48.3	24.0	-	-	-	.6
60000 TO 89999 POUNDS.	53	100.0	90.5	6.9	2.6	-	-	-	-
90000 POUNDS AND OVER.	935	100.0	48.8	51.2	-	-	-	-	-
500 TO 999 MILES........	834	100.0	80.1	14.4	5.4	-	-	-	-
UNDER 1000 POUNDS.....	2	100.0	1.8	90.9	-	4.2	-	1.8	1.3
1000 TO 9999 POUNDS...	15	100.0	17.0	81.6	.8	.2	-	-	.3
10000 TO 29999 POUNDS.	27	100.0	36.7	51.5	11.8	-	-	-	-
30000 TO 59999 POUNDS.	159	100.0	29.9	46.5	23.6	-	-	-	-
60000 TO 89999 POUNDS.	87	100.0	94.0	6.0	-	-	-	-	-
90000 POUNDS AND OVER.	542	100.0	97.0	2.3	.8	-	-	-	-
1000 TO 1499 MILES......	211	100.0	87.5	10.4	2.0	.1	-	-	-
UNDER 1000 POUNDS.....	-	100.0	-	84.9	-	15.1	-	-	-
1000 TO 9999 POUNDS...	2	100.0	-	87.8	12.2	-	-	-	-
10000 TO 29999 POUNDS.	9	100.0	30.7	64.1	5.2	-	-	-	-
30000 TO 59999 POUNDS.	26	100.0	49.8	37.3	12.9	-	-	-	-
60000 TO 89999 POUNDS.	44	100.0	92.6	7.4	-	-	-	-	-
90000 POUNDS AND OVER.	128	100.0	100.0	-	-	-	-	-	-
1500 MILES OR OVER......	191	100.0	89.5	8.0	2.0	.4	.1	-	-
UNDER 1000 POUNDS.....	2	100.0	8.7	60.2	-	29.8	.1	1.2	-
1000 TO 9999 POUNDS...	3	100.0	20.3	72.0	-	4.6	3.0	-	-
10000 TO 29999 POUNDS.	8	100.0	40.2	59.8	-	-	-	-	-
30000 TO 59999 POUNDS.	25	100.0	79.2	6.1	14.8	-	-	-	-
60000 TO 89999 POUNDS.	42	100.0	100.0	-	-	-	-	-	-
90000 POUNDS AND OVER.	108	100.0	95.7	4.3	-	-	-	-	-

Note: Detail may not add to total due to rounding. The introductory table shows the estimates of sampling variability for tons; sampling variability for ton-miles has not been estimated. See the map in the Introduction for the States comprising the geographic divisions of the United States.

Shipments excluded from the survey are those moving by pipeline (primarily petroleum products from refineries), parcel post shipments, and commodities moved by own power (motorized vehicles, aircraft, etc.) or towed (prefabricated buildings, etc.). Local shipments (commodities shipped less than 25 miles from the plant) and shipments within the same city are also excluded. Shipments to Alaska and Hawaii from the 48 conterminous States and the District of Columbia are included; however, no data were obtained for shipments originating in Alaska and Hawaii.

- Represents zero or rounds to zero.   (D) Withheld to avoid disclosing figures for individual companies.

[1]Production of this commodity is concentrated in the geographic divisions shown; figures and distributions for geographic divisions not shown are included in the total.

[2]Distances of shipments to foreign destinations are calculated only to the U.S. port of exit.

[3]Includes only shipments represented by bills of lading and invoices. Summary records which did not show individual weights of shipments are not included.

TCC 326. Pottery and Related Products

Comparisons of Tons and Ton-Miles of Shipments for
Geographic Divisions of Origin and for Sampling Variability: 1972 and 1967

Geographic division of origin	Estimates				Relative sampling variability in tons (percent)	
	1972		1967		1972	1967
	Tons (thousands)	Ton-miles (millions)	Tons (thousands)	Ton-miles (millions)		
U.S. total	1,017	634	1,195	692	9.6	24.4
New England	(D)	(D)	33	7	(*)	(*)
Middle Atlantic	286	186	288	185	17.7	(*)
East North Central	509	325	370	202	13.4	(*)
West North Central	(D)	(D)	12	5	(*)	(*)
South Atlantic	(D)	(D)	124	87	(*)	(*)
East South Central	(D)	(D)	261	129	(*)	(*)
West South Central	(D)	(D)	53	26	(*)	(*)
Mountain	(D)	(D)	7	6	(*)	(*)
Pacific	90	63	47	45	27.5	(*)

(D) Withheld to avoid disclosing figures for individual companies.   (*) Data not published.

TABLE 1. **TCC GROUP 326—Percent Distribution of Geographic Division of Origin and Distance Shipped, by Means of Transport: 1972**

Geographic division of origin[1] and distance shipped[2]	Number	Percent distribution by means of transport							
		All means of transport	Rail	Motor carrier	Private truck	Air	Water	Other	Unknown
TONS OF SHIPMENTS	(thousands of tons)								
U.S. TOTAL..........	1 017	100.0	14.2	55.5	29.4	.2	.2	.3	.2
MIDDLE ATLANTIC.........	286	100.0	14.2	68.9	16.1	.2	.2	.4	-
UNDER 100 MILES.......	42	100.0	2.3	62.3	34.5	-	-	.9	-
100 TO 199 MILES......	40	100.0	-	64.4	34.7	-	.5	.5	-
200 TO 299 MILES......	29	100.0	-	99.6	.1	.1	-	.3	-
300 TO 499 MILES......	52	100.0	9.2	77.0	13.1	.3	-	.4	-
500 TO 999 MILES......	68	100.0	24.5	64.4	10.4	.4	-	.3	-
1000 TO 1499 MILES....	25	100.0	33.2	61.7	4.5	.5	-	.1	-
1500 MILES OR OVER....	27	100.0	34.7	56.0	7.9	.3	1.0	.1	-
EAST NORTH CENTRAL......	509	100.0	18.5	54.3	26.4	.1	.2	.3	.1
UNDER 100 MILES.......	49	100.0	-	43.4	54.8	-	-	1.8	-
100 TO 199 MILES......	65	100.0	-	45.9	53.4	-	-	.7	-
200 TO 299 MILES......	44	100.0	2.6	55.9	41.2	-	-	.2	.1
300 TO 499 MILES......	117	100.0	8.7	66.0	24.9	.1	-	.2	.1
500 TO 999 MILES......	135	100.0	18.7	65.4	15.5	.1	-	-	.3
1000 TO 1499 MILES....	27	100.0	35.3	53.0	11.4	.3	-	-	-
1500 MILES OR OVER....	69	100.0	69.6	28.1	.4	.2	1.8	.1	-
PACIFIC................	90	100.0	4.4	53.4	39.6	.1	.6	.2	1.7
UNDER 100 MILES.......	23	100.0	-	25.3	74.3	-	-	.1	.3
100 TO 199 MILES......	5	100.0	-	26.7	73.1	-	-	.2	-
200 TO 299 MILES......	2	100.0	23.1	10.7	56.6	-	-	.2	9.5
300 TO 499 MILES......	21	100.0	.1	80.7	19.0	-	-	.2	.1
500 TO 999 MILES......	15	100.0	8.4	36.8	48.7	-	-	.1	6.1
1000 TO 1499 MILES....	4	100.0	14.1	82.6	2.8	.3	-	.1	-
1500 MILES OR OVER....	17	100.0	8.4	81.4	4.6	.3	3.0	.6	1.8
TON-MILES OF SHIPMENTS	(millions of ton-miles)								
U.S. TOTAL..........	634	100.0	29.1	53.8	15.0	.3	1.3	.2	.3
MIDDLE ATLANTIC.........	186	100.0	27.5	62.5	8.7	.3	.7	.2	-
UNDER 100 MILES.......	2	100.0	3.7	61.0	34.3	-	-	.9	-
100 TO 199 MILES......	6	100.0	-	63.8	35.2	-	.6	.4	-
200 TO 299 MILES......	7	100.0	-	99.6	.1	.1	-	.2	-
300 TO 499 MILES......	21	100.0	9.8	77.2	12.4	.3	-	.4	-
500 TO 999 MILES......	50	100.0	28.9	61.4	9.0	.3	-	.3	-
1000 TO 1499 MILES....	30	100.0	35.4	59.6	4.4	.5	-	.1	-
1500 MILES OR OVER....	67	100.0	35.0	55.8	7.0	.3	1.8	.1	-
EAST NORTH CENTRAL......	325	100.0	36.4	48.8	12.7	.1	1.7	.1	.1
UNDER 100 MILES.......	2	100.0	-	42.1	55.8	-	-	2.1	-
100 TO 199 MILES......	9	100.0	-	43.7	55.5	-	-	.8	-
200 TO 299 MILES......	11	100.0	2.8	56.2	40.8	-	-	.2	.1
300 TO 499 MILES......	45	100.0	8.8	64.6	26.2	.1	-	.2	.1
500 TO 999 MILES......	95	100.0	18.7	66.5	14.4	.1	-	-	.3
1000 TO 1499 MILES....	31	100.0	34.2	54.3	11.3	.3	-	-	-
1500 MILES OR OVER....	129	100.0	66.4	28.7	.4	.2	4.2	.1	-
PACIFIC................	63	100.0	7.8	69.3	17.4	.2	2.2	.4	2.7
UNDER 100 MILES.......	-	100.0	-	29.0	70.6	-	-	.1	.3
100 TO 199 MILES......	-	100.0	-	22.4	77.4	-	-	.2	-
200 TO 299 MILES......	-	100.0	23.1	11.1	53.8	-	-	.2	11.8
300 TO 499 MILES......	7	100.0	.1	82.3	17.4	-	-	.2	.1
500 TO 999 MILES......	12	100.0	7.8	35.3	50.6	-	-	.1	6.2
1000 TO 1499 MILES....	5	100.0	14.1	82.2	3.1	.4	-	.2	-
1500 MILES OR OVER....	35	100.0	8.5	79.6	4.6	.3	4.0	.6	2.4

See footnotes at end of table 4.

TABLE 2. **TCC GROUP 326—Percent Distribution of Geographic Division of Origin and Means of Transport, by Geographic Division of Destination: 1972**

Geographic division of origin[1] and means of transport	Number	Percent distribution by division of destination									
		U.S. total	New England	Middle Atlantic	East North Central	West North Central	South Atlantic	East South Central	West South Central	Mountain	Pacific
TONS OF SHIPMENTS	(thousands of tons)										
U.S. TOTAL..............	1 017	100.0	3.6	16.7	22.6	9.1	15.1	7.2	8.5	5.8	11.5
RAIL.................	144	100.0	.1	3.0	1.6	10.2	13.8	8.4	16.2	23.4	23.3
MOTOR CARRIER.........	564	100.0	5.5	20.7	22.0	5.7	18.5	5.4	9.9	3.6	8.8
PRIVATE TRUCK.........	298	100.0	1.8	15.7	34.2	15.0	9.3	10.2	2.5	1.5	9.8
AIR..................	1	100.0	5.7	11.5	20.6	3.4	25.4	9.9	6.9	1.1	15.4
WATER................	2	100.0	-	11.7	-	-	-	-	-	-	88.3
OTHER................	3	100.0	8.9	18.3	36.5	11.7	11.8	6.7	1.5	.3	4.2
UNKNOWN..............	2	100.0	3.6	2.5	.1	-	13.4	-	5.9	-	74.5

See footnotes at end of table 4.

TABLE 2. **TCC GROUP 326—Percent Distribution of Geographic Division of Origin and Means of Transport, by Geographic Division of Destination: 1972**—Continued

Geographic division of origin[1] and means of transport	Number	Percent distribution by division of destination									
		U.S. total	New England	Middle Atlantic	East North Central	West North Central	South Atlantic	East South Central	West South Central	Mountain	Pacific
TONS OF SHIPMENTS	(thousands of tons)										
MIDDLE ATLANTIC	286	100.0	5.4	28.7	19.0	6.7	15.4	5.1	9.0	3.3	7.4
RAIL	40	100.0	-	2.4	4.3	22.5	17.9	2.7	21.4	11.0	17.6
MOTOR CARRIER	197	100.0	7.0	27.5	22.5	3.9	16.9	5.8	8.0	2.6	5.8
PRIVATE TRUCK	46	100.0	3.0	56.8	17.6	4.9	6.6	3.9	2.4	-	4.7
AIR	-	100.0	6.3	4.9	26.8	3.9	9.1	23.1	13.4	1.2	11.3
WATER	-	100.0	-	42.8	-	-	-	-	-	-	57.2
OTHER	1	100.0	17.9	33.7	13.6	4.4	20.8	5.7	2.9	.2	.9
UNKNOWN	-	100.0	-	55.6	-	-	44.4	-	-	-	-
EAST NORTH CENTRAL	509	100.0	2.9	14.9	28.4	8.4	16.1	5.8	9.1	7.6	6.9
RAIL	94	100.0	-	3.3	-	5.9	11.2	11.6	14.1	29.7	24.2
MOTOR CARRIER	277	100.0	4.9	18.7	23.7	7.8	22.2	3.4	11.5	3.8	3.8
PRIVATE TRUCK	134	100.0	1.0	15.4	58.1	11.3	6.9	6.6	.5	-	.2
AIR	-	100.0	5.6	17.6	12.9	-	33.8	1.1	3.9	.5	24.5
WATER	1	100.0	-	-	-	-	-	-	-	-	100.0
OTHER	1	100.0	3.1	8.9	57.0	18.2	6.9	2.5	.2	-	3.1
UNKNOWN	-	100.0	14.4	8.4	-	-	53.2	-	24.0	-	-
PACIFIC	90	100.0	1.0	1.9	6.7	1.8	4.9	2.9	8.7	11.1	61.1
RAIL	3	100.0	3.0	5.2	14.1	1.6	12.3	.9	25.4	31.7	5.8
MOTOR CARRIER	48	100.0	1.5	2.7	10.8	2.9	7.4	5.2	7.1	8.6	53.8
PRIVATE TRUCK	35	100.0	-	.3	.7	.3	1.2	.1	9.5	12.9	75.1
AIR	-	100.0	13.5	33.3	27.0	24.6	-	.1	.1	-	1.3
WATER	-	100.0	-	-	-	-	-	-	-	-	100.0
OTHER	-	100.0	6.1	12.8	18.0	9.0	8.6	2.5	-	4.3	38.6
UNKNOWN	1	100.0	-	-	-	-	-	-	-	-	100.0
TON-MILES OF SHIPMENTS	(millions of ton-miles)										
U.S. TOTAL	634	100.0	2.8	7.6	10.9	7.9	14.0	5.7	13.7	13.4	24.1
RAIL	184	100.0	.2	.9	.9	6.0	7.0	4.2	13.7	28.4	38.7
MOTOR CARRIER	341	100.0	4.5	10.2	13.8	6.0	16.9	5.3	16.4	8.7	18.1
PRIVATE TRUCK	95	100.0	1.8	12.0	20.9	19.2	18.2	10.2	5.7	2.8	9.2
AIR	1	100.0	4.1	8.6	12.6	3.3	26.5	6.0	7.8	1.7	99.4
WATER	8	100.0	-	.6	-	-	-	-	-	-	99.4
OTHER	1	100.0	10.6	13.1	23.7	12.1	13.4	6.3	5.0	.6	15.1
UNKNOWN	2	100.0	1.5	.5	.1	-	9.2	-	5.5	-	83.3
MIDDLE ATLANTIC	186	100.0	2.5	6.0	12.8	8.4	11.2	5.1	15.4	8.9	29.8
RAIL	51	100.0	-	.2	1.1	16.0	9.6	1.5	19.5	14.6	37.5
MOTOR CARRIER	116	100.0	3.7	7.2	16.8	5.0	12.6	6.3	14.7	7.8	25.9
PRIVATE TRUCK	16	100.0	1.5	16.3	21.0	9.6	6.6	7.6	8.3	-	29.1
AIR	-	100.0	2.5	1.3	15.8	4.5	8.1	16.6	18.5	2.5	30.3
WATER	1	100.0	-	3.0	-	-	-	-	-	-	97.0
OTHER	-	100.0	14.6	7.4	23.5	10.6	17.4	9.4	10.1	.9	6.2
UNKNOWN	-	100.0	-	7.6	-	-	92.4	-	-	-	-
EAST NORTH CENTRAL	325	100.0	2.7	8.7	7.7	6.9	14.4	4.5	14.1	19.0	22.0
RAIL	118	100.0	-	.9	-	2.3	4.7	5.9	11.6	37.4	37.1
MOTOR CARRIER	159	100.0	5.1	11.6	8.0	7.5	20.9	2.6	19.8	11.0	13.5
PRIVATE TRUCK	41	100.0	1.9	20.6	29.2	18.4	18.5	8.5	1.6	-	1.3
AIR	-	100.0	4.4	9.4	4.9	-	27.4	.4	3.8	.9	100.0
WATER	5	100.0	-	-	-	-	-	-	-	-	100.0
OTHER	-	100.0	6.6	12.7	23.3	15.9	9.0	2.7	1.1	.2	28.5
UNKNOWN	-	100.0	9.0	2.7	-	-	55.1	-	33.2	-	-
PACIFIC	63	100.0	3.4	6.3	17.8	3.5	15.3	7.3	13.0	9.4	24.1
RAIL	4	100.0	6.2	10.0	20.8	1.9	21.6	1.2	20.4	13.6	4.3
MOTOR CARRIER	43	100.0	4.1	7.1	22.1	4.4	17.5	10.2	9.3	6.0	19.2
PRIVATE TRUCK	11	100.0	-	2.3	3.9	1.4	8.3	.4	28.4	23.9	31.5
AIR	-	100.0	16.8	39.3	26.1	17.0	-	.1	.1	-	.6
WATER	1	100.0	-	-	-	-	-	-	-	-	100.0
OTHER	-	100.0	11.9	23.3	25.5	10.6	14.6	3.4	-	1.2	9.5
UNKNOWN	1	100.0	-	-	-	-	-	-	-	-	100.0

See footnotes at end of table 4.

TABLE 3. **TCC GROUP 326**—Percent Distribution of Geographic Division of Destination and Means of Transport, by Geographic Division of Origin: 1972

Geographic division of destination and means of transport	Number	Percent distribution by division of origin[1]									
		U.S. total	New England	Middle Atlantic	East North Central	West North Central	South Atlantic	East South Central	West South Central	Mountain	Pacific
TONS OF SHIPMENTS	(thousands of tons)										
U.S. TOTAL..............	1 017	100.0	(D)	28.2	50.1	(D)	(D)	(D)	(D)	(D)	8.9
RAIL.................	144	100.0	(D)	28.1	65.4	(D)	(D)	(D)	(D)	(D)	2.7
MOTOR CARRIER........	564	100.0	(D)	35.0	49.0	(D)	(D)	(D)	(D)	(D)	8.5
PRIVATE TRUCK........	298	100.0	(D)	15.5	45.0	(D)	(D)	(D)	(D)	(D)	11.9
AIR..................	1	100.0	(D)	41.6	29.3	(D)	(D)	(D)	(D)	(D)	3.7
WATER................	2	100.0	(D)	20.3	53.9	(D)	(D)	(D)	(D)	(D)	22.8
OTHER................	3	100.0	(D)	35.0	53.0	(D)	(D)	(D)	(D)	(D)	5.7
UNKNOWN..............	2	100.0	(D)	.5	24.7	(D)	(D)	(D)	(D)	(D)	74.5
NEW ENGLAND.............	36	100.0	(D)	42.1	40.7	(D)	(D)	(D)	(D)	(D)	2.3
RAIL.................	-	100.0	(D)	-	-	(D)	(D)	(D)	(D)	(D)	100.0
MOTOR CARRIER........	30	100.0	(D)	45.0	43.7	(D)	(D)	(D)	(D)	(D)	2.3
PRIVATE TRUCK........	5	100.0	(D)	25.4	25.0	(D)	(D)	(D)	(D)	(D)	-
AIR..................	-	100.0	(D)	45.6	28.9	(D)	(D)	(D)	(D)	(D)	8.9
WATER................	-	100.0	(D)	-	-	(D)	(D)	(D)	(D)	(D)	-
OTHER................	-	100.0	(D)	70.2	18.4	(D)	(D)	(D)	(D)	(D)	3.9
UNKNOWN..............	-	100.0	(D)	-	100.0	(D)	(D)	(D)	(D)	(D)	-
MIDDLE ATLANTIC.........	169	100.0	(D)	48.5	44.9	(D)	(D)	(D)	(D)	(D)	1.0
RAIL.................	4	100.0	(D)	22.6	72.7	(D)	(D)	(D)	(D)	(D)	4.8
MOTOR CARRIER........	117	100.0	(D)	46.5	44.4	(D)	(D)	(D)	(D)	(D)	1.1
PRIVATE TRUCK........	47	100.0	(D)	55.8	43.9	(D)	(D)	(D)	(D)	(D)	.2
AIR..................	-	100.0	(D)	17.8	44.9	(D)	(D)	(D)	(D)	(D)	10.8
WATER................	-	100.0	(D)	74.5	-	(D)	(D)	(D)	(D)	(D)	-
OTHER................	-	100.0	(D)	64.6	25.9	(D)	(D)	(D)	(D)	(D)	4.0
UNKNOWN..............	-	100.0	(D)	11.1	83.0	(D)	(D)	(D)	(D)	(D)	-
EAST NORTH CENTRAL......	230	100.0	(D)	23.7	62.9	(D)	(D)	(D)	(D)	(D)	2.6
RAIL.................	2	100.0	(D)	75.9	-	(D)	(D)	(D)	(D)	(D)	24.1
MOTOR CARRIER........	124	100.0	(D)	35.8	52.9	(D)	(D)	(D)	(D)	(D)	4.2
PRIVATE TRUCK........	102	100.0	(D)	8.0	76.4	(D)	(D)	(D)	(D)	(D)	.2
AIR..................	-	100.0	(D)	54.1	18.4	(D)	(D)	(D)	(D)	(D)	4.9
WATER................	-	100.0	(D)	-	-	(D)	(D)	(D)	(D)	(D)	-
OTHER................	1	100.0	(D)	13.0	82.8	(D)	(D)	(D)	(D)	(D)	2.8
UNKNOWN..............	-	100.0	(D)	-	-	(D)	(D)	(D)	(D)	(D)	-
WEST NORTH CENTRAL......	92	100.0	(D)	20.9	46.4	(D)	(D)	(D)	(D)	(D)	1.7
RAIL.................	14	100.0	(D)	61.9	37.7	(D)	(D)	(D)	(D)	(D)	.4
MOTOR CARRIER........	32	100.0	(D)	24.3	67.2	(D)	(D)	(D)	(D)	(D)	4.3
PRIVATE TRUCK........	44	100.0	(D)	5.0	34.0	(D)	(D)	(D)	(D)	(D)	.2
AIR..................	-	100.0	(D)	48.4	-	(D)	(D)	(D)	(D)	(D)	27.1
WATER................	-	100.0	(D)	-	-	(D)	(D)	(D)	(D)	(D)	-
OTHER................	-	100.0	(D)	13.2	82.1	(D)	(D)	(D)	(D)	(D)	4.4
UNKNOWN..............	-	100.0	(D)	-	-	(D)	(D)	(D)	(D)	(D)	-
SOUTH ATLANTIC..........	153	100.0	(D)	28.8	53.5	(D)	(D)	(D)	(D)	(D)	2.9
RAIL.................	19	100.0	(D)	36.7	53.2	(D)	(D)	(D)	(D)	(D)	2.5
MOTOR CARRIER........	104	100.0	(D)	32.0	58.9	(D)	(D)	(D)	(D)	(D)	3.4
PRIVATE TRUCK........	27	100.0	(D)	11.1	33.4	(D)	(D)	(D)	(D)	(D)	1.5
AIR..................	-	100.0	(D)	14.9	38.9	(D)	(D)	(D)	(D)	(D)	-
WATER................	-	100.0	(D)	-	-	(D)	(D)	(D)	(D)	(D)	-
OTHER................	-	100.0	(D)	61.6	30.9	(D)	(D)	(D)	(D)	(D)	4.2
UNKNOWN..............	-	100.0	(D)	1.7	98.3	(D)	(D)	(D)	(D)	(D)	-
EAST SOUTH CENTRAL......	73	100.0	(D)	19.7	40.0	(D)	(D)	(D)	(D)	(D)	3.5
RAIL.................	12	100.0	(D)	9.1	90.6	(D)	(D)	(D)	(D)	(D)	.3
MOTOR CARRIER........	30	100.0	(D)	37.2	31.0	(D)	(D)	(D)	(D)	(D)	8.2
PRIVATE TRUCK........	30	100.0	(D)	5.9	29.2	(D)	(D)	(D)	(D)	(D)	.1
AIR..................	-	100.0	(D)	96.6	3.4	(D)	(D)	(D)	(D)	(D)	-
WATER................	-	100.0	(D)	-	-	(D)	(D)	(D)	(D)	(D)	-
OTHER................	-	100.0	(D)	29.7	19.7	(D)	(D)	(D)	(D)	(D)	2.2
UNKNOWN..............	-	100.0	(D)	-	-	(D)	(D)	(D)	(D)	(D)	-
WEST SOUTH CENTRAL......	86	100.0	(D)	29.8	53.2	(D)	(D)	(D)	(D)	(D)	9.0
RAIL.................	23	100.0	(D)	37.2	57.0	(D)	(D)	(D)	(D)	(D)	4.3
MOTOR CARRIER........	55	100.0	(D)	28.5	57.5	(D)	(D)	(D)	(D)	(D)	6.1
PRIVATE TRUCK........	7	100.0	(D)	15.2	9.5	(D)	(D)	(D)	(D)	(D)	46.1
AIR..................	-	100.0	(D)	80.6	16.5	(D)	(D)	(D)	(D)	(D)	.1
WATER................	-	100.0	(D)	-	-	(D)	(D)	(D)	(D)	(D)	-
OTHER................	-	100.0	(D)	69.1	7.8	(D)	(D)	(D)	(D)	(D)	-
UNKNOWN..............	-	100.0	(D)	-	100.0	(D)	(D)	(D)	(D)	(D)	-
MOUNTAIN................	58	100.0	(D)	16.4	66.0	(D)	(D)	(D)	(D)	(D)	17.1
RAIL.................	33	100.0	(D)	13.2	83.0	(D)	(D)	(D)	(D)	(D)	3.7
MOTOR CARRIER........	20	100.0	(D)	25.4	52.7	(D)	(D)	(D)	(D)	(D)	20.6
PRIVATE TRUCK........	4	100.0	(D)	-	-	(D)	(D)	(D)	(D)	(D)	100.0
AIR..................	-	100.0	(D)	45.9	12.9	(D)	(D)	(D)	(D)	(D)	-
WATER................	-	100.0	(D)	-	-	(D)	(D)	(D)	(D)	(D)	-
OTHER................	-	100.0	(D)	19.2	4.0	(D)	(D)	(D)	(D)	(D)	76.9
UNKNOWN..............	-	100.0	(D)	-	-	(D)	(D)	(D)	(D)	(D)	-
PACIFIC.................	116	100.0	(D)	18.1	30.1	(D)	(D)	(D)	(D)	(D)	47.2
RAIL.................	33	100.0	(D)	21.2	67.7	(D)	(D)	(D)	(D)	(D)	.7
MOTOR CARRIER........	49	100.0	(D)	22.9	21.3	(D)	(D)	(D)	(D)	(D)	52.0
PRIVATE TRUCK........	29	100.0	(D)	7.5	.9	(D)	(D)	(D)	(D)	(D)	91.6
AIR..................	-	100.0	(D)	30.5	46.5	(D)	(D)	(D)	(D)	(D)	.3
WATER................	2	100.0	(D)	13.1	61.0	(D)	(D)	(D)	(D)	(D)	25.9
OTHER................	-	100.0	(D)	7.7	39.1	(D)	(D)	(D)	(D)	(D)	52.2
UNKNOWN..............	1	100.0	(D)	-	-	(D)	(D)	(D)	(D)	(D)	100.0

See footnotes at end of table 4.

TABLE 3. **TCC GROUP 326—Percent Distribution of Geographic Division of Destination and Means of Transport, by Geographic Division of Origin: 1972**—Continued

Geographic division of destination and means of transport	Number	Percent distribution by division of origin[1]									
		U.S. total	New England	Middle Atlantic	East North Central	West North Central	South Atlantic	East South Central	West South Central	Mountain	Pacific
TON-MILES OF SHIPMENTS	(millions of ton-miles)										
U.S. TOTAL..............	634	100.0	(D)	29.4	51.4	(D)	(D)	(D)	(D)	(D)	10.0
RAIL...................	184	100.0	(D)	27.8	64.1	(D)	(D)	(D)	(D)	(D)	2.7
MOTOR CARRIER..........	341	100.0	(D)	34.2	46.6	(D)	(D)	(D)	(D)	(D)	12.9
PRIVATE TRUCK..........	95	100.0	(D)	17.1	43.5	(D)	(D)	(D)	(D)	(D)	11.6
AIR....................	1	100.0	(D)	35.5	26.7	(D)	(D)	(D)	(D)	(D)	7.3
WATER..................	8	100.0	(D)	15.7	66.8	(D)	(D)	(D)	(D)	(D)	17.4
OTHER..................	1	100.0	(D)	36.6	36.8	(D)	(D)	(D)	(D)	(D)	21.9
UNKNOWN................	2	100.0	(D)	.1	16.4	(D)	(D)	(D)	(D)	(D)	83.3
NEW ENGLAND............	17	100.0	(D)	26.7	50.9	(D)	(D)	(D)	(D)	(D)	12.4
RAIL...................	-	100.0	(D)	-	-	(D)	(D)	(D)	(D)	(D)	100.0
MOTOR CARRIER..........	15	100.0	(D)	28.5	52.8	(D)	(D)	(D)	(D)	(D)	11.9
PRIVATE TRUCK..........	1	100.0	(D)	14.5	45.3	(D)	(D)	(D)	(D)	(D)	-
AIR....................	-	100.0	(D)	21.2	28.4	(D)	(D)	(D)	(D)	(D)	29.8
WATER..................	-	100.0	(D)	-	-	(D)	(D)	(D)	(D)	(D)	-
OTHER..................	-	100.0	(D)	50.1	23.0	(D)	(D)	(D)	(D)	(D)	24.6
UNKNOWN................	-	100.0	(D)	-	100.0	(D)	(D)	(D)	(D)	(D)	-
MIDDLE ATLANTIC........	48	100.0	(D)	23.2	58.5	(D)	(D)	(D)	(D)	(D)	8.2
RAIL...................	1	100.0	(D)	4.7	65.9	(D)	(D)	(D)	(D)	(D)	29.4
MOTOR CARRIER..........	34	100.0	(D)	24.1	53.2	(D)	(D)	(D)	(D)	(D)	9.0
PRIVATE TRUCK..........	11	100.0	(D)	23.2	74.6	(D)	(D)	(D)	(D)	(D)	2.2
AIR....................	-	100.0	(D)	5.3	29.0	(D)	(D)	(D)	(D)	(D)	33.3
WATER..................	-	100.0	(D)	77.6	-	(D)	(D)	(D)	(D)	(D)	-
OTHER..................	-	100.0	(D)	20.8	35.6	(D)	(D)	(D)	(D)	(D)	39.0
UNKNOWN................	-	100.0	(D)	2.1	93.7	(D)	(D)	(D)	(D)	(D)	-
EAST NORTH CENTRAL.....	69	100.0	(D)	34.5	36.2	(D)	(D)	(D)	(D)	(D)	16.3
RAIL...................	1	100.0	(D)	36.4	-	(D)	(D)	(D)	(D)	(D)	63.6
MOTOR CARRIER..........	47	100.0	(D)	41.7	27.2	(D)	(D)	(D)	(D)	(D)	20.7
PRIVATE TRUCK..........	19	100.0	(D)	17.2	60.7	(D)	(D)	(D)	(D)	(D)	2.1
AIR....................	-	100.0	(D)	44.8	10.3	(D)	(D)	(D)	(D)	(D)	15.2
WATER..................	-	100.0	(D)	-	-	(D)	(D)	(D)	(D)	(D)	-
OTHER..................	-	100.0	(D)	36.2	36.2	(D)	(D)	(D)	(D)	(D)	23.6
UNKNOWN................	-	100.0	(D)	-	-	(D)	(D)	(D)	(D)	(D)	-
WEST NORTH CENTRAL.....	50	100.0	(D)	31.2	44.8	(D)	(D)	(D)	(D)	(D)	4.4
RAIL...................	11	100.0	(D)	74.2	25.0	(D)	(D)	(D)	(D)	(D)	.8
MOTOR CARRIER..........	20	100.0	(D)	28.1	58.2	(D)	(D)	(D)	(D)	(D)	9.3
PRIVATE TRUCK..........	18	100.0	(D)	8.5	41.8	(D)	(D)	(D)	(D)	(D)	.8
AIR....................	-	100.0	(D)	48.0	-	(D)	(D)	(D)	(D)	(D)	37.7
WATER..................	-	100.0	(D)	-	-	(D)	(D)	(D)	(D)	(D)	-
OTHER..................	-	100.0	(D)	31.9	48.2	(D)	(D)	(D)	(D)	(D)	19.1
UNKNOWN................	-	100.0	(D)	-	-	(D)	(D)	(D)	(D)	(D)	-
SOUTH ATLANTIC.........	88	100.0	(D)	23.5	52.8	(D)	(D)	(D)	(D)	(D)	11.0
RAIL...................	12	100.0	(D)	38.4	43.5	(D)	(D)	(D)	(D)	(D)	8.3
MOTOR CARRIER..........	57	100.0	(D)	25.5	57.6	(D)	(D)	(D)	(D)	(D)	13.4
PRIVATE TRUCK..........	17	100.0	(D)	6.2	44.1	(D)	(D)	(D)	(D)	(D)	5.3
AIR....................	-	100.0	(D)	10.8	27.6	(D)	(D)	(D)	(D)	(D)	-
WATER..................	-	100.0	(D)	-	-	(D)	(D)	(D)	(D)	(D)	-
OTHER..................	-	100.0	(D)	47.5	24.7	(D)	(D)	(D)	(D)	(D)	23.8
UNKNOWN................	-	100.0	(D)	1.3	98.7	(D)	(D)	(D)	(D)	(D)	-
EAST SOUTH CENTRAL.....	35	100.0	(D)	26.3	40.7	(D)	(D)	(D)	(D)	(D)	12.8
RAIL...................	7	100.0	(D)	9.7	89.6	(D)	(D)	(D)	(D)	(D)	.7
MOTOR CARRIER..........	18	100.0	(D)	40.2	22.5	(D)	(D)	(D)	(D)	(D)	24.7
PRIVATE TRUCK..........	9	100.0	(D)	12.7	36.2	(D)	(D)	(D)	(D)	(D)	.4
AIR....................	-	100.0	(D)	98.2	1.7	(D)	(D)	(D)	(D)	(D)	.1
WATER..................	-	100.0	(D)	-	-	(D)	(D)	(D)	(D)	(D)	-
OTHER..................	-	100.0	(D)	54.4	16.0	(D)	(D)	(D)	(D)	(D)	12.0
UNKNOWN................	-	100.0	(D)	-	-	(D)	(D)	(D)	(D)	(D)	-
WEST SOUTH CENTRAL.....	87	100.0	(D)	32.9	52.3	(D)	(D)	(D)	(D)	(D)	9.5
RAIL...................	25	100.0	(D)	39.6	54.3	(D)	(D)	(D)	(D)	(D)	4.0
MOTOR CARRIER..........	56	100.0	(D)	30.6	56.2	(D)	(D)	(D)	(D)	(D)	7.3
PRIVATE TRUCK..........	5	100.0	(D)	24.5	12.4	(D)	(D)	(D)	(D)	(D)	57.2
AIR....................	-	100.0	(D)	84.7	12.9	(D)	(D)	(D)	(D)	(D)	.1
WATER..................	-	100.0	(D)	-	-	(D)	(D)	(D)	(D)	(D)	-
OTHER..................	-	100.0	(D)	74.1	8.2	(D)	(D)	(D)	(D)	(D)	-
UNKNOWN................	-	100.0	(D)	-	100.0	(D)	(D)	(D)	(D)	(D)	-
MOUNTAIN...............	84	100.0	(D)	19.5	72.9	(D)	(D)	(D)	(D)	(D)	7.0
RAIL...................	52	100.0	(D)	14.3	84.5	(D)	(D)	(D)	(D)	(D)	1.3
MOTOR CARRIER..........	29	100.0	(D)	30.5	59.0	(D)	(D)	(D)	(D)	(D)	8.9
PRIVATE TRUCK..........	2	100.0	(D)	-	-	(D)	(D)	(D)	(D)	(D)	100.0
AIR....................	-	100.0	(D)	54.5	13.8	(D)	(D)	(D)	(D)	(D)	-
WATER..................	-	100.0	(D)	-	-	(D)	(D)	(D)	(D)	(D)	-
OTHER..................	-	100.0	(D)	50.4	9.2	(D)	(D)	(D)	(D)	(D)	40.3
UNKNOWN................	-	100.0	(D)	-	-	(D)	(D)	(D)	(D)	(D)	-
PACIFIC................	152	100.0	(D)	36.4	47.0	(D)	(D)	(D)	(D)	(D)	10.0
RAIL...................	71	100.0	(D)	26.9	61.4	(D)	(D)	(D)	(D)	(D)	.3
MOTOR CARRIER..........	61	100.0	(D)	48.8	34.7	(D)	(D)	(D)	(D)	(D)	13.7
PRIVATE TRUCK..........	8	100.0	(D)	54.2	6.1	(D)	(D)	(D)	(D)	(D)	39.0
AIR....................	-	100.0	(D)	36.4	44.3	(D)	(D)	(D)	(D)	(D)	.1
WATER..................	8	100.0	(D)	15.3	67.2	(D)	(D)	(D)	(D)	(D)	17.5
OTHER..................	-	100.0	(D)	15.0	69.2	(D)	(D)	(D)	(D)	(D)	13.8
UNKNOWN................	1	100.0	(D)	-	-	(D)	(D)	(D)	(D)	(D)	100.0

See footnotes at end of table 4.

TABLE 4. **TCC GROUP 326**—Percent Distribution of Distance Shipped and Weight of Shipment, by Means of Transport: 1972

Distance shipped and weight of shipment[2][3]	Number	Percent distribution by means of transport							
		All means of transport	Rail	Motor carrier	Private truck	Air	Water	Other	Unknown
TONS OF SHIPMENTS	(thousands of tons)								
U.S. TOTAL.........	782	100.0	15.2	64.6	19.3	.2	.1	.3	.3
UNDER 100 MILES.........	94	100.0	1.0	55.3	43.0	-	-	.5	.1
UNDER 1000 POUNDS.....	8	100.0	-	75.2	19.4	.1	-	4.5	.8
1000 TO 9999 POUNDS...	41	100.0	-	50.2	49.5	-	-	.3	-
10000 TO 29999 POUNDS.	27	100.0	-	59.6	40.4	-	-	-	-
30000 TO 59999 POUNDS.	15	100.0	6.2	50.5	43.3	-	-	-	-
60000 TO 89999 POUNDS.	-	100.0	-	-	-	-	-	-	-
90000 POUNDS AND OVER.	-	100.0	-	-	-	-	-	-	-
100 TO 199 MILES........	101	100.0	-	61.3	37.6	-	.3	.8	-
UNDER 1000 POUNDS.....	7	100.0	-	89.2	6.0	.1	-	4.7	-
1000 TO 9999 POUNDS...	24	100.0	-	57.6	40.8	-	1.1	.5	-
10000 TO 29999 POUNDS.	31	100.0	-	63.6	35.5	-	-	.9	-
30000 TO 59999 POUNDS.	33	100.0	-	61.3	38.7	-	-	-	-
60000 TO 89999 POUNDS.	3	100.0	-	-	100.0	-	-	-	-
90000 POUNDS AND OVER.	-	100.0	-	-	-	-	-	-	-
200 TO 299 MILES........	73	100.0	2.4	74.2	22.7	-	-	.2	.4
UNDER 1000 POUNDS.....	8	100.0	-	93.3	4.3	.3	-	1.6	.5
1000 TO 9999 POUNDS...	24	100.0	.8	83.5	14.7	-	-	-	1.0
10000 TO 29999 POUNDS.	22	100.0	4.4	73.1	22.4	-	-	-	-
30000 TO 59999 POUNDS.	18	100.0	3.4	54.0	42.6	-	-	-	-
60000 TO 89999 POUNDS.	-	100.0	-	-	-	-	-	-	-
90000 POUNDS AND OVER.	-	100.0	-	-	-	-	-	-	-
300 TO 499 MILES........	154	100.0	7.3	75.4	16.7	.2	-	.3	.1
UNDER 1000 POUNDS.....	14	100.0	.1	94.2	1.1	1.7	-	2.9	.1
1000 TO 9999 POUNDS...	36	100.0	-	93.6	5.8	.2	-	.2	.2
10000 TO 29999 POUNDS.	54	100.0	3.2	73.8	23.0	-	-	-	-
30000 TO 59999 POUNDS.	42	100.0	21.8	51.8	26.4	-	-	-	-
60000 TO 89999 POUNDS.	8	100.0	4.4	95.6	-	-	-	-	-
90000 POUNDS AND OVER.	-	100.0	-	-	-	-	-	-	-
500 TO 999 MILES........	209	100.0	17.9	69.2	11.9	.2	-	.2	.6
UNDER 1000 POUNDS.....	15	100.0	.9	93.2	.5	2.9	-	2.1	.5
1000 TO 9999 POUNDS...	41	100.0	1.9	91.7	5.9	-	-	-	.4
10000 TO 29999 POUNDS.	53	100.0	15.3	69.2	13.5	-	-	-	2.0
30000 TO 59999 POUNDS.	81	100.0	33.8	47.4	18.7	-	-	-	-
60000 TO 89999 POUNDS.	16	100.0	-	100.0	-	-	-	-	-
90000 POUNDS AND OVER.	-	100.0	100.0	-	-	-	-	-	-
1000 TO 1499 MILES......	51	100.0	32.9	62.5	3.6	.8	-	.1	-
UNDER 1000 POUNDS.....	4	100.0	1.0	93.7	.4	3.9	-	.9	-
1000 TO 9999 POUNDS...	10	100.0	5.3	92.1	.2	2.3	-	-	-
10000 TO 29999 POUNDS.	5	100.0	-	97.9	2.1	-	-	-	-
30000 TO 59999 POUNDS.	29	100.0	50.9	43.3	5.9	-	-	-	-
60000 TO 89999 POUNDS.	-	100.0	-	-	-	-	-	-	-
90000 POUNDS AND OVER.	1	100.0	100.0	-	-	-	-	-	-
1500 MILES OR OVER......	97	100.0	51.9	43.7	2.8	.3	.8	.1	.3
UNDER 1000 POUNDS.....	11	100.0	8.4	86.4	1.5	2.5	-	1.2	-
1000 TO 9999 POUNDS...	11	100.0	11.7	79.4	3.0	-	3.1	-	2.7
10000 TO 29999 POUNDS.	5	100.0	23.6	68.5	-	-	7.9	-	-
30000 TO 59999 POUNDS.	39	100.0	62.9	31.5	5.6	-	-	-	-
60000 TO 89999 POUNDS.	29	100.0	74.4	25.6	-	-	-	-	-
90000 POUNDS AND OVER.	-	100.0	-	-	-	-	-	-	-
TON-MILES OF SHIPMENTS	(millions of ton-miles)								
U.S. TOTAL.........	512	100.0	30.1	59.3	9.1	.3	.5	.2	.4
UNDER 100 MILES.........	4	100.0	1.6	54.6	43.1	-	-	.6	-
UNDER 1000 POUNDS.....	-	100.0	-	81.8	12.7	.1	-	4.9	.5
1000 TO 9999 POUNDS...	1	100.0	-	53.7	46.2	-	-	.2	-
10000 TO 29999 POUNDS.	1	100.0	-	53.0	47.0	-	-	-	-
30000 TO 59999 POUNDS.	1	100.0	7.7	45.8	46.5	-	-	-	-
60000 TO 89999 POUNDS.	-	100.0	-	-	-	-	-	-	-
90000 POUNDS AND OVER.	-	100.0	-	-	-	-	-	-	-
100 TO 199 MILES........	15	100.0	-	60.2	38.7	-	.3	.8	-
UNDER 1000 POUNDS.....	1	100.0	-	89.0	6.2	.1	-	4.7	-
1000 TO 9999 POUNDS...	3	100.0	-	61.4	36.8	-	1.3	.5	-
10000 TO 29999 POUNDS.	4	100.0	-	62.4	36.6	-	-	1.1	-
30000 TO 59999 POUNDS.	5	100.0	-	56.2	43.8	-	-	-	-
60000 TO 89999 POUNDS.	-	100.0	-	-	100.0	-	-	-	-
90000 POUNDS AND OVER.	-	100.0	-	-	-	-	-	-	-

See footnotes at end of table 4.

TABLE 4. **TCC GROUP 326—Percent Distribution of Distance Shipped and Weight of Shipment, by Means of Transport: 1972**—Continued

Distance shipped and weight of shipment[2] [3]	Number	Percent distribution by means of transport							
		All means of transport	Rail	Motor carrier	Private truck	Air	Water	Other	Unknown
TON-MILES OF SHIPMENTS	(millions of ton-miles)								
200 TO 299 MILES........	19	100.0	2.5	74.2	22.7	-	-	.2	.4
UNDER 1000 POUNDS.....	2	100.0	-	93.3	4.4	.3	-	1.5	.4
1000 TO 9999 POUNDS...	6	100.0	.8	82.5	15.4	-	-	-	1.2
10000 TO 29999 POUNDS.	5	100.0	4.7	74.3	21.0	-	-	-	-
30000 TO 59999 POUNDS.	4	100.0	3.0	55.0	42.0	-	-	-	-
60000 TO 89999 POUNDS.	-	100.0	-	-	-	-	-	-	-
90000 POUNDS AND OVER.	-	100.0	-	-	-	-	-	-	-
300 TO 499 MILES........	60	100.0	8.0	75.0	16.4	.2	-	.3	.1
UNDER 1000 POUNDS.....	5	100.0	.1	94.2	1.0	1.7	-	2.9	.1
1000 TO 9999 POUNDS...	13	100.0	-	93.9	5.5	.2	-	.2	.2
10000 TO 29999 POUNDS.	21	100.0	3.0	73.9	23.1	-	-	-	-
30000 TO 59999 POUNDS.	16	100.0	24.3	51.1	24.6	-	-	-	-
60000 TO 89999 POUNDS.	2	100.0	5.3	94.7	-	-	-	-	-
90000 POUNDS AND OVER.	-	100.0	-	-	-	-	-	-	-
500 TO 999 MILES........	151	100.0	19.5	68.6	10.8	.2	-	.2	.7
UNDER 1000 POUNDS.....	11	100.0	1.0	92.9	.5	3.0	-	2.0	.6
1000 TO 9999 POUNDS...	29	100.0	2.3	90.7	6.5	-	-	-	.5
10000 TO 29999 POUNDS.	36	100.0	17.3	67.0	13.3	-	-	-	2.4
30000 TO 59999 POUNDS.	61	100.0	35.9	48.6	15.5	-	-	-	-
60000 TO 89999 POUNDS.	11	100.0	-	100.0	-	-	-	-	-
90000 POUNDS AND OVER.	-	100.0	100.0	-	-	-	-	-	-
1000 TO 1499 MILES......	61	100.0	33.4	62.1	3.5	.9	-	.1	-
UNDER 1000 POUNDS.....	5	100.0	1.0	93.7	.5	3.9	-	.9	-
1000 TO 9999 POUNDS...	12	100.0	5.9	91.2	.2	2.7	-	-	-
10000 TO 29999 POUNDS.	6	100.0	-	98.2	1.8	-	-	-	-
30000 TO 59999 POUNDS.	34	100.0	51.6	42.7	5.7	-	-	-	-
60000 TO 89999 POUNDS.	-	100.0	-	-	-	-	-	-	-
90000 POUNDS AND OVER.	2	100.0	100.0	-	-	-	-	-	-
1500 MILES OR OVER......	199	100.0	49.6	45.3	2.9	.3	1.3	.1	.4
UNDER 1000 POUNDS.....	23	100.0	8.7	86.0	1.4	2.6	-	1.2	-
1000 TO 9999 POUNDS...	24	100.0	12.0	75.5	3.0	-	6.1	-	3.4
10000 TO 29999 POUNDS.	11	100.0	23.2	66.5	-	-	10.3	-	-
30000 TO 59999 POUNDS.	86	100.0	59.2	35.4	5.4	-	-	-	-
60000 TO 89999 POUNDS.	54	100.0	74.4	25.6	-	-	-	-	-
90000 POUNDS AND OVER.	-	100.0	-	-	-	-	-	-	-

Note: Detail may not add to total due to rounding. The introductory table shows the estimates of sampling variability for tons; sampling variability for ton-miles has not been estimated. See the map in the Introduction for the States comprising the geographic divisions of the United States.

Shipments excluded from the survey are those moving by pipeline (primarily petroleum products from refineries), parcel post shipments, and commodities moved by own power (motorized vehicles, aircraft, etc.) or towed (prefabricated buildings, etc.). Local shipments (commodities shipped less than 25 miles from the plant) and shipments within the same city are also excluded. Shipments to Alaska and Hawaii from the 48 conterminous States and the District of Columbia are included; however, no data were obtained for shipments originating in Alaska and Hawaii.

- Represents zero or rounds to zero. (D) Withheld to avoid disclosing figures for individual companies.

[1] Production of this commodity is concentrated in the geographic divisions shown; figures and distributions for geographic divisions not shown are included in the total.

[2] Distances of shipments to foreign destinations are calculated only to the U.S. port of exit.

[3] Includes only shipments represented by bills of lading and invoices. Summary records which did not show individual weights of shipments are not included.

TCC 327. Concrete, Gypsum, and Plaster Products

Comparisons of Tons and Ton-Miles of Shipments for
Geographic Divisions of Origin and for Sampling Variability: 1972 and 1967

Geographic division of origin	Estimates				Relative sampling variability in tons (percent)	
	1972		1967		1972	1967
	Tons (thousands)	Ton-miles (millions)	Tons (thousands)	Ton-miles (millions)		
U.S. total	41,717	6,167	27,243	4,890	13.6	11.2
New England	678	38	827	55	37.4	(*)
Middle Atlantic	7,620	699	3,670	381	21.5	(*)
East North Central	6,026	600	4,409	767	27.6	(*)
West North Central	3,732	739	3,983	945	24.1	(*)
South Atlantic	8,165	829	5,724	739	31.5	(*)
East South Central	2,584	307	368	42	37.5	(*)
West South Central	7,312	2,046	3,297	1,099	44.4	(*)
Mountain	1,676	255	987	379	46.2	(*)
Pacific	3,919	650	3,978	483	33.5	(*)

(D) Withheld to avoid disclosing figures for individual companies.   (*) Data not published.

TABLE 1. **TCC GROUP 327**—Percent Distribution of Geographic Division of Origin and Distance Shipped, by Means of Transport: 1972

Geographic division of origin[1] and distance shipped[2]	Number	Percent distribution by means of transport							
		All means of transport	Rail	Motor carrier	Private truck	Air	Water	Other	Unknown
TONS OF SHIPMENTS	(thousands of tons)								
U.S. TOTAL..........	41 717	100.0	16.8	48.0	33.6	-	1.4	.1	.2
NEW ENGLAND.............	678	100.0	-	29.8	70.2	-	-	-	-
UNDER 100 MILES.......	559	100.0	-	16.8	83.2	-	-	-	-
100 TO 199 MILES......	104	100.0	-	94.1	5.9	-	-	-	-
200 TO 299 MILES......	14	100.0	-	67.3	32.7	-	-	-	-
300 TO 499 MILES......	-	100.0	-	-	-	-	-	-	-
500 TO 999 MILES......	-	100.0	-	-	-	-	-	-	-
1000 TO 1499 MILES....	-	100.0	-	-	-	-	-	-	-
1500 MILES OR OVER....	-	100.0	-	-	-	-	-	-	-
MIDDLE ATLANTIC.........	7 620	100.0	5.7	61.5	32.4	-	-	-	.3
UNDER 100 MILES.......	5 322	100.0	.7	58.2	40.8	-	-	-	.4
100 TO 199 MILES......	1 623	100.0	16.6	70.9	12.3	-	-	-	.3
200 TO 299 MILES......	461	100.0	2.5	83.4	14.0	-	-	-	-
300 TO 499 MILES......	107	100.0	29.9	51.1	19.0	-	-	-	-
500 TO 999 MILES......	74	100.0	80.2	3.1	16.0	-	-	-	.7
1000 TO 1499 MILES....	26	100.0	99.8	.2	-	-	-	-	-
1500 MILES OR OVER....	4	100.0	100.0	-	-	-	-	-	-
EAST NORTH CENTRAL......	6 026	100.0	7.7	58.9	33.2	-	-	.2	.1
UNDER 100 MILES.......	3 995	100.0	1.4	56.0	42.3	-	-	.2	.1
100 TO 199 MILES......	1 524	100.0	3.8	76.8	19.3	-	-	-	.2
200 TO 299 MILES......	215	100.0	55.2	37.6	7.2	-	-	-	-
300 TO 499 MILES......	116	100.0	66.6	32.0	1.4	-	-	-	-
500 TO 999 MILES......	141	100.0	85.8	13.1	1.0	-	-	-	-
1000 TO 1499 MILES....	32	100.0	98.8	.8	-	-	-	.4	-
1500 MILES OR OVER....	-	100.0	-	28.1	-	-	-	71.9	-
WEST NORTH CENTRAL......	3 732	100.0	45.9	33.7	19.8	-	-	-	.6
UNDER 100 MILES.......	1 100	100.0	21.3	32.5	45.7	-	-	-	.5
100 TO 199 MILES......	1 038	100.0	38.4	40.6	19.8	-	-	-	1.2
200 TO 299 MILES......	937	100.0	64.9	31.6	3.0	-	-	-	.5
300 TO 499 MILES......	431	100.0	76.8	23.2	-	-	-	-	-
500 TO 999 MILES......	211	100.0	60.9	38.1	1.0	-	-	-	-
1000 TO 1499 MILES....	13	100.0	100.0	-	-	-	-	-	-
1500 MILES OR OVER....	-	100.0	-	-	-	-	-	-	-
SOUTH ATLANTIC..........	8 165	100.0	11.3	37.3	51.2	-	-	-	.1
UNDER 100 MILES.......	5 420	100.0	3.5	24.7	71.8	-	-	.1	-
100 TO 199 MILES......	1 312	100.0	17.7	68.6	13.3	-	-	-	.4
200 TO 299 MILES......	1 224	100.0	31.7	60.3	8.0	-	-	-	-
300 TO 499 MILES......	190	100.0	58.5	37.5	4.0	-	-	-	-
500 TO 999 MILES......	17	100.0	31.1	10.1	58.8	-	-	-	-
1000 TO 1499 MILES....	-	100.0	-	-	-	-	-	-	-
1500 MILES OR OVER....	-	100.0	-	-	-	-	-	-	-
EAST SOUTH CENTRAL......	2 584	100.0	17.4	12.1	64.0	-	6.2	.3	-
UNDER 100 MILES.......	1 516	100.0	14.1	9.3	66.4	-	10.1	.1	-
100 TO 199 MILES......	651	100.0	9.1	17.9	70.9	-	1.0	1.0	.1
200 TO 299 MILES......	236	100.0	34.5	20.0	45.5	-	-	-	-
300 TO 499 MILES......	129	100.0	42.6	1.8	55.7	-	-	-	-
500 TO 999 MILES......	51	100.0	77.5	8.0	14.5	-	-	-	-
1000 TO 1499 MILES....	-	100.0	-	-	-	-	-	-	-
1500 MILES OR OVER....	-	100.0	-	-	-	-	-	-	-
WEST SOUTH CENTRAL......	7 312	100.0	23.5	59.7	11.9	-	4.6	-	.2
UNDER 100 MILES.......	2 098	100.0	3.7	45.0	35.9	-	15.5	-	-
100 TO 199 MILES......	1 285	100.0	28.5	62.8	7.6	-	1.2	-	-
200 TO 299 MILES......	1 203	100.0	6.7	92.1	1.2	-	-	-	-
300 TO 499 MILES......	1 725	100.0	26.6	73.3	-	-	-	-	-
500 TO 999 MILES......	871	100.0	70.3	27.9	-	-	-	-	1.8
1000 TO 1499 MILES....	86	100.0	96.2	1.5	2.2	-	-	-	-
1500 MILES OR OVER....	42	100.0	99.0	.1	.9	-	-	-	-
MOUNTAIN................	1 676	100.0	51.9	7.2	40.8	-	-	-	-
UNDER 100 MILES.......	891	100.0	37.3	.3	62.5	-	-	-	-
100 TO 199 MILES......	132	100.0	18.8	33.5	47.7	-	-	-	-
200 TO 299 MILES......	371	100.0	83.9	14.2	1.9	-	-	-	-
300 TO 499 MILES......	262	100.0	73.6	6.3	20.1	-	-	-	-
500 TO 999 MILES......	18	100.0	47.3	27.3	25.4	-	-	-	-
1000 TO 1499 MILES....	-	100.0	-	-	-	-	-	-	-
1500 MILES OR OVER....	-	100.0	-	-	-	-	-	-	-
PACIFIC.................	3 919	100.0	11.0	62.8	24.3	-	1.7	.2	.1
UNDER 100 MILES.......	2 587	100.0	3.7	65.5	29.6	-	.9	.1	.1
100 TO 199 MILES......	674	100.0	17.7	69.6	12.6	-	-	.1	-
200 TO 299 MILES......	263	100.0	14.9	52.1	33.0	-	-	-	-
300 TO 499 MILES......	182	100.0	31.6	63.8	4.1	-	-	-	.4
500 TO 999 MILES......	94	100.0	63.8	28.0	6.1	-	-	2.1	-
1000 TO 1499 MILES....	15	100.0	74.5	24.9	.1	-	-	.6	-
1500 MILES OR OVER....	100	100.0	44.3	13.7	-	-	42.1	-	-

See footnotes at end of table 4.

TABLE 1. **TCC GROUP 327—Percent Distribution of Geographic Division of Origin and Distance Shipped, by Means of Transport: 1972**—Continued

Geographic division of origin[1] and distance shipped[2]	Number	Percent distribution by means of transport							
		All means of transport	Rail	Motor carrier	Private truck	Air	Water	Other	Unknown
TON-MILES OF SHIPMENTS	(millions of ton-miles)								
U.S. TOTAL..........	6 167	100.0	37.2	45.1	15.1	-	2.2	.1	.3
NEW ENGLAND.............	38	100.0	-	51.1	48.9	-	-	-	-
UNDER 100 MILES.......	21	100.0	-	21.6	78.4	-	-	-	-
100 TO 199 MILES......	13	100.0	-	93.8	6.2	-	-	-	-
200 TO 299 MILES......	3	100.0	-	69.6	30.4	-	-	-	-
300 TO 499 MILES......	-	100.0	-	-	-	-	-	-	-
500 TO 999 MILES......	-	100.0	-	-	-	-	-	-	-
1000 TO 1499 MILES....	-	100.0	-	-	-	-	-	-	-
1500 MILES OR OVER....	-	100.0	-	-	-	-	-	-	-
MIDDLE ATLANTIC.........	699	100.0	19.1	59.0	21.6	-	-	-	.3
UNDER 100 MILES.......	242	100.0	.6	60.3	38.7	-	-	-	.5
100 TO 199 MILES......	214	100.0	16.0	71.5	12.3	-	-	-	.2
200 TO 299 MILES......	110	100.0	2.9	84.2	12.9	-	-	-	-
300 TO 499 MILES......	38	100.0	34.5	48.9	16.6	-	-	-	-
500 TO 999 MILES......	50	100.0	76.1	3.0	20.3	-	-	-	.6
1000 TO 1499 MILES....	32	100.0	99.8	.1	-	-	-	-	-
1500 MILES OR OVER....	10	100.0	100.0	-	-	-	-	-	-
EAST NORTH CENTRAL......	600	100.0	33.9	47.8	18.0	-	-	.2	.1
UNDER 100 MILES.......	153	100.0	2.3	56.1	41.3	-	-	.1	.1
100 TO 199 MILES......	203	100.0	4.5	76.2	19.1	-	-	-	.2
200 TO 299 MILES......	52	100.0	54.9	37.9	7.3	-	-	-	-
300 TO 499 MILES......	49	100.0	72.0	26.6	1.4	-	-	-	-
500 TO 999 MILES....	103	100.0	87.2	11.7	1.0	-	-	-	-
1000 TO 1499 MILES....	37	100.0	98.7	.9	-	-	-	.5	-
1500 MILES OR OVER....	-	100.0	-	25.9	-	-	-	74.1	-
WEST NORTH CENTRAL......	739	100.0	59.3	31.9	8.4	-	-	-	.4
UNDER 100 MILES.......	53	100.0	24.6	29.8	45.1	-	-	-	.6
100 TO 199 MILES......	160	100.0	37.5	42.9	18.3	-	-	-	1.2
200 TO 299 MILES......	222	100.0	65.0	31.7	2.9	-	-	-	.4
300 TO 499 MILES......	165	100.0	77.9	22.1	-	-	-	-	-
500 TO 999 MILES....	123	100.0	63.1	35.6	1.3	-	-	-	-
1000 TO 1499 MILES....	13	100.0	100.0	-	-	-	-	-	-
1500 MILES OR OVER....	-	100.0	-	-	-	-	-	-	-
SOUTH ATLANTIC.........	829	100.0	22.9	48.1	28.9	-	-	-	.1
UNDER 100 MILES.......	260	100.0	4.9	23.8	71.3	-	-	-	-
100 TO 199 MILES......	203	100.0	19.9	67.9	11.9	-	-	-	.3
200 TO 299 MILES......	291	100.0	32.5	59.9	7.6	-	-	-	-
300 TO 499 MILES......	62	100.0	58.6	37.7	3.8	-	-	-	-
500 TO 999 MILES....	12	100.0	42.9	7.8	49.3	-	-	-	-
1000 TO 1499 MILES....	-	100.0	-	-	-	-	-	-	-
1500 MILES OR OVER....	-	100.0	-	-	-	-	-	-	-
EAST SOUTH CENTRAL......	307	100.0	27.5	12.6	55.1	-	4.5	.3	-
UNDER 100 MILES.......	78	100.0	17.6	8.5	57.3	-	16.6	.1	-
100 TO 199 MILES......	93	100.0	8.8	18.5	70.8	-	1.0	.8	-
200 TO 299 MILES......	55	100.0	32.5	19.8	47.8	-	-	-	.1
300 TO 499 MILES......	47	100.0	43.3	1.7	55.0	-	-	-	-
500 TO 999 MILES....	31	100.0	74.7	9.3	16.0	-	-	-	-
1000 TO 1499 MILES....	-	100.0	-	-	-	-	-	-	-
1500 MILES OR OVER....	-	100.0	-	-	-	-	-	-	-
WEST SOUTH CENTRAL......	2 046	100.0	42.8	52.8	2.9	-	1.0	-	.5
UNDER 100 MILES.......	107	100.0	2.2	46.1	35.0	-	16.8	-	-
100 TO 199 MILES......	199	100.0	29.7	62.0	7.5	-	.9	-	-
200 TO 299 MILES......	290	100.0	6.8	91.9	1.4	-	-	-	-
300 TO 499 MILES......	674	100.0	28.5	71.5	-	-	-	-	-
500 TO 999 MILES....	587	100.0	71.6	26.7	-	-	-	-	1.7
1000 TO 1499 MILES....	112	100.0	96.2	1.6	2.2	-	-	-	-
1500 MILES OR OVER....	73	100.0	99.1	.1	.8	-	-	-	-
MOUNTAIN................	255	100.0	64.8	10.9	24.3	-	-	-	-
UNDER 100 MILES.......	38	100.0	18.8	.4	80.8	-	-	-	-
100 TO 199 MILES......	19	100.0	22.2	36.9	40.9	-	-	-	-
200 TO 299 MILES......	93	100.0	84.5	13.6	1.9	-	-	-	-
300 TO 499 MILES......	94	100.0	75.0	5.6	19.4	-	-	-	-
500 TO 999 MILES....	10	100.0	45.5	25.9	28.6	-	-	-	-
1000 TO 1499 MILES....	-	100.0	-	-	-	-	-	-	-
1500 MILES OR OVER....	-	100.0	-	-	-	-	-	-	-
PACIFIC.................	650	100.0	31.1	43.0	9.7	-	15.9	.3	.1
UNDER 100 MILES.......	110	100.0	2.6	74.1	22.6	-	.5	-	.2
100 TO 199 MILES......	102	100.0	19.1	67.4	13.3	-	-	.2	-
200 TO 299 MILES......	60	100.0	16.6	53.6	29.9	-	-	-	-
300 TO 499 MILES......	65	100.0	34.3	61.3	4.0	-	-	-	.4
500 TO 999 MILES....	64	100.0	65.5	26.5	5.8	-	-	2.2	-
1000 TO 1499 MILES....	17	100.0	74.8	24.4	.1	-	-	.7	-
1500 MILES OR OVER....	229	100.0	39.8	15.3	-	-	44.9	-	-

See footnotes at end of table 4.

TABLE 2. **TCC GROUP 327**—Percent Distribution of Geographic Division of Origin and Means of Transport, by Geographic Division of Destination: 1972

Geographic division of origin[1] and means of transport	Number (thousands of tons)	Percent distribution by division of destination								
		U.S. total	New England	Middle Atlantic	East North Central	West North Central	South Atlantic	East South Central	West South Central	Mountain	Pacific
TONS OF SHIPMENTS											
U.S. TOTAL..............	41 717	100.0	3.4	16.9	17.2	3.5	24.7	8.3	11.7	3.9	10.3
RAIL................	7 011	100.0	1.7	7.1	14.5	3.2	23.1	14.9	13.0	10.2	12.3
MOTOR CARRIER........	20 007	100.0	4.0	21.1	19.6	3.4	19.8	5.6	13.3	1.0	12.2
PRIVATE TRUCK........	14 026	100.0	3.6	16.6	15.8	3.8	33.7	7.9	7.0	5.0	6.6
AIR.................	-	100.0	-	-	-	-	88.0	-	-	-	12.0
WATER...............	565	100.0	-	-	-	-	-	-	27.1	61.2	-	11.7
OTHER...............	28	100.0	.1	-	34.2	.4	12.6	27.3	.1	.1	25.1
UNKNOWN.............	78	100.0	3.1	27.8	35.7	10.8	6.0	.7	11.5	.9	3.5
NEW ENGLAND............	678	100.0	85.2	14.8	-	-	-	-	-	-	-
RAIL................	-	100.0	-	-	-	-	-	-	-	-	-
MOTOR CARRIER........	202	100.0	53.0	47.0	-	-	-	-	-	-	-
PRIVATE TRUCK........	476	100.0	98.9	1.1	-	-	-	-	-	-	-
AIR.................	-	100.0	-	-	-	-	-	-	-	-	-
WATER...............	-	100.0	-	-	-	-	-	-	-	-	-
OTHER...............	-	100.0	-	-	-	-	-	-	-	-	-
UNKNOWN.............	-	100.0	-	-	-	-	-	-	-	-	-
MIDDLE ATLANTIC........	7 620	100.0	9.9	81.6	1.5	.2	6.5	.2	-	.1	.1
RAIL................	437	100.0	10.4	67.1	-	-	16.5	3.8	.2	.9	1.0
MOTOR CARRIER........	4 689	100.0	14.3	77.9	1.8	-	6.0	-	-	-	-
PRIVATE TRUCK........	2 468	100.0	1.2	91.2	1.4	.5	5.7	-	-	-	-
AIR.................	-	100.0	-	-	-	-	88.0	-	-	-	12.0
WATER...............	-	100.0	-	-	-	-	-	-	-	-	-
OTHER...............	-	100.0	-	50.8	49.2	-	-	-	-	-	-
UNKNOWN.............	24	100.0	9.7	88.2	-	-	-	2.1	-	-	-
EAST NORTH CENTRAL......	6 026	100.0	1.2	7.0	87.4	.5	2.6	.3	.9	.1	-
RAIL................	461	100.0	13.0	31.9	21.4	1.2	15.0	4.0	11.8	1.7	-
MOTOR CARRIER........	3 547	100.0	.3	7.3	89.9	.2	2.2	-	-	-	-
PRIVATE TRUCK........	2 000	100.0	-	.7	98.0	.7	.5	-	-	-	-
AIR.................	-	100.0	-	-	-	-	-	-	-	-	-
WATER...............	-	100.0	-	-	-	-	-	-	-	-	-
OTHER...............	10	100.0	-	-	94.4	.2	.9	-	.4	.4	3.8
UNKNOWN.............	6	100.0	-	.4	99.6	-	-	-	-	-	-
WEST NORTH CENTRAL......	3 732	100.0	.2	1.9	44.9	33.5	1.2	13.1	4.7	.4	-
RAIL................	1 714	100.0	.5	.9	49.4	9.9	2.7	27.3	8.7	.7	-
MOTOR CARRIER........	1 256	100.0	-	4.6	47.1	46.3	-	1.5	.3	.2	-
PRIVATE TRUCK........	739	100.0	-	-	29.5	67.4	-	-	3.1	-	-
AIR.................	-	100.0	-	-	-	-	-	-	-	-	-
WATER...............	-	100.0	-	-	-	-	-	-	-	-	-
OTHER...............	-	100.0	-	-	-	-	-	-	-	-	-
UNKNOWN.............	22	100.0	-	-	96.2	3.8	-	-	-	-	-
SOUTH ATLANTIC.........	8 165	100.0	.1	3.0	.1	.1	96.2	.6	-	-	-
RAIL................	925	100.0	.5	3.6	-	.4	95.3	.2	-	-	-
MOTOR CARRIER........	3 048	100.0	-	5.2	.4	-	93.9	.5	-	-	-
PRIVATE TRUCK........	4 182	100.0	-	1.2	-	-	98.0	.7	-	-	-
AIR.................	-	100.0	-	-	-	-	-	-	-	-	-
WATER...............	-	100.0	-	-	-	-	-	-	-	-	-
OTHER...............	3	100.0	-	-	-	-	99.9	.1	-	-	-
UNKNOWN.............	4	100.0	-	-	-	-	100.0	-	-	-	-
EAST SOUTH CENTRAL......	2 584	100.0	-	.2	.7	.2	24.7	70.4	3.8	-	-
RAIL................	450	100.0	-	-	4.1	-	19.3	76.6	-	-	-
MOTOR CARRIER........	311	100.0	-	1.3	.2	-	22.3	76.0	.1	-	-
PRIVATE TRUCK........	1 655	100.0	-	-	-	.3	29.1	65.0	5.6	-	-
AIR.................	-	100.0	-	-	-	-	-	-	-	-	-
WATER...............	159	100.0	-	-	-	-	-	96.1	3.9	-	-
OTHER...............	7	100.0	-	-	-	-	-	100.0	-	-	-
UNKNOWN.............	-	100.0	-	-	-	-	-	6.4	93.6	-	-
WEST SOUTH CENTRAL......	7 312	100.0	-	-	1.1	2.0	15.3	14.4	62.1	3.8	1.3
RAIL................	1 720	100.0	-	.1	1.9	2.4	26.4	11.3	39.6	12.9	5.4
MOTOR CARRIER........	4 368	100.0	-	-	1.1	2.2	15.2	19.5	60.7	1.3	-
PRIVATE TRUCK........	867	100.0	-	-	-	-	-	.2	.9	98.8	-	-
AIR.................	-	100.0	-	-	-	-	-	-	-	-	-
WATER...............	339	100.0	-	-	-	-	-	-	100.0	-	-
OTHER...............	-	100.0	28.8	-	43.2	-	25.9	2.1	-	-	-
UNKNOWN.............	15	100.0	-	-	-	48.1	-	-	51.9	-	-
MOUNTAIN...............	1 676	100.0	-	-	-	-	-	-	.5	64.3	35.2
RAIL................	870	100.0	-	-	-	-	-	-	.6	44.0	55.4
MOTOR CARRIER........	121	100.0	-	-	-	-	-	-	-	22.6	77.4
PRIVATE TRUCK........	684	100.0	-	-	-	-	-	-	.5	97.5	2.1
AIR.................	-	100.0	-	-	-	-	-	-	-	-	-
WATER...............	-	100.0	-	-	-	-	-	-	-	-	-
OTHER...............	-	100.0	-	-	-	-	-	-	-	-	-
UNKNOWN.............	-	100.0	-	-	-	-	-	-	-	-	-
PACIFIC................	3 919	100.0	-	.2	.7	.1	.3	-	.4	6.0	92.4
RAIL................	429	100.0	.3	1.8	5.2	.7	2.3	-	3.8	19.9	66.1
MOTOR CARRIER........	2 461	100.0	-	-	.2	-	-	-	-	4.6	95.2
PRIVATE TRUCK........	951	100.0	-	-	-	-	-	-	-	3.7	96.3
AIR.................	-	100.0	-	-	-	-	-	-	-	-	-
WATER...............	66	100.0	-	-	-	-	-	-	-	-	100.0
OTHER...............	6	100.0	-	-	-	1.3	-	-	-	-	98.7
UNKNOWN.............	3	100.0	-	-	-	-	-	-	-	21.2	78.8

See footnotes at end of table 4.

TABLE 2. TCC GROUP 327—Percent Distribution of Geographic Division of Origin and Means of Transport, by Geographic Division of Destination: 1972—Continued

Geographic division of origin[1] and means of transport	Number	Percent distribution by division of destination									
		U.S. total	New England	Middle Atlantic	East North Central	West North Central	South Atlantic	East South Central	West South Central	Mountain	Pacific
TON-MILES OF SHIPMENTS	(millions of ton-miles)										
U.S. TOTAL................	6 167	100.0	3.5	9.8	13.0	4.0	26.9	10.2	14.1	5.6	12.9
RAIL..................	2 293	100.0	3.2	4.8	11.6	3.3	26.2	12.5	12.8	9.6	16.0
MOTOR CARRIER.........	2 781	100.0	4.1	13.1	14.5	4.3	25.9	9.2	17.2	2.1	9.5
PRIVATE TRUCK.........	934	100.0	2.6	13.4	13.8	5.2	35.6	8.2	7.9	7.1	6.2
AIR...................	-	100.0	-	-	-	-	75.8	-	-	-	24.2
WATER.................	137	100.0	-	-	-	-	-	9.5	15.1	-	75.4
OTHER.................	3	100.0	1.2	.1	5.9	3.5	6.9	21.3	.7	1.4	59.0
UNKNOWN...............	16	100.0	.8	8.6	21.4	32.3	4.1	1.9	28.0	1.6	1.2
NEW ENGLAND..............	38	100.0	65.4	34.6	-	-	-	-	-	-	-
RAIL..................	-	100.0	-	-	-	-	-	-	-	-	-
MOTOR CARRIER.........	19	100.0	38.0	62.0	-	-	-	-	-	-	-
PRIVATE TRUCK.........	18	100.0	94.0	6.0	-	-	-	-	-	-	-
AIR...................	-	100.0	-	-	-	-	-	-	-	-	-
WATER.................	-	100.0	-	-	-	-	-	-	-	-	-
OTHER.................	-	100.0	-	-	-	-	-	-	-	-	-
UNKNOWN...............	-	100.0	-	-	-	-	-	-	-	-	-
MIDDLE ATLANTIC..........	699	100.0	18.4	58.3	3.0	1.5	14.3	2.0	.2	.8	1.5
RAIL..................	133	100.0	17.8	27.0	-	-	31.6	10.4	.9	4.4	7.8
MOTOR CARRIER.........	412	100.0	24.0	61.8	4.6	-	9.5	-	-	-	-
PRIVATE TRUCK.........	150	100.0	3.5	76.3	1.1	6.8	12.3	-	-	-	-
AIR...................	-	100.0	-	-	-	-	75.8	-	-	-	24.2
WATER.................	-	100.0	-	-	-	-	-	-	-	-	-
OTHER.................	-	100.0	-	21.4	78.6	-	-	-	-	-	-
UNKNOWN...............	1	100.0	7.6	75.9	-	-	-	16.5	-	-	-
EAST NORTH CENTRAL......	600	100.0	7.5	14.6	54.6	1.3	10.3	.9	8.8	1.8	.1
RAIL..................	203	100.0	18.1	19.8	5.6	1.0	22.0	2.4	25.9	5.2	-
MOTOR CARRIER.........	287	100.0	2.6	15.9	74.8	1.2	5.3	-	.1	.2	-
PRIVATE TRUCK.........	108	100.0	.7	1.5	93.8	2.3	1.6	.2	-	-	-
AIR...................	-	100.0	-	-	-	-	-	-	-	-	-
WATER.................	-	100.0	-	-	-	-	-	-	-	-	-
OTHER.................	1	100.0	-	-	18.8	.7	11.4	-	2.5	4.9	61.7
UNKNOWN...............	-	100.0	-	3.6	96.4	-	-	-	-	-	-
WEST NORTH CENTRAL......	739	100.0	1.1	5.5	44.5	19.8	3.4	14.0	10.4	1.3	-
RAIL..................	438	100.0	1.9	2.1	40.4	9.1	5.8	22.8	16.1	1.9	-
MOTOR CARRIER.........	235	100.0	-	13.4	52.0	31.7	-	1.4	1.0	.6	-
PRIVATE TRUCK.........	61	100.0	-	-	42.5	51.3	-	-	6.2	-	-
AIR...................	-	100.0	-	-	-	-	-	-	-	-	-
WATER.................	-	100.0	-	-	-	-	-	-	-	-	-
OTHER.................	-	100.0	-	-	-	-	-	-	-	-	-
UNKNOWN...............	3	100.0	-	-	98.0	2.0	-	-	-	-	-
SOUTH ATLANTIC..........	829	100.0	.3	3.5	.2	.5	93.6	1.9	-	-	-
RAIL..................	189	100.0	.8	2.2	-	1.8	94.2	.9	-	-	-
MOTOR CARRIER.........	398	100.0	.2	4.4	.4	-	93.7	1.2	-	-	-
PRIVATE TRUCK.........	240	100.0	.1	2.9	-	.4	92.9	3.7	-	-	-
AIR...................	-	100.0	-	-	-	-	-	-	-	-	-
WATER.................	-	100.0	-	-	-	-	-	-	-	-	-
OTHER.................	-	100.0	-	-	-	-	99.3	.7	-	-	-
UNKNOWN...............	-	100.0	-	-	-	-	100.0	-	-	-	-
EAST SOUTH CENTRAL......	307	100.0	-	1.0	2.9	1.0	42.8	47.7	4.7	-	-
RAIL..................	84	100.0	-	-	10.3	-	41.0	48.8	-	-	-
MOTOR CARRIER.........	38	100.0	-	7.6	.4	-	26.3	65.6	.1	-	-
PRIVATE TRUCK.........	169	100.0	-	-	-	1.8	51.3	39.0	7.9	-	-
AIR...................	-	100.0	-	-	-	-	-	-	-	-	-
WATER.................	13	100.0	-	-	-	-	-	93.6	6.4	-	-
OTHER.................	-	100.0	-	-	-	-	-	100.0	-	-	-
UNKNOWN...............	-	100.0	-	-	-	-	-	-	2.6	97.4	-
WEST SOUTH CENTRAL......	2 046	100.0	-	.1	3.2	3.5	26.3	17.0	34.6	8.0	7.2
RAIL..................	875	100.0	-	.1	3.2	2.9	28.9	14.2	17.8	16.2	16.8
MOTOR CARRIER.........	1 080	100.0	-	-	3.5	3.9	26.1	20.5	43.8	2.1	.1
PRIVATE TRUCK.........	59	100.0	-	1.0	-	-	-	4.2	1.8	93.1	-
AIR...................	-	100.0	-	-	-	-	-	-	-	-	-
WATER.................	19	100.0	-	-	-	-	-	-	100.0	-	-
OTHER.................	-	100.0	44.1	-	27.1	-	27.7	1.1	-	-	-
UNKNOWN...............	10	100.0	-	-	-	53.8	-	-	46.2	-	-
MOUNTAIN................	255	100.0	-	-	-	-	-	-	.7	33.9	65.4
RAIL..................	165	100.0	-	-	-	-	-	-	.7	14.6	84.6
MOTOR CARRIER.........	27	100.0	-	-	-	-	-	-	-	18.1	81.9
PRIVATE TRUCK.........	62	100.0	-	-	-	-	-	-	1.1	92.3	6.6
AIR...................	-	100.0	-	-	-	-	-	-	-	-	-
WATER.................	-	100.0	-	-	-	-	-	-	-	-	-
OTHER.................	-	100.0	-	-	-	-	-	-	-	-	-
UNKNOWN...............	-	100.0	-	-	-	-	-	-	-	-	-
PACIFIC.................	650	100.0	.5	2.9	7.4	.7	3.5	-	2.1	10.7	72.2
RAIL..................	201	100.0	1.4	9.2	20.1	2.1	11.1	.1	6.2	15.0	34.7
MOTOR CARRIER.........	279	100.0	.2	-	2.6	-	-	-	.5	10.7	86.0
PRIVATE TRUCK.........	62	100.0	-	-	-	-	-	-	-	14.5	85.5
AIR...................	-	100.0	-	-	-	-	-	-	-	-	-
WATER.................	103	100.0	-	-	-	-	-	-	-	-	100.0
OTHER.................	1	100.0	-	.2	-	7.3	-	-	-	.1	92.4
UNKNOWN...............	-	100.0	-	-	-	-	-	-	-	57.4	42.6

See footnotes at end of table 4.

TABLE 3. **TCC GROUP 327—Percent Distribution of Geographic Division of Destination and Means of Transport, by Geographic Division of Origin: 1972**

Geographic division of destination and means of transport	Number	Percent distribution by division of origin[1]									
		U.S. total	New England	Middle Atlantic	East North Central	West North Central	South Atlantic	East South Central	West South Central	Mountain	Pacific
TONS OF SHIPMENTS	(thousands of tons)										
U.S. TOTAL	41 717	100.0	1.6	18.3	14.4	8.9	19.6	6.2	17.5	4.0	9.4
RAIL	7 011	100.0	–	6.2	6.6	24.5	13.2	6.4	24.5	12.4	6.1
MOTOR CARRIER	20 007	100.0	1.0	23.4	17.7	6.3	15.2	1.6	21.8	.6	12.3
PRIVATE TRUCK	14 026	100.0	3.4	17.6	14.3	5.3	29.8	11.8	6.2	4.9	6.8
AIR	–	100.0	–	100.0	–	–	–	–	–	–	–
WATER	565	100.0	–	–	–	–	–	28.2	60.1	–	11.7
OTHER	28	100.0	–	–	36.0	–	12.2	27.3	.4	–	24.1
UNKNOWN	78	100.0	–	31.5	8.4	28.4	6.0	1.1	20.2	–	4.4
NEW ENGLAND	1 418	100.0	40.7	53.0	5.1	.6	.6	–	–	–	.1
RAIL	119	100.0	–	38.2	50.0	6.7	4.1	–	–	–	1.0
MOTOR CARRIER	793	100.0	13.5	84.8	1.4	–	.2	–	–	–	–
PRIVATE TRUCK	503	100.0	93.5	6.0	.2	–	.3	–	–	–	–
AIR	–	100.0	–	–	–	–	–	–	–	–	–
WATER	–	100.0	–	–	–	–	–	–	–	–	–
OTHER	–	100.0	–	–	–	–	–	–	100.0	–	–
UNKNOWN	2	100.0	–	100.0	–	–	–	–	–	–	–
MIDDLE ATLANTIC	7 070	100.0	1.4	88.0	5.9	1.0	3.4	.1	–	–	.1
RAIL	497	100.0	–	59.1	29.6	3.0	6.6	–	.2	–	1.6
MOTOR CARRIER	4 227	100.0	2.2	86.4	6.1	1.4	3.7	.1	–	–	–
PRIVATE TRUCK	2 323	100.0	.2	96.9	.6	–	2.2	–	–	–	–
AIR	–	100.0	–	–	–	–	–	–	–	–	–
WATER	–	100.0	–	–	–	–	–	–	–	–	–
OTHER	–	100.0	–	15.2	–	–	–	–	–	–	84.8
UNKNOWN	21	100.0	–	99.9	.1	–	–	–	–	–	–
EAST NORTH CENTRAL	7 194	100.0	–	1.6	73.2	23.3	.2	.3	1.1	–	.4
RAIL	1 017	100.0	–	–	9.7	83.2	–	1.8	3.1	–	2.2
MOTOR CARRIER	3 925	100.0	–	2.1	81.2	15.1	.3	–	1.2	–	.1
PRIVATE TRUCK	2 213	100.0	–	1.6	88.6	9.8	–	–	–	–	–
AIR	–	100.0	–	–	–	–	–	–	–	–	–
WATER	–	100.0	–	–	–	–	–	–	–	–	–
OTHER	9	100.0	–	–	99.5	–	–	–	.5	–	–
UNKNOWN	28	100.0	–	–	23.4	76.6	–	–	–	–	–
WEST NORTH CENTRAL	1 449	100.0	–	.8	1.9	86.3	.3	.4	10.1	–	.2
RAIL	222	100.0	–	–	2.5	76.0	1.6	–	18.6	–	1.3
MOTOR CARRIER	686	100.0	–	–	1.2	84.7	–	–	14.1	–	–
PRIVATE TRUCK	530	100.0	–	2.2	2.7	93.9	.2	1.0	. –	–	–
AIR	–	100.0	–	–	–	–	–	–	–	–	–
WATER	–	100.0	–	–	–	–	–	–	–	–	–
OTHER	–	100.0	–	–	17.6	–	–	–	–	–	82.4
UNKNOWN	8	100.0	–	–	–	9.9	–	–	90.1	–	–
SOUTH ATLANTIC	10 320	100.0	–	4.8	1.5	.4	76.1	6.2	10.9	–	.1
RAIL	1 621	100.0	–	4.5	4.3	2.8	54.4	5.3	28.0	–	.6
MOTOR CARRIER	3 957	100.0	–	7.1	2.0	–	72.3	1.8	16.8	–	–
PRIVATE TRUCK	4 733	100.0	–	3.0	.2	–	86.6	10.2	–	–	–
AIR	–	100.0	–	100.0	–	–	–	–	–	–	–
WATER	–	100.0	–	–	–	–	–	–	–	–	–
OTHER	3	100.0	–	–	2.7	–	96.4	–	.9	–	–
UNKNOWN	4	100.0	–	–	–	–	100.0	–	–	–	–
EAST SOUTH CENTRAL	3 443	100.0	–	.5	.6	14.2	1.4	52.8	30.6	–	–
RAIL	1 045	100.0	–	1.6	1.8	44.8	.2	33.0	18.6	–	–
MOTOR CARRIER	1 122	100.0	–	–	–	1.7	1.4	21.1	75.8	–	–
PRIVATE TRUCK	1 114	100.0	–	–	–	–	2.7	96.6	.7	–	–
AIR	–	100.0	–	–	–	–	–	–	–	–	–
WATER	152	100.0	–	–	–	–	–	100.0	–	–	–
OTHER	7	100.0	–	–	–	–	–	99.9	–	–	–
UNKNOWN	–	100.0	–	90.0	–	–	–	10.0	–	–	–
WEST SOUTH CENTRAL	4 896	100.0	–	–	1.1	3.6	–	2.0	92.7	.2	.4
RAIL	908	100.0	–	.1	6.0	16.5	–	–	75.0	.6	1.8
MOTOR CARRIER	2 657	100.0	–	–	–	.2	–	–	99.8	–	–
PRIVATE TRUCK	975	100.0	–	–	–	2.3	–	9.4	87.9	.3	–
AIR	–	100.0	–	–	–	–	–	–	–	–	–
WATER	346	100.0	–	–	–	–	–	1.8	98.2	–	–
OTHER	–	100.0	–	–	100.0	–	–	–	–	–	–
UNKNOWN	9	100.0	–	–	–	–	–	9.3	90.7	–	–
MOUNTAIN	1 615	100.0	–	.3	.5	.9	–	–	17.2	66.7	14.5
RAIL	714	100.0	–	.6	1.1	1.7	–	–	31.1	53.6	11.9
MOTOR CARRIER	197	100.0	–	–	.2	1.1	–	–	28.0	13.8	56.9
PRIVATE TRUCK	702	100.0	–	–	–	–	–	–	–	95.0	5.0
AIR	–	100.0	–	–	–	–	–	–	–	–	–
WATER	–	100.0	–	–	–	–	–	–	–	–	–
OTHER	–	100.0	–	–	94.7	–	–	–	–	–	5.3
UNKNOWN	–	100.0	–	–	–	–	–	–	–	–	100.0
PACIFIC	4 309	100.0	–	.1	–	–	–	–	2.2	13.7	84.0
RAIL	863	100.0	–	.5	–	–	–	–	10.8	55.8	32.8
MOTOR CARRIER	2 438	100.0	–	–	–	–	–	–	–	3.8	96.1
PRIVATE TRUCK	930	100.0	–	–	–	–	–	–	–	1.5	98.5
AIR	–	100.0	–	100.0	–	–	–	–	–	–	–
WATER	66	100.0	–	–	–	–	–	–	–	–	100.0
OTHER	7	100.0	–	–	5.4	–	–	–	–	–	94.6
UNKNOWN	2	100.0	–	–	–	–	–	–	–	–	100.0

See footnotes at end of table 4.

TABLE 3. **TCC GROUP 327—Percent Distribution of Geographic Division of Destination and Means of Transport, by Geographic Division of Origin: 1972**—Continued

Geographic division of destination and means of transport	Number	Percent distribution by division of origin[1]									
		U.S. total	New England	Middle Atlantic	East North Central	West North Central	South Atlantic	East South Central	West South Central	Mountain	Pacific
TON-MILES OF SHIPMENTS	(millions of ton-miles)										
U.S. TOTAL	6 167	100.0	.6	11.3	9.7	12.0	13.5	5.0	33.2	4.2	10.5
RAIL	2 293	100.0	-	5.8	8.9	19.1	8.3	3.7	38.2	7.2	8.8
MOTOR CARRIER	2 781	100.0	.7	14.8	10.3	8.5	14.3	1.4	38.8	1.0	10.1
PRIVATE TRUCK	934	100.0	2.0	16.2	11.6	6.6	25.7	18.1	6.4	6.7	6.7
AIR	-	100.0	-	100.0	-	-	-	-	-	-	-
WATER	137	100.0	-	-	-	-	-	10.2	14.4	-	75.4
OTHER	3	100.0	-	-	27.7	-	3.0	21.2	2.6	-	45.4
UNKNOWN	16	100.0	-	11.2	3.0	19.0	4.1	.5	59.4	-	2.7
NEW ENGLAND	212	100.0	11.9	60.2	21.1	3.9	1.2	-	-	-	1.6
RAIL	73	100.0	-	32.4	50.3	11.3	2.1	-	-	-	3.9
MOTOR CARRIER	115	100.0	6.5	85.9	6.4	-	.7	-	-	-	.5
PRIVATE TRUCK	24	100.0	73.7	21.9	3.0	-	1.4	-	-	-	-
AIR	-	100.0	-	-	-	-	-	-	-	-	-
WATER	-	100.0	-	-	-	-	-	-	-	-	-
OTHER	-	100.0	-	-	-	-	-	-	100.0	-	-
UNKNOWN	-	100.0	-	100.0	-	-	-	-	-	-	-
MIDDLE ATLANTIC	602	100.0	2.2	67.7	14.5	6.8	4.8	.5	.4	-	3.1
RAIL	109	100.0	-	32.9	36.7	8.4	3.9	-	1.2	-	17.0
MOTOR CARRIER	365	100.0	3.3	69.8	12.5	8.6	4.8	.8	.1	-	-
PRIVATE TRUCK	125	100.0	.9	91.8	1.3	-	5.6	-	.5	-	-
AIR	-	100.0	-	-	-	-	-	-	-	-	-
WATER	-	100.0	-	.4	-	-	-	-	-	-	-
OTHER	-	100.0	-	.4	-	-	-	-	-	-	99.6
UNKNOWN	1	100.0	-	98.8	1.2	-	-	-	-	-	-
EAST NORTH CENTRAL	803	100.0	-	2.6	40.9	41.0	.2	1.1	8.2	-	6.0
RAIL	266	100.0	-	-	4.3	66.6	-	3.3	10.6	-	15.3
MOTOR CARRIER	403	100.0	-	4.7	53.2	30.4	.4	-	9.4	-	1.8
PRIVATE TRUCK	129	100.0	-	1.3	78.4	20.3	-	-	-	-	-
AIR	-	100.0	-	-	-	-	-	-	-	-	-
WATER	-	100.0	-	-	-	-	-	-	-	-	-
OTHER	-	100.0	-	-	87.9	-	-	-	12.1	-	-
UNKNOWN	3	100.0	-	-	13.3	86.7	-	-	-	-	-
WEST NORTH CENTRAL	248	100.0	-	4.2	3.2	58.9	1.7	1.2	29.1	-	1.7
RAIL	74	100.0	-	-	2.8	53.2	4.6	-	33.7	-	5.6
MOTOR CARRIER	119	100.0	-	-	2.8	62.4	-	-	34.7	-	-
PRIVATE TRUCK	48	100.0	-	21.2	5.2	65.4	1.8	6.4	-	-	-
AIR	-	100.0	-	-	-	-	-	-	-	-	-
WATER	-	100.0	-	-	-	-	-	-	-	-	-
OTHER	-	100.0	-	-	5.3	-	-	-	-	-	94.7
UNKNOWN	5	100.0	-	-	-	1.2	-	-	98.8	-	-
SOUTH ATLANTIC	1 656	100.0	-	6.0	3.7	1.5	46.9	7.9	32.5	-	1.4
RAIL	601	100.0	-	7.0	7.4	4.2	29.7	5.7	42.1	-	3.7
MOTOR CARRIER	721	100.0	-	5.4	2.1	-	51.9	1.4	39.1	-	-
PRIVATE TRUCK	332	100.0	-	5.6	.5	-	67.1	26.1	.7	-	-
AIR	-	100.0	-	100.0	-	-	-	-	-	-	-
WATER	-	100.0	-	-	-	-	-	-	-	-	-
OTHER	-	100.0	-	-	45.9	-	43.5	-	10.6	-	-
UNKNOWN	-	100.0	-	-	-	-	100.0	-	-	-	-
EAST SOUTH CENTRAL	631	100.0	-	2.2	.8	16.4	2.4	23.2	54.9	-	-
RAIL	285	100.0	-	4.8	1.7	35.0	.6	14.4	43.4	-	-
MOTOR CARRIER	255	100.0	-	-	-	1.3	1.9	10.0	86.8	-	-
PRIVATE TRUCK	76	100.0	-	-	.2	-	11.7	86.6	1.4	-	-
AIR	-	100.0	-	-	-	-	-	-	-	-	-
WATER	13	100.0	-	-	-	-	-	100.0	-	-	-
OTHER	-	100.0	-	-	-	-	.1	99.8	.1	-	-
UNKNOWN	-	100.0	-	99.3	-	-	-	-	.7	-	-
WEST SOUTH CENTRAL	869	100.0	-	.1	6.1	8.8	-	1.7	81.5	.2	1.6
RAIL	293	100.0	-	.4	18.0	24.0	-	-	52.9	.4	4.3
MOTOR CARRIER	477	100.0	-	-	.1	.5	-	-	99.1	-	.3
PRIVATE TRUCK	73	100.0	-	-	-	5.2	-	18.2	75.6	.9	-
AIR	-	100.0	-	-	-	-	-	-	-	-	-
WATER	20	100.0	-	-	-	-	-	4.3	95.7	-	-
OTHER	-	100.0	-	-	100.0	-	-	-	-	-	-
UNKNOWN	4	100.0	-	-	-	-	-	1.8	98.2	-	-
MOUNTAIN	346	100.0	-	1.7	3.2	2.7	-	-	47.3	25.0	20.1
RAIL	220	100.0	-	2.7	4.8	3.7	-	-	64.1	11.0	13.7
MOTOR CARRIER	59	100.0	-	-	.8	2.2	-	-	37.9	8.5	50.7
PRIVATE TRUCK	66	100.0	-	-	-	-	-	-	-	86.3	13.7
AIR	-	100.0	-	-	-	-	-	-	-	-	-
WATER	-	100.0	-	-	-	-	-	-	-	-	-
OTHER	-	100.0	-	-	96.2	-	-	-	-	-	3.8
UNKNOWN	-	100.0	-	-	-	-	-	-	-	-	100.0
PACIFIC	796	100.0	-	1.3	.1	-	-	-	18.6	21.0	59.0
RAIL	367	100.0	-	2.8	-	-	-	-	39.9	38.2	19.1
MOTOR CARRIER	264	100.0	-	-	-	-	-	-	.4	8.6	91.0
PRIVATE TRUCK	57	100.0	-	-	-	-	-	-	-	7.1	92.9
AIR	-	100.0	-	100.0	-	-	-	-	-	-	-
WATER	103	100.0	-	-	-	-	-	-	-	-	100.0
OTHER	2	100.0	-	-	29.0	-	-	-	-	-	71.0
UNKNOWN	-	100.0	-	-	-	-	-	-	-	-	100.0

See footnotes at end of table 4.

TABLE 4. TCC GROUP 327—Percent Distribution of Distance Shipped and Weight of Shipment, by Means of Transport: 1972

Distance shipped and weight of shipment [2] [3]	Number	Percent distribution by means of transport							
		All means of transport	Rail	Motor carrier	Private truck	Air	Water	Other	Unknown
TONS OF SHIPMENTS	(thousands of tons)								
U.S. TOTAL	38 659	100.0	17.1	47.9	33.3	-	1.4	.1	.2
UNDER 100 MILES	21 298	100.0	4.9	41.3	51.2	-	2.3	.1	.1
UNDER 1000 POUNDS	7	100.0	-	15.4	84.1	-	.1	.3	.1
1000 TO 9999 POUNDS	267	100.0	-	17.0	82.4	-	-	.5	.1
10000 TO 29999 POUNDS	3 074	100.0	-	34.1	65.8	-	-	-	.1
30000 TO 59999 POUNDS	12 295	100.0	-	54.5	45.2	-	-	.1	.2
60000 TO 89999 POUNDS	700	100.0	3.4	37.8	58.5	-	.1	-	.1
90000 POUNDS AND OVER	4 953	100.0	20.6	14.8	54.5	-	10.0	-	-
100 TO 199 MILES	7 764	100.0	18.2	63.7	17.4	-	.3	.1	.3
UNDER 1000 POUNDS	1	100.0	5.2	65.3	29.4	-	-	.1	-
1000 TO 9999 POUNDS	36	100.0	-	31.3	64.4	-	-	4.2	.1
10000 TO 29999 POUNDS	321	100.0	-	48.0	51.4	-	-	.3	.3
30000 TO 59999 POUNDS	5 271	100.0	.2	84.7	14.7	-	-	.1	.4
60000 TO 89999 POUNDS	332	100.0	13.2	74.0	12.6	-	-	-	.2
90000 POUNDS AND OVER	1 801	100.0	75.6	3.8	19.2	-	1.2	-	.1
200 TO 299 MILES	4 790	100.0	33.5	58.2	8.3	-	-	-	.1
UNDER 1000 POUNDS	-	100.0	-	93.3	6.6	-	-	.1	-
1000 TO 9999 POUNDS	10	100.0	-	76.9	23.1	-	-	-	-
10000 TO 29999 POUNDS	80	100.0	-	65.5	34.5	-	-	-	-
30000 TO 59999 POUNDS	2 939	100.0	.5	88.6	10.8	-	-	-	.1
60000 TO 89999 POUNDS	152	100.0	81.3	12.9	5.8	-	-	-	-
90000 POUNDS AND OVER	1 606	100.0	91.3	6.2	2.5	-	-	-	-
300 TO 499 MILES	3 079	100.0	42.5	52.3	5.2	-	-	-	-
UNDER 1000 POUNDS	1	100.0	-	96.2	1.8	-	-	1.9	-
1000 TO 9999 POUNDS	15	100.0	-	89.6	10.4	-	-	-	-
10000 TO 29999 POUNDS	72	100.0	2.0	97.4	.6	-	-	-	-
30000 TO 59999 POUNDS	1 664	100.0	2.9	90.7	6.3	-	-	-	-
60000 TO 89999 POUNDS	288	100.0	97.5	2.5	-	-	-	-	-
90000 POUNDS AND OVER	1 037	100.0	94.3	.6	5.1	-	-.	-	-
500 TO 999 MILES	1 427	100.0	69.2	26.6	2.9	-	-	.1	1.2
UNDER 1000 POUNDS	1	100.0	-	86.9	3.0	.1	-	8.1	1.9
1000 TO 9999 POUNDS	9	100.0	17.7	76.5	5.9	-	-	-	-
10000 TO 29999 POUNDS	28	100.0	10.8	68.0	14.1	-	-	7.1	-
30000 TO 59999 POUNDS	341	100.0	10.2	79.1	10.5	-	-	-	.2
60000 TO 89999 POUNDS	228	100.0	95.7	3.9	.4	-	-	-	-
90000 POUNDS AND OVER	818	100.0	89.2	8.9	-	-	-	-	1.9
1000 TO 1499 MILES	164	100.0	95.3	3.4	1.2	-	-	.2	-
UNDER 1000 POUNDS	-	100.0	-	42.6	5.0	3.8	-	48.6	-
1000 TO 9999 POUNDS	3	100.0	11.6	84.1	-	-	-	4.4	-
10000 TO 29999 POUNDS	2	100.0	47.3	52.7	-	-	-	-	-
30000 TO 59999 POUNDS	14	100.0	80.8	5.9	13.3	-	-	-	-
60000 TO 89999 POUNDS	62	100.0	100.0	-	-	-	-	-	-
90000 POUNDS AND OVER	80	100.0	100.0	-	-	-	-	-	-
1500 MILES OR OVER	133	100.0	68.0	2.7	.3	-	28.7	.3	-
UNDER 1000 POUNDS	-	100.0	5.2	16.2	-	.3	6.2	72.1	-
1000 TO 9999 POUNDS	5	100.0	86.2	11.6	-	-	-	2.2	-
10000 TO 29999 POUNDS	4	100.0	95.7	-	-	-	4.3	-	-
30000 TO 59999 POUNDS	51	100.0	23.5	5.6	.7	-	70.2	-	-
60000 TO 89999 POUNDS	29	100.0	94.2	-	-	-	5.8	-	-
90000 POUNDS AND OVER	41	100.0	100.0	-	-	-	-	-	-
TON-MILES OF SHIPMENTS	(millions of ton-miles)								
U.S. TOTAL	5 849	100.0	37.8	45.0	14.6	-	2.2	.1	.3
UNDER 100 MILES	973	100.0	4.8	41.6	50.1	-	3.2	-	.2
UNDER 1000 POUNDS	-	100.0	-	26.7	72.7	-	.1	.3	.2
1000 TO 9999 POUNDS	9	100.0	-	12.9	86.4	-	-	.6	.1
10000 TO 29999 POUNDS	103	100.0	.1	26.9	72.9	-	-	-	.1
30000 TO 59999 POUNDS	556	100.0	-	57.1	42.6	-	-	-	.3
60000 TO 89999 POUNDS	38	100.0	3.5	40.7	55.5	-	.2	-	.1
90000 POUNDS AND OVER	264	100.0	17.1	16.2	54.9	-	11.8	-	-
100 TO 199 MILES	1 122	100.0	19.3	63.2	16.9	-	.2	.1	.3
UNDER 1000 POUNDS	-	100.0	6.7	67.0	26.2	-	-	.1	-
1000 TO 9999 POUNDS	5	100.0	-	32.6	63.8	-	-	3.5	.1
10000 TO 29999 POUNDS	44	100.0	-	49.3	50.1	-	-	.4	.2
30000 TO 59999 POUNDS	754	100.0	.2	85.1	14.2	-	-	.1	.4
60000 TO 89999 POUNDS	45	100.0	16.9	68.8	14.1	-	-	-	.2
90000 POUNDS AND OVER	272	100.0	76.3	4.4	18.3	-	1.0	-	.1

See footnotes at end of table 4.

TABLE 4. **TCC GROUP 327—Percent Distribution of Distance Shipped and Weight of Shipment, by Means of Transport: 1972**—Continued

Distance shipped and weight of shipment[2][3]	Number	Percent distribution by means of transport							
		All means of transport	Rail	Motor carrier	Private truck	Air	Water	Other	Unknown
TON-MILES OF SHIPMENTS	(millions of ton-miles)								
200 TO 299 MILES	1 147	100.0	33.9	58.1	7.9	-	-	-	.1
UNDER 1000 POUNDS	-	100.0	-	92.5	7.4	-	-	.1	-
1000 TO 9999 POUNDS	2	100.0	-	75.5	24.5	-	-	-	-
10000 TO 29999 POUNDS	18	100.0	-	65.2	34.8	-	-	-	-
30000 TO 59999 POUNDS	698	100.0	.5	89.3	10.1	-	-	-	.1
60000 TO 89999 POUNDS	36	100.0	82.2	12.4	5.4	-	-	-	-
90000 POUNDS AND OVER	389	100.0	91.1	6.1	2.8	-	-	-	-
300 TO 499 MILES	1 175	100.0	43.9	51.3	4.8	-	-	-	-
UNDER 1000 POUNDS	-	100.0	-	96.3	1.7	-	-	2.0	-
1000 TO 9999 POUNDS	5	100.0	-	90.1	9.9	-	-	-	-
10000 TO 29999 POUNDS	28	100.0	1.7	97.6	.7	-	-	-	-
30000 TO 59999 POUNDS	621	100.0	3.1	90.9	5.9	-	-	-	-
60000 TO 89999 POUNDS	107	100.0	97.6	2.4	-	-	-	-	-
90000 POUNDS AND OVER	412	100.0	94.9	.5	4.5	-	-	-	-
500 TO 999 MILES	949	100.0	70.8	24.9	3.1	-	-	.2	1.1
UNDER 1000 POUNDS	1	100.0	-	87.4	3.0	.1	-	7.8	1.7
1000 TO 9999 POUNDS	6	100.0	20.5	74.4	5.1	-	-	-	-
10000 TO 29999 POUNDS	18	100.0	13.9	64.9	13.6	-	-	7.7	-
30000 TO 59999 POUNDS	226	100.0	11.7	76.8	11.3	-	-	-	.1
60000 TO 89999 POUNDS	158	100.0	96.8	2.9	.3	-	-	-	-
90000 POUNDS AND OVER	538	100.0	90.6	7.6	-	-	-	-	1.9
1000 TO 1499 MILES	203	100.0	95.4	3.2	1.2	-	-	.2	-
UNDER 1000 POUNDS	-	100.0	-	36.3	5.8	3.2	-	54.6	-
1000 TO 9999 POUNDS	4	100.0	13.7	81.4	-	-	-	4.9	-
10000 TO 29999 POUNDS	3	100.0	52.0	48.0	-	-	-	-	-
30000 TO 59999 POUNDS	18	100.0	80.8	5.8	13.4	-	-	-	-
60000 TO 89999 POUNDS	78	100.0	100.0	-	-	-	-	-	-
90000 POUNDS AND OVER	98	100.0	100.0	-	-	-	-	-	-
1500 MILES OR OVER	278	100.0	62.6	3.0	.2	-	34.0	.2	-
UNDER 1000 POUNDS	-	100.0	4.9	16.6	-	.4	7.0	71.2	-
1000 TO 9999 POUNDS	11	100.0	86.8	11.4	-	-	-	1.9	-
10000 TO 29999 POUNDS	9	100.0	94.5	-	-	-	5.5	-	-
30000 TO 59999 POUNDS	121	100.0	20.2	5.8	.5	-	73.5	-	-
60000 TO 89999 POUNDS	54	100.0	91.4	-	-	-	8.6	-	-
90000 POUNDS AND OVER	81	100.0	100.0	-	-	-	-	-	-

Note: Detail may not add to total due to rounding. The introductory tables shows the estimates of sampling variability for tons; sampling variability for ton-miles has not been estimated. See the map in the Introduction for the States comprising the geographic divisions of the United States.

Shipments excluded from the survey are those moving by pipeline (primarily petroleum products from refineries), parcel post shipments, and commodities moved by own power (motorized vehicles, aircraft, etc.) or towed (prefabricated buildings, etc.). Local shipments (commodities shipped less than 25 miles from the plant) and shipments within the same city are also excluded. Shipments to Alaska and Hawaii from the 48 conterminous States and the District of Columbia are included; however, no data were obtained for shipments originating in Alaska and Hawaii.

- Represents zero or rounds to zero.

[1]Production of this commodity is concentrated in the geographic divisions shown; figures and distributions for geographic divisions not shown are included in the total.

[2]Distances of shipments to foreign destinations are calculated only to the U.S. port of exit.

[3]Includes only shipments represented by bills of lading and invoices. Summary records which did not show individual weights of shipments are not included.

TCC 329. Abrasives and Asbestos Products

Comparisons of Tons and Ton-Miles of Shipments for
Geographic Divisions of Origin and for Sampling Variability: 1972 and 1967

Geographic division of origin	Estimates				Relative sampling variability in tons (percent)	
	1972		1967		1972	1967
	Tons (thousands)	Ton-miles (millions)	Tons (thousands)	Ton-miles (millions)		
U.S. total	20,679	9,824	13,578	3,903	21.4	23.6
New England	(D)	(D)	340	190	(*)	(*)
Middle Atlantic	2,758	806	1,685	612	32.9	(*)
East North Central	3,277	1,108	6,893	1,397	21.2	(*)
West North Central	(D)	(D)	257	162	(*)	(*)
South Atlantic	2,863	960	1,347	481	24.6	(*)
East South Central	(D)	(D)	181	71	(*)	(*)
West South Central	(D)	(D)	838	299	(*)	(*)
Mountain	(D)	(D)	1,091	234	(*)	(*)
Pacific	945	669	946	457	21.2	(*)

(D) Withheld to avoid disclosing figures for individual companies.   (*) Data not published.

TABLE 1. TCC GROUP 329—Percent Distribution of Geographic Division of Origin and Distance Shipped, by Means of Transport: 1972

Geographic division of origin[1] and distance shipped[2]	Number	Percent distribution by means of transport							
		All means of transport	Rail	Motor carrier	Private truck	Air	Water	Other	Unknown
TONS OF SHIPMENTS	(thousands of tons)								
U.S. TOTAL.........	20 679	100.0	53.9	30.7	10.1	-	5.1	-	.1
MIDDLE ATLANTIC.........	2 758	100.0	43.0	49.3	7.4	-	-	.1	.1
UNDER 100 MILES.......	854	100.0	40.5	47.6	11.5	.1	-	.1	.1
100 TO 199 MILES......	693	100.0	44.2	47.8	7.9	-	-	.1	.3
200 TO 299 MILES......	346	100.0	19.6	72.7	7.5	-	-	.1	-
300 TO 499 MILES......	401	100.0	50.0	46.6	3.3	-	-	.2	-
500 TO 999 MILES......	357	100.0	60.9	37.7	1.0	-	-	.2	-
1000 TO 1499 MILES....	64	100.0	50.6	33.0	11.3	.3	-	.1	-
1500 MILES OR OVER....	40	100.0	34.1	62.5	2.9	3.4	1.2	.5	-
EAST NORTH CENTRAL......	3 277	100.0	31.0	52.5	16.4	.1	-	-	-
UNDER 100 MILES.......	544	100.0	1.0	70.2	28.8	-	-	-	-
100 TO 199 MILES......	841	100.0	23.5	50.5	25.9	-	-	-	-
200 TO 299 MILES......	664	100.0	31.0	55.8	13.2	-	-	-	.1
300 TO 499 MILES......	588	100.0	36.6	54.9	8.3	.1	-	-	-
500 TO 999 MILES......	477	100.0	56.5	39.2	3.6	.7	-	-	.1
1000 TO 1499 MILES....	80	100.0	57.6	31.7	10.5	-	-	-	.1
1500 MILES OR OVER....	80	100.0	92.4	7.1	.3	.1	-	-	.1
SOUTH ATLANTIC..........	2 863	100.0	89.4	7.6	2.7	-	.2	-	-
UNDER 100 MILES.......	1 536	100.0	97.4	1.7	.9	-	-	-	-
100 TO 199 MILES......	144	100.0	60.6	15.3	24.1	-	-	-	-
200 TO 299 MILES......	101	100.0	38.2	60.6	.7	-	-	-	.4
300 TO 499 MILES......	357	100.0	83.7	14.6	1.7	-	-	-	-
500 TO 999 MILES......	416	100.0	82.7	12.2	5.1	-	-	-	-
1000 TO 1499 MILES....	271	100.0	99.1	.9	-	-	-	-	-
1500 MILES OR OVER....	34	100.0	72.1	9.8	2.2	.1	15.8	-	-
PACIFIC.................	945	100.0	26.5	59.8	12.4	-	.8	.5	-
UNDER 100 MILES.......	214	100.0	.4	73.6	25.2	-	-	.8	-
100 TO 199 MILES......	102	100.0	-	90.1	9.7	-	-	.8	-
200 TO 299 MILES......	42	100.0	16.3	68.3	14.8	-	-	.2	-
300 TO 499 MILES......	188	100.0	2.4	76.6	20.4	-	-	.7	-
500 TO 999 MILES......	182	100.0	32.2	62.8	4.1	-	-	.5	-
1000 TO 1499 MILES....	36	100.0	63.5	36.2	-	.3	-	.8	-
1500 MILES OR OVER....	180	100.0	86.9	8.3	.6	-	4.0	.1	-
TON-MILES OF SHIPMENTS	(millions of ton-miles)								
U.S. TOTAL.........	9 824	100.0	74.5	21.1	3.2	.1	1.0	-	.1
MIDDLE ATLANTIC.........	806	100.0	47.9	46.6	4.7	.5	.1	.1	-
UNDER 100 MILES.......	46	100.0	44.5	45.1	10.1	-	-	.1	.2
100 TO 199 MILES......	108	100.0	47.9	45.5	6.5	-	-	.1	-
200 TO 299 MILES......	84	100.0	19.2	72.4	8.1	-	-	.1	-
300 TO 499 MILES......	160	100.0	50.5	46.5	2.8	-	-	.2	-
500 TO 999 MILES......	238	100.0	61.1	37.3	1.1	.3	-	.1	-
1000 TO 1499 MILES....	78	100.0	51.2	31.2	12.7	3.1	1.4	.4	-
1500 MILES OR OVER....	89	100.0	34.4	62.3	2.9	.4	-	-	-
EAST NORTH CENTRAL......	1 108	100.0	48.6	41.7	9.3	.3	-	-	-
UNDER 100 MILES.......	31	100.0	.9	66.7	32.3	-	-	-	-
100 TO 199 MILES......	121	100.0	23.7	51.0	25.2	-	-	-	.1
200 TO 299 MILES......	160	100.0	29.9	56.8	13.3	-	-	-	-
300 TO 499 MILES......	229	100.0	37.3	54.6	7.9	-	-	-	.1
500 TO 999 MILES......	324	100.0	57.1	38.1	3.9	.9	-	-	.1
1000 TO 1499 MILES....	88	100.0	57.1	32.5	10.2	-	.1	-	-
1500 MILES OR OVER....	152	100.0	92.1	7.2	.6	.1	-	-	.1
SOUTH ATLANTIC..........	960	100.0	87.5	8.8	2.3	-	1.3	-	-
UNDER 100 MILES.......	117	100.0	98.0	1.0	.9	-	-	-	-
100 TO 199 MILES......	21	100.0	62.8	16.4	20.9	-	-	-	-
200 TO 299 MILES......	25	100.0	38.8	60.1	.7	-	-	-	-
300 TO 499 MILES......	137	100.0	83.1	15.1	1.7	-	-	-	.5
500 TO 999 MILES......	293	100.0	84.2	11.5	4.3	-	-	-	-
1000 TO 1499 MILES....	292	100.0	99.0	1.0	-	-	-	-	-
1500 MILES OR OVER....	72	100.0	70.3	9.8	2.3	.1	17.4	-	-
PACIFIC.................	669	100.0	59.7	32.7	4.3	.1	2.9	.3	-
UNDER 100 MILES.......	11	100.0	.5	70.4	28.6	-	-	.5	-
100 TO 199 MILES......	15	100.0	-	89.5	10.3	-	-	.1	-
200 TO 299 MILES......	10	100.0	14.8	70.9	13.6	-	-	.6	-
300 TO 499 MILES......	67	100.0	2.4	76.6	20.5	-	-	.5	-
500 TO 999 MILES......	140	100.0	32.9	61.5	4.6	-	-	1.0	-
1000 TO 1499 MILES....	46	100.0	64.7	35.0	-	.3	-	-	-
1500 MILES OR OVER....	377	100.0	84.7	9.4	.6	-	5.2	.1	-

See footnotes at end of table 4.

TABLE 2. TCC GROUP 329—Percent Distribution of Geographic Division of Origin and Means of Transport, by Geographic Division of Destination: 1972

Geographic division of origin[1] and means of transport	Number	Percent distribution by division of destination								
		U.S. total	New England	Middle Atlantic	East North Central	West North Central	South Atlantic	East South Central	West South Central	Mountain	Pacific
TONS OF SHIPMENTS	(thousands of tons)										
U.S. TOTAL	20 679	100.0	3.3	10.9	23.5	5.7	17.6	11.5	20.2	2.5	4.9
RAIL	11 153	100.0	2.6	7.7	23.7	5.7	23.3	11.8	19.5	2.0	3.7
MOTOR CARRIER	6 350	100.0	5.7	19.4	24.2	6.6	14.1	5.9	13.6	3.1	7.3
PRIVATE TRUCK	2 088	100.0	1.1	7.1	32.1	5.6	6.2	32.9	4.5	4.4	6.0
AIR	8	100.0	.8	5.4	15.5	26.7	10.9	.4	35.5	2.0	2.7
WATER	1 044	100.0	-	-	-	-	-	-	98.8	-	1.2
OTHER	9	100.0	2.9	19.0	12.0	1.6	7.3	2.7	2.8	7.2	44.6
UNKNOWN	25	100.0	-	8.4	6.1	39.5	-	.9	44.6	.4	-
MIDDLE ATLANTIC	2 758	100.0	13.7	43.6	10.2	.8	26.1	2.8	1.3	.4	1.1
RAIL	1 185	100.0	12.2	37.3	8.6	.6	34.3	4.5	1.4	.1	1.1
MOTOR CARRIER	1 358	100.0	15.6	46.9	12.1	.9	20.1	1.8	.8	.7	1.2
PRIVATE TRUCK	204	100.0	10.0	59.5	6.8	.6	19.0	-	3.4	.2	.6
AIR	3	100.0	.1	8.1	10.1	55.9	19.8	.3	1.8	2.5	1.4
WATER	-	100.0	-	5.6	-	-	-	-	94.4	-	-
OTHER	3	100.0	6.2	46.8	18.3	2.5	13.8	5.0	7.0	-	.3
UNKNOWN	2	100.0	-	100.0	-	-	-	-	-	-	-
EAST NORTH CENTRAL	3 277	100.0	2.3	12.3	58.7	7.5	7.2	4.9	3.6	1.2	2.4
RAIL	1 014	100.0	4.6	17.0	46.3	6.5	5.3	4.4	6.2	2.7	7.1
MOTOR CARRIER	1 719	100.0	1.7	12.5	60.1	6.6	10.1	5.8	2.3	.6	.3
PRIVATE TRUCK	537	100.0	-	3.1	77.7	12.1	1.5	2.7	2.5	.3	-
AIR	3	100.0	1.0	2.0	12.5	4.4	3.5	.3	73.5	.1	2.6
WATER	-	100.0	-	67.5	-	-	32.5	-	-	-	-
OTHER	-	100.0	2.5	17.1	57.0	4.3	5.3	10.2	1.5	-	2.1
UNKNOWN	1	100.0	-	-	78.5	-	-	16.3	-	5.2	-
SOUTH ATLANTIC	2 863	100.0	.2	1.3	3.9	2.0	66.5	6.9	17.0	1.0	1.1
RAIL	2 560	100.0	.1	.4	2.2	2.0	69.1	5.5	18.9	1.1	.8
MOTOR CARRIER	218	100.0	1.6	11.1	19.7	3.2	38.6	22.3	1.8	.3	1.5
PRIVATE TRUCK	77	100.0	.1	6.0	17.8	-	62.4	12.7	-	-	1.0
AIR	-	100.0	11.2	11.8	10.7	5.4	12.4	-	16.2	4.6	27.8
WATER	5	100.0	-	-	-	-	-	-	-	-	100.0
OTHER	-	100.0	4.9	23.6	22.5	.2	25.8	8.3	-	2.4	12.5
UNKNOWN	-	100.0	-	-	100.0	-	-	-	-	-	-
PACIFIC	945	100.0	.7	9.3	4.1	.7	.4	2.4	6.2	19.0	57.2
RAIL	250	100.0	.5	35.1	14.4	2.3	1.1	9.0	15.3	12.5	9.8
MOTOR CARRIER	565	100.0	.9	-	.2	.1	.2	.1	3.5	23.7	71.3
PRIVATE TRUCK	117	100.0	-	-	1.0	-	-	-	-	11.8	87.3
AIR	-	100.0	2.9	5.8	3.4	3.2	6.0	3.7	43.9	27.3	4.0
WATER	7	100.0	-	-	-	-	-	-	-	-	100.0
OTHER	4	100.0	-	-	.2	.2	3.0	-	-	13.4	83.2
UNKNOWN	-	100.0	-	-	-	-	-	-	-	-	-
TON-MILES OF SHIPMENTS	(millions of ton-miles)										
U.S. TOTAL	9 824	100.0	3.5	8.1	28.4	6.5	10.9	8.6	22.2	3.5	8.3
RAIL	7 323	100.0	3.2	7.6	31.3	5.4	9.7	9.1	24.0	2.4	7.4
MOTOR CARRIER	2 068	100.0	5.2	10.8	20.6	9.7	15.6	7.0	15.1	6.2	9.7
PRIVATE TRUCK	312	100.0	1.4	6.8	24.3	10.4	11.1	11.4	12.3	11.5	10.9
AIR	7	100.0	.7	3.1	9.6	30.9	9.3	.4	36.8	3.4	5.9
WATER	99	100.0	-	.1	-	-	.1	-	67.4	-	32.4
OTHER	3	100.0	1.5	7.4	9.5	3.0	13.3	4.8	7.3	5.7	47.6
UNKNOWN	9	100.0	-	1.2	4.5	79.4	-	.3	13.1	1.5	-
MIDDLE ATLANTIC	806	100.0	13.3	17.2	16.9	2.7	26.9	6.1	5.6	2.3	8.9
RAIL	386	100.0	13.2	14.6	14.1	1.9	33.8	8.6	5.7	.4	7.6
MOTOR CARRIER	375	100.0	13.9	19.0	20.6	3.0	21.1	4.2	3.3	4.4	10.5
PRIVATE TRUCK	38	100.0	10.0	28.0	10.9	2.4	16.0	-	24.6	1.4	6.8
AIR	3	100.0	-	1.6	6.6	63.7	16.9	.2	2.2	5.4	3.5
WATER	1	100.0	-	-	-	-	-	-	100.0	-	-
OTHER	1	100.0	3.8	18.5	20.3	5.9	15.3	12.1	21.9	.1	2.1
UNKNOWN	-	100.0	-	100.0	-	-	-	-	-	-	-
EAST NORTH CENTRAL	1 108	100.0	5.1	15.2	29.6	8.3	9.5	5.8	9.1	3.9	13.5
RAIL	538	100.0	7.0	15.9	21.3	6.4	5.3	3.2	9.7	5.7	25.5
MOTOR CARRIER	462	100.0	4.2	16.6	34.0	8.9	15.5	9.0	7.0	2.4	2.3
PRIVATE TRUCK	102	100.0	-	5.6	54.0	15.2	4.8	5.4	12.7	1.3	.9
AIR	3	100.0	.8	1.2	3.3	2.6	1.7	.2	83.6	.1	6.3
WATER	-	100.0	-	55.1	-	-	44.9	-	-	-	-
OTHER	-	100.0	4.2	22.9	26.1	7.1	8.4	13.4	3.9	.3	13.6
UNKNOWN	-	100.0	-	-	70.2	-	-	6.9	-	22.9	-
SOUTH ATLANTIC	960	100.0	.6	1.2	6.6	5.8	24.3	7.2	43.7	3.7	6.9
RAIL	840	100.0	.3	.5	4.5	6.1	24.9	4.8	49.5	4.1	5.3
MOTOR CARRIER	84	100.0	3.1	8.6	21.8	5.6	20.2	27.1	4.1	1.1	8.2
PRIVATE TRUCK	22	100.0	.2	2.4	32.2	-	33.5	24.1	-	-	7.5
AIR	-	100.0	6.8	6.4	5.0	4.7	4.9	-	14.5	6.1	51.6
WATER	12	100.0	-	-	-	-	-	-	-	-	100.0
OTHER	-	100.0	4.9	14.1	19.5	.2	6.5	7.0	-	4.9	42.9
UNKNOWN	-	100.0	-	-	100.0	-	-	-	-	-	-
PACIFIC	669	100.0	2.5	29.1	10.8	1.4	1.4	5.8	10.4	14.7	24.0
RAIL	399	100.0	.9	48.7	16.9	2.0	1.5	9.4	11.8	5.1	3.7
MOTOR CARRIER	218	100.0	6.1	.1	1.0	.5	1.4	.5	10.1	33.5	47.0
PRIVATE TRUCK	28	100.0	-	-	7.8	-	-	-	-	15.6	76.6
AIR	-	100.0	5.4	9.8	4.6	3.0	8.8	4.9	41.9	16.2	5.4
WATER	19	100.0	-	-	-	-	-	-	-	-	100.0
OTHER	2	100.0	-	-	.8	.7	12.9	.1	-	9.3	76.1
UNKNOWN	-	100.0	-	-	-	-	-	-	-	-	-

See footnotes at end of table 4.

TABLE 3. **TCC GROUP 329—Percent Distribution of Geographic Division of Destination and Means of Transport, by Geographic Division of Origin: 1972**

Geographic division of destination and means of transport	Number	Percent distribution by division of origin[1]									
		U.S. total	New England	Middle Atlantic	East North Central	West North Central	South Atlantic	East South Central	West South Central	Mountain	Pacific
TONS OF SHIPMENTS	(thousands of tons)										
U.S. TOTAL.............	20 679	100.0	(D)	13.3	15.8	(D)	13.8	(D)	(D)	(D)	4.6
RAIL...................	11 153	100.0	(D)	10.6	9.1	(D)	23.0	(D)	(D)	(D)	2.2
MOTOR CARRIER..........	6 350	100.0	(D)	21.4	27.1	(D)	3.4	(D)	(D)	(D)	8.9
PRIVATE TRUCK..........	2 088	100.0	(D)	9.8	25.7	(D)	3.7	(D)	(D)	(D)	5.6
AIR....................	8	100.0	(D)	43.2	45.0	(D)	1.6	(D)	(D)	(D)	3.0
WATER.................	1 044	100.0	(D)	.1	-	(D)	.5	(D)	(D)	(D)	.7
OTHER.................	9	100.0	(D)	36.7	7.7	(D)	.6	(D)	(D)	(D)	53.1
UNKNOWN...............	25	100.0	(D)	8.4	5.6	(D)	1.7	(D)	(D)	(D)	-
NEW ENGLAND............	674	100.0	(D)	55.9	11.2	(D)	1.0	(D)	(D)	(D)	1.0
RAIL..................	286	100.0	(D)	50.4	16.4	(D)	1.0	(D)	(D)	(D)	.5
MOTOR CARRIER.........	364	100.0	(D)	58.2	7.9	(D)	.9	(D)	(D)	(D)	1.4
PRIVATE TRUCK.........	23	100.0	(D)	88.0	-	(D)	.5	(D)	(D)	(D)	-
AIR...................	-	100.0	(D)	6.2	58.1	(D)	22.0	(D)	(D)	(D)	10.9
WATER.................	-	100.0	(D)	-	-	(D)	-	(D)	(D)	(D)	-
OTHER.................	-	100.0	(D)	78.7	6.7	(D)	1.0	(D)	(D)	(D)	-
UNKNOWN...............	-	100.0	(D)	-	-	(D)	-	(D)	(D)	(D)	-
MIDDLE ATLANTIC........	2 251	100.0	(D)	53.5	17.9	(D)	1.7	(D)	(D)	(D)	3.9
RAIL..................	863	100.0	(D)	51.1	20.0	(D)	1.1	(D)	(D)	(D)	10.2
MOTOR CARRIER.........	1 235	100.0	(D)	51.6	17.4	(D)	2.0	(D)	(D)	(D)	-
PRIVATE TRUCK.........	147	100.0	(D)	82.2	11.1	(D)	3.2	(D)	(D)	(D)	-
AIR...................	-	100.0	(D)	64.6	16.2	(D)	3.4	(D)	(D)	(D)	3.2
WATER.................	-	100.0	(D)	35.5	64.5	(D)	-	(D)	(D)	(D)	-
OTHER.................	1	100.0	(D)	90.5	6.9	(D)	.7	(D)	(D)	(D)	-
UNKNOWN...............	2	100.0	(D)	100.0	-	(D)	-	(D)	(D)	(D)	-
EAST NORTH CENTRAL.....	4 854	100.0	(D)	5.8	39.6	(D)	2.3	(D)	(D)	(D)	.8
RAIL..................	2 646	100.0	(D)	3.9	17.7	(D)	2.1	(D)	(D)	(D)	1.4
MOTOR CARRIER.........	1 534	100.0	(D)	10.7	67.4	(D)	2.8	(D)	(D)	(D)	.1
PRIVATE TRUCK.........	669	100.0	(D)	2.1	62.4	(D)	2.1	(D)	(D)	(D)	.2
AIR...................	1	100.0	(D)	28.2	36.4	(D)	1.1	(D)	(D)	(D)	.7
WATER.................	-	100.0	(D)	-	-	(D)	-	(D)	(D)	(D)	-
OTHER.................	1	100.0	(D)	56.0	36.3	(D)	1.1	(D)	(D)	(D)	1.0
UNKNOWN...............	1	100.0	(D)	-	71.7	(D)	28.3	(D)	(D)	(D)	-
WEST NORTH CENTRAL.....	1 177	100.0	(D)	1.9	20.9	(D)	4.8	(D)	(D)	(D)	.6
RAIL..................	631	100.0	(D)	1.1	10.4	(D)	7.9	(D)	(D)	(D)	.9
MOTOR CARRIER.........	416	100.0	(D)	2.9	27.5	(D)	1.7	(D)	(D)	(D)	.2
PRIVATE TRUCK.........	117	100.0	(D)	1.0	55.6	(D)	-	(D)	(D)	(D)	-
AIR...................	2	100.0	(D)	90.4	7.4	(D)	.3	(D)	(D)	(D)	.4
WATER.................	-	100.0	(D)	-	-	(D)	-	(D)	(D)	(D)	-
OTHER.................	-	100.0	(D)	59.4	21.2	(D)	.1	(D)	(D)	(D)	6.8
UNKNOWN...............	10	100.0	(D)	-	-	(D)	-	(D)	(D)	(D)	-
SOUTH ATLANTIC.........	3 632	100.0	(D)	19.8	6.5	(D)	52.4	(D)	(D)	(D)	.1
RAIL..................	2 603	100.0	(D)	15.6	2.0	(D)	68.0	(D)	(D)	(D)	.1
MOTOR CARRIER.........	897	100.0	(D)	30.5	19.3	(D)	9.4	(D)	(D)	(D)	.2
PRIVATE TRUCK.........	130	100.0	(D)	29.9	6.3	(D)	37.3	(D)	(D)	(D)	-
AIR...................	-	100.0	(D)	78.1	14.6	(D)	1.8	(D)	(D)	(D)	1.6
WATER.................	-	100.0	(D)	-	100.0	(D)	-	(D)	(D)	(D)	-
OTHER.................	-	100.0	(D)	68.9	5.6	(D)	2.1	(D)	(D)	(D)	21.5
UNKNOWN...............	-	100.0	(D)	-	-	(D)	-	(D)	(D)	(D)	-
EAST SOUTH CENTRAL.....	2 376	100.0	(D)	3.2	6.7	(D)	8.4	(D)	(D)	(D)	1.0
RAIL..................	1 313	100.0	(D)	4.0	3.4	(D)	10.7	(D)	(D)	(D)	1.7
MOTOR CARRIER.........	375	100.0	(D)	6.4	26.8	(D)	13.0	(D)	(D)	(D)	.1
PRIVATE TRUCK.........	687	100.0	(D)	-	2.1	(D)	1.4	(D)	(D)	(D)	-
AIR...................	-	100.0	(D)	30.3	34.2	(D)	-	(D)	(D)	(D)	26.9
WATER.................	-	100.0	(D)	-	-	(D)	-	(D)	(D)	(D)	-
OTHER.................	-	100.0	(D)	67.1	28.4	(D)	1.8	(D)	(D)	(D)	.6
UNKNOWN...............	-	100.0	(D)	-	100.0	(D)	-	(D)	(D)	(D)	-
WEST SOUTH CENTRAL.....	4 181	100.0	(D)	.8	2.8	(D)	11.7	(D)	(D)	(D)	1.4
RAIL..................	2 173	100.0	(D)	.8	2.9	(D)	22.2	(D)	(D)	(D)	1.8
MOTOR CARRIER.........	866	100.0	(D)	1.2	4.5	(D)	.5	(D)	(D)	(D)	2.3
PRIVATE TRUCK.........	94	100.0	(D)	7.3	14.1	(D)	-	(D)	(D)	(D)	-
AIR...................	3	100.0	(D)	2.2	93.1	(D)	.7	(D)	(D)	(D)	3.7
WATER.................	1 031	100.0	(D)	.1	-	(D)	-	(D)	(D)	(D)	-
OTHER.................	-	100.0	(D)	92.8	4.1	(D)	-	(D)	(D)	(D)	-
UNKNOWN...............	11	100.0	(D)	-	-	(D)	-	(D)	(D)	(D)	-
MOUNTAIN...............	516	100.0	(D)	2.1	7.5	(D)	5.6	(D)	(D)	(D)	34.8
RAIL..................	223	100.0	(D)	.4	12.2	(D)	12.7	(D)	(D)	(D)	14.0
MOTOR CARRIER.........	199	100.0	(D)	4.8	4.9	(D)	.3	(D)	(D)	(D)	66.9
PRIVATE TRUCK.........	91	100.0	(D)	.4	1.7	(D)	-	(D)	(D)	(D)	15.0
AIR...................	-	100.0	(D)	53.7	2.2	(D)	3.5	(D)	(D)	(D)	39.9
WATER.................	-	100.0	(D)	-	-	(D)	-	(D)	(D)	(D)	-
OTHER.................	-	100.0	(D)	.2	.1	(D)	.2	(D)	(D)	(D)	99.5
UNKNOWN...............	-	100.0	(D)	-	74.1	(D)	-	(D)	(D)	(D)	-
PACIFIC................	1 015	100.0	(D)	2.9	7.7	(D)	3.0	(D)	(D)	(D)	53.3
RAIL..................	410	100.0	(D)	3.2	17.6	(D)	5.1	(D)	(D)	(D)	6.0
MOTOR CARRIER.........	461	100.0	(D)	3.4	1.2	(D)	.7	(D)	(D)	(D)	87.3
PRIVATE TRUCK.........	126	100.0	(D)	.9	.2	(D)	.6	(D)	(D)	(D)	81.1
AIR...................	-	100.0	(D)	22.8	43.8	(D)	16.3	(D)	(D)	(D)	4.4
WATER.................	12	100.0	(D)	-	-	(D)	43.1	(D)	(D)	(D)	56.9
OTHER.................	4	100.0	(D)	.3	.4	(D)	.2	(D)	(D)	(D)	99.1
UNKNOWN...............	-	100.0	(D)	-	-	(D)	-	(D)	(D)	(D)	-

See footnotes at end of table 4.

TABLE 3. TCC GROUP 329—Percent Distribution of Geographic Division of Destination and Means of Transport, by Geographic Division of Origin: 1972—Continued

Geographic division of destination and means of transport	Number	Percent distribution by division of origin [1]									
		U.S. total	New England	Middle Atlantic	East North Central	West North Central	South Atlantic	East South Central	West South Central	Mountain	Pacific
TON-MILES OF SHIPMENTS	(millions of ton-miles)										
U.S. TOTAL.............	9 824	100.0	(D)	8.2	11.3	(D)	9.8	(D)	(D)	(D)	6.8
RAIL..............	7 323	100.0	(D)	5.3	7.4	(D)	11.5	(D)	(D)	(D)	5.5
MOTOR CARRIER.........	2 068	100.0	(D)	18.1	22.4	(D)	4.1	(D)	(D)	(D)	10.6
PRIVATE TRUCK........	312	100.0	(D)	12.2	33.0	(D)	7.2	(D)	(D)	(D)	9.2
AIR.................	7	100.0	(D)	45.8	40.0	(D)	1.9	(D)	(D)	(D)	4.6
WATER...............	99	100.0	(D)	1.1	.1	(D)	12.7	(D)	(D)	(D)	19.7
OTHER...............	3	100.0	(D)	31.7	5.3	(D)	.9	(D)	(D)	(D)	59.9
UNKNOWN.............	9	100.0	(D)	1.2	4.4	(D)	1.4	(D)	(D)	(D)	-
NEW ENGLAND.............	347	100.0	(D)	30.8	16.4	(D)	1.6	(D)	(D)	(D)	4.9
RAIL..............	234	100.0	(D)	21.8	16.1	(D)	1.2	(D)	(D)	(D)	1.6
MOTOR CARRIER.........	108	100.0	(D)	48.0	17.7	(D)	2.5	(D)	(D)	(D)	12.3
PRIVATE TRUCK........	4	100.0	(D)	90.1	-	(D)	.9	(D)	(D)	(D)	-
AIR.................	-	100.0	(D)	2.1	45.9	(D)	18.1	(D)	(D)	(D)	33.6
WATER...............	-	100.0	(D)	-	-	(D)	-	(D)	(D)	(D)	-
OTHER...............	-	100.0	(D)	78.3	14.7	(D)	2.9	(D)	(D)	(D)	-
UNKNOWN.............	-	100.0	(D)	-	-	(D)	-	(D)	(D)	(D)	-
MIDDLE ATLANTIC.........	800	100.0	(D)	17.4	21.0	(D)	1.5	(D)	(D)	(D)	24.4
RAIL..............	555	100.0	(D)	10.2	15.4	(D)	.7	(D)	(D)	(D)	35.1
MOTOR CARRIER.........	223	100.0	(D)	32.0	34.4	(D)	3.3	(D)	(D)	(D)	.1
PRIVATE TRUCK........	21	100.0	(D)	50.4	27.2	(D)	2.5	(D)	(D)	(D)	14.5
AIR.................	-	100.0	(D)	23.0	15.8	(D)	4.1	(D)	(D)	(D)	-
WATER...............	-	100.0	(D)	.3	99.7	(D)	-	(D)	(D)	(D)	-
OTHER...............	-	100.0	(D)	79.5	16.7	(D)	1.7	(D)	(D)	(D)	-
UNKNOWN.............	-	100.0	(D)	100.0	-	(D)	-	(D)	(D)	(D)	-
EAST NORTH CENTRAL......	2 793	100.0	(D)	4.9	11.8	(D)	2.3	(D)	(D)	(D)	2.6
RAIL..............	2 288	100.0	(D)	2.4	5.0	(D)	1.6	(D)	(D)	(D)	3.0
MOTOR CARRIER.........	427	100.0	(D)	18.1	36.8	(D)	4.3	(D)	(D)	(D)	.5
PRIVATE TRUCK........	75	100.0	(D)	5.5	73.3	(D)	9.5	(D)	(D)	(D)	2.9
AIR.................	-	100.0	(D)	31.4	14.0	(D)	1.0	(D)	(D)	(D)	2.2
WATER...............	-	100.0	(D)	-	-	(D)	-	(D)	(D)	(D)	-
OTHER...............	-	100.0	(D)	68.1	14.8	(D)	1.9	(D)	(D)	(D)	5.4
UNKNOWN.............	-	100.0	(D)	-	69.3	(D)	30.7	(D)	(D)	(D)	-
WEST NORTH CENTRAL......	639	100.0	(D)	3.4	14.3	(D)	8.7	(D)	(D)	(D)	1.4
RAIL..............	396	100.0	(D)	1.8	8.7	(D)	12.9	(D)	(D)	(D)	2.0
MOTOR CARRIER.........	200	100.0	(D)	5.6	20.6	(D)	2.4	(D)	(D)	(D)	.6
PRIVATE TRUCK........	32	100.0	(D)	2.8	48.1	(D)	-	(D)	(D)	(D)	.4
AIR.................	2	100.0	(D)	94.5	3.3	(D)	.3	(D)	(D)	(D)	-
WATER...............	-	100.0	(D)	-	-	(D)	-	(D)	(D)	(D)	-
OTHER...............	-	100.0	(D)	62.1	12.6	(D)	.1	(D)	(D)	(D)	12.9
UNKNOWN.............	7	100.0	(D)	-	-	(D)	-	(D)	(D)	(D)	-
SOUTH ATLANTIC.........	1 066	100.0	(D)	20.3	9.9	(D)	21.9	(D)	(D)	(D)	.9
RAIL..............	707	100.0	(D)	18.5	4.0	(D)	29.6	(D)	(D)	(D)	.9
MOTOR CARRIER.........	322	100.0	(D)	24.5	22.2	(D)	5.3	(D)	(D)	(D)	.9
PRIVATE TRUCK........	34	100.0	(D)	17.6	14.2	(D)	21.6	(D)	(D)	(D)	-
AIR.................	-	100.0	(D)	83.6	7.4	(D)	1.0	(D)	(D)	(D)	4.4
WATER...............	-	100.0	(D)	-	100.0	(D)	-	(D)	(D)	(D)	-
OTHER...............	-	100.0	(D)	36.5	3.4	(D)	.4	(D)	(D)	(D)	58.2
UNKNOWN.............	-	100.0	(D)	-	-	(D)	-	(D)	(D)	(D)	-
EAST SOUTH CENTRAL......	845	100.0	(D)	5.8	7.6	(D)	8.2	(D)	(D)	(D)	4.6
RAIL..............	664	100.0	(D)	5.0	2.6	(D)	6.1	(D)	(D)	(D)	5.6
MOTOR CARRIER.........	145	100.0	(D)	11.0	28.7	(D)	15.8	(D)	(D)	(D)	.7
PRIVATE TRUCK........	35	100.0	(D)	-	15.7	(D)	15.2	(D)	(D)	(D)	-
AIR.................	-	100.0	(D)	19.5	22.9	(D)	-	(D)	(D)	(D)	52.2
WATER...............	-	100.0	(D)	-	-	(D)	-	(D)	(D)	(D)	-
OTHER...............	-	100.0	(D)	80.4	15.0	(D)	1.3	(D)	(D)	(D)	1.6
UNKNOWN.............	-	100.0	(D)	-	100.0	(D)	-	(D)	(D)	(D)	-
WEST SOUTH CENTRAL......	2 178	100.0	(D)	2.1	4.6	(D)	19.3	(D)	(D)	(D)	3.2
RAIL..............	1 756	100.0	(D)	1.3	3.0	(D)	23.7	(D)	(D)	(D)	2.7
MOTOR CARRIER.........	312	100.0	(D)	4.0	10.4	(D)	1.1	(D)	(D)	(D)	7.1
PRIVATE TRUCK........	38	100.0	(D)	24.5	34.2	(D)	-	(D)	(D)	(D)	5.2
AIR.................	2	100.0	(D)	2.7	90.8	(D)	.8	(D)	(D)	(D)	-
WATER...............	67	100.0	(D)	1.6	-	(D)	-	(D)	(D)	(D)	-
OTHER...............	-	100.0	(D)	95.3	2.9	(D)	-	(D)	(D)	(D)	-
UNKNOWN.............	1	100.0	(D)	-	-	(D)	-	(D)	(D)	(D)	-
MOUNTAIN...............	341	100.0	(D)	5.5	12.7	(D)	10.4	(D)	(D)	(D)	28.8
RAIL..............	176	100.0	(D)	.8	17.5	(D)	19.6	(D)	(D)	(D)	11.5
MOTOR CARRIER.........	128	100.0	(D)	12.8	8.6	(D)	.7	(D)	(D)	(D)	57.1
PRIVATE TRUCK........	35	100.0	(D)	1.4	3.8	(D)	-	(D)	(D)	(D)	12.5
AIR.................	-	100.0	(D)	72.9	1.4	(D)	3.5	(D)	(D)	(D)	22.0
WATER...............	-	100.0	(D)	-	-	(D)	-	(D)	(D)	(D)	-
OTHER...............	-	100.0	(D)	.8	.3	(D)	.8	(D)	(D)	(D)	98.2
UNKNOWN.............	-	100.0	(D)	-	66.9	(D)	-	(D)	(D)	(D)	-
PACIFIC...............	812	100.0	(D)	8.8	18.4	(D)	8.1	(D)	(D)	(D)	19.8
RAIL..............	542	100.0	(D)	5.4	25.4	(D)	8.2	(D)	(D)	(D)	2.7
MOTOR CARRIER.........	201	100.0	(D)	19.7	5.4	(D)	3.5	(D)	(D)	(D)	51.1
PRIVATE TRUCK........	33	100.0	(D)	7.7	2.8	(D)	4.9	(D)	(D)	(D)	64.8
AIR.................	-	100.0	(D)	26.9	42.7	(D)	17.0	(D)	(D)	(D)	4.2
WATER...............	32	100.0	(D)	-	-	(D)	39.2	(D)	(D)	(D)	60.8
OTHER...............	1	100.0	(D)	1.4	1.5	(D)	.8	(D)	(D)	(D)	96.0
UNKNOWN.............	-	100.0	(D)	-	-	(D)	-	(D)	(D)	(D)	-

See footnotes at end of table 4.

TABLE 4. TCC GROUP 329—Percent Distribution of Distance Shipped and Weight of Shipment, by Means of Transport: 1972

Distance shipped and weight of shipment [2] [3]	Number	Percent distribution by means of transport							
		All means of transport	Rail	Motor carrier	Private truck	Air	Water	Other	Unknown
TONS OF SHIPMENTS	(thousands of tons)								
U.S. TOTAL.........	18 558	100.0	54.2	29.2	10.7	-	5.6	-	.1
UNDER 100 MILES........	5 005	100.0	32.1	24.6	23.8	-	19.4	.1	-
UNDER 1000 POUNDS.....	22	100.0	.3	79.4	12.8	.1	.2	7.1	.1
1000 TO 9999 POUNDS...	263	100.0	2.6	70.7	25.8	-	-	.4	.5
10000 TO 29999 POUNDS.	484	100.0	7.9	73.3	18.6	-	-	-	.2
30000 TO 59999 POUNDS.	700	100.0	4.2	61.8	34.0	-	-	-	-
60000 TO 89999 POUNDS.	55	100.0	3.3	54.1	41.0	-	1.7	-	-
90000 POUNDS AND OVER.	3 479	100.0	43.9	6.1	22.1	-	27.9	-	-
100 TO 199 MILES........	2 148	100.0	24.8	55.9	16.0	-	2.8	-	.5
UNDER 1000 POUNDS.....	18	100.0	-	93.6	3.8	.5	-	2.1	-
1000 TO 9999 POUNDS...	256	100.0	4.9	85.3	9.6	.1	-	.1	-
10000 TO 29999 POUNDS.	439	100.0	8.7	77.5	13.6	.1	-	-	.1
30000 TO 59999 POUNDS.	726	100.0	1.3	64.5	34.2	-	-	-	-
60000 TO 89999 POUNDS.	32	100.0	60.2	29.8	10.0	-	-	-	-
90000 POUNDS AND OVER.	674	100.0	67.1	21.5	.9	-	8.8	-	1.7
200 TO 299 MILES........	2 382	100.0	50.2	44.2	5.5	-	-	-	-
UNDER 1000 POUNDS.....	14	100.0	-	92.6	2.7	.6	-	4.1	-
1000 TO 9999 POUNDS...	178	100.0	7.0	88.1	4.4	-	-	.3	.2
10000 TO 29999 POUNDS.	433	100.0	8.1	83.6	8.2	-	-	-	.1
30000 TO 59999 POUNDS.	536	100.0	5.0	78.8	16.2	-	-	-	-
60000 TO 89999 POUNDS.	591	100.0	96.4	3.3	.3	-	-	-	-
90000 POUNDS AND OVER.	626	100.0	87.8	12.2	-	-	-	-	-
300 TO 499 MILES........	2 032	100.0	44.3	45.0	10.6	-	-	.1	-
UNDER 1000 POUNDS.....	20	100.0	.3	91.7	2.5	1.2	-	4.3	-
1000 TO 9999 POUNDS...	199	100.0	18.5	78.5	2.4	.1	-	.5	-
10000 TO 29999 POUNDS.	558	100.0	23.9	65.8	10.2	-	-	-	-
30000 TO 59999 POUNDS.	642	100.0	21.2	55.3	23.5	-	-	-	-
60000 TO 89999 POUNDS.	65	100.0	85.4	12.3	2.4	-	-	-	-
90000 POUNDS AND OVER.	545	100.0	98.5	1.4	-	-	. -	-	.1
500 TO 999 MILES........	3 318	100.0	71.2	25.7	2.7	.1	-	.1	.3
UNDER 1000 POUNDS.....	26	100.0	.7	91.4	1.7	4.0	-	2.1	.1
1000 TO 9999 POUNDS...	115	100.0	31.5	62.6	5.3	.7	-	-	-
10000 TO 29999 POUNDS.	318	100.0	55.3	39.2	5.1	-	-	.5	-
30000 TO 59999 POUNDS.	670	100.0	20.6	68.1	9.8	-	-	-	1.5
60000 TO 89999 POUNDS.	556	100.0	93.7	5.7	-	.5	-	-	-
90000 POUNDS AND OVER.	1 631	100.0	91.3	8.7	-	-	-	-	-
1000 TO 1499 MILES......	2 879	100.0	96.6	2.8	.6	.1	-	-	-
UNDER 1000 POUNDS.....	6	100.0	.3	89.7	.9	4.0	-	5.1	-
1000 TO 9999 POUNDS...	21	100.0	38.4	60.8	.3	.3	.2	-	-
10000 TO 29999 POUNDS.	51	100.0	84.3	11.6	-	4.1	-	-	-
30000 TO 59999 POUNDS.	77	100.0	15.9	61.9	22.2	-	-	-	-
60000 TO 89999 POUNDS.	767	100.0	99.7	.3	-	-	-	-	-
90000 POUNDS AND OVER.	1 956	100.0	99.7	.3	-	-	-	-	-
1500 MILES OR OVER......	791	100.0	87.0	10.9	.4	.1	1.6	-	-
UNDER 1000 POUNDS.....	8	100.0	6.7	83.3	2.6	4.3	.5	2.3	.3
1000 TO 9999 POUNDS...	32	100.0	7.9	87.9	1.7	.2	2.3	-	-
10000 TO 29999 POUNDS.	28	100.0	51.5	34.6	1.5	-	12.3	-	-
30000 TO 59999 POUNDS.	40	100.0	70.0	18.1	4.6	-	7.3	-	-
60000 TO 89999 POUNDS.	249	100.0	99.3	-	-	-	.7	-	-
90000 POUNDS AND OVER.	431	100.0	91.4	7.8	-	-	.9	-	-
TON-MILES OF SHIPMENTS	(millions of ton-miles)								
U.S. TOTAL.........	9 122	100.0	76.7	18.8	3.2	.1	1.1	-	.1
UNDER 100 MILES........	294	100.0	41.5	22.8	15.5	-	20.1	-	-
UNDER 1000 POUNDS.....	1	100.0	.3	83.5	8.6	-	-	7.5	-
1000 TO 9999 POUNDS...	13	100.0	2.7	75.5	21.3	-	-	.2	.3
10000 TO 29999 POUNDS.	25	100.0	10.2	71.8	17.7	-	-	-	.3
30000 TO 59999 POUNDS.	39	100.0	5.2	60.7	34.1	-	-	-	-
60000 TO 89999 POUNDS.	2	100.0	1.6	66.6	29.8	-	1.9	-	-
90000 POUNDS AND OVER.	212	100.0	55.2	5.7	11.3	-	27.8	-	-
100 TO 199 MILES........	319	100.0	24.7	57.7	15.0	-	2.2	-	.4
UNDER 1000 POUNDS.....	2	100.0	-	93.3	4.0	.5	-	2.2	-
1000 TO 9999 POUNDS...	38	100.0	4.9	86.0	8.9	.1	-	.1	-
10000 TO 29999 POUNDS.	67	100.0	8.8	78.2	12.9	.1	-	-	-
30000 TO 59999 POUNDS.	106	100.0	1.3	66.4	32.3	-	-	-	-
60000 TO 89999 POUNDS.	5	100.0	60.1	32.1	7.8	-	-	-	-
90000 POUNDS AND OVER.	98	100.0	67.3	23.6	.8	-	7.1	-	1.2

See footnotes at end of table 4.

TABLE 4. **TCC GROUP 329—Percent Distribution of Distance Shipped and Weight of Shipment, by Means of Transport: 1972**—Continued

Distance shipped and weight of shipment [2] [3]	Number	Percent distribution by means of transport							
		All means of transport	Rail	Motor carrier	Private truck	Air	Water	Other	Unknown
TON-MILES OF SHIPMENTS	(millions of ton-miles)								
200 TO 299 MILES	583	100.0	49.8	44.5	5.6	-	-	-	-
UNDER 1000 POUNDS	3	100.0	-	92.5	2.8	.6	-	4.0	-
1000 TO 9999 POUNDS	43	100.0	7.3	87.8	4.3	-	-	.3	.3
10000 TO 29999 POUNDS	106	100.0	8.2	83.4	8.3	-	-	-	.1
30000 TO 59999 POUNDS	133	100.0	5.0	79.0	16.0	-	-	-	-
60000 TO 89999 POUNDS	145	100.0	96.2	3.4	.3	-	-	-	-
90000 POUNDS AND OVER	150	100.0	87.8	12.2	-	-	-	-	-
300 TO 499 MILES	771	100.0	44.2	45.2	10.4	-	-	.1	-
UNDER 1000 POUNDS	7	100.0	.3	91.7	2.4	1.3	-	4.4	-
1000 TO 9999 POUNDS	76	100.0	19.9	77.2	2.4	-	-	.4	-
10000 TO 29999 POUNDS	209	100.0	25.6	64.6	9.8	-	-	-	-
30000 TO 59999 POUNDS	251	100.0	20.8	56.4	22.8	-	-	-	-
60000 TO 89999 POUNDS	25	100.0	84.0	13.5	2.5	-	-	-	-
90000 POUNDS AND OVER	201	100.0	98.6	1.4	-	-	-	-	.1
500 TO 999 MILES	2 364	100.0	72.4	24.7	2.4	.2	-	.1	.3
UNDER 1000 POUNDS	18	100.0	.7	91.8	1.5	3.8	-	2.1	.1
1000 TO 9999 POUNDS	77	100.0	31.4	62.7	5.0	.9	-	-	-
10000 TO 29999 POUNDS	213	100.0	57.5	37.0	4.8	-	-	.7	-
30000 TO 59999 POUNDS	460	100.0	21.2	68.2	9.0	-	-	-	1.6
60000 TO 89999 POUNDS	404	100.0	94.1	5.2	-	.7	-	-	-
90000 POUNDS AND OVER	1 191	100.0	91.3	8.7	-	-	-	-	-
1000 TO 1499 MILES	3 292	100.0	96.4	2.9	.6	.1	-	-	-
UNDER 1000 POUNDS	7	100.0	.3	90.0	.9	4.2	-	4.6	-
1000 TO 9999 POUNDS	24	100.0	36.9	62.3	.3	.3	.2	-	-
10000 TO 29999 POUNDS	59	100.0	83.0	13.1	-	3.9	-	-	-
30000 TO 59999 POUNDS	91	100.0	15.7	61.4	22.9	-	-	-	-
60000 TO 89999 POUNDS	916	100.0	99.8	.2	-	-	-	-	-
90000 POUNDS AND OVER	2 192	100.0	99.7	.3	-	-	-	-	-
1500 MILES OR OVER	1 496	100.0	85.2	12.1	.4	.1	2.2	-	-
UNDER 1000 POUNDS	17	100.0	8.0	81.4	2.9	4.4	.7	2.3	.3
1000 TO 9999 POUNDS	70	100.0	7.4	88.2	1.8	.2	2.5	-	-
10000 TO 29999 POUNDS	60	100.0	42.4	40.0	1.6	-	16.0	-	-
30000 TO 59999 POUNDS	95	100.0	68.9	18.5	4.0	-	8.5	-	-
60000 TO 89999 POUNDS	416	100.0	99.0	-	-	-	1.0	-	-
90000 POUNDS AND OVER	835	100.0	91.5	7.5	-	-	1.0	-	-

Note: Detail may not add to total due to rounding. The introductory table shows the estimates of sampling variability for tons; sampling variability for ton-miles has not been estimated. See the map in the Introduction for the States comprising the geographic divisions of the United States.

Shipments excluded from the survey are those moving by pipeline (primarily petroleum products from refineries), parcel post shipments, and commodities moved by own power (motorized vehicles, aircraft, etc.) or towed (prefabricated buildings, etc.). Local shipments (commodities shipped less than 25 miles from the plant) and shipments within the same city are also excluded. Shipments to Alaska and Hawaii from the 48 conterminous States and the District of Columbia are included; however, no data were obtained for shipments originating in Alaska and Hawaii.

- Represents zero or rounds to zero. (D) Withheld to avoid disclosing figures for individual companies.

[1] Production of this commodity is concentrated in the geographic divisions shown; figures and distributions for geographic divisions not shown are included in the total.

[2] Distances of shipments to foreign destinations are calculated only to the U.S. port of exit.

[3] Includes only shipments represented by bills of lading and invoices. Summary records which did not show individual weights of shipments are not included.

Primary Metal Products

CONTENTS

[Page numbers listed here omit the State prefix number that appears as part of the number for each page]

TABLES   (The tables listed below are shown for each of the Transportation Commodity Classification groups in this report)

Comparisons of Tons and Ton-Miles of Shipments for Geographic Divisions of Origin and for Sampling Variability: 1972 and 1967

1. Percent Distribution of Geographic Division of Origin and Distance Shipped, by Means of Transport: 1972

2. Percent Distribution of Geographic Division of Origin and Means of Transport, by Geographic Division of Destination: 1972

3. Percent Distribution of Geographic Division of Destination and Means of Transport, by Geographic Division of Origin: 1972

4. Percent Distribution of Distance Shipped and Weight of Shipment, by Means of Transport: 1972

TCC 331. Steel Works and Rolling Mill Products

Comparisons of Tons and Ton-Miles of Shipments for
Geographic Divisions of Origin and for Sampling Variability: 1972 and 1967

Geographic division of origin	Estimates				Relative sampling variability in tons (percent)	
	1972		1967		1972	1967
	Tons (thousands)	Ton-miles (millions)	Tons (thousands)	Ton-miles (millions)		
U.S. total	114,166	31,668	112,167	34,049	4.7	4.0
New England	(D)	(D)	624	226	(*)	(*)
Middle Atlantic	24,243	7,380	27,905	9,246	3.7	(*)
East North Central	58,697	14,647	51,817	13,188	7.6	(*)
West North Central	(D)	(D)	1,166	497	(*)	(*)
South Atlantic	11,214	3,325	10,985	4,070	27.8	(*)
East South Central	7,091	2,045	8,462	3,190	16.9	(*)
West South Central	4,689	1,439	5,410	1,446	47.3	(*)
Mountain	(D)	(D)	2,208	1,177	(*)	(*)
Pacific	3,782	838	3,590	1,009	16.3	(*)

(D) Withheld to avoid disclosing figures for individual companies.   (*) Data not published.

TABLE 1. **TCC GROUP 331—Percent Distribution of Geographic Division of Origin and Distance Shipped, by Means of Transport: 1972**

Geographic division of origin [1] and distance shipped [2]	Number	Percent distribution by means of transport							
		All means of transport	Rail	Motor carrier	Private truck	Air	Water	Other	Unknown
TONS OF SHIPMENTS	(thousands of tons)								
U.S. TOTAL	114 166	100.0	43.7	46.3	4.5	-	5.5	-	.1
MIDDLE ATLANTIC.........	24 243	100.0	40.0	50.1	3.9	-	5.6	-	.4
UNDER 100 MILES.......	6 928	100.0	45.0	48.0	6.7	-	-	-	.2
100 TO 199 MILES.....	4 105	100.0	39.1	57.5	2.5	-	.2	-	.2
200 TO 299 MILES.....	5 024	100.0	39.2	54.4	4.3	-	1.9	-	.6
300 TO 499 MILES.....	4 565	100.0	30.3	54.7	1.9	-	12.6	-	.2
500 TO 999 MILES.....	2 538	100.0	39.7	34.4	2.4	-	23.1	-	.5
1000 TO 1499 MILES....	665	100.0	51.6	40.6	1.6	-	6.2	-	.4
1500 MILES OR OVER....	416	100.0	64.7	22.2	1.0	-	11.8	.1	.2
EAST NORTH CENTRAL......	58 697	100.0	41.4	49.5	3.4	-	5.7	-	.1
UNDER 100 MILES.......	17 953	100.0	34.9	58.6	5.6	-	.8	-	-
100 TO 199 MILES.....	13 830	100.0	38.3	47.2	3.1	-	11.2	.2	-
200 TO 299 MILES.....	11 577	100.0	44.1	52.5	1.7	-	1.7	-	-
300 TO 499 MILES.....	9 029	100.0	40.4	50.6	2.1	-	6.9	-	-
500 TO 999 MILES.....	4 693	100.0	53.5	25.5	3.2	-	17.5	-	.3
1000 TO 1499 MILES....	730	100.0	82.8	16.5	-	-	.7	-	-
1500 MILES OR OVER....	883	100.0	96.8	2.2	.9	-	-	.1	-
SOUTH ATLANTIC..........	11 214	100.0	56.7	32.8	6.8	-	3.6	-	.1
UNDER 100 MILES.......	1 962	100.0	42.6	42.9	14.4	-	-	-	-
100 TO 199 MILES.....	3 645	100.0	64.7	30.5	4.6	-	-	-	.1
200 TO 299 MILES.....	2 024	100.0	60.2	27.6	7.5	-	4.4	-	.3
300 TO 499 MILES.....	1 932	100.0	47.8	44.4	6.5	-	1.3	-	-
500 TO 999 MILES.....	1 086	100.0	72.1	25.2	2.7	-	-	-	-
1000 TO 1499 MILES....	402	100.0	24.6	2.7	-	-	72.7	-	-
1500 MILES OR OVER....	159	100.0	89.0	10.5	.1	.1	.3	-	-
EAST SOUTH CENTRAL......	7 091	100.0	57.8	34.2	2.7	-	5.2	-	-
UNDER 100 MILES.......	1 234	100.0	57.2	39.6	3.2	-	-	-	-
100 TO 199 MILES.....	2 252	100.0	53.3	37.5	2.9	-	6.3	-	-
200 TO 299 MILES.....	700	100.0	22.2	65.6	4.2	-	8.0	-	-
300 TO 499 MILES.....	1 852	100.0	69.6	26.5	2.2	-	1.6	-	-
500 TO 999 MILES.....	959	100.0	68.7	14.4	1.9	-	14.8	-	.1
1000 TO 1499 MILES....	10	100.0	81.5	18.5	-	-	-	-	-
1500 MILES OR OVER....	81	100.0	94.2	5.6	-	-	-	.2	-
WEST SOUTH CENTRAL......	4 689	100.0	45.4	33.3	5.1	-	16.2	-	-
UNDER 100 MILES.......	982	100.0	60.7	18.4	3.6	-	17.3	-	-
100 TO 199 MILES.....	301	100.0	15.9	60.5	23.6	-	-	-	-
200 TO 299 MILES.....	1 735	100.0	36.9	45.5	5.3	-	12.3	-	-
300 TO 499 MILES.....	1 110	100.0	40.0	23.2	2.9	-	33.9	-	-
500 TO 999 MILES.....	369	100.0	59.0	38.8	2.2	-	-	-	-
1000 TO 1499 MILES....	162	100.0	96.4	3.2	.5	-	-	-	-
1500 MILES OR OVER....	26	100.0	100.0	-	-	-	-	-	-
PACIFIC.................	3 782	100.0	28.1	63.8	8.0	-	.1	-	-
UNDER 100 MILES.......	2 170	100.0	24.1	64.2	11.7	-	-	-	-
100 TO 199 MILES.....	176	100.0	36.4	50.1	13.5	-	-	-	-
200 TO 299 MILES.....	71	100.0	38.5	44.7	16.8	-	-	-	-
300 TO 499 MILES.....	886	100.0	21.1	78.3	.5	-	-	-	-
500 TO 999 MILES.....	374	100.0	53.2	45.5	1.3	-	-	-	.1
1000 TO 1499 MILES....	61	100.0	66.7	33.3	-	-	-	-	-
1500 MILES OR OVER....	42	100.0	47.5	37.5	4.7	.2	10.1	-	-
TON-MILES OF SHIPMENTS	(millions of ton-miles)								
U.S. TOTAL..........	31 668	100.0	51.6	37.1	2.8	-	8.3	-	.1
MIDDLE ATLANTIC.........	7 380	100.0	42.1	43.9	2.4	-	11.2	-	.3
UNDER 100 MILES.......	311	100.0	41.3	52.1	6.2	-	-	-	.3
100 TO 199 MILES.....	627	100.0	39.3	57.3	2.5	-	.2	-	.6
200 TO 299 MILES.....	1 214	100.0	38.7	54.9	4.3	-	2.0	-	.2
300 TO 499 MILES.....	1 726	100.0	31.5	54.8	1.8	-	11.4	-	.5
500 TO 999 MILES.....	1 823	100.0	40.4	32.8	2.1	-	24.3	-	.4
1000 TO 1499 MILES....	784	100.0	53.5	39.1	1.5	-	6.0	-	-
1500 MILES OR OVER....	892	100.0	63.1	22.4	1.1	-	13.1	.1	.2
EAST NORTH CENTRAL......	14 647	100.0	51.9	38.1	2.3	-	7.6	-	.1
UNDER 100 MILES.......	829	100.0	32.4	62.3	4.9	-	.4	-	-
100 TO 199 MILES.....	1 931	100.0	38.2	49.2	3.1	-	9.4	.1	-
200 TO 299 MILES.....	2 773	100.0	44.2	52.2	1.7	-	1.8	-	-
300 TO 499 MILES.....	3 417	100.0	40.8	49.6	2.0	-	7.5	-	-
500 TO 999 MILES.....	3 198	100.0	52.5	25.1	3.1	-	19.1	-	.2
1000 TO 1499 MILES....	853	100.0	83.4	15.9	-	-	.7	-	-
1500 MILES OR OVER....	1 643	100.0	96.8	2.2	.9	-	-	.1	-
SOUTH ATLANTIC..........	3 325	100.0	58.6	26.7	4.0	-	10.5	-	.1
UNDER 100 MILES.......	86	100.0	35.5	53.8	10.7	-	-	-	.1
100 TO 199 MILES.....	507	100.0	61.7	33.6	4.6	-	-	.1	.1
200 TO 299 MILES.....	475	100.0	58.4	29.9	7.2	-	4.2	-	.2
300 TO 499 MILES.....	730	100.0	49.0	43.4	6.4	-	1.1	-	-
500 TO 999 MILES.....	750	100.0	75.2	22.1	2.7	-	-	-	-
1000 TO 1499 MILES....	432	100.0	23.1	2.6	-	-	74.2	-	-
1500 MILES OR OVER....	343	100.0	89.1	10.4	.2	.1	.3	-	-

See footnotes at end of table 4.

TABLE 1. **TCC GROUP 331**—Percent Distribution of Geographic Division of Origin and Distance Shipped, by Means of Transport: 1972—Continued

Geographic division of origin [1] and distance shipped [2]	Number	Percent distribution by means of transport							
		All means of transport	Rail	Motor carrier	Private truck	Air	Water	Other	Unknown
TON-MILES OF SHIPMENTS	(millions of ton-miles)								
EAST SOUTH CENTRAL	2 045	100.0	65.1	26.7	2.2	-	6.0	-	-
UNDER 100 MILES	50	100.0	56.9	40.8	2.3	-	-	-	-
100 TO 199 MILES	340	100.0	57.6	34.4	2.8	-	5.1	-	-
200 TO 299 MILES	175	100.0	23.3	65.9	3.9	-	6.9	-	-
300 TO 499 MILES	696	100.0	69.5	26.4	2.2	-	1.9	-	-
500 TO 999 MILES	593	100.0	69.7	14.8	2.0	-	13.4	-	.1
1000 TO 1499 MILES	13	100.0	81.4	18.6	-	-	-	-	-
1500 MILES OR OVER	176	100.0	89.7	10.1	-	-	-	.2	-
WEST SOUTH CENTRAL	1 439	100.0	53.2	28.6	3.6	-	14.6	-	-
UNDER 100 MILES	38	100.0	38.5	21.1	3.9	-	36.6	-	-
100 TO 199 MILES	48	100.0	17.1	60.7	22.2	-	-	-	-
200 TO 299 MILES	409	100.0	38.1	44.5	5.2	-	12.1	-	-
300 TO 499 MILES	440	100.0	40.8	23.2	2.6	-	33.4	-	-
500 TO 999 MILES	251	100.0	64.6	33.3	2.1	-	-	-	-
1000 TO 1499 MILES	205	100.0	96.4	3.1	.5	-	-	-	-
1500 MILES OR OVER	46	100.0	100.0	-	-	-	-	-	-
PACIFIC	838	100.0	37.7	57.7	3.3	-	1.3	-	-
UNDER 100 MILES	94	100.0	21.5	67.1	11.5	-	-	-	-
100 TO 199 MILES	26	100.0	36.7	50.6	12.7	-	-	-	-
200 TO 299 MILES	17	100.0	38.8	46.5	14.7	-	-	-	-
300 TO 499 MILES	308	100.0	21.7	77.5	.6	-	-	-	.1
500 TO 999 MILES	231	100.0	54.4	44.1	1.5	-	-	-	-
1000 TO 1499 MILES	75	100.0	64.6	35.4	-	-	-	-	-
1500 MILES OR OVER	84	100.0	44.3	36.7	6.4	.2	12.4	-	-

See footnotes at end of table 4.

TABLE 2. **TCC GROUP 331**—Percent Distribution of Geographic Division of Origin and Means of Transport, by Geographic Division of Destination: 1972

Geographic division of origin [1] and means of transport	Number	Percent distribution by division of destination									
		U.S. total	New England	Middle Atlantic	East North Central	West North Central	South Atlantic	East South Central	West South Central	Mountain	Pacific
TONS OF SHIPMENTS	(thousands of tons)										
U.S. TOTAL	114 166	100.0	2.1	15.5	44.4	6.0	9.7	7.1	7.6	1.8	5.7
RAIL	49 838	100.0	2.7	16.1	34.9	6.0	15.0	7.5	8.5	2.3	7.1
MOTOR CARRIER	52 826	100.0	1.8	16.3	55.6	5.8	5.2	4.4	4.7	1.1	4.9
PRIVATE TRUCK	5 104	100.0	1.1	17.7	34.9	6.2	15.8	6.8	6.4	6.7	6.6
AIR	1	100.0	3.9	22.3	16.3	5.2	15.7	6.8	4.9	1.1	23.8
WATER	6 233	100.0	-	2.2	32.7	7.6	1.6	29.2	25.9	-	.9
OTHER	29	100.0	1.1	9.6	81.8	.1	2.9	.5	.1	-	3.9
UNKNOWN	132	100.0	.1	18.3	36.8	7.3	15.4	9.3	10.1	1.5	1.4
MIDDLE ATLANTIC	24 243	100.0	5.0	37.9	32.2	1.8	9.5	6.9	4.7	.3	1.6
RAIL	9 699	100.0	7.8	41.6	24.5	2.2	12.5	3.7	4.6	.5	2.5
MOTOR CARRIER	12 151	100.0	3.5	37.3	42.0	1.7	7.8	3.7	3.1	.2	.7
PRIVATE TRUCK	943	100.0	2.1	60.8	17.2	1.5	12.9	3.8	1.3	-	.4
AIR	-	100.0	-	16.5	22.7	6.5	30.1	1.3	4.2	2.0	16.8
WATER	1 358	100.0	-	2.1	9.0	-	1.0	61.5	22.8	-	3.6
OTHER	3	100.0	7.6	69.9	7.0	-	2.1	.4	-	-	13.0
UNKNOWN	85	100.0	-	24.4	40.7	11.1	11.2	11.9	-	-	.9
EAST NORTH CENTRAL	58 697	100.0	.9	9.1	66.6	9.2	3.1	5.2	3.7	.8	1.5
RAIL	24 290	100.0	1.4	11.0	58.3	9.6	4.5	5.8	4.8	1.3	3.4
MOTOR CARRIER	29 034	100.0	.7	8.7	74.9	8.2	2.3	3.5	1.2	.5	.1
PRIVATE TRUCK	1 984	100.0	.5	6.8	74.3	10.3	1.3	4.2	1.8	.3	.4
AIR	-	100.0	5.5	47.8	14.4	2.9	12.4	14.8	.9	.9	.3
WATER	3 331	100.0	-	.1	50.5	14.2	1.1	16.4	17.8	-	1.9
OTHER	24	100.0	-	.3	97.5	-	-	-	.1	-	-
UNKNOWN	31	100.0	.1	8.5	43.4	.4	.1	6.5	41.1	-	-
SOUTH ATLANTIC	11 214	100.0	4.4	21.1	14.0	1.2	50.5	2.7	4.7	-	1.4
RAIL	6 362	100.0	3.2	14.1	5.7	2.1	65.6	3.0	4.1	-	2.2
MOTOR CARRIER	3 673	100.0	7.3	36.7	30.1	-	22.7	2.3	.3	-	.4
PRIVATE TRUCK	759	100.0	2.2	13.4	1.4	.1	79.6	3.0	.2	-	-
AIR	-	100.0	13.9	3.2	2.1	.4	-	.1	.5	-	79.7
WATER	407	100.0	-	3.9	22.1	-	9.5	2.1	62.2	-	.1
OTHER	-	100.0	-	.3	-	.1	99.4	.1	-	-	-
UNKNOWN	10	100.0	-	5.5	-	-	94.5	-	-	-	-
EAST SOUTH CENTRAL	7 091	100.0	.4	7.3	24.7	3.1	17.9	33.2	12.0	.2	1.2
RAIL	4 097	100.0	.7	8.6	10.6	4.5	22.7	36.3	14.3	.4	1.9
MOTOR CARRIER	2 428	100.0	-	3.4	47.1	1.5	11.2	29.7	6.8	-	.2
PRIVATE TRUCK	194	100.0	.2	-	14.4	-	28.9	46.3	10.2	-	-
AIR	-	100.0	-	-	43.3	18.9	-	28.0	9.3	.5	-
WATER	370	100.0	-	22.9	38.5	-	2.9	15.1	20.6	-	-
OTHER	-	100.0	8.6	6.3	1.7	-	19.5	20.7	.5	-	42.7
UNKNOWN	-	100.0	-	-	12.4	-	83.0	4.7	-	-	-

See footnotes at end of table 4.

TABLE 2. **TCC GROUP 331—Percent Distribution of Geographic Division of Origin and Means of Transport, by Geographic Division of Destination: 1972**—Continued

Geographic division of origin [1] and means of transport	Number	Percent distribution by division of destination									
		U.S. total	New England	Middle Atlantic	East North Central	West North Central	South Atlantic	East South Central	West South Central	Mountain	Pacific
TONS OF SHIPMENTS	(thousands of tons)										
WEST SOUTH CENTRAL	4 689	100.0	.2	2.0	.4	1.0	1.0	14.5	75.3	3.8	1.8
RAIL	2 130	100.0	.4	4.2	.7	.5	1.7	12.7	70.6	5.2	4.0
MOTOR CARRIER	1 559	100.0	-	.3	.2	2.3	.8	2.1	90.1	4.2	-
PRIVATE TRUCK	240	100.0	-	.3	-	-	-	.6	99.0	-	-
AIR	-	100.0	-	2.1	-	-	.5	-	94.4	-	3.0
WATER	758	100.0	-	-	-	-	-	49.5	50.5	-	-
OTHER	-	100.0	-	-	-	-	-	98.7	-	-	1.3
UNKNOWN	-	100.0	-	-	-	-	-	-	100.0	-	-
PACIFIC	3 782	100.0	-	.1	.5	.5	.1	-	1.5	4.9	92.4
RAIL	1 061	100.0	-	.1	1.1	1.5	.1	-	1.5	4.9	92.4
MOTOR CARRIER	2 415	100.0	-	.1	.3	.1	-	.2	3.6	3.7	90.1
PRIVATE TRUCK	300	100.0	-	-	.3	.1	.2	-	.8	6.0	92.5
AIR	-	100.0	-	-	-	-	-	-	-	.3	99.7
WATER	4	100.0	-	3.0	5.5	-	3.5	-	15.8	.2	72.0
OTHER	-	100.0	-	-	-	-	-	-	-	-	100.0
UNKNOWN	1	100.0	-	-	-	-	-	-	-	-	100.0
TON-MILES OF SHIPMENTS	(millions of ton-miles)										
U.S. TOTAL	31 668	100.0	2.8	9.8	26.2	8.6	9.4	9.0	15.5	3.5	15.1
RAIL	16 336	100.0	3.2	8.1	17.6	8.1	12.6	7.8	15.2	4.3	23.1
MOTOR CARRIER	11 754	100.0	3.0	13.6	42.2	9.5	6.0	6.2	9.8	3.1	6.8
PRIVATE TRUCK	894	100.0	2.3	13.5	22.1	11.3	17.5	7.6	11.4	5.8	8.4
AIR	1	100.0	4.0	9.5	7.5	4.2	8.3	2.7	4.3	5.8	57.8
WATER	2 633	100.0	-	2.1	9.9	6.5	2.8	29.7	44.1	1.6	4.9
OTHER	5	100.0	1.4	3.1	51.2	.2	2.7	1.1	.2	-	40.1
UNKNOWN	42	100.0	.1	5.9	24.3	16.8	10.0	11.2	17.0	10.3	4.4
MIDDLE ATLANTIC	7 380	100.0	5.2	14.0	27.4	4.5	8.5	11.5	16.3	1.4	11.3
RAIL	3 108	100.0	7.7	12.1	20.7	5.4	11.0	7.6	16.4	2.2	16.7
MOTOR CARRIER	3 238	100.0	4.2	18.4	40.0	4.5	7.4	6.7	12.3	1.0	5.6
PRIVATE TRUCK	178	100.0	3.2	27.2	21.2	6.1	20.9	8.6	7.2	-	5.5
AIR	-	100.0	-	2.3	12.5	8.0	16.3	.6	5.8	4.2	50.4
WATER	828	100.0	-	.8	4.4	-	.9	45.7	34.0	-	14.1
OTHER	1	100.0	3.3	6.9	7.8	-	2.9	.5	-	-	78.6
UNKNOWN	23	100.0	-	7.9	31.7	30.1	9.4	14.6	-	-	6.4
EAST NORTH CENTRAL	14 647	100.0	2.0	9.4	35.5	13.5	5.0	8.5	11.6	3.5	11.0
RAIL	7 607	100.0	2.3	8.7	25.2	11.7	6.2	8.2	12.4	4.8	20.5
MOTOR CARRIER	5 584	100.0	2.0	12.1	53.0	14.9	4.0	6.4	4.5	2.6	.7
PRIVATE TRUCK	333	100.0	2.4	10.5	39.0	22.8	3.1	9.4	6.4	1.8	4.6
AIR	-	100.0	9.6	49.1	6.9	2.6	16.4	10.5	1.9	1.7	1.2
WATER	1 107	100.0	-	-	16.7	15.6	2.0	21.7	44.0	-	-
OTHER	3	100.0	.2	1.7	73.8	.1	.2	-	.3	-	23.6
UNKNOWN	11	100.0	.3	4.4	24.7	.3	.1	11.7	58.6	-	-
SOUTH ATLANTIC	3 325	100.0	5.6	11.2	13.1	3.1	35.1	5.1	16.4	.1	10.3
RAIL	1 950	100.0	4.1	4.5	6.3	5.3	45.7	5.6	12.8	.1	15.7
MOTOR CARRIER	888	100.0	11.3	28.8	32.5	.1	16.4	5.5	1.4	.3	3.7
PRIVATE TRUCK	134	100.0	4.3	16.9	2.7	.4	67.4	7.0	1.0	-	.4
AIR	-	100.0	7.4	1.3	1.1	.2	-	-	.2	-	89.9
WATER	350	100.0	-	1.4	5.9	-	11.3	.8	80.4	-	.3
OTHER	-	100.0	-	.7	.1	.6	97.7	.9	-	-	-
UNKNOWN	1	100.0	-	6.6	-	-	93.4	-	-	-	-
EAST SOUTH CENTRAL	2 045	100.0	1.0	8.4	21.0	6.0	19.5	15.1	19.6	.9	8.6
RAIL	1 332	100.0	1.4	7.3	11.6	7.8	23.2	14.9	20.6	1.3	11.9
MOTOR CARRIER	545	100.0	-	5.6	45.9	3.5	12.2	16.2	13.1	.2	3.3
PRIVATE TRUCK	44	100.0	.8	.1	16.3	-	41.1	20.8	21.0	-	-
AIR	-	100.0	-	-	42.3	17.8	-	26.8	12.0	1.1	-
WATER	122	100.0	-	35.8	14.2	-	3.3	9.9	36.8	-	-
OTHER	-	100.0	6.8	2.8	.6	-	2.7	6.6	.3	-	80.2
UNKNOWN	-	100.0	-	-	10.4	-	86.8	2.8	-	-	-
WEST SOUTH CENTRAL	1 439	100.0	.8	7.5	1.1	1.8	2.9	19.0	49.4	8.1	9.1
RAIL	765	100.0	1.5	13.3	1.9	.7	4.3	14.6	35.7	10.8	17.1
MOTOR CARRIER	412	100.0	.1	1.3	.5	5.0	2.3	3.7	78.7	8.4	.1
PRIVATE TRUCK	51	100.0	-	1.8	.1	-	-	1.1	97.0	-	-
AIR	-	100.0	-	13.7	-	-	3.7	-	58.6	-	24.0
WATER	210	100.0	-	-	-	-	-	69.8	30.2	-	-
OTHER	-	100.0	-	-	-	-	-	96.2	-	-	3.8
UNKNOWN	-	100.0	-	-	-	-	-	-	100.0	-	-
PACIFIC	838	100.0	.1	.9	4.5	2.8	1.0	.1	8.1	11.5	71.0
RAIL	316	100.0	-	.5	7.3	6.2	-	-	14.1	8.6	63.3
MOTOR CARRIER	484	100.0	.2	1.2	3.1	.8	1.7	.2	4.8	14.2	73.9
PRIVATE TRUCK	27	100.0	-	-	.1	-	-	-	-	.6	99.4
AIR	-	100.0	-	3.5	4.5	-	3.9	-	10.7	-	77.3
WATER	10	100.0	-	-	-	-	-	-	-	-	100.0
OTHER	-	100.0	-	-	-	-	-	-	-	-	100.0
UNKNOWN	-	100.0	-	-	-	-	-	-	-	-	100.0

See footnotes at end of table 4.

TABLE 3. **TCC GROUP 331**—Percent Distribution of Geographic Division of Destination and Means of Transport, by Geographic Division of Origin: 1972

Geographic division of destination and means of transport	Number	Percent distribution by division of origin[1]									
		U.S. total	New England	Middle Atlantic	East North Central	West North Central	South Atlantic	East South Central	West South Central	Mountain	Pacific
TONS OF SHIPMENTS	(thousands of tons)										
U.S. TOTAL.............	114 166	100.0	(D)	21.2	51.4	(D)	9.8	6.2	4.1	(D)	3.3
RAIL..................	49 838	100.0	(D)	19.5	48.7	(D)	12.8	8.2	4.3	(D)	2.1
MOTOR CARRIER.........	52 826	100.0	(D)	23.0	55.0	(D)	7.0	4.6	3.0	(D)	4.6
PRIVATE TRUCK.........	5 104	100.0	(D)	18.5	38.9	(D)	14.9	3.8	4.7	(D)	5.9
AIR...................	1	100.0	(D)	38.1	32.0	(D)	15.5	5.4	1.4	(D)	6.9
WATER.................	6 233	100.0	(D)	21.8	53.4	(D)	6.5	5.9	12.2	(D)	.1
OTHER.................	29	100.0	(D)	13.0	82.1	(D)	2.1	1.3	.1	(D)	.1
UNKNOWN...............	132	100.0	(D)	64.9	23.8	(D)	8.1	.6	-	(D)	.8
NEW ENGLAND...........	2 353	100.0	(D)	51.4	23.3	(D)	20.7	1.2	.3	(D)	-
RAIL..................	1 328	100.0	(D)	57.2	24.8	(D)	15.3	2.0	.6	(D)	-
MOTOR CARRIER.........	968	100.0	(D)	44.3	21.6	(D)	27.7	-	-	(D)	-
PRIVATE TRUCK.........	56	100.0	(D)	35.4	18.1	(D)	29.4	.7	-	(D)	-
AIR...................	-	100.0	(D)	-	45.1	(D)	54.9	-	-	(D)	-
WATER.................	-	100.0	(D)	-	-	(D)	-	-	-	(D)	-
OTHER.................	-	100.0	(D)	86.5	2.9	(D)	-	9.6	-	(D)	-
UNKNOWN...............	-	100.0	(D)	2.1	31.1	(D)	-	-	-	(D)	-
MIDDLE ATLANTIC.......	17 727	100.0	(D)	51.9	30.1	(D)	13.3	2.9	.5	(D)	-
RAIL..................	8 040	100.0	(D)	50.2	33.1	(D)	11.2	4.4	1.1	(D)	-
MOTOR CARRIER.........	8 624	100.0	(D)	52.5	29.3	(D)	15.6	1.0	.1	(D)	-
PRIVATE TRUCK.........	901	100.0	(D)	63.7	15.0	(D)	11.3	-	.1	(D)	-
AIR...................	-	100.0	(D)	28.1	68.6	(D)	2.2	-	.1	(D)	.9
WATER.................	134	100.0	(D)	21.6	3.3	(D)	11.9	63.2	-	(D)	-
OTHER.................	2	100.0	(D)	94.4	2.9	(D)	.1	.8	-	(D)	-
UNKNOWN...............	24	100.0	(D)	86.5	11.1	(D)	2.4	-	-	(D)	-
EAST NORTH CENTRAL....	50 662	100.0	(D)	15.4	77.2	(D)	3.1	3.5	-	(D)	-
RAIL..................	17 374	100.0	(D)	13.7	81.5	(D)	2.1	2.5	.1	(D)	.1
MOTOR CARRIER.........	29 395	100.0	(D)	17.4	74.0	(D)	3.8	3.9	-	(D)	-
PRIVATE TRUCK.........	1 781	100.0	(D)	9.1	82.8	(D)	.6	1.6	-	(D)	-
AIR...................	-	100.0	(D)	53.1	28.3	(D)	2.0	14.3	-	(D)	2.3
WATER.................	2 037	100.0	(D)	6.0	82.6	(D)	4.4	7.0	-	(D)	-
OTHER.................	24	100.0	(D)	1.1	97.9	(D)	-	-	-	(D)	-
UNKNOWN...............	48	100.0	(D)	71.8	28.0	(D)	-	.2	-	(D)	-
WEST NORTH CENTRAL....	6 851	100.0	(D)	6.5	78.5	(D)	2.0	3.2	.7	(D)	.3
RAIL..................	2 976	100.0	(D)	7.2	78.3	(D)	4.6	6.2	.3	(D)	.5
MOTOR CARRIER.........	3 079	100.0	(D)	6.6	77.0	(D)	-	1.2	1.2	(D)	.1
PRIVATE TRUCK.........	315	100.0	(D)	4.4	65.2	(D)	.2	-	-	(D)	-
AIR...................	-	100.0	(D)	48.1	17.9	(D)	1.1	19.6	-	(D)	-
WATER.................	471	100.0	(D)	-	100.0	(D)	-	-	-	(D)	-
OTHER.................	-	100.0	(D)	1.7	62.3	(D)	2.0	-	-	(D)	-
UNKNOWN...............	9	100.0	(D)	98.8	1.2	(D)	-	-	-	(D)	-
SOUTH ATLANTIC........	11 128	100.0	(D)	20.8	16.3	(D)	50.9	11.4	.4	(D)	-
RAIL..................	7 453	100.0	(D)	16.3	14.7	(D)	56.0	12.5	.5	(D)	-
MOTOR CARRIER.........	2 747	100.0	(D)	34.6	24.0	(D)	30.4	9.9	.4	(D)	.1
PRIVATE TRUCK.........	808	100.0	(D)	15.1	3.2	(D)	74.8	6.9	-	(D)	-
AIR...................	-	100.0	(D)	73.1	25.3	(D)	-	-	-	(D)	1.6
WATER.................	98	100.0	(D)	13.2	35.6	(D)	39.5	10.9	-	(D)	-
OTHER.................	-	100.0	(D)	9.4	1.4	(D)	73.6	8.6	-	(D)	-
UNKNOWN...............	20	100.0	(D)	47.1	.1	(D)	49.8	3.0	-	(D)	-
EAST SOUTH CENTRAL....	8 093	100.0	(D)	20.8	37.7	(D)	3.8	29.1	8.4	(D)	-
RAIL..................	3 720	100.0	(D)	9.5	37.9	(D)	5.1	40.0	7.3	(D)	-
MOTOR CARRIER.........	2 300	100.0	(D)	19.4	43.8	(D)	3.7	31.4	1.4	(D)	-
PRIVATE TRUCK.........	238	100.0	(D)	15.0	34.8	(D)	9.4	37.7	.6	(D)	-
AIR...................	-	100.0	(D)	7.3	70.3	(D)	.2	22.2	-	(D)	-
WATER.................	1 821	100.0	(D)	45.9	29.9	(D)	.5	3.1	20.6	(D)	-
OTHER.................	-	100.0	(D)	9.1	3.6	(D)	.6	51.8	21.4	(D)	-
UNKNOWN...............	12	100.0	(D)	83.0	16.7	(D)	-	.3	-	(D)	-
WEST SOUTH CENTRAL....	8 693	100.0	(D)	13.2	24.8	(D)	6.1	9.8	40.6	(D)	.7
RAIL..................	4 240	100.0	(D)	10.6	27.3	(D)	6.1	13.8	35.5	(D)	.9
MOTOR CARRIER.........	2 495	100.0	(D)	15.0	14.4	(D)	.5	6.7	56.3	(D)	.7
PRIVATE TRUCK.........	327	100.0	(D)	3.7	10.8	(D)	.6	6.0	72.8	(D)	-
AIR...................	-	100.0	(D)	32.9	6.1	(D)	1.6	10.2	27.0	(D)	22.2
WATER.................	1 616	100.0	(D)	19.1	36.7	(D)	15.7	4.7	23.7	(D)	-
OTHER.................	-	100.0	(D)	-	90.0	(D)	-	9.9	.1	(D)	-
UNKNOWN...............	13	100.0	(D)	-	97.0	(D)	-	-	-	(D)	-
MOUNTAIN..............	2 095	100.0	(D)	3.4	21.7	(D)	.1	.8	8.4	(D)	8.9
RAIL..................	1 147	100.0	(D)	4.1	27.0	(D)	-	1.4	9.6	(D)	3.4
MOTOR CARRIER.........	606	100.0	(D)	3.9	22.8	(D)	.3	.1	10.8	(D)	23.9
PRIVATE TRUCK.........	340	100.0	(D)	-	1.9	(D)	-	-	-	(D)	.3
AIR...................	-	100.0	(D)	69.4	26.9	(D)	-	2.5	-	(D)	1.2
WATER.................	-	100.0	(D)	100.0	-	(D)	-	-	-	(D)	-
OTHER.................	-	100.0	(D)	-	-	(D)	-	-	-	(D)	-
UNKNOWN...............	2	100.0	(D)	-	-	(D)	-	-	-	(D)	-
PACIFIC...............	6 559	100.0	(D)	5.8	13.2	(D)	2.4	1.2	1.3	(D)	53.3
RAIL..................	3 556	100.0	(D)	6.8	23.5	(D)	4.0	2.2	2.4	(D)	26.9
MOTOR CARRIER.........	2 609	100.0	(D)	3.1	.7	(D)	.6	.2	-	(D)	85.6
PRIVATE TRUCK.........	335	100.0	(D)	1.2	2.4	(D)	.1	-	-	(D)	89.3
AIR...................	-	100.0	(D)	26.8	.4	(D)	51.7	-	.2	(D)	20.8
WATER.................	53	100.0	(D)	91.2	-	(D)	.8	-	-	(D)	8.0
OTHER.................	1	100.0	(D)	43.6	40.5	(D)	-	13.9	-	(D)	1.8
UNKNOWN...............	1	100.0	(D)	40.5	-	(D)	-	-	-	(D)	59.1

See footnotes at end of table 4.

TABLE 3. **TCC GROUP 331**—Percent Distribution of Geographic Division of Destination and Means of Transport, by Geographic Division of Origin: 1972—Continued

Geographic division of destination and means of transport	Number	Percent distribution by division of origin [1]									
		U.S. total	New England	Middle Atlantic	East North Central	West North Central	South Atlantic	East South Central	West South Central	Mountain	Pacific
TON-MILES OF SHIPMENTS	(millions of ton-miles)										
U.S. TOTAL	31 668	100.0	(D)	23.3	46.3	(D)	10.5	6.5	4.5	(D)	2.6
RAIL	16 336	100.0	(D)	19.0	46.6	(D)	11.9	8.2	4.7	(D)	1.9
MOTOR CARRIER	11 754	100.0	(D)	27.6	47.5	(D)	7.6	4.6	3.5	(D)	4.1
PRIVATE TRUCK	894	100.0	(D)	19.9	37.3	(D)	15.1	5.0	5.8	(D)	3.1
AIR	1	100.0	(D)	31.4	15.9	(D)	33.3	3.3	.2	(D)	15.2
WATER	2 633	100.0	(D)	31.5	42.1	(D)	13.3	4.7	8.0	(D)	.4
OTHER	5	100.0	(D)	24.6	63.2	(D)	.9	6.7	.2	(D)	.3
UNKNOWN	42	100.0	(D)	55.8	26.4	(D)	4.2	.9	-	(D)	.8
NEW ENGLAND	894	100.0	(D)	42.6	32.4	(D)	20.8	2.2	1.3	(D)	.1
RAIL	525	100.0	(D)	45.8	32.8	(D)	15.3	3.6	2.2	(D)	-
MOTOR CARRIER	348	100.0	(D)	38.6	31.4	(D)	28.8	-	.1	(D)	.3
PRIVATE TRUCK	20	100.0	(D)	28.5	39.1	(D)	28.6	1.7	-	(D)	-
AIR	-	100.0	(D)	-	38.3	(D)	61.7	-	-	(D)	-
WATER	-	100.0	(D)	-	-	(D)	-	-	-	(D)	-
OTHER	-	100.0	(D)	57.7	9.6	(D)	-	32.6	-	(D)	-
UNKNOWN	-	100.0	(D)	3.1	87.9	(D)	-	-	-	(D)	-
MIDDLE ATLANTIC	3 104	100.0	(D)	33.2	44.3	(D)	12.0	5.5	3.5	(D)	.2
RAIL	1 331	100.0	(D)	28.3	49.9	(D)	6.5	7.3	7.7	(D)	.1
MOTOR CARRIER	1 593	100.0	(D)	37.3	42.4	(D)	16.1	1.9	.3	(D)	.4
PRIVATE TRUCK	121	100.0	(D)	40.0	29.0	(D)	18.7	-	.8	(D)	-
AIR	-	100.0	(D)	7.6	82.0	(D)	4.5	-	.3	(D)	5.6
WATER	56	100.0	(D)	12.4	.4	(D)	8.8	78.4	-	(D)	-
OTHER	-	100.0	(D)	55.4	34.3	(D)	.2	6.2	-	(D)	-
UNKNOWN	2	100.0	(D)	75.1	20.0	(D)	4.8	-	-	(D)	-
EAST NORTH CENTRAL	8 304	100.0	(D)	24.3	62.6	(D)	5.3	5.2	.2	(D)	.5
RAIL	2 878	100.0	(D)	22.4	66.6	(D)	4.3	5.4	.5	(D)	.8
MOTOR CARRIER	4 954	100.0	(D)	26.1	59.8	(D)	5.8	5.1	-	(D)	.3
PRIVATE TRUCK	198	100.0	(D)	19.1	65.6	(D)	1.8	3.7	-	(D)	-
AIR	-	100.0	(D)	52.6	14.7	(D)	4.8	18.7	-	(D)	9.2
WATER	260	100.0	(D)	14.1	71.3	(D)	7.9	6.7	-	(D)	-
OTHER	2	100.0	(D)	3.7	91.1	(D)	-	.1	-	(D)	-
UNKNOWN	10	100.0	(D)	72.8	26.8	(D)	-	.4	-	(D)	-
WEST NORTH CENTRAL	2 710	100.0	(D)	12.3	72.8	(D)	3.8	4.5	1.0	(D)	.9
RAIL	1 315	100.0	(D)	12.8	67.9	(D)	7.8	7.9	.4	(D)	1.5
MOTOR CARRIER	1 113	100.0	(D)	13.1	74.7	(D)	.1	1.7	1.8	(D)	.3
PRIVATE TRUCK	101	100.0	(D)	10.6	75.0	(D)	.5	-	-	(D)	-
AIR	-	100.0	(D)	59.4	9.6	(D)	1.4	13.9	-	(D)	-
WATER	172	100.0	(D)	-	100.0	(D)	-	-	-	(D)	-
OTHER	-	100.0	(D)	2.2	36.0	(D)	3.4	-	-	(D)	-
UNKNOWN	7	100.0	(D)	99.6	.4	(D)	-	-	-	(D)	-
SOUTH ATLANTIC	2 987	100.0	(D)	21.1	24.3	(D)	39.1	13.3	1.4	(D)	.3
RAIL	2 052	100.0	(D)	16.7	23.1	(D)	43.4	15.1	1.6	(D)	-
MOTOR CARRIER	700	100.0	(D)	34.2	31.6	(D)	20.8	9.5	1.3	(D)	1.2
PRIVATE TRUCK	156	100.0	(D)	23.8	6.5	(D)	57.9	11.7	-	(D)	-
AIR	-	100.0	(D)	61.3	31.3	(D)	-	-	.1	(D)	7.2
WATER	73	100.0	(D)	9.9	30.1	(D)	53.3	5.5	-	(D)	-
OTHER	-	100.0	(D)	26.5	5.4	(D)	32.5	6.6	-	(D)	-
UNKNOWN	4	100.0	(D)	52.4	.2	(D)	39.6	7.8	-	(D)	-
EAST SOUTH CENTRAL	2 864	100.0	(D)	29.7	43.7	(D)	5.9	10.8	9.6	(D)	-
RAIL	1 281	100.0	(D)	18.4	48.6	(D)	8.5	15.5	8.7	(D)	-
MOTOR CARRIER	729	100.0	(D)	29.7	48.9	(D)	6.7	12.1	2.1	(D)	.1
PRIVATE TRUCK	68	100.0	(D)	22.6	46.0	(D)	13.8	13.6	.8	(D)	-
AIR	-	100.0	(D)	6.7	60.8	(D)	.3	32.2	-	(D)	-
WATER	780	100.0	(D)	48.6	30.7	(D)	.3	1.6	18.8	(D)	-
OTHER	-	100.0	(D)	10.6	1.9	(D)	.7	40.4	21.0	(D)	-
UNKNOWN	4	100.0	(D)	72.2	27.5	(D)	-	.2	-	(D)	-
WEST SOUTH CENTRAL	4 907	100.0	(D)	24.5	34.7	(D)	11.1	8.2	14.5	(D)	1.4
RAIL	2 485	100.0	(D)	20.5	37.8	(D)	10.1	11.0	11.0	(D)	1.8
MOTOR CARRIER	1 150	100.0	(D)	34.7	21.7	(D)	1.1	6.2	28.2	(D)	2.0
PRIVATE TRUCK	101	100.0	(D)	12.7	20.8	(D)	1.3	9.2	49.2	(D)	-
AIR	-	100.0	(D)	41.9	6.8	(D)	1.4	9.2	3.1	(D)	37.6
WATER	1 161	100.0	(D)	24.3	41.9	(D)	24.2	3.9	5.5	(D)	-
OTHER	-	100.0	(D)	-	91.9	(D)	-	8.1	-	(D)	-
UNKNOWN	7	100.0	(D)	-	91.0	(D)	-	-	-	(D)	-
MOUNTAIN	1 121	100.0	(D)	9.1	45.7	(D)	.2	1.6	10.4	(D)	8.6
RAIL	698	100.0	(D)	9.9	52.1	(D)	-	2.4	11.8	(D)	3.9
MOTOR CARRIER	366	100.0	(D)	9.0	38.9	(D)	.7	.3	9.4	(D)	18.8
PRIVATE TRUCK	51	100.0	(D)	-	11.9	(D)	-	-	-	(D)	.3
AIR	-	100.0	(D)	80.7	16.8	(D)	-	2.3	-	(D)	.2
WATER	-	100.0	(D)	100.0	-	(D)	-	-	-	(D)	-
OTHER	-	100.0	(D)	-	-	(D)	-	-	-	(D)	-
UNKNOWN	4	100.0	(D)	-	-	(D)	-	-	-	(D)	-
PACIFIC	4 772	100.0	(D)	17.4	33.8	(D)	7.1	3.7	2.8	(D)	12.5
RAIL	3 766	100.0	(D)	13.8	41.4	(D)	8.1	4.2	3.5	(D)	5.3
MOTOR CARRIER	797	100.0	(D)	22.7	4.6	(D)	4.2	2.2	-	(D)	44.8
PRIVATE TRUCK	75	100.0	(D)	13.0	20.2	(D)	.7	-	-	(D)	36.2
AIR	-	100.0	(D)	27.4	.3	(D)	51.7	-	.1	(D)	20.4
WATER	128	100.0	(D)	91.1	-	(D)	.7	-	-	(D)	8.2
OTHER	2	100.0	(D)	48.3	37.2	(D)	-	13.5	-	(D)	.7
UNKNOWN	1	100.0	(D)	80.7	-	(D)	-	-	-	(D)	18.3

See footnotes at end of table 4.

TABLE 4. TCC GROUP 331—Percent Distribution of Distance Shipped and Weight of Shipment, by Means of Transport: 1972

Distance shipped and weight of shipment [2] [3]	Number	Percent distribution by means of transport							
		All means of transport	Rail	Motor carrier	Private truck	Air	Water	Other	Unknown
TONS OF SHIPMENTS	(thousands of tons)								
U.S. TOTAL.........	107 099	100.0	41.3	48.2	4.5	-	5.8	-	.1
UNDER 100 MILES.........	31 087	100.0	38.3	53.2	7.4	-	1.0	-	.1
UNDER 1000 POUNDS.....	21	100.0	-	62.1	36.3	-	-	1.6	-
1000 TO 9999 POUNDS...	396	100.0	5.3	69.4	24.5	-	-	.7	-
10000 TO 29999 POUNDS.	1 768	100.0	4.0	76.6	19.4	-	-	-	-
30000 TO 59999 POUNDS.	13 257	100.0	1.9	86.8	11.2	-	-	-	.1
60000 TO 89999 POUNDS.	2 173	100.0	43.6	52.9	3.5	-	-	-	.1
90000 POUNDS AND OVER.	13 470	100.0	78.9	16.6	2.3	-	2.3	-	-
100 TO 199 MILES........	22 694	100.0	38.4	49.4	4.5	-	7.5	.1	.1
UNDER 1000 POUNDS....	22	100.0	.1	85.7	9.9	.7	-	3.3	.2
1000 TO 9999 POUNDS...	324	100.0	2.0	78.6	19.4	-	-	-	.1
10000 TO 29999 POUNDS.	1 310	100.0	3.5	81.2	14.8	-	.3	-	.2
30000 TO 59999 POUNDS.	9 787	100.0	3.2	89.6	6.6	-	-	.2	.3
60000 TO 89999 POUNDS.	1 229	100.0	39.7	58.6	1.7	-	-	-	-
90000 POUNDS AND OVER.	10 019	100.0	78.5	3.7	1.0	-	16.8	-	-
200 TO 299 MILES........	20 163	100.0	40.2	52.9	3.5	-	3.2	-	.1
UNDER 1000 POUNDS.....	12	100.0	-	92.9	5.1	.7	-	1.1	.1
1000 TO 9999 POUNDS...	245	100.0	2.1	86.7	10.9	-	-	-	.3
10000 TO 29999 POUNDS.	1 053	100.0	6.5	84.4	8.3	-	.7	-	.1
30000 TO 59999 POUNDS.	8 735	100.0	2.0	91.5	6.2	-	-	-	.2
60000 TO 89999 POUNDS.	1 330	100.0	30.6	68.6	.8	-	-	-	-
90000 POUNDS AND OVER.	8 785	100.0	84.8	7.4	.4	-	7.4	-	-
300 TO 499 MILES........	19 262	100.0	39.3	49.6	2.5	-	8.5	-	.2
UNDER 1000 POUNDS.....	22	100.0	.4	87.0	9.0	2.2	-	1.1	.4
1000 TO 9999 POUNDS...	381	100.0	5.5	90.8	3.5	-	.1	-	.1
10000 TO 29999 POUNDS.	1 400	100.0	6.3	88.6	4.2	-	.8	-	-
30000 TO 59999 POUNDS.	7 575	100.0	5.0	89.0	5.2	-	.5	-	.4
60000 TO 89999 POUNDS.	1 330	100.0	72.3	27.7	-	-	-	-	-
90000 POUNDS AND OVER.	8 553	100.0	71.5	9.8	.2	-	18.5	-	-
500 TO 999 MILES........	10 436	100.0	52.7	29.1	3.0	-	14.8	-	.2
UNDER 1000 POUNDS.....	22	100.0	1.0	92.7	2.2	1.4	-	2.7	-
1000 TO 9999 POUNDS...	208	100.0	3.3	82.9	10.6	-	2.2	-	1.0
10000 TO 29999 POUNDS.	558	100.0	10.3	73.8	11.4	-	4.5	-	-
30000 TO 59999 POUNDS.	2 996	100.0	13.2	74.0	7.7	-	4.8	-	.3
60000 TO 89999 POUNDS.	924	100.0	76.0	12.5	-	-	11.4	-	-
90000 POUNDS AND OVER.	5 725	100.0	75.8	1.7	-	-	22.2	-	.2
1000 TO 1499 MILES......	1 834	100.0	56.8	24.0	.6	-	18.6	-	-
UNDER 1000 POUNDS.....	8	100.0	7.2	75.8	10.8	.5	5.5	.2	-
1000 TO 9999 POUNDS...	48	100.0	14.0	82.4	-	-	3.6	-	-
10000 TO 29999 POUNDS.	133	100.0	22.5	76.4	.8	-	.3	-	-
30000 TO 59999 POUNDS.	273	100.0	22.9	63.4	3.4	-	10.3	-	-
60000 TO 89999 POUNDS.	209	100.0	91.7	5.1	-	-	3.2	-	-
90000 POUNDS AND OVER.	1 162	100.0	64.5	9.4	-	-	26.1	-	-
1500 MILES OR OVER......	1 620	100.0	86.6	9.5	1.0	-	2.5	.1	.2
UNDER 1000 POUNDS.....	5	100.0	14.9	82.2	.3	2.1	.2	.2	.1
1000 TO 9999 POUNDS...	51	100.0	41.8	48.5	.6	.4	.5	2.2	6.1
10000 TO 29999 POUNDS.	57	100.0	43.7	42.1	7.1	-	7.1	-	-
30000 TO 59999 POUNDS.	329	100.0	78.0	18.8	2.8	-	.4	-	-
60000 TO 89999 POUNDS.	320	100.0	91.6	.3	-	-	8.2	-	-
90000 POUNDS AND OVER.	855	100.0	94.2	4.4	.4	-	1.1	-	-
TON-MILES OF SHIPMENTS	(millions of ton-miles)								
U.S. TOTAL.........	29 350	100.0	49.1	39.0	2.9	-	8.9	-	.1
UNDER 100 MILES.........	1 409	100.0	34.4	57.3	7.0	-	1.2	-	.1
UNDER 1000 POUNDS.....	-	100.0	-	72.3	26.1	-	-	1.6	-
1000 TO 9999 POUNDS...	18	100.0	3.6	74.5	21.5	-	-	.4	-
10000 TO 29999 POUNDS.	98	100.0	5.1	76.9	17.9	-	-	-	-
30000 TO 59999 POUNDS.	625	100.0	1.8	89.1	8.9	-	-	-	.2
60000 TO 89999 POUNDS.	90	100.0	37.1	60.0	2.8	-	-	-	.1
90000 POUNDS AND OVER.	575	100.0	75.4	18.4	3.2	-	3.0	-	-
100 TO 199 MILES........	3 287	100.0	38.8	50.4	4.5	-	6.1	.1	.2
UNDER 1000 POUNDS.....	3	100.0	.1	86.1	9.7	.6	-	3.4	.1
1000 TO 9999 POUNDS...	48	100.0	2.0	80.0	18.0	-	-	-	.1
10000 TO 29999 POUNDS.	193	100.0	3.6	81.5	14.5	-	.3	-	.2
30000 TO 59999 POUNDS.	1 435	100.0	3.4	89.6	6.4	-	.1	.2	.3
60000 TO 89999 POUNDS.	192	100.0	40.9	57.7	1.4	-	-	-	-
90000 POUNDS AND OVER.	1 413	100.0	80.7	4.2	1.1	-	14.0	-	-
200 TO 299 MILES........	4 851	100.0	40.2	53.0	3.5	-	3.2	-	.1
UNDER 1000 POUNDS.....	3	100.0	-	93.1	5.1	.7	-	1.1	.1
1000 TO 9999 POUNDS...	59	100.0	2.1	86.7	10.8	-	-	-	.4
10000 TO 29999 POUNDS.	254	100.0	6.1	84.6	8.5	-	.7	-	.1
30000 TO 59999 POUNDS.	2 118	100.0	2.1	91.6	6.1	-	-	-	.2
60000 TO 89999 POUNDS.	316	100.0	31.9	67.3	.8	-	-	-	-
90000 POUNDS AND OVER.	2 099	100.0	85.1	7.1	.4	-	7.4	-	-

See footnotes at end of table 4.

TABLE 4. **TCC GROUP 331—Percent Distribution of Distance Shipped and Weight of Shipment, by Means of Transport: 1972**—Continued

Distance shipped and weight of shipment [2] [3]	Number	Percent distribution by means of transport							
		All means of transport	Rail	Motor carrier	Private truck	Air	Water	Other	Unknown
TON-MILES OF SHIPMENTS	(millions of ton-miles)								
300 TO 499 MILES.........	7 283	100.0	40.0	48.9	2.5	-	8.5	-	.1
UNDER 1000 POUNDS.....	8	100.0	.3	87.3	8.5	2.3	-	1.2	.3
1000 TO 9999 POUNDS...	145	100.0	5.0	91.4	3.4	-	.1	-	.1
10000 TO 29999 POUNDS.	524	100.0	7.0	88.4	4.0	-	.7	-	-
30000 TO 59999 POUNDS.	2 836	100.0	5.1	88.9	5.3	-	.4	-	.3
60000 TO 89999 POUNDS.	501	100.0	73.7	26.3	-	-	-	-	-
90000 POUNDS AND OVER.	3 266	100.0	72.1	9.3	.2	-	18.5	-	-
500 TO 999 MILES........	7 161	100.0	53.1	28.0	2.9	-	15.8	-	.2
UNDER 1000 POUNDS.....	15	100.0	1.3	92.2	2.5	1.5	-	2.5	-
1000 TO 9999 POUNDS...	141	100.0	3.2	82.6	11.1	-	2.2	-	.9
10000 TO 29999 POUNDS.	367	100.0	11.4	72.2	11.0	-	5.4	-	-
30000 TO 59999 POUNDS.	2 001	100.0	13.5	73.5	7.7	-	5.0	-	.4
60000 TO 89999 POUNDS.	644	100.0	75.0	12.2	-	-	12.8	-	-
90000 POUNDS AND OVER.	3 990	100.0	75.2	1.4	-	-	23.3	-	.2
1000 TO 1499 MILES......	2 102	100.0	57.7	23.8	.6	-	17.9	-	-
UNDER 1000 POUNDS.....	9	100.0	7.4	75.0	10.7	.5	6.1	.2	-
1000 TO 9999 POUNDS...	58	100.0	13.8	82.0	-	-	4.2	-	-
10000 TO 29999 POUNDS.	151	100.0	22.7	76.3	.8	-	.3	-	-
30000 TO 59999 POUNDS.	318	100.0	23.5	63.6	3.2	-	9.8	-	-
60000 TO 89999 POUNDS.	241	100.0	91.9	5.1	-	-	3.0	-	-
90000 POUNDS AND OVER.	1 323	100.0	66.0	8.7	-	-	25.3	-	-
1500 MILES OR OVER......	3 254	100.0	85.0	10.4	1.2	-	3.0	.1	.2
UNDER 1000 POUNDS.....	12	100.0	13.6	83.5	.2	2.2	.2	.2	.2
1000 TO 9999 POUNDS...	104	100.0	38.7	51.1	.7	.5	.6	2.1	6.3
10000 TO 29999 POUNDS.	130	100.0	43.0	39.6	9.9	-	7.5	-	-
30000 TO 59999 POUNDS.	675	100.0	74.7	21.9	3.0	-	.4	-	-
60000 TO 89999 POUNDS.	644	100.0	89.6	.3	-	-	10.1	-	-
90000 POUNDS AND OVER.	1 686	100.0	94.1	4.4	.3	-	1.2	-	-

Note: Detail may not add to total due to rounding. The introductory table shows the estimates of sampling variability for tons; sampling variability for ton-miles has not been estimated. See the map in the Introduction for the States comprising the geographic divisions of the United States. Shipments excluded from the survey are those moving by pipeline (primarily petroleum products from refineries), parcel post shipments, and commodities moved by own power (motorized vehicles, aircraft, etc.) or towed (prefabricated buildings, etc.). Local shipments (commodities shipped less than 25 miles from the plant) and shipments within the same city are also excluded. Shipments to Alaska and Hawaii from the 48 conterminous States and the District of Columbia are included; however, no data were obtained for shipments originating in Alaska and Hawaii.

- Represents zero or rounds to zero. (D) Withheld to avoid disclosing figures for individual companies.

[1]Production of this commodity is concentrated in the geographic divisions shown; figures and distributions for geographic divisions not shown are included in the total.

[2]Distances of shipments to foreign destinations are calculated only to the U.S. port of exit.

[3]Includes only shipments represented by bills of lading and invoices. Summary records which did not show individual weights of shipments are not included.

TCC 332. Iron and Steel Castings

Comparisons of Tons and Ton-Miles of Shipments for
Geographic Divisions of Origin and for Sampling Variability: 1972 and 1967

Geographic division of origin	Estimates				Relative sampling variability in tons (percent)	
	1972		1967		1972	1967
	Tons (thousands)	Ton-miles (millions)	Tons (thousands)	Ton-miles (millions)		
U.S. total	12,283	3,381	12,657	4,145	9.8	5.6
New England	217	39	119	47	47.2	(*)
Middle Atlantic	1,292	348	1,432	302	28.6	(*)
East North Central	6,191	1,143	5,502	956	11.5	(*)
West North Central	491	223	286	84	42.1	(*)
South Atlantic	732	214	820	311	12.4	(*)
East South Central	2,513	957	3,308	1,620	32.5	(*)
West South Central	698	392	336	155	7.5	(*)
Mountain	(D)	(D)	190	93	(*)	(*)
Pacific	(D)	(D)	664	577	(*)	(*)

(D) Withheld to avoid disclosing figures for individual companies.   (*) Data not published.

TABLE 1. **TCC GROUP 332—Percent Distribution of Geographic Division of Origin and Distance Shipped, by Means of Transport: 1972**

Geographic division of origin [1] and distance shipped [2]	Number	Percent distribution by means of transport							
		All means of transport	Rail	Motor carrier	Private truck	Air	Water	Other	Unknown
TONS OF SHIPMENTS	(thousands of tons)								
U.S. TOTAL	12 283	100.0	20.2	47.8	28.6	-	-	3.3	.1
NEW ENGLAND..............	217	100.0	.9	85.8	7.7	-	.2	5.2	.2
UNDER 100 MILES.......	157	100.0	-	82.6	10.2	-	-	7.2	-
100 TO 199 MILES......	26	100.0	-	98.2	1.8	-	-	-	-
200 TO 299 MILES......	12	100.0	-	98.1	1.9	-	-	-	-
300 TO 499 MILES......	2	100.0	-	99.4	-	.6	-	-	-
500 TO 999 MILES......	8	100.0	4.3	95.7	-	-	-	-	-
1000 TO 1499 MILES....	3	100.0	-	100.0	-	-	-	-	-
1500 MILES OR OVER....	6	100.0	26.3	61.3	-	-	6.2	-	6.2
MIDDLE ATLANTIC..........	1 292	100.0	44.2	37.9	17.8	-	-	-	.1
UNDER 100 MILES.......	501	100.0	48.0	23.6	28.4	-	-	-	-
100 TO 199 MILES......	282	100.0	33.8	49.2	16.7	-	-	-	.3
200 TO 299 MILES......	152	100.0	33.5	49.3	17.1	-	-	-	.1
300 TO 499 MILES......	178	100.0	38.4	55.0	6.5	-	-	-	.1
500 TO 999 MILES......	112	100.0	66.9	30.8	2.2	-	-	-	.1
1000 TO 1499 MILES....	28	100.0	24.1	74.5	1.3	.1	-	-	-
1500 MILES OR OVER....	36	100.0	93.1	6.8	.1	-	-	-	-
EAST NORTH CENTRAL......	6 191	100.0	21.5	47.7	30.7	-	-	-	.1
UNDER 100 MILES.......	2 383	100.0	4.4	52.4	43.1	-	-	-	.1
100 TO 199 MILES......	1 592	100.0	16.4	49.3	34.2	-	-	-	-
200 TO 299 MILES......	1 510	100.0	47.5	39.0	13.4	-	-	-	.1
300 TO 499 MILES......	436	100.0	33.0	49.2	17.7	-	-	.1	-
500 TO 999 MILES......	226	100.0	35.8	44.0	19.3	.1	-	.5	.2
1000 TO 1499 MILES....	14	100.0	41.0	36.9	22.0	-	-	.1	-
1500 MILES OR OVER....	28	100.0	70.9	27.3	1.4	.2	-	.2	-
WEST NORTH CENTRAL......	491	100.0	14.5	74.3	10.4	.1	.7	-	.1
UNDER 100 MILES.......	69	100.0	2.3	67.2	30.5	-	-	-	-
100 TO 199 MILES......	132	100.0	2.1	94.8	3.1	-	-	-	-
200 TO 299 MILES......	52	100.0	5.1	75.1	18.8	-	-	-	1.0
300 TO 499 MILES......	44	100.0	24.0	72.8	2.3	.9	-	-	-
500 TO 999 MILES......	130	100.0	8.0	80.6	11.4	-	-	-	-
1000 TO 1499 MILES....	33	100.0	45.1	44.1	.7	-	10.0	-	-
1500 MILES OR OVER....	29	100.0	95.7	4.3	-	-	-	-	-
SOUTH ATLANTIC..........	732	100.0	14.9	68.5	15.3	-	-	1.2	-
UNDER 100 MILES.......	136	100.0	5.2	82.2	8.1	-	-	4.6	-
100 TO 199 MILES......	156	100.0	-	74.5	25.5	-	-	-	-
200 TO 299 MILES......	115	100.0	14.5	67.2	18.4	-	-	-	-
300 TO 499 MILES......	225	100.0	27.9	56.3	15.7	-	-	-	-
500 TO 999 MILES......	95	100.0	23.8	68.8	5.0	-	-	2.4	-
1000 TO 1499 MILES....	1	100.0	-	98.7	-	1.3	-	-	-
1500 MILES OR OVER....	2	100.0	-	100.0	-	-	-	-	-
EAST SOUTH CENTRAL......	2 513	100.0	12.6	46.0	25.9	-	-	15.3	.3
UNDER 100 MILES.......	232	100.0	1.2	20.7	54.3	-	-	23.6	.1
100 TO 199 MILES......	743	100.0	-	31.0	24.9	-	-	44.1	-
200 TO 299 MILES......	158	100.0	6.5	53.0	40.4	-	-	-	-
300 TO 499 MILES......	547	100.0	17.0	69.4	12.5	-	-	.1	1.0
500 TO 999 MILES......	772	100.0	24.8	49.8	25.3	-	-	-	.1
1000 TO 1499 MILES....	40	100.0	14.9	67.0	18.1	-	-	-	-
1500 MILES OR OVER....	17	100.0	71.1	4.0	24.4	.5	-	-	-
WEST SOUTH CENTRAL......	698	100.0	9.0	17.7	73.4	-	-	-	-
UNDER 100 MILES.......	35	100.0	-	3.5	96.3	-	-	-	.2
100 TO 199 MILES......	67	100.0	-	13.8	86.2	-	-	-	-
200 TO 299 MILES......	154	100.0	20.1	19.9	60.0	-	-	-	-
300 TO 499 MILES......	89	100.0	25.0	4.6	70.4	-	-	-	-
500 TO 999 MILES......	269	100.0	-	16.9	83.0	-	-	-	-
1000 TO 1499 MILES....	73	100.0	12.5	30.8	56.8	-	-	-	-
1500 MILES OR OVER....	9	100.0	-	100.0	-	-	-	-	-
TON-MILES OF SHIPMENTS	(millions of ton-miles)								
U.S. TOTAL	3 381	100.0	27.1	46.8	24.2	-	.1	1.5	.1
NEW ENGLAND..............	39	100.0	11.6	80.5	1.3	-	2.5	1.6	2.5
UNDER 100 MILES.......	7	100.0	-	86.7	5.3	-	-	8.0	-
100 TO 199 MILES......	3	100.0	-	97.9	2.1	-	-	-	-
200 TO 299 MILES......	2	100.0	-	98.2	1.8	-	-	-	-
300 TO 499 MILES......	1	100.0	-	99.4	-	.6	-	-	-
500 TO 999 MILES......	6	100.0	5.4	94.6	-	-	-	-	-
1000 TO 1499 MILES....	4	100.0	-	100.0	-	-	-	-	-
1500 MILES OR OVER....	13	100.0	31.2	54.2	-	-	7.3	-	7.2

See footnotes at end of table 4.

TABLE 1. **TCC GROUP 332—Percent Distribution of Geographic Division of Origin and Distance Shipped, by Means of Transport: 1972**—Continued

Geographic division of origin [1] and distance shipped [2]	Number	Percent distribution by means of transport							
		All means of transport	Rail	Motor carrier	Private truck	Air	Water	Other	Unknown
TON-MILES OF SHIPMENTS	(millions of ton-miles)								
MIDDLE ATLANTIC.........	348	100.0	52.7	39.7	7.5	-	-	-	.1
UNDER 100 MILES.......	24	100.0	44.2	27.1	28.7	-	-	-	-
100 TO 199 MILES......	38	100.0	29.7	53.4	16.6	-	-	-	.2
200 TO 299 MILES......	36	100.0	32.7	49.7	17.5	-	-	-	.1
300 TO 499 MILES......	71	100.0	38.9	55.4	5.6	-	-	-	-
500 TO 999 MILES......	72	100.0	63.5	33.8	2.6	-	-	-	.1
1000 TO 1499 MILES....	32	100.0	23.5	75.2	1.3	.1	-	-	-
1500 MILES OR OVER....	73	100.0	93.1	6.7	.1	-	-	-	-
EAST NORTH CENTRAL......	1 143	100.0	34.5	44.2	21.1	-	-	.1	.1
UNDER 100 MILES.......	142	100.0	5.8	58.0	36.1	-	-	-	.1
100 TO 199 MILES......	228	100.0	15.1	50.4	34.5	-	-	-	-
200 TO 299 MILES......	374	100.0	48.5	38.4	13.0	-	-	-	.1
300 TO 499 MILES......	167	100.0	35.2	48.0	16.7	-	-	.1	-
500 TO 999 MILES......	160	100.0	41.7	39.0	18.4	.1	-	.6	.2
1000 TO 1499 MILES....	16	100.0	44.1	35.5	20.3	-	-	.1	-
1500 MILES OR OVER....	53	100.0	69.5	28.7	1.4	.2	-	.2	-
WEST NORTH CENTRAL......	223	100.0	33.0	59.5	5.8	.1	1.5	-	.1
UNDER 100 MILES.......	2	100.0	3.1	91.1	5.8	-	-	-	-
100 TO 199 MILES......	18	100.0	2.2	94.3	3.4	-	-	-	-
200 TO 299 MILES......	12	100.0	5.1	74.6	19.4	-	-	-	1.0
300 TO 499 MILES......	17	100.0	26.2	70.2	2.6	1.0	-	-	-
500 TO 999 MILES......	87	100.0	7.0	82.8	10.2	-	-	-	-
1000 TO 1499 MILES....	37	100.0	47.7	42.6	.7	-	9.1	-	-
1500 MILES OR OVER....	45	100.0	95.7	4.3	-	-	-	-	-
SOUTH ATLANTIC.........	214	100.0	19.6	65.5	14.2	-	-	.7	-
UNDER 100 MILES.......	8	100.0	5.5	83.3	9.4	-	-	1.8	-
100 TO 199 MILES......	22	100.0	-	73.6	26.4	-	-	-	-
200 TO 299 MILES......	29	100.0	14.8	66.3	19.0	-	-	-	-
300 TO 499 MILES......	88	100.0	27.9	55.6	16.4	-	-	-	-
500 TO 999 MILES......	59	100.0	21.3	70.3	6.2	-	-	2.2	-
1000 TO 1499 MILES....	1	100.0	-	98.7	-	1.3	-	-	-
1500 MILES OR OVER....	5	100.0	-	100.0	-	-	-	-	-
EAST SOUTH CENTRAL......	957	100.0	19.3	51.8	23.6	-	-	5.0	.3
UNDER 100 MILES.......	13	100.0	.6	24.3	62.7	-	-	12.2	.2
100 TO 199 MILES......	109	100.0	-	30.6	27.3	-	-	42.0	.1
200 TO 299 MILES......	39	100.0	6.3	53.4	40.2	-	-	-	-
300 TO 499 MILES......	216	100.0	17.0	69.2	12.8	-	-	.1	1.0
500 TO 999 MILES......	501	100.0	22.8	51.5	25.6	-	-	-	.1
1000 TO 1499 MILES....	44	100.0	15.1	66.0	18.9	-	-	-	-
1500 MILES OR OVER....	33	100.0	73.4	3.8	22.3	.5	-	.1	-
WEST SOUTH CENTRAL......	392	100.0	7.1	21.7	71.2	-	-	-	-
UNDER 100 MILES.......	3	100.0	-	3.3	96.5	-	-	-	.2
100 TO 199 MILES......	10	100.0	-	11.4	88.6	-	-	-	-
200 TO 299 MILES......	36	100.0	17.8	19.7	62.5	-	-	-	-
300 TO 499 MILES......	35	100.0	25.1	4.9	70.0	-	-	-	-
500 TO 999 MILES......	202	100.0	-	16.6	83.4	-	-	-	-
1000 TO 1499 MILES....	88	100.0	13.9	28.9	57.2	-	-	-	-
1500 MILES OR OVER....	16	100.0	-	100.0	-	-	-	-	-

See footnotes at end of table 4.

TABLE 2. **TCC GROUP 332—Percent Distribution of Geographic Division of Origin and Means of Transport, by Geographic Division of Destination: 1972**

Geographic division of origin [1] and means of transport	Number	Percent distribution by division of destination									
		U.S. total	New England	Middle Atlantic	East North Central	West North Central	South Atlantic	East South Central	West South Central	Mountain	Pacific
TONS OF SHIPMENTS	(thousands of tons)										
U.S. TOTAL	12 283	100.0	2.4	10.1	52.7	7.2	10.2	9.2	5.2	1.1	2.0
RAIL...................	2 478	100.0	.5	16.5	49.1	9.2	5.7	7.2	6.1	1.3	4.3
MOTOR CARRIER..........	5 871	100.0	4.0	8.9	55.6	7.5	13.9	4.6	3.7	.4	1.4
PRIVATE TRUCK..........	3 508	100.0	1.1	8.8	56.5	6.0	7.9	8.4	7.6	2.3	1.4
AIR....................	1	100.0	8.2	16.3	15.4	34.5	6.4	.2	5.2	.5	13.3
WATER..................	4	100.0	-	79.2	-	11.7	-	-	-	-	9.1
OTHER..................	405	100.0	2.8	-	.7	.2	1.6	94.4	.2	-	-
UNKNOWN................	13	100.0	1.0	7.1	38.7	.2	43.5	4.4	2.1	-	2.9

TABLE 2. **TCC GROUP 332—Percent Distribution of Geographic Division of Origin and Means of Transport, by Geographic Division of Destination: 1972**—Continued

Geographic division of origin [1] and means of transport	Number	Percent distribution by division of destination									
		U.S. total	New England	Middle Atlantic	East North Central	West North Central	South Atlantic	East South Central	West South Central	Mountain	Pacific
TONS OF SHIPMENTS	(thousands of tons)										
NEW ENGLAND	217	100.0	78.2	12.6	2.8	1.0	2.6	-	.5	.9	1.5
RAIL	2	100.0	-	-	-	-	19.0	-	-	-	81.0
MOTOR CARRIER	186	100.0	76.4	14.3	3.2	1.1	2.8	-	.6	1.0	.5
PRIVATE TRUCK	16	100.0	95.8	4.2	-	-	-	-	-	-	.5
AIR	-	100.0	-	94.8	-	-	5.2	-	-	-	-
WATER	-	100.0	-	-	-	-	-	-	-	-	100.0
OTHER	11	100.0	100.0	-	-	-	-	-	-	-	-
UNKNOWN	-	100.0	-	-	-	-	-	-	-	-	100.0
MIDDLE ATLANTIC	1 292	100.0	3.4	46.9	31.3	1.4	5.7	6.4	2.2	.5	2.3
RAIL	571	100.0	2.3	39.3	35.8	1.4	2.4	11.9	1.1	1.0	4.9
MOTOR CARRIER	489	100.0	5.1	39.5	36.1	1.8	9.9	2.7	4.3	.3	.3
PRIVATE TRUCK	230	100.0	3.0	81.4	9.5	.4	4.9	.6	.2	-	-
AIR	-	100.0	-	-	40.2	18.6	-	-	32.1	-	9.0
WATER	-	100.0	-	-	-	-	-	-	-	-	-
OTHER	-	100.0	4.9	63.6	30.2	-	-	-	1.3	-	-
UNKNOWN	1	100.0	1.8	8.4	69.5	-	20.3	-	-	-	-
EAST NORTH CENTRAL	6 191	100.0	.2	4.9	83.9	5.5	.9	3.1	.9	.2	.5
RAIL	1 334	100.0	-	12.9	64.7	12.1	.4	6.8	1.1	.4	1.5
MOTOR CARRIER	2 951	100.0	.3	3.4	86.8	4.5	1.4	2.1	.9	.2	.3
PRIVATE TRUCK	1 898	100.0	.1	1.7	92.8	2.4	.4	1.8	.6	-	-
AIR	-	100.0	11.8	32.9	26.8	2.3	11.6	.3	.1	.1	14.1
WATER	-	100.0	-	-	-	100.0	-	-	-	-	-
OTHER	2	100.0	.1	1.8	31.0	42.1	1.6	.3	19.9	.6	2.5
UNKNOWN	4	100.0	-	7.1	88.1	.5	4.3	-	-	-	-
WEST NORTH CENTRAL	491	100.0	2.5	8.4	34.6	35.9	2.6	2.5	2.0	5.5	5.9
RAIL	71	100.0	-	10.7	14.0	4.3	6.1	3.6	-	22.3	39.0
MOTOR CARRIER	364	100.0	3.4	8.3	33.1	46.2	2.1	.9	2.6	3.0	.3
PRIVATE TRUCK	51	100.0	-	-	76.1	8.6	1.8	13.0	.4	-	-
AIR	-	100.0	1.8	.4	-	97.8	-	-	-	-	-
WATER	3	100.0	-	100.0	-	-	-	-	-	-	-
OTHER	-	100.0	-	-	-	-	-	-	-	-	-
UNKNOWN	-	100.0	-	-	100.0	-	-	-	-	-	-
SOUTH ATLANTIC	732	100.0	2.1	16.3	30.8	1.5	43.9	5.0	.2	-	.3
RAIL	109	100.0	-	-	90.8	-	9.2	-	-	-	-
MOTOR CARRIER	502	100.0	2.8	16.3	24.0	2.2	52.2	1.9	.1	-	.4
PRIVATE TRUCK	112	100.0	1.1	33.1	2.8	-	38.5	23.7	.9	-	-
AIR	-	100.0	37.9	13.4	14.8	-	33.7	-	-	-	.3
WATER	-	100.0	-	-	-	-	-	-	-	-	-
OTHER	8	100.0	-	-	26.4	-	73.5	.1	-	-	-
UNKNOWN	-	100.0	-	100.0	-	-	-	-	-	-	-
EAST SOUTH CENTRAL	2 513	100.0	1.7	4.8	14.2	7.2	30.0	31.5	9.7	.2	.7
RAIL	316	100.0	-	1.7	12.4	10.5	33.6	4.8	31.1	1.9	3.9
MOTOR CARRIER	1 155	100.0	2.7	6.7	20.4	8.9	36.9	15.0	9.2	-	.1
PRIVATE TRUCK	650	100.0	1.8	5.8	12.5	6.9	32.9	33.4	6.0	-	.6
AIR	-	100.0	-	.2	.3	-	5.7	-	-	-	93.8
WATER	-	100.0	-	-	-	-	-	-	-	-	-
OTHER	383	100.0	-	-	-	-	-	99.9	.1	-	-
UNKNOWN	6	100.0	1.6	6.9	-	-	79.7	8.7	3.0	-	-
WEST SOUTH CENTRAL	698	100.0	-	2.8	13.9	20.0	3.6	1.8	41.7	11.2	4.9
RAIL	62	100.0	-	-	-	35.9	-	-	49.6	-	14.6
MOTOR CARRIER	123	100.0	.1	7.0	19.8	3.7	20.4	3.1	36.0	1.9	8.1
PRIVATE TRUCK	512	100.0	-	2.2	14.2	22.0	-	1.7	42.1	14.9	2.9
AIR	-	100.0	-	-	9.3	45.1	-	-	44.8	-	.8
WATER	-	100.0	-	-	-	-	-	-	-	-	-
OTHER	-	100.0	-	-	1.5	9.3	10.6	4.2	74.4	-	-
UNKNOWN	-	100.0	-	-	-	3.1	-	-	96.9	-	-
TON-MILES OF SHIPMENTS	(millions of ton-miles)										
U.S. TOTAL	3 381	100.0	2.9	10.5	35.3	12.6	11.8	7.0	8.1	3.8	8.1
RAIL	917	100.0	.6	8.2	29.6	13.2	7.3	7.7	9.1	4.6	19.7
MOTOR CARRIER	1 583	100.0	4.7	11.8	39.2	11.2	16.1	4.3	7.3	1.5	3.8
PRIVATE TRUCK	818	100.0	2.0	10.9	36.6	15.3	9.1	5.9	8.8	7.8	3.5
AIR	1	100.0	12.1	18.3	13.2	15.6	6.0	.3	7.0	.5	27.1
WATER	4	100.0	-	77.2	-	.4	-	-	-	-	22.4
OTHER	51	100.0	1.2	.1	2.8	1.2	.5	93.0	.8	-	.3
UNKNOWN	4	100.0	2.4	11.5	14.6	.1	46.8	1.7	2.9	-	20.0
NEW ENGLAND	39	100.0	23.0	14.2	10.1	6.2	11.9	.1	4.3	8.8	21.3
RAIL	4	100.0	-	-	-	-	7.5	-	-	-	92.5
MOTOR CARRIER	31	100.0	25.4	17.2	12.6	7.6	13.7	.2	5.4	11.0	7.0
PRIVATE TRUCK	-	100.0	76.8	23.2	-	-	-	-	-	-	-
AIR	-	100.0	-	90.0	-	-	10.0	-	-	-	-
WATER	-	100.0	-	-	-	-	-	-	-	-	100.0
OTHER	-	100.0	100.0	-	-	-	-	-	-	-	-
UNKNOWN	-	100.0	-	-	-	-	-	-	-	-	100.0

See footnotes at end of table 4.

TABLE 2. **TCC GROUP 332—Percent Distribution of Geographic Division of Origin and Means of Transport, by Geographic Division of Destination: 1972**—Continued

Geographic division of origin [1] and means of transport	Number	Percent distribution by division of destination									
		U.S. total	New England	Middle Atlantic	East North Central	West North Central	South Atlantic	East South Central	West South Central	Mountain	Pacific
TON-MILES OF SHIPMENTS	(millions of ton-miles)										
MIDDLE ATLANTIC..........	348	100.0	4.5	17.4	25.0	4.2	5.0	13.9	8.8	3.4	17.8
RAIL..............	183	100.0	3.0	10.2	18.3	3.5	2.4	21.5	3.8	5.1	32.2
MOTOR CARRIER.........	138	100.0	5.9	19.1	35.4	5.3	7.6	6.1	16.9	1.7	2.1
PRIVATE TRUCK..........	26	100.0	8.2	58.6	16.9	3.3	9.3	1.7	1.6	.1	.3
AIR.................	-	100.0	-	-	18.6	19.3	-	-	42.7	-	19.3
WATER...............	-	100.0	-	-	-	-	-	-	-	-	-
OTHER..............	-	100.0	7.6	26.2	57.4	-	-	-	8.8	-	-
UNKNOWN..............	-	100.0	4.7	8.7	44.5	-	42.1	-	-	-	-
EAST NORTH CENTRAL......	1 143	100.0	.8	9.3	61.3	12.4	2.4	4.6	3.4	1.2	4.6
RAIL..............	394	100.0	-	12.3	43.4	22.8	.8	6.3	3.4	1.8	9.4
MOTOR CARRIER.........	505	100.0	1.4	8.2	68.1	6.7	3.9	4.2	3.3	1.1	3.0
PRIVATE TRUCK..........	240	100.0	.8	6.7	76.6	7.2	1.6	3.0	3.8	.3	-
AIR.................	-	100.0	12.2	30.0	7.9	1.3	9.8	.1	.1	.1	38.4
WATER...............	-	100.0	-	-	-	100.0	-	-	-	-	-
OTHER..............	1	100.0	.1	1.7	12.4	48.3	1.4	.2	27.0	1.2	7.5
UNKNOWN..............	-	100.0	-	22.0	60.3	.5	17.1	-	-	-	-
WEST NORTH CENTRAL......	223	100.0	5.8	15.8	14.9	22.1	4.0	2.8	2.0	12.1	20.5
RAIL..............	73	100.0	-	5.8	4.4	.8	2.8	1.4	-	25.4	59.4
MOTOR CARRIER.........	132	100.0	9.7	20.7	17.1	36.0	4.5	1.0	3.3	6.2	1.5
PRIVATE TRUCK..........	12	100.0	-	.1	56.1	5.2	7.0	30.5	1.1	-	-
AIR.................	-	100.0	4.1	.9	-	95.0	-	-	-	-	-
WATER...............	3	100.0	-	100.0	-	-	-	-	-	-	-
OTHER..............	-	100.0	-	-	-	-	-	-	-	-	-
UNKNOWN..............	-	100.0	-	-	100.0	-	-	-	-	-	-
SOUTH ATLANTIC..........	214	100.0	3.9	13.7	44.9	4.3	27.3	2.8	.6	-	2.4
RAIL..............	42	100.0	-	-	97.1	-	2.9	-	-	-	-
MOTOR CARRIER.........	140	100.0	5.5	10.6	37.1	6.5	35.0	1.3	.2	.1	3.7
PRIVATE TRUCK..........	30	100.0	2.0	47.6	7.3	-	26.1	13.6	3.3	-	-
AIR.................	-	100.0	60.3	10.9	12.8	-	15.0	-	-	-	1.0
WATER...............	-	100.0	-	-	-	-	-	-	-	-	-
OTHER..............	1	100.0	-	-	86.9	-	12.9	.2	-	-	-
UNKNOWN..............	-	100.0	-	100.0	-	-	-	-	-	-	-
EAST SOUTH CENTRAL......	957	100.0	4.4	9.6	18.3	12.0	27.2	11.9	12.5	.7	3.5
RAIL..............	184	100.0	-	1.8	11.0	8.1	30.2	1.9	30.1	3.6	13.2
MOTOR CARRIER.........	495	100.0	6.1	11.9	22.1	13.9	28.8	6.7	10.2	-	.3
PRIVATE TRUCK..........	225	100.0	5.1	12.9	20.0	13.6	26.4	13.0	5.7	-	3.3
AIR.................	-	100.0	-	.1	.1	-	2.1	-	-	-	97.7
WATER...............	-	100.0	-	-	-	-	-	-	-	-	-
OTHER..............	47	100.0	-	-	-	-	.1	99.5	.2	-	.1
UNKNOWN..............	2	100.0	3.9	12.3	-	-	75.8	3.0	5.0	-	-
WEST SOUTH CENTRAL......	392	100.0	-	6.3	18.8	22.5	5.6	1.5	16.6	16.5	12.2
RAIL..............	27	100.0	-	-	-	32.4	-	-	23.6	-	44.0
MOTOR CARRIER.........	85	100.0	.2	12.8	20.9	3.9	25.7	2.9	11.6	2.9	19.1
PRIVATE TRUCK..........	279	100.0	-	4.9	20.0	27.2	-	1.2	17.5	22.4	6.9
AIR.................	-	100.0	-	-	9.1	44.7	-	-	43.9	-	2.2
WATER...............	-	100.0	-	-	-	-	-	-	-	-	-
OTHER..............	-	100.0	-	-	3.9	14.1	22.7	4.5	54.7	-	-
UNKNOWN..............	-	100.0	-	-	-	21.2	-	-	78.8	-	-

See footnotes at end of table 4.

TABLE 3. **TCC GROUP 332—Percent Distribution of Geographic Division of Destination and Means of Transport, by Geographic Division of Origin: 1972**

Geographic division of destination and means of transport	Number	Percent distribution by division of origin [1]									
		U.S. total	New England	Middle Atlantic	East North Central	West North Central	South Atlantic	East South Central	West South Central	Mountain	Pacific
TONS OF SHIPMENTS	(thousands of tons)										
U.S. TOTAL..............	12 283	100.0	1.8	10.5	50.4	4.0	6.0	20.5	5.7	(D)	(D)
RAIL..............	2 478	100.0	.1	23.1	53.8	2.9	4.4	12.8	2.5	(D)	(D)
MOTOR CARRIER.........	5 871	100.0	3.2	8.3	50.3	6.2	8.6	19.7	2.1	(D)	(D)
PRIVATE TRUCK.........	3 508	100.0	.5	6.6	54.1	1.5	3.2	18.6	14.6	(D)	(D)
AIR..............	1	100.0	1.3	2.5	33.8	33.8	3.2	7.7	.4	(D)	(D)
WATER..............	4	100.0	9.1	-	11.7	79.2	-	-	-	(D)	(D)
OTHER..............	405	100.0	2.8	-	.5	-	2.1	94.6	-	(D)	(D)
UNKNOWN..............	13	100.0	2.8	8.2	33.2	3.7	.6	50.7	.6	(D)	(D)
NEW ENGLAND..............	299	100.0	56.9	14.9	4.3	4.1	5.1	14.5	-	(D)	(D)
RAIL..............	12	100.0	-	100.0	-	-	-	-	-	(D)	(D)
MOTOR CARRIER.........	235	100.0	60.6	10.5	4.3	5.2	6.0	13.4	.1	(D)	(D)
PRIVATE TRUCK.........	38	100.0	41.4	17.8	7.2	-	3.2	30.5	-	(D)	(D)
AIR..............	-	100.0	-	-	48.5	7.2	14.7	-	-	(D)	(D)
WATER..............	-	100.0	-	-	-	-	-	-	-	(D)	(D)
OTHER..............	11	100.0	100.0	-	-	-	-	-	-	(D)	(D)
UNKNOWN..............	-	100.0	-	15.2	-	-	-	84.8	-	(D)	(D)
MIDDLE ATLANTIC.........	1 241	100.0	2.2	48.8	24.6	3.3	9.6	9.8	1.6	(D)	(D)
RAIL..............	409	100.0	-	54.9	41.9	1.9	-	1.3	-	(D)	(D)
MOTOR CARRIER.........	519	100.0	5.1	37.2	19.2	5.8	15.8	15.0	1.7	(D)	(D)
PRIVATE TRUCK.........	307	100.0	.2	61.0	10.7	-	12.1	12.3	3.6	(D)	(D)
AIR..............	-	100.0	7.5	-	68.1	.9	2.6	.1	-	(D)	(D)
WATER..............	3	100.0	-	-	-	100.0	-	-	-	(D)	(D)
OTHER..............	-	100.0	-	27.8	55.6	-	.2	16.5	-	(D)	(D)
UNKNOWN..............	-	100.0	-	9.7	33.0	-	8.0	49.3	-	(D)	(D)
EAST NORTH CENTRAL......	6 473	100.0	.1	6.2	80.2	2.6	3.5	5.5	1.5	(D)	(D)
RAIL..............	1 217	100.0	-	16.8	70.9	.8	8.2	3.2	-	(D)	(D)
MOTOR CARRIER.........	3 266	100.0	.2	5.4	78.5	3.7	3.7	7.2	.7	(D)	(D)
PRIVATE TRUCK.........	1 980	100.0	-	1.1	89.0	2.0	.2	4.1	3.7	(D)	(D)
AIR..............	-	100.0	-	6.6	58.6	-	3.0	.2	.2	(D)	(D)
WATER..............	-	100.0	-	-	-	-	-	-	-	(D)	(D)
OTHER..............	2	100.0	-	.3	21.5	-	76.8	1.3	-	(D)	(D)
UNKNOWN..............	5	100.0	-	14.8	75.6	9.7	-	-	-	(D)	(D)
WEST NORTH CENTRAL......	878	100.0	.2	2.0	39.0	20.1	1.2	20.6	15.9	(D)	(D)
RAIL..............	228	100.0	-	3.5	70.8	1.3	-	14.5	9.8	(D)	(D)
MOTOR CARRIER.........	438	100.0	.5	2.0	30.3	38.5	2.5	23.3	1.0	(D)	(D)
PRIVATE TRUCK.........	209	100.0	-	.5	22.1	2.1	-	21.4	53.9	(D)	(D)
AIR..............	-	100.0	-	1.4	2.3	95.9	-	-	.5	(D)	(D)
WATER..............	-	100.0	-	-	100.0	-	-	-	-	(D)	(D)
OTHER..............	-	100.0	-	-	96.9	-	-	2.7	.4	(D)	(D)
UNKNOWN..............	-	100.0	-	-	90.2	-	-	-	9.8	(D)	(D)
SOUTH ATLANTIC..........	1 247	100.0	.5	5.9	4.5	1.0	25.8	60.3	2.0	(D)	(D)
RAIL..............	140	100.0	.3	9.7	3.9	3.1	7.2	75.7	-	(D)	(D)
MOTOR CARRIER.........	817	100.0	.6	5.9	5.2	.9	32.1	52.2	-	(D)	(D)
PRIVATE TRUCK.........	277	100.0	-	4.0	2.7	.3	15.6	77.3	3.1	(D)	(D)
AIR..............	-	100.0	1.1	-	61.6	-	16.8	6.8	-	(D)	(D)
WATER..............	-	100.0	-	-	-	-	-	-	-	(D)	(D)
OTHER..............	6	100.0	-	-	.5	-	97.0	2.4	.1	(D)	(D)
UNKNOWN..............	5	100.0	-	3.8	3.3	-	-	92.9	-	(D)	(D)
EAST SOUTH CENTRAL......	1 125	100.0	-	7.4	16.8	1.1	3.2	70.3	1.1	(D)	(D)
RAIL..............	178	100.0	-	38.2	51.3	1.5	-	8.5	-	(D)	(D)
MOTOR CARRIER.........	267	100.0	-	5.0	23.7	1.2	3.7	65.0	1.4	(D)	(D)
PRIVATE TRUCK.........	295	100.0	-	.4	11.8	2.2	9.0	73.6	2.9	(D)	(D)
AIR..............	-	100.0	-	-	39.5	-	-	-	-	(D)	(D)
WATER..............	-	100.0	-	-	-	-	-	-	-	(D)	(D)
OTHER..............	383	100.0	-	-	-	-	-	100.0	-	(D)	(D)
UNKNOWN..............	-	100.0	-	-	-	-	-	100.0	-	(D)	(D)
WEST SOUTH CENTRAL......	636	100.0	.2	4.4	8.3	1.5	.2	38.4	45.8	(D)	(D)
RAIL..............	151	100.0	-	4.3	9.8	-	.2	65.1	20.5	(D)	(D)
MOTOR CARRIER.........	216	100.0	.5	9.8	12.3	4.4	.2	49.3	20.5	(D)	(D)
PRIVATE TRUCK.........	267	100.0	-	.1	4.2	.1	.4	14.5	80.7	(D)	(D)
AIR..............	-	100.0	-	15.7	.6	-	-	-	3.1	(D)	(D)
WATER..............	-	100.0	-	-	-	-	-	-	-	(D)	(D)
OTHER..............	-	100.0	-	.1	54.5	-	-	41.3	4.2	(D)	(D)
UNKNOWN..............	-	100.0	-	-	-	-	-	72.6	27.4	(D)	(D)
MOUNTAIN..............	140	100.0	1.4	4.9	7.9	19.1	-	4.4	56.0	(D)	(D)
RAIL..............	33	100.0	-	16.8	16.4	48.0	-	18.5	-	(D)	(D)
MOTOR CARRIER.........	24	100.0	7.6	5.4	20.8	44.0	.2	.1	9.3	(D)	(D)
PRIVATE TRUCK.........	82	100.0	-	-	.5	-	-	-	92.7	(D)	(D)
AIR..............	-	100.0	-	-	3.9	-	-	-	-	(D)	(D)
WATER..............	-	100.0	-	-	-	-	-	-	-	(D)	(D)
OTHER..............	-	100.0	-	-	70.9	-	-	29.1	-	(D)	(D)
UNKNOWN..............	-	100.0	-	-	-	-	-	-	-	(D)	(D)
PACIFIC..............	241	100.0	1.4	12.1	11.9	12.0	.9	7.2	14.1	(D)	(D)
RAIL..............	107	100.0	1.5	26.1	19.2	25.9	-	11.5	8.5	(D)	(D)
MOTOR CARRIER.........	83	100.0	1.0	1.5	9.6	1.5	2.6	.8	11.9	(D)	(D)
PRIVATE TRUCK.........	49	100.0	-	.1	-	-	-	8.5	30.1	(D)	(D)
AIR..............	-	100.0	-	1.7	35.9	-	.1	54.0	-	(D)	(D)
WATER..............	-	100.0	100.0	-	-	-	-	-	-	(D)	(D)
OTHER..............	-	100.0	-	-	66.0	-	-	9.7	-	(D)	(D)
UNKNOWN..............	-	100.0	97.9	-	-	-	-	-	-	(D)	(D)

See footnotes at end of table 4.

TABLE 3. **TCC GROUP 332**—Percent Distribution of Geographic Division of Destination and Means of Transport, by Geographic Division of Origin: 1972—Continued

Geographic division of destination and means of transport	Number	Percent distribution by division of origin [1]									
		U.S. total	New England	Middle Atlantic	East North Central	West North Central	South Atlantic	East South Central	West South Central	Mountain	Pacific
TON-MILES OF SHIPMENTS	(millions of ton-miles)										
U.S. TOTAL............	3 381	100.0	1.2	10.3	33.8	6.6	6.4	28.3	11.6	(D)	(D)
RAIL...............	917	100.0	.5	20.0	43.0	8.0	4.6	20.2	3.0	(D)	(D)
MOTOR CARRIER.........	1 583	100.0	2.0	8.7	31.9	8.4	8.9	31.3	5.4	(D)	(D)
PRIVATE TRUCK.........	818	100.0	.1	3.2	29.4	1.6	3.7	27.5	34.1	(D)	(D)
AIR.................	1	100.0	.6	2.7	27.1	15.4	2.4	15.5	.2	(D)	(D)
WATER...............	4	100.0	22.4	-	.4	77.2	-	-	-	(D)	(D)
OTHER...............	51	100.0	1.2	-	2.3	-	2.9	93.5	-	(D)	(D)
UNKNOWN.............	4	100.0	20.0	4.2	16.8	2.6	.6	55.6	.2	(D)	(D)
NEW ENGLAND..........	98	100.0	9.3	16.1	9.3	13.1	8.6	43.0	.2	(D)	(D)
RAIL...............	5	100.0	-	100.0	-	-	-	-	-	(D)	(D)
MOTOR CARRIER.........	75	100.0	10.8	10.9	9.6	17.1	10.4	40.5	.2	(D)	(D)
PRIVATE TRUCK.........	16	100.0	2.5	12.9	11.2	-	3.7	69.8	-	(D)	(D)
AIR.................	-	100.0	-	-	27.5	5.2	12.0	-	-	(D)	(D)
WATER...............	-	100.0	-	-	-	-	-	-	-	(D)	(D)
OTHER...............	-	100.0	99.4	.1	.2	-	-	.3	-	(D)	(D)
UNKNOWN.............	-	100.0	-	8.3	-	-	-	91.7	-	(D)	(D)
MIDDLE ATLANTIC........	355	100.0	1.6	17.0	30.0	9.9	8.3	25.9	6.9	(D)	(D)
RAIL...............	75	100.0	-	25.0	64.7	5.7	-	4.5	-	(D)	(D)
MOTOR CARRIER.........	186	100.0	2.9	14.1	22.1	14.7	8.0	31.7	5.9	(D)	(D)
PRIVATE TRUCK.........	89	100.0	.1	17.2	18.2	-	16.3	32.8	15.3	(D)	(D)
AIR.................	-	100.0	3.2	-	44.5	.8	1.4	.1	-	(D)	(D)
WATER...............	3	100.0	-	-	-	100.0	-	-	-	(D)	(D)
OTHER...............	-	100.0	-	5.2	67.5	-	.1	27.2	-	(D)	(D)
UNKNOWN.............	-	100.0	-	3.2	32.0	-	5.6	59.2	-	(D)	(D)
EAST NORTH CENTRAL......	1 193	100.0	.3	7.3	58.7	2.8	8.1	14.7	6.2	(D)	(D)
RAIL...............	271	100.0	-	12.4	63.0	1.2	15.0	7.5	-	(D)	(D)
MOTOR CARRIER.........	620	100.0	.7	7.9	55.5	3.7	8.4	17.7	2.9	(D)	(D)
PRIVATE TRUCK.........	299	100.0	-	1.5	61.5	2.4	.7	15.0	18.7	(D)	(D)
AIR.................	-	100.0	-	3.9	16.3	-	2.3	.1	.2	(D)	(D)
WATER...............	-	100.0	-	-	-	-	-	-	-	(D)	(D)
OTHER...............	1	100.0	-	.2	10.2	-	88.0	1.5	-	(D)	(D)
UNKNOWN.............	-	100.0	-	12.9	69.4	17.7	-	-	-	(D)	(D)
WEST NORTH CENTRAL......	424	100.0	.6	3.4	33.3	11.6	2.2	27.0	20.8	(D)	(D)
RAIL...............	120	100.0	-	5.3	74.3	.5	-	12.4	7.5	(D)	(D)
MOTOR CARRIER.........	177	100.0	1.4	4.1	19.1	27.0	5.2	38.8	1.9	(D)	(D)
PRIVATE TRUCK.........	125	100.0	-	.7	13.8	.5	-	24.4	60.6	(D)	(D)
AIR.................	-	100.0	-	3.4	2.2	93.7	-	-	.7	(D)	(D)
WATER...............	-	100.0	-	-	100.0	-	-	-	-	(D)	(D)
OTHER...............	-	100.0	-	-	97.5	-	-	2.2	.3	(D)	(D)
UNKNOWN.............	-	100.0	-	-	72.9	-	-	-	27.1	(D)	(D)
SOUTH ATLANTIC........	399	100.0	1.2	4.4	6.8	2.2	14.7	65.2	5.5	(D)	(D)
RAIL...............	67	100.0	.5	6.6	4.5	3.1	1.8	83.2	-	(D)	(D)
MOTOR CARRIER.........	254	100.0	1.7	4.1	7.8	2.4	19.3	56.0	8.6	(D)	(D)
PRIVATE TRUCK.........	74	100.0	-	3.3	5.3	1.2	10.6	79.6	-	(D)	(D)
AIR.................	-	100.0	1.1	-	44.7	-	6.1	5.4	-	(D)	(D)
WATER...............	-	100.0	-	-	-	-	-	-	-	(D)	(D)
OTHER...............	-	100.0	-	-	6.4	-	69.6	22.8	1.2	(D)	(D)
UNKNOWN.............	2	100.0	-	3.8	6.1	-	-	90.1	-	(D)	(D)
EAST SOUTH CENTRAL......	235	100.0	-	20.6	22.6	2.7	2.5	48.3	2.4	(D)	(D)
RAIL...............	70	100.0	-	55.8	34.9	1.4	-	5.1	-	(D)	(D)
MOTOR CARRIER.........	68	100.0	.1	12.3	31.2	1.9	2.7	48.4	3.6	(D)	(D)
PRIVATE TRUCK.........	48	100.0	-	.9	14.7	8.2	8.6	60.6	6.9	(D)	(D)
AIR.................	-	100.0	-	-	11.0	-	-	-	-	(D)	(D)
WATER...............	-	100.0	-	-	-	-	-	-	-	(D)	(D)
OTHER...............	47	100.0	-	-	-	-	-	100.0	-	(D)	(D)
UNKNOWN.............	-	100.0	-	-	-	-	-	100.0	-	(D)	(D)
WEST SOUTH CENTRAL......	272	100.0	.6	11.3	14.5	1.7	.5	43.8	23.9	(D)	(D)
RAIL...............	83	100.0	-	8.4	15.9	-	-	66.7	7.9	(D)	(D)
MOTOR CARRIER.........	115	100.0	1.5	20.2	14.4	3.8	.3	43.6	8.5	(D)	(D)
PRIVATE TRUCK.........	72	100.0	-	.6	12.6	.2	1.4	17.9	67.4	(D)	(D)
AIR.................	-	100.0	-	16.8	.4	-	-	-	1.5	(D)	(D)
WATER...............	-	100.0	-	-	-	-	-	-	-	(D)	(D)
OTHER...............	-	100.0	-	.1	74.2	-	-	23.9	1.8	(D)	(D)
UNKNOWN.............	-	100.0	-	-	-	-	-	95.8	4.2	(D)	(D)
MOUNTAIN.............	129	100.0	2.7	9.0	10.3	20.8	.1	5.2	50.1	(D)	(D)
RAIL...............	41	100.0	-	22.4	16.7	44.8	-	16.0	-	(D)	(D)
MOTOR CARRIER.........	23	100.0	14.7	9.6	23.6	34.6	.3	.1	10.3	(D)	(D)
PRIVATE TRUCK.........	63	100.0	-	-	1.2	-	-	-	97.8	(D)	(D)
AIR.................	-	100.0	-	-	5.7	-	-	-	-	(D)	(D)
WATER...............	-	100.0	-	-	-	-	-	-	-	(D)	(D)
OTHER...............	-	100.0	-	-	71.2	-	-	28.8	-	(D)	(D)
UNKNOWN.............	-	100.0	-	-	-	-	-	-	-	(D)	(D)
PACIFIC.............	273	100.0	3.1	22.8	19.2	16.7	1.9	12.2	17.5	(D)	(D)
RAIL...............	180	100.0	2.4	32.7	20.4	24.2	-	13.5	6.8	(D)	(D)
MOTOR CARRIER.........	60	100.0	3.7	4.7	25.3	3.2	8.5	2.1	26.7	(D)	(D)
PRIVATE TRUCK.........	29	100.0	-	.2	-	-	-	25.5	66.5	(D)	(D)
AIR.................	-	100.0	-	2.0	38.3	-	.1	55.9	-	(D)	(D)
WATER...............	-	100.0	100.0	-	-	-	-	-	-	(D)	(D)
OTHER...............	-	100.0	-	-	59.3	-	-	16.7	-	(D)	(D)
UNKNOWN.............	-	100.0	100.0	-	-	-	-	-	-	(D)	(D)

See footnotes at end of table 4.

TABLE 4. **TCC GROUP 332—Percent Distribution of Distance Shipped and Weight of Shipment, by Means of Transport: 1972**

Distance shipped and weight of shipment [2] [3]	Number	Percent distribution by means of transport							
		All means of transport	Rail	Motor carrier	Private truck	Air	Water	Other	Unknown
TONS OF SHIPMENTS	(thousands of tons)								
U.S. TOTAL..........	10 307	100.0	21.0	45.8	29.1	-	-	3.9	.1
UNDER 100 MILES.........	3 280	100.0	10.8	47.9	39.0	-	-	2.2	.1
UNDER 1000 POUNDS.....	35	100.0	-	70.0	29.0	-	-	1.0	-
1000 TO 9999 POUNDS...	368	100.0	-	61.4	38.1	-	-	.4	-
10000 TO 29999 POUNDS.	397	100.0	.9	50.7	31.6	-	-	16.5	.4
30000 TO 59999 POUNDS.	1 474	100.0	.7	66.4	32.4	-	-	.4	-
60000 TO 89999 POUNDS.	697	100.0	5.1	19.5	75.5	-	-	-	-
90000 POUNDS AND OVER.	307	100.0	98.7	1.1	-	-	.2	-	-
100 TO 199 MILES........	2 741	100.0	12.9	44.1	30.9	-	-	12.0	.1
UNDER 1000 POUNDS.....	24	100.0	.1	88.3	10.4	.1	-	1.1	.1
1000 TO 9999 POUNDS...	241	100.0	-	67.6	31.3	-	-	1.0	.1
10000 TO 29999 POUNDS.	536	100.0	.8	37.2	61.9	-	-	-	.1
30000 TO 59999 POUNDS.	1 404	100.0	.5	49.2	27.0	-	-	23.2	.1
60000 TO 89999 POUNDS.	63	100.0	16.2	78.2	5.6	-	-	-	-
90000 POUNDS AND OVER.	471	100.0	70.4	18.0	11.7	-	-	-	-
200 TO 299 MILES........	2 048	100.0	39.8	41.8	18.3	-	-	-	.1
UNDER 1000 POUNDS.....	13	100.0	.1	87.4	11.5	-	-	.9	.1
1000 TO 9999 POUNDS...	134	100.0	.1	87.8	12.1	-	-	-	.1
10000 TO 29999 POUNDS.	208	100.0	1.1	61.7	37.0	-	-	-	.2
30000 TO 59999 POUNDS.	835	100.0	1.7	65.4	32.8	-	-	-	.1
60000 TO 89999 POUNDS.	44	100.0	84.4	15.6	-	-	-	-	-
90000 POUNDS AND OVER.	812	100.0	93.7	5.5	.8	-	-	-	-
300 TO 499 MILES........	1 125	100.0	26.1	56.4	16.9	-	-	-	.5
UNDER 1000 POUNDS.....	10	100.0	-	85.3	11.1	.8	-	2.8	-
1000 TO 9999 POUNDS...	83	100.0	2.4	81.8	15.2	.5	-	-	.1
10000 TO 29999 POUNDS.	163	100.0	5.4	71.6	23.0	-	-	-	-
30000 TO 59999 POUNDS.	509	100.0	4.4	67.2	27.3	-	-	-	1.1
60000 TO 89999 POUNDS.	85	100.0	55.5	44.5	-	-	-	-	-
90000 POUNDS AND OVER.	272	100.0	78.0	22.0	-	-	-	-	-
500 TO 999 MILES........	891	100.0	26.4	41.2	31.9	-	-	.4	.1
UNDER 1000 POUNDS.....	9	100.0	.2	87.1	8.8	2.8	-	.9	.2
1000 TO 9999 POUNDS...	78	100.0	.9	76.8	22.0	-	-	-	.4
10000 TO 29999 POUNDS.	122	100.0	2.6	53.5	41.8	-	-	1.9	.1
30000 TO 59999 POUNDS.	424	100.0	2.4	48.7	48.5	-	-	.3	.1
60000 TO 89999 POUNDS.	60	100.0	53.1	32.2	14.6	-	-	-	-
90000 POUNDS AND OVER.	195	100.0	96.7	3.3	-	-	-	-	-
1000 TO 1499 MILES......	110	100.0	24.9	54.5	17.5	.1	3.0	-	-
UNDER 1000 POUNDS.....	-	100.0	-	84.0	12.4	1.9	-	1.7	-
1000 TO 9999 POUNDS...	11	100.0	.2	88.9	10.5	.5	-	-	-
10000 TO 29999 POUNDS.	10	100.0	23.7	45.2	31.1	-	-	-	-
30000 TO 59999 POUNDS.	55	100.0	1.8	65.2	26.9	-	6.1	-	-
60000 TO 89999 POUNDS.	30	100.0	73.0	27.0	-	-	-	-	-
90000 POUNDS AND OVER.	1	100.0	100.0	-	-	-	-	-	-
1500 MILES OR OVER......	109	100.0	78.7	15.8	4.5	.2	.4	.1	.4
UNDER 1000 POUNDS.....	1	100.0	3.2	77.9	1.5	13.2	-	4.3	-
1000 TO 9999 POUNDS...	7	100.0	23.3	62.6	13.3	.5	-	.3	-
10000 TO 29999 POUNDS.	5	100.0	14.8	85.2	-	-	-	-	-
30000 TO 59999 POUNDS.	27	100.0	57.2	25.2	14.7	-	1.4	-	1.4
60000 TO 89999 POUNDS.	41	100.0	100.0	-	-	-	-	-	-
90000 POUNDS AND OVER.	26	100.0	100.0	-	-	-	-	-	-
TON-MILES OF SHIPMENTS	(millions of ton-miles)								
U.S. TOTAL..........	2 474	100.0	30.0	43.8	23.8	-	.2	2.1	.2
UNDER 100 MILES.........	188	100.0	10.2	53.6	34.8	-	-	1.3	.1
UNDER 1000 POUNDS.....	1	100.0	-	74.9	23.9	-	-	1.1	-
1000 TO 9999 POUNDS...	19	100.0	-	67.7	32.0	-	-	.3	.1
10000 TO 29999 POUNDS.	21	100.0	.5	57.5	30.9	-	-	10.7	.4
30000 TO 59999 POUNDS.	99	100.0	.6	68.9	30.3	-	-	.1	-
60000 TO 89999 POUNDS.	30	100.0	7.8	19.2	73.0	-	-	-	-
90000 POUNDS AND OVER.	16	100.0	98.2	1.7	-	-	.1	-	-
100 TO 199 MILES........	396	100.0	11.5	44.9	31.9	-	-	11.6	-
UNDER 1000 POUNDS.....	3	100.0	.1	88.2	10.4	.1	-	1.2	-
1000 TO 9999 POUNDS...	34	100.0	-	68.4	30.5	-	-	1.0	-
10000 TO 29999 POUNDS.	76	100.0	.7	37.3	62.0	-	-	-	.1
30000 TO 59999 POUNDS.	205	100.0	.5	49.4	28.0	-	-	22.1	.1
60000 TO 89999 POUNDS.	9	100.0	15.5	78.0	6.5	-	-	-	-
90000 POUNDS AND OVER.	66	100.0	64.8	20.0	15.1	-	-	-	-
200 TO 299 MILES........	505	100.0	40.4	41.5	18.1	-	-	-	.1
UNDER 1000 POUNDS.....	3	100.0	.1	87.2	11.7	-	-	.9	.1
1000 TO 9999 POUNDS...	33	100.0	.1	87.8	12.0	-	-	-	.1
10000 TO 29999 POUNDS.	51	100.0	1.1	62.8	35.9	-	-	-	.2
30000 TO 59999 POUNDS.	204	100.0	2.0	65.2	32.8	-	-	-	.1
60000 TO 89999 POUNDS.	11	100.0	85.2	14.8	-	-	-	-	-
90000 POUNDS AND OVER.	202	100.0	93.9	5.3	.8	-	-	-	-

See footnotes at end of table 4.

TABLE 4. TCC GROUP 332—Percent Distribution of Distance Shipped and Weight of Shipment, by Means of Transport: 1972—Continued

Distance shipped and weight of shipment [2] [3]	Number	Percent distribution by means of transport							
		All means of transport	Rail	Motor carrier	Private truck	Air	Water	Other	Unknown
TON-MILES OF SHIPMENTS	(millions of ton-miles)								
300 TO 499 MILES.........	439	100.0	27.0	55.9	16.5	-	-	-	.5
UNDER 1000 POUNDS.....	4	100.0	-	84.9	11.4	.7	-	2.9	-
1000 TO 9999 POUNDS...	32	100.0	2.7	81.9	14.7	.5	-	-	.1
10000 TO 29999 POUNDS.	61	100.0	5.7	70.2	24.1	-	-	-	-
30000 TO 59999 POUNDS.	194	100.0	4.5	67.3	27.1	-	-	-	1.1
60000 TO 89999 POUNDS.	34	100.0	55.8	44.2	-	-	-	-	-
90000 POUNDS AND OVER.	112	100.0	76.6	23.4	-	-	-	-	-
500 TO 999 MILES........	613	100.0	26.1	40.5	32.9	-	-	.4	.1
UNDER 1000 POUNDS.....	6	100.0	.2	86.5	9.3	2.9	-	.9	.2
1000 TO 9999 POUNDS...	52	100.0	1.1	75.3	23.1	-	-	-	.5
10000 TO 29999 POUNDS.	82	100.0	2.4	54.9	41.0	-	-	1.6	.1
30000 TO 59999 POUNDS.	300	100.0	2.5	47.1	50.1	-	-	.3	.1
60000 TO 89999 POUNDS.	37	100.0	51.3	35.1	13.6	-	-	-	-
90000 POUNDS AND OVER.	134	100.0	97.6	2.4	-	-	-	-	-
1000 TO 1499 MILES......	125	100.0	26.1	53.5	17.6	.1	2.8	-	-
UNDER 1000 POUNDS.....	1	100.0	-	84.7	11.6	1.8	-	1.8	-
1000 TO 9999 POUNDS...	13	100.0	.2	89.4	9.9	.5	-	-	-
10000 TO 29999 POUNDS.	11	100.0	22.7	47.1	30.2	-	-	-	-
30000 TO 59999 POUNDS.	61	100.0	1.9	64.7	27.8	-	5.6	-	-
60000 TO 89999 POUNDS.	35	100.0	75.6	24.4	-	-	-	-	-
90000 POUNDS AND OVER.	1	100.0	100.0	-	-	-	-	-	-
1500 MILES OR OVER......	205	100.0	78.2	16.3	4.2	.2	.5	.1	.5
UNDER 1000 POUNDS.....	2	100.0	2.7	77.9	1.2	13.9	-	4.2	-
1000 TO 9999 POUNDS...	13	100.0	22.5	65.0	11.7	.5	-	.3	-
10000 TO 29999 POUNDS.	11	100.0	14.8	85.2	-	-	-	-	-
30000 TO 59999 POUNDS.	48	100.0	55.1	26.5	14.3	-	2.0	-	2.0
60000 TO 89999 POUNDS.	78	100.0	100.0	-	-	-	-	-	-
90000 POUNDS AND OVER.	51	100.0	100.0	-	-	-	-	-	-

Note: Detail may not add to total due to rounding. The introductory table shows the estimates of sampling variability for tons; sampling variability for ton-miles has not been estimated. See the map in the Introduction for the States comprising the geographic divisions of the United States.

Shipments excluded from the survey are those moving by pipeline (primarily petroleum products from refineries), parcel post shipments, and commodities moved by own power (motorized vehicles, aircraft, etc.) or towed (prefabricated buildings, etc.). Local shipments (commodities shipped less than 25 miles from the plant) and shipments within the same city are also excluded. Shipments to Alaska and Hawaii from the 48 conterminous States and the District of Columbia are included; however, no data were obtained for shipments originating in Alaska and Hawaii.

- Represents zero or rounds to zero. (D) Withheld to avoid disclosing figures for individual companies.

[1] Production of this commodity is concentrated in the geographic divisions shown; figures and distributions for geographic divisions not shown are included in the total.

[2] Distances of shipments to foreign destinations are calculated only to the U.S. port of exit.

[3] Includes only shipments represented by bills of lading and invoices. Summary records which did not show individual weights of shipments are not included.

TCC 333. Nonferrous Metal Primary Smelter Products

Comparisons of Tons and Ton-Miles of Shipments for
Geographic Divisions of Origin and for Sampling Variability: 1972 and 1967

Geographic division of origin	Estimates				Relative sampling variability in tons (percent)	
	1972		1967		1972	1967
	Tons (thousands)	Ton-miles (millions)	Tons (thousands)	Ton-miles (millions)	1972	1967
U.S. total	9,882	6,201	8,440	5,818	12.6	7.2
New England	(D)	(D)	34	5	(*)	(*)
Middle Atlantic	1,496	388	1,469	365	15.7	(*)
East North Central	1,306	359	1,555	424	15.8	(*)
West North Central	(D)	(D)	252	135	(*)	(*)
South Atlantic	(D)	(D)	219	71	(*)	(*)
East South Central	(D)	(D)	195	88	(*)	(*)
West South Central	2,404	1,498	1,959	1,678	25.9	(*)
Mountain	2,218	2,305	1,766	1,682	17.9	(*)
Pacific	669	922	991	1,370	4.7	(*)

(D) Withheld to avoid disclosing figures for individual companies.   (*) Data not published.

TABLE 1. TCC GROUP 333—Percent Distribution of Geographic Division of Origin and Distance Shipped, by Means of Transport: 1972

Geographic division of origin [1] and distance shipped [2]	Number	Percent distribution by means of transport							
		All means of transport	Rail	Motor carrier	Private truck	Air	Water	Other	Unknown
TONS OF SHIPMENTS	(thousands of tons)								
U.S. TOTAL	9 882	100.0	67.2	14.5	17.8	-	.2	-	.2
MIDDLE ATLANTIC.........	1 496	100.0	48.6	27.0	22.3	-	1.2	-	.9
UNDER 100 MILES.......	635	100.0	38.5	32.0	26.5	-	2.1	-	.9
100 TO 199 MILES......	191	100.0	42.5	40.2	16.6	-	-	-	.6
200 TO 299 MILES......	323	100.0	64.1	14.7	20.7	-	-	-	.6
300 TO 499 MILES......	175	100.0	58.6	24.3	14.5	-	2.5	-	-
500 TO 999 MILES......	104	100.0	45.8	16.0	38.2	-	-	-	-
1000 TO 1499 MILES....	16	100.0	9.1	76.2	7.4	.2	-	-	7.2
1500 MILES OR OVER....	49	100.0	84.4	9.0	.2	.1	-	-	6.3
EAST NORTH CENTRAL......	1 306	100.0	21.7	39.6	38.1	-	-	-	.5
UNDER 100 MILES.......	330	100.0	6.1	38.2	55.0	-	-	-	.7
100 TO 199 MILES......	338	100.0	7.4	31.7	60.5	-	-	-	.5
200 TO 299 MILES......	256	100.0	23.8	47.4	28.7	-	-	-	-
300 TO 499 MILES......	262	100.0	42.6	47.5	8.8	-	-	-	1.2
500 TO 999 MILES......	70	100.0	54.3	32.2	13.5	-	-	-	-
1000 TO 1499 MILES....	6	100.0	81.0	3.8	15.2	-	-	-	-
1500 MILES OR OVER....	41	100.0	54.4	35.5	10.0	-	-	-	-
WEST SOUTH CENTRAL......	2 404	100.0	64.3	8.2	27.4	-	.1	-	-
UNDER 100 MILES.......	108	100.0	7.2	41.9	50.8	-	-	-	-
100 TO 199 MILES......	644	100.0	13.7	2.8	83.5	-	-	-	-
200 TO 299 MILES......	103	100.0	50.6	7.4	42.0	-	-	-	-
300 TO 499 MILES......	130	100.0	74.7	17.2	8.1	-	-	-	-
500 TO 999 MILES......	1 026	100.0	92.6	6.4	1.0	-	-	-	-
1000 TO 1499 MILES....	271	100.0	86.1	12.5	.7	-	.8	-	-
1500 MILES OR OVER....	119	100.0	96.8	2.4	-	-	.8	-	-
MOUNTAIN................	2 218	100.0	98.5	1.4	.1	-	-	-	-
UNDER 100 MILES.......	71	100.0	87.9	12.1	-	-	-	-	-
100 TO 199 MILES......	557	100.0	100.0	-	-	-	-	-	-
200 TO 299 MILES......	12	100.0	100.0	-	-	-	-	-	-
300 TO 499 MILES......	87	100.0	95.1	4.4	.5	-	-	-	-
500 TO 999 MILES......	380	100.0	99.7	.3	-	-	-	-	-
1000 TO 1499 MILES....	425	100.0	96.5	3.2	.3	-	-	-	-
1500 MILES OR OVER....	683	100.0	99.4	.4	.1	-	-	-	.1
PACIFIC.................	669	100.0	88.4	4.3	6.2	-	.3	.7	-
UNDER 100 MILES.......	54	100.0	22.2	12.2	53.4	-	3.9	7.9	.2
100 TO 199 MILES......	13	100.0	57.6	41.4	.1	-	-	.7	.3
200 TO 299 MILES......	2	100.0	49.5	45.9	3.9	-	-	.7	-
300 TO 499 MILES......	20	100.0	49.0	2.7	48.2	-	-	-	-
500 TO 999 MILES......	146	100.0	90.7	7.5	1.7	-	-	.2	-
1000 TO 1499 MILES....	25	100.0	99.9	.1	-	-	-	-	-
1500 MILES OR OVER....	406	100.0	99.0	.9	-	-	-	-	-
TON-MILES OF SHIPMENTS	(millions of ton-miles)								
U.S. TOTAL	6 201	100.0	87.2	7.6	4.8	-	.1	-	.2
MIDDLE ATLANTIC.........	388	100.0	58.8	21.6	16.8	-	.6	-	2.2
UNDER 100 MILES.......	31	100.0	47.2	27.5	23.1	-	.8	-	1.3
100 TO 199 MILES......	32	100.0	45.5	37.9	15.9	-	-	-	.7
200 TO 299 MILES......	83	100.0	65.0	14.3	20.2	-	-	-	.6
300 TO 499 MILES......	70	100.0	60.5	22.5	14.1	-	2.9	-	-
500 TO 999 MILES......	69	100.0	47.5	17.2	35.3	-	-	-	-
1000 TO 1499 MILES....	18	100.0	9.2	75.4	7.7	.2	-	-	7.4
1500 MILES OR OVER....	83	100.0	81.3	11.3	.1	.1	.1	-	7.0
EAST NORTH CENTRAL......	359	100.0	38.2	39.3	22.1	-	-	-	.4
UNDER 100 MILES.......	17	100.0	8.5	42.5	48.4	-	-	-	.6
100 TO 199 MILES......	47	100.0	7.0	31.8	60.7	-	-	-	.4
200 TO 299 MILES......	65	100.0	25.3	46.3	28.3	-	-	-	-
300 TO 499 MILES......	99	100.0	43.0	46.7	9.2	-	-	-	1.1
500 TO 999 MILES......	47	100.0	55.8	31.7	12.5	-	-	-	-
1000 TO 1499 MILES....	7	100.0	81.0	4.2	14.8	-	-	-	-
1500 MILES OR OVER....	74	100.0	54.7	35.4	9.9	-	-	-	-
WEST SOUTH CENTRAL......	1 498	100.0	86.4	7.2	6.0	-	.3	-	-
UNDER 100 MILES.......	4	100.0	12.0	47.6	40.3	-	-	-	-
100 TO 199 MILES......	81	100.0	16.4	3.4	80.2	-	-	-	-
200 TO 299 MILES......	25	100.0	55.1	7.5	37.4	-	-	-	-
300 TO 499 MILES......	52	100.0	75.8	16.1	8.1	-	-	-	-
500 TO 999 MILES......	795	100.0	93.3	5.8	.9	-	-	-	-
1000 TO 1499 MILES....	319	100.0	85.4	13.1	.7	-	.9	-	-
1500 MILES OR OVER....	218	100.0	97.0	2.3	-	-	.7	-	-
MOUNTAIN................	2 305	100.0	98.8	1.0	.1	-	-	-	.1
UNDER 100 MILES.......	4	100.0	97.6	2.4	-	-	-	-	-
100 TO 199 MILES......	84	100.0	100.0	-	-	-	-	-	-
200 TO 299 MILES......	3	100.0	100.0	-	-	-	-	-	-
300 TO 499 MILES......	41	100.0	96.5	3.1	.4	-	-	-	-
500 TO 999 MILES......	316	100.0	99.7	.3	-	-	-	-	-
1000 TO 1499 MILES....	553	100.0	96.6	3.1	.3	-	-	-	-
1500 MILES OR OVER....	1 301	100.0	99.4	.3	.1	-	-	-	.1

See footnotes at end of table 4.

TABLE 1. **TCC GROUP 333—Percent Distribution of Geographic Division of Origin and Distance Shipped, by Means of Transport: 1972**—Continued

Geographic division of origin [1] and distance shipped [2]	Number	Percent distribution by means of transport							
		All means of transport	Rail	Motor carrier	Private truck	Air	Water	Other	Unknown
TON-MILES OF SHIPMENTS	(millions of ton-miles)								
PACIFIC..................	922	100.0	97.3	2.0	.7	-	-	-	-
UNDER 100 MILES.......	2	100.0	47.4	15.4	30.9	-	2.5	3.5	.2
100 TO 199 MILES......	1	100.0	56.7	42.1	.1	-	-	.9	.3
200 TO 299 MILES......	-	100.0	54.3	40.7	4.4	-	-	.5	-
300 TO 499 MILES......	8	100.0	57.3	2.2	40.5	-	-	-	-
500 TO 999 MILES......	125	100.0	90.5	7.8	1.5	-	-	.1	-
1000 TO 1499 MILES....	31	100.0	99.9	.1	-	-	-	-	-
1500 MILES OR OVER....	752	100.0	99.1	.9	-	-	-	-	-

See footnotes at end of table 4.

TABLE 2. **TCC GROUP 333—Percent Distribution of Geographic Division of Origin and Means of Transport, by Geographic Division of Destination: 1972**

Geographic division of origin [1] and means of transport	Number	Percent distribution by division of destination									
		U.S. total	New England	Middle Atlantic	East North Central	West North Central	South Atlantic	East South Central	West South Central	Mountain	Pacific
TONS OF SHIPMENTS	(thousands of tons)										
U.S. TOTAL	9 882	100.0	2.7	16.6	30.0	8.3	9.8	6.3	16.2	5.0	4.9
RAIL.................	6 637	100.0	2.9	13.6	28.0	10.4	12.1	7.2	12.6	7.2	5.8
MOTOR CARRIER........	1 431	100.0	2.6	28.9	37.2	6.2	7.4	5.6	7.9	.9	3.4
PRIVATE TRUCK........	1 761	100.0	2.0	17.1	32.2	2.2	3.3	3.6	36.9	-	2.6
AIR..................	-	100.0	36.7	18.3	19.2	.3	10.4	1.4	2.5	1.8	9.3
WATER................	22	100.0	5.6	65.9	-	-	-	19.0	-	-	9.5
OTHER................	4	100.0	-	.4	.1	-	-	-	-	4.6	94.9
UNKNOWN..............	24	100.0	-	42.5	36.8	1.9	5.4	-	12.7	-	.7
MIDDLE ATLANTIC.........	1 496	100.0	10.4	48.5	23.0	.2	11.0	2.6	3.5	.3	.4
RAIL.................	727	100.0	15.9	38.8	28.2	.4	7.9	3.0	5.1	.3	.4
MOTOR CARRIER........	404	100.0	6.0	51.9	20.3	.1	16.3	1.7	2.7	.3	.8
PRIVATE TRUCK........	333	100.0	4.4	63.4	17.3	.1	12.1	2.1	.6	.6	-
AIR..................	-	100.0	7.8	4.1	5.6	1.2	36.4	4.8	3.7	6.3	30.1
WATER................	17	100.0	2.0	73.3	-	-	-	24.5	-	-	.1
OTHER................	-	100.0	2.7	35.9	8.1	27.7	25.3	.2	-	-	-
UNKNOWN..............	13	100.0	-	67.5	-	-	9.0	-	23.5	-	-
EAST NORTH CENTRAL......	1 306	100.0	.3	11.8	67.6	7.6	1.8	4.6	2.9	.2	3.2
RAIL.................	284	100.0	.2	9.3	56.6	7.4	1.3	7.3	9.4	.5	7.9
MOTOR CARRIER........	517	100.0	.6	21.7	56.0	11.1	3.4	2.7	1.4	.3	2.8
PRIVATE TRUCK........	497	100.0	-	3.1	85.7	4.1	.5	5.1	.8	-	.8
AIR..................	-	100.0	-	100.0	-	-	-	-	-	-	-
WATER................	-	100.0	-	-	-	-	-	-	-	-	-
OTHER................	-	100.0	-	28.7	65.6	5.7	-	-	-	-	-
UNKNOWN..............	7	100.0	-	4.4	89.0	6.6	-	-	-	-	-
WEST SOUTH CENTRAL......	2 404	100.0	.4	6.2	21.1	11.4	6.5	9.9	41.6	.5	2.4
RAIL.................	1 545	100.0	.4	8.6	29.3	16.7	9.0	14.0	17.6	.8	3.6
MOTOR CARRIER........	196	100.0	1.2	7.1	24.7	8.5	6.8	7.2	43.7	-	.9
PRIVATE TRUCK........	659	100.0	-	.1	.8	.1	.5	.9	97.4	-	.1
AIR..................	-	100.0	-	-	-	-	-	-	-	-	-
WATER................	2	100.0	30.4	69.6	-	-	-	-	-	-	-
OTHER................	-	100.0	-	-	-	-	-	-	-	-	-
UNKNOWN..............	-	100.0	-	-	-	-	-	-	-	-	-
MOUNTAIN................	2 218	100.0	1.0	8.6	15.7	12.5	17.0	1.9	17.2	19.4	6.7
RAIL.................	2 185	100.0	1.0	8.6	15.3	12.6	17.2	2.0	17.4	19.3	6.5
MOTOR CARRIER........	30	100.0	.3	8.4	44.1	1.2	1.2	-	-	29.8	14.9
PRIVATE TRUCK........	2	100.0	-	-	28.1	23.5	28.3	-	-	-	20.1
AIR..................	-	100.0	34.1	64.0	-	-	-	-	-	-	1.9
WATER................	-	100.0	-	-	-	-	-	-	-	-	-
OTHER................	-	100.0	-	-	-	-	-	-	-	-	-
UNKNOWN..............	-	100.0	-	86.0	-	-	14.0	-	-	-	-
PACIFIC.................	669	100.0	1.6	5.2	32.5	6.9	2.7	10.4	3.7	6.0	31.0
RAIL.................	591	100.0	1.8	5.8	36.1	7.8	3.0	11.8	4.2	6.6	22.9
MOTOR CARRIER........	28	100.0	-	-	13.1	.1	.2	-	-	3.0	83.5
PRIVATE TRUCK........	41	100.0	-	-	.2	-	-	-	-	1.1	98.7
AIR..................	-	100.0	-	-	92.3	-	-	-	7.7	-	-
WATER................	2	100.0	-	-	-	-	-	-	-	-	100.0
OTHER................	4	100.0	-	-	-	-	-	-	-	4.6	95.4
UNKNOWN..............	-	100.0	-	-	-	-	-	-	-	.4	99.6

See footnotes at end of table 4.

TABLE 2. **TCC GROUP 333—Percent Distribution of Geographic Division of Origin and Means of Transport, by Geographic Division of Destination: 1972**—Continued

Geographic division of origin [1] and means of transport	Number	Percent distribution by division of destination									
		U.S. total	New England	Middle Atlantic	East North Central	West North Central	South Atlantic	East South Central	West South Central	Mountain	Pacific
TON-MILES OF SHIPMENTS	(millions of ton-miles)										
U.S. TOTAL	6 201	100.0	2.2	16.0	29.2	10.2	17.0	6.4	10.0	2.0	7.0
RAIL....................	5 409	100.0	2.2	15.6	28.3	10.9	18.4	6.4	9.2	2.2	6.8
MOTOR CARRIER..........	473	100.0	2.7	22.2	36.3	6.9	7.3	5.3	7.2	.9	11.0
PRIVATE TRUCK.........	298	100.0	1.0	12.9	34.4	3.4	7.3	7.0	29.0	.1	4.8
AIR....................	-	100.0	25.2	20.1	25.5	.2	7.8	.7	3.0	2.2	15.3
WATER..................	6	100.0	22.8	44.4	-	-	-	30.3	-	-	2.6
OTHER..................	-	100.0	-	4.7	.2	.4	.3	-	-	47.1	47.3
UNKNOWN................	13	100.0	-	23.4	17.9	1.3	12.1	-	45.1	-	.1
MIDDLE ATLANTIC........	388	100.0	5.3	25.2	30.7	.9	7.8	4.9	20.0	1.6	3.5
RAIL...................	228	100.0	6.3	27.2	30.4	1.2	1.6	3.6	25.3	1.7	2.7
MOTOR CARRIER.........	83	100.0	5.2	20.2	27.1	.5	16.5	5.3	14.3	2.3	8.6
PRIVATE TRUCK.........	65	100.0	3.0	26.9	41.8	.5	17.5	6.7	3.4	.2	-
AIR....................	-	100.0	1.4	.5	2.0	.8	28.5	2.6	3.1	7.9	53.2
WATER..................	2	100.0	1.0	9.0	-	-	-	84.9	-	-	5.0
OTHER..................	-	100.0	1.7	4.8	7.9	47.0	38.3	.4	-	-	-
UNKNOWN................	8	100.0	-	13.4	-	-	16.5	-	70.0	-	-
EAST NORTH CENTRAL......	359	100.0	.7	13.0	39.5	8.6	2.6	6.7	7.5	.8	20.7
RAIL...................	137	100.0	.4	8.5	30.5	5.8	2.1	7.7	14.1	1.0	29.8
MOTOR CARRIER.........	141	100.0	1.4	20.8	35.2	12.1	3.7	4.1	3.2	1.0	18.5
PRIVATE TRUCK.........	79	100.0	-	6.9	61.6	7.1	1.7	9.6	3.7	-	9.4
AIR....................	-	100.0	-	100.0	-	-	-	-	-	-	-
WATER..................	-	100.0	-	-	-	-	-	-	-	-	-
OTHER..................	-	100.0	-	46.0	47.5	6.5	-	-	-	-	-
UNKNOWN................	1	100.0	-	1.5	86.0	12.4	-	-	-	-	-
WEST SOUTH CENTRAL......	1 498	100.0	1.0	15.7	29.0	15.1	9.5	8.0	15.1	.6	6.0
RAIL...................	1 294	100.0	.7	16.5	29.9	16.9	10.0	8.5	10.3	.7	6.7
MOTOR CARRIER.........	108	100.0	3.4	17.0	40.0	7.8	9.4	6.9	12.7	-	2.8
PRIVATE TRUCK.........	90	100.0	-	.6	4.6	.3	2.3	2.8	88.3	-	1.1
AIR....................	-	100.0	-	-	-	-	-	-	-	-	-
WATER..................	4	100.0	35.2	64.8	-	-	-	-	-	-	-
OTHER..................	-	100.0	-	-	-	-	-	-	-	-	-
UNKNOWN................	-	100.0	-	-	-	-	-	-	-	-	-
MOUNTAIN...............	2 305	100.0	2.0	16.6	21.7	10.8	31.3	2.7	7.9	3.0	4.0
RAIL...................	2 276	100.0	2.0	16.5	21.2	10.9	31.6	2.7	8.0	3.1	3.9
MOTOR CARRIER.........	23	100.0	.6	16.8	69.6	1.8	2.4	-	-	1.2	7.6
PRIVATE TRUCK.........	2	100.0	-	-	31.0	19.3	44.3	-	-	-	5.4
AIR....................	-	100.0	36.4	63.0	-	-	-	-	-	-	.6
WATER..................	-	100.0	-	-	-	-	-	-	-	-	-
OTHER..................	-	100.0	-	-	-	-	-	-	-	-	-
UNKNOWN................	1	100.0	-	88.2	-	-	11.8	-	-	-	-
PACIFIC................	922	100.0	2.8	8.3	41.7	7.8	4.3	14.7	4.2	3.6	12.6
RAIL...................	897	100.0	2.8	8.5	42.1	8.1	4.4	15.1	4.3	3.7	11.0
MOTOR CARRIER.........	18	100.0	-	-	36.6	.2	.9	-	-	1.2	61.0
PRIVATE TRUCK.........	6	100.0	-	-	2.6	-	-	-	-	4.2	93.2
AIR....................	-	100.0	-	-	92.2	-	-	-	7.8	-	-
WATER..................	-	100.0	-	-	-	-	-	-	-	-	100.0
OTHER..................	-	100.0	-	-	-	-	-	-	-	55.1	44.9
UNKNOWN................	-	100.0	-	-	-	-	-	-	-	2.0	98.0

See footnotes at end of table 4.

TABLE 3. **TCC GROUP 333—Percent Distribution of Geographic Division of Destination and Means of Transport, by Geographic Division of Origin: 1972**

Geographic division of destination and means of transport	Number	Percent distribution by division of origin [1]									
		U.S. total	New England	Middle Atlantic	East North Central	West North Central	South Atlantic	East South Central	West South Central	Mountain	Pacific
TONS OF SHIPMENTS	(thousands of tons)										
U.S. TOTAL	9 882	100.0	(D)	15.1	13.2	(D)	(D)	(D)	24.3	22.5	6.8
RAIL	6 637	100.0	(D)	11.0	4.3	(D)	(D)	(D)	23.3	32.9	8.9
MOTOR CARRIER	1 431	100.0	(D)	28.3	36.2	(D)	(D)	(D)	13.7	2.1	2.0
PRIVATE TRUCK	1 761	100.0	(D)	18.9	28.3	(D)	(D)	(D)	37.5	.1	2.4
AIR	-	100.0	(D)	26.4	3.2	(D)	(D)	(D)	-	21.9	19.1
WATER	22	100.0	(D)	77.5	-	(D)	(D)	(D)	13.0	-	9.4
OTHER	4	100.0	(D)	.1	.1	(D)	(D)	(D)	-	-	99.3
UNKNOWN	24	100.0	(D)	54.1	28.9	(D)	(D)	(D)	-	3.6	.7
NEW ENGLAND	267	100.0	(D)	57.9	1.4	(D)	(D)	(D)	3.4	8.4	4.0
RAIL	194	100.0	(D)	59.6	.4	(D)	(D)	(D)	3.0	11.6	5.6
MOTOR CARRIER	36	100.0	(D)	66.1	8.1	(D)	(D)	(D)	6.7	.2	-
PRIVATE TRUCK	35	100.0	(D)	41.4	-	(D)	(D)	(D)	-	-	-
AIR	-	100.0	(D)	6.0	-	(D)	(D)	(D)	-	20.3	-
WATER	1	100.0	(D)	28.5	-	(D)	(D)	(D)	71.5	-	-
OTHER	-	100.0	(D)	100.0	-	(D)	(D)	(D)	-	-	-
UNKNOWN	-	100.0	(D)	-	-	(D)	(D)	(D)	-	-	-
MIDDLE ATLANTIC	1 640	100.0	(D)	44.2	9.4	(D)	(D)	(D)	9.1	11.6	2.1
RAIL	901	100.0	(D)	31.3	2.9	(D)	(D)	(D)	14.7	20.8	3.8
MOTOR CARRIER	413	100.0	(D)	50.8	27.2	(D)	(D)	(D)	3.4	.6	-
PRIVATE TRUCK	300	100.0	(D)	70.4	5.1	(D)	(D)	(D)	.2	-	-
AIR	-	100.0	(D)	6.3	17.3	(D)	(D)	(D)	-	76.3	-
WATER	15	100.0	(D)	86.2	-	(D)	(D)	(D)	13.8	-	-
OTHER	-	100.0	(D)	8.8	5.8	(D)	(D)	(D)	-	-	-
UNKNOWN	10	100.0	(D)	85.8	3.0	(D)	(D)	(D)	-	7.2	-
EAST NORTH CENTRAL	2 969	100.0	(D)	11.6	29.8	(D)	(D)	(D)	17.1	11.8	7.3
RAIL	1 860	100.0	(D)	11.0	8.6	(D)	(D)	(D)	24.3	18.0	11.5
MOTOR CARRIER	532	100.0	(D)	15.4	54.5	(D)	(D)	(D)	9.1	2.5	.7
PRIVATE TRUCK	567	100.0	(D)	10.2	75.1	(D)	(D)	(D)	.9	.1	-
AIR	-	100.0	(D)	8.3	-	(D)	(D)	(D)	-	-	91.7
WATER	-	100.0	(D)	-	-	(D)	(D)	(D)	-	-	-
OTHER	-	100.0	(D)	13.1	86.9	(D)	(D)	(D)	-	-	-
UNKNOWN	9	100.0	(D)	-	70.0	(D)	(D)	(D)	-	-	-
WEST NORTH CENTRAL	820	100.0	(D)	.5	12.1	(D)	(D)	(D)	33.5	33.7	5.6
RAIL	692	100.0	(D)	.4	3.0	(D)	(D)	(D)	37.3	39.8	6.7
MOTOR CARRIER	89	100.0	(D)	.5	64.6	(D)	(D)	(D)	18.7	.4	-
PRIVATE TRUCK	38	100.0	(D)	1.0	52.1	(D)	(D)	(D)	2.0	1.3	-
AIR	-	100.0	(D)	100.0	-	(D)	(D)	(D)	-	-	-
WATER	-	100.0	(D)	-	-	(D)	(D)	(D)	-	-	-
OTHER	-	100.0	(D)	85.5	14.5	(D)	(D)	(D)	-	-	-
UNKNOWN	-	100.0	(D)	-	100.0	(D)	(D)	(D)	-	-	-
SOUTH ATLANTIC	971	100.0	(D)	17.0	2.4	(D)	(D)	(D)	16.1	38.9	1.8
RAIL	806	100.0	(D)	7.2	.5	(D)	(D)	(D)	17.4	46.7	2.2
MOTOR CARRIER	105	100.0	(D)	62.0	16.7	(D)	(D)	(D)	12.6	.4	.1
PRIVATE TRUCK	57	100.0	(D)	69.4	4.0	(D)	(D)	(D)	5.8	1.1	-
AIR	-	100.0	(D)	100.0	-	(D)	(D)	(D)	-	-	-
WATER	-	100.0	(D)	-	-	(D)	(D)	(D)	-	-	-
OTHER	-	100.0	(D)	100.0	-	(D)	(D)	(D)	-	-	-
UNKNOWN	1	100.0	(D)	90.7	-	(D)	(D)	(D)	-	9.3	-
EAST SOUTH CENTRAL	626	100.0	(D)	6.3	9.6	(D)	(D)	(D)	37.9	6.8	11.2
RAIL	478	100.0	(D)	4.5	4.4	(D)	(D)	(D)	45.4	9.0	14.6
MOTOR CARRIER	79	100.0	(D)	8.5	17.6	(D)	(D)	(D)	17.7	-	-
PRIVATE TRUCK	63	100.0	(D)	10.8	39.6	(D)	(D)	(D)	9.6	-	-
AIR	-	100.0	(D)	100.0	-	(D)	(D)	(D)	-	-	-
WATER	4	100.0	(D)	100.0	-	(D)	(D)	(D)	-	-	-
OTHER	-	100.0	(D)	100.0	-	(D)	(D)	(D)	-	-	-
UNKNOWN	-	100.0	(D)	-	-	(D)	(D)	(D)	-	-	-
WEST SOUTH CENTRAL	1 605	100.0	(D)	3.3	2.4	(D)	(D)	(D)	62.3	23.7	1.5
RAIL	838	100.0	(D)	4.4	3.2	(D)	(D)	(D)	32.4	45.4	2.9
MOTOR CARRIER	112	100.0	(D)	9.7	6.5	(D)	(D)	(D)	76.2	-	-
PRIVATE TRUCK	650	100.0	(D)	.3	.6	(D)	(D)	(D)	98.8	-	-
AIR	-	100.0	(D)	42.0	-	(D)	(D)	(D)	-	-	58.0
WATER	-	100.0	(D)	-	-	(D)	(D)	(D)	-	-	-
OTHER	-	100.0	(D)	-	-	(D)	(D)	(D)	-	-	-
UNKNOWN	3	100.0	(D)	100.0	-	(D)	(D)	(D)	-	-	-
MOUNTAIN	492	100.0	(D)	.8	.6	(D)	(D)	(D)	2.5	87.6	8.2
RAIL	478	100.0	(D)	.5	.3	(D)	(D)	(D)	2.5	88.3	8.1
MOTOR CARRIER	13	100.0	(D)	9.3	11.0	(D)	(D)	(D)	-	67.9	6.7
PRIVATE TRUCK	-	100.0	(D)	18.1	-	(D)	(D)	(D)	-	-	81.9
AIR	-	100.0	(D)	100.0	-	(D)	(D)	(D)	-	-	-
WATER	-	100.0	(D)	-	-	(D)	(D)	(D)	-	-	-
OTHER	-	100.0	(D)	-	-	(D)	(D)	(D)	-	-	100.0
UNKNOWN	-	100.0	(D)	-	-	(D)	(D)	(D)	-	-	100.0
PACIFIC	489	100.0	(D)	1.2	8.4	(D)	(D)	(D)	11.9	30.2	42.4
RAIL	387	100.0	(D)	.7	5.8	(D)	(D)	(D)	14.4	36.9	35.0
MOTOR CARRIER	48	100.0	(D)	6.3	29.8	(D)	(D)	(D)	3.5	9.2	49.6
PRIVATE TRUCK	46	100.0	(D)	-	9.0	(D)	(D)	(D)	1.7	.9	88.4
AIR	-	100.0	(D)	91.5	-	(D)	(D)	(D)	-	4.5	-
WATER	2	100.0	(D)	1.1	-	(D)	(D)	(D)	-	-	98.9
OTHER	4	100.0	(D)	-	-	(D)	(D)	(D)	-	-	99.8
UNKNOWN	-	100.0	(D)	-	-	(D)	(D)	(D)	-	-	100.0

See footnotes at end of table 4.

TABLE 3. **TCC GROUP 333**—Percent Distribution of Geographic Division of Destination and Means of Transport, by Geographic Division of Origin: 1972—Continued

Geographic division of destination and means of transport	Number	Percent distribution by division of origin [1]									
		U.S. total	New England	Middle Atlantic	East North Central	West North Central	South Atlantic	East South Central	West South Central	Mountain	Pacific
TON-MILES OF SHIPMENTS	(millions of ton-miles)										
U.S. TOTAL	6 201	100.0	(D)	6.3	5.8	(D)	(D)	(D)	24.2	37.2	14.9
RAIL	5 409	100.0	(D)	4.2	2.5	(D)	(D)	(D)	23.9	42.1	16.6
MOTOR CARRIER	473	100.0	(D)	17.7	29.8	(D)	(D)	(D)	22.9	5.1	3.8
PRIVATE TRUCK	298	100.0	(D)	21.8	26.6	(D)	(D)	(D)	30.4	.9	2.1
AIR	-	100.0	(D)	27.4	.8	(D)	(D)	(D)	-	30.4	27.0
WATER	6	100.0	(D)	35.7	-	(D)	(D)	(D)	63.5	-	.8
OTHER	-	100.0	(D)	.8	.3	(D)	(D)	(D)	-	-	85.4
UNKNOWN	13	100.0	(D)	64.4	10.7	(D)	(D)	(D)	-	12.5	.1
NEW ENGLAND	135	100.0	(D)	15.3	1.8	(D)	(D)	(D)	10.7	34.0	18.8
RAIL	117	100.0	(D)	12.2	.4	(D)	(D)	(D)	7.8	38.9	21.6
MOTOR CARRIER	12	100.0	(D)	34.4	15.5	(D)	(D)	(D)	29.2	1.1	-
PRIVATE TRUCK	3	100.0	(D)	63.0	-	(D)	(D)	(D)	-	-	-
AIR	-	100.0	(D)	1.5	-	(D)	(D)	(D)	-	43.9	-
WATER	1	100.0	(D)	1.6	-	(D)	(D)	(D)	98.4	-	-
OTHER	-	100.0	(D)	100.0	-	(D)	(D)	(D)	-	-	-
UNKNOWN	-	100.0	(D)	-	-	(D)	(D)	(D)	-	-	-
MIDDLE ATLANTIC	994	100.0	(D)	9.9	4.7	(D)	(D)	(D)	23.6	38.4	7.7
RAIL	844	100.0	(D)	7.4	1.4	(D)	(D)	(D)	25.2	44.6	9.1
MOTOR CARRIER	105	100.0	(D)	16.1	27.9	(D)	(D)	(D)	17.5	3.8	-
PRIVATE TRUCK	38	100.0	(D)	45.6	14.3	(D)	(D)	(D)	1.4	-	-
AIR	-	100.0	(D)	.7	3.9	(D)	(D)	(D)	-	95.3	-
WATER	3	100.0	(D)	7.2	-	(D)	(D)	(D)	92.8	-	-
OTHER	-	100.0	(D)	.8	2.8	(D)	(D)	(D)	-	-	-
UNKNOWN	3	100.0	(D)	36.9	.7	(D)	(D)	(D)	-	47.0	-
EAST NORTH CENTRAL	1 809	100.0	(D)	6.6	7.8	(D)	(D)	(D)	24.0	27.7	21.3
RAIL	1 532	100.0	(D)	4.5	2.7	(D)	(D)	(D)	25.2	31.5	24.6
MOTOR CARRIER	171	100.0	(D)	13.2	29.0	(D)	(D)	(D)	25.3	9.7	3.9
PRIVATE TRUCK	102	100.0	(D)	26.5	47.8	(D)	(D)	(D)	4.1	.8	.2
AIR	-	100.0	(D)	2.1	-	(D)	(D)	(D)	-	-	97.9
WATER	-	100.0	(D)	-	-	(D)	(D)	(D)	-	-	-
OTHER	-	100.0	(D)	31.8	68.2	(D)	(D)	(D)	-	-	-
UNKNOWN	2	100.0	(D)	-	51.4	(D)	(D)	(D)	-	-	-
WEST NORTH CENTRAL	633	100.0	(D)	.6	4.9	(D)	(D)	(D)	35.8	39.2	11.4
RAIL	590	100.0	(D)	.5	1.4	(D)	(D)	(D)	37.0	41.9	12.3
MOTOR CARRIER	32	100.0	(D)	1.3	52.0	(D)	(D)	(D)	25.7	1.3	.1
PRIVATE TRUCK	10	100.0	(D)	3.3	54.8	(D)	(D)	(D)	2.6	5.3	-
AIR	-	100.0	(D)	100.0	-	(D)	(D)	(D)	-	-	-
WATER	-	100.0	(D)	-	-	(D)	(D)	(D)	-	-	-
OTHER	-	100.0	(D)	95.3	4.7	(D)	(D)	(D)	-	-	-
UNKNOWN	-	100.0	(D)	-	100.0	(D)	(D)	(D)	-	-	-
SOUTH ATLANTIC	1 054	100.0	(D)	2.9	.9	(D)	(D)	(D)	13.5	68.5	3.7
RAIL	995	100.0	(D)	.4	.3	(D)	(D)	(D)	13.1	72.3	3.9
MOTOR CARRIER	34	100.0	(D)	40.0	14.9	(D)	(D)	(D)	29.5	1.6	.5
PRIVATE TRUCK	21	100.0	(D)	52.4	6.3	(D)	(D)	(D)	9.5	5.7	-
AIR	-	100.0	(D)	100.0	-	(D)	(D)	(D)	-	-	-
WATER	-	100.0	(D)	-	-	(D)	(D)	(D)	-	-	-
OTHER	-	100.0	(D)	100.0	-	(D)	(D)	(D)	-	-	-
UNKNOWN	1	100.0	(D)	87.8	-	(D)	(D)	(D)	-	12.2	-
EAST SOUTH CENTRAL	394	100.0	(D)	4.8	6.1	(D)	(D)	(D)	30.3	15.7	34.5
RAIL	346	100.0	(D)	2.4	3.1	(D)	(D)	(D)	31.6	17.9	39.3
MOTOR CARRIER	25	100.0	(D)	17.6	23.0	(D)	(D)	(D)	29.6	-	-
PRIVATE TRUCK	20	100.0	(D)	20.7	36.3	(D)	(D)	(D)	12.0	-	-
AIR	-	100.0	(D)	100.0	-	(D)	(D)	(D)	-	-	-
WATER	2	100.0	(D)	100.0	-	(D)	(D)	(D)	-	-	-
OTHER	-	100.0	(D)	100.0	-	(D)	(D)	(D)	-	-	-
UNKNOWN	-	100.0	(D)	-	-	(D)	(D)	(D)	-	-	-
WEST SOUTH CENTRAL	622	100.0	(D)	12.5	4.3	(D)	(D)	(D)	36.5	29.3	6.2
RAIL	495	100.0	(D)	11.7	3.9	(D)	(D)	(D)	26.9	36.8	7.8
MOTOR CARRIER	34	100.0	(D)	35.1	13.1	(D)	(D)	(D)	40.3	-	-
PRIVATE TRUCK	86	100.0	(D)	2.5	3.4	(D)	(D)	(D)	92.6	-	-
AIR	-	100.0	(D)	29.1	-	(D)	(D)	(D)	-	-	70.9
WATER	-	100.0	(D)	-	-	(D)	(D)	(D)	-	-	-
OTHER	-	100.0	(D)	-	-	(D)	(D)	(D)	-	-	-
UNKNOWN	5	100.0	(D)	100.0	-	(D)	(D)	(D)	-	-	-
MOUNTAIN	123	100.0	(D)	4.9	2.3	(D)	(D)	(D)	7.2	56.6	27.2
RAIL	118	100.0	(D)	3.3	1.2	(D)	(D)	(D)	7.5	58.8	27.9
MOTOR CARRIER	4	100.0	(D)	42.9	32.6	(D)	(D)	(D)	-	6.6	5.0
PRIVATE TRUCK	-	100.0	(D)	36.7	-	(D)	(D)	(D)	-	-	63.3
AIR	-	100.0	(D)	100.0	-	(D)	(D)	(D)	-	-	-
WATER	-	100.0	(D)	-	-	(D)	(D)	(D)	-	-	-
OTHER	-	100.0	(D)	-	-	(D)	(D)	(D)	-	-	100.0
UNKNOWN	-	100.0	(D)	-	-	(D)	(D)	(D)	-	-	100.0
PACIFIC	435	100.0	(D)	3.1	17.1	(D)	(D)	(D)	20.7	21.0	26.7
RAIL	368	100.0	(D)	1.7	11.1	(D)	(D)	(D)	23.4	24.3	26.9
MOTOR CARRIER	52	100.0	(D)	13.8	50.2	(D)	(D)	(D)	5.8	3.5	21.3
PRIVATE TRUCK	14	100.0	(D)	-	51.7	(D)	(D)	(D)	6.9	1.1	40.4
AIR	-	100.0	(D)	95.1	-	(D)	(D)	(D)	-	1.2	-
WATER	-	100.0	(D)	69.5	-	(D)	(D)	(D)	-	-	30.5
OTHER	-	100.0	(D)	-	-	(D)	(D)	(D)	-	-	81.1
UNKNOWN	-	100.0	(D)	-	-	(D)	(D)	(D)	-	-	100.0

See footnotes at end of table 4.

TABLE 4. **TCC GROUP 333—Percent Distribution of Distance Shipped and Weight of Shipment, by Means of Transport: 1972**

Distance shipped and weight of shipment [2] [3]	Number	Percent distribution by means of transport							
		All means of transport	Rail	Motor carrier	Private truck	Air	Water	Other	Unknown
TONS OF SHIPMENTS	(thousands of tons)								
U.S. TOTAL	8 632	100.0	65.0	15.1	19.3	-	.3	.1	.3
UNDER 100 MILES	1 289	100.0	29.9	30.6	37.3	-	1.2	.3	.7
UNDER 1000 POUNDS	1	100.0	-	46.9	48.7	-	-	1.1	3.2
1000 TO 9999 POUNDS	31	100.0	.6	39.9	57.7	-	-	1.1	.6
10000 TO 29999 POUNDS	129	100.0	.3	22.0	72.6	-	4.5	-	.6
30000 TO 59999 POUNDS	613	100.0	2.1	46.0	50.3	-	.2	.6	.7
60000 TO 89999 POUNDS	28	100.0	54.3	21.9	23.8	-	-	-	-
90000 POUNDS AND OVER	484	100.0	73.5	13.3	10.8	-	1.7	-	.6
100 TO 199 MILES	1 830	100.0	44.4	11.7	43.8	-	-	-	.2
UNDER 1000 POUNDS	-	100.0	-	81.3	17.7	.4	-	.4	.3
1000 TO 9999 POUNDS	23	100.0	-	68.8	30.7	-	-	.4	.2
10000 TO 29999 POUNDS	62	100.0	-	40.0	60.0	-	-	-	-
30000 TO 59999 POUNDS	341	100.0	1.1	40.3	57.8	-	-	-	.8
60000 TO 89999 POUNDS	34	100.0	18.8	20.0	61.2	-	-	-	-
90000 POUNDS AND OVER	1 367	100.0	58.6	2.0	39.3	-	-	-	-
200 TO 299 MILES	887	100.0	53.4	23.9	22.4	-	-	-	.2
UNDER 1000 POUNDS	-	100.0	-	67.1	25.1	2.6	-	3.0	2.2
1000 TO 9999 POUNDS	9	100.0	-	79.2	20.5	-	-	-	.2
10000 TO 29999 POUNDS	23	100.0	.5	72.8	26.8	-	-	-	-
30000 TO 59999 POUNDS	330	100.0	5.9	46.2	47.4	-	-	-	.5
60000 TO 89999 POUNDS	32	100.0	54.3	42.6	3.0	-	-	-	-
90000 POUNDS AND OVER	491	100.0	88.9	4.3	6.8	-	-	-	-
300 TO 499 MILES	873	100.0	62.0	26.4	10.4	-	.5	-	.7
UNDER 1000 POUNDS	-	100.0	-	99.0	-	.7	-	.2	.1
1000 TO 9999 POUNDS	9	100.0	1.8	62.4	30.9	-	-	-	5.0
10000 TO 29999 POUNDS	36	100.0	-	49.5	50.5	-	-	-	-
30000 TO 59999 POUNDS	266	100.0	2.7	70.5	25.8	-	-	-	1.0
60000 TO 89999 POUNDS	34	100.0	68.0	31.1	.9	-	-	-	-
90000 POUNDS AND OVER	527	100.0	96.9	1.6	.2	-	.8	-	.5
500 TO 999 MILES	1 972	100.0	87.8	8.1	4.1	-	-	-	-
UNDER 1000 POUNDS	-	100.0	-	91.1	1.2	1.8	-	5.9	-
1000 TO 9999 POUNDS	7	100.0	1.7	66.6	27.9	1.0	-	2.7	-
10000 TO 29999 POUNDS	17	100.0	12.3	62.8	24.9	-	-	-	-
30000 TO 59999 POUNDS	187	100.0	8.9	53.3	37.8	-	-	-	-
60000 TO 89999 POUNDS	52	100.0	53.3	43.1	3.7	-	-	-	-
90000 POUNDS AND OVER	1 706	100.0	98.7	1.2	.1	-	-	-	-
1000 TO 1499 MILES	726	100.0	90.1	8.5	.8	-	.3	-	.2
UNDER 1000 POUNDS	-	100.0	-	58.8	23.0	18.2	-	.1	-
1000 TO 9999 POUNDS	1	100.0	7.8	81.7	10.5	-	-	-	-
10000 TO 29999 POUNDS	5	100.0	-	49.0	51.0	-	-	-	-
30000 TO 59999 POUNDS	32	100.0	16.0	70.9	9.1	-	2.7	-	1.3
60000 TO 89999 POUNDS	17	100.0	51.9	48.1	-	-	-	-	-
90000 POUNDS AND OVER	668	100.0	95.7	3.9	-	-	.2	-	.2
1500 MILES OR OVER	1 052	100.0	96.3	2.8	.4	-	.1	-	.4
UNDER 1000 POUNDS	-	100.0	-	67.1	-	19.6	9.5	3.9	-
1000 TO 9999 POUNDS	4	100.0	15.1	79.7	2.7	2.6	-	-	-
10000 TO 29999 POUNDS	8	100.0	7.5	81.1	10.0	-	-	-	1.5
30000 TO 59999 POUNDS	20	100.0	18.3	60.7	16.5	-	4.4	-	-
60000 TO 89999 POUNDS	21	100.0	85.1	14.9	-	-	-	-	-
90000 POUNDS AND OVER	997	100.0	99.3	.3	-	-	-	-	.4
TON-MILES OF SHIPMENTS	(millions of ton-miles)								
U.S. TOTAL	5 247	100.0	86.2	8.2	5.2	-	.1	-	.2
UNDER 100 MILES	66	100.0	37.5	29.0	32.1	-	.4	.1	.8
UNDER 1000 POUNDS	-	100.0	-	55.9	36.0	-	-	1.1	7.0
1000 TO 9999 POUNDS	1	100.0	.1	45.6	53.3	-	-	.5	.4
10000 TO 29999 POUNDS	5	100.0	.6	23.1	73.8	-	1.8	-	.7
30000 TO 59999 POUNDS	30	100.0	2.9	48.9	47.2	-	.1	.2	.8
60000 TO 89999 POUNDS	1	100.0	69.1	11.6	19.2	-	-	-	-
90000 POUNDS AND OVER	27	100.0	83.1	8.7	6.7	-	.7	-	.9
100 TO 199 MILES	257	100.0	47.3	12.5	40.0	-	-	-	.2
UNDER 1000 POUNDS	-	100.0	-	80.4	18.5	.4	-	.4	.2
1000 TO 9999 POUNDS	3	100.0	-	70.9	28.5	-	-	.5	.2
10000 TO 29999 POUNDS	9	100.0	-	39.9	60.1	-	-	-	-
30000 TO 59999 POUNDS	49	100.0	1.2	41.6	56.3	-	-	-	.9
60000 TO 89999 POUNDS	5	100.0	15.6	21.1	63.3	-	-	-	-
90000 POUNDS AND OVER	190	100.0	63.2	2.4	34.4	-	-	-	-
200 TO 299 MILES	223	100.0	54.6	23.4	21.7	-	-	-	.2
UNDER 1000 POUNDS	-	100.0	-	64.9	28.4	2.6	-	2.4	1.8
1000 TO 9999 POUNDS	2	100.0	-	79.8	20.0	-	-	-	.2
10000 TO 29999 POUNDS	5	100.0	.4	72.1	27.5	-	-	-	-
30000 TO 59999 POUNDS	82	100.0	6.2	46.2	46.9	-	-	-	.6
60000 TO 89999 POUNDS	8	100.0	57.8	39.7	2.5	-	-	-	-
90000 POUNDS AND OVER	124	100.0	89.9	4.0	6.1	-	-	-	-

See footnotes at end of table 4.

TABLE 4. TCC GROUP 333—Percent Distribution of Distance Shipped and Weight of Shipment, by Means of Transport: 1972—Continued

Distance shipped and weight of shipment [2] [3]	Number	Percent distribution by means of transport							
		All means of transport	Rail	Motor carrier	Private truck	Air	Water	Other	Unknown
TON-MILES OF SHIPMENTS	(millions of ton-miles)								
300 TO 499 MILES.........	355	100.0	64.0	24.8	10.0	-	.6	-	.6
UNDER 1000 POUNDS.....	-	100.0	-	99.0	-	.7	-	.2	.1
1000 TO 9999 POUNDS...	3	100.0	2.1	61.4	31.8	-	-	-	4.7
10000 TO 29999 POUNDS.	13	100.0	-	49.7	50.3	-	-	-	-
30000 TO 59999 POUNDS.	102	100.0	3.1	69.8	26.2	-	-	-	.9
60000 TO 89999 POUNDS.	13	100.0	70.1	29.1	.8	-	-	-	-
90000 POUNDS AND OVER.	221	100.0	96.9	1.4	.3	-	.9	-	.5
500 TO 999 MILES.........	1 497	100.0	89.3	7.3	3.4	-	-	-	-
UNDER 1000 POUNDS.....	-	100.0	-	90.6	.9	1.7	-	6.8	-
1000 TO 9999 POUNDS...	5	100.0	2.2	67.0	27.7	.9	-	2.2	-
10000 TO 29999 POUNDS.	11	100.0	14.6	59.8	25.5	-	-	-	-
30000 TO 59999 POUNDS.	125	100.0	10.7	53.7	35.6	-	-	-	-
60000 TO 89999 POUNDS.	36	100.0	50.2	46.0	3.7	-	-	-	-
90000 POUNDS AND OVER.	1 318	100.0	98.9	1.1	.1	-	-	-	-
1000 TO 1499 MILES......	892	100.0	90.3	8.4	.8	-	.3	-	.2
UNDER 1000 POUNDS.....	-	100.0	-	57.9	25.5	16.6	-	.1	-
1000 TO 9999 POUNDS...	2	100.0	7.6	81.3	11.0	-	-	-	-
10000 TO 29999 POUNDS.	6	100.0	-	49.7	50.3	-	-	-	-
30000 TO 59999 POUNDS.	37	100.0	16.6	70.0	8.9	-	3.2	-	1.3
60000 TO 89999 POUNDS.	21	100.0	53.1	46.9	-	-	-	-	-
90000 POUNDS AND OVER.	824	100.0	95.6	4.0	-	-	.2	-	.2
1500 MILES OR OVER......	1 955	100.0	96.3	2.8	.4	-	.1	-	.4
UNDER 1000 POUNDS.....	-	100.0	-	58.2	-	18.3	19.8	3.8	-
1000 TO 9999 POUNDS...	9	100.0	18.3	76.8	2.3	2.7	-	-	-
10000 TO 29999 POUNDS.	15	100.0	8.5	80.7	9.6	-	-	-	1.2
30000 TO 59999 POUNDS.	38	100.0	20.3	60.4	15.4	-	3.9	-	-
60000 TO 89999 POUNDS.	38	100.0	85.2	14.8	-	-	-	-	-
90000 POUNDS AND OVER.	1 852	100.0	90.3	.3	-	-	-	-	.4

Note: Detail may not add to total due to rounding. The introductory table shows the estimates of sampling variability for tons; sampling variability for ton-miles has not been estimated. See the map in the Introduction for the States comprising the geographic divisions of the United States.

Shipments excluded from the survey are those moving by pipeline (primarily petroleum products from refineries), parcel post shipments, and commodities moved by own power (motorized vehicles, aircraft, etc.) or towed (prefabricated buildings, etc.). Local shipments (commodities shipped less than 25 miles from the plant) and shipments within the same city are also excluded. Shipments to Alaska and Hawaii from the 48 conterminous States and the District of Columbia are included; however, no data were obtained for shipments originating in Alaska and Hawaii.

- Represents zero or rounds to zero.   (D) Withheld to avoid disclosing figures for individual companies.

[1]Production of this commodity is concentrated in the geographic divisions shown; figures and distributions for geographic divisions not shown are included in the total.

[2]Distances of shipments to foreign destinations are calculated only to the U.S. port of exit.

[3]Includes only shipments represented by bills of lading and invoices. Summary records which did not show individual weights of shipments are not included.

TCC 335. Nonferrous Metal Basic Shapes

Comparisons of Tons and Ton-Miles of Shipments for
Geographic Divisions of Origin and for Sampling Variability: 1972 and 1967

Geographic division of origin	Estimates				Relative sampling variability in tons (percent)	
	1972		1967		1972	1967
	Tons (thousands)	Ton-miles (millions)	Tons (thousands)	Ton-miles (millions)		
U.S. total	17,161	7,794	10,417	6,217	21.6	8.4
New England	1,077	699	1,163	841	13.5	(*)
Middle Atlantic	3,012	1,175	2,761	1,172	17.1	(*)
East North Central	4,371	1,866	3,284	2,164	27.4	(*)
West North Central	501	307	456	315	28.3	(*)
South Atlantic	917	416	1,011	425	21.7	(*)
East South Central	1,483	802	588	347	28.9	(*)
West South Central	(D)	(D)	329	203	(*)	(*)
Mountain	443	487	214	277	2.7	(*)
Pacific	(D)	(D)	611	473	(*)	(*)

(D) Withheld to avoid disclosing figures for individual companies.   (*) Data not published.

TABLE 1. **TCC GROUP 335—Percent Distribution of Geographic Division of Origin and Distance Shipped, by Means of Transport: 1972**

Geographic division of origin [1] and distance shipped [2]	Number	Percent distribution by means of transport							
		All means of transport	Rail	Motor carrier	Private truck	Air	Water	Other	Unknown
TONS OF SHIPMENTS	(thousands of tons)								
U.S. TOTAL	17 161	100.0	35.4	37.6	25.9	.1	.7	.2	.1
NEW ENGLAND.............	1 077	100.0	8.9	69.4	20.0	-	.7	.7	.3
UNDER 100 MILES.......	262	100.0	-	50.2	48.7	-	-	1.0	.1
100 TO 199 MILES......	129	100.0	-	82.8	16.5	-	-	-	.6
200 TO 299 MILES......	84	100.0	-	74.0	19.7	-	-	4.9	1.4
300 TO 499 MILES......	112	100.0	2.5	74.0	22.9	-	-	-	.6
500 TO 999 MILES......	289	100.0	3.0	92.2	4.5	.1	-	.2	.1
1000 TO 1499 MILES....	62	100.0	7.1	82.4	9.9	-	.5	-	.1
1500 MILES OR OVER....	138	100.0	57.6	33.0	3.9	.1	5.3	-	-
MIDDLE ATLANTIC.........	3 012	100.0	11.2	58.0	26.6	.1	3.7	.2	.2
UNDER 100 MILES.......	918	100.0	1.4	53.7	36.7	-	8.2	.1	-
100 TO 199 MILES......	485	100.0	1.3	55.9	42.3	-	-	.1	.5
200 TO 299 MILES......	432	100.0	12.7	70.2	17.0	-	-	.1	-
300 TO 499 MILES......	429	100.0	6.3	62.6	30.7	.2	-	.1	.1
500 TO 999 MILES......	467	100.0	22.3	68.2	8.7	.3	.3	.1	.2
1000 TO 1499 MILES....	157	100.0	34.3	48.8	5.6	.2	11.0	.1	-
1500 MILES OR OVER....	122	100.0	65.4	13.2	3.0	.9	13.2	1.8	2.5
EAST NORTH CENTRAL......	4 371	100.0	40.0	43.2	16.7	-	-	.1	-
UNDER 100 MILES.......	390	100.0	4.0	64.6	31.3	-	-	-	.1
100 TO 199 MILES......	826	100.0	14.3	51.7	33.9	-	-	.1	-
200 TO 299 MILES......	520	100.0	16.4	72.0	11.4	-	-	.1	-
300 TO 499 MILES......	1 355	100.0	56.9	30.6	12.4	-	-	-	-
500 TO 999 MILES......	1 070	100.0	60.1	31.4	8.3	.1	-	.1	-
1000 TO 1499 MILES....	95	100.0	40.7	48.9	10.1	.3	-	-	-
1500 MILES OR OVER....	112	100.0	66.7	31.4	1.6	.1	-	.2	-
WEST NORTH CENTRAL......	501	100.0	34.8	52.4	12.5	.2	-	.1	-
UNDER 100 MILES.......	14	100.0	5.2	89.4	4.9	-	-	.5	-
100 TO 199 MILES......	31	100.0	-	89.5	10.5	-	-	-	-
200 TO 299 MILES......	58	100.0	18.1	78.4	3.5	-	-	-	-
300 TO 499 MILES......	127	100.0	40.6	46.8	12.5	.1	-	.1	-
500 TO 999 MILES......	207	100.0	35.6	46.2	18.0	.1	-	.1	-
1000 TO 1499 MILES....	26	100.0	42.8	44.8	11.3	.7	-	.4	-
1500 MILES OR OVER....	35	100.0	74.0	24.2	1.0	.8	-	-	-
SOUTH ATLANTIC.........	917	100.0	24.6	47.6	27.7	-	-	-	-
UNDER 100 MILES.......	117	100.0	11.1	25.4	63.5	-	-	-	-
100 TO 199 MILES......	73	100.0	3.7	56.2	40.1	-	-	-	-
200 TO 299 MILES......	101	100.0	35.7	54.9	9.1	-	-	.2	-
300 TO 499 MILES......	352	100.0	15.5	61.9	22.6	-	-	-	-
500 TO 999 MILES......	231	100.0	39.2	35.9	24.9	-	-	-	-
1000 TO 1499 MILES....	16	100.0	75.8	18.3	5.5	.4	-	-	-
1500 MILES OR OVER....	24	100.0	66.4	22.3	11.2	.1	-	-	-
EAST SOUTH CENTRAL......	1 483	100.0	21.8	50.6	27.0	-	-	-	.5
UNDER 100 MILES.......	21	100.0	-	54.6	45.4	-	-	-	-
100 TO 199 MILES......	128	100.0	-	36.7	63.3	-	-	-	-
200 TO 299 MILES......	186	100.0	9.0	61.2	29.8	-	-	-	-
300 TO 499 MILES......	539	100.0	24.2	50.0	24.9	-	-	-	.9
500 TO 999 MILES......	497	100.0	17.9	57.6	23.9	-	-	-	.6
1000 TO 1499 MILES....	11	100.0	24.0	74.7	1.3	-	-	-	-
1500 MILES OR OVER....	98	100.0	86.4	12.9	.7	-	-	-	-
MOUNTAIN................	443	100.0	65.7	34.3	-	-	-	-	-
UNDER 100 MILES.......	29	100.0	-	100.0	-	-	-	-	-
100 TO 199 MILES......	18	100.0	93.2	6.8	-	-	-	-	-
200 TO 299 MILES......	2	100.0	29.9	70.1	-	-	-	-	-
300 TO 499 MILES......	18	100.0	3.3	96.7	-	-	-	-	-
500 TO 999 MILES......	92	100.0	46.5	53.5	-	-	-	-	-
1000 TO 1499 MILES....	190	100.0	87.1	12.9	-	-	-	-	-
1500 MILES OR OVER....	91	100.0	70.0	30.0	-	-	-	-	-

See footnotes at end of table 4.

TABLE 1. **TCC GROUP 335—Percent Distribution of Geographic Division of Origin and Distance Shipped, by Means of Transport: 1972**—Continued

Geographic division of origin[1] and distance shipped[2]	Number	Percent distribution by means of transport							
		All means of transport	Rail	Motor carrier	Private truck	Air	Water	Other	Unknown
TON-MILES OF SHIPMENTS	(millions of ton-miles)								
U.S. TOTAL	7 794	100.0	50.4	35.2	12.5	.2	1.2	.4	.2
NEW ENGLAND.............	699	100.0	28.9	60.5	7.5	.1	2.7	.2	.1
UNDER 100 MILES.......	12	100.0	-	55.7	43.5	-	-	.6	.2
100 TO 199 MILES......	18	100.0	-	83.3	16.2	-	-	-	.5
200 TO 299 MILES......	20	100.0	-	75.0	19.1	-	-	4.4	1.6
300 TO 499 MILES......	45	100.0	2.9	73.8	22.8	-	-	-	.5
500 TO 999 MILES......	216	100.0	2.9	92.0	4.7	.1	-	.2	.1
1000 TO 1499 MILES....	72	100.0	6.6	82.0	10.8	-	.5	-	.1
1500 MILES OR OVER....	313	100.0	60.6	29.7	3.7	.1	5.9	-	-
MIDDLE ATLANTIC..........	1 175	100.0	29.8	49.7	13.5	.4	5.5	.4	.7
UNDER 100 MILES.......	42	100.0	1.9	48.7	45.8	-	3.6	-	-
100 TO 199 MILES......	74	100.0	1.1	56.2	42.0	-	-	.1	.5
200 TO 299 MILES......	113	100.0	13.6	70.1	16.2	-	-	.1	-
300 TO 499 MILES......	157	100.0	7.5	63.1	29.0	.2	-	.1	.1
500 TO 999 MILES......	330	100.0	25.1	66.2	7.8	.3	.4	.1	.2
1000 TO 1499 MILES....	188	100.0	35.3	48.2	5.2	.2	10.9	.1	-
1500 MILES OR OVER....	268	100.0	63.9	12.6	3.2	1.1	15.1	1.4	2.7
EAST NORTH CENTRAL......	1 866	100.0	52.9	36.7	10.2	.1	-	.1	-
UNDER 100 MILES.......	23	100.0	2.9	66.5	30.5	-	-	-	.1
100 TO 199 MILES......	118	100.0	15.5	54.7	29.7	-	-	.1	-
200 TO 299 MILES......	129	100.0	16.6	71.7	11.6	-	-	.1	-
300 TO 499 MILES......	523	100.0	57.1	30.7	12.1	-	-	.1	-
500 TO 999 MILES......	750	100.0	61.4	30.8	7.5	.1	-	.1	-
1000 TO 1499 MILES....	113	100.0	41.3	49.0	9.2	.4	-	-	-
1500 MILES OR OVER....	208	100.0	67.5	30.8	1.4	.1	-	.2	-
WEST NORTH CENTRAL......	307	100.0	44.3	43.1	12.2	.3	-	.1	-
UNDER 100 MILES.......	-	100.0	5.9	91.6	2.0	-	-	.5	-
100 TO 199 MILES......	5	100.0	-	90.4	9.6	-	-	-	-
200 TO 299 MILES......	16	100.0	18.6	77.9	3.5	-	-	-	-
300 TO 499 MILES......	49	100.0	40.8	45.7	13.4	-	-	.1	-
500 TO 999 MILES......	145	100.0	37.7	44.4	17.6	.1	-	.1	-
1000 TO 1499 MILES....	32	100.0	46.3	41.5	10.9	.8	-	.5	-
1500 MILES OR OVER....	57	100.0	74.5	23.8	1.0	.7	-	-	-
SOUTH ATLANTIC...........	416	100.0	35.1	42.9	21.9	-	-	-	-
UNDER 100 MILES.......	7	100.0	7.7	30.5	61.8	-	-	-	-
100 TO 199 MILES......	11	100.0	4.1	57.4	38.4	-	-	-	-
200 TO 299 MILES......	24	100.0	34.4	56.4	8.9	-	-	.2	-
300 TO 499 MILES......	141	100.0	16.7	59.7	23.5	-	-	-	-
500 TO 999 MILES......	159	100.0	39.6	35.2	25.1	-	-	-	-
1000 TO 1499 MILES....	20	100.0	76.5	18.5	4.7	.4	-	-	-
1500 MILES OR OVER....	51	100.0	65.8	22.7	11.4	.1	-	-	-
EAST SOUTH CENTRAL......	802	100.0	34.2	45.9	19.5	-	-	-	.4
UNDER 100 MILES.......	1	100.0	-	62.7	37.3	-	-	-	-
100 TO 199 MILES......	18	100.0	-	36.9	63.1	-	-	-	-
200 TO 299 MILES......	47	100.0	9.3	61.1	29.6	-	-	-	-
300 TO 499 MILES......	205	100.0	25.4	49.8	24.1	-	-	-	.7
500 TO 999 MILES......	335	100.0	17.4	58.4	23.7	-	-	-	.5
1000 TO 1499 MILES....	13	100.0	23.3	75.6	1.1	-	-	-	-
1500 MILES OR OVER....	180	100.0	86.5	12.9	.6	-	-	-	-
MOUNTAIN................	487	100.0	74.1	25.9	-	-	-	-	-
UNDER 100 MILES.......	2	100.0	-	100.0	-	-	-	-	-
100 TO 199 MILES......	2	100.0	95.0	5.0	-	-	-	-	-
200 TO 299 MILES......	-	100.0	32.9	67.1	-	-	-	-	-
300 TO 499 MILES......	6	100.0	4.3	95.7	-	-	-	-	-
500 TO 999 MILES......	69	100.0	49.1	50.9	-	-	-	-	-
1000 TO 1499 MILES....	238	100.0	87.9	12.1	-	-	-	-	-
1500 MILES OR OVER....	166	100.0	68.5	31.5	-	-	-	-	-

See footnotes at end of table 4.

TABLE 2. TCC GROUP 335—Percent Distribution of Geographic Division of Origin and Means of Transport, by Geographic Division of Destination: 1972

Geographic division of origin[1] and means of transport	Number	Percent distribution by division of destination									
		U.S. total	New England	Middle Atlantic	East North Central	West North Central	South Atlantic	East South Central	West South Central	Mountain	Pacific
TONS OF SHIPMENTS	(thousands of tons)										
U.S. TOTAL	17 161	100.0	5.7	18.4	21.3	5.6	11.3	5.6	23.4	2.7	6.1
RAIL	6 079	100.0	1.8	16.2	12.7	7.4	12.5	6.2	28.3	5.4	9.4
MOTOR CARRIER	6 453	100.0	7.4	22.5	32.7	5.7	12.7	5.5	6.5	1.9	5.1
PRIVATE TRUCK	4 439	100.0	8.8	14.3	16.9	3.0	7.6	5.3	41.8	.1	2.2
AIR	12	100.0	6.5	8.8	7.1	12.6	6.4	6.2	7.1	2.3	43.0
WATER	126	100.0	-	59.6	-	-	9.4	-	13.5	-	17.5
OTHER	30	100.0	9.2	23.3	38.5	.6	4.2	.7	.9	6.9	15.6
UNKNOWN	19	100.0	17.6	10.3	42.2	1.8	4.6	4.1	3.8	-	15.7
NEW ENGLAND	1 077	100.0	21.9	26.5	22.7	2.4	8.6	3.5	4.5	1.6	8.3
RAIL	95	100.0	-	-	11.0	2.3	1.5	1.6	7.6	10.4	65.7
MOTOR CARRIER	747	100.0	16.1	27.0	30.6	2.6	11.2	4.1	5.2	1.0	2.2
PRIVATE TRUCK	215	100.0	52.0	35.6	2.2	1.9	3.0	2.8	.9	-	1.5
AIR	-	100.0	2.2	21.5	26.0	2.9	7.8	3.1	1.7	3.5	31.3
WATER	7	100.0	-	-	-	-	3.9	-	6.6	-	89.5
OTHER	7	100.0	35.4	57.7	1.5	.1	5.1	-	.1	-	.1
UNKNOWN	3	100.0	34.6	56.3	6.2	1.4	1.5	-	-	-	-
MIDDLE ATLANTIC	3 012	100.0	15.4	43.2	17.9	2.2	12.8	1.5	4.0	.1	2.9
RAIL	338	100.0	1.7	20.6	15.7	5.1	22.1	.7	17.6	.2	16.3
MOTOR CARRIER	1 748	100.0	12.2	42.5	22.7	2.6	14.5	2.0	2.8	.1	.6
PRIVATE TRUCK	800	100.0	30.2	51.6	10.8	.3	5.5	.7	.5	-	.5
AIR	3	100.0	2.2	18.7	13.9	4.3	12.3	17.0	2.5	.6	28.3
WATER	110	100.0	-	68.3	-	-	10.5	-	7.6	-	13.5
OTHER	4	100.0	4.3	18.3	8.1	1.4	16.4	1.7	1.2	45.0	3.7
UNKNOWN	6	100.0	34.0	-	.2	-	8.5	9.9	-	-	47.4
EAST NORTH CENTRAL	4 371	100.0	3.5	25.0	37.4	5.6	8.4	8.0	6.5	3.1	2.5
RAIL	1 748	100.0	4.5	43.9	9.4	2.1	10.5	8.5	10.1	6.7	4.3
MOTOR CARRIER	1 888	100.0	3.1	13.7	52.9	8.5	7.9	6.9	4.3	1.0	1.6
PRIVATE TRUCK	729	100.0	1.7	8.8	64.5	6.8	4.4	10.1	3.5	-	.2
AIR	1	100.0	37.9	5.8	5.0	.9	9.4	4.0	27.8	.6	8.6
WATER	-	100.0	-	100.0	-	-	-	-	-	-	-
OTHER	2	100.0	.9	42.4	47.3	.6	.7	.5	.1	.1	7.4
UNKNOWN	-	100.0	31.7	2.0	64.5	-	1.4	.5	-	-	-
WEST NORTH CENTRAL	501	100.0	3.0	14.2	31.2	14.6	13.1	7.8	5.1	2.7	8.3
RAIL	174	100.0	1.7	25.4	36.9	3.1	9.8	.9	2.1	2.2	18.0
MOTOR CARRIER	263	100.0	3.6	6.5	31.8	24.2	9.8	10.4	6.6	3.6	3.6
PRIVATE TRUCK	62	100.0	4.3	15.5	13.1	6.8	36.3	16.2	7.2	-	.6
AIR	-	100.0	.3	5.3	5.8	4.7	.2	-	13.7	19.5	50.5
WATER	-	100.0	-	-	-	-	-	-	-	-	-
OTHER	-	100.0	-	14.1	20.4	19.8	22.9	18.9	2.8	.5	.6
UNKNOWN	-	100.0	-	-	-	-	-	-	-	-	-
SOUTH ATLANTIC	917	100.0	8.5	18.9	15.8	5.5	32.5	10.2	4.3	1.5	2.7
RAIL	226	100.0	4.4	19.3	20.7	8.0	19.3	7.5	8.0	5.6	7.2
MOTOR CARRIER	436	100.0	14.0	24.1	15.2	5.3	30.3	7.1	2.7	.2	1.2
PRIVATE TRUCK	254	100.0	2.8	9.7	12.6	3.8	48.1	18.2	3.9	-	1.1
AIR	-	100.0	-	18.5	22.9	-	-	-	40.5	9.8	8.2
WATER	-	100.0	-	-	-	-	-	-	-	-	-
OTHER	-	100.0	4.2	82.8	4.6	2.6	3.6	-	-	2.3	-
UNKNOWN	-	100.0	-	98.2	-	-	-	1.8	-	-	-
EAST SOUTH CENTRAL	1 483	100.0	1.3	10.8	30.3	5.1	23.3	13.0	7.9	1.7	6.5
RAIL	323	100.0	-	1.9	22.0	1.8	31.6	5.2	8.0	3.3	26.1
MOTOR CARRIER	750	100.0	1.1	16.4	35.2	4.4	20.1	11.9	7.3	1.9	1.7
PRIVATE TRUCK	401	100.0	2.7	7.7	26.5	9.0	23.2	21.6	9.0	.2	-
AIR	-	100.0	-	91.8	1.2	-	6.9	-	-	-	-
WATER	-	100.0	-	-	-	-	-	-	-	-	-
OTHER	-	100.0	-	-	-	-	1.1	-	-	-	98.9
UNKNOWN	7	100.0	-	-	100.0	-	-	-	-	-	-
MOUNTAIN	443	100.0	3.0	7.3	30.7	10.0	6.3	2.9	6.3	15.5	17.9
RAIL	291	100.0	3.8	10.1	43.5	14.1	3.8	2.9	4.5	8.6	8.6
MOTOR CARRIER	152	100.0	1.6	2.1	6.0	2.1	11.0	3.0	9.9	28.7	35.6
PRIVATE TRUCK	-	100.0	-	-	-	-	-	-	-	100.0	-
AIR	-	100.0	-	-	-	-	-	-	-	10.1	89.9
WATER	-	100.0	-	-	-	-	-	-	-	-	-
OTHER	-	100.0	-	-	-	-	-	-	-	100.0	-
UNKNOWN	-	100.0	-	100.0	-	-	-	-	-	-	-

See footnotes at end of table 4.

TABLE 2. **TCC GROUP 335—Percent Distribution of Geographic Division of Origin and Means of Transport, by Geographic Division of Destination: 1972**—Continued

Geographic division of origin [1] and means of transport	Number	Percent distribution by division of destination									
		U.S. total	New England	Middle Atlantic	East North Central	West North Central	South Atlantic	East South Central	West South Central	Mountain	Pacific
TON-MILES OF SHIPMENTS	(millions of ton-miles)										
U.S. TOTAL	7 794	100.0	3.9	13.5	20.6	8.2	15.2	6.3	10.8	4.4	17.1
RAIL	3 929	100.0	2.3	13.0	14.8	9.2	16.3	6.8	8.5	6.0	23.0
MOTOR CARRIER	2 739	100.0	5.2	14.0	27.9	7.4	15.1	5.4	11.6	3.6	9.8
PRIVATE TRUCK	974	100.0	6.9	15.6	24.2	6.9	12.1	7.6	17.8	.3	8.6
AIR	15	100.0	4.0	3.1	3.3	14.2	4.6	3.0	6.4	1.8	59.8
WATER	92	100.0	-	1.8	-	-	13.3	-	22.5	-	62.4
OTHER	28	100.0	.5	11.6	68.7	.4	3.0	.5	.5	11.8	3.1
UNKNOWN	14	100.0	4.3	5.3	23.7	1.5	4.1	4.6	5.4	-	51.2
NEW ENGLAND	699	100.0	1.9	8.1	23.9	4.2	9.0	4.8	10.6	4.8	32.7
RAIL	202	100.0	-	-	3.3	1.2	.7	.7	5.6	9.5	79.0
MOTOR CARRIER	422	100.0	2.0	9.1	37.2	5.0	13.0	6.4	13.8	3.5	10.2
PRIVATE TRUCK	52	100.0	9.5	32.2	5.4	10.6	10.6	9.6	6.7	-	15.5
AIR	-	100.0	.3	3.1	16.2	2.6	4.7	2.4	2.0	4.7	63.9
WATER	18	100.0	-	-	-	-	1.8	-	4.3	-	93.9
OTHER	1	100.0	5.2	62.6	6.8	.8	23.2	-	.7	-	.7
UNKNOWN	-	100.0	13.4	60.8	17.9	5.8	2.1	-	-	-	.7
MIDDLE ATLANTIC	1 175	100.0	6.5	13.6	20.4	5.3	19.1	2.6	14.1	.6	17.9
RAIL	350	100.0	.2	4.9	8.7	4.4	19.2	.7	25.0	.4	36.6
MOTOR CARRIER	584	100.0	7.0	14.7	29.9	7.5	21.6	4.1	10.6	.4	4.2
PRIVATE TRUCK	158	100.0	21.4	34.7	21.3	1.5	11.0	2.0	2.8	-	5.4
AIR	4	100.0	.7	4.9	7.1	3.3	8.0	9.1	3.1	1.0	62.8
WATER	64	100.0	-	2.4	-	-	18.6	-	18.5	-	60.5
OTHER	4	100.0	1.0	1.5	4.1	1.3	8.1	1.2	1.5	72.8	8.5
UNKNOWN	8	100.0	4.5	-	.1	-	3.2	7.1	-	-	85.1
EAST NORTH CENTRAL	1 866	100.0	5.8	24.8	15.5	5.9	12.0	6.4	11.4	7.4	10.8
RAIL	987	100.0	6.0	33.8	3.0	1.3	12.5	4.9	12.7	11.5	14.2
MOTOR CARRIER	685	100.0	6.2	16.1	27.6	10.1	12.0	5.8	10.2	3.6	8.3
PRIVATE TRUCK	190	100.0	3.1	9.8	36.3	14.7	9.1	16.6	8.8	.6	1.5
AIR	1	100.0	33.1	4.6	1.2	.6	6.3	1.3	35.5	.9	16.5
WATER	-	100.0	-	100.0	-	-	-	-	-	-	-
OTHER	1	100.0	1.4	47.5	20.9	.6	.9	.3	.2	.1	28.1
UNKNOWN	-	100.0	76.3	4.1	16.9	-	1.9	.8	-	-	-
WEST NORTH CENTRAL	307	100.0	5.1	18.8	17.5	6.7	14.2	6.6	5.2	4.2	21.6
RAIL	136	100.0	2.1	25.6	18.7	1.6	9.0	.7	1.8	3.6	37.1
MOTOR CARRIER	132	100.0	7.4	10.9	19.5	12.9	12.4	11.2	8.5	6.0	11.2
PRIVATE TRUCK	37	100.0	8.5	22.1	7.0	3.3	39.9	12.0	5.7	-	1.5
AIR	-	100.0	.4	5.5	1.9	2.1	.2	-	8.6	11.5	69.8
WATER	-	100.0	-	-	-	-	-	-	-	-	-
OTHER	-	100.0	-	17.6	14.5	3.4	40.3	19.8	2.6	.5	1.3
UNKNOWN	-	100.0	-	-	-	-	-	-	-	-	-
SOUTH ATLANTIC	416	100.0	8.6	18.5	14.4	7.4	19.8	7.1	7.6	4.1	12.4
RAIL	146	100.0	3.8	20.2	12.8	6.0	8.4	4.8	9.8	10.9	23.3
MOTOR CARRIER	178	100.0	13.5	19.5	13.1	9.5	24.6	7.1	5.7	.6	6.4
PRIVATE TRUCK	91	100.0	6.7	13.8	19.5	5.8	28.9	11.1	7.7	-	6.5
AIR	-	100.0	-	8.2	12.6	-	-	-	44.4	16.6	18.3
WATER	-	100.0	-	-	-	-	-	-	-	-	-
OTHER	-	100.0	5.3	66.9	5.2	6.8	5.6	-	-	10.2	-
UNKNOWN	-	100.0	-	99.6	-	-	-	.4	-	-	-
EAST SOUTH CENTRAL	802	100.0	2.1	14.4	24.1	4.5	16.1	5.3	7.7	3.6	22.3
RAIL	274	100.0	-	2.0	10.8	1.2	18.7	1.6	4.7	4.1	56.9
MOTOR CARRIER	368	100.0	1.8	23.6	30.9	4.7	14.2	5.5	8.6	4.4	6.2
PRIVATE TRUCK	156	100.0	6.3	14.8	29.9	9.6	16.2	11.3	11.0	.8	-
AIR	-	100.0	-	93.2	.8	-	6.0	-	-	-	-
WATER	-	100.0	-	-	-	-	-	-	-	-	-
OTHER	-	100.0	-	-	-	-	.1	-	-	-	99.9
UNKNOWN	3	100.0	-	-	100.0	-	-	-	-	-	-
MOUNTAIN	487	100.0	5.6	12.1	37.0	10.3	10.7	3.8	6.1	3.9	10.4
RAIL	361	100.0	6.1	14.6	45.9	13.0	5.6	3.4	4.2	2.5	4.7
MOTOR CARRIER	126	100.0	4.3	5.1	11.5	2.6	25.3	5.1	11.5	7.9	26.7
PRIVATE TRUCK	-	100.0	-	-	-	-	-	-	-	100.0	-
AIR	-	100.0	-	-	-	-	-	-	-	4.8	95.2
WATER	-	100.0	-	-	-	-	-	-	-	-	-
OTHER	-	100.0	-	-	-	-	-	-	-	100.0	-
UNKNOWN	-	100.0	-	100.0	-	-	-	-	-	-	-

See footnotes at end of table 4.

TABLE 3. **TCC GROUP 335—Percent Distribution of Geographic Division of Destination and Means of Transport, by Geographic Division of Origin: 1972**

Geographic division of destination and means of transport	Number	Percent distribution by division of origin [1]									
		U.S. total	New England	Middle Atlantic	East North Central	West North Central	South Atlantic	East South Central	West South Central	Mountain	Pacific
TONS OF SHIPMENTS	(thousands of tons)										
U.S. TOTAL.............	17 161	100.0	6.3	17.6	25.5	2.9	5.3	8.6	(D)	2.6	(D)
RAIL...................	6 079	100.0	1.6	5.6	28.8	2.9	3.7	5.3	(D)	4.8	(D)
MOTOR CARRIER..........	6 453	100.0	11.6	27.1	29.3	4.1	6.8	11.6	(D)	2.4	(D)
PRIVATE TRUCK..........	4 439	100.0	4.9	18.0	16.4	1.4	5.7	9.0	(D)	-	(D)
AIR....................	12	100.0	4.2	32.1	14.9	6.7	1.5	.3	(D)	-	(D)
WATER.................	126	100.0	6.0	86.9	.3	-	-	-	(D)	-	(D)
OTHER.................	30	100.0	23.9	15.1	8.5	1.6	.9	.1	(D)	-	(D)
UNKNOWN...............	19	100.0	16.2	33.0	2.5	-	.3	39.5	(D)	-	(D)
NEW ENGLAND............	981	100.0	24.1	47.2	15.4	1.5	8.0	2.0	(D)	1.4	(D)
RAIL...................	108	100.0	-	5.4	72.5	2.7	9.2	-	(D)	10.2	(D)
MOTOR CARRIER..........	475	100.0	25.3	44.8	12.4	2.0	12.9	1.8	(D)	.5	(D)
PRIVATE TRUCK..........	389	100.0	28.8	62.1	3.1	.7	1.8	2.8	(D)	-	(D)
AIR....................	-	100.0	1.4	11.2	87.1	.3	-	-	(D)	-	(D)
WATER.................	-	100.0	-	-	-	-	-	-	(D)	-	(D)
OTHER.................	2	100.0	91.7	7.1	.8	-	.4	-	(D)	-	(D)
UNKNOWN...............	3	100.0	31.8	63.7	4.5	-	-	-	(D)	-	(D)
MIDDLE ATLANTIC........	3 163	100.0	9.0	41.2	34.5	2.3	5.5	5.1	(D)	1.0	(D)
RAIL...................	987	100.0	-	7.1	77.7	4.5	4.4	.6	(D)	3.0	(D)
MOTOR CARRIER..........	1 455	100.0	13.9	51.0	17.8	1.2	7.2	8.5	(D)	.2	(D)
PRIVATE TRUCK..........	635	100.0	12.1	65.0	10.1	1.5	3.9	4.9	(D)	-	(D)
AIR....................	1	100.0	10.1	68.0	9.8	4.0	3.2	2.8	(D)	-	(D)
WATER.................	75	100.0	-	99.5	.5	-	-	-	(D)	-	(D)
OTHER.................	7	100.0	59.1	11.8	15.5	1.0	3.1	-	(D)	-	(D)
UNKNOWN...............	2	100.0	88.5	-	.5	-	3.3	-	(D)	.4	(D)
EAST NORTH CENTRAL.....	3 652	100.0	6.7	14.7	44.8	4.3	4.0	12.3	(D)	3.7	(D)
RAIL...................	772	100.0	1.4	6.9	21.4	8.3	6.1	9.2	(D)	16.4	(D)
MOTOR CARRIER..........	2 110	100.0	10.8	18.8	47.4	4.0	3.1	12.5	(D)	.4	(D)
PRIVATE TRUCK..........	748	100.0	.6	11.5	62.9	1.1	4.3	14.2	(D)	-	(D)
AIR....................	-	100.0	15.2	62.9	10.6	5.5	5.0	-	(D)	-	(D)
WATER.................	-	100.0	-	-	-	-	-	-	(D)	-	(D)
OTHER.................	11	100.0	.9	3.2	10.5	.9	.1	-	(D)	-	(D)
UNKNOWN...............	8	100.0	2.4	.1	3.8	-	-	93.7	(D)	-	(D)
WEST NORTH CENTRAL.....	954	100.0	2.7	6.9	25.8	7.7	5.3	7.9	(D)	4.7	(D)
RAIL...................	448	100.0	.5	3.8	8.2	1.2	4.0	1.3	(D)	9.2	(D)
MOTOR CARRIER..........	368	100.0	5.2	12.4	43.4	17.2	6.3	9.0	(D)	.9	(D)
PRIVATE TRUCK..........	135	100.0	3.1	1.8	36.7	3.1	7.1	26.9	(D)	-	(D)
AIR....................	1	100.0	.9	11.0	1.1	2.5	-	-	(D)	-	(D)
WATER.................	-	100.0	-	-	-	-	-	-	(D)	-	(D)
OTHER.................	-	100.0	5.5	31.9	7.9	49.1	3.5	-	(D)	-	(D)
UNKNOWN...............	-	100.0	13.0	-	-	-	-	-	(D)	-	(D)
SOUTH ATLANTIC.........	1 931	100.0	4.8	20.0	18.9	3.4	15.4	17.9	(D)	1.4	(D)
RAIL...................	762	100.0	.2	9.8	24.1	2.2	5.7	13.4	(D)	1.5	(D)
MOTOR CARRIER..........	818	100.0	10.2	31.1	18.3	3.1	16.2	18.4	(D)	2.0	(D)
PRIVATE TRUCK..........	335	100.0	1.9	13.1	9.6	6.8	36.4	27.8	(D)	-	(D)
AIR....................	-	100.0	5.1	62.2	21.9	.2	-	.3	(D)	-	(D)
WATER.................	11	100.0	2.5	97.5	-	-	-	-	(D)	-	(D)
OTHER.................	1	100.0	29.2	58.9	1.5	8.8	.7	-	(D)	-	(D)
UNKNOWN...............	-	100.0	5.4	60.7	.8	-	-	-	(D)	-	(D)
EAST SOUTH CENTRAL.....	969	100.0	3.9	4.5	36.3	4.0	9.7	19.9	(D)	1.3	(D)
RAIL...................	378	100.0	.4	.6	39.1	.4	4.5	4.4	(D)	2.2	(D)
MOTOR CARRIER..........	352	100.0	8.6	9.8	36.8	7.7	8.8	25.3	(D)	1.3	(D)
PRIVATE TRUCK..........	236	100.0	2.5	2.4	31.1	4.3	19.5	36.5	(D)	-	(D)
AIR....................	-	100.0	2.1	88.0	9.5	-	-	-	(D)	-	(D)
WATER.................	-	100.0	-	-	-	-	-	-	(D)	-	(D)
OTHER.................	-	100.0	-	38.3	6.5	44.9	-	-	(D)	-	(D)
UNKNOWN...............	-	100.0	-	80.8	.3	-	.1	-	(D)	-	(D)
WEST SOUTH CENTRAL.....	4 010	100.0	1.2	3.0	7.1	.6	1.0	2.9	(D)	.7	(D)
RAIL...................	1 718	100.0	.4	3.5	10.3	.2	1.1	1.5	(D)	.8	(D)
MOTOR CARRIER..........	417	100.0	9.4	11.6	19.4	4.2	2.8	13.2	(D)	3.6	(D)
PRIVATE TRUCK..........	1 855	100.0	.1	.2	1.4	.2	.5	1.9	(D)	-	(D)
AIR....................	-	100.0	1.0	11.3	58.1	12.9	8.8	-	(D)	-	(D)
WATER.................	17	100.0	2.9	49.0	-	-	-	-	(D)	-	(D)
OTHER.................	-	100.0	2.9	20.7	1.1	5.0	-	-	(D)	-	(D)
UNKNOWN...............	-	100.0	-	.1	-	-	-	-	(D)	-	(D)
MOUNTAIN...............	459	100.0	3.8	.9	29.8	2.9	2.9	5.6	(D)	14.9	(D)
RAIL...................	328	100.0	3.0	.2	35.7	1.1	3.9	3.2	(D)	7.6	(D)
MOTOR CARRIER..........	125	100.0	6.0	1.0	15.7	7.6	.5	11.2	(D)	34.6	(D)
PRIVATE TRUCK..........	2	100.0	-	-	-	.1	-	30.4	(D)	.1	(D)
AIR....................	-	100.0	6.4	9.1	3.8	57.4	6.6	-	(D)	-	(D)
WATER.................	-	100.0	-	-	-	-	-	-	(D)	-	(D)
OTHER.................	2	100.0	-	98.9	.1	.1	.3	-	(D)	-	(D)
UNKNOWN...............	-	100.0	-	100.0	-	-	-	-	(D)	-	(D)
PACIFIC................	1 039	100.0	8.6	8.5	10.5	4.0	2.4	9.3	(D)	7.6	(D)
RAIL...................	574	100.0	10.9	9.6	13.1	5.5	2.8	14.8	(D)	4.4	(D)
MOTOR CARRIER..........	330	100.0	5.1	3.2	9.4	2.8	1.6	3.7	(D)	16.4	(D)
PRIVATE TRUCK..........	99	100.0	3.4	3.7	1.8	.4	2.8	-	(D)	-	(D)
AIR....................	5	100.0	3.0	21.1	3.0	7.9	.3	-	(D)	-	(D)
WATER.................	22	100.0	30.8	67.2	-	-	-	-	(D)	-	(D)
OTHER.................	4	100.0	.1	3.5	4.0	.1	-	.5	(D)	-	(D)
UNKNOWN...............	3	100.0	-	100.0	-	-	-	-	(D)	-	(D)

See footnotes at end of table 4.

TABLE 3. **TCC GROUP 335**—Percent Distribution of Geographic Division of Destination and Means of Transport, by Geographic Division of Origin: 1972—Continued

Geographic division of destination and means of transport	Number	Percent distribution by division of origin [1]									
		U.S. total	New England	Middle Atlantic	East North Central	West North Central	South Atlantic	East South Central	West South Central	Mountain	Pacific
TON-MILES OF SHIPMENTS	(millions of ton-miles)										
U.S. TOTAL	7 794	100.0	9.0	15.1	23.9	3.9	5.3	10.3	(D)	6.3	(D)
RAIL	3 929	100.0	5.2	8.9	25.1	3.5	3.7	7.0	(D)	9.2	(D)
MOTOR CARRIER	2 739	100.0	15.4	21.3	25.0	4.8	6.5	13.5	(D)	4.6	(D)
PRIVATE TRUCK	974	100.0	5.4	16.3	19.5	3.9	9.4	16.1	(D)	-	(D)
AIR	15	100.0	4.3	29.8	11.2	5.8	1.2	.2	(D)	-	(D)
WATER	92	100.0	20.3	69.4	.2	-	-	-	(D)	-	(D)
OTHER	28	100.0	4.9	16.1	4.3	1.2	.3	.1	(D)	-	(D)
UNKNOWN	14	100.0	6.0	60.1	1.1	-	.3	22.4	(D)	.1	(D)
NEW ENGLAND	301	100.0	4.5	25.1	35.7	5.2	11.9	5.5	(D)	9.1	(D)
RAIL	89	100.0	-	.6	65.5	3.1	6.2	-	(D)	24.6	(D)
MOTOR CARRIER	142	100.0	5.9	28.6	29.6	6.8	16.8	4.7	(D)	3.8	(D)
PRIVATE TRUCK	67	100.0	7.4	50.3	8.6	4.7	9.1	14.7	(D)	-	(D)
AIR	-	100.0	.4	5.4	93.6	.6	-	-	(D)	-	(D)
WATER	-	100.0	-	-	-	-	-	-	(D)	-	(D)
OTHER	-	100.0	51.6	32.4	12.3	-	3.6	-	(D)	-	(D)
UNKNOWN	-	100.0	18.5	62.7	18.8	-	-	-	(D)	-	(D)
MIDDLE ATLANTIC	1 055	100.0	5.4	15.2	43.9	5.5	7.3	11.0	(D)	5.6	(D)
RAIL	512	100.0	-	3.4	65.2	6.8	5.8	1.0	(D)	10.3	(D)
MOTOR CARRIER	384	100.0	10.0	22.4	28.7	3.8	9.1	22.7	(D)	1.7	(D)
PRIVATE TRUCK	152	100.0	11.1	36.1	12.2	5.4	8.3	15.2	(D)	-	(D)
AIR	-	100.0	4.4	47.7	16.9	10.6	3.2	5.4	(D)	-	(D)
WATER	1	100.0	-	91.6	8.4	-	-	-	(D)	-	(D)
OTHER	3	100.0	26.7	2.1	17.6	1.9	2.0	-	(D)	-	(D)
UNKNOWN	-	100.0	68.4	-	.8	-	6.4	-	(D)	1.6	(D)
EAST NORTH CENTRAL	1 605	100.0	10.4	14.9	18.0	3.4	3.7	12.1	(D)	11.2	(D)
RAIL	581	100.0	1.1	5.2	5.2	4.4	3.2	5.1	(D)	28.5	(D)
MOTOR CARRIER	764	100.0	20.6	22.8	24.7	3.4	3.1	14.9	(D)	1.9	(D)
PRIVATE TRUCK	235	100.0	1.2	14.4	29.3	1.1	7.6	19.9	(D)	-	(D)
AIR	-	100.0	21.5	63.9	4.0	3.4	4.6	-	(D)	-	(D)
WATER	-	100.0	-	-	-	-	-	-	(D)	-	(D)
OTHER	19	100.0	.5	.9	1.3	.3	-	-	(D)	-	(D)
UNKNOWN	3	100.0	4.5	.1	.8	-	-	94.6	(D)	-	(D)
WEST NORTH CENTRAL	635	100.0	4.6	9.7	17.3	3.2	4.9	5.6	(D)	7.9	(D)
RAIL	362	100.0	.7	4.3	3.6	.6	2.4	.9	(D)	12.9	(D)
MOTOR CARRIER	203	100.0	10.4	21.5	34.1	8.4	8.4	8.6	(D)	1.6	(D)
PRIVATE TRUCK	67	100.0	8.3	3.4	41.4	1.8	7.8	22.3	(D)	-	(D)
AIR	2	100.0	.8	7.0	.5	.9	-	-	(D)	-	(D)
WATER	-	100.0	-	-	-	-	-	-	(D)	-	(D)
OTHER	-	100.0	11.4	58.7	7.1	11.4	6.3	-	(D)	-	(D)
UNKNOWN	-	100.0	23.8	-	-	-	-	-	(D)	-	(D)
SOUTH ATLANTIC	1 188	100.0	5.3	18.9	18.8	3.7	7.0	10.9	(D)	4.4	(D)
RAIL	641	100.0	.2	10.5	19.3	1.9	1.9	8.0	(D)	3.2	(D)
MOTOR CARRIER	414	100.0	13.3	30.5	19.8	4.0	10.6	12.6	(D)	7.7	(D)
PRIVATE TRUCK	117	100.0	4.7	14.8	14.7	12.7	22.3	21.6	(D)	-	(D)
AIR	-	100.0	4.5	52.3	15.6	.2	-	.2	(D)	-	(D)
WATER	12	100.0	2.8	97.2	-	-	-	-	(D)	-	(D)
OTHER	-	100.0	37.7	42.8	1.3	16.4	.6	-	(D)	-	(D)
UNKNOWN	-	100.0	3.1	46.6	.5	-	-	-	(D)	-	(D)
EAST SOUTH CENTRAL	489	100.0	6.8	6.2	24.6	4.1	6.1	8.6	(D)	3.8	(D)
RAIL	267	100.0	.6	.9	18.2	.4	2.6	1.6	(D)	4.6	(D)
MOTOR CARRIER	147	100.0	18.2	16.2	27.1	10.0	8.6	13.7	(D)	4.4	(D)
PRIVATE TRUCK	73	100.0	6.8	4.3	43.0	6.1	13.7	24.1	(D)	-	(D)
AIR	-	100.0	3.5	90.5	4.7	-	-	-	(D)	-	(D)
WATER	-	100.0	-	-	-	-	-	-	(D)	-	(D)
OTHER	-	100.0	-	41.8	2.6	51.7	-	-	(D)	-	(D)
UNKNOWN	-	100.0	-	94.0	.2	-	-	-	(D)	-	(D)
WEST SOUTH CENTRAL	844	100.0	8.7	19.7	25.2	1.9	3.7	7.3	(D)	3.5	(D)
RAIL	332	100.0	3.4	26.3	37.9	.7	4.3	3.9	(D)	4.6	(D)
MOTOR CARRIER	316	100.0	18.4	19.6	22.1	3.6	3.2	10.0	(D)	4.6	(D)
PRIVATE TRUCK	173	100.0	2.0	2.6	9.7	1.2	4.1	10.0	(D)	-	(D)
AIR	-	100.0	1.3	14.2	61.8	7.8	8.4	-	(D)	-	(D)
WATER	20	100.0	3.9	57.1	-	-	-	-	(D)	-	(D)
OTHER	-	100.0	6.9	46.6	1.5	6.3	-	-	(D)	-	(D)
UNKNOWN	-	100.0	-	.1	-	-	-	-	(D)	-	(D)
MOUNTAIN	341	100.0	9.9	2.1	40.4	3.8	5.0	8.4	(D)	5.6	(D)
RAIL	236	100.0	8.1	.5	47.8	2.0	6.7	4.7	(D)	3.8	(D)
MOTOR CARRIER	98	100.0	15.0	2.5	25.4	8.1	1.0	16.5	(D)	10.2	(D)
PRIVATE TRUCK	3	100.0	-	-	-	.1	-	39.3	(D)	-	(D)
AIR	-	100.0	11.5	17.5	5.5	37.7	11.3	-	(D)	-	(D)
WATER	-	100.0	-	-	-	-	-	-	(D)	-	(D)
OTHER	3	100.0	-	99.2	.1	.1	.3	-	(D)	-	(D)
UNKNOWN	-	100.0	-	100.0	-	-	-	-	(D)	-	(D)
PACIFIC	1 330	100.0	17.2	15.8	15.1	5.0	3.9	13.5	(D)	3.8	(D)
RAIL	904	100.0	17.7	14.2	15.5	5.6	3.8	17.3	(D)	1.9	(D)
MOTOR CARRIER	267	100.0	16.1	9.1	21.4	5.5	4.3	8.6	(D)	12.6	(D)
PRIVATE TRUCK	83	100.0	9.8	10.2	3.5	.7	7.1	-	(D)	-	(D)
AIR	9	100.0	4.6	31.3	3.1	6.8	.4	-	(D)	-	(D)
WATER	57	100.0	30.6	67.3	-	-	-	-	(D)	-	(D)
OTHER	-	100.0	1.2	44.4	39.4	.5	-	4.4	(D)	-	(D)
UNKNOWN	7	100.0	-	100.0	-	-	-	-	(D)	-	(D)

See footnotes at end of table 4.

TABLE 4. **TCC GROUP 335—Percent Distribution of Distance Shipped and Weight of Shipment, by Means of Transport: 1972**

Distance shipped and weight of shipment[2][3]	Number	Percent distribution by means of transport							
		All means of transport	Rail	Motor carrier	Private truck	Air	Water	Other	Unknown
TONS OF SHIPMENTS	(thousands of tons)								
U.S. TOTAL..........	15 892	100.0	35.2	37.3	26.3	.1	.8	.2	.1
UNDER 100 MILES........	4 603	100.0	28.8	22.2	47.3	-	1.6	.2	-
UNDER 1000 POUNDS.....	30	100.0	-	78.7	19.4	.1	-	1.2	.5
1000 TO 9999 POUNDS...	273	100.0	-	60.2	38.7	-	-	1.0	-
10000 TO 29999 POUNDS.	324	100.0	.1	50.4	49.4	-	-	-	.1
30000 TO 59999 POUNDS.	973	100.0	.7	58.0	40.8	-	.1	.4	-
60000 TO 89999 POUNDS.	39	100.0	27.5	39.8	32.7	-	-	-	-
90000 POUNDS AND OVER.	2 962	100.0	44.1	3.0	50.4	-	2.5	-	-
100 TO 199 MILES........	1 903	100.0	9.6	54.8	35.4	-	-	-	.2
UNDER 1000 POUNDS.....	25	100.0	-	91.1	6.8	.7	-	1.4	.1
1000 TO 9999 POUNDS...	171	100.0	.1	84.0	15.3	-	-	.3	.3
10000 TO 29999 POUNDS.	272	100.0	.3	67.8	31.7	-	-	-	.2
30000 TO 59999 POUNDS.	1 103	100.0	1.5	51.4	47.0	-	-	-	.2
60000 TO 89999 POUNDS.	74	100.0	34.4	29.8	35.8	-	-	-	-
90000 POUNDS AND OVER.	256	100.0	54.4	39.8	5.9	-	-	-	-
200 TO 299 MILES........	1 428	100.0	15.0	58.0	26.5	-	-	.3	.1
UNDER 1000 POUNDS.....	17	100.0	-	93.7	3.8	1.7	-	.8	-
1000 TO 9999 POUNDS...	125	100.0	.5	83.9	14.9	-	-	.5	.2
10000 TO 29999 POUNDS.	232	100.0	2.2	74.6	22.3	-	-	.7	.1
30000 TO 59999 POUNDS.	633	100.0	2.1	76.5	20.9	-	-	.4	.1
60000 TO 89999 POUNDS.	67	100.0	27.4	49.6	23.1	-	-	-	-
90000 POUNDS AND OVER.	351	100.0	50.4	4.1	45.5	-	-	-	-
300 TO 499 MILES........	2 864	100.0	40.5	41.4	17.8	-	-	-	.2
UNDER 1000 POUNDS.....	26	100.0	-	93.6	3.5	1.9	-	.9	.1
1000 TO 9999 POUNDS...	187	100.0	1.8	86.6	11.0	.2	-	-	.4
10000 TO 29999 POUNDS.	319	100.0	2.6	70.0	27.3	-	-	-	.1
30000 TO 59999 POUNDS.	1 024	100.0	4.2	61.5	34.2	-	-	-	-
60000 TO 89999 POUNDS.	204	100.0	61.7	36.0	-	-	-	-	2.3
90000 POUNDS AND OVER.	1 101	100.0	89.0	6.5	4.5	-	-	-	-
500 TO 999 MILES........	3 281	100.0	44.6	43.8	11.0	.1	.3	.1	.1
UNDER 1000 POUNDS.....	36	100.0	1.0	88.6	5.2	3.7	-	.9	.5
1000 TO 9999 POUNDS...	231	100.0	3.4	83.6	12.0	.4	-	.2	.3
10000 TO 29999 POUNDS.	420	100.0	7.0	74.6	18.1	-	-	.2	-
30000 TO 59999 POUNDS.	1 258	100.0	13.6	66.1	19.8	-	.1	-	.3
60000 TO 89999 POUNDS.	264	100.0	82.6	17.4	-	-	-	-	-
90000 POUNDS AND OVER.	1 069	100.0	96.9	1.9	.4	-	.8	-	-
1000 TO 1499 MILES......	997	100.0	72.7	22.1	3.1	.2	1.8	-	.1
UNDER 1000 POUNDS.....	8	100.0	2.7	88.4	2.2	4.8	-	1.5	.5
1000 TO 9999 POUNDS...	52	100.0	5.1	85.2	4.3	3.4	1.5	-	.6
10000 TO 29999 POUNDS.	83	100.0	28.4	55.2	9.1	-	6.7	-	.7
30000 TO 59999 POUNDS.	213	100.0	33.7	51.2	9.8	-	5.3	-	-
60000 TO 89999 POUNDS.	29	100.0	71.3	28.7	-	-	-	-	-
90000 POUNDS AND OVER.	608	100.0	99.4	.6	-	-	-	-	-
1500 MILES OR OVER......	812	100.0	64.2	23.4	7.0	.5	2.9	1.6	.4
UNDER 1000 POUNDS.....	10	100.0	5.7	83.6	1.5	6.9	.8	1.5	-
1000 TO 9999 POUNDS...	61	100.0	15.1	77.6	1.3	4.9	.9	.3	-
10000 TO 29999 POUNDS.	81	100.0	35.5	46.4	9.9	-	8.2	-	-
30000 TO 59999 POUNDS.	230	100.0	39.2	33.0	19.4	-	7.2	1.2	-
60000 TO 89999 POUNDS.	145	100.0	82.1	13.5	2.3	-	-	-	2.1
90000 POUNDS AND OVER.	283	100.0	96.5	-	-	-	-	3.5	-
TON-MILES OF SHIPMENTS	(millions of ton-miles)								
U.S. TOTAL..........	7 056	100.0	50.5	35.5	11.9	.2	1.3	.4	.2
UNDER 100 MILES........	144	100.0	11.8	36.9	50.1	-	1.1	.1	-
UNDER 1000 POUNDS.....	1	100.0	-	86.0	12.2	.1	-	.9	.9
1000 TO 9999 POUNDS...	14	100.0	-	65.5	33.9	-	-	.5	.1
10000 TO 29999 POUNDS.	16	100.0	-	50.8	49.1	-	-	-	.1
30000 TO 59999 POUNDS.	53	100.0	.4	58.0	41.5	-	-	.1	-
60000 TO 89999 POUNDS.	2	100.0	36.6	26.4	37.0	-	-	-	-
90000 POUNDS AND OVER.	56	100.0	28.6	4.5	64.2	-	2.7	-	-
100 TO 199 MILES........	284	100.0	10.4	56.0	33.4	-	-	.1	.2
UNDER 1000 POUNDS.....	3	100.0	-	90.9	6.7	.8	-	1.5	.1
1000 TO 9999 POUNDS...	25	100.0	.1	83.3	16.0	-	-	.3	.2
10000 TO 29999 POUNDS.	40	100.0	.2	68.3	31.3	-	-	-	.2
30000 TO 59999 POUNDS.	160	100.0	1.7	53.7	44.4	-	-	-	.2
60000 TO 89999 POUNDS.	12	100.0	34.3	29.4	36.3	-	-	-	-
90000 POUNDS AND OVER.	41	100.0	54.1	40.3	5.6	-	-	-	-
200 TO 299 MILES........	354	100.0	15.7	58.4	25.4	-	-	.3	.1
UNDER 1000 POUNDS.....	4	100.0	-	93.7	3.8	1.7	-	.8	-
1000 TO 9999 POUNDS...	31	100.0	.6	84.0	14.6	-	-	.5	.2
10000 TO 29999 POUNDS.	57	100.0	2.3	74.1	22.8	-	-	.6	.2
30000 TO 59999 POUNDS.	159	100.0	2.2	76.7	20.7	-	-	.3	.1
60000 TO 89999 POUNDS.	16	100.0	28.0	51.2	20.7	-	-	-	-
90000 POUNDS AND OVER.	85	100.0	53.7	4.4	42.0	-	-	-	-

See footnotes at end of table 4.

TABLE 4. **TCC GROUP 335—Percent Distribution of Distance Shipped and Weight of Shipment, by Means of Transport: 1972**—Continued

Distance shipped and weight of shipment [2] [3]	Number	Percent distribution by means of transport							
		All means of transport	Rail	Motor carrier	Private truck	Air	Water	Other	Unknown
TON-MILES OF SHIPMENTS	(millions of ton-miles)								
300 TO 499 MILES.........	1 102	100.0	40.8	41.4	17.5	-	-	-	.2
UNDER 1000 POUNDS.....	10	100.0	-	93.5	3.6	1.7	-	1.0	.2
1000 TO 9999 POUNDS...	73	100.0	1.7	86.8	10.9	.2	-	-	.4
10000 TO 29999 POUNDS.	125	100.0	2.7	70.4	26.7	-	-	-	.1
30000 TO 59999 POUNDS.	396	100.0	4.4	61.4	34.2	-	-	-	-
60000 TO 89999 POUNDS.	77	100.0	64.4	33.7	-	-	-	-	1.9
90000 POUNDS AND OVER.	418	100.0	90.4	5.9	3.8	-	-	-	-
500 TO 999 MILES.........	2 364	100.0	46.7	42.5	10.2	.1	.4	.1	.1
UNDER 1000 POUNDS.....	25	100.0	1.0	88.8	5.0	3.8	-	.9	.5
1000 TO 9999 POUNDS...	161	100.0	3.4	84.0	11.6	.4	-	.3	.3
10000 TO 29999 POUNDS.	289	100.0	6.9	75.2	17.7	-	-	.2	-
30000 TO 59999 POUNDS.	883	100.0	14.7	66.0	18.8	-	.2	-	.3
60000 TO 89999 POUNDS.	191	100.0	83.5	16.5	-	-	-	-	-
90000 POUNDS AND OVER.	812	100.0	96.9	1.8	.3	-	1.0	-	-
1000 TO 1499 MILES......	1 226	100.0	73.6	21.4	2.9	.2	1.7	-	.1
UNDER 1000 POUNDS.....	10	100.0	2.7	88.2	2.2	4.9	-	1.4	.5
1000 TO 9999 POUNDS...	63	100.0	5.4	84.8	3.9	4.1	1.4	-	.5
10000 TO 29999 POUNDS.	99	100.0	30.3	54.1	8.9	-	6.0	-	.8
30000 TO 59999 POUNDS.	258	100.0	34.1	51.1	9.3	-	5.5	-	-
60000 TO 89999 POUNDS.	37	100.0	71.3	28.7	-	-	-	-	-
90000 POUNDS AND OVER.	757	100.0	99.5	.5	-	-	-	-	-
1500 MILES OR OVER......	1 580	100.0	63.7	23.0	6.9	.6	3.8	1.6	.5
UNDER 1000 POUNDS.....	22	100.0	5.9	82.4	1.8	6.7	1.7	1.5	-
1000 TO 9999 POUNDS...	125	100.0	15.4	76.0	1.1	5.9	1.3	.2	-
10000 TO 29999 POUNDS.	157	100.0	34.5	46.0	10.2	-	9.4	-	-
30000 TO 59999 POUNDS.	444	100.0	39.0	31.2	18.8	-	9.8	-	-
60000 TO 89999 POUNDS.	303	100.0	82.2	12.7	2.7	-	-	1.1	2.4
90000 POUNDS AND OVER.	527	100.0	96.4	-	-	-	-	3.6	-

Note: Detail may not add to total due to rounding. The introductory table shows the estimates of sampling variability for tons; sampling variability for ton-miles has not been estimated. See the map in the Introduction for the States comprising the geographic divisions of the United States.
Shipments excluded from the survey are those moving by pipeline (primarily petroleum products from refineries), parcel post shipments, and commodities moved by own power (motorized vehicles, aircraft, etc.) or towed prefabricated buildings, etc.). Local shipments (commodities shipped less than 25 miles from the plant) and shipments within the same city are also excluded. Shipments to Alaska and Hawaii from the 48 conterminous States and the District of Columbia are included; however, no data were obtained for shipments originating in Alaska and Hawaii.

- Represents zero or rounds to zero. (D) Withheld to avoid disclosing figures for individual companies.

[1] Production of this commodity is concentrated in the geographic divisions shown; figures and distributions for geographic divisions not shown are included in the total.
[2] Distances of shipments to foreign destinations are calculated only to the U.S. port of exit.
[3] Includes only shipments represented by bills of lading and invoices. Summary records which did not show individual weights of shipments are not included.

TCC 336. Nonferrous Metal Castings

Comparisons of Tons and Ton-Miles of Shipments for
Geographic Divisions of Origin and for Sampling Variability: 1972 and 1967

Geographic division of origin	Estimates				Relative sampling variability in tons (percent)	
	1972		1967		1972	1967
	Tons (thousands)	Ton-miles (millions)	Tons (thousands)	Ton-miles (millions)		
U.S. total	1,607	732	1,205	405	7.8	26.2
New England	25	10	8	3	46.4	(*)
Middle Atlantic	329	75	186	57	9.5	(*)
East North Central	638	165	612	158	11.4	(*)
West North Central	(D)	(D)	325	133	(*)	(*)
South Atlantic	(D)	(D)	8	10	(*)	(*)
East South Central	(D)	(D)	29	14	(*)	(*)
West South Central	(D)	(D)	10	4	(*)	(*)
Mountain	(D)	(D)	–	–	(*)	(*)
Pacific	(D)	(D)	27	26	(*)	(*)

(D) Withheld to avoid disclosing figures for individual companies.   (*) Data not published.

TABLE 1. TCC GROUP 336—Percent Distribution of Geographic Division of Origin and Distance Shipped, by Means of Transport: 1972

Geographic division of origin[1] and distance shipped[2]	Number	Percent distribution by means of transport							
		All means of transport	Rail	Motor carrier	Private truck	Air	Water	Other	Unknown
TONS OF SHIPMENTS	(thousands of tons)								
U.S. TOTAL	1 607	100.0	26.4	45.0	24.6	.2	3.7	.2	-
NEW ENGLAND	25	100.0	-	88.4	9.9	1.1	-	.6	-
UNDER 100 MILES	10	100.0	-	87.2	12.5	-	-	.3	-
100 TO 199 MILES	2	100.0	-	98.4	-	.2	-	1.3	-
200 TO 299 MILES	-	100.0	-	79.9	8.4	9.1	-	2.6	-
300 TO 499 MILES	1	100.0	-	99.0	-	.1	-	.8	-
500 TO 999 MILES	5	100.0	-	78.8	19.2	1.8	-	.3	-
1000 TO 1499 MILES	3	100.0	-	96.3	.5	2.6	-	.7	-
1500 MILES OR OVER	-	100.0	-	89.4	-	7.5	-	3.1	-
MIDDLE ATLANTIC	329	100.0	26.0	24.4	31.2	.4	17.7	.2	
UNDER 100 MILES	154	100.0	11.1	20.7	30.2	-	37.8	.2	.1
100 TO 199 MILES	43	100.0	16.7	26.8	56.4	-		.1	
200 TO 299 MILES	32	100.0	69.0	15.7	15.2	-		.1	-
300 TO 499 MILES	58	100.0	59.5	32.7	6.2	1.6		.1	-
500 TO 999 MILES	36	100.0	11.7	25.6	61.8	.6	-	.4	-
1000 TO 1499 MILES	2	100.0	-	83.8	14.2	1.2	-	.5	-
1500 MILES OR OVER	1	100.0	-	85.0	10.3	4.7	-	-	.3
EAST NORTH CENTRAL	638	100.0	7.7	61.0	30.8	.3	-	.3	-
UNDER 100 MILES	193	100.0	-	43.4	55.8	.2	-	.7	-
100 TO 199 MILES	144	100.0	-	65.9	34.0	.1	-	.1	-
200 TO 299 MILES	111	100.0	17.3	68.9	13.7	.1	-	-	-
300 TO 499 MILES	101	100.0	29.2	52.0	17.9	.8	-	.1	-
500 TO 999 MILES	65	100.0	-	90.5	8.5	.9	-	.1	-
1000 TO 1499 MILES	15	100.0	-	97.6	2.3	-	-	.2	-
1500 MILES OR OVER	5	100.0	.1	99.1	-	.7	-	.1	-
TON-MILES OF SHIPMENTS	(millions of ton-miles)								
U.S. TOTAL	732	100.0	46.9	40.6	11.7	.3	.3	.1	.1
NEW ENGLAND	10	100.0	-	88.5	8.7	2.1	-	.6	-
UNDER 100 MILES	-	100.0	-	88.3	11.3	-	-	.4	-
100 TO 199 MILES	-	100.0	-	98.6	-	.3	-	1.1	-
200 TO 299 MILES	-	100.0	-	80.4	9.4	7.8	-	2.4	-
300 TO 499 MILES	-	100.0	-	99.1	-	.2	-	.7	-
500 TO 999 MILES	4	100.0	-	79.1	18.9	1.8	-	.2	-
1000 TO 1499 MILES	3	100.0	-	96.1	.5	2.6	-	.8	-
1500 MILES OR OVER	-	100.0	-	90.6	-	7.5	-	2.0	-
MIDDLE ATLANTIC	75	100.0	33.7	30.0	33.5	1.0	1.5	.2	-
UNDER 100 MILES	5	100.0	14.1	34.1	29.7	-	21.9	.2	-
100 TO 199 MILES	6	100.0	18.9	25.8	55.1	.1	-	.1	-
200 TO 299 MILES	7	100.0	68.4	16.2	15.2	-	-	.1	-
300 TO 499 MILES	24	100.0	64.1	29.3	4.9	1.6	-	.1	-
500 TO 999 MILES	25	100.0	10.0	23.0	66.0	.6	-	.4	-
1000 TO 1499 MILES	2	100.0	-	85.0	13.0	1.1	-	.5	-
1500 MILES OR OVER	3	100.0	-	81.8	12.3	5.9	-	-	.4
EAST NORTH CENTRAL	165	100.0	9.1	73.9	16.3	.5	-	.1	-
UNDER 100 MILES	10	100.0	-	51.8	47.5	.2	-	.1	-
100 TO 199 MILES	21	100.0	-	67.3	32.5	.1	-	.4	-
200 TO 299 MILES	27	100.0	19.3	67.8	12.8	.1	-	.1	-
300 TO 499 MILES	37	100.0	25.6	53.2	20.2	1.0	-	-	-
500 TO 999 MILES	40	100.0	-	89.8	9.1	.9	-	.1	-
1000 TO 1499 MILES	16	100.0	-	97.8	2.1	-	-	.2	-
1500 MILES OR OVER	10	100.0	.1	99.1	-	.8	-	.1	-

See footnotes at end of table 4.

TABLE 2. TCC GROUP 336—Percent Distribution of Geographic Division of Origin and Means of Transport, by Geographic Division of Destination: 1972

Geographic division of origin[1] and means of transport	Number	Percent distribution by division of destination									
		U.S. total	New England	Middle Atlantic	East North Central	West North Central	South Atlantic	East South Central	West South Central	Mountain	Pacific
TONS OF SHIPMENTS	(thousands of tons)										
U.S. TOTAL	1 607	100.0	3.5	18.4	54.1	3.9	5.5	8.2	1.6	1.6	3.3
RAIL	423	100.0	1.7	12.4	76.8	2.4	.8	2.6	.6	1.6	3.3
MOTOR CARRIER	722	100.0	3.3	13.1	48.1	5.4	8.6	12.4	2.6	2.1	4.4
PRIVATE TRUCK	394	100.0	6.2	22.5	48.9	3.3	5.2	7.7	1.2	.1	4.9
AIR	3	100.0	5.3	6.0	26.7	19.4	27.7	4.7	5.2	.1	4.8
WATER	58	100.0	-	99.4	-	-	-	-	-	-	.6
OTHER	3	100.0	3.4	13.7	55.8	6.3	10.6	7.0	1.6	.3	1.3
UNKNOWN	-	100.0	-	27.2	8.3	1.0	4.7	12.2	4.8	2.4	39.3

See footnotes at end of table 4.

TABLE 2. **TCC GROUP 336—Percent Distribution of Geographic Division of Origin and Means of Transport, by Geographic Division of Destination: 1972**—Continued

Geographic division of origin [1] and means of transport	Number	Percent distribution by division of destination									
		U.S. total	New England	Middle Atlantic	East North Central	West North Central	South Atlantic	East South Central	West South Central	Mountain	Pacific
TONS OF SHIPMENTS	(thousands of tons)										
NEW ENGLAND..............	25	100.0	38.0	18.0	6.8	.1	11.4	24.8	.4	-	.5
RAIL..................	-	100.0	-	-	-	-	-	-	-	-	-
MOTOR CARRIER.........	22	100.0	36.9	19.5	2.6	-	12.6	27.7	.2	-	.6
PRIVATE TRUCK.........	2	100.0	52.3	2.6	42.1	-	2.3	.7	-	-	-
AIR...................	-	100.0	.1	26.3	28.4	1.0	.5	24.6	15.5	.4	3.3
WATER.................	-	100.0	-	-	-	-	-	-	-	-	-
OTHER.................	-	100.0	34.9	33.0	9.6	11.2	6.8	.1	4.3	-	-
UNKNOWN...............	-	100.0	-	-	-	-	-	-	-	-	-
MIDDLE ATLANTIC.........	329	100.0	9.4	60.4	22.9	.5	2.7	3.4	.3	.3	.3
RAIL..................	85	100.0	7.4	46.9	44.9	-	-	.8	-	-	-
MOTOR CARRIER.........	80	100.0	8.4	53.0	27.5	1.7	4.3	1.9	1.0	1.3	.7
PRIVATE TRUCK.........	102	100.0	17.1	55.6	13.9	.1	4.4	8.6	-	-	.1
AIR...................	1	100.0	.3	2.7	24.6	5.0	55.6	4.9	.4	-	6.5
WATER.................	58	100.0	-	100.0	-	-	-	-	-	-	-
OTHER.................	-	100.0	7.3	58.2	23.2	1.1	3.3	5.8	1.0	-	-
UNKNOWN...............	-	100.0	-	94.3	-	-	-	-	5.7	-	-
EAST NORTH CENTRAL......	638	100.0	1.3	7.0	71.8	4.7	5.4	5.9	1.6	1.5	.9
RAIL..................	49	100.0	.5	.3	95.8	3.3	.1	-	-	-	-
MOTOR CARRIER.........	389	100.0	2.0	9.7	63.5	5.4	5.3	8.0	2.2	2.5	1.4
PRIVATE TRUCK.........	196	100.0	-	3.3	82.4	3.3	6.8	3.3	.9	-	-
AIR...................	1	100.0	10.3	4.9	22.9	34.6	16.7	2.1	6.4	-	2.0
WATER.................	-	100.0	-	-	-	-	-	-	-	-	-
OTHER.................	1	100.0	.1	.8	90.1	1.8	5.3	1.1	.6	-	-
UNKNOWN...............	-	100.0	-	-	87.9	11.0	-	-	-	-	1.1
TON-MILES OF SHIPMENTS	(millions of ton-miles)										
U.S. TOTAL	732	100.0	2.2	11.6	55.9	4.1	8.9	7.7	2.1	2.9	4.8
RAIL..................	343	100.0	.4	8.8	84.4	.8	1.0	2.4	.5	1.6	.1
MOTOR CARRIER.........	297	100.0	2.8	12.7	29.3	7.7	17.9	12.4	3.9	5.3	8.1
PRIVATE TRUCK.........	85	100.0	6.7	18.1	36.4	4.9	8.8	12.8	2.1	.1	10.1
AIR...................	2	100.0	5.2	4.3	17.7	17.2	23.1	6.1	8.3	.2	18.0
WATER.................	2	100.0	-	52.5	-	-	-	-	-	-	47.5
OTHER.................	-	100.0	3.7	11.0	30.5	9.4	28.2	7.6	7.0	.5	2.0
UNKNOWN...............	-	100.0	-	.7	1.9	.3	10.7	21.9	3.3	.7	60.4
NEW ENGLAND..............	10	100.0	4.8	7.3	12.1	.3	16.1	55.1	1.1	-	3.3
RAIL..................	-	100.0	-	-	-	-	-	-	-	-	-
MOTOR CARRIER.........	9	100.0	4.7	7.8	4.6	-	17.6	61.2	.6	-	3.5
PRIVATE TRUCK.........	-	100.0	6.3	1.9	84.3	-	5.5	2.0	-	-	-
AIR...................	-	100.0	-	7.2	25.5	1.3	.3	31.8	21.9	1.1	10.8
WATER.................	-	100.0	-	-	-	-	-	-	-	-	-
OTHER.................	-	100.0	8.1	16.1	15.1	31.3	13.5	.1	15.9	-	-
UNKNOWN...............	-	100.0	-	-	-	-	-	-	-	-	-
MIDDLE ATLANTIC.........	75	100.0	6.7	21.6	49.0	1.7	3.1	11.6	1.4	2.2	2.6
RAIL..................	25	100.0	2.4	26.6	69.8	-	-	1.3	-	-	-
MOTOR CARRIER.........	22	100.0	7.1	18.2	40.4	5.1	6.3	5.1	4.3	7.4	6.2
PRIVATE TRUCK.........	25	100.0	11.2	16.6	38.9	.3	2.6	28.6	.3	-	1.5
AIR...................	-	100.0	.2	1.0	20.6	7.2	37.9	5.2	1.0	-	26.9
WATER.................	1	100.0	-	100.0	-	-	-	-	-	-	-
OTHER.................	-	100.0	4.0	11.6	53.9	4.1	5.9	16.2	4.3	-	-
UNKNOWN...............	-	100.0	-	23.7	-	-	-	-	76.3	-	-
EAST NORTH CENTRAL......	165	100.0	3.2	10.0	40.6	7.1	11.4	10.0	4.5	6.8	6.4
RAIL..................	15	100.0	.8	.5	94.8	3.7	.1	-	-	-	.1
MOTOR CARRIER.........	122	100.0	4.2	12.5	31.4	6.5	10.1	12.0	5.5	9.2	8.5
PRIVATE TRUCK.........	26	100.0	-	4.3	52.8	11.1	22.8	6.6	2.4	-	-
AIR...................	-	100.0	12.4	5.1	6.7	34.1	20.7	1.5	10.4	-	9.1
WATER.................	-	100.0	-	-	-	-	-	-	-	-	-
OTHER.................	-	100.0	.9	4.3	48.0	2.6	35.8	5.6	2.7	-	-
UNKNOWN...............	-	100.0	-	-	72.9	12.1	-	-	-	-	15.0

See footnotes at end of table 4.

TABLE 3. TCC GROUP 336—Percent Distribution of Geographic Division of Destination and Means of Transport, by Geographic Division of Origin: 1972

Geographic division of destination and means of transport	Number	Percent distribution by division of origin [1]									
		U.S. total	New England	Middle Atlantic	East North Central	West North Central	South Atlantic	East South Central	West South Central	Mountain	Pacific
TONS OF SHIPMENTS	(thousands of tons)										
U.S. TOTAL	1 607	100.0	1.6	20.5	39.7	(D)	(D)	(D)	(D)	(D)	(D)
RAIL	423	100.0	-	20.2	11.6	(D)	(D)	(D)	(D)	(D)	(D)
MOTOR CARRIER	722	100.0	3.1	11.1	53.9	(D)	(D)	(D)	(D)	(D)	(D)
PRIVATE TRUCK	394	100.0	.6	26.0	49.7	(D)	(D)	(D)	(D)	(D)	(D)
AIR	3	100.0	7.5	33.7	50.4	(D)	(D)	(D)	(D)	(D)	(D)
WATER	58	100.0	-	99.4	-	(D)	(D)	(D)	(D)	(D)	(D)
OTHER	3	100.0	5.1	17.9	55.5	(D)	(D)	(D)	(D)	(D)	(D)
UNKNOWN	-	100.0	-	28.9	9.5	(D)	(D)	(D)	(D)	(D)	(D)
NEW ENGLAND	55	100.0	17.4	55.3	14.4	(D)	(D)	(D)	(D)	(D)	(D)
RAIL	7	100.0	-	89.5	3.3	(D)	(D)	(D)	(D)	(D)	(D)
MOTOR CARRIER	23	100.0	35.1	28.6	32.1	(D)	(D)	(D)	(D)	(D)	(D)
PRIVATE TRUCK	24	100.0	5.4	71.7	-	(D)	(D)	(D)	(D)	(D)	(D)
AIR	-	100.0	.2	1.7	98.1	(D)	(D)	(D)	(D)	(D)	(D)
WATER	-	100.0	-	-	-	(D)	(D)	(D)	(D)	(D)	(D)
OTHER	-	100.0	51.5	38.1	2.0	(D)	(D)	(D)	(D)	(D)	(D)
UNKNOWN	-	100.0	-	-	-	(D)	(D)	(D)	(D)	(D)	(D)
MIDDLE ATLANTIC	295	100.0	1.6	67.3	15.1	(D)	(D)	(D)	(D)	(D)	(D)
RAIL	52	100.0	-	76.1	.3	(D)	(D)	(D)	(D)	(D)	(D)
MOTOR CARRIER	94	100.0	4.6	45.1	39.9	(D)	(D)	(D)	(D)	(D)	(D)
PRIVATE TRUCK	88	100.0	.1	64.3	7.3	(D)	(D)	(D)	(D)	(D)	(D)
AIR	-	100.0	32.9	14.9	41.3	(D)	(D)	(D)	(D)	(D)	(D)
WATER	58	100.0	-	100.0	-	(D)	(D)	(D)	(D)	(D)	(D)
OTHER	-	100.0	12.2	75.7	3.3	(D)	(D)	(D)	(D)	(D)	(D)
UNKNOWN	-	100.0	-	100.0	-	(D)	(D)	(D)	(D)	(D)	(D)
EAST NORTH CENTRAL	868	100.0	.2	8.7	52.7	(D)	(D)	(D)	(D)	(D)	(D)
RAIL	325	100.0	-	11.8	14.4	(D)	(D)	(D)	(D)	(D)	(D)
MOTOR CARRIER	347	100.0	.2	6.4	71.0	(D)	(D)	(D)	(D)	(D)	(D)
PRIVATE TRUCK	193	100.0	.5	7.4	83.9	(D)	(D)	(D)	(D)	(D)	(D)
AIR	1	100.0	8.0	31.1	43.3	(D)	(D)	(D)	(D)	(D)	(D)
WATER	-	100.0	-	-	-	(D)	(D)	(D)	(D)	(D)	(D)
OTHER	1	100.0	.9	7.4	89.8	(D)	(D)	(D)	(D)	(D)	(D)
UNKNOWN	-	100.0	-	-	100.0	(D)	(D)	(D)	(D)	(D)	(D)
WEST NORTH CENTRAL	63	100.0	-	2.5	47.3	(D)	(D)	(D)	(D)	(D)	(D)
RAIL	10	100.0	-	-	16.3	(D)	(D)	(D)	(D)	(D)	(D)
MOTOR CARRIER	39	100.0	-	3.6	53.7	(D)	(D)	(D)	(D)	(D)	(D)
PRIVATE TRUCK	13	100.0	-	.7	49.8	(D)	(D)	(D)	(D)	(D)	(D)
AIR	-	100.0	.4	8.8	89.8	(D)	(D)	(D)	(D)	(D)	(D)
WATER	-	100.0	-	-	-	(D)	(D)	(D)	(D)	(D)	(D)
OTHER	-	100.0	9.0	3.2	15.9	(D)	(D)	(D)	(D)	(D)	(D)
UNKNOWN	-	100.0	-	-	100.0	(D)	(D)	(D)	(D)	(D)	(D)
SOUTH ATLANTIC	87	100.0	3.3	10.0	39.3	(D)	(D)	(D)	(D)	(D)	(D)
RAIL	3	100.0	-	-	.8	(D)	(D)	(D)	(D)	(D)	(D)
MOTOR CARRIER	62	100.0	4.6	5.6	33.2	(D)	(D)	(D)	(D)	(D)	(D)
PRIVATE TRUCK	20	100.0	.3	22.2	64.9	(D)	(D)	(D)	(D)	(D)	(D)
AIR	1	100.0	.1	67.8	30.4	(D)	(D)	(D)	(D)	(D)	(D)
WATER	-	100.0	-	-	-	(D)	(D)	(D)	(D)	(D)	(D)
OTHER	-	100.0	3.3	5.6	28.2	(D)	(D)	(D)	(D)	(D)	(D)
UNKNOWN	-	100.0	-	-	-	(D)	(D)	(D)	(D)	(D)	(D)
EAST SOUTH CENTRAL	131	100.0	4.8	8.6	28.9	(D)	(D)	(D)	(D)	(D)	(D)
RAIL	11	100.0	-	6.3	-	(D)	(D)	(D)	(D)	(D)	(D)
MOTOR CARRIER	89	100.0	7.0	1.7	35.1	(D)	(D)	(D)	(D)	(D)	(D)
PRIVATE TRUCK	30	100.0	.1	29.3	21.4	(D)	(D)	(D)	(D)	(D)	(D)
AIR	-	100.0	39.2	34.7	22.8	(D)	(D)	(D)	(D)	(D)	(D)
WATER	-	100.0	-	-	-	(D)	(D)	(D)	(D)	(D)	(D)
OTHER	-	100.0	-	14.9	8.9	(D)	(D)	(D)	(D)	(D)	(D)
UNKNOWN	-	100.0	-	-	-	(D)	(D)	(D)	(D)	(D)	(D)
WEST SOUTH CENTRAL	26	100.0	.4	3.3	39.1	(D)	(D)	(D)	(D)	(D)	(D)
RAIL	2	100.0	-	-	-	(D)	(D)	(D)	(D)	(D)	(D)
MOTOR CARRIER	18	100.0	.2	4.3	44.9	(D)	(D)	(D)	(D)	(D)	(D)
PRIVATE TRUCK	4	100.0	-	1.0	37.3	(D)	(D)	(D)	(D)	(D)	(D)
AIR	-	100.0	22.5	2.8	61.8	(D)	(D)	(D)	(D)	(D)	(D)
WATER	-	100.0	-	-	-	(D)	(D)	(D)	(D)	(D)	(D)
OTHER	-	100.0	14.1	11.3	22.2	(D)	(D)	(D)	(D)	(D)	(D)
UNKNOWN	-	100.0	-	34.5	-	(D)	(D)	(D)	(D)	(D)	(D)
MOUNTAIN	26	100.0	-	4.1	37.4	(D)	(D)	(D)	(D)	(D)	(D)
RAIL	10	100.0	-	-	-	(D)	(D)	(D)	(D)	(D)	(D)
MOTOR CARRIER	15	100.0	-	7.1	65.4	(D)	(D)	(D)	(D)	(D)	(D)
PRIVATE TRUCK	-	100.0	-	1.7	-	(D)	(D)	(D)	(D)	(D)	(D)
AIR	-	100.0	41.1	-	-	(D)	(D)	(D)	(D)	(D)	(D)
WATER	-	100.0	-	-	-	(D)	(D)	(D)	(D)	(D)	(D)
OTHER	-	100.0	-	-	-	(D)	(D)	(D)	(D)	(D)	(D)
UNKNOWN	-	100.0	-	-	-	(D)	(D)	(D)	(D)	(D)	(D)
PACIFIC	52	100.0	.3	1.6	10.4	(D)	(D)	(D)	(D)	(D)	(D)
RAIL	-	100.0	-	-	2.1	(D)	(D)	(D)	(D)	(D)	(D)
MOTOR CARRIER	31	100.0	.4	1.9	17.1	(D)	(D)	(D)	(D)	(D)	(D)
PRIVATE TRUCK	19	100.0	-	.8	-	(D)	(D)	(D)	(D)	(D)	(D)
AIR	-	100.0	5.1	45.5	21.1	(D)	(D)	(D)	(D)	(D)	(D)
WATER	-	100.0	-	-	-	(D)	(D)	(D)	(D)	(D)	(D)
OTHER	-	100.0	-	-	-	(D)	(D)	(D)	(D)	(D)	(D)
UNKNOWN	-	100.0	-	-	.3	(D)	(D)	(D)	(D)	(D)	(D)

See footnotes at end of table 4.

TABLE 3. **TCC GROUP 336**—Percent Distribution of Geographic Division of Destination and Means of Transport, by Geographic Division of Origin: 1972—Continued

Geographic division of destination and means of transport	Number	Percent distribution by division of origin [1]									
		U.S. total	New England	Middle Atlantic	East North Central	West North Central	South Atlantic	East South Central	West South Central	Mountain	Pacific
TON-MILES OF SHIPMENTS	(millions of ton-miles)										
U.S. TOTAL............	732	100.0	1.4	10.3	22.6	(D)	(D)	(D)	(D)	(D)	(D)
RAIL..............	343	100.0	-	7.4	4.4	(D)	(D)	(D)	(D)	(D)	(D)
MOTOR CARRIER.......	297	100.0	3.1	7.6	41.1	(D)	(D)	(D)	(D)	(D)	(D)
PRIVATE TRUCK........	85	100.0	1.0	29.5	31.4	(D)	(D)	(D)	(D)	(D)	(D)
AIR................	2	100.0	10.3	36.1	41.1	(D)	(D)	(D)	(D)	(D)	(D)
WATER..............	2	100.0	-	52.5	-	(D)	(D)	(D)	(D)	(D)	(D)
OTHER..............	-	100.0	10.9	24.8	28.9	(D)	(D)	(D)	(D)	(D)	(D)
UNKNOWN............	-	100.0	-	3.1	2.6	(D)	(D)	(D)	(D)	(D)	(D)
NEW ENGLAND...........	15	100.0	3.1	32.1	34.0	(D)	(D)	(D)	(D)	(D)	(D)
RAIL..............	1	100.0	-	41.4	8.0	(D)	(D)	(D)	(D)	(D)	(D)
MOTOR CARRIER.......	8	100.0	5.1	19.2	60.8	(D)	(D)	(D)	(D)	(D)	(D)
PRIVATE TRUCK........	5	100.0	1.0	49.5	-	(D)	(D)	(D)	(D)	(D)	(D)
AIR................	-	100.0	.1	1.1	98.8	(D)	(D)	(D)	(D)	(D)	(D)
WATER..............	-	100.0	-	-	-	(D)	(D)	(D)	(D)	(D)	(D)
OTHER..............	-	100.0	23.5	26.6	7.0	(D)	(D)	(D)	(D)	(D)	(D)
UNKNOWN............	-	100.0	-	-	-	(D)	(D)	(D)	(D)	(D)	(D)
MIDDLE ATLANTIC........	84	100.0	.9	19.2	19.5	(D)	(D)	(D)	(D)	(D)	(D)
RAIL..............	30	100.0	-	22.4	.2	(D)	(D)	(D)	(D)	(D)	(D)
MOTOR CARRIER.......	37	100.0	1.9	10.9	40.3	(D)	(D)	(D)	(D)	(D)	(D)
PRIVATE TRUCK........	15	100.0	.1	27.2	7.5	(D)	(D)	(D)	(D)	(D)	(D)
AIR................	-	100.0	17.1	8.2	48.7	(D)	(D)	(D)	(D)	(D)	(D)
WATER..............	1	100.0	-	100.0	-	(D)	(D)	(D)	(D)	(D)	(D)
OTHER..............	-	100.0	16.0	26.2	11.4	(D)	(D)	(D)	(D)	(D)	(D)
UNKNOWN............	-	100.0	-	100.0	-	(D)	(D)	(D)	(D)	(D)	(D)
EAST NORTH CENTRAL......	408	100.0	.3	9.0	16.4	(D)	(D)	(D)	(D)	(D)	(D)
RAIL..............	290	100.0	-	6.1	4.9	(D)	(D)	(D)	(D)	(D)	(D)
MOTOR CARRIER.......	87	100.0	.5	10.5	44.1	(D)	(D)	(D)	(D)	(D)	(D)
PRIVATE TRUCK........	31	100.0	2.4	31.6	45.6	(D)	(D)	(D)	(D)	(D)	(D)
AIR................	-	100.0	14.8	41.8	15.4	(D)	(D)	(D)	(D)	(D)	(D)
WATER..............	-	100.0	-	-	-	(D)	(D)	(D)	(D)	(D)	(D)
OTHER..............	-	100.0	5.4	43.9	45.5	(D)	(D)	(D)	(D)	(D)	(D)
UNKNOWN............	-	100.0	-	-	100.0	(D)	(D)	(D)	(D)	(D)	(D)
WEST NORTH CENTRAL......	30	100.0	.1	4.3	39.3	(D)	(D)	(D)	(D)	(D)	(D)
RAIL..............	2	100.0	-	-	21.9	(D)	(D)	(D)	(D)	(D)	(D)
MOTOR CARRIER.......	22	100.0	-	5.0	34.9	(D)	(D)	(D)	(D)	(D)	(D)
PRIVATE TRUCK........	4	100.0	-	2.0	70.2	(D)	(D)	(D)	(D)	(D)	(D)
AIR................	-	100.0	.8	15.1	81.6	(D)	(D)	(D)	(D)	(D)	(D)
WATER..............	-	100.0	-	-	-	(D)	(D)	(D)	(D)	(D)	(D)
OTHER..............	-	100.0	36.1	10.8	8.0	(D)	(D)	(D)	(D)	(D)	(D)
UNKNOWN............	-	100.0	-	-	100.0	(D)	(D)	(D)	(D)	(D)	(D)
SOUTH ATLANTIC.........	64	100.0	2.5	3.7	28.9	(D)	(D)	(D)	(D)	(D)	(D)
RAIL..............	3	100.0	-	-	.5	(D)	(D)	(D)	(D)	(D)	(D)
MOTOR CARRIER.......	53	100.0	3.0	2.7	23.2	(D)	(D)	(D)	(D)	(D)	(D)
PRIVATE TRUCK........	7	100.0	.7	8.6	81.9	(D)	(D)	(D)	(D)	(D)	(D)
AIR................	-	100.0	.1	59.4	37.0	(D)	(D)	(D)	(D)	(D)	(D)
WATER..............	-	100.0	-	-	-	(D)	(D)	(D)	(D)	(D)	(D)
OTHER..............	-	100.0	5.2	5.2	36.7	(D)	(D)	(D)	(D)	(D)	(D)
UNKNOWN............	-	100.0	-	-	-	(D)	(D)	(D)	(D)	(D)	(D)
EAST SOUTH CENTRAL......	56	100.0	10.0	15.6	29.3	(D)	(D)	(D)	(D)	(D)	(D)
RAIL..............	8	100.0	-	4.0	-	(D)	(D)	(D)	(D)	(D)	(D)
MOTOR CARRIER.......	36	100.0	15.2	3.2	40.0	(D)	(D)	(D)	(D)	(D)	(D)
PRIVATE TRUCK........	10	100.0	.2	65.9	16.2	(D)	(D)	(D)	(D)	(D)	(D)
AIR................	-	100.0	53.9	31.2	9.9	(D)	(D)	(D)	(D)	(D)	(D)
WATER..............	-	100.0	-	-	-	(D)	(D)	(D)	(D)	(D)	(D)
OTHER..............	-	100.0	.1	53.0	21.4	(D)	(D)	(D)	(D)	(D)	(D)
UNKNOWN............	-	100.0	-	-	-	(D)	(D)	(D)	(D)	(D)	(D)
WEST SOUTH CENTRAL......	15	100.0	.7	7.1	49.4	(D)	(D)	(D)	(D)	(D)	(D)
RAIL..............	1	100.0	-	-	-	(D)	(D)	(D)	(D)	(D)	(D)
MOTOR CARRIER.......	11	100.0	.4	8.5	58.4	(D)	(D)	(D)	(D)	(D)	(D)
PRIVATE TRUCK........	1	100.0	-	4.1	35.6	(D)	(D)	(D)	(D)	(D)	(D)
AIR................	-	100.0	27.2	4.3	51.3	(D)	(D)	(D)	(D)	(D)	(D)
WATER..............	-	100.0	-	-	-	(D)	(D)	(D)	(D)	(D)	(D)
OTHER..............	-	100.0	24.6	15.3	11.1	(D)	(D)	(D)	(D)	(D)	(D)
UNKNOWN............	-	100.0	-	71.0	-	(D)	(D)	(D)	(D)	(D)	(D)
MOUNTAIN..............	21	100.0	-	7.8	52.5	(D)	(D)	(D)	(D)	(D)	(D)
RAIL..............	5	100.0	-	-	-	(D)	(D)	(D)	(D)	(D)	(D)
MOTOR CARRIER.......	15	100.0	-	10.6	71.3	(D)	(D)	(D)	(D)	(D)	(D)
PRIVATE TRUCK........	-	100.0	-	10.1	-	(D)	(D)	(D)	(D)	(D)	(D)
AIR................	-	100.0	68.2	-	-	(D)	(D)	(D)	(D)	(D)	(D)
WATER..............	-	100.0	-	-	-	(D)	(D)	(D)	(D)	(D)	(D)
OTHER..............	-	100.0	-	-	-	(D)	(D)	(D)	(D)	(D)	(D)
UNKNOWN............	-	100.0	-	-	-	(D)	(D)	(D)	(D)	(D)	(D)
PACIFIC...............	34	100.0	1.0	5.7	30.3	(D)	(D)	(D)	(D)	(D)	(D)
RAIL..............	-	100.0	-	-	3.1	(D)	(D)	(D)	(D)	(D)	(D)
MOTOR CARRIER.......	23	100.0	1.3	5.8	43.6	(D)	(D)	(D)	(D)	(D)	(D)
PRIVATE TRUCK........	8	100.0	-	4.3	-	(D)	(D)	(D)	(D)	(D)	(D)
AIR................	-	100.0	6.2	54.0	20.8	(D)	(D)	(D)	(D)	(D)	(D)
WATER..............	1	100.0	-	-	-	(D)	(D)	(D)	(D)	(D)	(D)
OTHER..............	-	100.0	-	-	-	(D)	(D)	(D)	(D)	(D)	(D)
UNKNOWN............	-	100.0	-	-	.6	(D)	(D)	(D)	(D)	(D)	(D)

See footnotes at end of table 4.

TABLE 4. **TCC GROUP 336**—Percent Distribution of Distance Shipped and Weight of Shipment, by Means of Transport: 1972

Distance shipped and weight of shipment [2] [3]	Number	Percent distribution by means of transport							
		All means of transport	Rail	Motor carrier	Private truck	Air	Water	Other	Unknown
TONS OF SHIPMENTS	(thousands of tons)								
U.S. TOTAL..........	1 410	100.0	28.4	43.3	23.7	.2	4.2	.2	-
UNDER 100 MILES.........	389	100.0	4.8	34.1	45.5	.1	15.0	.5	-
UNDER 1000 POUNDS.....	35	100.0	-	61.4	36.1	.8	-	1.6	-
1000 TO 9999 POUNDS...	119	100.0	-	53.0	46.5	-	-	.4	-
10000 TO 29999 POUNDS.	82	100.0	.3	28.6	70.2	-	-	.9	.1
30000 TO 59999 POUNDS.	70	100.0	2.6	30.5	66.9	-	-	-	-
60000 TO 89999 POUNDS.	-	100.0	-	-	-	-	-	-	-
90000 POUNDS AND OVER.	80	100.0	20.6	2.9	3.8	-	72.6	-	-
100 TO 199 MILES........	215	100.0	3.9	64.0	32.0	-	-	.1	-
UNDER 1000 POUNDS.....	20	100.0	-	91.8	6.9	.5	-	.9	-
1000 TO 9999 POUNDS...	89	100.0	-	83.9	16.1	-	-	-	-
10000 TO 29999 POUNDS.	60	100.0	-	49.0	51.0	-	-	-	-
30000 TO 59999 POUNDS.	30	100.0	6.3	23.5	70.2	-	-	-	-
60000 TO 89999 POUNDS.	5	100.0	-	100.0	-	-	-	-	-
90000 POUNDS AND OVER.	9	100.0	73.2	19.6	7.2	-	-	-	-
200 TO 299 MILES........	159	100.0	26.4	59.2	14.2	.1	-	.1	-
UNDER 1000 POUNDS.....	8	100.0	-	80.4	16.7	1.2	-	1.2	.5
1000 TO 9999 POUNDS...	38	100.0	1.0	77.9	20.9	.1	-	-	-
10000 TO 29999 POUNDS.	44	100.0	3.7	86.0	10.3	-	-	-	-
30000 TO 59999 POUNDS.	41	100.0	32.7	47.4	19.9	-	-	-	-
60000 TO 89999 POUNDS.	13	100.0	100.0	-	-	-	-	-	-
90000 POUNDS AND OVER.	13	100.0	95.1	1.6	3.3	-	-	-	-
300 TO 499 MILES........	210	100.0	48.8	37.9	12.7	.4	-	.1	-
UNDER 1000 POUNDS.....	11	100.0	-	89.5	.9	7.0	-	2.5	.1
1000 TO 9999 POUNDS...	36	100.0	.6	90.4	8.8	.1	-	-	-
10000 TO 29999 POUNDS.	31	100.0	1.5	58.1	40.4	-	-	-	-
30000 TO 59999 POUNDS.	58	100.0	53.6	29.6	16.9	-	-	-	-
60000 TO 89999 POUNDS.	39	100.0	100.0	-	-	-	-	-	-
90000 POUNDS AND OVER.	31	100.0	97.8	-	2.2	-	-	-	-
500 TO 999 MILES........	183	100.0	26.0	52.6	20.8	.5	-	.1	-
UNDER 1000 POUNDS.....	13	100.0	-	90.5	1.9	6.3	-	1.3	-
1000 TO 9999 POUNDS...	41	100.0	1.0	88.4	10.2	.4	-	-	-
10000 TO 29999 POUNDS.	51	100.0	.7	70.3	29.0	-	-	-	-
30000 TO 59999 POUNDS.	24	100.0	6.9	49.4	43.7	-	-	-	-
60000 TO 89999 POUNDS.	35	100.0	76.7	-	23.3	-	-	-	-
90000 POUNDS AND OVER.	18	100.0	100.0	-	-	-	-	-	-
1000 TO 1499 MILES......	188	100.0	89.3	10.2	.4	.1	-	-	-
UNDER 1000 POUNDS.....	2	100.0	-	84.0	9.2	4.9	-	1.6	.3
1000 TO 9999 POUNDS...	6	100.0	5.2	86.5	7.6	.7	-	-	-
10000 TO 29999 POUNDS.	11	100.0	4.5	95.5	-	-	-	-	-
30000 TO 59999 POUNDS.	1	100.0	52.7	47.3	-	-	-	-	-
60000 TO 89999 POUNDS.	3	100.0	100.0	-	-	-	-	-	-
90000 POUNDS AND OVER.	163	100.0	100.0	-	-	-	-	-	-
1500 MILES OR OVER......	64	100.0	20.1	78.5	.3	.2	.5	-	.4
UNDER 1000 POUNDS.....	6	100.0	.1	95.7	1.5	1.5	-	.1	1.1
1000 TO 9999 POUNDS...	9	100.0	-	93.3	.9	.5	3.6	-	1.7
10000 TO 29999 POUNDS.	3	100.0	-	100.0	-	.5	-	-	-
30000 TO 59999 POUNDS.	34	100.0	5.8	94.2	-	-	-	-	-
60000 TO 89999 POUNDS.	-	100.0	-	-	-	-	-	-	-
90000 POUNDS AND OVER.	10	100.0	100.0	-	-	-	-	-	-
TON-MILES OF SHIPMENTS	(millions of ton-miles)								
U.S. TOTAL..........	659	100.0	50.1	40.0	9.2	.2	.3	.1	.1
UNDER 100 MILES.........	16	100.0	4.7	45.0	42.8	.1	6.9	.4	-
UNDER 1000 POUNDS.....	1	100.0	-	70.3	26.9	1.4	-	1.5	-
1000 TO 9999 POUNDS...	5	100.0	-	59.6	40.0	-	-	.4	-
10000 TO 29999 POUNDS.	4	100.0	.2	36.3	63.1	-	-	.3	-
30000 TO 59999 POUNDS.	2	100.0	1.9	41.3	56.9	-	-	-	-
60000 TO 89999 POUNDS.	-	100.0	-	-	-	-	-	-	-
90000 POUNDS AND OVER.	2	100.0	32.6	7.5	8.5	-	51.4	-	-
100 TO 199 MILES........	31	100.0	4.8	62.9	32.2	-	-	.1	-
UNDER 1000 POUNDS.....	2	100.0	-	91.4	7.2	.5	-	1.0	-
1000 TO 9999 POUNDS...	12	100.0	-	82.8	17.2	-	-	-	-
10000 TO 29999 POUNDS.	8	100.0	-	49.9	50.1	-	-	-	-
30000 TO 59999 POUNDS.	4	100.0	6.6	24.7	68.7	-	-	-	-
60000 TO 89999 POUNDS.	-	100.0	-	100.0	-	-	-	-	-
90000 POUNDS AND OVER.	1	100.0	77.5	16.7	5.8	-	-	-	-
200 TO 299 MILES........	39	100.0	27.5	58.8	13.5	.1	-	.1	-
UNDER 1000 POUNDS.....	2	100.0	-	80.6	16.6	1.2	-	1.2	.4
1000 TO 9999 POUNDS...	9	100.0	1.0	78.6	20.3	.1	-	-	-
10000 TO 29999 POUNDS.	10	100.0	4.1	86.1	9.7	-	-	-	-
30000 TO 59999 POUNDS.	10	100.0	35.4	46.2	18.4	-	-	-	-
60000 TO 89999 POUNDS.	3	100.0	100.0	-	-	-	-	-	-
90000 POUNDS AND OVER.	3	100.0	95.7	1.4	3.0	-	-	-	-

See footnotes at end of table 4.

TABLE 4. **TCC GROUP 336—Percent Distribution of Distance Shipped and Weight of Shipment, by Means of Transport: 1972**—Continued

Distance shipped and weight of shipment [2] [3]	Number	Percent distribution by means of transport							
		All means of transport	Rail	Motor carrier	Private truck	Air	Water	Other	Unknown
TON-MILES OF SHIPMENTS	(millions of ton-miles)								
300 TO 499 MILES.........	81	100.0	49.3	37.2	12.9	.5	-	.1	-
UNDER 1000 POUNDS.....	4	100.0	-	89.2	.9	7.6	-	2.3	.1
1000 TO 9999 POUNDS...	14	100.0	.7	89.9	9.2	.1	-	-	-
10000 TO 29999 POUNDS.	12	100.0	1.7	56.6	41.7	-	-	-	-
30000 TO 59999 POUNDS.	20	100.0	51.4	30.8	17.8	-	-	-	-
60000 TO 89999 POUNDS.	15	100.0	100.0	-	-	-	-	-	-
90000 POUNDS AND OVER.	13	100.0	97.8	-	2.2	-	-	-	-
500 TO 999 MILES........	118	100.0	24.4	53.1	21.9	.5	-	.1	-
UNDER 1000 POUNDS.....	9	100.0	-	91.3	1.8	5.7	-	1.2	-
1000 TO 9999 POUNDS...	27	100.0	1.2	88.3	10.1	.4	-	-	-
10000 TO 29999 POUNDS.	30	100.0	1.0	69.9	29.0	-	-	-	-
30000 TO 59999 POUNDS.	17	100.0	5.7	51.3	43.0	-	-	-	-
60000 TO 89999 POUNDS.	22	100.0	69.6	-	30.4	-	-	-	-
90000 POUNDS AND OVER.	11	100.0	100.0	-	-	-	-	-	-
1000 TO 1499 MILES......	247	100.0	90.6	9.0	.3	.1	-	-	.3
UNDER 1000 POUNDS.....	3	100.0	-	84.7	8.6	4.8	-	1.5	.3
1000 TO 9999 POUNDS...	7	100.0	6.1	86.5	6.8	.6	-	-	-
10000 TO 29999 POUNDS.	13	100.0	5.6	94.4	-	-	-	-	-
30000 TO 59999 POUNDS.	1	100.0	51.0	49.0	-	-	-	-	-
60000 TO 89999 POUNDS.	4	100.0	100.0	-	-	-	-	-	-
90000 POUNDS AND OVER.	217	100.0	100.0	-	-	-	-	-	-
1500 MILES OR OVER......	124	100.0	19.4	78.8	.3	.3	.9	-	.3
UNDER 1000 POUNDS.....	12	100.0	.1	95.2	1.8	1.6	-	.1	1.1
1000 TO 9999 POUNDS...	18	100.0	-	91.3	1.1	.7	5.6	-	1.4
10000 TO 29999 POUNDS.	5	100.0	-	100.0	-	-	-	-	-
30000 TO 59999 POUNDS.	66	100.0	5.2	94.8	-	-	-	-	-
60000 TO 89999 POUNDS.	-	100.0	-	-	-	-	-	-	-
90000 POUNDS AND OVER.	20	100.0	100.0	-	-	-	-	-	-

Note: Detail may not add to total due to rounding. The introductory table shows the estimates of sampling variability for tons; sampling variability for ton-miles has not been estimated. See the map in the Introduction for the States comprising the geographic divisions of the United States.

Shipments excluded from the survey are those moving by pipeline (primarily petroleum products from refineries), parcel post shipments, and commodities moved by own power (motorized vehicles, aircraft, etc.) or towed (prefabricated buildings, etc.). Local shipments (commodities shipped less than 25 miles from the plant) and shipments within the same city are also excluded. Shipments to Alaska and Hawaii from the 48 conterminous States and the District of Columbia are included; however, no data were obtained for shipments originating in Alaska and Hawaii.

- Represents zero or rounds to zero.   (D) Withheld to avoid disclosing figures for individual companies.

[1]Production of this commodity is concentrated in the geographic divisions shown; figures and distributions for geographic divisions not shown are included in the total.

[2]Distances of shipments to foreign destinations are calculated only to the U.S. port of exit.

[3]Includes only shipments represented by bills of lading and invoices. Summary records which did not show individual weights of shipments are not included.

TCC 339. Miscellaneous Primary Metal Products

Comparisons of Tons and Ton-Miles of Shipments for
Geographic Divisions of Origin and for Sampling Variability: 1972 and 1967

Geographic division of origin	Estimates				Relative sampling variability in tons (percent)	
	1972		1967		1972	1967
	Tons (thousands)	Ton-miles (millions)	Tons (thousands)	Ton-miles (millions)		
U.S. total	3,353	1,162	3,491	1,121	16.1	10.2
New England	75	22	122	42	17.7	(*)
Middle Atlantic	414	135	642	206	18.9	(*)
East North Central	1,933	450	1,907	420	13.8	(*)
West North Central	(D)	(D)	69	44	(*)	(*)
South Atlantic	(D)	(D)	10	1	(*)	(*)
East South Central	(D)	(D)	437	96	(*)	(*)
West South Central	(D)	(D)	80	36	(*)	(*)
Mountain	(D)	(D)	1	1	(*)	(*)
Pacific	38	34	223	275	24.9	(*)

(D) Withheld to avoid disclosing figures for individual companies.   (*) Data not published.

TABLE 1. TCC GROUP 339—Percent Distribution of Geographic Division of Origin and Distance Shipped, by Means of Transport: 1972

Geographic division of origin [1] and distance shipped [2]	Number	Percent distribution by means of transport							
		All means of transport	Rail	Motor carrier	Private truck	Air	Water	Other	Unknown
TONS OF SHIPMENTS	(thousands of tons)								
U.S. TOTAL	3 353	100.0	35.8	50.1	13.3	.1	.3	.1	.1
NEW ENGLAND.............	75	100.0	5.1	48.9	45.7	.1	-	.1	-
UNDER 100 MILES.......	30	100.0	-	43.9	55.9	-	-	.1	-
100 TO 199 MILES......	22	100.0	12.4	44.1	43.5	.1	-	-	-
200 TO 299 MILES......	5	100.0	-	49.5	49.7	.3	-	-	.5
300 TO 499 MILES......	5	100.0	-	44.0	56.0	-	-	-	-
500 TO 999 MILES......	5	100.0	-	66.6	32.9	.1	-	.3	-
1000 TO 1499 MILES....	2	100.0	-	98.7	-	1.3	-	-	-
1500 MILES OR OVER....	3	100.0	29.1	69.9	-	.9	-	.1	-
MIDDLE ATLANTIC.........	414	100.0	29.2	54.5	14.4	-	1.7	-	.2
UNDER 100 MILES.......	108	100.0	42.1	37.9	19.4	-	-	-	.5
100 TO 199 MILES......	56	100.0	2.3	70.1	27.6	-	-	-	-
200 TO 299 MILES......	88	100.0	30.3	48.7	21.0	-	-	-	-
300 TO 499 MILES......	92	100.0	20.3	77.0	2.7	-	-	-	-
500 TO 999 MILES......	53	100.0	50.4	46.3	2.9	-	-	-	.4
1000 TO 1499 MILES....	6	100.0	8.9	63.0	7.7	-	20.5	-	-
1500 MILES OR OVER....	8	100.0	8.4	23.3	-	-	68.3	-	-
EAST NORTH CENTRAL......	1 933	100.0	22.0	65.2	12.3	.1	.2	.1	.1
UNDER 100 MILES.......	406	100.0	4.8	70.7	24.2	-	-	.2	.1
100 TO 199 MILES......	728	100.0	26.2	61.7	12.0	-	-	-	.1
200 TO 299 MILES......	355	100.0	29.0	61.5	9.5	-	-	-	.1
300 TO 499 MILES......	292	100.0	18.8	74.9	5.6	.2	-	-	.6
500 TO 999 MILES......	140	100.0	37.4	57.6	1.4	.9	2.6	-	-
1000 TO 1499 MILES....	2	100.0	5.5	91.7	-	2.8	-	-	-
1500 MILES OR OVER....	8	100.0	53.2	44.7	1.2	.8	-	-	-
PACIFIC.................	38	100.0	3.2	53.6	30.7	2.0	1.1	9.3	.1
UNDER 100 MILES.......	13	100.0	-	13.2	73.7	.2	-	13.0	-
100 TO 199 MILES......	1	100.0	-	81.0	19.0	-	-	-	-
200 TO 299 MILES......	-	100.0	-	99.6	-	-	-	.4	-
300 TO 499 MILES......	2	100.0	-	80.2	18.4	.1	-	1.3	-
500 TO 999 MILES......	4	100.0	24.6	63.2	11.3	.6	-	.4	-
1000 TO 1499 MILES....	3	100.0	-	85.7	12.0	1.6	-	.6	-
1500 MILES OR OVER....	12	100.0	.8	73.8	2.3	5.3	3.2	14.2	.4
TON-MILES OF SHIPMENTS	(millions of ton-miles)								
U.S. TOTAL	1 162	100.0	50.7	40.5	6.5	.3	1.6	.3	.1
NEW ENGLAND.............	22	100.0	14.6	61.9	22.7	.6	-	.1	-
UNDER 100 MILES.......	1	100.0	-	44.9	55.0	-	-	.1	-
100 TO 199 MILES......	3	100.0	15.0	43.7	41.2	.1	-	-	-
200 TO 299 MILES......	1	100.0	-	51.0	48.2	.3	-	-	.6
300 TO 499 MILES......	1	100.0	-	51.2	48.8	-	-	-	-
500 TO 999 MILES......	3	100.0	-	63.5	36.1	.2	-	.3	-
1000 TO 1499 MILES....	3	100.0	-	98.5	-	1.5	-	-	-
1500 MILES OR OVER....	7	100.0	36.0	62.8	-	1.1	-	.2	-
MIDDLE ATLANTIC.........	135	100.0	26.9	54.8	7.2	-	11.1	-	.1
UNDER 100 MILES.......	3	100.0	16.8	58.8	24.2	-	-	-	.2
100 TO 199 MILES......	8	100.0	1.6	72.5	25.8	-	-	-	-
200 TO 299 MILES......	21	100.0	31.9	48.2	19.9	-	-	-	-
300 TO 499 MILES......	39	100.0	20.8	76.5	2.7	-	-	-	-
500 TO 999 MILES......	36	100.0	51.4	45.7	2.6	-	-	-	.3
1000 TO 1499 MILES....	8	100.0	8.8	64.3	6.6	-	20.3	-	-
1500 MILES OR OVER....	18	100.0	6.3	22.5	-	-	71.1	-	-
EAST NORTH CENTRAL......	450	100.0	28.1	63.1	7.8	.3	.5	-	.2
UNDER 100 MILES.......	23	100.0	6.0	71.8	22.0	-	-	.1	.1
100 TO 199 MILES......	109	100.0	26.0	61.6	12.4	-	-	-	-
200 TO 299 MILES......	86	100.0	27.8	62.1	10.0	-	-	-	-
300 TO 499 MILES......	108	100.0	17.3	75.9	5.8	.2	-	-	.8
500 TO 999 MILES......	104	100.0	44.2	51.6	1.2	1.0	2.0	-	-
1000 TO 1499 MILES....	2	100.0	5.2	91.3	-	3.5	-	-	-
1500 MILES OR OVER....	15	100.0	50.9	46.9	1.3	.8	-	-	-
PACIFIC.................	34	100.0	3.4	72.3	6.0	4.2	2.9	10.9	.2
UNDER 100 MILES.......	-	100.0	-	9.4	72.6	.1	-	17.9	-
100 TO 199 MILES......	-	100.0	-	82.0	18.0	-	-	-	-
200 TO 299 MILES......	-	100.0	-	99.7	-	-	-	.3	-
300 TO 499 MILES......	-	100.0	-	79.8	18.5	.2	-	1.5	-
500 TO 999 MILES......	3	100.0	27.7	59.6	11.9	.4	-	.4	-
1000 TO 1499 MILES....	4	100.0	-	87.7	9.9	1.8	-	.7	-
1500 MILES OR OVER....	25	100.0	.8	72.7	2.4	5.4	4.1	14.4	.3

See footnotes at end of table 4.

TABLE 2. **TCC GROUP 339—Percent Distribution of Geographic Division of Origin and Means of Transport, by Geographic Division of Destination: 1972**

Geographic division of origin [1] and means of transport	Number	Percent distribution by division of destination									
		U.S. total	New England	Middle Atlantic	East North Central	West North Central	South Atlantic	East South Central	West South Central	Mountain	Pacific
TONS OF SHIPMENTS	(thousands of tons)										
U.S. TOTAL	3 353	100.0	2.3	10.9	50.8	6.5	2.7	4.9	6.9	13.7	1.3
RAIL	1 201	100.0	.1	5.9	35.4	6.4	3.1	4.6	7.2	36.9	.6
MOTOR CARRIER	1 681	100.0	2.9	13.5	62.1	7.5	2.9	6.2	3.0	.9	1.1
PRIVATE TRUCK	447	100.0	6.2	14.1	51.7	3.2	.9	.6	20.7	-	2.6
AIR	3	100.0	31.2	20.5	15.8	1.0	13.0	1.6	5.7	5.2	6.0
WATER	10	100.0	3.7	-	-	-	-	33.3	11.8	-	51.2
OTHER	4	100.0	1.2	32.0	26.0	.6	.2	1.0	2.3	.2	36.6
UNKNOWN	3	100.0	-	64.0	34.0	.8	.2	-	1.0	-	-
NEW ENGLAND	75	100.0	42.9	40.5	5.0	1.9	3.7	-	3.3	.2	2.4
RAIL	3	100.0	-	72.7	-	-	-	-	-	-	27.3
MOTOR CARRIER	36	100.0	37.2	36.7	8.9	3.8	4.2	.1	6.6	.4	2.0
PRIVATE TRUCK	34	100.0	54.1	41.1	1.3	-	3.6	-	-	-	-
AIR	-	100.0	-	34.8	1.3	.1	4.0	1.3	28.8	-	29.7
WATER	-	100.0	-	-	-	-	-	-	-	-	-
OTHER	-	100.0	55.5	13.7	19.8	.2	2.4	-	1.1	-	7.4
UNKNOWN	-	100.0	3.9	96.1	-	-	-	-	-	-	-
MIDDLE ATLANTIC	414	100.0	4.5	40.7	41.9	4.8	3.5	1.3	1.2	.2	1.8
RAIL	121	100.0	-	25.2	59.4	10.6	2.6	1.3	.5	.6	-
MOTOR CARRIER	225	100.0	4.3	42.0	42.5	3.1	4.4	1.8	1.2	-	.8
PRIVATE TRUCK	59	100.0	15.2	71.5	9.5	-	2.7	.1	1.0	-	-
AIR	-	100.0	27.3	9.5	55.3	4.4	-	.1	-	-	3.3
WATER	6	100.0	-	-	-	-	-	-	18.7	-	81.3
OTHER	-	100.0	10.3	86.7	.3	.7	.6	-	1.2	-	.1
UNKNOWN	-	100.0	-	74.4	25.6	-	-	-	-	-	-
EAST NORTH CENTRAL	1 933	100.0	1.4	7.8	74.4	5.6	2.0	5.9	2.4	.1	.4
RAIL	425	100.0	.2	8.8	72.2	3.6	1.9	3.3	8.8	-	1.0
MOTOR CARRIER	1 261	100.0	1.9	8.4	71.9	7.0	2.3	7.5	.6	.1	.2
PRIVATE TRUCK	237	100.0	-	2.0	93.8	2.4	.4	1.1	.3	-	-
AIR	1	100.0	52.5	18.0	3.5	-	18.3	.2	.1	4.3	3.2
WATER	3	100.0	-	-	-	-	-	100.0	-	-	-
OTHER	-	100.0	-	6.6	91.9	.2	.3	.4	.3	-	.4
UNKNOWN	2	100.0	-	62.0	35.6	1.0	-	-	1.3	-	-
PACIFIC	38	100.0	1.8	10.7	14.7	2.5	2.9	1.0	6.5	2.0	57.9
RAIL	1	100.0	-	-	-	-	8.0	-	-	-	92.0
MOTOR CARRIER	20	100.0	1.4	11.4	23.2	4.6	4.6	1.6	11.8	3.2	38.2
PRIVATE TRUCK	11	100.0	-	1.1	1.2	-	-	-	-	.9	96.8
AIR	-	100.0	-	22.7	47.8	.8	7.1	6.0	8.4	1.8	5.3
WATER	-	100.0	100.0	-	-	-	-	-	-	-	-
OTHER	3	100.0	.4	40.5	8.8	.5	.1	-	.1	.2	49.4
UNKNOWN	-	100.0	-	-	100.0	-	-	-	-	-	-
TON-MILES OF SHIPMENTS	(millions of ton-miles)										
U.S. TOTAL	1 162	100.0	2.5	9.3	29.2	7.9	4.9	5.6	9.9	26.5	4.2
RAIL	589	100.0	.1	2.0	16.9	7.5	5.8	4.3	10.0	51.3	2.0
MOTOR CARRIER	470	100.0	5.1	17.2	43.5	9.4	4.3	7.8	7.1	1.2	4.4
PRIVATE TRUCK	75	100.0	3.3	13.5	44.9	3.1	2.3	1.2	28.3	.1	3.2
AIR	3	100.0	24.9	20.0	22.0	.9	9.2	2.4	4.8	6.6	9.2
WATER	18	100.0	5.7	-	-	-	-	11.3	9.1	-	74.0
OTHER	4	100.0	1.1	76.7	15.2	.7	.3	.5	.8	.2	4.6
UNKNOWN	1	100.0	-	73.2	22.6	1.6	-	-	2.6	-	-
NEW ENGLAND	22	100.0	6.7	27.1	10.6	7.0	9.2	.1	16.8	1.5	21.0
RAIL	3	100.0	-	17.1	-	-	-	-	-	-	82.9
MOTOR CARRIER	13	100.0	4.5	18.7	14.4	11.3	8.0	.2	26.8	2.4	13.6
PRIVATE TRUCK	5	100.0	17.4	56.8	7.3	-	18.5	-	-	-	-
AIR	-	100.0	-	5.1	.6	.1	2.5	.9	32.6	-	58.3
WATER	-	100.0	-	-	-	-	-	-	-	-	-
OTHER	-	100.0	4.8	3.8	36.6	.5	4.0	-	3.9	-	46.4
UNKNOWN	-	100.0	.7	99.3	-	-	-	-	-	-	-
MIDDLE ATLANTIC	135	100.0	3.6	14.6	44.2	12.5	4.1	2.8	4.4	1.0	12.8
RAIL	36	100.0	-	1.4	55.9	28.5	6.1	2.8	1.9	3.3	-
MOTOR CARRIER	74	100.0	4.3	18.7	50.6	8.9	4.3	3.7	4.1	.2	5.3
PRIVATE TRUCK	9	100.0	16.8	55.5	20.0	-	1.0	.3	6.5	-	-
AIR	-	100.0	17.1	1.0	59.4	7.9	-	.2	-	-	14.4
WATER	15	100.0	-	-	-	-	-	-	10.9	-	89.1
OTHER	-	100.0	39.4	33.4	1.7	5.4	.9	-	16.6	-	2.6
UNKNOWN	-	100.0	-	6.4	93.6	-	-	-	-	-	-
EAST NORTH CENTRAL	450	100.0	4.6	11.8	50.3	7.6	3.2	9.4	9.5	.5	3.2
RAIL	126	100.0	.6	8.6	44.9	3.3	1.8	6.5	28.4	-	6.1
MOTOR CARRIER	284	100.0	6.8	13.9	49.1	10.1	4.0	10.9	2.3	.7	2.2
PRIVATE TRUCK	35	100.0	-	4.4	85.3	4.0	1.9	2.6	1.3	-	.6
AIR	1	100.0	59.6	10.0	1.3	-	13.2	.1	.1	7.8	8.0
WATER	2	100.0	-	-	-	-	-	100.0	-	-	-
OTHER	-	100.0	-	33.4	52.5	.6	2.5	1.2	2.8	-	7.0
UNKNOWN	-	100.0	-	87.8	7.1	1.9	-	-	3.1	-	-
PACIFIC	34	100.0	5.1	26.6	28.7	3.6	7.3	2.1	9.6	1.3	15.8
RAIL	1	100.0	-	-	-	-	16.3	-	-	-	83.7
MOTOR CARRIER	25	100.0	2.9	21.7	33.4	4.8	8.8	2.5	12.8	1.6	11.5
PRIVATE TRUCK	2	100.0	-	14.6	13.0	-	-	-	.1	2.7	69.6
AIR	1	100.0	-	29.3	48.1	.7	8.4	5.6	6.2	.6	1.0
WATER	1	100.0	100.0	-	-	-	-	-	-	-	-
OTHER	3	100.0	1.0	80.7	13.8	.6	.2	-	.1	.1	3.5
UNKNOWN	-	100.0	-	-	100.0	-	-	-	-	-	-

See footnotes at end of table 4.

TABLE 3. **TCC GROUP 339**—Percent Distribution of Geographic Division of Destination and Means of Transport, by Geographic Division of Origin: 1972

Geographic division of destination and means of transport	Number	Percent distribution by division of origin [1]									
		U.S. total	New England	Middle Atlantic	East North Central	West North Central	South Atlantic	East South Central	West South Central	Mountain	Pacific
TONS OF SHIPMENTS	(thousands of tons)										
U.S. TOTAL.............	3 353	100.0	2.3	12.4	57.7	(D)	(D)	(D)	(D)	(D)	1.1
RAIL...............	1 201	100.0	.3	10.1	35.4	(D)	(D)	(D)	(D)	(D)	.1
MOTOR CARRIER.........	1 681	100.0	2.2	13.4	75.0	(D)	(D)	(D)	(D)	(D)	1.2
PRIVATE TRUCK.........	447	100.0	7.7	13.3	53.2	(D)	(D)	(D)	(D)	(D)	2.6
AIR................	3	100.0	3.2	.9	57.8	(D)	(D)	(D)	(D)	(D)	22.2
WATER..............	10	100.0	-	63.0	33.3	(D)	(D)	(D)	(D)	(D)	3.7
OTHER..............	4	100.0	1.3	.9	20.0	(D)	(D)	(D)	(D)	(D)	72.9
UNKNOWN............	3	100.0	.8	21.1	76.7	(D)	(D)	(D)	(D)	(D)	1.2
NEW ENGLAND............	78	100.0	41.3	23.9	33.7	(D)	(D)	(D)	(D)	(D)	.9
RAIL...............	-	100.0	-	-	100.0	(D)	(D)	(D)	(D)	(D)	-
MOTOR CARRIER.........	48	100.0	28.4	20.0	50.5	(D)	(D)	(D)	(D)	(D)	.6
PRIVATE TRUCK.........	27	100.0	67.3	32.7	-	(D)	(D)	(D)	(D)	(D)	-
AIR................	1	100.0	-	.8	97.1	(D)	(D)	(D)	(D)	(D)	-
WATER..............	-	100.0	-	-	-	(D)	(D)	(D)	(D)	(D)	100.0
OTHER..............	-	100.0	60.2	7.7	-	(D)	(D)	(D)	(D)	(D)	27.2
UNKNOWN............	-	100.0	100.0	-	-	(D)	(D)	(D)	(D)	(D)	
MIDDLE ATLANTIC.........	365	100.0	8.4	46.1	41.2	(D)	(D)	(D)	(D)	(D)	1.1
RAIL...............	70	100.0	4.0	43.0	53.0	(D)	(D)	(D)	(D)	(D)	-
MOTOR CARRIER.........	227	100.0	6.0	41.8	46.7	(D)	(D)	(D)	(D)	(D)	1.0
PRIVATE TRUCK.........	62	100.0	22.5	67.7	7.4	(D)	(D)	(D)	(D)	(D)	.2
AIR................	-	100.0	5.4	.4	50.6	(D)	(D)	(D)	(D)	(D)	24.5
WATER..............	-	100.0	-	-	-	(D)	(D)	(D)	(D)	(D)	-
OTHER..............	1	100.0	.5	2.4	4.1	(D)	(D)	(D)	(D)	(D)	92.4
UNKNOWN............	2	100.0	1.1	24.5	74.4	(D)	(D)	(D)	(D)	(D)	-
EAST NORTH CENTRAL......	1 704	100.0	.2	10.2	84.4	(D)	(D)	(D)	(D)	(D)	.3
RAIL...............	425	100.0	-	16.9	72.2	(D)	(D)	(D)	(D)	(D)	-
MOTOR CARRIER.........	1 045	100.0	.3	9.2	86.8	(D)	(D)	(D)	(D)	(D)	.5
PRIVATE TRUCK.........	231	100.0	.2	2.4	96.4	(D)	(D)	(D)	(D)	(D)	.1
AIR................	-	100.0	.3	3.2	12.8	(D)	(D)	(D)	(D)	(D)	67.3
WATER..............	-	100.0	-	-	-	(D)	(D)	(D)	(D)	(D)	-
OTHER..............	1	100.0	1.0	-	70.7	(D)	(D)	(D)	(D)	(D)	24.7
UNKNOWN............	1	100.0	-	15.9	80.4	(D)	(D)	(D)	(D)	(D)	3.5
WEST NORTH CENTRAL......	216	100.0	.7	9.2	50.4	(D)	(D)	(D)	(D)	(D)	.4
RAIL...............	76	100.0	-	16.7	20.2	(D)	(D)	(D)	(D)	(D)	-
MOTOR CARRIER.........	125	100.0	1.1	5.6	70.1	(D)	(D)	(D)	(D)	(D)	.8
PRIVATE TRUCK.........	14	100.0	-	-	40.1	(D)	(D)	(D)	(D)	(D)	-
AIR................	-	100.0	.4	4.3	-	(D)	(D)	(D)	(D)	(D)	19.5
WATER..............	-	100.0	-	-	-	(D)	(D)	(D)	(D)	(D)	-
OTHER..............	-	100.0	.4	1.2	6.1	(D)	(D)	(D)	(D)	(D)	60.8
UNKNOWN............	-	100.0	-	-	100.0	(D)	(D)	(D)	(D)	(D)	-
SOUTH ATLANTIC.........	89	100.0	3.1	16.4	43.4	(D)	(D)	(D)	(D)	(D)	1.2
RAIL...............	37	100.0	-	8.3	22.2	(D)	(D)	(D)	(D)	(D)	.3
MOTOR CARRIER.........	47	100.0	3.2	20.7	61.0	(D)	(D)	(D)	(D)	(D)	2.0
PRIVATE TRUCK.........	3	100.0	31.7	42.1	24.5	(D)	(D)	(D)	(D)	(D)	-
AIR................	-	100.0	1.0	-	81.3	(D)	(D)	(D)	(D)	(D)	12.0
WATER..............	-	100.0	-	-	-	(D)	(D)	(D)	(D)	(D)	-
OTHER..............	-	100.0	15.1	2.7	25.9	(D)	(D)	(D)	(D)	(D)	31.7
UNKNOWN............	-	100.0	-	-	-	(D)	(D)	(D)	(D)	(D)	-
EAST SOUTH CENTRAL......	165	100.0	-	3.4	69.3	(D)	(D)	(D)	(D)	(D)	.2
RAIL...............	54	100.0	-	2.8	25.7	(D)	(D)	(D)	(D)	(D)	-
MOTOR CARRIER.........	103	100.0	-	3.8	90.6	(D)	(D)	(D)	(D)	(D)	.3
PRIVATE TRUCK.........	2	100.0	-	1.2	98.8	(D)	(D)	(D)	(D)	(D)	-
AIR................	-	100.0	2.5	.1	5.9	(D)	(D)	(D)	(D)	(D)	83.6
WATER..............	3	100.0	-	-	100.0	(D)	(D)	(D)	(D)	(D)	-
OTHER..............	-	100.0	-	-	7.8	(D)	(D)	(D)	(D)	(D)	-
UNKNOWN............	-	100.0	-	-	-	(D)	(D)	(D)	(D)	(D)	-
WEST SOUTH CENTRAL......	230	100.0	1.1	2.2	19.9	(D)	(D)	(D)	(D)	(D)	1.1
RAIL...............	86	100.0	-	.7	43.5	(D)	(D)	(D)	(D)	(D)	-
MOTOR CARRIER.........	50	100.0	4.8	5.2	15.3	(D)	(D)	(D)	(D)	(D)	4.8
PRIVATE TRUCK.........	92	100.0	-	.6	.8	(D)	(D)	(D)	(D)	(D)	-
AIR................	-	100.0	16.0	-	.8	(D)	(D)	(D)	(D)	(D)	32.8
WATER..............	1	100.0	-	100.0	-	(D)	(D)	(D)	(D)	(D)	-
OTHER..............	-	100.0	.6	.5	2.7	(D)	(D)	(D)	(D)	(D)	3.5
UNKNOWN............	-	100.0	-	-	100.0	(D)	(D)	(D)	(D)	(D)	-
MOUNTAIN..............	458	100.0	-	.2	.4	(D)	(D)	(D)	(D)	(D)	.2
RAIL...............	442	100.0	-	.2	-	(D)	(D)	(D)	(D)	(D)	-
MOTOR CARRIER.........	15	100.0	1.1	.7	10.5	(D)	(D)	(D)	(D)	(D)	4.2
PRIVATE TRUCK.........	-	100.0	-	-	11.2	(D)	(D)	(D)	(D)	(D)	63.4
AIR................	-	100.0	-	-	47.4	(D)	(D)	(D)	(D)	(D)	7.8
WATER..............	-	100.0	-	-	-	(D)	(D)	(D)	(D)	(D)	-
OTHER..............	-	100.0	-	-	-	(D)	(D)	(D)	(D)	(D)	72.9
UNKNOWN............	-	100.0	-	-	-	(D)	(D)	(D)	(D)	(D)	-
PACIFIC...............	44	100.0	4.1	16.5	17.4	(D)	(D)	(D)	(D)	(D)	49.8
RAIL...............	6	100.0	15.3	-	64.3	(D)	(D)	(D)	(D)	(D)	16.5
MOTOR CARRIER.........	18	100.0	4.1	9.4	17.2	(D)	(D)	(D)	(D)	(D)	43.1
PRIVATE TRUCK.........	11	100.0	-	-	.9	(D)	(D)	(D)	(D)	(D)	96.5
AIR................	-	100.0	15.6	.5	30.8	(D)	(D)	(D)	(D)	(D)	19.6
WATER..............	5	100.0	-	100.0	-	(D)	(D)	(D)	(D)	(D)	-
OTHER..............	1	100.0	.3	-	.2	(D)	(D)	(D)	(D)	(D)	98.4
UNKNOWN............	-	100.0	-	-	-	(D)	(D)	(D)	(D)	(D)	-

See footnotes at end of table 4.

TABLE 3. **TCC GROUP 339—Percent Distribution of Geographic Division of Destination and Means of Transport, by Geographic Division of Origin: 1972**—Continued

Geographic division of destination and means of transport	Number	Percent distribution by division of origin [1]									
		U.S. total	New England	Middle Atlantic	East North Central	West North Central	South Atlantic	East South Central	West South Central	Mountain	Pacific
TON-MILES OF SHIPMENTS	(millions of ton-miles)										
U.S. TOTAL..............	1 162	100.0	1.9	11.7	38.8	(D)	(D)	(D)	(D)	(D)	3.0
RAIL...................	589	100.0	.6	6.2	21.5	(D)	(D)	(D)	(D)	(D)	.2
MOTOR CARRIER..........	470	100.0	2.9	15.8	60.3	(D)	(D)	(D)	(D)	(D)	5.4
PRIVATE TRUCK..........	75	100.0	6.7	12.9	47.0	(D)	(D)	(D)	(D)	(D)	2.8
AIR....................	3	100.0	3.8	.5	40.5	(D)	(D)	(D)	(D)	(D)	39.6
WATER..................	18	100.0	-	83.0	11.3	(D)	(D)	(D)	(D)	(D)	5.7
OTHER..................	4	100.0	.6	.1	2.3	(D)	(D)	(D)	(D)	(D)	93.8
UNKNOWN................	1	100.0	.6	10.7	81.9	(D)	(D)	(D)	(D)	(D)	6.7
NEW ENGLAND............	29	100.0	5.1	16.6	71.4	(D)	(D)	(D)	(D)	(D)	6.1
RAIL...................	-	100.0	-	-	100.0	(D)	(D)	(D)	(D)	(D)	-
MOTOR CARRIER..........	24	100.0	2.6	13.3	80.3	(D)	(D)	(D)	(D)	(D)	3.0
PRIVATE TRUCK..........	2	100.0	35.0	65.0	-	(D)	(D)	(D)	(D)	(D)	-
AIR....................	-	100.0	-	.3	97.0	(D)	(D)	(D)	(D)	(D)	-
WATER..................	1	100.0	-	-	-	(D)	(D)	(D)	(D)	(D)	100.0
OTHER..................	-	100.0	2.6	3.2	-	(D)	(D)	(D)	(D)	(D)	87.1
UNKNOWN................	-	100.0	100.0	-	-	(D)	(D)	(D)	(D)	(D)	-
MIDDLE ATLANTIC........	107	100.0	5.6	18.4	49.2	(D)	(D)	(D)	(D)	(D)	8.6
RAIL...................	11	100.0	4.7	4.4	91.0	(D)	(D)	(D)	(D)	(D)	-
MOTOR CARRIER..........	80	100.0	3.2	17.2	48.8	(D)	(D)	(D)	(D)	(D)	6.8
PRIVATE TRUCK..........	10	100.0	28.3	53.1	15.2	(D)	(D)	(D)	(D)	(D)	3.0
AIR....................	-	100.0	1.0	-	20.2	(D)	(D)	(D)	(D)	(D)	58.1
WATER..................	-	100.0	-	-	-	(D)	(D)	(D)	(D)	(D)	-
OTHER..................	3	100.0	-	-	1.0	(D)	(D)	(D)	(D)	(D)	98.6
UNKNOWN................	-	100.0	.8	.9	98.3	(D)	(D)	(D)	(D)	(D)	-
EAST NORTH CENTRAL......	339	100.0	.7	17.7	66.7	(D)	(D)	(D)	(D)	(D)	2.9
RAIL...................	99	100.0	-	20.5	57.1	(D)	(D)	(D)	(D)	(D)	-
MOTOR CARRIER..........	204	100.0	1.0	18.4	68.1	(D)	(D)	(D)	(D)	(D)	4.1
PRIVATE TRUCK..........	33	100.0	1.1	5.7	89.2	(D)	(D)	(D)	(D)	(D)	.8
AIR....................	-	100.0	.1	1.2	2.4	(D)	(D)	(D)	(D)	(D)	86.5
WATER..................	-	100.0	-	-	-	(D)	(D)	(D)	(D)	(D)	-
OTHER..................	-	100.0	1.5	-	8.0	(D)	(D)	(D)	(D)	(D)	85.2
UNKNOWN................	-	100.0	-	44.2	25.7	(D)	(D)	(D)	(D)	(D)	29.6
WEST NORTH CENTRAL......	91	100.0	1.7	18.7	37.6	(D)	(D)	(D)	(D)	(D)	1.4
RAIL...................	44	100.0	-	23.5	9.3	(D)	(D)	(D)	(D)	(D)	-
MOTOR CARRIER..........	44	100.0	3.5	14.8	64.6	(D)	(D)	(D)	(D)	(D)	2.8
PRIVATE TRUCK..........	2	100.0	-	-	60.1	(D)	(D)	(D)	(D)	(D)	-
AIR....................	-	100.0	.4	4.0	-	(D)	(D)	(D)	(D)	(D)	28.5
WATER..................	-	100.0	-	-	-	(D)	(D)	(D)	(D)	(D)	-
OTHER..................	-	100.0	.5	.8	2.0	(D)	(D)	(D)	(D)	(D)	84.2
UNKNOWN................	-	100.0	-	-	100.0	(D)	(D)	(D)	(D)	(D)	-
SOUTH ATLANTIC..........	56	100.0	3.6	9.7	25.5	(D)	(D)	(D)	(D)	(D)	4.5
RAIL...................	34	100.0	-	6.5	6.5	(D)	(D)	(D)	(D)	(D)	.6
MOTOR CARRIER..........	20	100.0	5.5	15.6	55.9	(D)	(D)	(D)	(D)	(D)	11.0
PRIVATE TRUCK..........	1	100.0	55.1	6.0	38.7	(D)	(D)	(D)	(D)	(D)	-
AIR....................	-	100.0	1.0	-	57.9	(D)	(D)	(D)	(D)	(D)	36.1
WATER..................	-	100.0	-	-	-	(D)	(D)	(D)	(D)	(D)	-
OTHER..................	-	100.0	7.8	.3	18.7	(D)	(D)	(D)	(D)	(D)	57.1
UNKNOWN................	-	100.0	-	-	-	(D)	(D)	(D)	(D)	(D)	-
EAST SOUTH CENTRAL......	65	100.0	-	5.8	64.4	(D)	(D)	(D)	(D)	(D)	1.1
RAIL...................	25	100.0	-	4.0	31.9	(D)	(D)	(D)	(D)	(D)	-
MOTOR CARRIER..........	36	100.0	.1	7.4	84.4	(D)	(D)	(D)	(D)	(D)	1.7
PRIVATE TRUCK..........	-	100.0	-	2.8	97.2	(D)	(D)	(D)	(D)	(D)	-
AIR....................	-	100.0	1.4	-	1.1	(D)	(D)	(D)	(D)	(D)	94.0
WATER..................	2	100.0	-	-	100.0	(D)	(D)	(D)	(D)	(D)	-
OTHER..................	-	100.0	-	-	5.8	(D)	(D)	(D)	(D)	(D)	-
UNKNOWN................	-	100.0	-	-	-	(D)	(D)	(D)	(D)	(D)	-
WEST SOUTH CENTRAL......	115	100.0	3.2	5.2	37.2	(D)	(D)	(D)	(D)	(D)	2.9
RAIL...................	58	100.0	-	1.2	61.0	(D)	(D)	(D)	(D)	(D)	-
MOTOR CARRIER..........	33	100.0	11.1	9.2	19.6	(D)	(D)	(D)	(D)	(D)	9.8
PRIVATE TRUCK..........	21	100.0	-	3.0	2.2	(D)	(D)	(D)	(D)	(D)	-
AIR....................	-	100.0	25.8	-	.9	(D)	(D)	(D)	(D)	(D)	51.8
WATER..................	1	100.0	-	100.0	-	(D)	(D)	(D)	(D)	(D)	-
OTHER..................	-	100.0	2.9	1.9	7.9	(D)	(D)	(D)	(D)	(D)	14.3
UNKNOWN................	-	100.0	-	-	100.0	(D)	(D)	(D)	(D)	(D)	-
MOUNTAIN...............	308	100.0	.1	.4	.7	(D)	(D)	(D)	(D)	(D)	.2
RAIL...................	302	100.0	-	.4	-	(D)	(D)	(D)	(D)	(D)	-
MOTOR CARRIER..........	5	100.0	5.8	2.9	36.0	(D)	(D)	(D)	(D)	(D)	7.0
PRIVATE TRUCK..........	-	100.0	-	-	19.1	(D)	(D)	(D)	(D)	(D)	73.1
AIR....................	-	100.0	-	-	47.7	(D)	(D)	(D)	(D)	(D)	3.6
WATER..................	-	100.0	-	-	-	(D)	(D)	(D)	(D)	(D)	-
OTHER..................	-	100.0	-	-	-	(D)	(D)	(D)	(D)	(D)	62.3
UNKNOWN................	-	100.0	-	-	-	(D)	(D)	(D)	(D)	(D)	-
PACIFIC................	48	100.0	9.5	35.4	29.1	(D)	(D)	(D)	(D)	(D)	11.3
RAIL...................	11	100.0	22.7	-	65.0	(D)	(D)	(D)	(D)	(D)	8.5
MOTOR CARRIER..........	20	100.0	9.1	18.9	29.9	(D)	(D)	(D)	(D)	(D)	14.0
PRIVATE TRUCK..........	2	100.0	-	-	8.3	(D)	(D)	(D)	(D)	(D)	60.4
AIR....................	-	100.0	24.0	.7	35.2	(D)	(D)	(D)	(D)	(D)	4.2
WATER..................	13	100.0	-	100.0	-	(D)	(D)	(D)	(D)	(D)	-
OTHER..................	-	100.0	6.3	.1	3.5	(D)	(D)	(D)	(D)	(D)	71.6
UNKNOWN................	-	100.0	-	-	-	(D)	(D)	(D)	(D)	(D)	-

See footnotes at end of table 4.

TABLE 4. **TCC GROUP 339—Percent Distribution of Distance Shipped and Weight of Shipment, by Means of Transport: 1972**

Distance shipped and weight of shipment [2] [3]	Number	Percent distribution by means of transport							
		All means of transport	Rail	Motor carrier	Private truck	Air	Water	Other	Unknown
TONS OF SHIPMENTS	(thousands of tons)								
U.S. TOTAL..........	3 212	100.0	35.6	50.9	12.9	.1	.3	.2	.1
UNDER 100 MILES.........	499	100.0	6.8	67.5	24.9	-	-	.5	.2
UNDER 1000 POUNDS.....	10	100.0	-	40.4	50.4	.2	-	8.8	.2
1000 TO 9999 POUNDS...	90	100.0	-	40.0	58.0	-	-	1.8	.2
10000 TO 29999 POUNDS.	68	100.0	.2	73.5	26.3	-	-	-	-
30000 TO 59999 POUNDS.	277	100.0	-	84.2	15.4	-	-	-	.4
60000 TO 89999 POUNDS.	14	100.0	32.9	64.8	2.3	-	-	-	-
90000 POUNDS AND OVER.	37	100.0	77.5	8.1	14.4	-	-	-	-
100 TO 199 MILES........	828	100.0	23.5	62.1	14.3	-	-	-	-
UNDER 1000 POUNDS.....	4	100.0	-	91.6	5.0	1.4	-	1.9	.1
1000 TO 9999 POUNDS...	46	100.0	.2	77.0	22.7	-	-	.1	-
10000 TO 29999 POUNDS.	91	100.0	.3	75.2	24.5	-	-	-	-
30000 TO 59999 POUNDS.	452	100.0	.2	80.9	18.8	-	-	-	.1
60000 TO 89999 POUNDS.	61	100.0	40.1	59.7	.3	-	-	-	-
90000 POUNDS AND OVER.	171	100.0	98.7	1.3	-	-	-	-	-
200 TO 299 MILES........	565	100.0	22.7	52.1	25.2	-	-	-	-
UNDER 1000 POUNDS.....	4	100.0	-	92.6	4.0	.9	-	2.5	-
1000 TO 9999 POUNDS...	26	100.0	-	89.1	10.8	-	-	-	.1
10000 TO 29999 POUNDS.	46	100.0	1.5	88.5	10.0	-	-	-	-
30000 TO 59999 POUNDS.	271	100.0	.6	80.8	18.6	-	-	-	-
60000 TO 89999 POUNDS.	17	100.0	88.7	11.3	-	-	-	-	-
90000 POUNDS AND OVER.	198	100.0	55.5	2.2	42.3	-	-	-	-
300 TO 499 MILES........	477	100.0	31.7	63.1	4.6	.1	-	-	.4
UNDER 1000 POUNDS.....	4	100.0	.1	93.7	.1	3.7	-	2.3	.1
1000 TO 9999 POUNDS...	27	100.0	-	94.8	4.6	.4	-	.2	-
10000 TO 29999 POUNDS.	64	100.0	.8	89.8	8.9	.4	-	-	-
30000 TO 59999 POUNDS.	227	100.0	2.0	90.7	6.6	-	-	-	.8
60000 TO 89999 POUNDS.	40	100.0	83.5	16.5	-	-	-	-	-
90000 POUNDS AND OVER.	112	100.0	100.0	-	-	-	-	-	-
500 TO 999 MILES........	748	100.0	79.6	19.1	.8	.1	.5	-	-
UNDER 1000 POUNDS.....	6	100.0	-	94.6	1.0	2.2	-	1.6	.5
1000 TO 9999 POUNDS...	27	100.0	.4	94.1	4.5	.9	-	-	.1
10000 TO 29999 POUNDS.	23	100.0	-	89.0	10.1	-	-	-	.9
30000 TO 59999 POUNDS.	100	100.0	14.0	84.0	2.0	-	-	-	-
60000 TO 89999 POUNDS.	7	100.0	36.4	16.2	-	-	47.4	-	-
90000 POUNDS AND OVER.	583	100.0	99.1	.9	-	-	-	-	-
1000 TO 1499 MILES......	53	100.0	62.2	36.4	.8	.6	-	.1	-
UNDER 1000 POUNDS.....	2	100.0	-	85.4	1.3	12.1	-	1.3	-
1000 TO 9999 POUNDS...	6	100.0	-	100.0	-	-	-	-	-
10000 TO 29999 POUNDS.	5	100.0	2.6	97.4	-	-	-	-	-
30000 TO 59999 POUNDS.	14	100.0	55.9	41.3	2.8	-	-	-	-
60000 TO 89999 POUNDS.	-	100.0	-	-	-	-	-	-	-
90000 POUNDS AND OVER.	24	100.0	100.0	-	-	-	-	-	-
1500 MILES OR OVER......	41	100.0	16.0	64.3	.9	2.0	12.3	4.4	.1
UNDER 1000 POUNDS.....	2	100.0	3.5	69.5	.3	19.3	-	7.4	-
1000 TO 9999 POUNDS...	7	100.0	13.2	71.9	2.1	3.4	5.3	3.6	.6
10000 TO 29999 POUNDS.	3	100.0	9.6	83.8	6.6	-	-	-	-
30000 TO 59999 POUNDS.	18	100.0	24.5	68.3	-	-	-	7.2	-
60000 TO 89999 POUNDS.	2	100.0	31.6	68.4	-	-	-	-	-
90000 POUNDS AND OVER.	6	100.0	-	32.1	-	-	67.9	-	-
TON-MILES OF SHIPMENTS	(millions of ton-miles)								
U.S. TOTAL..........	1 129	100.0	51.1	40.7	6.3	.2	1.3	.4	.1
UNDER 100 MILES.........	27	100.0	5.7	71.1	22.5	-	-	.5	.1
UNDER 1000 POUNDS.....	-	100.0	-	42.7	49.9	.1	-	7.2	.1
1000 TO 9999 POUNDS...	4	100.0	-	40.6	57.1	-	-	2.1	.1
10000 TO 29999 POUNDS.	3	100.0	.1	78.1	21.8	-	-	-	-
30000 TO 59999 POUNDS.	15	100.0	-	86.4	13.5	-	-	-	.1
60000 TO 89999 POUNDS.	-	100.0	52.6	45.1	2.3	-	-	-	-
90000 POUNDS AND OVER.	1	100.0	77.6	11.0	11.4	-	-	-	-
100 TO 199 MILES........	122	100.0	23.7	61.9	14.4	-	-	-	-
UNDER 1000 POUNDS.....	-	100.0	-	91.5	4.9	1.7	-	1.7	.1
1000 TO 9999 POUNDS...	6	100.0	.2	77.7	22.0	-	-	-	-
10000 TO 29999 POUNDS.	12	100.0	.2	77.2	22.6	-	-	-	-
30000 TO 59999 POUNDS.	67	100.0	.2	80.3	19.4	-	-	-	.1
60000 TO 89999 POUNDS.	9	100.0	44.8	54.9	.3	-	-	-	-
90000 POUNDS AND OVER.	24	100.0	98.9	1.1	-	-	-	-	-
200 TO 299 MILES........	136	100.0	22.8	52.7	24.5	-	-	-	-
UNDER 1000 POUNDS.....	1	100.0	-	92.9	3.8	.8	-	2.3	-
1000 TO 9999 POUNDS...	6	100.0	-	89.9	10.0	-	-	-	.1
10000 TO 29999 POUNDS.	12	100.0	1.3	88.2	10.6	-	-	-	-
30000 TO 59999 POUNDS.	65	100.0	.6	80.4	19.0	-	-	-	-
60000 TO 89999 POUNDS.	4	100.0	88.7	11.3	-	-	-	-	-
90000 POUNDS AND OVER.	46	100.0	57.2	2.2	40.6	-	-	-	-

See footnotes at end of table 4.

TABLE 4. TCC GROUP 339—Percent Distribution of Distance Shipped and Weight of Shipment, by Means of Transport: 1972—Continued

Distance shipped and weight of shipment [2] [3]	Number	Percent distribution by means of transport							
		All means of transport	Rail	Motor carrier	Private truck	Air	Water	Other	Unknown
TON-MILES OF SHIPMENTS	(millions of ton-miles)								
300 TO 499 MILES........	183	100.0	31.1	63.7	4.6	.1	-	-	.5
UNDER 1000 POUNDS.....	1	100.0	.2	93.8	.1	3.6	-	2.3	.1
1000 TO 9999 POUNDS...	10	100.0	-	93.9	5.4	.4	-	.3	-
10000 TO 29999 POUNDS.	24	100.0	.8	89.0	9.7	.5	-	-	-
30000 TO 59999 POUNDS.	90	100.0	2.1	90.9	6.1	-	-	-	1.0
60000 TO 89999 POUNDS.	14	100.0	82.9	17.1	-	-	-	-	-
90000 POUNDS AND OVER.	43	100.0	100.0	-	-	-	-	-	-
500 TO 999 MILES........	510	100.0	79.3	19.4	.8	.1	.4	-	-
UNDER 1000 POUNDS.....	4	100.0	-	94.4	1.0	2.3	-	1.8	.4
1000 TO 9999 POUNDS...	17	100.0	.4	94.0	4.3	1.1	-	-	.2
10000 TO 29999 POUNDS.	15	100.0	-	89.4	9.8	-	-	-	.8
30000 TO 59999 POUNDS.	70	100.0	13.8	83.9	2.3	-	-	-	-
60000 TO 89999 POUNDS.	5	100.0	41.4	19.9	-	-	38.7	-	-
90000 POUNDS AND OVER.	397	100.0	98.8	1.2	-	-	-	-	-
1000 TO 1499 MILES......	65	100.0	62.7	36.0	.7	.6	-	.1	-
UNDER 1000 POUNDS.....	3	100.0	-	85.4	1.0	12.3	-	1.3	-
1000 TO 9999 POUNDS...	7	100.0	-	100.0	-	-	-	-	-
10000 TO 29999 POUNDS.	5	100.0	2.4	97.6	-	-	-	-	-
30000 TO 59999 POUNDS.	16	100.0	50.8	46.7	2.5	-	-	-	-
60000 TO 89999 POUNDS.	-	100.0	-	-	-	-	-	-	-
90000 POUNDS AND OVER.	32	100.0	100.0	-	-	-	-	-	-
1500 MILES OR OVER......	83	100.0	14.7	63.2	1.0	2.0	14.6	4.4	.1
UNDER 1000 POUNDS.....	5	100.0	3.3	70.3	.4	18.6	-	7.4	-
1000 TO 9999 POUNDS...	16	100.0	15.0	69.8	2.2	3.5	6.2	2.8	.5
10000 TO 29999 POUNDS.	6	100.0	10.2	83.4	6.4	-	-	-	-
30000 TO 59999 POUNDS.	35	100.0	21.7	70.5	-	-	-	7.9	-
60000 TO 89999 POUNDS.	3	100.0	31.4	68.6	-	-	-	-	-
90000 POUNDS AND OVER.	14	100.0	-	25.6	-	-	74.4	-	-

Note : Detail may not add to total due to rounding. The introductory table shows the estimates of sampling variability for tons; sampling variability for ton-miles has not been estimated. See the map in the Introduction for the States comprising the geographic divisions of the United States.

Shipments excluded from the survey are those moving by pipeline (primarily petroleum products from refineries), parcel post shipments, and commodities moved by own power (motorized vehicles, aircraft, etc. or towed (prefabricated buildings, etc.). Local shipments (commodities shipped less than 25 miles from the plant) and shipments withing the same city are also excluded. Shipments to Alaska and Hawaii from the 48 conterminous States and the District of Columbia are included; however, no data were obtained for shipments originating in Alaska and Hawaii.

- Represents zero or rounds to zero.   (D) Withheld to avoid disclosing figures for individual companies.

[1] Production of this commodity is concentrated in the geographic divisions shown; figures and distributions for geographic divisions not shown are included in the total.

[2] Distances of shipments to foreign destinations are calculated only to the U.S. port of exit.

[3] Includes only shipments represented by bills of lading and invoices. Summary records which did not show individual weights of shipments are not included.

Food and Kindred Products, Tobacco Products

CONTENTS

[Page numbers listed here omit the State prefix number that appears as part of the number for each page]

TABLES   (The tables listed below are shown for each of the Transportation Commodity Classification groups in this report)

Comparisons of Tons and Ton-Miles of Shipments for Geographic Divisions of Origin and for
Sampling Variability: 1972 and 1967

1. Percent Distribution of Geographic Division of Origin and Distance Shipped, by Means of
Transport: 1972

2. Percent Distribution of Geographic Division of Origin and Means of Transport, by Geographic
Division of Destination: 1972

3. Percent Distribution of Geographic Division of Destination and Means of Transport, by Geographic
Division of Origin: 1972

4. Percent Distribution of Distance Shipped and Weight of Shipment, by Means of Transport: 1972

TCC 201. Meat: Fresh, Chilled, Frozen

Comparisons of Tons and Ton-Miles of Shipments for
Geographic Divisions of Origin and for Sampling Variability: 1972 and 1967

Geographic division of origin	Estimates				Relative sampling variability in tons (percent)	
	1972		1967		1972	1967
	Tons (thousands)	Ton-miles (millions)	Tons (thousands)	Ton-miles (millions)		
U.S. total	31,417	14,101	26,799	12,479	5.3	10.6
New England	106	14	1,117	214	29.9	(*)
Middle Atlantic	2,068	314	1,387	292	21.2	(*)
East North Central	5,481	1,724	5,395	1,886	26.3	(*)
West North Central	11,880	7,271	9,574	6,450	13.1	(*)
South Atlantic	3,581	945	3,063	858	13.3	(*)
East South Central	2,242	762	1,585	414	16.2	(*)
West South Central	3,344	1,966	1,884	872	12.5	(*)
Mountain	1,184	767	1,098	934	25.9	(*)
Pacific	1,526	334	1,696	559	21.9	(*)

(D) Withheld to avoid disclosing figures for individual companies.   (*) Data not published.

TABLE 1. **TCC GROUP 201—Percent Distribution of Geographic Division of Origin and Distance Shipped, by Means of Transport: 1972**

Geographic division of origin[1] and distance shipped[2]	Number	Percent distribution by means of transport							
		All means of transport	Rail	Motor carrier	Private truck	Air	Water	Other	Unknown
TONS OF SHIPMENTS	(thousands of tons)								
U.S. TOTAL..........	31 417	100.0	18.7	44.6	36.1	-	.1	.2	.3
NEW ENGLAND.............	106	100.0	2.8	44.8	50.5	-	1.9	-	-
UNDER 100 MILES.......	64	100.0	-	42.6	56.2	-	1.1	-	-
100 TO 199 MILES......	20	100.0	3.0	38.6	52.1	-	6.2	-	-
200 TO 299 MILES......	9	100.0	18.6	79.6	1.6	-	.2	-	-
300 TO 499 MILES......	7	100.0	-	56.9	43.1	-	-	-	-
500 TO 999 MILES......	3	100.0	-	10.2	89.8	-	-	-	-
1000 TO 1499 MILES....	-	100.0	-	-	-	-	-	-	-
1500 MILES OR OVER....	-	100.0	100.0	-	-	-	-	-	-
MIDDLE ATLANTIC.........	2 068	100.0	2.3	16.7	80.8	-	.1	-	-
UNDER 100 MILES.......	1 092	100.0	-	11.1	88.7	-	.2	-	-
100 TO 199 MILES......	616	100.0	-	11.0	89.0	-	-	-	-
200 TO 299 MILES......	142	100.0	2.3	24.5	73.2	-	-	-	-
300 TO 499 MILES......	96	100.0	45.2	24.7	30.1	-	-	-	-
500 TO 999 MILES......	90	100.0	1.3	76.8	21.9	-	-	-	.1
1000 TO 1499 MILES....	20	100.0	-	97.2	2.7	-	-	-	-
1500 MILES OR OVER....	8	100.0	-	95.5	4.3	-	-	-	-
EAST NORTH CENTRAL......	5 481	100.0	32.0	36.8	29.6	-	.2	.8	.6
UNDER 100 MILES.......	1 634	100.0	20.7	31.1	45.9	-	-	2.2	.1
100 TO 199 MILES......	1 406	100.0	42.7	26.7	28.7	-	.1	.1	1.8
200 TO 299 MILES......	600	100.0	17.6	46.3	35.2	-	.1	.5	.2
300 TO 499 MILES......	630	100.0	45.4	41.6	12.7	-	-	.1	.1
500 TO 999 MILES......	1 026	100.0	33.9	48.6	15.9	-	.9	.2	.5
1000 TO 1499 MILES....	79	100.0	18.4	70.7	10.8	.1	-	-	.1
1500 MILES OR OVER....	102	100.0	56.3	38.1	5.1	-	-	-	.6
WEST NORTH CENTRAL......	11 880	100.0	26.2	57.1	16.3	-	-	.1	.3
UNDER 100 MILES.......	1 424	100.0	10.9	31.0	58.0	-	-	.2	-
100 TO 199 MILES......	1 010	100.0	12.3	54.0	33.7	-	-	-	-
200 TO 299 MILES......	1 627	100.0	16.0	73.3	10.5	-	-	.2	-
300 TO 499 MILES......	1 916	100.0	29.5	62.3	8.0	-	-	-	.2
500 TO 999 MILES......	2 957	100.0	30.3	62.3	6.8	-	-	.1	.5
1000 TO 1499 MILES....	2 812	100.0	38.4	52.5	8.3	-	-	.2	.6
1500 MILES OR OVER....	131	100.0	26.5	68.3	5.1	-	-	-	-
SOUTH ATLANTIC..........	3 581	100.0	10.3	29.8	58.9	-	.7	.2	.1
UNDER 100 MILES.......	1 139	100.0	6.4	7.8	83.3	-	1.9	.6	-
100 TO 199 MILES......	858	100.0	14.8	24.0	61.2	-	-	-	-
200 TO 299 MILES......	386	100.0	6.1	45.9	47.3	-	.2	-	.5
300 TO 499 MILES......	732	100.0	14.9	41.4	43.6	-	-	-	.1
500 TO 999 MILES......	402	100.0	8.2	66.9	24.8	-	-	-	-
1000 TO 1499 MILES....	33	100.0	4.6	54.1	40.9	-	-	.4	-
1500 MILES OR OVER....	29	100.0	2.1	19.7	69.2	-	9.0	-	-
EAST SOUTH CENTRAL......	2 242	100.0	3.8	47.6	48.5	-	-	-	.1
UNDER 100 MILES.......	556	100.0	.6	14.3	85.1	-	-	-	-
100 TO 199 MILES......	580	100.0	5.3	21.8	72.9	-	-	-	-
200 TO 299 MILES......	232	100.0	4.4	45.3	50.3	-	-	-	-
300 TO 499 MILES......	357	100.0	6.0	84.5	9.6	-	-	-	.1
500 TO 999 MILES......	428	100.0	2.7	91.4	5.9	-	-	-	-
1000 TO 1499 MILES....	13	100.0	46.7	53.3	-	-	-	-	-
1500 MILES OR OVER....	73	100.0	2.2	75.5	18.6	-	-	-	3.7
WEST SOUTH CENTRAL......	3 344	100.0	5.0	45.5	49.2	-	-	-	.2
UNDER 100 MILES.......	358	100.0	.2	8.4	91.1	-	-	-	.2
100 TO 199 MILES......	394	100.0	1.0	8.0	91.0	-	-	-	-
200 TO 299 MILES......	642	100.0	2.1	29.5	67.4	-	-	-	1.0
300 TO 499 MILES......	603	100.0	5.6	33.6	60.8	-	-	-	-
500 TO 999 MILES......	551	100.0	11.8	66.8	21.4	-	-	-	-
1000 TO 1499 MILES....	627	100.0	6.5	89.2	4.0	-	.3	-	-
1500 MILES OR OVER....	166	100.0	4.9	84.7	10.4	-	-	-	-
MOUNTAIN................	1 184	100.0	27.4	43.4	29.3	-	-	-	-
UNDER 100 MILES.......	202	100.0	3.0	28.3	68.6	-	-	-	-
100 TO 199 MILES......	134	100.0	14.6	19.6	65.9	-	-	-	-
200 TO 299 MILES......	33	100.0	6.9	26.9	66.1	-	-	-	-
300 TO 499 MILES......	158	100.0	5.1	83.8	11.1	-	-	-	-
500 TO 999 MILES......	428	100.0	38.5	47.3	14.1	-	-	-	.1
1000 TO 1499 MILES....	124	100.0	43.8	42.1	14.1	-	-	-	-
1500 MILES OR OVER....	102	100.0	66.8	31.7	1.5	-	-	-	-
PACIFIC.................	1 526	100.0	1.3	42.0	56.1	.2	.2	-	.2
UNDER 100 MILES.......	718	100.0	.6	31.5	67.5	-	-	-	.4
100 TO 199 MILES......	361	100.0	.5	23.8	75.7	-	-	-	-
200 TO 299 MILES......	148	100.0	-	73.2	26.7	-	-	-	-
300 TO 499 MILES......	146	100.0	1.5	81.8	16.6	-	-	-	-
500 TO 999 MILES......	99	100.0	6.4	61.4	32.2	-	-	-	-
1000 TO 1499 MILES....	29	100.0	13.5	82.1	4.4	-	-	-	-
1500 MILES OR OVER....	21	100.0	6.7	69.0	.9	12.4	11.0	-	-

See footnotes at end of table 4.

TABLE 1. TCC GROUP 201—Percent Distribution of Geographic Division of Origin and Distance Shipped, by Means of Transport: 1972—Continued

Geographic division of origin[1] and distance shipped[2]	Number	Percent distribution by means of transport							
		All means of transport	Rail	Motor carrier	Private truck	Air	Water	Other	Unknown
TON-MILES OF SHIPMENTS	(millions of ton-miles)								
U.S. TOTAL..........	14 101	100.0	25.9	56.3	17.1	.1	.2	.1	.4
NEW ENGLAND............	14	100.0	10.6	42.5	45.0	-	1.9	-	-
UNDER 100 MILES.......	2	100.0	-	52.3	47.0	-	.7	-	-
100 TO 199 MILES......	2	100.0	4.1	40.7	47.0	-	8.2	-	-
200 TO 299 MILES......	2	100.0	22.9	75.3	1.7	-	.2	-	-
300 TO 499 MILES......	2	100.0	-	51.2	48.8	-	-	-	-
500 TO 999 MILES......	2	100.0	-	12.1	87.9	-	-	-	-
1000 TO 1499 MILES....	-	100.0	-	-	-	-	-	-	-
1500 MILES OR OVER....	-	100.0	100.0	-	-	-	-	-	-
MIDDLE ATLANTIC.........	314	100.0	6.0	38.1	55.9	-	-	-	-
UNDER 100 MILES.......	54	100.0	-	10.0	90.0	-	-	-	-
100 TO 199 MILES......	82	100.0	-	12.4	87.6	-	-	-	-
200 TO 299 MILES......	35	100.0	2.2	24.5	73.3	-	-	-	-
300 TO 499 MILES......	38	100.0	45.2	24.6	30.2	-	-	-	-
500 TO 999 MILES......	63	100.0	1.3	75.8	22.8	-	-	-	.1
1000 TO 1499 MILES....	22	100.0	-	97.1	2.9	-	-	-	-
1500 MILES OR OVER....	16	100.0	-	95.0	4.9	-	-	.1	-
EAST NORTH CENTRAL......	1 724	100.0	36.6	43.7	18.4	-	.4	.3	.6
UNDER 100 MILES.......	96	100.0	21.8	35.9	39.2	-	-	2.9	.2
100 TO 199 MILES......	209	100.0	45.1	25.3	27.6	-	-	.1	2.0
200 TO 299 MILES......	156	100.0	18.6	45.8	34.8	-	.1	.5	.2
300 TO 499 MILES......	254	100.0	44.3	42.5	13.1	-	-	.1	.1
500 TO 999 MILES......	739	100.0	34.7	48.1	15.7	-	1.0	.1	.5
1000 TO 1499 MILES....	87	100.0	17.4	71.7	10.7	.1	-	-	.1
1500 MILES OR OVER....	180	100.0	57.3	37.4	4.8	-	-	-	.6
WEST NORTH CENTRAL......	7 271	100.0	32.9	57.6	8.9	-	-	.2	.5
UNDER 100 MILES.......	79	100.0	11.6	32.7	55.4	-	-	.2	-
100 TO 199 MILES......	157	100.0	13.1	56.4	30.6	-	-	-	-
200 TO 299 MILES......	400	100.0	17.0	72.5	10.4	-	-	.2	-
300 TO 499 MILES......	768	100.0	30.0	62.3	7.6	-	-	-	.2
500 TO 999 MILES......	2 250	100.0	30.2	62.7	6.3	-	-	.2	.6
1000 TO 1499 MILES....	3 383	100.0	38.7	51.8	8.8	-	-	.2	.6
1500 MILES OR OVER....	231	100.0	31.1	61.6	7.3	-	-	-	-
SOUTH ATLANTIC..........	945	100.0	11.0	43.3	44.8	-	.8	.1	.1
UNDER 100 MILES.......	65	100.0	9.5	8.3	81.7	-	.3	.3	-
100 TO 199 MILES......	129	100.0	13.1	25.1	61.8	-	-	-	-
200 TO 299 MILES......	97	100.0	5.8	46.6	47.0	-	.2	-	.4
300 TO 499 MILES......	284	100.0	16.7	40.8	42.4	-	-	-	.1
500 TO 999 MILES......	259	100.0	9.4	68.3	22.3	-	-	-	-
1000 TO 1499 MILES....	38	100.0	4.1	55.2	40.2	-	-	.4	-
1500 MILES OR OVER....	69	100.0	2.2	16.1	71.6	-	10.0	-	-
EAST SOUTH CENTRAL......	762	100.0	4.5	71.8	23.1	-	-	-	.6
UNDER 100 MILES.......	33	100.0	.3	12.5	87.2	-	-	-	-
100 TO 199 MILES......	91	100.0	5.9	20.8	73.3	-	-	-	-
200 TO 299 MILES......	56	100.0	4.2	47.8	47.8	-	-	-	.1
300 TO 499 MILES......	144	100.0	5.7	86.0	8.3	-	-	-	-
500 TO 999 MILES......	286	100.0	3.0	90.9	6.1	-	-	-	-
1000 TO 1499 MILES....	15	100.0	42.8	57.2	-	-	-	-	-
1500 MILES OR OVER....	133	100.0	2.3	77.0	17.3	-	-	-	3.4
WEST SOUTH CENTRAL......	1 966	100.0	6.7	69.4	23.7	-	.1	-	.1
UNDER 100 MILES.......	19	100.0	.4	10.7	88.8	-	-	-	.1
100 TO 199 MILES......	61	100.0	1.0	8.4	90.6	-	-	-	-
200 TO 299 MILES......	149	100.0	2.1	29.0	67.6	-	-	-	1.3
300 TO 499 MILES......	232	100.0	6.2	33.5	60.3	-	-	-	-
500 TO 999 MILES......	414	100.0	12.4	68.1	19.5	-	-	-	-
1000 TO 1499 MILES....	801	100.0	6.2	89.8	3.7	-	.3	-	-
1500 MILES OR OVER....	287	100.0	4.6	81.2	14.3	-	-	-	-
MOUNTAIN................	767	100.0	42.5	44.2	13.3	-	-	-	-
UNDER 100 MILES.......	12	100.0	3.2	15.1	81.7	-	-	-	-
100 TO 199 MILES......	16	100.0	12.8	21.4	65.8	-	-	-	-
200 TO 299 MILES......	8	100.0	7.6	30.5	61.9	-	-	-	-
300 TO 499 MILES......	57	100.0	6.3	82.9	10.8	-	-	-	-
500 TO 999 MILES......	362	100.0	39.7	47.2	13.1	-	-	-	.1
1000 TO 1499 MILES....	147	100.0	46.8	40.0	13.3	-	-	-	-
1500 MILES OR OVER....	162	100.0	65.6	32.7	1.6	-	-	-	-
PACIFIC.................	334	100.0	4.5	61.6	30.2	2.2	1.5	-	-
UNDER 100 MILES.......	39	100.0	.8	40.9	58.0	-	-	-	.3
100 TO 199 MILES......	49	100.0	.4	23.0	76.6	-	-	-	-
200 TO 299 MILES......	39	100.0	-	76.4	23.6	-	-	-	-
300 TO 499 MILES......	49	100.0	2.2	80.6	17.2	-	-	-	-
500 TO 999 MILES......	66	100.0	7.3	63.3	29.4	-	-	-	-
1000 TO 1499 MILES....	42	100.0	13.1	82.4	4.6	-	-	-	-
1500 MILES OR OVER....	46	100.0	6.1	66.6	.9	15.4	11.0	-	-

See footnotes at end of table 4.

TABLE 2. TCC GROUP 201—Percent Distribution of Geographic Division of Origin and Means of Transport, by Geographic Division of Destination: 1972

Geographic division of origin[1] and means of transport	Number	Percent distribution by division of destination									
		U.S. total	New England	Middle Atlantic	East North Central	West North Central	South Atlantic	East South Central	West South Central	Mountain	Pacific
TONS OF SHIPMENTS	(thousands of tons)										
U.S. TOTAL	31 417	100.0	4.1	16.3	24.5	12.4	15.0	6.2	10.0	2.4	9.0
RAIL	5 881	100.0	4.2	16.1	27.5	15.5	12.4	6.3	9.4	1.0	7.6
MOTOR CARRIER	14 007	100.0	4.5	15.6	29.1	12.1	14.3	5.4	7.0	2.1	9.8
PRIVATE TRUCK	11 328	100.0	3.6	17.5	17.0	11.3	17.0	7.3	13.9	3.4	8.9
AIR	3	100.0	.5	4.3	2.4	-	3.4	5.1	.1	.8	83.4
WATER	43	100.0	1.7	9.7	2.0	-	57.9	4.7	13.4	-	10.7
OTHER	66	100.0	-	.2	61.0	10.8	13.6	.2	5.9	-	8.2
UNKNOWN	86	100.0	4.0	14.6	33.0	9.4	25.0	3.4	2.8	.1	7.7
NEW ENGLAND	106	100.0	64.6	28.8	5.3	-	.7	-	.6	-	-
RAIL	2	100.0	-	79.9	-	-	-	-	20.1	-	-
MOTOR CARRIER	47	100.0	66.0	32.3	.8	-	.9	-	-	-	-
PRIVATE TRUCK	53	100.0	68.1	21.6	9.7	-	.6	-	-	-	-
AIR	-	100.0	-	-	-	-	-	-	-	-	-
WATER	2	100.0	36.7	63.3	-	-	-	-	-	-	-
OTHER	-	100.0	100.0	-	-	-	-	-	-	-	-
UNKNOWN	-	100.0	-	-	-	-	-	-	-	-	-
MIDDLE ATLANTIC	2 068	100.0	5.6	77.1	3.3	.3	12.6	.4	.4	.3	.1
RAIL	48	100.0	1.3	5.7	.6	-	92.4	-	-	-	-
MOTOR CARRIER	345	100.0	8.2	46.5	10.5	1.6	27.7	.9	2.2	1.9	.6
PRIVATE TRUCK	1 672	100.0	5.2	85.4	1.9	-	7.1	.3	-	-	-
AIR	-	100.0	1.4	88.7	4.7	-	.8	.5	-	3.8	-
WATER	1	100.0	-	100.0	-	-	-	-	-	-	-
OTHER	-	100.0	1.2	28.3	37.4	-	5.4	18.6	-	-	9.0
UNKNOWN	-	100.0	-	72.9	24.1	-	3.1	-	-	-	-
EAST NORTH CENTRAL	5 481	100.0	3.3	9.9	59.2	12.7	7.1	3.4	2.4	.2	1.9
RAIL	1 752	100.0	3.8	7.4	44.9	27.7	4.7	3.3	4.7	.2	3.3
MOTOR CARRIER	2 019	100.0	4.1	14.5	55.0	6.6	11.1	5.0	1.6	.2	1.9
PRIVATE TRUCK	1 621	100.0	1.8	7.3	78.7	4.7	4.8	1.6	.5	.2	.3
AIR	-	100.0	.5	.3	34.9	-	55.5	7.9	.3	-	.5
WATER	10	100.0	-	11.6	8.4	-	23.4	-	56.5	-	-
OTHER	42	100.0	-	-	95.1	1.1	3.8	-	-	-	-
UNKNOWN	35	100.0	-	2.5	77.1	.1	11.0	4.2	3.5	-	1.7
WEST NORTH CENTRAL	11 880	100.0	4.8	14.8	30.0	23.6	8.8	3.9	7.9	1.3	4.8
RAIL	3 114	100.0	5.3	22.6	24.2	12.8	9.7	5.9	11.8	.8	6.9
MOTOR CARRIER	6 781	100.0	4.9	14.9	34.9	20.3	9.7	3.9	5.9	1.8	3.7
PRIVATE TRUCK	1 934	100.0	3.8	2.0	22.9	52.4	3.3	.6	8.9	.7	5.3
AIR	-	100.0	11.9	34.9	1.8	.2	-	28.9	2.0	19.3	1.0
WATER	-	100.0	-	-	-	-	-	-	-	-	-
OTHER	15	100.0	-	-	.1	42.3	-	-	24.7	-	32.9
UNKNOWN	34	100.0	7.4	30.9	4.2	4.4	48.7	4.3	-	-	-
SOUTH ATLANTIC	3 581	100.0	6.9	21.7	6.0	.9	59.2	4.0	.5	.1	.7
RAIL	367	100.0	1.1	1.7	5.4	1.2	72.8	17.6	-	-	.2
MOTOR CARRIER	1 068	100.0	5.7	36.2	12.8	2.6	37.9	3.3	1.1	-	.3
PRIVATE TRUCK	2 109	100.0	8.6	18.1	2.8	-	67.2	2.0	.3	.2	.9
AIR	-	100.0	-	-	1.1	-	96.3	-	-	-	2.6
WATER	25	100.0	-	-	-	-	89.6	-	-	-	10.4
OTHER	7	100.0	-	1.9	-	-	96.1	1.9	-	-	.1
UNKNOWN	3	100.0	29.7	33.4	-	-	37.0	-	-	-	-
EAST SOUTH CENTRAL	2 242	100.0	.8	6.8	11.8	1.1	24.7	43.0	8.4	.2	3.2
RAIL	84	100.0	2.4	11.5	-	1.0	14.7	51.1	17.3	-	2.0
MOTOR CARRIER	1 067	100.0	1.5	13.3	21.4	1.6	29.1	18.4	9.2	.4	5.1
PRIVATE TRUCK	1 087	100.0	-	-	3.2	.6	21.2	66.8	6.9	-	1.3
AIR	-	100.0	-	-	100.0	-	-	-	-	-	-
WATER	-	100.0	-	-	-	-	-	-	-	-	-
OTHER	-	100.0	-	-	-	-	18.8	-	81.3	-	-
UNKNOWN	3	100.0	-	-	-	-	-	-	11.4	-	88.6
WEST SOUTH CENTRAL	3 344	100.0	2.2	4.9	6.3	8.6	9.9	5.5	51.3	2.8	8.5
RAIL	166	100.0	1.4	5.9	10.2	3.6	9.3	8.2	30.8	.8	29.9
MOTOR CARRIER	1 522	100.0	4.6	9.8	7.9	6.8	20.0	10.0	24.4	2.6	13.9
PRIVATE TRUCK	1 646	100.0	.1	.3	4.5	10.4	.7	1.1	78.5	3.2	1.3
AIR	-	100.0	-	-	-	-	-	-	-	-	-
WATER	1	100.0	-	-	-	-	-	-	-	-	100.0
OTHER	-	100.0	-	-	-	100.0	-	-	-	-	-
UNKNOWN	7	100.0	-	-	-	88.2	-	-	11.8	-	-
MOUNTAIN	1 184	100.0	1.1	8.8	9.7	4.3	1.3	1.0	8.1	32.1	33.5
RAIL	324	100.0	2.6	25.0	12.8	3.4	1.2	2.3	9.5	8.8	34.3
MOTOR CARRIER	513	100.0	.9	4.5	13.4	5.1	1.4	1.0	8.9	18.5	46.3
PRIVATE TRUCK	346	100.0	-	-	1.2	4.0	1.2	-	5.7	73.9	13.9
AIR	-	100.0	-	-	100.0	-	-	-	-	-	-
WATER	-	100.0	-	-	-	-	-	-	-	-	-
OTHER	-	100.0	-	-	-	-	-	-	-	-	-
UNKNOWN	-	100.0	-	-	-	-	-	-	-	13.3	86.7
PACIFIC	1 526	100.0	-	.3	.4	.7	.1	.1	1.9	5.7	90.7
RAIL	20	100.0	-	-	-	6.6	4.5	-	33.3	6.7	48.8
MOTOR CARRIER	641	100.0	-	.8	.9	1.5	-	-	3.3	4.5	88.9
PRIVATE TRUCK	856	100.0	-	-	-	-	-	-	.2	6.6	93.3
AIR	2	100.0	-	-	-	-	-	4.1	-	-	95.9
WATER	2	100.0	-	-	-	-	-	84.9	-	-	15.1
OTHER	-	100.0	-	-	-	-	-	-	-	-	100.0
UNKNOWN	3	100.0	-	-	-	-	-	-	-	.8	99.2

See footnotes at end of table 4.

TABLE 2. **TCC GROUP 201—Percent Distribution of Geographic Division of Origin and Means of Transport, by Geographic Division of Destination: 1972**—Continued

Geographic division of origin[1] and means of transport	Number	Percent distribution by division of destination									
		U.S. total	New England	Middle Atlantic	East North Central	West North Central	South Atlantic	East South Central	West South Central	Mountain	Pacific
TON-MILES OF SHIPMENTS	(millions of ton-miles)										
U.S. TOTAL...............	14 101	100.0	8.2	21.9	16.7	5.7	16.7	5.0	9.0	2.2	14.7
RAIL....................	3 653	100.0	8.0	28.5	13.4	5.8	12.0	5.6	9.9	1.1	15.8
MOTOR CARRIER...........	7 934	100.0	8.2	21.6	18.8	4.9	19.2	4.8	6.7	2.4	13.6
PRIVATE TRUCK...........	2 415	100.0	8.2	13.2	14.9	8.3	15.4	4.6	15.5	3.7	16.1
AIR.....................	7	100.0	.2	.6	.3	-	1.6	3.5	-	.3	93.5
WATER...................	22	100.0	.1	5.0	.8	-	8.3	18.9	21.6	-	45.3
OTHER...................	16	100.0	-	.9	22.7	7.2	6.7	.5	20.5	-	41.4
UNKNOWN.................	50	100.0	7.4	23.0	9.9	4.8	37.9	3.0	2.2	-	11.8
NEW ENGLAND.............	14	100.0	23.1	44.3	24.4	-	1.8	-	6.4	-	-
RAIL....................	1	100.0	-	39.5	-	-	-	-	60.5	-	-
MOTOR CARRIER...........	6	100.0	31.6	60.7	5.1	-	2.7	-	-	-	-
PRIVATE TRUCK...........	6	100.0	21.2	27.9	49.4	-	1.6	-	-	-	-
AIR.....................	-	100.0	-	-	-	-	-	-	-	-	-
WATER...................	-	100.0	6.8	93.2	-	-	-	-	-	-	-
OTHER...................	-	100.0	100.0	-	-	-	-	-	-	-	-
UNKNOWN.................	-	100.0	-	-	-	-	-	-	-	-	-
MIDDLE ATLANTIC.........	314	100.0	6.4	42.1	11.8	1.7	28.1	1.8	2.9	3.5	1.6
RAIL....................	18	100.0	.9	3.4	.7	-	95.0	-	-	-	-
MOTOR CARRIER...........	119	100.0	5.0	11.1	18.8	4.1	39.3	1.6	7.4	8.7	4.0
PRIVATE TRUCK...........	175	100.0	8.0	67.4	8.3	.3	13.3	2.2	.1	.3	.2
AIR.....................	-	100.0	3.2	10.1	19.7	-	1.2	3.2	-	62.7	-
WATER...................	-	100.0	-	100.0	-	-	-	-	-	-	-
OTHER...................	-	100.0	.3	4.1	30.5	-	3.9	25.8	-	-	35.4
UNKNOWN.................	-	100.0	-	28.0	69.5	-	2.4	-	-	-	-
EAST NORTH CENTRAL......	1 724	100.0	8.8	19.3	24.9	10.2	15.6	4.2	5.9	.7	10.4
RAIL....................	631	100.0	9.3	15.1	18.1	18.9	7.6	3.9	10.1	.6	16.3
MOTOR CARRIER...........	753	100.0	9.3	23.9	21.8	4.7	21.9	5.4	3.4	.7	8.9
PRIVATE TRUCK...........	317	100.0	6.9	17.6	45.0	6.6	15.9	2.0	2.1	1.1	2.7
AIR.....................	-	100.0	.5	.3	10.7	-	83.9	2.8	.4	-	1.3
WATER...................	7	100.0	-	11.7	2.4	-	20.3	-	65.6	-	-
OTHER...................	4	100.0	-	-	78.2	3.6	18.2	-	-	-	-
UNKNOWN.................	9	100.0	-	7.9	45.0	-	22.2	3.5	10.3	-	11.1
WEST NORTH CENTRAL......	7 271	100.0	9.8	26.0	18.6	5.8	14.6	4.3	8.0	1.8	11.1
RAIL....................	2 389	100.0	8.8	33.4	13.1	3.3	12.2	5.2	10.1	1.1	12.8
MOTOR CARRIER...........	4 189	100.0	9.9	24.9	22.1	5.8	16.2	4.3	6.3	2.3	8.2
PRIVATE TRUCK...........	648	100.0	13.7	5.8	17.3	15.4	11.5	1.2	11.3	1.2	22.7
AIR.....................	-	100.0	16.0	42.4	.8	-	-	21.8	1.1	16.0	1.8
WATER...................	-	100.0	-	-	-	-	-	-	-	-	-
OTHER...................	11	100.0	-	-	-	9.0	-	-	30.2	-	60.8
UNKNOWN.................	33	100.0	10.1	32.0	1.9	1.6	50.8	3.6	-	-	-
SOUTH ATLANTIC..........	945	100.0	11.1	24.7	12.9	2.9	33.7	6.0	1.3	.7	6.6
RAIL....................	103	100.0	3.2	1.1	13.7	3.6	47.7	29.3	-	-	1.5
MOTOR CARRIER...........	409	100.0	7.5	32.4	18.6	5.6	28.2	3.3	2.4	.2	1.8
PRIVATE TRUCK...........	423	100.0	16.7	23.5	7.5	.1	36.1	3.2	.6	1.3	11.0
AIR.....................	-	100.0	-	-	1.6	-	72.8	-	-	-	25.6
WATER...................	7	100.0	-	-	-	-	5.2	-	-	-	94.8
OTHER...................	-	100.0	.3	31.5	-	-	49.1	16.6	-	-	2.4
UNKNOWN.................	-	100.0	48.6	26.6	-	-	24.8	-	-	-	-
EAST SOUTH CENTRAL......	762	100.0	2.4	12.4	18.8	1.2	26.2	14.7	6.3	.8	17.3
RAIL....................	34	100.0	6.7	25.8	-	.7	18.1	26.2	13.5	-	9.0
MOTOR CARRIER...........	547	100.0	2.9	15.6	24.3	1.3	25.5	5.8	5.1	1.1	18.4
PRIVATE TRUCK...........	176	100.0	-	.1	5.7	.8	30.7	40.5	9.0	-	13.2
AIR.....................	-	100.0	-	-	100.0	-	-	-	-	-	-
WATER...................	-	100.0	-	-	-	-	-	-	-	-	-
OTHER...................	-	100.0	-	-	-	-	23.1	-	76.9	-	-
UNKNOWN.................	4	100.0	-	-	-	-	-	-	1.6	-	98.4
WEST SOUTH CENTRAL......	1 966	100.0	5.8	11.4	7.4	5.5	19.7	6.1	20.7	3.1	20.4
RAIL....................	132	100.0	3.2	9.4	9.8	1.0	11.9	4.6	16.8	1.0	42.4
MOTOR CARRIER...........	1 363	100.0	7.9	15.0	6.8	2.8	26.5	7.8	8.8	2.7	21.8
PRIVATE TRUCK...........	465	100.0	.4	1.3	8.6	14.2	2.5	1.7	56.7	4.9	9.7
AIR.....................	-	100.0	-	-	-	-	-	-	-	-	-
WATER...................	2	100.0	-	-	-	-	-	-	-	-	100.0
OTHER...................	-	100.0	-	-	-	100.0	-	-	-	-	-
UNKNOWN.................	1	100.0	-	-	-	98.6	-	-	1.4	-	-
MOUNTAIN................	767	100.0	2.9	20.8	13.9	4.6	3.0	2.0	10.2	5.8	36.8
RAIL....................	326	100.0	4.3	37.6	11.3	1.9	1.8	2.8	6.4	1.5	32.3
MOTOR CARRIER...........	339	100.0	2.3	10.7	19.1	5.6	3.5	1.9	13.8	3.0	40.2
PRIVATE TRUCK...........	102	100.0	-	.2	4.9	9.8	5.7	-	10.7	28.8	40.0
AIR.....................	-	100.0	-	-	100.0	-	-	-	-	-	-
WATER...................	-	100.0	-	-	-	-	-	-	-	-	-
OTHER...................	-	100.0	-	-	-	-	-	-	-	-	-
UNKNOWN.................	-	100.0	-	-	-	-	-	-	-	.9	99.1
PACIFIC.................	334	100.0	-	3.6	3.2	4.7	.8	1.4	11.1	12.2	63.0
RAIL....................	14	100.0	-	-	-	12.4	13.4	-	52.8	4.7	16.7
MOTOR CARRIER...........	206	100.0	-	5.8	5.2	6.7	.2	.1	13.2	9.5	59.2
PRIVATE TRUCK...........	100	100.0	-	-	-	.1	.2	-	1.9	20.4	77.3
AIR.....................	7	100.0	-	-	-	-	-	3.2	-	-	96.8
WATER...................	5	100.0	-	-	-	-	-	82.2	-	-	17.8
OTHER...................	-	100.0	-	-	-	-	-	-	-	-	100.0
UNKNOWN.................	-	100.0	-	-	-	-	-	-	-	5.4	94.6

See footnotes at end of table 4.

TABLE 3. **TCC GROUP 201**—Percent Distribution of Geographic Division of Destination and Means of Transport, by Geographic Division of Origin: 1972

Geographic division of destination and means of transport	Number	U.S. total	New England	Middle Atlantic	East North Central	West North Central	South Atlantic	East South Central	West South Central	Mountain	Pacific
TONS OF SHIPMENTS	(thousands of tons)										
U.S. TOTAL..............	31 417	100.0	.3	6.6	17.4	37.8	11.4	7.1	10.6	3.8	4.9
RAIL...................	5 881	100.0	.1	.8	29.8	53.0	6.3	1.4	2.8	5.5	.3
MOTOR CARRIER.........	14 007	100.0	.3	2.5	14.4	48.4	7.6	7.6	10.9	3.7	4.6
PRIVATE TRUCK.........	11 328	100.0	.5	14.8	14.3	17.1	18.6	9.6	14.5	3.1	7.6
AIR...................	3	100.0	-	3.4	6.0	3.6	.1	-	-	-	86.9
WATER.................	43	100.0	4.7	4.0	23.7	-	58.4	-	3.8	-	5.5
OTHER.................	66	100.0	-	.1	64.1	23.8	11.6	-	-	-	.3
UNKNOWN...............	86	100.0	-	.3	40.6	39.5	3.5	3.5	8.7	.3	3.6
NEW ENGLAND...........	1 291	100.0	5.3	8.9	13.8	44.6	19.2	1.4	5.7	1.0	-
RAIL...................	249	100.0	-	.3	26.5	66.4	1.7	.8	1.0	3.4	-
MOTOR CARRIER.........	628	100.0	5.0	4.5	13.2	53.0	9.7	2.6	11.1	.8	-
PRIVATE TRUCK.........	409	100.0	8.9	21.1	7.1	18.1	44.4	-	.3	-	-
AIR...................	-	100.0	-	9.6	6.4	84.0	-	-	-	-	-
WATER.................	-	100.0	100.0	-	-	-	-	-	-	-	-
OTHER.................	-	100.0	75.4	3.5	-	-	21.1	-	-	-	-
UNKNOWN...............	3	100.0	-	-	-	74.0	26.0	-	-	-	-
MIDDLE ATLANTIC.......	5 131	100.0	.6	31.1	10.6	34.4	15.1	3.0	3.2	2.0	.1
RAIL...................	945	100.0	.2	.3	13.7	74.4	.7	1.0	1.0	8.6	-
MOTOR CARRIER.........	2 184	100.0	.7	7.4	13.4	46.3	17.7	6.5	6.8	1.0	.2
PRIVATE TRUCK.........	1 984	100.0	.6	72.0	6.0	1.9	19.2	-	.2	-	-
AIR...................	-	100.0	-	70.5	.4	29.1	-	-	-	-	-
WATER.................	4	100.0	30.6	40.9	28.5	-	-	-	-	-	-
OTHER.................	-	100.0	-	8.1	.1	.3	91.5	-	-	-	-
UNKNOWN...............	12	100.0	-	1.6	6.9	83.6	7.9	-	-	-	-
EAST NORTH CENTRAL.....	7 695	100.0	.1	.9	42.1	46.3	2.8	3.4	2.8	1.5	.1
RAIL...................	1 618	100.0	-	-	48.6	46.5	1.2	-	1.0	2.6	-
MOTOR CARRIER.........	4 075	100.0	-	.9	27.2	58.1	3.4	5.6	3.0	1.7	.1
PRIVATE TRUCK.........	1 931	100.0	.3	1.7	66.1	23.0	3.1	1.8	3.9	.2	-
AIR...................	-	100.0	-	6.9	88.3	2.7	-	.8	-	1.3	-
WATER.................	-	100.0	-	-	100.0	-	-	-	-	-	-
OTHER.................	40	100.0	-	-	99.9	-	-	-	-	-	-
UNKNOWN...............	28	100.0	-	.2	94.7	5.1	-	-	-	-	-
WEST NORTH CENTRAL.....	3 906	100.0	-	.2	17.8	71.7	.8	.6	7.3	1.3	.3
RAIL...................	909	100.0	-	-	53.4	44.0	.5	.1	.7	1.2	.1
MOTOR CARRIER.........	1 700	100.0	-	.3	7.8	81.1	1.6	1.0	6.1	1.5	.6
PRIVATE TRUCK.........	1 281	100.0	-	-	6.0	79.1	-	.5	13.3	1.1	-
AIR...................	-	100.0	-	-	-	100.0	-	-	-	-	-
WATER.................	-	100.0	-	-	-	-	-	-	-	-	-
OTHER.................	7	100.0	-	-	6.6	93.3	-	-	-	-	-
UNKNOWN...............	8	100.0	-	-	.2	18.7	-	-	81.1	-	-
SOUTH ATLANTIC.........	4 717	100.0	-	5.5	8.3	22.1	45.0	11.7	7.0	.3	-
RAIL...................	729	100.0	-	6.1	11.2	41.5	36.7	1.7	2.1	.5	.1
MOTOR CARRIER.........	2 006	100.0	-	4.8	11.1	32.8	20.2	15.5	15.2	.4	-
PRIVATE TRUCK.........	1 925	100.0	-	6.2	4.1	3.4	73.6	12.0	.6	.2	-
AIR...................	-	100.0	-	.8	96.7	-	2.5	-	-	-	-
WATER.................	25	100.0	-	-	9.6	-	90.4	-	-	-	-
OTHER.................	9	100.0	-	-	18.0	-	82.0	-	-	-	-
UNKNOWN...............	21	100.0	-	-	17.8	77.1	5.1	-	-	-	-
EAST SOUTH CENTRAL.....	1 961	100.0	-	.4	9.5	23.5	7.2	49.2	9.4	.6	.1
RAIL...................	371	100.0	-	-	15.6	49.7	17.4	11.6	3.6	2.0	-
MOTOR CARRIER.........	755	100.0	-	.4	13.4	34.8	4.6	25.9	20.2	.7	-
PRIVATE TRUCK.........	828	100.0	-	.6	3.2	1.5	5.0	87.6	2.1	-	-
AIR...................	-	100.0	-	.3	9.2	20.3	-	-	-	-	70.1
WATER.................	2	100.0	-	-	-	-	-	-	-	-	100.0
OTHER.................	-	100.0	-	5.5	.4	-	92.4	1.7	-	-	-
UNKNOWN...............	2	100.0	-	-	49.7	50.3	-	-	-	-	-
WEST SOUTH CENTRAL.....	3 128	100.0	-	.2	4.2	30.1	.6	6.0	54.9	3.1	.9
RAIL...................	553	100.0	.1	-	15.0	66.2	-	2.6	9.2	5.5	1.2
MOTOR CARRIER.........	987	100.0	-	.8	3.3	40.3	1.2	9.9	37.7	4.6	2.1
PRIVATE TRUCK.........	1 574	100.0	-	-	.5	11.0	.3	4.8	82.1	1.3	.1
AIR...................	-	100.0	-	-	22.0	78.0	-	-	-	-	-
WATER.................	5	100.0	-	-	100.0	-	-	-	-	-	-
OTHER.................	3	100.0	-	-	-	100.0	-	-	-	-	-
UNKNOWN...............	2	100.0	-	-	49.9	-	-	14.1	36.0	-	-
MOUNTAIN...............	744	100.0	-	.9	1.5	21.1	.6	.6	12.6	51.0	11.6
RAIL...................	59	100.0	-	-	6.5	40.5	-	-	2.3	48.4	2.3
MOTOR CARRIER.........	299	100.0	-	2.2	1.4	40.2	.2	1.5	13.2	31.7	9.7
PRIVATE TRUCK.........	385	100.0	-	.1	.9	3.3	1.0	-	13.8	66.4	14.6
AIR...................	-	100.0	-	15.9	-	84.1	-	-	-	-	-
WATER.................	-	100.0	-	-	-	-	-	-	-	-	-
OTHER.................	-	100.0	-	-	-	100.0	-	-	-	-	-
UNKNOWN...............	-	100.0	-	-	-	-	-	-	-	59.7	40.3
PACIFIC................	2 840	100.0	-	.1	3.6	20.1	.9	2.5	10.0	14.0	48.8
RAIL...................	444	100.0	-	-	13.0	48.1	.1	.4	11.2	25.0	2.2
MOTOR CARRIER.........	1 368	100.0	-	.1	2.9	18.3	.3	4.0	15.5	17.4	41.6
PRIVATE TRUCK.........	1 007	100.0	-	-	.5	10.2	1.8	1.4	2.1	4.8	79.3
AIR...................	2	100.0	-	-	-	-	-	-	-	-	99.9
WATER.................	4	100.0	-	-	-	-	56.7	-	35.5	-	7.7
OTHER.................	5	100.0	-	.1	-	95.8	.1	-	-	-	4.1
UNKNOWN...............	6	100.0	-	-	9.2	-	-	40.5	-	3.7	46.5

See footnotes at end of table 4.

TABLE 3. TCC GROUP 201—Percent Distribution of Geographic Division of Destination and Means of Transport, by Geographic Division of Origin: 1972—Continued

Geographic division of destination and means of transport	Number	Percent distribution by division of origin[1]									
		U.S. total	New England	Middle Atlantic	East North Central	West North Central	South Atlantic	East South Central	West South Central	Mountain	Pacific
TON-MILES OF SHIPMENTS	(millions of ton-miles)										
U.S. TOTAL............	14 101	100.0	.1	2.2	12.2	51.6	6.7	5.4	13.9	5.4	2.4
RAIL................	3 653	100.0	-	.5	17.3	65.4	2.8	.9	3.6	8.9	.4
MOTOR CARRIER........	7 934	100.0	.1	1.5	9.5	52.8	5.2	6.9	17.2	4.3	2.6
PRIVATE TRUCK........	2 415	100.0	.3	7.3	13.1	26.8	17.5	7.3	19.3	4.2	4.2
AIR.................	7	100.0	-	.1	1.8	1.4	-	-	-	-	96.6
WATER...............	22	100.0	1.2	.1	32.9	-	32.6	-	10.3	-	23.0
OTHER...............	16	100.0	-	.2	29.0	67.9	2.9	-	-	-	-
UNKNOWN.............	50	100.0	-	.1	19.0	65.5	1.6	9.1	3.8	.5	.3
NEW ENGLAND..........	1 149	100.0	.3	1.8	13.1	62.3	9.1	1.6	9.9	1.9	-
RAIL................	293	100.0	-	.1	20.0	71.7	1.1	.8	1.4	4.8	-
MOTOR CARRIER........	653	100.0	.3	.9	10.7	63.3	4.7	2.4	16.5	1.2	-
PRIVATE TRUCK........	198	100.0	.7	7.0	11.1	44.7	35.6	-	1.0	-	-
AIR.................	-	100.0	-	1.9	3.9	94.2	-	-	-	-	-
WATER...............	-	100.0	100.0	-	-	-	-	-	-	-	-
OTHER...............	-	100.0	27.3	3.7	-	-	69.0	-	-	-	-
UNKNOWN.............	3	100.0	-	-	-	89.2	10.8	-	-	-	-
MIDDLE ATLANTIC......	3 083	100.0	.2	4.3	10.8	61.3	7.6	3.1	7.2	5.2	.4
RAIL................	1 039	100.0	.1	.1	9.1	76.7	.1	.9	1.2	11.8	-
MOTOR CARRIER........	1 711	100.0	.2	.8	10.5	60.9	7.8	5.0	12.0	2.1	.7
PRIVATE TRUCK........	319	100.0	.6	37.1	17.5	11.8	31.1	.1	1.9	.1	-
AIR.................	-	100.0	-	2.3	.9	96.9	-	-	-	-	-
WATER...............	1	100.0	21.8	1.5	76.7	-	.4	-	-	-	-
OTHER...............	-	100.0	-	.8	.1	-	98.8	-	-	-	-
UNKNOWN.............	11	100.0	-	.2	6.5	91.4	1.9	-	-	-	-
EAST NORTH CENTRAL......	2 349	100.0	.1	1.6	18.3	57.5	5.2	6.1	6.2	4.5	.5
RAIL................	490	100.0	-	-	23.3	63.6	2.9	-	2.7	7.5	-
MOTOR CARRIER........	1 490	100.0	-	1.5	11.0	62.1	5.1	8.9	6.2	4.3	.7
PRIVATE TRUCK........	359	100.0	.9	4.0	39.7	31.3	8.8	2.8	11.2	1.4	-
AIR.................	-	100.0	-	10.8	77.9	4.6	.1	1.4	-	5.3	-
WATER...............	-	100.0	-	-	100.0	-	-	-	-	-	-
OTHER...............	3	100.0	-	.2	99.7	.1	-	-	-	-	-
UNKNOWN.............	4	100.0	-	.9	86.7	12.5	-	-	-	-	-
WEST NORTH CENTRAL......	800	100.0	-	.7	22.0	53.1	3.4	1.1	13.4	4.4	2.0
RAIL................	212	100.0	-	-	56.2	37.5	1.8	.1	.6	2.9	.9
MOTOR CARRIER........	385	100.0	-	1.3	9.2	63.3	6.0	1.9	9.8	4.9	3.6
PRIVATE TRUCK........	199	100.0	-	.2	10.6	50.1	.3	.7	33.1	5.0	-
AIR.................	-	100.0	-	-	-	100.0	-	-	-	-	-
WATER...............	-	100.0	-	-	-	-	-	-	-	-	-
OTHER...............	1	100.0	-	-	14.7	85.2	-	-	.1	-	-
UNKNOWN.............	2	100.0	-	-	.1	21.9	-	-	78.0	-	-
SOUTH ATLANTIC..........	2 351	100.0	-	3.8	11.4	45.2	13.6	8.5	16.5	1.0	.1
RAIL................	436	100.0	-	4.1	11.0	66.7	11.3	1.4	3.6	1.3	.5
MOTOR CARRIER........	1 520	100.0	-	3.1	10.8	44.7	7.6	9.2	23.7	.8	-
PRIVATE TRUCK........	372	100.0	-	6.3	13.5	20.0	41.0	14.5	3.1	1.6	.1
AIR.................	-	100.0	-	.1	99.1	-	.8	-	-	-	-
WATER...............	1	100.0	-	-	79.8	-	20.2	-	-	-	-
OTHER...............	1	100.0	-	.1	78.8	-	21.1	-	-	-	-
UNKNOWN.............	19	100.0	-	-	11.2	87.8	1.1	-	-	-	-
EAST SOUTH CENTRAL......	699	100.0	-	.8	10.3	44.6	8.2	16.0	17.2	2.2	.7
RAIL................	202	100.0	-	-	12.2	60.8	15.0	4.5	3.0	4.5	-
MOTOR CARRIER........	379	100.0	-	.5	10.7	47.3	3.5	8.3	27.9	1.7	-
PRIVATE TRUCK........	110	100.0	-	3.5	5.8	7.0	12.0	64.3	7.3	-	-
AIR.................	-	100.0	-	.1	1.5	8.8	-	-	-	-	89.6
WATER...............	4	100.0	-	-	-	-	-	-	-	-	100.0
OTHER...............	-	100.0	-	8.3	.1	-	91.1	.6	-	-	-
UNKNOWN.............	1	100.0	-	-	22.3	77.7	-	-	-	-	-
WEST SOUTH CENTRAL......	1 275	100.0	.1	.7	8.0	45.6	1.0	3.8	31.9	6.2	2.9
RAIL................	361	100.0	.3	-	17.6	66.8	-	1.3	6.1	5.8	2.2
MOTOR CARRIER........	529	100.0	-	1.7	4.8	49.7	1.9	5.2	22.7	8.8	5.1
PRIVATE TRUCK........	375	100.0	-	.1	1.8	19.5	.7	4.2	70.4	2.9	.5
AIR.................	-	100.0	-	-	32.6	67.4	-	-	-	-	-
WATER...............	4	100.0	-	-	100.0	-	-	-	-	-	-
OTHER...............	3	100.0	-	-	-	100.0	-	-	-	-	-
UNKNOWN.............	1	100.0	-	-	90.8	-	-	6.6	2.5	-	-
MOUNTAIN..............	315	100.0	-	3.5	4.0	42.0	2.0	1.9	19.3	14.2	13.0
RAIL................	38	100.0	-	-	10.7	71.1	-	-	3.4	12.9	1.8
MOTOR CARRIER........	186	100.0	-	5.6	2.7	52.2	.5	3.3	19.7	5.5	10.5
PRIVATE TRUCK........	90	100.0	-	.5	3.9	8.5	6.2	-	25.3	32.7	22.9
AIR.................	-	100.0	-	27.7	-	72.3	-	-	-	-	-
WATER...............	-	100.0	-	-	-	-	-	-	-	-	-
OTHER...............	-	100.0	-	-	-	100.0	-	-	-	-	-
UNKNOWN.............	-	100.0	-	-	-	-	-	-	-	20.4	79.6
PACIFIC...............	2 076	100.0	-	.2	8.7	38.7	3.0	6.3	19.3	13.6	10.1
RAIL................	578	100.0	-	-	17.8	53.0	.3	.5	9.7	18.3	.4
MOTOR CARRIER........	1 079	100.0	-	.4	6.2	31.9	.7	9.3	27.5	12.6	11.3
PRIVATE TRUCK........	389	100.0	-	.1	2.2	37.7	11.9	6.0	11.5	10.5	20.1
AIR.................	6	100.0	-	-	-	-	-	-	-	-	99.9
WATER...............	10	100.0	-	-	-	-	68.2	-	22.7	-	9.1
OTHER...............	7	100.0	-	.1	-	99.6	.2	-	-	.9	.1
UNKNOWN.............	5	100.0	-	-	17.8	-	-	75.8	-	3.9	2.5

See footnotes at end of table 4.

TABLE 4. **TCC GROUP 201**—Percent Distribution of Distance Shipped and Weight of Shipment, by Means of Transport: 1972

Distance shipped and weight of shipment [2] [3]	Number	Percent distribution by means of transport							
		All means of transport	Rail	Motor carrier	Private truck	Air	Water	Other	Unknown
TONS OF SHIPMENTS	(thousands of tons)								
U.S. TOTAL..........	23 954	100.0	14.8	45.9	38.5	-	.2	.3	.3
UNDER 100 MILES.........	5 724	100.0	6.3	19.2	73.1	-	.4	.8	.1
UNDER 1000 POUNDS.....	975	100.0	-	5.5	94.3	-	-	.1	.1
1000 TO 9999 POUNDS...	1 313	100.0	-	12.7	86.2	-	-	.9	.2
10000 TO 29999 POUNDS.	1 124	100.0	.2	20.5	78.5	-	-	.5	.2
30000 TO 59999 POUNDS.	1 445	100.0	3.2	36.9	58.0	-	-	2.0	-
60000 TO 89999 POUNDS.	182	100.0	44.1	2.9	53.0	-	-	-	-
90000 POUNDS AND OVER.	683	100.0	34.4	16.1	46.3	-	3.2	-	-
100 TO 199 MILES........	4 053	100.0	7.2	28.6	63.6	-	-	-	.6
UNDER 1000 POUNDS.....	261	100.0	-	11.6	88.2	-	-	.1	.1
1000 TO 9999 POUNDS...	690	100.0	-	23.7	75.8	-	-	-	.4
10000 TO 29999 POUNDS.	946	100.0	-	27.6	71.1	-	-	.1	1.1
30000 TO 59999 POUNDS.	1 527	100.0	2.0	42.7	54.8	-	-	-	.5
60000 TO 89999 POUNDS.	145	100.0	42.5	3.4	51.2	-	-	-	2.9
90000 POUNDS AND OVER.	482	100.0	41.0	9.5	49.5	-	-	-	-
200 TO 299 MILES........	2 655	100.0	9.0	63.1	27.2	-	.1	.3	.3
UNDER 1000 POUNDS.....	89	100.0	-	18.2	81.7	-	-	-	.1
1000 TO 9999 POUNDS...	312	100.0	-	38.1	61.9	-	-	-	-
10000 TO 29999 POUNDS.	522	100.0	1.9	64.0	34.0	-	-	-	-
30000 TO 59999 POUNDS.	1 483	100.0	1.7	79.6	18.1	-	.1	.5	.2
60000 TO 89999 POUNDS.	94	100.0	71.1	25.5	3.4	-	-	-	-
90000 POUNDS AND OVER.	152	100.0	90.3	.1	5.2	-	-	-	4.3
300 TO 499 MILES........	3 357	100.0	19.1	58.3	22.6	-	-	-	.1
UNDER 1000 POUNDS.....	38	100.0	-	51.4	48.6	.1	-	-	-
1000 TO 9999 POUNDS...	199	100.0	.1	50.7	48.9	-	-	.3	-
10000 TO 29999 POUNDS.	809	100.0	.4	62.9	36.6	-	-	-	-
30000 TO 59999 POUNDS.	1 705	100.0	6.1	73.5	20.2	-	-	-	.2
60000 TO 89999 POUNDS.	147	100.0	73.4	26.4	.2	-	-	-	-
90000 POUNDS AND OVER.	456	100.0	92.8	7.1	.2	-	-	-	-
500 TO 999 MILES........	4 970	100.0	23.3	62.7	13.3	-	.2	.1	.4
UNDER 1000 POUNDS.....	18	100.0	1.0	80.3	17.6	.2	.1	.9	-
1000 TO 9999 POUNDS...	202	100.0	2.6	76.4	21.0	-	-	-	-
10000 TO 29999 POUNDS.	730	100.0	1.1	78.4	19.2	-	.5	.5	.1
30000 TO 59999 POUNDS.	3 112	100.0	12.9	71.6	14.7	-	.2	.1	.6
60000 TO 89999 POUNDS.	409	100.0	79.4	19.2	1.4	-	-	-	-
90000 POUNDS AND OVER.	498	100.0	83.8	13.5	2.7	-	-	-	-
1000 TO 1499 MILES......	2 701	100.0	28.6	60.6	9.9	-	.1	.2	.6
UNDER 1000 POUNDS.....	6	100.0	-	89.1	10.7	.2	-	-	-
1000 TO 9999 POUNDS...	92	100.0	.3	79.8	19.6	.1	-	.2	.1
10000 TO 29999 POUNDS.	257	100.0	5.0	82.2	11.6	-	-	.5	.7
30000 TO 59999 POUNDS.	2 023	100.0	22.5	65.7	10.8	-	.1	.2	.7
60000 TO 89999 POUNDS.	141	100.0	94.9	4.5	.6	-	-	-	-
90000 POUNDS AND OVER.	179	100.0	94.8	5.2	-	-	-	-	-
1500 MILES OR OVER......	491	100.0	18.2	69.8	10.3	.5	1.0	-	.1
UNDER 1000 POUNDS.....	4	100.0	-	35.4	57.6	1.3	5.6	.2	-
1000 TO 9999 POUNDS...	37	100.0	1.4	52.5	38.7	2.7	4.7	-	-
10000 TO 29999 POUNDS.	89	100.0	.1	73.2	26.2	.1	.3	-	-
30000 TO 59999 POUNDS.	299	100.0	11.0	85.1	3.5	-	.2	-	.2
60000 TO 89999 POUNDS.	37	100.0	86.4	4.6	-	3.2	5.8	-	-
90000 POUNDS AND OVER.	23	100.0	100.0	-	-	-	-	-	-
TON-MILES OF SHIPMENTS	(millions of ton-miles)								
U.S. TOTAL..........	10 730	100.0	22.1	58.7	18.3	.1	.2	.2	.4
UNDER 100 MILES.........	316	100.0	7.9	21.8	69.1	-	.1	1.0	.1
UNDER 1000 POUNDS.....	45	100.0	-	6.7	93.2	-	-	.1	.1
1000 TO 9999 POUNDS...	67	100.0	-	16.1	83.1	-	-	.6	.2
10000 TO 29999 POUNDS.	61	100.0	.3	20.4	78.5	-	-	.5	.3
30000 TO 59999 POUNDS.	84	100.0	3.9	39.3	53.8	-	-	2.9	-
60000 TO 89999 POUNDS.	9	100.0	46.9	2.6	50.5	-	-	-	-
90000 POUNDS AND OVER.	46	100.0	36.9	18.7	44.1	-	.4	-	-
100 TO 199 MILES........	599	100.0	7.0	30.0	62.3	-	-	-	.7
UNDER 1000 POUNDS.....	36	100.0	-	12.6	87.2	-	-	.1	.1
1000 TO 9999 POUNDS...	98	100.0	-	25.0	74.6	-	-	-	.4
10000 TO 29999 POUNDS.	140	100.0	-	28.8	69.8	-	-	.1	1.3
30000 TO 59999 POUNDS.	235	100.0	2.1	44.0	53.4	-	-	-	.5
60000 TO 89999 POUNDS.	23	100.0	35.9	2.2	59.1	-	-	-	2.9
90000 POUNDS AND OVER.	65	100.0	43.7	8.9	47.4	-	-	-	-

See footnotes at end of table 4.

TABLE 4. **TCC GROUP 201—Percent Distribution of Distance Shipped and Weight of Shipment, by Means of Transport: 1972**—Continued

Distance shipped and weight of shipment[2][3]	Number	Percent distribution by means of transport							
		All means of transport	Rail	Motor carrier	Private truck	Air	Water	Other	Unknown
TON-MILES OF SHIPMENTS	(millions of ton-miles)								
200 TO 299 MILES........	665	100.0	9.7	62.7	26.9	-	.1	.2	.4
UNDER 1000 POUNDS.....	21	100.0	-	19.2	80.7	-	-	-	.1
1000 TO 9999 POUNDS...	77	100.0	-	38.4	61.6	-	-	-	-
10000 TO 29999 POUNDS.	131	100.0	2.0	64.4	33.6	-	-	.1	-
30000 TO 59999 POUNDS.	370	100.0	1.8	79.2	18.3	-	.1	.4	.1
60000 TO 89999 POUNDS.	23	100.0	74.5	22.1	3.4	-	-	-	-
90000 POUNDS AND OVER.	41	100.0	91.2	.1	4.2	-	-	-	4.6
300 TO 499 MILES........	1 304	100.0	19.6	58.1	22.2	-	-	-	.1
UNDER 1000 POUNDS.....	14	100.0	-	51.9	48.0	.1	-	-	-
1000 TO 9999 POUNDS...	75	100.0	.1	51.1	48.5	-	-	.3	-
10000 TO 29999 POUNDS.	307	100.0	.5	63.4	36.1	-	-	-	-
30000 TO 59999 POUNDS.	669	100.0	6.4	73.4	20.1	-	-	-	.2
60000 TO 89999 POUNDS.	56	100.0	72.5	27.3	.2	-	-	-	-
90000 POUNDS AND OVER.	181	100.0	93.9	6.0	.2	-	-	-	-
500 TO 999 MILES........	3 689	100.0	24.3	62.7	12.3	-	.2	.1	.5
UNDER 1000 POUNDS.....	12	100.0	1.0	80.2	17.8	.2	.1	.7	-
1000 TO 9999 POUNDS...	143	100.0	3.4	76.7	19.9	-	-	-	-
10000 TO 29999 POUNDS.	513	100.0	1.2	79.6	17.8	-	.5	.7	.2
30000 TO 59999 POUNDS.	2 317	100.0	13.4	72.1	13.6	-	.2	-	.7
60000 TO 89999 POUNDS.	334	100.0	78.6	20.1	1.2	-	-	-	-
90000 POUNDS AND OVER.	367	100.0	84.5	12.5	3.0	-	-	-	-
1000 TO 1499 MILES......	3 270	100.0	28.4	60.6	10.2	-	.1	.2	.6
UNDER 1000 POUNDS.....	7	100.0	-	88.8	10.9	.2	-	-	-
1000 TO 9999 POUNDS...	109	100.0	.3	80.2	19.2	.1	-	.1	-
10000 TO 29999 POUNDS.	312	100.0	4.7	82.2	11.9	-	-	.6	.6
30000 TO 59999 POUNDS.	2 449	100.0	22.1	65.8	11.1	-	.1	.2	.7
60000 TO 89999 POUNDS.	170	100.0	95.5	3.8	.7	-	-	-	-
90000 POUNDS AND OVER.	220	100.0	95.3	4.7	-	-	-	-	-
1500 MILES OR OVER......	884	100.0	18.7	65.7	13.4	.8	1.4	-	.1
UNDER 1000 POUNDS.....	10	100.0	-	26.8	67.6	.9	4.5	.2	-
1000 TO 9999 POUNDS...	78	100.0	1.4	43.6	46.6	3.7	4.8	-	-
10000 TO 29999 POUNDS.	175	100.0	.1	66.5	32.8	.2	.5	-	-
30000 TO 59999 POUNDS.	500	100.0	11.5	84.6	3.4	-	.3	-	.2
60000 TO 89999 POUNDS.	78	100.0	84.3	4.7	-	-	6.8	-	-
90000 POUNDS AND OVER.	40	100.0	100.0	-	-	-	-	-	-

Note: Detail may not add to total due to rounding. The introductory table shows the estimates of sampling variability for tons; sampling variability for ton-miles has not been estimated. See the map in the Introduction for the States comprising the geographic divisions of the United States.
   Shipments excluded from the survey are those moving by pipeline (primarily petroleum products from refineries), parcel post shipments, and commodities moved by own power (motorized vehicles, aircraft, etc.) or towed (prefabricated buildings, etc.). Local shipments (commodities shipped less than 25 miles from the plant) and shipments within the same city are also excluded. Shipments to Alaska and Hawaii from the 48 conterminous States and the District of Columbia are included; however, no data were obtained for shipments originating in Alaska and Hawaii.

   - Represents zero or rounds to zero.

[1]Production of this commodity is concentrated in the geographic divisions shown; figures and distributions for geographic divisions not shown are included in the total.
   [2]Distances of shipments to foreign destinations are calculated only to the U.S. port of exit.
   [3]Includes only shipments represented by bills of lading and invoices. Summary records which did not show individual weights of shipments are not included.

TCC 202. Dairy Products

Comparisons of Tons and Ton-Miles of Shipments for
Geographic Divisions of Origin and for Sampling Variability: 1972 and 1967

Geographic division of origin	Estimates				Relative sampling variability in tons (percent)	
	1972		1967		1972	1967
	Tons (thousands)	Ton-miles (millions)	Tons (thousands)	Ton-miles (millions)		
U.S. total	10,236	3,235	10,049	2,424	9.0	18.6
New England	(D)	(D)	97	7	(*)	(*)
Middle Atlantic	1,007	203	932	142	31.2	(*)
East North Central	3,678	1,445	5,610	1,271	18.2	(*)
West North Central	2,656	1,095	1,021	430	33.0	(*)
South Atlantic	638	137	1,283	192	35.2	(*)
East South Central	332	57	478	154	43.1	(*)
West South Central	(D)	(D)	66	11	(*)	(*)
Mountain	(D)	(D)	187	95	(*)	(*)
Pacific	383	116	375	122	46.5	(*)

(D) Withheld to avoid disclosing figures for individual companies.   (*) Data not published.

TABLE 1. **TCC GROUP 202**—Percent Distribution of Geographic Division of Origin and Distance Shipped, by Means of Transport: 1972

Geographic division of origin[1] and distance shipped[2]	Number	Percent distribution by means of transport							
		All means of transport	Rail	Motor carrier	Private truck	Air	Water	Other	Unknown
TONS OF SHIPMENTS	(thousands of tons)								
U.S. TOTAL	10 236	100.0	19.4	35.0	45.5	-	-	-	.1
MIDDLE ATLANTIC	1 007	100.0	38.7	23.0	38.1	-	-	-	.1
UNDER 100 MILES	345	100.0	4.1	16.5	79.4	-	-	-	-
100 TO 199 MILES	255	100.0	30.3	37.6	32.1	-	-	-	-
200 TO 299 MILES	266	100.0	69.5	23.6	6.8	-	-	-	-
300 TO 499 MILES	73	100.0	82.1	8.5	9.3	-	-	-	-
500 TO 999 MILES	50	100.0	76.3	17.8	4.6	-	-	-	1.3
1000 TO 1499 MILES	14	100.0	95.6	4.3	-	-	-	.1	-
1500 MILES OR OVER	1	100.0	85.9	14.1	-	-	-	-	-
EAST NORTH CENTRAL	3 678	100.0	28.8	36.9	34.1	-	-	-	.2
UNDER 100 MILES	1 338	100.0	-	24.5	75.5	-	-	-	.1
100 TO 199 MILES	429	100.0	20.7	51.8	27.0	-	-	-	.5
200 TO 299 MILES	382	100.0	56.8	37.1	6.0	-	-	-	.2
300 TO 499 MILES	468	100.0	46.3	48.7	4.8	-	-	-	.2
500 TO 999 MILES	689	100.0	53.7	38.5	7.6	-	-	-	.1
1000 TO 1499 MILES	185	100.0	24.0	63.0	13.0	-	-	-	-
1500 MILES OR OVER	184	100.0	66.0	30.5	2.3	-	-	-	1.1
WEST NORTH CENTRAL	2 656	100.0	9.5	57.4	33.0	-	-	-	-
UNDER 100 MILES	997	100.0	1.1	49.2	49.7	-	-	-	-
100 TO 199 MILES	408	100.0	.5	62.9	36.5	-	-	-	-
200 TO 299 MILES	147	100.0	4.2	62.4	33.5	-	-	-	-
300 TO 499 MILES	338	100.0	14.9	49.0	35.7	-	-	-	.3
500 TO 999 MILES	367	100.0	24.5	59.7	15.8	-	-	-	-
1000 TO 1499 MILES	251	100.0	26.7	71.5	1.7	-	-	.2	-
1500 MILES OR OVER	145	100.0	18.2	81.8	-	-	-	-	-
SOUTH ATLANTIC	638	100.0	36.1	12.4	51.6	-	-	-	-
UNDER 100 MILES	114	100.0	-	10.6	89.4	-	-	-	-
100 TO 199 MILES	266	100.0	41.5	6.8	51.7	-	-	-	-
200 TO 299 MILES	160	100.0	42.9	8.1	49.0	-	-	-	-
300 TO 499 MILES	55	100.0	48.5	36.5	15.0	-	-	-	-
500 TO 999 MILES	42	100.0	57.1	36.6	6.3	-	-	-	-
1000 TO 1499 MILES	-	100.0	-	-	-	-	-	-	-
1500 MILES OR OVER	-	100.0	-	-	-	-	-	-	-
EAST SOUTH CENTRAL	332	100.0	2.0	6.0	92.0	-	-	-	-
UNDER 100 MILES	152	100.0	-	2.6	97.4	-	-	-	-
100 TO 199 MILES	50	100.0	5.3	.7	94.0	-	-	-	-
200 TO 299 MILES	83	100.0	-	.5	99.5	-	-	-	-
300 TO 499 MILES	28	100.0	7.1	31.9	61.0	-	-	-	-
500 TO 999 MILES	14	100.0	12.5	27.3	60.3	-	-	-	-
1000 TO 1499 MILES	-	100.0	-	100.0	-	-	-	-	-
1500 MILES OR OVER	1	100.0	-	100.0	-	-	-	-	-
PACIFIC	383	100.0	10.1	58.9	30.4	-	.6	-	-
UNDER 100 MILES	210	100.0	6.4	58.4	35.3	-	-	-	-
100 TO 199 MILES	38	100.0	-	59.9	40.1	-	-	-	-
200 TO 299 MILES	64	100.0	-	75.9	24.1	-	-	-	-
300 TO 499 MILES	15	100.0	-	43.8	56.2	-	-	-	-
500 TO 999 MILES	23	100.0	3.4	92.7	3.9	-	-	-	-
1000 TO 1499 MILES	8	100.0	95.1	4.7	.2	-	-	-	-
1500 MILES OR OVER	22	100.0	73.5	9.2	7.5	-	9.8	-	-
TON-MILES OF SHIPMENTS	(millions of ton-miles)								
U.S. TOTAL	3 235	100.0	35.1	47.1	17.5	-	.2	-	.2
MIDDLE ATLANTIC	203	100.0	61.2	22.0	16.6	-	-	-	.2
UNDER 100 MILES	19	100.0	3.6	21.2	75.2	-	-	-	-
100 TO 199 MILES	37	100.0	30.2	40.7	29.1	-	-	-	-
200 TO 299 MILES	69	100.0	71.0	23.0	6.0	-	-	-	-
300 TO 499 MILES	26	100.0	81.4	8.1	10.4	-	-	-	-
500 TO 999 MILES	32	100.0	75.8	18.9	4.2	-	-	-	1.0
1000 TO 1499 MILES	14	100.0	95.5	4.4	-	-	-	.1	-
1500 MILES OR OVER	3	100.0	83.6	16.3	-	-	-	.1	-
EAST NORTH CENTRAL	1 445	100.0	47.4	41.5	10.7	-	-	-	.3
UNDER 100 MILES	70	100.0	-	26.1	73.8	-	-	-	.1
100 TO 199 MILES	66	100.0	21.6	50.8	27.3	-	-	-	.4
200 TO 299 MILES	98	100.0	59.3	34.8	5.8	-	-	-	.1
300 TO 499 MILES	186	100.0	46.5	48.2	5.1	-	-	-	.2
500 TO 999 MILES	476	100.0	53.7	38.4	7.8	-	-	-	.1
1000 TO 1499 MILES	216	100.0	23.7	64.7	11.7	-	-	-	-
1500 MILES OR OVER	330	100.0	66.2	30.6	2.3	-	-	-	1.0
WEST NORTH CENTRAL	1 095	100.0	19.4	67.5	13.0	-	-	.1	-
UNDER 100 MILES	53	100.0	1.5	68.9	29.6	-	-	-	-
100 TO 199 MILES	59	100.0	.7	62.1	37.2	-	-	-	-
200 TO 299 MILES	37	100.0	4.2	63.4	32.4	-	-	-	-
300 TO 499 MILES	136	100.0	15.9	47.6	36.1	-	-	-	.3
500 TO 999 MILES	270	100.0	24.0	61.9	14.1	-	-	-	-
1000 TO 1499 MILES	312	100.0	26.1	72.2	1.6	-	-	.2	-
1500 MILES OR OVER	226	100.0	18.5	81.5	-	-	-	-	-

See footnotes at end of table 4.

TABLE 1. **TCC GROUP 202—Percent Distribution of Geographic Division of Origin and Distance Shipped, by Means of Transport: 1972**—Continued

Geographic division of origin[1] and distance shipped[2]	Number	Percent distribution by means of transport							
		All means of transport	Rail	Motor carrier	Private truck	Air	Water	Other	Unknown
TON-MILES OF SHIPMENTS	(millions of ton-miles)								
SOUTH ATLANTIC..........	137	100.0	46.1	17.8	36.1	-	-	-	-
UNDER 100 MILES.......	8	100.0	-	9.6	90.4	-	-	-	-
100 TO 199 MILES......	39	100.0	49.8	7.6	42.6	-	-	-	-
200 TO 299 MILES......	42	100.0	43.6	7.4	49.0	-	-	-	-
300 TO 499 MILES......	19	100.0	46.3	38.8	15.0	-	-	-	-
500 TO 999 MILES......	27	100.0	58.4	35.6	6.0	-	-	-	-
1000 TO 1499 MILES....	-	100.0	-	-	-	-	-	-	-
1500 MILES OR OVER....	-	100.0	-	-	-	-	-	-	-
EAST SOUTH CENTRAL.....	57	100.0	4.1	18.6	77.4	-	-	-	-
UNDER 100 MILES.......	4	100.0	-	3.5	96.5	-	-	-	-
100 TO 199 MILES......	7	100.0	4.5	.7	94.9	-	-	-	-
200 TO 299 MILES......	18	100.0	-	.5	99.5	-	-	-	-
300 TO 499 MILES......	11	100.0	6.7	33.2	60.1	-	-	-	-
500 TO 999 MILES......	10	100.0	11.2	26.9	61.9	-	-	-	-
1000 TO 1499 MILES....	-	100.0	-	100.0	-	-	-	-	-
1500 MILES OR OVER....	2	100.0	-	100.0	-	-	-	-	-
PACIFIC................	116	100.0	36.8	43.0	14.9	-	5.3	-	-
UNDER 100 MILES.......	12	100.0	3.1	61.5	35.4	-	-	-	-
100 TO 199 MILES......	4	100.0	-	61.7	38.3	-	-	-	-
200 TO 299 MILES......	17	100.0	-	79.3	20.7	-	-	-	-
300 TO 499 MILES......	5	100.0	-	42.2	57.8	-	-	-	-
500 TO 999 MILES......	19	100.0	2.2	94.1	3.6	-	-	-	-
1000 TO 1499 MILES....	11	100.0	95.1	4.7	.2	-	-	-	-
1500 MILES OR OVER....	45	100.0	68.4	10.2	7.8	-	13.6	-	-

See footnotes at end of table 4.

TABLE 2. **TCC GROUP 202—Percent Distribution of Geographic Division of Origin and Means of Transport, by Geographic Division of Destination: 1972**

Geographic division of origin[1] and means of transport	Number	Percent distribution by division of destination									
		U.S. total	New England	Middle Atlantic	East North Central	West North Central	South Atlantic	East South Central	West South Central	Mountain	Pacific
TONS OF SHIPMENTS	(thousands of tons)										
U.S. TOTAL..............	10 236	100.0	12.4	14.1	23.6	19.8	10.5	3.7	4.1	2.7	9.1
RAIL...................	1 986	100.0	3.5	30.3	15.8	8.3	18.1	5.7	5.8	2.9	9.6
MOTOR CARRIER..........	3 582	100.0	1.6	10.5	24.9	27.4	7.0	2.7	6.0	4.1	15.8
PRIVATE TRUCK..........	4 655	100.0	24.5	10.0	25.9	18.8	9.9	3.6	2.0	1.5	3.7
AIR....................	-	100.0	-	24.4	10.0	-	58.9	6.7	-	-	-
WATER..................	2	100.0	-	2.9	-	-	-	-	-	-	97.1
OTHER..................	-	100.0	56.0	17.5	16.1	1.6	5.3	1.4	.2	-	2.0
UNKNOWN................	9	100.0	-	21.9	8.3	12.7	17.8	-	10.8	21.0	7.5
MIDDLE ATLANTIC.........	1 007	100.0	5.0	75.6	8.4	.2	9.4	.2	1.0	.1	-
RAIL...................	390	100.0	7.8	67.6	8.7	.5	12.0	.6	2.4	.4	-
MOTOR CARRIER..........	231	100.0	4.2	76.1	9.9	-	9.4	-	.3	-	.1
PRIVATE TRUCK..........	384	100.0	2.7	83.4	7.2	-	6.7	-	-	-	-
AIR....................	-	100.0	-	-	1.8	-	98.2	-	-	-	-
WATER..................	-	100.0	-	100.0	-	.2	-	-	-	-	-
OTHER..................	-	100.0	11.1	49.4	19.0	.2	19.8	-	-	-	.5
UNKNOWN................	-	100.0	-	15.0	-	-	85.0	-	-	-	-
EAST NORTH CENTRAL......	3 678	100.0	1.6	9.9	55.2	10.3	8.1	4.9	3.1	2.1	4.9
RAIL...................	1 059	100.0	2.2	20.7	21.8	11.4	13.1	9.6	6.4	3.3	11.5
MOTOR CARRIER..........	1 358	100.0	1.7	7.3	53.1	13.6	9.3	4.9	3.2	3.0	4.0
PRIVATE TRUCK..........	1 252	100.0	.8	3.4	86.0	5.7	2.5	1.0	.2	.2	.3
AIR....................	-	100.0	-	60.2	23.3	-	-	16.5	-	-	-
WATER..................	-	100.0	-	-	-	-	-	-	-	-	-
OTHER..................	-	100.0	-	.7	75.4	9.0	3.6	9.0	.7	-	1.6
UNKNOWN................	7	100.0	-	28.4	8.8	17.4	15.4	-	-	28.8	1.4
WEST NORTH CENTRAL......	2 656	100.0	1.3	4.6	9.7	56.7	3.9	.7	9.4	3.4	10.2
RAIL...................	252	100.0	5.0	15.9	16.2	10.2	10.7	1.3	10.7	8.9	21.3
MOTOR CARRIER..........	1 524	100.0	1.4	4.9	9.3	52.1	4.1	.9	10.2	2.8	14.2
PRIVATE TRUCK..........	877	100.0	-	.8	8.5	78.3	1.4	.4	7.6	2.8	.1
AIR....................	-	100.0	-	-	-	-	100.0	-	-	-	-
WATER..................	-	100.0	-	-	-	-	-	-	-	-	-
OTHER..................	-	100.0	80.2	13.7	1.7	.3	2.2	-	-	-	1.9
UNKNOWN................	1	100.0	-	-	15.6	-	-	-	84.4	-	-
SOUTH ATLANTIC..........	638	100.0	.3	21.8	1.7	.3	71.2	4.3	.4	-	-
RAIL...................	230	100.0	-	33.5	2.6	-	62.2	1.7	-	-	-
MOTOR CARRIER..........	78	100.0	2.1	28.7	1.9	-	48.7	16.0	2.7	-	-
PRIVATE TRUCK..........	329	100.0	-	12.0	1.0	.6	82.9	3.3	.2	-	-
AIR....................	-	100.0	-	-	-	-	-	-	-	-	-
WATER..................	-	100.0	-	-	-	-	-	-	-	-	-
OTHER..................	-	100.0	-	-	-	-	-	-	-	-	-
UNKNOWN................	-	100.0	-	-	-	-	-	-	-	-	-

See footnotes at end of table 4.

TABLE 2. TCC GROUP 202—Percent Distribution of Geographic Division of Origin and Means of Transport, by Geographic Division of Destination: 1972—Continued

Geographic division of origin[1] and means of transport	Number	Percent distribution by division of destination									
		U.S. total	New England	Middle Atlantic	East North Central	West North Central	South Atlantic	East South Central	West South Central	Mountain	Pacific
TONS OF SHIPMENTS	(thousands of tons)										
EAST SOUTH CENTRAL	332	100.0	-	.7	4.8	5.3	36.1	45.2	7.1	.6	.4
RAIL	6	100.0	-	-	-	30.8	-	41.0	28.2	-	-
MOTOR CARRIER	19	100.0	-	6.1	3.8	8.4	11.3	23.7	34.2	6.5	5.9
PRIVATE TRUCK	305	100.0	-	.3	5.0	4.5	38.4	46.7	4.9	.2	-
AIR	-	100.0	-	-	-	-	-	-	-	-	-
WATER	-	100.0	-	-	-	-	-	-	-	-	-
OTHER	-	100.0	-	-	100.0	-	-	-	-	-	-
UNKNOWN	-	100.0	-	-	100.0	-	-	-	-	-	-
PACIFIC	383	100.0	.6	.2	1.1	4.0	1.0	-	.6	3.6	89.1
RAIL	38	100.0	5.6	-	6.0	38.7	8.7	-	4.4	-	36.7
MOTOR CARRIER	225	100.0	-	-	.6	-	-	-	.2	1.3	97.9
PRIVATE TRUCK	116	100.0	-	.6	.3	.2	.3	-	-	9.2	89.3
AIR	-	100.0	-	-	-	-	-	-	-	-	100.0
WATER	2	100.0	-	-	-	-	-	-	-	-	100.0
OTHER	-	100.0	-	-	23.9	-	6.1	-	5.7	1.3	63.0
UNKNOWN	-	100.0	-	-	-	-	-	-	-	-	100.0
TON-MILES OF SHIPMENTS	(millions of ton-miles)										
U.S. TOTAL	3 235	100.0	5.3	15.5	13.1	8.8	14.0	3.8	7.6	4.8	27.1
RAIL	1 134	100.0	4.2	23.1	8.3	6.6	14.0	4.7	7.6	5.2	26.4
MOTOR CARRIER	1 523	100.0	3.3	11.3	14.4	8.3	12.5	3.2	8.2	5.4	33.4
PRIVATE TRUCK	565	100.0	12.9	11.6	19.7	14.5	18.4	3.9	6.3	2.1	10.6
AIR	-	100.0	-	19.0	3.6	-	68.7	8.7	-	-	-
WATER	6	100.0	-	-	-	-	-	-	-	-	100.0
OTHER	-	100.0	70.5	13.9	5.7	.5	5.5	.3	.2	-	3.5
UNKNOWN	5	100.0	-	17.9	2.1	3.9	7.7	-	6.8	52.6	9.0
MIDDLE ATLANTIC	203	100.0	7.5	55.8	14.6	1.1	13.5	.6	5.3	1.5	.3
RAIL	124	100.0	8.0	48.8	13.7	1.7	16.4	1.0	8.1	2.4	-
MOTOR CARRIER	44	100.0	5.3	64.7	18.6	-	8.8	-	1.4	-	1.3
PRIVATE TRUCK	33	100.0	8.6	70.6	13.0	-	7.8	-	-	-	-
AIR	-	100.0	-	-	2.6	-	97.4	-	-	-	-
WATER	-	100.0	-	100.0	-	-	-	-	-	-	-
OTHER	-	100.0	10.6	32.9	14.3	.3	38.6	-	-	-	3.3
UNKNOWN	-	100.0	-	.7	-	-	99.3	-	-	-	-
EAST NORTH CENTRAL	1 445	100.0	3.2	15.4	18.6	6.0	14.9	6.3	6.7	6.4	22.3
RAIL	685	100.0	2.5	19.8	8.0	6.2	10.7	7.3	7.8	5.9	31.9
MOTOR CARRIER	600	100.0	3.6	10.3	24.4	5.7	18.9	5.9	7.0	8.0	16.1
PRIVATE TRUCK	155	100.0	5.1	15.8	43.7	6.8	18.4	3.8	1.4	.3	4.8
AIR	-	100.0	-	61.9	9.7	-	-	28.5	-	-	-
WATER	-	100.0	-	-	-	-	-	-	-	-	-
OTHER	-	100.0	-	1.7	67.0	8.1	6.2	5.5	1.4	-	10.1
UNKNOWN	4	100.0	-	22.3	.9	4.9	2.5	-	-	65.7	3.6
WEST NORTH CENTRAL	1 095	100.0	3.7	10.9	9.8	14.1	8.5	1.0	11.3	4.3	36.6
RAIL	212	100.0	6.8	18.4	8.1	3.4	10.3	.6	7.7	7.1	37.6
MOTOR CARRIER	739	100.0	3.4	10.0	8.0	12.3	8.2	1.1	10.4	3.6	43.1
PRIVATE TRUCK	142	100.0	-	4.2	21.9	39.4	7.5	1.3	20.9	3.7	1.0
AIR	-	100.0	-	-	-	-	100.0	-	-	-	-
WATER	-	100.0	-	-	-	-	-	-	-	-	-
OTHER	-	100.0	80.3	13.1	.9	-	2.6	-	-	-	3.0
UNKNOWN	-	100.0	-	-	17.2	-	-	-	82.8	-	-
SOUTH ATLANTIC	137	100.0	1.0	26.5	2.5	.8	62.8	5.2	1.2	-	-
RAIL	63	100.0	-	41.2	2.4	-	55.4	1.0	-	-	-
MOTOR CARRIER	24	100.0	5.4	29.4	3.5	-	41.3	15.9	4.4	-	-
PRIVATE TRUCK	49	100.0	-	6.3	2.2	2.3	82.8	5.3	1.1	-	-
AIR	-	100.0	-	-	-	-	-	-	-	-	-
WATER	-	100.0	-	-	-	-	-	-	-	-	-
OTHER	-	100.0	-	-	-	-	-	-	-	-	-
UNKNOWN	-	100.0	-	-	-	-	-	-	-	-	-
EAST SOUTH CENTRAL	57	100.0	-	2.8	6.4	11.8	36.9	21.6	12.7	3.9	3.9
RAIL	2	100.0	-	-	-	33.1	-	15.0	51.9	-	-
MOTOR CARRIER	10	100.0	-	8.2	3.1	7.6	11.9	4.4	27.7	16.2	21.0
PRIVATE TRUCK	44	100.0	-	1.6	7.6	11.6	44.9	26.0	7.0	1.2	-
AIR	-	100.0	-	-	-	-	-	-	-	-	-
WATER	-	100.0	-	-	-	-	-	-	-	-	-
OTHER	-	100.0	-	-	100.0	-	-	-	-	-	-
UNKNOWN	-	100.0	-	-	100.0	-	-	-	-	-	-
PACIFIC	116	100.0	4.9	1.4	5.8	19.6	7.5	-	2.5	3.7	54.5
RAIL	42	100.0	13.3	-	8.7	52.3	18.3	-	5.6	-	1.9
MOTOR CARRIER	50	100.0	-	-	5.0	-	-	-	1.1	2.8	91.1
PRIVATE TRUCK	17	100.0	-	9.5	3.0	2.5	5.3	-	.1	16.7	62.8
AIR	-	100.0	-	-	-	-	-	-	-	-	100.0
WATER	6	100.0	-	-	-	-	-	-	-	-	100.0
OTHER	-	100.0	-	-	52.2	-	17.0	-	11.1	.3	19.4
UNKNOWN	-	100.0	-	-	-	-	-	-	-	-	100.0

See footnotes at end of table 4.

TABLE 3. **TCC GROUP 202**—Percent Distribution of Geographic Division of Destination and Means of Transport, by Geographic Division of Origin: 1972

Geographic division of destination and means of transport	Number	Percent distribution by division of origin[1]									
		U.S. total	New England	Middle Atlantic	East North Central	West North Central	South Atlantic	East South Central	West South Central	Mountain	Pacific
TONS OF SHIPMENTS	(thousands of tons)										
U.S. TOTAL	10 236	100.0	(D)	9.8	35.9	26.0	6.2	3.2	(D)	(D)	3.7
RAIL	1 986	100.0	(D)	19.6	53.3	12.7	11.6	.3	(D)	(D)	2.0
MOTOR CARRIER	3 582	100.0	(D)	6.5	37.9	42.6	2.2	.6	(D)	(D)	6.3
PRIVATE TRUCK	4 655	100.0	(D)	8.3	26.9	18.9	7.1	6.6	(D)	(D)	2.5
AIR	-	100.0	(D)	29.4	40.6	30.0	-	-	(D)	(D)	-
WATER	2	100.0	(D)	2.9	-	-	-	-	(D)	(D)	97.1
OTHER	-	100.0	(D)	16.3	15.3	67.6	-	.1	(D)	(D)	.7
UNKNOWN	9	100.0	(D)	7.8	73.0	12.1	-	-	(D)	(D)	-
NEW ENGLAND	1 268	100.0	(D)	4.0	4.5	2.7	.1	-	(D)	(D)	.2
RAIL	68	100.0	(D)	44.0	34.6	18.2	-	-	(D)	(D)	3.2
MOTOR CARRIER	56	100.0	(D)	17.3	41.6	38.3	2.9	-	(D)	(D)	-
PRIVATE TRUCK	1 142	100.0	(D)	.9	.9	-	-	-	(D)	(D)	-
AIR	-	100.0	(D)	-	-	-	-	-	(D)	(D)	-
WATER	-	100.0	(D)	-	-	-	-	-	(D)	(D)	-
OTHER	-	100.0	(D)	3.2	-	96.8	-	-	(D)	(D)	-
UNKNOWN	-	100.0	(D)	-	-	-	-	-	(D)	(D)	-
MIDDLE ATLANTIC	1 443	100.0	(D)	52.7	25.2	8.5	9.6	.2	(D)	(D)	-
RAIL	601	100.0	(D)	43.9	36.6	6.7	12.8	-	(D)	(D)	-
MOTOR CARRIER	375	100.0	(D)	47.1	26.5	20.1	6.0	.3	(D)	(D)	-
PRIVATE TRUCK	465	100.0	(D)	68.8	9.2	1.6	8.5	.2	(D)	(D)	.1
AIR	-	100.0	(D)	-	100.0	-	-	-	(D)	(D)	-
WATER	-	100.0	(D)	100.0	-	-	-	-	(D)	(D)	-
OTHER	-	100.0	(D)	46.2	.6	53.2	-	-	(D)	(D)	-
UNKNOWN	2	100.0	(D)	5.3	94.7	-	-	-	(D)	(D)	-
EAST NORTH CENTRAL	2 411	100.0	(D)	3.5	84.2	10.7	.4	.7	(D)	(D)	.2
RAIL	314	100.0	(D)	10.8	73.6	13.0	1.9	-	(D)	(D)	.7
MOTOR CARRIER	891	100.0	(D)	2.6	80.9	15.9	.2	.1	(D)	(D)	.2
PRIVATE TRUCK	1 204	100.0	(D)	2.3	89.4	6.2	.3	1.3	(D)	(D)	-
AIR	-	100.0	(D)	5.3	94.7	-	-	-	(D)	(D)	-
WATER	-	100.0	(D)	-	-	-	-	-	(D)	(D)	-
OTHER	-	100.0	(D)	19.4	71.8	7.3	-	.5	(D)	(D)	1.0
UNKNOWN	-	100.0	(D)	-	77.1	22.7	-	.2	(D)	(D)	-
WEST NORTH CENTRAL	2 023	100.0	(D)	.1	18.7	74.4	.1	.9	(D)	(D)	.8
RAIL	165	100.0	(D)	1.3	72.8	15.6	-	1.2	(D)	(D)	9.1
MOTOR CARRIER	981	100.0	(D)	-	18.8	80.8	-	.2	(D)	(D)	-
PRIVATE TRUCK	875	100.0	(D)	-	8.2	78.5	.2	1.6	(D)	(D)	-
AIR	-	100.0	(D)	-	-	-	-	-	(D)	(D)	-
WATER	-	100.0	(D)	-	-	-	-	-	(D)	(D)	-
OTHER	-	100.0	(D)	1.9	85.9	12.2	-	-	(D)	(D)	-
UNKNOWN	1	100.0	(D)	-	100.0	-	-	-	(D)	(D)	-
SOUTH ATLANTIC	1 075	100.0	(D)	8.9	27.7	9.5	42.2	11.1	(D)	(D)	.4
RAIL	359	100.0	(D)	13.0	38.7	7.5	39.8	-	(D)	(D)	.9
MOTOR CARRIER	251	100.0	(D)	8.7	50.0	24.9	15.3	.9	(D)	(D)	-
PRIVATE TRUCK	462	100.0	(D)	5.6	6.9	2.7	59.0	25.4	(D)	(D)	.1
AIR	-	100.0	(D)	49.1	-	50.9	-	-	(D)	(D)	-
WATER	-	100.0	(D)	-	-	-	-	-	(D)	(D)	-
OTHER	-	100.0	(D)	60.9	10.3	28.0	-	-	(D)	(D)	.8
UNKNOWN	1	100.0	(D)	37.1	62.9	-	-	-	(D)	(D)	-
EAST SOUTH CENTRAL	380	100.0	(D)	.6	47.3	5.2	7.3	39.5	(D)	(D)	-
RAIL	113	100.0	(D)	2.1	89.2	2.9	3.5	2.4	(D)	(D)	-
MOTOR CARRIER	96	100.0	(D)	-	68.2	13.4	13.1	4.9	(D)	(D)	-
PRIVATE TRUCK	169	100.0	(D)	-	7.2	2.1	6.5	84.2	(D)	(D)	-
AIR	-	100.0	(D)	-	100.0	-	-	-	(D)	(D)	-
WATER	-	100.0	(D)	-	-	-	-	-	(D)	(D)	-
OTHER	-	100.0	(D)	-	100.0	-	-	-	(D)	(D)	-
UNKNOWN	-	100.0	(D)	-	-	-	-	-	(D)	(D)	-
WEST SOUTH CENTRAL	424	100.0	(D)	2.4	26.7	59.2	.6	5.6	(D)	(D)	.5
RAIL	116	100.0	(D)	8.2	58.5	23.3	-	1.6	(D)	(D)	1.5
MOTOR CARRIER	215	100.0	(D)	.3	20.0	72.4	1.0	3.2	(D)	(D)	.2
PRIVATE TRUCK	91	100.0	(D)	-	2.6	72.9	.7	16.3	(D)	(D)	-
AIR	-	100.0	(D)	-	-	-	-	-	(D)	(D)	-
WATER	-	100.0	(D)	-	-	-	-	-	(D)	(D)	-
OTHER	-	100.0	(D)	-	70.3	4.0	-	-	(D)	(D)	25.7
UNKNOWN	1	100.0	(D)	-	.1	94.4	-	-	(D)	(D)	-
MOUNTAIN	279	100.0	(D)	.5	28.0	32.1	-	.7	(D)	(D)	4.9
RAIL	58	100.0	(D)	2.5	59.2	38.3	-	-	(D)	(D)	-
MOTOR CARRIER	148	100.0	(D)	-	27.9	28.9	-	.9	(D)	(D)	2.0
PRIVATE TRUCK	70	100.0	(D)	-	.4	34.7	-	.7	(D)	(D)	15.2
AIR	-	100.0	(D)	-	-	-	-	-	(D)	(D)	-
WATER	-	100.0	(D)	-	-	-	-	-	(D)	(D)	-
OTHER	-	100.0	(D)	-	-	-	-	-	(D)	(D)	100.0
UNKNOWN	2	100.0	(D)	-	100.0	-	-	-	(D)	(D)	-
PACIFIC	931	100.0	(D)	-	19.3	29.2	-	.1	(D)	(D)	36.7
RAIL	190	100.0	(D)	-	64.1	28.3	-	-	(D)	(D)	7.5
MOTOR CARRIER	564	100.0	(D)	-	9.5	38.5	-	.2	(D)	(D)	39.1
PRIVATE TRUCK	173	100.0	(D)	-	2.4	.6	-	-	(D)	(D)	60.0
AIR	-	100.0	(D)	-	-	-	-	-	(D)	(D)	-
WATER	2	100.0	(D)	-	-	-	-	-	(D)	(D)	100.0
OTHER	-	100.0	(D)	4.2	12.2	62.1	-	-	(D)	(D)	21.5
UNKNOWN	-	100.0	(D)	-	13.5	-	-	-	(D)	(D)	.3

See footnotes at end of table 4.

TABLE 3. TCC GROUP 202—Percent Distribution of Geographic Division of Destination and Means of Transport, by Geographic Division of Origin: 1972—Continued

Geographic division of destination and means of transport	Number	Percent distribution by division of origin[1]									
		U.S. total	New England	Middle Atlantic	East North Central	West North Central	South Atlantic	East South Central	West South Central	Mountain	Pacific
TON-MILES OF SHIPMENTS	(millions of ton-miles)										
U.S. TOTAL	3 235	100.0	(D)	6.3	44.7	33.9	4.3	1.8	(D)	(D)	3.6
RAIL	1 134	100.0	(D)	11.0	60.5	18.7	5.6	.2	(D)	(D)	3.8
MOTOR CARRIER	1 523	100.0	(D)	2.9	39.4	48.6	1.6	.7	(D)	(D)	3.3
PRIVATE TRUCK	565	100.0	(D)	6.0	27.5	25.2	8.8	7.8	(D)	(D)	3.1
AIR	-	100.0	(D)	23.8	30.7	45.5	-	-	(D)	(D)	-
WATER	6	100.0	(D)	-	-	-	-	-	(D)	(D)	100.0
OTHER	-	100.0	(D)	7.2	5.3	86.8	-	-	(D)	(D)	.7
UNKNOWN	5	100.0	(D)	5.7	80.0	8.0	-	-	(D)	(D)	-
NEW ENGLAND	171	100.0	(D)	8.9	27.3	23.5	.8	-	(D)	(D)	3.3
RAIL	47	100.0	(D)	21.0	36.2	30.7	-	-	(D)	(D)	12.1
MOTOR CARRIER	50	100.0	(D)	4.7	42.8	49.9	2.6	-	(D)	(D)	-
PRIVATE TRUCK	72	100.0	(D)	4.0	10.9	-	-	-	(D)	(D)	-
AIR	-	100.0	(D)	-	-	-	-	-	(D)	(D)	-
WATER	-	100.0	(D)	-	-	-	-	-	(D)	(D)	-
OTHER	-	100.0	(D)	1.1	-	98.9	-	-	(D)	(D)	-
UNKNOWN	-	100.0	(D)	-	-	-	-	-	(D)	(D)	-
MIDDLE ATLANTIC	501	100.0	(D)	22.6	44.5	23.7	7.3	.3	(D)	(D)	.3
RAIL	261	100.0	(D)	23.2	51.9	15.0	10.0	-	(D)	(D)	-
MOTOR CARRIER	172	100.0	(D)	16.8	35.8	42.7	4.2	.5	(D)	(D)	-
PRIVATE TRUCK	65	100.0	(D)	36.2	37.2	9.2	4.7	1.1	(D)	(D)	2.5
AIR	-	100.0	(D)	-	100.0	-	-	-	(D)	(D)	-
WATER	-	100.0	(D)	100.0	-	-	-	-	(D)	(D)	-
OTHER	-	100.0	(D)	17.1	.6	82.2	-	-	(D)	(D)	-
UNKNOWN	1	100.0	(D)	.2	99.8	-	-	-	(D)	(D)	-
EAST NORTH CENTRAL	424	100.0	(D)	7.0	63.4	25.3	.8	.9	(D)	(D)	1.6
RAIL	94	100.0	(D)	18.1	58.1	18.3	1.6	-	(D)	(D)	3.9
MOTOR CARRIER	219	100.0	(D)	3.8	67.0	26.9	.4	.1	(D)	(D)	1.1
PRIVATE TRUCK	111	100.0	(D)	3.9	60.9	28.0	1.0	3.0	(D)	(D)	.5
AIR	-	100.0	(D)	17.4	82.6	-	-	-	(D)	(D)	-
WATER	-	100.0	(D)	-	-	-	-	-	(D)	(D)	-
OTHER	-	100.0	(D)	18.1	62.0	13.1	-	.2	(D)	(D)	6.6
UNKNOWN	-	100.0	(D)	-	35.3	64.5	-	.2	(D)	(D)	-
WEST NORTH CENTRAL	284	100.0	(D)	.8	30.8	54.3	.4	2.4	(D)	(D)	8.0
RAIL	74	100.0	(D)	2.9	56.5	9.7	-	1.0	(D)	(D)	30.0
MOTOR CARRIER	127	100.0	(D)	-	27.0	71.5	-	.6	(D)	(D)	-
PRIVATE TRUCK	81	100.0	(D)	-	12.9	68.5	1.4	6.3	(D)	(D)	.5
AIR	-	100.0	(D)	-	-	-	-	-	(D)	(D)	-
WATER	-	100.0	(D)	-	-	-	-	-	(D)	(D)	-
OTHER	-	100.0	(D)	5.0	89.9	5.1	-	-	(D)	(D)	-
UNKNOWN	-	100.0	(D)	-	100.0	-	-	-	(D)	(D)	-
SOUTH ATLANTIC	452	100.0	(D)	6.0	47.5	20.5	19.1	4.7	(D)	(D)	1.9
RAIL	158	100.0	(D)	12.9	46.1	13.8	22.2	-	(D)	(D)	4.9
MOTOR CARRIER	189	100.0	(D)	2.1	59.8	31.8	5.3	.7	(D)	(D)	-
PRIVATE TRUCK	104	100.0	(D)	2.5	27.4	10.2	39.5	19.0	(D)	(D)	.9
AIR	-	100.0	(D)	33.7	-	66.3	-	-	(D)	(D)	-
WATER	-	100.0	(D)	-	-	-	-	-	(D)	(D)	-
OTHER	-	100.0	(D)	50.6	5.9	41.2	-	-	(D)	(D)	2.2
UNKNOWN	-	100.0	(D)	73.7	26.3	-	-	-	(D)	(D)	-
EAST SOUTH CENTRAL	123	100.0	(D)	1.0	74.0	9.0	5.8	10.0	(D)	(D)	-
RAIL	53	100.0	(D)	2.2	93.7	2.3	1.2	.7	(D)	(D)	-
MOTOR CARRIER	48	100.0	(D)	-	73.8	16.6	8.1	1.0	(D)	(D)	-
PRIVATE TRUCK	21	100.0	(D)	-	26.8	8.7	12.1	52.4	(D)	(D)	-
AIR	-	100.0	(D)	-	100.0	-	-	-	(D)	(D)	-
WATER	-	100.0	(D)	-	-	-	-	-	(D)	(D)	-
OTHER	-	100.0	(D)	-	100.0	-	-	-	(D)	(D)	-
UNKNOWN	-	100.0	(D)	-	-	-	-	-	(D)	(D)	-
WEST SOUTH CENTRAL	247	100.0	(D)	4.3	39.4	49.8	.7	2.9	(D)	(D)	1.2
RAIL	85	100.0	(D)	11.7	62.1	19.0	-	1.4	(D)	(D)	2.8
MOTOR CARRIER	125	100.0	(D)	.5	33.5	61.4	.9	2.3	(D)	(D)	.4
PRIVATE TRUCK	35	100.0	(D)	-	6.1	83.0	1.5	8.7	(D)	(D)	.1
AIR	-	100.0	(D)	-	-	-	-	-	(D)	(D)	-
WATER	-	100.0	(D)	-	-	-	-	-	(D)	(D)	-
OTHER	-	100.0	(D)	-	46.7	4.0	-	-	(D)	(D)	49.2
UNKNOWN	-	100.0	(D)	-	.3	97.2	-	-	(D)	(D)	-
MOUNTAIN	155	100.0	(D)	1.9	59.4	30.1	-	1.4	(D)	(D)	2.8
RAIL	58	100.0	(D)	5.0	69.4	25.6	-	-	(D)	(D)	-
MOTOR CARRIER	81	100.0	(D)	-	58.9	32.4	-	2.1	(D)	(D)	1.7
PRIVATE TRUCK	11	100.0	(D)	-	3.6	44.5	-	4.4	(D)	(D)	24.3
AIR	-	100.0	(D)	-	-	-	-	-	(D)	(D)	-
WATER	-	100.0	(D)	-	-	-	-	-	(D)	(D)	-
OTHER	-	100.0	(D)	-	-	-	-	-	(D)	(D)	100.0
UNKNOWN	3	100.0	(D)	-	100.0	-	-	-	(D)	(D)	-
PACIFIC	875	100.0	(D)	.1	36.9	45.8	-	.3	(D)	(D)	7.3
RAIL	299	100.0	(D)	-	73.0	26.7	-	-	(D)	(D)	.3
MOTOR CARRIER	509	100.0	(D)	.1	19.0	62.7	-	.4	(D)	(D)	9.0
PRIVATE TRUCK	59	100.0	(D)	-	12.4	2.3	-	-	(D)	(D)	18.1
AIR	-	100.0	(D)	-	-	-	-	-	(D)	(D)	-
WATER	6	100.0	(D)	-	-	-	-	-	(D)	(D)	100.0
OTHER	-	100.0	(D)	6.8	15.1	74.2	-	-	(D)	(D)	4.0
UNKNOWN	-	100.0	(D)	-	32.0	-	-	-	(D)	(D)	.1

See footnotes at end of table 4.

TABLE 4. TCC GROUP 202—Percent Distribution of Distance Shipped and Weight of Shipment, by Means of Transport: 1972

Distance shipped and weight of shipment[2][3]	Number	Percent distribution by means of transport							
		All means of transport	Rail	Motor carrier	Private truck	Air	Water	Other	Unknown
TONS OF SHIPMENTS	(thousands of tons)								
U.S. TOTAL..........	8 804	100.0	20.7	36.8	42.4	-	-	-	.1
UNDER 100 MILES.........	3 838	100.0	1.0	26.7	72.3	-	-	-	-
UNDER 1000 POUNDS.....	193	100.0	-	1.6	98.4	-	-	-	-
1000 TO 9999 POUNDS...	191	100.0	-	21.4	78.5	-	-	-	.1
10000 TO 29999 POUNDS.	284	100.0	1.0	51.9	47.1	-	-	-	-
30000 TO 59999 POUNDS.	2 089	100.0	.2	31.2	68.6	-	-	-	-
60000 TO 89999 POUNDS.	79	100.0	26.0	10.3	63.7	-	-	-	-
90000 POUNDS AND OVER.	999	100.0	1.0	17.3	81.7	-	-	-	-
100 TO 199 MILES........	1 119	100.0	20.6	45.1	34.1	-	-	-	.2
UNDER 1000 POUNDS.....	40	100.0	-	6.5	93.2	-	-	.1	.1
1000 TO 9999 POUNDS...	58	100.0	-	42.3	57.7	-	-	-	-
10000 TO 29999 POUNDS.	114	100.0	-	68.5	30.6	-	-	-	.9
30000 TO 59999 POUNDS.	644	100.0	7.2	57.3	35.4	-	-	-	-
60000 TO 89999 POUNDS.	103	100.0	66.2	21.6	12.1	-	-	-	.1
90000 POUNDS AND OVER.	157	100.0	73.6	4.7	21.7	-	-	-	-
200 TO 299 MILES........	987	100.0	46.6	33.4	20.0	-	-	-	-
UNDER 1000 POUNDS.....	13	100.0	-	23.6	75.2	-	-	1.2	-
1000 TO 9999 POUNDS...	28	100.0	-	56.1	43.9	-	-	-	-
10000 TO 29999 POUNDS.	80	100.0	-	58.4	41.6	-	-	-	-
30000 TO 59999 POUNDS.	417	100.0	8.1	58.1	33.8	-	-	-	-
60000 TO 89999 POUNDS.	98	100.0	99.3	.7	-	-	-	-	-
90000 POUNDS AND OVER.	348	100.0	94.1	5.9	-	-	-	-	-
300 TO 499 MILES........	868	100.0	35.7	45.4	18.6	-	-	-	.2
UNDER 1000 POUNDS.....	7	100.0	.5	35.6	62.5	-	-	.8	.3
1000 TO 9999 POUNDS...	43	100.0	.1	52.1	47.7	.3	-	-	-
10000 TO 29999 POUNDS.	109	100.0	1.6	68.0	28.6	-	-	-	1.7
30000 TO 59999 POUNDS.	425	100.0	8.4	67.0	24.6	-	-	-	-
60000 TO 89999 POUNDS.	194	100.0	95.2	4.8	-	-	-	-	-
90000 POUNDS AND OVER.	87	100.0	100.0	-	-	-	-	-	-
500 TO 999 MILES........	1 252	100.0	40.4	44.7	14.7	-	-	-	.2
UNDER 1000 POUNDS.....	8	100.0	1.2	40.4	56.5	.2	-	.5	1.1
1000 TO 9999 POUNDS...	57	100.0	3.3	51.4	45.3	-	-	-	-
10000 TO 29999 POUNDS.	102	100.0	2.3	70.2	26.8	-	-	-	.7
30000 TO 59999 POUNDS.	633	100.0	10.1	69.8	19.9	-	-	-	.2
60000 TO 89999 POUNDS.	235	100.0	94.4	5.6	-	-	-	-	-
90000 POUNDS AND OVER.	215	100.0	99.9	.1	-	-	-	-	-
1000 TO 1499 MILES......	393	100.0	29.8	62.9	7.2	-	-	.1	-
UNDER 1000 POUNDS.....	-	100.0	-	82.8	12.9	-	-	4.1	.1
1000 TO 9999 POUNDS...	9	100.0	-	72.1	22.2	-	-	5.7	-
10000 TO 29999 POUNDS.	14	100.0	-	97.4	2.6	-	-	-	-
30000 TO 59999 POUNDS.	260	100.0	4.6	85.6	9.8	-	-	-	-
60000 TO 89999 POUNDS.	35	100.0	93.0	7.0	-	-	-	-	-
90000 POUNDS AND OVER.	71	100.0	100.0	-	-	-	-	-	-
1500 MILES OR OVER......	345	100.0	46.0	51.4	1.4	-	.6	-	.6
UNDER 1000 POUNDS.....	-	100.0	-	88.5	8.1	-	1.6	1.8	-
1000 TO 9999 POUNDS...	16	100.0	-	73.7	24.4	-	1.3	-	.6
10000 TO 29999 POUNDS.	10	100.0	-	92.0	.3	-	7.8	-	-
30000 TO 59999 POUNDS.	159	100.0	1.9	95.8	.3	-	.7	-	1.3
60000 TO 89999 POUNDS.	58	100.0	97.3	2.7	-	-	-	-	-
90000 POUNDS AND OVER.	98	100.0	100.0	-	-	-	-	-	-
TON-MILES OF SHIPMENTS	(millions of ton-miles)								
U.S. TOTAL..........	2 902	100.0	36.2	47.5	15.8	-	.2	-	.2
UNDER 100 MILES.........	202	100.0	.9	34.5	64.5	-	-	-	-
UNDER 1000 POUNDS.....	6	100.0	-	3.0	96.9	-	-	-	-
1000 TO 9999 POUNDS...	9	100.0	-	30.4	69.6	-	-	-	-
10000 TO 29999 POUNDS.	17	100.0	.9	60.5	38.6	-	-	-	-
30000 TO 59999 POUNDS.	123	100.0	.1	38.4	61.5	-	-	-	-
60000 TO 89999 POUNDS.	5	100.0	16.0	11.0	73.0	-	-	-	-
90000 POUNDS AND OVER.	39	100.0	1.6	20.9	77.4	-	-	-	-
100 TO 199 MILES........	166	100.0	22.2	44.8	32.8	-	-	-	.1
UNDER 1000 POUNDS.....	5	100.0	-	6.4	93.3	-	-	.1	.2
1000 TO 9999 POUNDS...	8	100.0	-	41.8	58.2	-	-	-	-
10000 TO 29999 POUNDS.	16	100.0	-	67.4	31.9	-	-	-	.7
30000 TO 59999 POUNDS.	94	100.0	8.0	58.1	33.8	-	-	-	.1
60000 TO 89999 POUNDS.	16	100.0	69.6	20.2	10.2	-	-	-	-
90000 POUNDS AND OVER.	24	100.0	74.2	4.7	21.2	-	-	-	-

See footnotes at end of table 4.

TABLE 4. TCC GROUP 202—Percent Distribution of Distance Shipped and Weight of Shipment, by Means of Transport: 1972—Continued

Distance shipped and weight of shipment [2] [3]	Number	Percent distribution by means of transport							
		All means of transport	Rail	Motor carrier	Private truck	Air	Water	Other	Unknown
TON-MILES OF SHIPMENTS	(millions of ton-miles)								
200 TO 299 MILES.........	255	100.0	48.4	32.7	18.9	-	-	-	-
UNDER 1000 POUNDS.....	3	100.0	-	25.2	73.4	-	-	1.3	-
1000 TO 9999 POUNDS...	7	100.0	-	57.7	42.3	-	-	-	-
10000 TO 29999 POUNDS.	20	100.0	-	60.4	39.6	-	-	-	-
30000 TO 59999 POUNDS.	104	100.0	8.8	57.7	33.5	-	-	-	-
60000 TO 89999 POUNDS.	26	100.0	99.4	.6	-	-	-	-	-
90000 POUNDS AND OVER.	94	100.0	93.7	6.3	-	-	-	-	-
300 TO 499 MILES........	343	100.0	35.5	45.2	19.1	-	-	-	.2
UNDER 1000 POUNDS.....	3	100.0	.6	33.4	64.6	.4	-	.7	.4
1000 TO 9999 POUNDS...	17	100.0	.2	51.9	48.0	-	-	-	-
10000 TO 29999 POUNDS.	45	100.0	1.2	68.5	28.6	-	-	-	1.8
30000 TO 59999 POUNDS.	165	100.0	8.2	66.5	25.3	-	-	-	-
60000 TO 89999 POUNDS.	77	100.0	95.7	4.3	-	-	-	-	-
90000 POUNDS AND OVER.	33	100.0	100.0	-	-	-	-	-	-
500 TO 999 MILES........	868	100.0	40.3	45.5	14.0	-	-	-	.2
UNDER 1000 POUNDS.....	5	100.0	1.5	39.8	56.8	.3	-	.6	1.0
1000 TO 9999 POUNDS...	41	100.0	3.0	54.5	42.4	-	-	-	-
10000 TO 29999 POUNDS.	74	100.0	2.3	71.4	25.5	-	-	-	.8
30000 TO 59999 POUNDS.	434	100.0	10.1	70.9	18.9	-	-	-	.2
60000 TO 89999 POUNDS.	163	100.0	94.5	5.5	-	-	-	-	-
90000 POUNDS AND OVER.	148	100.0	99.8	.2	-	-	-	-	-
1000 TO 1499 MILES......	480	100.0	29.0	64.7	6.2	-	-	.1	-
UNDER 1000 POUNDS.....	-	100.0	-	83.2	12.5	-	-	4.2	.1
1000 TO 9999 POUNDS...	11	100.0	-	72.9	21.9	-	-	5.2	-
10000 TO 29999 POUNDS.	15	100.0	-	96.8	3.2	-	-	-	-
30000 TO 59999 POUNDS.	323	100.0	4.1	87.5	8.3	-	-	-	-
60000 TO 89999 POUNDS.	39	100.0	92.1	7.9	-	-	-	-	-
90000 POUNDS AND OVER.	89	100.0	100.0	-	-	-	-	-	-
1500 MILES OR OVER......	585	100.0	47.3	49.6	1.5	-	1.1	-	.6
UNDER 1000 POUNDS.....	1	100.0	-	87.7	8.1	-	2.5	1.8	-
1000 TO 9999 POUNDS...	29	100.0	-	73.1	24.2	-	2.1	-	.6
10000 TO 29999 POUNDS.	19	100.0	-	87.8	.2	-	12.0	-	-
30000 TO 59999 POUNDS.	259	100.0	1.9	95.2	.5	-	1.2	-	1.2
60000 TO 89999 POUNDS.	103	100.0	97.3	2.7	-	-	-	-	-
90000 POUNDS AND OVER.	171	100.0	100.0	-	-	-	-	-	-

Note: Detail may not add to total due to rounding. The introductory table shows the estimates of sampling variability for tons; sampling variability for ton-miles has not been estimated. See the map in the Introduction for the States comprising the geographic divisions of the United States.

Shipments excluded from the survey are those moving by pipeline (primarily petroleum products from refineries), parcel post shipments, and commodities moved by own power (motorized vehicles, aircraft, etc.) or towed (prefabricated buildings, etc.). Local shipments (commodities shipped less than 25 miles from the plant) and shipments within the same city are also excluded. Shipments to Alaska and Hawaii from the 48 conterminous States and the District of Columbia are included; however, no data were obtained for shipments originating in Alaska and Hawaii.

- Represents zero or rounds to zero.   (D) Withheld to avoid disclosing figures for individual companies.

[1]Production of this commodity is concentrated in the geographic divisions shown; figures and distributions for geographic divisions not shown are included in the total.

[2]Distances of shipments to foreign destinations are calculated only to the U.S. port of exit.

[3]Includes only shipments represented by bills of lading and invoices. Summary records which did not show individual weights of shipments are not included.

TCC 203. Canned and Preserved Fruits, Vegetables, Seafood

Comparisons of Tons and Ton-Miles of Shipments for
Geographic Divisions of Origin and for Sampling Variability: 1972 and 1967

Geographic division of origin	Estimates				Relative sampling variability in tons (percent)	
	1972		1967		1972	1967
	Tons (thousands)	Ton-miles (millions)	Tons (thousands)	Ton-miles (millions)		
U.S. total	34,317	20,485	32,475	23,898	5.9	8.8
New England	(D)	(D)	1,216	535	(*)	(*)
Middle Atlantic	5,868	1,878	4,968	1,573	16.3	(*)
East North Central	7,307	2,665	6,376	2,402	16.9	(*)
West North Central	1,838	921	1,615	758	27.5	(*)
South Atlantic	4,982	2,716	4,761	3,860	26.5	(*)
East South Central	(D)	(D)	439	122	(*)	(*)
West South Central	3,496	2,048	1,114	564	34.5	(*)
Mountain	1,408	1,460	434	440	35.0	(*)
Pacific	7,945	8,170	11,552	13,643	11.2	(*)

(D) Withheld to avoid disclosing figures for individual companies.　　(*) Data not published.

TABLE 1. **TCC GROUP 203**—Percent Distribution of Geographic Division of Origin and Distance Shipped, by Means of Transport: 1972

Geographic division of origin[1] and distance shipped[2]	Number	Percent distribution by means of transport							
		All means of transport	Rail	Motor carrier	Private truck	Air	Water	Other	Unknown
TONS OF SHIPMENTS	(thousands of tons)								
U.S. TOTAL............	34 317	100.0	35.2	41.7	22.1	-	.4	-	.6
MIDDLE ATLANTIC..........	5 868	100.0	16.2	55.5	27.4	-	.4	-	.4
UNDER 100 MILES........	1 781	100.0	4.4	33.9	61.4	-	.2	.1	.1
100 TO 199 MILES......	1 127	100.0	15.6	61.8	22.3	-	-	-	.3
200 TO 299 MILES......	1 128	100.0	20.4	69.4	9.6	-	.1	-	.5
300 TO 499 MILES......	722	100.0	17.8	70.7	11.4	-	-	-	.1
500 TO 999 MILES......	769	100.0	28.6	60.9	8.4	-	.9	-	1.2
1000 TO 1499 MILES....	236	100.0	22.3	71.6	2.6	-	3.2	-	.4
1500 MILES OR OVER....	102	100.0	65.5	26.9	2.4	-	4.0	-	1.2
EAST NORTH CENTRAL......	7 307	100.0	36.3	33.8	29.5	-	-	.1	.4
UNDER 100 MILES........	1 078	100.0	19.7	35.4	44.5	-	-	.1	.2
100 TO 199 MILES......	1 627	100.0	22.0	40.2	37.1	-	-	.2	.4
200 TO 299 MILES......	1 368	100.0	24.0	31.7	44.0	-	-	-	.3
300 TO 499 MILES......	1 442	100.0	45.0	34.2	20.5	-	-	-	.3
500 TO 999 MILES......	1 496	100.0	63.8	25.4	10.1	-	-	-	.7
1000 TO 1499 MILES....	185	100.0	51.0	42.0	6.7	.1	-	-	.3
1500 MILES OR OVER....	108	100.0	48.3	41.8	6.8	.1	-	-	3.0
WEST NORTH CENTRAL......	1 838	100.0	42.5	29.6	26.8	-	-	-	1.1
UNDER 100 MILES........	196	100.0	7.1	47.8	45.1	-	-	-	-
100 TO 199 MILES......	250	100.0	24.7	24.7	48.7	-	-	.1	1.7
200 TO 299 MILES......	227	100.0	26.3	22.7	46.9	-	-	-	4.1
300 TO 499 MILES......	408	100.0	49.5	23.4	27.1	-	-	-	-
500 TO 999 MILES......	577	100.0	56.7	32.4	10.3	-	-	-	.5
1000 TO 1499 MILES....	153	100.0	67.0	29.1	2.1	-	-	-	1.8
1500 MILES OR OVER....	24	100.0	54.2	37.7	8.1	-	-	-	-
SOUTH ATLANTIC..........	4 982	100.0	19.8	60.2	18.9	-	1.1	-	.1
UNDER 100 MILES........	588	100.0	1.5	52.6	45.8	-	.1	-	-
100 TO 199 MILES......	1 259	100.0	4.7	71.0	24.0	-	.1	-	.2
200 TO 299 MILES......	453	100.0	23.2	48.7	28.1	-	-	-	-
300 TO 499 MILES......	615	100.0	15.1	64.1	20.6	-	-	-	.2
500 TO 999 MILES......	1 317	100.0	31.1	59.8	7.0	-	2.1	-	-
1000 TO 1499 MILES....	488	100.0	35.3	58.5	1.5	-	4.4	-	.2
1500 MILES OR OVER....	258	100.0	53.5	40.4	5.7	-	.3	-	-
WEST SOUTH CENTRAL......	3 496	100.0	22.4	47.7	26.9	-	-	-	2.9
UNDER 100 MILES........	196	100.0	13.6	20.2	63.9	-	-	-	2.3
100 TO 199 MILES......	275	100.0	18.3	28.7	45.7	-	-	-	7.2
200 TO 299 MILES......	529	100.0	19.4	46.6	32.5	-	-	-	1.5
300 TO 499 MILES......	768	100.0	30.9	39.4	27.9	-	-	-	1.7
500 TO 999 MILES......	1 162	100.0	23.2	59.6	15.3	-	-	-	1.9
1000 TO 1499 MILES....	463	100.0	13.0	63.8	21.8	-	-	-	1.3
1500 MILES OR OVER....	100	100.0	36.5	12.1	23.5	-	-	-	27.8
MOUNTAIN................	1 408	100.0	75.9	14.9	8.8	-	-	-	.3
UNDER 100 MILES........	271	100.0	86.3	4.3	9.4	-	-	-	-
100 TO 199 MILES......	54	100.0	41.8	24.7	33.5	-	-	-	-
200 TO 299 MILES......	15	100.0	9.4	15.6	75.0	-	-	-	-
300 TO 499 MILES......	46	100.0	33.8	40.7	25.5	-	-	-	-
500 TO 999 MILES......	255	100.0	43.5	34.2	22.3	-	-	-	-
1000 TO 1499 MILES....	361	100.0	85.7	14.3	-	-	-	-	-
1500 MILES OR OVER....	403	100.0	92.6	6.2	-	-	-	-	1.2
PACIFIC.................	7 945	100.0	54.5	34.1	10.4	-	.8	-	.1
UNDER 100 MILES........	1 543	100.0	9.6	56.7	32.7	-	.8	-	.1
100 TO 199 MILES......	424	100.0	20.4	57.9	21.4	-	-	.2	.1
200 TO 299 MILES......	312	100.0	13.8	63.1	23.1	-	-	-	-
300 TO 499 MILES......	1 057	100.0	47.4	46.1	6.4	-	-	-	-
500 TO 999 MILES......	1 097	100.0	51.5	45.0	3.4	-	-	-	.1
1000 TO 1499 MILES....	687	100.0	76.2	19.9	3.8	-	-	-	.1
1500 MILES OR OVER....	2 822	100.0	87.3	9.6	1.1	.1	1.8	-	.2
TON-MILES OF SHIPMENTS	(millions of ton-miles)								
U.S. TOTAL............	20 485	100.0	56.3	32.4	9.5	-	1.0	-	.7
MIDDLE ATLANTIC..........	1 878	100.0	26.7	59.0	12.2	-	1.3	-	.7
UNDER 100 MILES........	126	100.0	4.8	27.6	67.4	-	.1	.1	-
100 TO 199 MILES......	162	100.0	16.3	62.0	21.4	-	-	-	.3
200 TO 299 MILES......	278	100.0	20.7	69.2	9.5	-	.1	-	.5
300 TO 499 MILES......	270	100.0	17.5	70.8	11.6	-	-	-	.1
500 TO 999 MILES......	537	100.0	28.6	61.1	7.7	-	1.1	-	1.5
1000 TO 1499 MILES....	274	100.0	21.8	72.6	2.4	-	2.9	-	.3
1500 MILES OR OVER....	230	100.0	65.4	27.1	1.8	-	4.3	-	1.3
EAST NORTH CENTRAL......	2 665	100.0	48.4	31.7	19.2	-	-	-	.7
UNDER 100 MILES........	72	100.0	21.5	34.0	44.3	-	-	-	.2
100 TO 199 MILES......	230	100.0	22.1	40.3	36.9	-	-	.2	.4
200 TO 299 MILES......	344	100.0	24.8	31.2	43.7	-	-	-	.3
300 TO 499 MILES......	558	100.0	46.6	33.9	19.3	-	-	-	.3
500 TO 999 MILES......	1 048	100.0	64.2	24.6	10.4	-	-	-	.7
1000 TO 1499 MILES....	207	100.0	51.3	41.8	6.6	.1	-	-	.3
1500 MILES OR OVER....	203	100.0	47.8	42.3	6.6	.1	-	-	3.1

See footnotes at end of table 4.

TABLE 1. **TCC GROUP 203**—Percent Distribution of Geographic Division of Origin and Distance Shipped, by Means of Transport: 1972—Continued

Geographic division of origin[1] and distance shipped[2]	Number	Percent distribution by means of transport							
		All means of transport	Rail	Motor carrier	Private truck	Air	Water	Other	Unknown
TON-MILES OF SHIPMENTS	(millions of ton-miles)								
WEST NORTH CENTRAL......	921	100.0	54.1	29.5	15.4	-	-	-	1.0
UNDER 100 MILES.......	9	100.0	7.1	38.7	54.2	-	-	-	-
100 TO 199 MILES......	41	100.0	25.7	25.5	47.2	-	-	.1	1.5
200 TO 299 MILES......	58	100.0	25.3	22.6	47.6	-	-	-	4.6
300 TO 499 MILES......	162	100.0	49.2	23.8	27.0	-	-	-	-
500 TO 999 MILES.....	424	100.0	57.9	32.3	9.1	-	-	-	.6
1000 TO 1499 MILES....	186	100.0	67.4	28.8	2.1	-	-	-	1.7
1500 MILES OR OVER....	39	100.0	54.5	37.5	8.0	-	-	-	-
SOUTH ATLANTIC..........	2 716	100.0	33.6	55.6	8.7	-	2.0	-	.1
UNDER 100 MILES.......	29	100.0	2.2	53.1	44.5	-	.1	-	-
100 TO 199 MILES......	189	100.0	4.9	73.0	21.8	-	.1	.1	.1
200 TO 299 MILES......	112	100.0	24.6	47.4	27.9	-	-	-	-
300 TO 499 MILES......	237	100.0	16.4	63.1	20.3	-	-	-	.2
500 TO 999 MILES......	1 050	100.0	31.0	60.4	6.0	-	2.5	-	-
1000 TO 1499 MILES....	538	100.0	35.4	58.6	1.5	-	4.4	-	.2
1500 MILES OR OVER....	558	100.0	57.3	36.4	5.6	-	.7	-	-
WEST SOUTH CENTRAL......	2 048	100.0	22.3	51.9	21.8	-	-	-	4.1
UNDER 100 MILES.......	13	100.0	14.2	17.9	66.1	-	-	-	1.7
100 TO 199 MILES......	39	100.0	18.5	27.8	47.8	-	-	-	5.9
200 TO 299 MILES......	131	100.0	19.0	46.1	33.6	-	-	-	1.3
300 TO 499 MILES......	303	100.0	29.8	38.9	29.7	-	-	-	1.6
500 TO 999 MILES......	828	100.0	21.4	61.7	14.5	-	-	-	2.4
1000 TO 1499 MILES....	533	100.0	12.6	63.6	22.3	-	-	-	1.4
1500 MILES OR OVER....	198	100.0	43.4	10.7	22.4	-	-	-	23.5
MOUNTAIN...............	1 460	100.0	82.8	12.7	3.8	-	-	-	.6
UNDER 100 MILES.......	12	100.0	84.0	3.0	12.9	-	-	-	-
100 TO 199 MILES......	9	100.0	40.1	24.1	35.8	-	-	-	-
200 TO 299 MILES......	3	100.0	8.4	18.1	73.5	-	-	-	-
300 TO 499 MILES......	19	100.0	31.8	42.3	25.9	-	-	-	-
500 TO 999 MILES......	197	100.0	45.3	32.8	21.9	-	-	-	-
1000 TO 1499 MILES....	452	100.0	85.9	14.1	-	-	-	-	-
1500 MILES OR OVER....	765	100.0	92.9	5.9	-	-	-	-	1.2
PACIFIC................	8 170	100.0	78.8	17.0	2.5	.1	1.6	-	.1
UNDER 100 MILES.......	79	100.0	12.4	59.4	27.4	-	.7	-	.1
100 TO 199 MILES......	60	100.0	20.4	59.2	20.1	-	-	.3	.1
200 TO 299 MILES......	79	100.0	13.5	63.3	23.2	-	-	-	-
300 TO 499 MILES......	402	100.0	50.7	43.2	6.1	-	-	-	-
500 TO 999 MILES......	769	100.0	49.2	47.5	3.3	-	-	-	-
1000 TO 1499 MILES....	940	100.0	77.3	18.8	3.8	-	-	-	.1
1500 MILES OR OVER....	5 838	100.0	87.2	9.2	1.1	.1	2.2	-	.2

See footnotes at end of table 4.

TABLE 2. **TCC GROUP 203**—Percent Distribution of Geographic Division of Origin and Means of Transport, by Geographic Division of Destination: 1972

Geographic division of origin[1] and means of transport	Number	Percent distribution by division of destination									
		U.S. total	New England	Middle Atlantic	East North Central	West North Central	South Atlantic	East South Central	West South Central	Mountain	Pacific
TONS OF SHIPMENTS	(thousands of tons)										
U.S. TOTAL..............	34 317	100.0	4.2	20.5	20.4	9.3	14.4	5.5	7.9	4.1	13.6
RAIL..................	12 063	100.0	4.8	14.6	19.0	10.8	16.3	7.1	9.3	6.3	12.0
MOTOR CARRIER.........	14 313	100.0	4.4	23.8	20.3	8.6	13.9	3.6	6.1	3.0	16.4
PRIVATE TRUCK.........	7 594	100.0	3.1	23.4	23.1	8.6	12.4	7.0	8.9	2.8	10.7
AIR...................	3	100.0	3.1	13.4	16.6	13.1	21.0	5.3	5.4	8.5	13.8
WATER.................	137	100.0	11.9	44.7	-	-	12.8	-	-	-	30.5
OTHER.................	10	100.0	5.9	18.3	51.3	5.4	6.0	-	.1	9.7	3.2
UNKNOWN...............	194	100.0	1.7	12.7	24.5	9.5	6.4	.8	24.2	.7	19.5
MIDDLE ATLANTIC.........	5 868	100.0	11.1	52.1	11.4	2.8	16.7	2.1	1.8	.3	1.6
RAIL..................	953	100.0	25.0	15.1	10.4	3.8	32.0	2.7	3.8	.3	6.9
MOTOR CARRIER.........	3 259	100.0	10.4	49.4	14.1	3.3	17.0	2.7	2.2	.4	.7
PRIVATE TRUCK.........	1 608	100.0	4.7	80.1	7.0	.8	6.5	.8	-	.2	-
AIR...................	-	100.0	-	9.5	72.3	-	-	-	-	-	18.2
WATER.................	23	100.0	-	20.0	-	-	62.2	-	-	-	17.8
OTHER.................	1	100.0	-	99.4	.3	-	.2	-	-	-	-
UNKNOWN...............	22	100.0	2.3	44.4	2.3	39.6	6.0	-	-	-	5.3

See footnotes at end of table 4.

TABLE 2. **TCC GROUP 203**—Percent Distribution of Geographic Division of Origin and Means of Transport, by Geographic Division of Destination: 1972—Continued

Geographic division of origin[1] and means of transport	Number	Percent distribution by division of destination									
		U.S. total	New England	Middle Atlantic	East North Central	West North Central	South Atlantic	East South Central	West South Central	Mountain	Pacific
TONS OF SHIPMENTS	(thousands of tons)										
EAST NORTH CENTRAL......	7 307	100.0	1.2	10.9	49.7	12.3	9.5	7.7	6.5	.9	1.5
RAIL..................	2 649	100.0	1.9	19.4	32.4	11.9	13.7	7.3	9.8	1.5	2.0
MOTOR CARRIER.........	2 468	100.0	1.1	8.0	54.7	15.6	7.1	5.4	5.6	.7	1.8
PRIVATE TRUCK.........	2 152	100.0	.4	3.7	65.1	8.9	7.0	10.8	3.5	.3	.3
AIR...................	-	100.0	6.1	5.2	5.2	5.9	47.9	3.4	8.5	2.0	15.7
WATER.................	-	100.0	-	-	-	-	-	-	-	-	-
OTHER.................	5	100.0	.1	.7	94.6	4.1	.3	-	.2	-	-
UNKNOWN...............	31	100.0	3.9	4.5	48.2	8.1	9.0	3.5	10.0	2.4	10.5
WEST NORTH CENTRAL......	1 838	100.0	.7	9.2	23.6	37.7	6.6	2.9	10.9	4.5	3.7
RAIL..................	781	100.0	1.0	16.4	17.7	31.6	7.4	2.6	10.1	7.4	5.9
MOTOR CARRIER.........	544	100.0	.9	7.2	26.8	37.0	9.9	1.9	10.3	2.3	3.7
PRIVATE TRUCK.........	492	100.0	.2	.6	28.5	48.6	1.0	4.7	13.4	2.5	.6
AIR...................	-	100.0	-	-	-	-	-	-	-	-	100.0
WATER.................	-	100.0	-	-	-	-	-	-	-	-	-
OTHER.................	-	100.0	-	-	-	100.0	-	-	-	-	-
UNKNOWN...............	19	100.0	-	-	47.7	21.9	30.4	-	-	-	-
SOUTH ATLANTIC..........	4 982	100.0	4.7	35.7	10.7	3.8	31.8	4.6	3.5	1.6	3.4
RAIL..................	986	100.0	3.3	15.7	15.3	4.2	36.1	5.6	5.6	1.6	12.6
MOTOR CARRIER.........	2 997	100.0	5.2	41.5	11.5	4.5	26.8	3.9	3.4	1.8	1.4
PRIVATE TRUCK.........	939	100.0	3.8	36.5	4.0	1.0	44.8	6.2	2.1	1.0	.5
AIR...................	-	100.0	-	-	1.4	-	.3	97.5	-	-	.8
WATER.................	52	100.0	24.7	69.7	-	-	4.0	-	-	-	1.6
OTHER.................	-	100.0	-	5.2	-	-	94.8	-	-	-	-
UNKNOWN...............	4	100.0	24.8	10.8	7.5	10.5	46.3	-	-	-	-
WEST SOUTH CENTRAL......	3 496	100.0	.5	5.2	12.6	13.3	13.4	10.1	35.2	5.4	4.4
RAIL..................	783	100.0	.2	2.5	1.5	9.5	15.3	19.9	40.5	4.6	6.0
MOTOR CARRIER.........	1 669	100.0	.9	7.1	22.8	15.7	15.7	8.0	23.1	5.4	1.3
PRIVATE TRUCK.........	941	100.0	-	3.7	2.7	13.3	9.3	6.8	51.5	6.6	6.0
AIR...................	-	100.0	-	-	-	27.2	46.8	26.0	-	-	-
WATER.................	-	100.0	-	-	-	-	-	-	-	-	-
OTHER.................	-	100.0	-	-	-	-	-	-	-	-	-
UNKNOWN...............	101	100.0	-	5.5	20.9	2.1	-	-	43.1	.5	27.9
MOUNTAIN................	1 408	100.0	4.8	8.7	12.5	17.3	6.5	9.5	4.3	26.9	9.5
RAIL..................	1 069	100.0	5.6	10.6	14.0	14.0	8.3	12.1	4.4	25.0	5.9
MOTOR CARRIER.........	210	100.0	3.8	2.2	12.1	23.1	1.0	2.0	6.5	20.9	28.4
PRIVATE TRUCK.........	123	100.0	-	-	-	37.2	-	-	-	54.1	8.7
AIR...................	-	100.0	-	-	-	-	-	-	-	-	-
WATER.................	-	100.0	-	-	-	-	-	-	-	-	-
OTHER.................	-	100.0	-	-	-	-	-	-	-	-	-
UNKNOWN...............	4	100.0	-	100.0	-	-	-	-	-	-	-
PACIFIC.................	7 945	100.0	1.7	9.1	12.3	6.7	5.2	3.0	5.1	7.4	49.4
RAIL..................	4 333	100.0	2.9	14.9	19.7	10.0	8.8	5.3	6.8	7.7	23.9
MOTOR CARRIER.........	2 706	100.0	.2	1.9	4.2	3.0	1.1	.4	3.5	7.4	78.3
PRIVATE TRUCK.........	830	100.0	.2	.7	.6	2.5	.4	-	1.6	6.0	87.9
AIR...................	2	100.0	2.6	16.0	19.9	15.5	16.1	.9	5.0	10.5	13.6
WATER.................	62	100.0	5.6	32.8	-	-	2.0	-	-	-	59.6
OTHER.................	2	100.0	29.3	-	.6	-	5.0	-	-	48.9	16.3
UNKNOWN...............	7	100.0	2.8	21.7	12.2	-	.4	-	-	-	62.9
TON-MILES OF SHIPMENTS	(millions of ton-miles)										
U.S. TOTAL.............	20 485	100.0	4.8	19.0	19.3	9.8	15.4	6.1	9.0	4.2	12.4
RAIL..................	11 533	100.0	5.4	20.6	19.1	9.4	15.8	7.3	8.5	3.2	10.7
MOTOR CARRIER.........	6 642	100.0	4.3	16.8	20.1	10.3	15.9	4.0	9.1	5.5	14.1
PRIVATE TRUCK.........	1 946	100.0	2.9	14.7	19.4	11.6	13.0	7.4	13.0	6.3	11.6
AIR...................	6	100.0	3.7	19.3	17.6	12.3	22.7	2.5	4.4	4.0	13.5
WATER.................	205	100.0	11.5	42.1	-	-	8.5	-	-	-	37.9
OTHER.................	2	100.0	53.7	3.7	20.2	4.7	10.7	-	.4	6.1	.6
UNKNOWN...............	147	100.0	1.5	16.3	18.0	7.3	6.3	.3	7.8	.7	41.8

See footnotes at end of table 4.

TABLE 2. **TCC GROUP 203—Percent Distribution of Geographic Division of Origin and Means of Transport, by Geographic Division of Destination: 1972**—Continued

Geographic division of origin[1] and means of transport	Number	Percent distribution by division of destination									
		U.S. total	New England	Middle Atlantic	East North Central	West North Central	South Atlantic	East South Central	West South Central	Mountain	Pacific
TON-MILES OF SHIPMENTS	(millions of ton-miles)										
MIDDLE ATLANTIC.........	1 878	100.0	9.4	20.5	14.7	7.4	24.1	4.3	6.8	1.5	11.3
RAIL..................	501	100.0	12.3	5.3	9.3	6.0	25.2	3.0	8.3	1.1	29.5
MOTOR CARRIER.........	1 109	100.0	8.6	21.4	16.7	8.2	25.9	5.2	7.7	1.7	4.6
PRIVATE TRUCK.........	229	100.0	8.5	52.2	19.5	4.5	10.1	3.0	.3	1.8	.1
AIR...................	-	100.0	-	.5	46.8	-	-	-	-	-	52.6
WATER.................	24	100.0	-	1.8	-	-	57.4	-	-	-	40.8
OTHER.................	-	100.0	.1	91.5	2.4	.4	2.3	-	.7	.2	2.3
UNKNOWN...............	13	100.0	1.2	13.5	1.9	54.4	7.3	-	-	-	21.5
EAST NORTH CENTRAL......	2 665	100.0	2.5	15.3	22.3	12.7	15.2	7.7	14.2	2.6	7.5
RAIL..................	1 289	100.0	3.3	22.1	12.2	10.2	18.4	7.1	15.8	3.3	7.5
MOTOR CARRIER.........	844	100.0	2.2	10.7	24.7	17.0	14.2	6.4	12.8	2.2	9.9
PRIVATE TRUCK.........	512	100.0	1.0	6.3	43.8	11.9	9.2	11.3	12.4	1.5	2.5
AIR...................	-	100.0	4.3	3.2	1.2	1.6	39.7	1.5	7.0	1.8	39.7
WATER.................	-	100.0	-	-	-	-	-	-	-	-	-
OTHER.................	-	100.0	.6	3.0	80.5	12.7	1.6	-	1.5	.2	-
UNKNOWN...............	17	100.0	5.6	5.0	16.2	5.7	10.8	2.5	14.5	4.2	35.5
WEST NORTH CENTRAL......	921	100.0	1.7	17.1	19.6	16.4	12.5	3.3	12.1	6.1	11.2
RAIL..................	498	100.0	1.9	23.7	13.4	15.2	11.3	2.5	10.6	7.8	13.6
MOTOR CARRIER.........	271	100.0	2.0	13.4	22.2	13.0	18.4	2.3	14.5	3.1	11.1
PRIVATE TRUCK.........	141	100.0	.6	1.9	36.0	27.8	2.5	8.5	13.4	6.0	3.3
AIR...................	-	100.0	-	-	-	-	-	-	-	-	100.0
WATER.................	-	100.0	-	-	-	-	-	-	-	-	-
OTHER.................	-	100.0	-	-	-	100.0	-	-	-	-	-
UNKNOWN...............	9	100.0	-	-	29.0	7.0	64.0	-	-	-	-
SOUTH ATLANTIC..........	2 716	100.0	6.0	24.2	15.6	6.9	17.4	3.6	6.2	5.2	15.0
RAIL..................	913	100.0	4.0	15.1	14.1	4.5	18.1	2.4	6.5	3.2	32.1
MOTOR CARRIER.........	1 510	100.0	6.4	27.6	18.2	9.1	16.2	3.5	6.4	6.1	6.5
PRIVATE TRUCK.........	235	100.0	6.3	28.5	8.1	3.8	25.6	9.2	5.2	8.2	5.1
AIR...................	-	100.0	-	-	2.1	-	.3	95.0	-	-	2.6
WATER.................	54	100.0	26.9	65.3	-	-	.5	-	-	-	7.3
OTHER.................	-	100.0	-	4.5	-	-	95.5	-	-	-	-
UNKNOWN...............	2	100.0	23.0	24.8	8.9	30.2	13.1	.1	-	-	-
WEST SOUTH CENTRAL......	2 048	100.0	1.1	10.4	17.2	8.3	18.2	7.9	16.7	7.2	13.0
RAIL..................	455	100.0	.4	4.8	2.2	6.0	21.4	18.3	20.1	5.2	21.6
MOTOR CARRIER.........	1 064	100.0	2.0	13.5	28.6	9.6	19.6	5.5	10.8	7.3	3.2
PRIVATE TRUCK.........	445	100.0	.1	8.8	4.5	8.7	14.9	4.3	28.4	10.6	19.6
AIR...................	-	100.0	-	-	-	24.8	48.0	27.2	-	-	-
WATER.................	-	100.0	-	-	-	-	-	-	-	-	-
OTHER.................	-	100.0	-	-	-	-	-	-	-	-	-
UNKNOWN...............	83	100.0	-	8.4	23.1	1.0	-	-	10.6	.3	56.7
MOUNTAIN................	1 460	100.0	9.8	15.9	17.4	16.1	12.4	13.0	5.0	3.3	7.1
RAIL..................	1 209	100.0	10.6	17.7	17.9	12.6	14.7	15.2	4.7	1.6	5.0
MOTOR CARRIER.........	185	100.0	8.3	4.7	19.9	26.1	2.3	3.4	8.9	8.6	17.8
PRIVATE TRUCK.........	56	100.0	-	-	.1	60.0	-	-	-	22.7	17.2
AIR...................	-	100.0	-	-	-	-	-	-	-	-	-
WATER.................	-	100.0	-	-	-	-	-	-	-	-	-
OTHER.................	-	100.0	-	-	-	-	-	-	-	-	-
UNKNOWN...............	9	100.0	-	100.0	-	-	-	-	-	-	-
PACIFIC.................	8 170	100.0	4.2	21.4	21.7	9.4	11.5	5.4	7.3	4.4	14.7
RAIL..................	6 435	100.0	5.0	24.1	24.1	9.6	13.4	6.6	7.0	3.2	7.0
MOTOR CARRIER.........	1 387	100.0	.9	8.8	15.1	8.3	4.7	1.5	9.4	9.3	42.1
PRIVATE TRUCK.........	202	100.0	1.6	7.1	4.2	14.7	3.7	.1	9.2	11.6	47.8
AIR...................	5	100.0	3.7	22.0	20.1	14.1	20.9	.9	4.2	4.4	9.7
WATER.................	126	100.0	7.1	40.1	-	-	2.4	-	-	-	50.4
OTHER.................	2	100.0	78.9	-	1.1	-	10.3	-	-	8.9	.8
UNKNOWN...............	11	100.0	5.2	37.8	11.9	-	.7	-	-	-	44.4

See footnotes at end of table 4.

TABLE 3. **TCC GROUP 203**—Percent Distribution of Geographic Division of Destination and Means of Transport, by Geographic Division of Origin: 1972

Geographic division of destination and means of transport	Number	Percent distribution by division of origin[1]									
		U.S. total	New England	Middle Atlantic	East North Central	West North Central	South Atlantic	East South Central	West South Central	Mountain	Pacific
TONS OF SHIPMENTS	(thousands of tons)										
U.S. TOTAL	34 317	100.0	(D)	17.1	21.3	5.4	14.5	(D)	10.2	4.1	23.2
RAIL	12 063	100.0	(D)	7.9	22.0	6.5	8.2	(D)	6.5	8.9	35.9
MOTOR CARRIER	14 313	100.0	(D)	22.8	17.2	3.8	20.9	(D)	11.7	1.5	18.9
PRIVATE TRUCK	7 594	100.0	(D)	21.2	28.3	6.5	12.4	(D)	12.4	1.6	10.9
AIR	3	100.0	(D)	.2	17.6	.4	4.1	(D)	.1	-	77.6
WATER	137	100.0	(D)	16.7	-	-	38.1	(D)	-	-	45.2
OTHER	10	100.0	(D)	17.8	54.0	3.2	5.0	(D)	-	-	19.9
UNKNOWN	194	100.0	(D)	11.8	16.1	10.0	2.5	(D)	52.4	2.5	4.1
NEW ENGLAND	1 457	100.0	(D)	44.7	5.9	.9	16.2	(D)	1.1	4.7	9.3
RAIL	574	100.0	(D)	41.5	8.6	1.4	5.7	(D)	.2	10.5	21.7
MOTOR CARRIER	623	100.0	(D)	54.2	4.3	.8	24.8	(D)	2.4	1.3	.8
PRIVATE TRUCK	238	100.0	(D)	31.5	3.3	.3	14.8	(D)	.1	-	.5
AIR	-	100.0	(D)	-	35.1	-	-	(D)	-	-	64.9
WATER	16	100.0	(D)	-	-	-	78.8	(D)	-	-	21.2
OTHER	-	100.0	(D)	-	1.2	-	-	(D)	-	-	98.5
UNKNOWN	3	100.0	(D)	16.2	37.1	-	36.3	(D)	-	-	6.8
MIDDLE ATLANTIC	7 027	100.0	(D)	43.5	11.3	2.4	25.3	(D)	2.6	1.8	10.3
RAIL	1 755	100.0	(D)	8.2	29.3	7.3	8.8	(D)	1.1	6.5	36.9
MOTOR CARRIER	3 408	100.0	(D)	47.3	5.8	1.1	36.5	(D)	3.5	.1	1.5
PRIVATE TRUCK	1 775	100.0	(D)	72.5	4.5	.2	19.3	(D)	2.0	-	.3
AIR	-	100.0	(D)	.2	6.9	-	-	(D)	-	-	93.0
WATER	61	100.0	(D)	7.5	-	-	59.4	(D)	-	-	33.1
OTHER	1	100.0	(D)	96.6	1.9	-	1.4	(D)	-	-	-
UNKNOWN	24	100.0	(D)	41.2	5.7	-	2.1	(D)	22.6	19.3	7.0
EAST NORTH CENTRAL	7 005	100.0	(D)	9.6	51.8	6.2	7.6	(D)	6.3	2.5	13.9
RAIL	2 292	100.0	(D)	4.3	37.4	6.0	6.6	(D)	.5	6.5	37.2
MOTOR CARRIER	2 906	100.0	(D)	15.8	46.5	5.0	11.9	(D)	13.1	.9	4.0
PRIVATE TRUCK	1 752	100.0	(D)	6.4	80.0	8.0	2.2	(D)	1.5	-	.3
AIR	-	100.0	(D)	1.0	5.6	-	.4	(D)	-	-	93.1
WATER	-	100.0	(D)	-	-	-	-	(D)	-	-	-
OTHER	5	100.0	(D)	.1	99.7	-	-	(D)	-	-	.2
UNKNOWN	47	100.0	(D)	1.1	31.7	19.5	.8	(D)	44.8	-	2.0
WEST NORTH CENTRAL	3 206	100.0	(D)	5.1	27.9	21.6	5.8	(D)	14.5	7.6	16.7
RAIL	1 298	100.0	(D)	2.8	24.3	19.1	3.2	(D)	5.7	11.5	33.3
MOTOR CARRIER	1 236	100.0	(D)	8.7	31.2	16.3	10.9	(D)	21.2	3.9	6.6
PRIVATE TRUCK	651	100.0	(D)	1.9	29.4	36.7	1.5	(D)	19.2	7.1	3.2
AIR	-	100.0	(D)	-	7.9	-	-	(D)	.1	-	92.0
WATER	-	100.0	(D)	-	-	-	-	(D)	-	-	-
OTHER	-	100.0	(D)	.1	41.2	58.5	-	(D)	-	-	-
UNKNOWN	18	100.0	(D)	48.9	13.7	23.1	2.7	(D)	11.6	-	-
SOUTH ATLANTIC	4 928	100.0	(D)	19.8	14.0	2.5	32.2	(D)	9.5	1.9	8.4
RAIL	1 969	100.0	(D)	15.5	18.5	2.9	18.1	(D)	6.1	4.5	19.4
MOTOR CARRIER	1 983	100.0	(D)	27.9	8.8	2.7	40.5	(D)	13.2	.1	1.5
PRIVATE TRUCK	944	100.0	(D)	11.0	15.9	.5	44.6	(D)	9.3	-	.4
AIR	-	100.0	(D)	-	40.2	-	-	(D)	.1	-	59.6
WATER	17	100.0	(D)	81.1	-	-	11.9	(D)	-	-	7.0
OTHER	-	100.0	(D)	.6	2.6	-	80.2	(D)	-	-	16.6
UNKNOWN	12	100.0	(D)	11.1	22.5	47.6	18.0	(D)	-	-	.3
EAST SOUTH CENTRAL	1 894	100.0	(D)	6.6	29.6	2.8	12.1	(D)	18.7	7.1	12.8
RAIL	852	100.0	(D)	3.1	22.8	2.3	6.5	(D)	18.3	15.2	27.0
MOTOR CARRIER	509	100.0	(D)	17.0	26.1	2.1	22.9	(D)	26.3	.8	2.3
PRIVATE TRUCK	530	100.0	(D)	2.5	43.9	4.3	11.0	(D)	12.1	-	-
AIR	-	100.0	(D)	-	11.5	-	75.2	(D)	.3	-	13.0
WATER	-	100.0	(D)	-	-	-	-	(D)	-	-	-
OTHER	-	100.0	(D)	-	-	-	-	(D)	-	-	-
UNKNOWN	1	100.0	(D)	-	71.3	-	.1	(D)	-	-	-
WEST SOUTH CENTRAL	2 722	100.0	(D)	4.0	17.5	7.4	6.4	(D)	45.2	2.2	14.8
RAIL	1 123	100.0	(D)	3.2	23.2	7.0	4.9	(D)	28.3	4.2	26.4
MOTOR CARRIER	873	100.0	(D)	8.1	15.8	6.4	11.5	(D)	44.1	1.6	10.7
PRIVATE TRUCK	678	100.0	(D)	.1	11.0	9.7	2.9	(D)	71.5	-	2.0
AIR	-	100.0	(D)	-	28.0	-	-	(D)	-	-	72.0
WATER	-	100.0	(D)	-	-	-	-	(D)	-	-	-
OTHER	-	100.0	(D)	3.7	96.3	-	-	(D)	-	-	-
UNKNOWN	47	100.0	(D)	-	6.6	-	-	(D)	93.4	-	-
MOUNTAIN	1 397	100.0	(D)	1.3	4.6	5.9	5.7	(D)	13.4	27.1	41.8
RAIL	754	100.0	(D)	.4	5.3	7.6	2.1	(D)	4.8	35.5	44.1
MOTOR CARRIER	430	100.0	(D)	2.8	3.9	2.9	12.7	(D)	20.8	10.2	46.5
PRIVATE TRUCK	210	100.0	(D)	1.2	3.1	5.9	4.6	(D)	29.4	31.9	23.8
AIR	-	100.0	(D)	-	4.1	-	-	(D)	-	-	95.9
WATER	-	100.0	(D)	-	-	-	-	(D)	-	-	-
OTHER	1	100.0	(D)	-	.1	-	-	(D)	-	-	99.9
UNKNOWN	1	100.0	(D)	-	58.8	-	-	(D)	41.2	-	-
PACIFIC	4 677	100.0	(D)	2.0	2.3	1.5	3.7	(D)	3.3	2.8	84.0
RAIL	1 441	100.0	(D)	4.5	3.7	3.2	8.6	(D)	3.2	4.3	71.7
MOTOR CARRIER	2 341	100.0	(D)	.9	1.9	.9	1.8	(D)	.9	2.6	90.6
PRIVATE TRUCK	813	100.0	(D)	-	.8	.4	.6	(D)	6.9	1.3	89.8
AIR	-	100.0	(D)	.3	20.1	2.9	.2	(D)	-	-	76.4
WATER	42	100.0	(D)	9.7	-	-	1.9	(D)	-	-	88.3
OTHER	-	100.0	(D)	.3	-	-	-	(D)	-	-	99.7
UNKNOWN	37	100.0	(D)	3.2	8.7	-	-	(D)	74.8	-	13.3

See footnotes at end of table 4.

TABLE 3. **TCC GROUP 203—Percent Distribution of Geographic Division of Destination and Means of Transport, by Geographic Division of Origin: 1972**—Continued

Geographic division of destination and means of transport	Number	Percent distribution by division of origin[1]									
		U.S. total	New England	Middle Atlantic	East North Central	West North Central	South Atlantic	East South Central	West South Central	Mountain	Pacific
TON-MILES OF SHIPMENTS	(millions of ton-miles)										
U.S. TOTAL.............	20 485	100.0	(D)	9.2	13.0	4.5	13.3	(D)	10.0	7.1	39.9
RAIL................	11 533	100.0	(D)	4.3	11.2	4.3	7.9	(D)	4.0	10.5	55.8
MOTOR CARRIER........	6 642	100.0	(D)	16.7	12.7	4.1	22.7	(D)	16.0	2.8	20.9
PRIVATE TRUCK........	1 946	100.0	(D)	11.8	26.3	7.3	12.1	(D)	22.9	2.9	10.4
AIR.................	6	100.0	(D)	.1	11.9	.3	1.6	(D)	-	-	86.0
WATER...............	205	100.0	(D)	12.0	-	-	26.3	(D)	-	-	61.7
OTHER...............	2	100.0	(D)	3.0	24.1	1.5	3.4	(D)	-	-	67.9
UNKNOWN.............	147	100.0	(D)	9.5	12.1	6.2	1.4	(D)	56.5	6.2	7.7
NEW ENGLAND...........	987	100.0	(D)	17.9	6.8	1.6	16.5	(D)	2.3	14.5	35.2
RAIL................	618	100.0	(D)	10.0	6.9	1.6	5.9	(D)	.3	20.7	51.7
MOTOR CARRIER........	284	100.0	(D)	33.5	6.5	1.9	34.0	(D)	7.4	5.4	4.3
PRIVATE TRUCK........	57	100.0	(D)	34.1	9.4	1.5	26.0	(D)	.6	-	5.7
AIR.................	-	100.0	(D)	-	13.7	-	-	(D)	-	-	86.3
WATER...............	23	100.0	(D)	-	-	-	61.6	(D)	-	-	38.4
OTHER...............	1	100.0	(D)	-	.2	-	-	(D)	-	-	99.7
UNKNOWN.............	2	100.0	(D)	7.5	44.1	-	21.3	(D)	-	-	26.2
MIDDLE ATLANTIC.......	3 886	100.0	(D)	9.9	10.5	4.0	16.9	(D)	5.5	6.0	44.9
RAIL................	2 374	100.0	(D)	1.1	12.0	5.0	5.8	(D)	.9	9.0	65.4
MOTOR CARRIER........	1 114	100.0	(D)	21.3	8.1	3.3	37.3	(D)	12.9	.8	10.9
PRIVATE TRUCK........	285	100.0	(D)	41.9	11.3	.9	23.6	(D)	13.8	-	5.0
AIR.................	1	100.0	(D)	-	2.0	-	-	(D)	-	-	98.0
WATER...............	86	100.0	(D)	.5	-	-	40.7	(D)	-	-	58.7
OTHER...............	-	100.0	(D)	76.2	19.4	-	4.2	(D)	-	-	-
UNKNOWN.............	23	100.0	(D)	7.9	3.7	-	2.2	(D)	28.9	38.3	17.9
EAST NORTH CENTRAL....	3 949	100.0	(D)	7.0	15.0	4.6	10.7	(D)	8.9	6.4	44.8
RAIL................	2 204	100.0	(D)	2.1	7.2	3.0	5.9	(D)	.4	9.8	70.3
MOTOR CARRIER........	1 338	100.0	(D)	13.8	15.6	4.5	20.5	(D)	22.7	2.8	15.6
PRIVATE TRUCK........	377	100.0	(D)	11.8	59.3	13.5	5.0	(D)	5.3	-	2.3
AIR.................	1	100.0	(D)	.3	.8	-	.2	(D)	-	-	98.7
WATER...............	-	100.0	(D)	-	-	-	-	(D)	-	-	-
OTHER...............	-	100.0	(D)	.4	95.9	-	-	(D)	-	-	3.7
UNKNOWN.............	26	100.0	(D)	1.0	10.9	10.0	.7	(D)	72.3	-	5.1
WEST NORTH CENTRAL....	2 001	100.0	(D)	6.9	16.9	7.5	9.4	(D)	8.5	11.7	38.2
RAIL................	1 080	100.0	(D)	2.8	12.2	7.0	3.8	(D)	2.5	14.1	57.3
MOTOR CARRIER........	682	100.0	(D)	13.3	21.0	5.2	20.2	(D)	15.0	7.1	16.8
PRIVATE TRUCK........	226	100.0	(D)	4.6	27.0	17.4	4.0	(D)	17.2	14.8	13.2
AIR.................	-	100.0	(D)	-	1.5	-	-	(D)	.1	-	98.4
WATER...............	-	100.0	(D)	-	-	-	-	(D)	-	-	-
OTHER...............	-	100.0	(D)	.3	65.9	32.8	-	(D)	-	-	-
UNKNOWN.............	10	100.0	(D)	71.1	9.5	6.0	5.9	(D)	7.4	-	-
SOUTH ATLANTIC........	3 162	100.0	(D)	14.3	12.8	3.7	14.9	(D)	11.8	5.7	29.8
RAIL................	1 826	100.0	(D)	6.9	13.0	3.1	9.1	(D)	5.3	9.7	47.3
MOTOR CARRIER........	1 054	100.0	(D)	27.3	11.4	4.7	23.2	(D)	19.8	.4	6.2
PRIVATE TRUCK........	253	100.0	(D)	9.2	18.7	1.4	23.9	(D)	26.3	-	2.9
AIR.................	1	100.0	(D)	-	20.8	-	-	(D)	.1	-	79.1
WATER...............	17	100.0	(D)	81.2	-	-	1.6	(D)	-	-	17.2
OTHER...............	-	100.0	(D)	.6	3.6	-	30.6	(D)	-	-	65.2
UNKNOWN.............	9	100.0	(D)	11.1	20.9	63.2	3.0	(D)	-	-	.8
EAST SOUTH CENTRAL....	1 249	100.0	(D)	6.4	16.3	2.5	7.8	(D)	12.9	15.2	35.4
RAIL................	839	100.0	(D)	1.8	10.9	1.5	2.7	(D)	9.9	21.9	50.2
MOTOR CARRIER........	264	100.0	(D)	21.8	20.4	2.3	20.1	(D)	22.1	2.4	7.7
PRIVATE TRUCK........	143	100.0	(D)	4.8	40.3	8.4	15.1	(D)	13.4	-	.1
AIR.................	-	100.0	(D)	-	7.3	-	60.7	(D)	.4	-	31.7
WATER...............	-	100.0	(D)	-	-	-	-	(D)	-	-	-
OTHER...............	-	100.0	(D)	-	-	-	-	(D)	-	-	-
UNKNOWN.............	-	100.0	(D)	-	89.9	-	.2	(D)	-	-	-
WEST SOUTH CENTRAL....	1 848	100.0	(D)	6.9	20.4	6.0	9.1	(D)	18.5	4.0	32.4
RAIL................	981	100.0	(D)	4.2	20.7	5.4	6.0	(D)	9.3	5.8	45.9
MOTOR CARRIER........	602	100.0	(D)	14.1	18.0	6.5	16.1	(D)	19.1	2.7	21.7
PRIVATE TRUCK........	252	100.0	(D)	.3	25.2	7.5	4.8	(D)	50.2	-	7.4
AIR.................	-	100.0	(D)	-	18.8	-	-	(D)	-	-	81.2
WATER...............	-	100.0	(D)	-	-	-	-	(D)	-	-	-
OTHER...............	-	100.0	(D)	5.9	94.1	-	-	(D)	-	-	-
UNKNOWN.............	11	100.0	(D)	-	22.7	-	-	(D)	77.3	-	-
MOUNTAIN..............	853	100.0	(D)	3.4	8.2	6.5	16.5	(D)	17.4	5.6	42.1
RAIL................	366	100.0	(D)	1.4	11.8	10.6	7.9	(D)	6.4	5.1	56.1
MOTOR CARRIER........	362	100.0	(D)	5.3	5.1	2.4	25.5	(D)	21.3	4.4	35.7
PRIVATE TRUCK........	123	100.0	(D)	3.3	6.2	6.9	15.6	(D)	38.2	10.3	19.1
AIR.................	-	100.0	(D)	-	5.5	-	-	(D)	-	-	94.5
WATER...............	-	100.0	(D)	-	-	-	-	(D)	-	-	-
OTHER...............	-	100.0	(D)	.1	.6	-	-	(D)	-	-	99.3
UNKNOWN.............	1	100.0	(D)	-	73.6	-	-	(D)	26.4	-	-
PACIFIC...............	2 545	100.0	(D)	8.4	7.9	4.0	16.0	(D)	10.5	4.1	47.2
RAIL................	1 239	100.0	(D)	11.9	7.8	5.5	23.6	(D)	8.0	4.9	36.3
MOTOR CARRIER........	939	100.0	(D)	5.5	8.9	3.2	10.5	(D)	3.6	3.5	62.2
PRIVATE TRUCK........	226	100.0	(D)	.1	5.6	2.1	5.3	(D)	38.6	4.3	42.8
AIR.................	-	100.0	(D)	.4	35.0	2.5	.3	(D)	-	-	61.8
WATER...............	77	100.0	(D)	12.9	-	-	5.1	(D)	-	-	82.1
OTHER...............	-	100.0	(D)	11.3	-	-	-	(D)	-	-	88.7
UNKNOWN.............	61	100.0	(D)	4.9	10.3	-	-	(D)	76.6	-	8.2

See footnotes at end of table 4.

TABLE 4. TCC GROUP 203—Percent Distribution of Distance Shipped and Weight of Shipment, by Means of Transport: 1972

Distance shipped and weight of shipment[2][3]	Number	Percent distribution by means of transport							
		All means of transport	Rail	Motor carrier	Private truck	Air	Water	Other	Unknown
TONS OF SHIPMENTS	(thousands of tons)								
U.S. TOTAL..........	31 257	100.0	35.4	42.5	21.0	-	.4	-	.6
UNDER 100 MILES.........	5 279	100.0	13.7	38.3	47.5	-	.3	.1	.2
UNDER 1000 POUNDS.....	31	100.0	-	33.0	64.7	-	.2	.7	1.4
1000 TO 9999 POUNDS...	394	100.0	-	35.5	63.9	-	.2	.2	.2
10000 TO 29999 POUNDS.	852	100.0	4.3	40.2	55.3	-	.1	.2	-
30000 TO 59999 POUNDS.	2 575	100.0	9.0	50.6	39.9	-	.1	-	.3
60000 TO 89999 POUNDS.	263	100.0	64.5	25.0	10.3	-	.2	-	-
90000 POUNDS AND OVER.	1 160	100.0	24.4	13.8	60.9	-	.9	-	-
100 TO 199 MILES........	4 907	100.0	18.2	52.1	28.8	-	-	-	.8
UNDER 1000 POUNDS.....	21	100.0	-	82.7	16.6	-	-	.6	-
1000 TO 9999 POUNDS...	331	100.0	-	51.1	48.8	-	-	-	.1
10000 TO 29999 POUNDS.	802	100.0	.9	49.9	48.8	-	-	.2	.2
30000 TO 59999 POUNDS.	2 849	100.0	2.3	66.7	29.7	-	-	-	1.2
60000 TO 89999 POUNDS.	329	100.0	88.4	9.0	2.2	-	-	-	.4
90000 POUNDS AND OVER.	573	100.0	92.6	6.7	.7	-	.1	-	-
200 TO 299 MILES........	3 734	100.0	23.9	50.0	25.3	-	-	-	.7
UNDER 1000 POUNDS.....	12	100.0	.2	78.7	19.9	.3	-	.3	.6
1000 TO 9999 POUNDS...	236	100.0	.6	52.0	45.2	-	-	-	2.2
10000 TO 29999 POUNDS.	576	100.0	1.2	54.8	43.4	-	-	-	.6
30000 TO 59999 POUNDS.	2 041	100.0	6.0	65.2	28.2	-	.1	-	.5
60000 TO 89999 POUNDS.	366	100.0	87.2	11.7	1.2	-	-	-	-
90000 POUNDS AND OVER.	501	100.0	88.5	9.1	.9	-	-	-	1.4
300 TO 499 MILES........	4 838	100.0	35.6	45.9	18.1	-	-	-	.4
UNDER 1000 POUNDS.....	16	100.0	.7	74.5	22.8	.2	-	.3	1.5
1000 TO 9999 POUNDS...	266	100.0	1.2	58.4	39.8	-	-	.1	.6
10000 TO 29999 POUNDS.	686	100.0	4.4	63.0	32.2	-	-	-	.4
30000 TO 59999 POUNDS.	2 239	100.0	9.7	65.8	23.8	-	-	-	.7
60000 TO 89999 POUNDS.	610	100.0	83.5	14.5	2.0	-	-	-	-
90000 POUNDS AND OVER.	1 020	100.0	94.1	5.9	-	-	-	-	-
500 TO 999 MILES........	6 572	100.0	42.0	47.6	9.1	-	.5	-	.7
UNDER 1000 POUNDS.....	21	100.0	.4	84.4	12.5	1.6	.1	.4	.5
1000 TO 9999 POUNDS...	292	100.0	1.9	74.0	22.7	.1	.3	-	1.0
10000 TO 29999 POUNDS.	687	100.0	5.1	71.6	22.4	-	-	-	.8
30000 TO 59999 POUNDS.	3 148	100.0	12.0	74.4	11.9	-	.9	-	.9
60000 TO 89999 POUNDS.	942	100.0	94.0	5.5	-	-	.1	-	.4
90000 POUNDS AND OVER.	1 481	100.0	98.5	.5	.2	-	.4	-	.4
1000 TO 1499 MILES......	2 519	100.0	50.7	41.8	5.9	-	1.2	-	.5
UNDER 1000 POUNDS.....	7	100.0	14.8	70.0	13.5	1.4	-	-	.2
1000 TO 9999 POUNDS...	95	100.0	4.6	65.8	29.1	-	.2	-	.3
10000 TO 29999 POUNDS.	243	100.0	6.7	72.4	20.1	-	.5	-	.3
30000 TO 59999 POUNDS.	983	100.0	13.2	76.9	7.0	-	1.8	-	1.1
60000 TO 89999 POUNDS.	532	100.0	94.3	4.8	.4	-	.5	-	-
90000 POUNDS AND OVER.	657	100.0	94.8	4.1	-	-	1.1	-	-
1500 MILES OR OVER......	3 405	100.0	82.1	13.1	2.2	-	1.3	-	1.2
UNDER 1000 POUNDS.....	18	100.0	54.5	24.2	4.9	.7	1.0	.1	14.5
1000 TO 9999 POUNDS...	195	100.0	68.2	25.1	3.7	-	2.6	-	.4
10000 TO 29999 POUNDS.	192	100.0	39.1	43.7	15.1	-	1.7	-	.3
30000 TO 59999 POUNDS.	676	100.0	47.6	40.2	5.4	-	2.6	.1	4.2
60000 TO 89999 POUNDS.	614	100.0	94.6	2.6	.3	-	1.2	-	1.3
90000 POUNDS AND OVER.	1 708	100.0	98.0	1.3	-	-	.7	-	-
TON-MILES OF SHIPMENTS	(millions of ton-miles)								
U.S. TOTAL..........	18 647	100.0	55.9	33.4	9.0	-	1.0	-	.8
UNDER 100 MILES.........	323	100.0	14.1	35.3	50.2	-	.2	-	.2
UNDER 1000 POUNDS.....	1	100.0	-	40.9	57.1	-	.2	.6	1.2
1000 TO 9999 POUNDS...	18	100.0	-	34.8	64.6	-	.2	.1	.2
10000 TO 29999 POUNDS.	45	100.0	5.2	36.5	58.1	-	.1	.1	.1
30000 TO 59999 POUNDS.	142	100.0	8.3	51.8	39.5	-	.1	-	.3
60000 TO 89999 POUNDS.	15	100.0	69.6	24.2	5.9	-	.2	-	-
90000 POUNDS AND OVER.	99	100.0	20.7	13.1	65.7	-	.4	-	-
100 TO 199 MILES........	719	100.0	18.5	52.5	28.3	-	-	-	.7
UNDER 1000 POUNDS.....	3	100.0	-	83.1	16.2	-	-	.6	-
1000 TO 9999 POUNDS...	50	100.0	-	51.8	48.1	-	-	-	.1
10000 TO 29999 POUNDS.	119	100.0	.9	49.8	48.8	-	-	.2	.2
30000 TO 59999 POUNDS.	412	100.0	2.4	67.8	28.8	-	-	-	1.0
60000 TO 89999 POUNDS.	49	100.0	89.5	8.0	2.2	-	-	-	.4
90000 POUNDS AND OVER.	83	100.0	92.7	6.6	.6	-	.1	-	-

See footnotes at end of table 4.

TABLE 4. TCC GROUP 203—Percent Distribution of Distance Shipped and Weight of Shipment, by Means of Transport: 1972—Continued

Distance shipped and weight of shipment[2] [3]	Number	Percent distribution by means of transport							
		All means of transport	Rail	Motor carrier	Private truck	Air	Water	Other	Unknown
TON-MILES OF SHIPMENTS	(millions of ton-miles)								
200 TO 299 MILES........	929	100.0	24.3	49.5	25.4	-	-	-	.7
UNDER 1000 POUNDS.....	3	100.0	.2	78.4	20.1	.3	-	.3	.6
1000 TO 9999 POUNDS...	58	100.0	.6	51.9	45.2	-	-	-	2.3
10000 TO 29999 POUNDS.	142	100.0	1.3	54.9	43.2	-	-	-	.5
30000 TO 59999 POUNDS.	504	100.0	6.0	64.7	28.8	-	.1	-	.5
60000 TO 89999 POUNDS.	93	100.0	87.4	11.4	1.2	-	-	-	-
90000 POUNDS AND OVER.	127	100.0	88.4	9.0	1.0	-	-	-	1.6
300 TO 499 MILES........	1 861	100.0	36.3	45.2	18.2	-	-	-	.4
UNDER 1000 POUNDS.....	6	100.0	.8	74.9	22.3	.2	-	.3	1.5
1000 TO 9999 POUNDS...	102	100.0	1.3	58.1	40.0	-	-	-	.6
10000 TO 29999 POUNDS.	265	100.0	4.5	63.2	31.9	-	-	-	.4
30000 TO 59999 POUNDS.	852	100.0	10.1	65.0	24.3	-	-	-	.6
60000 TO 89999 POUNDS.	236	100.0	84.4	13.8	1.9	-	-	-	-
90000 POUNDS AND OVER.	397	100.0	94.4	5.5	.1	-	-	-	-
500 TO 999 MILES........	4 781	100.0	41.4	48.7	8.4	-	.7	-	.8
UNDER 1000 POUNDS.....	15	100.0	.4	85.2	11.8	1.6	.1	.4	.5
1000 TO 9999 POUNDS...	206	100.0	2.1	74.5	21.9	.1	.4	-	1.0
10000 TO 29999 POUNDS.	488	100.0	5.6	72.0	21.5	-	.1	-	.9
30000 TO 59999 POUNDS.	2 339	100.0	11.7	75.5	10.6	-	1.1	-	1.0
60000 TO 89999 POUNDS.	668	100.0	94.1	5.4	-	-	.1	-	.4
90000 POUNDS AND OVER.	1 062	100.0	98.3	.6	.1	-	.5	-	.5
1000 TO 1499 MILES......	3 051	100.0	52.6	40.1	5.8	-	1.0	-	.4
UNDER 1000 POUNDS.....	9	100.0	16.6	67.4	14.3	1.5	-	-	.2
1000 TO 9999 POUNDS...	115	100.0	4.9	66.6	28.0	-	.2	-	.3
10000 TO 29999 POUNDS.	283	100.0	7.0	72.1	20.1	-	.5	-	.3
30000 TO 59999 POUNDS.	1 149	100.0	14.1	75.8	7.3	-	1.7	-	1.1
60000 TO 89999 POUNDS.	654	100.0	94.5	4.7	.4	-	.4	-	-
90000 POUNDS AND OVER.	838	100.0	95.1	4.0	-	-	.9	-	-
1500 MILES OR OVER......	6 980	100.0	82.5	12.6	2.2	-	1.6	-	1.0
UNDER 1000 POUNDS.....	37	100.0	54.2	24.2	5.0	.9	1.3	.1	14.4
1000 TO 9999 POUNDS...	424	100.0	69.1	23.5	3.9	-	3.2	-	.3
10000 TO 29999 POUNDS.	400	100.0	42.3	40.0	15.4	-	2.1	-	.2
30000 TO 59999 POUNDS.	1 342	100.0	49.2	38.7	5.1	-	3.4	.1	3.5
60000 TO 89999 POUNDS.	1 263	100.0	94.3	2.6	.3	-	1.5	-	1.3
90000 POUNDS AND OVER.	3 511	100.0	97.6	1.6	-	-	.8	-	-

Note: Detail may not add to total due to rounding. The introductory table shows the estimates of sampling variability for tons; sampling variability for ton-miles has not been estimated. See the map in the Introduction for the States comprising the geographic divisions of the United States.

Shipments excluded from the survey are those moving by pipeline (primarily petroleum products from refineries), parcel post shipments, and commodities moved by own power (motorized vehicles, aircraft, etc.) or towed (prefabricated buildings, etc.). Local shipments (commodities shipped less than 25 miles from the plant) and shipments within the same city are also excluded. Shipments to Alaska and Hawaii from the 48 conterminous States and the District of Columbia are included; however, no data were obtained for shipments originating in Alaska and Hawaii.

- Represents zero or rounds to zero.   (D) Withheld to avoid disclosing figures for individual companies.

[1]Production of this commodity is concentrated in the geographic divisions shown; figures and distributions for geographic divisions not shown are included in the total.

[2]Distances of shipments to foreign destinations are calculated only to the U.S. port of exit.

[3]Includes only shipments represented by bills of lading and invoices. Summary records which did not show individual weights of shipments are not included.

TCC 204. Grain Mill Products

Comparisons of Tons and Ton-Miles of Shipments for
Geographic Divisions of Origin and for Sampling Variability: 1972 and 1967

Geographic division of origin	Estimates				Relative sampling variability in tons (percent)	
	1972		1967		1972	1967
	Tons (thousands)	Ton-miles (millions)	Tons (thousands)	Ton-miles (millions)		
U.S. total	63,521	20,730	72,012	21,862	4.5	12.6
New England	(D)	(D)	962	59	(*)	(*)
Middle Atlantic	7,075	1,179	7,307	1,290	32.6	(*)
East North Central	15,571	6,033	22,385	8,879	15.3	(*)
West North Central	19,449	8,048	17,258	6,500	17.1	(*)
South Atlantic	(D)	(D)	5,178	603	(*)	(*)
East South Central	3,953	881	3,685	584	41.1	(*)
West South Central	6,604	2,176	8,409	1,954	27.9	(*)
Mountain	(D)	(D)	1,032	228	(*)	(*)
Pacific	1,549	592	5,796	1,765	45.1	(*)

(D) Withheld to avoid disclosing figures for individual companies.   (*) Data not published.

TABLE 1. **TCC GROUP 204**—Percent Distribution of Geographic Division of Origin and Distance Shipped, by Means of Transport: 1972

Geographic division of origin[1] and distance shipped[2]	Number	Percent distribution by means of transport							
		All means of transport	Rail	Motor carrier	Private truck	Air	Water	Other	Unknown
TONS OF SHIPMENTS	(thousands of tons)								
U.S. TOTAL..........	63 521	100.0	61.9	10.1	27.8	-	-	-	.2
MIDDLE ATLANTIC.........	7 075	100.0	45.7	16.8	37.3	-	-	-	.2
UNDER 100 MILES.......	3 425	100.0	12.6	19.8	67.5	-	-	-	.1
100 TO 199 MILES......	1 314	100.0	71.6	14.7	13.7	-	-	-	-
200 TO 299 MILES......	1 301	100.0	74.4	16.7	8.1	-	-	-	.8
300 TO 499 MILES......	866	100.0	92.1	3.7	4.2	-	-	-	-
500 TO 999 MILES......	105	100.0	59.2	39.1	1.7	-	-	-	-
1000 TO 1499 MILES....	37	100.0	31.8	68.2	-	-	-	-	-
1500 MILES OR OVER....	25	100.0	77.3	22.7	-	-	-	-	-
EAST NORTH CENTRAL......	15 571	100.0	69.3	15.1	15.5	-	-	-	.1
UNDER 100 MILES.......	2 753	100.0	25.9	21.3	52.5	-	-	-	.3
100 TO 199 MILES......	2 588	100.0	52.2	23.9	23.6	-	-	-	.2
200 TO 299 MILES......	2 929	100.0	79.0	16.3	4.7	-	-	-	-
300 TO 499 MILES......	2 908	100.0	83.9	12.0	3.9	-	-	-	.2
500 TO 999 MILES......	3 662	100.0	90.9	7.3	1.8	-	-	-	-
1000 TO 1499 MILES....	288	100.0	82.7	9.5	7.7	-	-	-	-
1500 MILES OR OVER....	441	100.0	93.6	4.1	2.2	-	-	-	-
WEST NORTH CENTRAL......	19 449	100.0	67.9	9.0	22.8	-	-	-	.3
UNDER 100 MILES.......	4 478	100.0	21.9	10.7	66.7	-	-	-	.7
100 TO 199 MILES......	2 862	100.0	52.9	10.1	36.5	-	-	-	.4
200 TO 299 MILES......	2 904	100.0	83.3	8.3	8.3	-	-	-	.1
300 TO 499 MILES......	3 066	100.0	85.0	11.3	3.4	-	-	-	.4
500 TO 999 MILES......	4 086	100.0	91.1	7.7	1.1	-	-	-	.1
1000 TO 1499 MILES....	1 514	100.0	93.9	5.5	.5	-	-	.1	.1
1500 MILES OR OVER....	536	100.0	98.9	.3	-	-	-	-	.8
EAST SOUTH CENTRAL......	3 953	100.0	46.5	1.9	51.5	-	-	-	-
UNDER 100 MILES.......	1 600	100.0	17.3	-	82.6	-	-	-	-
100 TO 199 MILES......	649	100.0	41.8	9.4	48.8	-	-	-	-
200 TO 299 MILES......	874	100.0	87.1	1.1	11.9	-	-	-	-
300 TO 499 MILES......	393	100.0	72.6	1.3	26.1	-	-	-	-
500 TO 999 MILES......	412	100.0	59.3	-	40.7	-	-	-	-
1000 TO 1499 MILES....	23	100.0	-	-	100.0	-	-	-	-
1500 MILES OR OVER....	-	100.0	-	-	-	-	-	-	-
WEST SOUTH CENTRAL......	6 604	100.0	62.3	8.3	29.2	-	-	.1	-
UNDER 100 MILES.......	1 886	100.0	50.6	1.2	48.2	-	-	-	-
100 TO 199 MILES......	1 768	100.0	65.5	.9	33.4	-	-	.2	-
200 TO 299 MILES......	730	100.0	65.2	6.3	28.3	-	-	-	.2
300 TO 499 MILES......	783	100.0	90.3	5.0	4.6	-	-	-	-
500 TO 999 MILES......	923	100.0	69.4	27.9	2.7	-	-	-	-
1000 TO 1499 MILES....	358	100.0	30.4	31.0	38.5	-	.1	-	-
1500 MILES OR OVER....	153	100.0	46.4	37.9	15.2	-	.1	-	.5
PACIFIC................	1 549	100.0	80.4	10.5	8.6	.1	.3	-	.1
UNDER 100 MILES.......	740	100.0	81.8	4.4	13.6	-	.1	-	-
100 TO 199 MILES......	134	100.0	61.9	31.8	4.8	-	-	-	1.4
200 TO 299 MILES......	128	100.0	81.9	12.5	5.7	-	-	-	-
300 TO 499 MILES......	213	100.0	69.4	23.5	7.0	.1	-	-	-
500 TO 999 MILES......	184	100.0	92.2	5.5	2.0	.3	-	-	-
1000 TO 1499 MILES....	21	100.0	73.9	25.2	-	.2	.7	-	-
1500 MILES OR OVER....	127	100.0	92.3	4.7	.1	.6	2.3	-	-
TON-MILES OF SHIPMENTS	(millions of ton-miles)								
U.S. TOTAL..........	20 730	100.0	79.4	9.7	10.7	-	-	-	.1
MIDDLE ATLANTIC.........	1 179	100.0	68.4	16.4	14.9	-	-	-	.2
UNDER 100 MILES.......	169	100.0	15.9	20.2	63.9	-	-	-	.1
100 TO 199 MILES......	200	100.0	73.4	14.6	12.1	-	-	-	-
200 TO 299 MILES......	335	100.0	75.7	15.9	7.6	-	-	-	.8
300 TO 499 MILES......	313	100.0	91.2	3.7	5.1	-	-	-	-
500 TO 999 MILES......	72	100.0	58.7	39.0	2.3	-	-	-	-
1000 TO 1499 MILES....	40	100.0	32.8	67.2	-	-	-	-	-
1500 MILES OR OVER....	47	100.0	79.5	20.5	-	-	-	-	-
EAST NORTH CENTRAL......	6 033	100.0	84.1	10.4	5.4	-	-	-	.1
UNDER 100 MILES.......	160	100.0	28.8	21.8	49.0	-	-	-	.3
100 TO 199 MILES......	380	100.0	53.6	24.5	21.7	-	-	-	.2
200 TO 299 MILES......	705	100.0	78.7	16.5	4.7	-	-	-	-
300 TO 499 MILES......	1 188	100.0	85.0	11.3	3.5	-	-	-	.2
500 TO 999 MILES......	2 500	100.0	90.8	7.4	1.8	-	-	-	-
1000 TO 1499 MILES....	322	100.0	82.0	9.5	8.5	-	-	-	-
1500 MILES OR OVER....	775	100.0	93.6	4.2	2.2	-	-	-	-

See footnotes at end of table 4.

TABLE 1. TCC GROUP 204—Percent Distribution of Geographic Division of Origin and Distance Shipped, by Means of Transport: 1972—Continued

Geographic division of origin[1] and distance shipped[2]	Number	Percent distribution by means of transport							
		All means of transport	Rail	Motor carrier	Private truck	Air	Water	Other	Unknown
TON-MILES OF SHIPMENTS	(millions of ton-miles)								
WEST NORTH CENTRAL	8 048	100.0	86.9	7.4	5.4	-	-	-	.3
UNDER 100 MILES	240	100.0	22.3	12.9	63.9	-	-	-	.9
100 TO 199 MILES	405	100.0	53.9	9.7	36.0	-	-	-	.4
200 TO 299 MILES	663	100.0	83.0	8.6	8.3	-	-	-	.1
300 TO 499 MILES	1 236	100.0	84.4	11.7	3.5	-	-	-	.4
500 TO 999 MILES	2 836	100.0	91.2	7.6	1.1	-	-	-	.1
1000 TO 1499 MILES	1 801	100.0	93.6	5.7	.5	-	-	.1	.1
1500 MILES OR OVER	865	100.0	98.9	.3	-	-	-	-	.8
EAST SOUTH CENTRAL	881	100.0	60.5	1.5	38.1	-	-	-	-
UNDER 100 MILES	84	100.0	24.1	-	75.9	-	-	-	-
100 TO 199 MILES	92	100.0	40.2	9.9	50.0	-	-	-	-
200 TO 299 MILES	205	100.0	87.3	1.0	11.7	-	-	-	-
300 TO 499 MILES	146	100.0	74.6	1.1	24.3	-	-	-	-
500 TO 999 MILES	324	100.0	57.5	-	42.5	-	-	-	-
1000 TO 1499 MILES	27	100.0	-	-	100.0	-	-	-	-
1500 MILES OR OVER	-	100.0	-	-	-	-	-	-	-
WEST SOUTH CENTRAL	2 176	100.0	59.0	20.2	20.7	-	-	-	.1
UNDER 100 MILES	114	100.0	52.7	1.1	46.2	-	-	-	-
100 TO 199 MILES	270	100.0	67.1	1.0	31.6	-	-	.3	-
200 TO 299 MILES	182	100.0	64.9	6.4	28.5	-	-	-	.2
300 TO 499 MILES	313	100.0	90.5	5.4	4.1	-	-	-	-
500 TO 999 MILES	584	100.0	66.1	31.1	2.7	-	-	-	-
1000 TO 1499 MILES	454	100.0	28.4	29.1	42.4	-	.1	-	-
1500 MILES OR OVER	254	100.0	48.3	36.3	14.8	-	.1	-	.5
PACIFIC	592	100.0	86.5	9.3	2.5	.4	1.3	-	.1
UNDER 100 MILES	34	100.0	84.8	3.3	11.8	-	-	-	-
100 TO 199 MILES	22	100.0	64.3	29.6	4.5	-	-	-	1.6
200 TO 299 MILES	28	100.0	81.8	12.6	5.7	-	-	-	-
300 TO 499 MILES	75	100.0	71.0	22.6	6.2	.1	-	-	-
500 TO 999 MILES	130	100.0	92.4	5.1	2.3	.2	-	-	-
1000 TO 1499 MILES	26	100.0	76.1	23.0	-	.2	.2	.8	-
1500 MILES OR OVER	273	100.0	91.5	5.0	.1	-	.7	2.7	-

See footnotes at end of table 4.

TABLE 2. TCC GROUP 204—Percent Distribution of Geographic Division of Origin and Means of Transport, by Geographic Division of Destination: 1972

Geographic division of origin[1] and means of transport	Number	Percent distribution by division of destination									
		U.S. total	New England	Middle Atlantic	East North Central	West North Central	South Atlantic	East South Central	West South Central	Mountain	Pacific
TONS OF SHIPMENTS	(thousands of tons)										
U.S. TOTAL	63 521	100.0	5.9	15.8	19.3	14.8	14.9	8.4	14.0	2.1	4.7
RAIL	39 335	100.0	8.0	15.4	21.0	10.0	13.8	8.0	15.7	1.8	6.3
MOTOR CARRIER	6 421	100.0	3.2	18.2	29.7	17.8	7.5	4.6	7.7	6.5	4.9
PRIVATE TRUCK	17 629	100.0	2.3	15.7	11.7	24.3	20.2	10.7	12.6	1.3	1.1
AIR	3	100.0	2.9	8.4	45.6	2.4	2.0	-	4.2	8.3	26.1
WATER	4	100.0	2.4	21.0	-	3.3	-	-	-	-	73.2
OTHER	13	100.0	-	.1	.4	6.1	58.2	-	27.9	7.3	7.3
UNKNOWN	113	100.0	-	17.1	34.4	25.8	10.0	-	5.4	.1	7.3
MIDDLE ATLANTIC	7 075	100.0	13.4	69.9	1.7	.3	14.1	.2	-	.3	.1
RAIL	3 232	100.0	24.1	59.7	3.0	.3	11.8	.4	-	.5	.3
MOTOR CARRIER	1 192	100.0	9.1	74.8	1.8	.7	13.1	-	-	.4	.1
PRIVATE TRUCK	2 636	100.0	2.2	80.1	-	.1	17.6	-	-	-	-
AIR	-	100.0	-	100.0	-	-	-	-	-	-	-
WATER	-	100.0	-	-	-	-	-	-	-	-	-
OTHER	-	100.0	-	58.4	-	-	41.6	-	-	-	-
UNKNOWN	13	100.0	-	94.5	.1	-	5.5	-	-	-	-
EAST NORTH CENTRAL	15 571	100.0	4.4	16.9	41.3	8.3	9.9	11.1	4.4	.8	2.9
RAIL	10 798	100.0	6.1	22.6	31.4	5.8	11.7	12.0	5.5	1.0	3.8
MOTOR CARRIER	2 347	100.0	.9	6.4	60.7	13.9	8.6	6.1	2.4	.3	.8
PRIVATE TRUCK	2 406	100.0	.4	1.2	66.5	14.1	3.3	12.0	1.5	.3	.7
AIR	-	100.0	-	8.5	2.9	.5	-	-	-	4.8	83.3
WATER	-	100.0	-	-	-	-	-	-	-	-	-
OTHER	-	100.0	-	-	100.0	-	-	-	-	-	-
UNKNOWN	18	100.0	-	27.6	72.2	-	-	-	-	-	.2

See footnotes at end of table 4.

TABLE 2. TCC GROUP 204—Percent Distribution of Geographic Division of Origin and Means of Transport, by Geographic Division of Destination: 1972—Continued

Geographic division of origin[1] and means of transport	Number	U.S. total	New England	Middle Atlantic	East North Central	West North Central	South Atlantic	East South Central	West South Central	Mountain	Pacific
TONS OF SHIPMENTS	(thousands of tons)										
WEST NORTH CENTRAL	19 449	100.0	2.0	6.5	26.2	39.2	3.8	4.9	11.0	2.1	4.4
RAIL	13 197	100.0	2.9	9.5	32.8	22.4	5.4	6.8	12.7	1.4	6.1
MOTOR CARRIER	1 755	100.0	.4	.3	17.4	44.0	1.3	2.7	19.3	11.6	2.9
PRIVATE TRUCK	4 426	100.0	.1	-	9.6	87.0	.1	-	2.7	.5	.1
AIR	1	100.0	.4	-	99.3	-	-	-	-	.3	-
WATER	-	100.0	-	-	-	-	-	-	-	-	-
OTHER	1	100.0	-	.9	1.4	43.9	.3	.2	.5	52.8	-
UNKNOWN	66	100.0	-	1.9	38.8	44.0	-	-	7.1	-	8.2
EAST SOUTH CENTRAL	3 953	100.0	.6	4.2	3.0	1.8	24.6	62.4	3.3	-	-
RAIL	1 840	100.0	-	4.3	3.1	2.6	40.8	46.2	3.0	-	-
MOTOR CARRIER	76	100.0	-	-	35.2	-	4.8	58.5	1.6	-	-
PRIVATE TRUCK	2 037	100.0	1.1	4.3	1.7	1.2	10.7	77.2	3.7	-	-
AIR	-	100.0	-	-	-	-	-	-	-	-	-
WATER	-	100.0	-	-	-	-	-	-	-	-	-
OTHER	-	100.0	-	-	-	-	-	-	-	-	-
UNKNOWN	-	100.0	-	-	-	-	-	-	-	-	-
WEST SOUTH CENTRAL	6 604	100.0	.6	2.4	6.5	2.6	2.0	1.9	78.5	2.2	3.3
RAIL	4 117	100.0	-	.5	7.4	2.9	1.6	1.5	82.1	1.5	2.3
MOTOR CARRIER	550	100.0	3.9	4.2	21.9	6.3	10.0	10.0	17.0	9.5	17.3
PRIVATE TRUCK	1 929	100.0	.9	5.7	.1	.9	.5	.3	88.5	1.6	1.5
AIR	-	100.0	10.7	-	-	-	-	-	-	89.3	-
WATER	-	100.0	18.6	81.4	-	-	-	-	-	-	-
OTHER	3	100.0	-	-	-	-	-	-	100.0	-	-
UNKNOWN	2	100.0	-	-	-	-	-	-	61.3	-	38.7
PACIFIC	1 549	100.0	.9	3.5	1.8	1.6	.3	.2	.7	2.9	88.2
RAIL	1 245	100.0	1.0	4.1	2.2	1.9	.3	.2	.8	2.9	86.6
MOTOR CARRIER	163	100.0	.5	1.4	.7	.4	-	.1	.5	4.8	91.6
PRIVATE TRUCK	133	100.0	-	-	.1	-	-	-	-	.5	99.4
AIR	1	100.0	5.1	15.1	7.4	4.4	3.8	-	7.9	14.3	41.9
WATER	4	100.0	-	11.9	-	3.8	-	-	-	-	84.3
OTHER	-	100.0	-	-	-	-	-	-	-	-	100.0
UNKNOWN	1	100.0	-	-	-	-	-	-	-	3.1	96.9
TON-MILES OF SHIPMENTS	(millions of ton-miles)										
U.S. TOTAL	20 730	100.0	8.0	18.2	15.5	7.5	13.1	6.9	13.9	3.5	13.5
RAIL	16 465	100.0	9.0	19.0	15.3	5.6	12.8	7.0	13.9	2.6	14.7
MOTOR CARRIER	2 007	100.0	4.2	11.3	21.5	11.8	11.8	5.1	8.5	12.1	13.8
PRIVATE TRUCK	2 213	100.0	4.5	18.1	11.2	17.3	16.4	7.6	18.5	2.1	4.3
AIR	2	100.0	8.0	21.9	19.5	4.0	5.0	-	7.1	5.8	28.7
WATER	8	100.0	2.1	21.7	-	2.5	-	-	-	-	73.6
OTHER	2	100.0	-	.6	.4	2.0	12.8	.1	33.2	51.0	-
UNKNOWN	30	100.0	-	18.5	24.9	11.2	1.8	-	11.3	.1	32.3
MIDDLE ATLANTIC	1 179	100.0	27.4	48.4	3.7	1.7	13.6	.7	-	2.7	1.8
RAIL	807	100.0	34.3	45.1	4.0	1.2	9.0	1.0	-	3.0	2.4
MOTOR CARRIER	193	100.0	13.1	42.6	5.7	4.8	28.4	-	-	3.8	1.3
PRIVATE TRUCK	175	100.0	11.7	68.9	-	.9	18.5	-	.3	-	-
AIR	-	100.0	-	100.0	-	-	-	-	-	-	-
WATER	-	100.0	-	-	-	-	-	-	-	-	-
OTHER	-	100.0	-	48.7	-	-	51.3	-	-	-	-
UNKNOWN	2	100.0	-	95.1	.2	-	4.7	-	-	-	-
EAST NORTH CENTRAL	6 033	100.0	9.1	23.4	16.7	5.8	14.3	8.2	7.1	2.4	13.0
RAIL	5 075	100.0	10.3	25.7	12.9	4.2	14.5	8.3	7.3	2.5	14.2
MOTOR CARRIER	627	100.0	2.6	13.5	34.9	13.5	16.6	6.2	6.3	1.3	5.2
PRIVATE TRUCK	326	100.0	2.8	5.5	40.3	15.8	7.7	10.6	6.0	2.9	8.5
AIR	-	100.0	-	3.7	.3	.1	-	-	-	3.0	92.8
WATER	-	100.0	-	-	-	-	-	-	-	-	-
OTHER	-	100.0	-	-	100.0	-	-	-	-	-	-
UNKNOWN	3	100.0	-	57.6	40.7	-	-	-	-	-	1.7

See footnotes at end of table 4.

TABLE 2. **TCC GROUP 204—Percent Distribution of Geographic Division of Origin and Means of Transport, by Geographic Division of Destination: 1972**—Continued

Geographic division of origin[1] and means of transport	Number	Percent distribution by division of destination									
		U.S. total	New England	Middle Atlantic	East North Central	West North Central	South Atlantic	East South Central	West South Central	Mountain	Pacific
TON-MILES OF SHIPMENTS	(millions of ton-miles)										
WEST NORTH CENTRAL......	8 048	100.0	5.4	14.4	21.3	11.5	8.5	6.5	12.6	3.5	16.1
RAIL.................	6 995	100.0	6.1	16.5	21.6	7.3	9.4	7.2	12.5	1.9	17.4
MOTOR CARRIER.........	593	100.0	1.2	.7	16.9	19.9	4.3	4.3	18.3	22.9	11.4
PRIVATE TRUCK.........	436	100.0	.6	-	21.8	67.1	.5	.2	5.6	2.9	1.3
AIR..................	-	100.0	1.6	-	97.7	-	-	-	-	.7	-
WATER................	-	100.0	-	-	-	-	-	-	-	-	-
OTHER................	1	100.0	-	1.1	.5	3.6	.4	.1	.5	93.7	-
UNKNOWN..............	21	100.0	-	4.4	28.2	15.8	-	-	14.4	-	37.2
EAST SOUTH CENTRAL......	881	100.0	3.0	17.4	4.1	4.0	34.5	32.7	4.3	-	-
RAIL.................	533	100.0	-	14.0	3.6	4.0	45.4	29.5	3.5	-	-
MOTOR CARRIER.........	12	100.0	-	-	28.1	-	7.4	63.4	1.1	-	-
PRIVATE TRUCK.........	335	100.0	7.8	23.3	3.9	4.1	18.3	36.7	5.8	-	-
AIR..................	-	100.0	-	-	-	-	-	-	-	-	-
WATER................	-	100.0	-	-	-	-	-	-	-	-	-
OTHER................	-	100.0	-	-	-	-	-	-	-	-	-
UNKNOWN..............	-	100.0	-	-	-	-	-	-	-	-	-
WEST SOUTH CENTRAL......	2 176	100.0	2.6	9.6	13.2	3.8	5.4	3.2	42.9	4.1	15.1
RAIL.................	1 283	100.0	.2	2.0	15.2	4.5	4.9	2.9	55.4	3.3	11.5
MOTOR CARRIER.........	439	100.0	6.5	6.0	20.3	4.9	10.6	6.3	4.6	9.3	31.5
PRIVATE TRUCK.........	449	100.0	5.7	34.9	.5	.8	2.0	.8	44.9	1.1	9.4
AIR..................	-	100.0	16.5	-	-	-	-	-	-	83.5	-
WATER................	-	100.0	21.2	78.8	-	-	-	-	-	-	-
OTHER................	-	100.0	-	-	-	-	-	-	100.0	-	-
UNKNOWN..............	1	100.0	-	-	-	-	-	-	18.9	-	81.1
PACIFIC..............	592	100.0	6.0	21.2	9.3	6.3	1.5	.7	2.6	5.0	47.4
RAIL.................	512	100.0	6.5	23.1	10.2	7.0	1.7	.8	2.7	4.4	43.6
MOTOR CARRIER.........	54	100.0	4.0	10.2	4.0	1.8	.3	.3	1.9	12.6	64.9
PRIVATE TRUCK.........	14	100.0	-	-	1.9	-	-	-	-	1.6	96.5
AIR..................	2	100.0	9.6	26.8	10.6	5.0	6.2	-	8.8	6.5	26.6
WATER................	7	100.0	-	15.3	-	2.8	-	-	-	-	81.9
OTHER................	-	100.0	-	-	-	-	-	-	-	-	100.0
UNKNOWN..............	-	100.0	-	-	-	-	-	-	-	5.8	94.2

See footnotes at end of table 4.

TABLE 3. **TCC GROUP 204**—Percent Distribution of Geographic Division of Destination and Means of Transport, by Geographic Division of Origin: 1972

Geographic division of destination and means of transport	Number	Percent distribution by division of origin [1]								
		U.S. total	New England	Middle Atlantic	East North Central	West North Central	South Atlantic	East South Central	West South Central	Mountain	Pacific
TONS OF SHIPMENTS	(thousands of tons)										
U.S. TOTAL	63 521	100.0	(D)	11.1	24.5	30.6	(D)	6.2	10.4	(D)	2.4
RAIL	39 335	100.0	(D)	8.2	27.5	33.6	(D)	4.7	10.5	(D)	3.2
MOTOR CARRIER	6 421	100.0	(D)	18.6	36.6	27.3	(D)	1.2	8.6	(D)	2.5
PRIVATE TRUCK	17 629	100.0	(D)	15.0	13.7	25.1	(D)	11.6	10.9	(D)	.8
AIR	3	100.0	(D)	-	4.6	41.8	(D)	-	.4	(D)	53.2
WATER	4	100.0	(D)	-	-	-	(D)	-	13.1	(D)	86.9
OTHER	13	100.0	(D)	-	.2	13.8	(D)	-	27.8	(D)	-
UNKNOWN	113	100.0	(D)	12.2	16.2	58.6	(D)	-	1.9	(D)	1.8
NEW ENGLAND	3 748	100.0	(D)	25.2	18.5	10.4	(D)	.6	1.1	(D)	.4
RAIL	3 135	100.0	(D)	24.9	21.1	12.1	(D)	-	.1	(D)	.4
MOTOR CARRIER	205	100.0	(D)	52.7	10.4	3.6	(D)	-	10.5	(D)	.4
PRIVATE TRUCK	406	100.0	(D)	14.3	2.4	.6	(D)	5.6	4.1	(D)	-
AIR	-	100.0	(D)	-	-	5.6	(D)	-	1.4	(D)	93.0
WATER	-	100.0	(D)	-	-	-	(D)	-	100.0	(D)	-
OTHER	-	100.0	(D)	-	-	-	(D)	-	-	(D)	-
UNKNOWN	-	100.0	(D)	-	-	-	(D)	-	-	(D)	-
MIDDLE ATLANTIC	10 022	100.0	(D)	49.4	26.2	12.5	(D)	1.7	1.6	(D)	.5
RAIL	6 062	100.0	(D)	31.8	40.3	20.6	(D)	1.3	.4	(D)	.8
MOTOR CARRIER	1 165	100.0	(D)	76.5	12.8	.4	(D)	-	2.0	(D)	.2
PRIVATE TRUCK	2 773	100.0	(D)	76.2	1.0	-	(D)	3.1	4.0	(D)	-
AIR	-	100.0	(D)	-	4.6	-	(D)	-	-	(D)	95.3
WATER	-	100.0	(D)	-	-	-	(D)	-	-	(D)	-
OTHER	-	100.0	(D)	14.8	-	85.2	(D)	-	50.9	(D)	49.1
UNKNOWN	19	100.0	(D)	67.4	26.2	6.4	(D)	-	-	(D)	-
EAST NORTH CENTRAL	12 282	100.0	(D)	1.0	52.3	41.4	(D)	1.0	3.5	(D)	.2
RAIL	8 265	100.0	(D)	1.2	41.0	52.4	(D)	.7	3.7	(D)	.3
MOTOR CARRIER	1 906	100.0	(D)	1.1	74.7	16.0	(D)	1.4	6.3	(D)	.1
PRIVATE TRUCK	2 070	100.0	(D)	-	77.3	20.4	(D)	1.7	.1	(D)	.1
AIR	1	100.0	(D)	-	.3	91.0	(D)	-	-	(D)	8.7
WATER	-	100.0	(D)	-	-	-	(D)	-	-	(D)	-
OTHER	-	100.0	(D)	-	48.8	51.2	(D)	-	-	(D)	-
UNKNOWN	39	100.0	(D)	-	33.9	66.1	(D)	-	-	(D)	-
WEST NORTH CENTRAL	9 384	100.0	(D)	.2	13.8	81.1	(D)	.8	1.8	(D)	.3
RAIL	3 923	100.0	(D)	.2	16.0	75.5	(D)	1.2	3.0	(D)	.6
MOTOR CARRIER	1 145	100.0	(D)	.8	28.5	67.4	(D)	-	3.0	(D)	.1
PRIVATE TRUCK	4 284	100.0	(D)	-	7.9	89.9	(D)	.6	.4	(D)	-
AIR	-	100.0	(D)	-	.9	-	(D)	-	-	(D)	99.1
WATER	-	100.0	(D)	-	-	-	(D)	-	-	(D)	100.0
OTHER	-	100.0	(D)	-	-	100.0	(D)	-	-	(D)	-
UNKNOWN	29	100.0	(D)	-	-	100.0	(D)	-	-	(D)	-
SOUTH ATLANTIC	9 482	100.0	(D)	10.5	16.3	7.8	(D)	10.3	1.4	(D)	-
RAIL	5 415	100.0	(D)	7.0	23.4	13.2	(D)	13.9	1.2	(D)	.1
MOTOR CARRIER	482	100.0	(D)	32.3	41.7	4.7	(D)	.8	11.4	(D)	-
PRIVATE TRUCK	3 565	100.0	(D)	13.0	2.2	.1	(D)	6.1	.3	(D)	-
AIR	-	100.0	(D)	-	-	-	(D)	-	-	(D)	100.0
WATER	-	100.0	(D)	-	-	-	(D)	-	-	(D)	-
OTHER	7	100.0	(D)	-	-	.1	(D)	-	-	(D)	-
UNKNOWN	11	100.0	(D)	6.6	-	.1	(D)	-	-	(D)	-
EAST SOUTH CENTRAL	5 345	100.0	(D)	.2	32.3	17.8	(D)	46.2	2.3	(D)	-
RAIL	3 160	100.0	(D)	.4	41.0	28.6	(D)	26.9	2.0	(D)	.1
MOTOR CARRIER	292	100.0	(D)	-	48.8	16.5	(D)	15.2	18.8	(D)	-
PRIVATE TRUCK	1 893	100.0	(D)	-	15.2	.1	(D)	83.1	.4	(D)	-
AIR	-	100.0	(D)	-	-	-	(D)	-	-	(D)	-
WATER	-	100.0	(D)	-	-	-	(D)	-	-	(D)	-
OTHER	-	100.0	(D)	-	-	100.0	(D)	-	-	(D)	-
UNKNOWN	-	100.0	(D)	-	-	-	(D)	-	-	(D)	-
WEST SOUTH CENTRAL	8 900	100.0	(D)	-	7.7	24.1	(D)	1.5	58.3	(D)	.1
RAIL	6 179	100.0	(D)	-	9.6	27.2	(D)	.9	54.7	(D)	.2
MOTOR CARRIER	491	100.0	(D)	.1	11.6	68.8	(D)	.2	19.0	(D)	.2
PRIVATE TRUCK	2 219	100.0	(D)	-	1.6	5.4	(D)	3.4	76.9	(D)	-
AIR	-	100.0	(D)	-	-	-	(D)	-	-	(D)	100.0
WATER	-	100.0	(D)	-	-	-	(D)	-	-	(D)	-
OTHER	3	100.0	(D)	-	-	.2	(D)	-	99.8	(D)	-
UNKNOWN	6	100.0	(D)	-	-	78.1	(D)	-	21.9	(D)	-
MOUNTAIN	1 364	100.0	(D)	1.5	9.4	29.7	(D)	-	10.7	(D)	3.3
RAIL	718	100.0	(D)	2.1	15.7	25.1	(D)	-	8.9	(D)	5.0
MOTOR CARRIER	415	100.0	(D)	1.1	1.7	49.2	(D)	-	12.5	(D)	1.9
PRIVATE TRUCK	229	100.0	(D)	-	3.6	8.8	(D)	-	13.0	(D)	.3
AIR	-	100.0	(D)	-	2.6	1.7	(D)	-	4.2	(D)	91.4
WATER	-	100.0	(D)	-	-	-	(D)	-	-	(D)	-
OTHER	1	100.0	(D)	-	-	100.0	(D)	-	-	(D)	-
UNKNOWN	-	100.0	(D)	-	-	-	(D)	-	-	(D)	100.0
PACIFIC	2 989	100.0	(D)	.3	15.0	28.8	(D)	-	7.3	(D)	45.7
RAIL	2 475	100.0	(D)	.3	16.6	32.3	(D)	-	3.8	(D)	43.6
MOTOR CARRIER	316	100.0	(D)	.3	5.7	16.3	(D)	-	30.1	(D)	47.2
PRIVATE TRUCK	185	100.0	(D)	-	9.6	2.2	(D)	-	15.5	(D)	71.5
AIR	-	100.0	(D)	-	14.7	-	(D)	-	-	(D)	85.3
WATER	3	100.0	(D)	-	-	-	(D)	-	-	(D)	100.0
OTHER	-	100.0	(D)	-	-	-	(D)	-	-	(D)	100.0
UNKNOWN	8	100.0	(D)	-	.4	66.1	(D)	-	10.1	(D)	23.4

See footnotes at end of table 4.

TABLE 3. **TCC GROUP 204—Percent Distribution of Geographic Division of Destination and Means of Transport, by Geographic Division of Origin: 1972**—Continued

Geographic division of destination and means of transport	Number	Percent distribution by division of origin[1]									
		U.S. total	New England	Middle Atlantic	East North Central	West North Central	South Atlantic	East South Central	West South Central	Mountain	Pacific
TON-MILES OF SHIPMENTS	(millions of ton-miles)										
U.S. TOTAL	20 730	100.0	(D)	5.7	29.1	38.8	(D)	4.3	10.5	(D)	2.9
RAIL	16 465	100.0	(D)	4.9	30.8	42.5	(D)	3.2	7.8	(D)	3.1
MOTOR CARRIER	2 007	100.0	(D)	9.7	31.2	29.6	(D)	.6	21.9	(D)	2.7
PRIVATE TRUCK	2 213	100.0	(D)	7.9	14.8	19.7	(D)	15.2	20.3	(D)	.7
AIR	2	100.0	(D)	-	7.8	11.2	(D)	-	.4	(D)	80.7
WATER	8	100.0	(D)	-	-	-	(D)	-	10.1	(D)	89.9
OTHER	2	100.0	(D)	-	.1	54.5	(D)	-	32.9	(D)	-
UNKNOWN	30	100.0	(D)	9.0	11.9	71.1	(D)	-	5.5	(D)	1.2
NEW ENGLAND	1 662	100.0	(D)	19.4	33.1	26.2	(D)	1.6	3.5	(D)	2.1
RAIL	1 479	100.0	(D)	18.7	35.5	28.8	(D)	-	.2	(D)	2.3
MOTOR CARRIER	83	100.0	(D)	30.5	19.7	8.8	(D)	-	34.4	(D)	2.6
PRIVATE TRUCK	98	100.0	(D)	20.8	9.3	2.6	(D)	26.6	26.0	(D)	-
AIR	-	100.0	(D)	-	-	2.3	(D)	-	.8	(D)	96.9
WATER	-	100.0	(D)	-	-	-	(D)	-	100.0	(D)	-
OTHER	-	100.0	(D)	-	-	-	(D)	-	-	(D)	-
UNKNOWN	-	100.0	(D)	-	-	-	(D)	-	-	(D)	-
MIDDLE ATLANTIC	3 767	100.0	(D)	15.1	37.4	30.8	(D)	4.1	5.6	(D)	3.3
RAIL	3 132	100.0	(D)	11.6	41.7	36.9	(D)	2.4	.8	(D)	3.8
MOTOR CARRIER	226	100.0	(D)	36.5	37.2	1.9	(D)	-	11.6	(D)	2.5
PRIVATE TRUCK	400	100.0	(D)	30.2	4.5	-	(D)	19.5	39.1	(D)	-
AIR	-	100.0	(D)	-	1.3	-	(D)	-	-	(D)	98.7
WATER	1	100.0	(D)	-	-	-	(D)	-	36.5	(D)	63.5
OTHER	-	100.0	(D)	2.1	-	97.9	(D)	-	-	(D)	-
UNKNOWN	5	100.0	(D)	46.2	37.0	16.9	(D)	-	-	(D)	-
EAST NORTH CENTRAL	3 207	100.0	(D)	1.4	31.4	53.5	(D)	1.1	8.9	(D)	1.7
RAIL	2 520	100.0	(D)	1.3	26.0	60.1	(D)	.8	7.7	(D)	2.1
MOTOR CARRIER	430	100.0	(D)	2.6	50.8	23.3	(D)	.8	20.8	(D)	.5
PRIVATE TRUCK	247	100.0	(D)	-	53.2	38.4	(D)	5.3	.9	(D)	.1
AIR	-	100.0	(D)	-	.1	56.0	(D)	-	-	(D)	43.8
WATER	-	100.0	(D)	-	-	-	(D)	-	-	(D)	-
OTHER	-	100.0	(D)	-	18.2	81.8	(D)	-	-	(D)	-
UNKNOWN	7	100.0	(D)	.1	19.4	80.5	(D)	-	-	(D)	-
WEST NORTH CENTRAL	1 553	100.0	(D)	1.3	22.5	59.7	(D)	2.3	5.3	(D)	2.4
RAIL	929	100.0	(D)	1.0	22.9	55.1	(D)	2.3	6.2	(D)	3.8
MOTOR CARRIER	236	100.0	(D)	3.9	35.7	49.9	(D)	-	9.0	(D)	.4
PRIVATE TRUCK	382	100.0	(D)	.4	13.5	76.5	(D)	3.6	.9	(D)	-
AIR	-	100.0	(D)	-	.3	-	(D)	-	-	(D)	99.7
WATER	-	100.0	(D)	-	-	-	(D)	-	-	(D)	100.0
OTHER	-	100.0	(D)	-	-	100.0	(D)	-	-	(D)	-
UNKNOWN	3	100.0	(D)	-	-	100.0	(D)	-	-	(D)	-
SOUTH ATLANTIC	2 707	100.0	(D)	5.9	32.0	25.4	(D)	11.2	4.4	(D)	.3
RAIL	2 105	100.0	(D)	3.5	35.0	31.4	(D)	11.5	3.0	(D)	.4
MOTOR CARRIER	237	100.0	(D)	23.2	44.0	10.7	(D)	.4	19.6	(D)	.1
PRIVATE TRUCK	363	100.0	(D)	8.9	6.9	.6	(D)	16.9	2.5	(D)	-
AIR	-	100.0	(D)	-	-	-	(D)	-	-	(D)	100.0
WATER	-	100.0	(D)	-	-	-	(D)	-	-	(D)	-
OTHER	-	100.0	(D)	.1	-	1.9	(D)	-	-	(D)	-
UNKNOWN	-	100.0	(D)	23.4	-	1.4	(D)	-	-	(D)	-
EAST SOUTH CENTRAL	1 424	100.0	(D)	.6	34.8	37.0	(D)	20.3	4.8	(D)	.3
RAIL	1 154	100.0	(D)	.7	36.6	43.4	(D)	13.6	3.3	(D)	.4
MOTOR CARRIER	101	100.0	(D)	-	38.0	25.1	(D)	8.0	27.2	(D)	.2
PRIVATE TRUCK	167	100.0	(D)	-	20.7	.5	(D)	73.4	2.1	(D)	-
AIR	-	100.0	(D)	-	-	-	(D)	-	-	(D)	-
WATER	-	100.0	(D)	-	-	-	(D)	-	-	(D)	-
OTHER	-	100.0	(D)	-	-	100.0	(D)	-	-	(D)	-
UNKNOWN	-	100.0	(D)	-	-	-	(D)	-	-	(D)	-
WEST SOUTH CENTRAL	2 880	100.0	(D)	-	14.9	35.1	(D)	1.3	32.4	(D)	.5
RAIL	2 295	100.0	(D)	-	16.1	38.1	(D)	.8	31.0	(D)	.6
MOTOR CARRIER	170	100.0	(D)	.3	23.1	63.8	(D)	.1	11.7	(D)	.6
PRIVATE TRUCK	410	100.0	(D)	-	4.7	6.0	(D)	4.7	49.3	(D)	-
AIR	-	100.0	(D)	-	-	-	(D)	-	-	(D)	100.0
WATER	-	100.0	(D)	-	-	-	(D)	-	-	(D)	-
OTHER	-	100.0	(D)	-	-	.8	(D)	-	99.2	(D)	-
UNKNOWN	3	100.0	(D)	-	-	90.8	(D)	-	9.2	(D)	-
MOUNTAIN	722	100.0	(D)	4.3	19.9	39.3	(D)	-	12.3	(D)	4.1
RAIL	431	100.0	(D)	5.6	29.3	31.0	(D)	-	9.9	(D)	5.2
MOTOR CARRIER	242	100.0	(D)	3.0	3.3	56.1	(D)	-	16.9	(D)	2.9
PRIVATE TRUCK	46	100.0	(D)	-	20.2	26.9	(D)	-	10.5	(D)	.5
AIR	-	100.0	(D)	-	4.0	1.3	(D)	-	5.6	(D)	89.1
WATER	-	100.0	(D)	-	-	-	(D)	-	-	(D)	-
OTHER	1	100.0	(D)	-	-	100.0	(D)	-	-	(D)	-
UNKNOWN	-	100.0	(D)	-	-	-	(D)	-	-	(D)	100.0
PACIFIC	2 806	100.0	(D)	.8	27.9	46.3	(D)	-	11.7	(D)	10.0
RAIL	2 417	100.0	(D)	.8	29.9	50.4	(D)	-	6.1	(D)	9.3
MOTOR CARRIER	277	100.0	(D)	.9	11.7	24.3	(D)	-	49.9	(D)	12.9
PRIVATE TRUCK	94	100.0	(D)	-	29.3	6.1	(D)	-	44.6	(D)	15.0
AIR	-	100.0	(D)	-	25.1	-	(D)	-	-	(D)	74.9
WATER	6	100.0	(D)	-	-	-	(D)	-	-	(D)	100.0
OTHER	-	100.0	(D)	-	-	-	(D)	-	-	(D)	100.0
UNKNOWN	9	100.0	(D)	-	.6	82.0	(D)	-	13.7	(D)	3.6

See footnotes at end of table 4.

TABLE 4. TCC GROUP 204—Percent Distribution of Distance Shipped and Weight of Shipment, by Means of Transport: 1972

Distance shipped and weight of shipment[2][3]	Number	Percent distribution by means of transport							
		All means of transport	Rail	Motor carrier	Private truck	Air	Water	Other	Unknown
TONS OF SHIPMENTS	(thousands of tons)								
U.S. TOTAL	58 282	100.0	61.1	10.0	28.7	-	-	-	.2
UNDER 100 MILES	18 209	100.0	28.1	9.5	62.0	-	-	-	.3
UNDER 1000 POUNDS	42	100.0	-	5.4	94.5	-	-	.1	-
1000 TO 9999 POUNDS	1 130	100.0	.4	4.2	95.0	-	-	-	.3
10000 TO 29999 POUNDS	6 615	100.0	.7	9.4	89.7	-	-	.1	-
30000 TO 59999 POUNDS	5 300	100.0	16.2	18.9	64.2	-	-	-	.7
60000 TO 89999 POUNDS	1 770	100.0	97.5	.6	1.6	-	-	-	.3
90000 POUNDS AND OVER	3 350	100.0	74.1	1.4	24.5	-	-	-	-
100 TO 199 MILES	10 196	100.0	59.2	11.4	29.3	-	-	-	.2
UNDER 1000 POUNDS	11	100.0	17.3	22.6	59.3	.5	-	.1	.2
1000 TO 9999 POUNDS	326	100.0	12.2	12.2	75.6	-	-	-	-
10000 TO 29999 POUNDS	1 209	100.0	7.3	18.3	74.4	-	-	-	.1
30000 TO 59999 POUNDS	4 133	100.0	35.2	21.3	43.1	-	-	-	.4
60000 TO 89999 POUNDS	2 463	100.0	98.1	.3	1.5	-	-	-	-
90000 POUNDS AND OVER	2 051	100.0	98.9	.3	.8	-	-	-	-
200 TO 299 MILES	9 088	100.0	76.7	10.2	12.9	-	-	-	.1
UNDER 1000 POUNDS	2	100.0	.1	74.8	24.7	-	-	.4	-
1000 TO 9999 POUNDS	82	100.0	8.1	44.9	46.8	-	-	-	.1
10000 TO 29999 POUNDS	494	100.0	17.1	34.9	47.2	.3	-	-	.5
30000 TO 59999 POUNDS	2 656	100.0	39.3	26.9	33.6	-	-	-	.2
60000 TO 89999 POUNDS	2 133	100.0	99.7	-	-	-	-	-	.3
90000 POUNDS AND OVER	3 717	100.0	99.7	.1	.2	-	-	-	-
300 TO 499 MILES	8 180	100.0	83.3	11.0	5.5	-	-	-	.2
UNDER 1000 POUNDS	5	100.0	27.2	46.7	19.1	5.3	-	.5	1.2
1000 TO 9999 POUNDS	94	100.0	14.6	55.4	30.0	-	-	-	-
10000 TO 29999 POUNDS	268	100.0	31.8	39.5	28.4	-	-	-	.3
30000 TO 59999 POUNDS	1 985	100.0	53.5	33.7	12.3	-	-	-	.5
60000 TO 89999 POUNDS	2 208	100.0	98.8	.9	-	-	-	-	.3
90000 POUNDS AND OVER	3 618	100.0	96.1	1.3	2.7	-	-	-	-
500 TO 999 MILES	9 377	100.0	85.4	8.4	6.2	-	-	-	-
UNDER 1000 POUNDS	7	100.0	5.1	53.3	34.9	6.3	-	.4	-
1000 TO 9999 POUNDS	78	100.0	18.0	61.7	20.3	-	-	-	-
10000 TO 29999 POUNDS	320	100.0	38.6	37.9	23.5	-	-	-	-
30000 TO 59999 POUNDS	2 080	100.0	52.1	25.5	22.4	-	-	-	-
60000 TO 89999 POUNDS	1 977	100.0	99.5	-	.5	-	-	-	-
90000 POUNDS AND OVER	4 911	100.0	98.1	1.7	.2	-	-	-	-
1000 TO 1499 MILES	2 078	100.0	79.5	11.4	9.1	-	-	-	-
UNDER 1000 POUNDS	2	100.0	18.4	78.9	.4	2.0	-	.1	.2
1000 TO 9999 POUNDS	19	100.0	16.6	72.9	9.8	-	.8	-	-
10000 TO 29999 POUNDS	117	100.0	7.5	69.6	22.0	-	-	.9	-
30000 TO 59999 POUNDS	425	100.0	31.9	32.5	35.7	-	-	-	-
60000 TO 89999 POUNDS	437	100.0	97.8	-	2.2	-	-	-	-
90000 POUNDS AND OVER	1 075	100.0	100.0	-	-	-	-	-	-
1500 MILES OR OVER	1 151	100.0	88.4	7.7	3.1	.1	.2	-	.5
UNDER 1000 POUNDS	2	100.0	-	58.2	7.4	34.4	-	-	-
1000 TO 9999 POUNDS	22	100.0	2.5	94.6	-	1.0	1.8	-	.1
10000 TO 29999 POUNDS	54	100.0	27.8	46.5	17.9	-	3.6	-	4.2
30000 TO 59999 POUNDS	154	100.0	54.6	26.5	16.6	-	.3	-	2.0
60000 TO 89999 POUNDS	200	100.0	100.0	-	-	-	-	-	-
90000 POUNDS AND OVER	717	100.0	100.0	-	-	-	-	-	-
TON-MILES OF SHIPMENTS	(millions of ton-miles)								
U.S. TOTAL	18 778	100.0	78.6	9.8	11.4	-	-	-	.1
UNDER 100 MILES	964	100.0	31.3	10.1	58.3	-	-	-	.3
UNDER 1000 POUNDS	2	100.0	-	5.0	94.9	-	-	.1	-
1000 TO 9999 POUNDS	55	100.0	.6	4.6	94.5	-	-	-	.3
10000 TO 29999 POUNDS	322	100.0	.8	10.7	88.4	-	-	.1	-
30000 TO 59999 POUNDS	297	100.0	17.0	19.4	62.9	-	-	-	.8
60000 TO 89999 POUNDS	99	100.0	97.1	.6	1.9	-	-	-	.5
90000 POUNDS AND OVER	187	100.0	80.9	1.1	17.9	-	-	-	-
100 TO 199 MILES	1 504	100.0	60.9	11.3	27.6	-	-	-	.2
UNDER 1000 POUNDS	1	100.0	17.1	24.7	57.1	.7	-	.2	.3
1000 TO 9999 POUNDS	43	100.0	12.4	13.0	74.6	-	-	-	-
10000 TO 29999 POUNDS	170	100.0	7.3	18.3	74.3	-	-	-	.1
30000 TO 59999 POUNDS	594	100.0	35.7	22.2	41.8	-	-	-	.4
60000 TO 89999 POUNDS	372	100.0	98.3	.3	1.5	-	-	-	-
90000 POUNDS AND OVER	322	100.0	99.0	.3	.7	-	-	-	-

See footnotes at end of table 4.

TABLE 4. TCC GROUP 204—Percent Distribution of Distance Shipped and Weight of Shipment, by Means of Transport: 1972—Continued

Distance shipped and weight of shipment [2] [3]	Number (millions of ton-miles)	Percent distribution by means of transport							
		All means of transport	Rail	Motor carrier	Private truck	Air	Water	Other	Unknown
TON-MILES OF SHIPMENTS									
200 TO 299 MILES........	2 184	100.0	76.3	10.4	13.1	-	-	-	.2
UNDER 1000 POUNDS.....	-	100.0	.1	74.5	25.0	-	-	.4	-
1000 TO 9999 POUNDS...	20	100.0	9.1	45.9	44.9	-	-	-	.1
10000 TO 29999 POUNDS.	122	100.0	17.5	34.9	46.8	.3	-	-	.5
30000 TO 59999 POUNDS.	651	100.0	39.8	26.7	33.3	-	-	-	.2
60000 TO 89999 POUNDS.	535	100.0	99.7	.1	-	-	-	-	.3
90000 POUNDS AND OVER.	853	100.0	99.7	.1	.2	-	-	-	-
300 TO 499 MILES........	3 245	100.0	83.8	10.8	5.2	-	-	-	.2
UNDER 1000 POUNDS.....	2	100.0	31.4	44.5	17.9	4.7	-	.5	1.1
1000 TO 9999 POUNDS...	36	100.0	16.8	55.2	27.9	-	-	-	-
10000 TO 29999 POUNDS.	101	100.0	32.3	39.2	28.2	-	-	-	.3
30000 TO 59999 POUNDS.	780	100.0	53.4	34.1	12.0	-	-	-	.5
60000 TO 89999 POUNDS.	851	100.0	98.8	.8	-	-	-	-	.4
90000 POUNDS AND OVER.	1 473	100.0	96.5	1.0	2.5	-	-	-	-
500 TO 999 MILES........	6 407	100.0	85.1	8.7	6.2	-	-	-	-
UNDER 1000 POUNDS.....	5	100.0	5.1	46.7	42.1	5.6	-	.4	-
1000 TO 9999 POUNDS...	54	100.0	16.1	64.5	19.4	-	-	-	-
10000 TO 29999 POUNDS.	221	100.0	37.0	39.0	23.9	-	-	-	-
30000 TO 59999 POUNDS.	1 435	100.0	52.1	26.2	21.7	-	-	-	-
60000 TO 89999 POUNDS.	1 373	100.0	99.4	.6	.3	-	-	-	-
90000 POUNDS AND OVER.	3 317	100.0	98.0	1.7	.3	-	-	-	-
1000 TO 1499 MILES......	2 469	100.0	78.2	11.4	10.3	-	-	-	-
UNDER 1000 POUNDS.....	2	100.0	18.5	78.6	.4	2.2	-	.1	.2
1000 TO 9999 POUNDS...	23	100.0	17.4	70.9	10.8	-	.9	-	-
10000 TO 29999 POUNDS.	143	100.0	6.7	68.5	23.9	-	-	.8	-
30000 TO 59999 POUNDS.	527	100.0	29.8	31.2	39.0	-	-	-	-
60000 TO 89999 POUNDS.	528	100.0	97.8	-	2.2	-	-	-	-
90000 POUNDS AND OVER.	1 243	100.0	100.0	-	-	-	-	-	-
1500 MILES OR OVER......	2 001	100.0	88.7	7.5	3.0	.1	.4	-	.4
UNDER 1000 POUNDS.....	4	100.0	-	58.1	6.4	35.5	-	-	-
1000 TO 9999 POUNDS...	40	100.0	2.3	93.3	-	1.2	3.0	-	.2
10000 TO 29999 POUNDS.	91	100.0	29.4	43.8	17.7	-	5.3	-	3.8
30000 TO 59999 POUNDS.	271	100.0	56.6	25.5	15.8	-	.4	-	1.7
60000 TO 89999 POUNDS.	344	100.0	100.0	-	-	-	-	-	-
90000 POUNDS AND OVER.	1 249	100.0	100.0	-	-	-	-	-	-

Note: Detail may not add to total due to rounding. The introductory table shows the estimates of sampling variability for tons; sampling variability for ton-miles has not been estimated. See the map in the Introduction for the States comprising the geographic divisions of the United States.

Shipments excluded from the survey are those moving by pipeline (primarily petroleum products from refineries), parcel post shipments, and commodities moved by own power (motorized vehicles, aircraft, etc.) or towed (prefabricated buildings, etc.). Local shipments (commodities shipped less than 25 miles from the plant) and shipments within the same city are also excluded. Shipments to Alaska and Hawaii from the 48 conterminous States and the District of Columbia are included; however, no data were obtained for shipments originating in Alaska and Hawaii.

  - Represents zero or rounds to zero.   (D) Withheld to avoid disclosing figures for individual companies.

[1] Production of this commodity is concentrated in the geographic divisions shown; figures and distributions for geographic divisions not shown are included in the total.

[2] Distances of shipments to foreign destinations are calculated only to the U.S. port of exit.

[3] Includes only shipments represented by bills of lading and invoices. Summary records which did not show individual weights of shipments are not included.

TCC 205. Bakery Products

Comparisons of Tons and Ton-Miles of Shipments for
Geographic Divisions of Origin and for Sampling Variability: 1972 and 1967

Geographic division of origin	Estimates				Relative sampling variability in tons (percent)	
	1972		1967		1972	1967
	Tons (thousands)	Ton-miles (millions)	Tons (thousands)	Ton-miles (millions)		
U.S. total	2,351	1,042	(^{1})	(^{1})	12.0	(^{1})
New England	(D)	(D)	(^{1})	(^{1})	(*)	(^{1})
Middle Atlantic	560	269	(^{1})	(^{1})	14.0	(^{1})
East North Central	691	318	(^{1})	(^{1})	31.9	(^{1})
West North Central	(D)	(D)	(^{1})	(^{1})	(*)	(^{1})
South Atlantic	687	272	(^{1})	(^{1})	21.4	(^{1})
East South Central	(D)	(D)	(^{1})	(^{1})	(*)	(^{1})
West South Central	(D)	(D)	(^{1})	(^{1})	(*)	(^{1})
Mountain	—	—	(^{1})	(^{1})	—	(^{1})
Pacific	(D)	(D)	(^{1})	(^{1})	(*)	(^{1})

— Represents zero or rounds to zero.　　(D) Withheld to avoid disclosing figures for individual companies.
(*) Data not published.

[1] SIC 205 was out of scope to the 1967 survey. However, for the 1972 survey SIC 2052, cookies and crackers, was included while SIC 2051 remained out of scope to the survey.

TABLE 1. **TCC GROUP 205**—Percent Distribution of Geographic Division of Origin and Distance Shipped, by Means of Transport: 1972

Geographic division of origin[1] and distance shipped[2]	Number	Percent distribution by means of transport							
		All means of transport	Rail	Motor carrier	Private truck	Air	Water	Other	Unknown
TONS OF SHIPMENTS	(thousands of tons)								
U.S. TOTAL..........	2 351	100.0	13.6	34.4	49.9	-	2.0	.1	.1
MIDDLE ATLANTIC.........	560	100.0	11.7	45.7	34.7	-	7.8	.2	-
UNDER 100 MILES.......	193	100.0	-	28.0	71.6	-	-	.3	-
100 TO 199 MILES......	69	100.0	-	78.4	21.6	-	-	-	-
200 TO 299 MILES......	57	100.0	1.8	62.3	35.9	-	-	-	-
300 TO 499 MILES......	47	100.0	16.3	56.5	26.5	-	-	.6	-
500 TO 999 MILES......	125	100.0	33.4	60.0	4.4	-	2.0	.1	-
1000 TO 1499 MILES....	27	100.0	37.0	30.6	2.6	-	29.4	.5	-
1500 MILES OR OVER....	40	100.0	11.4	2.8	4.0	-	81.8	-	-
EAST NORTH CENTRAL......	691	100.0	24.2	39.4	35.9	-	.3	-	.1
UNDER 100 MILES.......	67	100.0	-	39.9	60.1	-	-	-	-
100 TO 199 MILES......	190	100.0	.6	24.6	74.8	-	-	-	-
200 TO 299 MILES......	92	100.0	12.4	50.2	37.0	-	-	-	.4
300 TO 499 MILES......	88	100.0	20.4	51.8	27.8	-	-	-	-
500 TO 999 MILES......	203	100.0	58.9	37.5	3.3	-	-	-	.2
1000 TO 1499 MILES....	21	100.0	39.2	60.8	-	-	-	-	-
1500 MILES OR OVER....	28	100.0	30.2	62.5	-	-	7.3	-	-
SOUTH ATLANTIC..........	687	100.0	2.5	24.0	73.5	-	-	-	-
UNDER 100 MILES.......	28	100.0	-	22.1	77.9	-	-	-	-
100 TO 199 MILES......	104	100.0	-	19.1	80.9	-	-	-	-
200 TO 299 MILES......	123	100.0	.8	31.2	68.0	-	-	-	-
300 TO 499 MILES......	277	100.0	.2	18.6	81.3	-	-	-	-
500 TO 999 MILES......	136	100.0	10.1	30.8	59.2	-	-	-	-
1000 TO 1499 MILES....	13	100.0	-	31.9	68.1	-	-	-	-
1500 MILES OR OVER....	4	100.0	45.6	54.4	-	-	-	-	-
TON-MILES OF SHIPMENTS	(millions of ton-miles)								
U.S. TOTAL..........	1 042	100.0	23.3	35.3	31.0	-	10.3	-	.1
MIDDLE ATLANTIC.........	269	100.0	20.6	35.2	9.4	-	34.7	.1	-
UNDER 100 MILES.......	8	100.0	-	38.7	61.2	-	-	.1	-
100 TO 199 MILES......	10	100.0	-	79.3	20.7	-	-	-	-
200 TO 299 MILES......	13	100.0	2.2	63.4	34.5	-	-	-	-
300 TO 499 MILES......	17	100.0	16.7	56.5	26.2	-	-	.6	-
500 TO 999 MILES......	89	100.0	34.3	58.6	4.5	-	2.6	.1	-
1000 TO 1499 MILES....	32	100.0	35.4	30.1	2.3	-	31.9	.4	-
1500 MILES OR OVER....	97	100.0	10.3	2.4	4.0	-	83.3	-	-
EAST NORTH CENTRAL......	318	100.0	39.4	43.8	13.9	-	2.8	-	.1
UNDER 100 MILES.......	4	100.0	-	49.3	50.7	-	-	-	-
100 TO 199 MILES......	28	100.0	.4	24.0	75.6	-	-	-	-
200 TO 299 MILES......	21	100.0	12.6	52.6	34.4	-	-	-	.3
300 TO 499 MILES......	33	100.0	22.2	53.2	24.5	-	-	-	-
500 TO 999 MILES......	149	100.0	60.5	36.3	3.0	-	-	-	.2
1000 TO 1499 MILES....	25	100.0	36.9	63.1	-	-	-	-	-
1500 MILES OR OVER....	55	100.0	27.9	56.1	-	-	16.0	-	-
SOUTH ATLANTIC..........	272	100.0	5.3	26.6	68.1	-	-	-	-
UNDER 100 MILES.......	2	100.0	-	20.8	79.2	-	-	-	-
100 TO 199 MILES......	16	100.0	-	17.5	82.5	-	-	-	-
200 TO 299 MILES......	30	100.0	.7	31.6	67.7	-	-	-	-
300 TO 499 MILES......	111	100.0	.2	18.1	81.7	-	-	-	-
500 TO 999 MILES......	88	100.0	11.1	33.4	55.5	-	-	-	-
1000 TO 1499 MILES....	14	100.0	-	33.9	66.1	-	-	-	-
1500 MILES OR OVER....	9	100.0	46.5	53.5	-	-	-	-	-

See footnotes at end of table 4.

TABLE 2. **TCC GROUP 205**—Percent Distribution of Geographic Division of Origin and Means of Transport, by Geographic Division of Destination: 1972

Geographic division of origin[1] and means of transport	Number	Percent distribution by division of destination									
		U.S. total	New England	Middle Atlantic	East North Central	West North Central	South Atlantic	East South Central	West South Central	Mountain	Pacific
TONS OF SHIPMENTS	(thousands of tons)										
U.S. TOTAL.............	2 351	100.0	4.3	16.0	23.1	6.5	22.1	8.2	6.4	1.9	11.6
RAIL.................	319	100.0	7.9	9.1	15.2	9.9	9.5	4.0	28.2	1.6	14.6
MOTOR CARRIER.........	807	100.0	7.0	16.3	24.2	6.3	21.2	7.5	3.7	4.6	9.3
PRIVATE TRUCK.........	1 173	100.0	1.6	18.3	25.4	5.9	26.6	10.2	1.8	.3	9.9
AIR..................	-	100.0	.5	55.9	32.7	-	.2	-	.1	.1	10.5
WATER...............	47	100.0	-	-	-	-	10.3	-	15.0	-	74.6
OTHER...............	1	100.0	-	42.6	18.4	5.2	10.4	23.4	-	-	-
UNKNOWN.............	2	100.0	-	3.6	15.0	31.4	19.9	-	30.1	-	-

See footnotes at end of table 4.

TABLE 2. **TCC GROUP 205—Percent Distribution of Geographic Division of Origin and Means of Transport, by Geographic Division of Destination: 1972**—Continued

Geographic division of origin[1] and means of transport	Number	Percent distribution by division of destination									
		U.S. total	New England	Middle Atlantic	East North Central	West North Central	South Atlantic	East South Central	West South Central	Mountain	Pacific
TONS OF SHIPMENTS	(thousands of tons)										
MIDDLE ATLANTIC	560	100.0	10.3	42.4	18.1	2.1	17.0	1.0	2.6	.2	6.5
RAIL	65	100.0	-	1.6	50.3	14.6	22.3	-	6.2	-	5.0
MOTOR CARRIER	256	100.0	15.8	33.8	22.6	.8	23.2	2.0	1.4	.2	.2
PRIVATE TRUCK	194	100.0	8.8	76.8	5.4	-	8.2	-	-	.3	.6
AIR	-	100.0	1.1	92.8	.7	.3	1.2	-	-	.3	3.7
WATER	43	100.0	-	-	-	-	11.3	-	16.4	-	72.3
OTHER	1	100.0	-	50.6	3.1	6.1	12.3	27.8	-	-	-
UNKNOWN	-	100.0	-	100.0	-	-	-	-	-	-	-
EAST NORTH CENTRAL	691	100.0	4.1	5.7	46.8	9.7	6.6	8.9	10.7	3.3	4.1
RAIL	167	100.0	14.0	13.5	6.4	9.9	7.7	7.6	34.1	1.7	5.1
MOTOR CARRIER	272	100.0	1.8	6.2	41.3	9.9	10.1	11.3	5.3	7.5	6.5
PRIVATE TRUCK	248	100.0	-	-	80.4	9.4	2.0	7.2	1.1	-	-
AIR	-	100.0	-	-	-	-	-	-	-	-	-
WATER	2	100.0	-	-	-	-	-	-	-	-	100.0
OTHER	-	100.0	-	-	100.0	-	-	-	-	-	-
UNKNOWN	-	100.0	-	-	43.1	-	56.9	-	-	-	-
SOUTH ATLANTIC	687	100.0	1.6	12.3	10.0	3.6	51.3	16.0	4.3	.3	.7
RAIL	17	100.0	2.4	16.3	20.1	-	8.6	-	40.0	-	12.6
MOTOR CARRIER	164	100.0	5.7	15.2	7.1	4.3	46.2	14.5	4.8	.6	1.5
PRIVATE TRUCK	505	100.0	.2	11.2	10.5	3.4	54.5	17.1	2.9	.2	-
AIR	-	100.0	-	9.9	90.1	-	-	-	-	-	-
WATER	-	100.0	-	-	-	-	-	-	-	-	-
OTHER	-	100.0	-	-	-	-	-	-	-	-	-
UNKNOWN	-	100.0	-	-	-	-	-	-	-	-	-
TON-MILES OF SHIPMENTS	(millions of ton-miles)										
U.S. TOTAL	1 042	100.0	4.2	9.5	17.1	6.7	18.6	6.6	11.5	3.9	21.9
RAIL	243	100.0	8.4	7.6	10.3	7.9	9.3	2.4	28.7	2.2	23.1
MOTOR CARRIER	367	100.0	5.5	9.5	21.3	6.6	19.8	6.3	7.0	8.7	15.3
PRIVATE TRUCK	322	100.0	1.0	14.3	23.0	8.2	28.9	12.2	4.3	1.0	7.1
AIR	-	100.0	.5	60.1	17.7	-	.2	-	-	.1	21.3
WATER	107	100.0	-	-	-	-	4.4	-	9.4	-	86.3
OTHER	-	100.0	-	2.3	22.8	12.1	35.5	27.3	-	-	-
UNKNOWN	-	100.0	-	.4	11.1	23.1	35.7	-	29.7	-	-
MIDDLE ATLANTIC	269	100.0	4.1	7.6	23.8	4.3	16.9	1.3	7.5	.9	33.6
RAIL	55	100.0	-	.5	36.4	17.1	21.4	-	10.0	-	14.6
MOTOR CARRIER	94	100.0	9.5	10.1	41.9	2.2	25.9	3.5	4.8	1.2	1.0
PRIVATE TRUCK	25	100.0	8.1	41.5	17.3	.2	17.4	-	-	4.7	10.7
AIR	-	100.0	1.3	73.6	.7	.5	2.6	-	-	1.4	20.0
WATER	93	100.0	-	-	-	-	5.0	-	10.8	-	84.2
OTHER	-	100.0	-	2.9	.6	15.5	45.7	35.2	-	-	-
UNKNOWN	-	100.0	-	100.0	-	-	-	-	-	-	-
EAST NORTH CENTRAL	318	100.0	7.4	7.6	16.1	8.5	8.5	7.0	19.7	8.0	17.3
RAIL	125	100.0	15.3	11.6	2.0	6.1	7.7	4.7	38.0	2.5	12.3
MOTOR CARRIER	139	100.0	3.1	6.8	14.2	7.9	11.3	9.4	9.2	16.0	22.1
PRIVATE TRUCK	44	100.0	-	-	65.2	18.7	3.3	7.7	5.1	-	-
AIR	-	100.0	-	-	-	-	-	-	-	-	-
WATER	8	100.0	-	-	-	-	-	-	-	-	100.0
OTHER	-	100.0	-	-	100.0	-	-	-	-	-	-
UNKNOWN	-	100.0	-	-	23.8	-	76.2	-	-	-	-
SOUTH ATLANTIC	272	100.0	3.1	16.0	11.9	5.6	37.6	14.0	7.6	.9	3.3
RAIL	14	100.0	2.4	14.6	14.0	-	2.8	-	36.4	-	29.7
MOTOR CARRIER	72	100.0	9.5	15.8	8.1	7.1	33.3	9.2	8.8	1.8	6.4
PRIVATE TRUCK	185	100.0	.7	16.2	13.2	5.4	42.0	17.0	4.9	.6	-
AIR	-	100.0	-	14.6	85.4	-	-	-	-	-	-
WATER	-	100.0	-	-	-	-	-	-	-	-	-
OTHER	-	100.0	-	-	-	-	-	-	-	-	-
UNKNOWN	-	100.0	-	-	-	-	-	-	-	-	-

See footnotes at end of table 4.

TABLE 3. **TCC GROUP 205**—Percent Distribution of Geographic Division of Destination and Means of Transport, by Geographic Division of Origin: 1972

Geographic division of destination and means of transport	Number	Percent distribution by division of origin[1]									
		U.S. total	New England	Middle Atlantic	East North Central	West North Central	South Atlantic	East South Central	West South Central	Mountain	Pacific
TONS OF SHIPMENTS	(thousands of tons)										
U.S. TOTAL..............	2 351	100.0	(D)	23.8	29.4	(D)	29.3	(D)	(D)	-	(D)
RAIL....................	319	100.0	(D)	20.5	52.6	(D)	5.4	(D)	(D)	-	(D)
MOTOR CARRIER..........	807	100.0	(D)	31.7	33.8	(D)	20.4	(D)	(D)	-	(D)
PRIVATE TRUCK..........	1 173	100.0	(D)	16.6	21.2	(D)	43.1	(D)	(D)	-	(D)
AIR....................	-	100.0	(D)	17.5	-	(D)	35.7	(D)	(D)	-	(D)
WATER..................	47	100.0	(D)	91.5	4.4	(D)	-	(D)	(D)	-	(D)
OTHER..................	1	100.0	(D)	84.2	5.1	(D)	-	(D)	(D)	-	(D)
UNKNOWN................	2	100.0	(D)	3.6	34.9	(D)	-	(D)	(D)	-	(D)
NEW ENGLAND............	100	100.0	(D)	57.4	28.5	(D)	10.8	(D)	(D)	-	(D)
RAIL....................	25	100.0	(D)	-	93.1	(D)	1.7	(D)	(D)	-	(D)
MOTOR CARRIER..........	56	100.0	(D)	71.3	8.9	(D)	16.5	(D)	(D)	-	(D)
PRIVATE TRUCK..........	18	100.0	(D)	93.9	-	(D)	5.9	(D)	(D)	-	(D)
AIR....................	-	100.0	(D)	42.3	-	(D)	-	(D)	(D)	-	(D)
WATER..................	-	100.0	(D)	-	-	(D)	-	(D)	(D)	-	(D)
OTHER..................	-	100.0	(D)	-	-	(D)	-	(D)	(D)	-	(D)
UNKNOWN................	-	100.0	(D)	-	-	(D)	-	(D)	(D)	.-	(D)
MIDDLE ATLANTIC........	375	100.0	(D)	63.2	10.6	(D)	22.5	(D)	(D)	-	(D)
RAIL....................	29	100.0	(D)	3.5	78.1	(D)	9.7	(D)	(D)	-	(D)
MOTOR CARRIER..........	131	100.0	(D)	65.7	12.9	(D)	19.1	(D)	(D)	-	(D)
PRIVATE TRUCK..........	214	100.0	(D)	69.6	-	(D)	26.5	(D)	(D)	-	(D)
AIR....................	-	100.0	(D)	29.0	-	(D)	6.3	(D)	(D)	-	(D)
WATER..................	-	100.0	(D)	-	-	(D)	-	(D)	(D)	-	(D)
OTHER..................	-	100.0	(D)	100.0	-	(D)	-	(D)	(D)	-	(D)
UNKNOWN................	-	100.0	(D)	100.0	-	(D)	-	(D)	(D)	-	(D)
EAST NORTH CENTRAL......	542	100.0	(D)	18.7	59.7	(D)	12.6	(D)	(D)	-	(D)
RAIL....................	48	100.0	(D)	68.0	22.1	(D)	7.2	(D)	(D)	-	(D)
MOTOR CARRIER..........	195	100.0	(D)	29.6	57.8	(D)	6.0	(D)	(D)	-	(D)
PRIVATE TRUCK..........	298	100.0	(D)	3.5	67.0	(D)	17.9	(D)	(D)	-	(D)
AIR....................	-	100.0	(D)	.3	-	(D)	98.4	(D)	(D)	-	(D)
WATER..................	-	100.0	(D)	-	-	(D)	-	(D)	(D)	-	(D)
OTHER..................	-	100.0	(D)	14.2	27.5	(D)	-	(D)	(D)	-	(D)
UNKNOWN................	-	100.0	(D)	-	100.0	(D)	-	(D)	(D)	-	(D)
WEST NORTH CENTRAL......	152	100.0	(D)	7.6	43.8	(D)	16.0	(D)	(D)	-	(D)
RAIL....................	31	100.0	(D)	30.3	52.4	(D)	-	(D)	(D)	-	(D)
MOTOR CARRIER..........	50	100.0	(D)	3.9	53.6	(D)	14.2	(D)	(D)	-	(D)
PRIVATE TRUCK..........	69	100.0	(D)	.1	33.3	(D)	24.8	(D)	(D)	-	(D)
AIR....................	-	100.0	(D)	100.0	-	(D)	-	(D)	(D)	-	(D)
WATER..................	-	100.0	(D)	-	-	(D)	-	(D)	(D)	-	(D)
OTHER..................	-	100.0	(D)	100.0	-	(D)	-	(D)	(D)	-	(D)
UNKNOWN................	-	100.0	(D)	-	-	(D)	-	(D)	(D)	-	(D)
SOUTH ATLANTIC..........	518	100.0	(D)	18.3	8.8	(D)	68.1	(D)	(D)	-	(D)
RAIL....................	30	100.0	(D)	48.2	42.7	(D)	4.9	(D)	(D)	-	(D)
MOTOR CARRIER..........	170	100.0	(D)	34.8	16.1	(D)	44.6	(D)	(D)	-	(D)
PRIVATE TRUCK..........	311	100.0	(D)	5.1	1.6	(D)	88.3	(D)	(D)	-	(D)
AIR....................	-	100.0	(D)	100.0	-	(D)	-	(D)	(D)	-	(D)
WATER..................	4	100.0	(D)	100.0	-	(D)	-	(D)	(D)	-	(D)
OTHER..................	-	100.0	(D)	100.0	-	(D)	-	(D)	(D)	-	(D)
UNKNOWN................	-	100.0	(D)	-	100.0	(D)	-	(D)	(D)	-	(D)
EAST SOUTH CENTRAL......	192	100.0	(D)	2.8	31.8	(D)	57.1	(D)	(D)	-	(D)
RAIL....................	12	100.0	(D)	-	100.0	(D)	-	(D)	(D)	-	(D)
MOTOR CARRIER..........	60	100.0	(D)	8.5	51.3	(D)	39.7	(D)	(D)	-	(D)
PRIVATE TRUCK..........	119	100.0	(D)	-	14.9	(D)	72.2	(D)	(D)	-	(D)
AIR....................	-	100.0	(D)	-	-	(D)	-	(D)	(D)	-	(D)
WATER..................	-	100.0	(D)	-	-	(D)	-	(D)	(D)	-	(D)
OTHER..................	-	100.0	(D)	100.0	-	(D)	-	(D)	(D)	-	(D)
UNKNOWN................	-	100.0	(D)	-	-	(D)	-	(D)	(D)	-	(D)
WEST SOUTH CENTRAL......	149	100.0	(D)	9.9	49.7	(D)	19.7	(D)	(D)	-	(D)
RAIL....................	89	100.0	(D)	4.6	63.7	(D)	7.7	(D)	(D)	-	(D)
MOTOR CARRIER..........	30	100.0	(D)	12.0	47.8	(D)	26.3	(D)	(D)	-	(D)
PRIVATE TRUCK..........	21	100.0	(D)	-	12.1	(D)	67.3	(D)	(D)	-	(D)
AIR....................	-	100.0	(D)	-	-	(D)	-	(D)	(D)	-	(D)
WATER..................	7	100.0	(D)	100.0	-	(D)	-	(D)	(D)	-	(D)
OTHER..................	-	100.0	(D)	-	-	(D)	-	(D)	(D)	-	(D)
UNKNOWN................	-	100.0	(D)	-	-	(D)	-	(D)	(D)	-	(D)
MOUNTAIN...............	45	100.0	(D)	2.5	51.2	(D)	4.2	(D)	(D)	-	(D)
RAIL....................	4	100.0	(D)	-	55.8	(D)	-	(D)	(D)	-	(D)
MOTOR CARRIER..........	36	100.0	(D)	1.6	55.3	(D)	2.9	(D)	(D)	-	(D)
PRIVATE TRUCK..........	3	100.0	(D)	15.3	-	(D)	24.9	(D)	(D)	-	(D)
AIR....................	-	100.0	(D)	100.0	-	(D)	-	(D)	(D)	-	(D)
WATER..................	-	100.0	(D)	-	-	(D)	-	(D)	(D)	-	(D)
OTHER..................	-	100.0	(D)	-	-	(D)	-	(D)	(D)	-	(D)
UNKNOWN................	-	100.0	(D)	-	-	(D)	-	(D)	(D)	-	(D)
PACIFIC................	273	100.0	(D)	13.2	10.3	(D)	1.7	(D)	(D)	-	(D)
RAIL....................	46	100.0	(D)	7.0	18.3	(D)	4.7	(D)	(D)	-	(D)
MOTOR CARRIER..........	75	100.0	(D)	.5	23.5	(D)	3.2	(D)	(D)	-	(D)
PRIVATE TRUCK..........	116	100.0	(D)	.9	-	(D)	-	(D)	(D)	-	(D)
AIR....................	-	100.0	(D)	6.1	-	(D)	-	(D)	(D)	-	(D)
WATER..................	35	100.0	(D)	88.6	5.8	(D)	-	(D)	(D)	-	(D)
OTHER..................	-	100.0	(D)	-	-	(D)	-	(D)	(D)	-	(D)
UNKNOWN................	-	100.0	(D)	-	-	(D)	-	(D)	(D)	-	(D)

See footnotes at end of table 4.

TABLE 3. **TCC GROUP 205** —Percent Distribution of Geographic Division of Destination and Means of Transport, by Geographic Division of Origin: 1972—Continued

Geographic division of destination and means of transport	Number	Percent distribution by division of origin[1]									
		U.S. total	New England	Middle Atlantic	East North Central	West North Central	South Atlantic	East South Central	West South Central	Mountain	Pacific
TON-MILES OF SHIPMENTS	(millions of ton-miles)										
U.S. TOTAL..............	1 042	100.0	(D)	25.9	30.5	(D)	26.2	(D)	(D)	-	(D)
RAIL................	243	100.0	(D)	22.8	51.6	(D)	6.0	(D)	(D)	-	(D)
MOTOR CARRIER.......	367	100.0	(D)	25.8	37.9	(D)	19.7	(D)	(D)	-	(D)
PRIVATE TRUCK.......	322	100.0	(D)	7.9	13.7	(D)	57.6	(D)	(D)	-	(D)
AIR.................	-	100.0	(D)	7.1	-	(D)	20.2	(D)	(D)	-	(D)
WATER...............	107	100.0	(D)	86.9	8.2	(D)	-	(D)	(D)	-	(D)
OTHER...............	-	100.0	(D)	77.6	2.6	(D)	-	(D)	(D)	-	(D)
UNKNOWN.............	-	100.0	(D)	.4	46.8	(D)	-	(D)	(D)	-	(D)
NEW ENGLAND............	44	100.0	(D)	25.2	53.2	(D)	19.2	(D)	(D)	-	(D)
RAIL................	20	100.0	(D)	-	93.7	(D)	1.7	(D)	(D)	-	(D)
MOTOR CARRIER.......	20	100.0	(D)	44.5	21.1	(D)	34.0	(D)	(D)	-	(D)
PRIVATE TRUCK.......	3	100.0	(D)	62.4	-	(D)	37.6	(D)	(D)	-	(D)
AIR.................	-	100.0	(D)	18.7	-	(D)	-	(D)	(D)	-	(D)
WATER...............	-	100.0	(D)	-	-	(D)	-	(D)	(D)	-	(D)
OTHER...............	-	100.0	(D)	-	-	(D)	-	(D)	(D)	-	(D)
UNKNOWN.............	-	100.0	(D)	-	-	(D)	-	(D)	(D)	-	(D)
MIDDLE ATLANTIC........	99	100.0	(D)	20.5	24.2	(D)	43.9	(D)	(D)	-	(D)
RAIL................	18	100.0	(D)	1.6	78.3	(D)	11.4	(D)	(D)	-	(D)
MOTOR CARRIER.......	34	100.0	(D)	27.4	27.3	(D)	32.9	(D)	(D)	-	(D)
PRIVATE TRUCK.......	45	100.0	(D)	22.9	-	(D)	65.3	(D)	(D)	-	(D)
AIR.................	-	100.0	(D)	8.7	-	(D)	4.9	(D)	(D)	-	(D)
WATER...............	-	100.0	(D)	-	-	(D)	-	(D)	(D)	-	(D)
OTHER...............	-	100.0	(D)	100.0	-	(D)	-	(D)	(D)	-	(D)
UNKNOWN.............	-	100.0	(D)	98.3	-	(D)	-	(D)	(D)	-	(D)
EAST NORTH CENTRAL......	177	100.0	(D)	36.1	28.8	(D)	18.2	(D)	(D)	-	(D)
RAIL................	25	100.0	(D)	80.4	9.8	(D)	8.1	(D)	(D)	-	(D)
MOTOR CARRIER.......	78	100.0	(D)	50.6	25.3	(D)	7.5	(D)	(D)	-	(D)
PRIVATE TRUCK.......	74	100.0	(D)	5.9	38.9	(D)	33.1	(D)	(D)	-	(D)
AIR.................	-	100.0	(D)	.3	-	(D)	97.3	(D)	(D)	-	(D)
WATER...............	-	100.0	(D)	-	-	(D)	-	(D)	(D)	-	(D)
OTHER...............	-	100.0	(D)	2.0	11.3	(D)	-	(D)	(D)	-	(D)
UNKNOWN.............	-	100.0	(D)	-	100.0	(D)	-	(D)	(D)	-	(D)
WEST NORTH CENTRAL......	70	100.0	(D)	16.7	38.4	(D)	21.8	(D)	(D)	-	(D)
RAIL................	19	100.0	(D)	49.7	40.2	(D)	-	(D)	(D)	-	(D)
MOTOR CARRIER.......	24	100.0	(D)	8.7	45.0	(D)	21.0	(D)	(D)	-	(D)
PRIVATE TRUCK.......	26	100.0	(D)	.2	31.4	(D)	38.3	(D)	(D)	-	(D)
AIR.................	-	100.0	(D)	100.0	-	(D)	-	(D)	(D)	-	(D)
WATER...............	-	100.0	(D)	-	-	(D)	-	(D)	(D)	-	(D)
OTHER...............	-	100.0	(D)	100.0	-	(D)	-	(D)	(D)	-	(D)
UNKNOWN.............	-	100.0	(D)	-	-	(D)	-	(D)	(D)	-	(D)
SOUTH ATLANTIC.........	193	100.0	(D)	23.6	14.0	(D)	53.0	(D)	(D)	-	(D)
RAIL................	22	100.0	(D)	52.7	42.7	(D)	1.8	(D)	(D)	-	(D)
MOTOR CARRIER.......	72	100.0	(D)	33.8	21.6	(D)	33.2	(D)	(D)	-	(D)
PRIVATE TRUCK.......	93	100.0	(D)	4.7	1.6	(D)	83.6	(D)	(D)	-	(D)
AIR.................	-	100.0	(D)	100.0	-	(D)	-	(D)	(D)	-	(D)
WATER...............	4	100.0	(D)	100.0	-	(D)	-	(D)	(D)	-	(D)
OTHER...............	-	100.0	(D)	100.0	-	(D)	-	(D)	(D)	-	(D)
UNKNOWN.............	-	100.0	(D)	-	100.0	(D)	-	(D)	(D)	-	(D)
EAST SOUTH CENTRAL......	68	100.0	(D)	4.9	32.6	(D)	55.7	(D)	(D)	-	(D)
RAIL................	5	100.0	(D)	-	100.0	(D)	-	(D)	(D)	-	(D)
MOTOR CARRIER.......	23	100.0	(D)	14.2	56.7	(D)	28.8	(D)	(D)	-	(D)
PRIVATE TRUCK.......	39	100.0	(D)	-	8.6	(D)	79.8	(D)	(D)	-	(D)
AIR.................	-	100.0	(D)	-	-	(D)	-	(D)	(D)	-	(D)
WATER...............	-	100.0	(D)	-	-	(D)	-	(D)	(D)	-	(D)
OTHER...............	-	100.0	(D)	100.0	-	(D)	-	(D)	(D)	-	(D)
UNKNOWN.............	-	100.0	(D)	-	-	(D)	-	(D)	(D)	-	(D)
WEST SOUTH CENTRAL......	119	100.0	(D)	16.8	52.3	(D)	17.3	(D)	(D)	-	(D)
RAIL................	69	100.0	(D)	8.0	68.1	(D)	7.6	(D)	(D)	-	(D)
MOTOR CARRIER.......	25	100.0	(D)	17.4	49.6	(D)	24.7	(D)	(D)	-	(D)
PRIVATE TRUCK.......	13	100.0	(D)	-	16.2	(D)	65.7	(D)	(D)	-	(D)
AIR.................	-	100.0	(D)	-	-	(D)	-	(D)	(D)	-	(D)
WATER...............	10	100.0	(D)	100.0	-	(D)	-	(D)	(D)	-	(D)
OTHER...............	-	100.0	(D)	-	-	(D)	-	(D)	(D)	-	(D)
UNKNOWN.............	-	100.0	(D)	-	-	(D)	-	(D)	(D)	-	(D)
MOUNTAIN...............	40	100.0	(D)	5.8	62.8	(D)	5.9	(D)	(D)	-	(D)
RAIL................	5	100.0	(D)	-	57.9	(D)	-	(D)	(D)	-	(D)
MOTOR CARRIER.......	31	100.0	(D)	3.6	70.0	(D)	4.1	(D)	(D)	-	(D)
PRIVATE TRUCK.......	3	100.0	(D)	37.3	-	(D)	33.8	(D)	(D)	-	(D)
AIR.................	-	100.0	(D)	100.0	-	(D)	-	(D)	(D)	-	(D)
WATER...............	-	100.0	(D)	-	-	(D)	-	(D)	(D)	-	(D)
OTHER...............	-	100.0	(D)	-	-	(D)	-	(D)	(D)	-	(D)
UNKNOWN.............	-	100.0	(D)	-	-	(D)	-	(D)	(D)	-	(D)
PACIFIC................	227	100.0	(D)	39.7	24.1	(D)	3.9	(D)	(D)	-	(D)
RAIL................	56	100.0	(D)	14.4	27.4	(D)	7.7	(D)	(D)	-	(D)
MOTOR CARRIER.......	56	100.0	(D)	1.7	55.0	(D)	8.3	(D)	(D)	-	(D)
PRIVATE TRUCK.......	22	100.0	(D)	11.9	-	(D)	-	(D)	(D)	-	(D)
AIR.................	-	100.0	(D)	6.7	-	(D)	-	(D)	(D)	-	(D)
WATER...............	92	100.0	(D)	84.8	9.5	(D)	-	(D)	(D)	-	(D)
OTHER...............	-	100.0	(D)	-	-	(D)	-	(D)	(D)	-	(D)
UNKNOWN.............	-	100.0	(D)	-	-	(D)	-	(D)	(D)	-	(D)

See footnotes at end of table 4.

TABLE 4. **TCC GROUP 205**—Percent Distribution of Distance Shipped and Weight of Shipment, by Means of Transport: 1972

Distance shipped and weight of shipment [2] [3]	Number	Percent distribution by means of transport							
		All means of transport	Rail	Motor carrier	Private truck	Air	Water	Other	Unknown
TONS OF SHIPMENTS	(thousands of tons)								
U.S. TOTAL..........	2 130	100.0	14.1	32.2	51.3	-	2.2	.1	.1
UNDER 100 MILES........	364	100.0	-	25.2	74.6	-	-	.2	-
UNDER 1000 POUNDS.....	45	100.0	-	2.8	96.0	-	-	1.2	-
1000 TO 9999 POUNDS...	117	100.0	-	6.5	93.4	-	-	-	.1
10000 TO 29999 POUNDS.	188	100.0	-	40.2	59.8	-	-	-	-
30000 TO 59999 POUNDS.	8	100.0	-	33.1	66.9	-	-	-	-
60000 TO 89999 POUNDS.	-	100.0	-	-	-	-	-	-	-
90000 POUNDS AND OVER.	4	100.0	-	100.0	-	-	-	-	-
100 TO 199 MILES........	365	100.0	.4	33.5	66.0	-	-	-	.1
UNDER 1000 POUNDS.....	14	100.0	-	17.8	81.7	-	-	.5	-
1000 TO 9999 POUNDS...	98	100.0	-	10.0	89.8	-	-	-	.1
10000 TO 29999 POUNDS.	230	100.0	.6	38.1	61.1	-	-	-	.2
30000 TO 59999 POUNDS.	21	100.0	-	100.0	-	-	-	-	-
60000 TO 89999 POUNDS.	-	100.0	-	-	-	-	-	-	-
90000 POUNDS AND OVER.	-	100.0	-	-	-	-	-	-	-
200 TO 299 MILES........	265	100.0	7.9	40.9	50.8	-	-	-	.4
UNDER 1000 POUNDS.....	5	100.0	-	26.1	73.9	-	-	-	-
1000 TO 9999 POUNDS...	46	100.0	.4	20.0	79.3	-	-	-	.3
10000 TO 29999 POUNDS.	190	100.0	8.4	42.0	49.1	-	-	-	.5
30000 TO 59999 POUNDS.	23	100.0	20.1	77.1	2.8	-	-	-	-
60000 TO 89999 POUNDS.	-	100.0	-	-	-	-	-	-	-
90000 POUNDS AND OVER.	-	100.0	-	-	-	-	-	-	-
300 TO 499 MILES........	476	100.0	9.5	23.5	66.8	-	-	.1	.1
UNDER 1000 POUNDS.....	7	100.0	-	55.4	44.5	-	-	-	-
1000 TO 9999 POUNDS...	70	100.0	-	15.7	83.9	-	-	.4	-
10000 TO 29999 POUNDS.	339	100.0	9.3	20.4	70.3	-	-	-	.1
30000 TO 59999 POUNDS.	54	100.0	19.5	49.8	30.7	-	-	-	-
60000 TO 89999 POUNDS.	3	100.0	100.0	-	-	-	-	-	-
90000 POUNDS AND OVER.	-	100.0	-	-	-	-	-	-	-
500 TO 999 MILES........	516	100.0	37.4	38.3	23.6	-	.5	-	.1
UNDER 1000 POUNDS.....	8	100.0	.2	66.5	33.1	-	-	.2	-
1000 TO 9999 POUNDS...	28	100.0	4.5	34.3	60.5	-	-	.7	-
10000 TO 29999 POUNDS.	295	100.0	41.7	30.7	26.6	-	.9	-	.2
30000 TO 59999 POUNDS.	126	100.0	42.2	39.2	18.6	-	-	-	-
60000 TO 89999 POUNDS.	1	100.0	100.0	-	-	-	-	-	-
90000 POUNDS AND OVER.	57	100.0	25.3	74.7	-	-	-	-	-
1000 TO 1499 MILES......	59	100.0	33.4	46.7	5.9	-	13.7	.2	-
UNDER 1000 POUNDS.....	1	100.0	-	96.4	3.6	-	-	-	-
1000 TO 9999 POUNDS...	3	100.0	15.2	61.3	19.7	-	-	3.8	-
10000 TO 29999 POUNDS.	39	100.0	46.0	31.0	2.3	-	20.7	-	-
30000 TO 59999 POUNDS.	15	100.0	8.4	79.2	12.5	-	-	-	-
60000 TO 89999 POUNDS.	-	100.0	-	-	-	-	-	-	-
90000 POUNDS AND OVER.	-	100.0	-	-	-	-	-	-	-
1500 MILES OR OVER......	82	100.0	22.7	30.6	2.3	-	44.4	-	-
UNDER 1000 POUNDS.....	1	100.0	-	43.5	54.6	.1	1.8	-	-
1000 TO 9999 POUNDS...	5	100.0	20.4	54.5	22.1	-	3.0	-	-
10000 TO 29999 POUNDS.	25	100.0	43.5	25.8	-	-	30.8	-	-
30000 TO 59999 POUNDS.	23	100.0	9.2	62.9	-	-	27.9	-	-
60000 TO 89999 POUNDS.	4	100.0	100.0	-	-	-	-	-	-
90000 POUNDS AND OVER.	21	100.0	-	-	-	-	100.0	-	-
TON-MILES OF SHIPMENTS	(millions of ton-miles)								
U.S. TOTAL..........	943	100.0	24.1	33.2	31.2	-	11.4	-	.1
UNDER 100 MILES........	17	100.0	-	31.2	68.7	-	-	.1	-
UNDER 1000 POUNDS.....	1	100.0	-	4.0	95.5	-	-	.5	-
1000 TO 9999 POUNDS...	5	100.0	-	8.2	91.7	-	-	-	-
10000 TO 29999 POUNDS.	9	100.0	-	48.0	52.0	-	-	-	-
30000 TO 59999 POUNDS.	-	100.0	-	28.4	71.6	-	-	-	-
60000 TO 89999 POUNDS.	-	100.0	-	-	-	-	-	-	-
90000 POUNDS AND OVER.	-	100.0	-	100.0	-	-	-	-	-
100 TO 199 MILES........	55	100.0	.4	32.0	67.4	-	-	-	.1
UNDER 1000 POUNDS.....	2	100.0	-	18.2	81.2	-	-	.5	-
1000 TO 9999 POUNDS...	14	100.0	-	10.0	90.0	-	-	-	.1
10000 TO 29999 POUNDS.	35	100.0	.7	36.2	63.0	-	-	-	.1
30000 TO 59999 POUNDS.	3	100.0	-	100.0	-	-	-	-	-
60000 TO 89999 POUNDS.	-	100.0	-	-	-	-	-	-	-
90000 POUNDS AND OVER.	-	100.0	-	-	-	-	-	-	-

See footnotes at end of table 4.

TABLE 4. **TCC GROUP 205—Percent Distribution of Distance Shipped and Weight of Shipment, by Means of Transport: 1972**—Continued

Distance shipped and weight of shipment [2] [3]	Number	Percent distribution by means of transport							
		All means of transport	Rail	Motor carrier	Private truck	Air	Water	Other	Unknown
TON-MILES OF SHIPMENTS	(millions of ton-miles)								
200 TO 299 MILES.........	63	100.0	8.1	41.5	50.0	-	-	-	.4
UNDER 1000 POUNDS......	1	100.0	-	26.8	73.2	-	-	-	-
1000 TO 9999 POUNDS...	10	100.0	.4	20.2	79.1	-	-	-	.3
10000 TO 29999 POUNDS.	46	100.0	8.5	42.5	48.5	-	-	-	.5
30000 TO 59999 POUNDS.	5	100.0	20.5	76.8	2.7	-	-	-	-
60000 TO 89999 POUNDS.	-	100.0	-	-	-	-	-	-	-
90000 POUNDS AND OVER.	-	100.0	-	-	-	-	-	-	-
300 TO 499 MILES.........	187	100.0	10.3	22.9	66.7	-	-	.1	-
UNDER 1000 POUNDS......	3	100.0	-	54.8	45.2	-	-	-	-
1000 TO 9999 POUNDS...	26	100.0	-	16.5	83.1	-	-	.4	-
10000 TO 29999 POUNDS.	133	100.0	9.6	19.5	70.8	-	-	-	.1
30000 TO 59999 POUNDS.	22	100.0	22.4	47.7	29.9	-	-	-	-
60000 TO 89999 POUNDS.	1	100.0	100.0	-	-	-	-	-	-
90000 POUNDS AND OVER.	-	100.0	-	-	-	-	-	-	-
500 TO 999 MILES.........	363	100.0	39.5	38.3	21.5	-	.6	-	.1
UNDER 1000 POUNDS......	5	100.0	.1	68.3	31.3	-	-	.3	-
1000 TO 9999 POUNDS...	19	100.0	5.5	33.3	60.6	-	-	.6	-
10000 TO 29999 POUNDS.	202	100.0	45.0	30.1	23.7	-	1.1	-	.1
30000 TO 59999 POUNDS.	91	100.0	41.3	40.3	18.5	-	-	-	-
60000 TO 89999 POUNDS.	-	100.0	100.0	-	-	-	-	-	-
90000 POUNDS AND OVER.	44	100.0	28.6	71.4	-	-	-	-	-
1000 TO 1499 MILES......	71	100.0	31.3	48.6	5.4	-	14.5	.2	-
UNDER 1000 POUNDS......	1	100.0	-	96.6	3.4	-	-	-	-
1000 TO 9999 POUNDS...	3	100.0	16.2	63.3	17.0	-	-	3.4	-
10000 TO 29999 POUNDS.	46	100.0	44.0	31.6	2.0	-	22.4	-	-
30000 TO 59999 POUNDS.	19	100.0	7.0	81.8	11.2	-	-	-	-
60000 TO 89999 POUNDS.	-	100.0	-	-	-	-	-	-	-
90000 POUNDS AND OVER.	-	100.0	-	-	-	-	-	-	-
1500 MILES OR OVER......	182	100.0	19.9	25.3	2.8	-	51.9	-	-
UNDER 1000 POUNDS......	2	100.0	-	39.7	57.7	-	2.6	-	-
1000 TO 9999 POUNDS...	13	100.0	21.0	48.3	26.9	-	3.9	-	-
10000 TO 29999 POUNDS.	53	100.0	39.7	22.3	-	-	38.0	-	-
30000 TO 59999 POUNDS.	50	100.0	8.5	52.4	-	-	39.1	-	-
60000 TO 89999 POUNDS.	7	100.0	100.0	-	-	-	-	-	-
90000 POUNDS AND OVER.	54	100.0	-	-	-	-	100.0	-	-

Note: Detail may not add to total due to rounding. The introductory table shows the estimates of sampling variability for tons; sampling variability for ton-miles has not been estimated. See the map in the Introduction for the States comprising the geographic divisions of the United States.

Shipments excluded from the survey are those moving by pipeling (primarily petroleum products from refineries), parcel post shipments, and commodities moved by own power (motorized vehicles, aircraft, etc.) or towed (prefabricated buildings, etc.). Local shipments (commodities shipped less than 25 miles from the plant) and shipments within the same city are also excluded. Shipments to Alaska and Hawaii from the 48 conterminous States and the District of Columbia are included; however, no data were obtained for shipments originating in Alaska and Hawaii.

- Represents zero or rounds to zero.   (D) Withheld to avoid disclosing figures for individual companies.

[1] Production of this commodity is concentrated in the geographic divisions shown; figures and distributions for geographic divisions not shown are included in the total.

[2] Distances of shipments to foreign destinations are calculated only to the U.S. port of exit.

[3] Includes only shipments represented by bills of lading and invoices. Summary records which did not show individual weights of shipments are not included.

TCC 206. Sugar, Beet and Cane

Comparisons of Tons and Ton-Miles of Shipments for
Geographic Divisions of Origin and for Sampling Variability: 1972 and 1967

Geographic division of origin	Estimates				Relative sampling variability in tons (percent)	
	1972		1967		1972	1967
	Tons (thousands)	Ton-miles (millions)	Tons (thousands)	Ton-miles (millions)		
U.S. total	11,787	5,289	12,168	4,905	10.8	20.6
New England	(D)	(D)	499	85	(*)	(*)
Middle Atlantic	2,462	374	1,123	272	3.3	(*)
East North Central	(D)	(D)	1,901	473	(*)	(*)
West North Central	(D)	(D)	1,379	675	(*)	(*)
South Atlantic	1,288	425	1,181	407	34.0	(*)
East South Central	(D)	(D)	—	—	(*)	(*)
West South Central	1,618	889	3,105	1,428	11.6	(*)
Mountain	2,013	1,330	978	620	49.2	(*)
Pacific	2,893	1,975	2,002	945	24.6	(*)

— Represents zero or rounds to zero.   (D) Withheld to avoid disclosing figures for individual companies.
(*) Data not published.

TABLE 1. TCC GROUP 206—Percent Distribution of Geographic Division of Origin and Distance Shipped, by Means of Transport: 1972

Geographic division of origin[1] and distance shipped[2]	Number	Percent distribution by means of transport							
		All means of transport	Rail	Motor carrier	Private truck	Air	Water	Other	Unknown
TONS OF SHIPMENTS	(thousands of tons)								
U.S. TOTAL..........	11 787	100.0	44.4	33.8	17.4	-	2.3	-	2.2
MIDDLE ATLANTIC.........	2 462	100.0	11.7	61.0	17.1	-	-	-	10.2
UNDER 100 MILES.......	1 296	100.0	5.0	59.6	25.5	-	-	-	9.9
100 TO 199 MILES......	500	100.0	9.0	75.0	5.1	-	-	-	10.9
200 TO 299 MILES......	329	100.0	20.2	70.9	1.0	-	-	-	8.0
300 TO 499 MILES......	219	100.0	26.1	50.3	8.9	-	-	-	14.6
500 TO 999 MILES......	114	100.0	47.7	9.3	35.0	-	-	-	8.0
1000 TO 1499 MILES....	1	100.0	4.6	-	95.4	-	-	-	-
1500 MILES OR OVER....	-	100.0	75.6	-	-	24.4	-	-	-
SOUTH ATLANTIC.........	1 288	100.0	52.5	30.0	11.0	-	6.5	-	-
UNDER 100 MILES.......	275	100.0	1.3	54.8	43.9	-	-	-	-
100 TO 199 MILES......	229	100.0	44.4	42.8	8.1	-	4.8	-	-
200 TO 299 MILES......	70	100.0	62.0	34.7	3.3	-	-	-	-
300 TO 499 MILES......	503	100.0	67.2	18.2	.1	-	14.4	-	-
500 TO 999 MILES......	138	100.0	84.5	15.5	-	-	-	-	-
1000 TO 1499 MILES....	71	100.0	100.0	-	-	-	-	-	-
1500 MILES OR OVER....	-	100.0	-	-	-	-	-	-	-
WEST SOUTH CENTRAL......	1 618	100.0	63.9	9.7	15.0	-	11.4	-	-
UNDER 100 MILES.......	178	100.0	9.6	24.0	66.3	-	-	-	-
100 TO 199 MILES......	84	100.0	44.2	28.8	27.0	-	-	-	-
200 TO 299 MILES......	51	100.0	78.2	1.7	20.0	-	-	-	-
300 TO 499 MILES......	392	100.0	77.6	11.1	11.3	-	-	-	-
500 TO 999 MILES......	836	100.0	71.3	5.3	5.5	-	17.9	-	-
1000 TO 1499 MILES....	19	100.0	91.0	-	9.0	.1	-	-	-
1500 MILES OR OVER....	55	100.0	37.9	-	.4	-	61.7	-	-
MOUNTAIN...............	2 013	100.0	58.4	22.8	18.5	-	-	-	.3
UNDER 100 MILES.......	511	100.0	5.4	44.6	49.3	-	-	-	.7
100 TO 199 MILES......	100	100.0	1.0	7.5	91.5	-	-	-	-
200 TO 299 MILES......	75	100.0	28.3	67.5	4.2	-	-	-	-
300 TO 499 MILES......	199	100.0	15.2	72.3	12.5	-	-	-	-
500 TO 999 MILES......	498	100.0	93.5	5.9	.3	-	-	-	.3
1000 TO 1499 MILES....	546	100.0	100.0	-	-	-	-	-	-
1500 MILES OR OVER....	83	100.0	100.0	-	-	-	-	-	-
PACIFIC................	2 893	100.0	55.0	37.8	7.2	-	-	-	-
UNDER 100 MILES.......	607	100.0	9.0	75.8	15.2	-	-	-	-
100 TO 199 MILES......	442	100.0	20.1	71.6	8.3	-	-	-	-
200 TO 299 MILES......	387	100.0	50.1	43.5	6.5	-	-	-	-
300 TO 499 MILES......	327	100.0	43.9	39.8	16.3	-	-	-	-
500 TO 999 MILES......	127	100.0	87.7	12.3	-	-	-	-	-
1000 TO 1499 MILES....	433	100.0	99.7	-	.3	-	-	-	-
1500 MILES OR OVER....	566	100.0	99.7	.3	-	-	-	-	-
TON-MILES OF SHIPMENTS	(millions of ton-miles)								
U.S. TOTAL..........	5 289	100.0	78.7	11.8	5.0	-	3.6	-	.8
MIDDLE ATLANTIC.........	374	100.0	24.1	50.3	14.0	.1	-	-	11.5
UNDER 100 MILES.......	55	100.0	8.9	50.7	26.1	-	-	-	14.2
100 TO 199 MILES......	76	100.0	9.9	73.8	4.5	-	-	-	11.8
200 TO 299 MILES......	84	100.0	21.0	70.2	1.0	-	-	-	7.8
300 TO 499 MILES......	87	100.0	29.5	44.1	10.5	-	-	-	15.9
500 TO 999 MILES......	68	100.0	48.6	9.6	33.6	-	-	-	8.3
1000 TO 1499 MILES....	1	100.0	4.8	-	95.2	-	-	-	-
1500 MILES OR OVER....	1	100.0	69.9	-	-	30.1	-	-	-
SOUTH ATLANTIC.........	425	100.0	74.4	17.0	1.8	-	6.8	-	-
UNDER 100 MILES.......	11	100.0	2.9	56.9	40.2	-	-	-	-
100 TO 199 MILES......	30	100.0	42.3	44.5	7.3	-	5.9	-	-
200 TO 299 MILES......	18	100.0	65.1	31.8	3.1	-	-	-	-
300 TO 499 MILES......	189	100.0	67.3	18.3	.1	-	14.3	-	-
500 TO 999 MILES......	99	100.0	87.9	12.1	-	-	-	-	-
1000 TO 1499 MILES....	75	100.0	100.0	-	-	-	-	-	-
1500 MILES OR OVER....	-	100.0	-	-	-	-	-	-	-
WEST SOUTH CENTRAL......	889	100.0	69.5	5.5	6.9	-	18.1	-	-
UNDER 100 MILES.......	5	100.0	17.6	15.9	66.5	-	-	-	-
100 TO 199 MILES......	12	100.0	45.1	28.8	26.1	-	-	-	-
200 TO 299 MILES......	13	100.0	79.5	1.6	18.9	-	-	-	-
300 TO 499 MILES......	157	100.0	78.6	10.8	10.6	-	-	-	-
500 TO 999 MILES......	585	100.0	71.8	4.6	5.5	-	18.0	-	-
1000 TO 1499 MILES....	20	100.0	91.0	-	8.9	.1	-	-	-
1500 MILES OR OVER....	93	100.0	40.1	-	.9	-	59.0	-	-
MOUNTAIN...............	1 330	100.0	90.6	7.0	2.3	-	-	-	.1
UNDER 100 MILES.......	20	100.0	9.1	47.7	42.8	-	-	-	.3
100 TO 199 MILES......	12	100.0	1.3	7.8	91.0	-	-	-	-
200 TO 299 MILES......	18	100.0	28.4	67.7	4.0	-	-	-	-
300 TO 499 MILES......	69	100.0	15.8	70.8	13.4	-	-	-	-
500 TO 999 MILES......	386	100.0	94.2	5.3	.2	-	-	-	.2
1000 TO 1499 MILES....	675	100.0	100.0	-	-	-	-	-	-
1500 MILES OR OVER....	148	100.0	100.0	-	-	-	-	-	-

See footnotes at end of table 4.

TABLE 1. TCC GROUP 206—Percent Distribution of Geographic Division of Origin and Distance Shipped, by Means of Transport: 1972—Continued

Geographic division of origin[1] and distance shipped[2]	Number	Percent distribution by means of transport							
		All means of transport	Rail	Motor carrier	Private truck	Air	Water	Other	Unknown
TON-MILES OF SHIPMENTS	(millions of ton-miles)								
PACIFIC..................	1 975	100.0	89.4	8.7	1.8	-	-	-	-
UNDER 100 MILES.......	30	100.0	9.0	73.2	17.7	-	-	-	-
100 TO 199 MILES.....	62	100.0	19.4	72.4	8.3	-	-	-	-
200 TO 299 MILES.....	101	100.0	48.9	45.0	6.1	-	-	-	-
300 TO 499 MILES.....	118	100.0	44.7	39.6	15.7	-	-	-	-
500 TO 999 MILES.....	87	100.0	90.0	10.0	-	-	-	-	-
1000 TO 1499 MILES....	594	100.0	99.8	-	.2	-	-	-	-
1500 MILES OR OVER....	981	100.0	99.6	.4	-	-	-	-	-

See footnotes at end of table 4.

TABLE 2. TCC GROUP 206—Percent Distribution of Geographic Division of Origin and Means of Transport, by Geographic Division of Destination: 1972

Geographic division of origin[1] and means of transport	Number	Percent distribution by division of destination									
		U.S. total	New England	Middle Atlantic	East North Central	West North Central	South Atlantic	East South Central	West South Central	Mountain	Pacific
TONS OF SHIPMENTS	(thousands of tons)										
U.S. TOTAL..............	11 787	100.0	3.9	19.1	21.3	11.9	12.4	4.1	4.5	6.9	16.0
RAIL...................	5 228	100.0	2.1	8.2	36.0	15.1	13.3	7.2	5.1	2.3	10.7
MOTOR CARRIER.........	3 986	100.0	4.9	32.5	6.8	3.1	11.3	1.0	3.0	9.3	28.1
PRIVATE TRUCK.........	2 047	100.0	6.6	16.5	12.5	19.7	8.9	3.2	6.8	15.7	10.0
AIR...................	-	100.0	-	7.1	-	-	-	-	-	92.9	-
WATER.................	267	100.0	-	12.8	26.0	29.9	31.3	-	-	-	-
OTHER.................	-	100.0	-	90.2	9.8	-	-	-	-	-	-
UNKNOWN...............	256	100.0	7.0	60.5	10.7	1.0	19.4	-	-	1.3	-
MIDDLE ATLANTIC.........	2 462	100.0	7.0	72.1	8.4	-	12.0	.4	.1	-	-
RAIL...................	288	100.0	12.9	35.3	22.9	-	26.0	2.8	-	.2	-
MOTOR CARRIER.........	1 502	100.0	6.3	80.3	3.5	-	9.8	-	-	-	-
PRIVATE TRUCK.........	420	100.0	5.6	74.2	14.0	-	5.7	.1	.3	-	-
AIR...................	-	100.0	-	-	-	-	-	-	-	100.0	-
WATER.................	-	100.0	-	-	-	-	-	-	-	-	-
OTHER.................	-	100.0	-	100.0	-	-	-	-	-	-	-
UNKNOWN...............	250	100.0	7.1	62.0	11.0	-	19.9	-	-	-	-
SOUTH ATLANTIC..........	1 288	100.0	-	11.9	15.5	-	68.3	4.3	-	-	-
RAIL...................	676	100.0	-	12.0	25.0	-	54.8	8.2	-	-	-
MOTOR CARRIER.........	386	100.0	-	18.6	7.9	-	73.5	-	-	-	-
PRIVATE TRUCK.........	142	100.0	-	-	-	-	100.0	-	-	-	-
AIR...................	-	100.0	-	-	-	-	-	-	-	-	-
WATER.................	83	100.0	-	-	-	-	100.0	-	-	-	-
OTHER.................	-	100.0	-	-	-	-	-	-	-	-	-
UNKNOWN...............	-	100.0	-	-	-	-	-	-	-	-	-
WEST SOUTH CENTRAL.....	1 618	100.0	-	3.7	20.8	9.7	17.3	25.5	21.8	-	1.3
RAIL...................	1 034	100.0	-	2.4	25.3	4.8	23.8	29.8	12.0	-	2.0
MOTOR CARRIER.........	156	100.0	-	-	.6	5.4	11.1	25.2	57.8	-	-
PRIVATE TRUCK.........	243	100.0	-	.1	1.7	7.6	6.9	26.7	56.9	-	.1
AIR...................	-	100.0	-	100.0	-	-	-	-	-	-	-
WATER.................	183	100.0	-	18.7	37.9	43.4	-	-	-	-	-
OTHER.................	-	100.0	-	-	-	-	-	-	-	-	-
UNKNOWN...............	-	100.0	-	-	-	-	-	-	-	-	-
MOUNTAIN................	2 013	100.0	1.7	.8	30.8	22.1	.2	.3	4.8	36.3	3.0
RAIL...................	1 176	100.0	2.9	1.4	51.7	31.3	.3	.4	5.7	4.9	1.3
MOTOR CARRIER.........	459	100.0	-	-	2.6	4.3	-	-	6.4	77.0	9.6
PRIVATE TRUCK.........	373	100.0	-	-	-	15.0	-	-	-	85.0	-
AIR...................	-	100.0	-	-	-	-	-	-	-	-	-
WATER.................	-	100.0	-	-	-	-	-	-	-	-	-
OTHER.................	-	100.0	-	-	-	-	-	-	-	-	-
UNKNOWN...............	5	100.0	-	-	-	32.6	-	-	-	67.4	-
PACIFIC.................	2 893	100.0	-	-	22.6	10.1	.1	-	2.0	2.9	62.4
RAIL...................	1 590	100.0	-	-	41.1	18.4	-	-	3.7	3.9	33.0
MOTOR CARRIER.........	1 093	100.0	-	-	-	-	.1	-	-	1.5	98.3
PRIVATE TRUCK.........	209	100.0	-	-	-	-	-	-	-	2.4	97.6
AIR...................	-	100.0	-	-	-	-	-	-	-	-	-
WATER.................	-	100.0	-	-	-	-	-	-	-	-	-
OTHER.................	-	100.0	-	-	-	-	-	-	-	-	-
UNKNOWN...............	-	100.0	-	-	-	-	-	-	-	-	100.0

See footnotes at end of table 4.

TABLE 2. TCC GROUP 206—Percent Distribution of Geographic Division of Origin and Means of Transport, by Geographic Division of Destination: 1972—Continued

Geographic division of origin[1] and means of transport	Number	Percent distribution by division of destination									
		U.S. total	New England	Middle Atlantic	East North Central	West North Central	South Atlantic	East South Central	West South Central	Mountain	Pacific
TON-MILES OF SHIPMENTS	(millions of ton-miles)										
U.S. TOTAL...............	5 289	100.0	2.4	7.9	45.2	17.5	8.4	4.1	4.4	2.4	7.8
RAIL.................	4 164	100.0	2.3	4.4	52.6	18.7	7.1	4.4	4.5	1.2	4.7
MOTOR CARRIER.........	624	100.0	3.3	22.3	11.9	4.2	14.6	1.5	5.2	8.4	28.6
PRIVATE TRUCK.........	266	100.0	2.9	8.5	20.9	26.7	6.9	8.3	5.0	7.4	13.4
AIR..................	-	100.0	-	4.0	-	-	-	-	-	96.0	-
WATER................	189	100.0	-	29.1	30.5	25.1	15.3	-	-	-	-
OTHER................	-	100.0	-	99.7	.3	-	-	-	-	-	-
UNKNOWN..............	44	100.0	6.2	37.7	28.7	2.3	24.9	-	-	.2	-
MIDDLE ATLANTIC.........	374	100.0	6.2	48.0	27.4	-	15.9	1.7	.5	.3	-
RAIL.................	90	100.0	6.9	22.2	39.4	-	24.1	6.5	.1	.9	-
MOTOR CARRIER.........	188	100.0	6.9	67.8	12.0	-	13.2	.1	-	-	-
PRIVATE TRUCK.........	52	100.0	2.5	28.9	60.7	-	4.2	.5	3.3	-	-
AIR..................	-	100.0	-	-	-	-	-	-	-	100.0	-
WATER................	-	100.0	-	-	-	-	-	-	-	-	-
OTHER................	-	100.0	-	100.0	-	-	-	-	-	-	-
UNKNOWN..............	42	100.0	6.3	38.7	29.5	-	25.5	-	-	-	-
SOUTH ATLANTIC..........	425	100.0	-	8.5	34.1	-	48.9	8.5	-	-	-
RAIL.................	316	100.0	-	9.2	41.1	-	38.2	11.5	-	-	-
MOTOR CARRIER.........	72	100.0	-	9.4	20.6	-	70.0	-	-	-	-
PRIVATE TRUCK.........	7	100.0	-	-	-	-	100.0	-	-	-	-
AIR..................	-	100.0	-	-	-	-	-	-	-	-	-
WATER................	29	100.0	-	-	-	-	100.0	-	-	-	-
OTHER................	-	100.0	-	-	-	-	-	-	-	-	-
UNKNOWN..............	-	100.0	-	-	-	-	-	-	-	-	-
WEST SOUTH CENTRAL......	889	100.0	-	9.1	28.8	11.6	18.7	18.8	8.8	-	4.3
RAIL.................	617	100.0	-	4.1	31.5	5.7	23.6	22.0	7.1	-	6.1
MOTOR CARRIER.........	48	100.0	-	-	1.3	10.7	23.9	18.2	45.9	-	-
PRIVATE TRUCK.........	61	100.0	-	.4	5.3	24.1	14.1	35.9	18.8	-	1.3
AIR..................	-	100.0	-	100.0	-	-	-	-	-	-	-
WATER................	160	100.0	-	34.4	36.0	29.6	-	-	-	-	-
OTHER................	-	100.0	-	-	-	-	-	-	-	-	-
UNKNOWN..............	-	100.0	-	-	-	-	-	-	-	-	-
MOUNTAIN................	1 330	100.0	5.3	2.0	54.4	24.9	.4	.4	5.0	5.8	1.7
RAIL.................	1 205	100.0	5.8	2.2	59.2	25.5	.5	.4	4.7	.9	.7
MOTOR CARRIER.........	93	100.0	-	-	11.1	11.0	-	-	10.8	51.1	16.0
PRIVATE TRUCK.........	30	100.0	-	-	-	41.1	-	-	-	58.9	-
AIR..................	-	100.0	-	-	-	-	-	-	-	-	-
WATER................	-	100.0	-	-	-	-	-	-	-	-	-
OTHER................	-	100.0	-	-	-	-	-	-	-	-	-
UNKNOWN..............	-	100.0	-	-	-	92.9	-	-	-	7.1	-
PACIFIC.................	1 975	100.0	-	-	55.0	20.9	.2	-	3.9	2.3	17.7
RAIL.................	1 766	100.0	-	-	61.5	23.4	-	-	4.4	2.2	8.5
MOTOR CARRIER.........	172	100.0	-	-	-	-	2.2	-	-	3.0	94.7
PRIVATE TRUCK.........	36	100.0	-	-	-	-	-	-	-	4.5	95.5
AIR..................	-	100.0	-	-	-	-	-	-	-	-	-
WATER................	-	100.0	-	-	-	-	-	-	-	-	-
OTHER................	-	100.0	-	-	-	-	-	-	-	-	-
UNKNOWN..............	-	100.0	-	-	-	-	-	-	-	-	100.0

See footnotes at end of table 4.

TABLE 3. TCC GROUP 206—Percent Distribution of Geographic Division of Destination and Means of Transport, by Geographic Division of Origin: 1972

Geographic division of destination and means of transport	Number	Percent distribution by division of origin[1]									
		U.S. total	New England	Middle Atlantic	East North Central	West North Central	South Atlantic	East South Central	West South Central	Mountain	Pacific
TONS OF SHIPMENTS	(thousands of tons)										
U.S. TOTAL	11 787	100.0	(D)	20.9	(D)	(D)	10.9	(D)	13.7	17.1	24.5
RAIL	5 228	100.0	(D)	5.5	(D)	(D)	12.9	(D)	19.8	22.5	30.4
MOTOR CARRIER	3 986	100.0	(D)	37.7	(D)	(D)	9.7	(D)	3.9	11.5	27.4
PRIVATE TRUCK	2 047	100.0	(D)	20.5	(D)	(D)	6.9	(D)	11.9	18.2	10.2
AIR	-	100.0	(D)	92.9	(D)	(D)	-	(D)	7.1	-	-
WATER	267	100.0	(D)	-	(D)	(D)	31.3	(D)	68.7	-	-
OTHER	-	100.0	(D)	90.2	(D)	(D)	-	(D)	-	-	-
UNKNOWN	256	100.0	(D)	97.7	(D)	(D)	-	(D)	-	2.0	-
NEW ENGLAND	459	100.0	(D)	37.7	(D)	(D)	-	(D)	-	7.5	-
RAIL	110	100.0	(D)	33.6	(D)	(D)	-	(D)	-	31.1	-
MOTOR CARRIER	195	100.0	(D)	48.5	(D)	(D)	-	(D)	-	-	-
PRIVATE TRUCK	135	100.0	(D)	17.4	(D)	(D)	-	(D)	-	-	-
AIR	-	100.0	(D)	-	(D)	(D)	-	(D)	-	-	-
WATER	-	100.0	(D)	-	(D)	(D)	-	(D)	-	-	-
OTHER	-	100.0	(D)	-	(D)	(D)	-	(D)	-	-	-
UNKNOWN	17	100.0	(D)	100.0	(D)	(D)	-	(D)	-	-	-
MIDDLE ATLANTIC	2 251	100.0	(D)	78.9	(D)	(D)	6.8	(D)	2.6	.7	-
RAIL	426	100.0	(D)	23.9	(D)	(D)	19.1	(D)	5.8	3.9	-
MOTOR CARRIER	1 297	100.0	(D)	93.0	(D)	(D)	5.5	(D)	.1	-	-
PRIVATE TRUCK	338	100.0	(D)	92.2	(D)	(D)	-	(D)	.1	-	-
AIR	-	100.0	(D)	-	(D)	(D)	-	(D)	100.0	-	-
WATER	34	100.0	(D)	-	(D)	(D)	-	(D)	100.0	-	-
OTHER	-	100.0	(D)	100.0	(D)	(D)	-	(D)	-	-	-
UNKNOWN	155	100.0	(D)	100.0	(D)	(D)	-	(D)	-	-	-
EAST NORTH CENTRAL	2 506	100.0	(D)	8.2	(D)	(D)	8.0	(D)	13.4	24.7	26.1
RAIL	1 882	100.0	(D)	3.5	(D)	(D)	9.0	(D)	13.9	32.3	34.7
MOTOR CARRIER	270	100.0	(D)	19.7	(D)	(D)	11.3	(D)	.3	4.4	-
PRIVATE TRUCK	256	100.0	(D)	23.0	(D)	(D)	-	(D)	1.6	-	-
AIR	-	100.0	(D)	-	(D)	(D)	-	(D)	-	-	-
WATER	69	100.0	(D)	-	(D)	(D)	-	(D)	100.0	-	-
OTHER	-	100.0	(D)	-	(D)	(D)	-	(D)	-	-	-
UNKNOWN	27	100.0	(D)	100.0	(D)	(D)	-	(D)	-	-	-
WEST NORTH CENTRAL	1 398	100.0	(D)	-	(D)	(D)	-	(D)	11.2	31.9	20.9
RAIL	790	100.0	(D)	-	(D)	(D)	-	(D)	6.3	46.6	37.0
MOTOR CARRIER	122	100.0	(D)	-	(D)	(D)	-	(D)	6.9	16.2	-
PRIVATE TRUCK	403	100.0	(D)	-	(D)	(D)	-	(D)	4.6	13.9	-
AIR	-	100.0	(D)	-	(D)	(D)	-	(D)	-	-	-
WATER	79	100.0	(D)	-	(D)	(D)	-	(D)	100.0	-	-
OTHER	-	100.0	(D)	-	(D)	(D)	-	(D)	-	-	-
UNKNOWN	2	100.0	(D)	-	(D)	(D)	-	(D)	-	67.1	-
SOUTH ATLANTIC	1 464	100.0	(D)	20.2	(D)	(D)	60.2	(D)	19.1	.2	.1
RAIL	696	100.0	(D)	10.8	(D)	(D)	53.2	(D)	35.3	.5	-
MOTOR CARRIER	450	100.0	(D)	32.7	(D)	(D)	63.1	(D)	3.8	-	.4
PRIVATE TRUCK	182	100.0	(D)	13.0	(D)	(D)	77.8	(D)	9.2	-	-
AIR	-	100.0	(D)	-	(D)	(D)	-	(D)	-	-	-
WATER	83	100.0	(D)	-	(D)	(D)	100.0	(D)	-	-	-
OTHER	-	100.0	(D)	-	(D)	(D)	-	(D)	-	-	-
UNKNOWN	49	100.0	(D)	100.0	(D)	(D)	-	(D)	-	-	-
EAST SOUTH CENTRAL	482	100.0	(D)	1.9	(D)	(D)	11.5	(D)	85.6	1.1	-
RAIL	376	100.0	(D)	2.1	(D)	(D)	14.7	(D)	81.8	1.4	-
MOTOR CARRIER	39	100.0	(D)	.8	(D)	(D)	-	(D)	99.1	-	-
PRIVATE TRUCK	65	100.0	(D)	.8	(D)	(D)	-	(D)	99.2	-	-
AIR	-	100.0	(D)	-	(D)	(D)	-	(D)	-	-	-
WATER	-	100.0	(D)	-	(D)	(D)	-	(D)	-	-	-
OTHER	-	100.0	(D)	-	(D)	(D)	-	(D)	-	-	-
UNKNOWN	-	100.0	(D)	-	(D)	(D)	-	(D)	-	-	-
WEST SOUTH CENTRAL	525	100.0	(D)	.3	(D)	(D)	-	(D)	67.2	18.5	11.1
RAIL	265	100.0	(D)	-	(D)	(D)	-	(D)	46.7	25.4	21.9
MOTOR CARRIER	119	100.0	(D)	-	(D)	(D)	-	(D)	75.3	24.7	-
PRIVATE TRUCK	140	100.0	(D)	1.0	(D)	(D)	-	(D)	99.0	-	-
AIR	-	100.0	(D)	-	(D)	(D)	-	(D)	-	-	-
WATER	-	100.0	(D)	-	(D)	(D)	-	(D)	-	-	-
OTHER	-	100.0	(D)	-	(D)	(D)	-	(D)	-	-	-
UNKNOWN	-	100.0	(D)	-	(D)	(D)	-	(D)	-	-	-
MOUNTAIN	815	100.0	(D)	.1	(D)	(D)	-	(D)	-	89.7	10.2
RAIL	119	100.0	(D)	.4	(D)	(D)	-	(D)	-	47.9	51.7
MOTOR CARRIER	370	100.0	(D)	-	(D)	(D)	-	(D)	-	95.5	4.5
PRIVATE TRUCK	322	100.0	(D)	-	(D)	(D)	-	(D)	-	98.5	1.5
AIR	-	100.0	(D)	100.0	(D)	(D)	-	(D)	-	-	-
WATER	-	100.0	(D)	-	(D)	(D)	-	(D)	-	-	-
OTHER	-	100.0	(D)	-	(D)	(D)	-	(D)	-	-	-
UNKNOWN	3	100.0	(D)	-	(D)	(D)	-	(D)	-	100.0	-
PACIFIC	1 885	100.0	(D)	-	(D)	(D)	-	(D)	1.1	3.2	95.7
RAIL	561	100.0	(D)	-	(D)	(D)	-	(D)	3.8	2.8	93.5
MOTOR CARRIER	1 119	100.0	(D)	-	(D)	(D)	-	(D)	-	4.0	96.0
PRIVATE TRUCK	204	100.0	(D)	-	(D)	(D)	-	(D)	.1	-	99.9
AIR	-	100.0	(D)	-	(D)	(D)	-	(D)	-	-	-
WATER	-	100.0	(D)	-	(D)	(D)	-	(D)	-	-	-
OTHER	-	100.0	(D)	-	(D)	(D)	-	(D)	-	-	-
UNKNOWN	-	100.0	(D)	-	(D)	(D)	-	(D)	-	-	100.0

See footnotes at end of table 4.

TABLE 3. **TCC GROUP 206**—Percent Distribution of Geographic Division of Destination and Means of Transport, by Geographic Division of Origin: 1972—Continued

Geographic division of destination and means of transport	Number	Percent distribution by division of origin[1]									
		U.S. total	New England	Middle Atlantic	East North Central	West North Central	South Atlantic	East South Central	West South Central	Mountain	Pacific
TON-MILES OF SHIPMENTS	(millions of ton-miles)										
U.S. TOTAL	5 289	100.0	(D)	7.1	(D)	(D)	8.1	(D)	16.8	25.2	37.4
RAIL	4 164	100.0	(D)	2.2	(D)	(D)	7.6	(D)	14.8	28.9	42.4
MOTOR CARRIER	624	100.0	(D)	30.2	(D)	(D)	11.6	(D)	7.8	14.9	27.6
PRIVATE TRUCK	266	100.0	(D)	19.7	(D)	(D)	2.8	(D)	22.9	11.6	13.7
AIR	-	100.0	(D)	96.0	(D)	(D)	-	(D)	4.0	-	-
WATER	189	100.0	(D)	-	(D)	(D)	15.3	(D)	84.7	-	-
OTHER	-	100.0	(D)	99.7	(D)	(D)	-	(D)	-	-	-
UNKNOWN	44	100.0	(D)	97.5	(D)	(D)	-	(D)	-	2.2	-
NEW ENGLAND	127	100.0	(D)	18.2	(D)	(D)	-	(D)	-	55.0	-
RAIL	96	100.0	(D)	6.4	(D)	(D)	-	(D)	-	72.7	-
MOTOR CARRIER	20	100.0	(D)	63.5	(D)	(D)	-	(D)	-	-	-
PRIVATE TRUCK	7	100.0	(D)	16.9	(D)	(D)	-	(D)	-	-	-
AIR	-	100.0	(D)	-	(D)	(D)	-	(D)	-	-	-
WATER	-	100.0	(D)	-	(D)	(D)	-	(D)	-	-	-
OTHER	-	100.0	(D)	-	(D)	(D)	-	(D)	-	-	-
UNKNOWN	2	100.0	(D)	100.0	(D)	(D)	-	(D)	-	-	-
MIDDLE ATLANTIC	415	100.0	(D)	43.2	(D)	(D)	8.7	(D)	19.4	6.5	-
RAIL	182	100.0	(D)	11.0	(D)	(D)	16.1	(D)	13.8	14.7	-
MOTOR CARRIER	139	100.0	(D)	91.8	(D)	(D)	4.9	(D)	-	-	-
PRIVATE TRUCK	22	100.0	(D)	67.1	(D)	(D)	-	(D)	1.1	-	-
AIR	-	100.0	(D)	-	(D)	(D)	-	(D)	100.0	-	-
WATER	55	100.0	(D)	-	(D)	(D)	-	(D)	100.0	-	-
OTHER	-	100.0	(D)	100.0	(D)	(D)	-	(D)	-	-	-
UNKNOWN	16	100.0	(D)	100.0	(D)	(D)	-	(D)	-	-	-
EAST NORTH CENTRAL	2 392	100.0	(D)	4.3	(D)	(D)	6.1	(D)	10.7	30.3	45.4
RAIL	2 192	100.0	(D)	1.6	(D)	(D)	5.9	(D)	8.9	32.6	49.5
MOTOR CARRIER	74	100.0	(D)	30.4	(D)	(D)	20.1	(D)	.9	13.9	-
PRIVATE TRUCK	55	100.0	(D)	57.1	(D)	(D)	-	(D)	5.8	-	-
AIR	-	100.0	(D)	-	(D)	(D)	-	(D)	-	-	-
WATER	57	100.0	(D)	-	(D)	(D)	-	(D)	100.0	-	-
OTHER	-	100.0	(D)	-	(D)	(D)	-	(D)	-	-	-
UNKNOWN	12	100.0	(D)	100.0	(D)	(D)	-	(D)	-	-	-
WEST NORTH CENTRAL	924	100.0	(D)	-	(D)	(D)	-	(D)	11.1	35.9	44.7
RAIL	778	100.0	(D)	-	(D)	(D)	-	(D)	4.5	39.5	53.1
MOTOR CARRIER	26	100.0	(D)	-	(D)	(D)	-	(D)	19.9	39.1	-
PRIVATE TRUCK	71	100.0	(D)	-	(D)	(D)	-	(D)	20.7	17.8	-
AIR	-	100.0	(D)	-	(D)	(D)	-	(D)	-	-	-
WATER	47	100.0	(D)	-	(D)	(D)	-	(D)	100.0	-	-
OTHER	-	100.0	(D)	-	(D)	(D)	-	(D)	-	-	-
UNKNOWN	1	100.0	(D)	-	(D)	(D)	-	(D)	-	87.8	-
SOUTH ATLANTIC	444	100.0	(D)	13.4	(D)	(D)	46.9	(D)	37.4	1.3	.9
RAIL	294	100.0	(D)	7.3	(D)	(D)	41.0	(D)	49.4	2.0	-
MOTOR CARRIER	91	100.0	(D)	27.2	(D)	(D)	55.7	(D)	12.8	-	-
PRIVATE TRUCK	18	100.0	(D)	12.0	(D)	(D)	40.7	(D)	47.3	-	4.2
AIR	-	100.0	(D)	-	(D)	(D)	-	(D)	-	-	-
WATER	29	100.0	(D)	-	(D)	(D)	100.0	(D)	-	-	-
OTHER	-	100.0	(D)	-	(D)	(D)	-	(D)	-	-	-
UNKNOWN	10	100.0	(D)	100.0	(D)	(D)	-	(D)	-	-	-
EAST SOUTH CENTRAL	214	100.0	(D)	2.9	(D)	(D)	16.9	(D)	77.6	2.5	-
RAIL	183	100.0	(D)	3.2	(D)	(D)	19.8	(D)	74.1	2.9	-
MOTOR CARRIER	9	100.0	(D)	1.8	(D)	(D)	-	(D)	97.9	-	-
PRIVATE TRUCK	22	100.0	(D)	1.2	(D)	(D)	-	(D)	98.8	-	-
AIR	-	100.0	(D)	-	(D)	(D)	-	(D)	-	-	-
WATER	-	100.0	(D)	-	(D)	(D)	-	(D)	-	-	-
OTHER	-	100.0	(D)	-	(D)	(D)	-	(D)	-	-	-
UNKNOWN	-	100.0	(D)	-	(D)	(D)	-	(D)	-	-	-
WEST SOUTH CENTRAL	234	100.0	(D)	.8	(D)	(D)	-	(D)	33.3	28.4	33.0
RAIL	188	100.0	(D)	-	(D)	(D)	-	(D)	23.3	30.0	41.0
MOTOR CARRIER	32	100.0	(D)	-	(D)	(D)	-	(D)	69.2	30.8	-
PRIVATE TRUCK	13	100.0	(D)	12.9	(D)	(D)	-	(D)	87.1	-	-
AIR	-	100.0	(D)	-	(D)	(D)	-	(D)	-	-	-
WATER	-	100.0	(D)	-	(D)	(D)	-	(D)	-	-	-
OTHER	-	100.0	(D)	-	(D)	(D)	-	(D)	-	-	-
UNKNOWN	-	100.0	(D)	-	(D)	(D)	-	(D)	-	-	-
MOUNTAIN	124	100.0	(D)	.9	(D)	(D)	-	(D)	-	61.9	37.2
RAIL	51	100.0	(D)	1.5	(D)	(D)	-	(D)	-	22.0	76.5
MOTOR CARRIER	52	100.0	(D)	-	(D)	(D)	-	(D)	-	90.1	9.9
PRIVATE TRUCK	19	100.0	(D)	-	(D)	(D)	-	(D)	-	91.8	8.2
AIR	-	100.0	(D)	100.0	(D)	(D)	-	(D)	-	-	-
WATER	-	100.0	(D)	-	(D)	(D)	-	(D)	-	-	-
OTHER	-	100.0	(D)	-	(D)	(D)	-	(D)	-	-	-
UNKNOWN	-	100.0	(D)	-	(D)	(D)	-	(D)	-	100.0	-
PACIFIC	410	100.0	(D)	-	(D)	(D)	-	(D)	9.4	5.6	85.1
RAIL	196	100.0	(D)	-	(D)	(D)	-	(D)	19.1	4.1	76.8
MOTOR CARRIER	178	100.0	(D)	-	(D)	(D)	-	(D)	-	8.4	91.6
PRIVATE TRUCK	35	100.0	(D)	-	(D)	(D)	-	(D)	2.3	-	97.7
AIR	-	100.0	(D)	-	(D)	(D)	-	(D)	-	-	-
WATER	-	100.0	(D)	-	(D)	(D)	-	(D)	-	-	-
OTHER	-	100.0	(D)	-	(D)	(D)	-	(D)	-	-	-
UNKNOWN	-	100.0	(D)	-	(D)	(D)	-	(D)	-	-	100.0

See footnotes at end of table 4.

TABLE 4. **TCC GROUP 206**—Percent Distribution of Distance Shipped and Weight of Shipment, by Means of Transport: 1972

Distance shipped and weight of shipment[2][3]	Number	Percent distribution by means of transport							
		All means of transport	Rail	Motor carrier	Private truck	Air	Water	Other	Unknown
TONS OF SHIPMENTS	(thousands of tons)								
U.S. TOTAL..........	7 785	100.0	47.2	31.0	18.3	-	3.1	-	.4
UNDER 100 MILES........	2 243	100.0	10.4	48.9	40.4	-	-	-	.4
UNDER 1000 POUNDS.....	-	100.0	-	51.2	47.3	-	-	1.4	-
1000 TO 9999 POUNDS...	29	100.0	-	49.8	50.2	-	-	-	-
10000 TO 29999 POUNDS.	249	100.0	-	45.9	54.1	-	-	-	-
30000 TO 59999 POUNDS.	1 710	100.0	4.5	54.0	41.0	-	-	-	.5
60000 TO 89999 POUNDS.	77	100.0	21.1	49.8	29.1	-	-	-	-
90000 POUNDS AND OVER.	175	100.0	79.2	2.6	18.2	-	-	-	-
100 TO 199 MILES........	951	100.0	14.4	57.7	25.5	-	-	-	2.4
UNDER 1000 POUNDS.....	-	100.0	-	72.2	27.8	-	-	-	-
1000 TO 9999 POUNDS...	6	100.0	-	54.4	45.6	-	-	-	-
10000 TO 29999 POUNDS.	53	100.0	-	83.0	17.0	-	-	-	-
30000 TO 59999 POUNDS.	717	100.0	1.7	67.5	27.6	-	-	-	3.2
60000 TO 89999 POUNDS.	32	100.0	37.6	40.5	21.9	-	-	-	-
90000 POUNDS AND OVER.	142	100.0	79.1	3.1	17.8	-	-	-	-
200 TO 299 MILES........	735	100.0	50.3	42.0	7.8	-	-	-	-
UNDER 1000 POUNDS.....	-	100.0	-	22.2	77.8	-	-	-	-
1000 TO 9999 POUNDS...	3	100.0	-	31.8	68.2	-	-	-	-
10000 TO 29999 POUNDS.	14	100.0	-	58.3	41.7	-	-	-	-
30000 TO 59999 POUNDS.	327	100.0	9.8	75.3	14.9	-	-	-	-
60000 TO 89999 POUNDS.	10	100.0	100.0	-	-	-	-	-	-
90000 POUNDS AND OVER.	379	100.0	86.2	13.8	-	-	-	-	-
300 TO 499 MILES........	1 202	100.0	52.9	31.2	11.0	-	4.8	-	-
UNDER 1000 POUNDS.....	-	100.0	8.1	85.2	6.7	-	-	-	-
1000 TO 9999 POUNDS...	3	100.0	5.2	68.6	26.2	-	-	-	-
10000 TO 29999 POUNDS.	27	100.0	.2	80.2	19.6	-	-	-	-
30000 TO 59999 POUNDS.	474	100.0	14.2	62.6	23.2	-	-	-	-
60000 TO 89999 POUNDS.	32	100.0	89.4	-	10.6	-	-	-	-
90000 POUNDS AND OVER.	663	100.0	81.4	8.0	2.0	-	8.7	-	-
500 TO 999 MILES........	1 410	100.0	77.6	5.9	5.8	-	10.6	-	.1
UNDER 1000 POUNDS.....	-	100.0	-	100.0	-	-	-	-	-
1000 TO 9999 POUNDS...	3	100.0	10.7	71.6	17.7	-	-	-	-
10000 TO 29999 POUNDS.	3	100.0	-	67.9	32.1	-	-	-	-
30000 TO 59999 POUNDS.	254	100.0	40.4	31.0	28.5	-	-	-	-
60000 TO 89999 POUNDS.	93	100.0	91.7	-	8.3	-	-	-	-
90000 POUNDS AND OVER.	1 055	100.0	85.7	-	-	-	14.2	-	.2
1000 TO 1499 MILES......	649	100.0	99.3	-	.7	-	-	-	-
UNDER 1000 POUNDS.....	-	100.0	85.0	-	-	15.0	-	-	-
1000 TO 9999 POUNDS...	-	100.0	-	-	-	-	-	-	-
10000 TO 29999 POUNDS.	2	100.0	4.7	-	95.3	-	-	-	-
30000 TO 59999 POUNDS.	10	100.0	84.2	-	15.8	-	-	-	-
60000 TO 89999 POUNDS.	-	100.0	-	-	-	-	-	-	-
90000 POUNDS AND OVER.	635	100.0	100.0	-	-	-	-	-	-
1500 MILES OR OVER......	593	100.0	93.9	.3	-	-	5.8	-	-
UNDER 1000 POUNDS.....	-	100.0	-	-	100.0	-	-	-	-
1000 TO 9999 POUNDS...	-	100.0	100.0	-	-	-	-	-	-
10000 TO 29999 POUNDS.	-	100.0	-	-	-	-	-	-	-
30000 TO 59999 POUNDS.	1	100.0	-	88.9	11.1	-	-	-	-
60000 TO 89999 POUNDS.	-	100.0	-	-	-	-	-	-	-
90000 POUNDS AND OVER.	590	100.0	94.2	-	-	-	5.8	-	-
TON-MILES OF SHIPMENTS	(millions of ton-miles)								
U.S. TOTAL..........	3 736	100.0	78.9	10.8	5.3	-	4.9	-	.1
UNDER 100 MILES........	115	100.0	14.2	47.8	37.6	-	-	-	.4
UNDER 1000 POUNDS.....	-	100.0	-	30.5	69.4	-	-	.1	-
1000 TO 9999 POUNDS...	1	100.0	-	51.6	48.4	-	-	-	-
10000 TO 29999 POUNDS.	10	100.0	-	45.1	54.9	-	-	-	-
30000 TO 59999 POUNDS.	86	100.0	7.0	53.5	39.0	-	-	-	.5
60000 TO 89999 POUNDS.	4	100.0	18.8	64.5	16.7	-	-	-	-
90000 POUNDS AND OVER.	11	100.0	78.5	1.6	19.9	-	-	-	-
100 TO 199 MILES........	136	100.0	15.1	58.9	23.6	-	-	-	2.5
UNDER 1000 POUNDS.....	-	100.0	-	70.3	29.7	-	-	-	-
1000 TO 9999 POUNDS...	-	100.0	-	57.6	42.4	-	-	-	-
10000 TO 29999 POUNDS.	7	100.0	-	84.2	15.8	-	-	-	-
30000 TO 59999 POUNDS.	102	100.0	1.5	69.4	25.8	-	-	-	3.3
60000 TO 89999 POUNDS.	4	100.0	39.4	34.5	26.1	-	-	-	-
90000 POUNDS AND OVER.	20	100.0	82.8	3.0	14.2	-	-	-	-

See footnotes at end of table 4.

TABLE 4. TCC GROUP 206—Percent Distribution of Distance Shipped and Weight of Shipment, by Means of Transport: 1972—Continued

Distance shipped and weight of shipment[2] [3]	Number	Percent distribution by means of transport							
		All means of transport	Rail	Motor carrier	Private truck	Air	Water	Other	Unknown
TON-MILES OF SHIPMENTS	(millions of ton-miles)								
200 TO 299 MILES.........	184	100.0	50.9	42.0	7.2	-	-	-	-
UNDER 1000 POUNDS.....	-	100.0	-	24.4	75.6	-	-	-	-
1000 TO 9999 POUNDS...	-	100.0	-	30.3	69.7	-	-	-	-
10000 TO 29999 POUNDS.	3	100.0	-	59.5	40.5	-	-	-	-
30000 TO 59999 POUNDS.	80	100.0	10.5	75.9	13.7	-	-	-	-
60000 TO 89999 POUNDS.	2	100.0	100.0	-	-	-	-	-	-
90000 POUNDS AND OVER.	95	100.0	86.0	14.0	-	-	-	-	-
300 TO 499 MILES.........	457	100.0	54.6	29.2	11.4	-	4.7	-	-
UNDER 1000 POUNDS.....	-	100.0	7.6	86.0	6.4	-	-	-	-
1000 TO 9999 POUNDS...	1	100.0	5.7	67.3	27.0	-	-	-	-
10000 TO 29999 POUNDS.	9	100.0	.2	78.4	21.4	-	-	-	-
30000 TO 59999 POUNDS.	177	100.0	15.3	59.8	24.9	-	-	-	-
60000 TO 89999 POUNDS.	11	100.0	90.6	-	9.4	-	-	-	-
90000 POUNDS AND OVER.	257	100.0	82.6	7.3	1.7	-	8.4	-	-
500 TO 999 MILES.........	989	100.0	78.8	5.3	5.1	-	10.7	-	.1
UNDER 1000 POUNDS.....	-	100.0	-	100.0	-	-	-	-	-
1000 TO 9999 POUNDS...	1	100.0	11.0	73.9	15.1	-	-	-	-
10000 TO 29999 POUNDS.	1	100.0	-	67.1	32.9	-	-	-	-
30000 TO 59999 POUNDS.	163	100.0	41.2	30.7	28.1	-	-	-	-
60000 TO 89999 POUNDS.	60	100.0	93.6	-	6.4	-	-	-	-
90000 POUNDS AND OVER.	761	100.0	86.0	-	-	-	13.9	-	.1
1000 TO 1499 MILES......	814	100.0	99.4	-	.6	-	-	-	-
UNDER 1000 POUNDS.....	-	100.0	86.0	-	-	14.0	-	-	-
1000 TO 9999 POUNDS...	-	100.0	-	-	-	-	-	-	-
10000 TO 29999 POUNDS.	3	100.0	4.6	-	95.4	-	-	-	-
30000 TO 59999 POUNDS.	11	100.0	84.4	-	15.6	-	-	-	-
60000 TO 89999 POUNDS.	-	100.0	-	-	-	-	-	-	-
90000 POUNDS AND OVER.	799	100.0	100.0	-	-	-	-	-	-
1500 MILES OR OVER......	1 038	100.0	94.2	.4	.1	-	5.3	-	-
UNDER 1000 POUNDS.....	-	100.0	-	-	100.0	-	-	-	-
1000 TO 9999 POUNDS...	-	100.0	100.0	-	-	-	-	-	-
10000 TO 29999 POUNDS.	-	100.0	-	-	-	-	-	-	-
30000 TO 59999 POUNDS.	4	100.0	-	82.7	17.3	-	-	-	-
60000 TO 89999 POUNDS.	-	100.0	-	-	-	-	-	-	-
90000 POUNDS AND OVER.	1 033	100.0	94.6	-	-	-	5.4	-	-

Note: Detail may not add to total due to rounding. The introductory table shows the estimates of sampling variability for tons; sampling variability for ton-miles has not been estimated. See the map in the Introduction for the States comprising the geographic divisions of the United States.

Shipments excluded from the survey are those moving by pipeline (primarily petroleum products from refineries), parcel post shipments, and commodities moved by own power (motorized vehicles, aircraft, etc.) or towed (prefabricated buildings, etc.). Local shipments (commodities shipped less than 25 miles from the plant) and shipments within the same city are also excluded. Shipments to Alaska and Hawaii from the 48 conterminous States and the District of Columbia are included; however, no data were obtained for shipments originating in Alaska and Hawaii.

- Represents zero or rounds to zero.   (D) Withheld to avoid disclosing figures for individual companies.

[1] Production of this commodity is concentrated in the geographic divisions shown; figures and distributions for geographic divisions not shown are included in the total.

[2] Distances of shipments to foreign destinations are calculated only to the U.S. port of exit.

[3] Includes only shipments represented by bills of lading and invoices. Summary records which did not show individual weights of shipments are not included.

TCC 207. Confectionery and Related Products

Comparisons of Tons and Ton-Miles of Shipments for
Geographic Divisions of Origin and for Sampling Variability: 1972 and 1967

Geographic division of origin	Estimates				Relative sampling variability in tons (percent)	
	1972		1967		1972	1967
	Tons (thousands)	Ton-miles (millions)	Tons (thousands)	Ton-miles (millions)		
U.S. total	3,489	1,929	4,292	2,469	13.2	10.2
New England	211	57	220	122	41.8	(*)
Middle Atlantic	665	305	1,910	1,143	19.9	(*)
East North Central	1,196	787	1,389	702	34.2	(*)
West North Central	56	38	91	64	31.1	(*)
South Atlantic	538	282	195	121	18.1	(*)
East South Central	(D)	(D)	120	94	(*)	(*)
West South Central	(D)	(D)	99	59	(*)	(*)
Mountain	—	—	55	53	—	(*)
Pacific	(D)	(D)	213	111	(*)	(*)

— Represents zero or rounds to zero.   (D) Withheld to avoid disclosing figures for individual companies.
(*) Data not published.

TABLE 1. TCC GROUP 207—Percent Distribution of Geographic Division of Origin and Distance Shipped, by Means of Transport: 1972

Geographic division of origin[1] and distance shipped[2]	Number	Percent distribution by means of transport							
		All means of transport	Rail	Motor carrier	Private truck	Air	Water	Other	Unknown
TONS OF SHIPMENTS	(thousands of tons)								
U.S. TOTAL.........	3 489	100.0	13.0	73.4	13.0	-	.3	.2	.1
NEW ENGLAND.............	211	100.0	7.7	91.3	1.0	-	-	-	-
UNDER 100 MILES.......	94	100.0	-	98.2	1.8	-	-	-	-
100 TO 199 MILES......	50	100.0	24.5	75.3	.2	-	-	-	-
200 TO 299 MILES......	12	100.0	-	100.0	-	-	-	-	-
300 TO 499 MILES......	23	100.0	-	98.3	1.7	-	-	-	-
500 TO 999 MILES....	18	100.0	-	100.0	-	-	-	-	-
1000 TO 1499 MILES....	5	100.0	69.3	30.7	-	-	-	-	-
1500 MILES OR OVER....	7	100.0	-	100.0	-	-	-	-	-
MIDDLE ATLANTIC.........	665	100.0	10.4	84.6	4.9	-	-	-	.1
UNDER 100 MILES.......	188	100.0	.8	90.0	9.2	-	-	-	-
100 TO 199 MILES......	95	100.0	.6	99.0	.3	-	-	-	-
200 TO 299 MILES......	100	100.0	14.6	84.6	.4	-	-	-	.4
300 TO 499 MILES......	80	100.0	44.8	48.4	6.8	-	-	-	-
500 TO 999 MILES....	115	100.0	9.3	83.0	7.8	-	-	-	-
1000 TO 1499 MILES....	43	100.0	8.6	91.4	-	-	-	-	-
1500 MILES OR OVER....	41	100.0	5.6	94.1	.2	-	-	-	-
EAST NORTH CENTRAL......	1 196	100.0	11.7	80.9	7.4	-	-	-	.1
UNDER 100 MILES.......	59	100.0	6.4	54.2	39.4	-	-	.1	-
100 TO 199 MILES......	84	100.0	2.7	90.4	6.8	-	-	-	-
200 TO 299 MILES......	155	100.0	14.4	71.4	13.5	-	-	-	.7
300 TO 499 MILES......	277	100.0	7.8	83.6	8.5	-	-	-	-
500 TO 999 MILES....	425	100.0	16.5	80.2	3.2	-	-	-	-
1000 TO 1499 MILES....	64	100.0	4.1	95.6	.4	-	-	-	-
1500 MILES OR OVER....	130	100.0	12.7	87.0	.1	-	-	-	.1
WEST NORTH CENTRAL......	56	100.0	-	92.7	7.3	-	-	-	-
UNDER 100 MILES.......	2	100.0	-	80.3	19.7	-	-	-	-
100 TO 199 MILES......	2	100.0	-	89.5	10.5	-	-	-	-
200 TO 299 MILES......	4	100.0	-	100.0	-	-	-	-	-
300 TO 499 MILES......	7	100.0	-	95.4	4.6	-	-	-	-
500 TO 999 MILES....	26	100.0	-	89.0	11.0	-	-	-	-
1000 TO 1499 MILES....	11	100.0	-	99.9	.1	-	-	-	-
1500 MILES OR OVER....	-	100.0	-	100.0	-	-	-	-	-
SOUTH ATLANTIC..........	538	100.0	25.1	44.2	30.6	-	-	-	-
UNDER 100 MILES.......	50	100.0	-	59.6	40.4	-	-	-	-
100 TO 199 MILES......	40	100.0	6.7	57.8	35.4	-	-	-	-
200 TO 299 MILES......	63	100.0	6.7	61.8	31.4	-	-	-	-
300 TO 499 MILES......	177	100.0	24.0	39.5	36.5	-	-	-	-
500 TO 999 MILES....	150	100.0	34.1	39.7	26.2	-	-	-	-
1000 TO 1499 MILES....	29	100.0	50.3	40.4	9.3	-	-	-	-
1500 MILES OR OVER....	26	100.0	74.5	13.6	11.9	-	-	-	-
TON-MILES OF SHIPMENTS	(millions of ton-miles)								
U.S. TOTAL.........	1 929	100.0	17.7	71.5	9.0	-	1.5	.3	-
NEW ENGLAND.............	57	100.0	12.8	86.9	.3	-	-	-	-
UNDER 100 MILES.......	3	100.0	-	98.7	1.3	-	-	-	-
100 TO 199 MILES......	8	100.0	26.4	73.4	.2	-	-	-	-
200 TO 299 MILES......	3	100.0	-	100.0	-	-	-	-	-
300 TO 499 MILES......	9	100.0	-	98.7	1.3	-	-	-	-
500 TO 999 MILES....	12	100.0	-	100.0	-	-	-	-	-
1000 TO 1499 MILES....	6	100.0	72.6	27.4	-	-	-	-	-
1500 MILES OR OVER....	13	100.0	-	100.0	-	-	-	-	-
MIDDLE ATLANTIC.........	305	100.0	10.4	86.5	3.1	-	-	-	-
UNDER 100 MILES.......	10	100.0	.3	94.2	5.5	-	-	-	-
100 TO 199 MILES......	14	100.0	.6	99.1	.3	-	-	-	-
200 TO 299 MILES......	24	100.0	13.8	85.5	.4	-	-	-	.3
300 TO 499 MILES......	29	100.0	39.4	53.0	7.6	-	-	-	-
500 TO 999 MILES....	80	100.0	8.9	83.4	7.8	-	-	-	-
1000 TO 1499 MILES....	50	100.0	8.3	91.7	-	-	-	-	-
1500 MILES OR OVER....	95	100.0	5.5	94.2	.2	-	-	-	-
EAST NORTH CENTRAL......	787	100.0	12.8	83.8	3.3	-	-	-	.1
UNDER 100 MILES.......	3	100.0	3.4	34.2	62.2	-	-	.1	-
100 TO 199 MILES......	12	100.0	2.0	91.6	6.4	-	-	-	-
200 TO 299 MILES......	38	100.0	13.6	72.7	13.0	-	-	-	.7
300 TO 499 MILES......	107	100.0	8.4	83.8	7.7	-	-	-	-
500 TO 999 MILES....	311	100.0	16.5	80.6	2.9	-	-	-	-
1000 TO 1499 MILES....	71	100.0	4.3	95.3	.4	-	-	-	-
1500 MILES OR OVER....	242	100.0	13.2	86.5	.1	-	-	-	.1
WEST NORTH CENTRAL......	38	100.0	-	94.9	5.1	-	-	-	-
UNDER 100 MILES.......	-	100.0	-	77.0	23.0	-	-	-	-
100 TO 199 MILES......	-	100.0	-	89.8	10.2	-	-	-	-
200 TO 299 MILES......	1	100.0	-	100.0	-	-	-	-	-
300 TO 499 MILES......	2	100.0	-	94.7	5.3	-	-	-	-
500 TO 999 MILES....	19	100.0	-	90.9	9.1	-	-	-	-
1000 TO 1499 MILES....	12	100.0	-	99.9	.1	-	-	-	-
1500 MILES OR OVER....	2	100.0	-	100.0	-	-	-	-	-

See footnotes at end of table 4.

TABLE 1. **TCC GROUP 207**—Percent Distribution of Geographic Division of Origin and Distance Shipped, by Means of Transport: 1972—Continued

Geographic division of origin[1] and distance shipped[2]	Number	Percent distribution by means of transport							
		All means of transport	Rail	Motor carrier	Private truck	Air	Water	Other	Unknown
TON-MILES OF SHIPMENTS	(millions of ton-miles)								
SOUTH ATLANTIC	282	100.0	39.2	36.8	24.0	-	-	-	-
UNDER 100 MILES	3	100.0	-	62.7	37.3	-	-	-	-
100 TO 199 MILES	6	100.0	8.1	56.4	35.4	-	-	-	-
200 TO 299 MILES	16	100.0	7.0	61.7	31.3	-	-	-	-
300 TO 499 MILES	66	100.0	21.2	42.6	36.2	-	-	-	-
500 TO 999 MILES	98	100.0	34.1	39.0	26.9	-	-	-	-
1000 TO 1499 MILES	34	100.0	50.5	40.3	9.2	-	-	-	-
1500 MILES OR OVER	58	100.0	76.2	14.1	9.7	-	-	-	-

See footnotes at end of table 4.

TABLE 2. **TCC GROUP 207**—Percent Distribution of Geographic Division of Origin and Means of Transport, by Geographic Division of Destination: 1972

Geographic division of origin[1] and means of transport	Number	Percent distribution by division of destination									
		U.S. total	New England	Middle Atlantic	East North Central	West North Central	South Atlantic	East South Central	West South Central	Mountain	Pacific
TONS OF SHIPMENTS	(thousands of tons)										
U.S. TOTAL	3 489	100.0	8.1	18.7	17.5	7.3	14.0	5.3	10.4	3.7	15.0
RAIL	454	100.0	11.3	24.2	14.1	4.0	7.3	8.1	10.7	1.2	19.2
MOTOR CARRIER	2 562	100.0	8.7	19.1	18.6	7.6	12.5	4.1	9.8	4.6	15.0
PRIVATE TRUCK	453	100.0	.7	11.7	15.4	9.0	30.0	9.5	14.3	1.0	8.3
AIR	-	100.0	-	7.9	9.9	-	8.2	6.0	-	-	67.9
WATER	12	100.0	-	-	-	-	-	-	-	-	100.0
OTHER	5	100.0	86.5	.3	1.1	.4	.3	.1	.1	6.4	4.7
UNKNOWN	1	100.0	-	26.2	63.1	-	-	-	-	-	10.7
NEW ENGLAND	211	100.0	45.8	35.2	3.8	2.6	8.9	-	3.1	-	.5
RAIL	16	100.0	-	75.2	-	24.8	-	-	-	-	-
MOTOR CARRIER	193	100.0	49.1	32.2	4.1	.8	9.8	-	3.4	-	.6
PRIVATE TRUCK	2	100.0	100.0	-	-	-	-	-	-	-	-
AIR	-	100.0	-	-	-	-	-	-	-	-	-
WATER	-	100.0	-	-	-	-	-	-	-	-	-
OTHER	-	100.0	-	-	-	-	-	-	-	-	-
UNKNOWN	-	100.0	-	-	-	-	-	-	-	-	-
MIDDLE ATLANTIC	665	100.0	19.4	36.2	16.4	3.6	13.9	1.6	2.4	1.6	4.7
RAIL	69	100.0	47.8	15.9	15.0	9.1	6.0	1.9	1.0	.9	2.4
MOTOR CARRIER	563	100.0	17.0	37.8	16.0	3.1	14.9	1.4	2.7	1.8	5.3
PRIVATE TRUCK	32	100.0	1.5	50.8	27.2	1.1	14.1	5.0	-	.2	.1
AIR	-	100.0	-	-	-	-	-	-	-	-	-
WATER	-	100.0	-	-	-	-	-	-	-	-	-
OTHER	-	100.0	-	38.8	-	-	-	-	-	61.2	-
UNKNOWN	-	100.0	-	100.0	-	-	-	-	-	-	-
EAST NORTH CENTRAL	1 196	100.0	2.6	14.1	25.0	12.3	13.2	5.9	13.0	3.1	10.9
RAIL	139	100.0	8.0	32.5	14.8	3.5	8.5	7.4	13.1	.3	11.9
MOTOR CARRIER	967	100.0	2.0	12.3	24.0	13.1	14.3	4.7	14.2	3.7	11.7
PRIVATE TRUCK	87	100.0	.2	5.0	51.2	17.7	8.8	16.3	-	.6	.2
AIR	-	100.0	-	-	-	-	-	-	-	-	-
WATER	-	100.0	-	-	-	-	-	-	-	-	-
OTHER	-	100.0	-	12.4	56.6	18.1	1.0	3.1	3.1	-	5.7
UNKNOWN	1	100.0	-	4.8	81.4	-	-	-	-	-	13.8
WEST NORTH CENTRAL	56	100.0	10.4	8.9	35.3	14.6	13.3	5.5	6.6	2.9	2.5
RAIL	-	100.0	-	-	-	-	-	-	-	-	-
MOTOR CARRIER	52	100.0	11.2	9.6	32.4	14.3	14.3	6.0	7.1	2.4	2.7
PRIVATE TRUCK	4	100.0	-	-	72.9	17.9	.2	-	.2	8.8	-
AIR	-	100.0	-	-	-	-	-	-	-	-	-
WATER	-	100.0	-	-	-	-	-	-	-	-	-
OTHER	-	100.0	-	-	-	-	-	66.7	-	-	33.3
UNKNOWN	-	100.0	-	-	-	-	-	-	-	-	-
SOUTH ATLANTIC	538	100.0	2.7	27.8	20.8	1.7	27.5	6.7	7.8	1.5	3.6
RAIL	135	100.0	5.2	29.4	20.6	2.3	12.6	4.6	10.9	3.0	11.4
MOTOR CARRIER	238	100.0	2.9	32.6	29.7	.8	22.7	5.9	3.6	.3	1.4
PRIVATE TRUCK	164	100.0	.2	19.6	8.0	2.4	46.5	9.6	11.1	2.1	.5
AIR	-	100.0	-	-	-	-	-	-	-	-	-
WATER	-	100.0	-	-	-	-	-	-	-	-	-
OTHER	-	100.0	-	-	-	-	100.0	-	-	-	-
UNKNOWN	-	100.0	-	-	-	-	-	-	-	-	-

See footnotes at end of table 4.

TABLE 2. **TCC GROUP 207—Percent Distribution of Geographic Division of Origin and Means of Transport, by Geographic Division of Destination: 1972**—Continued

Geographic division of origin[1] and means of transport	Number	Percent distribution by division of destination									
		U.S. total	New England	Middle Atlantic	East North Central	West North Central	South Atlantic	East South Central	West South Central	Mountain	Pacific
TON-MILES OF SHIPMENTS	(millions of ton-miles)										
U.S. TOTAL.............	1 929	100.0	3.8	11.7	12.9	6.1	13.4	4.5	11.4	6.3	29.9
RAIL.................	340	100.0	6.7	13.2	9.5	4.7	5.2	7.1	10.7	2.4	40.4
MOTOR CARRIER.........	1 379	100.0	3.3	11.8	14.1	6.2	13.6	3.5	11.4	7.7	28.4
PRIVATE TRUCK.........	174	100.0	.5	10.0	12.9	9.4	30.5	8.0	15.1	3.8	9.9
AIR..................	-	100.0	-	4.3	4.6	-	3.0	1.8	-	-	86.4
WATER...............	28	100.0	-	-	-	-	-	-	-	-	100.0
OTHER...............	5	100.0	94.1	.1	.1	-	.1	.1	.1	4.5	1.0
UNKNOWN.............	-	100.0	-	14.8	39.1	-	-	-	-	-	46.1
NEW ENGLAND...........	57	100.0	6.9	30.5	10.1	11.6	18.1	-	17.6	-	5.2
RAIL................	7	100.0	-	31.4	-	68.6	-	-	-	-	-
MOTOR CARRIER.........	49	100.0	7.6	30.5	11.7	3.2	20.9	-	20.2	-	5.9
PRIVATE TRUCK.........	-	100.0	100.0	-	-	-	-	-	-	-	-
AIR..................	-	100.0	-	-	-	-	-	-	-	-	-
WATER...............	-	100.0	-	-	-	-	-	-	-	-	-
OTHER...............	-	100.0	-	-	-	-	-	-	-	-	-
UNKNOWN.............	-	100.0	-	-	-	-	-	-	-	-	-
MIDDLE ATLANTIC.........	305	100.0	7.4	9.4	18.7	7.5	16.4	2.7	6.8	6.0	25.1
RAIL................	31	100.0	31.7	7.1	13.5	18.8	7.4	2.4	2.8	3.7	12.6
MOTOR CARRIER.........	264	100.0	4.7	9.8	18.2	6.3	17.1	2.4	7.6	6.5	27.5
PRIVATE TRUCK.........	9	100.0	1.0	5.9	49.9	3.8	27.1	9.9	-	1.2	1.2
AIR..................	-	100.0	-	-	-	-	-	-	-	-	-
WATER...............	-	100.0	-	-	-	-	-	-	-	-	-
OTHER...............	-	100.0	-	.9	-	-	-	-	-	99.1	-
UNKNOWN.............	-	100.0	-	100.0	-	-	-	-	-	-	-
EAST NORTH CENTRAL......	787	100.0	3.4	14.0	8.2	7.0	14.4	3.4	13.6	5.2	30.8
RAIL................	101	100.0	9.3	25.5	3.8	2.0	7.3	4.8	15.4	.4	31.6
MOTOR CARRIER.........	660	100.0	2.6	12.3	8.0	7.3	15.3	2.7	13.8	6.1	31.8
PRIVATE TRUCK.........	25	100.0	.6	10.6	29.9	19.5	19.2	17.0	-	2.2	1.0
AIR..................	-	100.0	-	-	-	-	-	-	-	-	-
WATER...............	-	100.0	-	-	-	-	-	-	-	-	-
OTHER...............	-	100.0	-	19.1	16.3	7.8	2.3	4.7	12.3	-	37.4
UNKNOWN.............	-	100.0	-	3.4	44.3	-	-	-	-	-	52.2
WEST NORTH CENTRAL......	38	100.0	16.1	12.7	25.2	4.4	18.4	5.4	6.6	3.4	7.8
RAIL................	-	100.0	-	-	-	-	-	-	-	-	-
MOTOR CARRIER.........	36	100.0	16.9	13.4	21.9	4.4	19.4	5.7	6.9	3.2	8.2
PRIVATE TRUCK.........	1	100.0	-	-	87.6	3.3	.4	-	.2	8.4	-
AIR..................	-	100.0	-	-	-	-	-	-	-	-	-
WATER...............	-	100.0	-	-	-	-	-	-	-	-	-
OTHER...............	-	100.0	-	-	-	-	-	54.0	-	-	46.0
UNKNOWN.............	-	100.0	-	-	-	-	-	-	-	-	-
SOUTH ATLANTIC.........	282	100.0	3.2	16.8	22.7	2.7	12.8	6.2	14.3	4.6	16.7
RAIL................	110	100.0	3.1	10.7	17.2	2.7	7.2	3.5	15.6	5.8	34.2
MOTOR CARRIER.........	104	100.0	4.9	20.7	35.3	1.7	11.2	8.0	9.7	.9	7.5
PRIVATE TRUCK.........	67	100.0	.6	20.6	12.2	4.3	24.4	8.1	19.1	8.3	2.3
AIR..................	-	100.0	-	-	-	-	-	-	-	-	-
WATER...............	-	100.0	-	-	-	-	-	-	-	-	-
OTHER...............	-	100.0	-	-	-	-	100.0	-	-	-	-
UNKNOWN.............	-	100.0	-	-	-	-	-	-	-	-	-

See footnotes at end of table 4.

TABLE 3. **TCC GROUP 207**—Percent Distribution of Geographic Division of Destination and Means of Transport, by Geographic Division of Origin: 1972

Geographic division of destination and means of transport	Number	Percent distribution by division of origin[1]									
		U.S. total	New England	Middle Atlantic	East North Central	West North Central	South Atlantic	East South Central	West South Central	Mountain	Pacific
TONS OF SHIPMENTS	(thousands of tons)										
U.S. TOTAL.............	3 489	100.0	6.1	19.1	34.3	1.6	15.4	(D)	(D)	-	(D)
RAIL..................	454	100.0	3.6	15.3	30.7	-	29.8	(D)	(D)	-	(D)
MOTOR CARRIER.........	2 562	100.0	7.5	22.0	37.8	2.0	9.3	(D)	(D)	-	(D)
PRIVATE TRUCK.........	453	100.0	.5	7.2	19.4	.9	36.3	(D)	(D)	-	(D)
AIR...................	-	100.0	-	-	-	-	-	(D)	(D)	-	(D)
WATER.................	12	100.0	-	-	-	-	-	(D)	(D)	-	(D)
OTHER.................	5	100.0	-	.2	2.0	.1	.3	(D)	(D)	-	(D)
UNKNOWN...............	1	100.0	-	22.5	77.5	-	-	(D)	(D)	-	(D)
NEW ENGLAND...........	282	100.0	34.4	45.9	10.9	2.1	5.1	(D)	(D)	-	(D)
RAIL..................	51	100.0	-	64.6	21.7	-	13.7	(D)	(D)	-	(D)
MOTOR CARRIER.........	222	100.0	42.6	43.0	8.7	2.6	3.1	(D)	(D)	-	(D)
PRIVATE TRUCK.........	3	100.0	66.8	15.6	5.5	-	12.1	(D)	(D)	-	(D)
AIR...................	-	100.0	-	-	-	-	-	(D)	(D)	-	(D)
WATER.................	-	100.0	-	-	-	-	-	(D)	(D)	-	(D)
OTHER.................	4	100.0	-	-	-	-	-	(D)	(D)	-	(D)
UNKNOWN...............	-	100.0	-	-	-	-	-	(D)	(D)	-	(D)
MIDDLE ATLANTIC.......	652	100.0	11.4	36.9	25.8	.8	22.9	(D)	(D)	-	(D)
RAIL..................	109	100.0	11.2	10.1	41.4	-	36.2	(D)	(D)	-	(D)
MOTOR CARRIER.........	489	100.0	12.7	43.5	24.2	1.0	15.9	(D)	(D)	-	(D)
PRIVATE TRUCK.........	53	100.0	-	31.1	8.2	-	60.7	(D)	(D)	-	(D)
AIR...................	-	100.0	-	-	-	-	-	(D)	(D)	-	(D)
WATER.................	-	100.0	-	-	-	-	-	(D)	(D)	-	(D)
OTHER.................	-	100.0	-	26.9	73.1	-	-	(D)	(D)	-	(D)
UNKNOWN...............	-	100.0	-	85.8	14.2	-	-	(D)	(D)	-	(D)
EAST NORTH CENTRAL....	612	100.0	1.3	17.9	48.8	3.2	18.3	(D)	(D)	-	(D)
RAIL..................	63	100.0	-	16.4	32.2	-	43.5	(D)	(D)	-	(D)
MOTOR CARRIER.........	477	100.0	1.7	18.9	48.6	3.5	14.8	(D)	(D)	-	(D)
PRIVATE TRUCK.........	70	100.0	-	12.6	64.3	4.2	18.8	(D)	(D)	-	(D)
AIR...................	-	100.0	-	-	-	-	-	(D)	(D)	-	(D)
WATER.................	-	100.0	-	-	-	-	-	(D)	(D)	-	(D)
OTHER.................	-	100.0	-	-	100.0	-	-	(D)	(D)	-	(D)
UNKNOWN...............	1	100.0	-	-	100.0	-	-	(D)	(D)	-	(D)
WEST NORTH CENTRAL....	253	100.0	2.2	9.5	58.0	3.2	3.5	(D)	(D)	-	(D)
RAIL..................	18	100.0	22.0	34.3	26.9	-	16.8	(D)	(D)	-	(D)
MOTOR CARRIER.........	194	100.0	.8	9.0	65.2	3.8	1.0	(D)	(D)	-	(D)
PRIVATE TRUCK.........	40	100.0	-	.9	38.1	1.8	9.5	(D)	(D)	-	(D)
AIR...................	-	100.0	-	-	-	-	-	(D)	(D)	-	(D)
WATER.................	-	100.0	-	-	-	-	-	(D)	(D)	-	(D)
OTHER.................	-	100.0	-	-	100.0	-	-	(D)	(D)	-	(D)
UNKNOWN...............	-	100.0	-	-	-	-	-	(D)	(D)	-	(D)
SOUTH ATLANTIC........	488	100.0	3.9	19.0	32.4	1.5	30.2	(D)	(D)	-	(D)
RAIL..................	32	100.0	-	12.6	35.8	-	51.7	(D)	(D)	-	(D)
MOTOR CARRIER.........	319	100.0	5.9	26.3	43.3	2.3	16.9	(D)	(D)	-	(D)
PRIVATE TRUCK.........	136	100.0	-	3.4	5.7	-	56.3	(D)	(D)	-	(D)
AIR...................	-	100.0	-	-	-	-	-	(D)	(D)	-	(D)
WATER.................	-	100.0	-	-	-	-	-	(D)	(D)	-	(D)
OTHER.................	-	100.0	-	-	6.9	-	93.1	(D)	(D)	-	(D)
UNKNOWN...............	-	100.0	-	-	-	-	-	(D)	(D)	-	(D)
EAST SOUTH CENTRAL....	184	100.0	-	6.0	38.2	1.7	19.6	(D)	(D)	-	(D)
RAIL..................	36	100.0	-	3.6	28.1	-	17.0	(D)	(D)	-	(D)
MOTOR CARRIER.........	104	100.0	-	7.7	43.8	3.0	13.5	(D)	(D)	-	(D)
PRIVATE TRUCK.........	43	100.0	-	3.7	33.3	-	36.7	(D)	(D)	-	(D)
AIR...................	-	100.0	-	-	-	-	-	(D)	(D)	-	(D)
WATER.................	-	100.0	-	-	-	-	-	(D)	(D)	-	(D)
OTHER.................	-	100.0	-	-	60.7	39.3	-	(D)	(D)	-	(D)
UNKNOWN...............	-	100.0	-	-	-	-	-	(D)	(D)	-	(D)
WEST SOUTH CENTRAL....	364	100.0	1.8	4.4	42.6	1.0	11.4	(D)	(D)	-	(D)
RAIL..................	48	100.0	-	1.4	37.5	-	30.3	(D)	(D)	-	(D)
MOTOR CARRIER.........	250	100.0	2.6	6.1	54.6	1.5	3.5	(D)	(D)	-	(D)
PRIVATE TRUCK.........	64	100.0	-	-	-	-	28.2	(D)	(D)	-	(D)
AIR...................	-	100.0	-	-	-	-	-	(D)	(D)	-	(D)
WATER.................	-	100.0	-	-	-	-	-	(D)	(D)	-	(D)
OTHER.................	-	100.0	-	-	100.0	-	-	(D)	(D)	-	(D)
UNKNOWN...............	-	100.0	-	-	-	-	-	(D)	(D)	-	(D)
MOUNTAIN..............	129	100.0	-	8.3	28.7	1.3	6.4	(D)	(D)	-	(D)
RAIL..................	5	100.0	-	11.1	8.2	-	74.6	(D)	(D)	-	(D)
MOTOR CARRIER.........	118	100.0	-	8.5	30.4	1.1	.6	(D)	(D)	-	(D)
PRIVATE TRUCK.........	4	100.0	-	1.2	11.3	7.9	77.2	(D)	(D)	-	(D)
AIR...................	-	100.0	-	-	-	-	-	(D)	(D)	-	(D)
WATER.................	-	100.0	-	-	-	-	-	(D)	(D)	-	(D)
OTHER.................	-	100.0	-	2.2	-	-	-	(D)	(D)	-	(D)
UNKNOWN...............	-	100.0	-	-	-	-	-	(D)	(D)	-	(D)
PACIFIC...............	522	100.0	.2	6.0	25.0	.3	3.8	(D)	(D)	-	(D)
RAIL..................	87	100.0	-	1.9	19.1	-	17.7	(D)	(D)	-	(D)
MOTOR CARRIER.........	384	100.0	.3	7.7	29.5	.4	.9	(D)	(D)	-	(D)
PRIVATE TRUCK.........	37	100.0	-	.1	.4	-	2.1	(D)	(D)	-	(D)
AIR...................	-	100.0	-	-	-	-	-	(D)	(D)	-	(D)
WATER.................	12	100.0	-	-	-	-	-	(D)	(D)	-	(D)
OTHER.................	-	100.0	-	-	2.4	.4	-	(D)	(D)	-	(D)
UNKNOWN...............	-	100.0	-	-	100.0	-	-	(D)	(D)	-	(D)

See footnotes at end of table 4.

TABLE 3. TCC GROUP 207—Percent Distribution of Geographic Division of Destination and Means of Transport, by Geographic Division of Origin: 1972—Continued

Geographic division of destination and means of transport	Number	Percent distribution by division of origin[1]									
		U.S. total	New England	Middle Atlantic	East North Central	West North Central	South Atlantic	East South Central	West South Central	Mountain	Pacific
TON-MILES OF SHIPMENTS	(millions of ton-miles)										
U.S. TOTAL	1 929	100.0	3.0	15.9	40.8	2.0	14.7	(D)	(D)	-	(D)
RAIL	340	100.0	2.2	9.3	29.7	-	32.5	(D)	(D)	-	(D)
MOTOR CARRIER	1 379	100.0	3.6	19.2	47.8	2.6	7.6	(D)	(D)	-	(D)
PRIVATE TRUCK	174	100.0	.1	5.4	14.8	1.1	39.0	(D)	(D)	-	(D)
AIR	-	100.0	-	-	-	-	-	(D)	(D)	-	(D)
WATER	28	100.0	-	-	-	-	-	(D)	(D)	-	(D)
OTHER	5	100.0	-	.3	.6	.1	-	(D)	(D)	-	(D)
UNKNOWN	-	100.0	-	11.7	88.3	-	-	(D)	(D)	-	(D)
NEW ENGLAND	73	100.0	5.4	30.6	36.6	8.4	12.2	(D)	(D)	-	(D)
RAIL	22	100.0	-	44.1	40.9	-	15.0	(D)	(D)	-	(D)
MOTOR CARRIER	45	100.0	8.5	27.4	38.7	13.7	11.4	(D)	(D)	-	(D)
PRIVATE TRUCK	-	100.0	21.9	11.2	18.0	-	48.9	(D)	(D)	-	(D)
AIR	-	100.0	-	-	-	-	-	(D)	(D)	-	(D)
WATER	-	100.0	-	-	-	-	-	(D)	(D)	-	(D)
OTHER	4	100.0	-	-	-	-	-	(D)	(D)	-	(D)
UNKNOWN	-	100.0	-	-	-	-	-	(D)	(D)	-	(D)
MIDDLE ATLANTIC	225	100.0	7.8	12.8	48.9	2.2	21.1	(D)	(D)	-	(D)
RAIL	45	100.0	5.1	5.0	57.2	-	26.2	(D)	(D)	-	(D)
MOTOR CARRIER	162	100.0	9.4	16.0	50.1	3.0	13.3	(D)	(D)	-	(D)
PRIVATE TRUCK	17	100.0	-	3.2	15.9	-	80.9	(D)	(D)	-	(D)
AIR	-	100.0	-	-	-	-	-	(D)	(D)	-	(D)
WATER	-	100.0	-	-	-	-	-	(D)	(D)	-	(D)
OTHER	-	100.0	-	-	2.3	97.7	-	(D)	(D)	-	(D)
UNKNOWN	-	100.0	-	79.5	20.5	-	-	(D)	(D)	-	(D)
EAST NORTH CENTRAL	248	100.0	2.3	23.0	26.0	3.9	25.8	(D)	(D)	-	(D)
RAIL	32	100.0	-	13.3	11.9	-	59.2	(D)	(D)	-	(D)
MOTOR CARRIER	193	100.0	3.0	24.8	27.3	4.1	19.0	(D)	(D)	-	(D)
PRIVATE TRUCK	22	100.0	-	21.0	34.4	7.7	37.0	(D)	(D)	-	(D)
AIR	-	100.0	-	-	-	-	-	(D)	(D)	-	(D)
WATER	-	100.0	-	-	-	-	-	(D)	(D)	-	(D)
OTHER	-	100.0	-	-	100.0	-	-	(D)	(D)	-	(D)
UNKNOWN	-	100.0	-	-	100.0	-	-	(D)	(D)	-	(D)
WEST NORTH CENTRAL	118	100.0	5.6	19.3	46.4	1.4	6.5	(D)	(D)	-	(D)
RAIL	16	100.0	31.5	37.2	12.5	-	18.8	(D)	(D)	-	(D)
MOTOR CARRIER	86	100.0	1.9	19.2	55.8	1.9	2.1	(D)	(D)	-	(D)
PRIVATE TRUCK	16	100.0	-	2.2	30.6	.4	18.0	(D)	(D)	-	(D)
AIR	-	100.0	-	-	-	-	-	(D)	(D)	-	(D)
WATER	-	100.0	-	-	-	-	-	(D)	(D)	-	(D)
OTHER	-	100.0	-	-	100.0	-	-	(D)	(D)	-	(D)
UNKNOWN	-	100.0	-	-	-	-	-	(D)	(D)	-	(D)
SOUTH ATLANTIC	258	100.0	4.0	19.4	44.0	2.7	14.0	(D)	(D)	-	(D)
RAIL	17	100.0	-	13.3	41.6	-	45.2	(D)	(D)	-	(D)
MOTOR CARRIER	187	100.0	5.6	24.1	54.1	3.8	6.2	(D)	(D)	-	(D)
PRIVATE TRUCK	53	100.0	-	4.8	9.3	-	31.2	(D)	(D)	-	(D)
AIR	-	100.0	-	-	-	-	-	(D)	(D)	-	(D)
WATER	-	100.0	-	-	-	-	-	(D)	(D)	-	(D)
OTHER	-	100.0	-	-	24.0	-	76.0	(D)	(D)	-	(D)
UNKNOWN	-	100.0	-	-	-	-	-	(D)	(D)	-	(D)
EAST SOUTH CENTRAL	86	100.0	-	9.5	31.4	2.4	20.5	(D)	(D)	-	(D)
RAIL	24	100.0	-	3.2	19.9	-	15.8	(D)	(D)	-	(D)
MOTOR CARRIER	48	100.0	-	13.4	37.2	4.3	17.2	(D)	(D)	-	(D)
PRIVATE TRUCK	13	100.0	-	6.7	31.5	-	39.7	(D)	(D)	-	(D)
AIR	-	100.0	-	-	-	-	-	(D)	(D)	-	(D)
WATER	-	100.0	-	-	-	-	-	(D)	(D)	-	(D)
OTHER	-	100.0	-	-	47.2	52.8	-	(D)	(D)	-	(D)
UNKNOWN	-	100.0	-	-	-	-	-	(D)	(D)	-	(D)
WEST SOUTH CENTRAL	220	100.0	4.6	9.5	48.4	1.2	18.3	(D)	(D)	-	(D)
RAIL	36	100.0	-	2.5	42.9	-	47.5	(D)	(D)	-	(D)
MOTOR CARRIER	157	100.0	6.4	12.7	57.7	1.6	6.4	(D)	(D)	-	(D)
PRIVATE TRUCK	26	100.0	-	-	-	-	49.3	(D)	(D)	-	(D)
AIR	-	100.0	-	-	-	-	-	(D)	(D)	-	(D)
WATER	-	100.0	-	-	-	-	-	(D)	(D)	-	(D)
OTHER	-	100.0	-	-	100.0	-	-	(D)	(D)	-	(D)
UNKNOWN	-	100.0	-	-	-	-	-	(D)	(D)	-	(D)
MOUNTAIN	121	100.0	-	15.2	33.7	1.1	10.6	(D)	(D)	-	(D)
RAIL	8	100.0	-	14.3	4.9	-	77.1	(D)	(D)	-	(D)
MOTOR CARRIER	106	100.0	-	16.1	37.5	1.1	.9	(D)	(D)	-	(D)
PRIVATE TRUCK	6	100.0	-	1.8	8.8	2.5	85.9	(D)	(D)	-	(D)
AIR	-	100.0	-	-	-	-	-	(D)	(D)	-	(D)
WATER	-	100.0	-	-	-	-	-	(D)	(D)	-	(D)
OTHER	-	100.0	-	6.5	-	-	-	(D)	(D)	-	(D)
UNKNOWN	-	100.0	-	-	-	-	-	(D)	(D)	-	(D)
PACIFIC	576	100.0	.5	13.3	42.1	.5	8.2	(D)	(D)	-	(D)
RAIL	137	100.0	-	2.9	23.2	-	27.5	(D)	(D)	-	(D)
MOTOR CARRIER	392	100.0	.8	18.5	53.5	.8	2.0	(D)	(D)	-	(D)
PRIVATE TRUCK	17	100.0	-	.6	1.5	-	9.1	(D)	(D)	-	(D)
AIR	-	100.0	-	-	-	-	-	(D)	(D)	-	(D)
WATER	28	100.0	-	-	-	-	-	(D)	(D)	-	(D)
OTHER	-	100.0	-	-	21.1	2.5	-	(D)	(D)	-	(D)
UNKNOWN	-	100.0	-	-	100.0	-	-	(D)	(D)	-	(D)

See footnotes at end of table 4.

TABLE 4. TCC GROUP 207—Percent Distribution of Distance Shipped and Weight of Shipment, by Means of Transport: 1972

Distance shipped and weight of shipment[2][3]	Number	Percent distribution by means of transport							
		All means of transport	Rail	Motor carrier	Private truck	Air	Water	Other	Unknown
TONS OF SHIPMENTS	(thousands of tons)								
U.S. TOTAL..........	2 917	100.0	10.6	77.2	11.6	-	.4	.2	.1
UNDER 100 MILES........	444	100.0	1.7	84.4	13.9	-	-	.1	-
UNDER 1000 POUNDS.....	63	100.0	.1	82.3	17.3	-	-	.3	-
1000 TO 9999 POUNDS...	89	100.0	-	83.9	16.1	-	-	-	-
10000 TO 29999 POUNDS.	137	100.0	-	75.1	24.9	-	-	-	-
30000 TO 59999 POUNDS.	92	100.0	4.9	92.7	2.4	-	-	-	-
60000 TO 89999 POUNDS.	61	100.0	4.7	95.3	-	-	-	-	-
90000 POUNDS AND OVER.	-	100.0	-	-	-	-	-	-	-
100 TO 199 MILES........	304	100.0	5.9	80.4	13.7	-	-	-	-
UNDER 1000 POUNDS.....	51	100.0	.1	99.4	.4	-	-	.1	-
1000 TO 9999 POUNDS...	92	100.0	-	96.2	3.7	-	-	-	-
10000 TO 29999 POUNDS.	54	100.0	-	37.2	62.8	-	-	-	-
30000 TO 59999 POUNDS.	92	100.0	6.0	90.1	3.9	-	-	-	-
60000 TO 89999 POUNDS.	12	100.0	100.0	-	-	-	-	-	-
90000 POUNDS AND OVER.	-	100.0	-	-	-	-	-	-	-
200 TO 299 MILES........	339	100.0	11.3	75.1	13.1	-	-	-	.5
UNDER 1000 POUNDS.....	52	100.0	2.7	94.9	2.5	-	-	-	-
1000 TO 9999 POUNDS...	115	100.0	.2	76.4	23.3	-	-	-	-
10000 TO 29999 POUNDS.	47	100.0	-	69.0	31.0	-	-	-	-
30000 TO 59999 POUNDS.	94	100.0	8.8	88.3	1.3	-	-	-	1.6
60000 TO 89999 POUNDS.	28	100.0	100.0	-	-	-	-	-	-
90000 POUNDS AND OVER.	-	100.0	-	-	-	-	-	-	-
300 TO 499 MILES........	663	100.0	10.7	74.1	15.2	-	-	-	-
UNDER 1000 POUNDS.....	94	100.0	.1	96.8	3.0	-	-	-	.1
1000 TO 9999 POUNDS...	191	100.0	.4	82.4	17.2	-	-	-	-
10000 TO 29999 POUNDS.	147	100.0	.9	61.3	37.8	-	-	-	-
30000 TO 59999 POUNDS.	183	100.0	12.7	82.2	5.0	-	-	-	-
60000 TO 89999 POUNDS.	45	100.0	98.5	1.5	-	-	-	-	-
90000 POUNDS AND OVER.	-	100.0	-	-	-	-	-	-	-
500 TO 999 MILES........	789	100.0	14.9	74.7	10.3	-	-	-	-
UNDER 1000 POUNDS.....	128	100.0	3.7	94.1	2.1	-	-	-	-
1000 TO 9999 POUNDS...	214	100.0	5.2	68.3	26.3	-	-	.2	-
10000 TO 29999 POUNDS.	58	100.0	7.1	69.7	23.2	-	-	-	-
30000 TO 59999 POUNDS.	333	100.0	14.6	83.0	2.5	-	-	-	-
60000 TO 89999 POUNDS.	53	100.0	91.7	8.3	-	-	-	-	-
90000 POUNDS AND OVER.	-	100.0	-	-	-	-	-	-	-
1000 TO 1499 MILES......	173	100.0	14.5	82.4	.4	-	-	2.7	-
UNDER 1000 POUNDS.....	23	100.0	2.4	96.5	1.1	-	-	-	-
1000 TO 9999 POUNDS...	39	100.0	6.7	81.1	-	-	-	12.1	-
10000 TO 29999 POUNDS.	3	100.0	-	100.0	-	-	-	-	-
30000 TO 59999 POUNDS.	79	100.0	-	99.5	.5	-	-	-	-
60000 TO 89999 POUNDS.	21	100.0	100.0	-	-	-	-	-	-
90000 POUNDS AND OVER.	5	100.0	-	100.0	-	-	-	-	-
1500 MILES OR OVER......	203	100.0	14.8	75.5	3.6	-	5.9	-	.1
UNDER 1000 POUNDS.....	29	100.0	4.9	94.6	.5	-	-	-	-
1000 TO 9999 POUNDS...	53	100.0	.2	63.3	13.5	-	22.6	-	.4
10000 TO 29999 POUNDS.	36	100.0	-	100.0	-	-	-	-	-
30000 TO 59999 POUNDS.	56	100.0	3.0	97.0	-	-	-	-	-
60000 TO 89999 POUNDS.	26	100.0	100.0	-	-	-	-	-	-
90000 POUNDS AND OVER.	-	100.0	-	-	-	-	-	-	-
TON-MILES OF SHIPMENTS	(millions of ton-miles)								
U.S. TOTAL..........	1 568	100.0	13.7	76.3	7.9	-	1.8	.3	-
UNDER 100 MILES........	20	100.0	1.2	87.7	11.0	-	-	-	-
UNDER 1000 POUNDS.....	2	100.0	.1	90.3	9.4	-	-	.2	-
1000 TO 9999 POUNDS...	4	100.0	-	85.3	14.6	-	-	-	-
10000 TO 29999 POUNDS.	4	100.0	-	73.4	26.6	-	-	-	-
30000 TO 59999 POUNDS.	3	100.0	4.4	93.4	2.2	-	-	-	-
60000 TO 89999 POUNDS.	4	100.0	1.7	98.3	-	-	-	-	-
90000 POUNDS AND OVER.	-	100.0	-	-	-	-	-	-	-
100 TO 199 MILES........	47	100.0	6.5	79.0	14.4	-	-	-	-
UNDER 1000 POUNDS.....	7	100.0	.1	99.4	.4	-	-	.1	-
1000 TO 9999 POUNDS...	14	100.0	-	95.8	4.2	-	-	-	-
10000 TO 29999 POUNDS.	9	100.0	-	36.1	63.9	-	-	-	-
30000 TO 59999 POUNDS.	14	100.0	5.6	91.1	3.3	-	-	-	-
60000 TO 89999 POUNDS.	2	100.0	100.0	-	-	-	-	-	-
90000 POUNDS AND OVER.	-	100.0	-	-	-	-	-	-	-

See footnotes at end of table 4.

TABLE 4. **TCC GROUP 207**—Percent Distribution of Distance Shipped and Weight of Shipment, by Means of Transport: 1972—Continued

Distance shipped and weight of shipment[2] [3]	Number	Percent distribution by means of transport							
		All means of transport	Rail	Motor carrier	Private truck	Air	Water	Other	Unknown
TON-MILES OF SHIPMENTS	(millions of ton-miles)								
200 TO 299 MILES.........	85	100.0	10.7	75.9	12.9	-	-	-	.4
UNDER 1000 POUNDS.....	13	100.0	2.4	95.2	2.4	-	-	-	-
1000 TO 9999 POUNDS...	29	100.0	.2	77.7	22.1	-	-	-	-
10000 TO 29999 POUNDS.	12	100.0	-	69.2	30.8	-	-	-	-
30000 TO 59999 POUNDS.	23	100.0	8.2	88.9	1.2	-	-	-	1.6
60000 TO 89999 POUNDS.	6	100.0	100.0	-	-	-	-	-	-
90000 POUNDS AND OVER.	-	100.0	-	-	-	-	-	-	-
300 TO 499 MILES.........	256	100.0	9.9	75.0	15.1	-	-	-	-
UNDER 1000 POUNDS.....	37	100.0	.1	96.8	3.1	-	-	-	.1
1000 TO 9999 POUNDS...	73	100.0	.4	80.8	18.8	-	-	-	-
10000 TO 29999 POUNDS.	57	100.0	.9	64.1	35.0	-	-	-	-
30000 TO 59999 POUNDS.	71	100.0	12.0	83.1	4.9	-	-	-	-
60000 TO 89999 POUNDS.	16	100.0	98.5	1.5	-	-	-	-	-
90000 POUNDS AND OVER.	-	100.0	-	-	-	-	-	-	-
500 TO 999 MILES.........	549	100.0	14.9	75.8	9.3	-	-	-	-
UNDER 1000 POUNDS.....	91	100.0	4.0	94.0	2.0	-	-	-	-
1000 TO 9999 POUNDS...	149	100.0	6.0	69.8	24.0	-	-	.1	-
10000 TO 29999 POUNDS.	41	100.0	7.3	74.1	18.6	-	-	-	-
30000 TO 59999 POUNDS.	231	100.0	14.7	82.8	2.4	-	-	-	-
60000 TO 89999 POUNDS.	35	100.0	88.8	11.2	-	-	-	-	-
90000 POUNDS AND OVER.	-	100.0	-	-	-	-	-	-	-
1000 TO 1499 MILES......	198	100.0	14.9	82.3	.4	-	-	2.4	-
UNDER 1000 POUNDS.....	29	100.0	2.2	96.8	1.1	-	-	-	-
1000 TO 9999 POUNDS...	45	100.0	6.9	82.3	-	-	-	10.7	-
10000 TO 29999 POUNDS.	4	100.0	-	100.0	-	-	-	-	-
30000 TO 59999 POUNDS.	88	100.0	-	99.5	.5	-	-	-	-
60000 TO 89999 POUNDS.	25	100.0	100.0	-	-	-	-	-	-
90000 POUNDS AND OVER.	5	100.0	-	100.0	-	-	-	-	-
1500 MILES OR OVER......	409	100.0	15.9	73.9	3.1	-	7.1	-	.1
UNDER 1000 POUNDS.....	55	100.0	5.2	94.2	.4	-	.1	-	-
1000 TO 9999 POUNDS...	111	100.0	.1	62.5	11.2	-	25.8	-	.3
10000 TO 29999 POUNDS.	69	100.0	-	100.0	-	-	-	-	-
30000 TO 59999 POUNDS.	113	100.0	3.1	96.9	-	-	-	-	-
60000 TO 89999 POUNDS.	58	100.0	100.0	-	-	-	-	-	-
90000 POUNDS AND OVER.	-	100.0	-	-	-	-	-	-	-

Note: Detail may not add to total due to rounding. The introductory table shows the estimates of sampling variability for tons; sampling variability for ton-miles has not been estimated. See the map in the Introduction for the States comprising the geographic divisions of the United States.

Shipments excluded from the survey are those moving by pipeline (primarily petroleum products from refineries), parcel post shipments, and commodities moved by own power (motorized vehicles, aircraft, etc.) or towed (prefabricated buildings, etc.). Local shipments (commodities shipped less than 25 miles from the plant) and shipments within the same city are also excluded. Shipments to Alaska and Hawaii from the 48 conterminous States and the District of Columbia are included; however, no data were obtained for shipments originating in Alaska and Hawaii.

- Represents zero or rounds to zero. (D) Withheld to avoid disclosing figures for individual companies.

[1]Production of this commodity is concentrated in the geographic divisions shown; figures and distributions for geographic divisions not shown are included in the total.

[2]Distances of shipments to foreign destinations are calculated only to the U.S. port of exit.

[3]Includes only shipments represented by bills of lading and invoices. Summary records which did not show individual weights of shipments are not included.

TCC 208. Beverages and Flavoring Extracts

Comparisons of Tons and Ton-Miles of Shipments for
Geographic Divisions of Origin and for Sampling Variability: 1972 and 1967

Geographic division of origin	Estimates				Relative sampling variability in tons (percent)	
	1972		1967		1972	1967
	Tons (thousands)	Ton-miles (millions)	Tons (thousands)	Ton-miles (millions)		
U.S. total	49,527	10,658	33,118	10,799	19.2	6.2
New England	947	180	748	106	13.6	(*)
Middle Atlantic	6,052	745	6,889	1,014	11.5	(*)
East North Central	10,450	3,009	8,363	2,814	23.6	(*)
West North Central	5,593	1,803	3,443	1,263	28.2	(*)
South Atlantic	3,807	576	2,021	496	31.4	(*)
East South Central	(D)	(D)	3,003	1,391	(*)	(*)
West South Central	2,418	695	2,965	783	13.2	(*)
Mountain	(D)	(D)	1,045	539	(*)	(*)
Pacific	5,972	2,571	4,641	2,393	11.4	(*)

(D) Withheld to avoid disclosing figures for individual companies.   (*) Data not published.

TABLE 1. TCC GROUP 208—Percent Distribution of Geographic Division of Origin and Distance Shipped, by Means of Transport: 1972

Geographic division of origin[1] and distance shipped[2]	Number	Percent distribution by means of transport							
		All means of transport	Rail	Motor carrier	Private truck	Air	Water	Other	Unknown
TONS OF SHIPMENTS	(thousands of tons)								
U.S. TOTAL............	49 527	100.0	15.3	19.7	64.6	-	.1	-	.2
NEW ENGLAND...............	947	100.0	6.1	48.2	45.7	-	-	-	-
UNDER 100 MILES........	590	100.0	-	45.9	54.1	-	-	-	-
100 TO 199 MILES......	145	100.0	3.2	44.8	52.1	-	-	-	-
200 TO 299 MILES......	55	100.0	-	49.0	51.0	-	-	-	-
300 TO 499 MILES......	48	100.0	-	81.0	19.0	-	-	-	-
500 TO 999 MILES......	72	100.0	53.6	46.4	-	-	-	-	-
1000 TO 1499 MILES....	27	100.0	35.1	64.9	-	-	-	-	-
1500 MILES OR OVER....	6	100.0	70.6	29.4	-	-	-	-	-
MIDDLE ATLANTIC.........	6 052	100.0	2.3	27.0	70.1	-	.5	.1	-
UNDER 100 MILES........	3 674	100.0	.1	19.1	80.7	-	.1	-	-
100 TO 199 MILES......	1 508	100.0	3.7	31.3	64.3	-	.1	-	-
200 TO 299 MILES......	527	100.0	3.4	51.5	45.1	-	.1	.4	.2
300 TO 499 MILES......	183	100.0	8.3	58.9	32.8	-	-	-	-
500 TO 999 MILES......	83	100.0	28.8	67.7	2.3	-	-	-	-
1000 TO 1499 MILES....	47	100.0	18.8	42.5	6.0	-	1.0	.1	.1
1500 MILES OR OVER....	27	100.0	52.4	15.6	9.6	-	32.7	-	-
							22.0	.4	
EAST NORTH CENTRAL......	10 450	100.0	21.9	32.1	45.8	-	-	-	-
UNDER 100 MILES........	2 253	100.0	1.3	21.6	77.1	-	-	-	.1
100 TO 199 MILES......	3 214	100.0	2.7	43.6	53.7	-	-	-	-
200 TO 299 MILES......	1 991	100.0	10.8	47.1	41.8	-	-	-	-
300 TO 499 MILES......	1 144	100.0	41.7	27.0	31.2	-	-	-	.2
500 TO 999 MILES......	1 633	100.0	80.8	11.7	7.4	-	-	-	.1
1000 TO 1499 MILES....	84	100.0	73.0	18.8	8.2	-	-	-	.1
1500 MILES OR OVER....	129	100.0	78.4	12.8	8.4	-	.3	-	-
WEST NORTH CENTRAL......	5 593	100.0	29.4	18.0	52.2	-	-	-	-
UNDER 100 MILES........	1 214	100.0	13.3	10.8	75.8	-	-	-	.4
100 TO 199 MILES......	1 098	100.0	7.8	21.7	70.5	-	-	-	-
200 TO 299 MILES......	1 222	100.0	14.9	24.4	59.1	-	-	-	-
300 TO 499 MILES......	1 051	100.0	37.2	22.2	40.6	-	-	-	1.7
500 TO 999 MILES......	772	100.0	78.0	12.7	9.3	-	-	-	-
1000 TO 1499 MILES....	174	100.0	92.9	3.9	3.1	-	-	-	-
1500 MILES OR OVER....	57	100.0	100.0	-	-	-	-	-	-
SOUTH ATLANTIC..........	3 807	100.0	14.9	12.3	71.0	-	.1	-	1.7
UNDER 100 MILES........	2 033	100.0	3.2	6.7	87.0	-	.1	-	3.2
100 TO 199 MILES......	685	100.0	21.1	20.1	58.7	-	-	-	.1
200 TO 299 MILES......	760	100.0	19.1	16.0	64.9	-	-	-	-
300 TO 499 MILES......	169	100.0	55.6	32.8	11.6	-	-	-	-
500 TO 999 MILES......	132	100.0	76.8	12.9	7.6	-	2.7	-	-
1000 TO 1499 MILES....	9	100.0	92.3	4.0	3.7	-	-	-	-
1500 MILES OR OVER....	16	100.0	44.0	3.4	51.2	-	1.4	-	-
WEST SOUTH CENTRAL......	2 418	100.0	45.8	8.4	45.5	-	-	-	.2
UNDER 100 MILES........	476	100.0	11.4	11.9	76.7	-	-	-	.7
100 TO 199 MILES......	675	100.0	42.5	11.0	45.7	-	-	-	-
200 TO 299 MILES......	514	100.0	47.9	10.7	41.4	-	-	-	-
300 TO 499 MILES......	387	100.0	50.8	3.3	45.7	-	-	-	-
500 TO 999 MILES......	291	100.0	86.6	.8	12.6	-	.2	-	-
1000 TO 1499 MILES....	71	100.0	94.9	3.2	1.2	-	-	-	.7
1500 MILES OR OVER....	1	100.0	99.4	.6	-	-	-	-	-
PACIFIC.................	5 972	100.0	18.2	40.9	39.9	-	.7	-	.3
UNDER 100 MILES........	2 734	100.0	.6	41.3	57.8	-	.7	.1	.1
100 TO 199 MILES......	781	100.0	.6	62.1	37.0	-	.2	-	.2
200 TO 299 MILES......	432	100.0	2.7	60.7	36.1	-	-	-	.5
300 TO 499 MILES......	751	100.0	15.4	52.8	31.8	-	-	-	-
500 TO 999 MILES......	500	100.0	52.8	25.7	20.8	-	-	-	.2
1000 TO 1499 MILES....	74	100.0	88.5	1.5	9.9	-	-	.6	1.8
1500 MILES OR OVER....	697	100.0	86.7	5.8	.9	.1	4.7	-	
TON-MILES OF SHIPMENTS	(millions of ton-miles)								
U.S. TOTAL............	10 658	100.0	48.6	19.8	30.0	-	1.2	-	.3
NEW ENGLAND...............	180	100.0	28.9	51.2	19.9	-	-	-	-
UNDER 100 MILES........	26	100.0	-	48.0	52.0	-	-	-	-
100 TO 199 MILES......	21	100.0	3.2	44.3	52.5	-	-	-	-
200 TO 299 MILES......	13	100.0	-	47.6	52.4	-	-	-	-
300 TO 499 MILES......	17	100.0	-	79.7	20.3	-	-	-	-
500 TO 999 MILES......	53	100.0	54.6	45.4	-	-	-	-	-
1000 TO 1499 MILES....	32	100.0	34.8	65.2	-	-	-	-	-
1500 MILES OR OVER....	15	100.0	70.6	29.4	-	-	-	-	-
MIDDLE ATLANTIC.........	745	100.0	10.8	38.5	45.7	-	4.8	.1	.1
UNDER 100 MILES........	156	100.0	.1	25.0	74.8	-	-	-	-
100 TO 199 MILES......	216	100.0	3.8	33.5	62.1	-	.1	.3	.2
200 TO 299 MILES......	128	100.0	3.5	51.0	45.5	-	-	-	-
300 TO 499 MILES......	67	100.0	9.3	60.6	30.1	-	-	-	-
500 TO 999 MILES......	58	100.0	30.4	65.5	2.6	-	1.4	-	-
1000 TO 1499 MILES....	54	100.0	17.2	41.7	6.3	-	34.8	.1	.1
1500 MILES OR OVER....	62	100.0	54.1	11.7	8.5	-	25.3	.4	-

See footnotes at end of table 4.

TABLE 1. TCC GROUP 208—Percent Distribution of Geographic Division of Origin and Distance Shipped, by Means of Transport: 1972—Continued

Geographic division of origin[1] and distance shipped[2]	Number (millions of ton-miles)	All means of transport	Rail	Motor carrier	Private truck	Air	Water	Other	Unknown
TON-MILES OF SHIPMENTS									
EAST NORTH CENTRAL......	3 009	100.0	48.2	24.9	26.7	-	.1	-	.1
UNDER 100 MILES.......	133	100.0	2.0	19.2	78.8	-	-	-	-
100 TO 199 MILES......	485	100.0	2.7	45.4	51.9	-	-	-	.3
200 TO 299 MILES......	474	100.0	11.5	45.3	43.0	-	-	-	.1
300 TO 499 MILES......	442	100.0	43.6	26.7	29.7	-	-	-	-
500 TO 999 MILES......	1 138	100.0	81.9	10.6	7.4	-	-	-	-
1000 TO 1499 MILES....	92	100.0	73.2	18.8	8.0	-	.8	-	-
1500 MILES OR OVER....	241	100.0	77.6	13.3	8.4	-	-	-	.3
WEST NORTH CENTRAL......	1 803	100.0	52.9	15.6	31.2	-	-	-	-
UNDER 100 MILES.......	57	100.0	6.7	14.7	78.5	-	-	-	-
100 TO 199 MILES......	168	100.0	7.8	20.3	71.9	-	-	-	1.9
200 TO 299 MILES......	298	100.0	15.0	24.3	58.8	-	-	-	-
300 TO 499 MILES......	405	100.0	37.8	23.0	39.2	-	-	-	-
500 TO 999 MILES......	559	100.0	78.9	11.3	9.8	-	-	-	-
1000 TO 1499 MILES....	216	100.0	92.8	4.3	3.0	-	-	-	-
1500 MILES OR OVER....	97	100.0	100.0	-	-	-	-	-	.6
SOUTH ATLANTIC..........	576	100.0	33.4	16.6	48.8	-	.7	-	3.2
UNDER 100 MILES.......	100	100.0	4.6	7.7	84.5	-	-	-	.1
100 TO 199 MILES......	102	100.0	23.7	21.7	54.5	-	-	-	-
200 TO 299 MILES......	173	100.0	19.3	18.6	62.1	-	-	-	-
300 TO 499 MILES......	63	100.0	56.7	32.2	11.2	-	-	-	-
500 TO 999 MILES......	90	100.0	75.5	12.4	8.9	-	3.3	-	-
1000 TO 1499 MILES....	10	100.0	92.5	3.7	3.8	-	-	-	-
1500 MILES OR OVER....	35	100.0	45.7	3.6	47.5	-	3.2	-	-
WEST SOUTH CENTRAL......	695	100.0	64.7	5.6	29.5	-	.1	-	.2
UNDER 100 MILES.......	26	100.0	13.4	16.7	69.9	-	-	-	.6
100 TO 199 MILES......	106	100.0	42.6	11.3	45.5	-	-	-	-
200 TO 299 MILES......	125	100.0	47.5	11.0	41.5	-	-	-	-
300 TO 499 MILES......	149	100.0	53.4	3.0	43.3	-	.3	-	-
500 TO 999 MILES......	201	100.0	88.7	.7	10.7	-	-	-	.7
1000 TO 1499 MILES....	84	100.0	95.0	3.2	1.0	-	-	-	-
1500 MILES OR OVER....	2	100.0	99.3	.7	-	-	-	-	-
PACIFIC.................	2 571	100.0	64.8	19.2	11.5	.1	3.3	.1	.9
UNDER 100 MILES.......	91	100.0	1.2	48.1	50.5	-	.1	-	.2
100 TO 199 MILES......	99	100.0	.7	62.5	36.5	-	-	-	.5
200 TO 299 MILES......	102	100.0	2.6	60.0	37.0	-	-	-	-
300 TO 499 MILES......	268	100.0	15.8	51.7	32.4	-	-	.1	.2
500 TO 999 MILES......	347	100.0	53.2	25.8	20.2	-	-	.6	-
1000 TO 1499 MILES....	103	100.0	89.3	1.5	9.2	-	-	-	.2
1500 MILES OR OVER....	1 558	100.0	86.2	6.1	.6	.2	5.5	-	1.4

See footnotes at end of table 4.

TABLE 2. TCC GROUP 208—Percent Distribution of Geographic Division of Origin and Means of Transport, by Geographic Division of Destination: 1972

Geographic division of origin[1] and means of transport	Number (thousands of tons)	U.S. total	New England	Middle Atlantic	East North Central	West North Central	South Atlantic	East South Central	West South Central	Mountain	Pacific
TONS OF SHIPMENTS											
U.S. TOTAL..............	49 527	100.0	3.6	13.2	15.1	8.0	10.0	13.0	5.7	21.5	9.8
RAIL.................	7 564	100.0	5.7	13.1	11.1	10.0	19.6	8.0	18.5	7.4	6.5
MOTOR CARRIER........	9 754	100.0	5.6	14.4	21.5	8.3	8.0	14.7	2.1	2.0	23.5
PRIVATE TRUCK........	32 004	100.0	2.6	12.9	14.2	7.5	8.2	13.8	3.6	31.0	6.3
AIR..................	1	100.0	-	2.7	.7	1.8	.8	-	1.7	-	92.3
WATER...............	72	100.0	-	9.5	-	-	15.5	-	16.5	-	58.5
OTHER................	9	100.0	-	1.5	.3	.1	60.4	.7	-	21.3	15.7
UNKNOWN..............	121	100.0	.5	.2	15.0	1.6	56.6	-	20.4	.8	4.9
NEW ENGLAND.............	947	100.0	72.0	13.4	4.6	.9	7.9	.5	.2	-	.6
RAIL.................	57	100.0	8.0	-	50.3	7.7	18.7	7.6	-	-	7.6
MOTOR CARRIER........	456	100.0	62.5	18.7	3.1	.8	14.1	-	.4	-	.4
PRIVATE TRUCK........	433	100.0	90.4	9.6	-	-	-	-	-	-	-
AIR..................	-	100.0	-	-	-	-	-	-	-	-	-
WATER...............	-	100.0	-	-	-	-	-	-	-	-	-
OTHER................	-	100.0	-	-	-	-	-	-	-	-	-
UNKNOWN..............	-	100.0	100.0	-	-	-	-	-	-	-	-
MIDDLE ATLANTIC.........	6 052	100.0	10.4	76.3	1.3	.4	10.7	.1	.3	.1	.3
RAIL.................	139	100.0	7.9	36.8	11.6	4.3	26.7	.1	2.3	.5	9.8
MOTOR CARRIER........	1 633	100.0	13.2	59.9	2.7	1.1	22.3	.3	.3	.2	-
PRIVATE TRUCK........	4 242	100.0	9.4	84.4	.5	-	5.5	-	-	.1	-
AIR..................	-	100.0	1.0	7.3	75.9	-	3.6	-	-	-	12.2
WATER...............	27	100.0	-	13.8	-	-	27.3	-	39.3	-	19.6
OTHER................	6	100.0	.1	2.0	-	.3	94.8	1.0	-	-	1.7
UNKNOWN..............	2	100.0	2.5	-	-	-	97.5	-	-	-	-

See footnotes at end of table 4.

TABLE 2. TCC GROUP 208—Percent Distribution of Geographic Division of Origin and Means of Transport, by Geographic Division of Destination: 1972—Continued

Geographic division of origin[1] and means of transport	Number	Percent distribution by division of destination									
		U.S. total	New England	Middle Atlantic	East North Central	West North Central	South Atlantic	East South Central	West South Central	Mountain	Pacific
TONS OF SHIPMENTS	(thousands of tons)										
EAST NORTH CENTRAL	10 450	100.0	2.1	9.0	56.1	8.1	5.2	15.3	2.3	.7	1.2
RAIL	2 293	100.0	8.0	25.4	13.4	13.4	18.9	6.8	7.7	2.3	4.1
MOTOR CARRIER	3 359	100.0	.5	3.3	47.6	7.4	2.0	37.3	.8	.5	.5
PRIVATE TRUCK	4 790	100.0	.4	5.1	82.5	6.0	1.0	3.9	.8	.1	.2
AIR	-	100.0	-	18.5	10.6	10.6	-	4.5	-	-	55.9
WATER	-	100.0	-	-	-	1.3	-	30.1	41.4	-	27.1
OTHER	-	100.0	-	-	-	-	-	-	-	-	100.0
UNKNOWN	6	100.0	-	-	86.1	13.8	-	-	-	-	-
WEST NORTH CENTRAL	5 593	100.0	1.2	3.1	19.6	52.9	3.2	9.4	4.3	4.5	1.8
RAIL	1 643	100.0	3.6	7.9	17.0	21.9	10.3	10.0	9.5	13.8	5.9
MOTOR CARRIER	1 006	100.0	.1	1.3	35.6	51.2	1.1	7.9	1.3	1.1	.4
PRIVATE TRUCK	2 922	100.0	.2	1.1	15.7	71.2	-	9.5	1.3	1.1	-
AIR	-	100.0	50.0	-	-	50.0	-	-	-	-	-
WATER	-	100.0	-	-	-	-	-	-	-	-	-
OTHER	-	100.0	-	-	-	-	-	-	-	-	-
UNKNOWN	20	100.0	-	-	-	-	4.8	-	95.2	-	-
SOUTH ATLANTIC	3 807	100.0	.8	11.4	1.5	.1	80.5	4.8	.5	-	.4
RAIL	567	100.0	1.0	3.7	2.5	.2	78.8	9.3	3.2	.3	.4
MOTOR CARRIER	468	100.0	4.8	40.8	3.3	.1	49.6	1.1	.2	-	1.0
PRIVATE TRUCK	2 702	100.0	-	8.2	1.0	-	85.7	1.1	.2	-	.1
AIR	-	100.0	-	90.4	-	-	-	4.7	-	-	.3
WATER	3	100.0	-	-	-	-	93.9	9.6	-	-	6.1
OTHER	-	100.0	-	100.0	-	-	-	-	-	-	-
UNKNOWN	65	100.0	-	-	-	-	100.0	-	-	-	-
WEST SOUTH CENTRAL	2 418	100.0	-	.2	-	.5	8.9	6.9	80.2	2.3	.9
RAIL	1 107	100.0	-	.3	-	.5	18.4	7.5	67.6	3.9	1.9
MOTOR CARRIER	203	100.0	-	.2	.2	1.1	4.0	24.2	69.8	.1	.4
PRIVATE TRUCK	1 101	100.0	-	-	-	.5	.4	3.2	94.7	1.2	-
AIR	-	100.0	-	-	-	-	-	-	-	-	-
WATER	-	100.0	-	-	-	-	-	-	-	-	-
OTHER	-	100.0	-	-	-	-	-	-	100.0	-	-
UNKNOWN	5	100.0	8.8	-	-	-	-	-	91.2	-	-
PACIFIC	5 972	100.0	2.8	2.4	3.3	.7	1.4	.3	1.1	12.4	75.4
RAIL	1 084	100.0	15.3	12.4	16.2	3.5	7.9	1.6	5.6	18.3	19.2
MOTOR CARRIER	2 443	100.0	-	.3	.4	-	-	-	-	6.4	92.7
PRIVATE TRUCK	2 381	100.0	-	-	-	.2	-	-	-	16.0	83.4
AIR	1	100.0	-	.9	-	1.8	.1	-	1.3	-	95.9
WATER	39	100.0	-	7.7	-	-	-	-	-	-	92.3
OTHER	3	100.0	-	-	-	-	-	-	-	60.0	40.0
UNKNOWN	19	100.0	-	-	64.9	-	-	-	-	4.6	30.5
TON-MILES OF SHIPMENTS	(millions of ton-miles)										
U.S. TOTAL	10 658	100.0	7.8	13.7	14.8	9.5	13.9	8.0	8.7	11.2	12.5
RAIL	5 183	100.0	12.4	16.3	10.3	5.6	18.4	5.2	11.6	8.5	11.7
MOTOR CARRIER	2 105	100.0	3.9	11.9	18.7	11.8	10.6	13.9	3.3	5.0	20.7
PRIVATE TRUCK	3 197	100.0	3.3	11.1	19.6	14.6	9.1	9.0	7.5	19.9	5.8
AIR	2	100.0	-	1.4	.2	1.3	.2	-	.9	-	96.0
WATER	128	100.0	-	5.8	-	-	7.3	-	11.7	-	75.1
OTHER	3	100.0	-	.5	.4	.2	18.6	1.6	.1	49.9	28.7
UNKNOWN	36	100.0	1.7	.2	64.2	2.0	10.4	-	17.1	2.2	2.1
NEW ENGLAND	180	100.0	24.6	13.6	17.5	5.1	26.2	2.7	1.5	.1	8.6
RAIL	52	100.0	1.3	-	43.0	10.4	14.5	9.4	-	-	21.4
MOTOR CARRIER	92	100.0	16.9	18.0	9.8	4.2	43.0	-	3.0	.2	4.8
PRIVATE TRUCK	35	100.0	78.2	21.8	-	-	-	-	-	-	-
AIR	-	100.0	-	-	-	-	-	-	-	-	-
WATER	-	100.0	-	-	-	-	-	-	-	-	-
OTHER	-	100.0	-	-	-	-	-	-	-	-	-
UNKNOWN	-	100.0	100.0	-	-	-	-	-	-	-	-
MIDDLE ATLANTIC	745	100.0	12.9	44.8	4.8	3.0	22.0	.6	3.4	1.9	6.7
RAIL	80	100.0	3.3	9.7	9.6	6.6	24.3	.1	4.3	1.4	40.7
MOTOR CARRIER	286	100.0	13.8	32.8	7.7	5.7	33.9	1.1	2.4	2.1	.4
PRIVATE TRUCK	340	100.0	15.8	68.1	1.7	.2	11.6	.4	-	2.0	.3
AIR	-	100.0	-	.6	2.4	53.5	-	2.0	.4	-	41.4
WATER	35	100.0	-	.1	-	-	17.8	-	40.6	-	41.5
OTHER	-	100.0	-	.9	1.2	.3	64.9	5.6	.4	-	26.7
UNKNOWN	-	100.0	1.5	-	-	-	98.5	-	-	-	-

See footnotes at end of table 4.

TABLE 2. **TCC GROUP 208—Percent Distribution of Geographic Division of Origin and Means of Transport, by Geographic Division of Destination: 1972**—Continued

Geographic division of origin[1] and means of transport	Number	Percent distribution by division of destination									
		U.S. total	New England	Middle Atlantic	East North Central	West North Central	South Atlantic	East South Central	West South Central	Mountain	Pacific
TON-MILES OF SHIPMENTS	(millions of ton-miles)										
EAST NORTH CENTRAL......	3 009	100.0	5.8	16.2	27.6	10.6	10.9	12.3	6.4	2.6	7.5
RAIL..................	1 451	100.0	10.0	25.5	5.0	9.8	19.0	4.9	9.8	3.9	12.0
MOTOR CARRIER.........	749	100.0	1.9	7.4	31.4	12.4	3.9	33.8	2.8	2.3	4.1
PRIVATE TRUCK.........	803	100.0	2.0	7.5	64.8	10.5	2.8	5.9	3.5	.5	2.5
AIR...................	-	100.0	-	-	.1	-	20.3	-	37.6	-	42.0
WATER.................	1	100.0	-	-	-	-	-	-	-	-	100.0
OTHER.................	-	100.0	-	3.2	3.7	4.2	-	1.5	-	-	87.3
UNKNOWN...............	2	100.0	-	-	75.2	24.7	-	-	-	-	-
WEST NORTH CENTRAL......	1 803	100.0	3.6	7.7	15.2	30.6	7.5	8.2	5.9	12.6	8.9
RAIL..................	954	100.0	6.1	10.4	10.6	6.2	13.2	7.1	8.7	21.8	15.9
MOTOR CARRIER.........	281	100.0	.3	4.1	32.1	45.0	2.9	7.5	2.3	3.0	2.9
PRIVATE TRUCK.........	561	100.0	.9	5.0	14.7	64.9	.1	10.5	2.1	1.8	-
AIR...................	-	100.0	71.5	-	28.5	-	-	-	-	-	-
WATER.................	-	100.0	-	-	-	-	-	-	-	-	-
OTHER.................	-	100.0	-	-	-	-	-	-	-	-	-
UNKNOWN...............	5	100.0	-	-	-	3.8	-	-	96.2	-	-
SOUTH ATLANTIC..........	576	100.0	1.8	12.6	4.0	.4	65.0	6.8	3.2	.5	5.7
RAIL..................	192	100.0	1.2	2.7	5.1	.7	58.7	14.2	9.0	1.4	7.1
MOTOR CARRIER.........	95	100.0	8.2	44.7	6.3	.5	35.0	3.1	.9	.1	1.3
PRIVATE TRUCK.........	281	100.0	.1	8.9	2.5	.1	79.1	3.1	.1	-	6.0
AIR...................	-	100.0	-	76.4	-	-	-	23.6	-	-	-
WATER.................	4	100.0	-	-	-	-	72.0	-	-	-	28.0
OTHER.................	-	100.0	-	100.0	-	-	-	-	-	-	-
UNKNOWN...............	3	100.0	-	-	-	-	100.0	-	-	-	-
WEST SOUTH CENTRAL......	695	100.0	.1	.7	-	1.0	23.2	7.7	57.1	5.9	4.3
RAIL..................	449	100.0	-	1.0	-	.8	34.9	7.4	42.1	7.4	6.4
MOTOR CARRIER.........	38	100.0	-	1.5	.7	2.0	6.9	22.3	63.2	.3	3.2
PRIVATE TRUCK.........	205	100.0	-	-	-	1.3	.7	5.8	88.5	3.7	-
AIR...................	-	100.0	-	-	-	-	-	-	100.0	-	-
WATER.................	-	100.0	-	-	-	-	-	-	-	-	-
OTHER.................	-	100.0	-	-	-	-	-	-	51.6	-	-
UNKNOWN...............	1	100.0	48.4	-	-	-	-	-	-	-	-
PACIFIC.................	2 571	100.0	16.7	13.4	13.9	2.6	8.0	1.3	3.6	12.5	28.0
RAIL..................	1 667	100.0	25.7	19.1	19.0	3.4	12.2	2.0	4.9	6.9	6.8
MOTOR CARRIER.........	493	100.0	.3	4.1	3.9	.3	.1	-	.1	14.0	77.2
PRIVATE TRUCK.........	296	100.0	-	.9	-	2.7	.1	-	3.3	45.6	48.3
AIR...................	2	100.0	-	.9	-	1.3	.1	-	.8	-	96.9
WATER.................	85	100.0	-	8.7	-	-	-	-	-	-	91.3
OTHER.................	2	100.0	-	-	-	-	-	-	-	72.6	27.4
UNKNOWN...............	23	100.0	-	-	93.3	-	-	-	-	3.4	3.3

See footnotes at end of table 4.

TABLE 3. **TCC GROUP 208**—Percent Distribution of Geographic Division of Destination and Means of Transport, by Geographic Division of Origin: 1972

Geographic division of destination and means of transport	Number	Percent distribution by division of origin[1]									
		U.S. total	New England	Middle Atlantic	East North Central	West North Central	South Atlantic	East South Central	West South Central	Mountain	Pacific
TONS OF SHIPMENTS	(thousands of tons)										
U.S. TOTAL.............	49 527	100.0	1.9	12.2	21.1	11.3	7.7	(D)	4.9	(D)	12.1
RAIL..............	7 564	100.0	.8	1.8	30.3	21.7	7.5	(D)	14.6	(D)	14.3
MOTOR CARRIER........	9 754	100.0	4.7	16.7	34.4	10.3	4.8	(D)	2.1	(D)	25.0
PRIVATE TRUCK........	32 004	100.0	1.4	13.3	15.0	9.1	8.4	(D)	3.4	(D)	.7.4
AIR.................	1	100.0	-	.9	.6	-	.1	(D)	-	(D)	95.9
WATER..............	72	100.0	-	38.6	.6	-	5.3	(D)	1.3	(D)	54.2
OTHER..............	9	100.0	-	63.7	.7	-	-	(D)	-	(D)	35.5
UNKNOWN............	121	100.0	-	2.4	5.4	17.2	54.3	(D)	4.4	(D)	16.0
NEW ENGLAND............	1 801	100.0	37.8	34.8	12.3	3.6	1.6	(D)	-	(D)	9.2
RAIL..............	433	100.0	1.1	2.5	42.3	13.7	1.3	(D)	-	(D)	38.2
MOTOR CARRIER........	547	100.0	52.0	39.4	3.3	.2	4.1	(D)	-	(D)	.1
PRIVATE TRUCK........	818	100.0	47.9	48.8	2.5	.5	.1	(D)	-	(D)	-
AIR.................	-	100.0	-	43.7	-	21.6	-	(D)	-	(D)	-
WATER..............	-	100.0	-	-	-	-	-	(D)	-	(D)	-
OTHER..............	-	100.0	-	100.0	-	-	-	(D)	-	(D)	-
UNKNOWN............	-	100.0	5.2	12.8	-	-	-	(D)	82.0	(D)	-
MIDDLE ATLANTIC.........	6 529	100.0	1.9	70.7	14.3	2.7	6.6	(D)	.1	(D)	2.2
RAIL..............	990	100.0	-	5.2	58.8	13.2	2.1	(D)	.3	(D)	13.6
MOTOR CARRIER........	1 406	100.0	6.1	69.6	7.9	.9	13.6	(D)	-	(D)	.6
PRIVATE TRUCK........	4 125	100.0	1.0	86.8	5.9	.8	5.4	(D)	-	(D)	-
AIR.................	-	100.0	-	2.5	-	-	3.2	(D)	-	(D)	31.7
WATER..............	6	100.0	-	56.1	-	-	-	(D)	-	(D)	43.9
OTHER..............	-	100.0	-	85.7	9.4	-	1.8	(D)	-	(D)	-
UNKNOWN............	-	100.0	-	-	-	-	-	(D)	-	(D)	-
EAST NORTH CENTRAL......	7 496	100.0	.6	1.1	78.2	14.6	.8	(D)	-	(D)	2.7
RAIL..............	838	100.0	3.5	1.9	3(.7	33.3	1.7	(D)	-	(D)	21.0
MOTOR CARRIER........	2 095	100.0	.7	2.1	76.4	17.1	.7	(D)	-	(D)	.5
PRIVATE TRUCK........	4 544	100.0	-	.5	87.0	10.1	.6	(D)	-	(D)	-
AIR.................	-	100.0	-	96.3	1.0	.6	-	(D)	-	(D)	-
WATER..............	-	100.0	-	-	-	-	-	(D)	-	(D)	-
OTHER..............	-	100.0	-	69.4	28.8	-	-	(D)	-	(D)	-
UNKNOWN............	18	100.0	-	-	31.1	-	-	(D)	-	(D)	68.9
WEST NORTH CENTRAL.....	3 963	100.0	.2	.6	21.4	74.6	.1	(D)	.3	(D)	1.1
RAIL..............	754	100.0	.6	.8	40.6	47.7	.2	(D)	.7	(D)	5.1
MOTOR CARRIER........	804	100.0	.5	2.2	31.1	64.0	.1	(D)	.3	(D)	.1
PRIVATE TRUCK........	2 401	100.0	-	-	12.0	86.7	-	(D)	.2	(D)	.2
AIR.................	-	100.0	-	-	-	-	-	(D)	-	(D)	100.0
WATER..............	-	100.0	-	-	-	-	-	(D)	-	(D)	-
OTHER..............	-	100.0	-	26.8	73.2	-	-	(D)	-	(D)	-
UNKNOWN............	1	100.0	-	-	47.8	52.2	-	(D)	-	(D)	-
SOUTH ATLANTIC.........	4 965	100.0	1.5	13.1	11.0	3.6	61.7	(D)	4.3	(D)	1.7
RAIL..............	1 486	100.0	.7	2.5	29.2	11.3	30.1	(D)	13.7	(D)	5.8
MOTOR CARRIER........	777	100.0	8.3	46.8	8.4	1.4	29.9	(D)	1.1	(D)	-
PRIVATE TRUCK........	2 616	100.0	-	8.9	1.8	-	88.5	(D)	.2	(D)	-
AIR.................	-	100.0	-	4.2	21.3	-	-	(D)	-	(D)	7.5
WATER..............	11	100.0	-	67.9	-	-	32.1	(D)	-	(D)	-
OTHER..............	5	100.0	-	100.0	-	-	-	(D)	-	(D)	-
UNKNOWN............	68	100.0	-	4.1	-	-	95.9	(D)	-	(D)	-
EAST SOUTH CENTRAL.....	6 461	100.0	.1	.1	24.7	8.1	2.9	(D)	2.6	(D)	.3
RAIL..............	608	100.0	.7	-	25.7	27.1	8.6	(D)	13.7	(D)	2.8
MOTOR CARRIER........	1 434	100.0	-	.3	87.5	5.5	.4	(D)	3.4	(D)	-
PRIVATE TRUCK........	4 418	100.0	-	-	4.2	6.3	2.9	(D)	.8	(D)	-
AIR.................	-	100.0	-	-	-	-	100.0	(D)	-	(D)	-
WATER..............	-	100.0	-	-	-	-	-	(D)	-	(D)	-
OTHER..............	-	100.0	-	95.3	4.7	-	-	(D)	-	(D)	-
UNKNOWN............	-	100.0	-	-	-	-	-	(D)	-	(D)	-
WEST SOUTH CENTRAL.....	2 802	100.0	.1	.7	8.6	8.6	.7	(D)	69.2	(D)	2.4
RAIL..............	1 400	100.0	-	.2	12.5	11.2	1.3	(D)	53.4	(D)	4.3
MOTOR CARRIER........	202	100.0	.9	2.7	13.6	6.4	.4	(D)	70.1	(D)	.1
PRIVATE TRUCK........	1 162	100.0	-	-	3.4	4.6	-	(D)	89.7	(D)	.6
AIR.................	-	100.0	-	-	13.8	-	-	(D)	-	(D)	77.1
WATER..............	11	100.0	-	92.0	-	-	-	(D)	8.0	(D)	-
OTHER..............	-	100.0	-	100.0	-	-	-	(D)	-	(D)	-
UNKNOWN............	24	100.0	-	-	-	-	80.1	(D)	19.6	(D)	-
MOUNTAIN...............	10 663	100.0	-	.1	.7	2.3	-	(D)	.5	(D)	6.9
RAIL..............	560	100.0	-	.1	9.6	40.6	.3	(D)	7.7	(D)	35.5
MOTOR CARRIER........	192	100.0	.1	2.0	8.3	5.6	-	(D)	.1	(D)	81.8
PRIVATE TRUCK........	9 907	100.0	-	-	-	.1	-	(D)	.1	(D)	3.9
AIR.................	-	100.0	-	-	-	-	-	(D)	-	(D)	-
WATER..............	-	100.0	-	-	-	-	-	(D)	-	(D)	-
OTHER..............	2	100.0	-	-	-	-	-	(D)	-	(D)	100.0
UNKNOWN............	-	100.0	-	-	-	-	-	(D)	-	(D)	90.0
PACIFIC................	4 845	100.0	.1	.4	2.5	2.1	.3	(D)	.4	(D)	93.0
RAIL..............	491	100.0	.9	2.8	19.0	19.6	1.2	(D)	4.2	(D)	42.3
MOTOR CARRIER........	2 294	100.0	.1	-	.7	.3	-	(D)	-	(D)	98.7
PRIVATE TRUCK........	2 008	100.0	-	-	.5	-	.4	(D)	-	(D)	98.9
AIR.................	-	100.0	-	.1	.2	-	.4	(D)	-	(D)	99.6
WATER..............	42	100.0	-	12.9	1.0	-	.6	(D)	-	(D)	85.6
OTHER..............	1	100.0	-	7.1	2.6	-	-	(D)	-	(D)	90.3
UNKNOWN............	5	100.0	-	-	-	-	-	(D)	-	(D)	100.0

See footnotes at end of table 4.

TABLE 3. TCC GROUP 208—Percent Distribution of Geographic Division of Destination and Means of Transport, by Geographic Division of Origin: 1972—Continued

Geographic division of destination and means of transport	Number	Percent distribution by division of origin[1]									
		U.S. total	New England	Middle Atlantic	East North Central	West North Central	South Atlantic	East South Central	West South Central	Mountain	Pacific
TON-MILES OF SHIPMENTS	(millions of ton-miles)										
U.S. TOTAL	10 658	100.0	1.7	7.0	28.2	16.9	5.4	(D)	6.5	(D)	24.1
RAIL	5 183	100.0	1.0	1.5	28.0	18.4	3.7	(D)	8.7	(D)	32.2
MOTOR CARRIER	2 105	100.0	4.4	13.6	35.6	13.3	4.5	(D)	1.8	(D)	23.4
PRIVATE TRUCK	3 197	100.0	1.1	10.7	25.1	17.6	8.8	(D)	6.4	(D)	9.3
AIR	2	100.0	-	.3	.3	-	-	(D)	-	(D)	98.8
WATER	128	100.0	-	28.0	1.4	-	3.2	(D)	.3	(D)	67.0
OTHER	3	100.0	-	28.7	2.5	-	-	(D)	-	(D)	68.7
UNKNOWN	36	100.0	-	1.3	5.8	15.7	9.0	(D)	3.3	(D)	64.1
NEW ENGLAND	830	100.0	5.4	11.6	21.2	7.8	1.3	(D)	.1	(D)	51.8
RAIL	641	100.0	.1	.4	22.7	9.1	.3	(D)	-	(D)	66.8
MOTOR CARRIER	83	100.0	18.8	47.7	16.7	.9	9.4	(D)	-	(D)	1.8
PRIVATE TRUCK	104	100.0	26.8	51.5	15.6	5.0	.3	(D)	-	(D)	-
AIR	-	100.0	-	27.6	-	31.7	-	(D)	-	(D)	-
WATER	-	100.0	-	-	-	-	-	(D)	-	(D)	-
OTHER	-	100.0	-	100.0	-	-	-	(D)	-	(D)	-
UNKNOWN	-	100.0	.1	1.1	-	-	-	(D)	98.7	(D)	-
MIDDLE ATLANTIC	1 457	100.0	1.7	22.9	33.4	9.5	5.0	(D)	.3	(D)	23.7
RAIL	843	100.0	-	.9	43.9	11.7	.6	(D)	.5	(D)	37.7
MOTOR CARRIER	250	100.0	6.7	37.6	22.2	4.6	17.0	(D)	.2	(D)	8.0
PRIVATE TRUCK	355	100.0	2.2	65.2	17.0	7.8	7.0	(D)	-	(D)	-
AIR	-	100.0	-	.5	-	-	.5	(D)	-	(D)	67.3
WATER	7	100.0	-	.5	-	-	-	(D)	-	(D)	99.5
OTHER	-	100.0	-	55.9	17.9	-	3.3	(D)	-	(D)	-
UNKNOWN	-	100.0	-	-	-	-	-	(D)	-	(D)	-
EAST NORTH CENTRAL	1 579	100.0	2.0	2.3	52.6	17.4	1.4	(D)	-	(D)	22.7
RAIL	535	100.0	4.2	1.4	13.6	18.9	1.8	(D)	-	(D)	59.3
MOTOR CARRIER	394	100.0	2.3	5.6	59.8	22.9	1.5	(D)	.1	(D)	4.8
PRIVATE TRUCK	626	100.0	-	.9	83.2	13.2	1.1	(D)	-	(D)	-
AIR	-	100.0	-	98.0	.2	.5	-	(D)	-	(D)	-
WATER	-	100.0	-	-	-	-	-	(D)	-	(D)	-
OTHER	-	100.0	-	78.5	21.3	-	-	(D)	-	(D)	-
UNKNOWN	23	100.0	-	-	6.8	-	-	(D)	-	(D)	93.2
WEST NORTH CENTRAL	1 007	100.0	.9	2.2	31.8	54.7	.2	(D)	.7	(D)	6.6
RAIL	288	100.0	1.9	1.8	49.4	20.6	.5	(D)	1.2	(D)	19.7
MOTOR CARRIER	249	100.0	1.6	6.5	37.3	50.7	.2	(D)	.3	(D)	1.7
PRIVATE TRUCK	468	100.0	-	.1	17.9	77.9	.1	(D)	-	(D)	100.0
AIR	-	100.0	-	-	-	-	-	(D)	-	(D)	-
WATER	-	100.0	-	46.4	53.6	-	-	(D)	-	(D)	-
OTHER	-	100.0	-	-	70.6	29.4	-	(D)	-	(D)	-
UNKNOWN	-	100.0	-	-	-	-	-	(D)	-	(D)	-
SOUTH ATLANTIC	1 482	100.0	3.2	11.0	22.1	9.1	25.3	(D)	10.9	(D)	13.8
RAIL	954	100.0	.8	2.0	28.9	13.2	11.8	(D)	16.5	(D)	21.3
MOTOR CARRIER	223	100.0	17.8	43.5	13.2	3.7	15.0	(D)	1.2	(D)	.3
PRIVATE TRUCK	290	100.0	-	13.6	7.7	.1	76.5	(D)	.5	(D)	.1
AIR	-	100.0	-	2.6	24.5	-	-	(D)	-	(D)	25.4
WATER	9	100.0	-	68.6	-	-	31.4	(D)	-	(D)	-
OTHER	-	100.0	-	100.0	-	-	-	(D)	-	(D)	-
UNKNOWN	3	100.0	-	12.8	-	-	87.2	(D)	-	(D)	-
EAST SOUTH CENTRAL	848	100.0	.6	.5	43.7	17.4	4.6	(D)	6.3	(D)	3.9
RAIL	267	100.0	1.8	-	26.5	25.3	10.2	(D)	12.5	(D)	12.5
MOTOR CARRIER	293	100.0	-	1.0	86.4	7.2	1.0	(D)	2.9	(D)	-
PRIVATE TRUCK	287	100.0	-	.5	16.3	20.5	3.0	(D)	4.1	(D)	-
AIR	-	100.0	-	-	-	-	100.0	(D)	-	(D)	-
WATER	-	100.0	-	-	-	-	-	(D)	-	(D)	-
OTHER	-	100.0	-	97.6	2.4	-	-	(D)	-	(D)	-
UNKNOWN	-	100.0	-	-	-	-	-	(D)	-	(D)	-
WEST SOUTH CENTRAL	931	100.0	.3	2.7	20.6	11.5	2.0	(D)	42.6	(D)	9.8
RAIL	601	100.0	-	.6	23.8	13.8	2.9	(D)	31.5	(D)	13.5
MOTOR CARRIER	68	100.0	4.1	10.2	30.9	9.5	1.3	(D)	35.6	(D)	.5
PRIVATE TRUCK	240	100.0	-	-	11.6	5.0	.2	(D)	75.7	(D)	4.1
AIR	-	100.0	-	-	10.4	-	-	(D)	-	(D)	85.0
WATER	15	100.0	-	97.0	-	-	-	(D)	3.0	(D)	-
OTHER	-	100.0	-	100.0	-	-	-	(D)	-	(D)	-
UNKNOWN	6	100.0	-	-	-	-	88.2	(D)	10.7	(D)	-
MOUNTAIN	1 189	100.0	-	1.2	6.5	19.0	.2	(D)	3.4	(D)	27.0
RAIL	442	100.0	-	.2	12.7	46.9	.6	(D)	7.5	(D)	25.9
MOTOR CARRIER	106	100.0	.2	5.8	16.1	7.9	.1	(D)	.1	(D)	65.1
PRIVATE TRUCK	637	100.0	-	1.0	.7	1.6	-	(D)	1.2	(D)	21.2
AIR	-	100.0	-	-	-	-	-	(D)	-	(D)	-
WATER	-	100.0	-	-	-	-	-	(D)	-	(D)	100.0
OTHER	1	100.0	-	-	-	-	-	(D)	-	(D)	99.3
UNKNOWN	-	100.0	-	-	.1	-	-	(D)	-	(D)	-
PACIFIC	1 331	100.0	1.2	3.7	17.0	12.0	2.5	(D)	2.2	(D)	54.1
RAIL	608	100.0	1.8	5.4	28.7	25.0	2.2	(D)	4.7	(D)	18.7
MOTOR CARRIER	436	100.0	1.0	.3	7.0	1.8	.3	(D)	.3	(D)	87.2
PRIVATE TRUCK	185	100.0	-	.5	10.9	-	9.2	(D)	-	(D)	77.2
AIR	2	100.0	-	.1	.1	-	-	(D)	-	(D)	99.7
WATER	96	100.0	-	15.5	1.9	-	1.2	(D)	-	(D)	81.4
OTHER	-	100.0	-	26.7	7.7	-	-	(D)	-	(D)	65.6
UNKNOWN	-	100.0	-	-	-	-	-	(D)	-	(D)	100.0

See footnotes at end of table 4.

TABLE 4. TCC GROUP 208—Percent Distribution of Distance Shipped and Weight of Shipment, by Means of Transport: 1972

Distance shipped and weight of shipment[2][3]	Number	Percent distribution by means of transport							
		All means of transport	Rail	Motor carrier	Private truck	Air	Water	Other	Unknown
TONS OF SHIPMENTS	(thousands of tons)								
U.S. TOTAL..........	39 379	100.0	16.7	17.2	65.6	-	.2	-	.3
UNDER 100 MILES.........	22 133	100.0	1.5	11.5	86.6	-	-	-	.3
UNDER 1000 POUNDS.....	379	100.0	-	3.6	89.2	-	-	-	7.2
1000 TO 9999 POUNDS...	1 327	100.0	-	11.3	87.2	-	-	-	1.5
10000 TO 29999 POUNDS.	13 505	100.0	-	3.0	97.0	-	-	-	-
30000 TO 59999 POUNDS.	6 241	100.0	.1	28.8	70.7	-	-	-	.3
60000 TO 89999 POUNDS.	274	100.0	42.8	14.5	42.7	-	.1	-	-
90000 POUNDS AND OVER.	403	100.0	51.8	37.5	10.6	-	-	-	-
100 TO 199 MILES........	5 861	100.0	11.2	25.6	63.0	-	-	.1	.1
UNDER 1000 POUNDS.....	44	100.0	-	17.3	82.6	-	-	-	.1
1000 TO 9999 POUNDS...	246	100.0	-	30.1	69.6	-	-	-	.2
10000 TO 29999 POUNDS.	1 275	100.0	-	10.1	89.8	-	-	-	-
30000 TO 59999 POUNDS.	3 460	100.0	.5	34.5	64.7	-	-	-	.2
60000 TO 89999 POUNDS.	477	100.0	69.9	13.1	17.0	-	-	.2	.2
90000 POUNDS AND OVER.	356	100.0	85.4	9.4	5.2	-	-	-	-
200 TO 299 MILES........	3 524	100.0	20.5	30.5	48.2	-	-	-	.8
UNDER 1000 POUNDS.....	8	100.0	-	61.8	38.1	-	-	.1	-
1000 TO 9999 POUNDS...	149	100.0	.1	44.3	55.6	-	-	-	-
10000 TO 29999 POUNDS.	286	100.0	.4	31.3	67.8	-	-	-	.5
30000 TO 59999 POUNDS.	2 239	100.0	1.9	35.6	62.4	-	-	-	.1
60000 TO 89999 POUNDS.	496	100.0	82.8	10.9	2.3	-	-	-	4.0
90000 POUNDS AND OVER.	343	100.0	78.6	17.5	2.6	-	-	-	1.3
300 TO 499 MILES........	3 223	100.0	40.0	31.5	28.4	-	-	-	-
UNDER 1000 POUNDS.....	6	100.0	.1	83.4	15.8	.1	.1	.5	-
1000 TO 9999 POUNDS...	109	100.0	.9	44.6	53.9	-	.3	.3	-
10000 TO 29999 POUNDS.	278	100.0	2.0	25.9	71.9	-	-	-	-
30000 TO 59999 POUNDS.	1 490	100.0	7.6	48.9	43.4	-	.1	-	.1
60000 TO 89999 POUNDS.	604	100.0	88.4	10.3	1.3	-	-	-	-
90000 POUNDS AND OVER.	734	100.0	86.6	13.3	-	-	-	-	.1
500 TO 999 MILES........	3 270	100.0	75.2	15.4	9.1	-	-	-	.1
UNDER 1000 POUNDS.....	7	100.0	.5	91.1	7.9	.3	.1	.1	.1
1000 TO 9999 POUNDS...	44	100.0	3.2	64.7	32.0	-	-	.3	-
10000 TO 29999 POUNDS.	97	100.0	10.3	48.2	40.0	-	-	.1	-
30000 TO 59999 POUNDS.	712	100.0	17.4	48.7	33.1	-	-	1.4	.1
60000 TO 89999 POUNDS.	1 274	100.0	95.5	4.1	.3	-	.5	.2	.1
90000 POUNDS AND OVER.	1 133	100.0	97.6	2.0	.4	-	.1	-	.1
1000 TO 1499 MILES......	489	100.0	78.8	12.2	5.9	-	3.1	-	-
UNDER 1000 POUNDS.....	-	100.0	.5	57.7	40.0	.5	-	1.2	.1
1000 TO 9999 POUNDS...	5	100.0	15.1	76.3	8.4	.2	-	-	-
10000 TO 29999 POUNDS.	23	100.0	24.1	54.7	19.7	-	1.5	-	-
30000 TO 59999 POUNDS.	84	100.0	18.3	47.1	27.2	-	7.4	-	-
60000 TO 89999 POUNDS.	177	100.0	97.4	1.0	.2	-	1.4	-	-
90000 POUNDS AND OVER.	197	100.0	96.4	.5	-	-	3.1	-	-
1500 MILES OR OVER......	877	100.0	83.9	7.6	2.6	.1	4.4	-	1.4
UNDER 1000 POUNDS.....	1	100.0	18.2	78.6	.8	2.4	-	-	-
1000 TO 9999 POUNDS...	8	100.0	52.6	26.2	7.6	10.9	2.6	.1	-
10000 TO 29999 POUNDS.	38	100.0	67.4	19.7	5.2	-	7.7	-	-
30000 TO 59999 POUNDS.	180	100.0	45.0	27.1	11.1	-	16.8	-	-
60000 TO 89999 POUNDS.	321	100.0	98.1	1.0	-	-	.8	-	-
90000 POUNDS AND OVER.	325	100.0	94.5	.9	-	-	.7	-	3.8
TON-MILES OF SHIPMENTS	(millions of ton-miles)								
U.S. TOTAL..........	8 606	100.0	53.0	17.8	27.3	-	1.5	-	.4
UNDER 100 MILES.........	964	100.0	1.7	12.9	85.1	-	-	-	.3
UNDER 1000 POUNDS.....	12	100.0	-	6.2	82.9	-	-	-	10.9
1000 TO 9999 POUNDS...	43	100.0	-	17.5	79.7	-	-	-	2.8
10000 TO 29999 POUNDS.	563	100.0	-	4.0	96.0	-	-	-	-
30000 TO 59999 POUNDS.	316	100.0	.2	27.9	71.8	-	-	-	-
60000 TO 89999 POUNDS.	15	100.0	53.8	12.6	33.7	-	-	-	.2
90000 POUNDS AND OVER.	12	100.0	58.8	24.9	16.4	-	-	-	-
100 TO 199 MILES........	823	100.0	12.6	26.2	61.0	-	-	-	-
UNDER 1000 POUNDS.....	6	100.0	-	18.7	81.2	-	-	.1	.1
1000 TO 9999 POUNDS...	33	100.0	-	30.9	68.8	-	-	.1	-
10000 TO 29999 POUNDS.	156	100.0	-	10.8	89.2	-	-	.1	.2
30000 TO 59999 POUNDS.	497	100.0	.5	34.8	64.4	-	-	-	.2
60000 TO 89999 POUNDS.	74	100.0	72.6	12.4	14.9	-	-	.1	.2
90000 POUNDS AND OVER.	54	100.0	85.6	9.3	5.1	-	-	-	-

See footnotes at end of table 4.

TABLE 4. **TCC GROUP 208—Percent Distribution of Distance Shipped and Weight of Shipment, by Means of Transport: 1972**—Continued

Distance shipped and weight of shipment [2] [3]	Number	Percent distribution by means of transport							
		All means of transport	Rail	Motor carrier	Private truck	Air	Water	Other	Unknown
TON-MILES OF SHIPMENTS	(millions of ton-miles)								
200 TO 299 MILES	843	100.0	20.8	30.9	47.4	-	-	-	.9
UNDER 1000 POUNDS	2	100.0	-	62.6	37.2	-	-	.1	
1000 TO 9999 POUNDS	35	100.0	.1	44.6	55.3	-	-	-	-
10000 TO 29999 POUNDS	67	100.0	.4	31.5	67.6	-	-	-	.5
30000 TO 59999 POUNDS	534	100.0	2.0	36.4	61.5	-	-	-	.1
60000 TO 89999 POUNDS	119	100.0	82.0	11.2	2.2	-	-	-	4.6
90000 POUNDS AND OVER	84	100.0	78.6	17.0	2.9	-	-	-	1.5
300 TO 499 MILES	1 223	100.0	41.0	31.1	27.8	-	.1	.5	-
UNDER 1000 POUNDS	2	100.0	.1	84.4	14.7	.1	.1	.5	-
1000 TO 9999 POUNDS	42	100.0	1.0	45.4	53.0	-	.3	.3	-
10000 TO 29999 POUNDS	104	100.0	2.3	27.7	69.9	-	-	-	.1
30000 TO 59999 POUNDS	556	100.0	7.8	48.7	43.5	-	.1	-	-
60000 TO 89999 POUNDS	239	100.0	88.7	10.2	1.1	-	-	-	-
90000 POUNDS AND OVER	278	100.0	87.3	12.5	-	-	-	-	.1
500 TO 999 MILES	2 300	100.0	76.0	14.5	9.1	-	.2	.1	.1
UNDER 1000 POUNDS	5	100.0	.5	92.2	6.8	.3	-	.3	-
1000 TO 9999 POUNDS	30	100.0	3.4	64.9	31.6	-	-	.1	-
10000 TO 29999 POUNDS	68	100.0	10.2	46.6	41.5	-	-	1.6	.1
30000 TO 59999 POUNDS	487	100.0	17.9	46.8	34.3	-	.6	.2	.2
60000 TO 89999 POUNDS	908	100.0	96.0	3.6	.2	-	.1	-	.1
90000 POUNDS AND OVER	800	100.0	97.7	2.0	.3	-	-	-	-
1000 TO 1499 MILES	589	100.0	79.5	11.6	5.6	-	3.2	-	-
UNDER 1000 POUNDS	-	100.0	.6	59.2	38.5	.4	-	1.2	.1
1000 TO 9999 POUNDS	6	100.0	16.1	75.7	7.9	.3	-	-	-
10000 TO 29999 POUNDS	28	100.0	26.3	53.3	18.7	-	1.7	-	-
30000 TO 59999 POUNDS	97	100.0	18.3	46.2	27.6	-	7.9	-	-
60000 TO 89999 POUNDS	212	100.0	97.6	1.0	.2	-	1.3	-	-
90000 POUNDS AND OVER	244	100.0	96.3	.5	-	-	3.2	-	-
1500 MILES OR OVER	1 862	100.0	83.2	7.8	2.2	.1	5.5	-	1.2
UNDER 1000 POUNDS	2	100.0	22.4	73.6	.8	3.2	-	-	-
1000 TO 9999 POUNDS	19	100.0	53.6	23.6	6.5	12.4	3.7	.1	-
10000 TO 29999 POUNDS	80	100.0	64.1	21.3	4.5	-	10.1	-	-
30000 TO 59999 POUNDS	394	100.0	43.3	27.2	9.0	-	20.5	-	-
60000 TO 89999 POUNDS	662	100.0	97.8	1.2	-	-	1.0	-	-
90000 POUNDS AND OVER	702	100.0	95.1	.9	-	-	.8	-	3.1

Note: Detail may not add to total due to rounding. The introductory table shows the estimates of sampling variability for tons; sampling variability for ton-miles has not been estimated. See the map in the Introduction for the States comprising the geographic divisions of the United States. Shipments excluded from the survey are those moving by pipeline (primarily petroleum products from refineries), parcel post shipments, and commodities moved by own power (motorized vehicles, aircraft, etc.) or towed (prefabricated buildings, etc.). Local shipments (commodities shipped less than 25 miles from the plant) and shipments within the same city are also excluded. Shipments to Alaska and Hawaii from the 48 conterminous States and the District of Columbia are included; however, no data were obtained for shipments originating in Alaska and Hawaii.

- Represents zero or rounds to zero.   (D) Withheld to avoid disclosing figures for individual companies.

[1] Production of this commodity is concentrated in the geographic divisions shown; figures and distributions for geographic divisions not shown are included in the total.

[2] Distances of shipments to foreign destinations are calculated only to the U.S. port of exit.

[3] Includes only shipments represented by bills of lading and invoices. Summary records which did not show individual weights of shipments are not included.

TCC 209. Miscellaneous Food Preparations

Comparisons of Tons and Ton-Miles of Shipments for
Geographic Divisions of Origin and for Sampling Variability: 1972 and 1967

Geographic division of origin	Estimates				Relative sampling variability in tons (percent)	
	1972		1967		1972	1967
	Tons (thousands)	Ton-miles (millions)	Tons (thousands)	Ton-miles (millions)		
U.S. total	45,516	15,873	39,714	12,909	14.3	28.2
New England	(D)	(D)	131	32	(*)	(*)
Middle Atlantic	2,165	553	2,411	653	12.8	(*)
East North Central	12,518	4,740	8,918	3,182	21.0	(*)
West North Central	8,338	2,925	11,262	2,914	37.7	(*)
South Atlantic	3,559	1,092	758	220	43.1	(*)
East South Central	(D)	(D)	2,197	668	(*)	(*)
West South Central	5,443	1,952	10,664	3,943	43.9	(*)
Mountain	(D)	(D)	6	3	(*)	(*)
Pacific	3,777	1,490	3,367	1,294	36.5	(*)

(D) Withheld to avoid disclosing figures for individual companies.   (*) Data not published.

TABLE 1. **TCC GROUP 209**—Percent Distribution of Geographic Division of Origin and Distance Shipped, by Means of Transport: 1972

Geographic division of origin[1] and distance shipped[2]	Number	Percent distribution by means of transport							
		All means of transport	Rail	Motor carrier	Private truck	Air	Water	Other	Unknown
TONS OF SHIPMENTS	(thousands of tons)								
U.S. TOTAL	45 516	100.0	46.9	16.6	18.6	-	17.6	-	.3
MIDDLE ATLANTIC	2 165	100.0	14.1	66.9	18.0	-	-	-	1.0
UNDER 100 MILES	881	100.0	3.8	70.0	26.1	-	-	-	-
100 TO 199 MILES	457	100.0	9.9	73.4	16.2	-	-	-	.5
200 TO 299 MILES	288	100.0	11.2	72.5	13.5	-	-	-	2.8
300 TO 499 MILES	255	100.0	35.9	53.2	7.2	-	-	-	3.7
500 TO 999 MILES	213	100.0	33.1	54.6	11.9	-	-	-	.5
1000 TO 1499 MILES	34	100.0	57.3	37.6	5.1	-	-	-	-
1500 MILES OR OVER	34	100.0	36.5	60.9	2.6	-	-	-	-
EAST NORTH CENTRAL	12 518	100.0	64.4	19.1	14.4	-	1.6	-	.4
UNDER 100 MILES	2 135	100.0	31.6	27.3	40.4	-	-	-	.7
100 TO 199 MILES	1 865	100.0	45.1	38.0	16.8	-	-	-	.1
200 TO 299 MILES	1 410	100.0	52.7	26.1	21.1	-	-	-	.1
300 TO 499 MILES	3 439	100.0	79.5	11.9	7.5	-	-	-	1.0
500 TO 999 MILES	3 389	100.0	83.3	8.6	2.0	-	6.0	-	-
1000 TO 1499 MILES	113	100.0	92.3	7.6	-	.1	-	-	-
1500 MILES OR OVER	165	100.0	86.0	13.3	.6	-	-	.1	-
WEST NORTH CENTRAL	8 338	100.0	66.0	11.5	22.3	-	-	.1	.1
UNDER 100 MILES	1 631	100.0	31.2	17.4	51.1	-	-	.2	-
100 TO 199 MILES	1 813	100.0	63.9	15.4	20.5	-	-	.1	-
200 TO 299 MILES	2 313	100.0	78.2	9.8	11.7	-	-	.1	.2
300 TO 499 MILES	896	100.0	63.9	9.4	26.5	-	-	.1	-
500 TO 999 MILES	854	100.0	74.6	8.2	16.5	-	-	-	.7
1000 TO 1499 MILES	746	100.0	98.9	.7	.4	-	-	-	-
1500 MILES OR OVER	82	100.0	95.3	4.7	-	-	-	-	-
SOUTH ATLANTIC	3 559	100.0	43.9	12.2	42.7	-	-	-	1.2
UNDER 100 MILES	908	100.0	25.1	7.6	63.1	-	-	-	4.2
100 TO 199 MILES	957	100.0	21.3	6.3	72.3	-	-	.1	-
200 TO 299 MILES	634	100.0	65.2	19.1	15.7	-	-	-	-
300 TO 499 MILES	503	100.0	58.5	17.3	23.8	-	-	.1	.3
500 TO 999 MILES	414	100.0	71.7	19.6	8.4	-	-	-	.3
1000 TO 1499 MILES	30	100.0	86.8	13.2	-	-	-	-	-
1500 MILES OR OVER	109	100.0	88.7	10.6	.7	-	-	-	-
WEST SOUTH CENTRAL	5 443	100.0	43.8	7.8	13.5	-	35.0	-	-
UNDER 100 MILES	660	100.0	60.2	8.4	31.4	-	-	-	-
100 TO 199 MILES	786	100.0	68.4	10.1	21.5	-	-	-	-
200 TO 299 MILES	672	100.0	58.2	8.8	27.3	-	5.7	-	-
300 TO 499 MILES	2 626	100.0	20.5	3.6	4.9	-	71.1	-	-
500 TO 999 MILES	495	100.0	72.8	19.7	7.5	-	-	-	-
1000 TO 1499 MILES	164	100.0	74.3	20.8	4.9	-	-	-	-
1500 MILES OR OVER	36	100.0	89.7	10.3	-	-	-	-	-
PACIFIC	3 777	100.0	28.0	33.1	20.6	-	18.1	.1	.1
UNDER 100 MILES	1 773	100.0	12.6	26.1	23.6	-	37.5	.2	-
100 TO 199 MILES	329	100.0	4.4	42.2	53.3	-	-	.1	-
200 TO 299 MILES	180	100.0	4.9	66.7	28.4	-	-	-	-
300 TO 499 MILES	625	100.0	45.6	39.0	14.9	-	.4	-	.1
500 TO 999 MILES	445	100.0	41.5	52.3	6.2	-	-	-	-
1000 TO 1499 MILES	65	100.0	80.0	13.5	6.6	-	-	-	-
1500 MILES OR OVER	356	100.0	80.6	12.4	1.4	-	4.6	-	.9
TON-MILES OF SHIPMENTS	(millions of ton-miles)								
U.S. TOTAL	15 873	100.0	59.3	13.5	9.7	-	17.2	-	.3
MIDDLE ATLANTIC	553	100.0	28.6	59.7	10.4	-	-	-	1.2
UNDER 100 MILES	34	100.0	3.8	69.1	27.1	-	-	-	-
100 TO 199 MILES	69	100.0	10.8	73.0	15.6	-	-	-	.6
200 TO 299 MILES	71	100.0	11.0	72.6	13.3	-	-	-	3.0
300 TO 499 MILES	102	100.0	36.9	53.1	6.7	-	-	-	3.3
500 TO 999 MILES	153	100.0	33.6	54.6	11.3	-	-	-	.6
1000 TO 1499 MILES	38	100.0	56.3	38.5	5.1	-	-	-	-
1500 MILES OR OVER	83	100.0	36.9	61.0	2.1	-	-	-	-
EAST NORTH CENTRAL	4 740	100.0	76.9	13.2	6.7	-	2.9	-	.3
UNDER 100 MILES	127	100.0	34.9	26.7	38.0	-	-	-	.3
100 TO 199 MILES	254	100.0	46.0	37.0	16.9	-	-	-	.1
200 TO 299 MILES	352	100.0	53.1	25.6	21.2	-	-	-	.1
300 TO 499 MILES	1 353	100.0	79.7	11.9	7.4	-	-	-	1.0
500 TO 999 MILES	2 219	100.0	82.8	8.7	2.2	-	6.3	-	-
1000 TO 1499 MILES	142	100.0	92.9	6.9	-	.1	-	-	-
1500 MILES OR OVER	291	100.0	85.2	14.1	.6	-	-	.1	-
WEST NORTH CENTRAL	2 925	100.0	80.5	7.0	12.3	-	-	-	.2
UNDER 100 MILES	91	100.0	28.4	18.4	53.2	-	-	-	-
100 TO 199 MILES	264	100.0	66.5	14.1	19.3	-	-	.1	-
200 TO 299 MILES	521	100.0	75.9	10.6	13.1	-	-	.1	.3
300 TO 499 MILES	340	100.0	63.9	10.1	25.9	-	-	.1	-
500 TO 999 MILES	552	100.0	72.6	8.6	17.9	-	-	-	.9
1000 TO 1499 MILES	1 026	100.0	99.1	.6	.3	-	-	-	-
1500 MILES OR OVER	127	100.0	94.9	5.0	-	-	-	-	-

See footnotes at end of table 4.

TABLE 1. **TCC GROUP 209**—Percent Distribution of Geographic Division of Origin and Distance Shipped, by Means of Transport: 1972—Continued

Geographic division of origin[1] and distance shipped[2]	Number	Percent distribution by means of transport							
		All means of transport	Rail	Motor carrier	Private truck	Air	Water	Other	Unknown
TON-MILES OF SHIPMENTS	(millions of ton-miles)								
SOUTH ATLANTIC............	1 092	100.0	64.3	15.2	20.0	-	-	-	.5
UNDER 100 MILES........	49	100.0	30.3	6.0	56.1	-	-	-	7.6
100 TO 199 MILES......	138	100.0	22.7	7.0	70.3	-	-	.1	-
200 TO 299 MILES......	155	100.0	63.1	20.9	15.9	-	-	-	-
300 TO 499 MILES......	199	100.0	60.7	16.3	22.6	-	-	.1	.3
500 TO 999 MILES......	282	100.0	72.3	19.9	7.5	-	-	-	.2
1000 TO 1499 MILES....	35	100.0	85.6	14.4	-	-	-	-	-
1500 MILES OR OVER....	231	100.0	87.6	11.7	.7	-	-	-	-
WEST SOUTH CENTRAL......	1 952	100.0	44.2	9.4	8.3	-	38.2	-	-
UNDER 100 MILES........	36	100.0	66.3	7.4	26.3	-	-	-	-
100 TO 199 MILES......	113	100.0	69.4	9.9	20.7	-	-	-	-
200 TO 299 MILES......	167	100.0	57.2	8.8	28.0	-	6.0	-	-
300 TO 499 MILES......	1 022	100.0	19.7	3.6	4.7	-	72.0	-	-
500 TO 999 MILES......	345	100.0	73.6	19.5	6.9	-	-	-	-
1000 TO 1499 MILES....	206	100.0	74.6	20.9	4.5	-	-	-	-
1500 MILES OR OVER....	59	100.0	88.3	11.7	-	-	-	-	-
PACIFIC.................	1 490	100.0	57.3	28.1	8.0	-	6.1	-	.5
UNDER 100 MILES........	94	100.0	17.9	16.6	14.4	-	51.0	.1	-
100 TO 199 MILES......	45	100.0	4.5	42.7	52.7	-	-	.1	-
200 TO 299 MILES......	40	100.0	5.1	65.2	29.8	-	-	-	-
300 TO 499 MILES......	223	100.0	44.9	39.5	15.2	-	.4	-	.1
500 TO 999 MILES......	307	100.0	41.4	52.4	6.2	-	-	-	-
1000 TO 1499 MILES....	87	100.0	80.5	13.4	6.1	-	-	-	-
1500 MILES OR OVER....	690	100.0	77.5	13.9	1.7	-	6.0	-	1.0

See footnotes at end of table 4.

TABLE 2. **TCC GROUP 209**—Percent Distribution of Geographic Division of Origin and Means of Transport, by Geographic Division of Destination: 1972

Geographic division of origin[1] and means of transport	Number	Percent distribution by division of destination									
		U.S. total	New England	Middle Atlantic	East North Central	West North Central	South Atlantic	East South Central	West South Central	Mountain	Pacific
TONS OF SHIPMENTS	(thousands of tons)										
U.S. TOTAL..............	45 516	100.0	2.4	11.0	16.9	12.3	11.9	9.6	24.6	2.3	9.1
RAIL..................	21 344	100.0	3.2	12.9	17.8	14.5	14.8	12.4	13.8	2.9	7.7
MOTOR CARRIER.........	7 558	100.0	4.4	17.9	29.0	12.3	10.9	3.6	4.3	2.8	14.8
PRIVATE TRUCK.........	8 448	100.0	.7	10.4	19.7	18.4	16.5	15.1	8.3	2.8	8.0
AIR...................	-	100.0	1.9	21.0	3.0	4.3	66.7	-	-	.4	2.7
WATER.................	8 014	100.0	-	-	-	-	-	1.5	90.0	-	8.5
OTHER.................	12	100.0	.4	.6	53.8	17.8	.4	.9	2.8	1.9	21.4
UNKNOWN...............	136	100.0	.4	19.1	17.5	4.1	8.3	42.0	1.3	4.2	3.1
MIDDLE ATLANTIC.........	2 165	100.0	12.1	57.2	11.9	.8	14.8	1.2	.4	.1	1.5
RAIL..................	305	100.0	14.2	22.5	34.7	3.2	19.5	.7	1.1	-	4.1
MOTOR CARRIER.........	1 448	100.0	13.3	60.3	8.1	.5	14.8	1.4	.3	.1	1.3
PRIVATE TRUCK.........	390	100.0	6.8	73.5	8.9	-	9.4	.8	.3	.2	.1
AIR...................	-	100.0	-	.1	-	12.7	33.9	-	-	20.8	32.4
WATER.................	-	100.0	-	100.0	-	-	-	-	-	-	-
OTHER.................	-	100.0	38.0	46.3	6.8	-	8.9	-	-	-	-
UNKNOWN...............	20	100.0	2.0	47.9	3.2	-	46.9	-	-	-	-
EAST NORTH CENTRAL......	12 518	100.0	5.0	22.5	40.4	3.8	14.7	7.0	4.5	.7	1.3
RAIL..................	8 065	100.0	7.1	28.4	28.1	2.0	19.5	8.7	3.5	1.0	1.8
MOTOR CARRIER.........	2 392	100.0	1.2	8.5	65.1	10.3	7.6	3.4	2.6	.4	.9
PRIVATE TRUCK.........	1 799	100.0	1.4	17.3	67.7	3.6	5.0	4.3	.6	-	.1
AIR...................	-	100.0	2.4	11.3	-	-	82.9	-	-	-	3.3
WATER.................	204	100.0	-	-	-	-	-	-	100.0	-	-
OTHER.................	-	100.0	-	.2	55.1	27.7	3.1	2.3	1.1	-	10.5
UNKNOWN...............	54	100.0	.3	29.7	34.5	-	.7	34.8	-	-	.1
WEST NORTH CENTRAL......	8 338	100.0	-	1.2	14.4	55.4	.3	3.7	10.9	5.0	9.0
RAIL..................	5 505	100.0	-	1.6	11.9	47.3	.2	5.1	14.4	5.9	13.5
MOTOR CARRIER.........	954	100.0	-	1.2	24.8	65.0	1.7	1.9	4.1	.7	.5
PRIVATE TRUCK.........	1 858	100.0	-	-	16.0	74.5	-	.7	4.4	4.3	.5
AIR...................	-	100.0	-	6.4	-	-	93.6	-	-	-	-
WATER.................	-	100.0	-	-	-	-	-	-	-	-	-
OTHER.................	8	100.0	-	.8	73.5	25.2	.4	-	-	-	-
UNKNOWN...............	11	100.0	-	-	-	48.3	-	2.8	-	48.9	-

See footnotes at end of table 4.

TABLE 2. **TCC GROUP 209—Percent Distribution of Geographic Division of Origin and Means of Transport, by Geographic Division of Destination: 1972**—Continued

Geographic division of origin¹ and means of transport	Number	Percent distribution by division of destination									
		U.S. total	New England	Middle Atlantic	East North Central	West North Central	South Atlantic	East South Central	West South Central	Mountain	Pacific
TONS OF SHIPMENTS	(thousands of tons)										
SOUTH ATLANTIC	3 559	100.0	1.9	11.0	5.9	.7	61.2	13.6	2.6	1.2	1.9
RAIL	1 561	100.0	2.9	8.1	8.3	1.3	56.9	11.2	5.1	2.7	3.5
MOTOR CARRIER	435	100.0	4.1	30.1	11.2	1.0	42.6	7.1	1.0	.2	2.7
PRIVATE TRUCK	1 521	100.0	.3	8.7	2.1	.1	72.5	15.7	.5	-	.1
AIR	-	100.0	-	-	-	-	52.6	-	11.8	-	35.5
WATER	-	100.0	-	-	-	-	-	-	-	-	-
OTHER	-	100.0	-	-	50.6	-	-	10.2	39.1	-	-
UNKNOWN	40	100.0	-	-	-	-	2.8	93.2	4.1	-	-
WEST SOUTH CENTRAL	5 443	100.0	.1	.7	5.9	5.8	3.8	8.9	72.0	1.1	1.7
RAIL	2 381	100.0	.1	.9	11.1	8.9	5.5	11.1	57.9	1.2	3.3
MOTOR CARRIER	423	100.0	.2	4.1	8.2	7.0	11.3	16.0	44.7	5.5	2.9
PRIVATE TRUCK	733	100.0	-	-	3.5	9.7	3.6	10.9	70.9	1.4	-
AIR	-	100.0	-	94.3	5.7	-	-	-	-	-	-
WATER	1 904	100.0	-	-	-	-	-	4.0	96.0	-	-
OTHER	-	100.0	-	-	-	-	-	-	-	-	-
UNKNOWN	-	100.0	-	-	-	-	-	-	100.0	-	-
PACIFIC	3 777	100.0	.2	.3	6.3	.7	.4	.3	2.7	9.6	79.6
RAIL	1 057	100.0	.4	.5	20.8	1.7	.8	.8	8.0	10.7	56.2
MOTOR CARRIER	1 252	100.0	.1	.2	1.1	.5	.5	.1	1.1	12.3	84.1
PRIVATE TRUCK	776	100.0	-	.6	.1	-	-	-	.6	12.1	86.6
AIR	-	100.0	-	3.4	33.0	55.9	-	-	-	-	7.7
WATER	684	100.0	-	-	-	-	-	-	-	-	100.0
OTHER	2	100.0	-	-	-	-	-	-	-	8.5	91.5
UNKNOWN	4	100.0	-	-	82.5	-	-	.4	-	-	17.1
TON-MILES OF SHIPMENTS	(millions of ton-miles)										
U.S. TOTAL	15 873	100.0	3.9	13.1	12.8	6.8	12.0	6.7	25.1	4.6	14.9
RAIL	9 409	100.0	5.3	16.1	13.7	7.1	14.3	8.0	11.3	5.0	19.2
MOTOR CARRIER	2 150	100.0	4.3	14.6	21.6	9.0	15.2	4.3	6.4	6.5	18.2
PRIVATE TRUCK	1 538	100.0	1.5	16.1	17.3	14.6	15.3	11.2	11.9	7.5	4.5
AIR	-	100.0	.9	25.2	5.5	6.9	55.3	-	-	.6	5.5
WATER	2 725	100.0	-	-	-	-	-	1.3	95.4	-	3.3
OTHER	2	100.0	.4	3.1	36.9	25.5	2.9	1.3	7.3	2.1	20.6
UNKNOWN	47	100.0	.4	16.6	18.9	3.1	10.2	24.5	1.4	10.4	14.6
MIDDLE ATLANTIC	553	100.0	10.0	19.6	24.5	2.9	22.4	3.6	2.1	.7	14.2
RAIL	158	100.0	8.3	6.5	34.5	5.7	22.0	1.2	2.5	.1	19.2
MOTOR CARRIER	330	100.0	11.3	22.7	19.0	2.0	23.0	4.8	1.9	.7	14.5
PRIVATE TRUCK	57	100.0	8.2	35.9	31.1	.2	15.7	3.6	2.2	2.1	.9
AIR	-	100.0	-	-	-	7.2	18.9	-	-	22.2	51.7
WATER	-	100.0	-	100.0	-	-	-	-	-	-	-
OTHER	-	100.0	34.2	19.9	29.5	-	16.4	-	-	-	-
UNKNOWN	6	100.0	.9	36.9	3.8	-	58.4	-	-	-	-
EAST NORTH CENTRAL	4 740	100.0	10.0	29.8	15.1	3.8	18.3	6.7	7.8	2.5	6.1
RAIL	3 646	100.0	12.0	33.5	10.4	2.0	20.4	7.2	4.7	2.9	6.8
MOTOR CARRIER	623	100.0	3.3	14.6	33.9	13.3	14.6	4.6	7.6	1.6	6.4
PRIVATE TRUCK	316	100.0	5.1	29.5	38.4	7.1	10.2	6.0	3.2	-	.5
AIR	-	100.0	1.9	8.0	-	-	84.5	-	-	-	5.6
WATER	138	100.0	-	-	-	-	-	-	100.0	-	-
OTHER	-	100.0	-	.1	5.6	28.5	3.3	1.9	1.1	-	59.5
UNKNOWN	14	100.0	.8	36.8	7.4	-	1.1	53.3	-	-	.5
WEST NORTH CENTRAL	2 925	100.0	-	3.2	10.9	22.2	.6	5.0	12.0	9.5	36.7
RAIL	2 355	100.0	-	3.6	7.1	17.3	.3	5.7	12.2	8.7	45.2
MOTOR CARRIER	203	100.0	.2	4.6	33.7	36.1	4.5	3.1	11.4	2.7	3.7
PRIVATE TRUCK	358	100.0	-	.1	22.9	46.5	.2	1.2	11.6	17.1	.3
AIR	-	100.0	-	10.9	-	-	89.1	-	-	-	-
WATER	-	100.0	-	-	-	-	-	-	-	-	.4
OTHER	1	100.0	.2	5.7	57.6	32.4	3.5	.1	-	-	-
UNKNOWN	6	100.0	-	-	-	22.6	-	1.5	-	75.9	-

See footnotes at end of table 4.

TABLE 2. **TCC GROUP 209—Percent Distribution of Geographic Division of Origin and Means of Transport, by Geographic Division of Destination: 1972**—Continued

Geographic division of origin[1] and means of transport	Number	Percent distribution by division of destination									
		U.S. total	New England	Middle Atlantic	East North Central	West North Central	South Atlantic	East South Central	West South Central	Mountain	Pacific
TON-MILES OF SHIPMENTS	(millions of ton-miles)										
SOUTH ATLANTIC............	1 092	100.0	3.0	10.9	11.3	2.4	35.2	9.7	6.2	6.7	14.6
RAIL....................	703	100.0	3.4	7.8	11.3	2.8	30.9	6.5	8.5	10.2	18.7
MOTOR CARRIER..........	166	100.0	3.8	22.6	19.8	2.9	25.4	7.0	1.6	.7	16.2
PRIVATE TRUCK..........	218	100.0	.8	12.3	5.3	.8	57.4	20.6	2.2	-	.7
AIR....................	-	100.0	-	-	-	-	29.2	-	8.1	-	62.6
WATER..................	-	100.0	-	-	-	-	-	-	-	-	-
OTHER..................	-	100.0	-	-	33.4	-	-	6.0	60.7	-	-
UNKNOWN................	5	100.0	-	-	-	-	12.9	74.8	12.4	-	-
WEST SOUTH CENTRAL......	1 952	100.0	.3	2.3	8.9	6.3	9.2	5.6	59.0	1.6	6.7
RAIL....................	862	100.0	.6	2.6	15.9	10.3	15.2	6.4	34.6	1.2	13.1
MOTOR CARRIER..........	183	100.0	.5	12.3	15.4	6.2	15.5	9.2	21.8	8.9	10.0
PRIVATE TRUCK..........	161	100.0	-	-	5.6	14.3	12.9	8.1	56.6	2.6	-
AIR....................	-	100.0	-	95.3	4.7	-	-	-	-	-	-
WATER..................	745	100.0	-	-	-	-	-	3.2	96.8	-	-
OTHER..................	-	100.0	-	-	-	-	-	-	-	-	-
UNKNOWN................	-	100.0	-	-	-	-	-	-	100.0	-	-
PACIFIC.................	1 490	100.0	1.0	2.1	29.5	2.6	2.2	1.1	9.2	12.6	39.6
RAIL....................	854	100.0	1.3	1.5	47.6	3.4	2.3	1.8	13.8	6.3	21.9
MOTOR CARRIER..........	419	100.0	.8	1.8	6.1	2.2	3.0	.4	3.4	22.7	59.6
PRIVATE TRUCK..........	119	100.0	-	8.9	.6	-	-	-	4.8	32.7	52.9
AIR....................	-	100.0	-	5.0	35.5	50.6	-	-	-	-	8.9
WATER..................	90	100.0	-	-	-	-	-	-	-	-	100.0
OTHER..................	-	100.0	-	-	-	-	-	-	-	35.9	64.1
UNKNOWN................	7	100.0	-	-	96.9	-	-	.4	-	-	2.8

See footnotes at end of table 4.

TABLE 3. **TCC GROUP 209**—Percent Distribution of Geographic Division of Destination and Means of Transport, by Geographic Division of Origin: 1972

Geographic division of destination and means of transport	Number	Percent distribution by division of origin[1]									
		U.S. total	New England	Middle Atlantic	East North Central	West North Central	South Atlantic	East South Central	West South Central	Mountain	Pacific
TONS OF SHIPMENTS	(thousands of tons)										
U.S. TOTAL..............	45 516	100.0	(D)	4.8	27.5	18.3	7.8	(D)	12.0	(D)	8.3
RAIL................	21 344	100.0	(D)	1.4	37.8	25.8	7.3	(D)	11.2	(D)	5.0
MOTOR CARRIER........	7 558	100.0	(D)	19.2	31.7	12.6	5.8	(D)	5.6	(D)	16.6
PRIVATE TRUCK........	8 448	100.0	(D)	4.6	21.3	22.0	18.0	(D)	8.7	(D)	9.2
AIR.................	–	100.0	(D)	1.7	43.5	31.9	.4	(D)	10.6	(D)	7.2
WATER...............	8 014	100.0	(D)	–	2.6	–	–	(D)	23.8	(D)	8.5
OTHER...............	12	100.0	(D)	.1	6.4	63.5	6.9	(D)	–	(D)	22.6
UNKNOWN.............	136	100.0	(D)	15.3	39.8	8.5	29.9	(D)	.1	(D)	3.0
NEW ENGLAND............	1 073	100.0	(D)	24.5	58.3	–	6.2	(D)	.3	(D)	.5
RAIL................	677	100.0	(D)	6.4	84.4	–	6.6	(D)	.4	(D)	.7
MOTOR CARRIER........	333	100.0	(D)	57.5	8.6	.1	5.3	(D)	.2	(D)	.4
PRIVATE TRUCK........	61	100.0	(D)	43.4	41.0	–	7.1	(D)	–	(D)	–
AIR.................	–	100.0	(D)	–	55.2	–	–	(D)	–	(D)	–
WATER...............	–	100.0	(D)	–	–	–	–	(D)	–	(D)	–
OTHER...............	–	100.0	(D)	9.0	–	4.4	–	(D)	–	(D)	–
UNKNOWN.............	–	100.0	(D)	73.8	26.2	–	–	(D)	–	(D)	–
MIDDLE ATLANTIC........	5 020	100.0	(D)	24.7	56.2	2.0	7.8	(D)	.8	(D)	.3
RAIL................	2 755	100.0	(D)	2.5	83.1	3.2	4.6	(D)	.8	(D)	.2
MOTOR CARRIER........	1 355	100.0	(D)	64.4	14.9	.9	9.7	(D)	1.3	(D)	.2
PRIVATE TRUCK........	882	100.0	(D)	32.5	35.3	.1	14.9	(D)	–	(D)	.5
AIR.................	–	100.0	(D)	–	23.4	9.8	–	(D)	47.6	(D)	1.2
WATER...............	–	100.0	(D)	25.8	–	–	–	(D)	–	(D)	–
OTHER...............	–	100.0	(D)	8.0	1.9	89.9	.2	(D)	–	(D)	–
UNKNOWN.............	26	100.0	(D)	38.2	61.7	–	–	(D)	–	(D)	–
EAST NORTH CENTRAL.....	7 686	100.0	(D)	3.4	65.8	15.6	2.7	(D)	4.2	(D)	3.1
RAIL................	3 804	100.0	(D)	2.8	59.5	17.3	3.4	(D)	6.9	(D)	5.8
MOTOR CARRIER........	2 189	100.0	(D)	5.4	71.2	10.8	2.2	(D)	1.6	(D)	.6
PRIVATE TRUCK........	1 661	100.0	(D)	2.1	73.3	17.9	1.9	(D)	1.5	(D)	–
AIR.................	–	100.0	(D)	–	–	–	–	(D)	20.4	(D)	79.6
WATER...............	–	100.0	(D)	–	–	–	–	(D)	–	(D)	–
OTHER...............	6	100.0	(D)	–	6.6	86.8	6.5	(D)	–	(D)	14.0
UNKNOWN.............	23	100.0	(D)	2.8	78.5	–	–	(D)	–	(D)	–
WEST NORTH CENTRAL.....	5 591	100.0	(D)	.3	8.5	82.6	.5	(D)	5.6	(D)	.4
RAIL................	3 096	100.0	(D)	.3	5.2	84.2	.7	(D)	6.9	(D)	.6
MOTOR CARRIER........	930	100.0	(D)	.7	26.5	66.7	.5	(D)	3.2	(D)	.7
PRIVATE TRUCK........	1 557	100.0	(D)	–	4.2	88.9	.1	(D)	4.6	(D)	–
AIR.................	–	100.0	(D)	5.1	–	–	–	(D)	–	(D)	94.9
WATER...............	–	100.0	(D)	–	–	–	–	(D)	–	(D)	–
OTHER...............	2	100.0	(D)	–	10.0	90.0	–	(D)	–	(D)	–
UNKNOWN.............	5	100.0	(D)	–	–	100.0	–	(D)	–	(D)	–
SOUTH ATLANTIC.........	5 394	100.0	(D)	5.9	34.2	.5	40.4	(D)	3.8	(D)	.3
RAIL................	3 161	100.0	(D)	1.9	49.8	.3	28.1	(D)	4.2	(D)	.3
MOTOR CARRIER........	823	100.0	(D)	26.1	22.1	2.0	22.5	(D)	5.8	(D)	.7
PRIVATE TRUCK........	1 397	100.0	(D)	2.6	6.4	.1	78.9	(D)	1.9	(D)	–
AIR.................	–	100.0	(D)	.9	54.1	44.8	.3	(D)	–	(D)	–
WATER...............	–	100.0	(D)	–	–	–	–	(D)	–	(D)	–
OTHER...............	–	100.0	(D)	2.1	45.3	52.6	–	(D)	–	(D)	–
UNKNOWN.............	11	100.0	(D)	86.8	3.2	–	10.0	(D)	–	(D)	–
EAST SOUTH CENTRAL.....	4 365	100.0	(D)	.6	20.1	7.2	11.1	(D)	11.2	(D)	.2
RAIL................	2 637	100.0	(D)	.1	26.5	10.7	6.6	(D)	10.0	(D)	.3
MOTOR CARRIER........	270	100.0	(D)	7.2	29.6	6.6	11.4	(D)	25.0	(D)	.3
PRIVATE TRUCK........	1 279	100.0	(D)	.3	6.1	1.0	18.7	(D)	6.3	(D)	–
AIR.................	–	100.0	(D)	–	–	–	–	(D)	62.8	(D)	–
WATER...............	120	100.0	(D)	–	17.3	1.8	80.8	(D)	–	(D)	–
OTHER...............	–	100.0	(D)	–	33.0	.6	66.4	(D)	–	(D)	–
UNKNOWN.............	57	100.0	(D)	–	–	–	–	(D)	–	(D)	–
WEST SOUTH CENTRAL.....	11 180	100.0	(D)	.1	5.0	8.2	.8	(D)	35.0	(D)	.9
RAIL................	2 946	100.0	(D)	.1	9.6	26.9	2.7	(D)	46.8	(D)	2.9
MOTOR CARRIER........	323	100.0	(D)	1.5	19.1	12.2	1.4	(D)	58.5	(D)	4.2
PRIVATE TRUCK........	699	100.0	(D)	.2	1.6	11.6	1.2	(D)	74.4	(D)	.7
AIR.................	–	100.0	(D)	–	–	–	100.0	(D)	–	(D)	–
WATER...............	7 208	100.0	(D)	–	2.8	–	–	(D)	25.4	(D)	–
OTHER...............	–	100.0	(D)	–	2.5	–	97.5	(D)	–	(D)	–
UNKNOWN.............	1	100.0	(D)	–	–	–	92.3	(D)	7.7	(D)	–
MOUNTAIN...............	1 063	100.0	(D)	.2	8.6	39.5	4.1	(D)	5.8	(D)	34.0
RAIL................	615	100.0	(D)	–	13.2	53.1	6.9	(D)	4.6	(D)	18.4
MOTOR CARRIER........	208	100.0	(D)	.7	4.9	3.3	.4	(D)	11.1	(D)	73.8
PRIVATE TRUCK........	232	100.0	(D)	.3	–	34.3	–	(D)	4.3	(D)	40.3
AIR.................	–	100.0	(D)	100.0	–	–	–	(D)	–	(D)	–
WATER...............	–	100.0	(D)	–	–	–	–	(D)	–	(D)	100.0
OTHER...............	–	100.0	(D)	–	–	100.0	–	(D)	–	(D)	–
UNKNOWN.............	5	100.0	(D)	–	–	–	–	(D)	–	(D)	–
PACIFIC................	4 139	100.0	(D)	.8	4.0	18.1	1.6	(D)	2.2	(D)	72.7
RAIL................	1 648	100.0	(D)	.8	8.6	45.2	3.3	(D)	4.7	(D)	36.1
MOTOR CARRIER........	1 122	100.0	(D)	1.7	1.9	.4	1.0	(D)	1.1	(D)	93.8
PRIVATE TRUCK........	677	100.0	(D)	–	.1	.1	.1	(D)	–	(D)	99.3
AIR.................	–	100.0	(D)	20.6	53.5	–	5.1	(D)	–	(D)	20.8
WATER...............	684	100.0	(D)	–	–	–	–	(D)	–	(D)	100.0
OTHER...............	2	100.0	(D)	–	3.2	.1	–	(D)	–	(D)	96.7
UNKNOWN.............	4	100.0	(D)	–	1.0	–	–	(D)	–	(D)	16.3

See footnotes at end of table 4.

TABLE 3. **TCC GROUP 209**—Percent Distribution of Geographic Division of Destination and Means of Transport, by Geographic Division of Origin: 1972—Continued

Geographic division of destination and means of transport	Number	Percent distribution by division of origin[1]									
		U.S. total	New England	Middle Atlantic	East North Central	West North Central	South Atlantic	East South Central	West South Central	Mountain	Pacific
TON-MILES OF SHIPMENTS	(millions of ton-miles)										
U.S. TOTAL................	15 873	100.0	(D)	3.5	29.9	18.4	6.9	(D)	12.3	(D)	9.4
RAIL..................	9 409	100.0	(D)	1.7	38.7	25.0	7.5	(D)	9.2	(D)	9.1
MOTOR CARRIER.........	2 150	100.0	(D)	15.4	29.0	9.5	7.7	(D)	8.5	(D)	19.5
PRIVATE TRUCK.........	1 538	100.0	(D)	3.8	20.6	23.3	14.2	(D)	10.5	(D)	7.8
AIR...................	-	100.0	(D)	2.8	46.2	17.5	.5	(D)	15.8	(D)	13.3
WATER.................	2 725	100.0	(D)	-	5.1	-	-	(D)	27.4	(D)	3.3
OTHER.................	2	100.0	(D)	.1	27.9	54.2	11.5	(D)	-	(D)	5.8
UNKNOWN...............	47	100.0	(D)	14.5	30.5	13.7	10.6	(D)	-	(D)	15.0
NEW ENGLAND............	617	100.0	(D)	8.9	77.1	.1	5.2	(D)	.9	(D)	2.4
RAIL..................	501	100.0	(D)	2.6	87.5	-	4.8	(D)	.9	(D)	2.3
MOTOR CARRIER.........	92	100.0	(D)	40.5	22.6	.4	6.9	(D)	1.1	(D)	3.8
PRIVATE TRUCK.........	23	100.0	(D)	20.4	70.5	-	7.6	(D)	-	(D)	-
AIR...................	-	100.0	(D)	-	98.9	-	-	(D)	-	(D)	-
WATER.................	-	100.0	(D)	-	-	-	-	(D)	-	(D)	-
OTHER.................	-	100.0	(D)	7.5	-	27.8	-	(D)	-	(D)	-
UNKNOWN...............	-	100.0	(D)	34.0	66.0	-	-	(D)	-	(D)	-
MIDDLE ATLANTIC........	2 085	100.0	(D)	5.2	67.7	4.5	5.7	(D)	2.2	(D)	1.5
RAIL..................	1 516	100.0	(D)	.7	80.6	5.5	3.6	(D)	1.5	(D)	.9
MOTOR CARRIER.........	313	100.0	(D)	24.0	29.0	3.0	12.0	(D)	7.2	(D)	2.4
PRIVATE TRUCK.........	247	100.0	(D)	8.4	37.7	.2	10.8	(D)	-	(D)	4.3
AIR...................	-	100.0	(D)	-	14.7	7.6	-	(D)	59.7	(D)	2.6
WATER.................	-	100.0	(D)	2.4	-	-	-	(D)	-	(D)	-
OTHER.................	-	100.0	(D)	.6	1.0	98.4	-	(D)	-	(D)	-
UNKNOWN...............	7	100.0	(D)	32.2	67.8	-	-	(D)	-	(D)	-
EAST NORTH CENTRAL.....	2 026	100.0	(D)	6.7	35.2	15.7	6.1	(D)	8.6	(D)	21.7
RAIL..................	1 286	100.0	(D)	4.2	29.6	12.9	6.2	(D)	10.6	(D)	31.6
MOTOR CARRIER.........	463	100.0	(D)	13.6	45.6	14.8	7.1	(D)	6.1	(D)	5.5
PRIVATE TRUCK.........	266	100.0	(D)	6.7	45.5	30.8	4.3	(D)	3.4	(D)	.3
AIR...................	-	100.0	(D)	-	-	-	-	(D)	13.6	(D)	86.4
WATER.................	-	100.0	(D)	-	-	-	-	(D)	-	(D)	-
OTHER.................	-	100.0	(D)	.1	4.3	84.7	10.4	(D)	-	(D)	-
UNKNOWN...............	8	100.0	(D)	2.9	11.9	-	-	(D)	-	(D)	76.7
WEST NORTH CENTRAL.....	1 084	100.0	(D)	1.5	16.5	59.9	2.4	(D)	11.4	(D)	3.6
RAIL..................	664	100.0	(D)	1.3	11.0	61.3	3.0	(D)	13.4	(D)	4.4
MOTOR CARRIER.........	193	100.0	(D)	3.5	43.0	38.0	2.5	(D)	5.9	(D)	4.8
PRIVATE TRUCK.........	224	100.0	(D)	.1	10.0	74.2	.7	(D)	10.2	(D)	-
AIR...................	-	100.0	(D)	2.9	-	-	-	(D)	-	(D)	97.1
WATER.................	-	100.0	(D)	-	-	-	-	(D)	-	(D)	-
OTHER.................	-	100.0	(D)	-	31.1	68.8	-	(D)	-	(D)	-
UNKNOWN...............	1	100.0	(D)	-	-	100.0	-	(D)	-	(D)	-
SOUTH ATLANTIC.........	1 911	100.0	(D)	6.5	45.3	.9	20.1	(D)	9.4	(D)	1.7
RAIL..................	1 344	100.0	(D)	2.6	55.2	.5	16.1	(D)	9.8	(D)	1.5
MOTOR CARRIER.........	325	100.0	(D)	23.4	27.9	2.8	12.9	(D)	8.7	(D)	3.9
PRIVATE TRUCK.........	236	100.0	(D)	3.8	13.7	.3	53.0	(D)	8.8	(D)	-
AIR...................	-	100.0	(D)	1.0	70.6	28.1	.3	(D)	-	(D)	-
WATER.................	-	100.0	(D)	-	-	-	-	(D)	-	(D)	-
OTHER.................	-	100.0	(D)	.5	32.6	66.9	-	(D)	-	(D)	-
UNKNOWN...............	4	100.0	(D)	83.1	3.4	-	13.5	(D)	-	(D)	-
EAST SOUTH CENTRAL.....	1 065	100.0	(D)	1.9	29.9	13.7	9.9	(D)	10.2	(D)	1.6
RAIL..................	755	100.0	(D)	.3	34.8	17.9	6.0	(D)	7.3	(D)	2.1
MOTOR CARRIER.........	91	100.0	(D)	17.2	31.5	6.9	12.6	(D)	18.5	(D)	1.6
PRIVATE TRUCK.........	172	100.0	(D)	1.2	11.0	2.6	26.0	(D)	7.6	(D)	-
AIR...................	-	100.0	(D)	-	-	-	-	(D)	-	(D)	-
WATER.................	34	100.0	(D)	-	-	-	-	(D)	68.7	(D)	-
OTHER.................	-	100.0	(D)	-	41.1	4.4	54.4	(D)	-	(D)	-
UNKNOWN...............	11	100.0	(D)	-	66.4	.9	32.5	(D)	-	(D)	.2
WEST SOUTH CENTRAL.....	3 985	100.0	(D)	.3	9.2	8.8	1.7	(D)	28.9	(D)	3.5
RAIL..................	1 061	100.0	(D)	.4	16.2	27.1	5.6	(D)	28.1	(D)	11.1
MOTOR CARRIER.........	138	100.0	(D)	4.6	34.0	16.7	2.0	(D)	28.9	(D)	10.2
PRIVATE TRUCK.........	183	100.0	(D)	.7	5.5	22.7	2.6	(D)	49.7	(D)	3.1
AIR...................	-	100.0	(D)	-	-	-	100.0	(D)	-	(D)	-
WATER.................	2 600	100.0	(D)	-	5.3	-	-	(D)	27.8	(D)	-
OTHER.................	-	100.0	(D)	-	4.0	-	96.0	(D)	-	(D)	-
UNKNOWN...............	-	100.0	(D)	-	-	-	96.9	(D)	3.1	(D)	-
MOUNTAIN...............	730	100.0	(D)	.5	15.9	37.9	10.0	(D)	4.3	(D)	25.7
RAIL..................	470	100.0	(D)	.1	22.5	43.6	15.2	(D)	2.3	(D)	11.4
MOTOR CARRIER.........	140	100.0	(D)	1.7	7.3	3.9	.9	(D)	11.7	(D)	67.6
PRIVATE TRUCK.........	114	100.0	(D)	1.1	-	53.4	-	(D)	3.6	(D)	34.2
AIR...................	-	100.0	(D)	100.0	-	-	-	(D)	-	(D)	-
WATER.................	-	100.0	(D)	-	-	-	-	(D)	-	(D)	-
OTHER.................	-	100.0	(D)	-	-	-	-	(D)	-	(D)	100.0
UNKNOWN...............	4	100.0	(D)	-	-	100.0	-	(D)	-	(D)	-
PACIFIC................	2 367	100.0	(D)	3.3	12.3	45.3	6.8	(D)	5.6	(D)	25.0
RAIL..................	1 808	100.0	(D)	1.7	13.7	58.8	7.3	(D)	6.3	(D)	10.3
MOTOR CARRIER.........	390	100.0	(D)	12.2	10.3	1.9	6.9	(D)	4.7	(D)	63.9
PRIVATE TRUCK.........	69	100.0	(D)	.7	2.4	1.6	2.2	(D)	-	(D)	90.8
AIR...................	-	100.0	(D)	26.0	46.4	-	6.2	(D)	-	(D)	21.3
WATER.................	90	100.0	(D)	-	-	-	-	(D)	-	(D)	100.0
OTHER.................	-	100.0	(D)	-	80.8	1.2	-	(D)	-	(D)	18.0
UNKNOWN...............	6	100.0	(D)	-	1.0	-	-	(D)	-	(D)	2.8

See footnotes at end of table 4.

TABLE 4. **TCC GROUP 209**—Percent Distribution of Distance Shipped and Weight of Shipment, by Means of Transport: 1972

Distance shipped and weight of shipment [2] [3]	Number	Percent distribution by means of transport							
		All means of transport	Rail	Motor carrier	Private truck	Air	Water	Other	Unknown
TONS OF SHIPMENTS	(thousands of tons)								
U.S. TOTAL	36 395	100.0	52.6	18.7	20.6	-	7.7	-	.4
UNDER 100 MILES	8 533	100.0	27.5	23.3	40.6	-	7.8	.1	.6
UNDER 1000 POUNDS	80	100.0	-	31.9	67.4	-	.2	.2	.2
1000 TO 9999 POUNDS	341	100.0	.1	35.3	63.9	-	.6	.1	.1
10000 TO 29999 POUNDS	1 272	100.0	.7	31.6	67.1	-	.1	.5	-
30000 TO 59999 POUNDS	3 334	100.0	2.4	35.1	62.5	-	-	-	-
60000 TO 89999 POUNDS	435	100.0	55.4	11.3	33.3	-	-	-	-
90000 POUNDS AND OVER	3 070	100.0	65.7	7.3	3.7	-	21.5	-	1.7
100 TO 199 MILES	6 226	100.0	46.8	26.0	27.1	-	-	-	.1
UNDER 1000 POUNDS	52	100.0	-	42.5	57.2	-	-	.3	-
1000 TO 9999 POUNDS	278	100.0	.8	49.3	49.4	-	-	.6	-
10000 TO 29999 POUNDS	837	100.0	.5	28.5	71.1	-	-	-	-
30000 TO 59999 POUNDS	1 818	100.0	6.2	45.5	48.1	-	-	-	.1
60000 TO 89999 POUNDS	403	100.0	96.7	2.9	.3	-	-	-	-
90000 POUNDS AND OVER	2 835	100.0	84.8	13.4	1.7	-	-	-	.1
200 TO 299 MILES	5 598	100.0	62.5	19.7	16.9	-	.7	-	.3
UNDER 1000 POUNDS	28	100.0	.6	54.5	44.7	-	-	.2	.3
1000 TO 9999 POUNDS	209	100.0	.9	41.3	57.8	-	-	-	-
10000 TO 29999 POUNDS	441	100.0	4.2	53.2	42.4	-	-	.1	.1
30000 TO 59999 POUNDS	1 427	100.0	7.0	50.8	41.8	-	-	-	.4
60000 TO 89999 POUNDS	320	100.0	96.0	4.0	-	-	-	-	-
90000 POUNDS AND OVER	3 172	100.0	96.7	1.0	.9	-	1.2	-	.3
300 TO 499 MILES	8 408	100.0	54.2	12.4	10.6	-	22.2	-	.6
UNDER 1000 POUNDS	24	100.0	.2	79.6	19.2	-	-	.8	.3
1000 TO 9999 POUNDS	201	100.0	3.2	50.6	46.0	-	-	.1	-
10000 TO 29999 POUNDS	471	100.0	5.7	45.3	48.4	-	.5	-	.1
30000 TO 59999 POUNDS	1 442	100.0	19.0	44.3	36.6	-	-	.1	.1
60000 TO 89999 POUNDS	678	100.0	93.8	5.0	1.0	-	-	-	.2
90000 POUNDS AND OVER	5 590	100.0	64.7	.6	.5	-	33.4	-	.8
500 TO 999 MILES	5 726	100.0	72.1	15.6	8.6	-	3.6	-	.2
UNDER 1000 POUNDS	26	100.0	5.4	88.3	5.2	.2	-	.4	.6
1000 TO 9999 POUNDS	150	100.0	10.8	59.0	30.0	-	-	.1	-
10000 TO 29999 POUNDS	255	100.0	10.8	53.8	35.0	-	-	-	.4
30000 TO 59999 POUNDS	1 259	100.0	29.4	42.5	27.7	-	-	-	.5
60000 TO 89999 POUNDS	706	100.0	96.9	3.1	-	-	-	-	-
90000 POUNDS AND OVER	3 328	100.0	91.0	2.6	.2	-	6.2	-	.1
1000 TO 1499 MILES	1 163	100.0	92.5	6.1	1.4	-	-	-	-
UNDER 1000 POUNDS	4	100.0	5.6	89.7	2.1	1.4	-	1.2	-
1000 TO 9999 POUNDS	12	100.0	8.3	57.2	33.6	1.0	-	-	-
10000 TO 29999 POUNDS	24	100.0	38.6	45.4	16.0	-	-	-	-
30000 TO 59999 POUNDS	85	100.0	43.9	48.4	7.7	-	-	-	-
60000 TO 89999 POUNDS	139	100.0	94.4	5.6	-	-	-	-	-
90000 POUNDS AND OVER	897	100.0	99.8	-	.2	-	-	-	-
1500 MILES OR OVER	737	100.0	83.9	13.0	.9	-	1.7	-	.5
UNDER 1000 POUNDS	5	100.0	5.2	79.5	2.5	.9	8.5	2.1	1.3
1000 TO 9999 POUNDS	20	100.0	5.8	56.5	5.5	-	32.2	-	-
10000 TO 29999 POUNDS	17	100.0	11.3	61.3	3.4	-	22.3	-	1.6
30000 TO 59999 POUNDS	97	100.0	47.0	46.6	4.8	-	1.6	-	-
60000 TO 89999 POUNDS	105	100.0	91.8	5.1	-	-	-	-	3.2
90000 POUNDS AND OVER	491	100.0	96.2	3.8	-	-	-	-	-
TON-MILES OF SHIPMENTS	(millions of ton-miles)								
U.S. TOTAL	12 727	100.0	66.7	14.9	10.5	-	7.6	-	.3
UNDER 100 MILES	461	100.0	31.1	19.2	38.3	-	10.5	-	.9
UNDER 1000 POUNDS	3	100.0	-	36.0	63.5	-	.1	.3	.1
1000 TO 9999 POUNDS	15	100.0	.1	38.7	60.8	-	.2	-	.1
10000 TO 29999 POUNDS	61	100.0	.6	30.9	68.3	-	-	.2	-
30000 TO 59999 POUNDS	169	100.0	2.9	30.6	66.5	-	-	-	-
60000 TO 89999 POUNDS	24	100.0	60.0	10.7	29.3	-	-	-	-
90000 POUNDS AND OVER	187	100.0	65.9	4.3	1.8	-	25.8	-	2.3
100 TO 199 MILES	893	100.0	48.6	25.1	26.2	-	-	-	.1
UNDER 1000 POUNDS	7	100.0	-	43.7	55.9	-	-	.3	-
1000 TO 9999 POUNDS	40	100.0	1.1	49.1	49.1	-	-	.7	-
10000 TO 29999 POUNDS	119	100.0	.5	29.2	70.3	-	-	-	-
30000 TO 59999 POUNDS	254	100.0	6.9	46.3	46.6	-	-	.1	.2
60000 TO 89999 POUNDS	62	100.0	97.4	2.4	.2	-	-	-	-
90000 POUNDS AND OVER	408	100.0	86.8	11.5	1.6	-	-	-	.1

See footnotes at end of table 4.

TABLE 4. **TCC GROUP 209—Percent Distribution of Distance Shipped and Weight of Shipment, by Means of Transport: 1972**—Continued

Distance shipped and weight of shipment[2][3]	Number	Percent distribution by means of transport							
		All means of transport	Rail	Motor carrier	Private truck	Air	Water	Other	Unknown
TON-MILES OF SHIPMENTS	(millions of ton-miles)								
200 TO 299 MILES.........	1 328	100.0	61.0	20.4	17.6	-	.8	-	.3
UNDER 1000 POUNDS.....	6	100.0	.7	55.7	43.4	-	-	.2	-
1000 TO 9999 POUNDS...	51	100.0	.9	40.9	58.2	-	-	-	.1
10000 TO 29999 POUNDS.	108	100.0	4.4	52.8	42.6	-	-	.1	.1
30000 TO 59999 POUNDS.	353	100.0	7.0	50.8	41.7	-	-	-	.4
60000 TO 89999 POUNDS.	81	100.0	96.6	3.4	-	-	-	-	-
90000 POUNDS AND OVER.	726	100.0	96.6	.9	.9	-	1.4	-	.3
300 TO 499 MILES.........	3 265	100.0	54.4	12.3	10.2	-	22.6	-	.5
UNDER 1000 POUNDS.....	9	100.0	.2	79.7	19.0	-	-	.8	.3
1000 TO 9999 POUNDS...	78	100.0	3.4	50.6	45.8	-	-	.1	-
10000 TO 29999 POUNDS.	179	100.0	5.5	45.6	48.4	-	.5	-	.1
30000 TO 59999 POUNDS.	546	100.0	19.2	45.2	35.5	-	-	.1	.1
60000 TO 89999 POUNDS.	256	100.0	94.0	4.7	1.1	-	-	-	.2
90000 POUNDS AND OVER.	2 194	100.0	64.5	.6	.6	-	33.5	-	.7
500 TO 999 MILES.........	3 837	100.0	71.8	15.9	8.5	-	3.6	-	.2
UNDER 1000 POUNDS.....	18	100.0	5.1	88.5	5.1	.2	-	.4	.7
1000 TO 9999 POUNDS...	101	100.0	11.6	58.5	29.8	-	-	.1	-
10000 TO 29999 POUNDS.	168	100.0	11.0	54.0	34.4	-	-	-	.6
30000 TO 59999 POUNDS.	860	100.0	29.8	42.4	27.2	-	-	-	.6
60000 TO 89999 POUNDS.	488	100.0	96.8	3.2	-	-	-	-	-
90000 POUNDS AND OVER.	2 201	100.0	90.6	2.9	.2	-	6.3	-	.1
1000 TO 1499 MILES......	1 545	100.0	93.1	5.6	1.2	-	-	-	-
UNDER 1000 POUNDS.....	5	100.0	5.4	90.1	1.8	1.6	-	1.1	-
1000 TO 9999 POUNDS...	13	100.0	8.2	58.8	32.0	1.0	-	-	-
10000 TO 29999 POUNDS.	30	100.0	37.5	46.4	16.1	-	-	-	-
30000 TO 59999 POUNDS.	104	100.0	44.3	48.3	7.4	-	-	-	-
60000 TO 89999 POUNDS.	172	100.0	94.2	5.8	-	-	-	-	-
90000 POUNDS AND OVER.	1 218	100.0	99.8	-	.2	-	-	-	-
1500 MILES OR OVER......	1 394	100.0	81.3	14.8	1.0	-	2.2	-	.6
UNDER 1000 POUNDS.....	10	100.0	5.0	76.9	2.5	.7	10.2	3.6	1.0
1000 TO 9999 POUNDS...	44	100.0	5.1	52.9	4.8	-	37.2	-	-
10000 TO 29999 POUNDS.	38	100.0	11.3	58.5	3.1	-	25.2	-	2.0
30000 TO 59999 POUNDS.	208	100.0	45.6	47.5	5.0	-	1.8	-	3.6
60000 TO 89999 POUNDS.	190	100.0	91.0	5.4	-	-	-	-	-
90000 POUNDS AND OVER.	902	100.0	95.2	4.8	-	-	-	-	-

Note: Detail may not add to total due to rounding. The introductory table shows the estimates of sampling variability for tons; sampling variability for ton-miles has not been estimated. See the map in the Introduction for the States comprising the geographic divisions of the United States.
Shipments excluded from the survey are those moving by pipeline (primarily petroleum products from refineries), parcel post shipments, and commodities moved by own power (motorized vehicles, aircraft, etc.) or towed (prefabricated buildings, etc.). Local shipments (commodities shipped less than 25 miles from the plant) and shipments within the same city are also excluded. Shipments to Alaska and Hawaii from the 48 conterminous States and the District of Columbia are included; however, no data were obtained for shipments originating in Alaska and Hawaii.

- Represents zero or rounds to zero.   (D) Withheld to avoid disclosing figures for individual companies.

[1]Production of this commodity is concentrated in the geographic divisions shown; figures and distributions for geographic divisions not shown are included in the total.
[2]Distances of shipments to foreign destinations are calculated only to the U.S. port of exit.
[3]Includes only shipments represented by bills of lading and invoices. Summary records which did not show individual weights of shipments are not included.

TCC 211. Cigarettes

Comparisons of Tons and Ton-Miles of Shipments for
Geographic Divisions of Origin and for Sampling Variability: 1972 and 1967

Geographic division of origin	Estimates				Relative sampling variability in tons (percent)	
	1972		1967		1972	1967
	Tons (thousands)	Ton-miles (millions)	Tons (thousands)	Ton-miles (millions)		
U.S. total	993	801	1,100	953	4.1	(*)
New England	–	–	(*)	(*)	–	(*)
Middle Atlantic	–	–	(*)	(*)	–	(*)
East North Central	–	–	(*)	(*)	–	(*)
West North Central	–	–	(*)	(*)	–	(*)
South Atlantic	787	653	(*)	(*)	4.9	(*)
East South Central	206	148	(*)	(*)	2.2	(*)
West South Central	–	–	(*)	(*)	–	(*)
Mountain	–	–	(*)	(*)	–	(*)
Pacific	–	–	(*)	(*)	–	(*)

– Represents or rounds to zero.   (D) Withheld to avoid disclosing figures for individual companies.   (*) Data not published.

TABLE 1. **TCC GROUP 211**—Percent Distribution of Geographic Division of Origin and Distance Shipped, by Means of Transport: 1972

Geographic division of origin[1] and distance shipped[2]	Number	Percent distribution by means of transport							
		All means of transport	Rail	Motor carrier	Private truck	Air	Water	Other	Unknown
TONS OF SHIPMENTS	(thousands of tons)								
U.S. TOTAL..........	993	100.0	51.3	47.6	.1	-	.1	.4	.5
SOUTH ATLANTIC..........	787	100.0	49.5	49.1	.1	-	.2	.5	.6
UNDER 100 MILES.......	54	100.0	-	98.2	1.8	-	-	-	-
100 TO 199 MILES......	60	100.0	1.0	98.4	-	-	-	-	.6
200 TO 299 MILES......	79	100.0	12.0	87.4	-	-	-	-	.5
300 TO 499 MILES......	165	100.0	45.7	51.8	-	-	-	-	2.4
500 TO 999 MILES......	231	100.0	67.4	30.8	-	-	-	1.8	-
1000 TO 1499 MILES....	46	100.0	45.2	54.8	-	-	-	-	-
1500 MILES OR OVER....	149	100.0	84.9	14.3	-	-	.8	-	-
EAST SOUTH CENTRAL......	206	100.0	58.3	41.7	-	-	-	-	-
UNDER 100 MILES.......	3	100.0	-	99.7	.3	-	-	-	-
100 TO 199 MILES......	11	100.0	15.2	84.8	-	-	-	-	-
200 TO 299 MILES......	24	100.0	61.2	38.8	-	-	-	-	-
300 TO 499 MILES......	58	100.0	44.6	55.4	-	-	-	-	-
500 TO 999 MILES......	68	100.0	66.1	33.9	-	-	-	-	-
1000 TO 1499 MILES....	4	100.0	75.7	24.3	-	-	-	-	-
1500 MILES OR OVER....	34	100.0	81.2	18.8	-	-	-	-	-
TON-MILES OF SHIPMENTS	(millions of ton-miles)								
U.S. TOTAL..........	801	100.0	68.2	30.3	-	-	.7	.5	.2
SOUTH ATLANTIC..........	653	100.0	67.8	30.4	-	-	.9	.6	.3
UNDER 100 MILES.......	3	100.0	-	99.6	.4	-	-	-	-
100 TO 199 MILES......	8	100.0	1.1	98.4	-	-	-	-	.5
200 TO 299 MILES......	20	100.0	12.8	86.6	-	-	-	-	.5
300 TO 499 MILES......	67	100.0	47.2	50.4	-	-	-	-	2.4
500 TO 999 MILES......	165	100.0	66.3	31.3	-	-	-	2.4	-
1000 TO 1499 MILES....	55	100.0	50.0	50.0	-	-	-	-	-
1500 MILES OR OVER....	332	100.0	81.6	16.7	-	-	1.7	-	-
EAST SOUTH CENTRAL......	148	100.0	70.0	30.0	-	-	-	-	-
UNDER 100 MILES.......	-	100.0	-	100.0	-	-	-	-	-
100 TO 199 MILES......	1	100.0	14.9	85.1	-	-	-	-	-
200 TO 299 MILES......	6	100.0	62.3	37.7	-	-	-	-	-
300 TO 499 MILES......	22	100.0	45.3	54.7	-	-	-	-	-
500 TO 999 MILES......	48	100.0	67.5	32.5	-	-	-	-	-
1000 TO 1499 MILES....	5	100.0	74.2	25.8	-	-	-	-	-
1500 MILES OR OVER....	63	100.0	82.7	17.3	-	-	-	-	-

See footnotes at end of table 4.

TABLE 2. **TCC GROUP 211**—Percent Distribution of Geographic Division of Origin and Means of Transport, by Geographic Division of Destination: 1972

Geographic division of origin[1] and means of transport	Number	Percent distribution by division of destination									
		U.S. total	New England	Middle Atlantic	East North Central	West North Central	South Atlantic	East South Central	West South Central	Mountain	Pacific
TONS OF SHIPMENTS	(thousands of tons)										
U.S. TOTAL..............	993	100.0	5.9	13.0	16.8	7.8	21.4	4.7	12.0	4.2	14.4
RAIL...................	509	100.0	8.0	10.3	16.9	6.6	9.1	3.1	15.9	7.2	23.0
MOTOR CARRIER..........	472	100.0	3.7	16.3	16.2	8.4	34.7	6.5	8.1	1.0	5.1
PRIVATE TRUCK..........	-	100.0	-	-	.9	-	99.1	-	-	-	-
AIR....................	-	100.0	-	-	-	-	-	-	-	-	100.0
WATER..................	1	100.0	-	-	-	-	-	-	-	-	100.0
OTHER..................	4	100.0	.1	.3	.6	97.8	1.0	.1	.1	-	-
UNKNOWN................	4	100.0	-	-	83.9	-	16.1	-	-	-	-
SOUTH ATLANTIC..........	787	100.0	6.7	13.0	14.0	7.4	24.5	4.1	11.8	4.2	14.4
RAIL...................	389	100.0	9.2	8.8	16.0	6.0	10.3	2.3	15.7	8.4	23.4
MOTOR CARRIER..........	386	100.0	4.3	17.7	11.4	7.9	39.0	6.0	8.2	-	5.5
PRIVATE TRUCK..........	-	100.0	-	-	-	-	100.0	-	-	-	-
AIR....................	-	100.0	-	-	-	-	-	-	-	-	100.0
WATER..................	1	100.0	-	-	-	-	-	-	-	-	-
OTHER..................	4	100.0	.1	.3	.6	97.8	1.0	.1	.1	-	-
UNKNOWN................	4	100.0	-	-	83.9	-	16.1	-	-	-	-
EAST SOUTH CENTRAL......	206	100.0	2.9	12.9	27.3	9.3	9.4	7.0	12.8	4.3	14.1
RAIL...................	120	100.0	4.1	15.0	19.8	8.5	4.9	5.9	16.5	3.4	21.9
MOTOR CARRIER..........	86	100.0	1.3	9.9	37.9	10.6	15.6	8.5	7.6	5.6	3.2
PRIVATE TRUCK..........	-	100.0	-	-	100.0	-	-	-	-	-	-
AIR....................	-	100.0	-	-	-	-	-	-	-	-	-
WATER..................	-	100.0	-	-	-	-	-	-	-	-	-
OTHER..................	-	100.0	-	-	-	-	-	-	100.0	-	-
UNKNOWN................	-	100.0	-	-	-	-	-	-	-	-	-

See footnotes at end of table 4.

TABLE 2. **TCC GROUP 211—Percent Distribution of Geographic Division of Origin and Means of Transport, by Geographic Division of Destination: 1972**—Continued

Geographic division of origin[1] and means of transport	Number	Percent distribution by division of destination									
		U.S. total	New England	Middle Atlantic	East North Central	West North Central	South Atlantic	East South Oentral	West South Central	Mountain	Pacific
TON-MILES OF SHIPMENTS	(millions of ton-miles)										
U.S. TOTAL................	801	100.0	4.0	6.7	8.6	7.6	7.0	2.0	15.2	8.3	40.6
RAIL....................	547	100.0	4.1	4.5	7.3	4.6	4.7	1.1	15.5	10.9	47.4
MOTOR CARRIER..........	243	100.0	3.8	12.0	11.4	13.0	12.5	4.0	15.3	2.9	25.0
PRIVATE TRUCK.........	-	100.0	-	-	.5	-	99.5	-	-	-	-
AIR....................	-	100.0	-	-	-	-	-	-	-	-	-
WATER.................	5	100.0	-	-	-	-	-	-	-	-	100.0
OTHER.................	3	100.0	.1	.1	.4	99.2	.2	-	.1	-	-
UNKNOWN...............	1	100.0	-	-	91.4	-	8.6	-	-	-	-
SOUTH ATLANTIC..........	653	100.0	4.2	5.9	8.3	7.7	6.9	1.8	15.6	8.3	41.4
RAIL....................	443	100.0	4.3	3.2	7.5	4.4	4.8	.9	15.5	12.2	47.2
MOTOR CARRIER..........	198	100.0	4.2	12.3	9.8	13.5	11.7	4.0	16.6	-	27.9
PRIVATE TRUCK.........	-	100.0	-	-	-	-	100.0	-	-	-	-
AIR....................	-	100.0	-	-	-	-	-	-	-	-	-
WATER.................	5	100.0	-	-	-	-	-	-	-	-	100.0
OTHER.................	3	100.0	.1	.1	.4	99.2	.2	-	.1	-	-
UNKNOWN...............	1	100.0	-	-	91.4	-	8.6	-	-	-	-
EAST SOUTH CENTRAL......	148	100.0	3.1	10.2	10.2	6.9	7.7	2.6	13.7	8.4	37.2
RAIL....................	103	100.0	3.6	9.9	6.5	5.2	4.0	2.1	15.3	5.3	48.0
MOTOR CARRIER.........	44	100.0	1.8	11.0	18.7	10.7	16.3	4.0	9.7	15.8	11.9
PRIVATE TRUCK.........	-	100.0	-	-	100.0	-	-	-	-	-	-
AIR....................	-	100.0	-	-	-	-	-	-	-	-	-
WATER.................	-	100.0	-	-	-	-	-	-	-	-	-
OTHER.................	-	100.0	-	-	-	-	-	-	100.0	-	-
UNKNOWN...............	-	100.0	-	-	-	-	-	-	-	-	-

See footnotes at end of table 4.

TABLE 3. **TCC GROUP 211**—Percent Distribution of Geographic Division of Destination and Means of Transport, by Geographic Division of Origin: 1972

Geographic division of destination and means of transport	Number	Percent distribution by division of origin[1]									
		U.S. total	New England	Middle Atlantic	East North Central	West North Central	South Atlantic	East South Central	West South Central	Mountain	Pacific
TONS OF SHIPMENTS	(thousands of tons)										
U.S. TOTAL...............	993	100.0	-	-	-	-	79.2	20.8	-	-	-
RAIL...................	509	100.0	-	-	-	-	76.4	23.6	-	-	-
MOTOR CARRIER.........	472	100.0	-	-	-	-	81.8	18.2	-	-	-
PRIVATE TRUCK.........	-	100.0	-	-	-	-	99.1	.9	-	-	-
AIR...................	-	100.0	-	-	-	-	-	-	-	-	-
WATER................	1	100.0	-	-	-	-	100.0	-	-	-	-
OTHER................	4	100.0	-	-	-	-	99.9	.1	-	-	-
UNKNOWN..............	4	100.0	-	-	-	-	100.0	-	-	-	-
NEW ENGLAND..............	58	100.0	-	-	-	-	89.7	10.3	-	-	-
RAIL...................	40	100.0	-	-	-	-	88.0	12.0	-	-	-
MOTOR CARRIER.........	17	100.0	-	-	-	-	93.9	6.1	-	-	-
PRIVATE TRUCK.........	-	100.0	-	-	-	-	-	-	-	-	-
AIR...................	-	100.0	-	-	-	-	-	-	-	-	-
WATER................	-	100.0	-	-	-	-	-	-	-	-	-
OTHER................	-	100.0	-	-	-	-	100.0	-	-	-	-
UNKNOWN..............	-	100.0	-	-	-	-	-	-	-	-	-
MIDDLE ATLANTIC.........	129	100.0	-	-	-	-	79.4	20.6	-	-	-
RAIL...................	52	100.0	-	-	-	-	65.5	34.5	-	-	-
MOTOR CARRIER.........	76	100.0	-	-	-	-	88.9	11.1	-	-	-
PRIVATE TRUCK.........	-	100.0	-	-	-	-	-	-	-	-	-
AIR...................	-	100.0	-	-	-	-	-	-	-	-	-
WATER................	-	100.0	-	-	-	-	-	-	-	-	-
OTHER................	-	100.0	-	-	-	-	100.0	-	-	-	-
UNKNOWN..............	-	100.0	-	-	-	-	-	-	-	-	-
EAST NORTH CENTRAL......	166	100.0	-	-	-	-	66.2	33.8	-	-	-
RAIL...................	85	100.0	-	-	-	-	72.3	27.7	-	-	-
MOTOR CARRIER.........	76	100.0	-	-	-	-	57.4	42.6	-	-	-
PRIVATE TRUCK.........	-	100.0	-	-	-	-	-	100.0	-	-	-
AIR...................	-	100.0	-	-	-	-	-	-	-	-	-
WATER................	-	100.0	-	-	-	-	-	-	-	-	-
OTHER................	-	100.0	-	-	-	-	100.0	-	-	-	-
UNKNOWN..............	4	100.0	-	-	-	-	100.0	-	-	-	-
WEST NORTH CENTRAL......	77	100.0	-	-	-	-	75.0	25.0	-	-	-
RAIL...................	33	100.0	-	-	-	-	69.5	30.5	-	-	-
MOTOR CARRIER.........	39	100.0	-	-	-	-	77.1	22.9	-	-	-
PRIVATE TRUCK.........	-	100.0	-	-	-	-	-	-	-	-	-
AIR...................	-	100.0	-	-	-	-	-	-	-	-	-
WATER................	-	100.0	-	-	-	-	-	-	-	-	-
OTHER................	4	100.0	-	-	-	-	100.0	-	-	-	-
UNKNOWN..............	-	100.0	-	-	-	-	-	-	-	-	-
SOUTH ATLANTIC..........	212	100.0	-	-	-	-	90.9	9.1	-	-	-
RAIL...................	46	100.0	-	-	-	-	87.3	12.7	-	-	-
MOTOR CARRIER.........	164	100.0	-	-	-	-	91.8	8.2	-	-	-
PRIVATE TRUCK.........	-	100.0	-	-	-	-	100.0	-	-	-	-
AIR...................	-	100.0	-	-	-	-	-	-	-	-	-
WATER................	-	100.0	-	-	-	-	-	-	-	-	-
OTHER................	-	100.0	-	-	-	-	100.0	-	-	-	-
UNKNOWN..............	-	100.0	-	-	-	-	100.0	-	-	-	-
EAST SOUTH CENTRAL......	46	100.0	-	-	-	-	69.1	30.9	-	-	-
RAIL...................	15	100.0	-	-	-	-	55.6	44.4	-	-	-
MOTOR CARRIER.........	30	100.0	-	-	-	-	76.2	23.8	-	-	-
PRIVATE TRUCK.........	-	100.0	-	-	-	-	-	-	-	-	-
AIR...................	-	100.0	-	-	-	-	-	-	-	-	-
WATER................	-	100.0	-	-	-	-	-	-	-	-	-
OTHER................	-	100.0	-	-	-	-	100.0	-	-	-	-
UNKNOWN..............	-	100.0	-	-	-	-	-	-	-	-	-
WEST SOUTH CENTRAL......	119	100.0	-	-	-	-	77.8	22.2	-	-	-
RAIL...................	80	100.0	-	-	-	-	75.4	24.6	-	-	-
MOTOR CARRIER.........	38	100.0	-	-	-	-	82.9	17.1	-	-	-
PRIVATE TRUCK.........	-	100.0	-	-	-	-	-	-	-	-	-
AIR...................	-	100.0	-	-	-	-	-	-	-	-	-
WATER................	-	100.0	-	-	-	-	-	-	-	-	-
OTHER................	-	100.0	-	-	-	-	50.7	49.3	-	-	-
UNKNOWN..............	-	100.0	-	-	-	-	-	-	-	-	-
MOUNTAIN................	41	100.0	-	-	-	-	78.7	21.3	-	-	-
RAIL...................	36	100.0	-	-	-	-	88.9	11.1	-	-	-
MOTOR CARRIER.........	4	100.0	-	-	-	-	-	100.0	-	-	-
PRIVATE TRUCK.........	-	100.0	-	-	-	-	-	-	-	-	-
AIR...................	-	100.0	-	-	-	-	-	-	-	-	-
WATER................	-	100.0	-	-	-	-	-	-	-	-	-
OTHER................	-	100.0	-	-	-	-	-	-	-	-	-
UNKNOWN..............	-	100.0	-	-	-	-	-	-	-	-	-
PACIFIC.................	142	100.0	-	-	-	-	79.6	20.4	-	-	-
RAIL...................	117	100.0	-	-	-	-	77.5	22.5	-	-	-
MOTOR CARRIER.........	24	100.0	-	-	-	-	88.6	11.4	-	-	-
PRIVATE TRUCK.........	-	100.0	-	-	-	-	-	-	-	-	-
AIR...................	-	100.0	-	-	-	-	-	-	-	-	-
WATER................	1	100.0	-	-	-	-	100.0	-	-	-	-
OTHER................	-	100.0	-	-	-	-	-	-	-	-	-
UNKNOWN..............	-	100.0	-	-	-	-	-	-	-	-	-

See footnotes at end of table 4.

TABLE 3. **TCC GROUP 211**—Percent Distribution of Geographic Division of Destination and Means of Transport, by Geographic Division of Origin: 1972—Continued

Geographic division of destination and means of transport	Number	Percent distribution by division of origin[1]									
		U.S. total	New England	Middle Atlantic	East North Central	West North Central	South Atlantic	East South Central	West South Central	Mountain	Pacific
TON-MILES OF SHIPMENTS	(millions of ton-miles)										
U.S. TOTAL.............	801	100.0	-	-	-	-	81.5	18.5	-	-	-
RAIL.................	547	100.0	-	-	-	-	81.1	18.9	-	-	-
MOTOR CARRIER.........	243	100.0	-	-	-	-	81.7	18.3	-	-	-
PRIVATE TRUCK.........	-	100.0	-	-	-	-	99.5	.5	-	-	-
AIR..................	-	100.0	-	-	-	-	-	-	-	-	-
WATER................	5	100.0	-	-	-	-	100.0	-	-	-	-
OTHER................	3	100.0	-	-	-	-	100.0	-	-	-	-
UNKNOWN..............	1	100.0	-	-	-	-	100.0	-	-	-	-
NEW ENGLAND.............	31	100.0	-	-	-	-	85.6	14.4	-	-	-
RAIL.................	22	100.0	-	-	-	-	83.4	16.6	-	-	-
MOTOR CARRIER.........	9	100.0	-	-	-	-	91.1	8.9	-	-	-
PRIVATE TRUCK.........	-	100.0	-	-	-	-	-	-	-	-	-
AIR..................	-	100.0	-	-	-	-	-	-	-	-	-
WATER................	-	100.0	-	-	-	-	-	-	-	-	-
OTHER................	-	100.0	-	-	-	-	100.0	-	-	-	-
UNKNOWN..............	-	100.0	-	-	-	-	-	-	-	-	-
MIDDLE ATLANTIC.........	53	100.0	-	-	-	-	71.9	28.1	-	-	-
RAIL.................	24	100.0	-	-	-	-	58.3	41.7	-	-	-
MOTOR CARRIER.........	29	100.0	-	-	-	-	83.3	16.7	-	-	-
PRIVATE TRUCK.........	-	100.0	-	-	-	-	-	-	-	-	-
AIR..................	-	100.0	-	-	-	-	-	-	-	-	-
WATER................	-	100.0	-	-	-	-	-	-	-	-	-
OTHER................	-	100.0	-	-	-	-	100.0	-	-	-	-
UNKNOWN..............	-	100.0	-	-	-	-	-	-	-	-	-
EAST NORTH CENTRAL......	69	100.0	-	-	-	-	78.2	21.8	-	-	-
RAIL.................	39	100.0	-	-	-	-	83.0	17.0	-	-	-
MOTOR CARRIER.........	27	100.0	-	-	-	-	70.0	30.0	-	-	-
PRIVATE TRUCK.........	-	100.0	-	-	-	-	-	100.0	-	-	-
AIR..................	-	100.0	-	-	-	-	-	-	-	-	-
WATER................	-	100.0	-	-	-	-	-	-	-	-	-
OTHER................	-	100.0	-	-	-	-	100.0	-	-	-	-
UNKNOWN..............	1	100.0	-	-	-	-	100.0	-	-	-	-
WEST NORTH CENTRAL......	60	100.0	-	-	-	-	83.2	16.8	-	-	-
RAIL.................	25	100.0	-	-	-	-	78.4	21.6	-	-	-
MOTOR CARRIER.........	31	100.0	-	-	-	-	84.9	15.1	-	-	-
PRIVATE TRUCK.........	-	100.0	-	-	-	-	-	-	-	-	-
AIR..................	-	100.0	-	-	-	-	-	-	-	-	-
WATER................	-	100.0	-	-	-	-	-	-	-	-	-
OTHER................	3	100.0	-	-	-	-	100.0	-	-	-	-
UNKNOWN..............	-	100.0	-	-	-	-	-	-	-	-	-
SOUTH ATLANTIC.........	56	100.0	-	-	-	-	79.7	20.3	-	-	-
RAIL.................	25	100.0	-	-	-	-	83.6	16.4	-	-	-
MOTOR CARRIER.........	30	100.0	-	-	-	-	76.2	23.8	-	-	-
PRIVATE TRUCK.........	-	100.0	-	-	-	-	100.0	-	-	-	-
AIR..................	-	100.0	-	-	-	-	-	-	-	-	-
WATER................	-	100.0	-	-	-	-	-	-	-	-	-
OTHER................	-	100.0	-	-	-	-	100.0	-	-	-	-
UNKNOWN..............	-	100.0	-	-	-	-	100.0	-	-	-	-
EAST SOUTH CENTRAL......	15	100.0	-	-	-	-	75.2	24.8	-	-	-
RAIL.................	5	100.0	-	-	-	-	63.9	36.1	-	-	-
MOTOR CARRIER.........	9	100.0	-	-	-	-	82.1	17.9	-	-	-
PRIVATE TRUCK.........	-	100.0	-	-	-	-	-	-	-	-	-
AIR..................	-	100.0	-	-	-	-	-	-	-	-	-
WATER................	-	100.0	-	-	-	-	-	-	-	-	-
OTHER................	-	100.0	-	-	-	-	100.0	-	-	-	-
UNKNOWN..............	-	100.0	-	-	-	-	-	-	-	-	-
WEST SOUTH CENTRAL......	122	100.0	-	-	-	-	83.4	16.6	-	-	-
RAIL.................	84	100.0	-	-	-	-	81.2	18.8	-	-	-
MOTOR CARRIER.........	37	100.0	-	-	-	-	88.4	11.6	-	-	-
PRIVATE TRUCK.........	-	100.0	-	-	-	-	-	-	-	-	-
AIR..................	-	100.0	-	-	-	-	-	-	-	-	-
WATER................	-	100.0	-	-	-	-	-	-	-	-	-
OTHER................	-	100.0	-	-	-	-	65.6	34.4	-	-	-
UNKNOWN..............	-	100.0	-	-	-	-	-	-	-	-	-
MOUNTAIN...............	66	100.0	-	-	-	-	81.2	18.8	-	-	-
RAIL.................	59	100.0	-	-	-	-	90.8	9.2	-	-	-
MOTOR CARRIER.........	7	100.0	-	-	-	-	-	100.0	-	-	-
PRIVATE TRUCK.........	-	100.0	-	-	-	-	-	-	-	-	-
AIR..................	-	100.0	-	-	-	-	-	-	-	-	-
WATER................	-	100.0	-	-	-	-	-	-	-	-	-
OTHER................	-	100.0	-	-	-	-	-	-	-	-	-
UNKNOWN..............	-	100.0	-	-	-	-	-	-	-	-	-
PACIFIC................	325	100.0	-	-	-	-	83.1	16.9	-	-	-
RAIL.................	259	100.0	-	-	-	-	80.8	19.2	-	-	-
MOTOR CARRIER.........	60	100.0	-	-	-	-	91.3	8.7	-	-	-
PRIVATE TRUCK.........	-	100.0	-	-	-	-	-	-	-	-	-
AIR..................	-	100.0	-	-	-	-	-	-	-	-	-
WATER................	5	100.0	-	-	-	-	100.0	-	-	-	-
OTHER................	-	100.0	-	-	-	-	-	-	-	-	-
UNKNOWN..............	-	100.0	-	-	-	-	-	-	-	-	-

See footnotes at end of table 4.

TABLE 4. TCC GROUP 211—Percent Distribution of Distance Shipped and Weight of Shipment, by Means of Transport: 1972

Distance shipped and weight of shipment[2][3]	Number	Percent distribution by means of transport							
		All means of transport	Rail	Motor carrier	Private truck	Air	Water	Other	Unknown
TONS OF SHIPMENTS	(thousands of tons)								
U.S. TOTAL	779	100.0	53.0	46.7	.1	-	.2	-	.1
UNDER 100 MILES	38	100.0	-	97.4	2.6	-	-	-	-
UNDER 1000 POUNDS	7	100.0	-	99.9	.1	-	-	-	-
1000 TO 9999 POUNDS	14	100.0	-	93.0	7.0	-	-	-	-
10000 TO 29999 POUNDS	14	100.0	-	100.0	-	-	-	-	-
30000 TO 59999 POUNDS	1	100.0	-	100.0	-	-	-	-	-
60000 TO 89999 POUNDS	1	100.0	-	100.0	-	-	-	-	-
90000 POUNDS AND OVER	-	100.0	-	-	-	-	-	-	-
100 TO 199 MILES	54	100.0	4.3	95.6	-	-	-	-	-
UNDER 1000 POUNDS	9	100.0	-	99.8	-	-	-	.2	-
1000 TO 9999 POUNDS	19	100.0	-	100.0	-	-	-	-	-
10000 TO 29999 POUNDS	4	100.0	-	100.0	-	-	-	-	-
30000 TO 59999 POUNDS	19	100.0	8.9	91.1	-	-	-	-	-
60000 TO 89999 POUNDS	-	100.0	100.0	-	-	-	-	-	-
90000 POUNDS AND OVER	-	100.0	-	-	-	-	-	-	-
200 TO 299 MILES	93	100.0	26.4	73.1	-	-	-	-	.4
UNDER 1000 POUNDS	7	100.0	-	94.0	-	-	-	.1	5.9
1000 TO 9999 POUNDS	18	100.0	-	100.0	-	-	-	-	-
10000 TO 29999 POUNDS	9	100.0	-	100.0	-	-	-	-	-
30000 TO 59999 POUNDS	24	100.0	25.7	74.3	-	-	-	-	-
60000 TO 89999 POUNDS	34	100.0	54.2	45.8	-	-	-	-	-
90000 POUNDS AND OVER	-	100.0	-	-	-	-	-	-	-
300 TO 499 MILES	187	100.0	47.4	52.6	-	-	-	-	-
UNDER 1000 POUNDS	2	100.0	-	99.9	-	-	-	.1	-
1000 TO 9999 POUNDS	3	100.0	-	100.0	-	-	-	-	-
10000 TO 29999 POUNDS	12	100.0	20.8	79.2	-	-	-	-	-
30000 TO 59999 POUNDS	96	100.0	22.4	77.6	-	-	-	-	-
60000 TO 89999 POUNDS	71	100.0	90.1	9.9	-	-	-	-	-
90000 POUNDS AND OVER	-	100.0	-	-	-	-	-	-	-
500 TO 999 MILES	235	100.0	73.1	26.9	-	-	-	-	-
UNDER 1000 POUNDS	-	100.0	-	100.0	-	-	-	-	-
1000 TO 9999 POUNDS	-	100.0	-	100.0	-	-	-	-	-
10000 TO 29999 POUNDS	11	100.0	10.6	89.4	-	-	-	-	-
30000 TO 59999 POUNDS	127	100.0	60.4	39.6	-	-	-	-	-
60000 TO 89999 POUNDS	94	100.0	98.7	1.3	-	-	-	-	-
90000 POUNDS AND OVER	-	100.0	-	-	-	-	-	-	-
1000 TO 1499 MILES	36	100.0	51.7	48.3	-	-	-	-	-
UNDER 1000 POUNDS	-	100.0	-	-	-	-	-	-	-
1000 TO 9999 POUNDS	-	100.0	-	-	-	-	-	-	-
10000 TO 29999 POUNDS	8	100.0	4.3	95.7	-	-	-	-	-
30000 TO 59999 POUNDS	13	100.0	31.7	68.3	-	-	-	-	-
60000 TO 89999 POUNDS	14	100.0	100.0	-	-	-	-	-	-
90000 POUNDS AND OVER	-	100.0	-	-	-	-	-	-	-
1500 MILES OR OVER	133	100.0	79.5	19.6	-	-	.9	-	-
UNDER 1000 POUNDS	-	100.0	-	100.0	-	-	-	-	-
1000 TO 9999 POUNDS	-	100.0	100.0	-	-	-	-	-	-
10000 TO 29999 POUNDS	4	100.0	34.6	41.6	-	-	23.7	-	-
30000 TO 59999 POUNDS	80	100.0	91.9	8.1	-	-	-	-	-
60000 TO 89999 POUNDS	47	100.0	63.2	36.8	-	-	-	-	-
90000 POUNDS AND OVER	-	100.0	-	-	-	-	-	-	-
TON-MILES OF SHIPMENTS	(millions of ton-miles)								
U.S. TOTAL	605	100.0	67.6	31.4	-	-	.9	-	-
UNDER 100 MILES	2	100.0	-	99.4	.6	-	-	-	-
UNDER 1000 POUNDS	-	100.0	-	100.0	-	-	-	-	-
1000 TO 9999 POUNDS	-	100.0	-	98.2	1.8	-	-	-	-
10000 TO 29999 POUNDS	1	100.0	-	100.0	-	-	-	-	-
30000 TO 59999 POUNDS	-	100.0	-	100.0	-	-	-	-	-
60000 TO 89999 POUNDS	-	100.0	-	100.0	-	-	-	-	-
90000 POUNDS AND OVER	-	100.0	-	-	-	-	-	-	-
100 TO 199 MILES	7	100.0	4.6	95.4	-	-	-	-	-
UNDER 1000 POUNDS	1	100.0	-	99.8	-	-	-	.2	-
1000 TO 9999 POUNDS	2	100.0	-	100.0	-	-	-	-	-
10000 TO 29999 POUNDS	-	100.0	-	100.0	-	-	-	-	-
30000 TO 59999 POUNDS	2	100.0	9.3	90.7	-	-	-	-	-
60000 TO 89999 POUNDS	-	100.0	100.0	-	-	-	-	-	-
90000 POUNDS AND OVER	-	100.0	-	-	-	-	-	-	-

See footnotes at end of table 4.

TABLE 4. TCC GROUP 211—Percent Distribution of Distance Shipped and Weight of Shipment, by Means of Transport: 1972—Continued

Distance shipped and weight of shipment[2][3]	Number	Percent distribution by means of transport							
		All means of transport	Rail	Motor carrier	Private truck	Air	Water	Other	Unknown
TON-MILES OF SHIPMENTS	(millions of ton-miles)								
200 TO 299 MILES.........	23	100.0	27.6	71.9	-	-	-	-	.5
UNDER 1000 POUNDS......	1	100.0	-	93.6	-	-	-	.1	6.2
1000 TO 9999 POUNDS...	4	100.0	-	100.0	-	-	-	-	-
10000 TO 29999 POUNDS.	2	100.0	-	100.0	-	-	-	-	-
30000 TO 59999 POUNDS.	6	100.0	27.7	72.3	-	-	-	-	-
60000 TO 89999 POUNDS.	9	100.0	54.2	45.8	-	-	-	-	-
90000 POUNDS AND OVER.	-	100.0	-	-	-	-	-	-	-
300 TO 499 MILES........	74	100.0	48.7	51.3	-	-	-	-	-
UNDER 1000 POUNDS......	-	100.0	-	99.9	-	-	-	.1	-
1000 TO 9999 POUNDS...	1	100.0	-	100.0	-	-	-	-	-
10000 TO 29999 POUNDS.	5	100.0	20.7	79.3	-	-	-	-	-
30000 TO 59999 POUNDS.	38	100.0	22.5	77.5	-	-	-	-	-
60000 TO 89999 POUNDS.	28	100.0	92.2	7.8	-	-	-	-	-
90000 POUNDS AND OVER.	-	100.0	-	-	-	-	-	-	-
500 TO 999 MILES........	164	100.0	73.9	26.1	-	-	-	-	-
UNDER 1000 POUNDS......	-	100.0	-	100.0	-	-	-	-	-
1000 TO 9999 POUNDS...	-	100.0	-	100.0	-	-	-	-	-
10000 TO 29999 POUNDS.	7	100.0	10.3	89.7	-	-	-	-	-
30000 TO 59999 POUNDS.	91	100.0	62.2	37.8	-	-	-	-	-
60000 TO 89999 POUNDS.	65	100.0	98.7	1.3	-	-	-	-	-
90000 POUNDS AND OVER.	-	100.0	-	-	-	-	-	-	-
1000 TO 1499 MILES......	45	100.0	56.3	43.7	-	-	-	-	-
UNDER 1000 POUNDS......	-	100.0	-	-	-	-	-	-	-
1000 TO 9999 POUNDS...	-	100.0	-	-	-	-	-	-	-
10000 TO 29999 POUNDS.	10	100.0	5.3	94.7	-	-	-	-	-
30000 TO 59999 POUNDS.	14	100.0	35.1	64.9	-	-	-	-	-
60000 TO 89999 POUNDS.	19	100.0	100.0	-	-	-	-	-	-
90000 POUNDS AND OVER.	-	100.0	-	-	-	-	-	-	-
1500 MILES OR OVER......	286	100.0	76.2	21.8	-	-	2.0	-	-
UNDER 1000 POUNDS......	-	100.0	-	100.0	-	-	-	-	-
1000 TO 9999 POUNDS...	-	100.0	100.0	-	-	-	-	-	-
10000 TO 29999 POUNDS.	12	100.0	28.9	27.0	-	-	44.1	-	-
30000 TO 59999 POUNDS.	171	100.0	90.4	9.6	-	-	-	-	-
60000 TO 89999 POUNDS.	101	100.0	58.5	41.5	-	-	-	-	-
90000 POUNDS AND OVER.	-	100.0	-	-	-	-	-	-	-

Note: Detail may not add to total due to rounding. The introductory table shows the estimates of sampling variability for tons; sampling variability for ton-miles has not been estimated. See the map in the Introduction for the States comprising the geographic divisions of the United States.

Shipments excluded from the survey are those moving by pipeline (primarily petroleum products from refineries), parcel post shipments, and commodities moved by own power (motorized vehicles, aircraft, etc.) or towed (prefabricated buildings, etc.). Local shipments (commodities shipped less than 25 miles from the plant) and shipments within the same city are also excluded. Shipments to Alaska and Hawaii from the 48 conterminous States and the District of Columbia are included; however, no data were obtained for shipments originating in Alaska and Hawaii.

- Represents zero or rounds to zero.

[1]Production of this commodity is concentrated in the geographic divisions shown; figures and distributions for geographic divisions not shown are included in the total.

[2]Distances of shipments to foreign destinations are calculated only to the U.S. port of exit.

[3]Includes only shipments represented by bills of lading and invoices. Summary records which did not show individual weights of shipments are not included.

TCC 212. Cigars

Comparisons of Tons and Ton-Miles of Shipments for
Geographic Divisions of Origin and for Sampling Variability: 1972 and 1967

Geographic division of origin	Estimates				Relative sampling variability in tons (percent)	
	1972		1967		1972	1967
	Tons (thousands)	Ton-miles (millions)	Tons (thousands)	Ton-miles (millions)		
U.S. total	63	43	62	38	10.1	(*)
New England	—	—	(*)	(*)	—	(*)
Middle Atlantic	48	34	(*)	(*)	13.1	(*)
East North Central	(D)	(D)	(*)	(*)	(*)	(*)
West North Central	—	—	(*)	(*)	—	(*)
South Atlantic	7	5	(*)	(*)	11.0	(*)
East South Central	(D)	(D)	(*)	(*)	(*)	(*)
West South Central	—	—	(*)	(*)	—	(*)
Mountain	—	—	(*)	(*)	—	(*)
Pacific	—	—	(*)	(*)	—	(*)

— Represents or rounds to zero.   (D) Withheld to avoid disclosing figures for individual companies.   (*) Data not published.

TABLE 1. TCC GROUP 212—Percent Distribution of Geographic Division of Origin and Distance Shipped, by Means of Transport: 1972

Geographic division of origin[1] and distance shipped[2]	Number	Percent distribution by means of transport							
		All means of transport	Rail	Motor carrier	Private truck	Air	Water	Other	Unknown
TONS OF SHIPMENTS	(thousands of tons)								
U.S. TOTAL	63	100.0	14.4	84.0	.2	.1	-	.9	.4
MIDDLE ATLANTIC	48	100.0	16.8	82.3	-	-	-	.9	-
UNDER 100 MILES	7	100.0	-	99.2	.1	-	-	.7	-
100 TO 199 MILES	15	100.0	-	99.5	-	-	-	.4	-
200 TO 299 MILES	1	100.0	-	88.9	-	-	-	11.1	-
300 TO 499 MILES	6	100.0	-	99.7	-	-	-	.3	-
500 TO 999 MILES	6	100.0	.8	98.3	-	-	-	.8	-
1000 TO 1499 MILES	1	100.0	36.7	61.3	-	.8	-	1.3	-
1500 MILES OR OVER	9	100.0	77.8	21.9	-	-	-	.3	-
SOUTH ATLANTIC	7	100.0	3.4	90.7	1.6	.3	-	.9	3.2
UNDER 100 MILES	-	100.0	-	39.2	57.8	-	-	2.7	.2
100 TO 199 MILES	-	100.0	-	94.3	-	-	-	5.7	-
200 TO 299 MILES	-	100.0	-	99.1	-	-	-	.9	-
300 TO 499 MILES	1	100.0	-	86.9	-	.1	-	.2	12.8
500 TO 999 MILES	2	100.0	-	99.3	-	-	-	.7	-
1000 TO 1499 MILES	1	100.0	-	98.6	-	.1	-	1.1	.3
1500 MILES OR OVER	-	100.0	78.7	15.9	-	5.4	-	-	-
TON-MILES OF SHIPMENTS	(millions of ton-miles)								
U.S. TOTAL	43	100.0	47.6	51.3	-	.1	-	.7	.2
MIDDLE ATLANTIC	34	100.0	54.4	45.0	-	-	-	.5	-
UNDER 100 MILES	-	100.0	-	99.3	-	-	-	.7	-
100 TO 199 MILES	1	100.0	-	99.6	-	-	-	.4	-
200 TO 299 MILES	-	100.0	-	90.3	-	-	-	9.7	-
300 TO 499 MILES	2	100.0	-	99.8	-	-	-	.2	-
500 TO 999 MILES	4	100.0	1.0	98.2	-	.1	-	.8	-
1000 TO 1499 MILES	1	100.0	40.0	58.1	-	.7	-	1.2	-
1500 MILES OR OVER	22	100.0	79.8	19.9	-	-	-	.3	-
SOUTH ATLANTIC	5	100.0	10.2	86.4	.2	.7	-	.8	1.8
UNDER 100 MILES	-	100.0	-	25.6	71.8	-	-	2.2	.4
100 TO 199 MILES	-	100.0	-	94.5	-	-	-	5.5	-
200 TO 299 MILES	-	100.0	-	99.2	-	-	-	.8	-
300 TO 499 MILES	-	100.0	-	87.1	-	.1	-	.2	12.6
500 TO 999 MILES	1	100.0	-	99.3	-	-	-	.7	-
1000 TO 1499 MILES	1	100.0	-	98.5	-	.1	-	1.2	.3
1500 MILES OR OVER	-	100.0	79.4	15.2	-	5.4	-	-	-

See footnotes at end of table 4.

TABLE 2. TCC GROUP 212—Percent Distribution of Geographic Division of Origin and Means of Transport, by Geographic Division of Destination: 1972

Geographic division of origin[1] and means of transport	Number	Percent distribution by division of destination									
		U.S. total	New England	Middle Atlantic	East North Central	West North Central	South Atlantic	East South Central	West South Central	Mountain	Pacific
TONS OF SHIPMENTS	(thousands of tons)										
U.S. TOTAL	63	100.0	3.3	37.7	20.7	3.6	11.0	3.4	3.4	1.2	15.7
RAIL	9	100.0	-	-	-	-	.5	-	5.8	1.0	92.6
MOTOR CARRIER	53	100.0	3.8	44.6	24.5	4.3	12.3	3.6	3.0	1.3	2.6
PRIVATE TRUCK	-	100.0	-	6.1	2.5	-	91.5	-	-	-	-
AIR	-	100.0	-	8.7	-	-	42.2	-	-	27.0	22.0
WATER	-	100.0	-	-	-	-	-	-	-	-	-
OTHER	-	100.0	7.4	24.7	10.4	5.2	36.0	2.9	2.7	-	10.7
UNKNOWN	-	100.0	-	2.0	-	-	12.8	85.1	-	-	.1
MIDDLE ATLANTIC	48	100.0	3.7	44.5	19.3	3.3	6.7	.9	1.8	1.3	18.5
RAIL	8	100.0	-	-	-	-	.6	-	6.5	-	92.9
MOTOR CARRIER	40	100.0	4.3	53.7	23.3	4.0	7.6	1.1	.8	1.6	3.4
PRIVATE TRUCK	-	100.0	-	100.0	-	-	-	-	-	-	-
AIR	-	100.0	-	11.4	-	-	85.3	-	-	-	3.3
WATER	-	100.0	-	-	-	-	-	-	-	-	-
OTHER	-	100.0	9.5	31.0	9.0	3.8	37.9	.7	1.3	-	6.8
UNKNOWN	-	100.0	-	-	-	-	-	-	-	-	100.0
SOUTH ATLANTIC	7	100.0	3.5	25.1	7.5	2.4	43.3	8.8	5.0	1.7	2.6
RAIL	-	100.0	-	-	-	-	-	-	-	35.4	64.6
MOTOR CARRIER	6	100.0	3.9	27.5	8.2	2.5	45.0	6.7	5.4	.4	.4
PRIVATE TRUCK	-	100.0	-	-	-	-	100.0	-	-	-	-
AIR	-	100.0	-	6.8	-	-	9.6	-	-	47.5	36.2
WATER	-	100.0	-	-	-	-	-	-	-	-	-
OTHER	-	100.0	.3	6.2	11.7	15.0	51.2	6.6	9.0	-	-
UNKNOWN	-	100.0	-	2.1	-	-	13.4	84.5	-	-	-

See footnotes at end of table 4.

TABLE 2. **TCC GROUP 212—Percent Distribution of Geographic Division of Origin and Means of Transport, by Geographic Division of Destination: 1972**—Continued

Geographic division of origin[1] and means of transport	Number	Percent distribution by division of destination									
		U.S. total	New England	Middle Atlantic	East North Central	West North Central	South Atlantic	East South Central	West South Central	Mountain	Pacific
TON-MILES OF SHIPMENTS	(millions of ton-miles)										
U.S. TOTAL...............	43	100.0	1.4	10.1	13.0	4.6	7.8	2.1	4.7	3.3	53.0
RAIL....................	20	100.0	-	-	-	-	.2	-	3.4	.9	95.5
MOTOR CARRIER.........	22	100.0	2.7	19.5	25.1	8.8	14.5	3.7	5.9	5.5	14.1
PRIVATE TRUCK.........	-	100.0	-	3.0	1.2	-	95.9	-	-	-	-
AIR....................	-	100.0	-	2.8	-	-	27.2	-	-	35.9	34.1
WATER.................	-	100.0	-	-	-	-	-	-	-	-	-
OTHER.................	-	100.0	3.9	7.5	11.1	9.4	19.8	1.9	5.0	-	41.4
UNKNOWN...............	-	100.0	-	5.0	-	-	12.2	82.4	-	-	.5
MIDDLE ATLANTIC.........	34	100.0	.9	6.9	13.0	4.5	5.2	1.1	3.5	3.4	61.4
RAIL....................	18	100.0	-	-	-	-	.2	-	3.7	-	96.0
MOTOR CARRIER.........	15	100.0	2.0	15.2	28.8	10.0	10.9	2.5	3.2	7.5	19.9
PRIVATE TRUCK.........	-	100.0	-	100.0	-	-	-	-	-	-	-
AIR....................	-	100.0	-	.9	-	-	90.9	-	-	-	8.2
WATER.................	-	100.0	-	-	-	-	-	-	-	-	-
OTHER.................	-	100.0	5.3	7.9	11.5	8.1	26.1	.9	3.5	.1	36.7
UNKNOWN...............	-	100.0	-	-	-	-	-	-	-	-	100.0
SOUTH ATLANTIC..........	5	100.0	5.4	33.3	9.5	3.6	24.6	5.6	5.2	4.7	8.2
RAIL....................	-	100.0	-	-	-	-	-	-	-	33.2	66.8
MOTOR CARRIER.........	4	100.0	6.2	38.3	10.8	3.9	27.8	4.7	5.9	1.1	1.2
PRIVATE TRUCK.........	-	100.0	-	-	-	-	100.0	-	-	-	-
AIR....................	-	100.0	-	3.6	-	-	1.8	-	-	50.2	44.4
WATER.................	-	100.0	-	-	-	-	-	-	-	-	-
OTHER.................	-	100.0	.5	9.7	19.4	28.5	19.8	6.0	16.1	-	-
UNKNOWN...............	-	100.0	-	5.1	-	-	12.5	82.4	-	-	-

See footnotes at end of table 4.

TABLE 3. **TCC GROUP 212**—Percent Distribution of Geographic Division of Destination and Means of Transport, by Geographic Division of Origin: 1972

Geographic division of destination and means of transport	Number	Percent distribution by division of origin [1]									
		U.S. total	New England	Middle Atlantic	East North Central	West North Central	South Atlantic	East South Central	West South Central	Mountain	Pacific
TONS OF SHIPMENTS	(thousands of tons)										
U.S. TOTAL.................	63	100.0	-	76.9	(D)	-	12.1	(D)	-	-	-
RAIL......................	9	100.0	-	89.4	(D)	-	2.9	(D)	-	-	-
MOTOR CARRIER.............	53	100.0	-	75.4	(D)	-	13.0	(D)	-	-	-
PRIVATE TRUCK.............	-	100.0	-	6.1	(D)	-	91.5	(D)	-	-	-
AIR.......................	-	100.0	-	43.1	(D)	-	56.9	(D)	-	-	-
WATER.....................	-	100.0	-	-	(D)	-	-	(D)	-	-	-
OTHER.....................	-	100.0	-	74.4	(D)	-	12.0	(D)	-	-	-
UNKNOWN...................	-	100.0	-	.1	(D)	-	95.4	(D)	-	-	-
NEW ENGLAND...............	2	100.0	-	86.5	(D)	-	13.2	(D)	-	-	-
RAIL......................	-	100.0	-	-	(D)	-	-	(D)	-	-	-
MOTOR CARRIER.............	2	100.0	-	86.3	(D)	-	13.4	(D)	-	-	-
PRIVATE TRUCK.............	-	100.0	-	-	(D)	-	-	(D)	-	-	-
AIR.......................	-	100.0	-	-	(D)	-	-	(D)	-	-	-
WATER.....................	-	100.0	-	-	(D)	-	-	(D)	-	-	-
OTHER.....................	-	100.0	-	95.3	(D)	-	.5	(D)	-	-	-
UNKNOWN...................	-	100.0	-	-	(D)	-	-	(D)	-	-	-
MIDDLE ATLANTIC...........	23	100.0	-	90.8	(D)	-	8.0	(D)	-	-	-
RAIL......................	-	100.0	-	100.0	(D)	-	-	(D)	-	-	-
MOTOR CARRIER.............	23	100.0	-	90.8	(D)	-	8.0	(D)	-	-	-
PRIVATE TRUCK.............	-	100.0	-	100.0	(D)	-	-	(D)	-	-	-
AIR.......................	-	100.0	-	56.0	(D)	-	44.0	(D)	-	-	-
WATER.....................	-	100.0	-	-	(D)	-	-	(D)	-	-	-
OTHER.....................	-	100.0	-	93.1	(D)	-	3.0	(D)	-	-	-
UNKNOWN...................	-	100.0	-	-	(D)	-	100.0	(D)	-	-	-
EAST NORTH CENTRAL........	13	100.0	-	71.7	(D)	-	4.4	(D)	-	-	-
RAIL......................	-	100.0	-	-	(D)	-	-	(D)	-	-	-
MOTOR CARRIER.............	13	100.0	-	71.7	(D)	-	4.3	(D)	-	-	-
PRIVATE TRUCK.............	-	100.0	-	-	(D)	-	-	(D)	-	-	-
AIR.......................	-	100.0	-	-	(D)	-	-	(D)	-	-	-
WATER.....................	-	100.0	-	-	(D)	-	-	(D)	-	-	-
OTHER.....................	-	100.0	-	64.2	(D)	-	13.6	(D)	-	-	-
UNKNOWN...................	-	100.0	-	-	(D)	-	-	(D)	-	-	-
WEST NORTH CENTRAL........	2	100.0	-	70.0	(D)	-	8.1	(D)	-	-	-
RAIL......................	-	100.0	-	-	(D)	-	-	(D)	-	-	-
MOTOR CARRIER.............	2	100.0	-	70.2	(D)	-	7.8	(D)	-	-	-
PRIVATE TRUCK.............	-	100.0	-	-	(D)	-	-	(D)	-	-	-
AIR.......................	-	100.0	-	-	(D)	-	-	(D)	-	-	-
WATER.....................	-	100.0	-	-	(D)	-	-	(D)	-	-	-
OTHER.....................	-	100.0	-	54.9	(D)	-	35.0	(D)	-	-	-
UNKNOWN...................	-	100.0	-	-	(D)	-	-	(D)	-	-	-
SOUTH ATLANTIC............	6	100.0	-	47.0	(D)	-	47.6	(D)	-	-	-
RAIL......................	-	100.0	-	100.0	(D)	-	-	(D)	-	-	-
MOTOR CARRIER.............	6	100.0	-	46.7	(D)	-	47.7	(D)	-	-	-
PRIVATE TRUCK.............	-	100.0	-	-	(D)	-	100.0	(D)	-	-	-
AIR.......................	-	100.0	-	87.1	(D)	-	12.9	(D)	-	-	-
WATER.....................	-	100.0	-	-	(D)	-	-	(D)	-	-	-
OTHER.....................	-	100.0	-	78.3	(D)	-	17.1	(D)	-	-	-
UNKNOWN...................	-	100.0	-	-	(D)	-	100.0	(D)	-	-	-
EAST SOUTH CENTRAL........	2	100.0	-	21.2	(D)	-	31.2	(D)	-	-	-
RAIL......................	-	100.0	-	-	(D)	-	-	(D)	-	-	-
MOTOR CARRIER.............	1	100.0	-	23.7	(D)	-	24.1	(D)	-	-	-
PRIVATE TRUCK.............	-	100.0	-	-	(D)	-	-	(D)	-	-	-
AIR.......................	-	100.0	-	-	(D)	-	-	(D)	-	-	-
WATER.....................	-	100.0	-	-	(D)	-	-	(D)	-	-	-
OTHER.....................	-	100.0	-	18.3	(D)	-	27.6	(D)	-	-	-
UNKNOWN...................	-	100.0	-	-	(D)	-	94.7	(D)	-	-	-
WEST SOUTH CENTRAL........	2	100.0	-	40.9	(D)	-	17.8	(D)	-	-	-
RAIL......................	-	100.0	-	100.0	(D)	-	-	(D)	-	-	-
MOTOR CARRIER.............	1	100.0	-	21.2	(D)	-	23.5	(D)	-	-	-
PRIVATE TRUCK.............	-	100.0	-	-	(D)	-	-	(D)	-	-	-
AIR.......................	-	100.0	-	-	(D)	-	-	(D)	-	-	-
WATER.....................	-	100.0	-	-	(D)	-	-	(D)	-	-	-
OTHER.....................	-	100.0	-	35.9	(D)	-	40.6	(D)	-	-	-
UNKNOWN...................	-	100.0	-	-	(D)	-	-	(D)	-	-	-
MOUNTAIN..................	-	100.0	-	80.9	(D)	-	16.8	(D)	-	-	-
RAIL......................	-	100.0	-	-	(D)	-	100.0	(D)	-	-	-
MOTOR CARRIER.............	-	100.0	-	93.0	(D)	-	4.3	(D)	-	-	-
PRIVATE TRUCK.............	-	100.0	-	-	(D)	-	-	(D)	-	-	-
AIR.......................	-	100.0	-	-	(D)	-	100.0	(D)	-	-	-
WATER.....................	-	100.0	-	-	(D)	-	-	(D)	-	-	-
OTHER.....................	-	100.0	-	100.0	(D)	-	-	(D)	-	-	-
UNKNOWN...................	-	100.0	-	-	(D)	-	-	(D)	-	-	-
PACIFIC...................	9	100.0	-	90.6	(D)	-	2.0	(D)	-	-	-
RAIL......................	8	100.0	-	89.7	(D)	-	2.0	(D)	-	-	-
MOTOR CARRIER.............	1	100.0	-	98.1	(D)	-	1.8	(D)	-	-	-
PRIVATE TRUCK.............	-	100.0	-	-	(D)	-	-	(D)	-	-	-
AIR.......................	-	100.0	-	6.5	(D)	-	93.5	(D)	-	-	-
WATER.....................	-	100.0	-	-	(D)	-	-	(D)	-	-	-
OTHER.....................	-	100.0	-	47.7	(D)	-	-	(D)	-	-	-
UNKNOWN...................	-	100.0	-	100.0	(D)	-	-	(D)	-	-	-

See footnotes at end of table 4.

TABLE 3. **TCC GROUP 212**—Percent Distribution of Geographic Division of Destination and Means of Transport, by Geographic Division of Origin: 1972—Continued

Geographic division of destination and means of transport	Number	Percent distribution by division of origin[1]									
		U.S. total	New England	Middle Atlantic	East North Central	West North Central	South Atlantic	East South Central	West South Central	Mountain	Pacific
TON-MILES OF SHIPMENTS	(millions of ton-miles)										
U.S. TOTAL...............	43	100.0	-	79.4	(D)	-	12.7	(D)	-	-	-
RAIL.................	20	100.0	-	90.8	(D)	-	2.7	(D)	-	-	-
MOTOR CARRIER.........	22	100.0	-	69.6	(D)	-	21.4	(D)	-	-	-
PRIVATE TRUCK.........	-	100.0	-	3.0	(D)	-	95.9	(D)	-	-	-
AIR..................	-	100.0	-	28.5	(D)	-	71.5	(D)	-	-	-
WATER................	-	100.0	-	-	(D)	-	-	(D)	-	-	-
OTHER................	-	100.0	-	60.3	(D)	-	13.7	(D)	-	-	-
UNKNOWN..............	-	100.0	-	.5	(D)	-	97.3	(D)	-	-	-
NEW ENGLAND............	-	100.0	-	51.4	(D)	-	47.6	(D)	-	-	-
RAIL.................	-	100.0	-	-	(D)	-	-	(D)	-	-	-
MOTOR CARRIER.........	-	100.0	-	50.8	(D)	-	48.5	(D)	-	-	-
PRIVATE TRUCK.........	-	100.0	-	-	(D)	-	-	(D)	-	-	-
AIR..................	-	100.0	-	-	(D)	-	-	(D)	-	-	-
WATER................	-	100.0	-	82.5	(D)	-	1.9	(D)	-	-	-
OTHER................	-	100.0	-	-	(D)	-	-	(D)	-	-	-
UNKNOWN..............	-	100.0	-		(D)			(D)			
MIDDLE ATLANTIC........	4	100.0	-	54.1	(D)	-	41.9	(D)	-	-	-
RAIL.................	-	100.0	-	100.0	(D)	-	-	(D)	-	-	-
MOTOR CARRIER.........	4	100.0	-	54.1	(D)	-	41.9	(D)	-	-	-
PRIVATE TRUCK.........	-	100.0	-	100.0	(D)	-	-	(D)	-	-	-
AIR..................	-	100.0	-	8.8	(D)	-	91.2	(D)	-	-	-
WATER................	-	100.0	-	-	(D)	-	-	(D)	-	-	-
OTHER................	-	100.0	-	64.1	(D)	-	17.7	(D)	-	-	-
UNKNOWN..............	-	100.0	-	-	(D)	-	100.0	(D)	-	-	-
EAST NORTH CENTRAL......	5	100.0	-	79.8	(D)	-	9.3	(D)	-	-	-
RAIL.................	-	100.0	-	-	(D)	-	-	(D)	-	-	-
MOTOR CARRIER.........	5	100.0	-	79.9	(D)	-	9.2	(D)	-	-	-
PRIVATE TRUCK.........	-	100.0	-	-	(D)	-	-	(D)	-	-	-
AIR..................	-	100.0	-	-	(D)	-	-	(D)	-	-	-
WATER................	-	100.0	-	-	(D)	-	-	(D)	-	-	-
OTHER................	-	100.0	-	62.6	(D)	-	23.9	(D)	-	-	-
UNKNOWN..............	-	100.0	-	-	(D)	-	-	(D)	-	-	-
WEST NORTH CENTRAL......	1	100.0	-	78.7	(D)	-	10.0	(D)	-	-	-
RAIL.................	-	100.0	-	-	(D)	-	-	(D)	-	-	-
MOTOR CARRIER.........	1	100.0	-	79.1	(D)	-	9.5	(D)	-	-	-
PRIVATE TRUCK.........	-	100.0	-	-	(D)	-	-	(D)	-	-	-
AIR..................	-	100.0	-	-	(D)	-	-	(D)	-	-	-
WATER................	-	100.0	-	-	(D)	-	-	(D)	-	-	-
OTHER................	-	100.0	-	51.9	(D)	-	41.4	(D)	-	-	-
UNKNOWN..............	-	100.0	-	-	(D)	-	-	(D)	-	-	-
SOUTH ATLANTIC.........	3	100.0	-	53.3	(D)	-	40.1	(D)	-	-	-
RAIL.................	-	100.0	-	100.0	(D)	-	-	(D)	-	-	-
MOTOR CARRIER.........	3	100.0	-	52.3	(D)	-	40.9	(D)	-	-	-
PRIVATE TRUCK.........	-	100.0	-	-	(D)	-	100.0	(D)	-	-	-
AIR..................	-	100.0	-	95.4	(D)	-	4.6	(D)	-	-	-
WATER................	-	100.0	-	-	(D)	-	-	(D)	-	-	-
OTHER................	-	100.0	-	79.5	(D)	-	13.7	(D)	-	-	-
UNKNOWN..............	-	100.0	-	-	(D)	-	100.0	(D)	-	-	-
EAST SOUTH CENTRAL......	-	100.0	-	42.0	(D)	-	33.6	(D)	-	-	-
RAIL.................	-	100.0	-	-	(D)	-	-	(D)	-	-	-
MOTOR CARRIER.........	-	100.0	-	46.3	(D)	-	27.1	(D)	-	-	-
PRIVATE TRUCK.........	-	100.0	-	-	(D)	-	-	(D)	-	-	-
AIR..................	-	100.0	-	-	(D)	-	-	(D)	-	-	-
WATER................	-	100.0	-	-	(D)	-	-	(D)	-	-	-
OTHER................	-	100.0	-	27.8	(D)	-	43.0	(D)	-	-	-
UNKNOWN..............	-	100.0	-	-	(D)	-	97.3	(D)	-	-	-
WEST SOUTH CENTRAL......	2	100.0	-	59.3	(D)	-	14.1	(D)	-	-	-
RAIL.................	-	100.0	-	100.0	(D)	-	-	(D)	-	-	-
MOTOR CARRIER.........	1	100.0	-	37.9	(D)	-	21.1	(D)	-	-	-
PRIVATE TRUCK.........	-	100.0	-	-	(D)	-	-	(D)	-	-	-
AIR..................	-	100.0	-	-	(D)	-	-	(D)	-	-	-
WATER................	-	100.0	-	41.8	(D)	-	44.1	(D)	-	-	-
OTHER................	-	100.0	-	-	(D)	-	-	(D)	-	-	-
UNKNOWN..............	-	100.0									
MOUNTAIN...............	1	100.0	-	80.6	(D)	-	18.0	(D)	-	-	-
RAIL.................	-	100.0	-	-	(D)	-	100.0	(D)	-	-	-
MOTOR CARRIER.........	1	100.0	-	94.1	(D)	-	4.3	(D)	-	-	-
PRIVATE TRUCK.........	-	100.0	-	-	(D)	-	100.0	(D)	-	-	-
AIR..................	-	100.0	-	-	(D)	-	-	(D)	-	-	-
WATER................	-	100.0	-	-	(D)	-	-	(D)	-	-	-
OTHER................	-	100.0	-	100.0	(D)	-	-	(D)	-	-	-
UNKNOWN..............	-	100.0	-	-	(D)	-	-	(D)	-	-	-
PACIFIC................	23	100.0	-	92.0	(D)	-	2.0	(D)	-	-	-
RAIL.................	19	100.0	-	91.3	(D)	-	1.9	(D)	-	-	-
MOTOR CARRIER.........	3	100.0	-	98.1	(D)	-	1.8	(D)	-	-	-
PRIVATE TRUCK.........	-	100.0	-	-	(D)	-	-	(D)	-	-	-
AIR..................	-	100.0	-	6.9	(D)	-	93.1	(D)	-	-	-
WATER................	-	100.0	-	-	(D)	-	-	(D)	-	-	-
OTHER................	-	100.0	-	53.4	(D)	-	-	(D)	-	-	-
UNKNOWN..............	-	100.0	-	100.0	(D)			(D)			

See footnotes at end of table 4.

TABLE 4. TCC GROUP 212—Percent Distribution of Distance Shipped and Weight of Shipment, by Means of Transport: 1972

Distance shipped and weight of shipment[2] [3]	Number	Percent distribution by means of transport							
		All means of transport	Rail	Motor carrier	Private truck	Air	Water	Other	Unknown
TONS OF SHIPMENTS	(thousands of tons)								
U.S. TOTAL..........	61	100.0	14.8	83.9	.2	.1	-	.6	.4
UNDER 100 MILES.........	8	100.0	-	98.2	1.5	-	-	.2	-
UNDER 1000 POUNDS.....	1	100.0	-	97.6	.5	.1	-	1.7	-
1000 TO 9999 POUNDS...	1	100.0	-	93.0	7.0	-	-	-	-
10000 TO 29999 POUNDS.	3	100.0	-	100.0	-	-	-	-	-
30000 TO 59999 POUNDS.	2	100.0	-	100.0	-	-	-	-	-
60000 TO 89999 POUNDS.	-	100.0	-	-	-	-	-	-	-
90000 POUNDS AND OVER.	-	100.0	-	-	-	-	-	-	-
100 TO 199 MILES........	17	100.0	-	99.7	-	-	-	.3	.1
UNDER 1000 POUNDS.....	2	100.0	-	97.7	-	-	-	1.9	.5
1000 TO 9999 POUNDS...	4	100.0	-	100.0	-	-	-	-	-
10000 TO 29999 POUNDS.	6	100.0	-	100.0	-	-	-	-	-
30000 TO 59999 POUNDS.	3	100.0	-	100.0	-	-	-	-	-
60000 TO 89999 POUNDS.	-	100.0	-	-	-	-	-	-	-
90000 POUNDS AND OVER.	-	100.0	-	-	-	-	-	-	-
200 TO 299 MILES........	2	100.0	-	94.4	-	-	-	5.6	-
UNDER 1000 POUNDS.....	1	100.0	-	90.6	-	-	-	9.4	-
1000 TO 9999 POUNDS...	-	100.0	-	100.0	-	-	-	-	-
10000 TO 29999 POUNDS.	-	100.0	-	100.0	-	-	-	-	-
30000 TO 59999 POUNDS.	-	100.0	-	-	-	-	-	-	-
60000 TO 89999 POUNDS.	-	100.0	-	-	-	-	-	-	-
90000 POUNDS AND OVER.	-	100.0	-	-	-	-	-	-	-
300 TO 499 MILES........	9	100.0	-	97.2	-	-	-	.2	2.5
UNDER 1000 POUNDS.....	2	100.0	-	97.3	-	-	-	.7	1.8
1000 TO 9999 POUNDS...	2	100.0	-	92.3	-	.1	-	-	7.7
10000 TO 29999 POUNDS.	2	100.0	-	100.0	-	-	-	-	-
30000 TO 59999 POUNDS.	1	100.0	-	100.0	-	-	-	-	-
60000 TO 89999 POUNDS.	-	100.0	-	-	-	-	-	-	-
90000 POUNDS AND OVER.	-	100.0	-	-	-	-	-	-	-
500 TO 999 MILES........	9	100.0	.5	98.7	-	-	-	.7	-
UNDER 1000 POUNDS.....	3	100.0	1.3	96.8	-	.1	-	1.9	-
1000 TO 9999 POUNDS...	4	100.0	-	100.0	-	-	-	-	-
10000 TO 29999 POUNDS.	1	100.0	-	100.0	-	-	-	-	-
30000 TO 59999 POUNDS.	-	100.0	-	-	-	-	-	-	-
60000 TO 89999 POUNDS.	-	100.0	-	-	-	-	-	-	-
90000 POUNDS AND OVER.	-	100.0	-	-	-	-	-	-	-
1000 TO 1499 MILES......	3	100.0	16.2	82.4	-	.4	-	.8	.2
UNDER 1000 POUNDS.....	1	100.0	1.2	96.3	-	.7	-	1.6	.3
1000 TO 9999 POUNDS...	-	100.0	39.2	60.8	-	-	-	-	-
10000 TO 29999 POUNDS.	-	100.0	28.6	71.4	-	-	-	-	-
30000 TO 59999 POUNDS.	-	100.0	-	-	-	-	-	-	-
60000 TO 89999 POUNDS.	-	100.0	-	-	-	-	-	-	-
90000 POUNDS AND OVER.	-	100.0	-	-	-	-	-	-	-
1500 MILES OR OVER......	10	100.0	80.7	18.5	-	.2	-	.6	-
UNDER 1000 POUNDS.....	-	100.0	53.4	38.6	-	1.9	-	6.1	-
1000 TO 9999 POUNDS...	3	100.0	55.5	44.5	-	-	-	-	-
10000 TO 29999 POUNDS.	1	100.0	96.5	3.5	-	-	-	-	-
30000 TO 59999 POUNDS.	4	100.0	100.0	-	-	-	-	-	-
60000 TO 89999 POUNDS.	-	100.0	-	-	-	-	-	-	-
90000 POUNDS AND OVER.	-	100.0	-	-	-	-	-	-	-
TON-MILES OF SHIPMENTS	(millions of ton-miles)								
U.S. TOTAL..........	42	100.0	48.9	50.1	-	.1	-	.6	.2
UNDER 100 MILES.........	-	100.0	-	98.4	1.4	-	-	.2	-
UNDER 1000 POUNDS.....	-	100.0	-	98.0	.2	.1	-	1.6	.1
1000 TO 9999 POUNDS...	-	100.0	-	93.8	6.2	-	-	-	-
10000 TO 29999 POUNDS.	-	100.0	-	100.0	-	-	-	-	-
30000 TO 59999 POUNDS.	-	100.0	-	100.0	-	-	-	-	-
60000 TO 89999 POUNDS.	-	100.0	-	-	-	-	-	-	-
90000 POUNDS AND OVER.	-	100.0	-	-	-	-	-	-	-
100 TO 199 MILES........	2	100.0	-	99.6	-	-	-	.3	.1
UNDER 1000 POUNDS.....	-	100.0	-	97.5	-	-	-	1.9	.6
1000 TO 9999 POUNDS...	-	100.0	-	100.0	-	-	-	-	-
10000 TO 29999 POUNDS.	-	100.0	-	100.0	-	-	-	-	-
30000 TO 59999 POUNDS.	-	100.0	-	100.0	-	-	-	-	-
60000 TO 89999 POUNDS.	-	100.0	-	-	-	-	-	-	-
90000 POUNDS AND OVER.	-	100.0	-	-	-	-	-	-	-

See footnotes at end of table 4.

TABLE 4. **TCC GROUP 212—Percent Distribution of Distance Shipped and Weight of Shipment,**
by Means of Transport: 1972—Continued

Distance shipped and weight of shipment[2] [3]	Number	Percent distribution by means of transport							
		All means of transport	Rail	Motor carrier	Private truck	Air	Water	Other	Unknown
TON-MILES OF SHIPMENTS	(millions of ton-miles)								
200 TO 299 MILES	-	100.0	-	95.1	-	-	-	4.9	-
UNDER 1000 POUNDS	-	100.0	-	91.7	-	-	-	8.3	-
1000 TO 9999 POUNDS	-	100.0	-	100.0	-	-	-	-	-
10000 TO 29999 POUNDS	-	100.0	-	100.0	-	-	-	-	-
30000 TO 59999 POUNDS	-	100.0	-	-	-	-	-	-	-
60000 TO 89999 POUNDS	-	100.0	-	-	-	-	-	-	-
90000 POUNDS AND OVER	-	100.0	-	-	-	-	-	-	-
300 TO 499 MILES	3	100.0	-	97.3	-	-	-	.2	2.4
UNDER 1000 POUNDS	1	100.0	-	97.2	-	.1	-	.8	1.9
1000 TO 9999 POUNDS	-	100.0	-	92.3	-	-	-	-	7.7
10000 TO 29999 POUNDS	1	100.0	-	100.0	-	-	-	-	-
30000 TO 59999 POUNDS	-	100.0	-	100.0	-	-	-	-	-
60000 TO 89999 POUNDS	-	100.0	-	-	-	-	-	-	-
90000 POUNDS AND OVER	-	100.0	-	-	-	-	-	-	-
500 TO 999 MILES	7	100.0	.6	98.6	-	-	-	.8	-
UNDER 1000 POUNDS	2	100.0	1.5	96.5	-	.1	-	1.9	-
1000 TO 9999 POUNDS	3	100.0	-	100.0	-	-	-	-	-
10000 TO 29999 POUNDS	-	100.0	-	100.0	-	-	-	-	-
30000 TO 59999 POUNDS	-	100.0	-	-	-	-	-	-	-
60000 TO 89999 POUNDS	-	100.0	-	-	-	-	-	-	-
90000 POUNDS AND OVER	-	100.0	-	-	-	-	-	-	-
1000 TO 1499 MILES	3	100.0	19.2	79.4	-	.4	-	.9	.1
UNDER 1000 POUNDS	1	100.0	1.6	95.8	-	.7	-	1.7	.3
1000 TO 9999 POUNDS	-	100.0	44.0	56.0	-	-	-	-	-
10000 TO 29999 POUNDS	-	100.0	34.1	65.9	-	-	-	-	-
30000 TO 59999 POUNDS	-	100.0	-	-	-	-	-	-	-
60000 TO 89999 POUNDS	-	100.0	-	-	-	-	-	-	-
90000 POUNDS AND OVER	-	100.0	-	-	-	-	-	-	-
1500 MILES OR OVER	24	100.0	82.2	17.2	-	.2	-	.5	-
UNDER 1000 POUNDS	2	100.0	56.4	36.0	-	1.8	-	5.8	-
1000 TO 9999 POUNDS	7	100.0	58.0	42.0	-	-	-	-	-
10000 TO 29999 POUNDS	4	100.0	96.6	3.4	-	-	-	-	-
30000 TO 59999 POUNDS	10	100.0	100.0	-	-	-	-	-	-
60000 TO 89999 POUNDS	-	100.0	-	-	-	-	-	-	-
90000 POUNDS AND OVER	-	100.0	-	-	-	-	-	-	-

Note: Detail may not add to total due to rounding. The introductory table shows the estimates of sampling variability for tons; sampling variability for ton-miles has not been estimated. See the map in the Introduction for the States comprising the geographic divisions of the United States.
Shipments excluded from the survey are those moving by pipeline (primarily petroleum products from refineries), parcel post shipments, and commodities moved by own power (motorized vehicles, aircraft, etc.) or towed (prefabricated buildings, etc.). Local shipments (commodities shipped less than 25 miles from the plant) and shipments within the same city are also excluded. Shipments to Alaska and Hawaii from the 48 conterminous States and the District of Columbia are included; however, no data were obtained for shipments originating in Alaska and Hawaii.

- Represents zero or rounds to zero.   (D) Withheld to avoid disclosing figures for individual companies.

[1] Production of this commodity is concentrated in the geographic divisions shown; figures and distributions for geographic divisions not shown are included in the total.
[2] Distances of shipments to foreign destinations are calculated only to the U.S. port of exit.
[3] Includes only shipments represented by bills of lading and invoices. Summary records which did not show individual weights of shipments are not included.

Chemicals and Allied Products

CONTENTS

[Page numbers listed here omit the State prefix number that appears as part of the number for each page]

TABLES   (The tables listed below are shown for each of the Transportation Commodity Classification groups in this report)

Comparisons of Tons and Ton-Miles of Shipments for Geographic Divisions of Origin and for Sampling Variability: 1972 and 1967

1. Percent Distribution of Geographic Division of Origin and Distance Shipped, by Means of Transport: 1972

2. Percent Distribution of Geographic Division of Origin and Means of Transport, by Geographic Division of Destination: 1972

3. Percent Distribution of Geographic Division of Destination and Means of Transport, by Geographic Division of Origin: 1972

4. Percent Distribution of Distance Shipped and Weight of Shipment, by Means of Transport: 1972

TCC 281. Industrial Inorganic and Organic Chemicals

Comparisons of Tons and Ton-Miles of Shipments for
Geographic Divisions of Origin and for Sampling Variability: 1972 and 1967

| Geographic division of origin | Estimates | | | | Relative sampling variability in tons (percent) | |
| | 1972 | | 1967 | | | |
	Tons (thousands)	Ton-miles (millions)	Tons (thousands)	Ton-miles (millions)	1972	1967
U.S. total	79,278	32,424	81,026	33,945	6.9	8.2
New England	(D)	(D)	2,321	1,395	(*)	(*)
Middle Atlantic	10,883	3,000	10,977	2,645	11.4	(*)
East North Central	13,499	3,638	14,376	4,862	16.8	(*)
West North Central	1,007	366	1,211	607	8.6	(*)
South Atlantic	7,527	2,579	10,127	3,382	6.7	(*)
East South Central	5,606	2,402	10,264	4,140	10.7	(*)
West South Central	34,409	18,540	23,420	13,623	14.8	(*)
Mountain	(D)	(D)	2,930	2,178	(*)	(*)
Pacific	3,000	630	5,400	1,113	26.9	(*)

(D) Withheld to avoid disclosing figures for individual companies.   (*) Data not published.

TABLE 1. TCC GROUP 281—Percent Distribution of Geographic Division of Origin and Distance Shipped, by Means of Transport: 1972

Geographic division of origin[1] and distance shipped[2]	Number	Percent distribution by means of transport							
		All means of transport	Rail	Motor carrier	Private truck	Air	Water	Other	Unknown
TONS OF SHIPMENTS	(thousands of tons)								
U.S. TOTAL	79 278	100.0	45.3	26.9	10.3	-	16.4	.8	.3
MIDDLE ATLANTIC	10 883	100.0	32.4	37.1	26.8	-	3.7	-	.1
UNDER 100 MILES	4 250	100.0	11.8	44.6	40.9	-	2.6	-	.1
100 TO 199 MILES	2 056	100.0	28.1	34.9	29.8	-	7.2	-	.1
200 TO 299 MILES	1 714	100.0	53.6	20.9	19.1	-	6.4	-	.1
300 TO 499 MILES	1 480	100.0	63.4	27.5	8.9	-	-	.1	.1
500 TO 999 MILES	902	100.0	32.4	56.8	10.4	-	.2	.1	.1
1000 TO 1499 MILES	186	100.0	55.2	37.8	3.5	-	3.4	-	-
1500 MILES OR OVER	291	100.0	65.0	26.1	.2	-	8.0	.3	.4
EAST NORTH CENTRAL	13 499	100.0	50.0	32.7	16.5	-	.4	.2	.2
UNDER 100 MILES	4 091	100.0	29.2	39.0	31.2	-	-	-	.6
100 TO 199 MILES	2 724	100.0	51.9	27.7	19.9	-	.6	-	-
200 TO 299 MILES	2 515	100.0	48.5	45.7	5.6	-	-	.1	-
300 TO 499 MILES	2 337	100.0	69.2	23.5	6.3	-	.8	.1	.1
500 TO 999 MILES	1 482	100.0	67.6	22.4	7.3	-	1.2	1.1	.3
1000 TO 1499 MILES	160	100.0	86.8	7.6	5.5	.1	-	-	-
1500 MILES OR OVER	187	100.0	85.7	13.5	.6	.1	-	.1	-
WEST NORTH CENTRAL	1 007	100.0	50.1	22.8	26.4	.7	-	-	-
UNDER 100 MILES	144	100.0	20.3	34.3	45.5	-	-	-	-
100 TO 199 MILES	247	100.0	48.3	27.9	23.8	-	-	-	-
200 TO 299 MILES	94	100.0	34.2	27.9	36.1	1.7	-	-	-
300 TO 499 MILES	282	100.0	59.2	11.3	29.1	.5	-	-	-
500 TO 999 MILES	198	100.0	63.8	22.4	12.6	1.2	-	-	-
1000 TO 1499 MILES	31	100.0	74.8	23.8	1.3	.1	-	-	-
1500 MILES OR OVER	8	100.0	70.6	15.4	-	14.0	-	-	-
SOUTH ATLANTIC	7 527	100.0	53.2	30.3	11.0	-	3.9	.1	1.6
UNDER 100 MILES	2 260	100.0	40.6	36.3	15.4	-	7.5	.2	-
100 TO 199 MILES	1 138	100.0	37.6	41.2	11.5	-	8.1	-	1.5
200 TO 299 MILES	1 075	100.0	57.5	33.7	8.7	-	-	-	.1
300 TO 499 MILES	1 489	100.0	59.0	27.1	13.0	-	-	-	.9
500 TO 999 MILES	1 163	100.0	72.0	16.0	4.5	-	.2	-	7.3
1000 TO 1499 MILES	267	100.0	85.8	10.2	3.2	-	.8	-	-
1500 MILES OR OVER	131	100.0	70.6	8.4	1.9	-	19.1	-	-
EAST SOUTH CENTRAL	5 606	100.0	68.4	17.6	2.8	-	10.9	-	.3
UNDER 100 MILES	442	100.0	50.1	22.8	5.9	-	20.9	-	.3
100 TO 199 MILES	943	100.0	68.0	18.9	2.5	-	10.5	-	-
200 TO 299 MILES	839	100.0	62.2	24.2	1.1	-	12.5	-	-
300 TO 499 MILES	2 105	100.0	72.2	15.3	3.5	-	8.2	-	.7
500 TO 999 MILES	977	100.0	65.3	17.4	2.5	-	14.5	-	.3
1000 TO 1499 MILES	28	100.0	74.9	25.1	-	-	-	-	-
1500 MILES OR OVER	269	100.0	99.0	1.0	-	-	-	-	-
WEST SOUTH CENTRAL	34 409	100.0	43.9	18.4	2.2	-	33.7	1.7	.1
UNDER 100 MILES	7 213	100.0	27.8	28.0	5.9	-	30.9	7.2	.2
100 TO 199 MILES	5 313	100.0	26.7	35.6	3.0	-	34.7	-	-
200 TO 299 MILES	3 321	100.0	46.7	22.2	1.7	-	27.1	2.4	-
300 TO 499 MILES	2 976	100.0	48.8	20.7	2.1	-	28.3	-	.1
500 TO 999 MILES	9 163	100.0	53.1	8.5	.5	-	37.9	-	-
1000 TO 1499 MILES	5 718	100.0	55.0	4.7	.1	-	40.2	-	.1
1500 MILES OR OVER	702	100.0	96.6	2.6	.2	-	.7	-	-
PACIFIC	3 000	100.0	22.5	55.2	21.0	-	1.0	.1	-
UNDER 100 MILES	1 478	100.0	9.3	57.7	32.9	-	-	.1	-
100 TO 199 MILES	424	100.0	12.6	72.9	7.9	-	6.6	-	-
200 TO 299 MILES	335	100.0	26.1	65.5	8.4	-	-	-	-
300 TO 499 MILES	532	100.0	49.2	39.9	10.7	-	-	-	.2
500 TO 999 MILES	172	100.0	53.7	31.2	15.1	-	-	-	-
1000 TO 1499 MILES	1	100.0	6.8	93.1	-	.1	-	-	-
1500 MILES OR OVER	55	100.0	77.2	13.3	-	.8	4.7	4.0	-
TON-MILES OF SHIPMENTS	(millions of ton-miles)								
U.S. TOTAL	32 424	100.0	57.6	15.8	3.8	-	22.2	.2	.4
MIDDLE ATLANTIC	3 000	100.0	48.5	34.8	12.6	-	3.9	.1	.1
UNDER 100 MILES	186	100.0	13.7	43.1	42.4	-	.8	-	-
100 TO 199 MILES	314	100.0	28.6	33.8	29.2	-	8.3	-	-
200 TO 299 MILES	424	100.0	53.5	21.2	19.6	-	5.5	-	.1
300 TO 499 MILES	561	100.0	62.5	28.2	9.1	-	-	.1	-
500 TO 999 MILES	617	100.0	32.9	56.2	10.4	-	.2	.1	.1
1000 TO 1499 MILES	231	100.0	56.7	36.4	3.3	-	3.6	-	-
1500 MILES OR OVER	664	100.0	64.2	26.6	.2	-	8.3	.3	.4
EAST NORTH CENTRAL	3 638	100.0	64.3	26.3	8.3	-	.5	.4	.2
UNDER 100 MILES	184	100.0	30.9	42.2	26.6	-	-	-	.3
100 TO 199 MILES	394	100.0	54.2	26.5	18.7	-	.6	-	-
200 TO 299 MILES	605	100.0	48.7	45.7	5.5	-	-	.1	-
300 TO 499 MILES	904	100.0	69.1	23.5	6.6	-	.7	.1	.1
500 TO 999 MILES	1 015	100.0	68.0	22.1	7.4	-	1.1	1.1	.4
1000 TO 1499 MILES	179	100.0	86.2	7.7	6.0	.1	-	-	-
1500 MILES OR OVER	354	100.0	85.9	13.3	.6	.1	-	.1	-

See footnotes at end of table 4.

TABLE 1. **TCC GROUP 281**—Percent Distribution of Geographic Division of Origin and Distance Shipped, by Means of Transport: 1972—Continued

Geographic division of origin[1] and distance shipped[2]	Number	Percent distribution by means of transport							
		All means of transport	Rail	Motor carrier	Private truck	Air	Water	Other	Unknown
TON-MILES OF SHIPMENTS	(millions of ton-miles)								
WEST NORTH CENTRAL	366	100.0	60.4	19.6	18.6	1.4	-	-	-
UNDER 100 MILES	7	100.0	24.7	31.7	43.7	-	-	-	-
100 TO 199 MILES	37	100.0	49.5	26.4	24.1	-	-	-	-
200 TO 299 MILES	22	100.0	33.9	29.2	35.0	1.9	-	-	-
300 TO 499 MILES	114	100.0	60.0	10.9	28.5	.6	-	-	-
500 TO 999 MILES	133	100.0	64.6	22.5	11.5	1.4	-	-	-
1000 TO 1499 MILES	37	100.0	76.0	22.7	1.1	.2	-	-	-
1500 MILES OR OVER	14	100.0	70.8	15.7	-	13.5	-	-	-
SOUTH ATLANTIC	2 579	100.0	65.9	20.8	6.8	-	3.2	-	3.3
UNDER 100 MILES	121	100.0	48.1	35.5	13.7	-	2.6	-	1.6
100 TO 199 MILES	162	100.0	36.2	42.2	10.3	-	9.6	-	.1
200 TO 299 MILES	272	100.0	58.7	32.8	8.4	-	-	-	.8
300 TO 499 MILES	572	100.0	60.1	27.3	11.8	-	-	-	.8
500 TO 999 MILES	844	100.0	71.7	14.7	4.3	-	.2	-	9.1
1000 TO 1499 MILES	319	100.0	86.4	9.9	2.9	-	.9	-	-
1500 MILES OR OVER	287	100.0	68.7	8.5	1.9	-	20.7	-	-
EAST SOUTH CENTRAL	2 402	100.0	75.0	13.7	2.3	-	8.7	-	.3
UNDER 100 MILES	29	100.0	49.8	16.2	5.5	-	28.5	-	.1
100 TO 199 MILES	140	100.0	68.3	18.1	2.5	-	11.2	-	-
200 TO 299 MILES	206	100.0	64.9	22.3	1.0	-	11.8	-	-
300 TO 499 MILES	826	100.0	73.2	14.7	3.9	-	7.5	-	.7
500 TO 999 MILES	666	100.0	64.8	17.8	2.3	-	14.9	-	.3
1000 TO 1499 MILES	34	100.0	75.7	24.3	-	-	-	-	-
1500 MILES OR OVER	499	100.0	99.1	.9	-	-	-	-	-
WEST SOUTH CENTRAL	18 540	100.0	53.8	8.8	.7	-	36.4	.3	-
UNDER 100 MILES	384	100.0	26.7	27.9	7.1	-	30.4	7.6	.3
100 TO 199 MILES	746	100.0	30.1	33.5	2.7	-	33.7	-	-
200 TO 299 MILES	842	100.0	47.4	21.5	1.7	-	26.9	2.4	-
300 TO 499 MILES	1 139	100.0	50.0	20.5	2.0	-	27.5	-	.1
500 TO 999 MILES	7 036	100.0	51.5	7.3	.5	-	40.7	-	-
1000 TO 1499 MILES	7 137	100.0	53.9	4.5	-	-	41.5	-	.1
1500 MILES OR OVER	1 253	100.0	96.9	2.3	.2	-	.6	-	-
PACIFIC	630	100.0	44.6	40.4	12.0	.2	1.9	.9	.1
UNDER 100 MILES	65	100.0	11.5	51.9	36.5	-	-	-	.1
100 TO 199 MILES	63	100.0	12.9	70.5	8.1	-	8.5	-	-
200 TO 299 MILES	81	100.0	28.0	63.8	8.2	-	-	-	-
300 TO 499 MILES	191	100.0	49.7	38.2	12.0	-	-	-	.2
500 TO 999 MILES	115	100.0	55.4	29.5	15.1	-	-	-	-
1000 TO 1499 MILES	1	100.0	6.0	93.9	-	.1	-	-	-
1500 MILES OR OVER	111	100.0	74.6	14.0	-	.9	5.7	4.8	-

See footnotes at end of table 4.

TABLE 2. **TCC GROUP 281**—Percent Distribution of Geographic Division of Origin and Means of Transport, by Geographic Division of Destination: 1972

Geographic division of origin[1] and means of transport	Number	Percent distribution by division of destination									
		U.S. total	New England	Middle Atlantic	East North Central	West North Central	South Atlantic	East South Central	West South Central	Mountain	Pacific
TONS OF SHIPMENTS	(thousands of tons)										
U.S. TOTAL	79 278	100.0	2.8	16.3	20.4	5.3	13.7	7.9	22.7	5.2	5.7
RAIL	35 947	100.0	2.1	13.8	19.5	7.1	18.5	10.8	17.0	5.7	5.5
MOTOR CARRIER	21 360	100.0	2.2	17.3	20.4	4.3	10.8	5.3	22.6	8.8	8.4
PRIVATE TRUCK	8 127	100.0	6.0	28.5	25.7	4.1	11.3	2.7	11.6	2.5	7.6
AIR	10	100.0	2.2	19.7	37.5	3.7	12.7	1.6	4.8	2.8	15.0
WATER	12 981	100.0	3.9	14.7	20.6	3.2	7.4	7.7	42.0	-	.6
OTHER	637	100.0	.1	.6	.6	.1	1.8	2.0	94.4	-	.4
UNKNOWN	213	100.0	5.8	12.1	21.1	.2	15.5	4.5	38.5	1.7	.7
MIDDLE ATLANTIC	10 883	100.0	10.1	57.8	10.6	1.2	13.8	2.4	1.4	.4	2.3
RAIL	3 521	100.0	10.1	50.1	16.0	1.9	11.0	2.9	2.4	.9	4.6
MOTOR CARRIER	4 038	100.0	7.9	58.9	11.3	1.3	14.0	3.2	1.5	.2	1.7
PRIVATE TRUCK	2 911	100.0	14.4	69.6	4.4	.3	9.9	1.0	.3	.1	-
AIR	-	100.0	1.8	14.8	45.1	.7	22.3	.5	1.3	2.5	11.0
WATER	401	100.0	-	28.0	-	-	64.7	-	1.4	-	5.8
OTHER	4	100.0	9.9	21.3	6.4	12.8	30.9	.3	1.6	.1	16.7
UNKNOWN	6	100.0	.5	59.1	15.5	4.7	2.4	.3	-	-	17.4
EAST NORTH CENTRAL	13 499	100.0	1.3	11.7	61.7	9.6	6.5	3.5	4.2	.3	1.3
RAIL	6 746	100.0	1.8	17.0	48.3	10.5	10.0	3.5	6.4	.2	2.3
MOTOR CARRIER	4 419	100.0	1.0	7.9	72.5	9.2	3.6	2.7	2.4	.3	.5
PRIVATE TRUCK	2 226	100.0	.6	2.7	82.2	8.4	1.8	2.7	1.2	.4	-
AIR	1	100.0	.1	6.8	65.8	.6	13.2	2.3	1.0	.5	9.7
WATER	51	100.0	-	35.7	-	-	-	64.3	-	-	.1
OTHER	21	100.0	.2	3.4	13.7	.2	1.0	57.8	22.4	.3	1.0
UNKNOWN	31	100.0	3.4	4.1	77.3	.5	4.3	6.8	2.9	.8	-

See footnotes at end of table 4.

TABLE 2. TCC GROUP 281—Percent Distribution of Geographic Division of Origin and Means of Transport, by Geographic Division of Destination: 1972—Continued

Geographic division of origin[1] and means of transport	Number	Percent distribution by division of destination									
		U.S. total	New England	Middle Atlantic	East North Central	West North Central	South Atlantic	East South Central	West South Central	Mountain	Pacific
TONS OF SHIPMENTS	(thousands of tons)										
WEST NORTH CENTRAL......	1 007	100.0	1.1	4.2	22.6	40.7	3.4	2.9	15.9	7.2	2.0
RAIL...................	504	100.0	1.3	5.4	16.1	45.3	4.4	2.6	12.0	9.6	3.3
MOTOR CARRIER.........	229	100.0	1.7	5.5	36.5	38.1	4.6	5.4	7.1	.2	1.0
PRIVATE TRUCK.........	266	100.0	.2	.5	22.6	35.1	.3	1.1	31.3	9.0	-
AIR...................	6	100.0	.3	21.9	32.7	5.3	10.6	1.5	6.2	3.3	18.3
WATER.................	-	100.0	-	-	-	-	-	-	-	-	-
OTHER.................	-	100.0	-	-	28.5	21.7	-	41.7	8.2	-	-
UNKNOWN...............	-	100.0	-	-	-	-	-	-	-	-	-
SOUTH ATLANTIC........	7 527	100.0	1.8	21.8	13.5	2.3	44.2	10.2	3.8	.8	1.6
RAIL...................	4 003	100.0	1.8	14.5	16.0	3.3	43.5	13.2	4.0	1.4	2.1
MOTOR CARRIER.........	2 281	100.0	2.6	28.6	13.9	1.0	44.0	7.6	1.8	.1	.4
PRIVATE TRUCK.........	829	100.0	.7	25.1	5.2	1.8	57.7	7.8	1.4	-	.3
AIR...................	-	100.0	1.6	46.8	24.9	2.1	3.0	8.2	8.1	.1	5.2
WATER.................	290	100.0	-	61.8	-	-	28.8	-	.7	-	8.7
OTHER.................	5	100.0	.9	1.3	3.7	.3	88.3	1.2	2.4	1.0	.9
UNKNOWN...............	116	100.0	.8	13.9	14.3	-	12.5	-	58.5	-	-
EAST SOUTH CENTRAL.....	5 606	100.0	.5	6.6	14.8	4.0	34.3	25.3	9.5	.2	4.8
RAIL...................	3 833	100.0	.5	4.9	15.4	2.2	37.0	23.6	9.1	.3	7.0
MOTOR CARRIER.........	984	100.0	1.0	6.2	13.9	13.9	32.9	26.0	5.6	.2	.3
PRIVATE TRUCK.........	158	100.0	.7	6.7	3.9	3.0	56.5	23.8	5.4	-	-
AIR...................	-	100.0	-	-	27.2	-	70.4	-	2.4	-	-
WATER.................	610	100.0	-	17.9	15.4	-	12.5	34.9	19.3	-	-
OTHER.................	-	100.0	6.2	21.2	41.4	9.2	7.3	1.5	5.2	-	7.9
UNKNOWN...............	19	100.0	-	1.9	.2	-	77.5	20.4	-	-	-
WEST SOUTH CENTRAL.....	34 409	100.0	2.0	8.0	13.0	5.4	9.0	9.6	46.5	4.9	1.6
RAIL...................	15 114	100.0	1.3	7.6	11.7	8.1	15.3	13.7	32.5	6.5	3.4
MOTOR CARRIER.........	6 326	100.0	.2	1.8	1.8	3.2	3.5	6.8	71.6	10.5	.7
PRIVATE TRUCK.........	757	100.0	-	-	1.6	2.8	1.8	3.6	84.7	5.3	.2
AIR...................	-	100.0	-	42.6	1.4	5.4	46.8	-	2.8	.9	.1
WATER.................	11 594	100.0	4.3	12.8	22.2	3.6	4.6	6.5	45.9	-	-
OTHER.................	596	100.0	-	-	-	-	-	-	100.0	-	-
UNKNOWN...............	20	100.0	-	11.9	-	-	8.8	16.6	62.8	-	-
PACIFIC...............	3 000	100.0	-	.3	.1	-	.5	.2	.6	9.4	88.9
RAIL...................	675	100.0	-	.6	.5	.1	2.1	.7	2.0	22.4	71.5
MOTOR CARRIER.........	1 657	100.0	.1	.1	-	-	-	.7	.2	6.8	92.7
PRIVATE TRUCK.........	631	100.0	-	-	-	-	-	-	.1	2.7	97.3
AIR...................	-	100.0	31.9	8.1	23.0	-	21.5	-	.3	.2	15.0
WATER.................	30	100.0	-	-	-	-	-	-	-	-	100.0
OTHER.................	3	100.0	-	54.5	1.9	-	-	-	-	.2	43.4
UNKNOWN...............	1	100.0	-	-	-	-	.8	-	-	71.5	27.6
TON-MILES OF SHIPMENTS	(millions of ton-miles)										
U.S. TOTAL............	32 424	100.0	4.7	17.5	20.3	6.6	16.0	8.3	11.8	4.8	10.0
RAIL...................	18 676	100.0	2.8	15.3	16.8	7.6	19.3	9.9	9.9	5.2	13.3
MOTOR CARRIER.........	5 117	100.0	3.0	13.7	18.5	6.3	13.7	7.7	16.3	10.3	10.5
PRIVATE TRUCK.........	1 216	100.0	8.1	16.2	19.9	8.5	18.0	6.1	12.8	4.2	6.3
AIR...................	8	100.0	5.7	18.4	19.0	1.8	13.9	1.0	4.2	4.1	31.9
WATER.................	7 185	100.0	10.4	26.6	31.2	4.4	8.8	4.8	12.0	-	1.8
OTHER.................	76	100.0	.2	7.6	1.1	.7	7.6	9.1	70.3	.2	3.3
UNKNOWN...............	142	100.0	18.0	7.5	11.0	.2	9.9	2.1	48.0	1.4	1.9
MIDDLE ATLANTIC.......	3 000	100.0	8.6	21.7	16.7	3.7	14.7	5.6	6.6	2.2	20.1
RAIL...................	1 454	100.0	7.3	21.5	16.3	3.7	9.5	4.4	7.6	3.5	26.2
MOTOR CARRIER.........	1 043	100.0	6.3	18.6	20.4	4.6	18.2	8.0	7.0	1.3	15.6
PRIVATE TRUCK.........	378	100.0	22.3	37.8	13.5	2.0	16.4	5.1	2.3	.5	.1
AIR...................	-	100.0	.5	3.9	30.8	.9	17.3	.5	2.1	5.9	38.1
WATER.................	116	100.0	-	1.3	-	-	44.6	-	6.4	-	47.7
OTHER.................	3	100.0	3.2	1.5	4.2	14.6	17.7	.3	3.2	.3	54.9
UNKNOWN...............	3	100.0	.1	10.3	11.2	7.3	3.4	.4	-	-	67.2
EAST NORTH CENTRAL.....	3 638	100.0	3.0	16.9	29.7	11.4	9.8	5.2	13.6	1.2	9.3
RAIL...................	2 339	100.0	3.2	19.1	22.1	10.0	11.4	4.3	16.6	.7	12.7
MOTOR CARRIER.........	956	100.0	2.6	14.5	44.1	13.0	7.2	4.5	8.2	1.8	4.0
PRIVATE TRUCK.........	302	100.0	2.4	6.6	46.7	18.9	6.0	8.0	7.6	3.2	.6
AIR...................	-	100.0	.2	7.8	31.5	.5	20.1	3.6	2.0	1.1	33.3
WATER.................	19	100.0	-	31.0	-	-	-	-	68.3	-	.7
OTHER.................	12	100.0	.3	4.0	3.2	.1	1.3	54.0	33.2	.4	3.4
UNKNOWN...............	5	100.0	16.5	16.5	12.5	.8	16.0	17.9	15.4	4.3	.1

See footnotes at end of table 4.

TABLE 2. **TCC GROUP 281—Percent Distribution of Geographic Division of Origin and Means of Transport, by Geographic Division of Destination: 1972**—Continued

Geographic division of origin[1] and means of transport	Number	Percent distribution by division of destination									
		U.S. total	New England	Middle Atlantic	East North Central	West North Central	South Atlantic	East South Central	West South Central	Mountain	Pacific
TON-MILES OF SHIPMENTS	(millions of ton-miles)										
WEST NORTH CENTRAL......	366	100.0	3.0	10.6	23.2	22.0	5.9	2.8	14.7	10.0	7.8
RAIL...................	221	100.0	2.8	11.7	18.1	24.7	6.4	2.0	12.8	11.1	10.4
MOTOR CARRIER.........	71	100.0	5.8	14.7	32.7	17.5	9.2	6.9	7.7	.5	5.0
PRIVATE TRUCK.........	68	100.0	.6	1.6	30.3	19.3	.5	1.3	29.4	17.0	-
AIR...................	4	100.0	.4	24.0	15.4	2.3	10.1	.5	4.0	3.9	39.4
WATER.................	-	100.0	-	-	-	-	-	-	-	-	-
OTHER.................	-	100.0	-	-	19.3	21.1	-	44.2	15.4	-	-
UNKNOWN...............	-	100.0	-	-	-	-	-	-	-	-	-
SOUTH ATLANTIC..........	2 579	100.0	2.4	12.8	19.6	6.1	21.7	12.6	10.8	3.4	10.5
RAIL...................	1 698	100.0	1.8	9.3	22.7	7.5	19.1	14.2	9.5	5.0	10.8
MOTOR CARRIER.........	537	100.0	5.5	23.5	17.6	3.3	26.1	12.4	6.9	.6	4.2
PRIVATE TRUCK.........	175	100.0	1.5	14.2	8.7	6.6	49.8	9.6	6.4	-	3.2
AIR...................	-	100.0	1.6	31.7	21.1	2.6	4.6	4.2	16.1	.2	17.8
WATER.................	82	100.0	-	23.0	-	.1	1.5	-	3.3	-	72.1
OTHER.................	-	100.0	5.0	5.0	18.3	2.6	11.5	5.7	19.9	13.5	18.5
UNKNOWN...............	84	100.0	.2	3.0	12.7	-	5.6	-	78.4	-	-
EAST SOUTH CENTRAL......	2 402	100.0	1.3	10.1	13.5	3.2	30.3	9.3	11.0	.6	20.8
RAIL...................	1 801	100.0	1.2	7.9	13.4	2.2	30.7	8.3	8.1	.6	27.4
MOTOR CARRIER.........	328	100.0	3.0	14.0	15.7	10.6	34.5	10.3	9.5	1.0	1.4
PRIVATE TRUCK.........	54	100.0	1.7	12.6	3.0	4.0	65.0	7.3	6.4	-	-
AIR...................	-	100.0	-	-	19.5	-	79.9	-	.6	-	-
WATER.................	209	100.0	-	21.9	13.7	-	9.1	16.2	39.1	-	-
OTHER.................	-	100.0	9.8	27.1	27.8	4.8	6.6	.4	2.7	-	20.8
UNKNOWN...............	7	100.0	-	4.1	.1	-	84.3	11.5	-	-	-
WEST SOUTH CENTRAL......	18 540	100.0	5.5	19.8	21.2	6.4	15.7	9.2	12.7	4.7	4.9
RAIL...................	9 981	100.0	2.6	16.7	16.0	7.9	21.7	12.5	8.9	5.2	8.4
MOTOR CARRIER.........	1 638	100.0	.8	9.3	6.7	4.4	10.1	9.2	35.4	20.4	3.7
PRIVATE TRUCK.........	123	100.0	-	-	7.4	9.2	8.1	7.5	53.7	12.3	1.6
AIR...................	._	100.0	-	45.7	1.0	1.4	49.8	-	1.0	.8	.2
WATER.................	6 739	100.0	11.0	27.3	32.8	4.7	8.3	4.4	11.4	-	-
OTHER.................	49	100.0	-	-	-	-	-	-	100.0	-	-
UNKNOWN...............	7	100.0	-	43.4	-	-	25.9	15.8	14.9	-	-
PACIFIC.................	630	100.0	.6	3.1	1.2	.3	5.1	1.7	4.5	18.3	65.2
RAIL...................	280	100.0	-	3.2	2.5	.6	11.2	3.0	8.1	21.9	49.6
MOTOR CARRIER.........	254	100.0	1.3	2.0	.1	-	.2	1.0	2.2	17.6	75.6
PRIVATE TRUCK.........	75	100.0	-	-	-	-	-	-	-	11.6	88.4
AIR...................	1	100.0	41.5	9.8	20.1	-	25.2	-	.2	.1	3.0
WATER.................	11	100.0	.3	-	-	-	-	-	-	-	99.7
OTHER.................	5	100.0	-	96.0	2.8	-	-	-	-	.1	1.1
UNKNOWN...............	-	100.0	-	-	-	-	5.8	-	-	82.1	12.1

See footnotes at end of table 4.

TABLE 3. **TCC GROUP 281—Percent Distribution of Geographic Division of Destination and Means of Transport, by Geographic Division of Origin: 1972**

Geographic division of destination and means of transport	Number	Percent distribution by division of origin[1]									
		U.S. total	New England	Middle Atlantic	East North Central	West North Central	South Atlantic	East South Central	West South Central	Mountain	Pacific
TONS OF SHIPMENTS	(thousands of tons)										
U.S. TOTAL	79 278	100.0	(D)	13.7	17.0	1.3	9.5	7.1	43.4	(D)	3.8
RAIL	35 947	100.0	(D)	9.8	18.8	1.4	11.1	10.7	42.0	(D)	1.9
MOTOR CARRIER	21 360	100.0	(D)	18.9	20.7	1.1	10.7	4.6	29.6	(D)	7.8
PRIVATE TRUCK	8 127	100.0	(D)	35.8	27.4	3.3	10.2	1.9	9.3	(D)	7.8
AIR	10	100.0	(D)	7.2	16.9	61.6	2.5	-	.5	(D)	5.0
WATER	12 981	100.0	(D)	3.1	.4	-	2.2	4.7	89.3	(D)	.2
OTHER	637	100.0	(D)	.7	3.4	-	.9	-	93.6	(D)	.6
UNKNOWN	213	100.0	(D)	3.0	15.0	-	54.8	9.1	9.6	(D)	.5
NEW ENGLAND	2 249	100.0	(D)	48.7	7.8	.5	6.2	1.4	31.3	(D)	.1
RAIL	768	100.0	(D)	46.3	15.5	.9	9.5	2.5	24.7	(D)	-
MOTOR CARRIER	472	100.0	(D)	67.8	9.0	.8	12.5	2.1	2.1	(D).	.3
PRIVATE TRUCK	491	100.0	(D)	85.5	2.6	.1	1.2	.2	-	(D)	-
AIR	-	100.0	(D)	5.9	1.1	8.6	1.8	-	-	(D)	72.5
WATER	503	100.0	(D)	-	-	-	-	-	100.0	(D)	-
OTHER	-	100.0	(D)	56.5	6.4	-	6.6	.4	-	(D)	-
UNKNOWN	12	100.0	(D)	.3	8.6	-	7.5	-	-	(D)	-
MIDDLE ATLANTIC	12 884	100.0	(D)	48.8	12.2	.3	12.7	2.9	21.4	(D)	.1
RAIL	4 944	100.0	(D)	35.7	23.2	.6	11.8	3.8	23.3	(D)	.1
MOTOR CARRIER	3 693	100.0	(D)	64.4	9.5	.3	17.7	1.6	3.1	(D)	.1
PRIVATE TRUCK	2 312	100.0	(D)	87.7	2.6	.1	9.0	.5	-	(D)	-
AIR	2	100.0	(D)	5.4	5.8	68.5	5.9	-	1.2	(D)	2.1
WATER	1 902	100.0	(D)	5.9	1.0	-	9.4	5.8	77.9	(D)	-
OTHER	3	100.0	(D)	23.4	18.8	-	2.0	.3	-	(D)	54.4
UNKNOWN	25	100.0	(D)	14.5	5.1	-	63.4	1.4	9.4	(D)	-
EAST NORTH CENTRAL	16 175	100.0	(D)	7.1	51.5	1.4	6.3	5.1	27.6	(D)	-
RAIL	7 009	100.0	(D)	8.0	46.5	1.2	9.2	8.4	25.2	(D)	.1
MOTOR CARRIER	4 356	100.0	(D)	10.5	73.5	1.9	7.3	3.1	2.7	(D)	-
PRIVATE TRUCK	2 086	100.0	(D)	6.2	87.7	2.9	2.1	.3	.6	(D)	-
AIR	4	100.0	(D)	8.6	29.6	53.7	1.6	-	-	(D)	3.1
WATER	2 670	100.0	(D)	-	-	-	-	3.5	96.5	(D)	-
OTHER	3	100.0	(D)	7.6	82.0	.7	5.9	.6	.1	(D)	2.0
UNKNOWN	45	100.0	(D)	2.2	54.7	-	37.1	.1	-	(D)	-
WEST NORTH CENTRAL	4 216	100.0	(D)	3.0	30.9	9.7	4.1	5.4	44.2	(D)	-
RAIL	2 549	100.0	(D)	2.6	27.8	9.0	5.2	3.3	48.0	(D)	-
MOTOR CARRIER	918	100.0	(D)	5.6	44.1	9.5	2.6	14.9	22.1	(D)	-
PRIVATE TRUCK	330	100.0	(D)	2.6	56.7	28.3	4.5	1.4	6.5	(D)	-
AIR	-	100.0	(D)	1.3	2.6	88.7	1.4	-	.8	(D)	-
WATER	416	100.0	(D)	-	-	-	-	-	100.0	(D)	-
OTHER	-	100.0	(D)	85.1	6.8	3.0	2.8	.7	-	(D)	.1
UNKNOWN	-	100.0	(D)	65.1	34.9	-	-	-	-	(D)	-
SOUTH ATLANTIC	10 858	100.0	(D)	13.8	8.1	.3	30.6	17.7	28.4	(D)	.1
RAIL	6 637	100.0	(D)	5.9	10.2	.3	26.2	21.4	34.8	(D)	.2
MOTOR CARRIER	2 301	100.0	(D)	24.6	6.9	.5	43.6	14.1	9.5	(D)	-
PRIVATE TRUCK	916	100.0	(D)	31.3	4.3	.1	52.2	9.7	1.5	(D)	-
AIR	1	100.0	(D)	12.6	17.6	51.4	.6	.1	2.0	(D)	8.5
WATER	957	100.0	(D)	27.1	-	-	8.7	7.9	56.2	(D)	-
OTHER	11	100.0	(D)	11.9	2.0	-	46.0	-	.2	(D)	-
UNKNOWN	32	100.0	(D)	.5	4.2	-	44.3	45.6	5.4	(D)	-
EAST SOUTH CENTRAL	6 270	100.0	(D)	4.1	7.5	.5	12.2	22.6	52.4	(D)	.1
RAIL	3 893	100.0	(D)	2.6	6.1	.3	13.6	23.3	53.2	(D)	.1
MOTOR CARRIER	1 132	100.0	(D)	11.3	10.7	1.1	15.3	22.6	37.9	(D)	.1
PRIVATE TRUCK	221	100.0	(D)	13.1	27.2	1.3	29.2	17.0	12.2	(D)	-
AIR	-	100.0	(D)	2.2	23.3	55.5	12.5	-	-	(D)	-
WATER	1 001	100.0	(D)	-	3.3	-	-	21.3	75.4	(D)	-
OTHER	12	100.0	(D)	.1	98.9	.3	.6	-	-	(D)	-
UNKNOWN	9	100.0	(D)	.2	22.6	-	-	41.5	35.7	(D)	-
WEST SOUTH CENTRAL	18 007	100.0	(D)	.9	3.1	.9	1.6	3.0	88.9	(D)	.1
RAIL	6 107	100.0	(D)	1.4	7.0	1.0	2.6	5.7	80.4	(D)	.2
MOTOR CARRIER	4 822	100.0	(D)	1.2	2.2	.3	.8	1.1	93.9	(D)	.1
PRIVATE TRUCK	944	100.0	(D)	.9	2.8	8.8	1.3	.9	67.9	(D)	.3
AIR	-	100.0	(D)	1.9	3.5	78.5	4.2	-	.3	(D)	.3
WATER	5 448	100.0	(D)	.1	-	-	-	2.2	97.7	(D)	-
OTHER	602	100.0	(D)	-	.8	-	-	-	99.1	(D)	-
UNKNOWN	82	100.0	(D)	-	1.1	-	83.2	-	15.6	(D)	-
MOUNTAIN	4 136	100.0	(D)	1.0	.8	1.8	1.4	.3	40.6	(D)	6.8
RAIL	2 054	100.0	(D)	1.6	.6	2.4	2.8	.5	47.5	(D)	7.4
MOTOR CARRIER	1 873	100.0	(D)	.4	.7	-	.1	.1	35.5	(D)	6.0
PRIVATE TRUCK	204	100.0	(D)	.8	3.8	11.7	-	-	19.8	(D)	8.4
AIR	-	100.0	(D)	6.4	3.1	73.1	.1	-	.2	(D)	.3
WATER	-	100.0	(D)	-	-	-	-	-	-	(D)	-
OTHER	-	100.0	(D)	3.9	45.3	-	44.9	-	-	(D)	5.6
UNKNOWN	3	100.0	(D)	-	7.4	-	-	-	-	(D)	23.0
PACIFIC	4 479	100.0	(D)	5.7	4.0	.5	2.7	6.0	12.5	(D)	59.5
RAIL	1 983	100.0	(D)	8.2	7.9	.8	4.3	13.5	26.1	(D)	24.3
MOTOR CARRIER	1 790	100.0	(D)	3.8	1.1	.1	.6	.1	2.4	(D)	85.9
PRIVATE TRUCK	618	100.0	(D)	-	.2	-	.4	-	.2	(D)	99.2
AIR	1	100.0	(D)	5.3	10.9	75.2	.9	-	-	(D)	5.0
WATER	81	100.0	(D)	28.8	-	-	31.0	-	-	(D)	37.6
OTHER	2	100.0	(D)	26.0	7.8	-	1.8	.1	-	(D)	61.4
UNKNOWN	1	100.0	(D)	77.7	.1	-	-	-	-	(D)	22.2

See footnotes at end of table 4.

TABLE 3. TCC GROUP 281—Percent Distribution of Geographic Division of Destination and Means of Transport, by Geographic Division of Origin: 1972—Continued

Geographic division of destination and means of transport	Number	Percent distribution by division of origin[1]									
		U.S. total	New England	Middle Atlantic	East North Central	West North Central	South Atlantic	East South Central	West South Central	Mountain	Pacific
TON-MILES OF SHIPMENTS	(millions of ton-miles)										
U.S. TOTAL	32 424	100.0	(D)	9.3	11.2	1.1	8.0	7.4	57.2	(D)	1.9
RAIL	18 676	100.0	(D)	7.8	12.5	1.2	9.1	9.6	53.4	(D)	1.5
MOTOR CARRIER	5 117	100.0	(D)	20.4	18.7	1.4	10.5	6.4	32.0	(D)	5.0
PRIVATE TRUCK	1 216	100.0	(D)	31.1	24.9	5.6	14.4	4.5	10.1	(D)	6.2
AIR	8	100.0	(D)	6.6	11.6	59.6	2.0	-	.8	(D)	12.9
WATER	7 185	100.0	(D)	1.6	.3	-	1.1	2.9	93.8	(D)	.2
OTHER	76	100.0	(D)	4.2	16.6	-	.8	-	64.5	(D)	7.0
UNKNOWN	142	100.0	(D)	2.8	3.9	-	59.5	5.3	5.0	(D)	.3
NEW ENGLAND	1 535	100.0	(D)	16.7	7.0	.7	4.1	2.1	66.5	(D)	.2
RAIL	513	100.0	(D)	20.7	14.5	1.2	6.0	4.1	51.1	(D)	-
MOTOR CARRIER	153	100.0	(D)	43.2	16.3	2.7	19.2	6.5	8.9	(D)	2.2
PRIVATE TRUCK	98	100.0	(D)	85.9	7.5	.4	2.7	.9	-	(D)	-
AIR	-	100.0	(D)	.5	.5	4.1	.6	-	-	(D)	93.3
WATER	744	100.0	(D)	-	-	-	-	-	100.0	(D)	-
OTHER	-	100.0	(D)	54.6	21.3	-	15.5	1.8	-	(D)	-
UNKNOWN	25	100.0	(D)	-	3.6	-	.8	-	-	(D)	-
MIDDLE ATLANTIC	5 678	100.0	(D)	11.5	10.8	.7	5.8	4.3	64.6	(D)	.3
RAIL	2 851	100.0	(D)	11.0	15.7	.9	5.5	5.0	58.6	(D)	.3
MOTOR CARRIER	699	100.0	(D)	27.8	19.9	1.5	18.1	6.6	21.7	(D)	.7
PRIVATE TRUCK	196	100.0	(D)	72.7	10.1	.5	12.6	3.5	-	(D)	-
AIR	1	100.0	(D)	1.4	4.9	77.8	3.5	-	2.1	(D)	6.9
WATER	1 913	100.0	(D)	.1	.3	-	1.0	2.4	96.2	(D)	-
OTHER	5	100.0	(D)	.9	8.9	-	.5	.2	-	(D)	89.4
UNKNOWN	10	100.0	(D)	3.9	8.7	-	24.1	2.9	29.3	(D)	-
EAST NORTH CENTRAL	6 591	100.0	(D)	7.6	16.4	1.3	7.7	4.9	59.5	(D)	.1
RAIL	3 145	100.0	(D)	7.6	16.4	1.3	12.3	7.7	50.7	(D)	.2
MOTOR CARRIER	947	100.0	(D)	22.4	44.5	2.5	10.0	5.4	11.5	(D)	-
PRIVATE TRUCK	241	100.0	(D)	21.0	58.5	8.6	6.3	.7	3.8	(D)	-
AIR	1	100.0	(D)	10.6	19.2	48.4	2.2	-	-	(D)	13.7
WATER	2 238	100.0	(D)	-	-	-	-	1.3	98.7	(D)	-
OTHER	-	100.0	(D)	15.9	48.3	.7	12.7	1.1	.3	(D)	17.6
UNKNOWN	15	100.0	(D)	2.9	4.5	-	68.5	-	-	(D)	-
WEST NORTH CENTRAL	2 152	100.0	(D)	5.1	19.3	3.7	7.3	3.6	55.3	(D)	.1
RAIL	1 410	100.0	(D)	3.8	16.6	3.9	9.0	2.8	56.0	(D)	.1
MOTOR CARRIER	322	100.0	(D)	14.9	38.6	3.9	5.5	10.8	22.5	(D)	-
PRIVATE TRUCK	103	100.0	(D)	7.4	55.4	12.8	11.3	2.1	11.0	(D)	-
AIR	-	100.0	(D)	3.3	3.0	74.9	3.0	-	.7	(D)	-
WATER	315	100.0	(D)	-	-	-	-	-	100.0	(D)	-
OTHER	-	100.0	(D)	89.4	3.6	1.2	2.9	.3	-	(D)	.3
UNKNOWN	-	100.0	(D)	87.1	12.9	-	-	-	-	(D)	-
SOUTH ATLANTIC	5 177	100.0	(D)	8.5	6.9	.4	10.8	14.1	56.0	(D)	.6
RAIL	3 604	100.0	(D)	3.8	7.4	.4	9.0	15.4	60.1	(D)	.9
MOTOR CARRIER	701	100.0	(D)	27.0	9.8	.9	20.0	16.1	23.5	(D)	.1
PRIVATE TRUCK	219	100.0	(D)	28.3	8.3	-	39.8	16.2	4.6	(D)	-
AIR	1	100.0	(D)	8.2	16.7	43.2	.7	.1	3.0	(D)	23.4
WATER	631	100.0	(D)	8.2	-	-	.2	3.0	88.5	(D)	-
OTHER	5	100.0	(D)	9.7	2.8	-	1.2	-	.4	(D)	-
UNKNOWN	14	100.0	(D)	1.0	6.4	-	34.1	45.2	13.2	(D)	.2
EAST SOUTH CENTRAL	2 676	100.0	(D)	6.3	7.0	.4	12.2	8.3	63.8	(D)	.4
RAIL	1 850	100.0	(D)	3.5	5.4	.2	13.1	8.1	67.4	(D)	.5
MOTOR CARRIER	394	100.0	(D)	21.2	10.8	1.3	16.8	8.5	38.4	(D)	.6
PRIVATE TRUCK	74	100.0	(D)	26.0	32.5	1.2	22.5	5.4	12.4	(D)	-
AIR	-	100.0	(D)	3.4	43.2	33.1	8.9	-	-	(D)	-
WATER	346	100.0	(D)	-	3.8	-	-	9.8	86.4	(D)	-
OTHER	6	100.0	(D)	.1	99.0	.2	.5	-	-	(D)	-
UNKNOWN	3	100.0	(D)	.5	33.3	-	-	28.6	37.6	(D)	-
WEST SOUTH CENTRAL	3 834	100.0	(D)	5.2	12.9	1.4	7.3	6.9	61.4	(D)	.7
RAIL	1 857	100.0	(D)	5.9	20.9	1.5	8.7	7.9	47.8	(D)	1.2
MOTOR CARRIER	835	100.0	(D)	8.7	9.4	.7	4.4	3.7	69.5	(D)	.7
PRIVATE TRUCK	155	100.0	(D)	5.5	14.7	12.9	7.2	2.2	42.5	(D)	.6
AIR	-	100.0	(D)	3.4	5.5	56.9	7.8	-	.2	(D)	-
WATER	863	100.0	(D)	.9	-	-	.3	9.5	89.3	(D)	-
OTHER	54	100.0	(D)	.2	7.8	-	.2	-	91.7	(D)	-
UNKNOWN	68	100.0	(D)	-	1.3	-	97.2	-	1.6	(D)	-
MOUNTAIN	1 545	100.0	(D)	4.3	2.8	2.4	5.7	.9	56.3	(D)	7.5
RAIL	966	100.0	(D)	5.2	1.7	2.5	8.8	1.2	53.9	(D)	6.4
MOTOR CARRIER	525	100.0	(D)	2.6	3.3	.1	.6	.6	63.4	(D)	8.5
PRIVATE TRUCK	50	100.0	(D)	4.1	19.0	22.9	.1	-	29.9	(D)	17.3
AIR	-	100.0	(D)	9.4	3.1	56.1	.1	-	.2	(D)	.2
WATER	-	100.0	(D)	-	-	-	-	-	-	(D)	-
OTHER	-	100.0	(D)	6.2	36.8	-	54.7	-	-	(D)	1.9
UNKNOWN	1	100.0	(D)	-	12.1	-	-	-	-	(D)	16.2
PACIFIC	3 232	100.0	(D)	18.7	10.5	.9	8.4	15.4	28.0	(D)	12.7
RAIL	2 477	100.0	(D)	15.4	12.0	.9	7.4	20.0	34.0	(D)	5.6
MOTOR CARRIER	537	100.0	(D)	30.2	7.2	.7	4.2	.9	11.3	(D)	35.8
PRIVATE TRUCK	76	100.0	(D)	.5	2.3	-	7.2	-	2.6	(D)	87.3
AIR	2	100.0	(D)	7.8	12.0	73.5	1.1	-	-	(D)	1.2
WATER	132	100.0	(D)	41.8	.1	-	45.0	-	-	(D)	8.8
OTHER	2	100.0	(D)	68.5	16.7	-	4.2	.3	-	(D)	2.3
UNKNOWN	2	100.0	(D)	98.2	.1	-	-	-	-	(D)	1.7

See footnotes at end of table 4.

TABLE 4. TCC GROUP 281—Percent Distribution of Distance Shipped and Weight of Shipment, by Means of Transport: 1972

Distance shipped and weight of shipment [2][3]	Number	Percent distribution by means of transport							
		All means of transport	Rail	Motor carrier	Private truck	Air	Water	Other	Unknown
TONS OF SHIPMENTS	(thousands of tons)								
U.S. TOTAL............	67 647	100.0	44.3	26.1	11.2	-	17.3	.9	.2
UNDER 100 MILES.........	17 533	100.0	21.2	37.6	24.3	-	13.7	3.0	.1
UNDER 1000 POUNDS.....	44	100.0	-	49.3	48.4	.1	.6	1.2	.4
1000 TO 9999 POUNDS...	498	100.0	-	27.3	72.3	-	.2	.2	-
10000 TO 29999 POUNDS.	1 193	100.0	.5	27.6	71.0	-	.2	.6	.1
30000 TO 59999 POUNDS.	7 859	100.0	2.5	62.9	34.5	-	-	-	.1
60000 TO 89999 POUNDS.	830	100.0	21.3	63.7	14.5	-	-	-	.5
90000 POUNDS AND OVER.	7 108	100.0	47.0	8.9	2.8	-	33.8	7.3	.1
100 TO 199 MILES........	11 747	100.0	35.8	33.9	13.1	-	17.0	-	.1
UNDER 1000 POUNDS.....	19	100.0	-	63.3	34.3	.7	.2	1.5	.1
1000 TO 9999 POUNDS...	145	100.0	-	50.0	49.6	.1	-	-	.3
10000 TO 29999 POUNDS.	453	100.0	.2	35.3	64.1	-	.1	-	.3
30000 TO 59999 POUNDS.	3 921	100.0	1.0	72.1	26.8	-	-	-	.1
60000 TO 89999 POUNDS.	469	100.0	51.2	25.4	23.5	-	-	-	-
90000 POUNDS AND OVER.	6 737	100.0	58.2	11.8	.2	-	29.6	-	.1
200 TO 299 MILES........	9 246	100.0	48.9	30.6	7.5	-	12.1	.9	-
UNDER 1000 POUNDS.....	14	100.0	-	86.6	5.1	6.6	-	1.6	-
1000 TO 9999 POUNDS...	112	100.0	.6	72.0	26.3	.8	-	-	.2
10000 TO 29999 POUNDS.	244	100.0	.5	67.4	31.7	.1	-	-	.3
30000 TO 59999 POUNDS.	2 586	100.0	3.4	75.4	21.0	-	-	.1	.1
60000 TO 89999 POUNDS.	789	100.0	43.0	55.7	1.3	-	-	-	-
90000 POUNDS AND OVER.	5 498	100.0	74.5	3.2	.6	-	20.3	1.4	-
300 TO 499 MILES........	9 851	100.0	61.9	21.3	7.1	-	9.3	-	.3
UNDER 1000 POUNDS.....	20	100.0	-	86.2	7.0	4.4	.1	2.2	-
1000 TO 9999 POUNDS...	134	100.0	.1	66.4	32.4	.6	.3	-	.2
10000 TO 29999 POUNDS.	299	100.0	2.4	56.1	40.7	-	-	-	.8
30000 TO 59999 POUNDS.	2 110	100.0	6.2	69.7	24.0	-	-	.1	.1
60000 TO 89999 POUNDS.	782	100.0	63.9	32.4	3.8	-	-	-	-
90000 POUNDS AND OVER.	6 503	100.0	84.0	1.6	-	-	14.0	-	.4
500 TO 999 MILES........	12 530	100.0	55.6	14.1	2.7	-	27.2	.1	.3
UNDER 1000 POUNDS.....	22	100.0	-	82.9	1.2	10.7	-	4.8	.3
1000 TO 9999 POUNDS...	124	100.0	2.8	77.2	18.3	.7	.1	.5	.5
10000 TO 29999 POUNDS.	287	100.0	9.3	70.3	19.5	-	-	.2	.6
30000 TO 59999 POUNDS.	1 853	100.0	14.6	71.6	12.8	-	.1	.9	.1
60000 TO 89999 POUNDS.	773	100.0	90.2	9.4	.4	-	-	-	-
90000 POUNDS AND OVER.	9 469	100.0	63.1	.5	.2	-	36.0	-	.3
1000 TO 1499 MILES......	5 309	100.0	60.9	4.6	.4	-	33.9	.1	.1
UNDER 1000 POUNDS.....	4	100.0	-	89.1	.9	5.8	-	4.2	.1
1000 TO 9999 POUNDS...	16	100.0	4.0	95.1	.9	-	-	.1	-
10000 TO 29999 POUNDS.	50	100.0	19.3	70.3	7.1	-	1.7	1.5	-
30000 TO 59999 POUNDS.	261	100.0	26.5	64.3	6.5	-	1.7	-	1.0
60000 TO 89999 POUNDS.	330	100.0	90.0	6.7	-	-	1.7	1.1	.5
90000 POUNDS AND OVER.	4 646	100.0	61.5	-	-	-	38.5	-	.1
1500 MILES OR OVER......	1 427	100.0	84.4	10.1	.2	.1	4.0	.2	.9
UNDER 1000 POUNDS.....	4	100.0	3.4	78.4	1.2	10.8	-	6.2	-
1000 TO 9999 POUNDS...	22	100.0	11.9	78.7	.5	4.6	.2	3.9	.2
10000 TO 29999 POUNDS.	32	100.0	22.8	65.6	6.8	-	1.3	-	3.4
30000 TO 59999 POUNDS.	132	100.0	36.0	38.7	.6	-	23.1	1.6	-
60000 TO 89999 POUNDS.	209	100.0	84.8	5.9	-	-	8.6	-	.8
90000 POUNDS AND OVER.	1 025	100.0	94.6	3.7	-	-	.8	-	1.0
TON-MILES OF SHIPMENTS	(millions of ton-miles)								
U.S. TOTAL............	27 152	100.0	57.3	15.2	4.1	-	22.8	.3	.3
UNDER 100 MILES.........	847	100.0	23.1	36.9	23.2	-	13.2	3.5	.2
UNDER 1000 POUNDS.....	1	100.0	-	57.8	40.8	.1	.2	.9	.3
1000 TO 9999 POUNDS...	20	100.0	-	29.7	70.1	-	.1	.1	.1
10000 TO 29999 POUNDS.	48	100.0	.9	28.5	70.2	-	.2	.2	-
30000 TO 59999 POUNDS.	381	100.0	3.0	61.2	35.6	-	-	-	.1
60000 TO 89999 POUNDS.	43	100.0	15.3	72.9	11.6	-	-	-	.2
90000 POUNDS AND OVER.	351	100.0	50.2	7.5	1.9	-	31.8	8.3	.2
100 TO 199 MILES........	1 695	100.0	37.5	32.5	12.8	-	17.0	-	.2
UNDER 1000 POUNDS.....	2	100.0	-	64.4	33.0	.8	.3	1.5	.1
1000 TO 9999 POUNDS...	20	100.0	-	51.7	47.9	.1	-	-	.2
10000 TO 29999 POUNDS.	64	100.0	.2	37.3	62.1	-	.1	-	.4
30000 TO 59999 POUNDS.	567	100.0	1.1	72.5	26.2	-	-	-	.2
60000 TO 89999 POUNDS.	67	100.0	52.3	25.2	22.6	-	-	-	-
90000 POUNDS AND OVER.	972	100.0	61.1	8.9	.2	-	29.6	-	.1

See footnotes at end of table 4.

TABLE 4. **TCC GROUP 281—Percent Distribution of Distance Shipped and Weight of Shipment, by Means of Transport: 1972**—Continued

Distance shipped and weight of shipment [2] [3]	Number	Percent distribution by means of transport							
		All means of transport	Rail	Motor carrier	Private truck	Air	Water	Other	Unknown
TON-MILES OF SHIPMENTS	(millions of ton-miles)								
200 TO 299 MILES.........	2 285	100.0	49.6	29.9	7.4	-	12.0	.9	-
UNDER 1000 POUNDS.....	3	100.0	-	87.0	4.7	6.8	-	1.6	-
1000 TO 9999 POUNDS...	27	100.0	.7	73.8	24.4	.9	-	-	.3
10000 TO 29999 POUNDS.	60	100.0	.5	69.0	30.2	.1	-	-	.3
30000 TO 59999 POUNDS.	633	100.0	3.6	74.8	21.4	-	-	.1	.1
60000 TO 89999 POUNDS.	189	100.0	43.3	55.6	1.1	-	-	-	-
90000 POUNDS AND OVER.	1 369	100.0	75.1	2.8	.5	-	20.0	1.5	-
300 TO 499 MILES........	3 789	100.0	62.5	21.0	7.1	-	9.0	-	.3
UNDER 1000 POUNDS.....	8	100.0	-	86.0	7.1	4.6	.1	2.2	-
1000 TO 9999 POUNDS...	54	100.0	.1	66.2	32.6	.7	.2	-	.2
10000 TO 29999 POUNDS.	118	100.0	2.6	53.8	42.8	-	-	-	.9
30000 TO 59999 POUNDS.	798	100.0	6.6	69.6	23.6	-	-	.1	.1
60000 TO 89999 POUNDS.	299	100.0	64.0	32.1	4.0	-	-	-	-
90000 POUNDS AND OVER.	2 511	100.0	84.4	1.6	-	-	13.6	-	.4
500 TO 999 MILES........	9 298	100.0	54.0	12.7	2.4	-	30.3	.1	.3
UNDER 1000 POUNDS.....	15	100.0	-	82.6	1.0	11.3	-	4.7	.3
1000 TO 9999 POUNDS...	84	100.0	3.1	79.6	15.3	.8	.1	.5	.6
10000 TO 29999 POUNDS.	200	100.0	9.5	70.4	19.1	-	-	.2	.9
30000 TO 59999 POUNDS.	1 244	100.0	14.7	71.3	13.0	-	.1	.8	.1
60000 TO 89999 POUNDS.	539	100.0	91.1	8.6	.3	-	-	-	-
90000 POUNDS AND OVER.	7 214	100.0	60.0	.4	.2	-	39.1	-	.3
1000 TO 1499 MILES......	6 471	100.0	60.4	4.6	.4	-	34.4	.1	.1
UNDER 1000 POUNDS.....	5	100.0	.1	88.8	.9	5.9	-	4.2	.1
1000 TO 9999 POUNDS...	19	100.0	4.3	94.8	.8	-	-	.1	-
10000 TO 29999 POUNDS.	60	100.0	20.0	70.2	6.9	-	1.5	1.5	-
30000 TO 59999 POUNDS.	312	100.0	26.1	65.1	5.9	-	1.9	-	1.0
60000 TO 89999 POUNDS.	409	100.0	90.1	6.5	-	-	1.9	1.0	.5
90000 POUNDS AND OVER.	5 664	100.0	60.9	-	-	-	39.1	-	.1
1500 MILES OR OVER......	2 766	100.0	82.5	11.1	.2	.1	4.8	.3	1.1
UNDER 1000 POUNDS.....	10	100.0	3.9	77.8	1.3	10.1	-	6.8	-
1000 TO 9999 POUNDS...	46	100.0	12.5	78.5	.5	3.7	.3	4.4	.2
10000 TO 29999 POUNDS.	66	100.0	22.3	66.6	5.7	-	1.4	-	4.0
30000 TO 59999 POUNDS.	273	100.0	34.8	37.2	.6	-	25.5	1.9	-
60000 TO 89999 POUNDS.	432	100.0	83.3	6.2	-	-	9.8	-	.8
90000 POUNDS AND OVER.	1 937	100.0	93.2	4.6	-	-	1.0	-	1.3

Note: Detail may not add to total due to rounding. The introductory table shows the estimates of sampling variability for tons; sampling variability for ton-miles has not been estimated. See the map in the Introduction for the States comprising the geographic divisions of the United States.
    Shipments excluded from the survey are those moving by pipeline (primarily petroleum products from refineries), parcel post shipments, and commodities moved by own power (motorized vehicles, aircraft, etc.) or towed (prefabricated buildings, etc.). Local shipments (commodities shipped less than 25 miles from the plant) and shipments within the same city are also excluded. Shipments to Alaska and Hawaii from the 48 conterminous States and the District of Columbia are included; however, no data were obtained for shipments originating in Alaska and Hawaii.

- Represents zero or rounds to zero.   (D) Withheld to avoid disclosing figures for individual companies.

[1]Production of this commodity is concentrated in the geographic divisions shown; figures and distributions for geographic divisions not shown are included in the total.
    [2]Distances of shipments to foreign destinations are calculated only to the U.S. port of exit.
    [3]Includes only shipments represented by bills of lading and invoices. Summary records which did not show individual weights of shipments are not included.

TCC 282. Plastics Materials

Comparisons of Tons and Ton-Miles of Shipments for
Geographic Divisions of Origin and for Sampling Variability: 1972 and 1967

Geographic division of origin	Estimates				Relative sampling variability in tons (percent)	
	1972		1967		1972	1967
	Tons (thousands)	Ton-miles (millions)	Tons (thousands)	Ton-miles (millions)		
U.S. total	24,426	13,901	12,442	7,344	8.8	8.0
New England	1,432	446	1,089	382	19.8	(*)
Middle Atlantic	3,090	1,235	1,933	691	25.2	(*)
East North Central	3,685	1,708	2,212	863	12.5	(*)
West North Central	(D)	(D)	22	12	(*)	(*)
South Atlantic	4,442	1,620	1,320	608	22.1	(*)
East South Central	1,982	932	1,432	686	21.7	(*)
West South Central	8,174	7,121	3,888	3,808	10.9	(*)
Mountain	(D)	(D)	–	–	(*)	(*)
Pacific	402	116	546	294	38.4	(*)

– Represents or rounds to zero.   (D) Withheld to avoid disclosing figures for individual companies.   (*) Data not published.

TABLE 1. **TCC GROUP 282—Percent Distribution of Geographic Division of Origin and Distance Shipped, by Means of Transport: 1972**

Geographic division of origin [1] and distance shipped [2]	Number	Percent distribution by means of transport							
		All means of transport	Rail	Motor carrier	Private truck	Air	Water	Other	Unknown
TONS OF SHIPMENTS	(thousands of tons)								
U.S. TOTAL	24 426	100.0	44.5	43.8	8.2	-	2.8	.5	.2
NEW ENGLAND	1 432	100.0	11.3	72.8	14.9	-	.3	.3	.5
UNDER 100 MILES	476	100.0	5.8	63.0	29.7	-	-	-	1.5
100 TO 199 MILES	325	100.0	-	89.7	10.3	-	-	-	-
200 TO 299 MILES	221	100.0	1.4	95.9	2.8	-	-	-	-
300 TO 499 MILES	125	100.0	9.2	88.7	2.0	-	-	-	-
500 TO 999 MILES	220	100.0	39.5	47.9	10.9	-	-	1.6	-
1000 TO 1499 MILES	34	100.0	66.5	25.1	8.4	-	-	-	-
1500 MILES OR OVER	27	100.0	34.1	43.1	8.0	.2	14.6	-	-
MIDDLE ATLANTIC	3 090	100.0	14.4	76.0	7.3	-	1.7	.3	.4
UNDER 100 MILES	1 015	100.0	10.0	78.1	9.8	-	1.4	.3	.4
100 TO 199 MILES	319	100.0	13.2	79.7	5.8	-	-	.1	1.3
200 TO 299 MILES	433	100.0	10.2	77.0	12.3	-	.3	-	.1
300 TO 499 MILES	489	100.0	18.7	76.5	4.7	-	-	-	-
500 TO 999 MILES	578	100.0	16.5	77.5	5.0	-	-	.6	.4
1000 TO 1499 MILES	113	100.0	21.2	61.6	1.8	.1	15.0	-	.2
1500 MILES OR OVER	140	100.0	32.4	52.4	-	.2	14.3	.7	-
EAST NORTH CENTRAL	3 685	100.0	45.3	42.1	10.1	-	-	2.2	.1
UNDER 100 MILES	433	100.0	30.6	55.3	12.3	-	-	1.8	.1
100 TO 199 MILES	484	100.0	29.6	66.5	3.5	-	-	.4	-
200 TO 299 MILES	524	100.0	31.1	53.8	11.1	-	-	4.1	-
300 TO 499 MILES	917	100.0	43.3	39.9	14.6	-	-	2.2	-
500 TO 999 MILES	1 064	100.0	59.0	28.6	9.7	-	-	2.7	-
1000 TO 1499 MILES	124	100.0	83.5	9.7	6.1	.1	-	.6	-
1500 MILES OR OVER	136	100.0	75.2	20.1	-	.2	-	1.3	3.3
SOUTH ATLANTIC	4 442	100.0	20.9	57.7	20.9	-	.2	.3	-
UNDER 100 MILES	867	100.0	3.4	68.2	28.3	-	-	-	.1
100 TO 199 MILES	929	100.0	16.4	62.4	19.2	-	.7	1.2	-
200 TO 299 MILES	818	100.0	18.7	54.9	26.2	-	-	.2	-
300 TO 499 MILES	846	100.0	26.5	50.4	23.0	-	-	-	-
500 TO 999 MILES	760	100.0	29.7	58.7	11.7	-	-	-	-
1000 TO 1499 MILES	60	100.0	48.6	40.0	11.4	-	-	-	-
1500 MILES OR OVER	159	100.0	70.2	28.3	.7	-	.8	-	-
EAST SOUTH CENTRAL	1 982	100.0	39.6	54.5	5.9	-	-	-	-
UNDER 100 MILES	75	100.0	-	86.4	13.6	-	-	-	-
100 TO 199 MILES	335	100.0	25.0	71.3	3.7	-	-	-	-
200 TO 299 MILES	396	100.0	23.6	67.4	9.0	-	-	-	-
300 TO 499 MILES	516	100.0	39.5	54.1	6.3	-	-	-	-
500 TO 999 MILES	534	100.0	57.1	38.1	4.8	-	-	-	-
1000 TO 1499 MILES	6	100.0	-	99.9	-	.1	-	-	-
1500 MILES OR OVER	117	100.0	84.3	15.6	-	-	-	-	-
WEST SOUTH CENTRAL	8 174	100.0	73.4	17.2	1.4	-	7.7	-	.2
UNDER 100 MILES	334	100.0	19.1	53.6	6.9	-	18.2	.5	1.7
100 TO 199 MILES	410	100.0	65.0	30.9	4.1	-	-	-	-
200 TO 299 MILES	544	100.0	76.2	22.8	1.0	-	-	-	-
300 TO 499 MILES	577	100.0	68.4	29.9	1.6	-	-	-	-
500 TO 999 MILES	3 017	100.0	83.4	13.8	1.6	-	1.0	-	.2
1000 TO 1499 MILES	2 797	100.0	69.0	11.7	.6	-	18.7	-	.1
1500 MILES OR OVER	492	100.0	84.1	13.0	-	.1	2.9	-	-
PACIFIC	402	100.0	14.7	78.8	4.4	.4	.3	1.4	-
UNDER 100 MILES	238	100.0	3.0	94.2	2.6	.2	-	-	-
100 TO 199 MILES	43	100.0	21.1	75.7	1.4	-	-	1.7	-
200 TO 299 MILES	15	100.0	79.9	19.8	-	-	-	.3	-
300 TO 499 MILES	44	100.0	33.5	66.5	-	-	-	-	-
500 TO 999 MILES	24	100.0	39.5	48.9	10.3	1.2	-	.1	-
1000 TO 1499 MILES	17	100.0	-	52.5	46.9	.3	-	-	.3
1500 MILES OR OVER	19	100.0	30.1	33.0	1.8	4.8	5.8	24.3	.1
TON-MILES OF SHIPMENTS	(millions of ton-miles)								
U.S. TOTAL	13 901	100.0	59.5	29.3	4.4	-	6.2	.4	.1
NEW ENGLAND	446	100.0	26.9	60.6	9.5	-	2.4	.5	.1
UNDER 100 MILES	27	100.0	6.8	64.8	26.3	-	-	-	2.1
100 TO 199 MILES	47	100.0	-	89.8	10.2	-	-	-	-
200 TO 299 MILES	56	100.0	1.5	95.9	2.6	-	-	-	-
300 TO 499 MILES	47	100.0	9.3	88.2	2.4	-	-	-	-
500 TO 999 MILES	160	100.0	40.9	46.1	11.7	-	-	1.3	-
1000 TO 1499 MILES	40	100.0	65.7	26.2	8.0	-	-	-	-
1500 MILES OR OVER	65	100.0	31.3	43.6	8.5	.3	16.3	-	-
MIDDLE ATLANTIC	1 235	100.0	20.8	68.4	4.2	.1	5.9	.4	.2
UNDER 100 MILES	48	100.0	11.0	78.6	8.6	-	1.4	.3	.2
100 TO 199 MILES	46	100.0	13.7	79.0	5.9	-	-	.1	1.3
200 TO 299 MILES	109	100.0	10.4	76.7	12.3	-	.4	-	.1
300 TO 499 MILES	189	100.0	18.8	76.5	4.5	.1	-	-	-
500 TO 999 MILES	400	100.0	16.7	77.0	5.2	-	-	.7	.4
1000 TO 1499 MILES	140	100.0	20.8	60.3	1.6	.1	17.1	-	.2
1500 MILES OR OVER	300	100.0	34.2	49.1	-	.2	16.0	.6	-

See footnotes at end of table 4.

TABLE 1. **TCC GROUP 282**—Percent Distribution of Geographic Division of Origin and Distance Shipped, by Means of Transport: 1972—Continued

Geographic division of origin [1] and distance shipped [2]	Number	Percent distribution by means of transport							
		All means of transport	Rail	Motor carrier	Private truck	Air	Water	Other	Unknown
TON-MILES OF SHIPMENTS	(millions of ton-miles)								
EAST NORTH CENTRAL......	1 708	100.0	56.9	31.5	8.9	.1	-	2.1	.5
UNDER 100 MILES.......	20	100.0	37.5	46.4	12.9	-	-	3.0	.1
100 TO 199 MILES......	69	100.0	32.0	63.8	3.7	-	-	.4	-
200 TO 299 MILES......	131	100.0	32.0	53.1	11.0	-	-	3.8	-
300 TO 499 MILES......	359	100.0	43.1	40.2	14.5	-	-	2.2	-
500 TO 999 MILES......	725	100.0	59.4	28.1	9.9	-	-	2.5	-
1000 TO 1499 MILES....	144	100.0	84.0	9.7	5.6	.1	-	.6	-
1500 MILES OR OVER....	256	100.0	75.3	20.2	-	.2	-	1.3	3.0
SOUTH ATLANTIC.........	1 620	100.0	34.6	50.3	14.8	-	.2	.1	-
UNDER 100 MILES.......	48	100.0	4.2	66.8	28.9	-	-	-	.2
100 TO 199 MILES......	142	100.0	18.5	60.8	18.8	-	.5	1.3	-
200 TO 299 MILES......	208	100.0	19.5	53.8	26.4	-	-	.2	-
300 TO 499 MILES......	330	100.0	26.1	51.5	22.4	-	-	-	-
500 TO 999 MILES......	500	100.0	29.2	58.8	11.9	-	-	-	-
1000 TO 1499 MILES....	66	100.0	48.4	40.4	11.2	-	-	-	-
1500 MILES OR OVER....	323	100.0	69.8	28.5	.7	-	.9	-	-
EAST SOUTH CENTRAL......	932	100.0	53.9	41.6	4.5	-	-	-	-
UNDER 100 MILES.......	3	100.0	-	84.3	15.7	-	-	-	-
100 TO 199 MILES......	53	100.0	27.8	68.7	3.5	-	-	-	-
200 TO 299 MILES......	99	100.0	22.1	69.2	8.7	-	-	-	-
300 TO 499 MILES......	202	100.0	40.7	52.0	7.3	-	-	-	-
500 TO 999 MILES......	355	100.0	58.4	37.0	4.6	-	-	-	-
1000 TO 1499 MILES....	7	100.0	-	99.9	-	.1	-	-	-
1500 MILES OR OVER....	209	100.0	83.6	16.4	-	-	-	-	-
WEST SOUTH CENTRAL......	7 121	100.0	74.8	13.4	.9	-	10.8	-	.1
UNDER 100 MILES.......	16	100.0	21.8	51.7	6.4	-	16.6	.9	2.7
100 TO 199 MILES......	64	100.0	66.5	28.9	4.6	-	-	-	-
200 TO 299 MILES......	137	100.0	76.8	22.3	.9	-	-	-	-
300 TO 499 MILES......	231	100.0	68.5	29.7	1.8	-	-	-	-
500 TO 999 MILES......	2 400	100.0	83.5	13.7	1.4	-	1.2	-	.2
1000 TO 1499 MILES....	3 449	100.0	67.1	11.5	.5	-	20.8	-	.1
1500 MILES OR OVER....	821	100.0	84.5	12.7	-	.1	2.7	-	-
PACIFIC................	116	100.0	27.3	47.0	11.9	2.1	2.8	8.9	.1
UNDER 100 MILES.......	7	100.0	3.7	92.5	3.7	.1	-	-	-
100 TO 199 MILES......	5	100.0	30.9	65.8	1.5	-	-	1.7	-
200 TO 299 MILES......	4	100.0	81.8	18.0	-	-	-	.3	-
300 TO 499 MILES......	14	100.0	31.8	68.2	-	-	-	-	-
500 TO 999 MILES......	19	100.0	44.0	46.5	8.1	1.2	-	.1	-
1000 TO 1499 MILES....	23	100.0	-	52.0	47.5	.3	-	-	.2
1500 MILES OR OVER....	41	100.0	31.3	29.5	1.7	5.2	7.7	24.5	.1

See footnotes at end of table 4.

TABLE 2. **TCC GROUP 282**—Percent Distribution of Geographic Division of Origin and Means of Transport, by Geographic Division of Destination: 1972

Geographic division of origin [1] and means of transport	Number	Percent distribution by division of destination									
		U.S. total	New England	Middle Atlantic	East North Central	West North Central	South Atlantic	East South Central	West South Central	Mountain	Pacific
TONS OF SHIPMENTS	(thousands of tons)										
U.S. TOTAL..............	24 426	100.0	7.5	19.3	22.0	4.4	22.5	7.3	9.7	1.4	5.9
RAIL..................	10 871	100.0	4.6	12.9	24.6	6.3	19.6	9.5	12.3	2.2	8.0
MOTOR CARRIER.........	10 691	100.0	9.8	22.5	22.4	2.9	23.8	5.2	7.6	.8	5.0
PRIVATE TRUCK.........	2 007	100.0	10.3	17.6	13.8	3.4	38.9	9.0	6.0	.4	.5
AIR...................	5	100.0	10.8	22.6	19.2	2.4	8.9	4.0	2.4	6.1	23.6
WATER.................	695	100.0	6.7	76.9	-	-	1.5	-	11.1	-	3.8
OTHER.................	115	100.0	8.4	12.5	27.5	9.0	25.2	7.0	7.3	.9	2.3
UNKNOWN...............	38	100.0	20.1	16.5	6.3	2.1	15.1	13.9	14.3	-	11.7
NEW ENGLAND............	1 432	100.0	36.5	33.3	11.3	2.5	11.6	2.1	1.2	-	1.6
RAIL..................	161	100.0	22.1	1.9	43.2	12.9	6.2	3.1	6.6	-	3.9
MOTOR CARRIER.........	1 042	100.0	32.8	41.4	7.1	1.1	14.7	1.4	.6	-	1.0
PRIVATE TRUCK.........	212	100.0	64.7	19.8	6.6	1.1	1.6	4.9	.3	-	1.0
AIR...................	-	100.0	18.2	9.1	17.1	-	13.3	-	1.3	-	41.0
WATER.................	4	100.0	-	-	-	-	-	-	-	-	100.0
OTHER.................	3	100.0	1.1	.4	98.5	-	-	-	-	-	-
UNKNOWN...............	7	100.0	100.0	-	-	-	-	-	-	-	-
MIDDLE ATLANTIC........	3 090	100.0	14.8	41.3	20.7	2.2	10.7	2.6	4.0	.5	3.3
RAIL..................	444	100.0	9.5	30.2	24.2	2.9	11.0	6.2	5.7	.4	9.8
MOTOR CARRIER.........	2 347	100.0	16.0	42.4	21.6	2.2	10.4	1.9	3.4	.5	1.6
PRIVATE TRUCK.........	224	100.0	17.1	55.4	10.0	1.2	12.9	2.7	.8	-	-
AIR...................	1	100.0	17.8	16.9	28.5	2.3	5.8	.4	4.8	2.6	20.9
WATER.................	52	100.0	-	24.0	-	-	6.5	-	31.1	-	38.4
OTHER.................	7	100.0	1.6	37.9	40.8	.1	6.2	.2	-	12.6	-
UNKNOWN...............	11	100.0	5.9	37.8	-	7.2	49.1	-	-	-	.6

See footnotes at end of table 4.

TABLE 2. TCC GROUP 282—Percent Distribution of Geographic Division of Origin and Means of Transport, by Geographic Division of Destination: 1972—Continued

Geographic division of origin[1] and means of transport	Number	Percent distribution by division of destination									
		U.S. total	New England	Middle Atlantic	East North Central	West North Central	South Atlantic	East South Central	West South Central	Mountain	Pacific
TONS OF SHIPMENTS	(thousands of tons)										
EAST NORTH CENTRAL........	3 685	100.0	5.6	15.5	39.6	6.6	14.1	7.5	6.2	1.3	3.6
RAIL.....................	1 671	100.0	5.8	12.4	29.8	8.0	19.5	8.0	8.2	2.4	6.0
MOTOR CARRIER...........	1 553	100.0	5.6	18.1	52.3	4.6	7.8	6.1	3.5	.3	1.7
PRIVATE TRUCK..........	372	100.0	3.3	19.1	33.4	8.1	16.3	11.0	8.2	.7	-
AIR....................	-	100.0	5.9	11.7	12.5	11.6	17.0	10.9	.2	.2	30.0
WATER..................	-	100.0	-	-	-	-	-	-	-	-	-
OTHER..................	82	100.0	9.6	13.9	30.2	12.7	14.8	9.8	6.9	-	2.1
UNKNOWN................	4	100.0	-	-	7.2	-	-	-	-	-	92.8
SOUTH ATLANTIC...........	4 442	100.0	4.9	13.3	9.3	1.4	55.7	8.1	3.7	.6	2.9
RAIL.....................	926	100.0	3.6	10.9	12.2	1.9	38.8	13.5	7.4	1.8	9.9
MOTOR CARRIER...........	2 563	100.0	6.5	15.1	9.8	1.1	56.5	6.2	2.9	.5	1.4
PRIVATE TRUCK..........	930	100.0	1.9	11.1	5.2	1.6	69.8	8.0	2.2	-	.1
AIR....................	-	100.0	.9	29.1	8.2	.5	52.2	.8	1.3	-	7.0
WATER..................	8	100.0	-	-	-	-	83.9	-	-	-	16.1
OTHER..................	13	100.0	12.3	.4	.1	-	87.3	-	-	-	-
UNKNOWN................	1	100.0	5.6	-	63.8	-	30.6	-	-	-	-
EAST SOUTH CENTRAL.......	1 982	100.0	3.3	15.9	22.0	1.8	34.3	11.4	5.3	.5	5.5
RAIL.....................	785	100.0	4.4	22.5	12.3	.9	27.8	12.3	7.1	.5	12.1
MOTOR CARRIER...........	1 079	100.0	2.8	12.1	26.6	2.6	40.4	10.0	3.4	.6	1.3
PRIVATE TRUCK..........	116	100.0	.7	5.6	43.7	.6	22.1	17.6	9.7	-	-
AIR....................	-	100.0	4.5	8.3	51.4	2.7	21.3	-	1.2	-	10.6
WATER..................	-	100.0	-	-	-	-	-	-	-	-	-
OTHER..................	-	100.0	-	-	11.3	-	75.0	13.7	-	-	-
UNKNOWN................	-	100.0	-	-	-	-	100.0	-	-	-	-
WEST SOUTH CENTRAL.......	8 174	100.0	3.6	15.8	22.9	5.8	13.3	9.7	20.2	2.2	6.6
RAIL.....................	5 999	100.0	3.8	11.3	25.7	6.6	16.0	10.6	16.5	2.3	7.2
MOTOR CARRIER...........	1 409	100.0	1.6	5.7	22.2	4.6	8.3	8.7	38.5	2.6	7.7
PRIVATE TRUCK..........	117	100.0	-	4.7	10.0	11.3	8.7	22.4	40.5	2.0	.4
AIR....................	-	100.0	22.1	25.9	39.4	.1	5.1	.4	1.9	.4	4.6
WATER..................	629	100.0	7.4	83.0	-	-	-	-	9.7	-	-
OTHER..................	2	100.0	.1	.2	.1	-	.1	.1	99.5	-	-
UNKNOWN................	14	100.0	-	14.9	9.8	-	-	37.1	38.2	-	-
PACIFIC..................	402	100.0	.2	1.3	1.6	.4	1.4	.1	3.6	4.1	87.3
RAIL.....................	59	100.0	-	6.3	3.1	-	.7	-	-	2.0	87.9
MOTOR CARRIER...........	317	100.0	.2	.2	1.5	.5	-	.1	2.0	3.9	91.5
PRIVATE TRUCK..........	17	100.0	-	-	-	-	2.0	-	45.5	14.1	38.3
AIR....................	1	100.0	3.8	33.4	3.9	-	2.6	7.1	3.3	15.9	30.0
WATER..................	1	100.0	-	-	-	-	-	-	-	-	100.0
OTHER..................	5	100.0	.2	.1	.1	-	84.7	-	-	-	14.9
UNKNOWN................	-	100.0	-	11.9	17.9	5.9	-	-	-	-	64.3
TON-MILES OF SHIPMENTS	(millions of ton-miles)										
U.S. TOTAL...............	13 901	100.0	7.1	19.8	20.8	4.9	17.1	6.3	7.3	2.7	14.0
RAIL.....................	8 275	100.0	6.2	15.4	22.0	5.3	17.5	6.8	6.7	3.2	16.9
MOTOR CARRIER...........	4 072	100.0	8.9	16.5	24.0	4.7	17.6	5.7	8.7	2.3	11.5
PRIVATE TRUCK..........	609	100.0	6.1	15.0	14.5	7.1	31.2	11.9	11.8	1.1	1.4
AIR....................	6	100.0	10.7	28.9	12.0	1.2	6.9	4.1	2.3	4.9	29.0
WATER..................	862	100.0	8.0	81.2	-	-	.2	-	3.0	-	7.5
OTHER..................	56	100.0	9.9	11.0	18.4	10.5	30.1	2.4	8.6	2.8	6.3
UNKNOWN................	19	100.0	3.9	16.6	7.5	4.2	9.8	15.3	2.3	-	40.4
NEW ENGLAND.............	446	100.0	10.4	18.6	24.1	7.9	14.5	6.2	5.3	.1	12.9
RAIL.....................	120	100.0	4.3	.7	43.0	17.4	4.3	4.8	12.3	-	13.1
MOTOR CARRIER...........	270	100.0	12.2	28.3	16.7	4.4	21.2	4.5	3.0	.1	9.5
PRIVATE TRUCK..........	42	100.0	18.2	13.4	20.0	6.0	5.0	22.9	1.9	-	12.6
AIR....................	-	100.0	.3	.9	7.9	-	9.7	-	1.3	-	79.9
WATER..................	10	100.0	-	-	-	-	-	-	-	-	100.0
OTHER..................	2	100.0	-	.1	99.7	-	-	-	.1	-	-
UNKNOWN................	-	100.0	100.0	-	-	-	-	-	-	-	-
MIDDLE ATLANTIC..........	1 235	100.0	9.1	9.3	27.3	5.1	10.5	4.4	12.9	2.1	19.2
RAIL.....................	257	100.0	3.8	5.9	20.1	4.6	7.3	7.0	11.4	1.0	39.0
MOTOR CARRIER...........	844	100.0	11.1	10.3	32.6	5.8	11.0	3.7	12.5	2.6	10.5
PRIVATE TRUCK..........	51	100.0	17.0	21.6	15.8	3.2	30.3	8.6	3.4	-	-
AIR....................	-	100.0	9.2	2.1	17.8	2.5	2.5	.3	7.1	4.7	53.9
WATER..................	73	100.0	-	1.2	-	-	1.3	-	31.7	-	65.8
OTHER..................	4	100.0	.6	4.0	56.7	.2	1.5	.3	-	34.3	2.4
UNKNOWN................	2	100.0	4.1	2.8	-	28.0	65.0	-	-	-	-

See footnotes at end of table 4.

TABLE 2. **TCC GROUP 282—Percent Distribution of Geographic Division of Origin and Means of Transport, by Geographic Division of Destination: 1972**—Continued

Geographic division of origin[1] and means of transport	Number	Percent distribution by division of destination									
		U.S. total	New England	Middle Atlantic	East North Central	West North Central	South Atlantic	East South Central	West South Central	Mountain	Pacific
TON-MILES OF SHIPMENTS	(millions of ton-miles)										
EAST NORTH CENTRAL......	1 708	100.0	7.9	14.5	15.9	7.1	17.4	7.5	11.4	3.4	14.7
RAIL..................	972	100.0	6.8	11.3	10.3	7.3	20.8	6.6	12.3	5.1	19.4
MOTOR CARRIER.........	538	100.0	10.2	20.1	26.0	5.4	11.2	8.4	8.3	1.0	9.5
PRIVATE TRUCK.........	152	100.0	6.2	15.4	17.4	10.2	19.8	11.9	17.4	1.8	-
AIR...................	-	100.0	5.1	7.7	3.5	5.2	17.9	4.7	.2	.2	55.6
WATER.................	-	100.0	-	-	-	-	-	-	-	-	-
OTHER.................	35	100.0	13.9	16.7	15.3	16.4	13.1	3.7	11.7	-	9.2
UNKNOWN...............	7	100.0	-	-	.2	-	-	-	-	-	99.8
SOUTH ATLANTIC..........	1 620	100.0	7.9	13.1	8.6	3.2	30.0	8.9	8.6	2.9	16.9
RAIL..................	559	100.0	3.5	7.5	7.1	3.1	16.9	11.9	10.6	4.8	34.6
MOTOR CARRIER.........	814	100.0	11.9	16.0	10.2	3.0	32.9	6.9	7.6	2.4	9.1
PRIVATE TRUCK.........	239	100.0	4.4	16.6	6.9	4.4	50.4	8.7	7.7	-	.9
AIR...................	-	100.0	1.1	21.3	8.1	.5	40.2	.6	2.3	-	25.7
WATER.................	3	100.0	-	-	-	-	20.7	-	-	-	79.3
OTHER.................	2	100.0	20.1	.3	.1	-	79.5	-	-	-	-
UNKNOWN...............	-	100.0	37.4	-	48.1	-	14.6	-	-	-	-
EAST SOUTH CENTRAL......	932	100.0	5.8	20.3	14.7	1.7	23.4	4.6	6.6	1.8	21.1
RAIL..................	502	100.0	5.5	21.5	7.6	.8	17.9	4.2	7.6	1.2	33.7
MOTOR CARRIER.........	387	100.0	6.7	20.0	21.3	3.0	30.4	4.6	4.3	2.7	7.1
PRIVATE TRUCK.........	42	100.0	1.6	9.4	38.2	.7	23.5	10.2	16.3	-	-
AIR...................	-	100.0	7.1	7.9	34.1	1.0	20.0	-	.7	-	29.3
WATER.................	-	100.0	-	-	-	-	-	-	-	-	-
OTHER.................	-	100.0	-	-.	6.5	-	92.3	1.2	-	-	-
UNKNOWN...............	-	100.0	-	-	-	-	100.0	-	-	-	-
WEST SOUTH CENTRAL......	7 121	100.0	6.5	24.4	25.1	4.9	14.0	6.6	5.2	2.3	11.0
RAIL..................	5 324	100.0	6.8	17.2	27.6	5.4	16.6	7.2	4.8	2.6	11.8
MOTOR CARRIER.........	954	100.0	3.7	11.4	31.8	5.1	10.9	6.9	11.0	2.6	16.6
PRIVATE TRUCK.........	61	100.0	-	11.9	17.5	18.1	14.6	23.8	10.2	3.3	.7
AIR...................	1	100.0	28.1	30.2	30.7	.1	3.9	.2	.4	.5	6.1
WATER.................	772	100.0	9.0	90.7	-	-	-	-	.4	-	-
OTHER.................	-	100.0	.4	1.3	.5	-	.2	.2	97.4	-	-
UNKNOWN...............	7	100.0	-	39.5	17.1	-	-	37.7	5.7	-	-
PACIFIC.................	116	100.0	1.4	10.5	9.9	1.9	10.2	1.0	17.4	7.5	40.3
RAIL..................	31	100.0	-	28.8	10.2	-	2.4	-	-	2.1	56.6
MOTOR CARRIER.........	54	100.0	2.6	3.1	14.9	3.9	.2	1.7	16.5	11.5	45.6
PRIVATE TRUCK.........	13	100.0	-	-	-	-	5.2	-	80.8	11.3	2.6
AIR...................	2	100.0	6.7	54.6	4.7	-	3.8	9.0	2.8	9.0	9.4
WATER.................	3	100.0	-	-	-	-	-	-	-	-	100.0
OTHER.................	10	100.0	.2	.1	.1	-	98.3	-	-	-	1.2
UNKNOWN...............	-	100.0	-	20.4	23.0	6.7	-	-	-	-	49.8

See footnotes at end of table 4.

TABLE 3. **TCC GROUP 282**—Percent Distribution of Geographic Division of Destination and Means of Transport, by Geographic Division of Origin: 1972

Geographic division of destination and means of transport	Number	Percent distribution by division of origin[1]									
		U.S. total	New England	Middle Atlantic	East North Central	West North Central	South Atlantic	East South Central	West South Central	Mountain	Pacific
TONS OF SHIPMENTS	(thousands of tons)										
U.S. TOTAL..............	24 426	100.0	5.9	12.7	15.1	(D)	18.2	8.1	33.5	(D)	1.6
RAIL....................	10 871	100.0	1.5	4.1	15.4	(D)	8.5	7.2	55.2	(D)	.5
MOTOR CARRIER..........	10 691	100.0	9.8	22.0	14.5	(D)	24.0	10.1	13.2	(D)	3.0
PRIVATE TRUCK..........	2 007	100.0	10.6	11.2	18.6	(D)	46.3	5.8	5.9	(D)	.9
AIR....................	5	100.0	2.7	18.6	16.1	(D)	3.7	3.6	16.4	(D)	29.5
WATER..................	695	100.0	.6	7.5	-	(D)	1.2	-	90.6	(D)	.2
OTHER..................	115	100.0	3.2	6.8	71.1	(D)	11.6	-	2.4	(D)	4.9
UNKNOWN................	38	100.0	18.3	28.8	12.5	(D)	2.6	.2	37.5	(D)	.2
NEW ENGLAND............	1 820	100.0	28.7	25.1	11.3	(D)	12.1	3.6	16.4	(D)	-
RAIL....................	498	100.0	7.2	8.5	19.6	(D)	6.6	7.0	45.8	(D)	-
MOTOR CARRIER..........	1 050	100.0	32.6	35.7	8.3	(D)	15.9	2.9	2.2	(D)	.1
PRIVATE TRUCK..........	206	100.0	66.5	18.5	6.0	(D)	8.5	.4	-	(D)	-
AIR....................	-	100.0	4.5	30.7	8.7	(D)	.3	1.5	33.5	(D)	10.4
WATER..................	46	100.0	-	-	-	(D)	-	-	100.0	(D)	-
OTHER..................	9	100.0	.4	1.3	81.2	(D)	17.0	-	-	(D)	.1
UNKNOWN................	7	100.0	90.8	8.5	-	(D)	.7	-	-	(D)	-
MIDDLE ATLANTIC........	4 716	100.0	10.1	27.0	12.1	(D)	12.6	6.7	27.3	(D)	.1
RAIL....................	1 400	100.0	.2	9.6	14.8	(D)	7.2	12.6	48.4	(D)	.3
MOTOR CARRIER..........	2 405	100.0	17.9	41.4	11.7	(D)	16.1	5.4	3.4	(D)	-
PRIVATE TRUCK..........	353	100.0	11.9	35.2	20.1	(D)	29.3	1.9	1.6	(D)	-
AIR....................	1	100.0	1.1	14.0	8.4	(D)	4.8	1.3	18.8	(D)	43.7
WATER..................	535	100.0	-	2.4	-	(D)	-	-	97.6	(D)	-
OTHER..................	14	100.0	.1	20.7	78.8	(D)	.3	-	-	(D)	-
UNKNOWN................	6	100.0	-	66.0	-	(D)	-	-	33.9	(D)	.2
EAST NORTH CENTRAL......	5 374	100.0	3.0	11.9	27.2	(D)	7.7	8.1	34.8	(D)	.1
RAIL....................	2 670	100.0	2.6	4.0	18.6	(D)	4.2	3.6	57.8	(D)	.1
MOTOR CARRIER..........	2 392	100.0	3.1	21.2	34.0	(D)	10.5	12.0	13.1	(D)	.2
PRIVATE TRUCK..........	276	100.0	5.1	8.1	45.0	(D)	17.5	18.4	4.2	(D)	-
AIR....................	1	100.0	2.4	27.6	10.5	(D)	1.6	9.5	33.6	(D)	5.9
WATER..................	-	100.0	-	-	-	(D)	-	-	-	(D)	-
OTHER..................	31	100.0	11.6	10.1	78.2	(D)	-	-	-	(D)	-
UNKNOWN................	2	100.0	-	.1	14.3	(D)	26.6	-	58.4	(D)	.6
WEST NORTH CENTRAL......	1 079	100.0	3.3	6.4	22.7	(D)	5.6	3.3	43.7	(D)	.2
RAIL....................	686	100.0	3.0	1.9	19.4	(D)	2.5	1.1	57.4	(D)	-
MOTOR CARRIER..........	312	100.0	3.8	16.8	22.7	(D)	9.3	8.9	20.7	(D)	.5
PRIVATE TRUCK..........	68	100.0	3.6	3.9	43.8	(D)	21.1	1.1	19.4	(D)	-
AIR....................	-	100.0	-	17.6	76.9	(D)	.7	3.9	.9	(D)	-
WATER..................	-	100.0	-	-	-	(D)	-	-	-	(D)	-
OTHER..................	10	100.0	-	.1	99.9	(D)	-	-	-	(D)	-
UNKNOWN................	-	100.0	-	99.4	-	(D)	-	-	-	(D)	.6
SOUTH ATLANTIC.........	5 502	100.0	3.0	6.0	9.4	(D)	45.0	12.4	19.8	(D)	.1
RAIL....................	2 135	100.0	.5	2.3	15.2	(D)	16.8	10.2	45.0	(D)	-
MOTOR CARRIER..........	2 539	100.0	6.0	9.6	4.8	(D)	57.0	17.2	4.6	(D)	-
PRIVATE TRUCK..........	780	100.0	.4	3.7	7.8	(D)	83.2	3.3	1.3	(D)	-
AIR....................	-	100.0	4.0	12.1	31.0	(D)	21.8	8.5	9.4	(D)	8.6
WATER..................	10	100.0	-	33.2	-	(D)	66.8	-	-	(D)	-
OTHER..................	29	100.0	-	1.7	41.7	(D)	40.1	-	-	(D)	16.5
UNKNOWN................	5	100.0	-	93.5	-	(D)	5.3	1.2	-	(D)	-
EAST SOUTH CENTRAL......	1 787	100.0	1.7	4.4	15.5	(D)	20.1	12.6	44.2	(D)	-
RAIL....................	1 033	100.0	.5	2.7	12.9	(D)	12.1	9.4	61.5	(D)	-
MOTOR CARRIER..........	559	100.0	2.6	8.1	17.0	(D)	28.6	19.4	21.9	(D)	.1
PRIVATE TRUCK..........	180	100.0	5.8	3.4	22.6	(D)	41.1	11.4	14.6	(D)	-
AIR....................	-	100.0	-	1.7	43.7	(D)	.8	-	1.5	(D)	52.4
WATER..................	-	100.0	-	-	-	(D)	-	-	-	(D)	-
OTHER..................	8	100.0	-	.2	99.7	(D)	-	-	-	(D)	-
UNKNOWN................	5	100.0	-	-	-	(D)	-	-	100.0	(D)	-
WEST SOUTH CENTRAL......	2 358	100.0	.7	5.2	9.7	(D)	6.9	4.4	69.9	(D)	.6
RAIL....................	1 337	100.0	.8	1.9	10.2	(D)	5.1	4.2	74.0	(D)	-
MOTOR CARRIER..........	808	100.0	.7	9.8	6.8	(D)	9.1	4.6	67.1	(D)	.8
PRIVATE TRUCK..........	120	100.0	.5	1.4	25.3	(D)	17.3	9.4	39.3	(D)	6.7
AIR....................	-	100.0	1.5	37.6	1.3	(D)	2.0	1.8	13.4	(D)	40.3
WATER..................	77	100.0	-	21.1	-	(D)	-	-	78.9	(D)	-
OTHER..................	8	100.0	-	-	67.4	(D)	-	-	32.6	(D)	-
UNKNOWN................	5	100.0	-	-	-	(D)	-	-	100.0	(D)	-
MOUNTAIN...............	337	100.0	.1	4.4	13.7	(D)	8.4	3.2	53.5	(D)	4.9
RAIL....................	238	100.0	-	.7	16.5	(D)	7.0	1.6	59.1	(D)	.5
MOTOR CARRIER..........	89	100.0	.2	13.9	4.8	(D)	12.9	7.8	41.8	(D)	13.9
PRIVATE TRUCK..........	8	100.0	-	-	30.4	(D)	-	-	28.8	(D)	30.4
AIR....................	-	100.0	-	8.0	.4	(D)	-	-	1.1	(D)	76.6
WATER..................	-	100.0	-	-	-	(D)	-	-	-	(D)	-
OTHER..................	-	100.0	-	99.8	-	(D)	-	-	-	(D)	.2
UNKNOWN................	-	100.0	-	-	-	(D)	-	-	-	(D)	-
PACIFIC................	1 450	100.0	1.6	6.9	9.2	(D)	8.9	7.6	37.2	(D)	24.3
RAIL....................	869	100.0	.7	5.0	11.5	(D)	10.5	10.9	49.4	(D)	6.0
MOTOR CARRIER..........	534	100.0	1.9	6.8	5.1	(D)	6.5	2.7	20.4	(D)	54.3
PRIVATE TRUCK..........	10	100.0	19.3	-	-	(D)	10.0	-	4.1	(D)	64.4
AIR....................	1	100.0	4.7	16.5	20.6	(D)	1.1	1.6	3.2	(D)	37.5
WATER..................	26	100.0	15.1	75.6	-	(D)	4.9	-	-	(D)	4.3
OTHER..................	2	100.0	-	1.8	66.1	(D)	-	-	-	(D)	32.1
UNKNOWN................	4	100.0	-	-	98.8	(D)	-	-	-	(D)	1.2

See footnotes at end of table 4.

TABLE 3. **TCC GROUP 282**—Percent Distribution of Geographic Division of Destination and Means of Transport, by Geographic Division of Origin: 1972—Continued

Geographic division of destination and means of transport	Number	Percent distribution by division of origin[1]									
		U.S. total	New England	Middle Atlantic	East North Central	West North Central	South Atlantic	East South Central	West South Central	Mountain	Pacific
TON-MILES OF SHIPMENTS	(millions of ton-miles)										
U.S. TOTAL...............	13 901	100.0	3.2	8.9	12.3	(D)	11.7	6.7	51.2	(D)	.8
RAIL..................	8 275	100.0	1.5	3.1	11.8	(D)	6.8	6.1	64.3	(D)	.4
MOTOR CARRIER.........	4 072	100.0	6.6	20.7	13.2	(D)	20.0	9.5	23.4	(D)	1.3
PRIVATE TRUCK.........	609	100.0	7.0	8.5	25.0	(D)	39.3	7.0	10.1	(D)	2.3
AIR...................	6	100.0	3.1	14.9	14.2	(D)	2.0	2.1	17.5	(D)	36.9
WATER.................	862	100.0	1.2	8.5	-	(D)	.4	-	89.5	(D)	.4
OTHER.................	56	100.0	3.9	8.3	63.9	(D)	4.3	-	1.2	(D)	18.5
UNKNOWN...............	19	100.0	3.1	14.8	40.2	(D)	.6	.1	40.6	(D)	.6
NEW ENGLAND...........	990	100.0	4.7	11.4	13.7	(D)	12.9	5.5	46.9	(D)	.2
RAIL..................	513	100.0	1.0	1.9	13.0	(D)	3.8	5.4	70.1	(D)	-
MOTOR CARRIER.........	364	100.0	9.1	25.7	15.0	(D)	26.5	7.1	9.6	(D)	.4
PRIVATE TRUCK.........	37	100.0	20.8	23.7	25.3	(D)	28.5	1.8	-	(D)	-
AIR...................	-	100.0	.1	12.8	6.8	(D)	.2	1.4	46.2	(D)	23.3
WATER.................	69	100.0	-	-	-	(D)	-	-	100.0	(D)	-
OTHER.................	5	100.0	-	.5	90.2	(D)	8.8	-	-	(D)	.5
UNKNOWN...............	-	100.0	78.5	15.7	-	(D)	5.8	-	-	(D)	-
MIDDLE ATLANTIC.......	2 750	100.0	3.0	4.2	9.0	(D)	7.7	6.9	63.2	(D)	.4
RAIL..................	1 276	100.0	.1	1.2	8.6	(D)	3.3	8.5	71.9	(D)	.7
MOTOR CARRIER.........	670	100.0	11.4	13.0	16.1	(D)	19.5	11.5	16.3	(D)	.3
PRIVATE TRUCK.........	91	100.0	6.2	12.3	25.6	(D)	43.5	4.4	8.0	(D)	-
AIR...................	1	100.0	.1	1.1	3.8	(D)	1.5	.6	18.3	(D)	69.7
WATER.................	700	100.0	-	.1	-	(D)	-	-	99.9	(D)	-
OTHER.................	6	100.0	-	3.0	96.5	(D)	.1	-	.1	(D)	.2
UNKNOWN...............	3	100.0	-	2.5	-	(D)	-	-	96.8	(D)	.7
EAST NORTH CENTRAL....	2 895	100.0	3.7	11.7	9.4	(D)	4.8	4.7	61.7	(D)	.4
RAIL..................	1 818	100.0	2.8	2.8	5.5	(D)	2.2	2.1	80.9	(D)	.2
MOTOR CARRIER.........	976	100.0	4.6	28.2	14.3	(D)	8.5	8.4	31.1	(D)	.8
PRIVATE TRUCK.........	88	100.0	9.6	9.3	30.0	(D)	18.7	18.4	12.2	(D)	-
AIR...................	-	100.0	2.1	22.1	4.2	(D)	1.4	5.8	44.7	(D)	14.5
WATER.................	-	100.0	-	-	-	(D)	-	-	-	(D)	-
OTHER.................	10	100.0	21.1	25.5	53.2	(D)	-	-	-	(D)	.1
UNKNOWN...............	1	100.0	-	.1	1.3	(D)	3.9	-	93.0	(D)	1.8
WEST NORTH CENTRAL....	677	100.0	5.2	9.3	17.9	(D)	7.7	2.4	51.1	(D)	.3
RAIL..................	436	100.0	4.8	2.7	16.3	(D)	4.0	.9	65.6	(D)	-
MOTOR CARRIER.........	191	100.0	6.3	25.4	15.2	(D)	12.8	6.0	25.5	(D)	1.1
PRIVATE TRUCK.........	42	100.0	6.0	3.9	36.0	(D)	24.6	.7	25.7	(D)	-
AIR...................	-	100.0	-	31.9	64.1	(D)	1.0	1.7	1.3	(D)	-
WATER.................	-	100.0	-	-	-	(D)	-	-	-	(D)	-
OTHER.................	5	100.0	-	.2	99.8	(D)	-	-	-	(D)	-
UNKNOWN...............	-	100.0	-	99.1	-	(D)	-	-	-	(D)	.9
SOUTH ATLANTIC........	2 375	100.0	2.7	5.5	12.5	(D)	20.5	9.2	41.9	(D)	.5
RAIL..................	1 447	100.0	.4	1.3	14.0	(D)	6.5	6.2	60.9	(D)	.1
MOTOR CARRIER.........	716	100.0	8.0	13.0	8.5	(D)	37.4	16.5	14.5	(D)	-
PRIVATE TRUCK.........	190	100.0	1.1	8.3	15.9	(D)	63.5	5.2	4.7	(D)	.4
AIR...................	-	100.0	4.4	5.3	36.7	(D)	11.7	6.0	10.0	(D)	20.2
WATER.................	1	100.0	-	55.3	-	(D)	44.7	-	-	(D)	-
OTHER.................	16	100.0	-	.4	27.9	(D)	11.4	-	-	(D)	60.3
UNKNOWN...............	1	100.0	-	97.9	-	(D)	.9	1.2	-	(D)	-
EAST SOUTH CENTRAL....	876	100.0	3.2	6.1	14.7	(D)	16.4	4.9	53.5	(D)	.1
RAIL..................	565	100.0	1.0	3.2	11.3	(D)	11.8	3.8	68.2	(D)	-
MOTOR CARRIER.........	234	100.0	5.2	13.3	19.3	(D)	24.0	7.6	28.1	(D)	.4
PRIVATE TRUCK.........	72	100.0	13.4	6.2	25.0	(D)	28.8	6.0	20.1	(D)	-
AIR...................	-	100.0	-	.9	16.4	(D)	.3	-	.7	(D)	81.7
WATER.................	-	100.0	-	-	-	(D)	-	-	-	(D)	-
OTHER.................	1	100.0	-	1.0	98.8	(D)	-	-	.1	(D)	-
UNKNOWN...............	2	100.0	-	-	-	(D)	-	-	100.0	(D)	-
WEST SOUTH CENTRAL....	1 011	100.0	2.3	15.8	19.3	(D)	13.8	6.1	36.6	(D)	2.0
RAIL..................	552	100.0	2.7	5.3	21.7	(D)	10.8	6.9	46.2	(D)	-
MOTOR CARRIER.........	355	100.0	2.3	29.6	12.5	(D)	17.4	4.7	29.5	(D)	2.5
PRIVATE TRUCK.........	71	100.0	1.1	2.5	36.9	(D)	25.5	9.6	8.7	(D)	15.5
AIR...................	-	100.0	1.8	45.7	1.0	(D)	2.0	.7	2.8	(D)	44.4
WATER.................	25	100.0	-	89.4	-	(D)	-	-	10.6	(D)	-
OTHER.................	4	100.0	-	-	86.8	(D)	-	-	13.1	(D)	-
UNKNOWN...............	-	100.0	-	-	-	(D)	-	-	100.0	(D)	-
MOUNTAIN..............	371	100.0	.1	7.1	15.6	(D)	12.5	4.4	44.8	(D)	2.4
RAIL..................	268	100.0	-	.9	18.6	(D)	9.9	2.2	51.9	(D)	.2
MOTOR CARRIER.........	93	100.0	.4	23.8	5.6	(D)	21.1	11.2	26.4	(D)	6.7
PRIVATE TRUCK.........	6	100.0	-	-	41.0	(D)	-	-	30.2	(D)	23.1
AIR...................	-	100.0	-	14.3	.4	(D)	-	-	1.6	(D)	67.7
WATER.................	-	100.0	-	-	-	(D)	-	-	-	(D)	-
OTHER.................	1	100.0	-	99.9	-	(D)	-	-	-	(D)	.1
UNKNOWN...............	-	100.0	-	-	-	(D)	-	-	-	(D)	-
PACIFIC...............	1 953	100.0	3.0	12.2	12.9	(D)	14.0	10.1	40.2	(D)	2.4
RAIL..................	1 396	100.0	1.1	7.2	13.5	(D)	13.9	12.1	44.9	(D)	1.3
MOTOR CARRIER.........	469	100.0	5.5	18.8	10.9	(D)	15.9	5.9	33.6	(D)	5.3
PRIVATE TRUCK.........	8	100.0	60.9	-	-	(D)	25.9	-	4.7	(D)	4.2
AIR...................	1	100.0	8.6	27.7	27.3	(D)	1.8	2.1	3.7	(D)	12.0
WATER.................	65	100.0	16.4	74.1	-	(D)	4.6	-	-	(D)	4.9
OTHER.................	3	100.0	-	3.1	93.3	(D)	-	-	-	(D)	3.5
UNKNOWN...............	7	100.0	-	-	99.3	(D)	-	-	-	(D)	.7

See footnotes at end of table 4.

TABLE 4. **TCC GROUP 282—Percent Distribution of Distance Shipped and Weight of Shipment, by Means of Transport: 1972**

Distance shipped and weight of shipment[2][3]	Number	Percent distribution by means of transport							
		All means of transport	Rail	Motor carrier	Private truck	Air	Water	Other	Unknown
TONS OF SHIPMENTS	(thousands of tons)								
U.S. TOTAL..........	22 717	100.0	44.9	43.3	8.2	-	2.9	.5	.2
UNDER 100 MILES.........	3 242	100.0	11.2	69.0	16.8	-	2.0	.4	.6
UNDER 1000 POUNDS.....	19	100.0	-	81.3	15.5	.8	.1	2.2	-
1000 TO 9999 POUNDS...	233	100.0	-	77.4	21.5	-	.1	.6	.5
10000 TO 29999 POUNDS.	595	100.0	.2	65.4	30.7	-	1.8	.7	1.2
30000 TO 59999 POUNDS.	1 754	100.0	2.8	78.6	17.5	-	.3	.4	.4
60000 TO 89999 POUNDS.	168	100.0	38.3	52.0	.4	-	7.4	-	1.9
90000 POUNDS AND OVER.	470	100.0	52.4	39.5	-	-	8.1	-	-
100 TO 199 MILES........	2 930	100.0	27.3	62.6	9.3	-	.2	.5	.1
UNDER 1000 POUNDS.....	12	100.0	-	91.1	5.7	.7	.2	1.4	1.0
1000 TO 9999 POUNDS...	142	100.0	.1	80.7	17.7	-	-	1.6	-
10000 TO 29999 POUNDS.	327	100.0	.4	75.6	23.0	-	.4	.5	-
30000 TO 59999 POUNDS.	1 461	100.0	1.5	85.7	11.7	-	.1	.7	.3
60000 TO 89999 POUNDS.	229	100.0	58.1	40.3	-	-	1.6	-	-
90000 POUNDS AND OVER.	756	100.0	84.8	15.2	-	-	-	-	-
200 TO 299 MILES........	2 858	100.0	33.4	54.2	11.6	-	-	.8	-
UNDER 1000 POUNDS.....	11	100.0	-	93.7	2.2	1.7	-	2.4	-
1000 TO 9999 POUNDS...	107	100.0	-	84.2	14.1	-	-	1.6	.1
10000 TO 29999 POUNDS.	296	100.0	1.7	78.8	17.6	-	-	1.9	.1
30000 TO 59999 POUNDS.	1 392	100.0	.6	79.3	18.9	-	-	1.1	-
60000 TO 89999 POUNDS.	204	100.0	61.6	38.4	-	-	-	-	-
90000 POUNDS AND OVER.	847	100.0	96.2	3.8	-	-	-	-	-
300 TO 499 MILES........	3 392	100.0	39.8	48.3	11.3	-	-	.6	-
UNDER 1000 POUNDS.....	13	100.0	.1	90.9	4.2	2.1	-	2.6	-
1000 TO 9999 POUNDS...	125	100.0	.9	83.3	13.7	.2	-	1.9	.1
10000 TO 29999 POUNDS.	385	100.0	1.6	71.0	25.4	-	-	2.0	-
30000 TO 59999 POUNDS.	1 388	100.0	5.2	76.5	17.6	-	-	.7	-
60000 TO 89999 POUNDS.	247	100.0	75.7	24.1	.3	-	-	-	-
90000 POUNDS AND OVER.	1 231	100.0	87.9	10.3	1.8	-	-	-	-
500 TO 999 MILES........	6 266	100.0	63.8	30.3	4.7	-	.5	.6	.1
UNDER 1000 POUNDS.....	15	100.0	.1	88.9	3.8	4.1	-	3.1	-
1000 TO 9999 POUNDS...	171	100.0	1.3	84.4	12.5	.5	-	1.3	-
10000 TO 29999 POUNDS.	355	100.0	2.1	79.1	17.6	-	-	1.1	.1
30000 TO 59999 POUNDS.	1 645	100.0	10.8	74.6	12.6	-	-	1.8	.1
60000 TO 89999 POUNDS.	461	100.0	79.7	20.3	-	-	-	-	-
90000 POUNDS AND OVER.	3 616	100.0	95.2	3.8	-	-	.9	-	.2
1000 TO 1499 MILES......	2 970	100.0	66.9	14.3	1.2	-	17.5	-	.1
UNDER 1000 POUNDS.....	3	100.0	.1	89.7	.5	9.1	-	.6	-
1000 TO 9999 POUNDS...	20	100.0	.3	90.2	3.5	1.1	4.6	-	.3
10000 TO 29999 POUNDS.	68	100.0	4.6	81.3	10.1	-	2.5	1.1	.4
30000 TO 59999 POUNDS.	322	100.0	11.2	67.8	8.8	-	12.2	-	-
60000 TO 89999 POUNDS.	210	100.0	68.2	31.8	-	-	-	-	-
90000 POUNDS AND OVER.	2 344	100.0	77.0	2.6	-	-	20.3	-	.1
1500 MILES OR OVER......	1 055	100.0	71.8	23.6	.4	.2	2.9	.7	.4
UNDER 1000 POUNDS.....	6	100.0	.4	79.0	.5	15.7	-	3.3	1.1
1000 TO 9999 POUNDS...	25	100.0	.8	88.7	6.6	3.2	.1	.7	-
10000 TO 29999 POUNDS.	39	100.0	3.3	91.2	1.7	-	3.8	-	-
30000 TO 59999 POUNDS.	193	100.0	23.5	65.5	.8	-	6.4	3.7	-
60000 TO 89999 POUNDS.	63	100.0	70.2	16.3	-	-	13.5	-	-
90000 POUNDS AND OVER.	728	100.0	91.5	6.8	-	-	1.2	-	.6
TON-MILES OF SHIPMENTS	(millions of ton-miles)								
U.S. TOTAL..........	12 860	100.0	59.8	29.0	4.4	-	6.3	.4	.1
UNDER 100 MILES.........	163	100.0	13.3	66.3	17.4	-	1.8	.6	.7
UNDER 1000 POUNDS.....	-	100.0	-	84.1	13.1	.5	.1	2.3	-
1000 TO 9999 POUNDS...	10	100.0	-	80.2	18.3	-	.1	.5	.8
10000 TO 29999 POUNDS.	32	100.0	-	68.6	27.3	-	1.5	.8	1.8
30000 TO 59999 POUNDS.	83	100.0	3.1	75.0	20.6	-	.3	.7	.3
60000 TO 89999 POUNDS.	8	100.0	36.8	53.1	.2	-	6.9	-	3.0
90000 POUNDS AND OVER.	26	100.0	60.8	33.3	-	-	5.9	-	-
100 TO 199 MILES........	443	100.0	29.6	60.2	9.4	-	.2	.5	.1
UNDER 1000 POUNDS.....	1	100.0	-	91.6	4.9	.7	.2	1.4	1.3
1000 TO 9999 POUNDS...	21	100.0	.2	81.4	17.1	-	-	1.3	-
10000 TO 29999 POUNDS.	46	100.0	.4	75.6	23.1	-	-	.3	.6	-
30000 TO 59999 POUNDS.	214	100.0	1.7	84.5	12.6	-	-	.1	.8	.3
60000 TO 89999 POUNDS.	37	100.0	62.4	36.5	-	-	1.1	-	-
90000 POUNDS AND OVER.	121	100.0	85.6	14.4	-	-	-	-	-

See footnotes at end of table 4.

TABLE 4. **TCC GROUP 282—Percent Distribution of Distance Shipped and Weight of Shipment, by Means of Transport: 1972**—Continued

Distance shipped and weight of shipment [2][3]	Number	Percent distribution by means of transport							
		All means of transport	Rail	Motor carrier	Private truck	Air	Water	Other	Unknown
TON-MILES OF SHIPMENTS	(millions of ton-miles)								
200 TO 299 MILES........	722	100.0	33.5	54.0	11.7	-	-	.8	-
UNDER 1000 POUNDS.....	2	100.0	-	93.4	2.3	1.8	-	2.4	-
1000 TO 9999 POUNDS...	26	100.0	-	84.0	14.3	-	-	1.6	.1
10000 TO 29999 POUNDS.	74	100.0	1.8	79.7	16.5	-	-	1.8	.1
30000 TO 59999 POUNDS.	353	100.0	.6	79.0	19.3	-	-	1.1	-
60000 TO 89999 POUNDS.	49	100.0	61.0	39.0	-	-	-	-	-
90000 POUNDS AND OVER.	216	100.0	96.6	3.4	-	-	-	-	-
300 TO 499 MILES........	1 325	100.0	39.8	48.3	11.3	-	-	.6	-
UNDER 1000 POUNDS.....	5	100.0	.1	91.1	3.8	2.4	-	2.6	-
1000 TO 9999 POUNDS...	49	100.0	.9	83.9	13.0	.2	-	2.0	-
10000 TO 29999 POUNDS.	148	100.0	1.6	71.5	24.8	-	-	2.1	-
30000 TO 59999 POUNDS.	540	100.0	5.2	76.5	17.6	-	-	.7	-
60000 TO 89999 POUNDS.	97	100.0	76.3	23.4	.2	-	-	-	-
90000 POUNDS AND OVER.	484	100.0	87.3	10.5	2.2	-	-	-	-
500 TO 999 MILES........	4 626	100.0	65.3	28.9	4.4	-	.6	.5	.1
UNDER 1000 POUNDS.....	10	100.0	.1	88.8	3.7	4.4	-	2.9	-
1000 TO 9999 POUNDS...	121	100.0	1.3	83.8	13.2	.5	-	1.1	-
10000 TO 29999 POUNDS.	246	100.0	1.8	79.1	17.9	-	-	1.0	.2
30000 TO 59999 POUNDS.	1 143	100.0	10.3	75.3	12.7	-	-	1.7	.1
60000 TO 89999 POUNDS.	340	100.0	78.8	21.2	-	-	-	-	-
90000 POUNDS AND OVER.	2 763	100.0	95.2	3.6	-	-	1.0	-	.2
1000 TO 1499 MILES......	3 638	100.0	65.2	14.0	1.2	-	19.5	-	.1
UNDER 1000 POUNDS.....	4	100.0	.1	89.7	.5	9.1	-	.6	-
1000 TO 9999 POUNDS...	24	100.0	.3	89.2	3.7	1.2	5.4	-	.2
10000 TO 29999 POUNDS.	80	100.0	4.6	82.3	9.0	-	2.6	1.1	.4
30000 TO 59999 POUNDS.	391	100.0	11.6	65.5	8.7	-	14.2	-	-
60000 TO 89999 POUNDS.	257	100.0	68.3	31.7	-	-	-	-	-
90000 POUNDS AND OVER.	2 878	100.0	74.6	2.7	-	-	22.6	-	.1
1500 MILES OR OVER......	1 940	100.0	70.5	24.4	.5	.2	3.3	.8	.4
UNDER 1000 POUNDS.....	13	100.0	.5	77.9	.6	16.7	-	3.4	.9
1000 TO 9999 POUNDS...	49	100.0	.9	88.3	7.0	3.1	.1	.6	-
10000 TO 29999 POUNDS.	78	100.0	3.6	89.8	1.8	-	4.8	-	-
30000 TO 59999 POUNDS.	396	100.0	24.1	64.0	1.0	-	7.2	3.7	-
60000 TO 89999 POUNDS.	121	100.0	72.0	15.0	-	-	13.0	-	-
90000 POUNDS AND OVER.	1 280	100.0	92.2	6.0	-	-	1.3	-	.6

Note: Detail may not add to total due to rounding. The introductory table shows the estimates of sampling variability for tons; sampling variability for ton-miles has not been estimated. See the Introduction for the States comprising the geographic divisions of the United States.

Shipments excluded from the survey are those moving by pipeline (primarily petroleum products from refineries), parcel post shipments, and commodities moved by own power (motorized vehicles, aircraft, etc.) or towed (prefabricated buildings, etc.). Local shipments (commodities shipped less than 25 miles from the plant) and shipments within the same city are also excluded. Shipments to Alaska and Hawaii from the 48 conterminous States and the District of Columbia are included; however, no data were obtained for shipments originating in Alaska and Hawaii.

- Represents zero or rounds to zero.   (D) Withheld to avoid disclosing figures for individual companies.

[1]Production of this commodity is concentrated in the geographic divisions shown; figures and distributions for geographic divisions not shown are included in the total.

[2]Distances of shipments to foreign destinations are calculated only to the U.S. port of exit.

[3]Includes only shipments represented by bills of lading and invoices. Summary records which did not show individual weights of shipments are not included.

TCC 283. Drugs (Biological and Botanical Products)

Comparisons of Tons and Ton-Miles of Shipments for
Geographic Divisions of Origin and for Sampling Variability: 1972 and 1967

| Geographic division of origin | Estimates | | | | Relative sampling variability in tons (percent) | |
| | 1972 | | 1967 | | 1972 | 1967 |
	Tons (thousands)	Ton-miles (millions)	Tons (thousands)	Ton-miles (millions)		
U.S. total	1,491	909	1,664	1,231	11.9	14.6
New England	18	12	5	4	19.3	(*)
Middle Atlantic	387	248	697	597	9.7	(*)
East North Central	298	183	411	308	12.6	(*)
West North Central	73	50	206	132	18.3	(*)
South Atlantic	221	136	142	86	10.4	(*)
East South Central	(D)	(D)	93	64	(*)	(*)
West South Central	(D)	(D)	16	5	(*)	(*)
Mountain	(D)	(D)	1	1	(*)	(*)
Pacific	(D)	(D)	93	34	(*)	(*)

(D) Withheld to avoid disclosing figures for individual companies.　　　　(*) Data not published.

TABLE 1. **TCC GROUP 283**—Percent Distribution of Geographic Division of Origin and Distance Shipped, by Means of Transport: 1972

Geographic division of origin [1] and distance shipped [2]	Number	Percent distribution by means of transport							
		All means of transport	Rail	Motor carrier	Private truck	Air	Water	Other	Unknown
TONS OF SHIPMENTS	(thousands of tons)								
U.S. TOTAL..........	1 491	100.0	25.1	53.9	17.6	.9	.7	1.6	.1
NEW ENGLAND.............	18	100.0	.8	87.5	7.4	.1	-	.8	3.5
UNDER 100 MILES.......	3	100.0	-	92.9	6.7	-	-	.4	-
100 TO 199 MILES......	6	100.0	-	98.1	1.6	-	-	.2	-
200 TO 299 MILES......	2	100.0	-	65.1	3.5	-	-	.3	31.1
300 TO 499 MILES......	1	100.0	-	27.5	72.1	-	-	.3	-
500 TO 999 MILES......	3	100.0	-	97.6	.8	.1	-	1.6	-
1000 TO 1499 MILES....	-	100.0	-	79.7	-	3.5	-	16.8	-
1500 MILES OR OVER....	2	100.0	5.9	84.3	9.1	.1	-	.7	-
MIDDLE ATLANTIC.........	387	100.0	10.3	74.8	9.2	1.8	2.0	1.8	.1
UNDER 100 MILES.......	110	100.0	.9	79.3	17.6	.3	-	2.0	-
100 TO 199 MILES......	38	100.0	-	72.6	24.1	.5	-	2.5	.3
200 TO 299 MILES......	30	100.0	1.9	83.1	3.5	5.0	3.4	3.0	.1
300 TO 499 MILES......	28	100.0	2.1	82.9	8.3	3.4	-	3.3	-
500 TO 999 MILES......	102	100.0	20.2	73.4	3.2	1.7	.3	1.1	-
1000 TO 1499 MILES....	33	100.0	8.4	78.0	1.0	2.8	8.7	1.0	.1
1500 MILES OR OVER....	44	100.0	32.6	55.7	-	2.8	7.7	.9	.2
EAST NORTH CENTRAL......	298	100.0	35.9	48.9	9.9	.6	-	4.4	.2
UNDER 100 MILES.......	25	100.0	3.3	43.6	48.2	.1	-	4.9	-
100 TO 199 MILES......	16	100.0	2.5	62.3	15.1	.1	-	20.0	.1
200 TO 299 MILES......	50	100.0	-	83.9	10.1	.3	-	5.2	.5
300 TO 499 MILES......	32	100.0	23.1	60.2	11.2	.7	-	4.9	-
500 TO 999 MILES......	130	100.0	49.0	43.1	4.7	.7	-	2.5	.1
1000 TO 1499 MILES....	21	100.0	89.8	8.5	-	.7	-	1.0	-
1500 MILES OR OVER....	20	100.0	72.6	20.0	.1	2.2	.3	4.5	.4
WEST NORTH CENTRAL......	73	100.0	29.7	61.7	6.6	1.0	-	1.0	-
UNDER 100 MILES.......	2	100.0	-	42.7	51.0	-	-	6.3	-
100 TO 199 MILES......	3	100.0	-	50.1	43.4	.1	-	6.5	-
200 TO 299 MILES......	5	100.0	.3	95.5	-	.9	-	3.2	-
300 TO 499 MILES......	19	100.0	39.5	56.8	2.3	.8	-	.5	-
500 TO 999 MILES......	22	100.0	27.1	65.6	6.2	.6	-	.5	-
1000 TO 1499 MILES....	15	100.0	31.6	63.6	3.2	1.5	-	.1	-
1500 MILES OR OVER....	3	100.0	69.7	26.8	-	3.5	-	.1	-
SOUTH ATLANTIC..........	221	100.0	38.8	57.1	3.2	.7	-	-	.2
UNDER 100 MILES.......	5	100.0	-	66.9	32.6	.2	.2	.1	-
100 TO 199 MILES......	6	100.0	-	79.2	17.0	3.7	-	.2	-
200 TO 299 MILES......	10	100.0	7.6	91.1	.1	1.0	-	.1	-
300 TO 499 MILES......	47	100.0	24.9	74.9	-	.1	-	.1	-
500 TO 999 MILES......	143	100.0	47.2	49.2	2.8	.5	-	-	.3
1000 TO 1499 MILES....	5	100.0	79.1	17.9	-	2.8	-	.2	-
1500 MILES OR OVER....	3	100.0	47.9	44.7	.9	6.0	-	.5	-
TON-MILES OF SHIPMENTS	(millions of ton-miles)								
U.S. TOTAL..........	909	100.0	35.6	51.5	8.5	1.4	1.6	1.2	.1
NEW ENGLAND.............	12	100.0	3.1	87.3	7.2	.1	-	1.0	1.2
UNDER 100 MILES.......	-	100.0	-	98.7	.9	-	-	.4	-
100 TO 199 MILES......	-	100.0	-	97.4	2.3	-	-	.3	-
200 TO 299 MILES......	-	100.0	-	63.8	4.1	-	-	.3	31.9
300 TO 499 MILES......	-	100.0	-	29.3	70.4	-	-	.3	-
500 TO 999 MILES......	2	100.0	-	97.6	.9	.1	-	1.5	-
1000 TO 1499 MILES....	-	100.0	-	79.9	-	3.5	-	16.6	-
1500 MILES OR OVER....	7	100.0	4.8	87.2	7.5	.1	-	.3	-
MIDDLE ATLANTIC.........	248	100.0	21.3	67.1	2.5	2.5	5.2	1.3	.1
UNDER 100 MILES.......	5	100.0	1.2	83.7	12.3	.2	-	2.6	-
100 TO 199 MILES......	5	100.0	-	75.2	21.5	.6	-	2.4	.3
200 TO 299 MILES......	7	100.0	2.3	82.1	3.6	5.6	3.3	3.1	.1
300 TO 499 MILES......	10	100.0	2.1	82.2	8.7	3.7	-	3.3	-
500 TO 999 MILES......	73	100.0	19.6	73.5	3.7	1.7	.3	1.2	-
1000 TO 1499 MILES....	40	100.0	8.8	76.6	1.1	2.9	9.5	1.0	.1
1500 MILES OR OVER....	104	100.0	32.9	55.0	-	2.9	8.1	1.0	.2
EAST NORTH CENTRAL......	183	100.0	53.7	37.0	4.5	1.1	.1	3.4	.2
UNDER 100 MILES.......	1	100.0	3.5	40.5	50.2	-	-	5.8	-
100 TO 199 MILES......	2	100.0	2.3	64.3	13.0	.1	-	20.2	-
200 TO 299 MILES......	11	100.0	-	84.2	9.5	.3	-	5.6	.5
300 TO 499 MILES......	13	100.0	23.1	59.2	12.6	.7	-	4.3	-
500 TO 999 MILES......	90	100.0	49.8	41.9	4.8	.7	-	2.6	.1
1000 TO 1499 MILES....	25	100.0	89.8	8.6	-	.7	-	.9	-
1500 MILES OR OVER....	37	100.0	72.0	19.7	.1	2.7	.7	4.5	.3

See footnotes at end of table 4.

TABLE 1. **TCC GROUP 283—Percent Distribution of Geographic Division of Origin and Distance Shipped, by Means of Transport: 1972**—Continued

Geographic division of origin[1] and distance shipped[2]	Number	Percent distribution by means of transport							
		All means of transport	Rail	Motor carrier	Private truck	Air	Water	Other	Unknown
TON-MILES OF SHIPMENTS	(millions of ton-miles)								
WEST NORTH CENTRAL	50	100.0	32.7	61.0	4.5	1.3	-	.4	-
UNDER 100 MILES	-	100.0	-	50.2	42.0	-	-	7.9	-
100 TO 199 MILES	-	100.0	-	50.1	44.2	.1	-	5.6	-
200 TO 299 MILES	1	100.0	.4	95.5	-	1.0	-	3.2	-
300 TO 499 MILES	7	100.0	34.6	61.0	2.9	.9	-	.5	-
500 TO 999 MILES	16	100.0	26.3	65.0	7.7	.5	-	.5	-
1000 TO 1499 MILES	18	100.0	28.7	66.6	2.9	1.6	-	.1	-
1500 MILES OR OVER	6	100.0	68.1	28.6	-	3.2	-	.1	-
SOUTH ATLANTIC	136	100.0	45.3	51.5	2.1	.9	-	.1	.2
UNDER 100 MILES	-	100.0	-	74.1	25.5	.1	.3	.1	-
100 TO 199 MILES	1	100.0	-	80.4	15.5	4.0	-	.1	-
200 TO 299 MILES	2	100.0	8.8	90.0	.1	.9	-	.1	-
300 TO 499 MILES	19	100.0	23.7	76.1	-	.1	-	.1	-
500 TO 999 MILES	99	100.0	48.7	48.0	2.5	.6	-	-	.3
1000 TO 1499 MILES	6	100.0	79.5	17.3	-	2.9	-	.3	-
1500 MILES OR OVER	7	100.0	49.3	43.3	1.0	6.0	-	.4	-

See footnotes at end of table 4.

TABLE 2. **TCC GROUP 283—Percent Distribution of Geographic Division of Origin and Means of Transport, by Geographic Division of Destination: 1972**

Geographic division of origin[1] and means of transport	Number	Percent distribution by division of destination									
		U.S. total	New England	Middle Atlantic	East North Central	West North Central	South Atlantic	East South Central	West South Central	Mountain	Pacific
TONS OF SHIPMENTS	(thousands of tons)										
U.S. TOTAL	1 491	100.0	4.3	23.6	19.8	5.8	20.3	7.3	8.7	1.5	8.7
RAIL	374	100.0	5.9	17.4	15.3	5.0	24.0	9.6	10.4	1.9	10.4
MOTOR CARRIER	804	100.0	4.2	27.8	22.1	7.4	15.3	5.0	9.4	1.6	7.2
PRIVATE TRUCK	263	100.0	2.4	20.2	18.8	2.6	31.0	11.6	2.6	.7	9.9
AIR	13	100.0	6.1	21.5	14.4	6.5	20.8	3.2	8.9	2.1	16.6
WATER	10	100.0	-	9.8	-	-	29.3	-	28.8	-	32.1
OTHER	23	100.0	3.3	18.9	32.7	6.9	9.3	7.6	14.6	.5	6.2
UNKNOWN	1	100.0	6.8	38.2	16.3	.8	.5	-	26.2	3.3	7.9
NEW ENGLAND	18	100.0	6.9	59.7	7.8	1.7	4.4	6.0	4.2	1.2	8.0
RAIL	-	100.0	-	-	-	-	-	-	-	-	100.0
MOTOR CARRIER	16	100.0	6.2	58.8	8.7	1.7	4.9	6.8	4.6	1.4	6.9
PRIVATE TRUCK	1	100.0	18.8	63.1	1.8	-	-	-	-	-	16.3
AIR	-	100.0	-	.4	15.2	69.4	1.7	-	-	-	13.2
WATER	-	100.0	-	-	-	-	-	-	-	-	-
OTHER	-	100.0	12.5	12.9	12.1	9.8	18.3	15.8	18.4	-	-
UNKNOWN	-	100.0	-	100.0	-	-	-	-	-	-	-
MIDDLE ATLANTIC	387	100.0	6.2	38.0	17.0	4.0	15.1	2.6	5.8	1.3	10.0
RAIL	40	100.0	1.1	.8	41.4	7.6	4.9	1.5	6.5	2.9	33.3
MOTOR CARRIER	289	100.0	7.6	39.1	14.8	4.0	18.3	2.4	5.4	1.3	7.1
PRIVATE TRUCK	35	100.0	.6	78.6	12.8	.1	1.2	5.8	.8	.-	-
AIR	6	100.0	6.5	19.1	13.4	7.3	21.6	3.6	10.4	1.7	16.3
WATER	7	100.0	-	13.8	-	-	4.3	-	37.5	-	44.5
OTHER	6	100.0	7.4	46.0	13.6	5.1	16.6	2.5	3.0	.5	5.4
UNKNOWN	-	100.0	49.5	7.4	-	4.6	-	-	7.3	3.3	27.9
EAST NORTH CENTRAL	298	100.0	4.3	23.6	29.3	6.3	15.3	2.4	10.2	1.9	6.7
RAIL	107	100.0	2.4	30.2	1.2	2.7	24.6	.8	20.5	3.9	13.6
MOTOR CARRIER	146	100.0	3.6	23.8	41.7	8.5	11.7	2.3	4.7	.9	2.7
PRIVATE TRUCK	29	100.0	15.2	5.5	61.9	8.9	3.2	5.1	.1	-	-
AIR	1	100.0	5.2	23.5	5.7	4.1	21.3	3.4	8.1	5.8	23.0
WATER	-	100.0	-	-	-	-	-	-	-	-	100.0
OTHER	13	100.0	1.8	9.1	49.8	6.0	5.7	10.8	10.0	.1	6.8
UNKNOWN	-	100.0	-	.2	56.6	.5	1.9	-	14.8	10.7	15.3
WEST NORTH CENTRAL	73	100.0	11.1	11.7	26.8	11.4	10.3	2.8	7.1	7.4	11.3
RAIL	21	100.0	23.9	7.8	35.9	-	12.2	-	7.4	.4	12.4
MOTOR CARRIER	45	100.0	5.1	13.9	24.6	11.9	8.9	4.4	7.5	11.9	11.9
PRIVATE TRUCK	4	100.0	10.6	12.3	9.6	50.7	16.8	-	-	-	-
AIR	-	100.0	14.7	7.1	15.7	8.5	10.6	-	3.1	10.7	1.2	28.4
WATER	-	100.0	-	-	-	-	-	-	-	-	-
OTHER	-	100.0	.2	.4	16.0	57.6	3.3	5.0	15.6	1.4	.6
UNKNOWN	-	100.0	-	-	96.7	3.3	-	-	-	-	-
SOUTH ATLANTIC	221	100.0	6.9	23.4	22.2	10.5	17.4	8.4	9.0	.9	1.3
RAIL	86	100.0	16.3	13.6	19.4	14.7	13.0	10.8	8.3	2.1	1.8
MOTOR CARRIER	126	100.0	1.0	29.8	24.4	8.3	18.8	7.0	9.6	.2	.9
PRIVATE TRUCK	7	100.0	-	30.8	21.2	-	41.3	6.2	-	-	.4
AIR	1	100.0	4.7	20.4	3.9	3.0	43.7	2.6	9.9	.4	11.4
WATER	-	100.0	-	-	-	-	100.0	-	-	-	-
OTHER	-	100.0	10.4	6.6	11.7	3.0	39.2	3.8	11.5	6.8	7.1
UNKNOWN	-	100.0	-	1.5	.1	-	-	-	98.4	-	-

See footnotes at end of table 4.

TABLE 2. **TCC GROUP 283—Percent Distribution of Geographic Division of Origin and Means of Transport, by Geographic Division of Destination: 1972**—Continued

Geographic division of origin[1] and means of transport	Number	Percent distribution by division of destination									
		U.S. total	New England	Middle Atlantic	East North Central	West North Central	South Atlantic	East South Central	West South Central	Mountain	Pacific
TON-MILES OF SHIPMENTS	(millions of ton-miles)										
U.S. TOTAL..............	909	100.0	4.4	16.8	14.2	6.5	18.5	5.8	10.5	2.9	20.3
RAIL..................	324	100.0	6.2	14.6	10.2	3.7	21.7	6.8	9.6	2.9	24.3
MOTOR CARRIER.........	468	100.0	3.0	18.5	17.0	9.1	14.6	4.9	11.0	3.0	18.9
PRIVATE TRUCK.........	77	100.0	6.1	20.0	17.0	3.5	32.3	8.3	8.0	3.4	1.5
AIR...................	13	100.0	4.0	14.4	11.8	5.3	13.6	2.4	10.2	2.8	35.4
WATER.................	14	100.0	-	1.7	-	-	12.8	-	26.5	-	59.0
OTHER.................	10	100.0	3.1	11.7	17.6	7.7	10.7	6.1	15.6	1.4	26.0
UNKNOWN...............	1	100.0	1.9	16.0	7.6	1.2	.5	-	36.5	6.4	29.8
NEW ENGLAND............	12	100.0	.8	12.3	9.4	2.7	4.0	7.5	10.3	3.6	49.5
RAIL..................	-	100.0	-	-	-	-	-	-	-	-	100.0
MOTOR CARRIER.........	10	100.0	.8	10.0	10.4	2.8	4.3	8.3	11.4	4.1	47.8
PRIVATE TRUCK.........	-	100.0	.7	31.2	2.4	-	-	-	-	-	65.7
AIR...................	-	100.0	-	-	9.5	64.1	.4	-	-	-	26.0
WATER.................	-	100.0	-	-	-	-	-	-	-	-	-
OTHER.................	-	100.0	1.0	3.1	10.3	14.0	18.1	20.1	33.3	-	-
UNKNOWN...............	-	100.0	-	100.0	-	-	-	-	-	-	-
MIDDLE ATLANTIC........	248	100.0	2.2	5.3	15.8	5.8	13.9	3.3	11.9	3.7	38.1
RAIL..................	52	100.0	.2	.1	21.0	4.7	1.6	.9	6.3	4.5	60.6
MOTOR CARRIER.........	166	100.0	2.9	6.0	15.4	6.7	19.2	3.3	12.4	3.8	30.2
PRIVATE TRUCK.........	6	100.0	1.7	33.5	24.8	.7	2.8	30.4	6.0	-	-
AIR...................	6	100.0	2.3	4.6	7.3	7.0	13.3	3.0	15.1	3.2	44.1
WATER.................	12	100.0	-	2.0	-	-	1.9	-	30.1	-	66.0
OTHER.................	3	100.0	3.6	12.0	16.8	10.6	13.6	3.6	8.4	2.4	29.0
UNKNOWN...............	-	100.0	7.7	2.0	-	4.2	-	-	9.6	6.0	70.6
EAST NORTH CENTRAL......	183	100.0	5.1	22.2	8.2	4.4	20.6	1.5	14.3	3.4	20.4
RAIL..................	98	100.0	1.7	18.9	.1	1.0	26.1	.4	19.8	4.5	27.5
MOTOR CARRIER.........	68	100.0	5.9	30.0	17.4	8.0	15.8	1.8	8.1	2.3	10.7
PRIVATE TRUCK.........	8	100.0	40.3	8.3	22.6	15.2	6.3	6.5	.5	-	.3
AIR...................	1	100.0	4.2	14.0	1.0	1.5	13.2	1.9	6.8	6.1	51.3
WATER.................	-	100.0	-	-	-	-	-	-	-	-	100.0
OTHER.................	6	100.0	2.8	11.6	19.0	5.5	8.4	7.2	17.9	.3	27.3
UNKNOWN...............	-	100.0	-	.1	20.0	.5	1.7	-	19.1	16.6	42.0
WEST NORTH CENTRAL......	50	100.0	17.4	15.6	13.1	4.1	10.1	1.7	5.8	7.6	24.5
RAIL..................	16	100.0	33.0	9.4	15.2	-	9.0	-	6.1	.6	26.6
MOTOR CARRIER.........	30	100.0	8.7	18.6	12.4	5.6	9.2	2.7	5.8	12.1	25.0
PRIVATE TRUCK.........	2	100.0	23.5	24.7	9.3	12.0	30.5	-	-	-	-
AIR...................	-	100.0	19.3	8.2	6.9	3.7	8.7	1.2	6.0	1.0	44.9
WATER.................	-	100.0	-	-	-	-	-	-	-	-	-
OTHER.................	-	100.0	.7	1.4	16.7	31.2	9.4	6.2	27.5	4.0	2.9
UNKNOWN...............	-	100.0	-	-	98.3	1.7	-	-	-	-	-
SOUTH ATLANTIC.........	136	100.0	9.8	24.7	19.6	11.4	9.2	7.0	11.2	2.2	4.9
RAIL..................	61	100.0	20.7	13.3	15.7	13.9	8.6	8.0	10.0	4.0	5.8
MOTOR CARRIER.........	70	100.0	.8	34.1	23.0	9.8	9.4	6.0	12.4	.7	3.8
PRIVATE TRUCK.........	2	100.0	-	49.1	27.1	-	9.2	12.0	.1	-	2.5
AIR...................	1	100.0	3.7	8.8	2.6	3.5	32.8	1.9	14.5	.7	31.5
WATER.................	-	100.0	-	-	-	-	100.0	-	-	-	-
OTHER.................	-	100.0	5.3	1.6	7.9	3.5	17.7	3.1	20.6	17.3	23.0
UNKNOWN...............	-	100.0	-	1.0	.1	-	-	-	98.9	-	-

See footnotes at end of table 4.

TABLE 3. **TCC GROUP 283—Percent Distribution of Geographic Division of Destination and Means of Transport, by Geographic Division of Origin: 1972**

Geographic division of destination and means of transport	Number	Percent distribution by division of origin [1]									
		U.S. total	New England	Middle Atlantic	East North Central	West North Central	South Atlantic	East South Central	West South Central	Mountain	Pacific
TONS OF SHIPMENTS	(thousands of tons)										
U.S. TOTAL............	1 491	100.0	1.3	26.0	20.0	4.9	14.9	(D)	(D)	(D)	(D)
RAIL............	374	100.0	-	10.7	28.6	5.8	23.0	(D)	(D)	(D)	(D)
MOTOR CARRIER........	804	100.0	2.1	36.0	18.2	5.6	15.8	(D)	(D)	(D)	(D)
PRIVATE TRUCK........	263	100.0	.5	13.6	11.3	1.8	2.7	(D)	(D)	(D)	(D)
AIR.................	13	100.0	.1	52.0	14.4	5.5	11.0	(D)	(D)	(D)	(D)
WATER...............	10	100.0	-	70.9	.5	-	.1	(D)	(D)	(D)	(D)
OTHER...............	23	100.0	.6	28.8	55.0	3.1	.4	(D)	(D)	(D)	(D)
UNKNOWN.............	1	100.0	36.8	13.8	26.2	.4	21.7	(D)	(D)	(D)	(D)
NEW ENGLAND..........	63	100.0	2.0	37.4	20.0	12.8	24.1	(D)	(D)	(D)	(D)
RAIL............	22	100.0	-	1.9	11.5	23.4	63.2	(D)	(D)	(D)	(D)
MOTOR CARRIER........	33	100.0	3.0	66.2	15.9	6.9	3.8	(D)	(D)	(D)	(D)
PRIVATE TRUCK........	6	100.0	4.1	3.5	70.9	8.0	-	(D)	(D)	(D)	(D)
AIR.................	-	100.0	-	55.0	12.4	13.1	8.5	(D)	(D)	(D)	(D)
WATER...............	-	100.0	-	-	-	-	-	(D)	(D)	(D)	(D)
OTHER...............	-	100.0	2.3	63.7	29.1	.2	1.4	(D)	(D)	(D)	(D)
UNKNOWN.............	-	100.0	-	100.0	-	-	-	(D)	(D)	(D)	(D)
MIDDLE ATLANTIC.........	351	100.0	3.2	41.9	20.0	2.4	14.8	(D)	(D)	(D)	(D)
RAIL............	65	100.0	-	.5	49.6	2.6	18.0	(D)	(D)	(D)	(D)
MOTOR CARRIER........	223	100.0	4.3	50.6	15.5	2.8	16.9	(D)	(D)	(D)	(D)
PRIVATE TRUCK........	53	100.0	1.7	52.8	3.0	1.1	4.0	(D)	(D)	(D)	(D)
AIR.................	2	100.0	-	46.4	15.8	1.8	10.5	(D)	(D)	(D)	(D)
WATER...............	1	100.0	-	100.0	-	-	-	(D)	(D)	(D)	(D)
OTHER...............	4	100.0	.4	70.1	26.6	.1	.2	(D)	(D)	(D)	(D)
UNKNOWN.............	-	100.0	96.3	2.7	.2	-	.9	(D)	(D)	(D)	(D)
EAST NORTH CENTRAL......	294	100.0	.5	22.4	29.7	6.6	16.7	(D)	(D)	(D)	(D)
RAIL............	57	100.0	-	29.0	2.2	13.6	29.2	(D)	(D)	(D)	(D)
MOTOR CARRIER........	177	100.0	.8	24.1	34.3	6.2	17.4	(D)	(D)	(D)	(D)
PRIVATE TRUCK........	49	100.0	.1	9.3	37.1	.9	3.0	(D)	(D)	(D)	(D)
AIR.................	1	100.0	.1	48.4	5.7	6.0	3.0	(D)	(D)	(D)	(D)
WATER...............	-	100.0	-	-	-	-	-	(D)	(D)	(D)	(D)
OTHER...............	7	100.0	.2	12.0	83.9	1.5	.2	(D)	(D)	(D)	(D)
UNKNOWN.............	-	100.0	-	-	90.9	2.5	.2	(D)	(D)	(D)	(D)
WEST NORTH CENTRAL......	87	100.0	.4	17.8	21.7	9.5	26.6	(D)	(D)	(D)	(D)
RAIL............	18	100.0	-	16.4	15.7	-	67.9	(D)	(D)	(D)	(D)
MOTOR CARRIER........	59	100.0	.5	19.5	21.1	9.1	17.7	(D)	(D)	(D)	(D)
PRIVATE TRUCK........	6	100.0	-	.7	39.3	36.3	-	(D)	(D)	(D)	(D)
AIR.................	-	100.0	1.1	58.5	9.1	7.1	5.1	(D)	(D)	(D)	(D)
WATER...............	-	100.0	-	-	-	-	-	(D)	(D)	(D)	(D)
OTHER...............	1	100.0	.9	21.2	47.4	26.2	.2	(D)	(D)	(D)	(D)
UNKNOWN.............	-	100.0	-	81.5	16.8	1.8	-	(D)	(D)	(D)	(D)
SOUTH ATLANTIC..........	302	100.0	.3	19.3	15.1	2.5	12.8	(D)	(D)	(D)	(D)
RAIL............	89	100.0	-	2.2	29.5	3.0	12.5	(D)	(D)	(D)	(D)
MOTOR CARRIER........	123	100.0	.7	43.0	13.9	3.2	19.3	(D)	(D)	(D)	(D)
PRIVATE TRUCK........	81	100.0	-	.5	1.2	1.0	3.5	(D)	(D)	(D)	(D)
AIR.................	2	100.0	-	54.1	14.8	2.8	23.1	(D)	(D)	(D)	(D)
WATER...............	3	100.0	-	10.3	-	-	.4	(D)	(D)	(D)	(D)
OTHER...............	2	100.0	1.2	51.7	33.8	1.1	1.9	(D)	(D)	(D)	(D)
UNKNOWN.............	-	100.0	-	-	98.3	-	-	(D)	(D)	(D)	(D)
EAST SOUTH CENTRAL......	109	100.0	1.0	9.1	6.6	1.9	17.2	(D)	(D)	(D)	(D)
RAIL............	35	100.0	-	1.7	2.4	-	25.8	(D)	(D)	(D)	(D)
MOTOR CARRIER........	40	100.0	2.8	17.0	8.5	4.9	22.3	(D)	(D)	(D)	(D)
PRIVATE TRUCK........	30	100.0	-	6.7	4.9	-	1.4	(D)	(D)	(D)	(D)
AIR.................	-	100.0	-	60.1	15.3	5.3	9.1	(D)	(D)	(D)	(D)
WATER...............	-	100.0	-	-	-	-	-	(D)	(D)	(D)	(D)
OTHER...............	1	100.0	1.3	9.3	78.0	2.0	.2	(D)	(D)	(D)	(D)
UNKNOWN.............	-	100.0	-	-	-	-	-	(D)	(D)	(D)	(D)
WEST SOUTH CENTRAL......	129	100.0	.6	17.3	23.4	4.0	15.3	(D)	(D)	(D)	(D)
RAIL............	38	100.0	-	6.7	56.3	4.1	18.4	(D)	(D)	(D)	(D)
MOTOR CARRIER........	75	100.0	1.0	20.8	9.1	4.5	16.1	(D)	(D)	(D)	(D)
PRIVATE TRUCK........	6	100.0	-	4.2	.6	-	-	(D)	(D)	(D)	(D)
AIR.................	1	100.0	-	61.2	13.1	6.6	12.3	(D)	(D)	(D)	(D)
WATER...............	3	100.0	-	92.1	-	-	-	(D)	(D)	(D)	(D)
OTHER...............	3	100.0	.8	5.9	37.8	3.4	.4	(D)	(D)	(D)	(D)
UNKNOWN.............	-	100.0	-	3.8	14.8	-	81.3	(D)	(D)	(D)	(D)
MOUNTAIN...............	22	100.0	1.1	22.8	25.7	24.5	9.5	(D)	(D)	(D)	(D)
RAIL............	7	100.0	-	16.1	58.2	1.1	24.6	(D)	(D)	(D)	(D)
MOTOR CARRIER........	12	100.0	1.9	29.4	10.3	42.2	2.4	(D)	(D)	(D)	(D)
PRIVATE TRUCK........	1	100.0	-	-	-	-	-	(D)	(D)	(D)	(D)
AIR.................	-	100.0	-	41.0	39.3	3.2	2.0	(D)	(D)	(D)	(D)
WATER...............	-	100.0	-	-	-	-	-	(D)	(D)	(D)	(D)
OTHER...............	-	100.0	-	29.4	12.3	8.1	5.8	(D)	(D)	(D)	(D)
UNKNOWN.............	-	100.0	-	14.1	85.9	-	-	(D)	(D)	(D)	(D)
PACIFIC................	130	100.0	1.2	29.9	15.4	6.4	2.2	(D)	(D)	(D)	(D)
RAIL............	38	100.0	.4	34.2	37.5	6.9	4.0	(D)	(D)	(D)	(D)
MOTOR CARRIER........	57	100.0	2.0	35.6	6.8	9.3	2.0	(D)	(D)	(D)	(D)
PRIVATE TRUCK........	26	100.0	.9	-	-	-	.1	(D)	(D)	(D)	(D)
AIR.................	2	100.0	.1	51.2	20.0	9.3	7.6	(D)	(D)	(D)	(D)
WATER...............	3	100.0	-	98.3	1.7	-	-	(D)	(D)	(D)	(D)
OTHER...............	1	100.0	-	24.9	60.1	.3	.5	(D)	(D)	(D)	(D)
UNKNOWN.............	-	100.0	-	49.0	51.0	-	-	(D)	(D)	(D)	(D)

See footnotes at end of table 4.

TABLE 3. TCC GROUP 283—Percent Distribution of Geographic Division of Destination and Means of Transport, by Geographic Division of Origin: 1972—Continued

Geographic division of destination and means of transport	Number	Percent distribution by division of origin [1]									
		U.S. total	New England	Middle Atlantic	East North Central	West North Central	South Atlantic	East South Central	West South Central	Mountain	Pacific
TON-MILES OF SHIPMENTS	(millions of ton-miles)										
U.S. TOTAL	909	100.0	1.4	27.3	20.2	5.6	15.0	(D)	(D)	(D)	(D)
RAIL	324	100.0	.1	16.3	30.4	5.1	19.1	(D)	(D)	(D)	(D)
MOTOR CARRIER	468	100.0	2.3	35.5	14.5	6.6	15.0	(D)	(D)	(D)	(D)
PRIVATE TRUCK	77	100.0	1.2	8.2	10.7	3.0	3.7	(D)	(D)	(D)	(D)
AIR	13	100.0	.1	48.3	15.1	5.2	9.6	(D)	(D)	(D)	(D)
WATER	14	100.0	-	86.6	1.8	-	-	(D)	(D)	(D)	(D)
OTHER	10	100.0	1.2	30.0	58.9	2.1	.7	(D)	(D)	(D)	(D)
UNKNOWN	1	100.0	15.2	24.6	29.8	.3	28.8	(D)	(D)	(D)	(D)
NEW ENGLAND	39	100.0	.2	13.5	23.4	22.3	33.9	(D)	(D)	(D)	(D)
RAIL	20	100.0	-	.6	8.4	27.2	63.7	(D)	(D)	(D)	(D)
MOTOR CARRIER	14	100.0	.7	34.6	28.5	19.1	4.0	(D)	(D)	(D)	(D)
PRIVATE TRUCK	4	100.0	.1	2.3	71.3	11.5	-	(D)	(D)	(D)	(D)
AIR	-	100.0	-	28.0	15.9	25.2	8.9	(D)	(D)	(D)	(D)
WATER	-	100.0	-	-	-	-	-	(D)	(D)	(D)	(D)
OTHER	-	100.0	.4	35.5	54.0	.5	1.3	(D)	(D)	(D)	(D)
UNKNOWN	-	100.0	-	100.0	-	-	-	(D)	(D)	(D)	(D)
MIDDLE ATLANTIC	153	100.0	1.0	8.6	26.6	5.2	22.1	(D)	(D)	(D)	(D)
RAIL	47	100.0	-	.1	39.5	3.3	17.4	(D)	(D)	(D)	(D)
MOTOR CARRIER	86	100.0	1.2	11.5	23.5	6.6	27.7	(D)	(D)	(D)	(D)
PRIVATE TRUCK	15	100.0	1.8	13.7	4.5	3.7	9.0	(D)	(D)	(D)	(D)
AIR	1	100.0	-	15.5	14.6	2.9	5.9	(D)	(D)	(D)	(D)
WATER	-	100.0	-	100.0	-	-	-	(D)	(D)	(D)	(D)
OTHER	1	100.0	.3	30.7	58.4	.3	.1	(D)	(D)	(D)	(D)
UNKNOWN	-	100.0	94.8	3.1	.2	-	1.9	(D)	(D)	(D)	(D)
EAST NORTH CENTRAL	129	100.0	.9	30.3	11.6	5.1	20.7	(D)	(D)	(D)	(D)
RAIL	33	100.0	-	33.5	.3	7.6	29.4	(D)	(D)	(D)	(D)
MOTOR CARRIER	79	100.0	1.4	32.2	14.8	4.8	20.3	(D)	(D)	(D)	(D)
PRIVATE TRUCK	13	100.0	.2	11.9	14.3	1.6	5.8	(D)	(D)	(D)	(D)
AIR	1	100.0	.1	29.9	1.3	3.0	2.1	(D)	(D)	(D)	(D)
WATER	-	100.0	-	-	-	-	-	(D)	(D)	(D)	(D)
OTHER	1	100.0	.7	28.7	63.5	2.0	.3	(D)	(D)	(D)	(D)
UNKNOWN	-	100.0	-	-	78.3	4.3	.4	(D)	(D)	(D)	(D)
WEST NORTH CENTRAL	58	100.0	.6	24.6	13.8	3.6	26.4	(D)	(D)	(D)	(D)
RAIL	12	100.0	-	20.4	8.4	-	71.2	(D)	(D)	(D)	(D)
MOTOR CARRIER	42	100.0	.7	26.3	12.8	4.1	16.2	(D)	(D)	(D)	(D)
PRIVATE TRUCK	2	100.0	-	1.6	46.9	10.2	-	(D)	(D)	(D)	(D)
AIR	-	100.0	1.7	63.8	4.1	3.6	6.3	(D)	(D)	(D)	(D)
WATER	-	100.0	-	-	-	-	-	(D)	(D)	(D)	(D)
OTHER	-	100.0	2.1	41.3	42.2	8.4	.3	(D)	(D)	(D)	(D)
UNKNOWN	-	100.0	-	87.2	12.3	.5	-	(D)	(D)	(D)	(D)
SOUTH ATLANTIC	168	100.0	.3	20.5	22.5	3.0	7.5	(D)	(D)	(D)	(D)
RAIL	70	100.0	-	1.2	36.6	2.1	7.6	(D)	(D)	(D)	(D)
MOTOR CARRIER	68	100.0	.7	46.7	15.8	4.2	9.7	(D)	(D)	(D)	(D)
PRIVATE TRUCK	25	100.0	-	.7	2.1	2.8	1.0	(D)	(D)	(D)	(D)
AIR	1	100.0	-	47.2	14.6	3.3	23.1	(D)	(D)	(D)	(D)
WATER	1	100.0	-	13.1	-	-	.1	(D)	(D)	(D)	(D)
OTHER	1	100.0	2.0	37.9	46.3	1.8	1.2	(D)	(D)	(D)	(D)
UNKNOWN	-	100.0	-	-	97.6	-	-	(D)	(D)	(D)	(D)
EAST SOUTH CENTRAL	52	100.0	1.8	15.6	5.2	1.6	18.2	(D)	(D)	(D)	(D)
RAIL	22	100.0	-	2.1	2.0	-	22.5	(D)	(D)	(D)	(D)
MOTOR CARRIER	22	100.0	3.9	24.0	5.4	3.6	18.4	(D)	(D)	(D)	(D)
PRIVATE TRUCK	6	100.0	-	30.0	8.4	-	5.3	(D)	(D)	(D)	(D)
AIR	-	100.0	-	60.3	12.0	2.6	7.7	(D)	(D)	(D)	(D)
WATER	-	100.0	-	-	-	-	-	(D)	(D)	(D)	(D)
OTHER	-	100.0	3.8	17.5	69.3	2.1	.4	(D)	(D)	(D)	(D)
UNKNOWN	-	100.0	-	-	-	-	-	(D)	(D)	(D)	(D)
WEST SOUTH CENTRAL	95	100.0	1.3	30.7	27.5	3.1	16.0	(D)	(D)	(D)	(D)
RAIL	31	100.0	-	10.7	62.6	3.3	19.8	(D)	(D)	(D)	(D)
MOTOR CARRIER	51	100.0	2.4	40.2	10.7	3.5	17.0	(D)	(D)	(D)	(D)
PRIVATE TRUCK	6	100.0	-	6.2	.6	-	-	(D)	(D)	(D)	(D)
AIR	1	100.0	-	71.4	10.1	3.1	13.7	(D)	(D)	(D)	(D)
WATER	3	100.0	-	98.3	-	-	-	(D)	(D)	(D)	(D)
OTHER	1	100.0	2.5	16.0	67.3	3.7	1.0	(D)	(D)	(D)	(D)
UNKNOWN	-	100.0	-	6.4	15.6	-	78.0	(D)	(D)	(D)	(D)
MOUNTAIN	26	100.0	1.7	34.0	23.2	14.5	11.1	(D)	(D)	(D)	(D)
RAIL	9	100.0	-	25.4	47.2	1.1	26.3	(D)	(D)	(D)	(D)
MOTOR CARRIER	14	100.0	3.1	45.4	11.1	26.6	3.3	(D)	(D)	(D)	(D)
PRIVATE TRUCK	2	100.0	-	-	-	-	-	(D)	(D)	(D)	(D)
AIR	-	100.0	-	54.8	32.4	1.9	2.5	(D)	(D)	(D)	(D)
WATER	-	100.0	-	-	-	-	-	(D)	(D)	(D)	(D)
OTHER	-	100.0	-	51.4	12.5	6.0	9.1	(D)	(D)	(D)	(D)
UNKNOWN	-	100.0	-	23.0	77.0	-	-	(D)	(D)	(D)	(D)
PACIFIC	185	100.0	3.3	51.1	20.3	6.7	3.7	(D)	(D)	(D)	(D)
RAIL	78	100.0	.5	40.6	34.4	5.6	4.6	(D)	(D)	(D)	(D)
MOTOR CARRIER	88	100.0	5.8	56.7	8.2	8.7	3.0	(D)	(D)	(D)	(D)
PRIVATE TRUCK	1	100.0	49.0	-	1.8	-	5.9	(D)	(D)	(D)	(D)
AIR	4	100.0	.1	60.0	21.8	6.5	8.5	(D)	(D)	(D)	(D)
WATER	8	100.0	-	97.0	3.0	-	-	(D)	(D)	(D)	(D)
OTHER	2	100.0	-	33.4	61.7	.2	.7	(D)	(D)	(D)	(D)
UNKNOWN	-	100.0	-	58.1	41.9	-	-	(D)	(D)	(D)	(D)

See footnotes at end of table 4.

TABLE 4. **TCC GROUP 283—Percent Distribution of Distance Shipped and Weight of Shipment, by Means of Transport: 1972**

Distance shipped and weight of shipment [2] [3]	Number	Percent distribution by means of transport							
		All means of transport	Rail	Motor carrier	Private truck	Air	Water	Other	Unknown
TONS OF SHIPMENTS	(thousands of tons)								
U.S. TOTAL.........	1 292	100.0	22.3	57.0	17.4	.8	.6	1.7	.1
UNDER 100 MILES........	171	100.0	.5	72.9	23.6	.1	-	2.9	-
UNDER 1000 POUNDS.....	23	100.0	-	74.5	12.2	1.0	-	12.3	-
1000 TO 9999 POUNDS...	41	100.0	-	46.5	52.7	-	.1	.7	-
10000 TO 29999 POUNDS.	60	100.0	-	95.1	4.9	-	-	-	-
30000 TO 59999 POUNDS.	33	100.0	-	55.5	39.1	-	-	5.4	-
60000 TO 89999 POUNDS.	4	100.0	16.2	83.8	-	-	-	-	-
90000 POUNDS AND OVER.	7	100.0	-	100.0	-	-	-	-	-
100 TO 199 MILES........	105	100.0	3.9	55.4	36.9	.3	-	3.4	.1
UNDER 1000 POUNDS.....	21	100.0	-	59.1	26.5	1.0	-	12.8	.6
1000 TO 9999 POUNDS...	41	100.0	-	41.1	56.7	.2	-	2.0	-
10000 TO 29999 POUNDS.	11	100.0	-	59.8	40.2	-	-	-	-
30000 TO 59999 POUNDS.	26	100.0	-	81.5	18.5	-	-	-	-
60000 TO 89999 POUNDS.	4	100.0	97.2	2.8	-	-	-	-	-
90000 POUNDS AND OVER.	-	100.0	-	-	-	-	-	-	-
200 TO 299 MILES........	138	100.0	4.2	53.8	36.4	1.3	.9	2.7	.7
UNDER 1000 POUNDS.....	26	100.0	.1	47.0	33.4	6.7	-	12.3	.5
1000 TO 9999 POUNDS...	57	100.0	-	33.7	63.1	-	2.2	.8	.2
10000 TO 29999 POUNDS.	23	100.0	6.4	78.6	15.0	-	-	-	-
30000 TO 59999 POUNDS.	29	100.0	11.8	80.9	5.1	-	-	-	2.2
60000 TO 89999 POUNDS.	-	100.0	85.6	14.4	-	-	-	-	-
90000 POUNDS AND OVER.	-	100.0	-	-	-	-	-	-	-
300 TO 499 MILES........	200	100.0	18.5	55.4	23.8	.8	-	1.4	-
UNDER 1000 POUNDS.....	32	100.0	.4	57.3	28.9	4.7	-	8.7	-
1000 TO 9999 POUNDS...	38	100.0	.1	54.4	45.2	.2	-	-	-
10000 TO 29999 POUNDS.	36	100.0	7.4	41.5	51.1	-	-	-	-
30000 TO 59999 POUNDS.	66	100.0	19.9	76.5	3.6	-	-	-	-
60000 TO 89999 POUNDS.	24	100.0	86.7	13.3	-	-	-	-	-
90000 POUNDS AND OVER.	1	100.0	-	100.0	-	-	-	-	-
500 TO 999 MILES........	494	100.0	34.1	55.0	8.6	.6	.6	1.0	.1
UNDER 1000 POUNDS.....	49	100.0	1.8	67.4	19.3	4.8	-	6.4	.2
1000 TO 9999 POUNDS...	58	100.0	.5	62.5	35.0	1.2	-	-	.7
10000 TO 29999 POUNDS.	44	100.0	6.7	79.7	13.0	-	.6	-	-
30000 TO 59999 POUNDS.	229	100.0	33.1	62.1	2.9	-	1.3	.7	-
60000 TO 89999 POUNDS.	82	100.0	79.5	20.5	-	-	-	-	-
90000 POUNDS AND OVER.	30	100.0	76.2	23.8	-	-	-	-	-
1000 TO 1499 MILES......	91	100.0	35.1	56.2	3.9	1.4	2.6	.8	-
UNDER 1000 POUNDS.....	11	100.0	1.0	79.2	4.2	8.7	-	6.6	.2
1000 TO 9999 POUNDS...	11	100.0	-	77.9	19.3	2.8	-	-	-
10000 TO 29999 POUNDS.	7	100.0	29.4	58.8	7.6	-	4.2	-	-
30000 TO 59999 POUNDS.	36	100.0	29.8	63.7	.9	-	5.7	-	-
60000 TO 89999 POUNDS.	19	100.0	96.0	4.0	-	-	-	-	-
90000 POUNDS AND OVER.	4	100.0	-	100.0	-	-	-	-	-
1500 MILES OR OVER......	90	100.0	43.6	49.2	1.7	2.4	1.4	1.5	.2
UNDER 1000 POUNDS.....	16	100.0	16.5	60.9	8.0	10.8	.4	2.5	.9
1000 TO 9999 POUNDS...	8	100.0	3.6	83.1	-	4.9	-	8.4	-
10000 TO 29999 POUNDS.	8	100.0	38.4	58.5	-	-	-	3.1	-
30000 TO 59999 POUNDS.	50	100.0	53.0	44.1	.4	-	2.4	-	-
60000 TO 89999 POUNDS.	2	100.0	93.5	6.5	-	-	-	-	-
90000 POUNDS AND OVER.	4	100.0	100.0	-	-	-	-	-	-
TON-MILES OF SHIPMENTS	(millions of ton-miles)								
U.S. TOTAL.........	786	100.0	32.2	54.5	9.5	1.3	1.1	1.3	.1
UNDER 100 MILES........	9	100.0	.6	71.5	24.2	.1	-	3.6	-
UNDER 1000 POUNDS.....	1	100.0	-	69.9	14.3	.6	-	15.1	-
1000 TO 9999 POUNDS...	2	100.0	-	40.2	58.8	-	-	1.0	-
10000 TO 29999 POUNDS.	3	100.0	-	96.9	3.1	-	-	-	-
30000 TO 59999 POUNDS.	1	100.0	-	54.3	37.7	-	-	8.1	-
60000 TO 89999 POUNDS.	-	100.0	14.3	85.7	-	-	-	-	-
90000 POUNDS AND OVER.	-	100.0	-	100.0	-	-	-	-	-
100 TO 199 MILES........	15	100.0	5.1	54.0	36.9	.3	-	3.6	.1
UNDER 1000 POUNDS.....	3	100.0	-	58.9	26.1	1.2	-	13.1	.6
1000 TO 9999 POUNDS...	6	100.0	-	41.8	55.7	.2	-	2.3	-
10000 TO 29999 POUNDS.	1	100.0	-	54.5	45.5	-	-	-	-
30000 TO 59999 POUNDS.	3	100.0	-	83.6	16.4	-	-	-	-
60000 TO 89999 POUNDS.	-	100.0	98.1	1.9	-	-	-	-	-
90000 POUNDS AND OVER.	-	100.0	-	-	-	-	-	-	-

See footnotes at end of table 4.

TABLE 4. **TCC GROUP 283—Percent Distribution of Distance Shipped and Weight of Shipment, by Means of Transport: 1972**—Continued

Distance shipped and weight of shipment[2][3]	Number	Percent distribution by means of transport							
		All means of transport	Rail	Motor carrier	Private truck	Air	Water	Other	Unknown
TON-MILES OF SHIPMENTS	(millions of ton-miles)								
200 TO 299 MILES.........	34	100.0	4.5	54.0	35.8	1.4	.9	2.8	.6
UNDER 1000 POUNDS.....	6	100.0	.1	47.3	32.8	7.2	-	12.1	.5
1000 TO 9999 POUNDS...	14	100.0	-	33.9	62.7	-	2.2	1.0	.2
10000 TO 29999 POUNDS.	5	100.0	5.7	80.7	13.7	-	-	-	-
30000 TO 59999 POUNDS.	7	100.0	13.2	80.2	4.6	-	-	-	2.0
60000 TO 89999 POUNDS.	-	100.0	85.8	14.2	-	-	-	-	-
90000 POUNDS AND OVER.	-	100.0	-	-	-	-	-	-	-
300 TO 499 MILES........	81	100.0	18.0	54.9	25.0	.8	-	1.3	-
UNDER 1000 POUNDS.....	12	100.0	.5	58.0	28.0	4.9	-	8.5	-
1000 TO 9999 POUNDS...	15	100.0	.2	52.7	47.0	.2	-	-	-
10000 TO 29999 POUNDS.	15	100.0	7.7	38.6	53.7	-	-	-	-
30000 TO 59999 POUNDS.	27	100.0	19.0	77.0	4.0	-	-	-	-
60000 TO 89999 POUNDS.	9	100.0	85.7	14.3	-	-	-	-	-
90000 POUNDS AND OVER.	-	100.0	-	100.0	-	-	-	-	-
500 TO 999 MILES........	345	100.0	35.0	54.9	7.9	.6	.5	1.0	.1
UNDER 1000 POUNDS.....	34	100.0	2.2	68.7	17.2	5.0	-	6.7	.3
1000 TO 9999 POUNDS...	39	100.0	.7	66.3	30.8	1.3	-	-	.8
10000 TO 29999 POUNDS.	32	100.0	6.9	79.0	13.5	-	.6	-	-
30000 TO 59999 POUNDS.	157	100.0	33.4	61.8	3.0	-	1.1	.7	-
60000 TO 89999 POUNDS.	59	100.0	80.0	20.0	-	-	-	-	-
90000 POUNDS AND OVER.	22	100.0	77.5	22.5	-	-	-	-	-
1000 TO 1499 MILES......	108	100.0	33.0	58.1	3.5	1.5	3.0	.8	-
UNDER 1000 POUNDS.....	13	100.0	1.1	79.1	4.1	8.8	-	6.6	.2
1000 TO 9999 POUNDS...	13	100.0	-	79.7	17.1	3.2	-	-	-
10000 TO 29999 POUNDS.	8	100.0	28.4	60.1	6.8	-	4.7	-	-
30000 TO 59999 POUNDS.	44	100.0	27.9	64.9	.9	-	6.3	-	-
60000 TO 89999 POUNDS.	21	100.0	94.9	5.1	-	-	-	-	-
90000 POUNDS AND OVER.	6	100.0	-	100.0	-	-	-	-	-
1500 MILES OR OVER......	190	100.0	41.8	50.7	1.4	2.6	1.8	1.5	.2
UNDER 1000 POUNDS.....	34	100.0	18.3	59.3	6.3	12.0	.8	2.4	.9
1000 TO 9999 POUNDS...	16	100.0	3.2	82.9	-	5.7	-	8.2	-
10000 TO 29999 POUNDS.	20	100.0	35.3	61.6	-	-	-	3.1	-
30000 TO 59999 POUNDS.	106	100.0	49.6	46.9	.6	-	2.9	-	-
60000 TO 89999 POUNDS.	5	100.0	93.1	6.9	-	-	-	-	-
90000 POUNDS AND OVER.	8	100.0	100.0	-	-	-	-	-	-

Note: Detail may not add to total due to rounding. The introductory table shows the estimates of sampling variability for tons; sampling variability for ton-miles has not been estimated. See the map in the Introduction for the States comprising the geographic divisions of the United States.

Shipments excluded from the survey are those moving by pipeline (primarily petroleum products from refineries), parcel post shipments, and commodities moved by own power (motorized vehicles, aircraft, etc.) or towed (prefabricated buildings, etc.). Local shipments (commodities shipped less than 25 miles from the plant) and shipments within the same city are also excluded. Shipments to Alaska and Hawaii from the 48 conterminous States and the District of Columbia are included; however, no data were obtained for shipments originating in Alaska and Hawaii.

- Represents zero or rounds to zero. (D) Withheld to avoid disclosing figures for individual companies.

[1]Production of this commodity is concentrated in the geographic divisions shown; figures and distributions for geographic divisions not shown are included in the total.
[2]Distances of shipments to foreign destinations are calculated only to the U.S. port of exit.
[3]Includes only shipments represented by bills of lading and invoices. Summary records which did not show individual weights of shipments are not included.

TCC 284. Soap and Other Detergents

Comparisons of Tons and Ton-Miles of Shipments for
Geographic Divisions of Origin and for Sampling Variability: 1972 and 1967

Geographic division of origin	Estimates				Relative sampling variability in tons (percent)	
	1972		1967		1972	1967
	Tons (thousands)	Ton-miles (millions)	Tons (thousands)	Ton-miles (millions)		
U.S. total	11,731	5,368	9,526	4,081	6.8	5.6
New England	679	599	612	309	13.2	(*)
Middle Atlantic	2,393	1,014	2,315	865	18.8	(*)
East North Central	3,965	1,768	2,610	1,317	16.0	(*)
West North Central	1,402	607	1,214	597	7.1	(*)
South Atlantic	1,139	380	1,123	320	10.7	(*)
East South Central	(D)	(D)	20	9	(*)	(*)
West South Central	841	459	369	132	37.3	(*)
Mountain	(D)	(D)	11	14	(*)	(*)
Pacific	1,190	504	1,252	518	23.0	(*)

(D) Withheld to avoid disclosing figures for individual companies.   (*) Data not published.

TABLE 1. TCC GROUP 284—Percent Distribution of Geographic Division of Origin and Distance Shipped, by Means of Transport: 1972

Geographic division of origin[1] and distance shipped[2]	Number	Percent distribution by means of transport							
		All means of transport	Rail	Motor carrier	Private truck	Air	Water	Other	Unknown
TONS OF SHIPMENTS	(thousands of tons)								
U.S. TOTAL..........	11 731	100.0	21.1	62.8	14.0	.1	1.2	.6	.1
NEW ENGLAND.............	679	100.0	18.1	69.8	4.3	-	5.6	1.8	.4
UNDER 100 MILES.......	97	100.0	-	95.7	3.8	-	.2	.2	-
100 TO 199 MILES......	84	100.0	-	88.3	8.9	-	.4	2.5	-
200 TO 299 MILES......	72	100.0	-	87.6	12.3	-	-	-	-
300 TO 499 MILES......	46	100.0	-	80.9	18.8	-	-	.2	-
500 TO 999 MILES....	167	100.0	15.7	78.6	.1	-	-	5.6	-
1000 TO 1499 MILES....	35	100.0	8.9	43.1	-	.7	39.7	.1	7.6
1500 MILES OR OVER....	176	100.0	53.0	33.3	-	-	13.4	.2	.1
MIDDLE ATLANTIC.........	2 393	100.0	15.9	61.8	17.6	-	3.4	1.1	.1
UNDER 100 MILES.......	670	100.0	-	60.1	38.9	-	.6	.4	-
100 TO 199 MILES......	495	100.0	-	78.8	21.0	-	-	.3	-
200 TO 299 MILES......	291	100.0	16.4	73.3	10.0	-	-	.3	-
300 TO 499 MILES......	187	100.0	3.2	89.6	5.4	.1	-	1.7	-
500 TO 999 MILES....	530	100.0	57.0	33.8	2.7	-	4.9	1.4	.1
1000 TO 1499 MILES....	116	100.0	11.9	54.8	3.4	.1	26.6	2.9	.1
1500 MILES OR OVER....	101	100.0	10.8	59.8	.1	.5	20.2	7.7	.7
EAST NORTH CENTRAL......	3 965	100.0	22.9	65.9	10.8	.1	-	-	.2
UNDER 100 MILES.......	574	100.0	.5	62.5	36.9	-	-	-	.1
100 TO 199 MILES......	690	100.0	1.7	80.7	17.4	-	-	-	.2
200 TO 299 MILES......	665	100.0	9.5	86.7	3.7	-	-	-	.1
300 TO 499 MILES......	733	100.0	25.8	71.4	2.8	.1	-	-	-
500 TO 999 MILES....	1 032	100.0	44.5	50.4	4.1	.3	.1	.1	.5
1000 TO 1499 MILES....	38	100.0	64.4	32.1	3.4	-	-	.1	-
1500 MILES OR OVER....	230	100.0	68.2	28.1	3.4	.2	-	.2	-
WEST NORTH CENTRAL......	1 402	100.0	23.1	72.6	4.1	-	-	.2	-
UNDER 100 MILES.......	58	100.0	1.4	69.6	28.5	-	-	.5	-
100 TO 199 MILES......	191	100.0	2.0	92.5	5.2	-	-	.2	-
200 TO 299 MILES......	283	100.0	4.6	91.5	3.9	-	-	.1	-
300 TO 499 MILES......	407	100.0	20.9	77.3	1.8	-	-	.1	-
500 TO 999 MILES....	394	100.0	45.4	52.5	1.8	-	-	.2	-
1000 TO 1499 MILES....	51	100.0	61.0	33.1	5.4	.1	-	.5	-
1500 MILES OR OVER....	15	100.0	64.6	16.8	15.8	-	-	2.9	-
SOUTH ATLANTIC.........	1 139	100.0	9.7	62.5	25.7	-	.4	1.8	-
UNDER 100 MILES.......	233	100.0	-	52.6	47.4	-	-	-	-
100 TO 199 MILES......	334	100.0	1.1	78.1	19.7	-	.1	1.0	-
200 TO 299 MILES......	129	100.0	12.7	51.2	34.2	-	-	1.9	-
300 TO 499 MILES......	225	100.0	13.5	71.9	11.4	-	-	3.2	-
500 TO 999 MILES....	172	100.0	28.5	51.1	16.4	-	.1	3.9	-
1000 TO 1499 MILES....	19	100.0	-	47.0	52.4	-	-	.5	.1
1500 MILES OR OVER....	24	100.0	43.5	10.8	31.5	-	13.9	.3	-
WEST SOUTH CENTRAL......	841	100.0	33.0	36.2	30.7	-	-	-	.1
UNDER 100 MILES.......	77	100.0	9.6	34.6	55.8	-	-	-	-
100 TO 199 MILES......	89	100.0	2.0	58.6	39.5	-	-	-	-
200 TO 299 MILES......	165	100.0	14.8	69.4	15.7	-	-	-	-
300 TO 499 MILES......	216	100.0	1.3	34.0	64.6	-	-	-	-
500 TO 999 MILES....	154	100.0	81.2	18.0	.9	-	-	-	-
1000 TO 1499 MILES....	121	100.0	82.8	6.7	9.7	.3	-	-	.5
1500 MILES OR OVER....	16	100.0	92.9	5.7	1.3	-	-	-	-
PACIFIC.................	1 190	100.0	28.9	60.6	7.8	.1	1.7	1.0	-
UNDER 100 MILES.......	309	100.0	-	68.0	25.6	-	2.8	3.6	-
100 TO 199 MILES......	66	100.0	16.6	70.4	12.5	-	-	.6	-
200 TO 299 MILES......	34	100.0	20.1	78.9	.8	-	-	.2	-
300 TO 499 MILES......	450	100.0	28.8	70.8	.3	-	.1	-	-
500 TO 999 MILES....	271	100.0	71.7	27.0	1.3	-	-	.1	-
1000 TO 1499 MILES....	12	100.0	-	99.6	-	.2	-	.2	-
1500 MILES OR OVER....	45	100.0	2.8	72.5	-	1.6	23.1	.1	-
TON-MILES OF SHIPMENTS	(millions of ton-miles)								
U.S. TOTAL..........	5 368	100.0	37.2	50.8	6.5	.1	4.2	1.0	.2
NEW ENGLAND.............	599	100.0	37.8	45.6	1.1	.1	13.3	1.4	.7
UNDER 100 MILES.......	5	100.0	-	96.9	2.8	-	.2	.1	-
100 TO 199 MILES......	11	100.0	-	88.3	9.0	-	.4	2.3	-
200 TO 299 MILES......	16	100.0	-	88.1	11.8	-	-	-	-
300 TO 499 MILES......	17	100.0	-	82.4	17.3	-	-	.2	-
500 TO 999 MILES....	123	100.0	19.4	74.6	.1	-	-	5.8	-
1000 TO 1499 MILES....	47	100.0	9.3	40.6	-	.6	41.4	.1	8.0
1500 MILES OR OVER....	377	100.0	52.6	31.2	-	-	15.9	.2	.1
MIDDLE ATLANTIC.........	1 014	100.0	27.0	54.1	4.9	.2	10.6	3.0	.2
UNDER 100 MILES.......	27	100.0	-	66.5	32.4	-	.5	.5	-
100 TO 199 MILES......	78	100.0	-	79.2	20.5	-	-	.3	-
200 TO 299 MILES......	70	100.0	14.1	77.0	8.6	-	-	.3	-
300 TO 499 MILES......	75	100.0	3.2	90.1	4.9	.1	-	1.8	-
500 TO 999 MILES......	386	100.0	57.3	33.2	2.5	-	5.4	1.5	.1
1000 TO 1499 MILES....	137	100.0	12.5	54.6	3.4	.2	26.2	3.0	.2
1500 MILES OR OVER....	238	100.0	9.8	59.7	.1	.6	21.3	7.9	.6

See footnotes at end of table 4.

TABLE 1. **TCC GROUP 284**—Percent Distribution of Geographic Division of Origin and Distance Shipped, by Means of Transport: 1972—Continued

Geographic division of origin[1] and distance shipped[2]	Number	Percent distribution by means of transport							
		All means of transport	Rail	Motor carrier	Private truck	Air	Water	Other	Unknown
TON-MILES OF SHIPMENTS	(millions of ton-miles)								
EAST NORTH CENTRAL	1 768	100.0	41.6	52.9	4.9	.2	-	.1	.3
UNDER 100 MILES	32	100.0	.8	67.9	31.2	-	-	-	.1
100 TO 199 MILES	99	100.0	1.8	79.7	18.2	-	-	-	.3
200 TO 299 MILES	163	100.0	9.3	87.0	3.6	-	-	-	.1
300 TO 499 MILES	267	100.0	25.9	71.1	2.9	.1	-	-	-
500 TO 999 MILES	732	100.0	44.3	50.6	4.1	.3	.1	.1	.6
1000 TO 1499 MILES	48	100.0	67.9	29.0	3.0	-	-	.1	-
1500 MILES OR OVER	423	100.0	68.8	27.6	3.3	.2	-	.2	-
WEST NORTH CENTRAL	607	100.0	34.5	61.9	3.3	-	-	.3	-
UNDER 100 MILES	1	100.0	4.0	62.2	32.6	-	-	1.2	-
100 TO 199 MILES	30	100.0	1.7	93.2	4.9	-	-	.2	-
200 TO 299 MILES	69	100.0	4.3	92.0	3.6	-	-	.1	-
300 TO 499 MILES	164	100.0	21.4	76.8	1.8	-	-	.1	-
500 TO 999 MILES	248	100.0	45.1	52.5	2.1	-	-	.3	-
1000 TO 1499 MILES	66	100.0	62.7	32.4	4.4	-	-	.5	-
1500 MILES OR OVER	25	100.0	65.0	16.0	16.2	-	-	2.7	-
SOUTH ATLANTIC	380	100.0	18.8	54.5	21.9	-	2.2	2.5	-
UNDER 100 MILES	17	100.0	-	55.4	44.5	-	-	-	-
100 TO 199 MILES	50	100.0	1.2	76.9	20.8	-	.1	1.0	-
200 TO 299 MILES	31	100.0	12.0	53.1	32.6	-	-	2.2	-
300 TO 499 MILES	87	100.0	13.2	73.3	9.9	-	-	3.6	-
500 TO 999 MILES	117	100.0	27.1	52.7	15.8	-	.1	4.3	-
1000 TO 1499 MILES	21	100.0	-	48.7	50.8	-	-	.5	.1
1500 MILES OR OVER	54	100.0	43.9	10.7	30.2	-	14.9	.3	-
WEST SOUTH CENTRAL	459	100.0	59.7	21.3	18.7	.1	-	-	.2
UNDER 100 MILES	2	100.0	10.4	49.9	39.7	-	-	-	-
100 TO 199 MILES	14	100.0	1.5	56.5	42.0	-	-	-	-
200 TO 299 MILES	40	100.0	16.8	67.7	15.5	-	-	-	-
300 TO 499 MILES	85	100.0	1.1	34.5	64.4	-	-	-	-
500 TO 999 MILES	127	100.0	84.4	14.8	.8	-	-	-	-
1000 TO 1499 MILES	161	100.0	83.1	6.7	9.5	.3	-	-	.5
1500 MILES OR OVER	26	100.0	93.0	5.7	1.3	-	-	-	-
PACIFIC	504	100.0	39.7	53.3	1.1	.3	5.5	.1	-
UNDER 100 MILES	11	100.0	-	80.1	16.9	-	1.3	1.7	-
100 TO 199 MILES	9	100.0	16.9	72.4	10.2	-	-	.5	-
200 TO 299 MILES	8	100.0	23.7	75.2	.9	-	-	.2	-
300 TO 499 MILES	158	100.0	28.9	70.7	.3	-	.1	-	-
500 TO 999 MILES	208	100.0	71.5	27.4	1.0	-	-	.1	-
1000 TO 1499 MILES	15	100.0	-	99.5	-	.2	-	.2	-
1500 MILES OR OVER	93	100.0	2.3	66.6	-	-	1.7	29.3	.1

See footnotes at end of table 4.

TABLE 2. **TCC GROUP 284**—Percent Distribution of Geographic Division of Origin and Means of Transport, by Geographic Division of Destination: 1972

Geographic division of origin[1] and means of transport	Number	Percent distribution by division of destination									
		U.S. total	New England	Middle Atlantic	East North Central	West North Central	South Atlantic	East South Central	West South Central	Mountain	Pacific
TONS OF SHIPMENTS	(thousands of tons)										
U.S. TOTAL	11 731	100.0	5.1	15.1	25.2	8.1	15.3	4.3	11.1	3.5	12.4
RAIL	2 474	100.0	4.4	6.5	21.4	4.7	15.5	1.9	16.4	8.8	20.5
MOTOR CARRIER	7 370	100.0	6.0	17.0	27.7	9.8	13.3	4.1	9.5	2.4	10.2
PRIVATE TRUCK	1 646	100.0	2.8	20.9	22.2	6.5	23.1	8.4	8.9	.8	6.5
AIR	6	100.0	30.7	12.2	10.0	7.5	15.9	2.8	4.6	.9	15.4
WATER	143	100.0	.2	3.5	-	-	28.5	-	21.1	-	46.7
OTHER	75	100.0	4.1	7.2	19.2	3.7	10.1	7.9	20.1	.8	27.0
UNKNOWN	14	100.0	-	4.8	22.0	.6	1.5	33.2	31.4	3.7	2.8
NEW ENGLAND	679	100.0	16.8	23.2	17.4	.5	11.4	.5	13.7	2.1	14.4
RAIL	123	100.0	-	-	10.1	-	10.0	1.3	35.7	.7	42.2
MOTOR CARRIER	474	100.0	23.0	28.9	20.4	.7	12.4	.4	6.8	2.8	4.6
PRIVATE TRUCK	28	100.0	9.0	68.7	.3	-	22.0	-	-	.1	-
AIR	-	100.0	-	9.9	.8	16.8	14.5	5.5	46.3	3.7	2.5
WATER	38	100.0	.6	.9	-	-	-	-	36.6	-	61.9
OTHER	12	100.0	17.7	2.1	74.7	-	2.4	-	.5	-	2.6
UNKNOWN	2	100.0	-	.3	.7	-	-	-	99.0	-	-
MIDDLE ATLANTIC	2 393	100.0	12.0	38.4	18.0	1.3	22.1	1.3	2.8	.5	3.5
RAIL	381	100.0	12.6	-	76.0	.6	4.7	.3	3.1	.9	1.8
MOTOR CARRIER	1 478	100.0	13.6	42.3	9.1	1.8	25.2	1.8	2.4	.5	3.3
PRIVATE TRUCK	422	100.0	9.0	68.0	.4	.1	22.0	.1	.4	-	-
AIR	1	100.0	1.2	6.6	5.6	5.6	15.9	2.4	12.3	.4	50.0
WATER	81	100.0	-	4.8	-	-	49.9	-	20.2	-	25.2
OTHER	27	100.0	3.2	14.4	16.2	6.6	16.0	9.1	6.3	1.0	27.3
UNKNOWN	1	100.0	-	1.0	2.8	-	4.1	38.6	.7	31.7	21.1

See footnotes at end of table 4.

TABLE 2. TCC GROUP 284—Percent Distribution of Geographic Division of Origin and Means of Transport, by Geographic Division of Destination: 1972—Continued

Geographic division of origin [1] and means of transport	Number	Percent distribution by division of destination									
		U.S. total	New England	Middle Atlantic	East North Central	West North Central	South Atlantic	East South Central	West South Central	Mountain	Pacific
TONS OF SHIPMENTS	(thousands of tons)										
EAST NORTH CENTRAL......	3 965	100.0	2.5	7.8	49.2	8.6	12.0	5.3	7.2	1.7	5.7
RAIL................	908	100.0	4.4	10.4	15.4	6.1	21.3	2.9	17.7	4.5	17.3
MOTOR CARRIER........	2 614	100.0	2.0	7.7	56.1	10.2	9.9	6.4	4.4	.9	2.3
PRIVATE TRUCK........	428	100.0	.7	2.3	79.4	4.8	5.0	3.0	2.0	1.0	1.8
AIR.................	3	100.0	51.4	10.4	1.9	8.6	13.7	3.6	.3	.3	9.9
WATER...............	-	100.0	-	100.0	-	-	-	-	-	-	-
OTHER...............	1	100.0	.4	39.4	22.7	.5	1.9	1.6	1.5	.6	31.4
UNKNOWN.............	8	100.0	-	-	34.8	-	1.5	46.2	17.3	-	.2
WEST NORTH CENTRAL......	1 402	100.0	.2	1.5	23.8	33.2	3.3	3.9	23.5	7.0	3.7
RAIL................	323	100.0	-	3.0	10.1	12.7	6.9	1.3	43.4	11.2	11.5
MOTOR CARRIER........	1 018	100.0	.2	.7	28.0	38.9	2.4	4.6	18.4	5.7	1.2
PRIVATE TRUCK........	57	100.0	1.9	6.9	27.2	45.6	.5	5.9	2.6	5.3	4.1
AIR.................	-	100.0	35.8	2.5	-	17.7	-	-	-	44.0	-
WATER...............	-	100.0	-	-	-	-	-	-	-	-	-
OTHER...............	2	100.0	.7	11.3	10.7	31.5	3.1	2.6	15.2	2.8	22.1
UNKNOWN.............	-	100.0	-	-	-	61.8	-	-	38.2	-	-
SOUTH ATLANTIC..........	1 139	100.0	8.1	24.6	5.2	1.0	45.3	7.4	6.3	.2	2.0
RAIL................	110	100.0	13.9	1.5	10.0	2.2	52.1	.9	9.5	-	9.8
MOTOR CARRIER........	711	100.0	10.6	37.3	5.8	1.1	33.1	6.0	5.7	.1	.3
PRIVATE TRUCK........	292	100.0	.4	4.3	2.2	.2	74.9	12.6	2.8	.4	2.2
AIR.................	-	100.0	27.1	-	15.6	-	-	2.5	-	-	54.7
WATER...............	4	100.0	.9	2.0	-	-	10.7	-	-	-	86.4
OTHER...............	20	100.0	.2	2.5	1.9	.4	13.9	16.3	64.5	.1	.3
UNKNOWN.............	-	100.0	-	47.6	-	-	52.4	-	-	-	-
WEST SOUTH CENTRAL......	841	100.0	.6	8.6	5.6	9.2	9.6	9.2	52.2	.2	4.7
RAIL................	277	100.0	1.6	19.8	15.0	5.7	25.9	4.4	13.9	.1	13.6
MOTOR CARRIER........	304	100.0	.3	2.0	1.4	.9	2.7	1.0	90.8	.5	.4
PRIVATE TRUCK........	258	100.0	.1	4.0	.4	22.8	.3	24.0	48.0	-	.3
AIR.................	-	100.0	-	.5	98.5	-	-	-	.2	-	.8
WATER...............	-	100.0	-	-	-	-	-	-	-	-	-
OTHER...............	-	100.0	35.0	-	-	32.3	-	-	32.7	-	-
UNKNOWN.............	-	100.0	-	99.6	-	-	-	-	.4	-	-
PACIFIC.................	1 190	100.0	.2	.4	.6	1.7	.4	.1	.8	17.9	78.0
RAIL................	343	100.0	-	-	.4	-	-	-	-	39.9	59.7
MOTOR CARRIER........	721	100.0	.3	.6	.9	2.7	.6	.2	1.3	10.0	83.6
PRIVATE TRUCK........	92	100.0	-	-	-	-	-	-	-	3.7	96.3
AIR.................	-	100.0	-	37.3	12.2	5.2	37.1	-	1.1	1.8	5.4
WATER...............	19	100.0	-	-	-	-	.2	-	-	-	99.8
OTHER...............	11	100.0	-	-	.1	.1	-	.1	.1	1.5	98.0
UNKNOWN.............	-	100.0	-	-	-	-	-	-	-	-	100.0
TON-MILES OF SHIPMENTS	(millions of ton-miles)										
U.S. TOTAL..............	5 368	100.0	3.5	8.7	16.8	6.7	14.7	3.2	14.9	5.8	25.6
RAIL................	1 995	100.0	2.6	7.0	16.1	3.0	12.3	1.0	15.2	7.7	35.1
MOTOR CARRIER........	2 727	100.0	4.6	10.2	19.4	9.6	15.5	3.7	14.6	5.4	17.0
PRIVATE TRUCK........	349	100.0	3.4	13.1	11.8	10.0	23.8	13.2	11.1	3.1	10.5
AIR.................	7	100.0	22.0	12.7	8.9	4.7	13.1	1.9	5.5	1.0	30.2
WATER...............	224	100.0	-	.3	-	-	16.4	-	17.9	-	65.5
OTHER...............	52	100.0	.8	2.3	19.4	3.8	7.4	4.8	19.7	1.4	40.4
UNKNOWN.............	11	100.0	-	6.3	4.6	.1	1.3	27.6	45.8	7.5	6.9
NEW ENGLAND.............	599	100.0	1.3	5.4	13.7	.6	8.8	.5	23.3	4.8	41.6
RAIL................	227	100.0	-	-	4.8	-	5.1	.6	29.8	.7	58.9
MOTOR CARRIER........	273	100.0	2.8	10.3	23.3	1.3	14.1	.6	17.6	10.0	19.9
PRIVATE TRUCK........	6	100.0	.8	63.2	.9	-	34.5	-	-	.6	-
AIR.................	-	100.0	-	1.8	.5	14.7	11.6	4.9	55.0	6.6	4.9
WATER...............	79	100.0	-	.1	-	-	-	-	24.5	-	75.4
OTHER...............	8	100.0	3.1	.6	82.9	-	2.1	.1	1.3	-	9.8
UNKNOWN.............	3	100.0	-	-	.3	-	-	-	99.7	-	-
MIDDLE ATLANTIC.........	1 014	100.0	5.7	8.4	27.8	3.0	21.5	2.3	8.5	2.0	20.7
RAIL................	274	100.0	3.6	-	75.9	.8	5.8	.4	5.4	1.8	6.2
MOTOR CARRIER........	548	100.0	7.4	12.9	12.8	4.8	25.3	3.6	8.4	2.6	22.1
PRIVATE TRUCK........	49	100.0	15.3	28.5	1.8	.5	48.7	.4	4.3	.5	-
AIR.................	1	100.0	.1	.1	2.3	3.2	5.5	1.1	9.7	.4	77.4
WATER...............	107	100.0	-	.1	-	-	33.8	-	19.0	-	47.1
OTHER...............	30	100.0	.4	1.2	9.0	5.7	8.9	6.2	7.2	1.7	59.6
UNKNOWN.............	2	100.0	-	-	1.0	-	2.0	16.6	.9	42.3	37.2

See footnotes at end of table 4.

TABLE 2. **TCC GROUP 284—Percent Distribution of Geographic Division of Origin and Means of Transport, by Geographic Division of Destination: 1972**—Continued

Geographic division of origin [1] and means of transport	Number	Percent distribution by division of destination									
		U.S. total	New England	Middle Atlantic	East North Central	West North Central	South Atlantic	East South Central	West South Central	Mountain	Pacific
TON-MILES OF SHIPMENTS	(millions of ton-miles)										
EAST NORTH CENTRAL......	1 768	100.0	4.2	9.9	18.9	7.4	15.1	3.7	12.9	4.3	23.7
RAIL.................	735	100.0	4.2	7.8	5.2	3.8	14.4	1.2	17.6	6.3	39.6
MOTOR CARRIER.........	935	100.0	4.3	12.0	28.1	10.2	15.8	5.4	9.8	2.7	11.9
PRIVATE TRUCK.........	87	100.0	2.6	5.4	36.5	8.9	14.7	3.6	7.7	4.7	16.0
AIR..................	3	100.0	52.2	7.7	.6	5.6	7.3	3.2	.3	.4	22.7
WATER................	-	100.0	-	100.0	-	-	-	-	-	-	-
OTHER................	1	100.0	.3	30.3	3.6	.3	2.4	1.2	1.4	.9	59.7
UNKNOWN..............	4	100.0	-	.1	10.3	-	2.0	59.1	27.9	-	.7
WEST NORTH CENTRAL......	607	100.0	.5	2.9	18.3	19.4	4.8	2.4	28.3	10.8	12.6
RAIL.................	209	100.0	-	4.0	5.8	8.4	7.3	.4	35.8	12.4	25.8
MOTOR CARRIER.........	375	100.0	.5	1.5	25.0	26.1	3.5	3.5	25.2	10.0	4.7
PRIVATE TRUCK.........	19	100.0	5.9	15.2	24.4	9.9	2.1	4.1	7.9	10.4	20.1
AIR..................	-	100.0	37.3	2.3	-	10.4	-	-	-	49.9	-
WATER................	-	100.0	-	-	-	-	-	-	-	-	-
OTHER................	1	100.0	1.0	14.9	5.0	7.1	4.2	2.0	14.0	3.5	48.4
UNKNOWN..............	-	100.0	-	-	-	19.0	-	-	81.0	-	-
SOUTH ATLANTIC..........	380	100.0	8.4	12.5	8.0	2.5	33.1	6.5	14.6	.8	13.5
RAIL.................	71	100.0	6.9	1.0	7.3	1.7	38.5	.5	10.7	-	33.5
MOTOR CARRIER.........	207	100.0	12.9	19.3	10.9	3.7	30.0	4.7	15.8	.4	2.3
PRIVATE TRUCK.........	83	100.0	.6	7.6	3.1	.8	42.1	17.1	9.0	2.6	17.2
AIR..................	-	100.0	6.5	-	5.7	-	-	1.3	-	-	86.5
WATER................	8	100.0	.4	.8	-	-	.9	-	-	-	97.9
OTHER................	9	100.0	.2	1.9	1.7	.7	8.6	5.4	79.7	.4	1.4
UNKNOWN..............	-	100.0	-	60.8	-	-	39.2	-	-	-	-
WEST SOUTH CENTRAL......	459	100.0	1.8	20.7	10.7	7.9	15.9	7.6	22.2	.3	12.9
RAIL.................	274	100.0	2.4	26.4	16.1	4.0	24.3	2.8	3.4	.1	20.6
MOTOR CARRIER.........	98	100.0	1.3	8.5	3.8	1.1	6.1	2.2	74.1	1.1	1.8
PRIVATE TRUCK.........	85	100.0	.5	15.9	1.1	28.0	.8	29.3	23.2	.1	1.1
AIR..................	-	100.0	-	.6	98.3	-	-	-	.1	-	1.1
WATER................	-	100.0	-	-	-	-	-	-	-	-	-
OTHER................	-	100.0	68.9	-	-	21.7	-	-	9.4	-	-
UNKNOWN..............	-	100.0	-	99.9	-	-	-	-	.1	-	-
PACIFIC.................	504	100.0	1.1	2.0	2.8	5.8	2.0	.4	2.0	23.1	60.7
RAIL.................	200	100.0	-	-	1.1	-	-	-	-	37.1	61.9
MOTOR CARRIER.........	269	100.0	2.1	3.5	4.3	10.8	3.6	.8	3.7	15.0	56.2
PRIVATE TRUCK.........	5	100.0	-	-	-	-	-	-	-	38.3	61.7
AIR..................	1	100.0	-	42.0	9.8	3.5	36.4	-	.7	.7	6.8
WATER................	27	100.0	-	-	-	-	.3	-	-	-	99.7
OTHER................	-	100.0	-	1.7	3.6	3.8	.4	2.5	3.0	15.7	69.2
UNKNOWN..............	-	100.0	-	-	-	-	-	-	-	-	100.0

See footnotes at end of table 4.

TABLE 3. **TCC GROUP 284—Percent Distribution of Geographic Division of Destination and Means of Transport, by Geographic Division of Origin: 1972**

Geographic division of destination and means of transport	Number	Percent distribution by division of origin[1]									
	(thousands of tons)	U.S. total	New England	Middle Atlantic	East North Central	West North Central	South Atlantic	East South Central	West South Central	Mountain	Pacific
TONS OF SHIPMENTS											
U.S. TOTAL	11 731	100.0	5.8	20.4	33.8	12.0	9.7	(D)	7.2	(D)	10.1
RAIL	2 474	100.0	5.0	15.4	36.7	13.1	4.5	(D)	11.2	(D)	13.9
MOTOR CARRIER	7 370	100.0	6.4	20.1	35.5	13.8	9.7	(D)	4.1	(D)	9.8
PRIVATE TRUCK	1 646	100.0	1.8	25.6	26.0	3.5	17.8	(D)	15.7	(D)	5.6
AIR	6	100.0	4.8	17.3	58.8	.6	.2	(D)	6.5	(D)	11.8
WATER	143	100.0	26.6	56.5	.5	-	2.8	(D)	-	(D)	13.7
OTHER	75	100.0	16.0	36.0	1.6	3.6	26.6	(D)	-	(D)	15.6
UNKNOWN	14	100.0	20.4	11.7	62.0	.9	.2	(D)	4.5	(D)	.2
NEW ENGLAND	602	100.0	18.9	47.9	16.1	.5	15.3	(D)	.9	(D)	.4
RAIL	107	100.0	-	44.5	37.1	-	14.3	(D)	4.0	(D)	-
MOTOR CARRIER	442	100.0	24.6	45.5	11.8	.4	17.0	(D)	.2	(D)	.5
PRIVATE TRUCK	46	100.0	5.6	81.9	6.8	2.4	2.7	(D)	.6	(D)	-
AIR	1	100.0	-	.7	98.4	.7	.2	(D)	-	(D)	-
WATER	-	100.0	86.6	-	-	-	13.4	(D)	-	(D)	-
OTHER	3	100.0	69.8	28.1	.2	.6	1.2	(D)	.2	(D)	-
UNKNOWN	-	100.0	-	-	-	-	-	(D)	-	(D)	-
MIDDLE ATLANTIC	1 766	100.0	8.9	52.1	17.4	1.2	15.9	(D)	4.1	(D)	.2
RAIL	161	100.0	-	58.8	6.0		1.1	(D)	34.1	(D)	-
MOTOR CARRIER	1 249	100.0	11.0	50.1	16.1	.5	21.2	(D)	.5	(D)	.3
PRIVATE TRUCK	343	100.0	5.8	83.5	2.9	1.1	3.6	(D)	3.0	(D)	-
AIR	-	100.0	3.9	9.4	50.2	.1	-	(D)	.2	(D)	36.2
WATER	4	100.0	6.6	78.3	13.5	-	1.6	(D)	-	(D)	.1
OTHER	5	100.0	4.6	71.8	8.7	5.6	9.0	(D)	-	(D)	.1
UNKNOWN	-	100.0	1.3	2.4	.6	-	2.2	(D)	93.5	(D)	-
EAST NORTH CENTRAL	2 950	100.0	4.0	14.6	66.1	11.3	2.0	(D)	1.6	(D)	.3
RAIL	528	100.0	2.4	54.8	26.4	6.2	2.1	(D)	7.9	(D)	.2
MOTOR CARRIER	2 038	100.0	4.7	6.6	72.0	14.0	2.0	(D)	.2	(D)	.3
PRIVATE TRUCK	365	100.0	-	.5	93.1	4.3	1.8	(D)	.3	(D)	-
AIR	-	100.0	.4	9.6	11.2	-	.3	(D)	64.1	(D)	14.3
WATER	-	100.0	-	-	-	-	-	(D)	-	(D)	-
OTHER	14	100.0	62.4	30.4	1.9	2.0	2.6	(D)	-	(D)	.1
UNKNOWN	3	100.0	.6	1.5	97.8	-	-	(D)	-	(D)	-
WEST NORTH CENTRAL	952	100.0	.4	3.3	35.9	48.8	1.1	(D)	8.1	(D)	2.1
RAIL	117	100.0	-	2.1	47.2	35.1	2.0	(D)	13.5	(D)	-
MOTOR CARRIER	725	100.0	.5	3.7	36.7	54.7	1.1	(D)	.4	(D)	2.7
PRIVATE TRUCK	106	100.0	-	.3	19.2	24.4	.4	(D)	55.2	(D)	-
AIR	-	100.0	10.6	12.9	67.0	1.4	-	(D)	-	(D)	8.1
WATER	-	100.0	-	-	-	-	-	(D)	-	(D)	-
OTHER	2	100.0	.1	64.1	.2	30.7	2.6	(D)	.2	(D)	.6
UNKNOWN	-	100.0	-	-	-	100.0	-	(D)	-	(D)	-
SOUTH ATLANTIC	1 791	100.0	4.3	29.5	26.5	2.6	28.8	(D)	4.5	(D)	.3
RAIL	382	100.0	3.2	4.7	50.7	5.8	15.1	(D)	18.8	(D)	-
MOTOR CARRIER	979	100.0	6.0	38.0	26.5	2.5	24.1	(D)	.8	(D)	.4
PRIVATE TRUCK	380	100.0	1.7	24.5	5.6	.1	57.7	(D)	.2	(D)	-
AIR	1	100.0	4.4	17.3	50.8	-	-	(D)	-	(D)	27.6
WATER	41	100.0	-	98.9	-	-	1.0	(D)	-	(D)	.1
OTHER	7	100.0	3.8	57.0	.3	1.1	36.6	(D)	-	(D)	-
UNKNOWN	-	100.0	-	30.7	58.1	-	7.3	(D)	-	(D)	-
EAST SOUTH CENTRAL	499	100.0	.7	6.4	42.4	10.9	16.8	(D)	15.4	(D)	.3
RAIL	46	100.0	3.5	2.6	56.7	8.7	2.2	(D)	26.2	(D)	-
MOTOR CARRIER	304	100.0	.6	8.9	55.4	15.4	14.1	(D)	1.0	(D)	.4
PRIVATE TRUCK	138	100.0	-	.2	9.3	2.4	26.6	(D)	44.9	(D)	-
AIR	-	100.0	9.5	14.8	75.5	-	.2	(D)	-	(D)	-
WATER	-	100.0	-	-	-	-	-	(D)	-	(D)	-
OTHER	6	100.0	.1	41.4	.3	1.2	54.8	(D)	-	(D)	.1
UNKNOWN	4	100.0	-	13.6	86.4	-	-	(D)	-	(D)	-
WEST SOUTH CENTRAL	1 304	100.0	7.1	5.1	21.9	25.3	5.5	(D)	33.7	(D)	.7
RAIL	405	100.0	10.8	2.9	39.6	34.6	2.6	(D)	9.5	(D)	-
MOTOR CARRIER	702	100.0	4.6	5.0	16.4	26.7	5.7	(D)	39.5	(D)	1.3
PRIVATE TRUCK	146	100.0	-	1.1	5.8	1.0	5.6	(D)	84.6	(D)	-
AIR	-	100.0	47.6	45.8	3.4	-	-	(D)	.3	(D)	2.9
WATER	30	100.0	46.1	53.9	-	-	-	(D)	-	(D)	-
OTHER	15	100.0	.4	11.2	.1	2.7	85.1	(D)	-	(D)	.1
UNKNOWN	4	100.0	64.4	.3	34.1	1.1	-	(D)	.1	(D)	-
MOUNTAIN	409	100.0	3.5	2.7	16.6	23.9	.5	(D)	.5	(D)	51.9
RAIL	218	100.0	.4	1.5	18.6	16.5	-	(D)	.2	(D)	62.8
MOTOR CARRIER	176	100.0	7.6	4.0	13.0	33.1	.3	(D)	.9	(D)	40.7
PRIVATE TRUCK	13	100.0	.2	1.1	31.7	23.0	10.0	(D)	.9	(D)	26.3
AIR	-	100.0	20.0	7.4	19.7	29.1	-	(D)	-	(D)	23.7
WATER	-	100.0	-	-	-	-	-	(D)	-	(D)	-
OTHER	-	100.0	-	50.0	1.3	13.5	3.8	(D)	-	(D)	31.3
UNKNOWN	-	100.0	-	100.0	-	-	-	(D)	-	(D)	-
PACIFIC	1 455	100.0	6.7	5.8	15.6	3.6	1.6	(D)	2.7	(D)	63.8
RAIL	507	100.0	10.2	1.4	31.0	7.3	2.1	(D)	7.5	(D)	40.4
MOTOR CARRIER	752	100.0	2.9	6.5	8.1	1.6	.3	(D)	.2	(D)	80.1
PRIVATE TRUCK	106	100.0	-	-	7.4	2.2	6.1	(D)	.7	(D)	83.6
AIR	-	100.0	.8	56.1	37.8	-	.8	(D)	.4	(D)	4.1
WATER	67	100.0	35.2	30.4	-	-	5.1	(D)	-	(D)	29.2
OTHER	20	100.0	1.5	36.4	1.9	2.9	.3	(D)	-	(D)	56.9
UNKNOWN	-	100.0	-	88.4	4.8	-	-	(D)	-	(D)	6.7

See footnotes at end of table 4.

TABLE 3. **TCC GROUP 284—Percent Distribution of Geographic Division of Destination and Means of Transport, by Geographic Division of Origin: 1972**—Continued

Geographic division of destination and means of transport	Number	Percent distribution by division of origin [1]									
		U.S. total	New England	Middle Atlantic	East North Central	West North Central	South Atlantic	East South Central	West South Central	Mountain	Pacific
TON-MILES OF SHIPMENTS	(millions of ton-miles)										
U.S. TOTAL	5 368	100.0	11.2	18.9	32.9	11.3	7.1	(D)	8.6	(D)	9.4
RAIL	1 995	100.0	11.4	13.7	36.9	10.5	3.6	(D)	13.8	(D)	10.0
MOTOR CARRIER	2 727	100.0	10.0	20.1	34.3	13.8	7.6	(D)	3.6	(D)	9.9
PRIVATE TRUCK	349	100.0	1.8	14.1	25.0	5.7	23.9	(D)	24.6	(D)	1.6
AIR	7	100.0	5.2	24.1	41.6	.5	.3	(D)	6.0	(D)	22.2
WATER	224	100.0	35.6	48.2	.2	-	3.7	(D)	-	(D)	12.4
OTHER	52	100.0	16.2	58.4	2.1	3.6	18.4	(D)	-	(D)	1.0
UNKNOWN	11	100.0	33.7	17.7	41.8	.4	.2	(D)	6.2	(D)	-
NEW ENGLAND	190	100.0	4.2	30.7	39.2	1.5	16.9	(D)	4.3	(D)	3.0
RAIL	52	100.0	-	19.2	58.7	-	9.5	(D)	12.6	(D)	-
MOTOR CARRIER	124	100.0	6.2	32.8	32.3	1.4	21.5	(D)	1.0	(D)	4.6
PRIVATE TRUCK	11	100.0	.4	63.4	18.9	9.8	3.9	(D)	3.6	(D)	-
AIR	1	100.0	-	.1	98.9	.9	.1	(D)	-	(D)	-
WATER	-	100.0	24.3	-	-	-	75.7	(D)	-	(D)	-
OTHER	-	100.0	59.9	28.3	.7	4.4	4.6	(D)	2.0	(D)	-
UNKNOWN	-	100.0	-	-	-	-	-	(D)	-	(D)	-
MIDDLE ATLANTIC	466	100.0	7.0	18.3	37.5	3.7	10.2	(D)	20.4	(D)	2.2
RAIL	138	100.0	-	-	41.2	6.1	.5	(D)	52.2	(D)	-
MOTOR CARRIER	277	100.0	10.2	25.4	40.3	2.0	14.5	(D)	3.0	(D)	3.4
PRIVATE TRUCK	45	100.0	8.8	30.6	10.3	6.5	13.8	(D)	29.9	(D)	-
AIR	-	100.0	.7	.2	25.2	.1	-	(D)	.3	(D)	73.5
WATER	-	100.0	7.3	20.5	61.9	-	10.4	(D)	-	(D)	.8
OTHER	1	100.0	4.2	29.4	27.5	23.0	14.8	(D)	-	(D)	-
UNKNOWN	-	100.0	.1	.1	.4	-	2.0	(D)	97.4	(D)	-
EAST NORTH CENTRAL	904	100.0	9.1	31.2	36.9	12.3	3.4	(D)	5.5	(D)	1.5
RAIL	321	100.0	3.4	64.7	12.0	3.8	1.6	(D)	13.8	(D)	.7
MOTOR CARRIER	530	100.0	12.0	13.3	49.5	17.7	4.3	(D)	.7	(D)	2.2
PRIVATE TRUCK	41	100.0	.1	2.2	77.3	11.8	6.3	(D)	2.3	(D)	-
AIR	-	100.0	.3	6.3	2.7	-	.2	(D)	66.1	(D)	24.4
WATER	-	100.0	-	-	-	-	-	(D)	-	(D)	-
OTHER	10	100.0	69.3	27.1	.4	.9	1.7	(D)	-	(D)	.2
UNKNOWN	-	100.0	2.0	4.0	94.0	-	-	(D)	-	(D)	-
WEST NORTH CENTRAL	359	100.0	1.0	8.6	36.4	32.8	2.7	(D)	10.1	(D)	8.1
RAIL	59	100.0	-	3.8	46.3	29.4	2.1	(D)	18.4	(D)	-
MOTOR CARRIER	262	100.0	1.4	10.1	36.2	37.5	2.9	(D)	.4	(D)	11.1
PRIVATE TRUCK	34	100.0	-	.7	22.3	5.6	2.0	(D)	69.1	(D)	-
AIR	-	100.0	16.3	16.4	49.6	1.1	-	(D)	-	(D)	16.6
WATER	-	100.0	-	-	-	-	-	(D)	-	(D)	-
OTHER	1	100.0	.2	88.0	.2	6.7	3.2	(D)	.1	(D)	1.0
UNKNOWN	-	100.0	-	-	-	100.0	-	(D)	-	(D)	-
SOUTH ATLANTIC	790	100.0	6.7	27.6	33.7	3.7	15.9	(D)	9.3	(D)	1.3
RAIL	244	100.0	4.8	6.5	43.2	6.2	11.3	(D)	27.2	(D)	-
MOTOR CARRIER	421	100.0	9.2	32.9	35.0	3.1	14.8	(D)	1.4	(D)	2.3
PRIVATE TRUCK	83	100.0	2.7	28.9	15.5	.5	42.2	(D)	.9	(D)	-
AIR	-	100.0	4.6	10.2	23.2	-	-	(D)	-	(D)	62.0
WATER	36	100.0	-	99.5	-	-	.2	(D)	-	(D)	.3
OTHER	3	100.0	4.7	70.2	.7	2.1	21.4	(D)	-	(D)	.1
UNKNOWN	-	100.0	-	27.4	65.3	-	6.3	(D)	-	(D)	-
EAST SOUTH CENTRAL	174	100.0	1.8	13.4	37.7	8.5	14.3	(D)	20.1	(D)	1.2
RAIL	20	100.0	6.6	4.8	44.1	4.5	1.7	(D)	38.2	(D)	-
MOTOR CARRIER	102	100.0	1.7	19.5	49.7	12.8	9.5	(D)	2.1	(D)	2.0
PRIVATE TRUCK	46	100.0	-	.4	6.8	1.7	30.9	(D)	54.7	(D)	-
AIR	-	100.0	13.6	14.8	71.4	-	.2	(D)	-	(D)	-
WATER	-	100.0	-	-	-	-	-	(D)	-	(D)	.5
OTHER	2	100.0	.2	75.3	.5	1.5	20.6	(D)	-	(D)	-
UNKNOWN	3	100.0	-	10.6	89.4	-	-	(D)	-	(D)	-
WEST SOUTH CENTRAL	797	100.0	17.5	10.8	28.7	21.5	7.0	(D)	12.8	(D)	1.2
RAIL	303	100.0	22.3	4.9	42.6	24.7	2.5	(D)	3.1	(D)	-
MOTOR CARRIER	398	100.0	12.1	11.6	22.9	23.8	8.2	(D)	18.2	(D)	2.5
PRIVATE TRUCK	38	100.0	-	5.5	17.3	4.0	19.2	(D)	51.2	(D)	2.8
AIR	-	100.0	52.5	42.5	2.0	-	-	(D)	.1	(D)	-
WATER	40	100.0	48.8	51.2	-	-	-	(D)	-	(D)	.2
OTHER	10	100.0	1.1	21.4	.1	2.6	74.5	(D)	-	(D)	-
UNKNOWN	5	100.0	73.5	.3	25.4	-	.8	(D)	-	(D)	-
MOUNTAIN	312	100.0	9.3	6.6	24.1	21.1	1.0	(D)	.5	(D)	37.3
RAIL	153	100.0	1.1	3.3	30.2	16.9	-	(D)	.1	(D)	48.4
MOTOR CARRIER	146	100.0	18.6	9.5	17.1	25.7	.6	(D)	.8	(D)	27.5
PRIVATE TRUCK	10	100.0	.4	2.1	37.3	18.7	20.1	(D)	.8	(D)	19.5
AIR	-	100.0	33.9	9.8	16.4	24.9	-	(D)	-	(D)	15.0
WATER	-	100.0	-	-	-	-	-	(D)	-	(D)	-
OTHER	-	100.0	-	73.1	1.4	9.0	4.9	(D)	-	(D)	11.6
UNKNOWN	-	100.0	-	100.0	-	-	-	(D)	-	(D)	-
PACIFIC	1 373	100.0	18.2	15.3	30.5	5.6	3.7	(D)	4.3	(D)	22.3
RAIL	701	100.0	19.1	2.4	41.6	7.7	3.4	(D)	8.1	(D)	17.7
MOTOR CARRIER	464	100.0	11.7	26.1	23.9	3.8	1.0	(D)	.4	(D)	32.5
PRIVATE TRUCK	36	100.0	-	-	38.0	10.9	39.1	(D)	2.5	(D)	9.4
AIR	2	100.0	.9	61.8	31.3	-	.8	(D)	.2	(D)	5.0
WATER	146	100.0	41.0	34.6	-	-	5.6	(D)	-	(D)	18.8
OTHER	21	100.0	3.9	86.2	3.1	4.3	.6	(D)	-	(D)	1.8
UNKNOWN	-	100.0	-	95.4	4.1	-	-	(D)	-	(D)	.4

See footnotes at end of table 4.

TABLE 4. **TCC GROUP 284**—Percent Distribution of Distance Shipped and Weight of Shipment, by Means of Transport: 1972

Distance shipped and weight of shipment [2] [3]	Number	Percent distribution by means of transport							
		All means of transport	Rail	Motor carrier	Private truck	Air	Water	Other	Unknown
TONS OF SHIPMENTS	(thousands of tons)								
U.S. TOTAL.........	9 860	100.0	20.2	62.3	15.4	-	1.1	.8	.1
UNDER 100 MILES........	1 780	100.0	.6	59.4	38.5	-	.6	.8	-
UNDER 1000 POUNDS.....	181	100.0	-	62.4	35.2	-	.1	2.2	-
1000 TO 9999 POUNDS...	351	100.0	-	53.1	46.4	-	.2	.1	.1
10000 TO 29999 POUNDS.	375	100.0	-	46.6	51.4	-	.3	1.7	-
30000 TO 59999 POUNDS.	811	100.0	.3	69.4	28.8	-	1.0	.4	-
60000 TO 89999 POUNDS.	25	100.0	6.6	78.0	15.4	-	-	-	-
90000 POUNDS AND OVER.	34	100.0	21.7	-	78.3	-	-	-	-
100 TO 199 MILES........	1 732	100.0	1.9	77.2	20.4	-	-	.5	.1
UNDER 1000 POUNDS.....	101	100.0	-	89.5	7.7	-	.3	2.4	.1
1000 TO 9999 POUNDS...	247	100.0	.2	76.3	22.8	-	.2	.2	.3
10000 TO 29999 POUNDS.	362	100.0	1.6	69.2	27.8	-	-	1.4	-
30000 TO 59999 POUNDS.	913	100.0	1.1	78.2	20.6	-	-	-	.1
60000 TO 89999 POUNDS.	49	100.0	10.4	89.6	-	-	-	-	-
90000 POUNDS AND OVER.	58	100.0	18.7	81.3	-	-	-	-	-
200 TO 299 MILES........	1 476	100.0	11.6	78.1	10.0	-	-	.2	-
UNDER 1000 POUNDS.....	74	100.0	.3	95.6	1.7	-	-	2.3	-
1000 TO 9999 POUNDS...	231	100.0	.4	90.1	8.7	-	-	.8	-
10000 TO 29999 POUNDS.	313	100.0	3.1	85.2	11.4	-	-	-	.2
30000 TO 59999 POUNDS.	754	100.0	9.5	78.5	12.0	-	-	-	-
60000 TO 89999 POUNDS.	47	100.0	72.3	27.7	-	-	-	-	-
90000 POUNDS AND OVER.	54	100.0	100.0	-	-	-	-	-	-
300 TO 499 MILES........	1 964	100.0	21.7	67.0	10.6	-	-	.5	-
UNDER 1000 POUNDS.....	93	100.0	1.4	93.1	1.6	.2	-	3.7	.1
1000 TO 9999 POUNDS...	219	100.0	2.5	93.8	3.0	.1	.2	.3	-
10000 TO 29999 POUNDS.	319	100.0	2.5	83.2	14.3	-	-	-	-
30000 TO 59999 POUNDS.	957	100.0	11.0	72.1	16.2	-	-	.7	-
60000 TO 89999 POUNDS.	223	100.0	78.1	21.9	-	-	-	-	-
90000 POUNDS AND OVER.	151	100.0	87.6	12.4	-	-	-	-	-
500 TO 999 MILES........	2 007	100.0	45.5	47.4	4.1	.1	1.3	1.2	.3
UNDER 1000 POUNDS.....	97	100.0	2.5	90.6	1.0	.2	.1	5.4	.2
1000 TO 9999 POUNDS...	236	100.0	4.1	89.1	4.3	.1	-	2.1	.3
10000 TO 29999 POUNDS.	266	100.0	6.5	81.5	9.4	-	.7	.8	1.1
30000 TO 59999 POUNDS.	765	100.0	35.5	53.1	6.1	.2	3.1	1.7	.3
60000 TO 89999 POUNDS.	412	100.0	92.9	7.1	-	-	-	-	-
90000 POUNDS AND OVER.	229	100.0	100.0	-	-	-	-	-	-
1000 TO 1499 MILES......	339	100.0	42.4	38.2	8.8	.1	8.4	1.1	1.0
UNDER 1000 POUNDS.....	27	100.0	1.4	83.4	4.2	1.5	-	9.3	.2
1000 TO 9999 POUNDS...	64	100.0	5.6	74.8	17.6	.1	-	1.0	1.0
10000 TO 29999 POUNDS.	26	100.0	1.6	82.7	13.8	-	-	1.9	-
30000 TO 59999 POUNDS.	80	100.0	17.0	43.9	17.0	-	22.1	-	-
60000 TO 89999 POUNDS.	28	100.0	95.0	5.0	-	-	-	-	-
90000 POUNDS AND OVER.	112	100.0	88.1	-	-	-	9.5	-	2.4
1500 MILES OR OVER......	558	100.0	52.6	35.5	2.5	.2	7.6	1.6	-
UNDER 1000 POUNDS.....	29	100.0	3.7	76.8	1.8	1.1	-	16.5	.1
1000 TO 9999 POUNDS...	83	100.0	4.0	84.2	2.9	1.2	2.7	4.8	.2
10000 TO 29999 POUNDS.	32	100.0	23.5	66.7	9.8	-	-	-	-
30000 TO 59999 POUNDS.	167	100.0	43.1	48.7	4.7	-	3.5	-	-
60000 TO 89999 POUNDS.	154	100.0	77.1	.8	-	-	22.1	-	-
90000 POUNDS AND OVER.	90	100.0	100.0	-	-	-	-	-	-
TON-MILES OF SHIPMENTS	(millions of ton-miles)								
U.S. TOTAL.........	4 444	100.0	36.4	51.2	7.2	.1	3.7	1.2	.2
UNDER 100 MILES........	88	100.0	.7	64.3	34.3	-	.2	.4	-
UNDER 1000 POUNDS.....	7	100.0	-	69.7	27.7	-	.1	2.5	-
1000 TO 9999 POUNDS...	15	100.0	-	55.3	44.4	-	.1	-	.1
10000 TO 29999 POUNDS.	17	100.0	-	53.8	45.2	-	.2	.8	-
30000 TO 59999 POUNDS.	44	100.0	.4	73.0	26.1	-	.3	.1	-
60000 TO 89999 POUNDS.	1	100.0	8.4	89.9	1.7	-	-	-	-
90000 POUNDS AND OVER.	2	100.0	13.7	-	86.3	-	-	-	-
100 TO 199 MILES........	261	100.0	1.8	76.5	21.1	-	-	.4	.1
UNDER 1000 POUNDS.....	15	100.0	-	90.6	6.6	-	.3	2.3	.1
1000 TO 9999 POUNDS...	37	100.0	.1	76.6	22.7	-	.2	.2	.2
10000 TO 29999 POUNDS.	56	100.0	1.3	68.2	29.2	-	-	1.2	-
30000 TO 59999 POUNDS.	137	100.0	1.1	77.6	21.2	-	-	-	.1
60000 TO 89999 POUNDS.	6	100.0	12.2	87.8	-	-	-	-	-
90000 POUNDS AND OVER.	7	100.0	20.5	79.5	-	-	-	-	-

See footnotes at end of table 4.

TABLE 4. **TCC GROUP 284—Percent Distribution of Distance Shipped and Weight of Shipment, by Means of Transport: 1972**—Continued

Distance shipped and weight of shipment [2] [3]	Number	Percent distribution by means of transport							
		All means of transport	Rail	Motor carrier	Private truck	Air	Water	Other	Unknown
TON-MILES OF SHIPMENTS	(millions of ton-miles)								
200 TO 299 MILES.........	360	100.0	11.3	78.8	9.6	-	-	.3	-
UNDER 1000 POUNDS.....	18	100.0	.3	95.6	1.7	-	-	2.3	-
1000 TO 9999 POUNDS...	57	100.0	.4	90.5	8.2	-	-	.9	-
10000 TO 29999 POUNDS.	77	100.0	3.1	85.2	11.5	-	-	-	.2
30000 TO 59999 POUNDS.	183	100.0	9.8	79.0	11.2	-	-	-	-
60000 TO 89999 POUNDS.	10	100.0	73.7	26.3	-	-	-	-	-
90000 POUNDS AND OVER.	11	100.0	100.0	-	-	-	-	-	-
300 TO 499 MILES........	740	100.0	21.3	67.2	10.8	-	-	.6	-
UNDER 1000 POUNDS.....	36	100.0	1.5	92.9	1.5	.2	-	3.9	.1
1000 TO 9999 POUNDS...	84	100.0	2.6	93.7	3.0	.1	.2	.3	-
10000 TO 29999 POUNDS.	116	100.0	2.7	84.2	13.1	-	-	-	-
30000 TO 59999 POUNDS.	366	100.0	11.4	71.1	16.8	-	-	.8	-
60000 TO 89999 POUNDS.	81	100.0	77.3	22.7	-	-	-	-	-
90000 POUNDS AND OVER.	53	100.0	87.4	12.6	-	-	-	-	-
500 TO 999 MILES........	1 431	100.0	45.5	47.4	3.9	.1	1.5	1.3	.3
UNDER 1000 POUNDS.....	69	100.0	2.4	90.6	1.0	.2	.1	5.5	.1
1000 TO 9999 POUNDS...	167	100.0	4.3	89.2	4.0	.1	-	2.2	.2
10000 TO 29999 POUNDS.	181	100.0	6.2	82.0	8.9	-	.9	.7	1.3
30000 TO 59999 POUNDS.	544	100.0	33.7	54.4	5.8	.3	3.6	1.9	.4
60000 TO 89999 POUNDS.	302	100.0	93.2	6.8	-	-	-	-	-
90000 POUNDS AND OVER.	165	100.0	100.0	-	-	-	-	-	-
1000 TO 1499 MILES......	431	100.0	44.8	36.6	8.3	.1	8.1	1.0	1.0
UNDER 1000 POUNDS.....	32	100.0	1.4	83.2	4.2	1.6	-	9.2	.3
1000 TO 9999 POUNDS...	74	100.0	5.5	75.2	17.1	.1	-	1.1	1.0
10000 TO 29999 POUNDS.	30	100.0	1.4	83.2	13.5	-	-	1.8	-
30000 TO 59999 POUNDS.	99	100.0	15.3	47.3	17.4	-	20.1	-	-
60000 TO 89999 POUNDS.	38	100.0	94.9	5.1	-	-	-	-	-
90000 POUNDS AND OVER.	155	100.0	88.0	-	-	-	9.6	-	2.4
1500 MILES OR OVER......	1 130	100.0	50.5	35.6	2.4	.3	9.4	1.9	-
UNDER 1000 POUNDS.....	60	100.0	4.2	74.2	1.5	1.2	-	18.8	.1
1000 TO 9999 POUNDS...	180	100.0	4.6	82.7	2.4	1.3	3.4	5.4	.1
10000 TO 29999 POUNDS.	68	100.0	19.4	72.6	8.0	-	-	-	-
30000 TO 59999 POUNDS.	319	100.0	42.0	48.4	5.0	-	4.5	-	-
60000 TO 89999 POUNDS.	320	100.0	72.2	1.0	-	-	26.8	-	-
90000 POUNDS AND OVER.	180	100.0	100.0	-	-	-	-	-	-

Note: Detail may not add to total due to rounding. The introductory table shows the estimates of sampling variability for tons; sampling variability for ton-miles has not been estimated. See the map in the Introduction for the States comprising the geographic divisions of the United States.
Shipments excluded from the survey are those moving by pipeline (primarily petroleum products from refineries), parcel post shipments, and commodities moved by own power (motorized vehicles, aircraft, etc.) or towed (prefabricated buildings, etc.). Local shipments (commodities shipped less than 25 miles from the plant) and shipments within the same city are also excluded. Shipments to Alaska and Hawaii from the 48 conterminous States and the District of Columbia are included; however, no data were obtained for shipments originating in Alaska and Hawaii.

- Represents zero or rounds to zero.   (D) Withheld to avoid disclosing figures for individual companies.

[1] Production of this commodity is concentrated in the geographic divisions shown; figures and distributions for geographic divisions not shown are included in the total.
[2] Distances of shipments to foreign destinations are calculated only to the U.S. port of exit.
[3] Includes only shipments represented by bills of lading and invoices. Summary records which did not show individual weights of shipments are not included.

TCC 285. Paints, Enamels, Lacquers, Shellacs, and Allied Products

Comparisons of Tons and Ton-Miles of Shipments for
Geographic Divisions of Origin and for Sampling Variability: 1972 and 1967

Geographic division of origin	Estimates				Relative sampling variability in tons (percent)	
	1972		1967		1972	1967
	Tons (thousands)	Ton-miles (millions)	Tons (thousands)	Ton-miles (millions)	1972	1967
U.S. total	6,382	2,452	5,474	1,869	10.9	10.4
New England	(D)	(D)	145	32	(*)	(*)
Middle Atlantic	1,377	440	916	259	23.6	(*)
East North Central	1,488	502	1,732	570	19.3	(*)
West North Central	360	172	371	158	26.0	(*)
South Atlantic	1,623	554	615	207	47.8	(*)
East South Central	162	52	543	169	36.7	(*)
West South Central	1,065	570	778	340	27.0	(*)
Mountain	(D)	(D)	10	4	(*)	(*)
Pacific	220	122	364	130	22.3	(*)

(D) Withheld to avoid disclosing figures for individual companies.   (*) Data not published.

TABLE 1. TCC GROUP 285—Percent Distribution of Geographic Division of Origin and Distance Shipped, by Means of Transport: 1972

Geographic division of origin[1] and distance shipped[2]	Number	Percent distribution by means of transport							
		All means of transport	Rail	Motor carrier	Private truck	Air	Water	Other	Unknown
TONS OF SHIPMENTS	(thousands of tons)								
U.S. TOTAL...........	6 382	100.0	8.9	66.6	18.7	-	5.2	.4	.2
MIDDLE ATLANTIC.........	1 377	100.0	1.6	73.9	22.7	-	.5	1.0	.2
UNDER 100 MILES.......	509	100.0	.7	67.3	32.0	-	-	-	-
100 TO 199 MILES......	287	100.0	.4	65.5	29.8	-	-	3.4	.9
200 TO 299 MILES......	199	100.0	1.0	86.6	12.2	-	-	.1	.1
300 TO 499 MILES......	120	100.0	4.9	87.3	6.6	-	-	1.2	-
500 TO 999 MILES......	151	100.0	1.3	78.0	17.0	-	2.5	1.2	-
1000 TO 1499 MILES....	73	100.0	4.2	92.0	3.8	-	-	-	-
1500 MILES OR OVER....	36	100.0	11.8	65.9	11.8	-	10.3	.1	-
EAST NORTH CENTRAL......	1 488	100.0	17.0	68.2	14.1	-	-	.4	.3
UNDER 100 MILES.......	432	100.0	8.7	63.2	27.0	-	-	.5	.6
100 TO 199 MILES......	225	100.0	.9	78.5	19.8	-	-	.7	.1
200 TO 299 MILES......	205	100.0	7.1	88.4	4.5	-	-	-	-
300 TO 499 MILES......	236	100.0	26.1	70.4	3.4	.1	-	-	-
500 TO 999 MILES......	330	100.0	39.4	51.8	7.9	.2	-	.6	.2
1000 TO 1499 MILES....	21	100.0	21.6	72.8	5.6	-	-	-	-
1500 MILES OR OVER....	37	100.0	8.3	82.1	9.6	-	-	-	-
WEST NORTH CENTRAL......	360	100.0	11.9	61.9	25.2	.1	-	.2	.7
UNDER 100 MILES.......	19	100.0	-	61.4	36.6	-	-	2.0	-
100 TO 199 MILES......	65	100.0	4.2	61.7	34.0	-	-	-	-
200 TO 299 MILES......	54	100.0	7.6	46.9	44.9	-	-	.6	-
300 TO 499 MILES......	108	100.0	14.9	73.0	12.1	-	-	-	-
500 TO 999 MILES......	68	100.0	25.9	53.3	17.5	-	-	-	3.3
1000 TO 1499 MILES....	36	100.0	3.3	63.5	32.6	-	-	-	.6
1500 MILES OR OVER....	7	100.0	13.5	83.6	-	3.0	-	-	-
SOUTH ATLANTIC..........	1 623	100.0	1.2	81.0	17.1	-	.4	.3	-
UNDER 100 MILES.......	207	100.0	-	65.8	31.8	-	-	2.3	-
100 TO 199 MILES......	509	100.0	-	85.8	12.9	-	1.2	.1	-
200 TO 299 MILES......	159	100.0	1.8	68.0	30.1	-	-	.1	-
300 TO 499 MILES......	408	100.0	2.0	86.8	11.1	-	-	-	-
500 TO 999 MILES......	324	100.0	2.5	81.3	16.1	-	-	-	-
1000 TO 1499 MILES....	3	100.0	2.3	97.7	-	-	-	-	-
1500 MILES OR OVER....	10	100.0	.1	99.9	-	-	-	-	-
EAST SOUTH CENTRAL......	162	100.0	7.1	70.4	22.2	-	-	.2	-
UNDER 100 MILES.......	20	100.0	-	68.7	31.3	-	-	-	-
100 TO 199 MILES......	35	100.0	-	74.8	25.2	-	-	-	-
200 TO 299 MILES......	31	100.0	-	89.8	10.2	-	-	-	-
300 TO 499 MILES......	41	100.0	-	69.5	30.3	-	-	.2	-
500 TO 999 MILES......	33	100.0	34.7	49.8	14.5	-	-	1.0	-
1000 TO 1499 MILES....	-	100.0	-	100.0	-	-	-	-	-
1500 MILES OR OVER....	-	100.0	-	51.3	48.7	-	-	-	-
WEST SOUTH CENTRAL......	1 065	100.0	18.4	32.0	20.1	-	29.4	-	.2
UNDER 100 MILES.......	164	100.0	6.1	8.8	84.1	-	-	-	1.0
100 TO 199 MILES......	81	100.0	.4	74.1	25.5	-	-	-	-
200 TO 299 MILES......	213	100.0	1.3	41.7	.8	-	56.2	-	-
300 TO 499 MILES......	158	100.0	18.0	63.3	18.7	-	-	-	-
500 TO 999 MILES......	347	100.0	20.4	18.1	6.1	-	55.4	-	-
1000 TO 1499 MILES....	93	100.0	89.5	8.0	2.5	-	-	-	-
1500 MILES OR OVER....	6	100.0	-	99.3	-	.7	-	-	-
PACIFIC.................	220	100.0	9.7	63.5	23.3	.2	3.3	.1	-
UNDER 100 MILES.......	89	100.0	-	55.5	44.3	-	.1	.1	-
100 TO 199 MILES......	16	100.0	-	65.5	34.4	-	-	.1	-
200 TO 299 MILES......	18	100.0	50.3	42.7	7.0	-	-	.1	-
300 TO 499 MILES......	22	100.0	-	81.0	18.9	-	-	.1	-
500 TO 999 MILES......	31	100.0	11.9	87.8	.1	-	-	.1	.1
1000 TO 1499 MILES....	9	100.0	-	99.6	-	.3	-	.1	-
1500 MILES OR OVER....	32	100.0	26.4	49.4	.6	1.0	22.6	-	-
TON-MILES OF SHIPMENTS	(millions of ton-miles)								
U.S. TOTAL...........	2 452	100.0	15.8	62.6	11.1	.1	10.1	.2	.1
MIDDLE ATLANTIC.........	440	100.0	3.8	79.3	13.3	-	2.7	.8	.1
UNDER 100 MILES.......	24	100.0	.7	74.3	24.9	-	-	-	-
100 TO 199 MILES......	40	100.0	.5	65.9	29.0	-	-	3.8	.8
200 TO 299 MILES......	49	100.0	.9	86.7	12.3	-	-	.1	.1
300 TO 499 MILES......	47	100.0	5.7	86.1	6.9	-	-	1.2	-
500 TO 999 MILES......	109	100.0	.9	78.4	16.8	-	2.8	1.1	-
1000 TO 1499 MILES....	85	100.0	4.3	92.4	3.3	-	-	-	-
1500 MILES OR OVER....	83	100.0	10.4	66.6	12.0	-	10.8	.1	-
EAST NORTH CENTRAL......	502	100.0	25.0	66.7	7.7	.1	-	.4	.2
UNDER 100 MILES.......	19	100.0	16.5	63.7	18.6	-	-	.7	.5
100 TO 199 MILES......	32	100.0	1.1	78.7	19.5	-	-	.6	.1
200 TO 299 MILES......	50	100.0	7.2	88.3	4.4	-	-	-	-
300 TO 499 MILES......	95	100.0	28.5	68.3	3.1	.1	-	-	-
500 TO 999 MILES......	210	100.0	38.7	52.9	7.2	.2	-	.7	.3
1000 TO 1499 MILES....	23	100.0	19.3	74.3	6.4	-	-	-	-
1500 MILES OR OVER....	70	100.0	7.8	82.6	9.5	-	-	-	-

See footnotes at end of table 4.

TABLE 1. **TCC GROUP 285—Percent Distribution of Geographic Division of Origin and Distance Shipped, by Means of Transport: 1972**—Continued

Geographic division of origin[1] and distance shipped[2]	Number	Percent distribution by means of transport							
		All means of transport	Rail	Motor carrier	Private truck	Air	Water	Other	Unknown
TON-MILES OF SHIPMENTS	(millions of ton-miles)								
WEST NORTH CENTRAL	172	100.0	13.7	63.6	21.1	.2	-	.1	1.2
UNDER 100 MILES	1	100.0	-	78.4	19.9	.2	-	1.6	-
100 TO 199 MILES	9	100.0	4.5	59.3	36.2	-	-	-	-
200 TO 299 MILES	13	100.0	7.8	46.5	45.1	-	-	.5	-
300 TO 499 MILES	41	100.0	16.4	71.7	11.9	-	-	-	-
500 TO 999 MILES	44	100.0	26.7	53.9	15.1	-	-	-	4.3
1000 TO 1499 MILES	49	100.0	3.5	65.5	30.5	-	-	-	.5
1500 MILES OR OVER	12	100.0	13.8	83.4	-	2.9	-	-	-
SOUTH ATLANTIC	554	100.0	2.0	82.5	15.3	-	.2	-	-
UNDER 100 MILES	10	100.0	-	64.9	34.6	-	-	.5	-
100 TO 199 MILES	85	100.0	-	86.3	12.4	-	1.2	.1	-
200 TO 299 MILES	40	100.0	2.0	67.5	30.4	-	-	.1	-
300 TO 499 MILES	165	100.0	2.0	87.2	10.7	-	-	-	-
500 TO 999 MILES	224	100.0	3.0	79.0	18.0	-	-	-	-
1000 TO 1499 MILES	4	100.0	2.1	97.9	-	-	-	-	-
1500 MILES OR OVER	23	100.0	.1	99.9	-	-	-	-	-
EAST SOUTH CENTRAL	52	100.0	12.8	66.2	20.5	-	-	.5	-
UNDER 100 MILES	1	100.0	-	68.4	31.6	-	-	-	-
100 TO 199 MILES	5	100.0	-	76.0	24.0	-	-	-	-
200 TO 299 MILES	7	100.0	-	89.4	10.6	-	-	-	-
300 TO 499 MILES	14	100.0	-	69.2	30.6	-	-	.2	-
500 TO 999 MILES	21	100.0	30.6	53.9	14.3	-	-	1.1	-
1000 TO 1499 MILES	-	100.0	-	100.0	-	-	-	-	-
1500 MILES OR OVER	1	100.0	-	53.0	47.0	-	-	-	-
WEST SOUTH CENTRAL	570	100.0	31.6	23.9	6.6	-	37.8	-	-
UNDER 100 MILES	7	100.0	7.7	9.6	81.8	-	-	-	.9
100 TO 199 MILES	12	100.0	.4	77.5	22.1	-	-	-	-
200 TO 299 MILES	58	100.0	1.4	37.4	.7	-	60.6	-	-
300 TO 499 MILES	59	100.0	16.2	65.5	18.2	-	-	-	-
500 TO 999 MILES	298	100.0	19.7	14.9	5.0	-	60.4	-	-
1000 TO 1499 MILES	122	100.0	89.9	7.8	2.3	-	-	-	-
1500 MILES OR OVER	11	100.0	-	98.4	-	1.6	-	-	-
PACIFIC	122	100.0	18.6	62.8	3.4	.7	14.4	.1	-
UNDER 100 MILES	3	100.0	-	66.7	33.2	-	-	.1	-
100 TO 199 MILES	2	100.0	-	69.3	30.6	-	-	.1	-
200 TO 299 MILES	4	100.0	48.6	44.2	7.0	-	-	.1	-
300 TO 499 MILES	7	100.0	-	80.5	19.5	-	-	.1	-
500 TO 999 MILES	23	100.0	11.2	88.5	.1	-	-	-	-
1000 TO 1499 MILES	11	100.0	-	99.6	-	.3	-	.1	.1
1500 MILES OR OVER	69	100.0	26.1	46.5	.6	1.2	25.5	-	-

See footnotes at end of table 4.

TABLE 2. **TCC GROUP 285—Percent Distribution of Geographic Division of Origin and Means of Transport, by Geographic Division of Destination: 1972**

Geographic division of origin[1] and means of transport	Number	Percent distribution by division of destination									
		U.S. total	New England	Middle Atlantic	East North Central	West North Central	South Atlantic	East South Central	West South Central	Mountain	Pacific
TONS OF SHIPMENTS	(thousands of tons)										
U.S. TOTAL	6 382	100.0	5.1	18.1	21.7	6.9	23.0	6.1	12.3	1.6	5.2
RAIL	566	100.0	.4	14.1	20.7	18.7	16.2	2.3	15.0	1.4	11.3
MOTOR CARRIER	4 249	100.0	5.9	17.7	19.7	6.6	27.1	7.1	9.4	1.9	4.6
PRIVATE TRUCK	1 194	100.0	5.5	25.3	19.5	4.3	17.5	6.3	15.2	1.4	5.1
AIR	1	100.0	7.5	23.7	2.9	14.9	2.2	9.4	6.3	-	33.0
WATER	333	100.0	-	-	57.7	-	3.0	-	36.0	-	3.3
OTHER	25	100.0	8.2	45.3	15.0	3.3	23.5	3.1	.6	.4	.7
UNKNOWN	10	100.0	2.0	43.8	26.8	.5	3.9	.3	15.5	7.1	.2
MIDDLE ATLANTIC	1 377	100.0	16.6	47.0	7.6	2.2	17.3	3.2	3.8	.5	1.8
RAIL	21	100.0	9.2	15.4	38.4	-	11.7	-	14.6	-	10.7
MOTOR CARRIER	1 018	100.0	16.1	42.0	9.0	3.0	20.4	2.6	4.8	.5	1.5
PRIVATE TRUCK	313	100.0	19.7	65.0	1.3	-	7.3	5.4	-	.3	1.1
AIR	-	100.0	40.8	-	15.5	2.7	.4	20.4	11.9	-	8.3
WATER	7	100.0	-	-	-	-	50.2	-	-	-	49.8
OTHER	13	100.0	4.8	71.5	11.3	-	6.2	5.8	-	-	.4
UNKNOWN	2	100.0	7.9	88.2	-	-	3.9	-	-	-	-
EAST NORTH CENTRAL	1 488	100.0	1.9	8.5	55.3	14.4	9.0	4.0	3.5	.9	2.5
RAIL	253	100.0	-	4.8	21.1	38.3	25.7	-	8.9	.9	1.2
MOTOR CARRIER	1 015	100.0	2.6	9.1	59.1	10.9	6.2	5.5	2.4	1.2	3.0
PRIVATE TRUCK	209	100.0	.1	9.6	78.9	2.9	2.7	1.5	2.1	.6	1.6
AIR	-	100.0	.1	48.1	1.1	30.8	.5	16.3	2.4	-	.8
WATER	-	100.0	-	-	-	-	-	-	-	-	-
OTHER	5	100.0	26.1	27.5	41.7	1.2	.7	-	2.6	-	.2
UNKNOWN	3	100.0	-	1.6	77.3	.7	-	-	-	20.4	-

See footnotes at end of table 4.

TABLE 2. TCC GROUP 285—Percent Distribution of Geographic Division of Origin and Means of Transport, by Geographic Division of Destination: 1972—Continued

Geographic division of origin [1] and means of transport	Number	Percent distribution by division of destination									
		U.S. total	New England	Middle Atlantic	East North Central	West North Central	South Atlantic	East South Central	West South Central	Mountain	Pacific
TONS OF SHIPMENTS	(thousands of tons)										
WEST NORTH CENTRAL......	360	100.0	.6	3.4	26.5	31.0	3.8	3.8	16.4	5.1	9.5
RAIL...................	42	100.0	-	6.7	21.0	13.6	8.4	-	27.1	17.9	5.3
MOTOR CARRIER.........	223	100.0	.2	1.5	26.2	29.5	2.9	5.1	17.5	4.7	12.5
PRIVATE TRUCK........	90	100.0	2.0	4.0	31.1	43.5	3.6	2.5	9.2	-	4.1
AIR..................	-	100.0	1.0	6.4	.4	-	.3	-	-	-	91.9
WATER................	-	100.0	-	-	-	-	-	-	-	-	-
OTHER................	-	100.0	-	.2	2.2	96.8	.1	.8	-	-	-
UNKNOWN..............	2	100.0	-	90.0	-	1.4	8.5	.1	-	-	-
SOUTH ATLANTIC..........	1 623	100.0	.2	17.5	2.6	3.1	62.5	10.8	2.7	-	.6
RAIL...................	19	100.0	.3	57.6	9.6	.1	17.0	9.7	5.4	.1	-
MOTOR CARRIER.........	1 315	100.0	.2	15.5	2.1	3.8	63.4	11.3	2.9	-	.8
PRIVATE TRUCK........	277	100.0	-	24.9	4.4	-	60.1	8.8	1.8	-	-
AIR..................	-	100.0	48.9	-	19.6	-	3.8	-	27.7	-	-
WATER................	6	100.0	-	-	1.1	-	98.9	-	-	-	-
OTHER................	5	100.0	-	5.3	-	-	94.6	-	-	-	-
UNKNOWN..............	-	100.0	-	-	-	-	100.0	-	-	-	-
EAST SOUTH CENTRAL......	162	100.0	4.9	5.8	46.7	3.9	14.6	17.5	6.1	.1	.4
RAIL...................	11	100.0	-	-	-	25.1	37.4	37.5	-	-	-
MOTOR CARRIER.........	114	100.0	6.2	4.8	47.1	2.9	15.5	20.1	2.9	.1	.3
PRIVATE TRUCK........	36	100.0	2.5	10.1	60.9	-	4.4	15.0	6.4	-	.8
AIR..................	-	100.0	-	-	-	-	100.0	-	-	-	-
WATER................	-	100.0	-	-	-	-	-	-	-	-	-
OTHER................	-	100.0	-	53.5	.5	19.1	5.4	.1	-	21.4	-
UNKNOWN..............	-	100.0	-	-	-	-	-	-	-	-	-
WEST SOUTH CENTRAL......	1 065	100.0	.3	5.3	21.6	1.2	3.6	6.3	52.6	4.6	4.4
RAIL...................	195	100.0	-	25.6	18.4	-	6.5	5.7	21.6	-	22.1
MOTOR CARRIER.........	340	100.0	.9	1.2	.3	2.1	4.9	9.8	69.0	10.6	1.1
PRIVATE TRUCK........	214	100.0	.2	.9	.2	2.4	4.0	10.7	75.4	6.1	-
AIR..................	-	100.0	-	6.7	5.4	-	-	-	-	-	87.9
WATER................	312	100.0	-	-	61.6	-	-	-	38.4	-	-
OTHER................	-	100.0	-	-	-	-	-	-	-	-	-
UNKNOWN..............	1	100.0	-	-	-	-	-	1.4	98.6	-	-
PACIFIC.................	220	100.0	.7	1.6	5.2	.8	1.0	.5	4.8	7.1	78.3
RAIL...................	21	100.0	-	-	39.8	-	-	-	-	-	60.2
MOTOR CARRIER.........	139	100.0	1.1	2.5	2.2	1.3	1.5	.7	7.5	10.7	72.4
PRIVATE TRUCK........	51	100.0	-	-	-	-	-	-	-	1.4	98.6
AIR..................	-	100.0	11.1	.4	1.2	3.3	4.9	2.9	12.3	-	63.9
WATER................	7	100.0	-	-	-	-	-	-	-	-	100.0
OTHER................	-	100.0	-	.2	.6	-	2.0	-	-	10.8	86.4
UNKNOWN..............	-	100.0	-	14.8	-	-	-	-	-	-	85.2
TON-MILES OF SHIPMENTS	(millions of ton-miles)										
U.S. TOTAL..............	2 452	100.0	3.4	12.3	18.7	8.0	21.0	6.7	12.9	3.3	13.7
RAIL...................	387	100.0	.1	20.5	15.9	13.4	14.4	3.2	12.3	1.0	19.1
MOTOR CARRIER.........	1 535	100.0	4.5	9.9	11.7	8.5	25.6	7.9	13.9	4.3	13.6
PRIVATE TRUCK........	271	100.0	4.5	24.3	13.4	4.5	22.4	10.9	7.3	3.9	8.7
AIR..................	2	100.0	6.3	14.1	1.2	7.4	2.6	3.5	6.0	-	58.8
WATER................	246	100.0	-	-	73.3	-	1.7	-	14.3	-	10.8
OTHER................	6	100.0	22.1	34.4	15.1	2.2	10.1	10.1	1.6	1.4	3.1
UNKNOWN..............	3	100.0	1.0	64.1	4.0	.3	7.7	.1	2.0	20.3	.5
MIDDLE ATLANTIC.........	440	100.0	9.5	13.5	11.0	6.7	20.2	7.4	14.9	2.6	14.2
RAIL...................	16	100.0	2.5	1.1	22.6	-	12.8	-	27.5	-	33.5
MOTOR CARRIER.........	349	100.0	9.5	12.3	12.1	8.4	20.6	5.5	17.5	2.8	11.4
PRIVATE TRUCK........	58	100.0	13.9	24.6	3.0	.1	19.7	21.7	-	3.4	13.6
AIR..................	-	100.0	11.6	-	11.0	3.3	.3	23.4	23.3	-	27.1
WATER................	12	100.0	-	-	-	-	25.4	-	-	-	74.6
OTHER................	3	100.0	2.7	44.4	20.0	-	12.2	17.1	.2	-	3.4
UNKNOWN..............	-	100.0	9.4	87.3	.1	-	3.3	-	-	-	-
EAST NORTH CENTRAL......	502	100.0	3.6	10.5	20.7	19.8	15.0	4.5	8.9	3.1	13.7
RAIL...................	125	100.0	-	4.6	5.6	38.8	30.2	-	16.4	-	4.4
MOTOR CARRIER.........	334	100.0	5.1	11.6	25.2	14.1	10.1	6.6	6.4	3.9	17.1
PRIVATE TRUCK........	38	100.0	.2	20.0	31.8	8.9	9.4	1.6	6.9	4.6	16.4
AIR..................	-	100.0	.1	56.5	.2	29.1	.7	8.2	2.8	.1	2.3
WATER................	-	100.0	-	-	-	-	-	-	-	-	-
OTHER................	1	100.0	65.0	16.8	10.5	.5	1.1	.1	4.9	-	1.0
UNKNOWN..............	-	100.0	-	1.1	16.1	1.0	-	-	-	81.8	-

See footnotes at end of table 4.

TABLE 2. **TCC GROUP 285—Percent Distribution of Geographic Division of Origin and Means of Transport, by Geographic Division of Destination: 1972**—Continued

Geographic division of origin[1] and means of transport	Number	Percent distribution by division of destination									
		U.S. total	New England	Middle Atlantic	East North Central	West North Central	South Atlantic	East South Central	West South Central	Mountain	Pacific
TON-MILES OF SHIPMENTS	(millions of ton-miles)										
WEST NORTH CENTRAL......	172	100.0	1.8	6.9	20.2	11.7	6.0	3.1	15.1	6.2	29.0
RAIL.....................	23	100.0	-	10.3	14.8	5.8	10.5	-	26.9	16.7	14.9
MOTOR CARRIER..........	109	100.0	.4	2.8	18.6	11.1	3.8	4.4	15.2	6.2	37.5
PRIVATE TRUCK.........	36	100.0	7.3	12.3	29.9	18.0	9.4	1.2	8.1	.1	13.7
AIR....................	-	100.0	.7	4.1	.1	-	.1	-	-	-	95.0
WATER..................	-	100.0	-	-	-	-	-	-	-	-	-
OTHER..................	-	100.0	-	1.3	7.0	86.1	.8	4.8	-	-	-
UNKNOWN...............	2	100.0	-	89.3	-	.1	10.5	-	-	-	-
SOUTH ATLANTIC..........	554	100.0	.2	16.2	3.6	4.3	53.5	10.8	7.3	-	4.2
RAIL.....................	11	100.0	.6	64.5	6.7	.2	9.1	9.6	9.1	.2	-
MOTOR CARRIER..........	457	100.0	.2	10.4	2.9	5.2	56.5	11.6	8.0	-	5.1
PRIVATE TRUCK.........	84	100.0	.1	41.1	6.9	-	42.0	6.9	3.1	-	-
AIR....................	-	100.0	44.5	-	14.9	-	2.9	-	37.7	-	-
WATER..................	1	100.0	-	-	2.8	-	97.2	-	-	-	-
OTHER..................	-	100.0	-	22.5	.4	-	77.1	-	-	-	-
UNKNOWN...............	-	100.0	-	-	-	-	100.0	-	-	-	-
EAST SOUTH CENTRAL......	52	100.0	11.5	10.1	29.9	6.2	19.4	10.8	9.7	.3	2.1
RAIL.....................	6	100.0	-	-	-	26.7	33.0	-	40.3	-	-
MOTOR CARRIER..........	34	100.0	15.6	8.2	31.3	4.1	21.0	13.9	4.0	.2	1.7
PRIVATE TRUCK.........	10	100.0	5.8	21.4	44.8	-	5.7	8.0	9.3	-	4.9
AIR....................	-	100.0	-	-	-	-	100.0	-	-	-	-
WATER..................	-	100.0	-	-	-	-	-	-	-	-	-
OTHER..................	-	100.0	-	56.2	.1	10.1	5.7	-	-	27.9	-
UNKNOWN...............	-	100.0	-	-	-	-	-	-	-	-	-
WEST SOUTH CENTRAL......	570	100.0	1.0	12.6	36.8	1.1	4.6	6.4	20.8	6.0	10.8
RAIL.....................	180	100.0	-	35.4	15.6	-	5.6	6.4	6.8	-	30.3
MOTOR CARRIER..........	136	100.0	3.8	4.3	.6	2.9	7.2	11.4	44.4	20.4	5.0
PRIVATE TRUCK.........	37	100.0	1.5	5.9	.9	5.5	16.2	24.5	28.1	17.4	-
AIR....................	-	100.0	-	2.4	1.1	-	-	-	-	-	96.5
WATER..................	215	100.0	-	-	83.7	-	-	-	16.3	-	-
OTHER..................	-	100.0	-	-	-	-	-	-	-	-	-
UNKNOWN...............	-	100.0	-	-	-	-	-	4.2	95.8	-	-
PACIFIC.................	122	100.0	3.2	7.0	19.5	2.1	3.6	1.5	12.5	7.4	43.1
RAIL.....................	22	100.0	-	-	79.6	-	-	-	-	-	20.4
MOTOR CARRIER..........	77	100.0	4.9	11.2	7.5	3.4	5.7	2.4	19.8	11.4	33.7
PRIVATE TRUCK.........	4	100.0	-	-	-	-	-	-	-	6.3	93.7
AIR....................	-	100.0	11.4	.4	.9	1.6	4.6	2.0	7.4	-	71.9
WATER..................	17	100.0	-	-	-	-	-	-	-	-	100.0
OTHER..................	-	100.0	-	1.0	2.2	-	11.3	-	-	13.5	71.9
UNKNOWN...............	-	100.0	-	31.0	-	-	-	-	-	-	69.0

See footnotes at end of table 4.

TABLE 3. **TCC GROUP 285**—Percent Distribution of Geographic Division of Destination and Means of Transport, by Geographic Division of Origin: 1972

Geographic division of destination and means of transport	Number	Percent distribution by division of origin[1]									
		U.S. total	New England	Middle Atlantic	East North Central	West North Central	South Atlantic	East South Central	West South Central	Mountain	Pacific
TONS OF SHIPMENTS	(thousands of tons)										
U.S. TOTAL	6 382	100.0	(D)	21.6	23.3	5.7	25.4	2.6	16.7	(D)	3.4
RAIL	566	100.0	(D)	3.8	44.8	7.6	3.4	2.0	34.6	(D)	3.8
MOTOR CARRIER	4 249	100.0	(D)	24.0	23.9	5.3	31.0	2.7	8.0	(D)	3.3
PRIVATE TRUCK	1 194	100.0	(D)	26.2	17.5	7.6	23.2	3.0	17.9	(D)	4.3
AIR	1	100.0	(D)	6.3	45.6	15.9	4.5	.6	3.4	(D)	22.7
WATER	333	100.0	(D)	2.3	-	-	1.8	-	93.7	(D)	2.2
OTHER	25	100.0	(D)	52.2	21.7	2.9	21.1	1.6	-	(D)	.5
UNKNOWN	10	100.0	(D)	25.8	34.7	22.6	1.0	-	15.7	(D)	.2
NEW ENGLAND	322	100.0	(D)	71.1	8.6	.7	1.1	2.5	1.1	(D)	.5
RAIL	2	100.0	(D)	97.0	-	-	3.0	-	-	(D)	-
MOTOR CARRIER	252	100.0	(D)	65.2	10.3	.2	1.3	2.8	1.3	(D)	.6
PRIVATE TRUCK	65	100.0	(D)	93.9	.2	2.8	.1	1.4	.6	(D)	-
AIR	-	100.0	(D)	34.5	.3	2.1	29.4	-	-	(D)	33.7
WATER	-	100.0	(D)	-	-	-	-	-	-	(D)	-
OTHER	2	100.0	(D)	30.6	69.1	-	-	-	-	(D)	-
UNKNOWN	-	100.0	(D)	100.0	-	-	-	-	-	(D)	-
MIDDLE ATLANTIC	1 152	100.0	(D)	56.2	11.0	1.1	24.7	.8	4.9	(D)	.3
RAIL	79	100.0	(D)	4.2	15.4	3.6	13.9	-	63.0	(D)	-
MOTOR CARRIER	753	100.0	(D)	56.9	12.3	.4	27.1	.7	.6	(D)	.5
PRIVATE TRUCK	302	100.0	(D)	67.4	6.6	1.2	22.9	1.2	.7	(D)	-
AIR	-	100.0	(D)	-	92.4	4.3	-	-	1.0	(D)	.4
WATER	-	100.0	(D)	-	-	-	-	-	-	(D)	-
OTHER	11	100.0	(D)	82.5	13.2	-	2.5	1.8	-	(D)	-
UNKNOWN	4	100.0	(D)	52.1	1.3	46.5	-	-	-	(D)	.1
EAST NORTH CENTRAL	1 388	100.0	(D)	7.6	59.4	6.9	3.0	5.5	16.6	(D)	.8
RAIL	117	100.0	(D)	7.1	45.6	7.7	1.6	-	30.7	(D)	7.3
MOTOR CARRIER	838	100.0	(D)	10.9	71.6	7.0	3.3	6.4	.1	(D)	.4
PRIVATE TRUCK	233	100.0	(D)	1.7	70.8	12.1	5.2	9.4	.2	(D)	.4
AIR	-	100.0	(D)	33.8	17.8	2.2	30.4	-	6.4	(D)	9.1
WATER	192	100.0	(D)	-	-	-	-	-	100.0	(D)	-
OTHER	3	100.0	(D)	39.2	60.3	.4	-	.1	-	(D)	-
UNKNOWN	2	100.0	(D)	-	100.0	-	-	-	-	(D)	-
WEST NORTH CENTRAL	437	100.0	(D)	7.1	49.0	25.6	11.5	1.4	2.9	(D)	.4
RAIL	105	100.0	(D)	-	91.7	5.5	-	2.7	-	(D)	-
MOTOR CARRIER	279	100.0	(D)	11.0	39.7	23.5	18.0	1.2	2.6	(D)	.7
PRIVATE TRUCK	50	100.0	(D)	.1	11.8	77.8	-	-	10.3	(D)	-
AIR	-	100.0	(D)	1.2	93.8	-	-	-	-	(D)	5.1
WATER	-	100.0	(D)	-	-	-	-	-	-	(D)	-
OTHER	-	100.0	(D)	.2	8.1	82.9	-	8.9	-	(D)	-
UNKNOWN	-	100.0	(D)	-	43.6	56.4	-	-	-	(D)	-
SOUTH ATLANTIC	1 470	100.0	(D)	16.2	9.1	.9	69.1	1.6	2.6	(D)	.1
RAIL	91	100.0	(D)	2.8	71.1	3.9	3.6	4.7	14.0	(D)	-
MOTOR CARRIER	1 153	100.0	(D)	18.0	5.5	.6	72.3	1.5	1.4	(D)	.2
PRIVATE TRUCK	208	100.0	(D)	10.9	2.8	1.6	79.9	.8	4.1	(D)	-
AIR	-	100.0	(D)	1.1	10.4	2.2	7.7	28.4	-	(D)	49.9
WATER	9	100.0	(D)	38.4	-	-	61.6	-	-	(D)	-
OTHER	6	100.0	(D)	13.8	.6	-	85.2	.4	-	(D)	-
UNKNOWN	-	100.0	(D)	25.9	-	49.5	24.6	-	-	(D)	-
EAST SOUTH CENTRAL	389	100.0	(D)	11.3	15.3	3.5	44.9	7.3	17.4	(D)	.3
RAIL	13	100.0	(D)	-	-	-	14.2	-	85.8	(D)	-
MOTOR CARRIER	300	100.0	(D)	8.8	18.7	3.8	49.5	7.7	11.1	(D)	.3
PRIVATE TRUCK	74	100.0	(D)	22.4	4.2	3.0	32.5	7.2	30.6	(D)	-
AIR	-	100.0	(D)	13.8	79.2	-	-	-	-	(D)	7.0
WATER	-	100.0	(D)	-	-	-	-	-	-	(D)	-
OTHER	-	100.0	(D)	98.5	.8	.7	-	-	-	(D)	-
UNKNOWN	-	100.0	(D)	-	-	12.2	-	-	87.8	(D)	-
WEST SOUTH CENTRAL	788	100.0	(D)	6.6	6.6	7.5	5.5	1.3	71.1	(D)	1.3
RAIL	85	100.0	(D)	3.7	26.5	13.7	1.2	5.1	49.8	(D)	-
MOTOR CARRIER	399	100.0	(D)	12.2	6.2	9.8	9.4	.8	58.8	(D)	2.6
PRIVATE TRUCK	181	100.0	(D)	-	2.4	4.6	2.7	1.3	89.0	(D)	-
AIR	-	100.0	(D)	11.9	17.1	-	19.7	-	-	(D)	44.1
WATER	120	100.0	(D)	-	-	-	-	-	100.0	(D)	-
OTHER	-	100.0	(D)	3.4	96.6	-	-	-	-	(D)	-
UNKNOWN	1	100.0	(D)	-	-	-	-	-	100.0	(D)	-
MOUNTAIN	103	100.0	(D)	6.1	13.6	17.6	.1	.1	47.4	(D)	15.1
RAIL	7	100.0	(D)	.1	-	99.8	.2	-	-	(D)	-
MOTOR CARRIER	79	100.0	(D)	6.7	15.2	13.3	.1	.1	45.7	(D)	18.9
PRIVATE TRUCK	16	100.0	(D)	6.3	8.2	.2	-	-	81.0	(D)	4.4
AIR	-	100.0	(D)	-	69.4	-	-	-	-	(D)	30.6
WATER	-	100.0	(D)	-	-	-	-	-	-	(D)	-
OTHER	-	100.0	(D)	.3	-	-	-	84.9	-	(D)	14.9
UNKNOWN	-	100.0	(D)	-	100.0	-	-	-	-	(D)	-
PACIFIC	330	100.0	(D)	7.4	11.1	10.3	3.0	.2	14.3	(D)	52.1
RAIL	63	100.0	(D)	3.6	4.8	3.6	-	-	67.9	(D)	20.1
MOTOR CARRIER	193	100.0	(D)	7.7	15.5	14.4	5.2	.2	1.9	(D)	52.2
PRIVATE TRUCK	61	100.0	(D)	5.4	5.5	6.0	-	.5	-	(D)	82.6
AIR	-	100.0	(D)	1.6	1.1	44.2	-	-	9.1	(D)	43.9
WATER	11	100.0	(D)	33.9	-	-	-	-	-	(D)	66.1
OTHER	-	100.0	(D)	27.6	5.6	-	-	-	-	(D)	66.8
UNKNOWN	-	100.0	(D)	-	-	-	-	-	-	(D)	100.0

See footnotes at end of table 4.

TABLE 3. **TCC GROUP 285**—Percent Distribution of Geographic Division of Destination and Means of Transport, by Geographic Division of Origin: 1972—Continued

Geographic division of destination and means of transport	Number	Percent distribution by division of origin [1]									
		U.S. total	New England	Middle Atlantic	East North Central	West North Central	South Atlantic	East South Central	West South Central	Mountain	Pacific
TON-MILES OF SHIPMENTS	(millions of ton-miles)										
U.S. TOTAL..............	2 452	100.0	(D)	18.0	20.5	7.0	22.6	2.1	23.3	(D)	5.0
RAIL................	387	100.0	(D)	4.3	32.5	6.1	2.9	1.7	46.6	(D)	5.9
MOTOR CARRIER........	1 535	100.0	(D)	22.7	21.8	7.1	29.8	2.2	8.9	(D)	5.0
PRIVATE TRUCK........	271	100.0	(D)	21.6	14.2	13.4	31.2	3.9	13.9	(D)	1.5
AIR.................	2	100.0	(D)	3.3	22.8	18.4	1.9	.4	9.1	(D)	43.2
WATER...............	246	100.0	(D)	4.9	-	-	.4	-	87.5	(D)	7.2
OTHER...............	6	100.0	(D)	58.3	31.5	1.8	2.9	4.5	-	(D)	1.0
UNKNOWN.............	3	100.0	(D)	10.9	24.8	60.6	.9	-	2.0	(D)	.8
NEW ENGLAND.............	83	100.0	(D)	50.2	22.0	3.7	1.6	7.2	6.8	(D)	4.7
RAIL................	-	100.0	(D)	86.1	-	-	13.9	-	-	(D)	-
MOTOR CARRIER........	68	100.0	(D)	47.9	24.6	.6	1.7	7.8	7.4	(D)	5.5
PRIVATE TRUCK........	12	100.0	(D)	66.9	.7	21.8	.6	5.1	4.6	(D)	-
AIR.................	-	100.0	(D)	6.1	.2	2.0	13.6	-	-	(D)	78.1
WATER...............	-	100.0	(D)	-	-	-	-	-	-	(D)	-
OTHER...............	1	100.0	(D)	7.1	92.9	-	-	-	-	(D)	-
UNKNOWN.............	-	100.0	(D)	100.0	-	-	-	-	-	(D)	-
MIDDLE ATLANTIC........	302	100.0	(D)	19.6	17.5	3.9	29.7	1.7	23.8	(D)	2.9
RAIL................	79	100.0	(D)	.2	7.3	3.1	9.0	-	80.5	(D)	-
MOTOR CARRIER........	152	100.0	(D)	28.1	25.4	2.0	31.3	1.8	3.9	(D)	5.7
PRIVATE TRUCK........	65	100.0	(D)	21.8	11.7	6.8	52.8	3.5	3.4	(D)	-
AIR.................	-	100.0	(D)	-	91.0	5.3	-	-	1.5	(D)	1.2
WATER...............	-	100.0	(D)	-	-	-	-	-	-	(D)	-
OTHER...............	2	100.0	(D)	75.2	15.4	.1	1.9	7.3	-	(D)	-
UNKNOWN.............	2	100.0	(D)	14.8	.4	84.4	-	-	-	(D)	.4
EAST NORTH CENTRAL......	458	100.0	(D)	10.6	22.7	7.6	4.3	3.4	45.8	(D)	5.2
RAIL................	61	100.0	(D)	6.2	11.4	5.7	1.2	-	45.9	(D)	29.5
MOTOR CARRIER........	179	100.0	(D)	23.6	47.0	11.3	7.4	6.0	.5	(D)	3.2
PRIVATE TRUCK........	36	100.0	(D)	4.9	33.6	29.9	16.0	13.1	1.0	(D)	-
AIR.................	-	100.0	(D)	30.4	4.4	1.8	23.7	-	8.5	(D)	30.7
WATER...............	180	100.0	(D)	-	-	-	-	-	100.0	(D)	-
OTHER...............	-	100.0	(D)	77.1	21.8	.8	.1	-	-	(D)	.2
UNKNOWN.............	-	100.0	(D)	.1	99.9	-	-	-	-	(D)	-
WEST NORTH CENTRAL......	195	100.0	(D)	15.0	51.1	10.3	12.2	1.7	3.1	(D)	1.3
RAIL................	52	100.0	(D)	-	93.9	2.7	-	3.4	-	(D)	-
MOTOR CARRIER........	130	100.0	(D)	22.4	36.1	9.3	18.2	1.1	3.0	(D)	2.0
PRIVATE TRUCK........	12	100.0	(D)	.3	28.3	54.1	-	-	17.3	(D)	-
AIR.................	-	100.0	(D)	1.5	89.3	-	-	-	-	(D)	9.3
WATER...............	-	100.0	(D)	-	-	-	-	-	-	(D)	-
OTHER...............	-	100.0	(D)	1.0	8.0	70.1	-	20.9	-	(D)	-
UNKNOWN.............	-	100.0	(D)	-	74.0	26.0	-	-	-	(D)	-
SOUTH ATLANTIC..........	515	100.0	(D)	17.3	14.7	2.0	57.6	2.0	5.0	(D)	.9
RAIL................	55	100.0	(D)	3.8	68.0	4.5	1.8	3.9	18.0	(D)	-
MOTOR CARRIER........	393	100.0	(D)	18.3	8.6	1.1	65.8	1.8	2.5	(D)	1.1
PRIVATE TRUCK........	60	100.0	(D)	18.9	5.9	5.6	58.4	1.0	10.1	(D)	-
AIR.................	-	100.0	(D)	.3	6.3	1.0	2.1	14.0	-	(D)	76.1
WATER...............	4	100.0	(D)	75.1	-	-	24.9	-	-	(D)	-
OTHER...............	-	100.0	(D)	70.4	3.5	.1	22.3	2.5	-	(D)	1.2
UNKNOWN.............	-	100.0	(D)	4.7	-	83.1	12.1	-	-	(D)	-
EAST SOUTH CENTRAL......	164	100.0	(D)	19.7	13.8	3.2	36.4	3.4	22.1	(D)	1.1
RAIL................	12	100.0	(D)	-	-	-	8.4	-	91.6	(D)	-
MOTOR CARRIER........	121	100.0	(D)	15.8	18.1	4.0	43.6	3.9	12.8	(D)	1.5
PRIVATE TRUCK........	29	100.0	(D)	42.7	2.1	1.5	19.6	2.9	31.2	(D)	-
AIR.................	-	100.0	(D)	22.4	53.3	-	-	-	-	(D)	24.3
WATER...............	-	100.0	(D)	-	-	-	-	-	-	(D)	-
OTHER...............	-	100.0	(D)	98.9	.3	.8	-	-	-	(D)	-
UNKNOWN.............	-	100.0	(D)	-	-	13.1	-	-	86.9	(D)	-
WEST SOUTH CENTRAL......	316	100.0	(D)	20.7	14.2	8.2	12.7	1.6	37.5	(D)	4.9
RAIL................	47	100.0	(D)	9.7	43.5	13.4	2.1	5.7	25.6	(D)	-
MOTOR CARRIER........	213	100.0	(D)	28.6	10.1	7.8	17.2	.6	28.4	(D)	7.2
PRIVATE TRUCK........	19	100.0	(D)	-	13.4	14.9	13.2	5.0	53.5	(D)	-
AIR.................	-	100.0	(D)	12.9	10.7	-	11.9	-	-	(D)	53.0
WATER...............	35	100.0	(D)	-	-	-	-	-	100.0	(D)	-
OTHER...............	-	100.0	(D)	6.1	93.9	-	-	-	-	(D)	-
UNKNOWN.............	-	100.0	(D)	-	-	-	-	-	100.0	(D)	-
MOUNTAIN................	81	100.0	(D)	14.2	19.0	13.2	.2	.2	42.1	(D)	11.1
RAIL................	3	100.0	(D)	.1	-	99.3	.6	-	-	(D)	-
MOTOR CARRIER........	66	100.0	(D)	14.5	19.6	10.2	.2	.1	42.0	(D)	13.3
PRIVATE TRUCK........	10	100.0	(D)	18.7	16.8	.3	-	-	61.8	(D)	2.4
AIR.................	-	100.0	(D)	-	80.2	-	-	-	-	(D)	19.8
WATER...............	-	100.0	(D)	-	-	-	-	-	-	(D)	-
OTHER...............	-	100.0	(D)	.7	-	-	-	-	89.4	(D)	9.9
UNKNOWN.............	-	100.0	(D)	-	100.0	-	-	-	-	(D)	-
PACIFIC.................	335	100.0	(D)	18.6	20.6	14.9	6.9	.3	18.4	(D)	15.8
RAIL................	73	100.0	(D)	7.6	7.4	4.8	-	-	73.9	(D)	6.3
MOTOR CARRIER........	209	100.0	(D)	18.9	27.3	19.6	11.1	.3	3.3	(D)	12.4
PRIVATE TRUCK........	23	100.0	(D)	33.7	26.7	21.1	-	2.2	-	(D)	16.3
AIR.................	1	100.0	(D)	1.5	.9	29.7	-	-	14.9	(D)	52.8
WATER...............	26	100.0	(D)	33.7	-	-	-	-	-	(D)	66.3
OTHER...............	-	100.0	(D)	65.5	10.2	-	-	-	-	(D)	24.2
UNKNOWN.............	-	100.0	(D)	-	-	-	-	-	-	(D)	100.0

See footnotes at end of table 4.

TABLE 4. TCC GROUP 285—Percent Distribution of Distance Shipped and Weight of Shipment, by Means of Transport: 1972

Distance shipped and weight of shipment[2][3]	Number	Percent distribution by means of transport							
		All means of transport	Rail	Motor carrier	Private truck	Air	Water	Other	Unknown
TONS OF SHIPMENTS	(thousands of tons)								
U.S. TOTAL...........	6 044	100.0	8.5	66.4	19.0	-	5.5	.4	.2
UNDER 100 MILES.........	1 402	100.0	3.6	58.1	37.4	-	-	.5	.3
UNDER 1000 POUNDS.....	116	100.0	-	65.9	30.3	-	-	3.6	.2
1000 TO 9999 POUNDS...	530	100.0	-	51.7	47.6	-	-	.3	.3
10000 TO 29999 POUNDS.	380	100.0	-	62.9	36.1	-	-	.4	.6
30000 TO 59999 POUNDS.	345	100.0	10.9	60.9	28.2	-	-	-	-
60000 TO 89999 POUNDS.	8	100.0	37.2	47.4	15.5	-	-	-	-
90000 POUNDS AND OVER.	19	100.0	50.3	49.7	-	-	-	-	-
100 TO 199 MILES........	1 205	100.0	.5	76.8	21.0	-	.5	.9	.2
UNDER 1000 POUNDS.....	79	100.0	.1	86.5	10.2	.1	-	3.0	.1
1000 TO 9999 POUNDS...	299	100.0	.3	80.6	19.0	-	-	-	.1
10000 TO 29999 POUNDS.	255	100.0	1.0	66.1	31.4	-	-	.5	.9
30000 TO 59999 POUNDS.	319	100.0	.4	61.7	33.7	-	1.9	2.3	-
60000 TO 89999 POUNDS.	17	100.0	8.8	91.2	-	-	-	-	-
90000 POUNDS AND OVER.	234	100.0	-	100.0	-	-	-	-	-
200 TO 299 MILES........	846	100.0	4.2	68.4	13.1	-	14.2	.1	-
UNDER 1000 POUNDS.....	47	100.0	.1	93.8	4.9	-	-	1.2	-
1000 TO 9999 POUNDS...	200	100.0	-	91.3	8.6	-	-	-	.1
10000 TO 29999 POUNDS.	187	100.0	2.0	76.7	21.1	-	-	.1	-
30000 TO 59999 POUNDS.	259	100.0	7.6	72.3	20.1	-	-	-	-
60000 TO 89999 POUNDS.	20	100.0	59.1	40.9	-	-	-	-	-
90000 POUNDS AND OVER.	131	100.0	-	8.8	-	-	91.2	-	-
300 TO 499 MILES........	1 056	100.0	10.7	79.0	10.1	-	-	.1	-
UNDER 1000 POUNDS.....	51	100.0	.1	81.0	15.7	.4	-	2.7	.1
1000 TO 9999 POUNDS...	243	100.0	-	88.7	11.2	-	-	-	-
10000 TO 29999 POUNDS.	191	100.0	1.3	82.2	16.5	-	-	-	-
30000 TO 59999 POUNDS.	425	100.0	11.3	79.2	9.5	-	-	-	-
60000 TO 89999 POUNDS.	55	100.0	60.3	39.7	-	-	-	-	-
90000 POUNDS AND OVER.	89	100.0	31.4	68.6	-	-	-	-	-
500 TO 999 MILES........	1 222	100.0	18.6	54.2	10.6	.1	16.1	.2	.2
UNDER 1000 POUNDS.....	48	100.0	.1	85.8	9.9	1.4	-	2.8	-
1000 TO 9999 POUNDS...	167	100.0	.6	93.4	5.2	-	-	.8	-
10000 TO 29999 POUNDS.	192	100.0	2.0	90.8	.7.1	-	-	.1	-
30000 TO 59999 POUNDS.	435	100.0	20.9	54.8	23.2	-	.9	-	.2
60000 TO 89999 POUNDS.	122	100.0	57.6	41.3	1.0	-	-	-	-
90000 POUNDS AND OVER.	255	100.0	23.8	-	-	-	75.3	-	.9
1000 TO 1499 MILES......	203	100.0	32.3	58.5	9.0	-	-	-	.1
UNDER 1000 POUNDS.....	10	100.0	2.1	92.6	2.5	.5	-	.2	2.1
1000 TO 9999 POUNDS...	32	100.0	-	89.7	10.3	-	-	-	-
10000 TO 29999 POUNDS.	19	100.0	4.8	84.8	10.4	-	-	-	-
30000 TO 59999 POUNDS.	72	100.0	23.1	59.3	17.6	-	-	-	-
60000 TO 89999 POUNDS.	23	100.0	39.7	60.3	-	-	-	-	-
90000 POUNDS AND OVER.	45	100.0	84.5	15.5	-	-	-	-	-
1500 MILES OR OVER......	106	100.0	15.9	71.3	5.5	.5	6.8	-	-
UNDER 1000 POUNDS.....	5	100.0	.4	88.9	.1	9.4	1.1	.2	.1
1000 TO 9999 POUNDS...	24	100.0	.2	90.7	6.4	.1	2.5	-	-
10000 TO 29999 POUNDS.	29	100.0	4.9	83.8	9.7	-	1.6	-	-
30000 TO 59999 POUNDS.	34	100.0	17.5	70.7	4.1	-	7.7	-	-
60000 TO 89999 POUNDS.	10	100.0	84.4	-	-	-	15.6	-	-
90000 POUNDS AND OVER.	2	100.0	30.7	-	-	-	69.3	-	-
TON-MILES OF SHIPMENTS	(millions of ton-miles)								
U.S. TOTAL...........	2 238	100.0	14.9	62.9	11.1	.1	10.6	.2	.2
UNDER 100 MILES.........	65	100.0	6.0	62.2	31.2	-	-	.3	.3
UNDER 1000 POUNDS.....	5	100.0	-	76.8	21.4	-	-	1.5	.2
1000 TO 9999 POUNDS...	23	100.0	-	58.9	40.6	-	-	.1	.3
10000 TO 29999 POUNDS.	15	100.0	-	66.0	32.8	-	-	.6	.5
30000 TO 59999 POUNDS.	18	100.0	17.3	59.3	23.4	-	-	-	-
60000 TO 89999 POUNDS.	-	100.0	38.6	36.8	24.6	-	-	-	-
90000 POUNDS AND OVER.	1	100.0	36.6	63.4	-	-	-	-	-
100 TO 199 MILES........	186	100.0	.6	78.0	19.8	-	.5	.9	.2
UNDER 1000 POUNDS.....	11	100.0	.1	87.5	.9.2	.1	-	3.0	.1
1000 TO 9999 POUNDS...	43	100.0	.3	81.8	17.8	-	-	-	.1
10000 TO 29999 POUNDS.	37	100.0	1.3	65.9	31.6	-	-	.4	.9
30000 TO 59999 POUNDS.	48	100.0	.4	61.5	33.6	-	2.1	2.5	-
60000 TO 89999 POUNDS.	2	100.0	8.9	91.1	-	-	-	-	-
90000 POUNDS AND OVER.	42	100.0	-	100.0	-	-	-	-	-

See footnotes at end of table 4.

TABLE 4. **TCC GROUP 285—Percent Distribution of Distance Shipped and Weight of Shipment, by Means of Transport: 1972**—Continued

Distance shipped and weight of shipment [2] [3]	Number	Percent distribution by means of transport							
		All means of transport	Rail	Motor carrier	Private truck	Air	Water	Other	Unknown
TON-MILES OF SHIPMENTS	(millions of ton-miles)								
200 TO 299 MILES.........	215	100.0	4.1	66.5	13.0	-	16.3	.1	-
UNDER 1000 POUNDS.....	11	100.0	.1	93.9	4.8	-	-	1.2	-
1000 TO 9999 POUNDS...	49	100.0	-	91.3	8.6	-	-	-	.1
10000 TO 29999 POUNDS.	46	100.0	2.0	76.2	21.7	-	-	.1	-
30000 TO 59999 POUNDS.	64	100.0	7.8	71.9	20.3	-	-	-	-
60000 TO 89999 POUNDS.	4	100.0	57.1	42.9	-	-	-	-	-
90000 POUNDS AND OVER.	38	100.0	-	8.6	-	-	91.4	-	-
300 TO 499 MILES.........	416	100.0	11.2	78.9	9.8	-	-	.1	.1
UNDER 1000 POUNDS.....	19	100.0	.1	81.0	15.7	.4	-	2.8	.1
1000 TO 9999 POUNDS...	94	100.0	-	89.2	10.7	-	-	-	-
10000 TO 29999 POUNDS.	76	100.0	1.3	82.5	16.2	-	-	-	-
30000 TO 59999 POUNDS.	165	100.0	13.4	77.5	9.2	-	-	-	-
60000 TO 89999 POUNDS.	21	100.0	57.1	42.9	-	-	-	-	-
90000 POUNDS AND OVER.	39	100.0	28.6	71.4	-	-	-	-	-
500 TO 999 MILES.........	884	100.0	17.7	50.9	10.0	.1	20.8	.2	.3
UNDER 1000 POUNDS.....	32	100.0	.1	86.0	9.5	1.5	-	2.8	.1
1000 TO 9999 POUNDS...	116	100.0	.5	93.3	5.3	-	-	.9	-
10000 TO 29999 POUNDS.	125	100.0	1.9	91.4	6.6	-	-	.1	-
30000 TO 59999 POUNDS.	300	100.0	20.6	54.7	23.4	-	1.0	-	.2
60000 TO 89999 POUNDS.	75	100.0	54.1	44.8	1.1	-	-	-	-
90000 POUNDS AND OVER.	233	100.0	21.7	-	-	-	77.4	-	.8
1000 TO 1499 MILES......	249	100.0	32.9	58.1	8.9	-	-	-	.1
UNDER 1000 POUNDS.....	11	100.0	2.3	92.5	2.6	.5	-	.2	1.9
1000 TO 9999 POUNDS...	38	100.0	-	89.9	10.1	-	-	-	-
10000 TO 29999 POUNDS.	24	100.0	5.1	86.7	8.3	-	-	-	-
30000 TO 59999 POUNDS.	85	100.0	23.3	57.8	18.9	-	-	-	-
60000 TO 89999 POUNDS.	31	100.0	39.2	60.8	-	-	-	-	-
90000 POUNDS AND OVER.	58	100.0	82.7	17.3	-	-	-	-	-
1500 MILES OR OVER......	219	100.0	15.5	70.5	5.3	.6	8.1	-	-
UNDER 1000 POUNDS.....	11	100.0	.3	87.1	-	11.0	1.3	.2	.1
1000 TO 9999 POUNDS...	50	100.0	.2	90.4	6.3	.1	2.9	-	-
10000 TO 29999 POUNDS.	60	100.0	4.7	83.5	9.6	-	2.2	-	-
30000 TO 59999 POUNDS.	68	100.0	15.9	70.8	3.9	-	9.5	-	-
60000 TO 89999 POUNDS.	21	100.0	82.8	-	-	-	17.2	-	-
90000 POUNDS AND OVER.	6	100.0	31.0	-	-	-	69.0	-	-

Note: Detail may not add to total due to rounding. The introductory table shows the estimates of sampling variability for tons; sampling variability for ton-miles has not been estimated. See the map in the Introduction for the States comprising the geographic divisions of the United States.

Shipments excluded from the survey are those moving by pipeline (primarily petroleum products from refineries), parcel post shipments, and commodities moved by own power (motorized vehicles, aircraft, etc.) or towed (prefabricated buildings, etc.). Local shipments (commodities shipped less than 25 miles from the plant) and shipments within the same city are also excluded. Shipments to Alaska and Hawaii from the 48 conterminous States and the District of Columbia are included; however, no data were obtained for shipments originating in Alaska and Hawaii.

- Represents zero or rounds to zero.   (D) Withheld to avoid disclosing figures for individual companies.

[1] Production of this commodity is concentrated in the geographic divisions shown; figures and distributions for geographic divisions not shown are included in the total.

[2] Distances of shipments to foreign destinations are calculated only to the U.S. port of exit.

[3] Includes only shipments represented by bills of lading and invoices. Summary records which did not show individual weights of shipments are not included.

TCC 287. Agricultural Chemicals

Comparisons of Tons and Ton-Miles of Shipments for
Geographic Divisions of Origin and for Sampling Variability: 1972 and 1967

Geographic division of origin	Estimates				Relative sampling variability in tons (percent)	
	1972		1967		1972	1967
	Tons (thousands)	Ton-miles (millions)	Tons (thousands)	Ton-miles (millions)		
U.S. total	26,422	7,380	37,010	8,620	11.0	13.6
New England	(D)	(D)	471	36	(*)	(*)
Middle Atlantic	2,245	470	1,391	237	(*)	(*)
East North Central	2,931	775	3,123	758	41.0	(*)
West North Central	2,023	400	3,437	729	41.6	(*)
South Atlantic	10,230	2,963	21,674	4,530	20.5	(*)
East South Central	2,164	492	1,964	698	29.4	(*)
West South Central	4,697	1,765	4,305	1,428	43.8	(*)
Mountain	(D)	(D)	361	158	(*)	(*)
Pacific	1,415	258	284	46	31.6	(*)

(D) Withheld to avoid disclosing figures for individual companies.   (*) Data not published.

TABLE 1. TCC GROUP 287—Percent Distribution of Geographic Division of Origin and Distance Shipped, by Means of Transport: 1972

Geographic division of origin[1] and distance shipped[2]	Number	Percent distribution by means of transport							
		All means of transport	Rail	Motor carrier	Private truck	Air	Water	Other	Unknown
TONS OF SHIPMENTS	(thousands of tons)								
U.S. TOTAL	26 422	100.0	56.0	24.9	13.7	-	5.2	.1	.1
MIDDLE ATLANTIC	2 245	100.0	42.1	47.5	10.0	-	.3	-	-
UNDER 100 MILES	704	100.0	-	76.3	23.6	.1	-	-	-
100 TO 199 MILES	779	100.0	54.5	38.1	7.3	-	-	-	-
200 TO 299 MILES	419	100.0	77.8	22.1	.1	-	-	-	-
300 TO 499 MILES	207	100.0	87.4	12.5	.1	-	-	-	-
500 TO 999 MILES	73	100.0	8.7	86.8	1.6	-	2.1	.8	-
1000 TO 1499 MILES	43	100.0	7.5	80.5	-	-	12.0	-	-
1500 MILES OR OVER	17	100.0	19.6	79.7	-	-	.7	-	-
EAST NORTH CENTRAL	2 931	100.0	28.1	38.3	4.7	-	28.8	-	-
UNDER 100 MILES	522	100.0	12.6	75.6	11.8	-	-	-	-
100 TO 199 MILES	962	100.0	22.9	37.4	4.9	-	34.9	-	-
200 TO 299 MILES	355	100.0	60.8	34.3	4.9	-	-	-	-
300 TO 499 MILES	845	100.0	19.3	20.0	.4	-	60.2	-	-
500 TO 999 MILES	192	100.0	59.0	37.2	3.8	-	-	.1	-
1000 TO 1499 MILES	18	100.0	96.2	2.9	.8	-	-	-	-
1500 MILES OR OVER	33	100.0	83.0	17.0	-	-	-	-	-
WEST NORTH CENTRAL	2 023	100.0	48.1	41.3	10.3	-	-	-	.3
UNDER 100 MILES	654	100.0	11.8	75.8	12.1	-	-	-	.3
100 TO 199 MILES	631	100.0	47.1	45.0	7.9	-	-	-	-
200 TO 299 MILES	310	100.0	77.2	9.8	13.0	-	-	-	-
300 TO 499 MILES	324	100.0	82.2	6.2	11.6	-	-	-	-
500 TO 999 MILES	92	100.0	88.7	5.3	2.5	-	-	-	3.5
1000 TO 1499 MILES	7	100.0	100.0	-	-	-	-	-	-
1500 MILES OR OVER	3	100.0	100.0	-	-	-	-	-	-
SOUTH ATLANTIC	10 230	100.0	71.9	10.4	15.9	-	1.5	.2	.1
UNDER 100 MILES	5 200	100.0	68.2	10.0	20.4	-	1.3	-	.1
100 TO 199 MILES	1 803	100.0	56.3	23.0	20.6	-	-	.1	-
200 TO 299 MILES	449	100.0	85.9	3.9	6.8	-	-	3.3	-
300 TO 499 MILES	448	100.0	93.0	3.6	3.5	-	-	-	-
500 TO 999 MILES	1 595	100.0	87.4	4.6	8.0	-	-	-	.5
1000 TO 1499 MILES	679	100.0	81.5	2.7	2.7	-	12.6	-	.5
1500 MILES OR OVER	53	100.0	77.5	11.6	-	-	-	-	10.9
EAST SOUTH CENTRAL	2 164	100.0	42.9	17.6	23.1	-	15.8	-	.6
UNDER 100 MILES	724	100.0	10.8	18.1	59.3	-	11.8	-	-
100 TO 199 MILES	510	100.0	57.6	29.5	10.4	-	-	-	2.5
200 TO 299 MILES	277	100.0	84.4	13.4	2.1	-	-	-	-
300 TO 499 MILES	500	100.0	35.8	10.7	2.1	-	51.4	-	-
500 TO 999 MILES	143	100.0	95.7	4.3	-	-	-	-	-
1000 TO 1499 MILES	-	100.0	-	99.9	-	-	-	.1	-
1500 MILES OR OVER	7	100.0	68.3	31.7	-	-	-	-	-
WEST SOUTH CENTRAL	4 697	100.0	67.4	22.6	9.6	-	.4	-	-
UNDER 100 MILES	709	100.0	29.6	45.6	24.8	-	-	-	-
100 TO 199 MILES	724	100.0	44.3	44.0	11.7	-	-	-	-
200 TO 299 MILES	654	100.0	50.6	35.3	13.6	-	.5	-	-
300 TO 499 MILES	1 376	100.0	86.1	6.5	6.9	-	.5	-	-
500 TO 999 MILES	1 107	100.0	91.0	7.7	.6	-	.6	-	-
1000 TO 1499 MILES	95	100.0	90.9	9.1	-	-	-	-	-
1500 MILES OR OVER	30	100.0	87.0	13.0	-	-	-	-	-
PACIFIC	1 415	100.0	3.2	66.8	30.0	-	-	-	-
UNDER 100 MILES	689	100.0	-	66.7	33.3	-	-	-	-
100 TO 199 MILES	333	100.0	-	52.6	47.4	-	-	-	-
200 TO 299 MILES	157	100.0	-	97.8	2.2	-	-	-	-
300 TO 499 MILES	146	100.0	-	84.6	15.4	-	-	-	-
500 TO 999 MILES	68	100.0	41.9	42.8	15.2	-	-	-	-
1000 TO 1499 MILES	6	100.0	93.8	.7	5.5	-	-	-	-
1500 MILES OR OVER	11	100.0	85.6	12.2	-	-	2.2	-	-
TON-MILES OF SHIPMENTS	(millions of ton-miles)								
U.S. TOTAL	7 380	100.0	70.6	16.3	6.6	-	6.0	.1	.3
MIDDLE ATLANTIC	470	100.0	48.8	45.7	3.5	-	1.9	.1	-
UNDER 100 MILES	32	100.0	-	79.6	20.4	-	-	-	-
100 TO 199 MILES	109	100.0	56.4	35.3	8.3	-	-	-	-
200 TO 299 MILES	103	100.0	77.9	22.0	.1	-	-	-	-
300 TO 499 MILES	79	100.0	87.9	12.0	.1	-	-	-	-
500 TO 999 MILES	55	100.0	9.0	86.6	1.1	-	2.6	.8	-
1000 TO 1499 MILES	49	100.0	6.7	79.0	-	-	14.3	-	-
1500 MILES OR OVER	40	100.0	21.0	78.2	-	-	.7	-	-

See footnotes at end of table 4.

TABLE 1. TCC GROUP 287—Percent Distribution of Geographic Division of Origin and Distance Shipped, by Means of Transport: 1972—Continued

Geographic division of origin[1] and distance shipped[2]	Number	Percent distribution by means of transport							
		All means of transport	Rail	Motor carrier	Private truck	Air	Water	Other	Unknown
TON-MILES OF SHIPMENTS	(millions of ton-miles)								
EAST NORTH CENTRAL	775	100.0	39.1	28.3	2.7	-	29.9	-	-
UNDER 100 MILES	25	100.0	15.4	70.7	13.9	-	-	-	-
100 TO 199 MILES	128	100.0	26.4	40.4	5.8	-	27.5	-	-
200 TO 299 MILES	86	100.0	60.3	34.9	4.7	-	-	-	-
300 TO 499 MILES	322	100.0	18.3	20.3	.4	-	61.0	-	-
500 TO 999 MILES	127	100.0	62.4	33.8	3.8	-	-	.1	-
1000 TO 1499 MILES	21	100.0	96.1	3.0	.8	-	-	-	-
1500 MILES OR OVER	63	100.0	84.4	15.6	-	-	-	-	-
WEST NORTH CENTRAL	400	100.0	69.6	20.2	9.4	-	-	-	.8
UNDER 100 MILES	33	100.0	13.8	73.2	12.4	-	-	-	.5
100 TO 199 MILES	93	100.0	50.1	41.6	8.3	-	-	-	-
200 TO 299 MILES	76	100.0	77.5	9.5	13.0	-	-	-	-
300 TO 499 MILES	121	100.0	82.3	5.8	11.9	-	-	-	-
500 TO 999 MILES	59	100.0	87.7	5.4	2.1	-	-	-	4.7
1000 TO 1499 MILES	10	100.0	100.0	-	-	-	-	-	-
1500 MILES OR OVER	5	100.0	100.0	-	-	-	-	-	-
SOUTH ATLANTIC	2 963	100.0	81.8	6.5	7.8	-	3.1	.1	.7
UNDER 100 MILES	284	100.0	69.1	11.1	18.2	-	1.4	-	.2
100 TO 199 MILES	250	100.0	57.9	22.1	20.0	-	-	.1	-
200 TO 299 MILES	105	100.0	86.6	4.0	6.6	-	-	2.8	-
300 TO 499 MILES	186	100.0	93.0	3.7	3.3	-	-	-	-
500 TO 999 MILES	1 258	100.0	87.5	4.7	7.7	-	-	-	-
1000 TO 1499 MILES	782	100.0	82.7	2.7	2.7	-	11.3	-	.6
1500 MILES OR OVER	95	100.0	71.5	14.1	-	-	-	-	14.4
EAST SOUTH CENTRAL	492	100.0	59.2	13.7	6.7	-	20.0	-	.5
UNDER 100 MILES	40	100.0	10.4	18.4	51.2	-	20.0	-	-
100 TO 199 MILES	80	100.0	59.9	28.1	8.8	-	-	-	3.1
200 TO 299 MILES	70	100.0	85.1	12.9	2.0	-	-	-	-
300 TO 499 MILES	184	100.0	39.1	10.1	2.0	-	48.9	-	-
500 TO 999 MILES	101	100.0	95.6	4.4	-	-	-	-	-
1000 TO 1499 MILES	-	100.0	-	99.9	-	-	-	.1	-
1500 MILES OR OVER	14	100.0	67.7	32.3	-	-	-	-	-
WEST SOUTH CENTRAL	1 765	100.0	81.2	13.2	5.0	-	.6	-	-
UNDER 100 MILES	38	100.0	26.7	48.5	24.8	-	-	-	-
100 TO 199 MILES	105	100.0	42.6	45.4	12.0	-	-	-	-
200 TO 299 MILES	161	100.0	49.3	35.1	15.1	-	.4	-	-
300 TO 499 MILES	521	100.0	86.4	6.1	6.9	-	.5	-	-
500 TO 999 MILES	772	100.0	90.4	7.9	.8	-	.8	-	-
1000 TO 1499 MILES	104	100.0	90.0	10.0	-	-	-	-	-
1500 MILES OR OVER	61	100.0	89.8	10.2	-	-	-	-	-
PACIFIC	258	100.0	16.8	62.3	20.6	-	.2	-	-
UNDER 100 MILES	42	100.0	-	64.1	35.9	-	-	-	-
100 TO 199 MILES	49	100.0	-	54.8	45.2	-	-	-	-
200 TO 299 MILES	36	100.0	-	97.8	2.2	-	-	-	-
300 TO 499 MILES	60	100.0	-	85.3	14.7	-	-	-	-
500 TO 999 MILES	37	100.0	41.7	42.7	15.6	-	-	-	-
1000 TO 1499 MILES	9	100.0	94.9	.7	4.3	-	-	-	-
1500 MILES OR OVER	23	100.0	82.7	14.6	-	-	2.7	-	-

See footnotes at end of table 4.

TABLE 2. TCC GROUP 287—Percent Distribution of Geographic Division of Origin and Means of Transport, by Geographic Division of Destination: 1972

Geographic division of origin[1] and means of transport	Number	Percent distribution by division of destination									
		U.S. total	New England	Middle Atlantic	East North Central	West North Central	South Atlantic	East South Central	West South Central	Mountain	Pacific
TONS OF SHIPMENTS	(thousands of tons)										
U.S. TOTAL	26 422	100.0	1.1	8.5	14.8	10.8	32.4	10.4	12.5	3.6	6.0
RAIL	14 801	100.0	1.6	6.9	12.8	12.9	38.9	10.4	11.0	4.2	1.3
MOTOR CARRIER	6 587	100.0	.5	15.4	17.2	11.0	17.0	6.8	14.5	2.8	14.8
PRIVATE TRUCK	3 612	100.0	.7	5.6	3.8	5.9	43.6	15.1	10.2	4.0	11.2
AIR	-	100.0	.8	79.5	.1	3.0	13.1	1.2	1.5	.7	-
WATER	1 365	100.0	-	-	54.1	-	5.0	14.6	26.2	-	.1
OTHER	21	100.0	.2	1.0	3.5	.2	95.0	.1	-	-	-
UNKNOWN	33	100.0	2.7	9.7	-	6.1	15.4	38.0	10.9	-	17.3
MIDDLE ATLANTIC	2 245	100.0	8.2	82.7	1.4	.8	4.1	1.2	.9	.3	.5
RAIL	945	100.0	16.5	81.4	.4	.8	.6	-	-	-	.4
MOTOR CARRIER	1 066	100.0	2.5	83.3	2.4	1.0	5.6	2.5	1.3	.6	.8
PRIVATE TRUCK	225	100.0	.6	87.8	.5	-	11.1	-	-	-	-
AIR	-	100.0	-	97.6	.1	-	-	1.4	-	.9	-
WATER	6	100.0	-	-	-	-	22.2	-	76.1	-	1.7
OTHER	-	100.0	1.4	2.2	95.0	.2	1.2	-	-	-	-
UNKNOWN	-	100.0	-	-	-	-	-	-	-	-	-

See footnotes at end of table 4.

TABLE 2. **TCC GROUP 287—Percent Distribution of Geographic Division of Origin and Means of Transport, by Geographic Division of Destination: 1972**—Continued

Geographic division of origin[1] and means of transport	Number	Percent distribution by division of destination									
		U.S. total	New England	Middle Atlantic	East North Central	West North Central	South Atlantic	East South Central	West South Central	Mountain	Pacific
TONS OF SHIPMENTS	(thousands of tons)										
EAST NORTH CENTRAL	2 931	100.0	.5	4.7	71.5	9.9	3.4	6.9	1.3	.6	1.2
RAIL	824	100.0	1.2	2.6	50.9	25.9	4.7	5.3	4.2	1.8	3.4
MOTOR CARRIER	1 123	100.0	.5	10.2	73.3	6.6	5.2	3.2	.3	.1	.5
PRIVATE TRUCK	137	100.0	-	1.1	88.7	2.4	1.2	5.5	1.0	.1	-
AIR	-	100.0	15.9	-	-	55.8	-	-	28.3	-	-
WATER	845	100.0	-	-	86.5	-	-	13.5	-	-	-
OTHER	-	100.0	7.2	40.7	34.1	8.1	7.6	-	2.4	-	-
UNKNOWN	-	100.0	25.8	22.6	-	-	51.6	-	-	-	-
WEST NORTH CENTRAL	2 023	100.0	-	.3	17.8	72.0	.8	2.7	5.6	.1	.5
RAIL	973	100.0	-	.3	14.7	68.5	1.7	5.7	8.0	-	1.1
MOTOR CARRIER	836	100.0	-	-	24.7	71.1	-	-	3.9	.3	-
PRIVATE TRUCK	209	100.0	-	-	5.4	92.9	-	-	1.7	-	-
AIR	-	100.0	-	-	-	-	-	-	-	-	-
WATER	-	100.0	-	-	-	-	-	-	-	-	-
OTHER	-	100.0	-	-	-	-	100.0	-	-	-	-
UNKNOWN	5	100.0	-	61.1	-	38.9	-	-	-	-	-
SOUTH ATLANTIC	10 230	100.0	.1	1.2	7.7	5.1	76.4	5.6	3.6	.1	.1
RAIL	7 355	100.0	.1	1.5	10.6	6.8	71.4	6.3	3.2	.1	-
MOTOR CARRIER	1 065	100.0	-	.7	.8	1.5	90.5	4.0	1.9	-	.5
PRIVATE TRUCK	1 625	100.0	-	.1	.1	.7	93.1	4.2	1.8	-	-
AIR	-	100.0	-	-	-	-	-	100.0	-	-	-
WATER	152	100.0	-	-	-	-	43.8	-	56.2	-	-
OTHER	17	100.0	-	-	.1	-	99.8	.1	-	-	-
UNKNOWN	14	100.0	-	.3	-	-	35.1	-	25.0	-	39.6
EAST SOUTH CENTRAL	2 164	100.0	-	1.5	7.5	3.9	8.1	61.8	16.8	.1	.3
RAIL	928	100.0	-	3.6	17.0	8.7	12.4	50.4	7.4	.2	.4
MOTOR CARRIER	381	100.0	-	-	1.4	.7	7.2	80.7	9.4	-	.7
PRIVATE TRUCK	499	100.0	-	-	-	-	6.6	93.0	.5	-	-
AIR	-	100.0	-	-	-	-	-	-	-	-	-
WATER	342	100.0	-	-	-	-	-	25.0	75.0	-	-
OTHER	-	100.0	-	28.6	-	-	-	71.4	-	-	-
UNKNOWN	12	100.0	-	-	-	-	-	100.0	-	-	-
WEST SOUTH CENTRAL	4 697	100.0	.1	1.6	9.9	9.2	7.2	11.6	50.7	9.0	.7
RAIL	3 168	100.0	.1	2.3	12.4	12.7	10.5	16.0	37.8	7.4	.8
MOTOR CARRIER	1 059	100.0	-	.2	6.2	2.2	.5	3.1	79.7	7.5	.7
PRIVATE TRUCK	452	100.0	-	-	-	1.1	-	1.2	73.1	24.7	-
AIR	-	100.0	-	46.8	-	-	53.2	-	-	-	-
WATER	17	100.0	-	-	41.1	-	-	-	58.9	-	-
OTHER	-	100.0	-	-	-	-	-	-	-	-	-
UNKNOWN	-	100.0	-	-	-	-	-	-	-	-	-
PACIFIC	1 415	100.0	-	.1	-	-	-	.4	.1	.7	97.0
RAIL	45	100.0	-	-	-	1.1	13.4	4.4	21.9	-	59.2
MOTOR CARRIER	945	100.0	-	.1	-	-	-	-	-	.5	99.3
PRIVATE TRUCK	424	100.0	-	-	-	-	-	-	-	4.3	95.7
AIR	-	100.0	-	-	-	-	-	-	-	-	-
WATER	-	100.0	-	-	-	-	-	-	-	-	100.0
OTHER	-	100.0	-	-	-	-	-	-	-	-	-
UNKNOWN	-	100.0	-	-	-	-	-	-	-	-	-
TON-MILES OF SHIPMENTS	(millions of ton-miles)										
U.S. TOTAL	7 380	100.0	1.4	7.2	19.7	17.6	18.3	10.4	14.8	3.9	6.7
RAIL	5 213	100.0	1.8	7.2	20.5	21.5	19.2	9.6	12.4	3.7	4.0
MOTOR CARRIER	1 203	100.0	.8	11.8	14.2	10.7	14.1	10.2	15.9	4.2	18.0
PRIVATE TRUCK	486	100.0	.5	2.6	3.6	10.6	33.4	14.9	15.8	8.1	10.5
AIR	-	100.0	2.8	15.7	.3	4.1	58.4	4.5	7.5	6.8	-
WATER	443	100.0	-	-	44.5	-	1.2	15.2	38.7	-	.4
OTHER	8	100.0	.3	1.0	6.1	.4	92.1	-	.1	-	-
UNKNOWN	24	100.0	.2	11.4	-	.7	3.5	10.0	19.2	-	55.0
MIDDLE ATLANTIC	470	100.0	14.5	52.0	3.6	4.1	7.0	5.4	4.8	2.6	6.0
RAIL	229	100.0	27.2	65.0	.8	3.0	.4	-	-	-	3.7
MOTOR CARRIER	215	100.0	2.6	38.7	6.6	5.7	12.6	11.9	7.2	5.6	9.1
PRIVATE TRUCK	16	100.0	1.8	73.4	3.6	-	21.2	-	-	-	-
AIR	-	100.0	-	32.6	1.5	-	-	25.8	-	40.1	-
WATER	8	100.0	-	-	-	-	16.2	-	80.4	-	3.3
OTHER	-	100.0	.3	.5	98.1	.3	.7	-	-	-	.2
UNKNOWN	-	100.0	-	-	-	-	-	-	-	-	-

See footnotes at end of table 4.

TABLE 2. **TCC GROUP 287—Percent Distribution of Geographic Division of Origin and Means of Transport, by Geographic Division of Destination: 1972**—Continued

Geographic division of origin[1] and means of transport	Number	Percent distribution by division of destination									
		U.S. total	New England	Middle Atlantic	East North Central	West North Central	South Atlantic	East South Central	West South Central	Mountain	Pacific
TON-MILES OF SHIPMENTS	(millions of ton-miles)										
EAST NORTH CENTRAL......	775	100.0	1.4	8.1	48.0	12.4	5.9	9.4	4.4	2.2	8.2
RAIL..................	303	100.0	2.1	3.9	25.2	23.2	7.9	4.8	10.0	5.2	17.8
MOTOR CARRIER.........	219	100.0	2.1	23.2	41.4	11.3	9.2	6.3	1.4	.6	4.6
PRIVATE TRUCK.........	21	100.0	-	1.7	67.1	4.8	5.5	16.3	4.4	.3	-
AIR..................	-	100.0	19.4	-	-	28.7	-	-	51.9	-	-
WATER.................	231	100.0	-	-	82.3	-	-	17.7	-	-	-
OTHER.................	-	100.0	12.1	38.6	19.7	14.6	10.4	-	4.6	-	-
UNKNOWN...............	-	100.0	26.6	5.1	-	-	68.3	-	-	-	-
WEST NORTH CENTRAL......	400	100.0	-	1.4	13.8	62.2	3.4	6.1	8.7	.5	3.9
RAIL..................	278	100.0	-	1.0	15.0	55.4	4.9	8.7	9.4	-	5.6
MOTOR CARRIER.........	80	100.0	-	.1	14.8	73.8	-	-	8.8	2.5	-
PRIVATE TRUCK.........	37	100.0	-	-	4.0	92.4	-	-	3.6	-	-
AIR..................	-	100.0	-	-	-	-	-	-	-	-	-
WATER.................	-	100.0	-	-	-	-	-	-	-	-	-
OTHER.................	-	100.0	-	-	-	100.0	-	-	-	-	-
UNKNOWN...............	3	100.0	-	93.9	-	6.1	-	-	-	-	-
SOUTH ATLANTIC..........	2 963	100.0	.4	3.1	22.2	20.7	30.8	9.8	11.6	.3	1.1
RAIL..................	2 423	100.0	.5	3.7	27.0	24.2	26.7	8.8	8.5	.4	.2
MOTOR CARRIER.........	192	100.0	-	.7	2.0	8.3	54.0	18.0	9.9	.3	6.7
PRIVATE TRUCK.........	232	100.0·	-	.2	.5	4.9	65.2	17.9	11.2	-	-
AIR..................	-	100.0	-	-	-	-	-	100.0	-	-	-
WATER.................	92	100.0	-	-	-	-	4.3	-	95.7	-	-
OTHER.................	3	100.0	-	-	.2	-	99.7	-	-	-	-
UNKNOWN...............	19	100.0	-	-	-	-	4.6	-	24.7	-	70.7
EAST SOUTH CENTRAL......	492	100.0	-	5.3	10.9	9.6	12.5	35.1	23.7	.5	2.5
RAIL..................	291	100.0	-	9.0	18.0	15.6	15.9	27.3	10.8	.8	2.6
MOTOR CARRIER.........	67	100.0	-	-	1.6	2.3	12.9	57.3	18.8	-	7.0
PRIVATE TRUCK.........	32	100.0	-	-	-	-	19.1	79.9	1.0	-	-
AIR..................	-	100.0	-	-	-	-	-	-	-	-	-
WATER.................	98	100.0	-	-	-	-	-	26.5	73.5	-	-
OTHER.................	-	100.0	-	84.4	-	-	-	15.6	-	-	-
UNKNOWN...............	2	100.0	-	-	-	-	-	100.0	-	-	-
WEST SOUTH CENTRAL......	1 765	100.0	.3	4.5	16.8	13.4	14.6	9.9	29.6	7.1	3.8
RAIL..................	1 433	100.0	.4	5.4	16.8	15.5	17.7	11.4	23.8	5.1	3.9
MOTOR CARRIER.........	233	100.0	-	1.0	20.8	4.7	1.9	4.0	55.8	7.1	4.8
PRIVATE TRUCK.........	88	100.0	-	-	-	4.7	-	1.0	54.2	40.2	-
AIR..................	-	100.0	-	60.6	-	-	39.4	-	-	-	-
WATER.................	9	100.0	-	-	65.0	-	-	-	35.0	-	-
OTHER.................	-	100.0	-	-	-	-	-	-	-	-	-
UNKNOWN...............	-	100.0	-	-	-	-	-	-	-	-	-
PACIFIC...............	258	100.0	-	1.1	.2	.3	5.0	1.2	5.0	1.8	85.4
RAIL..................	43	100.0	-	-	-	1.5	29.8	7.1	29.7	-	31.9
MOTOR CARRIER.........	161	100.0	-	1.8	.3	-	-	-	-	1.4	96.4
PRIVATE TRUCK.........	53	100.0	-	-	-	-	-	-	-	4.6	95.4
AIR..................	-	100.0	-	-	-	-	-	-	-	-	-
WATER.................	-	100.0	-	-	-	-	-	-	-	-	100.0
OTHER.................	-	100.0	-	-	-	-	-	-	-	-	-
UNKNOWN...............	-	100.0	-	-	-	-	-	-	-	-	-

See footnotes at end of table 4.

TABLE 3. **TCC GROUP 287—Percent Distribution of Geographic Division of Destination and Means of Transport, by Geographic Division of Origin: 1972**

Geographic division of destination and means of transport	Number	Percent distribution by division of origin[1]									
		U.S. total	New England	Middle Atlantic	East North Central	West North Central	South Atlantic	East South Central	West South Central	Mountain	Pacific
TONS OF SHIPMENTS	(thousands of tons)										
U.S. TOTAL	26 422	100.0	(D)	8.5	11.1	7.7	38.7	8.2	17.8	(D)	5.4
RAIL	14 801	100.0	(D)	6.4	5.6	6.6	49.7	6.3	21.4	(D)	.3
MOTOR CARRIER	6 587	100.0	(D)	16.2	17.1	12.7	16.2	5.8	16.1	(D)	14.3
PRIVATE TRUCK	3 612	100.0	(D)	6.2	3.8	5.8	45.0	13.8	12.5	(D)	11.8
AIR	-	100.0	(D)	79.6	5.3	-	.1	-	4.1	(D)	-
WATER	1 365	100.0	(D)	.5	61.9	-	11.2	25.1	1.3	(D)	-
OTHER	21	100.0	(D)	2.8	2.3	-	79.6	-	-	(D)	-
UNKNOWN	33	100.0	(D)	-	-	15.7	43.7	38.0	-	(D)	-
NEW ENGLAND	295	100.0	(D)	62.6	5.4	-	3.2	-	1.3	(D)	-
RAIL	234	100.0	(D)	66.7	4.3	-	3.9	-	1.6	(D)	-
MOTOR CARRIER	32	100.0	(D)	81.6	17.4	-	.9	-	-	(D)	-
PRIVATE TRUCK	26	100.0	(D)	4.8	-	-	-	-	-	(D)	-
AIR	-	100.0	(D)	-	100.0	-	-	-	-	(D)	-
WATER	-	100.0	(D)	-	-	-	-	-	-	(D)	-
OTHER	-	100.0	(D)	19.1	80.9	-	-	-	-	(D)	-
UNKNOWN	-	100.0	(D)	-	.1	-	-	-	-	(D)	-
MIDDLE ATLANTIC	2 242	100.0	(D)	82.8	6.2	.3	5.5	1.5	3.3	(D)	.1
RAIL	1 022	100.0	(D)	75.3	2.1	.3	11.1	3.2	7.0	(D)	-
MOTOR CARRIER	1 014	100.0	(D)	87.6	11.3	-	.7	-	.2	(D)	.1
PRIVATE TRUCK	201	100.0	(D)	98.4	.8	-	.8	-	-	(D)	-
AIR	-	100.0	(D)	97.6	-	-	-	-	2.4	(D)	-
WATER	-	100.0	(D)	-	-	-	-	-	-	(D)	-
OTHER	-	100.0	(D)	6.3	93.6	-	-	-	-	(D)	-
UNKNOWN	3	100.0	(D)	-	-	98.7	1.3	-	-	(D)	-
EAST NORTH CENTRAL	3 907	100.0	(D)	.8	53.6	9.2	20.2	4.2	11.9	(D)	-
RAIL	1 896	100.0	(D)	.2	22.1	7.5	41.1	8.3	20.7	(D)	-
MOTOR CARRIER	1 135	100.0	(D)	2.2	72.5	18.2	.7	.5	5.8	(D)	-
PRIVATE TRUCK	135	100.0	(D)	.9	89.4	8.3	1.4	-	-	(D)	-
AIR	-	100.0	(D)	100.0	-	-	-	-	-	(D)	-
WATER	738	100.0	(D)	-	99.0	-	-	-	1.0	(D)	-
OTHER	-	100.0	(D)	76.4	22.0	-	1.6	-	-	(D)	-
UNKNOWN	-	100.0	(D)	-	-	-	-	-	-	(D)	-
WEST NORTH CENTRAL	2 855	100.0	(D)	.6	10.2	51.1	18.4	2.9	15.1	(D)	-
RAIL	1 913	100.0	(D)	.4	11.2	34.9	26.0	4.2	21.1	(D)	-
MOTOR CARRIER	726	100.0	(D)	1.5	10.2	81.9	2.2	.3	3.3	(D)	-
PRIVATE TRUCK	213	100.0	(D)	-	1.5	91.1	5.1	-	2.2	(D)	-
AIR	-	100.0	(D)	-	100.0	-	-	-	-	(D)	-
WATER	-	100.0	(D)	-	-	-	-	-	-	(D)	-
OTHER	-	100.0	(D)	2.6	90.2	7.2	-	-	-	(D)	-
UNKNOWN	2	100.0	(D)	-	-	100.0	-	-	-	(D)	-
SOUTH ATLANTIC	8 549	100.0	(D)	1.1	1.2	.2	91.4	2.0	3.9	(D)	.1
RAIL	5 762	100.0	(D)	.1	.7	.3	91.1	2.0	5.8	(D)	.1
MOTOR CARRIER	1 118	100.0	(D)	5.3	5.3	-	86.1	2.4	.5	(D)	-
PRIVATE TRUCK	1 573	100.0	(D)	1.6	.1	-	96.2	2.1	-	(D)	-
AIR	-	100.0	(D)	-	-	-	-	-	16.7	(D)	-
WATER	68	100.0	(D)	2.2	-	-	97.8	-	-	(D)	-
OTHER	20	100.0	(D)	-	.2	-	83.7	-	-	(D)	-
UNKNOWN	5	100.0	(D)	-	-	-	100.0	-	-	(D)	-
EAST SOUTH CENTRAL	2 748	100.0	(D)	1.0	7.3	2.0	21.0	48.7	19.8	(D)	.1
RAIL	1 544	100.0	(D)	-	2.8	3.6	30.2	30.3	32.8	(D)	.1
MOTOR CARRIER	447	100.0	(D)	5.9	8.2	-	9.6	68.8	7.2	(D)	-
PRIVATE TRUCK	544	100.0	(D)	-	1.4	-	12.5	85.2	1.0	(D)	-
AIR	-	100.0	(D)	94.7	-	-	5.3	-	-	(D)	-
WATER	199	100.0	(D)	-	57.1	-	-	42.9	-	(D)	-
OTHER	-	100.0	(D)	-	-	-	99.5	.5	-	(D)	-
UNKNOWN	12	100.0	(D)	-	-	-	-	100.0	-	(D)	-
WEST SOUTH CENTRAL	3 306	100.0	(D)	.6	1.2	3.4	11.2	11.0	72.1	(D)	.3
RAIL	1 622	100.0	(D)	-	2.1	4.8	14.4	4.3	73.8	(D)	.6
MOTOR CARRIER	955	100.0	(D)	1.5	.3	3.4	2.1	3.8	88.4	(D)	-
PRIVATE TRUCK	366	100.0	(D)	-	.4	1.0	7.9	.6	90.1	(D)	-
AIR	-	100.0	(D)	-	100.0	-	-	-	-	(D)	-
WATER	358	100.0	(D)	1.5	-	-	23.9	71.8	2.9	(D)	-
OTHER	-	100.0	(D)	-	100.0	-	-	-	-	(D)	-
UNKNOWN	3	100.0	(D)	-	-	-	100.0	-	-	(D)	-
MOUNTAIN	944	100.0	(D)	.6	1.8	.3	.6	.2	45.0	(D)	2.5
RAIL	617	100.0	(D)	-	2.5	-	.9	.2	38.0	(D)	-
MOTOR CARRIER	183	100.0	(D)	3.2	.7	1.4	.2	-	43.0	(D)	2.7
PRIVATE TRUCK	143	100.0	(D)	-	.1	-	-	-	77.7	(D)	12.7
AIR	-	100.0	(D)	100.0	-	-	-	-	-	(D)	-
WATER	-	100.0	(D)	-	-	-	-	-	-	(D)	-
OTHER	-	100.0	(D)	-	-	-	-	-	-	(D)	-
UNKNOWN	-	100.0	(D)	-	-	-	-	-	-	(D)	-
PACIFIC	1 573	100.0	(D)	.8	2.1	.7	.9	.4	2.2	(D)	87.2
RAIL	187	100.0	(D)	1.9	15.0	5.8	1.1	2.1	14.1	(D)	14.3
MOTOR CARRIER	973	100.0	(D)	.9	.6	-	.6	.3	.8	(D)	96.4
PRIVATE TRUCK	406	100.0	(D)	-	-	-	-	-	-	(D)	100.0
AIR	-	100.0	(D)	-	-	-	-	-	-	(D)	-
WATER	-	100.0	(D)	15.1	-	-	-	-	-	(D)	33.7
OTHER	-	100.0	(D)	100.0	-	-	-	-	-	(D)	-
UNKNOWN	5	100.0	(D)	-	-	-	100.0	-	-	(D)	-

See footnotes at end of table 4.

TABLE 3. TCC GROUP 287—Percent Distribution of Geographic Division of Destination and Means of Transport, by Geographic Division of Origin: 1972—Continued

Geographic division of destination and means of transport	Number	Percent distribution by division of origin[1]									
		U.S. total	New England	Middle Atlantic	East North Central	West North Central	South Atlantic	East South Central	West South Central	Mountain	Pacific
TON-MILES OF SHIPMENTS	(millions of ton-miles)										
U.S. TOTAL	7 380	100.0	(D)	6.4	10.5	5.4	40.2	6.7	23.9	(D)	3.5
RAIL	5 213	100.0	(D)	4.4	5.8	5.3	46.5	5.6	27.5	(D)	.8
MOTOR CARRIER	1 203	100.0	(D)	17.9	18.2	6.7	16.0	5.6	19.4	(D)	13.4
PRIVATE TRUCK	486	100.0	(D)	3.4	4.4	7.7	47.8	6.8	18.2	(D)	11.0
AIR	-	100.0	(D)	16.9	14.4	-	.1	-	16.9	(D)	-
WATER	443	100.0	(D)	2.0	52.3	-	20.9	22.2	2.2	(D)	.1
OTHER	8	100.0	(D)	5.7	2.4	-	45.4	-	-	(D)	-
UNKNOWN	24	100.0	(D)	-	-	12.1	77.7	10.0	-	(D)	-
NEW ENGLAND	105	100.0	(D)	64.5	10.5	-	10.7	-	5.2	(D)	-
RAIL	92	100.0	(D)	67.3	6.9	-	12.1	-	5.9	(D)	-
MOTOR CARRIER	10	100.0	(D)	53.8	45.3	-	.9	-	-	(D)	-
PRIVATE TRUCK	2	100.0	(D)	10.9	-	-	-	-	-	(D)	-
AIR	-	100.0	(D)	-	100.0	-	-	-	-	(D)	-
WATER	-	100.0	(D)	-	-	-	-	-	-	(D)	-
OTHER	-	100.0	(D)	6.3	93.7	-	-	-	-	(D)	-
UNKNOWN	-	100.0	(D)	-	.9	-	-	-	-	(D)	-
MIDDLE ATLANTIC	532	100.0	(D)	45.9	11.9	1.1	17.4	4.9	15.0	(D)	.6
RAIL	374	100.0	(D)	39.8	3.2	.8	24.2	7.0	20.6	(D)	-
MOTOR CARRIER	141	100.0	(D)	58.8	35.8	.1	1.0	-	1.6	(D)	2.1
PRIVATE TRUCK	12	100.0	(D)	93.4	2.7	-	3.8	-	-	(D)	-
AIR	-	100.0	(D)	35.0	-	-	-	-	65.0	(D)	-
WATER	-	100.0	(D)	-	-	-	-	-	-	(D)	-
OTHER	-	100.0	(D)	2.7	97.2	-	-	.1	-	(D)	-
UNKNOWN	2	100.0	(D)	-	-	99.7	.3	-	-	(D)	-
EAST NORTH CENTRAL	1 456	100.0	(D)	1.2	25.5	3.8	45.3	3.7	20.4	(D)	-
RAIL	1 069	100.0	(D)	.2	7.1	3.9	61.2	4.9	22.6	(D)	-
MOTOR CARRIER	171	100.0	(D)	8.3	52.9	7.0	2.3	.6	28.3	(D)	.3
PRIVATE TRUCK	17	100.0	(D)	3.4	81.2	8.6	6.8	-	-	(D)	-
AIR	-	100.0	(D)	100.0	-	-	-	-	-	(D)	-
WATER	197	100.0	(D)	-	96.7	-	-	-	3.3	(D)	-
OTHER	-	100.0	(D)	90.6	7.8	-	1.5	-	-	(D)	-
UNKNOWN	-	100.0	(D)	-	-	-	-	-	-	(D)	-
WEST NORTH CENTRAL	1 299	100.0	(D)	1.5	7.4	19.2	47.2	3.6	18.3	(D)	.1
RAIL	1 119	100.0	(D)	.6	6.3	13.8	52.3	4.1	19.9	(D)	.1
MOTOR CARRIER	128	100.0	(D)	9.5	19.3	46.5	12.4	1.2	8.5	(D)	.1
PRIVATE TRUCK	51	100.0	(D)	-	2.0	67.6	22.4	-	8.1	(D)	-
AIR	-	100.0	(D)	-	100.0	-	-	-	-	(D)	-
WATER	-	100.0	(D)	-	-	-	-	-	-	(D)	-
OTHER	-	100.0	(D)	4.4	95.4	.2	-	-	-	(D)	-
UNKNOWN	-	100.0	(D)	-	-	100.0	-	-	-	(D)	-
SOUTH ATLANTIC	1 347	100.0	(D)	2.4	3.4	1.0	67.6	4.6	19.1	(D)	1.0
RAIL	1 001	100.0	(D)	.1	2.4	1.4	64.7	4.6	25.3	(D)	1.3
MOTOR CARRIER	169	100.0	(D)	16.0	11.9	-	61.1	5.1	2.6	(D)	-
PRIVATE TRUCK	162	100.0	(D)	2.1	.7	-	93.3	3.9	-	(D)	-
AIR	-	100.0	(D)	-	-	-	-	-	11.4	(D)	-
WATER	5	100.0	(D)	26.5	-	-	73.5	-	-	(D)	-
OTHER	7	100.0	(D)	-	.3	-	49.2	-	-	(D)	-
UNKNOWN	-	100.0	(D)	-	.2	-	99.8	-	-	(D)	-
EAST SOUTH CENTRAL	766	100.0	(D)	3.3	9.5	3.2	37.9	22.6	22.7	(D)	.4
RAIL	501	100.0	(D)	-	2.9	4.8	42.7	15.9	32.7	(D)	.6
MOTOR CARRIER	122	100.0	(D)	20.8	11.2	-	28.2	31.4	7.6	(D)	-
PRIVATE TRUCK	72	100.0	(D)	-	4.8	-	57.6	36.4	1.2	(D)	-
AIR	-	100.0	(D)	97.5	-	-	2.5	-	-	(D)	-
WATER	67	100.0	(D)	-	61.1	-	-	38.9	-	(D)	-
OTHER	-	100.0	(D)	-	-	-	99.5	.5	-	(D)	-
UNKNOWN	2	100.0	(D)	-	-	-	-	100.0	-	(D)	-
WEST SOUTH CENTRAL	1 093	100.0	(D)	2.1	3.1	3.2	31.6	10.7	47.8	(D)	1.2
RAIL	648	100.0	(D)	-	4.7	4.0	31.8	4.8	52.5	(D)	2.0
MOTOR CARRIER	191	100.0	(D)	8.1	1.5	3.7	9.9	6.6	68.0	(D)	-
PRIVATE TRUCK	76	100.0	(D)	-	1.2	1.7	33.9	.4	62.7	(D)	-
AIR	-	100.0	(D)	-	100.0	-	-	-	-	(D)	-
WATER	171	100.0	(D)	4.1	-	-	51.7	42.1	2.0	(D)	-
OTHER	-	100.0	(D)	-	100.0	-	-	-	-	(D)	-
UNKNOWN	4	100.0	(D)	-	-	-	100.0	-	-	(D)	-
MOUNTAIN	284	100.0	(D)	4.2	6.0	.7	3.2	.8	44.0	(D)	1.7
RAIL	194	100.0	(D)	-	8.0	-	4.5	1.2	37.7	(D)	-
MOTOR CARRIER	51	100.0	(D)	23.5	2.7	4.0	1.0	-	32.2	(D)	4.4
PRIVATE TRUCK	39	100.0	(D)	-	.2	-	-	-	90.5	(D)	6.2
AIR	-	100.0	(D)	100.0	-	-	-	-	-	(D)	-
WATER	-	100.0	(D)	-	-	-	-	-	-	(D)	-
OTHER	-	100.0	(D)	-	-	-	-	-	-	(D)	-
UNKNOWN	-	100.0	(D)	-	-	-	-	-	-	(D)	-
PACIFIC	494	100.0	(D)	5.7	12.9	3.1	6.4	2.5	13.5	(D)	44.7
RAIL	210	100.0	(D)	4.0	25.6	7.4	2.3	3.6	26.4	(D)	6.6
MOTOR CARRIER	217	100.0	(D)	9.0	4.6	-	6.0	2.2	5.1	(D)	71.6
PRIVATE TRUCK	50	100.0	(D)	-	-	-	-	-	-	(D)	100.0
AIR	-	100.0	(D)	-	-	-	-	-	-	(D)	-
WATER	1	100.0	(D)	15.4	-	-	-	-	-	(D)	33.0
OTHER	-	100.0	(D)	100.0	-	-	-	-	-	(D)	-
UNKNOWN	13	100.0	(D)	-	-	-	100.0	-	-	(D)	-

See footnotes at end of table 4.

TABLE 4. TCC GROUP 287—Percent Distribution of Distance Shipped and Weight of Shipment, by Means of Transport: 1972

Distance shipped and weight of shipment[2][3]	Number	Percent distribution by means of transport							
		All means of transport	Rail	Motor carrier	Private truck	Air	Water	Other	Unknown
TONS OF SHIPMENTS	(thousands of tons)								
U.S. TOTAL.........	24 942	100.0	56.7	23.5	14.1	-	5.5	.1	.1
UNDER 100 MILES.........	8 864	100.0	45.0	28.6	24.5	-	1.7	-	.1
UNDER 1000 POUNDS.....	24	100.0	-	61.3	38.1	-	-	.7	-
1000 TO 9999 POUNDS...	277	100.0	.3	23.2	76.3	.2	-	-	-
10000 TO 29999 POUNDS.	734	100.0	1.2	18.9	80.0	-	-	-	-
30000 TO 59999 POUNDS.	3 536	100.0	2.5	62.4	35.0	-	-	-	.1
60000 TO 89999 POUNDS.	121	100.0	61.4	27.3	11.4	-	-	-	-
90000 POUNDS AND OVER.	4 170	100.0	91.6	1.9	2.7	-	3.7	-	.1
100 TO 199 MILES........	5 365	100.0	45.8	32.6	15.1	-	6.3	-	.2
UNDER 1000 POUNDS.....	14	100.0	-	69.1	29.8	-	-	.8	.3
1000 TO 9999 POUNDS...	110	100.0	-	41.4	57.0	-	-	1.6	-
10000 TO 29999 POUNDS.	207	100.0	2.3	38.3	59.4	-	-	-	-
30000 TO 59999 POUNDS.	2 174	100.0	2.1	70.2	27.7	-	-	-	-
60000 TO 89999 POUNDS.	68	100.0	65.4	32.6	2.0	-	-	-	-
90000 POUNDS AND OVER.	2 789	100.0	84.7	2.3	.5	-	12.0	-	.5
200 TO 299 MILES........	2 439	100.0	65.2	26.3	7.7	-	.1	.6	-
UNDER 1000 POUNDS.....	9	100.0	-	80.3	19.3	-	-	.3	-
1000 TO 9999 POUNDS...	37	100.0	4.3	63.9	31.9	-	-	-	-
10000 TO 29999 POUNDS.	58	100.0	1.5	42.2	56.3	-	-	-	-
30000 TO 59999 POUNDS.	706	100.0	1.4	76.6	19.9	-	-	2.1	-
60000 TO 89999 POUNDS.	32	100.0	72.4	27.6	-	-	-	-	-
90000 POUNDS AND OVER.	1 595	100.0	97.5	2.3	-	-	.2	-	-
300 TO 499 MILES........	3 863	100.0	62.4	12.8	4.8	-	20.0	-	-
UNDER 1000 POUNDS.....	7	100.0	-	87.1	8.9	.2	-	3.7	-
1000 TO 9999 POUNDS...	29	100.0	-	86.7	13.3	-	-	-	-
10000 TO 29999 POUNDS.	79	100.0	.8	68.1	31.2	-	-	-	-
30000 TO 59999 POUNDS.	503	100.0	8.2	62.6	29.2	-	-	-	-
60000 TO 89999 POUNDS.	71	100.0	84.2	15.8	-	-	-	-	-
90000 POUNDS AND OVER.	3 173	100.0	72.8	2.5	.3	-	24.4	-	-
500 TO 999 MILES........	3 378	100.0	85.0	10.0	4.6	-	.3	-	.1
UNDER 1000 POUNDS.....	9	100.0	-	81.6	8.0	.3	-	10.1	-
1000 TO 9999 POUNDS...	33	100.0	-	89.7	7.7	-	-	1.0	1.7
10000 TO 29999 POUNDS.	64	100.0	-	74.4	25.6	-	-	-	-
30000 TO 59999 POUNDS.	543	100.0	31.9	42.9	24.9	-	.3	-	-
60000 TO 89999 POUNDS.	107	100.0	84.3	12.7	-	-	-	-	3.0
90000 POUNDS AND OVER.	2 620	100.0	99.5	.2	-	-	.3	-	-
1000 TO 1499 MILES......	862	100.0	79.0	7.4	2.2	-	10.5	.4	.4
UNDER 1000 POUNDS.....	1	100.0	-	84.5	13.5	1.5	-	.5	-
1000 TO 9999 POUNDS...	9	100.0	-	93.8	5.5	.7	-	-	-
10000 TO 29999 POUNDS.	27	100.0	3.2	57.6	14.2	-	19.2	5.7	-
30000 TO 59999 POUNDS.	88	100.0	43.0	38.9	16.1	-	-	2.0	-
60000 TO 89999 POUNDS.	16	100.0	80.9	19.1	-	-	-	-	-
90000 POUNDS AND OVER.	718	100.0	87.6	-	-	-	11.9	-	.5
1500 MILES OR OVER......	168	100.0	77.5	18.6	-	-	.5	-	3.5
UNDER 1000 POUNDS.....	-	100.0	-	71.4	-	.8	27.7	.1	-
1000 TO 9999 POUNDS...	4	100.0	-	95.3	-	-	4.7	-	-
10000 TO 29999 POUNDS.	8	100.0	23.5	76.5	-	-	-	-	-
30000 TO 59999 POUNDS.	35	100.0	30.9	51.6	-	-	1.1	-	16.4
60000 TO 89999 POUNDS.	34	100.0	100.0	-	-	-	-	-	-
90000 POUNDS AND OVER.	84	100.0	98.5	1.5	-	-	-	-	-
TON-MILES OF SHIPMENTS	(millions of ton-miles)								
U.S. TOTAL.........	7 110	100.0	71.1	15.5	6.7	-	6.2	.1	.4
UNDER 100 MILES.........	480	100.0	45.7	28.7	22.9	-	2.5	-	.1
UNDER 1000 POUNDS.....	1	100.0	-	67.3	31.8	-	-	.9	-
1000 TO 9999 POUNDS...	12	100.0	.3	27.0	72.7	.1	-	-	-
10000 TO 29999 POUNDS.	33	100.0	1.2	20.5	78.3	-	-	-	-
30000 TO 59999 POUNDS.	195	100.0	2.7	62.7	34.5	-	-	-	.1
60000 TO 89999 POUNDS.	4	100.0	77.0	14.4	8.6	-	-	-	-
90000 POUNDS AND OVER.	232	100.0	90.3	1.5	2.9	-	5.2	-	.2
100 TO 199 MILES........	759	100.0	47.5	32.4	15.1	-	4.6	-	.3
UNDER 1000 POUNDS.....	2	100.0	-	70.5	28.2	-	-	.9	.4
1000 TO 9999 POUNDS...	16	100.0	-	42.1	56.0	-	-	1.9	-
10000 TO 29999 POUNDS.	30	100.0	2.3	38.9	58.8	-	-	-	-
30000 TO 59999 POUNDS.	304	100.0	2.1	70.1	27.9	-	-	-	-
60000 TO 89999 POUNDS.	9	100.0	60.4	37.9	1.7	-	-	-	-
90000 POUNDS AND OVER.	397	100.0	87.7	2.2	.6	-	8.9	-	.6

See footnotes at end of table 4.

TABLE 4. **TCC GROUP 287—Percent Distribution of Distance Shipped and Weight of Shipment, by Means of Transport: 1972**—Continued

Distance shipped and weight of shipment[2][3]	Number	Percent distribution by means of transport							
		All means of transport	Rail	Motor carrier	Private truck	Air	Water	Other	Unknown
TON-MILES OF SHIPMENTS	(millions of ton-miles)								
200 TO 299 MILES.........	595	100.0	65.2	26.2	8.0	-	.1	.5	-
UNDER 1000 POUNDS.....	2	100.0	-	81.9	17.8	-	-	.3	-
1000 TO 9999 POUNDS...	9	100.0	5.0	63.5	31.5	-	-	-	-
10000 TO 29999 POUNDS.	13	100.0	1.5	44.7	53.8	-	-	-	-
30000 TO 59999 POUNDS.	172	100.0	1.3	75.6	21.4	-	-	1.7	-
60000 TO 89999 POUNDS.	8	100.0	70.3	29.7	-	-	-	-	-
90000 POUNDS AND OVER.	389	100.0	97.5	2.3	-	-	.2	-	-
300 TO 499 MILES......	1 492	100.0	63.2	12.7	4.7	-	19.4	-	-
UNDER 1000 POUNDS.....	2	100.0	-	87.7	8.3	.2	-	3.8	-
1000 TO 9999 POUNDS...	10	100.0	-	88.2	11.8	-	-	-	-
10000 TO 29999 POUNDS.	31	100.0	.6	67.7	31.7	-	-	-	-
30000 TO 59999 POUNDS.	189	100.0	8.4	61.9	29.7	-	-	-	-
60000 TO 89999 POUNDS.	26	100.0	84.4	15.6	-	-	-	-	-
90000 POUNDS AND OVER.	1 230	100.0	73.5	2.7	.2	-	23.5	-	-
500 TO 999 MILES........	2 475	100.0	85.2	9.6	4.7	-	.3	-	.1
UNDER 1000 POUNDS.....	5	100.0	-	79.4	9.0	.3	-	11.3	-
1000 TO 9999 POUNDS...	23	100.0	-	89.8	7.5	-	-	.8	1.9
10000 TO 29999 POUNDS.	46	100.0	-	71.5	28.5	-	-	-	-
30000 TO 59999 POUNDS.	395	100.0	31.9	42.5	25.2	-	.4	-	-
60000 TO 89999 POUNDS.	77	100.0	86.8	9.6	-	-	-	-	3.6
90000 POUNDS AND OVER.	1 924	100.0	99.5	.2	-	-	.3	-	-
1000 TO 1499 MILES......	989	100.0	80.0	7.3	2.2	-	9.7	.4	.5
UNDER 1000 POUNDS.....	1	100.0	-	86.0	12.1	1.4	-	.5	-
1000 TO 9999 POUNDS...	11	100.0	-	94.4	5.0	.6	-	-	-
10000 TO 29999 POUNDS.	31	100.0	3.1	55.7	13.6	-	22.1	5.5	-
30000 TO 59999 POUNDS.	100	100.0	43.1	38.7	16.2	-	-	2.0	-
60000 TO 89999 POUNDS.	19	100.0	84.1	15.9	-	-	-	-	-
90000 POUNDS AND OVER.	824	100.0	88.6	-	-	-	10.8	-	.6
1500 MILES OR OVER......	317	100.0	75.6	19.5	-	-	.6	-	4.3
UNDER 1000 POUNDS.....	1	100.0	-	72.5	-	.7	26.8	.1	-
1000 TO 9999 POUNDS...	11	100.0	-	95.1	-	-	4.9	-	-
10000 TO 29999 POUNDS.	18	100.0	20.6	79.4	-	-	-	-	-
30000 TO 59999 POUNDS.	69	100.0	31.1	47.8	-	-	1.4	-	19.7
60000 TO 89999 POUNDS.	70	100.0	100.0	-	-	-	-	-	-
90000 POUNDS AND OVER.	146	100.0	98.7	1.3	-	-	-	-	-

Note: Detail may not add to total due to rounding. The introductory table shows the estimates of sampling variability for tons; sampling variability for ton-miles has not been estimated. See the map in the Introduction for the States comprising the geographic divisions of the United States.

Shipments excluded from the survey are those moving by pipeline (primarily petroleum products from refineries), parcel post shipments, and commodities moved by own power (motorized vehicles, aircraft, etc.) or towed (prefabricated buildings, etc.). Local shipments (commodities shipped less than 25 miles from the plant) and shipments within the same city are also excluded. Shipments to Alaska and Hawaii from the 48 conterminous States and the District of Columbia are included; however, no data were obtained for shipments originating in Alaska and Hawaii.

- Represents zero or rounds to zero. (D) Withheld to avoid disclosing figures for individual companies.

[1]Production of this commodity is concentrated in the geographic divisions shown; figures and distributions for geographic divisions not shown are included in the total.

[2]Distances of shipments to foreign destinations are calculated only to the U.S. port of exit.

[3]Includes only shipments represented by bills of lading and invoices. Summary records which did not show individual weights of shipments are not included.

TCC 289. Miscellaneous Chemical Products

Comparisons of Tons and Ton-Miles of Shipments for
Geographic Divisions of Origin and for Sampling Variability: 1972 and 1967

Geographic division of origin	Estimates				Relative sampling variability in tons (percent)	
	1972		1967		1972	1967
	Tons (thousands)	Ton-miles (millions)	Tons (thousands)	Ton-miles (millions)		
U.S. total	21,536	12,372	11,073	4,740	11.9	14.0
New England	446	163	167	77	28.2	(*)
Middle Atlantic	2,785	998	1,747	514	38.6	(*)
East North Central	3,274	1,266	3,484	984	14.0	(*)
West North Central	(D)	(D)	732	296	(*)	(*)
South Atlantic	1,308	424	305	154	43.5	(*)
East South Central	333	177	919	661	17.2	(*)
West South Central	(D)	(D)	2,232	1,642	(*)	(*)
Mountain	73	24	3	–	29.4	(*)
Pacific	1,371	492	1,484	412	47.2	(*)

– Represents or rounds to zero.   (D) Withheld to avoid disclosing figures for individual companies.   (*) Data not published.

TABLE 1. **TCC GROUP 289**—Percent Distribution of Geographic Division of Origin and Distance Shipped, by Means of Transport: 1972

Geographic division of origin[1] and distance shipped[2]	Number	Percent distribution by means of transport							
		All means of transport	Rail	Motor carrier	Private truck	Air	Water	Other	Unknown
TONS OF SHIPMENTS	(thousands of tons)								
U.S. TOTAL..........	21 536	100.0	30.1	28.9	11.5	-	29.2	.1	.1
NEW ENGLAND..............	446	100.0	2.1	73.9	20.7	.1	1.8	.6	.7
UNDER 100 MILES.......	169	100.0	-	58.3	37.6	-	2.1	1.3	.6
100 TO 199 MILES.....	56	100.0	-	99.2	-	-	-	.1	.6
200 TO 299 MILES......	36	100.0	-	77.5	18.9	-	-	.1	3.6
300 TO 499 MILES......	65	100.0	-	95.0	4.8	.1	-	.1	-
500 TO 999 MILES.....	76	100.0	3.8	74.5	20.8	-	-	.1	.7
1000 TO 1499 MILES....	21	100.0	.3	67.8	12.3	.6	19.1	.3	-
1500 MILES OR OVER....	20	100.0	32.1	63.5	1.2	.2	2.0	1.1	-
MIDDLE ATLANTIC.........	2 785	100.0	25.6	55.2	17.8	-	1.3	.1	-
UNDER 100 MILES.......	567	100.0	5.9	58.9	34.8	-	.3	.1	-
100 TO 199 MILES.....	895	100.0	23.9	54.9	21.3	-	-	-	-
200 TO 299 MILES......	409	100.0	39.0	55.0	5.9	-	-	-	-
300 TO 499 MILES......	370	100.0	23.4	60.3	16.1	-	-	.1	-
500 TO 999 MILES.....	326	100.0	38.0	55.6	5.4	.2	.7	.1	-
1000 TO 1499 MILES....	130	100.0	46.4	44.6	3.8	.1	5.0	.1	-
1500 MILES OR OVER....	85	100.0	40.4	26.3	2.3	.1	30.6	.1	.3
EAST NORTH CENTRAL......	3 274	100.0	31.7	53.9	13.6	-	-	.5	.2
UNDER 100 MILES.......	547	100.0	3.5	69.3	26.6	-	-	.6	-
100 TO 199 MILES.....	772	100.0	6.8	77.6	15.6	-	-	-	-
200 TO 299 MILES......	445	100.0	28.1	53.8	17.1	-	-	.7	.3
300 TO 499 MILES......	657	100.0	47.5	41.9	10.2	-	-	.3	.1
500 TO 999 MILES.....	681	100.0	58.7	34.3	4.9	.1	-	1.4	.8
1000 TO 1499 MILES....	17	100.0	43.8	46.8	8.5	.1	-	.1	.8
1500 MILES OR OVER....	151	100.0	80.3	19.1	.5	.1	-	-	-
SOUTH ATLANTIC..........	1 308	100.0	51.0	28.1	20.5	.1	.2	-	-
UNDER 100 MILES.......	364	100.0	27.7	34.9	37.4	-	-	-	-
100 TO 199 MILES.....	263	100.0	51.0	21.7	27.3	-	-	-	-
200 TO 299 MILES......	216	100.0	70.8	13.6	15.5	-	-	-	-
300 TO 499 MILES......	204	100.0	62.5	34.1	3.0	-	-	.1	.3
500 TO 999 MILES.....	222	100.0	56.5	34.7	8.6	.2	-	-	-
1000 TO 1499 MILES....	11	100.0	26.2	41.7	-	10.9	21.2	-	-
1500 MILES OR OVER....	24	100.0	92.1	7.2	.3	.4	-	-	-
EAST SOUTH CENTRAL......	333	100.0	64.0	29.4	6.6	-	-	-	-
UNDER 100 MILES.......	19	100.0	24.0	75.9	-	-	-	-	-
100 TO 199 MILES.....	23	100.0	16.7	61.3	22.0	-	-	-	-
200 TO 299 MILES......	43	100.0	80.1	19.8	.1	-	-	-	-
300 TO 499 MILES......	91	100.0	64.4	17.3	18.3	-	-	-	-
500 TO 999 MILES.....	137	100.0	72.2	27.8	-	-	-	-	-
1000 TO 1499 MILES....	5	100.0	23.0	77.0	-	-	-	-	-
1500 MILES OR OVER....	12	100.0	83.3	16.7	-	-	-	-	-
MOUNTAIN................	73	100.0	9.7	65.0	25.3	-	-	-	-
UNDER 100 MILES.......	35	100.0	10.5	58.8	30.7	-	-	-	-
100 TO 199 MILES.....	7	100.0	-	98.1	1.9	-	-	-	-
200 TO 299 MILES......	4	100.0	-	96.6	2.8	-	-	-	.6
300 TO 499 MILES......	6	100.0	-	5.5	94.5	-	-	-	-
500 TO 999 MILES.....	16	100.0	7.4	85.9	6.7	-	-	-	-
1000 TO 1499 MILES....	1	100.0	-	99.9	-	.1	-	-	-
1500 MILES OR OVER....	2	100.0	90.2	9.8	-	-	-	-	-
PACIFIC.................	1 371	100.0	31.5	43.8	24.3	-	.4	-	-
UNDER 100 MILES.......	380	100.0	3.3	50.7	45.7	-	.2	.1	-
100 TO 199 MILES.....	115	100.0	11.1	46.4	42.2	-	.3	-	-
200 TO 299 MILES......	48	100.0	-	54.9	45.0	-	-	-	-
300 TO 499 MILES......	434	100.0	20.3	60.5	19.2	-	-	-	-
500 TO 999 MILES.....	375	100.0	84.5	14.0	1.5	-	-	-	-
1000 TO 1499 MILES....	2	100.0	-	96.6	-	3.2	-	.1	-
1500 MILES OR OVER....	15	100.0	5.1	69.0	.1	.4	25.4	.1	-
TON-MILES OF SHIPMENTS	(millions of ton-miles)								
U.S. TOTAL..........	12 372	100.0	27.9	17.4	5.3	-	49.3	.1	.1
NEW ENGLAND..............	163	100.0	8.1	75.3	11.8	.2	3.6	.5	.5
UNDER 100 MILES.......	7	100.0	-	61.2	35.1	-	1.7	1.5	.5
100 TO 199 MILES.....	8	100.0	-	99.4	-	-	-	.1	.5
200 TO 299 MILES......	8	100.0	-	77.7	19.2	-	-	.1	3.0
300 TO 499 MILES......	22	100.0	-	95.3	4.5	.1	-	.1	-
500 TO 999 MILES.....	54	100.0	4.1	74.9	19.9	-	-	.2	.9
1000 TO 1499 MILES....	24	100.0	-	69.1	11.2	.6	18.9	.3	-
1500 MILES OR OVER....	37	100.0	29.2	64.7	1.5	.2	2.9	1.5	-
MIDDLE ATLANTIC.........	998	100.0	34.4	48.2	9.4	.1	7.7	.1	-
UNDER 100 MILES.......	29	100.0	7.4	56.4	36.0	-	.2	-	-
100 TO 199 MILES.....	147	100.0	26.4	52.6	21.0	-	-	-	-
200 TO 299 MILES......	103	100.0	40.5	53.8	5.6	-	-	-	-
300 TO 499 MILES......	144	100.0	23.1	60.5	16.3	-	-	.1	-
500 TO 999 MILES.....	224	100.0	37.4	55.6	5.7	.2	1.0	.1	-
1000 TO 1499 MILES....	158	100.0	46.4	43.9	3.8	.1	5.7	.1	-
1500 MILES OR OVER....	190	100.0	36.6	26.2	2.3	.1	34.4	.1	.2

See footnotes at end of table 4.

TABLE 1. **TCC GROUP 289—Percent Distribution of Geographic Division of Origin and Distance Shipped, by Means of Transport: 1972**—Continued

Geographic division of origin[1] and distance shipped[2]	Number	Percent distribution by means of transport							
		All means of transport	Rail	Motor carrier	Private truck	Air	Water	Other	Unknown
TON-MILES OF SHIPMENTS	(millions of ton-miles)								
EAST NORTH CENTRAL......	1 266	100.0	51.7	39.8	7.4	-	-	.7	.4
UNDER 100 MILES.......	29	100.0	1.7	76.0	21.7	-	-	.6	-
100 TO 199 MILES......	120	100.0	6.4	79.8	13.7	-	-	-	-
200 TO 299 MILES......	113	100.0	29.0	53.5	16.6	-	-	.6	.2
300 TO 499 MILES......	260	100.0	48.5	41.2	9.9	-	-	.3	.1
500 TO 999 MILES......	452	100.0	58.5	33.9	5.1	.1	-	1.5	.9
1000 TO 1499 MILES....	18	100.0	42.0	48.1	8.6	.1	-	.1	1.0
1500 MILES OR OVER....	271	100.0	79.2	20.3	.5	.1	-	-	-
SOUTH ATLANTIC..........	424	100.0	62.4	27.2	9.1	.4	.8	-	.1
UNDER 100 MILES.......	24	100.0	36.2	40.6	23.3	-	-	-	-
100 TO 199 MILES......	39	100.0	54.1	20.9	25.0	-	-	-	-
200 TO 299 MILES......	54	100.0	72.4	13.8	13.8	-	-	-	-
300 TO 499 MILES......	82	100.0	64.3	32.3	3.0	-	-	.1	.3
500 TO 999 MILES......	159	100.0	58.4	33.3	8.1	.1	-	-	-
1000 TO 1499 MILES....	13	100.0	22.9	42.4	-	10.5	24.2	-	-
1500 MILES OR OVER....	49	100.0	91.3	7.9	.3	.4	-	-	-
EAST SOUTH CENTRAL......	177	100.0	69.0	27.1	4.0	-	-	-	-
UNDER 100 MILES.......	1	100.0	26.9	73.0	-	-	-	-	-
100 TO 199 MILES......	3	100.0	17.0	58.2	24.8	-	-	-	-
200 TO 299 MILES......	11	100.0	79.5	20.4	.1	-	-	-	-
300 TO 499 MILES......	37	100.0	67.3	16.6	16.2	-	-	-	-
500 TO 999 MILES......	93	100.0	70.5	29.5	-	-	-	-	-
1000 TO 1499 MILES....	6	100.0	25.9	74.1	-	-	-	-	-
1500 MILES OR OVER....	22	100.0	83.3	16.6	-	-	-	-	-
MOUNTAIN................	24	100.0	20.7	63.5	15.8	-	-	-	-
UNDER 100 MILES.......	1	100.0	17.3	60.0	22.6	-	-	-	-
100 TO 199 MILES......	1	100.0	-	98.1	1.9	-	-	-	-
200 TO 299 MILES......	1	100.0	-	96.9	2.6	-	-	-	.5
300 TO 499 MILES......	2	100.0	-	6.3	93.7	-	-	-	-
500 TO 999 MILES.....	11	100.0	9.1	83.7	7.2	-	-	-	-
1000 TO 1499 MILES....	1	100.0	-	99.9	-	.1	-	-	-
1500 MILES OR OVER....	4	100.0	89.7	10.3	-	-	-	-	-
PACIFIC.................	492	100.0	51.7	35.8	10.4	-	2.1	-	-
UNDER 100 MILES.......	16	100.0	5.7	49.9	44.3	-	.1	.1	-
100 TO 199 MILES......	17	100.0	11.5	45.3	43.0	-	.2	-	-
200 TO 299 MILES......	11	100.0	-	54.7	45.2	-	-	-	-
300 TO 499 MILES......	146	100.0	21.0	60.1	18.9	-	-	-	-
500 TO 999 MILES......	260	100.0	84.3	14.4	1.2	-	-	-	-
1000 TO 1499 MILES....	2	100.0	-	97.1	-	2.7	-	.1	-
1500 MILES OR OVER....	37	100.0	4.8	67.3	.1	.3	27.5	.1	-

See footnotes at end of table 4.

TABLE 2. **TCC GROUP 289—Percent Distribution of Geographic Division of Origin and Means of Transport, by Geographic Division of Destination: 1972**

Geographic division of origin[1] and means of transport	Number	Percent distribution by division of destination									
		U.S. total	New England	Middle Atlantic	East North Central	West North Central	South Atlantic	East South Central	West South Central	Mountain	Pacific
TONS OF SHIPMENTS	(thousands of tons)										
U.S. TOTAL..............	21 536	100.0	3.2	12.9	45.0	8.6	7.1	3.8	7.9	3.2	8.2
RAIL..................	6 491	100.0	4.8	11.1	26.3	14.1	7.9	4.9	14.1	5.7	11.0
MOTOR CARRIER.........	6 228	100.0	4.4	25.3	23.6	8.8	8.0	5.3	9.6	4.0	11.1
PRIVATE TRUCK.........	2 477	100.0	4.1	18.4	26.0	15.7	9.4	4.8	4.8	3.3	13.6
AIR...................	4	100.0	.7	31.5	13.9	29.7	7.3	1.0	7.8	2.9	5.3
WATER.................	6 291	100.0	.1	-	93.2	-	4.3	.8	1.1	-	.5
OTHER.................	27	100.0	11.5	37.4	22.1	3.6	4.2	1.2	16.7	.1	3.2
UNKNOWN...............	14	100.0	18.7	34.9	24.6	4.1	11.8	.6	1.8	2.2	1.2
NEW ENGLAND.............	446	100.0	35.4	31.9	10.1	1.9	12.7	1.8	4.4	.7	1.1
RAIL..................	9	100.0	-	30.6	-	-	-	-	61.8	-	7.6
MOTOR CARRIER.........	330	100.0	26.0	41.0	12.1	2.5	11.7	1.5	3.2	.9	1.0
PRIVATE TRUCK.........	92	100.0	69.0	7.7	2.6	-	14.3	3.3	3.0	-	.2
AIR...................	-	100.0	-	30.2	1.8	-	.8	-	52.3	3.5	11.4
WATER.................	8	100.0	43.4	.1	-	-	51.4	-	-	-	5.1
OTHER.................	2	100.0	80.3	4.5	2.8	1.7	1.7	.5	1.1	-	7.4
UNKNOWN...............	3	100.0	83.1	-	.4	-	16.6	-	-	-	-
MIDDLE ATLANTIC.........	2 785	100.0	10.5	50.9	13.3	1.9	12.4	3.5	4.7	.5	2.3
RAIL..................	713	100.0	20.1	36.0	11.6	4.1	13.1	2.3	9.2	1.3	2.5
MOTOR CARRIER.........	1 536	100.0	7.7	51.7	16.9	1.4	14.0	3.3	3.5	.3	1.1
PRIVATE TRUCK.........	496	100.0	6.2	73.2	5.6	.3	7.6	6.0	.7	-	1.4
AIR...................	-	100.0	.1	2.7	2.8	58.2	11.5	.1	18.1	5.1	1.4
WATER.................	36	100.0	-	5.1	-	-	.3	-	23.9	-	70.7
OTHER.................	1	100.0	7.0	27.2	15.0	5.3	29.1	9.8	2.2	.1	4.2
UNKNOWN...............	-	100.0	.5	.3	1.4	-	-	-	-	97.8	-

See footnotes at end of table 4.

TABLE 2. **TCC GROUP 289—Percent Distribution of Geographic Division of Origin and Means of Transport, by Geographic Division of Destination: 1972**—Continued

Geographic division of origin[1] and means of transport	Number	Percent distribution by division of destination									
		U.S. total	New England	Middle Atlantic	East North Central	West North Central	South Atlantic	East South Central	West South Central	Mountain	Pacific
TONS OF SHIPMENTS	(thousands of tons)										
EAST NORTH CENTRAL......	3 274	100.0	3.5	21.9	41.6	10.2	7.4	7.6	2.9	1.1	3.6
RAIL................	1 038	100.0	5.9	17.1	22.9	16.6	12.2	7.3	6.1	3.1	8.7
MOTOR CARRIER........	1 765	100.0	2.7	26.3	46.0	8.4	5.5	8.0	1.4	.2	1.6
PRIVATE TRUCK........	444	100.0	1.0	13.7	68.8	2.9	4.2	7.1	1.8	.4	.2
AIR.................	-	100.0	.1	41.7	28.9	2.3	6.7	3.7	2.4	-	14.1
WATER...............	-	100.0	-	83.8	16.2	-	-	-	-	-	-
OTHER...............	17	100.0	4.8	55.5	32.5	3.3	3.3	.2	.3	-	-
UNKNOWN.............	7	100.0	.7	68.5	2.8	8.1	15.9	1.3	1.4	.7	.6
SOUTH ATLANTIC..........	1 308	100.0	6.5	21.0	28.8	3.0	23.5	11.0	4.3	.9	1.0
RAIL................	667	100.0	11.4	19.0	33.2	4.1	13.0	10.1	5.7	1.6	1.7
MOTOR CARRIER........	367	100.0	2.2	35.1	26.7	2.7	19.3	10.3	3.0	.3	.3
PRIVATE TRUCK........	267	100.0	.1	6.7	20.5	.7	55.8	14.5	1.5	-	-
AIR.................	1	100.0	1.6	60.0	18.7	2.5	9.4	.6	3.7	-	3.5
WATER...............	2	100.0	-	-	-	-	.1	-	99.9	-	-
OTHER...............	-	100.0	.9	28.1	12.4	-	20.9	35.8	.1	1.3	.5
UNKNOWN.............	-	100.0	-	-	100.0	-	-	-	-	-	-
EAST SOUTH CENTRAL......	333	100.0	.6	4.3	20.7	1.8	14.8	3.4	50.2	.5	3.6
RAIL................	213	100.0	-	5.5	16.1	1.7	9.3	2.2	59.9	.6	4.7
MOTOR CARRIER........	98	100.0	2.2	2.7	30.3	2.7	24.4	1.4	33.6	.6	2.1
PRIVATE TRUCK........	21	100.0	-	.1	22.4	-	25.0	23.5	29.0	-	-
AIR.................	-	100.0	8.2	-	33.2	-	17.3	-	39.5	1.9	-
WATER...............	-	100.0	-	-	-	-	-	-	-	-	100.0
OTHER...............	-	100.0	-	100.0	-	-	-	-	-	-	-
UNKNOWN.............	-	100.0	-	16.7	83.3	-	-	-	-	-	-
MOUNTAIN...............	73	100.0	.4	-	1.2	2.0	1.3	2.6	1.5	74.9	16.0
RAIL................	7	100.0	4.5	-	3.0	-	-	27.0	-	51.5	13.9
MOTOR CARRIER........	47	100.0	-	-	1.4	3.1	2.0	-	2.4	69.1	22.0
PRIVATE TRUCK........	18	100.0	-	-	-	-	-	-	-	98.9	1.1
AIR.................	-	100.0	16.7	-	-	67.7	13.4	-	-	-	2.2
WATER...............	-	100.0	-	-	-	-	-	-	-	-	-
OTHER...............	-	100.0	-	-	-	-	-	-	-	-	100.0
UNKNOWN.............	-	100.0	-	-	-	-	-	-	-	100.0	-
PACIFIC................	1 371	100.0	-	.2	.1	-	.1	-	.2	8.5	90.9
RAIL................	431	100.0	-	.1	.1	-	-	-	.1	20.7	79.0
MOTOR CARRIER........	600	100.0	-	.4	.2	-	.1	-	.4	4.0	94.9
PRIVATE TRUCK........	333	100.0	-	-	-	-	-	-	-	1.1	98.9
AIR.................	-	100.0	2.3	1.2	14.4	.9	17.7	1.7	.1	51.1	10.7
WATER...............	5	100.0	-	-	-	-	-	-	-	-	100.0
OTHER...............	-	100.0	.5	.2	1.7	.8	.5	-	3.1	1.0	92.2
UNKNOWN.............	-	100.0	-	-	-	-	-	-	-	-	100.0
TON-MILES OF SHIPMENTS	(millions of ton-miles)										
U.S. TOTAL.............	12 372	100.0	2.3	6.4	56.9	5.2	6.7	3.0	5.6	3.7	10.1
RAIL................	3 447	100.0	5.1	10.5	17.5	10.7	9.5	4.7	12.1	7.8	22.1
MOTOR CARRIER........	2 153	100.0	4.1	16.3	21.8	8.6	10.1	6.1	10.3	6.8	15.8
PRIVATE TRUCK........	653	100.0	2.5	10.9	36.3	14.3	7.3	6.5	5.6	6.6	9.9
AIR.................	3	100.0	1.2	35.7	11.1	15.8	6.9	.7	11.0	4.8	12.8
WATER...............	6 095	100.0	-	-	93.9	-	3.9	.6	.3	-	1.3
OTHER...............	11	100.0	7.2	58.1	8.9	2.9	6.5	1.5	3.0	.3	11.7
UNKNOWN.............	7	100.0	5.2	52.8	15.1	2.4	12.2	.7	3.0	7.3	1.2
NEW ENGLAND............	163	100.0	5.5	17.2	17.7	5.2	22.1	4.1	17.1	3.5	7.6
RAIL................	13	100.0	-	-	16.9	-	-	-	68.6	-	14.5
MOTOR CARRIER........	123	100.0	4.8	21.3	20.3	6.9	18.7	3.7	12.8	4.7	6.8
PRIVATE TRUCK........	19	100.0	13.0	9.3	8.9	-	40.5	11.2	14.6	-	2.4
AIR.................	-	100.0	-	9.0	1.3	-	.9	-	55.2	5.7	27.9
WATER...............	5	100.0	2.0	-	-	-	79.1	-	-	-	18.8
OTHER...............	-	100.0	12.5	3.3	5.9	5.8	4.5	1.6	5.6	.1	60.7
UNKNOWN.............	-	100.0	39.9	-	.9	-	59.2	-	-	-	-
MIDDLE ATLANTIC........	998	100.0	8.5	18.7	15.8	4.6	12.8	5.8	16.4	2.2	15.2
RAIL................	343	100.0	13.7	12.9	10.8	6.8	12.3	2.8	24.5	3.9	12.2
MOTOR CARRIER........	481	100.0	6.1	21.4	23.1	4.3	15.2	6.7	13.3	1.7	8.3
PRIVATE TRUCK........	94	100.0	8.8	41.7	9.3	1.8	12.3	16.7	4.6	-	4.7
AIR.................	-	100.0	.1	.3	1.8	51.7	7.8	.1	24.3	10.2	3.7
WATER...............	76	100.0	-	.1	-	-	.1	-	14.7	-	85.1
OTHER...............	-	100.0	4.4	5.3	13.8	11.3	22.0	13.7	6.1	.6	22.9
UNKNOWN.............	-	100.0	-	-	.7	-	-	-	-	99.2	-

See footnotes at end of table 4.

TABLE 2. **TCC GROUP 289—Percent Distribution of Geographic Division of Origin and Means of Transport, by Geographic Division of Destination: 1972**—Continued

Geographic division of origin[1] and means of transport	Number	Percent distribution by division of destination									
		U.S. total	New England	Middle Atlantic	East North Central	West North Central	South Atlantic	East South Central	West South Central	Mountain	Pacific
TON-MILES OF SHIPMENTS	(millions of ton-miles)										
EAST NORTH CENTRAL......	1 266	100.0	6.4	19.3	17.4	12.6	9.8	6.3	6.5	4.4	17.4
RAIL...................	654	100.0	6.6	13.1	9.7	13.9	10.2	4.9	8.7	7.8	25.2
MOTOR CARRIER.........	504	100.0	6.8	25.0	23.7	12.6	9.6	7.0	3.9	.7	10.7
PRIVATE TRUCK.........	93	100.0	3.3	22.9	39.1	4.6	9.1	12.2	5.9	1.8	1.3
AIR...................	-	100.0	.1	37.9	11.2	1.7	4.4	3.0	4.1	-	37.6
WATER.................	-	100.0	-	90.9	9.1	-	-	-	-	-	-
OTHER.................	8	100.0	7.7	74.3	9.3	2.0	5.8	.2	.7	-	.1
UNKNOWN...............	4	100.0	.9	79.7	.9	3.7	8.1	1.1	2.6	1.5	1.6
SOUTH ATLANTIC..........	424	100.0	9.3	15.8	20.9	6.7	11.5	12.2	11.7	5.4	6.5
RAIL...................	264	100.0	13.2	12.5	20.2	6.9	7.7	9.2	13.1	8.0	9.2
MOTOR CARRIER.........	115	100.0	3.7	25.8	21.0	7.3	13.5	16.8	7.8	1.7	2.4
PRIVATE TRUCK.........	38	100.0	.3	7.5	27.3	4.1	33.0	20.2	7.2	-	.4
AIR...................	1	100.0	1.9	61.1	15.6	3.3	6.3	.3	3.4	-	8.1
WATER.................	3	100.0	-	-	-	-	-	-	100.0	-	-
OTHER.................	-	100.0	1.7	32.0	13.3	-	8.8	34.4	.4	6.4	3.1
UNKNOWN...............	-	100.0	-	-	100.0	-	-	-	-	-	-
EAST SOUTH CENTRAL......	177	100.0	1.4	7.4	14.9	2.5	8.5	.9	50.6	1.2	12.5
RAIL...................	122	100.0	-	8.6	13.4	2.3	5.4	.3	53.5	1.3	15.1
MOTOR CARRIER.........	47	100.0	5.2	5.4	16.7	3.6	13.4	.7	46.2	1.1	7.7
PRIVATE TRUCK.........	7	100.0	-	.2	27.2	-	27.8	13.4	31.4	-	-
AIR...................	-	100.0	16.0	-	36.0	-	14.4	-	30.4	3.2	-
WATER.................	-	100.0	-	-	-	-	-	-	-	-	100.0
OTHER.................	-	100.0	-	100.0	-	-	-	-	-	-	-
UNKNOWN...............	-	100.0	-	70.6	29.4	-	-	-	-	-	-
MOUNTAIN...............	24	100.0	2.3	.1	3.4	3.5	6.0	12.7	4.2	32.3	35.6
RAIL...................	4	100.0	11.2	-	3.8	-	-	61.4	-	6.0	17.5
MOTOR CARRIER.........	15	100.0	-	.1	4.1	5.5	9.4	-	6.6	25.2	49.1
PRIVATE TRUCK.........	3	100.0	-	-	-	-	-	-	-	95.1	4.9
AIR...................	-	100.0	26.2	-	-	55.3	17.5	-	-	-	1.0
WATER.................	-	100.0	-	-	-	-	-	-	-	-	-
OTHER.................	-	100.0	-	-	-	-	-	-	-	-	100.0
UNKNOWN...............	-	100.0	-	-	-	-	-	-	-	100.0	-
PACIFIC................	492	100.0	-	1.3	.6	.1	.4	-	.7	16.3	80.6
RAIL...................	254	100.0	-	.4	.3	-	-	-	.1	24.6	74.6
MOTOR CARRIER.........	176	100.0	-	3.0	1.3	.2	1.0	-	1.7	9.6	83.2
PRIVATE TRUCK.........	51	100.0	-	-	-	-	.1	-	-	1.7	98.2
AIR...................	-	100.0	4.2	2.0	18.6	.9	28.2	2.1	.1	38.2	5.6
WATER.................	10	100.0	-	-	-	-	-	-	-	-	100.0
OTHER.................	-	100.0	5.2	1.4	12.7	5.2	4.0	-	17.0	1.7	52.8
UNKNOWN...............	-	100.0	-	-	-	-	-	-	-	-	100.0

See footnotes at end of table 4.

TABLE 3. **TCC GROUP 289**—Percent Distribution of Geographic Division of Destination and Means of Transport, by Geographic Division of Origin: 1972

Geographic division of destination and means of transport	Number	Percent distribution by division of origin[1]									
		U.S. total	New England	Middle Atlantic	East North Central	West North Central	South Atlantic	East South Central	West South Central	Mountain	Pacific
TONS OF SHIPMENTS	(thousands of tons)										
U.S. TOTAL..............	21 536	100.0	2.1	12.9	15.2	(D)	6.1	1.5	(D)	.3	6.4
RAIL.................	6 491	100.0	.1	11.0	16.0	(D)	10.3	3.3	(D)	.1	6.7
MOTOR CARRIER.........	6 228	100.0	5.3	24.7	28.3	(D)	5.9	1.6	(D)	.8	9.6
PRIVATE TRUCK.........	2 477	100.0	3.7	20.0	17.9	(D)	10.8	.9	(D)	.8	13.4
AIR..................	4	100.0	5.0	17.3	18.3	(D)	35.9	.3	(D)	-	3.1
WATER................	6 291	100.0	.1	.6	-	(D)	-	-	(D)	-	.1
OTHER................	27	100.0	10.1	5.5	63.2	(D)	1.3	-	(D)	-	1.1
UNKNOWN..............	14	100.0	22.1	1.8	51.0	(D)	4.4	-	(D)	.2	.9
NEW ENGLAND...........	696	100.0	22.7	42.0	16.4	(D)	12.1	.3	(D)	-	-
RAIL.................	314	100.0	-	45.5	19.6	(D)	24.1	-	(D)	.1	-
MOTOR CARRIER.........	271	100.0	31.7	43.7	17.3	(D)	3.0	.8	(D)	-	-
PRIVATE TRUCK.........	100	100.0	63.3	30.5	4.2	(D)	.4	-	(D)	-	-
AIR..................	-	100.0	.1	3.2	2.4	(D)	80.2	2.9	(D)	1.2	10.0
WATER................	3	100.0	100.0	-	-	(D)	-	-	(D)	-	-
OTHER................	3	100.0	70.1	3.3	26.4	(D)	.1	-	(D)	-	.1
UNKNOWN..............	2	100.0	98.1	-	1.8	(D)	-	-	(D)	-	-
MIDDLE ATLANTIC.........	2 774	100.0	5.1	51.1	25.9	(D)	9.9	.5	(D)	-	.1
RAIL.................	723	100.0	-	35.4	24.6	(D)	17.6	1.6	(D)	-	.1
MOTOR CARRIER.........	1 577	100.0	8.6	50.4	29.4	(D)	8.2	.2	(D)	-	.1
PRIVATE TRUCK.........	454	100.0	1.6	79.9	13.4	(D)	3.9	-	(D)	-	.1
AIR..................	1	100.0	4.8	1.5	24.2	(D)	68.5	-	(D)	-	.1
WATER................	2	100.0	.4	94.0	5.6	(D)	-	-	(D)	-	-
OTHER................	10	100.0	1.2	4.0	93.7	(D)	1.0	-	(D)	-	-
UNKNOWN..............	5	100.0	-	-	100.0	(D)	-	-	(D)	-	-
EAST NORTH CENTRAL......	9 695	100.0	.5	3.8	14.1	(D)	3.9	.7	(D)	-	-
RAIL.................	1 708	100.0	.2	4.9	13.9	(D)	13.0	2.0	(D)	-	-
MOTOR CARRIER.........	1 469	100.0	2.7	17.7	55.3	(D)	6.7	2.0	(D)	-	.1
PRIVATE TRUCK.........	644	100.0	.4	4.3	47.4	(D)	8.5	.8	(D)	-	-
AIR..................	-	100.0	.6	3.5	38.0	(D)	48.1	.6	(D)	-	3.2
WATER................	5 863	100.0	-	-	-	(D)	-	-	(D)	-	-
OTHER................	6	100.0	1.3	3.7	92.9	(D)	.7	-	(D)	-	.1
UNKNOWN..............	3	100.0	.3	.1	5.8	(D)	17.9	-	(D)	-	-
WEST NORTH CENTRAL......	1 852	100.0	.5	2.9	18.1	(D)	2.1	.3	(D)	.1	-
RAIL.................	915	100.0	-	3.2	18.8	(D)	3.0	.4	(D)	.3	-
MOTOR CARRIER.........	545	100.0	1.5	4.0	27.2	(D)	1.8	.5	(D)	.3	-
PRIVATE TRUCK.........	387	100.0	-	.4	3.4	(D)	.5	-	(D)	-	-
AIR..................	1	100.0	-	33.8	1.4	(D)	3.0	-	(D)	.1	.1
WATER................	-	100.0	-	-	-	(D)	-	-	(D)	-	-
OTHER................	-	100.0	4.8	8.1	58.8	(D)	-	-	(D)	-	.3
UNKNOWN..............	-	100.0	-	-	100.0	(D)	-	-	(D)	-	-
SOUTH ATLANTIC..........	1 520	100.0	3.7	22.8	16.0	(D)	20.2	3.2	(D)	.1	.1
RAIL.................	512	100.0	-	18.2	24.7	(D)	17.0	3.9	(D)	.2	-
MOTOR CARRIER.........	501	100.0	7.7	42.9	19.2	(D)	14.2	4.8	(D)	.2	.2
PRIVATE TRUCK.........	232	100.0	5.7	16.2	8.1	(D)	64.3	2.4	(D)	-	-
AIR..................	-	100.0	.6	27.3	16.8	(D)	46.5	.6	(D)	.1	7.6
WATER................	271	100.0	1.5	-	-	(D)	-	-	(D)	-	-
OTHER................	1	100.0	4.1	38.1	49.0	(D)	6.4	-	(D)	-	.1
UNKNOWN..............	1	100.0	31.1	-	68.9	(D)	-	-	(D)	-	-
EAST SOUTH CENTRAL......	813	100.0	1.0	11.9	30.7	(D)	17.8	1.4	(D)	.2	-
RAIL.................	318	100.0	-	5.1	23.9	(D)	21.2	1.5	(D)	.6	-
MOTOR CARRIER.........	327	100.0	1.5	15.5	43.3	(D)	11.5	.4	(D)	-	-
PRIVATE TRUCK.........	119	100.0	2.6	24.7	26.6	(D)	32.4	4.3	(D)	-	-
AIR..................	-	100.0	-	1.7	70.6	(D)	22.2	-	(D)	-	5.4
WATER................	47	100.0	-	-	-	(D)	-	-	(D)	-	-
OTHER................	-	100.0	4.5	45.7	10.8	(D)	39.1	-	(D)	-	-
UNKNOWN..............	-	100.0	-	-	100.0	(D)	-	-	(D)	-	-
WEST SOUTH CENTRAL......	1 709	100.0	1.1	7.7	5.6	(D)	3.3	9.8	(D)	.1	.2
RAIL.................	916	100.0	.6	7.1	6.9	(D)	4.2	13.9	(D)	-	-
MOTOR CARRIER.........	597	100.0	1.8	9.0	4.0	(D)	1.9	5.5	(D)	.2	.4
PRIVATE TRUCK.........	118	100.0	2.3	2.9	6.6	(D)	3.5	5.4	(D)	-	-
AIR..................	-	100.0	33.7	40.3	5.8	(D)	17.1	1.3	(D)	-	-
WATER................	71	100.0	-	12.4	-	(D)	3.5	-	(D)	-	-
OTHER................	4	100.0	.7	.7	1.3	(D)	-	-	(D)	-	.2
UNKNOWN..............	-	100.0	-	-	39.3	(D)	-	-	(D)	-	-
MOUNTAIN..............	696	100.0	.4	2.0	5.3	(D)	1.7	.3	(D)	7.9	16.8
RAIL.................	367	100.0	-	2.5	8.8	(D)	3.0	.3	(D)	1.0	24.3
MOTOR CARRIER.........	247	100.0	1.2	1.9	1.1	(D)	.4	.2	(D)	13.4	9.6
PRIVATE TRUCK.........	81	100.0	-	-	2.0	(D)	-	-	(D)	22.7	4.7
AIR..................	-	100.0	6.0	30.5	.1	(D)	-	.2	(D)	-	55.1
WATER................	-	100.0	-	-	-	(D)	-	-	(D)	-	-
OTHER................	-	100.0	2.5	7.6	1.1	(D)	18.1	-	(D)	-	13.1
UNKNOWN..............	-	100.0	-	77.6	15.6	(D)	-	-	(D)	6.9	-
PACIFIC..............	1 775	100.0	.3	3.5	6.7	(D)	.7	.7	(D)	.7	70.2
RAIL.................	713	100.0	.1	2.5	12.6	(D)	1.6	1.4	(D)	.1	47.8
MOTOR CARRIER.........	690	100.0	.5	2.4	4.1	(D)	.2	.3	(D)	1.5	82.6
PRIVATE TRUCK.........	337	100.0	.1	.6	.2	(D)	-	-	(D)	.1	97.5
AIR..................	-	100.0	10.8	4.5	49.0	(D)	24.2	-	(D)	-	6.3
WATER................	31	100.0	1.3	82.1	-	(D)	-	-	(D)	-	16.6
OTHER................	-	100.0	23.1	7.2	.5	(D)	.2	-	(D)	-	32.7
UNKNOWN..............	-	100.0	-	-	26.4	(D)	-	-	(D)	-	73.6

See footnotes at end of table 4.

TABLE 3. **TCC GROUP 289**—Percent Distribution of Geographic Division of Destination and Means of Transport, by Geographic Division of Origin: 1972—Continued

Geographic division of destination and means of transport	Number	Percent distribution by division of origin[1]									
		U.S. total	New England	Middle Atlantic	East North Central	West North Central	South Atlantic	East South Central	West South Central	Mountain	Pacific
TON-MILES OF SHIPMENTS	(millions of ton-miles)										
U.S. TOTAL................	12 372	100.0	1.3	8.1	10.2	(D)	3.4	1.4	(D)	.2	4.0
RAIL..................	3 447	100.0	.4	10.0	19.0	(D)	7.7	3.5	(D)	.1	7.4
MOTOR CARRIER.........	2 153	100.0	5.7	22.4	23.4	(D)	5.3	2.2	(D)	.7	8.2
PRIVATE TRUCK.........	653	100.0	3.0	14.4	14.3	(D)	5.9	1.1	(D)	.6	7.8
AIR...................	3	100.0	6.5	20.3	14.8	(D)	47.4	.2	(D)	.1	5.4
WATER.................	6 095	100.0	.1	1.3	-	(D)	.1	-	(D)	-	.2
OTHER.................	11	100.0	7.7	6.3	76.7	(D)	1.1	-	(D)	-	.8
UNKNOWN...............	7	100.0	11.7	6.3	66.3	(D)	3.9	-	(D)	.1	.1
NEW ENGLAND..............	284	100.0	3.2	29.8	28.5	(D)	13.8	.9	(D)	.2	-
RAIL..................	177	100.0	-	26.5	24.2	(D)	19.7	-	(D)	.3	-
MOTOR CARRIER.........	89	100.0	6.6	33.0	38.6	(D)	4.8	2.8	(D)	-	-
PRIVATE TRUCK.........	16	100.0	15.2	50.2	18.4	(D)	.7	-	(D)	-	-
AIR...................	-	100.0	-	1.0	1.1	(D)	74.7	2.3	(D)	1.8	19.0
WATER.................	-	100.0	100.0	-	-	(D)	-	-	(D)	-	-
OTHER.................	-	100.0	13.4	3.8	82.0	(D)	.3	-	(D)	-	.5
UNKNOWN...............	-	100.0	88.9	.1	11.1	(D)	-	-	(D)	-	-
MIDDLE ATLANTIC..........	795	100.0	3.5	23.5	30.7	(D)	8.4	1.7	(D)	-	.8
RAIL..................	360	100.0	-	12.3	23.8	(D)	9.2	2.9	(D)	-	.3
MOTOR CARRIER.........	351	100.0	7.5	29.3	35.9	(D)	8.5	.7	(D)	-	1.5
PRIVATE TRUCK.........	71	100.0	2.5	55.2	30.1	(D)	4.1	-	(D)	-	-
AIR...................	1	100.0	1.6	.2	15.7	(D)	81.1	-	(D)	-	.3
WATER.................	-	100.0	1.5	46.2	52.3	(D)	-	-	(D)	-	-
OTHER.................	6	100.0	.4	.6	98.1	(D)	.6	-	(D)	-	-
UNKNOWN...............	3	100.0	-	-	100.0	(D)	-	-	(D)	-	-
EAST NORTH CENTRAL......	7 038	100.0	.4	2.2	3.1	(D)	1.3	.4	(D)	-	-
RAIL..................	602	100.0	.4	6.1	10.5	(D)	8.9	2.7	(D)	-	.1
MOTOR CARRIER.........	470	100.0	5.3	23.7	25.4	(D)	5.1	1.7	(D)	.1	.5
PRIVATE TRUCK.........	237	100.0	.7	3.7	15.4	(D)	4.4	.8	(D)	-	-
AIR...................	-	100.0	.8	3.4	14.8	(D)	66.6	.6	(D)	-	9.1
WATER.................	5 726	100.0	-	-	-	(D)	-	-	(D)	-	-
OTHER.................	-	100.0	5.1	9.7	80.1	(D)	1.7	-	(D)	-	1.1
UNKNOWN...............	1	100.0	.7	.3	3.9	(D)	25.6	-	(D)	-	-
WEST NORTH CENTRAL......	647	100.0	1.3	7.1	24.6	(D)	4.4	.7	(D)	.1	.1
RAIL..................	368	100.0	-	6.4	24.7	(D)	5.0	.7	(D)	-	-
MOTOR CARRIER.........	184	100.0	4.6	11.1	34.5	(D)	4.6	.9	(D)	.5	.2
PRIVATE TRUCK.........	93	100.0	-	1.8	4.6	(D)	1.7	-	(D)	-	-
AIR...................	-	100.0	-	66.6	1.6	(D)	9.8	-	(D)	.3	.3
WATER.................	-	100.0	-	-	-	(D)	-	-	(D)	-	-
OTHER.................	-	100.0	15.3	24.2	52.1	(D)	-	-	(D)	-	1.4
UNKNOWN...............	-	100.0	-	-	100.0	(D)	-	-	(D)	-	-
SOUTH ATLANTIC...........	831	100.0	4.3	15.3	14.9	(D)	5.9	1.8	(D)	.2	.2
RAIL..................	328	100.0	-	12.9	20.3	(D)	6.2	2.0	(D)	-	-
MOTOR CARRIER.........	217	100.0	10.6	33.7	22.1	(D)	7.1	2.9	(D)	.7	.8
PRIVATE TRUCK.........	47	100.0	16.4	24.2	17.7	(D)	26.6	4.1	(D)	-	.1
AIR...................	-	100.0	.8	22.9	9.4	(D)	43.5	.4	(D)	.2	22.2
WATER.................	235	100.0	2.0	-	-	(D)	-	-	(D)	-	-
OTHER.................	-	100.0	5.4	21.2	68.0	(D)	1.5	-	(D)	-	.5
UNKNOWN...............	-	100.0	56.4	-	43.6	(D)	-	-	(D)	-	-
EAST SOUTH CENTRAL......	374	100.0	1.8	15.4	21.1	(D)	13.8	.4	(D)	.8	-
RAIL..................	161	100.0	-	6.0	19.9	(D)	15.1	.2	(D)	1.9	-
MOTOR CARRIER.........	131	100.0	3.5	24.3	26.9	(D)	14.6	.3	(D)	-	-
PRIVATE TRUCK.........	42	100.0	5.1	37.3	26.9	(D)	18.6	2.2	(D)	-	-
AIR...................	-	100.0	-	2.0	60.7	(D)	21.2	-	(D)	-	16.1
WATER.................	38	100.0	-	-	-	(D)	-	-	(D)	-	-
OTHER.................	-	100.0	8.1	57.0	8.9	(D)	26.0	-	(D)	-	-
UNKNOWN...............	-	100.0	-	-	100.0	(D)	-	-	(D)	-	-
WEST SOUTH CENTRAL......	697	100.0	4.0	23.5	11.8	(D)	7.1	12.9	(D)	.1	.5
RAIL..................	417	100.0	2.2	20.2	13.6	(D)	8.3	15.6	(D)	-	.1
MOTOR CARRIER.........	222	100.0	7.1	28.7	8.9	(D)	4.1	9.9	(D)	.5	1.3
PRIVATE TRUCK.........	36	100.0	7.7	11.8	15.0	(D)	7.6	6.0	(D)	-	-
AIR...................	-	100.0	32.9	45.1	5.6	(D)	14.9	.5	(D)	-	.1
WATER.................	19	100.0	-	59.6	-	(D)	17.2	-	(D)	-	-
OTHER.................	-	100.0	14.6	12.9	17.0	(D)	.1	-	(D)	-	4.3
UNKNOWN...............	-	100.0	-	-	57.5	(D)	-	-	(D)	-	-
MOUNTAIN.................	457	100.0	1.3	4.8	12.2	(D)	5.0	.5	(D)	1.7	17.6
RAIL..................	267	100.0	-	5.0	19.0	(D)	7.9	.6	(D)	.1	23.4
MOTOR CARRIER.........	145	100.0	4.0	5.5	2.3	(D)	1.3	.4	(D)	2.6	11.6
PRIVATE TRUCK.........	42	100.0	-	-	3.9	(D)	-	-	(D)	8.4	2.0
AIR...................	-	100.0	7.7	43.1	.1	(D)	-	.1	(D)	-	43.3
WATER.................	-	100.0	-	-	-	(D)	-	-	(D)	-	-
OTHER.................	-	100.0	3.9	14.3	.9	(D)	27.9	-	(D)	-	4.9
UNKNOWN...............	-	100.0	-	85.3	13.7	(D)	-	-	(D)	.9	-
PACIFIC..................	1 246	100.0	1.0	12.2	17.7	(D)	2.2	1.8	(D)	.7	31.9
RAIL..................	762	100.0	.3	5.5	21.6	(D)	3.2	2.4	(D)	.1	24.9
MOTOR CARRIER.........	340	100.0	2.5	11.7	15.9	(D)	.8	1.1	(D)	2.2	43.0
PRIVATE TRUCK.........	64	100.0	.7	6.9	1.9	(D)	.3	-	(D)	.3	77.8
AIR...................	-	100.0	14.3	5.9	43.5	(D)	30.0	-	(D)	-	2.4
WATER.................	76	100.0	1.4	85.2	-	(D)	-	-	(D)	-	13.3
OTHER.................	1	100.0	40.3	12.3	.6	(D)	.3	-	(D)	-	3.4
UNKNOWN...............	-	100.0	-	-	92.8	(D)	-	-	(D)	-	7.2

See footnotes at end of table 4.

TABLE 4. TCC GROUP 289—Percent Distribution of Distance Shipped and Weight of Shipment, by Means of Transport: 1972

Distance shipped and weight of shipment [2] [3]	Number	Percent distribution by means of transport							
		All means of transport	Rail	Motor carrier	Private truck	Air	Water	Other	Unknown
TONS OF SHIPMENTS	(thousands of tons)								
U.S. TOTAL..........	11 666	100.0	37.9	42.0	18.7	-	1.1	.2	.1
UNDER 100 MILES.........	2 436	100.0	30.5	42.5	25.8	-	.7	.4	-
UNDER 1000 POUNDS.....	61	100.0	.2	79.6	18.5	-	-	1.5	.1
1000 TO 9999 POUNDS...	248	100.0	-	68.2	31.3	-	.2	.2	.1
10000 TO 29999 POUNDS.	532	100.0	.2	37.1	61.1	-	.8	.6	.2
30000 TO 59999 POUNDS.	737	100.0	1.3	70.6	27.7	-	.2	.2	-
60000 TO 89999 POUNDS.	60	100.0	13.6	75.8	10.5	-	-	-	-
90000 POUNDS AND OVER.	797	100.0	90.9	6.7	.5	-	1.3	.5	-
100 TO 199 MILES........	2 146	100.0	23.4	52.3	24.2	-	-	-	-
UNDER 1000 POUNDS.....	33	100.0	.4	94.2	4.1	.1	-	.9	.3
1000 TO 9999 POUNDS...	161	100.0	1.1	84.6	13.6	.5	-	.1	.1
10000 TO 29999 POUNDS.	249	100.0	1.8	57.7	40.5	-	-	-	-
30000 TO 59999 POUNDS.	1 158	100.0	1.8	64.5	33.7	-	-	-	-
60000 TO 89999 POUNDS.	49	100.0	58.2	34.5	7.3	-	-	-	-
90000 POUNDS AND OVER.	493	100.0	90.5	9.1	.4	-	-	-	-
200 TO 299 MILES........	1 429	100.0	37.5	44.8	17.2	-	-	.2	.3
UNDER 1000 POUNDS.....	24	100.0	2.2	94.6	.5	.7	.1	1.9	.1
1000 TO 9999 POUNDS...	115	100.0	.7	90.2	7.8	-	-	.1	1.1
10000 TO 29999 POUNDS.	170	100.0	2.6	72.3	23.8	-	-	1.0	.3
30000 TO 59999 POUNDS.	612	100.0	5.9	61.7	31.8	-	-	.2	.4
60000 TO 89999 POUNDS.	114	100.0	97.4	2.0	.6	-	-	-	-
90000 POUNDS AND OVER.	391	100.0	97.7	2.3	-	-	-	-	-
300 TO 499 MILES........	2 119	100.0	37.6	43.6	18.6	-	-	.1	.1
UNDER 1000 POUNDS.....	30	100.0	1.0	89.2	4.6	.9	.4	3.3	.5
1000 TO 9999 POUNDS...	140	100.0	.4	90.8	8.5	-	-	-	.3
10000 TO 29999 POUNDS.	200	100.0	2.6	72.4	24.2	-	-	.9	-
30000 TO 59999 POUNDS.	820	100.0	3.5	56.2	40.1	-	.1	-	.1
60000 TO 89999 POUNDS.	244	100.0	75.9	23.9	.3	-	-	-	-
90000 POUNDS AND OVER.	683	100.0	84.3	15.5	.3	-	-	-	-
500 TO 999 MILES........	2 565	100.0	46.9	35.5	14.3	-	2.6	.4	.2
UNDER 1000 POUNDS.....	34	100.0	1.8	91.2	3.1	1.2	-	2.1	.7
1000 TO 9999 POUNDS...	129	100.0	1.9	91.9	4.3	.5	.1	.7	.6
10000 TO 29999 POUNDS.	192	100.0	3.8	65.1	30.5	-	.1	.4	-
30000 TO 59999 POUNDS.	937	100.0	13.4	54.2	31.5	-	.1	.8	-
60000 TO 89999 POUNDS.	381	100.0	77.0	20.6	.7	-	.4	-	1.3
90000 POUNDS AND OVER.	890	100.0	87.0	5.4	.5	-	7.2	-	-
1000 TO 1499 MILES......	634	100.0	66.8	28.7	2.2	.3	2.1	-	-
UNDER 1000 POUNDS.....	10	100.0	3.0	86.8	2.6	5.4	-	1.7	.5
1000 TO 9999 POUNDS...	31	100.0	.6	96.6	1.0	1.5	-	-	.3
10000 TO 29999 POUNDS.	43	100.0	3.8	92.4	3.8	-	-	-	-
30000 TO 59999 POUNDS.	148	100.0	18.1	64.9	7.7	.4	8.9	-	-
60000 TO 89999 POUNDS.	63	100.0	94.7	5.3	-	-	-	-	-
90000 POUNDS AND OVER.	336	100.0	99.4	.6	-	-	-	-	-
1500 MILES OR OVER......	333	100.0	64.7	24.4	2.2	.1	8.4	.2	.1
UNDER 1000 POUNDS.....	6	100.0	.7	84.7	6.3	3.7	1.6	2.3	.7
1000 TO 9999 POUNDS...	26	100.0	2.3	82.2	7.8	.4	5.4	1.7	-
10000 TO 29999 POUNDS.	33	100.0	19.3	77.1	1.9	-	1.0	-	.7
30000 TO 59999 POUNDS.	59	100.0	41.7	46.3	7.0	-	5.1	-	-
60000 TO 89999 POUNDS.	63	100.0	63.0	.5	-	-	36.5	-	-
90000 POUNDS AND OVER.	143	100.0	100.0	-	-	-	-	-	-
TON-MILES OF SHIPMENTS	(millions of ton-miles)								
U.S. TOTAL..........	4 856	100.0	48.0	36.1	12.4	.1	3.0	.2	.1
UNDER 100 MILES.........	132	100.0	34.4	43.4	21.4	-	.5	.3	-
UNDER 1000 POUNDS.....	2	100.0	.3	86.1	11.7	.1	-	1.7	.1
1000 TO 9999 POUNDS...	10	100.0	-	75.1	24.8	-	.1	-	.1
10000 TO 29999 POUNDS.	24	100.0	.1	42.1	56.6	-	.6	.5	.1
30000 TO 59999 POUNDS.	42	100.0	.7	73.0	26.0	-	-	.3	-
60000 TO 89999 POUNDS.	3	100.0	14.6	80.3	5.0	-	-	-	-
90000 POUNDS AND OVER.	48	100.0	92.3	6.1	.3	-	1.1	.2	-
100 TO 199 MILES........	342	100.0	26.4	50.9	22.6	-	-	.8	.3
UNDER 1000 POUNDS.....	5	100.0	.4	94.9	3.4	.1	-	.8	.3
1000 TO 9999 POUNDS...	24	100.0	1.0	85.7	12.6	.5	-	.1	.1
10000 TO 29999 POUNDS.	34	100.0	2.0	58.6	39.3	-	-	-	-
30000 TO 59999 POUNDS.	182	100.0	1.7	65.6	32.7	-	-	-	-
60000 TO 89999 POUNDS.	7	100.0	62.6	30.0	7.4	-	-	-	-
90000 POUNDS AND OVER.	88	100.0	92.0	7.8	.2	-	-	-	-

See footnotes at end of table 4.

TABLE 4. **TCC GROUP 289—Percent Distribution of Distance Shipped and Weight of Shipment, by Means of Transport: 1972**—Continued

Distance shipped and weight of shipment[2][3]	Number	Percent distribution by means of transport							
		All means of transport	Rail	Motor carrier	Private truck	Air	Water	Other	Unknown
TON-MILES OF SHIPMENTS	(millions of ton-miles)								
200 TO 299 MILES.........	355	100.0	38.5	44.5	16.4	-	-	.2	.3
UNDER 1000 POUNDS.....	6	100.0	2.2	94.7	.4	.7	.1	1.9	.1
1000 TO 9999 POUNDS...	28	100.0	.7	90.2	7.9	-	-	.1	1.0
10000 TO 29999 POUNDS.	42	100.0	2.8	72.9	23.0	-	-	1.0	.2
30000 TO 59999 POUNDS.	148	100.0	6.4	62.0	30.9	-	-	.1	.5
60000 TO 89999 POUNDS.	28	100.0	97.7	1.7	.5	-	-	-	-
90000 POUNDS AND OVER.	100	100.0	97.7	2.3	-	-	-	-	-
300 TO 499 MILES........	805	100.0	38.9	43.3	17.6	-	-	.1	.1
UNDER 1000 POUNDS.....	11	100.0	1.0	89.4	4.5	.9	.4	3.2	.5
1000 TO 9999 POUNDS...	53	100.0	.4	90.8	8.5	-	-	-	.3
10000 TO 29999 POUNDS.	77	100.0	2.9	71.9	24.3	-	-	.9	-
30000 TO 59999 POUNDS.	304	100.0	3.7	57.7	38.5	-	.1	-	.1
60000 TO 89999 POUNDS.	101	100.0	75.4	24.4	.3	-	-	-	-
90000 POUNDS AND OVER.	256	100.0	86.8	12.9	.2	-	-	-	-
500 TO 999 MILES........	1 814	100.0	46.2	35.1	14.8	-	3.2	.4	.3
UNDER 1000 POUNDS.....	23	100.0	2.2	90.8	2.9	1.2	-	2.1	.7
1000 TO 9999 POUNDS...	89	100.0	1.9	91.0	5.1	.5	.1	.7	.7
10000 TO 29999 POUNDS.	137	100.0	3.7	62.3	33.6	-	.1	.5	-
30000 TO 59999 POUNDS.	664	100.0	12.7	54.6	31.8	-	.1	.8	-
60000 TO 89999 POUNDS.	279	100.0	77.0	20.4	.7	-	.5	-	1.3
90000 POUNDS AND OVER.	619	100.0	85.9	4.6	.6	-	8.9	-	-
1000 TO 1499 MILES......	769	100.0	67.1	28.4	2.0	.2	2.2	-	-
UNDER 1000 POUNDS.....	12	100.0	3.2	86.5	2.9	5.2	-	1.6	.6
1000 TO 9999 POUNDS...	37	100.0	.6	96.7	1.0	1.4	-	-	.3
10000 TO 29999 POUNDS.	51	100.0	3.5	93.0	3.5	-	-	-	-
30000 TO 59999 POUNDS.	179	100.0	18.2	64.7	7.2	.4	9.4	-	-
60000 TO 89999 POUNDS.	75	100.0	94.8	5.2	-	-	-	-	-
90000 POUNDS AND OVER.	411	100.0	99.4	.6	-	-	-	-	-
1500 MILES OR OVER......	637	100.0	61.3	25.2	2.1	.1	11.1	.2	.1
UNDER 1000 POUNDS.....	13	100.0	.9	83.8	6.7	3.7	1.9	2.4	.6
1000 TO 9999 POUNDS...	52	100.0	2.2	79.8	8.6	.4	7.3	1.7	-
10000 TO 29999 POUNDS.	64	100.0	17.7	78.3	1.8	-	1.5	-	.7
30000 TO 59999 POUNDS.	118	100.0	40.2	47.6	5.6	-	6.6	-	-
60000 TO 89999 POUNDS.	136	100.0	57.3	.4	-	-	42.3	-	-
90000 POUNDS AND OVER.	252	100.0	100.0	-	-	-	-	-	-

Note: Detail may not add to total due to rounding. The introductory table shows the estimates of sampling variability for tons; sampling variability for ton-miles has not been estimated. See the map in the Introduction for the States comprising the geographic divisions of the United States.

Shipments excluded from the survey are those moving by pipeline (primarily petroleum products from refiners), parcel post shipments, and commodities moved by own power (motorized vehicles, aircraft, etc.) or towed (prefabricated buildings, etc.). Local shipments (commodities shipped less than 25 miles from the plant) and shipments within the same city are also excluded. Shipments to Alaska and Hawaii from the 48 conterminous States and the District of Columbia are included; however, no data were obtained for shipments originating in Alaska and Hawaii.

- Represents zero or rounds to zero.   (D) Withheld to avoid disclosing figures for individual companies.

[1]Production of this commodity is concentrated in the geographic divisions shown; figures and distributions for geographic divisions not shown are included in the total.

[2]Distances of shipments to foreign destinations are calculated only to the U.S. port of exit.

[3]Includes only shipments represented by bills of lading and invoices. Summary records which did not show individual weights of shipments are not included.

Petroleum and Coal Products

CONTENTS

[Page numbers listed here omit the State prefix number that appears as part of the number for each page]

TABLES (The tables listed below are shown for each of the Transportation Commodity Classification groups in this report)

Comparisons of Tons and Ton-Miles of Shipments for Geographic Divisions of Origin and for Sampling Variability: 1972 and 1967

1. Percent Distribution of Geographic Division of Origin and Distance Shipped, by Means of Transport: 1972

2. Percent Distribution of Geographic Division of Origin and Means of Transport, by Geographic Division of Destination: 1972

3. Percent Distribution of Geographic Division of Destination and Means of Transport, by Geographic Division of Origin: 1972

4. Percent Distribution of Distance Shipped and Weight of Shipment, by Means of Transport: 1972

TCC 291. Products of Petroleum Refining

Comparisons of Tons and Ton-Miles of Shipments for
Geographic Divisions of Origin and for Sampling Variability: 1972 and 1967

Geographic division of origin	Estimates				Relative sampling variability in tons (percent)	
	1972		1967		1972	1967
	Tons (thousands)	Ton-miles (millions)	Tons (thousands)	Ton-miles (millions)		
U.S. total	310,196	177,627	[1] 277,033	([2])	7.1	([2])
New England	(D)	(D)	1,430	96	(*)	(*)
Middle Atlantic	34,790	3,669	[1] 34,717	([2])	11.9	(*)
East North Central	21,590	3,069	32,116	4,309	22.2	(*)
West North Central	6,620	948	7,395	1,082	27.1	(*)
South Atlantic	(D)	(D)	4,074	1,177	(*)	(*)
East South Central	23,693	4,510	21,626	8,793	46.4	(*)
West South Central	173,846	148,574	[1] 131,553	([2])	11.6	(*)
Mountain	11,209	3,276	6,955	1,078	46.4	(*)
Pacific	24,063	10,060	37,167	16,965	9.9	(*)

(D) Withheld to avoid disclosing figures for individual companies.   (*) Data not published.

[1] Revised from 1967 published data.   [2] Revised data not available.

TABLE 1. **TCC GROUP 291**—Percent Distribution of Geographic Division of Origin and Distance Shipped, by Means of Transport: 1972

Geographic division of origin[1] and distance shipped[2]	Number	Percent distribution by means of transport							
		All means of transport	Rail	Motor carrier	Private truck	Air	Water	Other	Unknown
TONS OF SHIPMENTS	(thousands of tons)								
U.S. TOTAL..........	310 196	100.0	8.3	15.0	7.5	-	68.7	.1	.3
MIDDLE ATLANTIC.........	34 790	100.0	5.7	28.8	13.3	-	52.2	-	.1
UNDER 100 MILES.......	26 456	100.0	.9	29.6	15.6	-	53.8	-	-
100 TO 199 MILES......	2 847	100.0	7.5	28.1	11.6	-	52.8	-	-
200 TO 299 MILES......	3 393	100.0	5.6	23.2	3.3	-	67.9	.1	.1
300 TO 499 MILES......	1 039	100.0	63.0	32.5	3.8	-	-	.4	.4
500 TO 999 MILES......	762	100.0	57.8	29.0	1.7	.1	11.3	.1	-
1000 TO 1499 MILES....	210	100.0	82.9	9.7	1.9	-	5.4	-	-
1500 MILES OR OVER....	81	100.0	64.7	25.0	2.8	-	6.3	1.3	-
EAST NORTH CENTRAL......	21 590	100.0	8.9	49.4	14.2	-	27.4	-	-
UNDER 100 MILES.......	11 893	100.0	2.6	68.1	20.1	-	9.2	-	-
100 TO 199 MILES......	4 405	100.0	7.6	34.2	10.8	-	47.4	-	-
200 TO 299 MILES......	2 783	100.0	13.2	18.1	4.2	-	64.5	-	-
300 TO 499 MILES......	1 565	100.0	40.9	23.5	3.7	-	31.9	-	-
500 TO 999 MILES......	835	100.0	23.7	19.8	3.5	-	53.1	-	-
1000 TO 1499 MILES....	51	100.0	58.5	31.7	9.7	-	-	-	.1
1500 MILES OR OVER....	55	100.0	85.8	13.7	.5	-	-	-	-
WEST NORTH CENTRAL......	6 620	100.0	16.1	56.1	27.7	-	-	.1	-
UNDER 100 MILES.......	3 707	100.0	4.7	64.6	30.7	-	-	.1	-
100 TO 199 MILES......	1 758	100.0	20.1	52.4	27.2	-	-	.3	-
200 TO 299 MILES......	393	100.0	27.4	51.4	21.2	-	-	-	.1
300 TO 499 MILES......	264	100.0	46.2	33.3	20.3	-	-	-	.2
500 TO 999 MILES......	453	100.0	63.1	23.3	13.1	-	-	.5	-
1000 TO 1499 MILES....	29	100.0	70.8	5.2	24.0	-	-	-	-
1500 MILES OR OVER....	14	100.0	-	3.8	96.2	-	-	-	-
EAST SOUTH CENTRAL......	23 693	100.0	3.3	16.3	6.5	-	73.9	.1	-
UNDER 100 MILES.......	7 736	100.0	3.4	29.2	14.0	-	52.9	.4	-
100 TO 199 MILES......	9 809	100.0	2.1	16.0	3.8	-	78.1	-	-
200 TO 299 MILES......	953	100.0	3.6	1.9	5.9	-	88.7	-	-
300 TO 499 MILES......	4 406	100.0	4.2	.2	.4	-	95.3	-	-
500 TO 999 MILES......	788	100.0	10.5	-	-	-	89.5	-	-
1000 TO 1499 MILES....	-	100.0	-	-	-	-	-	-	-
1500 MILES OR OVER....	-	100.0	-	-	-	-	-	-	-
WEST SOUTH CENTRAL......	173 846	100.0	7.3	4.3	2.9	-	84.8	-	.6
UNDER 100 MILES.......	18 275	100.0	12.1	20.1	17.5	-	49.6	-	.7
100 TO 199 MILES......	14 978	100.0	13.1	10.6	8.6	-	62.5	-	5.1
200 TO 299 MILES......	6 834	100.0	12.6	16.6	5.3	-	65.5	-	-
300 TO 499 MILES......	15 195	100.0	9.5	3.4	1.4	-	85.6	-	.1
500 TO 999 MILES......	42 400	100.0	12.8	1.1	.1	-	85.7	-	.2
1000 TO 1499 MILES....	58 739	100.0	1.2	.1	-	-	98.6	-	-
1500 MILES OR OVER....	17 422	100.0	.7	.2	-	-	99.1	-	-
MOUNTAIN...............	11 209	100.0	43.8	40.6	15.7	-	-	-	-
UNDER 100 MILES.......	3 774	100.0	2.1	74.4	23.5	-	-	-	-
100 TO 199 MILES......	2 638	100.0	33.2	43.5	23.4	-	-	-	-
200 TO 299 MILES......	1 774	100.0	67.8	24.3	7.9	-	-	-	-
300 TO 499 MILES......	730	100.0	64.1	21.2	14.7	-	-	-	-
500 TO 999 MILES......	824	100.0	98.6	.6	.8	-	-	-	-
1000 TO 1499 MILES....	1 461	100.0	100.0	-	-	-	-	-	-
1500 MILES OR OVER....	4	100.0	100.0	-	-	-	-	-	-
PACIFIC.................	24 063	100.0	7.8	24.0	20.4	-	46.1	1.7	-
UNDER 100 MILES.......	8 391	100.0	4.1	48.6	32.7	-	9.7	4.8	-
100 TO 199 MILES......	2 857	100.0	7.1	38.9	9.6	-	44.4	-	-
200 TO 299 MILES......	4 117	100.0	1.9	7.8	35.6	-	54.7	-	-
300 TO 499 MILES......	2 157	100.0	34.3	7.9	13.2	-	44.6	-	-
500 TO 999 MILES......	3 744	100.0	8.0	1.5	3.0	-	87.4	-	-
1000 TO 1499 MILES....	1 294	100.0	2.2	1.6	.3	-	96.0	-	-
1500 MILES OR OVER....	1 499	100.0	11.5	1.4	2.0	-	85.0	-	-
TON-MILES OF SHIPMENTS	(millions of ton-miles)								
U.S. TOTAL..........	177 627	100.0	6.7	2.9	1.3	-	89.0	-	.1
MIDDLE ATLANTIC.........	3 669	100.0	27.6	26.0	6.5	-	39.7	.1	.1
UNDER 100 MILES.......	1 015	100.0	1.4	28.7	13.0	-	57.0	-	-
100 TO 199 MILES......	407	100.0	8.8	28.2	12.0	-	51.0	-	-
200 TO 299 MILES......	834	100.0	6.0	23.2	3.3	-	67.4	.1	.1
300 TO 499 MILES......	431	100.0	64.4	31.5	3.3	-	-	.4	.3
500 TO 999 MILES......	545	100.0	56.5	27.2	1.5	-	14.5	.2	-
1000 TO 1499 MILES....	247	100.0	82.8	9.6	1.8	-	5.8	-	-
1500 MILES OR OVER....	187	100.0	64.5	25.0	2.5	-	6.8	1.2	-
EAST NORTH CENTRAL......	3 069	100.0	22.1	31.3	7.7	-	38.9	-	-
UNDER 100 MILES.......	493	100.0	3.4	66.5	19.4	-	10.7	-	-
100 TO 199 MILES......	608	100.0	7.1	34.8	10.7	-	47.3	-	-
200 TO 299 MILES......	653	100.0	13.0	18.2	4.2	-	64.7	-	-
300 TO 499 MILES......	626	100.0	43.5	22.6	3.6	-	30.3	-	-
500 TO 999 MILES......	525	100.0	26.7	23.8	3.8	-	45.7	-	-
1000 TO 1499 MILES....	63	100.0	59.9	30.6	9.4	-	-	-	.1
1500 MILES OR OVER....	98	100.0	84.4	15.0	.6	-	-	-	-

See footnotes at end of table 4.

TABLE 1. **TCC GROUP 291**—Percent Distribution of Geographic Division of Origin and Distance Shipped, by Means of Transport: 1972—Continued

Geographic division of origin [1] and distance shipped [2]	Number	Percent distribution by means of transport							
		All means of transport	Rail	Motor carrier	Private truck	Air	Water	Other	Unknown
TON-MILES OF SHIPMENTS	(millions of ton-miles)								
WEST NORTH CENTRAL......	948	100.0	34.5	40.1	25.2	-	-	.2	-
UNDER 100 MILES.......	155	100.0	5.1	59.0	35.9	-	-	-	-
100 TO 199 MILES......	239	100.0	20.4	51.2	28.2	-	-	.2	-
200 TO 299 MILES......	95	100.0	28.6	51.9	19.3	-	-	-	.1
300 TO 499 MILES......	107	100.0	44.5	34.6	20.7	-	-	-	.2
500 TO 999 MILES......	289	100.0	58.3	26.3	15.0	-	-	.4	.2
1000 TO 1499 MILES....	36	100.0	72.6	4.9	22.5	-	-	-	-
1500 MILES OR OVER....	24	100.0	-	3.8	96.2	-	-	-	-
EAST SOUTH CENTRAL......	4 510	100.0	3.8	7.7	2.7	-	85.8	.1	-
UNDER 100 MILES.......	410	100.0	3.5	31.4	13.6	-	50.9	.6	-
100 TO 199 MILES......	1 522	100.0	2.0	13.7	3.1	-	81.1	-	-
200 TO 299 MILES......	218	100.0	3.6	1.9	5.9	-	88.5	-	-
300 TO 499 MILES......	1 810	100.0	3.9	.2	.4	-	95.6	-	-
500 TO 999 MILES......	549	100.0	8.7	-	-	-	91.3	-	-
1000 TO 1499 MILES....	-	100.0	-	-	-	-	-	-	-
1500 MILES OR OVER....	-	100.0	-	-	-	-	-	-	-
WEST SOUTH CENTRAL......	148 574	100.0	4.0	1.0	.4	-	94.6	-	.1
UNDER 100 MILES.......	1 092	100.0	10.9	18.5	15.5	-	54.5	-	.6
100 TO 199 MILES......	2 284	100.0	11.3	10.8	7.4	-	66.4	-	4.1
200 TO 299 MILES......	1 719	100.0	13.3	15.9	5.2	-	65.7	-	-
300 TO 499 MILES......	6 313	100.0	9.3	3.2	1.3	-	86.1	-	.1
500 TO 999 MILES......	31 734	100.0	11.5	.9	.1	-	87.1	-	.3
1000 TO 1499 MILES....	76 680	100.0	1.1	.1	-	-	98.8	-	-
1500 MILES OR OVER....	28 748	100.0	.8	.4	-	-	98.8	-	-
MOUNTAIN................	3 276	100.0	81.2	12.8	6.0	-	-	-	-
UNDER 100 MILES.......	138	100.0	2.6	71.1	26.3	-	-	-	-
100 TO 199 MILES......	372	100.0	34.6	43.9	21.5	-	-	-	-
200 TO 299 MILES......	431	100.0	68.6	23.4	8.0	-	-	-	-
300 TO 499 MILES......	284	100.0	67.2	19.1	13.7	-	-	-	-
500 TO 999 MILES......	537	100.0	98.4	.6	1.0	-	-	-	-
1000 TO 1499 MILES....	1 503	100.0	100.0	-	-	-	-	-	-
1500 MILES OR OVER....	7	100.0	100.0	-	-	-	-	-	-
PACIFIC.................	10 060	100.0	9.0	5.4	7.0	-	78.3	.2	-
UNDER 100 MILES.......	338	100.0	7.5	43.7	29.4	-	13.3	6.0	-
100 TO 199 MILES......	404	100.0	8.1	37.5	9.0	-	45.4	-	-
200 TO 299 MILES......	928	100.0	2.1	8.0	35.3	-	54.6	-	-
300 TO 499 MILES......	802	100.0	34.1	7.5	13.1	-	45.4	-	-
500 TO 999 MILES......	2 618	100.0	8.0	1.6	2.8	-	87.6	-	-
1000 TO 1499 MILES....	1 371	100.0	2.1	1.8	.3	-	95.7	-	-
1500 MILES OR OVER....	3 597	100.0	8.9	1.3	1.7	-	88.1	-	-

See footnotes at end of table 4.

TABLE 2. **TCC GROUP 291**—Percent Distribution of Geographic Division of Origin and Means of Transport, by Geographic Division of Destination: 1972

Geographic division of origin [1] and means of transport	Number	Percent distribution by division of destination									
		U.S. total	New England	Middle Atlantic	East North Central	West North Central	South Atlantic	East South Central	West South Central	Mountain	Pacific
TONS OF SHIPMENTS	(thousands of tons)										
U.S. TOTAL..............	310 196	100.0	13.8	17.1	11.6	4.2	21.1	9.0	11.8	3.5	7.8
RAIL.................	25 838	100.0	.9	3.6	17.2	14.3	12.0	12.2	19.4	12.9	7.6
MOTOR CARRIER........	46 422	100.0	1.1	19.0	21.9	9.4	2.9	8.5	13.6	11.5	12.0
PRIVATE TRUCK........	23 292	100.0	.6	18.2	12.0	10.0	3.1	5.8	19.3	10.1	20.9
AIR..................	3	100.0	1.9	5.0	75.6	2.1	14.1	.3	.2	-	.6
WATER................	213 145	100.0	19.7	18.4	8.6	1.2	28.3	8.8	9.6	-	5.4
OTHER................	450	100.0	.6	.3	1.1	1.7	6.4	-	-	.1	90.0
UNKNOWN..............	1 044	100.0	.2	1.5	10.2	1.5	.1	73.1	13.0	-	.4
MIDDLE ATLANTIC.........	34 790	100.0	13.3	62.0	3.2	.4	19.6	.8	.5	-	.2
RAIL.................	1 972	100.0	8.4	19.8	33.4	4.5	14.1	10.3	7.2	.1	2.1
MOTOR CARRIER........	10 013	100.0	4.7	82.8	3.8	.3	7.2	.8	.1	-	.2
PRIVATE TRUCK........	4 620	100.0	2.5	89.3	1.2	.2	6.6	.2	.1	-	.2
AIR..................	-	100.0	-	-	3.0	-	95.0	-	1.2	-	.8
WATER................	18 157	100.0	21.4	48.1	-	-	30.4	-	.1	-	-
OTHER................	8	100.0	30.6	13.2	30.0	12.8	-	-	.6	5.9	6.8
UNKNOWN..............	19	100.0	11.9	83.4	.2	-	4.6	-	-	-	-
EAST NORTH CENTRAL......	21 590	100.0	.1	4.7	85.1	6.7	1.3	.7	.6	.4	.2
RAIL.................	1 928	100.0	.9	5.7	60.4	11.3	9.5	2.8	3.6	3.3	2.5
MOTOR CARRIER........	10 666	100.0	.1	3.9	88.1	5.3	.9	.9	.5	.3	-
PRIVATE TRUCK........	3 072	100.0	.1	1.6	81.9	15.5	.2	.1	.4	.1	-
AIR..................	2	100.0	2.3	6.0	91.3	-	-	.4	-	-	-
WATER................	5 915	100.0	-	7.5	89.5	3.0	-	-	-	-	-
OTHER................	-	100.0	.7	15.5	32.4	9.6	17.9	24.0	-	-	-
UNKNOWN..............	3	100.0	-	-	98.9	-	1.1	-	-	-	-

See footnotes at end of table 4.

TABLE 2. TCC GROUP 291—Percent Distribution of Geographic Division of Origin and Means of Transport, by Geographic Division of Destination: 1972—Continued

Geographic division of origin[1] and means of transport	Number	Percent distribution by division of destination									
		U.S. total	New England	Middle Atlantic	East North Central	West North Central	South Atlantic	East South Central	West South Central	Mountain	Pacific
TONS OF SHIPMENTS	(thousands of tons)										
WEST NORTH CENTRAL......	6 620	100.0	.2	.2	5.1	85.3	1.4	.5	5.8	1.3	.3
RAIL....................	1 063	100.0	.7	.3	10.7	78.8	1.7	1.7	3.5	2.2	.4
MOTOR CARRIER..........	3 716	100.0	-	-	3.9	87.1	1.6	.1	6.7	.6	-
PRIVATE TRUCK..........	1 832	100.0	.1	.3	4.0	85.5	.8	.7	5.5	2.2	.8
AIR....................	-	100.0	-	-	-	-	-	-	-	-	-
WATER..................	-	100.0	-	-	-	-	-	-	-	-	-
OTHER..................	8	100.0	-	-	25.0	75.0	-	-	-	-	-
UNKNOWN................	-	100.0	-	-	55.6	44.4	-	-	-	-	-
EAST SOUTH CENTRAL......	23 693	100.0	-	11.5	21.6	.7	28.0	31.1	7.2	-	-
RAIL....................	777	100.0	-	10.4	7.0	.4	24.6	54.6	3.1	-	-
MOTOR CARRIER..........	3 855	100.0	-	-	2.7	.2	3.7	92.5	.9	-	-
PRIVATE TRUCK..........	1 529	100.0	-	-	4.7	3.6	7.4	70.3	13.9	-	-
AIR....................	-	100.0	-	-	-	-	-	-	-	-	-
WATER..................	17 502	100.0	-	15.1	27.9	.5	35.2	13.1	8.2	-	-
OTHER..................	28	100.0	-	-	-	-	100.0	-	-	-	-
UNKNOWN................	-	100.0	-	-	-	-	-	-	-	-	-
WEST SOUTH CENTRAL......	173 846	100.0	16.4	14.1	5.3	2.7	29.1	11.5	19.5	1.0	.4
RAIL....................	12 774	100.0	.2	1.3	6.4	14.8	17.4	18.6	34.9	4.0	2.3
MOTOR CARRIER..........	7 478	100.0	-	.2	1.8	5.1	1.7	2.2	79.6	8.6	.8
PRIVATE TRUCK..........	5 116	100.0	-	-	.4	1.9	.1	3.9	81.4	12.3	-
AIR....................	-	100.0	-	1.1	-	41.5	-	-	.3	-	57.2
WATER..................	147 461	100.0	19.3	16.5	5.6	1.6	32.7	11.1	13.0	-	.2
OTHER..................	-	100.0	-	8.7	25.6	-	5.7	-	60.0	-	-
UNKNOWN................	1 015	100.0	-	-	10.0	1.5	-	75.1	13.3	-	-
MOUNTAIN................	11 209	100.0	-	-	13.8	7.9	-	-	1.2	72.4	4.6
RAIL....................	4 905	100.0	-	-	31.6	12.8	-	-	2.8	42.4	10.3
MOTOR CARRIER..........	4 548	100.0	-	-	-	3.1	-	-	-	96.9	-
PRIVATE TRUCK..........	1 755	100.0	-	-	-	6.6	-	-	.1	93.0	.3
AIR....................	-	100.0	-	-	-	-	-	-	-	-	-
WATER..................	-	100.0	-	-	-	-	-	-	-	-	-
OTHER..................	-	100.0	-	-	-	-	-	-	-	-	-
UNKNOWN................	-	100.0	-	-	-	-	-	-	-	100.0	-
PACIFIC................	24 063	100.0	-	.2	.2	.1	-	-	.5	3.7	95.3
RAIL....................	1 871	100.0	-	1.3	1.9	1.0	-	-	5.1	33.5	57.2
MOTOR CARRIER..........	5 779	100.0	-	.1	.1	-	.1	-	.4	4.0	95.3
PRIVATE TRUCK..........	4 913	100.0	-	.2	.4	-	.1	-	.1	.7	98.6
AIR....................	-	100.0	.8	5.3	.4	86.0	-	-	-	.5	7.0
WATER..................	11 088	100.0	-	-	-	-	-	-	-	-	100.0
OTHER..................	404	100.0	-	-	-	-	-	-	-	-	100.0
UNKNOWN................	4	100.0	-	-	6.0	2.4	1.8	-	4.4	-	85.5
TON-MILES OF SHIPMENTS	(millions of ton-miles)										
U.S. TOTAL.............	177 627	100.0	27.1	20.0	6.9	2.1	28.2	4.9	3.4	1.2	6.1
RAIL....................	11 887	100.0	1.0	3.7	24.3	12.9	15.2	10.7	11.9	10.0	10.3
MOTOR CARRIER..........	5 130	100.0	1.3	12.0	17.3	10.4	7.5	9.4	16.8	13.2	11.9
PRIVATE TRUCK..........	2 352	100.0	1.1	8.6	11.2	10.7	3.8	6.5	18.2	11.7	28.2
AIR....................	-	100.0	4.7	9.7	36.9	12.0	31.1	.5	.8	-	4.3
WATER..................	158 021	100.0	30.3	21.7	5.1	.9	30.3	4.2	2.1	-	5.3
OTHER..................	30	100.0	3.3	1.0	7.3	4.9	8.6	.1	.2	2.9	71.6
UNKNOWN................	203	100.0	.5	.5	46.0	3.2	.2	45.7	3.8	-	.1
MIDDLE ATLANTIC........	3 669	100.0	21.5	30.8	13.0	3.0	15.8	5.4	5.7	.3	4.5
RAIL....................	1 012	100.0	4.2	5.6	30.7	7.8	9.3	14.5	17.2	.5	10.2
MOTOR CARRIER..........	954	100.0	6.0	48.5	15.7	2.8	15.2	5.1	1.6	.4	4.6
PRIVATE TRUCK..........	240	100.0	6.3	65.6	5.8	2.2	15.1	1.3	1.7	.7	1.3
AIR....................	-	100.0	-	-	2.5	-	91.5	-	2.6	-	3.5
WATER..................	1 455	100.0	46.1	31.1	-	-	20.9	-	1.0	-	.9
OTHER..................	5	100.0	18.3	5.2	18.7	16.3	-	-	1.3	16.4	23.8
UNKNOWN................	2	100.0	43.9	43.7	.7	-	11.7	-	-	-	-
EAST NORTH CENTRAL......	3 069	100.0	.6	13.6	63.0	7.5	4.4	1.6	2.9	3.4	3.0
RAIL....................	678	100.0	1.5	8.3	35.1	10.3	13.1	2.5	6.8	10.2	12.2
MOTOR CARRIER..........	959	100.0	.6	11.2	63.7	8.7	4.6	3.3	3.6	3.3	.9
PRIVATE TRUCK..........	236	100.0	1.0	5.3	68.7	18.0	.5	.5	3.7	2.1	.2
AIR....................	-	100.0	9.1	17.5	72.3	-	-	.9	-	-	.1
WATER..................	1 192	100.0	-	20.1	77.2	2.7	-	-	-	-	-
OTHER..................	-	100.0	.8	13.0	14.2	10.7	30.1	31.2	-	-	-
UNKNOWN................	-	100.0	-	-	85.8	-	14.2	-	-	-	-
WEST NORTH CENTRAL......	948	100.0	1.4	1.0	9.2	61.5	8.2	1.6	8.4	5.5	3.2
RAIL....................	327	100.0	3.3	1.0	14.4	60.3	5.2	3.5	6.5	4.1	1.8
MOTOR CARRIER..........	380	100.0	-	.4	3.2	66.2	12.9	.2	12.9	3.9	.3
PRIVATE TRUCK..........	238	100.0	1.2	1.8	10.9	55.8	4.8	1.3	4.1	10.1	10.0
AIR....................	-	100.0	-	-	-	-	-	-	-	-	-
WATER..................	-	100.0	-	-	-	-	-	-	-	-	-
OTHER..................	1	100.0	-	.1	65.7	34.2	-	-	-	-	-
UNKNOWN................	-	100.0	-	-	70.3	29.7	-	-	-	-	-

See footnotes at end of table 4.

TABLE 2. **TCC GROUP 291—Percent Distribution of Geographic Division of Origin and Means of Transport, by Geographic Division of Destination: 1972**—Continued

Geographic division of origin [1] and means of transport	Number	Percent distribution by division of destination									
		U.S. total	New England	Middle Atlantic	East North Central	West North Central	South Atlantic	East South Central	West South Central	Mountain	Pacific
TON-MILES OF SHIPMENTS	(millions of ton-miles)										
EAST SOUTH CENTRAL......	4 510	100.0	-	16.2	19.1	.7	40.2	15.6	8.1	-	-
RAIL..................	171	100.0	-	19.5	1.5	1.2	17.2	55.0	5.7	-	-
MOTOR CARRIER.........	345	100.0	-	-	2.1	.3	3.1	93.5	1.0	-	-
PRIVATE TRUCK.........	122	100.0	-	-	3.5	5.6	6.8	71.9	12.1	-	-
AIR...................	-	100.0	-	-	-	-	-	-	-	-	-
WATER.................	3 868	100.0	-	18.0	21.9	.6	45.6	5.2	8.8		-
OTHER.................	2	100.0	-	-	-	-	-	100.0	-	-	-
UNKNOWN...............	-	100.0	-	-	-	-	-	-	-	-	-
WEST SOUTH CENTRAL......	148 574	100.0	29.9	22.1	4.8	1.6	31.8	5.1	3.4	.4	.7
RAIL..................	5 913	100.0	.7	3.4	10.8	14.1	25.4	16.5	15.6	6.3	7.2
MOTOR CARRIER.........	1 430	100.0	.2	1.6	6.7	8.7	5.2	4.0	51.1	12.4	10.0
PRIVATE TRUCK.........	550	100.0	.3	-	2.5	4.8	.5	8.1	69.1	14.5	.1
AIR...................	-	100.0	-	1.1	-	18.7	-	-	-	-	80.2
WATER.................	140 480	100.0	31.6	23.2	4.5	1.0	32.5	4.6	2.1	-	.4
OTHER.................	-	100.0	-	20.1	38.1	-	12.5	-	29.3	-	-
UNKNOWN...............	199	100.0	-	.1	46.4	3.1	-	46.7	3.7	-	-
MOUNTAIN...............	3 276	100.0	.1	.1	48.3	12.5	.1	-	1.5	29.3	8.2
RAIL..................	2 660	100.0	.1	.1	59.4	12.4	.1	-	1.8	16.2	9.9
MOTOR CARRIER.........	420	100.0	-	-	-	10.3	-	-	-	89.6	.1
PRIVATE TRUCK.........	195	100.0	-	-	-	19.2	-	-	.6	78.1	2.1
AIR...................	-	100.0	-	-	-	-	-	-	-	-	-
WATER.................	-	100.0	-	-	-	-	-	-	-	-	-
OTHER.................	-	100.0	-	-	-	-	-	-	-	-	-
UNKNOWN...............	-	100.0	-	-	-	-	-	-	-	100.0	-
PACIFIC................	10 060	100.0	-	.9	1.1	.3	.1	-	1.8	3.6	92.3
RAIL..................	907	100.0	-	6.5	7.0	3.0	-	-	16.2	30.0	37.2
MOTOR CARRIER.........	547	100.0	-	2.6	1.2	.6	1.2	-	4.9	13.5	75.9
PRIVATE TRUCK.........	708	100.0	-	2.7	5.1	.1	.7	-	.6	1.7	89.1
AIR...................	-	100.0	1.3	7.6	.5	89.1	-	-	-	.3	1.2
WATER.................	7 875	100.0	-	-	-	-	-	-	-	-	100.0
OTHER.................	20	100.0	-	-	.2	-	-	-	-	-	99.7
UNKNOWN...............	1	100.0	-	-	33.4	11.5	11.0	-	23.6	-	20.5

See footnotes at end of table 4.

TABLE 3. **TCC GROUP 291—Percent Distribution of Geographic Division of Destination and Means of Transport, by Geographic Division of Origin: 1972**

Geographic division of destination and means of transport	Number (thousands of tons)	Percent distribution by division of origin[1]									
		U.S. total	New England	Middle Atlantic	East North Central	West North Central	South Atlantic	East South Central	West South Central	Mountain	Pacific
TONS OF SHIPMENTS											
U.S. TOTAL	310 196	100.0	(D)	11.2	7.0	2.1	(D)	7.6	56.0	3.6	7.8
RAIL	25 838	100.0	(D)	7.6	7.5	4.1	(D)	3.0	49.4	19.0	7.2
MOTOR CARRIER	46 422	100.0	(D)	21.6	23.0	8.0	(D)	8.3	16.1	9.8	12.5
PRIVATE TRUCK	23 292	100.0	(D)	19.8	13.2	7.9	(D)	6.6	22.0	7.5	21.1
AIR	3	100.0	(D)	12.9	82.4	-	(D)	-	.7	-	2.1
WATER	213 145	100.0	(D)	8.5	2.8	-	(D)	8.2	69.2	-	5.2
OTHER	450	100.0	(D)	1.8	.1	1.9	(D)	6.3	-	-	89.9
UNKNOWN	1 044	100.0	(D)	1.8	.4	.1	(D)	-	97.3	-	.4
NEW ENGLAND	42 926	100.0	(D)	10.8	.1	-	(D)	-	66.4	-	-
RAIL	245	100.0	(D)	67.3	6.9	3.0	(D)	-	12.3	.8	.1
MOTOR CARRIER	492	100.0	(D)	96.2	1.7	-	(D)	-	.3	-	-
PRIVATE TRUCK	136	100.0	(D)	85.8	2.1	2.0	(D)	-	.8	-	-
AIR	-	100.0	(D)	-	99.2	-	(D)	-	-	-	.8
WATER	42 046	100.0	(D)	9.2	-	-	(D)	-	67.7	-	-
OTHER	2	100.0	(D)	99.8	.1	-	(D)	-	-	-	-
UNKNOWN	2	100.0	(D)	100.0	-	-	(D)	-	-	-	-
MIDDLE ATLANTIC	53 125	100.0	(D)	40.6	1.9	-	(D)	5.1	46.2	-	.1
RAIL	933	100.0	(D)	41.9	11.8	.3	(D)	8.7	17.9	.2	2.7
MOTOR CARRIER	8 815	100.0	(D)	94.1	4.8	-	(D)	-	.2	-	.1
PRIVATE TRUCK	4 247	100.0	(D)	97.1	1.2	.1	(D)	-	-	-	.2
AIR	-	100.0	(D)	-	97.7	-	(D)	-	.1	-	2.2
WATER	39 113	100.0	(D)	22.3	1.1	-	(D)	6.7	62.3	-	-
OTHER	1	100.0	(D)	94.4	5.3	.1	(D)	-	.1	-	-
UNKNOWN	15	100.0	(D)	99.3	-	-	(D)	-	.7	-	-
EAST NORTH CENTRAL	35 934	100.0	(D)	3.1	51.1	.9	(D)	14.2	25.9	4.3	.2
RAIL	4 438	100.0	(D)	14.8	26.3	2.6	(D)	1.2	18.4	34.9	.8
MOTOR CARRIER	10 179	100.0	(D)	3.8	92.3	1.4	(D)	1.0	1.3	-	.8
PRIVATE TRUCK	2 791	100.0	(D)	1.9	90.1	2.6	(D)	2.6	.7	-	.7
AIR	2	100.0	(D)	.5	99.5	-	(D)	-	-	-	-
WATER	18 411	100.0	(D)	-	28.8	-	(D)	26.5	44.7	-	-
OTHER	4	100.0	(D)	51.5	2.6	45.3	(D)	-	.1	-	.5
UNKNOWN	106	100.0	(D)	-	3.6	.5	(D)	-	95.6	-	.3
WEST NORTH CENTRAL	13 022	100.0	(D)	1.0	11.1	43.4	(D)	1.2	36.3	6.8	.2
RAIL	3 688	100.0	(D)	2.4	5.9	22.7	(D)	.1	51.3	17.0	.5
MOTOR CARRIER	4 371	100.0	(D)	.8	13.0	74.1	(D)	.1	8.7	3.2	.1
PRIVATE TRUCK	2 319	100.0	(D)	.3	20.6	67.5	(D)	2.4	4.1	5.0	-
AIR	-	100.0	(D)	-	-	-	(D)	-	13.5	-	86.5
WATER	2 619	100.0	(D)	-	6.8	-	(D)	3.5	89.7	-	-
OTHER	7	100.0	(D)	13.9	.5	85.6	(D)	-	-	-	-
UNKNOWN	15	100.0	(D)	-	-	2.4	(D)	-	96.9	-	.7
SOUTH ATLANTIC	65 442	100.0	(D)	10.4	.4	.1	(D)	10.1	77.2	-	-
RAIL	3 091	100.0	(D)	9.0	5.9	.6	(D)	6.2	72.0	-	-
MOTOR CARRIER	1 358	100.0	(D)	52.8	7.2	4.5	(D)	10.6	9.2	-	.3
PRIVATE TRUCK	726	100.0	(D)	41.8	.8	2.0	(D)	15.7	.8	-	.4
AIR	-	100.0	(D)	86.6	-	-	(D)	-	-	-	-
WATER	60 235	100.0	(D)	9.2	-	-	(D)	10.2	80.0	-	-
OTHER	28	100.0	(D)	-	.2	-	(D)	98.9	-	-	8.0
UNKNOWN	-	100.0	(D)	87.5	4.5	-	(D)	-	-	-	-
EAST SOUTH CENTRAL	27 919	100.0	(D)	1.0	.5	.1	(D)	26.4	71.3	-	-
RAIL	3 141	100.0	(D)	6.5	1.7	.6	(D)	13.5	75.7	-	-
MOTOR CARRIER	3 952	100.0	(D)	2.0	2.4	.1	(D)	90.2	4.2	-	-
PRIVATE TRUCK	1 355	100.0	(D)	.5	.2	1.0	(D)	79.3	14.7	-	-
AIR	-	100.0	(D)	-	100.0	-	(D)	-	-	-	-
WATER	18 705	100.0	(D)	-	-	-	(D)	12.3	87.7	-	-
OTHER	-	100.0	(D)	-	97.7	-	(D)	-	-	-	-
UNKNOWN	763	100.0	(D)	-	-	-	(D)	-	100.0	-	-
WEST SOUTH CENTRAL	36 545	100.0	(D)	.5	.4	1.1	(D)	4.7	92.6	.4	.3
RAIL	5 012	100.0	(D)	2.8	1.4	.7	(D)	.5	89.1	2.7	1.9
MOTOR CARRIER	6 322	100.0	(D)	.2	.8	3.9	(D)	.5	94.1	-	.4
PRIVATE TRUCK	4 505	100.0	(D)	.1	.3	2.2	(D)	4.7	92.4	-	.1
AIR	-	100.0	(D)	98.7	-	-	(D)	-	1.3	-	-
WATER	20 568	100.0	(D)	.1	-	-	(D)	7.0	93.0	-	-
OTHER	-	100.0	(D)	83.6	-	.2	(D)	-	15.7	-	.4
UNKNOWN	135	100.0	(D)	-	-	-	(D)	-	99.9	-	.1
MOUNTAIN	11 010	100.0	(D)	.1	.9	.8	(D)	-	16.3	73.8	8.1
RAIL	3 323	100.0	(D)	.1	1.9	.7	(D)	-	15.3	62.6	18.9
MOTOR CARRIER	5 336	100.0	(D)	-	.5	.4	(D)	-	12.1	82.6	4.4
PRIVATE TRUCK	2 341	100.0	(D)	-	-	.2	(D)	1.7	26.9	69.8	1.4
AIR	-	100.0	(D)	-	-	-	(D)	-	100.0	-	-
WATER	8	100.0	(D)	99.0	-	-	(D)	-	-	-	1.0
OTHER	-	100.0	(D)	-	-	-	(D)	-	-	100.0	-
UNKNOWN	-	100.0	(D)	-	-	-	(D)	-	-	100.0	-
PACIFIC	24 270	100.0	(D)	.3	.2	.1	(D)	-	2.9	2.1	94.4
RAIL	1 963	100.0	(D)	2.1	2.4	.2	(D)	-	14.8	25.8	54.6
MOTOR CARRIER	5 592	100.0	(D)	.3	.1	-	(D)	-	1.1	-	98.5
PRIVATE TRUCK	4 867	100.0	(D)	-	-	.3	(D)	-	-	.1	99.6
AIR	-	100.0	(D)	16.0	1.1	-	(D)	-	60.2	-	22.7
WATER	11 437	100.0	(D)	-	-	-	(D)	-	3.0	-	96.9
OTHER	405	100.0	(D)	.1	-	-	(D)	-	-	-	99.9
UNKNOWN	3	100.0	(D)	-	-	-	(D)	-	-	-	100.0

See footnotes at end of table 4.

TABLE 3. TCC GROUP 291—Percent Distribution of Geographic Division of Destination and Means of Transport, by Geographic Division of Origin: 1972—Continued

Geographic division of destination and means of transport	Number	Percent distribution by division of origin [1]									
		U.S. total	New England	Middle Atlantic	East North Central	West North Central	South Atlantic	East South Central	West South Central	Mountain	Pacific
TON-MILES OF SHIPMENTS	(millions of ton-miles)										
U.S. TOTAL	177 627	100.0	(D)	2.1	1.7	.5	(D)	2.5	83.6	1.8	5.7
RAIL	11 887	100.0	(D)	8.5	5.7	2.8	(D)	1.4	49.7	22.4	7.6
MOTOR CARRIER	5 130	100.0	(D)	18.6	18.7	7.4	(D)	6.7	27.9	8.2	10.7
PRIVATE TRUCK	2 352	100.0	(D)	10.2	10.1	10.2	(D)	5.2	23.4	8.3	30.1
AIR	-	100.0	(D)	31.7	49.8	-	(D)	-	3.7	-	12.7
WATER	158 021	100.0	(D)	.9	.8	-	(D)	2.4	88.9	-	5.0
OTHER	30	100.0	(D)	17.7	.5	5.7	(D)	8.2	-	-	67.6
UNKNOWN	203	100.0	(D)	1.1	.2	.2	(D)	-	97.9	-	.7
NEW ENGLAND	48 159	100.0	(D)	1.6	-	-	(D)	-	92.4	-	-
RAIL	119	100.0	(D)	35.2	8.5	9.0	(D)	-	36.2	2.7	.3
MOTOR CARRIER	67	100.0	(D)	85.0	8.8	-	(D)	-	3.6	-	-
PRIVATE TRUCK	25	100.0	(D)	59.8	8.9	11.2	(D)	-	6.1	-	-
AIR	-	100.0	(D)	-	96.5	-	(D)	-	-	-	3.5
WATER	47 945	100.0	(D)	1.4	-	-	(D)	-	92.7	-	-
OTHER	-	100.0	(D)	99.9	.1	-	(D)	-	-	-	-
UNKNOWN	-	100.0	(D)	100.0	-	-	(D)	-	-	-	-
MIDDLE ATLANTIC	35 544	100.0	(D)	3.2	1.2	-	(D)	2.1	92.4	-	.3
RAIL	435	100.0	(D)	13.0	13.0	.7	(D)	7.7	46.5	.7	13.6
MOTOR CARRIER	617	100.0	(D)	74.9	17.4	.3	(D)	-	3.6	-	2.3
PRIVATE TRUCK	202	100.0	(D)	78.0	6.2	2.2	(D)	-	.1	-	9.5
AIR	-	100.0	(D)	-	89.7	-	(D)	-	.4	-	9.9
WATER	34 288	100.0	(D)	1.3	.7	-	(D)	2.0	95.1	-	-
OTHER	-	100.0	(D)	92.7	6.3	.4	(D)	-	.6	-	-
UNKNOWN	1	100.0	(D)	88.5	-	-	(D)	-	11.5	-	-
EAST NORTH CENTRAL	12 231	100.0	(D)	3.9	15.8	.7	(D)	7.0	58.6	12.9	.9
RAIL	2 891	100.0	(D)	10.8	8.2	1.6	(D)	.1	22.0	54.7	2.2
MOTOR CARRIER	886	100.0	(D)	16.9	69.0	1.4	(D)	.8	10.9	-	.8
PRIVATE TRUCK	263	100.0	(D)	5.3	61.8	9.9	(D)	1.7	5.1	-	13.8
AIR	-	100.0	(D)	2.1	97.7	-	(D)	-	-	-	.2
WATER	8 094	100.0	(D)	-	11.4	-	(D)	10.4	78.2	-	-
OTHER	2	100.0	(D)	45.4	.9	51.2	(D)	-	.1	-	2.3
UNKNOWN	93	100.0	(D)	-	.3	.2	(D)	-	98.9	-	.5
WEST NORTH CENTRAL	3 790	100.0	(D)	3.0	6.0	15.4	(D)	.8	63.1	10.8	.8
RAIL	1 538	100.0	(D)	5.1	4.5	12.8	(D)	.1	54.1	21.4	1.8
MOTOR CARRIER	535	100.0	(D)	5.1	15.6	47.0	(D)	.2	23.2	8.1	.6
PRIVATE TRUCK	252	100.0	(D)	2.1	16.9	52.8	(D)	2.7	10.5	14.9	.1
AIR	-	100.0	(D)	-	-	-	(D)	-	5.7	-	94.3
WATER	1 455	100.0	(D)	-	2.2	-	(D)	1.5	96.3	-	-
OTHER	1	100.0	(D)	59.2	1.0	39.7	(D)	-	-	-	-
UNKNOWN	6	100.0	(D)	-	-	1.5	(D)	-	96.0	-	2.5
SOUTH ATLANTIC	50 097	100.0	(D)	1.2	.3	.2	(D)	3.6	94.4	-	-
RAIL	1 808	100.0	(D)	5.2	4.9	.9	(D)	1.6	82.9	.1	-
MOTOR CARRIER	383	100.0	(D)	37.8	11.6	12.8	(D)	2.8	19.6	-	1.7
PRIVATE TRUCK	88	100.0	(D)	40.8	1.3	12.9	(D)	9.5	3.4	-	5.6
AIR	-	100.0	(D)	93.3	-	-	(D)	-	-	-	-
WATER	47 813	100.0	(D)	.6	-	-	(D)	3.7	95.6	-	-
OTHER	2	100.0	(D)	-	1.7	-	(D)	94.8	-	-	-
UNKNOWN	-	100.0	(D)	56.0	10.5	-	(D)	-	-	-	33.6
EAST SOUTH CENTRAL	8 673	100.0	(D)	2.3	.6	.2	(D)	8.1	88.1	-	-
RAIL	1 275	100.0	(D)	11.5	1.3	.9	(D)	7.4	76.5	-	-
MOTOR CARRIER	484	100.0	(D)	10.1	6.6	.2	(D)	66.7	11.9	-	-
PRIVATE TRUCK	153	100.0	(D)	2.1	.7	2.0	(D)	57.5	29.0	-	-
AIR	-	100.0	(D)	-	100.0	-	(D)	-	-	-	-
WATER	6 666	100.0	(D)	-	-	-	(D)	3.0	97.0	-	-
OTHER	-	100.0	(D)	-	99.6	-	(D)	-	-	-	-
UNKNOWN	93	100.0	(D)	-	-	-	(D)	-	100.0	-	-
WEST SOUTH CENTRAL	6 057	100.0	(D)	3.4	1.5	1.3	(D)	6.1	83.1	.8	2.9
RAIL	1 408	100.0	(D)	12.4	3.3	1.5	(D)	.7	65.3	3.5	10.5
MOTOR CARRIER	864	100.0	(D)	1.7	4.0	5.7	(D)	.4	84.6	-	3.1
PRIVATE TRUCK	427	100.0	(D)	.9	2.1	2.3	(D)	3.5	88.9	.3	1.0
AIR	-	100.0	(D)	100.0	-	-	(D)	-	-	-	-
WATER	3 348	100.0	(D)	.4	-	-	(D)	10.1	89.4	-	-
OTHER	-	100.0	(D)	96.0	-	.1	(D)	-	3.4	-	.5
UNKNOWN	7	100.0	(D)	-	-	-	(D)	-	95.8	-	4.2
MOUNTAIN	2 155	100.0	(D)	.5	4.9	2.4	(D)	-	29.9	44.5	16.6
RAIL	1 189	100.0	(D)	.4	5.8	1.1	(D)	-	31.5	36.1	22.9
MOTOR CARRIER	678	100.0	(D)	.6	4.6	2.2	(D)	-	26.1	55.5	10.9
PRIVATE TRUCK	275	100.0	(D)	.6	1.8	8.8	(D)	-	29.1	55.4	4.4
AIR	-	100.0	(D)	-	-	-	(D)	-	-	-	100.0
WATER	11	100.0	(D)	-	-	-	(D)	-	100.0	-	-
OTHER	-	100.0	(D)	99.8	-	-	(D)	-	-	-	.2
UNKNOWN	-	100.0	(D)	-	-	-	(D)	-	-	100.0	-
PACIFIC	10 917	100.0	(D)	1.5	.8	.3	(D)	-	9.9	2.5	85.0
RAIL	1 221	100.0	(D)	8.4	6.8	.5	(D)	-	35.1	21.6	27.7
MOTOR CARRIER	612	100.0	(D)	7.1	1.4	.2	(D)	-	23.4	-	67.8
PRIVATE TRUCK	663	100.0	(D)	.5	.1	3.6	(D)	-	.1	.6	95.1
AIR	-	100.0	(D)	25.9	1.2	-	(D)	-	69.3	-	3.6
WATER	8 397	100.0	(D)	.2	-	-	(D)	-	6.1	-	93.8
OTHER	21	100.0	(D)	5.9	-	-	(D)	-	-	-	94.1
UNKNOWN	-	100.0	(D)	-	-	-	(D)	-	-	-	100.0

See footnotes at end of table 4.

TABLE 4. **TCC GROUP 291—Percent Distribution of Distance Shipped and Weight of Shipment, by Means of Transport: 1972**

Distance shipped and weight of shipment [2] [3]	Number	Percent distribution by means of transport							
		All means of transport	Rail	Motor carrier	Private truck	Air	Water	Other	Unknown
TONS OF SHIPMENTS	(thousands of tons)								
U.S. TOTAL.........	219 551	100.0	7.7	14.7	8.4	-	68.4	.2	.5
UNDER 100 MILES.........	64 044	100.0	4.5	36.2	19.6	-	38.7	.7	.2
UNDER 1000 POUNDS.....	43	100.0	-	20.8	78.3	-	.1	.4	.3
1000 TO 9999 POUNDS...	377	100.0	.3	43.4	55.6	-	.5	.1	.2
10000 TO 29999 POUNDS.	2 726	100.0	.3	37.0	62.4	-	-	-	.2
30000 TO 59999 POUNDS.	27 266	100.0	.7	65.7	33.5	-	-	-	.1
60000 TO 89999 POUNDS.	3 974	100.0	17.6	51.0	31.3	-	.1	-	-
90000 POUNDS AND OVER.	29 655	100.0	6.7	7.0	.8	-	83.6	1.5	.4
100 TO 199 MILES........	29 431	100.0	10.0	16.0	9.4	-	62.0	-	2.6
UNDER 1000 POUNDS.....	14	100.0	-	56.3	43.1	-	-	.6	-
1000 TO 9999 POUNDS...	97	100.0	1.5	58.8	38.6	-	.2	.7	.1
10000 TO 29999 POUNDS.	545	100.0	.1	57.8	39.7	-	1.8	.3	.2
30000 TO 59999 POUNDS.	6 104	100.0	3.0	61.4	35.3	-	.1	-	-
60000 TO 89999 POUNDS.	907	100.0	45.9	40.1	13.4	-	.6	-	-
90000 POUNDS AND OVER.	21 762	100.0	10.7	1.0	1.1	-	83.7	-	3.5
200 TO 299 MILES........	14 042	100.0	16.2	16.5	15.2	-	52.1	-	-
UNDER 1000 POUNDS.....	13	100.0	.1	67.8	31.8	-	-	.3	-
1000 TO 9999 POUNDS...	76	100.0	.6	72.9	25.9	-	.2	-	.3
10000 TO 29999 POUNDS.	256	100.0	.7	69.2	29.4	-	.3	.4	-
30000 TO 59999 POUNDS.	2 891	100.0	4.0	68.6	27.3	-	-	-	.1
60000 TO 89999 POUNDS.	276	100.0	82.5	11.0	5.9	-	.6	-	-
90000 POUNDS AND OVER.	10 527	100.0	18.3	.6	11.7	-	69.5	-	-
300 TO 499 MILES........	20 367	100.0	12.9	6.1	3.5	-	77.3	-	.1
UNDER 1000 POUNDS.....	13	100.0	.1	72.7	20.9	1.2	-	1.3	3.8
1000 TO 9999 POUNDS...	82	100.0	1.3	49.3	48.9	-	-	.6	-
10000 TO 29999 POUNDS.	176	100.0	3.1	67.5	29.2	-	.2	-	-
30000 TO 59999 POUNDS.	1 613	100.0	8.4	61.8	28.2	-	-	.2	1.3
60000 TO 89999 POUNDS.	471	100.0	83.5	16.3	.2	-	-	-	-
90000 POUNDS AND OVER.	18 010	100.0	11.6	-	.9	-	87.5	-	-
500 TO 999 MILES........	32 977	100.0	11.7	2.2	.8	-	85.0	-	.3
UNDER 1000 POUNDS.....	16	100.0	.9	87.2	11.0	.5	-	.3	.1
1000 TO 9999 POUNDS...	84	100.0	2.9	49.5	47.5	-	-	.1	.1
10000 TO 29999 POUNDS.	75	100.0	16.9	69.9	9.5	.5	1.8	1.4	-
30000 TO 59999 POUNDS.	984	100.0	33.5	45.5	20.8	-	-	.2	-
60000 TO 89999 POUNDS.	933	100.0	91.4	8.1	-	-	.6	-	-
90000 POUNDS AND OVER.	30 883	100.0	8.6	.3	-	-	90.8	-	.3
1000 TO 1499 MILES......	43 040	100.0	4.8	.2	-	-	95.0	-	-
UNDER 1000 POUNDS.....	5	100.0	.6	92.7	6.1	.1	-	.6	-
1000 TO 9999 POUNDS...	21	100.0	2.9	62.4	33.6	-	.4	-	.7
10000 TO 29999 POUNDS.	21	100.0	28.4	59.4	11.1	-	1.1	-	-
30000 TO 59999 POUNDS.	119	100.0	43.3	51.9	4.5	-	.4	-	-
60000 TO 89999 POUNDS.	108	100.0	95.9	2.8	1.4	-	-	-	-
90000 POUNDS AND OVER.	42 764	100.0	4.4	-	-	-	95.6	-	-
1500 MILES OR OVER......	15 647	100.0	2.0	.5	.3	-	97.2	-	-
UNDER 1000 POUNDS.....	2	100.0	1.7	90.8	4.5	.3	-	2.7	-
1000 TO 9999 POUNDS...	21	100.0	2.8	24.1	68.8	.3	2.0	.1	1.9
10000 TO 29999 POUNDS.	28	100.0	29.7	26.3	39.8	-	-	3.4	.8
30000 TO 59999 POUNDS.	125	100.0	23.1	52.3	16.0	-	8.6	-	-
60000 TO 89999 POUNDS.	41	100.0	100.0	-	-	-	-	-	-
90000 POUNDS AND OVER.	15 427	100.0	1.5	-	-	-	98.5	-	-
TON-MILES OF SHIPMENTS	(millions of ton-miles)								
U.S. TOTAL.........	125 117	100.0	6.1	2.7	1.5	-	89.4	-	.2
UNDER 100 MILES.........	2 819	100.0	5.7	32.7	17.5	-	42.9	.8	.2
UNDER 1000 POUNDS.....	2	100.0	-	23.8	75.4	-	-	.4	.4
1000 TO 9999 POUNDS...	15	100.0	.3	43.7	55.5	-	.3	-	.2
10000 TO 29999 POUNDS.	96	100.0	.4	42.3	57.1	-	.1	-	-
30000 TO 59999 POUNDS.	1 090	100.0	.9	64.3	34.7	-	-	-	-
60000 TO 89999 POUNDS.	149	100.0	26.3	48.4	25.2	-	.1	-	-
90000 POUNDS AND OVER.	1 466	100.0	7.6	6.9	.9	-	82.6	1.5	.4
100 TO 199 MILES........	4 378	100.0	9.4	14.9	8.3	-	65.3	-	2.1
UNDER 1000 POUNDS.....	2	100.0	-	57.3	42.2	-	-	.5	-
1000 TO 9999 POUNDS...	14	100.0	1.8	59.5	37.8	-	.1	.6	.1
10000 TO 29999 POUNDS.	75	100.0	.1	57.0	40.6	-	1.8	.3	.2
30000 TO 59999 POUNDS.	824	100.0	3.0	62.4	34.5	-	.1	-	-
60000 TO 89999 POUNDS.	127	100.0	45.2	42.0	12.4	-	.4	-	-
90000 POUNDS AND OVER.	3 335	100.0	9.8	.9	.9	-	85.6	-	2.8

See footnotes at end of table 4.

TABLE 4. **TCC GROUP 291—Percent Distribution of Distance Shipped and Weight of Shipment, by Means of Transport: 1972**—Continued

Distance shipped and weight of shipment [2] [3]	Number	Percent distribution by means of transport							
		All means of transport	Rail	Motor carrier	Private truck	Air	Water	Other	Unknown
TON-MILES OF SHIPMENTS	(millions of ton-miles)								
200 TO 299 MILES.........	3 392	100.0	16.7	16.2	14.5	-	52.5	-	-
UNDER 1000 POUNDS.....	3	100.0	.1	68.5	31.0	-	-	.3	-
1000 TO 9999 POUNDS...	18	100.0	.7	72.7	26.1	-	.2	-	.3
10000 TO 29999 POUNDS.	62	100.0	.7	67.4	31.2	-	.3	.4	-
30000 TO 59999 POUNDS.	689	100.0	3.9	68.4	27.6	-	-	-	.1
60000 TO 89999 POUNDS.	68	100.0	83.2	10.9	5.4	-	.6	-	-
90000 POUNDS AND OVER.	2 550	100.0	18.9	.6	10.7	-	69.9	-	-
300 TO 499 MILES.........	8 389	100.0	12.6	5.7	3.2	-	78.3	-	.1
UNDER 1000 POUNDS.....	5	100.0	.1	72.1	20.5	1.4	-	1.3	4.6
1000 TO 9999 POUNDS...	32	100.0	1.0	48.1	50.2	-	-	.7	-
10000 TO 29999 POUNDS.	68	100.0	2.9	68.8	28.1	-	.2	-	-
30000 TO 59999 POUNDS.	620	100.0	8.9	62.4	27.1	-	-	.3	1.4
60000 TO 89999 POUNDS.	180	100.0	84.5	15.3	.2	-	-	-	-
90000 POUNDS AND OVER.	7 482	100.0	11.3	-	.8	-	87.9	-	-
500 TO 999 MILES.........	24 189	100.0	11.1	2.0	.7	-	85.8	-	.4
UNDER 1000 POUNDS.....	11	100.0	1.1	86.3	11.7	.4	-	.3	.1
1000 TO 9999 POUNDS...	60	100.0	3.0	49.8	47.1	-	-	.1	-
10000 TO 29999 POUNDS.	52	100.0	17.4	69.7	9.0	.5	1.8	1.6	-
30000 TO 59999 POUNDS.	670	100.0	34.7	44.7	20.5	-	-	.2	-
60000 TO 89999 POUNDS.	679	100.0	92.2	7.1	-	-	.7	-	-
90000 POUNDS AND OVER.	22 713	100.0	8.0	.2	-	-	91.4	-	.4
1000 TO 1499 MILES......	54 795	100.0	4.0	.2	-	-	95.7	-	-
UNDER 1000 POUNDS.....	6	100.0	.5	93.3	5.5	.1	-	.6	-
1000 TO 9999 POUNDS...	26	100.0	2.6	64.1	32.2	-	.4	-	.6
10000 TO 29999 POUNDS.	25	100.0	30.7	56.8	11.3	-	1.2	-	-
30000 TO 59999 POUNDS.	144	100.0	44.7	50.5	4.4	-	.4	-	-
60000 TO 89999 POUNDS.	125	100.0	95.6	3.0	1.4	-	-	-	-
90000 POUNDS AND OVER.	54 466	100.0	3.7	-	-	-	96.3	-	-
1500 MILES OR OVER......	27 152	100.0	2.1	.8	.3	-	96.7	-	-
UNDER 1000 POUNDS.....	5	100.0	1.9	89.7	4.3	.4	-	3.6	-
1000 TO 9999 POUNDS...	38	100.0	3.3	25.7	65.7	.2	3.2	.1	1.8
10000 TO 29999 POUNDS.	60	100.0	30.5	26.1	39.4	-	-	3.3	.7
30000 TO 59999 POUNDS.	301	100.0	16.4	61.7	13.2	-	8.8	-	-
60000 TO 89999 POUNDS.	79	100.0	100.0	-	-	-	-	-	-
90000 POUNDS AND OVER.	26 667	100.0	1.6	-	-	-	98.4	-	-

Note: Detail may not add to total due to rounding. The introductory table shows the estimates of sampling variability for tons; sampling variability for ton-miles has not been estimated. See the map in the Introduction for the States comprising the geographic divisions of the United States.
  Shipments excluded from the survey are those moving by pipeline (primarily petroleum products from refineries), parcel post shipments, and commodities moved by own power (motorized vehicles, aircraft, etc.) or towed (prefabricated buildings, etc.). Local shipments (commodities shipped less than 25 miles from the plant) and shipments within the same city are also excluded. Shipments to Alaska and Hawaii from the 48 conterminous States and the District of Columbia are included; however, no data were obtained for shipments originating in Alaska and Hawaii.

  - Represents zero or rounds to zero.   (D) Withheld to avoid disclosing figures for individual companies.

[1] Production of this commodity is concentrated in the geographic divisions shown; figures and distributions for geographic divisions not shown are included in the total.
[2] Distances of shipments to foreign destinations are calculated only to the U.S. port of exit.
[3] Includes only shipments represented by bills of lading and invoices. Summary records which did not show individual weights of shipments are not included.

TCC 295. Asphalt Paving and Roofing Material

Comparisons of Tons and Ton-Miles of Shipments for
Geographic Divisions of Origin and for Sampling Variability: 1972 and 1967

Geographic division of origin	Estimates				Relative sampling variability in tons (percent)	
	1972		1967		1972	1967
	Tons (thousands)	Ton-miles (millions)	Tons (thousands)	Ton-miles (millions)		
U.S. total	21,273	4,807	11,116	2,026	11.5	7.2
New England	409	36	336	27	12.3	(*)
Middle Atlantic	1,961	248	1,913	150	16.6	(*)
East North Central	6,126	1,223	2,741	449	12.3	(*)
West North Central	1,194	213	196	40	47.2	(*)
South Atlantic	2,173	335	1,094	184	24.6	(*)
East South Central	(D)	(D)	301	76	(*)	(*)
West South Central	6,684	2,141	2,205	576	24.1	(*)
Mountain	(D)	(D)	456	195	(*)	(*)
Pacific	1,172	354	1,874	329	24.6	(*)

(D) Withheld to avoid disclosing figures for individual companies.   (*) Data not published.

TABLE 1. **TCC GROUP 295**—Percent Distribution of Geographic Division of Origin and Distance Shipped,
by Means of Transport: 1972

Geographic division of origin[1] and distance shipped[2]	Number	Percent distribution by means of transport							
		All means of transport	Rail	Motor carrier	Private truck	Air	Water	Other	Unknown
TONS OF SHIPMENTS	(thousands of tons)								
U.S. TOTAL..........	21 273	100.0	20.8	35.8	23.4	-	19.9	-	.2
NEW ENGLAND.............	409	100.0	3.6	83.3	12.1	-	-	-	1.0
UNDER 100 MILES.......	279	100.0	1.2	81.8	17.0	-	-	-	-
100 TO 199 MILES......	110	100.0	8.0	86.4	1.9	-	-	-	3.7
200 TO 299 MILES......	10	100.0	-	100.0	-	-	-	-	-
300 TO 499 MILES......	1	100.0	-	100.0	-	-	-	-	-
500 TO 999 MILES......	5	100.0	46.1	53.9	-	-	-	-	-
1000 TO 1499 MILES....	-	100.0	-	-	-	-	-	-	-
1500 MILES OR OVER....	1	100.0	-	100.0	-	-	-	-	-
MIDDLE ATLANTIC.........	1 961	100.0	5.9	53.7	20.7	-	19.5	-	.2
UNDER 100 MILES.......	1 153	100.0	.6	50.0	33.9	-	15.5	-	-
100 TO 199 MILES......	321	100.0	5.4	91.2	3.1	-	-	-	.3
200 TO 299 MILES......	365	100.0	9.6	37.8	.5	-	51.6	-	.5
300 TO 499 MILES......	57	100.0	30.9	67.8	.7	-	-	-	.5
500 TO 999 MILES......	53	100.0	67.6	12.0	.7	-	19.7	-	-
1000 TO 1499 MILES....	3	100.0	-	37.5	62.5	-	-	-	-
1500 MILES OR OVER....	7	100.0	41.4	3.8	-	-	54.9	-	-
EAST NORTH CENTRAL......	6 126	100.0	10.2	41.4	12.8	-	35.3	-	.2
UNDER 100 MILES.......	1 737	100.0	1.2	59.7	29.8	-	9.2	-	-
100 TO 199 MILES......	2 200	100.0	13.1	35.0	6.3	-	45.4	.1	-
200 TO 299 MILES......	730	100.0	17.6	71.9	10.1	-	.5	-	-
300 TO 499 MILES......	1 293	100.0	7.0	11.8	3.9	-	77.3	-	-
500 TO 999 MILES......	149	100.0	60.8	29.5	2.7	-	-	-	7.0
1000 TO 1499 MILES....	3	100.0	54.9	35.6	9.5	-	-	-	-
1500 MILES OR OVER....	11	100.0	62.8	28.0	9.3	-	-	-	-
WEST NORTH CENTRAL......	1 194	100.0	8.8	40.2	51.0	-	-	-	-
UNDER 100 MILES.......	185	100.0	-	44.7	55.3	-	-	-	-
100 TO 199 MILES......	624	100.0	9.2	37.9	52.9	-	-	-	-
200 TO 299 MILES......	243	100.0	-	56.8	43.2	-	-	-	-
300 TO 499 MILES......	118	100.0	37.1	12.8	50.1	-	-	-	-
500 TO 999 MILES......	22	100.0	16.5	33.0	50.5	-	-	-	-
1000 TO 1499 MILES....	-	100.0	-	-	-	-	-	-	-
1500 MILES OR OVER....	-	100.0	-	-	-	-	-	-	-
SOUTH ATLANTIC..........	2 173	100.0	29.5	35.5	34.7	-	.2	-	.1
UNDER 100 MILES.......	843	100.0	5.7	44.2	49.8	-	-	-	.3
100 TO 199 MILES......	720	100.0	38.9	26.3	34.4	-	.5	-	-
200 TO 299 MILES......	345	100.0	55.8	29.6	14.7	-	-	-	-
300 TO 499 MILES......	245	100.0	42.6	42.5	14.8	-	-	-	-
500 TO 999 MILES......	6	100.0	58.2	41.8	-	-	-	-	-
1000 TO 1499 MILES....	11	100.0	100.0	-	-	-	-	-	-
1500 MILES OR OVER....	-	100.0	-	-	-	-	-	-	-
WEST SOUTH CENTRAL......	6 684	100.0	36.2	12.3	26.7	-	24.7	-	.1
UNDER 100 MILES.......	1 747	100.0	28.5	12.9	58.2	-	-	-	.4
100 TO 199 MILES......	717	100.0	21.5	30.2	48.3	-	-	-	-
200 TO 299 MILES......	552	100.0	20.1	34.3	45.4	-	-	.3	-
300 TO 499 MILES......	2 393	100.0	65.3	5.2	4.7	-	24.7	-	.1
500 TO 999 MILES......	1 244	100.0	7.0	4.8	3.3	-	85.0	-	-
1000 TO 1499 MILES....	23	100.0	31.9	23.4	44.7	-	-	-	-
1500 MILES OR OVER....	5	100.0	-	6.2	93.8	-	-	-	-
PACIFIC.................	1 172	100.0	13.1	48.8	35.8	-	2.1	-	.3
UNDER 100 MILES.......	422	100.0	.3	66.0	33.7	-	-	-	-
100 TO 199 MILES......	232	100.0	8.8	34.6	55.3	-	-	-	1.2
200 TO 299 MILES......	92	100.0	8.5	25.3	66.1	-	-	-	-
300 TO 499 MILES......	225	100.0	16.3	60.1	23.6	-	-	-	-
500 TO 999 MILES......	151	100.0	48.2	29.4	22.4	-	-	-	-
1000 TO 1499 MILES....	18	100.0	74.0	26.0	-	-	-	-	-
1500 MILES OR OVER....	29	100.0	-	14.3	-	-	83.4	-	2.3
TON-MILES OF SHIPMENTS	(millions of ton-miles)								
U.S. TOTAL..........	4 807	100.0	30.0	23.9	13.2	-	32.6	-	.3
NEW ENGLAND.............	36	100.0	8.3	87.1	3.1	-	-	-	1.5
UNDER 100 MILES.......	11	100.0	2.1	90.3	7.5	-	-	-	-
100 TO 199 MILES......	14	100.0	10.1	84.7	1.5	-	-	-	3.7
200 TO 299 MILES......	2	100.0	-	100.0	-	-	-	-	-
300 TO 499 MILES......	-	100.0	-	100.0	-	-	-	-	-
500 TO 999 MILES......	2	100.0	44.0	56.0	-	-	-	-	-
1000 TO 1499 MILES....	-	100.0	-	-	-	-	-	-	-
1500 MILES OR OVER....	3	100.0	-	100.0	-	-	-	-	-
MIDDLE ATLANTIC.........	248	100.0	19.6	51.6	6.0	-	22.5	-	.3
UNDER 100 MILES.......	40	100.0	1.0	69.7	26.1	-	3.1	-	.4
100 TO 199 MILES......	48	100.0	4.2	92.3	3.1	-	-	-	.4
200 TO 299 MILES......	81	100.0	10.5	42.0	.5	-	46.4	-	.5
300 TO 499 MILES......	20	100.0	30.5	68.3	.6	-	-	-	.6
500 TO 999 MILES......	35	100.0	68.4	12.4	.7	-	18.5	-	-
1000 TO 1499 MILES....	3	100.0	-	39.7	60.3	-	-	-	-
1500 MILES OR OVER....	17	100.0	39.1	3.3	-	-	57.6	-	-

See footnotes at end of table 4.

TABLE 1. **TCC GROUP 295**—Percent Distribution of Geographic Division of Origin and Distance Shipped, by Means of Transport: 1972—Continued

Geographic division of origin [1] and distance shipped [2]	Number	Percent distribution by means of transport							
		All means of transport	Rail	Motor carrier	Private truck	Air	Water	Other	Unknown
TON-MILES OF SHIPMENTS	(millions of ton-miles)								
EAST NORTH CENTRAL......	1 223	100.0	14.8	31.6	7.2	-	45.5	-	.8
UNDER 100 MILES........	86	100.0	1.3	64.8	29.7	.1	4.1	-	-
100 TO 199 MILES......	311	100.0	13.4	36.4	6.1	-	44.0	.1	-
200 TO 299 MILES......	177	100.0	18.0	71.4	10.2	-	.4	-	-
300 TO 499 MILES......	526	100.0	6.3	10.7	4.0	-	79.1	-	-
500 TO 999 MILES......	99	100.0	59.9	27.8	2.6	-	-	-	9.7
1000 TO 1499 MILES....	3	100.0	54.7	36.9	8.4	-	-	-	-
1500 MILES OR OVER....	19	100.0	61.8	28.0	10.2	-	-	-	-
WEST NORTH CENTRAL......	213	100.0	12.5	40.7	46.8	-	-	-	-
UNDER 100 MILES........	7	100.0	-	65.0	35.0	-	-	-	-
100 TO 199 MILES......	88	100.0	9.5	40.5	50.0	-	-	-	-
200 TO 299 MILES......	58	100.0	-	59.6	40.4	-	-	-	-
300 TO 499 MILES......	41	100.0	38.2	14.0	47.8	-	-	-	-
500 TO 999 MILES......	17	100.0	13.2	32.1	54.8	-	-	-	-
1000 TO 1499 MILES....	-	100.0	-	-	-	-	-	-	-
1500 MILES OR OVER....	-	100.0	-	-	-	-	-	-	-
SOUTH ATLANTIC..........	335	100.0	43.4	32.0	24.5	-	.2	-	.4
UNDER 100 MILES........	39	100.0	9.4	40.4	49.8	-	-	.1	.4
100 TO 199 MILES......	104	100.0	38.2	26.1	35.2	-	.5	-	-
200 TO 299 MILES......	82	100.0	55.5	29.7	14.8	-	-	-	-
300 TO 499 MILES......	90	100.0	44.1	41.3	14.6	-	-	-	-
500 TO 999 MILES......	3	100.0	56.1	43.9	-	-	-	-	-
1000 TO 1499 MILES....	13	100.0	100.0	-	-	-	-	-	-
1500 MILES OR OVER....	-	100.0	-	-	-	-	-	-	-
WEST SOUTH CENTRAL......	2 141	100.0	38.5	8.7	11.1	-	41.7	-	-
UNDER 100 MILES........	58	100.0	23.5	21.4	54.7	-	-	-	.3
100 TO 199 MILES......	112	100.0	21.0	29.4	49.6	-	-	-	-
200 TO 299 MILES......	138	100.0	20.7	33.9	45.1	-	-	.3	-
300 TO 499 MILES......	1 051	100.0	65.3	4.6	3.7	-	26.4	-	.1
500 TO 999 MILES......	745	100.0	8.5	5.1	3.9	-	82.5	-	-
1000 TO 1499 MILES....	26	100.0	28.9	26.2	44.8	-	-	-	-
1500 MILES OR OVER....	9	100.0	-	5.8	94.2	-	-	-	-
PACIFIC.................	354	100.0	25.3	34.6	22.6	-	16.8	-	.6
UNDER 100 MILES........	17	100.0	.6	71.8	27.7	-	-	-	-
100 TO 199 MILES......	31	100.0	9.6	38.0	51.4	-	-	-	1.0
200 TO 299 MILES......	23	100.0	9.7	22.6	67.7	-	-	-	-
300 TO 499 MILES......	78	100.0	19.0	57.0	24.1	-	-	-	-
500 TO 999 MILES......	104	100.0	47.9	28.9	23.2	-	-	-	-
1000 TO 1499 MILES....	26	100.0	73.7	26.3	-	-	-	-	-
1500 MILES OR OVER....	72	100.0	-	15.2	-	-	82.5	-	2.3

See footnotes at end of table 4.

TABLE 2. **TCC GROUP 295**—Percent Distribution of Geographic Division of Origin and Means of Transport, by Geographic Division of Destination: 1972

Geographic division of origin [1] and means of transport	Number	Percent distribution by division of destination									
		U.S. total	New England	Middle Atlantic	East North Central	West North Central	South Atlantic	East South Central	West South Central	Mountain	Pacific
TONS OF SHIPMENTS	(thousands of tons)										
U.S. TOTAL..............	21 273	100.0	3.4	7.6	26.0	7.0	21.8	14.6	12.6	2.2	4.8
RAIL.................	4 422	100.0	1.2	1.3	10.3	4.3	50.6	11.5	15.3	3.1	2.3
MOTOR CARRIER.........	7 610	100.0	5.6	12.3	29.8	8.0	12.6	15.2	7.8	1.7	7.0
PRIVATE TRUCK.........	4 976	100.0	1.2	8.8	12.9	13.7	15.7	9.0	28.1	3.6	7.1
AIR..................	-	100.0	-	2.6	93.5	1.0	2.9	-	-	-	-
WATER................	4 224	100.0	4.5	4.2	51.2	-	15.9	23.5	-	-	.7
OTHER................	5	100.0	.5	.1	50.3	-	5.8	19.3	23.9	-	-
UNKNOWN..............	32	100.0	12.4	9.4	.3	-	9.2	5.1	21.2	31.6	10.9
NEW ENGLAND.............	409	100.0	93.7	4.6	.5	-	.8	-	-	.4	-
RAIL.................	14	100.0	73.1	10.5	-	-	16.3	-	-	-	-
MOTOR CARRIER.........	341	100.0	93.5	5.1	.6	-	.3	-	-	.5	-
PRIVATE TRUCK.........	49	100.0	100.0	-	-	-	-	-	-	-	-
AIR..................	-	100.0	-	-	-	-	-	-	-	-	-
WATER................	-	100.0	-	-	-	-	-	-	-	-	-
OTHER................	-	100.0	100.0	-	-	-	-	-	-	-	-
UNKNOWN..............	4	100.0	100.0	-	-	-	-	-	-	-	-
MIDDLE ATLANTIC.........	1 961	100.0	15.7	69.3	2.1	.3	12.1	.1	-	-	.4
RAIL.................	116	100.0	10.0	30.2	28.9	.3	27.4	.4	-	.3	2.5
MOTOR CARRIER.........	1 053	100.0	9.7	71.6	.7	.3	17.5	.1	-	-	-
PRIVATE TRUCK.........	405	100.0	1.2	95.6	-	.5	2.6	.1	-	-	-
AIR..................	-	100.0	-	72.9	-	27.1	-	-	-	-	-
WATER................	382	100.0	49.3	46.8	-	-	2.8	-	-	-	1.1
OTHER................	-	100.0	20.0	10.0	50.0	10.0	10.0	-	-	-	-
UNKNOWN..............	3	100.0	-	96.7	3.3	-	-	-	-	-	-

See footnotes at end of table 4.

TABLE 2. **TCC GROUP 295—Percent Distribution of Geographic Division of Origin and Means of Transport, by Geographic Division of Destination: 1972**—Continued

Geographic division of origin [1] and means of transport	Number	Percent distribution by division of destination									
		U.S. total	New England	Middle Atlantic	East North Central	West North Central	South Atlantic	East South Central	West South Central	Mountain	Pacific
TONS OF SHIPMENTS	(thousands of tons)										
EAST NORTH CENTRAL......	6 126	100.0	.6	2.9	86.7	3.0	1.7	4.3	.3	.4	-
RAIL....................	627	100.0	5.0	2.8	58.3	9.7	6.4	14.3	1.3	2.1	.1
MOTOR CARRIER..........	2 535	100.0	.1	5.2	84.6	4.7	.7	4.3	.2	.1	-
PRIVATE TRUCK..........	785	100.0	.1	3.8	80.3	.5	6.2	8.6	.4	.1	-
AIR....................	-	100.0	-	-	97.0	-	3.0	-	-	-	-
WATER..................	2 164	100.0	-	-	100.0	-	-	-	-	-	-
OTHER..................	2	100.0	-	.2	99.5	-	.2	-	-	-	-
UNKNOWN................	10	100.0	-	-	-	-	-	-	-	100.0	-
WEST NORTH CENTRAL......	1 194	100.0	-	-	12.7	81.7	.1	-	.1	5.4	-
RAIL....................	105	100.0	-	-	46.9	38.1	-	-	-	15.0	-
MOTOR CARRIER..........	480	100.0	-	-	20.5	78.6	-	-	-	.9	-
PRIVATE TRUCK..........	608	100.0	-	-	.6	91.7	.1	-	.3	7.3	-
AIR....................	-	100.0	-	-	-	-	-	-	-	-	-
WATER..................	-	100.0	-	-	-	-	-	-	-	-	-
OTHER..................	-	100.0	-	-	-	-	-	-	-	-	-
UNKNOWN................	-	100.0	-	-	-	-	-	-	-	-	-
SOUTH ATLANTIC..........	2 173	100.0	.2	2.6	.1	-	92.0	4.6	.4	.1	-
RAIL....................	641	100.0	-	.3	.3	-	91.2	6.4	1.5	.3	-
MOTOR CARRIER..........	771	100.0	-	4.6	.1	-	92.1	3.1	-	-	-
PRIVATE TRUCK..........	754	100.0	.5	2.4	-	-	92.5	4.6	-	-	-
AIR....................	-	100.0	-	-	-	-	-	-	-	-	-
WATER..................	3	100.0	-	-	-	-	100.0	-	-	-	-
OTHER..................	-	100.0	-	-	-	-	100.0	-	-	-	-
UNKNOWN................	2	100.0	-	-	-	-	100.0	-	-	-	-
WEST SOUTH CENTRAL......	6 684	100.0	-	-	.3	4.5	31.7	23.2	37.8	2.4	.2
RAIL....................	2 420	100.0	-	-	-	3.4	59.6	9.2	25.4	2.4	-
MOTOR CARRIER..........	820	100.0	-	.1	1.6	13.2	1.2	11.0	65.2	7.3	.3
PRIVATE TRUCK..........	1 782	100.0	-	-	.3	6.1	.2	13.7	76.7	2.3	.7
AIR....................	-	100.0	-	-	-	-	-	-	-	-	-
WATER..................	1 649	100.0	-	-	-	-	39.9	60.1	-	-	-
OTHER..................	2	100.0	-	-	.1	-	.1	44.6	55.2	-	-
UNKNOWN................	8	100.0	-	-	-	-	-	19.3	80.7	-	-
PACIFIC................	1 172	100.0	-	-	-	.5	-	-	1.1	13.3	85.1
RAIL....................	153	100.0	-	-	-	3.7	-	-	5.1	26.9	64.3
MOTOR CARRIER..........	571	100.0	-	-	-	-	-	-	.8	6.4	92.8
PRIVATE TRUCK..........	419	100.0	-	-	-	-	-	-	-	18.8	81.2
AIR....................	-	100.0	-	-	-	-	-	-	-	-	-
WATER..................	24	100.0	-	-	-	-	-	-	-	-	100.0
OTHER..................	-	100.0	-	-	-	-	-	-	-	-	-
UNKNOWN................	3	100.0	-	-	-	-	-	-	-	-	100.0
TON-MILES OF SHIPMENTS	(millions of ton-miles)										
U.S. TOTAL..............	4 807	100.0	2.3	3.0	21.0	6.5	31.2	18.4	6.3	5.0	6.2
RAIL....................	1 444	100.0	1.7	1.1	6.5	4.9	60.3	9.1	6.2	6.5	3.8
MOTOR CARRIER..........	1 149	100.0	3.7	9.6	26.5	11.1	13.6	12.6	8.8	5.0	9.3
PRIVATE TRUCK..........	633	100.0	.5	2.9	8.7	17.9	15.5	13.4	18.1	12.5	10.5
AIR....................	-	100.0	-	1.5	72.4	9.3	16.7	-	-	-	-
WATER..................	1 565	100.0	2.4	.1	35.6	-	24.0	33.5	-	-	4.5
OTHER..................	-	100.0	.1	.1	41.2	-	3.1	28.6	26.9	-	-
UNKNOWN................	14	100.0	3.8	4.9	.4	-	3.7	4.8	1.3	67.3	13.7
NEW ENGLAND............	36	100.0	71.6	10.2	3.3	-	4.9	-	-	10.1	-
RAIL....................	3	100.0	47.8	9.9	-	-	42.2	-	-	-	-
MOTOR CARRIER..........	31	100.0	72.3	10.7	3.8	-	1.6	-	-	11.6	-
PRIVATE TRUCK..........	1	100.0	100.0	-	-	-	-	-	-	-	-
AIR....................	-	100.0	-	-	-	-	-	-	-	-	-
WATER..................	-	100.0	-	-	-	-	-	-	-	-	-
OTHER..................	-	100.0	100.0	-	-	-	-	-	-	-	-
UNKNOWN................	-	100.0	100.0	-	-	-	-	-	-	-	-

See footnotes at end of table 4.

TABLE 2. **TCC GROUP 295**—Percent Distribution of Geographic Division of Origin and Means of Transport, by Geographic Division of Destination: 1972—Continued

Geographic division of origin[1] and means of transport	Number	Percent distribution by division of destination									
		U.S. total	New England	Middle Atlantic	East North Central	West North Central	South Atlantic	East South Central	West South Central	Mountain	Pacific
TON-MILES OF SHIPMENTS	(millions of ton-miles)										
MIDDLE ATLANTIC.........	248	100.0	24.2	34.3	8.9	2.1	22.6	.4	.2	.5	6.7
RAIL...................	48	100.0	10.1	10.7	38.9	.7	24.4	.7	-	1.1	13.2
MOTOR CARRIER.........	128	100.0	13.0	52.7	2.5	2.2	28.3	.4	.3	.6	-
PRIVATE TRUCK.........	14	100.0	4.9	70.8	-	13.7	9.0	.9	.7	-	-
AIR...................	-	100.0	-	14.1	-	85.9	-	-	-	-	-
WATER.................	55	100.0	67.6	2.2	-	-	11.8	-	-	-	18.4
OTHER.................	-	100.0	20.9	.6	44.7	19.6	14.3	-	-	-	-
UNKNOWN...............	-	100.0	-	93.0	7.0	-	-	-	-	-	-
EAST NORTH CENTRAL......	1 223	100.0	1.7	4.2	76.4	5.2	3.8	5.0	.9	2.7	.2
RAIL...................	180	100.0	10.1	4.7	34.6	12.6	12.5	12.5	3.2	8.9	.9
MOTOR CARRIER.........	386	100.0	.5	9.3	68.7	10.2	1.6	7.3	.8	1.2	.3
PRIVATE TRUCK.........	88	100.0	.3	7.3	55.4	1.3	19.4	11.7	2.4	2.2	-
AIR...................	-	100.0	-	-	81.2	.1	18.7	-	-	-	-
WATER.................	557	100.0	-	-	100.0	-	-	-	-	-	-
OTHER.................	-	100.0	-	.3	98.8	-	.7	.1	-	-	-
UNKNOWN...............	9	100.0	-	-	-	-	-	-	-	100.0	-
WEST NORTH CENTRAL......	213	100.0	-	-	15.7	70.8	.3	-	.1	13.0	-
RAIL...................	26	100.0	-	-	36.6	43.7	-	-	-	19.8	-
MOTOR CARRIER.........	86	100.0	-	-	26.7	68.8	-	-	-	4.5	-
PRIVATE TRUCK.........	99	100.0	-	-	.5	79.9	.7	-	.3	18.7	-
AIR...................	-	100.0	-	-	-	-	-	-	-	-	-
WATER.................	-	100.0	-	-	-	-	-	-	-	-	-
OTHER.................	-	100.0	-	-	-	-	-	-	-	-	-
UNKNOWN...............	-	100.0	-	-	-	-	-	-	-	-	-
SOUTH ATLANTIC..........	335	100.0	.4	1.6	.3	-	85.3	8.3	3.2	.8	-
RAIL...................	145	100.0	-	.8	.1	-	80.4	9.2	7.5	1.9	-
MOTOR CARRIER.........	107	100.0	-	2.7	.7	-	89.3	7.2	-	-	-
PRIVATE TRUCK.........	82	100.0	1.6	1.6	-	-	88.7	8.1	-	-	-
AIR...................	-	100.0	-	-	-	-	-	-	-	-	-
WATER.................	-	100.0	-	-	-	-	100.0	-	-	-	-
OTHER.................	-	100.0	-	-	-	-	100.0	-	-	-	-
UNKNOWN...............	-	100.0	-	-	-	-	100.0	-	-	-	-
WEST SOUTH CENTRAL......	2 141	100.0	-	-	.7	3.7	47.4	31.0	11.5	4.6	.9
RAIL...................	823	100.0	-	-	-	3.3	77.8	6.8	6.6	5.5	-
MOTOR CARRIER.........	185	100.0	.3	.4	5.3	13.3	3.1	15.6	45.2	14.9	1.9
PRIVATE TRUCK.........	238	100.0	-	-	2.2	11.7	.6	22.4	45.3	11.1	6.9
AIR...................	-	100.0	-	-	-	-	-	-	-	-	-
WATER.................	892	100.0	-	-	-	-	41.2	58.8	-	-	-
OTHER.................	-	100.0	-	-	.5	-	.6	50.9	48.1	-	-
UNKNOWN...............	-	100.0	-	-	-	.1	-	78.0	22.0	-	-
PACIFIC.................	354	100.0	-	-	-	2.2	-	-	5.2	19.0	73.5
RAIL...................	89	100.0	-	-	-	8.9	-	-	12.9	25.4	52.9
MOTOR CARRIER.........	122	100.0	-	-	-	-	-	-	5.7	11.5	82.8
PRIVATE TRUCK.........	80	100.0	-	-	-	-	-	-	-	38.0	62.0
AIR...................	-	100.0	-	-	-	-	-	-	-	-	-
WATER.................	59	100.0	-	-	-	-	-	-	-	-	100.0
OTHER.................	-	100.0	-	-	-	-	-	-	-	-	-
UNKNOWN...............	1	100.0	-	-	-	-	-	-	-	-	100.0

See footnotes at end of table 4.

TABLE 3. **TCC GROUP 295**—Percent Distribution of Geographic Division of Destination and Means of Transport, by Geographic Division of Origin: 1972

Geographic division of destination and means of transport	Number	Percent distribution by division of origin[1]									
		U.S. total	New England	Middle Atlantic	East North Central	West North Central	South Atlantic	East South Central	West South Central	Mountain	Pacific
TONS OF SHIPMENTS	(thousands of tons)										
U.S. TOTAL...............	21 273	100.0	1.9	9.2	28.8	5.6	10.2	(D)	31.4	(D)	5.5
RAIL...............	4 422	100.0	.3	2.6	14.2	2.4	14.5	(D)	54.7	(D)	3.5
MOTOR CARRIER.........	7 610	100.0	4.5	13.8	33.3	6.3	10.1	(D)	10.8	(D)	7.5
PRIVATE TRUCK.........	4 976	100.0	1.0	8.1	15.8	12.2	15.2	(D)	35.8	(D)	8.4
AIR.................	-	100.0	-	3.6	96.4	-	-	(D)	-	(D)	-
WATER...............	4 224	100.0	-	9.1	51.2	-	.1	(D)	39.1	(D)	.6
OTHER...............	5	100.0	.5	-	50.5	-	5.6	(D)	43.4	(D)	-
UNKNOWN.............	32	100.0	12.4	9.7	31.6	-	6.7	(D)	26.2	(D)	10.9
NEW ENGLAND..............	730	100.0	52.5	42.1	4.8	-	.5	(D)	.1	(D)	-
RAIL...............	53	100.0	19.7	21.5	58.8	-	-	(D)	-	(D)	-
MOTOR CARRIER.........	424	100.0	75.1	24.1	.7	-	-	(D)	.1	(D)	-
PRIVATE TRUCK.........	58	100.0	84.3	8.5	.9	-	6.4	(D)	-	(D)	-
AIR.................	-	100.0	-	-	-	-	-	(D)	-	(D)	-
WATER...............	188	100.0	-	100.0	-	-	-	(D)	-	(D)	-
OTHER...............	-	100.0	98.3	1.7	-	-	-	(D)	-	(D)	-
UNKNOWN.............	4	100.0	100.0	-	-	-	-	(D)	-	(D)	-
MIDDLE ATLANTIC.........	1 614	100.0	1.2	84.2	11.1	-	3.5	(D)	-	(D)	-
RAIL...............	56	100.0	2.7	62.5	31.3	-	3.3	(D)	.2	(D)	-
MOTOR CARRIER.........	939	100.0	1.9	80.2	14.1	-	3.8	(D)	.1	(D)	-
PRIVATE TRUCK.........	436	100.0	-	88.9	6.9	-	4.2	(D)	-	(D)	-
AIR.................	-	100.0	-	100.0	-	-	-	(D)	-	(D)	-
WATER...............	179	100.0	-	100.0	-	-	-	(D)	-	(D)	-
OTHER...............	-	100.0	-	3.7	96.3	-	-	(D)	-	(D)	-
UNKNOWN.............	3	100.0	-	100.0	-	-	-	(D)	-	(D)	-
EAST NORTH CENTRAL......	5 535	100.0	-	.7	95.9	2.7	.1	(D)	.4	(D)	-
RAIL...............	456	100.0	-	7.4	80.1	10.8	.4	(D)	-	(D)	-
MOTOR CARRIER.........	2 268	100.0	.1	.3	94.6	4.3	-	(D)	.6	(D)	-
PRIVATE TRUCK.........	642	100.0	-	-	98.2	.6	-	(D)	1.0	(D)	-
AIR.................	-	100.0	-	-	100.0	-	-	(D)	-	(D)	-
WATER...............	2 164	100.0	-	-	100.0	-	-	(D)	-	(D)	-
OTHER...............	2	100.0	-	-	99.8	-	-	(D)	.1	(D)	-
UNKNOWN.............	-	100.0	-	100.0	-	-	-	(D)	-	(D)	-
WEST NORTH CENTRAL......	1 485	100.0	-	.4	12.5	65.7	-	(D)	20.1	(D)	.4
RAIL...............	191	100.0	-	.2	31.8	20.9	-	(D)	42.3	(D)	2.9
MOTOR CARRIER.........	609	100.0	-	.6	19.7	61.9	-	(D)	17.8	(D)	-
PRIVATE TRUCK.........	683	100.0	-	.3	.6	81.6	-	(D)	15.9	(D)	-
AIR.................	-	100.0	-	97.9	2.1	-	-	(D)	-	(D)	-
WATER...............	-	100.0	-	-	-	-	-	(D)	-	(D)	-
OTHER...............	-	100.0	-	100.0	-	-	-	(D)	-	(D)	-
UNKNOWN.............	-	100.0	-	-	-	-	-	(D)	100.0	(D)	-
SOUTH ATLANTIC.........	4 648	100.0	.1	5.1	2.3	-	43.0	(D)	45.5	(D)	-
RAIL...............	2 236	100.0	.1	1.4	1.8	-	26.2	(D)	64.5	(D)	-
MOTOR CARRIER.........	956	100.0	.1	19.3	1.7	-	74.3	(D)	1.1	(D)	-
PRIVATE TRUCK.........	778	100.0	-	1.4	6.2	.1	89.6	(D)	.5	(D)	-
AIR.................	-	100.0	-	-	100.0	-	-	(D)	-	(D)	-
WATER...............	672	100.0	-	1.6	-	-	.5	(D)	97.9	(D)	-
OTHER...............	-	100.0	-	.1	1.8	-	97.2	(D)	.9	(D)	-
UNKNOWN.............	3	100.0	-	-	-	-	73.2	(D)	-	(D)	-
EAST SOUTH CENTRAL......	3 105	100.0	-	.1	8.6	-	3.2	(D)	49.9	(D)	-
RAIL...............	510	100.0	-	.1	17.5	-	8.0	(D)	43.4	(D)	-
MOTOR CARRIER.........	1 155	100.0	-	.1	9.5	-	2.1	(D)	7.8	(D)	-
PRIVATE TRUCK.........	445	100.0	-	.1	15.1	-	7.7	(D)	54.6	(D)	-
AIR.................	-	100.0	-	-	-	-	-	(D)	-	(D)	-
WATER...............	991	100.0	-	-	-	-	-	(D)	100.0	(D)	-
OTHER...............	1	100.0	-	-	-	-	.1	(D)	99.9	(D)	-
UNKNOWN.............	1	100.0	-	-	-	-	-	(D)	100.0	(D)	-
WEST SOUTH CENTRAL......	2 675	100.0	-	-	.6	.1	.4	(D)	94.4	(D)	.5
RAIL...............	675	100.0	-	-	1.2	-	1.4	(D)	91.2	(D)	1.2
MOTOR CARRIER.........	594	100.0	-	.1	.7	-	-	(D)	90.0	(D)	.8
PRIVATE TRUCK.........	1 397	100.0	-	-	.2	.1	-	(D)	97.9	(D)	-
AIR.................	-	100.0	-	-	-	-	-	(D)	-	(D)	-
WATER...............	-	100.0	-	-	-	-	-	(D)	-	(D)	-
OTHER...............	1	100.0	-	-	-	-	-	(D)	100.0	(D)	-
UNKNOWN.............	6	100.0	-	-	-	-	-	(D)	100.0	(D)	-
MOUNTAIN.................	458	100.0	.4	.2	6.0	14.1	.5	(D)	34.8	(D)	34.1
RAIL...............	138	100.0	-	.3	9.3	11.4	1.5	(D)	42.2	(D)	29.8
MOTOR CARRIER.........	128	100.0	1.4	.3	2.4	3.4	-	(D)	47.0	(D)	28.4
PRIVATE TRUCK.........	181	100.0	-	-	.6	24.5	-	(D)	22.5	(D)	43.4
AIR.................	-	100.0	-	-	-	-	-	(D)	-	(D)	-
WATER...............	-	100.0	-	-	-	-	-	(D)	-	(D)	-
OTHER...............	-	100.0	-	-	-	-	-	(D)	-	(D)	-
UNKNOWN.............	10	100.0	-	-	100.0	-	-	(D)	-	(D)	-
PACIFIC.................	1 020	100.0	-	.7	.2	-	-	(D)	1.4	(D)	97.8
RAIL...............	102	100.0	-	2.8	.9	-	-	(D)	-	(D)	96.3
MOTOR CARRIER.........	533	100.0	-	-	.1	-	-	(D)	.4	(D)	99.4
PRIVATE TRUCK.........	352	100.0	-	-	-	-	-	(D)	3.3	(D)	96.7
AIR.................	-	100.0	-	-	-	-	-	(D)	-	(D)	-
WATER...............	28	100.0	-	14.9	-	-	-	(D)	-	(D)	85.1
OTHER...............	-	100.0	-	-	-	-	-	(D)	-	(D)	-
UNKNOWN.............	3	100.0	-	-	-	-	-	(D)	-	(D)	100.0

See footnotes at end of table 4.

TABLE 3. **TCC GROUP 295—Percent Distribution of Geographic Division of Destination and Means of Transport, by Geographic Division of Origin: 1972**—Continued

Geographic division of destination and means of transport	Number	Percent distribution by division of origin [1]									
		U.S. total	New England	Middle Atlantic	East North Central	West North Central	South Atlantic	East South Central	West South Central	Mountain	Pacific
TON-MILES OF SHIPMENTS	(millions of ton-miles)										
U.S. TOTAL..............	4 807	100.0	.8	5.2	25.5	4.4	7.0	(D)	44.5	(D)	7.4
RAIL.................	1 444	100.0	.2	3.4	12.5	1.8	10.1	(D)	57.0	(D)	6.2
MOTOR CARRIER........	1 149	100.0	2.7	11.2	33.7	7.6	9.3	(D)	16.2	(D)	10.7
PRIVATE TRUCK........	633	100.0	.2	2.4	14.0	15.7	13.0	(D)	37.7	(D)	12.7
AIR.................	-	100.0	-	10.8	89.2	-	-	(D)	-	(D)	-
WATER...............	1 565	100.0	-	3.6	35.6	-	-	(D)	57.0	(D)	3.8
OTHER...............	-	100.0	-	.1	41.4	-	2.4	(D)	56.0	(D)	-
UNKNOWN.............	14	100.0	3.8	5.2	67.3	-	1.0	(D)	6.1	(D)	13.7
NEW ENGLAND.............	108	100.0	23.9	55.4	18.9	-	1.2	(D)	.6	(D)	-
RAIL.................	24	100.0	5.9	20.1	74.0	-	-	(D)	-	(D)	-
MOTOR CARRIER........	42	100.0	54.2	39.5	4.9	-	-	(D)	1.4	(D)	-
PRIVATE TRUCK........	3	100.0	32.7	21.3	7.0	-	38.9	(D)	-	(D)	-
AIR.................	-	100.0	-	-	-	-	-	(D)	-	(D)	-
WATER...............	37	100.0	-	100.0	-	-	-	(D)	-	(D)	-
OTHER...............	-	100.0	69.7	30.3	-	-	-	(D)	-	(D)	-
UNKNOWN.............	-	100.0	100.0	-	-	-	-	(D)	-	(D)	-
MIDDLE ATLANTIC.........	146	100.0	2.5	58.4	34.9	-	3.7	(D)	.6	(D)	-
RAIL.................	15	100.0	1.9	33.9	55.4	-	7.8	(D)	.9	(D)	-
MOTOR CARRIER........	110	100.0	3.1	61.2	32.5	-	2.6	(D)	.6	(D)	-
PRIVATE TRUCK........	18	100.0	-	57.6	35.3	-	7.2	(D)	-	(D)	-
AIR.................	-	100.0	-	100.0	-	-	-	(D)	-	(D)	-
WATER...............	1	100.0	-	100.0	-	-	-	(D)	-	(D)	-
OTHER...............	-	100.0	-	.4	99.6	-	-	(D)	-	(D)	-
UNKNOWN.............	-	100.0	-	100.0	-	-	-	(D)	-	(D)	-
EAST NORTH CENTRAL......	1 010	100.0	.1	2.2	92.5	3.3	.1	(D)	1.5	(D)	-
RAIL.................	93	100.0	-	20.2	66.8	10.4	.2	(D)	-	(D)	-
MOTOR CARRIER........	304	100.0	.4	1.1	87.4	7.6	.3	(D)	3.3	(D)	-
PRIVATE TRUCK........	55	100.0	-	-	88.6	.9	-	(D)	9.3	(D)	-
AIR.................	-	100.0	-	-	100.0	-	-	(D)	-	(D)	-
WATER...............	557	100.0	-	-	100.0	-	-	(D)	-	(D)	-
OTHER...............	-	100.0	-	.1	99.3	-	-	(D)	.6	(D)	-
UNKNOWN.............	-	100.0	-	100.0	-	-	-	(D)	-	(D)	-
WEST NORTH CENTRAL......	310	100.0	-	1.7	20.5	48.6	-	(D)	25.7	(D)	2.6
RAIL.................	70	100.0	-	.5	32.5	16.5	-	(D)	38.7	(D)	11.3
MOTOR CARRIER........	127	100.0	-	2.3	31.2	47.0	-	(D)	19.5	(D)	-
PRIVATE TRUCK........	113	100.0	-	1.8	1.0	70.3	-	(D)	24.6	(D)	-
AIR.................	-	100.0	-	99.1	.9	-	-	(D)	-	(D)	-
WATER...............	-	100.0	-	-	-	-	-	(D)	-	(D)	-
OTHER...............	-	100.0	-	100.0	-	-	-	(D)	-	(D)	-
UNKNOWN.............	-	100.0	-	-	-	-	-	(D)	100.0	(D)	-
SOUTH ATLANTIC..........	1 500	100.0	.1	3.7	3.1	-	19.1	(D)	67.7	(D)	-
RAIL.................	870	100.0	.1	1.4	2.6	-	13.4	(D)	73.6	(D)	-
MOTOR CARRIER........	156	100.0	.3	23.2	3.9	-	61.2	(D)	3.7	(D)	-
PRIVATE TRUCK........	97	100.0	-	1.4	17.5	.7	74.4	(D)	1.4	(D)	-
AIR.................	-	100.0	-	-	100.0	-	-	(D)	-	(D)	-
WATER...............	375	100.0	-	1.8	-	-	.1	(D)	98.1	(D)	-
OTHER...............	-	100.0	-	.5	10.1	-	79.1	(D)	10.3	(D)	-
UNKNOWN.............	-	100.0	-	-	-	-	27.4	(D)	-	(D)	-
EAST SOUTH CENTRAL......	885	100.0	-	.1	6.9	-	3.1	(D)	74.9	(D)	-
RAIL.................	130	100.0	-	.3	17.3	-	10.3	(D)	42.6	(D)	-
MOTOR CARRIER........	144	100.0	-	.4	19.5	-	5.4	(D)	20.0	(D)	-
PRIVATE TRUCK........	84	100.0	-	.2	12.3	-	7.8	(D)	62.8	(D)	-
AIR.................	-	100.0	-	-	-	-	-	(D)	-	(D)	-
WATER...............	524	100.0	-	-	-	-	-	(D)	100.0	(D)	-
OTHER...............	-	100.0	-	-	.1	-	-	(D)	99.9	(D)	-
UNKNOWN.............	-	100.0	-	-	-	-	-	(D)	100.0	(D)	-
WEST SOUTH CENTRAL......	305	100.0	-	.2	3.6	.1	3.6	(D)	80.7	(D)	6.1
RAIL.................	89	100.0	-	-	6.4	-	12.1	(D)	60.3	(D)	12.9
MOTOR CARRIER........	100	100.0	-	.4	3.1	-	-	(D)	83.4	(D)	6.9
PRIVATE TRUCK........	114	100.0	-	.1	1.9	.3	-	(D)	94.4	(D)	-
AIR.................	-	100.0	-	-	-	-	-	(D)	-	(D)	-
WATER...............	-	100.0	-	-	-	-	-	(D)	-	(D)	-
OTHER...............	-	100.0	-	-	-	-	-	(D)	100.0	(D)	-
UNKNOWN.............	-	100.0	-	-	-	-	-	(D)	100.0	(D)	-
MOUNTAIN................	239	100.0	1.5	.5	13.6	11.6	1.1	(D)	41.5	(D)	28.1
RAIL.................	93	100.0	-	.6	17.3	5.6	2.9	(D)	48.4	(D)	24.4
MOTOR CARRIER........	57	100.0	6.4	1.2	8.5	6.8	-	(D)	48.7	(D)	24.8
PRIVATE TRUCK........	79	100.0	-	-	2.5	23.4	-	(D)	33.2	(D)	38.3
AIR.................	-	100.0	-	-	-	-	-	(D)	-	(D)	-
WATER...............	-	100.0	-	-	-	-	-	(D)	-	(D)	-
OTHER...............	-	100.0	-	-	-	-	-	(D)	-	(D)	-
UNKNOWN.............	9	100.0	-	-	100.0	-	-	(D)	-	(D)	-
PACIFIC.................	300	100.0	-	5.6	.9	-	-	(D)	6.7	(D)	86.8
RAIL.................	55	100.0	-	11.6	2.9	-	-	(D)	-	(D)	85.6
MOTOR CARRIER........	106	100.0	-	-	1.2	-	-	(D)	3.3	(D)	95.6
PRIVATE TRUCK........	66	100.0	-	-	-	-	-	(D)	25.0	(D)	75.0
AIR.................	-	100.0	-	-	-	-	-	(D)	-	(D)	-
WATER...............	70	100.0	-	14.7	-	-	-	(D)	-	(D)	85.3
OTHER...............	-	100.0	-	-	-	-	-	(D)	-	(D)	-
UNKNOWN.............	1	100.0	-	-	-	-	-	(D)	-	(D)	100.0

See footnotes at end of table 4.

TABLE 4. **TCC GROUP 295—Percent Distribution of Distance Shipped and Weight of Shipment, by Means of Transport: 1972**

Distance shipped and weight of shipment[2][3]	Number	Percent distribution by means of transport							
		All means of transport	Rail	Motor carrier	Private truck	Air	Water	Other	Unknown
TONS OF SHIPMENTS	(thousands of tons)								
U.S. TOTAL.........	12 495	100.0	15.3	46.0	21.9	-	16.5	-	.2
UNDER 100 MILES.........	4 040	100.0	2.8	58.3	34.2	-	4.4	-	.2
UNDER 1000 POUNDS.....	2	100.0	.1	47.3	51.4	.7	-	.2	.2
1000 TO 9999 POUNDS...	67	100.0	1.0	36.8	61.2	-	.1	.3	.6
10000 TO 29999 POUNDS.	494	100.0	.3	36.4	62.9	-	-	.2	.2
30000 TO 59999 POUNDS.	3 014	100.0	.2	68.6	31.0	-	-	-	.2
60000 TO 89999 POUNDS.	98	100.0	23.0	33.3	43.7	-	-	-	-
90000 POUNDS AND OVER.	363	100.0	23.1	13.9	13.7	-	49.3	-	-
100 TO 199 MILES........	2 835	100.0	21.7	56.1	21.7	-	.1	.1	.3
UNDER 1000 POUNDS.....	2	100.0	.4	97.0	2.6	-	-	-	-
1000 TO 9999 POUNDS...	21	100.0	.6	40.2	59.2	-	-	-	-
10000 TO 29999 POUNDS.	174	100.0	3.4	56.1	40.6	-	-	-	-
30000 TO 59999 POUNDS.	1 948	100.0	1.2	72.2	26.2	-	-	.1	.2
60000 TO 89999 POUNDS.	257	100.0	71.9	19.4	7.1	-	-	-	1.6
90000 POUNDS AND OVER.	429	100.0	93.2	5.6	.4	-	.8	-	-
200 TO 299 MILES........	2 042	100.0	21.2	52.1	17.2	-	9.4	.1	.1
UNDER 1000 POUNDS.....	1	100.0	2.1	92.9	4.9	-	-	.1	-
1000 TO 9999 POUNDS...	15	100.0	4.7	64.5	30.8	-	-	-	-
10000 TO 29999 POUNDS.	103	100.0	12.4	48.2	39.5	-	-	-	-
30000 TO 59999 POUNDS.	1 313	100.0	1.2	75.4	22.9	-	.3	.1	.1
60000 TO 89999 POUNDS.	107	100.0	88.3	11.7	-	-	-	-	-
90000 POUNDS AND OVER.	501	100.0	61.4	-	1.0	-	37.6	-	-
300 TO 499 MILES........	1 876	100.0	23.5	29.7	15.1	-	31.6	-	.1
UNDER 1000 POUNDS.....	6	100.0	-	93.5	6.5	-	-	-	-
1000 TO 9999 POUNDS...	13	100.0	.5	72.3	27.2	-	-	-	-
10000 TO 29999 POUNDS.	44	100.0	1.7	57.2	40.0	-	-	.9	.2
30000 TO 59999 POUNDS.	722	100.0	2.6	61.5	35.6	-	-	-	.3
60000 TO 89999 POUNDS.	86	100.0	93.1	5.5	1.4	-	-	-	-
90000 POUNDS AND OVER.	1 002	100.0	34.0	6.7	.3	-	59.1	-	-
500 TO 999 MILES........	1 597	100.0	16.9	9.9	5.7	-	66.9	-	.7
UNDER 1000 POUNDS.....	5	100.0	-	99.0	.6	.1	-	.2	-
1000 TO 9999 POUNDS...	18	100.0	4.0	73.6	22.3	.1	-	-	-
10000 TO 29999 POUNDS.	22	100.0	.6	64.7	34.7	-	-	-	-
30000 TO 59999 POUNDS.	213	100.0	7.9	55.3	36.8	-	-	-	-
60000 TO 89999 POUNDS.	79	100.0	87.0	-	-	-	-	-	13.0
90000 POUNDS AND OVER.	1 257	100.0	14.5	.5	-	-	84.9	-	-
1000 TO 1499 MILES......	47	100.0	57.0	24.3	18.7	-	-	-	-
UNDER 1000 POUNDS.....	1	100.0	7.3	92.5	-	-	-	.2	-
1000 TO 9999 POUNDS...	2	100.0	-	96.1	3.9	-	-	-	-
10000 TO 29999 POUNDS.	1	100.0	-	72.9	27.1	-	-	-	-
30000 TO 59999 POUNDS.	15	100.0	-	45.9	54.1	-	-	-	-
60000 TO 89999 POUNDS.	3	100.0	100.0	-	-	-	-	-	-
90000 POUNDS AND OVER.	23	100.0	100.0	-	-	-	-	-	-
1500 MILES OR OVER......	56	100.0	18.6	17.2	11.3	-	51.6	-	1.2
UNDER 1000 POUNDS.....	-	100.0	-	100.0	-	-	-	-	-
1000 TO 9999 POUNDS...	-	100.0	-	100.0	-	-	-	-	-
10000 TO 29999 POUNDS.	6	100.0	-	7.7	83.6	-	8.7	-	-
30000 TO 59999 POUNDS.	24	100.0	4.7	34.1	4.3	-	54.2	-	2.7
60000 TO 89999 POUNDS.	7	100.0	41.2	-	-	-	58.8	-	-
90000 POUNDS AND OVER.	16	100.0	36.9	-	-	-	63.1	-	-
TON-MILES OF SHIPMENTS	(millions of ton-miles)								
U.S. TOTAL.........	3 021	100.0	20.3	31.8	14.1	-	33.4	-	.5
UNDER 100 MILES.........	191	100.0	4.1	62.9	32.1	-	.7	-	.1
UNDER 1000 POUNDS.....	-	100.0	.2	60.7	37.3	1.2	-	.1	.5
1000 TO 9999 POUNDS...	2	100.0	2.3	41.9	55.1	-	-	.3	.4
10000 TO 29999 POUNDS.	18	100.0	.7	44.4	54.6	-	-	.2	.1
30000 TO 59999 POUNDS.	156	100.0	.3	68.9	30.7	-	-	-	.1
60000 TO 89999 POUNDS.	4	100.0	34.3	41.5	24.2	-	-	-	-
90000 POUNDS AND OVER.	9	100.0	57.3	17.4	12.5	-	12.8	-	-
100 TO 199 MILES........	417	100.0	21.4	57.2	21.0	-	.1	.1	.3
UNDER 1000 POUNDS.....	-	100.0	.3	97.5	2.2	-	-	-	-
1000 TO 9999 POUNDS...	3	100.0	.5	39.7	59.8	-	-	-	-
10000 TO 29999 POUNDS.	25	100.0	3.7	55.3	40.9	-	-	-	-
30000 TO 59999 POUNDS.	288	100.0	1.1	73.4	25.2	-	-	.1	.2
60000 TO 89999 POUNDS.	37	100.0	73.8	19.3	5.4	-	-	-	1.5
90000 POUNDS AND OVER.	62	100.0	92.0	6.6	.5	-	.9	-	-

See footnotes at end of table 4.

TABLE 4. **TCC GROUP 295—Percent Distribution of Distance Shipped and Weight of Shipment, by Means of Transport: 1972**—Continued

Distance shipped and weight of shipment[2] [3]	Number	Percent distribution by means of transport							
		All means of transport	Rail	Motor carrier	Private truck	Air	Water	Other	Unknown
TON-MILES OF SHIPMENTS	(millions of ton-miles)								
200 TO 299 MILES........	494	100.0	21.8	52.5	17.7	–	7.8	.1	.1
UNDER 1000 POUNDS.....	–	100.0	2.0	93.2	4.8	–	–	.1	–
1000 TO 9999 POUNDS...	3	100.0	4.3	64.0	31.7	–	–	–	–
10000 TO 29999 POUNDS.	24	100.0	11.6	47.8	40.6	–	–	–	–
30000 TO 59999 POUNDS.	322	100.0	1.2	75.0	23.3	–	.2	.1	.1
60000 TO 89999 POUNDS.	26	100.0	88.8	11.2	–	–	–	–	–
90000 POUNDS AND OVER.	116	100.0	66.2	–	1.3	–	32.5	–	–
300 TO 499 MILES........	755	100.0	22.9	26.8	13.5	–	36.7	–	.1
UNDER 1000 POUNDS.....	2	100.0	–	93.8	6.2	–	–	–	–
1000 TO 9999 POUNDS...	5	100.0	.5	73.7	25.8	–	–	–	–
10000 TO 29999 POUNDS.	16	100.0	2.0	57.9	39.0	–	–	.8	.3
30000 TO 59999 POUNDS.	263	100.0	2.8	61.8	35.1	–	–	–	.3
60000 TO 89999 POUNDS.	35	100.0	94.5	4.5	1.0	–	–	–	–
90000 POUNDS AND OVER.	432	100.0	30.5	5.2	.2	–	64.1	–	–
500 TO 999 MILES........	979	100.0	18.4	10.5	6.7	–	63.5	–	1.0
UNDER 1000 POUNDS.....	3	100.0	–	99.1	.6	.2	–	.2	–
1000 TO 9999 POUNDS...	12	100.0	4.1	73.2	22.6	.1	–	–	–
10000 TO 29999 POUNDS.	15	100.0	.6	62.9	36.5	–	–	–	–
30000 TO 59999 POUNDS.	141	100.0	7.4	52.6	40.1	–	–	–	–
60000 TO 89999 POUNDS.	54	100.0	82.3	–	–	–	–	–	17.7
90000 POUNDS AND OVER.	751	100.0	16.5	.7	–	–	82.7	–	–
1000 TO 1499 MILES......	61	100.0	57.9	25.5	16.7	–	–	–	–
UNDER 1000 POUNDS.....	1	100.0	8.4	91.4	–	–	–	.2	–
1000 TO 9999 POUNDS...	2	100.0	–	95.8	4.2	–	–	–	–
10000 TO 29999 POUNDS.	1	100.0	–	77.2	22.8	–	–	–	–
30000 TO 59999 POUNDS.	20	100.0	–	51.4	48.6	–	–	–	–
60000 TO 89999 POUNDS.	3	100.0	100.0	–	–	–	–	–	–
90000 POUNDS AND OVER.	31	100.0	100.0	–	–	–	–	–	–
1500 MILES OR OVER......	121	100.0	15.4	17.1	8.7	–	57.4	–	1.3
UNDER 1000 POUNDS.....	–	100.0	–	100.0	–	–	–	–	–
1000 TO 9999 POUNDS...	–	100.0	–	100.0	–	–	–	–	–
10000 TO 29999 POUNDS.	11	100.0	–	7.9	78.6	–	13.5	–	–
30000 TO 59999 POUNDS.	60	100.0	3.6	31.1	3.3	–	59.3	–	2.7
60000 TO 89999 POUNDS.	16	100.0	38.4	–	–	–	61.6	–	–
90000 POUNDS AND OVER.	32	100.0	31.1	–	–	–	68.9	–	–

Note: Detail may not add to total due to rounding. The introductory table shows the estimates of sampling variability for tons; sampling variability for ton-miles has not been estimated. See the map in the Introduction for the States comprising the geographic divisions of the United States.

Shipments excluded from the survey are those moving by pipeline (primarily petroleum products from refineries), parcel post shipments, and commodities moved by own power (motorized vehicles, aircraft, etc.) or towed (prefabricated buildings, etc.). Local shipments (commodities shipped less than 25 miles from the plant) and shipments within the same city are also excluded. Shipments to Alaska and Hawaii from the 48 conterminous States and the District of Columbia are included; however, no data were obtained for shipments originating in Alaska and Hawaii.

- Represents zero or rounds to zero.   (D) Withheld to avoid disclosing figures for individual companies.

[1]Production of this commodity is concentrated in the geographic divisions shown; figures and distributions for geographic divisions not shown are included in the total.

[2]Distances of shipments to foreign destinations are calculated only to the U.S. port of exit.

[3]Includes only shipments represented by bills of lading and invoices. Summary records which did not show individual weights of shipments are not included.

TCC 299. Miscellaneous Petroleum and Coal Products

Comparisons of Tons and Ton-Miles of Shipments for
Geographic Divisions of Origin and for Sampling Variability: 1972 and 1967

Geographic division of origin	Estimates				Relative sampling variability in tons (percent)	
	1972		1967		1972	1967
	Tons (thousands)	Ton-miles (millions)	Tons (thousands)	Ton-miles (millions)		
U.S. total	12,951	4,240	8,916	2,097	33.7	(*)
New England	–	–	(*)	(*)	(*)	(*)
Middle Atlantic	1,524	376	(*)	(*)	20.0	(*)
East North Central	(D)	(D)	(*)	(*)	(*)	(*)
West North Central	228	108	(*)	(*)	5.1	(*)
South Atlantic	274	29	(*)	(*)	38.9	(*)
East South Central	2,511	1,044	(*)	(*)	31.7	(*)
West South Central	(D)	(D)	(*)	(*)	(*)	(*)
Mountain	(D)	(D)	(*)	(*)	(*)	(*)
Pacific	(D)	(D)	(*)	(*)	(*)	(*)

– Represents or rounds to zero.   (D) Withheld to avoid disclosing figures for individual companies.   (*) Data not published.

TABLE 1. **TCC GROUP 299**—Percent Distribution of Geographic Division of Origin and Distance Shipped, by Means of Transport: 1972

Geographic division of origin[1] and distance shipped[2]	Number	Percent distribution by means of transport							
		All means of transport	Rail	Motor carrier	Private truck	Air	Water	Other	Unknown
TONS OF SHIPMENTS	(thousands of tons)								
U.S. TOTAL	12 951	100.0	70.1	10.9	2.0	-	16.8	-	.1
NEW ENGLAND	-	100.0	2.8	96.0	-	-	-	1.2	-
UNDER 100 MILES	-	100.0	-	100.0	-	-	-	-	-
100 TO 199 MILES	-	100.0	-	100.0	-	-	-	-	-
200 TO 299 MILES	-	100.0	-	-	-	-	-	-	-
300 TO 499 MILES	-	100.0	-	100.0	-	-	-	-	-
500 TO 999 MILES	-	100.0	-	100.0	-	-	-	-	-
1000 TO 1499 MILES	-	100.0	-	86.7	-	-	-	13.3	-
1500 MILES OR OVER	-	100.0	40.1	59.9	-	-	-	-	-
MIDDLE ATLANTIC	1 524	100.0	69.7	24.0	6.0	-	-	-	.2
UNDER 100 MILES	195	100.0	-	73.8	25.8	-	-	-	.4
100 TO 199 MILES	783	100.0	91.2	6.4	2.4	-	.1	-	.1
200 TO 299 MILES	247	100.0	77.4	18.3	4.1	-	-	-	.2
300 TO 499 MILES	128	100.0	49.2	50.0	.7	-	-	-	-
500 TO 999 MILES	149	100.0	58.5	33.1	7.3	-	-	-	1.0
1000 TO 1499 MILES	9	100.0	9.8	84.4	5.8	-	-	-	-
1500 MILES OR OVER	10	100.0	53.7	44.3	2.0	-	-	-	-
WEST NORTH CENTRAL	228	100.0	71.6	27.4	1.0	-	-	-	-
UNDER 100 MILES	24	100.0	33.5	65.8	.6	-	-	-	-
100 TO 199 MILES	38	100.0	83.1	16.9	-	-	-	-	-
200 TO 299 MILES	63	100.0	56.0	40.6	3.3	-	-	-	-
300 TO 499 MILES	36	100.0	83.9	16.1	-	-	-	-	-
500 TO 999 MILES	25	100.0	72.7	27.3	-	-	-	-	-
1000 TO 1499 MILES	38	100.0	96.7	3.3	-	-	-	-	-
1500 MILES OR OVER	1	100.0	96.4	3.6	-	-	-	-	-
SOUTH ATLANTIC	274	100.0	20.6	45.2	34.2	-	-	-	-
UNDER 100 MILES	219	100.0	19.4	47.9	32.7	-	-	-	-
100 TO 199 MILES	-	100.0	-	100.0	-	-	-	-	-
200 TO 299 MILES	40	100.0	1.9	43.7	54.4	-	-	-	-
300 TO 499 MILES	2	100.0	66.2	33.8	-	-	-	-	-
500 TO 999 MILES	11	100.0	99.8	.2	-	-	-	-	-
1000 TO 1499 MILES	-	100.0	-	-	-	-	-	-	-
1500 MILES OR OVER	-	100.0	-	-	-	-	-	-	-
EAST SOUTH CENTRAL	2 511	100.0	95.8	3.6	.6	-	-	-	-
UNDER 100 MILES	2	100.0	83.5	-	16.5	-	-	-	-
100 TO 199 MILES	877	100.0	99.5	.5	-	-	-	-	-
200 TO 299 MILES	51	100.0	-	95.6	4.4	-	-	-	-
300 TO 499 MILES	110	100.0	66.7	25.0	8.4	-	-	-	-
500 TO 999 MILES	1 463	100.0	99.1	.7	.2	-	-	-	-
1000 TO 1499 MILES	-	100.0	-	-	-	-	-	-	-
1500 MILES OR OVER	5	100.0	100.0	-	-	-	-	-	-
TON-MILES OF SHIPMENTS	(millions of ton-miles)								
U.S. TOTAL	4 240	100.0	77.9	5.0	1.0	-	15.5	-	.5
NEW ENGLAND	-	100.0	15.3	81.4	-	-	-	3.3	-
UNDER 100 MILES	-	100.0	-	100.0	-	-	-	-	-
100 TO 199 MILES	-	100.0	-	100.0	-	-	-	-	-
200 TO 299 MILES	-	100.0	-	-	-	-	-	-	-
300 TO 499 MILES	-	100.0	-	100.0	-	-	-	-	-
500 TO 999 MILES	-	100.0	-	100.0	-	-	-	-	-
1000 TO 1499 MILES	-	100.0	-	87.1	-	-	-	12.9	-
1500 MILES OR OVER	-	100.0	52.2	47.8	-	-	-	-	-
MIDDLE ATLANTIC	376	100.0	67.3	28.0	4.4	-	-	-	.3
UNDER 100 MILES	9	100.0	-	69.8	29.7	-	-	-	.5
100 TO 199 MILES	100	100.0	88.4	8.4	3.2	-	-	-	.1
200 TO 299 MILES	68	100.0	79.2	17.0	3.6	-	-	-	.2
300 TO 499 MILES	50	100.0	50.2	49.1	.7	-	-	-	-
500 TO 999 MILES	111	100.0	63.2	30.0	6.1	-	-	-	.8
1000 TO 1499 MILES	10	100.0	10.0	84.6	5.4	-	-	-	-
1500 MILES OR OVER	25	100.0	52.9	45.1	2.1	-	-	-	-
WEST NORTH CENTRAL	108	100.0	83.3	16.2	.5	-	-	-	-
UNDER 100 MILES	1	100.0	32.7	67.1	.2	-	-	-	-
100 TO 199 MILES	6	100.0	82.5	17.5	-	-	-	-	-
200 TO 299 MILES	15	100.0	59.3	37.3	3.4	-	-	-	-
300 TO 499 MILES	15	100.0	84.6	15.4	-	-	-	-	-
500 TO 999 MILES	18	100.0	67.9	32.1	-	-	-	-	-
1000 TO 1499 MILES	46	100.0	96.8	3.2	-	-	-	-	-
1500 MILES OR OVER	5	100.0	98.3	1.7	-	-	-	-	-
SOUTH ATLANTIC	29	100.0	37.5	30.0	32.5	-	-	-	-
UNDER 100 MILES	10	100.0	29.1	36.1	34.8	-	-	-	-
100 TO 199 MILES	-	100.0	-	100.0	-	-	-	-	-
200 TO 299 MILES	10	100.0	2.0	43.2	54.8	-	-	-	-
300 TO 499 MILES	-	100.0	59.6	40.4	-	-	-	-	-
500 TO 999 MILES	7	100.0	99.8	.2	-	-	-	-	-
1000 TO 1499 MILES	-	100.0	-	-	-	-	-	-	-
1500 MILES OR OVER	-	100.0	-	-	-	-	-	-	-

See footnotes at end of table 4.

TABLE 1. TCC GROUP 299—Percent Distribution of Geographic Division of Origin and Distance Shipped, by Means of Transport: 1972—Continued

Geographic division of origin[1] and distance shipped[2]	Number	Percent distribution by means of transport							
		All means of transport	Rail	Motor carrier	Private truck	Air	Water	Other	Unknown
TON-MILES OF SHIPMENTS	(millions of ton-miles)								
EAST SOUTH CENTRAL......	1 044	100.0	96.5	3.0	.5	-	-	-	-
UNDER 100 MILES......	-	100.0	95.1	-	4.9	-	-	-	-
100 TO 199 MILES......	129	100.0	99.4	.6	-	-	-	-	-
200 TO 299 MILES......	13	100.0	-	95.8	4.2	-	-	-	-
300 TO 499 MILES......	40	100.0	64.1	27.5	8.4	-	-	-	-
500 TO 999 MILES......	849	100.0	99.0	.8	.2	-	-	-	-
1000 TO 1499 MILES....	-	100.0	-	-	-	-	-	-	-
1500 MILES OR OVER....	11	100.0	100.0	-	-	-	-	-	-

See footnotes at end of table 4.

TABLE 2. TCC GROUP 299—Percent Distribution of Geographic Division of Origin and Means of Transport, by Geographic Division of Destination: 1972

Geographic division of origin[1] and means of transport	Number	Percent distribution by division of destination									
		U.S. total	New England	Middle Atlantic	East North Central	West North Central	South Atlantic	East South Central	West South Central	Mountain	Pacific
TONS OF SHIPMENTS	(thousands of tons)										
U.S. TOTAL..............	12 951	100.0	.2	11.4	46.0	1.7	6.2	13.0	15.7	2.1	3.7
RAIL.................	9 083	100.0	.1	10.0	58.7	1.4	5.9	13.3	6.1	2.8	1.6
MOTOR CARRIER.........	1 409	100.0	1.1	20.8	39.5	3.0	9.3	1.3	2.5	.3	22.2
PRIVATE TRUCK.........	264	100.0	.2	19.9	20.4	4.0	40.3	3.8	1.7	.1	9.5
AIR..................	-	100.0	-	17.4	71.7	.6	2.4	-	.7	5.0	2.2
WATER................	2 177	100.0	-	10.0	.7	1.5	1.2	20.6	66.0	-	-
OTHER................	-	100.0	8.1	25.1	22.9	5.3	23.7	.9	2.1	1.8	10.2
UNKNOWN..............	17	100.0	-	1.0	6.1	8.7	5.2	-	-	79.0	-
NEW ENGLAND............	-	100.0	58.0	8.2	8.3	11.7	-	2.8	8.2	-	2.8
RAIL.................	-	100.0	-	-	-	-	-	-	-	-	100.0
MOTOR CARRIER.........	-	100.0	60.5	8.5	8.6	10.9	-	2.9	8.5	-	-
PRIVATE TRUCK.........	-	100.0	-	-	-	-	-	-	-	-	-
AIR..................	-	100.0	-	-	-	-	-	-	-	-	-
WATER................	-	100.0	-	-	-	-	-	-	-	-	-
OTHER................	-	100.0	-	-	-	100.0	-	-	-	-	-
UNKNOWN..............	-	100.0	-	-	-	-	-	-	-	-	-
MIDDLE ATLANTIC........	1 524	100.0	.8	66.7	7.2	1.5	20.8	1.8	.5	-	.7
RAIL.................	1 062	100.0	-	72.9	4.8	1.4	19.5	.8	.1	-	.5
MOTOR CARRIER.........	365	100.0	3.3	51.6	10.4	.3	26.4	4.6	2.0	.1	1.2
PRIVATE TRUCK.........	91	100.0	.7	56.8	21.4	5.0	13.7	2.1	-	-	.2
AIR..................	-	100.0	-	73.3	-	-	-	-	26.7	-	-
WATER................	-	100.0	-	100.0	-	-	-	-	-	-	-
OTHER................	-	100.0	11.4	29.5	26.7	-	29.9	1.3	1.2	-	-
UNKNOWN..............	3	100.0	-	5.3	20.4	46.5	27.7	-	-	-	-
WEST NORTH CENTRAL......	228	100.0	.2	10.6	31.0	44.4	1.7	.6	2.4	4.0	5.2
RAIL.................	163	100.0	.3	10.9	23.0	48.4	2.2	.3	2.5	5.2	7.2
MOTOR CARRIER.........	62	100.0	.1	10.1	49.4	35.7	.4	1.4	2.1	.8	.1
PRIVATE TRUCK.........	2	100.0	-	-	99.6	.1	-	.4	-	-	-
AIR..................	-	100.0	-	-	-	-	-	-	-	-	-
WATER................	-	100.0	-	-	-	-	-	-	-	-	-
OTHER................	-	100.0	-	100.0	-	-	-	-	-	-	-
UNKNOWN..............	-	100.0	-	-	-	-	-	-	-	-	-
SOUTH ATLANTIC.........	274	100.0	-	50.5	-	-	49.1	.4	-	-	-
RAIL.................	56	100.0	-	78.1	-	-	21.9	-	-	-	-
MOTOR CARRIER.........	123	100.0	-	76.1	-	-	23.8	-	-	-	-
PRIVATE TRUCK.........	93	100.0	-	-	-	-	99.0	1.0	-	-	-
AIR..................	-	100.0	-	-	-	-	-	-	-	-	-
WATER................	-	100.0	-	-	-	-	-	-	-	-	-
OTHER................	-	100.0	-	-	-	-	-	-	-	-	-
UNKNOWN..............	-	100.0	-	-	-	-	-	-	-	-	-
EAST SOUTH CENTRAL......	2 511	100.0	-	.4	60.6	1.8	1.0	35.1	.9	-	.2
RAIL.................	2 405	100.0	-	.4	60.4	.9	1.1	36.4	.7	-	.2
MOTOR CARRIER.........	90	100.0	-	-	75.0	18.6	-	-	6.4	-	-
PRIVATE TRUCK.........	14	100.0	-	-	12.7	39.4	-	47.9	-	-	-
AIR..................	-	100.0	-	-	-	-	-	-	-	-	-
WATER................	-	100.0	-	-	-	-	-	-	-	-	-
OTHER................	-	100.0	-	-	-	-	-	-	-	-	-
UNKNOWN..............	-	100.0	-	-	-	-	-	-	-	-	-

See footnotes at end of table 4.

TABLE 2. **TCC GROUP 299—Percent Distribution of Geographic Division of Origin and Means of Transport, by Geographic Division of Destination: 1972**—Continued

Geographic division of origin [1] and means of transport	Number	Percent distribution by division of destination									
		U.S. total	New England	Middle Atlantic	East North Central	West North Central	South Atlantic	East South Central	West South Central	Mountain	Pacific
TON-MILES OF SHIPMENTS	(millions of ton-miles)										
U.S. TOTAL...............	4 240	100.0	.2	10.9	48.2	2.2	6.0	11.6	8.8	4.6	7.5
RAIL....................	3 303	100.0	.2	5.7	59.3	1.7	5.5	8.9	4.9	5.2	8.6
MOTOR CARRIER..........	214	100.0	1.9	15.1	28.6	5.3	18.6	6.9	8.0	2.2	13.5
PRIVATE TRUCK..........	43	100.0	.4	14.2	18.0	13.9	24.8	7.7	12.3	.2	8.6
AIR....................	-	100.0	-	23.3	52.4	2.0	10.2	-	2.2	6.5	3.5
WATER..................	656	100.0	-	36.1	2.0	2.6	3.0	27.3	28.9	-	-
OTHER..................	-	100.0	6.5	18.4	20.8	11.4	25.9	2.6	8.5	4.2	1.7
UNKNOWN................	22	100.0	-	-	.2	3.7	.9	-	-	95.2	-
NEW ENGLAND.............	-	100.0	9.5	6.0	12.8	26.7	-	4.0	25.7	-	15.3
RAIL....................	-	100.0	-	-	-	-	-	-	-	-	100.0
MOTOR CARRIER..........	-	100.0	11.7	7.4	15.7	28.8	-	4.9	31.6	-	-
PRIVATE TRUCK..........	-	100.0	-	-	-	-	-	-	-	-	-
AIR....................	-	100.0	-	-	-	-	-	-	-	-	-
WATER..................	-	100.0	-	-	-	-	-	-	-	-	-
OTHER..................	-	100.0	-	-	-	100.0	-	-	-	-	-
UNKNOWN................	-	100.0	-	-	-	-	-	-	-	-	-
MIDDLE ATLANTIC.........	376	100.0	.7	40.4	10.1	4.7	29.3	5.6	2.5	.4	6.4
RAIL....................	253	100.0	-	48.7	8.0	5.0	30.1	2.5	.4	.2	5.1
MOTOR CARRIER..........	105	100.0	2.2	21.3	12.7	.8	30.9	13.2	7.9	.9	10.1
PRIVATE TRUCK..........	16	100.0	1.0	36.7	26.4	18.4	8.5	5.7	-	-	3.2
AIR....................	-	100.0	-	29.8	-	-	-	-	70.2	-	-
WATER..................	-	100.0	-	100.0	-	-	-	-	-	-	-
OTHER..................	-	100.0	8.9	16.1	32.8	-	31.5	4.6	6.1	-	-
UNKNOWN................	1	100.0	-	1.0	4.0	77.1	18.0	-	-	-	-
WEST NORTH CENTRAL......	108	100.0	.7	25.0	24.8	20.2	2.5	.9	5.5	4.5	15.9
RAIL....................	90	100.0	.8	24.0	20.8	21.7	2.8	.7	5.0	5.2	19.0
MOTOR CARRIER..........	17	100.0	.2	30.7	42.6	13.1	1.2	2.0	8.2	1.5	.5
PRIVATE TRUCK..........	-	100.0	-	-	99.6	.1	-	.4	-	-	-
AIR....................	-	100.0	-	-	-	-	-	-	-	-	-
WATER..................	-	100.0	-	-	-	-	-	-	-	-	-
OTHER..................	-	100.0	-	100.0	-	-	-	-	-	-	-
UNKNOWN................	-	100.0	-	-	-	-	-	-	-	-	-
SOUTH ATLANTIC..........	29	100.0	-	21.7	-	-	77.3	1.0	-	-	-
RAIL....................	10	100.0	-	31.7	-	-	68.3	-	-	-	-
MOTOR CARRIER..........	8	100.0	-	32.7	-	-	67.1	.2	-	-	-
PRIVATE TRUCK..........	9	100.0	-	-	-	-	97.1	2.9	-	-	-
AIR....................	-	100.0	-	-	-	-	-	-	-	-	-
WATER..................	-	100.0	-	-	-	-	-	-	-	-	-
OTHER..................	-	100.0	-	-	-	-	-	-	-	-	-
UNKNOWN................	-	100.0	-	-	-	-	-	-	-	-	-
EAST SOUTH CENTRAL......	1 044	100.0	-	.6	81.1	2.2	1.0	12.5	1.6	-	1.1
RAIL....................	1 007	100.0	-	.6	82.0	1.2	1.0	12.8	1.3	-	1.1
MOTOR CARRIER..........	31	100.0	-	-	63.7	23.1	-	-	13.1	-	-
PRIVATE TRUCK..........	5	100.0	-	-	8.5	53.3	-	38.2	-	-	-
AIR....................	-	100.0	-	-	-	-	-	-	-	-	-
WATER..................	-	100.0	-	-	-	-	-	-	-	-	-
OTHER..................	-	100.0	-	-	-	-	-	-	-	-	-
UNKNOWN................	-	100.0	-	-	-	-	-	-	-	-	-

See footnotes at end of table 4.

TABLE 3. TCC GROUP 299—Percent Distribution of Geographic Division of Destination and Means of Transport, by Geographic Division of Origin: 1972

Geographic division of destination and means of transport	Number (thousands of tons)	Percent distribution by division of origin [1]									
		U.S. total	New England	Middle Atlantic	East North Central	West North Central	South Atlantic	East South Central	West South Central	Mountain	Pacific
TONS OF SHIPMENTS											
U.S. TOTAL	12 951	100.0	-	11.8	(D)	1.8	2.1	19.4	(D)	(D)	(D)
RAIL	9 083	100.0	-	11.7	(D)	1.8	.6	26.5	(D)	(D)	(D)
MOTOR CARRIER	1 409	100.0	-	26.0	(D)	4.4	8.8	6.5	(D)	(D)	(D)
PRIVATE TRUCK	264	100.0	-	34.8	(D)	.9	35.5	5.7	(D)	(D)	(D)
AIR	-	100.0	-	2.6	(D)	-	-	-	(D)	(D)	(D)
WATER	2 177	100.0	-	-	(D)	-	-	-	(D)	(D)	(D)
OTHER	-	100.0	1.8	64.7	(D)	1.8	-	-	(D)	(D)	(D)
UNKNOWN	17	100.0	-	18.7	(D)	-	-	-	(D)	(D)	(D)
NEW ENGLAND	20	100.0	.5	63.1	(D)	2.4	-	-	(D)	(D)	(D)
RAIL	4	100.0	-	-	(D)	9.6	-	-	(D)	(D)	(D)
MOTOR CARRIER	14	100.0	.7	82.0	(D)	.2	-	-	(D)	(D)	(D)
PRIVATE TRUCK	-	100.0	-	100.0	(D)	-	-	-	(D)	(D)	(D)
AIR	-	100.0	-	-	(D)	-	-	-	(D)	(D)	(D)
WATER	-	100.0	-	-	(D)	-	-	-	(D)	(D)	(D)
OTHER	-	100.0	-	91.4	(D)	-	-	-	(D)	(D)	(D)
UNKNOWN	-	100.0	-	-	(D)	-	-	-	(D)	(D)	(D)
MIDDLE ATLANTIC	1 474	100.0	-	68.9	(D)	1.6	9.4	.6	(D)	(D)	(D)
RAIL	910	100.0	-	85.1	(D)	2.0	4.8	1.0	(D)	(D)	(D)
MOTOR CARRIER	293	100.0	-	64.3	(D)	2.2	32.1	-	(D)	(D)	(D)
PRIVATE TRUCK	52	100.0	-	99.5	(D)	-	-	-	(D)	(D)	(D)
AIR	-	100.0	-	11.0	(D)	-	-	-	(D)	(D)	(D)
WATER	216	100.0	-	.1	(D)	-	-	-	(D)	(D)	(D)
OTHER	-	100.0	-	76.1	(D)	7.2	-	-	(D)	(D)	(D)
UNKNOWN	-	100.0	-	100.0	(D)	-	-	-	(D)	(D)	(D)
EAST NORTH CENTRAL	5 958	100.0	-	1.8	(D)	1.2	-	25.6	(D)	(D)	(D)
RAIL	5 330	100.0	-	1.0	(D)	.7	-	27.2	(D)	(D)	(D)
MOTOR CARRIER	556	100.0	-	6.9	(D)	5.6	-	12.3	(D)	(D)	(D)
PRIVATE TRUCK	53	100.0	-	36.6	(D)	4.2	-	3.5	(D)	(D)	(D)
AIR	-	100.0	-	-	(D)	-	-	-	(D)	(D)	(D)
WATER	15	100.0	-	-	(D)	-	-	-	(D)	(D)	(D)
OTHER	-	100.0	-	75.3	(D)	-	-	-	(D)	(D)	(D)
UNKNOWN	1	100.0	-	62.3	(D)	-	-	-	(D)	(D)	(D)
WEST NORTH CENTRAL	215	100.0	-	10.4	(D)	47.2	-	20.5	(D)	(D)	(D)
RAIL	128	100.0	-	11.7	(D)	61.5	-	16.6	(D)	(D)	(D)
MOTOR CARRIER	42	100.0	-	2.4	(D)	53.1	-	40.1	(D)	(D)	(D)
PRIVATE TRUCK	10	100.0	-	44.0	(D)	-	-	56.0	(D)	(D)	(D)
AIR	-	100.0	-	-	(D)	-	-	-	(D)	(D)	(D)
WATER	32	100.0	34.2	-	(D)	-	-	-	(D)	(D)	(D)
OTHER	-	100.0	-	-	(D)	-	-	-	(D)	(D)	(D)
UNKNOWN	1	100.0	-	100.0	(D)	-	-	-	(D)	(D)	(D)
SOUTH ATLANTIC	801	100.0	-	39.6	(D)	.5	16.8	3.2	(D)	(D)	(D)
RAIL	536	100.0	-	38.7	(D)	.7	2.3	4.7	(D)	(D)	(D)
MOTOR CARRIER	130	100.0	-	73.8	(D)	.2	22.6	-	(D)	(D)	(D)
PRIVATE TRUCK	106	100.0	-	11.8	(D)	-	87.1	-	(D)	(D)	(D)
AIR	-	100.0	-	-	(D)	-	-	-	(D)	(D)	(D)
WATER	26	100.0	-	81.7	(D)	-	-	-	(D)	(D)	(D)
OTHER	-	100.0	-	100.0	(D)	-	-	-	(D)	(D)	(D)
UNKNOWN	-	100.0	-	-	(D)	-	-	-	(D)	(D)	(D)
EAST SOUTH CENTRAL	1 689	100.0	-	1.6	(D)	.1	.1	52.3	(D)	(D)	(D)
RAIL	1 212	100.0	-	.7	(D)	-	-	72.2	(D)	(D)	(D)
MOTOR CARRIER	18	100.0	-	90.1	(D)	4.7	.1	-	(D)	(D)	(D)
PRIVATE TRUCK	10	100.0	-	19.4	(D)	.1	9.4	71.1	(D)	(D)	(D)
AIR	-	100.0	-	-	(D)	-	-	-	(D)	(D)	(D)
WATER	448	100.0	-	-	(D)	-	-	-	(D)	(D)	(D)
OTHER	-	100.0	-	100.0	(D)	-	-	-	(D)	(D)	(D)
UNKNOWN	-	100.0	-	-	(D)	-	-	-	(D)	(D)	(D)
WEST SOUTH CENTRAL	2 034	100.0	-	.4	(D)	.3	-	1.1	(D)	(D)	(D)
RAIL	558	100.0	-	.2	(D)	.7	-	2.8	(D)	(D)	(D)
MOTOR CARRIER	34	100.0	-	20.9	(D)	3.8	-	16.7	(D)	(D)	(D)
PRIVATE TRUCK	4	100.0	-	-	(D)	-	-	-	(D)	(D)	(D)
AIR	-	100.0	-	100.0	(D)	-	-	-	(D)	(D)	(D)
WATER	1 436	100.0	-	-	(D)	-	-	-	(D)	(D)	(D)
OTHER	-	100.0	-	36.6	(D)	-	-	-	(D)	(D)	(D)
UNKNOWN	-	100.0	-	-	(D)	-	-	-	(D)	(D)	(D)
MOUNTAIN	275	100.0	-	.3	(D)	3.3	-	-	(D)	(D)	(D)
RAIL	256	100.0	-	.1	(D)	3.3	-	-	(D)	(D)	(D)
MOTOR CARRIER	4	100.0	-	9.8	(D)	10.5	-	-	(D)	(D)	(D)
PRIVATE TRUCK	-	100.0	-	-	(D)	-	-	-	(D)	(D)	(D)
AIR	-	100.0	-	-	(D)	-	-	-	(D)	(D)	(D)
WATER	-	100.0	-	-	(D)	-	-	-	(D)	(D)	(D)
OTHER	-	100.0	-	-	(D)	-	-	-	(D)	(D)	(D)
UNKNOWN	13	100.0	-	-	(D)	-	-	-	(D)	(D)	(D)
PACIFIC	483	100.0	-	2.1	(D)	2.5	-	1.2	(D)	(D)	(D)
RAIL	145	100.0	-	3.8	(D)	8.1	-	4.0	(D)	(D)	(D)
MOTOR CARRIER	312	100.0	-	1.4	(D)	-	-	-	(D)	(D)	(D)
PRIVATE TRUCK	25	100.0	-	.8	(D)	-	-	-	(D)	(D)	(D)
AIR	-	100.0	-	-	(D)	-	-	-	(D)	(D)	(D)
WATER	-	100.0	-	-	(D)	-	-	-	(D)	(D)	(D)
OTHER	-	100.0	-	-	(D)	-	-	-	(D)	(D)	(D)
UNKNOWN	-	100.0	-	-	(D)	-	-	-	(D)	(D)	(D)

See footnotes at end of table 4.

TABLE 3. **TCC GROUP 299**—Percent Distribution of Geographic Division of Destination and Means of Transport, by Geographic Division of Origin: 1972—Continued

Geographic division of destination and means of transport	Number	Percent distribution by division of origin[1]									
		U.S. total	New England	Middle Atlantic	East North Central	West North Central	South Atlantic	East South Central	West South Central	Mountain	Pacific
TON-MILES OF SHIPMENTS	(millions of ton-miles)										
U.S. TOTAL	4 240	100.0	-	8.9	(D)	2.6	.7	24.6	(D)	(D)	(D)
RAIL	3 303	100.0	-	7.7	(D)	2.7	.3	30.5	(D)	(D)	(D)
MOTOR CARRIER	214	100.0	-	49.2	(D)	8.2	4.1	14.6	(D)	(D)	(D)
PRIVATE TRUCK	43	100.0	-	38.3	(D)	1.2	21.6	12.8	(D)	(D)	(D)
AIR	-	100.0	-	3.1	(D)	-	-	-	(D)	(D)	(D)
WATER	656	100.0	-	-	(D)	-	-	-	(D)	(D)	(D)
OTHER	-	100.0	7.2	56.4	(D)	4.1	-	-	(D)	(D)	(D)
UNKNOWN	22	100.0	-	4.8	(D)	-	-	-	(D)	(D)	(D)
NEW ENGLAND	10	100.0	.1	24.6	(D)	7.0	-	-	(D)	(D)	(D)
RAIL	5	100.0	-	-	(D)	11.6	-	-	(D)	(D)	(D)
MOTOR CARRIER	4	100.0	.2	57.0	(D)	.8	-	-	(D)	(D)	(D)
PRIVATE TRUCK	-	100.0	-	100.0	(D)	-	-	-	(D)	(D)	(D)
AIR	-	100.0	-	-	(D)	-	-	-	(D)	(D)	(D)
WATER	-	100.0	-	-	(D)	-	-	-	(D)	(D)	(D)
OTHER	-	100.0	-	77.4	(D)	-	-	-	(D)	(D)	(D)
UNKNOWN	-	100.0	-	-	(D)	-	-	-	(D)	(D)	(D)
MIDDLE ATLANTIC	463	100.0	-	32.8	(D)	5.8	1.4	1.3	(D)	(D)	(D)
RAIL	187	100.0	-	65.8	(D)	11.5	1.8	3.1	(D)	(D)	(D)
MOTOR CARRIER	32	100.0	-	69.5	(D)	16.7	8.8	-	(D)	(D)	(D)
PRIVATE TRUCK	6	100.0	-	99.2	(D)	-	-	-	(D)	(D)	(D)
AIR	-	100.0	-	4.0	(D)	-	-	-	(D)	(D)	(D)
WATER	237	100.0	-	-	(D)	-	-	-	(D)	(D)	(D)
OTHER	-	100.0	-	49.2	(D)	22.0	-	-	(D)	(D)	(D)
UNKNOWN	-	100.0	-	100.0	(D)	-	-	-	(D)	(D)	(D)
EAST NORTH CENTRAL	2 042	100.0	-	1.9	(D)	1.3	-	41.4	(D)	(D)	(D)
RAIL	1 959	100.0	-	1.0	(D)	1.0	-	42.1	(D)	(D)	(D)
MOTOR CARRIER	61	100.0	-	21.9	(D)	12.2	-	32.5	(D)	(D)	(D)
PRIVATE TRUCK	7	100.0	-	56.4	(D)	6.8	-	6.0	(D)	(D)	(D)
AIR	-	100.0	-	-	(D)	-	-	-	(D)	(D)	(D)
WATER	13	100.0	-	-	(D)	-	-	-	(D)	(D)	(D)
OTHER	-	100.0	-	88.7	(D)	-	-	-	(D)	(D)	(D)
UNKNOWN	-	100.0	-	85.4	(D)	-	-	-	(D)	(D)	(D)
WEST NORTH CENTRAL	91	100.0	-	19.2	(D)	24.0	-	24.8	(D)	(D)	(D)
RAIL	55	100.0	-	22.9	(D)	35.0	-	22.3	(D)	(D)	(D)
MOTOR CARRIER	11	100.0	.2	7.3	(D)	20.4	-	63.9	(D)	(D)	(D)
PRIVATE TRUCK	6	100.0	-	50.8	(D)	-	-	49.1	(D)	(D)	(D)
AIR	-	100.0	-	-	(D)	-	-	-	(D)	(D)	(D)
WATER	17	100.0	-	-	(D)	-	-	-	(D)	(D)	(D)
OTHER	-	100.0	63.2	-	(D)	-	-	-	(D)	(D)	(D)
UNKNOWN	-	100.0	-	100.0	(D)	-	-	-	(D)	(D)	(D)
SOUTH ATLANTIC	253	100.0	-	43.7	(D)	1.1	8.9	4.0	(D)	(D)	(D)
RAIL	182	100.0	-	41.9	(D)	1.4	4.1	5.5	(D)	(D)	(D)
MOTOR CARRIER	39	100.0	-	81.8	(D)	.5	14.7	-	(D)	(D)	(D)
PRIVATE TRUCK	10	100.0	-	13.2	(D)	-	84.6	-	(D)	(D)	(D)
AIR	-	100.0	-	-	(D)	-	-	-	(D)	(D)	(D)
WATER	19	100.0	-	-	(D)	-	-	-	(D)	(D)	(D)
OTHER	-	100.0	-	68.7	(D)	-	-	-	(D)	(D)	(D)
UNKNOWN	-	100.0	-	100.0	(D)	-	-	-	(D)	(D)	(D)
EAST SOUTH CENTRAL	492	100.0	-	4.3	(D)	.2	.1	26.6	(D)	(D)	(D)
RAIL	294	100.0	-	2.1	(D)	.2	-	43.7	(D)	(D)	(D)
MOTOR CARRIER	14	100.0	-	94.0	(D)	2.4	.1	-	(D)	(D)	(D)
PRIVATE TRUCK	3	100.0	-	28.5	(D)	.1	8.1	63.4	(D)	(D)	(D)
AIR	-	100.0	-	-	(D)	-	-	-	(D)	(D)	(D)
WATER	179	100.0	-	-	(D)	-	-	-	(D)	(D)	(D)
OTHER	-	100.0	-	100.0	(D)	-	-	-	(D)	(D)	(D)
UNKNOWN	-	100.0	-	-	(D)	-	-	-	(D)	(D)	(D)
WEST SOUTH CENTRAL	374	100.0	-	2.5	(D)	1.6	-	4.5	(D)	(D)	(D)
RAIL	162	100.0	-	.6	(D)	2.8	-	7.8	(D)	(D)	(D)
MOTOR CARRIER	17	100.0	.1	48.4	(D)	8.4	-	23.9	(D)	(D)	(D)
PRIVATE TRUCK	5	100.0	-	-	(D)	-	-	-	(D)	(D)	(D)
AIR	-	100.0	-	100.0	(D)	-	-	-	(D)	(D)	(D)
WATER	189	100.0	-	-	(D)	-	-	-	(D)	(D)	(D)
OTHER	-	100.0	-	40.8	(D)	-	-	-	(D)	(D)	(D)
UNKNOWN	-	100.0	-	-	(D)	-	-	-	(D)	(D)	(D)
MOUNTAIN	196	100.0	-	.7	(D)	2.5	-	-	(D)	(D)	(D)
RAIL	170	100.0	-	.3	(D)	2.7	-	-	(D)	(D)	(D)
MOTOR CARRIER	4	100.0	-	19.9	(D)	5.7	-	-	(D)	(D)	(D)
PRIVATE TRUCK	-	100.0	-	-	(D)	-	-	-	(D)	(D)	(D)
AIR	-	100.0	-	-	(D)	-	-	-	(D)	(D)	(D)
WATER	-	100.0	-	-	(D)	-	-	-	(D)	(D)	(D)
OTHER	-	100.0	-	-	(D)	-	-	-	(D)	(D)	(D)
UNKNOWN	21	100.0	-	-	(D)	-	-	-	(D)	(D)	(D)
PACIFIC	316	100.0	-	7.6	(D)	5.4	-	3.6	(D)	(D)	(D)
RAIL	283	100.0	-	4.5	(D)	6.0	-	4.0	(D)	(D)	(D)
MOTOR CARRIER	28	100.0	-	37.0	(D)	.3	-	-	(D)	(D)	(D)
PRIVATE TRUCK	3	100.0	-	14.1	(D)	-	-	-	(D)	(D)	(D)
AIR	-	100.0	-	-	(D)	-	-	-	(D)	(D)	(D)
WATER	-	100.0	-	-	(D)	-	-	-	(D)	(D)	(D)
OTHER	-	100.0	-	-	(D)	-	-	-	(D)	(D)	(D)
UNKNOWN	-	100.0	-	-	(D)	-	-	-	(D)	(D)	(D)

See footnotes at end of table 4.

TABLE 4. TCC GROUP 299—Percent Distribution of Distance Shipped and Weight of Shipment, by Means of Transport: 1972

Distance shipped and weight of shipment [2] [3]	Number	Percent distribution by means of transport							
		All means of transport	Rail	Motor carrier	Private truck	Air	Water	Other	Unknown
TONS OF SHIPMENTS	(thousands of tons)								
U.S. TOTAL	10 113	100.0	83.1	10.5	2.6	-	3.7	-	.2
UNDER 100 MILES	1 063	100.0	29.3	55.6	15.0	-	-	-	.1
UNDER 1000 POUNDS	3	100.0	-	55.4	42.9	-	-	.7	.9
1000 TO 9999 POUNDS	27	100.0	-	37.7	62.3	-	-	-	-
10000 TO 29999 POUNDS	74	100.0	-	44.7	54.1	-	.2	-	1.0
30000 TO 59999 POUNDS	539	100.0	.2	81.1	18.7	-	-	-	-
60000 TO 89999 POUNDS	37	100.0	96.1	3.9	-	-	-	-	-
90000 POUNDS AND OVER	380	100.0	72.0	28.0	-	-	-	-	-
100 TO 199 MILES	1 989	100.0	91.8	6.9	1.2	-	-	-	-
UNDER 1000 POUNDS	1	100.0	-	90.7	8.7	-	-	.6	-
1000 TO 9999 POUNDS	6	100.0	-	47.6	45.2	-	-	-	7.3
10000 TO 29999 POUNDS	26	100.0	-	92.0	8.0	-	-	-	-
30000 TO 59999 POUNDS	115	100.0	3.4	79.6	17.0	-	-	-	-
60000 TO 89999 POUNDS	171	100.0	90.1	9.9	-	-	-	-	-
90000 POUNDS AND OVER	1 668	100.0	100.0	-	-	-	-	-	-
200 TO 299 MILES	3 493	100.0	95.0	3.8	1.1	-	-	-	-
UNDER 1000 POUNDS	1	100.0	-	79.7	6.0	5.1	-	4.2	4.9
1000 TO 9999 POUNDS	9	100.0	1.3	52.0	46.7	-	-	-	-
10000 TO 29999 POUNDS	32	100.0	11.6	71.3	16.8	-	-	-	.3
30000 TO 59999 POUNDS	147	100.0	12.9	66.4	20.6	-	-	-	.2
60000 TO 89999 POUNDS	98	100.0	93.1	6.9	-	-	-	-	-
90000 POUNDS AND OVER	3 205	100.0	100.0	-	-	-	-	-	-
300 TO 499 MILES	916	100.0	46.1	11.6	1.8	-	40.5	-	-
UNDER 1000 POUNDS	-	100.0	-	93.9	-	-	-	3.0	3.1
1000 TO 9999 POUNDS	3	100.0	-	88.2	11.8	-	-	-	-
10000 TO 29999 POUNDS	10	100.0	6.5	89.0	4.5	-	-	-	-
30000 TO 59999 POUNDS	125	100.0	14.0	73.6	12.5	-	-	-	-
60000 TO 89999 POUNDS	119	100.0	99.0	.7	.3	-	-	-	-
90000 POUNDS AND OVER	656	100.0	43.5	-	-	-	56.5	-	-
500 TO 999 MILES	2 376	100.0	96.2	3.1	.6	-	-	-	.1
UNDER 1000 POUNDS	-	100.0	1.5	90.6	.7	2.2	-	1.5	3.5
1000 TO 9999 POUNDS	5	100.0	19.1	52.7	28.2	-	-	-	-
10000 TO 29999 POUNDS	23	100.0	12.8	66.4	14.2	-	-	-	6.6
30000 TO 59999 POUNDS	83	100.0	22.9	66.4	10.7	-	-	-	-
60000 TO 89999 POUNDS	61	100.0	100.0	-	-	-	-	-	-
90000 POUNDS AND OVER	2 202	100.0	100.0	-	-	-	-	-	-
1000 TO 1499 MILES	69	100.0	76.5	16.3	7.2	-	-	-	-
UNDER 1000 POUNDS	-	100.0	-	88.5	10.3	-	-	1.2	-
1000 TO 9999 POUNDS	-	100.0	-	100.0	-	-	-	-	-
10000 TO 29999 POUNDS	-	100.0	-	-	-	-	-	-	-
30000 TO 59999 POUNDS	17	100.0	13.6	57.9	28.5	-	-	-	-
60000 TO 89999 POUNDS	28	100.0	100.0	-	-	-	-	-	-
90000 POUNDS AND OVER	22	100.0	100.0	-	-	-	-	-	-
1500 MILES OR OVER	204	100.0	90.2	2.9	.1	-	-	-	6.8
UNDER 1000 POUNDS	-	100.0	4.4	93.7	-	1.9	-	-	-
1000 TO 9999 POUNDS	2	100.0	1.4	89.2	9.4	-	-	-	-
10000 TO 29999 POUNDS	1	100.0	10.2	89.8	-	-	-	-	-
30000 TO 59999 POUNDS	2	100.0	11.9	88.1	-	-	-	-	-
60000 TO 89999 POUNDS	55	100.0	100.0	-	-	-	-	-	-
90000 POUNDS AND OVER	141	100.0	90.2	-	-	-	-	-	9.8
TON-MILES OF SHIPMENTS	(millions of ton-miles)								
U.S. TOTAL	3 451	100.0	88.5	5.5	1.3	-	4.1	-	.6
UNDER 100 MILES	45	100.0	42.4	39.4	18.1	-	-	-	.1
UNDER 1000 POUNDS	-	100.0	-	65.5	31.2	-	-	1.2	2.0
1000 TO 9999 POUNDS	1	100.0	-	47.7	52.3	-	-	-	-
10000 TO 29999 POUNDS	3	100.0	-	40.9	58.0	-	-	-	1.1
30000 TO 59999 POUNDS	18	100.0	.1	69.6	30.3	-	-	-	-
60000 TO 89999 POUNDS	2	100.0	97.9	2.1	-	-	-	-	-
90000 POUNDS AND OVER	20	100.0	84.1	15.9	-	-	-	-	-
100 TO 199 MILES	293	100.0	92.0	6.6	1.4	-	-	-	-
UNDER 1000 POUNDS	-	100.0	-	90.8	8.5	-	-	.7	-
1000 TO 9999 POUNDS	1	100.0	-	44.4	48.7	-	-	-	6.9
10000 TO 29999 POUNDS	3	100.0	-	92.5	7.5	-	-	-	-
30000 TO 59999 POUNDS	15	100.0	2.6	77.0	20.4	-	-	-	-
60000 TO 89999 POUNDS	27	100.0	88.0	12.0	-	-	-	-	-
90000 POUNDS AND OVER	244	100.0	100.0	-	-	-	-	-	-

See footnotes at end of table 4.

TABLE 4. **TCC GROUP 299—Percent Distribution of Distance Shipped and Weight of Shipment, by Means of Transport: 1972**—Continued

Distance shipped and weight of shipment [2] [3]	Number	Percent distribution by means of transport							
		All means of transport	Rail	Motor carrier	Private truck	Air	Water	Other	Unknown
TON-MILES OF SHIPMENTS	(millions of ton-miles)								
200 TO 299 MILES.........	850	100.0	94.8	4.0	1.2	-	-	-	-
UNDER 1000 POUNDS.....	-	100.0	-	78.3	6.0	6.1	-	4.2	5.3
1000 TO 9999 POUNDS...	2	100.0	1.2	52.0	46.8	-	-	-	-
10000 TO 29999 POUNDS.	7	100.0	10.8	71.2	17.6	-	-	-	.4
30000 TO 59999 POUNDS.	37	100.0	11.9	67.2	20.7	-	-	-	.2
60000 TO 89999 POUNDS.	21	100.0	93.2	6.8	-	-	-	-	-
90000 POUNDS AND OVER.	781	100.0	100.0	-	-	-	-	-	-
300 TO 499 MILES.........	348	100.0	46.2	11.9	1.7	-	40.2	-	-
UNDER 1000 POUNDS.....	-	100.0	-	94.5	.1	-	-	2.9	2.5
1000 TO 9999 POUNDS...	1	100.0	-	89.0	11.0	-	-	-	-
10000 TO 29999 POUNDS.	3	100.0	8.2	87.9	3.9	-	-	-	-
30000 TO 59999 POUNDS.	48	100.0	13.5	75.2	11.3	-	-	-	-
60000 TO 89999 POUNDS.	44	100.0	99.1	.6	.3	-	-	-	-
90000 POUNDS AND OVER.	249	100.0	43.9	-	-	-	56.1	-	-
500 TO 999 MILES.........	1 439	100.0	95.8	3.5	.6	-	-	-	.1
UNDER 1000 POUNDS.....	-	100.0	1.6	91.0	.6	2.2	-	1.3	3.4
1000 TO 9999 POUNDS...	4	100.0	19.2	53.6	27.2	-	-	-	-
10000 TO 29999 POUNDS.	17	100.0	11.9	70.4	12.9	-	-	-	4.9
30000 TO 59999 POUNDS.	55	100.0	25.0	65.7	9.3	-	-	-	-
60000 TO 89999 POUNDS.	41	100.0	100.0	-	-	-	-	-	-
90000 POUNDS AND OVER.	1 321	100.0	100.0	-	-	-	-	-	-
1000 TO 1499 MILES......	86	100.0	78.2	15.0	6.8	-	-	-	-
UNDER 1000 POUNDS.....	-	100.0	-	89.8	9.0	-	-	1.2	-
1000 TO 9999 POUNDS...	1	100.0	-	100.0	-	-	-	-	-
10000 TO 29999 POUNDS.	-	100.0	-	-	-	-	-	-	-
30000 TO 59999 POUNDS.	20	100.0	15.1	55.9	29.0	-	-	-	-
60000 TO 89999 POUNDS.	36	100.0	100.0	-	-	-	-	-	-
90000 POUNDS AND OVER.	28	100.0	100.0	-	-	-	-	-	-
1500 MILES OR OVER......	387	100.0	90.8	3.6	.1	-	-	-	5.5
UNDER 1000 POUNDS.....	-	100.0	5.2	92.9	-	1.9	-	-	-
1000 TO 9999 POUNDS...	5	100.0	1.3	88.5	10.2	-	-	-	-
10000 TO 29999 POUNDS.	4	100.0	10.5	89.5	-	-	-	-	-
30000 TO 59999 POUNDS.	5	100.0	12.6	87.4	-	-	-	-	-
60000 TO 89999 POUNDS.	102	100.0	100.0	-	-	-	-	-	-
90000 POUNDS AND OVER.	269	100.0	92.1	-	-	-	-	-	7.9

Note: Detail may not add to total due to rounding. The introductory table shows the estimates of sampling variability for tons; sampling variability for ton-miles has not been estimated. See the map in the Introduction for the States comprising the geographic divisions of the United States.

Shipments excluded from the survey are those moving by pipeline (primarily petroleum products from refineries, parcel post shipments, and commodities moved by own power (motorized vehicles, aircraft, etc.) or towed (prefabricated buildings, etc.). Local shipments (commodities shipped less than 25 miles from the plant) and shipments within the same city are also excluded. Shipments to Alaska and Hawaii from the 48 conterminous States and the District of Columbia are included; however, no data were obtained for shipments originating in Alaska and Hawaii.

- Represents zero or rounds to zero.   (D) Withheld to avoid disclosing figures for individual companies.

[1]Production of this commodity is concentrated in the geographic divisions shown; figures and distributions for geographic divisions not shown are included in the total.

[2]Distances of shipments to foreign destinations are calculated only to the U.S. port of exit.

[3]Includes only shipments represented by bills of lading and invoices. Summary records which did not show individual weights of shipments are not included.

Leather and Leather Products

CONTENTS

[Page numbers listed here omit the State prefix number that appears as part of the number for each page]

TABLES   (The tables listed below are shown for each of the Transportation Commodity Classification groups in this report)

        Comparisons of Tons and Ton-Miles of Shipments for Geographic Divisions of Origin and for
           Sampling Variability: 1972 and 1967

      1. Percent Distribution of Geographic Division of Origin and Distance Shipped, by Means of
         Transport: 1972

      2. Percent Distribution of Geographic Division of Origin and Means of Transport, by Geographic
         Division of Destination: 1972

      3. Percent Distribution of Geographic Division of Destination and Means of Transport, by Geographic
         Division of Origin: 1972

      4. Percent Distribution of Distance Shipped and Weight of Shipment, by Means of Transport: 1972

TCC 311. Leather

Comparisons of Tons and Ton-Miles of Shipments for
Geographic Divisions of Origin and for Sampling Variability: 1972 and 1967

Geographic division of origin	Estimates				Relative sampling variability in tons (percent)	
	1972		1967		1972	1967
	Tons (thousands)	Ton-miles (millions)	Tons (thousands)	Ton-miles (millions)		
U.S. total	327	143	610	191	22.0	(*)
New England	122	44	(*)	(*)	47.9	(*)
Middle Atlantic	35	20	(*)	(*)	43.6	(*)
East North Central	66	29	(*)	(*)	39.9	(*)
West North Central	(D)	(D)	(*)	(*)	(*)	(*)
South Atlantic	(D)	(D)	(*)	(*)	(*)	(*)
East South Central	(D)	(D)	(*)	(*)	(*)	(*).
West South Central	(D)	(D)	(*)	(*)	(*)	(*)
Mountain	(D)	(D)	(*)	(*)	(*)	(*)
Pacific	(D)	(D)	(*)	(*)	(*)	(*)

— Represents or rounds to zero.   (D) Withheld to avoid disclosing figures for individual companies.   (*) Data not published.

TABLE 1. **TCC GROUP 311—Percent Distribution of Geographic Division of Origin and Distance Shipped, by Means of Transport: 1972**

Geographic division of origin[1] and distance shipped[2]	Number	Percent distribution by means of transport							
		All means of transport	Rail	Motor carrier	Private truck	Air	Water	Other	Unknown
TONS OF SHIPMENTS	(thousands of tons)								
U.S. TOTAL.........	327	100.0	4.6	53.2	37.8	.2	-	2.8	1.4
NEW ENGLAND............	122	100.0	-	68.6	30.6	.4	-	-	.4
UNDER 100 MILES......	26	100.0	-	79.4	20.6	-	-	-	-
100 TO 199 MILES......	51	100.0	-	40.6	59.3	-	-	.1	-
200 TO 299 MILES......	7	100.0	-	95.1	.1	-	-	.1	4.7
300 TO 499 MILES......	7	100.0	-	96.5	3.0	-	-	.1	.4
500 TO 999 MILES......	18	100.0	-	96.4	2.9	.3	-	-	.5
1000 TO 1499 MILES....	7	100.0	-	83.3	11.1	5.5	-	.1	-
1500 MILES OR OVER....	3	100.0	-	99.9	-	-	-	.1	-
MIDDLE ATLANTIC.........	35	100.0	9.3	66.9	23.6	.1	-	-	-
UNDER 100 MILES......	2	100.0	-	77.0	23.0	-	-	-	-
100 TO 199 MILES......	8	100.0	-	50.2	49.7	-	-	-	.1
200 TO 299 MILES......	3	100.0	-	90.4	9.6	-	-	-	-
300 TO 499 MILES......	3	100.0	14.6	47.8	37.6	-	-	-	-
500 TO 999 MILES......	12	100.0	22.4	63.9	13.4	.3	-	-	-
1000 TO 1499 MILES....	-	100.0	-	99.7	-	.3	-	-	-
1500 MILES OR OVER....	3	100.0	-	100.0	-	-	-	-	-
EAST NORTH CENTRAL......	66	100.0	13.3	47.8	19.4	.2	-	13.3	6.0
UNDER 100 MILES......	17	100.0	44.6	37.1	12.6	-	-	5.8	-
100 TO 199 MILES......	5	100.0	-	79.9	.7	.2	-	19.2	-
200 TO 299 MILES......	5	100.0	-	6.0	94.0	-	-	-	-
300 TO 499 MILES......	7	100.0	-	49.9	12.4	-	-	37.7	-
500 TO 999 MILES......	28	100.0	3.1	52.6	16.5	.2	-	13.6	14.0
1000 TO 1499 MILES....	1	100.0	-	97.2	-	2.8	-	-	-
1500 MILES OR OVER....	-	100.0	-	82.9	15.4	1.8	-	-	-
TON-MILES OF SHIPMENTS	(millions of ton-miles)								
U.S. TOTAL.........	143	100.0	4.4	62.4	26.9	.5	-	3.3	2.5
NEW ENGLAND............	44	100.0	-	85.9	12.6	1.1	-	.1	.4
UNDER 100 MILES......	1	100.0	-	64.6	35.3	-	-	-	-
100 TO 199 MILES......	6	100.0	-	45.7	54.3	-	-	-	-
200 TO 299 MILES......	1	100.0	-	95.9	.1	-	-	-	3.9
300 TO 499 MILES......	2	100.0	-	96.6	2.9	-	-	.1	.4
500 TO 999 MILES......	15	100.0	-	96.7	2.6	.2	-	.1	.5
1000 TO 1499 MILES....	8	100.0	-	83.8	11.3	4.9	-	-	-
1500 MILES OR OVER....	7	100.0	-	99.9	-	-	-	.1	-
MIDDLE ATLANTIC.........	20	100.0	10.0	77.0	12.8	.2	-	-	-
UNDER 100 MILES......	-	100.0	-	76.9	23.1	-	-	-	-
100 TO 199 MILES......	1	100.0	-	53.9	45.9	-	-	-	-
200 TO 299 MILES......	-	100.0	-	90.3	9.7	-	-	-	.2
300 TO 499 MILES......	1	100.0	17.5	39.3	43.3	-	-	-	-
500 TO 999 MILES......	7	100.0	21.9	62.2	15.6	.4	-	-	-
1000 TO 1499 MILES....	1	100.0	-	99.7	-	.3	-	-	-
1500 MILES OR OVER....	7	100.0	-	100.0	-	-	-	-	-
EAST NORTH CENTRAL......	29	100.0	4.9	50.7	16.9	.4	-	15.5	11.7
UNDER 100 MILES......	1	100.0	48.6	37.3	8.2	-	-	5.9	-
100 TO 199 MILES......	-	100.0	-	81.8	1.0	.1	-	17.1	-
200 TO 299 MILES......	1	100.0	-	6.2	93.8	-	-	-	-
300 TO 499 MILES......	2	100.0	-	51.2	13.8	-	-	35.0	-
500 TO 999 MILES......	20	100.0	3.7	48.4	15.0	.2	-	16.0	16.7
1000 TO 1499 MILES....	1	100.0	-	97.2	-	2.8	-	-	-
1500 MILES OR OVER....	-	100.0	-	83.3	15.0	1.6	-	-	-

See footnotes at end of table 4.

TABLE 2. **TCC GROUP 311—Percent Distribution of Geographic Division of Origin and Means of Transport, by Geographic Division of Destination: 1972**

Geographic division of origin[1] and means of transport	Number	Percent distribution by division of destination									
		U.S. total	New England	Middle Atlantic	East North Central	West North Central	South Atlantic	East South Central	West South Central	Mountain	Pacific
TONS OF SHIPMENTS	(thousands of tons)										
U.S. TOTAL..............	327	100.0	35.7	15.5	21.2	5.5	3.9	9.6	3.6	.7	4.3
RAIL...................	15	100.0	22.1	-	77.9	-	-	-	-	-	-
MOTOR CARRIER..........	174	100.0	26.1	19.4	17.7	5.3	6.8	9.0	6.4	1.3	8.0
PRIVATE TRUCK..........	123	100.0	48.7	13.2	19.8	5.0	.5	12.1	.5	-	.2
AIR....................	-	100.0	7.8	8.6	7.8	67.1	.7	.2	6.6	.6	.6
WATER..................	-	100.0	-	-	-	-	-	-	-	-	-
OTHER..................	9	100.0	35.4	6.6	23.6	23.6	1.3	8.4	.6	-	.4
UNKNOWN................	4	100.0	97.2	1.0	1.8	-	-	-	-	-	-

See footnotes at end of table 4.

TABLE 2. **TCC GROUP 311—Percent Distribution of Geographic Division of Origin and Means of Transport, by Geographic Division of Destination: 1972**—Continued

Geographic division of origin[1] and means of transport	Number	Percent distribution by division of destination									
		U.S. total	New England	Middle Atlantic	East North Central	West North Central	South Atlantic	East South Central	West South Central	Mountain	Pacific
TONS OF SHIPMENTS	(thousands of tons)										
NEW ENGLAND............	122	100.0	60.3	15.9	8.7	2.8	2.1	5.3	3.9	.2	.9
RAIL.................	-	100.0	-	-	-	-	-	-	-	-	-
MOTOR CARRIER.........	84	100.0	44.7	22.9	11.9	2.9	2.9	7.7	5.5	.3	1.3
PRIVATE TRUCK.........	37	100.0	95.7	.6	1.3	1.4	.4	.1	.5	-	-
AIR..................	-	100.0	-	-	9.2	89.6	.8	.2	-	-	.2
WATER................	-	100.0	-	-	-	-	-	-	-	-	-
OTHER................	-	100.0	54.2	16.9	7.6	9.5	3.1	3.1	4.8	-	.8
UNKNOWN..............	-	100.0	76.1	6.6	17.3	-	-	-	-	-	-
MIDDLE ATLANTIC........	35	100.0	14.7	20.3	30.0	5.4	6.1	12.5	2.1	.8	8.1
RAIL.................	3	100.0	-	-	100.0	-	-	-	-	-	-
MOTOR CARRIER.........	23	100.0	20.9	25.4	8.6	1.0	9.1	18.7	3.1	1.2	12.1
PRIVATE TRUCK.........	8	100.0	3.1	13.9	63.4	19.6	.1	-	-	-	-
AIR..................	-	100.0	-	1.8	-	91.5	-	-	6.7	-	-
WATER................	-	100.0	-	-	-	-	-	-	-	-	-
OTHER................	-	100.0	-	-	-	-	-	-	-	-	-
UNKNOWN..............	-	100.0	-	100.0	-	-	-	-	-	-	-
EAST NORTH CENTRAL......	66	100.0	22.1	9.1	43.1	6.3	10.4	3.7	4.8	.1	.5
RAIL.................	8	100.0	10.0	-	90.0	-	-	-	-	-	-
MOTOR CARRIER.........	32	100.0	7.1	14.8	36.4	5.7	20.5	4.6	9.8	.1	.9
PRIVATE TRUCK.........	13	100.0	33.3	5.8	53.8	2.3	2.9	1.4	-	-	.4
AIR..................	-	100.0	45.6	3.8	8.3	-	.6	-	36.0	3.7	2.0
WATER................	-	100.0	-	-	-	-	-	-	-	-	-
OTHER................	8	100.0	36.6	6.8	24.0	23.2	-	8.7	.6	-	-
UNKNOWN..............	4	100.0	100.0	-	-	-	-	-	-	-	-
TON-MILES OF SHIPMENTS	(millions of ton-miles)										
U.S. TOTAL............	143	100.0	24.8	10.9	18.3	8.5	5.6	9.7	10.2	1.6	10.6
RAIL.................	6	100.0	53.7	-	46.3	-	-	-	-	-	-
MOTOR CARRIER.........	89	100.0	7.6	13.1	15.7	7.5	8.3	13.4	15.4	2.6	16.5
PRIVATE TRUCK.........	38	100.0	49.3	8.4	23.2	11.2	1.2	3.9	1.8	-	1.0
AIR..................	-	100.0	5.7	18.2	4.6	62.4	.4	.2	6.8	.9	.9
WATER................	-	100.0	-	-	-	-	-	-	-	-	-
OTHER................	4	100.0	58.4	9.0	5.1	15.0	1.9	7.5	1.1	-	1.8
UNKNOWN..............	3	100.0	97.6	.4	2.0	-	-	-	-	-	-
NEW ENGLAND............	44	100.0	16.2	12.3	20.4	8.1	5.1	14.1	16.6	1.0	6.2
RAIL.................	-	100.0	-	-	-	-	-	-	-	-	-
MOTOR CARRIER.........	37	100.0	8.0	14.0	22.5	6.8	5.5	16.2	18.6	1.2	7.3
PRIVATE TRUCK.........	5	100.0	73.2	1.5	6.6	10.0	2.6	.8	5.2	-	-
AIR..................	-	100.0	-	-	7.0	91.8	.5	.2	-	-	.5
WATER................	-	100.0	-	-	-	-	-	-	-	-	-
OTHER................	-	100.0	16.2	12.5	13.5	22.9	6.3	6.9	17.4	-	4.3
UNKNOWN..............	-	100.0	46.3	7.2	46.4	-	-	-	-	-	-
MIDDLE ATLANTIC........	20	100.0	6.4	4.2	21.0	7.4	5.3	14.8	4.8	2.4	33.7
RAIL.................	2	100.0	-	-	100.0	-	-	-	-	-	-
MOTOR CARRIER.........	15	100.0	7.7	4.5	7.2	1.4	6.9	19.2	6.2	3.2	43.8
PRIVATE TRUCK.........	2	100.0	4.0	5.4	42.6	48.0	-	-	10.5	-	-
AIR..................	-	100.0	-	-	-	89.5	-	-	-	-	-
WATER................	-	100.0	-	-	-	-	-	-	-	-	-
OTHER................	-	100.0	-	-	-	-	-	-	-	-	-
UNKNOWN..............	-	100.0	-	100.0	-	-	-	-	-	-	-
EAST NORTH CENTRAL......	29	100.0	39.8	13.0	12.1	4.9	14.6	3.8	9.5	.2	2.1
RAIL.................	1	100.0	53.2	-	46.8	-	-	-	-	-	-
MOTOR CARRIER.........	14	100.0	12.6	20.5	9.1	4.5	26.7	4.5	18.1	.4	3.5
PRIVATE TRUCK.........	4	100.0	55.6	6.6	26.3	1.5	6.2	1.7	-	-	2.0
AIR..................	-	100.0	40.6	2.4	1.2	-	.3	-	45.0	6.4	4.0
WATER................	-	100.0	-	-	-	-	-	-	-	-	-
OTHER................	4	100.0	61.6	9.5	5.0	15.0	-	7.9	1.1	-	-
UNKNOWN..............	3	100.0	100.0	-	-	-	-	-	-	-	-

See footnotes at end of table 4.

TABLE 3. **TCC GROUP 311**—Percent Distribution of Geographic Division of Destination and Means of Transport, by Geographic Division of Origin: 1972

Geographic division of destination and means of transport	Number	Percent distribution by division of origin[1]									
		U.S. total	New England	Middle Atlantic	East North Central	West North Central	South Atlantic	East South Central	West South Central	Mountain	Pacific
TONS OF SHIPMENTS	(thousands of tons)										
U.S. TOTAL............	327	100.0	37.5	10.7	20.4	(D)	(D)	(D)	(D)	(D)	(D)
RAIL.................	15	100.0	-	21.6	59.2	(D)	(D)	(D)	(D)	(D)	(D)
MOTOR CARRIER........	174	100.0	48.3	13.5	18.4	(D)	(D)	(D)	(D)	(D)	(D)
PRIVATE TRUCK........	123	100.0	30.4	6.7	10.5	(D)	(D)	(D)	(D)	(D)	(D)
AIR..................	-	100.0	69.0	5.9	17.2	(D)	(D)	(D)	(D)	(D)	(D)
WATER................	-	100.0	-	-	-	(D)	(D)	(D)	(D)	(D)	(D)
OTHER................	9	100.0	.5	-	95.8	(D)	(D)	(D)	(D)	(D)	(D)
UNKNOWN..............	4	100.0	10.5	.3	89.2	(D)	(D)	(D)	(D)	(D)	(D)
NEW ENGLAND..........	116	100.0	63.4	4.4	12.7	(D)	(D)	(D)	(D)	(D)	(D)
RAIL.................	3	100.0	-	-	26.8	(D)	(D)	(D)	(D)	(D)	(D)
MOTOR CARRIER........	45	100.0	82.7	10.8	5.0	(D)	(D)	(D)	(D)	(D)	(D)
PRIVATE TRUCK........	60	100.0	59.7	.4	7.2	(D)	(D)	(D)	(D)	(D)	(D)
AIR..................	-	100.0	-	-	100.0	(D)	(D)	(D)	(D)	(D)	(D)
WATER................	-	100.0	-	-	-	(D)	(D)	(D)	(D)	(D)	(D)
OTHER................	3	100.0	.8	-	99.1	(D)	(D)	(D)	(D)	(D)	(D)
UNKNOWN..............	4	100.0	8.2	-	91.8	(D)	(D)	(D)	(D)	(D)	(D)
MIDDLE ATLANTIC......	50	100.0	38.4	14.0	12.0	(D)	(D)	(D)	(D)	(D)	(D)
RAIL.................	-	100.0	-	-	-	(D)	(D)	(D)	(D)	(D)	(D)
MOTOR CARRIER........	33	100.0	57.0	17.7	14.0	(D)	(D)	(D)	(D)	(D)	(D)
PRIVATE TRUCK........	16	100.0	1.4	7.0	4.6	(D)	(D)	(D)	(D)	(D)	(D)
AIR..................	-	100.0	-	1.2	7.6	(D)	(D)	(D)	(D)	(D)	(D)
WATER................	-	100.0	-	-	-	(D)	(D)	(D)	(D)	(D)	(D)
OTHER................	-	100.0	1.4	-	98.3	(D)	(D)	(D)	(D)	(D)	(D)
UNKNOWN..............	-	100.0	73.0	27.0	-	(D)	(D)	(D)	(D)	(D)	(D)
EAST NORTH CENTRAL...	69	100.0	15.3	15.1	41.5	(D)	(D)	(D)	(D)	(D)	(D)
RAIL.................	11	100.0	-	27.8	68.4	(D)	(D)	(D)	(D)	(D)	(D)
MOTOR CARRIER........	30	100.0	32.5	6.5	37.8	(D)	(D)	(D)	(D)	(D)	(D)
PRIVATE TRUCK........	24	100.0	2.0	21.4	28.5	(D)	(D)	(D)	(D)	(D)	(D)
AIR..................	-	100.0	81.6	-	18.4	(D)	(D)	(D)	(D)	(D)	(D)
WATER................	-	100.0	-	-	-	(D)	(D)	(D)	(D)	(D)	(D)
OTHER................	2	100.0	.2	-	97.5	(D)	(D)	(D)	(D)	(D)	(D)
UNKNOWN..............	-	100.0	100.0	-	-	(D)	(D)	(D)	(D)	(D)	(D)
WEST NORTH CENTRAL...	18	100.0	18.8	10.4	23.2	(D)	(D)	(D)	(D)	(D)	(D)
RAIL.................	-	100.0	-	-	-	(D)	(D)	(D)	(D)	(D)	(D)
MOTOR CARRIER........	9	100.0	26.5	2.4	19.8	(D)	(D)	(D)	(D)	(D)	(D)
PRIVATE TRUCK........	6	100.0	8.3	26.3	4.8	(D)	(D)	(D)	(D)	(D)	(D)
AIR..................	-	100.0	92.0	8.0	-	(D)	(D)	(D)	(D)	(D)	(D)
WATER................	-	100.0	-	-	-	(D)	(D)	(D)	(D)	(D)	(D)
OTHER................	2	100.0	.2	-	94.2	(D)	(D)	(D)	(D)	(D)	(D)
UNKNOWN..............	-	100.0	-	-	-	(D)	(D)	(D)	(D)	(D)	(D)
SOUTH ATLANTIC.......	12	100.0	20.6	16.8	54.9	(D)	(D)	(D)	(D)	(D)	(D)
RAIL.................	-	100.0	-	-	-	(D)	(D)	(D)	(D)	(D)	(D)
MOTOR CARRIER........	11	100.0	20.7	17.9	55.3	(D)	(D)	(D)	(D)	(D)	(D)
PRIVATE TRUCK........	-	100.0	21.3	.7	57.6	(D)	(D)	(D)	(D)	(D)	(D)
AIR..................	-	100.0	85.3	-	14.7	(D)	(D)	(D)	(D)	(D)	(D)
WATER................	-	100.0	-	-	-	(D)	(D)	(D)	(D)	(D)	(D)
OTHER................	-	100.0	1.3	-	-	(D)	(D)	(D)	(D)	(D)	(D)
UNKNOWN..............	-	100.0	-	-	-	(D)	(D)	(D)	(D)	(D)	(D)
EAST SOUTH CENTRAL...	31	100.0	20.6	13.9	7.8	(D)	(D)	(D)	(D)	(D)	(D)
RAIL.................	-	100.0	-	-	-	(D)	(D)	(D)	(D)	(D)	(D)
MOTOR CARRIER........	15	100.0	41.1	27.9	9.5	(D)	(D)	(D)	(D)	(D)	(D)
PRIVATE TRUCK........	15	100.0	.3	-	1.2	(D)	(D)	(D)	(D)	(D)	(D)
AIR..................	-	100.0	73.6	-	-	(D)	(D)	(D)	(D)	(D)	(D)
WATER................	-	100.0	-	-	-	(D)	(D)	(D)	(D)	(D)	(D)
OTHER................	-	100.0	.2	-	99.8	(D)	(D)	(D)	(D)	(D)	(D)
UNKNOWN..............	-	100.0	-	-	-	(D)	(D)	(D)	(D)	(D)	(D)
WEST SOUTH CENTRAL...	11	100.0	40.7	6.2	27.4	(D)	(D)	(D)	(D)	(D)	(D)
RAIL.................	-	100.0	-	-	-	(D)	(D)	(D)	(D)	(D)	(D)
MOTOR CARRIER........	11	100.0	41.4	6.6	28.2	(D)	(D)	(D)	(D)	(D)	(D)
PRIVATE TRUCK........	-	100.0	34.3	-	-	(D)	(D)	(D)	(D)	(D)	(D)
AIR..................	-	100.0	-	6.0	94.0	(D)	(D)	(D)	(D)	(D)	(D)
WATER................	-	100.0	-	-	-	(D)	(D)	(D)	(D)	(D)	(D)
OTHER................	-	100.0	4.0	-	91.8	(D)	(D)	(D)	(D)	(D)	(D)
UNKNOWN..............	-	100.0	-	-	-	(D)	(D)	(D)	(D)	(D)	(D)
MOUNTAIN.............	2	100.0	9.7	12.6	2.1	(D)	(D)	(D)	(D)	(D)	(D)
RAIL.................	-	100.0	-	-	-	(D)	(D)	(D)	(D)	(D)	(D)
MOTOR CARRIER........	2	100.0	9.7	12.6	1.9	(D)	(D)	(D)	(D)	(D)	(D)
PRIVATE TRUCK........	-	100.0	-	-	-	(D)	(D)	(D)	(D)	(D)	(D)
AIR..................	-	100.0	-	-	100.0	(D)	(D)	(D)	(D)	(D)	(D)
WATER................	-	100.0	-	-	-	(D)	(D)	(D)	(D)	(D)	(D)
OTHER................	-	100.0	-	-	-	(D)	(D)	(D)	(D)	(D)	(D)
UNKNOWN..............	-	100.0	-	-	-	(D)	(D)	(D)	(D)	(D)	(D)
PACIFIC..............	14	100.0	7.5	20.0	2.4	(D)	(D)	(D)	(D)	(D)	(D)
RAIL.................	-	100.0	-	-	-	(D)	(D)	(D)	(D)	(D)	(D)
MOTOR CARRIER........	13	100.0	7.6	20.4	2.0	(D)	(D)	(D)	(D)	(D)	(D)
PRIVATE TRUCK........	-	100.0	-	-	26.6	(D)	(D)	(D)	(D)	(D)	(D)
AIR..................	-	100.0	21.6	-	55.2	(D)	(D)	(D)	(D)	(D)	(D)
WATER................	-	100.0	-	-	-	(D)	(D)	(D)	(D)	(D)	(D)
OTHER................	-	100.0	1.0	-	-	(D)	(D)	(D)	(D)	(D)	(D)
UNKNOWN..............	-	100.0	-	-	-	(D)	(D)	(D)	(D)	(D)	(D)

See footnotes at end of table 4.

TABLE 3. **TCC GROUP 311**—Percent Distribution of Geographic Division of Destination and Means of Transport, by Geographic Division of Origin: 1972—Continued

Geographic division of destination and means of transport	Number (millions of ton-miles)	Percent distribution by division of origin [1]									
		U.S. total	New England	Middle Atlantic	East North Central	West North Central	South Atlantic	East South Central	West South Central	Mountain	Pacific
TON-MILES OF SHIPMENTS											
U.S. TOTAL.............	143	100.0	30.7	14.0	20.2	(D)	(D)	(D)	(D)	(D)	(D)
RAIL..............	6	100.0	-	31.8	22.4	(D)	(D)	(D)	(D)	(D)	(D)
MOTOR CARRIER.........	89	100.0	42.3	17.3	16.4	(D)	(D)	(D)	(D)	(D)	(D)
PRIVATE TRUCK.........	38	100.0	14.4	6.7	12.7	(D)	(D)	(D)	(D)	(D)	(D)
AIR................	-	100.0	63.3	4.7	14.0	(D)	(D)	(D)	(D)	(D)	(D)
WATER..............	-	100.0	-	-	-	(D)	(D)	(D)	(D)	(D)	(D)
OTHER..............	4	100.0	.5	-	94.6	(D)	(D)	(D)	(D)	(D)	(D)
UNKNOWN............	3	100.0	4.4	.1	95.6	(D)	(D)	(D)	(D)	(D)	(D)
NEW ENGLAND............	35	100.0	20.1	3.6	32.5	(D)	(D)	(D)	(D)	(D)	(D)
RAIL..............	3	100.0	-	-	22.2	(D)	(D)	(D)	(D)	(D)	(D)
MOTOR CARRIER.........	6	100.0	44.5	17.5	27.4	(D)	(D)	(D)	(D)	(D)	(D)
PRIVATE TRUCK.........	19	100.0	21.3	.5	14.3	(D)	(D)	(D)	(D)	(D)	(D)
AIR................	-	100.0	-	-	100.0	(D)	(D)	(D)	(D)	(D)	(D)
WATER..............	-	100.0	-	-	-	(D)	(D)	(D)	(D)	(D)	(D)
OTHER..............	2	100.0	.1	-	99.8	(D)	(D)	(D)	(D)	(D)	(D)
UNKNOWN............	3	100.0	2.1	-	97.9	(D)	(D)	(D)	(D)	(D)	(D)
MIDDLE ATLANTIC.........	15	100.0	34.8	5.4	24.2	(D)	(D)	(D)	(D)	(D)	(D)
RAIL..............	-	100.0	-	-	-	(D)	(D)	(D)	(D)	(D)	(D)
MOTOR CARRIER.........	11	100.0	45.2	5.9	25.6	(D)	(D)	(D)	(D)	(D)	(D)
PRIVATE TRUCK.........	3	100.0	2.6	4.3	10.0	(D)	(D)	(D)	(D)	(D)	(D)
AIR................	-	100.0	-	-	1.9	(D)	(D)	(D)	(D)	(D)	(D)
WATER..............	-	100.0	-	-	-	(D)	(D)	(D)	(D)	(D)	(D)
OTHER..............	-	100.0	.7	-	99.2	(D)	(D)	(D)	(D)	(D)	(D)
UNKNOWN............	-	100.0	83.9	16.1	-	(D)	(D)	(D)	(D)	(D)	(D)
EAST NORTH CENTRAL......	26	100.0	34.3	16.1	13.4	(D)	(D)	(D)	(D)	(D)	(D)
RAIL..............	2	100.0	-	68.8	22.7	(D)	(D)	(D)	(D)	(D)	(D)
MOTOR CARRIER.........	14	100.0	60.8	7.9	9.6	(D)	(D)	(D)	(D)	(D)	(D)
PRIVATE TRUCK.........	8	100.0	4.1	12.3	14.4	(D)	(D)	(D)	(D)	(D)	(D)
AIR................	-	100.0	96.3	-	3.7	(D)	(D)	(D)	(D)	(D)	(D)
WATER..............	-	100.0	-	-	-	(D)	(D)	(D)	(D)	(D)	(D)
OTHER..............	-	100.0	1.3	-	91.8	(D)	(D)	(D)	(D)	(D)	(D)
UNKNOWN............	-	100.0	100.0	-	-	(D)	(D)	(D)	(D)	(D)	(D)
WEST NORTH CENTRAL......	12	100.0	29.3	12.2	11.6	(D)	(D)	(D)	(D)	(D)	(D)
RAIL..............	-	100.0	-	-	-	(D)	(D)	(D)	(D)	(D)	(D)
MOTOR CARRIER.........	6	100.0	38.4	3.2	9.9	(D)	(D)	(D)	(D)	(D)	(D)
PRIVATE TRUCK.........	4	100.0	12.9	28.6	1.8	(D)	(D)	(D)	(D)	(D)	(D)
AIR................	-	100.0	93.2	6.8	-	(D)	(D)	(D)	(D)	(D)	(D)
WATER..............	-	100.0	-	-	-	(D)	(D)	(D)	(D)	(D)	(D)
OTHER..............	-	100.0	.8	-	94.1	(D)	(D)	(D)	(D)	(D)	(D)
UNKNOWN............	-	100.0	-	-	-	(D)	(D)	(D)	(D)	(D)	(D)
SOUTH ATLANTIC..........	8	100.0	28.0	13.5	52.9	(D)	(D)	(D)	(D)	(D)	(D)
RAIL..............	-	100.0	-	-	-	(D)	(D)	(D)	(D)	(D)	(D)
MOTOR CARRIER.........	7	100.0	28.1	14.5	52.8	(D)	(D)	(D)	(D)	(D)	(D)
PRIVATE TRUCK.........	-	100.0	31.0	.1	65.0	(D)	(D)	(D)	(D)	(D)	(D)
AIR................	-	100.0	88.2	-	11.8	(D)	(D)	(D)	(D)	(D)	(D)
WATER..............	-	100.0	-	-	-	(D)	(D)	(D)	(D)	(D)	(D)
OTHER..............	-	100.0	1.7	-	-	(D)	(D)	(D)	(D)	(D)	(D)
UNKNOWN............	-	100.0	-	-	-	(D)	(D)	(D)	(D)	(D)	(D)
EAST SOUTH CENTRAL......	13	100.0	44.7	21.4	7.9	(D)	(D)	(D)	(D)	(D)	(D)
RAIL..............	-	100.0	-	-	-	(D)	(D)	(D)	(D)	(D)	(D)
MOTOR CARRIER.........	12	100.0	51.2	24.7	5.5	(D)	(D)	(D)	(D)	(D)	(D)
PRIVATE TRUCK.........	1	100.0	3.0	-	5.5	(D)	(D)	(D)	(D)	(D)	(D)
AIR................	-	100.0	60.4	-	-	(D)	(D)	(D)	(D)	(D)	(D)
WATER..............	-	100.0	-	-	-	(D)	(D)	(D)	(D)	(D)	(D)
OTHER..............	-	100.0	.5	-	99.5	(D)	(D)	(D)	(D)	(D)	(D)
UNKNOWN............	-	100.0	-	-	-	(D)	(D)	(D)	(D)	(D)	(D)
WEST SOUTH CENTRAL......	14	100.0	50.2	6.6	18.9	(D)	(D)	(D)	(D)	(D)	(D)
RAIL..............	-	100.0	-	-	-	(D)	(D)	(D)	(D)	(D)	(D)
MOTOR CARRIER.........	13	100.0	51.1	7.0	19.4	(D)	(D)	(D)	(D)	(D)	(D)
PRIVATE TRUCK.........	-	100.0	40.8	-	-	(D)	(D)	(D)	(D)	(D)	(D)
AIR................	-	100.0	-	7.3	92.7	(D)	(D)	(D)	(D)	(D)	(D)
WATER..............	-	100.0	-	-	-	(D)	(D)	(D)	(D)	(D)	(D)
OTHER..............	-	100.0	7.7	-	87.0	(D)	(D)	(D)	(D)	(D)	(D)
UNKNOWN............	-	100.0	-	-	-	(D)	(D)	(D)	(D)	(D)	(D)
MOUNTAIN...............	2	100.0	19.1	21.4	3.0	(D)	(D)	(D)	(D)	(D)	(D)
RAIL..............	-	100.0	-	-	-	(D)	(D)	(D)	(D)	(D)	(D)
MOTOR CARRIER.........	2	100.0	19.1	21.5	2.7	(D)	(D)	(D)	(D)	(D)	(D)
PRIVATE TRUCK.........	-	100.0	-	-	100.0	(D)	(D)	(D)	(D)	(D)	(D)
AIR................	-	100.0	-	-	-	(D)	(D)	(D)	(D)	(D)	(D)
WATER..............	-	100.0	-	-	-	(D)	(D)	(D)	(D)	(D)	(D)
OTHER..............	-	100.0	-	-	-	(D)	(D)	(D)	(D)	(D)	(D)
UNKNOWN............	-	100.0	-	-	-	(D)	(D)	(D)	(D)	(D)	(D)
PACIFIC................	15	100.0	18.1	44.6	4.0	(D)	(D)	(D)	(D)	(D)	(D)
RAIL..............	-	100.0	-	-	-	(D)	(D)	(D)	(D)	(D)	(D)
MOTOR CARRIER.........	14	100.0	18.6	46.0	3.4	(D)	(D)	(D)	(D)	(D)	(D)
PRIVATE TRUCK.........	-	100.0	-	-	27.0	(D)	(D)	(D)	(D)	(D)	(D)
AIR................	-	100.0	34.5	-	60.4	(D)	(D)	(D)	(D)	(D)	(D)
WATER..............	-	100.0	-	-	-	(D)	(D)	(D)	(D)	(D)	(D)
OTHER..............	-	100.0	1.2	-	-	(D)	(D)	(D)	(D)	(D)	(D)
UNKNOWN............	-	100.0	-	-	-	(D)	(D)	(D)	(D)	(D)	(D)

See footnotes at end of table 4.

TABLE 4. **TCC GROUP 311—Percent Distribution of Distance Shipped and Weight of Shipment, by Means of Transport: 1972**

Distance shipped and weight of shipment [2] [3]	Number	Percent distribution by means of transport							
		All means of transport	Rail	Motor carrier	Private truck	Air	Water	Other	Unknown
TONS OF SHIPMENTS	(thousands of tons)								
U.S. TOTAL..........	259	100.0	5.8	54.8	33.8	.3	-	3.6	1.7
UNDER 100 MILES.........	56	100.0	14.2	56.4	27.5	-	-	1.9	-
UNDER 1000 POUNDS.....	4	100.0	-	91.3	8.7	-	-	-	-
1000 TO 9999 POUNDS...	21	100.0	-	78.7	21.3	-	-	-	-
10000 TO 29999 POUNDS.	10	100.0	-	14.2	75.8	-	-	10.0	-
30000 TO 59999 POUNDS.	10	100.0	42.7	33.9	23.4	-	-	-	-
60000 TO 89999 POUNDS.	6	100.0	54.2	45.8	-	-	-	-	-
90000 POUNDS AND OVER.	2	100.0	-	100.0	-	-	-	-	-
100 TO 199 MILES........	32	100.0	-	65.8	30.8	-	-	3.4	.1
UNDER 1000 POUNDS.....	4	100.0	-	83.1	16.2	-	-	.3	.4
1000 TO 9999 POUNDS...	20	100.0	-	65.5	34.3	-	-	.2	-
10000 TO 29999 POUNDS.	6	100.0	-	51.0	32.6	-	-	16.4	-
30000 TO 59999 POUNDS.	-	100.0	-	100.0	-	-	-	-	-
60000 TO 89999 POUNDS.	-	100.0	-	-	-	-	-	-	-
90000 POUNDS AND OVER.	-	100.0	-	-	-	-	-	-	-
200 TO 299 MILES........	30	100.0	-	46.6	51.8	-	-	.3	1.2
UNDER 1000 POUNDS.....	2	100.0	-	85.0	11.2	-	-	3.8	-
1000 TO 9999 POUNDS...	9	100.0	-	72.8	23.5	-	-	-	3.7
10000 TO 29999 POUNDS.	9	100.0	-	46.4	53.6	-	-	-	-
30000 TO 59999 POUNDS.	7	100.0	-	-	100.0	-	-	-	-
60000 TO 89999 POUNDS.	-	100.0	-	-	-	-	-	-	-
90000 POUNDS AND OVER.	-	100.0	-	-	-	-	-	-	-
300 TO 499 MILES........	26	100.0	2.1	66.6	20.2	-	-	11.0	.1
UNDER 1000 POUNDS.....	4	100.0	-	90.7	6.9	-	-	1.6	.7
1000 TO 9999 POUNDS...	13	100.0	-	82.5	17.5	-	-	-	-
10000 TO 29999 POUNDS.	4	100.0	-	11.3	27.7	-	-	60.9	-
30000 TO 59999 POUNDS.	4	100.0	12.9	53.3	33.8	-	-	-	-
60000 TO 89999 POUNDS.	-	100.0	-	-	-	-	-	-	-
90000 POUNDS AND OVER.	-	100.0	-	-	-	-	-	-	-
500 TO 999 MILES........	89	100.0	4.5	44.7	41.5	.2	-	4.5	4.6
UNDER 1000 POUNDS.....	6	100.0	-	87.4	8.1	1.3	-	1.9	1.2
1000 TO 9999 POUNDS...	17	100.0	2.5	69.1	26.6	.3	-	1.4	-
10000 TO 29999 POUNDS.	21	100.0	3.4	31.6	45.1	-	-	14.1	5.8
30000 TO 59999 POUNDS.	40	100.0	6.7	31.1	54.0	-	-	1.5	6.7
60000 TO 89999 POUNDS.	2	100.0	2.5	97.5	-	-	-	-	-
90000 POUNDS AND OVER.	-	100.0	100.0	-	-	-	-	-	-
1000 TO 1499 MILES......	14	100.0	16.5	53.1	27.2	3.2	-	.1	-
UNDER 1000 POUNDS.....	2	100.0	-	72.1	23.0	4.5	-	.4	-
1000 TO 9999 POUNDS...	7	100.0	-	87.1	7.6	5.3	-	-	-
10000 TO 29999 POUNDS.	-	100.0	-	100.0	-	-	-	-	-
30000 TO 59999 POUNDS.	2	100.0	-	-	100.0	-	-	-	-
60000 TO 89999 POUNDS.	2	100.0	100.0	-	-	-	-	-	-
90000 POUNDS AND OVER.	-	100.0	-	-	-	-	-	-	-
1500 MILES OR OVER......	9	100.0	-	97.1	1.9	.6	-	.4	-
UNDER 1000 POUNDS.....	2	100.0	-	99.5	-	.3	-	.1	-
1000 TO 9999 POUNDS...	6	100.0	-	95.6	2.9	.9	-	.6	-
10000 TO 29999 POUNDS.	1	100.0	-	100.0	-	-	-	-	-
30000 TO 59999 POUNDS.	-	100.0	-	-	-	-	-	-	-
60000 TO 89999 POUNDS.	-	100.0	-	-	-	-	-	-	-
90000 POUNDS AND OVER.	-	100.0	-	-	-	-	-	-	-
TON-MILES OF SHIPMENTS	(millions of ton-miles)								
U.S. TOTAL..........	123	100.0	5.1	59.9	27.6	.6	-	3.9	2.9
UNDER 100 MILES.........	2	100.0	25.2	52.2	19.5	-	-	3.1	-
UNDER 1000 POUNDS.....	-	100.0	-	93.7	6.2	-	-	.1	-
1000 TO 9999 POUNDS...	-	100.0	-	78.3	21.7	-	-	-	-
10000 TO 29999 POUNDS.	-	100.0	-	25.7	56.8	-	-	17.5	-
30000 TO 59999 POUNDS.	-	100.0	52.4	37.2	10.4	-	-	-	-
60000 TO 89999 POUNDS.	-	100.0	72.6	27.4	-	-	-	-	-
90000 POUNDS AND OVER.	-	100.0	-	100.0	-	-	-	-	-
100 TO 199 MILES........	4	100.0	-	69.0	28.0	-	-	3.0	.1
UNDER 1000 POUNDS.....	-	100.0	-	86.1	13.1	-	-	.3	.4
1000 TO 9999 POUNDS...	3	100.0	-	69.6	30.3	-	-	.2	-
10000 TO 29999 POUNDS.	1	100.0	-	53.0	33.3	-	-	13.7	-
30000 TO 59999 POUNDS.	-	100.0	-	100.0	-	-	-	-	-
60000 TO 89999 POUNDS.	-	100.0	-	-	-	-	-	-	-
90000 POUNDS AND OVER.	-	100.0	-	-	-	-	-	-	-

See footnotes at end of table 4.

TABLE 4. **TCC GROUP 311—Percent Distribution of Distance Shipped and Weight of Shipment, by Means of Transport: 1972**—Continued

Distance shipped and weight of shipment[2][3]	Number	Percent distribution by means of transport							
		All means of transport	Rail	Motor carrier	Private truck	Air	Water	Other	Unknown
TON-MILES OF SHIPMENTS	(millions of ton-miles)								
200 TO 299 MILES	6	100.0	-	49.3	49.3	-	-	.4	1.0
UNDER 1000 POUNDS	-	100.0	-	84.9	11.0	-	-	4.2	-
1000 TO 9999 POUNDS	2	100.0	-	75.1	21.8	-	-	-	3.2
10000 TO 29999 POUNDS	2	100.0	-	51.4	48.6	-	-	-	-
30000 TO 59999 POUNDS	1	100.0	-	-	100.0	-	-	-	-
60000 TO 89999 POUNDS	-	100.0	-	-	-	-	-	-	-
90000 POUNDS AND OVER	-	100.0	-	-	-	-	-	-	-
300 TO 499 MILES	10	100.0	2.7	64.1	22.7	-	-	10.4	.1
UNDER 1000 POUNDS	1	100.0	-	90.9	6.6	-	-	1.7	.7
1000 TO 9999 POUNDS	5	100.0	-	80.2	19.8	-	-	-	-
10000 TO 29999 POUNDS	1	100.0	-	10.7	30.6	-	-	58.7	-
30000 TO 59999 POUNDS	1	100.0	16.5	44.2	39.3	-	-	-	-
60000 TO 89999 POUNDS	-	100.0	-	-	-	-	-	-	-
90000 POUNDS AND OVER	-	100.0	-	-	-	-	-	-	-
500 TO 999 MILES	59	100.0	4.6	48.1	35.8	.2	-	5.6	5.8
UNDER 1000 POUNDS	4	100.0	-	87.5	7.7	1.4	-	1.9	1.5
1000 TO 9999 POUNDS	11	100.0	2.1	73.0	22.9	.4	-	1.6	-
10000 TO 29999 POUNDS	14	100.0	3.6	30.9	40.2	-	-	17.8	7.5
30000 TO 59999 POUNDS	26	100.0	7.1	35.0	47.3	-	-	1.9	8.7
60000 TO 89999 POUNDS	2	100.0	1.7	98.3	-	-	-	-	-
90000 POUNDS AND OVER	-	100.0	100.0	-	-	-	-	-	-
1000 TO 1499 MILES	16	100.0	15.8	54.6	26.7	2.9	-	.1	-
UNDER 1000 POUNDS	2	100.0	-	70.9	24.6	4.0	-	.4	-
1000 TO 9999 POUNDS	8	100.0	-	87.7	7.6	4.7	-	-	-
10000 TO 29999 POUNDS	-	100.0	-	100.0	-	-	-	-	-
30000 TO 59999 POUNDS	3	100.0	-	-	100.0	-	-	-	-
60000 TO 89999 POUNDS	2	100.0	100.0	-	-	-	-	-	-
90000 POUNDS AND OVER	-	100.0	-	-	-	-	-	-	-
1500 MILES OR OVER	21	100.0	-	97.2	1.7	.7	-	.4	-
UNDER 1000 POUNDS	5	100.0	-	99.6	-	.3	-	.1	-
1000 TO 9999 POUNDS	13	100.0	-	95.7	2.7	1.0	-	.6	-
10000 TO 29999 POUNDS	2	100.0	-	100.0	-	-	-	-	-
30000 TO 59999 POUNDS	-	100.0	-	-	-	-	-	-	-
60000 TO 89999 POUNDS	-	100.0	-	-	-	-	-	-	-
90000 POUNDS AND OVER	-	100.0	-	-	-	-	-	-	-

Note: Detail may not add to total due to rounding. The introductory table shows the estimates of sampling variability for tons; sampling variability for ton-miles has not been estimated. See the map in the Introduction for the States comprising the geographic divisions of the United States.

Shipments excluded from the survey are those moving by pipeline (primarily petroleum products from refineries), parcel post shipments, and commodities moved by own power (motorized vehicles, aircraft, etc.) or towed (prefabricated buildings, etc.). Local shipments (commodities shipped less than 25 miles from the plant) and shipments within the same city are also excluded. Shipments to Alaska and Hawaii from the 48 conterminous States and the District of Columbia are included; however, no data were obtained for shipments originating in Alaska and Hawaii.

- Represents zero or rounds to zero.   (D) Withheld to avoid disclosing figures for individual companies.

[1]Production of this commodity is concentrated in the geographic divisions shown; figures and distributions for geographic divisions not shown are included in the total.

[2]Distances of shipments to foreign destinations are calculated only to the U.S. port of exit.

[3]Includes only shipments represented by bills of lading and invoices. Summary records which did not show individual weights of shipments are not included.

TCC 314. Footwear, Leather and Similar Materials

Comparisons of Tons and Ton-Miles of Shipments for
Geographic Divisions of Origin and for Sampling Variability: 1972 and 1967

Geographic division of origin	Estimates				Relative sampling variability in tons (percent)	
	1972		1967		1972	1967
	Tons (thousands)	Ton-miles (millions)	Tons (thousands)	Ton-miles (millions)		
U.S. total	614	285	404	238	11.9	16.0
New England	137	70	189	152	29.2	(*)
Middle Atlantic	73	46	33	16	33.8	(*)
East North Central	94	41	100	34	42.7	(*)
West North Central	48	9	23	9	39.2	(*)
South Atlantic	(D)	(D)	10	7	(*)	(*)
East South Central	112	30	38	12	34.6	(*)
West South Central	(D)	(D)	8	6	(*)	(*)
Mountain	—	—	—	—	—	—
Pacific	(D)	(D)	3	2	(*)	(*)

— Represents or rounds to zero.   (D) Withheld to avoid disclosing figures for individual companies.   (*) Data not published.

TABLE 1. TCC GROUP 314—Percent Distribution of Geographic Division of Origin and Distance Shipped, by Means of Transport: 1972

Geographic division of origin[1] and distance shipped[2]	Number	All means of transport	Rail	Motor carrier	Private truck	Air	Water	Other	Unknown
TONS OF SHIPMENTS	(thousands of tons)								
U.S. TOTAL	614	100.0	1.6	56.6	37.0	.2	-	4.0	.5
NEW ENGLAND	137	100.0	.1	64.8	20.2	.1	-	13.2	1.6
UNDER 100 MILES	56	100.0	-	68.3	25.1	-	-	3.9	2.8
100 TO 199 MILES	8	100.0	-	49.4	25.7	-	-	24.9	-
200 TO 299 MILES	8	100.0	-	69.4	13.3	-	-	16.3	1.0
300 TO 499 MILES	15	100.0	-	34.5	47.4	.1	-	14.3	3.6
500 TO 999 MILES	23	100.0	.2	72.2	3.9	-	-	23.6	.1
1000 TO 1499 MILES	14	100.0	-	68.9	13.2	-	-	17.9	-
1500 MILES OR OVER	11	100.0	.1	76.9	1.8	.5	-	20.4	.3
MIDDLE ATLANTIC	73	100.0	-	64.3	34.3	1.3	-	.1	.1
UNDER 100 MILES	10	100.0	-	42.6	56.9	-	-	.5	-
100 TO 199 MILES	8	100.0	-	95.2	4.4	-	-	-	.5
200 TO 299 MILES	8	100.0	-	100.0	-	-	-	-	-
300 TO 499 MILES	7	100.0	-	88.1	11.5	.4	-	-	-
500 TO 999 MILES	25	100.0	-	29.8	69.3	.9	-	-	-
1000 TO 1499 MILES	6	100.0	-	96.6	-	3.4	-	-	-
1500 MILES OR OVER	6	100.0	-	92.8	-	7.2	-	-	-
EAST NORTH CENTRAL	94	100.0	1.6	59.2	35.8	-	-	3.4	-
UNDER 100 MILES	16	100.0	-	1.0	93.6	-	-	5.4	-
100 TO 199 MILES	22	100.0	-	14.9	84.3	-	-	.8	-
200 TO 299 MILES	11	100.0	-	97.1	-	-	-	2.9	-
300 TO 499 MILES	11	100.0	-	96.2	-	-	-	3.8	-
500 TO 999 MILES	24	100.0	.8	94.0	-	.1	-	5.0	-
1000 TO 1499 MILES	1	100.0	4.6	77.5	-	-	-	17.9	-
1500 MILES OR OVER	7	100.0	16.0	84.0	-	-	-	-	-
WEST NORTH CENTRAL	48	100.0	.1	18.9	77.9	-	-	3.1	-
UNDER 100 MILES	31	100.0	-	.4	99.4	-	-	.2	-
100 TO 199 MILES	6	100.0	-	5.0	92.5	-	-	2.5	-
200 TO 299 MILES	2	100.0	-	90.2	-	-	-	9.8	-
300 TO 499 MILES	1	100.0	-	76.4	.6	-	-	23.0	-
500 TO 999 MILES	4	100.0	.9	81.6	2.2	.1	-	15.2	-
1000 TO 1499 MILES	1	100.0	-	89.5	2.5	-	-	8.0	-
1500 MILES OR OVER	-	100.0	-	88.8	11.2	-	-	-	-
EAST SOUTH CENTRAL	112	100.0	7.5	29.0	63.1	-	-	.3	.1
UNDER 100 MILES	37	100.0	-	8.6	91.4	-	-	-	-
100 TO 199 MILES	9	100.0	89.9	10.0	-	-	-	-	-
200 TO 299 MILES	39	100.0	-	5.7	94.1	-	-	.2	-
300 TO 499 MILES	6	100.0	-	96.7	-	-	-	1.4	1.9
500 TO 999 MILES	17	100.0	-	99.3	-	-	-	.5	.2
1000 TO 1499 MILES	-	100.0	-	100.0	-	-	-	-	-
1500 MILES OR OVER	1	100.0	-	96.7	-	-	-	3.3	-
TON-MILES OF SHIPMENTS	(millions of ton-miles)								
U.S. TOTAL	285	100.0	1.4	78.4	13.5	.8	-	5.6	.3
NEW ENGLAND	70	100.0	.1	70.9	10.6	.2	-	17.6	.6
UNDER 100 MILES	2	100.0	-	77.3	17.3	-	-	1.3	4.1
100 TO 199 MILES	1	100.0	-	47.0	26.9	-	-	26.1	-
200 TO 299 MILES	1	100.0	-	68.6	13.0	-	-	17.5	.9
300 TO 499 MILES	5	100.0	-	36.5	45.8	.1	-	14.0	3.6
500 TO 999 MILES	17	100.0	.2	72.0	4.8	-	-	22.8	.1
1000 TO 1499 MILES	16	100.0	-	67.2	14.7	-	-	18.0	-
1500 MILES OR OVER	24	100.0	.1	81.5	1.9	.5	-	15.6	.3
MIDDLE ATLANTIC	46	100.0	-	70.0	26.6	3.4	-	-	-
UNDER 100 MILES	-	100.0	-	66.5	32.5	-	-	.9	-
100 TO 199 MILES	1	100.0	-	95.0	4.5	-	-	-	.5
200 TO 299 MILES	2	100.0	-	100.0	-	-	-	-	-
300 TO 499 MILES	2	100.0	-	87.8	11.7	.5	-	-	-
500 TO 999 MILES	17	100.0	-	31.1	68.0	.9	-	-	-
1000 TO 1499 MILES	7	100.0	-	96.3	-	3.7	-	-	-
1500 MILES OR OVER	14	100.0	-	92.4	-	7.6	-	-	-
EAST NORTH CENTRAL	41	100.0	5.7	83.3	7.4	-	-	3.5	-
UNDER 100 MILES	1	100.0	-	1.3	91.8	-	-	6.9	-
100 TO 199 MILES	2	100.0	-	19.9	79.0	-	-	1.1	-
200 TO 299 MILES	2	100.0	-	96.9	-	-	-	3.1	-
300 TO 499 MILES	4	100.0	-	95.8	-	-	-	4.2	-
500 TO 999 MILES	15	100.0	.8	93.4	-	.1	-	5.7	-
1000 TO 1499 MILES	1	100.0	5.4	78.0	-	-	-	16.7	-
1500 MILES OR OVER	14	100.0	15.2	84.8	-	-	-	-	-
WEST NORTH CENTRAL	9	100.0	.3	65.1	26.1	-	-	8.4	-
UNDER 100 MILES	1	100.0	-	.6	99.3	-	-	.2	-
100 TO 199 MILES	-	100.0	-	5.8	91.5	-	-	2.7	-
200 TO 299 MILES	-	100.0	-	91.0	-	-	-	9.0	-
300 TO 499 MILES	-	100.0	-	76.5	.7	-	-	22.8	-
500 TO 999 MILES	2	100.0	1.1	81.9	1.7	.1	-	15.1	-
1000 TO 1499 MILES	1	100.0	-	90.6	2.1	-	-	7.3	-
1500 MILES OR OVER	1	100.0	-	88.8	11.2	-	-	-	-

See footnotes at end of table 4.

TABLE 1. TCC GROUP 314—Percent Distribution of Geographic Division of Origin and Distance Shipped, by Means of Transport: 1972—Continued

Geographic division of origin[1] and distance shipped[2]	Number	Percent distribution by means of transport							
		All means of transport	Rail	Motor carrier	Private truck	Air	Water	Other	Unknown
TON-MILES OF SHIPMENTS	(millions of ton-miles)								
EAST SOUTH CENTRAL......	30	100.0	4.9	63.6	30.6	-	-	.7	.3
UNDER 100 MILES......	1	100.0	-	9.2	90.8	-	-	-	-
100 TO 199 MILES......	1	100.0	90.7	9.2	-	-	-	-	-
200 TO 299 MILES......	8	100.0	-	6.8	93.0	-	-	.2	-
300 TO 499 MILES......	2	100.0	-	96.3	-	-	-	1.5	2.2
500 TO 999 MILES......	11	100.0	-	99.3	-	-	-	.5	.2
1000 TO 1499 MILES....	1	100.0	-	100.0	-	-	-	-	-
1500 MILES OR OVER....	3	100.0	-	97.0	-	-	-	3.0	-

See footnotes at end of table 4.

TABLE 2. TCC GROUP 314—Percent Distribution of Geographic Division of Origin and Means of Transport, by Geographic Division of Destination: 1972

Geographic division of origin[1] and means of transport	Number	Percent distribution by division of destination									
		U.S. total	New England	Middle Atlantic	East North Central	West North Central	South Atlantic	East South Central	West South Central	Mountain	Pacific
TONS OF SHIPMENTS	(thousands of tons)										
U.S. TOTAL............	614	100.0	14.1	11.5	16.0	12.3	10.1	16.1	6.1	1.6	12.2
RAIL............	10	100.0	-	-	.5	.4	1.9	83.9	-	.6	12.6
MOTOR CARRIER........	347	100.0	18.4	14.3	13.6	8.1	10.9	5.1	6.2	2.7	20.8
PRIVATE TRUCK........	226	100.0	7.5	6.7	19.9	20.5	8.6	31.3	5.4	.1	-
AIR.................	1	100.0	-	1.2	27.8	.4	10.9	-	18.2	.7	40.8
WATER..............	-	100.0	-	-	-	-	-	-	-	-	-
OTHER..............	24	100.0	16.2	21.2	23.0	4.7	13.2	6.0	13.7	.9	1.0
UNKNOWN............	3	100.0	52.7	13.1	3.6	-	25.4	-	4.1	-	1.0
NEW ENGLAND..........	137	100.0	46.7	15.4	11.0	6.5	9.9	1.5	3.5	.7	4.8
RAIL............	-	100.0	-	2.7	77.4	-	-	-	-	-	19.9
MOTOR CARRIER........	89	100.0	47.9	9.2	12.0	8.5	11.6	.8	2.0	.9	7.1
PRIVATE TRUCK........	27	100.0	57.8	30.9	3.3	3.8	1.4	.9	1.2	.6	.1
AIR.................	-	100.0	-	-	6.0	-	22.0	-	-	1.2	70.9
WATER..............	-	100.0	-	-	-	-	-	-	-	-	-
OTHER..............	18	100.0	20.9	23.8	18.7	1.8	13.2	6.3	14.2	.1	1.0
UNKNOWN............	2	100.0	69.5	3.5	1.0	-	24.7	-	-	-	1.4
MIDDLE ATLANTIC........	73	100.0	12.7	21.7	36.1	4.2	11.1	1.5	4.1	1.2	7.6
RAIL............	-	100.0	-	-	-	-	-	-	-	-	-
MOTOR CARRIER........	47	100.0	17.9	19.7	18.0	6.6	17.0	2.3	5.9	1.8	10.8
PRIVATE TRUCK........	25	100.0	3.3	25.9	70.7	-	-	-	-	.9	48.5
AIR.................	-	100.0	-	-	19.0	.6	11.5	-	19.5	.9	48.5
WATER..............	-	100.0	-	-	-	-	-	-	-	-	-
OTHER..............	-	100.0	-	91.1	-	.2	-	8.4	-	.3	-
UNKNOWN............	-	100.0	-	100.0	-	-	-	-	-	-	-
EAST NORTH CENTRAL......	94	100.0	1.7	19.1	30.9	27.7	3.5	3.8	4.1	.9	8.3
RAIL............	1	100.0	-	-	2.9	10.1	-	-	4.0	83.1	
MOTOR CARRIER........	56	100.0	2.6	31.8	22.0	13.5	4.7	6.3	6.2	1.1	11.8
PRIVATE TRUCK........	33	100.0	-	-	46.1	53.9	-	-	100.0	-	-
AIR.................	-	100.0	-	-	-	-	-	-	-	-	-
WATER..............	-	100.0	-	-	-	-	-	-	-	-	-
OTHER..............	3	100.0	4.8	9.2	40.4	11.9	16.1	2.7	10.1	4.9	-
UNKNOWN............	-	100.0	-	-	-	-	-	-	-	-	-
WEST NORTH CENTRAL......	48	100.0	.3	1.5	29.3	58.6	1.7	1.1	3.5	1.3	2.7
RAIL............	-	100.0	-	-	-	-	100.0	-	-	-	-
MOTOR CARRIER........	9	100.0	1.6	6.9	33.2	10.8	8.4	4.3	15.2	6.1	13.5
PRIVATE TRUCK........	37	100.0	-	-	27.9	71.7	-	-	-	.1	.2
AIR.................	-	100.0	-	-	-	-	100.0	-	-	-	-
WATER..............	-	100.0	-	-	-	-	-	-	-	-	-
OTHER..............	1	100.0	-	4.7	42.0	21.9	1.8	7.9	21.5	.2	-
UNKNOWN............	-	100.0	-	-	-	-	-	-	-	-	-
EAST SOUTH CENTRAL......	112	100.0	7.7	2.0	3.4	2.2	4.5	75.0	2.9	.8	1.5
RAIL............	8	100.0	-	-	-	-	-	100.0	-	-	-
MOTOR CARRIER........	32	100.0	26.5	7.0	11.3	7.5	15.0	15.3	9.8	2.5	5.0
PRIVATE TRUCK........	70	100.0	-	-	-	-	-	100.0	-	-	-
AIR.................	-	100.0	-	-	-	-	-	-	-	-	-
WATER..............	-	100.0	-	-	-	-	-	-	-	-	-
OTHER..............	-	100.0	2.2	6.2	10.1	13.3	23.4	10.6	13.5	12.3	8.3
UNKNOWN............	-	100.0	-	-	57.5	-	42.5	-	-	-	-

See footnotes at end of table 4.

TABLE 2. **TCC GROUP 314—Percent Distribution of Geographic Division of Origin and Means of Transport, by Geographic Division of Destination: 1972**—Continued

Geographic division of origin[1] and means of transport	Number	Percent distribution by division of destination									
		U.S. total	New England	Middle Atlantic	East North Central	West North Central	South Atlantic	East South Central	West South Central	Mountain	Pacific
TON-MILES OF SHIPMENTS	(millions of ton-miles)										
U.S. TOTAL..............	285	100.0	5.5	10.4	14.2	9.7	8.9	6.3	9.4	4.6	30.9
RAIL....................	3	100.0	-	-	1.0	.6	3.1	37.5	-	2.2	55.6
MOTOR CARRIER..........	223	100.0	6.3	10.9	10.2	9.7	9.4	2.4	8.1	5.5	37.5
PRIVATE TRUCK..........	38	100.0	2.8	8.2	36.4	14.0	3.0	25.1	8.8	1.2	.5
AIR....................	2	100.0	-	.6	21.9	.2	6.9	-	14.3	.8	55.5
WATER..................	-	100.0	-	-	-	-	-	-	-	-	-
OTHER..................	15	100.0	2.9	12.2	20.2	4.7	15.3	8.8	30.8	1.7	3.3
UNKNOWN................	-	100.0	14.4	19.6	7.3	-	34.7	-	15.1	-	8.9
NEW ENGLAND............	70	100.0	5.3	9.3	16.1	15.1	13.2	3.2	10.6	2.8	24.5
RAIL...................	-	100.0	-	.9	52.2	-	-	-	-	-	46.9
MOTOR CARRIER..........	50	100.0	5.1	4.4	15.7	17.5	14.0	1.5	5.7	3.0	33.0
PRIVATE TRUCK..........	7	100.0	10.1	39.0	11.1	19.5	3.7	3.8	6.6	5.4	.8
AIR....................	-	100.0	-	-	2.1	-	4.9	-	-	1.3	91.6
WATER..................	-	100.0	-	-	-	-	-	-	-	-	-
OTHER..................	12	100.0	2.5	11.5	21.1	3.2	14.5	9.8	33.2	.4	3.8
UNKNOWN................	-	100.0	23.0	4.0	4.4	-	49.6	-	-	-	19.0
MIDDLE ATLANTIC........	46	100.0	5.3	3.1	34.1	5.9	10.5	1.6	8.3	3.2	28.1
RAIL...................	-	100.0	-	-	-	-	-	-	-	-	-
MOTOR CARRIER..........	32	100.0	6.5	3.6	12.1	8.4	14.7	2.2	11.1	4.5	36.8
PRIVATE TRUCK..........	12	100.0	2.8	1.8	95.4	-	-	-	-	-	-
AIR....................	1	100.0	-	-	6.9	.2	5.9	-	15.9	1.0	70.0
WATER..................	-	100.0	-	-	-	-	-	-	-	-	-
OTHER..................	-	100.0	-	51.8	-	1.1	-	43.2	-	3.9	-
UNKNOWN................	-	100.0	-	100.0	-	-	-	-	-	-	-
EAST NORTH CENTRAL.....	41	100.0	3.0	24.5	10.4	11.1	4.5	2.4	7.2	2.4	34.6
RAIL...................	2	100.0	-	-	-	1.1	3.8	-	-	3.7	91.5
MOTOR CARRIER..........	34	100.0	3.2	28.9	8.3	7.5	4.1	2.8	7.7	2.2	35.2
PRIVATE TRUCK..........	3	100.0	-	-	40.3	59.7	-	-	-	-	-
AIR....................	-	100.0	-	-	-	-	-	-	100.0	-	-
WATER..................	-	100.0	-	-	-	-	-	-	-	-	-
OTHER..................	1	100.0	8.1	12.4	11.5	10.3	25.9	2.6	19.2	10.0	-
UNKNOWN................	-	100.0	-	-	-	-	-	-	-	-	-
WEST NORTH CENTRAL.....	9	100.0	1.9	7.3	16.4	25.7	7.5	2.9	12.2	5.7	20.3
RAIL...................	-	100.0	-	-	-	-	100.0	-	-	-	-
MOTOR CARRIER..........	6	100.0	2.9	10.2	17.5	4.7	10.5	3.2	13.8	7.8	29.2
PRIVATE TRUCK..........	2	100.0	-	.1	10.0	82.7	-	-	-	2.2	5.0
AIR....................	-	100.0	-	-	-	-	100.0	-	-	-	-
WATER..................	-	100.0	-	-	-	-	-	-	-	-	-
OTHER..................	-	100.0	-	7.8	28.1	12.0	3.8	9.9	38.3	.3	-
UNKNOWN................	-	100.0	-	-	-	-	-	-	-	-	-
EAST SOUTH CENTRAL.....	30	100.0	19.2	5.7	5.8	5.4	8.0	37.4	4.6	3.8	10.2
RAIL...................	1	100.0	-	-	-	-	-	100.0	-	-	-
MOTOR CARRIER..........	19	100.0	30.1	8.9	8.8	8.4	12.3	3.1	7.1	5.6	15.8
PRIVATE TRUCK..........	9	100.0	-	-	-	-	-	100.0	-	-	-
AIR....................	-	100.0	-	-	-	-	-	-	-	-	-
WATER..................	-	100.0	-	-	-	-	-	-	-	-	-
OTHER..................	-	100.0	3.0	5.9	4.8	6.6	15.7	4.3	11.2	27.0	21.6
UNKNOWN................	-	100.0	-	-	59.5	-	40.5	-	-	-	-

See footnotes at end of table 4.

TABLE 3. **TCC GROUP 314**—Percent Distribution of Geographic Division of Destination and Means of Transport, by Geographic Division of Origin: 1972

Geographic division of destination and means of transport	Number (thousands of tons)	Percent distribution by division of origin[1]									
		U.S. total	New England	Middle Atlantic	East North Central	West North Central	South Atlantic	East South Central	West South Central	Mountain	Pacific
TONS OF SHIPMENTS											
U.S. TOTAL	614	100.0	22.4	12.0	15.4	7.9	(D)	18.3	(D)	(D)	(D)
RAIL	10	100.0	.7	-	15.0	.4	(D)	83.9	(D)	(D)	(D)
MOTOR CARRIER	347	100.0	25.7	13.7	16.1	2.6	(D)	9.4	(D)	(D)	(D)
PRIVATE TRUCK	226	100.0	12.3	11.2	15.0	16.6	(D)	31.2	(D)	(D)	(D)
AIR	1	100.0	5.1	65.9	2.0	.2	(D)	-	(D)	(D)	(D)
WATER	-	100.0	-	-	-	-	(D)	-	(D)	(D)	(D)
OTHER	24	100.0	73.6	.3	13.2	6.1	(D)	1.3	(D)	(D)	(D)
UNKNOWN	3	100.0	74.1	1.3	-	-	(D)	5.1	(D)	(D)	(D)
NEW ENGLAND	86	100.0	74.4	10.8	1.9	.2	(D)	10.0	(D)	(D)	(D)
RAIL	-	100.0	-	-	-	-	(D)	-	(D)	(D)	(D)
MOTOR CARRIER	63	100.0	67.0	13.3	2.3	.2	(D)	13.5	(D)	(D)	(D)
PRIVATE TRUCK	16	100.0	95.0	5.0	-	-	(D)	-	(D)	(D)	(D)
AIR	-	100.0	-	-	-	-	(D)	-	(D)	(D)	(D)
WATER	-	100.0	-	-	-	-	(D)	-	(D)	(D)	(D)
OTHER	4	100.0	94.9	-	3.9	-	(D)	.2	(D)	(D)	(D)
UNKNOWN	1	100.0	97.7	-	-	-	(D)	-	(D)	(D)	(D)
MIDDLE ATLANTIC	70	100.0	30.0	22.7	25.7	1.0	(D)	3.3	(D)	(D)	(D)
RAIL	-	100.0	100.0	-	-	-	(D)	-	(D)	(D)	(D)
MOTOR CARRIER	49	100.0	16.4	18.8	35.8	1.3	(D)	4.6	(D)	(D)	(D)
PRIVATE TRUCK	15	100.0	56.7	43.3	-	-	(D)	-	(D)	(D)	(D)
AIR	-	100.0	-	-	-	-	(D)	-	(D)	(D)	(D)
WATER	-	100.0	-	-	-	-	(D)	-	(D)	(D)	(D)
OTHER	5	100.0	82.8	1.1	5.7	1.3	(D)	.4	(D)	(D)	(D)
UNKNOWN	-	100.0	19.6	9.7	-	-	(D)	-	(D)	(D)	(D)
EAST NORTH CENTRAL	98	100.0	15.4	27.1	29.8	14.4	(D)	3.9	(D)	(D)	(D)
RAIL	-	100.0	100.0	-	-	-	(D)	-	(D)	(D)	(D)
MOTOR CARRIER	47	100.0	22.7	18.1	26.2	6.4	(D)	7.8	(D)	(D)	(D)
PRIVATE TRUCK	45	100.0	2.0	39.8	34.8	23.4	(D)	-	(D)	(D)	(D)
AIR	-	100.0	1.1	44.9	-	-	(D)	-	(D)	(D)	(D)
WATER	-	100.0	-	-	-	-	(D)	-	(D)	(D)	(D)
OTHER	5	100.0	59.8	-	23.1	11.1	(D)	.6	(D)	(D)	(D)
UNKNOWN	-	100.0	20.0	-	-	-	(D)	80.0	(D)	(D)	(D)
WEST NORTH CENTRAL	75	100.0	11.9	4.1	34.8	37.5	(D)	3.3	(D)	(D)	(D)
RAIL	-	100.0	-	-	100.0	-	(D)	-	(D)	(D)	(D)
MOTOR CARRIER	28	100.0	27.1	11.1	27.1	3.5	(D)	8.7	(D)	(D)	(D)
PRIVATE TRUCK	46	100.0	2.3	-	39.4	58.3	(D)	-	(D)	(D)	(D)
AIR	-	100.0	-	100.0	-	-	(D)	-	(D)	(D)	(D)
WATER	-	100.0	-	-	-	-	(D)	-	(D)	(D)	(D)
OTHER	1	100.0	28.8	-	33.3	28.3	(D)	3.6	(D)	(D)	(D)
UNKNOWN	-	100.0	-	-	-	-	(D)	-	(D)	(D)	(D)
SOUTH ATLANTIC	61	100.0	22.2	13.3	5.3	1.3	(D)	8.2	(D)	(D)	(D)
RAIL	-	100.0	-	-	80.6	19.4	(D)	-	(D)	(D)	(D)
MOTOR CARRIER	37	100.0	27.4	21.4	6.9	2.0	(D)	13.0	(D)	(D)	(D)
PRIVATE TRUCK	19	100.0	1.9	-	-	-	(D)	-	(D)	(D)	(D)
AIR	-	100.0	10.3	69.3	-	1.9	(D)	-	(D)	(D)	(D)
WATER	-	100.0	-	-	-	-	(D)	-	(D)	(D)	(D)
OTHER	3	100.0	73.3	-	16.0	.8	(D)	2.2	(D)	(D)	(D)
UNKNOWN	-	100.0	72.1	-	-	-	(D)	8.5	(D)	(D)	(D)
EAST SOUTH CENTRAL	98	100.0	2.1	1.1	3.7	.5	(D)	85.3	(D)	(D)	(D)
RAIL	8	100.0	-	-	-	-	(D)	100.0	(D)	(D)	(D)
MOTOR CARRIER	17	100.0	4.1	6.1	19.8	2.2	(D)	28.0	(D)	(D)	(D)
PRIVATE TRUCK	71	100.0	.3	-	-	-	(D)	99.7	(D)	(D)	(D)
AIR	-	100.0	-	-	-	-	(D)	-	(D)	(D)	(D)
WATER	-	100.0	-	-	-	-	(D)	-	(D)	(D)	(D)
OTHER	1	100.0	76.4	.4	5.8	8.0	(D)	2.2	(D)	(D)	(D)
UNKNOWN	-	100.0	-	-	-	-	(D)	-	(D)	(D)	(D)
WEST SOUTH CENTRAL	37	100.0	12.7	8.0	10.3	4.5	(D)	8.6	(D)	(D)	(D)
RAIL	-	100.0	-	-	-	-	(D)	-	(D)	(D)	(D)
MOTOR CARRIER	21	100.0	8.4	13.1	16.3	6.4	(D)	14.8	(D)	(D)	(D)
PRIVATE TRUCK	12	100.0	2.8	-	-	-	(D)	-	(D)	(D)	(D)
AIR	-	100.0	-	70.6	11.1	-	(D)	-	(D)	(D)	(D)
WATER	-	100.0	-	-	-	-	(D)	-	(D)	(D)	(D)
OTHER	3	100.0	76.5	-	9.7	9.6	(D)	1.3	(D)	(D)	(D)
UNKNOWN	-	100.0	-	-	-	-	(D)	-	(D)	(D)	(D)
MOUNTAIN	9	100.0	9.8	8.7	8.4	6.2	(D)	8.7	(D)	(D)	(D)
RAIL	-	100.0	-	-	100.0	-	(D)	-	(D)	(D)	(D)
MOTOR CARRIER	9	100.0	8.2	9.1	6.5	5.9	(D)	8.8	(D)	(D)	(D)
PRIVATE TRUCK	-	100.0	77.1	-	-	22.9	(D)	-	(D)	(D)	(D)
AIR	-	100.0	9.0	91.0	-	-	(D)	-	(D)	(D)	(D)
WATER	-	100.0	-	-	-	-	(D)	-	(D)	(D)	(D)
OTHER	-	100.0	11.6	.1	69.9	1.3	(D)	17.1	(D)	(D)	(D)
UNKNOWN	-	100.0	-	-	-	-	(D)	-	(D)	(D)	(D)
PACIFIC	74	100.0	8.9	7.5	10.5	1.8	(D)	2.2	(D)	(D)	(D)
RAIL	1	100.0	1.1	-	98.9	-	(D)	-	(D)	(D)	(D)
MOTOR CARRIER	72	100.0	8.8	7.1	9.1	1.7	(D)	2.3	(D)	(D)	(D)
PRIVATE TRUCK	-	100.0	21.9	-	-	78.1	(D)	-	(D)	(D)	(D)
AIR	-	100.0	8.9	78.4	-	-	(D)	-	(D)	(D)	(D)
WATER	-	100.0	-	-	-	-	(D)	-	(D)	(D)	(D)
OTHER	-	100.0	74.4	-	-	-	(D)	-	(D)	(D)	(D)
UNKNOWN	-	100.0	100.0	-	-	-	(D)	10.8	(D)	(D)	(D)

See footnotes at end of table 4.

TABLE 3. **TCC GROUP 314**—Percent Distribution of Geographic Division of Destination and Means of Transport, by Geographic Division of Origin: 1972—Continued

Geographic division of destination and means of transport	Number	Percent distribution by division of origin[1]									
	(millions of ton-miles)	U.S. total	New England	Middle Atlantic	East North Central	West North Central	South Atlantic	East South Central	West South Central	Mountain	Pacific
TON-MILES OF SHIPMENTS											
U.S. TOTAL	285	100.0	24.9	16.1	14.7	3.4	(D)	10.8	(D)	(D)	(D)
RAIL	3	100.0	1.9	-	59.8	.8	(D)	37.5	(D)	(D)	(D)
MOTOR CARRIER	223	100.0	22.5	14.4	15.6	2.8	(D)	8.7	(D)	(D)	(D)
PRIVATE TRUCK	38	100.0	19.5	31.8	8.1	6.5	(D)	24.4	(D)	(D)	(D)
AIR	2	100.0	6.3	66.9	.9	.1	(D)	-	(D)	(D)	(D)
WATER	-	100.0	-	-	-	-	(D)	-	(D)	(D)	(D)
OTHER	15	100.0	78.7	.1	9.3	5.0	(D)	1.4	(D)	(D)	(D)
UNKNOWN	-	100.0	47.0	.7	-	-	(D)	8.8	(D)	(D)	(D)
NEW ENGLAND	15	100.0	23.6	15.4	7.9	1.2	(D)	37.4	(D)	(D)	(D)
RAIL	-	100.0	-	-	-	-	(D)	-	(D)	(D)	(D)
MOTOR CARRIER	14	100.0	18.2	14.8	8.0	1.3	(D)	41.8	(D)	(D)	(D)
PRIVATE TRUCK	1	100.0	69.1	30.9	-	-	(D)	-	(D)	(D)	(D)
AIR	-	100.0	-	-	-	-	(D)	-	(D)	(D)	(D)
WATER	-	100.0	-	-	-	-	(D)	-	(D)	(D)	(D)
OTHER	-	100.0	67.4	-	25.9	-	(D)	1.5	(D)	(D)	(D)
UNKNOWN	-	100.0	75.1	-	-	-	(D)	-	(D)	(D)	(D)
MIDDLE ATLANTIC	29	100.0	22.2	4.7	34.4	2.4	(D)	5.9	(D)	(D)	(D)
RAIL	-	100.0	100.0	-	-	-	(D)	-	(D)	(D)	(D)
MOTOR CARRIER	24	100.0	9.0	4.8	41.1	2.6	(D)	7.2	(D)	(D)	(D)
PRIVATE TRUCK	3	100.0	92.9	7.0	-	.1	(D)	-	(D)	(D)	(D)
AIR	-	100.0	-	-	-	-	(D)	-	(D)	(D)	(D)
WATER	-	100.0	-	-	-	-	(D)	.7	(D)	(D)	(D)
OTHER	1	100.0	74.2	.2	9.5	3.2	(D)	.7	(D)	(D)	(D)
UNKNOWN	-	100.0	9.6	3.5	-	-	(D)	-	(D)	(D)	(D)
EAST NORTH CENTRAL	40	100.0	28.1	38.6	10.7	3.9	(D)	4.4	(D)	(D)	(D)
RAIL	-	100.0	100.0	-	-	-	(D)	-	(D)	(D)	(D)
MOTOR CARRIER	22	100.0	34.7	17.1	12.8	4.8	(D)	7.5	(D)	(D)	(D)
PRIVATE TRUCK	14	100.0	6.0	83.3	9.0	1.8	(D)	-	(D)	(D)	(D)
AIR	-	100.0	.6	21.1	-	-	(D)	-	(D)	(D)	(D)
WATER	-	100.0	-	-	-	-	(D)	-	(D)	(D)	(D)
OTHER	3	100.0	81.9	-	5.3	7.0	(D)	.3	(D)	(D)	(D)
UNKNOWN	-	100.0	28.2	-	-	-	(D)	71.8	(D)	(D)	(D)
WEST NORTH CENTRAL	27	100.0	38.5	9.8	16.7	8.8	(D)	6.0	(D)	(D)	(D)
RAIL	-	100.0	-	-	100.0	-	(D)	-	(D)	(D)	(D)
MOTOR CARRIER	21	100.0	40.8	12.5	12.1	1.4	(D)	7.6	(D)	(D)	(D)
PRIVATE TRUCK	5	100.0	27.2	-	34.5	38.3	(D)	-	(D)	(D)	(D)
AIR	-	100.0	-	100.0	-	-	(D)	-	(D)	(D)	(D)
WATER	-	100.0	-	-	-	-	(D)	-	(D)	(D)	(D)
OTHER	-	100.0	54.0	-	20.3	12.8	(D)	2.0	(D)	(D)	(D)
UNKNOWN	-	100.0	-	-	-	-	(D)	-	(D)	(D)	(D)
SOUTH ATLANTIC	25	100.0	37.0	19.1	7.5	2.8	(D)	9.8	(D)	(D)	(D)
RAIL	-	100.0	-	-	74.0	26.0	(D)	-	(D)	(D)	(D)
MOTOR CARRIER	21	100.0	33.4	22.5	6.8	3.1	(D)	11.4	(D)	(D)	(D)
PRIVATE TRUCK	1	100.0	24.6	-	-	-	(D)	-	(D)	(D)	(D)
AIR	-	100.0	4.5	57.8	-	1.7	(D)	-	(D)	(D)	(D)
WATER	-	100.0	-	-	-	-	(D)	-	(D)	(D)	(D)
OTHER	2	100.0	74.6	-	15.6	1.2	(D)	1.5	(D)	(D)	(D)
UNKNOWN	-	100.0	67.2	-	-	-	(D)	10.2	(D)	(D)	(D)
EAST SOUTH CENTRAL	18	100.0	12.6	4.0	5.6	1.6	(D)	63.9	(D)	(D)	(D)
RAIL	1	100.0	-	-	-	-	(D)	100.0	(D)	(D)	(D)
MOTOR CARRIER	5	100.0	13.8	13.3	17.8	3.7	(D)	11.0	(D)	(D)	(D)
PRIVATE TRUCK	9	100.0	3.0	-	-	-	(D)	97.0	(D)	(D)	(D)
AIR	-	100.0	-	-	-	-	(D)	-	(D)	(D)	(D)
WATER	-	100.0	-	-	-	-	(D)	-	(D)	(D)	(D)
OTHER	1	100.0	87.3	.3	2.7	5.6	(D)	.7	(D)	(D)	(D)
UNKNOWN	-	100.0	-	-	-	-	(D)	-	(D)	(D)	(D)
WEST SOUTH CENTRAL	26	100.0	28.1	14.3	11.2	4.3	(D)	5.2	(D)	(D)	(D)
RAIL	-	100.0	-	-	-	-	(D)	-	(D)	(D)	(D)
MOTOR CARRIER	18	100.0	15.9	19.9	14.9	4.8	(D)	7.6	(D)	(D)	(D)
PRIVATE TRUCK	3	100.0	14.7	-	-	-	(D)	-	(D)	(D)	(D)
AIR	-	100.0	-	74.4	6.2	-	(D)	-	(D)	(D)	(D)
WATER	-	100.0	-	-	-	-	(D)	-	(D)	(D)	(D)
OTHER	4	100.0	84.9	-	5.8	6.3	(D)	.5	(D)	(D)	(D)
UNKNOWN	-	100.0	-	-	-	-	(D)	-	(D)	(D)	(D)
MOUNTAIN	13	100.0	15.3	11.2	7.6	4.2	(D)	8.9	(D)	(D)	(D)
RAIL	-	100.0	-	-	100.0	-	(D)	-	(D)	(D)	(D)
MOTOR CARRIER	12	100.0	12.5	11.8	6.2	4.0	(D)	9.0	(D)	(D)	(D)
PRIVATE TRUCK	-	100.0	88.2	-	-	11.8	(D)	-	(D)	(D)	(D)
AIR	-	100.0	10.5	89.5	-	-	(D)	-	(D)	(D)	(D)
WATER	-	100.0	-	-	-	-	(D)	-	(D)	(D)	(D)
OTHER	-	100.0	20.5	.1	55.4	1.0	(D)	23.0	(D)	(D)	(D)
UNKNOWN	-	100.0	-	-	-	-	(D)	-	(D)	(D)	(D)
PACIFIC	88	100.0	19.7	14.7	16.4	2.2	(D)	3.6	(D)	(D)	(D)
RAIL	2	100.0	1.6	-	98.4	-	(D)	-	(D)	(D)	(D)
MOTOR CARRIER	83	100.0	19.8	14.1	14.6	2.2	(D)	3.7	(D)	(D)	(D)
PRIVATE TRUCK	-	100.0	32.2	-	-	67.8	(D)	-	(D)	(D)	(D)
AIR	1	100.0	10.4	84.5	-	-	(D)	-	(D)	(D)	(D)
WATER	-	100.0	-	-	-	-	(D)	-	(D)	(D)	(D)
OTHER	-	100.0	88.7	-	-	-	(D)	9.2	(D)	(D)	(D)
UNKNOWN	-	100.0	100.0	-	-	-	(D)	-	(D)	(D)	(D)

See footnotes at end of table 4.

TABLE 4. **TCC GROUP 314**—Percent Distribution of Distance Shipped and Weight of Shipment, by Means of Transport: 1972

Distance shipped and weight of shipment [2] [3]	Number	Percent distribution by means of transport							
		All means of transport	Rail	Motor carrier	Private truck	Air	Water	Other	Unknown
TONS OF SHIPMENTS	(thousands of tons)								
U.S. TOTAL.........	355	100.0	.4	80.9	11.1	.4	-	6.3	.8
UNDER 100 MILES.........	73	100.0	-	62.0	32.6	-	-	3.2	2.1
UNDER 1000 POUNDS.....	9	100.0	-	67.1	6.5	-	-	24.9	1.5
1000 TO 9999 POUNDS...	57	100.0	-	56.6	40.9	-	-	-	2.5
10000 TO 29999 POUNDS.	6	100.0	-	100.0	-	-	-	-	-
30000 TO 59999 POUNDS.	-	100.0	-	-	-	-	-	-	-
60000 TO 89999 POUNDS.	-	100.0	-	-	-	-	-	-	-
90000 POUNDS AND OVER.	-	100.0	-	-	-	-	-	-	-
100 TO 199 MILES........	26	100.0	-	79.6	10.8	-	-	9.4	.3
UNDER 1000 POUNDS.....	15	100.0	-	71.6	12.0	-	-	15.9	.5
1000 TO 9999 POUNDS...	10	100.0	-	90.6	9.4	-	-	-	-
10000 TO 29999 POUNDS.	-	100.0	-	100.0	-	-	-	-	-
30000 TO 59999 POUNDS.	-	100.0	-	-	-	-	-	-	-
60000 TO 89999 POUNDS.	-	100.0	-	-	-	-	-	-	-
90000 POUNDS AND OVER.	-	100.0	-	-	-	-	-	-	-
200 TO 299 MILES........	38	100.0	-	92.3	2.8	-	-	4.7	.2
UNDER 1000 POUNDS.....	19	100.0	-	87.2	3.5	-	-	9.3	-
1000 TO 9999 POUNDS...	18	100.0	-	97.3	2.3	-	-	-	.4
10000 TO 29999 POUNDS.	1	100.0	-	100.0	-	-	-	-	-
30000 TO 59999 POUNDS.	-	100.0	-	-	-	-	-	-	-
60000 TO 89999 POUNDS.	-	100.0	-	-	-	-	-	-	-
90000 POUNDS AND OVER.	-	100.0	-	-	-	-	-	-	-
300 TO 499 MILES........	52	100.0	-	76.5	15.4	.2	-	6.6	1.4
UNDER 1000 POUNDS.....	35	100.0	-	70.8	18.4	.3	-	9.8	.8
1000 TO 9999 POUNDS...	17	100.0	-	87.8	9.5	-	-	-	2.7
10000 TO 29999 POUNDS.	-	100.0	-	-	-	-	-	-	-
30000 TO 59999 POUNDS.	-	100.0	-	-	-	-	-	-	-
60000 TO 89999 POUNDS.	-	100.0	-	-	-	-	-	-	-
90000 POUNDS AND OVER.	-	100.0	-	-	-	-	-	-	-
500 TO 999 MILES........	90	100.0	.3	89.7	1.1	.3	-	8.1	.5
UNDER 1000 POUNDS.....	52	100.0	.4	84.0	.3	.5	-	13.9	.8
1000 TO 9999 POUNDS...	35	100.0	.2	97.5	2.4	-	-	-	-
10000 TO 29999 POUNDS.	2	100.0	-	100.0	-	-	-	-	-
30000 TO 59999 POUNDS.	-	100.0	-	-	-	-	-	-	-
60000 TO 89999 POUNDS.	-	100.0	-	-	-	-	-	-	-
90000 POUNDS AND OVER.	-	100.0	-	-	-	-	-	-	-
1000 TO 1499 MILES......	32	100.0	.2	84.3	5.8	.8	-	8.9	-
UNDER 1000 POUNDS.....	17	100.0	.3	80.0	2.2	1.5	-	16.0	.1
1000 TO 9999 POUNDS...	11	100.0	-	87.3	12.7	-	-	-	-
10000 TO 29999 POUNDS.	2	100.0	-	100.0	-	-	-	-	-
30000 TO 59999 POUNDS.	-	100.0	-	-	-	-	-	-	-
60000 TO 89999 POUNDS.	-	100.0	-	-	-	-	-	-	-
90000 POUNDS AND OVER.	-	100.0	-	-	-	-	-	-	-
1500 MILES OR OVER......	40	100.0	3.1	88.6	.7	2.0	-	5.3	.2
UNDER 1000 POUNDS.....	23	100.0	5.4	81.0	1.2	2.9	-	9.2	.4
1000 TO 9999 POUNDS...	12	100.0	-	99.1	-	.9	-	-	-
10000 TO 29999 POUNDS.	4	100.0	-	100.0	-	-	-	-	-
30000 TO 59999 POUNDS.	-	100.0	-	-	-	-	-	-	-
60000 TO 89999 POUNDS.	-	100.0	-	-	-	-	-	-	-
90000 POUNDS AND OVER.	-	100.0	-	-	-	-	-	-	-
TON-MILES OF SHIPMENTS	(millions of ton-miles)								
U.S. TOTAL.........	219	100.0	1.1	86.8	3.9	1.1	-	6.7	.4
UNDER 100 MILES.........	3	100.0	-	70.8	24.8	-	-	1.4	2.9
UNDER 1000 POUNDS.....	-	100.0	-	80.1	7.6	-	-	10.8	1.6
1000 TO 9999 POUNDS...	2	100.0	-	66.0	30.5	-	-	-	3.5
10000 TO 29999 POUNDS.	-	100.0	-	100.0	-	-	-	-	-
30000 TO 59999 POUNDS.	-	100.0	-	-	-	-	-	-	-
60000 TO 89999 POUNDS.	-	100.0	-	-	-	-	-	-	-
90000 POUNDS AND OVER.	-	100.0	-	-	-	-	-	-	-
100 TO 199 MILES........	4	100.0	-	79.5	10.8	-	-	9.4	.3
UNDER 1000 POUNDS.....	2	100.0	-	70.3	12.8	-	-	16.4	.5
1000 TO 9999 POUNDS...	1	100.0	-	91.5	8.5	-	-	-	-
10000 TO 29999 POUNDS.	-	100.0	-	100.0	-	-	-	-	-
30000 TO 59999 POUNDS.	-	100.0	-	-	-	-	-	-	-
60000 TO 89999 POUNDS.	-	100.0	-	-	-	-	-	-	-
90000 POUNDS AND OVER.	-	100.0	-	-	-	-	-	-	-

See footnotes at end of table 4.

TABLE 4. **TCC GROUP 314—Percent Distribution of Distance Shipped and Weight of Shipment,**
by Means of Transport: 1972—Continued

Distance shipped and weight of shipment [2] [3]	Number	Percent distribution by means of transport							
		All means of transport	Rail	Motor carrier	Private truck	Air	Water	Other	Unknown
TON-MILES OF SHIPMENTS	(millions of ton-miles)								
200 TO 299 MILES.........	9	100.0	-	92.2	2.7	-	-	4.9	.2
UNDER 1000 POUNDS.....	4	100.0	-	87.2	3.1	-	-	9.7	-
1000 TO 9999 POUNDS...	4	100.0	-	97.1	2.5	-	-	-	.4
10000 TO 29999 POUNDS.	-	100.0	-	100.0	-	-	-	-	-
30000 TO 59999 POUNDS.	-	100.0	-	-	-	-	-	-	-
60000 TO 89999 POUNDS.	-	100.0	-	-	-	-	-	-	-
90000 POUNDS AND OVER.	-	100.0	-	-	-	-	-	-	-
300 TO 499 MILES.........	19	100.0	-	76.4	15.2	.2	-	6.8	1.5
UNDER 1000 POUNDS.....	13	100.0	-	71.8	17.3	.2	-	9.8	.8
1000 TO 9999 POUNDS...	6	100.0	-	86.4	10.7	-	-	-	2.9
10000 TO 29999 POUNDS.	-	100.0	-	-	-	-	-	-	-
30000 TO 59999 POUNDS.	-	100.0	-	-	-	-	-	-	-
60000 TO 89999 POUNDS.	-	100.0	-	-	-	-	-	-	-
90000 POUNDS AND OVER.	-	100.0	-	-	-	-	-	-	-
500 TO 999 MILES.........	62	100.0	.3	89.1	1.4	.3	-	8.4	.5
UNDER 1000 POUNDS.....	37	100.0	.4	84.1	.3	.5	-	13.9	.8
1000 TO 9999 POUNDS...	23	100.0	.2	96.5	3.3	-	-	-	-
10000 TO 29999 POUNDS.	1	100.0	-	100.0	-	-	-	-	-
30000 TO 59999 POUNDS.	-	100.0	-	-	-	-	-	-	-
60000 TO 89999 POUNDS.	-	100.0	-	-	-	-	-	-	-
90000 POUNDS AND OVER.	-	100.0	-	-	-	-	-	-	-
1000 TO 1499 MILES......	38	100.0	.2	83.4	6.6	.9	-	8.9	-
UNDER 1000 POUNDS.....	21	100.0	.3	79.9	2.5	1.6	-	15.6	.1
1000 TO 9999 POUNDS...	13	100.0	-	85.1	14.9	-	-	-	-
10000 TO 29999 POUNDS.	3	100.0	-	100.0	-	-	-	-	-
30000 TO 59999 POUNDS.	-	100.0	-	-	-	-	-	-	-
60000 TO 89999 POUNDS.	-	100.0	-	-	-	-	-	-	-
90000 POUNDS AND OVER.	-	100.0	-	-	-	-	-	-	-
1500 MILES OR OVER......	82	100.0	2.7	89.7	.7	2.1	-	4.5	.2
UNDER 1000 POUNDS.....	46	100.0	4.7	82.4	1.3	3.2	-	8.0	.4
1000 TO 9999 POUNDS...	27	100.0	-	99.0	-	1.0	-	-	-
10000 TO 29999 POUNDS.	8	100.0	-	100.0	-	-	-	-	-
30000 TO 59999 POUNDS.	-	100.0	-	-	-	-	-	-	-
60000 TO 89999 POUNDS.	-	100.0	-	-	-	-	-	-	-
90000 POUNDS AND OVER.	-	100.0	-	-	-	-	-	-	-

Note: Detail may not add to total due to rounding. The introductory table shows the estimates of sampling variability for tons; sampling variability for ton-miles has not been estimated. See the map in the Introduction for the States comprising the geographic divisions of the United States.

Shipments excluded from the survey are those moving by pipeline (primarily petroleum products from refineries), parcel post shipments, and commodities moved by own power (motorized vehicles, aircraft, etc.) or towed (prefabricated buildings, etc.). Local shipments (commodities shipped less than 25 miles from the plant) and shipments within the same city are also excluded. Shipments to Alaska and Hawaii from the 48 conterminous States and the District of Columbia are included; however, no data were obtained for shipments originating in Alaska and Hawaii.

- Represents zero or rounds to zero.   (D) Withheld to avoid disclosing figures for individual companies.

[1]Production of this commodity is concentrated in the geographic divisions shown; figures and distributions for geographic divisions not shown are included in the total.

[2]Distances of shipments to foreign destinations are calculated only to the U.S. port of exit.

[3]Includes only shipments represented by bills of lading and invoices. Summary records which did not show individual weights of shipments are not included.

TCC 316. Luggage, Handbags, and Other Personal Leather Goods

Comparisons of Tons and Ton-Miles of Shipments for
Geographic Divisions of Origin and for Sampling Variability: 1972 and 1967

Geographic division of origin	Estimates				Relative sampling variability in tons (percent)	
	1972		1967		1972	1967
	Tons (thousands)	Ton-miles (millions)	Tons (thousands)	Ton-miles (millions)		
U.S. total	104	78	205	159	21.4	22.4
New England	7	4	27	25	47.2	(*)
Middle Atlantic	54	43	93	85	31.4	(*)
East North Central	(D)	(D)	9	5	(*)	(*)
West North Central	(D)	(D)	13	4	(*)	(*)
South Atlantic	(D)	(D)	12	8	(*)	(*)
East South Central	(D)	(D)	22	13	(*)	(*)
West South Central	(D)	(D)	—	—	(*)	—
Mountain	—	—	14	15	—	(*)
Pacific	(D)	(D)	15	4	(*)	(*)

— Represents or rounds to zero.   (D) Withheld to avoid disclosing figures for individual companies.   (*) Data not published.

TABLE 1. **TCC GROUP 316**—Percent Distribution of Geographic Division of Origin and Distance Shipped, by Means of Transport: 1972

Geographic division of origin[1] and distance shipped[2]	Number	Percent distribution by means of transport							
		All means of transport	Rail	Motor carrier	Private truck	Air	Water	Other	Unknown
TONS OF SHIPMENTS	(thousands of tons)								
U.S. TOTAL..........	104	100.0	2.4	81.6	3.4	1.0	.1	10.8	.7
NEW ENGLAND..............	7	100.0	-	64.9	17.9	.7	-	16.3	.2
UNDER 100 MILES.......	1	100.0	-	91.0	-	-	-	9.0	-
100 TO 199 MILES......	1	100.0	-	56.4	36.7	-	-	7.0	-
200 TO 299 MILES......	-	100.0	-	66.5	-	-	-	33.5	-
300 TO 499 MILES......	-	100.0	-	82.1	5.8	-	-	12.1	-
500 TO 999 MILES......	1	100.0	-	37.9	27.2	1.0	-	33.8	-
1000 TO 1499 MILES....	-	100.0	-	60.0	4.6	.1	-	33.6	1.7
1500 MILES OR OVER....	1	100.0	-	70.1	20.1	3.6	-	6.3	-
MIDDLE ATLANTIC.........	54	100.0	4.3	88.7	.3	.6	.2	4.9	1.0
UNDER 100 MILES.......	9	100.0	-	94.5	1.1	-	.9	3.3	.1
100 TO 199 MILES......	6	100.0	-	95.3	-	.3	-	4.3	-
200 TO 299 MILES......	3	100.0	-	92.8	-	2.6	-	4.6	-
300 TO 499 MILES......	5	100.0	.5	93.2	.5	.3	-	5.3	.2
500 TO 999 MILES......	13	100.0	3.3	84.7	.1	.2	-	8.1	3.6
1000 TO 1499 MILES....	8	100.0	9.9	85.1	.2	.8	-	3.8	.3
1500 MILES OR OVER....	7	100.0	12.4	83.1	.4	1.2	.2	2.5	.2
TON-MILES OF SHIPMENTS	(millions of ton-miles)								
U.S. TOTAL..........	78	100.0	5.3	80.2	2.5	2.0	.1	9.2	.7
NEW ENGLAND..............	4	100.0	-	63.9	17.4	2.3	-	16.1	.3
UNDER 100 MILES.......	-	100.0	-	88.7	-	-	-	11.3	-
100 TO 199 MILES......	-	100.0	-	56.9	36.5	-	-	6.5	-
200 TO 299 MILES......	-	100.0	-	65.8	-	-	-	34.2	-
300 TO 499 MILES......	-	100.0	-	81.6	6.2	-	-	12.2	-
500 TO 999 MILES......	-	100.0	-	35.9	27.3	1.2	-	35.6	-
1000 TO 1499 MILES....	-	100.0	-	60.0	4.3	.1	-	33.7	2.1
1500 MILES OR OVER....	2	100.0	-	72.8	18.3	4.0	-	4.9	-
MIDDLE ATLANTIC.........	43	100.0	8.8	84.7	.3	1.0	.2	4.1	1.0
UNDER 100 MILES.......	-	100.0	-	93.8	1.5	-	.2	4.2	.3
100 TO 199 MILES......	-	100.0	-	95.8	-	.3	-	3.9	-
200 TO 299 MILES......	-	100.0	-	93.0	-	2.5	-	4.5	-
300 TO 499 MILES......	2	100.0	.5	93.7	.5	.3	-	4.7	.3
500 TO 999 MILES......	9	100.0	3.4	85.2	.1	.2	-	7.5	3.7
1000 TO 1499 MILES....	10	100.0	10.4	84.8	.1	.8	-	3.6	.3
1500 MILES OR OVER....	18	100.0	13.1	82.0	.4	1.5	.4	2.4	.2

See footnotes at end of table 4.

TABLE 2. **TCC GROUP 316**—Percent Distribution of Geographic Division of Origin and Means of Transport, by Geographic Division of Destination: 1972

Geographic division of origin[1] and means of transport	Number	Percent distribution by division of destination									
		U.S. total	New England	Middle Atlantic	East North Central	West North Central	South Atlantic	East South Central	West South Central	Mountain	Pacific
TONS OF SHIPMENTS	(thousands of tons)										
U.S. TOTAL...............	104	100.0	7.0	19.9	19.3	7.7	18.6	3.6	11.7	2.8	9.5
RAIL.....................	2	100.0	-	-	14.8	2.9	3.3	1.2	32.7	2.5	42.7
MOTOR CARRIER..........	85	100.0	7.0	19.9	19.9	7.7	19.5	2.9	11.1	2.7	9.3
PRIVATE TRUCK..........	3	100.0	14.6	47.5	8.8	13.2	7.7	.4	1.5	3.5	2.9
AIR......................	1	100.0	26.0	17.6	16.2	2.4	6.1	1.4	9.8	1.2	19.4
WATER....................	-	100.0	-	83.6	-	-	-	-	-	-	16.4
OTHER....................	11	100.0	4.4	16.5	19.7	8.0	16.9	10.6	15.9	3.5	4.3
UNKNOWN..................	-	100.0	-	2.5	18.3	-	62.1	5.1	5.0	1.3	5.6
NEW ENGLAND..............	7	100.0	2.5	45.0	12.9	4.2	13.7	4.2	4.1	2.7	10.7
RAIL.....................	-	100.0	-	-	-	-	-	-	-	-	-
MOTOR CARRIER..........	4	100.0	1.3	48.8	8.8	4.7	14.9	2.8	3.5	1.2	13.9
PRIVATE TRUCK..........	1	100.0	3.0	49.6	21.2	1.6	5.7	1.0	2.7	9.4	5.8
AIR......................	-	100.0	-	-	21.2	.7	2.1	-	.2	-	75.8
WATER....................	-	100.0	-	-	-	-	-	-	-	-	-
OTHER....................	1	100.0	6.6	27.6	19.8	5.2	18.1	13.8	7.0	1.5	.5
UNKNOWN..................	-	100.0	-	-	-	-	-	-	100.0	-	-
MIDDLE ATLANTIC.........	54	100.0	6.9	22.8	18.2	7.7	18.0	2.5	10.3	3.2	10.5
RAIL.....................	2	100.0	-	-	15.8	3.1	3.5	1.3	34.9	2.7	38.8
MOTOR CARRIER..........	48	100.0	7.3	24.2	18.1	8.1	17.7	2.4	9.4	3.3	9.4
PRIVATE TRUCK..........	-	100.0	.3	56.0	19.9	7.1	.7	-	1.5	.5	14.1
AIR......................	-	100.0	1.0	19.6	22.9	4.7	5.8	-	14.2	2.9	28.9
WATER....................	-	100.0	-	83.6	-	-	-	-	-	-	16.4
OTHER....................	2	100.0	8.2	16.0	24.4	6.8	26.5	6.0	5.1	2.4	4.5
UNKNOWN..................	-	100.0	-	2.5	10.8	-	79.9	-	4.5	-	2.4

See footnotes at end of table 4.

TABLE 2. **TCC GROUP 316—Percent Distribution of Geographic Division of Origin and Means of Transport, by Geographic Division of Destination: 1972**—Continued

Geographic division of origin[1] and means of transport	Number	Percent distribution by division of destination									
		U.S. total	New England	Middle Atlantic	East North Central	West North Central	South Atlantic	East South Central	West South Central	Mountain	Pacific
TON-MILES OF SHIPMENTS	(millions of ton-miles)										
U.S. TOTAL	78	100.0	5.0	7.5	13.7	7.6	15.1	2.6	14.6	6.0	28.1
RAIL	4	100.0	-	-	6.2	1.6	2.0	.6	25.8	3.2	60.8
MOTOR CARRIER	62	100.0	4.7	6.2	14.2	8.3	16.0	2.1	14.2	6.0	28.3
PRIVATE TRUCK	1	100.0	19.3	34.1	11.2	2.9	3.1	.7	3.8	11.5	13.4
AIR	1	100.0	20.4	17.0	11.3	1.8	4.6	1.8	7.7	1.5	33.9
WATER	-	100.0	-	1.1	-	-	-	-	-	-	98.9
OTHER	7	100.0	3.5	14.2	14.8	7.6	16.4	8.9	17.4	6.6	10.7
UNKNOWN	-	100.0	-	.7	13.1	-	58.9	.8	7.9	2.6	16.1
NEW ENGLAND	4	100.0	.3	8.9	13.2	6.5	9.6	6.2	9.0	7.3	39.1
RAIL	-	100.0	-	-	-	-	-	-	-	-	-
MOTOR CARRIER	3	100.0	.1	8.6	8.7	7.3	8.4	4.4	7.7	3.2	51.6
PRIVATE TRUCK	-	100.0	.8	12.2	23.2	2.4	4.8	1.6	7.2	26.1	21.6
AIR	-	100.0	-	-	8.3	.4	.8	-	.1	-	90.4
WATER	-	100.0	-	-	-	-	-	-	-	-	-
OTHER	-	100.0	.9	8.1	21.0	8.3	21.0	19.1	15.4	4.3	1.8
UNKNOWN	-	100.0	-	-	-	-	-	-	100.0	-	-
MIDDLE ATLANTIC	43	100.0	1.4	2.7	13.6	9.4	13.1	2.5	17.3	7.4	32.7
RAIL	3	100.0	-	-	6.6	1.7	2.1	.6	27.7	3.4	57.9
MOTOR CARRIER	36	100.0	1.6	3.0	14.0	10.4	13.3	2.5	16.8	8.0	30.6
PRIVATE TRUCK	-	100.0	-	4.6	16.9	11.1	.6	-	3.1	1.1	62.7
AIR	-	100.0	.2	3.6	7.7	3.7	3.5	-	14.7	4.7	62.0
WATER	-	100.0	-	1.1	-	-	-	-	-	-	98.9
OTHER	1	100.0	2.1	2.5	22.0	11.1	21.0	8.3	9.8	6.3	16.8
UNKNOWN	-	100.0	-	.3	9.2	-	76.5	-	6.6	-	7.4

See footnotes at end of table 4.

TABLE 3. TCC GROUP 316—Percent Distribution of Geographic Division of Destination and Means of Transport, by Geographic Division of Origin: 1972

Geographic division of destination and means of transport	Number	Percent distribution by division of origin[1]								
		U.S. total	New England	Middle Atlantic	East North Central	West North Central	South Atlantic	East South Central	West South Central	Mountain	Pacific
TONS OF SHIPMENTS	(thousands of tons)										
U.S. TOTAL............	104	100.0	6.8	52.1	(D)	(D)	(D)	(D)	(D)	(D)	(D)
RAIL.................	2	100.0	-	93.6	(D)	(D)	(D)	(D)	(D)	(D)	(D)
MOTOR CARRIER........	85	100.0	5.4	56.7	(D)	(D)	(D)	(D)	(D)	(D)	(D)
PRIVATE TRUCK........	3	100.0	36.5	5.4	(D)	(D)	(D)	(D)	(D)	(D)	(D)
AIR..................	1	100.0	4.9	28.4	(D)	(D)	(D)	(D)	(D)	(D)	(D)
WATER................	-	100.0	-	100.0	(D)	(D)	(D)	(D)	(D)	(D)	(D)
OTHER................	11	100.0	10.3	23.4	(D)	(D)	(D)	(D)	(D)	(D)	(D)
UNKNOWN..............	-	100.0	1.7	74.6	(D)	(D)	(D)	(D)	(D)	(D)	(D)
NEW ENGLAND..........	7	100.0	2.4	51.5	(D)	(D)	(D)	(D)	(D)	(D)	(D)
RAIL.................	-	100.0	-	-	(D)	(D)	(D)	(D)	(D)	(D)	(D)
MOTOR CARRIER........	5	100.0	1.0	59.0	(D)	(D)	(D)	(D)	(D)	(D)	(D)
PRIVATE TRUCK........	-	100.0	7.4	.1	(D)	(D)	(D)	(D)	(D)	(D)	(D)
AIR..................	-	100.0	-	1.1	(D)	(D)	(D)	(D)	(D)	(D)	(D)
WATER................	-	100.0	-	-	(D)	(D)	(D)	(D)	(D)	(D)	(D)
OTHER................	-	100.0	15.2	43.2	(D)	(D)	(D)	(D)	(D)	(D)	(D)
UNKNOWN..............	-	100.0	-	-	(D)	(D)	(D)	(D)	(D)	(D)	(D)
MIDDLE ATLANTIC......	20	100.0	15.5	59.6	(D)	(D)	(D)	(D)	(D)	(D)	(D)
RAIL.................	-	100.0	-	-	(D)	(D)	(D)	(D)	(D)	(D)	(D)
MOTOR CARRIER........	16	100.0	13.3	69.0	(D)	(D)	(D)	(D)	(D)	(D)	(D)
PRIVATE TRUCK........	1	100.0	38.1	6.3	(D)	(D)	(D)	(D)	(D)	(D)	(D)
AIR..................	-	100.0	-	31.8	(D)	(D)	(D)	(D)	(D)	(D)	(D)
WATER................	-	100.0	-	100.0	(D)	(D)	(D)	(D)	(D)	(D)	(D)
OTHER................	1	100.0	17.2	22.7	(D)	(D)	(D)	(D)	(D)	(D)	(D)
UNKNOWN..............	-	100.0	-	73.9	(D)	(D)	(D)	(D)	(D)	(D)	(D)
EAST NORTH CENTRAL...	20	100.0	4.6	49.0	(D)	(D)	(D)	(D)	(D)	(D)	(D)
RAIL.................	-	100.0	-	100.0	(D)	(D)	(D)	(D)	(D)	(D)	(D)
MOTOR CARRIER........	17	100.0	2.4	51.4	(D)	(D)	(D)	(D)	(D)	(D)	(D)
PRIVATE TRUCK........	-	100.0	87.7	12.1	(D)	(D)	(D)	(D)	(D)	(D)	(D)
AIR..................	-	100.0	6.4	40.1	(D)	(D)	(D)	(D)	(D)	(D)	(D)
WATER................	-	100.0	-	-	(D)	(D)	(D)	(D)	(D)	(D)	(D)
OTHER................	2	100.0	10.3	28.8	(D)	(D)	(D)	(D)	(D)	(D)	(D)
UNKNOWN..............	-	100.0	-	43.9	(D)	(D)	(D)	(D)	(D)	(D)	(D)
WEST NORTH CENTRAL...	8	100.0	3.7	52.2	(D)	(D)	(D)	(D)	(D)	(D)	(D)
RAIL.................	-	100.0	-	100.0	(D)	(D)	(D)	(D)	(D)	(D)	(D)
MOTOR CARRIER........	6	100.0	3.3	59.6	(D)	(D)	(D)	(D)	(D)	(D)	(D)
PRIVATE TRUCK........	-	100.0	4.4	2.9	(D)	(D)	(D)	(D)	(D)	(D)	(D)
AIR..................	-	100.0	1.5	54.5	(D)	(D)	(D)	(D)	(D)	(D)	(D)
WATER................	-	100.0	-	-	(D)	(D)	(D)	(D)	(D)	(D)	(D)
OTHER................	-	100.0	6.7	19.8	(D)	(D)	(D)	(D)	(D)	(D)	(D)
UNKNOWN..............	-	100.0	-	-	(D)	(D)	(D)	(D)	(D)	(D)	(D)
SOUTH ATLANTIC.......	19	100.0	5.0	50.6	(D)	(D)	(D)	(D)	(D)	(D)	(D)
RAIL.................	-	100.0	-	100.0	(D)	(D)	(D)	(D)	(D)	(D)	(D)
MOTOR CARRIER........	16	100.0	4.2	51.6	(D)	(D)	(D)	(D)	(D)	(D)	(D)
PRIVATE TRUCK........	-	100.0	27.1	.5	(D)	(D)	(D)	(D)	(D)	(D)	(D)
AIR..................	-	100.0	1.6	27.1	(D)	(D)	(D)	(D)	(D)	(D)	(D)
WATER................	-	100.0	-	-	(D)	(D)	(D)	(D)	(D)	(D)	(D)
OTHER................	1	100.0	11.0	36.6	(D)	(D)	(D)	(D)	(D)	(D)	(D)
UNKNOWN..............	-	100.0	-	95.9	(D)	(D)	(D)	(D)	(D)	(D)	(D)
EAST SOUTH CENTRAL...	3	100.0	8.1	36.4	(D)	(D)	(D)	(D)	(D)	(D)	(D)
RAIL.................	-	100.0	-	100.0	(D)	(D)	(D)	(D)	(D)	(D)	(D)
MOTOR CARRIER........	2	100.0	5.3	48.0	(D)	(D)	(D)	(D)	(D)	(D)	(D)
PRIVATE TRUCK........	-	100.0	100.0	-	(D)	(D)	(D)	(D)	(D)	(D)	(D)
AIR..................	-	100.0	-	-	(D)	(D)	(D)	(D)	(D)	(D)	(D)
WATER................	-	100.0	-	-	(D)	(D)	(D)	(D)	(D)	(D)	(D)
OTHER................	1	100.0	13.3	13.3	(D)	(D)	(D)	(D)	(D)	(D)	(D)
UNKNOWN..............	-	100.0	-	-	(D)	(D)	(D)	(D)	(D)	(D)	(D)
WEST SOUTH CENTRAL...	12	100.0	2.4	45.5	(D)	(D)	(D)	(D)	(D)	(D)	(D)
RAIL.................	-	100.0	-	100.0	(D)	(D)	(D)	(D)	(D)	(D)	(D)
MOTOR CARRIER........	9	100.0	1.7	48.2	(D)	(D)	(D)	(D)	(D)	(D)	(D)
PRIVATE TRUCK........	-	100.0	67.3	5.5	(D)	(D)	(D)	(D)	(D)	(D)	(D)
AIR..................	-	100.0	.1	41.3	(D)	(D)	(D)	(D)	(D)	(D)	(D)
WATER................	-	100.0	-	-	(D)	(D)	(D)	(D)	(D)	(D)	(D)
OTHER................	1	100.0	4.5	7.5	(D)	(D)	(D)	(D)	(D)	(D)	(D)
UNKNOWN..............	-	100.0	33.4	66.6	(D)	(D)	(D)	(D)	(D)	(D)	(D)
MOUNTAIN.............	2	100.0	6.6	59.6	(D)	(D)	(D)	(D)	(D)	(D)	(D)
RAIL.................	-	100.0	-	100.0	(D)	(D)	(D)	(D)	(D)	(D)	(D)
MOTOR CARRIER........	2	100.0	2.4	69.3	(D)	(D)	(D)	(D)	(D)	(D)	(D)
PRIVATE TRUCK........	-	100.0	99.3	.7	(D)	(D)	(D)	(D)	(D)	(D)	(D)
AIR..................	-	100.0	-	71.4	(D)	(D)	(D)	(D)	(D)	(D)	(D)
WATER................	-	100.0	-	-	(D)	(D)	(D)	(D)	(D)	(D)	(D)
OTHER................	-	100.0	4.3	16.1	(D)	(D)	(D)	(D)	(D)	(D)	(D)
UNKNOWN..............	-	100.0	-	-	(D)	(D)	(D)	(D)	(D)	(D)	(D)
PACIFIC..............	9	100.0	7.7	57.7	(D)	(D)	(D)	(D)	(D)	(D)	(D)
RAIL.................	1	100.0	-	85.1	(D)	(D)	(D)	(D)	(D)	(D)	(D)
MOTOR CARRIER........	7	100.0	8.1	56.9	(D)	(D)	(D)	(D)	(D)	(D)	(D)
PRIVATE TRUCK........	-	100.0	72.9	26.4	(D)	(D)	(D)	(D)	(D)	(D)	(D)
AIR..................	-	100.0	19.0	42.3	(D)	(D)	(D)	(D)	(D)	(D)	(D)
WATER................	-	100.0	-	100.0	(D)	(D)	(D)	(D)	(D)	(D)	(D)
OTHER................	-	100.0	1.1	24.2	(D)	(D)	(D)	(D)	(D)	(D)	(D)
UNKNOWN..............	-	100.0	-	31.5	(D)	(D)	(D)	(D)	(D)	(D)	(D)

See footnotes at end of table 4.

TABLE 3. **TCC GROUP 316—Percent Distribution of Geographic Division of Destination and Means of Transport, by Geographic Division of Origin: 1972**—Continued

Geographic division of destination and means of transport	Number	Percent distribution by division of origin[1]									
		U.S. total	New England	Middle Atlantic	East North Central	West North Central	South Atlantic	East South Central	West South Central	Mountain	Pacific
TON-MILES OF SHIPMENTS	(millions of ton-miles)										
U.S. TOTAL..............	78	100.0	6.3	55.6	(D)	(D)	(D)	(D)	(D)	(D)	(D)
RAIL...................	4	100.0	-	93.0	(D)	(D)	(D)	(D)	(D)	(D)	(D)
MOTOR CARRIER.........	62	100.0	5.1	58.8	(D)	(D)	(D)	(D)	(D)	(D)	(D)
PRIVATE TRUCK.........	1	100.0	43.8	6.3	(D)	(D)	(D)	(D)	(D)	(D)	(D)
AIR...................	1	100.0	7.5	26.8	(D)	(D)	(D)	(D)	(D)	(D)	(D)
WATER.................	-	100.0	-	100.0	(D)	(D)	(D)	(D)	(D)	(D)	(D)
OTHER.................	7	100.0	11.1	24.6	(D)	(D)	(D)	(D)	(D)	(D)	(D)
UNKNOWN...............	-	100.0	2.9	74.6	(D)	(D)	(D)	(D)	(D)	(D)	(D)
NEW ENGLAND.............	3	100.0	.4	16.3	(D)	(D)	(D)	(D)	(D)	(D)	(D)
RAIL...................	-	100.0	-	-	(D)	(D)	(D)	(D)	(D)	(D)	(D)
MOTOR CARRIER.........	2	100.0	.1	20.2	(D)	(D)	(D)	(D)	(D)	(D)	(D)
PRIVATE TRUCK.........	-	100.0	1.9	-	(D)	(D)	(D)	(D)	(D)	(D)	(D)
AIR...................	-	100.0	-	.3	(D)	(D)	(D)	(D)	(D)	(D)	(D)
WATER.................	-	100.0	-	-	(D)	(D)	(D)	(D)	(D)	(D)	(D)
OTHER.................	-	100.0	2.9	14.8	(D)	(D)	(D)	(D)	(D)	(D)	(D)
UNKNOWN...............	-	100.0	-	-	(D)	(D)	(D)	(D)	(D)	(D)	(D)
MIDDLE ATLANTIC..........	5	100.0	7.5	19.9	(D)	(D)	(D)	(D)	(D)	(D)	(D)
RAIL...................	-	100.0	-	-	(D)	(D)	(D)	(D)	(D)	(D)	(D)
MOTOR CARRIER.........	3	100.0	7.0	28.2	(D)	(D)	(D)	(D)	(D)	(D)	(D)
PRIVATE TRUCK.........	-	100.0	15.7	.8	(D)	(D)	(D)	(D)	(D)	(D)	(D)
AIR...................	-	100.0	-	5.6	(D)	(D)	(D)	(D)	(D)	(D)	(D)
WATER.................	-	100.0	-	100.0	(D)	(D)	(D)	(D)	(D)	(D)	(D)
OTHER.................	1	100.0	6.3	4.3	(D)	(D)	(D)	(D)	(D)	(D)	(D)
UNKNOWN...............	-	100.0	-	29.0	(D)	(D)	(D)	(D)	(D)	(D)	(D)
EAST NORTH CENTRAL......	10	100.0	6.1	55.2	(D)	(D)	(D)	(D)	(D)	(D)	(D)
RAIL...................	-	100.0	-	100.0	(D)	(D)	(D)	(D)	(D)	(D)	(D)
MOTOR CARRIER.........	8	100.0	3.1	58.0	(D)	(D)	(D)	(D)	(D)	(D)	(D)
PRIVATE TRUCK.........	-	100.0	90.6	9.4	(D)	(D)	(D)	(D)	(D)	(D)	(D)
AIR...................	-	100.0	5.5	18.3	(D)	(D)	(D)	(D)	(D)	(D)	(D)
WATER.................	-	100.0	-	-	(D)	(D)	(D)	(D)	(D)	(D)	(D)
OTHER.................	1	100.0	15.7	36.6	(D)	(D)	(D)	(D)	(D)	(D)	(D)
UNKNOWN...............	-	100.0	-	52.3	(D)	(D)	(D)	(D)	(D)	(D)	(D)
WEST NORTH CENTRAL......	5	100.0	5.4	69.3	(D)	(D)	(D)	(D)	(D)	(D)	(D)
RAIL...................	-	100.0	-	100.0	(D)	(D)	(D)	(D)	(D)	(D)	(D)
MOTOR CARRIER.........	5	100.0	4.5	73.0	(D)	(D)	(D)	(D)	(D)	(D)	(D)
PRIVATE TRUCK.........	-	100.0	36.4	24.0	(D)	(D)	(D)	(D)	(D)	(D)	(D)
AIR...................	-	100.0	1.6	54.4	(D)	(D)	(D)	(D)	(D)	(D)	(D)
WATER.................	-	100.0	-	-	(D)	(D)	(D)	(D)	(D)	(D)	(D)
OTHER.................	-	100.0	12.0	35.8	(D)	(D)	(D)	(D)	(D)	(D)	(D)
UNKNOWN...............	-	100.0	-	-	(D)	(D)	(D)	(D)	(D)	(D)	(D)
SOUTH ATLANTIC..........	11	100.0	4.1	48.3	(D)	(D)	(D)	(D)	(D)	(D)	(D)
RAIL...................	-	100.0	-	100.0	(D)	(D)	(D)	(D)	(D)	(D)	(D)
MOTOR CARRIER.........	10	100.0	2.7	48.7	(D)	(D)	(D)	(D)	(D)	(D)	(D)
PRIVATE TRUCK.........	-	100.0	68.8	1.1	(D)	(D)	(D)	(D)	(D)	(D)	(D)
AIR...................	-	100.0	1.3	20.1	(D)	(D)	(D)	(D)	(D)	(D)	(D)
WATER.................	-	100.0	-	-	(D)	(D)	(D)	(D)	(D)	(D)	(D)
OTHER.................	1	100.0	14.2	31.4	(D)	(D)	(D)	(D)	(D)	(D)	(D)
UNKNOWN...............	-	100.0	-	96.9	(D)	(D)	(D)	(D)	(D)	(D)	(D)
EAST SOUTH CENTRAL......	1	100.0	15.3	54.2	(D)	(D)	(D)	(D)	(D)	(D)	(D)
RAIL...................	-	100.0	-	100.0	(D)	(D)	(D)	(D)	(D)	(D)	(D)
MOTOR CARRIER.........	1	100.0	10.7	70.8	(D)	(D)	(D)	(D)	(D)	(D)	(D)
PRIVATE TRUCK.........	-	100.0	100.0	-	(D)	(D)	(D)	(D)	(D)	(D)	(D)
AIR...................	-	100.0	-	-	(D)	(D)	(D)	(D)	(D)	(D)	(D)
WATER.................	-	100.0	-	-	(D)	(D)	(D)	(D)	(D)	(D)	(D)
OTHER.................	-	100.0	23.8	23.0	(D)	(D)	(D)	(D)	(D)	(D)	(D)
UNKNOWN...............	-	100.0	-	-	(D)	(D)	(D)	(D)	(D)	(D)	(D)
WEST SOUTH CENTRAL......	11	100.0	3.9	65.6	(D)	(D)	(D)	(D)	(D)	(D)	(D)
RAIL...................	1	100.0	-	100.0	(D)	(D)	(D)	(D)	(D)	(D)	(D)
MOTOR CARRIER.........	8	100.0	2.7	69.5	(D)	(D)	(D)	(D)	(D)	(D)	(D)
PRIVATE TRUCK.........	-	100.0	83.5	5.1	(D)	(D)	(D)	(D)	(D)	(D)	(D)
AIR...................	-	100.0	.1	51.1	(D)	(D)	(D)	(D)	(D)	(D)	(D)
WATER.................	-	100.0	-	-	(D)	(D)	(D)	(D)	(D)	(D)	(D)
OTHER.................	1	100.0	9.8	13.9	(D)	(D)	(D)	(D)	(D)	(D)	(D)
UNKNOWN...............	-	100.0	37.1	62.9	(D)	(D)	(D)	(D)	(D)	(D)	(D)
MOUNTAIN................	4	100.0	7.8	68.8	(D)	(D)	(D)	(D)	(D)	(D)	(D)
RAIL...................	-	100.0	-	100.0	(D)	(D)	(D)	(D)	(D)	(D)	(D)
MOTOR CARRIER.........	3	100.0	2.7	77.6	(D)	(D)	(D)	(D)	(D)	(D)	(D)
PRIVATE TRUCK.........	-	100.0	99.4	.6	(D)	(D)	(D)	(D)	(D)	(D)	(D)
AIR...................	-	100.0	-	86.4	(D)	(D)	(D)	(D)	(D)	(D)	(D)
WATER.................	-	100.0	-	-	(D)	(D)	(D)	(D)	(D)	(D)	(D)
OTHER.................	-	100.0	7.3	23.7	(D)	(D)	(D)	(D)	(D)	(D)	(D)
UNKNOWN...............	-	100.0	-	-	(D)	(D)	(D)	(D)	(D)	(D)	(D)
PACIFIC.................	21	100.0	8.8	64.8	(D)	(D)	(D)	(D)	(D)	(D)	(D)
RAIL...................	2	100.0	-	88.5	(D)	(D)	(D)	(D)	(D)	(D)	(D)
MOTOR CARRIER.........	17	100.0	9.2	63.6	(D)	(D)	(D)	(D)	(D)	(D)	(D)
PRIVATE TRUCK.........	-	100.0	70.7	29.2	(D)	(D)	(D)	(D)	(D)	(D)	(D)
AIR...................	-	100.0	19.9	49.1	(D)	(D)	(D)	(D)	(D)	(D)	(D)
WATER.................	-	100.0	-	100.0	(D)	(D)	(D)	(D)	(D)	(D)	(D)
OTHER.................	-	100.0	1.9	38.6	(D)	(D)	(D)	(D)	(D)	(D)	(D)
UNKNOWN...............	-	100.0	-	34.4	(D)	(D)	(D)	(D)	(D)	(D)	(D)

See footnotes at end of table 4.

TABLE 4. TCC GROUP 316—Percent Distribution of Distance Shipped and Weight of Shipment, by Means of Transport: 1972

Distance shipped and weight of shipment[2][3]	Number	Percent distribution by means of transport							
		All means of transport	Rail	Motor carrier	Private truck	Air	Water	Other	Unknown
TONS OF SHIPMENTS	(thousands of tons)								
U.S. TOTAL.........	101	100.0	2.5	81.1	3.4	1.0	.1	11.1	.7
UNDER 100 MILES........	12	100.0	-	88.5	5.4	-	.7	5.1	.3
UNDER 1000 POUNDS.....	10	100.0	-	90.4	2.2	-	.8	6.1	.4
1000 TO 9999 POUNDS...	2	100.0	-	79.4	20.6	-	-	-	-
10000 TO 29999 POUNDS.	-	100.0	-	-	-	-	-	-	-
30000 TO 59999 POUNDS.	-	100.0	-	-	-	-	-	-	-
60000 TO 89999 POUNDS.	-	100.0	-	-	-	-	-	-	-
90000 POUNDS AND OVER.	-	100.0	-	-	-	-	-	-	-
100 TO 199 MILES........	9	100.0	-	85.3	7.3	.2	-	7.2	-
UNDER 1000 POUNDS.....	6	100.0	-	84.2	5.0	.3	-	10.5	-
1000 TO 9999 POUNDS...	-	100.0	-	58.2	41.8	-	-	-	-
10000 TO 29999 POUNDS.	-	100.0	-	-	-	-	-	-	-
30000 TO 59999 POUNDS.	2	100.0	-	100.0	-	-	-	-	-
60000 TO 89999 POUNDS.	-	100.0	-	-	-	-	-	-	-
90000 POUNDS AND OVER.	-	100.0	-	-	-	-	-	-	-
200 TO 299 MILES........	5	100.0	-	84.8	-	1.4	-	13.8	-
UNDER 1000 POUNDS.....	5	100.0	-	82.3	-	1.6	-	16.1	-
1000 TO 9999 POUNDS...	-	100.0	-	100.0	-	-	-	-	-
10000 TO 29999 POUNDS.	-	100.0	-	-	-	-	-	-	-
30000 TO 59999 POUNDS.	-	100.0	-	-	-	-	-	-	-
60000 TO 89999 POUNDS.	-	100.0	-	-	-	-	-	-	-
90000 POUNDS AND OVER.	-	100.0	-	-	-	-	-	-	-
300 TO 499 MILES........	15	100.0	.2	84.3	.5	.2	-	14.3	.6
UNDER 1000 POUNDS.....	10	100.0	.3	77.5	.4	.3	-	20.7	.8
1000 TO 9999 POUNDS...	2	100.0	-	98.9	1.1	-	-	-	-
10000 TO 29999 POUNDS.	2	100.0	-	100.0	-	-	-	-	-
30000 TO 59999 POUNDS.	-	100.0	-	-	-	-	-	-	-
60000 TO 89999 POUNDS.	-	100.0	-	-	-	-	-	-	-
90000 POUNDS AND OVER.	-	100.0	-	-	-	-	-	-	-
500 TO 999 MILES........	31	100.0	1.4	74.6	5.6	.3	-	16.5	1.6
UNDER 1000 POUNDS.....	22	100.0	2.0	73.8	1.6	.4	-	20.0	2.3
1000 TO 9999 POUNDS...	7	100.0	-	71.2	19.8	-	-	8.9	-
10000 TO 29999 POUNDS.	1	100.0	-	100.0	-	-	-	-	-
30000 TO 59999 POUNDS.	-	100.0	-	-	-	-	-	-	-
60000 TO 89999 POUNDS.	-	100.0	-	-	-	-	-	-	-
90000 POUNDS AND OVER.	-	100.0	-	-	-	-	-	-	-
1000 TO 1499 MILES......	13	100.0	6.3	82.0	.3	3.4	-	7.7	.3
UNDER 1000 POUNDS.....	10	100.0	2.9	83.9	.5	2.1	-	10.2	.4
1000 TO 9999 POUNDS...	3	100.0	16.5	76.3	-	7.2	-	-	-
10000 TO 29999 POUNDS.	-	100.0	-	-	-	-	-	-	-
30000 TO 59999 POUNDS.	-	100.0	-	-	-	-	-	-	-
60000 TO 89999 POUNDS.	-	100.0	-	-	-	-	-	-	-
90000 POUNDS AND OVER.	-	100.0	-	-	-	-	-	-	-
1500 MILES OR OVER......	12	100.0	9.4	80.4	2.1	2.9	.1	4.7	.4
UNDER 1000 POUNDS.....	10	100.0	5.7	83.1	2.4	2.9	.2	5.2	.4
1000 TO 9999 POUNDS...	1	100.0	32.9	63.1	-	3.0	-	1.0	-
10000 TO 29999 POUNDS.	-	100.0	-	-	-	-	-	-	-
30000 TO 59999 POUNDS.	-	100.0	-	-	-	-	-	-	-
60000 TO 89999 POUNDS.	-	100.0	-	-	-	-	-	-	-
90000 POUNDS AND OVER.	-	100.0	-	-	-	-	-	-	-
TON-MILES OF SHIPMENTS	(millions of ton-miles)								
U.S. TOTAL.........	76	100.0	5.4	79.8	2.6	1.9	.1	9.4	.8
UNDER 100 MILES........	-	100.0	-	88.0	5.0	.1	.2	6.3	.4
UNDER 1000 POUNDS.....	-	100.0	-	90.4	1.1	.1	.2	7.8	.5
1000 TO 9999 POUNDS...	-	100.0	-	77.8	22.2	-	-	-	-
10000 TO 29999 POUNDS.	-	100.0	-	-	-	-	-	-	-
30000 TO 59999 POUNDS.	-	100.0	-	-	-	-	-	-	-
60000 TO 89999 POUNDS.	-	100.0	-	-	-	-	-	-	-
90000 POUNDS AND OVER.	-	100.0	-	-	-	-	-	-	-
100 TO 199 MILES........	1	100.0	-	86.1	7.2	.2	-	6.5	-
UNDER 1000 POUNDS.....	1	100.0	-	85.2	5.1	.3	-	9.4	-
1000 TO 9999 POUNDS...	-	100.0	-	57.0	43.0	-	-	-	-
10000 TO 29999 POUNDS.	-	100.0	-	-	-	-	-	-	-
30000 TO 59999 POUNDS.	-	100.0	-	100.0	-	-	-	-	-
60000 TO 89999 POUNDS.	-	100.0	-	-	-	-	-	-	-
90000 POUNDS AND OVER.	-	100.0	-	-	-	-	-	-	-

See footnotes at end of table 4.

TABLE 4. TCC GROUP 316—Percent Distribution of Distance Shipped and Weight of Shipment, by Means of Transport: 1972—Continued

Distance shipped and weight of shipment[2] [3]	Number	Percent distribution by means of transport							
		All means of transport	Rail	Motor carrier	Private truck	Air	Water	Other	Unknown
TON-MILES OF SHIPMENTS	(millions of ton-miles)								
200 TO 299 MILES........	1	100.0	-	85.0	-	1.4	-	13.6	-
UNDER 1000 POUNDS.....	1	100.0	-	82.4	-	1.6	-	16.0	-
1000 TO 9999 POUNDS...	-	100.0	-	100.0	-	-	-	-	-
10000 TO 29999 POUNDS.	-	100.0	-	-	-	-	-	-	-
30000 TO 59999 POUNDS.	-	100.0	-	-	-	-	-	-	-
60000 TO 89999 POUNDS.	-	100.0	-	-	-	-	-	-	-
90000 POUNDS AND OVER.	-	100.0	-	-	-	-	-	-	-
300 TO 499 MILES........	6	100.0	.2	84.8	.4	.2	-	13.8	.6
UNDER 1000 POUNDS.....	4	100.0	.3	77.7	.4	.3	-	20.4	.9
1000 TO 9999 POUNDS...	1	100.0	-	98.8	1.2	-	-	-	-
10000 TO 29999 POUNDS.	1	100.0	-	100.0	-	-	-	-	-
30000 TO 59999 POUNDS.	-	100.0	-	-	-	-	-	-	-
60000 TO 89999 POUNDS.	-	100.0	-	-	-	-	-	-	-
90000 POUNDS AND OVER.	-	100.0	-	-	-	-	-	-	-
500 TO 999 MILES........	22	100.0	1.5	75.4	5.3	.3	-	15.9	1.7
UNDER 1000 POUNDS.....	16	100.0	2.1	73.7	1.6	.5	-	19.8	2.4
1000 TO 9999 POUNDS...	5	100.0	-	74.3	18.0	-	-	7.7	-
10000 TO 29999 POUNDS.	1	100.0	-	100.0	-	-	-	-	-
30000 TO 59999 POUNDS.	-	100.0	-	-	-	-	-	-	-
60000 TO 89999 POUNDS.	-	100.0	-	-	-	-	-	-	-
90000 POUNDS AND OVER.	-	100.0	-	-	-	-	-	-	-
1000 TO 1499 MILES......	16	100.0	6.8	82.0	.3	3.1	-	7.5	.3
UNDER 1000 POUNDS.....	12	100.0	3.2	83.9	.4	2.1	-	10.0	.4
1000 TO 9999 POUNDS...	4	100.0	17.8	75.9	-	6.3	-	-	-
10000 TO 29999 POUNDS.	-	100.0	-	-	-	-	-	-	-
30000 TO 59999 POUNDS.	-	100.0	-	-	-	-	-	-	-
60000 TO 89999 POUNDS.	-	100.0	-	-	-	-	-	-	-
90000 POUNDS AND OVER.	-	100.0	-	-	-	-	-	-	-
1500 MILES OR OVER......	26	100.0	10.0	80.2	2.1	3.2	.3	4.0	.4
UNDER 1000 POUNDS.....	23	100.0	6.2	83.2	2.4	3.1	.3	4.4	.4
1000 TO 9999 POUNDS...	3	100.0	35.2	60.1	-	3.5	-	1.2	-
10000 TO 29999 POUNDS.	-	100.0	-	-	-	-	-	-	-
30000 TO 59999 POUNDS.	-	100.0	-	-	-	-	-	-	-
60000 TO 89999 POUNDS.	-	100.0	-	-	-	-	-	-	-
90000 POUNDS AND OVER.	-	100.0	-	-	-	-	-	-	-

Note: Detail may not add to total due to rounding. The introductory table shows the estimates of sampling variability for tons; sampling variability for ton-miles has not been estimated. See the map in the Introduction for the States comprising the geographic divisions of the United States.

Shipments excluded from the survey are those moving by pipeline (primarily petroleum products from refineries), parcel post shipments, and commodities moved by own power (motorized vehicles, aircraft, etc.) or towed (prefabricated buildings, etc.). Local shipments (commodities shipped less than 25 miles from the plant) and shipments within the same city are also excluded. Shipments to Alaska and Hawaii from the 48 conterminous States and the District of Columbia are included; however, no data were obtained for shipments originating in Alaska and Hawaii.

- Represents zero or rounds to zero.   (D) Withheld to avoid disclosing figures for individual companies.

[1]Production of this commodity is concentrated in the geographic divisions shown; figures and distributions for geographic divisions not shown are included in the total.

[2]Distances of shipments to foreign destinations are calculated only to the U.S. port or exit.

[3]Includes only shipments represented by bills of lading and invoices. Summary records which did not show individual weights of shipments are not included.

Fabricated Metal Products, Except Ordnance, Machinery, and Transportation

CONTENTS

[Page numbers listed here omit the State prefix number that appears as part of the number for each page]

TABLES

(The tables listed below are shown for each of the Transportation Commodity Classification groups in this report)

Comparisons of Tons and Ton-Miles of Shipments for Geographic Divisions of Origin and for Sampling Variability: 1972 and 1967

1. Percent Distribution of Geographic Division of Origin and Distance Shipped, by Means of Transport: 1972

2. Percent Distribution of Geographic Division of Origin and Means of Transport, by Geographic Division of Destination: 1972

3. Percent Distribution of Geographic Division of Destination and Means of Transport, by Geographic Division of Origin: 1972

4. Percent Distribution of Distance Shipped and Weight of Shipment, by Means of Transport: 1972

TCC 341. Metal Cans

Comparisons of Tons and Ton-Miles of Shipments for
Geographic Divisions of Origin and for Sampling Variability: 1972 and 1967

Geographic division of origin	Estimates				Relative sampling variability in tons (percent)	
	1972		1967		1972	1967
	Tons (thousands)	Ton-miles (millions)	Tons (thousands)	Ton-miles (millions)		
U.S. total	3,701	863	3,845	851	8.3	8.4
New England	(D)	(D)	71	10	(*)	(*)
Middle Atlantic	550	87	897	154	2.6	(*)
East North Central	1,431	398	1,096	292	17.6	(*)
West North Central	208	37	288	59	23.3	(*)
South Atlantic	356	67	343	65	2.9	(*)
East South Central	(D)	(D)	114	76	(*)	(*)
West South Central	128	51	219	47	3.7	(*)
Mountain	(D)	(D)	—	—	(*)	(*)
Pacific	727	154	817	148	20.8	(*)

— Represents or rounds to zero.   (D) Withheld to avoid disclosing figures for individual companies.   (*) Data not published.

TABLE 1. TCC GROUP 341—Percent Distribution of Geographic Division of Origin and Distance Shipped, by Means of Transport: 1972

Geographic division of origin[1] and distance shipped[2]	Number	Percent distribution by means of transport							
		All means of transport	Rail	Motor carrier	Private truck	Air	Water	Other	Unknown
TONS OF SHIPMENTS	(thousands of tons)								
U.S. TOTAL...........	3 701	100.0	18.9	45.5	35.2	-	.2	.2	.1
MIDDLE ATLANTIC.........	550	100.0	8.8	69.6	20.9	-	-	.6	-
UNDER 100 MILES.......	310	100.0	1.1	68.7	29.6	-	-	.4	-
100 TO 199 MILES......	117	100.0	22.8	63.8	13.1	-	-	.3	-
200 TO 299 MILES......	55	100.0	5.1	83.4	9.1	-	-	2.4	-
300 TO 499 MILES......	29	100.0	5.3	90.7	4.0	-	-	.1	-
500 TO 999 MILES......	29	100.0	28.9	65.6	5.1	.2	-	.1	-
1000 TO 1499 MILES....	5	100.0	58.6	36.2	4.7	-	-	.5	-
1500 MILES OR OVER....	2	100.0	71.6	26.9	.8	-	-	.8	-
EAST NORTH CENTRAL......	1 431	100.0	24.7	40.4	34.9	-	-	-	-
UNDER 100 MILES.......	542	100.0	2.5	36.3	61.2	-	-	-	-
100 TO 199 MILES......	290	100.0	9.0	53.9	37.0	-	-	.1	.1
200 TO 299 MILES......	184	100.0	26.5	62.9	10.6	-	-	-	-
300 TO 499 MILES......	194	100.0	44.5	39.8	15.7	-	-	-	-
500 TO 999 MILES......	155	100.0	75.1	18.6	6.0	-	-	.2	-
1000 TO 1499 MILES....	9	100.0	89.0	4.0	6.0	-	-	1.0	-
1500 MILES OR OVER....	54	100.0	96.8	3.0	.2	-	-	-	-
WEST NORTH CENTRAL......	208	100.0	17.1	42.7	39.3	-	-	.9	-
UNDER 100 MILES.......	97	100.0	5.7	47.5	46.4	-	-	.4	-
100 TO 199 MILES......	48	100.0	13.8	25.6	58.2	-	-	2.3	-
200 TO 299 MILES......	31	100.0	38.5	48.2	13.3	-	-	-	-
300 TO 499 MILES......	17	100.0	32.2	45.4	22.4	-	-	-	-
500 TO 999 MILES......	10	100.0	50.7	47.4	2.0	-	-	-	-
1000 TO 1499 MILES....	3	100.0	19.1	68.7	-	-	-	12.2	-
1500 MILES OR OVER....	-	100.0	-	-	-	-	-	-	-
SOUTH ATLANTIC..........	356	100.0	8.0	47.3	44.3	-	.1	.2	.1
UNDER 100 MILES.......	157	100.0	.1	50.0	49.4	-	-	.3	.2
100 TO 199 MILES......	104	100.0	5.2	51.9	42.7	-	.2	.1	-
200 TO 299 MILES......	37	100.0	3.2	36.2	60.3	-	.1	.3	-
300 TO 499 MILES......	28	100.0	14.6	53.3	32.1	-	-	-	-
500 TO 999 MILES......	26	100.0	57.0	27.2	15.2	-	-	.2	.4
1000 TO 1499 MILES....	-	100.0	61.2	37.6	1.2	-	-	-	-
1500 MILES OR OVER....	2	100.0	76.0	5.2	18.8	-	-	-	-
WEST SOUTH CENTRAL......	128	100.0	39.6	19.9	40.5	-	-	-	-
UNDER 100 MILES.......	34	100.0	10.0	26.4	63.6	-	-	-	-
100 TO 199 MILES......	20	100.0	19.4	33.8	46.8	-	-	-	-
200 TO 299 MILES......	28	100.0	34.0	21.7	44.3	-	-	-	-
300 TO 499 MILES......	18	100.0	60.4	7.9	31.7	-	-	-	-
500 TO 999 MILES......	9	100.0	67.3	14.7	18.0	-	-	-	-
1000 TO 1499 MILES....	11	100.0	97.2	1.9	.9	-	-	-	-
1500 MILES OR OVER....	5	100.0	88.4	5.5	6.0	-	-	-	-
PACIFIC.................	727	100.0	9.5	53.5	35.9	-	1.0	-	.1
UNDER 100 MILES.......	502	100.0	.4	50.5	48.9	-	-	-	.2
100 TO 199 MILES......	73	100.0	-	90.3	9.7	-	-	-	-
200 TO 299 MILES......	7	100.0	-	87.9	12.1	-	-	-	-
300 TO 499 MILES......	72	100.0	17.7	73.3	8.8	-	-	-	.1
500 TO 999 MILES......	40	100.0	77.5	20.7	1.8	-	-	-	-
1000 TO 1499 MILES....	2	100.0	98.7	1.3	-	-	-	-	-
1500 MILES OR OVER....	29	100.0	70.6	5.5	-	-	23.9	-	-
TON-MILES OF SHIPMENTS	(millions of ton-miles)								
U.S. TOTAL...........	863	100.0	48.9	32.4	16.7	-	1.7	.2	-
MIDDLE ATLANTIC.........	87	100.0	22.1	67.5	9.8	-	-	.6	-
UNDER 100 MILES.......	11	100.0	1.5	68.0	30.3	-	-	.2	.1
100 TO 199 MILES......	16	100.0	21.1	65.7	12.9	-	-	.3	-
200 TO 299 MILES......	13	100.0	5.5	83.5	8.6	-	-	2.4	-
300 TO 499 MILES......	10	100.0	5.6	90.5	3.9	-	-	.1	-
500 TO 999 MILES......	21	100.0	27.0	68.8	3.9	.2	-	.1	-
1000 TO 1499 MILES....	7	100.0	59.8	35.0	4.7	-	-	.5	-
1500 MILES OR OVER....	6	100.0	70.1	28.5	.6	-	-	.8	-
EAST NORTH CENTRAL......	398	100.0	59.1	27.7	13.1	-	-	.1	-
UNDER 100 MILES.......	21	100.0	4.0	35.5	60.5	-	-	-	-
100 TO 199 MILES......	42	100.0	10.2	53.9	35.9	-	-	.1	.1
200 TO 299 MILES......	45	100.0	27.3	62.2	10.5	-	-	-	-
300 TO 499 MILES......	74	100.0	45.5	38.9	15.5	-	-	-	-
500 TO 999 MILES......	103	100.0	75.8	17.9	6.0	-	-	.2	-
1000 TO 1499 MILES....	10	100.0	88.2	3.8	6.8	-	-	1.2	-
1500 MILES OR OVER....	100	100.0	96.4	3.2	.4	-	-	-	-
WEST NORTH CENTRAL......	37	100.0	28.4	45.8	24.4	-	-	1.5	-
UNDER 100 MILES.......	5	100.0	8.5	50.8	40.5	-	-	.2	-
100 TO 199 MILES......	7	100.0	14.8	25.7	57.3	-	-	2.2	-
200 TO 299 MILES......	7	100.0	39.0	48.1	12.8	-	-	-	-
300 TO 499 MILES......	6	100.0	32.2	43.9	24.0	-	-	-	-
500 TO 999 MILES......	7	100.0	46.3	51.8	2.0	-	-	-	-
1000 TO 1499 MILES....	3	100.0	19.5	68.6	-	-	-	11.9	-
1500 MILES OR OVER....	-	100.0	-	-	-	-	-	-	-

See footnotes at end of table 4.

TABLE 1. TCC GROUP 341—Percent Distribution of Geographic Division of Origin and Distance Shipped, by Means of Transport: 1972—Continued

Geographic division of origin[1] and distance shipped[2]	Number	Percent distribution by means of transport							
		All means of transport	Rail	Motor carrier	Private truck	Air	Water	Other	Unknown
TON-MILES OF SHIPMENTS	(millions of ton-miles)								
SOUTH ATLANTIC............	67	100.0	27.9	38.4	33.4	-	.1	.2	.1
UNDER 100 MILES........	8	100.0	.2	48.8	50.4	-	-	.4	.2
100 TO 199 MILES......	15	100.0	5.0	51.7	42.9	-	.2	.1	-
200 TO 299 MILES......	8	100.0	3.7	37.0	59.0	-	.1	.3	-
300 TO 499 MILES......	11	100.0	17.2	51.7	31.1	-	-	-	-
500 TO 999 MILES......	18	100.0	61.2	24.5	13.8	-	-	.2	.3
1000 TO 1499 MILES....	1	100.0	64.0	34.9	1.1	-	-	-	-
1500 MILES OR OVER....	4	100.0	76.1	5.7	18.1	-	-	-	-
WEST SOUTH CENTRAL......	51	100.0	69.9	10.6	19.5	-	-	-	-
UNDER 100 MILES........	1	100.0	12.5	20.6	66.9	-	-	-	-
100 TO 199 MILES......	3	100.0	23.8	33.6	42.6	-	-	-	-
200 TO 299 MILES......	6	100.0	32.9	21.5	45.6	-	-	-	-
300 TO 499 MILES......	7	100.0	62.6	8.1	29.3	-	-	-	-
500 TO 999 MILES......	6	100.0	70.4	14.9	14.7	-	-	-	-
1000 TO 1499 MILES....	15	100.0	97.4	1.9	.7	-	-	-	-
1500 MILES OR OVER....	10	100.0	81.5	6.8	11.7	-	-	-	-
PACIFIC..................	154	100.0	46.0	33.0	11.4	-	9.6	-	.1
UNDER 100 MILES........	27	100.0	.2	48.6	51.0	-	-	-	.2
100 TO 199 MILES......	9	100.0	-	90.9	9.1	-	-	-	-
200 TO 299 MILES......	1	100.0	-	88.5	11.5	-	-	-	-
300 TO 499 MILES......	25	100.0	20.8	70.7	8.4	-	-	-	.1
500 TO 999 MILES......	27	100.0	78.7	19.4	1.9	-	-	-	-
1000 TO 1499 MILES....	3	100.0	98.6	1.4	-	-	-	-	-
1500 MILES OR OVER....	59	100.0	68.9	6.3	-	-	24.8	-	-

See footnotes at end of table 4.

TABLE 2. TCC GROUP 341—Percent Distribution of Geographic Division of Origin and Means of Transport, by Geographic Division of Destination: 1972

Geographic division of origin[1] and means of transport	Number	Percent distribution by division of destination									
		U.S. total	New England	Middle Atlantic	East North Central	West North Central	South Atlantic	East South Central	West South Central	Mountain	Pacific
TONS OF SHIPMENTS	(thousands of tons)										
U.S. TOTAL..............	3 701	100.0	3.8	15.9	29.2	7.9	11.2	3.5	5.9	1.5	21.2
RAIL...................	698	100.0	1.9	9.6	16.8	15.0	18.7	6.4	14.2	3.0	14.3
MOTOR CARRIER..........	1 684	100.0	3.9	21.6	30.3	6.3	10.1	2.1	2.4	.8	22.4
PRIVATE TRUCK..........	1 303	100.0	4.6	11.7	34.6	6.2	8.8	3.9	5.9	1.5	22.8
AIR....................	-	100.0	1.1	34.6	43.4	1.7	5.7	9.9	1.7	.8	1.1
WATER..................	7	100.0	-	-	-	-	3.4	-	-	-	96.6
OTHER..................	6	100.0	13.2	40.2	8.4	22.1	13.0	1.0	.4	1.4	.3
UNKNOWN................	1	100.0	-	16.7	13.3	-	14.0	-	-	-	56.0
MIDDLE ATLANTIC.........	550	100.0	7.4	72.3	5.9	1.0	11.2	.8	1.0	.1	.4
RAIL...................	48	100.0	2.6	43.0	12.1	1.7	27.4	1.3	8.2	.7	3.1
MOTOR CARRIER..........	383	100.0	9.3	72.2	6.3	1.2	9.5	.9	.4	-	.2
PRIVATE TRUCK..........	115	100.0	2.5	85.1	1.8	.1	10.0	.2	.1	-	-
AIR....................	-	100.0	-	-	99.0	-	.8	.2	-	-	-
WATER..................	-	100.0	-	-	-	-	-	-	-	-	-
OTHER..................	3	100.0	24.8	62.6	4.7	.3	6.2	.2	.7	.1	.6
UNKNOWN................	-	100.0	-	100.0	-	-	-	-	-	-	-
EAST NORTH CENTRAL......	1 431	100.0	1.0	4.2	68.4	9.5	5.1	4.7	2.9	.4	3.8
RAIL...................	353	100.0	2.4	5.6	21.6	23.6	13.5	7.5	9.1	1.7	15.0
MOTOR CARRIER..........	577	100.0	.5	4.5	80.2	6.9	3.8	3.1	.8	-	.3
PRIVATE TRUCK..........	499	100.0	.5	2.8	88.1	2.5	.5	4.5	.9	-	-
AIR....................	-	100.0	1.9	67.0	10.0	3.3	.9	16.3	-	-	.6
WATER..................	-	100.0	-	-	-	-	-	-	-	-	-
OTHER..................	-	100.0	9.5	13.5	34.0	1.2	27.8	.6	.4	12.9	.1
UNKNOWN................	-	100.0	.3	-	99.7	-	-	-	-	-	-
WEST NORTH CENTRAL......	208	100.0	-	1.8	12.4	71.0	1.0	2.4	9.5	1.9	.1
RAIL...................	35	100.0	-	2.5	7.8	48.3	.6	10.7	19.1	11.0	-
MOTOR CARRIER..........	88	100.0	-	3.2	18.1	68.4	1.6	1.0	7.4	.1	.1
PRIVATE TRUCK..........	81	100.0	-	-	8.3	83.6	-	.4	7.7	-	-
AIR....................	-	100.0	44.4	-	55.6	-	-	-	-	-	-
WATER..................	-	100.0	-	-	-	-	-	-	-	-	-
OTHER..................	1	100.0	-	-	5.3	74.5	20.2	-	-	-	-
UNKNOWN................	-	100.0	-	-	-	-	-	-	-	-	-
SOUTH ATLANTIC..........	356	100.0	.6	26.3	2.1	.3	58.9	7.6	3.6	.1	.5
RAIL...................	28	100.0	.8	19.6	4.8	1.5	28.3	2.5	36.4	-	6.2
MOTOR CARRIER..........	168	100.0	.7	28.5	2.9	.3	61.8	5.1	.7	.3	.1
PRIVATE TRUCK..........	158	100.0	.5	25.0	.8	-	61.5	11.1	.8	-	-
AIR....................	-	100.0	-	-	-	-	78.0	22.0	-	-	-
WATER..................	-	100.0	-	-	-	-	100.0	-	-	-	-
OTHER..................	-	100.0	-	74.5	8.7	.1	9.1	7.6	-	-	-
UNKNOWN................	-	100.0	-	38.2	-	-	61.8	-	-	-	-

See footnotes at end of table 4.

TABLE 2. TCC GROUP 341—Percent Distribution of Geographic Division of Origin and Means of Transport, by Geographic Division of Destination: 1972—Continued

Geographic division of origin[1] and means of transport	Number	Percent distribution by division of destination									
		U.S. total	New England	Middle Atlantic	East North Central	West North Central	South Atlantic	East South Central	West South Central	Mountain	Pacific
TONS OF SHIPMENTS	(thousands of tons)										
WEST SOUTH CENTRAL......	128	100.0	1.0	4.0	.8	1.3	4.5	11.9	68.9	1.2	6.4
RAIL............	50	100.0	2.4	10.1	1.1	2.4	10.1	13.5	43.6	2.2	14.6
MOTOR CARRIER........	25	100.0	-	-	1.1	1.7	2.4	3.0	88.4	1.4	1.9
PRIVATE TRUCK.......	51	100.0	-	-	.3	-	.1	14.8	83.9	.2	.6
AIR...............	-	100.0	-	-	-	-	-	-	51.8	45.6	2.6
WATER.............	-	100.0	-	-	-	-	-	-	-	-	-
OTHER.............	-	100.0	-	-	-	-	-	-	-	-	-
UNKNOWN...........	-	100.0	-	-	-	-	-	-	-	-	-
PACIFIC..............	727	100.0	-	1.2	1.7	.1	-	-	.4	3.4	93.2
RAIL............	69	100.0	-	10.7	18.0	1.0	-	-	3.6	14.0	52.7
MOTOR CARRIER........	389	100.0	-	.3	-	-	-	-	-	3.5	96.1
PRIVATE TRUCK.......	260	100.0	-	-	-	-	-	-	-	.5	99.5
AIR...............	-	100.0	-	-	56.2	-	-	-	22.7	-	21.1
WATER.............	6	100.0	-	-	-	-	-	-	-	-	100.0
OTHER.............	-	100.0	-	-	40.8	-	-	-	-	-	59.2
UNKNOWN...........	1	100.0	-	-	-	-	-	-	-	-	100.0
TON-MILES OF SHIPMENTS	(millions of ton-miles)										
U.S. TOTAL..........	863	100.0	3.4	11.6	19.1	9.9	11.9	4.6	9.7	2.9	27.0
RAIL............	422	100.0	1.8	9.5	11.7	11.5	11.4	4.3	13.6	3.8	32.5
MOTOR CARRIER........	279	100.0	5.0	15.9	29.0	8.7	13.3	4.4	4.1	2.2	17.4
PRIVATE TRUCK.......	144	100.0	5.2	10.2	23.7	8.5	11.8	6.0	10.3	1.8	22.5
AIR...............	-	100.0	1.6	33.5	47.9	2.0	3.2	6.6	2.4	.8	2.2
WATER.............	14	100.0	-	-	-	-	.3	-	-	-	99.7
OTHER.............	1	100.0	13.3	18.8	6.4	11.3	34.5	2.9	1.8	8.0	3.0
UNKNOWN...........	-	100.0	.3	8.6	15.1	-	36.2	-	-	-	39.9
MIDDLE ATLANTIC........	87	100.0	11.5	31.5	15.4	5.4	18.1	3.7	7.7	.6	6.1
RAIL............	19	100.0	1.9	12.7	17.1	3.2	17.0	2.1	25.0	2.3	18.7
MOTOR CARRIER........	58	100.0	15.2	33.5	16.3	6.6	18.0	4.6	2.9	.1	2.9
PRIVATE TRUCK.......	8	100.0	6.1	59.8	5.9	1.9	22.1	1.6	2.2	.4	-
AIR...............	-	100.0	-	-	98.7	-	1.1	.2	-	-	-
WATER.............	-	100.0	-	-	-	-	-	-	-	-	-
OTHER.............	-	100.0	31.7	36.2	6.9	1.7	8.2	.8	5.2	.8	8.6
UNKNOWN...........	-	100.0	-	100.0	-	-	-	-	-	-	-
EAST NORTH CENTRAL......	398	100.0	2.1	6.1	27.9	15.1	8.8	4.7	8.5	1.6	25.2
RAIL............	235	100.0	2.0	3.4	6.8	17.9	10.5	4.4	11.4	2.6	41.0
MOTOR CARRIER........	110	100.0	1.7	10.1	57.0	12.2	8.3	4.9	2.9	.1	2.9
PRIVATE TRUCK.......	52	100.0	3.0	10.1	61.7	9.1	2.6	5.5	7.2	-	.8
AIR...............	-	100.0	2.9	74.5	5.5	4.4	.5	10.1	-	-	2.1
WATER.............	-	100.0	-	-	-	-	-	-	-	-	-
OTHER.............	-	100.0	12.0	14.4	9.5	.9	29.6	.5	.5	32.2	.5
UNKNOWN...........	-	100.0	1.8	-	98.2	-	-	-	-	-	-
WEST NORTH CENTRAL......	37	100.0	-	9.8	16.0	44.5	4.8	4.6	13.0	6.8	.5
RAIL............	10	100.0	-	8.2	6.8	27.8	1.4	11.8	20.6	23.4	-
MOTOR CARRIER........	17	100.0	-	16.3	25.4	36.5	7.5	1.6	11.3	.4	1.0
PRIVATE TRUCK.......	9	100.0	-	-	9.7	80.0	-	1.9	8.3	.1	-
AIR...............	-	100.0	70.6	-	29.4	-	-	-	-	-	-
WATER.............	-	100.0	-	-	-	-	-	-	-	-	-
OTHER.............	-	100.0	-	-	2.4	29.4	68.2	-	-	-	-
UNKNOWN...........	-	100.0	-	-	-	-	-	-	-	-	-
SOUTH ATLANTIC..........	67	100.0	1.5	18.8	5.3	1.0	43.0	7.8	15.5	1.3	5.8
RAIL............	18	100.0	.4	10.5	4.1	1.6	15.2	2.5	46.3	-	19.4
MOTOR CARRIER........	26	100.0	2.5	24.7	8.5	1.3	52.2	6.1	3.4	-	1.1
PRIVATE TRUCK.......	22	100.0	1.3	18.8	2.5	-	55.6	14.1	3.9	3.8	-
AIR...............	-	100.0	-	-	-	-	56.7	43.3	-	-	-
WATER.............	-	100.0	-	-	-	-	100.0	-	-	-	-
OTHER.............	-	100.0	-	47.2	12.7	.4	5.0	34.5	-	-	.2
UNKNOWN...........	-	100.0	-	8.2	-	-	91.8	-	-	-	-
WEST SOUTH CENTRAL......	51	100.0	3.6	13.2	1.4	2.0	10.0	10.4	29.1	2.2	28.1
RAIL............	36	100.0	5.1	18.9	1.2	2.4	12.8	9.6	13.9	2.2	34.1
MOTOR CARRIER........	5	100.0	-	.2	3.6	3.4	9.1	4.7	57.0	4.1	17.8
PRIVATE TRUCK.......	10	100.0	-	-	1.0	.1	.3	16.6	68.6	1.0	12.3
AIR...............	-	100.0	-	-	-	-	-	-	42.1	51.2	6.7
WATER.............	-	100.0	-	-	-	-	-	-	-	-	-
OTHER.............	-	100.0	-	-	-	-	-	-	-	-	-
UNKNOWN...........	-	100.0	-	-	-	-	-	-	-	-	-
PACIFIC..............	154	100.0	-	13.6	14.5	.7	.2	-	2.2	8.0	60.8
RAIL............	71	100.0	-	25.0	31.3	1.5	-	-	4.7	8.3	29.2
MOTOR CARRIER........	51	100.0	-	6.4	.4	.1	.5	-	-	11.4	81.2
PRIVATE TRUCK.......	17	100.0	-	-	-	-	-	-	.5	3.3	96.2
AIR...............	-	100.0	-	-	66.6	-	-	-	20.3	-	13.1
WATER.............	14	100.0	-	-	-	-	-	-	-	-	100.0
OTHER.............	-	100.0	-	-	81.6	-	-	-	-	-	18.4
UNKNOWN...........	-	100.0	-	-	-	-	-	-	-	-	100.0

See footnotes at end of table 4.

TABLE 3. **TCC GROUP 341**—Percent Distribution of Geographic Division of Destination and Means of Transport, by Geographic Division of Origin: 1972

Geographic division of destination and means of transport	Number	Percent distribution by division of origin [1]								
		U.S. total	New England	Middle Atlantic	East North Central	West North Central	South Atlantic	East South Central	West South Central	Mountain	Pacific
TONS OF SHIPMENTS	(thousands of tons)										
U.S. TOTAL.............	3 701	100.0	(D)	14.9	38.7	5.6	9.6	(D)	3.5	(D)	19.7
RAIL..................	698	100.0	(D)	7.0	50.6	5.1	4.1	(D)	7.3	(D)	9.9
MOTOR CARRIER.........	1 684	100.0	(D)	22.8	34.3	5.3	10.0	(D)	1.5	(D)	23.1
PRIVATE TRUCK.........	1 303	100.0	(D)	8.9	38.3	6.3	12.1	(D)	4.0	(D)	20.0
AIR...................	-	100.0	(D)	36.5	51.6	.3	6.4	(D)	1.7	(D)	3.5
WATER.................	7	100.0	(D)	-	-	-	3.4	(D)	-	(D)	96.6
OTHER.................	6	100.0	(D)	49.1	10.8	29.3	10.8	(D)	-	(D)	-
UNKNOWN...............	1	100.0	(D)	8.1	13.3	-	22.6	(D)	-	(D)	56.0
NEW ENGLAND...........	140	100.0	(D)	28.9	9.8	-	1.6	(D)	.9	(D)	-
RAIL..................	13	100.0	(D)	9.5	63.2	-	1.7	(D)	9.3	(D)	-
MOTOR CARRIER.........	66	100.0	(D)	54.0	4.0	-	1.7	(D)	-	(D)	-
PRIVATE TRUCK.........	60	100.0	(D)	4.8	4.4	-	1.4	(D)	-	(D)	-
AIR...................	-	100.0	(D)	-	87.3	12.7	-	(D)	-	(D)	-
WATER.................	-	100.0	(D)	-	-	-	-	(D)	-	(D)	-
OTHER.................	-	100.0	(D)	92.2	7.8	-	-	(D)	-	(D)	-
UNKNOWN...............	-	100.0	(D)	-	100.0	-	-	(D)	-	(D)	-
MIDDLE ATLANTIC.......	586	100.0	(D)	67.8	10.2	.6	16.0	(D)	.9	(D)	1.5
RAIL..................	67	100.0	(D)	31.0	29.3	1.3	8.3	(D)	7.6	(D)	11.0
MOTOR CARRIER.........	364	100.0	(D)	76.0	7.1	.8	13.2	(D)	-	(D)	.4
PRIVATE TRUCK.........	151	100.0	(D)	64.6	9.4	-	26.0	(D)	-	(D)	-
AIR...................	-	100.0	(D)	-	100.0	-	-	(D)	-	(D)	-
WATER.................	-	100.0	(D)	-	-	-	-	(D)	-	(D)	-
OTHER.................	2	100.0	(D)	76.4	3.6	-	20.0	(D)	-	(D)	-
UNKNOWN...............	-	100.0	(D)	48.4	-	-	51.6	(D)	-	(D)	-
EAST NORTH CENTRAL....	1 079	100.0	(D)	3.0	90.8	2.4	.7	(D)	.1	(D)	1.2
RAIL..................	117	100.0	(D)	5.0	65.1	2.4	1.2	(D)	.5	(D)	10.7
MOTOR CARRIER.........	510	100.0	(D)	4.7	90.6	3.2	1.0	(D)	.1	(D)	-
PRIVATE TRUCK.........	450	100.0	(D)	.5	97.7	1.5	.3	(D)	-	(D)	-
AIR...................	-	100.0	(D)	83.2	11.8	.4	-	(D)	-	(D)	4.5
WATER.................	-	100.0	(D)	-	-	-	-	(D)	-	(D)	-
OTHER.................	-	100.0	(D)	27.0	43.6	18.2	11.1	(D)	-	(D)	-
UNKNOWN...............	-	100.0	(D)	-	100.0	-	-	(D)	-	(D)	-
WEST NORTH CENTRAL....	293	100.0	(D)	1.9	46.3	50.4	.3	(D)	.6	(D)	.2
RAIL..................	104	100.0	(D)	.8	79.8	16.5	.4	(D)	1.2	(D)	.6
MOTOR CARRIER.........	106	100.0	(D)	4.3	37.5	57.3	.4	(D)	.4	(D)	-
PRIVATE TRUCK.........	81	100.0	(D)	.2	15.6	84.2	-	(D)	-	(D)	-
AIR...................	-	100.0	(D)	-	100.0	-	-	(D)	-	(D)	-
WATER.................	-	100.0	(D)	-	-	-	-	(D)	-	(D)	-
OTHER.................	1	100.0	(D)	.6	.6	98.8	-	(D)	-	(D)	-
UNKNOWN...............	-	100.0	(D)	-	-	-	-	(D)	-	(D)	-
SOUTH ATLANTIC........	416	100.0	(D)	14.8	17.5	.5	50.5	(D)	1.4	(D)	-
RAIL..................	130	100.0	(D)	10.2	36.5	.2	6.2	(D)	4.0	(D)	-
MOTOR CARRIER.........	169	100.0	(D)	21.5	13.0	.8	61.4	(D)	.4	(D)	.1
PRIVATE TRUCK.........	114	100.0	(D)	10.1	2.3	-	85.0	(D)	-	(D)	-
AIR...................	-	100.0	(D)	5.3	7.9	-	86.8	(D)	-	(D)	-
WATER.................	-	100.0	(D)	-	-	-	100.0	(D)	-	(D)	-
OTHER.................	-	100.0	(D)	23.4	23.2	45.8	7.6	(D)	-	(D)	-
UNKNOWN...............	-	100.0	(D)	-	-	-	100.0	(D)	-	(D)	-
EAST SOUTH CENTRAL....	130	100.0	(D)	3.2	51.2	3.9	20.6	(D)	11.7	(D)	-
RAIL..................	44	100.0	(D)	1.4	58.7	8.5	1.6	(D)	15.3	(D)	-
MOTOR CARRIER.........	35	100.0	(D)	9.2	50.7	2.5	24.3	(D)	2.2	(D)	-
PRIVATE TRUCK.........	50	100.0	(D)	.6	45.0	.7	34.8	(D)	15.2	(D)	-
AIR...................	-	100.0	(D)	.7	85.1	-	14.2	(D)	-	(D)	-
WATER.................	-	100.0	(D)	-	-	-	-	(D)	-	(D)	-
OTHER.................	-	100.0	(D)	9.4	6.6	-	84.0	(D)	-	(D)	-
UNKNOWN...............	-	100.0	(D)	-	-	-	-	(D)	-	(D)	-
WEST SOUTH CENTRAL....	216	100.0	(D)	2.6	19.2	9.1	5.9	(D)	40.8	(D)	1.2
RAIL..................	99	100.0	(D)	4.0	32.5	6.9	10.4	(D)	22.3	(D)	2.5
MOTOR CARRIER.........	39	100.0	(D)	3.6	11.3	16.6	2.9	(D)	57.0	(D)	-
PRIVATE TRUCK.........	77	100.0	(D)	.2	6.1	8.1	1.7	(D)	56.3	(D)	.1
AIR...................	-	100.0	(D)	-	-	-	-	(D)	52.4	(D)	47.6
WATER.................	-	100.0	(D)	-	-	-	-	(D)	-	(D)	-
OTHER.................	-	100.0	(D)	89.4	10.6	-	-	(D)	-	(D)	-
UNKNOWN...............	-	100.0	(D)	-	-	-	-	(D)	-	(D)	-
MOUNTAIN..............	54	100.0	(D)	.7	11.3	7.4	.8	(D)	2.9	(D)	44.6
RAIL..................	21	100.0	(D)	1.6	28.7	18.5	-	(D)	5.2	(D)	46.0
MOTOR CARRIER.........	14	100.0	(D)	.2	.4	.9	-	(D)	2.5	(D)	96.0
PRIVATE TRUCK.........	19	100.0	(D)	.1	-	.1	2.2	(D)	.5	(D)	6.7
AIR...................	-	100.0	(D)	-	-	-	-	(D)	100.0	(D)	-
WATER.................	-	100.0	(D)	-	-	-	-	(D)	-	(D)	-
OTHER.................	-	100.0	(D)	2.3	97.7	-	-	(D)	-	(D)	-
UNKNOWN...............	-	100.0	(D)	-	-	-	-	(D)	-	(D)	-
PACIFIC...............	783	100.0	(D)	.3	7.0	-	.2	(D)	1.1	(D)	86.6
RAIL..................	100	100.0	(D)	1.5	52.9	-	1.8	(D)	7.4	(D)	36.4
MOTOR CARRIER.........	377	100.0	(D)	.2	.4	-	-	(D)	.1	(D)	99.1
PRIVATE TRUCK.........	297	100.0	(D)	-	-	-	-	(D)	.1	(D)	87.3
AIR...................	-	100.0	(D)	-	29.2	-	-	(D)	3.9	(D)	66.9
WATER.................	6	100.0	(D)	-	-	-	-	(D)	-	(D)	100.0
OTHER.................	-	100.0	(D)	92.3	5.2	-	.6	(D)	-	(D)	1.9
UNKNOWN...............	1	100.0	(D)	-	-	-	-	(D)	-	(D)	100.0

See footnotes at end of table 4.

TABLE 3. **TCC GROUP 341**—Percent Distribution of Geographic Division of Destination and Means of Transport, by Geographic Division of Origin: 1972—Continued

Geographic division of destination and means of transport	Number	Percent distribution by division of origin[1]									
		U.S. total	New England	Middle Atlantic	East North Central	West North Central	South Atlantic	East South Central	West South Central	Mountain	Pacific
TON-MILES OF SHIPMENTS	(millions of ton-miles)										
U.S. TOTAL	863	100.0	(D)	10.1	46.2	4.4	7.9	(D)	6.0	(D)	17.9
RAIL	422	100.0	(D)	4.6	55.8	2.5	4.5	(D)	8.6	(D)	16.9
MOTOR CARRIER	279	100.0	(D)	21.1	39.4	6.2	9.3	(D)	2.0	(D)	18.3
PRIVATE TRUCK	144	100.0	(D)	5.9	36.2	6.4	15.7	(D)	7.0	(D)	12.2
AIR	-	100.0	(D)	40.2	45.0	.3	4.5	(D)	1.5	(D)	8.5
WATER	14	100.0	(D)	-	-	-	.3	(D)	-	(D)	99.7
OTHER	1	100.0	(D)	32.9	24.2	35.6	7.3	(D)	-	(D)	-
UNKNOWN	-	100.0	(D)	5.4	15.4	-	39.4	(D)	-	(D)	39.9
NEW ENGLAND	29	100.0	(D)	34.4	28.6	-	3.6	(D)	6.3	(D)	-
RAIL	7	100.0	(D)	5.0	64.8	-	1.0	(D)	24.9	(D)	-
MOTOR CARRIER	14	100.0	(D)	63.9	13.5	-	4.7	(D)	-	(D)	-
PRIVATE TRUCK	7	100.0	(D)	7.0	21.1	-	4.0	(D)	-	(D)	-
AIR	-	100.0	(D)	-	85.1	14.9	-	(D)	-	(D)	-
WATER	-	100.0	(D)	-	-	-	-	(D)	-	(D)	-
OTHER	-	100.0	(D)	78.3	21.7	-	-	(D)	-	(D)	-
UNKNOWN	-	100.0	(D)	-	100.0	-	-	(D)	-	(D)	-
MIDDLE ATLANTIC	99	100.0	(D)	27.5	24.4	3.7	12.8	(D)	6.9	(D)	21.1
RAIL	40	100.0	(D)	6.1	19.8	2.2	4.9	(D)	17.1	(D)	44.2
MOTOR CARRIER	44	100.0	(D)	44.3	24.8	6.4	14.5	(D)	-	(D)	7.3
PRIVATE TRUCK	14	100.0	(D)	34.8	36.0	-	29.1	(D)	-	(D)	-
AIR	-	100.0	(D)	-	100.0	-	-	(D)	-	(D)	-
WATER	-	100.0	(D)	-	-	-	-	(D)	-	(D)	-
OTHER	-	100.0	(D)	63.3	18.5	-	18.2	(D)	-	(D)	-
UNKNOWN	-	100.0	(D)	62.5	-	-	37.5	(D)	-	(D)	-
EAST NORTH CENTRAL	164	100.0	(D)	8.2	67.3	3.7	2.2	(D)	.4	(D)	13.6
RAIL	49	100.0	(D)	6.7	32.3	1.5	1.6	(D)	.9	(D)	45.1
MOTOR CARRIER	81	100.0	(D)	11.8	77.4	5.4	2.7	(D)	.2	(D)	.2
PRIVATE TRUCK	34	100.0	(D)	1.5	94.0	2.6	1.7	(D)	.3	(D)	-
AIR	-	100.0	(D)	82.8	5.2	.2	-	(D)	-	(D)	11.9
WATER	-	100.0	(D)	-	-	-	-	(D)	-	(D)	-
OTHER	-	100.0	(D)	35.4	36.2	13.3	14.5	(D)	-	(D)	.5
UNKNOWN	-	100.0	(D)	-	100.0	-	-	(D)	-	(D)	-
WEST NORTH CENTRAL	85	100.0	(D)	5.5	70.9	19.8	.8	(D)	1.2	(D)	1.3
RAIL	48	100.0	(D)	1.3	87.1	6.2	.6	(D)	1.8	(D)	2.2
MOTOR CARRIER	24	100.0	(D)	16.0	55.4	26.2	1.4	(D)	.8	(D)	.2
PRIVATE TRUCK	12	100.0	(D)	1.3	38.5	60.1	-	(D)	.1	(D)	-
AIR	-	100.0	(D)	-	100.0	-	-	(D)	-	(D)	-
WATER	-	100.0	(D)	-	-	-	-	(D)	-	(D)	-
OTHER	-	100.0	(D)	4.9	1.9	92.9	.3	(D)	-	(D)	-
UNKNOWN	-	100.0	(D)	-	-	-	-	(D)	-	(D)	-
SOUTH ATLANTIC	103	100.0	(D)	15.4	34.2	1.8	28.4	(D)	5.0	(D)	.2
RAIL	48	100.0	(D)	6.8	51.0	.3	5.9	(D)	9.6	(D)	-
MOTOR CARRIER	37	100.0	(D)	28.6	24.5	3.5	36.7	(D)	1.3	(D)	.7
PRIVATE TRUCK	16	100.0	(D)	11.1	8.1	-	74.4	(D)	.2	(D)	-
AIR	-	100.0	(D)	13.4	6.9	-	79.7	(D)	-	(D)	-
WATER	-	100.0	(D)	-	-	-	100.0	(D)	-	(D)	-
OTHER	-	100.0	(D)	7.8	20.8	70.4	1.0	(D)	-	(D)	-
UNKNOWN	-	100.0	(D)	-	-	-	100.0	(D)	-	(D)	-
EAST SOUTH CENTRAL	39	100.0	(D)	8.3	47.7	4.4	13.5	(D)	13.8	(D)	-
RAIL	18	100.0	(D)	2.2	57.1	6.9	2.6	(D)	19.0	(D)	-
MOTOR CARRIER	12	100.0	(D)	21.9	44.0	2.3	13.0	(D)	2.1	(D)	-
PRIVATE TRUCK	8	100.0	(D)	1.6	33.2	2.0	36.9	(D)	19.4	(D)	-
AIR	-	100.0	(D)	1.4	69.0	-	29.6	(D)	-	(D)	-
WATER	-	100.0	(D)	-	-	-	-	(D)	-	(D)	-
OTHER	-	100.0	(D)	9.0	4.0	-	87.0	(D)	-	(D)	-
UNKNOWN	-	100.0	(D)	-	-	-	-	(D)	-	(D)	-
WEST SOUTH CENTRAL	83	100.0	(D)	8.1	40.3	5.9	12.6	(D)	18.1	(D)	4.2
RAIL	57	100.0	(D)	8.4	46.8	3.9	15.3	(D)	8.8	(D)	5.9
MOTOR CARRIER	11	100.0	(D)	14.9	27.9	17.1	7.8	(D)	27.3	(D)	-
PRIVATE TRUCK	14	100.0	(D)	1.3	25.1	5.2	5.9	(D)	46.7	(D)	.6
AIR	-	100.0	(D)	-	-	-	-	(D)	26.9	(D)	73.1
WATER	-	100.0	(D)	-	-	-	-	(D)	-	(D)	-
OTHER	-	100.0	(D)	93.1	6.9	-	-	(D)	-	(D)	-
UNKNOWN	-	100.0	(D)	-	-	-	-	(D)	-	(D)	-
MOUNTAIN	24	100.0	(D)	2.1	25.6	10.4	3.5	(D)	4.5	(D)	49.7
RAIL	15	100.0	(D)	2.8	39.0	15.9	-	(D)	5.0	(D)	37.4
MOTOR CARRIER	6	100.0	(D)	.7	1.0	1.0	-	(D)	3.6	(D)	93.6
PRIVATE TRUCK	2	100.0	(D)	1.3	-	.4	33.0	(D)	4.0	(D)	21.8
AIR	-	100.0	(D)	-	-	-	-	(D)	100.0	(D)	-
WATER	-	100.0	(D)	-	-	-	-	(D)	-	(D)	-
OTHER	-	100.0	(D)	3.1	96.9	-	-	(D)	-	(D)	-
UNKNOWN	-	100.0	(D)	-	-	-	-	(D)	-	(D)	-
PACIFIC	233	100.0	(D)	2.3	43.0	.1	1.7	(D)	6.3	(D)	40.4
RAIL	137	100.0	(D)	2.6	70.5	-	2.7	(D)	9.0	(D)	15.2
MOTOR CARRIER	48	100.0	(D)	3.5	6.6	.4	.6	(D)	2.0	(D)	85.5
PRIVATE FATE TRUCK	32	100.0	(D)	-	1.3	-	-	(D)	3.8	(D)	52.1
AIR	-	100.0	(D)	-	43.7	-	-	(D)	4.7	(D)	51.7
WATER	14	100.0	(D)	-	-	-	-	(D)	-	(D)	100.0
OTHER	-	100.0	(D)	95.2	4.0	-	.5	(D)	-	(D)	.3
UNKNOWN	-	100.0	(D)	-	-	-	-	(D)	-	(D)	100.0

See footnotes at end of table 4.

TABLE 4. TCC GROUP 341—Percent Distribution of Distance Shipped and Weight of Shipment, by Means of Transport: 1972

Distance shipped and weight of shipment[2][3]	Number	Percent distribution by means of transport							
		All means of transport	Rail	Motor carrier	Private truck	Air	Water	Other	Unknown
TONS OF SHIPMENTS	(thousands of tons)								
U.S. TOTAL..........	2 939	100.0	20.2	·41.3	38.1	-	.2	-	-
UNDER 100 MILES.........	1 367	100.0	2.5	40.5	56.9	-	-	-	.1
UNDER 1000 POUNDS.....	3	100.0	-	56.8	42.2	-	-	1.0	-
1000 TO 9999 POUNDS...	152	100.0	.3	58.4	40.9	-	-	.3	.1
10000 TO 29999 POUNDS.	832	100.0	3.5	44.3	52.1	-	-	-	.1
30000 TO 59999 POUNDS.	343	100.0	1.2	19.9	78.9	-	-	-	-
60000 TO 89999 POUNDS.	26	100.0	-	63.0	37.0	-	-	-	-
90000 POUNDS AND OVER.	10	100.0	-	100.0	-	-	-	-	-
100 TO 199 MILES........	552	100.0	12.5	52.3	35.1	-	-	-	-
UNDER 1000 POUNDS.....	1	100.0	-	62.0	31.7	-	4.3	1.5	.5
1000 TO 9999 POUNDS...	39	100.0	1.7	52.1	45.6	-	.4	.1	-
10000 TO 29999 POUNDS.	397	100.0	12.5	51.0	36.4	-	-	-	.1
30000 TO 59999 POUNDS.	93	100.0	6.0	60.5	33.5	-	-	-	-
60000 TO 89999 POUNDS.	20	100.0	57.2	42.8	-	-	-	-	-
90000 POUNDS AND OVER.	1	100.0	100.0	-	-	-	-	-	-
200 TO 299 MILES........	328	100.0	32.3	53.1	14.5	-	-	-	-
UNDER 1000 POUNDS.....	1	100.0	-	85.4	10.2	.1	1.6	2.6	-
1000 TO 9999 POUNDS...	40	100.0	9.2	59.1	31.5	.1	-	.3	-
10000 TO 29999 POUNDS.	237	100.0	40.0	48.5	11.5	-	-	-	-
30000 TO 59999 POUNDS.	46	100.0	13.8	70.1	16.0	-	-	-	-
60000 TO 89999 POUNDS.	1	100.0	-	100.0	-	-	-	-	-
90000 POUNDS AND OVER.	-	100.0	100.0	-	-	-	-	-	-
300 TO 499 MILES........	343	100.0	39.2	40.6	20.1	-	-	-	-
UNDER 1000 POUNDS.....	-	100.0	-	86.2	8.3	2.3	-	3.1	-
1000 TO 9999 POUNDS...	41	100.0	14.2	71.2	14.6	-	-	-	-
10000 TO 29999 POUNDS.	225	100.0	47.2	33.7	19.0	-	-	-	-
30000 TO 59999 POUNDS.	63	100.0	23.6	45.0	31.4	-	-	-	-
60000 TO 89999 POUNDS.	5	100.0	66.5	33.5	-	-	-	-	-
90000 POUNDS AND OVER.	6	100.0	60.6	39.4	-	-	-	-	-
500 TO 999 MILES........	248	100.0	66.7	21.1	12.1	-	-	.1	-
UNDER 1000 POUNDS.....	1	100.0	.2	87.3	3.2	.7	-	8.5	.1
1000 TO 9999 POUNDS...	21	100.0	10.4	73.7	15.3	.4	-	.2	-
10000 TO 29999 POUNDS.	162	100.0	70.0	15.7	14.3	-	-	-	-
30000 TO 59999 POUNDS.	25	100.0	49.8	36.5	13.7	-	-	-	-
60000 TO 89999 POUNDS.	11	100.0	100.0	-	-	-	-	-	-
90000 POUNDS AND OVER.	26	100.0	95.8	4.2	-	-	-	-	-
1000 TO 1499 MILES......	16	100.0	79.3	15.4	5.2	-	-	.1	-
UNDER 1000 POUNDS.....	-	100.0	-	71.6	12.0	-	-	16.4	-
1000 TO 9999 POUNDS...	-	100.0	10.9	59.0	30.1	-	-	-	-
10000 TO 29999 POUNDS.	8	100.0	70.6	22.7	6.7	-	-	-	-
30000 TO 59999 POUNDS.	2	100.0	100.0	-	-	-	-	-	-
60000 TO 89999 POUNDS.	-	100.0	-	-	-	-	-	-	-
90000 POUNDS AND OVER.	4	100.0	100.0	-	-	-	-	-	-
1500 MILES OR OVER......	83	100.0	87.0	3.7	.9	-	8.4	-	-
UNDER 1000 POUNDS.....	-	100.0	5.1	85.3	.4	1.2	-	7.9	-
1000 TO 9999 POUNDS...	2	100.0	14.6	50.9	29.2	-	5.4	-	-
10000 TO 29999 POUNDS.	31	100.0	96.5	2.3	-	-	1.2	-	-
30000 TO 59999 POUNDS.	5	100.0	27.6	17.1	1.9	-	53.4	-	-
60000 TO 89999 POUNDS.	5	100.0	77.9	-	-	-	22.1	-	-
90000 POUNDS AND OVER.	38	100.0	93.5	-	-	-	6.5	-	-
TON-MILES OF SHIPMENTS	(millions of ton-miles)								
U.S. TOTAL..........	697	100.0	50.7	29.6	17.5	-	2.1	-	-
UNDER 100 MILES.........	63	100.0	2.8	40.1	57.0	-	-	.1	.1
UNDER 1000 POUNDS.....	-	100.0	-	68.3	30.2	-	-	1.5	-
1000 TO 9999 POUNDS...	5	100.0	.4	49.2	49.7	-	-	.6	.1
10000 TO 29999 POUNDS.	41	100.0	3.8	41.8	54.3	-	-	-	.1
30000 TO 59999 POUNDS.	14	100.0	1.3	26.4	72.3	-	-	-	-
60000 TO 89999 POUNDS.	1	100.0	-	67.5	32.5	-	-	-	-
90000 POUNDS AND OVER.	-	100.0	-	100.0	-	-	-	-	-
100 TO 199 MILES........	80	100.0	13.6	51.4	34.9	-	-	-	-
UNDER 1000 POUNDS.....	-	100.0	-	60.7	32.9	-	4.6	1.3	.5
1000 TO 9999 POUNDS...	5	100.0	1.9	50.0	47.5	-	.5	.2	-
10000 TO 29999 POUNDS.	57	100.0	14.6	49.1	36.3	-	-	-	.1
30000 TO 59999 POUNDS.	13	100.0	5.3	62.5	32.3	-	-	-	-
60000 TO 89999 POUNDS.	2	100.0	47.7	52.3	-	-	-	-	-
90000 POUNDS AND OVER.	-	100.0	100.0	-	-	-	-	-	-

See footnotes at end of table 4.

TABLE 4. TCC GROUP 341—Percent Distribution of Distance Shipped and Weight of Shipment, by Means of Transport: 1972—Continued

Distance shipped and weight of shipment²³	Number	Percent distribution by means of transport							
		All means of transport	Rail	Motor carrier	Private truck	Air	Water	Other	Unknown
TON-MILES OF SHIPMENTS	(millions of ton-miles)								
200 TO 299 MILES........	80	100.0	32.5	53.1	14.3	-	-	-	-
UNDER 1000 POUNDS.....	-	100.0	-	85.7	9.8	.1	1.7	2.6	-
1000 TO 9999 POUNDS...	10	100.0	9.3	59.7	30.7	-	-	.3	-
10000 TO 29999 POUNDS.	58	100.0	40.1	48.7	11.2	-	-	-	-
30000 TO 59999 POUNDS.	11	100.0	14.8	69.0	16.2	-	-	-	-
60000 TO 89999 POUNDS.	-	100.0	-	100.0	-	-	-	-	-
90000 POUNDS AND OVER.	-	100.0	100.0	-	-	-	-	-	-
300 TO 499 MILES........	129	100.0	40.2	39.7	20.1	-	-	-	-
UNDER 1000 POUNDS.....	-	100.0	-	86.6	7.8	2.3	-	3.2	-
1000 TO 9999 POUNDS...	15	100.0	15.3	71.3	13.3	-	-	-	-
10000 TO 29999 POUNDS.	82	100.0	47.2	33.0	19.7	-	-	-	-
30000 TO 59999 POUNDS.	25	100.0	27.1	43.5	29.4	-	-	-	-
60000 TO 89999 POUNDS.	2	100.0	72.8	27.2	-	-	-	-	-
90000 POUNDS AND OVER.	2	100.0	68.6	31.4	-	-	-	-	-
500 TO 999 MILES........	165	100.0	67.8	21.6	10.5	-	-	.1	-
UNDER 1000 POUNDS.....	-	100.0	.2	86.8	3.3	.9	-	8.8	.1
1000 TO 9999 POUNDS...	14	100.0	9.2	73.7	16.5	.4	-	.2	-
10000 TO 29999 POUNDS.	110	100.0	71.8	16.3	11.9	-	-	-	-
30000 TO 59999 POUNDS.	15	100.0	50.4	37.3	12.2	-	-	-	-
60000 TO 89999 POUNDS.	8	100.0	100.0	-	-	-	-	-	-
90000 POUNDS AND OVER.	16	100.0	95.6	4.4	-	-	-	-	-
1000 TO 1499 MILES......	19	100.0	79.3	15.1	5.4	-	-	.1	-
UNDER 1000 POUNDS.....	-	100.0	-	72.0	11.4	-	-	16.6	-
1000 TO 9999 POUNDS...	1	100.0	9.7	58.1	32.2	-	-	-	-
10000 TO 29999 POUNDS.	9	100.0	70.5	22.4	7.1	-	-	-	-
30000 TO 59999 POUNDS.	2	100.0	100.0	-	-	-	-	-	-
60000 TO 89999 POUNDS.	-	100.0	-	-	-	-	-	-	-
90000 POUNDS AND OVER.	5	100.0	100.0	-	-	-	-	-	-
1500 MILES OR OVER......	159	100.0	85.1	4.1	1.4	-	9.3	-	-
UNDER 1000 POUNDS.....	-	100.0	6.0	83.2	.5	1.1	-	9.2	-
1000 TO 9999 POUNDS...	5	100.0	14.7	46.0	34.5	-	4.9	-	-
10000 TO 29999 POUNDS.	60	100.0	96.0	2.7	-	-	1.4	-	-
30000 TO 59999 POUNDS.	11	100.0	23.5	16.9	1.9	-	57.8	-	-
60000 TO 89999 POUNDS.	9	100.0	77.1	-	-	-	22.9	-	-
90000 POUNDS AND OVER.	71	100.0	93.1	-	-	-	6.9	-	-

Note: Detail may not add to total due to rounding. The introductory table shows the estimates of sampling variability for tons; sampling variability for ton-miles has not been estimated. See the map in the Introduction for the States comprising the geographic divisions of the United States.

Shipments excluded from the survey are those moving by pipeline (primarily petroleum products from refineries), parcel post shipments, and commodities moved by own power (motorized vehicles, aircraft, etc.) or towed (prefabricated buildings, etc.). Local shipments (commodities shipped less than 25 miles from the plant) and shipments within the same city are also excluded. Shipments to Alaska and Hawaii from the 48 conterminous States and the District of Columbia are included; however, no data were obtained for shipments originating in Alaska and Hawaii.

- Represents zero or rounds to zero.   (D) Withheld to avoid disclosing figures for individual companies.

¹Production of this commodity is concentrated in the geographic divisions shown; figures and distributions for geographic divisions not shown are included in the total.

²Distances of shipments to foreign destinations are calculated only to the U.S. port of exit.

³Includes only shipments represented by bills of lading and invoices. Summary records which did not show individual weights of shipments are not included.

TCC 342. Cutlery, Hand Tools and General Hardware

Comparisons of Tons and Ton-Miles of Shipments for
Geographic Divisions of Origin and for Sampling Variability: 1972 and 1967

Geographic division of origin	Estimates				Relative sampling variability in tons (percent)	
	1972		1967		1972	1967
	Tons (thousands)	Ton-miles (millions)	Tons (thousands)	Ton-miles (millions)		
U.S. total	1,557	1,008	1,616	1,118	4.9	14.2
New England	232	182	269	304	18.6	(*)
Middle Atlantic	328	170	189	114	19.1	(*)
East North Central	550	263	820	454	11.1	(*)
West North Central	100	63	13	11	30.6	(*)
South Atlantic	106	63	48	52	23.7	(*)
East South Central	(D)	(D)	57	25	(*)	(*)
West South Central	33	24	126	68	49.4	(*)
Mountain	(D)	(D)	1	2	(*)	(*)
Pacific	152	203	93	88	24.7	(*)

(D) Withheld to avoid disclosing figures for individual companies.   (*) Data not published.

TABLE 1. TCC GROUP 342—Percent Distribution of Geographic Division of Origin and Distance Shipped, by Means of Transport: 1972

Geographic division of origin[1] and distance shipped[2]	Number	Percent distribution by means of transport							
		All means of transport	Rail	Motor carrier	Private truck	Air	Water	Other	Unknown
TONS OF SHIPMENTS	(thousands of tons)								
U.S. TOTAL...........	1 557	100.0	9.1	74.8	12.9	.3	.1	2.4	.4
NEW ENGLAND.............	232	100.0	8.8	64.6	18.2	.6	.1	7.1	.5
UNDER 100 MILES.......	45	100.0	-	63.9	33.1	-	-	1.3	1.6
100 TO 199 MILES......	40	100.0	-	44.1	54.5	.1	.3	.9	-
200 TO 299 MILES......	7	100.0	.7	87.1	5.5	.4	-	6.3	-
300 TO 499 MILES......	11	100.0	.1	85.9	6.8	4.4	-	2.9	-
500 TO 999 MILES.....	55	100.0	13.7	65.4	7.4	1.0	-	12.1	.4
1000 TO 1499 MILES....	25	100.0	.7	74.9	-	.2	-	23.3	.9
1500 MILES OR OVER....	47	100.0	26.3	68.0	.1	.6	-	4.8	.2
MIDDLE ATLANTIC.........	328	100.0	12.5	70.9	14.6	.3	-	1.5	.1
UNDER 100 MILES.......	75	100.0	-	70.4	27.8	-	-	1.8	-
100 TO 199 MILES......	58	100.0	11.8	75.9	10.5	-	-	1.4	.4
200 TO 299 MILES......	34	100.0	16.0	67.6	14.9	.1	-	1.4	-
300 TO 499 MILES......	53	100.0	14.4	71.8	12.2	.5	-	1.0	-
500 TO 999 MILES.....	59	100.0	16.9	65.1	15.6	.5	-	1.9	-
1000 TO 1499 MILES....	21	100.0	9.5	88.6	-	.4	-	1.1	.4
1500 MILES OR OVER....	26	100.0	34.5	62.8	-	.6	.1	1.8	.3
EAST NORTH CENTRAL......	550	100.0	11.3	71.1	14.9	.4	-	1.8	.5
UNDER 100 MILES.......	84	100.0	10.4	43.2	44.6	-	-	1.8	-
100 TO 199 MILES......	101	100.0	14.1	69.4	15.3	.1	-	1.1	-
200 TO 299 MILES......	81	100.0	2.8	76.5	16.0	.4	-	.9	3.4
300 TO 499 MILES......	103	100.0	13.4	79.5	5.0	.1	-	2.0	-
500 TO 999 MILES.....	118	100.0	11.1	77.1	8.3	.7	.1	2.8	.1
1000 TO 1499 MILES....	19	100.0	5.2	91.1	.3	.6	-	2.8	-
1500 MILES OR OVER....	41	100.0	21.3	74.1	1.5	1.4	-	1.6	-
WEST NORTH CENTRAL......	100	100.0	10.8	84.3	2.5	.1	.4	1.6	.2
UNDER 100 MILES.......	14	100.0	-	96.7	3.2	-	-	.2	-
100 TO 199 MILES......	5	100.0	.1	96.5	-	-	-	3.3	-
200 TO 299 MILES......	9	100.0	.1	91.2	7.0	.4	-	1.3	-
300 TO 499 MILES......	17	100.0	3.2	86.9	5.6	-	2.1	2.0	.2
500 TO 999 MILES.....	37	100.0	18.6	78.8	.1	-	-	2.3	.2
1000 TO 1499 MILES....	10	100.0	4.2	93.1	-	.4	-	1.3	1.0
1500 MILES OR OVER....	6	100.0	43.8	48.8	6.1	.5	.8	-	-
SOUTH ATLANTIC..........	106	100.0	4.1	80.0	14.9	.1	-	.9	.1
UNDER 100 MILES.......	5	100.0	-	80.2	18.3	-	-	1.5	-
100 TO 199 MILES......	12	100.0	30.4	61.7	6.9	-	-	.9	-
200 TO 299 MILES......	19	100.0	-	79.2	20.1	-	-	.6	-
300 TO 499 MILES......	24	100.0	-	86.2	12.9	.1	-	.8	-
500 TO 999 MILES.....	33	100.0	-	78.6	20.5	-	-	.8	-
1000 TO 1499 MILES....	2	100.0	-	97.2	-	.1	-	2.6	-
1500 MILES OR OVER....	9	100.0	7.6	89.0	.8	.3	-	.9	1.5
WEST SOUTH CENTRAL......	33	100.0	6.3	73.1	15.8	-	-	3.7	1.2
UNDER 100 MILES.......	1	100.0	-	29.0	63.3	-	-	7.7	-
100 TO 199 MILES......	-	100.0	-	94.7	-	-	-	5.3	-
200 TO 299 MILES......	10	100.0	20.3	62.4	16.0	-	-	1.3	-
300 TO 499 MILES......	2	100.0	-	67.5	32.1	-	-	.1	.4
500 TO 999 MILES.....	6	100.0	-	77.5	11.3	-	-	5.8	5.3
1000 TO 1499 MILES....	9	100.0	-	85.3	9.1	-	-	5.6	.1
1500 MILES OR OVER....	1	100.0	-	97.4	-	.1	-	.7	1.8
PACIFIC.................	152	100.0	.4	94.9	1.9	.3	.5	1.3	.5
UNDER 100 MILES.......	16	100.0	-	85.0	11.1	-	-	3.9	-
100 TO 199 MILES......	5	100.0	-	96.5	.4	-	-	3.0	-
200 TO 299 MILES......	3	100.0	.1	96.2	-	-	-	3.3	.3
300 TO 499 MILES......	8	100.0	-	94.0	-	.2	.2	5.7	-
500 TO 999 MILES.....	14	100.0	1.0	96.4	1.0	.1	-	1.2	.4
1000 TO 1499 MILES....	21	100.0	-	97.6	1.6	.7	-	.1	-
1500 MILES OR OVER....	81	100.0	.6	95.9	.7	.4	.9	.5	.9
TON-MILES OF SHIPMENTS	(millions of ton-miles)								
U.S. TOTAL...........	1 008	100.0	12.2	78.6	4.9	.5	.3	3.1	.4
NEW ENGLAND.............	182	100.0	18.5	66.0	3.8	.7	-	10.5	.4
UNDER 100 MILES.......	2	100.0	-	66.4	29.7	-	-	1.0	2.8
100 TO 199 MILES......	5	100.0	-	51.2	47.3	.1	.2	1.1	-
200 TO 299 MILES......	1	100.0	.7	87.0	5.7	.4	-	6.3	-
300 TO 499 MILES......	4	100.0	.1	84.7	7.8	4.4	-	3.0	-
500 TO 999 MILES.....	40	100.0	13.3	64.9	7.5	1.1	-	12.7	.4
1000 TO 1499 MILES....	31	100.0	.7	72.5	-	.2	-	25.9	.7
1500 MILES OR OVER....	96	100.0	29.1	64.0	.2	.6	-	5.8	.2
MIDDLE ATLANTIC.........	170	100.0	22.1	68.6	7.0	.5	-	1.6	.2
UNDER 100 MILES.......	3	100.0	-	78.1	20.4	-	-	1.5	-
100 TO 199 MILES......	8	100.0	13.6	75.3	9.2	-	-	1.4	.5
200 TO 299 MILES......	8	100.0	15.2	69.6	13.6	.1	-	1.5	-
300 TO 499 MILES......	21	100.0	13.7	71.0	13.7	.6	-	1.0	-
500 TO 999 MILES.....	42	100.0	19.1	63.5	15.1	.5	-	1.9	-
1000 TO 1499 MILES....	25	100.0	10.2	87.9	-	.4	-	1.1	.4
1500 MILES OR OVER....	61	100.0	35.3	61.9	-	.6	.1	1.9	.2

See footnotes at end of table 4.

TABLE 1. TCC GROUP 342—Percent Distribution of Geographic Division of Origin and Distance Shipped, by Means of Transport: 1972—Continued

Geographic division of origin[1] and distance shipped[2]	Number	Percent distribution by means of transport							
		All means of transport	Rail	Motor carrier	Private truck	Air	Water	Other	Unknown
TON-MILES OF SHIPMENTS	(millions of ton-miles)								
EAST NORTH CENTRAL	263	100.0	14.1	76.9	6.1	.7	-	2.0	.3
UNDER 100 MILES	4	100.0	10.8	47.7	39.7	-	-	1.7	-
100 TO 199 MILES	14	100.0	14.5	70.1	14.1	.1	-	1.2	-
200 TO 299 MILES	20	100.0	2.4	77.6	15.6	.4	-	.9	3.0
300 TO 499 MILES	41	100.0	14.2	79.1	4.7	.1	-	1.8	-
500 TO 999 MILES	81	100.0	11.4	78.2	6.9	.6	.1	2.8	.1
1000 TO 1499 MILES	22	100.0	6.0	90.4	.4	.7	-	2.6	-
1500 MILES OR OVER	77	100.0	22.2	73.4	1.4	1.4	-	1.5	-
WEST NORTH CENTRAL	63	100.0	17.5	77.8	2.0	.2	.6	1.6	.3
UNDER 100 MILES	1	100.0	-	97.5	2.4	-	-	.1	-
100 TO 199 MILES	-	100.0	.1	96.3	-	-	-	3.6	-
200 TO 299 MILES	2	100.0	.1	90.9	7.4	.4	-	1.2	-
300 TO 499 MILES	6	100.0	3.6	85.4	6.3	-	2.5	1.9	.3
500 TO 999 MILES	29	100.0	20.0	77.4	.1	-	-	2.3	.2
1000 TO 1499 MILES	12	100.0	3.6	93.9	-	.3	-	1.2	.9
1500 MILES OR OVER	10	100.0	43.0	48.6	5.8	.5	2.1	-	-
SOUTH ATLANTIC	63	100.0	3.1	83.4	12.1	.1	-	.9	.3
UNDER 100 MILES	-	100.0	-	80.1	18.9	-	-	1.0	-
100 TO 199 MILES	1	100.0	29.0	61.9	8.2	-	-	.8	-
200 TO 299 MILES	4	100.0	-	79.6	19.7	-	-	.7	-
300 TO 499 MILES	9	100.0	-	86.2	12.9	.1	-	.8	-
500 TO 999 MILES	24	100.0	-	78.4	20.8	-	-	.8	-
1000 TO 1499 MILES	3	100.0	-	97.2	-	.2	-	2.7	-
1500 MILES OR OVER	18	100.0	7.6	89.3	.8	.3	-	.9	1.1
WEST SOUTH CENTRAL	24	100.0	2.4	81.4	10.6	-	-	4.2	1.4
UNDER 100 MILES	-	100.0	-	34.1	54.3	-	-	11.5	-
100 TO 199 MILES	-	100.0	-	95.1	-	-	-	4.9	-
200 TO 299 MILES	2	100.0	22.4	61.0	15.3	-	-	1.2	-
300 TO 499 MILES	1	100.0	-	65.0	34.5	-	-	.1	.5
500 TO 999 MILES	4	100.0	-	76.0	12.9	-	-	5.5	5.5
1000 TO 1499 MILES	12	100.0	-	85.7	8.8	-	-	5.4	.1
1500 MILES OR OVER	2	100.0	-	97.5	-	.1	-	.7	1.8
PACIFIC	203	100.0	.6	95.6	1.0	.4	1.1	.6	.7
UNDER 100 MILES	-	100.0	-	88.6	7.0	-	-	4.4	-
100 TO 199 MILES	-	100.0	-	96.4	.5	-	-	3.0	-
200 TO 299 MILES	-	100.0	.1	96.2	-	-	-	3.3	.3
300 TO 499 MILES	3	100.0	-	93.9	-	.2	.1	5.8	-
500 TO 999 MILES	11	100.0	1.2	96.0	1.1	.1	-	1.3	.4
1000 TO 1499 MILES	27	100.0	-	97.6	1.6	.7	-	.1	-
1500 MILES OR OVER	160	100.0	.7	95.3	.9	.4	1.4	.5	.9

See footnotes at end of table 4.

TABLE 2. TCC GROUP 342—Percent Distribution of Geographic Division of Origin and Means of Transport, by Geographic Division of Destination: 1972

Geographic division of origin[1] and means of transport	Number	Percent distribution by division of destination									
		U.S. total	New England	Middle Atlantic	East North Central	West North Central	South Atlantic	East South Central	West South Central	Mountain	Pacific
TONS OF SHIPMENTS	(thousands of tons)										
U.S. TOTAL	1 557	100.0	6.0	18.4	29.4	8.9	11.6	5.3	7.2	3.6	9.5
RAIL	141	100.0	4.6	8.4	29.1	10.3	12.7	4.6	7.7	2.0	20.6
MOTOR CARRIER	1 164	100.0	4.8	19.0	26.8	9.6	12.9	5.7	7.5	4.4	9.4
PRIVATE TRUCK	200	100.0	14.8	22.9	43.8	5.0	4.5	3.7	3.6	.1	1.6
AIR	5	100.0	3.4	7.1	29.7	6.1	18.2	4.0	8.8	5.2	17.5
WATER	1	100.0	-	8.6	24.9	-	5.3	-	-	-	61.1
OTHER	37	100.0	3.9	15.0	30.1	7.0	7.9	3.1	19.2	1.4	12.4
UNKNOWN	6	100.0	.1	14.8	61.6	1.8	1.7	5.5	1.3	9.7	3.5
NEW ENGLAND	232	100.0	22.1	19.8	12.4	3.1	8.1	7.9	8.2	10.1	8.2
RAIL	20	100.0	-	.3	3.5	.8	1.7	31.8	20.0	.8	41.1
MOTOR CARRIER	150	100.0	17.8	20.1	13.7	3.9	10.7	6.5	6.4	15.4	5.5
PRIVATE TRUCK	42	100.0	57.1	32.8	1.9	1.6	2.5	3.9	-	-	.1
AIR	1	100.0	.6	9.2	35.7	2.0	30.1	1.5	5.5	12.0	3.3
WATER	-	100.0	-	87.9	-	-	-	-	-	-	12.1
OTHER	16	100.0	2.8	6.2	36.2	2.6	5.8	1.1	32.3	.5	12.6
UNKNOWN	1	100.0	.2	58.9	14.1	-	1.0	17.7	.7	-	7.5
MIDDLE ATLANTIC	328	100.0	5.5	38.6	23.6	5.1	11.7	3.3	4.5	.6	7.0
RAIL	41	100.0	1.7	13.3	22.9	15.1	21.3	-	4.1	1.1	20.5
MOTOR CARRIER	233	100.0	5.5	39.7	22.2	4.3	11.8	4.6	5.2	.7	6.0
PRIVATE TRUCK	48	100.0	9.2	55.6	31.1	.1	2.7	-	1.4	-	-
AIR	-	100.0	1.5	2.8	49.1	.8	13.3	4.9	12.4	.9	14.3
WATER	-	100.0	-	-	-	-	-	-	-	-	100.0
OTHER	5	100.0	6.5	41.6	21.7	3.9	12.1	2.6	2.8	.8	8.1
UNKNOWN		100.0	.3	18.7	41.3	11.7	.4	-	9.7	18.0	-

See footnotes at end of table 4.

TABLE 2. TCC GROUP 342—Percent Distribution of Geographic Division of Origin and Means of Transport, by Geographic Division of Destination: 1972—Continued

Geographic division of origin [1] and means of transport	Number	Percent distribution by division of destination									
		U.S. total	New England	Middle Atlantic	East North Central	West North Central	South Atlantic	East South Central	West South Central	Mountain	Pacific
TONS OF SHIPMENTS	(thousands of tons)										
EAST NORTH CENTRAL	550	100.0	2.1	10.8	49.2	11.9	8.7	3.5	5.0	1.5	7.3
RAIL	62	100.0	4.7	9.8	44.1	13.1	12.0	-	.6	1.5	14.1
MOTOR CARRIER	391	100.0	1.9	12.4	43.7	12.4	9.0	4.6	6.6	1.9	7.5
PRIVATE TRUCK	81	100.0	.9	3.5	80.3	8.3	5.1	.9	.2	-	.8
AIR	2	100.0	6.7	7.0	19.2	9.4	11.4	5.6	11.4	1.6	27.8
WATER	-	100.0	-	-	-	-	100.0	-	-	-	-
OTHER	9	100.0	4.0	18.0	34.0	15.7	7.6	5.4	8.5	.3	6.6
UNKNOWN	2	100.0	-	-	94.9	2.3	.2	-	.2	1.7	.6
WEST NORTH CENTRAL	100	100.0	3.8	14.7	13.6	26.5	7.0	6.2	13.6	4.0	10.6
RAIL	10	100.0	26.8	2.6	-	.1	9.2	-	24.8	10.1	26.4
MOTOR CARRIER	84	100.0	1.0	16.7	15.1	29.5	7.0	7.2	11.5	3.4	8.6
PRIVATE TRUCK	2	100.0	-	-	.6	51.1	1.6	-	31.0	-	15.6
AIR	-	100.0	-	.6	37.5	-	31.8	.9	.7	-	28.5
WATER	-	100.0	-	-	86.7	-	-	-	-	-	13.3
OTHER	1	100.0	1.8	13.1	24.6	22.9	3.5	3.1	24.6	5.6	.8
UNKNOWN	-	100.0	-	44.5	17.5	-	-	24.3	13.7	-	-
SOUTH ATLANTIC	106	100.0	2.8	11.3	20.3	7.5	30.8	9.4	8.5	3.8	5.7
RAIL	4	100.0	-	-	83.9	-	-	-	-	3.3	12.8
MOTOR CARRIER	85	100.0	3.3	12.5	14.3	9.3	36.6	6.4	6.9	4.4	6.3
PRIVATE TRUCK	15	100.0	.9	7.6	34.7	-	9.1	28.3	19.0	-	.4
AIR	-	100.0	.7	24.0	22.9	-	.6	1.9	5.0	4.8	40.1
WATER	-	100.0	-	-	-	-	-	-	-	-	-
OTHER	-	100.0	6.7	19.2	22.5	1.9	18.0	9.6	13.8	1.8	6.6
UNKNOWN	-	100.0	-	-	-	-	-	-	-	100.0	-
WEST SOUTH CENTRAL	33	100.0	3.0	8.8	6.2	6.9	6.6	12.9	30.1	4.8	20.7
RAIL	2	100.0	-	-	-	-	-	-	100.0	-	-
MOTOR CARRIER	24	100.0	3.6	7.8	5.9	7.3	5.8	15.3	21.9	5.1	27.4
PRIVATE TRUCK	5	100.0	-	16.0	8.6	9.5	11.8	9.5	43.7	-	.9
AIR	-	100.0	-	-	-	19.4	-	-	22.4	-	58.3
WATER	-	100.0	-	-	-	-	-	-	-	-	-
OTHER	1	100.0	11.0	17.5	14.1	1.7	13.3	6.9	24.0	.4	11.1
UNKNOWN	-	100.0	-	-	2.8	-	-	.8	-	85.6	10.7
PACIFIC	152	100.0	1.4	5.4	22.6	6.7	17.5	3.4	9.1	7.4	26.5
RAIL	-	100.0	-	4.3	2.9	-	69.9	-	-	3.7	19.2
MOTOR CARRIER	144	100.0	1.4	5.4	23.2	6.9	17.7	3.5	9.4	7.5	24.9
PRIVATE TRUCK	2	100.0	.8	8.7	1.0	3.5	8.7	.2	9.4	.6	67.1
AIR	-	100.0	2.8	8.0	12.1	17.2	21.0	4.9	5.8	9.6	18.6
WATER	-	100.0	-	-	-	-	-	-	-	-	100.0
OTHER	2	100.0	.2	1.9	5.0	.7	10.4	1.1	1.5	12.9	66.2
UNKNOWN	-	100.0	-	-	81.1	-	10.7	-	-	.9	7.3
TON-MILES OF SHIPMENTS	(millions of ton-miles)										
U.S. TOTAL	1 008	100.0	3.2	10.8	18.0	7.9	13.4	5.2	10.8	7.2	23.4
RAIL	123	100.0	4.7	3.6	7.3	8.3	7.5	3.7	9.3	3.1	52.6
MOTOR CARRIER	792	100.0	2.8	12.0	18.2	8.0	14.9	5.4	10.6	8.4	19.6
PRIVATE TRUCK	49	100.0	7.7	13.7	38.3	9.6	8.9	8.1	9.0	.1	4.7
AIR	5	100.0	2.9	4.4	17.6	5.0	13.4	2.6	10.0	9.6	34.6
WATER	2	100.0	-	.5	6.2	-	1.8	-	-	-	91.5
OTHER	31	100.0	2.4	7.3	20.2	4.6	7.1	2.2	28.8	1.6	25.8
UNKNOWN	3	100.0	-	5.0	51.3	1.7	5.5	6.8	2.0	17.9	9.7
NEW ENGLAND	182	100.0	2.2	4.0	11.4	4.3	7.0	8.0	14.7	21.9	26.5
RAIL	33	100.0	-	1.7	.5	.9	13.5	18.7	1.0	63.7	
MOTOR CARRIER	120	100.0	1.6	4.5	11.9	5.4	9.1	7.0	10.6	32.5	17.5
PRIVATE TRUCK	6	100.0	31.0	21.3	9.7	9.7	8.9	17.1	.1	-	2.2
AIR	1	100.0	-	2.6	32.2	2.5	13.1	1.4	9.3	29.6	9.3
WATER	-	100.0	-	23.3	-	-	-	-	-	-	76.7
OTHER	19	100.0	.1	1.1	23.9	2.6	3.9	.9	39.1	.9	27.4
UNKNOWN	-	100.0	-	9.9	20.9	-	1.4	31.9	1.7	-	34.3
MIDDLE ATLANTIC	170	100.0	2.0	8.2	20.9	9.2	9.6	4.4	10.7	2.4	32.5
RAIL	37	100.0	.4	2.5	10.8	14.7	8.6	-	6.0	2.5	54.3
MOTOR CARRIER	117	100.0	2.0	9.4	18.7	8.5	10.8	6.3	12.9	2.5	28.7
PRIVATE TRUCK	12	100.0	6.6	14.8	73.4	.2	.9	-	4.1	-	-
AIR	-	100.0	.2	.8	27.7	.7	7.9	4.0	19.7	1.5	37.4
WATER	-	100.0	-	-	-	-	-	-	-	-	100.0
OTHER	2	100.0	2.6	6.6	23.1	6.6	9.7	3.6	7.2	2.2	38.3
UNKNOWN	-	100.0	-	4.5	9.9	17.3	-	-	15.5	52.7	.1
EAST NORTH CENTRAL	263	100.0	3.5	12.4	17.0	11.1	11.3	3.2	9.3	3.8	28.4
RAIL	37	100.0	7.6	8.6	10.3	12.2	10.7	-	1.0	3.6	46.2
MOTOR CARRIER	202	100.0	2.7	13.3	16.1	10.4	11.3	3.9	11.4	4.2	26.8
PRIVATE TRUCK	15	100.0	4.4	8.5	44.7	18.2	13.5	2.6	.7	-	7.3
AIR	1	100.0	5.9	4.2	5.1	5.2	9.8	2.0	10.0	2.2	55.7
WATER	-	100.0	-	-	-	-	100.0	-	-	-	-
OTHER	5	100.0	6.1	22.5	9.3	11.3	9.1	4.3	14.6	.7	22.1
UNKNOWN	-	100.0	-	-	85.0	2.2	.6	-	.6	7.3	4.3

See footnotes at end of table 4.

TABLE 2. **TCC GROUP 342—Percent Distribution of Geographic Division of Origin and Means of Transport, by Geographic Division of Destination: 1972**—Continued

Geographic division of origin[1] and means of transport	Number	Percent distribution by division of destination									
		U.S. total	New England	Middle Atlantic	East North Central	West North Central	South Atlantic	East South Central	West South Central	Mountain	Pacific
TON-MILES OF SHIPMENTS	(millions of ton-miles)										
WEST NORTH CENTRAL......	63	100.0	6.1	21.2	8.2	7.1	8.1	4.2	14.1	5.3	25.9
RAIL...................	11	100.0	25.6	2.1	-	-	6.3	-	16.9	7.9	41.3
MOTOR CARRIER.........	49	100.0	2.0	26.1	9.7	8.1	8.7	5.3	13.1	4.9	22.1
PRIVATE TRUCK.........	1	100.0	-	-	.3	30.3	1.9	-	19.0	.1	48.4
AIR...................	-	100.0	-	.7	11.3	-	37.2	.5	.6	-	49.7
WATER.................	-	100.0	-	-	43.8	-	-	-	-	-	56.2
OTHER.................	1	100.0	3.8	19.1	17.7	9.3	5.5	3.7	31.9	7.5	1.6
UNKNOWN...............	-	100.0	-	61.4	10.3	-	-	18.7	9.7	-	-
SOUTH ATLANTIC..........	63	100.0	2.8	7.6	10.4	9.1	17.1	8.2	13.4	9.9	21.5
RAIL...................	1	100.0	-	-	26.8	-	-	-	-	13.4	59.8
MOTOR CARRIER.........	52	100.0	3.1	8.2	8.0	10.9	19.8	5.5	10.5	10.9	22.9
PRIVATE TRUCK.........	7	100.0	1.2	5.5	22.5	-	3.8	28.9	36.3	-	1.9
AIR...................	-	100.0	.4	8.6	10.6	-	.3	1.2	5.0	5.9	68.0
WATER.................	-	100.0	-	-	-	-	-	-	-	-	-
OTHER.................	-	100.0	5.0	7.7	17.6	2.5	8.5	6.7	22.8	5.3	23.8
UNKNOWN...............	-	100.0	-	-	-	-	-	-	-	100.0	-
WEST SOUTH CENTRAL......	24	100.0	6.2	14.4	6.2	2.5	8.9	5.1	11.4	5.4	40.1
RAIL...................	-	100.0	-	-	-	-	-	-	100.0	-	-
MOTOR CARRIER.........	19	100.0	6.5	10.9	5.9	2.4	7.3	5.2	8.6	5.3	47.7
PRIVATE TRUCK.........	2	100.0	-	41.5	9.0	4.1	21.8	5.0	16.3	-	2.3
AIR...................	-	100.0	-	-	-	11.0	-	-	6.2	-	82.8
WATER.................	-	100.0	-	-	-	-	-	-	-	-	-
OTHER.................	1	100.0	19.9	24.9	10.1	1.1	15.5	6.3	4.2	.5	17.4
UNKNOWN...............	-	100.0	-	-	1.7	-	-	.2	-	79.4	18.8
PACIFIC.................	203	100.0	2.6	9.5	30.9	6.9	26.8	4.4	8.5	3.3	7.0
RAIL...................	1	100.0	-	5.3	2.8	-	81.2	-	-	1.6	9.1
MOTOR CARRIER.........	194	100.0	2.7	9.5	31.5	7.1	26.8	4.6	8.6	3.4	5.8
PRIVATE TRUCK.........	1	100.0	3.0	31.6	2.6	5.4	30.6	.5	17.6	.4	8.3
AIR...................	-	100.0	3.8	10.5	12.3	13.5	25.3	4.9	4.2	5.1	20.5
WATER.................	2	100.0	-	-	-	-	-	3.3	-	-	100.0
OTHER.................	1	100.0	.7	7.3	15.3	1.7	36.7	3.3	2.9	9.1	22.9
UNKNOWN...............	1	100.0	-	-	83.0	-	13.9	-	-	.3	2.8

See footnotes at end of table 4.

TABLE 3. TCC GROUP 342—Percent Distribution of Geographic Division of Destination and Means of Transport, by Geographic Division of Origin: 1972

Geographic division of destination and means of transport	Number	Percent distribution by division of origin [1]									
		U.S. total	New England	Middle Atlantic	East North Central	West North Central	South Atlantic	East South Central	West South Central	Mountain	Pacific
TONS OF SHIPMENTS	(thousands of tons)										
U.S. TOTAL.............	1 557	100.0	14.9	21.1	35.3	6.4	6.8	(D)	2.2	(D)	9.8
RAIL................	141	100.0	14.4	29.0	44.0	7.6	3.1	(D)	1.5	(D)	.5
MOTOR CARRIER........	1 164	100.0	12.9	20.0	33.6	7.2	7.3	(D)	2.1	(D)	12.4
PRIVATE TRUCK........	200	100.0	21.2	24.0	40.8	1.3	7.9	(D)	2.7	(D)	1.5
AIR.................	5	100.0	28.5	16.6	40.1	2.3	1.1	(D)	-	(D)	9.6
WATER...............	1	100.0	9.8	1.0	5.3	28.7	-	(D)	-	(D)	55.1
OTHER...............	37	100.0	43.8	13.2	26.1	4.3	2.5	(D)	3.3	(D)	5.3
UNKNOWN.............	6	100.0	20.3	6.3	47.2	3.7	2.2	(D)	6.4	(D)	13.0
NEW ENGLAND............	94	100.0	54.8	19.3	12.3	4.0	3.2	(D)	1.1	(D)	2.2
RAIL................	6	100.0	-	10.4	45.2	44.3	-	(D)	-	(D)	-
MOTOR CARRIER........	56	100.0	47.7	22.6	13.0	1.5	5.0	(D)	1.6	(D)	3.6
PRIVATE TRUCK........	29	100.0	81.9	14.9	2.6	-	.5	(D)	-	(D)	.1
AIR.................	-	100.0	4.9	7.4	79.5	-	.2	(D)	-	(D)	7.9
WATER...............	-	100.0	-	-	-	-	-	(D)	-	(D)	-
OTHER...............	1	100.0	30.9	21.9	26.9	2.0	4.2	(D)	9.3	(D)	.2
UNKNOWN.............	-	100.0	70.4	29.6	-	-	-	(D)	-	(D)	-
MIDDLE ATLANTIC........	286	100.0	16.1	44.3	20.8	5.1	4.2	(D)	1.0	(D)	2.9
RAIL................	11	100.0	.4	45.9	51.1	2.3	-	(D)	-	(D)	.2
MOTOR CARRIER........	221	100.0	13.6	41.7	21.9	6.4	4.8	(D)	.9	(D)	3.5
PRIVATE TRUCK........	45	100.0	30.4	58.4	6.2	-	2.6	(D)	1.9	(D)	.6
AIR.................	-	100.0	36.9	6.5	39.5	.2	3.8	(D)	-	(D)	10.9
WATER...............	-	100.0	100.0	-	-	-	-	(D)	-	(D)	-
OTHER...............	5	100.0	18.1	36.6	31.3	3.8	3.2	(D)	3.8	(D)	.7
UNKNOWN.............	-	100.0	81.1	7.9	-	11.0	-	(D)	-	(D)	-
EAST NORTH CENTRAL......	458	100.0	6.3	17.0	59.1	3.0	4.7	(D)	.5	(D)	7.5
RAIL................	41	100.0	1.7	22.8	66.6	-	8.8	(D)	-	(D)	-
MOTOR CARRIER........	312	100.0	6.6	16.6	54.9	4.1	3.9	(D)	.5	(D)	10.8
PRIVATE TRUCK........	87	100.0	.9	17.0	74.8	-	6.3	(D)	.5	(D)	-
AIR.................	1	100.0	34.2	27.5	25.9	2.9	.9	(D)	-	(D)	3.9
WATER...............	-	100.0	-	-	-	100.0	-	(D)	-	(D)	-
OTHER...............	11	100.0	52.7	9.5	29.4	3.5	1.9	(D)	1.5	(D)	.9
UNKNOWN.............	3	100.0	4.7	4.2	72.7	1.0	-	(D)	.3	(D)	17.1
WEST NORTH CENTRAL......	139	100.0	5.2	11.9	46.9	19.0	5.7	(D)	1.7	(D)	7.3
RAIL................	14	100.0	1.0	42.7	56.1	.1	-	(D)	-	(D)	-
MOTOR CARRIER........	111	100.0	5.3	9.1	43.5	22.3	7.1	(D)	1.6	(D)	8.9
PRIVATE TRUCK........	10	100.0	6.7	.3	67.4	12.7	-	(D)	5.0	(D)	1.0
AIR.................	-	100.0	9.4	2.1	61.3	-	-	(D)	.2	(D)	27.0
WATER...............	-	100.0	-	-	-	-	-	(D)	-	(D)	-
OTHER...............	2	100.0	16.1	7.3	58.5	14.2	.7	(D)	.8	(D)	.6
UNKNOWN.............	-	100.0	-	40.1	59.9	-	-	(D)	-	(D)	-
SOUTH ATLANTIC.........	180	100.0	10.4	21.2	26.5	3.9	18.2	(D)	1.2	(D)	14.8
RAIL................	18	100.0	1.9	48.5	41.4	5.5	-	(D)	-	(D)	2.6
MOTOR CARRIER........	149	100.0	10.7	18.4	23.5	3.9	20.8	(D)	1.0	(D)	17.1
PRIVATE TRUCK........	8	100.0	12.0	14.3	46.5	.5	16.2	(D)	7.1	(D)	2.9
AIR.................	-	100.0	47.0	12.1	25.2	4.0	-	(D)	-	(D)	11.0
WATER...............	-	100.0	-	-	100.0	-	-	(D)	-	(D)	-
OTHER...............	2	100.0	32.2	20.3	25.0	1.9	5.7	(D)	5.5	(D)	7.1
UNKNOWN.............	-	100.0	11.6	1.5	4.7	-	-	(D)	-	(D)	82.2
EAST SOUTH CENTRAL......	82	100.0	22.5	13.3	23.6	7.6	12.3	(D)	5.4	(D)	6.3
RAIL................	6	100.0	100.0	-	-	-	-	(D)	-	(D)	-
MOTOR CARRIER........	66	100.0	14.9	16.2	27.0	9.2	8.2	(D)	5.7	(D)	7.7
PRIVATE TRUCK........	7	100.0	22.3	-	10.1	-	59.9	(D)	6.8	(D)	.1
AIR.................	-	100.0	10.9	20.5	55.8	.5	.5	(D)	-	(D)	11.8
WATER...............	-	100.0	-	-	-	-	-	(D)	-	(D)	-
OTHER...............	1	100.0	16.2	10.9	45.0	4.3	7.7	(D)	7.3	(D)	1.9
UNKNOWN.............	-	100.0	65.1	-	-	16.1	-	(D)	.9	(D)	-
WEST SOUTH CENTRAL......	112	100.0	17.0	13.2	24.4	12.1	8.0	(D)	9.1	(D)	12.3
RAIL................	10	100.0	37.2	15.3	3.6	24.3	-	(D)	19.5	(D)	-
MOTOR CARRIER........	86	100.0	11.1	14.1	29.9	11.2	6.8	(D)	6.3	(D)	15.6
PRIVATE TRUCK........	7	100.0	.1	9.0	1.8	10.7	41.4	(D)	32.3	(D)	3.8
AIR.................	-	100.0	17.8	23.3	51.6	.2	.6	(D)	.1	(D)	6.3
WATER...............	-	100.0	-	-	-	-	-	(D)	-	(D)	-
OTHER...............	7	100.0	73.6	1.9	11.5	5.5	1.8	(D)	4.1	(D)	.4
UNKNOWN.............	-	100.0	10.0	45.8	6.6	37.7	-	(D)	-	(D)	-
MOUNTAIN...............	55	100.0	42.5	3.8	15.0	7.2	7.2	(D)	2.9	(D)	20.2
RAIL................	2	100.0	6.1	16.0	33.0	38.9	5.1	(D)	-	(D)	.9
MOTOR CARRIER........	51	100.0	45.4	3.1	14.3	5.6	7.3	(D)	2.5	(D)	21.3
PRIVATE TRUCK........	-	100.0	-	-	-	.3	-	(D)	-	(D)	6.2
AIR.................	-	100.0	65.9	2.9	12.6	-	1.0	(D)	-	(D)	17.6
WATER...............	-	100.0	-	-	-	-	-	(D)	-	(D)	-
OTHER...............	-	100.0	15.6	7.2	5.6	17.2	3.2	(D)	1.0	(D)	49.4
UNKNOWN.............	-	100.0	-	11.5	8.5	-	22.2	(D)	56.6	(D)	1.2
PACIFIC................	148	100.0	12.8	15.5	27.0	7.2	4.1	(D)	4.7	(D)	27.2
RAIL................	29	100.0	28.7	29.0	30.2	9.7	1.9	(D)	-	(D)	.5
MOTOR CARRIER........	109	100.0	7.6	12.9	26.8	6.7	4.9	(D)	6.2	(D)	32.9
PRIVATE TRUCK........	3	100.0	1.9	-	21.1	12.1	2.2	(D)	1.5	(D)	61.2
AIR.................	-	100.0	5.4	13.6	63.9	3.8	2.6	(D)	.2	(D)	10.2
WATER...............	-	100.0	1.9	1.6	-	6.3	-	(D)	-	(D)	90.2
OTHER...............	4	100.0	44.3	8.6	13.9	.3	1.3	(D)	2.9	(D)	28.4
UNKNOWN.............	-	100.0	44.0	-	8.7	-	-	(D)	19.9	(D)	27.4

See footnotes at end of table 4.

TABLE 3. TCC GROUP 342—Percent Distribution of Geographic Division of Destination and Means of Transport, by Geographic Division of Origin: 1972—Continued

Geographic division of destination and means of transport	Number	Percent distribution by division of origin[1]									
		U.S. total	New England	Middle Atlantic	East North Central	West North Central	South Atlantic	East South Central	West South Central	Mountain	Pacific
TON-MILES OF SHIPMENTS	(millions of ton-miles)										
U.S. TOTAL..............	1 008	100.0	18.1	16.9	26.1	6.3	6.3	(D)	2.4	(D)	20.2
RAIL..................	123	100.0	27.4	30.5	30.0	9.0	1.6	(D)	.5	(D)	1.0
MOTOR CARRIER.........	792	100.0	15.2	14.8	25.5	6.2	6.7	(D)	2.5	(D)	24.6
PRIVATE TRUCK.........	49	100.0	13.9	24.4	32.5	2.6	15.7	(D)	5.3	(D)	4.0
AIR...................	5	100.0	25.8	15.4	37.3	2.0	1.4	(D)	.1	(D)	17.1
WATER.................	2	100.0	2.0	2.5	1.8	14.3	-	(D)	-	(D)	79.5
OTHER.................	31	100.0	61.3	8.7	16.7	3.2	1.9	(D)	3.3	(D)	3.9
UNKNOWN...............	3	100.0	18.2	7.5	18.2	4.7	5.6	(D)	8.8	(D)	37.0
NEW ENGLAND...........	32	100.0	12.4	10.5	28.7	11.8	5.4	(D)	4.6	(D)	16.2
RAIL..................	5	100.0	-	2.9	48.3	48.8	-	(D)	-	(D)	-
MOTOR CARRIER.........	22	100.0	8.5	10.8	24.4	4.4	7.4	(D)	5.9	(D)	23.5
PRIVATE TRUCK.........	3	100.0	56.3	20.9	18.9	-	2.4	(D)	-	(D)	1.6
AIR...................	-	100.0	-	1.1	76.1	-	.2	(D)	-	(D)	22.6
WATER.................	-	100.0	-	-	-	-	-	(D)	-	(D)	-
OTHER.................	-	100.0	3.0	9.4	41.9	4.9	3.8	(D)	26.6	(D)	1.1
UNKNOWN...............	-	100.0	43.8	56.2	-	-	-	(D)	-	(D)	-
MIDDLE ATLANTIC.......	109	100.0	6.6	12.8	29.9	12.3	4.4	(D)	3.2	(D)	17.7
RAIL..................	4	100.0	.3	21.3	71.7	5.3	-	(D)	-	(D)	1.5
MOTOR CARRIER.........	95	100.0	5.7	11.6	28.2	13.5	4.6	(D)	2.3	(D)	19.4
PRIVATE TRUCK.........	6	100.0	21.7	26.4	20.2	-	6.3	(D)	16.1	(D)	9.3
AIR...................	-	100.0	15.3	2.7	35.8	.3	2.8	(D)	-	(D)	41.0
WATER.................	-	100.0	100.0	-	-	-	-	(D)	-	(D)	-
OTHER.................	2	100.0	9.2	7.8	51.9	8.5	2.0	(D)	11.2	(D)	3.9
UNKNOWN...............	-	100.0	35.7	6.7	-	57.6	-	(D)	-	(D)	-
EAST NORTH CENTRAL....	181	100.0	11.4	19.6	24.6	2.8	3.6	(D)	.8	(D)	34.7
RAIL..................	8	100.0	6.3	45.2	42.3	-	5.8	(D)	-	(D)	.4
MOTOR CARRIER.........	144	100.0	9.9	15.2	22.5	3.3	2.9	(D)	.8	(D)	42.5
PRIVATE TRUCK.........	18	100.0	3.5	46.9	38.0	-	9.2	(D)	1.2	(D)	.3
AIR...................	-	100.0	47.2	24.3	10.8	1.3	.8	(D)	-	(D)	12.0
WATER.................	-	100.0	-	-	-	100.0	-	(D)	-	(D)	-
OTHER.................	6	100.0	72.8	10.0	7.7	2.8	1.6	(D)	1.6	(D)	2.9
UNKNOWN...............	1	100.0	7.4	1.5	30.1	.9	-	(D)	.3	(D)	59.8
WEST NORTH CENTRAL....	79	100.0	9.9	19.7	36.6	5.6	7.3	(D)	.8	(D)	17.7
RAIL..................	10	100.0	1.5	54.3	44.1	-	-	(D)	-	(D)	-
MOTOR CARRIER.........	63	100.0	10.3	15.8	33.4	6.4	9.2	(D)	.8	(D)	22.0
PRIVATE TRUCK.........	4	100.0	14.1	.4	61.7	8.2	-	(D)	2.3	(D)	2.3
AIR...................	-	100.0	12.8	2.2	38.6	-	-	(D)	.1	(D)	46.2
WATER.................	-	100.0	-	-	-	-	-	(D)	-	(D)	-
OTHER.................	1	100.0	35.2	12.5	41.0	6.6	1.0	(D)	.8	(D)	1.5
UNKNOWN...............	-	100.0	-	76.2	23.8	-	-	(D)	-	(D)	-
SOUTH ATLANTIC........	135	100.0	9.4	12.1	22.0	3.8	8.0	(D)	1.6	(D)	40.4
RAIL..................	9	100.0	3.2	35.3	43.0	7.5	-	(D)	-	(D)	10.9
MOTOR CARRIER.........	118	100.0	9.2	10.7	19.3	3.6	8.9	(D)	1.2	(D)	44.0
PRIVATE TRUCK.........	4	100.0	13.8	2.6	49.3	.6	6.7	(D)	13.0	(D)	13.8
AIR...................	-	100.0	25.3	9.0	27.4	5.6	-	(D)	-	(D)	32.3
WATER.................	-	100.0	-	-	100.0	-	-	(D)	-	(D)	-
OTHER.................	2	100.0	33.7	11.8	21.4	2.5	2.2	(D)	7.1	(D)	19.9
UNKNOWN...............	-	100.0	4.7	-	1.8	-	-	(D)	-	(D)	93.5
EAST SOUTH CENTRAL....	52	100.0	27.6	14.3	16.2	5.0	9.8	(D)	2.4	(D)	17.1
RAIL..................	4	100.0	100.0	-	-	-	-	(D)	-	(D)	-
MOTOR CARRIER.........	43	100.0	19.5	17.1	18.2	6.0	6.7	(D)	2.4	(D)	20.7
PRIVATE TRUCK.........	3	100.0	29.6	-	10.5	-	56.1	(D)	3.3	(D)	.3
AIR...................	-	100.0	13.8	24.3	28.3	.4	.7	(D)	-	(D)	32.5
WATER.................	-	100.0	-	-	-	-	-	(D)	-	(D)	-
OTHER.................	-	100.0	25.5	14.0	32.3	5.5	5.7	(D)	9.4	(D)	5.8
UNKNOWN...............	-	100.0	85.8	-	-	13.0	-	(D)	.3	(D)	-
WEST SOUTH CENTRAL....	109	100.0	24.4	16.8	22.4	8.1	7.8	(D)	2.6	(D)	15.8
RAIL..................	11	100.0	55.2	19.9	3.2	16.4	-	(D)	5.2	(D)	-
MOTOR CARRIER.........	83	100.0	15.2	18.1	27.4	7.7	6.7	(D)	2.1	(D)	20.1
PRIVATE TRUCK.........	4	100.0	.1	11.1	2.4	5.5	62.8	(D)	9.6	(D)	7.8
AIR...................	-	100.0	24.1	30.6	37.3	.1	.7	(D)	-	(D)	7.1
WATER.................	-	100.0	-	-	-	-	-	(D)	-	(D)	-
OTHER.................	9	100.0	83.1	2.2	8.5	3.6	1.5	(D)	.5	(D)	.4
UNKNOWN...............	-	100.0	15.1	57.3	5.2	22.5	-	(D)	-	(D)	-
MOUNTAIN..............	72	100.0	55.3	5.7	13.9	4.6	8.7	(D)	1.8	(D)	9.4
RAIL..................	3	100.0	9.2	25.0	35.1	23.2	7.0	(D)	-	(D)	.5
MOTOR CARRIER.........	66	100.0	58.5	4.4	12.9	3.6	8.7	(D)	1.6	(D)	9.9
PRIVATE TRUCK.........	-	100.0	-	-	-	1.6	-	(D)	-	(D)	16.3
AIR...................	-	100.0	79.3	2.4	8.5	-	.9	(D)	-	(D)	9.0
WATER.................	-	100.0	-	-	-	-	-	(D)	-	(D)	-
OTHER.................	-	100.0	34.9	12.3	7.2	15.2	6.2	(D)	.9	(D)	22.3
UNKNOWN...............	-	100.0	-	22.1	7.4	-	31.0	(D)	38.9	(D)	.6
PACIFIC...............	235	100.0	20.5	23.5	31.7	6.9	5.8	(D)	4.2	(D)	6.1
RAIL..................	64	100.0	33.1	31.5	26.3	7.1	1.8	(D)	-	(D)	.2
MOTOR CARRIER.........	155	100.0	13.5	21.6	34.8	7.0	7.8	(D)	6.1	(D)	7.3
PRIVATE TRUCK.........	2	100.0	6.6	-	50.5	26.9	6.3	(D)	2.7	(D)	7.1
AIR...................	1	100.0	6.9	16.7	60.2	2.9	2.8	(D)	.1	(D)	10.1
WATER.................	2	100.0	1.6	2.7	-	8.8	-	(D)	-	(D)	86.9
OTHER.................	8	100.0	65.0	12.9	14.3	.2	1.7	(D)	2.2	(D)	3.4
UNKNOWN...............	-	100.0	64.3	.1	8.0	-	-	(D)	16.9	(D)	10.7

See footnotes at end of table 4.

TABLE 4. **TCC GROUP 342**—Percent Distribution of Distance Shipped and Weight of Shipment, by Means of Transport: 1972

Distance shipped and weight of shipment [2] [3]	Number	Percent distribution by means of transport							
		All means of transport	Rail	Motor carrier	Private truck	Air	Water	Other	Unknown
TONS OF SHIPMENTS	(thousands of tons)								
U.S. TOTAL..........	1 472	100.0	9.5	74.5	12.7	.3	.1	2.4	.4
UNDER 100 MILES.........	226	100.0	3.9	64.4	29.5	-	-	1.8	.4
UNDER 1000 POUNDS.....	50	100.0	.1	80.5	10.8	.1	-	8.1	.5
1000 TO 9999 POUNDS...	93	100.0	.6	73.1	25.6	-	-	.1	.6
10000 TO 29999 POUNDS.	37	100.0	-	53.2	46.8	-	-	-	-
30000 TO 59999 POUNDS.	33	100.0	15.2	25.5	59.3	-	-	-	-
60000 TO 89999 POUNDS.	10	100.0	28.3	71.7	-	-	-	-	-
90000 POUNDS AND OVER.	-	100.0	-	100.0	-	-	-	-	-
100 TO 199 MILES........	220	100.0	11.3	67.3	19.9	.1	.1	1.2	.1
UNDER 1000 POUNDS.....	49	100.0	-	91.1	3.0	.3	.1	5.5	-
1000 TO 9999 POUNDS...	74	100.0	1.6	89.7	8.2	-	.1	.1	-
10000 TO 29999 POUNDS.	40	100.0	16.5	48.0	35.5	-	-	.1	.3
30000 TO 59999 POUNDS.	41	100.0	10.8	37.1	52.0	-	-	-	-
60000 TO 89999 POUNDS.	5	100.0	75.0	25.0	-	-	-	-	-
90000 POUNDS AND OVER.	8	100.0	100.0	-	-	-	-	-	-
200 TO 299 MILES........	168	100.0	6.0	76.1	14.8	.2	-	1.2	1.7
UNDER 1000 POUNDS.....	47	100.0	.1	93.5	1.7	.7	-	3.9	.2
1000 TO 9999 POUNDS...	64	100.0	1.5	87.4	6.4	.1	-	.4	4.3
10000 TO 29999 POUNDS.	40	100.0	13.6	48.0	38.5	-	-	-	-
30000 TO 59999 POUNDS.	13	100.0	16.4	50.0	33.7	-	-	-	-
60000 TO 89999 POUNDS.	2	100.0	51.6	48.4	-	-	-	-	-
90000 POUNDS AND OVER.	-	100.0	-	-	-	-	-	-	-
300 TO 499 MILES........	225	100.0	9.9	80.2	7.8	.4	.2	1.5	-
UNDER 1000 POUNDS.....	67	100.0	.1	92.1	2.3	.6	-	4.8	-
1000 TO 9999 POUNDS...	99	100.0	2.1	91.6	5.3	.6	.4	.1	.1
10000 TO 29999 POUNDS.	33	100.0	35.1	63.5	1.4	-	-	-	-
30000 TO 59999 POUNDS.	21	100.0	25.7	27.2	47.1	-	-	-	-
60000 TO 89999 POUNDS.	2	100.0	100.0	-	-	-	-	-	-
90000 POUNDS AND OVER.	-	100.0	-	-	-	-	-	-	-
500 TO 999 MILES........	330	100.0	11.3	75.1	9.4	.4	-	3.5	.2
UNDER 1000 POUNDS.....	111	100.0	2.1	90.6	.9	.9	.1	5.1	.3
1000 TO 9999 POUNDS...	114	100.0	2.0	89.8	7.1	.4	-	.5	.3
10000 TO 29999 POUNDS.	34	100.0	37.6	41.2	21.2	-	-	-	-
30000 TO 59999 POUNDS.	56	100.0	10.7	54.0	25.9	-	-	9.3	-
60000 TO 89999 POUNDS.	14	100.0	100.0	-	-	-	-	-	-
90000 POUNDS AND OVER.	-	100.0	-	-	-	-	-	-	-
1000 TO 1499 MILES......	111	100.0	3.2	88.4	1.2	.4	-	6.7	.2
UNDER 1000 POUNDS.....	38	100.0	6.0	86.1	.6	.8	-	6.1	.5
1000 TO 9999 POUNDS...	46	100.0	2.6	94.6	2.3	.2	-	.3	-
10000 TO 29999 POUNDS.	8	100.0	-	100.0	-	-	-	-	-
30000 TO 59999 POUNDS.	18	100.0	-	72.4	-	-	-	27.6	-
60000 TO 89999 POUNDS.	-	100.0	-	-	-	-	-	-	-
90000 POUNDS AND OVER.	-	100.0	-	100.0	-	-	-	-	-
1500 MILES OR OVER......	190	100.0	17.5	77.8	.9	.7	.4	2.0	.6
UNDER 1000 POUNDS.....	48	100.0	9.8	81.3	.7	1.9	.4	5.3	.7
1000 TO 9999 POUNDS...	65	100.0	14.9	79.4	1.9	.7	1.0	1.9	-
10000 TO 29999 POUNDS.	45	100.0	28.1	70.2	.3	-	-	-	1.4
30000 TO 59999 POUNDS.	28	100.0	22.1	77.5	-	-	-	-	.3
60000 TO 89999 POUNDS.	3	100.0	-	100.0	-	-	-	-	-
90000 POUNDS AND OVER.	-	100.0	-	-	-	-	-	-	-
TON-MILES OF SHIPMENTS	(millions of ton-miles)								
U.S. TOTAL..........	937	100.0	12.8	77.7	5.1	.5	.3	3.2	.4
UNDER 100 MILES.........	11	100.0	4.6	68.7	24.5	-	-	1.5	.6
UNDER 1000 POUNDS.....	2	100.0	.2	84.3	7.3	-	-	7.5	.7
1000 TO 9999 POUNDS...	4	100.0	.3	75.9	22.7	.1	-	-	1.1
10000 TO 29999 POUNDS.	1	100.0	-	60.4	39.6	-	-	-	-
30000 TO 59999 POUNDS.	1	100.0	18.1	32.4	49.5	-	-	-	-
60000 TO 89999 POUNDS.	-	100.0	20.6	79.4	-	-	-	-	-
90000 POUNDS AND OVER.	-	100.0	-	100.0	-	-	-	-	-
100 TO 199 MILES........	30	100.0	12.2	69.1	17.2	.1	-	1.3	.1
UNDER 1000 POUNDS.....	7	100.0	-	91.2	2.9	.3	.1	5.6	-
1000 TO 9999 POUNDS...	11	100.0	1.5	90.2	7.8	-	.1	.1	.4
10000 TO 29999 POUNDS.	5	100.0	20.3	48.4	31.3	-	-	-	-
30000 TO 59999 POUNDS.	5	100.0	11.9	38.1	50.0	-	-	-	-
60000 TO 89999 POUNDS.	-	100.0	73.9	26.1	-	-	-	-	-
90000 POUNDS AND OVER.	1	100.0	100.0	-	-	-	-	-	-

See footnotes at end of table 4.

TABLE 4. **TCC GROUP 342**—Percent Distribution of Distance Shipped and Weight of Shipment, by Means of Transport: 1972—Continued

Distance shipped and weight of shipment[2] [3]	Number	Percent distribution by means of transport							
		All means of transport	Rail	Motor carrier	Private truck	Air	Water	Other	Unknown
TON-MILES OF SHIPMENTS	(millions of ton-miles)								
200 TO 299 MILES.........	41	100.0	5.8	77.0	14.3	.2	-	1.2	1.5
UNDER 1000 POUNDS.....	12	100.0	.1	93.5	1.6	.8	-	3.8	.1
1000 TO 9999 POUNDS...	15	100.0	1.5	88.0	6.4	.1	-	.3	3.7
10000 TO 29999 POUNDS.	9	100.0	12.7	49.5	37.8	-	-	-	-
30000 TO 59999 POUNDS.	3	100.0	19.3	49.3	31.4	-	-	-	-
60000 TO 89999 POUNDS.	-	100.0	50.6	49.4	-	-	-	-	-
90000 POUNDS AND OVER.	-	100.0	-	-	-	-	-	-	-
300 TO 499 MILES........	89	100.0	10.2	79.5	8.2	.5	.2	1.4	-
UNDER 1000 POUNDS.....	26	100.0	.1	91.9	2.5	.7	-	4.7	.1
1000 TO 9999 POUNDS...	39	100.0	2.0	91.4	5.4	.6	.5	.1	-
10000 TO 29999 POUNDS.	13	100.0	35.9	62.9	1.1	-	-	-	-
30000 TO 59999 POUNDS.	9	100.0	26.1	27.2	46.7	-	-	-	-
60000 TO 89999 POUNDS.	1	100.0	100.0	-	-	-	-	-	-
90000 POUNDS AND OVER.	-	100.0	-	-	-	-	-	-	-
500 TO 999 MILES........	240	100.0	11.8	75.1	8.8	.4	-	3.6	.2
UNDER 1000 POUNDS.....	80	100.0	2.2	90.4	1.0	.8	.1	5.1	.3
1000 TO 9999 POUNDS...	81	100.0	2.1	88.8	7.7	.5	-	.5	.3
10000 TO 29999 POUNDS.	25	100.0	39.8	40.3	19.9	-	-	-	-
30000 TO 59999 POUNDS.	43	100.0	11.8	57.7	21.0	-	-	9.4	-
60000 TO 89999 POUNDS.	9	100.0	100.0	-	-	-	-	-	-
90000 POUNDS AND OVER.	-	100.0	-	-	-	-	-	-	-
1000 TO 1499 MILES......	136	100.0	3.3	87.7	1.2	.4	-	7.3	.2
UNDER 1000 POUNDS.....	47	100.0	6.1	86.0	.6	.8	-	6.0	.5
1000 TO 9999 POUNDS...	56	100.0	2.8	94.3	2.4	.2	-	.2	-
10000 TO 29999 POUNDS.	9	100.0	-	100.0	-	-	-	-	-
30000 TO 59999 POUNDS.	23	100.0	-	69.7	-	-	-	30.3	-
60000 TO 89999 POUNDS.	-	100.0	-	-	-	-	-	-	-
90000 POUNDS AND OVER.	-	100.0	-	100.0	-	-	-	-	-
1500 MILES OR OVER......	385	100.0	18.5	76.5	.9	.7	.6	2.3	.5
UNDER 1000 POUNDS.....	101	100.0	10.0	80.8	.6	1.8	.5	5.5	.7
1000 TO 9999 POUNDS...	133	100.0	15.9	77.7	1.9	.8	1.5	2.4	-
10000 TO 29999 POUNDS.	90	100.0	30.4	68.0	.3	-	-	-	1.3
30000 TO 59999 POUNDS.	53	100.0	22.8	76.9	-	-	-	-	.4
60000 TO 89999 POUNDS.	6	100.0	-	100.0	-	-	-	-	-
90000 POUNDS AND OVER.	-	100.0	-	-	-	-	-	-	-

Note: Detail may not add to total due to rounding. The introductory table shows the estimates of sampling variability for tons; sampling variability for ton-miles has not been estimated. See the map in the Introduction for the States comprising the geographic divisions of the United States.
　Shipments excluded from the survey are those moving by pipeline (primarily petroleum products from refineries), parcel post shipments, and commodities moved by own power (motorized vehicles, aircraft, etc.) or towed (prefabricated buildings, etc.). Local shipments (commodities shipped less than 25 miles from the plant) and shipments within the same city are also excluded. Shipments to Alaska and Hawaii from the 48 conterminous States and the District of Columbia are included; however, no data were obtained for shipments originating in Alaska and Hawaii.

　- Represents zero or rounds to zero.　　(D) Withheld to avoid disclosing figures for individual companies.

[1]Production of this commodity is concentrated in the geographic divisions shown; figures and distributions for geographic divisions not shown are included in the total.
[2]Distances of shipments to foreign destinations are calculated only to the U.S. port of exit.
[3]Includes only shipments represented by bills of lading and invoices. Summary records which did not show individual weights of shipments are not included.

TCC 343. Plumbing Fixtures and Heating Apparatus

Comparisons of Tons and Ton-Miles of Shipments for
Geographic Divisions of Origin and for Sampling Variability: 1972 and 1967

Geographic division of origin	Estimates				Relative sampling variability in tons (percent)	
	1972		1967		1972	1967
	Tons (thousands)	Ton-miles (millions)	Tons (thousands)	Ton-miles (millions)		
U.S. total	1,972	1,026	1,681	913	19.0	12.0
New England	15	9	53	27	39.8	(*)
Middle Atlantic	(D)	(D)	433	230	(*)	(*)
East North Central	698	417	746	403	11.1	(*)
West North Central	88	66	71	42	25.8	(*)
South Atlantic	78	32	82	30	21.1	(*)
East South Central	251	143	170	104	15.0	(*)
West South Central	(D)	(D)	19	10	(*)	(*)
Mountain	(D)	(D)	—	—	(*)	(*)
Pacific	90	103	107	67	27.6	(*)

— Represents or rounds to zero.   (D) Withheld to avoid disclosing figures for individual companies.   (*) Data not published.

TABLE 1. TCC GROUP 343—Percent Distribution of Geographic Division of Origin and Distance Shipped, by Means of Transport: 1972

Geographic division of origin[1] and distance shipped[2]	Number	Percent distribution by means of transport							
		All means of transport	Rail	Motor carrier	Private truck	Air	Water	Other	Unknown
TONS OF SHIPMENTS	(thousands of tons)								
U.S. TOTAL	1 972	100.0	16.8	57.5	23.7	.1	-	.4	1.4
NEW ENGLAND	15	100.0	-	84.1	5.0	.1	-	10.5	.4
UNDER 100 MILES	2	100.0	-	72.2	26.7	-	-	1.0	-
100 TO 199 MILES	1	100.0	-	94.6	-	.1	-	3.5	1.8
200 TO 299 MILES	1	100.0	-	99.6	-	-	-	.4	-
300 TO 499 MILES	3	100.0	-	99.3	-	.3	-	.5	-
500 TO 999 MILES	3	100.0	-	87.8	-	.1	-	12.1	-
1000 TO 1499 MILES	1	100.0	-	79.3	5.6	-	-	15.1	-
1500 MILES OR OVER	1	100.0	-	27.0	-	.1	-	69.5	3.4
EAST NORTH CENTRAL	698	100.0	26.8	64.1	8.1	.2	.1	.6	.2
UNDER 100 MILES	66	100.0	5.1	68.5	24.3	-	-	1.1	1.1
100 TO 199 MILES	71	100.0	4.4	85.6	9.4	.1	-	.5	-
200 TO 299 MILES	66	100.0	7.3	76.0	15.6	-	-	1.0	.1
300 TO 499 MILES	129	100.0	13.4	79.6	5.8	.1	.5	.6	-
500 TO 999 MILES	265	100.0	35.3	59.1	4.7	.2	-	.5	.1
1000 TO 1499 MILES	49	100.0	57.9	37.6	4.1	.2	-	.2	-
1500 MILES OR OVER	48	100.0	73.8	23.1	1.8	.7	-	.7	-
WEST NORTH CENTRAL	88	100.0	6.8	50.1	13.7	.1	-	.6	28.7
UNDER 100 MILES	6	100.0	-	24.0	68.2	-	-	.5	7.3
100 TO 199 MILES	2	100.0	-	55.6	43.8	-	-	-	-
200 TO 299 MILES	5	100.0	-	97.4	1.6	-	-	1.0	-
300 TO 499 MILES	14	100.0	-	40.4	-	-	-	.9	58.7
500 TO 999 MILES	43	100.0	13.7	47.4	15.3	.1	-	.4	23.1
1000 TO 1499 MILES	7	100.0	-	95.7	2.4	.5	-	1.1	.2
1500 MILES OR OVER	9	100.0	-	30.4	-	.4	-	.1	69.1
SOUTH ATLANTIC	78	100.0	2.2	64.6	32.8	.1	-	.3	-
UNDER 100 MILES	4	100.0	-	91.2	8.7	-	-	.1	-
100 TO 199 MILES	25	100.0	2.2	85.8	11.9	-	-	.1	-
200 TO 299 MILES	5	100.0	-	52.9	46.9	-	-	.2	-
300 TO 499 MILES	24	100.0	-	63.3	36.6	-	-	.1	-
500 TO 999 MILES	17	100.0	4.7	31.2	62.9	.1	-	1.0	-
1000 TO 1499 MILES	-	100.0	-	96.4	-	-	-	3.6	-
1500 MILES OR OVER	2	100.0	17.1	63.4	18.4	1.0	-	.1	-
EAST SOUTH CENTRAL	251	100.0	31.2	46.1	22.3	-	-	.4	-
UNDER 100 MILES	43	100.0	52.7	21.7	25.6	-	-	-	-
100 TO 199 MILES	24	100.0	25.6	24.6	49.8	-	-	-	-
200 TO 299 MILES	13	100.0	27.1	60.1	6.0	-	-	6.4	.4
300 TO 499 MILES	39	100.0	15.6	51.2	32.9	.1	-	.1	-
500 TO 999 MILES	90	100.0	17.4	63.1	19.4	-	-	-	-
1000 TO 1499 MILES	22	100.0	74.5	25.5	-	-	-	-	-
1500 MILES OR OVER	17	100.0	40.0	52.3	7.5	-	-	-	.2
PACIFIC	90	100.0	35.5	54.0	9.9	.1	.2	.1	.3
UNDER 100 MILES	10	100.0	6.8	38.5	52.2	.1	1.3	.5	.6
100 TO 199 MILES	5	100.0	-	86.2	13.7	-	-	.1	-
200 TO 299 MILES	2	100.0	-	75.6	24.2	-	-	.2	-
300 TO 499 MILES	6	100.0	-	66.1	32.9	.8	-	.2	-
500 TO 999 MILES	18	100.0	64.4	34.6	.7	.1	-	-	.2
1000 TO 1499 MILES	11	100.0	67.2	32.4	.2	-	-	-	.3
1500 MILES OR OVER	35	100.0	32.5	67.0	-	.1	.1	-	.3
TON-MILES OF SHIPMENTS	(millions of ton-miles)								
U.S. TOTAL	1 026	100.0	29.5	57.0	10.1	.2	-	.6	2.5
NEW ENGLAND	9	100.0	-	68.0	1.2	.1	-	29.7	.9
UNDER 100 MILES	-	100.0	-	71.2	27.7	-	-	1.1	-
100 TO 199 MILES	-	100.0	-	95.4	-	.1	-	3.3	1.3
200 TO 299 MILES	-	100.0	-	99.6	-	-	-	.4	-
300 TO 499 MILES	1	100.0	-	99.3	-	.2	-	.4	-
500 TO 999 MILES	2	100.0	-	86.9	-	.1	-	13.0	-
1000 TO 1499 MILES	1	100.0	-	80.6	4.6	-	-	14.8	-
1500 MILES OR OVER	2	100.0	-	20.9	-	.2	-	75.8	3.0
EAST NORTH CENTRAL	417	100.0	43.1	51.1	4.8	.3	.1	.5	.1
UNDER 100 MILES	3	100.0	3.4	74.9	19.7	-	-	1.2	.8
100 TO 199 MILES	9	100.0	4.5	85.3	9.6	.1	-	.6	-
200 TO 299 MILES	16	100.0	7.5	76.2	15.1	-	-	1.1	.1
300 TO 499 MILES	50	100.0	13.8	78.7	6.2	.1	.6	.5	-
500 TO 999 MILES	186	100.0	37.0	57.3	4.9	.2	-	.5	.1
1000 TO 1499 MILES	56	100.0	56.7	39.1	3.8	.2	-	.2	-
1500 MILES OR OVER	94	100.0	74.4	22.5	1.8	.6	-	.7	-
WEST NORTH CENTRAL	66	100.0	7.3	46.0	8.8	.3	-	.5	37.1
UNDER 100 MILES	-	100.0	-	32.5	39.1	-	-	.9	27.5
100 TO 199 MILES	-	100.0	-	56.1	43.3	-	-	.6	-
200 TO 299 MILES	1	100.0	-	97.5	1.4	-	-	1.1	-
300 TO 499 MILES	5	100.0	-	40.7	-	-	-	.7	58.5
500 TO 999 MILES	30	100.0	16.2	46.3	18.0	.1	-	.5	18.8
1000 TO 1499 MILES	8	100.0	-	96.0	2.2	.6	-	1.1	.2
1500 MILES OR OVER	20	100.0	-	22.9	-	.6	-	.1	76.4

See footnotes at end of table 4.

TABLE 1. **TCC GROUP 343**—Percent Distribution of Geographic Division of Origin and Distance Shipped, by Means of Transport: 1972—Continued

Geographic division of origin[1] and distance shipped[2]	Number	Percent distribution by means of transport							
		All means of transport	Rail	Motor carrier	Private truck	Air	Water	Other	Unknown
TON-MILES OF SHIPMENTS	(millions of ton-miles)								
SOUTH ATLANTIC	32	100.0	4.6	52.9	41.8	.2	-	.5	-
UNDER 100 MILES	-	100.0	-	90.0	9.8	-	-	.2	-
100 TO 199 MILES	4	100.0	2.4	86.5	11.0	-	-	.1	-
200 TO 299 MILES	1	100.0	-	53.5	46.2	-	-	.2	-
300 TO 499 MILES	8	100.0	-	62.5	37.4	-	-	.1	-
500 TO 999 MILES	13	100.0	5.0	28.2	65.7	.1	-	.9	-
1000 TO 1499 MILES	-	100.0	-	96.6	-	-	-	3.4	-
1500 MILES OR OVER	4	100.0	15.9	65.8	17.2	1.0	-	.1	-
EAST SOUTH CENTRAL	143	100.0	33.2	51.3	15.3	-	-	.2	.1
UNDER 100 MILES	1	100.0	55.3	20.7	24.0	-	-	-	-
100 TO 199 MILES	3	100.0	30.2	22.2	47.7	-	-	-	-
200 TO 299 MILES	3	100.0	30.0	57.6	5.7	-	-	6.3	.4
300 TO 499 MILES	16	100.0	15.5	50.1	34.2	.1	-	.1	-
500 TO 999 MILES	58	100.0	16.0	64.4	19.5	-	-	-	-
1000 TO 1499 MILES	26	100.0	74.0	26.0	-	-	-	-	-
1500 MILES OR OVER	33	100.0	39.5	52.9	7.3	-	-	-	.2
PACIFIC	103	100.0	43.0	55.2	1.3	.1	.1	-	.3
UNDER 100 MILES	-	100.0	5.9	39.3	52.3	-	.6	.7	1.0
100 TO 199 MILES	-	100.0	-	88.5	11.5	-	-	.1	-
200 TO 299 MILES	-	100.0	-	72.6	27.3	-	-	.2	-
300 TO 499 MILES	2	100.0	-	66.1	33.0	.8	-	.2	-
500 TO 999 MILES	16	100.0	69.8	29.4	.6	.1	-	-	.1
1000 TO 1499 MILES	14	100.0	66.5	33.0	.1	-	-	-	.3
1500 MILES OR OVER	68	100.0	34.3	65.1	-	.1	.1	-	.4

See footnotes at end of table 4.

TABLE 2. **TCC GROUP 343**—Percent Distribution of Geographic Division of Origin and Means of Transport, by Geographic Division of Destination: 1972

Geographic division of origin[1] and means of transport	Number	Percent distribution by division of destination									
		U.S. total	New England	Middle Atlantic	East North Central	West North Central	South Atlantic	East South Central	West South Central	Mountain	Pacific
TONS OF SHIPMENTS	(thousands of tons)										
U.S. TOTAL	1 972	100.0	8.2	16.4	25.4	5.3	12.0	6.4	16.3	4.2	5.9
RAIL	330	100.0	4.1	5.2	7.3	9.0	12.5	12.4	20.9	16.0	12.5
MOTOR CARRIER	1 134	100.0	10.8	18.7	35.1	5.7	13.4	4.6	4.5	2.5	4.8
PRIVATE TRUCK	467	100.0	5.2	19.5	16.0	1.5	7.4	6.0	41.5	.5	2.4
AIR	1	100.0	2.7	26.5	12.9	2.8	22.6	1.2	3.1	3.3	24.9
WATER	-	100.0	-	78.3	-	-	4.4	-	-	-	17.2
OTHER	8	100.0	3.1	9.9	26.9	7.8	12.5	17.9	3.2	1.0	17.6
UNKNOWN	27	100.0	.4	1.8	3.6	11.2	23.6	9.9	24.8	.4	24.3
NEW ENGLAND	15	100.0	14.8	41.0	18.0	2.5	8.4	4.5	3.6	1.3	6.0
RAIL	-	100.0	-	-	-	-	-	-	-	-	-
MOTOR CARRIER	12	100.0	12.3	47.8	19.7	2.6	7.3	5.2	3.6	1.2	.4
PRIVATE TRUCK	-	100.0	81.0	10.0	-	-	9.0	-	-	-	-
AIR	-	100.0	4.1	64.4	22.6	-	-	-	-	-	9.0
WATER	-	100.0	-	-	-	-	-	-	-	-	-
OTHER	1	100.0	2.7	2.6	13.3	2.8	17.3	1.4	5.5	-	54.3
UNKNOWN	-	100.0	34.4	-	-	-	-	-	-	65.6	-
EAST NORTH CENTRAL	698	100.0	7.6	15.6	28.2	8.7	13.6	5.8	9.5	4.9	5.9
RAIL	187	100.0	7.0	3.5	6.1	13.7	12.7	7.5	20.8	12.7	15.8
MOTOR CARRIER	447	100.0	8.9	21.0	34.0	7.6	14.3	4.9	4.8	2.2	2.3
PRIVATE TRUCK	56	100.0	.6	12.3	54.0	1.4	11.5	7.6	10.4	.5	1.5
AIR	1	100.0	4.2	33.3	9.7	4.1	13.8	1.7	3.1	3.9	26.2
WATER	-	100.0	-	100.0	-	-	-	-	-	-	-
OTHER	4	100.0	3.3	13.5	43.3	8.6	10.7	8.0	3.3	1.1	8.3
UNKNOWN	1	100.0	-	3.9	66.2	.4	27.3	-	2.2	-	-
WEST NORTH CENTRAL	88	100.0	.7	4.7	16.3	10.0	19.5	4.4	28.8	2.6	13.0
RAIL	5	100.0	-	-	-	-	-	-	100.0	-	-
MOTOR CARRIER	44	100.0	1.1	9.1	21.1	11.6	24.9	2.4	13.5	5.2	11.1
PRIVATE TRUCK	12	100.0	.7	-	40.6	3.1	-	.5	55.1	-	-
AIR	-	100.0	-	24.0	32.3	.1	1.6	-	-	-	42.1
WATER	-	100.0	-	-	-	-	-	-	-	-	-
OTHER	-	100.0	7.4	11.4	16.4	37.0	12.3	7.9	4.1	1.5	2.0
UNKNOWN	25	100.0	-	-	-	12.3	24.1	10.8	26.9	-	25.9
SOUTH ATLANTIC	78	100.0	3.9	27.8	20.0	1.4	35.5	3.9	4.4	.6	2.4
RAIL	1	100.0	-	32.1	-	-	34.6	-	12.3	-	21.0
MOTOR CARRIER	50	100.0	3.7	31.3	7.7	.6	48.1	4.3	1.0	1.0	2.3
PRIVATE TRUCK	25	100.0	4.5	20.6	45.7	2.9	10.7	3.4	10.7	-	1.5
AIR	-	100.0	-	25.9	20.7	-	-	-	-	-	53.3
WATER	-	100.0	-	-	-	-	-	-	-	-	-
OTHER	-	100.0	13.0	24.4	15.5	6.8	23.4	10.0	4.5	1.9	.5
UNKNOWN	-	100.0	-	-	-	-	-	-	-	-	-

See footnotes at end of table 4.

TABLE 2. **TCC GROUP 343—Percent Distribution of Geographic Division of Origin and Means of Transport, by Geographic Division of Destination: 1972**—Continued

Geographic division of origin[1] and means of transport	Number	Percent distribution by division of destination									
		U.S. total	New England	Middle Atlantic	East North Central	West North Central	South Atlantic	East South Central	West South Central	Mountain	Pacific
TONS OF SHIPMENTS	(thousands of tons)										
EAST SOUTH CENTRAL......	251	100.0	1.6	11.4	15.6	8.3	18.4	24.2	5.5	8.7	6.4
RAIL................	78	100.0	.4	4.3	10.9	3.3	12.9	31.9	6.4	21.9	8.0
MOTOR CARRIER.......	115	100.0	2.4	18.8	11.4	11.7	23.6	13.8	7.0	4.1	7.2
PRIVATE TRUCK.......	55	100.0	1.6	6.2	31.1	8.4	15.3	33.7	1.4	-	2.3
AIR.................	-	100.0	-	-	100.0	-	-	-	-	-	-
WATER...............	-	100.0	-	-	-	-	-	-	-	-	-
OTHER...............	-	100.0	.1	1.1	3.6	.8	2.0	92.0	-	-	.4
UNKNOWN.............	-	100.0	-	-	-	-	56.6	-	-	4.0	39.4
PACIFIC................	90	100.0	-	1.6	16.1	.8	4.0	5.7	23.9	19.1	28.6
RAIL................	31	100.0	-	.7	2.4	-	.4	-	56.9	35.6	4.0
MOTOR CARRIER.......	48	100.0	-	2.5	28.3	1.5	7.1	10.6	6.8	8.9	34.3
PRIVATE TRUCK.......	8	100.0	-	-	-	-	-	-	.2	16.8	83.0
AIR.................	-	100.0	.5	-	22.4	1.3	.6	.7	1.3	11.9	61.3
WATER...............	-	100.0	-	-	-	-	-	-	-	-	100.0
OTHER...............	-	100.0	.1	.1	.1	.1	-	.3	-	3.0	96.3
UNKNOWN.............	-	100.0	.1	-	6.4	-	25.0	2.2	13.7	7.1	45.5
TON-MILES OF SHIPMENTS	(millions of ton-miles)										
U.S. TOTAL.............	1 026	100.0	7.0	12.0	18.1	6.0	11.6	4.4	14.3	8.9	17.6
RAIL................	303	100.0	3.4	4.6	2.7	6.0	8.3	4.2	25.1	20.1	25.7
MOTOR CARRIER.......	585	100.0	9.2	15.6	26.5	6.4	13.2	4.3	6.8	5.0	13.0
PRIVATE TRUCK.......	103	100.0	7.1	15.7	21.2	4.6	11.7	5.7	26.2	1.3	6.5
AIR.................	1	100.0	2.0	20.1	7.7	1.4	11.2	.8	3.3	3.9	49.6
WATER...............	-	100.0	-	79.3	-	-	2.1	-	-	-	18.6
OTHER...............	6	100.0	3.1	6.8	9.1	4.2	11.9	10.5	4.1	1.3	48.9
UNKNOWN.............	25	100.0	.2	.5	.7	4.2	14.7	3.7	14.1	.5	61.5
NEW ENGLAND............	9	100.0	1.8	19.2	19.6	5.0	11.4	6.3	8.5	3.8	24.6
RAIL................	-	100.0	-	-	-	-	-	-	-	-	-
MOTOR CARRIER.......	6	100.0	1.9	27.9	26.2	6.5	11.9	8.9	10.5	4.2	2.0
PRIVATE TRUCK.......	-	100.0	34.4	4.9	-	-	60.8	-	-	-	-
AIR.................	-	100.0	-	29.5	14.6	-	-	-	-	-	55.8
WATER...............	-	100.0	-	-	-	-	-	-	-	-	-
OTHER...............	2	100.0	.1	.3	5.9	1.7	8.6	.7	4.5	-	78.0
UNKNOWN.............	-	100.0	2.7	-	-	-	-	-	-	97.3	-
EAST NORTH CENTRAL......	417	100.0	8.9	13.3	8.0	8.0	12.8	4.8	14.5	10.2	19.5
RAIL................	179	100.0	5.6	2.0	1.2	8.4	8.3	5.0	20.4	16.4	32.7
MOTOR CARRIER.......	213	100.0	12.5	22.7	12.7	8.3	16.1	4.1	8.4	5.9	9.2
PRIVATE TRUCK.......	20	100.0	1.3	13.2	19.7	1.6	16.7	8.8	28.5	1.8	8.4
AIR.................	1	100.0	3.0	24.2	2.6	1.6	10.7	.9	2.7	4.6	49.7
WATER...............	-	100.0	-	100.0	-	-	-	-	-	-	-
OTHER...............	2	100.0	5.7	14.9	14.8	6.1	13.4	8.6	5.0	2.7	28.8
UNKNOWN.............	-	100.0	-	5.7	15.4	1.0	71.6	-	6.4	-	-
WEST NORTH CENTRAL......	66	100.0	1.0	5.4	4.8	4.1	17.4	2.4	26.4	3.4	35.3
RAIL................	4	100.0	-	-	-	-	-	-	100.0	-	-
MOTOR CARRIER.......	30	100.0	1.7	11.5	9.8	4.9	26.3	1.8	11.7	7.3	25.0
PRIVATE TRUCK.......	5	100.0	1.5	-	2.8	1.1	-	.7	94.0	-	-
AIR.................	-	100.0	-	16.3	14.4	-	.8	-	-	-	68.5
WATER...............	-	100.0	-	-	-	-	-	-	-	-	-
OTHER...............	-	100.0	14.0	16.7	10.9	16.4	19.7	9.9	5.5	2.0	4.7
UNKNOWN.............	24	100.0	-	-	-	4.4	13.9	3.8	14.5	-	63.4
SOUTH ATLANTIC.........	32	100.0	4.0	17.7	25.3	2.6	20.1	4.2	10.3	2.5	13.3
RAIL................	1	100.0	-	6.5	-	-	29.4	-	13.9	-	50.3
MOTOR CARRIER.......	17	100.0	4.5	25.5	10.7	1.5	29.2	5.9	2.5	4.6	15.7
PRIVATE TRUCK.......	13	100.0	3.7	9.0	46.8	4.3	7.7	2.5	19.9	-	6.0
AIR.................	-	100.0	-	9.7	9.5	-	-	-	-	-	80.8
WATER...............	-	100.0	-	-	-	-	-	-	-	-	-
OTHER...............	-	100.0	15.4	25.9	16.9	8.5	12.7	6.9	7.4	4.4	1.9
UNKNOWN.............	-	100.0	-	-	-	-	-	-	-	-	-
EAST SOUTH CENTRAL......	143	100.0	2.7	13.4	10.9	8.2	15.4	3.9	5.7	17.8	22.0
RAIL................	47	100.0	.7	3.9	5.1	2.6	10.1	3.7	6.4	41.5	25.9
MOTOR CARRIER.......	73	100.0	3.8	20.5	8.5	9.5	17.9	2.4	6.8	7.8	22.8
PRIVATE TRUCK.......	21	100.0	3.4	10.6	31.5	15.7	18.5	8.4	.8	-	11.1
AIR.................	-	100.0	-	-	100.0	-	-	-	-	-	-
WATER...............	-	100.0	-	-	-	-	-	-	-	-	-
OTHER...............	-	100.0	.2	3.3	6.4	1.5	3.3	82.4	.1	-	2.9
UNKNOWN.............	-	100.0	-	-	-	-	15.5	-	-	6.0	78.4
PACIFIC................	103	100.0	.1	3.4	25.8	1.0	7.2	8.9	33.6	13.4	6.6
RAIL................	44	100.0	-	1.3	3.4	-	.6	-	69.0	24.5	1.3
MOTOR CARRIER.......	57	100.0	.1	5.1	44.1	1.7	12.4	16.1	7.1	4.2	9.2
PRIVATE TRUCK.......	1	100.0	-	-	-	-	-	-	1.5	40.7	57.8
AIR.................	-	100.0	1.7	.1	53.4	2.4	2.1	1.8	2.3	12.6	23.6
WATER...............	-	100.0	-	-	-	-	-	-	-	-	100.0
OTHER...............	-	100.0	.8	.8	1.2	1.0	-	3.3	-	8.3	84.8
UNKNOWN.............	-	100.0	.1	-	7.9	-	39.2	2.8	13.7	3.5	32.8

See footnotes at end of table 4.

TABLE 3. **TCC GROUP 343**—Percent Distribution of Geographic Division of Destination and Means of Transport, by Geographic Division of Origin: 1972

Geographic division of destination and means of transport	Number	Percent distribution by division of origin [1]									
		U.S. total	New England	Middle Atlantic	East North Central	West North Central	South Atlantic	East South Central	West South Central	Mountain	Pacific
TONS OF SHIPMENTS	(thousands of tons)										
U.S. TOTAL.............	1 972	100.0	.8	(D)	35.4	4.5	4.0	12.7	(D)	(D)	4.6
RAIL................	330	100.0	-	(D)	56.6	1.8	.5	23.7	(D)	(D)	9.7
MOTOR CARRIER........	1 134	100.0	1.1	(D)	39.4	3.9	4.5	10.2	(D)	(D)	4.3
PRIVATE TRUCK........	467	100.0	.2	(D)	12.0	2.6	5.5	12.0	(D)	(D)	1.9
AIR.................	1	100.0	.8	(D)	61.6	5.7	2.1	3.0	(D)	(D)	5.8
WATER...............	-	100.0	-	(D)	78.3	-	-	-	(D)	(D)	17.2
OTHER...............	8	100.0	18.8	(D)	50.7	6.1	3.1	11.0	(D)	(D)	.9
UNKNOWN.............	27	100.0	.2	(D)	4.2	91.4	-	.4	(D)	(D)	.9
NEW ENGLAND...........	161	100.0	1.4	(D)	33.1	.4	1.9	2.5	(D)	(D)	-
RAIL................	13	100.0	-	(D)	97.5	-	-	2.5	(D)	(D)	-
MOTOR CARRIER........	122	100.0	1.3	(D)	32.3	.4	1.5	2.2	(D)	(D)	-
PRIVATE TRUCK........	24	100.0	2.5	(D)	1.5	.3	4.8	3.7	(D)	(D)	-
AIR.................	-	100.0	1.2	(D)	97.7	-	-	-	(D)	(D)	1.1
WATER...............	-	100.0	-	(D)	-	-	-	-	(D)	(D)	-
OTHER...............	-	100.0	15.9	(D)	53.2	14.3	12.8	.2	(D)	(D)	-
UNKNOWN.............	-	100.0	19.2	(D)	-	-	-	-	(D)	(D)	.2
MIDDLE ATLANTIC.......	322	100.0	1.9	(D)	33.8	1.3	6.8	8.9	(D)	(D)	.4
RAIL................	17	100.0	-	(D)	38.3	-	3.2	19.8	(D)	(D)	1.4
MOTOR CARRIER........	212	100.0	2.9	(D)	44.3	1.9	7.5	10.3	(D)	(D)	.6
PRIVATE TRUCK........	91	100.0	.1	(D)	7.6	-	5.8	3.8	(D)	(D)	-
AIR.................	-	100.0	1.9	(D)	77.3	5.2	2.1	-	(D)	(D)	-
WATER...............	-	100.0	-	(D)	100.0	-	-	-	(D)	(D)	-
OTHER...............	-	100.0	5.0	(D)	69.2	7.0	7.6	1.2	(D)	(D)	-
UNKNOWN.............	-	100.0	-	(D)	9.1	-	-	-	(D)	(D)	-
EAST NORTH CENTRAL.....	500	100.0	.5	(D)	39.3	2.9	3.2	7.8	(D)	(D)	2.9
RAIL................	24	100.0	-	(D)	47.1	-	-	35.0	(D)	(D)	3.1
MOTOR CARRIER........	397	100.0	.6	(D)	38.3	2.4	1.0	3.3	(D)	(D)	3.5
PRIVATE TRUCK........	74	100.0	-	(D)	40.6	6.6	15.8	23.2	(D)	(D)	-
AIR.................	-	100.0	1.3	(D)	46.2	14.3	3.4	23.0	(D)	(D)	10.0
WATER...............	-	100.0	-	(D)	-	-	-	-	(D)	(D)	-
OTHER...............	2	100.0	9.3	(D)	81.5	3.7	1.8	1.5	(D)	(D)	-
UNKNOWN.............	-	100.0	-	(D)	77.6	-	-	-	(D)	(D)	1.6
WEST NORTH CENTRAL.....	104	100.0	.4	(D)	58.1	8.4	1.0	19.8	(D)	(D)	.7
RAIL................	29	100.0	-	(D)	86.4	-	-	8.7	(D)	(D)	-
MOTOR CARRIER........	64	100.0	.5	(D)	52.9	8.0	.5	21.0	(D)	(D)	1.2
PRIVATE TRUCK........	7	100.0	-	(D)	11.5	5.3	10.7	66.5	(D)	(D)	-
AIR.................	-	100.0	-	(D)	89.1	.1	-	-	(D)	(D)	2.6
WATER...............	-	100.0	-	(D)	-	-	-	-	(D)	(D)	-
OTHER...............	-	100.0	6.8	(D)	55.8	28.8	2.7	1.1	(D)	(D)	-
UNKNOWN.............	3	100.0	-	(D)	.1	99.7	-	-	(D)	(D)	-
SOUTH ATLANTIC........	236	100.0	.5	(D)	40.3	7.3	11.8	19.5	(D)	(D)	1.5
RAIL................	41	100.0	-	(D)	57.2	-	1.4	24.4	(D)	(D)	.3
MOTOR CARRIER........	152	100.0	.6	(D)	42.1	7.3	16.1	18.0	(D)	(D)	2.3
PRIVATE TRUCK........	34	100.0	.2	(D)	18.6	-	8.0	24.7	(D)	(D)	-
AIR.................	-	100.0	-	(D)	37.5	.4	-	-	(D)	(D)	.2
WATER...............	-	100.0	-	(D)	-	-	-	-	(D)	(D)	-
OTHER...............	1	100.0	26.0	(D)	43.2	5.9	5.8	1.8	(D)	(D)	-
UNKNOWN.............	6	100.0	-	(D)	4.8	93.4	-	.9	(D)	(D)	.9
EAST SOUTH CENTRAL.....	125	100.0	.5	(D)	32.3	3.1	2.5	48.3	(D)	(D)	4.1
RAIL................	41	100.0	-	(D)	34.2	-	-	60.6	(D)	(D)	-
MOTOR CARRIER........	51	100.0	1.3	(D)	42.1	2.0	4.2	30.8	(D)	(D)	9.9
PRIVATE TRUCK........	28	100.0	-	(D)	15.2	.2	3.1	67.1	(D)	(D)	-
AIR.................	-	100.0	-	(D)	89.5	-	-	-	(D)	(D)	3.4
WATER...............	-	100.0	-	(D)	-	-	-	-	(D)	(D)	-
OTHER...............	1	100.0	1.5	(D)	22.7	2.7	1.7	56.3	(D)	(D)	-
UNKNOWN.............	2	100.0	-	(D)	-	99.8	-	-	(D)	(D)	.2
WEST SOUTH CENTRAL.....	321	100.0	.2	(D)	20.7	7.9	1.1	4.3	(D)	(D)	6.7
RAIL................	69	100.0	-	(D)	56.5	8.7	.3	7.3	(D)	(D)	26.3
MOTOR CARRIER........	50	100.0	.9	(D)	42.0	11.8	1.0	15.9	(D)	(D)	6.5
PRIVATE TRUCK........	194	100.0	-	(D)	3.0	3.5	1.4	.4	(D)	(D)	-
AIR.................	-	100.0	-	(D)	61.4	-	-	-	(D)	(D)	2.5
WATER...............	-	100.0	-	(D)	-	-	-	-	(D)	(D)	-
OTHER...............	-	100.0	31.7	(D)	51.6	7.6	4.3	.1	(D)	(D)	.5
UNKNOWN.............	6	100.0	-	(D)	.4	99.2	-	-	(D)	(D)	-
MOUNTAIN..............	83	100.0	.2	(D)	41.0	2.8	.6	26.1	(D)	(D)	20.6
RAIL................	53	100.0	-	(D)	45.0	-	-	32.3	(D)	(D)	21.4
MOTOR CARRIER........	28	100.0	.5	(D)	35.9	8.2	1.8	16.8	(D)	(D)	15.4
PRIVATE TRUCK........	2	100.0	-	(D)	12.2	-	-	-	(D)	(D)	62.7
AIR.................	-	100.0	-	(D)	73.4	-	-	-	(D)	(D)	21.0
WATER...............	-	100.0	-	(D)	-	-	-	-	(D)	(D)	-
OTHER...............	-	100.0	-	(D)	53.2	9.3	5.7	-	(D)	(D)	2.7
UNKNOWN.............	-	100.0	38.6	(D)	-	-	-	3.6	(D)	(D)	15.9
PACIFIC...............	116	100.0	.8	(D)	35.7	9.9	1.7	13.8	(D)	(D)	22.2
RAIL................	41	100.0	-	(D)	71.6	-	.9	15.2	(D)	(D)	3.1
MOTOR CARRIER........	54	100.0	.1	(D)	18.9	9.0	2.1	15.3	(D)	(D)	30.5
PRIVATE TRUCK........	11	100.0	-	(D)	7.8	-	3.5	11.6	(D)	(D)	66.9
AIR.................	-	100.0	.3	(D)	65.0	9.7	4.6	-	(D)	(D)	14.3
WATER...............	-	100.0	-	(D)	-	-	-	-	(D)	(D)	100.0
OTHER...............	1	100.0	58.0	(D)	23.9	.7	.1	.3	(D)	(D)	4.8
UNKNOWN.............	6	100.0	-	(D)	-	97.4	-	.6	(D)	(D)	1.6

See footnotes at end of table 4.

TABLE 3. **TCC GROUP 343**—Percent Distribution of Geographic Division of Destination and Means of Transport, by Geographic Division of Origin: 1972—Continued

Geographic division of destination and means of transport	Number	Percent distribution by division of origin [1]								
		U.S. total	New England	Middle Atlantic	East North Central	West North Central	South Atlantic	East South Central	West South Central	Mountain	Pacific
TON-MILES OF SHIPMENTS	(millions of ton-miles)										
U.S. TOTAL.............	1 026	100.0	.9	(D)	40.6	6.5	3.2	13.9	(D)	(D)	10.1
RAIL.................	303	100.0	-	(D)	59.3	1.6	.5	15.6	(D)	(D)	14.7
MOTOR CARRIER........	585	100.0	1.1	(D)	36.4	5.3	3.0	12.5	(D)	(D)	9.8
PRIVATE TRUCK........	103	100.0	.1	(D)	19.5	5.6	13.3	21.1	(D)	(D)	1.3
AIR..................	1	100.0	.7	(D)	65.0	11.4	3.3	1.3	(D)	(D)	4.7
WATER................	-	100.0	-	(D)	79.3	-	-	-	(D)	(D)	18.6
OTHER................	6	100.0	42.1	(D)	33.2	4.9	2.4	4.1	(D)	(D)	.2
UNKNOWN..............	25	100.0	.3	(D)	1.2	95.3	-	.4	(D)	(D)	1.4
NEW ENGLAND............	72	100.0	.2	(D)	51.4	.9	1.8	5.3	(D)	(D)	.1
RAIL.................	10	100.0	-	(D)	96.7	-	-	3.3	(D)	(D)	-
MOTOR CARRIER........	54	100.0	.2	(D)	49.2	1.0	1.5	5.1	(D)	(D)	.1
PRIVATE TRUCK........	7	100.0	.5	(D)	3.6	1.2	7.0	10.2	(D)	(D)	-
AIR..................	-	100.0	-	(D)	96.0	-	-	-	(D)	(D)	4.0
WATER................	-	100.0	-	(D)	-	-	-	-	(D)	(D)	-
OTHER................	-	100.0	2.0	(D)	61.6	22.4	12.3	.3	(D)	(D)	.1
UNKNOWN..............	-	100.0	5.3	(D)	-	-	-	-	(D)	(D)	1.2
MIDDLE ATLANTIC........	122	100.0	1.5	(D)	45.4	2.9	4.7	15.6	(D)	(D)	2.8
RAIL.................	14	100.0	-	(D)	26.0	-	.7	13.1	(D)	(D)	4.0
MOTOR CARRIER........	91	100.0	1.9	(D)	53.1	3.9	4.9	16.5	(D)	(D)	3.2
PRIVATE TRUCK........	16	100.0	-	(D)	16.4	-	7.6	14.3	(D)	(D)	-
AIR..................	-	100.0	1.0	(D)	77.9	9.3	1.6	-	(D)	(D)	-
WATER................	-	100.0	-	(D)	100.0	-	-	-	(D)	(D)	-
OTHER................	-	100.0	2.0	(D)	72.9	12.0	9.2	2.0	(D)	(D)	-
UNKNOWN..............	-	100.0	-	(D)	13.0	-	-	-	(D)	(D)	-
EAST NORTH CENTRAL.....	185	100.0	1.0	(D)	18.0	1.7	4.5	8.4	(D)	(D)	14.4
RAIL.................	8	100.0	-	(D)	25.7	-	-	30.2	(D)	(D)	18.7
MOTOR CARRIER........	154	100.0	1.1	(D)	17.5	1.9	1.2	4.0	(D)	(D)	16.3
PRIVATE TRUCK........	22	100.0	-	(D)	18.1	.7	29.3	31.2	(D)	(D)	-
AIR..................	-	100.0	1.3	(D)	21.7	21.3	4.1	17.2	(D)	(D)	32.9
WATER................	-	100.0	-	(D)	-	-	-	-	(D)	(D)	-
OTHER................	-	100.0	27.3	(D)	53.8	5.8	4.5	2.9	(D)	(D)	-
UNKNOWN..............	-	100.0	-	(D)	25.9	-	-	-	(D)	(D)	15.2
WEST NORTH CENTRAL.....	61	100.0	.8	(D)	54.3	4.4	1.4	19.0	(D)	(D)	1.6
RAIL.................	18	100.0	-	(D)	84.0	-	-	6.8	(D)	(D)	-
MOTOR CARRIER........	37	100.0	1.1	(D)	47.6	4.1	.7	18.8	(D)	(D)	2.6
PRIVATE TRUCK........	4	100.0	-	(D)	6.7	1.3	12.4	72.8	(D)	(D)	-
AIR..................	-	100.0	-	(D)	74.1	.2	-	-	(D)	(D)	8.0
WATER................	-	100.0	-	(D)	-	-	-	-	(D)	(D)	-
OTHER................	-	100.0	17.4	(D)	47.8	18.9	4.9	1.4	(D)	(D)	-
UNKNOWN..............	1	100.0	-	(D)	.3	99.3	-	-	(D)	(D)	-
SOUTH ATLANTIC.........	119	100.0	.9	(D)	44.6	9.7	5.5	18.4	(D)	(D)	6.3
RAIL.................	25	100.0	-	(D)	59.0	-	1.8	19.1	(D)	(D)	1.0
MOTOR CARRIER........	77	100.0	1.0	(D)	44.5	10.5	6.6	17.0	(D)	(D)	9.2
PRIVATE TRUCK........	12	100.0	.6	(D)	28.0	-	8.8	33.4	(D)	(D)	.9
AIR..................	-	100.0	-	(D)	62.4	.8	-	-	(D)	(D)	.9
WATER................	-	100.0	-	(D)	-	-	-	-	(D)	(D)	-
OTHER................	-	100.0	30.4	(D)	37.4	8.1	2.6	1.1	(D)	(D)	3.7
UNKNOWN..............	3	100.0	-	(D)	5.8	90.1	-	.4	(D)	(D)	3.7
EAST SOUTH CENTRAL.....	45	100.0	1.3	(D)	43.8	3.5	3.0	12.4	(D)	(D)	20.3
RAIL.................	12	100.0	-	(D)	71.7	-	-	13.9	(D)	(D)	-
MOTOR CARRIER........	25	100.0	2.2	(D)	35.0	2.2	4.0	7.1	(D)	(D)	36.6
PRIVATE TRUCK........	5	100.0	-	(D)	30.1	.7	5.9	31.1	(D)	(D)	11.0
AIR..................	-	100.0	-	(D)	75.1	-	-	-	(D)	(D)	-
WATER................	-	100.0	-	(D)	-	-	-	-	(D)	(D)	-
OTHER................	-	100.0	3.0	(D)	27.4	4.6	1.6	32.1	(D)	(D)	.1
UNKNOWN..............	-	100.0	-	(D)	-	98.9	-	-	(D)	(D)	1.1
WEST SOUTH CENTRAL.....	147	100.0	.5	(D)	41.2	12.0	2.3	5.6	(D)	(D)	23.7
RAIL.................	76	100.0	-	(D)	48.3	6.4	.3	4.0	(D)	(D)	40.4
MOTOR CARRIER........	39	100.0	1.7	(D)	44.8	9.0	1.1	12.4	(D)	(D)	10.1
PRIVATE TRUCK........	27	100.0	-	(D)	21.2	20.3	10.1	.6	(D)	(D)	.1
AIR..................	-	100.0	-	(D)	53.0	-	-	-	(D)	(D)	3.3
WATER................	-	100.0	-	(D)	-	-	-	-	(D)	(D)	-
OTHER................	-	100.0	46.2	(D)	39.8	6.6	4.4	.1	(D)	(D)	1.3
UNKNOWN..............	3	100.0	-	(D)	.5	98.1	-	-	(D)	(D)	1.3
MOUNTAIN...............	91	100.0	.4	(D)	46.5	2.5	.9	27.7	(D)	(D)	15.1
RAIL.................	60	100.0	-	(D)	48.3	-	-	32.3	(D)	(D)	17.9
MOTOR CARRIER........	29	100.0	.9	(D)	43.6	7.7	2.8	19.7	(D)	(D)	8.2
PRIVATE TRUCK........	1	100.0	-	(D)	26.1	-	-	-	(D)	(D)	41.1
AIR..................	-	100.0	-	(D)	76.8	-	-	-	(D)	(D)	15.3
WATER................	-	100.0	-	(D)	-	-	-	-	(D)	(D)	-
OTHER................	-	100.0	-	(D)	68.9	7.8	8.4	-	(D)	(D)	1.3
UNKNOWN..............	-	100.0	71.0	(D)	-	-	-	4.9	(D)	(D)	10.2
PACIFIC................	180	100.0	1.3	(D)	45.0	13.0	2.4	17.4	(D)	(D)	3.8
RAIL.................	77	100.0	-	(D)	75.5	-	1.0	15.8	(D)	(D)	.8
MOTOR CARRIER........	76	100.0	.2	(D)	25.8	10.1	3.6	21.9	(D)	(D)	6.9
PRIVATE TRUCK........	6	100.0	-	(D)	25.3	-	12.2	35.8	(D)	(D)	11.7
AIR..................	-	100.0	.8	(D)	65.2	15.8	5.4	-	(D)	(D)	2.3
WATER................	-	100.0	-	(D)	-	-	-	-	(D)	(D)	100.0
OTHER................	3	100.0	67.1	(D)	19.5	.5	.1	.2	(D)	(D)	.4
UNKNOWN..............	15	100.0	-	(D)	-	98.3	-	.5	(D)	(D)	.7

See footnotes at end of table 4.

TABLE 4. **TCC GROUP 343**—Percent Distribution of Distance Shipped and Weight of Shipment, by Means of Transport: 1972

Distance shipped and weight of shipment [2] [3]	Number	Percent distribution by means of transport							
		All means of transport	Rail	Motor carrier	Private truck	Air	Water	Other	Unknown
TONS OF SHIPMENTS	(thousands of tons)								
U.S. TOTAL..........	1 933	100.0	16.9	57.1	24.1	.1	-	.3	1.4
UNDER 100 MILES........	344	100.0	7.4	22.8	69.0	-	-	.3	.4
UNDER 1000 POUNDS.....	19	100.0	-	76.1	19.0	.1	-	4.4	.4
1000 TO 9999 POUNDS...	43	100.0	1.9	41.4	54.5	.4	.3	.1	1.5
10000 TO 29999 POUNDS.	87	100.0	20.7	39.5	39.3	-	-	-	.6
30000 TO 59999 POUNDS.	31	100.0	21.6	36.8	41.6	-	-	-	-
60000 TO 89999 POUNDS.	163	100.0	-	-	100.0	-	-	-	-
90000 POUNDS AND OVER.	-	100.0	-	-	-	-	-	-	-
100 TO 199 MILES........	216	100.0	4.6	54.2	40.9	-	-	.2	.1
UNDER 1000 POUNDS.....	21	100.0	-	82.5	14.9	.2	.2	2.2	-
1000 TO 9999 POUNDS...	57	100.0	-	56.6	43.2	-	-	-	.3
10000 TO 29999 POUNDS.	105	100.0	2.7	47.8	49.5	-	-	-	-
30000 TO 59999 POUNDS.	23	100.0	16.9	71.1	12.0	-	-	-	-
60000 TO 89999 POUNDS.	8	100.0	36.1	-	63.9	-	-	-	-
90000 POUNDS AND OVER.	-	100.0	-	100.0	-	-	-	-	-
200 TO 299 MILES........	195	100.0	4.3	77.3	17.5	.3	-	.8	.1
UNDER 1000 POUNDS.....	15	100.0	-	94.1	1.1	.3	-	4.1	.5
1000 TO 9999 POUNDS...	37	100.0	-	78.8	20.6	.1	-	.4	.2
10000 TO 29999 POUNDS.	74	100.0	6.4	67.0	25.4	-	-	1.1	-
30000 TO 59999 POUNDS.	64	100.0	5.6	83.0	11.4	-	-	-	-
60000 TO 89999 POUNDS.	-	100.0	-	-	-	-	-	-	-
90000 POUNDS AND OVER.	3	100.0	-	100.0	-	-	-	-	-
300 TO 499 MILES........	437	100.0	5.8	81.8	9.9	.1	.2	.2	2.0
UNDER 1000 POUNDS.....	27	100.0	-	92.2	2.5	.9	-	3.6	.8
1000 TO 9999 POUNDS...	62	100.0	2.1	84.3	11.8	.3	1.1	-	.4
10000 TO 29999 POUNDS.	133	100.0	8.8	65.0	20.0	-	-	-	6.2
30000 TO 59999 POUNDS.	207	100.0	6.0	89.8	4.2	-	-	-	-
60000 TO 89999 POUNDS.	4	100.0	-	100.0	-	-	-	-	-
90000 POUNDS AND OVER.	1	100.0	-	100.0	-	-	-	-	-
500 TO 999 MILES........	492	100.0	27.5	59.0	10.8	.1	-	.4	2.2
UNDER 1000 POUNDS.....	46	100.0	-	92.1	3.2	1.3	-	3.2	.2
1000 TO 9999 POUNDS...	72	100.0	1.5	93.4	4.4	-	-	.7	-
10000 TO 29999 POUNDS.	205	100.0	24.7	54.4	15.9	-	-	-	5.0
30000 TO 59999 POUNDS.	152	100.0	45.7	43.9	10.3	-	-	-	.1
60000 TO 89999 POUNDS.	2	100.0	88.7	11.3	-	-	-	-	-
90000 POUNDS AND OVER.	13	100.0	92.9	7.1	-	-	-	-	-
1000 TO 1499 MILES......	120	100.0	54.6	40.9	4.2	.1	-	.2	-
UNDER 1000 POUNDS.....	10	100.0	.1	92.8	3.0	1.2	-	2.7	.2
1000 TO 9999 POUNDS...	26	100.0	.7	93.9	5.2	-	-	-	.1
10000 TO 29999 POUNDS.	35	100.0	70.3	24.5	5.2	-	-	-	-
30000 TO 59999 POUNDS.	32	100.0	78.6	16.7	4.7	-	-	-	-
60000 TO 89999 POUNDS.	1	100.0	86.8	13.2	-	-	-	-	-
90000 POUNDS AND OVER.	14	100.0	97.2	2.8	-	-	-	-	-
1500 MILES OR OVER......	127	100.0	43.9	47.3	2.6	.4	-	.4	5.4
UNDER 1000 POUNDS.....	10	100.0	1.4	86.5	4.4	2.6	.2	3.7	1.2
1000 TO 9999 POUNDS...	16	100.0	2.6	91.4	3.5	1.0	-	.9	.6
10000 TO 29999 POUNDS.	45	100.0	25.4	57.7	2.3	-	-	-	14.6
30000 TO 59999 POUNDS.	38	100.0	82.1	14.9	3.1	-	-	-	-
60000 TO 89999 POUNDS.	6	100.0	36.5	63.5	-	-	-	-	-
90000 POUNDS AND OVER.	10	100.0	100.0	-	-	-	-	-	-
TON-MILES OF SHIPMENTS	(millions of ton-miles)								
U.S. TOTAL..........	1 008	100.0	30.0	56.6	10.2	.2	-	.4	2.6
UNDER 100 MILES........	20	100.0	5.8	22.3	71.2	-	-	.3	.4
UNDER 1000 POUNDS.....	-	100.0	-	79.6	14.6	.1	-	5.2	.5
1000 TO 9999 POUNDS...	2	100.0	1.7	46.7	48.7	.3	.1	.1	2.5
10000 TO 29999 POUNDS.	4	100.0	18.7	44.6	36.1	-	-	-	.5
30000 TO 59999 POUNDS.	1	100.0	16.1	41.8	42.1	-	-	-	-
60000 TO 89999 POUNDS.	11	100.0	-	-	100.0	-	-	-	-
90000 POUNDS AND OVER.	-	100.0	-	-	-	-	-	-	-
100 TO 199 MILES........	31	100.0	5.2	54.5	40.0	-	-	.2	.1
UNDER 1000 POUNDS.....	3	100.0	-	82.7	14.6	.2	.2	2.2	-
1000 TO 9999 POUNDS...	8	100.0	-	57.3	42.5	-	-	-	.2
10000 TO 29999 POUNDS.	15	100.0	3.2	47.2	49.6	-	-	-	-
30000 TO 59999 POUNDS.	3	100.0	18.4	70.3	11.3	-	-	-	-
60000 TO 89999 POUNDS.	1	100.0	39.3	-	60.7	-	-	-	-
90000 POUNDS AND OVER.	-	100.0	-	100.0	-	-	-	-	-

See footnotes at end of table 4.

TABLE 4. **TCC GROUP 343—Percent Distribution of Distance Shipped and Weight of Shipment, by Means of Transport: 1972**—Continued

Distance shipped and weight of shipment [2] [3]	Number	Percent distribution by means of transport							
		All means of transport	Rail	Motor carrier	Private truck	Air	Water	Other	Unknown
TON-MILES OF SHIPMENTS	(millions of ton-miles)								
200 TO 299 MILES.........	48	100.0	4.7	77.9	16.5	-	-	.9	.1
UNDER 1000 POUNDS.....	3	100.0	-	94.1	1.1	.3	-	4.0	.5
1000 TO 9999 POUNDS...	9	100.0	-	79.2	20.1	.1	-	.4	.2
10000 TO 29999 POUNDS.	18	100.0	7.6	66.9	24.3	-	-	1.2	-
30000 TO 59999 POUNDS.	16	100.0	5.4	84.2	10.4	-	-	-	-
60000 TO 89999 POUNDS.	-	100.0	-	-	-	-	-	-	-
90000 POUNDS AND OVER.	-	100.0	-	100.0	-	-	-	-	-
300 TO 499 MILES........	168	100.0	6.1	81.3	10.1	.1	.2	.2	2.1
UNDER 1000 POUNDS.....	10	100.0	-	92.1	2.9	.9	-	3.3	.8
1000 TO 9999 POUNDS...	24	100.0	2.3	83.8	12.0	.3	1.2	-	.4
10000 TO 29999 POUNDS.	52	100.0	9.7	64.1	19.9	-	-	-	6.3
30000 TO 59999 POUNDS.	78	100.0	5.9	89.9	4.2	-	-	-	-
60000 TO 89999 POUNDS.	2	100.0	-	100.0	-	-	-	-	-
90000 POUNDS AND OVER.	-	100.0	-	100.0	-	-	-	-	-
500 TO 999 MILES........	343	100.0	29.4	57.2	11.1	.1	-	.4	1.8
UNDER 1000 POUNDS.....	32	100.0	-	92.0	3.2	1.4	-	3.2	.2
1000 TO 9999 POUNDS...	50	100.0	1.9	93.3	4.1	-	-	.7	-
10000 TO 29999 POUNDS.	135	100.0	25.8	53.0	16.8	-	-	-	4.3
30000 TO 59999 POUNDS.	111	100.0	46.7	42.2	11.0	-	-	-	.1
60000 TO 89999 POUNDS.	1	100.0	91.8	8.2	-	-	-	-	-
90000 POUNDS AND OVER.	11	100.0	96.0	4.0	-	-	-	-	-
1000 TO 1499 MILES......	143	100.0	53.2	42.1	4.3	.1	-	.2	.1
UNDER 1000 POUNDS.....	12	100.0	.1	92.7	3.1	1.2	-	2.6	.2
1000 TO 9999 POUNDS...	33	100.0	.6	93.8	5.5	-	-	-	.1
10000 TO 29999 POUNDS.	42	100.0	70.2	24.1	5.7	-	-	-	-
30000 TO 59999 POUNDS.	37	100.0	78.0	17.8	4.3	-	-	-	-
60000 TO 89999 POUNDS.	1	100.0	85.2	14.8	-	-	-	-	-
90000 POUNDS AND OVER.	15	100.0	96.6	3.4	-	-	-	-	-
1500 MILES OR OVER......	251	100.0	43.5	46.7	2.5	.4	-	.4	6.5
UNDER 1000 POUNDS.....	20	100.0	1.8	85.8	4.3	3.1	.3	3.4	1.3
1000 TO 9999 POUNDS...	31	100.0	2.9	90.4	3.8	1.0	-	1.2	.8
10000 TO 29999 POUNDS.	92	100.0	23.7	57.2	2.1	-	-	-	17.0
30000 TO 59999 POUNDS.	74	100.0	81.6	15.3	3.2	-	-	-	-
60000 TO 89999 POUNDS.	10	100.0	37.0	63.0	-	-	-	-	-
90000 POUNDS AND OVER.	21	100.0	100.0	-	-	-	-	-	-

Note: Detail may not add to total due to rounding. The introductory table shows the estimates of sampling variability for tons; sampling variability for ton-miles has not been estimated. See the map in the Introduction for the States comprising the geographic divisions of the United States.

Shipments excluded from the survey are those moving by pipeline (primarily petroleum products from refineries), parcel post shipments, and commodities moved by own power (motorized vehicles, aircraft, etc.) or towed (prefabricated buildings, etc.). Local shipments (commodities shipped less than 25 miles from the plant) and shipments within the same city are also excluded. Shipments to Alaska and Hawaii from the 48 conterminous States and the District of Columbia are included; however, no data were obtained for shipments originating in Alaska and Hawaii.

- Represents zero or rounds to zero.   (D) Withheld to avoid disclosing figures for individual companies.

[1] Production of this commodity is concentrated in the geographic divisions shown; figures and distributions for geographic divisions not shown are included in the total.
[2] Distances of shipments to foreign destinations are calculated only to the U.S. port of exit.
[3] Includes only shipments represented by bills of lading and invoices. Summary records which did not show individual weights of shipments are not included.

TCC 344. Fabricated Structural Metal Products

Comparisons of Tons and Ton-Miles of Shipments for
Geographic Divisions of Origin and for Sampling Variability: 1972 and 1967

Geographic division of origin	Estimates				Relative sampling variability in tons (percent)	
	1972		1967		1972	1967
	Tons (thousands)	Ton-miles (millions)	Tons (thousands)	Ton-miles (millions)		
U.S. total	13,475	5,924	14,991	4,835	12.3	11.8
New England	91	24	343	121	40.8	(*)
Middle Atlantic	2,946	1,158	4,348	1,275	6.4	(*)
East North Central	4,585	1,553	3,758	1,260	30.6	(*)
West North Central	(D)	(D)	1,013	476	(*)	(*)
South Atlantic	1,629	701	1,964	422	40.8	(*)
East South Central	261	124	1,042	336	43.8	(*)
West South Central	2,235	1,284	1,364	606	36.2	(*)
Mountain	(D)	(D)	151	71	(*)	(*)
Pacific	(D)	(D)	1,008	268	(*)	(*)

(D) Withheld to avoid disclosing figures for individual companies.   (*) Data not published.

TABLE 1. TCC GROUP 344—Percent Distribution of Geographic Division of Origin and Distance Shipped, by Means of Transport: 1972

Geographic division of origin[1] and distance shipped[2]	Number	Percent distribution by means of transport							
		All means of transport	Rail	Motor carrier	Private truck	Air	Water	Other	Unknown
TONS OF SHIPMENTS	(thousands of tons)								
U.S. TOTAL..........	13 475	100.0	20.3	50.0	27.4	.1	2.1	.1	-
NEW ENGLAND.............	91	100.0	3.8	43.2	52.6	.5	-	-	-
UNDER 100 MILES.......	53	100.0	-	11.6	88.1	.3	-	-	-
100 TO 199 MILES......	5	100.0	-	86.6	13.4	-	-	-	-
200 TO 299 MILES.....	12	100.0	-	96.2	3.7	.1	-	-	-
300 TO 499 MILES.....	2	100.0	-	88.1	7.8	4.0	-	-	-
500 TO 999 MILES.....	14	100.0	22.5	76.6	.3	.5	-	-	-
1000 TO 1499 MILES....	2	100.0	-	98.1	-	1.9	-	-	-
1500 MILES OR OVER....	1	100.0	15.3	82.5	-	2.2	-	-	-
MIDDLE ATLANTIC.........	2 946	100.0	50.0	34.1	13.7	.1	2.1	.1	-
UNDER 100 MILES.......	926	100.0	31.8	46.1	22.0	-	-	.1	-
100 TO 199 MILES......	487	100.0	45.3	37.1	17.5	-	.1	-	-
200 TO 299 MILES.....	422	100.0	54.7	34.9	7.9	.1	2.3	.2	-
300 TO 499 MILES.....	529	100.0	60.7	29.5	5.1	.2	4.4	-	.2
500 TO 999 MILES.....	299	100.0	55.9	20.4	17.6	.1	6.0	-	-
1000 TO 1499 MILES....	128	100.0	82.5	14.8	-	.1	2.5	-	-
1500 MILES OR OVER....	152	100.0	86.0	8.4	.3	-	4.9	-	.4
EAST NORTH CENTRAL......	4 585	100.0	11.9	50.5	35.0	-	2.6	-	-
UNDER 100 MILES.......	1 259	100.0	1.6	33.4	64.9	-	-	.1	-
100 TO 199 MILES......	796	100.0	6.9	54.3	36.2	-	2.5	-	-
200 TO 299 MILES.....	570	100.0	3.6	68.0	26.9	-	1.2	-	.3
300 TO 499 MILES.....	982	100.0	18.1	53.5	27.0	.1	1.3	-	-
500 TO 999 MILES.....	721	100.0	28.0	51.0	10.7	-	10.2	-	-
1000 TO 1499 MILES....	139	100.0	14.0	81.4	1.5	-	3.0	-	.1
1500 MILES OR OVER....	116	100.0	41.3	58.1	.4	.2	-	.1	-
SOUTH ATLANTIC..........	1 629	100.0	9.2	48.0	42.3	-	.4	.1	-
UNDER 100 MILES.......	223	100.0	2.3	32.0	65.3	-	-	.4	-
100 TO 199 MILES......	297	100.0	6.7	37.5	55.8	-	-	-	.1
200 TO 299 MILES.....	231	100.0	.7	57.8	40.7	-	.6	-	.1
300 TO 499 MILES.....	391	100.0	2.2	67.7	30.1	-	-	-	-
500 TO 999 MILES.....	382	100.0	11.2	47.5	40.7	-	.6	-	-
1000 TO 1499 MILES....	53	100.0	52.8	27.7	19.5	-	-	-	-
1500 MILES OR OVER....	49	100.0	88.3	5.8	-	-	5.8	-	-
EAST SOUTH CENTRAL......	261	100.0	51.5	19.6	28.2	-	.1	.6	-
UNDER 100 MILES.......	22	100.0	15.6	9.8	74.6	-	-	-	-
100 TO 199 MILES......	33	100.0	31.7	36.8	31.5	-	-	-	-
200 TO 299 MILES.....	25	100.0	25.0	38.6	36.4	-	-	-	-
300 TO 499 MILES.....	80	100.0	52.0	24.8	22.1	-	.3	.7	-
500 TO 999 MILES.....	91	100.0	70.2	7.3	21.5	-	-	1.0	-
1000 TO 1499 MILES....	4	100.0	98.7	1.3	-	-	-	-	-
1500 MILES OR OVER....	4	100.0	93.2	6.2	-	.6	-	-	-
WEST SOUTH CENTRAL......	2 235	100.0	8.0	58.9	28.1	.7	4.2	.2	-
UNDER 100 MILES.......	145	100.0	-	27.3	72.1	-	-	.6	-
100 TO 199 MILES......	287	100.0	1.8	61.0	37.0	-	-	.1	.1
200 TO 299 MILES.....	296	100.0	10.4	32.0	56.3	-	1.2	.1	-
300 TO 499 MILES.....	530	100.0	7.3	63.5	28.8	.1	.2	.1	-
500 TO 999 MILES.....	638	100.0	10.3	64.0	14.7	.9	9.9	.2	-
1000 TO 1499 MILES....	239	100.0	6.8	77.8	1.8	2.7	10.5	.4	-
1500 MILES OR OVER....	97	100.0	21.8	76.0	-	2.2	-	-	-
TON-MILES OF SHIPMENTS	(millions of ton-miles)								
U.S. TOTAL..........	5 924	100.0	29.0	52.3	14.5	.3	3.8	.1	-
NEW ENGLAND.............	24	100.0	12.6	75.0	11.6	.8	-	-	-
UNDER 100 MILES.......	2	100.0	-	14.5	85.4	.2	-	-	-
100 TO 199 MILES......	-	100.0	-	86.2	13.8	-	-	-	-
200 TO 299 MILES.....	3	100.0	-	97.1	2.9	.1	-	-	-
300 TO 499 MILES.....	-	100.0	-	89.9	6.6	3.5	-	-	-
500 TO 999 MILES.....	10	100.0	24.8	74.4	.2	.6	-	-	-
1000 TO 1499 MILES....	3	100.0	-	98.3	-	1.7	-	-	-
1500 MILES OR OVER....	2	100.0	15.7	82.7	-	1.6	-	-	-
MIDDLE ATLANTIC.........	1 158	100.0	68.0	20.5	6.7	.1	4.5	-	.2
UNDER 100 MILES.......	52	100.0	34.6	44.1	21.2	-	-	.1	-
100 TO 199 MILES......	67	100.0	45.0	36.1	18.8	-	.1	-	-
200 TO 299 MILES.....	105	100.0	55.8	33.8	7.8	.1	2.4	.1	-
300 TO 499 MILES.....	204	100.0	61.0	28.7	4.9	.2	5.1	-	.2
500 TO 999 MILES.....	225	100.0	56.8	20.2	15.5	.1	7.4	-	-
1000 TO 1499 MILES....	149	100.0	81.6	15.4	-	.1	2.9	-	-
1500 MILES OR OVER....	354	100.0	86.5	7.8	.3	-	5.0	-	.4
EAST NORTH CENTRAL......	1 553	100.0	21.3	56.2	18.1	.1	4.2	-	-
UNDER 100 MILES.......	73	100.0	1.1	29.6	69.3	-	-	.1	-
100 TO 199 MILES......	118	100.0	6.5	54.7	36.3	-	2.4	-	-
200 TO 299 MILES.....	144	100.0	3.6	67.7	27.2	-	1.2	-	.3
300 TO 499 MILES.....	365	100.0	17.6	55.0	25.9	.1	1.4	-	-
500 TO 999 MILES.....	479	100.0	27.9	50.8	10.5	-	10.7	-	-
1000 TO 1499 MILES....	155	100.0	17.1	78.1	1.7	-	3.0	-	.1
1500 MILES OR OVER....	216	100.0	42.8	56.5	.4	.2	-	.1	-

See footnotes at end of table 4.

TABLE 1. **TCC GROUP 344**—Percent Distribution of Geographic Division of Origin and Distance Shipped, by Means of Transport: 1972—Continued

Geographic division of origin[1] and distance shipped[2]	Number	Percent distribution by means of transport							
		All means of transport	Rail	Motor carrier	Private truck	Air	Water	Other	Unknown
TON-MILES OF SHIPMENTS	(millions of ton-miles)								
SOUTH ATLANTIC..........	701	100.0	21.2	43.8	33.6	-	1.4	-	-
UNDER 100 MILES........	13	100.0	1.4	36.5	61.8	-	-	.4	-
100 TO 199 MILES......	45	100.0	6.4	34.8	58.7	-	-	-	.1
200 TO 299 MILES......	58	100.0	.7	57.2	41.2	-	.7	-	.1
300 TO 499 MILES......	150	100.0	2.1	69.4	28.5	-	-	-	-
500 TO 999 MILES......	277	100.0	10.7	44.7	43.9	-	.7	-	-
1000 TO 1499 MILES....	62	100.0	50.0	30.9	19.1	-	-	-	-
1500 MILES OR OVER....	93	100.0	86.5	5.8	-	-	7.7	-	-
EAST SOUTH CENTRAL......	124	100.0	65.5	13.2	20.5	-	.1	.8	-
UNDER 100 MILES........	-	100.0	22.1	16.1	61.8	-	-	-	-
100 TO 199 MILES......	5	100.0	34.6	34.7	30.6	-	-	-	-
200 TO 299 MILES......	6	100.0	25.0	36.7	38.2	-	-	-	-
300 TO 499 MILES......	32	100.0	53.7	22.6	22.6	-	.4	.8	-
500 TO 999 MILES......	65	100.0	71.6	6.5	20.8	-	-	1.1	-
1000 TO 1499 MILES....	5	100.0	98.8	1.1	-	-	-	-	-
1500 MILES OR OVER....	9	100.0	93.9	5.4	-	.6	-	-	-
WEST SOUTH CENTRAL......	1 284	100.0	9.5	67.4	14.9	1.3	6.8	.2	-
UNDER 100 MILES........	6	100.0	-	39.1	59.8	-	-	1.0	-
100 TO 199 MILES......	46	100.0	1.2	61.7	37.0	-	-	.1	.1
200 TO 299 MILES......	70	100.0	10.6	32.1	56.1	-	1.0	.1	-
300 TO 499 MILES......	219	100.0	6.9	65.5	27.1	.1	.2	.1	-
500 TO 999 MILES......	491	100.0	9.5	65.3	13.3	1.0	10.6	.2	-
1000 TO 1499 MILES....	294	100.0	6.2	77.4	1.8	2.9	11.3	.4	-
1500 MILES OR OVER....	154	100.0	21.4	76.5	-	2.1	-	-	-

See footnotes at end of table 4.

TABLE 2. **TCC GROUP 344**—Percent Distribution of Geographic Division of Origin and Means of Transport, by Geographic Division of Destination: 1972

Geographic division of origin[1] and means of transport	Number	Percent distribution by division of destination									
		U.S. total	New England	Middle Atlantic	East North Central	West North Central	South Atlantic	East South Central	West South Central	Mountain	Pacific
TONS OF SHIPMENTS	(thousands of tons)										
U.S. TOTAL..............	13 475	100.0	4.1	17.7	26.4	6.3	14.2	4.2	12.6	4.5	9.9
RAIL................	2 729	100.0	4.3	19.7	18.7	5.9	23.4	5.4	9.7	6.5	6.4
MOTOR CARRIER........	6 732	100.0	4.5	19.9	22.5	5.0	11.6	4.6	12.2	3.8	15.9
PRIVATE TRUCK........	3 688	100.0	3.5	12.9	38.3	9.3	12.7	2.3	14.3	4.7	2.1
AIR.................	19	100.0	13.2	15.2	18.0	.7	19.9	2.3	4.6	1.4	24.7
WATER...............	283	100.0	-	9.1	39.2	2.8	8.2	6.7	29.3	-	4.7
OTHER...............	18	100.0	.5	7.3	12.0	25.2	12.9	1.1	20.8	16.1	4.2
UNKNOWN.............	4	100.0	19.2	1.0	42.4	.3	15.8	-	5.3	.8	15.3
NEW ENGLAND.............	91	100.0	51.9	26.5	10.7	.8	6.3	2.3	.6	.2	.8
RAIL................	3	100.0	-	-	68.9	-	26.4	-	-	.9	3.8
MOTOR CARRIER........	39	100.0	10.0	49.1	18.4	1.8	12.3	5.2	1.4	.4	1.5
PRIVATE TRUCK........	48	100.0	90.1	9.8	.1	-	-	-	-	-	-
AIR.................	-	100.0	35.6	25.6	15.6	-	2.1	15.6	3.8	1.6	-
WATER...............	-	100.0	-	-	-	-	-	-	-	-	-
OTHER...............	-	100.0	25.3	19.2	31.8	5.4	14.5	.1	-	-	3.6
UNKNOWN.............	-	100.0	-	100.0	-	-	-	-	-	-	-
MIDDLE ATLANTIC.........	2 946	100.0	5.8	42.3	17.7	2.5	20.6	2.8	2.9	.9	4.4
RAIL................	1 472	100.0	5.4	29.3	20.8	1.5	27.1	3.6	3.3	1.2	7.8
MOTOR CARRIER........	1 003	100.0	4.7	58.0	16.4	1.0	14.5	1.9	1.7	1.0	.8
PRIVATE TRUCK........	402	100.0	10.7	57.5	6.3	10.2	14.9	.2	-	-	.1
AIR.................	1	100.0	6.3	18.5	3.2	6.9	56.3	.3	6.5	-	1.9
WATER...............	62	100.0	-	1.0	40.0	-	2.7	12.9	32.7	-	10.7
OTHER...............	1	100.0	2.2	46.1	43.6	.2	7.0	.2	.4	-	.3
UNKNOWN.............	1	100.0	54.5	-	7.0	-	-	-	-	-	38.4
EAST NORTH CENTRAL......	4 585	100.0	3.2	15.6	51.8	7.2	8.1	4.2	6.6	1.6	1.8
RAIL................	543	100.0	2.8	16.4	26.4	11.2	10.3	5.2	15.0	3.9	8.6
MOTOR CARRIER........	2 315	100.0	5.1	21.1	40.5	6.9	9.9	6.2	6.7	2.2	1.4
PRIVATE TRUCK........	1 604	100.0	.6	8.6	79.1	6.4	4.1	.6	.4	.2	-
AIR.................	1	100.0	.4	1.6	65.9	.2	9.5	.3	.8	7.1	14.3
WATER...............	117	100.0	-	-	18.1	6.7	17.6	7.2	50.3	-	-
OTHER...............	1	100.0	2.6	7.6	68.0	6.9	5.2	3.8	1.2	.1	4.7
UNKNOWN.............	1	100.0	-	2.2	92.8	-	5.1	-	-	-	-
SOUTH ATLANTIC..........	1 629	100.0	5.3	16.7	13.6	13.7	38.9	4.7	3.2	3.4	.5
RAIL................	149	100.0	.2	1.0	14.9	12.9	15.5	5.1	19.1	28.9	2.5
MOTOR CARRIER........	781	100.0	7.1	22.7	13.3	10.3	38.3	4.7	1.7	1.6	.2
PRIVATE TRUCK........	690	100.0	4.4	13.4	13.5	17.8	44.8	4.6	1.5	-	-
AIR.................	-	100.0	65.6	.2	15.9	-	18.2	-	-	-	.1
WATER...............	6	100.0	-	-	22.2	-	11.1	22.2	-	-	44.4
OTHER...............	1	100.0	.1	1.4	-	-	96.9	1.4	-	-	.1
UNKNOWN.............	-	100.0	-	.7	-	-	99.3	-	-	-	-

See footnotes at end of table 4.

TABLE 2. TCC GROUP 344—Percent Distribution of Geographic Division of Origin and Means of Transport, by Geographic Division of Destination: 1972—Continued

Geographic division of origin [1] and means of transport	Number	Percent distribution by division of destination									
		U.S. total	New England	Middle Atlantic	East North Central	West North Central	South Atlantic	East South Central	West South Central	Mountain	Pacific
TONS OF SHIPMENTS	(thousands of tons)										
EAST SOUTH CENTRAL	261	100.0	.9	5.9	13.0	11.2	26.5	23.1	14.0	3.5	1.8
RAIL	134	100.0	-	6.3	15.8	9.5	24.8	15.0	18.6	6.8	3.3
MOTOR CARRIER	51	100.0	4.5	2.7	4.7	1.9	41.1	30.9	13.6	.3	.4
PRIVATE TRUCK	73	100.0	-	7.7	13.4	20.1	19.9	33.2	5.7	-	-
AIR	-	100.0	-	1.1	3.5	-	9.5	-	-	-	85.9
WATER	-	100.0	-	-	100.0	-	-	-	-	-	-
OTHER	1	100.0	-	-	14.7	49.6	6.9	.8	28.0	-	-
UNKNOWN	-	100.0	-	-	-	-	-	-	-	-	-
WEST SOUTH CENTRAL	2 235	100.0	4.4	4.6	15.8	4.2	5.3	5.6	50.9	5.9	3.3
RAIL	178	100.0	11.9	1.5	5.6	4.0	12.1	16.2	29.7	17.8	1.0
MOTOR CARRIER	1 316	100.0	5.6	5.3	20.7	4.4	5.6	5.8	43.6	3.8	5.2
PRIVATE TRUCK	628	100.0	.1	.2	.8	4.6	3.2	3.1	80.2	7.9	-
AIR	14	100.0	15.0	16.5	16.4	.1	18.0	2.5	4.9	1.2	25.6
WATER	92	100.0	-	27.2	68.0	-	-	1.1	3.8	-	-
OTHER	4	100.0	.6	6.7	9.5	4.5	25.7	1.2	51.7	.1	-
UNKNOWN	-	100.0	-	-	-	-	-	-	85.9	14.1	-
TON-MILES OF SHIPMENTS	(millions of ton-miles)										
U.S. TOTAL	5 924	100.0	5.4	10.5	16.2	7.8	13.8	4.6	13.8	7.5	20.4
RAIL	1 716	100.0	3.6	6.6	11.9	5.3	23.0	5.1	10.9	11.0	22.7
MOTOR CARRIER	3 095	100.0	7.2	12.0	15.6	5.0	9.9	4.8	14.1	6.4	24.9
PRIVATE TRUCK	858	100.0	3.5	11.4	23.3	24.0	10.8	3.7	15.7	6.7	.8
AIR	19	100.0	17.6	17.6	12.2	.6	14.8	1.6	2.6	1.6	31.3
WATER	223	100.0	-	15.0	30.6	2.4	9.0	2.4	26.1	-	14.5
OTHER	8	100.0	.9	9.6	7.7	14.5	18.9	1.0	21.6	2.6	23.1
UNKNOWN	2	100.0	14.5	1.0	16.3	.1	10.1	-	2.5	.9	54.5
NEW ENGLAND	24	100.0	10.9	19.1	25.8	3.2	19.8	8.9	3.4	1.5	7.4
RAIL	3	100.0	-	-	59.8	-	27.8	-	-	1.9	10.5
MOTOR CARRIER	18	100.0	1.6	22.9	23.9	4.2	21.7	11.5	4.4	1.6	8.1
PRIVATE TRUCK	2	100.0	83.5	15.6	.8	-	-	-	-	-	-
AIR	-	100.0	2.4	17.9	31.7	-	1.3	27.0	12.6	7.1	-
WATER	-	100.0	-	-	-	-	-	-	-	-	-
OTHER	-	100.0	2.0	4.7	46.8	12.2	16.8	.1	-	-	17.3
UNKNOWN	-	100.0	-	100.0	-	-	-	-	-	-	-
MIDDLE ATLANTIC	1 158	100.0	3.5	10.2	18.4	4.8	17.5	5.7	9.0	3.8	27.3
RAIL	788	100.0	2.4	5.7	16.9	2.3	19.5	6.2	8.2	3.5	35.4
MOTOR CARRIER	237	100.0	4.5	22.8	25.6	3.7	15.6	6.0	7.7	6.6	7.5
PRIVATE TRUCK	78	100.0	12.6	24.6	10.8	36.4	13.4	.6	-	-	1.5
AIR	-	100.0	7.4	8.7	2.9	12.2	40.8	.2	17.9	.1	9.7
WATER	51	100.0	-	.1	20.7	-	2.7	4.1	40.3	-	31.9
OTHER	-	100.0	3.9	47.1	26.1	1.5	12.3	.5	2.7	.2	5.7
UNKNOWN	1	100.0	20.9	-	.8	-	-	-	-	-	78.3
EAST NORTH CENTRAL	1 553	100.0	5.2	16.6	21.8	8.7	10.1	4.8	15.7	6.7	10.3
RAIL	331	100.0	3.2	16.0	12.1	7.5	5.6	3.8	15.6	8.8	27.4
MOTOR CARRIER	873	100.0	7.4	18.1	16.9	6.2	11.5	6.6	17.3	8.2	7.9
PRIVATE TRUCK	281	100.0	2.1	16.7	52.2	17.7	7.0	1.2	1.6	1.3	.2
AIR	-	100.0	.4	1.2	30.8	.1	9.6	.2	.9	15.1	41.6
WATER	65	100.0	-	-	5.3	8.1	27.5	3.5	55.5	-	-
OTHER	-	100.0	4.6	8.2	25.8	7.9	11.4	5.6	4.2	.4	32.0
UNKNOWN	-	100.0	-	4.2	77.3	-	18.4	-	-	-	-
SOUTH ATLANTIC	701	100.0	5.9	12.7	10.1	24.2	19.1	4.4	7.4	13.6	2.7
RAIL	148	100.0	.1	.7	4.6	8.4	6.6	2.3	19.6	52.3	5.4
MOTOR CARRIER	307	100.0	9.9	21.0	10.0	18.1	26.7	3.8	3.5	5.7	1.1
PRIVATE TRUCK	235	100.0	4.6	9.8	13.4	43.2	17.5	6.5	5.0	-	-
AIR	-	100.0	66.8	.3	11.7	-	20.8	-	-	-	.3
WATER	9	100.0	-	-	15.0	-	5.4	4.3	-	-	75.3
OTHER	-	100.0	.6	12.9	.4	-	78.4	3.5	-	-	4.1
UNKNOWN	-	100.0	-	2.5	-	-	97.5	-	-	-	-
EAST SOUTH CENTRAL	124	100.0	1.4	10.1	13.3	15.4	24.2	8.4	12.6	7.4	7.1
RAIL	81	100.0	-	9.2	14.0	10.6	24.3	6.0	14.4	11.0	10.4
MOTOR CARRIER	16	100.0	10.7	5.2	5.1	3.1	37.3	20.1	15.1	1.3	2.1
PRIVATE TRUCK	25	100.0	-	16.7	16.3	36.8	16.0	9.1	5.1	-	-
AIR	-	100.0	-	.6	.8	-	3.6	-	-	-	95.1
WATER	-	100.0	-	-	100.0	-	-	-	-	-	-
OTHER	-	100.0	-	-	11.0	61.0	7.0	.3	20.7	-	-
UNKNOWN	-	100.0	-	-	-	-	-	-	-	-	-
WEST SOUTH CENTRAL	1 284	100.0	11.6	9.9	22.3	3.5	8.3	4.5	24.2	7.6	8.2
RAIL	121	100.0	26.7	2.5	6.8	4.9	14.0	9.9	12.7	19.8	2.8
MOTOR CARRIER	865	100.0	12.9	9.9	25.4	3.3	7.9	4.1	20.5	5.0	11.1
PRIVATE TRUCK	190	100.0	.6	.7	1.8	5.8	9.0	5.4	60.8	15.9	-
AIR	16	100.0	19.9	19.4	11.9	-	14.5	1.5	1.8	.9	30.0
WATER	86	100.0	-	38.4	60.2	-	-	.6	.8	-	-
OTHER	2	100.0	1.5	14.1	12.1	2.2	46.6	.9	22.5	.1	-
UNKNOWN	-	100.0	-	-	-	-	-	-	59.8	40.2	-

See footnotes at end of table 4.

TABLE 3. **TCC GROUP 344**—Percent Distribution of Geographic Division of Destination and Means of Transport, by Geographic Division of Origin: 1972

Geographic division of destination and means of transport	Number	Percent distribution by division of origin[1]									
		U.S. total	New England	Middle Atlantic	East North Central	West North Central	South Atlantic	East South Central	West South Central	Mountain	Pacific
TONS OF SHIPMENTS	(thousands of tons)										
U.S. TOTAL.............	13 475	100.0	.7	21.9	34.0	(D)	12.1	1.9	16.6	(D)	(D)
RAIL................	2 729	100.0	.1	34.0	19.9	(D)	5.5	4.9	6.5	(D)	(D)
MOTOR CARRIER........	6 732	100.0	.6	14.9	34.4	(D)	11.6	.8	19.5	(D)	(D)
PRIVATE TRUCK........	3 688	100.0	1.3	10.9	43.5	(D)	18.7	2.0	17.0	(D)	(D)
AIR.................	19	100.0	2.2	9.4	7.2	(D)	.5	.2	76.4	(D)	(D)
WATER...............	283	100.0	-	22.1	41.5	(D)	2.3	.1	32.8	(D)	(D)
OTHER...............	18	100.0	-	8.2	7.2	(D)	5.4	8.2	23.9	(D)	(D)
UNKNOWN.............	4	100.0	-	35.1	43.0	(D)	12.3	-	5.4	(D)	(D)
NEW ENGLAND............	552	100.0	8.6	31.0	26.2	(D)	15.6	.4	17.9	(D)	(D)
RAIL................	116	100.0	-	68.4	13.1	(D)	.3	-	18.2	(D)	(D)
MOTOR CARRIER........	304	100.0	1.3	15.5	39.2	(D)	18.2	.8	24.4	(D)	(D)
PRIVATE TRUCK........	128	100.0	34.0	33.7	7.9	(D)	23.8	-	.7	(D)	(D)
AIR.................	2	100.0	5.9	4.5	.2	(D)	2.3	-	87.0	(D)	(D)
WATER...............	-	100.0	-	-	-	(D)	-	-	-	(D)	(D)
OTHER...............	-	100.0	1.7	33.9	35.2	(D)	1.2	-	28.1	(D)	(D)
UNKNOWN.............	-	100.0	-	99.8	-	(D)	-	-	-	(D)	(D)
MIDDLE ATLANTIC........	2 382	100.0	1.0	52.3	30.0	(D)	11.4	.7	4.3	(D)	(D)
RAIL................	536	100.0	-	80.3	16.7	(D)	.3	1.6	.5	(D)	(D)
MOTOR CARRIER........	1 341	100.0	1.5	43.4	36.4	(D)	13.2	.1	5.2	(D)	(D)
PRIVATE TRUCK........	474	100.0	1.0	48.7	28.9	(D)	19.5	1.2	.2	(D)	(D)
AIR.................	2	100.0	3.7	11.5	.7	(D)	-	-	82.9	(D)	(D)
WATER...............	25	100.0	-	2.3	-	(D)	-	-	97.7	(D)	(D)
OTHER...............	1	100.0	.1	52.3	7.5	(D)	1.0	-	22.1	(D)	(D)
UNKNOWN.............	-	100.0	.9	-	90.3	(D)	8.8	-	-	(D)	(D)
EAST NORTH CENTRAL......	3 555	100.0	.3	14.7	66.8	(D)	6.2	1.0	9.9	(D)	(D)
RAIL................	510	100.0	.5	59.9	28.1	(D)	4.4	4.2	2.0	(D)	(D)
MOTOR CARRIER........	1 513	100.0	.5	10.9	61.9	(D)	6.9	.2	18.0	(D)	(D)
PRIVATE TRUCK........	1 412	100.0	-	1.8	89.8	(D)	6.6	.7	.3	(D)	(D)
AIR.................	3	100.0	1.9	1.7	26.3	(D)	.4	-	69.4	(D)	(D)
WATER...............	111	100.0	-	22.5	19.1	(D)	1.3	.3	56.8	(D)	(D)
OTHER...............	2	100.0	.1	29.9	40.8	(D)	-	10.1	18.9	(D)	(D)
UNKNOWN.............	1	100.0	-	5.8	94.2	(D)	-	-	-	(D)	(D)
WEST NORTH CENTRAL......	855	100.0	.1	8.6	38.7	(D)	26.1	3.4	11.0	(D)	(D)
RAIL................	161	100.0	-	13.7	37.7	(D)	11.9	7.9	4.5	(D)	(D)
MOTOR CARRIER........	339	100.0	.2	3.1	46.9	(D)	23.8	.3	17.0	(D)	(D)
PRIVATE TRUCK........	341	100.0	-	12.0	30.0	(D)	36.0	4.3	8.4	(D)	(D)
AIR.................	-	100.0	-	87.8	1.7	(D)	-	-	5.7	(D)	(D)
WATER...............	7	100.0	-	-	100.0	(D)	-	-	-	(D)	(D)
OTHER...............	4	100.0	-	.1	2.0	(D)	-	16.1	4.2	(D)	(D)
UNKNOWN.............	-	100.0	-	-	-	(D)	-	-	-	(D)	(D)
SOUTH ATLANTIC.........	1 916	100.0	.3	31.7	19.4	(D)	33.1	3.6	6.2	(D)	(D)
RAIL................	638	100.0	.1	62.4	8.8	(D)	3.7	5.2	3.4	(D)	(D)
MOTOR CARRIER........	778	100.0	.6	18.7	29.5	(D)	38.5	2.7	9.5	(D)	(D)
PRIVATE TRUCK........	469	100.0	-	12.8	14.1	(D)	65.8	3.1	4.3	(D)	(D)
AIR.................	3	100.0	.2	26.6	3.4	(D)	.4	.1	69.1	(D)	(D)
WATER...............	23	100.0	-	7.3	89.6	(D)	3.1	-	-	(D)	(D)
OTHER...............	2	100.0	-	4.5	2.9	(D)	40.5	4.4	47.6	(D)	(D)
UNKNOWN.............	-	100.0	-	-	13.8	(D)	77.1	-	-	(D)	(D)
EAST SOUTH CENTRAL......	561	100.0	.4	14.5	34.1	(D)	13.8	10.8	22.4	(D)	(D)
RAIL................	146	100.0	-	36.6	19.4	(D)	5.2	13.8	19.7	(D)	(D)
MOTOR CARRIER........	308	100.0	.7	6.2	46.7	(D)	11.8	5.1	24.7	(D)	(D)
PRIVATE TRUCK........	86	100.0	-	1.1	11.8	(D)	36.5	28.2	22.2	(D)	(D)
AIR.................	-	100.0	14.7	1.1	.9	(D)	-	-	82.8	(D)	(D)
WATER...............	19	100.0	-	42.4	44.7	(D)	7.5	-	5.4	(D)	(D)
OTHER...............	-	100.0	-	1.4	24.0	(D)	6.7	6.0	26.2	(D)	(D)
UNKNOWN.............	-	100.0	-	-	100.0	(D)	-	-	-	(D)	(D)
WEST SOUTH CENTRAL......	1 703	100.0	-	5.1	17.7	(D)	3.1	2.1	66.8	(D)	(D)
RAIL................	265	100.0	-	18.5	30.7	(D)	10.8	9.4	19.9	(D)	(D)
MOTOR CARRIER........	823	100.0	.1	2.0	18.8	(D)	1.6	.8	69.8	(D)	(D)
PRIVATE TRUCK........	526	100.0	-	-	1.2	(D)	2.0	.8	95.7	(D)	(D)
AIR.................	-	100.0	1.8	13.3	1.2	(D)	-	-	80.8	(D)	(D)
WATER...............	82	100.0	-	24.6	71.1	(D)	-	-	4.2	(D)	(D)
OTHER...............	3	100.0	-	.2	.4	(D)	-	11.1	59.4	(D)	(D)
UNKNOWN.............	-	100.0	-	-	-	(D)	-	-	86.8	(D)	(D)
MOUNTAIN...............	611	100.0	-	4.4	12.3	(D)	9.2	1.5	21.4	(D)	(D)
RAIL................	178	100.0	-	9.6	11.9	(D)	24.2	5.1	17.7	(D)	(D)
MOTOR CARRIER........	256	100.0	.1	3.8	19.7	(D)	5.0	.1	19.3	(D)	(D)
PRIVATE TRUCK........	172	100.0	-	-	1.7	(D)	-	-	28.7	(D)	(D)
AIR.................	-	100.0	2.4	.2	35.3	(D)	-	-	61.9	(D)	(D)
WATER...............	-	100.0	-	-	-	(D)	-	-	-	(D)	(D)
OTHER...............	3	100.0	-	-	-	(D)	-	-	.2	(D)	(D)
UNKNOWN.............	-	100.0	-	-	-	(D)	-	-	100.0	(D)	(D)
PACIFIC................	1 336	100.0	.1	9.8	6.1	(D)	.6	.3	5.5	(D)	(D)
RAIL................	173	100.0	.1	66.6	27.0	(D)	2.1	2.5	1.1	(D)	(D)
MOTOR CARRIER........	1 067	100.0	.1	.7	3.1	(D)	.2	-	6.4	(D)	(D)
PRIVATE TRUCK........	75	100.0	-	.7	.4	(D)	-	-	-	(D)	(D)
AIR.................	4	100.0	-	.7	4.2	(D)	-	.6	79.4	(D)	(D)
WATER...............	13	100.0	-	50.8	-	(D)	21.8	-	-	(D)	(D)
OTHER...............	-	100.0	-	.6	8.1	(D)	.2	-	-	(D)	(D)
UNKNOWN.............	-	100.0	-	88.3	-	(D)	-	-	-	(D)	(D)

See footnotes at end of table 4.

TABLE 3. **TCC GROUP 344—Percent Distribution of Geographic Division of Destination and Means of Transport, by Geographic Division of Origin: 1972**—Continued

Geographic division of destination and means of transport	Number	Percent distribution by division of origin [1]									
		U.S. total	New England	Middle Atlantic	East North Central	West North Central	South Atlantic	East South Central	West South Central	Mountain	Pacific
TON-MILES OF SHIPMENTS	(millions of ton-miles)										
U.S. TOTAL..............	5 924	100.0	.4	19.6	26.2	(D)	11.8	2.1	21.7	(D)	(D)
RAIL................	1 716	100.0	.2	45.9	19.3	(D)	8.7	4.7	7.1	(D)	(D)
MOTOR CARRIER........	3 095	100.0	.6	7.7	28.2	(D)	9.9	.5	27.9	(D)	(D)
PRIVATE TRUCK........	858	100.0	.3	9.1	32.8	(D)	27.5	3.0	22.2	(D)	(D)
AIR.................	19	100.0	1.0	4.3	5.0	(D)	.3	.3	85.5	(D)	(D)
WATER...............	223	100.0	-	23.3	29.5	(D)	4.3	.1	39.0	(D)	(D)
OTHER...............	8	100.0	-	3.6	4.8	(D)	1.0	11.7	35.0	(D)	(D)
UNKNOWN.............	2	100.0	-	69.1	20.4	(D)	4.4	-	2.4	(D)	(D)
NEW ENGLAND.............	319	100.0	.8	12.5	25.4	(D)	13.0	.5	46.4	(D)	(D)
RAIL................	62	100.0	-	30.7	16.9	(D)	.3	-	52.1	(D)	(D)
MOTOR CARRIER........	223	100.0	.1	4.8	28.9	(D)	13.6	.8	49.8	(D)	(D)
PRIVATE TRUCK........	30	100.0	7.8	32.8	19.7	(D)	36.2	-	3.5	(D)	(D)
AIR.................	3	100.0	.1	1.8	.1	(D)	1.0	-	96.7	(D)	(D)
WATER...............	-	100.0	-	-	-	(D)	-	-	-	(D)	(D)
OTHER...............	-	100.0	.1	15.9	25.0	(D)	.6	-	58.4	(D)	(D)
UNKNOWN.............	-	100.0	-	99.3	-	(D)	-	-	-	(D)	(D)
MIDDLE ATLANTIC.........	619	100.0	.7	19.1	41.7	(D)	14.3	2.0	20.5	(D)	(D)
RAIL................	112	100.0	-	39.5	47.1	(D)	.9	6.7	2.7	(D)	(D)
MOTOR CARRIER........	371	100.0	1.1	14.6	42.6	(D)	17.4	.2	23.0	(D)	(D)
PRIVATE TRUCK........	97	100.0	.5	19.7	48.1	(D)	23.7	4.3	1.3	(D)	(D)
AIR.................	3	100.0	1.0	2.1	.3	(D)	-	-	94.2	(D)	(D)
WATER...............	33	100.0	-	.2	-	(D)	-	-	99.8	(D)	(D)
OTHER...............	-	100.0	-	17.5	4.1	(D)	1.3	-	51.3	(D)	(D)
UNKNOWN.............	-	100.0	.5	-	88.1	(D)	11.4	-	-	(D)	(D)
EAST NORTH CENTRAL......	960	100.0	.7	22.2	35.3	(D)	7.4	1.7	29.8	(D)	(D)
RAIL................	204	100.0	.9	65.1	19.5	(D)	3.4	5.6	4.0	(D)	(D)
MOTOR CARRIER........	484	100.0	.9	12.6	30.4	(D)	6.4	.2	45.3	(D)	(D)
PRIVATE TRUCK........	199	100.0	-	4.2	73.6	(D)	15.8	2.1	1.7	(D)	(D)
AIR.................	2	100.0	2.6	1.0	12.6	(D)	.3	-	82.9	(D)	(D)
WATER...............	68	100.0	-	15.8	5.2	(D)	2.1	.2	76.8	(D)	(D)
OTHER...............	-	100.0	.3	12.1	16.0	(D)	.1	16.7	54.6	(D)	(D)
UNKNOWN.............	-	100.0	-	3.5	96.5	(D)	-	-	-	(D)	(D)
WEST NORTH CENTRAL......	459	100.0	.2	12.0	29.3	(D)	37.0	4.2	9.9	(D)	(D)
RAIL................	91	100.0	-	19.4	27.4	(D)	13.7	9.5	6.5	(D)	(D)
MOTOR CARRIER........	155	100.0	.5	5.7	34.9	(D)	35.9	.3	18.3	(D)	(D)
PRIVATE TRUCK........	205	100.0	-	13.8	24.2	(D)	49.4	4.6	5.4	(D)	(D)
AIR.................	-	100.0	-	87.0	.9	(D)	-	-	5.1	(D)	(D)
WATER...............	5	100.0	-	-	100.0	(D)	-	-	-	(D)	(D)
OTHER...............	1	100.0	-	.4	2.6	(D)	-	49.6	5.4	(D)	(D)
UNKNOWN.............	-	100.0	-	-	-	(D)	-	-	-	(D)	(D)
SOUTH ATLANTIC..........	816	100.0	.6	24.8	19.2	(D)	16.4	3.7	13.0	(D)	(D)
RAIL................	394	100.0	.2	39.0	4.7	(D)	2.5	5.0	4.3	(D)	(D)
MOTOR CARRIER........	305	100.0	1.3	12.2	32.9	(D)	26.9	2.0	22.3	(D)	(D)
PRIVATE TRUCK........	92	100.0	-	11.3	21.2	(D)	44.4	4.4	18.6	(D)	(D)
AIR.................	2	100.0	.1	11.8	3.3	(D)	.4	.1	84.1	(D)	(D)
WATER...............	20	100.0	-	7.0	90.4	(D)	2.5	-	-	(D)	(D)
OTHER...............	1	100.0	-	2.3	2.9	(D)	4.0	4.4	86.1	(D)	(D)
UNKNOWN.............	-	100.0	-	-	37.1	(D)	42.8	-	-	(D)	(D)
EAST SOUTH CENTRAL......	273	100.0	.8	24.0	27.6	(D)	11.3	3.8	21.3	(D)	(D)
RAIL................	86	100.0	-	56.0	14.4	(D)	3.9	5.6	13.8	(D)	(D)
MOTOR CARRIER........	148	100.0	1.4	9.6	38.5	(D)	7.9	2.2	23.6	(D)	(D)
PRIVATE TRUCK........	31	100.0	-	1.5	10.3	(D)	48.2	7.2	32.5	(D)	(D)
AIR.................	-	100.0	16.5	.5	.6	(D)	-	-	81.2	(D)	(D)
WATER...............	5	100.0	-	40.2	43.0	(D)	7.7	-	9.1	(D)	(D)
OTHER...............	-	100.0	-	1.9	26.6	(D)	3.4	3.2	31.7	(D)	(D)
UNKNOWN.............	-	100.0	-	-	100.0	(D)	-	-	-	(D)	(D)
WEST SOUTH CENTRAL......	819	100.0	.1	12.7	29.8	(D)	6.3	1.9	37.9	(D)	(D)
RAIL................	186	100.0	-	34.6	27.7	(D)	15.6	6.3	8.2	(D)	(D)
MOTOR CARRIER........	437	100.0	.2	4.2	34.6	(D)	2.5	.6	40.5	(D)	(D)
PRIVATE TRUCK........	134	100.0	-	-	3.4	(D)	8.8	1.0	86.1	(D)	(D)
AIR.................	-	100.0	4.8	29.1	1.8	(D)	-	-	57.6	(D)	(D)
WATER...............	58	100.0	-	35.9	62.8	(D)	-	-	1.3	(D)	(D)
OTHER...............	1	100.0	-	.4	.9	(D)	-	11.3	36.4	(D)	(D)
UNKNOWN.............	-	100.0	-	-	-	(D)	-	-	57.2	(D)	(D)
MOUNTAIN................	443	100.0	.1	9.8	23.5	(D)	21.5	2.1	22.0	(D)	(D)
RAIL................	188	100.0	-	14.8	15.6	(D)	41.3	4.8	12.8	(D)	(D)
MOTOR CARRIER........	197	100.0	.1	8.0	36.1	(D)	8.9	.1	21.8	(D)	(D)
PRIVATE TRUCK........	57	100.0	-	-	6.2	(D)	-	-	52.7	(D)	(D)
AIR.................	-	100.0	4.3	.3	46.0	(D)	-	-	49.2	(D)	(D)
WATER...............	-	100.0	-	-	-	(D)	-	-	-	(D)	(D)
OTHER...............	-	100.0	-	.2	.7	(D)	-	-	1.2	(D)	(D)
UNKNOWN.............	-	100.0	-	-	-	(D)	-	-	100.0	(D)	(D)
PACIFIC.................	1 210	100.0	.1	26.1	13.2	(D)	1.6	.7	8.7	(D)	(D)
RAIL................	390	100.0	.1	71.5	23.2	(D)	2.1	2.2	.9	(D)	(D)
MOTOR CARRIER........	771	100.0	.2	2.3	8.9	(D)	.5	-	12.5	(D)	(D)
PRIVATE TRUCK........	7	100.0	-	16.2	8.4	(D)	.5	-	-	(D)	(D)
AIR.................	6	100.0	-	1.3	6.6	(D)	-	.9	82.1	(D)	(D)
WATER...............	32	100.0	-	51.1	-	(D)	22.1	-	-	(D)	(D)
OTHER...............	1	100.0	-	.9	6.6	(D)	.2	-	-	(D)	(D)
UNKNOWN.............	1	100.0	-	99.4	-	(D)	-	-	-	(D)	(D)

See footnotes at end of table 4.

TABLE 4. **TCC GROUP 344**—Percent Distribution of Distance Shipped and Weight of Shipment, by Means of Transport: 1972

Distance shipped and weight of shipment[2][3]	Number	Percent distribution by means of transport							
		All means of transport	Rail	Motor carrier	Private truck	Air	Water	Other	Unknown
TONS OF SHIPMENTS	(thousands of tons)								
U.S. TOTAL..........	11 830	100.0	21.9	47.4	29.1	.2	1.3	.1	-
UNDER 100 MILES.........	2 707	100.0	12.0	37.9	50.0	-	-	.2	-
UNDER 1000 POUNDS.....	68	100.0	-	42.8	54.2	-	-	2.8	.2
1000 TO 9999 POUNDS...	519	100.0	-	25.6	73.6	-	-	.8	-
10000 TO 29999 POUNDS.	796	100.0	.6	17.3	82.0	-	-	-	-
30000 TO 59999 POUNDS.	877	100.0	3.0	74.9	22.1	-	-	-	-
60000 TO 89999 POUNDS.	119	100.0	62.5	12.8	24.7	-	-	-	-
90000 POUNDS AND OVER.	324	100.0	66.9	15.9	17.2	-	-	-	-
100 TO 199 MILES........	1 896	100.0	15.8	49.1	33.9	-	1.0	.1	-
UNDER 1000 POUNDS.....	37	100.0	.2	67.1	30.1	-	-	1.5	1.0
1000 TO 9999 POUNDS...	283	100.0	.8	47.0	51.9	-	-	.2	-
10000 TO 29999 POUNDS.	370	100.0	4.6	37.3	57.7	-	-	.4	-
30000 TO 59999 POUNDS.	676	100.0	4.2	75.3	20.6	-	-	-	-
60000 TO 89999 POUNDS.	180	100.0	63.0	10.3	26.8	-	-	-	-
90000 POUNDS AND OVER.	347	100.0	39.9	30.4	24.0	-	5.7	-	-
200 TO 299 MILES........	1 499	100.0	18.0	51.1	30.0	-	.7	.1	.1
UNDER 1000 POUNDS.....	28	100.0	-	76.3	20.8	1.2	-	1.5	.1
1000 TO 9999 POUNDS...	241	100.0	.3	68.4	30.4	-	-	.3	.6
10000 TO 29999 POUNDS.	337	100.0	6.5	56.3	37.2	-	-	-	-
30000 TO 59999 POUNDS.	562	100.0	5.0	64.9	30.0	-	-	-	.1
60000 TO 89999 POUNDS.	124	100.0	83.3	5.1	11.0	-	.6	-	-
90000 POUNDS AND OVER.	204	100.0	56.4	8.5	30.5	-	4.6	-	-
300 TO 499 MILES........	2 547	100.0	25.0	51.5	22.8	.1	.5	.1	-
UNDER 1000 POUNDS.....	66	100.0	.8	75.7	18.2	3.9	-	1.3	-
1000 TO 9999 POUNDS...	362	100.0	2.0	69.4	28.5	-	-	.1	-
10000 TO 29999 POUNDS.	509	100.0	11.6	49.4	39.0	-	-	-	-
30000 TO 59999 POUNDS.	833	100.0	9.1	67.3	23.5	-	.1	-	-
60000 TO 89999 POUNDS.	196	100.0	44.9	26.7	27.6	-	.8	-	-
90000 POUNDS AND OVER.	578	100.0	70.2	25.1	2.8	-	1.9	-	-
500 TO 999 MILES........	2 094	100.0	26.5	49.7	19.1	.3	4.3	.2	-
UNDER 1000 POUNDS.....	62	100.0	1.2	69.6	20.0	6.3	-	2.7	.1
1000 TO 9999 POUNDS...	550	100.0	.7	73.0	25.6	.4	-	.3	-
10000 TO 29999 POUNDS.	392	100.0	18.8	51.3	29.7	-	.1	.1	-
30000 TO 59999 POUNDS.	558	100.0	20.3	61.5	17.2	-	.9	-	-
60000 TO 89999 POUNDS.	117	100.0	89.5	.7	6.6	-	3.3	-	-
90000 POUNDS AND OVER.	413	100.0	62.4	12.0	6.3	-	19.3	-	-
1000 TO 1499 MILES......	539	100.0	30.3	64.0	3.0	1.2	1.4	.2	-
UNDER 1000 POUNDS.....	23	100.0	.3	90.6	.2	6.9	-	2.0	-
1000 TO 9999 POUNDS...	161	100.0	.1	96.1	.6	3.1	-	-	.1
10000 TO 29999 POUNDS.	59	100.0	10.0	66.9	21.7	-	1.4	-	-
30000 TO 59999 POUNDS.	147	100.0	32.0	65.6	1.1	-	.9	.4	-
60000 TO 89999 POUNDS.	42	100.0	93.6	5.4	1.0	-	-	-	-
90000 POUNDS AND OVER.	105	100.0	66.3	28.7	-	-	5.0	-	-
1500 MILES OR OVER......	545	100.0	63.4	33.9	.2	.5	1.9	.1	.1
UNDER 1000 POUNDS.....	14	100.0	2.1	91.2	.7	5.6	-	.5	-
1000 TO 9999 POUNDS...	85	100.0	1.2	96.0	-	2.0	.1	.7	-
10000 TO 29999 POUNDS.	54	100.0	43.4	54.3	1.3	-	-	-	1.0
30000 TO 59999 POUNDS.	122	100.0	47.4	47.9	-	-	4.7	-	-
60000 TO 89999 POUNDS.	148	100.0	98.5	.4	-	-	1.1	-	-
90000 POUNDS AND OVER.	119	100.0	97.6	-	-	-	2.4	-	-
TON-MILES OF SHIPMENTS	(millions of ton-miles)								
U.S. TOTAL..........	4 978	100.0	33.1	47.9	16.3	.4	2.2	.2	-
UNDER 100 MILES.........	150	100.0	12.9	36.1	50.7	-	-	.3	-
UNDER 1000 POUNDS.....	3	100.0	-	43.7	53.1	.1	-	3.1	.1
1000 TO 9999 POUNDS...	26	100.0	-	21.9	77.0	-	-	1.1	-
10000 TO 29999 POUNDS.	47	100.0	.4	13.4	86.2	-	-	-	-
30000 TO 59999 POUNDS.	48	100.0	2.7	78.3	19.0	-	-	-	-
60000 TO 89999 POUNDS.	5	100.0	74.5	9.9	15.6	-	-	-	-
90000 POUNDS AND OVER.	19	100.0	72.3	10.9	16.7	-	-	-	-
100 TO 199 MILES........	281	100.0	14.6	48.7	35.5	-	1.0	.1	-
UNDER 1000 POUNDS.....	5	100.0	.2	67.7	29.3	-	-	1.6	1.1
1000 TO 9999 POUNDS...	45	100.0	.9	44.9	54.1	-	-	.2	-
10000 TO 29999 POUNDS.	56	100.0	4.9	38.2	56.6	-	-	.3	-
30000 TO 59999 POUNDS.	94	100.0	4.0	75.2	20.9	-	-	-	-
60000 TO 89999 POUNDS.	26	100.0	59.5	11.9	28.6	-	-	-	-
90000 POUNDS AND OVER.	53	100.0	34.5	32.8	27.4	-	5.4	-	-

See footnotes at end of table 4.

TABLE 4. TCC GROUP 344—Percent Distribution of Distance Shipped and Weight of Shipment, by Means of Transport: 1972—Continued

Distance shipped and weight of shipment [2] [3]	Number	Percent distribution by means of transport							
		All means of transport	Rail	Motor carrier	Private truck	Air	Water	Other	Unknown
TON-MILES OF SHIPMENTS	(millions of ton-miles)								
200 TO 299 MILES.........	373	100.0	18.2	51.0	29.9	-	.7	.1	.1
UNDER 1000 POUNDS.....	7	100.0	-	77.3	20.1	1.1	-	1.5	.1
1000 TO 9999 POUNDS...	60	100.0	.3	69.7	29.1	-	-	.3	.6
10000 TO 29999 POUNDS.	84	100.0	5.8	55.4	38.7	-	-	-	-
30000 TO 59999 POUNDS.	139	100.0	4.9	64.7	30.3	-	-	-	.1
60000 TO 89999 POUNDS.	31	100.0	83.6	5.2	10.6	-	.6	-	-
90000 POUNDS AND OVER.	49	100.0	58.4	8.0	28.7	-	4.9	-	-
300 TO 499 MILES.........	987	100.0	24.9	52.7	21.7	.1	.5	.1	-
UNDER 1000 POUNDS.....	25	100.0	.8	74.9	19.3	3.7	-	1.3	-
1000 TO 9999 POUNDS...	139	100.0	2.1	70.2	27.5	-	-	.2	-
10000 TO 29999 POUNDS.	195	100.0	12.3	50.6	37.1	-	-	-	-
30000 TO 59999 POUNDS.	321	100.0	9.3	68.5	22.1	-	.1	-	-
60000 TO 89999 POUNDS.	80	100.0	45.2	27.6	26.4	-	.8	-	-
90000 POUNDS AND OVER.	225	100.0	67.7	27.5	2.9	-	1.9	-	-
500 TO 999 MILES.........	1 498	100.0	26.2	49.7	19.2	.3	4.4	.2	-
UNDER 1000 POUNDS.....	43	100.0	1.4	67.7	20.6	7.3	-	2.9	.1
1000 TO 9999 POUNDS...	421	100.0	.7	72.5	26.1	.4	-	.3	-
10000 TO 29999 POUNDS.	282	100.0	19.1	51.5	29.2	-	.1	.1	-
30000 TO 59999 POUNDS.	374	100.0	21.4	60.6	16.9	-	1.1	-	-
60000 TO 89999 POUNDS.	87	100.0	87.8	.6	8.3	-	3.3	-	-
90000 POUNDS AND OVER.	288	100.0	62.0	12.6	5.2	-	20.3	-	-
1000 TO 1499 MILES......	638	100.0	30.0	64.1	2.9	1.4	1.4	.2	-
UNDER 1000 POUNDS.....	28	100.0	.2	90.0	.2	7.4	-	2.1	-
1000 TO 9999 POUNDS...	196	100.0	.1	95.9	.5	3.4	-	-	-
10000 TO 29999 POUNDS.	73	100.0	9.5	69.2	20.1	-	1.2	-	-
30000 TO 59999 POUNDS.	163	100.0	33.6	63.6	1.3	-	1.1	.4	-
60000 TO 89999 POUNDS.	57	100.0	94.1	4.8	1.1	-	-	-	-
90000 POUNDS AND OVER.	119	100.0	62.7	32.0	-	-	5.3	-	-
1500 MILES OR OVER......	1 048	100.0	65.5	31.2	.2	.4	2.4	.2	.1
UNDER 1000 POUNDS.....	28	100.0	2.3	91.7	.7	4.8	-	.5	-
1000 TO 9999 POUNDS...	146	100.0	1.4	95.5	-	1.8	.2	1.2	-
10000 TO 29999 POUNDS.	93	100.0	40.5	56.3	1.7	-	-	-	1.5
30000 TO 59999 POUNDS.	236	100.0	49.1	45.2	-	-	5.7	-	-
60000 TO 89999 POUNDS.	335	100.0	98.2	.5	-	-	1.3	-	-
90000 POUNDS AND OVER.	207	100.0	96.5	-	-	-	3.5	-	-

Note: Detail may not add to total due to rounding. The introductory table shows the estimates of sampling variability for tons; sampling variability for ton-miles has not been estimated. See the map in the Introduction for the States comprising the geographic divisions of the United States.

Shipments excluded from the survey are those moving by pipeline (primarily petroleum products from refineries), parcel post shipments, and commodities moved by own power (motorized vehicles, aircraft, etc.) or towed (prefabricated buildings, etc.). Local shipments (commodities shipped less than 25 miles from the plant) and shipments within the same city are also excluded. Shipments to Alaska and Hawaii from the 48 conterminous States and the District of Columbia are included; however, no data were obtained for shipments originating in Alaska and Hawaii.

\- Represents zero or rounds to zero.   (D) Withheld to avoid disclosing figures for individual companies.

[1] Production of this commodity is concentrated in the geographic divisions shown; figures and distributions for geographic divisions not shown are included in the total.

[2] Distances of shipments to foreign destinations are calculated only to the U.S. port of exit.

[3] Includes only shipments represented by bills of lading and invoices. Summary records which did not show individual weights of shipments are not included.

TCC 345. Bolts, Nuts, Screws, Rivets, and Washers

Comparisons of Tons and Ton-Miles of Shipments for
Geographic Divisions of Origin and for Sampling Variability: 1972 and 1967

Geographic division of origin	Estimates				Relative sampling variability in tons (percent)	
	1972		1967		1972	1967
	Tons (thousands)	Ton-miles (millions)	Tons (thousands)	Ton-miles (millions)		
U.S. total	1,336	469	2,174	783	17.1	14.0
New England	36	24	142	45	37.8	(*)
Middle Atlantic	275	102	349	167	30.2	(*)
East North Central	852	251	1,188	332	25.1	(*)
West North Central	(D)	(D)	34	19	(*)	(*)
South Atlantic	(D)	(D)	3	2	(*)	(*)
East South Central	(D)	(D)	14	3	(*)	(*)
West South Central	(D)	(D)	—	—	(*)	(*)
Mountain	(D)	(D)	11	4	(*)	(*)
Pacific	30	24	433	211	29.8	(*)

— Represents or rounds to zero.   (D) Withheld to avoid disclosing figures for individual companies.   (*) Data not published.

TABLE 1. TCC GROUP 345—Percent Distribution of Geographic Division of Origin and Distance Shipped, by Means of Transport: 1972

Geographic division of origin [1] and distance shipped [2]	Number	Percent distribution by means of transport							
		All means of transport	Rail	Motor carrier	Private truck	Air	Water	Other	Unknown
TONS OF SHIPMENTS	(thousands of tons)								
U.S. TOTAL	1 336	100.0	2.0	88.6	7.5	.7	-	.7	.5
NEW ENGLAND	36	100.0	-	82.2	4.6	3.2	-	.1	9.9
UNDER 100 MILES	6	100.0	-	87.7	7.3	.2	-	.1	4.7
100 TO 199 MILES	4	100.0	-	99.1	.1	.8	-	-	-
200 TO 299 MILES	2	100.0	-	97.3	-	1.8	-	-	.8
300 TO 499 MILES	3	100.0	.3	83.7	1.4	14.5	-	.1	-
500 TO 999 MILES	12	100.0	-	96.8	-	3.2	-	-	-
1000 TO 1499 MILES	2	100.0	-	42.8	53.6	3.3	-	.3	-
1500 MILES OR OVER	3	100.0	-	14.8	-	2.8	-	-	82.5
MIDDLE ATLANTIC	275	100.0	.8	85.1	12.9	.3	-	.9	-
UNDER 100 MILES	53	100.0	-	74.9	21.2	-	-	4.0	-
100 TO 199 MILES	34	100.0	-	99.2	-	.5	-	.3	-
200 TO 299 MILES	51	100.0	2.2	93.3	4.1	.3	-	.1	-
300 TO 499 MILES	55	100.0	.8	96.5	2.4	.2	-	.1	-
500 TO 999 MILES	76	100.0	.2	72.3	27.2	.2	-	.1	-
1000 TO 1499 MILES	2	100.0	-	97.3	-	2.0	-	.7	-
1500 MILES OR OVER	2	100.0	18.6	78.1	.9	2.0	-	.5	-
EAST NORTH CENTRAL	852	100.0	2.8	89.7	6.1	.5	-	.5	.4
UNDER 100 MILES	224	100.0	2.2	77.5	18.9	.1	-	.4	.9
100 TO 199 MILES	155	100.0	-	96.5	2.4	.3	-	.3	.5
200 TO 299 MILES	195	100.0	2.3	95.4	1.7	.4	-	.3	-
300 TO 499 MILES	140	100.0	-	96.4	1.6	1.1	-	.7	.2
500 TO 999 MILES	105	100.0	9.2	88.2	.6	1.0	.1	.9	-
1000 TO 1499 MILES	8	100.0	-	99.3	-	.2	-	.5	-
1500 MILES OR OVER	21	100.0	21.4	75.9	-	1.9	-	.5	.3
PACIFIC	30	100.0	.5	71.0	22.2	4.5	.9	.4	.5
UNDER 100 MILES	10	100.0	-	34.3	63.5	.2	-	.5	1.5
100 TO 199 MILES	-	100.0	-	94.3	4.5	.6	-	.6	-
200 TO 299 MILES	-	100.0	-	98.0	-	-	-	2.0	-
300 TO 499 MILES	6	100.0	-	97.4	.1	2.4	-	.1	-
500 TO 999 MILES	-	100.0	-	62.3	-	37.4	-	.3	-
1000 TO 1499 MILES	4	100.0	4.0	91.4	.8	3.6	-	.2	-
1500 MILES OR OVER	7	100.0	-	87.1	-	8.7	3.6	.5	-
TON-MILES OF SHIPMENTS	(millions of ton-miles)								
U.S. TOTAL	469	100.0	3.9	87.3	4.8	1.4	.2	.6	1.8
NEW ENGLAND	24	100.0	-	56.8	6.4	3.8	-	.1	33.0
UNDER 100 MILES	-	100.0	-	91.2	1.6	-	-	.1	7.0
100 TO 199 MILES	-	100.0	-	98.8	.1	1.1	-	-	-
200 TO 299 MILES	-	100.0	-	97.6	-	1.6	-	-	.9
300 TO 499 MILES	1	100.0	.2	81.7	1.6	16.4	-	.1	-
500 TO 999 MILES	8	100.0	-	96.5	-	3.5	-	-	-
1000 TO 1499 MILES	2	100.0	-	38.7	58.3	2.7	-	.3	-
1500 MILES OR OVER	9	100.0	-	15.2	-	2.8	-	-	81.9
MIDDLE ATLANTIC	102	100.0	1.6	82.4	15.3	.4	-	.3	-
UNDER 100 MILES	2	100.0	-	62.9	31.9	-	-	5.2	-
100 TO 199 MILES	4	100.0	-	99.3	-	.4	-	.3	-
200 TO 299 MILES	12	100.0	2.7	92.9	4.0	.3	-	.2	-
300 TO 499 MILES	21	100.0	.9	96.6	2.1	.2	-	.1	-
500 TO 999 MILES	51	100.0	.2	73.0	26.5	.2	-	.1	-
1000 TO 1499 MILES	2	100.0	-	97.0	-	2.1	-	.9	-
1500 MILES OR OVER	5	100.0	18.5	78.1	.7	2.1	-	.6	-
EAST NORTH CENTRAL	251	100.0	6.5	90.3	1.4	1.0	-	.6	.2
UNDER 100 MILES	11	100.0	1.8	89.4	7.0	.1	-	.4	1.3
100 TO 199 MILES	22	100.0	-	95.4	3.3	.3	-	.3	.6
200 TO 299 MILES	47	100.0	2.2	95.2	1.9	.4	-	.3	-
300 TO 499 MILES	51	100.0	-	96.7	1.3	1.1	-	.7	.2
500 TO 999 MILES	70	100.0	10.4	86.8	.5	1.0	.2	1.0	-
1000 TO 1499 MILES	9	100.0	-	99.2	-	.2	-	.5	-
1500 MILES OR OVER	37	100.0	20.2	77.0	-	2.1	-	.5	.3
PACIFIC	24	100.0	.8	87.1	1.0	7.7	3.0	.4	-
UNDER 100 MILES	-	100.0	-	39.6	59.5	.1	-	.2	.6
100 TO 199 MILES	-	100.0	-	95.4	3.6	.5	-	.5	-
200 TO 299 MILES	-	100.0	-	98.2	-	-	-	1.8	-
300 TO 499 MILES	2	100.0	-	97.6	.1	2.2	-	.2	-
500 TO 999 MILES	-	100.0	-	58.5	-	41.3	-	.2	-
1000 TO 1499 MILES	5	100.0	3.7	92.1	.8	3.2	-	.2	-
1500 MILES OR OVER	16	100.0	-	86.4	-	8.4	4.6	.6	-

See footnotes at end of table 4.

TABLE 2. **TCC GROUP 345—Percent Distribution of Geographic Division of Origin and Means of Transport, by Geographic Division of Destination: 1972**

Geographic division of origin [1] and means of transport	Number	Percent distribution by division of destination									
		U.S. total	New England	Middle Atlantic	East North Central	West North Central	South Atlantic	East South Central	West South Central	Mountain	Pacific
TONS OF SHIPMENTS	(thousands of tons)										
U.S. TOTAL	1 336	100.0	2.1	14.7	55.7	4.2	9.2	4.8	3.6	2.5	3.2
RAIL	26	100.0	-	4.3	38.8	12.4	8.2	-	17.2	-	19.1
MOTOR CARRIER	1 184	100.0	2.3	14.9	55.8	4.2	9.4	5.1	3.3	2.8	2.2
PRIVATE TRUCK	100	100.0	.5	13.5	65.5	.7	7.4	2.4	3.3	-	6.7
AIR	8	100.0	1.2	17.4	27.0	25.8	9.9	2.5	1.8	.8	13.6
WATER	-	100.0	-	36.1	-	-	-	-	.1	-	63.8
OTHER	8	100.0	3.0	33.3	28.5	8.9	10.5	5.3	6.5	1.2	2.9
UNKNOWN	6	100.0	-	4.4	43.5	.7	.7	.1	-	-	50.5
NEW ENGLAND	36	100.0	16.3	26.1	29.5	1.4	9.8	2.1	3.9	-	10.9
RAIL	-	100.0	-	94.6	5.4	-	-	-	-	-	-
MOTOR CARRIER	29	100.0	18.2	30.4	34.5	1.4	10.2	2.5	.9	-	1.9
PRIVATE TRUCK	1	100.0	28.2	.2	2.8	-	-	-	68.9	-	-
AIR	1	100.0	1.3	7.6	32.6	5.7	41.2	2.2	-	-	9.2
WATER	-	100.0	-	-	-	-	-	-	-	-	-
OTHER	-	100.0	30.6	23.0	16.1	28.3	.4	-	1.6	-	-
UNKNOWN	3	100.0	-	8.4	-	-	.7	-	-	-	90.8
MIDDLE ATLANTIC	275	100.0	3.4	33.1	39.4	2.7	17.1	2.8	.6	.2	.6
RAIL	2	100.0	-	50.6	27.3	-	-	-	-	-	22.1
MOTOR CARRIER	234	100.0	3.9	31.6	38.6	3.1	18.0	3.3	.6	.2	.5
PRIVATE TRUCK	35	100.0	-	38.1	47.7	-	14.2	-	-	.1	-
AIR	-	100.0	.1	45.5	33.7	5.4	2.1	.4	5.4	1.1	6.3
WATER	-	100.0	-	-	-	-	-	-	100.0	-	-
OTHER	2	100.0	2.5	89.5	4.8	.3	1.3	.4	.6	-	.5
UNKNOWN	-	100.0	-	-	-	-	-	-	-	-	-
EAST NORTH CENTRAL	852	100.0	1.1	9.9	70.1	4.4	5.7	3.8	2.0	.5	2.4
RAIL	23	100.0	-	-	40.1	13.6	9.0	-	18.2	-	19.0
MOTOR CARRIER	765	100.0	1.2	10.8	69.7	4.2	5.9	3.9	1.6	.6	2.0
PRIVATE TRUCK	52	100.0	-	.1	93.6	.5	1.1	4.7	-	-	-
AIR	4	100.0	1.2	18.5	38.9	22.0	4.9	3.5	1.7	-	9.2
WATER	-	100.0	-	100.0	-	-	-	-	-	-	-
OTHER	4	100.0	3.0	10.1	46.4	15.3	10.8	7.6	3.4	1.0	2.4
UNKNOWN	3	100.0	-	-	96.2	1.5	.2	.3	-	-	1.8
PACIFIC	30	100.0	1.2	6.9	9.5	1.5	4.8	.5	12.4	14.9	48.4
RAIL	-	100.0	-	-	-	-	-	-	100.0	-	-
MOTOR CARRIER	21	100.0	1.5	8.6	13.1	1.0	6.2	.5	16.3	20.9	31.9
PRIVATE TRUCK	6	100.0	-	-	-	-	-	-	.5	-	99.5
AIR	1	100.0	1.6	17.6	4.6	16.6	7.1	2.7	2.9	1.8	45.2
WATER	-	100.0	-	-	-	-	-	-	-	-	100.0
OTHER	-	100.0	-	3.3	2.8	5.0	27.8	.2	1.0	1.8	58.1
UNKNOWN	-	100.0	-	-	-	-	-	-	-	.1	99.9
TON-MILES OF SHIPMENTS	(millions of ton-miles)										
U.S. TOTAL	469	100.0	2.8	13.0	37.9	6.6	11.6	5.2	7.1	3.8	12.0
RAIL	18	100.0	-	1.9	8.4	13.9	7.9	-	20.0	-	48.0
MOTOR CARRIER	410	100.0	3.1	13.9	39.5	6.5	11.4	5.6	6.7	4.3	8.9
PRIVATE TRUCK	22	100.0	-	6.6	56.5	1.5	22.8	3.1	8.4	.2	1.0
AIR	6	100.0	1.7	19.1	14.1	22.3	10.1	2.4	2.5	1.1	26.7
WATER	-	100.0	-	14.1	-	-	-	-	-	-	85.9
OTHER	2	100.0	6.1	21.8	17.5	9.0	16.0	6.5	7.8	4.1	11.3
UNKNOWN	8	100.0	-	.3	4.0	.2	.1	-	-	-	95.4
NEW ENGLAND	24	100.0	1.4	8.1	30.0	2.1	8.2	2.5	7.6	.1	40.1
RAIL	-	100.0	-	91.9	8.1	-	-	-	-	-	-
MOTOR CARRIER	13	100.0	2.4	14.0	50.5	3.1	12.6	4.3	2.3	.1	10.6
PRIVATE TRUCK	1	100.0	.4	-	1.5	-	-	-	98.2	-	-
AIR	-	100.0	-	2.1	31.5	7.5	26.1	2.4	-	-	30.4
WATER	-	100.0	-	-	-	-	-	-	-	-	-
OTHER	-	100.0	2.1	13.4	20.8	58.7	.8	-	4.2	-	-
UNKNOWN	8	100.0	-	.3	-	-	.1	-	-	-	99.6

See footnotes at end of table 4.

TABLE 2. **TCC GROUP 345—Percent Distribution of Geographic Division of Origin and Means of Transport, by Geographic Division of Destination: 1972**—Continued

Geographic division of origin[1] and means of transport	Number	Percent distribution by division of destination									
		U.S. total	New England	Middle Atlantic	East North Central	West North Central	South Atlantic	East South Central	West South Central	Mountain	Pacific
TON-MILES OF SHIPMENTS	(millions of ton-miles)										
MIDDLE ATLANTIC	102	100.0	1.9	10.9	55.2	5.9	15.0	4.0	2.1	1.1	4.0
RAIL	1	100.0	-	20.1	16.7	-	-	-	-	-	63.2
MOTOR CARRIER	84	100.0	2.3	10.8	54.2	7.1	13.6	4.9	2.4	1.3	3.5
PRIVATE TRUCK	15	100.0	-	9.4	65.8	-	24.6	-	-	.2	-
AIR	-	100.0	-	16.4	28.8	8.6	2.5	.4	12.8	3.9	26.6
WATER	-	100.0	-	-	-	-	-	-	100.0	-	-
OTHER	-	100.0	4.4	53.5	17.4	1.5	3.2	2.2	7.4	-	10.5
UNKNOWN	-	100.0	-	-	-	-	-	-	-	-	-
EAST NORTH CENTRAL	251	100.0	2.8	14.4	37.1	7.4	10.7	5.2	5.6	2.1	14.7
RAIL	16	100.0	-	-	7.7	15.5	8.8	-	21.1	-	47.0
MOTOR CARRIER	226	100.0	3.0	15.5	39.0	6.7	10.9	5.4	4.6	2.3	12.4
PRIVATE TRUCK	3	100.0	-	.3	66.4	4.7	8.4	20.2	-	-	-
AIR	2	100.0	1.7	21.3	16.2	16.6	5.8	2.7	2.5	-	33.2
WATER	-	100.0	-	100.0	-	-	-	-	-	-	-
OTHER	1	100.0	6.0	14.9	17.2	14.9	16.6	8.8	6.9	3.4	11.2
UNKNOWN	-	100.0	-	-	73.4	3.5	.7	.8	-	-	21.5
PACIFIC	24	100.0	3.6	20.3	21.7	2.6	12.9	.9	19.6	6.5	11.9
RAIL	-	100.0	-	-	-	-	-	-	100.0	-	-
MOTOR CARRIER	21	100.0	3.9	20.6	24.4	1.4	13.5	.8	21.2	7.3	6.9
PRIVATE TRUCK	-	100.0	-	-	-	-	-	-	15.9	-	84.1
AIR	1	100.0	2.8	30.2	6.0	18.2	10.1	3.4	2.6	.8	25.9
WATER	-	100.0	-	-	-	-	-	-	-	-	100.0
OTHER	-	100.0	-	8.8	5.6	6.5	69.8	.4	1.5	1.2	6.2
UNKNOWN	-	100.0	-	-	-	-	-	-	-	3.6	96.4

See footnotes at end of table 4.

TABLE 3. **TCC GROUP 345—Percent Distribution of Geographic Division of Destination and Means of Transport, by Geographic Division of Origin: 1972**

Geographic division of destination and means of transport	Number (thousands of tons)	Percent distribution by division of origin [1]									
		U.S. total	New England	Middle Atlantic	East North Central	West North Central	South Atlantic	East South Central	West South Central	Mountain	Pacific
TONS OF SHIPMENTS											
U.S. TOTAL	1 336	100.0	2.7	20.6	63.8	(D)	(D)	(D)	(D)	(D)	2.3
RAIL	26	100.0	-	8.4	90.9	(D)	(D)	(D)	(D)	(D)	.6
MOTOR CARRIER	1 184	100.0	2.5	19.8	64.6	(D)	(D)	(D)	(D)	(D)	1.8
PRIVATE TRUCK	100	100.0	1.7	35.4	51.8	(D)	(D)	(D)	(D)	(D)	6.8
AIR	8	100.0	13.2	7.8	49.6	(D)	(D)	(D)	(D)	(D)	15.4
WATER	-	100.0	-	.1	36.1	(D)	(D)	(D)	(D)	(D)	63.8
OTHER	8	100.0	.3	28.2	46.7	(D)	(D)	(D)	(D)	(D)	1.4
UNKNOWN	6	100.0	52.2	-	45.3	(D)	(D)	(D)	(D)	(D)	2.3
NEW ENGLAND	28	100.0	20.6	32.5	34.0	(D)	(D)	(D)	(D)	(D)	1.2
RAIL	-	100.0	-	100.0	-	(D)	(D)	(D)	(D)	(D)	-
MOTOR CARRIER	27	100.0	19.5	33.2	34.3	(D)	(D)	(D)	(D)	(D)	1.2
PRIVATE TRUCK	-	100.0	100.0	-	-	(D)	(D)	(D)	(D)	(D)	-
AIR	-	100.0	14.6	.4	51.8	(D)	(D)	(D)	(D)	(D)	20.0
WATER	-	100.0	-	-	-	(D)	(D)	(D)	(D)	(D)	-
OTHER	-	100.0	3.0	22.9	45.9	(D)	(D)	(D)	(D)	(D)	-
UNKNOWN	-	100.0	100.0	-	-	(D)	(D)	(D)	(D)	(D)	-
MIDDLE ATLANTIC	196	100.0	4.8	46.5	42.9	(D)	(D)	(D)	(D)	(D)	1.1
RAIL	1	100.0	.8	99.0	-	(D)	(D)	(D)	(D)	(D)	-
MOTOR CARRIER	176	100.0	5.1	42.0	46.9	(D)	(D)	(D)	(D)	(D)	1.1
PRIVATE TRUCK	13	100.0	-	99.6	.3	(D)	(D)	(D)	(D)	(D)	-
AIR	1	100.0	5.8	20.3	52.7	(D)	(D)	(D)	(D)	(D)	15.6
WATER	-	100.0	-	-	100.0	(D)	(D)	(D)	(D)	(D)	-
OTHER	2	100.0	.2	75.7	14.2	(D)	(D)	(D)	(D)	(D)	.1
UNKNOWN	-	100.0	100.0	-	-	(D)	(D)	(D)	(D)	(D)	-
EAST NORTH CENTRAL	744	100.0	1.4	14.6	80.3	(D)	(D)	(D)	(D)	(D)	.4
RAIL	10	100.0	-	5.9	94.1	(D)	(D)	(D)	(D)	(D)	-
MOTOR CARRIER	660	100.0	1.6	13.7	80.7	(D)	(D)	(D)	(D)	(D)	.4
PRIVATE TRUCK	66	100.0	.1	25.8	74.1	(D)	(D)	(D)	(D)	(D)	-
AIR	2	100.0	16.0	9.7	71.5	(D)	(D)	(D)	(D)	(D)	2.6
WATER	-	100.0	-	-	-	(D)	(D)	(D)	(D)	(D)	-
OTHER	2	100.0	.2	4.8	76.1	(D)	(D)	(D)	(D)	(D)	.1
UNKNOWN	2	100.0	-	-	100.0	(D)	(D)	(D)	(D)	(D)	-
WEST NORTH CENTRAL	56	100.0	.9	13.2	66.6	(D)	(D)	(D)	(D)	(D)	.8
RAIL	3	100.0	-	-	100.0	(D)	(D)	(D)	(D)	(D)	-
MOTOR CARRIER	49	100.0	.9	15.0	65.7	(D)	(D)	(D)	(D)	(D)	.4
PRIVATE TRUCK	-	100.0	-	-	37.7	(D)	(D)	(D)	(D)	(D)	-
AIR	2	100.0	2.9	1.6	42.2	(D)	(D)	(D)	(D)	(D)	9.9
WATER	-	100.0	-	-	-	(D)	(D)	(D)	(D)	(D)	-
OTHER	-	100.0	.9	1.1	80.1	(D)	(D)	(D)	(D)	(D)	.8
UNKNOWN	-	100.0	-	-	100.0	(D)	(D)	(D)	(D)	(D)	-
SOUTH ATLANTIC	122	100.0	2.9	38.6	39.8	(D)	(D)	(D)	(D)	(D)	1.2
RAIL	2	100.0	-	-	100.0	(D)	(D)	(D)	(D)	(D)	-
MOTOR CARRIER	111	100.0	2.7	38.0	40.9	(D)	(D)	(D)	(D)	(D)	1.2
PRIVATE TRUCK	7	100.0	-	68.2	7.9	(D)	(D)	(D)	(D)	(D)	-
AIR	-	100.0	54.9	1.7	24.4	(D)	(D)	(D)	(D)	(D)	11.0
WATER	-	100.0	-	-	-	(D)	(D)	(D)	(D)	(D)	-
OTHER	-	100.0	-	3.4	48.0	(D)	(D)	(D)	(D)	(D)	3.6
UNKNOWN	-	100.0	50.5	-	14.3	(D)	(D)	(D)	(D)	(D)	-
EAST SOUTH CENTRAL	64	100.0	1.2	12.3	51.0	(D)	(D)	(D)	(D)	(D)	.2
RAIL	-	100.0	-	-	-	(D)	(D)	(D)	(D)	(D)	-
MOTOR CARRIER	60	100.0	1.2	12.9	48.9	(D)	(D)	(D)	(D)	(D)	.2
PRIVATE TRUCK	2	100.0	-	-	99.7	(D)	(D)	(D)	(D)	(D)	-
AIR	-	100.0	11.7	1.2	70.5	(D)	(D)	(D)	(D)	(D)	16.5
WATER	-	100.0	-	-	-	(D)	(D)	(D)	(D)	(D)	-
OTHER	-	100.0	-	2.3	67.6	(D)	(D)	(D)	(D)	(D)	.1
UNKNOWN	-	100.0	-	-	100.0	(D)	(D)	(D)	(D)	(D)	-
WEST SOUTH CENTRAL	47	100.0	2.9	3.3	35.0	(D)	(D)	(D)	(D)	(D)	7.9
RAIL	4	100.0	-	-	96.3	(D)	(D)	(D)	(D)	(D)	3.7
MOTOR CARRIER	39	100.0	.6	3.9	31.0	(D)	(D)	(D)	(D)	(D)	9.0
PRIVATE TRUCK	3	100.0	35.0	-	-	(D)	(D)	(D)	(D)	(D)	1.0
AIR	-	100.0	-	23.8	48.8	(D)	(D)	(D)	(D)	(D)	25.7
WATER	-	100.0	-	100.0	-	(D)	(D)	(D)	(D)	(D)	-
OTHER	-	100.0	.1	2.8	23.9	(D)	(D)	(D)	(D)	(D)	.2
UNKNOWN	-	100.0	-	-	-	(D)	(D)	(D)	(D)	(D)	-
MOUNTAIN	32	100.0	-	1.8	13.6	(D)	(D)	(D)	(D)	(D)	13.9
RAIL	-	100.0	-	-	-	(D)	(D)	(D)	(D)	(D)	-
MOTOR CARRIER	32	100.0	-	1.7	13.6	(D)	(D)	(D)	(D)	(D)	13.9
PRIVATE TRUCK	-	100.0	-	100.0	-	(D)	(D)	(D)	(D)	(D)	-
AIR	-	100.0	-	10.6	-	(D)	(D)	(D)	(D)	(D)	33.8
WATER	-	100.0	-	-	-	(D)	(D)	(D)	(D)	(D)	-
OTHER	-	100.0	-	-	41.9	(D)	(D)	(D)	(D)	(D)	2.1
UNKNOWN	-	100.0	-	-	-	(D)	(D)	(D)	(D)	(D)	100.0
PACIFIC	42	100.0	9.2	4.2	48.2	(D)	(D)	(D)	(D)	(D)	35.0
RAIL	5	100.0	-	9.7	90.3	(D)	(D)	(D)	(D)	(D)	-
MOTOR CARRIER	25	100.0	2.2	4.8	60.4	(D)	(D)	(D)	(D)	(D)	27.3
PRIVATE TRUCK	6	100.0	-	-	-	(D)	(D)	(D)	(D)	(D)	100.0
AIR	1	100.0	9.0	3.6	33.6	(D)	(D)	(D)	(D)	(D)	51.2
WATER	-	100.0	-	-	-	(D)	(D)	(D)	(D)	(D)	100.0
OTHER	-	100.0	-	5.4	39.3	(D)	(D)	(D)	(D)	(D)	27.6
UNKNOWN	3	100.0	93.8	-	1.6	(D)	(D)	(D)	(D)	(D)	4.5

See footnotes at end of table 4.

TABLE 3. **TCC GROUP 345**—Percent Distribution of Geographic Division of Destination and Means of Transport, by Geographic Division of Origin: 1972—Continued

Geographic division of destination and means of transport	Number	Percent distribution by division of origin [1]									
		U.S. total	New England	Middle Atlantic	East North Central	West North Central	South Atlantic	East South Central	West South Central	Mountain	Pacific
TON-MILES OF SHIPMENTS	(millions of ton-miles)										
U.S. TOTAL............	469	100.0	5.2	21.8	53.5	(D)	(D)	(D)	(D)	(D)	5.3
RAIL..................	18	100.0	-	9.1	89.8	(D)	(D)	(D)	(D)	(D)	1.1
MOTOR CARRIER.........	410	100.0	3.4	20.6	55.3	(D)	(D)	(D)	(D)	(D)	5.3
PRIVATE TRUCK.........	22	100.0	7.0	69.8	15.6	(D)	(D)	(D)	(D)	(D)	1.1
AIR...................	6	100.0	14.3	6.0	37.0	(D)	(D)	(D)	(D)	(D)	29.8
WATER.................	-	100.0	-	-	14.1	(D)	(D)	(D)	(D)	(D)	85.9
OTHER.................	2	100.0	.5	10.6	52.2	(D)	(D)	(D)	(D)	(D)	3.7
UNKNOWN...............	8	100.0	94.5	-	5.4	(D)	(D)	(D)	(D)	(D)	-
NEW ENGLAND...........	12	100.0	2.7	14.9	54.4	(D)	(D)	(D)	(D)	(D)	7.0
RAIL..................	-	100.0	-	100.0	-	(D)	(D)	(D)	(D)	(D)	-
MOTOR CARRIER.........	12	100.0	2.7	15.2	54.6	(D)	(D)	(D)	(D)	(D)	6.7
PRIVATE TRUCK.........	-	100.0	100.0	-	-	(D)	(D)	(D)	(D)	(D)	-
AIR...................	-	100.0	.1	.1	36.6	(D)	(D)	(D)	(D)	(D)	49.0
WATER.................	-	100.0	-	-	-	(D)	(D)	(D)	(D)	(D)	-
OTHER.................	-	100.0	.2	7.6	51.4	(D)	(D)	(D)	(D)	(D)	-
UNKNOWN...............	-	100.0	100.0	-	-	(D)	(D)	(D)	(D)	(D)	-
MIDDLE ATLANTIC.......	60	100.0	3.3	18.3	59.2	(D)	(D)	(D)	(D)	(D)	8.3
RAIL..................	-	100.0	1.0	98.3	-	(D)	(D)	(D)	(D)	(D)	-
MOTOR CARRIER.........	57	100.0	3.4	15.9	61.6	(D)	(D)	(D)	(D)	(D)	7.8
PRIVATE TRUCK.........	1	100.0	-	98.9	.7	(D)	(D)	(D)	(D)	(D)	-
AIR...................	1	100.0	1.5	5.2	41.3	(D)	(D)	(D)	(D)	(D)	47.1
WATER.................	-	100.0	-	-	100.0	(D)	(D)	(D)	(D)	(D)	-
OTHER.................	-	100.0	.3	26.0	35.9	(D)	(D)	(D)	(D)	(D)	1.5
UNKNOWN...............	-	100.0	100.0	-	-	(D)	(D)	(D)	(D)	(D)	-
EAST NORTH CENTRAL....	178	100.0	4.1	31.7	52.2	(D)	(D)	(D)	(D)	(D)	3.0
RAIL..................	1	100.0	-	18.0	82.0	(D)	(D)	(D)	(D)	(D)	-
MOTOR CARRIER.........	162	100.0	4.4	28.2	54.6	(D)	(D)	(D)	(D)	(D)	3.3
PRIVATE TRUCK.........	12	100.0	.2	81.3	18.3	(D)	(D)	(D)	(D)	(D)	-
AIR...................	-	100.0	32.0	12.4	42.7	(D)	(D)	(D)	(D)	(D)	12.7
WATER.................	-	100.0	-	-	-	(D)	(D)	(D)	(D)	(D)	-
OTHER.................	-	100.0	.6	10.5	51.6	(D)	(D)	(D)	(D)	(D)	1.2
UNKNOWN...............	-	100.0	-	-	100.0	(D)	(D)	(D)	(D)	(D)	-
WEST NORTH CENTRAL....	31	100.0	1.6	19.3	59.9	(D)	(D)	(D)	(D)	(D)	2.1
RAIL..................	2	100.0	-	-	100.0	(D)	(D)	(D)	(D)	(D)	-
MOTOR CARRIER.........	26	100.0	1.6	22.5	57.7	(D)	(D)	(D)	(D)	(D)	1.1
PRIVATE TRUCK.........	-	100.0	-	-	49.8	(D)	(D)	(D)	(D)	(D)	-
AIR...................	1	100.0	4.8	2.3	27.5	(D)	(D)	(D)	(D)	(D)	24.3
WATER.................	-	100.0	-	-	-	(D)	(D)	(D)	(D)	(D)	-
OTHER.................	-	100.0	3.2	1.7	86.4	(D)	(D)	(D)	(D)	(D)	2.7
UNKNOWN...............	-	100.0	-	-	100.0	(D)	(D)	(D)	(D)	(D)	-
SOUTH ATLANTIC........	54	100.0	3.7	28.3	49.2	(D)	(D)	(D)	(D)	(D)	5.9
RAIL..................	1	100.0	-	-	100.0	(D)	(D)	(D)	(D)	(D)	-
MOTOR CARRIER.........	46	100.0	3.8	24.7	52.8	(D)	(D)	(D)	(D)	(D)	6.3
PRIVATE TRUCK.........	5	100.0	-	75.3	5.8	(D)	(D)	(D)	(D)	(D)	-
AIR...................	-	100.0	37.1	1.5	21.4	(D)	(D)	(D)	(D)	(D)	29.8
WATER.................	-	100.0	-	-	-	(D)	(D)	(D)	(D)	(D)	-
OTHER.................	-	100.0	-	2.1	54.3	(D)	(D)	(D)	(D)	(D)	16.0
UNKNOWN...............	-	100.0	55.5	-	27.3	(D)	(D)	(D)	(D)	(D)	-
EAST SOUTH CENTRAL....	24	100.0	2.6	17.0	54.4	(D)	(D)	(D)	(D)	(D)	1.0
RAIL..................	-	100.0	-	-	-	(D)	(D)	(D)	(D)	(D)	-
MOTOR CARRIER.........	23	100.0	2.6	17.7	52.9	(D)	(D)	(D)	(D)	(D)	.7
PRIVATE TRUCK.........	-	100.0	-	-	100.0	(D)	(D)	(D)	(D)	(D)	-
AIR...................	-	100.0	14.4	1.1	41.8	(D)	(D)	(D)	(D)	(D)	42.7
WATER.................	-	100.0	-	-	-	(D)	(D)	(D)	(D)	(D)	-
OTHER.................	-	100.0	-	3.5	71.6	(D)	(D)	(D)	(D)	(D)	.3
UNKNOWN...............	-	100.0	-	-	100.0	(D)	(D)	(D)	(D)	(D)	-
WEST SOUTH CENTRAL....	33	100.0	5.6	6.4	42.0	(D)	(D)	(D)	(D)	(D)	14.5
RAIL..................	3	100.0	-	-	94.7	(D)	(D)	(D)	(D)	(D)	5.3
MOTOR CARRIER.........	27	100.0	1.2	7.5	38.0	(D)	(D)	(D)	(D)	(D)	16.6
PRIVATE TRUCK.........	1	100.0	81.7	-	-	(D)	(D)	(D)	(D)	(D)	2.2
AIR...................	-	100.0	-	30.7	37.5	(D)	(D)	(D)	(D)	(D)	30.7
WATER.................	-	100.0	-	100.0	-	(D)	(D)	(D)	(D)	(D)	-
OTHER.................	-	100.0	.3	10.0	46.1	(D)	(D)	(D)	(D)	(D)	.7
UNKNOWN...............	-	100.0	-	-	-	(D)	(D)	(D)	(D)	(D)	-
MOUNTAIN..............	17	100.0	.1	6.2	29.6	(D)	(D)	(D)	(D)	(D)	9.0
RAIL..................	-	100.0	-	-	-	(D)	(D)	(D)	(D)	(D)	-
MOTOR CARRIER.........	17	100.0	.1	6.0	29.7	(D)	(D)	(D)	(D)	(D)	9.0
PRIVATE TRUCK.........	-	100.0	-	100.0	-	(D)	(D)	(D)	(D)	(D)	-
AIR...................	-	100.0	-	21.6	-	(D)	(D)	(D)	(D)	(D)	21.2
WATER.................	-	100.0	-	-	-	(D)	(D)	(D)	(D)	(D)	-
OTHER.................	-	100.0	-	-	42.7	(D)	(D)	(D)	(D)	(D)	1.1
UNKNOWN...............	-	100.0	-	-	-	(D)	(D)	(D)	(D)	(D)	100.0
PACIFIC...............	56	100.0	17.5	7.3	65.4	(D)	(D)	(D)	(D)	(D)	5.2
RAIL..................	8	100.0	-	11.9	88.1	(D)	(D)	(D)	(D)	(D)	-
MOTOR CARRIER.........	36	100.0	4.1	8.0	77.1	(D)	(D)	(D)	(D)	(D)	4.1
PRIVATE TRUCK.........	-	100.0	-	-	-	(D)	(D)	(D)	(D)	(D)	100.0
AIR...................	1	100.0	16.3	6.0	46.0	(D)	(D)	(D)	(D)	(D)	28.9
WATER.................	-	100.0	-	-	-	(D)	(D)	(D)	(D)	(D)	100.0
OTHER.................	-	100.0	-	9.8	51.8	(D)	(D)	(D)	(D)	(D)	2.0
UNKNOWN...............	8	100.0	98.8	-	1.2	(D)	(D)	(D)	(D)	(D)	-

See footnotes at end of table 4.

TABLE 4. TCC GROUP 345—Percent Distribution of Distance Shipped and Weight of Shipment, by Means of Transport: 1972

Distance shipped and weight of shipment [2] [3]	Number	Percent distribution by means of transport							
		All means of transport	Rail	Motor carrier	Private truck	Air	Water	Other	Unknown
TONS OF SHIPMENTS	(thousands of tons)								
U.S. TOTAL	1 289	100.0	2.0	88.7	7.7	.6	-	.6	.4
UNDER 100 MILES	314	100.0	1.6	77.3	19.6	.1	-	1.0	.4
UNDER 1000 POUNDS	37	100.0	-	80.4	14.3	.4	-	3.6	1.3
1000 TO 9999 POUNDS	110	100.0	-	75.3	22.4	-	-	1.8	.6
10000 TO 29999 POUNDS	70	100.0	-	63.1	36.9	-	-	-	-
30000 TO 59999 POUNDS	75	100.0	-	92.5	7.5	-	-	-	-
60000 TO 89999 POUNDS	15	100.0	-	100.0	-	-	-	-	-
90000 POUNDS AND OVER	5	100.0	100.0	-	-	-	-	-	-
100 TO 199 MILES	204	100.0	-	96.8	2.6	.3	-	.3	-
UNDER 1000 POUNDS	25	100.0	-	90.4	6.0	1.1	-	2.2	.2
1000 TO 9999 POUNDS	79	100.0	-	95.0	4.6	.4	-	-	-
10000 TO 29999 POUNDS	36	100.0	-	100.0	-	-	-	-	-
30000 TO 59999 POUNDS	58	100.0	-	100.0	-	-	-	-	-
60000 TO 89999 POUNDS	5	100.0	-	100.0	-	-	-	-	-
90000 POUNDS AND OVER	-	100.0	-	-	-	-	-	-	-
200 TO 299 MILES	257	100.0	2.2	94.9	2.1	.3	-	.5	-
UNDER 1000 POUNDS	29	100.0	-	92.5	1.1	2.2	-	4.2	.1
1000 TO 9999 POUNDS	94	100.0	1.2	94.7	3.9	.2	-	-	-
10000 TO 29999 POUNDS	63	100.0	-	97.9	2.1	-	-	-	-
30000 TO 59999 POUNDS	66	100.0	-	100.0	-	-	-	-	-
60000 TO 89999 POUNDS	4	100.0	100.0	-	-	-	-	-	-
90000 POUNDS AND OVER	-	100.0	-	-	-	-	-	-	-
300 TO 499 MILES	222	100.0	.2	96.8	1.6	.8	-	.5	.1
UNDER 1000 POUNDS	40	100.0	.1	93.0	2.1	1.6	-	2.7	.5
1000 TO 9999 POUNDS	101	100.0	.4	97.0	1.4	1.1	-	-	-
10000 TO 29999 POUNDS	30	100.0	-	95.7	4.3	-	-	-	-
30000 TO 59999 POUNDS	46	100.0	-	100.0	-	-	-	-	-
60000 TO 89999 POUNDS	4	100.0	-	100.0	-	-	-	-	-
90000 POUNDS AND OVER	-	100.0	-	-	-	-	-	-	-
500 TO 999 MILES	223	100.0	4.4	84.0	9.8	1.1	.1	.6	-
UNDER 1000 POUNDS	41	100.0	-	90.8	.1	5.9	-	3.2	-
1000 TO 9999 POUNDS	99	100.0	.2	96.0	3.6	.1	.2	-	-
10000 TO 29999 POUNDS	40	100.0	-	100.0	-	-	-	-	-
30000 TO 59999 POUNDS	36	100.0	17.9	31.1	50.9	-	-	-	-
60000 TO 89999 POUNDS	6	100.0	49.1	50.9	-	-	-	-	-
90000 POUNDS AND OVER	-	100.0	-	-	-	-	-	-	-
1000 TO 1499 MILES	28	100.0	.6	93.7	4.2	1.1	-	.5	-
UNDER 1000 POUNDS	7	100.0	-	94.0	.4	3.9	-	1.7	-
1000 TO 9999 POUNDS	15	100.0	-	92.7	7.3	-	-	-	-
10000 TO 29999 POUNDS	1	100.0	-	100.0	-	-	-	-	-
30000 TO 59999 POUNDS	-	100.0	-	100.0	-	-	-	-	-
60000 TO 89999 POUNDS	2	100.0	6.4	93.6	-	-	-	-	-
90000 POUNDS AND OVER	-	100.0	-	-	-	-	-	-	-
1500 MILES OR OVER	38	100.0	12.8	74.9	.1	2.9	.7	.4	8.3
UNDER 1000 POUNDS	9	100.0	-	88.4	.2	9.7	-	1.6	-
1000 TO 9999 POUNDS	17	100.0	.2	98.7	-	1.1	-	-	-
10000 TO 29999 POUNDS	3	100.0	12.7	79.5	-	-	7.8	-	-
30000 TO 59999 POUNDS	3	100.0	-	5.1	-	-	-	-	94.9
60000 TO 89999 POUNDS	5	100.0	84.1	15.9	-	-	-	-	-
90000 POUNDS AND OVER	-	100.0	-	-	-	-	-	-	-
TON-MILES OF SHIPMENTS	(millions of ton-miles)								
U.S. TOTAL	450	100.0	4.0	87.5	4.8	1.2	.2	.6	1.8
UNDER 100 MILES	16	100.0	1.3	84.9	12.0	.1	-	1.3	.5
UNDER 1000 POUNDS	1	100.0	-	87.1	7.3	.4	-	3.4	1.9
1000 TO 9999 POUNDS	5	100.0	-	86.3	10.3	.1	-	2.5	.8
10000 TO 29999 POUNDS	3	100.0	-	73.1	26.9	-	-	-	-
30000 TO 59999 POUNDS	4	100.0	-	95.4	4.6	-	-	-	-
60000 TO 89999 POUNDS	-	100.0	-	100.0	-	-	-	-	-
90000 POUNDS AND OVER	-	100.0	100.0	-	-	-	-	-	-
100 TO 199 MILES	29	100.0	-	95.9	3.4	.3	-	.3	-
UNDER 1000 POUNDS	3	100.0	-	89.2	7.4	1.0	-	2.3	.2
1000 TO 9999 POUNDS	11	100.0	-	93.4	6.2	.4	-	-	-
10000 TO 29999 POUNDS	5	100.0	-	100.0	-	-	-	-	-
30000 TO 59999 POUNDS	8	100.0	-	100.0	-	-	-	-	-
60000 TO 89999 POUNDS	-	100.0	-	100.0	-	-	-	-	-
90000 POUNDS AND OVER	-	100.0	-	-	-	-	-	-	-

See footnotes at end of table 4.

TABLE 4. **TCC GROUP 345—Percent Distribution of Distance Shipped and Weight of Shipment, by Means of Transport: 1972**—Continued

Distance shipped and weight of shipment [2] [3]	Number	Percent distribution by means of transport							
		All means of transport	Rail	Motor carrier	Private truck	Air	Water	Other	Unknown
TON-MILES OF SHIPMENTS	(millions of ton-miles)								
200 TO 299 MILES........	62	100.0	2.2	94.8	2.2	.3	-	.5	-
UNDER 1000 POUNDS.....	7	100.0	-	92.3	1.1	2.2	-	4.3	.1
1000 TO 9999 POUNDS...	23	100.0	1.4	94.1	4.3	.2	-	-	-
10000 TO 29999 POUNDS.	15	100.0	-	98.0	2.0	-	-	-	-
30000 TO 59999 POUNDS.	15	100.0	-	100.0	-	-	-	-	-
60000 TO 89999 POUNDS.	1	100.0	100.0	-	-	-	-	-	-
90000 POUNDS AND OVER.	-	100.0	-	-	-	-	-	-	-
300 TO 499 MILES........	84	100.0	.2	97.0	1.4	.8	-	.5	.1
UNDER 1000 POUNDS.....	15	100.0	.1	93.6	1.7	1.5	-	2.8	.4
1000 TO 9999 POUNDS...	39	100.0	.5	97.2	1.3	1.1	-	-	-
10000 TO 29999 POUNDS.	11	100.0	-	96.6	3.4	-	-	-	-
30000 TO 59999 POUNDS.	15	100.0	-	100.0	-	-	-	-	-
60000 TO 89999 POUNDS.	1	100.0	-	100.0	-	-	-	-	-
90000 POUNDS AND OVER.	-	100.0	-	-	-	-	-	-	-
500 TO 999 MILES........	149	100.0	5.0	83.5	9.6	1.2	.1	.7	-
UNDER 1000 POUNDS.....	29	100.0	-	90.6	.1	5.9	-	3.5	-
1000 TO 9999 POUNDS...	64	100.0	.1	96.3	3.3	.1	.2	-	-
10000 TO 29999 POUNDS.	26	100.0	-	100.0	-	-	-	-	-
30000 TO 59999 POUNDS.	25	100.0	19.2	32.6	48.2	-	-	-	-
60000 TO 89999 POUNDS.	4	100.0	55.0	45.0	-	-	-	-	-
90000 POUNDS AND OVER.	-	100.0	-	-	-	-	-	-	-
1000 TO 1499 MILES......	32	100.0	.6	93.1	4.8	1.1	-	.5	-
UNDER 1000 POUNDS.....	9	100.0	-	94.0	.4	3.9	-	1.7	-
1000 TO 9999 POUNDS...	18	100.0	-	91.5	8.5	-	-	-	-
10000 TO 29999 POUNDS.	1	100.0	-	100.0	-	-	-	-	-
30000 TO 59999 POUNDS.	1	100.0	-	100.0	-	-	-	-	-
60000 TO 89999 POUNDS.	3	100.0	5.7	94.3	-	-	-	-	-
90000 POUNDS AND OVER.	-	100.0	-	-	-	-	-	-	-
1500 MILES OR OVER......	75	100.0	11.5	73.4	-	3.0	1.0	.4	10.7
UNDER 1000 POUNDS.....	18	100.0	-	88.4	.2	9.9	-	1.5	-
1000 TO 9999 POUNDS...	32	100.0	.2	98.6	-	1.2	-	-	-
10000 TO 29999 POUNDS.	6	100.0	14.8	73.7	-	-	11.5	-	-
30000 TO 59999 POUNDS.	8	100.0	-	4.4	-	-	-	-	95.6
60000 TO 89999 POUNDS.	9	100.0	80.7	19.3	-	-	-	-	-
90000 POUNDS AND OVER.	-	100.0	-	-	-	-	-	-	-

Note: Detail may not add to total due to rounding. The introductory table shows the estimates of sampling variability for tons; sampling variability for ton-miles has not been estimated. See the map in the Introduction for the States comprising the geographic divisions of the United States.

Shipments excluded from the survey are those moving by pipeline (primarily petroleum products from refineries), parcel post shipments, and commodities moved by own power (motorized vehicles, aircraft, etc.) or towed (prefabricated buildings, etc.). Local shipments (commodities shipped less than 25 miles from the plant) and shipments within the same city are also excluded. Shipments to Alaska and Hawaii from the 48 conterminous States and the District of Columbia are included; however, no data were obtained for shipments originating in Alaska and Hawaii.

- Represents zero or rounds to zero.   (D) Withheld to avoid disclosing figures for individual companies.

[1] Production of this commodity is concentrated in the geographic divisions shown; figures and distributions for geographic divisions not shown are included in the total.

[2] Distances of shipments to foreign destinations are calculated only to the U.S. port of exit.

[3] Includes only shipments represented by bills of lading and invoices. Summary records which did not show individual weights of shipments are not included.

TCC 346. Metal Stampings

Comparisons of Tons and Ton-Miles of Shipments for
Geographic Divisions of Origin and for Sampling Variability: 1972 and 1967

Geographic division of origin	Estimates				Relative sampling variability in tons (percent)	
	1972		1967		1972	1967
	Tons (thousands)	Ton-miles (millions)	Tons (thousands)	Ton-miles (millions)	1972	1967
U.S. total	7,916	3,396	5,750	2,013	6.2	15.8
New England	211	120	81	41	49.4	(*)
Middle Atlantic	739	365	891	432	13.1	(*)
East North Central	6,586	2,702	4,169	1,335	7.5	(*)
West North Central	93	34	91	45	32.9	(*)
South Atlantic	105	69	262	76	24.8	(*)
East South Central	61	37	157	56	48.0	(*)
West South Central	(D)	(D)	14	10	(*)	(*)
Mountain	(D)	(D)	—	—	(*)	(*)
Pacific	88	58	85	18	27.6	(*)

— Represents or rounds to zero.   (D) Withheld to avoid disclosing figures for individual companies.   (*) Data not published.

TABLE 1. TCC GROUP 346—Percent Distribution of Geographic Division of Origin and Distance Shipped, by Means of Transport: 1972

Geographic division of origin[1] and distance shipped[2]	Number	Percent distribution by means of transport							
		All means of transport	Rail	Motor carrier	Private truck	Air	Water	Other	Unknown
TONS OF SHIPMENTS	(thousands of tons)								
U.S. TOTAL	7 916	100.0	53.4	35.5	10.3	.3	-	.2	.2
NEW ENGLAND	211	100.0	16.5	61.8	19.5	.8	.5	.6	.3
UNDER 100 MILES	24	100.0	-	56.5	38.5	-	4.4	.6	-
100 TO 199 MILES	24	100.0	.2	86.8	8.8	-	-	4.2	-
200 TO 299 MILES	39	100.0	-	95.5	4.3	.2	-	-	-
300 TO 499 MILES	10	100.0	-	62.8	37.0	-	-	.1	-
500 TO 999 MILES	86	100.0	28.4	43.2	27.6	.2	-	-	.7
1000 TO 1499 MILES	21	100.0	47.2	45.6	.1	7.2	-	-	-
1500 MILES OR OVER	3	100.0	4.0	92.9	1.2	.8	-	1.2	-
MIDDLE ATLANTIC	739	100.0	47.7	46.5	4.9	.5	-	.4	-
UNDER 100 MILES	109	100.0	.4	80.6	16.9	.5	-	1.7	-
100 TO 199 MILES	103	100.0	34.0	63.4	2.3	.2	-	.1	-
200 TO 299 MILES	142	100.0	66.3	32.4	1.3	.1	-	-	-
300 TO 499 MILES	155	100.0	46.9	50.8	1.8	.4	-	-	-
500 TO 999 MILES	155	100.0	61.1	31.9	5.9	1.0	-	.1	-
1000 TO 1499 MILES	22	100.0	56.3	36.4	6.4	.6	-	.3	-
1500 MILES OR OVER	50	100.0	83.6	14.1	.3	1.4	-	.6	-
EAST NORTH CENTRAL	6 586	100.0	57.6	31.8	10.0	.2	-	.2	.2
UNDER 100 MILES	1 381	100.0	47.4	31.0	21.5	-	-	.1	.1
100 TO 199 MILES	1 279	100.0	52.6	32.9	14.4	-	-	.1	-
200 TO 299 MILES	860	100.0	44.3	51.4	3.0	-	-	.1	1.1
300 TO 499 MILES	1 317	100.0	68.6	23.0	7.6	.4	.2	.1	.1
500 TO 999 MILES	1 218	100.0	64.3	31.4	3.8	.2	-	.3	-
1000 TO 1499 MILES	112	100.0	53.5	41.1	4.2	.2	-	1.0	.1
1500 MILES OR OVER	416	100.0	81.0	17.0	.6	1.2	-	.3	-
WEST NORTH CENTRAL	93	100.0	7.5	72.1	19.4	-	-	.9	-
UNDER 100 MILES	17	100.0	.2	61.7	38.0	-	-	.1	-
100 TO 199 MILES	12	100.0	8.7	60.2	30.3	-	-	.8	-
200 TO 299 MILES	28	100.0	4.5	75.9	19.5	-	-	.1	-
300 TO 499 MILES	15	100.0	8.9	89.8	1.2	-	-	.1	-
500 TO 999 MILES	13	100.0	21.9	66.2	11.6	-	-	.3	-
1000 TO 1499 MILES	2	100.0	7.6	79.3	12.8	-	-	.2	-
1500 MILES OR OVER	2	100.0	3.0	73.2	.1	.1	-	23.6	-
SOUTH ATLANTIC	105	100.0	21.1	62.4	14.2	1.8	-	.4	.1
UNDER 100 MILES	13	100.0	.4	76.8	22.3	-	-	.1	.4
100 TO 199 MILES	14	100.0	3.4	85.1	11.5	-	-	.1	-
200 TO 299 MILES	8	100.0	4.6	64.8	30.6	-	-	-	-
300 TO 499 MILES	10	100.0	22.4	73.0	4.6	-	-	-	-
500 TO 999 MILES	39	100.0	35.4	41.7	18.4	3.9	-	.6	-
1000 TO 1499 MILES	9	100.0	-	96.6	.7	.6	-	2.1	-
1500 MILES OR OVER	10	100.0	47.7	48.5	.8	2.9	-	.1	-
EAST SOUTH CENTRAL	61	100.0	11.7	70.0	18.2	-	-	-	-
UNDER 100 MILES	6	100.0	-	12.0	88.0	-	-	-	-
100 TO 199 MILES	3	100.0	-	100.0	-	-	-	-	-
200 TO 299 MILES	6	100.0	-	19.5	80.5	-	-	-	-
300 TO 499 MILES	10	100.0	-	100.0	-	-	-	-	-
500 TO 999 MILES	23	100.0	18.1	81.9	-	-	-	-	-
1000 TO 1499 MILES	8	100.0	37.1	62.9	-	-	-	-	-
1500 MILES OR OVER	2	100.0	-	100.0	-	-	-	-	-
PACIFIC	88	100.0	12.4	66.4	20.1	.5	-	.2	.5
UNDER 100 MILES	30	100.0	-	67.1	32.5	.2	-	.2	-
100 TO 199 MILES	4	100.0	-	76.4	23.1	-	-	.5	-
200 TO 299 MILES	-	100.0	-	23.1	76.9	-	-	-	-
300 TO 499 MILES	17	100.0	9.5	87.9	2.0	.4	-	.2	-
500 TO 999 MILES	14	100.0	53.4	43.1	.1	.3	-	.2	2.9
1000 TO 1499 MILES	2	100.0	-	98.7	-	1.2	-	.1	-
1500 MILES OR OVER	18	100.0	9.1	57.3	32.3	1.2	-	-	-
TON-MILES OF SHIPMENTS	(millions of ton-miles)								
U.S. TOTAL	3 396	100.0	61.9	31.4	5.5	.7	-	.3	.1
NEW ENGLAND	120	100.0	25.8	52.9	18.7	2.0	-	.3	.3
UNDER 100 MILES	1	100.0	-	56.0	42.5	-	.7	.8	-
100 TO 199 MILES	4	100.0	.1	86.9	8.1	-	-	4.9	-
200 TO 299 MILES	9	100.0	-	95.1	4.6	.2	-	-	-
300 TO 499 MILES	4	100.0	-	57.1	42.8	-	-	.1	-
500 TO 999 MILES	67	100.0	27.8	42.9	28.5	.2	-	-	.6
1000 TO 1499 MILES	25	100.0	47.8	43.3	.1	8.8	-	-	-
1500 MILES OR OVER	8	100.0	4.5	92.4	1.0	.9	-	1.1	-
MIDDLE ATLANTIC	365	100.0	64.7	31.2	3.1	.9	-	.3	-
UNDER 100 MILES	3	100.0	.7	79.4	18.6	.2	-	1.1	-
100 TO 199 MILES	17	100.0	35.9	61.8	1.9	.2	-	.1	-
200 TO 299 MILES	35	100.0	67.0	31.7	1.3	.1	-	-	-
300 TO 499 MILES	64	100.0	50.8	46.9	1.9	.4	-	-	-
500 TO 999 MILES	110	100.0	62.1	30.8	6.0	1.0	-	.1	-
1000 TO 1499 MILES	25	100.0	56.5	36.8	5.8	.6	-	.3	-
1500 MILES OR OVER	109	100.0	83.4	14.2	.4	1.5	-	.6	-

See footnotes at end of table 4.

TABLE 1. TCC GROUP 346—Percent Distribution of Geographic Division of Origin and Distance Shipped, by Means of Transport: 1972—Continued

Geographic division of origin[1] and distance shipped[2]	Number	Percent distribution by means of transport							
		All means of transport	Rail	Motor carrier	Private truck	Air	Water	Other	Unknown
TON-MILES OF SHIPMENTS	(millions of ton-miles)								
EAST NORTH CENTRAL	2 702	100.0	66.5	28.0	4.6	.6	-	.2	.1
UNDER 100 MILES	61	100.0	40.9	34.7	24.3	-	-	.1	.1
100 TO 199 MILES	178	100.0	51.3	34.3	14.4	-	-	.1	-
200 TO 299 MILES	210	100.0	44.8	51.0	2.9	-	-	.2	1.0
300 TO 499 MILES	546	100.0	70.0	21.6	7.6	.4	.2	.1	.1
500 TO 999 MILES	763	100.0	62.4	33.6	3.5	.2	-	.3	-
1000 TO 1499 MILES	127	100.0	54.3	40.6	3.8	.2	-	.9	.1
1500 MILES OR OVER	814	100.0	80.7	17.1	.6	1.4	-	.2	-
WEST NORTH CENTRAL	34	100.0	10.6	73.9	12.0	-	-	3.5	-
UNDER 100 MILES	1	100.0	.1	59.8	40.1	-	-	-	-
100 TO 199 MILES	1	100.0	10.4	56.4	32.1	-	-	1.0	-
200 TO 299 MILES	6	100.0	4.2	76.5	19.1	-	-	.1	-
300 TO 499 MILES	7	100.0	8.6	90.2	1.1	-	-	.1	-
500 TO 999 MILES	9	100.0	22.0	64.1	13.5	-	-	.4	-
1000 TO 1499 MILES	3	100.0	8.9	76.9	13.9	-	-	.2	-
1500 MILES OR OVER	4	100.0	2.7	73.5	.1	.1	-	23.7	-
SOUTH ATLANTIC	69	100.0	29.1	57.5	10.1	2.7	-	.6	-
UNDER 100 MILES	-	100.0	.4	65.4	33.5	-	-	-	.7
100 TO 199 MILES	2	100.0	4.4	84.2	11.4	-	-	.1	-
200 TO 299 MILES	2	100.0	4.5	70.3	25.2	-	-	-	-
300 TO 499 MILES	3	100.0	19.0	76.9	4.1	-	-	-	-
500 TO 999 MILES	26	100.0	30.7	43.5	20.9	4.2	-	.6	-
1000 TO 1499 MILES	10	100.0	-	96.6	.7	.6	-	2.1	-
1500 MILES OR OVER	23	100.0	47.4	48.9	.7	2.9	-	.1	-
EAST SOUTH CENTRAL	37	100.0	18.7	76.6	4.7	-	-	-	-
UNDER 100 MILES	-	100.0	-	12.5	87.5	-	-	-	-
100 TO 199 MILES	-	100.0	-	100.0	-	-	-	-	-
200 TO 299 MILES	1	100.0	-	22.7	77.3	-	-	-	-
300 TO 499 MILES	4	100.0	-	100.0	-	-	-	-	-
500 TO 999 MILES	16	100.0	17.3	82.7	-	-	-	-	-
1000 TO 1499 MILES	10	100.0	41.1	58.9	-	-	-	-	-
1500 MILES OR OVER	3	100.0	-	100.0	-	-	-	-	-
PACIFIC	58	100.0	14.1	62.6	21.6	.9	-	.1	.7
UNDER 100 MILES	1	100.0	-	75.7	24.0	.1	-	.1	-
100 TO 199 MILES	-	100.0	-	76.9	22.6	-	-	.6	-
200 TO 299 MILES	-	100.0	-	23.2	76.8	-	-	-	-
300 TO 499 MILES	6	100.0	12.4	84.8	2.2	.4	-	.2	-
500 TO 999 MILES	8	100.0	48.0	46.8	.1	.4	-	.2	4.4
1000 TO 1499 MILES	3	100.0	-	98.7	-	1.3	-	.1	-
1500 MILES OR OVER	37	100.0	8.3	59.2	31.4	1.1	-	-	-

See footnotes at end of table 4.

TABLE 2. TCC GROUP 346—Percent Distribution of Geographic Division of Origin and Means of Transport, by Geographic Division of Destination: 1972

Geographic division of origin[1] and means of transport	Number	Percent distribution by division of destination									
		U.S. total	New England	Middle Atlantic	East North Central	West North Central	South Atlantic	East South Central	West South Central	Mountain	Pacific
TONS OF SHIPMENTS	(thousands of tons)										
U.S. TOTAL	7 916	100.0	1.9	13.5	47.8	11.7	11.1	3.5	3.4	.4	6.7
RAIL	4 230	100.0	1.0	11.5	43.6	15.7	14.1	1.4	3.6	.2	9.1
MOTOR CARRIER	2 813	100.0	3.2	17.5	49.2	7.4	8.4	5.5	3.5	.9	4.4
PRIVATE TRUCK	818	100.0	2.0	9.3	66.2	6.0	5.2	7.4	2.1	.1	1.7
AIR	21	100.0	2.4	28.6	13.6	6.0	7.1	3.1	10.0	.4	28.7
WATER	3	100.0	29.1	67.6	-	-	.7	2.7	-	-	-
OTHER	16	100.0	3.0	25.7	20.2	10.4	13.9	8.0	4.4	1.1	13.3
UNKNOWN	12	100.0	-	.5	83.7	6.2	1.6	4.6	-	-	3.4
NEW ENGLAND	211	100.0	11.3	32.6	37.5	7.5	5.4	2.8	1.6	.2	1.1
RAIL	34	100.0	.1	-	54.6	28.7	16.2	-	-	-	.4
MOTOR CARRIER	130	100.0	10.2	48.8	25.2	4.5	4.2	3.9	1.4	.3	1.6
PRIVATE TRUCK	41	100.0	22.3	10.1	66.0	-	.7	.7	.1	-	-
AIR	1	100.0	-	5.0	7.8	-	-	-	85.5	.1	1.7
WATER	1	100.0	100.0	-	-	-	-	-	-	-	-
OTHER	1	100.0	7.4	86.7	.9	-	1.1	.2	-	3.7	.1
UNKNOWN	-	100.0	-	-	-	-	-	100.0	-	-	-
MIDDLE ATLANTIC	739	100.0	4.4	28.2	32.1	11.3	11.0	3.8	2.8	.3	6.0
RAIL	352	100.0	.9	12.5	33.8	20.1	12.8	4.6	4.7	.1	10.5
MOTOR CARRIER	343	100.0	8.1	41.4	31.4	2.8	9.6	3.2	1.2	.6	1.7
PRIVATE TRUCK	36	100.0	3.5	54.8	25.1	7.6	8.5	-	-	-	.5
AIR	3	100.0	6.9	20.1	25.3	6.0	10.4	10.4	3.0	.5	17.4
WATER	-	100.0	-	-	-	-	100.0	-	-	-	-
OTHER	2	100.0	4.5	71.7	4.7	.8	3.4	.8	2.7	1.9	9.5
UNKNOWN	-	100.0	-	-	8.1	-	91.9	-	-	-	-

See footnotes at end of table 4.

TABLE 2. TCC GROUP 346—Percent Distribution of Geographic Division of Origin and Means of Transport, by Geographic Division of Destination: 1972—Continued

Geographic division of origin[1] and means of transport	Number	Percent distribution by division of destination									
		U.S. total	New England	Middle Atlantic	East North Central	West North Central	South Atlantic	East South Central	West South Central	Mountain	Pacific
TONS OF SHIPMENTS	(thousands of tons)										
EAST NORTH CENTRAL	6 586	100.0	1.3	11.6	51.3	11.6	11.2	3.3	3.3	.1	6.2
RAIL	3 794	100.0	1.0	11.5	44.6	15.2	14.3	1.1	3.5	-	8.8
MOTOR CARRIER	2 093	100.0	2.0	12.9	56.6	7.7	7.5	6.0	3.6	.4	3.3
PRIVATE TRUCK	660	100.0	.9	7.4	74.3	3.8	4.7	7.2	1.3	-	.4
AIR	13	100.0	1.5	39.1	3.9	5.1	7.7	2.0	3.2	.1	37.5
WATER	2	100.0	-	96.2	-	-	-	3.8	-	-	-
OTHER	10	100.0	2.6	11.0	28.3	10.7	18.9	11.6	5.5	.8	10.7
UNKNOWN	11	100.0	-	-	91.2	6.8	1.7	-	-	-	.3
WEST NORTH CENTRAL	93	100.0	.4	2.7	29.7	45.4	3.9	2.8	7.8	3.7	3.5
RAIL	7	100.0	-	.4	51.2	21.8	-	3.7	18.3	.8	3.8
MOTOR CARRIER	67	100.0	.2	3.5	33.9	39.7	3.1	3.2	7.8	5.1	3.5
PRIVATE TRUCK	18	100.0	1.5	.4	7.1	77.6	8.5	.9	3.9	-	-
AIR	-	100.0	-	-	27.5	33.5	-	-	7.8	-	31.3
WATER	-	100.0	-	-	-	-	-	-	-	-	-
OTHER	-	100.0	-	.5	4.5	12.9	4.2	1.1	1.7	-	75.1
UNKNOWN	-	100.0	-	-	-	-	-	-	-	-	-
SOUTH ATLANTIC	105	100.0	4.3	14.0	28.3	7.0	30.9	3.1	2.1	.5	9.7
RAIL	22	100.0	-	13.6	31.3	17.4	7.9	6.9	-	-	22.8
MOTOR CARRIER	65	100.0	6.8	13.2	22.5	4.8	39.1	2.4	3.3	.8	7.2
PRIVATE TRUCK	14	100.0	.3	19.5	45.9	.3	32.8	.5	.1	-	.5
AIR	1	100.0	2.9	1.6	57.5	15.3	3.7	.1	2.3	.2	16.5
WATER	-	100.0	-	-	-	-	-	-	-	-	-
OTHER	-	100.0	1.5	8.9	33.8	6.5	32.5	14.6	-	-	2.1
UNKNOWN	-	100.0	-	100.0	-	-	-	-	-	-	-
EAST SOUTH CENTRAL	61	100.0	4.6	6.2	36.7	4.4	7.9	24.8	6.0	6.2	3.3
RAIL	7	100.0	-	7.5	51.3	-	-	-	-	41.2	-
MOTOR CARRIER	43	100.0	6.5	7.6	43.8	6.2	11.3	9.4	8.5	2.0	4.7
PRIVATE TRUCK	11	100.0	-	-	-	-	-	100.0	-	-	-
AIR	-	100.0	-	-	-	-	-	-	100.0	-	-
WATER	-	100.0	-	-	-	-	-	-	-	-	-
OTHER	-	100.0	-	-	-	-	-	66.1	33.9	-	-
UNKNOWN	-	100.0	-	-	-	-	-	-	-	-	-
PACIFIC	88	100.0	.9	.5	10.6	.3	7.6	1.4	2.5	12.2	64.1
RAIL	11	100.0	-	-	15.4	-	-	-	-	28.2	56.3
MOTOR CARRIER	58	100.0	1.4	.7	2.5	.3	11.4	2.2	3.7	12.4	65.4
PRIVATE TRUCK	17	100.0	-	-	33.8	-	-	-	-	1.8	64.5
AIR	-	100.0	-	7.1	37.9	6.8	3.0	-	3.1	11.7	30.4
WATER	-	100.0	-	-	-	-	-	-	-	-	-
OTHER	-	100.0	-	2.9	2.7	1.7	-	-	-	1.5	91.2
UNKNOWN	-	100.0	-	-	-	-	-	-	-	-	100.0
TON-MILES OF SHIPMENTS	(millions of ton-miles)										
U.S. TOTAL	3 396	100.0	2.2	10.8	19.5	14.2	13.1	3.7	7.4	.9	28.1
RAIL	2 103	100.0	1.3	9.6	13.4	17.5	13.7	1.1	7.3	.3	35.7
MOTOR CARRIER	1 067	100.0	4.0	12.8	26.8	9.1	12.5	7.5	8.2	2.1	16.9
PRIVATE TRUCK	187	100.0	2.4	11.8	47.2	8.0	11.6	11.7	3.8	.2	3.3
AIR	23	100.0	1.3	11.1	8.4	3.4	4.0	1.5	11.8	.4	58.1
WATER	1	100.0	.7	93.7	-	-	.4	5.2	-	-	-
OTHER	9	100.0	2.5	9.9	7.5	5.1	19.0	8.0	6.0	2.8	39.2
UNKNOWN	3	100.0	-	.1	62.3	10.3	4.0	10.6	-	-	12.7
NEW ENGLAND	120	100.0	1.2	12.7	51.1	15.5	5.5	4.3	4.2	.6	4.9
RAIL	31	100.0	-	-	48.5	38.6	11.7	-	-	-	1.3
MOTOR CARRIER	63	100.0	1.2	22.4	40.4	10.6	4.5	7.1	4.5	.9	8.4
PRIVATE TRUCK	22	100.0	2.7	3.3	91.5	.1	.7	1.3	.2	-	.2
AIR	2	100.0	-	.9	4.8	-	-	-	91.1	.1	3.2
WATER	-	100.0	100.0	-	-	-	-	-	-	-	-
OTHER	-	100.0	2.3	62.4	2.3	-	2.1	.6	-	29.6	.7
UNKNOWN	-	100.0	-	-	-	-	-	100.0	-	-	-
MIDDLE ATLANTIC	365	100.0	2.1	8.3	22.5	17.5	10.3	4.3	7.0	1.1	26.9
RAIL	236	100.0	.6	5.3	14.9	22.5	9.0	3.8	8.8	.3	34.9
MOTOR CARRIER	113	100.0	5.2	14.5	36.3	7.0	12.5	5.9	4.2	2.7	11.7
PRIVATE TRUCK	11	100.0	2.4	9.7	44.3	23.2	16.6	-	-	-	3.7
AIR	3	100.0	3.0	2.4	18.1	6.3	6.6	7.8	4.3	1.4	50.1
WATER	-	100.0	-	-	-	-	100.0	-	-	-	-
OTHER	-	100.0	1.5	6.4	7.6	1.9	4.7	2.0	8.7	8.3	58.8
UNKNOWN	-	100.0	-	-	5.5	-	94.5	-	-	-	-
EAST NORTH CENTRAL	2 702	100.0	2.1	11.4	16.8	14.2	13.9	3.6	7.8	.4	29.9
RAIL	1 795	100.0	1.4	10.4	12.3	16.7	14.7	.7	7.4	-	36.4
MOTOR CARRIER	756	100.0	3.6	12.8	24.4	9.7	12.3	8.4	9.4	1.4	18.0
PRIVATE TRUCK	124	100.0	2.5	16.1	36.3	8.2	13.0	15.7	4.1	.2	3.9
AIR	15	100.0	1.0	15.7	.8	2.1	4.2	.7	2.2	.1	73.2
WATER	1	100.0	-	94.8	-	-	-	5.2	-	-	-
OTHER	6	100.0	3.2	9.7	6.8	6.0	25.0	10.5	7.2	1.4	30.2
UNKNOWN	2	100.0	-	-	79.8	13.2	4.8	-	-	-	2.2

See footnotes at end of table 4.

TABLE 2. **TCC GROUP 346—Percent Distribution of Geographic Division of Origin and Means of Transport, by Geographic Division of Destination: 1972**—Continued

Geographic division of origin [1] and means of transport	Number	Percent distribution by division of destination									
		U.S. total	New England	Middle Atlantic	East North Central	West North Central	South Atlantic	East South Central	West South Central	Mountain	Pacific
TON-MILES OF SHIPMENTS	(millions of ton-miles)										
WEST NORTH CENTRAL......	34	100.0	1.5	6.8	32.1	17.5	9.2	2.4	9.4	5.3	15.8
RAIL....................	3	100.0	-	.8	60.9	8.5	-	1.7	16.7	1.0	10.5
MOTOR CARRIER..........	25	100.0	.6	8.7	33.4	14.8	7.1	2.9	10.0	7.1	15.4
PRIVATE TRUCK..........	4	100.0	8.6	2.0	7.6	46.6	32.2	.9	2.0	-	.1
AIR....................	-	100.0	-	-	15.8	10.2	-	-	7.1	-	66.9
WATER..................	-	100.0	-	-	-	-	-	-	-	-	-
OTHER..................	1	100.0	-	.4	1.0	1.4	2.9	.4	.5	-	93.5
UNKNOWN................	-	100.0	-	-	-	-	-	-	-	-	-
SOUTH ATLANTIC..........	69	100.0	5.3	7.2	30.8	9.7	9.0	1.8	2.5	1.2	32.5
RAIL....................	20	100.0	-	8.9	17.3	14.4	2.6	2.2	-	-	54.7
MOTOR CARRIER..........	40	100.0	9.0	7.2	28.9	8.8	11.3	1.8	4.1	2.2	26.7
PRIVATE TRUCK..........	7	100.0	.6	3.5	76.5	.6	15.6	.6	.3	-	2.3
AIR....................	1	100.0	2.5	1.4	44.8	10.0	2.5	-	2.5	.2	36.0
WATER..................	-	100.0	-	-	-	-	-	-	-	-	-
OTHER..................	-	100.0	2.3	6.6	42.7	9.3	21.4	12.2	-	-	5.5
UNKNOWN................	-	100.0	-	100.0	-	-	-	-	-	-	-
EAST SOUTH CENTRAL......	37	100.0	9.1	8.1	38.8	3.1	5.6	6.9	4.5	14.1	9.7
RAIL....................	7	100.0	-	4.2	36.1	-	-	-	-	59.7	-
MOTOR CARRIER..........	28	100.0	11.9	9.5	41.8	4.1	7.4	2.9	5.9	3.8	12.7
PRIVATE TRUCK..........	1	100.0	-	-	-	-	-	100.0	-	-	-
AIR....................	-	100.0	-	-	-	-	-	-	100.0	-	-
WATER..................	-	100.0	-	-	-	-	-	-	-	-	-
OTHER..................	-	100.0	-	-	-	-	84.0	16.0	-	-	-
UNKNOWN................	-	100.0	-	-	-	-	-	-	-	-	-
PACIFIC.................	58	100.0	3.5	1.6	30.9	.5	24.6	4.0	4.7	10.2	19.9
RAIL....................	8	100.0	-	-	37.8	-	-	-	-	22.1	40.1
MOTOR CARRIER..........	36	100.0	5.6	2.4	7.6	.7	39.2	6.4	7.5	10.8	19.8
PRIVATE TRUCK..........	12	100.0	-	-	94.1	-	-	-	-	1.0	4.9
AIR....................	-	100.0	-	13.8	56.7	8.4	5.5	-	3.3	5.9	6.4
WATER..................	-	100.0	-	-	-	-	-	-	-	-	-
OTHER..................	-	100.0	-	17.4	11.7	6.3	-	-	-	1.3	63.4
UNKNOWN................	-	100.0	-	-	-	-	-	-	-	-	100.0

See footnotes at end of table 4.

TABLE 3. **TCC GROUP 346**—Percent Distribution of Geographic Division of Destination and Means of Transport, by Geographic Division of Origin: 1972

Geographic division of destination and means of transport	Number	Percent distribution by division of origin[1]									
		U.S. total	New England	Middle Atlantic	East North Central	West North Central	South Atlantic	East South Central	West South Central	Mountain	Pacific
TONS OF SHIPMENTS	(thousands of tons)										
U.S. TOTAL..............	7 916	100.0	2.7	9.3	83.2	1.2	1.3	.8	(D)	(D)	1.1
RAIL..................	4 230	100.0	.8	8.3	89.7	.2	.5	.2	(D)	(D)	.3
MOTOR CARRIER.........	2 813	100.0	4.6	12.2	74.4	2.4	2.3	1.5	(D)	(D)	2.1
PRIVATE TRUCK.........	818	100.0	5.1	4.4	80.7	2.2	1.8	1.4	(D)	(D)	2.2
AIR...................	21	100.0	8.4	18.5	61.9	.1	8.9	-	(D)	(D)	2.0
WATER.................	3	100.0	29.1	.7	70.2	-	-	-	(D)	(D)	-
OTHER.................	16	100.0	7.8	16.2	64.0	5.4	2.8	-	(D)	(D)	.9
UNKNOWN...............	12	100.0	4.6	-	91.7	-	.5	-	(D)	(D)	3.2
NEW ENGLAND...........	150	100.0	15.9	21.7	56.7	.3	3.0	1.9	(D)	(D)	.5
RAIL..................	41	100.0	.1	7.7	92.2	-	-	-	(D)	(D)	-
MOTOR CARRIER.........	90	100.0	14.8	30.8	45.3	.1	4.9	3.1	(D)	(D)	.9
PRIVATE TRUCK.........	16	100.0	55.9	7.7	34.4	1.7	.3	-	(D)	(D)	-
AIR...................	-	100.0	-	52.1	37.3	-	10.6	-	(D)	(D)	-
WATER.................	1	100.0	100.0	-	-	-	-	-	(D)	(D)	-
OTHER.................	-	100.0	19.0	24.2	55.4	-	1.4	-	(D)	(D)	-
UNKNOWN...............	-	100.0	-	-	-	-	-	-	(D)	(D)	-
MIDDLE ATLANTIC.......	1 065	100.0	6.5	19.6	71.8	.2	1.4	.4	(D)	(D)	-
RAIL..................	485	100.0	-	9.1	90.1	-	.6	.1	(D)	(D)	-
MOTOR CARRIER.........	491	100.0	13.0	28.9	55.1	.5	1.8	.7	(D)	(D)	.1
PRIVATE TRUCK.........	76	100.0	5.5	26.1	64.5	.1	3.8	-	(D)	(D)	-
AIR...................	6	100.0	1.5	13.0	84.5	-	.5	-	(D)	(D)	.5
WATER.................	2	100.0	-	-	100.0	-	-	-	(D)	(D)	-
OTHER.................	4	100.0	26.2	45.2	27.5	.1	1.0	-	(D)	(D)	.1
UNKNOWN...............	-	100.0	-	-	-	-	100.0	-	(D)	(D)	-
EAST NORTH CENTRAL....	3 787	100.0	2.1	6.3	89.3	.7	.8	.6	(D)	(D)	.2
RAIL..................	1 846	100.0	1.0	6.5	91.6	.2	.4	.2	(D)	(D)	.1
MOTOR CARRIER.........	1 382	100.0	2.4	7.8	85.6	1.7	1.1	1.4	(D)	(D)	.1
PRIVATE TRUCK.........	541	100.0	5.0	1.7	90.7	.2	1.3	-	(D)	(D)	1.1
AIR...................	2	100.0	4.8	34.4	17.6	.1	37.5	-	(D)	(D)	5.6
WATER.................	-	100.0	-	-	-	-	-	-	(D)	(D)	-
OTHER.................	3	100.0	.3	3.8	89.9	1.2	4.7	-	(D)	(D)	.1
UNKNOWN...............	10	100.0	-	-	100.0	-	-	-	(D)	(D)	-
WEST NORTH CENTRAL....	924	100.0	1.7	9.0	82.7	4.6	.8	.3	(D)	(D)	-
RAIL..................	663	100.0	1.5	10.7	87.0	.2	.6	-	(D)	(D)	-
MOTOR CARRIER.........	208	100.0	2.8	4.6	76.7	12.8	1.5	1.3	(D)	(D)	.1
PRIVATE TRUCK.........	48	100.0	-	5.6	51.9	28.8	.1	-	(D)	(D)	-
AIR...................	1	100.0	-	18.6	52.5	.3	22.7	-	(D)	(D)	2.3
WATER.................	-	100.0	-	-	-	-	-	-	(D)	(D)	-
OTHER.................	1	100.0	-	1.2	66.0	6.7	1.8	-	(D)	(D)	.1
UNKNOWN...............	-	100.0	-	-	100.0	-	-	-	(D)	(D)	-
SOUTH ATLANTIC........	878	100.0	1.3	9.3	83.7	.4	3.7	.6	(D)	(D)	.8
RAIL..................	596	100.0	.9	7.5	91.2	-	.3	-	(D)	(D)	-
MOTOR CARRIER.........	236	100.0	2.3	13.9	66.8	.9	10.9	2.1	(D)	(D)	2.8
PRIVATE TRUCK.........	42	100.0	.7	7.3	73.5	3.7	11.6	-	(D)	(D)	-
AIR...................	1	100.0	-	27.0	67.0	-	4.6	-	(D)	(D)	.9
WATER.................	-	100.0	-	100.0	-	-	-	-	(D)	(D)	-
OTHER.................	2	100.0	.6	4.0	87.2	1.6	6.6	-	(D)	(D)	-
UNKNOWN...............	-	100.0	-	2.4	97.6	-	-	-	(D)	(D)	-
EAST SOUTH CENTRAL....	276	100.0	2.2	10.1	78.0	1.0	1.2	5.6	(D)	(D)	.5
RAIL..................	58	100.0	-	28.0	68.9	.4	2.6	-	(D)	(D)	-
MOTOR CARRIER.........	154	100.0	3.3	7.2	81.7	1.4	1.0	2.6	(D)	(D)	.8
PRIVATE TRUCK.........	60	100.0	.5	-	78.0	.3	.1	18.6	(D)	(D)	-
AIR...................	-	100.0	-	61.2	38.5	-	.3	-	(D)	(D)	-
WATER.................	-	100.0	-	-	100.0	-	-	-	(D)	(D)	-
OTHER.................	1	100.0	.2	1.6	92.4	.7	5.1	-	(D)	(D)	-
UNKNOWN...............	-	100.0	100.0	-	-	-	-	-	(D)	(D)	-
WEST SOUTH CENTRAL....	269	100.0	1.2	7.7	80.7	2.7	.8	1.4	(D)	(D)	.8
RAIL..................	150	100.0	-	10.9	88.0	.9	-	-	(D)	(D)	-
MOTOR CARRIER.........	98	100.0	1.8	4.1	76.7	5.3	2.2	3.7	(D)	(D)	2.2
PRIVATE TRUCK.........	17	100.0	.2	-	48.1	4.1	.1	-	(D)	(D)	-
AIR...................	2	100.0	72.0	5.5	19.8	-	2.0	-	(D)	(D)	.6
WATER.................	-	100.0	-	-	-	-	-	-	(D)	(D)	-
OTHER.................	-	100.0	-	10.0	78.7	2.1	-	-	(D)	(D)	-
UNKNOWN...............	-	100.0	-	-	-	-	-	-	(D)	(D)	-
MOUNTAIN..............	33	100.0	1.1	7.6	29.0	10.4	1.5	11.4	(D)	(D)	32.0
RAIL..................	6	100.0	-	7.1	1.2	.8	-	44.6	(D)	(D)	46.2
MOTOR CARRIER.........	26	100.0	1.3	7.7	35.5	13.2	1.9	3.3	(D)	(D)	28.1
PRIVATE TRUCK.........	-	100.0	-	-	51.0	-	-	-	(D)	(D)	49.0
AIR...................	-	100.0	1.1	23.6	16.0	-	3.2	-	(D)	(D)	55.3
WATER.................	-	100.0	-	-	-	-	-	-	(D)	(D)	-
OTHER.................	-	100.0	26.3	27.9	44.5	-	-	-	(D)	(D)	1.3
UNKNOWN...............	-	100.0	-	-	-	-	-	-	(D)	(D)	-
PACIFIC...............	530	100.0	.4	8.3	77.6	.6	1.9	.4	(D)	(D)	10.7
RAIL..................	383	100.0	-	9.6	87.3	.1	1.3	-	(D)	(D)	1.6
MOTOR CARRIER.........	124	100.0	1.7	4.8	55.1	1.9	3.8	1.6	(D)	(D)	31.0
PRIVATE TRUCK.........	14	100.0	.1	1.2	17.0	-	.6	-	(D)	(D)	81.1
AIR...................	6	100.0	.5	11.2	81.0	.1	5.1	-	(D)	(D)	2.1
WATER.................	-	100.0	-	-	-	-	-	-	(D)	(D)	-
OTHER.................	2	100.0	-	11.5	51.3	30.5	.4	-	(D)	(D)	6.2
UNKNOWN...............	-	100.0	-	-	7.3	-	-	-	(D)	(D)	92.7

See footnotes at end of table 4.

TABLE 3. **TCC GROUP 346**—Percent Distribution of Geographic Division of Destination and Means of Transport, by Geographic Division of Origin: 1972—Continued

Geographic division of destination and means of transport	Number	Percent distribution by division of origin[1]									
		U.S. total	New England	Middle Atlantic	East North Central	West North Central	South Atlantic	East South Central	West South Central	Mountain	Pacific
TON-MILES OF SHIPMENTS	(millions of ton-miles)										
U.S. TOTAL..............	3 396	100.0	3.6	10.8	79.6	1.0	2.1	1.1	(D)	(D)	1.7
RAIL...................	2 103	100.0	1.5	11.2	85.4	.2	1.0	.3	(D)	(D)	.4
MOTOR CARRIER..........	1 067	100.0	6.0	10.7	70.8	2.4	3.8	2.7	(D)	(D)	3.4
PRIVATE TRUCK..........	187	100.0	12.0	6.0	66.6	2.2	3.8	.9	(D)	(D)	6.7
AIR....................	23	100.0	10.5	13.5	65.5	-	8.1	-	(D)	(D)	2.2
WATER..................	1	100.0	.7	.4	98.9	-	-	-	(D)	(D)	-
OTHER..................	9	100.0	3.5	9.9	68.7	12.8	4.3	-	(D)	(D)	.6
UNKNOWN................	3	100.0	10.6	.2	78.1	-	.1	-	(D)	(D)	11.0
NEW ENGLAND............	75	100.0	1.8	10.3	75.0	.7	4.9	4.5	(D)	(D)	2.7
RAIL...................	27	100.0	-	5.1	94.8	-	-	-	(D)	(D)	-
MOTOR CARRIER..........	43	100.0	1.8	13.9	63.0	.4	8.4	7.9	(D)	(D)	4.8
PRIVATE TRUCK..........	4	100.0	13.8	6.1	71.1	8.1	1.0	-	(D)	(D)	-
AIR....................	-	100.0	-	31.2	52.6	-	16.2	-	(D)	(D)	-
WATER..................	-	100.0	100.0	-	-	-	-	-	(D)	(D)	-
OTHER..................	-	100.0	3.1	5.8	87.1	-	4.0	-	(D)	(D)	-
UNKNOWN................	-	100.0	-	-	-	-	-	-	(D)	(D)	-
MIDDLE ATLANTIC........	366	100.0	4.2	8.3	84.2	.6	1.4	.8	(D)	(D)	.3
RAIL...................	202	100.0	-	6.2	92.4	-	.9	.1	(D)	(D)	-
MOTOR CARRIER..........	136	100.0	10.5	12.1	70.9	1.6	2.1	2.0	(D)	(D)	.6
PRIVATE TRUCK..........	22	100.0	3.3	4.9	90.3	.4	1.1	-	(D)	(D)	-
AIR....................	2	100.0	.8	2.9	92.6	-	1.0	-	(D)	(D)	2.7
WATER..................	1	100.0	-	-	100.0	-	-	-	(D)	(D)	-
OTHER..................	-	100.0	21.9	6.4	67.2	.5	2.9	-	(D)	(D)	1.1
UNKNOWN................	-	100.0	-	-	-	-	100.0	-	(D)	(D)	-
EAST NORTH CENTRAL......	661	100.0	9.3	12.4	68.4	1.7	3.3	2.2	(D)	(D)	2.7
RAIL...................	282	100.0	5.3	12.5	78.1	.8	1.2	.9	(D)	(D)	1.1
MOTOR CARRIER..........	286	100.0	9.0	14.4	64.3	3.0	4.0	4.2	(D)	(D)	1.0
PRIVATE TRUCK..........	88	100.0	23.3	5.6	51.2	.4	6.1	-	(D)	(D)	13.4
AIR....................	1	100.0	6.0	29.2	6.5	.1	43.4	-	(D)	(D)	14.7
WATER..................	-	100.0	-	-	-	-	-	-	(D)	(D)	-
OTHER..................	-	100.0	1.1	10.0	61.9	1.6	24.5	-	(D)	(D)	.9
UNKNOWN................	2	100.0	-	-	100.0	-	-	-	(D)	(D)	-
WEST NORTH CENTRAL......	480	100.0	3.9	13.3	79.7	1.3	1.4	.2	(D)	(D)	.1
RAIL...................	367	100.0	3.3	14.5	81.4	.1	.8	-	(D)	(D)	-
MOTOR CARRIER..........	96	100.0	7.0	8.2	75.5	3.9	3.7	1.2	(D)	(D)	.3
PRIVATE TRUCK..........	15	100.0	.1	17.3	68.3	12.9	.3	-	(D)	(D)	-
AIR....................	-	100.0	-	25.4	41.3	.1	24.3	-	(D)	(D)	5.4
WATER..................	-	100.0	-	-	-	-	-	-	(D)	(D)	-
OTHER..................	-	100.0	-	3.8	81.8	3.5	8.0	-	(D)	(D)	.8
UNKNOWN................	-	100.0	-	-	100.0	-	-	-	(D)	(D)	-
SOUTH ATLANTIC.........	446	100.0	1.5	8.4	83.9	.7	1.4	.5	(D)	(D)	3.2
RAIL...................	288	100.0	1.3	7.4	91.1	-	.2	-	(D)	(D)	-
MOTOR CARRIER..........	133	100.0	2.1	10.7	69.7	1.4	3.4	1.6	(D)	(D)	10.7
PRIVATE TRUCK..........	21	100.0	.7	8.6	74.9	6.2	5.1	-	(D)	(D)	-
AIR....................	-	100.0	-	22.4	68.5	-	5.1	-	(D)	(D)	3.0
WATER..................	-	100.0	-	100.0	-	-	-	-	(D)	(D)	-
OTHER..................	1	100.0	.4	2.5	90.3	2.0	4.9	-	(D)	(D)	-
UNKNOWN................	-	100.0	-	4.2	95.8	-	-	-	(D)	(D)	-
EAST SOUTH CENTRAL......	126	100.0	4.1	12.6	77.0	.7	1.0	2.1	(D)	(D)	1.8
RAIL...................	22	100.0	-	40.0	57.8	.3	2.0	-	(D)	(D)	-
MOTOR CARRIER..........	80	100.0	5.7	8.3	79.4	.9	.9	1.0	(D)	(D)	2.9
PRIVATE TRUCK..........	21	100.0	1.3	-	89.4	.2	.2	8.0	(D)	(D)	-
AIR....................	-	100.0	-	70.2	29.5	-	.3	-	(D)	(D)	-
WATER..................	-	100.0	-	-	100.0	-	-	-	(D)	(D)	-
OTHER..................	-	100.0	.3	2.5	90.0	.7	6.6	-	(D)	(D)	-
UNKNOWN................	-	100.0	100.0	-	-	-	-	-	(D)	(D)	-
WEST SOUTH CENTRAL......	252	100.0	2.0	10.2	82.9	1.3	.7	.7	(D)	(D)	1.1
RAIL...................	154	100.0	-	13.4	86.1	.4	-	-	(D)	(D)	-
MOTOR CARRIER..........	87	100.0	3.3	5.4	80.5	2.9	1.9	1.9	(D)	(D)	3.1
PRIVATE TRUCK..........	7	100.0	.6	-	70.6	1.2	.3	-	(D)	(D)	-
AIR....................	2	100.0	80.7	4.9	12.1	-	1.7	-	(D)	(D)	.6
WATER..................	-	100.0	-	-	-	-	-	-	(D)	(D)	-
OTHER..................	-	100.0	-	14.4	83.4	1.0	-	-	(D)	(D)	-
UNKNOWN................	-	100.0	-	-	-	-	-	-	(D)	(D)	-
MOUNTAIN...............	30	100.0	2.3	13.3	37.4	6.1	2.8	17.3	(D)	(D)	19.4
RAIL...................	6	100.0	-	11.6	1.4	.5	-	60.3	(D)	(D)	26.2
MOTOR CARRIER..........	22	100.0	2.6	13.7	48.0	8.0	3.8	4.8	(D)	(D)	17.3
PRIVATE TRUCK..........	-	100.0	-	-	69.2	-	-	-	(D)	(D)	30.8
AIR....................	-	100.0	2.2	43.7	20.1	-	4.3	-	(D)	(D)	29.2
WATER..................	-	100.0	-	-	-	-	-	-	(D)	(D)	-
OTHER..................	-	100.0	36.4	29.1	34.2	-	-	-	(D)	(D)	.3
UNKNOWN................	-	100.0	-	-	-	-	-	-	(D)	(D)	-
PACIFIC................	955	100.0	.6	10.3	84.5	.6	2.4	.4	(D)	(D)	1.2
RAIL...................	751	100.0	.1	11.0	87.0	.1	1.5	-	(D)	(D)	.4
MOTOR CARRIER..........	180	100.0	3.0	7.4	75.5	2.2	5.9	2.0	(D)	(D)	4.0
PRIVATE TRUCK..........	6	100.0	.8	6.7	79.7	-	2.7	-	(D)	(D)	10.1
AIR....................	13	100.0	.6	11.6	82.5	-	5.0	-	(D)	(D)	.2
WATER..................	-	100.0	-	-	-	-	-	-	(D)	(D)	-
OTHER..................	3	100.0	.1	14.8	53.0	30.5	.6	-	(D)	(D)	1.0
UNKNOWN................	-	100.0	-	-	13.4	-	-	-	(D)	(D)	86.6

See footnotes at end of table 4.

TABLE 4. TCC GROUP 346—Percent Distribution of Distance Shipped and Weight of Shipment, by Means of Transport: 1972

Distance shipped and weight of shipment[2][3]	Number	Percent distribution by means of transport							
		All means of transport	Rail	Motor carrier	Private truck	Air	Water	Other	Unknown
TONS OF SHIPMENTS	(thousands of tons)								
U.S. TOTAL...........	5 512	100.0	48.8	42.7	7.7	.3	-	.3	.2
UNDER 100 MILES.........	931	100.0	35.3	42.2	22.0	.1	-	.3	.1
UNDER 1000 POUNDS.....	70	100.0	.1	79.1	17.1	.2	-	3.3	.1
1000 TO 9999 POUNDS...	276	100.0	1.2	68.2	30.0	-	-	.2	.3
10000 TO 29999 POUNDS.	219	100.0	23.3	39.1	37.4	.2	-	-	-
30000 TO 59999 POUNDS.	210	100.0	56.8	29.9	13.3	-	-	-	-
60000 TO 89999 POUNDS.	92	100.0	99.7	.3	-	-	-	-	-
90000 POUNDS AND OVER.	61	100.0	100.0	-	-	-	-	-	-
100 TO 199 MILES........	1 164	100.0	53.3	40.4	6.1	-	-	.2	-
UNDER 1000 POUNDS.....	42	100.0	.1	90.9	5.7	.5	.1	2.7	-
1000 TO 9999 POUNDS...	190	100.0	2.2	89.1	8.6	-	-	-	-
10000 TO 29999 POUNDS.	281	100.0	41.9	50.9	6.9	-	-	.4	-
30000 TO 59999 POUNDS.	456	100.0	67.5	25.3	7.2	-	-	-	-
60000 TO 89999 POUNDS.	103	100.0	98.2	1.8	-	-	-	-	-
90000 POUNDS AND OVER.	90	100.0	99.0	1.0	-	-	-	-	-
200 TO 299 MILES........	696	100.0	28.0	67.5	2.9	.1	-	.2	1.4
UNDER 1000 POUNDS.....	30	100.0	.1	94.4	1.0	.5	-	3.1	.8
1000 TO 9999 POUNDS...	143	100.0	1.2	96.1	2.3	.1	-	.2	-
10000 TO 29999 POUNDS.	162	100.0	15.2	81.4	3.4	-	-	-	-
30000 TO 59999 POUNDS.	226	100.0	25.9	68.3	4.8	-	-	-	1.0
60000 TO 89999 POUNDS.	79	100.0	85.3	5.8	-	-	-	-	8.9
90000 POUNDS AND OVER.	54	100.0	77.2	22.8	-	-	-	-	-
300 TO 499 MILES........	1 189	100.0	61.9	32.7	4.6	.4	.2	.1	.1
UNDER 1000 POUNDS.....	50	100.0	.3	94.6	1.3	2.0	-	1.9	-
1000 TO 9999 POUNDS...	208	100.0	2.1	89.4	6.1	1.8	.5	.2	.5
10000 TO 29999 POUNDS.	220	100.0	45.6	46.0	7.9	-	.5	-	-
30000 TO 59999 POUNDS.	434	100.0	83.9	10.4	5.3	.3	-	-	-
60000 TO 89999 POUNDS.	152	100.0	96.9	2.2	.9	-	-	-	-
90000 POUNDS AND OVER.	123	100.0	96.6	3.4	-	-	-	-	-
500 TO 999 MILES........	1 054	100.0	50.1	43.1	5.8	.5	-	.4	.1
UNDER 1000 POUNDS.....	79	100.0	.8	88.5	1.7	4.7	-	4.1	.1
1000 TO 9999 POUNDS...	236	100.0	1.8	91.5	5.3	.6	-	.3	.4
10000 TO 29999 POUNDS.	196	100.0	55.1	36.0	8.8	-	-	-	-
30000 TO 59999 POUNDS.	335	100.0	63.3	27.7	9.0	-	-	-	-
60000 TO 89999 POUNDS.	109	100.0	96.7	3.3	-	-	-	-	-
90000 POUNDS AND OVER.	95	100.0	100.0	-	-	-	-	-	-
1000 TO 1499 MILES.....	122	100.0	32.4	63.7	1.5	1.6	-	.8	.1
UNDER 1000 POUNDS.....	18	100.0	2.9	91.9	.9	1.4	-	2.5	.4
1000 TO 9999 POUNDS...	49	100.0	5.5	89.4	.6	3.5	-	.9	-
10000 TO 29999 POUNDS.	21	100.0	60.2	33.2	6.6	-	-	-	-
30000 TO 59999 POUNDS.	23	100.0	60.5	39.5	-	-	-	-	-
60000 TO 89999 POUNDS.	4	100.0	96.0	4.0	-	-	-	-	-
90000 POUNDS AND OVER.	4	100.0	100.0	-	-	-	-	-	-
1500 MILES OR OVER......	352	100.0	68.4	28.3	2.5	.5	-	.4	-
UNDER 1000 POUNDS.....	19	100.0	7.5	81.9	2.1	5.6	-	2.8	.2
1000 TO 9999 POUNDS...	62	100.0	9.4	88.7	.6	.9	-	.5	-
10000 TO 29999 POUNDS.	47	100.0	39.2	56.5	4.3	-	-	-	-
30000 TO 59999 POUNDS.	89	100.0	91.6	1.0	6.6	-	-	.7	-
60000 TO 89999 POUNDS.	85	100.0	99.8	.2	-	-	-	-	-
90000 POUNDS AND OVER.	48	100.0	98.7	1.3	-	-	-	-	-
TON-MILES OF SHIPMENTS	(millions of ton-miles)								
U.S. TOTAL...........	2 399	100.0	54.5	39.9	4.5	.5	-	.3	.2
UNDER 100 MILES.........	47	100.0	34.3	45.6	19.8	-	-	.2	.1
UNDER 1000 POUNDS.....	3	100.0	.1	84.5	13.2	.1	-	2.0	.1
1000 TO 9999 POUNDS...	14	100.0	1.0	75.0	23.6	-	-	.2	.3
10000 TO 29999 POUNDS.	10	100.0	16.7	44.5	38.7	.1	-	-	-
30000 TO 59999 POUNDS.	7	100.0	50.6	34.3	15.1	-	-	-	-
60000 TO 89999 POUNDS.	6	100.0	99.8	.2	-	-	-	-	-
90000 POUNDS AND OVER.	3	100.0	100.0	-	-	-	-	-	-
100 TO 199 MILES........	167	100.0	51.8	41.8	6.2	-	-	.2	-
UNDER 1000 POUNDS.....	6	100.0	.1	90.8	5.8	.6	.1	2.6	-
1000 TO 9999 POUNDS...	27	100.0	2.1	89.9	8.0	-	-	-	-
10000 TO 29999 POUNDS.	38	100.0	39.3	52.7	7.5	-	-	.5	-
30000 TO 59999 POUNDS.	64	100.0	63.6	28.9	7.6	-	-	-	-
60000 TO 89999 POUNDS.	16	100.0	98.4	1.6	-	-	-	-	-
90000 POUNDS AND OVER.	14	100.0	99.1	.9	-	-	-	-	-

See footnotes at end of table 4.

TABLE 4. TCC GROUP 346—Percent Distribution of Distance Shipped and Weight of Shipment, by Means of Transport: 1972—Continued

Distance shipped and weight of shipment [2] [3]	Number	Percent distribution by means of transport							
		All means of transport	Rail	Motor carrier	Private truck	Air	Water	Other	Unknown
TON-MILES OF SHIPMENTS	(millions of ton-miles)								
200 TO 299 MILES.........	169	100.0	28.2	67.4	2.9	.1	-	.2	1.3
UNDER 1000 POUNDS......	7	100.0	.1	94.2	1.0	.5	-	3.2	.9
1000 TO 9999 POUNDS...	34	100.0	1.3	95.9	2.4	.2	-	.3	-
10000 TO 29999 POUNDS.	40	100.0	15.7	81.1	3.2	-	-	-	-
30000 TO 59999 POUNDS.	55	100.0	26.1	68.0	4.9	-	-	-	1.0
60000 TO 89999 POUNDS.	19	100.0	87.0	5.2	-	-	-	-	7.8
90000 POUNDS AND OVER.	12	100.0	77.8	22.2	-	-	-	-	-
300 TO 499 MILES.........	480	100.0	63.4	31.4	4.3	.4	.2	.1	.1
UNDER 1000 POUNDS.....	19	100.0	.3	94.2	1.6	2.0	-	2.0	-
1000 TO 9999 POUNDS...	83	100.0	2.1	89.0	6.4	1.8	-	.2	.6
10000 TO 29999 POUNDS.	86	100.0	46.9	44.5	8.0	-	.6	-	-
30000 TO 59999 POUNDS.	170	100.0	85.6	9.6	4.5	-	.4	-	-
60000 TO 89999 POUNDS.	67	100.0	96.9	2.3	.8	-	-	-	-
90000 POUNDS AND OVER.	52	100.0	97.1	2.9	-	-	-	-	-
500 TO 999 MILES.........	701	100.0	48.3	44.4	6.2	.5	-	.4	.1
UNDER 1000 POUNDS.....	56	100.0	.9	88.6	1.6	4.7	-	3.9	.2
1000 TO 9999 POUNDS...	165	100.0	1.6	91.6	5.5	.6	-	.2	.4
10000 TO 29999 POUNDS.	127	100.0	52.1	37.9	10.0	-	-	-	-
30000 TO 59999 POUNDS.	213	100.0	62.5	27.7	9.8	-	-	-	-
60000 TO 89999 POUNDS.	76	100.0	96.8	3.2	-	-	-	-	-
90000 POUNDS AND OVER.	61	100.0	100.0	-	-	-	-	-	-
1000 TO 1499 MILES......	141	100.0	33.4	62.5	1.4	1.9	-	.8	.1
UNDER 1000 POUNDS.....	21	100.0	3.3	91.4	.9	1.4	-	2.6	.4
1000 TO 9999 POUNDS...	56	100.0	6.2	87.9	.6	4.3	-	1.0	-
10000 TO 29999 POUNDS.	26	100.0	64.2	30.3	5.5	-	-	-	-
30000 TO 59999 POUNDS.	27	100.0	60.6	39.4	-	-	-	-	-
60000 TO 89999 POUNDS.	4	100.0	94.8	5.2	-	-	-	-	-
90000 POUNDS AND OVER.	4	100.0	100.0	-	-	-	-	-	-
1500 MILES OR OVER......	692	100.0	67.5	29.0	2.5	.6	-	.4	-
-UNDER 1000 POUNDS.....	40	100.0	7.9	79.2	2.2	8.1	-	2.4	.2
1000 TO 9999 POUNDS...	127	100.0	10.6	87.5	.6	.9	-	.4	-
10000 TO 29999 POUNDS.	92	100.0	38.1	57.5	4.4	-	-	-	-
30000 TO 59999 POUNDS.	174	100.0	91.8	.9	6.6	-	-	.6	-
60000 TO 89999 POUNDS.	163	100.0	99.8	.2	-	-	-	-	-
90000 POUNDS AND OVER.	93	100.0	98.6	1.4	-	-	-	-	-

Note: Detail may not add to total due to rounding. The introductory table shows the estimates of sampling variability for tons; sampling variability for ton-miles has not been estimated. See the map in the Introduction for the States comprising the geographic divisions of the United States.

Shipments excluded from the survey are those moving by pipeline (primarily petroleum products from refineries), parcel post shipments, and commodities moved by own power (motorized vehicles, aircraft, etc.) or towed (prefabricated buildings, etc.). Local shipments (commodities shipped less than 25 miles from the plant) and shipments within the same city are also excluded. Shipments to Alaska and Hawaii from the 48 conterminous States and the District of Columbia are included; however, no data were obtained for shipments originating in Alaska and Hawaii.

- Represents zero or rounds to zero.   (D) Withheld to avoid disclosing figures for individual companies.

[1] Production of this commodity is concentrated in the geographic divisions shown; figures and distributions for geographic divisions not shown are included in the total.

[2] Distances of shipments to foreign destinations are calculated only to the U.S. port of exit.

[3] Includes only shipments represented by bills of lading and invoices. Summary records which did not show individual weights of shipments are not included.

TCC 348. Miscellaneous Fabricated Wire Products

Comparisons of Tons and Ton-Miles of Shipments for
Geographic Divisions of Origin and for Sampling Variability: 1972 and 1967

Geographic division of origin	Estimates				Relative sampling variability in tons (percent)	
	1972		1967		1972	1967
	Tons (thousands)	Ton-miles (millions)	Tons (thousands)	Ton-miles (millions)		
U.S. total	2,905	1,224	2,808	946	11.5	19.4
New England	127	66	98	47	43.0	(*)
Middle Atlantic	515	228	208	114	33.0	(*)
East North Central	1,123	439	1,267	422	17.7	(*)
West North Central	377	136	445	114	21.9	(*)
South Atlantic	122	58	117	35	42.9	(*)
East South Central	(D)	(D)	76	25	(*)	(*)
West South Central	(D)	(D)	401	101	(*)	(*)
Mountain	(D)	(D)	94	31	(*)	(*)
Pacific	(D)	(D)	102	57	(*)	(*)

(D) Withheld to avoid disclosing figures for individual companies.   (*) Data not published.

TABLE 1. TCC GROUP 348—Percent Distribution of Geographic Division of Origin and Distance Shipped, by Means of Transport: 1972

Geographic division of origin[1] and distance shipped[2]	Number	Percent distribution by means of transport							
		All means of transport	Rail	Motor carrier	Private truck	Air	Water	Other	Unknown
TONS OF SHIPMENTS	(thousands of tons)								
U.S. TOTAL............	2 905	100.0	18.3	64.1	14.9	.1	1.4	.4	.9
NEW ENGLAND..............	127	100.0	1.2	58.1	34.5	.6	.8	3.1	1.6
UNDER 100 MILES........	41	100.0	-	61.1	35.5	.2	.2	2.9	.1
100 TO 199 MILES.......	33	100.0	-	45.9	47.6	-	2.5	4.0	-
200 TO 299 MILES.......	6	100.0	.6	63.7	32.9	.3	-	2.5	-
300 TO 499 MILES.......	6	100.0	-	93.4	1.2	.1	-	5.3	-
500 TO 999 MILES.......	21	100.0	.8	45.3	51.3	1.0	-	1.5	-
1000 TO 1499 MILES.....	4	100.0	5.0	82.8	.7	1.4	1.8	8.4	-
1500 MILES OR OVER.....	13	100.0	8.3	70.7	1.7	2.8	-	1.7	14.8
MIDDLE ATLANTIC..........	515	100.0	8.3	65.6	20.0	-	1.4	.2	4.5
UNDER 100 MILES........	115	100.0	-	42.9	56.4	-	-	.4	.3
100 TO 199 MILES.......	115	100.0	1.5	72.4	7.8	-	-	.1	18.2
200 TO 299 MILES.......	53	100.0	-	94.0	4.8	-	-	.2	1.0
300 TO 499 MILES.......	80	100.0	-	75.0	23.8	-	-	.2	1.0
500 TO 999 MILES.......	93	100.0	33.4	60.6	5.7	-	-	.1	.3
1000 TO 1499 MILES.....	35	100.0	27.0	46.2	6.6	-	20.0	.2	-
1500 MILES OR OVER.....	22	100.0	-	99.7	-	.1	-	.2	-
EAST NORTH CENTRAL.......	1 123	100.0	25.9	65.0	7.7	.1	.9	.4	-
UNDER 100 MILES........	215	100.0	15.1	64.2	19.8	-	-	.9	-
100 TO 199 MILES.......	201	100.0	3.7	84.9	11.1	.1	-	.2	-
200 TO 299 MILES.......	177	100.0	17.4	76.9	4.5	.1	-	1.1	-
300 TO 499 MILES.......	247	100.0	28.4	67.8	3.6	.1	-	.1	-
500 TO 999 MILES.......	208	100.0	45.1	47.8	2.3	-	4.6	.1	-
1000 TO 1499 MILES.....	29	100.0	59.4	40.5	-	.1	-	-	-
1500 MILES OR OVER.....	43	100.0	87.2	12.7	.1	.1	-	-	-
WEST NORTH CENTRAL.......	377	100.0	16.8	57.9	24.6	-	-	.6	-
UNDER 100 MILES........	36	100.0	-	73.4	24.1	-	-	2.1	.3
100 TO 199 MILES.......	87	100.0	25.5	48.1	25.9	-	-	.5	-
200 TO 299 MILES.......	88	100.0	1.5	66.7	31.1	-	-	.6	-
300 TO 499 MILES.......	80	100.0	20.2	55.1	24.4	-	-	.3	-
500 TO 999 MILES.......	70	100.0	33.3	50.1	16.4	-	-	.2	-
1000 TO 1499 MILES.....	10	100.0	-	75.2	24.6	.2	-	.1	-
1500 MILES OR OVER.....	2	100.0	-	100.0	-	-	-	-	-
SOUTH ATLANTIC..........	122	100.0	4.0	52.6	37.9	-	4.8	.4	.2
UNDER 100 MILES........	6	100.0	-	65.0	12.2	-	21.9	.9	-
100 TO 199 MILES.......	34	100.0	-	66.1	33.4	-	-	.5	-
200 TO 299 MILES.......	13	100.0	-	72.0	25.1	-	-	.8	2.1
300 TO 499 MILES.......	29	100.0	16.9	47.9	35.1	-	-	.1	-
500 TO 999 MILES.......	27	100.0	-	37.9	61.9	.1	-	.2	-
1000 TO 1499 MILES.....	5	100.0	-	41.9	57.8	.2	-	.2	-
1500 MILES OR OVER.....	5	100.0	-	12.6	-	.3	87.1	-	-
TON-MILES OF SHIPMENTS	(millions of ton-miles)								
U.S. TOTAL............	1 224	100.0	26.5	58.4	9.8	.2	4.2	.3	.7
NEW ENGLAND..............	66	100.0	4.8	66.1	16.9	1.8	.3	2.4	7.6
UNDER 100 MILES........	2	100.0	-	70.3	26.1	.1	.1	3.2	.1
100 TO 199 MILES.......	4	100.0	-	50.4	42.4	-	2.8	4.4	-
200 TO 299 MILES.......	1	100.0	.6	61.3	35.1	.3	-	2.6	-
300 TO 499 MILES.......	2	100.0	-	93.2	1.2	.1	-	5.5	-
500 TO 999 MILES.......	15	100.0	.8	47.3	49.2	1.0	-	1.5	.1
1000 TO 1499 MILES.....	5	100.0	4.5	84.3	.6	1.3	1.6	7.7	-
1500 MILES OR OVER.....	33	100.0	8.2	71.8	1.1	2.8	-	1.4	14.8
MIDDLE ATLANTIC..........	228	100.0	15.5	69.6	9.0	-	4.0	.2	1.7
UNDER 100 MILES........	6	100.0	-	38.0	61.5	-	-	.2	.3
100 TO 199 MILES.......	17	100.0	1.9	71.6	7.8	-	-	.1	18.5
200 TO 299 MILES.......	13	100.0	-	93.5	5.3	-	-	.2	1.0
300 TO 499 MILES.......	30	100.0	-	75.8	22.9	-	-	.2	1.1
500 TO 999 MILES.......	66	100.0	33.6	59.6	6.4	-	-	.1	.3
1000 TO 1499 MILES.....	44	100.0	28.9	43.6	6.7	-	20.6	.2	-
1500 MILES OR OVER.....	49	100.0	-	99.6	-	.2	-	.2	-
EAST NORTH CENTRAL.......	439	100.0	44.6	50.3	3.2	.1	1.6	.2	-
UNDER 100 MILES........	12	100.0	25.0	56.2	17.9	-	-	.8	-
100 TO 199 MILES.......	30	100.0	3.8	83.7	12.3	.1	-	.2	-
200 TO 299 MILES.......	45	100.0	17.7	76.5	4.6	.1	-	1.1	-
300 TO 499 MILES.......	92	100.0	27.7	68.8	3.2	.1	-	.1	-
500 TO 999 MILES.......	144	100.0	48.3	44.7	2.1	-	4.7	.1	-
1000 TO 1499 MILES.....	36	100.0	57.4	42.5	-	-	.1	-	-
1500 MILES OR OVER.....	77	100.0	86.7	13.1	.1	.1	-	-	-
WEST NORTH CENTRAL.......	136	100.0	19.9	58.7	21.1	-	-	.3	-
UNDER 100 MILES........	2	100.0	-	73.2	25.0	-	-	1.8	-
100 TO 199 MILES.......	12	100.0	23.5	49.9	26.0	-	-	.5	-
200 TO 299 MILES.......	22	100.0	1.5	68.2	29.7	-	-	.6	-
300 TO 499 MILES.......	33	100.0	20.9	55.0	23.8	-	-	.3	-
500 TO 999 MILES.......	50	100.0	33.9	50.9	15.0	-	-	.2	-
1000 TO 1499 MILES.....	12	100.0	-	75.9	23.9	.1	-	.1	-
1500 MILES OR OVER.....	4	100.0	-	100.0	-	-	-	-	-

See footnotes at end of table 4.

TABLE 1. **TCC GROUP 348**—Percent Distribution of Geographic Division of Origin and Distance Shipped, by Means of Transport: 1972—Continued

Geographic division of origin [1] and distance shipped [2]	Number	Percent distribution by means of transport							
		All means of transport	Rail	Motor carrier	Private truck	Air	Water	Other	Unknown
TON-MILES OF SHIPMENTS	(millions of ton-miles)								
SOUTH ATLANTIC...........	58	100.0	2.9	39.1	39.3	.1	18.2	.2	.1
UNDER 100 MILES.......	-	100.0	-	59.0	17.4	-	22.6	1.0	-
100 TO 199 MILES......	5	100.0	-	62.6	37.0	-	-	.4	-
200 TO 299 MILES......	3	100.0	-	71.1	25.6	-	-	.7	2.5
300 TO 499 MILES......	10	100.0	15.6	48.7	35.6	-	-	.2	-
500 TO 999 MILES......	19	100.0	-	37.4	62.3	.1	-	.2	-
1000 TO 1499 MILES....	6	100.0	-	42.4	57.3	.2	-	.2	-
1500 MILES OR OVER....	11	100.0	-	11.7	-	.3	88.0	-	-

See footnotes at end of table 4.

TABLE 2. **TCC GROUP 348**—Percent Distribution of Geographic Division of Origin and Means of Transport, by Geographic Division of Destination: 1972

Geographic division of origin [1] and means of transport	Number	Percent distribution by division of destination									
		U.S. total	New England	Middle Atlantic	East North Central	West North Central	South Atlantic	East South Central	West South Central	Mountain	Pacific
TONS OF SHIPMENTS	(thousands of tons)										
U.S. TOTAL...............	2 905	100.0	3.2	11.0	30.8	14.8	13.8	6.6	6.3	5.6	7.9
RAIL.................	531	100.0	1.0	5.0	27.8	19.9	14.9	6.1	10.1	6.5	8.6
MOTOR CARRIER........	1 861	100.0	2.5	10.9	33.1	14.1	13.8	7.0	4.5	5.1	9.0
PRIVATE TRUCK........	431	100.0	9.1	19.9	29.1	13.1	9.0	6.6	5.4	7.7	.2
AIR..................	2	100.0	4.0	13.0	36.9	5.0	6.7	3.4	8.3	1.0	21.9
WATER...............	40	100.0	.2	2.7	-	-	12.5	-	55.0	-	29.6
OTHER...............	12	100.0	7.4	22.2	23.2	32.9	6.6	2.3	3.3	.6	1.3
UNKNOWN.............	25	100.0	.5	4.1	2.5	.5	83.4	.9	-	-	8.0
NEW ENGLAND.............	127	100.0	33.4	34.2	8.0	.8	3.4	7.4	2.7	.1	9.9
RAIL.................	1	100.0	-	2.8	10.6	7.6	5.9	1.5	10.9	2.6	58.2
MOTOR CARRIER........	74	100.0	22.7	43.7	9.5	1.0	4.9	2.0	3.6	.1	12.5
PRIVATE TRUCK........	44	100.0	56.1	18.6	5.9	-	.9	18.0	.5	-	-
AIR..................	-	100.0	9.9	3.5	26.3	4.0	1.4	.4	8.2	.3	46.0
WATER...............	1	100.0	8.8	82.8	-	-	8.4	-	-	-	-
OTHER...............	3	100.0	20.2	53.9	6.9	3.4	3.7	.8	7.4	.5	3.1
UNKNOWN.............	2	100.0	1.7	.6	-	-	.1	.5	-	-	97.1
MIDDLE ATLANTIC.........	515	100.0	5.6	32.6	15.1	3.8	28.4	3.4	5.1	2.2	3.8
RAIL.................	42	100.0	-	4.2	31.7	17.2	.2	7.9	19.6	19.3	-
MOTOR CARRIER........	338	100.0	5.1	26.8	17.1	3.6	34.7	3.4	2.5	1.0	5.8
PRIVATE TRUCK........	103	100.0	11.0	71.7	5.1	-	7.7	2.2	2.3	-	-
AIR..................	-	100.0	5.0	2.5	21.3	-	7.6	16.4	-	-	47.3
WATER...............	7	100.0	-	-	-	-	-	-	100.0	-	-
OTHER...............	1	100.0	7.1	50.8	12.5	2.8	15.1	3.3	4.5	-	3.8
UNKNOWN.............	22	100.0	.4	4.5	2.8	-	91.3	1.0	-	-	-
EAST NORTH CENTRAL......	1 123	100.0	1.3	5.9	48.0	15.8	11.0	7.3	4.1	2.7	3.9
RAIL.................	290	100.0	1.8	8.0	24.5	15.6	15.9	5.0	11.8	4.4	13.1
MOTOR CARRIER........	730	100.0	1.2	5.7	54.2	17.2	9.5	8.4	.8	2.4	.8
PRIVATE TRUCK........	86	100.0	.7	.7	80.0	5.3	5.5	7.3	.5	-	-
AIR..................	-	100.0	.1	29.0	36.4	3.1	12.3	7.7	6.8	-	4.5
WATER...............	9	100.0	-	2.5	-	-	35.7	-	61.8	-	-
OTHER...............	4	100.0	.9	1.3	51.0	40.2	2.8	3.3	.3	.2	.1
UNKNOWN.............	-	100.0	-	-	13.2	-	-	-	-	86.8	-
WEST NORTH CENTRAL......	377	100.0	.1	1.5	27.1	47.9	3.2	3.1	9.2	6.4	1.4
RAIL.................	63	100.0	-	-	.9	67.7	9.9	13.3	2.9	5.4	-
MOTOR CARRIER........	218	100.0	.2	2.6	31.9	40.2	2.7	.9	12.9	6.6	2.1
PRIVATE TRUCK........	93	100.0	-	-	34.2	51.4	-	1.6	5.2	6.8	.7
AIR..................	-	100.0	-	4.6	64.6	12.8	-	-	-	11.1	6.9
WATER...............	-	100.0	-	-	-	-	-	-	-	-	-
OTHER...............	2	100.0	-	-	1.3	94.5	2.2	-	.3	1.7	-
UNKNOWN.............	-	100.0	-	-	-	100.0	-	-	-	-	-
SOUTH ATLANTIC..........	122	100.0	2.7	10.1	9.1	1.0	50.6	13.9	8.5	-	4.0
RAIL.................	4	100.0	-	-	-	-	100.0	-	-	-	-
MOTOR CARRIER........	64	100.0	1.4	19.1	12.4	1.9	47.1	11.1	6.1	-	.8
PRIVATE TRUCK........	46	100.0	5.2	-	6.7	-	53.0	21.2	13.9	-	-
AIR..................	-	100.0	-	9.9	-	-	30.5	-	32.0	8.2	19.5
WATER...............	5	100.0	-	-	-	-	25.3	-	-	-	74.7
OTHER...............	-	100.0	3.6	10.5	7.3	2.6	65.2	9.4	1.3	.2	-
UNKNOWN.............	-	100.0	-	-	-	-	100.0	-	-	-	-

See footnotes at end of table 4.

TABLE 2. **TCC GROUP 348—Percent Distribution of Geographic Division of Origin and Means of Transport, by Geographic Division of Destination: 1972**—Continued

Geographic division of origin[1] and means of transport	Number	Percent distribution by division of destination									
		U.S. total	New England	Middle Atlantic	East North Central	West North Central	South Atlantic	East South Central	West South Central	Mountain	Pacific
TON-MILES OF SHIPMENTS	(millions of ton-miles)										
U.S. TOTAL..............	1 224	100.0	2.2	7.6	18.8	11.1	14.4	6.1	10.4	9.2	20.3
RAIL...................	323	100.0	1.4	4.8	15.9	10.8	16.6	4.4	13.0	9.8	23.3
MOTOR CARRIER..........	714	100.0	2.0	9.1	21.4	11.8	13.8	6.3	7.6	9.2	18.8
PRIVATE TRUCK..........	119	100.0	6.4	9.0	20.2	13.1	14.2	12.3	11.3	12.6	.8
AIR....................	1	100.0	.2	6.1	19.0	3.5	3.7	1.8	9.1	1.4	55.3
WATER..................	51	100.0	-	.6	-	-	6.1	-	32.5	-	60.8
OTHER..................	3	100.0	3.2	11.6	13.8	30.0	9.9	3.6	13.6	2.4	11.9
UNKNOWN................	9	100.0	.3	2.0	3.2	.1	36.8	2.1	-	-	55.4
NEW ENGLAND............	66	100.0	4.3	11.1	10.4	1.7	4.5	11.4	7.3	.5	48.7
RAIL...................	3	100.0	-	.3	3.9	4.1	3.6	.8	8.5	2.5	76.3
MOTOR CARRIER..........	43	100.0	2.5	12.3	11.4	1.9	5.6	3.4	8.6	.4	54.0
PRIVATE TRUCK..........	11	100.0	15.0	13.4	12.5	-	2.1	53.8	3.2	-	-
AIR....................	1	100.0	.2	.5	13.2	3.2	.4	.2	7.2	.4	74.7
WATER..................	-	100.0	1.5	56.8	-	-	41.7	-	-	-	-
OTHER..................	1	100.0	3.5	21.6	12.4	9.3	6.3	1.9	24.1	2.2	18.8
UNKNOWN................	5	100.0	-	-	-	-	-	.2	-	-	99.7
MIDDLE ATLANTIC........	228	100.0	3.7	8.2	16.6	6.7	18.9	5.2	13.5	7.3	19.8
RAIL...................	35	100.0	-	.9	23.8	15.0	.2	4.9	23.6	31.5	-
MOTOR CARRIER..........	159	100.0	2.5	7.8	17.3	6.3	22.0	5.6	6.5	3.6	28.4
PRIVATE TRUCK..........	20	100.0	21.7	28.1	7.8	-	23.0	4.9	14.5	-	-
AIR....................	-	100.0	.8	.4	5.7	-	2.1	11.3	-	-	79.8
WATER..................	9	100.0	-	-	-	-	-	-	100.0	-	-
OTHER..................	-	100.0	4.1	5.0	16.9	8.4	14.1	7.9	14.0	-	29.5
UNKNOWN................	3	100.0	.7	4.6	7.3	-	82.4	4.7	-	-	.2
EAST NORTH CENTRAL.....	439	100.0	2.6	8.1	18.4	13.4	17.3	6.6	7.9	8.1	17.6
RAIL...................	196	100.0	2.2	7.0	7.3	8.1	17.3	2.4	13.4	8.0	34.3
MOTOR CARRIER..........	221	100.0	3.0	9.7	26.6	18.6	16.4	10.0	2.1	9.0	4.6
PRIVATE TRUCK..........	14	100.0	3.5	1.7	52.0	8.8	18.4	13.5	1.8	-	.4
AIR....................	-	100.0	.2	26.4	16.1	2.9	13.1	6.6	15.4	.1	19.2
WATER..................	6	100.0	-	2.5	-	-	43.5	-	54.0	-	-
OTHER..................	-	100.0	3.4	2.3	19.9	58.3	6.9	6.1	1.2	.9	1.0
UNKNOWN................	-	100.0	-	-	.3	-	-	-	-	99.7	-
WEST NORTH CENTRAL.....	136	100.0	.4	3.4	21.8	29.8	6.7	6.2	11.6	15.2	5.1
RAIL...................	27	100.0	-	-	.8	43.9	15.7	22.3	5.5	11.8	-
MOTOR CARRIER..........	80	100.0	.7	5.7	27.1	20.2	6.0	1.6	15.8	15.3	7.5
PRIVATE TRUCK..........	28	100.0	-	-	27.0	42.4	-	3.6	5.6	18.3	3.0
AIR....................	-	100.0	-	8.6	49.4	3.2	-	-	-	21.4	17.5
WATER..................	-	100.0	-	-	-	-	-	-	-	-	-
OTHER..................	-	100.0	-	-	3.8	78.5	9.1	-	1.7	6.9	-
UNKNOWN................	-	100.0	-	-	-	100.0	-	-	-	-	-
SOUTH ATLANTIC.........	58	100.0	2.7	3.8	9.4	2.2	31.8	11.2	18.6	-	20.2
RAIL...................	1	100.0	-	-	-	-	100.0	-	-	-	-
MOTOR CARRIER..........	22	100.0	2.2	9.7	16.5	5.5	34.5	7.9	18.2	.1	5.4
PRIVATE TRUCK..........	22	100.0	4.7	-	7.4	-	38.1	20.6	29.2	-	-
AIR....................	-	100.0	-	5.3	-	-	19.7	-	24.5	13.1	37.4
WATER..................	10	100.0	-	-	-	-	.8	-	-	-	99.2
OTHER..................	-	100.0	6.3	13.4	16.0	10.0	41.8	5.7	4.9	1.8	-
UNKNOWN................	-	100.0	-	-	-	-	100.0	-	-	-	-

See footnotes at end of table 4.

TABLE 3. **TCC GROUP 348**—Percent Distribution of Geographic Division of Destination and Means of Transport, by Geographic Division of Origin: 1972

Geographic division of destination and means of transport	Number	Percent distribution by division of origin[1]									
		U.S. total	New England	Middle Atlantic	East North Central	West North Central	South Atlantic	East South Central	West South Central	Mountain	Pacific
TONS OF SHIPMENTS	(thousands of tons)										
U.S. TOTAL	2 905	100.0	4.4	17.8	38.7	13.0	4.2	(D)	(D)	(D)	(D)
RAIL	531	100.0	.3	8.0	54.7	12.0	.9	(D)	(D)	(D)	(D)
MOTOR CARRIER	1 861	100.0	4.0	18.2	39.2	11.8	3.5	(D)	(D)	(D)	(D)
PRIVATE TRUCK	431	100.0	10.2	23.9	20.1	21.6	10.8	(D)	(D)	(D)	(D)
AIR	2	100.0	38.0	3.3	35.0	4.3	2.7	(D)	(D)	(D)	(D)
WATER	40	100.0	2.5	17.8	24.0	-	14.7	(D)	(D)	(D)	(D)
OTHER	12	100.0	31.6	8.6	38.0	17.1	3.4	(D)	(D)	(D)	(D)
UNKNOWN	25	100.0	8.2	90.2	-	.4	1.1	(D)	(D)	(D)	(D)
NEW ENGLAND	91	100.0	46.4	31.5	16.3	.5	3.6	(D)	(D)	(D)	(D)
RAIL	5	100.0	-	-	100.0	-	-	(D)	(D)	(D)	(D)
MOTOR CARRIER	46	100.0	36.6	37.7	19.5	1.1	2.0	(D)	(D)	(D)	(D)
PRIVATE TRUCK	39	100.0	63.3	29.1	1.4	-	6.1	(D)	(D)	(D)	(D)
AIR	-	100.0	94.9	4.1	1.0	-	-	(D)	(D)	(D)	(D)
WATER	-	100.0	100.0	-	-	-	-	(D)	(D)	(D)	(D)
OTHER	-	100.0	85.7	8.1	4.4	-	1.7	(D)	(D)	(D)	(D)
UNKNOWN	-	100.0	29.1	70.9	-	-	-	(D)	(D)	(D)	(D)
MIDDLE ATLANTIC	319	100.0	13.7	52.5	20.5	1.7	3.9	(D)	(D)	(D)	(D)
RAIL	26	100.0	.2	6.7	87.2	-	-	(D)	(D)	(D)	(D)
MOTOR CARRIER	202	100.0	16.0	44.9	20.5	2.8	6.1	(D)	(D)	(D)	(D)
PRIVATE TRUCK	86	100.0	9.5	86.1	.7	-	-	(D)	(D)	(D)	(D)
AIR	-	100.0	10.3	.6	78.5	1.5	2.0	(D)	(D)	(D)	(D)
WATER	1	100.0	77.9	-	22.1	-	-	(D)	(D)	(D)	(D)
OTHER	2	100.0	76.6	19.5	2.1	-	1.6	(D)	(D)	(D)	(D)
UNKNOWN	1	100.0	1.2	98.8	-	-	-	(D)	(D)	(D)	(D)
EAST NORTH CENTRAL	893	100.0	1.1	8.7	60.3	11.5	1.3	(D)	(D)	(D)	(D)
RAIL	147	100.0	.1	9.2	48.1	.4	-	(D)	(D)	(D)	(D)
MOTOR CARRIER	615	100.0	1.1	9.4	64.3	11.4	1.3	(D)	(D)	(D)	(D)
PRIVATE TRUCK	125	100.0	2.1	4.2	55.2	25.4	2.5	(D)	(D)	(D)	(D)
AIR	-	100.0	27.1	1.9	34.6	7.5	-	(D)	(D)	(D)	(D)
WATER	-	100.0	-	-	-	-	-	(D)	(D)	(D)	(D)
OTHER	2	100.0	9.5	4.6	83.5	1.0	1.1	(D)	(D)	(D)	(D)
UNKNOWN	-	100.0	-	100.0	-	-	-	(D)	(D)	(D)	(D)
WEST NORTH CENTRAL	430	100.0	.2	4.6	41.2	42.0	.3	(D)	(D)	(D)	(D)
RAIL	105	100.0	.1	6.9	42.8	40.6	-	(D)	(D)	(D)	(D)
MOTOR CARRIER	263	100.0	.3	4.7	47.7	33.4	.5	(D)	(D)	(D)	(D)
PRIVATE TRUCK	56	100.0	-	-	8.1	84.4	-	(D)	(D)	(D)	(D)
AIR	-	100.0	30.6	-	21.8	11.0	-	(D)	(D)	(D)	(D)
WATER	-	100.0	-	-	-	-	-	(D)	(D)	(D)	(D)
OTHER	4	100.0	3.3	.7	46.4	49.1	.3	(D)	(D)	(D)	(D)
UNKNOWN	-	100.0	-	.7	-	82.3	-	(D)	(D)	(D)	(D)
SOUTH ATLANTIC	401	100.0	1.1	36.5	30.8	3.0	15.5	(D)	(D)	(D)	(D)
RAIL	79	100.0	.1	.1	58.1	7.9	6.2	(D)	(D)	(D)	(D)
MOTOR CARRIER	256	100.0	1.4	45.8	27.0	2.3	11.9	(D)	(D)	(D)	(D)
PRIVATE TRUCK	38	100.0	1.0	20.3	12.3	-	63.2	(D)	(D)	(D)	(D)
AIR	-	100.0	7.9	3.7	64.3	-	12.2	(D)	(D)	(D)	(D)
WATER	5	100.0	1.7	-	68.6	-	29.7	(D)	(D)	(D)	(D)
OTHER	-	100.0	17.7	19.5	16.0	5.5	33.8	(D)	(D)	(D)	(D)
UNKNOWN	21	100.0	-	98.6	-	-	1.3	(D)	(D)	(D)	(D)
EAST SOUTH CENTRAL	192	100.0	4.9	9.0	42.7	6.2	8.9	(D)	(D)	(D)	(D)
RAIL	32	100.0	.1	10.4	44.3	26.0	-	(D)	(D)	(D)	(D)
MOTOR CARRIER	131	100.0	1.1	8.7	46.7	1.4	5.5	(D)	(D)	(D)	(D)
PRIVATE TRUCK	28	100.0	28.1	8.2	22.3	5.4	34.8	(D)	(D)	(D)	(D)
AIR	-	100.0	4.0	16.0	80.0	-	-	(D)	(D)	(D)	(D)
WATER	-	100.0	-	-	-	-	-	(D)	(D)	(D)	(D)
OTHER	-	100.0	10.7	12.2	53.2	-	13.8	(D)	(D)	(D)	(D)
UNKNOWN	-	100.0	4.4	95.6	-	-	-	(D)	(D)	(D)	(D)
WEST SOUTH CENTRAL	183	100.0	1.9	14.4	25.3	19.0	5.7	(D)	(D)	(D)	(D)
RAIL	53	100.0	.3	15.5	63.7	3.4	-	(D)	(D)	(D)	(D)
MOTOR CARRIER	83	100.0	3.2	10.1	6.8	33.7	4.7	(D)	(D)	(D)	(D)
PRIVATE TRUCK	23	100.0	1.0	10.2	1.8	21.0	27.8	(D)	(D)	(D)	(D)
AIR	-	100.0	37.3	-	28.7	-	10.3	(D)	(D)	(D)	(D)
WATER	22	100.0	-	32.4	27.0	-	-	(D)	(D)	(D)	(D)
OTHER	-	100.0	70.9	11.7	3.8	1.5	1.3	(D)	(D)	(D)	(D)
UNKNOWN	-	100.0	-	-	-	-	-	(D)	(D)	(D)	(D)
MOUNTAIN	163	100.0	.1	7.1	18.4	14.9	-	(D)	(D)	(D)	(D)
RAIL	34	100.0	.1	23.9	37.2	10.0	-	(D)	(D)	(D)	(D)
MOTOR CARRIER	95	100.0	.1	3.5	18.1	15.1	-	(D)	(D)	(D)	(D)
PRIVATE TRUCK	33	100.0	-	-	-	19.1	-	(D)	(D)	(D)	(D)
AIR	-	100.0	11.4	-	1.1	49.8	23.1	(D)	(D)	(D)	(D)
WATER	-	100.0	-	-	-	-	-	(D)	(D)	(D)	(D)
OTHER	-	100.0	27.7	-	10.2	47.7	1.3	(D)	(D)	(D)	(D)
UNKNOWN	-	100.0	-	-	100.0	-	-	(D)	(D)	(D)	(D)
PACIFIC	229	100.0	5.5	8.6	19.1	2.3	2.2	(D)	(D)	(D)	(D)
RAIL	45	100.0	2.0	-	83.8	-	-	(D)	(D)	(D)	(D)
MOTOR CARRIER	168	100.0	5.5	11.6	3.3	2.7	.3	(D)	(D)	(D)	(D)
PRIVATE TRUCK	-	100.0	-	-	3.5	82.2	-	(D)	(D)	(D)	(D)
AIR	-	100.0	79.9	7.1	7.3	1.3	2.4	(D)	(D)	(D)	(D)
WATER	11	100.0	-	-	-	-	37.0	(D)	(D)	(D)	(D)
OTHER	-	100.0	72.3	24.5	3.2	-	-	(D)	(D)	(D)	(D)
UNKNOWN	2	100.0	99.8	.2	-	-	-	(D)	(D)	(D)	(D)

See footnotes at end of table 4.

TABLE 3. **TCC GROUP 348**—Percent Distribution of Geographic Division of Destination and Means of Transport, by Geographic Division of Origin: 1972—Continued

Geographic division of destination and means of transport	Number	Percent distribution by division of origin[1]								
		U.S. total	New England	Middle Atlantic	East North Central	West North Central	South Atlantic	East South Central	West South Central	Mountain	Pacific
TON-MILES OF SHIPMENTS	(millions of ton-miles)										
U.S. TOTAL	1 224	100.0	5.4	18.7	35.9	11.2	4.8	(D)	(D)	(D)	(D)
RAIL	323	100.0	1.0	10.9	60.5	8.4	.5	(D)	(D)	(D)	(D)
MOTOR CARRIER	714	100.0	6.1	22.3	31.0	11.3	3.2	(D)	(D)	(D)	(D)
PRIVATE TRUCK	119	100.0	9.3	17.2	11.8	24.1	19.1	(D)	(D)	(D)	(D)
AIR	1	100.0	61.4	4.9	16.8	2.4	3.2	(D)	(D)	(D)	(D)
WATER	51	100.0	.4	17.6	13.3	-	20.6	(D)	(D)	(D)	(D)
OTHER	3	100.0	46.1	10.1	26.3	11.6	3.3	(D)	(D)	(D)	(D)
UNKNOWN	9	100.0	55.4	43.6	-	-	.9	(D)	(D)	(D)	(D)
NEW ENGLAND	26	100.0	10.8	32.1	43.7	2.0	6.0	(D)	(D)	(D)	(D)
RAIL	4	100.0	-	-	100.0	-	-	(D)	(D)	(D)	(D)
MOTOR CARRIER	14	100.0	7.8	28.0	46.8	3.8	3.5	(D)	(D)	(D)	(D)
PRIVATE TRUCK	7	100.0	21.7	58.0	6.3	-	14.0	(D)	(D)	(D)	(D)
AIR	-	100.0	63.3	19.0	17.7	-	-	(D)	(D)	(D)	(D)
WATER	-	100.0	100.0	-	-	-	-	(D)	(D)	(D)	(D)
OTHER	-	100.0	50.0	13.1	27.7	-	6.4	(D)	(D)	(D)	(D)
UNKNOWN	-	100.0	6.7	93.3	-	-	-	(D)	(D)	(D)	(D)
MIDDLE ATLANTIC	92	100.0	7.9	20.3	38.6	5.0	2.4	(D)	(D)	(D)	(D)
RAIL	15	100.0	.1	2.1	87.8	-	-	(D)	(D)	(D)	(D)
MOTOR CARRIER	65	100.0	8.2	19.1	33.0	7.1	3.4	(D)	(D)	(D)	(D)
PRIVATE TRUCK	10	100.0	13.9	53.8	2.2	-	-	(D)	(D)	(D)	(D)
AIR	-	100.0	5.4	.3	73.3	3.4	2.7	(D)	(D)	(D)	(D)
WATER	-	100.0	43.0	-	57.0	-	-	(D)	(D)	(D)	(D)
OTHER	-	100.0	85.9	4.4	5.3	-	3.8	(D)	(D)	(D)	(D)
UNKNOWN	-	100.0	1.1	98.9	-	-	-	(D)	(D)	(D)	(D)
EAST NORTH CENTRAL	229	100.0	3.0	16.5	35.2	13.0	2.4	(D)	(D)	(D)	(D)
RAIL	51	100.0	.2	16.4	27.7	.4	-	(D)	(D)	(D)	(D)
MOTOR CARRIER	152	100.0	3.3	18.0	38.6	14.3	2.5	(D)	(D)	(D)	(D)
PRIVATE TRUCK	24	100.0	5.8	6.7	30.5	32.2	7.1	(D)	(D)	(D)	(D)
AIR	-	100.0	42.6	1.5	14.3	6.3	-	(D)	(D)	(D)	(D)
WATER	-	100.0	-	-	-	-	-	(D)	(D)	(D)	(D)
OTHER	-	100.0	41.5	12.4	38.1	3.2	3.8	(D)	(D)	(D)	(D)
UNKNOWN	-	100.0	-	100.0	-	-	-	(D)	(D)	(D)	(D)
WEST NORTH CENTRAL	136	100.0	.8	11.3	43.2	29.9	.9	(D)	(D)	(D)	(D)
RAIL	35	100.0	.4	15.2	45.2	34.2	-	(D)	(D)	(D)	(D)
MOTOR CARRIER	84	100.0	1.0	11.9	49.0	19.3	1.5	(D)	(D)	(D)	(D)
PRIVATE TRUCK	15	100.0	-	-	7.9	77.7	-	(D)	(D)	(D)	(D)
AIR	-	100.0	56.6	-	14.0	2.2	-	(D)	(D)	(D)	(D)
WATER	-	100.0	-	-	-	-	-	(D)	(D)	(D)	(D)
OTHER	1	100.0	14.2	2.8	51.2	30.3	1.1	(D)	(D)	(D)	(D)
UNKNOWN	-	100.0	-	9.4	-	13.4	-	(D)	(D)	(D)	(D)
SOUTH ATLANTIC	176	100.0	1.7	24.5	43.0	5.2	10.5	(D)	(D)	(D)	(D)
RAIL	53	100.0	.2	-	63.3	8.0	3.1	(D)	(D)	(D)	(D)
MOTOR CARRIER	98	100.0	2.5	35.5	36.7	4.9	8.0	(D)	(D)	(D)	(D)
PRIVATE TRUCK	17	100.0	1.4	27.8	15.3	-	51.2	(D)	(D)	(D)	(D)
AIR	-	100.0	6.9	2.7	58.7	-	16.6	(D)	(D)	(D)	(D)
WATER	3	100.0	3.0	-	94.4	-	2.6	(D)	(D)	(D)	(D)
OTHER	-	100.0	29.3	14.5	18.5	10.7	13.8	(D)	(D)	(D)	(D)
UNKNOWN	3	100.0	-	97.5	-	-	2.4	(D)	(D)	(D)	(D)
EAST SOUTH CENTRAL	74	100.0	10.2	16.1	39.0	11.4	8.8	(D)	(D)	(D)	(D)
RAIL	14	100.0	.2	12.2	33.3	43.2	-	(D)	(D)	(D)	(D)
MOTOR CARRIER	44	100.0	3.3	20.0	49.4	2.9	4.0	(D)	(D)	(D)	(D)
PRIVATE TRUCK	14	100.0	40.8	6.9	13.0	7.1	32.0	(D)	(D)	(D)	(D)
AIR	-	100.0	7.3	30.7	62.0	-	-	(D)	(D)	(D)	(D)
WATER	-	100.0	-	-	-	-	-	(D)	(D)	(D)	(D)
OTHER	-	100.0	23.6	22.0	43.9	-	5.2	(D)	(D)	(D)	(D)
UNKNOWN	-	100.0	4.1	95.9	-	-	-	(D)	(D)	(D)	(D)
WEST SOUTH CENTRAL	127	100.0	3.8	24.2	27.3	12.4	8.5	(D)	(D)	(D)	(D)
RAIL	42	100.0	.6	19.9	62.4	3.5	-	(D)	(D)	(D)	(D)
MOTOR CARRIER	54	100.0	6.9	19.1	8.4	23.4	7.6	(D)	(D)	(D)	(D)
PRIVATE TRUCK	13	100.0	2.7	22.0	1.9	11.8	49.1	(D)	(D)	(D)	(D)
AIR	-	100.0	48.4	-	28.4	-	8.5	(D)	(D)	(D)	(D)
WATER	16	100.0	-	54.2	22.0	-	-	(D)	(D)	(D)	(D)
OTHER	-	100.0	81.7	10.4	2.4	1.4	1.2	(D)	(D)	(D)	(D)
UNKNOWN	-	100.0	-	-	-	-	-	(D)	(D)	(D)	(D)
MOUNTAIN	112	100.0	.3	15.0	31.5	18.6	-	(D)	(D)	(D)	(D)
RAIL	31	100.0	.3	35.3	49.4	10.2	-	(D)	(D)	(D)	(D)
MOTOR CARRIER	65	100.0	.3	8.6	30.2	18.8	-	(D)	(D)	(D)	(D)
PRIVATE TRUCK	15	100.0	-	-	-	35.1	-	(D)	(D)	(D)	(D)
AIR	-	100.0	15.9	-	1.4	37.7	30.4	(D)	(D)	(D)	(D)
WATER	-	100.0	-	-	-	-	-	(D)	(D)	(D)	(D)
OTHER	-	100.0	42.2	-	9.3	33.0	2.4	(D)	(D)	(D)	(D)
UNKNOWN	-	100.0	-	-	100.0	-	-	(D)	(D)	(D)	(D)
PACIFIC	248	100.0	13.0	18.2	31.1	2.8	4.7	(D)	(D)	(D)	(D)
RAIL	75	100.0	3.2	-	88.8	-	-	(D)	(D)	(D)	(D)
MOTOR CARRIER	134	100.0	17.6	33.6	7.6	4.5	.9	(D)	(D)	(D)	(D)
PRIVATE TRUCK	-	100.0	-	-	5.4	94.2	-	(D)	(D)	(D)	(D)
AIR	1	100.0	83.0	7.0	5.8	.8	2.1	(D)	(D)	(D)	(D)
WATER	31	100.0	-	-	-	-	33.6	(D)	(D)	(D)	(D)
OTHER	-	100.0	72.7	25.1	2.2	-	-	(D)	(D)	(D)	(D)
UNKNOWN	5	100.0	99.8	.2	-	-	-	(D)	(D)	(D)	(D)

See footnotes at end of table 4.

TABLE 4. **TCC GROUP 348**—Percent Distribution of Distance Shipped and Weight of Shipment, by Means of Transport: 1972

Distance shipped and weight of shipment [2] [3]	Number	Percent distribution by means of transport							
		All means of transport	Rail	Motor carrier	Private truck	Air	Water	Other	Unknown
TONS OF SHIPMENTS	(thousands of tons)								
U.S. TOTAL..........	2 394	100.0	17.9	62.7	16.4	.1	1.5	.4	1.1
UNDER 100 MILES.........	405	100.0	8.0	57.2	33.4	-	.4	.9	.1
UNDER 1000 POUNDS.....	36	100.0	-	63.6	28.2	.1	.2	7.0	.9
1000 TO 9999 POUNDS...	101	100.0	-	49.8	48.9	-	-	1.0	.2
10000 TO 29999 POUNDS.	116	100.0	1.8	54.1	42.8	-	1.3	-	-
30000 TO 59999 POUNDS.	99	100.0	1.1	77.0	21.9	-	-	-	-
60000 TO 89999 POUNDS.	19	100.0	18.3	63.9	17.7	-	-	-	-
90000 POUNDS AND OVER.	31	100.0	81.6	18.4	-	-	-	-	-
100 TO 199 MILES........	459	100.0	9.4	67.7	17.7	-	.2	.5	4.6
UNDER 1000 POUNDS.....	34	100.0	-	76.4	17.7	.2	.1	5.3	.4
1000 TO 9999 POUNDS...	76	100.0	3.1	71.0	22.3	-	1.1	.6	1.9
10000 TO 29999 POUNDS.	130	100.0	7.3	69.8	19.5	-	-	-	3.4
30000 TO 59999 POUNDS.	165	100.0	5.8	65.4	19.7	-	-	-	9.0
60000 TO 89999 POUNDS.	9	100.0	-	100.0	-	-	-	-	-
90000 POUNDS AND OVER.	43	100.0	50.1	49.9	-	-	-	-	-
200 TO 299 MILES........	373	100.0	11.2	71.1	17.2	-	-	.3	.2
UNDER 1000 POUNDS.....	16	100.0	.3	82.2	12.3	.7	-	2.9	1.6
1000 TO 9999 POUNDS...	61	100.0	.7	76.1	21.2	.1	-	.9	1.0
10000 TO 29999 POUNDS.	103	100.0	9.4	66.4	24.2	-	-	-	-
30000 TO 59999 POUNDS.	179	100.0	12.4	74.3	13.3	-	-	-	-
60000 TO 89999 POUNDS.	9	100.0	100.0	-	-	-	-	-	-
90000 POUNDS AND OVER.	2	100.0	-	100.0	-	-	-	-	-
300 TO 499 MILES........	568	100.0	23.1	63.5	11.5	.1	1.6	.2	.1
UNDER 1000 POUNDS.....	23	100.0	-	90.8	4.2	1.0	-	3.1	1.0
1000 TO 9999 POUNDS...	84	100.0	2.3	86.3	10.4	.1	-	.3	.6
10000 TO 29999 POUNDS.	169	100.0	43.0	47.6	9.4	-	-	-	-
30000 TO 59999 POUNDS.	264	100.0	16.3	68.8	14.9	-	-	-	-
60000 TO 89999 POUNDS.	1	100.0	-	100.0	-	-	-	-	-
90000 POUNDS AND OVER.	25	100.0	55.1	9.1	-	-	35.8	-	-
500 TO 999 MILES........	435	100.0	32.7	55.4	9.5	.1	2.1	.2	.1
UNDER 1000 POUNDS.....	26	100.0	.7	91.5	3.8	1.3	-	2.1	.5
1000 TO 9999 POUNDS...	67	100.0	1.0	89.6	9.1	-	-	.2	.2
10000 TO 29999 POUNDS.	80	100.0	22.2	56.2	21.6	-	-	-	-
30000 TO 59999 POUNDS.	191	100.0	31.6	58.1	8.9	-	1.5	-	-
60000 TO 89999 POUNDS.	58	100.0	89.1	-	-	-	10.9	-	-
90000 POUNDS AND OVER.	11	100.0	100.0	-	-	-	-	-	-
1000 TO 1499 MILES......	87	100.0	25.6	60.2	5.3	.1	8.3	.5	-
UNDER 1000 POUNDS.....	9	100.0	2.6	90.9	.5	.9	.9	4.2	-
1000 TO 9999 POUNDS...	16	100.0	-	95.9	3.8	-	-	.3	-
10000 TO 29999 POUNDS.	8	100.0	15.7	76.7	7.6	-	-	-	-
30000 TO 59999 POUNDS.	26	100.0	15.2	63.7	12.1	-	9.0	-	-
60000 TO 89999 POUNDS.	17	100.0	47.1	26.1	-	-	26.9	-	-
90000 POUNDS AND OVER.	8	100.0	100.0	-	-	-	-	-	-
1500 MILES OR OVER......	65	100.0	23.2	60.9	.4	.7	11.4	.4	3.1
UNDER 1000 POUNDS.....	7	100.0	10.7	80.9	-	5.4	-	3.0	.1
1000 TO 9999 POUNDS...	17	100.0	1.7	85.1	1.5	-	-	-	11.7
10000 TO 29999 POUNDS.	5	100.0	-	41.3	-	-	58.7	-	-
30000 TO 59999 POUNDS.	32	100.0	36.4	50.6	-	-	13.0	-	-
60000 TO 89999 POUNDS.	2	100.0	100.0	-	-	-	-	-	-
90000 POUNDS AND OVER.		100.0	-	-	-	-	-	-	-
TON-MILES OF SHIPMENTS	(millions of ton-miles)								
U.S. TOTAL..........	968	100.0	24.5	60.1	9.8	.2	4.2	.3	.9
UNDER 100 MILES.........	22	100.0	13.8	50.3	34.6	-	.4	.8	.1
UNDER 1000 POUNDS.....	1	100.0	-	72.8	19.6	.1	.2	6.7	.7
1000 TO 9999 POUNDS...	6	100.0	-	50.7	48.1	-	-	1.0	.2
10000 TO 29999 POUNDS.	6	100.0	2.5	47.4	48.8	-	1.2	-	-
30000 TO 59999 POUNDS.	4	100.0	2.1	69.2	28.7	-	-	-	-
60000 TO 89999 POUNDS.	1	100.0	28.4	63.0	8.6	-	-	-	-
90000 POUNDS AND OVER.	2	100.0	96.2	3.8	-	-	-	-	-
100 TO 199 MILES........	67	100.0	8.7	68.4	17.4	-	.2	.5	4.8
UNDER 1000 POUNDS.....	5	100.0	-	76.6	17.5	.1	.1	5.3	.4
1000 TO 9999 POUNDS...	10	100.0	3.8	72.7	19.7	-	1.1	.6	2.0
10000 TO 29999 POUNDS.	19	100.0	8.7	71.4	16.2	-	-	-	3.6
30000 TO 59999 POUNDS.	24	100.0	4.1	64.0	22.7	-	-	-	9.2
60000 TO 89999 POUNDS.	1	100.0	-	100.0	-	-	-	-	-
90000 POUNDS AND OVER.	6	100.0	45.7	54.3	-	-	-	-	-

See footnotes at end of table 4.

TABLE 4. TCC GROUP 348—Percent Distribution of Distance Shipped and Weight of Shipment, by Means of Transport: 1972—Continued

Distance shipped and weight of shipment[2] [3]	Number	Percent distribution by means of transport							
		All means of transport	Rail	Motor carrier	Private truck	Air	Water	Other	Unknown
TON-MILES OF SHIPMENTS	(millions of ton-miles)								
200 TO 299 MILES........	93	100.0	11.6	70.7	17.2	-	-	.3	.2
UNDER 1000 POUNDS.....	4	100.0	.3	82.8	11.6	.7	-	2.9	1.7
1000 TO 9999 POUNDS...	14	100.0	.8	76.2	21.0	.1	-	.9	1.1
10000 TO 29999 POUNDS.	27	100.0	9.5	66.8	23.7	-	-	-	-
30000 TO 59999 POUNDS.	44	100.0	12.5	73.8	13.6	-	-	-	-
60000 TO 89999 POUNDS.	2	100.0	100.0	-	-	-	-	-	-
90000 POUNDS AND OVER.	-	100.0	-	100.0	-	-	-	-	-
300 TO 499 MILES........	227	100.0	24.2	62.8	10.9	.1	1.8	.2	.1
UNDER 1000 POUNDS.....	9	100.0	-	90.8	4.4	1.0	-	2.9	.9
1000 TO 9999 POUNDS...	33	100.0	2.6	85.6	10.7	.2	-	.2	.8
10000 TO 29999 POUNDS.	70	100.0	44.1	47.7	8.2	-	-	-	-
30000 TO 59999 POUNDS.	103	100.0	17.2	68.3	14.5	-	-	-	-
60000 TO 89999 POUNDS.	-	100.0	-	100.0	-	-	-	-	-
90000 POUNDS AND OVER.	10	100.0	51.5	9.0	-	-	39.5	-	-
500 TO 999 MILES........	306	100.0	34.7	53.5	9.4	.1	2.1	.2	.1
UNDER 1000 POUNDS.....	18	100.0	.7	92.0	3.3	1.4	-	2.1	.5
1000 TO 9999 POUNDS...	46	100.0	.8	91.2	7.6	-	-	.2	.3
10000 TO 29999 POUNDS.	56	100.0	20.6	56.5	22.9	-	-	-	-
30000 TO 59999 POUNDS.	132	100.0	35.0	54.8	8.8	-	1.3	-	-
60000 TO 89999 POUNDS.	44	100.0	89.2	-	-	-	10.8	-	-
90000 POUNDS AND OVER.	8	100.0	100.0	-	-	-	-	-	-
1000 TO 1499 MILES......	105	100.0	26.1	59.4	5.2	.1	8.7	.5	-
UNDER 1000 POUNDS.....	11	100.0	2.4	91.4	.4	.9	.8	4.1	-
1000 TO 9999 POUNDS...	19	100.0	-	96.3	3.4	-	-	.3	-
10000 TO 29999 POUNDS.	10	100.0	15.4	76.0	8.6	-	-	-	-
30000 TO 59999 POUNDS.	31	100.0	15.3	62.6	12.4	-	9.7	-	-
60000 TO 89999 POUNDS.	22	100.0	43.8	28.7	-	-	27.4	-	-
90000 POUNDS AND OVER.	11	100.0	100.0	-	-	-	-	-	-
1500 MILES OR OVER......	144	100.0	19.9	60.9	.3	.7	14.4	.3	3.5
UNDER 1000 POUNDS.....	15	100.0	12.8	77.6	-	6.5	-	3.1	.1
1000 TO 9999 POUNDS...	38	100.0	2.0	83.9	1.1	-	-	-	13.0
10000 TO 29999 POUNDS.	14	100.0	-	39.9	-	-	60.1	-	-
30000 TO 59999 POUNDS.	71	100.0	30.9	52.5	-	-	16.6	-	-
60000 TO 89999 POUNDS.	3	100.0	100.0	-	-	-	-	-	-
90000 POUNDS AND OVER.	-	100.0	-	-	-	-	-	-	-

Note: Detail may not add to total due to rounding. The introductory table shows the estimates of sampling variability for tons; sampling variability for ton-miles has not been estimated. See the map in the Introduction for the States comprising the geographic divisions of the United States.

Shipments excluded from the survey are those moving by pipeline (primarily petroleum products from refineries), parcel post shipments, and commodities moved by own power (motorized vehicles, aircraft, etc.) or towed (prefabricated buildings, etc.). Local shipments (commodities shipped less than 25 miles from the plant) and shipments within the same city are also excluded. Shipments to Alaska and Hawaii from the 48 conterminous States and the District of Columbia are included; however, no data were obtained for shipments originating in Alaska and Hawaii.

- Represents zero or rounds to zero. (D) Withheld to avoid disclosing figures for individual companies.

[1]Production of this commodity is concentrated in the geographic divisions shown; figures and distributions for geographic divisions not shown are included in the total.
[2]Distances of shipments to foreign destinations are calculated only to the U.S. port of exit.
[3]Includes only shipments represented by bills of lading and invoices. Summary records which did not show individual weights of shipments are not included.

TCC 349. Miscellaneous Fabricated Metal Products

Comparisons of Tons and Ton-Miles of Shipments for
Geographic Divisions of Origin and for Sampling Variability: 1972 and 1967

Geographic division of origin	Estimates				Relative sampling variability in tons (percent)	
	1972		1967		1972	1967
	Tons (thousands)	Ton-miles (millions)	Tons (thousands)	Ton-miles (millions)		
U.S. total	6,671	2,646	5,495	2,803	17.2	9.6
New England	102	63	158	76	25.6	(*)
Middle Atlantic	1,037	319	1,267	603	37.7	(*)
East North Central	2,642	1,428	1,582	538	41.5	(*)
West North Central	141	73	235	98	25.7	(*)
South Atlantic	604	134	227	93	46.5	(*)
East South Central	426	144	1,088	579	38.8	(*)
West South Central	(D)	(D)	238	127	(*)	(*)
Mountain	(D)	(D)	4	3	(*)	(*)
Pacific	(D)	(D)	696	686	(*)	(*)

(D) Withheld to avoid disclosing figures for individual companies.   (*) Data not published.

TABLE 1. TCC GROUP 349—Percent Distribution of Geographic Division of Origin and Distance Shipped, by Means of Transport: 1972

Geographic division of origin [1] and distance shipped [2]	Number	Percent distribution by means of transport							
		All means of transport	Rail	Motor carrier	Private truck	Air	Water	Other	Unknown
TONS OF SHIPMENTS	(thousands of tons)								
U.S. TOTAL..........	6 671	100.0	18.2	43.2	36.7	.2	.5	.9	.2
NEW ENGLAND..............	102	100.0	3.6	82.4	8.3	1.4	.3	2.0	2.0
UNDER 100 MILES.......	38	100.0	-	82.2	14.8	.1	.7	2.1	-
100 TO 199 MILES......	12	100.0	.5	89.7	6.6	.3	-	2.9	-
200 TO 299 MILES......	4	100.0	-	97.1	-	.1	-	2.8	-
300 TO 499 MILES......	2	100.0	-	91.9	-	1.3	-	6.8	-
500 TO 999 MILES......	23	100.0	10.3	69.9	8.8	.9	-	1.7	8.4
1000 TO 1499 MILES....	3	100.0	10.0	60.6	-	25.2	-	4.2	-
1500 MILES OR OVER....	16	100.0	4.6	94.5	-	.5	-	.3	-
MIDDLE ATLANTIC.........	1 037	100.0	2.3	44.2	51.0	.1	.9	1.5	.1
UNDER 100 MILES.......	457	100.0	.5	20.4	77.7	-	.2	1.2	.1
100 TO 199 MILES......	170	100.0	1.7	38.8	57.5	-	.9	1.0	.1
200 TO 299 MILES......	115	100.0	-	56.0	43.1	.1	-	.7	-
300 TO 499 MILES......	111	100.0	1.5	83.8	12.4	.2	-	1.9	.1
500 TO 999 MILES....	106	100.0	6.4	82.6	7.4	.2	-	3.2	.2
1000 TO 1499 MILES....	40	100.0	11.7	65.8	6.4	.3	11.6	4.2	-
1500 MILES OR OVER....	35	100.0	14.4	72.8	4.3	.4	5.7	2.0	.4
EAST NORTH CENTRAL......	2 642	100.0	36.1	46.5	15.9	.1	-	1.3	.1
UNDER 100 MILES.......	678	100.0	2.9	47.7	46.4	-	-	2.9	-
100 TO 199 MILES......	275	100.0	11.1	58.3	27.3	-	-	3.2	-
200 TO 299 MILES......	229	100.0	9.5	84.8	5.0	.3	-	.5	-
300 TO 499 MILES......	391	100.0	34.0	63.7	1.3	.1	-	.7	.2
500 TO 999 MILES......	693	100.0	65.3	32.5	1.7	.2	-	.2	.2
1000 TO 1499 MILES....	48	100.0	55.5	42.9	.9	.4	-	.2	-
1500 MILES OR OVER....	325	100.0	82.9	16.3	.4	.3	-	.1	-
WEST NORTH CENTRAL......	141	100.0	1.3	75.7	17.1	.8	-	5.0	-
UNDER 100 MILES.......	7	100.0	-	26.1	37.2	-	-	36.7	.1
100 TO 199 MILES......	15	100.0	-	70.6	26.8	-	-	2.6	-
200 TO 299 MILES......	21	100.0	-	58.0	37.8	.1	-	4.0	.1
300 TO 499 MILES......	40	100.0	1.4	90.2	6.2	-	-	2.2	-
500 TO 999 MILES......	40	100.0	3.0	76.6	13.9	2.4	-	4.0	-
1000 TO 1499 MILES....	13	100.0	-	87.5	8.0	.6	-	3.9	-
1500 MILES OR OVER....	2	100.0	-	93.5	-	.7	-	5.8	-
SOUTH ATLANTIC..........	604	100.0	3.1	65.9	30.5	-	.3	.1	-
UNDER 100 MILES.......	223	100.0	.7	53.2	45.7	-	-	.3	-
100 TO 199 MILES......	125	100.0	4.0	78.3	16.7	-	1.0	-	-
200 TO 299 MILES......	120	100.0	.9	71.8	27.3	-	-	-	-
300 TO 499 MILES......	72	100.0	6.2	66.0	27.9	-	-	-	-
500 TO 999 MILES......	56	100.0	7.9	77.0	14.6	-	.5	-	-
1000 TO 1499 MILES....	3	100.0	-	97.5	2.5	-	-	-	-
1500 MILES OR OVER....	2	100.0	79.5	20.4	-	.1	-	-	-
EAST SOUTH CENTRAL......	426	100.0	27.2	25.4	42.8	-	4.5	.1	-
UNDER 100 MILES.......	122	100.0	.2	9.5	90.3	-	-	-	-
100 TO 199 MILES......	27	100.0	-	67.7	32.2	-	-	.1	-
200 TO 299 MILES......	89	100.0	10.1	22.7	45.7	-	21.4	-	-
300 TO 499 MILES......	82	100.0	38.8	40.0	20.9	.1	-	.1	-
500 TO 999 MILES......	93	100.0	70.6	23.9	5.2	-	-	.2	-
1000 TO 1499 MILES....	2	100.0	91.8	8.0	-	-	-	.2	-
1500 MILES OR OVER....	8	100.0	78.0	21.6	-	.1	-	.3	-
TON-MILES OF SHIPMENTS	(millions of ton-miles)								
U.S. TOTAL..........	2 646	100.0	43.0	43.9	10.5	.6	1.1	.6	.3
NEW ENGLAND..............	63	100.0	6.4	84.9	2.7	2.4	-	1.2	2.3
UNDER 100 MILES.......	1	100.0	-	86.2	11.3	.1	.5	1.9	-
100 TO 199 MILES......	1	100.0	.5	89.3	7.1	.2	-	2.9	-
200 TO 299 MILES......	1	100.0	-	96.9	-	.1	-	2.9	-
300 TO 499 MILES......	-	100.0	-	92.2	-	1.2	-	6.6	-
500 TO 999 MILES......	17	100.0	11.6	69.4	7.8	.9	-	1.6	8.8
1000 TO 1499 MILES....	4	100.0	10.5	62.7	-	22.9	-	3.8	-
1500 MILES OR OVER....	35	100.0	4.4	94.5	.1	.6	-	.4	-
MIDDLE ATLANTIC.........	319	100.0	7.4	68.3	18.1	.2	3.4	2.4	.2
UNDER 100 MILES.......	20	100.0	.7	28.5	69.3	-	.2	1.3	.1
100 TO 199 MILES......	25	100.0	1.8	43.2	52.9	.1	1.1	1.0	.1
200 TO 299 MILES......	27	100.0	-	56.5	42.6	.1	-	.7	-
300 TO 499 MILES......	42	100.0	1.5	83.4	12.6	.2	-	2.2	.1
500 TO 999 MILES......	77	100.0	6.6	81.1	8.8	.3	-	3.1	.2
1000 TO 1499 MILES....	48	100.0	12.2	65.0	6.1	.3	12.2	4.1	-
1500 MILES OR OVER....	76	100.0	14.9	72.4	4.1	.4	5.9	2.0	.4
EAST NORTH CENTRAL......	1 428	100.0	65.2	31.3	2.9	.2	-	.3	.1
UNDER 100 MILES.......	29	100.0	3.9	42.3	52.2	-	-	1.5	-
100 TO 199 MILES......	38	100.0	9.4	58.5	29.0	-	-	3.1	-
200 TO 299 MILES......	54	100.0	10.1	84.5	4.6	.3	-	.5	-
300 TO 499 MILES......	151	100.0	35.4	62.5	1.1	.1	-	.7	.2
500 TO 999 MILES......	515	100.0	68.9	29.0	1.5	.2	-	.2	.2
1000 TO 1499 MILES....	56	100.0	55.5	42.9	.8	.5	-	.2	-
1500 MILES OR OVER....	581	100.0	82.4	16.7	.4	.3	-	.1	-

See footnotes at end of table 4.

TABLE 1. **TCC GROUP 349**—Percent Distribution of Geographic Division of Origin and Distance Shipped, by Means of Transport: 1972—Continued

Geographic division of origin[1] and distance shipped[2]	Number	Percent distribution by means of transport							
		All means of transport	Rail	Motor carrier	Private truck	Air	Water	Other	Unknown
TON-MILES OF SHIPMENTS	(millions of ton-miles)								
WEST NORTH CENTRAL......	73	100.0	1.8	81.7	11.3	1.4	-	3.8	-
UNDER 100 MILES.......	-	100.0	-	33.5	23.4	-	-	43.1	.1
100 TO 199 MILES......	2	100.0	-	76.5	21.2	-	-	2.2	-
200 TO 299 MILES......	5	100.0	-	59.2	36.4	.1	-	4.1	.1
300 TO 499 MILES......	15	100.0	1.6	90.6	5.7	-	-	2.1	-
500 TO 999 MILES.....	29	100.0	3.7	76.4	12.6	3.1	-	4.3	-
1000 TO 1499 MILES....	15	100.0	-	88.0	7.8	.6	-	3.6	-
1500 MILES OR OVER....	4	100.0	-	93.8	-	.6	-	5.6	-
SOUTH ATLANTIC..........	134	100.0	8.2	70.8	20.6	-	.4	.1	-
UNDER 100 MILES.......	10	100.0	.2	59.7	39.4	-	-	.7	-
100 TO 199 MILES......	19	100.0	3.9	78.7	16.2	-	1.2	-	-
200 TO 299 MILES......	29	100.0	.8	75.1	24.1	-	-	-	-
300 TO 499 MILES......	26	100.0	5.7	67.1	27.2	-	-	-	-
500 TO 999 MILES.....	37	100.0	8.9	74.3	16.0	-	.7	-	-
1000 TO 1499 MILES....	4	100.0	-	98.0	2.0	-	-	-	-
1500 MILES OR OVER....	6	100.0	79.0	20.9	-	.1	-	-	-
EAST SOUTH CENTRAL......	144	100.0	51.4	28.0	17.1	-	3.3	.2	-
UNDER 100 MILES.......	5	100.0	.1	8.0	91.9	-	-	-	-
100 TO 199 MILES......	4	100.0	-	74.0	25.9	-	-	.1	-
200 TO 299 MILES......	21	100.0	10.8	23.5	44.0	-	21.6	-	-
300 TO 499 MILES......	32	100.0	40.0	41.0	18.7	.1	-	.1	-
500 TO 999 MILES.....	61	100.0	71.4	23.8	4.6	-	-	.2	-
1000 TO 1499 MILES....	2	100.0	90.7	9.0	-	-	-	.2	-
1500 MILES OR OVER....	16	100.0	78.4	21.2	-	.1	-	.3	-

See footnotes at end of table 4.

TABLE 2. **TCC GROUP 349**—Percent Distribution of Geographic Division of Origin and Means of Transport, by Geographic Division of Destination: 1972

Geographic division of origin[1] and means of transport	Number	Percent distribution by division of destination									
		U.S. total	New England	Middle Atlantic	East North Central	West North Central	South Atlantic	East South Central	West South Central	Mountain	Pacific
TONS OF SHIPMENTS	(thousands of tons)										
U.S. TOTAL..............	6 671	100.0	2.3	13.1	23.8	4.4	13.2	5.7	18.2	1.0	18.4
RAIL................	1 214	100.0	1.8	3.5	8.2	9.7	8.5	5.3	34.8	1.0	27.1
MOTOR CARRIER........	2 883	100.0	2.9	13.8	32.9	4.9	17.9	7.2	8.0	1.5	10.8
PRIVATE TRUCK........	2 446	100.0	1.8	17.0	20.4	1.0	10.4	4.2	21.7	.3	23.2
AIR.................	13	100.0	4.8	29.8	12.3	3.0	19.1	2.1	9.4	2.5	16.9
WATER...............	35	100.0	.7	8.1	.3	-	2.9	-	66.6	-	21.3
OTHER...............	62	100.0	3.7	13.1	52.8	11.6	7.9	1.9	3.6	1.5	3.8
UNKNOWN.............	12	100.0	9.6	7.5	21.2	5.2	2.8	.9	.7	2.3	49.8
NEW ENGLAND............	102	100.0	30.4	24.5	12.1	1.4	5.8	7.8	8.8	.7	8.6
RAIL................	3	100.0	-	1.7	49.2	3.1	.3	17.6	17.8	.7	9.6
MOTOR CARRIER........	84	100.0	29.6	27.4	8.9	1.4	3.6	8.7	9.8	.8	9.8
PRIVATE TRUCK........	8	100.0	59.2	16.0	8.4	-	16.4	-	-	-	.1
AIR.................	1	100.0	3.3	4.4	8.6	.7	75.2	.2	1.5	-	6.1
WATER...............	-	100.0	100.0	-	-	-	-	-	-	-	-
OTHER...............	2	100.0	39.8	22.6	10.3	4.3	19.3	-	1.0	-	2.8
UNKNOWN.............	2	100.0	-	-	100.0	-	-	-	-	-	-
MIDDLE ATLANTIC.........	1 037	100.0	5.9	53.5	15.7	4.2	12.3	1.6	3.6	.7	2.6
RAIL................	23	100.0	-	19.0	18.0	15.6	4.0	4.3	13.6	8.4	17.0
MOTOR CARRIER........	458	100.0	5.2	33.2	31.1	7.2	9.6	2.9	5.5	1.1	4.3
PRIVATE TRUCK........	528	100.0	6.9	73.7	2.5	.9	14.9	.3	.5	.1	.2
AIR.................	-	100.0	6.0	24.6	15.6	6.2	19.8	8.2	6.4	1.5	11.6
WATER...............	9	100.0	-	17.7	-	-	8.5	-	51.9	-	21.9
OTHER...............	15	100.0	6.8	38.1	18.3	7.5	16.1	3.0	7.3	.7	2.3
UNKNOWN.............	-	100.0	.2	51.3	4.1	-	29.5	-	-	14.8	-
EAST NORTH CENTRAL......	2 642	100.0	1.1	5.7	41.3	6.6	10.0	6.9	15.6	.5	12.2
RAIL................	954	100.0	1.2	3.1	6.2	11.8	6.0	5.4	37.8	.2	28.2
MOTOR CARRIER........	1 227	100.0	1.3	8.6	50.0	4.3	16.5	10.2	4.1	.9	4.2
PRIVATE TRUCK........	420	100.0	.2	3.1	92.7	1.0	1.1	1.5	.2	-	.3
AIR.................	3	100.0	4.3	13.0	19.6	8.5	6.0	3.2	14.5	3.2	27.6
WATER...............	-	100.0	-	-	100.0	-	-	-	-	-	-
OTHER...............	33	100.0	.8	2.6	80.5	10.7	2.1	.9	1.3	-	1.1
UNKNOWN.............	2	100.0	45.0	17.7	13.1	22.5	.5	-	-	.3	.8
WEST NORTH CENTRAL......	141	100.0	2.6	10.5	35.7	16.3	8.1	8.7	11.9	2.0	4.2
RAIL................	1	100.0	-	-	31.5	-	-	.7	67.9	-	-
MOTOR CARRIER........	107	100.0	3.3	10.5	40.1	10.6	8.1	11.2	9.0	1.9	5.3
PRIVATE TRUCK........	24	100.0	-	9.1	17.5	38.8	8.6	.3	23.4	2.3	-
AIR.................	1	100.0	.6	59.1	2.3	-	29.9	1.8	1.0	1.4	4.0
WATER...............	-	100.0	-	-	-	-	-	-	-	-	-
OTHER...............	7	100.0	2.0	11.2	37.4	31.7	5.3	2.7	3.6	3.3	2.8
UNKNOWN.............	-	100.0	-	-	-	100.0	-	-	-	-	-

See footnotes at end of table 4.

TABLE 2. TCC GROUP 349—Percent Distribution of Geographic Division of Origin and Means of Transport, by Geographic Division of Destination: 1972—Continued

Geographic division of origin [1] and means of transport	Number	U.S. total	New England	Middle Atlantic	East North Central	West North Central	South Atlantic	East South Central	West South Central	Mountain	Pacific
TONS OF SHIPMENTS	(thousands of tons)										
SOUTH ATLANTIC	604	100.0	1.3	15.5	10.2	1.1	64.4	5.3	1.3	.5	.5
RAIL	19	100.0	3.0	.6	8.9	-	46.8	11.5	16.7	-	12.5
MOTOR CARRIER	398	100.0	1.3	21.0	12.6	1.3	55.8	6.7	.4	.7	.1
PRIVATE TRUCK	184	100.0	1.0	4.8	5.1	.6	85.1	1.8	1.5	-	-
AIR	-	100.0	1.0	-	72.9	-	15.8	1.8	-	-	8.5
WATER	1	100.0	-	82.3	-	-	17.7	-	-	-	-
OTHER	-	100.0	-	.3	.1	-	99.4	.1	-	-	-
UNKNOWN	-	100.0	-	-	-	-	100.0	-	-	-	-
EAST SOUTH CENTRAL	426	100.0	.8	2.5	38.1	4.0	11.0	25.8	15.2	.6	1.9
RAIL	116	100.0	-	3.0	27.8	1.1	19.4	8.0	33.1	2.0	5.6
MOTOR CARRIER	108	100.0	3.0	6.6	48.2	13.2	12.8	8.8	5.6	.3	1.5
PRIVATE TRUCK	182	100.0	-	-	42.8	.9	5.8	50.0	.6	-	-
AIR	-	100.0	-	7.9	7.0	1.3	17.9	-	62.9	-	3.0
WATER	19	100.0	-	-	-	-	-	-	100.0	-	-
OTHER	-	100.0	1.5	11.1	16.6	8.8	19.6	13.8	21.7	-	6.9
UNKNOWN	-	100.0	-	-	-	-	-	-	-	-	-
TON-MILES OF SHIPMENTS	(millions of ton-miles)										
U.S. TOTAL	2 646	100.0	2.7	7.2	12.1	5.7	11.1	4.8	22.8	2.4	31.3
RAIL	1 137	100.0	1.7	2.4	2.3	4.6	5.1	2.9	30.8	1.1	49.0
MOTOR CARRIER	1 160	100.0	3.5	10.8	20.4	7.2	16.6	6.4	12.6	3.9	18.6
PRIVATE TRUCK	278	100.0	3.1	11.1	18.1	3.7	13.2	6.3	33.1	1.6	9.7
AIR	15	100.0	5.8	34.0	10.4	1.7	15.6	1.1	5.6	2.4	23.5
WATER	29	100.0	-	1.7	-	-	1.0	-	35.8	-	61.4
OTHER	16	100.0	4.2	10.4	22.7	15.7	12.9	3.8	13.4	3.1	13.8
UNKNOWN	7	100.0	12.5	3.6	27.6	3.7	4.7	.6	.8	4.4	42.2
NEW ENGLAND	63	100.0	2.6	6.0	13.3	2.4	6.9	9.5	21.5	2.3	35.6
RAIL	4	100.0	-	.2	34.3	3.3	.1	14.8	23.5	1.3	22.5
MOTOR CARRIER	54	100.0	2.5	6.6	9.0	2.4	3.9	10.1	23.5	2.6	39.5
PRIVATE TRUCK	1	100.0	12.6	8.3	27.5	-	50.4	-	-	-	1.1
AIR	1	100.0	.1	.9	5.8	.7	75.6	.1	2.1	-	14.6
WATER	-	100.0	100.0	-	-	-	-	-	-	-	-
OTHER	-	100.0	6.7	10.4	18.8	12.5	28.9	.1	3.5	-	19.0
UNKNOWN	1	100.0	-	-	100.0	-	-	-	-	-	-
MIDDLE ATLANTIC	319	100.0	4.4	14.2	18.5	11.2	10.7	3.4	13.9	4.1	19.6
RAIL	23	100.0	-	2.0	8.5	16.3	1.2	2.9	15.6	13.7	39.7
MOTOR CARRIER	218	100.0	3.2	10.5	23.3	11.9	8.8	3.8	13.9	3.9	20.8
PRIVATE TRUCK	57	100.0	11.5	36.7	8.4	7.9	22.6	2.5	5.2	1.7	3.7
AIR	-	100.0	1.6	7.2	10.7	7.7	16.7	8.5	10.3	2.9	34.4
WATER	10	100.0	-	2.5	-	-	.4	-	55.2	-	41.9
OTHER	7	100.0	3.3	7.0	19.5	15.7	14.5	4.6	20.3	2.8	12.3
UNKNOWN	-	100.0	.1	5.1	3.5	-	39.1	-	-	52.2	-
EAST NORTH CENTRAL	1 428	100.0	1.4	4.6	8.0	5.3	9.1	5.1	24.8	1.1	40.5
RAIL	930	100.0	.8	1.4	.9	5.2	3.4	3.1	33.4	.2	51.6
MOTOR CARRIER	447	100.0	2.5	10.8	17.0	5.7	21.5	9.0	9.5	3.0	21.0
PRIVATE TRUCK	41	100.0	1.1	7.6	68.4	3.2	2.5	9.3	2.1	-	5.8
AIR	3	100.0	3.3	8.1	5.2	4.5	4.0	1.4	13.1	4.5	55.9
WATER	-	100.0	-	-	100.0	-	-	-	-	-	-
OTHER	4	100.0	3.7	7.7	34.6	20.0	7.0	2.5	8.6	.3	15.5
UNKNOWN	1	100.0	60.8	15.2	4.9	15.4	.4	-	-	.7	2.7
WEST NORTH CENTRAL	73	100.0	6.0	16.9	22.8	6.9	12.8	6.9	12.5	2.9	12.3
RAIL	1	100.0	-	-	18.8	-	-	.9	80.3	-	-
MOTOR CARRIER	60	100.0	7.0	16.2	25.2	4.9	11.5	8.2	10.0	2.5	14.4
PRIVATE TRUCK	8	100.0	-	16.6	10.8	21.5	22.8	.5	22.9	4.6	.1
AIR	1	100.0	.7	59.2	.7	-	30.1	1.2	.6	1.1	6.3
WATER	-	100.0	-	-	-	-	-	-	-	-	-
OTHER	2	100.0	5.8	25.3	18.2	12.5	11.2	3.3	5.9	6.8	11.1
UNKNOWN	-	100.0	-	-	-	100.0	-	-	-	-	-
SOUTH ATLANTIC	134	100.0	2.9	12.9	20.6	3.8	41.6	5.6	4.8	2.9	4.8
RAIL	11	100.0	4.0	.1	5.1	-	13.7	7.5	22.6	-	46.9
MOTOR CARRIER	95	100.0	2.3	15.1	25.0	4.6	40.2	5.9	1.4	4.1	1.4
PRIVATE TRUCK	27	100.0	4.3	10.1	12.0	2.7	57.2	4.0	9.6	-	-
AIR	-	100.0	1.0	-	68.3	-	2.0	1.1	-	-	27.5
WATER	-	100.0	-	45.5	-	-	54.5	-	-	-	-
OTHER	-	100.0	-	.8	1.1	-	96.9	.2	-	-	1.0
UNKNOWN	-	100.0	-	-	-	-	100.0	-	-	-	-
EAST SOUTH CENTRAL	144	100.0	1.7	4.2	24.8	5.3	15.3	10.5	25.5	1.9	10.9
RAIL	74	100.0	-	2.4	18.6	.7	16.9	3.2	38.0	3.2	16.9
MOTOR CARRIER	40	100.0	6.0	10.6	31.3	15.8	14.6	5.1	7.9	1.0	7.7
PRIVATE TRUCK	24	100.0	-	-	37.3	2.7	14.6	43.2	2.1	-	-
AIR	-	100.0	-	9.8	7.2	1.7	18.6	-	50.2	-	12.5
WATER	4	100.0	-	-	-	-	-	-	100.0	-	-
OTHER	-	100.0	1.8	10.8	9.3	8.2	11.6	9.1	25.7	-	23.4
UNKNOWN	-	100.0	-	-	-	-	-	-	-	-	-

See footnotes at end of table 4.

TABLE 3. **TCC GROUP 349**—Percent Distribution of Geographic Division of Destination and Means of Transport, by Geographic Division of Origin: 1972

Geographic division of destination and means of transport	Number	Percent distribution by division of origin [1]								
		U.S. total	New England	Middle Atlantic	East North Central	West North Central	South Atlantic	East South Central	West South Central	Mountain	Pacific
TONS OF SHIPMENTS	(thousands of tons)										
U.S. TOTAL..............	6 671	100.0	1.5	15.5	39.6	2.1	9.1	6.4	(D)	(D)	(D)
RAIL.................	1 214	100.0	.3	1.9	78.6	.1	1.6	9.6	(D)	(D)	(D)
MOTOR CARRIER.........	2 883	100.0	2.9	15.9	42.6	3.7	13.8	3.7	(D)	(D)	(D)
PRIVATE TRUCK.........	2 446	100.0	.3	21.6	17.2	1.0	7.5	7.5	(D)	(D)	(D)
AIR..................	13	100.0	10.3	7.2	24.2	8.1	.3	1.1	(D)	(D)	(D)
WATER................	35	100.0	.7	25.5	.3	-	4.4	53.4	(D)	(D)	(D)
OTHER................	62	100.0	3.3	25.0	54.0	11.3	1.2	.6	(D)	(D)	(D)
UNKNOWN..............	12	100.0	16.0	7.2	21.4	.2	-	-	(D)	(D)	(D)
NEW ENGLAND............	153	100.0	20.4	39.9	19.8	2.4	5.0	2.1	(D)	(D)	(D)
RAIL.................	21	100.0	-	-	55.1	-	2.7	-	(D)	(D)	(D)
MOTOR CARRIER.........	83	100.0	29.9	28.4	19.5	4.2	6.3	3.9	(D)	(D)	(D)
PRIVATE TRUCK.........	43	100.0	11.5	82.7	1.6	-	4.2	-	(D)	(D)	(D)
AIR..................	-	100.0	7.0	8.9	21.6	1.0	.1	-	(D)	(D)	(D)
WATER................	-	100.0	100.0	-	-	-	-	-	(D)	(D)	(D)
OTHER................	2	100.0	35.5	45.8	11.1	6.2	-	.2	(D)	(D)	(D)
UNKNOWN..............	1	100.0	-	.2	99.8	-	-	-	(D)	(D)	(D)
MIDDLE ATLANTIC.........	874	100.0	2.9	63.4	17.2	1.7	10.7	1.2	(D)	(D)	(D)
RAIL.................	42	100.0	.1	10.4	68.9	-	.3	8.2	(D)	(D)	(D)
MOTOR CARRIER.........	399	100.0	5.8	38.1	26.6	2.8	20.9	1.8	(D)	(D)	(D)
PRIVATE TRUCK.........	416	100.0	.3	93.6	3.2	.5	2.1	-	(D)	(D)	(D)
AIR..................	4	100.0	1.5	5.9	10.6	16.0	-	.3	(D)	(D)	(D)
WATER................	2	100.0	-	55.4	-	-	44.6	-	(D)	(D)	(D)
OTHER................	8	100.0	5.7	73.0	10.7	9.7	-	.5	(D)	(D)	(D)
UNKNOWN..............	-	100.0	-	49.2	50.3	-	-	-	(D)	(D)	(D)
EAST NORTH CENTRAL......	1 585	100.0	.8	10.3	68.8	3.2	3.9	10.2	(D)	(D)	(D)
RAIL.................	99	100.0	1.8	4.2	59.4	.6	1.7	32.2	(D)	(D)	(D)
MOTOR CARRIER.........	949	100.0	.8	15.0	64.6	4.5	5.3	5.5	(D)	(D)	(D)
PRIVATE TRUCK.........	498	100.0	.1	2.7	78.1	.9	1.9	15.6	(D)	(D)	(D)
AIR..................	1	100.0	7.2	9.1	38.6	1.5	1.6	.6	(D)	(D)	(D)
WATER................	-	100.0	-	-	100.0	-	-	-	(D)	(D)	(D)
OTHER................	33	100.0	.6	8.7	82.2	8.0	-	.2	(D)	(D)	(D)
UNKNOWN..............	2	100.0	75.5	1.4	13.2	-	-	-	(D)	(D)	(D)
WEST NORTH CENTRAL......	291	100.0	.5	14.7	59.8	7.9	2.2	5.9	(D)	(D)	(D)
RAIL.................	117	100.0	.1	3.1	95.7	-	-	1.1	(D)	(D)	(D)
MOTOR CARRIER.........	142	100.0	.9	23.4	37.3	8.0	3.8	10.0	(D)	(D)	(D)
PRIVATE TRUCK.........	23	100.0	-	21.0	17.6	40.2	4.9	6.6	(D)	(D)	(D)
AIR..................	-	100.0	2.3	14.8	68.4	.1	-	.5	(D)	(D)	(D)
WATER................	-	100.0	-	-	-	-	-	-	(D)	(D)	(D)
OTHER................	7	100.0	1.2	16.3	49.9	30.9	-	.5	(D)	(D)	(D)
UNKNOWN..............	-	100.0	-	-	92.2	4.2	-	-	(D)	(D)	(D)
SOUTH ATLANTIC.........	883	100.0	.7	14.4	30.0	1.3	44.1	5.3	(D)	(D)	(D)
RAIL.................	103	100.0	-	.9	54.7	-	8.6	21.6	(D)	(D)	(D)
MOTOR CARRIER.........	515	100.0	.6	8.5	39.3	1.7	43.1	2.7	(D)	(D)	(D)
PRIVATE TRUCK.........	255	100.0	.5	30.9	1.7	.8	61.5	4.2	(D)	(D)	(D)
AIR..................	2	100.0	40.5	7.4	7.6	12.6	.2	1.0	(D)	(D)	(D)
WATER................	1	100.0	-	73.6	-	-	26.4	-	(D)	(D)	(D)
OTHER................	4	100.0	8.1	51.2	14.1	7.6	15.5	1.5	(D)	(D)	(D)
UNKNOWN..............	-	100.0	-	76.9	3.7	-	.5	-	(D)	(D)	(D)
EAST SOUTH CENTRAL......	378	100.0	2.1	4.4	48.4	3.3	8.5	29.0	(D)	(D)	(D)
RAIL.................	64	100.0	1.0	1.6	79.7	-	3.4	14.3	(D)	(D)	(D)
MOTOR CARRIER.........	208	100.0	3.5	6.3	59.9	5.8	12.9	4.6	(D)	(D)	(D)
PRIVATE TRUCK.........	103	100.0	-	1.6	5.9	.1	3.2	87.9	(D)	(D)	(D)
AIR..................	-	100.0	.8	28.0	36.6	6.9	.2	-	(D)	(D)	(D)
WATER................	-	100.0	-	-	-	-	-	-	(D)	(D)	(D)
OTHER................	1	100.0	.1	39.2	26.6	15.9	.1	4.4	(D)	(D)	(D)
UNKNOWN..............	-	100.0	-	-	-	-	-	-	(D)	(D)	(D)
WEST SOUTH CENTRAL......	1 212	100.0	.7	3.0	34.0	1.4	.6	5.4	(D)	(D)	(D)
RAIL.................	422	100.0	.2	.8	85.4	.3	.8	9.1	(D)	(D)	(D)
MOTOR CARRIER.........	230	100.0	3.6	10.9	21.7	4.2	.7	2.6	(D)	(D)	(D)
PRIVATE TRUCK.........	532	100.0	-	.5	.2	1.1	.5	.2	(D)	(D)	(D)
AIR..................	1	100.0	1.7	4.9	37.2	.9	-	7.3	(D)	(D)	(D)
WATER................	23	100.0	-	19.8	-	-	-	80.2	(D)	(D)	(D)
OTHER................	2	100.0	.9	49.8	19.6	11.2	-	3.6	(D)	(D)	(D)
UNKNOWN..............	-	100.0	-	-	.1	-	-	-	(D)	(D)	(D)
MOUNTAIN...............	63	100.0	1.1	12.0	19.9	4.6	4.3	4.0	(D)	(D)	(D)
RAIL.................	12	100.0	.2	16.5	16.1	-	-	19.0	(D)	(D)	(D)
MOTOR CARRIER.........	43	100.0	1.5	11.2	24.6	4.8	6.4	.6	(D)	(D)	(D)
PRIVATE TRUCK.........	6	100.0	-	8.9	-	8.2	-	-	(D)	(D)	(D)
AIR..................	-	100.0	-	4.2	30.8	4.5	-	-	(D)	(D)	(D)
WATER................	-	100.0	-	-	-	-	-	-	(D)	(D)	(D)
OTHER................	-	100.0	-	11.4	1.3	24.3	-	-	(D)	(D)	(D)
UNKNOWN..............	-	100.0	-	47.0	2.8	-	-	-	(D)	(D)	(D)
PACIFIC...............	1 228	100.0	.7	2.2	26.3	.5	.2	.7	(D)	(D)	(D)
RAIL.................	329	100.0	.1	1.2	81.8	-	.7	2.0	(D)	(D)	(D)
MOTOR CARRIER.........	312	100.0	2.6	6.3	16.3	1.8	.2	.5	(D)	(D)	(D)
PRIVATE TRUCK.........	567	100.0	-	.2	.2	-	-	-	(D)	(D)	(D)
AIR..................	2	100.0	3.7	4.9	39.5	1.9	.1	.2	(D)	(D)	(D)
WATER................	7	100.0	-	26.2	-	-	-	-	(D)	(D)	(D)
OTHER................	2	100.0	2.4	14.8	15.2	8.3	-	1.1	(D)	(D)	(D)
UNKNOWN..............	6	100.0	-	-	.4	-	-	-	(D)	(D)	(D)

See footnotes at end of table 4.

TABLE 3. **TCC GROUP 349**—Percent Distribution of Geographic Division of Destination and Means of Transport, by Geographic Division of Origin: 1972—Continued

Geographic division of destination and means of transport	Number	Percent distribution by division of origin[1]									
		U.S. total	New England	Middle Atlantic	East North Central	West North Central	South Atlantic	East South Central	West South Central	Mountain	Pacific
TON-MILES OF SHIPMENTS	(millions of ton-miles)										
U.S. TOTAL...............	2 646	100.0	2.4	12.1	54.0	2.8	5.1	5.5	(D)	(D)	(D)
RAIL...................	1 137	100.0	.4	2.1	81.8	.1	1.0	6.6	(D)	(D)	(D)
MOTOR CARRIER..........	1 160	100.0	4.7	18.8	38.5	5.2	8.2	3.5	(D)	(D)	(D)
PRIVATE TRUCK..........	278	100.0	.6	20.7	14.8	3.0	9.9	8.9	(D)	(D)	(D)
AIR....................	15	100.0	9.5	5.0	20.2	6.6	.2	.4	(D)	(D)	(D)
WATER..................	29	100.0	-	36.2	-	-	1.6	15.8	(D)	(D)	(D)
OTHER..................	16	100.0	4.7	44.6	27.4	16.7	.4	1.3	(D)	(D)	(D)
UNKNOWN................	7	100.0	20.2	7.1	20.6	.1	-	-	(D)	(D)	(D)
NEW ENGLAND.............	71	100.0	2.3	19.6	28.4	6.2	5.5	3.4	(D)	(D)	(D)
RAIL...................	19	100.0	-	-	37.9	-	2.3	-	(D)	(D)	(D)
MOTOR CARRIER..........	40	100.0	3.3	17.4	27.4	10.5	5.5	6.1	(D)	(D)	(D)
PRIVATE TRUCK..........	8	100.0	2.5	77.8	5.5	-	14.1	-	(D)	(D)	(D)
AIR....................	-	100.0	.1	1.4	11.4	.8	-	-	(D)	(D)	(D)
WATER..................	-	100.0	100.0	-	-	-	-	-	(D)	(D)	(D)
OTHER..................	-	100.0	7.4	35.3	24.2	23.1	-	.6	(D)	(D)	(D)
UNKNOWN................	-	100.0	-	-	100.0	-	-	-	(D)	(D)	(D)
MIDDLE ATLANTIC.........	191	100.0	2.0	23.7	34.3	6.5	9.1	3.2	(D)	(D)	(D)
RAIL...................	27	100.0	-	1.7	48.3	-	-	6.5	(D)	(D)	(D)
MOTOR CARRIER..........	125	100.0	2.8	18.2	38.8	7.8	11.5	3.4	(D)	(D)	(D)
PRIVATE TRUCK..........	30	100.0	.5	68.4	10.1	4.5	9.0	-	(D)	(D)	(D)
AIR....................	5	100.0	.3	1.1	4.8	11.4	-	.1	(D)	(D)	(D)
WATER..................	-	100.0	-	55.3	-	-	44.7	-	(D)	(D)	(D)
OTHER..................	1	100.0	4.7	29.9	20.3	40.7	-	1.4	(D)	(D)	(D)
UNKNOWN................	-	100.0	-	10.0	87.0	-	-	-	(D)	(D)	(D)
EAST NORTH CENTRAL......	320	100.0	2.6	18.5	35.6	5.3	8.6	11.2	(D)	(D)	(D)
RAIL...................	26	100.0	5.4	7.7	30.6	1.0	2.1	53.1	(D)	(D)	(D)
MOTOR CARRIER..........	236	100.0	2.1	21.5	32.2	6.4	10.1	5.4	(D)	(D)	(D)
PRIVATE TRUCK..........	50	100.0	.9	9.6	55.8	1.8	6.6	18.3	(D)	(D)	(D)
AIR....................	1	100.0	5.4	5.2	10.2	.4	1.1	.3	(D)	(D)	(D)
WATER..................	-	100.0	-	-	100.0	-	-	-	(D)	(D)	(D)
OTHER..................	3	100.0	3.9	38.2	41.8	13.4	-	.5	(D)	(D)	(D)
UNKNOWN................	2	100.0	73.3	.9	3.6	-	-	-	(D)	(D)	(D)
WEST NORTH CENTRAL......	149	100.0	1.0	23.8	50.8	3.4	3.4	5.1	(D)	(D)	(D)
RAIL...................	52	100.0	.3	7.3	91.4	-	-	1.0	(D)	(D)	(D)
MOTOR CARRIER..........	83	100.0	1.6	31.1	30.3	3.6	5.3	7.7	(D)	(D)	(D)
PRIVATE TRUCK..........	10	100.0	-	43.6	12.6	17.2	7.2	6.5	(D)	(D)	(D)
AIR....................	-	100.0	4.3	23.1	54.6	.1	-	.4	(D)	(D)	(D)
WATER..................	-	100.0	-	-	-	-	-	-	(D)	(D)	(D)
OTHER..................	2	100.0	3.7	44.6	35.0	13.3	-	.7	(D)	(D)	(D)
UNKNOWN................	-	100.0	-	-	86.3	2.3	-	-	(D)	(D)	(D)
SOUTH ATLANTIC..........	292	100.0	1.5	11.6	44.3	3.2	19.1	7.6	(D)	(D)	(D)
RAIL...................	57	100.0	-	.5	55.5	-	2.6	21.8	(D)	(D)	(D)
MOTOR CARRIER..........	192	100.0	1.1	10.0	49.9	3.6	19.8	3.1	(D)	(D)	(D)
PRIVATE TRUCK..........	36	100.0	2.3	35.4	2.8	5.2	42.9	9.8	(D)	(D)	(D)
AIR....................	2	100.0	46.2	5.3	5.1	12.7	-	.5	(D)	(D)	(D)
WATER..................	-	100.0	-	13.0	-	-	87.0	-	(D)	(D)	(D)
OTHER..................	2	100.0	10.4	50.0	14.9	14.4	3.2	1.2	(D)	(D)	(D)
UNKNOWN................	-	100.0	-	58.2	1.9	-	-	-	(D)	(D)	(D)
EAST SOUTH CENTRAL......	126	100.0	4.8	8.6	57.7	4.0	6.0	12.0	(D)	(D)	(D)
RAIL...................	33	100.0	1.8	2.1	86.5	-	2.5	7.1	(D)	(D)	(D)
MOTOR CARRIER..........	74	100.0	7.3	11.2	53.7	6.6	7.5	2.8	(D)	(D)	(D)
PRIVATE TRUCK..........	17	100.0	-	8.1	22.0	.3	6.4	61.1	(D)	(D)	(D)
AIR....................	-	100.0	.9	37.4	24.6	7.0	.2	-	(D)	(D)	(D)
WATER..................	-	100.0	-	-	-	-	-	-	(D)	(D)	(D)
OTHER..................	-	100.0	.1	54.6	18.2	14.5	-	3.2	(D)	(D)	(D)
UNKNOWN................	-	100.0	-	-	-	-	-	-	(D)	(D)	(D)
WEST SOUTH CENTRAL......	603	100.0	2.3	7.4	58.8	1.5	1.1	6.1	(D)	(D)	(D)
RAIL...................	350	100.0	.3	1.1	88.6	.3	.7	8.1	(D)	(D)	(D)
MOTOR CARRIER..........	146	100.0	8.7	20.7	29.1	4.1	.9	2.2	(D)	(D)	(D)
PRIVATE TRUCK..........	92	100.0	-	3.2	1.0	2.1	2.9	.6	(D)	(D)	(D)
AIR....................	-	100.0	3.5	9.1	46.9	.7	-	3.9	(D)	(D)	(D)
WATER..................	10	100.0	-	55.8	-	-	-	44.2	(D)	(D)	(D)
OTHER..................	2	100.0	1.2	67.8	17.6	7.4	-	2.5	(D)	(D)	(D)
UNKNOWN................	-	100.0	-	-	.2	-	-	-	(D)	(D)	(D)
MOUNTAIN................	62	100.0	2.3	21.0	25.0	3.4	6.1	4.4	(D)	(D)	(D)
RAIL...................	11	100.0	.4	27.2	19.2	-	-	19.7	(D)	(D)	(D)
MOTOR CARRIER..........	45	100.0	3.1	18.7	29.3	3.4	8.5	.9	(D)	(D)	(D)
PRIVATE TRUCK..........	4	100.0	-	21.6	-	8.6	-	-	(D)	(D)	(D)
AIR....................	-	100.0	-	6.2	38.6	3.1	-	-	(D)	(D)	(D)
WATER..................	-	100.0	-	-	-	-	-	-	(D)	(D)	(D)
OTHER..................	-	100.0	.1	40.3	3.1	36.8	-	-	(D)	(D)	(D)
UNKNOWN................	-	100.0	-	84.4	3.2	-	-	-	(D)	(D)	(D)
PACIFIC.................	827	100.0	2.7	7.6	69.9	1.1	.8	1.9	(D)	(D)	(D)
RAIL...................	557	100.0	.2	1.7	86.1	-	.9	2.3	(D)	(D)	(D)
MOTOR CARRIER..........	216	100.0	9.9	20.9	43.4	4.0	.6	1.4	(D)	(D)	(D)
PRIVATE TRUCK..........	27	100.0	.1	7.9	8.7	-	-	-	(D)	(D)	(D)
AIR....................	3	100.0	5.9	7.3	47.9	1.8	.2	.2	(D)	(D)	(D)
WATER..................	18	100.0	-	24.7	-	-	-	-	(D)	(D)	(D)
OTHER..................	2	100.0	6.4	39.6	30.6	13.5	-	2.2	(D)	(D)	(D)
UNKNOWN................	3	100.0	-	-	1.3	-	-	-	(D)	(D)	(D)

See footnotes at end of table 4.

TABLE 4. **TCC GROUP 349—Percent Distribution of Distance Shipped and Weight of Shipment, by Means of Transport: 1972**

Distance shipped and weight of shipment[2][3]	Number	Percent distribution by means of transport							
		All means of transport	Rail	Motor carrier	Private truck	Air	Water	Other	Unknown
TONS OF SHIPMENTS	(thousands of tons)								
U.S. TOTAL..........	6 524	100.0	18.0	42.9	37.2	.2	.6	.9	.2
UNDER 100 MILES.........	2 280	100.0	1.1	29.3	68.2	-	.1	1.3	.1
UNDER 1000 POUNDS.....	138	100.0	-	29.6	62.6	.1	-	7.4	.2
1000 TO 9999 POUNDS...	922	100.0	-	19.7	78.9	-	-	1.4	-
10000 TO 29999 POUNDS.	524	100.0	1.0	26.5	71.4	-	-	1.0	-
30000 TO 59999 POUNDS.	539	100.0	1.7	43.8	53.9	-	.1	.3	.1
60000 TO 89999 POUNDS.	94	100.0	3.2	68.0	28.7	-	-	-	-
90000 POUNDS AND OVER.	61	100.0	11.7	9.7	78.6	-	-	-	-
100 TO 199 MILES........	818	100.0	4.5	49.5	44.1	-	.4	1.4	-
UNDER 1000 POUNDS.....	54	100.0	.1	86.2	5.8	.3	-	7.2	.4
1000 TO 9999 POUNDS...	221	100.0	.4	65.0	34.0	-	.6	-	-
10000 TO 29999 POUNDS.	208	100.0	2.3	42.4	53.1	-	-	2.1	-
30000 TO 59999 POUNDS.	179	100.0	.7	69.6	27.0	-	.9	1.8	-
60000 TO 89999 POUNDS.	18	100.0	9.1	5.6	85.3	-	-	-	-
90000 POUNDS AND OVER.	136	100.0	20.9	-	79.1	-	-	-	-
200 TO 299 MILES........	900	100.0	4.7	53.5	39.2	.1	2.1	.3	-
UNDER 1000 POUNDS.....	45	100.0	.4	86.9	5.6	1.5	-	5.5	.1
1000 TO 9999 POUNDS...	171	100.0	.5	78.2	20.9	.1	-	.3	-
10000 TO 29999 POUNDS.	165	100.0	3.5	38.0	58.5	-	-	-	-
30000 TO 59999 POUNDS.	315	100.0	3.2	76.5	20.3	-	-	-	-
60000 TO 89999 POUNDS.	43	100.0	36.8	9.4	53.8	-	-	-	-
90000 POUNDS AND OVER.	160	100.0	6.1	-	81.9	-	12.0	-	-
300 TO 499 MILES........	800	100.0	22.0	63.8	12.7	.1	-	.8	.6
UNDER 1000 POUNDS.....	60	100.0	1.0	86.6	3.4	1.3	-	7.5	.2
1000 TO 9999 POUNDS...	150	100.0	1.4	87.4	9.3	.2	-	.1	1.7
10000 TO 29999 POUNDS.	157	100.0	29.2	51.6	18.2	-	-	-	1.0
30000 TO 59999 POUNDS.	280	100.0	7.1	83.5	8.6	-	-	.6	.2
60000 TO 89999 POUNDS.	104	100.0	96.2	3.5	.3	-	-	-	-
90000 POUNDS AND OVER.	46	100.0	14.5	15.5	70.0	-	-	-	-
500 TO 999 MILES........	1 081	100.0	49.8	44.5	4.1	.4	-	.6	.5
UNDER 1000 POUNDS.....	79	100.0	.7	85.0	2.9	2.7	-	8.1	.6
1000 TO 9999 POUNDS...	159	100.0	4.3	84.8	8.2	1.1	-	.2	1.5
10000 TO 29999 POUNDS.	142	100.0	20.0	68.6	9.2	.4	.2	-	1.7
30000 TO 59999 POUNDS.	350	100.0	47.6	47.8	4.6	-	-	-	-
60000 TO 89999 POUNDS.	203	100.0	96.2	3.8	-	-	-	-	-
90000 POUNDS AND OVER.	146	100.0	95.7	4.3	-	-	-	-	-
1000 TO 1499 MILES......	187	100.0	32.2	58.8	3.9	1.1	2.5	1.4	-
UNDER 1000 POUNDS.....	33	100.0	1.2	89.2	.8	2.7	-	6.0	.1
1000 TO 9999 POUNDS...	58	100.0	-	89.6	9.2	.2	-	1.1	-
10000 TO 29999 POUNDS.	10	100.0	13.6	76.8	-	9.6	-	-	-
30000 TO 59999 POUNDS.	43	100.0	54.2	30.9	4.1	-	10.8	-	-
60000 TO 89999 POUNDS.	19	100.0	62.4	37.6	-	-	-	-	-
90000 POUNDS AND OVER.	22	100.0	100.0	-	-	-	-	-	-
1500 MILES OR OVER......	453	100.0	65.2	30.7	1.0	1.1	1.7	.3	.1
UNDER 1000 POUNDS.....	24	100.0	3.0	84.0	.9	5.6	1.0	4.5	.9
1000 TO 9999 POUNDS...	50	100.0	2.0	83.8	3.2	6.8	3.4	.3	.5
10000 TO 29999 POUNDS.	26	100.0	4.0	88.2	7.8	-	-	-	-
30000 TO 59999 POUNDS.	139	100.0	57.4	37.9	.6	-	4.1	-	-
60000 TO 89999 POUNDS.	94	100.0	100.0	-	-	-	-	-	-
90000 POUNDS AND OVER.	118	100.0	100.0	-	-	-	-	-	-
TON-MILES OF SHIPMENTS	(millions of ton-miles)								
U.S. TOTAL..........	2 587	100.0	43.0	43.8	10.6	.6	1.2	.6	.3
UNDER 100 MILES.........	87	100.0	1.5	32.6	64.6	-	.1	1.1	-
UNDER 1000 POUNDS.....	4	100.0	-	48.8	42.6	.2	-	8.1	.2
1000 TO 9999 POUNDS...	34	100.0	-	27.1	71.7	-	-	1.2	-
10000 TO 29999 POUNDS.	24	100.0	1.1	29.5	68.6	-	-	.7	-
30000 TO 59999 POUNDS.	20	100.0	3.0	42.4	54.2	-	.2	.1	.1
60000 TO 89999 POUNDS.	1	100.0	8.1	55.5	36.3	-	-	-	-
90000 POUNDS AND OVER.	1	100.0	14.6	2.3	83.1	-	-	-	-
100 TO 199 MILES........	119	100.0	3.9	51.3	43.0	-	.4	1.3	-
UNDER 1000 POUNDS.....	8	100.0	.1	87.1	5.3	.3	-	6.9	.3
1000 TO 9999 POUNDS...	32	100.0	.3	65.8	33.2	-	.7	-	-
10000 TO 29999 POUNDS.	30	100.0	2.2	45.5	50.7	-	-	1.6	-
30000 TO 59999 POUNDS.	26	100.0	.8	70.6	25.7	-	1.0	2.0	-
60000 TO 89999 POUNDS.	3	100.0	5.9	5.9	88.1	-	-	-	-
90000 POUNDS AND OVER.	18	100.0	18.5	-	81.5	-	-	-	-

See footnotes at end of table 4.

TABLE 4. **TCC GROUP 349—Percent Distribution of Distance Shipped and Weight of Shipment, by Means of Transport: 1972**—Continued

Distance shipped and weight of shipment[2] [3]	Number	Percent distribution by means of transport							
		All means of transport	Rail	Motor carrier	Private truck	Air	Water	Other	Unknown
TON-MILES OF SHIPMENTS	(millions of ton-miles)								
200 TO 299 MILES.........	213	100.0	5.1	54.3	38.0	.1	2.2	.3	-
UNDER 1000 POUNDS.....	11	100.0	.4	87.2	5.3	1.6	-	5.4	.1
1000 TO 9999 POUNDS...	41	100.0	.5	79.5	19.6	.1	-	.3	-
10000 TO 29999 POUNDS.	39	100.0	3.5	38.4	58.0	-	-	-	-
30000 TO 59999 POUNDS.	73	100.0	3.5	77.7	18.7	-	-	-	-
60000 TO 89999 POUNDS.	10	100.0	37.9	9.2	52.9	-	-	-	-
90000 POUNDS AND OVER.	37	100.0	6.9	-	80.4	-	12.7	-	-
300 TO 499 MILES.........	306	100.0	23.0	63.8	11.7	.1	-	.8	.6
UNDER 1000 POUNDS.....	23	100.0	1.1	86.3	3.3	1.3	-	7.7	.2
1000 TO 9999 POUNDS...	57	100.0	1.5	87.7	8.8	.2	-	.1	1.7
10000 TO 29999 POUNDS.	61	100.0	30.4	52.0	16.8	-	-	-	.9
30000 TO 59999 POUNDS.	105	100.0	7.6	83.4	8.4	-	-	.5	.2
60000 TO 89999 POUNDS.	41	100.0	95.8	4.0	.3	-	-	-	-
90000 POUNDS AND OVER.	15	100.0	15.0	16.8	68.2	-	-	-	-
500 TO 999 MILES.........	786	100.0	52.7	41.8	3.8	.5	-	.6	.6
UNDER 1000 POUNDS.....	57	100.0	.7	85.1	2.9	2.8	-	7.9	.7
1000 TO 9999 POUNDS...	110	100.0	4.4	84.9	7.4	1.5	-	.2	1.6
10000 TO 29999 POUNDS.	95	100.0	19.1	69.1	8.9	.3	.3	-	2.2
30000 TO 59999 POUNDS.	248	100.0	50.7	44.5	4.8	-	-	-	.1
60000 TO 89999 POUNDS.	159	100.0	96.7	3.3	-	-	-	-	-
90000 POUNDS AND OVER.	114	100.0	96.6	3.4	-	-	-	-	-
1000 TO 1499 MILES......	230	100.0	33.5	57.6	4.0	1.0	2.6	1.3	-
UNDER 1000 POUNDS.....	40	100.0	1.3	89.1	.9	2.8	-	5.9	.1
1000 TO 9999 POUNDS...	71	100.0	-	89.0	9.9	.2	-	.9	-
10000 TO 29999 POUNDS.	12	100.0	15.5	75.8	-	8.7	-	-	-
30000 TO 59999 POUNDS.	53	100.0	56.2	28.9	3.6	-	11.2	-	-
60000 TO 89999 POUNDS.	26	100.0	66.2	33.8	-	-	-	-	-
90000 POUNDS AND OVER.	27	100.0	100.0	-	-	-	-	-	-
1500 MILES OR OVER......	843	100.0	63.2	32.0	1.1	1.1	2.2	.3	.1
UNDER 1000 POUNDS.....	47	100.0	3.4	82.4	.9	6.3	1.3	4.7	1.0
1000 TO 9999 POUNDS...	102	100.0	1.8	84.0	3.1	5.9	4.3	.4	.4
10000 TO 29999 POUNDS.	51	100.0	3.9	89.1	7.0	-	-	-	-
30000 TO 59999 POUNDS.	262	100.0	56.4	37.7	.8	-	5.1	-	-
60000 TO 89999 POUNDS.	169	100.0	100.0	-	-	-	-	-	-
90000 POUNDS AND OVER.	209	100.0	100.0	-	-	-	-	-	-

Note: Detail may not add to total due to rounding. The introductory table shows the estimates of sampling variability for tons; sampling varia-bility for ton-miles has not been estimated. See the map in the Introduction for the States comprising the geographic divisions of the United States.
Shipments excluded from the survey are those moving by pipeline (primarily petroleum products from refineries), parcel post shipments, and com-modities moved by own power (motorized vehicles, aircraft, etc.) or towed (prefabricated buildings, etc.). Local shipments (commodities shipped less than 25 miles from the plant) and shipments within the same city are also excluded. Shipments to Alaska and Hawaii from the 48 conterminous States and the District of Columbia are included; however, no data were obtained for shipments originating in Alaska and Hawaii.

- Represents zero or rounds to zero.   (D) Withheld to avoid disclosing figures for individual companies.

[1]Production of this commodity is concentrated in the geographic divisions shown; figures and distributions for geographic divisions not shown are included in the total.
[2]Distances of shipments to foreign destinations are calculated only to the U.S. port of exit.
[3]Includes only shipments represented by bills of lading and invoices. Summary records which did not show individual weights of shipments are not included.

Machinery, Except Electrical

CONTENTS

[Page numbers listed here omit the State prefix number that appears as part of the number for each page]

TABLES   (The tables listed below are shown for each of the Transportation Commodity Classification groups in this report)

Comparisons of Tons and Ton-Miles of Shipments for Geographic Divisions of Origin and for Sampling Variability: 1972 and 1967

1. Percent Distribution of Geographic Division of Origin and Distance Shipped, by Means of Transport: 1972

2. Percent Distribution of Geographic Division of Origin and Means of Transport, by Geographic Division of Destination: 1972

3. Percent Distribution of Geographic Division of Destination and Means of Transport, by Geographic Division of Origin: 1972

4. Percent Distribution of Distance Shipped and Weight of Shipment, by Means of Transport: 1972

TCC 351. Engines and Turbines

Comparisons of Tons and Ton-Miles of Shipments for
Geographic Divisions of Origin and for Sampling Variability: 1972 and 1967

Geographic division of origin	Estimates				Relative sampling variability in tons (percent)	
	1972		1967		1972	1967
	Tons (thousands)	Ton-miles (millions)	Tons (thousands)	Ton-miles (millions)	1972	1967
U.S. total	1,304	643	1,107	630	8.0	6.2
New England	(D)	(D)	30	17	(*)	(*)
Middle Atlantic	277	217	163	124	14.8	(*)
East North Central	837	298	815	419	5.9	(*)
West North Central	(D)	(D)	13	8	(*)	(*)
South Atlantic	41	32	4	1	10.5	(*)
East South Central	(D)	(D)	23	7	(*)	(*)
West South Central	(D)	(D)	51	41	(*)	(*)
Mountain	(D)	(D)	—	—	(*)	(*)
Pacific	19	25	8	13	26.4	(*)

— Represents or rounds to zero.   (D) Withheld to avoid disclosing figures for individual companies.   (*) Data not published.

TABLE 1. TCC GROUP 351—Percent Distribution of Geographic Division of Origin and Distance Shipped, by Means of Transport: 1972

Geographic division of origin[1] and distance shipped[2]	Number	Percent distribution by means of transport							
		All means of transport	Rail	Motor carrier	Private truck	Air	Water	Other	Unknown
TONS OF SHIPMENTS	(thousands of tons)								
U.S. TOTAL..........	1 304	100.0	21.5	41.0	33.8	2.3	-	.2	1.1
MIDDLE ATLANTIC.........	277	100.0	56.2	27.0	2.0	9.6	-	-	5.2
UNDER 100 MILES.......	15	100.0	15.9	79.2	4.8	-	-	-	-
100 TO 199 MILES......	22	100.0	53.5	34.9	11.1	.4	-	.1	-
200 TO 299 MILES......	34	100.0	59.1	37.9	2.7	.2	-	.1	-
300 TO 499 MILES......	49	100.0	71.5	26.6	1.7	.1	-	-	-
500 TO 999 MILES.....	56	100.0	48.2	25.3	.7	.5	-	-	25.3
1000 TO 1499 MILES....	72	100.0	52.7	11.3	-	35.9	-	-	-
1500 MILES OR OVER....	26	100.0	77.6	21.8	-	.6	-	-	-
EAST NORTH CENTRAL.........	837	100.0	8.6	41.3	49.6	.2	-	.4	-
UNDER 100 MILES.......	347	100.0	.2	11.8	87.6	-	-	.4	-
100 TO 199 MILES......	123	100.0	-	76.0	23.8	.1	-	.1	-
200 TO 299 MILES......	61	100.0	.1	70.3	28.5	.1	-	1.1	-
300 TO 499 MILES......	93	100.0	17.6	54.4	27.7	.1	-	.2	-
500 TO 999 MILES.....	137	100.0	17.7	58.3	23.1	.6	-	.4	-
1000 TO 1499 MILES....	30	100.0	16.9	66.8	15.3	.5	-	.5	-
1500 MILES OR OVER....	43	100.0	60.2	36.8	2.6	.4	-	.1	-
SOUTH ATLANTIC.........	41	100.0	67.2	30.6	2.1	.1	-	-	-
UNDER 100 MILES.......	2	100.0	38.8	57.4	3.8	-	-	-	-
100 TO 199 MILES......	2	100.0	64.0	34.2	1.8	-	-	-	-
200 TO 299 MILES......	4	100.0	74.6	25.4	-	-	-	-	-
300 TO 499 MILES......	13	100.0	66.2	33.6	-	.2	-	-	-
500 TO 999 MILES.....	12	100.0	60.3	33.7	5.8	.2	-	-	-
1000 TO 1499 MILES....	-	100.0	83.5	16.4	-	-	-	-	-
1500 MILES OR OVER....	5	100.0	92.3	7.5	-	-	-	.2	-
PACIFIC.................	19	100.0	8.5	89.5	-	1.9	-	-	-
UNDER 100 MILES.......	3	100.0	-	99.8	-	-	-	.2	-
100 TO 199 MILES......	-	100.0	-	94.6	-	5.4	-	-	-
200 TO 299 MILES......	-	100.0	-	91.3	-	8.7	-	-	-
300 TO 499 MILES......	2	100.0	-	99.9	-	.1	-	-	-
500 TO 999 MILES.....	-	100.0	-	92.5	-	7.5	-	-	-
1000 TO 1499 MILES....	2	100.0	-	95.8	-	4.2	-	-	-
1500 MILES OR OVER....	10	100.0	16.7	81.0	-	2.3	-	-	-
TON-MILES OF SHIPMENTS	(millions of ton-miles)								
U.S. TOTAL..........	643	100.0	41.2	41.8	10.0	5.4	-	.2	1.5
MIDDLE ATLANTIC.........	217	100.0	62.0	18.7	.6	14.3	-	-	4.4
UNDER 100 MILES.......	-	100.0	19.5	74.9	5.5	-	-	.1	-
100 TO 199 MILES......	3	100.0	58.1	31.9	9.5	.4	-	.1	-
200 TO 299 MILES......	8	100.0	59.8	36.8	3.1	.2	-	.1	-
300 TO 499 MILES......	19	100.0	73.9	24.7	1.3	.1	-	-	-
500 TO 999 MILES.....	42	100.0	52.7	23.5	.7	.5	-	-	22.6
1000 TO 1499 MILES....	90	100.0	54.3	11.8	-	33.8	-	-	-
1500 MILES OR OVER....	52	100.0	79.7	19.6	-	.7	-	.1	-
EAST NORTH CENTRAL......	298	100.0	25.9	52.9	20.4	.4	-	.3	-
UNDER 100 MILES.......	15	100.0	.2	15.2	84.1	-	-	.5	-
100 TO 199 MILES......	18	100.0	-	73.1	26.8	-	-	.1	-
200 TO 299 MILES......	15	100.0	.1	71.2	27.6	.1	-	1.1	-
300 TO 499 MILES......	36	100.0	17.1	55.2	27.5	.1	-	.2	-
500 TO 999 MILES.....	95	100.0	17.7	59.0	22.3	.6	-	.4	-
1000 TO 1499 MILES....	36	100.0	17.6	66.7	14.7	.6	-	.5	-
1500 MILES OR OVER....	79	100.0	59.6	37.5	2.3	.5	-	.1	-
SOUTH ATLANTIC..........	32	100.0	79.1	19.1	1.7	.1	-	-	-
UNDER 100 MILES.......	-	100.0	56.7	41.2	2.1	-	-	-	-
100 TO 199 MILES......	-	100.0	64.1	33.7	2.2	-	-	-	-
200 TO 299 MILES......	1	100.0	74.5	25.4	-	-	-	-	-
300 TO 499 MILES......	5	100.0	68.8	31.0	-	-	-	-	-
500 TO 999 MILES.....	9	100.0	61.1	32.9	5.8	.3	-	-	-
1000 TO 1499 MILES....	-	100.0	81.5	18.5	-	.2	-	-	-
1500 MILES OR OVER....	15	100.0	94.6	5.3	-	-	-	.1	-
PACIFIC.................	25	100.0	14.0	83.6	-	2.4	-	-	-
UNDER 100 MILES.......	-	100.0	-	99.9	-	-	-	-	-
100 TO 199 MILES......	-	100.0	-	94.0	-	6.0	-	.1	-
200 TO 299 MILES......	-	100.0	-	90.8	-	9.2	-	-	-
300 TO 499 MILES......	1	100.0	-	99.9	-	.1	-	-	-
500 TO 999 MILES.....	-	100.0	.1	92.9	-	7.1	-	-	-
1000 TO 1499 MILES....	3	100.0	-	96.0	-	4.0	-	-	-
1500 MILES OR OVER....	20	100.0	17.3	80.4	-	2.3	-	-	-

See footnotes at end of table 4.

TABLE 2. TCC GROUP 351—Percent Distribution of Geographic Division of Origin and Means of Transport, by Geographic Division of Destination: 1972

Geographic division of origin[1] and means of transport	Number	Percent distribution by division of destination									
		U.S. total	New England	Middle Atlantic	East North Central	West North Central	South Atlantic	East South Central	West South Central	Mountain	Pacific
TONS OF SHIPMENTS	(thousands of tons)										
U.S. TOTAL...............	1 304	100.0	1.5	13.0	44.5	6.0	13.9	5.2	9.6	.9	5.5
RAIL.....................	280	100.0	1.0	13.0	6.8	3.5	33.4	7.9	18.2	1.5	14.6
MOTOR CARRIER...........	535	100.0	2.1	20.1	35.9	8.9	11.5	6.9	7.8	1.5	5.3
PRIVATE TRUCK..........	441	100.0	1.1	5.5	82.9	4.7	2.3	1.8	1.4	-	.3
AIR.....................	29	100.0	.1	2.9	2.2	.6	1.6	.7	89.6	.3	1.9
WATER...................	-	100.0	-	80.2	-	-	19.8	-	-	-	-
OTHER...................	3	100.0	5.4	3.2	70.1	2.0	10.9	1.3	3.7	.8	2.6
UNKNOWN.................	14	100.0	-	-	.1	-	99.8	-	-	-	-
MIDDLE ATLANTIC.........	277	100.0	1.5	17.9	6.6	.6	36.2	3.6	28.8	1.1	3.7
RAIL.....................	155	100.0	.2	13.5	4.1	-	44.2	3.7	27.6	1.0	5.7
MOTOR CARRIER...........	74	100.0	5.1	31.2	15.6	2.2	22.3	5.3	14.8	1.8	1.7
PRIVATE TRUCK..........	5	100.0	.3	92.4	.2	1.3	3.2	2.5	-	-	-
AIR.....................	26	100.0	-	.6	.5	-	.5	.4	97.4	.1	.5
WATER...................	-	100.0	-	-	-	-	100.0	-	-	-	-
OTHER...................	-	100.0	5.2	27.1	20.6	6.1	6.3	7.3	17.3	1.7	8.4
UNKNOWN.................	14	100.0	-	-	-	-	100.0	-	-	-	-
EAST NORTH CENTRAL......	837	100.0	.5	6.4	62.9	8.2	5.7	6.1	4.1	.9	5.2
RAIL.....................	72	100.0	-	9.0	5.3	10.0	15.0	17.8	3.7	3.4	35.8
MOTOR CARRIER...........	345	100.0	1.1	8.0	48.9	12.1	7.8	8.7	7.4	1.4	4.7
PRIVATE TRUCK..........	415	100.0	-	4.5	84.7	4.8	2.3	1.9	1.4	-	.3
AIR.....................	1	100.0	.3	20.3	13.0	1.5	15.2	6.9	26.2	3.4	13.2
WATER...................	-	100.0	-	-	-	-	-	-	-	-	-
OTHER...................	3	100.0	5.5	2.4	72.6	1.9	11.1	1.1	3.3	.6	1.7
UNKNOWN.................	-	100.0	-	25.9	74.1	-	-	-	-	-	-
SOUTH ATLANTIC..........	41	100.0	6.8	30.0	8.5	8.3	25.5	5.7	2.4	1.1	11.6
RAIL.....................	27	100.0	8.0	23.1	8.5	8.4	26.0	6.3	2.4	.8	16.5
MOTOR CARRIER...........	12	100.0	3.8	45.5	9.2	5.8	25.1	4.8	2.6	1.6	1.5
PRIVATE TRUCK..........	-	100.0	11.4	28.0	-	44.5	16.1	-	-	-	-
AIR.....................	-	100.0	-	30.5	.5	-	38.4	19.8	8.6	.2	1.9
WATER...................	-	100.0	-	-	-	-	-	-	-	-	-
OTHER...................	-	100.0	.5	2.3	1.6	.2	2.2	2.4	.9	86.4	3.5
UNKNOWN.................	-	100.0	-	-	-	-	-	-	-	-	-
PACIFIC.................	19	100.0	6.7	7.3	34.7	.8	1.2	.4	13.6	1.1	34.3
RAIL.....................	1	100.0	-	-	100.0	-	-	-	-	-	-
MOTOR CARRIER...........	17	100.0	7.4	8.0	28.7	.6	1.2	.3	14.5	1.2	38.0
PRIVATE TRUCK..........	-	100.0	-	-	-	-	-	-	-	-	-
AIR.....................	-	100.0	6.0	2.5	21.1	12.7	2.9	3.0	35.6	2.4	13.8
WATER...................	-	100.0	-	-	-	-	-	-	-	-	-
OTHER...................	-	100.0	-	-	-	-	29.6	-	-	-	70.4
UNKNOWN.................	-	100.0	-	-	-	-	-	-	-	-	-
TON-MILES OF SHIPMENTS	(millions of ton-miles)										
U.S. TOTAL...............	643	100.0	1.5	10.2	13.0	5.5	16.6	6.1	23.9	2.6	20.6
RAIL.....................	264	100.0	.5	5.2	5.2	2.1	19.0	5.3	27.6	2.1	33.0
MOTOR CARRIER...........	268	100.0	2.8	15.1	16.5	7.7	13.8	7.4	16.7	4.2	15.7
PRIVATE TRUCK..........	64	100.0	.4	15.7	38.7	13.3	13.8	8.3	6.8	-	3.0
AIR.....................	34	100.0	.2	2.9	1.5	.7	1.4	.5	90.0	.3	2.6
WATER...................	-	100.0	-	28.1	-	-	71.9	-	-	-	-
OTHER...................	1	100.0	13.9	4.1	26.4	3.0	25.4	2.5	10.1	3.6	11.0
UNKNOWN.................	9	100.0	-	-	-	-	99.9	-	-	-	-
MIDDLE ATLANTIC.........	217	100.0	.2	3.9	4.1	.6	25.7	2.9	48.5	2.5	11.4
RAIL.....................	134	100.0	-	3.0	2.8	-	28.6	2.8	44.7	2.2	15.9
MOTOR CARRIER...........	40	100.0	1.2	8.7	12.5	3.2	18.4	5.6	36.6	6.4	7.5
PRIVATE TRUCK..........	1	100.0	.4	74.4	.5	4.5	10.1	9.7	-	-	.5
AIR.....................	31	100.0	-	.1	.3	-	.3	.3	97.9	.1	1.0
WATER...................	-	100.0	-	-	-	-	100.0	-	-	-	-
OTHER...................	-	100.0	1.9	5.6	11.8	7.7	6.4	5.9	27.8	3.5	29.5
UNKNOWN.................	9	100.0	-	-	-	.1	99.9	-	-	-	-

See footnotes at end of table 4.

TABLE 2. **TCC GROUP 351—Percent Distribution of Geographic Division of Origin and Means of Transport, by Geographic Division of Destination: 1972**—Continued

Geographic division of origin[1] and means of transport	Number	Percent distribution by division of destination									
		U.S. total	New England	Middle Atlantic	East North Central	West North Central	South Atlantic	East South Central	West South Central	Mountain	Pacific
TON-MILES OF SHIPMENTS	(millions of ton-miles)										
EAST NORTH CENTRAL......	298	100.0	1.0	9.2	17.1	9.6	12.8	9.9	10.5	2.9	26.9
RAIL.................	77	100.0	-	5.3	1.7	4.0	9.3	10.8	4.5	2.9	61.5
MOTOR CARRIER.........	157	100.0	1.8	9.0	16.3	11.0	13.9	10.1	14.6	3.9	19.4
PRIVATE TRUCK.........	60	100.0	-	14.6	38.8	13.5	14.4	8.5	7.1	-	3.1
AIR..................	1	100.0	.3	14.0	2.0	.7	15.9	4.7	26.6	5.4	30.4
WATER................	-	100.0	-	-	-	-	-	-	-	-	-
OTHER................	-	100.0	15.2	4.1	28.4	2.7	27.1	2.3	9.0	2.4	8.9
UNKNOWN..............	-	100.0	-	59.3	40.7	-	-	-	-	-	-
SOUTH ATLANTIC..........	32	100.0	5.2	17.9	8.2	9.7	7.2	2.4	2.9	2.4	44.2
RAIL.................	25	100.0	4.8	12.1	7.0	8.5	7.1	2.3	2.5	1.6	54.1
MOTOR CARRIER.........	6	100.0	5.9	40.9	13.9	11.0	7.7	3.0	4.7	5.9	7.0
PRIVATE TRUCK.........	-	100.0	14.7	31.4	-	52.1	1.9	-	-	-	-
AIR..................	-	100.0	-	35.1	.3	-	31.7	10.7	13.8	.4	7.9
WATER................	-	100.0	-	-	-	-	-	-	-	-	-
OTHER................	-	100.0	.2	.7	.6	.1	.5	.5	.5	91.9	4.9
UNKNOWN..............	-	100.0	-	-	-	-	-	-	-	-	-
PACIFIC................	25	100.0	13.5	13.4	49.9	.9	2.0	.5	13.4	.5	5.9
RAIL.................	3	100.0	-	-	100.0	-	-	-	-	-	-
MOTOR CARRIER.........	21	100.0	15.9	16.0	42.3	.8	2.3	.5	15.2	.5	6.5
PRIVATE TRUCK.........	-	100.0	-	-	-	-	-	-	-	-	-
AIR..................	-	100.0	9.2	3.8	22.3	11.1	3.9	3.2	27.7	.9	17.9
WATER................	-	100.0	-	-	-	-	-	-	-	-	-
OTHER................	-	100.0	-	-	-	-	98.7	-	-	-	1.3
UNKNOWN..............	-	100.0	-	-	-	-	-	-	-	-	-

See footnotes at end of table 4.

TABLE 3. TCC GROUP 351—Percent Distribution of Geographic Division of Destination and Means of Transport, by Geographic Division of Origin: 1972

Geographic division of destination and means of transport	Number	Percent distribution by division of origin[1]									
		U.S. total	New England	Middle Atlantic	East North Central	West North Central	South Atlantic	East South Central	West South Central	Mountain	Pacific
TONS OF SHIPMENTS	(thousands of tons)										
U.S. TOTAL..............	1 304	100.0	(D)	21.3	64.2	(D)	3.2	(D)	(D)	(D)	1.5
RAIL...................	280	100.0	(D)	55.5	25.8	(D)	10.0	(D)	(D)	(D)	.6
MOTOR CARRIER.........	535	100.0	(D)	14.0	64.6	(D)	2.4	(D)	(D)	(D)	3.3
PRIVATE TRUCK.........	441	100.0	(D)	1.2	94.1	(D)	.2	(D)	(D)	(D)	-
AIR...................	29	100.0	(D)	89.9	4.7	(D)	.2	(D)	(D)	(D)	1.3
WATER.................	-	100.0	(D)	19.8	-	(D)	-	(D)	(D)	(D)	-
OTHER.................	3	100.0	(D)	3.1	95.6	(D)	.3	(D)	(D)	(D)	.3
UNKNOWN...............	14	100.0	(D)	99.9	.1	(D)	-	(D)	(D)	(D)	-
NEW ENGLAND............	19	100.0	(D)	21.7	21.1	(D)	14.8	(D)	(D)	(D)	7.0
RAIL...................	2	100.0	(D)	10.8	-	(D)	78.9	(D)	(D)	(D)	-
MOTOR CARRIER.........	11	100.0	(D)	33.5	33.8	(D)	4.3	(D)	(D)	(D)	11.6
PRIVATE TRUCK.........	4	100.0	(D)	.3	-	(D)	2.1	(D)	(D)	(D)	-
AIR...................	-	100.0	(D)	11.0	11.3	(D)	-	(D)	(D)	(D)	53.5
WATER.................	-	100.0	(D)	-	-	(D)	-	(D)	(D)	(D)	-
OTHER.................	-	100.0	(D)	3.0	96.3	(D)	-	(D)	(D)	(D)	-
UNKNOWN...............	-	100.0	(D)	-	-	(D)	-	(D)	(D)	(D)	-
MIDDLE ATLANTIC........	169	100.0	(D)	29.3	31.5	(D)	7.4	(D)	(D)	(D)	.9
RAIL...................	36	100.0	(D)	57.7	17.8	(D)	17.6	(D)	(D)	(D)	-
MOTOR CARRIER.........	107	100.0	(D)	21.8	25.8	(D)	5.4	(D)	(D)	(D)	1.3
PRIVATE TRUCK.........	24	100.0	(D)	20.6	77.0	(D)	1.0	(D)	(D)	(D)	-
AIR...................	-	100.0	(D)	20.0	33.2	(D)	2.1	(D)	(D)	(D)	1.1
WATER.................	-	100.0	(D)	-	-	(D)	-	(D)	(D)	(D)	-
OTHER.................	-	100.0	(D)	26.8	72.3	(D)	.2	(D)	(D)	(D)	-
UNKNOWN...............	-	100.0	(D)	-	100.0	(D)	-	(D)	(D)	(D)	-
EAST NORTH CENTRAL......	580	100.0	(D)	3.1	90.8	(D)	.6	(D)	(D)	(D)	1.2
RAIL...................	19	100.0	(D)	33.7	20.2	(D)	12.5	(D)	(D)	(D)	9.0
MOTOR CARRIER.........	192	100.0	(D)	6.1	87.8	(D)	.6	(D)	(D)	(D)	2.7
PRIVATE TRUCK.........	365	100.0	(D)	-	96.0	(D)	-	(D)	(D)	(D)	-
AIR...................	-	100.0	(D)	19.2	27.6	(D)	-	(D)	(D)	(D)	12.3
WATER.................	-	100.0	(D)	-	-	(D)	-	(D)	(D)	(D)	-
OTHER.................	2	100.0	(D)	.9	99.0	(D)	-	(D)	(D)	(D)	-
UNKNOWN...............	-	100.0	(D)	-	100.0	(D)	-	(D)	(D)	(D)	-
WEST NORTH CENTRAL......	78	100.0	(D)	2.3	88.2	(D)	4.4	(D)	(D)	(D)	.2
RAIL...................	9	100.0	(D)	.5	72.5	(D)	23.5	(D)	(D)	(D)	-
MOTOR CARRIER.........	47	100.0	(D)	3.4	87.7	(D)	1.6	(D)	(D)	(D)	.2
PRIVATE TRUCK.........	20	100.0	(D)	.3	97.7	(D)	1.9	(D)	(D)	(D)	-
AIR...................	-	100.0	(D)	5.8	11.3	(D)	-	(D)	(D)	(D)	25.3
WATER.................	-	100.0	(D)	-	-	(D)	-	(D)	(D)	(D)	-
OTHER.................	-	100.0	(D)	9.4	90.5	(D)	-	(D)	(D)	(D)	-
UNKNOWN...............	-	100.0	(D)	100.0	-	(D)	-	(D)	(D)	(D)	-
SOUTH ATLANTIC.........	180	100.0	(D)	55.5	26.6	(D)	5.9	(D)	(D)	(D)	.1
RAIL...................	93	100.0	(D)	73.5	11.6	(D)	7.7	(D)	(D)	(D)	-
MOTOR CARRIER.........	61	100.0	(D)	27.1	43.6	(D)	5.2	(D)	(D)	(D)	.4
PRIVATE TRUCK.........	10	100.0	(D)	1.7	96.9	(D)	1.4	(D)	(D)	(D)	-
AIR...................	-	100.0	(D)	26.6	44.4	(D)	4.8	(D)	(D)	(D)	2.3
WATER.................	-	100.0	(D)	100.0	-	(D)	-	(D)	(D)	(D)	-
OTHER.................	-	100.0	(D)	1.8	97.2	(D)	.1	(D)	(D)	(D)	.7
UNKNOWN...............	14	100.0	(D)	100.0	-	(D)	-	(D)	(D)	(D)	-
EAST SOUTH CENTRAL......	67	100.0	(D)	14.8	75.7	(D)	3.6	(D)	(D)	(D)	.1
RAIL...................	22	100.0	(D)	25.8	58.3	(D)	8.0	(D)	(D)	(D)	-
MOTOR CARRIER.........	36	100.0	(D)	10.9	81.5	(D)	1.7	(D)	(D)	(D)	.2
PRIVATE TRUCK.........	8	100.0	(D)	1.7	97.8	(D)	-	(D)	(D)	(D)	.2
AIR...................	-	100.0	(D)	43.5	44.0	(D)	5.4	(D)	(D)	(D)	5.2
WATER.................	-	100.0	(D)	-	-	(D)	-	(D)	(D)	(D)	-
OTHER.................	-	100.0	(D)	18.0	81.5	(D)	.5	(D)	(D)	(D)	-
UNKNOWN...............	-	100.0	(D)	-	-	(D)	-	(D)	(D)	(D)	-
WEST SOUTH CENTRAL......	125	100.0	(D)	63.6	27.5	(D)	.8	(D)	(D)	(D)	2.2
RAIL...................	51	100.0	(D)	84.0	5.3	(D)	1.3	(D)	(D)	(D)	-
MOTOR CARRIER.........	41	100.0	(D)	26.5	60.9	(D)	.8	(D)	(D)	(D)	6.2
PRIVATE TRUCK.........	6	100.0	(D)	-	95.9	(D)	-	(D)	(D)	(D)	-
AIR...................	26	100.0	(D)	97.7	1.4	(D)	-	(D)	(D)	(D)	.5
WATER.................	-	100.0	(D)	-	-	(D)	-	(D)	(D)	(D)	-
OTHER.................	-	100.0	(D)	14.7	84.9	(D)	.1	(D)	(D)	(D)	-
UNKNOWN...............	-	100.0	(D)	-	-	(D)	-	(D)	(D)	(D)	-
MOUNTAIN...............	12	100.0	(D)	23.7	59.1	(D)	3.6	(D)	(D)	(D)	1.8
RAIL...................	4	100.0	(D)	36.5	58.0	(D)	5.4	(D)	(D)	(D)	-
MOTOR CARRIER.........	8	100.0	(D)	16.9	59.6	(D)	2.5	(D)	(D)	(D)	2.6
PRIVATE TRUCK.........	-	100.0	(D)	-	-	(D)	-	(D)	(D)	(D)	-
AIR...................	-	100.0	(D)	23.6	60.1	(D)	.2	(D)	(D)	(D)	11.3
WATER.................	-	100.0	(D)	-	-	(D)	-	(D)	(D)	(D)	-
OTHER.................	-	100.0	(D)	6.3	63.5	(D)	28.5	(D)	(D)	(D)	-
UNKNOWN...............	-	100.0	(D)	-	-	(D)	-	(D)	(D)	(D)	-
PACIFIC................	71	100.0	(D)	14.4	61.0	(D)	6.8	(D)	(D)	(D)	9.6
RAIL...................	41	100.0	(D)	21.5	63.0	(D)	11.2	(D)	(D)	(D)	-
MOTOR CARRIER.........	28	100.0	(D)	4.6	57.5	(D)	.7	(D)	(D)	(D)	24.0
PRIVATE TRUCK.........	1	100.0	(D)	.2	86.0	(D)	-	(D)	(D)	(D)	-
AIR...................	-	100.0	(D)	23.7	33.2	(D)	.2	(D)	(D)	(D)	9.5
WATER.................	-	100.0	(D)	-	-	(D)	-	(D)	(D)	(D)	-
OTHER.................	-	100.0	(D)	10.0	60.7	(D)	.4	(D)	(D)	(D)	7.2
UNKNOWN...............	-	100.0	(D)	-	-	(D)	-	(D)	(D)	(D)	-

See footnotes at end of table 4.

TABLE 3. **TCC GROUP 351—Percent Distribution of Geographic Division of Destination and Means of Transport, by Geographic Division of Origin: 1972**—Continued

Geographic division of destination and means of transport	Number	Percent distribution by division of origin[1]									
		U.S. total	New England	Middle Atlantic	East North Central	West North Central	South Atlantic	East South Central	West South Central	Mountain	Pacific
TON-MILES OF SHIPMENTS	(millions of ton-miles)										
U.S. TOTAL..............	643	100.0	(D)	33.8	46.4	(D)	5.1	(D)	(D)	(D)	4.0
RAIL...................	264	100.0	(D)	50.9	29.1	(D)	9.7	(D)	(D)	(D)	1.3
MOTOR CARRIER.........	268	100.0	(D)	15.1	58.8	(D)	2.3	(D)	(D)	(D)	7.9
PRIVATE TRUCK..........	64	100.0	(D)	1.9	94.5	(D)	.9	(D)	(D)	(D)	-
AIR...................	34	100.0	(D)	90.1	3.5	(D)	.1	(D)	(D)	(D)	1.8
WATER.................	-	100.0	(D)	71.9	-	(D)	-	(D)	(D)	(D)	-
OTHER.................	1	100.0	(D)	7.2	89.6	(D)	1.3	(D)	(D)	(D)	.5
UNKNOWN...............	9	100.0	(D)	99.9	.1	(D)	-	(D)	(D)	(D)	-
NEW ENGLAND............	9	100.0	(D)	5.6	32.3	(D)	17.9	(D)	(D)	(D)	36.5
RAIL...................	1	100.0	(D)	3.1	-	(D)	92.5	(D)	(D)	(D)	-
MOTOR CARRIER.........	7	100.0	(D)	6.2	38.1	(D)	4.8	(D)	(D)	(D)	44.5
PRIVATE TRUCK..........	-	100.0	(D)	1.8	.1	(D)	32.0	(D)	(D)	(D)	-
AIR...................	-	100.0	(D)	1.6	5.0	(D)	-	(D)	(D)	(D)	70.9
WATER.................	-	100.0	(D)	-	-	(D)	-	(D)	(D)	(D)	-
OTHER.................	-	100.0	(D)	1.0	98.0	(D)	-	(D)	(D)	(D)	-
UNKNOWN...............	-	100.0	(D)	-	-	(D)	-	(D)	(D)	(D)	-
MIDDLE ATLANTIC.........	65	100.0	(D)	13.1	41.9	(D)	8.9	(D)	(D)	(D)	5.2
RAIL...................	13	100.0	(D)	29.8	29.6	(D)	22.7	(D)	(D)	(D)	-
MOTOR CARRIER.........	40	100.0	(D)	8.7	35.1	(D)	6.3	(D)	(D)	(D)	8.3
PRIVATE TRUCK..........	10	100.0	(D)	8.9	88.0	(D)	1.7	(D)	(D)	(D)	-
AIR...................	-	100.0	(D)	3.4	17.3	(D)	1.2	(D)	(D)	(D)	2.4
WATER.................	-	100.0	(D)	-	-	(D)	-	(D)	(D)	(D)	-
OTHER.................	-	100.0	(D)	9.9	89.4	(D)	.2	(D)	(D)	(D)	-
UNKNOWN...............	-	100.0	(D)	-	100.0	(D)	-	(D)	(D)	(D)	-
EAST NORTH CENTRAL......	83	100.0	(D)	10.7	60.9	(D)	3.2	(D)	(D)	(D)	15.1
RAIL...................	13	100.0	(D)	27.5	9.8	(D)	13.1	(D)	(D)	(D)	25.8
MOTOR CARRIER.........	44	100.0	(D)	11.5	58.1	(D)	2.0	(D)	(D)	(D)	20.3
PRIVATE TRUCK..........	24	100.0	(D)	-	94.8	(D)	-	(D)	(D)	(D)	-
AIR...................	-	100.0	(D)	15.2	4.8	(D)	-	(D)	(D)	(D)	26.7
WATER.................	-	100.0	(D)	-	-	(D)	-	(D)	(D)	(D)	-
OTHER.................	-	100.0	(D)	3.2	96.2	(D)	-	(D)	(D)	(D)	-
UNKNOWN...............	-	100.0	(D)	-	100.0	(D)	-	(D)	(D)	(D)	-
WEST NORTH CENTRAL......	35	100.0	(D)	4.0	81.9	(D)	9.0	(D)	(D)	(D)	.7
RAIL...................	5	100.0	(D)	.9	55.9	(D)	39.1	(D)	(D)	(D)	-
MOTOR CARRIER.........	20	100.0	(D)	6.2	84.0	(D)	3.3	(D)	(D)	(D)	.8
PRIVATE TRUCK..........	8	100.0	(D)	.6	95.9	(D)	3.3	(D)	(D)	(D)	-
AIR...................	-	100.0	(D)	3.9	3.9	(D)	-	(D)	(D)	(D)	30.2
WATER.................	-	100.0	(D)	-	-	(D)	-	(D)	(D)	(D)	-
OTHER.................	-	100.0	(D)	18.7	81.3	(D)	-	(D)	(D)	(D)	-
UNKNOWN...............	-	100.0	(D)	100.0	-	(D)	-	(D)	(D)	(D)	-
SOUTH ATLANTIC..........	106	100.0	(D)	52.4	35.9	(D)	2.2	(D)	(D)	(D)	.5
RAIL...................	50	100.0	(D)	76.7	14.2	(D)	3.7	(D)	(D)	(D)	-
MOTOR CARRIER.........	37	100.0	(D)	20.2	59.1	(D)	1.3	(D)	(D)	(D)	1.3
PRIVATE TRUCK..........	8	100.0	(D)	1.4	98.5	(D)	.1	(D)	(D)	(D)	-
AIR...................	-	100.0	(D)	17.7	40.1	(D)	2.2	(D)	(D)	(D)	4.9
WATER.................	-	100.0	(D)	100.0	-	(D)	-	(D)	(D)	(D)	-
OTHER.................	-	100.0	(D)	1.8	95.7	(D)	-	(D)	(D)	(D)	2.1
UNKNOWN...............	9	100.0	(D)	100.0	-	(D)	-	(D)	(D)	(D)	-
EAST SOUTH CENTRAL......	39	100.0	(D)	15.8	74.9	(D)	2.0	(D)	(D)	(D)	.3
RAIL...................	13	100.0	(D)	26.7	59.9	(D)	4.3	(D)	(D)	(D)	-
MOTOR CARRIER.........	19	100.0	(D)	11.5	79.8	(D)	.9	(D)	(D)	(D)	.6
PRIVATE TRUCK..........	5	100.0	(D)	2.2	97.0	(D)	-	(D)	(D)	(D)	-
AIR...................	-	100.0	(D)	49.7	33.9	(D)	2.2	(D)	(D)	(D)	11.9
WATER.................	-	100.0	(D)	-	-	(D)	-	(D)	(D)	(D)	-
OTHER.................	-	100.0	(D)	17.0	82.7	(D)	.3	(D)	(D)	(D)	-
UNKNOWN...............	-	100.0	(D)	-	-	(D)	-	(D)	(D)	(D)	-
WEST SOUTH CENTRAL......	153	100.0	(D)	68.7	20.3	(D)	.6	(D)	(D)	(D)	2.2
RAIL...................	73	100.0	(D)	82.3	4.8	(D)	.9	(D)	(D)	(D)	-
MOTOR CARRIER.........	44	100.0	(D)	33.2	51.3	(D)	.6	(D)	(D)	(D)	7.2
PRIVATE TRUCK..........	4	100.0	(D)	-	98.9	(D)	-	(D)	(D)	(D)	-
AIR...................	31	100.0	(D)	98.1	1.0	(D)	-	(D)	(D)	(D)	.6
WATER.................	-	100.0	(D)	-	-	(D)	-	(D)	(D)	(D)	-
OTHER.................	-	100.0	(D)	19.9	79.7	(D)	.1	(D)	(D)	(D)	-
UNKNOWN...............	-	100.0	(D)	-	-	(D)	-	(D)	(D)	(D)	-
MOUNTAIN...............	17	100.0	(D)	32.5	50.0	(D)	4.7	(D)	(D)	(D)	.7
RAIL...................	5	100.0	(D)	52.6	39.9	(D)	7.5	(D)	(D)	(D)	-
MOTOR CARRIER.........	11	100.0	(D)	22.8	54.8	(D)	3.2	(D)	(D)	(D)	1.0
PRIVATE TRUCK..........	-	100.0	(D)	-	-	(D)	-	(D)	(D)	(D)	-
AIR...................	-	100.0	(D)	32.3	61.6	(D)	.1	(D)	(D)	(D)	5.2
WATER.................	-	100.0	(D)	-	-	(D)	-	(D)	(D)	(D)	-
OTHER.................	-	100.0	(D)	7.0	58.8	(D)	33.4	(D)	(D)	(D)	-
UNKNOWN...............	-	100.0	(D)	-	-	(D)	-	(D)	(D)	(D)	-
PACIFIC................	132	100.0	(D)	18.7	60.6	(D)	10.8	(D)	(D)	(D)	1.1
RAIL...................	87	100.0	(D)	24.5	54.2	(D)	15.9	(D)	(D)	(D)	-
MOTOR CARRIER.........	42	100.0	(D)	7.2	72.3	(D)	1.0	(D)	(D)	(D)	3.3
PRIVATE TRUCK, EXCEPT..	1	100.0	(D)	.3	96.5	(D)	-	(D)	(D)	(D)	-
AIR...................	-	100.0	(D)	35.7	41.9	(D)	.3	(D)	(D)	(D)	12.4
WATER.................	-	100.0	(D)	-	-	(D)	-	(D)	(D)	(D)	-
OTHER.................	-	100.0	(D)	19.5	72.4	(D)	.6	(D)	(D)	(D)	.1
UNKNOWN...............	-	100.0	(D)	-	-	(D)	-	(D)	(D)	(D)	-

See footnotes at end of table 4.

TABLE 4. TCC GROUP 351—Percent Distribution of Distance Shipped and Weight of Shipment, by Means of Transport: 1972

Distance shipped and weight of shipment[2][3]	Number	Percent distribution by means of transport							
		All means of transport	Rail	Motor carrier	Private truck	Air	Water	Other	Unknown
TONS OF SHIPMENTS	(thousands of tons)								
U.S. TOTAL	1 017	100.0	26.6	49.6	19.4	2.8	-	.2	1.4
UNDER 100 MILES	156	100.0	2.6	37.9	59.2	-	-	.3	.1
UNDER 1000 POUNDS	2	100.0	-	60.3	33.3	3.1	-	3.1	.1
1000 TO 9999 POUNDS	11	100.0	-	36.5	63.5	-	-	-	-
10000 TO 29999 POUNDS	65	100.0	3.5	19.7	76.2	-	-	.6	-
30000 TO 59999 POUNDS	61	100.0	-	65.2	34.8	-	-	-	-
60000 TO 89999 POUNDS	1	100.0	65.2	34.8	-	-	-	-	-
90000 POUNDS AND OVER	14	100.0	4.3	2.4	93.3	-	-	-	-
100 TO 199 MILES	144	100.0	9.4	71.9	18.5	.1	-	.1	-
UNDER 1000 POUNDS	2	100.0	-	81.2	6.7	6.7	1.0	4.0	.4
1000 TO 9999 POUNDS	15	100.0	-	87.0	13.0	-	-	-	-
10000 TO 29999 POUNDS	29	100.0	1.1	76.3	22.7	-	-	-	-
30000 TO 59999 POUNDS	80	100.0	2.9	74.7	22.4	-	-	-	-
60000 TO 89999 POUNDS	15	100.0	59.3	40.7	-	-	-	-	-
90000 POUNDS AND OVER	1	100.0	100.0	-	-	-	-	-	-
200 TO 299 MILES	133	100.0	18.1	67.5	13.9	.1	-	.5	-
UNDER 1000 POUNDS	3	100.0	1.2	93.2	.5	2.4	-	2.7	.1
1000 TO 9999 POUNDS	11	100.0	.3	86.7	11.3	-	-	1.7	-
10000 TO 29999 POUNDS	39	100.0	-	72.3	26.7	-	-	1.0	-
30000 TO 59999 POUNDS	45	100.0	2.2	82.9	14.9	-	-	-	-
60000 TO 89999 POUNDS	7	100.0	57.6	42.4	-	-	-	-	-
90000 POUNDS AND OVER	26	100.0	69.9	30.1	-	-	-	-	-
300 TO 499 MILES	164	100.0	39.6	46.6	13.7	.1	-	.1	-
UNDER 1000 POUNDS	4	100.0	.1	90.4	2.9	3.1	-	3.5	-
1000 TO 9999 POUNDS	16	100.0	.7	92.7	6.5	.1	-	-	-
10000 TO 29999 POUNDS	39	100.0	10.6	49.6	39.8	-	-	-	-
30000 TO 59999 POUNDS	40	100.0	7.2	79.2	13.6	-	-	-	-
60000 TO 89999 POUNDS	16	100.0	93.2	6.8	-	-	-	-	-
90000 POUNDS AND OVER	46	100.0	90.8	9.2	-	-	-	-	-
500 TO 999 MILES	213	100.0	29.7	48.0	14.7	.6	-	.2	6.7
UNDER 1000 POUNDS	10	100.0	3.0	83.1	2.0	8.5	-	3.5	.1
1000 TO 9999 POUNDS	28	100.0	3.3	87.4	7.2	1.5	-	.6	-
10000 TO 29999 POUNDS	48	100.0	1.3	62.8	35.9	-	-	-	-
30000 TO 59999 POUNDS	77	100.0	34.8	50.0	15.2	-	-	-	-
60000 TO 89999 POUNDS	15	100.0	100.0	-	-	-	-	-	-
90000 POUNDS AND OVER	33	100.0	57.2	-	-	-	-	-	42.8
1000 TO 1499 MILES	109	100.0	37.2	34.4	4.4	23.9	-	.1	-
UNDER 1000 POUNDS	3	100.0	3.4	80.7	2.2	11.5	.2	1.8	.1
1000 TO 9999 POUNDS	6	100.0	5.0	90.6	1.8	1.2	-	1.4	-
10000 TO 29999 POUNDS	16	100.0	7.8	64.3	27.9	-	-	-	-
30000 TO 59999 POUNDS	27	100.0	34.6	65.4	-	-	-	-	-
60000 TO 89999 POUNDS	10	100.0	100.0	-	-	-	-	-	-
90000 POUNDS AND OVER	44	100.0	42.6	-	-	57.4	-	-	-
1500 MILES OR OVER	94	100.0	62.3	35.8	1.2	.6	-	.1	-
UNDER 1000 POUNDS	3	100.0	13.0	67.0	.1	18.2	-	1.7	-
1000 TO 9999 POUNDS	10	100.0	8.2	91.5	-	.3	-	-	-
10000 TO 29999 POUNDS	16	100.0	28.5	71.5	-	-	-	-	-
30000 TO 59999 POUNDS	31	100.0	63.0	33.5	3.5	-	-	-	-
60000 TO 89999 POUNDS	12	100.0	100.0	-	-	-	-	-	-
90000 POUNDS AND OVER	20	100.0	100.0	-	-	-	-	-	-
TON-MILES OF SHIPMENTS	(millions of ton-miles)								
U.S. TOTAL	604	100.0	42.5	42.0	8.3	5.5	-	.2	1.6
UNDER 100 MILES	7	100.0	3.8	42.7	53.1	.1	-	.3	-
UNDER 1000 POUNDS	-	100.0	-	63.0	28.7	4.1	-	4.1	.1
1000 TO 9999 POUNDS	-	100.0	-	39.9	60.1	-	-	-	-
10000 TO 29999 POUNDS	3	100.0	5.8	21.5	72.2	-	-	.5	-
30000 TO 59999 POUNDS	3	100.0	-	71.1	28.9	-	-	-	-
60000 TO 89999 POUNDS	-	100.0	60.4	39.6	-	-	-	-	-
90000 POUNDS AND OVER	-	100.0	8.3	1.1	90.6	-	-	-	-
100 TO 199 MILES	21	100.0	10.4	68.5	20.9	.1	-	.1	-
UNDER 1000 POUNDS	-	100.0	-	81.8	7.1	5.8	.7	4.0	.4
1000 TO 9999 POUNDS	2	100.0	-	85.4	14.6	-	-	-	-
10000 TO 29999 POUNDS	4	100.0	.9	76.5	22.7	-	-	-	-
30000 TO 59999 POUNDS	11	100.0	2.1	71.6	26.3	-	-	-	-
60000 TO 89999 POUNDS	2	100.0	72.6	27.4	-	-	-	-	-
90000 POUNDS AND OVER	-	100.0	100.0	-	-	-	-	-	-

See footnotes at end of table 4.

TABLE 4. TCC GROUP 351—Percent Distribution of Distance Shipped and Weight of Shipment, by Means of Transport: 1972—Continued

Distance shipped and weight of shipment[2] [3]	Number	Percent distribution by means of transport							
		All means of transport	Rail	Motor carrier	Private truck	Air	Water	Other	Unknown
TON-MILES OF SHIPMENTS	(millions of ton-miles)								
200 TO 299 MILES.........	33	100.0	17.8	68.3	13.4	.1	-	.5	-
UNDER 1000 POUNDS......	-	100.0	1.3	93.4	.4	2.2	-	2.5	.1
1000 TO 9999 POUNDS...	2	100.0	.4	87.0	11.0	-	-	1.6	-
10000 TO 29999 POUNDS.	9	100.0	-	72.4	26.6	-	-	1.0	-
30000 TO 59999 POUNDS.	11	100.0	2.0	84.3	13.7	-	-	-	-
60000 TO 89999 POUNDS.	1	100.0	52.2	47.8	-	-	-	-	-
90000 POUNDS AND OVER.	7	100.0	69.6	30.4	-	-	-	-	-
300 TO 499 MILES.........	64	100.0	40.7	45.9	13.2	.1	-	.1	-
UNDER 1000 POUNDS......	1	100.0	.1	90.8	2.5	3.1	-	3.5	-
1000 TO 9999 POUNDS...	6	100.0	.8	92.6	6.5	.2	-	-	-
10000 TO 29999 POUNDS.	14	100.0	10.0	50.5	39.5	-	-	-	-
30000 TO 59999 POUNDS.	15	100.0	7.5	78.6	13.9	-	-	-	-
60000 TO 89999 POUNDS.	6	100.0	94.1	5.9	-	-	-	-	-
90000 POUNDS AND OVER.	18	100.0	90.9	9.1	-	-	-	-	-
500 TO 999 MILES.........	153	100.0	31.8	47.4	13.7	.6	-	.2	6.2
UNDER 1000 POUNDS......	7	100.0	2.8	83.7	2.0	8.1	-	3.2	.1
1000 TO 9999 POUNDS...	20	100.0	3.1	86.3	8.2	1.7	-	.7	-
10000 TO 29999 POUNDS.	33	100.0	1.2	64.6	34.2	-	-	-	-
30000 TO 59999 POUNDS.	55	100.0	36.0	49.8	14.2	-	-	-	-
60000 TO 89999 POUNDS.	11	100.0	100.0	-	-	-	-	-	-
90000 POUNDS AND OVER.	25	100.0	62.8	-	-	-	-	-	37.2
1000 TO 1499 MILES......	135	100.0	39.1	33.8	4.1	22.8	-	.1	-
UNDER 1000 POUNDS......	4	100.0	3.4	79.5	2.4	12.4	.2	2.0	.1
1000 TO 9999 POUNDS...	8	100.0	4.8	90.7	1.9	1.4	-	1.3	-
10000 TO 29999 POUNDS.	19	100.0	8.5	64.0	27.5	-	-	-	-
30000 TO 59999 POUNDS.	35	100.0	35.5	64.5	-	-	-	-	-
60000 TO 89999 POUNDS.	11	100.0	100.0	-	-	-	-	-	-
90000 POUNDS AND OVER.	56	100.0	47.0	-	-	53.0	-	-	-
1500 MILES OR OVER......	187	100.0	64.0	34.3	1.0	.7	-	.1	-
UNDER 1000 POUNDS......	5	100.0	12.8	65.7	.1	19.6	-	1.8	-
1000 TO 9999 POUNDS...	20	100.0	7.7	91.9	-	.3	-	-	-
10000 TO 29999 POUNDS.	30	100.0	27.3	72.7	-	-	-	-	-
30000 TO 59999 POUNDS.	62	100.0	65.8	31.3	3.0	-	-	-	-
60000 TO 89999 POUNDS.	28	100.0	100.0	-	-	-	-	-	-
90000 POUNDS AND OVER.	40	100.0	100.0	-	-	-	-	-	-

Note: Detail may not add to total due to rounding. The introductory table shows the estimates of sampling variability for tons; sampling variability for ton-miles has not been estimated. See the map in the Introduction for the States comprising the geographic divisions of the United States.
Shipments excluded from the survey are those moving by pipeline (primarily petroleum products from refineries), parcel post shipments, and commodities moved by own power (motorized vehicles, aircraft, etc.) or towed (prefabricated buildings, etc.). Local shipments (commodities shipped less than 25 miles from the plant) and shipments within the same city are also excluded. Shipments to Alaska and Hawaii from the 48 conterminous States and the District of Columbia are included; however, no data were obtained for shipments originating in Alaska and Hawaii.

- Represents zero or rounds to zero.   (D) Withheld to avoid disclosing figures for individual companies.

[1] Production of this commodity is concentrated in the geographic divisions shown; figures and distributions for geographic divisions not shown are included in the total.
[2] Distances of shipments to foreign destinations are calculated only to the U.S. port of exit.
[3] Includes only shipments represented by bills of lading and invoices. Summary records which did not show individual weights of shipments are not included.

TCC 352. Farm Machinery and Equipment

Comparisons of Tons and Ton-Miles of Shipments for
Geographic Divisions of Origin and for Sampling Variability: 1972 and 1967

Geographic division of origin	Estimates				Relative sampling variability in tons (percent)	
	1972		1967		1972	1967
	Tons (thousands)	Ton-miles (millions)	Tons (thousands)	Ton-miles (millions)		
U.S. total	3,836	1,905	3,958	1,801	7.4	9.0
New England	—	—	—	—	—	(*)
Middle Atlantic	150	105	127	83	23.3	(*)
East North Central	1,781	805	2,029	899	5.7	(*)
West North Central	1,195	580	1,413	649	18.7	(*)
South Atlantic	(D)	(D)	95	38	(*)	(*)
East South Central	297	139	74	43	28.8	(*)
West South Central	49	18	181	71	47.2	(*)
Mountain	(D)	(D)	—	—	(*)	(*)
Pacific	(D)	(D)	39	18	(*)	(*)

— Represents or rounds to zero.   (D) Withheld to avoid disclosing figures for individual companies.   (*) Data not published.

TABLE 1. **TCC GROUP 352**—Percent Distribution of Geographic Division of Origin and Distance Shipped, by Means of Transport: 1972

Geographic division of origin[1] and distance shipped[2]	Number	Percent distribution by means of transport							
		All means of transport	Rail	Motor carrier	Private truck	Air	Water	Other	Unknown
TONS OF SHIPMENTS	(thousands of tons)								
U.S. TOTAL..........	3 836	100.0	24.8	52.1	21.2	.1	-	.9	.9
MIDDLE ATLANTIC.........	150	100.0	30.7	35.4	33.7	.1	-	-	-
UNDER 100 MILES.......	17	100.0	-	55.2	44.2	.6	-	-	-
100 TO 199 MILES......	12	100.0	7.8	19.8	72.1	-	-	-	-
200 TO 299 MILES......	19	100.0	2.4	28.9	68.7	-	-	.1	.2
300 TO 499 MILES......	20	100.0	26.7	26.6	46.6	.1	-	-	-
500 TO 999 MILES......	35	100.0	42.7	47.1	10.2	.1	-	-	-
1000 TO 1499 MILES....	31	100.0	56.8	27.9	15.3	-	-	-	-
1500 MILES OR OVER....	12	100.0	45.5	35.5	19.0	-	-	-	-
EAST NORTH CENTRAL......	1 781	100.0	28.4	55.1	15.2	.1	-	1.1	.1
UNDER 100 MILES.......	204	100.0	8.5	75.9	13.7	.3	-	1.7	-
100 TO 199 MILES......	243	100.0	8.3	61.9	27.3	.2	-	2.3	-
200 TO 299 MILES......	294	100.0	23.3	58.0	17.9	-	-	.3	.5
300 TO 499 MILES......	390	100.0	18.9	57.5	22.2	.1	-	1.3	-
500 TO 999 MILES......	533	100.0	45.2	47.6	6.4	.1	-	.7	-
1000 TO 1499 MILES....	73	100.0	72.1	25.5	1.7	.2	-	.5	-
1500 MILES OR OVER....	40	100.0	77.7	17.8	4.2	.3	-	.1	-
WEST NORTH CENTRAL......	1 195	100.0	20.1	45.2	30.7	-	-	1.2	2.8
UNDER 100 MILES.......	112	100.0	-	35.6	64.1	-	-	.2	.1
100 TO 199 MILES......	215	100.0	2.0	33.5	63.0	-	-	1.3	.2
200 TO 299 MILES......	152	100.0	5.6	41.3	33.2	-	-	4.4	15.5
300 TO 499 MILES......	203	100.0	26.0	51.4	22.4	-	-	.3	-
500 TO 999 MILES......	384	100.0	37.6	47.3	12.5	-	-	.3	2.3
1000 TO 1499 MILES....	119	100.0	23.8	61.5	11.8	-	-	2.8	-
1500 MILES OR OVER....	8	100.0	16.8	63.8	18.9	.4	-	.2	-
EAST SOUTH CENTRAL......	297	100.0	20.7	75.0	4.2	-	-	.1	-
UNDER 100 MILES.......	8	100.0	38.2	12.5	49.2	-	-	.1	-
100 TO 199 MILES......	20	100.0	10.4	74.1	15.2	-	-	.4	-
200 TO 299 MILES......	56	100.0	1.1	96.1	2.6	-	-	.2	-
300 TO 499 MILES......	96	100.0	14.2	83.9	1.9	-	-	.1	-
500 TO 999 MILES......	104	100.0	31.6	66.5	1.8	-	-	.1	-
1000 TO 1499 MILES....	5	100.0	77.1	22.9	-	-	-	-	-
1500 MILES OR OVER....	5	100.0	86.6	13.0	-	.1	-	.3	-
WEST SOUTH CENTRAL......	49	100.0	8.5	9.1	80.2	-	-	-	2.1
UNDER 100 MILES.......	5	100.0	-	4.0	95.9	-	-	.1	-
100 TO 199 MILES......	7	100.0	-	5.2	94.7	-	-	.1	-
200 TO 299 MILES......	17	100.0	-	.9	99.1	-	-	-	-
300 TO 499 MILES......	10	100.0	-	25.7	64.5	-	-	-	9.8
500 TO 999 MILES......	3	100.0	-	22.9	77.0	-	-	-	-
1000 TO 1499 MILES....	2	100.0	78.7	4.2	17.1	-	-	-	-
1500 MILES OR OVER....	2	100.0	99.6	-	-	.4	-	-	-
TON-MILES OF SHIPMENTS	(millions of ton-miles)								
U.S. TOTAL..........	1 905	100.0	37.1	48.4	12.9	.1	-	.7	.7
MIDDLE ATLANTIC.........	105	100.0	46.7	33.3	20.0	-	-	-	-
UNDER 100 MILES.......	-	100.0	-	30.0	69.4	.6	-	-	-
100 TO 199 MILES......	1	100.0	8.7	19.1	71.9	-	-	.1	.2
200 TO 299 MILES......	4	100.0	2.4	29.5	68.2	-	-	-	-
300 TO 499 MILES......	8	100.0	29.4	25.7	44.8	.1	-	-	-
500 TO 999 MILES......	25	100.0	46.6	43.3	10.1	-	-	-	-
1000 TO 1499 MILES....	37	100.0	59.1	27.0	13.9	-	-	-	-
1500 MILES OR OVER....	27	100.0	46.4	36.8	16.8	-	-	-	-
EAST NORTH CENTRAL......	805	100.0	43.1	45.6	10.3	.1	-	.8	.1
UNDER 100 MILES.......	8	100.0	13.4	65.8	18.6	.1	-	2.1	-
100 TO 199 MILES......	36	100.0	8.5	62.5	26.6	.2	-	2.1	-
200 TO 299 MILES......	74	100.0	23.4	59.0	16.6	-	-	.3	.6
300 TO 499 MILES......	155	100.0	20.0	57.6	21.2	.1	-	1.2	-
500 TO 999 MILES......	373	100.0	47.4	45.7	6.0	.1	-	.8	-
1000 TO 1499 MILES....	85	100.0	71.7	25.9	1.6	.2	-	.6	-
1500 MILES OR OVER....	71	100.0	77.7	17.5	4.4	.3	-	.1	-
WEST NORTH CENTRAL......	580	100.0	27.1	51.4	18.0	-	-	1.2	2.2
UNDER 100 MILES.......	6	100.0	-	33.1	66.5	-	-	.3	.1
100 TO 199 MILES......	32	100.0	2.4	33.0	63.0	-	-	1.3	.2
200 TO 299 MILES......	36	100.0	5.7	41.0	34.4	-	-	4.4	14.5
300 TO 499 MILES......	79	100.0	24.9	52.5	22.3	-	-	.3	-
500 TO 999 MILES......	273	100.0	36.6	49.0	11.3	-	-	.3	2.8
1000 TO 1499 MILES....	138	100.0	23.3	62.3	11.4	-	-	3.0	-
1500 MILES OR OVER....	13	100.0	16.8	62.7	19.9	.5	-	.2	-
EAST SOUTH CENTRAL......	139	100.0	31.4	66.4	2.0	-	-	.1	-
UNDER 100 MILES.......	-	100.0	37.5	16.7	45.7	-	-	.1	-
100 TO 199 MILES......	2	100.0	8.4	76.6	14.6	-	-	.4	-
200 TO 299 MILES......	15	100.0	.9	96.5	2.4	-	-	.2	-
300 TO 499 MILES......	35	100.0	15.0	82.7	2.2	-	-	.1	-
500 TO 999 MILES......	68	100.0	35.9	62.6	1.4	-	-	.1	-
1000 TO 1499 MILES....	6	100.0	77.0	23.0	-	-	-	.1	-
1500 MILES OR OVER....	10	100.0	83.5	15.8	-	.1	-	.7	-

See footnotes at end of table 4.

TABLE 1. **TCC GROUP 352—Percent Distribution of Geographic Division of Origin and Distance Shipped, by Means of Transport: 1972**—Continued

Geographic division of origin[1] and distance shipped[2]	Number	Percent distribution by means of transport							
		All means of transport	Rail	Motor carrier	Private truck	Air	Water	Other	Unknown
TON-MILES OF SHIPMENTS	(millions of ton-miles)								
WEST SOUTH CENTRAL......	18	100.0	32.2	12.8	53.1	.1	-	-	1.8
UNDER 100 MILES........	-	100.0	-	5.4	94.5	-	-	.1	-
100 TO 199 MILES.......	1	100.0	-	5.7	94.2	-	-	.1	-
200 TO 299 MILES......	4	100.0	-	.9	99.1	-	-	-	-
300 TO 499 MILES......	3	100.0	-	32.5	59.2	-	-	-	8.3
500 TO 999 MILES......	2	100.0	-	33.2	66.8	-	-	-	-
1000 TO 1499 MILES....	2	100.0	77.3	4.8	17.9	-	-	-	-
1500 MILES OR OVER....	3	100.0	99.6	-	-	.4	-	-	-

See footnotes at end of table 4.

TABLE 2. **TCC GROUP 352—Percent Distribution of Geographic Division of Origin and Means of Transport, by Geographic Division of Destination: 1972**

Geographic division of origin[1] and means of transport	Number	Percent distribution by division of destination									
		U.S. total	New England	Middle Atlantic	East North Central	West North Central	South Atlantic	East South Central	West South Central	Mountain	Pacific
TONS OF SHIPMENTS	(thousands of tons)										
U.S. TOTAL..............	3 836	100.0	2.0	8.0	30.6	24.0	9.5	8.1	10.3	4.3	3.1
RAIL.................	950	100.0	1.2	5.3	20.9	20.5	8.7	8.1	20.5	9.0	5.9
MOTOR CARRIER........	2 000	100.0	2.8	9.9	33.2	22.7	10.5	9.4	6.7	2.3	2.4
PRIVATE TRUCK........	811	100.0	.7	7.1	33.4	31.8	7.5	5.3	8.3	4.3	1.6
AIR..................	2	100.0	.7	9.4	47.1	4.7	8.8	5.2	5.4	4.1	14.7
WATER...............	-	100.0	-	100.0	-	-	-	-	-	-	-
OTHER...............	34	100.0	9.1	2.1	38.5	36.2	5.9	.6	1.1	.3	6.2
UNKNOWN.............	36	100.0	-	.4	69.0	2.7	24.4	3.5	-	-	-
MIDDLE ATLANTIC.........	150	100.0	2.7	27.9	20.8	22.0	8.6	4.3	5.1	4.9	3.7
RAIL.................	46	100.0	-	6.2	24.4	38.3	1.6	4.7	11.6	5.9	7.1
MOTOR CARRIER........	53	100.0	2.6	30.4	22.8	17.3	9.0	5.1	4.4	4.1	4.2
PRIVATE TRUCK........	50	100.0	5.3	44.8	15.4	12.2	14.5	2.9	-	4.8	-
AIR..................	-	100.0	-	87.3	12.7	-	-	-	-	-	-
WATER...............	-	100.0	-	-	-	-	-	-	-	-	-
OTHER...............	-	100.0	-	-	97.7	-	-	-	-	2.3	-
UNKNOWN.............	-	100.0	-	-	-	-	100.0	-	-	-	-
EAST NORTH CENTRAL......	1 781	100.0	1.6	8.2	35.9	23.6	7.0	9.2	8.9	3.9	1.6
RAIL.................	505	100.0	.6	4.2	16.8	22.3	11.2	6.2	23.4	11.3	4.0
MOTOR CARRIER........	981	100.0	2.1	9.4	41.4	23.3	6.5	12.1	3.2	1.1	.8
PRIVATE TRUCK........	270	100.0	.7	11.5	51.6	25.8	1.6	4.7	3.1	.7	.3
AIR..................	1	100.0	.2	4.7	60.6	4.6	7.6	5.9	5.7	5.0	5.8
WATER...............	-	100.0	-	100.0	-	-	-	-	-	-	-
OTHER...............	19	100.0	16.5	1.5	31.6	46.0	2.7	.5	.8	.1	.2
UNKNOWN.............	1	100.0	-	6.4	79.0	2.8	.6	11.3	-	-	-
WEST NORTH CENTRAL......	1 195	100.0	1.3	6.5	32.1	32.2	6.2	5.7	8.5	4.5	2.9
RAIL.................	240	100.0	1.7	5.8	40.0	13.5	5.5	13.8	12.2	4.5	3.0
MOTOR CARRIER........	540	100.0	1.9	11.2	25.2	31.5	9.0	4.5	9.3	3.6	3.7
PRIVATE TRUCK........	367	100.0	.4	1.0	33.0	48.3	.6	2.8	6.0	6.3	1.6
AIR..................	-	100.0	5.4	18.5	8.2	12.2	18.2	1.5	11.1	3.9	21.0
WATER...............	-	100.0	-	-	-	-	-	-	-	-	-
OTHER...............	14	100.0	.1	2.6	49.5	25.6	8.1	-	.9	.5	12.7
UNKNOWN.............	33	100.0	-	-	70.6	2.8	26.5	-	-	-	-
EAST SOUTH CENTRAL......	297	100.0	2.8	5.9	30.7	11.2	11.9	15.4	18.4	1.9	1.9
RAIL.................	61	100.0	7.3	9.9	10.6	17.3	2.8	12.5	24.6	7.1	7.8
MOTOR CARRIER........	223	100.0	1.8	5.2	37.2	10.0	13.0	15.3	16.7	.5	.4
PRIVATE TRUCK........	12	100.0	-	-	13.0	2.4	35.4	30.8	18.3	-	-
AIR..................	-	100.0	-	-	-	-	-	78.9	-	-	21.1
WATER...............	-	100.0	-	-	-	-	-	-	-	-	-
OTHER...............	-	100.0	-	-	4.3	7.4	52.0	16.5	15.0	-	4.7
UNKNOWN.............	-	100.0	-	-	-	-	-	-	-	-	-
WEST SOUTH CENTRAL......	49	100.0	.1	1.5	.2	4.2	1.2	30.9	54.4	2.9	4.7
RAIL.................	4	100.0	-	-	-	45.1	-	-	-	-	54.9
MOTOR CARRIER........	4	100.0	1.1	16.2	-	.2	4.5	7.2	70.9	-	-
PRIVATE TRUCK........	39	100.0	-	-	.3	.4	1.0	35.0	59.7	3.6	-
AIR..................	-	100.0	-	-	-	-	-	-	-	-	100.0
WATER...............	-	100.0	-	-	-	-	-	-	-	-	-
OTHER...............	-	100.0	-	-	-	-	2.5	-	73.6	23.9	-
UNKNOWN.............	1	100.0	-	-	.1	-	-	99.9	-	-	-

See footnotes at end of table 4.

TABLE 2. **TCC GROUP 352—Percent Distribution of Geographic Division of Origin and Means of Transport, by Geographic Division of Destination: 1972**—Continued

Geographic division of origin[1] and means of transport	Number	Percent distribution by division of destination									
		U.S. total	New England	Middle Atlantic	East North Central	West North Central	South Atlantic	East South Central	West South Central	Mountain	Pacific
TON-MILES OF SHIPMENTS	(millions of ton-miles)										
U.S. TOTAL............	1 905	100.0	3.6	10.3	16.7	19.3	10.4	7.0	14.2	8.6	10.0
RAIL.................	707	100.0	1.6	5.7	12.1	16.1	8.8	5.7	21.7	13.6	14.7
MOTOR CARRIER........	921	100.0	5.5	14.5	17.9	19.7	12.2	8.0	10.2	4.5	7.5
PRIVATE TRUCK........	246	100.0	1.9	8.7	23.4	27.6	5.4	7.6	9.7	10.5	5.3
AIR..................	1	100.0	1.1	7.3	9.6	3.0	14.8	4.5	7.2	7.7	44.8
WATER................	-	100.0	-	100.0	-	-	-	-	-	-	-
OTHER................	14	100.0	18.3	4.6	21.2	21.0	13.7	.6	1.6	.5	18.6
UNKNOWN..............	13	100.0	-	.4	40.9	1.6	53.8	3.4	-	-	-
MIDDLE ATLANTIC.......	105	100.0	1.2	5.9	15.2	34.4	4.8	4.0	8.8	13.1	12.6
RAIL.................	49	100.0	-	1.6	14.2	40.6	1.1	3.4	13.1	10.6	15.5
MOTOR CARRIER........	35	100.0	.8	5.2	17.7	28.1	7.4	5.1	8.0	11.6	16.1
PRIVATE TRUCK........	21	100.0	4.5	17.3	13.4	30.6	9.3	3.4	-	21.5	-
AIR..................	-	100.0	-	40.9	59.1	-	-	-	-	-	-
WATER................	-	100.0	-	-	-	-	-	-	-	-	-
OTHER................	-	100.0	-	-	77.7	-	-	-	-	22.3	-
UNKNOWN..............	-	100.0	-	-	-	-	100.0	-	-	-	-
EAST NORTH CENTRAL.....	805	100.0	2.8	10.3	13.4	21.7	10.7	8.7	15.6	10.2	6.5
RAIL.................	346	100.0	.8	4.4	5.5	15.5	11.7	4.8	27.3	19.5	10.5
MOTOR CARRIER........	367	100.0	4.3	14.4	17.2	25.8	11.4	12.7	7.3	3.2	3.7
PRIVATE TRUCK........	83	100.0	1.9	17.6	29.6	29.0	3.4	8.4	4.8	3.3	1.9
AIR..................	-	100.0	.3	8.2	14.0	4.7	12.9	7.9	11.3	14.2	26.4
WATER................	-	100.0	-	100.0	-	-	-	-	-	-	-
OTHER................	6	100.0	38.7	2.3	12.3	33.8	8.4	.7	2.0	.6	1.3
UNKNOWN..............	-	100.0	-	6.1	67.5	3.5	.9	22.0	-	-	-
WEST NORTH CENTRAL.....	580	100.0	3.2	13.0	24.4	15.2	12.0	6.3	10.7	7.2	7.9
RAIL.................	157	100.0	2.9	8.7	35.5	8.3	8.4	11.5	12.4	6.5	5.8
MOTOR CARRIER........	298	100.0	4.0	19.5	16.7	13.7	15.3	4.0	12.1	5.6	9.1
PRIVATE TRUCK........	104	100.0	2.0	3.0	27.6	32.2	2.0	6.2	6.1	14.2	6.8
AIR..................	-	100.0	5.8	17.0	4.2	3.5	17.7	.9	8.8	3.6	38.5
WATER................	-	100.0	-	-	-	-	-	-	-	-	-
OTHER................	7	100.0	.2	6.1	30.3	9.6	18.3	.1	.5	.4	34.4
UNKNOWN..............	12	100.0	-	.1	40.6	1.5	57.8	-	-	-	-
EAST SOUTH CENTRAL.....	139	100.0	4.9	8.0	22.7	13.6	10.0	8.0	21.0	4.3	7.4
RAIL.................	43	100.0	8.4	13.0	7.9	12.8	2.1	4.1	21.6	10.8	19.4
MOTOR CARRIER........	92	100.0	3.5	6.0	29.7	14.3	12.7	9.6	21.0	1.4	1.9
PRIVATE TRUCK........	2	100.0	-	-	25.6	1.4	45.8	16.1	11.0	-	-
AIR..................	-	100.0	-	-	-	-	-	35.3	-	-	64.7
WATER................	-	100.0	-	-	-	-	-	-	-	-	-
OTHER................	-	100.0	-	-	2.6	12.6	26.0	6.4	17.6	-	34.8
UNKNOWN..............	-	100.0	-	-	-	-	-	-	-	-	-
WEST SOUTH CENTRAL.....	18	100.0	.4	3.9	.5	11.4	3.3	22.5	32.7	4.0	21.4
RAIL.................	5	100.0	-	-	-	33.8	-	-	-	-	66.2
MOTOR CARRIER........	2	100.0	2.8	30.1	-	.1	7.7	5.3	53.9	-	-
PRIVATE TRUCK........	9	100.0	-	-	.9	.9	4.4	37.8	48.6	7.5	-
AIR..................	-	100.0	-	-	-	-	-	-	-	-	100.0
WATER................	-	100.0	-	-	-	-	-	-	-	-	-
OTHER................	-	100.0	-	-	-	-	17.0	-	40.7	42.3	-
UNKNOWN..............	-	100.0	-	-	.1	-	.1	99.8	-	-	-

See footnotes at end of table 4.

TABLE 3. TCC GROUP 352—Percent Distribution of Geographic Division of Destination and Means of Transport, by Geographic Division of Origin: 1972

Geographic division of destination and means of transport	Number	Percent distribution by division of origin[1]									
		U.S. total	New England	Middle Atlantic	East North Central	West North Central	South Atlantic	East South Central	West South Central	Mountain	Pacific
TONS OF SHIPMENTS	(thousands of tons)										
U.S. TOTAL	3 836	100.0	(D)	3.9	46.4	31.2	(D)	7.8	1.3	(D)	(D)
RAIL	950	100.0	(D)	4.9	53.2	25.3	(D)	6.5	.4	(D)	(D)
MOTOR CARRIER	2 000	100.0	(D)	2.7	49.1	27.0	(D)	11.1	.2	(D)	(D)
PRIVATE TRUCK	811	100.0	(D)	6.2	33.4	45.3	(D)	1.5	4.9	(D)	(D)
AIR	2	100.0	(D)	4.6	74.3	10.1	(D)	.9	.4	(D)	(D)
WATER	-	100.0	(D)	-	100.0	-	(D)	-	-	(D)	(D)
OTHER	34	100.0	(D)	-	54.8	42.3	(D)	1.0	-	(D)	(D)
UNKNOWN	36	100.0	(D)	.1	5.3	91.7	(D)	-	2.9	(D)	(D)
NEW ENGLAND	76	100.0	(D)	5.4	37.3	20.8	(D)	11.0	.1	(D)	(D)
RAIL	11	100.0	(D)	-	27.0	34.3	(D)	38.7	-	(D)	(D)
MOTOR CARRIER	55	100.0	(D)	2.5	36.5	18.8	(D)	7.1	.1	(D)	(D)
PRIVATE TRUCK	6	100.0	(D)	44.6	31.9	23.5	(D)	-	-	(D)	(D)
AIR	-	100.0	(D)	-	18.8	81.2	(D)	-	-	(D)	(D)
WATER	-	100.0	(D)	-	-	-	(D)	-	-	(D)	(D)
OTHER	3	100.0	(D)	-	98.8	.4	(D)	-	-	(D)	(D)
UNKNOWN	-	100.0	(D)	-	-	-	(D)	-	-	(D)	(D)
MIDDLE ATLANTIC	307	100.0	(D)	13.6	47.3	25.4	(D)	5.8	.2	(D)	(D)
RAIL	50	100.0	(D)	5.7	42.3	27.6	(D)	12.1	-	(D)	(D)
MOTOR CARRIER	198	100.0	(D)	8.1	46.6	30.3	(D)	5.8	.4	(D)	(D)
PRIVATE TRUCK	57	100.0	(D)	39.5	54.0	6.4	(D)	-	-	(D)	(D)
AIR	-	100.0	(D)	43.1	37.0	20.0	(D)	-	-	(D)	(D)
WATER	-	100.0	(D)	-	100.0	-	(D)	-	-	(D)	(D)
OTHER	-	100.0	(D)	-	39.6	52.4	(D)	-	-	(D)	(D)
UNKNOWN	-	100.0	(D)	-	91.5	8.5	(D)	-	-	(D)	(D)
EAST NORTH CENTRAL	1 174	100.0	(D)	2.7	54.5	32.7	(D)	7.8	-	(D)	(D)
RAIL	198	100.0	(D)	5.7	42.7	48.3	(D)	3.3	-	(D)	(D)
MOTOR CARRIER	664	100.0	(D)	1.8	61.2	20.5	(D)	12.5	-	(D)	(D)
PRIVATE TRUCK	271	100.0	(D)	2.9	51.5	44.7	(D)	.6	-	(D)	(D)
AIR	1	100.0	(D)	1.3	95.6	1.8	(D)	-	-	(D)	(D)
WATER	-	100.0	(D)	-	-	-	(D)	-	-	(D)	(D)
OTHER	13	100.0	(D)	.1	45.0	54.4	(D)	.1	-	(D)	(D)
UNKNOWN	24	100.0	(D)	-	6.1	93.9	(D)	-	-	(D)	(D)
WEST NORTH CENTRAL	920	100.0	(D)	3.6	45.7	41.8	(D)	3.6	.2	(D)	(D)
RAIL	194	100.0	(D)	9.1	57.8	16.7	(D)	5.5	1.0	(D)	(D)
MOTOR CARRIER	454	100.0	(D)	2.0	50.5	37.5	(D)	4.9	-	(D)	(D)
PRIVATE TRUCK	258	100.0	(D)	2.4	27.0	68.7	(D)	.1	.1	(D)	(D)
AIR	-	100.0	(D)	-	73.5	26.5	(D)	-	-	(D)	(D)
WATER	-	100.0	(D)	-	-	-	(D)	-	-	(D)	(D)
OTHER	12	100.0	(D)	-	69.6	29.9	(D)	.2	-	(D)	(D)
UNKNOWN	-	100.0	(D)	-	5.4	94.6	(D)	-	-	(D)	(D)
SOUTH ATLANTIC	364	100.0	(D)	3.5	34.3	20.3	(D)	9.7	.2	(D)	(D)
RAIL	82	100.0	(D)	.9	68.8	15.9	(D)	2.1	-	(D)	(D)
MOTOR CARRIER	210	100.0	(D)	2.3	30.2	23.2	(D)	13.8	.1	(D)	(D)
PRIVATE TRUCK	61	100.0	(D)	12.0	7.2	3.4	(D)	7.2	.6	(D)	(D)
AIR	-	100.0	(D)	-	63.9	21.0	(D)	-	-	(D)	(D)
WATER	-	100.0	(D)	-	-	-	(D)	-	-	(D)	(D)
OTHER	2	100.0	(D)	-	25.4	58.4	(D)	9.1	-	(D)	(D)
UNKNOWN	8	100.0	(D)	.3	.1	99.6	(D)	-	-	(D)	(D)
EAST SOUTH CENTRAL	310	100.0	(D)	2.1	52.6	21.9	(D)	14.7	4.9	(D)	(D)
RAIL	76	100.0	(D)	2.9	41.0	43.2	(D)	10.0	-	(D)	(D)
MOTOR CARRIER	188	100.0	(D)	1.5	62.8	12.9	(D)	18.1	.2	(D)	(D)
PRIVATE TRUCK	43	100.0	(D)	3.4	29.9	23.8	(D)	8.9	32.3	(D)	(D)
AIR	-	100.0	(D)	-	83.1	2.8	(D)	14.0	-	(D)	(D)
WATER	-	100.0	(D)	-	-	-	(D)	-	-	(D)	(D)
OTHER	-	100.0	(D)	-	43.7	3.2	(D)	26.9	-	(D)	(D)
UNKNOWN	1	100.0	(D)	-	16.9	-	(D)	-	83.1	(D)	(D)
WEST SOUTH CENTRAL	396	100.0	(D)	2.0	40.1	25.7	(D)	13.8	6.8	(D)	(D)
RAIL	194	100.0	(D)	2.8	60.9	15.0	(D)	7.8	-	(D)	(D)
MOTOR CARRIER	133	100.0	(D)	1.8	23.7	37.5	(D)	27.8	2.4	(D)	(D)
PRIVATE TRUCK	67	100.0	(D)	-	12.5	32.8	(D)	3.4	35.3	(D)	(D)
AIR	-	100.0	(D)	-	78.7	20.9	(D)	-	-	(D)	(D)
WATER	-	100.0	(D)	-	-	-	(D)	-	-	(D)	(D)
OTHER	-	100.0	(D)	-	39.8	36.9	(D)	14.2	3.1	(D)	(D)
UNKNOWN	-	100.0	(D)	-	-	-	(D)	-	-	(D)	(D)
MOUNTAIN	166	100.0	(D)	4.4	42.0	32.4	(D)	3.3	.9	(D)	(D)
RAIL	85	100.0	(D)	3.2	67.0	12.8	(D)	5.2	-	(D)	(D)
MOTOR CARRIER	46	100.0	(D)	4.7	23.4	42.1	(D)	2.5	-	(D)	(D)
PRIVATE TRUCK	34	100.0	(D)	7.0	5.6	67.2	(D)	-	4.2	(D)	(D)
AIR	-	100.0	(D)	-	90.4	9.6	(D)	-	-	(D)	(D)
WATER	-	100.0	(D)	-	-	-	(D)	-	-	(D)	(D)
OTHER	-	100.0	(D)	.2	25.7	67.7	(D)	-	3.6	(D)	(D)
UNKNOWN	-	100.0	(D)	-	-	-	(D)	-	-	(D)	(D)
PACIFIC	119	100.0	(D)	4.6	24.4	29.2	(D)	4.7	2.0	(D)	(D)
RAIL	56	100.0	(D)	5.9	35.7	13.0	(D)	8.6	4.1	(D)	(D)
MOTOR CARRIER	47	100.0	(D)	4.7	17.1	41.3	(D)	1.7	-	(D)	(D)
PRIVATE TRUCK	12	100.0	(D)	-	6.2	45.4	(D)	-	-	(D)	(D)
AIR	-	100.0	(D)	-	29.5	14.5	(D)	1.3	2.5	(D)	(D)
WATER	-	100.0	(D)	-	-	-	(D)	-	-	(D)	(D)
OTHER	2	100.0	(D)	-	2.0	87.4	(D)	.8	-	(D)	(D)
UNKNOWN	-	100.0	(D)	-	-	-	(D)	-	-	(D)	(D)

See footnotes at end of table 4.

TABLE 3. **TCC GROUP 352**—Percent Distribution of Geographic Division of Destination and Means of Transport, by Geographic Division of Origin: 1972—Continued

Geographic division of destination and means of transport	Number	Percent distribution by division of origin[1]									
		U.S. total	New England	Middle Atlantic	East North Central	West North Central	South Atlantic	East South Central	West South Central	Mountain	Pacific
TON-MILES OF SHIPMENTS	(millions of ton-miles)										
U.S. TOTAL	1 905	100.0	(D)	5.6	42.3	30.5	(D)	7.3	1.0	(D)	(D)
RAIL	707	100.0	(D)	7.0	49.0	22.2	(D)	6.2	.8	(D)	(D)
MOTOR CARRIER	921	100.0	(D)	3.8	39.9	32.4	(D)	10.0	.3	(D)	(D)
PRIVATE TRUCK	246	100.0	(D)	8.6	33.8	42.3	(D)	1.1	4.0	(D)	(D)
AIR	1	100.0	(D)	.9	50.5	16.5	(D)	1.0	1.1	(D)	(D)
WATER	-	100.0	(D)	-	100.0	-	(D)	-	-	(D)	(D)
OTHER	14	100.0	(D)	-	46.7	49.7	(D)	1.4	-	(D)	(D)
UNKNOWN	13	100.0	(D)	-	4.6	93.0	(D)	-	2.4	(D)	(D)
NEW ENGLAND	68	100.0	(D)	1.8	33.1	27.3	(D)	10.0	.1	(D)	(D)
RAIL	11	100.0	(D)	-	25.8	41.0	(D)	33.2	-	(D)	(D)
MOTOR CARRIER	50	100.0	(D)	.6	31.2	24.0	(D)	6.4	.1	(D)	(D)
PRIVATE TRUCK	4	100.0	(D)	20.7	34.0	45.3	(D)	-	-	(D)	(D)
AIR	-	100.0	(D)	-	14.8	85.2	(D)	-	-	(D)	(D)
WATER	-	100.0	(D)	-	-	-	(D)	-	-	(D)	(D)
OTHER	2	100.0	(D)	-	98.5	.6	(D)	-	-	(D)	(D)
UNKNOWN	-	100.0	(D)	-	-	-	(D)	-	-	(D)	(D)
MIDDLE ATLANTIC	196	100.0	(D)	3.2	42.3	38.4	(D)	5.7	.4	(D)	(D)
RAIL	40	100.0	(D)	1.9	37.5	33.6	(D)	14.0	-	(D)	(D)
MOTOR CARRIER	133	100.0	(D)	1.4	39.7	43.7	(D)	4.1	.5	(D)	(D)
PRIVATE TRUCK	21	100.0	(D)	17.0	68.3	14.5	(D)	-	-	(D)	(D)
AIR	-	100.0	(D)	5.0	56.5	38.5	(D)	-	-	(D)	(D)
WATER	-	100.0	(D)	-	100.0	-	(D)	-	-	(D)	(D)
OTHER	-	100.0	(D)	-	23.2	66.0	(D)	-	-	(D)	(D)
UNKNOWN	-	100.0	(D)	-	77.5	22.5	(D)	-	-	(D)	(D)
EAST NORTH CENTRAL	317	100.0	(D)	5.1	34.1	44.7	(D)	10.0	-	(D)	(D)
RAIL	85	100.0	(D)	8.2	22.3	65.5	(D)	4.0	-	(D)	(D)
MOTOR CARRIER	165	100.0	(D)	3.8	38.2	30.1	(D)	16.6	-	(D)	(D)
PRIVATE TRUCK	57	100.0	(D)	4.9	42.8	49.9	(D)	1.2	.2	(D)	(D)
AIR	-	100.0	(D)	5.5	73.9	7.2	(D)	-	-	(D)	(D)
WATER	-	100.0	(D)	-	-	-	(D)	-	-	(D)	(D)
OTHER	3	100.0	(D)	.1	27.1	71.1	(D)	.2	-	(D)	(D)
UNKNOWN	5	100.0	(D)	-	7.6	92.4	(D)	-	-	(D)	(D)
WEST NORTH CENTRAL	367	100.0	(D)	9.9	47.7	24.1	(D)	5.2	.6	(D)	(D)
RAIL	114	100.0	(D)	17.6	47.0	11.4	(D)	4.9	1.8	(D)	(D)
MOTOR CARRIER	181	100.0	(D)	5.5	52.2	22.5	(D)	7.3	-	(D)	(D)
PRIVATE TRUCK	67	100.0	(D)	9.6	35.6	49.5	(D)	.1	.1	(D)	(D)
AIR	-	100.0	(D)	-	80.6	19.4	(D)	-	-	(D)	(D)
WATER	-	100.0	(D)	-	-	-	(D)	-	-	(D)	(D)
OTHER	2	100.0	(D)	-	75.1	22.8	(D)	.8	-	(D)	(D)
UNKNOWN	-	100.0	(D)	-	10.2	89.8	(D)	-	-	(D)	(D)
SOUTH ATLANTIC	197	100.0	(D)	2.6	43.5	35.2	(D)	7.1	.3	(D)	(D)
RAIL	62	100.0	(D)	.9	65.4	21.1	(D)	1.5	-	(D)	(D)
MOTOR CARRIER	112	100.0	(D)	2.3	37.1	40.5	(D)	10.4	.2	(D)	(D)
PRIVATE TRUCK	13	100.0	(D)	15.0	21.4	15.9	(D)	9.5	3.3	(D)	(D)
AIR	-	100.0	(D)	-	43.9	19.8	(D)	-	-	(D)	(D)
WATER	-	100.0	(D)	-	-	-	(D)	-	-	(D)	(D)
OTHER	1	100.0	(D)	-	28.5	66.7	(D)	2.6	-	(D)	(D)
UNKNOWN	7	100.0	(D)	.1	.1	99.9	(D)	-	-	(D)	(D)
EAST SOUTH CENTRAL	133	100.0	(D)	3.2	52.9	27.4	(D)	8.4	3.1	(D)	(D)
RAIL	40	100.0	(D)	4.2	41.2	45.0	(D)	4.5	-	(D)	(D)
MOTOR CARRIER	73	100.0	(D)	2.5	63.3	16.1	(D)	12.1	.2	(D)	(D)
PRIVATE TRUCK	18	100.0	(D)	3.8	37.5	34.5	(D)	2.4	20.0	(D)	(D)
AIR	-	100.0	(D)	-	89.2	3.3	(D)	7.5	-	(D)	(D)
WATER	-	100.0	(D)	-	-	-	(D)	-	-	(D)	(D)
OTHER	-	100.0	(D)	-	59.0	5.7	(D)	16.2	-	(D)	(D)
UNKNOWN	-	100.0	(D)	-	30.1	-	(D)	-	69.9	(D)	(D)
WEST SOUTH CENTRAL	271	100.0	(D)	3.4	46.3	22.9	(D)	10.8	2.2	(D)	(D)
RAIL	153	100.0	(D)	4.2	61.6	12.7	(D)	6.1	-	(D)	(D)
MOTOR CARRIER	93	100.0	(D)	3.0	28.6	38.8	(D)	20.8	1.4	(D)	(D)
PRIVATE TRUCK	23	100.0	(D)	-	16.9	26.6	(D)	1.3	20.1	(D)	(D)
AIR	-	100.0	(D)	-	79.4	20.1	(D)	-	-	(D)	(D)
WATER	-	100.0	(D)	-	-	-	(D)	-	-	(D)	(D)
OTHER	-	100.0	(D)	-	60.0	16.0	(D)	15.4	.6	(D)	(D)
UNKNOWN	-	100.0	(D)	-	-	-	(D)	-	-	(D)	(D)
MOUNTAIN	164	100.0	(D)	8.5	50.1	25.6	(D)	3.6	.5	(D)	(D)
RAIL	96	100.0	(D)	5.4	70.3	10.7	(D)	4.9	-	(D)	(D)
MOTOR CARRIER	41	100.0	(D)	9.8	28.1	40.3	(D)	3.0	-	(D)	(D)
PRIVATE TRUCK	25	100.0	(D)	17.6	10.5	56.9	(D)	-	2.9	(D)	(D)
AIR	-	100.0	(D)	-	92.3	7.7	(D)	-	-	(D)	(D)
WATER	-	100.0	(D)	-	-	-	(D)	-	-	(D)	(D)
OTHER	-	100.0	(D)	.7	54.1	41.6	(D)	-	1.9	(D)	(D)
UNKNOWN	-	100.0	(D)	-	-	-	(D)	-	-	(D)	(D)
PACIFIC	189	100.0	(D)	7.0	27.5	24.2	(D)	5.4	2.1	(D)	(D)
RAIL	104	100.0	(D)	7.3	35.1	8.8	(D)	8.1	3.8	(D)	(D)
MOTOR CARRIER	69	100.0	(D)	8.2	19.9	39.1	(D)	2.5	-	(D)	(D)
PRIVATE TRUCK	13	100.0	(D)	-	12.4	54.2	(D)	-	-	(D)	(D)
AIR	-	100.0	(D)	-	29.8	14.2	(D)	1.4	2.5	(D)	(D)
WATER	-	100.0	(D)	-	-	-	(D)	-	-	(D)	(D)
OTHER	2	100.0	(D)	-	3.2	92.0	(D)	2.6	-	(D)	(D)
UNKNOWN	-	100.0	(D)	-	-	-	(D)	-	-	(D)	(D)

See footnotes at end of table 4.

TABLE 4. TCC GROUP 352—Percent Distribution of Distance Shipped and Weight of Shipment, by Means of Transport: 1972

Distance shipped and weight of shipment [2] [3]	Number	Percent distribution by means of transport							
		All means of transport	Rail	Motor carrier	Private truck	Air	Water	Other	Unknown
TONS OF SHIPMENTS	(thousands of tons)								
U.S. TOTAL..........	3 584	100.0	25.2	53.3	19.5	.1	-	1.0	1.0
UNDER 100 MILES........	358	100.0	5.8	64.4	28.6	.2	-	1.0	-
UNDER 1000 POUNDS.....	15	100.0	.1	48.2	44.8	1.9	-	4.9	.1
1000 TO 9999 POUNDS...	68	100.0	-	34.8	62.9	.5	-	1.7	.2
10000 TO 29999 POUNDS.	139	100.0	2.6	59.1	37.0	-	-	1.3	-
30000 TO 59999 POUNDS.	114	100.0	7.1	92.0	.9	-	-	-	-
60000 TO 89999 POUNDS.	15	100.0	23.8	76.2	-	-	-	-	-
90000 POUNDS AND OVER.	5	100.0	100.0	-	-	-	-	-	-
100 TO 199 MILES........	506	100.0	5.4	52.1	40.6	.1	-	1.7	.1
UNDER 1000 POUNDS.....	20	100.0	.1	60.6	32.8	1.6	-	3.8	1.1
1000 TO 9999 POUNDS...	142	100.0	-	36.1	62.4	.2	-	1.3	-
10000 TO 29999 POUNDS.	262	100.0	3.5	54.0	40.2	-	-	2.2	.1
30000 TO 59999 POUNDS.	80	100.0	22.7	72.1	5.2	-	-	-	-
60000 TO 89999 POUNDS.	-	100.0	-	-	-	-	-	-	-
90000 POUNDS AND OVER.	-	100.0	-	-	-	-	-	-	-
200 TO 299 MILES........	532	100.0	14.3	55.4	24.1	-	-	1.4	4.7
UNDER 1000 POUNDS.....	17	100.0	.9	73.0	21.0	.7	-	4.2	.2
1000 TO 9999 POUNDS...	102	100.0	1.3	46.0	45.9	-	-	6.2	.6
10000 TO 29999 POUNDS.	210	100.0	16.4	60.2	22.5	-	-	.3	.7
30000 TO 59999 POUNDS.	177	100.0	20.0	50.1	16.9	-	-	-	13.0
60000 TO 89999 POUNDS.	-	100.0	100.0	-	-	-	-	-	-
90000 POUNDS AND OVER.	24	100.0	19.4	80.6	-	-	-	-	-
300 TO 499 MILES........	709	100.0	20.8	57.7	20.6	-	-	.8	-
UNDER 1000 POUNDS.....	19	100.0	.9	77.2	17.0	1.0	-	3.3	.6
1000 TO 9999 POUNDS...	120	100.0	3.0	67.1	29.8	-	-	-	-
10000 TO 29999 POUNDS.	303	100.0	19.2	57.4	23.3	-	-	.1	-
30000 TO 59999 POUNDS.	249	100.0	29.9	53.6	14.7	-	-	1.8	-
60000 TO 89999 POUNDS.	13	100.0	71.6	28.4	-	-	-	-	-
90000 POUNDS AND OVER.	3	100.0	37.0	63.0	-	-	-	-	-
500 TO 999 MILES........	1 142	100.0	39.8	50.8	8.1	-	-	.4	.8
UNDER 1000 POUNDS.....	32	100.0	1.8	86.1	7.3	.9	.2	3.2	.4
1000 TO 9999 POUNDS...	101	100.0	4.0	75.6	20.2	.1	-	-	.2
10000 TO 29999 POUNDS.	510	100.0	30.1	59.1	10.0	-	-	.8	-
30000 TO 59999 POUNDS.	409	100.0	53.7	42.5	3.9	-	-	-	-
60000 TO 89999 POUNDS.	22	100.0	60.4	-	-	-	-	-	39.6
90000 POUNDS AND OVER.	65	100.0	95.8	-	4.2	-	-	-	-
1000 TO 1499 MILES......	234	100.0	47.7	42.1	8.5	.1	-	1.6	-
UNDER 1000 POUNDS.....	8	100.0	1.1	91.7	3.2	1.8	-	2.2	.1
1000 TO 9999 POUNDS...	28	100.0	7.8	78.0	10.6	-	-	3.5	-
10000 TO 29999 POUNDS.	100	100.0	41.2	44.6	11.7	-	-	2.5	-
30000 TO 59999 POUNDS.	79	100.0	72.6	21.3	6.2	-	-	-	-
60000 TO 89999 POUNDS.	15	100.0	57.5	42.5	-	-	-	-	-
90000 POUNDS AND OVER.	1	100.0	100.0	-	-	-	-	-	-
1500 MILES OR OVER......	101	100.0	64.5	29.9	5.2	.3	-	.1	-
UNDER 1000 POUNDS.....	8	100.0	2.1	91.8	1.9	3.0	-	1.2	-
1000 TO 9999 POUNDS...	9	100.0	15.0	68.6	16.2	.2	-	-	-
10000 TO 29999 POUNDS.	21	100.0	35.8	50.4	13.8	-	-	-	-
30000 TO 59999 POUNDS.	57	100.0	90.3	8.7	1.0	-	-	-	-
60000 TO 89999 POUNDS.	1	100.0	100.0	-	-	-	-	-	-
90000 POUNDS AND OVER.	2	100.0	100.0	-	-	-	-	-	-
TON-MILES OF SHIPMENTS	(millions of ton-miles)								
U.S. TOTAL..........	1 780	100.0	37.7	48.6	12.1	.1	-	.8	.8
UNDER 100 MILES........	15	100.0	8.3	52.8	37.5	.1	-	1.2	.1
UNDER 1000 POUNDS.....	-	100.0	.1	51.5	42.2	.9	-	5.1	.2
1000 TO 9999 POUNDS...	4	100.0	-	31.4	66.9	.2	-	1.2	.2
10000 TO 29999 POUNDS.	6	100.0	4.2	49.1	45.1	-	-	1.6	-
30000 TO 59999 POUNDS.	3	100.0	14.0	83.5	2.5	-	-	-	-
60000 TO 89999 POUNDS.	-	100.0	44.6	55.4	-	-	-	-	-
90000 POUNDS AND OVER.	-	100.0	100.0	-	-	-	-	-	-
100 TO 199 MILES........	75	100.0	5.6	52.3	40.3	.1	-	1.6	.1
UNDER 1000 POUNDS.....	2	100.0	.1	61.7	31.4	1.5	-	3.8	1.4
1000 TO 9999 POUNDS...	20	100.0	-	36.2	62.5	.2	-	1.1	-
10000 TO 29999 POUNDS.	40	100.0	3.8	53.4	40.5	-	-	2.1	.1
30000 TO 59999 POUNDS.	12	100.0	21.9	72.6	5.5	-	-	-	-
60000 TO 89999 POUNDS.	-	100.0	-	-	-	-	-	-	-
90000 POUNDS AND OVER.	-	100.0	-	-	-	-	-	-	-

See footnotes at end of table 4.

TABLE 4. **TCC GROUP 352—Percent Distribution of Distance Shipped and Weight of Shipment, by Means of Transport: 1972**—Continued

Distance shipped and weight of shipment[2][3]	Number	Percent distribution by means of transport							
		All means of transport	Rail	Motor carrier	Private truck	Air	Water	Other	Unknown
TON-MILES OF SHIPMENTS	(millions of ton-miles)								
200 TO 299 MILES	134	100.0	14.5	56.6	23.2	-	-	1.4	4.3
UNDER 1000 POUNDS	4	100.0	.9	73.3	20.7	.7	-	4.2	.2
1000 TO 9999 POUNDS	25	100.0	1.3	46.2	46.0	-	-	5.9	.6
10000 TO 29999 POUNDS	53	100.0	16.4	61.0	21.5	-	-	.3	.8
30000 TO 59999 POUNDS	44	100.0	20.5	51.9	15.9	-	-	-	11.7
60000 TO 89999 POUNDS	-	100.0	100.0	-	-	-	-	-	-
90000 POUNDS AND OVER	6	100.0	18.8	81.2	-	-	-	-	-
300 TO 499 MILES	277	100.0	21.3	57.8	20.1	-	-	.7	-
UNDER 1000 POUNDS	7	100.0	.8	77.2	17.2	1.1	-	3.2	.6
1000 TO 9999 POUNDS	47	100.0	3.1	68.4	28.5	-	-	-	-
10000 TO 29999 POUNDS	119	100.0	19.3	57.5	23.1	-	-	.1	-
30000 TO 59999 POUNDS	96	100.0	31.4	52.9	14.0	-	-	1.7	-
60000 TO 89999 POUNDS	5	100.0	73.0	27.0	-	-	-	-	-
90000 POUNDS AND OVER	1	100.0	31.0	69.0	-	-	-	-	-
500 TO 999 MILES	808	100.0	41.1	50.0	7.4	-	-	.5	1.0
UNDER 1000 POUNDS	23	100.0	1.8	85.8	7.7	1.0	.2	3.1	.3
1000 TO 9999 POUNDS	71	100.0	4.2	76.2	19.4	-	-	-	.2
10000 TO 29999 POUNDS	356	100.0	31.3	58.7	9.1	-	-	.9	-
30000 TO 59999 POUNDS	295	100.0	55.7	40.9	3.4	-	-	-	-
60000 TO 89999 POUNDS	17	100.0	58.1	-	-	-	-	-	41.9
90000 POUNDS AND OVER	43	100.0	95.9	-	4.1	-	-	-	-
1000 TO 1499 MILES	275	100.0	47.7	42.4	8.1	.1	-	1.7	-
UNDER 1000 POUNDS	10	100.0	1.1	91.9	3.0	1.8	-	2.2	.1
1000 TO 9999 POUNDS	34	100.0	7.7	77.1	11.1	-	-	4.1	-
10000 TO 29999 POUNDS	117	100.0	41.5	44.9	11.1	-	-	2.5	-
30000 TO 59999 POUNDS	92	100.0	73.7	20.6	5.7	-	-	-	-
60000 TO 89999 POUNDS	18	100.0	52.1	47.9	-	-	-	-	-
90000 POUNDS AND OVER	2	100.0	100.0	-	-	-	-	-	-
1500 MILES OR OVER	193	100.0	64.2	30.5	4.9	.3	-	.1	-
UNDER 1000 POUNDS	18	100.0	1.6	92.2	1.7	3.1	-	1.3	-
1000 TO 9999 POUNDS	17	100.0	13.8	70.0	16.0	.2	-	-	-
10000 TO 29999 POUNDS	40	100.0	37.0	49.5	13.5	-	-	-	-
30000 TO 59999 POUNDS	110	100.0	89.7	9.4	.9	-	-	-	-
60000 TO 89999 POUNDS	3	100.0	100.0	-	-	-	-	-	-
90000 POUNDS AND OVER	3	100.0	100.0	-	-	-	-	-	-

Note: Detail may not add to total due to rounding. The introductory table shows the estimates of sampling variability for tons; sampling variability for ton-miles has not been estimated. See the map in the Introduction for the States comprising the geographic divisions of the United States.

Shipments excluded from the survey are those moving by pipeline (primarily petroleum products from refineries), parcel post shipments, and commodities moved by own power (motorized vehicles, aircraft, etc.) or towed (prefabricated buildings, etc.). Local shipments (commodities shipped less than 25 miles from the plant) and shipments within the same city are also excluded. Shipments to Alaska and Hawaii from the 48 conterminous States and the District of Columbia are included; however, no data were obtained for shipments originating in Alaska and Hawaii.

- Represents zero or rounds to zero.   (D) Withheld to avoid disclosing figures for individual companies.

[1]Production of this commodity is concentrated in the geographic divisions shown; figures and distributions for geographic divisions not shown are included in the total.

[2]Distances of shipments to foreign destinations are calculated only to the U.S. port of exit.

[3]Includes only shipment represented by bills of lading and invoices. Summary records which did not show individual weights of shipments are not included.

TCC 353. Contruction, Mining, Materials Handling Machinery and Equipment

Comparisons of Tons and Ton-Miles of Shipments for
Geographic Divisions of Origin and for Sampling Variability: 1972 and 1967

Geographic division of origin	Estimates				Relative sampling variability in tons (percent)	
	1972		1967		1972	1967
	Tons (thousands)	Ton-miles (millions)	Tons (thousands)	Ton-miles (millions)		
U.S. total	5,628	3,584	5,549	3,675	5.3	6.0
New England	16	14	31	22	26.7	(*)
Middle Atlantic	675	554	757	515	17.6	(*)
East North Central	3,391	2,324	3,215	2,058	4.8	(*)
West North Central	737	482	556	367	3.9	(*)
South Atlantic	(D)	(D)	95	35	(*)	(*)
East South Central	(D)	(D)	221	197	(*)	(*)
West South Central	270	177	431	288	16.8	(*)
Mountain	(D)	(D)	24	23	(*)	(*)
Pacific	133	136	219	170	19.2	(*)

(D) Withheld to avoid disclosing figures for individual companies.   (*) Data not published.

TABLE 1. **TCC GROUP 353**—Percent Distribution of Geographic Division of Origin and Distance Shipped, by Means of Transport: 1972

Geographic division of origin [1] and distance shipped [2]	Number	Percent distribution by means of transport							
		All means of transport	Rail	Motor carrier	Private truck	Air	Water	Other	Unknown
TONS OF SHIPMENTS	(thousands of tons)								
U.S. TOTAL...........	5 628	100.0	34.3	47.4	16.6	.3	.3	.9	.2
NEW ENGLAND.............	16	100.0	38.6	57.6	2.5	.6	.6	.1	-
UNDER 100 MILES.......	1	100.0	-	76.0	23.4	-	-	.6	-
100 TO 199 MILES......	-	100.0	-	98.9	.1	.9	-	.2	-
200 TO 299 MILES......	-	100.0	-	75.4	24.4	.2	-	-	-
300 TO 499 MILES......	2	100.0	-	94.5	-	.3	5.2	-	-
500 TO 999 MILES......	8	100.0	59.5	40.2	-	.2	-	-	-
1000 TO 1499 MILES....	1	100.0	-	99.7	-	.3	-	-	-
1500 MILES OR OVER....	1	100.0	69.9	27.0	-	3.1	-	-	-
MIDDLE ATLANTIC.........	675	100.0	19.4	66.2	12.6	.1	1.0	.6	-
UNDER 100 MILES.......	77	100.0	.3	62.0	34.7	-	-	3.0	-
100 TO 199 MILES......	65	100.0	1.3	78.1	19.9	.1	.2	.4	-
200 TO 299 MILES......	69	100.0	3.0	76.9	19.6	.1	-	.1	.2
300 TO 499 MILES......	95	100.0	8.6	86.5	4.7	.1	-	.1	-
500 TO 999 MILES......	138	100.0	11.5	69.3	18.3	.1	-	.8	.1
1000 TO 1499 MILES....	121	100.0	15.4	81.6	.9	.2	1.9	-	-
1500 MILES OR OVER....	106	100.0	79.8	15.1	.6	.2	4.3	-	-
EAST NORTH CENTRAL......	3 391	100.0	47.7	39.3	11.2	.2	.2	1.2	.2
UNDER 100 MILES.......	305	100.0	17.3	34.6	47.0	.1	.4	.2	.3
100 TO 199 MILES......	333	100.0	9.1	47.2	38.8	-	-	4.8	.2
200 TO 299 MILES......	227	100.0	21.3	65.0	12.7	.1	-	.4	.5
300 TO 499 MILES......	468	100.0	24.2	65.8	6.8	.6	-	2.0	.5
500 TO 999 MILES......	1 371	100.0	60.2	35.7	2.4	.2	.4	.9	.2
1000 TO 1499 MILES....	310	100.0	74.1	23.6	2.0	.2	-	-	-
1500 MILES OR OVER....	374	100.0	84.5	13.9	1.3	.2	-	.1	-
WEST NORTH CENTRAL......	737	100.0	16.3	64.8	18.2	.3	-	.1	.3
UNDER 100 MILES.......	54	100.0	-	67.8	30.6	.2	-	.2	1.3
100 TO 199 MILES......	34	100.0	2.9	49.7	47.3	-	-	.1	.1
200 TO 299 MILES......	84	100.0	.8	80.6	18.4	-	-	.1	.1
300 TO 499 MILES......	123	100.0	29.6	40.4	29.5	.3	-	.3	-
500 TO 999 MILES......	296	100.0	12.0	76.6	10.6	.2	-	.1	.5
1000 TO 1499 MILES....	118	100.0	32.1	52.6	14.4	.9	-	-	-
1500 MILES OR OVER....	25	100.0	32.4	63.7	3.7	.1	-	-	.1
WEST SOUTH CENTRAL......	270	100.0	2.3	57.2	38.1	.7	.6	1.0	-
UNDER 100 MILES.......	6	100.0	-	61.6	37.7	-	-	.7	-
100 TO 199 MILES......	15	100.0	-	44.6	34.9	.2	10.3	9.7	.3
200 TO 299 MILES......	32	100.0	7.2	83.7	8.4	.3	-	.4	-
300 TO 499 MILES......	83	100.0	.1	56.5	42.3	.6	-	.4	-
500 TO 999 MILES......	75	100.0	4.7	38.5	55.8	.8	-	.3	-
1000 TO 1499 MILES....	52	100.0	.7	68.7	28.4	1.1	-	1.0	.1
1500 MILES OR OVER....	5	100.0	-	95.0	2.9	2.0	-	-	-
PACIFIC.................	133	100.0	14.3	70.1	11.2	1.7	.2	2.2	.3
UNDER 100 MILES.......	17	100.0	-	58.9	38.5	.1	1.2	1.2	.1
100 TO 199 MILES......	6	100.0	10.9	78.1	9.5	-	-	.3	1.2
200 TO 299 MILES......	17	100.0	-	94.0	5.7	-	-	.2	.1
300 TO 499 MILES......	17	100.0	5.5	80.3	13.7	.2	-	.4	-
500 TO 999 MILES......	18	100.0	10.8	81.4	2.7	.8	-	4.0	.3
1000 TO 1499 MILES....	13	100.0	1.8	93.2	2.0	2.0	-	.1	.8
1500 MILES OR OVER....	42	100.0	35.3	47.1	8.5	4.3	.1	4.4	.2
TON-MILES OF SHIPMENTS	(millions of ton-miles)								
U.S. TOTAL...........	3 854	100.0	49.6	41.1	7.5	.4	.7	.6	.1
NEW ENGLAND.............	14	100.0	49.6	48.5	.3	1.3	.3	-	-
UNDER 100 MILES.......	-	100.0	-	83.9	15.6	-	-	.5	-
100 TO 199 MILES......	-	100.0	-	99.0	.1	.7	-	.2	-
200 TO 299 MILES......	-	100.0	-	77.9	21.9	.2	-	-	-
300 TO 499 MILES......	-	100.0	-	94.7	-	.3	5.0	-	-
500 TO 999 MILES......	7	100.0	60.7	39.2	-	.1	-	-	-
1000 TO 1499 MILES....	2	100.0	-	99.7	-	.3	-	-	-
1500 MILES OR OVER....	3	100.0	69.4	26.5	-	4.1	-	-	-
MIDDLE ATLANTIC.........	554	100.0	42.4	48.0	5.1	.2	4.0	.2	-
UNDER 100 MILES.......	4	100.0	.4	59.3	36.7	-	-	3.6	-
100 TO 199 MILES......	9	100.0	1.4	79.3	18.5	.1	.2	.4	-
200 TO 299 MILES......	16	100.0	2.8	76.5	20.1	.1	-	.1	.3
300 TO 499 MILES......	36	100.0	8.4	86.8	4.6	.1	-	.1	-
500 TO 999 MILES......	94	100.0	11.8	68.9	18.3	.1	-	.8	.1
1000 TO 1499 MILES....	141	100.0	16.2	80.5	1.0	.2	2.2	-	-
1500 MILES OR OVER....	250	100.0	78.8	12.9	.5	.2	7.7	-	-
EAST NORTH CENTRAL......	2 324	100.0	64.3	30.8	3.6	.2	.2	.7	.1
UNDER 100 MILES.......	14	100.0	12.7	41.6	44.6	.1	.3	.3	.4
100 TO 199 MILES......	48	100.0	9.9	48.1	36.8	-	-	4.9	.2
200 TO 299 MILES......	57	100.0	21.9	64.1	12.9	.1	-	.4	.5
300 TO 499 MILES......	190	100.0	24.7	65.5	6.7	.6	-	2.1	.4
500 TO 999 MILES......	988	100.0	61.0	35.0	2.4	.3	.4	.8	.2
1000 TO 1499 MILES....	363	100.0	74.5	23.4	1.9	.2	-	-	-
1500 MILES OR OVER....	661	100.0	84.0	14.2	1.4	.2	-	.1	-

See footnotes at end of table 4.

TABLE 1. **TCC GROUP 353—Percent Distribution of Geographic Division of Origin and Distance Shipped, by Means of Transport: 1972**—Continued

Geographic division of origin[1] and distance shipped[2]	Number	Percent distribution by means of transport							
		All means of transport	Rail	Motor carrier	Private truck	Air	Water	Other	Unknown
TON-MILES OF SHIPMENTS	(millions of ton-miles)								
WEST NORTH CENTRAL......	482	100.0	21.2	64.2	13.8	.4	-	.1	.3
UNDER 100 MILES.......	3	100.0	-	70.9	27.4	.2	-	.2	1.2
100 TO 199 MILES......	5	100.0	2.4	49.4	48.0	-	-	.1	.1
200 TO 299 MILES......	21	100.0	.7	81.5	17.6	-	-	.1	.1
300 TO 499 MILES......	51	100.0	32.7	38.2	28.6	.3	-	.2	-
500 TO 999 MILES......	221	100.0	13.2	75.1	10.9	.2	-	.1	.6
1000 TO 1499 MILES....	137	100.0	31.2	53.9	14.0	.9	-	-	-
1500 MILES OR OVER....	42	100.0	31.1	65.1	3.6	.1	-	-	.1
WEST SOUTH CENTRAL......	177	100.0	2.5	56.0	39.9	.9	.1	.6	-
UNDER 100 MILES.......	-	100.0	-	75.6	23.7	-	-	.7	-
100 TO 199 MILES......	2	100.0	-	45.5	38.0	.3	7.9	8.0	.3
200 TO 299 MILES......	8	100.0	8.0	82.3	9.0	.3	-	.4	-
300 TO 499 MILES......	35	100.0	.1	53.7	45.2	.6	-	.4	-
500 TO 999 MILES......	59	100.0	5.4	35.5	58.2	.7	-	.2	-
1000 TO 1499 MILES....	63	100.0	.7	68.5	28.7	1.1	-	.9	.1
1500 MILES OR OVER....	7	100.0	-	95.0	2.8	2.1	-	.1	-
PACIFIC................	136	100.0	26.0	59.7	6.3	3.4	.1	4.3	.3
UNDER 100 MILES.......	-	100.0	-	53.6	43.6	-	1.8	.9	-
100 TO 199 MILES......	-	100.0	9.8	79.1	9.3	-	-	.3	1.5
200 TO 299 MILES......	4	100.0	-	94.4	5.3	-	-	.1	.1
300 TO 499 MILES......	6	100.0	4.9	81.4	13.0	.2	-	.5	-
500 TO 999 MILES......	15	100.0	9.7	82.4	2.3	.8	-	4.5	.2
1000 TO 1499 MILES....	17	100.0	1.9	93.1	1.9	2.1	-	.1	.8
1500 MILES OR OVER....	91	100.0	36.4	46.1	7.1	4.5	.1	5.6	.2

See footnotes at end of table 4.

TABLE 2. **TCC GROUP 353—Percent Distribution of Geographic Division of Origin and Means of Transport, by Geographic Division of Destination: 1972**

Geographic division of origin[1] and means of transport	Number	Percent distribution by division of destination									
		U.S. total	New England	Middle Atlantic	East North Central	West North Central	South Atlantic	East South Central	West South Central	Mountain	Pacific
TONS OF SHIPMENTS	(thousands of tons)										
U.S. TOTAL..............	5 628	100.0	2.7	12.4	22.9	6.8	21.8	5.1	11.6	6.3	10.4
RAIL...................	1 933	100.0	1.3	10.5	8.4	4.3	28.6	3.9	12.6	9.6	20.7
MOTOR CARRIER..........	2 665	100.0	4.3	15.4	25.3	8.5	15.7	6.9	12.9	5.0	5.9
PRIVATE TRUCK..........	934	100.0	1.2	7.5	44.9	7.6	25.0	2.4	5.9	3.5	2.2
AIR....................	16	100.0	5.4	27.0	12.0	10.4	14.8	3.1	15.4	5.1	6.9
WATER..................	16	100.0	-	2.8	7.6	-	33.3	-	32.3	-	24.1
OTHER..................	51	100.0	.4	12.6	45.3	2.5	23.7	3.5	5.4	1.7	4.9
UNKNOWN................	11	100.0	10.5	17.2	32.1	9.7	18.6	7.2	2.4	.7	1.5
NEW ENGLAND.............	16	100.0	6.5	15.1	30.7	6.3	13.4	15.7	1.8	9.7	.8
RAIL...................	6	100.0	-	-	41.9	-	12.4	24.6	-	21.2	-
MOTOR CARRIER..........	9	100.0	9.5	22.4	25.2	10.9	14.7	10.7	3.0	2.2	1.3
PRIVATE TRUCK..........	-	100.0	39.4	60.6	-	-	-	-	-	-	-
AIR....................	-	100.0	6.4	7.0	-	-	21.3	-	3.5	50.8	10.9
WATER..................	-	100.0	-	100.0	-	-	-	-	-	-	-
OTHER..................	-	100.0	66.3	-	-	-	33.7	-	-	-	-
UNKNOWN................	-	100.0	-	-	-	-	-	-	-	-	-
MIDDLE ATLANTIC.........	675	100.0	4.6	21.4	21.0	2.3	13.5	5.4	15.3	3.2	13.2
RAIL...................	131	100.0	1.2	4.7	5.5	4.0	7.0	1.1	11.8	5.1	59.7
MOTOR CARRIER..........	446	100.0	5.3	24.2	23.2	2.0	14.2	7.7	18.7	3.2	1.6
PRIVATE TRUCK..........	85	100.0	6.8	32.2	35.2	1.8	21.3	.7	1.3	.4	.3
AIR....................	-	100.0	2.9	17.9	8.5	2.6	29.1	3.5	12.3	3.8	19.4
WATER..................	6	100.0	-	1.6	-	-	-	-	46.6	-	51.8
OTHER..................	3	100.0	1.4	64.2	22.0	5.4	4.2	1.9	.4	.1	.4
UNKNOWN................	-	100.0	57.7	.9	-	40.5	-	.1	-	.8	-
EAST NORTH CENTRAL......	3 391	100.0	2.7	12.6	26.0	5.4	22.3	4.9	9.5	6.2	10.5
RAIL...................	1 616	100.0	1.3	11.3	8.6	3.0	30.9	4.0	12.1	10.1	18.7
MOTOR CARRIER..........	1 333	100.0	5.0	16.2	31.5	8.4	16.9	6.8	8.4	3.2	3.7
PRIVATE TRUCK..........	378	100.0	1.1	5.0	77.6	5.7	3.3	2.1	3.2	.7	1.2
AIR....................	8	100.0	1.6	34.2	15.8	10.9	13.1	3.4	10.1	3.7	7.2
WATER..................	7	100.0	-	2.9	16.6	-	72.7	-	5.9	-	1.8
OTHER..................	39	100.0	.2	9.5	55.3	1.3	28.5	3.6	.4	.1	1.1
UNKNOWN................	7	100.0	1.9	16.1	46.7	3.6	26.6	3.7	1.2	.2	-
WEST NORTH CENTRAL......	737	100.0	3.0	9.0	20.2	18.6	17.6	6.0	11.8	8.2	5.7
RAIL...................	120	100.0	1.0	5.4	7.3	21.1	22.3	2.6	22.6	8.9	8.8
MOTOR CARRIER..........	477	100.0	3.9	9.2	19.5	16.2	18.6	7.5	10.5	8.8	5.7
PRIVATE TRUCK..........	134	100.0	.6	11.5	34.4	24.7	9.8	3.7	6.7	5.7	2.9
AIR....................	2	100.0	19.1	15.4	12.7	7.3	27.4	1.7	8.2	3.9	4.3
WATER..................	-	100.0	-	-	-	-	-	-	-	-	-
OTHER..................	-	100.0	3.8	6.0	24.2	48.5	9.2	3.4	2.7	1.4	.8
UNKNOWN................	2	100.0	39.0	.9	3.2	31.4	.4	23.8	.6	-	.8

See footnotes at end of table 4.

TABLE 2. **TCC GROUP 353—Percent Distribution of Geographic Division of Origin and Means of Transport, by Geographic Division of Destination: 1972**—Continued

Geographic division of origin[1] and means of transport	Number	Percent distribution by division of destination									
		U.S. total	New England	Middle Atlantic	East North Central	West North Central	South Atlantic	East South Central	West South Central	Mountain	Pacific
TONS OF SHIPMENTS	(millions of ton-miles)										
WEST SOUTH CENTRAL......	270	100.0	.7	6.3	11.1	7.7	10.1	4.7	40.4	14.5	4.4
RAIL..................	6	100.0	-	-	3.2	.9	54.2	-	38.4	1.1	2.3
MOTOR CARRIER.........	154	100.0	1.0	5.9	9.5	5.9	4.5	6.5	47.4	12.2	7.2
PRIVATE TRUCK.........	103	100.0	-	7.4	14.4	11.1	16.0	2.5	28.4	19.6	.6
AIR..................	1	100.0	14.0	6.0	9.0	8.7	8.1	4.4	35.6	11.4	2.8
WATER................	1	100.0	-	-	-	-	-	-	100.0	-	-
OTHER................	2	100.0	.1	.5	3.8	2.0	15.2	4.0	72.8	.9	.7
UNKNOWN..............	-	100.0	-	-	-	-	-	.8	50.6	-	48.6
PACIFIC.................	133	100.0	1.1	9.9	7.5	2.5	4.4	3.2	11.8	9.2	50.5
RAIL..................	19	100.0	2.6	38.5	15.3	3.8	6.0	9.9	5.4	9.4	9.0
MOTOR CARRIER.........	93	100.0	1.0	5.1	5.7	1.7	3.9	1.7	14.9	9.5	56.5
PRIVATE TRUCK.........	14	100.0	-	.1	11.4	3.6	5.7	5.1	.1	4.5	69.5
AIR..................	2	100.0	.2	40.9	1.1	17.9	3.6	.5	26.7	4.9	4.2
WATER................	-	100.0	-	6.7	-	-	-	-	-	-	93.3
OTHER................	2	100.0	.3	.8	1.6	.3	.9	.4	.3	26.5	68.8
UNKNOWN..............	-	100.0	-	-	.9	-	20.1	-	32.6	16.8	29.7
TON-MILES OF SHIPMENTS	(millions of ton-miles)										
U.S. TOTAL..............	3 854	100.0	3.1	11.0	8.5	4.2	20.0	3.8	13.5	10.2	25.7
RAIL..................	1 910	100.0	1.2	8.0	2.1	2.3	22.2	2.1	11.1	11.7	39.3
MOTOR CARRIER.........	1 582	100.0	5.6	14.4	12.1	6.0	17.4	5.9	17.1	8.9	12.6
PRIVATE TRUCK.........	288	100.0	1.9	11.9	30.3	8.0	19.2	3.9	10.0	9.0	5.8
AIR..................	15	100.0	6.1	29.6	5.2	7.6	14.5	2.0	15.6	6.1	13.3
WATER................	27	100.0	-	1.0	.2	-	13.3	-	19.3	-	66.3
OTHER................	24	100.0	.7	8.7	22.0	2.5	32.2	2.8	3.5	3.3	24.2
UNKNOWN..............	5	100.0	18.2	19.6	14.5	4.8	27.4	7.7	4.6	1.1	2.0
NEW ENGLAND............	14	100.0	.5	4.8	29.5	8.6	10.1	17.9	3.2	22.7	2.6
RAIL..................	7	100.0	-	-	31.7	-	8.2	21.6	-	38.4	-
MOTOR CARRIER.........	6	100.0	1.1	8.7	28.4	17.6	12.3	14.9	6.6	5.9	4.5
PRIVATE TRUCK.........	-	100.0	7.8	92.2	-	-	-	-	-	-	-
AIR..................	-	100.0	.4	1.1	-	-	6.8	-	2.8	60.5	28.3
WATER................	-	100.0	-	100.0	-	-	-	-	-	-	-
OTHER................	-	100.0	14.3	-	-	-	85.7	-	-	-	-
UNKNOWN..............	-	100.0	-	-	-	-	-	-	-	-	-
MIDDLE ATLANTIC........	554	100.0	1.6	4.2	12.3	2.5	7.3	4.0	22.0	6.6	39.4
RAIL..................	235	100.0	.3	.8	2.0	1.7	2.6	.4	8.4	5.8	78.0
MOTOR CARRIER.........	266	100.0	2.6	6.7	17.6	3.1	11.3	7.8	36.1	8.5	6.2
PRIVATE TRUCK.........	28	100.0	3.9	10.3	57.7	4.6	13.3	1.3	5.0	1.9	2.1
AIR..................	-	100.0	.8	3.8	4.2	2.5	19.7	2.5	15.0	6.8	44.8
WATER................	22	100.0	-	.1	-	-	-	-	20.7	-	79.2
OTHER................	1	100.0	.9	18.3	47.0	18.0	5.1	5.3	1.5	.6	3.1
UNKNOWN..............	-	100.0	34.2	.2	-	61.8	-	.3	.1	3.5	-
EAST NORTH CENTRAL.....	2 324	100.0	3.3	11.4	6.1	3.2	23.5	3.3	11.3	10.5	27.4
RAIL..................	1 495	100.0	1.3	8.5	1.6	1.5	25.4	2.1	10.9	12.8	35.8
MOTOR CARRIER.........	715	100.0	7.6	17.5	11.5	5.9	20.2	5.7	12.2	6.8	12.5
PRIVATE TRUCK.........	84	100.0	3.7	9.3	36.7	9.3	9.9	5.0	12.1	3.5	10.5
AIR..................	5	100.0	1.9	30.3	6.5	5.9	14.2	2.8	12.5	6.5	19.4
WATER................	4	100.0	-	3.5	1.0	-	80.0	-	9.7	-	5.7
OTHER................	15	100.0	.6	11.4	29.5	1.4	46.7	3.3	.8	.3	6.0
UNKNOWN..............	3	100.0	2.9	21.3	24.1	4.0	41.5	2.7	2.7	.7	.1
WEST NORTH CENTRAL.....	482	100.0	4.8	11.9	8.5	8.5	23.3	4.6	13.5	11.4	13.4
RAIL..................	102	100.0	1.2	5.8	3.3	11.6	26.5	1.7	23.7	10.1	16.1
MOTOR CARRIER.........	309	100.0	6.2	11.6	7.1	7.7	23.8	5.7	11.4	12.6	13.9
PRIVATE TRUCK.........	66	100.0	1.7	22.8	23.0	8.0	16.6	3.6	8.3	8.7	7.4
AIR..................	1	100.0	22.5	14.9	6.1	1.8	33.2	1.3	7.3	5.3	7.5
WATER................	-	100.0	-	-	-	-	-	-	-	-	-
OTHER................	-	100.0	8.0	10.9	20.6	29.9	16.4	5.0	3.1	3.4	2.7
UNKNOWN..............	1	100.0	65.5	1.3	1.2	3.0	.5	25.7	.6	-	2.2
WEST SOUTH CENTRAL.....	177	100.0	1.3	11.3	12.6	6.7	15.6	3.5	19.8	19.6	9.5
RAIL..................	4	100.0	-	-	4.5	1.1	73.6	-	16.0	1.1	3.7
MOTOR CARRIER.........	99	100.0	2.0	11.7	11.6	5.5	6.6	4.2	23.7	18.7	15.9
PRIVATE TRUCK.........	71	100.0	-	11.7	14.8	8.9	24.4	2.6	14.2	22.5	1.0
AIR..................	1	100.0	24.3	9.9	9.5	6.6	9.9	3.5	18.7	12.5	5.1
WATER................	-	100.0	-	-	-	-	-	-	100.0	-	-
OTHER................	1	100.0	.5	1.5	9.3	2.6	43.0	5.8	32.7	1.9	2.7
UNKNOWN..............	-	100.0	-	-	-	-	-	.6	10.1	-	89.3
PACIFIC.................	136	100.0	2.7	23.7	13.4	3.5	9.7	5.8	16.7	5.6	18.9
RAIL..................	35	100.0	3.6	50.7	14.9	3.1	7.5	10.2	5.2	2.4	2.5
MOTOR CARRIER.........	81	100.0	3.0	14.6	12.2	2.7	10.2	3.7	24.2	6.8	22.7
PRIVATE TRUCK.........	8	100.0	-	.2	34.7	8.8	21.1	14.5	.3	4.2	16.2
AIR..................	4	100.0	.3	51.6	1.0	14.2	4.5	.4	23.9	2.0	1.9
WATER................	-	100.0	-	31.6	-	-	-	-	-	-	68.4
OTHER................	5	100.0	.4	1.0	1.4	.2	1.1	.4	.2	11.9	83.3
UNKNOWN..............	-	100.0	-	-	1.4	-	44.0	-	40.5	9.6	4.6

See footnotes at end of table 4.

TABLE 3. **TCC GROUP 353**—Percent Distribution of Geographic Division of Destination and Means of Transport, by Geographic Division of Origin: 1972

Geographic division of destination and means of transport	Number	Percent distribution by division of origin[1]									
		U.S. total	New England	Middle Atlantic	East North Central	West North Central	South Atlantic	East South Central	West South Central	Mountain	Pacific
TONS OF SHIPMENTS	(thousands of tons)										
U.S. TOTAL..............	5 628	100.0	.3	12.0	60.2	13.1	(D)	(D)	4.8	(D)	2.4
RAIL................	1 933	100.0	.3	6.8	83.6	6.2	(D)	(D)	.3	(D)	1.0
MOTOR CARRIER........	2 665	100.0	.4	16.8	50.0	17.9	(D)	(D)	5.8	(D)	3.5
PRIVATE TRUCK........	934	100.0	-	9.1	40.5	14.4	(D)	(D)	11.0	(D)	1.6
AIR.................	16	100.0	.6	5.0	49.5	13.8	(D)	(D)	12.0	(D)	14.4
WATER...............	16	100.0	.7	42.2	45.7	-	(D)	(D)	9.9	(D)	1.5
OTHER...............	51	100.0	-	7.7	77.3	1.6	(D)	(D)	5.5	(D)	5.8
UNKNOWN.............	11	100.0	-	2.7	67.3	19.7	(D)	(D)	.9	(D)	3.1
NEW ENGLAND............	153	100.0	.7	20.3	60.5	14.3	(D)	(D)	1.2	(D)	1.0
RAIL................	25	100.0	-	6.3	85.1	4.8	(D)	(D)	-	(D)	1.9
MOTOR CARRIER........	114	100.0	.8	20.5	58.0	16.2	(D)	(D)	1.3	(D)	.8
PRIVATE TRUCK........	10	100.0	1.5	52.5	38.5	7.6	(D)	(D)	-	(D)	-
AIR.................	-	100.0	.7	2.7	14.9	48.9	(D)	(D)	31.0	(D)	.5
WATER...............	-	100.0	-	-	-	-	(D)	(D)	-	(D)	-
OTHER...............	-	100.0	3.8	25.7	45.8	14.7	(D)	(D)	1.8	(D)	3.9
UNKNOWN.............	1	100.0	-	14.6	12.3	73.1	(D)	(D)	-	(D)	-
MIDDLE ATLANTIC........	698	100.0	.4	20.7	61.0	9.5	(D)	(D)	2.4	(D)	1.9
RAIL................	203	100.0	-	3.0	89.9	3.2	(D)	(D)	-	(D)	3.6
MOTOR CARRIER........	411	100.0	.5	26.3	52.5	10.7	(D)	(D)	2.2	(D)	1.2
PRIVATE TRUCK........	69	100.0	.4	39.3	27.0	22.1	(D)	(D)	11.0	(D)	-
AIR.................	4	100.0	.2	3.3	62.6	7.9	(D)	(D)	2.7	(D)	21.8
WATER...............	-	100.0	23.7	24.5	48.2	-	(D)	(D)	-	(D)	3.7
OTHER...............	6	100.0	-	39.0	58.4	.8	(D)	(D)	.2	(D)	.4
UNKNOWN.............	1	100.0	-	.1	62.8	1.0	(D)	(D)	-	(D)	-
EAST NORTH CENTRAL.....	1 286	100.0	.4	11.0	68.4	11.6	(D)	(D)	2.3	(D)	.8
RAIL................	162	100.0	1.7	4.5	85.4	5.4	(D)	(D)	.1	(D)	1.8
MOTOR CARRIER........	674	100.0	.4	15.4	62.2	13.8	(D)	(D)	2.2	(D)	.8
PRIVATE TRUCK........	419	100.0	-	7.1	70.0	11.0	(D)	(D)	3.5	(D)	.4
AIR.................	1	100.0	-	3.5	65.0	14.6	(D)	(D)	9.0	(D)	1.4
WATER...............	1	100.0	-	-	100.0	-	(D)	(D)	-	(D)	-
OTHER...............	23	100.0	-	3.7	94.2	.9	(D)	(D)	.5	(D)	.2
UNKNOWN.............	3	100.0	-	-	97.9	2.0	(D)	(D)	-	(D)	.1
WEST NORTH CENTRAL.....	384	100.0	.3	4.1	47.7	35.6	(D)	(D)	5.4	(D)	.8
RAIL................	83	100.0	-	6.2	57.7	30.5	(D)	(D)	.1	(D)	.9
MOTOR CARRIER........	226	100.0	.5	3.9	49.6	34.1	(D)	(D)	4.0	(D)	.7
PRIVATE TRUCK........	71	100.0	-	2.1	30.4	46.6	(D)	(D)	16.0	(D)	.8
AIR.................	1	100.0	-	1.2	51.8	9.6	(D)	(D)	10.0	(D)	24.7
WATER...............	-	100.0	-	-	-	-	(D)	(D)	-	(D)	-
OTHER...............	1	100.0	-	17.0	42.2	32.3	(D)	(D)	4.5	(D)	.7
UNKNOWN.............	1	100.0	-	11.0	24.8	63.4	(D)	(D)	-	(D)	-
SOUTH ATLANTIC.........	1 226	100.0	.2	7.4	61.6	10.6	(D)	(D)	2.2	(D)	.5
RAIL................	553	100.0	.1	1.7	90.1	4.8	(D)	(D)	.6	(D)	.2
MOTOR CARRIER........	417	100.0	.3	15.2	53.9	21.3	(D)	(D)	1.7	(D)	.9
PRIVATE TRUCK........	233	100.0	-	7.8	5.3	5.6	(D)	(D)	7.1	(D)	.4
AIR.................	2	100.0	.9	9.8	43.8	25.6	(D)	(D)	6.5	(D)	3.6
WATER...............	5	100.0	-	-	100.0	-	(D)	(D)	-	(D)	-
OTHER...............	12	100.0	-	1.4	93.1	.6	(D)	(D)	3.5	(D)	.2
UNKNOWN.............	2	100.0	-	-	96.2	.4	(D)	(D)	-	(D)	3.4
EAST SOUTH CENTRAL.....	285	100.0	.9	12.8	57.8	15.6	(D)	(D)	4.5	(D)	1.5
RAIL................	74	100.0	2.1	1.9	86.3	4.1	(D)	(D)	-	(D)	2.5
MOTOR CARRIER........	184	100.0	.6	18.6	48.9	19.4	(D)	(D)	5.5	(D)	.9
PRIVATE TRUCK........	22	100.0	-	2.7	35.7	22.0	(D)	(D)	11.3	(D)	3.3
AIR.................	-	100.0	-	5.8	55.2	7.8	(D)	(D)	17.4	(D)	2.4
WATER...............	-	100.0	-	-	-	-	(D)	(D)	-	(D)	-
OTHER...............	1	100.0	-	4.3	80.0	1.6	(D)	(D)	6.4	(D)	.6
UNKNOWN.............	-	100.0	-	-	34.6	65.3	(D)	(D)	.1	(D)	-
WEST SOUTH CENTRAL.....	653	100.0	-	15.8	49.1	13.2	(D)	(D)	16.7	(D)	2.4
RAIL................	243	100.0	-	6.3	80.1	11.1	(D)	(D)	1.0	(D)	.4
MOTOR CARRIER........	344	100.0	.1	24.2	32.5	14.6	(D)	(D)	21.3	(D)	4.0
PRIVATE TRUCK........	54	100.0	-	2.1	22.4	16.5	(D)	(D)	53.4	(D)	-
AIR.................	2	100.0	.1	4.0	32.5	7.4	(D)	(D)	27.8	(D)	25.0
WATER...............	5	100.0	-	60.9	8.4	-	(D)	(D)	30.7	(D)	-
OTHER...............	2	100.0	-	.5	5.2	.8	(D)	(D)	74.4	(D)	.4
UNKNOWN.............	-	100.0	-	-	34.2	5.0	(D)	(D)	19.1	(D)	41.6
MOUNTAIN...............	354	100.0	.5	6.0	58.9	17.0	(D)	(D)	11.1	(D)	3.5
RAIL................	186	100.0	.7	3.6	87.8	5.8	(D)	(D)	-	(D)	1.0
MOTOR CARRIER........	134	100.0	.2	10.7	31.4	31.3	(D)	(D)	14.1	(D)	6.6
PRIVATE TRUCK........	32	100.0	-	1.0	8.4	23.4	(D)	(D)	62.1	(D)	2.1
AIR.................	-	100.0	6.2	3.8	36.6	10.6	(D)	(D)	27.0	(D)	13.9
WATER...............	-	100.0	-	-	-	-	(D)	(D)	-	(D)	-
OTHER...............	-	100.0	-	.4	5.0	1.3	(D)	(D)	2.7	(D)	89.8
UNKNOWN.............	-	100.0	-	3.2	21.5	-	(D)	(D)	-	(D)	75.3
PACIFIC................	584	100.0	-	15.3	61.2	7.2	(D)	(D)	2.1	(D)	11.5
RAIL................	399	100.0	-	19.5	75.7	2.6	(D)	(D)	-	(D)	.4
MOTOR CARRIER........	156	100.0	.1	4.5	31.4	17.5	(D)	(D)	7.1	(D)	33.7
PRIVATE TRUCK........	20	100.0	-	1.2	23.1	19.5	(D)	(D)	3.3	(D)	51.7
AIR.................	1	100.0	1.0	14.1	52.2	8.7	(D)	(D)	5.0	(D)	8.8
WATER...............	3	100.0	-	90.6	3.5	-	(D)	(D)	-	(D)	5.8
OTHER...............	2	100.0	-	.6	16.9	.3	(D)	(D)	.8	(D)	81.1
UNKNOWN.............	-	100.0	-	-	1.2	10.0	(D)	(D)	29.0	(D)	59.8

See footnotes at end of table 4.

TABLE 3. **TCC GROUP 353—Percent Distribution of Geographic Division of Destination and Means of Transport, by Geographic Division of Origin: 1972**—Continued

Geographic division of destination and means of transport	Number	Percent distribution by division of origin[1]									
		U.S. total	New England	Middle Atlantic	East North Central	West North Central	South Atlantic	East South Central	West South Central	Mountain	Pacific
TON-MILES OF SHIPMENTS	(millions of ton-miles)										
U.S. TOTAL............	3 854	100.0	.4	14.4	60.3	12.5	(D)	(D)	4.6	(D)	3.5
RAIL.................	1 910	100.0	.4	12.3	78.3	5.4	(D)	(D)	.2	(D)	1.9
MOTOR CARRIER........	1 582	100.0	.4	16.8	45.2	19.6	(D)	(D)	6.3	(D)	5.1
PRIVATE TRUCK........	288	100.0	-	9.8	29.2	23.1	(D)	(D)	24.6	(D)	3.0
AIR.................	15	100.0	1.2	5.4	36.1	12.4	(D)	(D)	9.9	(D)	29.5
WATER...............	27	100.0	.1	82.1	16.6	-	(D)	(D)	.7	(D)	.5
OTHER...............	24	100.0	-	4.7	62.8	1.6	(D)	(D)	4.5	(D)	24.0
UNKNOWN.............	5	100.0	-	2.7	58.6	23.8	(D)	(D)	1.2	(D)	6.8
NEW ENGLAND...........	119	100.0	.1	7.4	64.8	19.2	(D)	(D)	2.0	(D)	3.1
RAIL.................	22	100.0	-	2.6	84.7	5.5	(D)	(D)	-	(D)	5.5
MOTOR CARRIER........	89	100.0	.1	7.9	61.2	21.7	(D)	(D)	2.3	(D)	2.7
PRIVATE TRUCK........	5	100.0	.1	20.5	58.4	21.1	(D)	(D)	-	(D)	-
AIR.................	-	100.0	.1	.7	11.1	46.0	(D)	(D)	39.6	(D)	1.3
WATER...............	-	100.0	-	-	-	-	(D)	(D)	-	(D)	-
OTHER...............	-	100.0	.3	6.5	52.1	18.8	(D)	(D)	3.5	(D)	13.1
UNKNOWN.............	-	100.0	-	5.0	9.3	85.7	(D)	(D)	-	(D)	-
MIDDLE ATLANTIC.........	424	100.0	.2	5.4	62.5	13.6	(D)	(D)	4.7	(D)	7.6
RAIL.................	153	100.0	-	1.3	83.0	3.8	(D)	(D)	-	(D)	11.7
MOTOR CARRIER........	228	100.0	.3	7.9	55.0	15.8	(D)	(D)	5.1	(D)	5.2
PRIVATE TRUCK........	34	100.0	.1	8.5	22.7	44.2	(D)	(D)	24.2	(D)	.1
AIR.................	4	100.0	-	.7	37.0	6.2	(D)	(D)	3.3	(D)	51.4
WATER...............	-	100.0	15.4	8.0	60.5	-	(D)	(D)	-	(D)	16.1
OTHER...............	2	100.0	-	9.8	82.5	2.0	(D)	(D)	.7	(D)	2.8
UNKNOWN.............	1	100.0	-	-	63.5	1.6	(D)	(D)	-	(D)	-
EAST NORTH CENTRAL......	327	100.0	1.3	20.9	43.6	12.5	(D)	(D)	6.9	(D)	5.6
RAIL.................	40	100.0	5.5	11.5	58.9	8.3	(D)	(D)	.5	(D)	13.0
MOTOR CARRIER........	192	100.0	1.0	24.4	42.7	11.5	(D)	(D)	6.0	(D)	5.1
PRIVATE TRUCK........	87	100.0	-	18.7	35.4	17.5	(D)	(D)	12.0	(D)	3.4
AIR.................	-	100.0	-	4.3	45.0	14.4	(D)	(D)	18.0	(D)	5.8
WATER...............	-	100.0	-	-	100.0	-	(D)	(D)	-	(D)	-
OTHER...............	5	100.0	-	10.0	84.1	1.5	(D)	(D)	1.9	(D)	1.5
UNKNOWN.............	-	100.0	-	-	97.3	2.0	(D)	(D)	-	(D)	.6
WEST NORTH CENTRAL......	162	100.0	.7	8.7	45.1	25.3	(D)	(D)	7.3	(D)	2.9
RAIL.................	43	100.0	-	9.5	52.3	27.3	(D)	(D)	.1	(D)	2.5
MOTOR CARRIER........	94	100.0	1.3	8.9	44.7	25.3	(D)	(D)	5.8	(D)	2.4
PRIVATE TRUCK........	23	100.0	-	5.7	34.1	23.2	(D)	(D)	27.4	(D)	3.3
AIR.................	1	100.0	-	1.8	28.1	2.9	(D)	(D)	8.6	(D)	55.2
WATER...............	-	100.0	-	-	-	-	(D)	(D)	-	(D)	-
OTHER...............	-	100.0	-	33.3	34.9	18.6	(D)	(D)	4.6	(D)	2.2
UNKNOWN.............	-	100.0	-	34.5	49.4	15.1	(D)	(D)	-	(D)	-
SOUTH ATLANTIC..........	770	100.0	.2	5.2	70.9	14.6	(D)	(D)	3.6	(D)	1.7
RAIL.................	424	100.0	.1	1.4	89.6	6.4	(D)	(D)	.8	(D)	.6
MOTOR CARRIER........	275	100.0	.3	10.9	52.6	26.7	(D)	(D)	2.4	(D)	3.0
PRIVATE TRUCK........	55	100.0	-	6.8	15.0	20.0	(D)	(D)	31.2	(D)	3.3
AIR.................	2	100.0	.6	7.4	35.2	28.3	(D)	(D)	6.8	(D)	9.2
WATER...............	3	100.0	-	-	100.0	-	(D)	(D)	-	(D)	-
OTHER...............	7	100.0	-	.7	91.1	.8	(D)	(D)	5.9	(D)	.8
UNKNOWN.............	1	100.0	-	-	88.7	.4	(D)	(D)	-	(D)	10.9
EAST SOUTH CENTRAL......	146	100.0	1.7	15.3	53.1	15.2	(D)	(D)	4.2	(D)	5.4
RAIL.................	40	100.0	3.8	2.4	78.6	4.3	(D)	(D)	-	(D)	8.9
MOTOR CARRIER........	93	100.0	1.1	22.4	43.9	19.0	(D)	(D)	4.5	(D)	3.2
PRIVATE TRUCK........	11	100.0	-	3.3	37.3	21.1	(D)	(D)	16.6	(D)	11.0
AIR.................	-	100.0	-	6.8	49.9	8.3	(D)	(D)	17.3	(D)	6.4
WATER...............	-	100.0	-	-	-	-	(D)	(D)	-	(D)	-
OTHER...............	-	100.0	-	9.0	74.2	2.9	(D)	(D)	9.3	(D)	3.4
UNKNOWN.............	-	100.0	-	.1	20.8	79.1	(D)	(D)	.1	(D)	-
WEST SOUTH CENTRAL......	519	100.0	.1	23.5	50.5	12.5	(D)	(D)	6.8	(D)	4.4
RAIL.................	211	100.0	-	9.3	77.3	11.4	(D)	(D)	.3	(D)	.9
MOTOR CARRIER........	270	100.0	.2	35.6	32.3	13.0	(D)	(D)	8.7	(D)	7.3
PRIVATE TRUCK........	28	100.0	-	4.9	35.7	19.3	(D)	(D)	35.0	(D)	.1
AIR.................	2	100.0	.2	5.2	28.8	5.8	(D)	(D)	11.8	(D)	45.1
WATER...............	5	100.0	-	88.0	8.4	-	(D)	(D)	3.6	(D)	-
OTHER...............	-	100.0	-	2.0	14.3	1.4	(D)	(D)	41.4	(D)	1.7
UNKNOWN.............	-	100.0	-	.1	34.4	3.1	(D)	(D)	2.7	(D)	59.8
MOUNTAIN..............	391	100.0	.8	9.4	62.3	14.1	(D)	(D)	8.9	(D)	1.9
RAIL.................	223	100.0	1.2	6.1	85.9	4.6	(D)	(D)	-	(D)	.4
MOTOR CARRIER........	140	100.0	.3	16.1	34.6	27.8	(D)	(D)	13.3	(D)	4.0
PRIVATE TRUCK........	26	100.0	-	2.0	11.4	22.2	(D)	(D)	61.2	(D)	1.4
AIR.................	-	100.0	11.6	6.1	38.5	10.8	(D)	(D)	20.4	(D)	9.8
WATER...............	-	100.0	-	-	-	-	(D)	(D)	-	(D)	-
OTHER...............	-	100.0	-	.9	6.3	1.6	(D)	(D)	2.6	(D)	87.3
UNKNOWN.............	-	100.0	-	8.2	34.7	-	(D)	(D)	-	(D)	57.1
PACIFIC...............	992	100.0	-	22.0	64.1	6.5	(D)	(D)	1.7	(D)	2.6
RAIL.................	750	100.0	-	24.5	71.3	2.2	(D)	(D)	-	(D)	.1
MOTOR CARRIER........	199	100.0	.2	8.2	45.1	21.6	(D)	(D)	8.0	(D)	9.3
PRIVATE TRUCK........	16	100.0	-	3.6	52.9	29.5	(D)	(D)	4.2	(D)	8.3
AIR.................	2	100.0	2.5	18.2	52.6	7.0	(D)	(D)	3.8	(D)	4.3
WATER...............	18	100.0	-	98.1	1.4	-	(D)	(D)	-	(D)	.5
OTHER...............	5	100.0	-	.6	15.6	.2	(D)	(D)	.5	(D)	82.6
UNKNOWN.............	-	100.0	-	-	3.3	25.9	(D)	(D)	55.0	(D)	15.8

See footnotes at end of table 4.

TABLE 4. TCC GROUP 353—Percent Distribution of Distance Shipped and Weight of Shipment, by Means of Transport: 1972

Distance shipped and weight of shipment[2][3]	Number	Percent distribution by means of transport							
		All means of transport	Rail	Motor carrier	Private truck	Air	Water	Other	Unknown
TONS OF SHIPMENTS	(thousands of tons)								
U.S. TOTAL..........	4 889	100.0	36.1	46.8	15.7	.3	.2	.7	.2
UNDER 100 MILES.........	441	100.0	2.0	35.7	60.8	.1	.3	.7	.4
UNDER 1000 POUNDS.....	17	100.0	-	79.6	10.9	1.2	-	8.0	.3
1000 TO 9999 POUNDS...	70	100.0	-	39.5	55.7	-	1.8	1.9	1.0
10000 TO 29999 POUNDS.	237	100.0	.1	23.4	76.4	-	-	-	-
30000 TO 59999 POUNDS.	96	100.0	3.6	56.3	38.8	-	-	.5	.7
60000 TO 89999 POUNDS.	4	100.0	4.4	90.9	.7	-	4.0	-	-
90000 POUNDS AND OVER.	14	100.0	33.9	11.8	53.7	-	-	-	.6
100 TO 199 MILES........	405	100.0	8.0	51.4	39.9	.1	-	.5	.2
UNDER 1000 POUNDS.....	17	100.0	.8	89.6	4.6	1.2	.1	3.6	.2
1000 TO 9999 POUNDS...	121	100.0	.4	41.9	57.2	-	-	.3	.1
10000 TO 29999 POUNDS.	111	100.0	1.3	55.9	42.9	-	-	-	-
30000 TO 59999 POUNDS.	112	100.0	7.0	58.6	33.3	-	.1	1.0	-
60000 TO 89999 POUNDS.	31	100.0	45.0	44.6	10.4	-	-	-	-
90000 POUNDS AND OVER.	12	100.0	68.4	2.0	25.2	-	-	-	4.4
200 TO 299 MILES........	433	100.0	12.9	67.4	19.0	.1	-	.3	.3
UNDER 1000 POUNDS.....	18	100.0	-	90.2	4.5	1.8	-	2.6	.9
1000 TO 9999 POUNDS...	65	100.0	.2	70.6	28.2	-	-	-	.9
10000 TO 29999 POUNDS.	147	100.0	2.6	72.2	24.8	-	-	.4	-
30000 TO 59999 POUNDS.	149	100.0	25.0	59.6	15.2	-	-	-	.1
60000 TO 89999 POUNDS.	29	100.0	28.6	59.1	12.1	-	-	-	.1
90000 POUNDS AND OVER.	22	100.0	26.9	70.1	.9	-	-	-	2.1
300 TO 499 MILES........	735	100.0	20.8	62.6	14.6	.4	-	1.4	.3
UNDER 1000 POUNDS.....	39	100.0	-	92.8	.9	3.4	-	2.8	-
1000 TO 9999 POUNDS...	90	100.0	1.3	83.5	11.7	1.4	.1	.6	1.3
10000 TO 29999 POUNDS.	138	100.0	5.1	69.9	24.1	-	-	.4	.4
30000 TO 59999 POUNDS.	284	100.0	14.6	62.4	21.3	-	-	1.7	-
60000 TO 89999 POUNDS.	66	100.0	53.4	39.0	2.9	-	-	4.6	-
90000 POUNDS AND OVER.	115	100.0	58.0	41.0	.6	-	-	-	.4
500 TO 999 MILES........	1 782	100.0	47.0	45.6	5.8	.2	.3	.8	.2
UNDER 1000 POUNDS.....	54	100.0	1.4	88.7	1.1	5.2	.3	3.1	.1
1000 TO 9999 POUNDS...	137	100.0	3.5	82.5	11.3	.8	.1	.5	1.3
10000 TO 29999 POUNDS.	345	100.0	9.2	76.9	13.5	-	.1	.1	.2
30000 TO 59999 POUNDS.	621	100.0	39.2	54.1	5.9	-	-	.6	.2
60000 TO 89999 POUNDS.	334	100.0	87.9	8.9	1.1	-	-	2.1	-
90000 POUNDS AND OVER.	288	100.0	91.3	6.7	.1	-	1.9	-	.1
1000 TO 1499 MILES......	553	100.0	48.6	43.7	6.6	.4	.4	.1	-
UNDER 1000 POUNDS.....	14	100.0	1.9	84.9	1.3	10.3	-	1.6	-
1000 TO 9999 POUNDS...	46	100.0	5.8	83.6	8.5	1.1	-	.8	.1
10000 TO 29999 POUNDS.	90	100.0	13.7	65.0	20.7	.4	-	-	.1
30000 TO 59999 POUNDS.	198	100.0	38.6	54.5	6.4	-	.4	-	-
60000 TO 89999 POUNDS.	92	100.0	89.3	8.3	.9	-	1.6	-	-
90000 POUNDS AND OVER.	110	100.0	85.5	14.2	.2	-	-	-	-
1500 MILES OR OVER......	537	100.0	75.7	21.3	1.6	.5	.4	.4	-
UNDER 1000 POUNDS.....	15	100.0	20.1	71.6	.2	6.6	.2	1.2	.2
1000 TO 9999 POUNDS...	35	100.0	15.6	71.0	6.3	5.0	.9	1.0	.2
10000 TO 29999 POUNDS.	52	100.0	46.1	48.1	5.2	-	.6	-	-
30000 TO 59999 POUNDS.	180	100.0	70.4	26.6	1.2	-	.7	1.0	-
60000 TO 89999 POUNDS.	104	100.0	95.2	4.7	.1	-	-	-	-
90000 POUNDS AND OVER.	148	100.0	99.1	-	.9	-	-	-	-
TON-MILES OF SHIPMENTS	(millions of ton-miles)								
U.S. TOTAL..........	3 431	100.0	51.6	40.0	6.9	.4	.4	.6	.1
UNDER 100 MILES.........	21	100.0	2.3	40.7	55.3	.1	.3	1.0	.4
UNDER 1000 POUNDS.....	-	100.0	-	82.1	8.0	1.3	-	8.2	.4
1000 TO 9999 POUNDS...	3	100.0	-	39.9	55.3	-	1.1	2.7	.9
10000 TO 29999 POUNDS.	10	100.0	.2	31.6	68.1	-	-	-	-
30000 TO 59999 POUNDS.	5	100.0	1.7	55.1	41.9	-	-	.6	.7
60000 TO 89999 POUNDS.	-	100.0	6.9	88.3	.3	-	4.6	-	-
90000 POUNDS AND OVER.	-	100.0	40.5	5.7	53.0	-	-	-	.8
100 TO 199 MILES........	59	100.0	8.7	51.9	38.6	.1	-	.5	.2
UNDER 1000 POUNDS.....	2	100.0	.6	89.5	4.6	1.4	.1	3.7	.2
1000 TO 9999 POUNDS...	17	100.0	.4	45.0	54.1	-	-	.4	.1
10000 TO 29999 POUNDS.	16	100.0	1.5	56.1	42.3	-	-	-	-
30000 TO 59999 POUNDS.	16	100.0	7.0	57.7	34.5	-	.1	.7	-
60000 TO 89999 POUNDS.	4	100.0	51.6	40.7	7.7	-	-	-	-
90000 POUNDS AND OVER.	1	100.0	73.5	2.5	18.7	-	-	-	5.3

See footnotes at end of table 4.

TABLE 4. **TCC GROUP 353—Percent Distribution of Distance Shipped and Weight of Shipment, by Means of Transport: 1972**—Continued

Distance shipped and weight of shipment[2] [3]	Number	Percent distribution by means of transport							
		All means of transport	Rail	Motor carrier	Private truck	Air	Water	Other	Unknown
TON-MILES OF SHIPMENTS	(millions of ton-miles)								
200 TO 299 MILES.........	109	100.0	13.1	66.8	19.3	.1	-	.3	.3
UNDER 1000 POUNDS......	4	100.0	-	89.8	4.8	1.8	-	2.5	1.0
1000 TO 9999 POUNDS...	16	100.0	.3	68.9	29.9	-	-	-	.9
10000 TO 29999 POUNDS.	37	100.0	2.4	72.5	24.6	-	-	.4	-
30000 TO 59999 POUNDS.	37	100.0	26.2	58.0	15.7	-	-	-	.1
60000 TO 89999 POUNDS.	6	100.0	27.6	60.8	11.4	-	-	-	.2
90000 POUNDS AND OVER.	5	100.0	27.2	70.2	.7	-	-	-	1.9
300 TO 499 MILES.........	297	100.0	21.7	61.5	14.7	.4	-	1.4	.3
UNDER 1000 POUNDS.....	15	100.0	-	92.9	.9	3.4	-	2.8	-
1000 TO 9999 POUNDS...	35	100.0	1.5	82.8	11.9	1.7	.1	.6	1.3
10000 TO 29999 POUNDS.	54	100.0	5.3	69.2	24.7	-	-	.5	.4
30000 TO 59999 POUNDS.	116	100.0	15.1	61.9	21.3	-	-	1.7	-
60000 TO 89999 POUNDS.	26	100.0	52.9	39.0	2.8	-	-	5.3	-
90000 POUNDS AND OVER.	48	100.0	60.8	38.4	.5	-	-	-	.3
500 TO 999 MILES.........	1 286	100.0	47.6	44.9	6.0	.2	.3	.7	.2
UNDER 1000 POUNDS.....	38	100.0	1.4	88.3	1.1	5.6	.3	3.1	.1
1000 TO 9999 POUNDS...	98	100.0	3.6	81.6	12.2	.8	.1	.6	1.2
10000 TO 29999 POUNDS.	250	100.0	9.4	76.4	13.8	-	.2	.1	.1
30000 TO 59999 POUNDS.	449	100.0	40.2	52.7	6.3	-	-	.6	.2
60000 TO 89999 POUNDS.	240	100.0	88.7	8.5	1.0	-	-	1.7	-
90000 POUNDS AND OVER.	209	100.0	91.2	7.0	-	-	1.7	-	.1
1000 TO 1499 MILES......	649	100.0	48.4	43.9	6.6	.4	.5	.1	-
UNDER 1000 POUNDS.....	17	100.0	2.0	84.8	1.4	10.2	-	1.6	-
1000 TO 9999 POUNDS...	56	100.0	5.4	85.0	7.8	1.0	-	.8	.1
10000 TO 29999 POUNDS.	105	100.0	14.6	64.8	20.1	.4	-	-	.1
30000 TO 59999 POUNDS.	235	100.0	39.0	53.7	6.8	-	.5	-	-
60000 TO 89999 POUNDS.	106	100.0	89.4	7.8	.9	-	1.8	-	-
90000 POUNDS AND OVER.	127	100.0	84.8	14.9	.2	-	-	-	-
1500 MILES OR OVER......	1 008	100.0	75.5	21.2	1.6	.6	.6	.6	-
UNDER 1000 POUNDS.....	29	100.0	19.6	70.9	.2	7.5	.2	1.3	.2
1000 TO 9999 POUNDS...	67	100.0	15.4	70.3	5.7	5.5	1.7	1.2	.2
10000 TO 29999 POUNDS.	105	100.0	48.6	46.1	4.7	-	.5	-	-
30000 TO 59999 POUNDS.	348	100.0	71.0	25.2	1.2	-	1.2	1.4	-
60000 TO 89999 POUNDS.	188	100.0	95.3	4.6	.1	-	-	-	-
90000 POUNDS AND OVER.	268	100.0	99.1	-	.9	-	-	-	-

Note: Detail may not add to total due to rounding. The introductory table shows the estimates of sampling variability for tons; sampling variability for ton-miles has not been estimated. See the map in the Introduction for the States comprising the geographic divisions of the United States.
    Shipments excluded from the survey are those moving by pipeline (primarily petroleum products from refineries), parcel post shipments, and commodities moved by own power (motorized vehicles, aircraft, etc.) or towed (prefabricated buildings, etc.). Local shipments (commodities shipped less than 25 miles from the plant) and shipments within the same city are also excluded. Shipments to Alaska and Hawaii from the 48 conterminous States and the District of Columbia are included; however, no data were obtained for shipments originating in Alaska and Hawaii.

    - Represents zero or rounds to zero.   (D) Withheld to avoid disclosing figures for individual companies.

[1]Production of this commodity is concentrated in the geographic divisions shown; figures and distributions for geographic divisions not shown are included in the total.
[2]Distances of shipments to foreign destinations are calculated only to the U.S. port of exit.
[3]Includes only shipments represented by bills of lading and invoices. Summary records which did not show individual weights of shipments are not included.

TCC 354. Metalworkng Machinery and Equipment

Comparisons of Tons and Ton-Miles of Shipments for
Geographic Divisions of Origin and for Sampling Variability: 1972 and 1967

Geographic division of origin	Estimates				Relative sampling variability in tons (percent)	
	1972		1967		1972	1967
	Tons (thousands)	Ton-miles (millions)	Tons (thousands)	Ton-miles (millions)		
U.S. total	1,798	826	2,135	1,107	9.3	22.2
New England	136	101	153	101	7.7	(*)
Middle Atlantic	200	61	905	445	18.8	(*)
East North Central	1,047	338	934	395	10.4	(*)
West North Central	(D)	(D)	27	20	(*)	(*)
South Atlantic	235	137	24	10	43.2	(*)
East South Central	8	5	7	4	49.3	(*)
West South Central	(D)	(D)	9	6	(*)	(*)
Mountain	(D)	(D)	—	—	(*)	(*)
Pacific	(D)	(D)	76	126	(*)	(*)

— Represents or rounds to zero.   (D) Withheld to avoid disclosing figures for individual companies.   (*) Data not published.

TABLE 1. **TCC GROUP 354**—Percent Distribution of Geographic Division of Origin and Distance Shipped, by Means of Transport: 1972

Geographic division of origin[1] and distance shipped[2]	Number	Percent distribution by means of transport							
		All means of transport	Rail	Motor carrier	Private truck	Air	Water	Other	Unknown
TONS OF SHIPMENTS	(thousands of tons)								
U.S. TOTAL	1 798	100.0	8.5	79.6	9.7	.6	-	1.4	.1
NEW ENGLAND	136	100.0	.9	94.3	1.9	1.0	-	1.9	-
UNDER 100 MILES	23	100.0	2.5	86.6	9.4	.1	-	1.4	-
100 TO 199 MILES	12	100.0	-	97.2	1.1	.5	.1	1.2	-
200 TO 299 MILES	6	100.0	-	94.0	4.5	.4	-	1.1	-
300 TO 499 MILES	9	100.0	-	97.2	-	1.2	-	1.6	-
500 TO 999 MILES	55	100.0	1.1	95.4	-	1.1	-	2.3	-
1000 TO 1499 MILES	6	100.0	-	91.6	.1	2.7	-	5.7	-
1500 MILES OR OVER	22	100.0	.1	97.4	.1	1.6	-	.8	-
MIDDLE ATLANTIC	200	100.0	10.5	61.1	25.4	.7	.1	2.3	-
UNDER 100 MILES	31	100.0	4.1	69.0	19.6	.1	-	6.9	.3
100 TO 199 MILES	57	100.0	3.1	67.0	29.3	-	-	.6	-
200 TO 299 MILES	33	100.0	41.9	54.8	1.3	.2	.4	1.3	-
300 TO 499 MILES	52	100.0	.5	51.3	46.4	.8	-	1.0	-
500 TO 999 MILES	17	100.0	8.5	71.5	12.1	3.3	-	4.6	-
1000 TO 1499 MILES	5	100.0	38.4	46.1	12.6	1.1	.1	1.7	-
1500 MILES OR OVER	3	100.0	5.6	70.8	9.0	8.8	.4	5.3	-
EAST NORTH CENTRAL	1 047	100.0	9.9	79.1	8.7	.8	-	1.4	.1
UNDER 100 MILES	331	100.0	9.1	72.5	17.6	.1	-	.4	.2
100 TO 199 MILES	167	100.0	5.0	81.9	12.3	.1	-	.7	-
200 TO 299 MILES	166	100.0	12.5	81.2	2.1	.7	-	3.5	-
300 TO 499 MILES	164	100.0	16.8	78.6	1.5	1.5	-	1.6	.1
500 TO 999 MILES	166	100.0	7.0	86.8	3.3	1.7	-	1.1	-
1000 TO 1499 MILES	23	100.0	4.0	88.3	1.3	.4	-	3.3	2.7
1500 MILES OR OVER	27	100.0	15.6	77.2	1.7	3.3	-	2.2	-
SOUTH ATLANTIC	235	100.0	11.2	76.9	11.3	.2	-	.3	-
UNDER 100 MILES	43	100.0	-	85.0	15.0	-	-	-	.1
100 TO 199 MILES	24	100.0	16.8	56.3	23.9	-	-	3.1	-
200 TO 299 MILES	31	100.0	-	87.8	12.2	-	-	-	-
300 TO 499 MILES	17	100.0	-	96.7	2.4	.8	-	-	-
500 TO 999 MILES	95	100.0	12.5	77.0	10.2	.3	-	-	-
1000 TO 1499 MILES	8	100.0	10.9	88.6	.4	-	-	.1	-
1500 MILES OR OVER	13	100.0	69.6	28.3	1.7	.3	-	.1	-
EAST SOUTH CENTRAL	8	100.0	-	72.6	27.3	.1	-	-	-
UNDER 100 MILES	-	100.0	-	98.1	1.9	-	-	-	-
100 TO 199 MILES	-	100.0	-	76.6	23.4	-	-	-	-
200 TO 299 MILES	-	100.0	-	100.0	-	-	-	-	-
300 TO 499 MILES	-	100.0	-	75.6	24.3	.2	-	-	-
500 TO 999 MILES	6	100.0	-	69.9	30.0	.1	-	-	-
1000 TO 1499 MILES	-	100.0	-	100.0	-	-	-	-	-
1500 MILES OR OVER	-	100.0	-	-	-	-	-	-	-
TON-MILES OF SHIPMENTS	(millions of ton-miles)								
U.S. TOTAL	826	100.0	8.8	84.2	4.4	1.0	-	1.4	.1
NEW ENGLAND	101	100.0	.6	95.6	.3	1.5	-	1.9	-
UNDER 100 MILES	1	100.0	2.1	86.4	10.1	.1	-	1.3	-
100 TO 199 MILES	1	100.0	-	97.1	.9	.6	.1	1.3	-
200 TO 299 MILES	1	100.0	-	93.8	4.7	.4	-	1.2	-
300 TO 499 MILES	3	100.0	-	96.8	-	1.5	-	1.7	-
500 TO 999 MILES	38	100.0	1.5	95.1	-	.9	-	2.5	-
1000 TO 1499 MILES	8	100.0	-	91.6	.1	2.4	-	5.8	-
1500 MILES OR OVER	46	100.0	.1	97.0	.1	1.9	-	.9	-
MIDDLE ATLANTIC	61	100.0	12.2	59.6	23.4	2.2	.2	2.5	-
UNDER 100 MILES	1	100.0	7.5	68.6	12.6	.1	-	11.0	.3
100 TO 199 MILES	8	100.0	3.3	65.8	30.4	-	-	.6	-
200 TO 299 MILES	8	100.0	41.8	55.1	1.2	.2	.4	1.3	-
300 TO 499 MILES	18	100.0	.6	50.4	46.9	.9	-	1.1	-
500 TO 999 MILES	10	100.0	7.7	72.4	11.5	4.0	-	4.4	-
1000 TO 1499 MILES	6	100.0	37.2	47.1	12.9	1.0	.1	1.7	-
1500 MILES OR OVER	7	100.0	5.6	70.0	9.0	9.0	.8	5.6	-
EAST NORTH CENTRAL	338	100.0	10.6	82.4	3.5	1.5	-	1.7	.3
UNDER 100 MILES	16	100.0	11.4	71.6	16.0	.1	-	.5	.4
100 TO 199 MILES	24	100.0	5.7	81.7	11.9	.1	-	.7	-
200 TO 299 MILES	40	100.0	13.0	80.9	2.1	.8	-	3.2	-
300 TO 499 MILES	61	100.0	15.2	79.8	1.5	1.9	-	1.6	.1
500 TO 999 MILES	119	100.0	7.2	87.7	2.6	1.4	-	1.1	-
1000 TO 1499 MILES	26	100.0	4.6	86.9	1.5	.4	-	3.4	3.1
1500 MILES OR OVER	49	100.0	16.7	75.5	1.8	3.8	-	2.2	-
SOUTH ATLANTIC	137	100.0	20.1	73.7	5.8	.3	-	.1	-
UNDER 100 MILES	1	100.0	-	91.7	8.2	-	-	-	.1
100 TO 199 MILES	3	100.0	13.0	62.1	22.4	-	-	2.5	-
200 TO 299 MILES	7	100.0	-	87.9	12.1	-	-	-	-
300 TO 499 MILES	6	100.0	-	96.2	2.9	.9	-	-	-
500 TO 999 MILES	81	100.0	10.4	82.6	6.7	.3	-	-	-
1000 TO 1499 MILES	9	100.0	12.9	86.7	.4	-	-	.1	-
1500 MILES OR OVER	26	100.0	66.4	31.5	1.6	.3	-	.1	-

See footnotes at end of table 4.

TABLE 1. TCC GROUP 354—Percent Distribution of Geographic Division of Origin and Distance Shipped, by Means of Transport: 1972—Continued

Geographic division of origin[1] and distance shipped[2]	Number	Percent distribution by means of transport							
		All means of transport	Rail	Motor carrier	Private truck	Air	Water	Other	Unknown
TON-MILES OF SHIPMENTS	(millions of ton-miles)								
EAST SOUTH CENTRAL......	5	100.0	-	66.7	33.2	.1	-	-	-
UNDER 100 MILES.......	-	100.0	-	99.1	.9	-	-	-	-
100 TO 199 MILES......	-	100.0	-	76.2	23.8	-	-	-	-
200 TO 299 MILES......	-	100.0	-	100.0	-	-	-	-	-
300 TO 499 MILES......	-	100.0	-	71.2	28.6	.2	-	-	-
500 TO 999 MILES......	5	100.0	-	65.4	34.5	.1	-	-	-
1000 TO 1499 MILES....	-	100.0	-	100.0	-	-	-	-	-
1500 MILES OR OVER....	-	100.0	-	-	-	-	-	-	-

See footnotes at end of table 4.

TABLE 2. TCC GROUP 354—Percent Distribution of Geographic Division of Origin and Means of Transport, by Geographic Division of Destination: 1972

Geographic division of origin[1] and means of transport	Number	Percent distribution by division of destination									
		U.S. total	New England	Middle Atlantic	East North Central	West North Central	South Atlantic	East South Central	West South Central	Mountain	Pacific
TONS OF SHIPMENTS	(thousands of tons)										
U.S. TOTAL..............	1 798	100.0	3.2	21.8	46.4	4.6	10.9	3.3	4.6	1.4	3.8
RAIL.................	153	100.0	-	27.8	40.8	8.8	7.7	.3	5.2	4.6	4.7
MOTOR CARRIER........	1 431	100.0	3.6	20.0	48.2	4.2	10.5	3.6	4.9	1.1	3.9
PRIVATE TRUCK........	174	100.0	1.6	33.1	38.1	3.0	18.4	3.1	1.8	.4	.6
AIR..................	11	100.0	13.9	9.4	26.8	21.3	6.8	3.3	4.0	1.0	13.5
WATER................	-	100.0	-	89.9	-	-	1.9	-	-	-	8.2
OTHER................	25	100.0	4.0	19.6	47.1	5.6	7.1	5.6	4.0	1.6	5.5
UNKNOWN..............	1	100.0	.2	7.5	50.7	-	8.0	-	-	32.1	1.5
NEW ENGLAND..............	136	100.0	8.8	25.5	17.9	1.9	22.9	3.9	9.1	1.9	8.0
RAIL.................	1	100.0	-	46.9	52.0	.2	-	-	-	-	.9
MOTOR CARRIER........	128	100.0	7.1	26.2	17.6	1.8	24.1	3.5	9.6	2.0	8.1
PRIVATE TRUCK........	2	100.0	96.8	1.4	.5	-	.2	.2	.1	.2	.6
AIR..................	1	100.0	1.0	8.8	48.8	2.0	10.2	1.2	3.8	.3	24.0
WATER................	-	100.0	-	67.2	-	-	-	-	-	-	32.8
OTHER................	2	100.0	12.1	11.9	19.8	12.0	4.5	30.9	3.7	.5	4.6
UNKNOWN..............	-	100.0	88.8	-	-	11.2	-	-	-	-	-
MIDDLE ATLANTIC..........	200	100.0	1.4	56.0	11.7	1.2	22.8	1.3	3.9	.5	1.1
RAIL.................	20	100.0	-	71.3	11.7	4.9	.9	.9	9.4	-	.9
MOTOR CARRIER........	122	100.0	2.1	59.0	14.7	.9	16.2	1.2	4.2	.6	1.2
PRIVATE TRUCK........	50	100.0	.1	43.9	2.9	-	50.0	1.3	1.3	.4	.1
AIR..................	1	100.0	.5	8.8	28.6	15.7	10.1	13.4	3.0	2.9	17.0
WATER................	-	100.0	-	89.1	-	-	3.0	-	-	-	7.9
OTHER................	4	100.0	6.0	53.0	25.1	2.1	4.0	4.0	1.8	.1	3.9
UNKNOWN..............	-	100.0	.1	92.3	6.7	-	.1	-	-	-	.9
EAST NORTH CENTRAL......	1 047	100.0	2.7	17.1	57.4	4.8	6.7	3.9	4.0	.8	2.6
RAIL.................	103	100.0	-	25.3	50.9	7.9	6.3	.3	4.9	.3	4.1
MOTOR CARRIER........	828	100.0	3.2	15.0	58.3	4.2	7.3	4.4	4.3	.8	2.5
PRIVATE TRUCK........	90	100.0	-	28.0	59.5	5.5	1.5	4.4	.3	.2	.5
AIR..................	7	100.0	19.5	9.7	21.7	27.2	4.2	2.0	3.8	.7	11.1
WATER................	-	100.0	-	100.0	-	-	-	-	-	-	-
OTHER................	14	100.0	2.7	11.9	59.1	6.2	8.3	2.2	4.0	1.2	4.2
UNKNOWN..............	1	100.0	.1	2.9	56.0	-	4.8	-	-	35.9	.3
SOUTH ATLANTIC..........	235	100.0	4.8	21.1	46.3	2.8	16.0	1.4	1.7	3.0	2.8
RAIL.................	26	100.0	-	-	24.9	16.5	19.2	-	3.7	25.4	10.4
MOTOR CARRIER........	181	100.0	6.2	22.1	50.3	1.2	15.0	1.5	1.7	.2	2.0
PRIVATE TRUCK........	26	100.0	.4	36.7	39.1	.7	19.9	2.2	.1	.6	.3
AIR..................	-	100.0	.9	-	44.7	-	33.6	.1	12.3	-	8.3
WATER................	-	100.0	-	-	-	-	-	-	-	-	-
OTHER................	-	100.0	.5	.7	95.9	-	1.0	-	-	-	1.8
UNKNOWN..............	-	100.0	-	-	-	-	100.0	-	-	-	-
EAST SOUTH CENTRAL......	8	100.0	-	9.7	13.2	18.0	5.2	8.3	45.7	-	-
RAIL.................	-	100.0	-	-	-	-	-	-	-	-	-
MOTOR CARRIER........	6	100.0	-	12.9	15.6	24.8	7.1	10.6	28.9	-	-
PRIVATE TRUCK........	2	100.0	-	.9	6.8	-	-	2.1	90.3	-	-
AIR..................	-	100.0	-	83.3	16.7	-	-	-	-	-	-
WATER................	-	100.0	-	-	-	-	-	-	-	-	-
OTHER................	-	100.0	-	100.0	-	-	-	-	-	-	-
UNKNOWN..............	-	100.0	-	-	-	-	-	-	-	-	-

See footnotes at end of table 4.

TABLE 2. **TCC GROUP 354—Percent Distribution of Geographic Division of Origin and Means of Transport, by Geographic Division of Destination: 1972**—Continued

Geographic division of origin[1] and means of transport	Number	Percent distribution by division of destination									
		U.S. total	New England	Middle Atlantic	East North Central	West North Central	South Atlantic	East South Central	West South Central	Mountain	Pacific
TON-MILES OF SHIPMENTS	(millions of ton-miles)										
U.S. TOTAL.............	826	100.0	4.1	16.2	28.5	6.2	13.2	3.6	10.0	3.9	14.4
RAIL.................	72	100.0	.1	17.3	15.7	8.6	9.6	.4	11.4	15.8	21.3
MOTOR CARRIER........	695	100.0	4.6	15.9	30.4	5.8	12.9	3.9	10.1	2.6	13.8
PRIVATE TRUCK........	36	100.0	.9	23.9	22.8	6.5	28.0	3.8	7.7	2.9	3.6
AIR.................	8	100.0	9.3	5.4	14.4	15.8	5.9	2.6	5.3	1.8	39.5
WATER...............	-	100.0	-	47.5	-	-	3.4	-	-	-	49.1
OTHER...............	11	100.0	3.5	12.1	26.1	7.5	11.4	8.6	7.4	4.4	19.2
UNKNOWN.............	1	100.0	.1	2.2	9.4	-	10.7	-	-	74.5	2.9
NEW ENGLAND............	101	100.0	1.0	5.2	15.1	2.9	21.5	4.0	18.3	4.4	27.7
RAIL.................	-	100.0	-	4.7	90.2	.4	-	-	-	.1	4.7
MOTOR CARRIER........	96	100.0	.8	5.3	14.5	2.6	22.3	3.5	18.9	4.5	27.7
PRIVATE TRUCK........	-	100.0	73.4	1.3	3.3	.1	.5	1.7	1.4	4.5	13.7
AIR.................	1	100.0	-	1.8	25.2	2.1	9.3	.9	4.9	.4	55.4
WATER...............	-	100.0	-	11.3	-	-	-	-	-	-	88.7
OTHER...............	1	100.0	1.0	3.2	17.1	19.7	3.5	31.6	7.1	1.4	15.5
UNKNOWN.............	-	100.0	29.8	-	-	70.2	-	-	-	-	-
MIDDLE ATLANTIC........	61	100.0	1.0	33.2	14.1	3.2	21.3	2.5	13.1	3.4	8.3
RAIL.................	7	100.0	-	47.6	5.9	7.8	.5	1.4	31.2	.2	5.5
MOTOR CARRIER........	36	100.0	1.4	37.6	18.2	3.0	11.2	2.2	12.9	4.1	9.4
PRIVATE TRUCK........	14	100.0	.1	19.6	6.2	-	61.2	2.6	5.7	3.5	1.2
AIR.................	1	100.0	.2	2.3	13.4	14.7	6.3	10.7	4.1	5.4	42.9
WATER...............	-	100.0	-	30.5	-	-	5.8	-	-	-	63.7
OTHER...............	1	100.0	4.8	12.8	31.2	4.6	4.3	7.6	6.3	.6	27.8
UNKNOWN.............	-	100.0	.2	38.3	37.2	-	1.2	-	-	-	23.1
EAST NORTH CENTRAL......	338	100.0	6.5	18.8	24.2	5.6	12.0	4.4	11.2	2.7	14.6
RAIL.................	35	100.0	-	23.2	23.4	4.4	11.0	.4	12.9	1.4	23.2
MOTOR CARRIER........	279	100.0	7.5	18.7	24.1	4.8	12.4	4.9	11.6	2.6	13.3
PRIVATE TRUCK........	11	100.0	-	18.6	36.6	19.0	7.3	7.1	1.4	2.2	7.8
AIR.................	5	100.0	15.3	6.4	8.3	22.0	4.2	1.2	5.3	1.4	35.9
WATER...............	-	100.0	-	100.0	-	-	-	-	-	-	-
OTHER...............	5	100.0	4.5	10.4	29.2	6.2	15.8	2.9	9.0	3.6	18.5
UNKNOWN.............	-	100.0	.1	2.0	8.6	-	9.2	-	-	79.2	.9
SOUTH ATLANTIC.........	137	100.0	3.1	9.3	49.5	4.6	10.6	.7	3.1	8.4	10.8
RAIL.................	27	100.0	-	-	7.0	14.7	10.5	-	4.5	39.4	23.9
MOTOR CARRIER........	101	100.0	4.1	8.9	62.1	2.0	10.9	.8	2.8	.4	7.9
PRIVATE TRUCK........	8	100.0	1.2	46.3	36.4	2.0	7.2	1.2	.4	3.2	2.1
AIR.................	-	100.0	.5	-	47.7	-	15.7	.1	13.0	-	23.0
WATER...............	-	100.0	-	-	-	-	-	-	-	-	-
OTHER...............	-	100.0	3.4	3.9	63.6	-	.8	-	-	-	28.4
UNKNOWN.............	-	100.0	-	-	-	-	100.0	-	-	-	-
EAST SOUTH CENTRAL......	5	100.0	-	10.0	11.2	15.9	2.2	3.3	57.4	-	-
RAIL.................	-	100.0	-	-	-	-	-	-	-	-	-
MOTOR CARRIER........	3	100.0	-	14.6	15.0	23.9	3.3	4.7	38.4	-	-
PRIVATE TRUCK........	1	100.0	-	.6	3.5	-	-	.3	95.6	-	-
AIR.................	-	100.0	-	87.2	12.8	-	-	-	-	-	-
WATER...............	-	100.0	-	-	-	-	-	-	-	-	-
OTHER...............	-	100.0	-	100.0	-	-	-	-	-	-	-
UNKNOWN.............	-	100.0	-	-	-	-	-	-	-	-	-

See footnotes at end of table 4.

TABLE 3. **TCC GROUP 354**—Percent Distribution of Geographic Division of Destination and Means of Transport, by Geographic Division of Origin: 1972

Geographic division of destination and means of transport	Number	Percent distribution by division of origin[1]									
		U.S. total	New England	Middle Atlantic	East North Central	West North Central	South Atlantic	East South Central	West South Central	Mountain	Pacific
TONS OF SHIPMENTS	(thousands of tons)										
U.S. TOTAL.............	1 798	100.0	7.6	11.1	58.3	(D)	13.1	.5	(D)	(D)	(D)
RAIL...................	153	100.0	.8	13.7	67.7	(D)	17.2	-	(D)	(D)	(D)
MOTOR CARRIER.........	1 431	100.0	9.0	8.6	57.9	(D)	12.7	.4	(D)	(D)	(D)
PRIVATE TRUCK.........	174	100.0	1.5	29.2	52.2	(D)	15.3	1.3	(D)	(D)	(D)
AIR...................	11	100.0	11.9	12.6	69.9	(D)	3.9	.1	(D)	(D)	(D)
WATER.................	-	100.0	9.7	63.6	26.7	(D)	-	-	(D)	(D)	(D)
OTHER.................	25	100.0	10.2	18.0	56.8	(D)	3.1	-	(D)	(D)	(D)
UNKNOWN...............	1	100.0	.1	5.4	89.3	(D)	1.9	-	(D)	(D)	(D)
NEW ENGLAND...........	57	100.0	21.0	5.0	49.3	(D)	19.8	-	(D)	(D)	(D)
RAIL...................	-	100.0	-	-	-	(D)	-	-	(D)	(D)	(D)
MOTOR CARRIER.........	51	100.0	17.7	4.9	50.7	(D)	21.6	-	(D)	(D)	(D)
PRIVATE TRUCK.........	2	100.0	94.6	1.1	-	(D)	4.3	-	(D)	(D)	(D)
AIR...................	1	100.0	.8	.5	98.0	(D)	.3	-	(D)	(D)	(D)
WATER.................	-	100.0	-	-	-	(D)	-	-	(D)	(D)	(D)
OTHER.................	1	100.0	30.6	26.9	38.8	(D)	.4	-	(D)	(D)	(D)
UNKNOWN...............	-	100.0	30.3	2.0	67.7	(D)	-	-	(D)	(D)	(D)
MIDDLE ATLANTIC........	392	100.0	8.8	28.6	45.6	(D)	12.7	.2	(D)	(D)	(D)
RAIL...................	42	100.0	1.3	35.1	61.8	(D)	-	-	(D)	(D)	(D)
MOTOR CARRIER.........	285	100.0	11.8	25.3	43.5	(D)	14.0	.3	(D)	(D)	(D)
PRIVATE TRUCK.........	57	100.0	.1	38.7	44.2	(D)	16.9	-	(D)	(D)	(D)
AIR...................	1	100.0	11.1	11.8	72.1	(D)	-	.5	(D)	(D)	(D)
WATER.................	-	100.0	7.2	63.1	29.7	(D)	-	-	(D)	(D)	(D)
OTHER.................	4	100.0	6.1	48.7	34.4	(D)	.1	-	(D)	(D)	(D)
UNKNOWN...............	-	100.0	-	66.1	33.9	(D)	-	-	(D)	(D)	(D)
EAST NORTH CENTRAL......	834	100.0	2.9	2.8	72.0	(D)	13.1	.1	(D)	(D)	(D)
RAIL...................	62	100.0	1.0	3.9	84.5	(D)	10.5	-	(D)	(D)	(D)
MOTOR CARRIER.........	689	100.0	3.3	2.6	70.0	(D)	13.2	.1	(D)	(D)	(D)
PRIVATE TRUCK.........	66	100.0	-	2.2	81.6	(D)	15.7	.2	(D)	(D)	(D)
AIR...................	3	100.0	21.6	13.4	56.6	(D)	6.5	-	(D)	(D)	(D)
WATER.................	-	100.0	-	-	-	(D)	-	-	(D)	(D)	(D)
OTHER.................	11	100.0	4.3	9.6	71.4	(D)	6.3	-	(D)	(D)	(D)
UNKNOWN...............	-	100.0	-	.7	98.6	(D)	-	-	(D)	(D)	(D)
WEST NORTH CENTRAL......	82	100.0	3.2	3.0	61.2	(D)	8.1	1.8	(D)	(D)	(D)
RAIL...................	13	100.0	-	7.5	60.2	(D)	32.2	-	(D)	(D)	(D)
MOTOR CARRIER.........	60	100.0	3.8	1.8	57.2	(D)	3.6	2.5	(D)	(D)	(D)
PRIVATE TRUCK.........	5	100.0	-	-	95.6	(D)	3.5	-	(D)	(D)	(D)
AIR...................	2	100.0	1.1	9.3	89.5	(D)	-	-	(D)	(D)	(D)
WATER.................	-	100.0	-	-	-	(D)	-	-	(D)	(D)	(D)
OTHER.................	1	100.0	21.7	6.8	62.8	(D)	-	-	(D)	(D)	(D)
UNKNOWN...............	-	100.0	53.6	-	46.4	(D)	-	-	(D)	(D)	(D)
SOUTH ATLANTIC.........	196	100.0	15.9	23.3	35.6	(D)	19.2	.2	(D)	(D)	(D)
RAIL...................	11	100.0	-	1.7	55.3	(D)	42.7	-	(D)	(D)	(D)
MOTOR CARRIER.........	149	100.0	20.7	13.2	40.3	(D)	18.1	.3	(D)	(D)	(D)
PRIVATE TRUCK.........	32	100.0	-	79.2	4.3	(D)	16.5	-	(D)	(D)	(D)
AIR...................	-	100.0	17.8	18.7	43.4	(D)	19.4	-	(D)	(D)	(D)
WATER.................	-	100.0	-	100.0	-	(D)	-	-	(D)	(D)	(D)
OTHER.................	1	100.0	6.5	10.1	66.9	(D)	.4	-	(D)	(D)	(D)
UNKNOWN...............	-	100.0	-	.1	53.9	(D)	23.6	-	(D)	(D)	(D)
EAST SOUTH CENTRAL......	58	100.0	9.0	4.5	70.1	(D)	5.5	1.2	(D)	(D)	(D)
RAIL...................	-	100.0	-	37.5	62.5	(D)	-	-	(D)	(D)	(D)
MOTOR CARRIER.........	51	100.0	8.7	2.8	71.3	(D)	5.2	1.3	(D)	(D)	(D)
PRIVATE TRUCK.........	5	100.0	.1	11.7	74.4	(D)	10.6	.9	(D)	(D)	(D)
AIR...................	-	100.0	4.2	51.8	43.6	(D)	.1	-	(D)	(D)	(D)
WATER.................	-	100.0	-	-	-	(D)	-	-	(D)	(D)	(D)
OTHER.................	1	100.0	56.3	12.9	22.3	(D)	-	-	(D)	(D)	(D)
UNKNOWN...............	-	100.0	-	-	-	(D)	-	-	(D)	(D)	(D)
WEST SOUTH CENTRAL......	82	100.0	15.0	9.5	51.0	(D)	4.9	4.6	(D)	(D)	(D)
RAIL...................	8	100.0	-	24.6	63.3	(D)	12.1	-	(D)	(D)	(D)
MOTOR CARRIER.........	70	100.0	17.5	7.2	51.2	(D)	4.3	2.5	(D)	(D)	(D)
PRIVATE TRUCK.........	3	100.0	.1	21.0	9.9	(D)	1.0	66.8	(D)	(D)	(D)
AIR...................	-	100.0	11.2	9.5	65.3	(D)	12.0	-	(D)	(D)	(D)
WATER.................	-	100.0	-	-	-	(D)	-	-	(D)	(D)	(D)
OTHER.................	1	100.0	9.4	8.1	57.6	(D)	-	-	(D)	(D)	(D)
UNKNOWN...............	-	100.0	-	-	-	(D)	-	-	(D)	(D)	(D)
MOUNTAIN...............	24	100.0	10.4	3.9	32.7	(D)	28.8	-	(D)	(D)	(D)
RAIL...................	7	100.0	-	.1	5.1	(D)	94.8	-	(D)	(D)	(D)
MOTOR CARRIER.........	15	100.0	16.0	4.3	42.4	(D)	1.7	-	(D)	(D)	(D)
PRIVATE TRUCK.........	-	100.0	1.0	36.2	28.6	(D)	24.8	-	(D)	(D)	(D)
AIR...................	-	100.0	3.4	38.3	51.2	(D)	-	-	(D)	(D)	(D)
WATER.................	-	100.0	-	-	-	(D)	-	-	(D)	(D)	(D)
OTHER.................	-	100.0	3.3	1.6	44.9	(D)	-	-	(D)	(D)	(D)
UNKNOWN...............	-	100.0	-	-	100.0	(D)	-	-	(D)	(D)	(D)
PACIFIC................	67	100.0	16.1	3.2	39.9	(D)	9.6	-	(D)	(D)	(D)
RAIL...................	7	100.0	.2	2.5	59.2	(D)	38.1	-	(D)	(D)	(D)
MOTOR CARRIER.........	56	100.0	18.5	2.6	36.8	(D)	6.5	-	(D)	(D)	(D)
PRIVATE TRUCK.........	1	100.0	1.4	6.8	42.5	(D)	7.3	-	(D)	(D)	(D)
AIR...................	1	100.0	21.1	15.9	57.6	(D)	2.4	-	(D)	(D)	(D)
WATER.................	-	100.0	38.7	61.3	-	(D)	-	-	(D)	(D)	(D)
OTHER.................	1	100.0	8.6	12.8	44.2	(D)	1.0	-	(D)	(D)	(D)
UNKNOWN...............	-	100.0	-	3.3	16.1	(D)	-	-	(D)	(D)	(D)

See footnotes at end of table 4.

TABLE 3. TCC GROUP 354—Percent Distribution of Geographic Division of Destination and Means of Transport, by Geographic Division of Origin: 1972—Continued

Geographic division of destination and means of transport	Number	Percent distribution by division of origin[1]									
		U.S. total	New England	Middle Atlantic	East North Central	West North Central	South Atlantic	East South Central	West South Central	Mountain	Pacific
TON-MILES OF SHIPMENTS	(millions of ton-miles)										
U.S. TOTAL............	826	100.0	12.3	7.4	41.0	(D)	16.7	.7	(D)	(D)	(D)
RAIL..............	72	100.0	.9	10.4	49.6	(D)	38.2	-	(D)	(D)	(D)
MOTOR CARRIER........	695	100.0	13.9	5.3	40.1	(D)	14.6	.5	(D)	(D)	(D)
PRIVATE TRUCK........	36	100.0	.8	39.3	32.0	(D)	22.0	5.1	(D)	(D)	(D)
AIR..............	8	100.0	17.3	15.8	59.6	(D)	4.5	-	(D)	(D)	(D)
WATER.............	-	100.0	13.4	58.4	28.2	(D)	-	-	(D)	(D)	(D)
OTHER.............	11	100.0	17.0	13.0	50.2	(D)	1.2	-	(D)	(D)	(D)
UNKNOWN...........	1	100.0	-	.8	94.1	(D)	.3	-	(D)	(D)	(D)
NEW ENGLAND...........	33	100.0	2.9	1.8	65.5	(D)	12.8	-	(D)	(D)	(D)
RAIL..............	-	100.0	-	-	-	(D)	-	-	(D)	(D)	(D)
MOTOR CARRIER........	31	100.0	2.3	1.6	65.5	(D)	13.1	-	(D)	(D)	(D)
PRIVATE TRUCK........	-	100.0	68.1	2.9	-	(D)	28.9	-	(D)	(D)	(D)
AIR..............	-	100.0	.1	.3	98.0	(D)	.3	-	(D)	(D)	(D)
WATER.............	-	100.0	-	-	-	(D)	-	-	(D)	(D)	(D)
OTHER.............	-	100.0	4.8	18.0	65.2	(D)	1.2	-	(D)	(D)	(D)
UNKNOWN...........	-	100.0	3.8	1.5	94.7	(D)	-	-	(D)	(D)	(D)
MIDDLE ATLANTIC........	134	100.0	3.9	15.2	47.5	(D)	9.5	.4	(D)	(D)	(D)
RAIL..............	12	100.0	.2	28.5	66.6	(D)	-	-	(D)	(D)	(D)
MOTOR CARRIER........	110	100.0	4.6	12.4	47.1	(D)	8.1	.5	(D)	(D)	(D)
PRIVATE TRUCK........	8	100.0	-	32.2	24.9	(D)	42.7	.1	(D)	(D)	(D)
AIR..............	-	100.0	5.7	6.9	71.0	(D)	-	.7	(D)	(D)	(D)
WATER.............	-	100.0	3.2	37.5	59.3	(D)	-	-	(D)	(D)	(D)
OTHER.............	1	100.0	4.5	13.8	43.3	(D)	.4	-	(D)	(D)	(D)
UNKNOWN...........	-	100.0	-	13.9	86.1	(D)	-	-	(D)	(D)	(D)
EAST NORTH CENTRAL......	235	100.0	6.5	3.7	34.9	(D)	29.0	.3	(D)	(D)	(D)
RAIL..............	11	100.0	5.0	3.9	74.1	(D)	17.0	-	(D)	(D)	(D)
MOTOR CARRIER........	211	100.0	6.6	3.1	31.8	(D)	29.8	.3	(D)	(D)	(D)
PRIVATE TRUCK........	8	100.0	.1	10.7	51.4	(D)	35.2	.8	(D)	(D)	(D)
AIR..............	1	100.0	30.3	14.7	34.6	(D)	14.9	-	(D)	(D)	(D)
WATER.............	-	100.0	-	-	-	(D)	-	-	(D)	(D)	(D)
OTHER.............	3	100.0	11.2	15.5	56.2	(D)	2.9	-	(D)	(D)	(D)
UNKNOWN...........	-	100.0	-	3.2	85.6	(D)	-	-	(D)	(D)	(D)
WEST NORTH CENTRAL......	51	100.0	5.7	3.8	36.9	(D)	12.4	1.8	(D)	(D)	(D)
RAIL..............	6	100.0	-	9.4	25.2	(D)	65.3	-	(D)	(D)	(D)
MOTOR CARRIER........	40	100.0	6.2	2.7	33.7	(D)	5.2	2.2	(D)	(D)	(D)
PRIVATE TRUCK........	2	100.0	-	-	93.0	(D)	6.9	-	(D)	(D)	(D)
AIR..............	1	100.0	2.3	14.7	82.9	(D)	-	-	(D)	(D)	(D)
WATER.............	-	100.0	-	-	-	(D)	-	-	(D)	(D)	(D)
OTHER.............	-	100.0	44.8	8.1	42.0	(D)	-	-	(D)	(D)	(D)
UNKNOWN...........	-	100.0	81.4	-	18.6	(D)	-	-	(D)	(D)	(D)
SOUTH ATLANTIC........	108	100.0	20.0	12.0	37.3	(D)	13.5	.1	(D)	(D)	(D)
RAIL..............	6	100.0	-	.5	57.1	(D)	42.1	-	(D)	(D)	(D)
MOTOR CARRIER........	89	100.0	24.0	4.6	38.5	(D)	12.4	.1	(D)	(D)	(D)
PRIVATE TRUCK........	10	100.0	-	86.0	8.3	(D)	5.7	-	(D)	(D)	(D)
AIR..............	-	100.0	27.2	16.8	42.7	(D)	11.9	-	(D)	(D)	(D)
WATER.............	-	100.0	-	100.0	-	(D)	-	-	(D)	(D)	(D)
OTHER.............	1	100.0	5.2	4.9	69.6	(D)	.1	-	(D)	(D)	(D)
UNKNOWN...........	-	100.0	-	.1	80.2	(D)	2.5	-	(D)	(D)	(D)
EAST SOUTH CENTRAL......	29	100.0	13.4	5.2	50.4	(D)	3.1	.6	(D)	(D)	(D)
RAIL..............	-	100.0	-	39.7	60.3	(D)	-	-	(D)	(D)	(D)
MOTOR CARRIER........	26	100.0	12.5	3.0	51.2	(D)	3.0	.7	(D)	(D)	(D)
PRIVATE TRUCK........	1	100.0	.4	26.7	60.3	(D)	7.0	.5	(D)	(D)	(D)
AIR..............	-	100.0	6.0	64.8	28.3	(D)	.1	-	(D)	(D)	(D)
WATER.............	-	100.0	-	-	-	(D)	-	-	(D)	(D)	(D)
OTHER.............	-	100.0	62.9	11.6	16.9	(D)	-	-	(D)	(D)	(D)
UNKNOWN...........	-	100.0	-	-	-	(D)	-	-	(D)	(D)	(D)
WEST SOUTH CENTRAL......	82	100.0	22.4	9.7	46.1	(D)	5.1	3.9	(D)	(D)	(D)
RAIL..............	8	100.0	-	28.5	56.5	(D)	15.0	-	(D)	(D)	(D)
MOTOR CARRIER........	70	100.0	26.0	6.7	46.3	(D)	4.1	2.1	(D)	(D)	(D)
PRIVATE TRUCK........	2	100.0	.2	28.9	5.9	(D)	1.2	63.5	(D)	(D)	(D)
AIR..............	-	100.0	16.1	12.1	59.7	(D)	11.1	-	(D)	(D)	(D)
WATER.............	-	100.0	-	-	-	(D)	-	-	(D)	(D)	(D)
OTHER.............	-	100.0	16.2	11.0	60.8	(D)	-	-	(D)	(D)	(D)
UNKNOWN...........	-	100.0	-	-	-	(D)	-	-	(D)	(D)	(D)
MOUNTAIN..............	32	100.0	13.8	6.5	28.6	(D)	36.0	-	(D)	(D)	(D)
RAIL..............	11	100.0	-	.1	4.5	(D)	95.4	-	(D)	(D)	(D)
MOTOR CARRIER........	18	100.0	24.0	8.2	40.4	(D)	2.4	-	(D)	(D)	(D)
PRIVATE TRUCK........	1	100.0	1.3	47.6	24.3	(D)	24.5	-	(D)	(D)	(D)
AIR..............	-	100.0	4.2	47.1	45.6	(D)	-	-	(D)	(D)	(D)
WATER.............	-	100.0	-	-	-	(D)	-	-	(D)	(D)	(D)
OTHER.............	-	100.0	5.3	1.8	41.0	(D)	-	-	(D)	(D)	(D)
UNKNOWN...........	-	100.0	-	-	100.0	(D)	-	-	(D)	(D)	(D)
PACIFIC..............	118	100.0	23.6	4.3	41.5	(D)	12.6	-	(D)	(D)	(D)
RAIL..............	15	100.0	.2	2.7	54.1	(D)	43.0	-	(D)	(D)	(D)
MOTOR CARRIER........	96	100.0	27.9	3.6	38.6	(D)	8.3	-	(D)	(D)	(D)
PRIVATE TRUCK........	1	100.0	3.1	13.3	69.8	(D)	12.6	-	(D)	(D)	(D)
AIR..............	3	100.0	24.3	17.2	54.2	(D)	2.6	-	(D)	(D)	(D)
WATER.............	-	100.0	24.2	75.8	-	(D)	-	-	(D)	(D)	(D)
OTHER.............	2	100.0	13.7	18.8	48.4	(D)	1.7	-	(D)	(D)	(D)
UNKNOWN...........	-	100.0	-	6.4	28.1	(D)	-	-	(D)	(D)	(D)

See footnotes at end of table 4.

TABLE 4. **TCC GROUP 354**—Percent Distribution of Distance Shipped and Weight of Shipment, by Means of Transport: 1972

Distance shipped and weight of shipment[2] [3]	Number	Percent distribution by means of transport							
		All means of transport	Rail	Motor carrier	Private truck	Air	Water	Other	Unknown
TONS OF SHIPMENTS	(thousands of tons)								
U.S. TOTAL.........	1 693	100.0	9.0	79.1	10.0	.6	-	1.1	.1
UNDER 100 MILES.........	421	100.0	7.6	73.9	17.2	.1	-	.9	.2
UNDER 1000 POUNDS.....	33	100.0	-	59.3	31.9	.7	-	8.0	.1
1000 TO 9999 POUNDS...	88	100.0	-	63.8	33.6	.1	-	1.5	1.0
10000 TO 29999 POUNDS.	105	100.0	-	76.7	23.3	-	-	-	-
30000 TO 59999 POUNDS.	126	100.0	8.4	85.6	6.0	-	-	-	-
60000 TO 89999 POUNDS.	27	100.0	33.7	66.3	-	-	-	-	-
90000 POUNDS AND OVER.	40	100.0	30.3	69.7	-	-	-	-	-
100 TO 199 MILES........	244	100.0	5.8	76.1	17.1	-	-	.9	-
UNDER 1000 POUNDS.....	27	100.0	-	86.1	8.1	.4	.1	5.3	-
1000 TO 9999 POUNDS...	59	100.0	-	60.6	39.4	-	-	-	-
10000 TO 29999 POUNDS.	40	100.0	-	58.5	39.6	-	-	1.9	-
30000 TO 59999 POUNDS.	91	100.0	1.5	98.0	.6	-	-	-	-
60000 TO 89999 POUNDS.	8	100.0	55.3	44.7	-	-	-	-	-
90000 POUNDS AND OVER.	17	100.0	45.5	54.5	-	-	-	-	-
200 TO 299 MILES........	228	100.0	15.2	79.7	3.4	.5	.1	1.1	-
UNDER 1000 POUNDS.....	27	100.0	-	82.4	4.2	4.3	-	9.1	-
1000 TO 9999 POUNDS...	40	100.0	-	90.8	8.7	.2	.3	-	-
10000 TO 29999 POUNDS.	28	100.0	-	97.2	2.8	-	-	-	-
30000 TO 59999 POUNDS.	79	100.0	17.6	79.5	2.9	-	-	-	-
60000 TO 89999 POUNDS.	14	100.0	25.7	74.3	-	-	-	-	-
90000 POUNDS AND OVER.	38	100.0	44.3	55.7	-	-	-	-	-
300 TO 499 MILES........	228	100.0	12.2	73.2	11.9	1.2	-	1.4	-
UNDER 1000 POUNDS.....	26	100.0	.1	74.5	5.6	9.7	-	9.8	.4
1000 TO 9999 POUNDS...	40	100.0	.1	92.2	6.0	-	-	1.7	-
10000 TO 29999 POUNDS.	54	100.0	-	71.6	28.4	-	-	-	-
30000 TO 59999 POUNDS.	58	100.0	4.0	83.0	13.0	-	-	-	-
60000 TO 89999 POUNDS.	15	100.0	34.1	65.0	-	.9	-	-	-
90000 POUNDS AND OVER.	32	100.0	62.2	37.8	-	-	-	-	-
500 TO 999 MILES........	394	100.0	6.5	86.6	4.8	1.0	-	1.1	-
UNDER 1000 POUNDS.....	38	100.0	.1	81.3	1.4	8.7	.2	8.4	-
1000 TO 9999 POUNDS...	82	100.0	-	95.0	3.7	.9	-	.4	-
10000 TO 29999 POUNDS.	78	100.0	1.3	90.1	7.7	-	-	.9	-
30000 TO 59999 POUNDS.	85	100.0	5.4	83.9	10.7	-	-	-	-
60000 TO 89999 POUNDS.	34	100.0	26.2	73.8	-	-	-	-	-
90000 POUNDS AND OVER.	74	100.0	14.6	85.4	-	-	-	-	-
1000 TO 1499 MILES......	64	100.0	6.1	87.7	1.6	.6	-	3.1	1.0
UNDER 1000 POUNDS.....	21	100.0	-	92.2	.5	1.2	-	6.0	-
1000 TO 9999 POUNDS...	29	100.0	-	93.2	2.0	.4	-	2.2	2.1
10000 TO 29999 POUNDS.	4	100.0	13.0	84.3	2.6	-	-	-	-
30000 TO 59999 POUNDS.	4	100.0	23.0	72.8	4.2	-	-	-	-
60000 TO 89999 POUNDS.	-	100.0	100.0	-	-	-	-	-	-
90000 POUNDS AND OVER.	3	100.0	48.0	52.0	-	-	-	-	-
1500 MILES OR OVER......	113	100.0	12.3	85.2	1.0	.7	-	.8	-
UNDER 1000 POUNDS.....	25	100.0	.3	92.5	2.3	1.8	-	2.9	.1
1000 TO 9999 POUNDS...	41	100.0	.1	97.7	.9	.9	-	.4	-
10000 TO 29999 POUNDS.	14	100.0	-	99.2	.8	-	-	-	-
30000 TO 59999 POUNDS.	7	100.0	39.6	60.4	-	-	-	-	-
60000 TO 89999 POUNDS.	4	100.0	56.3	43.7	-	-	-	-	-
90000 POUNDS AND OVER.	19	100.0	41.5	58.5	-	-	-	-	-
TON-MILES OF SHIPMENTS	(millions of ton-miles)								
U.S. TOTAL.........	777	100.0	9.2	84.0	4.6	.8	-	1.2	.1
UNDER 100 MILES.........	20	100.0	9.6	74.1	14.7	.1	-	1.2	.3
UNDER 1000 POUNDS.....	1	100.0	-	65.9	23.7	.7	-	9.5	.1
1000 TO 9999 POUNDS...	4	100.0	-	69.2	27.6	.2	-	1.6	1.4
10000 TO 29999 POUNDS.	4	100.0	-	75.9	24.1	-	-	-	-
30000 TO 59999 POUNDS.	6	100.0	13.5	82.6	3.9	-	-	-	-
60000 TO 89999 POUNDS.	1	100.0	43.0	57.0	-	-	-	-	-
90000 POUNDS AND OVER.	2	100.0	24.1	75.9	-	-	-	-	-
100 TO 199 MILES........	35	100.0	5.9	76.3	17.0	.1	-	.8	-
UNDER 1000 POUNDS.....	3	100.0	-	87.1	7.0	.5	.1	5.3	-
1000 TO 9999 POUNDS...	8	100.0	-	59.1	40.9	-	-	-	-
10000 TO 29999 POUNDS.	5	100.0	-	59.0	39.5	-	-	1.4	-
30000 TO 59999 POUNDS.	14	100.0	1.8	97.6	.6	-	-	-	-
60000 TO 89999 POUNDS.	1	100.0	50.8	49.2	-	-	-	-	-
90000 POUNDS AND OVER.	2	100.0	50.5	49.5	-	-	-	-	-

See footnotes at end of table 4.

TABLE 4. **TCC GROUP 354—Percent Distribution of Distance Shipped and Weight of Shipment, by Means of Transport: 1972**—Continued

Distance shipped and weight of shipment[2] [3]	Number	Percent distribution by means of transport							
		All means of transport	Rail	Motor carrier	Private truck	Air	Water	Other	Unknown
TON-MILES OF SHIPMENTS	(millions of ton-miles)								
200 TO 299 MILES........	55	100.0	15.6	79.3	3.3	.6	.1	1.1	-
UNDER 1000 POUNDS.....	6	100.0	-	81.5	4.8	4.9	-	8.8	-
1000 TO 9999 POUNDS...	9	100.0	-	91.1	8.5	.2	.3	-	-
10000 TO 29999 POUNDS.	6	100.0	-	97.6	2.4	-	-	-	-
30000 TO 59999 POUNDS.	19	100.0	17.4	79.9	2.6	-	-	-	-
60000 TO 89999 POUNDS.	3	100.0	26.3	73.7	-	-	-	-	-
90000 POUNDS AND OVER.	9	100.0	47.2	52.8	-	-	-	-	-
300 TO 499 MILES........	83	100.0	11.3	74.0	11.7	1.5	-	1.5	-
UNDER 1000 POUNDS.....	10	100.0	.1	72.7	5.6	11.5	-	9.7	.4
1000 TO 9999 POUNDS...	16	100.0	.1	92.4	5.9	-	-	1.6	-
10000 TO 29999 POUNDS.	20	100.0	-	72.4	27.6	-	-	-	-
30000 TO 59999 POUNDS.	20	100.0	4.0	83.0	13.0	-	-	-	-
60000 TO 89999 POUNDS.	5	100.0	32.7	66.1	-	1.2	-	-	-
90000 POUNDS AND OVER.	11	100.0	61.6	38.4	-	-	-	-	-
500 TO 999 MILES........	286	100.0	6.4	87.7	3.9	.9	-	1.0	-
UNDER 1000 POUNDS.....	27	100.0	.1	83.0	1.3	7.5	.2	8.0	-
1000 TO 9999 POUNDS...	60	100.0	-	95.6	3.1	.9	-	.4	-
10000 TO 29999 POUNDS.	66	100.0	.9	92.1	6.1	-	-	.8	-
30000 TO 59999 POUNDS.	60	100.0	4.7	87.2	8.1	-	-	-	-
60000 TO 89999 POUNDS.	26	100.0	25.3	74.7	-	-	-	-	-
90000 POUNDS AND OVER.	43	100.0	18.5	81.5	-	-	-	-	-
1000 TO 1499 MILES......	76	100.0	6.3	87.2	1.7	.6	-	3.1	1.1
UNDER 1000 POUNDS.....	25	100.0	-	92.2	.5	1.2	-	6.1	-
1000 TO 9999 POUNDS...	34	100.0	-	92.7	2.2	.4	-	2.4	2.4
10000 TO 29999 POUNDS.	5	100.0	14.2	83.0	2.8	-	-	-	-
30000 TO 59999 POUNDS.	5	100.0	23.0	72.2	4.8	-	-	-	-
60000 TO 89999 POUNDS.	-	100.0	100.0	-	-	-	-	-	-
90000 POUNDS AND OVER.	4	100.0	45.8	54.2	-	-	-	-	-
1500 MILES OR OVER......	218	100.0	12.0	85.4	1.0	.9	-	.8	-
UNDER 1000 POUNDS.....	52	100.0	.4	92.5	2.3	1.9	-	2.8	.1
1000 TO 9999 POUNDS...	80	100.0	-	97.5	.9	1.1	-	.4	-
10000 TO 29999 POUNDS.	25	100.0	-	99.1	.9	-	-	-	-
30000 TO 59999 POUNDS.	15	100.0	42.9	57.1	-	-	-	-	-
60000 TO 89999 POUNDS.	9	100.0	56.4	43.6	-	-	-	-	-
90000 POUNDS AND OVER.	35	100.0	39.2	60.8	-	-	-	-	-

Note: Detail may not add to total due to rounding. The introductory table shows the estimates of sampling variability for tons; sampling variability for ton-miles has not been estimated. See the map in the Introduction for the States comprising the geographic divisions of the United States.

Shipments excluded from the survey are those moving by pipeline (primarily petroleum products from refineries), parcel post shipments, and commodities moved by own power (motorized vehicles, aircraft, etc.) or towed (prefabricated buildings, etc.). Local shipments (commodities shipped less than 25 miles from the plant) and shipments within the same city are also excluded. Shipments to Alaska and Hawaii from the 48 conterminous States and the District of Columbia are included; however, no data were obtained for shipments originating in Alaska and Hawaii.

- Represents zero or rounds to zero.   (D) Withheld to avoid disclosing figures for individual companies.

[1]Production of this commodity is concentrated in the geographic divisions shown; figures and distributions for geographic divisions not shown are included in the total.

[2]Distances of shipments to foreign destinations are calculated only to the U.S. port of exit.

[3]Includes only shipments represented by bills of lading and invoices. Summary records which did not show individual weights of shipments are not included.

TCC 355. Special Industry Machinery

Comparisons of Tons and Ton-Miles of Shipments for
Geographic Divisions of Origin and for Sampling Variability: 1972 and 1967

Geographic division of origin	Estimates				Relative sampling variability in tons (percent)	
	1972		1967		1972	1967
	Tons (thousands)	Ton-miles (millions)	Tons (thousands)	Ton-miles (millions)		
U.S. total	2,306	1,733	1,479	828	19.4	16.2
New England	315	232	135	80	42.5	(*)
Middle Atlantic	216	94	372	199	31.1	(*)
East North Central	1,075	587	543	307	32.5	(*)
West North Central	31	21	145	82	35.9	(*)
South Atlantic	331	154	122	33	48.3	(*)
East South Central	(D)	(D)	13	8	(*)	(*)
West South Central	22	11	90	55	26.2	(*)
Mountain	(D)	(D)	17	14	(*)	(*)
Pacific	(D)	(D)	42	50	(*)	(*)

(D) Withheld to avoid disclosing figures for individual companies.   (*) Data not published.

TABLE 1. TCC GROUP 355—Percent Distribution of Geographic Division of Origin and Distance Shipped, by Means of Transport: 1972

Geographic division of origin[1] and distance shipped[2]	Number	Percent distribution by means of transport							
		All means of transport	Rail	Motor carrier	Private truck	Air	Water	Other	Unknown
TONS OF SHIPMENTS	(thousands of tons)								
U.S. TOTAL	2 306	100.0	8.1	78.2	10.7	.6	.2	2.1	.2
NEW ENGLAND	315	100.0	15.5	70.3	1.2	.3	.3	11.3	1.1
UNDER 100 MILES	20	100.0	-	81.4	5.4	.1	5.1	.4	7.7
100 TO 199 MILES	56	100.0	-	98.4	-	.3	.1	.1	1.1
200 TO 299 MILES	18	100.0	-	99.8	-	-	-	.2	
300 TO 499 MILES	6	100.0	12.4	85.3	.1	1.6	-	.5	.1
500 TO 999 MILES	126	100.0	34.5	35.6	1.8	.1	-	27.8	
1000 TO 1499 MILES	56	100.0	7.2	92.3	.1	.2	-	.1	.1
1500 MILES OR OVER	29	100.0	.5	93.8	1.0	.7	-	.1	3.9
MIDDLE ATLANTIC	216	100.0	4.7	91.0	3.0	.6	-	.7	-
UNDER 100 MILES	55	100.0	.6	91.9	5.2	.7	-	1.6	-
100 TO 199 MILES	40	100.0	-	99.8	-	-	-	.2	-
200 TO 299 MILES	14	100.0	-	95.2	2.4	1.7	-	.7	-
300 TO 499 MILES	49	100.0	-	99.2	.1	.5	-	.2	.1
500 TO 999 MILES	35	100.0	12.1	80.5	6.7	.2	-	.5	-
1000 TO 1499 MILES	5	100.0	11.1	84.2	-	3.6	-	1.1	-
1500 MILES OR OVER	15	100.0	32.4	60.6	5.9	.8	-	.3	-
EAST NORTH CENTRAL	1 075	100.0	8.2	88.9	1.2	.8	.4	.6	.1
UNDER 100 MILES	90	100.0	1.7	89.1	5.9	2.9	-	.3	-
100 TO 199 MILES	154	100.0	13.7	85.2	.7	-	-	.2	.1
200 TO 299 MILES	177	100.0	1.9	97.6	.3	.1	-	.2	-
300 TO 499 MILES	175	100.0	5.1	92.2	2.0	.2	-	.5	-
500 TO 999 MILES	330	100.0	12.3	84.5	.4	.7	1.2	.8	.1
1000 TO 1499 MILES	83	100.0	3.2	95.4	.4	.5	-	.5	-
1500 MILES OR OVER	63	100.0	15.0	77.8	.3	3.6	-	3.3	-
WEST NORTH CENTRAL	31	100.0	15.0	65.5	12.1	.6	-	6.7	.1
UNDER 100 MILES	-	100.0	27.8	12.1	59.5	-	-	.6	
100 TO 199 MILES	2	100.0	-	11.3	20.0	.3	-	68.4	-
200 TO 299 MILES	2	100.0	-	81.5	18.0	.1	-	.5	-
300 TO 499 MILES	3	100.0	-	66.0	32.7	.1	-	.7	.5
500 TO 999 MILES	16	100.0	26.8	66.5	6.4	.1	-	.2	-
1000 TO 1499 MILES	4	100.0	5.3	86.1	5.6	2.9	-	-	-
1500 MILES OR OVER	1	100.0	-	98.0	-	1.3	-	.7	-
SOUTH ATLANTIC	331	100.0	8.3	28.5	62.7	.1	-	.4	-
UNDER 100 MILES	64	100.0	-	28.3	71.1	-	-	.6	-
100 TO 199 MILES	31	100.0	4.1	58.8	36.4	-	-	.7	-
200 TO 299 MILES	39	100.0	1.7	69.6	28.5	-	-	.3	-
300 TO 499 MILES	42	100.0	3.9	29.3	65.7	.1	-	.8	.1
500 TO 999 MILES	124	100.0	9.6	10.4	79.8	.1	-	.1	-
1000 TO 1499 MILES	15	100.0	8.9	15.6	74.7	.5	-	.4	-
1500 MILES OR OVER	13	100.0	81.1	18.7	-	.1	-	.1	-
WEST SOUTH CENTRAL	22	100.0	6.2	74.7	18.8	.1	-	.2	-
UNDER 100 MILES	5	100.0	-	61.4	38.5	-	-	-	-
100 TO 199 MILES	4	100.0	-	79.2	20.8	-	-	-	-
200 TO 299 MILES	1	100.0	86.6	13.4	-	-	-	-	-
300 TO 499 MILES	2	100.0	-	51.1	48.5	.1	-	.3	-
500 TO 999 MILES	3	100.0	8.8	84.5	5.8	.3	-	.6	-
1000 TO 1499 MILES	5	100.0	-	99.8	-	.1	-	-	-
1500 MILES OR OVER	-	100.0	-	88.8	-	11.2	-	-	-
TON-MILES OF SHIPMENTS	(millions of ton-miles)								
U.S. TOTAL	1 733	100.0	8.3	82.5	6.0	.8	.2	2.0	.2
NEW ENGLAND	232	100.0	14.6	71.5	1.1	.3	-	11.3	1.2
UNDER 100 MILES	-	100.0	-	81.9	2.0	-	3.8	.4	11.9
100 TO 199 MILES	9	100.0	-	98.8	-	.4	.1	.1	.7
200 TO 299 MILES	4	100.0	-	99.8	-	-	-	.2	-
300 TO 499 MILES	2	100.0	11.0	86.4	.1	1.9	-	.5	.1
500 TO 999 MILES	92	100.0	31.4	38.3	1.9	.2	-	28.2	
1000 TO 1499 MILES	65	100.0	6.6	92.9	.1	.2	-	.1	.2
1500 MILES OR OVER	57	100.0	.6	92.9	1.2	.8	-	.1	4.4
MIDDLE ATLANTIC	94	100.0	17.5	77.3	3.9	.8	-	.5	-
UNDER 100 MILES	2	100.0	.5	92.7	3.9	.3	-	2.6	-
100 TO 199 MILES	5	100.0	-	99.7	-	-	-	.3	-
200 TO 299 MILES	3	100.0	-	95.4	2.1	1.9	-	.7	-
300 TO 499 MILES	17	100.0	-	99.0	.1	.6	-	.3	.1
500 TO 999 MILES	24	100.0	15.6	77.6	6.0	.2	-	.5	
1000 TO 1499 MILES	5	100.0	13.3	81.6	-	4.1	-	1.0	-
1500 MILES OR OVER	35	100.0	33.5	59.7	5.8	.8	-	.3	-
EAST NORTH CENTRAL	587	100.0	9.3	87.3	.6	1.1	.5	1.2	-
UNDER 100 MILES	5	100.0	2.4	88.5	7.9	.8	-	.4	-
100 TO 199 MILES	23	100.0	10.8	88.2	.7	-	-	.2	.1
200 TO 299 MILES	44	100.0	1.8	97.7	.3	-	-	.2	-
300 TO 499 MILES	64	100.0	5.5	91.7	2.0	.1	-	.5	.1
500 TO 999 MILES	227	100.0	12.1	84.5	.3	.7	1.4	.9	.1
1000 TO 1499 MILES	103	100.0	3.0	95.8	.4	.4	-	.4	-
1500 MILES OR OVER	117	100.0	14.1	78.8	.3	3.5	-	3.3	-

See footnotes at end of table 4.

TABLE 1. **TCC GROUP 355—Percent Distribution of Geographic Division of Origin and Distance Shipped, by Means of Transport: 1972**—Continued

Geographic division of origin[1] and distance shipped[2]	Number	Percent distribution by means of transport							
		All means of transport	Rail	Motor carrier	Private truck	Air	Water	Other	Unknown
TON-MILES OF SHIPMENTS	(millions of ton-miles)								
WEST NORTH CENTRAL......	21	100.0	17.1	71.9	8.0	1.0	-	2.0	-
UNDER 100 MILES.......	-	100.0	33.1	14.4	51.8	-	-	.7	-
100 TO 199 MILES......	-	100.0	-	9.2	18.9	.3	-	71.5	-
200 TO 299 MILES......	-	100.0	-	81.1	18.3	.1	-	.5	-
300 TO 499 MILES......	1	100.0	-	67.9	30.8	.1	-	.7	.5
500 TO 999 MILES......	11	100.0	29.2	64.1	6.2	.1	-	.3	-
1000 TO 1499 MILES....	5	100.0	5.2	86.0	5.6	3.1	-	-	-
1500 MILES OR OVER....	1	100.0	-	97.9	-	1.3	-	.7	-
SOUTH ATLANTIC.........	154	100.0	21.2	20.2	58.2	.1	-	.3	-
UNDER 100 MILES.......	3	100.0	-	27.4	71.9	-	-	.6	-
100 TO 199 MILES......	4	100.0	4.2	54.4	40.8	-	-	.6	-
200 TO 299 MILES......	9	100.0	1.9	68.6	29.3	-	-	.2	-
300 TO 499 MILES......	16	100.0	4.3	27.6	67.0	.1	-	.8	.1
500 TO 999 MILES......	74	100.0	11.8	11.1	76.9	.1	-	.1	-
1000 TO 1499 MILES....	18	100.0	9.7	14.8	74.7	.4	-	.4	-
1500 MILES OR OVER....	26	100.0	80.0	19.8	-	.1	-	.1	-
WEST SOUTH CENTRAL......	11	100.0	4.2	88.9	6.6	.2	-	.2	-
UNDER 100 MILES.......	-	100.0	-	74.5	25.5	-	-	-	-
100 TO 199 MILES......	-	100.0	-	70.5	29.5	-	-	-	-
200 TO 299 MILES......	-	100.0	85.9	14.0	-	-	-	-	-
300 TO 499 MILES......	-	100.0	-	57.3	42.2	.2	-	.3	-
500 TO 999 MILES......	2	100.0	7.2	86.7	5.1	.3	-	.6	-
1000 TO 1499 MILES....	6	100.0	-	99.8	-	.1	-	.1	-
1500 MILES OR OVER....	-	100.0	-	78.6	-	21.4	-	-	-

See footnotes at end of table 4.

TABLE 2. **TCC GROUP 355—Percent Distribution of Geographic Division of Origin and Means of Transport, by Geographic Division of Destination: 1972**

Geographic division of origin[1] and means of transport	Number	Percent distribution by division of destination									
		U.S. total	New England	Middle Atlantic	East North Central	West North Central	South Atlantic	East South Central	West South Central	Mountain	Pacific
TONS OF SHIPMENTS	(thousands of tons)										
U.S. TOTAL.............	2 306	100.0	3.9	17.0	24.7	4.7	23.9	7.0	11.3	3.1	4.3
RAIL................	186	100.0	1.1	15.1	31.1	4.2	20.2	2.6	9.8	3.6	12.3
MOTOR CARRIER........	1 803	100.0	4.6	19.6	27.5	5.2	21.8	4.0	10.3	3.5	3.6
PRIVATE TRUCK........	246	100.0	.5	2.2	4.6	2.6	31.6	33.7	21.0	.5	3.3
AIR.................	13	100.0	7.6	24.0	24.9	1.9	13.8	1.4	6.5	1.0	18.9
WATER...............	5	100.0	20.9	.6	-	-	44.7	-	31.2	-	2.5
OTHER...............	47	100.0	.5	3.8	3.0	1.4	78.9	4.9	2.9	.5	4.1
UNKNOWN.............	4	100.0	48.4	14.8	4.8	1.0	1.4	1.3	.7	26.5	1.0
NEW ENGLAND............	315	100.0	9.1	22.3	14.1	4.8	27.1	11.1	6.8	3.7	1.2
RAIL................	48	100.0	-	1.1	56.5	.3	33.5	8.3	-	-	.3
MOTOR CARRIER........	221	100.0	11.0	31.2	7.5	6.7	14.2	13.8	9.6	4.6	1.5
PRIVATE TRUCK........	3	100.0	28.9	-	-	1.6	53.9	7.6	-	8.0	-
AIR.................	-	100.0	2.1	29.1	15.3	5.7	17.2	4.7	10.2	2.6	13.0
WATER...............	1	100.0	97.0	3.0	-	-	-	-	-	-	-
OTHER...............	35	100.0	.2	.3	.1	-	99.2	-	-	-	.1
UNKNOWN.............	3	100.0	58.8	5.3	.1	1.2	.2	.1	.9	32.2	1.2
MIDDLE ATLANTIC........	216	100.0	4.3	56.4	11.8	1.2	14.3	1.8	3.5	.5	6.2
RAIL................	10	100.0	-	3.3	-	-	-	-	47.9	-	48.8
MOTOR CARRIER........	197	100.0	4.6	59.5	12.4	1.3	14.9	1.6	1.3	.5	3.8
PRIVATE TRUCK........	6	100.0	.2	46.8	8.4	1.9	20.2	8.6	-	-	13.8
AIR.................	1	100.0	14.1	37.1	17.6	.6	5.1	2.9	13.6	-	9.0
WATER...............	-	100.0	-	-	-	-	-	-	-	-	-
OTHER...............	1	100.0	3.7	63.4	10.9	1.3	14.0	1.5	2.3	.2	2.6
UNKNOWN.............	-	100.0	-	-	-	-	100.0	-	-	-	-
EAST NORTH CENTRAL......	1 075	100.0	4.6	16.6	44.3	7.3	8.5	3.1	6.1	4.2	5.4
RAIL................	87	100.0	2.1	29.0	31.5	7.2	10.7	.1	6.2	2.4	10.8
MOTOR CARRIER........	955	100.0	4.9	15.7	45.7	7.4	8.2	3.1	5.9	4.5	4.6
PRIVATE TRUCK........	12	100.0	-	3.8	58.4	2.8	.2	23.1	7.2	2.9	1.6
AIR.................	8	100.0	9.8	13.9	35.1	.9	3.2	1.2	7.2	.8	27.8
WATER...............	3	100.0	-	-	-	-	58.8	-	41.2	-	-
OTHER...............	6	100.0	1.1	9.8	15.9	7.8	14.8	1.8	18.5	3.5	26.8
UNKNOWN.............	-	100.0	-	68.1	27.9	.6	3.3	.1	-	-	-
WEST NORTH CENTRAL......	31	100.0	1.0	7.7	23.1	11.0	18.9	15.7	14.8	2.6	5.2
RAIL................	4	100.0	-	7.4	-	3.4	62.1	-	27.1	-	-
MOTOR CARRIER........	20	100.0	1.5	9.1	32.8	10.7	14.6	11.2	9.7	2.9	7.5
PRIVATE TRUCK........	3	100.0	-	1.4	10.6	28.5	-	17.1	35.5	5.5	1.3
AIR.................	-	100.0	.3	76.8	7.6	.8	3.2	.2	2.2	2.1	6.9
WATER...............	-	100.0	-	-	-	-	-	-	-	-	-
OTHER...............	2	100.0	.5	.6	3.2	.7	.5	94.0	.2	-	.3
UNKNOWN.............	-	100.0	-	12.2	87.8	-	.5	-	-	-	-

See footnotes at end of table 4.

TABLE 2. TCC GROUP 355—Percent Distribution of Geographic Division of Origin and Means of Transport, by Geographic Division of Destination: 1972—Continued

Geographic division of origin[1] and means of transport	Number	Percent distribution by division of destination									
		U.S. total	New England	Middle Atlantic	East North Central	West North Central	South Atlantic	East South Central	West South Central	Mountain	Pacific
TONS OF SHIPMENTS	(thousands of tons)										
SOUTH ATLANTIC	331	100.0	.3	3.4	3.2	2.5	45.3	25.4	15.9	1.5	2.4
RAIL	27	100.0	-	5.1	9.6	4.3	25.3	1.4	15.6	15.8	22.8
MOTOR CARRIER	94	100.0	1.1	8.4	5.3	2.0	72.4	5.1	2.9	.8	1.9
PRIVATE TRUCK	207	100.0	-	.9	1.4	2.4	35.7	37.8	21.9	-	-
AIR	-	100.0	1.3	26.2	16.7	25.9	10.7	6.3	8.7	.2	3.9
WATER	-	100.0	-	-	-	-	-	-	-	-	-
OTHER	1	100.0	.9	6.2	3.0	6.9	65.5	14.7	1.9	-	.9
UNKNOWN	-	100.0	-	-	7.3	-	-	-	92.7	-	-
WEST SOUTH CENTRAL	22	100.0	-	17.1	9.7	2.7	6.4	3.2	58.2	2.7	.1
RAIL	1	100.0	-	-	-	-	-	23.0	77.0	-	-
MOTOR CARRIER	16	100.0	-	22.7	12.8	3.6	8.6	2.3	46.3	3.6	.1
PRIVATE TRUCK	4	100.0	-	-	-	-	-	-	100.0	-	-
AIR	-	100.0	-	70.5	2.8	7.0	.1	-	15.4	-	4.1
WATER	-	100.0	-	-	-	-	-	-	-	-	-
OTHER	-	100.0	1.0	6.9	61.1	8.4	-	1.1	21.5	-	-
UNKNOWN	-	100.0	-	-	-	-	-	-	-	-	-
TON-MILES OF SHIPMENTS	(millions of ton-miles)										
U.S. TOTAL	1 733	100.0	2.5	9.0	8.8	3.5	35.4	5.9	18.8	5.7	10.2
RAIL	144	100.0	1.6	10.7	15.9	2.8	18.5	3.3	10.9	6.7	29.7
MOTOR CARRIER	1 430	100.0	2.9	9.5	8.8	3.7	38.0	3.9	18.8	5.9	8.5
PRIVATE TRUCK	103	100.0	.1	.9	2.9	3.3	11.3	40.5	36.6	1.4	3.1
AIR	14	100.0	4.8	25.6	2.9	1.6	23.6	1.0	6.9	1.0	32.6
WATER	3	100.0	1.1	.1	-	-	52.0	-	39.3	-	7.4
OTHER	34	100.0	.3	1.5	1.0	1.0	79.2	1.5	3.4	1.1	10.9
UNKNOWN	3	100.0	5.4	7.6	1.1	1.8	1.1	.6	1.1	77.7	3.5
NEW ENGLAND	232	100.0	.9	6.1	12.8	7.9	27.5	16.4	13.6	10.7	4.0
RAIL	33	100.0	-	.6	50.6	.4	34.9	12.6	-	-	1.0
MOTOR CARRIER	166	100.0	1.2	8.3	7.5	10.9	14.7	20.2	18.9	13.1	5.2
PRIVATE TRUCK	2	100.0	.7	-	-	2.7	58.4	11.1	-	27.1	-
AIR	-	100.0	.1	6.5	10.1	6.9	14.7	5.0	16.8	5.9	34.1
WATER	-	100.0	88.0	12.0	-	-	-	-	-	-	-
OTHER	26	100.0	-	.1	.1	-	99.3	-	-	-	.3
UNKNOWN	2	100.0	6.0	.7	.1	2.0	.3	.1	1.3	85.8	3.9
MIDDLE ATLANTIC	94	100.0	2.3	17.8	13.4	2.8	15.6	2.8	8.9	1.7	34.6
RAIL	16	100.0	-	.1	-	-	-	-	27.7	-	72.2
MOTOR CARRIER	73	100.0	2.9	22.7	16.7	3.4	19.0	3.0	4.9	2.2	25.1
PRIVATE TRUCK	3	100.0	.1	3.6	8.2	2.9	18.0	11.4	-	-	55.7
AIR	-	100.0	6.4	3.4	13.4	1.1	4.6	3.7	30.8	.1	36.5
WATER	-	100.0	-	-	-	-	-	-	-	-	-
OTHER	-	100.0	3.3	17.7	14.9	3.9	23.5	3.8	10.1	1.4	21.4
UNKNOWN	-	100.0	-	-	-	-	100.0	-	-	-	-
EAST NORTH CENTRAL	587	100.0	6.2	17.8	15.8	5.5	13.0	2.8	10.4	9.9	18.5
RAIL	54	100.0	3.3	26.3	7.6	5.2	14.6	.1	9.4	3.1	30.5
MOTOR CARRIER	513	100.0	6.7	17.3	17.1	5.7	12.7	3.0	10.2	10.8	16.4
PRIVATE TRUCK	3	100.0	-	7.0	22.7	5.9	.6	28.6	14.7	10.6	9.9
AIR	6	100.0	9.4	10.1	1.4	.5	2.6	1.0	9.4	1.1	64.3
WATER	3	100.0	-	-	-	-	56.9	-	43.1	-	-
OTHER	6	100.0	.7	5.0	2.8	3.4	13.4	.9	16.0	5.6	52.1
UNKNOWN	-	100.0	-	84.7	8.9	.5	5.8	.1	-	-	.1
WEST NORTH CENTRAL	21	100.0	1.7	11.7	17.1	4.2	25.0	11.2	13.8	3.8	11.4
RAIL	3	100.0	-	9.7	-	.3	63.9	-	26.1	-	-
MOTOR CARRIER	15	100.0	2.4	12.3	23.2	4.0	19.5	11.3	8.4	3.8	15.1
PRIVATE TRUCK	1	100.0	-	2.9	4.6	16.0	-	17.2	41.6	13.3	4.2
AIR	-	100.0	.2	81.4	1.9	.2	2.9	.1	1.3	2.3	9.7
WATER	-	100.0	-	-	-	-	-	-	-	-	-
OTHER	-	100.0	2.4	2.3	2.5	.8	1.7	86.6	1.0	-	2.7
UNKNOWN	-	100.0	-	25.7	74.3	-	-	-	-	-	-
SOUTH ATLANTIC	154	100.0	.4	3.1	3.6	3.6	17.1	27.1	27.9	5.7	11.4
RAIL	32	100.0	-	1.9	4.5	3.4	11.5	.7	13.5	23.4	41.0
MOTOR CARRIER	31	100.0	1.8	11.6	8.0	5.2	42.7	5.0	8.7	3.9	13.2
PRIVATE TRUCK	89	100.0	-	.6	1.7	3.1	10.2	44.4	40.0	-	-
AIR	-	100.0	1.4	19.0	12.9	35.1	5.0	5.3	10.0	.4	11.0
WATER	-	100.0	-	-	-	-	-	-	-	-	-
OTHER	-	100.0	1.7	11.1	5.9	20.8	32.1	17.4	5.3	.1	5.7
UNKNOWN	-	100.0	-	-	13.1	-	-	-	86.9	-	-
WEST SOUTH CENTRAL	11	100.0	-	41.5	17.4	2.4	11.8	3.0	18.7	4.9	.3
RAIL	-	100.0	-	-	-	-	-	41.3	58.7	-	-
MOTOR CARRIER	9	100.0	-	46.5	19.4	2.7	13.3	1.4	10.9	5.5	.3
PRIVATE TRUCK	-	100.0	-	-	-	-	-	-	100.0	-	-
AIR	-	100.0	-	76.2	2.6	3.2	-	-	4.2	-	13.7
WATER	-	100.0	-	-	-	-	-	-	-	-	-
OTHER	-	100.0	2.0	13.1	71.1	5.3	.1	1.1	7.3	-	-
UNKNOWN	-	100.0	-	-	-	-	-	-	-	-	-

See footnotes at end of table 4.

TABLE 3. TCC GROUP 355—Percent Distribution of Geographic Division of Destination and Means of Transport, by Geographic Division of Origin: 1972

Geographic division of destination and means of transport	Number	Percent distribution by division of origin[1]									
		U.S. total	New England	Middle Atlantic	East North Central	West North Central	South Atlantic	East South Central	West South Central	Mountain	Pacific
TONS OF SHIPMENTS	(thousands of tons)										
U.S. TOTAL	2 306	100.0	13.7	9.4	46.6	1.4	14.4	(D)	1.0	(D)	(D)
RAIL	186	100.0	26.1	5.4	47.1	2.5	14.8	(D)	.7	(D)	(D)
MOTOR CARRIER	1 803	100.0	12.3	10.9	53.0	1.1	5.2	(D)	.9	(D)	(D)
PRIVATE TRUCK	246	100.0	1.5	2.7	5.0	1.5	84.3	(D)	1.7	(D)	(D)
AIR	13	100.0	6.0	9.5	60.8	1.4	2.0	(D)	.2	(D)	(D)
WATER	5	100.0	21.6	-	75.9	-	-	(D)	-	(D)	(D)
OTHER	47	100.0	75.1	3.1	14.6	4.4	2.6	(D)	.1	(D)	(D)
UNKNOWN	4	100.0	82.2	.7	15.3	.5	1.3	(D)	-	(D)	(D)
NEW ENGLAND	89	100.0	31.8	10.4	54.7	.4	1.2	(D)	-	(D)	(D)
RAIL	2	100.0	-	-	85.0	-	-	(D)	-	(D)	(D)
MOTOR CARRIER	82	100.0	29.6	11.1	56.5	.4	1.2	(D)	-	(D)	(D)
PRIVATE TRUCK	1	100.0	93.9	1.4	-	-	4.7	(D)	-	(D)	(D)
AIR	1	100.0	1.7	17.6	78.2	-	.4	(D)	-	(D)	(D)
WATER	1	100.0	100.0	-	-	-	-	(D)	-	(D)	(D)
OTHER	-	100.0	32.8	24.4	32.6	4.5	4.7	(D)	.1	(D)	(D)
UNKNOWN	2	100.0	100.0	-	-	-	-	(D)	-	(D)	(D)
MIDDLE ATLANTIC	392	100.0	17.9	31.1	45.5	.6	2.9	(D)	1.0	(D)	(D)
RAIL	28	100.0	2.0	1.2	90.6	1.2	5.0	(D)	-	(D)	(D)
MOTOR CARRIER	353	100.0	19.5	33.2	42.5	.5	2.3	(D)	1.1	(D)	(D)
PRIVATE TRUCK	5	100.0	-	56.3	8.6	1.0	34.1	(D)	-	(D)	(D)
AIR	3	100.0	7.3	14.8	35.2	4.6	2.2	(D)	.5	(D)	(D)
WATER	-	100.0	100.0	-	-	-	-	(D)	-	(D)	(D)
OTHER	1	100.0	5.1	52.2	37.6	.7	4.2	(D)	.1	(D)	(D)
UNKNOWN	-	100.0	29.3	-	70.3	.4	-	(D)	-	(D)	(D)
EAST NORTH CENTRAL	569	100.0	7.8	4.5	83.5	1.3	1.9	(D)	.4	(D)	(D)
RAIL	57	100.0	47.5	-	47.8	-	4.6	(D)	-	(D)	(D)
MOTOR CARRIER	495	100.0	3.3	5.0	88.1	1.4	1.0	(D)	.4	(D)	(D)
PRIVATE TRUCK	11	100.0	-	4.9	64.1	3.6	26.0	(D)	-	(D)	(D)
AIR	3	100.0	3.7	6.7	85.9	.4	1.4	(D)	-	(D)	(D)
WATER	-	100.0	-	-	-	-	-	(D)	-	(D)	(D)
OTHER	1	100.0	3.6	11.3	76.3	4.6	2.6	(D)	1.5	(D)	(D)
UNKNOWN	-	100.0	.9	-	88.7	8.5	1.9	(D)	-	(D)	(D)
WEST NORTH CENTRAL	108	100.0	13.9	2.4	71.9	3.2	7.5	(D)	.6	(D)	(D)
RAIL	7	100.0	1.7	-	81.1	2.0	15.2	(D)	-	(D)	(D)
MOTOR CARRIER	93	100.0	15.9	2.7	75.9	2.3	2.0	(D)	.6	(D)	(D)
PRIVATE TRUCK	6	100.0	.9	1.9	5.3	16.5	75.3	(D)	-	(D)	(D)
AIR	-	100.0	18.2	3.0	30.9	.7	28.4	(D)	.6	(D)	(D)
WATER	-	100.0	-	-	-	-	-	(D)	-	(D)	(D)
OTHER	-	100.0	1.6	2.8	80.2	2.2	12.7	(D)	.4	(D)	(D)
UNKNOWN	-	100.0	91.7	-	8.3	-	-	(D)	-	(D)	(D)
SOUTH ATLANTIC	550	100.0	15.5	5.6	16.6	1.1	27.3	(D)	.3	(D)	(D)
RAIL	37	100.0	43.4	-	25.0	7.8	18.6	(D)	-	(D)	(D)
MOTOR CARRIER	393	100.0	8.0	7.5	19.9	.8	17.3	(D)	.4	(D)	(D)
PRIVATE TRUCK	77	100.0	2.6	1.7	-	-	95.1	(D)	-	(D)	(D)
AIR	1	100.0	7.5	3.5	14.0	.3	1.6	(D)	-	(D)	(D)
WATER	2	100.0	-	-	100.0	-	-	(D)	-	(D)	(D)
OTHER	37	100.0	94.5	.6	2.7	-	2.2	(D)	-	(D)	(D)
UNKNOWN	-	100.0	14.2	50.1	35.7	-	-	(D)	-	(D)	(D)
EAST SOUTH CENTRAL	162	100.0	21.5	2.3	20.3	3.0	51.7	(D)	.4	(D)	(D)
RAIL	4	100.0	83.6	-	1.7	-	8.0	(D)	6.6	(D)	(D)
MOTOR CARRIER	72	100.0	42.3	4.4	41.4	3.2	6.7	(D)	.5	(D)	(D)
PRIVATE TRUCK	82	100.0	.4	.7	3.4	.8	94.6	(D)	-	(D)	(D)
AIR	-	100.0	20.4	20.0	50.3	.2	9.2	(D)	-	(D)	(D)
WATER	-	100.0	-	-	-	-	-	(D)	-	(D)	(D)
OTHER	2	100.0	.6	1.0	5.5	85.1	7.9	(D)	-	(D)	(D)
UNKNOWN	-	100.0	5.7	-	.9	-	93.5	(D)	-	(D)	(D)
WEST SOUTH CENTRAL	260	100.0	8.2	3.0	25.3	1.8	20.2	(D)	5.0	(D)	(D)
RAIL	18	100.0	-	26.6	29.7	7.0	23.4	(D)	5.9	(D)	(D)
MOTOR CARRIER	186	100.0	11.4	1.4	30.0	1.1	1.5	(D)	4.2	(D)	(D)
PRIVATE TRUCK	51	100.0	-	-	1.7	2.6	87.6	(D)	8.1	(D)	(D)
AIR	-	100.0	9.4	19.9	67.0	.5	2.7	(D)	.4	(D)	(D)
WATER	1	100.0	-	-	100.0	-	-	(D)	-	(D)	(D)
OTHER	1	100.0	1.0	2.6	93.6	.4	1.7	(D)	.5	(D)	(D)
UNKNOWN	-	100.0	100.0	-	-	-	-	(D)	-	(D)	(D)
MOUNTAIN	72	100.0	16.0	1.4	63.0	1.1	7.0	(D)	.8	(D)	(D)
RAIL	6	100.0	-	-	31.0	-	64.0	(D)	-	(D)	(D)
MOTOR CARRIER	62	100.0	16.1	1.6	68.2	.9	1.2	(D)	1.0	(D)	(D)
PRIVATE TRUCK	1	100.0	24.0	-	28.6	16.5	-	(D)	-	(D)	(D)
AIR	-	100.0	16.0	.3	51.3	3.1	.5	(D)	-	(D)	(D)
WATER	-	100.0	-	-	-	-	-	(D)	-	(D)	(D)
OTHER	-	100.0	-	1.3	98.6	-	.1	(D)	-	(D)	(D)
UNKNOWN	1	100.0	100.0	-	-	-	-	(D)	-	(D)	(D)
PACIFIC	99	100.0	3.6	13.5	57.7	1.6	8.1	(D)	-	(D)	(D)
RAIL	22	100.0	.6	21.6	41.3	-	27.3	(D)	-	(D)	(D)
MOTOR CARRIER	64	100.0	5.2	11.7	68.3	2.4	2.8	(D)	-	(D)	(D)
PRIVATE TRUCK	8	100.0	-	11.2	2.4	.6	-	(D)	-	(D)	(D)
AIR	2	100.0	4.1	4.5	89.2	.5	.4	(D)	-	(D)	(D)
WATER	-	100.0	-	-	-	-	-	(D)	-	(D)	(D)
OTHER	1	100.0	1.6	2.0	95.3	.4	.6	(D)	-	(D)	(D)
UNKNOWN	-	100.0	97.5	-	.3	-	-	(D)	-	(D)	(D)

See footnotes at end of table 4.

TABLE 3. **TCC GROUP 355—Percent Distribution of Geographic Division of Destination and Means of Transport, by Geographic Division of Origin: 1972**—Continued

Geographic division of destination and means of transport	Number	Percent distribution by division of origin[1]									
		U.S. total	New England	Middle Atlantic	East North Central	West North Central	South Atlantic	East South Central	West South Central	Mountain	Pacific
TON-MILES OF SHIPMENTS	(millions of ton-miles)										
U.S. TOTAL.............	1 733	100.0	13.4	5.5	33.9	1.2	8.9	(D)	.6	(D)	(D)
RAIL................	144	100.0	23.5	11.5	37.7	2.5	22.6	(D)	.3	(D)	(D)
MOTOR CARRIER.......	1 430	100.0	11.6	5.1	35.9	1.1	2.2	(D)	.7	(D)	(D)
PRIVATE TRUCK.......	103	100.0	2.5	3.6	3.4	1.6	86.7	(D)	.7	(D)	(D)
AIR.................	14	100.0	5.5	5.3	44.1	1.5	1.5	(D)	.2	(D)	(D)
WATER...............	3	100.0	1.2	-	91.3	-	-	(D)	-	(D)	(D)
OTHER...............	34	100.0	76.3	1.3	19.8	1.2	1.2	(D)	.1	(D)	(D)
UNKNOWN.............	3	100.0	90.6	.4	8.2	.3	.6	(D)	-	(D)	(D)
NEW ENGLAND............	44	100.0	5.0	5.0	83.1	.8	1.4	(D)	-	(D)	(D)
RAIL................	2	100.0	-	-	81.0	-	-	(D)	-	(D)	(D)
MOTOR CARRIER.......	40	100.0	4.8	5.2	83.7	.9	1.3	(D)	-	(D)	(D)
PRIVATE TRUCK.......	-	100.0	31.8	6.6	-	-	61.6	(D)	-	(D)	(D)
AIR.................	-	100.0	.1	7.2	86.7	.1	.5	(D)	-	(D)	(D)
WATER...............	-	100.0	100.0	-	-	-	-	(D)	-	(D)	(D)
OTHER...............	-	100.0	4.3	16.0	55.3	10.9	7.5	(D)	.5	(D)	(D)
UNKNOWN.............	-	100.0	100.0	-	-	-	-	(D)	-	(D)	(D)
MIDDLE ATLANTIC........	156	100.0	9.0	10.8	66.7	1.6	3.1	(D)	3.0	(D)	(D)
RAIL................	15	100.0	1.3	.1	92.4	2.2	4.1	(D)	-	(D)	(D)
MOTOR CARRIER.......	135	100.0	10.2	12.3	65.4	1.4	2.6	(D)	3.4	(D)	(D)
PRIVATE TRUCK.......	-	100.0	-	13.8	25.8	5.2	55.2	(D)	-	(D)	(D)
AIR.................	3	100.0	1.4	.7	17.4	4.8	1.1	(D)	.5	(D)	(D)
WATER...............	-	100.0	100.0	-	-	-	-	(D)	-	(D)	(D)
OTHER...............	-	100.0	3.7	15.8	68.2	1.9	9.1	(D)	.6	(D)	(D)
UNKNOWN.............	-	100.0	8.2	-	90.8	1.0	-	(D)	-	(D)	(D)
EAST NORTH CENTRAL......	153	100.0	19.5	8.3	60.8	2.4	3.6	(D)	1.3	(D)	(D)
RAIL................	22	100.0	75.0	-	18.0	-	6.5	(D)	-	(D)	(D)
MOTOR CARRIER.......	126	100.0	9.9	9.7	69.5	2.8	2.0	(D)	1.5	(D)	(D)
PRIVATE TRUCK.......	2	100.0	-	10.3	27.0	2.6	50.2	(D)	-	(D)	(D)
AIR.................	-	100.0	19.3	24.7	21.9	1.0	6.8	(D)	.1	(D)	(D)
WATER...............	-	100.0	-	-	-	-	-	(D)	-	(D)	(D)
OTHER...............	-	100.0	10.9	19.0	54.7	3.0	6.9	(D)	4.5	(D)	(D)
UNKNOWN.............	-	100.0	5.7	-	66.6	20.7	7.1	(D)	-	(D)	(D)
WEST NORTH CENTRAL......	60	100.0	30.1	4.4	53.4	1.5	9.2	(D)	.4	(D)	(D)
RAIL................	4	100.0	3.1	-	69.3	.2	27.4	(D)	-	(D)	(D)
MOTOR CARRIER.......	52	100.0	34.1	4.8	55.4	1.1	3.1	(D)	.5	(D)	(D)
PRIVATE TRUCK.......	3	100.0	2.0	3.2	6.1	7.9	80.7	(D)	-	(D)	(D)
AIR.................	-	100.0	23.8	3.5	15.0	.2	33.3	(D)	.3	(D)	(D)
WATER...............	-	100.0	-	-	-	-	-	(D)	-	(D)	(D)
OTHER...............	-	100.0	3.6	4.9	66.1	.9	24.2	(D)	.3	(D)	(D)
UNKNOWN.............	-	100.0	97.9	-	2.1	-	-	(D)	-	(D)	(D)
SOUTH ATLANTIC.........	614	100.0	10.4	2.4	12.4	.9	4.3	(D)	.2	(D)	(D)
RAIL................	26	100.0	44.5	-	29.7	8.6	14.1	(D)	-	(D)	(D)
MOTOR CARRIER.......	543	100.0	4.5	2.6	12.0	.5	2.4	(D)	.2	(D)	(D)
PRIVATE TRUCK.......	11	100.0	12.8	5.7	.2	-	78.4	(D)	-	(D)	(D)
AIR.................	3	100.0	3.4	1.0	4.9	.2	.3	(D)	-	(D)	(D)
WATER...............	1	100.0	-	-	100.0	-	-	(D)	-	(D)	(D)
OTHER...............	27	100.0	95.7	.4	3.3	-	.5	(D)	-	(D)	(D)
UNKNOWN.............	-	100.0	25.2	33.0	41.7	-	-	(D)	-	(D)	(D)
EAST SOUTH CENTRAL......	102	100.0	37.2	2.6	15.9	2.3	40.6	(D)	.3	(D)	(D)
RAIL................	4	100.0	90.1	-	1.3	-	4.5	(D)	4.1	(D)	(D)
MOTOR CARRIER.......	55	100.0	60.6	4.0	27.4	3.1	2.8	(D)	.2	(D)	(D)
PRIVATE TRUCK.......	41	100.0	.7	1.0	2.4	.7	95.2	(D)	-	(D)	(D)
AIR.................	-	100.0	27.7	19.8	44.2	.1	8.2	(D)	-	(D)	(D)
WATER...............	-	100.0	-	-	-	-	-	(D)	-	(D)	(D)
OTHER...............	-	100.0	2.5	3.3	12.0	68.6	13.7	(D)	-	(D)	(D)
UNKNOWN.............	-	100.0	12.5	-	1.5	-	85.9	(D)	-	(D)	(D)
WEST SOUTH CENTRAL......	326	100.0	9.7	2.6	18.7	.9	13.2	(D)	.6	(D)	(D)
RAIL................	15	100.0	-	29.2	32.4	5.9	28.1	(D)	1.7	(D)	(D)
MOTOR CARRIER.......	269	100.0	11.7	1.3	19.5	.5	1.0	(D)	.4	(D)	(D)
PRIVATE TRUCK.......	37	100.0	-	-	1.4	1.9	94.8	(D)	1.9	(D)	(D)
AIR.................	-	100.0	13.5	23.8	60.1	.3	2.2	(D)	.1	(D)	(D)
WATER...............	1	100.0	-	-	100.0	-	-	(D)	-	(D)	(D)
OTHER...............	1	100.0	1.5	3.8	91.9	.3	1.9	(D)	.1	(D)	(D)
UNKNOWN.............	-	100.0	100.0	-	-	-	-	(D)	-	(D)	(D)
MOUNTAIN...............	98	100.0	25.4	1.7	59.2	.8	9.0	(D)	.6	(D)	(D)
RAIL................	9	100.0	-	-	17.3	-	78.9	(D)	-	(D)	(D)
MOTOR CARRIER.......	84	100.0	25.9	1.9	66.1	.7	1.4	(D)	.7	(D)	(D)
PRIVATE TRUCK.......	1	100.0	48.5	-	26.2	15.7	-	(D)	-	(D)	(D)
AIR.................	-	100.0	32.8	.5	50.4	3.5	.6	(D)	-	(D)	(D)
WATER...............	-	100.0	-	-	-	-	-	(D)	-	(D)	(D)
OTHER...............	-	100.0	-	1.6	98.2	-	.1	(D)	-	(D)	(D)
UNKNOWN.............	2	100.0	100.0	-	-	-	-	(D)	-	(D)	(D)
PACIFIC................	176	100.0	5.3	18.6	61.6	1.4	9.9	(D)	-	(D)	(D)
RAIL................	42	100.0	.8	28.0	38.7	-	31.3	(D)	-	(D)	(D)
MOTOR CARRIER.......	121	100.0	7.1	15.1	69.2	1.9	3.4	(D)	-	(D)	(D)
PRIVATE TRUCK.......	3	100.0	-	64.2	10.9	2.2	-	(D)	-	(D)	(D)
AIR.................	4	100.0	5.8	5.9	86.8	.5	.5	(D)	.1	(D)	(D)
WATER...............	-	100.0	-	-	-	-	-	(D)	-	(D)	(D)
OTHER...............	3	100.0	2.1	2.6	94.5	.3	.6	(D)	-	(D)	(D)
UNKNOWN.............	-	100.0	99.8	-	.2	-	-	(D)	-	(D)	(D)

See footnotes at end of table 4.

TABLE 4. TCC GROUP 355—Percent Distribution of Distance Shipped and Weight of Shipment, by Means of Transport: 1972

Distance shipped and weight of shipment[2][3]	Number	Percent distribution by means of transport							
		All means of transport	Rail	Motor carrier	Private truck	Air	Water	Other	Unknown
TONS OF SHIPMENTS	(thousands of tons)								
U.S. TOTAL	1 854	100.0	7.4	77.4	12.0	.5	.1	2.4	.2
UNDER 100 MILES	218	100.0	.8	76.0	21.4	-	.5	.6	.7
UNDER 1000 POUNDS	24	100.0	-	90.1	6.3	.3	-	3.0	.3
1000 TO 9999 POUNDS	100	100.0	.2	83.0	15.9	-	-	.6	.4
10000 TO 29999 POUNDS	61	100.0	.7	67.5	28.4	-	1.7	-	1.8
30000 TO 59999 POUNDS	30	100.0	3.8	57.5	38.7	-	-	-	-
60000 TO 89999 POUNDS	1	100.0	-	100.0	-	-	-	-	-
90000 POUNDS AND OVER	-	100.0	-	-	-	-	-	-	-
100 TO 199 MILES	228	100.0	1.2	91.9	5.3	.1	-	1.1	.4
UNDER 1000 POUNDS	33	100.0	-	96.5	1.0	.6	.1	1.6	.3
1000 TO 9999 POUNDS	95	100.0	-	93.7	5.4	.1	-	-	.8
10000 TO 29999 POUNDS	30	100.0	2.5	81.7	9.4	-	-	6.4	-
30000 TO 59999 POUNDS	42	100.0	1.2	90.2	8.6	-	-	-	-
60000 TO 89999 POUNDS	1	100.0	93.9	6.1	-	-	-	-	-
90000 POUNDS AND OVER	24	100.0	-	100.0	-	-	-	-	-
200 TO 299 MILES	120	100.0	3.9	85.3	10.2	.3	-	.4	-
UNDER 1000 POUNDS	21	100.0	-	94.5	1.6	1.7	-	2.2	-
1000 TO 9999 POUNDS	33	100.0	-	93.4	6.6	-	-	-	-
10000 TO 29999 POUNDS	42	100.0	5.6	76.1	18.3	-	-	-	-
30000 TO 59999 POUNDS	20	100.0	5.8	84.1	10.1	-	-	-	-
60000 TO 89999 POUNDS	1	100.0	-	100.0	-	-	-	-	-
90000 POUNDS AND OVER	1	100.0	56.9	43.1	-	-	-	-	-
300 TO 499 MILES	252	100.0	4.4	82.2	12.6	.2	-	.5	.1
UNDER 1000 POUNDS	26	100.0	.1	93.7	.2	2.1	-	3.4	.6
1000 TO 9999 POUNDS	102	100.0	-	93.5	6.1	.1	-	.2	.1
10000 TO 29999 POUNDS	74	100.0	-	86.8	13.2	-	-	-	-
30000 TO 59999 POUNDS	38	100.0	24.3	53.2	22.5	-	-	-	-
60000 TO 89999 POUNDS	5	100.0	27.9	11.0	61.2	-	-	-	-
90000 POUNDS AND OVER	4	100.0	6.0	8.5	85.5	-	-	-	-
500 TO 999 MILES	545	100.0	15.4	57.7	19.4	.5	-	7.0	.1
UNDER 1000 POUNDS	58	100.0	-	93.3	.5	2.0	-	4.1	-
1000 TO 9999 POUNDS	156	100.0	.2	94.5	4.0	.9	-	.3	-
10000 TO 29999 POUNDS	74	100.0	16.1	68.1	15.4	-	-	-	.4
30000 TO 59999 POUNDS	170	100.0	12.6	33.2	46.6	-	-	7.6	-
60000 TO 89999 POUNDS	49	100.0	39.1	9.2	6.7	-	-	45.1	-
90000 POUNDS AND OVER	36	100.0	85.0	.8	14.1	-	-	-	-
1000 TO 1499 MILES	105	100.0	8.0	78.8	11.8	.9	-	.5	.1
UNDER 1000 POUNDS	17	100.0	-	93.0	.3	3.5	-	2.7	.5
1000 TO 9999 POUNDS	36	100.0	-	97.3	1.7	.8	-	.2	-
10000 TO 29999 POUNDS	19	100.0	16.1	67.8	16.0	.1	-	-	-
30000 TO 59999 POUNDS	15	100.0	25.7	17.3	57.0	-	-	-	-
60000 TO 89999 POUNDS	16	100.0	1.3	98.7	-	-	-	-	-
90000 POUNDS AND OVER	1	100.0	100.0	-	-	-	-	-	-
1500 MILES OR OVER	382	100.0	6.6	91.4	.4	1.0	-	.3	.3
UNDER 1000 POUNDS	17	100.0	.3	91.4	.2	3.8	-	4.0	.2
1000 TO 9999 POUNDS	37	100.0	.5	88.8	3.7	6.3	-	.7	-
10000 TO 29999 POUNDS	15	100.0	14.7	71.6	.9	4.7	.8	-	7.3
30000 TO 59999 POUNDS	44	100.0	18.3	81.7	-	-	-	-	-
60000 TO 89999 POUNDS	41	100.0	20.9	79.1	-	-	-	-	-
90000 POUNDS AND OVER	226	100.0	2.6	97.3	.1	-	-	-	-
TON-MILES OF SHIPMENTS	(millions of ton-miles)								
U.S. TOTAL	1 477	100.0	8.4	81.7	6.8	.8	-	2.1	.2
UNDER 100 MILES	11	100.0	1.2	75.3	21.4	-	.3	.8	1.0
UNDER 1000 POUNDS	1	100.0	-	93.1	3.2	.2	-	3.4	.2
1000 TO 9999 POUNDS	5	100.0	.2	82.5	15.9	-	-	.9	.5
10000 TO 29999 POUNDS	3	100.0	1.0	59.8	35.5	-	1.1	-	2.6
30000 TO 59999 POUNDS	1	100.0	6.5	64.0	29.5	-	-	-	-
60000 TO 89999 POUNDS	-	100.0	-	100.0	-	-	-	-	-
90000 POUNDS AND OVER	-	100.0	-	-	-	-	-	-	-
100 TO 199 MILES	34	100.0	1.2	91.8	5.3	.1	-	1.3	.3
UNDER 1000 POUNDS	5	100.0	-	96.8	.9	.6	.1	1.4	.2
1000 TO 9999 POUNDS	14	100.0	-	94.7	4.7	.1	-	-	.6
10000 TO 29999 POUNDS	4	100.0	2.7	78.2	10.4	-	-	8.7	-
30000 TO 59999 POUNDS	6	100.0	1.2	87.9	10.9	-	-	-	-
60000 TO 89999 POUNDS	-	100.0	95.1	4.9	-	-	-	-	-
90000 POUNDS AND OVER	4	100.0	-	100.0	-	-	-	-	-

See footnotes at end of table 4.

TABLE 4. TCC GROUP 355—Percent Distribution of Distance Shipped and Weight of Shipment, by Means of Transport: 1972—Continued

Distance shipped and weight of shipment[2][3]	Number	Percent distribution by means of transport							
		All means of transport	Rail	Motor carrier	Private truck	Air	Water	Other	Unknown
TON-MILES OF SHIPMENTS	(millions of ton-miles)								
200 TO 299 MILES.........	29	100.0	3.9	84.7	10.7	.3	-	.4	-
UNDER 1000 POUNDS.....	5	100.0	-	94.0	1.9	1.8	-	2.2	-
1000 TO 9999 POUNDS...	7	100.0	-	93.6	6.4	-	-	-	-
10000 TO 29999 POUNDS.	10	100.0	5.3	75.8	19.0	-	-	-	-
30000 TO 59999 POUNDS.	5	100.0	6.3	83.4	10.4	-	-	-	-
60000 TO 89999 POUNDS.	-	100.0	-	100.0	-	-	-	-	-
90000 POUNDS AND OVER.	-	100.0	60.2	39.8	-	-	-	-	-
300 TO 499 MILES........	92	100.0	4.9	80.5	13.8	.3	-	.5	.1
UNDER 1000 POUNDS.....	9	100.0	-	93.5	.2	2.3	-	3.4	.6
1000 TO 9999 POUNDS...	35	100.0	-	93.8	5.8	.1	-	.3	-
10000 TO 29999 POUNDS.	27	100.0	-	87.3	12.7	-	-	-	-
30000 TO 59999 POUNDS.	16	100.0	23.5	51.7	24.7	-	-	-	-
60000 TO 89999 POUNDS.	2	100.0	26.7	9.3	64.1	-	-	-	-
90000 POUNDS AND OVER.	2	100.0	5.0	6.9	88.2	-	-	-	-
500 TO 999 MILES........	365	100.0	16.0	58.9	16.8	.5	-	7.7	.1
UNDER 1000 POUNDS.....	39	100.0	-	92.8	.5	2.0	-	4.7	-
1000 TO 9999 POUNDS...	105	100.0	.2	94.8	3.6	1.0	-	.4	-
10000 TO 29999 POUNDS.	52	100.0	17.8	68.4	13.5	-	-	-	.3
30000 TO 59999 POUNDS.	109	100.0	13.9	35.5	41.7	-	-	8.8	-
60000 TO 89999 POUNDS.	35	100.0	39.5	9.4	4.9	-	-	46.1	-
90000 POUNDS AND OVER.	22	100.0	86.5	.9	12.7	-	-	-	-
1000 TO 1499 MILES......	127	100.0	7.5	79.7	11.4	.9	-	.5	.1
UNDER 1000 POUNDS.....	21	100.0	-	93.4	.3	3.5	-	2.3	.5
1000 TO 9999 POUNDS...	44	100.0	-	97.5	1.6	.7	-	.2	-
10000 TO 29999 POUNDS.	21	100.0	15.9	67.7	16.2	.1	-	-	-
30000 TO 59999 POUNDS.	17	100.0	24.4	17.7	57.9	-	-	-	-
60000 TO 89999 POUNDS.	20	100.0	1.2	98.8	-	-	-	-	-
90000 POUNDS AND OVER.	1	100.0	100.0	-	-	-	-	-	-
1500 MILES OR OVER......	816	100.0	6.1	91.9	.4	1.0	-	.2	.3
UNDER 1000 POUNDS.....	34	100.0	.3	91.3	.2	4.2	-	3.8	.3
1000 TO 9999 POUNDS...	74	100.0	.7	87.2	4.1	7.4	-	.7	-
10000 TO 29999 POUNDS.	31	100.0	13.1	73.4	.8	4.4	.8	-	7.6
30000 TO 59999 POUNDS.	92	100.0	15.4	84.6	-	-	-	-	-
60000 TO 89999 POUNDS.	91	100.0	20.0	80.0	-	-	-	-	-
90000 POUNDS AND OVER.	492	100.0	2.6	97.4	.1	-	-	-	-

Note: Detail may not add to total due to rounding. The introductory table shows the estimates of sampling variability for tons; sampling variability for ton-miles has not been estimated. See the map in the Introduction for the States comprising the geographic divisions of the United States.

Shipments excluded from the survey are those moving by pipeline (primarily petroleum products from refineries), parcel post shipments, and commodities moved by own power (motorized vehicles, aircraft, etc.) or towed (prefabricated buildings, etc.). Local shipments (commodities shipped less than 25 miles from the plant) and shipments within the same city are also excluded. Shipments to Alaska and Hawaii from the 48 conterminous States and the District of Columbia are included; however, no data were obtained for shipments originating in Alaska and Hawaii.

- Represents zero or rounds to zero. (D) Withheld to avoid disclosing figures for individual companies.

[1]Production of this commodity is concentrated in the geographic divisions shown; figures and distributions for geographic divisions not shown are included in the total.
[2]Distances of shipments to foreign destinations are calculated only to the U.S. port of exit.
[3]Includes only shipments represented by bills of lading and invoices. Summary records which did not show individual weights of shipments are not included.

TCC 356. General Industrial Machinery and Equipment

Comparisons of Tons and Ton-Miles of Shipments for
Geographic Divisions of Origin and for Sampling Variability: 1972 and 1967

Geographic division of origin	Estimates				Relative sampling variability in tons (percent)	
	1972		1967		1972	1967
	Tons (thousands)	Ton-miles (millions)	Tons (thousands)	Ton-miles (millions)		
U.S. total	2,512	1,398	2,932	2,067	10.9	17.8
New England	187	149	189	108	32.5	(*)
Middle Atlantic	427	233	668	360	14.3	(*)
East North Central	1,171	557	1,620	1,174	20.4	(*)
West North Central	160	81	157	105	30.9	(*)
South Atlantic	149	107	40	29	41.3	(*)
East South Central	276	124	73	45	44.9	(*)
West South Central	44	40	27	24	39.9	(*)
Mountain	(D)	(D)	24	25	(*)	(*)
Pacific	(D)	(D)	134	197	(*)	(*)

(D) Withheld to avoid disclosing figures for individual companies.   (*) Data not published.

TABLE 1. TCC GROUP 356—Percent Distribution of Geographic Division of Origin and Distance Shipped, by Means of Transport: 1972

Geographic division of origin[1] and distance shipped[2]	Number	Percent distribution by means of transport							
		All means of transport	Rail	Motor carrier	Private truck	Air	Water	Other	Unknown
TONS OF SHIPMENTS	(thousands of tons)								
U.S. TOTAL..........	2 512	100.0	6.5	79.9	11.2	.9	.2	1.1	.2
NEW ENGLAND..............	187	100.0	5.1	87.8	2.7	1.2	.1	3.2	-
UNDER 100 MILES.......	17	100.0	-	88.1	5.1	.4	1.4	4.9	.1
100 TO 199 MILES......	16	100.0	-	82.6	10.0	.6	-	6.8	-
200 TO 299 MILES......	10	100.0	-	97.6	-	.6	-	1.8	.1
300 TO 499 MILES......	13	100.0	-	95.4	-	1.6	-	3.0	-
500 TO 999 MILES......	82	100.0	-	94.0	2.6	.9	-	2.4	.1
1000 TO 1499 MILES....	30	100.0	27.2	67.6	.8	.7	-	3.6	-
1500 MILES OR OVER....	15	100.0	7.5	85.8	-	5.1	-	1.6	-
MIDDLE ATLANTIC.........	427	100.0	7.2	88.2	2.7	.7	.5	.5	-
UNDER 100 MILES.......	57	100.0	5.8	84.6	8.3	.7	.1	.5	-
100 TO 199 MILES......	46	100.0	.7	89.9	8.4	.1	-	1.0	-
200 TO 299 MILES......	59	100.0	.4	91.3	2.5	1.0	3.8	1.0	-
300 TO 499 MILES......	91	100.0	6.3	92.7	.3	.3	-	.4	.1
500 TO 999 MILES......	113	100.0	5.5	92.9	.6	.8	-	.2	-
1000 TO 1499 MILES....	34	100.0	23.6	74.1	.7	1.3	-	.2	-
1500 MILES OR OVER....	25	100.0	28.3	67.8	1.6	1.5	-	.8	-
EAST NORTH CENTRAL......	1 171	100.0	7.8	86.6	4.1	.5	-	.7	.2
UNDER 100 MILES.......	151	100.0	21.6	66.7	9.8	.1	-	1.0	.7
100 TO 199 MILES......	160	100.0	10.9	83.0	5.4	.1	-	.5	.2
200 TO 299 MILES......	161	100.0	.9	96.2	1.6	.3	-	.8	.2
300 TO 499 MILES......	301	100.0	3.6	92.0	3.6	.4	-	.5	-
500 TO 999 MILES......	291	100.0	7.1	88.4	2.5	1.0	.2	.8	.1
1000 TO 1499 MILES....	39	100.0	4.0	93.3	.9	.6	-	.9	.2
1500 MILES OR OVER....	66	100.0	11.1	81.2	5.2	1.4	-	1.1	-
WEST NORTH CENTRAL......	160	100.0	.8	53.2	42.9	1.1	-	1.9	.2
UNDER 100 MILES.......	29	100.0	-	17.6	80.9	-	-	1.5	-
100 TO 199 MILES......	8	100.0	-	51.0	46.6	1.3	-	1.0	-
200 TO 299 MILES......	18	100.0	-	40.5	57.9	.1	-	1.1	.3
300 TO 499 MILES......	27	100.0	-	66.2	32.0	.1	-	1.7	-
500 TO 999 MILES......	59	100.0	1.9	56.9	36.2	2.5	-	2.5	-
1000 TO 1499 MILES....	17	100.0	.6	94.2	1.7	.7	-	1.7	1.2
1500 MILES OR OVER....	-	100.0	5.1	81.8	.6	2.9	-	9.5	-
SOUTH ATLANTIC..........	149	100.0	10.2	72.7	15.3	.5	-	.5	.8
UNDER 100 MILES.......	8	100.0	-	68.9	30.5	-	-	.1	.4
100 TO 199 MILES......	10	100.0	-	96.0	4.0	-	-	.1	-
200 TO 299 MILES......	15	100.0	5.3	92.7	1.8	-	-	.2	-
300 TO 499 MILES......	43	100.0	1.4	66.1	32.1	.2	-	.1	-
500 TO 999 MILES......	42	100.0	-	85.0	9.8	1.3	-	1.1	2.8
1000 TO 1499 MILES....	9	100.0	13.0	77.1	9.0	.3	-	.7	-
1500 MILES OR OVER....	20	100.0	60.7	34.1	4.1	.5	-	.7	-
EAST SOUTH CENTRAL......	276	100.0	2.8	52.3	41.7	1.0	-	2.2	-
UNDER 100 MILES.......	58	100.0	-	39.0	60.7	-	-	.3	-
100 TO 199 MILES......	15	100.0	-	44.7	52.5	-	-	2.8	-
200 TO 299 MILES......	50	100.0	-	19.4	76.9	.2	-	3.5	-
300 TO 499 MILES......	56	100.0	4.7	71.6	20.4	1.1	-	2.2	-
500 TO 999 MILES......	74	100.0	1.0	67.1	28.7	2.4	-	.8	-
1000 TO 1499 MILES....	9	100.0	46.3	46.4	-	.8	-	6.4	-
1500 MILES OR OVER....	12	100.0	-	89.1	-	1.2	-	9.2	.5
WEST SOUTH CENTRAL......	44	100.0	12.5	61.9	18.5	.7	4.9	1.4	-
UNDER 100 MILES.......	-	100.0	-	80.9	15.5	-	-	3.6	-
100 TO 199 MILES......	1	100.0	-	68.5	31.3	-	-	.2	-
200 TO 299 MILES......	1	100.0	-	78.0	6.5	.4	14.6	.5	-
300 TO 499 MILES......	9	100.0	-	34.8	43.7	.2	21.1	.1	-
500 TO 999 MILES......	11	100.0	42.9	34.0	20.8	1.1	-	1.2	-
1000 TO 1499 MILES....	18	100.0	-	90.7	6.1	.8	-	2.3	-
1500 MILES OR OVER....	-	100.0	81.9	16.1	-	.6	-	1.3	-
TON-MILES OF SHIPMENTS	(millions of ton-miles)								
U.S. TOTAL..........	1 398	100.0	8.9	81.0	6.7	1.8	.1	1.3	.1
NEW ENGLAND..............	149	100.0	8.8	85.5	1.3	1.8	-	2.5	-
UNDER 100 MILES.......	1	100.0	-	90.1	3.7	.3	2.1	3.8	.1
100 TO 199 MILES......	2	100.0	-	83.1	8.7	.8	-	7.4	-
200 TO 299 MILES......	2	100.0	-	97.5	-	.6	-	1.9	-
300 TO 499 MILES......	5	100.0	-	95.2	-	1.8	-	3.0	-
500 TO 999 MILES......	62	100.0	-	94.7	2.1	.8	-	2.3	.1
1000 TO 1499 MILES....	37	100.0	25.7	69.2	.9	.7	-	3.6	-
1500 MILES OR OVER....	38	100.0	9.5	84.4	-	4.7	-	1.4	-
MIDDLE ATLANTIC.........	233	100.0	14.7	82.4	1.2	1.0	.2	.5	-
UNDER 100 MILES.......	2	100.0	7.3	84.0	7.4	.6	-	.6	-
100 TO 199 MILES......	7	100.0	.8	90.8	7.4	.1	-	.9	-
200 TO 299 MILES......	15	100.0	.4	92.0	2.2	.9	3.6	.9	-
300 TO 499 MILES......	36	100.0	6.6	92.4	.2	.3	-	.4	.1
500 TO 999 MILES......	73	100.0	5.8	92.5	.5	.8	-	.3	-
1000 TO 1499 MILES....	41	100.0	24.8	72.9	.8	1.3	-	.2	-
1500 MILES OR OVER....	55	100.0	30.5	65.3	1.7	1.6	-	.8	-

See footnotes at end of table 4.

TABLE 1. TCC GROUP 356—Percent Distribution of Geographic Division of Origin and Distance Shipped, by Means of Transport: 1972—Continued

Geographic division of origin[1] and distance shipped[2]	Number	Percent distribution by means of transport							
		All means of transport	Rail	Motor carrier	Private truck	Air	Water	Other	Unknown
TON-MILES OF SHIPMENTS	(millions of ton-miles)								
EAST NORTH CENTRAL......	557	100.0	6.2	88.7	3.3	.9	.1	.8	.1
UNDER 100 MILES.......	7	100.0	12.8	74.2	11.4	.1	-	.7	.8
100 TO 199 MILES......	23	100.0	9.4	85.0	4.8	.1	-	.5	.2
200 TO 299 MILES......	40	100.0	.9	96.2	1.6	.3	-	.8	.2
300 TO 499 MILES......	113	100.0	3.6	91.6	3.9	.4	-	.5	-
500 TO 999 MILES......	200	100.0	6.0	89.5	2.3	1.1	.2	.8	.1
1000 TO 1499 MILES....	46	100.0	3.5	93.7	.9	.7	-	1.0	.2
1500 MILES OR OVER....	125	100.0	10.4	82.0	5.2	1.4	-	1.0	-
WEST NORTH CENTRAL......	81	100.0	1.2	65.8	28.6	1.8	-	2.3	.3
UNDER 100 MILES.......	1	100.0	-	17.8	80.7	-	-	1.5	-
100 TO 199 MILES......	1	100.0	-	57.8	39.2	1.7	-	1.3	-
200 TO 299 MILES......	4	100.0	-	39.5	59.0	.1	-	1.1	.3
300 TO 499 MILES......	11	100.0	-	64.1	34.2	.1	-	1.5	-
500 TO 999 MILES......	41	100.0	1.8	57.7	34.7	2.9	-	2.9	-
1000 TO 1499 MILES....	19	100.0	.7	94.0	1.7	.8	-	1.7	1.2
1500 MILES OR OVER....	1	100.0	4.6	80.7	.5	4.6	-	9.5	-
SOUTH ATLANTIC..........	107	100.0	28.7	59.2	10.1	.6	-	.7	.7
UNDER 100 MILES.......	-	100.0	-	51.9	47.4	-	-	.2	.5
100 TO 199 MILES......	1	100.0	-	96.7	3.2	-	-	.1	-
200 TO 299 MILES......	3	100.0	6.0	92.1	1.6	-	-	.2	-
300 TO 499 MILES......	16	100.0	1.3	67.5	30.7	.3	-	.1	-
500 TO 999 MILES......	27	100.0	-	85.7	9.2	1.2	-	1.1	2.8
1000 TO 1499 MILES....	10	100.0	16.0	73.5	9.5	.4	-	.7	-
1500 MILES OR OVER....	45	100.0	62.5	32.4	4.0	.5	-	.7	-
EAST SOUTH CENTRAL......	124	100.0	5.1	65.7	24.3	1.5	-	3.3	.1
UNDER 100 MILES.......	1	100.0	-	43.4	56.0	-	-	.6	-
100 TO 199 MILES......	2	100.0	-	39.5	58.0	-	-	2.6	-
200 TO 299 MILES......	13	100.0	-	19.4	77.2	.2	-	3.2	-
300 TO 499 MILES......	22	100.0	4.9	71.9	20.0	1.0	-	2.1	-
500 TO 999 MILES......	49	100.0	1.3	68.4	26.9	2.5	-	.8	-
1000 TO 1499 MILES....	10	100.0	44.4	48.6	-	.9	-	6.1	-
1500 MILES OR OVER....	25	100.0	-	90.4	-	1.1	-	8.1	.4
WEST SOUTH CENTRAL......	40	100.0	12.2	71.0	12.4	.8	1.7	1.9	-
UNDER 100 MILES.......	-	100.0	-	81.9	13.1	-	-	4.9	-
100 TO 199 MILES......	-	100.0	-	64.6	35.3	-	-	.2	-
200 TO 299 MILES......	-	100.0	-	77.4	7.0	.5	14.6	.5	-
300 TO 499 MILES......	3	100.0	-	31.5	50.5	.2	17.8	.1	-
500 TO 999 MILES......	7	100.0	37.0	38.4	21.4	1.5	-	1.7	-
1000 TO 1499 MILES....	26	100.0	-	91.0	5.8	.8	-	2.3	-
1500 MILES OR OVER....	2	100.0	90.8	7.8	-	.8	-	.7	-

See footnotes at end of table 4.

TABLE 2. TCC GROUP 356—Percent Distribution of Geographic Division of Origin and Means of Transport, by Geographic Division of Destination: 1972

Geographic division of origin[1] and means of transport	Number	Percent distribution by division of destination									
		U.S. total	New England	Middle Atlantic	East North Central	West North Central	South Atlantic	East South Central	West South Central	Mountain	Pacific
TONS OF SHIPMENTS	(thousands of tons)										
U.S. TOTAL..............	2 512	100.0	2.7	16.7	37.4	7.6	12.1	8.0	7.5	2.3	5.6
RAIL.................	162	100.0	-	8.7	34.3	6.5	14.5	8.2	7.7	4.6	15.4
MOTOR CARRIER........	2 007	100.0	3.1	17.6	38.0	6.9	12.6	6.9	7.4	2.4	5.2
PRIVATE TRUCK........	281	100.0	.9	14.2	36.3	13.8	7.8	16.6	8.0	.3	2.1
AIR..................	23	100.0	3.7	20.5	36.9	4.0	10.8	4.5	6.5	2.5	10.5
WATER................	5	100.0	4.8	52.2	-	-	-	-	41.3	-	1.7
OTHER................	28	100.0	8.2	16.0	29.4	9.7	10.4	6.4	6.5	2.0	11.4
UNKNOWN..............	3	100.0	.8	12.6	62.6	2.8	10.5	.6	6.8	-	3.2
NEW ENGLAND.............	187	100.0	6.7	20.1	31.9	10.6	10.4	7.7	5.5	1.6	5.5
RAIL.................	9	100.0	-	.1	-	87.4	-	-	.7	-	11.8
MOTOR CARRIER........	164	100.0	6.3	20.9	33.4	6.6	11.4	8.7	5.8	1.7	5.2
PRIVATE TRUCK........	5	100.0	17.9	33.7	43.6	4.8	-	-	-	-	-
AIR..................	2	100.0	2.9	9.5	34.2	5.6	5.7	5.3	10.4	1.2	25.2
WATER................	-	100.0	99.8	.2	-	-	-	-	-	-	-
OTHER................	5	100.0	15.6	22.9	30.1	8.1	12.1	1.3	7.0	.9	2.0
UNKNOWN..............	-	100.0	18.9	16.8	50.9	.1	11.0	-	-	-	2.3
MIDDLE ATLANTIC.........	427	100.0	3.7	28.3	31.6	3.8	15.7	4.3	7.1	2.2	3.2
RAIL.................	30	100.0	.2	12.3	19.9	1.2	16.1	1.4	26.9	6.8	15.3
MOTOR CARRIER........	377	100.0	4.0	28.1	33.1	4.1	16.1	4.8	5.7	1.9	2.2
PRIVATE TRUCK........	11	100.0	3.3	63.6	21.4	-	5.8	.3	2.2	-	3.4
AIR..................	3	100.0	3.5	17.2	35.7	7.5	12.4	2.1	12.0	2.9	6.8
WATER................	2	100.0	-	100.0	-	-	-	-	-	-	-
OTHER................	2	100.0	8.8	35.7	28.7	2.2	9.5	3.5	2.5	.2	8.8
UNKNOWN..............	-	100.0	.3	4.5	5.1	-	90.0	-	.1	-	-

See footnotes at end of table 4.

TABLE 2. TCC GROUP 356—Percent Distribution of Geographic Division of Origin and Means of Transport, by Geographic Division of Destination: 1972—Continued

Geographic division of origin[1] and means of transport	Number	Percent distribution by division of destination									
		U.S. total	New England	Middle Atlantic	East North Central	West North Central	South Atlantic	East South Central	West South Central	Mountain	Pacific
TONS OF SHIPMENTS	(thousands of tons)										
EAST NORTH CENTRAL	1 171	100.0	1.8	12.8	47.4	6.1	11.7	6.7	6.3	1.8	5.5
RAIL	91	100.0	-	9.9	52.5	-	19.3	8.1	2.1	-	8.0
MOTOR CARRIER	1 015	100.0	2.0	13.3	46.7	6.7	11.2	6.3	6.8	2.0	5.1
PRIVATE TRUCK	47	100.0	.2	5.9	58.0	4.7	6.0	14.0	4.0	-	7.2
AIR	6	100.0	6.7	23.3	11.7	3.6	22.6	5.1	9.6	4.6	12.9
WATER	-	100.0	-	97.2	-	-	-	-	-	-	2.8
OTHER	8	100.0	2.3	17.3	37.4	9.7	10.9	5.5	5.0	3.7	8.4
UNKNOWN	2	100.0	.4	12.9	55.6	3.9	13.6	1.0	12.3	.1	.2
WEST NORTH CENTRAL	160	100.0	1.9	10.7	35.2	30.8	2.6	.9	13.4	1.7	2.8
RAIL	1	100.0	.7	35.7	54.4	-	-	-	-	-	9.3
MOTOR CARRIER	85	100.0	2.6	15.7	38.7	19.8	4.6	1.7	9.2	3.0	4.8
PRIVATE TRUCK	68	100.0	-	2.6	31.6	46.0	-	-	19.7	-	-
AIR	1	100.0	.1	69.3	12.7	.6	2.3	.8	2.7	4.9	6.6
WATER	-	100.0	-	-	-	-	-	-	-	-	-
OTHER	3	100.0	27.2	3.9	24.1	27.6	5.5	1.6	2.7	3.6	3.7
UNKNOWN	-	100.0	4.1	72.8	22.9	-	.1	-	.2	-	-
SOUTH ATLANTIC	149	100.0	4.2	23.6	18.5	5.3	23.2	5.9	3.9	5.2	10.1
RAIL	15	100.0	-	-	3.9	-	5.3	-	-	19.1	71.7
MOTOR CARRIER	108	100.0	5.4	21.1	18.6	7.0	27.5	8.2	5.3	4.1	2.8
PRIVATE TRUCK	22	100.0	1.6	53.6	21.5	.7	16.5	-	.7	1.8	3.6
AIR	-	100.0	2.6	9.4	60.9	.6	7.0	1.1	1.5	4.5	12.5
WATER	-	100.0	-	-	-	-	-	-	-	-	-
OTHER	-	100.0	5.3	6.2	46.3	15.7	5.0	1.6	1.5	.3	18.1
UNKNOWN	1	100.0	-	-	94.7	2.1	3.2	-	-	-	-
EAST SOUTH CENTRAL	276	100.0	1.6	13.1	28.1	8.2	12.2	25.3	5.8	1.3	4.4
RAIL	7	100.0	-	9.0	-	24.7	.2	6.9	27.2	31.9	-
MOTOR CARRIER	144	100.0	2.8	14.6	23.1	11.2	12.5	19.2	8.3	.7	7.5
PRIVATE TRUCK	115	100.0	-	11.8	36.8	3.3	12.6	34.7	.7	-	-
AIR	2	100.0	7.1	25.6	17.9	10.0	9.2	17.6	6.6	1.0	5.0
WATER	-	100.0	-	-	-	-	-	-	-	-	-
OTHER	5	100.0	1.6	3.3	24.2	5.9	14.0	18.7	13.4	-	18.9
UNKNOWN	-	100.0	-	-	-	-	-	-	-	-	100.0
WEST SOUTH CENTRAL	44	100.0	2.0	37.3	6.1	2.0	2.3	12.2	34.1	1.6	2.3
RAIL	5	100.0	-	-	-	-	-	89.0	-	-	11.0
MOTOR CARRIER	27	100.0	1.1	56.8	7.2	.9	3.0	1.7	26.7	1.4	1.3
PRIVATE TRUCK	8	100.0	7.3	5.4	7.1	7.5	.9	-	67.7	4.0	-
AIR	-	100.0	-	28.7	15.2	3.8	30.2	-	9.7	.2	12.2
WATER	2	100.0	-	-	-	-	-	-	100.0	-	-
OTHER	-	100.0	1.6	63.6	15.1	3.2	5.4	1.6	7.1	.3	2.3
UNKNOWN	-	100.0	-	-	-	-	-	-	-	-	-
TON-MILES OF SHIPMENTS	(millions of ton-miles)										
U.S. TOTAL	1 398	100.0	2.9	13.2	22.6	7.9	11.8	5.5	11.9	5.4	18.8
RAIL	125	100.0	-	3.6	6.1	9.5	9.1	6.0	11.0	10.7	44.0
MOTOR CARRIER	1 133	100.0	3.3	13.7	23.3	7.9	12.7	5.6	11.8	5.3	16.6
PRIVATE TRUCK	93	100.0	2.1	19.2	33.1	7.7	6.4	5.4	15.4	.9	9.8
AIR	24	100.0	2.9	16.0	39.6	2.9	8.2	2.5	6.8	3.3	17.8
WATER	1	100.0	1.4	50.4	-	-	-	-	39.0	-	9.2
OTHER	17	100.0	6.8	12.9	17.8	8.0	9.9	3.8	10.4	3.3	27.2
UNKNOWN	1	100.0	1.0	18.3	49.6	2.7	5.2	.7	14.1	.1	8.3
NEW ENGLAND	149	100.0	.7	4.5	27.7	15.4	9.6	9.0	10.1	3.6	19.4
RAIL	13	100.0	-	-	-	72.4	-	-	.9	-	26.7
MOTOR CARRIER	127	100.0	.7	4.9	29.9	9.7	10.8	10.3	11.0	4.1	18.5
PRIVATE TRUCK	1	100.0	2.4	10.2	70.6	16.8	-	-	-	-	-
AIR	2	100.0	.1	1.8	18.2	5.3	2.8	4.3	12.8	1.8	52.9
WATER	-	100.0	99.9	.1	-	-	-	-	-	-	-
OTHER	3	100.0	1.6	6.0	33.6	14.8	15.0	2.1	15.5	2.6	8.7
UNKNOWN	-	100.0	1.0	4.4	69.2	.2	15.8	-	-	-	9.5
MIDDLE ATLANTIC	233	100.0	1.8	7.9	26.8	6.2	13.5	4.8	16.7	8.1	14.2
RAIL	34	100.0	.1	.9	11.0	.8	6.6	1.2	31.6	14.3	33.6
MOTOR CARRIER	191	100.0	2.1	8.7	30.0	7.2	14.9	5.6	14.1	7.2	10.2
PRIVATE TRUCK	2	100.0	2.7	27.7	13.2	-	10.6	.7	12.5	-	32.6
AIR	2	100.0	1.7	1.9	19.1	9.4	11.3	2.1	21.5	7.7	25.4
WATER	-	100.0	-	100.0	-	-	-	-	-	-	-
OTHER	1	100.0	3.9	12.5	21.3	4.1	5.8	4.8	5.8	.7	41.0
UNKNOWN	-	100.0	.2	.2	2.9	-	96.3	-	.4	-	-
EAST NORTH CENTRAL	557	100.0	2.8	12.3	19.5	6.9	14.5	6.2	11.4	4.6	21.8
RAIL	34	100.0	-	9.5	9.2	-	25.7	12.3	5.6	-	37.8
MOTOR CARRIER	494	100.0	3.0	12.5	20.4	7.5	13.9	5.5	11.9	5.1	20.1
PRIVATE TRUCK	18	100.0	.4	8.9	19.8	5.0	7.3	15.0	8.8	-	34.9
AIR	4	100.0	6.1	17.3	2.5	1.8	19.5	3.2	10.5	8.1	30.9
WATER	-	100.0	-	93.1	-	-	-	-	-	-	6.9
OTHER	4	100.0	2.8	17.9	10.1	6.4	12.4	5.0	8.3	8.2	28.9
UNKNOWN	-	100.0	1.1	17.6	14.7	4.9	9.0	2.3	48.3	.3	1.8

See footnotes at end of table 4.

TABLE 2. **TCC-GROUP 356—Percent Distribution of Geographic Division of Origin and Means of Transport, by Geographic Division of Destination: 1972**—Continued

Geographic division of origin[1] and means of transport	Number	Percent distribution by division of destination									
		U.S. total	New England	Middle Atlantic	East North Central	West North Central	South Atlantic	East South Central	West South Central	Mountain	Pacific
TON-MILES OF SHIPMENTS	(millions of ton-miles)										
WEST NORTH CENTRAL......	81	100.0	4.0	21.4	32.5	8.9	4.5	.8	17.9	2.6	7.3
RAIL..................	-	100.0	.9	32.5	48.3	-	-	-	-	-	18.3
MOTOR CARRIER.........	53	100.0	4.6	26.0	30.7	7.7	6.5	1.2	9.6	3.7	10.1
PRIVATE TRUCK.........	23	100.0	-	7.9	39.3	12.9	-	-	39.9	-	-
AIR...................	1	100.0	.1	72.6	5.6	.3	2.3	.2	2.6	3.7	12.6
WATER.................	-	100.0	-	-	-	-	-	-	-	-	-
OTHER.................	1	100.0	41.6	5.8	18.5	7.8	8.0	1.5	3.6	4.3	9.0
UNKNOWN...............	-	100.0	4.6	89.2	6.0	-	.1	-	.1	-	-
SOUTH ATLANTIC.........	107	100.0	3.5	13.6	14.5	7.4	7.3	3.6	4.6	14.0	31.5
RAIL..................	30	100.0	-	-	.7	-	.8	-	-	18.7	79.8
MOTOR CARRIER.........	63	100.0	5.3	15.9	17.8	12.1	11.0	6.1	7.5	13.5	10.9
PRIVATE TRUCK.........	10	100.0	3.2	41.3	25.3	1.5	5.6	.1	1.2	5.5	16.4
AIR...................	-	100.0	2.2	6.4	43.3	.6	5.0	.5	1.6	8.1	32.4
WATER.................	-	100.0	-	-	-	-	-	-	-	-	-
OTHER.................	-	100.0	2.1	3.6	30.7	16.8	1.6	.9	1.3	.5	42.7
UNKNOWN...............	-	100.0	-	-	96.8	2.9	.2	-	-	-	-
EAST SOUTH CENTRAL......	124	100.0	3.3	17.7	21.5	12.5	9.0	4.6	8.1	3.1	20.3
RAIL..................	6	100.0	-	9.7	-	31.8	.2	2.8	14.2	41.3	-
MOTOR CARRIER.........	82	100.0	4.8	15.1	16.0	13.2	8.6	3.5	9.5	1.4	27.9
PRIVATE TRUCK.........	30	100.0	-	28.3	42.6	7.7	12.1	7.4	1.8	-	-
AIR...................	1	100.0	8.2	23.3	19.5	9.2	7.3	9.3	7.0	2.4	13.7
WATER.................	-	100.0	-	-	-	-	-	-	-	-	-
OTHER.................	4	100.0	1.9	2.3	8.7	4.8	7.9	6.3	18.0	-	50.1
UNKNOWN...............	-	100.0	-	-	-	-	-	-	-	-	100.0
WEST SOUTH CENTRAL......	40	100.0	3.3	58.1	6.2	1.4	2.5	7.4	13.2	1.2	6.7
RAIL..................	4	100.0	-	-	-	-	-	56.2	-	-	43.8
MOTOR CARRIER.........	28	100.0	1.5	77.6	6.5	.5	2.8	.7	7.8	1.0	1.6
PRIVATE TRUCK.........	4	100.0	17.9	10.8	10.4	7.8	1.7	-	48.1	3.4	-
AIR...................	-	100.0	-	35.7	14.8	2.9	24.4	-	3.2	.2	18.8
WATER.................	-	100.0	-	-	-	-	-	-	100.0	-	-
OTHER.................	-	100.0	2.1	75.3	11.7	2.0	4.4	.8	.8	.2	2.7
UNKNOWN...............	-	100.0	-	-	-	-	-	-	-	-	-

See footnotes at end of table 4.

TABLE 3. TCC GROUP 356—Percent Distribution of Geographic Division of Destination and Means of Transport, by Geographic Division of Origin: 1972

Geographic division of destination and means of transport	Number (thousands of tons)	Percent distribution by division of origin[1] U.S. total	New England	Middle Atlantic	East North Central	West North Central	South Atlantic	East South Central	West South Central	Mountain	Pacific
TONS OF SHIPMENTS											
U.S. TOTAL................	2 512	100.0	7.5	17.0	46.6	6.4	6.0	11.0	1.8	(D)	(D)
RAIL..................	162	100.0	5.8	19.1	56.6	.8	9.4	4.8	3.4	(D)	(D)
MOTOR CARRIER.........	2 007	100.0	8.2	18.8	50.6	4.2	5.4	7.2	1.4	(D)	(D)
PRIVATE TRUCK.........	281	100.0	1.8	4.1	17.0	24.4	8.1	40.9	2.9	(D)	(D)
AIR...................	23	100.0	9.4	13.3	25.7	7.5	3.4	11.8	1.4	(D)	(D)
WATER.................	5	100.0	4.8	43.7	8.7	-	-	-	41.3	(D)	(D)
OTHER.................	28	100.0	21.0	7.9	29.7	10.6	2.7	21.1	2.3	(D)	(D)
UNKNOWN...............	3	100.0	1.8	2.0	55.2	6.8	31.0	1.5	-	(D)	(D)
NEW ENGLAND..............	67	100.0	18.5	23.4	31.1	4.4	9.2	6.4	1.3	(D)	(D)
RAIL..................	-	100.0	-	87.6	-	12.4	-	-	-	(D)	(D)
MOTOR CARRIER.........	61	100.0	16.9	24.5	33.0	3.5	9.4	6.5	.5	(D)	(D)
PRIVATE TRUCK.........	2	100.0	35.2	15.0	4.2	-	13.9	-	23.6	(D)	(D)
AIR...................	-	100.0	7.2	12.4	46.0	.1	2.3	22.5	-	(D)	(D)
WATER.................	-	100.0	100.0	-	-	-	-	-	-	(D)	(D)
OTHER.................	2	100.0	40.0	8.5	8.3	35.4	1.8	4.3	.4	(D)	(D)
UNKNOWN...............	-	100.0	41.2	.7	24.0	34.1	-	-	-	(D)	(D)
MIDDLE ATLANTIC..........	420	100.0	9.0	28.8	35.7	4.1	8.4	8.6	3.9	(D)	(D)
RAIL..................	14	100.0	-	27.0	64.7	3.2	-	5.0	-	(D)	(D)
MOTOR CARRIER.........	353	100.0	9.7	30.0	38.0	3.8	6.5	6.0	4.4	(D)	(D)
PRIVATE TRUCK.........	40	100.0	4.2	18.5	7.0	4.5	30.7	33.9	1.1	(D)	(D)
AIR...................	4	100.0	4.3	11.2	29.1	25.2	1.6	14.7	1.9	(D)	(D)
WATER.................	2	100.0	-	83.8	16.2	-	-	-	-	(D)	(D)
OTHER.................	4	100.0	30.1	17.6	32.2	2.6	1.1	4.4	9.1	(D)	(D)
UNKNOWN...............	-	100.0	2.4	.7	56.2	39.4	-	-	-	(D)	(D)
EAST NORTH CENTRAL......	939	100.0	6.4	14.4	59.1	6.0	3.0	8.3	.3	(D)	(D)
RAIL..................	55	100.0	-	11.1	86.6	1.2	1.1	-	-	(D)	(D)
MOTOR CARRIER.........	762	100.0	7.2	16.4	62.2	4.3	2.7	4.4	.3	(D)	(D)
PRIVATE TRUCK.........	102	100.0	2.1	2.4	27.2	21.3	4.8	41.5	.6	(D)	(D)
AIR...................	8	100.0	8.7	12.9	8.1	2.6	5.6	5.7	.6	(D)	(D)
WATER.................	-	100.0	-	-	-	-	-	-	-	(D)	(D)
OTHER.................	8	100.0	21.5	7.7	37.8	8.7	4.3	17.4	1.2	(D)	(D)
UNKNOWN...............	2	100.0	1.4	.2	49.0	2.5	46.9	-	-	(D)	(D)
WEST NORTH CENTRAL......	191	100.0	10.4	8.4	37.2	25.8	4.1	11.8	.5	(D)	(D)
RAIL..................	10	100.0	78.3	3.4	-	-	-	18.2	-	(D)	(D)
MOTOR CARRIER.........	138	100.0	7.8	11.2	49.1	12.2	5.5	11.8	.2	(D)	(D)
PRIVATE TRUCK.........	38	100.0	.6	-	5.8	81.4	.4	9.9	1.6	(D)	(D)
AIR...................	-	100.0	13.2	24.9	23.2	1.2	.5	29.5	1.3	(D)	(D)
WATER.................	-	100.0	-	-	-	-	-	-	-	(D)	(D)
OTHER.................	2	100.0	17.5	1.8	29.5	30.1	4.4	12.8	.7	(D)	(D)
UNKNOWN...............	-	100.0	-	-	76.6	-	23.4	-	-	(D)	(D)
SOUTH ATLANTIC..........	304	100.0	6.4	22.1	44.9	1.4	11.4	11.1	.3	(D)	(D)
RAIL..................	23	100.0	-	21.1	75.3	-	3.4	.1	-	(D)	(D)
MOTOR CARRIER.........	252	100.0	7.4	24.1	44.8	1.6	11.8	7.2	.3	(D)	(D)
PRIVATE TRUCK.........	21	100.0	-	3.1	13.0	-	17.3	66.2	.3	(D)	(D)
AIR...................	2	100.0	4.9	15.3	53.8	1.6	2.2	10.0	3.8	(D)	(D)
WATER.................	-	100.0	-	-	-	-	-	-	-	(D)	(D)
OTHER.................	2	100.0	24.5	7.2	31.0	5.6	1.3	28.5	1.2	(D)	(D)
UNKNOWN...............	-	100.0	1.9	17.2	71.5	-	9.4	-	-	(D)	(D)
EAST SOUTH CENTRAL......	200	100.0	7.2	9.2	39.3	.7	4.4	34.9	2.7	(D)	(D)
RAIL..................	13	100.0	-	3.2	55.6	-	-	4.0	37.1	(D)	(D)
MOTOR CARRIER.........	137	100.0	10.4	13.0	46.5	1.0	6.5	20.3	.3	(D)	(D)
PRIVATE TRUCK.........	46	100.0	-	.1	14.3	-	-	85.6	-	(D)	(D)
AIR...................	1	100.0	11.0	6.1	28.9	1.3	.9	45.6	-	(D)	(D)
WATER.................	-	100.0	-	-	-	-	-	-	-	(D)	(D)
OTHER.................	1	100.0	4.1	4.3	25.4	2.7	.7	61.6	.6	(D)	(D)
UNKNOWN...............	-	100.0	-	-	100.0	-	-	-	-	(D)	(D)
WEST SOUTH CENTRAL......	189	100.0	5.4	16.1	39.0	11.4	3.1	8.5	8.0	(D)	(D)
RAIL..................	12	100.0	.5	67.1	15.3	-	-	17.1	-	(D)	(D)
MOTOR CARRIER.........	148	100.0	6.4	14.5	46.3	5.3	3.9	8.1	5.0	(D)	(D)
PRIVATE TRUCK.........	22	100.0	-	1.2	8.6	60.2	.7	3.8	24.9	(D)	(D)
AIR...................	1	100.0	14.9	24.5	37.6	3.1	.8	11.9	2.0	(D)	(D)
WATER.................	2	100.0	-	-	-	-	-	-	100.0	(D)	(D)
OTHER.................	1	100.0	22.7	3.0	22.7	4.5	.6	43.5	2.5	(D)	(D)
UNKNOWN...............	-	100.0	-	-	99.8	.2	-	-	-	(D)	(D)
MOUNTAIN................	57	100.0	5.1	16.3	36.7	4.8	13.7	6.2	1.2	(D)	(D)
RAIL..................	7	100.0	-	27.9	-	-	38.8	33.2	-	(D)	(D)
MOTOR CARRIER.........	47	100.0	5.9	14.9	42.8	5.3	9.4	2.2	.8	(D)	(D)
PRIVATE TRUCK.........	-	100.0	-	-	-	-	49.0	-	40.2	(D)	(D)
AIR...................	-	100.0	4.6	15.5	47.0	14.8	6.1	4.6	.1	(D)	(D)
WATER.................	-	100.0	-	-	-	-	-	-	-	(D)	(D)
OTHER.................	-	100.0	9.2	.9	53.1	18.8	.4	-	.3	(D)	(D)
UNKNOWN...............	-	100.0	-	-	100.0	-	-	-	-	(D)	(D)
PACIFIC.................	141	100.0	7.3	9.8	45.4	3.2	10.7	8.7	.7	(D)	(D)
RAIL..................	24	100.0	4.5	19.0	29.6	.5	43.9	-	2.5	(D)	(D)
MOTOR CARRIER.........	104	100.0	8.1	7.9	49.5	3.9	2.9	10.4	.3	(D)	(D)
PRIVATE TRUCK.........	5	100.0	-	6.8	59.2	.1	14.1	-	-	(D)	(D)
AIR...................	2	100.0	22.6	8.6	31.7	4.7	4.1	5.6	1.6	(D)	(D)
WATER.................	-	100.0	-	-	13.8	-	-	-	-	(D)	(D)
OTHER.................	3	100.0	3.7	6.1	22.0	3.5	4.3	35.0	.5	(D)	(D)
UNKNOWN...............	-	100.0	1.3	-	4.3	-	-	45.6	-	(D)	(D)

See footnotes at end of table 4.

TABLE 3. **TCC GROUP 356**—Percent Distribution of Geographic Division of Destination and Means of Transport, by Geographic Division of Origin: 1972—Continued

Geographic division of destination and means of transport	Number	Percent distribution by division of origin[1]									
		U.S. total	New England	Middle Atlantic	East North Central	West North Central	South Atlantic	East South Central	West South Central	Mountain	Pacific
TON-MILES OF SHIPMENTS	(millions of ton-miles)										
U.S. TOTAL................	1 398	100.0	10.7	16.7	39.9	5.8	7.7	8.9	2.9	(D)	(D)
RAIL..................	125	100.0	10.6	27.4	27.5	.8	24.7	5.1	3.9	(D)	(D)
MOTOR CARRIER.........	1 133	100.0	11.3	16.9	43.6	4.7	5.6	7.2	2.5	(D)	(D)
PRIVATE TRUCK.........	93	100.0	2.0	3.0	19.8	24.7	11.5	32.3	5.3	(D)	(D)
AIR...................	24	100.0	10.9	9.4	19.9	5.9	2.7	7.6	1.4	(D)	(D)
WATER.................	1	100.0	1.4	32.2	19.5	-	-	-	39.0	(D)	(D)
OTHER.................	17	100.0	21.1	6.2	25.1	10.8	4.0	23.1	4.3	(D)	(D)
UNKNOWN...............	1	100.0	2.3	2.1	29.2	13.9	44.3	6.0	-	(D)	(D)
NEW ENGLAND..............	41	100.0	2.5	10.1	37.5	7.9	9.1	10.1	3.3	(D)	(D)
RAIL..................	-	100.0	-	72.1	-	27.9	-	-	-	(D)	(D)
MOTOR CARRIER.........	37	100.0	2.4	10.7	40.2	6.6	9.1	10.5	1.2	(D)	(D)
PRIVATE TRUCK.........	1	100.0	2.3	3.8	4.1	-	17.4	-	45.1	(D)	(D)
AIR...................	-	100.0	.4	5.5	41.9	.2	2.0	21.5	-	(D)	(D)
WATER.................	-	100.0	100.0	-	-	-	-	-	-	(D)	(D)
OTHER.................	1	100.0	5.0	3.5	10.3	65.6	1.2	6.3	1.3	(D)	(D)
UNKNOWN...............	-	100.0	2.3	.4	33.4	63.9	-	-	-	(D)	(D)
MIDDLE ATLANTIC..........	185	100.0	3.7	10.0	37.1	9.4	7.9	12.0	12.6	(D)	(D)
RAIL..................	4	100.0	-	6.9	72.4	6.9	-	13.8	-	(D)	(D)
MOTOR CARRIER.........	155	100.0	4.1	10.7	39.8	9.0	6.5	8.0	14.2	(D)	(D)
PRIVATE TRUCK.........	18	100.0	1.1	4.3	9.1	10.1	24.7	47.7	3.0	(D)	(D)
AIR...................	3	100.0	1.2	1.1	21.5	26.7	1.1	11.1	3.0	(D)	(D)
WATER.................	-	100.0	-	63.9	36.1	-	-	-	-	(D)	(D)
OTHER.................	2	100.0	9.9	6.0	35.0	4.9	1.1	4.2	25.2	(D)	(D)
UNKNOWN...............	-	100.0	.5	-	28.2	67.6	-	-	-	(D)	(D)
EAST NORTH CENTRAL......	316	100.0	13.1	19.7	34.3	8.4	4.9	8.5	.8	(D)	(D)
RAIL..................	7	100.0	-	49.6	41.5	6.0	2.9	-	-	(D)	(D)
MOTOR CARRIER.........	263	100.0	14.5	21.8	38.3	6.2	4.3	5.0	.7	(D)	(D)
PRIVATE TRUCK.........	31	100.0	4.3	1.2	11.8	29.4	8.8	41.7	1.7	(D)	(D)
AIR...................	9	100.0	5.0	4.5	1.3	.8	2.9	3.7	.5	(D)	(D)
WATER.................	-	100.0	-	-	-	-	-	-	-	(D)	(D)
OTHER.................	3	100.0	40.0	7.4	14.3	11.2	7.0	11.3	2.8	(D)	(D)
UNKNOWN...............	-	100.0	3.2	.1	8.6	1.7	86.4	-	-	(D)	(D)
WEST NORTH CENTRAL......	110	100.0	20.8	13.1	34.8	6.6	7.2	14.1	.5	(D)	(D)
RAIL..................	11	100.0	80.6	2.2	-	-	-	17.1	-	(D)	(D)
MOTOR CARRIER.........	89	100.0	13.9	15.6	41.6	4.6	8.6	12.2	.2	(D)	(D)
PRIVATE TRUCK.........	7	100.0	4.4	-	12.8	41.3	2.2	32.3	5.3	(D)	(D)
AIR...................	-	100.0	19.8	30.2	12.5	.7	.5	23.9	1.3	(D)	(D)
WATER.................	-	100.0	-	-	-	-	-	-	-	(D)	(D)
OTHER.................	1	100.0	38.9	3.2	20.1	10.5	8.5	14.0	1.1	(D)	(D)
UNKNOWN...............	-	100.0	.1	-	52.3	-	47.5	-	-	(D)	(D)
SOUTH ATLANTIC..........	164	100.0	8.7	19.1	48.9	2.2	4.8	6.8	.6	(D)	(D)
RAIL..................	11	100.0	-	20.0	77.7	-	2.1	.1	-	(D)	(D)
MOTOR CARRIER.........	143	100.0	9.6	19.9	47.9	2.4	4.9	4.9	.5	(D)	(D)
PRIVATE TRUCK.........	6	100.0	-	5.0	22.6	.1	10.0	61.1	1.4	(D)	(D)
AIR...................	2	100.0	3.8	13.1	47.7	1.6	1.6	6.8	4.1	(D)	(D)
WATER.................	-	100.0	-	-	-	-	-	-	-	(D)	(D)
OTHER.................	1	100.0	32.2	3.6	31.5	8.7	.7	18.5	1.9	(D)	(D)
UNKNOWN...............	-	100.0	6.9	39.7	51.0	.3	2.1	-	-	(D)	(D)
EAST SOUTH CENTRAL......	76	100.0	17.5	14.6	45.1	.8	5.1	7.4	3.9	(D)	(D)
RAIL..................	7	100.0	-	5.4	55.7	-	-	2.4	36.4	(D)	(D)
MOTOR CARRIER.........	62	100.0	21.0	17.0	43.4	1.0	6.2	4.5	.3	(D)	(D)
PRIVATE TRUCK.........	5	100.0	-	.4	55.0	-	.1	44.4	-	(D)	(D)
AIR...................	-	100.0	18.5	7.8	25.4	.5	.5	28.1	-	(D)	(D)
WATER.................	-	100.0	-	-	-	-	-	-	-	(D)	(D)
OTHER.................	-	100.0	11.6	7.8	33.1	4.3	1.0	38.6	.9	(D)	(D)
UNKNOWN...............	-	100.0	-	-	100.0	-	-	-	-	(D)	(D)
WEST SOUTH CENTRAL......	165	100.0	9.1	23.4	38.3	8.7	3.0	6.1	3.2	(D)	(D)
RAIL..................	13	100.0	.8	78.7	13.9	-	-	6.6	-	(D)	(D)
MOTOR CARRIER.........	133	100.0	10.5	20.4	44.2	3.9	3.6	5.8	1.7	(D)	(D)
PRIVATE TRUCK.........	14	100.0	-	2.4	11.3	64.0	.9	3.8	16.5	(D)	(D)
AIR...................	1	100.0	20.5	30.0	30.9	2.3	.6	7.9	.6	(D)	(D)
WATER.................	-	100.0	-	-	-	-	-	-	100.0	(D)	(D)
OTHER.................	1	100.0	31.4	3.5	20.1	3.7	.5	39.9	.3	(D)	(D)
UNKNOWN...............	-	100.0	-	.1	99.8	.1	-	-	-	(D)	(D)
MOUNTAIN................	75	100.0	7.2	25.2	34.5	2.8	20.0	5.1	.6	(D)	(D)
RAIL..................	13	100.0	-	36.8	-	-	43.4	19.8	-	(D)	(D)
MOTOR CARRIER.........	59	100.0	8.8	23.3	42.2	3.3	14.4	2.0	.5	(D)	(D)
PRIVATE TRUCK.........	-	100.0	-	.1	-	-	71.4	-	20.5	(D)	(D)
AIR...................	-	100.0	5.8	22.1	48.9	6.6	6.5	5.6	.1	(D)	(D)
WATER.................	-	100.0	-	-	-	-	-	-	-	(D)	(D)
OTHER.................	-	100.0	16.8	1.4	62.4	14.0	.6	-	.3	(D)	(D)
UNKNOWN...............	-	100.0	-	-	100.0	-	-	-	-	(D)	(D)
PACIFIC.................	262	100.0	11.0	12.6	46.4	2.3	12.9	9.7	1.0	(D)	(D)
RAIL..................	55	100.0	6.4	20.9	23.6	.3	44.8	-	3.9	(D)	(D)
MOTOR CARRIER.........	188	100.0	12.6	10.4	52.7	2.9	3.7	12.2	.2	(D)	(D)
PRIVATE TRUCK.........	9	100.0	-	10.0	70.2	.1	19.2	-	-	(D)	(D)
AIR...................	4	100.0	32.3	13.5	34.5	4.2	4.9	5.8	1.4	(D)	(D)
WATER.................	-	100.0	-	-	14.6	-	-	-	-	(D)	(D)
OTHER.................	4	100.0	6.8	9.4	26.7	3.6	6.4	42.7	.4	(D)	(D)
UNKNOWN...............	-	100.0	2.6	-	6.3	-	-	73.0	-	(D)	(D)

See footnotes at end of table 4.

TABLE 4. **TCC GROUP 356**—Percent Distribution of Distance Shipped and Weight of Shipment, by Means of Transport: 1972

Distance shipped and weight of shipment[2][3]	Number	Percent distribution by means of transport							
		All means of transport	Rail	Motor carrier	Private truck	Air	Water	Other	Unknown
TONS OF SHIPMENTS	(thousands of tons)								
U.S. TOTAL............	2 066	100.0	4.3	82.2	11.2	.8	.1	1.2	.1
UNDER 100 MILES.........	252	100.0	1.2	67.7	29.3	.4	.1	1.3	-
UNDER 1000 POUNDS.....	47	100.0	-	73.4	19.6	1.4	.1	5.2	.3
1000 TO 9999 POUNDS...	126	100.0	-	59.5	39.8	.2	.2	.3	-
10000 TO 29999 POUNDS.	48	100.0	-	83.2	16.0	-	-	.8	-
30000 TO 59999 POUNDS.	24	100.0	11.8	61.7	26.4	-	-	-	-
60000 TO 89999 POUNDS.	4	100.0	-	99.2	.8	-	-	-	-
90000 POUNDS AND OVER.	-	100.0	-	-	-	-	-	-	-
100 TO 199 MILES........	214	100.0	2.1	87.7	8.5	.2	-	1.3	.1
UNDER 1000 POUNDS.....	40	100.0	-	89.0	3.3	.8	-	6.8	.1
1000 TO 9999 POUNDS...	89	100.0	.3	90.1	9.2	-	-	-	.3
10000 TO 29999 POUNDS.	52	100.0	-	88.8	11.2	-	-	-	-
30000 TO 59999 POUNDS.	24	100.0	-	88.7	11.3	-	-	-	-
60000 TO 89999 POUNDS.	-	100.0	-	79.0	21.0	-	-	-	-
90000 POUNDS AND OVER.	6	100.0	65.2	34.8	-	-	-	-	-
200 TO 299 MILES........	286	100.0	.9	79.7	17.6	.4	.1	1.2	.1
UNDER 1000 POUNDS.....	48	100.0	.1	90.0	2.1	1.4	-	6.2	.2
1000 TO 9999 POUNDS...	82	100.0	-	90.7	7.9	.5	-	.7	.2
10000 TO 29999 POUNDS.	100	100.0	.3	65.9	33.7	-	-	-	.1
30000 TO 59999 POUNDS.	39	100.0	5.3	75.6	19.1	-	-	-	-
60000 TO 89999 POUNDS.	13	100.0	-	100.0	-	-	-	-	-
90000 POUNDS AND OVER.	1	100.0	-	-	81.9	-	18.1	-	-
300 TO 499 MILES........	436	100.0	4.2	84.6	9.4	.5	.4	.8	-
UNDER 1000 POUNDS.....	71	100.0	-	88.8	3.8	2.5	-	4.8	.1
1000 TO 9999 POUNDS...	164	100.0	.1	93.6	5.9	.2	-	.1	-
10000 TO 29999 POUNDS.	128	100.0	5.0	82.0	13.0	-	-	-	-
30000 TO 59999 POUNDS.	65	100.0	8.8	72.8	18.5	-	-	-	-
60000 TO 89999 POUNDS.	4	100.0	100.0	-	-	-	-	-	-
90000 POUNDS AND OVER.	3	100.0	37.8	-	-	-	62.2	-	-
500 TO 999 MILES........	601	100.0	4.6	85.8	6.8	1.4	.1	1.1	.2
UNDER 1000 POUNDS.....	121	100.0	.1	89.2	2.4	4.2	-	4.0	.2
1000 TO 9999 POUNDS...	226	100.0	.6	91.6	5.3	1.4	.2	.8	.1
10000 TO 29999 POUNDS.	164	100.0	1.4	84.0	14.0	-	-	-	.7
30000 TO 59999 POUNDS.	78	100.0	17.2	79.1	3.8	-	-	-	-
60000 TO 89999 POUNDS.	5	100.0	100.0	-	-	-	-	-	-
90000 POUNDS AND OVER.	5	100.0	93.9	6.1	-	-	-	-	-
1000 TO 1499 MILES......	151	100.0	14.2	80.9	2.0	.9	-	1.7	.2
UNDER 1000 POUNDS.....	36	100.0	.3	88.9	1.2	3.3	-	5.7	.6
1000 TO 9999 POUNDS...	55	100.0	2.5	93.8	2.4	.2	-	1.1	.2
10000 TO 29999 POUNDS.	23	100.0	23.7	70.6	5.7	.1	-	-	-
30000 TO 59999 POUNDS.	18	100.0	63.1	36.9	-	-	-	-	-
60000 TO 89999 POUNDS.	-	100.0	90.7	9.3	-	-	-	-	-
90000 POUNDS AND OVER.	17	100.0	11.3	88.7	-	-	-	-	-
1500 MILES OR OVER......	124	100.0	9.1	82.5	3.7	2.5	-	2.1	.1
UNDER 1000 POUNDS.....	31	100.0	1.2	83.5	2.0	9.4	-	3.6	.2
1000 TO 9999 POUNDS...	46	100.0	1.8	90.8	3.7	.4	-	3.2	-
10000 TO 29999 POUNDS.	26	100.0	5.8	85.9	8.4	-	-	-	-
30000 TO 59999 POUNDS.	19	100.0	43.0	57.0	-	-	-	-	-
60000 TO 89999 POUNDS.	-	100.0	-	-	-	-	100.0	-	-
90000 POUNDS AND OVER.	-	100.0	-	-	-	-	-	-	-
TON-MILES OF SHIPMENTS	(millions of ton-miles)								
U.S. TOTAL............	1 139	100.0	6.8	83.6	6.6	1.4	.1	1.4	.1
UNDER 100 MILES.........	12	100.0	1.5	71.0	25.7	.3	.2	1.3	-
UNDER 1000 POUNDS.....	2	100.0	-	78.2	15.5	1.1	-	5.0	.2
1000 TO 9999 POUNDS...	5	100.0	-	62.5	36.3	.3	.4	.4	-
10000 TO 29999 POUNDS.	2	100.0	-	87.0	12.7	-	-	.3	-
30000 TO 59999 POUNDS.	1	100.0	12.5	64.4	23.0	-	-	-	-
60000 TO 89999 POUNDS.	-	100.0	-	96.3	3.7	-	-	-	-
90000 POUNDS AND OVER.	-	100.0	-	-	-	-	-	-	-
100 TO 199 MILES........	31	100.0	2.5	88.2	7.7	.2	-	1.3	.2
UNDER 1000 POUNDS.....	6	100.0	-	89.3	3.0	.9	-	6.6	.1
1000 TO 9999 POUNDS...	13	100.0	.4	91.3	8.0	-	-	-	.3
10000 TO 29999 POUNDS.	7	100.0	-	88.1	11.9	-	-	-	-
30000 TO 59999 POUNDS.	3	100.0	-	92.1	7.9	-	-	-	-
60000 TO 89999 POUNDS.	-	100.0	-	82.9	17.1	-	-	-	-
90000 POUNDS AND OVER.	1	100.0	71.1	28.9	-	-	-	-	-

See footnotes at end of table 4.

TABLE 4. **TCC GROUP 356—Percent Distribution of Distance Shipped and Weight of Shipment, by Means of Transport: 1972**—Continued

Distance shipped and weight of shipment[2] [3]	Number	Percent distribution by means of transport							
		All means of transport	Rail	Motor carrier	Private truck	Air	Water	Other	Unknown
TON-MILES OF SHIPMENTS	(millions of ton-miles)								
200 TO 299 MILES........	72	100.0	.9	79.3	18.0	.4	.1	1.2	.1
UNDER 1000 POUNDS.....	12	100.0	.1	90.1	2.2	1.4	-	6.0	.2
1000 TO 9999 POUNDS...	20	100.0	-	90.2	8.5	.5	-	.6	.2
10000 TO 29999 POUNDS.	25	100.0	.3	65.4	34.2	-	-	-	.1
30000 TO 59999 POUNDS.	10	100.0	5.5	75.3	19.2	-	-	-	-
60000 TO 89999 POUNDS.	3	100.0	-	100.0	-	-	-	-	-
90000 POUNDS AND OVER.	-	100.0	-	-	83.9	-	16.1	-	-
300 TO 499 MILES........	173	100.0	4.3	84.4	9.7	.5	.4	.8	-
UNDER 1000 POUNDS.....	28	100.0	-	88.7	4.0	2.5	-	4.8	.1
1000 TO 9999 POUNDS...	64	100.0	.1	93.4	6.1	.2	-	.1	-
10000 TO 29999 POUNDS.	51	100.0	5.1	81.5	13.4	-	-	-	-
30000 TO 59999 POUNDS.	25	100.0	8.8	72.7	18.5	-	-	-	-
60000 TO 89999 POUNDS.	1	100.0	100.0	-	-	-	-	-	-
90000 POUNDS AND OVER.	1	100.0	44.6	-	-	-	55.4	-	-
500 TO 999 MILES........	410	100.0	3.9	86.7	6.4	1.5	.1	1.2	.3
UNDER 1000 POUNDS.....	84	100.0	.1	89.2	2.3	4.2	-	4.0	.2
1000 TO 9999 POUNDS...	160	100.0	.6	92.1	4.6	1.6	.2	.9	.1
10000 TO 29999 POUNDS.	111	100.0	1.3	84.4	13.6	-	-	-	.7
30000 TO 59999 POUNDS.	48	100.0	16.2	79.8	4.1	-	-	-	-
60000 TO 89999 POUNDS.	2	100.0	100.0	-	-	-	-	-	-
90000 POUNDS AND OVER.	2	100.0	94.4	5.6	-	-	-	-	-
1000 TO 1499 MILES......	184	100.0	14.0	81.1	2.1	.9	-	1.7	.2
UNDER 1000 POUNDS.....	43	100.0	.3	88.9	1.3	3.4	-	5.5	.5
1000 TO 9999 POUNDS...	67	100.0	2.9	93.2	2.4	.2	-	1.1	.2
10000 TO 29999 POUNDS.	27	100.0	23.9	69.5	6.5	.1	-	-	-
30000 TO 59999 POUNDS.	22	100.0	63.3	36.7	-	-	-	-	-
60000 TO 89999 POUNDS.	1	100.0	91.8	8.2	-	-	-	-	-
90000 POUNDS AND OVER.	23	100.0	8.7	91.3	-	-	-	-	-
1500 MILES OR OVER......	255	100.0	10.5	81.3	3.6	2.6	.1	2.0	.1
UNDER 1000 POUNDS.....	63	100.0	1.3	83.0	2.2	9.7	-	3.6	.2
1000 TO 9999 POUNDS...	94	100.0	2.1	90.8	3.8	.4	-	2.9	-
10000 TO 29999 POUNDS.	53	100.0	5.5	86.6	7.9	-	-	-	-
30000 TO 59999 POUNDS.	43	100.0	48.7	51.3	-	-	-	-	-
60000 TO 89999 POUNDS.	-	100.0	-	-	-	-	100.0	-	-
90000 POUNDS AND OVER.	-	100.0	-	-	-	-	-	-	-

Note: Detail may not add to total due to rounding. The introductory table shows the estimates of sampling variability for tons; sampling variability for ton-miles has not been estimated. See the map in the Introduction for the States comprising the geographic divisions of the United States.
Shipments excluded from the survey are those moving by pipeline (primarily petroleum products from refineries), parcel post shipments, and commodities moved by own power (motorized vehicles, aircraft, etc.) or towed (prefabricated buildings, etc.). Local shipments (commodities shipped less than 25 miles from the plant) and shipments within the same city are also excluded. Shipments to Alaska and Hawaii from the 48 conterminous States and the District of Columbia are included; however, no data were obtained for shipments originating in Alaska and Hawaii.

- Represents zero or rounds to zero. (D) Withheld to avoid disclosing figures for individual companies.

[1]Production of this commodity is concentrated in the geographic divisions shown; figures and distributions for geographic divisions not shown are included in the total.
[2]Distances of shipments to foreign destinations are calculated only to the U.S. port of exit.
[3]Includes only shipments represented by bills of lading and invoices. Summary records which did not show individual weights of shipments are not included.

TCC 357. Office, Computing, and Accounting Machines

Comparisons of Tons and Ton-Miles of Shipments for
Geographic Divisions of Origin and for Sampling Variability: 1972 and 1967

Geographic division of origin	Estimates				Relative sampling variability in tons (percent)	
	1972		1967		1972	1967
	Tons (thousands)	Ton-miles (millions)	Tons (thousands)	Ton-miles (millions)		
U.S. total	379	392	463	439	7.8	11.0
New England	16	16	40	26	14.1	(*)
Middle Atlantic	71	45	173	166	15.8	(*)
East North Central	78	49	113	75	17.6	(*)
West North Central	11	7	11	25	21.5	(*)
South Atlantic . . . . , ...	(D)	(D)	35	10	(*)	(*)
East South Central	(D)	(D)	1	30	(*)	(*)
West South Central	12	12	14	1	14.7	(*)
Mountain	6	6	48	15	31.2	(*)
Pacific	(D)	(D)	28	91	(*)	(*)

(D) Withheld to avoid disclosing figures for individual companies.   (*) Data not published.

TABLE 1. **TCC GROUP 357—Percent Distribution of Geographic Division of Origin and Distance Shipped, by Means of Transport: 1972**

Geographic division of origin[1] and distance shipped[2]	Number	Percent distribution by means of transport							
		All means of transport	Rail	Motor carrier	Private truck	Air	Water	Other	Unknown
TONS OF SHIPMENTS	(thousands of tons)								
U.S. TOTAL..........	379	100.0	2.5	78.2	5.8	10.3	-	1.9	1.2
NEW ENGLAND.............	16	100.0	25.2	60.4	1.2	12.2	-	1.0	-
UNDER 100 MILES.......	2	100.0	-	85.5	3.8	7.1	-	3.6	-
100 TO 199 MILES......	2	100.0	-	94.6	1.5	3.7	-	.2	-
200 TO 299 MILES.....	-	100.0	-	85.6	8.3	5.7	-	.4	-
300 TO 499 MILES.....	1	100.0	-	88.2	-	11.0	-	.8	-
500 TO 999 MILES.....	3	100.0	56.4	41.4	-	1.8	-	.5	-
1000 TO 1499 MILES....	1	100.0	54.5	42.1	-	2.8	-	.5	-
1500 MILES OR OVER....	4	100.0	23.0	43.3	-	32.8	-	.9	-
MIDDLE ATLANTIC.........	71	100.0	4.1	89.4	2.7	3.4	-	.4	-
UNDER 100 MILES.......	11	100.0	-	88.0	7.6	3.6	-	.8	-
100 TO 199 MILES......	12	100.0	-	88.8	8.5	2.1	-	.6	-
200 TO 299 MILES.....	7	100.0	-	95.6	-	4.2	-	.2	-
300 TO 499 MILES.....	8	100.0	-	98.7	-	1.2	-	.1	-
500 TO 999 MILES.....	17	100.0	-	96.4	-	3.3	-	.3	-
1000 TO 1499 MILES....	5	100.0	.6	90.7	-	8.6	-	.1	-
1500 MILES OR OVER....	8	100.0	35.7	60.5	-	3.1	-	.7	-
EAST NORTH CENTRAL......	78	100.0	3.2	73.1	11.6	2.0	.1	4.7	5.2
UNDER 100 MILES.......	6	100.0	-	89.5	1.3	.7	-	2.7	5.7
100 TO 199 MILES......	8	100.0	-	70.5	22.0	1.2	-	3.2	3.1
200 TO 299 MILES.....	10	100.0	-	43.8	53.1	.4	-	2.3	.5
300 TO 499 MILES.....	8	100.0	-	81.7	-	4.2	-	4.6	9.5
500 TO 999 MILES.....	31	100.0	-	86.0	2.0	2.2	-	2.1	7.7
1000 TO 1499 MILES....	3	100.0	4.2	76.0	8.1	3.7	-	3.0	5.0
1500 MILES OR OVER....	8	100.0	27.0	43.8	4.8	1.8	1.3	21.3	-
WEST NORTH CENTRAL......	11	100.0	-	64.5	17.5	17.2	-	.8	-
UNDER 100 MILES.......	-	100.0	-	99.6	-	.1	-	.3	-
100 TO 199 MILES......	2	100.0	-	5.4	94.5	-	-	-	-
200 TO 299 MILES.....	-	100.0	-	89.5	-	10.0	-	.5	-
300 TO 499 MILES.....	1	100.0	-	94.0	-	4.2	-	1.8	-
500 TO 999 MILES.....	4	100.0	-	63.5	-	35.5	-	.9	-
1000 TO 1499 MILES....	1	100.0	-	93.4	-	5.7	-	.8	-
1500 MILES OR OVER....	-	100.0	-	82.9	-	16.0	-	1.1	-
WEST SOUTH CENTRAL......	12	100.0	.1	83.3	2.6	11.7	-	-	2.2
UNDER 100 MILES.......	-	100.0	-	98.1	.1	1.6	-	.1	.1
100 TO 199 MILES......	-	100.0	-	68.8	27.9	3.3	-	-	-
200 TO 299 MILES.....	-	100.0	-	60.0	5.1	8.6	-	-	26.3
300 TO 499 MILES.....	-	100.0	-	92.0	4.8	3.2	-	-	-
500 TO 999 MILES.....	3	100.0	-	94.3	-	1.9	-	.1	3.8
1000 TO 1499 MILES....	5	100.0	.3	82.0	1.9	14.2	-	-	1.7
1500 MILES OR OVER....	1	100.0	-	65.1	-	34.9	-	-	-
MOUNTAIN................	6	100.0	-	73.9	1.8	22.0	-	1.2	1.2
UNDER 100 MILES.......	-	100.0	-	90.2	6.3	.6	-	2.9	-
100 TO 199 MILES......	-	100.0	-	100.0	-	-	-	-	-
200 TO 299 MILES.....	-	100.0	-	91.7	-	2.0	-	-	6.4
300 TO 499 MILES.....	-	100.0	-	96.2	-	1.0	-	1.3	1.5
500 TO 999 MILES.....	1	100.0	-	69.4	7.6	19.8	-	3.3	-
1000 TO 1499 MILES....	-	100.0	-	80.9	-	18.2	-	.9	-
1500 MILES OR OVER....	2	100.0	-	59.3	-	40.0	-	.4	.2
TON-MILES OF SHIPMENTS	(millions of ton-miles)								
U.S. TOTAL..........	392	100.0	4.2	74.6	1.7	17.1	.1	1.7	.7
NEW ENGLAND.............	16	100.0	32.0	42.6	.2	24.4	-	.8	-
UNDER 100 MILES.......	-	100.0	-	86.2	3.7	7.7	-	2.4	-
100 TO 199 MILES......	-	100.0	-	94.4	1.3	4.1	-	.2	-
200 TO 299 MILES.....	-	100.0	-	84.5	9.0	6.1	-	.4	-
300 TO 499 MILES.....	-	100.0	-	88.0	-	11.1	-	.9	-
500 TO 999 MILES.....	2	100.0	53.0	44.7	-	1.8	-	.5	-
1000 TO 1499 MILES....	2	100.0	57.6	39.4	-	2.6	-	.5	-
1500 MILES OR OVER....	10	100.0	24.4	38.3	-	36.4	-	.9	-
MIDDLE ATLANTIC.........	45	100.0	14.8	80.1	.4	4.2	-	.5	-
UNDER 100 MILES.......	-	100.0	-	82.8	7.9	8.4	-	.9	-
100 TO 199 MILES......	1	100.0	-	88.0	9.0	2.4	-	.6	-
200 TO 299 MILES.....	1	100.0	-	95.8	-	4.0	-	.2	-
300 TO 499 MILES.....	3	100.0	-	98.7	-	1.2	-	.1	-
500 TO 999 MILES.....	11	100.0	-	95.8	-	3.9	-	.3	-
1000 TO 1499 MILES....	6	100.0	.6	89.6	-	9.7	-	.1	-
1500 MILES OR OVER....	19	100.0	34.6	61.5	-	3.1	-	.8	-
EAST NORTH CENTRAL......	49	100.0	8.8	67.6	6.3	2.3	1.0	9.2	4.7
UNDER 100 MILES.......	-	100.0	-	91.8	1.1	.8	-	5.1	1.2
100 TO 199 MILES......	1	100.0	-	70.6	21.9	1.0	-	3.2	3.2
200 TO 299 MILES.....	2	100.0	-	48.2	48.6	.4	-	2.4	.4
300 TO 499 MILES.....	3	100.0	-	82.8	-	4.2	-	4.6	8.5
500 TO 999 MILES.....	20	100.0	-	85.0	1.6	2.4	-	2.4	8.6
1000 TO 1499 MILES....	4	100.0	4.6	74.0	9.4	3.8	-	2.9	5.2
1500 MILES OR OVER....	16	100.0	24.6	43.6	5.0	1.9	3.0	21.9	-

See footnotes at end of table 4.

TABLE 1. TCC GROUP 357—Percent Distribution of Geographic Division of Origin and Distance Shipped, by Means of Transport: 1972—Continued

Geographic division of origin[1] and distance shipped[2]	Number	Percent distribution by means of transport							
		All means of transport	Rail	Motor carrier	Private truck	Air	Water	Other	Unknown
TON-MILES OF SHIPMENTS	(millions of ton-miles)								
WEST NORTH CENTRAL	7	100.0	-	69.4	5.0	24.7	-	.9	-
UNDER 100 MILES	-	100.0	-	99.8	-	.1	-	.1	-
100 TO 199 MILES	-	100.0	-	4.3	95.7	-	-	-	-
200 TO 299 MILES	-	100.0	-	90.3	-	9.2	-	.5	-
300 TO 499 MILES	-	100.0	-	94.0	-	4.1	-	1.9	-
500 TO 999 MILES	4	100.0	-	59.7	-	39.4	-	.8	-
1000 TO 1499 MILES	1	100.0	-	94.2	-	5.1	-	.7	-
1500 MILES OR OVER	1	100.0	-	81.1	-	17.9	-	1.1	-
WEST SOUTH CENTRAL	12	100.0	.2	80.1	1.3	16.5	-	-	2.0
UNDER 100 MILES	-	100.0	-	99.2	-	.7	-	-	.1
100 TO 199 MILES	-	100.0	-	71.8	24.4	3.8	-	-	-
200 TO 299 MILES	-	100.0	-	58.5	4.7	8.4	-	-	28.5
300 TO 499 MILES	-	100.0	-	90.8	5.8	3.4	-	-	-
500 TO 999 MILES	2	100.0	-	93.7	-	2.1	-	.1	4.2
1000 TO 1499 MILES	6	100.0	.3	81.1	1.6	15.2	-	-	1.8
1500 MILES OR OVER	2	100.0	-	61.1	-	38.9	-	-	-
MOUNTAIN	6	100.0	-	68.2	1.0	29.4	-	.9	.5
UNDER 100 MILES	-	100.0	-	82.8	8.9	.6	-	7.7	-
100 TO 199 MILES	-	100.0	-	100.0	-	-	-	-	-
200 TO 299 MILES	-	100.0	-	91.7	-	2.0	-	-	6.4
300 TO 499 MILES	-	100.0	-	96.0	-	1.1	-	1.4	1.5
500 TO 999 MILES	1	100.0	-	70.0	6.4	20.3	-	3.2	-
1000 TO 1499 MILES	1	100.0	-	80.1	-	18.8	-	1.1	-
1500 MILES OR OVER	4	100.0	-	62.0	-	37.3	-	.4	.3

See footnotes at end of table 4.

TABLE 2. TCC GROUP 357—Percent Distribution of Geographic Division of Origin and Means of Transport, by Geographic Division of Destination: 1972

Geographic division of origin[1] and means of transport	Number	Percent distribution by division of destination									
		U.S. total	New England	Middle Atlantic	East North Central	West North Central	South Atlantic	East South Central	West South Central	Mountain	Pacific
TONS OF SHIPMENTS	(thousands of tons)										
U.S. TOTAL	379	100.0	7.5	27.1	19.0	4.2	14.5	2.6	10.3	3.2	11.6
RAIL	9	100.0	-	-	23.0	-	-	-	9.9	17.2	49.9
MOTOR CARRIER	296	100.0	7.2	28.1	18.8	3.7	15.3	2.9	11.7	2.7	9.5
PRIVATE TRUCK	22	100.0	.7	11.0	36.2	10.0	21.3	2.8	1.0	4.7	12.3
AIR	39	100.0	16.0	39.2	8.2	5.3	6.5	.8	6.1	2.4	15.3
WATER	-	100.0	-	-	-	-	-	-	-	-	100.0
OTHER	7	100.0	6.5	11.3	23.6	7.0	13.9	2.4	4.2	.9	30.1
UNKNOWN	4	100.0	8.8	16.0	27.6	3.6	25.0	.7	11.1	5.3	1.9
NEW ENGLAND	16	100.0	13.5	19.2	20.6	1.4	7.0	3.0	8.4	8.6	18.2
RAIL	4	100.0	-	-	52.9	-	.1	-	21.8	.1	25.1
MOTOR CARRIER	10	100.0	19.6	28.3	11.3	2.2	10.3	5.0	4.3	14.0	5.0
PRIVATE TRUCK	-	100.0	46.1	53.9	-	-	-	-	-	-	-
AIR	2	100.0	4.6	11.4	3.0	.7	6.1	-	2.6	1.0	70.6
WATER	-	100.0	-	-	-	-	-	-	-	-	-
OTHER	-	100.0	50.4	6.7	7.0	1.1	4.1	3.9	4.0	.5	22.4
UNKNOWN	-	100.0	5.4	-	-	-	-	-	94.6	-	-
MIDDLE ATLANTIC	71	100.0	2.0	33.7	24.6	3.3	19.7	.4	5.1	2.6	8.7
RAIL	2	100.0	-	-	-	-	-	-	1.3	51.1	47.6
MOTOR CARRIER	64	100.0	2.2	33.0	26.7	2.8	21.8	.4	5.4	.5	7.2
PRIVATE TRUCK	1	100.0	-	99.2	.7	-	.1	-	-	-	-
AIR	2	100.0	.4	38.7	17.6	23.8	3.0	1.3	5.6	1.6	8.1
WATER	-	100.0	-	-	-	-	-	-	-	-	-
OTHER	-	100.0	5.4	48.6	4.5	5.3	14.5	1.0	.5	.6	19.6
UNKNOWN	-	100.0	-	-	-	-	-	-	-	-	-
EAST NORTH CENTRAL	78	100.0	6.2	21.5	31.2	5.3	9.9	6.0	5.4	3.8	10.7
RAIL	2	100.0	-	-	-	-	-	-	-	6.2	93.8
MOTOR CARRIER	57	100.0	7.3	27.4	25.4	6.7	10.3	6.9	5.9	4.0	6.1
PRIVATE TRUCK	9	100.0	-	.5	84.8	-	-	6.9	-	3.3	4.5
AIR	1	100.0	13.5	17.4	13.4	3.2	22.1	.4	14.9	5.0	10.2
WATER	-	100.0	-	-	-	-	-	-	-	-	100.0
OTHER	3	100.0	2.5	3.8	20.4	4.7	12.0	2.5	3.5	.7	49.9
UNKNOWN	4	100.0	8.7	17.2	29.9	2.7	25.7	.7	12.0	3.1	-
WEST NORTH CENTRAL	11	100.0	13.4	10.6	13.3	34.3	9.8	2.3	4.3	3.3	8.6
RAIL	-	100.0	-	-	-	-	-	-	-	-	-
MOTOR CARRIER	7	100.0	2.5	14.5	19.4	25.4	14.3	3.5	5.1	3.5	11.8
PRIVATE TRUCK	2	100.0	-	-	-	100.0	-	-	-	-	-
AIR	1	100.0	68.6	6.3	3.4	1.6	2.6	.3	6.0	5.8	5.5
WATER	-	100.0	-	-	-	-	-	-	-	-	-
OTHER	-	100.0	3.2	17.9	29.7	21.0	15.0	.6	4.4	.6	7.5
UNKNOWN	-	100.0	-	100.0	-	-	-	-	-	-	-

See footnotes at end of table 4.

TABLE 2. **TCC GROUP 357** —Percent Distribution of Geographic Division of Origin and Means of Transport, by Geographic Division of Destination: 1972—Continued

Geographic division of origin[1] and means of transport	Number	Percent distribution by division of destination									
		U.S. total	New England	Middle Atlantic	East North Central	West North Central	South Atlantic	East South Central	West South Central	Mountain	Pacific
TONS OF SHIPMENTS	(thousands of tons)										
WEST SOUTH CENTRAL......	12	100.0	4.6	22.2	13.7	5.6	19.6	2.6	12.3	10.1	9.4
RAIL................	-	100.0	-	-	-	-	-	-	-	-	100.0
MOTOR CARRIER.........	10	100.0	4.4	20.7	15.5	5.6	21.0	3.1	12.5	10.6	6.6
PRIVATE TRUCK.........	-	100.0	-	-	-	-	34.1	-	54.5	11.4	-
AIR.................	1	100.0	6.0	42.0	6.3	3.8	6.2	-	4.0	.5	31.2
WATER...............	-	100.0	-	-	-	-	-	-	-	-	-
OTHER...............	-	100.0	-	12.7	29.9	3.0	32.1	9.4	10.7	2.2	-
UNKNOWN.............	-	100.0	11.5	.8	.6	18.3	21.7	1.7	.1	39.7	5.6
MOUNTAIN.............	6	100.0	1.8	29.2	8.6	7.2	5.5	.1	11.2	4.2	32.1
RAIL................	-	100.0	-	-	-	-	-	-	-	-	-
MOTOR CARRIER.........	4	100.0	1.3	25.2	7.8	7.0	3.6	-	13.9	4.8	36.3
PRIVATE TRUCK.........	-	100.0	-	-	-	86.2	-	-	-	13.8	-
AIR.................	1	100.0	3.0	47.4	12.4	2.3	12.7	.5	4.3	1.6	15.8
WATER...............	-	100.0	-	-	-	-	-	-	-	-	-
OTHER...............	-	100.0	2.3	9.8	7.6	2.3	5.8	-	1.6	9.5	61.0
UNKNOWN.............	-	100.0	7.6	-	-	-	-	-	-	-	92.4
TON-MILES OF SHIPMENTS	(millions of ton-miles)										
U.S. TOTAL...........	392	100.0	7.0	34.8	13.7	2.7	10.7	1.8	12.2	3.9	13.2
RAIL................	16	100.0	-	-	8.9	-	-	-	8.1	21.9	61.0
MOTOR CARRIER.........	292	100.0	5.4	35.5	15.4	2.4	12.0	2.0	14.8	3.3	9.2
PRIVATE TRUCK.........	6	100.0	1.6	11.3	29.4	9.4	15.3	5.0	1.5	10.8	15.8
AIR.................	66	100.0	16.4	46.3	7.0	4.0	6.6	.8	3.6	1.4	13.9
WATER...............	-	100.0	-	-	-	-	-	-	-	-	100.0
OTHER...............	6	100.0	5.5	5.6	6.5	3.9	11.8	1.4	4.4	1.2	59.7
UNKNOWN.............	2	100.0	14.0	16.4	9.8	1.3	31.4	.7	14.7	10.2	1.6
NEW ENGLAND..........	16	100.0	.7	3.5	13.7	1.5	3.4	2.7	12.0	16.2	46.4
RAIL................	5	100.0	-	-	27.4	-	.1	-	23.9	.1	48.5
MOTOR CARRIER.........	7	100.0	1.5	7.2	10.8	3.2	6.8	6.2	8.8	37.3	18.1
PRIVATE TRUCK.........	-	100.0	11.2	88.6	-	.1	.1	-	-	-	-
AIR.................	4	100.0	-	1.1	1.1	.4	1.8	-	2.0	1.0	92.7
WATER...............	-	100.0	-	-	-	-	-	-	-	-	-
OTHER...............	-	100.0	1.6	2.5	5.6	1.5	4.4	4.2	7.5	1.1	71.5
UNKNOWN.............	-	100.0	.1	-	-	-	-	-	99.9	-	-
MIDDLE ATLANTIC.........	45	100.0	.6	5.4	22.5	5.4	13.8	.5	9.3	8.9	33.6
RAIL................	6	100.0	-	-	-	-	-	-	.8	50.3	48.9
MOTOR CARRIER.........	36	100.0	.7	5.8	27.3	4.8	17.1	.5	11.0	1.6	31.1
PRIVATE TRUCK.........	-	100.0	-	99.2	.7	-	.1	-	-	-	-
AIR.................	1	100.0	.1	7.2	13.9	35.4	2.0	1.5	9.7	4.0	26.2
WATER...............	-	100.0	-	-	-	-	-	-	-	-	-
OTHER...............	-	100.0	1.4	5.9	3.7	7.1	9.4	1.2	1.0	1.5	68.8
UNKNOWN.............	-	100.0	-	-	-	-	-	-	-	-	-
EAST NORTH CENTRAL......	49	100.0	7.1	18.5	8.2	4.2	9.9	4.1	7.6	7.8	32.8
RAIL................	4	100.0	-	-	-	-	-	-	-	4.9	95.1
MOTOR CARRIER.........	33	100.0	9.0	25.4	6.3	5.8	10.7	4.8	9.1	8.6	20.2
PRIVATE TRUCK.........	3	100.0	-	.2	48.1	-	-	10.5	-	14.2	26.9
AIR.................	1	100.0	11.6	10.3	2.6	2.7	20.4	.2	16.6	8.6	27.0
WATER...............	-	100.0	-	-	-	-	-	-	-	-	100.0
OTHER...............	4	100.0	1.7	1.9	3.1	1.5	7.1	1.1	2.3	.9	80.4
UNKNOWN.............	2	100.0	13.2	18.2	10.7	.9	32.4	.6	16.4	7.5	-
WEST NORTH CENTRAL......	7	100.0	19.7	14.0	8.8	10.9	14.1	2.6	6.3	3.9	19.7
RAIL................	-	100.0	-	-	-	-	-	-	-	-	-
MOTOR CARRIER.........	5	100.0	3.9	17.8	12.0	8.0	19.2	3.8	7.1	3.5	24.6
PRIVATE TRUCK.........	-	100.0	-	-	-	100.0	-	-	-	-	-
AIR.................	1	100.0	68.5	5.8	1.2	.8	2.3	.1	5.4	5.9	10.0
WATER...............	-	100.0	-	-	-	-	-	-	-	-	-
OTHER...............	-	100.0	5.1	23.3	20.7	9.8	18.3	.7	5.2	1.0	15.8
UNKNOWN.............	-	100.0	-	100.0	-	-	-	-	-	-	-
WEST SOUTH CENTRAL......	12	100.0	7.1	30.1	12.2	3.5	21.2	1.3	3.0	8.0	13.6
RAIL................	-	100.0	-	-	-	-	-	-	-	-	100.0
MOTOR CARRIER.........	9	100.0	6.9	28.5	14.2	3.7	23.6	1.6	3.4	8.8	9.3
PRIVATE TRUCK.........	-	100.0	-	-	-	-	72.8	-	16.1	11.1	-
AIR.................	2	100.0	6.9	43.9	5.0	2.7	5.4	-	.8	.3	35.1
WATER...............	-	100.0	-	-	-	-	-	-	-	-	-
OTHER...............	-	100.0	-	20.9	33.8	1.7	30.2	9.9	1.7	1.7	-
UNKNOWN.............	-	100.0	19.0	1.1	.7	5.5	26.8	1.5	-	36.8	8.5
MOUNTAIN.............	6	100.0	3.3	48.6	10.0	6.9	8.7	.2	9.0	.3	13.0
RAIL................	-	100.0	-	-	-	-	-	-	-	-	-
MOTOR CARRIER.........	4	100.0	2.6	48.1	9.2	7.9	6.1	-	11.9	.1	14.1
PRIVATE TRUCK.........	-	100.0	-	-	-	99.2	-	-	-	.8	-
AIR.................	1	100.0	4.3	53.4	12.3	1.6	15.3	.5	3.0	.6	9.0
WATER...............	-	100.0	-	-	-	-	-	-	-	-	-
OTHER...............	-	100.0	5.5	18.2	10.2	1.8	10.0	-	1.3	.7	52.3
UNKNOWN.............	-	100.0	38.5	-	-	-	-	-	-	-	61.5

See footnotes at end of table 4.

TABLE 3. **TCC GROUP 357**—Percent Distribution of Geographic Division of Destination and Means of Transport, by Geographic Division of Origin: 1972

Geographic division of destination and means of transport	Number	Percent distribution by division of origin [1]									
		U.S. total	New England	Middle Atlantic	East North Central	West North Central	South Atlantic	East South Central	West South Central	Mountain	Pacific
TONS OF SHIPMENTS	(thousands of tons)										
U.S. TOTAL..............	379	100.0	4.4	18.9	20.7	3.0	(D)	(D)	3.2	1.6	(D)
RAIL...................	9	100.0	43.4	30.4	26.0	-	(D)	(D)	.2	-	(D)
MOTOR CARRIER..........	296	100.0	3.4	21.7	19.4	2.5	(D)	(D)	3.4	1.5	(D)
PRIVATE TRUCK..........	22	100.0	.9	8.6	41.0	9.1	(D)	(D)	1.4	.5	(D)
AIR....................	39	100.0	5.2	6.3	4.0	5.1	(D)	(D)	3.6	3.4	(D)
WATER.................	-	100.0	-	-	100.0	-	(D)	(D)	-	-	(D)
OTHER.................	7	100.0	2.4	4.2	52.8	1.3	(D)	(D)	-	1.0	(D)
UNKNOWN...............	4	100.0	-	-	92.1	-	(D)	(D)	6.0	1.6	(D)
NEW ENGLAND..............	28	100.0	7.9	5.0	17.0	5.4	(D)	(D)	2.0	.4	(D)
RAIL...................	-	100.0	-	-	-	-	(D)	(D)	-	-	(D)
MOTOR CARRIER..........	21	100.0	9.3	6.6	19.8	.9	(D)	(D)	2.1	.3	(D)
PRIVATE TRUCK..........	-	100.0	57.2	-	-	-	(D)	(D)	-	-	(D)
AIR....................	6	100.0	1.5	.1	3.4	21.8	(D)	(D)	1.3	.6	(D)
WATER.................	-	100.0	-	-	-	-	(D)	(D)	-	-	(D)
OTHER.................	-	100.0	18.5	3.5	20.0	.7	(D)	(D)	-	.4	(D)
UNKNOWN...............	-	100.0	-	-	90.7	-	(D)	(D)	7.9	1.4	(D)
MIDDLE ATLANTIC.........	102	100.0	3.1	23.6	16.4	1.2	(D)	(D)	2.6	1.7	(D)
RAIL...................	-	100.0	-	-.	-	-	(D)	(D)	-	-	(D)
MOTOR CARRIER..........	83	100.0	3.4	25.4	18.8	1.3	(D)	(D)	2.5	1.4	(D)
PRIVATE TRUCK..........	2	100.0	4.4	77.8	1.8	-	(D)	(D)	-	-	(D)
AIR....................	15	100.0	1.5	6.2	1.8	.8	(D)	(D)	3.9	4.2	(D)
WATER.................	-	100.0	-	-	-	-	(D)	(D)	-	-	(D)
OTHER.................	-	100.0	1.4	18.3	17.6	2.1	(D)	(D)	-	.9	(D)
UNKNOWN...............	-	100.0	-	-	99.3	.2	(D)	(D)	.3	-	(D)
EAST NORTH CENTRAL......	72	100.0	4.7	24.4	33.9	2.1	(D)	(D)	2.3	.7	(D)
RAIL...................	2	100.0	100.0	-	-	-	(D)	(D)	-	-	(D)
MOTOR CARRIER..........	55	100.0	2.0	30.8	26.1	2.6	(D)	(D)	2.8	.6	(D)
PRIVATE TRUCK..........	8	100.0	-	.2	96.0	-	(D)	(D)	-	-	(D)
AIR....................	3	100.0	1.9	13.4	6.5	2.1	(D)	(D)	2.8	5.2	(D)
WATER.................	-	100.0	-	-	-	-	(D)	(D)	-	-	(D)
OTHER.................	1	100.0	.7	.8	45.5	1.7	(D)	(D)	-	.3	(D)
UNKNOWN...............	1	100.0	-	-	99.7	-	(D)	(D)	.1	-	(D)
WEST NORTH CENTRAL......	15	100.0	1.5	15.1	26.5	25.0	(D)	(D)	4.2	2.8	(D)
RAIL...................	-	100.0	100.0	-	-	-	(D)	(D)	-	-	(D)
MOTOR CARRIER..........	10	100.0	2.1	16.4	35.5	17.4	(D)	(D)	5.2	2.9	(D)
PRIVATE TRUCK..........	2	100.0	-	-	-	90.5	(D)	(D)	-	4.1	(D)
AIR....................	2	100.0	.6	28.0	2.4	1.5	(D)	(D)	2.6	1.5	(D)
WATER.................	-	100.0	-	-	-	-	(D)	(D)	-	-	(D)
OTHER.................	-	100.0	.4	3.2	35.6	4.0	(D)	(D)	-	.3	(D)
UNKNOWN...............	-	100.0	-	-	69.3	-	(D)	(D)	30.7	-	(D)
SOUTH ATLANTIC..........	54	100.0	2.1	25.7	14.2	2.1	(D)	(D)	4.3	.6	(D)
RAIL...................	-	100.0	100.0	-	-	-	(D)	(D)	-	-	(D)
MOTOR CARRIER..........	45	100.0	2.3	30.8	13.0	2.3	(D)	(D)	4.6	.4	(D)
PRIVATE TRUCK..........	4	100.0	-	-	-	-	(D)	(D)	2.2	-	(D)
AIR....................	2	100.0	4.9	2.9	13.6	2.1	(D)	(D)	3.4	6.7	(D)
WATER.................	-	100.0	-	-	-	-	(D)	(D)	-	-	(D)
OTHER.................	1	100.0	.7	4.4	45.7	1.4	(D)	(D)	.1	.4	(D)
UNKNOWN...............	1	100.0	-	-	94.8	-	(D)	(D)	5.2	-	(D)
EAST SOUTH CENTRAL......	9	100.0	5.1	3.1	47.9	2.7	(D)	(D)	3.2	.1	(D)
RAIL...................	-	100.0	-	-	-	-	(D)	(D)	-	-	(D)
MOTOR CARRIER..........	8	100.0	5.8	3.1	45.6	3.0	(D)	(D)	3.5	-	(D)
PRIVATE TRUCK..........	-	100.0	-	-	100.0	-	(D)	(D)	-	-	(D)
AIR....................	-	100.0	-	9.7	1.8	1.8	(D)	(D)	.2	2.3	(D)
WATER.................	-	100.0	-	-	-	-	(D)	(D)	-	-	(D)
OTHER.................	-	100.0	3.9	1.7	54.2	.4	(D)	(D)	.1	-	(D)
UNKNOWN...............	-	100.0	-	-	86.1	-	(D)	(D)	13.9	-	(D)
WEST SOUTH CENTRAL......	39	100.0	3.6	9.3	10.9	1.3	(D)	(D)	3.8	1.7	(D)
RAIL...................	-	100.0	95.5	4.0	-	-	(D)	(D)	-	-	(D)
MOTOR CARRIER..........	34	100.0	1.2	10.0	9.8	1.1	(D)	(D)	3.6	1.8	(D)
PRIVATE TRUCK..........	-	100.0	-	-	-	-	(D)	(D)	74.2	-	(D)
AIR....................	2	100.0	2.2	5.7	9.7	5.0	(D)	(D)	2.4	2.4	(D)
WATER.................	-	100.0	-	-	-	-	(D)	(D)	-	-	(D)
OTHER.................	-	100.0	2.3	.5	43.5	1.4	(D)	(D)	.1	.4	(D)
UNKNOWN...............	-	100.0	-	-	99.8	-	(D)	(D)	.1	-	(D)
MOUNTAIN................	12	100.0	11.9	15.3	24.8	3.1	(D)	(D)	10.1	2.1	(D)
RAIL...................	1	100.0	.2	90.4	9.4	-	(D)	(D)	-	-	(D)
MOTOR CARRIER..........	8	100.0	17.4	3.8	28.3	3.2	(D)	(D)	13.1	2.6	(D)
PRIVATE TRUCK..........	1	100.0	-	-	29.1	-	(D)	(D)	3.4	1.4	(D)
AIR....................	-	100.0	2.1	4.0	8.2	12.0	(D)	(D)	.7	2.3	(D)
WATER.................	-	100.0	-	-	-	-	(D)	(D)	-	-	(D)
OTHER.................	-	100.0	1.2	2.6	42.8	.9	(D)	(D)	.1	10.4	(D)
UNKNOWN...............	-	100.0	-	-	54.0	-	(D)	(D)	45.2	-	(D)
PACIFIC.................	44	100.0	6.9	14.2	19.0	2.2	(D)	(D)	2.6	4.4	(D)
RAIL...................	4	100.0	21.8	29.0	48.9	-	(D)	(D)	.3	-	(D)
MOTOR CARRIER..........	28	100.0	1.8	16.3	12.4	3.1	(D)	(D)	2.3	5.8	(D)
PRIVATE TRUCK..........	2	100.0	-	-	15.1	-	(D)	(D)	-	-	(D)
AIR....................	5	100.0	24.0	3.3	2.7	1.8	(D)	(D)	7.3	3.6	(D)
WATER.................	-	100.0	-	-	100.0	-	(D)	(D)	-	-	(D)
OTHER.................	2	100.0	1.8	2.8	87.5	.3	(D)	(D)	-	2.0	(D)
UNKNOWN...............	-	100.0	-	-	-	-	(D)	(D)	17.3	77.4	(D)

See footnotes at end of table 4.

TABLE 3. **TCC GROUP 357**—Percent Distribution of Geographic Division of Destination and Means of Transport, by Geographic Division of Origin: 1972—Continued

Geographic division of destination and means of transport	Number	Percent distribution by division of origin [1]									
		U.S. total	New England	Middle Atlantic	East North Central	West North Central	South Atlantic	East South Central	West South Central	Mountain	Pacific
TON-MILES OF SHIPMENTS	(millions of ton-miles)										
U.S. TOTAL...............	392	100.0	4.2	11.6	12.5	2.0	(D)	(D)	3.1	1.7	(D)
RAIL.................	16	100.0	32.5	41.0	26.4	-	(D)	(D)	.1	-	(D)
MOTOR CARRIER.........	292	100.0	2.4	12.4	11.4	1.8	(D)	(D)	3.3	1.5	(D)
PRIVATE TRUCK.........	6	100.0	.4	2.9	47.2	5.9	(D)	(D)	2.4	1.0	(D)
AIR..................	66	100.0	6.1	2.9	1.7	2.9	(D)	(D)	3.0	2.9	(D)
WATER................	-	100.0	-	-	100.0	-	(D)	(D)	-	-	(D)
OTHER................	6	100.0	2.0	3.2	68.4	1.0	(D)	(D)	-	.9	(D)
UNKNOWN..............	2	100.0	-	-	89.1	-	(D)	(D)	9.3	1.3	(D)
NEW ENGLAND.............	27	100.0	.4	1.0	12.7	5.5	(D)	(D)	3.1	.8	(D)
RAIL.................	-	100.0	-	-	-	-	(D)	(D)	-	-	(D)
MOTOR CARRIER.........	15	100.0	.7	1.7	19.0	1.3	(D)	(D)	4.3	.8	(D)
PRIVATE TRUCK.........	-	100.0	3.0	-	-	-	(D)	(D)	-	-	(D)
AIR..................	10	100.0	-	-	1.2	11.9	(D)	(D)	1.3	.8	(D)
WATER................	-	100.0	-	-	-	-	(D)	(D)	-	-	(D)
OTHER................	-	100.0	.6	.8	20.9	1.0	(D)	(D)	-	.9	(D)
UNKNOWN..............	-	100.0	-	-	84.0	-	(D)	(D)	12.6	3.5	(D)
MIDDLE ATLANTIC.........	136	100.0	.4	1.8	6.7	.8	(D)	(D)	2.7	2.4	(D)
RAIL.................	-	100.0	-	-	-	-	(D)	(D)	-	-	(D)
MOTOR CARRIER.........	104	100.0	.5	2.0	8.1	.9	(D)	(D)	2.7	2.1	(D)
PRIVATE TRUCK.........	-	100.0	3.3	25.9	.8	-	(D)	(D)	-	-	(D)
AIR..................	30	100.0	.1	.4	.4	.4	(D)	(D)	2.8	3.3	(D)
WATER................	-	100.0	-	-	-	-	(D)	(D)	-	-	(D)
OTHER................	-	100.0	.9	3.4	23.6	4.3	(D)	(D)	.1	3.0	(D)
UNKNOWN..............	-	100.0	-	-	98.5	.3	(D)	(D)	.6	-	(D)
EAST NORTH CENTRAL......	53	100.0	4.2	18.9	7.5	1.3	(D)	(D)	2.8	1.2	(D)
RAIL.................	1	100.0	100.0	-	-	-	(D)	(D)	-	-	(D)
MOTOR CARRIER.........	45	100.0	1.7	22.0	4.7	1.4	(D)	(D)	3.1	.9	(D)
PRIVATE TRUCK.........	1	100.0	-	.1	77.3	-	(D)	(D)	-	-	(D)
AIR..................	4	100.0	.9	5.7	.6	.5	(D)	(D)	2.1	5.1	(D)
WATER................	-	100.0	-	-	-	-	(D)	(D)	-	-	(D)
OTHER................	-	100.0	1.7	1.8	32.8	3.3	(D)	(D)	.2	1.4	(D)
UNKNOWN..............	-	100.0	-	-	97.6	-	(D)	(D)	.6	-	(D)
WEST NORTH CENTRAL......	10	100.0	2.3	22.9	19.2	7.9	(D)	(D)	4.0	4.2	(D)
RAIL.................	-	100.0	100.0	-	-	-	(D)	(D)	-	-	(D)
MOTOR CARRIER.........	7	100.0	3.2	24.7	27.2	6.1	(D)	(D)	5.1	5.0	(D)
PRIVATE TRUCK.........	-	100.0	-	-	-	62.7	(D)	(D)	-	10.4	(D)
AIR..................	2	100.0	.6	25.3	1.1	.5	(D)	(D)	2.0	1.1	(D)
WATER................	-	100.0	-	-	-	-	(D)	(D)	-	-	(D)
OTHER................	-	100.0	.8	5.7	26.6	2.6	(D)	(D)	-	.4	(D)
UNKNOWN..............	-	100.0	-	-	62.0	-	(D)	(D)	38.0	-	(D)
SOUTH ATLANTIC..........	42	100.0	1.3	14.9	11.6	2.6	(D)	(D)	6.1	1.4	(D)
RAIL.................	-	100.0	100.0	-	-	-	(D)	(D)	-	-	(D)
MOTOR CARRIER.........	35	100.0	1.4	17.7	10.1	2.9	(D)	(D)	6.6	.8	(D)
PRIVATE TRUCK.........	1	100.0	-	-	-	-	(D)	(D)	11.2	-	(D)
AIR..................	4	100.0	1.6	.9	5.3	1.0	(D)	(D)	2.5	6.7	(D)
WATER................	-	100.0	-	-	-	-	(D)	(D)	-	-	(D)
OTHER................	-	100.0	.7	2.5	41.1	1.6	(D)	(D)	.1	.8	(D)
UNKNOWN..............	-	100.0	-	-	92.1	-	(D)	(D)	7.9	-	(D)
EAST SOUTH CENTRAL......	6	100.0	6.5	3.2	29.0	3.0	(D)	(D)	2.3	.1	(D)
RAIL.................	-	100.0	-	-	-	-	(D)	(D)	-	-	(D)
MOTOR CARRIER.........	5	100.0	7.5	3.2	27.0	3.4	(D)	(D)	2.6	-	(D)
PRIVATE TRUCK.........	-	100.0	-	-	99.9	-	(D)	(D)	-	-	(D)
AIR..................	-	100.0	-	5.6	.5	.5	(D)	(D)	.1	2.0	(D)
WATER................	-	100.0	-	-	-	-	(D)	(D)	-	-	(D)
OTHER................	-	100.0	6.0	2.8	51.7	.5	(D)	(D)	.2	-	(D)
UNKNOWN..............	-	100.0	-	-	79.2	-	(D)	(D)	20.8	-	(D)
WEST SOUTH CENTRAL......	47	100.0	4.2	8.9	7.8	1.0	(D)	(D)	.8	1.2	(D)
RAIL.................	1	100.0	95.5	3.9	-	-	(D)	(D)	-	-	(D)
MOTOR CARRIER.........	43	100.0	1.4	9.2	7.0	.9	(D)	(D)	.8	1.2	(D)
PRIVATE TRUCK.........	-	100.0	-	-	-	-	(D)	(D)	26.1	-	(D)
AIR..................	2	100.0	3.4	7.6	7.9	4.3	(D)	(D)	.6	2.4	(D)
WATER................	-	100.0	-	-	-	-	(D)	(D)	-	-	(D)
OTHER................	-	100.0	3.4	.7	36.2	1.2	(D)	(D)	-	.3	(D)
UNKNOWN..............	-	100.0	.1	-	99.8	-	(D)	(D)	-	-	(D)
MOUNTAIN................	15	100.0	17.8	26.6	25.2	2.0	(D)	(D)	6.4	.1	(D)
RAIL.................	3	100.0	.2	93.9	5.9	-	(D)	(D)	-	-	(D)
MOTOR CARRIER.........	9	100.0	27.7	6.0	29.8	2.0	(D)	(D)	9.0	.1	(D)
PRIVATE TRUCK.........	-	100.0	-	-	62.4	-	(D)	(D)	2.4	.1	(D)
AIR..................	-	100.0	4.2	8.3	10.6	12.2	(D)	(D)	.5	1.3	(D)
WATER................	-	100.0	-	-	-	-	(D)	(D)	-	.6	(D)
OTHER................	-	100.0	1.9	3.9	48.4	.9	(D)	(D)	-	-	(D)
UNKNOWN..............	-	100.0	-	-	65.9	-	(D)	(D)	33.5	-	(D)
PACIFIC.................	51	100.0	15.0	29.5	31.2	3.0	(D)	(D)	3.2	1.7	(D)
RAIL.................	10	100.0	25.9	32.8	41.1	-	(D)	(D)	.2	-	(D)
MOTOR CARRIER.........	26	100.0	4.8	42.1	25.0	4.9	(D)	(D)	3.4	2.4	(D)
PRIVATE TRUCK.........	1	100.0	-	-	80.3	-	(D)	(D)	-	-	(D)
AIR..................	9	100.0	40.5	5.4	3.4	2.0	(D)	(D)	7.6	1.9	(D)
WATER................	-	100.0	-	-	100.0	-	(D)	(D)	-	-	(D)
OTHER................	3	100.0	2.4	3.6	92.1	.3	(D)	(D)	-	.8	(D)
UNKNOWN..............	-	100.0	-	-	-	-	(D)	(D)	50.5	49.4	(D)

See footnotes at end of table 4.

TABLE 4. **TCC GROUP 357—Percent Distribution of Distance Shipped and Weight of Shipment, by Means of Transport: 1972**

Distance shipped and weight of shipment[2][3]	Number	Percent distribution by means of transport							
		All means of transport	Rail	Motor carrier	Private truck	Air	Water	Other	Unknown
TONS OF SHIPMENTS	(thousands of tons)								
U.S. TOTAL..........	236	100.0	3.0	76.5	8.2	7.8	-	2.7	1.8
UNDER 100 MILES.........	29	100.0	-	68.7	23.9	4.7	-	1.5	1.2
UNDER 1000 POUNDS.....	7	100.0	-	70.7	13.8	8.6	-	5.4	1.6
1000 TO 9999 POUNDS...	11	100.0	-	82.6	8.2	6.7	-	.4	2.1
10000 TO 29999 POUNDS.	8	100.0	-	63.7	36.3	-	-	-	-
30000 TO 59999 POUNDS.	1	100.0	-	-	100.0	-	-	-	-
60000 TO 89999 POUNDS.	-	100.0	-	-	-	-	-	-	-
90000 POUNDS AND OVER.	-	100.0	-	-	-	-	-	-	-
100 TO 199 MILES........	25	100.0	-	76.0	19.0	1.8	-	2.3	.9
UNDER 1000 POUNDS.....	4	100.0	-	79.3	3.5	3.5	-	12.4	1.4
1000 TO 9999 POUNDS...	14	100.0	-	91.8	5.1	2.0	-	-	1.1
10000 TO 29999 POUNDS.	6	100.0	-	38.1	61.9	-	-	-	-
30000 TO 59999 POUNDS.	-	100.0	-	-	100.0	-	-	-	-
60000 TO 89999 POUNDS.	-	100.0	-	-	-	-	-	-	-
90000 POUNDS AND OVER.	-	100.0	-	-	-	-	-	-	-
200 TO 299 MILES........	18	100.0	-	64.6	30.0	2.0	-	2.8	.5
UNDER 1000 POUNDS.....	3	100.0	-	82.5	.3	2.5	-	13.5	1.3
1000 TO 9999 POUNDS...	9	100.0	-	37.3	59.2	3.0	-	-	.5
10000 TO 29999 POUNDS.	5	100.0	-	100.0	-	-	-	-	-
30000 TO 59999 POUNDS.	-	100.0	-	-	100.0	-	-	-	-
60000 TO 89999 POUNDS.	-	100.0	-	-	-	-	-	-	-
90000 POUNDS AND OVER.	-	100.0	-	-	-	-	-	-	-
300 TO 499 MILES........	31	100.0	-	88.1	2.7	2.9	-	3.7	2.6
UNDER 1000 POUNDS.....	10	100.0	-	77.6	.6	9.1	-	11.6	1.1
1000 TO 9999 POUNDS...	9	100.0	-	97.8	.5	-	-	-	1.6
10000 TO 29999 POUNDS.	11	100.0	-	90.7	4.5	-	-	-	4.8
30000 TO 59999 POUNDS.	1	100.0	-	78.1	21.9	-	-	-	-
60000 TO 89999 POUNDS.	-	100.0	-	-	-	-	-	-	-
90000 POUNDS AND OVER.	-	100.0	-	-	-	-	-	-	-
500 TO 999 MILES........	70	100.0	3.1	85.8	.4	5.6	-	1.6	3.5
UNDER 1000 POUNDS.....	15	100.0	-	81.0	.1	10.2	-	7.3	1.4
1000 TO 9999 POUNDS...	22	100.0	-	81.5	1.1	10.5	-	-	6.9
10000 TO 29999 POUNDS.	26	100.0	8.3	88.8	-	-	-	-	2.8
30000 TO 59999 POUNDS.	6	100.0	-	100.0	-	-	-	-	-
60000 TO 89999 POUNDS.	-	100.0	-	-	-	-	-	-	-
90000 POUNDS AND OVER.	-	100.0	-	-	-	-	-	-	-
1000 TO 1499 MILES......	31	100.0	3.0	78.1	.8	16.4	-	.8	.9
UNDER 1000 POUNDS.....	9	100.0	.4	64.5	1.1	31.2	-	1.8	.9
1000 TO 9999 POUNDS...	11	100.0	-	81.9	1.1	14.7	-	.7	1.6
10000 TO 29999 POUNDS.	10	100.0	8.7	86.9	-	4.4	-	-	-
30000 TO 59999 POUNDS.	-	100.0	-	-	100.0	-	-	-	-
60000 TO 89999 POUNDS.	-	100.0	-	-	-	-	-	-	-
90000 POUNDS AND OVER.	-	100.0	-	-	-	-	-	-	-
1500 MILES OR OVER......	28	100.0	13.7	55.1	2.6	20.9	-	7.7	-
UNDER 1000 POUNDS.....	8	100.0	2.1	46.2	.7	46.9	-	4.1	-
1000 TO 9999 POUNDS...	12	100.0	4.9	61.6	5.6	14.1	-	13.8	-
10000 TO 29999 POUNDS.	6	100.0	27.6	68.4	-	1.8	-	2.1	-
30000 TO 59999 POUNDS.	1	100.0	100.0	-	-	-	-	-	-
60000 TO 89999 POUNDS.	-	100.0	-	-	-	-	-	-	-
90000 POUNDS AND OVER.	-	100.0	-	-	-	-	-	-	-
TON-MILES OF SHIPMENTS	(millions of ton-miles)								
U.S. TOTAL..........	171	100.0	7.0	71.5	2.7	13.6	-	3.6	1.5
UNDER 100 MILES........	1	100.0	-	61.0	31.2	5.4	-	2.2	.3
UNDER 1000 POUNDS.....	-	100.0	-	76.1	5.9	9.0	-	8.3	.6
1000 TO 9999 POUNDS...	-	100.0	-	86.2	5.0	8.3	-	.2	.3
10000 TO 29999 POUNDS.	-	100.0	-	37.5	62.5	-	-	-	-
30000 TO 59999 POUNDS.	-	100.0	-	-	100.0	-	-	-	-
60000 TO 89999 POUNDS.	-	100.0	-	-	-	-	-	-	-
90000 POUNDS AND OVER.	-	100.0	-	-	-	-	-	-	-
100 TO 199 MILES........	3	100.0	-	74.3	20.7	1.8	-	2.3	.9
UNDER 1000 POUNDS.....	-	100.0	-	78.7	3.6	3.6	-	12.4	1.6
1000 TO 9999 POUNDS...	2	100.0	-	91.8	5.0	2.1	-	-	1.1
10000 TO 29999 POUNDS.	1	100.0	-	36.0	64.0	-	-	-	-
30000 TO 59999 POUNDS.	-	100.0	-	-	100.0	-	-	-	-
60000 TO 89999 POUNDS.	-	100.0	-	-	-	-	-	-	-
90000 POUNDS AND OVER.	-	100.0	-	-	-	-	-	-	-

See footnotes at end of table 4.

TABLE 4. TCC GROUP 357—Percent Distribution of Distance Shipped and Weight of Shipment, by Means of Transport: 1972—Continued

Distance shipped and weight of shipment[2] [3]	Number	Percent distribution by means of transport							
		All means of transport	Rail	Motor carrier	Private truck	Air	Water	Other	Unknown
TON-MILES OF SHIPMENTS	(millions of ton-miles)								
200 TO 299 MILES	4	100.0	-	67.2	27.1	2.0	-	3.1	.6
UNDER 1000 POUNDS	-	100.0	-	82.4	.2	2.5	-	13.7	1.1
1000 TO 9999 POUNDS	2	100.0	-	39.6	56.6	3.1	-	-	.7
10000 TO 29999 POUNDS	1	100.0	-	100.0	-	-	-	-	-
30000 TO 59999 POUNDS	-	100.0	-	-	100.0	-	-	-	-
60000 TO 89999 POUNDS	-	100.0	-	-	-	-	-	-	-
90000 POUNDS AND OVER	-	100.0	-	-	-	-	-	-	-
300 TO 499 MILES	12	100.0	-	88.5	2.6	3.0	-	3.6	2.3
UNDER 1000 POUNDS	3	100.0	-	77.4	.7	9.4	-	11.2	1.3
1000 TO 9999 POUNDS	3	100.0	-	98.0	.5	-	-	-	1.6
10000 TO 29999 POUNDS	4	100.0	-	91.5	4.4	-	-	-	4.0
30000 TO 59999 POUNDS	-	100.0	-	81.4	18.6	-	-	-	-
60000 TO 89999 POUNDS	-	100.0	-	-	-	-	-	-	-
90000 POUNDS AND OVER	-	100.0	-	-	-	-	-	-	-
500 TO 999 MILES	50	100.0	2.9	84.7	.4	6.8	-	1.6	3.6
UNDER 1000 POUNDS	11	100.0	-	80.1	.1	11.5	-	7.1	1.3
1000 TO 9999 POUNDS	16	100.0	-	79.2	1.1	12.8	-	-	6.9
10000 TO 29999 POUNDS	18	100.0	8.0	89.1	-	-	-	-	2.9
30000 TO 59999 POUNDS	4	100.0	-	100.0	-	-	-	-	-
60000 TO 89999 POUNDS	-	100.0	-	-	-	-	-	-	-
90000 POUNDS AND OVER	-	100.0	-	-	-	-	-	-	-
1000 TO 1499 MILES	37	100.0	3.5	77.4	.8	16.5	-	.9	1.0
UNDER 1000 POUNDS	11	100.0	.5	64.6	1.0	31.2	-	1.8	.9
1000 TO 9999 POUNDS	13	100.0	-	81.6	1.0	14.7	-	.8	1.9
10000 TO 29999 POUNDS	12	100.0	10.2	85.1	-	4.7	-	-	-
30000 TO 59999 POUNDS	-	100.0	-	-	100.0	-	-	-	-
60000 TO 89999 POUNDS	-	100.0	-	-	-	-	-	-	-
90000 POUNDS AND OVER	-	100.0	-	-	-	-	-	-	-
1500 MILES OR OVER	61	100.0	15.0	54.0	2.6	21.3	-	7.2	-
UNDER 1000 POUNDS	18	100.0	2.4	42.6	.8	49.7	-	4.5	-
1000 TO 9999 POUNDS	26	100.0	5.4	62.2	5.3	14.6	-	12.5	-
10000 TO 29999 POUNDS	13	100.0	30.3	66.4	-	1.4	-	1.8	-
30000 TO 59999 POUNDS	3	100.0	100.0	-	-	-	-	-	-
60000 TO 89999 POUNDS	-	100.0	-	-	-	-	-	-	-
90000 POUNDS AND OVER	-	100.0	-	-	-	-	-	-	-

Note: Detail may not add to total due to rounding. The introductory table shows the estimates of sampling variability for tons; sampling variability for ton-miles has not been estimated. See the map in the Introduction for the States comprising the geographic divisions of the United States.
Shipments excluded from the survey are those moving by pipeline (primarily petroleum products from refineries), parcel post shipments, and commodities moved by own power (motorized vehicles, aircraft, etc.) or towed (prefabricated buildings, etc.). Local shipments (commodities shipped less than 25 miles from the plant) and shipments within the same city are also excluded. Shipments to Alaska and Hawaii from the 48 conterminous States and the District of Columbia are included; however, no data were obtained for shipments originating in Alaska and Hawaii.

- Represents zero or rounds to zero.   (D) Withheld to avoid disclosing figures for individual companies.

[1]Production of this commodity is concentrated in the geographic divisions shown; figures and distributions for geographic divisions not shown are included in the total.
[2]Distances of shipments to foreign destinations are calculated only to the U.S. port of exit.
[3]Includes only shipments represented by bills of lading and invoices. Summary records which did not show individual weights of shipments are not included.

TCC 358. Refrigeration and Service Industry Machines

Comparisons of Tons and Ton-Miles of Shipments for
Geographic Divisions of Origin and for Sampling Variability: 1972 and 1967

Geographic division of origin	Estimates				Relative sampling variability in tons (percent)	
	1972		1967		1972	1967
	Tons (thousands)	Ton-miles (millions)	Tons (thousands)	Ton-miles (millions)		
U.S. total	3,322	2,146	2,596	1,521	9.3	16.2
New England	(D)	(D)	37	27	(*)	(*)
Middle Atlantic	590	447	523	406	35.3	(*)
East North Central	1,418	803	774	403	14.5	(*)
West North Central	174	110	159	118	37.3	(*)
South Atlantic	99	42	85	44	22.5	(*)
East South Central	590	353	123	82	31.4	(*)
West South Central	277	195	569	345	48.2	(*)
Mountain	(D)	(D)	—	—	(*)	(*)
Pacific	(D)	(D)	326	96	(*)	(*)

— Represents or rounds to zero.   (D) Withheld to avoid disclosing figures for individual companies.   (*) Data not published.

TABLE 1. **TCC GROUP 358—Percent Distribution of Geographic Division of Origin and Distance Shipped, by Means of Transport: 1972**

Geographic division of origin[1] and distance shipped[2]	Number	Percent distribution by means of transport							
		All means of transport	Rail	Motor carrier	Private truck	Air	Water	Other	Unknown
TONS OF SHIPMENTS	(thousands of tons)								
U.S. TOTAL..........	3 322	100.0	22.4	65.1	10.6	.1	.1	1.5	.2
MIDDLE ATLANTIC.........	590	100.0	28.5	64.9	5.7	.2	.1	.4	.1
UNDER 100 MILES.......	47	100.0	1.1	78.1	19.5	-	-	1.3	-
100 TO 199 MILES......	48	100.0	-	89.6	10.1	.1	-	.3	-
200 TO 299 MILES.....	54	100.0	.7	93.9	4.5	.1	-	.8	-
300 TO 499 MILES.....	148	100.0	65.1	30.3	3.9	.1	.2	.1	.2
500 TO 999 MILES.....	129	100.0	19.8	72.2	7.5	.1	.2	.2	-
1000 TO 1499 MILES....	74	100.0	31.1	66.4	1.0	.5	.4	.6	-
1500 MILES OR OVER....	85	100.0	25.4	72.9	.6	.2	-	.3	.5
EAST NORTH CENTRAL......	1 418	100.0	19.3	68.1	9.5	.1	-	3.0	.1
UNDER 100 MILES.......	129	100.0	16.4	52.9	30.6	-	-	.2	-
100 TO 199 MILES......	153	100.0	3.1	71.3	24.8	-	-	.7	-
200 TO 299 MILES.....	235	100.0	7.3	82.7	9.9	-	-	.2	-
300 TO 499 MILES.....	299	100.0	19.4	79.9	.4	-	-	.2	-
500 TO 999 MILES.....	396	100.0	30.2	63.8	4.6	.2	-	1.2	-
1000 TO 1499 MILES....	89	100.0	14.0	43.5	10.3	-	-	32.2	-
1500 MILES OR OVER....	114	100.0	35.7	53.8	3.8	.1	-	5.8	.8
WEST NORTH CENTRAL......	174	100.0	16.3	75.4	4.0	.2	-	2.0	2.0
UNDER 100 MILES.......	3	100.0	-	87.3	11.8	-	-	.8	-
100 TO 199 MILES......	16	100.0	-	98.8	1.1	-	-	.1	-
200 TO 299 MILES.....	34	100.0	10.4	87.7	1.4	-	-	.5	-
300 TO 499 MILES.....	25	100.0	13.6	79.7	3.6	-	-	3.0	-
500 TO 999 MILES.....	62	100.0	17.1	65.9	8.1	.3	-	2.9	5.7
1000 TO 1499 MILES....	18	100.0	12.3	86.0	.1	.4	-	1.1	.1
1500 MILES OR OVER....	13	100.0	63.2	32.2	-	.8	.5	3.4	-
SOUTH ATLANTIC..........	99	100.0	13.2	65.0	21.2	.1	-	.5	-
UNDER 100 MILES.......	6	100.0	-	64.7	33.7	.1	-	1.5	-
100 TO 199 MILES......	33	100.0	23.1	61.1	14.9	-	-	.9	-
200 TO 299 MILES.....	22	100.0	6.3	64.1	29.3	-	-	.2	-
300 TO 499 MILES.....	10	100.0	36.2	45.6	17.6	-	-	.6	-
500 TO 999 MILES.....	13	100.0	-	65.8	33.8	.2	-	.2	-
1000 TO 1499 MILES....	5	100.0	-	100.0	-	-	-	-	-
1500 MILES OR OVER....	5	100.0	-	90.6	9.2	.2	-	-	-
EAST SOUTH CENTRAL......	590	100.0	38.6	56.1	5.2	.1	-	.1	-
UNDER 100 MILES.......	45	100.0	38.1	32.1	29.9	-	-	-	-
100 TO 199 MILES......	43	100.0	27.2	69.0	3.7	-	-	.1	-
200 TO 299 MILES.....	65	100.0	24.9	67.2	7.6	.2	-	-	-
300 TO 499 MILES.....	151	100.0	35.4	61.2	3.2	-	-	.1	-
500 TO 999 MILES.....	218	100.0	38.3	59.0	2.6	-	-	.1	-
1000 TO 1499 MILES....	13	100.0	50.3	49.5	-	-	-	.1	-
1500 MILES OR OVER....	52	100.0	73.0	26.7	-	.2	-	.1	-
WEST SOUTH CENTRAL......	277	100.0	4.9	55.0	40.0	.1	-	-	-
UNDER 100 MILES.......	29	100.0	-	29.6	70.3	-	-	-	-
100 TO 199 MILES......	17	100.0	-	81.9	18.1	-	-	-	-
200 TO 299 MILES.....	26	100.0	-	67.9	32.1	-	-	-	-
300 TO 499 MILES.....	38	100.0	-	36.1	63.9	-	-	-	-
500 TO 999 MILES.....	94	100.0	11.1	55.1	33.7	.1	-	-	-
1000 TO 1499 MILES....	61	100.0	3.9	59.2	36.7	-	-	.1	-
1500 MILES OR OVER....	9	100.0	5.6	94.3	-	.1	-	-	-
TON-MILES OF SHIPMENTS	(millions of ton-miles)								
U.S. TOTAL..........	2 146	100.0	26.0	63.5	7.0	.2	.4	2.7	.2
MIDDLE ATLANTIC..........	447	100.0	29.7	66.2	3.1	.3	.2	.3	.2
UNDER 100 MILES.......	2	100.0	1.2	76.6	21.0	.1	-	1.2	-
100 TO 199 MILES......	6	100.0	-	89.9	9.7	.1	-	.3	-
200 TO 299 MILES.....	13	100.0	.8	93.7	4.5	.1	-	.8	-
300 TO 499 MILES.....	52	100.0	61.7	33.3	4.3	.1	.2	.1	.2
500 TO 999 MILES.....	100	100.0	22.1	69.3	8.0	.1	.3	.2	-
1000 TO 1499 MILES....	93	100.0	31.7	66.1	.8	.4	.3	.6	-
1500 MILES OR OVER....	178	100.0	27.4	70.9	.6	.3	-	.3	.5
EAST NORTH CENTRAL......	803	100.0	24.1	63.2	5.9	.1	-	6.5	.2
UNDER 100 MILES.......	7	100.0	13.5	58.8	27.6	-	-	.1	-
100 TO 199 MILES......	22	100.0	3.3	74.0	21.9	.1	-	.7	-
200 TO 299 MILES.....	60	100.0	6.9	83.1	9.8	-	-	.2	-
300 TO 499 MILES.....	118	100.0	21.1	78.2	.5	-	-	.2	-
500 TO 999 MILES.....	263	100.0	28.7	64.1	5.6	.2	-	1.4	-
1000 TO 1499 MILES....	106	100.0	13.8	42.8	10.0	-	-	33.4	-
1500 MILES OR OVER....	224	100.0	32.1	57.5	3.9	.1	-	5.7	.8
WEST NORTH CENTRAL......	110	100.0	24.5	67.3	3.4	.4	.2	2.4	1.8
UNDER 100 MILES.......	-	100.0	-	86.0	13.3	-	-	.7	-
100 TO 199 MILES......	2	100.0	-	98.8	1.1	-	-	.1	-
200 TO 299 MILES.....	8	100.0	10.9	87.3	1.3	-	-	.5	-
300 TO 499 MILES.....	10	100.0	15.5	78.0	3.5	-	-	2.9	-
500 TO 999 MILES.....	46	100.0	18.3	67.4	6.9	.3	-	2.9	4.2
1000 TO 1499 MILES....	21	100.0	13.2	85.0	.1	.5	-	1.1	.1
1500 MILES OR OVER....	21	100.0	62.5	31.9	-	.9	1.2	3.4	-

See footnotes at end of table 4.

TABLE 1. **TCC GROUP 358**—Percent Distribution of Geographic Division of Origin and Distance Shipped, by Means of Transport: 1972—Continued

Geographic division of origin[1] and distance shipped[2]	Number	Percent distribution by means of transport							
		All means of transport	Rail	Motor carrier	Private truck	Air	Water	Other	Unknown
TON-MILES OF SHIPMENTS	(millions of ton-miles)								
SOUTH ATLANTIC	42	100.0	7.4	74.4	17.8	.1	-	.3	-
UNDER 100 MILES	-	100.0	-	71.2	27.2	-	-	1.5	-
100 TO 199 MILES	5	100.0	24.9	59.4	14.9	-	-	.8	-
200 TO 299 MILES	5	100.0	7.0	63.5	29.3	-	-	.2	-
300 TO 499 MILES	4	100.0	33.9	46.7	18.8	-	-	.6	-
500 TO 999 MILES	10	100.0	-	69.2	30.3	.3	-	.2	-
1000 TO 1499 MILES	6	100.0	-	100.0	-	-	-	-	-
1500 MILES OR OVER	10	100.0	-	88.8	10.9	.2	-	.1	-
EAST SOUTH CENTRAL	353	100.0	45.8	52.0	2.0	.1	-	.1	-
UNDER 100 MILES	2	100.0	38.9	29.9	31.2	-	-	-	-
100 TO 199 MILES	6	100.0	29.4	66.1	4.4	-	-	.1	-
200 TO 299 MILES	16	100.0	24.0	67.5	8.2	.2	-	-	-
300 TO 499 MILES	58	100.0	32.6	64.4	2.8	-	-	.1	-
500 TO 999 MILES	155	100.0	37.9	60.0	2.0	-	-	-	-
1000 TO 1499 MILES	17	100.0	52.2	47.6	-	-	-	.1	.3
1500 MILES OR OVER	96	100.0	70.4	29.2	-	.2	-	.1	-
WEST SOUTH CENTRAL	195	100.0	6.2	59.3	34.4	.1	-	.1	-
UNDER 100 MILES	1	100.0	-	32.6	67.4	-	-	-	-
100 TO 199 MILES	3	100.0	-	81.8	18.2	-	-	-	-
200 TO 299 MILES	6	100.0	-	68.7	31.3	-	-	-	-
300 TO 499 MILES	16	100.0	-	35.2	64.8	-	-	-	-
500 TO 999 MILES	74	100.0	11.4	56.3	32.1	.1	-	-	-
1000 TO 1499 MILES	76	100.0	3.6	58.4	37.9	-	-	.1	-
1500 MILES OR OVER	16	100.0	5.2	94.7	-	.1	-	-	-

See footnotes at end of table 4.

TABLE 2. **TCC GROUP 358**—Percent Distribution of Geographic Division of Origin and Means of Transport, by Geographic Division of Destination: 1972

Geographic division of origin[1] and means of transport	Number	Percent distribution by division of destination									
		U.S. total	New England	Middle Atlantic	East North Central	West North Central	South Atlantic	East South Central	West South Central	Mountain	Pacific
TONS OF SHIPMENTS	(thousands of tons)										
U.S. TOTAL	3 322	100.0	2.8	18.1	22.1	8.0	14.5	8.9	12.9	4.4	8.3
RAIL	744	100.0	2.2	28.9	13.6	5.6	18.3	6.7	6.9	4.9	12.7
MOTOR CARRIER	2 163	100.0	3.3	16.2	23.4	9.9	14.2	9.1	12.3	4.7	6.9
PRIVATE TRUCK	353	100.0	1.2	8.6	35.5	2.4	10.3	14.0	20.4	1.8	5.7
AIR	3	100.0	1.1	20.1	12.2	21.2	11.8	2.3	9.0	5.1	17.2
WATER	3	100.0	-	1.2	8.7	-	16.5	-	-	-	73.6
OTHER	49	100.0	1.4	5.0	4.6	1.8	3.9	.8	67.2	.6	14.6
UNKNOWN	5	100.0	.1	7.6	.6	-	.2	.1	65.5	6.7	19.3
MIDDLE ATLANTIC	590	100.0	4.7	35.2	12.0	3.2	14.8	5.5	9.7	7.8	7.2
RAIL	168	100.0	-	54.8	3.8	-	14.5	6.8	2.8	6.2	11.0
MOTOR CARRIER	383	100.0	6.7	26.7	15.3	4.6	13.0	5.0	13.6	9.0	6.1
PRIVATE TRUCK	33	100.0	5.4	34.2	15.1	2.6	35.8	5.2	-	.7	.9
AIR	-	100.0	1.4	10.4	11.2	39.7	15.0	.1	1.1	1.7	19.3
WATER	-	100.0	-	-	34.8	-	65.2	-	-	-	-
OTHER	2	100.0	13.5	39.0	10.2	3.7	6.2	-	16.4	9.6	.4
UNKNOWN	-	100.0	-	43.4	1.0	-	.2	.9	-	43.4	12.2
EAST NORTH CENTRAL	1 418	100.0	1.4	16.7	31.8	9.6	12.4	8.8	9.7	2.3	7.2
RAIL	274	100.0	1.2	28.6	13.4	10.4	18.0	7.2	5.0	3.7	12.5
MOTOR CARRIER	965	100.0	1.7	15.8	32.8	10.9	13.0	10.6	7.1	2.4	5.8
PRIVATE TRUCK	134	100.0	-	3.6	72.4	1.5	.5	2.2	16.5	-	3.2
AIR	1	100.0	2.2	40.2	7.2	18.6	5.3	3.9	11.3	.6	10.7
WATER	-	100.0	-	-	-	-	100.0	-	-	-	-
OTHER	42	100.0	.3	1.8	3.1	1.3	1.6	.5	75.7	.1	15.6
UNKNOWN	-	100.0	-	-	2.7	-	.1	.7	-	-	96.5
WEST NORTH CENTRAL	174	100.0	4.2	17.3	15.5	29.2	6.9	4.2	11.5	2.7	8.5
RAIL	28	100.0	.8	32.2	1.0	12.3	5.9	1.8	12.9	1.1	31.8
MOTOR CARRIER	131	100.0	5.2	15.4	18.8	35.3	7.0	5.0	6.4	3.0	3.9
PRIVATE TRUCK	7	100.0	-	-	18.1	11.7	5.2	.7	59.3	4.7	.3
AIR	-	100.0	-	21.9	2.7	.2	20.6	6.9	1.6	18.5	27.5
WATER	-	100.0	-	-	-	-	-	-	-	-	100.0
OTHER	3	100.0	6.4	19.8	19.4	6.8	19.7	2.9	10.6	1.0	13.4
UNKNOWN	3	100.0	-	1.4	-	-	.2	.7	98.4	-	-
SOUTH ATLANTIC	99	100.0	8.6	31.8	2.0	2.4	33.6	7.0	9.0	3.6	2.1
RAIL	13	100.0	41.1	58.9	-	-	-	-	-	-	-
MOTOR CARRIER	64	100.0	4.5	35.7	1.8	3.0	31.6	2.3	13.4	5.5	2.4
PRIVATE TRUCK	21	100.0	1.5	3.7	3.9	2.1	59.6	25.6	1.2	-	2.4
AIR	-	100.0	-	5.9	6.5	20.0	40.1	14.2	-	-	13.3
WATER	-	100.0	-	-	-	-	-	-	-	-	-
OTHER	-	100.0	.3	6.1	2.1	.1	80.6	6.5	3.8	.3	.2
UNKNOWN	-	100.0	-	-	-	-	.2	-	-	-	-

See footnotes at end of table 4.

TABLE 2. TCC GROUP 358—Percent Distribution of Geographic Division of Origin and Means of Transport, by Geographic Division of Destination: 1972—Continued

Geographic division of origin[1] and means of transport	Number	Percent distribution by division of destination									
		U.S. total	New England	Middle Atlantic	East North Central	West North Central	South Atlantic	East South Central	West South Central	Mountain	Pacific
TONS OF SHIPMENTS	(thousands of tons)										
EAST SOUTH CENTRAL......	590	100.0	3.7	10.7	22.9	7.1	17.5	13.9	13.3	3.3	7.6
RAIL.................	227	100.0	3.4	12.2	25.6	4.3	17.5	8.1	9.2	6.1	13.7
MOTOR CARRIER........	331	100.0	4.2	10.6	21.6	9.6	18.9	14.2	15.2	1.7	4.1
PRIVATE TRUCK........	30	100.0	-	-	18.2	-	2.4	55.3	24.1	-	-
AIR.................	-	100.0	.5	-	12.0	36.4	24.5	-	-	-	26.5
WATER...............	-	100.0	-	-	-	-	-	-	-	-	-
OTHER...............	-	100.0	1.8	4.8	10.1	8.3	7.9	4.2	43.2	2.8	16.8
UNKNOWN.............	-	100.0	46.0	-	-	-	-	-	-	-	54.0
WEST SOUTH CENTRAL......	277	100.0	2.1	7.7	8.6	3.6	18.9	14.3	29.8	7.3	7.8
RAIL.................	13	100.0	-	-	-	-	90.0	-	-	-	10.0
MOTOR CARRIER........	152	100.0	2.3	5.2	5.4	3.7	19.9	11.5	29.5	10.3	12.3
PRIVATE TRUCK........	111	100.0	2.0	11.9	14.0	3.9	8.9	20.0	33.8	4.2	1.3
AIR.................	-	100.0	-	9.2	81.0	-	-	-	1.5	1.1	7.1
WATER...............	-	100.0	-	-	-	-	-	-	-	-	-
OTHER...............	-	100.0	-	81.4	-	-	-	6.7	1.9	-	10.0
UNKNOWN.............	-	100.0	-	-	-	-	-	-	-	-	-
TON-MILES OF SHIPMENTS	(millions of ton-miles)										
U.S. TOTAL..............	2 146	100.0	3.0	13.7	10.9	5.9	14.8	5.1	15.7	8.8	22.2
RAIL.................	558	100.0	2.1	17.8	4.5	4.1	19.4	3.5	7.2	9.3	32.1
MOTOR CARRIER........	1 363	100.0	3.5	12.6	13.1	7.2	13.8	5.3	16.1	9.5	18.9
PRIVATE TRUCK........	151	100.0	2.5	14.2	19.3	3.5	12.3	11.2	23.5	3.3	10.2
AIR.................	3	100.0	.7	14.3	8.4	14.7	8.1	1.1	9.8	5.8	37.0
WATER...............	7	100.0	-	.1	1.5	-	7.3	-	-	-	91.2
OTHER...............	57	100.0	.7	2.2	1.1	.5	2.1	.3	68.0	1.0	24.0
UNKNOWN.............	4	100.0	.1	3.5	.1	-	.1	.1	41.2	12.0	42.9
MIDDLE ATLANTIC.........	447	100.0	1.7	10.6	8.6	3.8	13.2	5.3	16.5	18.0	22.3
RAIL.................	133	100.0	-	22.7	2.2	-	18.8	7.0	4.7	12.1	32.5
MOTOR CARRIER........	295	100.0	2.3	5.4	11.2	5.2	8.7	4.5	22.7	21.3	18.6
PRIVATE TRUCK........	13	100.0	3.4	8.3	13.6	5.9	51.7	9.5	-	2.7	4.9
AIR.................	1	100.0	.5	1.9	6.4	32.6	8.4	.1	1.1	2.7	46.3
WATER...............	-	100.0	-	-	17.1	-	82.9	-	-	-	-
OTHER...............	1	100.0	4.1	7.8	8.7	5.2	6.3	.9	33.6	32.0	1.4
UNKNOWN.............	-	100.0	-	12.7	.3	-	-	-	-	59.9	27.2
EAST NORTH CENTRAL......	803	100.0	1.8	15.3	10.3	7.9	11.9	5.3	16.5	5.4	25.7
RAIL.................	193	100.0	1.2	21.1	2.5	8.5	15.8	4.5	6.4	7.6	32.4
MOTOR CARRIER........	507	100.0	2.4	15.6	13.0	9.0	12.6	6.4	11.7	5.6	23.7
PRIVATE TRUCK........	47	100.0	-	4.6	25.4	1.6	.5	2.3	47.3	-	18.2
AIR.................	-	100.0	2.1	33.6	2.0	14.0	4.0	3.0	14.1	.9	26.3
WATER...............	-	100.0	-	-	-	-	100.0	-	-	-	-
OTHER...............	52	100.0	.2	.9	.5	.2	1.0	.2	72.6	.1	24.3
UNKNOWN.............	1	100.0	-	-	.2	-	-	.2	-	-	99.6
WEST NORTH CENTRAL......	110	100.0	7.3	22.9	8.7	11.5	9.4	2.8	12.5	3.7	21.2
RAIL.................	27	100.0	.9	28.2	.3	3.6	4.2	.5	8.2	1.5	52.7
MOTOR CARRIER........	74	100.0	10.2	22.9	11.8	15.4	11.3	3.9	9.1	4.5	10.7
PRIVATE TRUCK........	3	100.0	-	-	11.5	4.7	6.6	.3	69.8	6.2	.8
AIR.................	-	100.0	-	14.5	.8	-	14.4	3.2	1.3	21.3	44.5
WATER...............	-	100.0	-	-	-	-	-	-	-	-	100.0
OTHER...............	2	100.0	8.3	21.1	9.9	3.1	18.3	2.0	8.0	1.0	28.4
UNKNOWN.............	1	100.0	-	2.4	-	-	.3	-	97.4	-	-
SOUTH ATLANTIC..........	42	100.0	7.0	16.1	2.4	4.5	21.3	3.8	20.8	13.4	10.6
RAIL.................	3	100.0	56.9	43.1	-	-	-	-	-	-	-
MOTOR CARRIER........	31	100.0	2.8	15.6	1.9	4.8	17.1	1.8	27.4	18.0	10.7
PRIVATE TRUCK........	7	100.0	3.6	7.3	5.7	5.1	47.1	14.1	2.4	-	14.8
AIR.................	-	100.0	-	6.6	2.1	25.5	23.9	2.7	-	-	39.3
WATER...............	-	100.0	-	-	-	-	-	-	-	-	-
OTHER...............	-	100.0	.5	8.8	3.7	.3	57.9	10.2	13.9	2.9	1.9
UNKNOWN.............	-	100.0	-	-	-	-	-	-	-	-	-
EAST SOUTH CENTRAL......	353	100.0	5.6	12.2	11.5	5.6	16.7	3.3	13.4	7.7	24.0
RAIL.................	161	100.0	4.6	11.9	10.6	3.3	12.9	.9	8.3	12.2	35.4
MOTOR CARRIER........	183	100.0	6.7	13.0	11.9	7.8	20.7	4.6	16.4	4.0	14.9
PRIVATE TRUCK........	7	100.0	-	-	22.8	-	2.9	22.9	51.3	-	-
AIR.................	-	100.0	.8	-	4.3	11.5	21.5	-	-	-	61.9
WATER...............	-	100.0	-	-	-	-	-	-	-	-	-
OTHER...............	-	100.0	2.2	4.1	3.4	4.6	5.4	1.8	25.4	5.8	47.3
UNKNOWN.............	-	100.0	17.4	-	-	-	-	-	-	-	82.6
WEST SOUTH CENTRAL......	195	100.0	4.1	14.1	9.8	3.2	24.0	11.0	8.3	9.1	16.5
RAIL.................	12	100.0	-	-	-	-	84.2	-	-	-	15.8
MOTOR CARRIER........	116	100.0	4.2	8.5	5.5	2.7	25.9	8.4	8.5	11.8	24.4
PRIVATE TRUCK........	67	100.0	4.6	26.1	18.8	4.6	9.9	17.6	9.5	6.0	3.0
AIR.................	-	100.0	-	13.4	71.8	-	-	-	.2	1.4	13.3
WATER...............	-	100.0	-	-	-	-	-	-	-	-	-
OTHER...............	-	100.0	-	85.4	-	-	-	-	2.8	.5	11.3
UNKNOWN.............	-	100.0	-	-	-	-	-	-	-	-	-

See footnotes at end of table 4.

TABLE 3. **TCC GROUP 358**—Percent Distribution of Geographic Division of Destination and Means of Transport, by Geographic Division of Origin: 1972

Geographic division of destination and means of transport	Number (thousands of tons)	Percent distribution by division of origin[1]									
		U.S. total	New England	Middle Atlantic	East North Central	West North Central	South Atlantic	East South Central	West South Central	Mountain	Pacific
TONS OF SHIPMENTS											
U.S. TOTAL...............	3 322	100.0	(D)	17.8	42.7	5.3	3.0	17.8	8.3	(D)	(D)
RAIL.................	744	100.0	(D)	22.6	36.8	3.8	1.8	30.6	1.8	(D)	(D)
MOTOR CARRIER.........	2 163	100.0	(D)	17.7	44.6	6.1	3.0	15.3	7.1	(D)	(D)
PRIVATE TRUCK.........	353	100.0	(D)	9.5	38.0	2.0	6.0	8.7	31.5	(D)	(D)
AIR..................	3	100.0	(D)	28.0	31.3	10.6	2.0	10.4	4.1	(D)	(D)
WATER................	3	100.0	(D)	25.1	.1	1.9	-	-	-	(D)	(D)
OTHER................	49	100.0	(D)	4.7	86.2	6.9	1.1	.8	.2	(D)	(D)
UNKNOWN..............	5	100.0	(D)	15.4	17.9	66.5	-	.2	-	(D)	(D)
NEW ENGLAND..............	92	100.0	(D)	29.8	21.6	7.9	9.2	23.3	6.2	(D)	(D)
RAIL.................	16	100.0	(D)	-	19.7	1.4	32.5	46.4	-	(D)	(D)
MOTOR CARRIER.........	71	100.0	(D)	35.9	23.3	9.7	4.0	19.5	5.0	(D)	(D)
PRIVATE TRUCK.........	4	100.0	(D)	42.0	-	-	7.2	-	50.4	(D)	(D)
AIR..................	-	100.0	(D)	34.3	60.5	-	-	4.9	-	(D)	(D)
WATER................	-	100.0	(D)	-	-	-	-	-	-	(D)	(D)
OTHER................	-	100.0	(D)	45.7	20.8	32.3	.2	1.1	-	(D)	(D)
UNKNOWN..............	-	100.0	(D)	-	-	-	-	100.0	-	(D)	(D)
MIDDLE ATLANTIC..........	600	100.0	(D)	34.5	39.5	5.0	5.3	10.5	3.6	(D)	(D)
RAIL.................	215	100.0	(D)	42.8	36.4	4.3	3.6	12.9	-	(D)	(D)
MOTOR CARRIER.........	351	100.0	(D)	29.1	43.4	5.8	6.6	10.0	2.3	(D)	(D)
PRIVATE TRUCK.........	30	100.0	(D)	37.8	15.9	-	2.5	-	43.8	(D)	(D)
AIR..................	-	100.0	(D)	14.5	62.6	11.5	.6	-	1.9	(D)	(D)
WATER................	-	100.0	(D)	-	-	-	-	-	-	(D)	(D)
OTHER................	2	100.0	(D)	36.2	30.7	27.3	1.3	.8	3.3	(D)	(D)
UNKNOWN..............	-	100.0	(D)	87.8	.1	12.2	-	-	-	(D)	(D)
EAST NORTH CENTRAL.......	735	100.0	(D)	9.6	61.4	3.7	.3	18.4	3.2	(D)	(D)
RAIL.................	101	100.0	(D)	6.3	36.0	.3	-	57.3	3.2	(D)	(D)
MOTOR CARRIER.........	505	100.0	(D)	11.6	62.6	4.9	.2	14.1	1.6	(D)	(D)
PRIVATE TRUCK.........	125	100.0	(D)	4.0	77.5	1.0	.7	4.5	12.4	(D)	(D)
AIR..................	-	100.0	(D)	25.8	18.4	2.3	1.1	10.3	27.5	(D)	(D)
WATER................	-	100.0	(D)	100.0	-	-	-	-	-	(D)	(D)
OTHER................	2	100.0	(D)	10.2	58.1	29.1	.5	1.8	-	(D)	(D)
UNKNOWN..............	-	100.0	(D)	23.6	76.4	-	-	-	-	(D)	(D)
WEST NORTH CENTRAL.......	266	100.0	(D)	7.2	51.3	19.2	.9	15.7	3.7	(D)	(D)
RAIL.................	41	100.0	(D)	-	68.0	8.4	-	23.6	-	(D)	(D)
MOTOR CARRIER.........	213	100.0	(D)	8.3	49.2	21.8	.9	14.9	2.6	(D)	(D)
PRIVATE TRUCK.........	8	100.0	(D)	10.4	24.3	9.7	5.1	-	50.4	(D)	(D)
AIR..................	-	100.0	(D)	52.6	27.5	.1	1.9	17.9	-	(D)	(D)
WATER................	-	100.0	(D)	-	-	-	-	-	-	(D)	(D)
OTHER................	-	100.0	(D)	9.5	60.8	25.9	-	3.8	-	(D)	(D)
UNKNOWN..............	-	100.0	(D)	-	-	-	-	-	-	(D)	(D)
SOUTH ATLANTIC...........	482	100.0	(D)	18.1	36.5	2.5	6.9	21.4	10.9	(D)	(D)
RAIL.................	136	100.0	(D)	17.9	36.3	1.2	-	29.2	8.9	(D)	(D)
MOTOR CARRIER.........	306	100.0	(D)	16.3	40.9	3.0	6.7	20.4	9.9	(D)	(D)
PRIVATE TRUCK.........	36	100.0	(D)	32.9	1.8	1.0	34.5	2.0	27.2	(D)	(D)
AIR..................	-	100.0	(D)	35.6	14.0	18.4	6.8	21.6	-	(D)	(D)
WATER................	-	100.0	(D)	99.3	.7	-	-	-	-	(D)	(D)
OTHER................	1	100.0	(D)	7.4	34.1	34.8	21.9	1.7	-	(D)	(D)
UNKNOWN..............	-	100.0	(D)	-	9.4	90.6	-	-	-	(D)	(D)
EAST SOUTH CENTRAL.......	296	100.0	(D)	11.0	42.1	2.5	2.3	27.8	13.4	(D)	(D)
RAIL.................	50	100.0	(D)	22.8	39.5	1.0	-	36.7	-	(D)	(D)
MOTOR CARRIER.........	196	100.0	(D)	9.8	51.8	3.4	.8	23.9	8.9	(D)	(D)
PRIVATE TRUCK.........	49	100.0	(D)	3.5	5.9	.1	10.9	34.4	45.1	(D)	(D)
AIR..................	-	100.0	(D)	1.7	53.5	32.4	12.5	-	-	(D)	(D)
WATER................	-	100.0	(D)	-	-	-	-	-	-	(D)	(D)
OTHER................	-	100.0	(D)	5.3	53.2	26.1	9.1	4.6	1.8	(D)	(D)
UNKNOWN..............	-	100.0	(D)	-	100.0	-	-	-	-	(D)	(D)
WEST SOUTH CENTRAL.......	427	100.0	(D)	13.4	32.1	4.7	2.1	18.4	19.3	(D)	(D)
RAIL.................	51	100.0	(D)	9.3	26.6	7.1	-	40.6	-	(D)	(D)
MOTOR CARRIER.........	266	100.0	(D)	19.6	25.8	3.2	3.2	18.8	16.9	(D)	(D)
PRIVATE TRUCK.........	72	100.0	(D)	-	30.8	5.8	.4	10.3	52.2	(D)	(D)
AIR..................	-	100.0	(D)	3.3	39.2	1.9	-	-	.7	(D)	(D)
WATER................	-	100.0	(D)	-	-	-	-	-	-	(D)	(D)
OTHER................	33	100.0	(D)	1.1	97.1	1.1	.1	.5	-	(D)	(D)
UNKNOWN..............	3	100.0	(D)	-	-	100.0	-	-	-	(D)	(D)
MOUNTAIN.................	145	100.0	(D)	31.4	22.7	3.3	2.4	13.3	14.0	(D)	(D)
RAIL.................	36	100.0	(D)	28.7	27.5	.9	-	37.8	-	(D)	(D)
MOTOR CARRIER.........	101	100.0	(D)	33.8	22.6	3.9	3.5	5.4	15.4	(D)	(D)
PRIVATE TRUCK.........	6	100.0	(D)	3.8	-	5.2	-	-	72.0	(D)	(D)
AIR..................	-	100.0	(D)	9.6	3.7	38.7	-	-	.9	(D)	(D)
WATER................	-	100.0	(D)	-	-	-	-	-	-	(D)	(D)
OTHER................	-	100.0	(D)	69.6	15.7	10.2	.5	3.7	-	(D)	(D)
UNKNOWN..............	-	100.0	(D)	100.0	-	-	-	-	-	(D)	(D)
PACIFIC..................	275	100.0	(D)	15.4	37.0	5.4	.7	16.3	7.8	(D)	(D)
RAIL.................	94	100.0	(D)	19.6	36.3	9.6	-	33.1	1.4	(D)	(D)
MOTOR CARRIER.........	149	100.0	(D)	15.5	37.3	3.5	1.0	9.0	12.5	(D)	(D)
PRIVATE TRUCK.........	20	100.0	(D)	1.4	21.5	.1	2.5	-	7.2	(D)	(D)
AIR..................	-	100.0	(D)	31.5	19.6	17.0	1.5	16.1	1.7	(D)	(D)
WATER................	2	100.0	(D)	-	-	2.6	-	-	-	(D)	(D)
OTHER................	7	100.0	(D)	.1	91.9	6.3	-	1.0	.1	(D)	(D)
UNKNOWN..............	1	100.0	(D)	9.7	89.8	-	-	.4	-	(D)	(D)

See footnotes at end of table 4.

TABLE 3. **TCC GROUP 358—Percent Distribution of Geographic Division of Destination and Means of Transport, by Geographic Division of Origin: 1972**—Continued

Geographic division of destination and means of transport	Number	Percent distribution by division of origin[1]									
		U.S. total	New England	Middle Atlantic	East North Central	West North Central	South Atlantic	East South Central	West South Central	Mountain	Pacific
TON-MILES OF SHIPMENTS	(millions of ton-miles)										
U.S. TOTAL.............	2 146	100.0	(D)	20.8	37.5	5.2	2.0	16.5	9.1	(D)	(D)
RAIL..................	558	100.0	(D)	23.8	34.7	4.9	.6	29.0	2.2	(D)	(D)
MOTOR CARRIER.........	1 363	100.0	(D)	21.7	37.2	5.5	2.3	13.5	8.5	(D)	(D)
PRIVATE TRUCK.........	151	100.0	(D)	9.2	31.4	2.5	5.0	4.7	44.6	(D)	(D)
AIR...................	3	100.0	(D)	31.5	22.8	11.5	1.4	7.8	3.4	(D)	(D)
WATER.................	7	100.0	(D)	8.7	-	3.3	-	-	-	(D)	(D)
OTHER.................	57	100.0	(D)	2.6	91.8	4.6	.2	.5	.2	(D)	(D)
UNKNOWN...............	4	100.0	(D)	20.0	37.2	42.3	-	-	-	(D)	(D)
NEW ENGLAND............	63	100.0	(D)	11.6	22.7	12.6	4.7	31.0	12.6	(D)	(D)
RAIL..................	11	100.0	(D)	-	20.2	2.0	15.4	62.5	-	(D)	(D)
MOTOR CARRIER.........	47	100.0	(D)	14.3	25.1	15.9	1.9	26.0	10.3	(D)	(D)
PRIVATE TRUCK.........	3	100.0	(D)	12.5	-	-	7.2	-	80.3	(D)	(D)
AIR...................	-	100.0	(D)	21.3	68.7	-	-	9.0	-	(D)	(D)
WATER.................	-	100.0	(D)	-	-	-	-	-	-	(D)	(D)
OTHER.................	-	100.0	(D)	15.0	30.1	53.2	.1	1.5	-	(D)	(D)
UNKNOWN...............	-	100.0	(D)	-	-	-	-	100.0	-	(D)	(D)
MIDDLE ATLANTIC.........	293	100.0	(D)	16.2	41.8	8.7	2.4	14.7	9.4	(D)	(D)
RAIL..................	99	100.0	(D)	30.4	41.1	7.7	1.4	19.4	-	(D)	(D)
MOTOR CARRIER.........	171	100.0	(D)	9.3	46.2	10.0	2.9	14.0	5.7	(D)	(D)
PRIVATE TRUCK.........	21	100.0	(D)	5.4	10.1	-	2.6	-	81.9	(D)	(D)
AIR...................	-	100.0	(D)	4.1	53.6	11.7	.7	-	3.2	(D)	(D)
WATER.................	-	100.0	(D)	-	-	-	-	-	-	(D)	(D)
OTHER.................	1	100.0	(D)	9.2	37.2	43.7	.8	.9	6.8	(D)	(D)
UNKNOWN...............	-	100.0	(D)	71.5	.1	28.4	-	-	-	(D)	(D)
EAST NORTH CENTRAL......	233	100.0	(D)	16.5	35.5	4.1	.4	17.4	8.2	(D)	(D)
RAIL..................	25	100.0	(D)	11.8	19.0	.4	-	68.9	-	(D)	(D)
MOTOR CARRIER.........	178	100.0	(D)	18.7	36.9	4.9	.3	12.3	3.6	(D)	(D)
PRIVATE TRUCK.........	29	100.0	(D)	6.5	41.4	1.5	1.5	5.6	43.4	(D)	(D)
AIR...................	-	100.0	(D)	24.0	5.4	1.1	.4	4.0	28.6	(D)	(D)
WATER.................	-	100.0	(D)	100.0	-	-	-	-	-	(D)	(D)
OTHER.................	-	100.0	(D)	20.1	36.4	39.9	.6	1.5	-	(D)	(D)
UNKNOWN...............	-	100.0	(D)	44.3	55.7	-	-	-	-	(D)	(D)
WEST NORTH CENTRAL......	127	100.0	(D)	13.2	49.7	10.0	1.5	15.5	4.9	(D)	(D)
RAIL..................	22	100.0	(D)	-	72.3	4.3	-	23.4	-	(D)	(D)
MOTOR CARRIER.........	98	100.0	(D)	15.7	46.5	11.7	1.5	14.6	3.2	(D)	(D)
PRIVATE TRUCK.........	5	100.0	(D)	15.9	14.4	3.4	7.4	-	59.0	(D)	(D)
AIR...................	-	100.0	(D)	69.7	21.7	-	2.4	6.1	-	(D)	(D)
WATER.................	-	100.0	(D)	-	-	-	-	-	-	(D)	(D)
OTHER.................	-	100.0	(D)	26.7	41.3	27.4	.1	4.5	-	(D)	(D)
UNKNOWN...............	-	100.0	(D)	-	-	-	-	-	-	(D)	(D)
SOUTH ATLANTIC..........	317	100.0	(D)	18.5	30.1	3.3	2.9	18.6	14.8	(D)	(D)
RAIL..................	108	100.0	(D)	23.1	28.3	1.1	-	19.2	9.4	(D)	(D)
MOTOR CARRIER.........	188	100.0	(D)	13.7	34.0	4.5	2.9	20.2	16.0	(D)	(D)
PRIVATE TRUCK.........	18	100.0	(D)	38.8	1.3	1.3	19.3	1.1	35.7	(D)	(D)
AIR...................	-	100.0	(D)	32.5	11.3	20.5	4.2	20.8	-	(D)	(D)
WATER.................	-	100.0	(D)	99.5	.5	-	-	-	-	(D)	(D)
OTHER.................	1	100.0	(D)	8.1	44.1	41.0	5.4	1.3	-	(D)	(D)
UNKNOWN...............	-	100.0	(D)	-	8.1	91.9	-	-	-	(D)	(D)
EAST SOUTH CENTRAL......	108	100.0	(D)	22.0	39.1	2.9	1.5	10.6	19.8	(D)	(D)
RAIL..................	19	100.0	(D)	47.6	44.7	.7	-	7.1	-	(D)	(D)
MOTOR CARRIER.........	71	100.0	(D)	18.4	45.3	4.1	.8	11.8	13.5	(D)	(D)
PRIVATE TRUCK.........	16	100.0	(D)	7.8	6.6	.1	6.3	9.6	69.7	(D)	(D)
AIR...................	-	100.0	(D)	2.2	61.3	33.1	3.4	-	-	(D)	(D)
WATER.................	-	100.0	(D)	-	-	-	-	-	-	(D)	(D)
OTHER.................	-	100.0	(D)	8.5	48.0	31.8	6.8	3.2	1.7	(D)	(D)
UNKNOWN...............	-	100.0	(D)	-	100.0	-	-	-	-	(D)	(D)
WEST SOUTH CENTRAL......	336	100.0	(D)	22.0	39.4	4.1	2.7	14.0	4.8	(D)	(D)
RAIL..................	40	100.0	(D)	15.5	30.7	5.6	-	33.2	-	(D)	(D)
MOTOR CARRIER.........	219	100.0	(D)	30.6	27.1	3.1	4.0	13.7	4.5	(D)	(D)
PRIVATE TRUCK.........	35	100.0	(D)	-	63.3	7.4	.5	10.3	18.0	(D)	(D)
AIR...................	-	100.0	(D)	3.5	32.8	1.6	-	-	.1	(D)	(D)
WATER.................	-	100.0	(D)	-	-	-	-	-	-	(D)	(D)
OTHER.................	38	100.0	(D)	1.3	97.9	.5	-	.2	-	(D)	(D)
UNKNOWN...............	1	100.0	(D)	-	-	100.0	-	-	-	(D)	(D)
MOUNTAIN................	188	100.0	(D)	42.9	23.0	2.2	3.0	14.5	9.4	(D)	(D)
RAIL..................	51	100.0	(D)	31.1	28.3	.8	-	38.3	-	(D)	(D)
MOTOR CARRIER.........	129	100.0	(D)	48.6	22.0	2.6	4.4	5.7	10.6	(D)	(D)
PRIVATE TRUCK.........	5	100.0	(D)	7.5	-	4.7	-	-	80.6	(D)	(D)
AIR...................	-	100.0	(D)	14.6	3.6	42.1	-	-	.8	(D)	(D)
WATER.................	-	100.0	(D)	-	-	-	-	-	-	(D)	(D)
OTHER.................	-	100.0	(D)	81.5	10.6	4.5	.5	2.8	-	(D)	(D)
UNKNOWN...............	-	100.0	(D)	100.0	-	-	-	-	-	(D)	(D)
PACIFIC.................	476	100.0	(D)	20.9	43.3	4.9	1.0	17.8	6.8	(D)	(D)
RAIL..................	179	100.0	(D)	24.1	34.9	8.0	-	31.9	1.1	(D)	(D)
MOTOR CARRIER.........	257	100.0	(D)	21.4	46.7	3.1	1.3	10.6	11.0	(D)	(D)
PRIVATE TRUCK.........	15	100.0	(D)	4.5	56.4	.2	7.3	-	13.2	(D)	(D)
AIR...................	1	100.0	(D)	39.4	16.2	13.9	1.5	13.1	1.2	(D)	(D)
WATER.................	7	100.0	(D)	-	-	3.7	-	-	-	(D)	(D)
OTHER.................	13	100.0	(D)	.2	93.2	5.5	-	1.0	.1	(D)	(D)
UNKNOWN...............	1	100.0	(D)	12.7	86.3	-	-	1.0	-	(D)	(D)

See footnotes at end of table 4.

TABLE 4. **TCC GROUP 358—Percent Distribution of Distance Shipped and Weight of Shipment, by Means of Transport: 1972**

Distance shipped and weight of shipment[2][3]	Number	Percent distribution by means of transport							
		All means of transport	Rail	Motor carrier	Private truck	Air	Water	Other	Unknown
TONS OF SHIPMENTS	(thousands of tons)								
U.S. TOTAL.........	3 212	100.0	22.3	66.0	9.9	.1	.1	1.5	.2
UNDER 100 MILES.........	259	100.0	15.0	53.5	31.2	-	-	.4	-
UNDER 1000 POUNDS.....	18	100.0	-	70.4	26.1	.1	-	3.4	-
1000 TO 9999 POUNDS...	76	100.0	-	68.8	30.8	-	-	.4	-
10000 TO 29999 POUNDS.	88	100.0	20.4	37.7	41.9	-	-	-	-
30000 TO 59999 POUNDS.	75	100.0	27.7	52.1	20.2	-	-	-	-
60000 TO 89999 POUNDS.	-	100.0	-	-	-	-	-	-	-
90000 POUNDS AND OVER.	-	100.0	-	-	-	-	-	-	-
100 TO 199 MILES........	312	100.0	7.8	74.6	17.0	-	-	.5	-
UNDER 1000 POUNDS.....	28	100.0	-	93.4	2.7	.2	.1	3.6	-
1000 TO 9999 POUNDS...	100	100.0	-	89.4	10.0	.1	-	.5	-
10000 TO 29999 POUNDS.	124	100.0	10.4	78.6	11.0	-	-	-	-
30000 TO 59999 POUNDS.	58	100.0	19.3	32.0	48.7	-	-	-	-
60000 TO 89999 POUNDS.	-	100.0	-	-	-	-	-	-	-
90000 POUNDS AND OVER.	-	100.0	-	-	-	-	-	-	-
200 TO 299 MILES........	432	100.0	9.0	81.0	9.7	.1	-	.3	-
UNDER 1000 POUNDS.....	24	100.0	-	95.0	.9	.9	-	3.1	-
1000 TO 9999 POUNDS...	90	100.0	-	87.0	12.6	-	-	.4	-
10000 TO 29999 POUNDS.	180	100.0	13.8	75.8	10.4	-	-	-	-
30000 TO 59999 POUNDS.	130	100.0	8.4	82.8	8.8	-	-	-	-
60000 TO 89999 POUNDS.	6	100.0	50.1	49.9	-	-	-	-	-
90000 POUNDS AND OVER.	-	100.0	-	-	-	-	-	-	-
300 TO 499 MILES........	685	100.0	31.7	62.9	5.1	-	-	.2	.1
UNDER 1000 POUNDS.....	46	100.0	.3	95.1	.9	.6	-	3.1	-
1000 TO 9999 POUNDS...	149	100.0	.6	92.9	6.0	-	.2	.1	.2
10000 TO 29999 POUNDS.	270	100.0	19.0	71.6	9.4	-	-	-	-
30000 TO 59999 POUNDS.	116	100.0	53.3	46.7	-	-	-	-	-
60000 TO 89999 POUNDS.	11	100.0	100.0	-	-	-	-	-	-
90000 POUNDS AND OVER.	91	100.0	100.0	-	-	-	-	-	-
500 TO 999 MILES........	902	100.0	26.9	64.1	7.7	.2	-	.7	.4
UNDER 1000 POUNDS.....	80	100.0	2.6	91.8	.6	1.3	-	3.6	-
1000 TO 9999 POUNDS...	256	100.0	3.0	91.5	4.1	.1	-	1.3	-
10000 TO 29999 POUNDS.	358	100.0	27.0	62.9	9.0	-	.1	-	1.0
30000 TO 59999 POUNDS.	156	100.0	67.8	18.4	13.8	-	-	-	-
60000 TO 89999 POUNDS.	50	100.0	59.7	31.0	9.3	-	-	-	-
90000 POUNDS AND OVER.	-	100.0	-	-	-	-	-	-	-
1000 TO 1499 MILES......	295	100.0	16.1	63.1	10.5	.2	.1	10.0	-
UNDER 1000 POUNDS.....	22	100.0	.9	93.0	.1	2.6	-	3.4	.1
1000 TO 9999 POUNDS...	73	100.0	3.0	95.4	1.0	.2	-	.5	-
10000 TO 29999 POUNDS.	154	100.0	15.7	51.5	14.2	-	.2	18.4	-
30000 TO 59999 POUNDS.	39	100.0	39.3	39.4	21.3	-	-	-	-
60000 TO 89999 POUNDS.	5	100.0	100.0	-	-	-	-	-	-
90000 POUNDS AND OVER.	-	100.0	-	-	-	-	-	-	-
1500 MILES OR OVER......	325	100.0	32.9	61.7	1.7	.2	.8	2.2	.4
UNDER 1000 POUNDS.....	21	100.0	.9	86.5	.3	2.9	1.7	7.7	-
1000 TO 9999 POUNDS...	76	100.0	11.1	77.0	2.8	.2	1.2	7.1	.6
10000 TO 29999 POUNDS.	137	100.0	34.8	64.2	-	-	.3	-	.7
30000 TO 59999 POUNDS.	71	100.0	52.4	41.7	4.7	-	1.1	-	-
60000 TO 89999 POUNDS.	12	100.0	100.0	-	-	-	-	-	-
90000 POUNDS AND OVER.	4	100.0	-	100.0	-	-	-	-	-
TON-MILES OF SHIPMENTS	(millions of ton-miles)								
U.S. TOTAL.........	2 068	100.0	25.2	64.6	6.7	.2	.4	2.7	.2
UNDER 100 MILES.........	14	100.0	13.0	57.2	29.4	-	-	.4	-
UNDER 1000 POUNDS.....	1	100.0	-	80.0	16.5	.2	-	3.3	-
1000 TO 9999 POUNDS...	4	100.0	-	71.9	27.7	-	-	.4	-
10000 TO 29999 POUNDS.	4	100.0	19.0	39.1	42.0	-	-	-	-
30000 TO 59999 POUNDS.	3	100.0	24.4	56.2	19.3	-	-	-	-
60000 TO 89999 POUNDS.	-	100.0	-	-	-	-	-	-	-
90000 POUNDS AND OVER.	-	100.0	-	-	-	-	-	-	-
100 TO 199 MILES........	47	100.0	8.6	75.2	15.6	-	-	.5	-
UNDER 1000 POUNDS.....	4	100.0	-	93.5	2.7	.2	.1	3.5	-
1000 TO 9999 POUNDS...	15	100.0	-	89.8	9.7	.1	-	.5	-
10000 TO 29999 POUNDS.	18	100.0	11.8	76.9	11.4	-	-	-	-
30000 TO 59999 POUNDS.	8	100.0	22.4	34.3	43.3	-	-	-	-
60000 TO 89999 POUNDS.	-	100.0	-	-	-	-	-	-	-
90000 POUNDS AND OVER.	-	100.0	-	-	-	-	-	-	-

See footnotes at end of table 4.

TABLE 4. **TCC GROUP 358—Percent Distribution of Distance Shipped and Weight of Shipment, by Means of Transport: 1972**—Continued

Distance shipped and weight of shipment[2] [3]	Number	Percent distribution by means of transport							
		All means of transport	Rail	Motor carrier	Private truck	Air	Water	Other	Unknown
TON-MILES OF SHIPMENTS	(millions of ton-miles)								
200 TO 299 MILES.........	109	100.0	8.8	81.0	9.9	.1	-	.3	-
UNDER 1000 POUNDS.....	6	100.0	-	94.9	1.0	.9	-	3.2	-
1000 TO 9999 POUNDS...	22	100.0	-	87.2	12.4	-	-	.4	-
10000 TO 29999 POUNDS.	44	100.0	13.6	75.5	10.9	-	-	-	-
30000 TO 59999 POUNDS.	34	100.0	7.9	83.1	8.9	-	-	-	-
60000 TO 89999 POUNDS.	1	100.0	56.1	43.9	-	-	-	-	-
90000 POUNDS AND OVER.	-	100.0	-	-	-	-	-	-	-
300 TO 499 MILES.........	263	100.0	30.2	63.9	5.4	-	-	.2	-
UNDER 1000 POUNDS.....	18	100.0	.2	95.2	.8	.6	-	3.1	-
1000 TO 9999 POUNDS...	57	100.0	.6	92.9	5.9	-	.2	.1	.2
10000 TO 29999 POUNDS.	107	100.0	19.3	70.6	10.1	-	-	-	-
30000 TO 59999 POUNDS.	46	100.0	51.6	48.4	-	-	-	-	-
60000 TO 89999 POUNDS.	4	100.0	100.0	-	-	-	-	-	-
90000 POUNDS AND OVER.	29	100.0	100.0	-	-	-	-	-	-
500 TO 999 MILES.........	639	100.0	26.4	64.3	8.1	.2	-	.7	.3
UNDER 1000 POUNDS.....	56	100.0	2.9	91.3	.7	1.5	-	3.7	-
1000 TO 9999 POUNDS...	181	100.0	3.5	91.0	3.9	.1	-	1.5	-
10000 TO 29999 POUNDS.	261	100.0	25.8	64.4	8.9	-	.1	-	.7
30000 TO 59999 POUNDS.	110	100.0	68.5	16.4	15.1	-	-	-	-
60000 TO 89999 POUNDS.	30	100.0	58.9	27.1	14.0	-	-	-	-
90000 POUNDS AND OVER.	-	100.0	-	-	-	-	-	-	-
1000 TO 1499 MILES......	361	100.0	16.4	62.5	10.7	.2	.1	10.1	-
UNDER 1000 POUNDS.....	26	100.0	.8	93.3	.1	2.4	-	3.2	.1
1000 TO 9999 POUNDS...	87	100.0	3.1	95.3	1.0	.2	-	.5	-
10000 TO 29999 POUNDS.	192	100.0	15.7	51.3	14.6	-	.2	18.2	-
30000 TO 59999 POUNDS.	48	100.0	42.0	38.4	19.6	-	-	-	-
60000 TO 89999 POUNDS.	5	100.0	100.0	-	-	-	-	-	-
90000 POUNDS AND OVER.	-	100.0	-	-	-	-	-	-	-
1500 MILES OR OVER......	633	100.0	31.3	63.0	1.8	.3	1.1	2.2	.4
UNDER 1000 POUNDS.....	43	100.0	.8	85.1	.3	3.5	2.7	7.6	-
1000 TO 9999 POUNDS...	142	100.0	9.7	77.4	3.1	.2	1.7	7.3	.6
10000 TO 29999 POUNDS.	262	100.0	32.8	66.1	-	-	-	.4	.7
30000 TO 59999 POUNDS.	145	100.0	46.7	47.0	4.7	-	1.6	-	-
60000 TO 89999 POUNDS.	29	100.0	100.0	-	-	-	-	-	-
90000 POUNDS AND OVER.	9	100.0	-	100.0	-	-	-	-	-

Note: Detail may not add to total due to rounding. The introductory table shows the estimates of sampling variability for tons; sampling variability for ton-miles has not been estimated. See the map in the Introduction for the States comprising the geographic divisions of the United States.

Shipments excluded from the survey are those moving by pipeline (primarily petroleum products from refineries), parcel post shipments, and commodities moved by own power (motorized vehicles, aircraft, etc.) or towed (prefabricated buildings, etc.). Local shipments (commodities shipped less than 25 miles from the plant) and shipments within the same city are also excluded. Shipments to Alaska and Hawaii from the 48 conterminous States and the District of Columbia are included; however, no data were obtained for shipments originating in Alaska and Hawaii.

- Represents zero or rounds to zero.   (D) Withheld to avoid disclosing figures for individual companies.

[1]Production of this commodity is concentrated in the geographic divisions shown; figures and distributions for geographic divisions not shown are included in the total.

[2]Distances of shipments to foreign destinations are calculated only to the U.S. port of exit.

[3]Includes only shipments represented by bills of lading and invoices. Summary records which did not show individual weights of shipments are not included.

TCC 359. Miscellaneous Machinery and Parts

Comparisons of Tons and Ton-Miles of Shipments for
Geographic Divisions of Origin and for Sampling Variability: 1972 and 1967

Geographic division of origin	Estimates				Relative sampling variability in tons (percent)	
	1972		1967		1972	1967
	Tons (thousands)	Ton-miles (millions)	Tons (thousands)	Ton-miles (millions)		
U.S. total	733	343	693	273	10.3	26.2
New England	19	6	40	21	27.1	(*)
Middle Atlantic	75	36	92	45	27.5	(*)
East North Central	365	124	418	118	11.5	(*)
West North Central	(D)	(D)	31	19	(*)	(*)
South Atlantic	(D)	(D)	33	14	(*)	(*)
East South Central	68	34	13	5	39.9	(*)
West South Central	(D)	(D)	24	11	(*)	(*)
Mountain	(D)	(D)	—	—	(*)	(*)
Pacific	35	45	42	45	22.9	(*)

— Represents or rounds to zero.   (D) Withheld to avoid disclosing figures for individual companies.   (*) Data not published.

TABLE 1. TCC GROUP 359—Percent Distribution of Geographic Division of Origin and Distance Shipped, by Means of Transport: 1972

Geographic division of origin[1] and distance shipped[2]	Number	Percent distribution by means of transport							
		All means of transport	Rail	Motor carrier	Private truck	Air	Water	Other	Unknown
TONS OF SHIPMENTS	(thousands of tons)								
U.S. TOTAL..........	733	100.0	8.6	71.8	15.4	1.2	.2	2.6	.2
NEW ENGLAND..............	19	100.0	.3	85.9	11.3	1.2	.1	1.2	-
UNDER 100 MILES.......	8	100.0	-	74.7	23.6	.1	.1	1.4	-
100 TO 199 MILES......	3	100.0	-	92.3	4.8	.3	-	2.7	-
200 TO 299 MILES......	-	100.0	-	93.9	1.7	2.9	-	1.5	-
300 TO 499 MILES......	1	100.0	-	99.0	-	.5	-	.5	-
500 TO 999 MILES.....	4	100.0	.3	98.0	-	1.6	-	.1	-
1000 TO 1499 MILES....	-	100.0	7.8	81.9	.2	7.8	-	2.4	-
1500 MILES OR OVER....	-	100.0	2.6	55.5	4.1	33.4	3.7	.7	-
MIDDLE ATLANTIC.........	75	100.0	7.7	78.8	8.7	2.6	.2	1.9	.1
UNDER 100 MILES.......	18	100.0	13.6	60.2	21.4	3.5	-	1.1	.2
100 TO 199 MILES......	10	100.0	-	96.0	.8	1.2	-	1.9	-
200 TO 299 MILES......	11	100.0	-	77.4	19.1	.9	1.6	1.0	-
300 TO 499 MILES......	10	100.0	-	95.7	.6	1.3	-	2.4	-
500 TO 999 MILES.....	11	100.0	-	91.7	1.7	3.0	-	3.4	.1
1000 TO 1499 MILES....	8	100.0	21.0	74.5	-	2.7	-	1.7	-
1500 MILES OR OVER....	4	100.0	35.1	53.4	-	8.2	-	3.3	-
EAST NORTH CENTRAL......	365	100.0	10.3	62.3	22.4	1.1	-	3.8	.2
UNDER 100 MILES.......	135	100.0	1.2	49.8	47.7	.6	-	.4	.2
100 TO 199 MILES......	67	100.0	-	86.5	12.5	-	-	.8	.1
200 TO 299 MILES......	40	100.0	7.0	65.7	13.8	.6	-	12.8	-
300 TO 499 MILES......	47	100.0	25.3	63.6	2.6	.7	-	7.8	-
500 TO 999 MILES.....	51	100.0	17.6	68.1	3.6	3.5	-	6.8	.3
1000 TO 1499 MILES....	5	100.0	.2	89.4	.5	4.9	-	4.4	.6
1500 MILES OR OVER....	17	100.0	67.7	29.0	-	2.0	-	.8	.5
EAST SOUTH CENTRAL......	68	100.0	-	97.8	.1	.8	-	1.0	.3
UNDER 100 MILES.......	-	100.0	-	88.1	2.0	-	-	9.9	-
100 TO 199 MILES......	11	100.0	-	99.5	.1	-	-	.4	-
200 TO 299 MILES......	2	100.0	-	95.4	2.7	-	-	1.9	-
300 TO 499 MILES......	27	100.0	-	97.5	-	.9	-	.8	.8
500 TO 999 MILES.....	22	100.0	-	97.8	-	1.1	-	1.0	-
1000 TO 1499 MILES....	1	100.0	-	99.5	-	-	-	.5	-
1500 MILES OR OVER....	2	100.0	-	95.5	-	1.1	-	3.4	-
PACIFIC.................	35	100.0	12.9	70.5	6.4	3.0	4.2	3.0	-
UNDER 100 MILES.......	5	100.0	-	39.8	36.1	.4	18.3	5.3	-
100 TO 199 MILES......	2	100.0	-	96.9	1.6	.3	-	1.3	-
200 TO 299 MILES......	-	100.0	-	64.8	25.6	-	-	9.6	-
300 TO 499 MILES......	6	100.0	-	88.9	4.2	.2	4.9	1.8	-
500 TO 999 MILES.....	1	100.0	-	98.1	-	.6	-	1.2	.1
1000 TO 1499 MILES....	-	100.0	41.4	57.6	.1	.7	-	.2	-
1500 MILES OR OVER....	18	100.0	23.0	67.1	-	5.4	1.2	3.2	-
TON-MILES OF SHIPMENTS	(millions of ton-miles)								
U.S. TOTAL..........	343	100.0	16.6	71.8	6.3	2.2	.2	2.7	.1
NEW ENGLAND..............	6	100.0	1.1	91.6	1.7	4.4	.6	.7	-
UNDER 100 MILES.......	-	100.0	-	67.2	29.7	.2	.1	2.6	.1
100 TO 199 MILES......	-	100.0	-	93.8	3.7	.3	-	2.2	-
200 TO 299 MILES......	-	100.0	-	93.6	1.7	3.1	-	1.6	-
300 TO 499 MILES......	-	100.0	-	98.9	-	.5	-	.6	-
500 TO 999 MILES.....	3	100.0	.3	98.1	-	1.5	-	.1	-
1000 TO 1499 MILES....	-	100.0	7.2	82.8	.2	7.7	-	2.2	-
1500 MILES OR OVER....	-	100.0	2.8	49.7	2.8	35.9	8.1	.7	-
MIDDLE ATLANTIC.........	36	100.0	14.7	76.4	2.4	3.9	.1	2.4	-
UNDER 100 MILES.......	1	100.0	16.5	67.8	12.8	1.9	-	1.0	-
100 TO 199 MILES......	1	100.0	-	95.3	1.1	1.5	-	2.1	-
200 TO 299 MILES......	2	100.0	-	76.8	19.7	1.0	1.5	1.0	-
300 TO 499 MILES......	3	100.0	-	95.7	.5	1.4	-	2.5	-
500 TO 999 MILES.....	7	100.0	-	92.1	1.3	3.1	-	3.4	.1
1000 TO 1499 MILES....	10	100.0	19.6	75.9	-	2.8	-	1.7	-
1500 MILES OR OVER....	8	100.0	36.1	52.1	-	8.7	-	3.1	-
EAST NORTH CENTRAL......	124	100.0	29.6	56.5	7.1	2.0	-	4.6	.3
UNDER 100 MILES.......	8	100.0	.6	49.6	48.8	.6	-	.3	.2
100 TO 199 MILES......	10	100.0	-	84.7	14.5	-	-	.8	-
200 TO 299 MILES......	9	100.0	7.2	64.6	14.5	.6	-	13.0	-
300 TO 499 MILES......	19	100.0	25.7	65.0	2.2	.7	-	6.4	-
500 TO 999 MILES.....	33	100.0	16.7	68.0	3.7	3.6	-	7.7	.3
1000 TO 1499 MILES....	6	100.0	.2	89.3	.5	4.9	-	4.4	.7
1500 MILES OR OVER....	36	100.0	70.2	26.6	-	2.0	-	.7	.4
EAST SOUTH CENTRAL......	34	100.0	-	97.5	.1	.9	-	1.3	.3
UNDER 100 MILES.......	-	100.0	-	93.5	.8	-	-	5.7	-
100 TO 199 MILES......	1	100.0	-	99.3	.1	-	-	.5	-
200 TO 299 MILES......	-	100.0	-	95.0	2.9	-	-	2.0	-
300 TO 499 MILES......	11	100.0	-	97.6	-	.8	-	.7	.8
500 TO 999 MILES.....	14	100.0	-	97.9	-	1.0	-	1.1	-
1000 TO 1499 MILES....	1	100.0	-	99.5	-	-	-	.5	-
1500 MILES OR OVER....	5	100.0	-	95.0	-	1.3	-	3.7	-

See footnotes at end of table 4.

TABLE 1. **TCC GROUP 359**—Percent Distribution of Geographic Division of Origin and Distance Shipped, by Means of Transport: 1972—Continued

Geographic division of origin[1] and distance shipped[2]	Number	Percent distribution by means of transport							
		All means of transport	Rail	Motor carrier	Private truck	Air	Water	Other	Unknown
TON-MILES OF SHIPMENTS	(millions of ton-miles)								
PACIFIC..................	45	100.0	23.0	67.6	.4	4.8	1.6	2.6	-
UNDER 100 MILES........	-	100.0	-	45.6	32.6	.4	12.5	8.9	-
100 TO 199 MILES......	-	100.0	-	97.5	1.2	.3	-	.9	-
200 TO 299 MILES......	-	100.0	-	67.4	22.8	-	-	9.7	-
300 TO 499 MILES......	2	100.0	-	89.4	3.9	.2	4.9	1.6	-
500 TO 999 MILES......	1	100.0	-	98.1	-	.6	-	1.2	.1
1000 TO 1499 MILES....	1	100.0	45.7	53.5	-	.6	-	.2	-
1500 MILES OR OVER....	39	100.0	25.0	65.4	-	5.4	1.4	2.8	-

See footnotes at end of table 4.

TABLE 2. **TCC GROUP 359**—Percent Distribution of Geographic Division of Origin and Means of Transport, by Geographic Division of Destination: 1972

Geographic division of origin[1] and means of transport	Number	Percent distribution by division of destination									
		U.S. total	New England	Middle Atlantic	East North Central	West North Central	South Atlantic	East South Central	West South Central	Mountain	Pacific
TONS OF SHIPMENTS	(thousands of tons)										
U.S. TOTAL..............	733	100.0	3.2	14.1	41.3	14.0	7.8	4.1	7.3	1.9	6.2
RAIL.................	63	100.0	-	18.6	36.0	12.9	5.8	.6	3.9	2.8	19.2
MOTOR CARRIER........	526	100.0	3.5	15.3	44.4	7.9	8.2	4.8	9.1	1.9	4.9
PRIVATE TRUCK........	112	100.0	4.0	5.4	30.0	45.7	5.5	2.8	1.3	1.2	4.0
AIR..................	8	100.0	4.1	25.8	22.1	6.1	13.7	5.2	10.0	4.2	8.7
WATER................	1	100.0	.7	10.7	.6	-	.9	-	-	-	87.2
OTHER................	18	100.0	2.2	12.2	52.1	5.1	15.2	1.6	6.1	1.2	4.2
UNKNOWN..............	1	100.0	.6	5.4	46.6	.6	36.0	-	1.1	2.6	7.2
NEW ENGLAND.............	19	100.0	49.7	19.7	9.4	1.2	12.4	5.2	1.6	.2	.5
RAIL.................	-	100.0	-	-	12.5	41.2	11.8	-	26.7	-	7.8
MOTOR CARRIER........	17	100.0	44.2	21.9	10.8	1.2	14.0	5.9	1.6	.1	.3
PRIVATE TRUCK........	2	100.0	93.4	6.2	-	-	-	-	.3	-	-
AIR..................	-	100.0	4.7	15.5	9.4	1.0	25.4	8.3	10.9	8.8	16.0
WATER................	-	100.0	64.2	.3	-	-	-	-	-	-	35.5
OTHER................	-	100.0	84.0	7.2	1.3	5.1	1.8	-	.1	-	.5
UNKNOWN..............	-	100.0	100.0	-	-	-	-	-	-	-	-
MIDDLE ATLANTIC.........	75	100.0	3.0	40.7	22.5	3.7	10.4	3.2	11.0	2.2	3.1
RAIL.................	5	100.0	-	44.1	-	-	-	-	31.1	7.5	17.3
MOTOR CARRIER........	59	100.0	3.5	37.1	26.2	4.3	10.8	4.0	10.5	1.8	1.8
PRIVATE TRUCK........	6	100.0	.3	72.7	11.4	.1	15.6	-	-	-	-
AIR..................	1	100.0	1.8	39.1	9.8	6.3	15.3	2.4	7.8	7.0	10.6
WATER................	-	100.0	-	100.0	-	-	-	-	-	-	-
OTHER................	1	100.0	9.1	24.6	32.4	7.2	8.7	2.4	6.5	4.5	4.6
UNKNOWN..............	-	100.0	-	75.9	24.1	-	-	-	-	-	-
EAST NORTH CENTRAL......	365	100.0	2.0	10.5	54.3	17.6	5.6	2.5	2.1	1.0	4.4
RAIL.................	37	100.0	-	13.7	22.2	21.8	9.8	.2	-	3.7	28.6
MOTOR CARRIER........	227	100.0	3.1	12.9	66.8	2.7	5.5	2.8	3.2	.9	2.1
PRIVATE TRUCK........	81	100.0	-	1.0	34.2	60.2	1.4	3.0	.1	-	-
AIR..................	3	100.0	7.3	28.1	28.5	2.5	8.6	6.8	6.2	5.2	6.8
WATER................	-	100.0	-	21.5	78.5	-	-	-	-	-	-
OTHER................	13	100.0	.3	12.0	61.9	5.2	18.0	.9	.6	.2	1.0
UNKNOWN..............	-	100.0	.6	3.9	60.0	1.0	14.6	-	2.1	5.1	12.6
EAST SOUTH CENTRAL......	68	100.0	.8	11.1	37.6	5.2	5.6	17.1	17.5	.9	4.2
RAIL.................	-	100.0	-	-	87.4	9.3	3.3	-	-	-	-
MOTOR CARRIER........	66	100.0	.8	10.8	37.5	5.2	5.6	17.3	17.8	.9	4.1
PRIVATE TRUCK........	-	100.0	-	-	-	-	-	100.0	-	-	-
AIR..................	-	100.0	-	46.3	37.6	-	7.9	.2	1.9	-	6.2
WATER................	-	100.0	-	-	-	-	-	-	-	-	-
OTHER................	-	100.0	2.9	15.2	28.4	8.9	8.0	8.2	12.5	.9	15.0
UNKNOWN..............	-	100.0	-	-	100.0	-	-	-	-	-	-
PACIFIC.................	35	100.0	.5	18.1	8.7	3.5	9.7	4.6	8.0	2.9	44.1
RAIL.................	4	100.0	-	84.3	1.1	-	-	-	6.6	8.0	45.5
MOTOR CARRIER........	25	100.0	.7	10.0	12.1	4.8	12.0	4.8	6.4	3.7	45.5
PRIVATE TRUCK........	2	100.0	-	-	-	-	-	-	-	-	100.0
AIR..................	1	100.0	.7	5.5	.8	2.5	38.7	7.6	34.6	.2	9.5
WATER................	1	100.0	-	-	-	-	.9	-	-	-	99.1
OTHER................	1	100.0	-	.1	.9	1.0	3.4	2.5	47.0	7.7	37.4
UNKNOWN..............	-	100.0	-	29.8	-	12.4	-	-	-	25.8	32.0

See footnotes at end of table 4.

TABLE 2. TCC GROUP 359—Percent Distribution of Geographic Division of Origin and Means of Transport, by Geographic Division of Destination: 1972—Continued

Geographic division of origin[1] and means of transport	Number	Percent distribution by division of destination									
		U.S. total	New England	Middle Atlantic	East North Central	West North Central	South Atlantic	East South Central	West South Central	Mountain	Pacific
TON-MILES OF SHIPMENTS	(millions of ton-miles)										
U.S. TOTAL..............	343	100.0	3.1	15.9	23.2	9.5	11.9	4.0	10.3	4.1	18.0
RAIL....................	57	100.0	-	21.7	9.3	6.9	3.9	1.1	5.0	4.8	47.3
MOTOR CARRIER..........	246	100.0	3.0	15.9	26.7	9.3	13.3	4.7	12.0	3.7	11.5
PRIVATE TRUCK..........	21	100.0	13.1	4.5	23.0	23.4	9.9	4.0	2.2	5.5	14.4
AIR....................	7	100.0	3.4	13.4	7.3	4.1	20.2	5.5	15.9	8.7	21.4
WATER..................	-	100.0	-	5.9	.1	-	3.9	-	-	-	90.1
OTHER..................	9	100.0	1.1	10.8	31.3	4.7	24.5	2.0	13.7	2.5	9.3
UNKNOWN................	-	100.0	.7	3.5	25.5	1.0	22.0	-	2.3	9.5	35.5
NEW ENGLAND............	6	100.0	7.0	12.4	20.2	4.0	28.9	14.2	7.4	1.3	4.5
RAIL....................	-	100.0	-	-	6.2	36.7	7.9	-	32.4	-	16.8
MOTOR CARRIER..........	5	100.0	6.0	13.1	21.7	3.7	30.6	15.3	6.8	.6	2.2
PRIVATE TRUCK..........	-	100.0	74.6	13.1	-	-	.3	.7	11.2	-	-
AIR....................	-	100.0	.2	2.9	5.5	.9	18.2	5.6	13.1	16.5	37.1
WATER..................	-	100.0	.6	-	-	-	-	-	-	-	99.4
OTHER..................	-	100.0	39.7	8.7	5.4	33.0	4.8	-	1.1	-	7.4
UNKNOWN................	-	100.0	100.0	-	-	-	-	-	-	-	-
MIDDLE ATLANTIC........	36	100.0	1.3	10.5	17.0	6.3	9.4	4.6	27.1	8.5	15.4
RAIL....................	5	100.0	-	3.3	-	-	-	-	37.2	15.2	44.3
MOTOR CARRIER..........	27	100.0	1.6	11.0	20.4	7.5	10.5	5.8	27.2	6.8	9.3
PRIVATE TRUCK..........	-	100.0	.2	49.6	17.0	.5	32.6	-	-	-	-
AIR....................	1	100.0	.6	3.5	6.3	7.8	11.2	2.5	13.9	20.2	34.0
WATER..................	-	100.0	-	100.0	-	-	-	-	-	-	-
OTHER..................	-	100.0	3.1	6.1	28.0	11.3	5.9	2.5	12.9	12.1	18.2
UNKNOWN................	-	100.0	-	4.8	95.2	-	-	-	-	-	-
EAST NORTH CENTRAL.....	124	100.0	4.3	14.6	22.7	8.7	10.0	3.1	5.5	4.0	27.1
RAIL....................	36	100.0	-	7.5	5.9	10.6	5.9	.1	-	5.3	64.6
MOTOR CARRIER..........	70	100.0	7.2	19.5	29.8	3.4	10.1	4.3	9.2	3.7	12.8
PRIVATE TRUCK..........	8	100.0	-	2.9	32.6	47.7	9.0	7.0	.9	-	-
AIR....................	2	100.0	8.5	23.8	4.9	1.7	10.2	7.1	8.6	12.4	22.8
WATER..................	-	100.0	-	80.9	19.1	-	-	-	-	-	-
OTHER..................	5	100.0	.5	14.6	37.7	4.6	35.5	.9	1.4	.5	4.4
UNKNOWN................	-	100.0	.9	3.5	6.2	1.2	26.7	-	3.2	13.1	45.2
EAST SOUTH CENTRAL.....	34	100.0	1.4	13.3	32.4	4.9	5.9	5.0	20.4	2.1	14.6
RAIL....................	-	100.0	-	-	81.9	15.3	2.8	-	-	-	-
MOTOR CARRIER..........	34	100.0	1.4	13.1	32.6	5.0	5.9	5.0	20.7	2.1	14.2
PRIVATE TRUCK..........	-	100.0	-	-	-	-	-	100.0	-	-	-
AIR....................	-	100.0	-	46.2	24.2	-	5.2	.1	2.4	-	21.8
WATER..................	-	100.0	-	-	-	-	-	-	-	-	-
OTHER..................	-	100.0	2.9	10.8	13.4	6.3	5.0	4.5	14.4	1.4	41.4
UNKNOWN................	-	100.0	-	-	100.0	-	-	-	-	-	-
PACIFIC................	45	100.0	1.0	34.3	13.2	4.2	18.2	7.0	10.6	1.3	10.3
RAIL....................	10	100.0	-	88.1	1.0	-	-	-	5.6	5.3	-
MOTOR CARRIER..........	30	100.0	1.4	20.2	19.0	6.0	23.3	7.8	8.7	1.9	11.8
PRIVATE TRUCK..........	-	100.0	-	-	-	-	-	-	-	-	100.0
AIR....................	2	100.0	.8	6.6	.7	1.9	44.4	7.5	31.3	.1	6.8
WATER..................	-	100.0	-	-	-	-	4.3	-	-	-	95.7
OTHER..................	1	100.0	.1	.2	1.6	1.5	7.3	4.5	77.9	2.5	4.5
UNKNOWN................	-	100.0	-	58.0	-	14.8	-	-	-	18.1	9.1

See footnotes at end of table 4.

TABLE 3. **TCC GROUP 359—Percent Distribution of Geographic Division of Destination and Means of Transport, by Geographic Division of Origin: 1972**

Geographic division of destination and means of transport	Number	Percent distribution by division of origin[1]									
		U.S. total	New England	Middle Atlantic	East North Central	West North Central	South Atlantic	East South Central	West South Central	Mountain	Pacific
TONS OF SHIPMENTS	(thousands of tons)										
U.S. TOTAL	733	100.0	2.7	10.3	49.8	(D)	(D)	9.3	(D)	(D)	4.9
RAIL	63	100.0	.1	9.1	59.1	(D)	(D)	-	(D)	(D)	7.3
MOTOR CARRIER	526	100.0	3.2	11.3	43.3	(D)	(D)	12.7	(D)	(D)	4.8
PRIVATE TRUCK	112	100.0	2.0	5.8	72.6	(D)	(D)	.1	(D)	(D)	2.1
AIR	8	100.0	2.7	22.0	43.9	(D)	(D)	6.0	(D)	(D)	12.1
WATER	1	100.0	1.1	10.5	.7	(D)	(D)	-	(D)	(D)	87.5
OTHER	18	100.0	1.3	7.6	74.1	(D)	(D)	3.5	(D)	(D)	5.8
UNKNOWN	1	100.0	.3	4.4	49.0	(D)	(D)	16.0	(D)	(D)	.5
NEW ENGLAND	23	100.0	41.7	9.6	30.9	(D)	(D)	2.4	(D)	(D)	.7
RAIL	-	100.0	-	-	38.0	(D)	(D)	-	(D)	(D)	-
MOTOR CARRIER	18	100.0	41.2	11.4	38.2	(D)	(D)	3.0	(D)	(D)	.9
PRIVATE TRUCK	4	100.0	46.1	.4	-	(D)	(D)	-	(D)	(D)	-
AIR	-	100.0	3.1	9.7	78.4	(D)	(D)	-	(D)	(D)	2.0
WATER	-	100.0	100.0	-	-	(D)	(D)	-	(D)	(D)	-
OTHER	-	100.0	49.7	31.3	8.8	(D)	(D)	4.5	(D)	(D)	.1
UNKNOWN	-	100.0	49.9	-	50.1	(D)	(D)	-	(D)	(D)	-
MIDDLE ATLANTIC	103	100.0	3.8	29.7	37.0	(D)	(D)	7.3	(D)	(D)	6.3
RAIL	11	100.0	-	21.6	43.4	(D)	(D)	-	(D)	(D)	32.9
MOTOR CARRIER	80	100.0	4.6	27.3	36.6	(D)	(D)	9.0	(D)	(D)	3.2
PRIVATE TRUCK	6	100.0	2.3	77.6	13.9	(D)	(D)	-	(D)	(D)	-
AIR	2	100.0	1.6	33.3	47.7	(D)	(D)	10.8	(D)	(D)	2.6
WATER	-	100.0	-	98.6	1.4	(D)	(D)	-	(D)	(D)	-
OTHER	2	100.0	.8	15.4	72.8	(D)	(D)	4.3	(D)	(D)	-
UNKNOWN	-	100.0	-	62.0	35.5	(D)	(D)	-	(D)	(D)	2.5
EAST NORTH CENTRAL	302	100.0	.6	5.6	65.6	(D)	(D)	8.5	(D)	(D)	1.0
RAIL	22	100.0	-	-	36.5	(D)	(D)	.1	(D)	(D)	.2
MOTOR CARRIER	233	100.0	.8	6.6	65.0	(D)	(D)	10.7	(D)	(D)	1.3
PRIVATE TRUCK	33	100.0	-	2.2	82.8	(D)	(D)	-	(D)	(D)	-
AIR	1	100.0	1.1	9.8	56.5	(D)	(D)	10.3	(D)	(D)	.4
WATER	-	100.0	-	-	100.0	(D)	(D)	-	(D)	(D)	-
OTHER	9	100.0	-	4.8	88.0	(D)	(D)	1.9	(D)	(D)	.1
UNKNOWN	-	100.0	-	2.3	63.1	(D)	(D)	34.4	(D)	(D)	-
WEST NORTH CENTRAL	102	100.0	.2	2.7	62.6	(D)	(D)	3.4	(D)	(D)	1.2
RAIL	8	100.0	.3	-	99.7	(D)	(D)	-	(D)	(D)	-
MOTOR CARRIER	41	100.0	.5	6.2	14.8	(D)	(D)	8.4	(D)	(D)	2.9
PRIVATE TRUCK	51	100.0	-	-	95.5	(D)	(D)	-	(D)	(D)	-
AIR	-	100.0	.4	23.0	18.1	(D)	(D)	-	(D)	(D)	5.0
WATER	-	100.0	-	-	-	(D)	(D)	-	(D)	(D)	-
OTHER	-	100.0	1.3	10.8	75.7	(D)	(D)	6.0	(D)	(D)	1.2
UNKNOWN	-	100.0	-	-	90.0	(D)	(D)	-	(D)	(D)	10.0
SOUTH ATLANTIC	57	100.0	4.3	13.7	35.5	(D)	(D)	6.6	(D)	(D)	6.1
RAIL	3	100.0	.2	-	99.7	(D)	(D)	-	(D)	(D)	-
MOTOR CARRIER	43	100.0	5.5	14.9	29.3	(D)	(D)	8.6	(D)	(D)	7.0
PRIVATE TRUCK	6	100.0	-	16.4	18.7	(D)	(D)	-	(D)	(D)	-
AIR	1	100.0	4.9	24.5	27.5	(D)	(D)	3.4	(D)	(D)	33.9
WATER	-	100.0	-	-	-	(D)	(D)	-	(D)	(D)	89.9
OTHER	2	100.0	.2	4.4	87.9	(D)	(D)	1.8	(D)	(D)	1.3
UNKNOWN	-	100.0	-	-	19.9	(D)	(D)	-	(D)	(D)	-
EAST SOUTH CENTRAL	29	100.0	3.4	8.2	30.9	(D)	(D)	39.3	(D)	(D)	5.5
RAIL	-	100.0	-	.1	18.6	(D)	(D)	-	(D)	(D)	81.3
MOTOR CARRIER	25	100.0	3.9	9.2	24.7	(D)	(D)	45.3	(D)	(D)	4.8
PRIVATE TRUCK	3	100.0	-	-	78.9	(D)	(D)	2.6	(D)	(D)	-
AIR	-	100.0	4.2	10.3	57.4	(D)	(D)	.2	(D)	(D)	17.5
WATER	-	100.0	-	-	-	(D)	(D)	-	(D)	(D)	-
OTHER	-	100.0	-	11.0	39.5	(D)	(D)	17.5	(D)	(D)	8.9
UNKNOWN	-	100.0	-	-	-	(D)	(D)	-	(D)	(D)	-
WEST SOUTH CENTRAL	53	100.0	.6	15.4	14.6	(D)	(D)	22.2	(D)	(D)	5.3
RAIL	2	100.0	.7	72.3	.3	(D)	(D)	-	(D)	(D)	14.8
MOTOR CARRIER	47	100.0	.6	13.0	15.5	(D)	(D)	24.9	(D)	(D)	3.4
PRIVATE TRUCK	1	100.0	.5	-	6.7	(D)	(D)	-	(D)	(D)	-
AIR	-	100.0	2.9	17.2	27.2	(D)	(D)	1.1	(D)	(D)	41.8
WATER	-	100.0	-	-	-	(D)	(D)	-	(D)	(D)	-
OTHER	1	100.0	-	8.2	7.5	(D)	(D)	7.1	(D)	(D)	44.8
UNKNOWN	-	100.0	-	-	96.2	(D)	(D)	-	(D)	(D)	-
MOUNTAIN	14	100.0	.3	12.0	25.9	(D)	(D)	4.5	(D)	(D)	7.3
RAIL	1	100.0	-	24.1	75.9	(D)	(D)	-	(D)	(D)	-
MOTOR CARRIER	10	100.0	.2	10.3	19.7	(D)	(D)	6.1	(D)	(D)	9.2
PRIVATE TRUCK	1	100.0	-	-	-	(D)	(D)	-	(D)	(D)	-
AIR	-	100.0	5.5	36.1	54.2	(D)	(D)	-	(D)	(D)	.5
WATER	-	100.0	-	-	-	(D)	(D)	-	(D)	(D)	-
OTHER	-	100.0	-	28.0	10.0	(D)	(D)	2.4	(D)	(D)	35.8
UNKNOWN	-	100.0	-	-	95.5	(D)	(D)	-	(D)	(D)	4.5
PACIFIC	45	100.0	.2	5.1	34.9	(D)	(D)	6.2	(D)	(D)	34.6
RAIL	12	100.0	-	8.2	88.1	(D)	(D)	-	(D)	(D)	-
MOTOR CARRIER	25	100.0	.2	4.1	18.3	(D)	(D)	10.5	(D)	(D)	44.5
PRIVATE TRUCK	4	100.0	-	-	-	(D)	(D)	-	(D)	(D)	51.2
AIR	-	100.0	4.9	26.6	34.1	(D)	(D)	4.3	(D)	(D)	13.1
WATER	1	100.0	.5	-	-	(D)	(D)	-	(D)	(D)	99.5
OTHER	-	100.0	.2	8.3	18.0	(D)	(D)	12.3	(D)	(D)	50.9
UNKNOWN	-	100.0	-	-	85.7	(D)	(D)	-	(D)	(D)	2.0

See footnotes at end of table 4.

TABLE 3. **TCC GROUP 359—Percent Distribution of Geographic Division of Destination and Means of Transport, by Geographic Division of Origin: 1972**—Continued

Geographic division of destination and means of transport	Number	Percent distribution by division of origin[1]									
		U.S. total	New England	Middle Atlantic	East North Central	West North Central	South Atlantic	East South Central	West South Central	Mountain	Pacific
TON-MILES OF SHIPMENTS	(millions of ton-miles)										
U.S. TOTAL	343	100.0	1.9	10.5	36.4	(D)	(D)	10.2	(D)	(D)	13.3
RAIL	57	100.0	.1	9.3	64.7	(D)	(D)	-	(D)	(D)	18.3
MOTOR CARRIER	246	100.0	2.4	11.2	28.6	(D)	(D)	13.8	(D)	(D)	12.5
PRIVATE TRUCK	21	100.0	.5	4.0	40.9	(D)	(D)	.1	(D)	(D)	.8
AIR	7	100.0	3.7	18.9	33.1	(D)	(D)	4.1	(D)	(D)	28.9
WATER	-	100.0	4.4	5.7	.3	(D)	(D)	-	(D)	(D)	89.6
OTHER	9	100.0	.5	9.6	62.4	(D)	(D)	5.0	(D)	(D)	12.9
UNKNOWN	-	100.0	.1	2.1	70.3	(D)	(D)	19.1	(D)	(D)	1.6
NEW ENGLAND	10	100.0	4.2	4.6	50.2	(D)	(D)	4.6	(D)	(D)	4.2
RAIL	-	100.0	-	-	28.0	(D)	(D)	-	(D)	(D)	-
MOTOR CARRIER	7	100.0	4.7	6.1	68.8	(D)	(D)	6.5	(D)	(D)	5.8
PRIVATE TRUCK	2	100.0	2.8	.1	-	(D)	(D)	-	(D)	(D)	-
AIR	-	100.0	.2	3.4	82.3	(D)	(D)	-	(D)	(D)	6.9
WATER	-	100.0	100.0	-	-	(D)	(D)	-	(D)	(D)	-
OTHER	-	100.0	17.6	27.8	27.1	(D)	(D)	13.7	(D)	(D)	1.0
UNKNOWN	-	100.0	7.8	-	92.2	(D)	(D)	-	(D)	(D)	-
MIDDLE ATLANTIC	54	100.0	1.4	6.9	33.3	(D)	(D)	8.5	(D)	(D)	28.5
RAIL	12	100.0	-	1.4	22.3	(D)	(D)	-	(D)	(D)	74.6
MOTOR CARRIER	39	100.0	2.0	7.7	35.1	(D)	(D)	11.4	(D)	(D)	15.8
PRIVATE TRUCK	-	100.0	1.4	43.6	25.7	(D)	(D)	-	(D)	(D)	-
AIR	1	100.0	.8	4.9	58.6	(D)	(D)	14.2	(D)	(D)	14.1
WATER	-	100.0	-	95.9	4.1	(D)	(D)	-	(D)	(D)	-
OTHER	-	100.0	.4	5.4	84.8	(D)	(D)	5.0	(D)	(D)	.2
UNKNOWN	-	100.0	-	2.9	70.9	(D)	(D)	-	(D)	(D)	26.2
EAST NORTH CENTRAL	79	100.0	1.6	7.7	35.7	(D)	(D)	14.2	(D)	(D)	7.5
RAIL	5	100.0	.1	-	41.0	(D)	(D)	.1	(D)	(D)	2.0
MOTOR CARRIER	65	100.0	1.9	8.6	32.0	(D)	(D)	16.8	(D)	(D)	8.9
PRIVATE TRUCK	4	100.0	-	3.0	57.9	(D)	(D)	-	(D)	(D)	-
AIR	-	100.0	2.8	16.1	22.3	(D)	(D)	13.7	(D)	(D)	2.7
WATER	-	100.0	-	-	100.0	(D)	(D)	-	(D)	(D)	-
OTHER	2	100.0	.1	8.5	75.0	(D)	(D)	2.1	(D)	(D)	.7
UNKNOWN	-	100.0	-	7.9	17.1	(D)	(D)	74.9	(D)	(D)	-
WEST NORTH CENTRAL	32	100.0	.8	7.0	33.2	(D)	(D)	5.2	(D)	(D)	5.8
RAIL	3	100.0	.7	-	99.3	(D)	(D)	-	(D)	(D)	-
MOTOR CARRIER	22	100.0	.9	9.0	10.5	(D)	(D)	7.3	(D)	(D)	8.1
PRIVATE TRUCK	5	100.0	-	.1	83.2	(D)	(D)	-	(D)	(D)	-
AIR	-	100.0	.8	36.1	13.4	(D)	(D)	-	(D)	(D)	13.1
WATER	-	100.0	-	-	-	(D)	(D)	-	(D)	(D)	-
OTHER	-	100.0	3.3	22.9	60.9	(D)	(D)	6.6	(D)	(D)	4.0
UNKNOWN	-	100.0	-	-	77.4	(D)	(D)	-	(D)	(D)	22.6
SOUTH ATLANTIC	40	100.0	4.5	8.3	30.6	(D)	(D)	5.0	(D)	(D)	20.2
RAIL	2	100.0	.3	-	99.6	(D)	(D)	-	(D)	(D)	-
MOTOR CARRIER	32	100.0	5.5	8.9	21.8	(D)	(D)	6.2	(D)	(D)	22.0
PRIVATE TRUCK	2	100.0	-	13.2	37.1	(D)	(D)	-	(D)	(D)	-
AIR	1	100.0	3.4	10.5	16.8	(D)	(D)	1.1	(D)	(D)	63.7
WATER	-	100.0	-	-	-	(D)	(D)	-	(D)	(D)	99.2
OTHER	2	100.0	.1	2.3	90.4	(D)	(D)	1.0	(D)	(D)	3.8
UNKNOWN	-	100.0	-	-	85.1	(D)	(D)	-	(D)	(D)	-
EAST SOUTH CENTRAL	13	100.0	6.6	12.2	28.7	(D)	(D)	12.7	(D)	(D)	23.3
RAIL	-	100.0	-	-	6.7	(D)	(D)	-	(D)	(D)	93.2
MOTOR CARRIER	11	100.0	7.7	13.9	26.2	(D)	(D)	14.7	(D)	(D)	20.6
PRIVATE TRUCK	-	100.0	.1	-	72.2	(D)	(D)	2.3	(D)	(D)	-
AIR	-	100.0	3.8	8.5	42.7	(D)	(D)	.1	(D)	(D)	39.5
WATER	-	100.0	-	-	-	(D)	(D)	-	(D)	(D)	-
OTHER	-	100.0	-	11.7	28.5	(D)	(D)	11.0	(D)	(D)	28.4
UNKNOWN	-	100.0	-	-	-	(D)	(D)	-	(D)	(D)	-
WEST SOUTH CENTRAL	35	100.0	1.3	27.8	19.5	(D)	(D)	20.2	(D)	(D)	13.7
RAIL	2	100.0	.8	69.7	.3	(D)	(D)	-	(D)	(D)	19.4
MOTOR CARRIER	29	100.0	1.3	25.5	21.9	(D)	(D)	23.9	(D)	(D)	9.0
PRIVATE TRUCK	-	100.0	2.6	-	16.6	(D)	(D)	-	(D)	(D)	-
AIR	1	100.0	3.1	16.5	17.9	(D)	(D)	.6	(D)	(D)	56.7
WATER	-	100.0	-	-	-	(D)	(D)	-	(D)	(D)	-
OTHER	1	100.0	-	8.9	6.2	(D)	(D)	5.2	(D)	(D)	73.0
UNKNOWN	-	100.0	-	-	99.2	(D)	(D)	-	(D)	(D)	-
MOUNTAIN	13	100.0	.6	22.1	35.4	(D)	(D)	5.2	(D)	(D)	4.3
RAIL	2	100.0	-	29.2	70.8	(D)	(D)	-	(D)	(D)	-
MOTOR CARRIER	9	100.0	.4	20.7	28.7	(D)	(D)	8.0	(D)	(D)	6.3
PRIVATE TRUCK	1	100.0	-	-	-	(D)	(D)	-	(D)	(D)	-
AIR	-	100.0	7.0	43.7	46.9	(D)	(D)	-	(D)	(D)	.2
WATER	-	100.0	-	-	-	(D)	(D)	-	(D)	(D)	-
OTHER	-	100.0	-	45.5	12.2	(D)	(D)	2.7	(D)	(D)	12.7
UNKNOWN	-	100.0	-	-	97.0	(D)	(D)	-	(D)	(D)	3.0
PACIFIC	61	100.0	.5	9.0	54.9	(D)	(D)	8.3	(D)	(D)	7.6
RAIL	27	100.0	-	8.7	88.4	(D)	(D)	-	(D)	(D)	-
MOTOR CARRIER	28	100.0	.5	9.1	32.1	(D)	(D)	17.1	(D)	(D)	12.9
PRIVATE TRUCK	3	100.0	-	-	-	(D)	(D)	-	(D)	(D)	5.5
AIR	1	100.0	6.4	30.0	35.2	(D)	(D)	4.2	(D)	(D)	9.2
WATER	-	100.0	4.9	-	-	(D)	(D)	-	(D)	(D)	95.1
OTHER	-	100.0	.4	18.8	29.5	(D)	(D)	22.1	(D)	(D)	6.2
UNKNOWN	-	100.0	-	-	89.6	(D)	(D)	-	(D)	(D)	.4

See footnotes at end of table 4.

TABLE 4. **TCC GROUP 359**—Percent Distribution of Distance Shipped and Weight of Shipment, by Means of Transport: 1972

Distance shipped and weight of shipment[2][3]	Number	Percent distribution by means of transport							
		All means of transport	Rail	Motor carrier	Private truck	Air	Water	Other	Unknown
TONS OF SHIPMENTS	(thousands of tons)								
U.S. TOTAL..........	618	100.0	10.2	77.5	7.8	1.3	.2	2.9	.2
UNDER 100 MILES.........	116	100.0	3.6	78.4	14.5	1.2	.7	1.0	.5
UNDER 1000 POUNDS.....	22	100.0	-	78.8	14.8	.6	.1	5.4	.3
1000 TO 9999 POUNDS...	49	100.0	-	88.9	8.3	1.5	.1	-	1.2
10000 TO 29999 POUNDS.	17	100.0	7.3	71.7	18.2	2.8	-	-	-
30000 TO 59999 POUNDS.	22	100.0	7.4	63.0	27.9	-	1.7	-	-
60000 TO 89999 POUNDS.	4	100.0	26.3	65.0	-	-	8.7	-	-
90000 POUNDS AND OVER.	-	100.0	-	-	-	-	-	-	-
100 TO 199 MILES........	108	100.0	-	88.4	10.6	.2	-	.8	-
UNDER 1000 POUNDS.....	11	100.0	-	89.7	2.7	1.5	-	5.7	.4
1000 TO 9999 POUNDS...	24	100.0	-	90.6	8.3	-	-	1.0	-
10000 TO 29999 POUNDS.	22	100.0	-	97.6	2.4	-	-	-	-
30000 TO 59999 POUNDS.	41	100.0	-	79.5	20.5	-	-	-	-
60000 TO 89999 POUNDS.	4	100.0	-	100.0	-	-	-	-	-
90000 POUNDS AND OVER.	3	100.0	-	100.0	-	-	-	-	-
200 TO 299 MILES........	81	100.0	21.0	62.4	9.0	.5	.2	6.9	-
UNDER 1000 POUNDS.....	10	100.0	-	88.4	1.8	3.1	-	6.6	.1
1000 TO 9999 POUNDS...	27	100.0	-	91.3	4.0	.3	.6	3.8	-
10000 TO 29999 POUNDS.	19	100.0	8.9	45.3	25.8	-	-	20.0	-
30000 TO 59999 POUNDS.	11	100.0	25.7	64.6	9.7	-	-	-	-
60000 TO 89999 POUNDS.	-	100.0	-	100.0	-	-	-	-	-
90000 POUNDS AND OVER.	12	100.0	100.0	-	-	-	-	-	-
300 TO 499 MILES........	112	100.0	10.9	78.8	4.9	1.1	.3	3.8	.2
UNDER 1000 POUNDS.....	23	100.0	.8	88.0	1.7	4.0	-	4.6	.9
1000 TO 9999 POUNDS...	37	100.0	.2	93.6	3.0	.7	-	2.5	-
10000 TO 29999 POUNDS.	23	100.0	1.9	73.5	13.3	-	1.4	10.0	-
30000 TO 59999 POUNDS.	13	100.0	-	93.2	6.8	-	-	-	-
60000 TO 89999 POUNDS.	13	100.0	83.6	16.4	-	-	-	-	-
90000 POUNDS AND OVER.	1	100.0	-	100.0	-	-	-	-	-
500 TO 999 MILES........	127	100.0	7.5	83.4	3.8	1.8	-	3.4	.1
UNDER 1000 POUNDS.....	33	100.0	.6	91.4	.2	4.4	-	3.3	.1
1000 TO 9999 POUNDS...	54	100.0	1.5	91.5	3.7	1.6	-	1.6	.2
10000 TO 29999 POUNDS.	20	100.0	2.2	75.7	10.3	-	-	11.8	-
30000 TO 59999 POUNDS.	12	100.0	10.8	84.4	4.8	-	-	-	-
60000 TO 89999 POUNDS.	6	100.0	100.0	-	-	-	-	-	-
90000 POUNDS AND OVER.	-	100.0	-	-	-	-	-	-	-
1000 TO 1499 MILES......	33	100.0	6.7	83.4	7.0	1.7	-	1.2	.1
UNDER 1000 POUNDS.....	7	100.0	.5	89.2	.7	6.6	-	2.7	.4
1000 TO 9999 POUNDS...	16	100.0	.2	97.5	.5	.6	-	1.2	-
10000 TO 29999 POUNDS.	4	100.0	25.6	73.7	.7	-	-	-	-
30000 TO 59999 POUNDS.	3	100.0	-	43.7	56.3	-	-	-	-
60000 TO 89999 POUNDS.	-	100.0	100.0	-	-	-	-	-	-
90000 POUNDS AND OVER.	-	100.0	-	-	-	-	-	-	-
1500 MILES OR OVER.....	38	100.0	45.6	47.1	-	4.4	.2	2.6	-
UNDER 1000 POUNDS.....	10	100.0	.8	74.3	.1	15.3	.3	9.1	.1
1000 TO 9999 POUNDS...	4	100.0	16.5	77.7	-	3.2	1.1	1.4	-
10000 TO 29999 POUNDS.	6	100.0	36.9	63.1	-	-	-	-	-
30000 TO 59999 POUNDS.	11	100.0	72.8	27.2	-	-	-	-	-
60000 TO 89999 POUNDS.	-	100.0	-	-	-	-	-	-	-
90000 POUNDS AND OVER.	6	100.0	100.0	-	-	-	-	-	-
TON-MILES OF SHIPMENTS	(millions of ton-miles)								
U.S. TOTAL..........	292	100.0	19.1	71.0	4.4	2.3	.1	2.9	.1
UNDER 100 MILES.........	6	100.0	3.6	85.6	8.0	1.0	.2	1.1	.4
UNDER 1000 POUNDS.....	1	100.0	-	83.8	9.5	.4	.1	6.1	.1
1000 TO 9999 POUNDS...	2	100.0	-	94.3	3.3	1.5	-	-	.8
10000 TO 29999 POUNDS.	-	100.0	9.5	73.0	16.0	1.4	-	-	-
30000 TO 59999 POUNDS.	-	100.0	5.0	80.0	14.7	-	.3	-	-
60000 TO 89999 POUNDS.	-	100.0	38.5	56.6	-	-	4.8	-	-
90000 POUNDS AND OVER.	-	100.0	-	-	-	-	-	-	-
100 TO 199 MILES........	16	100.0	-	86.6	12.3	.2	-	.8	-
UNDER 1000 POUNDS.....	1	100.0	-	89.5	2.5	1.8	-	5.8	.3
1000 TO 9999 POUNDS...	3	100.0	-	90.3	8.7	-	-	1.0	-
10000 TO 29999 POUNDS.	3	100.0	-	97.2	2.8	-	-	-	-
30000 TO 59999 POUNDS.	6	100.0	-	77.1	22.9	-	-	-	-
60000 TO 89999 POUNDS.	-	100.0	-	100.0	-	-	-	-	-
90000 POUNDS AND OVER.	-	100.0	-	100.0	-	-	-	-	-

See footnotes at end of table 4.

TABLE 4. **TCC GROUP 359—Percent Distribution of Distance Shipped and Weight of Shipment, by Means of Transport: 1972**—Continued

Distance shipped and weight of shipment [2] [3]	Number	Percent distribution by means of transport							
		All means of transport	Rail	Motor carrier	Private truck	Air	Water	Other	Unknown
TON-MILES OF SHIPMENTS	(millions of ton-miles)								
200 TO 299 MILES........	19	100.0	18.5	64.3	9.5	.5	.2	7.0	-
UNDER 1000 POUNDS.....	2	100.0	-	88.3	1.6	3.3	-	6.6	.1
1000 TO 9999 POUNDS...	6	100.0	-	91.2	4.1	.3	.7	3.7	-
10000 TO 29999 POUNDS.	4	100.0	8.8	45.7	26.1	-	-	19.5	-
30000 TO 59999 POUNDS.	2	100.0	25.1	65.3	9.6	-	-	-	-
60000 TO 89999 POUNDS.	-	100.0	-	100.0	-	-	-	-	-
90000 POUNDS AND OVER.	2	100.0	100.0	-	-	-	-	-	-
300 TO 499 MILES........	45	100.0	11.3	79.4	4.6	1.1	.3	3.2	.2
UNDER 1000 POUNDS.....	9	100.0	.8	88.2	1.6	4.0	-	4.3	1.0
1000 TO 9999 POUNDS...	14	100.0	.2	93.8	3.0	.7	-	2.1	-
10000 TO 29999 POUNDS.	9	100.0	2.2	76.9	11.8	-	1.3	7.8	-
30000 TO 59999 POUNDS.	5	100.0	-	93.6	6.4	-	-	-	-
60000 TO 89999 POUNDS.	5	100.0	84.3	15.7	-	-	-	-	-
90000 POUNDS AND OVER.	-	100.0	-	100.0	-	-	-	-	-
500 TO 999 MILES........	86	100.0	7.0	83.4	3.9	1.8	-	3.8	.1
UNDER 1000 POUNDS.....	23	100.0	.5	91.6	.2	4.3	-	3.2	.1
1000 TO 9999 POUNDS...	37	100.0	1.6	90.7	4.2	1.3	-	1.9	.2
10000 TO 29999 POUNDS.	13	100.0	2.3	74.8	9.4	-	-	13.5	-
30000 TO 59999 POUNDS.	7	100.0	13.2	81.2	5.7	-	-	-	-
60000 TO 89999 POUNDS.	4	100.0	100.0	-	-	-	-	-	-
90000 POUNDS AND OVER.	-	100.0	-	-	-	-	-	-	-
1000 TO 1499 MILES......	39	100.0	6.5	82.7	7.7	1.8	-	1.1	.1
UNDER 1000 POUNDS.....	8	100.0	.6	89.1	.7	6.7	-	2.5	.4
1000 TO 9999 POUNDS...	19	100.0	.1	97.5	.5	.7	-	1.2	-
10000 TO 29999 POUNDS.	5	100.0	26.2	73.0	.8	-	-	-	-
30000 TO 59999 POUNDS.	4	100.0	-	40.8	59.2	-	-	-	-
60000 TO 89999 POUNDS.	-	100.0	100.0	-	-	-	-	-	-
90000 POUNDS AND OVER.	-	100.0	-	-	-	-	-	-	-
1500 MILES OR OVER......	79	100.0	48.5	44.3	-	4.6	.2	2.4	-
UNDER 1000 POUNDS.....	19	100.0	.8	73.1	.1	16.7	.4	8.8	.1
1000 TO 9999 POUNDS...	8	100.0	15.3	78.2	-	4.1	1.2	1.3	-
10000 TO 29999 POUNDS.	11	100.0	33.3	66.7	-	-	-	-	-
30000 TO 59999 POUNDS.	25	100.0	75.7	24.3	-	-	-	-	-
60000 TO 89999 POUNDS.	-	100.0	-	-	-	-	-	-	-
90000 POUNDS AND OVER.	13	100.0	100.0	-	-	-	-	-	-

Note: Detail may not add to total due to rounding. The introductory table shows the estimates of sampling variability for tons; sampling variability for ton-miles has not been estimated. See the map in the Introduction for the States comprising the geographic divisions of the United States.
Shipments excluded from the survey are those moving by pipeline (primarily petroleum products from refineries), parcel post shipments, and commodities moved by own power (motorized vehicles, aircraft, etc.) or towed (prefabricated buildings, etc.). Local shipments (commodities shipped less than 25 miles from the plant) and shipments within the same city are also excluded. Shipments to Alaska and Hawaii from the 48 conterminous States and the District of Columbia are included; however, no data were obtained for shipments originating in Alaska and Hawaii.

- Represents zero or rounds to zero.   (D) Withheld to avoid disclosing figures for individual companies.

[1] Production of this commodity is concentrated in the geographic divisions shown; figures and distributions for geographic divisions not shown are included in the total.
[2] Distances of shipments to foreign destinations are calculated only to the U.S. port of exit.
[3] Includes only shipments represented by bills of lading and invoices. Summary records which did not show individual weights of shipments are not included.

Electrical Machinery, Equipment, and Supplies

CONTENTS

[Page numbers listed here omit the State prefix number that appears as part of the number for each page]

TABLES   (The tables listed below are shown for each of the Transportation Commodity Classification groups in this report)

Comparisons of Tons and Ton-Miles of Shipments for Geographic Divisions of Origin and for Sampling Variability: 1972 and 1967

1. Percent Distribution of Geographic Division of Origin and Distance Shipped, by Means of Transport: 1972

2. Percent Distribution of Geographic Division of Origin and Means of Transport, by Geographic Division of Destination: 1972

3. Percent Distribution of Geographic Division of Destination and Means of Transport, by Geographic Division of Origin: 1972

4. Percent Distribution of Distance Shipped and Weight of Shipment, by Means of Transport: 1972

TCC 361. Electrical Transmission Equipment

Comparisons of Tons and Ton-Miles of Shipments for
Geographic Divisions of Origin and for Sampling Variability: 1972 and 1967

Geographic division of origin	Estimates				Relative sampling variability in tons (percent)	
	1972		1967		1972	1967
	Tons (thousands)	Ton-miles (millions)	Tons (thousands)	Ton-miles (millions)		
U.S. total	1,719	1,086	1,601	1,023	6.4	12.6
New England	(D)	(D)	177	201	(*)	(*)
Middle Atlantic	437	268	583	320	11.4	(*)
East North Central	529	260	495	301	15.2	(*)
West North Central	85	54	153	71	27.1	(*)
South Atlantic	182	104	73	44	19.8	(*)
East South Central	86	57	59	54	21.3	(*)
West South Central	85	64	22	17	24.2	(*)
Mountain	(D)	(D)	1	1	(*)	(*)
Pacific	64	44	38	14	43.2	(*)

(D) Withheld to avoid disclosing figures for individual companies.   (*) Data not published.

TABLE 1. **TCC GROUP 361**—Percent Distribution of Geographic Division of Origin and Distance Shipped, by Means of Transport: 1972

Geographic division of origin[1] and distance shipped[2]	Number	Percent distribution by means of transport							
		All means of transport	Rail	Motor carrier	Private truck	Air	Water	Other	Unknown
TONS OF SHIPMENTS	(thousands of tons)								
U.S. TOTAL	1 719	100.0	15.3	61.4	20.8	1.0	.2	1.0	.2
MIDDLE ATLANTIC	437	100.0	17.7	71.1	10.0	.4	-	.6	.2
UNDER 100 MILES	61	100.0	1.4	83.3	14.4	.1	-	.7	.1
100 TO 199 MILES	34	100.0	8.8	87.8	2.1	.1	-	.9	.2
200 TO 299 MILES	81	100.0	24.4	53.0	21.9	.3	-	.4	-
300 TO 499 MILES	87	100.0	11.6	82.7	4.3	.8	-	.7	-
500 TO 999 MILES	86	100.0	31.7	57.7	9.5	.6	-	.6	-
1000 TO 1499 MILES	43	100.0	19.8	69.9	9.6	.4	-	.4	-
1500 MILES OR OVER	43	100.0	17.9	78.6	.5	.6	.1	.6	1.7
EAST NORTH CENTRAL	529	100.0	10.0	51.9	36.3	.9	.1	.7	.1
UNDER 100 MILES	62	100.0	-	35.0	64.3	.2	-	.3	.2
100 TO 199 MILES	106	100.0	2.2	49.5	47.8	.1	-	.4	-
200 TO 299 MILES	61	100.0	6.7	74.1	18.0	.3	-	.8	-
300 TO 499 MILES	103	100.0	.4	71.2	27.1	.5	-	.8	.1
500 TO 999 MILES	139	100.0	15.7	40.3	42.4	.7	-	.9	-
1000 TO 1499 MILES	17	100.0	10.4	71.2	4.0	11.9	-	2.6	-
1500 MILES OR OVER	39	100.0	57.7	32.5	6.3	2.3	.8	.4	-
WEST NORTH CENTRAL	85	100.0	5.9	84.7	6.1	.9	-	2.2	.3
UNDER 100 MILES	1	100.0	-	72.9	9.2	.2	-	1.1	16.6
100 TO 199 MILES	7	100.0	46.6	52.8	-	-	-	.6	-
200 TO 299 MILES	9	100.0	-	71.7	24.4	-	-	3.8	-
300 TO 499 MILES	20	100.0	-	85.8	10.8	.1	-	3.2	-
500 TO 999 MILES	34	100.0	4.8	92.0	.6	.6	-	2.0	-
1000 TO 1499 MILES	10	100.0	-	93.6	-	5.5	-	.9	-
1500 MILES OR OVER	2	100.0	-	83.3	14.4	.8	-	.2	1.3
SOUTH ATLANTIC	182	100.0	12.7	75.6	10.4	.4	.3	.5	-
UNDER 100 MILES	7	100.0	-	39.9	59.4	-	-	.8	-
100 TO 199 MILES	34	100.0	-	84.9	14.8	-	.2	-	-
200 TO 299 MILES	12	100.0	-	99.8	.1	-	-	.2	-
300 TO 499 MILES	27	100.0	9.4	85.4	4.4	.3	-	.6	-
500 TO 999 MILES	84	100.0	24.2	64.3	9.8	.6	.3	.7	-
1000 TO 1499 MILES	4	100.0	-	99.5	-	.1	-	.4	-
1500 MILES OR OVER	11	100.0	.5	95.1	.2	1.5	2.4	.3	-
EAST SOUTH CENTRAL	86	100.0	11.6	26.7	58.8	.3	-	.1	2.5
UNDER 100 MILES	3	100.0	-	22.1	77.9	-	-	-	-
100 TO 199 MILES	11	100.0	-	39.9	60.0	-	-	.1	-
200 TO 299 MILES	2	100.0	-	30.8	68.1	.5	-	.6	-
300 TO 499 MILES	15	100.0	-	23.8	76.0	.1	-	.1	-
500 TO 999 MILES	27	100.0	35.8	10.0	53.4	.6	-	.2	-
1000 TO 1499 MILES	17	100.0	-	17.0	70.8	-	-	-	12.2
1500 MILES OR OVER	7	100.0	-	96.7	2.4	.8	-	.2	-
WEST SOUTH CENTRAL	85	100.0	3.4	77.1	17.2	2.2	-	-	-
UNDER 100 MILES	1	100.0	-	57.3	39.3	3.4	-	-	-
100 TO 199 MILES	7	100.0	.1	61.7	38.1	-	-	-	-
200 TO 299 MILES	6	100.0	7.4	73.0	19.5	.1	-	-	-
300 TO 499 MILES	12	100.0	5.0	69.7	24.2	1.1	-	-	-
500 TO 999 MILES	32	100.0	5.6	76.9	14.1	3.3	-	.1	-
1000 TO 1499 MILES	21	100.0	-	88.9	9.7	1.4	-	-	-
1500 MILES OR OVER	3	100.0	-	79.7	11.0	9.1	-	.2	-
PACIFIC	64	100.0	4.1	75.8	.4	6.5	4.3	8.7	.2
UNDER 100 MILES	20	100.0	-	83.6	.7	.4	-	15.3	-
100 TO 199 MILES	7	100.0	-	94.0	1.4	.2	-	3.2	1.2
200 TO 299 MILES	7	100.0	-	98.6	-	.5	-	.9	-
300 TO 499 MILES	8	100.0	-	75.9	-	9.0	-	15.0	-
500 TO 999 MILES	2	100.0	4.6	72.8	-	9.2	-	13.4	-
1000 TO 1499 MILES	3	100.0	17.5	71.4	-	10.8	-	.3	-
1500 MILES OR OVER	14	100.0	13.5	45.0	-	18.8	18.8	3.7	.3
TON-MILES OF SHIPMENTS	(millions of ton-miles)								
U.S. TOTAL	1 086	100.0	21.4	61.0	13.8	1.9	.9	.7	.4
MIDDLE ATLANTIC	268	100.0	20.6	71.7	5.9	.5	.1	.6	.6
UNDER 100 MILES	3	100.0	2.3	88.0	9.0	-	-	.4	.2
100 TO 199 MILES	4	100.0	9.3	87.1	2.1	.1	-	1.1	.3
200 TO 299 MILES	20	100.0	21.9	53.9	23.5	.3	-	.4	-
300 TO 499 MILES	33	100.0	11.3	83.2	3.9	.9	-	.6	-
500 TO 999 MILES	56	100.0	30.4	60.6	7.7	.6	-	.6	-
1000 TO 1499 MILES	51	100.0	20.8	69.6	8.8	.4	.3	.6	1.6
1500 MILES OR OVER	98	100.0	18.9	77.5	.5	.6	.3	.6	

See footnotes at end of table 4.

TABLE 1. **TCC GROUP 361**—Percent Distribution of Geographic Division of Origin and Distance Shipped, by Means of Transport: 1972—Continued

Geographic division of origin[1] and distance shipped[2]	Number	Percent distribution by means of transport							
		All means of transport	Rail	Motor carrier	Private truck	Air	Water	Other	Unknown
TON-MILES OF SHIPMENTS	(millions of ton-miles)								
EAST NORTH CENTRAL......	260	100.0	22.5	47.7	26.5	1.9	.5	.9	-
UNDER 100 MILES........	3	100.0	-	38.4	60.9	.2	-	.3	.2
100 TO 199 MILES......	14	100.0	2.7	51.8	44.9	.2	-	.4	-
200 TO 299 MILES......	15	100.0	6.1	74.2	18.6	.3	-	.9	-
300 TO 499 MILES......	40	100.0	.5	66.9	31.3	.4	-	.8	.1
500 TO 999 MILES......	97	100.0	16.2	41.0	41.3	.7	-	.9	-
1000 TO 1499 MILES....	19	100.0	11.4	70.7	4.3	11.1	-	2.5	-
1500 MILES OR OVER....	69	100.0	56.5	32.8	5.5	2.8	1.9	.5	-
WEST NORTH CENTRAL......	54	100.0	3.4	88.5	4.3	1.6	-	1.8	.3
UNDER 100 MILES........	-	100.0	-	61.8	10.4	.2	-	1.0	26.6
100 TO 199 MILES......	1	100.0	51.3	48.1	-	-	-	.6	-
200 TO 299 MILES......	2	100.0	-	70.5	25.8	-	-	3.7	-
300 TO 499 MILES......	8	100.0	-	85.8	10.9	.1	-	3.2	-
500 TO 999 MILES......	25	100.0	4.9	91.8	.8	.6	-	1.9	-
1000 TO 1499 MILES....	12	100.0	-	93.6	-	5.6	-	.8	-
1500 MILES OR OVER....	4	100.0	-	82.7	13.3	.8	-	.1	3.1
SOUTH ATLANTIC..........	104	100.0	13.7	78.2	6.1	.7	.8	.5	-
UNDER 100 MILES........	-	100.0	-	43.9	55.4	-	-	.7	-
100 TO 199 MILES......	5	100.0	-	83.9	15.8	-	.2	-	-
200 TO 299 MILES......	3	100.0	-	99.8	.1	-	-	.2	-
300 TO 499 MILES......	10	100.0	9.6	85.5	3.9	.3	-	.7	-
500 TO 999 MILES......	56	100.0	23.1	66.6	8.6	.7	.4	.6	-
1000 TO 1499 MILES....	5	100.0	-	99.5	-	.1	-	.4	-
1500 MILES OR OVER....	22	100.0	.5	94.8	.2	1.5	2.6	.3	-
EAST SOUTH CENTRAL......	57	100.0	12.3	34.3	49.1	.4	-	.1	3.8
UNDER 100 MILES........	-	100.0	-	33.4	66.6	-	-	-	-
100 TO 199 MILES......	2	100.0	-	39.4	60.5	-	-	.1	-
200 TO 299 MILES......	-	100.0	-	30.6	68.2	.6	-	.7	-
300 TO 499 MILES......	5	100.0	-	22.6	77.2	.1	-	.1	-
500 TO 999 MILES......	17	100.0	40.1	11.0	48.0	.7	-	.2	-
1000 TO 1499 MILES....	18	100.0	-	17.2	71.0	-	-	-	11.9
1500 MILES OR OVER....	12	100.0	-	96.4	2.6	.7	-	.2	-
WEST SOUTH CENTRAL......	64	100.0	2.7	80.9	13.4	2.9	-	.1	-
UNDER 100 MILES........	-	100.0	-	66.5	31.8	1.7	-	-	-
100 TO 199 MILES......	1	100.0	.1	66.5	33.4	-	-	-	-
200 TO 299 MILES......	1	100.0	6.9	74.9	18.1	.1	-	-	-
300 TO 499 MILES......	5	100.0	5.0	70.7	23.1	1.1	-	-	-
500 TO 999 MILES......	23	100.0	5.9	77.0	14.0	3.0	-	.1	-
1000 TO 1499 MILES....	26	100.0	-	88.3	10.3	1.3	-	-	-
1500 MILES OR OVER....	6	100.0	-	76.9	10.6	12.4	-	.2	-
PACIFIC.................	44	100.0	11.2	52.0	.1	16.2	15.9	4.3	.3
UNDER 100 MILES........	-	100.0	-	92.3	.5	.3	-	6.9	-
100 TO 199 MILES......	1	100.0	-	94.0	1.6	.2	-	2.9	1.3
200 TO 299 MILES......	1	100.0	-	98.3	-	.5	-	1.2	-
300 TO 499 MILES......	3	100.0	-	75.8	-	10.7	-	13.5	-
500 TO 999 MILES......	1	100.0	4.6	71.3	-	8.7	-	15.3	-
1000 TO 1499 MILES....	3	100.0	19.4	68.7	-	11.6	-	.4	-
1500 MILES OR OVER....	31	100.0	12.9	41.6	-	19.5	22.0	3.5	.3

See footnotes at end of table 4.

TABLE 2. **TCC GROUP 361**—Percent Distribution of Geographic Division of Origin and Means of Transport, by Geographic Division of Destination: 1972

Geographic division of origin[1] and means of transport	Number	Percent distribution by division of destination									
		U.S. total	New England	Middle Atlantic	East North Central	West North Central	South Atlantic	East South Central	West South Central	Mountain	Pacific
TONS OF SHIPMENTS	(thousands of tons)										
U.S. TOTAL..............	1 719	100.0	2.9	16.4	29.5	5.2	19.5	5.2	9.6	2.7	9.1
RAIL.................	263	100.0	1.6	8.5	30.6	8.1	22.3	1.8	12.6	3.3	11.2
MOTOR CARRIER........	1 056	100.0	3.6	17.3	25.6	5.4	18.6	5.1	10.7	3.3	10.4
PRIVATE TRUCK........	357	100.0	.8	19.3	42.2	2.6	21.5	8.2	4.0	.2	1.2
AIR..................	16	100.0	4.1	17.8	11.2	6.1	9.4	6.4	17.5	5.4	22.1
WATER................	3	100.0	-	7.6	-	-	-	-	1.7	-	90.7
OTHER................	17	100.0	17.0	14.3	15.0	4.6	8.3	3.3	5.8	2.1	29.7
UNKNOWN..............	3	100.0	.7	64.1	5.0	4.6	.9	-	.3	6.3	18.0

See footnotes at end of table 4.

TABLE 2. **TCC GROUP 361—Percent Distribution of Geographic Division of Origin and Means of Transport, by Geographic Division of Destination: 1972**—Continued

Geographic division of origin[1] and means of transport	Number	Percent distribution by division of destination									
		U.S. total	New England	Middle Atlantic	East North Central	West North Central	South Atlantic	East South Central	West South Central	Mountain	Pacific
TONS OF SHIPMENTS	(thousands of tons)										
MIDDLE ATLANTIC	437	100.0	4.7	24.7	23.1	3.4	20.6	3.8	9.4	2.8	7.4
RAIL	77	100.0	5.3	5.7	36.5	5.8	24.1	2.6	8.3	2.7	8.8
MOTOR CARRIER	311	100.0	5.0	29.0	18.2	3.2	18.0	4.5	11.1	3.1	7.8
PRIVATE TRUCK	43	100.0	1.0	27.7	35.9	.8	33.8	.3	-	-	.5
AIR	1	100.0	1.5	7.3	7.0	5.8	24.0	35.6	6.2	3.9	8.7
WATER	-	100.0	-	1.3	-	-	-	-	-	-	98.7
OTHER	2	100.0	8.3	35.4	19.2	3.8	15.5	2.4	5.6	2.5	7.3
UNKNOWN	-	100.0	1.1	11.3	2.2	-	2.8	-	-	25.3	57.3
EAST NORTH CENTRAL	529	100.0	2.0	15.3	42.9	4.9	13.2	6.9	6.4	1.1	7.3
RAIL	53	100.0	-	20.1	12.0	1.7	8.4	4.2	10.9	-	42.5
MOTOR CARRIER	274	100.0	3.3	15.2	47.6	6.7	9.2	5.1	6.6	1.9	4.4
PRIVATE TRUCK	192	100.0	.6	14.3	45.7	3.3	20.5	10.4	3.8	.2	1.3
AIR	4	100.0	4.2	9.1	13.1	1.3	7.6	1.7	43.9	.8	18.3
WATER	-	100.0	-	4.3	-	-	-	-	-	-	95.7
OTHER	3	100.0	6.2	13.3	29.1	11.3	15.0	7.2	12.6	1.2	4.3
UNKNOWN	-	100.0	-	42.9	47.1	-	-	-	4.1	-	5.8
WEST NORTH CENTRAL	85	100.0	1.6	11.9	21.8	18.5	20.7	9.6	6.2	3.8	5.7
RAIL	5	100.0	-	18.4	67.3	-	8.0	3.3	3.1	-	-
MOTOR CARRIER	72	100.0	1.8	11.6	18.5	20.0	23.5	7.8	6.7	4.5	5.6
PRIVATE TRUCK	5	100.0	-	4.3	25.9	19.1	-	43.2	-	-	7.5
AIR	-	100.0	1.3	36.0	2.1	.5	4.8	.2	.5	2.0	52.6
WATER	-	100.0	-	-	-	-	-	-	-	-	-
OTHER	1	100.0	3.1	18.6	26.2	10.5	14.2	9.1	18.1	-	.2
UNKNOWN	-	100.0	-	.4	7.4	76.1	-	-	-	-	16.1
SOUTH ATLANTIC	182	100.0	2.3	12.5	21.9	4.5	31.9	7.6	12.7	2.5	4.0
RAIL	23	100.0	-	22.6	56.6	8.3	7.2	-	5.1	-	.2
MOTOR CARRIER	137	100.0	3.0	8.9	16.7	4.6	34.0	10.1	14.6	3.3	4.8
PRIVATE TRUCK	19	100.0	.2	22.6	18.7	-	49.9	.1	8.5	-	.1
AIR	-	100.0	1.8	12.9	23.3	7.8	7.6	.2	24.7	.3	21.5
WATER	-	100.0	-	44.7	-	-	-	-	10.6	-	44.7
OTHER	-	100.0	1.9	51.0	23.0	3.2	11.2	2.2	3.4	2.8	1.3
UNKNOWN	-	100.0	-	-	85.7	-	14.3	-	-	-	-
EAST SOUTH CENTRAL	86	100.0	.1	23.6	42.3	.9	13.2	8.9	2.0	.3	8.6
RAIL	10	100.0	-	-	72.0	-	28.0	-	-	-	-
MOTOR CARRIER	22	100.0	.3	18.2	25.9	1.2	7.4	7.6	7.0	.8	31.5
PRIVATE TRUCK	50	100.0	-	27.4	45.9	1.0	13.5	11.7	.2	-	.4
AIR	-	100.0	5.1	60.7	7.1	.6	-	.6	1.1	17.5	7.2
WATER	-	100.0	-	-	-	-	-	-	-	-	-
OTHER	2	100.0	11.0	2.8	26.9	11.0	17.9	13.4	4.2	.1	12.7
UNKNOWN	2	100.0	-	100.0	-	-	-	-	-	-	-
WEST SOUTH CENTRAL	85	100.0	2.5	7.9	13.7	8.3	22.2	3.3	26.2	5.5	10.5
RAIL	2	100.0	-	-	-	-	75.0	-	25.0	-	-
MOTOR CARRIER	65	100.0	1.6	9.6	15.6	8.2	19.6	2.3	24.7	6.5	11.8
PRIVATE TRUCK	14	100.0	6.9	.7	8.0	7.6	25.7	7.2	36.2	2.2	5.4
AIR	1	100.0	.1	12.4	12.3	30.3	7.2	11.3	3.1	4.5	18.9
WATER	-	100.0	-	-	-	-	-	-	-	-	-
OTHER	-	100.0	8.8	35.7	25.5	10.4	13.7	3.9	1.9	-	-
UNKNOWN	-	100.0	-	-	21.7	54.6	-	-	-	-	23.7
PACIFIC	64	100.0	1.0	3.7	6.0	.9	4.9	.9	2.4	10.1	70.2
RAIL	2	100.0	.3	10.5	16.4	-	37.5	9.2	22.0	-	4.1
MOTOR CARRIER	49	100.0	.4	1.6	5.5	.8	3.4	.4	1.4	12.4	74.0
PRIVATE TRUCK	-	100.0	1.0	.9	-	-	-	-	.4	-	97.8
AIR	4	100.0	8.6	27.3	11.4	3.6	9.5	2.3	6.3	5.6	25.4
WATER	2	100.0	-	-	-	-	-	-	-	-	100.0
OTHER	5	100.0	.8	2.9	4.3	.2	.9	.5	.1	4.0	86.3
UNKNOWN	-	100.0	12.6	10.0	3.6	-	6.9	-	.1	-	66.9
TON-MILES OF SHIPMENTS	(millions of ton-miles)										
U.S. TOTAL	1 086	100.0	2.5	11.3	16.4	5.5	17.6	3.3	15.7	5.6	22.2
RAIL	232	100.0	.7	5.8	17.4	9.1	16.3	1.4	18.6	6.6	24.1
MOTOR CARRIER	662	100.0	3.2	9.4	14.2	5.0	16.7	3.5	17.2	6.5	24.2
PRIVATE TRUCK	149	100.0	1.5	25.8	27.6	2.5	26.5	5.2	5.8	.6	4.4
AIR	20	100.0	6.1	22.0	7.6	4.1	8.7	3.3	15.6	2.8	29.7
WATER	9	100.0	-	2.7	-	-	-	-	.1	-	97.2
OTHER	7	100.0	9.0	17.5	15.4	5.3	13.3	3.8	11.1	3.9	20.7
UNKNOWN	4	100.0	1.1	53.9	.6	.4	.6	-	.3	11.0	32.0

See footnotes at end of table 4.

TABLE 2. TCC GROUP 361—Percent Distribution of Geographic Division of Origin and Means of Transport, by Geographic Division of Destination: 1972—Continued

Geographic division of origin[1] and means of transport	Number	Percent distribution by division of destination									
		U.S. total	New England	Middle Atlantic	East North Central	West North Central	South Atlantic	East South Central	West South Central	Mountain	Pacific
TON-MILES OF SHIPMENTS	(millions of ton-miles)										
MIDDLE ATLANTIC	268	100.0	3.0	5.6	13.6	4.8	15.1	3.6	17.4	7.7	29.1
RAIL	55	100.0	2.7	1.8	23.3	7.9	11.9	1.6	14.3	6.0	30.5
MOTOR CARRIER	192	100.0	3.4	6.6	9.8	4.2	12.5	4.3	20.0	8.7	30.5
PRIVATE TRUCK	15	100.0	.2	8.1	27.1	1.5	59.8	.5	-	-	2.9
AIR	1	100.0	.5	1.9	4.9	7.2	14.5	23.5	11.0	9.8	26.8
WATER	-	100.0	-	-	-	-	-	-	-	-	100.0
OTHER	1	100.0	4.5	9.7	14.6	6.1	14.9	2.6	11.6	7.2	28.9
UNKNOWN	1	100.0	.1	.8	.3	-	.3	-	-	28.2	70.3
EAST NORTH CENTRAL	260	100.0	3.1	17.6	14.3	4.2	15.0	4.8	12.2	2.6	26.2
RAIL	58	100.0	-	12.7	2.3	.8	5.4	2.9	9.2	-	66.7
MOTOR CARRIER	123	100.0	5.5	16.1	21.0	6.1	10.7	4.1	14.0	4.9	17.5
PRIVATE TRUCK	68	100.0	1.2	25.9	13.9	4.0	31.6	8.0	9.2	.6	5.5
AIR	5	100.0	3.3	4.9	2.7	.5	4.9	.7	43.7	1.0	38.1
WATER	1	100.0	-	.8	-	-	-	-	-	-	99.2
OTHER	2	100.0	8.0	12.3	9.1	8.1	19.1	5.1	20.3	2.4	15.7
UNKNOWN	-	100.0	-	51.8	8.1	-	-	-	11.5	-	28.6
WEST NORTH CENTRAL	54	100.0	2.9	15.6	10.6	11.8	26.4	6.6	6.8	5.4	13.9
RAIL	1	100.0	-	39.7	34.0	-	13.6	6.2	6.5	-	-
MOTOR CARRIER	48	100.0	3.1	14.6	9.6	12.7	28.8	5.1	7.1	6.1	12.9
PRIVATE TRUCK	2	100.0	-	8.1	15.0	10.4	-	40.3	-	-	26.1
AIR	-	100.0	1.2	31.0	.8	.1	2.9	.1	.3	1.5	62.1
WATER	-	100.0	-	-	-	-	-	-	-	-	-
OTHER	-	100.0	6.1	26.8	17.6	6.0	19.5	6.0	17.3	-	.7
UNKNOWN	-	100.0	-	.5	.5	10.3	-	-	-	-	88.7
SOUTH ATLANTIC	104	100.0	3.1	12.0	21.1	6.8	13.3	3.5	18.0	7.3	15.0
RAIL	14	100.0	-	24.5	53.2	11.7	4.3	-	5.5	-	.8
MOTOR CARRIER	81	100.0	4.0	7.5	15.1	6.5	14.8	4.5	20.6	9.2	17.8
PRIVATE TRUCK	6	100.0	.4	35.7	30.8	-	16.7	-	15.5	-	.8
AIR	-	100.0	1.4	9.4	12.4	6.7	5.4	.1	19.6	.4	44.6
WATER	-	100.0	-	29.6	-	-	-	-	1.3	-	69.0
OTHER	-	100.0	2.6	49.6	20.7	4.1	3.0	1.5	5.2	7.4	5.9
UNKNOWN	-	100.0	-	-	91.0	-	9.0	-	-	-	-
EAST SOUTH CENTRAL	57	100.0	.1	35.5	27.7	.5	10.5	2.5	.9	.6	21.5
RAIL	7	100.0	-	-	71.1	-	28.9	-	-	-	-
MOTOR CARRIER	19	100.0	.3	20.1	8.6	.6	4.1	1.6	2.4	1.4	60.9
PRIVATE TRUCK	28	100.0	-	50.1	32.6	.7	11.3	4.0	.2	-	1.2
AIR	-	100.0	5.1	47.8	2.5	.4	-	.1	.5	29.8	13.8
WATER	-	100.0	-	-	-	-	-	-	-	-	-
OTHER	-	100.0	16.3	3.2	13.6	9.1	15.8	3.7	3.3	.2	34.9
UNKNOWN	2	100.0	-	100.0	-	-	-	-	-	-	-
WEST SOUTH CENTRAL	64	100.0	4.4	12.1	12.3	6.9	24.6	1.2	10.0	7.6	20.9
RAIL	1	100.0	-	-	-	-	89.4	-	10.6	-	-
MOTOR CARRIER	52	100.0	2.9	14.2	13.4	7.2	21.5	1.0	9.4	8.6	21.9
PRIVATE TRUCK	8	100.0	15.8	1.6	8.7	3.9	33.8	2.3	15.3	4.2	14.3
AIR	1	100.0	.1	14.0	9.1	18.3	7.0	5.4	.3	3.7	42.0
WATER	-	100.0	-	-	-	-	-	-	-	-	-
OTHER	-	100.0	15.2	41.2	18.2	4.9	17.4	3.1	.2	-	-
UNKNOWN	-	100.0	-	-	15.8	37.0	-	-	-	-	47.2
PACIFIC	44	100.0	3.8	12.8	16.0	1.8	15.7	2.4	4.5	6.2	36.7
RAIL	4	100.0	.4	13.0	16.6	-	44.1	8.8	15.4	-	1.7
MOTOR CARRIER	23	100.0	2.4	7.9	21.5	2.4	15.9	1.7	3.7	10.9	33.7
PRIVATE TRUCK	-	100.0	18.2	14.1	-	-	.5	-	4.8	-	62.4
AIR	7	100.0	13.1	39.1	12.4	3.3	13.1	2.4	5.1	2.1	9.3
WATER	7	100.0	-	-	-	-	-	-	-	-	100.0
OTHER	1	100.0	6.1	20.1	22.3	.7	6.1	2.8	.5	4.7	36.6
UNKNOWN	-	100.0	35.7	27.3	7.0	-	17.7	-	.1	-	12.1

See footnotes at end of table 4.

TABLE 3. **TCC GROUP 361**—Percent Distribution of Geographic Division of Destination and Means of Transport, by Geographic Division of Origin: 1972

Geographic division of destination and means of transport	Number	Percent distribution by division of origin[1]									
		U.S. total	New England	Middle Atlantic	East North Central	West North Central	South Atlantic	East South Central	West South Central	Mountain	Pacific
TONS OF SHIPMENTS	(thousands of tons)										
U.S. TOTAL..............	1 719	100.0	(D)	25.5	30.8	5.0	10.6	5.0	5.0	(D)	3.8
RAIL................	263	100.0	(D)	29.4	20.1	1.9	8.8	3.8	1.1	(D)	1.0
MOTOR CARRIER.........	1 056	100.0	(D)	29.4	26.0	6.9	13.0	2.2	6.2	(D)	4.7
PRIVATE TRUCK........	357	100.0	(D)	12.2	53.8	1.5	5.3	14.2	4.1	(D)	.1
AIR.................	16	100.0	(D)	11.1	28.5	4.7	4.7	1.5	11.3	(D)	25.1
WATER...............	3	100.0	(D)	1.7	8.6	-	16.1	-	-	(D)	73.6
OTHER...............	17	100.0	(D)	14.6	21.4	10.5	5.1	.6	.2	(D)	31.7
UNKNOWN.............	3	100.0	(D)	24.8	7.6	6.0	-	57.6	.1	(D)	3.6
NEW ENGLAND..........	49	100.0	(D)	41.8	21.6	2.8	8.6	.2	4.3	(D)	1.3
RAIL................	4	100.0	(D)	99.8	-	-	-	-	-	(D)	.2
MOTOR CARRIER.........	38	100.0	(D)	40.8	23.6	3.4	10.8	.2	2.8	(D)	.6
PRIVATE TRUCK........	2	100.0	(D)	16.2	40.3	-	1.2	-	37.0	(D)	.1
AIR.................	-	100.0	(D)	4.1	29.8	1.5	2.1	1.9	.2	(D)	53.5
WATER...............	-	100.0	(D)	-	-	-	-	-	-	(D)	-
OTHER...............	3	100.0	(D)	7.1	7.8	1.9	.6	.4	.1	(D)	1.5
UNKNOWN.............	-	100.0	(D)	37.4	-	-	-	-	-	(D)	62.6
MIDDLE ATLANTIC........	282	100.0	(D)	38.3	28.7	3.6	8.0	7.2	2.4	(D)	.8
RAIL................	22	100.0	(D)	19.7	47.4	4.1	23.2	-	-	(D)	1.3
MOTOR CARRIER.........	182	100.0	(D)	49.5	22.9	4.6	6.8	2.3	3.5	(D)	.4
PRIVATE TRUCK........	69	100.0	(D)	17.5	39.8	.3	6.2	20.1	.2	(D)	-
AIR.................	3	100.0	(D)	4.6	14.6	9.5	3.4	5.1	7.9	(D)	38.4
WATER...............	-	100.0	(D)	.3	4.9	-	94.8	-	-	(D)	-
OTHER...............	2	100.0	(D)	36.0	19.9	13.6	18.3	.1	.6	(D)	6.4
UNKNOWN.............	2	100.0	(D)	4.4	5.1	-	-	89.9	-	(D)	.6
EAST NORTH CENTRAL......	506	100.0	(D)	20.0	44.8	3.7	7.9	7.2	2.3	(D)	.8
RAIL................	80	100.0	(D)	35.1	7.9	4.2	16.2	8.9	-	(D)	.5
MOTOR CARRIER.........	270	100.0	(D)	20.9	48.3	4.9	8.5	2.2	3.8	(D)	1.0
PRIVATE TRUCK........	150	100.0	(D)	10.4	58.3	.9	2.4	15.4	.8	(D)	-
AIR.................	1	100.0	(D)	7.0	33.4	.9	9.7	1.0	12.4	(D)	25.5
WATER...............	-	100.0	(D)	-	-	-	-	-	-	(D)	-
OTHER...............	2	100.0	(D)	18.7	41.5	18.4	7.9	1.1	.4	(D)	9.1
UNKNOWN.............	-	100.0	(D)	11.0	72.4	9.0	.2	-	.3	(D)	2.6
WEST NORTH CENTRAL......	89	100.0	(D)	16.8	29.1	17.7	9.3	.9	7.9	(D)	.6
RAIL................	21	100.0	(D)	21.1	4.3	-	9.0	-	-	(D)	-
MOTOR CARRIER.........	56	100.0	(D)	17.5	32.3	25.6	11.1	.5	9.5	(D)	.7
PRIVATE TRUCK........	9	100.0	(D)	3.8	67.9	10.7	-	5.4	12.1	(D)	-
AIR.................	1	100.0	(D)	10.6	6.2	.4	5.9	.1	56.2	(D)	14.9
WATER...............	-	100.0	(D)	-	-	-	-	-	-	(D)	-
OTHER...............	-	100.0	(D)	12.1	52.9	24.1	3.6	1.4	.5	(D)	1.1
UNKNOWN.............	-	100.0	(D)	.1	-	99.0	-	-	.9	(D)	-
SOUTH ATLANTIC.........	335	100.0	(D)	26.9	20.9	5.3	17.4	3.4	5.7	(D)	.9
RAIL................	58	100.0	(D)	31.8	7.6	.7	2.8	4.8	3.7	(D)	1.7
MOTOR CARRIER.........	196	100.0	(D)	28.4	12.8	8.7	23.8	.9	6.6	(D)	.9
PRIVATE TRUCK........	76	100.0	(D)	19.3	51.3	-	12.4	8.9	4.9	(D)	-
AIR.................	1	100.0	(D)	28.4	23.0	2.4	3.8	-	8.7	(D)	25.3
WATER...............	-	100.0	(D)	-	-	-	-	-	-	(D)	-
OTHER...............	1	100.0	(D)	27.2	38.7	17.9	6.9	1.3	.4	(D)	3.5
UNKNOWN.............	-	100.0	(D)	73.7	-	-	.1	-	-	(D)	26.1
EAST SOUTH CENTRAL......	89	100.0	(D)	18.8	40.9	9.2	15.6	8.6	3.1	(D)	.7
RAIL................	4	100.0	(D)	43.1	47.2	3.4	-	-	-	(D)	5.2
MOTOR CARRIER.........	53	100.0	(D)	25.9	26.1	10.5	25.8	3.3	2.8	(D)	.4
PRIVATE TRUCK........	29	100.0	(D)	.4	68.1	7.7	-	20.2	3.6	(D)	-
AIR.................	1	100.0	(D)	61.8	7.7	.1	.1	.1	19.8	(D)	9.0
WATER...............	-	100.0	(D)	-	-	-	-	-	-	(D)	-
OTHER...............	-	100.0	(D)	10.7	46.0	28.5	3.5	2.4	.3	(D)	4.7
UNKNOWN.............	-	100.0	(D)	-	-	-	-	-	-	(D)	-
WEST SOUTH CENTRAL......	164	100.0	(D)	25.1	20.5	3.2	14.1	1.0	13.6	(D)	.9
RAIL................	33	100.0	(D)	19.4	17.4	.5	3.5	-	2.2	(D)	1.8
MOTOR CARRIER.........	112	100.0	(D)	30.6	16.0	4.3	17.8	1.4	14.4	(D)	.6
PRIVATE TRUCK........	14	100.0	(D)	-	50.9	-	11.2	.6	37.2	(D)	-
AIR.................	2	100.0	(D)	3.9	71.5	.1	6.6	.1	2.0	(D)	9.1
WATER...............	-	100.0	(D)	-	-	-	100.0	-	-	(D)	-
OTHER...............	1	100.0	(D)	14.2	46.6	32.9	3.0	.4	.1	(D)	.8
UNKNOWN.............	-	100.0	(D)	-	99.0	-	-	-	-	(D)	1.0
MOUNTAIN.............	45	100.0	(D)	26.6	12.4	7.1	10.0	.5	10.3	(D)	14.4
RAIL................	8	100.0	(D)	23.8	.2	-	-	-	-	(D)	-
MOTOR CARRIER.........	34	100.0	(D)	27.9	15.0	9.3	13.1	.6	12.4	(D)	17.5
PRIVATE TRUCK........	-	100.0	(D)	-	47.6	-	-	-	45.0	(D)	-
AIR.................	-	100.0	(D)	8.1	4.1	1.8	.2	4.8	9.3	(D)	25.8
WATER...............	-	100.0	(D)	-	-	-	-	-	-	(D)	-
OTHER...............	-	100.0	(D)	17.3	12.3	.2	7.0	-	-	(D)	61.2
UNKNOWN.............	-	100.0	(D)	99.8	-	-	-	-	-	(D)	-
PACIFIC..............	156	100.0	(D)	20.6	24.5	3.1	4.6	4.7	5.7	(D)	29.0
RAIL................	29	100.0	(D)	23.2	76.3	-	.2	-	-	(D)	.4
MOTOR CARRIER.........	109	100.0	(D)	22.1	11.0	3.7	6.1	6.6	7.1	(D)	33.1
PRIVATE TRUCK........	4	100.0	(D)	5.0	57.0	9.1	.5	4.2	18.5	(D)	5.7
AIR.................	3	100.0	(D)	4.4	23.7	11.2	4.5	.5	9.7	(D)	28.9
WATER...............	3	100.0	(D)	1.9	9.1	-	7.9	-	-	(D)	81.1
OTHER...............	5	100.0	(D)	3.6	3.1	.1	.2	.3	-	(D)	92.3
UNKNOWN.............	-	100.0	(D)	78.9	2.5	5.4	-	-	.1	(D)	13.2

See footnotes at end of table 4.

TABLE 3. **TCC GROUP 361**—Percent Distribution of Geográphic Division of Destination and Means of Transport, by Geographic Division of Origin: 1972—Continued

Geographic division of destination and means of transport	Number	Percent distribution by division of origin[1]									
		U.S. total	New England	Middle Atlantic	East North Central	West North Central	South Atlantic	East South Central	West South Central	Mountain	Pacific
TON-MILES OF SHIPMENTS	(millions of ton-miles)										
U.S. TOTAL	1 086	100.0	(D)	24.7	23.9	5.0	9.6	5.3	6.0	(D)	4.1
RAIL	232	100.0	(D)	23.8	25.2	.8	6.1	3.0	.8	(D)	2.1
MOTOR CARRIER	662	100.0	(D)	29.1	18.7	7.3	12.3	3.0	7.9	(D)	3.5
PRIVATE TRUCK	149	100.0	(D)	10.6	46.0	1.6	4.3	18.8	5.8	(D)	-
AIR	20	100.0	(D)	7.2	24.8	4.4	3.8	1.1	9.4	(D)	35.7
WATER	9	100.0	(D)	3.1	14.0	-	8.8	-	-	(D)	74.1
OTHER	7	100.0	(D)	19.3	28.7	12.5	6.5	.9	.5	(D)	24.8
UNKNOWN	4	100.0	(D)	39.1	2.4	3.9	-	51.6	-	(D)	2.9
NEW ENGLAND	26	100.0	(D)	30.4	30.0	5.9	12.3	.3	10.8	(D)	6.3
RAIL	1	100.0	(D)	98.7	-	-	-	-	-	(D)	1.3
MOTOR CARRIER	20	100.0	(D)	31.1	32.7	7.2	15.4	.3	7.2	(D)	2.6
PRIVATE TRUCK	2	100.0	(D)	1.4	36.7	-	1.2	-	59.9	(D)	.3
AIR	1	100.0	(D)	.6	13.5	.8	.9	.9	.2	(D)	76.5
WATER	-	100.0	(D)	-	-	-	-	-	-	(D)	-
OTHER	-	100.0	(D)	9.6	25.5	8.4	1.9	1.6	.8	(D)	17.0
UNKNOWN	-	100.0	(D)	3.5	-	-	-	-	-	(D)	96.5
MIDDLE ATLANTIC	122	100.0	(D)	12.3	37.3	7.0	10.2	16.5	6.4	(D)	4.6
RAIL	13	100.0	(D)	7.3	55.4	5.5	25.9	-	-	(D)	4.8
MOTOR CARRIER	62	100.0	(D)	20.2	31.9	11.3	9.8	6.3	11.9	(D)	2.9
PRIVATE TRUCK	38	100.0	(D)	3.3	46.2	.5	5.9	36.5	.4	(D)	-
AIR	4	100.0	(D)	.6	5.6	6.3	1.6	2.5	6.0	(D)	63.3
WATER	-	100.0	(D)	-	3.9	-	96.1	-	-	(D)	-
OTHER	1	100.0	(D)	10.8	20.2	19.1	18.4	.2	1.1	(D)	28.5
UNKNOWN	2	100.0	(D)	.6	2.3	-	-	95.6	-.	(D)	1.5
EAST NORTH CENTRAL	178	100.0	(D)	20.4	20.9	3.3	12.4	8.9	4.5	(D)	4.0
RAIL	40	100.0	(D)	31.8	3.3	1.6	18.7	12.3	-	(D)	2.0
MOTOR CARRIER	93	100.0	(D)	20.2	27.8	4.9	13.1	1.8	7.5	(D)	5.3
PRIVATE TRUCK	41	100.0	(D)	10.4	23.1	.9	4.8	22.1	1.8	(D)	5.3
AIR	1	100.0	(D)	4.7	8.9	.5	6.2	.4	11.2	(D)	58.6
WATER	-	100.0	(D)	-	-	-	-	-	-	(D)	-
OTHER	1	100.0	(D)	18.2	16.9	14.2	8.7	.8	.6	(D)	35.9
UNKNOWN	-	100.0	(D)	16.2	29.9	2.8	.3	-	1.1	(D)	31.4
WEST NORTH CENTRAL	59	100.0	(D)	21.5	18.4	10.9	11.9	.5	7.5	(D)	1.3
RAIL	21	100.0	(D)	20.6	2.2	-	7.9	-	-	(D)	-
MOTOR CARRIER	33	100.0	(D)	24.0	22.6	18.5	16.0	.4	11.3	(D)	1.7
PRIVATE TRUCK	3	100.0	(D)	6.3	73.2	6.5	-	4.9	9.0	(D)	-
AIR	-	100.0	(D)	12.8	3.3	.1	6.2	.1	42.2	(D)	28.5
WATER	-	100.0	(D)	-	-	-	-	-	-	(D)	-
OTHER	-	100.0	(D)	22.3	44.0	14.3	5.1	1.5	.4	(D)	3.3
UNKNOWN	-	100.0	(D)	1.0	-	95.1	-	-	3.9	(D)	-
SOUTH ATLANTIC	190	100.0	(D)	21.3	20.4	7.6	7.3	3.2	8.3	(D)	3.6
RAIL	37	100.0	(D)	17.3	8.3	.7	1.6	5.3	4.2	(D)	5.8
MOTOR CARRIER	110	100.0	(D)	21.9	12.1	12.7	11.0	.7	10.2	(D)	3.3
PRIVATE TRUCK	39	100.0	(D)	24.0	54.9	-	2.7	8.0	7.4	(D)	-
AIR	1	100.0	(D)	11.9	14.1	1.5	2.4	-	7.6	(D)	53.3
WATER	-	100.0	(D)	-	-	-	-	-	-	(D)	-
OTHER	1	100.0	(D)	21.7	41.3	18.3	1.5	1.0	.6	(D)	11.5
UNKNOWN	-	100.0	(D)	18.6	-	-	-	-	-	(D)	81.4
EAST SOUTH CENTRAL	35	100.0	(D)	27.5	35.2	10.3	10.5	4.1	2.3	(D)	3.0
RAIL	3	100.0	(D)	27.7	53.1	3.7	-	-	-	(D)	14.0
MOTOR CARRIER	23	100.0	(D)	35.8	21.9	10.7	15.8	1.3	2.2	(D)	1.7
PRIVATE TRUCK	7	100.0	(D)	1.0	70.0	12.2	-	14.3	2.6	(D)	-
AIR	-	100.0	(D)	50.9	5.4	.1	.1	-	15.4	(D)	25.7
WATER	-	100.0	(D)	-	-	-	-	-	-	(D)	-
OTHER	-	100.0	(D)	12.9	38.4	19.3	2.5	.8	.4	(D)	18.3
UNKNOWN	-	100.0	(D)	-	-	-	-	-	-	(D)	-
WEST SOUTH CENTRAL	170	100.0	(D)	27.5	18.6	2.2	11.0	.3	3.8	(D)	1.2
RAIL	43	100.0	(D)	18.3	12.5	.3	1.8	-	.4	(D)	1.8
MOTOR CARRIER	114	100.0	(D)	33.7	15.2	3.0	14.7	.4	4.3	(D)	.8
PRIVATE TRUCK	8	100.0	(D)	-	72.7	-	11.3	.7	15.2	(D)	-
AIR	3	100.0	(D)	5.1	69.6	.1	4.8	-	.2	(D)	11.7
WATER	-	100.0	(D)	-	-	-	100.0	-	-	(D)	-
OTHER	-	100.0	(D)	20.1	52.6	19.4	3.0	.3	-	(D)	1.2
UNKNOWN	-	100.0	(D)	-	98.4	-	-	-	-	(D)	1.6
MOUNTAIN	60	100.0	(D)	34.2	11.0	4.9	12.4	.6	8.1	(D)	4.5
RAIL	15	100.0	(D)	21.5	.1	-	-	-	-	(D)	-
MOTOR CARRIER	43	100.0	(D)	38.9	14.1	6.8	17.4	.6	10.4	(D)	5.8
PRIVATE TRUCK	-	100.0	(D)	-	48.8	-	-	-	40.1	(D)	-
AIR	-	100.0	(D)	24.7	8.5	2.3	.5	11.9	12.2	(D)	26.8
WATER	-	100.0	(D)	-	-	-	-	-	-	(D)	-
OTHER	-	100.0	(D)	35.4	17.5	.1	12.3	-	-	(D)	29.6
UNKNOWN	-	100.0	(D)	100.0	-	-	-	-	-	(D)	-
PACIFIC	241	100.0	(D)	32.4	28.2	3.2	6.5	5.1	5.6	(D)	6.7
RAIL	56	100.0	(D)	30.0	69.6	-	.2	-	-	(D)	.2
MOTOR CARRIER	160	100.0	(D)	36.6	13.5	3.9	9.0	7.4	7.1	(D)	4.8
PRIVATE TRUCK	6	100.0	(D)	7.2	58.0	9.5	.8	5.1	19.0	(D)	.3
AIR	5	100.0	(D)	6.5	31.9	9.3	5.7	.5	13.3	(D)	11.2
WATER	9	100.0	(D)	3.2	14.3	-	6.3	-	-	(D)	76.2
OTHER	1	100.0	(D)	27.0	21.7	.4	1.9	1.5	-	(D)	43.9
UNKNOWN	1	100.0	(D)	85.9	2.1	10.8	-	-	.1	(D)	1.1

See footnotes at end of table 4.

TABLE 4. TCC GROUP 361—Percent Distribution of Distance Shipped and Weight of Shipment, by Means of Transport: 1972

Distance shipped and weight of shipment[2][3]	Number	Percent distribution by means of transport							
		All means of transport	Rail	Motor carrier	Private truck	Air	Water	Other	Unknown
TONS OF SHIPMENTS	(thousands of tons)								
U.S. TOTAL..........	1 467	100.0	15.4	67.1	14.9	1.1	.2	1.1	.3
UNDER 100 MILES.........	115	100.0	1.2	76.3	16.9	.6	-	4.6	.3
UNDER 1000 POUNDS.....	25	100.0	-	69.8	13.3	1.1	-	15.6	.3
1000 TO 9999 POUNDS...	47	100.0	.1	83.8	11.8	.9	-	2.7	.6
10000 TO 29999 POUNDS.	33	100.0	3.9	71.3	24.8	-	-	-	-
30000 TO 59999 POUNDS.	8	100.0	-	72.0	28.0	-	-	-	-
60000 TO 89999 POUNDS.	-	100.0	-	-	-	-	-	-	-
90000 POUNDS AND OVER.	-	100.0	-	100.0	-	-	-	-	-
100 TO 199 MILES........	180	100.0	4.8	74.9	19.0	.1	-	1.0	.1
UNDER 1000 POUNDS.....	20	100.0	-	88.0	6.0	1.0	-	4.3	.6
1000 TO 9999 POUNDS...	54	100.0	-	89.6	8.5	.1	-	1.8	.1
10000 TO 29999 POUNDS.	48	100.0	1.0	77.4	21.5	-	-	-	-
30000 TO 59999 POUNDS.	48	100.0	3.9	62.5	33.6	-	-	-	-
60000 TO 89999 POUNDS.	2	100.0	28.9	-	71.1	-	-	-	-
90000 POUNDS AND OVER.	5	100.0	99.1	-	-	-	.9	-	-
200 TO 299 MILES........	164	100.0	16.1	66.3	16.5	.3	-	.8	-
UNDER 1000 POUNDS.....	17	100.0	.1	86.4	3.1	2.9	-	7.3	.1
1000 TO 9999 POUNDS...	49	100.0	.4	87.0	12.5	-	-	-	-
10000 TO 29999 POUNDS.	31	100.0	5.1	59.8	35.2	-	-	-	-
30000 TO 59999 POUNDS.	37	100.0	8.9	65.9	25.2	-	-	-	-
60000 TO 89999 POUNDS.	11	100.0	60.2	39.8	-	-	-	-	-
90000 POUNDS AND OVER.	17	100.0	81.9	18.1	-	-	-	-	-
300 TO 499 MILES........	283	100.0	8.7	71.7	17.7	.7	-	1.2	-
UNDER 1000 POUNDS.....	32	100.0	.1	79.9	5.7	4.5	-	9.9	-
1000 TO 9999 POUNDS...	76	100.0	-	86.1	12.8	.9	-	.1	.2
10000 TO 29999 POUNDS.	63	100.0	5.7	80.1	14.2	-	-	-	-
30000 TO 59999 POUNDS.	90	100.0	5.2	61.9	32.9	-	-	-	-
60000 TO 89999 POUNDS.	7	100.0	34.0	66.0	-	-	-	-	-
90000 POUNDS AND OVER.	13	100.0	100.0	-	-	-	-	-	-
500 TO 999 MILES........	424	100.0	21.5	61.1	15.8	.9	.1	.7	-
UNDER 1000 POUNDS.....	40	100.0	.7	74.3	10.8	7.4	-	6.8	-
1000 TO 9999 POUNDS...	96	100.0	3.1	74.2	21.5	.9	-	.3	-
10000 TO 29999 POUNDS.	72	100.0	6.4	80.5	13.0	-	-	-	-
30000 TO 59999 POUNDS.	144	100.0	15.7	61.8	22.5	-	-	-	-
60000 TO 89999 POUNDS.	37	100.0	72.8	27.2	-	-	-	-	-
90000 POUNDS AND OVER.	33	100.0	99.0	.2	-	-	.8	-	-
1000 TO 1499 MILES......	160	100.0	27.1	57.2	12.0	2.0	-	.4	1.3
UNDER 1000 POUNDS.....	13	100.0	.6	78.8	4.8	10.8	-	5.0	-
1000 TO 9999 POUNDS...	32	100.0	.5	86.0	8.1	5.3	-	-	-
10000 TO 29999 POUNDS.	44	100.0	12.6	66.7	20.7	-	-	-	-
30000 TO 59999 POUNDS.	42	100.0	29.1	49.8	16.1	-	-	-	5.0
60000 TO 89999 POUNDS.	2	100.0	100.0	-	-	-	-	-	-
90000 POUNDS AND OVER.	24	100.0	90.6	9.4	-	-	-	-	-
1500 MILES OR OVER......	139	100.0	21.7	70.3	1.1	3.6	1.9	.7	.6
UNDER 1000 POUNDS.....	15	100.0	3.4	61.7	3.1	24.7	.3	6.3	.4
1000 TO 9999 POUNDS...	30	100.0	1.8	82.1	2.2	3.5	7.8	-	2.6
10000 TO 29999 POUNDS.	31	100.0	19.3	80.7	-	-	-	-	-
30000 TO 59999 POUNDS.	48	100.0	29.5	69.8	.8	-	-	-	-
60000 TO 89999 POUNDS.	1	100.0	86.1	13.9	-	-	-	-	-
90000 POUNDS AND OVER.	10	100.0	67.2	30.3	-	-	2.5	-	-
TON-MILES OF SHIPMENTS	(millions of ton-miles)								
U.S. TOTAL..........	952	100.0	19.5	65.8	10.8	1.9	.9	.7	.4
UNDER 100 MILES.........	6	100.0	1.5	81.5	13.1	.5	-	2.8	.5
UNDER 1000 POUNDS.....	1	100.0	-	78.7	12.8	1.1	-	7.0	.4
1000 TO 9999 POUNDS...	2	100.0	.1	86.7	8.4	.7	-	3.2	.9
10000 TO 29999 POUNDS.	1	100.0	5.2	75.1	19.6	-	-	-	-
30000 TO 59999 POUNDS.	-	100.0	-	82.5	17.5	-	-	-	-
60000 TO 89999 POUNDS.	-	100.0	-	-	-	-	-	-	-
90000 POUNDS AND OVER.	-	100.0	-	100.0	-	-	-	-	-
100 TO 199 MILES........	26	100.0	5.4	73.5	19.7	.1	-	1.0	.1
UNDER 1000 POUNDS.....	3	100.0	-	87.6	6.3	1.2	-	4.3	.7
1000 TO 9999 POUNDS...	8	100.0	-	88.9	9.1	.1	-	1.8	.1
10000 TO 29999 POUNDS.	7	100.0	1.4	77.9	20.7	-	-	-	-
30000 TO 59999 POUNDS.	7	100.0	2.9	60.7	36.4	-	-	-	-
60000 TO 89999 POUNDS.	-	100.0	31.7	-	68.3	-	-	-	-
90000 POUNDS AND OVER.	1	100.0	99.2	-	-	-	.8	-	-

See footnotes at end of table 4.

TABLE 4. TCC GROUP 361—Percent Distribution of Distance Shipped and Weight of Shipment, by Means of Transport: 1972—Continued

Distance shipped and weight of shipment[2][3]	Number	All means of transport	Rail	Motor carrier	Private truck	Air	Water	Other	Unknown
TON-MILES OF SHIPMENTS	(millions of ton-miles)								
200 TO 299 MILES	41	100.0	14.8	67.0	17.1	.3	-	.8	-
UNDER 1000 POUNDS	4	100.0	.1	86.6	3.1	2.8	-	7.2	.1
1000 TO 9999 POUNDS	12	100.0	.4	87.5	12.0	-	-	-	-
10000 TO 29999 POUNDS	7	100.0	4.8	58.7	36.5	-	-	-	-
30000 TO 59999 POUNDS	9	100.0	8.5	64.4	27.2	-	-	-	-
60000 TO 89999 POUNDS	2	100.0	57.9	42.1	-	-	-	-	-
90000 POUNDS AND OVER	4	100.0	78.8	21.2	-	-	-	-	-
300 TO 499 MILES	110	100.0	9.0	70.4	18.6	.8	-	1.1	-
UNDER 1000 POUNDS	12	100.0	.1	79.8	5.8	4.8	-	9.5	-
1000 TO 9999 POUNDS	29	100.0	-	84.8	13.9	1.0	-	.1	.2
10000 TO 29999 POUNDS	24	100.0	5.9	80.6	13.5	-	-	-	-
30000 TO 59999 POUNDS	36	100.0	5.3	60.5	34.2	-	-	-	-
60000 TO 89999 POUNDS	2	100.0	38.5	61.5	-	-	-	-	-
90000 POUNDS AND OVER	5	100.0	100.0	-	-	-	-	-	-
500 TO 999 MILES	296	100.0	20.1	62.9	15.2	.9	.1	.7	-
UNDER 1000 POUNDS	28	100.0	.7	74.1	10.3	7.9	-	6.9	-
1000 TO 9999 POUNDS	63	100.0	3.2	77.0	18.7	.9	-	.2	-
10000 TO 29999 POUNDS	51	100.0	7.2	81.6	11.2	-	-	-	-
30000 TO 59999 POUNDS	107	100.0	15.0	62.3	22.7	-	-	-	-
60000 TO 89999 POUNDS	23	100.0	72.2	27.8	-	-	-	-	-
90000 POUNDS AND OVER	20	100.0	98.5	.3	-	-	1.2	-	-
1000 TO 1499 MILES	186	100.0	27.0	58.2	11.3	1.9	-	.4	1.2
UNDER 1000 POUNDS	16	100.0	.6	79.0	4.9	10.8	-	4.7	-
1000 TO 9999 POUNDS	37	100.0	.5	87.0	7.6	4.8	-	-	-
10000 TO 29999 POUNDS	51	100.0	12.1	68.5	19.4	-	-	-	-
30000 TO 59999 POUNDS	49	100.0	28.6	51.6	15.3	-	-	-	4.4
60000 TO 89999 POUNDS	3	100.0	100.0	-	-	-	-	-	-
90000 POUNDS AND OVER	28	100.0	90.8	9.2	-	-	-	-	-
1500 MILES OR OVER	284	100.0	20.4	70.6	1.0	3.9	2.8	.7	.7
UNDER 1000 POUNDS	32	100.0	3.4	60.1	2.9	.26.2	.6	6.4	.5
1000 TO 9999 POUNDS	66	100.0	1.8	79.6	1.8	3.6	10.6	-	2.6
10000 TO 29999 POUNDS	63	100.0	17.2	82.8	-	-	-	-	-
30000 TO 59999 POUNDS	94	100.0	28.4	70.9	.6	-	-	-	-
60000 TO 89999 POUNDS	3	100.0	86.5	13.5	-	-	-	-	-
90000 POUNDS AND OVER	23	100.0	63.1	34.4	-	-	2.5	-	-

Note: Detail may not add to total due to rounding. The introductory table shows the estimates of sampling variability for tons; sampling variability for ton-miles has not been estimated. See the map in the Introduction for the States comprising the geographic divisions of the United States.

Shipments excluded from the survey are those moving by pipeline (primarily petroleum products from refineries), parcel post shipments, and commodities moved by own power (motorized vehicles, aircraft, etc.) or towed (prefabricated buildings, etc.). Local shipments (commodities shipped less than 25 miles from the plant) and shipments within the same city are also excluded. Shipments to Alaska and Hawaii from the 48 conterminous States and the District of Columbia are included; however, no data were obtained for shipments originating in Alaska and Hawaii.

- Represents zero or rounds to zero.   (D) Withheld to avoid disclosing figures for individual companies.

[1]Production of this commodity is concentrated in the geographic divisions shown; figures and distributions for geographic divisions not shown are included in the total.

[2]Distances of shipments to foreign destinations are calculated only to the U.S. port of exit.

[3]Includes only shipments represented by bills of lading and invoices. Summary records which did not show individual weights of shipments are not included.

TCC 362. Electrical Industrial Apparatus

Comparisons of Tons and Ton-Miles of Shipments for
Geographic Divisions of Origin and for Sampling Variability: 1972 and 1967

Geographic division of origin	Estimates				Relative sampling variability in tons (percent)	
	1972		1967		1972	1967
	Tons (thousands)	Ton-miles (millions)	Tons (thousands)	Ton-miles (millions)		
U.S. total	2,075	1,125	2,100	1,094	16.5	13.6
New England	15	6	63	40	17.8	(*)
Middle Atlantic	533	326	691	397	12.2	(*)
East North Central	565	239	803	360	7.2	(*)
West North Central	86	46	177	77	9.3	(*)
South Atlantic	106	83	135	91	25.5	(*)
East South Central	(D)	(D)	178	60	(*)	(*)
West South Central	125	47	15	15	28.1	(*)
Mountain	(D)	(D)	—	—	(*)	—
Pacific	18	18	38	54	43.8	(*)

— Represents or rounds to zero.   (D) Withheld to avoid disclosing figures for individual companies.   *Data not published.

TABLE 1. TCC GROUP 362—Percent Distribution of Geographic Division of Origin and Distance Shipped, by Means of Transport: 1972

Geographic division of origin[1] and distance shipped[2]	Number	Percent distribution by means of transport							
		All means of transport	Rail	Motor carrier	Private truck	Air	Water	Other	Unknown
TONS OF SHIPMENTS	(thousands of tons)								
U.S. TOTAL..........	2 075	100.0	21.6	54.9	21.2	.9	.1	.7	.5
NEW ENGLAND..............	15	100.0	.2	68.8	17.6	3.9	6.0	2.4	1.1
UNDER 100 MILES.......	5	100.0	-	41.2	35.6	.9	17.1	2.2	3.1
100 TO 199 MILES......	1	100.0	-	97.9	-	.1	-	2.0	-
200 TO 299 MILES......	1	100.0	-	97.9	-	.8	-	1.3	-
300 TO 499 MILES......	1	100.0	-	92.9	.4	3.9	-	2.7	-
500 TO 999 MILES.....	3	100.0	-	89.6	1.7	5.7	-	3.0	-
1000 TO 1499 MILES....	-	100.0	-	58.2	9.0	31.5	-	1.3	-
1500 MILES OR OVER....	1	100.0	3.0	28.4	59.2	5.4	-	4.0	-
MIDDLE ATLANTIC.........	533	100.0	24.9	68.6	4.9	1.0	-	.5	-
UNDER 100 MILES.......	48	100.0	24.0	67.2	5.9	2.7	-	.2	-
100 TO 199 MILES......	94	100.0	9.3	86.9	3.6	.1	-	.2	-
200 TO 299 MILES......	64	100.0	7.1	86.1	6.2	.3	-	.2	-
300 TO 499 MILES......	81	100.0	42.5	54.4	2.4	.3	-	.4	-
500 TO 999 MILES.....	154	100.0	22.7	69.5	7.0	.4	-	.5	-
1000 TO 1499 MILES....	33	100.0	23.8	64.8	9.1	1.9	-	.4	-
1500 MILES OR OVER....	54	100.0	54.8	38.9	.1	4.4	.3	1.5	-
EAST NORTH CENTRAL......	565	100.0	2.1	62.7	30.8	1.9	-	1.9	.5
UNDER 100 MILES.......	88	100.0	-	64.6	33.3	-	-	1.1	.9
100 TO 199 MILES......	116	100.0	-	56.9	41.6	-	.1	1.1	.7
200 TO 299 MILES......	85	100.0	-	65.4	30.6	.8	-	.7	-
300 TO 499 MILES......	121	100.0	3.6	68.8	24.1	2.3	-	1.6	.1
500 TO 999 MILES.....	114	100.0	4.2	60.4	26.6	.7	-	2.1	.7
1000 TO 1499 MILES....	9	100.0	7.8	69.3	13.0	4.5	-	3.3	1.1
1500 MILES OR OVER....	28	100.0	7.9	54.7	30.9	4.6	-	5.1	.3
						4.3	-	2.2	.1
WEST NORTH CENTRAL......	86	100.0	2.5	50.2	46.5	.4	-	.1	.3
UNDER 100 MILES.......	5	100.0	-	10.6	89.3	-	-	-	-
100 TO 199 MILES......	21	100.0	-	1.9	98.1	-	-	-	-
200 TO 299 MILES......	7	100.0	-	61.2	38.7	-	-	.1	-
300 TO 499 MILES......	18	100.0	5.9	52.5	41.6	.1	-	-	-
500 TO 999 MILES.....	20	100.0	5.0	78.9	15.3	.6	-	.2	-
1000 TO 1499 MILES....	7	100.0	.6	89.8	8.5	.8	-	.3	-
1500 MILES OR OVER....	5	100.0	-	92.3	-	2.5	-	-	5.2
SOUTH ATLANTIC.........	106	100.0	17.8	51.7	28.1	1.1	-	1.3	-
UNDER 100 MILES.......	16	100.0	-	9.2	90.7	-	-	.1	-
100 TO 199 MILES......	4	100.0	-	42.1	57.7	-	-	.2	-
200 TO 299 MILES......	18	100.0	-	51.7	48.0	.3	-	.1	-
300 TO 499 MILES......	25	100.0	-	86.0	12.2	1.1	-	.6	-
500 TO 999 MILES.....	13	100.0	.9	85.2	3.9	4.6	-	5.4	-
1000 TO 1499 MILES....	5	100.0	-	92.3	-	-	-	7.7	-
1500 MILES OR OVER....	23	100.0	81.4	17.3	-	.9	-	.4	-
WEST SOUTH CENTRAL......	125	100.0	25.3	9.4	65.2	.1	-	-	-
UNDER 100 MILES.......	9	100.0	-	2.9	97.0	-	-	-	-
100 TO 199 MILES......	26	100.0	-	1.9	98.1	-	-	.1	-
200 TO 299 MILES......	28	100.0	-	14.6	85.4	-	-	-	-
300 TO 499 MILES......	13	100.0	-	25.6	74.3	-	-	-	-
500 TO 999 MILES.....	45	100.0	69.2	5.9	24.8	.1	-	-	-
1000 TO 1499 MILES....	-	100.0	-	69.3	19.8	10.4	-	.5	-
1500 MILES OR OVER....	-	100.0	-	93.4	2.6	4.0	-	-	-
PACIFIC.................	18	100.0	-	87.1	2.5	2.0	7.0	1.0	.3
UNDER 100 MILES.......	1	100.0	-	71.0	25.5	.2	-	3.4	-
100 TO 199 MILES......	3	100.0	-	98.4	-	.1	-	1.5	-
200 TO 299 MILES......	3	100.0	-	100.0			-	-	-
300 TO 499 MILES......	1	100.0	-	98.1	-	.4	-	1.5	-
500 TO 999 MILES.....	1	100.0	-	97.7	-	2.2	-	.1	-
1000 TO 1499 MILES....	-	100.0	-	91.9	-	3.2	-	4.9	-
1500 MILES OR OVER....	7	100.0	-	75.3	-	4.6	18.7	.5	.8
TON-MILES OF SHIPMENTS	(millions of ton-miles)								
U.S. TOTAL..........	1 125	100.0	31.2	51.9	13.6	1.6	.3	.9	.4
NEW ENGLAND..............	6	100.0	1.1	66.8	20.0	7.8	.9	3.3	.2
UNDER 100 MILES.......	-	100.0	-	45.2	25.5	.7	23.0	1.0	4.7
100 TO 199 MILES......	-	100.0	-	98.0	-	.1	-	1.9	-
200 TO 299 MILES......	-	100.0	-	97.8	-	.8	-	1.4	-
300 TO 499 MILES......	-	100.0	-	92.3	.4	4.5	-	2.8	-
500 TO 999 MILES.....	2	100.0	-	89.6	1.7	5.7	-	3.0	-
1000 TO 1499 MILES....	-	100.0	-	59.6	10.5	28.6	-	1.3	-
1500 MILES OR OVER....	2	100.0	3.5	31.8	53.5	6.1	-	5.1	-
MIDDLE ATLANTIC.........	326	100.0	34.3	58.3	4.3	2.1	.1	.8	-
UNDER 100 MILES.......	2	100.0	28.0	64.6	6.0	1.2	-	.2	-
100 TO 199 MILES......	13	100.0	7.9	87.9	3.8	.1	-	.3	-
200 TO 299 MILES......	16	100.0	7.9	84.9	6.7	.3	-	.2	-
300 TO 499 MILES......	33	100.0	45.6	51.4	2.3	.3	-	.4	-
500 TO 999 MILES.....	106	100.0	24.2	67.2	7.6	.4	-	.5	-
1000 TO 1499 MILES....	39	100.0	24.8	64.5	8.4	1.9	-	.4	-
1500 MILES OR OVER....	114	100.0	50.7	42.4	.1	4.8	.4	1.6	-

See footnotes at end of table 4.

TABLE 1. **TCC GROUP 362**—Percent Distribution of Geographic Division of Origin and Distance Shipped, by Means of Transport: 1972—Continued

Geographic division of origin[1] and distance shipped[2]	Number	Percent distribution by means of transport							
		All means of transport	Rail	Motor carrier	Private truck	Air	Water	Other	Unknown
TON-MILES OF SHIPMENTS	(millions of ton-miles)								
EAST NORTH CENTRAL......	239	100.0	4.1	61.9	28.1	2.9	-	2.4	.6
UNDER 100 MILES.......	4	100.0	-	72.8	25.5	-	.1	1.0	.6
100 TO 199 MILES......	17	100.0	-	55.8	42.6	.9	-	.7	-
200 TO 299 MILES......	21	100.0	-	65.1	30.7	2.5	-	1.6	.1
300 TO 499 MILES......	46	100.0	4.2	66.5	25.6	.7	-	2.2	.9
500 TO 999 MILES......	79	100.0	3.9	62.6	25.2	3.9	-	3.2	1.1
1000 TO 1499 MILES....	11	100.0	7.1	70.4	12.0	5.3	-	4.9	.3
1500 MILES OR OVER....	57	100.0	6.8	55.2	32.0	3.8	-	2.2	.1
WEST NORTH CENTRAL......	46	100.0	2.5	72.8	22.7	.9	-	.1	1.1
UNDER 100 MILES.......	-	100.0	-	10.5	89.5	-	-	-	-
100 TO 199 MILES......	3	100.0	-	2.0	98.0	-	-	-	-
200 TO 299 MILES......	1	100.0	-	63.1	36.8	-	-	.1	-
300 TO 499 MILES......	7	100.0	6.9	51.1	41.8	.1	-	-	-
500 TO 999 MILES......	14	100.0	4.1	79.2	15.9	.7	-	.2	-
1000 TO 1499 MILES....	9	100.0	.6	90.6	7.6	.9	-	.3	-
1500 MILES OR OVER....	9	100.0	-	92.4	-	2.3	-	-	5.3
SOUTH ATLANTIC..........	83	100.0	49.8	41.4	6.3	1.1	-	1.4	-
UNDER 100 MILES.......	1	100.0	-	6.2	93.8	-	-	-	-
100 TO 199 MILES......	-	100.0	-	42.6	57.1	-	-	.2	-
200 TO 299 MILES......	4	100.0	-	49.9	49.7	.3	-	.1	-
300 TO 499 MILES......	10	100.0	-	86.6	11.5	1.1	-	.7	-
500 TO 999 MILES......	9	100.0	.8	86.2	3.7	4.1	-	5.1	-
1000 TO 1499 MILES....	7	100.0	-	93.8	-	-	-	6.2	-
1500 MILES OR OVER....	50	100.0	81.7	17.0	-	.9	-	.4	-
WEST SOUTH CENTRAL......	47	100.0	41.2	10.9	47.7	.2	-	-	-
UNDER 100 MILES.......	-	100.0	-	6.9	92.7	-	-	.4	-
100 TO 199 MILES......	4	100.0	-	2.0	98.0	-	-	-	-
200 TO 299 MILES......	7	100.0	-	14.9	85.1	-	-	-	-
300 TO 499 MILES......	6	100.0	-	24.2	75.8	-	-	-	-
500 TO 999 MILES......	28	100.0	69.8	6.0	24.1	.1	-	-	-
1000 TO 1499 MILES....	-	100.0	-	70.3	18.1	11.1	-	.5	-
1500 MILES OR OVER....	-	100.0	-	93.3	2.5	4.2	-	-	-
PACIFIC.................	18	100.0	-	79.0	-	4.3	15.1	.6	.9
UNDER 100 MILES.......	-	100.0	-	85.0	10.8	.1	-	4.1	-
100 TO 199 MILES......	-	100.0	-	98.9	-	.1	-	1.0	-
200 TO 299 MILES......	-	100.0	-	100.0	-	-	-	-	-
300 TO 499 MILES......	-	100.0	-	98.2	-	.4	-	1.3	-
500 TO 999 MILES......	-	100.0	-	97.4	-	2.4	-	.2	-
1000 TO 1499 MILES....	-	100.0	-	91.3	-	3.5	-	5.1	-
1500 MILES OR OVER....	15	100.0	-	75.1	-	5.0	18.4	.5	1.0

See footnotes at end of table 4.

TABLE 2. **TCC GROUP 362**—Percent Distribution of Geographic Division of Origin and Means of Transport, by Geographic Division of Destination: 1972

Geographic division of origin[1] and means of transport	Number	Percent distribution by division of destination									
		U.S. total	New England	Middle Atlantic	East North Central	West North Central	South Atlantic	East South Central	West South Central	Mountain	Pacific
TONS OF SHIPMENTS	(thousands of tons)										
U.S. TOTAL...............	2 075	100.0	2.6	17.1	33.4	8.8	10.4	10.4	8.0	2.7	6.6
RAIL.................	448	100.0	1.5	6.1	12.3	10.3	11.3	17.2	17.8	8.5	15.0
MOTOR CARRIER.........	1 139	100.0	3.4	24.3	37.5	4.1	12.0	7.3	5.3	1.5	4.7
PRIVATE TRUCK.........	439	100.0	1.7	8.2	45.6	19.8	6.0	11.3	5.3	.1	2.2
AIR..................	19	100.0	2.3	36.7	21.4	3.0	5.1	3.4	3.0	4.3	20.8
WATER................	2	100.0	-	36.4	2.5	-	-	-	-	-	61.1
OTHER................	15	100.0	6.1	22.1	27.4	11.2	9.7	7.2	5.3	2.0	9.1
UNKNOWN..............	10	100.0	.4	24.5	25.4	8.4	.8	33.7	2.8	.2	3.7
NEW ENGLAND.............	15	100.0	31.2	30.0	18.7	3.3	6.8	1.5	5.6	.2	2.8
RAIL.................	-	100.0	-	-	-	-	-	-	-	-	100.0
MOTOR CARRIER.........	10	100.0	25.5	32.7	24.6	2.7	8.6	1.8	2.2	.1	1.8
PRIVATE TRUCK.........	2	100.0	71.1	.2	2.2	.1	-	-	22.1	.1	4.2
AIR..................	-	100.0	6.6	3.3	22.8	34.2	15.7	4.5	4.5	1.1	7.3
WATER................	-	100.0	-	100.0	-	-	-	-	-	-	-
OTHER................	-	100.0	37.0	13.2	20.4	2.6	11.2	2.8	.8	-	11.9
UNKNOWN..............	-	100.0	-	100.0	-	-	-	-	-	-	-
MIDDLE ATLANTIC.........	533	100.0	5.2	25.6	27.1	2.8	16.6	7.1	5.3	3.8	6.4
RAIL.................	132	100.0	4.6	10.9	13.3	3.6	22.4	15.1	7.6	11.2	11.3
MOTOR CARRIER.........	365	100.0	5.8	30.2	31.3	2.1	15.7	4.6	4.6	1.4	4.4
PRIVATE TRUCK.........	26	100.0	1.4	36.2	42.1	10.3	4.7	2.4	2.6	.1	.1
AIR..................	5	100.0	.9	27.5	12.0	1.0	3.8	5.8	3.1	6.0	39.8
WATER................	-	100.0	-	-	-	-	-	-	-	-	100.0
OTHER................	2	100.0	5.8	11.5	30.2	2.2	11.5	4.2	4.8	8.9	20.8
UNKNOWN..............	-	100.0	-	62.5	-	37.5	-	-	-	-	-

See footnotes at end of table 4.

TABLE 2. **TCC GROUP 362—Percent Distribution of Geographic Division of Origin and Means of Transport, by Geographic Division of Destination: 1972**—Continued

Geographic division of origin[1] and means of transport	Number	Percent distribution by division of destination									
		U.S. total	New England	Middle Atlantic	East North Central	West North Central	South Atlantic	East South Central	West South Central	Mountain	Pacific
TONS OF SHIPMENTS	(thousands of tons)										
EAST NORTH CENTRAL......	565	100.0	2.6	12.9	48.0	4.9	7.1	13.5	5.2	.8	4.9
RAIL........................	12	100.0	3.2	17.8	1.0	20.9	19.7	1.9	10.7	6.1	18.6
MOTOR CARRIER..........	354	100.0	2.5	11.0	49.8	5.7	8.6	12.3	4.9	.9	4.1
PRIVATE TRUCK.........	174	100.0	2.7	13.6	50.2	1.6	3.3	17.9	5.5	-	5.1
AIR.....................	10	100.0	2.2	43.9	28.0	2.6	3.0	2.5	3.3	4.3	10.2
WATER..................	-	100.0	-	-	100.0	-	-	-	-	-	-
OTHER..................	10	100.0	4.1	23.4	30.8	11.4	10.5	8.2	5.4	.6	5.7
UNKNOWN................	3	100.0	1.3	29.4	26.3	28.0	2.8	1.0	9.5	.8	.9
WEST NORTH CENTRAL.....	86	100.0	2.4	9.2	23.8	32.6	7.9	5.8	9.8	2.1	6.5
RAIL........................	2	100.0	.4	7.9	-	.4	50.6	-	40.8	-	-
MOTOR CARRIER..........	43	100.0	4.7	13.0	26.5	9.6	12.2	6.7	10.7	4.2	12.3
PRIVATE TRUCK.........	40	100.0	-	5.0	22.4	59.7	.6	4.9	7.4	-	-
AIR.....................	-	100.0	4.0	20.2	5.5	.3	53.7	13.2	.6	.1	2.4
WATER..................	-	100.0	-	-	-	-	-	-	-	-	-
OTHER..................	-	100.0	1.5	3.6	22.0	9.2	.4	26.5	32.8	3.8	.2
UNKNOWN................	-	100.0	-	-	-	-	-	-	-	-	100.0
SOUTH ATLANTIC.........	106	100.0	.6	19.5	13.6	2.1	24.3	10.4	7.4	5.1	17.0
RAIL........................	18	100.0	-	-	-	-	-	.6	-	23.6	75.8
MOTOR CARRIER..........	55	100.0	.7	35.3	18.6	3.2	17.7	2.2	14.3	1.8	6.3
PRIVATE TRUCK.........	29	100.0	-	.8	13.3	-	53.4	32.4	-	-	-
AIR.....................	1	100.0	2.6	46.8	22.9	.6	7.0	1.5	1.4	1.3	15.9
WATER..................	-	100.0	-	-	-	-	-	-	-	-	-
OTHER..................	1	100.0	14.1	38.1	4.1	29.2	2.2	3.3	2.1	-	6.7
UNKNOWN................	-	100.0	-	-	-	-	-	-	-	-	-
WEST SOUTH CENTRAL.....	125	100.0	-	.1	18.9	72.5	.3	1.3	6.4	.2	.2
RAIL........................	31	100.0	-	-	-	100.0	-	-	-	-	-
MOTOR CARRIER..........	11	100.0	-	.4	15.3	32.6	1.0	14.2	31.8	2.3	2.4
PRIVATE TRUCK.........	81	100.0	-	-	26.8	67.7	.2	-	5.2	-	-
AIR.....................	-	100.0	.2	40.7	21.5	5.6	11.2	6.0	2.7	1.4	10.6
WATER..................	-	100.0	-	-	-	-	-	-	-	-	-
OTHER..................	-	100.0	-	1.3	13.8	-	2.0	1.1	81.8	-	-
UNKNOWN................	-	100.0	-	-	-	-	-	-	-	-	-
PACIFIC.................	18	100.0	.4	2.6	1.6	1.7	1.6	.1	.8	11.9	79.4
RAIL........................	-	100.0	-	42.5	-	-	57.5	-	-	-	-
MOTOR CARRIER..........	16	100.0	-	1.9	1.8	1.8	1.5	.1	.8	13.4	78.6
PRIVATE TRUCK.........	-	100.0	-	-	-	-	-	-	-	-	100.0
AIR.....................	-	100.0	14.4	40.8	.7	3.3	15.7	1.1	1.0	7.2	15.8
WATER..................	1	100.0	-	-	-	-	-	-	-	-	100.0
OTHER..................	-	100.0	4.9	7.6	2.6	6.1	2.3	-	2.3	5.7	68.6
UNKNOWN................	-	100.0	-	-	-	-	.2	-	-	-	99.8
TON-MILES OF SHIPMENTS	(millions of ton-miles)										
U.S. TOTAL.............	1 125	100.0	2.0	13.2	21.3	6.7	9.4	5.9	10.1	7.3	24.2
RAIL........................	351	100.0	.3	2.6	7.6	7.9	6.9	5.9	12.9	16.4	39.6
MOTOR CARRIER..........	584	100.0	2.9	19.9	25.2	4.6	12.3	5.2	9.2	3.8	16.9
PRIVATE TRUCK.........	153	100.0	2.6	10.4	40.0	12.4	5.0	8.7	8.3	.2	12.3
AIR.....................	18	100.0	2.3	21.9	8.2	2.3	5.0	2.9	3.3	7.3	46.7
WATER..................	3	100.0	-	1.8	.2	-	-	-	-	-	98.0
OTHER..................	10	100.0	4.9	16.8	11.6	10.9	8.9	6.0	8.1	5.0	27.8
UNKNOWN................	4	100.0	.6	36.0	20.9	9.4	1.5	9.0	5.8	.8	16.1
NEW ENGLAND............	6	100.0	4.3	12.4	28.6	7.7	8.3	2.7	19.9	.7	15.4
RAIL........................	-	100.0	-	-	-	-	-	-	-	-	100.0
MOTOR CARRIER..........	4	100.0	4.8	16.7	39.2	6.7	10.4	3.4	7.7	.6	10.5
PRIVATE TRUCK.........	1	100.0	4.9	.1	2.9	.2	-	-	70.8	.6	20.4
AIR.....................	-	100.0	.2	.7	13.6	38.5	13.5	3.9	6.8	2.2	20.5
WATER..................	-	100.0	-	100.0	-	-	-	-	-	-	-
OTHER..................	-	100.0	3.7	4.1	23.4	4.0	9.5	4.2	1.7	-	49.4
UNKNOWN................	-	100.0	-	100.0	-	-	-	-	-	-	-
MIDDLE ATLANTIC........	326	100.0	1.4	6.4	21.8	4.2	13.0	8.0	10.2	10.7	24.3
RAIL........................	112	100.0	.6	1.3	9.0	3.3	11.2	12.3	10.4	22.0	29.9
MOTOR CARRIER..........	190	100.0	2.1	9.2	27.8	3.7	15.0	6.0	10.8	4.8	20.5
PRIVATE TRUCK.........	14	100.0	.4	12.0	50.5	20.3	6.3	4.1	5.5	.4	.5
AIR.....................	6	100.0	.2	1.1	6.0	.7	2.2	5.0	3.2	7.9	73.7
WATER..................	-	100.0	-	-	-	-	-	-	-	-	100.0
OTHER..................	2	100.0	1.2	1.8	16.8	1.6	6.0	2.8	6.7	15.4	47.6
UNKNOWN................	-	100.0	-	6.4	-	93.6	-	-	-	-	-
EAST NORTH CENTRAL.....	239	100.0	4.6	15.2	19.0	5.6	9.3	9.9	10.8	2.3	23.3
RAIL........................	9	100.0	3.2	11.4	.5	13.1	10.4	1.8	11.4	8.2	40.0
MOTOR CARRIER..........	148	100.0	4.6	12.7	21.2	6.6	11.9	9.2	10.8	2.6	20.4
PRIVATE TRUCK.........	67	100.0	5.0	17.7	18.6	1.9	4.0	13.8	11.5	-	27.4
AIR.....................	6	100.0	2.9	38.1	10.7	1.5	2.8	1.5	4.4	9.9	28.3
WATER..................	-	100.0	-	-	100.0	-	-	-	-	-	-
OTHER..................	5	100.0	4.9	22.5	10.4	10.5	12.1	8.0	9.5	1.5	20.6
UNKNOWN................	1	100.0	1.8	38.9	2.4	28.6	4.4	.5	17.8	2.3	3.2

See footnotes at end of table 4.

TABLE 2. **TCC GROUP 362**—Percent Distribution of Geographic Division of Origin and Means of Transport, by Geographic Division of Destination: 1972—Continued

Geographic division of origin[1] and means of transport	Number	Percent distribution by division of destination									
		U.S. total	New England	Middle Atlantic	East North Central	West North Central	South Atlantic	East South Central	West South Central	Mountain	Pacific
TON-MILES OF SHIPMENTS	(millions of ton-miles)										
WEST NORTH CENTRAL......	46	100.0	4.7	15.8	18.8	11.5	12.7	4.9	7.7	3.7	20.1
RAIL....................	1	100.0	.7	11.1	-	.3	44.8	-	43.1	-	-
MOTOR CARRIER..........	33	100.0	6.4	15.4	14.6	3.5	14.4	6.0	8.4	5.1	26.1
PRIVATE TRUCK..........	10	100.0	-	18.5	35.9	39.5	2.2	1.8	2.0	-	-
AIR....................	-	100.0	3.8	14.7	2.1	.1	66.0	9.7	.3	.1	3.2
WATER..................	-	100.0	-	-	-	-	-	-	-	-	-
OTHER..................	-	100.0	2.2	4.4	15.1	2.1	.5	25.5	46.4	3.2	.5
UNKNOWN................	-	100.0	-	-	-	-	-	-	-	-	100.0
SOUTH ATLANTIC..........	83	100.0	.5	9.9	7.5	2.4	4.6	3.4	10.0	11.2	50.5
RAIL....................	41	100.0	-	-	-	-	-	.2	-	18.5	81.3
MOTOR CARRIER..........	34	100.0	.8	22.0	14.2	4.5	6.2	1.4	24.1	4.6	22.3
PRIVATE TRUCK..........	5	100.0	-	.5	23.9	-	32.1	43.4	.2	-	-
AIR....................	-	100.0	1.6	30.8	12.7	.6	5.9	.7	1.1	2.8	44.0
WATER..................	-	100.0	-	-	-	-	-	-	-	-	-
OTHER..................	1	100.0	12.5	26.1	2.2	35.9	.6	2.4	2.3	-	17.9
UNKNOWN................	-	100.0	-	-	-	-	-	-	-	-	-
WEST SOUTH CENTRAL......	47	100.0	-	.2	25.9	65.6	.6	1.1	4.9	.6	1.0
RAIL....................	19	100.0	-	-	-	100.0	-	-	-	-	-
MOTOR CARRIER..........	5	100.0	.1	1.2	18.7	25.8	1.7	9.7	28.3	5.8	8.7
PRIVATE TRUCK......:...	22	100.0	-	-	50.0	45.3	.9	-	3.9	-	-
AIR....................	-	100.0	.3	48.8	14.4	3.4	11.2	2.8	1.0	.9	17.1
WATER..................	-	100.0	-	-	-	-	-	-	-	-	-
OTHER..................	-	100.0	-	6.3	57.7	-	5.8	1.5	28.7	-	-
UNKNOWN................	-	100.0	-	-	-	-	-	-	-	-	-
PACIFIC.................	18	100.0	1.0	6.1	3.1	2.6	3.6	.1	1.3	6.5	75.8
RAIL....................	-	100.0	-	45.0	-	-	55.0	-	-	-	-
MOTOR CARRIER..........	14	100.0	.1	5.0	3.8	3.0	3.5	.1	1.5	8.0	74.9
PRIVATE TRUCK..........	-	100.0	-	-	-	-	-	-	-	-	100.0
AIR....................	-	100.0	17.9	45.7	.6	2.4	17.2	1.0	.6	2.2	12.4
WATER..................	2	100.0	-	-	-	-	-	-	-	-	100.0
OTHER..................	-	100.0	20.4	30.1	7.6	12.5	8.0	-	4.9	3.3	13.1
UNKNOWN................	-	100.0	-	-	-	-	.1	-	-	-	99.9

See footnotes at end of table 4.

TABLE 3. TCC GROUP 362—Percent Distribution of Geographic Division of Destination and Means of Transport, by Geographic Division of Origin: 1972

Geographic division of destination and means of transport	Number	Percent distribution by division of origin[1]									
		U.S. total	New England	Middle Atlantic	East North Central	West North Central	South Atlantic	East South Central	West South Central	Mountain	Pacific
TONS OF SHIPMENTS	(thousands of tons)										
U.S. TOTAL	2 075	100.0	.7	25.7	27.2	4.2	5.1	(D)	6.0	(D)	.9
RAIL	448	100.0	-	29.6	2.7	.5	4.2	(D)	7.0	(D)	-
MOTOR CARRIER	1 139	100.0	.9	32.1	31.1	3.8	4.8	(D)	1.0	(D)	1.4
PRIVATE TRUCK	439	100.0	.6	6.0	39.6	9.1	6.8	(D)	18.6	(D)	.1
AIR	19	100.0	3.0	27.5	53.8	1.7	5.8	(D)	.5	(D)	1.9
WATER	2	100.0	36.4	7.3	2.5	-	-	(D)	-	(D)	53.8
OTHER	15	100.0	2.3	16.5	69.1	.5	9.3	(D)	.1	(D)	1.2
UNKNOWN	10	100.0	1.6	-	29.8	2.9	-	(D)	-	(D)	.6
NEW ENGLAND	53	100.0	8.7	51.6	27.5	3.8	1.1	(D)	-	(D)	.1
RAIL	6	100.0	-	93.9	6.0	.1	-	(D)	-	(D)	-
MOTOR CARRIER	38	100.0	6.8	54.7	23.4	5.3	1.0	(D)	-	(D)	-
PRIVATE TRUCK	7	100.0	25.4	5.1	63.5	-	-	(D)	-	(D)	-
AIR	-	100.0	8.6	11.1	51.8	3.0	6.5	(D)	-	(D)	12.1
WATER	-	100.0	-	-	-	-	-	(D)	-	(D)	-
OTHER	-	100.0	14.3	15.9	47.0	.1	21.6	(D)	-	(D)	1.0
UNKNOWN	-	100.0	-	-	100.0	-	-	(D)	-	(D)	-
MIDDLE ATLANTIC	354	100.0	1.3	38.5	20.6	2.2	5.9	(D)	-	(D)	.1
RAIL	27	100.0	-	53.2	7.9	.6	-	(D)	-	(D)	-
MOTOR CARRIER	276	100.0	1.2	40.0	14.2	2.0	7.0	(D)	-	(D)	.1
PRIVATE TRUCK	36	100.0	-	26.3	65.9	5.6	.7	(D)	-	(D)	-
AIR	7	100.0	.3	20.7	64.3	1.0	7.4	(D)	.5	(D)	2.2
WATER	-	100.0	100.0	-	-	-	-	(D)	-	(D)	-
OTHER	3	100.0	1.4	8.6	73.3	.1	16.0	(D)	-	(D)	.4
UNKNOWN	2	100.0	6.5	-	35.7	-	-	(D)	-	(D)	-
EAST NORTH CENTRAL	693	100.0	.4	20.9	39.2	3.0	2.1	(D)	3.4	(D)	-
RAIL	55	100.0	-	32.1	.2	-	-	(D)	-	(D)	-
MOTOR CARRIER	426	100.0	.6	26.8	41.4	2.7	2.4	(D)	.4	(D)	.1
PRIVATE TRUCK	200	100.0	-	5.5	43.6	4.5	2.0	(D)	10.9	(D)	-
AIR	4	100.0	3.2	15.5	70.3	.4	6.2	(D)	.5	(D)	.1
WATER	-	100.0	-	-	100.0	-	-	(D)	-	(D)	-
OTHER	4	100.0	1.7	18.2	77.5	.4	1.4	(D)	-	(D)	.1
UNKNOWN	2	100.0	-	-	30.9	-	-	(D)	-	(D)	-
WEST NORTH CENTRAL	182	100.0	.3	8.3	15.2	15.4	1.2	(D)	49.6	(D)	.2
RAIL	46	100.0	-	10.2	5.5	-	-	(D)	68.2	(D)	-
MOTOR CARRIER	46	100.0	.6	16.2	43.5	9.0	3.8	(D)	8.3	(D)	.7
PRIVATE TRUCK	86	100.0	-	3.1	3.2	27.6	-	(D)	63.6	(D)	-
AIR	-	100.0	33.9	8.9	46.5	.2	1.2	(D)	.9	(D)	2.1
WATER	-	100.0	-	-	-	-	-	(D)	-	(D)	-
OTHER	1	100.0	.5	3.2	69.9	.4	24.2	(D)	-	(D)	.6
UNKNOWN	-	100.0	-	-	100.0	-	-	(D)	-	(D)	-
SOUTH ATLANTIC	216	100.0	.5	41.1	18.6	3.1	11.9	(D)	.1	(D)	.1
RAIL	50	100.0	-	58.3	4.7	2.1	-	(D)	-	(D)	-
MOTOR CARRIER	136	100.0	.6	42.0	22.4	3.9	7.2	(D)	.1	(D)	.2
PRIVATE TRUCK	26	100.0	-	4.7	22.2	.9	60.7	(D)	.7	(D)	-
AIR	-	100.0	9.3	20.7	31.9	18.6	8.0	(D)	1.1	(D)	6.0
WATER	-	100.0	-	-	-	-	-	(D)	-	(D)	-
OTHER	1	100.0	2.7	19.7	74.8	-	2.1	(D)	-	(D)	.3
UNKNOWN	-	100.0	-	-	99.9	-	-	(D)	-	(D)	.1
EAST SOUTH CENTRAL	215	100.0	.1	17.5	35.4	2.3	5.1	(D)	.8	(D)	-
RAIL	77	100.0	-	25.9	.3	-	.1	(D)	-	(D)	-
MOTOR CARRIER	83	100.0	.2	20.0	52.4	3.5	1.4	(D)	2.0	(D)	-
PRIVATE TRUCK	49	100.0	-	1.3	63.0	4.0	19.5	(D)	.9	(D)	-
AIR	-	100.0	3.9	46.7	38.7	6.8	2.5	(D)	.9	(D)	.6
WATER	-	100.0	-	-	-	-	-	(D)	-	(D)	-
OTHER	1	100.0	.9	9.6	78.6	1.9	4.3	(D)	-	(D)	-
UNKNOWN	3	100.0	-	-	.9	-	-	(D)	-	(D)	-
WEST SOUTH CENTRAL	165	100.0	.5	17.0	18.0	5.1	4.8	(D)	4.9	(D)	.1
RAIL	79	100.0	-	12.7	1.6	1.1	-	(D)	6.2	(D)	-
MOTOR CARRIER	60	100.0	.4	28.1	29.0	7.7	13.0	(D)	6.2	(D)	.2
PRIVATE TRUCK	23	100.0	2.5	3.0	41.3	12.7	.1	(D)	18.4	(D)	-
AIR	-	100.0	4.6	28.5	60.6	.4	2.7	(D)	.5	(D)	.6
WATER	-	100.0	-	-	-	-	-	(D)	-	(D)	-
OTHER	-	100.0	.4	15.1	70.5	3.2	3.8	(D)	1.5	(D)	.5
UNKNOWN	-	100.0	-	-	100.0	-	-	(D)	-	(D)	-
MOUNTAIN	56	100.0	-	36.4	7.8	3.2	9.7	(D)	.5	(D)	4.0
RAIL	37	100.0	-	39.1	2.0	-	11.8	(D)	-	(D)	-
MOTOR CARRIER	16	100.0	.1	30.0	18.3	10.7	5.8	(D)	1.6	(D)	13.1
PRIVATE TRUCK	-	100.0	1.6	11.6	.6	-	-	(D)	-	(D)	-
AIR	-	100.0	.7	38.9	54.0	-	1.8	(D)	.2	(D)	3.3
WATER	-	100.0	-	-	-	-	-	(D)	-	(D)	-
OTHER	-	100.0	-	73.7	21.4	1.0	-	(D)	-	(D)	3.4
UNKNOWN	-	100.0	-	-	100.0	-	-	(D)	-	(D)	-
PACIFIC	138	100.0	.3	24.6	19.9	4.1	13.1	(D)	.2	(D)	10.8
RAIL	67	100.0	-	22.2	3.3	-	21.3	(D)	-	(D)	24.0
MOTOR CARRIER	53	100.0	.3	30.0	27.3	9.9	6.5	(D)	.5	(D)	24.0
PRIVATE TRUCK	9	100.0	1.2	.3	93.4	-	-	(D)	.1	(D)	5.0
AIR	4	100.0	1.1	52.5	26.3	.2	4.4	(D)	.2	(D)	1.5
WATER	1	100.0	-	11.9	-	-	-	(D)	-	(D)	88.1
OTHER	1	100.0	3.1	37.9	43.1	-	6.9	(D)	-	(D)	9.0
UNKNOWN	-	100.0	-	-	7.4	77.4	-	(D)	-	(D)	15.1

See footnotes at end of table 4.

TABLE 3. **TCC GROUP 362**—Percent Distribution of Geographic Division of Destination and Means of Transport, by Geographic Division of Origin: 1972—Continued

Geographic division of destination and means of transport	Number	Percent distribution by division of origin[1]									
		U.S. total	New England	Middle Atlantic	East North Central	West North Central	South Atlantic	East South Central	West South Central	Mountain	Pacific
TON-MILES OF SHIPMENTS	(millions of ton-miles)										
U.S. TOTAL	1 125	100.0	.6	29.0	21.3	4.1	7.4	(D)	4.2	(D)	1.6
RAIL	351	100.0	-	31.9	2.8	.3	11.9	(D)	5.6	(D)	-
MOTOR CARRIER	584	100.0	.8	32.6	25.3	5.8	5.9	(D)	.9	(D)	2.5
PRIVATE TRUCK	153	100.0	.9	9.2	43.9	6.8	3.4	(D)	14.8	(D)	-
AIR	18	100.0	3.0	38.6	38.7	2.3	5.2	(D)	.6	(D)	4.4
WATER	3	100.0	1.8	13.8	.2	-	-	(D)	-	(D)	84.2
OTHER	10	100.0	2.2	26.8	57.1	.6	11.5	(D)	-	(D)	1.1
UNKNOWN	4	100.0	.3	-	32.9	11.4	-	(D)	-	(D)	3.6
NEW ENGLAND	22	100.0	1.3	20.7	48.3	9.5	1.9	(D)	-	(D)	.8
RAIL	-	100.0	-	66.1	33.0	.9	-	(D)	-	(D)	-
MOTOR CARRIER	17	100.0	1.3	23.5	40.3	12.7	1.5	(D)	-	(D)	.1
PRIVATE TRUCK	3	100.0	1.7	1.4	85.1	-	-	(D)	-	(D)	-
AIR	-	100.0	.3	3.4	47.4	3.7	3.5	(D)	.1	(D)	33.3
WATER	-	100.0	-	-	-	-	-	(D)	-	(D)	-
OTHER	-	100.0	1.7	6.7	57.1	.3	29.7	(D)	-	(D)	4.6
UNKNOWN	-	100.0	-	-	100.0	-	-	(D)	-	(D)	-
MIDDLE ATLANTIC	149	100.0	.6	14.0	24.4	4.9	5.5	(D)	.1	(D)	.7
RAIL	9	100.0	-	16.4	12.1	1.4	-	(D)	-	(D)	-
MOTOR CARRIER	116	100.0	.7	15.1	16.2	4.5	6.5	(D)	.1	(D)	.6
PRIVATE TRUCK	15	100.0	-	10.6	74.6	12.2	.2	(D)	-	(D)	-
AIR	3	100.0	.1	1.9	67.2	1.5	7.3	(D)	1.3	(D)	9.1
WATER	-	100.0	100.0	-	-	-	-	(D)	-	(D)	-
OTHER	1	100.0	.5	2.9	76.4	.2	17.9	(D)	-	(D)	2.0
UNKNOWN	1	100.0	.8	-	35.6	-	-	(D)	-	(D)	-
EAST NORTH CENTRAL	239	100.0	.8	29.7	19.0	3.6	2.6	(D)	5.2	(D)	.2
RAIL	26	100.0	-	37.5	.2	-	-	(D)	-	(D)	-
MOTOR CARRIER	147	100.0	1.2	35.9	21.3	3.3	3.3	(D)	.7	(D)	.4
PRIVATE TRUCK	61	100.0	.1	11.7	20.5	6.2	2.0	(D)	18.6	(D)	-
AIR	1	100.0	4.9	28.4	50.7	.6	8.1	(D)	1.0	(D)	.3
WATER	-	100.0	-	-	100.0	-	-	(D)	-	(D)	-
OTHER	1	100.0	4.4	38.9	51.5	.8	2.2	(D)	.2	(D)	.7
UNKNOWN	-	100.0	-	-	3.8	-	-	(D)	-	(D)	-
WEST NORTH CENTRAL	75	100.0	.7	18.2	17.9	7.1	2.7	(D)	41.6	(D)	.6
RAIL	27	100.0	-	13.3	4.6	-	-	(D)	71.0	(D)	-
MOTOR CARRIER	26	100.0	1.1	26.5	36.8	4.4	5.9	(D)	5.1	(D)	1.6
PRIVATE TRUCK	19	100.0	-	15.1	6.6	21.8	-	(D)	54.1	(D)	-
AIR	-	100.0	48.9	11.6	24.8	.1	1.3	(D)	.8	(D)	4.5
WATER	-	100.0	-	-	-	-	-	(D)	-	(D)	-
OTHER	1	100.0	.8	4.0	54.9	.1	38.1	(D)	-	(D)	1.2
UNKNOWN	-	100.0	-	.1	99.9	-	-	(D)	-	(D)	-
SOUTH ATLANTIC	105	100.0	.5	40.2	21.1	5.6	3.7	(D)	.3	(D)	.6
RAIL	24	100.0	-	52.0	4.2	2.1	-	(D)	-	(D)	-
MOTOR CARRIER	71	100.0	.7	39.9	24.6	6.8	3.0	(D)	.1	(D)	.7
PRIVATE TRUCK	7	100.0	-	11.6	34.9	3.0	21.8	(D)	2.5	(D)	-
AIR	-	100.0	7.9	16.6	21.3	29.5	6.1	(D)	1.3	(D)	14.9
WATER	-	100.0	-	-	-	-	-	(D)	-	(D)	-
OTHER	-	100.0	2.3	18.1	77.4	-	.8	(D)	-	(D)	1.0
UNKNOWN	-	100.0	-	-	99.7	-	-	(D)	-	(D)	.3
EAST SOUTH CENTRAL	66	100.0	.3	39.5	35.7	3.4	4.3	(D)	.8	(D)	-
RAIL	20	100.0	-	66.2	.8	-	.4	(D)	-	(D)	-
MOTOR CARRIER	30	100.0	.5	37.4	44.5	6.6	1.5	(D)	1.7	(D)	.1
PRIVATE TRUCK	13	100.0	-	4.3	69.5	1.4	16.9	(D)	-	(D)	-
AIR	-	100.0	3.9	66.0	19.5	7.4	1.2	(D)	.5	(D)	1.4
WATER	-	100.0	-	-	-	-	-	(D)	-	(D)	-
OTHER	-	100.0	1.5	12.7	76.8	2.5	4.7	(D)	-	(D)	-
UNKNOWN	-	100.0	-	-	1.9	-	-	(D)	-	(D)	-
WEST SOUTH CENTRAL	113	100.0	1.2	29.5	22.9	3.2	7.4	(D)	2.1	(D)	.2
RAIL	45	100.0	-	25.8	2.5	1.1	-	(D)	-	(D)	-
MOTOR CARRIER	53	100.0	.7	38.3	29.7	5.3	15.6	(D)	2.8	(D)	.4
PRIVATE TRUCK	12	100.0	7.5	6.0	60.6	1.7	.1	(D)	6.8	(D)	-
AIR	-	100.0	6.1	37.6	51.7	.2	1.7	(D)	.2	(D)	.7
WATER	-	100.0	-	-	-	-	-	(D)	-	(D)	-
OTHER	-	100.0	.4	22.0	66.4	3.3	3.3	(D)	.1	(D)	.7
UNKNOWN	-	100.0	-	-	100.0	-	-	(D)	-	(D)	-
MOUNTAIN	82	100.0	.1	42.4	6.7	2.1	11.4	(D)	.4	(D)	1.4
RAIL	57	100.0	-	42.7	1.4	-	13.4	(D)	-	(D)	-
MOTOR CARRIER	22	100.0	.1	41.5	17.5	7.8	7.1	(D)	1.4	(D)	5.2
PRIVATE TRUCK	-	100.0	2.1	14.5	.5	-	-	(D)	-	(D)	-
AIR	1	100.0	.9	42.0	52.8	-	2.0	(D)	.1	(D)	1.3
WATER	-	100.0	-	-	-	-	-	(D)	-	(D)	-
OTHER	-	100.0	-	81.8	17.1	.4	-	(D)	-	(D)	.7
UNKNOWN	-	100.0	-	-	100.0	-	-	(D)	-	(D)	-
PACIFIC	271	100.0	.4	29.2	20.5	3.4	15.5	(D)	.2	(D)	5.1
RAIL	139	100.0	.1	24.1	2.8	-	24.4	(D)	-	(D)	-
MOTOR CARRIER	98	100.0	.5	39.5	30.5	8.9	7.8	(D)	.5	(D)	11.0
PRIVATE TRUCK	18	100.0	1.5	.4	98.0	-	-	(D)	.1	(D)	-
AIR	8	100.0	1.3	60.9	23.4	.2	4.9	(D)	.2	(D)	1.2
WATER	3	100.0	-	14.1	-	-	-	(D)	-	(D)	85.9
OTHER	2	100.0	3.9	45.9	42.3	-	7.4	(D)	-	(D)	.5
UNKNOWN	-	100.0	-	-	6.6	71.3	-	(D)	-	(D)	22.1

See footnotes at end of table 4.

TABLE 4. **TCC GROUP 362—Percent Distribution of Distance Shipped and Weight of Shipment, by Means of Transport: 1972**

Distance shipped and weight of shipment[2][3]	Number	Percent distribution by means of transport							
		All means of transport	Rail	Motor carrier	Private truck	Air	Water	Other	Unknown
TONS OF SHIPMENTS	(thousands of tons)								
U.S. TOTAL	1 826	100.0	24.5	58.5	14.6	1.0	.1	.8	.5
UNDER 100 MILES	190	100.0	18.4	52.3	26.2	.7	.5	.6	1.2
UNDER 1000 POUNDS	19	100.0	-	60.9	32.8	.3	-	5.8	.1
1000 TO 9999 POUNDS	60	100.0	-	75.0	22.0	2.1	.2	.2	.5
10000 TO 29999 POUNDS	40	100.0	-	48.3	49.8	-	1.9	-	-
30000 TO 59999 POUNDS	34	100.0	-	66.2	28.0	-	-	-	5.8
60000 TO 89999 POUNDS	-	100.0	-	-	46.9	-	53.1	-	-
90000 POUNDS AND OVER	35	100.0	99.5	-	.5	-	-	-	-
100 TO 199 MILES	240	100.0	13.2	63.2	22.1	.4	-	.4	.7
UNDER 1000 POUNDS	18	100.0	-	81.2	11.4	2.0	-	5.3	-
1000 TO 9999 POUNDS	59	100.0	-	65.6	33.5	.9	-	-	-
10000 TO 29999 POUNDS	32	100.0	-	57.6	42.4	-	-	-	-
30000 TO 59999 POUNDS	95	100.0	-	83.3	14.9	-	-	-	1.7
60000 TO 89999 POUNDS	10	100.0	76.1	-	23.9	-	-	-	-
90000 POUNDS AND OVER	24	100.0	96.0	-	4.0	-	-	-	-
200 TO 299 MILES	185	100.0	8.3	70.3	19.4	1.2	-	.8	-
UNDER 1000 POUNDS	15	100.0	.1	75.8	2.4	11.5	-	9.9	.2
1000 TO 9999 POUNDS	50	100.0	-	82.9	16.2	.9	-	-	-
10000 TO 29999 POUNDS	47	100.0	-	68.5	31.5	-	-	-	-
30000 TO 59999 POUNDS	51	100.0	-	75.3	24.7	-	-	-	-
60000 TO 89999 POUNDS	14	100.0	77.3	22.7	-	-	-	-	-
90000 POUNDS AND OVER	6	100.0	54.6	45.4	-	-	-	-	-
300 TO 499 MILES	422	100.0	30.2	55.1	13.0	.3	-	.7	.6
UNDER 1000 POUNDS	32	100.0	.6	81.6	4.7	4.4	-	8.7	.1
1000 TO 9999 POUNDS	52	100.0	.1	80.0	19.8	.1	-	-	-
10000 TO 29999 POUNDS	63	100.0	1.7	74.9	23.4	-	-	-	-
30000 TO 59999 POUNDS	141	100.0	6.0	72.6	19.6	-	-	-	1.8
60000 TO 89999 POUNDS	35	100.0	80.1	18.1	1.9	-	-	-	-
90000 POUNDS AND OVER	96	100.0	91.9	8.1	-	-	-	-	-
500 TO 999 MILES	564	100.0	22.2	64.9	10.3	1.2	-	.9	.5
UNDER 1000 POUNDS	40	100.0	2.4	72.0	5.1	8.0	-	12.3	.2
1000 TO 9999 POUNDS	86	100.0	2.1	75.8	20.1	1.7	-	-	.3
10000 TO 29999 POUNDS	73	100.0	.4	81.1	13.7	3.2	-	.4	1.1
30000 TO 59999 POUNDS	247	100.0	3.1	84.9	11.4	-	-	-	.6
60000 TO 89999 POUNDS	22	100.0	96.5	3.1	.2	-	-	.2	-
90000 POUNDS AND OVER	94	100.0	97.8	1.8	.4	-	-	-	-
1000 TO 1499 MILES	70	100.0	29.4	62.1	5.8	1.2	-	1.5	-
UNDER 1000 POUNDS	8	100.0	3.1	71.9	5.2	7.6	-	11.9	.3
1000 TO 9999 POUNDS	17	100.0	4.6	89.2	4.8	1.1	-	.2	-
10000 TO 29999 POUNDS	13	100.0	-	78.7	21.3	-	-	-	-
30000 TO 59999 POUNDS	12	100.0	5.9	94.1	-	-	-	-	-
60000 TO 89999 POUNDS	-	100.0	-	100.0	-	-	-	-	-
90000 POUNDS AND OVER	18	100.0	100.0	-	-	-	-	-	-
1500 MILES OR OVER	152	100.0	60.6	28.6	6.3	3.0	.3	1.0	.2
UNDER 1000 POUNDS	13	100.0	2.9	57.1	5.6	26.4	.4	5.2	2.4
1000 TO 9999 POUNDS	27	100.0	4.8	83.1	4.4	4.0	.7	2.8	.2
10000 TO 29999 POUNDS	8	100.0	9.4	65.8	22.4	-	2.0	.4	-
30000 TO 59999 POUNDS	17	100.0	25.8	41.6	32.6	-	-	-	-
60000 TO 89999 POUNDS	20	100.0	100.0	-	-	-	-	-	-
90000 POUNDS AND OVER	65	100.0	100.0	-	-	-	-	-	-
TON-MILES OF SHIPMENTS	(millions of ton-miles)								
U.S. TOTAL	1 027	100.0	34.1	52.6	10.2	1.6	.1	.9	.4
UNDER 100 MILES	10	100.0	17.5	55.6	24.1	.3	.6	.5	1.3
UNDER 1000 POUNDS	1	100.0	-	65.6	29.3	.2	-	4.9	-
1000 TO 9999 POUNDS	3	100.0	-	80.0	18.3	.9	.3	.1	.4
10000 TO 29999 POUNDS	2	100.0	-	47.1	50.4	-	2.5	-	-
30000 TO 59999 POUNDS	1	100.0	-	66.4	27.5	-	-	-	6.1
60000 TO 89999 POUNDS	-	100.0	-	-	50.8	-	49.2	-	-
90000 POUNDS AND OVER	1	100.0	99.1	-	.9	-	-	-	-
100 TO 199 MILES	35	100.0	10.8	64.4	23.3	.5	-	.4	.7
UNDER 1000 POUNDS	2	100.0	-	81.9	10.8	2.3	-	5.0	-
1000 TO 9999 POUNDS	9	100.0	-	64.5	34.4	1.1	-	-	-
10000 TO 29999 POUNDS	5	100.0	-	60.2	39.8	-	-	-	-
30000 TO 59999 POUNDS	13	100.0	-	82.1	16.2	-	-	-	1.7
60000 TO 89999 POUNDS	1	100.0	72.0	-	28.0	-	-	-	-
90000 POUNDS AND OVER	3	100.0	95.3	-	4.7	-	-	-	-

See footnotes at end of table 4.

TABLE 4. TCC GROUP 362—Percent Distribution of Distance Shipped and Weight of Shipment, by Means of Transport: 1972—Continued

Distance shipped and weight of shipment[2] [3]	Number	Percent distribution by means of transport							
		All means of transport	Rail	Motor carrier	Private truck	Air	Water	Other	Unknown
TON-MILES OF SHIPMENTS	(millions of ton-miles)								
200 TO 299 MILES	47	100.0	8.9	69.4	19.6	1.3	-	.8	-
UNDER 1000 POUNDS	3	100.0	.1	75.1	2.3	12.3	-	9.9	.2
1000 TO 9999 POUNDS	12	100.0	-	82.0	16.9	1.0	-	-	.2
10000 TO 29999 POUNDS	11	100.0	-	68.6	31.4	-	-	-	-
30000 TO 59999 POUNDS	12	100.0	-	74.6	25.4	-	-	-	-
60000 TO 89999 POUNDS	3	100.0	79.1	20.9	-	-	-	-	-
90000 POUNDS AND OVER	1	100.0	58.8	41.2	-	-	-	-	-
300 TO 499 MILES	170	100.0	31.8	53.4	13.1	.3	-	.7	.8
UNDER 1000 POUNDS	12	100.0	.6	81.2	4.9	4.3	-	8.9	.1
1000 TO 9999 POUNDS	20	100.0	.2	80.3	19.4	.1	-	-	.1
10000 TO 29999 POUNDS	25	100.0	1.3	75.8	22.9	-	-	-	-
30000 TO 59999 POUNDS	57	100.0	6.3	71.0	20.4	-	-	-	2.2
60000 TO 89999 POUNDS	15	100.0	83.1	15.1	1.8	-	-	-	-
90000 POUNDS AND OVER	40	100.0	93.9	6.1	-	-	-	-	-
500 TO 999 MILES	369	100.0	21.7	65.3	10.3	1.2	-	1.0	.5
UNDER 1000 POUNDS	27	100.0	2.7	72.1	5.1	8.0	-	11.8	.3
1000 TO 9999 POUNDS	61	100.0	1.9	77.9	18.4	1.4	-	.1	.3
10000 TO 29999 POUNDS	51	100.0	.5	83.1	12.3	2.6	-	.4	1.1
30000 TO 59999 POUNDS	154	100.0	3.1	83.9	12.3	-	-	-	.7
60000 TO 89999 POUNDS	15	100.0	96.4	3.3	.2	-	-	.1	-
90000 POUNDS AND OVER	59	100.0	97.6	2.0	.4	-	-	-	-
1000 TO 1499 MILES	84	100.0	30.8	61.3	5.4	1.2	-	1.3	-
UNDER 1000 POUNDS	9	100.0	3.6	72.3	5.2	7.6	-	11.0	.3
1000 TO 9999 POUNDS	20	100.0	4.7	89.1	4.8	1.2	-	.2	-
10000 TO 29999 POUNDS	15	100.0	-	80.1	19.9	-	-	-	-
30000 TO 59999 POUNDS	14	100.0	5.3	94.7	-	-	-	-	-
60000 TO 89999 POUNDS	-	100.0	-	100.0	-	-	-	-	-
90000 POUNDS AND OVER	23	100.0	100.0	-	-	-	-	-	-
1500 MILES OR OVER	309	100.0	58.2	30.6	6.4	3.2	.4	1.0	.2
UNDER 1000 POUNDS	27	100.0	2.9	55.5	.5.5	28.4	.4	5.3	2.0
1000 TO 9999 POUNDS	59	100.0	4.3	84.2	3.8	3.8	.9	2.8	.3
10000 TO 29999 POUNDS	17	100.0	8.2	68.3	20.6	-	2.5	.4	-
30000 TO 59999 POUNDS	37	100.0	20.7	46.1	33.1	-	-	-	-
60000 TO 89999 POUNDS	48	100.0	100.0	-	-	-	-	-	-
90000 POUNDS AND OVER	119	100.0	100.0	-	-	-	-	-	-

Note: Detail may not add to total due to rounding. The introductory table shows the estimates of sampling variability for tons; sampling variability for ton-miles has not been estimated. See the map in the Introduction for the States comprising the geographic divisions of the United States.
Shipments excluded from the survey are those moving by pipeline (primarily petroleum products from refineries), parcel post shipments, and commodities moved by own power (motorized vehicles, aircraft, etc.) or towed (prefabricated buildings, etc.). Local shipments (commodities shipped less than 25 miles from the plant) and shipments within the same city are also excluded. Shipments to Alaska and Hawaii from the 48 conterminous States and the District of Columbia are included; however, no data were obtained for shipments originating in Alaska and Hawaii.

- Represents zero or rounds to zero.   (D) Withheld to avoid disclosing figures for individual companies.

[1]Production of this commodity is concentrated in the geographic divisions shown; figures and distributions for geographic divisions not shown are included in the total.
[2]Distances of shipments to foreign destinations are calculated only to the U.S. port of exit.
[3]Includes only shipments represented by bills of lading and invoices. Summary records which did not show individual weights of shipments are not included.

TCC 363. Household Appliances

Comparisons of Tons and Ton-Miles of Shipments for
Geographic Divisions of Origin and for Sampling Variability: 1972 and 1967

Geographic division of origin	Estimates				Relative sampling variability in tons (percent)	
	1972		1967		1972	1967
	Tons (thousands)	Ton-miles (millions)	Tons (thousands)	Ton-miles (millions)		
U.S. total	5,088	3,133	4,311	3,063	3.4	23.0
New England	70	38	62	57	24.5	(*)
Middle Atlantic . . . . : .	83	44	210	125	12.2	(*)
East North Central	2,603	1,558	1,971	1,329	2.8	(*)
West North Central	245	193	439	345	14.4	(*)
South Atlantic	431	199	22	21	16.5	(*)
East South Central	(D)	(D)	729	484	(*)	(*)
West South Central	123	79	777	614	24.1	(*)
Mountain	(D)	(D)	—	—	(*)	—
Pacific	158	154	101	88	11.5	(*)

— Represents or rounds to zero.   (D) Withheld to avoid disclosing figures for individual companies.   * Data not published.

TABLE 1. TCC GROUP 363—Percent Distribution of Geographic Division of Origin and Distance Shipped, by Means of Transport: 1972

Geographic division of origin[1] and distance shipped[2]	Number	Percent distribution by means of transport							
		All means of transport	Rail	Motor carrier	Private truck	Air	Water	Other	Unknown
TONS OF SHIPMENTS	(thousands of tons)								
U.S. TOTAL.........	5 088	100.0	58.3	35.1	6.0	.1	.1	.2	.2
NEW ENGLAND...........	70	100.0	9.6	73.2	15.6	.3	1.1	.3	-
UNDER 100 MILES......	25	100.0	-	58.1	41.9	-	-	-	-
100 TO 199 MILES......	9	100.0	-	96.2	3.6	-	-	.3	-
200 TO 299 MILES......	3	100.0	-	99.5	-	-	-	.5	-
300 TO 499 MILES......	5	100.0	6.8	92.4	-	-	-	.8	-
500 TO 999 MILES......	13	100.0	26.6	72.5	-	.3	-	.6	-
1000 TO 1499 MILES....	7	100.0	20.7	69.7	.1	.7	7.9	.9	-
1500 MILES OR OVER....	6	100.0	20.5	75.4	-	1.2	2.9	-	-
MIDDLE ATLANTIC.........	83	100.0	13.5	62.9	22.8	.3	-	.3	.1
UNDER 100 MILES......	24	100.0	-	56.1	43.1	-	-	.5	.2
100 TO 199 MILES......	10	100.0	20.9	53.6	25.0	-	-	.4	.1
200 TO 299 MILES......	6	100.0	13.4	84.3	1.7	.3	-	.2	-
300 TO 499 MILES......	9	100.0	23.5	70.8	4.2	1.1	-	.4	-
500 TO 999 MILES......	14	100.0	16.4	56.4	26.0	.9	-	.4	-
1000 TO 1499 MILES....	12	100.0	16.9	78.9	3.8	.1	-	.1	.1
1500 MILES OR OVER....	5	100.0	26.6	52.0	21.3	.1	-	-	.1
EAST NORTH CENTRAL......	2 603	100.0	61.6	34.5	3.5	.1	-	.3	.1
UNDER 100 MILES......	286	100.0	34.2	58.2	7.4	-	-	.2	-
100 TO 199 MILES......	177	100.0	19.6	68.8	11.2	-	-	.2	.2
200 TO 299 MILES......	279	100.0	46.6	46.8	6.3	-	-	.2	.1
300 TO 499 MILES......	539	100.0	63.5	32.0	4.0	.3	-	.3	-
500 TO 999 MILES......	968	100.0	75.7	23.0	.7	-	-	.4	.1
1000 TO 1499 MILES....	138	100.0	89.2	10.1	.6	-	-	.1	-
1500 MILES OR OVER....	213	100.0	66.5	32.3	.8	-	-	.4	-
WEST NORTH CENTRAL......	245	100.0	67.0	26.7	3.7	.1	-	.7	1.8
UNDER 100 MILES......	3	100.0	-	92.3	7.6	-	-	.1	-
100 TO 199 MILES......	5	100.0	-	53.6	45.7	-	-	.6	-
200 TO 299 MILES......	23	100.0	62.6	19.1	10.5	-	-	.2	7.6
300 TO 499 MILES......	34	100.0	51.6	40.1	7.8	.1	-	.4	-
500 TO 999 MILES......	121	100.0	82.7	15.8	.8	.2	-	.6	-
1000 TO 1499 MILES....	34	100.0	34.8	57.0	.2	.1	-	.4	7.4
1500 MILES OR OVER....	23	100.0	87.3	10.1	.1	-	-	2.5	-
SOUTH ATLANTIC.........	431	100.0	28.0	69.8	1.8	-	-	.1	.2
UNDER 100 MILES......	79	100.0	15.7	83.8	.1	-	-	.3	-
100 TO 199 MILES......	123	100.0	14.2	85.2	.5	-	-	-	-
200 TO 299 MILES......	50	100.0	27.2	72.7	-	-	-	.1	-
300 TO 499 MILES......	66	100.0	33.9	63.4	2.4	-	-	.1	-
500 TO 999 MILES......	68	100.0	40.3	50.3	8.0	.1	-	.1	1.3
1000 TO 1499 MILES....	10	100.0	57.9	42.0	-	-	-	.1	-
1500 MILES OR OVER....	32	100.0	63.5	36.4	-	-	-	-	-
WEST SOUTH CENTRAL......	123	100.0	55.9	24.1	19.7	-	-	.3	-
UNDER 100 MILES......	1	100.0	-	28.1	67.9	-	-	4.0	-
100 TO 199 MILES......	8	100.0	-	19.1	80.6	-	-	.3	-
200 TO 299 MILES......	8	100.0	46.4	25.9	27.7	-	-	-	-
300 TO 499 MILES......	32	100.0	55.4	28.2	16.4	-	-	-	-
500 TO 999 MILES......	51	100.0	63.1	20.1	16.3	-	-	.4	-
1000 TO 1499 MILES....	16	100.0	73.8	25.2	.9	-	-	-	-
1500 MILES OR OVER....	4	100.0	54.8	43.3	-	-	-	1.9	-
PACIFIC.................	158	100.0	48.8	40.1	8.4	.1	1.7	.3	.5
UNDER 100 MILES......	15	100.0	-	52.9	44.4	-	.4	2.0	.2
100 TO 199 MILES......	10	100.0	44.2	28.9	21.2	-	-	.1	5.6
200 TO 299 MILES......	2	100.0	-	99.8	-	-	-	.2	-
300 TO 499 MILES......	27	100.0	41.1	57.5	1.3	-	-	-	-
500 TO 999 MILES......	22	100.0	53.8	46.2	-	-	-	-	-
1000 TO 1499 MILES....	49	100.0	92.7	6.8	-	-	-	.1	.3
1500 MILES OR OVER....	31	100.0	12.5	65.1	12.8	.5	8.6	.4	-
TON-MILES OF SHIPMENTS	(millions of ton-miles)								
U.S. TOTAL.........	3 133	100.0	67.7	27.9	3.6	.1	.3	.3	.2
NEW ENGLAND...........	38	100.0	20.4	74.0	1.1	.7	3.3	.4	-
UNDER 100 MILES......	1	100.0	-	67.1	32.9	-	-	-	-
100 TO 199 MILES......	1	100.0	-	96.4	3.3	-	-	.3	-
200 TO 299 MILES......	-	100.0	-	99.5	-	-	-	.5	-
300 TO 499 MILES......	1	100.0	6.5	92.7	-	-	-	.8	-
500 TO 999 MILES......	9	100.0	27.0	72.0	-	.3	-	.6	-
1000 TO 1499 MILES....	9	100.0	20.9	68.8	.1	.7	8.7	.8	-
1500 MILES OR OVER....	14	100.0	22.4	73.0	-	1.3	3.3	-	-
MIDDLE ATLANTIC.........	44	100.0	19.1	65.5	14.8	.4	-	.2	.1
UNDER 100 MILES......	1	100.0	-	61.8	37.4	-	-	.5	.2
100 TO 199 MILES......	1	100.0	20.2	53.9	25.3	-	-	.4	.1
200 TO 299 MILES......	1	100.0	15.1	82.5	1.9	.3	-	.2	-
300 TO 499 MILES......	3	100.0	26.1	69.1	3.4	.9	-	.4	-
500 TO 999 MILES......	10	100.0	16.1	55.5	27.1	.9	-	.4	-
1000 TO 1499 MILES....	14	100.0	17.3	78.1	4.2	.1	-	.1	.1
1500 MILES OR OVER....	11	100.0	24.0	56.5	19.4	.1	-	-	-

See footnotes at end of table 4.

TABLE 1. **TCC GROUP 363**—Percent Distribution of Geographic Division of Origin and Distance Shipped, by Means of Transport: 1972—Continued

Geographic division of origin[1] and distance shipped[2]	Number	Percent distribution by means of transport							
		All means of transport	Rail	Motor carrier	Private truck	Air	Water	Other	Unknown
TON-MILES OF SHIPMENTS	(millions of ton-miles)								
EAST NORTH CENTRAL	1 558	100.0	70.4	27.3	1.8	-	-	.3	.1
UNDER 100 MILES	13	100.0	39.6	51.4	8.9	-	-	.1	-
100 TO 199 MILES	27	100.0	19.8	69.4	10.3	-	-	.3	.2
200 TO 299 MILES	70	100.0	46.4	47.1	6.1	-	-	.2	.1
300 TO 499 MILES	216	100.0	65.1	30.7	3.7	.2	-	.2	-
500 TO 999 MILES	671	100.0	75.5	23.2	.7	-	-	.4	.1
1000 TO 1499 MILES	165	100.0	89.7	9.7	.5	-	-	.1	-
1500 MILES OR OVER	393	100.0	65.5	32.5	1.6	-	-	.4	-
WEST NORTH CENTRAL	193	100.0	70.8	25.2	1.4	.1	-	.9	1.6
UNDER 100 MILES	-	100.0	-	93.1	6.7	-	-	.2	-
100 TO 199 MILES	-	100.0	-	56.8	42.6	-	-	.6	-
200 TO 299 MILES	5	100.0	65.0	17.4	9.4	-	-	.2	8.0
300 TO 499 MILES	14	100.0	53.8	37.4	8.4	.1	-	.4	-
500 TO 999 MILES	95	100.0	84.5	14.2	.5	.1	-	.6	-
1000 TO 1499 MILES	41	100.0	33.4	59.6	.2	.1	-	.4	6.3
1500 MILES OR OVER	35	100.0	86.9	10.4	.1	-	-	2.6	-
SOUTH ATLANTIC	199	100.0	45.8	51.4	2.3	-	-	-	.4
UNDER 100 MILES	5	100.0	16.9	82.7	.2	-	-	.3	-
100 TO 199 MILES	20	100.0	14.3	85.1	.6	-	-	-	-
200 TO 299 MILES	12	100.0	27.7	72.2	-	-	-	.1	-
300 TO 499 MILES	25	100.0	35.5	62.2	2.1	-	-	.1	.2
500 TO 999 MILES	47	100.0	41.1	49.0	8.2	.1	-	.1	1.5
1000 TO 1499 MILES	12	100.0	58.2	41.6	-	-	-	.1	-
1500 MILES OR OVER	74	100.0	63.9	36.0	-	-	-	-	-
WEST SOUTH CENTRAL	79	100.0	62.1	25.8	11.4	-	-	.7	-
UNDER 100 MILES	-	100.0	-	34.1	64.7	-	-	1.2	-
100 TO 199 MILES	1	100.0	-	20.3	79.3	-	-	.4	-
200 TO 299 MILES	2	100.0	46.3	26.8	26.9	-	-	-	-
300 TO 499 MILES	13	100.0	58.2	27.5	14.2	-	-	-	-
500 TO 999 MILES	37	100.0	64.1	21.0	14.5	-	-	.5	-
1000 TO 1499 MILES	19	100.0	72.0	26.9	1.0	-	-	-	-
1500 MILES OR OVER	7	100.0	49.4	45.9	-	-	-	4.7	-
PACIFIC	154	100.0	50.1	39.1	5.3	.3	4.8	.2	.2
UNDER 100 MILES	-	100.0	-	68.0	30.3	-	.5	1.1	.1
100 TO 199 MILES	1	100.0	43.8	30.8	20.3	-	-	.1	5.0
200 TO 299 MILES	-	100.0	-	99.8	-	-	-	.2	-
300 TO 499 MILES	9	100.0	41.0	57.6	1.3	-	-	-	-
500 TO 999 MILES	15	100.0	51.2	48.8	-	-	-	-	-
1000 TO 1499 MILES	62	100.0	92.5	7.1	-	-	-	.1	.4
1500 MILES OR OVER	63	100.0	10.6	64.5	12.1	.6	11.6	.4	-

See footnotes at end of table 4.

TABLE 2. **TCC GROUP 363**—Percent Distribution of Geographic Division of Origin and Means of Transport, by Geographic Division of Destination: 1972

Geographic division of origin[1] and means of transport	Number	Percent distribution by division of destination									
		U.S. total	New England	Middle Atlantic	East North Central	West North Central	South Atlantic	East South Central	West South Central	Mountain	Pacific
TONS OF SHIPMENTS	(thousands of tons)										
U.S. TOTAL	5 088	100.0	4.7	15.7	22.3	6.8	21.4	5.3	8.6	7.7	7.4
RAIL	2 967	100.0	3.6	13.8	13.8	7.3	28.6	4.9	10.8	10.9	6.5
MOTOR CARRIER	1 788	100.0	7.1	19.0	35.7	6.8	12.8	5.4	4.6	2.4	6.3
PRIVATE TRUCK	305	100.0	.8	15.8	27.2	2.4	3.0	9.5	9.7	9.3	22.3
AIR	3	100.0	1.3	9.4	9.9	3.3	12.4	44.7	8.7	1.5	8.8
WATER	3	100.0	-	1.0	-	-	-	-	15.7	-	83.4
OTHER	11	100.0	2.8	15.4	21.7	6.4	23.2	3.8	7.8	2.7	16.4
UNKNOWN	9	100.0	1.3	4.6	5.9	22.7	17.2	4.1	36.6	.3	7.2
NEW ENGLAND	70	100.0	20.4	35.9	13.3	2.4	10.9	2.5	5.7	4.3	4.5
RAIL	6	100.0	-	-	34.2	5.7	21.3	5.4	13.2	2.8	17.3
MOTOR CARRIER	51	100.0	25.9	29.7	13.5	2.4	11.9	2.7	5.0	5.6	3.4
PRIVATE TRUCK	10	100.0	9.4	90.6	-	-	-	-	-	-	-
AIR	-	100.0	2.0	-	22.6	20.4	7.6	.8	2.1	5.5	38.9
WATER	-	100.0	-	-	-	-	-	-	74.3	-	25.7
OTHER	-	100.0	7.6	15.4	26.5	2.6	36.0	2.4	9.4	-	-
UNKNOWN	-	100.0	-	-	-	-	-	-	-	-	-
MIDDLE ATLANTIC	83	100.0	5.2	40.2	13.3	4.9	22.8	2.8	6.2	.5	4.2
RAIL	11	100.0	3.9	12.9	20.1	6.3	33.0	6.8	10.8	.7	5.5
MOTOR CARRIER	52	100.0	5.8	36.4	13.7	4.9	25.9	2.9	5.4	.6	4.4
PRIVATE TRUCK	18	100.0	4.4	66.4	8.0	4.2	8.6	.1	5.5	-	2.8
AIR	-	100.0	.5	44.1	31.8	1.5	.6	14.4	4.7	-	2.4
WATER	-	100.0	-	-	-	-	-	-	-	-	-
OTHER	-	100.0	8.3	55.4	11.6	3.2	13.3	6.9	.5	.1	.7
UNKNOWN	-	100.0	10.9	65.1	3.4	-	20.7	-	-	-	-

See footnotes at end of table 4.

TABLE 2. **TCC GROUP 363**—Percent Distribution of Geographic Division of Origin and Means of Transport, by Geographic Division of Destination: 1972—Continued

Geographic division of origin[1] and means of transport	Number	Percent distribution by division of destination									
		U.S. total	New England	Middle Atlantic	East North Central	West North Central	South Atlantic	East South Central	West South Central	Mountain	Pacific
TONS OF SHIPMENTS	(thousands of tons)										
EAST NORTH CENTRAL......	2 603	100.0	4.3	15.2	26.8	7.4	19.8	6.8	8.1	5.3	6.4
RAIL..................	1 603	100.0	4.1	17.5	14.1	8.4	24.3	6.7	10.9	7.2	6.9
MOTOR CARRIER.........	897	100.0	5.2	11.4	46.5	5.7	13.1	5.8	3.9	2.4	6.0
PRIVATE TRUCK.........	90	100.0	.3	11.0	58.1	3.8	5.8	18.5	.4	.1	1.9
AIR...................	1	100.0	2.0	8.4	8.5	1.6	2.9	72.4	1.7	-	2.6
WATER.................	-	100.0	-	-	-	-	-	-	-	-	100.0
OTHER.................	7	100.0	2.7	18.2	24.7	7.8	19.3	3.7	8.9	3.8	10.9
UNKNOWN...............	1	100.0	-	18.8	28.8	16.0	34.7	-	-	1.6	-
WEST NORTH CENTRAL......	245	100.0	6.4	17.3	21.6	13.8	10.3	4.9	10.7	3.8	11.1
RAIL..................	164	100.0	2.8	22.8	15.3	12.8	11.1	5.8	11.6	5.1	12.7
MOTOR CARRIER.........	65	100.0	16.9	7.5	31.3	13.6	9.8	3.9	6.5	1.6	9.0
PRIVATE TRUCK.........	9	100.0	-	-	76.7	21.6	.9	-	-	.3	.3
AIR...................	-	100.0	-	2.8	-	1.8	-	-	81.9	13.5	-
WATER.................	-	100.0	-	-	-	-	-	-	-	-	-
OTHER.................	1	100.0	2.8	5.7	11.2	4.7	31.0	2.9	3.4	.2	38.1
UNKNOWN...............	4	100.0	-	-	-	41.0	-	-	58.9	-	.1
SOUTH ATLANTIC..........	431	100.0	14.6	43.5	7.9	3.5	16.2	3.6	3.2	1.7	5.9
RAIL..................	120	100.0	11.5	23.8	12.1	5.0	15.9	8.2	6.2	2.2	15.1
MOTOR CARRIER.........	301	100.0	16.3	52.0	4.6	3.0	16.4	1.9	2.0	1.6	2.3
PRIVATE TRUCK.........	7	100.0	-	28.3	69.2	-	1.7	.1	.7	-	-
AIR...................	-	100.0	-	-	13.4	-	57.4	-	-	-	29.2
WATER.................	-	100.0	-	100.0	-	-	-	-	-	-	-
OTHER.................	-	100.0	1.9	11.0	12.0	.9	68.6	2.2	2.8	.2	.5
UNKNOWN...............	1	100.0	10.7	-	-	.4	88.9	-	-	-	-
WEST SOUTH CENTRAL......	123	100.0	.5	7.0	34.1	6.1	13.6	3.5	21.5	7.9	5.8
RAIL..................	69	100.0	-	8.3	45.0	7.5	17.9	2.9	3.9	7.4	7.1
MOTOR CARRIER.........	29	100.0	2.1	9.6	30.7	7.1	14.3	6.1	20.6	2.8	6.7
PRIVATE TRUCK.........	24	100.0	-	-	7.9	1.0	.1	2.0	72.6	15.8	.6
AIR...................	-	100.0	-	-	-	-	-	-	-	-	-
WATER.................	-	100.0	-	-	-	-	-	-	-	-	-
OTHER.................	-	100.0	-	.2	3.8	-	54.3	7.7	13.0	-	21.0
UNKNOWN...............	-	100.0	-	-	-	-	-	-	-	-	-
PACIFIC................	158	100.0	.8	4.1	8.4	5.2	1.0	1.0	31.5	16.4	31.6
RAIL..................	77	100.0	-	-	1.5	9.0	-	.5	56.2	21.9	10.9
MOTOR CARRIER.........	63	100.0	1.6	9.8	13.6	1.9	2.2	2.0	9.9	14.2	44.7
PRIVATE TRUCK.........	13	100.0	1.6	1.1	26.0	-	1.3	-	-	-	70.0
AIR...................	-	100.0	-	.4	-	-	-	16.5	-	.3	82.7
WATER.................	2	100.0	-	-	-	-	-	-	-	-	100.0
OTHER.................	-	100.0	.1	-	27.3	-	.1	.1	7.4	.5	64.5
UNKNOWN...............	-	100.0	-	1.2	-	-	-	-	19.7	-	79.1
TON-MILES OF SHIPMENTS	(millions of ton-miles)										
U.S. TOTAL.............	3 133	100.0	4.9	12.2	10.0	5.6	18.5	3.3	11.7	15.7	18.2
RAIL..................	2 122	100.0	3.7	11.3	5.7	5.1	21.5	2.8	13.3	19.6	17.0
MOTOR CARRIER.........	872	100.0	8.4	14.3	19.2	7.2	13.0	4.1	7.5	7.0	19.2
PRIVATE TRUCK.........	113	100.0	1.0	12.8	22.5	2.7	4.4	5.8	12.3	11.9	26.6
AIR...................	2	100.0	1.2	6.7	6.8	3.7	16.1	22.2	8.8	2.6	31.8
WATER.................	8	100.0	-	.1	-	-	-	-	9.2	-	90.8
OTHER.................	8	100.0	2.9	13.1	9.9	3.2	19.9	2.6	9.3	3.8	35.3
UNKNOWN...............	5	100.0	.7	5.1	1.6	11.9	21.4	2.8	54.5	.7	1.3
NEW ENGLAND............	38	100.0	2.7	7.5	14.7	5.0	14.4	4.3	15.1	15.7	20.5
RAIL..................	7	100.0	-	-	18.9	5.5	13.4	4.5	16.3	4.4	37.0
MOTOR CARRIER.........	28	100.0	3.3	9.0	14.5	5.1	15.4	4.5	13.0	19.9	15.2
PRIVATE TRUCK.........	-	100.0	24.1	73.9	-	-	.4	1.6	-	-	-
AIR...................	-	100.0	.1	-	10.5	14.5	5.4	.5	1.6	6.8	60.5
WATER.................	1	100.0	-	-	-	-	-	-	62.5	-	37.5
OTHER.................	-	100.0	1.4	5.5	25.7	3.9	39.8	3.7	19.8	-	.1
UNKNOWN...............	-	100.0	-	-	-	-	-	-	-	-	-
MIDDLE ATLANTIC.........	44	100.0	1.7	6.7	13.7	9.0	28.0	4.2	15.9	1.8	19.1
RAIL..................	8	100.0	.8	2.3	13.9	9.6	24.5	8.3	21.1	1.9	17.7
MOTOR CARRIER.........	29	100.0	1.8	6.9	12.9	8.3	31.8	3.8	12.8	2.1	19.5
PRIVATE TRUCK.........	6	100.0	2.3	11.3	15.8	11.7	16.2	.2	23.0	-	19.5
AIR...................	-	100.0	.3	21.7	40.0	1.9	.2	18.2	8.8	-	8.8
WATER.................	-	100.0	-	-	-	-	-	-	-	-	-
OTHER.................	-	100.0	4.4	17.6	21.3	11.5	19.4	17.7	2.1	.3	5.7
UNKNOWN...............	-	100.0	6.3	9.7	5.1	-	78.9	-	-	-	-
EAST NORTH CENTRAL......	1 558	100.0	5.4	13.9	7.4	5.6	19.9	4.3	11.2	12.1	20.3
RAIL..................	1 097	100.0	4.6	14.7	3.6	5.7	21.8	3.7	13.1	13.9	19.0
MOTOR CARRIER.........	425	100.0	7.8	12.0	15.6	5.4	16.0	4.6	7.0	8.3	23.4
PRIVATE TRUCK.........	28	100.0	1.0	13.2	28.7	4.7	9.6	18.9	1.2	.4	22.2
AIR...................	-	100.0	3.4	13.0	6.0	1.2	6.1	55.1	3.3	.1	11.8
WATER.................	-	100.0	-	-	-	-	-	-	-	-	100.0
OTHER.................	5	100.0	3.1	18.1	6.6	4.1	17.5	2.8	12.0	5.9	30.0
UNKNOWN...............	1	100.0	-	25.5	8.7	18.4	43.7	-	-	3.7	-

See footnotes at end of table 4.

TABLE 2. **TCC GROUP 363—Percent Distribution of Geographic Division of Origin and Means of Transport, by Geographic Division of Destination: 1972**—Continued

Geographic division of origin[1] and means of transport	Number	Percent distribution by division of destination									
		U.S. total	New England	Middle Atlantic	East North Central	West North Central	South Atlantic	East South Central	West South Central	Mountain	Pacific
TON-MILES OF SHIPMENTS	(millions of ton-miles)										
WEST NORTH CENTRAL	193	100.0	9.6	19.3	12.3	5.0	12.0	4.4	10.9	4.6	21.8
RAIL	136	100.0	3.6	24.0	9.6	5.1	12.0	5.1	11.4	5.8	23.5
MOTOR CARRIER	48	100.0	28.0	9.2	17.1	4.0	12.9	3.0	5.5	2.0	18.3
PRIVATE TRUCK	2	100.0	-	.1	82.0	12.1	3.1	-	-	1.0	1.8
AIR	-	100.0	-	4.4	-	1.0	-	-	75.1	19.4	-
WATER	-	100.0	-	-	-	-	-	-	-	-	-
OTHER	1	100.0	3.0	4.9	4.1	1.3	24.8	1.5	2.3	.2	58.0
UNKNOWN	3	100.0	-	-	-	15.6	-	-	84.3	-	.1
SOUTH ATLANTIC	199	100.0	12.2	15.3	10.1	6.8	8.0	3.2	7.0	7.2	30.2
RAIL	91	100.0	5.3	5.3	10.1	5.5	8.3	4.5	8.6	5.5	46.9
MOTOR CARRIER	102	100.0	19.0	24.4	6.8	8.3	7.3	2.3	6.0	9.1	16.9
PRIVATE TRUCK	4	100.0	-	13.9	84.8	-	.4	-	.8	-	-
AIR	-	100.0	-	-	5.8	-	42.2	-	-	-	52.0
WATER	-	100.0	-	100.0	-	-	-	-	-	-	-
OTHER	-	100.0	3.3	10.4	26.4	3.7	31.2	4.6	14.4	1.0	4.9
UNKNOWN	-	100.0	5.0	-	-	.5	94.5	-	-	-	-
WEST SOUTH CENTRAL	79	100.0	1.1	11.8	27.8	3.3	19.3	2.3	9.5	10.8	14.1
RAIL	49	100.0	-	12.0	32.3	3.0	23.6	2.0	2.1	10.6	14.4
MOTOR CARRIER	20	100.0	4.3	16.7	24.6	5.4	17.2	3.0	7.9	3.8	17.1
PRIVATE TRUCK	9	100.0	-	-	11.8	.8	.2	2.0	54.3	28.6	2.2
AIR	-	100.0	-	-	-	-	-	-	-	-	-
WATER	-	100.0	-	-	-	-	-	-	-	-	-
OTHER	-	100.0	-	.2	1.9	-	32.7	1.2	.2	-	63.9
UNKNOWN	-	100.0	-	-	-	-	-	-	-	-	-
PACIFIC	154	100.0	2.1	9.7	15.6	6.4	2.1	1.8	40.7	9.0	12.5
RAIL	77	100.0	-	2.5	-	10.5	.1	.9	71.6	11.4	2.9
MOTOR CARRIER	60	100.0	4.3	24.2	25.7	3.0	4.7	3.5	12.0	8.3	14.2
PRIVATE TRUCK	8	100.0	6.9	4.3	77.0	-	4.8	-	-	-	7.1
AIR	-	100.0	-	.4	-	-	-	10.6	-	-	89.0
WATER	7	100.0	-	-	-	-	-	-	-	-	100.0
OTHER	-	100.0	.3	-	79.8	-	.5	.2	14.0	.3	5.0
UNKNOWN	-	100.0	-	7.7	-	-	-	-	70.5	-	21.9

See footnotes at end of table 4.

TABLE 3. TCC GROUP 363—Percent Distribution of Geographic Division of Destination and Means of Transport, by Geographic Division of Origin: 1972

Geographic division of destination and means of transport	Number	Percent distribution by division of origin[1]									
		U.S. total	New England	Middle Atlantic	East North Central	West North Central	South Atlantic	East South Central	West South Central	Mountain	Pacific
TONS OF SHIPMENTS	(thousands of tons)										
U.S. TOTAL	5 088	100.0	1.4	1.6	51.2	4.8	8.5	(D)	2.4	(D)	3.1
RAIL	2 967	100.0	.2	.4	54.1	5.5	4.1	(D)	2.3	(D)	2.6
MOTOR CARRIER	1 788	100.0	2.9	2.9	50.2	3.7	16.8	(D)	1.7	(D)	3.6
PRIVATE TRUCK	305	100.0	3.6	6.2	29.5	3.0	2.6	(D)	8.0	(D)	4.4
AIR	3	100.0	5.8	9.0	58.9	8.6	1.7	(D)	-	(D)	4.6
WATER	3	100.0	21.1	-	.1	-	1.0	(D)	-	(D)	77.9
OTHER	11	100.0	2.0	2.4	68.4	14.2	3.6	(D)	3.3	(D)	4.3
UNKNOWN	9	100.0	-	1.0	20.3	47.4	11.2	(D)	-	(D)	9.1
NEW ENGLAND	237	100.0	6.1	1.8	47.6	6.7	26.6	(D)	.3	(D)	.5
RAIL	106	100.0	-	.4	61.7	4.4	13.0	(D)	-	(D)	-
MOTOR CARRIER	127	100.0	10.5	2.4	36.5	8.7	38.6	(D)	.5	(D)	.8
PRIVATE TRUCK	2	100.0	43.3	35.0	12.5	-	-	(D)	-	(D)	9.2
AIR	-	100.0	8.9	3.1	88.0	-	-	(D)	-	(D)	-
WATER	-	100.0	-	-	-	-	-	(D)	-	(D)	-
OTHER	-	100.0	5.6	7.2	65.9	14.3	2.5	(D)	-	(D)	.1
UNKNOWN	-	100.0	-	8.4	-	-	91.6	(D)	-	(D)	-
MIDDLE ATLANTIC	800	100.0	3.2	4.2	49.3	5.3	23.4	(D)	1.1	(D)	.8
RAIL	409	100.0	-	.4	68.4	9.1	7.0	(D)	1.4	(D)	-
MOTOR CARRIER	340	100.0	4.5	5.6	30.2	1.4	46.0	(D)	.8	(D)	1.8
PRIVATE TRUCK	48	100.0	20.6	26.1	20.6	-	4.6	(D)	-	(D)	.3
AIR	-	100.0	-	42.3	52.6	2.6	-	(D)	-	(D)	.2
WATER	-	100.0	-	-	-	-	100.0	(D)	-	(D)	-
OTHER	1	100.0	2.0	8.6	80.8	5.3	2.5	(D)	-	(D)	-
UNKNOWN	-	100.0	-	14.5	83.1	-	-	(D)	-	(D)	2.4
EAST NORTH CENTRAL	1 133	100.0	.8	1.0	61.7	4.7	3.0	(D)	3.7	(D)	1.2
RAIL	408	100.0	.6	.6	55.2	6.2	3.6	(D)	7.6	(D)	.3
MOTOR CARRIER	637	100.0	1.1	1.1	65.5	3.2	2.2	(D)	1.4	(D)	1.4
PRIVATE TRUCK	83	100.0	-	1.8	62.9	8.4	6.5	(D)	2.3	(D)	4.2
AIR	-	100.0	13.3	29.0	50.8	-	2.3	(D)	-	(D)	-
WATER	-	100.0	-	-	-	-	-	(D)	-	(D)	-
OTHER	2	100.0	2.5	1.3	78.1	7.3	2.0	(D)	.6	(D)	5.5
UNKNOWN	-	100.0	-	.6	99.3	-	-	(D)	-	(D)	-
WEST NORTH CENTRAL	346	100.0	.5	1.2	55.3	9.8	4.3	(D)	2.2	(D)	2.4
RAIL	215	100.0	.2	.3	62.9	9.8	2.8	(D)	2.4	(D)	3.2
MOTOR CARRIER	120	100.0	1.0	2.1	42.7	7.4	7.4	(D)	1.8	(D)	1.0
PRIVATE TRUCK	7	100.0	-	10.9	47.3	27.1	-	(D)	3.3	(D)	-
AIR	-	100.0	35.9	4.1	28.4	4.7	-	(D)	-	(D)	-
WATER	-	100.0	-	-	-	-	-	(D)	-	(D)	-
OTHER	-	100.0	.8	1.2	84.3	10.5	.5	(D)	-	(D)	-
UNKNOWN	2	100.0	-	-	14.3	85.5	.2	(D)	-	(D)	-
SOUTH ATLANTIC	1 091	100.0	.7	1.7	47.2	2.3	6.4	(D)	1.5	(D)	.1
RAIL	848	100.0	.2	.4	46.0	2.1	2.3	(D)	1.5	(D)	-
MOTOR CARRIER	228	100.0	2.7	5.9	51.3	2.8	21.6	(D)	1.9	(D)	.6
PRIVATE TRUCK	9	100.0	-	17.8	56.5	.9	1.5	(D)	.2	(D)	1.9
AIR	-	100.0	3.6	.5	13.9	-	7.9	(D)	-	(D)	-
WATER	-	100.0	-	-	-	-	-	(D)	-	(D)	-
OTHER	2	100.0	3.1	1.4	56.8	18.9	10.6	(D)	7.7	(D)	-
UNKNOWN	1	100.0	-	1.2	40.9	-	57.8	(D)	-	(D)	-
EAST SOUTH CENTRAL	271	100.0	.7	.9	65.1	4.5	5.7	(D)	1.6	(D)	.6
RAIL	144	100.0	.3	.5	73.9	6.6	6.9	(D)	1.4	(D)	.2
MOTOR CARRIER	96	100.0	1.4	1.6	54.0	2.7	5.9	(D)	1.9	(D)	1.3
PRIVATE TRUCK	28	100.0	-	.1	57.4	-	-	(D)	1.7	(D)	-
AIR	1	100.0	.1	2.9	95.3	-	-	(D)	-	(D)	1.7
WATER	-	100.0	-	-	-	-	-	(D)	-	(D)	-
OTHER	-	100.0	1.3	4.4	66.3	11.0	2.1	(D)	6.8	(D)	.1
UNKNOWN	-	100.0	-	-	-	-	-	(D)	-	(D)	-
WEST SOUTH CENTRAL	436	100.0	.9	1.2	48.3	6.0	3.1	(D)	6.1	(D)	11.5
RAIL	319	100.0	.3	.4	54.7	6.0	2.4	(D)	.8	(D)	13.6
MOTOR CARRIER	81	100.0	3.1	3.5	42.7	5.2	7.4	(D)	7.5	(D)	7.7
PRIVATE TRUCK	29	100.0	-	3.5	1.3	-	.2	(D)	59.4	(D)	-
AIR	-	100.0	1.4	4.9	11.3	81.0	-	(D)	-	(D)	-
WATER	-	100.0	100.0	-	-	-	-	(D)	-	(D)	-
OTHER	-	100.0	2.4	.1	78.5	6.2	1.3	(D)	5.6	(D)	4.1
UNKNOWN	3	100.0	-	-	-	76.2	-	(D)	-	(D)	4.9
MOUNTAIN	393	100.0	.8	.1	34.7	2.4	1.9	(D)	2.5	(D)	6.6
RAIL	322	100.0	.1	-	35.7	2.6	.8	(D)	1.6	(D)	5.3
MOTOR CARRIER	42	100.0	6.7	.7	49.6	2.4	11.1	(D)	2.0	(D)	21.1
PRIVATE TRUCK	28	100.0	-	-	.4	.1	-	(D)	13.5	(D)	-
AIR	-	100.0	21.3	-	1.3	76.6	-	(D)	-	(D)	.9
WATER	-	100.0	-	-	-	-	-	(D)	-	(D)	-
OTHER	-	100.0	-	.1	97.6	1.2	.2	(D)	-	(D)	.8
UNKNOWN	-	100.0	-	-	100.0	-	-	(D)	-	(D)	-
PACIFIC	378	100.0	.8	.9	44.0	7.2	6.7	(D)	1.9	(D)	13.3
RAIL	191	100.0	.6	.3	57.4	10.9	9.5	(D)	2.6	(D)	4.4
MOTOR CARRIER	112	100.0	1.5	2.1	47.7	5.2	6.2	(D)	1.8	(D)	25.3
PRIVATE TRUCK	68	100.0	-	.8	2.5	-	-	(D)	.2	(D)	13.8
AIR	-	100.0	25.7	2.4	17.1	-	5.6	(D)	-	(D)	43.6
WATER	2	100.0	6.5	-	.1	-	-	(D)	-	(D)	93.4
OTHER	1	100.0	-	.1	45.5	32.9	.1	(D)	4.2	(D)	17.1
UNKNOWN	-	100.0	-	-	-	.4	-	(D)	-	(D)	99.6

See footnotes at end of table 4.

TABLE 3. **TCC GROUP 363—Percent Distribution of Geographic Division of Destination and Means of Transport, by Geographic Division of Origin: 1972**—Continued

Geographic division of destination and means of transport	Number	Percent distribution by division of origin[1]									
		U.S. total	New England	Middle Atlantic	East North Central	West North Central	South Atlantic	East South Central	West South Central	Mountain	Pacific
TON-MILES OF SHIPMENTS	(millions of ton-miles)										
U.S. TOTAL..............	3 133	100.0	1.2	1.4	49.7	6.2	6.4	(D)	2.6	(D)	4.9
RAIL................	2 122	100.0	.4	.4	51.7	6.4	4.3	(D)	2.3	(D)	3.6
MOTOR CARRIER........	872	100.0	3.3	3.3	48.7	5.6	11.7	(D)	2.4	(D)	6.9
PRIVATE TRUCK........	113	100.0	.4	5.8	24.9	2.5	4.1	(D)	8.0	(D)	7.3
AIR.................	2	100.0	13.2	7.5	34.2	8.7	3.1	(D)	-	(D)	18.1
WATER...............	8	100.0	14.7	-	.1	-	.1	(D)	-	(D)	85.2
OTHER...............	8	100.0	1.9	1.0	63.2	20.6	1.2	(D)	6.3	(D)	4.0
UNKNOWN.............	5	100.0	-.	.4	18.1	54.4	13.9	(D)	-	(D)	5.6
NEW ENGLAND..............	154	100.0	.7	.5	54.3	12.0	15.8	(D)	.6	(D)	2.1
RAIL................	79	100.0	-	.1	63.5	6.2	6.2	(D)	-	(D)	-
MOTOR CARRIER........	73	100.0	1.3	.7	44.8	18.5	26.4	(D)	1.2	(D)	3.6
PRIVATE TRUCK........	1	100.0	9.4	13.7	25.8	-	-	(D)	-	(D)	51.1
AIR.................	-	100.0	1.1	1.8	97.1	-	-	(D)	-	(D)	-
WATER...............	-	100.0	-	-	-	-	-	(D)	-	(D)	-
OTHER...............	-	100.0	.9	1.5	67.7	21.5	1.4	(D)	-	(D)	.4
UNKNOWN.............	-	100.0	-	3.9	-	-	96.1	(D)	-	(D)	-
MIDDLE ATLANTIC.........	381	100.0	.8	.8	56.9	9.8	8.0	(D)	2.5	(D)	3.9
RAIL................	240	100.0	-	.1	66.9	13.6	2.0	(D)	2.5	(D)	11.7
MOTOR CARRIER........	124	100.0	2.1	1.6	40.9	3.6	20.1	(D)	2.8	(D)	2.5
PRIVATE TRUCK........	14	100.0	2.2	5.1	25.6	-	4.4	(D)		(D)	1.1
AIR.................	-	100.0	-	24.2	66.0	5.7	-	(D)	-	(D)	-
WATER...............	-	100.0	-	-	-	-	100.0	(D)	-	(D)	-
OTHER...............	1	100.0	.8	1.4	87.4	7.7	.9	(D)	.1	(D)	-
UNKNOWN.............	-	100.0	-	.8	90.6	-	-	(D)	-	(D)	8.5
EAST NORTH CENTRAL......	314	100.0	1.8	1.9	36.5	7.6	6.4	(D)	7.1	(D)	7.7
RAIL................	119	100.0	1.2	1.0	33.3	10.9	7.7	(D)	13.4	(D)	1.6
MOTOR CARRIER........	167	100.0	2.5	2.3	39.5	5.0	4.2	(D)	3.0	(D)	9.2
PRIVATE TRUCK........	25	100.0	-	4.1	31.7	9.0	15.3	(D)	4.2	(D)	24.9
AIR.................	-	100.0	20.4	44.0	30.0	-	2.7	(D)	-	(D)	-
WATER...............	-	100.0	-	-	-	-	-	(D)	-	(D)	-
OTHER...............	-	100.0	4.9	2.2	41.9	8.4	3.1	(D)	1.2	(D)	32.1
UNKNOWN.............	-	100.0	-	1.4	98.2	-	-	(D)	-	(D)	-
WEST NORTH CENTRAL......	175	100.0	1.1	2.3	49.8	5.5	7.7	(D)	1.5	(D)	5.7
RAIL................	108	100.0	.4	.8	57.6	6.4	4.6	(D)	1.4	(D)	7.5
MOTOR CARRIER........	63	100.0	2.3	3.9	36.8	3.1	13.6	(D)	1.8	(D)	2.8
PRIVATE TRUCK........	3	100.0	-	25.4	44.0	11.1	-	(D)	2.4	(D)	-
AIR.................	-	100.0	52.1	4.0	11.0	2.5	-	(D)	-	(D)	-
WATER...............	-	100.0	-	-	-	-	-	(D)	-	(D)	-
OTHER...............	-	100.0	2.3	3.6	81.2	8.4	1.4	(D)	-	(D)	-
UNKNOWN.............	-	100.0	-	-	28.0	71.4	.6	(D)	-	(D)	-
SOUTH ATLANTIC..........	578	100.0	1.0	2.2	53.8	4.0	2.7	(D)	2.7	(D)	.6
RAIL................	456	100.0	.2	.5	52.4	3.6	1.7	(D)	2.6	(D)	-
MOTOR CARRIER........	113	100.0	3.9	8.2	59.7	5.5	6.6	(D)	3.1	(B)	2.5
PRIVATE TRUCK........	4	100.0	-	21.4	53.9	1.7	.4	(D)	.3	(D)	7.9
AIR.................	-	100.0	4.4	.1	12.9	-	8.2	(D)	-	(D)	-
WATER...............	-	100.0	-	-	-	-	-	(D)	-	(D)	-
OTHER...............	1	100.0	3.8	1.0	55.4	25.7	1.8	(D)	10.4	(D)	.1
UNKNOWN.............	1	100.0	-	1.6	37.0	-	61.4	(D)	-	(D)	-
EAST SOUTH CENTRAL......	102	100.0	1.6	1.8	64.9	8.3	6.3	(D)	1.8	(D)	2.8
RAIL................	59	100.0	.6	1.2	69.2	11.8	6.9	(D)	1.7	(D)	1.1
MOTOR CARRIER........	35	100.0	3.7	3.1	54.9	4.1	6.5	(D)	1.7	(D)	6.0
PRIVATE TRUCK........	6	100.0	.1	.2	80.5	-	-	(D)	2.8	(D)	-
AIR.................	-	100.0	.3	6.2	84.9	-	-	(D)	-	(D)	8.7
WATER...............	-	100.0	-	-	-	-	-	(D)	-	(D)	-
OTHER...............	-	100.0	2.7	6.8	67.2	11.6	2.1	(D)	2.8	(D)	.2
UNKNOWN.............	-	100.0	-	-	-	-	-	(D)	-	(D)	-
WEST SOUTH CENTRAL......	365	100.0	1.6	1.9	47.8	5.7	3.8	(D)	2.1	(D)	17.2
RAIL................	281	100.0	.5	.6	51.1	5.5	2.8	(D)	.4	(D)	19.7
MOTOR CARRIER........	65	100.0	5.7	5.7	45.6	4.1	9.4	(D)	2.5	(D)	11.1
PRIVATE TRUCK........	13	100.0	-	10.9	2.4	-	.3	(D)	35.4	(D)	-
AIR.................	-	100.0	2.4	7.5	12.9	74.6	-	(D)	-	(D)	-
WATER...............	-	100.0	100.0	-	-	-	-	(D)	-	(D)	-
OTHER...............	-	100.0	4.0	.2	81.4	5.0	1.8	(D)	.1	(D)	6.0
UNKNOWN.............	3	100.0	-	-	-	84.1	-	(D)	-	(D)	7.3
MOUNTAIN................	491	100.0	1.2	.2	38.3	1.8	2.9	(D)	1.8	(D)	2.8
RAIL................	416	100.0	.1	-	36.5	1.9	1.2	(D)	1.3	(D)	2.1
MOTOR CARRIER........	61	100.0	9.3	1.0	57.8	1.6	15.1	(D)	1.3	(D)	8.2
PRIVATE TRUCK........	13	100.0	-	-	.9	.2	-	(D)	19.3	(D)	-
AIR.................	-	100.0	34.0	-	1.5	64.2	-	(D)	-	(D)	.3
WATER...............	-	100.0	-	-	-	-	-	(D)	-	(D)	-
OTHER...............	-	100.0	-	.1	98.3	.9	.3	(D)	-	(D)	.3
UNKNOWN.............	-	100.0	-	-	100.0	-	-	(D)	-	(D)	-
PACIFIC.................	570	100.0	1.4	1.5	55.3	7.4	10.5	(D)	2.0	(D)	3.4
RAIL................	361	100.0	.8	.4	57.6	8.9	11.9	(D)	2.0	(D)	.6
MOTOR CARRIER........	167	100.0	2.6	3.4	59.3	5.3	10.3	(D)	2.1	(D)	5.1
PRIVATE TRUCK........	30	100.0	-	4.3	20.7	.2	-	(D)	.7	(D)	1.9
AIR.................	-	100.0	25.0	2.1	12.7	-	5.1	(D)	-	(D)	50.6
WATER...............	7	100.0	6.1	-	.1	-	-	(D)	-	(D)	93.8
OTHER...............	2	100.0	-	.2	53.7	33.9	.2	(D)	11.4	(D)	.6
UNKNOWN.............	-	100.0	-	-	-	5.4	-	(D)	-	(D)	94.6

See footnotes at end of table 4.

TABLE 4. TCC GROUP 363—Percent Distribution of Distance Shipped and Weight of Shipment, by Means of Transport: 1972

Distance shipped and weight of shipment[2][3]	Number	Percent distribution by means of transport							
		All means of transport	Rail	Motor carrier	Private truck	Air	Water	Other	Unknown
TONS OF SHIPMENTS	(thousands of tons)								
U.S. TOTAL..........	5 006	100.0	58.1	35.5	5.8	.1	.1	.2	.2
UNDER 100 MILES........	434	100.0	24.1	64.4	11.2	-	-	.3	-
UNDER 1000 POUNDS.....	25	100.0	.1	69.4	25.6	-	-	4.4	.4
1000 TO 9999 POUNDS...	70	100.0	1.3	70.5	28.0	-	.1	.1	-
10000 TO 29999 POUNDS.	316	100.0	31.9	61.0	7.1	-	-	-	-
30000 TO 59999 POUNDS.	7	100.0	37.5	62.5	-	-	-	-	-
60000 TO 89999 POUNDS.	-	100.0	-	-	-	-	-	-	-
90000 POUNDS AND OVER.	14	100.0	-	100.0	-	-	-	-	-
100 TO 199 MILES........	404	100.0	17.8	71.5	10.3	-	-	.1	.2
UNDER 1000 POUNDS.....	22	100.0	1.9	85.1	10.4	.1	.2	2.2	.1
1000 TO 9999 POUNDS...	104	100.0	2.3	87.0	10.1	-	-	.1	.6
10000 TO 29999 POUNDS.	253	100.0	24.3	66.0	9.6	-	-	-	.1
30000 TO 59999 POUNDS.	13	100.0	55.5	14.3	30.2	-	-	-	-
60000 TO 89999 POUNDS.	1	100.0	-	68.7	31.3	-	-	-	-
90000 POUNDS AND OVER.	9	100.0	-	100.0	-	-	-	-	-
200 TO 299 MILES........	499	100.0	39.0	47.8	12.6	-	-	.2	.4
UNDER 1000 POUNDS.....	20	100.0	.1	93.8	1.9	.4	-	3.8	-
1000 TO 9999 POUNDS...	112	100.0	3.5	68.8	27.7	-	-	-	-
10000 TO 29999 POUNDS.	353	100.0	50.4	40.1	8.9	-	-	-	.6
30000 TO 59999 POUNDS.	13	100.0	100.0	-	-	-	-	-	-
60000 TO 89999 POUNDS.	-	100.0	-	-	-	-	-	-	-
90000 POUNDS AND OVER.	-	100.0	-	-	-	-	-	-	-
300 TO 499 MILES........	1 310	100.0	66.8	28.7	4.2	.1	-	.1	.1
UNDER 1000 POUNDS.....	33	100.0	.5	90.7	2.7	.9	-	4.9	.2
1000 TO 9999 POUNDS...	183	100.0	5.3	82.9	11.1	.7	-	-	.1
10000 TO 29999 POUNDS.	868	100.0	74.4	21.7	3.8	-	-	-	.1
30000 TO 59999 POUNDS.	202	100.0	97.1	2.7	.2	-	-	-	-
60000 TO 89999 POUNDS.	12	100.0	100.0	-	-	-	-	-	-
90000 POUNDS AND OVER.	9	100.0	100.0	-	-	-	-	-	-
500 TO 999 MILES........	1 552	100.0	68.9	25.8	4.8	.1	-	.3	.1
UNDER 1000 POUNDS.....	67	100.0	2.9	87.9	2.2	.8	-	5.9	.2
1000 TO 9999 POUNDS...	213	100.0	11.7	77.1	10.1	.2	-	.5	.4
10000 TO 29999 POUNDS.	1 155	100.0	81.6	13.9	4.4	-	-	-	.1
30000 TO 59999 POUNDS.	110	100.0	84.8	14.1	1.1	-	-	-	-
60000 TO 89999 POUNDS.	-	100.0	-	-	-	-	-	-	-
90000 POUNDS AND OVER.	6	100.0	97.0	3.0	-	-	-	-	-
1000 TO 1499 MILES......	445	100.0	83.6	15.2	.3	-	.1	.1	.6
UNDER 1000 POUNDS.....	16	100.0	3.6	90.5	2.5	.7	-	2.4	.3
1000 TO 9999 POUNDS...	38	100.0	14.9	83.3	1.1	-	.3	-	.4
10000 TO 29999 POUNDS.	257	100.0	94.3	4.3	.3	-	.2	-	1.0
30000 TO 59999 POUNDS.	128	100.0	92.5	7.5	-	-	-	-	-
60000 TO 89999 POUNDS.	4	100.0	100.0	-	-	-	-	-	-
90000 POUNDS AND OVER.	-	100.0	-	-	-	-	-	-	-
1500 MILES OR OVER......	358	100.0	61.7	35.0	1.9	.1	.8	.5	-
UNDER 1000 POUNDS.....	16	100.0	12.0	76.9	2.7	1.9	1.2	5.3	.1
1000 TO 9999 POUNDS...	62	100.0	20.6	71.8	4.8	-	1.5	1.3	-
10000 TO 29999 POUNDS.	217	100.0	76.4	21.7	1.0	-	.8	-	-
30000 TO 59999 POUNDS.	57	100.0	69.0	28.8	2.2	-	-	-	-
60000 TO 89999 POUNDS.	5	100.0	16.3	83.7	-	-	-	-	-
90000 POUNDS AND OVER.	-	100.0	-	-	-	-	-	-	-
TON-MILES OF SHIPMENTS	(millions of ton-miles)								
U.S. TOTAL..........	3 089	100.0	67.5	28.1	3.6	.1	.3	.3	.2
UNDER 100 MILES........	22	100.0	27.0	62.9	9.9	-	-	.1	-
UNDER 1000 POUNDS.....	1	100.0	.1	77.9	19.3	-	.1	2.4	.3
1000 TO 9999 POUNDS...	3	100.0	.2	71.6	28.1	-	.1	-	-
10000 TO 29999 POUNDS.	16	100.0	36.1	58.0	5.8	-	-	-	-
30000 TO 59999 POUNDS.	-	100.0	54.3	45.7	-	-	-	-	-
60000 TO 89999 POUNDS.	-	100.0	-	-	-	-	-	-	-
90000 POUNDS AND OVER.	-	100.0	-	100.0	-	-	-	-	-
100 TO 199 MILES........	61	100.0	17.3	72.8	9.6	-	-	.2	.2
UNDER 1000 POUNDS.....	3	100.0	1.4	85.2	10.5	.2	.2	2.4	.1
1000 TO 9999 POUNDS...	15	100.0	2.7	87.4	9.4	-	-	.1	.4
10000 TO 29999 POUNDS.	39	100.0	23.2	67.7	9.0	-	-	-	.1
30000 TO 59999 POUNDS.	2	100.0	55.9	17.0	27.1	-	-	-	-
60000 TO 89999 POUNDS.	-	100.0	-	61.4	38.6	-	-	-	-
90000 POUNDS AND OVER.	1	100.0	-	100.0	-	-	-	-	-

See footnotes at end of table 4.

TABLE 4. TCC GROUP 363—Percent Distribution of Distance Shipped and Weight of Shipment, by Means of Transport: 1972—Continued

Distance shipped and weight of shipment[2] [3]	Number	Percent distribution by means of transport							
		All means of transport	Rail	Motor carrier	Private truck	Air	Water	Other	Unknown
TON-MILES OF SHIPMENTS	(millions of ton-miles)								
200 TO 299 MILES	126	100.0	39.6	47.7	12.1	-	-	.2	.4
UNDER 1000 POUNDS	5	100.0	.1	93.8	2.0	.4	-	3.8	-
1000 TO 9999 POUNDS	27	100.0	3.7	69.6	26.7	-	-	-	-
10000 TO 29999 POUNDS	89	100.0	50.8	40.0	8.6	-	-	-	.6
30000 TO 59999 POUNDS	3	100.0	100.0	-	-	-	-	-	-
60000 TO 89999 POUNDS	-	100.0	-	-	-	-	-	-	-
90000 POUNDS AND OVER	-	100.0	-	-	-	-	-	-	-
300 TO 499 MILES	534	100.0	68.5	27.4	3.8	.1	-	.1	.1
UNDER 1000 POUNDS	13	100.0	.6	90.7	2.8	.8	-	4.9	.2
1000 TO 9999 POUNDS	71	100.0	5.4	83.6	10.4	.6	-	-	.1
10000 TO 29999 POUNDS	352	100.0	75.7	20.7	3.5	-	-	-	.1
30000 TO 59999 POUNDS	88	100.0	97.2	2.6	.1	-	-	-	-
60000 TO 89999 POUNDS	5	100.0	100.0	-	-	-	-	-	-
90000 POUNDS AND OVER	4	100.0	100.0	-	-	-	-	-	-
500 TO 999 MILES	1 096	100.0	69.4	25.4	4.6	.1	-	.3	.1
UNDER 1000 POUNDS	48	100.0	3.1	87.9	2.3	.8	-	5.7	.2
1000 TO 9999 POUNDS	151	100.0	11.9	77.3	9.6	.2	-	.6	.4
10000 TO 29999 POUNDS	812	100.0	82.6	13.2	4.2	-	-	-	.1
30000 TO 59999 POUNDS	77	100.0	83.9	14.9	1.1	-	-	-	-
60000 TO 89999 POUNDS	-	100.0	-	-	-	-	-	-	-
90000 POUNDS AND OVER	5	100.0	97.4	2.6	-	-	-	-	-
1000 TO 1499 MILES	560	100.0	84.4	14.5	.3	-	.1	.1	.5
UNDER 1000 POUNDS	19	100.0	3.9	89.9	2.6	.7	-	2.5	.3
1000 TO 9999 POUNDS	45	100.0	15.3	82.8	1.2	-	.3	-	.5
10000 TO 29999 POUNDS	316	100.0	94.4	4.4	.2	-	.2	-	.8
30000 TO 59999 POUNDS	171	100.0	93.1	6.9	-	-	-	-	-
60000 TO 89999 POUNDS	6	100.0	100.0	-	-	-	-	-	-
90000 POUNDS AND OVER	-	100.0	-	-	-	-	-	-	-
1500 MILES OR OVER	687	100.0	60.8	35.1	2.4	.1	1.1	.5	-
UNDER 1000 POUNDS	31	100.0	13.9	74.4	2.6	2.4	1.7	5.0	.1
1000 TO 9999 POUNDS	123	100.0	23.1	68.8	4.7	-	2.0	1.3	-
10000 TO 29999 POUNDS	417	100.0	75.3	21.8	1.8	-	1.2	-	-
30000 TO 59999 POUNDS	103	100.0	67.1	30.8	2.1	-	-	-	-
60000 TO 89999 POUNDS	11	100.0	12.4	87.6	-	-	-	-	-
90000 POUNDS AND OVER	-	100.0	-	-	-	-	-	-	-

Note: Detail may not add to total due to rounding. The introductory table shows the estimates of sampling variability for tons; sampling variability for ton-miles has not been estimated. See the map in the Introduction for the States comprising the geographic divisions of the United States.

Shipments excluded from the survey are those moving by pipeline (primarily petroleum products from refineries), parcel post shipments, and commodities moved by own power (motorized vehicles, aircraft, etc.) or towed (prefabricated buildings, etc.). Local shipments (commodities shipped less than 25 miles from the plant) and shipments within the same city are also excluded. Shipments to Alaska and Hawaii from the 48 conterminous States and the District of Columbia are included; however, no data were obtained for shipments originating in Alaska and Hawaii.

- Represents zero or rounds to zero.   (D) Withheld to avoid disclosing figures for individual companies.

[1]Production of this commodity is concentrated in the geographic divisions shown; figures and distributions for geographic divisions not shown are included in the total.

[2]Distances of shipments to foreign destinations are calculated only to the U.S. port of exit.

[3]Includes only shipments represented by bills of lading and invoices. Summary records which did not show individual weights of shipments are not included.

TCC 364. Electric Lighting and Wiring Equipment

Comparisons of Tons and Ton-Miles of Shipments for
Geographic Divisions of Origin and for Sampling Variability: 1972 and 1967

Geographic division of origin	Estimates				Relative sampling variability in tons (percent)	
	1972		1967		1972	1967
	Tons (thousands)	Ton-miles (millions)	Tons (thousands)	Ton-miles (millions)		
U.S. total	2,177	1,526	2,215	1,519	10.3	15.2
New England	149	122	344	382	30.1	(*)
Middle Atlantic	470	330	847	465	20.5	(*)
East North Central	612	283	416	225	10.7	(*)
West North Central	(D)	(D)	189	123	(*)	(*)
South Atlantic	(D)	(D)	133	89	(*)	(*)
East South Central	(D)	(D)	201	160	(*)	(*)
West South Central	(D)	(D)	20	17	(*)	(*)
Mountain	—	—	—	—	—	—
Pacific	211	276	65	58	33.7	(*)

— Represents or rounds to zero.   (D) Withheld to avoid disclosing figures for individual companies.   * Data not published.

TABLE 1. TCC GROUP 364—Percent Distribution of Geographic Division of Origin and Distance Shipped, by Means of Transport: 1972

Geographic division of origin[1] and distance shipped[2]	Number	Percent distribution by means of transport							
		All means of transport	Rail	Motor carrier	Private truck	Air	Water	Other	Unknown
TONS OF SHIPMENTS	(thousands of tons)								
U.S. TOTAL..........	2 177	100.0	18.7	63.7	14.4	1.1	.4	1.6	.1
NEW ENGLAND.............	149	100.0	27.2	63.8	7.6	1.0	-	.4	-
UNDER 100 MILES.......	13	100.0	.1	91.1	7.4	.5	-	.9	-
100 TO 199 MILES......	21	100.0	-	80.9	18.7	-	-	.3	-
200 TO 299 MILES......	7	100.0	-	86.7	12.5	.1	-	.7	-
300 TO 499 MILES......	24	100.0	34.7	59.5	5.0	.6	-	.2	-
500 TO 999 MILES......	44	100.0	28.9	60.5	8.3	1.9	-	.4	-
1000 TO 1499 MILES....	16	100.0	26.4	68.8	3.1	1.4	-	.3	.1
1500 MILES OR OVER....	22	100.0	66.9	31.9	-	.8	-	.5	-
MIDDLE ATLANTIC.........	470	100.0	13.7	71.0	9.4	1.0	1.5	3.4	.1
UNDER 100 MILES.......	80	100.0	.2	88.6	9.1	.2	-	1.8	.1
100 TO 199 MILES......	58	100.0	10.8	82.8	5.0	.3	-	1.1	-
200 TO 299 MILES......	55	100.0	1.2	81.3	15.6	.7	-	1.0	.2
300 TO 499 MILES......	66	100.0	8.4	53.4	35.8	.8	-	1.6	-
500 TO 999 MILES......	98	100.0	28.8	57.6	.4	.7	6.1	6.3	.1
1000 TO 1499 MILES....	45	100.0	38.6	55.4	.1	2.1	2.2	1.3	.3
1500 MILES OR OVER....	64	100.0	9.1	78.5	1.3	2.6	-	8.5	-
EAST NORTH CENTRAL......	612	100.0	23.8	62.8	10.9	.9	-	1.4	.2
UNDER 100 MILES.......	118	100.0	23.4	52.1	23.9	-	-	.6	-
100 TO 199 MILES......	59	100.0	5.7	91.9	.7	1.0	-	.8	-
200 TO 299 MILES......	96	100.0	17.5	64.8	14.2	2.4	-	1.0	.2
300 TO 499 MILES......	135	100.0	31.6	50.4	15.4	.6	-	1.7	.4
500 TO 999 MILES......	151	100.0	27.3	67.9	1.9	.8	-	2.0	.3
1000 TO 1499 MILES....	16	100.0	15.1	78.8	.5	1.5	-	4.0	-
1500 MILES OR OVER....	34	100.0	32.2	62.1	2.1	.9	-	2.2	.5
PACIFIC.................	211	100.0	-	80.7	13.8	4.0	.5	.9	.1
UNDER 100 MILES.......	28	100.0	-	44.3	50.3	.1	-	5.3	-
100 TO 199 MILES......	6	100.0	-	97.7	-	-	-	.6	1.7
200 TO 299 MILES......	4	100.0	-	99.9	-	-	-	.1	-
300 TO 499 MILES......	25	100.0	-	99.7	-	.2	-	.1	-
500 TO 999 MILES......	9	100.0	-	98.5	-	1.4	-	.1	-
1000 TO 1499 MILES....	11	100.0	-	94.0	.2	5.6	-	.1	-
1500 MILES OR OVER....	123	100.0	-	80.9	11.9	6.2	.9	.2	-
TON-MILES OF SHIPMENTS	(millions of ton-miles)								
U.S. TOTAL..........	1 526	100.0	22.2	63.5	9.5	2.2	.6	2.0	.1
NEW ENGLAND.............	122	100.0	45.3	49.1	4.1	1.1	-	.4	-
UNDER 100 MILES.......	-	100.0	.1	96.2	2.2	.6	-	.9	-
100 TO 199 MILES......	3	100.0	-	77.4	22.3	-	-	.3	-
200 TO 299 MILES......	1	100.0	-	85.6	13.6	.1	-	.7	-
300 TO 499 MILES......	10	100.0	37.2	57.7	4.5	.5	-	.2	-
500 TO 999 MILES......	33	100.0	29.7	59.6	8.6	1.7	-	.3	-
1000 TO 1499 MILES....	19	100.0	26.0	68.9	3.4	1.3	-	.3	.1
1500 MILES OR OVER....	52	100.0	69.1	29.6	-	.8	-	.5	-
MIDDLE ATLANTIC.........	330	100.0	17.4	68.8	4.0	1.8	2.1	6.0	.1
UNDER 100 MILES.......	4	100.0	.2	92.0	6.4	.3	-	1.1	.1
100 TO 199 MILES......	8	100.0	9.3	85.3	4.3	.2	-	.9	-
200 TO 299 MILES......	13	100.0	1.2	82.2	14.7	.7	-	1.0	.2
300 TO 499 MILES......	24	100.0	10.1	53.9	33.6	.8	-	1.6	-
500 TO 999 MILES......	72	100.0	27.3	56.9	.4	.7	7.9	6.7	-
1000 TO 1499 MILES....	54	100.0	39.6	54.9	.1	2.1	1.9	1.3	.2
1500 MILES OR OVER....	151	100.0	8.2	79.0	1.3	2.6	-	8.9	-
EAST NORTH CENTRAL......	283	100.0	26.9	64.4	5.7	.9	-	1.8	.3
UNDER 100 MILES.......	6	100.0	25.2	60.1	14.1	-	-	.6	-
100 TO 199 MILES......	8	100.0	7.3	90.3	.6	1.0	-	.8	-
200 TO 299 MILES......	24	100.0	17.5	64.4	14.6	2.4	-	.9	.2
300 TO 499 MILES......	52	100.0	33.0	49.0	15.5	.5	-	1.5	.4
500 TO 999 MILES......	107	100.0	25.5	69.9	1.8	.7	-	1.7	.3
1000 TO 1499 MILES....	18	100.0	15.2	78.9	.5	1.4	-	4.0	-
1500 MILES OR OVER....	64	100.0	33.9	60.4	2.3	.8	-	2.2	.4
PACIFIC.................	276	100.0	-	82.6	9.4	6.8	1.1	.2	-
UNDER 100 MILES.......	-	100.0	-	59.8	35.6	.1	-	4.5	-
100 TO 199 MILES......	-	100.0	-	97.7	-	-	-	.6	1.6
200 TO 299 MILES......	1	100.0	-	99.9	-	-	-	.1	-
300 TO 499 MILES......	9	100.0	-	99.7	-	.2	-	.1	-
500 TO 999 MILES......	7	100.0	-	98.2	-	1.6	-	.1	-
1000 TO 1499 MILES....	14	100.0	-	94.2	.2	5.4	-	.1	-
1500 MILES OR OVER....	242	100.0	-	80.7	10.5	7.4	1.2	.2	-

See footnotes at end of table 4.

TABLE 2. **TCC GROUP 364**—Percent Distribution of Geographic Division of Origin and Means of Transport, by Geographic Division of Destination: 1972

Geographic division of origin[1] and means of transport	Number	U.S. total	New England	Middle Atlantic	East North Central	West North Central	South Atlantic	East South Central	West South Central	Mountain	Pacific
TONS OF SHIPMENTS	(thousands of tons)										
U.S. TOTAL...............	2 177	100.0	4.2	17.5	25.6	7.5	19.1	5.3	7.8	2.2	10.8
RAIL....................	407	100.0	1.4	9.8	21.4	14.9	20.0	2.9	10.9	2.4	16.4
MOTOR CARRIER..........	1 387	100.0	5.8	19.9	25.1	6.5	17.9	4.3	8.4	2.6	9.5
PRIVATE TRUCK..........	312	100.0	1.2	17.4	35.7	2.9	20.0	13.2	1.8	.5	7.3
AIR....................	23	100.0	3.2	33.5	10.2	6.1	13.1	1.5	8.3	2.1	21.9
WATER..................	8	100.0	-	.4	-	-	85.7	-	-	-	14.0
OTHER..................	35	100.0	2.9	10.4	23.1	4.5	31.3	2.0	2.3	.7	22.8
UNKNOWN................	1	100.0	2.3	21.1	12.8	28.8	18.5	.7	.8	-	15.0
NEW ENGLAND............	149	100.0	7.0	24.2	29.4	4.1	15.7	2.0	5.6	1.3	10.8
RAIL....................	40	100.0	-	3.2	37.4	7.0	12.5	.1	7.5	2.8	29.6
MOTOR CARRIER..........	95	100.0	9.9	31.0	25.7	3.2	17.6	2.9	4.9	.8	4.1
PRIVATE TRUCK..........	11	100.0	8.6	44.5	30.5	.4	12.0	-	4.0	-	-
AIR....................	1	100.0	2.2	8.7	42.5	8.1	14.0	8.3	5.4	.3	10.6
WATER..................	-	100.0	-	-	-	-	-	-	-	-	-
OTHER..................	-	100.0	9.2	28.4	18.5	3.5	15.2	3.2	5.7	1.9	14.5
UNKNOWN................	-	100.0	-	-	8.7	70.5	20.8	-	-	-	-
MIDDLE ATLANTIC........	470	100.0	8.4	32.8	12.9	4.7	20.2	1.6	6.0	1.6	11.9
RAIL....................	64	100.0	.2	.5	18.5	12.8	40.6	-	17.5	4.6	5.2
MOTOR CARRIER..........	333	100.0	10.9	34.2	12.3	3.9	16.9	2.1	4.8	1.2	13.5
PRIVATE TRUCK..........	44	100.0	5.3	84.5	4.8	-	3.3	.2	-	-	1.8
AIR....................	4	100.0	4.5	6.9	8.5	7.7	20.0	2.3	13.3	7.7	29.2
WATER..................	7	100.0	-	-	-	-	99.9	-	-	-	.1
OTHER..................	16	100.0	1.9	11.4	30.4	1.6	17.1	1.8	1.7	.2	34.0
UNKNOWN................	-	100.0	-	35.6	15.0	-	48.3	-	-	-	1.2
EAST NORTH CENTRAL.....	612	100.0	2.8	18.3	40.0	9.8	11.8	5.8	5.1	1.1	5.4
RAIL....................	145	100.0	2.9	19.0	34.3	11.8	14.8	4.7	4.9	-	7.6
MOTOR CARRIER..........	384	100.0	3.1	18.9	39.3	8.6	12.4	5.2	5.8	1.6	5.1
PRIVATE TRUCK..........	66	100.0	.5	14.0	59.7	11.1	.2	12.6	.9	-	1.1
AIR....................	5	100.0	.7	18.8	15.0	13.5	32.7	1.4	11.8	.9	5.4
WATER..................	-	100.0	-	-	-	-	-	-	-	-	-
OTHER..................	8	100.0	6.6	14.5	32.4	14.4	13.2	3.8	4.6	1.8	8.7
UNKNOWN................	1	100.0	3.5	20.0	14.5	39.1	8.1	1.0	1.0	-	12.8
PACIFIC................	211	100.0	1.5	9.6	25.5	4.2	15.3	3.1	3.8	5.1	31.8
RAIL....................	-	100.0	-	-	51.3	48.7	-	-	-	-	-
MOTOR CARRIER..........	170	100.0	1.6	8.1	22.8	5.1	18.8	3.8	4.4	6.3	29.1
PRIVATE TRUCK..........	29	100.0	-	-	49.9	.1	-	.3	-	-	49.7
AIR....................	8	100.0	4.4	75.5	4.7	2.3	1.4	.5	7.2	.7	3.3
WATER..................	1	100.0	-	-	-	-	-	-	-	-	100.0
OTHER..................	1	100.0	1.0	.6	4.3	1.4	4.6	.4	.4	.5	86.9
UNKNOWN................	-	100.0	-	-	-	-	-	.1	-	-	99.9
TON-MILES OF SHIPMENTS	(millions of ton-miles)										
U.S. TOTAL...............	1 526	100.0	3.6	12.3	19.9	6.5	17.9	3.4	8.5	3.5	24.5
RAIL....................	338	100.0	1.3	7.4	8.8	9.4	15.9	1.2	12.5	4.3	39.2
MOTOR CARRIER..........	968	100.0	5.0	13.3	20.7	6.4	18.7	3.5	8.4	3.7	20.3
PRIVATE TRUCK..........	144	100.0	.5	10.9	46.4	1.9	16.4	8.8	1.8	1.7	11.7
AIR....................	33	100.0	3.3	47.2	4.6	3.4	4.4	.9	6.5	2.4	27.2
WATER..................	9	100.0	-	.3	-	-	69.3	-	-	-	30.4
OTHER..................	30	100.0	1.8	3.5	14.4	3.1	21.4	1.4	2.9	1.1	50.4
UNKNOWN................	1	100.0	3.4	19.6	6.9	22.1	18.2	.6	1.1	-	28.0
NEW ENGLAND............	122	100.0	.6	5.9	23.7	5.7	14.6	2.2	10.4	3.0	34.0
RAIL....................	55	100.0	-	1.0	18.0	5.8	6.6	.1	8.4	3.8	56.2
MOTOR CARRIER..........	59	100.0	1.2	9.2	26.3	5.9	22.2	4.2	12.1	2.6	16.3
PRIVATE TRUCK..........	5	100.0	.3	20.7	53.4	.9	12.5	-	12.2	-	-
AIR....................	1	100.0	.1	2.7	31.2	9.8	11.4	7.0	8.1	.5	29.3
WATER..................	-	100.0	-	-	-	-	-	-	-	-	-
OTHER..................	-	100.0	1.3	3.9	16.0	5.1	10.3	3.1	10.5	4.8	45.0
UNKNOWN................	-	100.0	-	-	7.4	85.6	7.0	-	-	-	-

See footnotes at end of table 4.

TABLE 2. **TCC GROUP 364—Percent Distribution of Geographic Division of Origin and Means of Transport, by Geographic Division of Destination: 1972**—Continued

Geographic division of origin[1] and means of transport	Number	Percent distribution by division of destination									
		U.S. total	New England	Middle Atlantic	East North Central	West North Central	South Atlantic	East South Central	West South Central	Mountain	Pacific
TON-MILES OF SHIPMENTS	(millions of ton-miles)										
MIDDLE ATLANTIC.........	330	100.0	2.4	7.2	10.2	6.0	15.9	1.9	11.1	4.1	41.3
RAIL..................	57	100.0	-	.1	11.6	12.6	27.6	-	25.3	9.6	13.2
MOTOR CARRIER.........	227	100.0	3.1	6.2	9.8	5.3	12.1	2.5	9.3	3.2	48.4
PRIVATE TRUCK.........	13	100.0	4.0	71.4	7.8	-	1.5	.5	.2	-	14.5
AIR...................	5	100.0	1.0	.9	3.5	5.9	8.5	1.5	12.8	10.7	55.2
WATER.................	6	100.0	-	-	-	-	99.4	-	-	-	.6
OTHER.................	19	100.0	.4	.8	17.4	1.3	8.7	1.2	1.8	.3	68.2
UNKNOWN...............	-	100.0	-	14.4	15.7	-	64.3	-	-	-	5.7
EAST NORTH CENTRAL......	283	100.0	4.0	19.5	13.7	9.8	12.5	5.5	10.2	2.9	21.9
RAIL..................	76	100.0	3.4	17.0	9.7	11.4	15.5	4.6	9.5	-	28.9
MOTOR CARRIER.........	182	100.0	4.4	20.8	13.8	8.8	12.2	4.6	11.0	4.4	20.0
PRIVATE TRUCK.........	16	100.0	1.2	19.9	32.5	12.0	.7	21.2	3.2	.1	9.1
AIR...................	2	100.0	1.1	14.4	5.9	14.4	18.2	1.1	22.0	2.2	20.8
WATER.................	-	100.0	-	-	-	-	-	-	-	-	-
OTHER.................	5	100.0	7.4	11.3	12.3	11.9	16.0	2.5	7.6	3.7	27.3
UNKNOWN...............	-	100.0	4.5	21.3	5.3	25.6	8.1	.8	1.3	-	33.1
PACIFIC.................	276	100.0	2.7	17.0	33.9	4.6	25.3	3.9	3.9	2.1	6.7
RAIL..................	-	100.0	-	-	63.5	36.5	-	-	-	-	-
MOTOR CARRIER.........	228	100.0	2.8	13.8	29.6	5.4	30.5	4.6	4.4	2.5	6.4
PRIVATE TRUCK.........	25	100.0	-	-	98.0	.1	-	.6	-	-	1.3
AIR...................	18	100.0	4.8	81.7	3.7	1.5	1.4	.4	4.0	.3	2.1
WATER.................	2	100.0	-	-	-	-	-	-	-	-	100.0
OTHER.................	-	100.0	8.9	4.8	28.2	7.0	34.6	2.4	1.7	.8	11.6
UNKNOWN...............	-	100.0	-	-	-	-	-	1.2	-	-	98.8

See footnotes at end of table 4.

TABLE 3. TCC GROUP 364—Percent Distribution of Geographic Division of Destination and Means of Transport, by Geographic Division of Origin: 1972

Geographic division of destination and means of transport	Number	Percent distribution by division of origin[1]									
		U.S. total	New England	Middle Atlantic	East North Central	West North Central	South Atlantic	East South Central	West South Central	Mountain	Pacific
TONS OF SHIPMENTS	(thousands of tons)										
U.S. TOTAL...............	2 177	100.0	6.9	21.6	28.2	(D)	(D)	(D)	(D)	(D)	9.7
RAIL.................	407	100.0	10.0	15.8	35.7	(D)	(D)	(D)	(D)	(D)	-
MOTOR CARRIER........	1 387	100.0	6.9	24.0	27.7	(D)	(D)	(D)	(D)	(D)	12.3
PRIVATE TRUCK........	312	100.0	3.6	14.1	21.4	(D)	(D)	(D)	(D)	(D)	9.3
AIR..................	23	100.0	6.2	19.0	22.8	(D)	(D)	(D)	(D)	(D)	35.6
WATER................	8	100.0	-	85.8	-	(D)	(D)	(D)	(D)	(D)	13.9
OTHER................	35	100.0	1.7	45.6	25.0	(D)	(D)	(D)	(D)	(D)	5.2
UNKNOWN..............	1	100.0	.7	20.3	66.5	(D)	(D)	(D)	(D)	(D)	6.3
NEW ENGLAND.............	91	100.0	11.5	43.2	18.8	(D)	(D)	(D)	(D)	(D)	3.5
RAIL.................	5	100.0	.2	2.7	74.1	(D)	(D)	(D)	(D)	(D)	-
MOTOR CARRIER........	79	100.0	11.8	45.5	15.0	(D)	(D)	(D)	(D)	(D)	-
PRIVATE TRUCK........	3	100.0	27.0	64.5	8.5	(D)	(D)	(D)	(D)	(D)	3.5
AIR..................	-	100.0	4.3	26.4	5.1	(D)	(D)	(D)	(D)	(D)	48.6
WATER................	-	100.0	-	-	-	(D)	(D)	(D)	(D)	(D)	-
OTHER................	1	100.0	5.3	29.8	56.2	(D)	(D)	(D)	(D)	(D)	1.7
UNKNOWN..............	-	100.0	-	-	100.0	(D)	(D)	(D)	(D)	(D)	-
MIDDLE ATLANTIC.........	382	100.0	9.5	40.3	29.4	(D)	(D)	(D)	(D)	(D)	5.3
RAIL.................	39	100.0	3.2	.8	69.7	(D)	(D)	(D)	(D)	(D)	-
MOTOR CARRIER........	275	100.0	10.7	41.4	26.4	(D)	(D)	(D)	(D)	(D)	5.0
PRIVATE TRUCK........	54	100.0	9.2	68.2	17.2	(D)	(D)	(D)	(D)	(D)	-
AIR..................	7	100.0	1.6	3.9	12.8	(D)	(D)	(D)	(D)	(D)	80.3
WATER................	-	100.0	-	-	-	(D)	(D)	(D)	(D)	(D)	-
OTHER................	3	100.0	4.6	50.0	35.1	(D)	(D)	(D)	(D)	(D)	.3
UNKNOWN..............	-	100.0	-	34.3	63.1	(D)	(D)	(D)	(D)	(D)	-
EAST NORTH CENTRAL......	557	100.0	7.9	10.8	43.9	(D)	(D)	(D)	(D)	(D)	9.7
RAIL.................	87	100.0	17.5	13.7	57.3	(D)	(D)	(D)	(D)	(D)	-
MOTOR CARRIER........	348	100.0	7.0	11.8	43.4	(D)	(D)	(D)	(D)	(D)	11.2
PRIVATE TRUCK........	111	100.0	3.1	1.9	35.8	(D)	(D)	(D)	(D)	(D)	13.0
AIR..................	2	100.0	25.8	15.8	33.5	(D)	(D)	(D)	(D)	(D)	16.4
WATER................	-	100.0	-	-	-	(D)	(D)	(D)	(D)	(D)	-
OTHER................	8	100.0	1.4	60.0	35.1	(D)	(D)	(D)	(D)	(D)	1.0
UNKNOWN..............	-	100.0	.5	23.8	75.7	(D)	(D)	(D)	(D)	(D)	-
WEST NORTH CENTRAL......	164	100.0	3.7	13.4	36.6	(D)	(D)	(D)	(D)	(D)	5.5
RAIL.................	60	100.0	4.7	13.6	28.3	(D)	(D)	(D)	(D)	(D)	-
MOTOR CARRIER........	90	100.0	3.4	14.5	36.5	(D)	(D)	(D)	(D)	(D)	9.6
PRIVATE TRUCK........	9	100.0	.5	.1	80.6	(D)	(D)	(D)	(D)	(D)	.3
AIR..................	1	100.0	8.2	24.1	50.4	(D)	(D)	(D)	(D)	(D)	13.3
WATER................	-	100.0	-	-	-	(D)	(D)	(D)	(D)	(D)	-
OTHER................	1	100.0	1.3	15.7	80.0	(D)	(D)	(D)	(D)	(D)	1.6
UNKNOWN..............	-	100.0	1.6	-	90.1	(D)	(D)	(D)	(D)	(D)	-
SOUTH ATLANTIC..........	414	100.0	5.7	22.9	17.5	(D)	(D)	(D)	(D)	(D)	7.8
RAIL.................	81	100.0	6.2	32.1	26.4	(D)	(D)	(D)	(D)	(D)	-
MOTOR CARRIER........	249	100.0	6.7	22.6	19.2	(D)	(D)	(D)	(D)	(D)	12.9
PRIVATE TRUCK........	62	100.0	2.2	2.3	.2	(D)	(D)	(D)	(D)	(D)	-
AIR..................	3	100.0	6.6	29.1	56.7	(D)	(D)	(D)	(D)	(D)	3.8
WATER................	7	100.0	-	100.0	-	(D)	(D)	(D)	(D)	(D)	-
OTHER................	11	100.0	.8	24.9	10.5	(D)	(D)	(D)	(D)	(D)	.8
UNKNOWN..............	-	100.0	.7	53.0	29.1	(D)	(D)	(D)	(D)	(D)	-
EAST SOUTH CENTRAL......	114	100.0	2.6	6.7	31.1	(D)	(D)	(D)	(D)	(D)	5.8
RAIL.................	11	100.0	.3	-	58.2	(D)	(D)	(D)	(D)	(D)	-
MOTOR CARRIER........	60	100.0	4.6	11.9	33.0	(D)	(D)	(D)	(D)	(D)	10.8
PRIVATE TRUCK........	41	100.0	-	.2	20.4	(D)	(D)	(D)	(D)	(D)	.2
AIR..................	-	100.0	33.3	28.7	20.3	(D)	(D)	(D)	(D)	(D)	11.7
WATER................	-	100.0	-	-	-	(D)	(D)	(D)	(D)	(D)	-
OTHER................	-	100.0	2.7	41.9	47.5	(D)	(D)	(D)	(D)	(D)	1.0
UNKNOWN..............	-	100.0	-	-	98.9	(D)	(D)	(D)	(D)	(D)	1.1
WEST SOUTH CENTRAL......	169	100.0	4.9	16.7	18.3	(D)	(D)	(D)	(D)	(D)	4.8
RAIL.................	44	100.0	6.9	25.4	16.2	(D)	(D)	(D)	(D)	(D)	-
MOTOR CARRIER........	116	100.0	4.0	13.8	19.0	(D)	(D)	(D)	(D)	(D)	6.4
PRIVATE TRUCK........	5	100.0	8.1	.4	10.6	(D)	(D)	(D)	(D)	(D)	-
AIR..................	1	100.0	4.0	30.3	32.2	(D)	(D)	(D)	(D)	(D)	30.9
WATER................	-	100.0	-	-	-	(D)	(D)	(D)	(D)	(D)	-
OTHER................	-	100.0	4.2	33.1	50.5	(D)	(D)	(D)	(D)	(D)	.9
UNKNOWN..............	-	100.0	-	-	83.4	(D)	(D)	(D)	(D)	(D)	-
MOUNTAIN................	47	100.0	4.0	15.6	13.5	(D)	(D)	(D)	(D)	(D)	22.5
RAIL.................	9	100.0	11.5	30.4	-	(D)	(D)	(D)	(D)	(D)	29.9
MOTOR CARRIER........	35	100.0	2.1	11.5	17.4	(D)	(D)	(D)	(D)	(D)	-
PRIVATE TRUCK........	1	100.0	-	-	.5	(D)	(D)	(D)	(D)	(D)	12.1
AIR..................	-	100.0	.8	68.2	9.1	(D)	(D)	(D)	(D)	(D)	-
WATER................	-	100.0	-	-	-	(D)	(D)	(D)	(D)	(D)	3.7
OTHER................	-	100.0	4.5	12.8	64.5	(D)	(D)	(D)	(D)	(D)	-
UNKNOWN..............	-	100.0	-	-	-	(D)	(D)	(D)	(D)	(D)	-
PACIFIC.................	235	100.0	6.9	23.8	13.9	(D)	(D)	(D)	(D)	(D)	28.5
RAIL.................	66	100.0	18.1	5.0	16.6	(D)	(D)	(D)	(D)	(D)	-
MOTOR CARRIER........	131	100.0	3.0	34.3	15.0	(D)	(D)	(D)	(D)	(D)	37.6
PRIVATE TRUCK........	22	100.0	-	3.6	3.2	(D)	(D)	(D)	(D)	(D)	63.8
AIR..................	5	100.0	3.0	25.4	5.6	(D)	(D)	(D)	(D)	(D)	5.4
WATER................	1	100.0	-	.8	-	(D)	(D)	(D)	(D)	(D)	99.2
OTHER................	8	100.0	1.1	67.9	9.5	(D)	(D)	(D)	(D)	(D)	19.9
UNKNOWN..............	-	100.0	-	1.6	56.4	(D)	(D)	(D)	(D)	(D)	42.0

See footnotes at end of table 4.

TABLE 3. **TCC GROUP 364**—Percent Distribution of Geographic Division of Destination and Means of Transport, by Geographic Division of Origin: 1972—Continued

Geographic division of destination and means of transport	Number	Percent distribution by division of origin[1]									
		U.S. total	New England	Middle Atlantic	East North Central	West North Central	South Atlantic	East South Central	West South Central	Mountain	Pacific
TON-MILES OF SHIPMENTS	(millions of ton-miles)										
U.S. TOTAL	1 526	100.0	8.0	21.6	18.5	(D)	(D)	(D)	(D)	(D)	18.1
RAIL	338	100.0	16.4	17.0	22.5	(D)	(D)	(D)	(D)	(D)	-
MOTOR CARRIER	968	100.0	6.2	23.5	18.8	(D)	(D)	(D)	(D)	(D)	23.6
PRIVATE TRUCK	144	100.0	3.5	9.1	11.2	(D)	(D)	(D)	(D)	(D)	17.9
AIR	33	100.0	3.9	17.5	7.6	(D)	(D)	(D)	(D)	(D)	55.9
WATER	9	100.0	-	69.7	-	(D)	(D)	(D)	(D)	(D)	30.0
OTHER	30	100.0	1.6	64.9	17.0	(D)	(D)	(D)	(D)	(D)	1.7
UNKNOWN	1	100.0	1.3	17.2	76.4	(D)	(D)	(D)	(D)	(D)	1.8
NEW ENGLAND	55	100.0	1.3	14.2	20.5	(D)	(D)	(D)	(D)	(D)	13.4
RAIL	4	100.0	-	.6	58.1	(D)	(D)	(D)	(D)	(D)	-
MOTOR CARRIER	48	100.0	1.5	14.8	16.7	(D)	(D)	(D)	(D)	(D)	13.3
PRIVATE TRUCK	-	100.0	2.1	70.6	27.1	(D)	(D)	(D)	(D)	(D)	-
AIR	1	100.0	.1	5.5	2.6	(D)	(D)	(D)	(D)	(D)	81.7
WATER	-	100.0	-	-	-	(D)	(D)	(D)	(D)	(D)	-
OTHER	-	100.0	1.2	14.4	70.0	(D)	(D)	(D)	(D)	(D)	8.7
UNKNOWN	-	100.0	-	-	100.0	(D)	(D)	(D)	(D)	(D)	-
MIDDLE ATLANTIC	187	100.0	3.8	12.7	29.5	(D)	(D)	(D)	(D)	(D)	25.1
RAIL	25	100.0	2.3	.1	51.4	(D)	(D)	(D)	(D)	(D)	-
MOTOR CARRIER	128	100.0	4.3	11.0	29.5	(D)	(D)	(D)	(D)	(D)	24.4
PRIVATE TRUCK	15	100.0	6.6	59.8	20.4	(D)	(D)	(D)	(D)	(D)	-
AIR	15	100.0	.2	.3	2.3	(D)	(D)	(D)	(D)	(D)	96.7
WATER	-	100.0	-	-	-	(D)	(D)	(D)	(D)	(D)	-
OTHER	1	100.0	1.8	13.9	54.5	(D)	(D)	(D)	(D)	(D)	2.4
UNKNOWN	-	100.0	-	12.6	83.2	(D)	(D)	(D)	(D)	(D)	-
EAST NORTH CENTRAL	303	100.0	9.5	11.1	12.8	(D)	(D)	(D)	(D)	(D)	30.9
RAIL	29	100.0	33.3	22.2	24.8	(D)	(D)	(D)	(D)	(D)	-
MOTOR CARRIER	200	100.0	7.9	11.1	12.6	(D)	(D)	(D)	(D)	(D)	33.7
PRIVATE TRUCK	67	100.0	4.0	1.5	7.9	(D)	(D)	(D)	(D)	(D)	37.9
AIR	1	100.0	26.3	13.5	9.6	(D)	(D)	(D)	(D)	(D)	44.8
WATER	-	100.0	-	-	-	(D)	(D)	(D)	(D)	(D)	-
OTHER	4	100.0	1.8	78.3	14.5	(D)	(D)	(D)	(D)	(D)	3.4
UNKNOWN	-	100.0	1.4	39.2	59.4	(D)	(D)	(D)	(D)	(D)	-
WEST NORTH CENTRAL	98	100.0	7.0	20.2	28.1	(D)	(D)	(D)	(D)	(D)	12.8
RAIL	31	100.0	10.1	22.8	27.5	(D)	(D)	(D)	(D)	(D)	-
MOTOR CARRIER	62	100.0	5.7	19.5	25.7	(D)	(D)	(D)	(D)	(D)	19.8
PRIVATE TRUCK	2	100.0	1.7	.2	72.8	(D)	(D)	(D)	(D)	(D)	1.3
AIR	1	100.0	11.1	29.9	31.8	(D)	(D)	(D)	(D)	(D)	24.5
WATER	-	100.0	-	-	-	(D)	(D)	(D)	(D)	(D)	-
OTHER	-	100.0	2.6	26.6	65.2	(D)	(D)	(D)	(D)	(D)	3.9
UNKNOWN	-	100.0	5.2	-	88.4	(D)	(D)	(D)	(D)	(D)	-
SOUTH ATLANTIC	273	100.0	6.5	19.3	13.0	(D)	(D)	(D)	(D)	(D)	25.7
RAIL	53	100.0	6.8	29.5	21.9	(D)	(D)	(D)	(D)	(D)	-
MOTOR CARRIER	180	100.0	7.4	15.2	12.3	(D)	(D)	(D)	(D)	(D)	38.5
PRIVATE TRUCK	23	100.0	2.7	.8	.5	(D)	(D)	(D)	(D)	(D)	.1
AIR	1	100.0	10.1	34.2	31.6	(D)	(D)	(D)	(D)	(D)	18.5
WATER	6	100.0	-	100.0	-	(D)	(D)	(D)	(D)	(D)	-
OTHER	6	100.0	.8	26.3	12.7	(D)	(D)	(D)	(D)	(D)	2.8
UNKNOWN	-	100.0	.5	60.7	34.0	(D)	(D)	(D)	(D)	(D)	-
EAST SOUTH CENTRAL	51	100.0	5.1	11.9	30.0	(D)	(D)	(D)	(D)	(D)	21.0
RAIL	4	100.0	.9	-	84.5	(D)	(D)	(D)	(D)	(D)	-
MOTOR CARRIER	34	100.0	7.4	16.9	24.5	(D)	(D)	(D)	(D)	(D)	31.1
PRIVATE TRUCK	12	100.0	-	.5	27.1	(D)	(D)	(D)	(D)	(D)	1.1
AIR	-	100.0	30.4	30.0	9.4	(D)	(D)	(D)	(D)	(D)	25.1
WATER	-	100.0	-	-	-	(D)	(D)	(D)	(D)	(D)	-
OTHER	-	100.0	3.6	56.8	30.5	(D)	(D)	(D)	(D)	(D)	3.1
UNKNOWN	-	100.0	-	-	96.5	(D)	(D)	(D)	(D)	(D)	3.5
WEST SOUTH CENTRAL	129	100.0	9.8	28.4	22.3	(D)	(D)	(D)	(D)	(D)	8.4
RAIL	42	100.0	11.0	34.4	17.1	(D)	(D)	(D)	(D)	(D)	-
MOTOR CARRIER	81	100.0	9.0	26.0	24.7	(D)	(D)	(D)	(D)	(D)	12.5
PRIVATE TRUCK	2	100.0	23.8	1.2	20.2	(D)	(D)	(D)	(D)	(D)	-
AIR	2	100.0	4.8	34.1	25.5	(D)	(D)	(D)	(D)	(D)	34.3
WATER	-	100.0	-	-	-	(D)	(D)	(D)	(D)	(D)	-
OTHER	-	100.0	5.8	40.4	44.9	(D)	(D)	(D)	(D)	(D)	1.0
UNKNOWN	-	100.0	-	-	89.5	(D)	(D)	(D)	(D)	(D)	-
MOUNTAIN	54	100.0	6.8	24.8	15.3	(D)	(D)	(D)	(D)	(D)	10.5
RAIL	14	100.0	14.6	38.0	-	(D)	(D)	(D)	(D)	(D)	-
MOTOR CARRIER	36	100.0	4.3	20.1	22.3	(D)	(D)	(D)	(D)	(D)	15.7
PRIVATE TRUCK	2	100.0	-	-	.6	(D)	(D)	(D)	(D)	(D)	-
AIR	-	100.0	.8	76.5	6.7	(D)	(D)	(D)	(D)	(D)	6.0
WATER	-	100.0	-	-	-	(D)	(D)	(D)	(D)	(D)	-
OTHER	-	100.0	6.9	19.4	56.7	(D)	(D)	(D)	(D)	(D)	1.3
UNKNOWN	-	100.0	-	-	-	(D)	(D)	(D)	(D)	(D)	-
PACIFIC	374	100.0	11.1	36.4	16.6	(D)	(D)	(D)	(D)	(D)	4.9
RAIL	132	100.0	23.5	5.7	16.6	(D)	(D)	(D)	(D)	(D)	-
MOTOR CARRIER	197	100.0	5.0	55.8	18.5	(D)	(D)	(D)	(D)	(D)	7.5
PRIVATE TRUCK	16	100.0	-	11.3	8.7	(D)	(D)	(D)	(D)	(D)	2.0
AIR	9	100.0	4.2	35.5	5.8	(D)	(D)	(D)	(D)	(D)	4.4
WATER	2	100.0	-	1.4	-	(D)	(D)	(D)	(D)	(D)	98.6
OTHER	15	100.0	1.4	87.8	9.2	(D)	(D)	(D)	(D)	(D)	.4
UNKNOWN	-	100.0	-	3.5	90.1	(D)	(D)	(D)	(D)	(D)	6.4

See footnotes at end of table 4.

TABLE 4. TCC GROUP 364—Percent Distribution of Distance Shipped and Weight of Shipment, by Means of Transport: 1972

Distance shipped and weight of shipment[2][3]	Number	Percent distribution by means of transport							
		All means of transport	Rail	Motor carrier	Private truck	Air	Water	Other	Unknown
TONS OF SHIPMENTS	(thousands of tons)								
U.S. TOTAL..........	2 028	100.0	17.9	64.2	15.0	1.1	.4	1.3	.1
UNDER 100 MILES........	228	100.0	12.1	67.4	19.1	.1	-	1.2	-
UNDER 1000 POUNDS.....	44	100.0	-	86.0	7.2	.3	-	6.4	.2
1000 TO 9999 POUNDS...	75	100.0	-	57.6	42.4	-	-	-	-
10000 TO 29999 POUNDS.	46	100.0	11.6	84.1	4.3	-	-	-	-
30000 TO 59999 POUNDS.	43	100.0	14.7	71.2	14.1	-	-	-	-
60000 TO 89999 POUNDS.	15	100.0	88.7	11.3	-	-	-	-	-
90000 POUNDS AND OVER.	2	100.0	100.0	-	-	-	-	-	-
100 TO 199 MILES........	187	100.0	4.7	89.6	4.6	.4	-	.6	.1
UNDER 1000 POUNDS.....	39	100.0	-	94.2	2.4	1.0	-	2.0	.4
1000 TO 9999 POUNDS...	59	100.0	-	93.5	5.3	.6	-	.7	-
10000 TO 29999 POUNDS.	57	100.0	15.2	76.9	7.9	-	-	-	-
30000 TO 59999 POUNDS.	17	100.0	-	100.0	-	-	-	-	-
60000 TO 89999 POUNDS.	-	100.0	-	-	-	-	-	-	-
90000 POUNDS AND OVER.	12	100.0	-	100.0	-	-	-	-	-
200 TO 299 MILES........	240	100.0	8.3	62.8	27.0	1.1	-	.6	.1
UNDER 1000 POUNDS.....	35	100.0	-	92.2	1.9	1.3	-	3.8	.8
1000 TO 9999 POUNDS...	57	100.0	.2	79.5	19.1	1.2	-	-	-
10000 TO 29999 POUNDS.	95	100.0	16.9	32.4	49.0	1.7	-	-	-
30000 TO 59999 POUNDS.	37	100.0	-	82.4	17.6	-	-	-	-
60000 TO 89999 POUNDS.	1	100.0	100.0	-	-	-	-	-	-
90000 POUNDS AND OVER.	13	100.0	14.1	85.9	-	-	-	-	-
300 TO 499 MILES........	373	100.0	17.6	52.5	28.0	.4	-	1.4	.1
UNDER 1000 POUNDS.....	51	100.0	.2	89.3	2.5	2.4	-	5.5	.1
1000 TO 9999 POUNDS...	87	100.0	.7	84.5	11.9	.4	-	2.6	-
10000 TO 29999 POUNDS.	148	100.0	36.7	33.4	29.6	-	-	-	.3
30000 TO 59999 POUNDS.	75	100.0	7.6	27.1	65.3	-	-	-	-
60000 TO 89999 POUNDS.	7	100.0	60.5	39.5	-	-	-	-	-
90000 POUNDS AND OVER.	2	100.0	-	100.0	-	-	-	-	-
500 TO 999 MILES........	517	100.0	25.7	59.8	11.0	.5	1.2	1.7	.1
UNDER 1000 POUNDS.....	80	100.0	.9	88.9	2.0	2.9	-	4.6	.6
1000 TO 9999 POUNDS...	140	100.0	.7	76.4	21.9	.2	-	.8	-
10000 TO 29999 POUNDS.	169	100.0	55.0	30.8	14.2	-	-	-	-
30000 TO 59999 POUNDS.	61	100.0	31.3	51.5	.8	-	9.8	6.6	-
60000 TO 89999 POUNDS.	26	100.0	62.2	37.8	-	-	-	-	-
90000 POUNDS AND OVER.	37	100.0	5.3	94.7	-	-	-	-	-
1000 TO 1499 MILES......	190	100.0	27.0	68.9	.3	2.6	.5	.6	.1
UNDER 1000 POUNDS.....	31	100.0	1.7	82.9	.6	11.5	-	3.1	.1
1000 TO 9999 POUNDS...	39	100.0	10.0	82.4	1.1	3.2	2.5	.5	.3
10000 TO 29999 POUNDS.	56	100.0	70.8	29.2	-	-	-	-	-
30000 TO 59999 POUNDS.	49	100.0	10.9	89.1	-	-	-.	-	-
60000 TO 89999 POUNDS.	-	100.0	-	-	-	-	-	-	-
90000 POUNDS AND OVER.	12	100.0	10.0	90.0	-	-	-	-	-
1500 MILES OR OVER......	290	100.0	19.6	66.3	8.4	3.3	.4	2.0	.1
UNDER 1000 POUNDS.....	45	100.0	3.9	74.4	2.5	13.8	1.5	3.5	.4
1000 TO 9999 POUNDS...	60	100.0	3.4	75.1	14.5	5.6	.7	.8	-
10000 TO 29999 POUNDS.	64	100.0	41.3	54.4	-	-	-	4.3	-
30000 TO 59999 POUNDS.	107	100.0	18.0	67.4	13.6	-	-	1.0	-
60000 TO 89999 POUNDS.	8	100.0	85.7	14.3	-	-	-	-	-
90000 POUNDS AND OVER.	5	100.0	-	100.0	-	-	-	-	-
TON-MILES OF SHIPMENTS	(millions of ton-miles)								
U.S. TOTAL..........	1 438	100.0	22.0	63.3	10.0	2.2	.7	1.7	.1
UNDER 100 MILES........	12	100.0	13.1	75.7	10.2	-	-	.9	-
UNDER 1000 POUNDS.....	2	100.0	-	91.3	2.9	.3	-	5.3	.2
1000 TO 9999 POUNDS...	3	100.0	-	76.8	23.2	-	-	-	-
10000 TO 29999 POUNDS.	2	100.0	13.7	85.0	1.3	-	-	-	-
30000 TO 59999 POUNDS.	2	100.0	14.2	73.8	11.9	-	-	-	-
60000 TO 89999 POUNDS.	-	100.0	84.7	15.3	-	-	-	-	-
90000 POUNDS AND OVER.	-	100.0	100.0	-	-	-	-	-	-
100 TO 199 MILES........	28	100.0	4.5	89.6	4.9	.4	-	.5	.1
UNDER 1000 POUNDS.....	5	100.0	-	94.2	2.5	1.0	-	1.9	.4
1000 TO 9999 POUNDS...	8	100.0	-	94.3	4.6	.6	-	.5	-
10000 TO 29999 POUNDS.	9	100.0	14.2	76.5	9.3	-	-	-	-
30000 TO 59999 POUNDS.	2	100.0	-	100.0	-	-	-	-	-
60000 TO 89999 POUNDS.	-	100.0	-	-	-	-	-	-	-
90000 POUNDS AND OVER.	2	100.0	-	100.0	-	-	-	-	-

See footnotes at end of table 4.

TABLE 4. **TCC GROUP 364—Percent Distribution of Distance Shipped and Weight of Shipment, by Means of Transport: 1972**—Continued

Distance shipped and weight of shipment[2][3]	Number	Percent distribution by means of transport							
		All means of transport	Rail	Motor carrier	Private truck	Air	Water	Other	Unknown
TON-MILES OF SHIPMENTS	(millions of ton-miles)								
200 TO 299 MILES........	59	100.0	8.5	62.7	26.9	1.2	-	.6	.1
UNDER 1000 POUNDS.....	8	100.0	-	92.3	1.8	1.3	-	3.7	.8
1000 TO 9999 POUNDS...	14	100.0	.2	79.5	19.0	1.3	-	-	-
10000 TO 29999 POUNDS.	23	100.0	17.3	32.5	48.6	1.6	-	-	-
30000 TO 59999 POUNDS.	9	100.0	-	81.7	18.3	-	-	-	-
60000 TO 89999 POUNDS.	-	100.0	100.0	-	-	-	-	-	-
90000 POUNDS AND OVER.	3	100.0	15.7	84.3	-	-	-	-	-
300 TO 499 MILES........	147	100.0	18.7	51.0	28.4	.4	-	1.3	.1
UNDER 1000 POUNDS.....	19	100.0	.2	89.7	2.5	2.4	-	5.2	-
1000 TO 9999 POUNDS...	33	100.0	.6	83.3	12.8	.4	-	2.8	-
10000 TO 29999 POUNDS.	59	100.0	38.1	31.9	29.7	-	-	-	.3
30000 TO 59999 POUNDS.	29	100.0	8.3	25.9	65.8	-	-	-	-
60000 TO 89999 POUNDS.	3	100.0	58.1	41.9	-	-	-	-	-
90000 POUNDS AND OVER.	1	100.0	-	100.0	-	-	-	-	-
500 TO 999 MILES........	366	100.0	26.1	59.6	10.4	.5	1.6	1.8	.1
UNDER 1000 POUNDS.....	57	100.0	1.0	88.9	2.1	3.1	-	4.3	.6
1000 TO 9999 POUNDS...	101	100.0	.7	78.8	19.4	.2	-	1.0	-
10000 TO 29999 POUNDS.	122	100.0	55.7	30.5	13.7	-	-	-	-
30000 TO 59999 POUNDS.	44	100.0	32.1	47.6	.8	-	12.8	6.7	-
60000 TO 89999 POUNDS.	18	100.0	56.0	44.0	-	-	-	-	-
90000 POUNDS AND OVER.	21	100.0	5.1	94.9	-	-	-	-	-
1000 TO 1499 MILES......	227	100.0	27.7	68.2	.4	2.7	.5	.6	.1
UNDER 1000 POUNDS.....	37	100.0	1.8	82.8	.6	11.7	-	2.9	.1
1000 TO 9999 POUNDS...	48	100.0	10.7	81.9	1.3	3.3	2.1	.4	.2
10000 TO 29999 POUNDS.	67	100.0	72.3	27.7	-	-	-	-	-
30000 TO 59999 POUNDS.	55	100.0	12.1	87.9	-	-	-	-	-
60000 TO 89999 POUNDS.	-	100.0	-	-	-	-	-	-	-
90000 POUNDS AND OVER.	17	100.0	7.3	92.7	-	-	-	-	-
1500 MILES OR OVER......	595	100.0	20.4	65.4	7.5	3.8	.5	2.4	-
UNDER 1000 POUNDS.....	94	100.0	4.0	71.8	2.7	15.7	1.8	3.8	.3
1000 TO 9999 POUNDS...	122	100.0	3.4	74.7	13.6	6.3	1.0	.9	-
10000 TO 29999 POUNDS.	129	100.0	43.0	51.7	-	-	-	5.3	-
30000 TO 59999 POUNDS.	224	100.0	19.3	68.3	11.3	-	-	1.1	-
60000 TO 89999 POUNDS.	16	100.0	88.6	11.4	-	-	-	-	-
90000 POUNDS AND OVER.	8	100.0	-	100.0	-	-	-	-	-

Note: Detail may not add to total due to rounding. The introductory table shows the estimates of sampling variability for tons; sampling variability for ton-miles has not been estimated. See the map in the Introduction for the States comprising the geographic divisions of the United States.

Shipments excluded from the survey are those moving by pipeline (primarily petroleum products from refineries), parcel post shipments, and commodities moved by own power (motorized vehicles, aircraft, etc.) or towed (prefabricated buildings, etc.). Local shipments (commodities shipped less than 25 miles from the plant) and shipments within the same city are also excluded. Shipments to Alaska and Hawaii from the 48 conterminous States and the District of Columbia are included; however, no data were obtained for shipments originating in Alaska and Hawaii.

- Represents zero or rounds to zero.   (D) Withheld to avoid disclosing figures for individual companies.

[1]Production of this commodity is concentrated in the geographic divisions shown; figures and distributions for geographic divisions not shown are included in the total.

[2]Distances of shipments to foreign destinations are calculated only to the U.S. port of exit.

[3]Includes only shipments represented by bills of lading and invoices. Summary records which did not show individual weights of shipments are not included.

TCC 365. Radio and Television Receiving Sets

Comparisons of Tons and Ton-Miles of Shipments for
Geographic Divisions of Origin and for Sampling Variability: 1972 and 1967

Geographic division of origin	Estimates				Relative sampling variability in tons (percent)	
	1972		1967		1972	1967
	Tons (thousands)	Ton-miles (millions)	Tons (thousands)	Ton-miles (millions)		
U.S. total	774	541	1,110	693	7.1	8.4
New England	10	8	22	16	41.0	(*)
Middle Atlantic	160	90	409	242	15.9	(*)
East North Central	300	182	504	290	5.6	(*)
West North Central	1	—	14	9	46.9	(*)
South Atlantic	(D)	(D)	7	4	(*)	(*)
East South Central	105	72	89	63	25.9	(*)
West South Central	(D)	(D)	25	20	(*)	(*)
Mountain	—	—	—	—	—	—
Pacific	100	127	40	49	37.6	(*)

— Represents or rounds to zero.   (D) Withheld to avoid disclosing figures for individual companies.   * Data not published.

TABLE 1. TCC GROUP 365—Percent Distribution of Geographic Division of Origin and Distance Shipped, by Means of Transport: 1972

Geographic division of origin[1] and distance shipped[2]	Number	Percent distribution by means of transport							
		All means of transport	Rail	Motor carrier	Private truck	Air	Water	Other	Unknown
TONS OF SHIPMENTS	(thousands of tons)								
U.S. TOTAL..........	774	100.0	18.7	60.2	13.0	2.4	-	5.4	.2
NEW ENGLAND..............	10	100.0	6.4	91.5	1.0	1.0	-	-	-
UNDER 100 MILES.......	-	100.0	-	85.5	14.5	-	-	-	-
100 TO 199 MILES......	2	100.0	-	99.8	.1	-	-	-	-
200 TO 299 MILES......	-	100.0	-	99.8	-	.2	-	-	-
300 TO 499 MILES......	1	100.0	-	100.0	-	-	-	-	-
500 TO 999 MILES......	1	100.0	2.3	92.4	.6	4.5	-	-	.2
1000 TO 1499 MILES....	-	100.0	4.1	94.4	-	1.5	-	-	-
1500 MILES OR OVER....	2	100.0	27.8	71.6	-	.6	-	-	-
MIDDLE ATLANTIC.........	160	100.0	7.4	69.9	12.6	2.7	.2	6.4	.8
UNDER 100 MILES.......	32	100.0	-	56.5	23.7	.2	-	18.1	1.6
100 TO 199 MILES......	19	100.0	1.9	86.5	3.7	2.2	-	5.7	-
200 TO 299 MILES......	12	100.0	.1	93.6	1.2	1.3	2.0	1.9	-
300 TO 499 MILES......	33	100.0	6.6	62.7	27.2	2.0	-	1.5	-
500 TO 999 MILES......	36	100.0	6.2	82.3	3.8	5.0	-	2.4	.3
1000 TO 1499 MILES....	14	100.0	14.7	63.9	8.0	6.7	-	2.0	4.7
1500 MILES OR OVER....	11	100.0	43.8	40.2	2.4	1.5	-	11.9	.1
EAST NORTH CENTRAL......	300	100.0	18.3	61.1	9.2	1.6	-	9.9	-
UNDER 100 MILES.......	38	100.0	21.1	51.6	26.9	-	-	.5	-
100 TO 199 MILES......	19	100.0	.1	89.8	9.0	.5	-	.4	.1
200 TO 299 MILES......	55	100.0	6.3	77.3	15.7	.5	-	.2	-
300 TO 499 MILES......	32	100.0	12.6	60.6	9.3	2.5	-	15.0	-
500 TO 999 MILES......	120	100.0	21.0	54.9	1.9	2.1	-	20.0	-
1000 TO 1499 MILES....	8	100.0	25.2	56.4	16.6	1.6	-	.2	-
1500 MILES OR OVER....	25	100.0	45.9	49.8	.2	3.2	-	.9	-
WEST NORTH CENTRAL......	1	100.0	58.0	35.9	2.1	.9	-	3.2	-
UNDER 100 MILES.......	-	100.0	95.5	-	4.4	-	-	-	-
100 TO 199 MILES......	-	100.0	-	67.2	16.9	-	-	15.9	-
200 TO 299 MILES......	-	100.0	99.1	.9	-	-	-	-	-
300 TO 499 MILES......	-	100.0	-	97.9	-	.1	-	2.0	-
500 TO 999 MILES......	-	100.0	-	49.8	.5	4.7	-	44.9	-
1000 TO 1499 MILES....	-	100.0	-	59.1	-	12.5	-	28.4	-
1500 MILES OR OVER....	-	100.0	-	-	-	98.8	-	1.2	-
EAST SOUTH CENTRAL......	105	100.0	30.6	35.6	32.0	1.2	-	.7	-
UNDER 100 MILES.......	2	100.0	-	10.4	88.4	-	-	1.2	-
100 TO 199 MILES......	4	100.0	-	52.0	47.1	-	-	.9	-
200 TO 299 MILES......	13	100.0	3.8	43.4	52.5	-	-	.3	-
300 TO 499 MILES......	26	100.0	43.5	16.2	39.8	-	-	.4	-
500 TO 999 MILES......	44	100.0	34.4	37.2	24.8	2.8	-	.9	-
1000 TO 1499 MILES....	1	100.0	35.5	40.8	21.3	-	-	2.4	-
1500 MILES OR OVER....	12	100.0	35.9	60.4	3.6	-	-	.1	-
PACIFIC.................	100	100.0	-	84.1	7.1	8.2	-	.5	.1
UNDER 100 MILES.......	10	100.0	-	70.5	25.1	2.6	.3	1.5	-
100 TO 199 MILES......	8	100.0	-	72.1	27.4	-	-	.1	.4
200 TO 299 MILES......	1	100.0	-	91.8	6.9	1.0	-	-	.2
300 TO 499 MILES......	7	100.0	-	99.2	.6	.1	-	.1	-
500 TO 999 MILES......	11	100.0	-	94.0	2.7	1.4	-	1.7	.2
1000 TO 1499 MILES....	14	100.0	-	95.3	.8	3.8	-	.1	-
1500 MILES OR OVER....	46	100.0	-	80.8	3.5	15.5	-	.2	-
TON-MILES OF SHIPMENTS	(millions of ton-miles)								
U.S. TOTAL..........	541	100.0	24.3	59.3	6.8	4.6	-	4.8	.2
NEW ENGLAND..............	8	100.0	16.8	82.1	.1	1.0	-	-	-
UNDER 100 MILES.......	-	100.0	-	84.3	15.7	-	-	-	-
100 TO 199 MILES......	-	100.0	-	99.8	.1	-	-	-	-
200 TO 299 MILES......	-	100.0	-	99.8	-	.2	-	-	-
300 TO 499 MILES......	-	100.0	-	100.0	-	-	-	-	-
500 TO 999 MILES......	1	100.0	2.5	93.0	.6	3.7	-	-	.2
1000 TO 1499 MILES....	-	100.0	4.2	94.3	-	1.5	-	-	-
1500 MILES OR OVER....	5	100.0	26.5	73.1	-	.4	-	-	-
MIDDLE ATLANTIC.........	90	100.0	19.0	62.6	8.3	3.7	.1	5.3	.9
UNDER 100 MILES.......	1	100.0	-	58.5	29.9	.1	-	10.7	.8
100 TO 199 MILES......	2	100.0	2.3	85.6	3.6	2.0	-	6.5	-
200 TO 299 MILES......	3	100.0	.1	93.5	1.0	1.3	2.3	1.9	-
300 TO 499 MILES......	13	100.0	5.7	62.0	28.6	2.0	-	1.7	-
500 TO 999 MILES......	26	100.0	6.1	82.0	3.9	5.3	-	2.4	.3
1000 TO 1499 MILES....	16	100.0	15.7	63.5	8.2	6.5	-	2.0	4.1
1500 MILES OR OVER....	26	100.0	45.8	37.4	2.5	1.9	-	12.2	.1
EAST NORTH CENTRAL......	182	100.0	27.7	55.2	3.9	2.1	-	11.1	-
UNDER 100 MILES.......	2	100.0	24.9	57.4	17.1	-	-	.5	-
100 TO 199 MILES......	2	100.0	.1	90.2	8.5	.6	-	.5	.1
200 TO 299 MILES......	13	100.0	7.0	76.3	15.9	.6	-	.2	-
300 TO 499 MILES......	13	100.0	14.1	59.4	9.1	2.3	-	15.2	-
500 TO 999 MILES......	86	100.0	21.0	55.0	1.7	1.9	-	20.4	-
1000 TO 1499 MILES....	10	100.0	25.7	56.3	16.3	1.5	-	.2	-
1500 MILES OR OVER....	53	100.0	49.1	47.1	.1	2.9	-	.8	-

See footnotes at end of table 4.

TABLE 1. **TCC GROUP 365**—Percent Distribution of Geographic Division of Origin and Distance Shipped, by Means of Transport: 1972—Continued

Geographic division of origin[1] and distance shipped[2]	Number	Percent distribution by means of transport							
		All means of transport	Rail	Motor carrier	Private truck	Air	Water	Other	Unknown
TON-MILES OF SHIPMENTS	(millions of ton-miles)								
WEST NORTH CENTRAL......	-	100.0	32.2	52.9	.7	5.5	-	8.7	-
UNDER 100 MILES......	-	100.0	93.9	-	6.1	-	-	-	-
100 TO 199 MILES......	-	100.0	-	65.6	13.4	-	-	21.0	-
200 TO 299 MILES......	-	100.0	99.1	.8	-	-	-	-	-
300 TO 499 MILES......	-	100.0	-	97.3	-	.1	-	2.6	-
500 TO 999 MILES......	-	100.0	-	53.3	.4	3.9	-	42.5	-
1000 TO 1499 MILES....	-	100.0	-	62.7	-	11.1	-	26.2	-
1500 MILES OR OVER....	-	100.0	-	-	-	99.4	-	.6	-
EAST SOUTH CENTRAL......	72	100.0	35.9	41.3	20.8	1.5	-	.5	-
UNDER 100 MILES......	-	100.0	-	8.3	90.9	-	-	.8	-
100 TO 199 MILES......	-	100.0	-	52.4	46.7	-	-	.9	-
200 TO 299 MILES......	3	100.0	3.5	43.7	52.6	-	-	.3	-
300 TO 499 MILES......	10	100.0	46.1	15.3	38.2	-	-	.5	-
500 TO 999 MILES......	31	100.0	34.8	37.9	23.1	3.4	-	.8	-
1000 TO 1499 MILES....	2	100.0	35.6	45.6	16.7	-	-	2.2	-
1500 MILES OR OVER....	23	100.0	39.6	56.7	3.7	-	-	.1	-
PACIFIC.................	127	100.0	-	83.2	3.4	13.1	-	.3	.1
UNDER 100 MILES......	-	100.0	-	62.7	31.6	3.1	.2	2.4	-
100 TO 199 MILES......	1	100.0	-	66.8	32.5	-	-	.1	.6
200 TO 299 MILES......	-	100.0	-	90.7	8.1	1.0	-	-	.2
300 TO 499 MILES......	2	100.0	-	99.3	.5	.1	-	.1	-
500 TO 999 MILES......	9	100.0	-	94.2	2.4	1.5	-	1.8	.2
1000 TO 1499 MILES....	18	100.0	-	95.2	.9	3.8	-	.1	-
1500 MILES OR OVER....	95	100.0	-	79.6	3.6	16.5	-	.2	-

See footnotes at end of table 4.

TABLE 2. **TCC GROUP 365**—Percent Distribution of Geographic Division of Origin and Means of Transport, by Geographic Division of Destination: 1972

Geographic division of origin[1] and means of transport	Number	Percent distribution by division of destination									
		U.S. total	New England	Middle Atlantic	East North Central	West North Central	South Atlantic	East South Central	West South Central	Mountain	Pacific
TONS OF SHIPMENTS	(thousands of tons)										
U.S. TOTAL..............	774	100.0	5.1	20.8	24.5	5.4	12.2	7.7	10.2	3.2	10.8
RAIL..................	145	100.0	2.6	13.3	13.9	7.2	9.0	12.3	17.3	7.9	16.6
MOTOR CARRIER.........	466	100.0	5.3	21.9	26.7	5.6	11.8	5.9	9.1	2.8	10.8
PRIVATE TRUCK.........	100	100.0	3.4	15.9	37.8	4.3	18.3	11.6	2.5	.3	5.8
AIR...................	18	100.0	2.4	25.2	27.7	3.4	15.8	3.6	11.4	1.1	9.5
WATER.................	-	100.0	-	89.9	-	-	-	-	-	-	10.1
OTHER.................	41	100.0	16.2	43.4	3.3	.8	10.8	4.2	16.6	.1	4.6
UNKNOWN...............	1	100.0	-	35.1	7.9	.1	48.1	-	3.3	.2	5.3
NEW ENGLAND.............	10	100.0	7.1	38.1	12.3	3.3	15.5	2.0	3.1	6.5	12.0
RAIL..................	-	100.0	-	6.2	1.9	.7	-	-	15.4	43.7	32.1
MOTOR CARRIER.........	9	100.0	6.9	41.6	12.3	3.4	16.8	2.0	2.2	4.0	10.9
PRIVATE TRUCK.........	-	100.0	86.4	3.4	10.2	-	-	-	-	-	-
AIR...................	-	100.0	-	2.2	54.0	9.8	-	22.9	9.5	-	1.6
WATER.................	-	100.0	-	-	-	-	-	-	-	-	-
OTHER.................	-	100.0	-	-	-	-	-	-	-	-	-
UNKNOWN...............	-	100.0	-	-	-	-	100.0	-	-	-	-
MIDDLE ATLANTIC.........	160	100.0	10.3	28.4	22.7	4.0	20.5	2.4	4.8	.8	6.1
RAIL..................	11	100.0	.1	3.2	32.5	4.4	1.1	3.4	13.7	-	41.6
MOTOR CARRIER.........	112	100.0	14.0	26.8	25.1	4.4	18.7	2.5	4.6	1.1	2.8
PRIVATE TRUCK.........	20	100.0	1.5	35.1	11.2	2.7	44.4	.9	2.8	-	1.3
AIR...................	4	100.0	1.3	15.9	24.4	5.3	38.2	6.3	4.5	.7	3.3
WATER.................	-	100.0	-	100.0	-	-	-	-	-	-	-
OTHER.................	10	100.0	5.1	63.7	8.8	1.5	5.1	1.4	1.5	.1	12.7
UNKNOWN...............	1	100.0	-	39.6	7.2	.1	52.0	-	-	-	1.0
EAST NORTH CENTRAL......	300	100.0	4.3	19.3	32.4	4.5	8.2	8.6	12.0	2.4	8.4
RAIL..................	54	100.0	2.0	14.5	3.8	3.1	5.3	17.5	24.8	7.8	21.3
MOTOR CARRIER.........	183	100.0	2.7	20.0	39.7	4.7	8.3	7.8	8.5	1.6	6.8
PRIVATE TRUCK.........	27	100.0	1.5	1.6	78.6	10.1	7.1	.4	.6	-	.1
AIR...................	4	100.0	4.1	28.3	11.4	3.9	20.3	7.7	6.2	.6	17.5
WATER.................	-	100.0	-	-	-	-	-	-	-	-	-
OTHER.................	29	100.0	20.9	39.1	.8	.4	11.5	5.2	21.3	-	.8
UNKNOWN...............	-	100.0	-	.1	27.1	-	18.0	-	46.9	-	7.9
WEST NORTH CENTRAL......	1	100.0	1.4	.6	31.8	62.0	1.9	.4	.4	.3	1.1
RAIL..................	-	100.0	-	-	-	100.0	-	-	-	-	-
MOTOR CARRIER.........	-	100.0	2.7	.6	86.7	4.0	3.1	-	-	.7	2.2
PRIVATE TRUCK.........	-	100.0	-	-	-	99.3	-	.7	-	-	-
AIR...................	-	100.0	-	-	.8	4.1	14.2	-	47.8	-	33.0
WATER.................	-	100.0	-	-	-	-	-	-	-	-	-
OTHER.................	-	100.0	14.0	12.2	22.6	15.5	22.0	11.1	.7	-	1.9
UNKNOWN...............	-	100.0	-	-	-	-	-	-	-	-	-

See footnotes at end of table 4.

TABLE 2. TCC GROUP 365—Percent Distribution of Geographic Division of Origin and Means of Transport, by Geographic Division of Destination: 1972—Continued

Geographic division of origin[1] and means of transport	Number	Percent distribution by division of destination									
		U.S. total	New England	Middle Atlantic	East North Central	West North Central	South Atlantic	East South Central	West South Central	Mountain	Pacific
TONS OF SHIPMENTS	(thousands of tons)										
EAST SOUTH CENTRAL	105	100.0	5.3	17.7	15.5	5.2	15.1	15.4	13.0	1.5	11.3
RAIL	32	100.0	8.0	21.7	7.2	7.0	5.1	13.9	22.0	2.3	12.8
MOTOR CARRIER	37	100.0	1.0	20.6	5.0	7.0	19.3	16.0	9.4	2.1	19.8
PRIVATE TRUCK	33	100.0	7.5	11.3	35.5	1.8	20.7	17.0	5.0	.1	1.2
AIR	1	100.0	.1	3.9	.2	-	-	-	95.4	-	.3
WATER	-	100.0	-	-	-	-	-	-	-	-	-
OTHER	-	100.0	8.7	4.5	25.7	5.4	13.5	5.2	33.7	1.7	1.6
UNKNOWN	-	100.0	-	-	-	-	-	-	-	-	-
PACIFIC	100	100.0	.7	13.6	19.5	8.5	6.7	.8	10.1	8.1	31.9
RAIL	-	100.0	-	-	-	-	-	-	-	-	-
MOTOR CARRIER	84	100.0	.5	12.2	19.0	9.4	7.1	.9	11.4	9.0	30.4
PRIVATE TRUCK	7	100.0	1.1	9.8	1.3	5.8	5.3	.1	.8	4.6	71.1
AIR	8	100.0	2.4	32.5	42.0	2.3	4.3	.2	4.8	1.8	9.8
WATER	-	100.0	-	-	-	-	-	-	-	-	100.0
OTHER	-	100.0	.4	4.7	6.4	3.9	2.5	2.4	2.1	1.1	76.6
UNKNOWN	-	100.0	-	-	-	-	15.0	-	12.4	3.2	69.4
TON-MILES OF SHIPMENTS	(millions of ton-miles)										
U.S. TOTAL	541	100.0	4.0	17.6	16.6	6.0	12.0	3.2	12.4	5.9	22.2
RAIL	131	100.0	2.2	7.6	7.3	4.4	6.1	2.9	14.3	14.8	40.3
MOTOR CARRIER	320	100.0	3.2	20.1	19.4	7.1	13.2	3.2	11.8	3.7	18.2
PRIVATE TRUCK	36	100.0	6.3	16.4	26.5	8.0	24.4	5.6	6.6	.7	5.5
AIR	25	100.0	2.6	29.7	30.1	2.5	11.2	1.6	8.1	.8	13.3
WATER	-	100.0	-	99.3	-	-	-	-	-	-	.7
OTHER	26	100.0	21.4	26.6	2.8	1.0	7.5	3.2	22.9	.2	14.5
UNKNOWN	-	100.0	-	1.5	7.5	.2	77.6	-	4.7	.1	8.4
NEW ENGLAND	8	100.0	.5	9.3	11.2	4.5	10.3	2.4	5.7	16.8	39.4
RAIL	1	100.0	-	-	-	2.3	1.0	.3	11.0	47.8	37.6
MOTOR CARRIER	7	100.0	.5	11.3	12.5	5.1	12.4	2.6	4.5	10.7	40.3
PRIVATE TRUCK	-	100.0	27.3	4.5	68.1	-	-	-	-	-	-
AIR	-	100.0	-	.6	40.3	15.2	-	20.0	18.7	-	5.2
WATER	-	100.0	-	-	-	-	-	-	-	-	-
OTHER	-	100.0	-	-	-	-	-	-	-	-	-
UNKNOWN	-	100.0	-	-	-	-	100.0	-	-	-	-
MIDDLE ATLANTIC	90	100.0	3.9	5.5	21.2	6.9	19.9	3.0	10.8	2.3	26.5
RAIL	17	100.0	-	.4	11.4	3.1	.6	1.3	12.5	-	70.5
MOTOR CARRIER	56	100.0	6.0	6.7	27.1	8.2	20.1	3.6	11.4	3.5	13.4
PRIVATE TRUCK	7	100.0	.7	6.9	8.9	8.2	55.3	1.7	9.6	-	8.8
AIR	3	100.0	.2	3.9	18.1	7.0	41.2	7.1	7.4	1.6	13.6
WATER	-	100.0	-	100.0	-	-	-	-	-	-	-
OTHER	4	100.0	1.6	6.8	10.7	3.2	5.3	2.5	4.3	.6	65.1
UNKNOWN	-	100.0	-	1.7	8.4	.2	85.5	-	-	-	4.2
EAST NORTH CENTRAL	182	100.0	6.1	20.1	9.4	3.1	9.3	3.3	15.1	4.2	29.3
RAIL	50	100.0	2.0	8.7	.2	1.7	4.8	2.8	18.5	8.9	52.3
MOTOR CARRIER	100	100.0	4.1	24.4	13.8	3.3	10.7	3.7	12.1	3.1	24.8
PRIVATE TRUCK	7	100.0	4.2	3.8	42.7	18.6	27.4	.5	1.7	-	1.0
AIR	3	100.0	4.4	22.9	4.2	2.0	15.5	3.2	5.9	.9	40.9
WATER	-	100.0	-	-	-	-	-	-	-	-	-
OTHER	20	100.0	27.1	32.6	.2	.3	6.8	3.4	27.6	-	2.1
UNKNOWN	-	100.0	-	-	4.3	-	10.3	-	45.9	-	39.5
WEST NORTH CENTRAL	-	100.0	6.1	2.3	40.1	34.0	6.4	.8	1.7	.8	7.9
RAIL	-	100.0	-	-	-	100.0	-	-	-	-	-
MOTOR CARRIER	-	100.0	8.1	1.6	72.9	1.2	6.9	-	-	1.6	7.7
PRIVATE TRUCK	-	100.0	-	-	-	95.0	-	5.0	-	-	-
AIR	-	100.0	-	-	.3	.8	5.6	-	29.2	-	64.1
WATER	-	100.0	-	-	-	-	-	-	-	-	-
OTHER	-	100.0	20.6	16.8	17.2	4.3	28.1	8.3	.9	-	3.7
UNKNOWN	-	100.0	-	-	-	-	-	-	-	-	-
EAST SOUTH CENTRAL	72	100.0	5.4	13.9	9.1	4.9	9.5	7.1	15.4	3.1	31.6
RAIL	25	100.0	6.7	12.4	3.9	6.4	3.5	7.2	21.9	4.3	33.8
MOTOR CARRIER	29	100.0	1.0	16.0	2.0	5.0	13.3	5.4	9.3	3.6	44.3
PRIVATE TRUCK	14	100.0	11.8	13.2	32.8	2.4	13.0	11.0	10.1	.2	5.5
AIR	1	100.0	.2	3.3	.1	-	-	-	95.8	-	.7
WATER	-	100.0	-	-	-	-	-	-	-	-	-
OTHER	-	100.0	11.2	4.2	21.6	7.1	6.9	1.6	38.4	3.6	5.4
UNKNOWN	-	100.0	-	-	-	-	-	-	-	-	-
PACIFIC	127	100.0	1.4	25.6	28.0	9.7	12.0	1.2	10.1	4.0	7.9
RAIL	-	100.0	-	-	-	-	-	-	-	-	-
MOTOR CARRIER	106	100.0	1.1	23.2	27.2	10.7	12.8	1.4	11.5	4.5	7.7
PRIVATE TRUCK	4	100.0	4.7	37.5	4.2	14.7	20.4	.2	1.9	5.4	10.8
AIR	16	100.0	2.9	38.7	39.9	1.7	5.0	.2	3.1	.8	7.8
WATER	-	100.0	-	-	-	-	-	-	-	-	100.0
OTHER	-	100.0	1.2	14.2	14.4	6.9	6.8	5.2	3.8	.8	46.7
UNKNOWN	-	100.0	-	-	-	.1	42.3	-	24.7	.9	32.1

See footnotes at end of table 4.

TABLE 3. **TCC GROUP 365**—Percent Distribution of Geographic Division of Destination and Means of Transport, by Geographic Division of Origin: 1972

Geographic division of destination and means of transport	Number	Percent distribution by division of origin[1]									
		U.S. total	New England	Middle Atlantic	East North Central	West North Central	South Atlantic	East South Central	West South Central	Mountain	Pacific
TONS OF SHIPMENTS	(thousands of tons)										
U.S. TOTAL	774	100.0	1.3	20.7	38.8	.2	(D)	13.7	(D)	(D)	13.0
RAIL	145	100.0	.4	8.2	37.8	.6	(D)	22.3	(D)	(D)	-
MOTOR CARRIER	466	100.0	2.0	24.1	39.4	.1	(D)	8.1	(D)	(D)	18.1
PRIVATE TRUCK	100	100.0	.1	20.2	27.4	-	(D)	33.7	(D)	(D)	7.1
AIR	18	100.0	.6	22.9	24.9	.1	(D)	6.6	(D)	(D)	43.7
WATER	-	100.0	-	89.9	-	-	(D)	-	(D)	(D)	10.1
OTHER	41	100.0	-	24.4	70.9	.1	(D)	1.7	(D)	(D)	1.2
UNKNOWN	1	100.0	.2	88.6	5.6	-	(D)	-	(D)	(D)	5.6
NEW ENGLAND	39	100.0	1.8	42.1	32.5	.1	(D)	14.1	(D)	(D)	1.8
RAIL	3	100.0	-	.4	28.5	-	(D)	68.2	(D)	(D)	-
MOTOR CARRIER	24	100.0	2.6	62.9	19.7	.1	(D)	1.5	(D)	(D)	1.8
PRIVATE TRUCK	3	100.0	2.4	8.9	12.3	-	(D)	74.0	(D)	(D)	2.4
AIR	-	100.0	-	12.8	43.1	-	(D)	.4	(D)	(D)	43.6
WATER	-	100.0	-	-	-	-	(D)	-	(D)	(D)	-
OTHER	6	100.0	-	7.7	91.3	.1	(D)	.9	(D)	(D)	-
UNKNOWN	-	100.0	-	-	-	-	(D)	-	(D)	(D)	-
MIDDLE ATLANTIC	161	100.0	2.4	28.3	36.0	-	(D)	11.6	(D)	(D)	8.5
RAIL	19	100.0	-	2.0	41.0	-	(D)	36.3	(D)	(D)	-
MOTOR CARRIER	102	100.0	3.8	29.4	35.9	-	(D)	7.6	(D)	(D)	10.1
PRIVATE TRUCK	15	100.0	-	44.7	2.8	-	(D)	24.1	(D)	(D)	4.4
AIR	4	100.0	-	14.5	28.1	-	(D)	1.0	(D)	(D)	56.4
WATER	-	100.0	-	100.0	-	-	(D)	-	(D)	(D)	-
OTHER	18	100.0	-	35.8	63.8	-	(D)	.2	(D)	(D)	.1
UNKNOWN	-	100.0	-	100.0	-	-	(D)	-	(D)	(D)	-
EAST NORTH CENTRAL	189	100.0	.7	19.2	51.4	.2	(D)	8.7	(D)	(D)	10.4
RAIL	20	100.0	.2	19.2	10.3	-	(D)	11.5	(D)	(D)	-
MOTOR CARRIER	124	100.0	.9	22.6	58.4	.3	(D)	1.5	(D)	(D)	12.9
PRIVATE TRUCK	38	100.0	-	6.0	57.1	-	(D)	31.7	(D)	(D)	.2
AIR	5	100.0	1.1	20.2	10.2	-	(D)	.1	(D)	(D)	66.2
WATER	-	100.0	-	-	-	-	(D)	-	(D)	(D)	-
OTHER	1	100.0	-	64.5	17.9	.7	(D)	12.8	(D)	(D)	2.2
UNKNOWN	-	100.0	-	80.8	19.2	-	(D)	-	(D)	(D)	-
WEST NORTH CENTRAL	42	100.0	.8	15.2	31.8	2.1	(D)	13.1	(D)	(D)	20.4
RAIL	10	100.0	.1	5.0	16.3	7.8	(D)	21.7	(D)	(D)	-
MOTOR CARRIER	26	100.0	1.2	18.8	32.7	.1	(D)	10.0	(D)	(D)	30.2
PRIVATE TRUCK	4	100.0	-	12.5	63.6	.7	(D)	13.7	(D)	(D)	9.5
AIR	-	100.0	1.6	36.3	28.6	.1	(D)	-	(D)	(D)	29.6
WATER	-	100.0	-	-	-	-	(D)	-	(D)	(D)	-
OTHER	-	100.0	-	44.6	36.5	2.0	(D)	10.8	(D)	(D)	5.4
UNKNOWN	-	100.0	-	98.4	-	-	(D)	-	(D)	(D)	1.6
SOUTH ATLANTIC	94	100.0	1.7	34.8	25.9	-	(D)	16.9	(D)	(D)	7.1
RAIL	12	100.0	-	1.0	22.2	-	(D)	12.7	(D)	(D)	-
MOTOR CARRIER	55	100.0	2.8	38.0	27.8	-	(D)	13.2	(D)	(D)	10.9
PRIVATE TRUCK	18	100.0	-	48.9	10.6	-	(D)	38.0	(D)	(D)	2.1
AIR	2	100.0	-	55.5	32.2	.1	(D)	-	(D)	(D)	11.8
WATER	-	100.0	-	-	-	-	(D)	-	(D)	(D)	-
OTHER	4	100.0	-	11.6	75.6	.2	(D)	2.1	(D)	(D)	.3
UNKNOWN	-	100.0	.5	95.7	2.1	-	(D)	-	(D)	(D)	1.7
EAST SOUTH CENTRAL	59	100.0	.3	6.4	43.7	-	(D)	27.5	(D)	(D)	1.4
RAIL	17	100.0	-	2.3	54.1	-	(D)	25.3	(D)	(D)	-
MOTOR CARRIER	27	100.0	.7	10.3	52.1	-	(D)	21.9	(D)	(D)	2.9
PRIVATE TRUCK	11	100.0	-	1.5	.9	-	(D)	49.2	(D)	(D)	-
AIR	-	100.0	3.5	40.4	53.6	-	(D)	-	(D)	(D)	2.5
WATER	-	100.0	-	-	-	-	(D)	-	(D)	(D)	-
OTHER	1	100.0	-	8.4	88.6	.3	(D)	2.1	(D)	(D)	.7
UNKNOWN	-	100.0	-	-	-	-	(D)	-	(D)	(D)	-
WEST SOUTH CENTRAL	78	100.0	.4	9.7	45.7	-	(D)	17.4	(D)	(D)	12.8
RAIL	25	100.0	.4	6.5	54.3	-	(D)	28.4	(D)	(D)	-
MOTOR CARRIER	42	100.0	.5	12.2	37.0	-	(D)	8.4	(D)	(D)	22.8
PRIVATE TRUCK	2	100.0	-	22.9	6.2	-	(D)	68.5	(D)	(D)	2.4
AIR	2	100.0	.5	9.0	13.6	.3	(D)	55.1	(D)	(D)	18.2
WATER	-	100.0	-	-	-	-	(D)	-	(D)	(D)	-
OTHER	6	100.0	-	2.2	91.0	-	(D)	3.4	(D)	(D)	.1
UNKNOWN	-	100.0	-	-	79.1	-	(D)	-	(D)	(D)	20.9
MOUNTAIN	25	100.0	2.6	5.0	28.6	-	(D)	6.2	(D)	(D)	32.3
RAIL	11	100.0	2.5	-	37.2	-	(D)	6.6	(D)	(D)	-
MOTOR CARRIER	13	100.0	2.8	9.3	22.1	-	(D)	6.0	(D)	(D)	58.2
PRIVATE TRUCK	-	100.0	-	-	-	-	(D)	5.7	(D)	(D)	94.3
AIR	-	100.0	-	14.1	12.9	-	(D)	-	(D)	(D)	73.1
WATER	-	100.0	-	-	-	-	(D)	-	(D)	(D)	-
OTHER	-	100.0	-	38.8	14.7	-	(D)	32.0	(D)	(D)	14.3
UNKNOWN	-	100.0	-	-	.8	-	(D)	-	(D)	(D)	99.2
PACIFIC	83	100.0	1.4	11.7	30.0	-	(D)	14.3	(D)	(D)	38.1
RAIL	24	100.0	.9	20.7	48.7	-	(D)	17.2	(D)	(D)	-
MOTOR CARRIER	50	100.0	2.0	6.3	24.7	-	(D)	14.8	(D)	(D)	51.0
PRIVATE TRUCK	5	100.0	-	4.7	.7	-	(D)	7.2	(D)	(D)	87.5
AIR	1	100.0	.1	8.0	45.9	.2	(D)	.2	(D)	(D)	44.9
WATER	-	100.0	-	-	-	-	(D)	-	(D)	(D)	100.0
OTHER	1	100.0	-	68.0	12.1	-	(D)	.6	(D)	(D)	19.3
UNKNOWN	-	100.0	-	17.5	8.4	-	(D)	-	(D)	(D)	74.0

See footnotes at end of table 4.

TABLE 3. **TCC GROUP 365**—Percent Distribution of Geographic Division of Destination and Means of Transport, by Geographic Division of Origin: 1972—Continued

Geographic division of destination and means of transport	Number	Percent distribution by division of origin[1]									
		U.S. total	New England	Middle Atlantic	East North Central	West North Central	South Atlantic	East South Central	West South Central	Mountain	Pacific
TON-MILES OF SHIPMENTS	(millions of ton-miles)										
U.S. TOTAL..............	541	100.0	1.6	16.8	33.6	.1	(D)	13.3	(D)	(D)	23.6
RAIL..................	131	100.0	1.1	13.2	38.5	.1	(D)	19.7	(D)	(D)	-
MOTOR CARRIER.........	320	100.0	2.2	17.7	31.3	.1	(D)	9.3	(D)	(D)	33.2
PRIVATE TRUCK.........	36	100.0	-	20.6	19.3	-	(D)	40.7	(D)	(D)	11.6
AIR...................	25	100.0	.3	13.4	14.9	.1	(D)	4.2	(D)	(D)	66.4
WATER.................	-	100.0	-	99.3	-	-	(D)	-	(D)	(D)	.7
OTHER.................	26	100.0	-	18.5	77.0	.1	(D)	1.5	(D)	(D)	1.5
UNKNOWN...............	-	100.0	.3	86.1	6.4	-	(D)	-	(D)	(D)	7.2
NEW ENGLAND............	21	100.0	.2	16.2	50.9	.1	(D)	17.7	(D)	(D)	8.4
RAIL..................	2	100.0	-	.2	35.3	-	(D)	60.1	(D)	(D)	-
MOTOR CARRIER.........	10	100.0	.4	32.8	40.2	.2	(D)	2.9	(D)	(D)	11.1
PRIVATE TRUCK.........	2	100.0	.1	2.1	12.8	-	(D)	76.2	(D)	(D)	8.7
AIR...................	-	100.0	-	1.1	25.1	-	(D)	.3	(D)	(D)	73.4
WATER.................	-	100.0	-	-	-	-	(D)	-	(D)	(D)	-
OTHER.................	5	100.0	-	1.4	97.6	.1	(D)	.8	(D)	(D)	.1
UNKNOWN...............	-	100.0	-	-	-	-	(D)	-	(D)	(D)	-
MIDDLE ATLANTIC........	95	100.0	.9	5.2	38.5	-	(D)	10.5	(D)	(D)	34.4
RAIL..................	10	100.0	-	.7	44.0	-	(D)	32.1	(D)	(D)	-
MOTOR CARRIER.........	64	100.0	1.3	5.9	38.0	-	(D)	7.4	(D)	(D)	38.1
PRIVATE TRUCK.........	6	100.0	-	8.6	4.5	-	(D)	32.8	(D)	(D)	26.7
AIR...................	7	100.0	-	1.8	11.5	-	(D)	.5	(D)	(D)	86.3
WATER.................	-	100.0	-	100.0	-	-	(D)	-	(D)	(D)	-
OTHER.................	6	100.0	-	4.7	94.1	.1	(D)	.2	(D)	(D)	.8
UNKNOWN...............	-	100.0	-	99.9	.1	-	(D)	-	(D)	(D)	-
EAST NORTH CENTRAL.....	89	100.0	1.1	21.5	19.1	.2	(D)	7.3	(D)	(D)	39.9
RAIL..................	9	100.0	.4	20.6	1.0	-	(D)	10.5	(D)	(D)	-
MOTOR CARRIER.........	62	100.0	1.4	24.8	22.3	.2	(D)	.9	(D)	(D)	46.5
PRIVATE TRUCK.........	9	100.0	.1	6.9	31.0	-	(D)	50.2	(D)	(D)	1.9
AIR...................	7	100.0	.5	8.0	2.1	-	(D)	-	(D)	(D)	88.1
WATER.................	-	100.0	-	-	-	-	(D)	-	(D)	(D)	-
OTHER.................	-	100.0	-	71.2	6.1	.8	(D)	11.6	(D)	(D)	7.6
UNKNOWN...............	-	100.0	-	96.3	3.7	-	(D)	-	(D)	(D)	-
WEST NORTH CENTRAL.....	32	100.0	1.2	19.3	17.3	.4	(D)	10.9	(D)	(D)	38.3
RAIL..................	5	100.0	.3	9.1	14.9	2.1	(D)	28.3	(D)	(D)	-
MOTOR CARRIER.........	22	100.0	1.6	20.7	14.5	-	(D)	6.6	(D)	(D)	50.5
PRIVATE TRUCK.........	2	100.0	-	21.0	45.0	.1	(D)	12.4	(D)	(D)	21.5
AIR...................	-	100.0	2.0	37.8	12.0	-	(D)	-	(D)	(D)	44.6
WATER.................	-	100.0	-	-	-	-	(D)	-	(D)	(D)	-
OTHER.................	-	100.0	-	58.5	19.8	.5	(D)	10.4	(D)	(D)	10.0
UNKNOWN...............	-	100.0	-	97.8	-	-	(D)	-	(D)	(D)	2.2
SOUTH ATLANTIC.........	64	100.0	1.4	27.8	26.2	-	(D)	10.5	(D)	(D)	23.8
RAIL..................	8	100.0	.1	1.4	30.1	-	(D)	11.1	(D)	(D)	
MOTOR CARRIER.........	42	100.0	2.1	26.9	25.2	-	(D)	9.3	(D)	(D)	32.
PRIVATE TRUCK.........	9	100.0	-	46.6	21.6	-	(D)	21.7	(D)	(D)	9.
AIR...................	2	100.0	-	49.3	20.8	-	(D)	-	(D)	(D)	29.5
WATER.................	-	100.0	-	-	-	-	(D)	-	(D)	(D)	-
OTHER.................	1	100.0	-	13.1	69.4	.5	(D)	1.4	(D)	(D)	1.3
UNKNOWN...............	-	100.0	.4	94.8	.8	-	(D)	-	(D)	(D)	3.9
EAST SOUTH CENTRAL.....	17	100.0	1.2	15.8	34.2	-	(D)	29.6	(D)	(D)	8.7
RAIL..................	3	100.0	-	6.2	37.7	-	(D)	49.3	(D)	(D)	-
MOTOR CARRIER.........	10	100.0	1.8	19.7	35.7	-	(D)	15.7	(D)	(D)	14.0
PRIVATE TRUCK.........	2	100.0	-	6.2	1.9	-	(D)	80.3	(D)	(D)	.3
AIR...................	-	100.0	4.2	58.5	29.4	-	(D)	-	(D)	(D)	7.9
WATER.................	-	100.0	-	-	-	-	(D)	-	(D)	(D)	-
OTHER.................	-	100.0	-	14.5	82.0	.3	(D)	.8	(D)	(D)	2.4
UNKNOWN...............	-	100.0	-	-	-	-	(D)	-	(D)	(D)	-
WEST SOUTH CENTRAL.....	67	100.0	.7	14.6	40.8	-	(D)	16.5	(D)	(D)	19.1
RAIL..................	18	100.0	.9	11.5	49.7	-	(D)	30.2	(D)	(D)	-
MOTOR CARRIER.........	37	100.0	.8	17.1	32.1	-	(D)	7.3	(D)	(D)	32.3
PRIVATE TRUCK.........	2	100.0	-	29.8	5.0	-	(D)	61.8	(D)	(D)	3.3
AIR...................	2	100.0	.8	12.1	10.9	.3	(D)	49.9	(D)	(D)	25.1
WATER.................	-	100.0	-	-	-	-	(D)	-	(D)	(D)	-
OTHER.................	5	100.0	-	3.5	92.8	-	(D)	2.5	(D)	(D)	.2
UNKNOWN...............	-	100.0	-	-	62.3	-	(D)	-	(D)	(D)	37.7
MOUNTAIN...............	31	100.0	4.6	6.5	24.0	-	(D)	7.0	(D)	(D)	16.0
RAIL..................	19	100.0	3.6	-	23.1	-	(D)	5.7	(D)	(D)	-
MOTOR CARRIER.........	11	100.0	6.4	16.8	26.3	-	(D)	9.0	(D)	(D)	39.7
PRIVATE TRUCK.........	-	100.0	-	-	-	-	(D)	12.4	(D)	(D)	87.6
AIR...................	-	100.0	-	24.4	15.5	-	(D)	-	(D)	(D)	60.0
WATER.................	-	100.0	-	-	-	-	(D)	-	(D)	(D)	-
OTHER.................	-	100.0	-	52.8	14.4	-	(D)	27.0	(D)	(D)	5.7
UNKNOWN...............	-	100.0	-	-	4.4	-	(D)	-	(D)	(D)	95.6
PACIFIC................	120	100.0	2.9	20.0	44.4	-	(D)	18.9	(D)	(D)	8.4
RAIL..................	52	100.0	1.0	23.0	50.0	-	(D)	16.5	(D)	(D)	-
MOTOR CARRIER.........	58	100.0	5.0	13.1	42.8	-	(D)	22.6	(D)	(D)	14.0
PRIVATE TRUCK.........	2	100.0	-	33.1	3.5	-	(D)	40.4	(D)	(D)	23.0
AIR...................	3	100.0	.1	13.6	45.9	.4	(D)	.2	(D)	(D)	39.1
WATER.................	-	100.0	-	-	-	-	(D)	-	(D)	(D)	100.0
OTHER.................	3	100.0	-	83.4	11.3	-	(D)	.6	(D)	(D)	4.7
UNKNOWN...............	-	100.0	-	42.6	30.0	-	(D)	-	(D)	(D)	27.4

See footnotes at end of table 4.

TABLE 4. **TCC GROUP 365—Percent Distribution of Distance Shipped and Weight of Shipment, by Means of Transport: 1972**

Distance shipped and weight of shipment [2] [3]	Number	Percent distribution by means of transport							
		All means of transport	Rail	Motor carrier	Private truck	Air	Water	Other	Unknown
TONS OF SHIPMENTS	(thousands of tons)								
U.S. TOTAL............	713	100.0	19.9	58.3	14.0	1.8	-	5.8	.2
UNDER 100 MILES.........	91	100.0	12.5	48.5	31.2	.4	-	6.8	.6
UNDER 1000 POUNDS.....	11	100.0	-	64.5	21.0	2.8	.3	8.8	2.6
1000 TO 9999 POUNDS...	30	100.0	-	70.2	23.8	.1	-	5.2	.7
10000 TO 29999 POUNDS.	45	100.0	23.3	31.8	37.0	-	-	7.9	-
30000 TO 59999 POUNDS.	3	100.0	20.9	28.0	51.0	-	-	-	-
60000 TO 89999 POUNDS.	-	100.0	-	-	-	-	-	-	-
90000 POUNDS AND OVER.	-	100.0	-	-	-	-	-	-	-
100 TO 199 MILES........	54	100.0	3.4	80.8	12.3	1.0	-	2.5	.1
UNDER 1000 POUNDS.....	16	100.0	-	81.8	11.3	.9	-	5.8	.2
1000 TO 9999 POUNDS...	23	100.0	-	81.2	15.5	1.6	-	1.7	-
10000 TO 29999 POUNDS.	7	100.0	24.2	73.0	2.8	-	-	-	-
30000 TO 59999 POUNDS.	6	100.0	-	85.6	14.4	-	-	-	-
60000 TO 89999 POUNDS.	-	100.0	-	-	-	-	-	-	-
90000 POUNDS AND OVER.	-	100.0	-	-	-	-	-	-	-
200 TO 299 MILES........	83	100.0	6.9	72.5	19.1	.6	.3	.5	-
UNDER 1000 POUNDS.....	14	100.0	.8	85.7	7.8	2.7	-	2.9	-
1000 TO 9999 POUNDS...	23	100.0	1.8	89.2	7.9	.7	.5	-	-
10000 TO 29999 POUNDS.	41	100.0	12.6	58.3	28.7	-	.3	-	-
30000 TO 59999 POUNDS.	4	100.0	-	75.0	25.0	-	-	-	-
60000 TO 89999 POUNDS.	-	100.0	-	-	-	-	-	-	-
90000 POUNDS AND OVER.	-	100.0	-	-	-	-	-	-	-
300 TO 499 MILES........	120	100.0	22.4	50.0	21.8	1.2	-	4.6	-
UNDER 1000 POUNDS.....	23	100.0	11.4	65.9	13.9	4.9	-	3.8	.1
1000 TO 9999 POUNDS...	42	100.0	12.8	62.4	23.8	.9	-	-	-
10000 TO 29999 POUNDS.	40	100.0	32.2	40.8	23.8	-	-	3.3	-
30000 TO 59999 POUNDS.	14	100.0	41.0	12.4	23.0	-	-	23.5	-
60000 TO 89999 POUNDS.	-	100.0	-	-	-	-	-	-	-
90000 POUNDS AND OVER.	-	100.0	-	-	-	-	-	-	-
500 TO 999 MILES........	246	100.0	25.5	54.7	6.9	2.3	-	10.5	.1
UNDER 1000 POUNDS.....	37	100.0	16.5	58.5	9.6	10.5	-	4.4	.4
1000 TO 9999 POUNDS...	70	100.0	11.4	69.8	15.4	2.7	-	.8	-
10000 TO 29999 POUNDS.	105	100.0	33.4	48.1	2.3	-	-	16.2	-
30000 TO 59999 POUNDS.	26	100.0	50.6	24.4	-	-	-	25.0	-
60000 TO 89999 POUNDS.	6	100.0	-	100.0	-	-	-	-	-
90000 POUNDS AND OVER.	-	100.0	-	-	-	-	-	-	-
1000 TO 1499 MILES......	35	100.0	15.1	68.9	8.6	4.4	-	1.1	1.9
UNDER 1000 POUNDS.....	9	100.0	7.8	64.4	9.8	14.0	-	4.0	-
1000 TO 9999 POUNDS...	12	100.0	2.3	85.2	5.4	1.8	-	-	5.4
10000 TO 29999 POUNDS.	10	100.0	21.9	63.9	14.2	-	-	-	-
30000 TO 59999 POUNDS.	3	100.0	65.7	34.3	-	-	-	-	-
60000 TO 89999 POUNDS.	-	100.0	-	-	-	-	-	-	-
90000 POUNDS AND OVER.	-	100.0	-	-	-	-	-	-	-
1500 MILES OR OVER......	82	100.0	33.7	58.2	2.9	3.2	-	2.0	-
UNDER 1000 POUNDS.....	11	100.0	21.3	54.4	6.1	11.8	-	6.1	.3
1000 TO 9999 POUNDS...	23	100.0	17.3	66.3	7.0	5.3	-	4.1	-
10000 TO 29999 POUNDS.	21	100.0	56.3	43.7	-	-	-	-	-
30000 TO 59999 POUNDS.	21	100.0	43.1	56.9	-	-	-	-	-
60000 TO 89999 POUNDS.	-	100.0	-	-	-	-	-	-	-
90000 POUNDS AND OVER.	4	100.0	-	100.0	-	-	-	-	-
TON-MILES OF SHIPMENTS	(millions of ton-miles)								
U.S. TOTAL............	471	100.0	26.6	57.3	7.8	2.7	-	5.5	.2
UNDER 100 MILES.........	4	100.0	14.9	50.7	29.7	.2	-	4.2	.3
UNDER 1000 POUNDS.....	-	100.0	-	66.8	21.6	2.1	.1	7.6	1.8
1000 TO 9999 POUNDS...	1	100.0	-	71.0	26.1	.1	-	2.7	.3
10000 TO 29999 POUNDS.	2	100.0	28.7	35.0	31.3	-	-	5.0	-
30000 TO 59999 POUNDS.	-	100.0	14.9	26.5	58.6	-	-	-	-
60000 TO 89999 POUNDS.	-	100.0	-	-	-	-	-	-	-
90000 POUNDS AND OVER.	-	100.0	-	-	-	-	-	-	-
100 TO 199 MILES........	8	100.0	4.0	79.7	12.5	.9	-	2.8	.1
UNDER 1000 POUNDS.....	2	100.0	-	82.1	10.6	.9	-	6.1	.3
1000 TO 9999 POUNDS...	3	100.0	-	80.8	15.8	1.4	-	2.0	-
10000 TO 29999 POUNDS.	1	100.0	27.3	70.1	2.6	-	-	-	-
30000 TO 59999 POUNDS.	-	100.0	-	81.4	18.6	-	-	-	-
60000 TO 89999 POUNDS.	-	100.0	-	-	-	-	-	-	-
90000 POUNDS AND OVER.	-	100.0	-	-	-	-	-	-	-

See footnotes at end of table 4.

TABLE 4. TCC GROUP 365—Percent Distribution of Distance Shipped and Weight of Shipment, by Means of Transport: 1972—Continued

Distance shipped and weight of shipment [2] [3]	Number	Percent distribution by means of transport							
		All means of transport	Rail	Motor carrier	Private truck	Air	Water	Other	Unknown
TON-MILES OF SHIPMENTS	(millions of ton-miles)								
200 TO 299 MILES.........	20	100.0	7.3	71.4	19.8	.6	.4	.5	-
UNDER 1000 POUNDS.....	3	100.0	.8	85.7	7.9	2.6	-	2.9	-
1000 TO 9999 POUNDS...	5	100.0	1.9	88.9	8.1	.7	.6	-	-
10000 TO 29999 POUNDS.	10	100.0	13.6	56.2	29.8	-	.4	-	-
30000 TO 59999 POUNDS.	1	100.0	-	74.3	25.7	-	-	-	-
60000 TO 89999 POUNDS.	-	100.0	-	-	-	-	-	-	-
90000 POUNDS AND OVER.	-	100.0	-	-	-	-	-	-	-
300 TO 499 MILES........	48	100.0	22.6	49.3	22.1	1.2	-	4.7	-
UNDER 1000 POUNDS.....	9	100.0	12.2	64.5	14.3	4.9	-	4.0	.1
1000 TO 9999 POUNDS...	16	100.0	13.5	62.4	23.2	.8	-	-	-
10000 TO 29999 POUNDS.	16	100.0	30.9	40.6	24.6	-	-	3.8	-
30000 TO 59999 POUNDS.	5	100.0	41.5	12.4	23.9	-	-	22.1	-
60000 TO 89999 POUNDS.	-	100.0	-	-	-	-	-	-	-
90000 POUNDS AND OVER.	-	100.0	-	-	-	-	-	-	-
500 TO 999 MILES........	172	100.0	25.2	55.1	6.3	2.5	-	10.9	.1
UNDER 1000 POUNDS.....	26	100.0	15.9	58.9	9.2	11.3	-	4.3	.4
1000 TO 9999 POUNDS...	49	100.0	10.8	71.3	14.4	2.7	-	.8	-
10000 TO 29999 POUNDS.	73	100.0	34.3	48.0	1.9	-	-	15.8	-
30000 TO 59999 POUNDS.	18	100.0	47.4	22.4	-	-	-	30.2	-
60000 TO 89999 POUNDS.	5	100.0	-	100.0	-	-	-	-	-
90000 POUNDS AND OVER.	-	100.0	-	-	-	-	-	-	-
1000 TO 1499 MILES......	42	100.0	15.5	69.2	8.3	4.3	-	1.0	1.6
UNDER 1000 POUNDS.....	11	100.0	8.1	65.3	9.4	13.4	-	3.8	-
1000 TO 9999 POUNDS...	14	100.0	2.5	86.4	4.6	1.8	-	-	4.6
10000 TO 29999 POUNDS.	12	100.0	21.8	63.7	14.4	-	-	-	-
30000 TO 59999 POUNDS.	3	100.0	68.6	31.4	-	-	-	-	-
60000 TO 89999 POUNDS.	-	100.0	-	-	-	-	-	-	-
90000 POUNDS AND OVER.	-	100.0	-	-	-	-	-	-	-
1500 MILES OR OVER......	174	100.0	35.4	56.1	2.9	3.3	-	2.2	-
UNDER 1000 POUNDS.....	24	100.0	20.9	52.9	6.4	13.1	-	6.4	.3
1000 TO 9999 POUNDS...	49	100.0	17.1	65.9	7.0	5.4	-	4.7	-
10000 TO 29999 POUNDS.	45	100.0	61.1	38.9	-	-	-	-	-
30000 TO 59999 POUNDS.	46	100.0	43.4	56.6	-	-	-	-	-
60000 TO 89999 POUNDS.	-	100.0	-	-	-	-	-	-	-
90000 POUNDS AND OVER.	8	100.0	-	100.0	-	-	-	-	-

Note: Detail may not add to total due to rounding. The introductory table shows the estimates of sampling variability for tons; sampling variability for ton-miles has not been estimated. See the map in the Introduction for the States comprising the geographic divisions of the United States.

Shipments excluded from the survey are those moving by pipeline (primarily petroleum products from refineries), parcel post shipments, and commodities moved by own power (motorized vehicles, aircraft, etc.) or towed (prefabricated buildings, etc.). Local shipments (commodities shipped less than 25 miles from the plant) and shipments within the same city are also excluded. Shipments to Alaska and Hawaii from the 48 conterminous States and the District of Columbia are included; however, no data were obtained for shipments originating in Alaska and Hawaii.

- Represents zero or rounds to zero.   (D) Withheld to avoid disclosing figures for individual companies.

[1]Production of this commodity is concentrated in the geographic divisions shown; figures and distributions for geographic divisions not shown are included in the total.

[2]Distances of shipments to foreign destinations are calculated only to the U.S. port of exit.

[3]Includes only shipments represented by bills of lading and invoices. Summary records which did not show individual weights of shipments are not included.

TCC 366. Communication Equipment

Comparisons of Tons and Ton-Miles of Shipments for
Geographic Divisions of Origin and for Sampling Variability: 1972 and 1967

Geographic division of origin	Estimates				Relative sampling variability in tons (percent)	
	1972		1967		1972	1967
	Tons (thousands)	Ton-miles (millions)	Tons (thousands)	Ton-miles (millions)		
U.S. total	547	363	375	311	9.2	11.0
New England	17	8	13	9	36.2	(*)
Middle Atlantic	(D)	(D)	55	55	(*)	(*)
East North Central	185	124	204	145	18.9	(*)
West North Central	(D)	(D)	20	17	(*)	(*)
South Atlantic	49	31	15	11	39.9	(*)
East South Central	18	15	2	2	15.5	(*)
West South Central	(D)	(D)	50	48	(*)	(*)
Mountain	(D)	(D)	7	11	(*)	(*)
Pacific	36	47	9	13	20.9	(*)

(D) Withheld to avoid disclosing figures for individual companies.   (*) Data not published.

TABLE 1. **TCC GROUP 366—Percent Distribution of Geographic Division of Origin and Distance Shipped, by Means of Transport: 1972**

Geographic division of origin[1] and distance shipped[2]	Number	Percent distribution by means of transport							
		All means of transport	Rail	Motor carrier	Private truck	Air	Water	Other	Unknown
TONS OF SHIPMENTS	(thousands of tons)								
U.S. TOTAL	547	100.0	8.7	76.0	7.6	4.8	.3	2.6	.1
NEW ENGLAND	17	100.0	-	88.1	4.1	3.7	-	4.1	-
UNDER 100 MILES	6	100.0	-	86.6	11.3	-	-	2.1	-
100 TO 199 MILES	-	100.0	-	89.1	.2	3.8	-	6.9	-
200 TO 299 MILES	4	100.0	-	96.6	-	1.0	-	2.4	-
300 TO 499 MILES	1	100.0	-	92.2	-	1.9	-	5.9	-
500 TO 999 MILES	1	100.0	-	83.8	.1	3.1	-	13.1	-
1000 TO 1499 MILES	1	100.0	-	82.9	-	8.7	-	8.2	.2
1500 MILES OR OVER	1	100.0	-	77.6	.1	21.5	-	.8	-
EAST NORTH CENTRAL	185	100.0	17.3	55.8	18.7	5.8	.4	2.1	-
UNDER 100 MILES	11	100.0	-	59.8	36.0	-	-	4.2	-
100 TO 199 MILES	5	100.0	-	91.2	6.4	1.2	-	1.2	-
200 TO 299 MILES	32	100.0	.9	34.6	60.4	1.5	-	2.6	-
300 TO 499 MILES	24	100.0	.6	62.1	28.5	2.7	-	6.0	-
500 TO 999 MILES	84	100.0	29.3	57.5	4.5	7.7	-	1.1	-
1000 TO 1499 MILES	12	100.0	47.8	45.6	-	6.3	-	.3	-
1500 MILES OR OVER	15	100.0	5.6	74.8	.2	14.0	4.6	.8	-
SOUTH ATLANTIC	49	100.0	-	86.0	1.2	2.5	-	9.8	.5
UNDER 100 MILES	1	100.0	-	77.5	3.1	.4	-	18.9	-
100 TO 199 MILES	13	100.0	-	97.8	.5	.1	-	1.5	-
200 TO 299 MILES	7	100.0	-	96.8	-	.3	-	3.0	-
300 TO 499 MILES	8	100.0	-	85.7	.2	1.5	-	12.4	.1
500 TO 999 MILES	10	100.0	.1	74.3	3.8	5.1	-	16.8	-
1000 TO 1499 MILES	3	100.0	-	61.7	-	5.1	-	33.2	-
1500 MILES OR OVER	5	100.0	-	83.6	1.1	6.9	-	4.3	4.2
EAST SOUTH CENTRAL	18	100.0	4.3	88.7	2.2	1.1	1.9	1.8	-
UNDER 100 MILES	-	100.0	-	99.1	.2	-	-	.7	-
100 TO 199 MILES	-	100.0	-	92.1	-	-	-	7.9	-
200 TO 299 MILES	1	100.0	-	84.0	15.6	-	-	.4	-
300 TO 499 MILES	3	100.0	-	83.3	3.5	.6	10.4	2.3	-
500 TO 999 MILES	8	100.0	-	96.3	.1	1.0	-	2.7	-
1000 TO 1499 MILES	1	100.0	-	99.0	-	.7	-	.3	-
1500 MILES OR OVER	3	100.0	23.9	73.4	-	2.6	-	-	-
PACIFIC	36	100.0	.6	82.9	2.7	10.1	.9	2.9	-
UNDER 100 MILES	6	100.0	-	83.1	7.0	2.4	-	7.6	-
100 TO 199 MILES	-	100.0	-	60.8	11.9	10.4	-	16.8	-
200 TO 299 MILES	-	100.0	-	7.5	89.6	1.3	-	1.6	-
300 TO 499 MILES	1	100.0	.7	88.6	.2	7.2	-	3.3	-
500 TO 999 MILES	2	100.0	3.8	72.0	-	22.1	-	2.1	-
1000 TO 1499 MILES	13	100.0	.1	98.0	.5	1.4	-	-	-
1500 MILES OR OVER	12	100.0	.9	70.0	.9	22.2	2.6	3.3	.1
TON-MILES OF SHIPMENTS	(millions of ton-miles)								
U.S. TOTAL	363	100.0	10.1	74.4	3.6	8.1	1.1	2.5	.2
NEW ENGLAND	8	100.0	-	83.5	.4	11.0	-	5.0	.1
UNDER 100 MILES	-	100.0	-	89.9	8.4	-	-	1.7	-
100 TO 199 MILES	-	100.0	-	87.7	.2	4.8	-	7.3	-
200 TO 299 MILES	-	100.0	-	96.2	-	1.2	-	2.7	-
300 TO 499 MILES	-	100.0	-	92.3	-	1.8	-	5.8	-
500 TO 999 MILES	1	100.0	-	83.4	.1	3.3	-	13.2	-
1000 TO 1499 MILES	2	100.0	-	83.3	-	8.8	-	7.7	.2
1500 MILES OR OVER	3	100.0	-	77.8	.1	21.3	-	.8	-
EAST NORTH CENTRAL	124	100.0	21.5	58.4	7.8	8.4	2.5	1.4	-
UNDER 100 MILES	-	100.0	-	61.0	33.7	.1	-	5.2	-
100 TO 199 MILES	-	100.0	-	90.6	7.0	1.2	-	1.2	-
200 TO 299 MILES	7	100.0	.9	36.0	59.0	1.6	-	2.5	-
300 TO 499 MILES	9	100.0	.6	65.1	25.5	2.9	-	5.9	-
500 TO 999 MILES	58	100.0	30.6	57.0	3.8	7.4	-	1.2	-
1000 TO 1499 MILES	14	100.0	49.0	44.4	-	6.4	-	.3	-
1500 MILES OR OVER	32	100.0	4.8	70.0	.1	14.8	9.5	.7	-
SOUTH ATLANTIC	31	100.0	-	80.8	1.6	4.7	-	11.1	1.8
UNDER 100 MILES	-	100.0	-	77.2	1.0	.5	-	21.3	-
100 TO 199 MILES	2	100.0	-	97.9	.4	.1	-	1.5	-
200 TO 299 MILES	1	100.0	-	96.5	-	.3	-	3.2	-
300 TO 499 MILES	3	100.0	-	85.4	.2	1.6	-	12.8	.1
500 TO 999 MILES	8	100.0	.1	74.3	4.3	5.4	-	16.0	-
1000 TO 1499 MILES	3	100.0	-	64.4	-	4.7	-	30.9	-
1500 MILES OR OVER	12	100.0	-	84.0	1.0	6.5	-	3.9	4.5
EAST SOUTH CENTRAL	15	100.0	9.9	85.4	.9	1.8	.9	1.1	-
UNDER 100 MILES	-	100.0	-	99.4	.2	-	-	.4	-
100 TO 199 MILES	-	100.0	-	90.8	-	-	-	9.2	-
200 TO 299 MILES	-	100.0	-	84.3	15.4	-	-	.4	-
300 TO 499 MILES	1	100.0	-	85.1	3.7	.6	8.7	2.0	-
500 TO 999 MILES	4	100.0	-	96.3	-	1.1	-	2.5	-
1000 TO 1499 MILES	1	100.0	-	99.2	-	.6	-	.2	-
1500 MILES OR OVER	6	100.0	21.9	75.0	-	3.0	-	-	-

See footnotes at end of table 4.

TABLE 1. **TCC GROUP 366**—Percent Distribution of Geographic Division of Origin and Distance Shipped, by Means of Transport: 1972—Continued

Geographic division of origin[1] and distance shipped[2]	Number	Percent distribution by means of transport							
		All means of transport	Rail	Motor carrier	Private truck	Air	Water	Other	Unknown
TON-MILES OF SHIPMENTS	(millions of ton-miles)								
PACIFIC..................	47	100.0	.7	80.6	1.0	13.7	1.7	2.3	.1
UNDER 100 MILES.......	-	100.0	-	83.5	6.6	1.5	-	8.5	-
100 TO 199 MILES......	-	100.0	-	60.1	15.2	9.3	-	15.3	-
200 TO 299 MILES......	-	100.0	-	7.8	89.2	1.4	-	1.6	-
300 TO 499 MILES......	-	100.0	.6	88.8	.2	7.3	-	3.1	-
500 TO 999 MILES......	1	100.0	3.8	71.0	-	23.0	-	2.2	-
1000 TO 1499 MILES....	19	100.0	.1	98.2	.5	1.2	-	-	-
1500 MILES OR OVER....	24	100.0	1.0	67.3	1.0	23.3	3.3	4.0	.1

See footnotes at end of table 4.

TABLE 2. **TCC GROUP 366**—Percent Distribution of Geographic Division of Origin and Means of Transport, by Geographic Division of Destination: 1972

Geographic division of origin[1] and means of transport	Number	Percent distribution by division of destination									
		U.S. total	New England	Middle Atlantic	East North Central	West North Central	South Atlantic	East South Central	West South Central	Mountain	Pacific
TONS OF SHIPMENTS	(thousands of tons)										
U.S. TOTAL..............	547	100.0	4.2	24.6	25.9	4.9	16.0	3.4	11.1	2.5	7.5
RAIL...................	47	100.0	1.0	19.1	23.6	4.0	23.7	.4	16.7	7.8	3.7
MOTOR CARRIER.........	415	100.0	4.6	27.9	23.8	4.8	16.1	2.6	10.7	1.9	7.6
PRIVATE TRUCK.........	41	100.0	1.7	3.6	60.7	1.1	3.6	15.5	11.8	.1	2.1
AIR....................	26	100.0	3.9	21.9	11.2	10.4	20.7	.9	8.2	5.4	17.5
WATER.................	1	100.0	-	-	-	-	-	-	25.4	-	74.6
OTHER.................	13	100.0	11.3	15.5	22.0	15.2	13.9	4.8	7.4	1.7	8.2
UNKNOWN...............	-	100.0	-	.9	34.7	.2	29.9	-	.8	-	33.5
NEW ENGLAND............	17	100.0	37.4	29.0	5.9	3.8	8.9	4.4	6.0	2.0	2.6
RAIL...................	-	100.0	-	-	-	-	-	-	-	-	-
MOTOR CARRIER.........	15	100.0	37.1	31.1	5.4	3.5	8.8	4.8	6.2	.5	2.5
PRIVATE TRUCK.........	-	100.0	93.4	6.2	-	-	.3	-	-	-	.1
AIR....................	-	100.0	-	9.4	7.5	9.1	10.9	-	10.8	43.2	9.0
WATER.................	-	100.0	-	-	-	-	-	-	-	-	-
OTHER.................	-	100.0	20.8	23.3	20.1	10.6	17.0	4.1	3.6	-	.5
UNKNOWN...............	-	100.0	-	-	-	-	-	-	100.0	-	-
EAST NORTH CENTRAL......	185	100.0	1.7	17.8	25.5	6.8	14.9	5.0	16.7	3.2	8.3
RAIL...................	32	100.0	1.5	27.2	.9	.4	32.8	-	22.8	11.6	2.7
MOTOR CARRIER.........	103	100.0	1.9	19.3	20.3	10.4	13.9	2.7	18.3	1.9	11.2
PRIVATE TRUCK.........	34	100.0	-	1.0	69.4	1.3	-	18.4	9.8	.1	-
AIR....................	10	100.0	4.7	33.2	4.5	2.3	23.9	.4	9.4	1.6	20.1
WATER.................	-	100.0	-	-	-	-	-	-	-	-	100.0
OTHER.................	3	100.0	5.2	12.3	37.6	25.9	5.3	1.0	8.5	1.3	2.9
UNKNOWN...............	-	100.0	-	-	9.7	-	-	-	-	-	90.3
SOUTH ATLANTIC..........	49	100.0	9.4	37.2	12.3	3.0	18.7	2.1	5.3	2.3	9.8
RAIL...................	-	100.0	-	10.7	-	-	89.3	-	-	-	-
MOTOR CARRIER.........	42	100.0	9.4	40.7	11.9	1.9	19.5	1.0	3.9	2.0	9.7
PRIVATE TRUCK.........	-	100.0	2.9	.3	.6	-	20.8	.1	66.0	-	9.3
AIR....................	1	100.0	13.1	23.6	15.2	6.1	3.3	5.4	3.3	12.0	18.1
WATER.................	-	100.0	-	-	-	-	-	-	-	-	100.0
OTHER.................	4	100.0	9.6	16.5	16.8	12.5	16.2	11.1	10.4	3.2	3.7
UNKNOWN...............	-	100.0	-	2.8	-	-	-	-	1.1	-	96.1
EAST SOUTH CENTRAL......	18	100.0	1.0	8.0	22.9	10.4	24.0	3.9	7.8	7.0	15.1
RAIL...................	-	100.0	-	-	-	-	-	-	-	-	100.0
MOTOR CARRIER.........	16	100.0	1.1	8.8	22.8	11.6	26.6	4.3	5.3	7.8	11.6
PRIVATE TRUCK.........	-	100.0	-	-	47.7	-	-	.3	52.0	-	-
AIR....................	-	100.0	1.6	9.3	20.6	2.1	17.4	.1	1.4	2.3	45.2
WATER.................	-	100.0	-	-	-	-	-	-	100.0	-	-
OTHER.................	-	100.0	.9	3.0	80.4	3.6	9.2	.6	1.8	-	.5
UNKNOWN...............	-	100.0	-	-	-	-	-	-	-	-	-
PACIFIC.................	36	100.0	1.6	4.6	4.5	1.0	8.0	12.0	39.1	3.9	25.3
RAIL...................	-	100.0	1.0	19.0	12.9	-	18.7	1.5	4.3	.1	42.5
MOTOR CARRIER.........	30	100.0	1.0	1.9	2.4	.7	7.1	14.4	45.6	4.0	22.9
PRIVATE TRUCK.........	-	100.0	-	3.6	-	-	6.2	-	7.8	-	82.3
AIR....................	3	100.0	6.5	25.0	23.3	3.8	12.5	.6	10.3	5.3	12.5
WATER.................	-	100.0	-	-	-	-	-	-	-	-	100.0
OTHER.................	1	100.0	4.8	9.8	2.2	.4	21.5	-	.1	.8	60.4
UNKNOWN...............	-	100.0	.4	-	88.7	9.1	-	-	-	-	1.9

See footnotes at end of table 4.

TABLE 2. **TCC GROUP 366**—Percent Distribution of Geographic Division of Origin and Means of Transport, by Geographic Division of Destination: 1972—Continued

Geographic division of origin[1] and means of transport	Number	Percent distribution by division of destination								
		U.S. total	New England	Middle Atlantic	East North Central	West North Central	South Atlantic	East South Central	West South Central	Mountain	Pacific
TON-MILES OF SHIPMENTS	(millions of ton-miles)										
U.S. TOTAL...............	363	100.0	4.1	17.1	15.3	5.1	17.3	3.8	15.2	4.1	18.0
RAIL...................	36	100.0	1.1	16.8	13.6	5.6	29.0	.2	16.0	9.5	8.4
MOTOR CARRIER..........	270	100.0	4.6	18.2	15.3	4.7	16.5	4.1	15.8	3.3	17.6
PRIVATE TRUCK..........	13	100.0	.3	3.0	42.0	1.5	7.6	17.5	25.8	.3	2.0
AIR....................	29	100.0	4.2	17.6	8.9	7.3	17.6	.7	7.1	7.2	29.3
WATER..................	4	100.0	-	-	-	-	-	-	3.3	-	96.7
OTHER..................	8	100.0	9.1	11.3	14.3	17.9	16.7	4.2	9.7	3.4	13.4
UNKNOWN................	-	100.0	-	.3	16.3	.2	8.9	-	.8	-	73.5
NEW ENGLAND.............	8	100.0	4.3	13.2	8.8	10.8	11.2	10.9	19.6	7.7	13.6
RAIL...................	-	100.0	-	-	-	-	-	-	-	-	-
MOTOR CARRIER..........	6	100.0	4.7	14.9	8.5	10.6	11.0	12.6	21.4	2.3	13.9
PRIVATE TRUCK..........	-	100.0	82.6	5.1	-	-	4.4	-	-	-	8.0
AIR....................	-	100.0	-	1.4	4.1	7.5	6.7	-	11.2	52.5	16.3
WATER..................	-	100.0	-	-	-	-	-	-	-	-	-
OTHER..................	-	100.0	2.2	10.6	24.1	21.8	23.6	6.9	8.7	-	2.2
UNKNOWN................	-	100.0	-	-	-	-	-	-	100.0	-	-
EAST NORTH CENTRAL......	124	100.0	1.8	15.9	7.4	5.2	17.5	2.7	18.7	5.1	25.6
RAIL...................	26	100.0	1.4	21.5	.3	.2	37.1	-	20.7	13.1	5.7
MOTOR CARRIER..........	72	100.0	1.8	15.6	5.2	7.9	13.5	1.4	20.3	3.4	30.8
PRIVATE TRUCK..........	9	100.0	-	2.7	51.2	2.0	-	23.5	20.1	.4	-
AIR....................	10	100.0	3.8	20.9	1.2	1.0	18.6	.2	7.6	2.0	44.8
WATER..................	3	100.0	-	-	-	-	-	-	-	-	100.0
OTHER..................	1	100.0	9.8	13.8	15.1	22.9	6.9	.9	15.1	3.8	11.8
UNKNOWN................	-	100.0	-	-	.9	-	-	-	-	-	99.1
SOUTH ATLANTIC..........	31	100.0	4.9	14.8	9.9	4.4	13.0	1.8	8.9	5.7	36.7
RAIL...................	-	100.0	-	3.5	-	-	96.5	-	-	-	-
MOTOR CARRIER..........	25	100.0	4.4	16.1	9.6	2.6	14.9	.9	7.5	5.2	38.9
PRIVATE TRUCK..........	-	100.0	1.1	-	.6	-	2.1	.1	70.4	-	25.6
AIR....................	1	100.0	7.9	15.8	9.0	4.8	1.6	3.3	3.0	17.9	36.7
WATER..................	-	100.0	-	-	-	-	-	-	-	-	100.0
OTHER..................	3	100.0	8.4	9.3	15.2	19.1	8.0	8.1	14.1	6.0	11.8
UNKNOWN................	-	100.0	-	.4	-	-	-	-	.4	-	99.2
EAST SOUTH CENTRAL......	15	100.0	1.3	5.3	14.3	6.0	15.9	.5	4.4	13.6	38.9
RAIL...................	1	100.0	-	-	-	-	-	-	-	-	100.0
MOTOR CARRIER..........	12	100.0	1.4	6.0	15.0	6.9	18.4	.6	3.6	15.9	32.3
PRIVATE TRUCK..........	-	100.0	-	-	56.4	-	-	.1	43.5	-	-
AIR....................	-	100.0	1.2	6.1	7.9	1.1	6.4	-	.6	2.0	74.7
WATER..................	-	100.0	-	-	-	-	-	-	100.0	-	-
OTHER..................	-	100.0	2.1	3.5	80.9	3.8	5.0	.2	2.7	-	1.8
UNKNOWN................	-	100.0	-	-	-	-	-	-	-	-	-
PACIFIC.................	47	100.0	3.2	8.5	6.3	1.1	14.7	15.7	43.6	2.2	4.8
RAIL...................	-	100.0	1.5	29.2	15.5	-	28.0	1.9	3.4	-	20.4
MOTOR CARRIER..........	38	100.0	2.0	3.7	3.5	.8	13.3	19.3	52.5	2.4	2.5
PRIVATE TRUCK..........	-	100.0	-	17.1	-	-	33.1	-	22.2	-	27.6
AIR....................	6	100.0	9.4	34.1	23.4	3.3	16.4	.6	7.3	2.0	3.6
WATER..................	-	100.0	-	-	-	-	-	-	-	-	100.0
OTHER..................	1	100.0	11.3	22.6	3.6	.6	54.3	-	.1	.3	7.1
UNKNOWN................	-	100.0	.6	-	92.2	7.2	-	-	-	-	.1

See footnotes at end of table 4.

TABLE 3. TCC GROUP 366—Percent Distribution of Geographic Division of Destination and Means of Transport, by Geographic Division of Origin: 1972

Geographic division of destination and means of transport	Number	Percent distribution by division of origin[1]									
		U.S. total	New England	Middle Atlantic	East North Central	West North Central	South Atlantic	East South Central	West South Central	Mountain	Pacific
TONS OF SHIPMENTS	(thousands of tons)										
U.S. TOTAL	547	100.0	3.1	(D)	34.0	(D)	9.0	3.4	(D)	(D)	6.7
RAIL	47	100.0	-	(D)	67.1	(D)	-	1.7	(D)	(D)	.4
MOTOR CARRIER	415	100.0	3.7	(D)	24.9	(D)	10.2	4.0	(D)	(D)	7.3
PRIVATE TRUCK	41	100.0	1.7	(D)	83.8	(D)	1.5	1.0	(D)	(D)	2.3
AIR	26	100.0	2.4	(D)	41.0	(D)	4.7	.8	(D)	(D)	14.0
WATER	1	100.0	-	(D)	51.6	(D)	-	25.4	(D)	(D)	23.0
OTHER	13	100.0	5.0	(D)	28.0	(D)	34.6	2.4	(D)	(D)	7.4
UNKNOWN	-	100.0	.4	(D)	.5	(D)	32.6	-	(D)	(D)	2.4
NEW ENGLAND	22	100.0	28.2	(D)	13.8	(D)	20.2	.8	(D)	(D)	2.6
RAIL	-	100.0	-	(D)	99.6	(D)	-	-	(D)	(D)	.4
MOTOR CARRIER	19	100.0	29.5	(D)	10.3	(D)	20.8	1.0	(D)	(D)	1.6
PRIVATE TRUCK	-	100.0	96.4	(D)	-	(D)	2.6	-	(D)	(D)	-
AIR	1	100.0	-	(D)	50.4	(D)	16.0	.3	(D)	(D)	23.8
WATER	-	100.0	-	(D)	-	(D)	-	-	(D)	(D)	-
OTHER	1	100.0	9.3	(D)	12.9	(D)	29.6	.2	(D)	(D)	3.1
UNKNOWN	-	100.0	-	(D)	-	(D)	-	-	(D)	(D)	100.0
MIDDLE ATLANTIC	134	100.0	3.7	(D)	24.7	(D)	13.7	1.1	(D)	(D)	1.2
RAIL	9	100.0	-	(D)	95.6	(D)	-	-	(D)	(D)	.4
MOTOR CARRIER	115	100.0	4.1	(D)	17.3	(D)	14.9	1.3	(D)	(D)	.5
PRIVATE TRUCK	1	100.0	3.0	(D)	24.5	(D)	.1	-	(D)	(D)	2.4
AIR	5	100.0	1.0	(D)	62.2	(D)	5.1	.3	(D)	(D)	16.1
WATER	-	100.0	-	(D)	-	(D)	-	-	(D)	(D)	-
OTHER	2	100.0	7.6	(D)	22.3	(D)	36.9	.5	(D)	(D)	4.7
UNKNOWN	-	100.0	-	(D)	-	(D)	100.0	-	(D)	(D)	-
EAST NORTH CENTRAL	141	100.0	.7	(D)	33.5	(D)	4.3	3.0	(D)	(D)	1.2
RAIL	11	100.0	-	(D)	2.7	(D)	-	-	(D)	(D)	.2
MOTOR CARRIER	99	100.0	.8	(D)	21.3	(D)	5.1	3.8	(D)	(D)	.7
PRIVATE TRUCK	25	100.0	-	(D)	95.8	(D)	-	.8	(D)	(D)	-
AIR	2	100.0	1.6	(D)	16.5	(D)	6.4	1.4	(D)	(D)	29.3
WATER	-	100.0	-	(D)	-	(D)	-	-	(D)	(D)	-
OTHER	3	100.0	4.6	(D)	47.9	(D)	26.5	8.8	(D)	(D)	.7
UNKNOWN	-	100.0	-	(D)	.1	(D)	-	-	(D)	(D)	6.1
WEST NORTH CENTRAL	27	100.0	2.4	(D)	46.5	(D)	5.5	7.2	(D)	(D)	1.3
RAIL	1	100.0	-	(D)	6.1	(D)	-	-	(D)	(D)	-
MOTOR CARRIER	19	100.0	2.6	(D)	54.2	(D)	4.0	9.7	(D)	(D)	1.1
PRIVATE TRUCK	-	100.0	-	(D)	100.0	(D)	-	-	(D)	(D)	-
AIR	2	100.0	2.1	(D)	9.0	(D)	2.8	.2	(D)	(D)	5.2
WATER	-	100.0	-	(D)	-	(D)	-	-	(D)	(D)	-
OTHER	2	100.0	3.5	(D)	47.9	(D)	28.4	.6	(D)	(D)	.2
UNKNOWN	-	100.0	-	(D)	-	(D)	-	-	(D)	(D)	99.7
SOUTH ATLANTIC	87	100.0	1.7	(D)	31.8	(D)	10.6	5.2	(D)	(D)	3.3
RAIL	11	100.0	-	(D)	93.1	(D)	.1	-	(D)	(D)	.3
MOTOR CARRIER	66	100.0	2.0	(D)	21.6	(D)	12.3	6.6	(D)	(D)	3.2
PRIVATE TRUCK	1	100.0	.1	(D)	-	(D)	8.3	-	(D)	(D)	4.0
AIR	5	100.0	1.3	(D)	47.2	(D)	.7	.6	(D)	(D)	8.5
WATER	-	100.0	-	(D)	-	(D)	-	-	(D)	(D)	-
OTHER	1	100.0	6.1	(D)	10.6	(D)	40.3	1.6	(D)	(D)	11.5
UNKNOWN	-	100.0	-	(D)	-	(D)	.1	-	(D)	(D)	-
EAST SOUTH CENTRAL	18	100.0	4.1	(D)	50.3	(D)	5.5	3.9	(D)	(D)	23.7
RAIL	-	100.0	-	(D)	-	(D)	-	-	(D)	(D)	1.5
MOTOR CARRIER	10	100.0	6.7	(D)	25.6	(D)	3.8	6.6	(D)	(D)	40.0
PRIVATE TRUCK	6	100.0	-	(D)	99.4	(D)	-	-	(D)	(D)	-
AIR	-	100.0	.1	(D)	16.2	(D)	28.4	.1	(D)	(D)	9.3
WATER	-	100.0	-	(D)	-	(D)	-	-	(D)	(D)	-
OTHER	-	100.0	4.3	(D)	5.7	(D)	80.3	.3	(D)	(D)	-
UNKNOWN	-	100.0	-	(D)	-	(D)	-	-	(D)	(D)	-
WEST SOUTH CENTRAL	60	100.0	1.7	(D)	51.2	(D)	4.3	2.4	(D)	(D)	23.4
RAIL	7	100.0	-	(D)	91.8	(D)	-	-	(D)	(D)	.1
MOTOR CARRIER	44	100.0	2.1	(D)	42.9	(D)	3.7	2.0	(D)	(D)	31.0
PRIVATE TRUCK	4	100.0	-	(D)	69.9	(D)	8.2	4.4	(D)	(D)	1.6
AIR	2	100.0	3.2	(D)	47.3	(D)	1.9	.1	(D)	(D)	17.7
WATER	-	100.0	-	(D)	-	(D)	-	100.0	(D)	(D)	-
OTHER	1	100.0	2.5	(D)	32.2	(D)	48.5	.6	(D)	(D)	.1
UNKNOWN	-	100.0	54.9	(D)	-	(D)	45.1	-	(D)	(D)	-
MOUNTAIN	13	100.0	2.6	(D)	44.1	(D)	8.6	9.7	(D)	(D)	10.5
RAIL	3	100.0	-	(D)	100.0	(D)	-	-	(D)	(D)	-
MOTOR CARRIER	8	100.0	1.0	(D)	24.5	(D)	10.6	16.1	(D)	(D)	15.0
PRIVATE TRUCK	-	100.0	-	(D)	86.4	(D)	-	-	(D)	(D)	-
AIR	1	100.0	19.2	(D)	11.7	(D)	10.5	.3	(D)	(D)	13.8
WATER	-	100.0	-	(D)	-	(D)	-	-	(D)	(D)	-
OTHER	-	100.0	-	(D)	20.8	(D)	62.6	-	(D)	(D)	3.5
UNKNOWN	-	100.0	-	(D)	-	(D)	100.0	-	(D)	(D)	-
PACIFIC	41	100.0	1.1	(D)	37.7	(D)	11.7	6.9	(D)	(D)	22.4
RAIL	1	100.0	-	(D)	49.1	(D)	-	45.6	(D)	(D)	4.9
MOTOR CARRIER	31	100.0	1.2	(D)	37.0	(D)	13.1	6.2	(D)	(D)	22.0
PRIVATE TRUCK	-	100.0	.1	(D)	-	(D)	6.6	-	(D)	(D)	93.3
AIR	4	100.0	1.2	(D)	47.0	(D)	4.9	1.9	(D)	(D)	10.0
WATER	1	100.0	-	(D)	69.1	(D)	-	-	(D)	(D)	30.9
OTHER	1	100.0	.3	(D)	10.0	(D)	15.6	.1	(D)	(D)	54.8
UNKNOWN	-	100.0	-	(D)	1.4	(D)	93.6	-	(D)	(D)	.1

See footnotes at end of table 4.

TABLE 3. **TCC GROUP 366**—Percent Distribution of Geographic Division of Destination and Means of Transport, by Geographic Division of Origin: 1972—Continued

Geographic division of destination and means of transport	Number	Percent distribution by division of origin [1]									
		U.S. total	New England	Middle Atlantic	East North Central	West North Central	South Atlantic	East South Central	West South Central	Mountain	Pacific
TON-MILES OF SHIPMENTS	(millions of ton-miles)										
U.S. TOTAL................	363	100.0	2.3	(D)	34.1	(D)	8.8	4.1	(D)	(D)	13.0
RAIL.................	36	100.0	-	(D)	72.3	(D)	-	4.0	(D)	(D)	.9
MOTOR CARRIER........	270	100.0	2.6	(D)	26.8	(D)	9.5	4.7	(D)	(D)	14.1
PRIVATE TRUCK........	13	100.0	.2	(D)	73.8	(D)	3.9	1.1	(D)	(D)	3.6
AIR..................	29	100.0	3.1	(D)	35.6	(D)	5.2	.9	(D)	(D)	22.1
WATER................	4	100.0	-	(D)	76.1	(D)	-	3.3	(D)	(D)	20.5
OTHER................	8	100.0	4.7	(D)	19.6	(D)	39.3	1.8	(D)	(D)	12.1
UNKNOWN..............	-	100.0	.5	(D)	.7	(D)	71.3	-	(D)	(D)	3.4
NEW ENGLAND............	14	100.0	2.4	(D)	15.3	(D)	10.5	1.3	(D)	(D)	10.1
RAIL.................	-	100.0	-	(D)	98.7	(D)	-	-	(D)	(D)	1.3
MOTOR CARRIER........	12	100.0	2.6	(D)	10.7	(D)	9.2	1.5	(D)	(D)	6.2
PRIVATE TRUCK........	-	100.0	77.5	(D)	-	(D)	17.2	-	(D)	(D)	-
AIR..................	1	100.0	-	(D)	31.9	(D)	9.7	.3	(D)	(D)	48.9
WATER................	-	100.0	-	(D)	-	(D)	-	-	(D)	(D)	-
OTHER................	-	100.0	1.1	(D)	20.9	(D)	36.2	.4	(D)	(D)	15.1
UNKNOWN..............	-	100.0	-	(D)	-	(D)	-	-	(D)	(D)	100.0
MIDDLE ATLANTIC.........	62	100.0	1.8	(D)	31.8	(D)	7.6	1.3	(D)	(D)	6.5
RAIL.................	6	100.0	-	(D)	92.5	(D)	-	-	(D)	(D)	1.5
MOTOR CARRIER........	49	100.0	2.1	(D)	23.0	(D)	8.4	1.6	(D)	(D)	2.8
PRIVATE TRUCK........	-	100.0	.4	(D)	66.3	(D)	.1	-	(D)	(D)	20.3
AIR..................	5	100.0	.3	(D)	42.2	(D)	4.6	.3	(D)	(D)	42.7
WATER................	-	100.0	-	(D)	-	(D)	-	-	(D)	(D)	-
OTHER................	1	100.0	4.4	(D)	23.8	(D)	32.1	.5	(D)	(D)	24.3
UNKNOWN..............	-	100.0	-	(D)	-	(D)	100.0	-	(D)	(D)	-
EAST NORTH CENTRAL.....	55	100.0	1.3	(D)	16.4	(D)	5.6	3.8	(D)	(D)	5.3
RAIL.................	5	100.0	-	(D)	1.4	(D)	-	-	(D)	(D)	1.0
MOTOR CARRIER........	41	100.0	1.4	(D)	9.1	(D)	6.0	4.6	(D)	(D)	3.3
PRIVATE TRUCK........	5	100.0	-	(D)	90.0	(D)	.1	1.4	(D)	(D)	-
AIR..................	2	100.0	1.4	(D)	4.6	(D)	5.2	.8	(D)	(D)	57.9
WATER................	-	100.0	-	(D)	-	(b)	-	-	(D)	(D)	-
OTHER................	1	100.0	7.8	(D)	20.6	(D)	41.6	10.1	(D)	(D)	3.0
UNKNOWN..............	-	100.0	-	(D)	-	(D)	-	-	(D)	(D)	19.3
WEST NORTH CENTRAL.....	18	100.0	4.8	(D)	34.8	(D)	7.5	4.8	(D)	(D)	2.8
RAIL.................	2	100.0	-	(D)	2.3	(D)	-	-	(D)	(D)	-
MOTOR CARRIER........	12	100.0	5.8	(D)	45.4	(D)	5.2	7.0	(D)	(D)	2.4
PRIVATE TRUCK........	-	100.0	-	(D)	100.0	(D)	-	-	(D)	(D)	-
AIR..................	2	100.0	3.2	(D)	4.8	(D)	3.4	.1	(D)	(D)	9.9
WATER................	-	100.0	-	(D)	-	(D)	-	-	(D)	(D)	-
OTHER................	1	100.0	5.7	(D)	25.1	(D)	42.1	.4	(D)	(D)	.4
UNKNOWN..............	-	100.0	-	(D)	-	(D)	-	-	(D)	(D)	99.7
SOUTH ATLANTIC.........	63	100.0	1.5	(D)	34.5	(D)	6.6	3.8	(D)	(D)	11.0
RAIL.................	10	100.0	-	(D)	92.5	(D)	.1	-	(D)	(D)	.8
MOTOR CARRIER........	44	100.0	1.7	(D)	21.9	(D)	8.6	5.3	(D)	(D)	11.3
PRIVATE TRUCK........	-	100.0	.1	(D)	-	(D)	1.1	-	(D)	(D)	15.5
AIR..................	5	100.0	1.2	(D)	37.6	(D)	.5	.3	(D)	(D)	20.7
WATER................	-	100.0	-	(D)	-	(D)	-	-	(D)	(D)	-
OTHER................	1	100.0	6.6	(D)	8.1	(D)	18.9	.5	(D)	(D)	39.5
UNKNOWN..............	-	100.0	-	(D)	-	(D)	.1	-	(D)	(D)	-
EAST SOUTH CENTRAL.....	13	100.0	6.5	(D)	23.9	(D)	4.1	.5	(D)	(D)	53.1
RAIL.................	-	100.0	-	(D)	-	(D)	-	-	(D)	(D)	9.8
MOTOR CARRIER........	11	100.0	7.9	(D)	9.5	(D)	2.1	.7	(D)	(D)	66.7
PRIVATE TRUCK........	2	100.0	-	(D)	99.0	(D)	-	-	(D)	(D)	-
AIR..................	-	100.0	.1	(D)	9.2	(D)	25.7	-	(D)	(D)	19.3
WATER................	-	100.0	-	(D)	-	(D)	-	-	(D)	(D)	-
OTHER................	-	100.0	7.7	(D)	4.2	(D)	76.8	.1	(D)	(D)	.1
UNKNOWN..............	-	100.0	-	(D)	-	(D)	-	-	(D)	(D)	-
WEST SOUTH CENTRAL.....	55	100.0	3.0	(D)	42.1	(D)	5.1	1.2	(D)	(D)	37.4
RAIL.................	5	100.0	-	(D)	93.6	(D)	-	-	(D)	(D)	.2
MOTOR CARRIER........	42	100.0	3.5	(D)	34.3	(D)	4.5	1.1	(D)	(D)	46.8
PRIVATE TRUCK........	3	100.0	-	(D)	57.7	(D)	10.6	1.8	(D)	(D)	3.1
AIR..................	2	100.0	4.9	(D)	38.0	(D)	2.2	.1	(D)	(D)	22.8
WATER................	-	100.0	-	(D)	-	(D)	-	100.0	(D)	(D)	-
OTHER................	-	100.0	4.2	(D)	30.4	(D)	56.9	.5	(D)	(D)	.1
UNKNOWN..............	-	100.0	64.3	(D)	-	(D)	35.7	-	(D)	(D)	-
MOUNTAIN...............	14	100.0	4.3	(D)	42.1	(D)	12.1	13.7	(D)	(D)	7.0
RAIL.................	3	100.0	-	(D)	100.0	(D)	-	-	(D)	(D)	-
MOTOR CARRIER........	8	100.0	1.8	(D)	27.5	(D)	14.8	22.7	(D)	(D)	10.3
PRIVATE TRUCK........	-	100.0	-	(D)	99.9	(D)	-	-	(D)	(D)	-
AIR..................	2	100.0	22.6	(D)	9.7	(D)	12.8	.3	(D)	(D)	6.0
WATER................	-	100.0	-	(D)	-	(D)	-	-	(D)	(D)	-
OTHER................	-	100.0	-	(D)	21.9	(D)	69.6	-	(D)	(D)	1.2
UNKNOWN..............	-	100.0	-	(D)	-	(D)	100.0	-	(D)	(D)	-
PACIFIC................	65	100.0	1.7	(D)	48.6	(D)	17.9	8.9	(D)	(D)	3.5
RAIL.................	3	100.0	-	(D)	49.2	(D)	-	48.2	(D)	(D)	2.1
MOTOR CARRIER........	47	100.0	2.0	(D)	46.8	(D)	21.0	8.7	(D)	(D)	2.0
PRIVATE TRUCK........	-	100.0	.9	(D)	-	(D)	49.8	-	(D)	(D)	49.3
AIR..................	8	100.0	1.7	(D)	54.4	(D)	6.5	2.4	(D)	(D)	2.7
WATER................	3	100.0	-	(D)	78.8	(D)	-	-	(D)	(D)	21.2
OTHER................	1	100.0	.8	(D)	17.2	(D)	34.4	.2	(D)	(D)	6.4
UNKNOWN..............	-	100.0	-	(D)	1.0	(D)	96.2	-	(D)	(D)	-

See footnotes at end of table 4.

TABLE 4. TCC GROUP 366—Percent Distribution of Distance Shipped and Weight of Shipment, by Means of Transport: 1972

Distance shipped and weight of shipment [2] [3]	Number	All means of transport	Rail	Motor carrier	Private truck	Air	Water	Other	Unknown
TONS OF SHIPMENTS	(thousands of tons)								
U.S. TOTAL..........	397	100.0	9.3	70.8	10.3	5.8	.4	3.3	.2
UNDER 100 MILES.........	31	100.0	-	75.7	17.8	.8	-	5.7	-
UNDER 1000 POUNDS.....	7	100.0	.1	71.1	4.5	.8	-	23.4	-
1000 TO 9999 POUNDS...	15	100.0	-	65.1	33.5	1.2	-	.2	-
10000 TO 29999 POUNDS.	3	100.0	-	100.0	-	-	-	-	-
30000 TO 59999 POUNDS.	5	100.0	-	100.0	-	-	-	-	-
60000 TO 89999 POUNDS.	-	100.0	-	-	-	-	-	-	-
90000 POUNDS AND OVER.	-	100.0	-	-	-	-	-	-	-
100 TO 199 MILES........	20	100.0	.1	92.4	2.6	1.0	-	3.9	-
UNDER 1000 POUNDS....	4	100.0	.5	69.7	6.3	5.0	-	18.5	-
1000 TO 9999 POUNDS...	7	100.0	-	96.7	3.3	-	-	-	-
10000 TO 29999 POUNDS.	8	100.0	-	100.0	-	-	-	-	-
30000 TO 59999 POUNDS.	-	100.0	-	100.0	-	-	-	-	-
60000 TO 89999 POUNDS.	-	100.0	-	-	-	-	-	-	-
90000 POUNDS AND OVER.	-	100.0	-	-	-	-	-	-	-
200 TO 299 MILES........	57	100.0	1.3	59.1	35.4	1.4	-	2.4	.3
UNDER 1000 POUNDS.....	6	100.0	4.8	58.8	4.6	12.1	-	19.7	-
1000 TO 9999 POUNDS...	29	100.0	-	40.2	59.2	-	-	-	.6
10000 TO 29999 POUNDS.	15	100.0	3.1	79.0	17.2	-	-	.8	-
30000 TO 59999 POUNDS.	6	100.0	-	100.0	-	-	-	-	-
60000 TO 89999 POUNDS.	-	100.0	-	-	-	-	-	-	-
90000 POUNDS AND OVER.	-	100.0	-	-	-	-	-	-	-
300 TO 499 MILES........	45	100.0	.3	72.4	17.0	2.9	.8	6.2	.4
UNDER 1000 POUNDS.....	11	100.0	.3	64.7	1.2	11.2	-	22.6	-
1000 TO 9999 POUNDS...	19	100.0	.6	90.9	6.2	.1	.6	.8	.9
10000 TO 29999 POUNDS.	11	100.0	-	56.1	41.8	-	2.1	-	-
30000 TO 59999 POUNDS.	2	100.0	-	38.9	61.1	-	-	-	-
60000 TO 89999 POUNDS.	-	100.0	-	-	-	-	-	-	-
90000 POUNDS AND OVER.	-	100.0	-	-	-	-	-	-	-
500 TO 999 MILES........	136	100.0	19.1	66.9	3.7	7.7	-	2.5	-
UNDER 1000 POUNDS.....	26	100.0	3.3	67.0	1.3	17.0	-	11.4	.1
1000 TO 9999 POUNDS...	40	100.0	6.0	73.7	6.2	12.8	-	1.2	.1
10000 TO 29999 POUNDS.	31	100.0	24.9	66.4	5.7	3.0	-	-	-
30000 TO 59999 POUNDS.	38	100.0	38.9	60.1	1.0	-	-	-	-
60000 TO 89999 POUNDS.	-	100.0	-	-	-	-	-	-	-
90000 POUNDS AND OVER.	-	100.0	-	-	-	-	-	-	-
1000 TO 1499 MILES......	58	100.0	13.9	76.0	2.3	4.8	-	3.0	.1
UNDER 1000 POUNDS.....	7	100.0	2.0	52.7	.3	28.2	-	16.5	.3
1000 TO 9999 POUNDS...	9	100.0	23.3	64.2	2.9	7.3	-	2.0	.3
10000 TO 29999 POUNDS.	10	100.0	2.5	84.8	10.1	-	-	2.7	-
30000 TO 59999 POUNDS.	19	100.0	-	100.0	-	-	-	-	-
60000 TO 89999 POUNDS.	11	100.0	49.1	50.9	-	-	-	-	-
90000 POUNDS AND OVER.	-	100.0	-	100.0	-	-	-	-	-
1500 MILES OR OVER......	46	100.0	3.9	75.7	.4	15.2	2.3	2.0	.5
UNDER 1000 POUNDS.....	13	100.0	1.0	52.5	.8	39.4	.2	5.9	.1
1000 TO 9999 POUNDS...	14	100.0	6.7	76.5	.6	8.6	6.0	-	1.6
10000 TO 29999 POUNDS.	7	100.0	1.5	94.5	-	-	2.2	1.9	-
30000 TO 59999 POUNDS.	5	100.0	10.7	79.6	-	9.7	-	-	-
60000 TO 89999 POUNDS.	5	100.0	-	100.0	'-	-	-	-	-
90000 POUNDS AND OVER.	-	100.0	-	-	-	-	-	-	-
TON-MILES OF SHIPMENTS	(millions of ton-miles)								
U.S. TOTAL...........	303	100.0	10.6	72.0	4.3	8.8	1.3	2.7	.3
UNDER 100 MILES.........	1	100.0	-	75.6	16.7	1.4	-	6.2	-
UNDER 1000 POUNDS.....	-	100.0	.1	69.7	3.5	1.1	-	25.6	-
1000 TO 9999 POUNDS...	-	100.0	-	66.7	31.1	2.2	-	-	-
10000 TO 29999 POUNDS.	-	100.0	-	100.0	-	-	-	-	-
30000 TO 59999 POUNDS.	-	100.0	-	100.0	-	-	-	-	-
60000 TO 89999 POUNDS.	-	100.0	-	-	-	-	-	-	-
90000 POUNDS AND OVER.	-	100.0	-	-	-	-	-	-	-
100 TO 199 MILES........	3	100.0	.1	92.7	2.7	1.1	-	3.5	-
UNDER 1000 POUNDS.....	-	100.0	.4	70.5	6.9	5.2	-	17.0	-
1000 TO 9999 POUNDS...	1	100.0	-	96.7	3.3	-	-	-	-
10000 TO 29999 POUNDS.	1	100.0	-	100.0	-	-	-	-	-
30000 TO 59999 POUNDS.	-	100.0	-	100.0	-	-	-	-	-
60000 TO 89999 POUNDS.	-	100.0	-	-	-	-	-	-	-
90000 POUNDS AND OVER.	-	100.0	-	-	-	-	-	-	-

See footnotes at end of table 4.

TABLE 4. **TCC GROUP 366—Percent Distribution of Distance Shipped and Weight of Shipment, by Means of Transport: 1972**—Continued

Distance shipped and weight of shipment [2] [3]	Number	Percent distribution by means of transport							
		All means of transport	Rail	Motor carrier	Private truck	Air	Water	Other	Unknown
TON-MILES OF SHIPMENTS	(millions of ton-miles)								
200 TO 299 MILES........	13	100.0	1.4	59.3	35.1	1.4	-	2.4	.3
UNDER 1000 POUNDS.....	1	100.0	4.6	60.9	4.3	11.8	-	18.5	-
1000 TO 9999 POUNDS...	7	100.0	-	41.5	57.9	-	-	-	.6
10000 TO 29999 POUNDS.	3	100.0	3.5	78.0	17.6	-	-	.8	-
30000 TO 59999 POUNDS.	1	100.0	-	100.0	-	-	-	-	-
60000 TO 89999 POUNDS.	-	100.0	-	-	-	-	-	-	-
90000 POUNDS AND OVER.	-	100.0	-	-	-	-	-	-	-
300 TO 499 MILES........	18	100.0	.3	74.5	15.2	2.9	.7	6.0	.4
UNDER 1000 POUNDS.....	4	100.0	.3	64.5	1.4	11.2	-	22.5	-
1000 TO 9999 POUNDS...	8	100.0	.6	91.5	5.8	.1	.5	.6	.9
10000 TO 29999 POUNDS.	4	100.0	-	59.1	38.8	-	2.1	-	-
30000 TO 59999 POUNDS.	1	100.0	-	46.8	53.2	-	-	-	-
60000 TO 89999 POUNDS.	-	100.0	-	-	-	-	-	-	-
90000 POUNDS AND OVER.	-	100.0	-	-	-	-	-	-	-
500 TO 999 MILES........	98	100.0	19.4	66.9	3.2	7.9	-	2.6	-
UNDER 1000 POUNDS.....	18	100.0	3.3	65.7	1.2	17.8	-	11.9	.1
1000 TO 9999 POUNDS...	28	100.0	7.0	74.3	5.4	12.3	-	.9	.1
10000 TO 29999 POUNDS.	23	100.0	23.8	68.0	4.3	3.8	-	-	-
30000 TO 59999 POUNDS.	27	100.0	39.2	59.5	1.3	-	-	-	-
60000 TO 89999 POUNDS.	-	100.0	-	-	-	-	-	-	-
90000 POUNDS AND OVER.	-	100.0	-	-	-	-	-	-	-
1000 TO 1499 MILES......	75	100.0	12.6	78.1	2.0	4.5	-	2.7	.1
UNDER 1000 POUNDS.....	9	100.0	1.9	53.7	.3	27.8	-	16.0	.3
1000 TO 9999 POUNDS...	10	100.0	22.3	65.5	2.8	7.4	-	1.8	.2
10000 TO 29999 POUNDS.	13	100.0	2.2	86.7	8.8	-	-	2.3	-
30000 TO 59999 POUNDS.	26	100.0	-	100.0	-	-	-	-	-
60000 TO 89999 POUNDS.	14	100.0	45.0	55.0	-	-	-	-	-
90000 POUNDS AND OVER.	-	100.0	-	100.0	-	-	-	-	-
1500 MILES OR OVER......	92	100.0	3.5	73.0	.5	15.9	4.2	2.3	.6
UNDER 1000 POUNDS.....	27	100.0	1.0	51.1	.9	40.0	.4	6.5	.1
1000 TO 9999 POUNDS...	30	100.0	5.5	72.5	.6	8.6	11.0	-	1.9
10000 TO 29999 POUNDS.	14	100.0	1.6	93.0	-	-	3.1	2.3	-
30000 TO 59999 POUNDS.	9	100.0	11.1	79.0	-	9.9	-	-	-
60000 TO 89999 POUNDS.	9	100.0	-	100.0	-	-	-	-	-
90000 POUNDS AND OVER.	-	100.0	-	-	-	-	-	-	-

Note: Detail may not add to total due to rounding. The introductory table shows the estimates of sampling variability for tons; sampling variability for ton-miles has not been estimated. See the map in the Introduction for the States comprising the geographic divisions of the United States.

Shipments excluded from the survey are those moving by pipeline (primarily petroleum products from refineries), parcel post shipments, and commodities moved by own power (motorized vehicles, aircraft, etc.) or towed (prefabricated buildings, etc.). Local shipments (commodities shipped less than 25 miles from the plant) and shipments within the same city are also excluded. Shipments to Alaska and Hawaii from the 48 conterminous States and the District of Columbia are included; however, no data were obtained for shipments originating in Alaska and Hawaii.

- Represents zero or rounds to zero.   (D) Withheld to avoid disclosing figures for individual companies.

[1]Production of this commodity is concentrated in the geographic divisions shown; figures and distributions for geographic divisions not shown are included in the total.

[2]Distances of shipments to foreign destinations are calculated only to the U.S. port of exit.

[3]Includes only shipments represented by bills of lading and invoices. Summary records which did not show individual weights of shipments are not included.

TCC 367. Electronic Components and Accessories

Comparisons of Tons and Ton-Miles of Shipments for
Geographic Divisions of Origin and for Sampling Variability: 1972 and 1967

Geographic division of origin	Estimates				Relative sampling variability in tons (percent)	
	1972		1967		1972	1967
	Tons (thousands)	Ton-miles (millions)	Tons (thousands)	Ton-miles (millions)		
U.S. total	710	439	681	407	21.7	10.8
New England	25	14	34	·22	22.1	(*)
Middle Atlantic	159	142	196	111	22.3	(*)
East North Central	322	113	250	125	44.1	(*)
West North Central	(D)	(D)	46	25	(*)	(*)
South Atlantic	33	12	19	14	31.0	(*)
East South Central	(D)	(D)	56	29	(*)	(*)
West South Central	(D)	(D)	2	2	(*)	(*)
Mountain	(D)	(D)	1	1	(*)	(*)
Pacific	34	44	77	78	40.1	(*)

(D) Withheld to avoid disclosing figures for individual companies.   (*) Data not published.

TABLE 1. **TCC GROUP 367**—Percent Distribution of Geographic Division of Origin and Distance Shipped, by Means of Transport: 1972

Geographic division of origin[1] and distance shipped[2]	Number	Percent distribution by means of transport							
		All means of transport	Rail	Motor carrier	Private truck	Air	Water	Other	Unknown
TONS OF SHIPMENTS	(thousands of tons)								
U.S. TOTAL..........	710	100.0	8.3	65.8	10.8	11.4	-	2.7	1.0
NEW ENGLAND.............	25	100.0	.1	73.2	1.5	13.3	-	11.9	-
UNDER 100 MILES.......	5	100.0	-	66.0	3.5	14.8	-	15.8	-
100 TO 199 MILES......	4	100.0	-	85.4	-	5.0	-	9.7	-
200 TO 299 MILES......	4	100.0	-	96.5	-	1.4	-	2.0	-
300 TO 499 MILES......	1	100.0	.1	57.4	10.6	13.9	-	18.0	-
500 TO 999 MILES......	5	100.0	-	66.6	-	13.9	-	19.5	-
1000 TO 1499 MILES....	1	100.0	1.2	70.2	-	13.9	-	14.7	-
1500 MILES OR OVER....	2	100.0	.4	42.3	2.4	48.3	-	6.7	-
MIDDLE ATLANTIC.........	159	100.0	17.6	56.7	17.8	4.3	-	3.3	.2
UNDER 100 MILES.......	25	100.0	.4	40.9	52.2	.4	-	6.2	-
100 TO 199 MILES......	12	100.0	-	71.1	19.3	3.9	-	5.7	-
200 TO 299 MILES......	9	100.0	-	72.6	14.3	4.0	-	5.7	3.5
300 TO 499 MILES......	11	100.0	6.4	39.2	40.4	9.2	-	4.8	-
500 TO 999 MILES......	59	100.0	25.1	58.5	10.9	3.2	-	2.2	-
1000 TO 1499 MILES....	2	100.0	2.7	49.1	-	37.1	-	11.2	-
1500 MILES OR OVER....	38	100.0	32.1	61.6	.6	5.0	-	.7	-
EAST NORTH CENTRAL......	322	100.0	7.2	75.9	9.3	5.8	-	.9	.9
UNDER 100 MILES.......	86	100.0	-	97.3	1.0	.1	-	.7	.9
100 TO 199 MILES......	57	100.0	1.1	75.4	22.3	.6	-	.7	-
200 TO 299 MILES......	65	100.0	.6	91.7	6.7	.4	-	.6	-
300 TO 499 MILES......	30	100.0	10.1	65.5	21.4	2.0	-	.9	-
500 TO 999 MILES......	51	100.0	16.9	38.5	10.1	32.4	-	1.7	.3
1000 TO 1499 MILES....	23	100.0	29.4	61.2	-	.4	-	.4	8.6
1500 MILES OR OVER....	7	100.0	50.3	38.6	-	7.6	-	3.5	-
SOUTH ATLANTIC..........	33	100.0	-	76.2	13.3	6.1	-	4.3	.1
UNDER 100 MILES.......	11	100.0	-	67.2	32.3	-	-	.4	-
100 TO 199 MILES......	1	100.0	-	72.0	20.5	1.3	-	6.2	-
200 TO 299 MILES......	-	100.0	-	74.1	.4	16.9	-	8.6	-
300 TO 499 MILES......	3	100.0	-	81.6	10.5	.8	-	7.2	-
500 TO 999 MILES......	15	100.0	-	82.2	-	12.1	-	5.5	.2
1000 TO 1499 MILES....	-	100.0	-	88.4	-	2.9	-	8.1	.6
1500 MILES OR OVER....	-	100.0	-	26.1	-	29.1	-	44.9	-
PACIFIC.................	34	100.0	-	23.2	8.9	61.6	-	2.9	3.4
UNDER 100 MILES.......	6	100.0	-	21.4	37.7	32.2	-	8.7	-
100 TO 199 MILES......	2	100.0	-	44.4	14.7	34.2	-	6.7	-
200 TO 299 MILES......	-	100.0	-	35.2	-	64.3	-	.5	-
300 TO 499 MILES......	4	100.0	-	41.8	7.2	48.9	-	2.1	-
500 TO 999 MILES......	-	100.0	-	42.0	-	57.7	-	.3	-
1000 TO 1499 MILES....	2	100.0	.2	39.9	2.8	57.1	-	-	-
1500 MILES OR OVER....	18	100.0	-	13.2	-	79.3	-	1.1	6.4
TON-MILES OF SHIPMENTS	(millions of ton-miles)								
U.S. TOTAL..........	439	100.0	14.2	54.6	5.5	21.3	-	2.4	1.9
NEW ENGLAND.............	14	100.0	.4	59.6	1.4	27.0	-	11.6	-
UNDER 100 MILES.......	-	100.0	-	71.0	2.9	11.1	-	15.0	-
100 TO 199 MILES......	-	100.0	-	87.4	-	4.6	-	7.9	-
200 TO 299 MILES......	1	100.0	-	96.2	-	1.6	-	2.2	-
300 TO 499 MILES......	-	100.0	.1	58.1	10.4	13.8	-	17.5	-
500 TO 999 MILES......	3	100.0	-	65.0	-	14.9	-	20.1	-
1000 TO 1499 MILES....	2	100.0	1.4	71.3	-	13.4	-	13.8	-
1500 MILES OR OVER....	5	100.0	.4	40.7	2.6	49.4	-	7.0	-
MIDDLE ATLANTIC.........	142	100.0	27.7	60.1	5.0	5.5	-	1.7	.1
UNDER 100 MILES.......	1	100.0	.2	56.1	39.0	.3	-	4.4	-
100 TO 199 MILES......	1	100.0	-	69.6	19.1	4.7	-	6.7	-
200 TO 299 MILES......	2	100.0	-	73.1	14.3	3.7	-	5.2	3.8
300 TO 499 MILES......	4	100.0	7.8	39.7	38.7	9.2	-	4.6	-
500 TO 999 MILES......	37	100.0	24.7	58.9	10.3	3.7	-	2.4	-
1000 TO 1499 MILES....	3	100.0	2.7	47.5	-	39.0	-	10.8	-
1500 MILES OR OVER....	91	100.0	32.4	61.6	.4	4.8	-	.7	-
EAST NORTH CENTRAL......	113	100.0	20.0	59.0	7.1	10.4	-	1.3	2.4
UNDER 100 MILES.......	4	100.0	-	97.0	1.5	.1	-	.4	.9
100 TO 199 MILES......	8	100.0	1.1	74.1	23.5	.6	-	.7	-
200 TO 299 MILES......	15	100.0	.7	92.5	5.9	.4	-	.6	-
300 TO 499 MILES......	11	100.0	12.7	64.7	19.6	1.9	-	.9	-
500 TO 999 MILES......	31	100.0	16.6	38.9	9.1	33.1	-	2.0	.3
1000 TO 1499 MILES....	29	100.0	29.6	61.0	-	.4	-	.3	8.7
1500 MILES OR OVER....	13	100.0	52.2	37.5	-	7.1	-	3.2	-

See footnotes at end of table 4.

TABLE 1. **TCC GROUP 367**—Percent Distribution of Geographic Division of Origin and Distance Shipped, by Means of Transport: 1972—Continued

Geographic division of origin[1] and distance shipped[2]	Number	Percent distribution by means of transport							
		All means of transport	Rail	Motor carrier	Private truck	Air	Water	Other	Unknown
TON-MILES OF SHIPMENTS	(millions of ton-miles)								
SOUTH ATLANTIC	12	100.0	-	77.3	3.1	11.8	-	7.6	.2
UNDER 100 MILES	-	100.0	-	77.0	22.7	-	-	.4	-
100 TO 199 MILES	-	100.0	-	72.7	19.5	1.3	-	6.4	-
200 TO 299 MILES	-	100.0	-	76.2	.4	15.5	-	7.8	-
300 TO 499 MILES	1	100.0	-	80.7	11.5	.7	-	7.1	-
500 TO 999 MILES	8	100.0	-	78.2	-	15.0	-	6.5	.2
1000 TO 1499 MILES	-	100.0	-	89.4	-	3.3	-	6.7	.6
1500 MILES OR OVER	-	100.0	-	23.7	-	28.8	-	47.5	-
PACIFIC	44	100.0	-	17.6	.7	75.2	-	1.2	5.3
UNDER 100 MILES	-	100.0	-	33.0	27.3	23.3	-	16.3	-
100 TO 199 MILES	-	100.0	-	36.3	17.4	38.6	-	7.7	-
200 TO 299 MILES	-	100.0	-	34.5	-	65.0	-	.5	-
300 TO 499 MILES	1	100.0	-	42.8	6.7	48.4	-	2.1	-
500 TO 999 MILES	-	100.0	-	47.6	-	52.1	-	.3	-
1000 TO 1499 MILES	2	100.0	.2	39.3	2.9	57.6	-	-	-
1500 MILES OR OVER	38	100.0	-	14.3	-	78.5	-	1.1	6.0

See footnotes at end of table 4.

TABLE 2. **TCC GROUP 367**—Percent Distribution of Geographic Division of Origin and Means of Transport, by Geographic Division of Destination: 1972

Geographic division of origin[1] and means of transport	Number	Percent distribution by division of destination									
		U.S. total	New England	Middle Atlantic	East North Central	West North Central	South Atlantic	East South Central	West South Central	Mountain	Pacific
TONS OF SHIPMENTS	(thousands of tons)										
U.S. TOTAL	710	100.0	2.6	17.5	44.1	4.4	8.0	3.8	7.5	3.2	9.0
RAIL	58	100.0	-	14.9	21.4	15.3	4.8	2.5	14.3	-	26.8
MOTOR CARRIER	467	100.0	1.5	13.3	56.2	3.2	5.7	3.3	5.9	3.8	7.0
PRIVATE TRUCK	77	100.0	3.1	28.8	28.8	1.2	8.2	12.1	13.0	.4	4.5
AIR	81	100.0	8.4	29.7	12.7	5.9	23.6	.7	3.7	3.9	11.4
WATER	-	100.0									
OTHER	18	100.0	9.8	22.4	19.6	6.8	8.2	1.9	11.5	7.2	12.5
UNKNOWN	7	100.0	5.4	34.3	23.5	4.0	.7	-	29.9	-	2.2
NEW ENGLAND	25	100.0	23.5	37.8	14.5	4.1	7.0	1.9	3.2	1.1	6.9
RAIL	-	100.0	-	4.5	-	-	5.0	-	60.5	19.5	10.5
MOTOR CARRIER	18	100.0	22.1	45.9	13.1	4.0	6.6	.8	3.4	.4	3.6
PRIVATE TRUCK	-	100.0	36.4	14.3	-	-	34.1	-	-	-	15.3
AIR	3	100.0	24.7	10.2	13.1	4.9	8.0	4.1	3.4	5.6	26.2
WATER	-	100.0									
OTHER	3	100.0	28.8	22.1	26.2	4.8	5.1	6.7	1.3	.1	4.7
UNKNOWN	-	100.0	36.8	63.2	-	-	-	-	-	-	-
MIDDLE ATLANTIC	159	100.0	3.4	28.2	22.8	3.1	5.9	10.1	2.8	1.1	22.6
RAIL	28	100.0	-	.3	42.5	-	4.3	3.7	5.6	.1	43.6
MOTOR CARRIER	90	100.0	2.4	25.7	20.4	3.5	7.8	12.2	2.2	1.3	24.5
PRIVATE TRUCK	28	100.0	7.4	65.3	.13.3	-	-	13.2	.7	-	.1
AIR	6	100.0	10.6	5.2	22.1	13.8	9.4	2.2	8.6	7.8	20.3
WATER	-	100.0									
OTHER	5	100.0	7.6	45.6	14.5	15.0	9.0	.9	2.5	.7	4.2
UNKNOWN	-	100.0	-	95.8	.5	-	-	-	-	-	3.6
EAST NORTH CENTRAL	322	100.0	.3	7.0	67.7	1.4	9.2	2.8	9.4	.1	2.2
RAIL	23	100.0	-	37.3	2.7	6.4	7.1	1.8	29.4	-	15.4
MOTOR CARRIER	244	100.0	.2	4.0	80.9	1.0	4.3	1.3	7.2	.1	1.1
PRIVATE TRUCK	29	100.0	-	8.7	56.2	.7	5.5	17.5	11.3	-	-
AIR	18	100.0	1.1	5.6	4.2	1.5	83.0	.9	.5	.6	2.8
WATER	-	100.0									
OTHER	2	100.0	5.1	15.5	47.9	4.3	10.8	2.5	4.1	1.2	8.6
UNKNOWN	2	100.0	-	.5	26.8	-	-	-	72.7	-	-
SOUTH ATLANTIC	33	100.0	4.5	42.8	31.8	2.5	14.7	2.7	.6	.2	.5
RAIL	-	100.0	-	100.0	-	-	-	-	-	-	-
MOTOR CARRIER	25	100.0	.3	53.5	38.7	2.3	2.8	2.1	.3	.1	.1
PRIVATE TRUCK	4	100.0	-	.5	5.7	-	86.1	7.7	-	-	-
AIR	2	100.0	59.8	17.1	4.8	5.8	8.7	-	.3	1.5	2.1
WATER	-	100.0									
OTHER	1	100.0	13.5	21.3	29.7	9.7	11.3	.7	7.4	.3	6.0
UNKNOWN	-	100.0	-	-	-	-	89.5	-	10.5	-	-
PACIFIC	34	100.0	6.3	14.9	19.1	6.3	8.1	.3	3.7	5.5	35.9
RAIL	-	100.0	-	47.9	-	39.1	3.0	-	-	-	10.1
MOTOR CARRIER	7	100.0	.6	13.2	1.8	9.2	14.4	-	1.2	5.3	54.3
PRIVATE TRUCK	3	100.0	-	-	-	-	-	-	1.9	-	98.0
AIR	21	100.0	8.3	18.9	26.1	6.6	7.6	.5	5.2	6.8	19.9
WATER	-	100.0									
OTHER	-	100.0	6.1	5.9	1.4	3.6	2.5	-	.1	.4	80.0
UNKNOWN	1	100.0	25.0	-	75.0	-	-	-	-	-	-

See footnotes at end of table 4.

TABLE 2. **TCC GROUP 367—Percent Distribution of Geographic Division of Origin and Means of Transport, by Geographic Division of Destination: 1972**—Continued

Geographic division of origin[1] and means of transport	Number	Percent distribution by division of destination									
		U.S. total	New England	Middle Atlantic	East North Central	West North Central	South Atlantic	East South Central	West South Central	Mountain	Pacific
TON-MILES OF SHIPMENTS	(millions of ton-miles)										
U.S. TOTAL...............	439	100.0	3.0	16.4	20.7	3.4	8.4	3.1	10.9	7.4	26.6
RAIL....................	62	100.0	-	8.3	11.4	1.9	2.2	1.0	16.2	.1	58.8
MOTOR CARRIER.........	239	100.0	.6	9.6	25.6	3.3	7.6	3.6	10.2	12.0	27.4
PRIVATE TRUCK.........	24	100.0	4.4	15.6	24.5	1.2	5.3	14.3	28.9	1.0	4.9
AIR....................	93	100.0	9.7	37.9	14.2	4.9	15.7	.6	3.0	2.9	11.1
WATER.................	-	100.0	-	-	-	-	-	-	-	-	-
OTHER.................	10	100.0	7.8	13.2	16.3	9.4	10.4	2.5	9.4	5.4	25.8
UNKNOWN...............	8	100.0	10.7	36.5	19.3	.6	.4	-	30.8	-	1.7
NEW ENGLAND..............	14	100.0	2.6	14.0	18.2	8.3	8.7	3.2	8.7	3.8	32.5
RAIL....................	-	100.0	-	1.1	-	-	3.2	-	54.4	24.6	16.7
MOTOR CARRIER.........	8	100.0	3.1	21.2	19.7	9.8	10.5	1.7	11.5	1.7	20.7
PRIVATE TRUCK.........	-	100.0	2.6	1.2	-	-	23.9	-	-	-	72.2
AIR....................	3	100.0	.9	1.9	8.8	4.6	4.9	3.5	4.7	9.8	60.9
WATER.................	-	100.0	-	-	-	-	-	-	-	-	-
OTHER.................	1	100.0	3.5	7.2	35.4	9.9	6.6	10.7	3.4	.4	22.9
UNKNOWN...............	-	100.0	1.5	98.5	-	-	-	-	-	-	-
MIDDLE ATLANTIC.........	142	100.0	1.1	3.5	15.3	2.9	3.4	6.4	3.4	2.3	61.7
RAIL....................	39	100.0	-	-	17.8	-	1.6	1.4	3.7	.1	75.4
MOTOR CARRIER.........	85	100.0	.5	3.6	13.1	3.1	4.2	7.5	2.5	2.5	63.2
PRIVATE TRUCK.........	7	100.0	13.0	21.9	31.8	-	-	27.7	4.8	-	.8
AIR....................	7	100.0	2.4	1.0	11.5	11.9	4.3	1.5	10.0	13.8	43.7
WATER.................	-	100.0	-	-	-	-	-	-	-	-	-
OTHER.................	2	100.0	3.4	9.1	17.9	23.5	11.2	1.6	7.7	2.8	22.8
UNKNOWN...............	-	100.0	-	75.0	1.0	.1	-	-	.1	.1	23.7
EAST NORTH CENTRAL......	113	100.0	.5	11.7	27.5	2.0	14.9	2.5	28.6	.3	11.9
RAIL....................	22	100.0	-	22.9	.4	3.2	3.4	.5	38.3	-	31.2
MOTOR CARRIER.........	66	100.0	.5	8.6	41.9	1.9	8.7	1.9	28.6	.3	7.6
PRIVATE TRUCK.........	8	100.0	-	17.3	34.8	.6	7.0	17.8	22.4	-	.1
AIR....................	11	100.0	1.3	5.5	1.1	.9	81.2	.4	.7	1.1	7.8
WATER.................	-	100.0	-	-	-	-	-	-	-	-	-
OTHER.................	1	100.0	8.1	19.0	12.4	3.4	16.2	1.9	6.4	2.8	29.9
UNKNOWN...............	2	100.0	-	.3	1.4	-	-	-	98.3	-	-
SOUTH ATLANTIC..........	12	100.0	8.5	30.0	40.5	7.5	5.7	2.9	1.6	.6	2.7
RAIL....................	-	100.0	-	100.0	-	-	-	-	-	-	-
MOTOR CARRIER.........	9	100.0	.5	35.3	48.7	7.4	3.1	3.3	.9	.3	.5
PRIVATE TRUCK.........	-	100.0	-	.7	26.0	-	63.9	9.4	-	-	-
AIR....................	1	100.0	60.7	12.1	3.6	6.9	6.8	-	.4	3.3	6.3
WATER.................	-	100.0	-	-	-	-	-	-	-	-	-
OTHER.................	-	100.0	13.3	15.8	20.8	13.3	5.0	.7	10.4	.6	20.1
UNKNOWN...............	-	100.0	-	-	-	-	80.5	-	19.5	-	-
PACIFIC.................	44	100.0	12.7	29.0	26.9	7.2	13.6	.5	3.9	2.2	4.1
RAIL....................	-	100.0	-	63.8	-	31.0	3.5	-	-	-	1.7
MOTOR CARRIER.........	7	100.0	1.6	34.4	3.6	12.6	31.3	-	1.6	4.3	10.5
PRIVATE TRUCK.........	-	100.0	.9	.2	-	-	-	-	28.5	-	70.4
AIR....................	33	100.0	13.8	30.0	30.1	6.4	10.6	.7	4.5	1.8	2.2
WATER.................	-	100.0	-	-	-	-	-	-	-	-	-
OTHER.................	-	100.0	30.0	27.3	5.0	10.5	10.7	-	.2	.4	15.9
UNKNOWN...............	2	100.0	32.1	-	67.9	-	-	-	-	-	-

See footnotes at end of table 4.

TABLE 3. **TCC GROUP 367**—Percent Distribution of Geographic Division of Destination and Means of Transport, by Geographic Division of Origin: 1972

Geographic division of destination and means of transport	Number	Percent distribution by division of origin[1]									
		U.S. total	New England	Middle Atlantic	East. North Central	West North Central	South Atlantic	East South Central	West South Central	Mountain	Pacific
TONS OF SHIPMENTS	(thousands of tons)										
U.S. TOTAL............	710	100.0	3.6	22.4	45.4	(D)	4.7	(D)	(D)	(D)	4.8
RAIL...............	58	100.0	.1	47.5	39.5	(D)	-	(D)	(D)	(D)	-
MOTOR CARRIER.........	467	100.0	4.0	19.4	52.4	(D)	5.4	(D)	(D)	(D)	1.7
PRIVATE TRUCK........	77	100.0	.5	36.9	38.9	(D)	5.7	(D)	(D)	(D)	4.0
AIR.................	81	100.0	4.2	8.5	23.0	(D)	2.5	(D)	(D)	(D)	26.1
WATER...............	-	100.0	-	-	-	(D)	-	(D)	(D)	(D)	-
OTHER...............	18	100.0	16.3	27.9	14.9	(D)	7.6	(D)	(D)	(D)	5.3
UNKNOWN..............	7	100.0	-	5.0	40.9	(D)	.6	(D)	(D)	(D)	16.0
NEW ENGLAND..........	18	100.0	32.6	29.1	4.5	(D)	8.0	(D)	(D)	(D)	11.6
RAIL...............	-	100.0	-	-	-	(D)	-	(D)	(D)	(D)	-
MOTOR CARRIER........	7	100.0	58.7	30.5	6.8	(D)	1.0	(D)	(D)	(D)	.7
PRIVATE TRUCK........	2	100.0	5.8	89.0	-	(D)	-	(D)	(D)	(D)	-
AIR.................	6	100.0	12.3	10.8	2.9	(D)	17.9	(D)	(D)	(D)	25.8
WATER...............	-	100.0	-	-	-	(D)	-	(D)	(D)	(D)	-
OTHER...............	1	100.0	47.8	21.5	7.7	(D)	10.4	(D)	(D)	(D)	3.3
UNKNOWN..............	-	100.0	.1	-	-	(D)	-	(D)	(D)	(D)	73.6
MIDDLE ATLANTIC........	124	100.0	7.8	36.3	18.2	(D)	11.5	(D)	(D)	(D)	4.1
RAIL...............	8	100.0	-	1.0	98.9	(D)	-	(D)	(D)	(D)	-
MOTOR CARRIER........	62	100.0	13.9	37.3	15.8	(D)	21.7	(D)	(D)	(D)	1.7
PRIVATE TRUCK........	22	100.0	.2	83.6	11.7	(D)	.1	(D)	(D)	(D)	-
AIR.................	24	100.0	1.4	1.5	4.3	(D)	1.4	(D)	(D)	(D)	16.7
WATER...............	-	100.0	-	-	-	(D)	-	(D)	(D)	(D)	-
OTHER...............	4	100.0	16.0	56.8	10.3	(D)	7.2	(D)	(D)	(D)	1.4
UNKNOWN..............	2	100.0	-	14.0	.6	(D)	-	(D)	(D)	(D)	-
EAST NORTH CENTRAL......	313	100.0	1.2	11.6	69.7	(D)	3.4	(D)	(D)	(D)	2.1
RAIL...............	12	100.0	-	94.4	4.9	(D)	-	(D)	(D)	(D)	-
MOTOR CARRIER........	262	100.0	.9	7.0	75.4	(D)	3.7	(D)	(D)	(D)	.1
PRIVATE TRUCK........	22	100.0	-	17.0	75.9	(D)	1.1	(D)	(D)	(D)	-
AIR.................	10	100.0	4.3	14.8	7.5	(D)	.9	(D)	(D)	(D)	53.5
WATER...............	-	100.0	-	-	-	(D)	-	(D)	(D)	(D)	-
OTHER...............	3	100.0	21.8	20.7	36.5	(D)	11.5	(D)	(D)	(D)	.4
UNKNOWN..............	1	100.0	-	.1	46.5	(D)	-	(D)	(D)	(D)	50.9
WEST NORTH CENTRAL......	31	100.0	3.4	15.6	14.6	(D)	2.7	(D)	(D)	(D)	6.9
RAIL...............	9	100.0	-	-	16.6	(D)	-	(D)	(D)	(D)	-
MOTOR CARRIER........	14	100.0	5.0	20.9	16.5	(D)	3.8	(D)	(D)	(D)	4.9
PRIVATE TRUCK........	-	100.0	-	.1	23.9	(D)	-	(D)	(D)	(D)	-
AIR.................	4	100.0	3.5	20.1	5.7	(D)	2.5	(D)	(D)	(D)	29.3
WATER...............	-	100.0	-	-	-	(D)	-	(D)	(D)	(D)	-
OTHER...............	1	100.0	11.4	61.2	9.4	(D)	10.8	(D)	(D)	(D)	2.8
UNKNOWN..............	-	100.0	-	-	-	(D)	-	(D)	(D)	(D)	-
SOUTH ATLANTIC..........	56	100.0	3.2	16.7	52.4	(D)	8.6	(D)	(D)	(D)	4.9
RAIL...............	2	100.0	.1	42.2	57.7	(D)	-	(D)	(D)	(D)	-
MOTOR CARRIER........	26	100.0	4.7	26.7	39.6	(D)	2.6	(D)	(D)	(D)	4.3
PRIVATE TRUCK........	6	100.0	2.0	.1	26.1	(D)	60.5	(D)	(D)	(D)	-
AIR.................	19	100.0	1.4	3.4	80.8	(D)	.9	(D)	(D)	(D)	8.4
WATER...............	-	100.0	-	-	-	(D)	-	(D)	(D)	(D)	-
OTHER...............	1	100.0	10.2	30.5	19.5	(D)	10.4	(D)	(D)	(D)	1.6
UNKNOWN..............	-	100.0	-	-	-	(D)	72.1	(D)	(D)	(D)	-
EAST SOUTH CENTRAL......	27	100.0	1.8	58.8	32.8	(D)	3.2	(D)	(D)	(D)	.4
RAIL...............	1	100.0	-	71.8	28.2	(D)	-	(D)	(D)	(D)	-
MOTOR CARRIER........	15	100.0	1.0	71.3	19.7	(D)	3.4	(D)	(D)	(D)	-
PRIVATE TRUCK........	9	100.0	-	40.1	56.3	(D)	3.6	(D)	(D)	(D)	-
AIR.................	-	100.0	22.9	25.1	26.5	(D)	-	(D)	(D)	(D)	18.6
WATER...............	-	100.0	-	-	-	(D)	-	(D)	(D)	(D)	-
OTHER...............	-	100.0	57.5	13.3	19.7	(D)	2.9	(D)	(D)	(D)	-
UNKNOWN..............	-	100.0	-	-	-	(D)	-	(D)	(D)	(D)	-
WEST SOUTH CENTRAL......	53	100.0	1.5	8.3	56.4	(D)	.4	(D)	(D)	(D)	2.4
RAIL...............	8	100.0	.2	18.5	81.2	(D)	-	(D)	(D)	(D)	-
MOTOR CARRIER........	27	100.0	2.3	7.1	63.4	(D)	.3	(D)	(D)	(D)	.3
PRIVATE TRUCK........	10	100.0	-	2.1	33.9	(D)	-	(D)	(D)	(D)	.6
AIR.................	2	100.0	3.8	20.0	3.1	(D)	.2	(D)	(D)	(D)	37.1
WATER...............	-	100.0	-	-	-	(D)	-	(D)	(D)	(D)	-
OTHER...............	2	100.0	1.8	6.1	5.3	(D)	4.9	(D)	(D)	(D)	.1
UNKNOWN..............	2	100.0	-	-	99.4	(D)	.2	(D)	(D)	(D)	-
MOUNTAIN..............	22	100.0	1.2	7.8	1.5	(D)	.2	(D)	(D)	(D)	8.3
RAIL...............	-	100.0	28.6	71.4	-	(D)	-	(D)	(D)	(D)	-
MOTOR CARRIER........	17	100.0	.4	6.6	1.1	(D)	.1	(D)	(D)	(D)	2.4
PRIVATE TRUCK........	-	100.0	-	-	-	(D)	-	(D)	(D)	(D)	-
AIR.................	3	100.0	6.0	17.0	3.4	(D)	1.0	(D)	(D)	(D)	45.5
WATER...............	-	100.0	-	-	-	(D)	-	(D)	(D)	(D)	-
OTHER...............	1	100.0	.3	2.7	2.5	(D)	.3	(D)	(D)	(D)	.3
UNKNOWN..............	-	100.0	-	100.0	-	(D)	-	(D)	(D)	(D)	-
PACIFIC...............	63	100.0	2.8	56.4	11.1	(D)	.2	(D)	(D)	(D)	19.3
RAIL...............	15	100.0	-	77.3	22.7	(D)	-	(D)	(D)	(D)	-
MOTOR CARRIER........	32	100.0	2.1	67.4	8.3	(D)	.1	(D)	(D)	(D)	13.2
PRIVATE TRUCK........	3	100.0	1.7	.7	.1	(D)	-	(D)	(D)	(D)	86.7
AIR.................	9	100.0	9.7	15.2	5.6	(D)	.5	(D)	(D)	(D)	45.7
WATER...............	-	100.0	-	-	-	(D)	-	(D)	(D)	(D)	-
OTHER...............	2	100.0	6.2	9.4	10.2	(D)	3.7	(D)	(D)	(D)	33.9
UNKNOWN..............	-	100.0	-	8.3	-	(D)	-	(D)	(D)	(D)	.2

See footnotes at end of table 4.

TABLE 3. TCC GROUP 367—Percent Distribution of Geographic Division of Destination and Means of Transport, by Geographic Division of Origin: 1972—Continued

Geographic division of destination and means of transport	Number	Percent distribution by division of origin [1]									
		U.S. total	New England	Middle Atlantic	East North Central	West North Central	South Atlantic	East South Central	West South Central	Mountain	Pacific
TON-MILES OF SHIPMENTS	(millions of ton-miles)										
U.S. TOTAL...............	439	100.0	3.2	32.4	25.8	(D)	2.9	(D)	(D)	(D)	10.0
RAIL....................	62	100.0	.1	63.0	36.1	(D)	-	(D)	(D)	(D)	-
MOTOR CARRIER..........	239	100.0	3.5	35.6	27.8	(D)	4.1	(D)	(D)	(D)	3.2
PRIVATE TRUCK..........	24	100.0	.8	29.6	33.2	(D)	1.6	(D)	(D)	(D)	1.2
AIR....................	93	100.0	4.1	8.3	12.6	(D)	1.6	(D)	(D)	(D)	35.4
WATER..................	-	100.0	-	-	-	(D)	-	(D)	(D)	(D)	-
OTHER..................	10	100.0	15.6	22.6	13.5	(D)	9.1	(D)	(D)	(D)	5.0
UNKNOWN................	8	100.0	-	1.5	31.2	(D)	.3	(D)	(D)	(D)	27.2
NEW ENGLAND.............	13	100.0	2.7	11.9	4.6	(D)	8.1	(D)	(D)	(D)	42.0
RAIL....................	-	100.0	-	-	-	(D)	-	(D)	(D)	(D)	-
MOTOR CARRIER..........	1	100.0	18.6	27.7	24.7	(D)	3.1	(D)	(D)	(D)	8.5
PRIVATE TRUCK..........	1	100.0	.5	87.8	-	(D)	-	(D)	(D)	(D)	.2
AIR....................	9	100.0	.4	2.0	1.7	(D)	10.0	(D)	(D)	(D)	50.1
WATER..................	-	100.0	-	-	-	(D)	-	(D)	(D)	(D)	-
OTHER..................	-	100.0	7.1	9.8	14.1	(D)	15.7	(D)	(D)	(D)	19.2
UNKNOWN................	-	100.0	-	-	-	(D)	-	(D)	(D)	(D)	81.9
MIDDLE ATLANTIC.........	72	100.0	2.7	6.9	18.4	(D)	5.3	(D)	(D)	(D)	17.7
RAIL....................	5	100.0	-	-	99.8	(D)	-	(D)	(D)	(D)	.2
MOTOR CARRIER..........	23	100.0	7.7	13.1	24.9	(D)	15.0	(D)	(D)	(D)	11.6
PRIVATE TRUCK..........	3	100.0	.1	41.7	36.8	(D)	.1	(D)	(D)	(D)	-
AIR....................	35	100.0	.2	.2	1.8	(D)	.5	(D)	(D)	(D)	28.1
WATER..................	-	100.0	-	-	-	(D)	-	(D)	(D)	(D)	-
OTHER..................	1	100.0	8.4	15.6	19.5	(D)	11.0	(D)	(D)	(D)	10.3
UNKNOWN................	3	100.0	-	3.1	.2	(D)	-	(D)	(D)	(D)	-
EAST NORTH CENTRAL......	91	100.0	2.8	23.9	34.2	(D)	5.6	(D)	(D)	(D)	13.0
RAIL....................	7	100.0	-	98.1	1.3	(D)	-	(D)	(D)	(D)	-
MOTOR CARRIER..........	61	100.0	2.7	18.2	45.5	(D)	7.8	(D)	(D)	(D)	.5
PRIVATE TRUCK..........	5	100.0	-	38.5	47.2	(D)	1.7	(D)	(D)	(D)	-
AIR....................	13	100.0	2.5	6.7	1.0	(D)	.4	(D)	(D)	(D)	75.1
WATER..................	-	100.0	-	-	-	(D)	-	(D)	(D)	(D)	-
OTHER..................	1	100.0	33.9	24.8	10.3	(D)	11.7	(D)	(D)	(D)	1.5
UNKNOWN................	1	100.0	-	.1	2.2	(D)	-	(D)	(D)	(D)	95.6
WEST NORTH CENTRAL......	14	100.0	7.8	27.4	14.9	(D)	6.4	(D)	(D)	(D)	21.1
RAIL....................	1	100.0	-	-	60.5	(D)	-	(D)	(D)	(D)	.4
MOTOR CARRIER..........	7	100.0	10.6	33.5	16.5	(D)	9.3	(D)	(D)	(D)	12.6
PRIVATE TRUCK..........	-	100.0	-	.4	15.3	(D)	-	(D)	(D)	(D)	-
AIR....................	4	100.0	3.8	20.0	2.4	(D)	2.2	(D)	(D)	(D)	45.8
WATER..................	-	100.0	-	-	-	(D)	-	(D)	(D)	(D)	-
OTHER..................	-	100.0	16.5	56.7	4.9	(D)	13.0	(D)	(D)	(D)	5.6
UNKNOWN................	-	100.0	-	.2	-	(D)	-	(D)	(D)	(D)	-
SOUTH ATLANTIC..........	36	100.0	3.3	13.1	45.9	(D)	2.0	(D)	(D)	(D)	16.3
RAIL....................	1	100.0	.1	44.5	55.3	(D)	-	(D)	(D)	(D)	-
MOTOR CARRIER..........	18	100.0	4.8	19.6	31.6	(D)	1.7	(D)	(D)	(D)	13.3
PRIVATE TRUCK..........	1	100.0	3.8	.3	44.2	(D)	19.8	(D)	(D)	(D)	-
AIR....................	14	100.0	1.3	2.2	64.9	(D)	.7	(D)	(D)	(D)	23.8
WATER..................	-	100.0	-	-	-	(D)	-	(D)	(D)	(D)	-
OTHER..................	1	100.0	9.9	24.3	21.1	(D)	4.4	(D)	(D)	(D)	5.1
UNKNOWN................	-	100.0	-	-	-	(D)	56.5	(D)	(D)	(D)	-
EAST SOUTH CENTRAL......	13	100.0	3.3	66.9	21.2	(D)	2.7	(D)	(D)	(D)	1.6
RAIL....................	-	100.0	-	84.3	15.7	(D)	-	(D)	(D)	(D)	-
MOTOR CARRIER..........	8	100.0	1.6	74.0	14.6	(D)	3.8	(D)	(D)	(D)	-
PRIVATE TRUCK..........	3	100.0	-	57.4	41.5	(D)	1.1	(D)	(D)	(D)	-
AIR....................	-	100.0	23.5	21.0	9.4	(D)	-	(D)	(D)	(D)	38.8
WATER..................	-	100.0	-	-	-	(D)	-	(D)	(D)	(D)	-
OTHER..................	-	100.0	67.7	15.0	10.6	(D)	2.5	(D)	(D)	(D)	.1
UNKNOWN................	-	100.0	-	-	-	(D)	-	(D)	(D)	(D)	-
WEST SOUTH CENTRAL......	48	100.0	2.6	10.2	67.3	(D)	.4	(D)	(D)	(D)	3.6
RAIL....................	10	100.0	.3	14.5	85.2	(D)	-	(D)	(D)	(D)	-
MOTOR CARRIER..........	24	100.0	4.0	8.6	77.7	(D)	.4	(D)	(D)	(D)	.5
PRIVATE TRUCK..........	6	100.0	-	4.9	25.8	(D)	-	(D)	(D)	(D)	1.2
AIR....................	2	100.0	6.5	28.0	2.9	(D)	.2	(D)	(D)	(D)	54.2
WATER..................	-	100.0	-	-	-	(D)	-	(D)	(D)	(D)	-
OTHER..................	-	100.0	5.6	18.5	9.2	(D)	10.1	(D)	(D)	(D)	.1
UNKNOWN................	2	100.0	-	-	99.7	(D)	.2	(D)	(D)	(D)	-
MOUNTAIN................	32	100.0	1.7	10.2	1.1	(D)	.3	(D)	(D)	(D)	2.9
RAIL....................	-	100.0	30.0	70.0	-	(D)	-	(D)	(D)	(D)	-
MOTOR CARRIER..........	28	100.0	.5	7.4	.7	(D)	.1	(D)	(D)	(D)	1.2
PRIVATE TRUCK..........	-	100.0	-	-	-	(D)	-	(D)	(D)	(D)	-
AIR....................	2	100.0	13.9	40.1	4.7	(D)	1.8	(D)	(D)	(D)	22.9
WATER..................	-	100.0	-	-	-	(D)	-	(D)	(D)	(D)	-
OTHER..................	-	100.0	1.2	11.6	6.9	(D)	1.0	(D)	(D)	(D)	.4
UNKNOWN................	-	100.0	-	100.0	-	(D)	-	(D)	(D)	(D)	-
PACIFIC.................	116	100.0	3.9	75.0	11.5	(D)	.3	(D)	(D)	(D)	1.6
RAIL....................	36	100.0	-	80.8	19.2	(D)	-	(D)	(D)	(D)	-
MOTOR CARRIER..........	65	100.0	2.7	82.2	7.7	(D)	.1	(D)	(D)	(D)	1.2
PRIVATE TRUCK..........	1	100.0	12.3	4.8	.5	(D)	-	(D)	(D)	(D)	16.9
AIR....................	10	100.0	22.2	32.5	8.8	(D)	.9	(D)	(D)	(D)	6.9
WATER..................	-	100.0	-	-	-	(D)	-	(D)	(D)	(D)	-
OTHER..................	2	100.0	13.8	19.9	15.6	(D)	7.1	(D)	(D)	(D)	3.1
UNKNOWN................	-	100.0	-	21.3	-	(D)	-	(D)	(D)	(D)	-

See footnotes at end of table 4.

TABLE 4. TCC GROUP 367—Percent Distribution of Distance Shipped and Weight of Shipment, by Means of Transport: 1972

Distance shipped and weight of shipment[2][3]	Number	Percent distribution by means of transport							
		All means of transport	Rail	Motor carrier	Private truck	Air	Water	Other	Unknown
TONS OF SHIPMENTS	(thousands of tons)								
U.S. TOTAL.........	652	100.0	8.9	68.2	9.6	10.0	-	2.6	.7
UNDER 100 MILES.........	145	100.0	5.2	76.5	12.9	2.1	-	2.6	.7
UNDER 1000 POUNDS.....	20	100.0	-	42.4	29.6	11.6	-	16.4	-
1000 TO 9999 POUNDS...	18	100.0	-	81.8	14.8	3.2	-	.2	-
10000 TO 29999 POUNDS.	94	100.0	4.7	83.4	10.4	-	-	.4	1.1
30000 TO 59999 POUNDS.	11	100.0	28.7	71.3	-	-	-	-	-
60000 TO 89999 POUNDS.	-	100.0	-	-	-	-	-	-	-
90000 POUNDS AND OVER.	-	100.0	-	-	-	-	-	-	-
100 TO 199 MILES........	76	100.0	.8	76.0	17.8	3.1	-	2.3	-
UNDER 1000 POUNDS.....	14	100.0	-	74.6	3.0	9.9	-	12.5	-
1000 TO 9999 POUNDS...	25	100.0	-	86.8	9.5	3.7	-	-	-
10000 TO 29999 POUNDS.	34	100.0	1.8	71.8	26.4	-	-	-	-
30000 TO 59999 POUNDS.	2	100.0	-	20.4	79.6	-	-	-	-
60000 TO 89999 POUNDS.	-	100.0	-	-	-	-	-	-	-
90000 POUNDS AND OVER.	-	100.0	-	-	-	-	-	-	-
200 TO 299 MILES........	78	100.0	.5	90.9	6.1	1.2	-	1.2	-
UNDER 1000 POUNDS.....	6	100.0	-	62.4	8.6	14.0	-	15.0	-
1000 TO 9999 POUNDS...	10	100.0	3.9	91.9	3.7	.4	-	-	-
10000 TO 29999 POUNDS.	11	100.0	-	67.3	32.7	-	-	-	-
30000 TO 59999 POUNDS.	49	100.0	-	100.0	-	-	-	-	-
60000 TO 89999 POUNDS.	-	100.0	-	-	-	-	-	-	-
90000 POUNDS AND OVER.	-	100.0	-	-	-	-	-	-	-
300 TO 499 MILES........	84	100.0	3.8	75.4	11.6	4.6	-	4.4	.1
UNDER 1000 POUNDS.....	13	100.0	-	48.6	7.3	24.7	-	18.4	.9
1000 TO 9999 POUNDS...	22	100.0	.4	76.2	14.6	2.9	-	6.0	-
10000 TO 29999 POUNDS.	45	100.0	3.3	84.2	12.5	-	-	-	-
30000 TO 59999 POUNDS.	4	100.0	40.8	59.2	-	-	-	-	-
60000 TO 89999 POUNDS.	-	100.0	-	-	-	-	-	-	-
90000 POUNDS AND OVER.	-	100.0	-	-	-	-	-	-	-
500 TO 999 MILES........	134	100.0	17.5	52.4	8.9	18.1	-	2.9	.2
UNDER 1000 POUNDS.....	30	100.0	-	59.4	5.7	22.0	-	12.6	.3
1000 TO 9999 POUNDS...	35	100.0	-	85.0	7.7	6.8	-	-	.4
10000 TO 29999 POUNDS.	24	100.0	9.0	68.1	22.9	-	-	-	-
30000 TO 59999 POUNDS.	43	100.0	48.9	12.3	4.2	34.7	-	-	-
60000 TO 89999 POUNDS.	-	100.0	-	-	-	-	-	-	-
90000 POUNDS AND OVER.	-	100.0	-	-	-	-	-	-	-
1000 TO 1499 MILES......	51	100.0	13.5	49.7	5.7	23.5	-	3.7	4.0
UNDER 1000 POUNDS.....	16	100.0	.1	42.0	.7	45.7	-	11.3	.1
1000 TO 9999 POUNDS...	7	100.0	.2	42.2	1.3	56.2	-	-	-
10000 TO 29999 POUNDS.	8	100.0	29.2	70.8	-	-	-	-	-
30000 TO 59999 POUNDS.	18	100.0	24.4	50.4	14.4	-	-	-	10.8
60000 TO 89999 POUNDS.	-	100.0	-	-	-	-	-	-	-
90000 POUNDS AND OVER.	-	100.0	-	-	-	-	-	-	-
1500 MILES OR OVER......	82	100.0	19.2	54.6	.6	22.5	-	1.4	1.7
UNDER 1000 POUNDS.....	18	100.0	.2	24.4	1.8	64.7	-	6.3	2.7
1000 TO 9999 POUNDS...	13	100.0	2.3	39.6	1.4	50.3	-	-	6.5
10000 TO 29999 POUNDS.	39	100.0	36.4	63.6	-	-	-	-	-
30000 TO 59999 POUNDS.	11	100.0	10.7	89.3	-	-	-	-	-
60000 TO 89999 POUNDS.	-	100.0	-	-	-	-	-	-	-
90000 POUNDS AND OVER.	-	100.0	-	-	-	-	-	-	-
TON-MILES OF SHIPMENTS	(millions of ton-miles)								
U.S. TOTAL.........	396	100.0	15.6	57.3	4.8	18.5	-	2.4	1.4
UNDER 100 MILES.........	6	100.0	6.9	80.6	8.6	1.0	-	2.1	.8
UNDER 1000 POUNDS.....	-	100.0	-	46.9	28.9	6.0	-	18.1	-
1000 TO 9999 POUNDS...	1	100.0	-	88.8	9.4	1.8	-	-	-
10000 TO 29999 POUNDS.	4	100.0	6.4	86.1	6.1	-	-	.2	1.2
30000 TO 59999 POUNDS.	-	100.0	33.9	66.1	-	-	-	-	-
60000 TO 89999 POUNDS.	-	100.0	-	-	-	-	-	-	-
90000 POUNDS AND OVER.	-	100.0	-	-	-	-	-	-	-
100 TO 199 MILES........	10	100.0	.8	74.4	18.8	3.5	-	2.4	-
UNDER 1000 POUNDS.....	2	100.0	-	74.7	2.8	9.8	-	12.7	-
1000 TO 9999 POUNDS...	3	100.0	-	85.1	10.4	4.6	-	-	-
10000 TO 29999 POUNDS.	4	100.0	1.9	70.2	27.9	-	-	-	-
30000 TO 59999 POUNDS.	-	100.0	-	13.0	87.0	-	-	-	-
60000 TO 89999 POUNDS.	-	100.0	-	-	-	-	-	-	-
90000 POUNDS AND OVER.	-	100.0	-	-	-	-	-	-	-

See footnotes at end of table 4.

TABLE 4. TCC GROUP 367—Percent Distribution of Distance Shipped and Weight of Shipment, by Means of Transport: 1972—Continued

Distance shipped and weight of shipment[2] [3]	Number	Percent distribution by means of transport							
		All means of transport	Rail	Motor carrier	Private truck	Air	Water	Other	Unknown
TON-MILES OF SHIPMENTS	(millions of ton-miles)								
200 TO 299 MILES.........	18	100.0	.5	91.5	5.4	1.3	-	1.2	-
UNDER 1000 POUNDS.....	1	100.0	-	63.6	8.3	14.1	-	14.0	-
1000 TO 9999 POUNDS...	2	100.0	3.9	92.4	3.3	.4	-	-	-
10000 TO 29999 POUNDS.	2	100.0	-	70.0	30.0	-	-	-	-
30000 TO 59999 POUNDS.	11	100.0	-	100.0	-	-	-	-	-
60000 TO 89999 POUNDS.	-	100.0	-	-	-	-	-	-	-
90000 POUNDS AND OVER.	-	100.0	-	-	-	-	-	-	-
300 TO 499 MILES........	32	100.0	4.7	76.2	10.6	4.3	-	4.1	.1
UNDER 1000 POUNDS.....	4	100.0	-	50.1	7.5	22.7	-	18.7	.9
1000 TO 9999 POUNDS...	8	100.0	.5	77.7	14.0	3.1	-	4.6	-
10000 TO 29999 POUNDS.	17	100.0	4.2	85.1	10.7	-	-	-	-
30000 TO 59999 POUNDS.	1	100.0	47.8	52.2	-	-	-	-	-
60000 TO 89999 POUNDS.	-	100.0	-	-	-	-	-	-	-
90000 POUNDS AND OVER.	-	100.0	-	-	-	-	-	-	-
500 TO 999 MILES........	85	100.0	16.8	52.6	8.6	18.5	-	3.3	.2
UNDER 1000 POUNDS.....	21	100.0	-	57.5	5.6	23.4	-	13.2	.3
1000 TO 9999 POUNDS...	22	100.0	-	83.6	8.8	7.1	-	-	.4
10000 TO 29999 POUNDS.	15	100.0	7.9	70.6	21.5	-	-	-	-
30000 TO 59999 POUNDS.	27	100.0	48.6	13.4	3.6	34.4	-	-	-
60000 TO 89999 POUNDS.	-	100.0	-	-	-	-	-	-	-
90000 POUNDS AND OVER.	-	100.0	-	-	-	-	-	-	-
1000 TO 1499 MILES......	65	100.0	13.3	48.9	5.5	24.9	-	3.5	3.9
UNDER 1000 POUNDS.....	21	100.0	.1	41.1	.7	47.2	-	10.8	.1
1000 TO 9999 POUNDS...	10	100.0	.2	40.6	1.1	58.0	-	-	-
10000 TO 29999 POUNDS.	10	100.0	29.7	70.3	-	-	-	-	-
30000 TO 59999 POUNDS.	23	100.0	24.4	50.6	14.2	-	-	-	10.8
60000 TO 89999 POUNDS.	-	100.0	-	-	-	-	-	-	-
90000 POUNDS AND OVER.	-	100.0	-	-	-	-	-	-	-
1500 MILES OR OVER......	175	100.0	20.9	53.5	.6	22.1	-	1.3	1.6
UNDER 1000 POUNDS.....	38	100.0	.2	23.2	1.8	65.7	-	6.1	3.1
1000 TO 9999 POUNDS...	27	100.0	2.7	40.5	1.3	49.7	-	-	5.8
10000 TO 29999 POUNDS.	81	100.0	40.3	59.7	-	-	-	-	-
30000 TO 59999 POUNDS.	27	100.0	10.3	89.7	-	-	-	-	-
60000 TO 89999 POUNDS.	-	100.0	-	-	-	-	-	-	-
90000 POUNDS AND OVER.	-	100.0	-	-	-	-	-	-	-

Note: Detail may not add to total due to rounding. The introductory table shows the estimates of sampling variability for tons; sampling variability for ton-miles has not been estimated. See the map in the Introduction for the States comprising the geographic divisions of the United States.

Shipments excluded from the survey are those moving by pipeline (primarily petroleum products from refineries), parcel post shipments, and commodities moved by own power (motorized vehicles, aircraft, etc.) or towed (prefabricated buildings, etc.). Local shipments (commodities shipped less than 25 miles from the plant) and shipments within the same city are also excluded. Shipments to Alaska and Hawaii from the 48 conterminous States and the District of Columbia are included; however, no data were obtained for shipments originating in Alaska and Hawaii.

- Represents zero or rounds to zero.   (D) Withheld to avoid disclosing figures for individual companies.

[1]Production of this commodity is concentrated in the geographic divisions shown; figures and distributions for geographic divisions not shown are included in the total.

[2]Distances of shipments to foreign destinations are calculated only to the U.S. port of exit.

[3]Includes only shipments represented by bills of lading and invoices. Summary records which did not show individual weights of shipments are not included.

TCC 369. Miscellaneous Electrical Machinery, Equipment, and Supplies

Comparisons of Tons and Ton-Miles of Shipments for
Geographic Divisions of Origin and for Sampling Variability: 1972 and 1967

Geographic division of origin	Estimates				Relative sampling variability in tons (percent)	
	1972		1967		1972	1967
	Tons (thousands)	Ton-miles (millions)	Tons (thousands)	Ton-miles (millions)		
U.S. total	1,789	765	1,803	671	12.0	24.6
New England	(D)	(D)	85	30	(*)	(*)
Middle Atlantic	233	87	345	146	30.3	(*)
East North Central	898	396	956	319	16.8	(*)
West North Central	172	69	123	56	34.9	(*)
South Atlantic	103	54	118	25	46.6	(*)
East South Central	(D)	(D)	22	29	(*)	(*)
West South Central	(D)	(D)	115	35	(*)	(*)
Mountain	(D)	(D)	6	8	(*)	(*)
Pacific	184	84	33	23	47.6	(*)

(D) Withheld to avoid disclosing figures for individual companies.   (*) Data not published.

TABLE 1. **TCC GROUP 369—Percent Distribution of Geographic Division of Origin and Distance Shipped, by Means of Transport: 1972**

Geographic division of origin[1] and distance shipped[2]	Number	Percent distribution by means of transport							
		All means of transport	Rail	Motor carrier	Private truck	Air	Water	Other	Unknown
TONS OF SHIPMENTS	(thousands of tons)								
U.S. TOTAL..........	1 789	100.0	9.3	65.4	22.9	.6	.2	1.3	.2
MIDDLE ATLANTIC.........	233	100.0	10.5	81.5	7.7	.2	-	.1	-
UNDER 100 MILES.......	86	100.0	25.9	62.3	11.8	-	-	-	-
100 TO 199 MILES......	34	100.0	-	97.5	2.3	.1	-	.1	-
200 TO 299 MILES......	37	100.0	-	98.8	1.1	.1	-	-	-
300 TO 499 MILES......	19	100.0	-	89.6	10.1	.1	-	.2	-
500 TO 999 MILES.....	31	100.0	-	88.6	10.6	.5	-	.3	-
1000 TO 1499 MILES....	12	100.0	-	90.1	9.2	.5	-	.2	-
1500 MILES OR OVER....	10	100.0	18.7	77.6	1.0	1.5	.9	.2	-
EAST NORTH CENTRAL......	898	100.0	9.7	66.0	20.7	.4	.2	2.5	.4
UNDER 100 MILES.......	161	100.0	4.6	45.9	49.3	-	-	.2	-
100 TO 199 MILES......	141	100.0	-	80.7	18.7	.1	-	.2	.2
200 TO 299 MILES......	166	100.0	7.8	71.4	20.3	.2	-	.4	-
300 TO 499 MILES......	151	100.0	13.7	68.5	16.9	.5	-	.3	.2
500 TO 999 MILES.....	199	100.0	15.8	68.7	6.1	1.1	-	8.0	.3
1000 TO 1499 MILES....	28	100.0	5.3	62.4	29.8	1.3	-	1.1	-
1500 MILES OR OVER....	49	100.0	26.3	54.9	.7	.6	4.1	8.7	4.7
WEST NORTH CENTRAL......	172	100.0	18.5	66.6	14.6	-		-	.2
UNDER 100 MILES.......	30	100.0	-	81.9	18.1	-		-	-
100 TO 199 MILES......	15	100.0	3.8	49.4	46.5	-		-	.2
200 TO 299 MILES......	27	100.0	19.5	55.0	24.1	-		-	1.4
300 TO 499 MILES......	40	100.0	44.1	49.3	6.6	-		-	-
500 TO 999 MILES.....	52	100.0	12.6	81.1	6.3	-		-	-
1000 TO 1499 MILES....	6	100.0	23.3	76.6	-	.1		-	-
1500 MILES OR OVER....	-	100.0	-	99.5	-	.4		-	-
SOUTH ATLANTIC..........	103	100.0	18.5	69.4	11.5	.3	-	.1	.2
UNDER 100 MILES.......	14	100.0	-	83.7	16.0	-	-	.2	-
100 TO 199 MILES......	6	100.0	.1	95.5	4.3	-	-	.2	-
200 TO 299 MILES......	9	100.0	42.1	52.6	4.7	-	-	-	.6
300 TO 499 MILES......	37	100.0	1.2	77.7	20.7	.1	-	-	.3
500 TO 999 MILES.....	25	100.0	44.2	53.3	1.5	.7	-	.2	-
1000 TO 1499 MILES....	1	100.0	.3	67.0	31.7	1.0	-	-	-
1500 MILES OR OVER....	7	100.0	44.1	51.5	3.2	1.2	-	-	-
PACIFIC.................	184	100.0	2.1	64.2	32.6	.5	.5	-	.1
UNDER 100 MILES.......	50	100.0	-	41.2	58.5	.3	-	.1	-
100 TO 199 MILES......	22	100.0	-	88.1	11.8	.1	-	-	-
200 TO 299 MILES......	11	100.0	-	60.9	39.1	-	-	-	-
300 TO 499 MILES......	55	100.0	6.9	56.4	36.6	.1	-	-	-
500 TO 999 MILES.....	20	100.0	-	91.6	7.7	.7	-	-	-
1000 TO 1499 MILES....	13	100.0	-	98.6	-	1.0	-	-	.3
1500 MILES OR OVER....	10	100.0	-	69.0	16.4	3.9	9.1	.4	1.3
TON-MILES OF SHIPMENTS	(millions of ton-miles)								
U.S. TOTAL..........	765	100.0	12.9	67.7	13.2	1.2	1.5	2.7	.7
MIDDLE ATLANTIC.........	87	100.0	7.4	85.6	5.7	.6	.5	.2	-
UNDER 100 MILES.......	5	100.0	31.5	61.9	6.6	-	-	-	-
100 TO 199 MILES......	4	100.0	-	96.8	2.9	.1	-	.1	-
200 TO 299 MILES......	9	100.0	-	98.8	1.1	.1	-	-	-
300 TO 499 MILES......	7	100.0	-	90.7	9.0	.1	-	.2	-
500 TO 999 MILES.....	21	100.0	-	90.4	8.8	.5	-	.3	-
1000 TO 1499 MILES....	14	100.0	-	90.0	9.4	.5	-	.2	-
1500 MILES OR OVER....	24	100.0	19.7	75.0	1.8	1.5	1.9	.2	-
EAST NORTH CENTRAL......	396	100.0	14.8	64.9	11.2	.8	2.2	5.0	1.2
UNDER 100 MILES.......	7	100.0	2.7	56.8	40.3	-	-	.2	-
100 TO 199 MILES......	21	100.0	-	79.6	19.8	.2	-	.2	.1
200 TO 299 MILES......	39	100.0	7.6	73.4	18.4	.2	-	.4	-
300 TO 499 MILES......	61	100.0	14.0	67.4	17.7	.5	-	.3	.1
500 TO 999 MILES.....	137	100.0	13.5	70.7	6.1	1.1	-	8.3	.3
1000 TO 1499 MILES....	31	100.0	5.9	61.5	30.1	1.3	-	1.2	-
1500 MILES OR OVER....	96	100.0	27.5	50.1	.7	.7	8.9	7.9	4.2
WEST NORTH CENTRAL......	69	100.0	21.5	69.8	8.5	-	-	-	.1
UNDER 100 MILES.......	-	100.0	-	66.4	33.6	-	-	-	-
100 TO 199 MILES......	2	100.0	4.3	49.1	46.4	-	-	-	.2
200 TO 299 MILES......	6	100.0	19.9	54.4	24.4	-	-	-	1.3
300 TO 499 MILES......	16	100.0	43.2	49.6	7.2	-	-	-	-
500 TO 999 MILES.....	35	100.0	12.5	82.6	4.9	-	-	-	-
1000 TO 1499 MILES....	7	100.0	26.7	73.2	-	.1	-	-	-
1500 MILES OR OVER....	-	100.0	-	99.5	-	.4	-	-	-
SOUTH ATLANTIC..........	54	100.0	31.3	59.4	8.5	.6	-	.1	.1
UNDER 100 MILES.......	-	100.0	-	54.5	44.9	-	-	.6	-
100 TO 199 MILES......	1	100.0	.1	94.8	4.9	-	-	.1	-
200 TO 299 MILES......	2	100.0	43.0	51.8	4.7	-	-	-	.5
300 TO 499 MILES......	14	100.0	1.4	77.4	20.8	.1	-	-	.3
500 TO 999 MILES.....	17	100.0	47.5	50.2	1.4	.7	-	.2	-
1000 TO 1499 MILES....	1	100.0	.3	64.4	34.3	1.0	-	-	-
1500 MILES OR OVER....	16	100.0	44.5	51.3	3.0	1.2	-	-	-

See footnotes at end of table 4.

TABLE 1. **TCC GROUP 369**—Percent Distribution of Geographic Division of Origin and Distance Shipped, by Means of Transport: 1972—Continued

Geographic division of origin[1] and distance shipped[2]	Number	Percent distribution by means of transport							
		All means of transport	Rail	Motor carrier	Private truck	Air	Water	Other	Unknown
TON-MILES OF SHIPMENTS	(millions of ton-miles)								
PACIFIC	84	100.0	1.7	75.7	17.7	1.4	3.0	.1	.4
UNDER 100 MILES	1	100.0	-	49.9	49.9	.1	-	-	-
100 TO 199 MILES	3	100.0	-	89.7	10.2	.1	-	-	-
200 TO 299 MILES	2	100.0	-	62.0	38.0	-	-	-	-
300 TO 499 MILES	19	100.0	7.5	56.6	35.8	.1	-	-	-
500 TO 999 MILES	15	100.0	-	93.0	6.4	.6	-	-	-
1000 TO 1499 MILES	17	100.0	-	98.6	-	1.1	-	-	.3
1500 MILES OR OVER	24	100.0	-	65.4	19.2	3.6	10.4	.4	1.1

See footnotes at end of table 4.

TABLE 2. **TCC GROUP 369**—Percent Distribution of Geographic Division of Origin and Means of Transport, by Geographic Division of Destination: 1972

Geographic division of origin[1] and means of transport	Number	Percent distribution by division of destination									
		U.S. total	New England	Middle Atlantic	East North Central	West North Central	South Atlantic	East South Central	West South Central	Mountain	Pacific
TONS OF SHIPMENTS	(thousands of tons)										
U.S. TOTAL	1 789	100.0	3.9	13.4	32.4	11.1	11.7	7.3	5.9	2.7	11.6
RAIL	166	100.0	6.5	5.6	28.1	11.5	23.4	8.7	2.1	-	14.2
MOTOR CARRIER	1 170	100.0	4.4	16.9	30.2	10.6	12.2	5.6	6.6	3.1	10.5
PRIVATE TRUCK	410	100.0	1.4	6.0	43.1	13.4	4.6	11.6	5.0	2.6	12.3
AIR	10	100.0	8.0	29.0	12.9	4.1	15.5	5.3	9.0	2.3	13.9
WATER	3	100.0	-	.8	-	-	.1	-	-	-	99.0
OTHER	24	100.0	.7	14.5	6.2	1.4	32.4	11.4	13.3	.9	19.1
UNKNOWN	4	100.0	1.6	15.2	16.8	10.2	1.6	-	1.3	-	53.4
MIDDLE ATLANTIC	233	100.0	10.4	38.0	9.5	2.8	29.9	1.7	3.5	.4	3.8
RAIL	24	100.0	-	-	-	-	92.1	-	-	-	7.9
MOTOR CARRIER	189	100.0	12.6	42.7	11.4	2.9	20.8	1.5	4.2	.5	3.5
PRIVATE TRUCK	17	100.0	1.5	40.8	2.7	6.1	41.8	6.4	.2	-	.6
AIR	-	100.0	2.4	13.0	20.7	2.3	12.6	7.9	6.1	9.2	25.8
WATER	-	100.0	-	-	-	-	-	-	-	-	100.0
OTHER	-	100.0	2.1	33.1	25.5	11.6	6.4	8.1	3.1	4.6	5.4
UNKNOWN	-	100.0	-	58.1	-	-	41.9	-	-	-	-
EAST NORTH CENTRAL	898	100.0	2.8	11.0	48.9	8.5	9.9	6.9	5.3	1.3	5.4
RAIL	87	100.0	10.8	10.7	23.4	11.2	10.3	16.0	2.5	.1	15.0
MOTOR CARRIER	592	100.0	2.4	13.6	46.4	9.7	11.0	5.7	4.8	1.9	4.4
PRIVATE TRUCK	186	100.0	.2	2.1	76.2	4.5	3.8	5.9	7.0	.1	.2
AIR	4	100.0	12.2	38.2	13.3	8.1	11.4	3.8	4.9	.6	7.5
WATER	2	100.0	-	-	-	-	-	-	-	-	100.0
OTHER	22	100.0	.5	12.6	5.3	1.4	34.2	12.1	13.9	.9	19.2
UNKNOWN	3	100.0	1.9	16.0	16.1	.5	.1	-	-	-	65.4
WEST NORTH CENTRAL	172	100.0	.5	3.1	38.0	40.9	5.4	1.8	6.6	2.3	1.4
RAIL	31	100.0	-	-	66.5	18.5	10.2	-	-	-	4.8
MOTOR CARRIER	114	100.0	.8	4.7	34.0	39.1	5.3	2.7	9.4	3.5	.7
PRIVATE TRUCK	25	100.0	-	-	21.2	76.6	-	.1	2.1	-	-
AIR	-	100.0	.6	-	2.7	5.4	14.0	-	69.2	-	8.0
WATER	-	100.0	-	-	-	-	-	-	-	-	-
OTHER	-	100.0	3.9	15.5	17.9	28.7	16.0	1.9	15.7	-	.5
UNKNOWN	-	100.0	-	-	-	100.0	-	-	-	-	-
SOUTH ATLANTIC	103	100.0	2.2	13.7	11.7	4.5	34.8	20.8	5.3	.3	6.7
RAIL	19	100.0	7.0	-	27.2	18.0	21.9	2.3	6.9	-	16.7
MOTOR CARRIER	71	100.0	1.0	17.6	8.4	1.1	40.4	20.5	5.8	.5	4.8
PRIVATE TRUCK	11	100.0	1.1	11.7	6.5	3.3	22.6	53.0	-	.1	1.9
AIR	-	100.0	13.1	18.7	14.7	2.0	14.2	1.5	6.9	4.5	24.5
WATER	-	100.0	-	-	-	-	-	-	-	-	-
OTHER	-	100.0	1.5	14.2	2.9	-	62.4	4.3	13.9	.4	.4
UNKNOWN	-	100.0	-	50.0	12.9	-	35.6	-	-	-	1.4
PACIFIC	184	100.0	-	1.1	1.7	3.2	.7	.1	4.0	15.1	74.1
RAIL	3	100.0	-	-	-	-	-	-	-	.1	99.9
MOTOR CARRIER	118	100.0	-	1.6	2.5	5.0	.8	.1	6.1	14.6	69.2
PRIVATE TRUCK	60	100.0	-	-	-	-	.2	-	-	17.3	82.6
AIR	-	100.0	.8	6.5	8.4	4.1	21.0	8.3	13.0	16.2	21.7
WATER	-	100.0	-	-	-	-	-	-	-	-	100.0
OTHER	-	100.0	1.3	.2	8.7	-	36.3	-	-	16.3	37.2
UNKNOWN	-	100.0	-	-	75.3	-	-	-	24.2	-	.6

See footnotes at end of table 4.

TABLE 2. **TCC GROUP 369—Percent Distribution of Geographic Division of Origin and Means of Transport, by Geographic Division of Destination: 1972**—Continued

Geographic division of origin[1] and means of transport	Number	Percent distribution by division of destination									
		U.S. total	New England	Middle Atlantic	East North Central	West North Central	South Atlantic	East South Central	West South Central	Mountain	Pacific
TON-MILES OF SHIPMENTS	(millions of ton-miles)										
U.S. TOTAL	765	100.0	3.8	10.3	17.6	9.8	13.1	6.3	10.3	4.3	24.6
RAIL	98	100.0	6.1	5.0	15.5	10.2	11.0	5.8	3.4	.1	42.9
MOTOR CARRIER	517	100.0	4.0	12.6	17.8	9.2	14.5	5.0	11.0	5.4	20.5
PRIVATE TRUCK	101	100.0	1.2	4.2	25.6	16.4	7.0	14.1	14.5	4.1	12.8
AIR	9	100.0	5.5	15.2	7.8	2.7	16.6	5.5	13.2	2.7	30.7
WATER	11	100.0	-	-	-	-	-	-	-	-	100.0
OTHER	20	100.0	.5	10.4	2.0	.8	25.7	7.1	12.6	1.3	39.5
UNKNOWN	5	100.0	.8	8.8	7.8	1.9	.3	-	1.1	-	79.3
MIDDLE ATLANTIC	87	100.0	6.6	10.1	14.1	7.8	19.4	3.4	11.8	1.9	24.8
RAIL	6	100.0	-	-	-	-	26.2	-	-	-	73.8
MOTOR CARRIER	74	100.0	7.6	11.2	16.1	7.2	18.1	2.9	13.7	2.1	21.1
PRIVATE TRUCK	4	100.0	1.2	8.9	4.1	27.4	34.0	15.0	.7	-	8.7
AIR	-	100.0	.5	1.7	11.5	1.8	8.5	5.7	6.4	12.7	51.3
WATER	-	100.0	-	-	-	-	-	-	-	-	100.0
OTHER	-	100.0	.6	5.2	23.0	16.8	5.7	9.2	6.3	13.6	19.7
UNKNOWN	-	100.0	-	16.9	-	-	83.1	-	-	-	-
EAST NORTH CENTRAL	396	100.0	4.3	11.7	16.5	8.1	15.5	6.4	10.4	3.2	23.9
RAIL	58	100.0	8.8	8.4	5.5	9.4	9.8	9.3	3.5	.1	45.2
MOTOR CARRIER	257	100.0	4.3	14.2	17.9	8.8	17.8	5.2	9.1	4.7	18.1
PRIVATE TRUCK	44	100.0	.9	2.9	35.7	8.7	9.9	11.1	28.9	.5	1.4
AIR	3	100.0	13.4	33.7	3.8	4.4	11.8	2.5	6.8	1.0	22.6
WATER	8	100.0	-	-	-	-	-	-	-	-	100.0
OTHER	19	100.0	.5	10.8	1.1	.7	26.7	7.4	13.0	1.2	38.6
UNKNOWN	4	100.0	.9	8.9	2.7	.1	-	-	-	-	87.5
WEST NORTH CENTRAL	69	100.0	1.6	7.3	44.6	15.6	10.9	2.4	8.5	4.4	4.7
RAIL	14	100.0	-	-	60.9	9.6	15.1	-	-	-	14.3
MOTOR CARRIER	48	100.0	2.3	10.4	41.2	11.4	11.0	3.4	11.6	6.4	2.3
PRIVATE TRUCK	5	100.0	-	-	31.8	63.9	-	.2	4.1	-	-
AIR	-	100.0	1.1	-	1.8	3.3	23.1	-	55.6	-	15.1
WATER	-	100.0	-	-	-	-	-	-	-	-	-
OTHER	-	100.0	8.1	26.6	14.7	13.9	20.5	2.2	12.9	-	1.1
UNKNOWN	-	100.0	-	-	-	100.0	-	-	-	-	-
SOUTH ATLANTIC	54	100.0	2.8	12.2	12.1	8.0	14.5	12.6	7.4	1.1	29.3
RAIL	17	100.0	5.1	-	17.8	18.3	6.6	1.5	7.7	-	43.1
MOTOR CARRIER	32	100.0	1.7	18.3	9.8	2.5	19.8	13.1	8.4	1.8	24.6
PRIVATE TRUCK	4	100.0	1.7	14.3	7.5	9.8	5.7	50.4	-	.3	10.3
AIR	-	100.0	6.3	8.7	8.4	2.1	10.5	.6	5.6	6.7	51.1
WATER	-	100.0	-	-	-	-	-	-	-	-	-
OTHER	-	100.0	1.6	15.8	4.2	-	41.4	4.6	28.8	1.6	2.0
UNKNOWN	-	100.0	-	58.9	14.6	-	18.7	-	-	.1	7.7
PACIFIC	84	100.0	.1	5.6	7.1	9.4	3.2	.5	10.7	15.0	48.6
RAIL	1	100.0	-	-	-	-	-	-	.3	-	99.7
MOTOR CARRIER	63	100.0	.1	7.2	8.7	12.3	3.1	.4	13.8	13.7	40.8
PRIVATE TRUCK	14	100.0	-	-	-	-	1.5	-	-	25.5	73.0
AIR	1	100.0	1.5	12.1	11.2	4.1	36.6	11.9	13.0	7.8	1.8
WATER	2	100.0	-	-	-	-	-	-	-	-	100.0
OTHER	-	100.0	3.0	.4	14.8	-	76.1	-	-	5.2	.5
UNKNOWN	-	100.0	-	-	83.3	-	-	-	16.6	-	-

See footnotes at end of table 4.

TABLE 3. **TCC GROUP 369**—Percent Distribution of Geographic Division of Destination and Means of Transport, by Geographic Division of Origin: 1972

Geographic division of destination and means of transport	Number	Percent distribution by division of origin[1]									
		U.S. total	New England	Middle Atlantic	East North Central	West North Central	South Atlantic	East South Central	West South Central	Mountain	Pacific
TONS OF SHIPMENTS	(thousands of tons)										
U.S. TOTAL	1 789	100.0	(D)	13.0	50.2	9.6	5.8	(D)	(D)	(D)	10.3
RAIL	166	100.0	(D)	14.7	52.4	19.2	11.5	(D)	(D)	(D)	2.3
MOTOR CARRIER	1 170	100.0	(D)	16.2	50.6	9.8	6.1	(D)	(D)	(D)	10.1
PRIVATE TRUCK	410	100.0	(D)	4.4	45.4	6.1	2.9	(D)	(D)	(D)	14.7
AIR	10	100.0	(D)	4.2	37.2	.3	2.7	(D)	(D)	(D)	8.2
WATER	3	100.0	(D)	2.9	64.7	-	-	(D)	(D)	(D)	30.2
OTHER	24	100.0	(D)	1.0	93.2	-	.5	(D)	(D)	(D)	.3
UNKNOWN	4	100.0	(D)	.3	81.4	9.7	3.8	(D)	(D)	(D)	4.3
NEW ENGLAND	69	100.0	(D)	35.1	35.7	1.3	3.2	(D)	(D)	(D)	-
RAIL	10	100.0	(D)	-	87.6	-	12.4	(D)	(D)	(D)	-
MOTOR CARRIER	51	100.0	(D)	46.5	27.5	1.8	1.4	(D)	(D)	(D)	-
PRIVATE TRUCK	5	100.0	(D)	4.5	7.9	-	2.2	(D)	(D)	(D)	-
AIR	-	100.0	(D)	1.2	56.9	-	4.5	(D)	(D)	(D)	.8
WATER	-	100.0	(D)	-	-	-	-	(D)	(D)	(D)	-
OTHER	-	100.0	(D)	3.1	75.4	.1	1.1	(D)	(D)	(D)	.7
UNKNOWN	-	100.0	(D)	-	99.9	-	-	(D)	(D)	(D)	-
MIDDLE ATLANTIC	239	100.0	(D)	37.0	41.4	2.2	5.9	(D)	(D)	(D)	.8
RAIL	9	100.0	(D)	-	100.0	-	-	(D)	(D)	(D)	-
MOTOR CARRIER	197	100.0	(D)	41.0	40.8	2.7	6.4	(D)	(D)	(D)	1.0
PRIVATE TRUCK	24	100.0	(D)	29.8	15.8	-	5.6	(D)	(D)	(D)	-
AIR	3	100.0	(D)	1.9	49.0	-	1.7	(D)	(D)	(D)	1.8
WATER	-	100.0	(D)	-	-	-	-	(D)	(D)	(D)	-
OTHER	3	100.0	(D)	2.3	80.6	-	.5	(D)	(D)	(D)	-
UNKNOWN	-	100.0	(D)	1.3	85.6	-	12.4	(D)	(D)	(D)	-
EAST NORTH CENTRAL	580	100.0	(D)	3.8	75.8	11.3	2.1	(D)	(D)	(D)	.5
RAIL	46	100.0	(D)	-	43.6	45.4	11.1	(D)	(D)	(D)	-
MOTOR CARRIER	353	100.0	(D)	6.1	77.9	11.0	1.7	(D)	(D)	(D)	.8
PRIVATE TRUCK	176	100.0	(D)	.3	80.3	3.0	.4	(D)	(D)	(D)	-
AIR	1	100.0	(D)	6.7	38.4	.1	3.1	(D)	(D)	(D)	5.3
WATER	-	100.0	(D)	-	-	-	-	(D)	(D)	(D)	-
OTHER	1	100.0	(D)	4.2	80.1	-	.2	(D)	(D)	(D)	.5
UNKNOWN	-	100.0	(D)	-	77.9	-	2.9	(D)	(D)	(D)	19.2
WEST NORTH CENTRAL	198	100.0	(D)	3.3	38.5	35.4	2.3	(D)	(D)	(D)	3.0
RAIL	19	100.0	(D)	-	51.1	30.9	18.0	(D)	(D)	(D)	-
MOTOR CARRIER	123	100.0	(D)	4.4	46.7	36.2	.7	(D)	(D)	(D)	4.8
PRIVATE TRUCK	54	100.0	(D)	2.0	15.2	35.1	.7	(D)	(D)	(D)	-
AIR	-	100.0	(D)	2.3	74.4	.5	1.4	(D)	(D)	(D)	8.4
WATER	-	100.0	(D)	-	-	-	-	(D)	(D)	(D)	-
OTHER	-	100.0	(D)	8.3	88.1	.2	-	(D)	(D)	(D)	-
UNKNOWN	-	100.0	(D)	-	4.1	95.9	-	(D)	(D)	(D)	-
SOUTH ATLANTIC	210	100.0	(D)	33.1	42.5	4.4	17.1	(D)	(D)	(D)	.6
RAIL	38	100.0	(D)	57.8	23.1	8.3	10.7	(D)	(D)	(D)	-
MOTOR CARRIER	142	100.0	(D)	27.7	45.6	4.2	20.2	(D)	(D)	(D)	.6
PRIVATE TRUCK	18	100.0	(D)	39.8	37.7	-	14.2	(D)	(D)	(D)	.5
AIR	1	100.0	(D)	3.4	27.3	.3	2.5	(D)	(D)	(D)	11.2
WATER	-	100.0	(D)	-	-	-	-	(D)	(D)	(D)	-
OTHER	7	100.0	(D)	.2	98.3	-	1.0	(D)	(D)	(D)	.4
UNKNOWN	-	100.0	(D)	8.8	3.0	-	85.8	(D)	(D)	(D)	-
EAST SOUTH CENTRAL	131	100.0	(D)	3.1	47.0	2.4	16.3	(D)	(D)	(D)	.2
RAIL	14	100.0	(D)	-	97.0	-	3.0	(D)	(D)	(D)	-
MOTOR CARRIER	65	100.0	(D)	4.3	51.3	4.7	22.3	(D)	(D)	(D)	.2
PRIVATE TRUCK	47	100.0	(D)	2.4	23.1	-	13.2	(D)	(D)	(D)	-
AIR	-	100.0	(D)	6.2	26.9	-	.8	(D)	(D)	(D)	12.9
WATER	-	100.0	(D)	-	-	-	-	(D)	(D)	(D)	-
OTHER	2	100.0	(D)	.7	98.5	-	.2	(D)	(D)	(D)	-
UNKNOWN	-	100.0	(D)	-	-	-	-	(D)	(D)	(D)	-
WEST SOUTH CENTRAL	105	100.0	(D)	7.7	44.8	10.7	5.2	(D)	(D)	(D)	7.1
RAIL	3	100.0	(D)	-	62.5	-	37.4	(D)	(D)	(D)	.1
MOTOR CARRIER	77	100.0	(D)	10.4	37.2	13.9	5.3	(D)	(D)	(D)	9.4
PRIVATE TRUCK	20	100.0	(D)	.2	63.7	2.6	-	(D)	(D)	(D)	-
AIR	-	100.0	(D)	2.8	20.0	2.6	2.1	(D)	(D)	(D)	11.8
WATER	-	100.0	(D)	-	-	-	-	(D)	(D)	(D)	-
OTHER	3	100.0	(D)	.2	97.1	-	.5	(D)	(D)	(D)	-
UNKNOWN	-	100.0	(D)	-	-	-	-	(D)	(D)	81.5
MOUNTAIN	47	100.0	(D)	2.0	25.2	8.3	.7	(D)	(D)	(D)	58.3
RAIL	-	100.0	(D)	-	99.3	-	.7	(D)	(D)	(D)	-
MOTOR CARRIER	36	100.0	(D)	2.5	31.5	10.8	.9	(D)	(D)	(D)	47.4
PRIVATE TRUCK	10	100.0	(D)	-	2.1	-	.1	(D)	(D)	(D)	97.0
AIR	-	100.0	(D)	16.9	10.3	-	5.3	(D)	(D)	(D)	58.3
WATER	-	100.0	(D)	-	-	-	-	(D)	(D)	(D)	-
OTHER	-	100.0	(D)	5.2	88.4	-	.2	(D)	(D)	(D)	6.1
UNKNOWN	-	100.0	(D)	-	-	-	100.0	(D)	(D)	(D)	-
PACIFIC	208	100.0	(D)	4.2	23.3	1.1	3.3	(D)	(D)	(D)	65.7
RAIL	23	100.0	(D)	8.2	55.4	6.5	13.5	(D)	(D)	(D)	16.3
MOTOR CARRIER	122	100.0	(D)	5.4	21.3	.6	2.8	(D)	(D)	(D)	67.1
PRIVATE TRUCK	50	100.0	(D)	.2	.7	-	.4	(D)	(D)	(D)	98.1
AIR	1	100.0	(D)	7.8	20.1	.2	4.8	(D)	(D)	(D)	12.8
WATER	3	100.0	(D)	3.0	65.4	-	-	(D)	(D)	(D)	30.5
OTHER	4	100.0	(D)	.3	93.6	-	-	(D)	(D)	(D)	.7
UNKNOWN	2	100.0	(D)	-	99.7	-	.1	(D)	(D)	(D)	-

See footnotes at end of table 4.

TABLE 3. **TCC GROUP 369**—Percent Distribution of Geographic Division of Destination and Means of Transport, by Geographic Division of Origin: 1972—Continued

Geographic division of destination and means of transport	Number	Percent distribution by division of origin[1]									
		U.S. total	New England	Middle Atlantic	East North Central	West North Central	South Atlantic	East South Central	West South Central	Mountain	Pacific
TON-MILES OF SHIPMENTS	(millions of ton-miles)										
U.S. TOTAL..............	765	100.0	(D)	11.4	51.8	9.0	7.1	(D)	(D)	(D)	11.0
RAIL..................	98	100.0	(D)	6.5	59.6	15.1	17.3	(D)	(D)	(D)	1.5
MOTOR CARRIER.........	517	100.0	(D)	14.5	49.7	9.3	6.2	(D)	(D)	(D)	12.3
PRIVATE TRUCK.........	101	100.0	(D)	4.9	43.7	5.8	4.6	(D)	(D)	(D)	14.7
AIR...................	9	100.0	(D)	5.8	32.0	.3	3.5	(D)	(D)	(D)	12.2
WATER.................	11	100.0	(D)	3.9	73.7	-	-	(D)	(D)	(D)	21.6
OTHER.................	20	100.0	(D)	.8	94.2	-	.3	(D)	(D)	(D)	.4
UNKNOWN...............	5	100.0	(D)	-	90.3	1.8	1.3	(D)	(D)	(D)	6.2
NEW ENGLAND............	28	100.0	(D)	20.1	59.7	3.9	5.3	(D)	(D)	(D)	.3
RAIL..................	6	100.0	(D)	-	85.6	-	14.4	(D)	(D)	(D)	-
MOTOR CARRIER.........	20	100.0	(D)	27.4	53.0	5.4	2.7	(D)	(D)	(D)	.3
PRIVATE TRUCK.........	1	100.0	(D)	4.7	32.5	-	6.4	(D)	(D)	(D)	.1
AIR...................	-	100.0	(D)	.5	77.7	-	3.9	(D)	(D)	(D)	3.3
WATER.................	-	100.0	(D)	-	-	-	-	(D)	(D)	(D)	-
OTHER.................	-	100.0	(D)	.9	92.1	.1	.8	(D)	(D)	(D)	2.6
UNKNOWN...............	-	100.0	(D)	-	100.0	-	-	(D)	(D)	(D)	-
MIDDLE ATLANTIC........	78	100.0	(D)	11.3	58.8	6.4	8.5	(D)	(D)	(D)	6.0
RAIL..................	4	100.0	(D)	-	100.0	-	-	(D)	(D)	(D)	-
MOTOR CARRIER.........	65	100.0	(D)	12.8	55.8	7.7	9.0	(D)	(D)	(D)	7.0
PRIVATE TRUCK.........	4	100.0	(D)	10.4	30.5	-	15.7	(D)	(D)	(D)	-
AIR...................	1	100.0	(D)	.6	70.8	-	2.0	(D)	(D)	(D)	9.6
WATER.................	-	100.0	(D)	-	-	-	-	(D)	(D)	(D)	-
OTHER.................	2	100.0	(D)	.4	97.8	-	.4	(D)	(D)	(D)	-
UNKNOWN...............	-	100.0	(D)	.1	91.0	-	8.8	(D)	(D)	(D)	-
EAST NORTH CENTRAL.....	134	100.0	(D)	9.2	48.5	22.9	4.9	(D)	(D)	(D)	4.4
RAIL..................	15	100.0	(D)	-	21.0	59.2	19.7	(D)	(D)	(D)	-
MOTOR CARRIER.........	92	100.0	(D)	13.1	50.0	21.6	3.4	(D)	(D)	(D)	6.0
PRIVATE TRUCK.........	25	100.0	(D)	.8	60.9	7.2	1.3	(D)	(D)	(D)	-
AIR...................	-	100.0	(D)	8.6	15.7	.1	3.7	(D)	(D)	(D)	17.4
WATER.................	-	100.0	(D)	-	-	-	-	(D)	(D)	(D)	-
OTHER.................	-	100.0	(D)	8.6	51.0	.1	.5	(D)	(D)	(D)	3.2
UNKNOWN...............	-	100.0	(D)	-	30.8	-	2.5	(D)	(D)	(D)	66.7
WEST NORTH CENTRAL.....	74	100.0	(D)	9.1	43.1	14.4	5.8	(D)	(D)	(D)	10.6
RAIL..................	10	100.0	(D)	-	54.8	14.2	31.0	(D)	(D)	(D)	-
MOTOR CARRIER.........	47	100.0	(D)	11.3	47.5	11.5	1.7	(D)	(D)	(D)	16.5
PRIVATE TRUCK.........	16	100.0	(D)	8.2	23.1	22.6	2.7	(D)	(D)	(D)	-
AIR...................	-	100.0	(D)	3.9	51.2	.3	2.7	(D)	(D)	(D)	18.4
WATER.................	-	100.0	(D)	-	-	-	-	(D)	(D)	(D)	-
OTHER.................	-	100.0	(D)	16.2	80.0	.1	-	(D)	(D)	(D)	-
UNKNOWN...............	-	100.0	(D)	-	4.3	95.7	-	(D)	(D)	(D)	-
SOUTH ATLANTIC.........	100	100.0	(D)	17.0	61.6	7.6	7.9	(D)	(D)	(D)	2.7
RAIL..................	10	100.0	(D)	15.6	53.1	20.8	10.4	(D)	(D)	(D)	-
MOTOR CARRIER.........	75	100.0	(D)	18.0	61.1	7.0	8.5	(D)	(D)	(D)	2.6
PRIVATE TRUCK.........	7	100.0	(D)	23.8	61.7	-	3.7	(D)	(D)	(D)	3.1
AIR...................	1	100.0	(D)	3.0	22.6	.3	2.2	(D)	(D)	(D)	26.7
WATER.................	-	100.0	(D)	-	-	-	-	(D)	(D)	(D)	-
OTHER.................	5	100.0	(D)	.2	98.0	-	.4	(D)	(D)	(D)	1.3
UNKNOWN...............	-	100.0	(D)	8.0	5.3	-	83.0	(D)	(D)	(D)	-
EAST SOUTH CENTRAL.....	48	100.0	(D)	6.2	52.4	3.4	14.2	(D)	(D)	(D)	.8
RAIL..................	5	100.0	(D)	-	95.6	-	4.4	(D)	(D)	(D)	-
MOTOR CARRIER.........	26	100.0	(D)	8.4	50.9	6.3	16.2	(D)	(D)	(D)	.9
PRIVATE TRUCK.........	14	100.0	(D)	5.2	34.5	.1	16.3	(D)	(D)	(D)	-
AIR...................	-	100.0	(D)	6.0	14.7	-	.4	(D)	(D)	(D)	26.2
WATER.................	-	100.0	(D)	-	-	-	-	(D)	(D)	(D)	-
OTHER.................	1	100.0	(D)	1.0	98.2	-	.2	(D)	(D)	(D)	-
UNKNOWN...............	-	100.0	(D)	-	-	-	-	(D)	(D)	(D)	-
WEST SOUTH CENTRAL.....	78	100.0	(D)	13.2	52.1	7.4	5.1	(D)	(D)	(D)	11.5
RAIL..................	3	100.0	(D)	-	61.2	-	38.7	(D)	(D)	(D)	.1
MOTOR CARRIER.........	56	100.0	(D)	18.1	41.2	9.9	4.8	(D)	(D)	(D)	15.5
PRIVATE TRUCK.........	14	100.0	(D)	.2	87.2	1.6	-	(D)	(D)	(D)	-
AIR...................	1	100.0	(D)	2.8	16.6	1.1	1.5	(D)	(D)	(D)	12.0
WATER.................	-	100.0	(D)	-	-	-	-	(D)	(D)	(D)	-
OTHER.................	2	100.0	(D)	.4	96.8	-	.6	(D)	(D)	(D)	-
UNKNOWN...............	-	100.0	(D)	-	-	-	-	(D)	(D)	(D)	95.5
MOUNTAIN...............	32	100.0	(D)	5.0	38.9	9.4	1.8	(D)	(D)	(D)	38.5
RAIL..................	-	100.0	(D)	-	99.2	-	.8	(D)	(D)	(D)	-
MOTOR CARRIER.........	28	100.0	(D)	5.5	43.4	10.9	2.0	(D)	(D)	(D)	31.1
PRIVATE TRUCK.........	4	100.0	(D)	-	5.1	-	.3	(D)	(D)	(D)	92.1
AIR...................	-	100.0	(D)	27.7	12.1	-	8.8	(D)	(D)	(D)	35.8
WATER.................	-	100.0	(D)	-	-	-	-	(D)	(D)	(D)	-
OTHER.................	-	100.0	(D)	8.1	89.7	-	.3	(D)	(D)	(D)	1.8
UNKNOWN...............	-	100.0	(D)	-	-	-	100.0	(D)	(D)	(D)	-
PACIFIC................	188	100.0	(D)	11.5	50.4	1.7	8.5	(D)	(D)	(D)	21.7
RAIL..................	42	100.0	(D)	11.2	62.8	5.0	17.3	(D)	(D)	(D)	3.4
MOTOR CARRIER.........	106	100.0	(D)	14.9	44.0	1.1	7.5	(D)	(D)	(D)	24.6
PRIVATE TRUCK.........	13	100.0	(D)	3.3	4.9	-	3.7	(D)	(D)	(D)	83.5
AIR...................	2	100.0	(D)	9.7	23.6	.1	5.8	(D)	(D)	(D)	.7
WATER.................	11	100.0	(D)	3.9	73.7	-	-	(D)	(D)	(D)	21.6
OTHER.................	8	100.0	(D)	.4	92.0	-	-	(D)	(D)	(D)	-
UNKNOWN...............	4	100.0	(D)	-	99.6	-	.1	(D)	(D)	(D)	-

See footnotes at end of table 4.

TABLE 4. **TCC GROUP 369—Percent Distribution of Distance Shipped and Weight of Shipment, by Means of Transport: 1972**

Distance shipped and weight of shipment [2] [3]	Number	Percent distribution by means of transport							
		All means of transport	Rail	Motor carrier	Private truck	Air	Water	Other	Unknown
TONS OF SHIPMENTS	(thousands of tons)								
U.S. TOTAL............	1 331	100.0	8.4	64.7	25.2	.7	.2	.4	.3
UNDER 100 MILES.........	269	100.0	2.8	46.5	50.2	.2	-	.3	-
UNDER 1000 POUNDS.....	19	100.0	-	62.1	30.2	3.5	-	4.0	.3
1000 TO 9999 POUNDS...	71	100.0	-	67.1	32.9	-	-	.1	-
10000 TO 29999 POUNDS.	81	100.0	-	34.1	65.9	-	-	-	-
30000 TO 59999 POUNDS.	75	100.0	-	30.7	69.3	-	-	-	-
60000 TO 89999 POUNDS.	21	100.0	34.2	65.8	-	-	-	-	-
90000 POUNDS AND OVER.	-	100.0	-	-	-	-	-	-	-
100 TO 199 MILES........	190	100.0	.3	74.2	24.7	.5	-	.2	.1
UNDER 1000 POUNDS.....	18	100.0	-	81.4	11.5	4.5	.1	1.3	1.0
1000 TO 9999 POUNDS...	74	100.0	.8	75.3	23.7	-	-	.1	.1
10000 TO 29999 POUNDS.	51	100.0	-	69.0	31.0	-	-	-	-
30000 TO 59999 POUNDS.	41	100.0	-	73.2	26.8	-	-	-	-
60000 TO 89999 POUNDS.	3	100.0	-	100.0	-	-	-	-	-
90000 POUNDS AND OVER.	-	100.0	-	-	-	-	-	-	-
200 TO 299 MILES........	218	100.0	5.3	71.2	22.7	.2	-	.3	.2
UNDER 1000 POUNDS.....	18	100.0	.5	88.7	5.7	1.7	-	3.2	.3
1000 TO 9999 POUNDS...	79	100.0	.5	84.2	15.1	-	-	-	-
10000 TO 29999 POUNDS.	43	100.0	.3	57.3	41.4	.2	-	-	1.0
30000 TO 59999 POUNDS.	66	100.0	9.1	63.0	27.9	-	-	-	-
60000 TO 89999 POUNDS.	9	100.0	42.6	57.4	-	-	-	-	-
90000 POUNDS AND OVER.	-	100.0	100.0	-	-	-	-	-	-
300 TO 499 MILES........	246	100.0	10.9	60.4	27.9	.5	-	.2	.2
UNDER 1000 POUNDS.....	20	100.0	.2	83.4	8.8	5.0	-	2.4	.1
1000 TO 9999 POUNDS...	79	100.0	1.6	72.7	25.0	.3	-	-	.5
10000 TO 29999 POUNDS.	53	100.0	1.8	59.3	39.0	-	-	-	-
30000 TO 59999 POUNDS.	85	100.0	20.4	49.1	30.5	-	-	-	-
60000 TO 89999 POUNDS.	4	100.0	94.0	6.0	-	-	-	-	-
90000 POUNDS AND OVER.	2	100.0	100.0	-	-	-	-	-	-
500 TO 999 MILES........	282	100.0	15.8	74.3	7.8	1.3	-	.6	.2
UNDER 1000 POUNDS.....	34	100.0	.4	83.8	3.7	6.0	-	4.5	1.7
1000 TO 9999 POUNDS...	88	100.0	1.4	88.9	7.7	1.7	-	.2	.1
10000 TO 29999 POUNDS.	49	100.0	3.2	86.3	10.6	-	-	-	-
30000 TO 59999 POUNDS.	92	100.0	30.4	60.4	9.3	-	-	-	-
60000 TO 89999 POUNDS.	9	100.0	65.3	34.7	-	-	-	-	-
90000 POUNDS AND OVER.	7	100.0	100.0	-	-	-	-	-	-
1000 TO 1499 MILES......	51	100.0	5.9	71.6	19.2	2.5	-	.7	.1
UNDER 1000 POUNDS.....	10	100.0	1.3	82.9	2.1	10.9	-	2.4	.4
1000 TO 9999 POUNDS...	12	100.0	10.7	86.6	1.2	.8	-	.7	-
10000 TO 29999 POUNDS.	3	100.0	-	59.5	40.5	-	-	-	-
30000 TO 59999 POUNDS.	16	100.0	6.1	44.4	49.5	-	-	-	-
60000 TO 89999 POUNDS.	-	100.0	100.0	-	-	-	-	-	-
90000 POUNDS AND OVER.	7	100.0	-	100.0	-	-	-	-	-
1500 MILES OR OVER......	72	100.0	25.1	60.6	3.6	2.1	4.3	1.1	3.2
UNDER 1000 POUNDS.....	12	100.0	3.4	76.0	3.6	11.0	.8	5.2	.1
1000 TO 9999 POUNDS...	17	100.0	1.5	91.4	3.7	.6	2.1	.8	-
10000 TO 29999 POUNDS.	20	100.0	28.4	39.8	7.4	-	13.1	-	11.4
30000 TO 59999 POUNDS.	17	100.0	45.0	55.0	-	-	-	-	-
60000 TO 89999 POUNDS.	3	100.0	100.0	-	-	-	-	-	-
90000 POUNDS AND OVER.	-	100.0	-	-	-	-	-	-	-
TON-MILES OF SHIPMENTS	(millions of ton-miles)								
U.S. TOTAL............	600	100.0	14.1	67.4	13.7	1.4	2.0	.6	.8
UNDER 100 MILES.........	12	100.0	1.7	54.5	43.4	.2	-	.2	-
UNDER 1000 POUNDS.....	-	100.0	-	69.5	24.8	2.7	-	2.8	.2
1000 TO 9999 POUNDS...	3	100.0	-	70.4	29.6	-	-	-	-
10000 TO 29999 POUNDS.	3	100.0	-	38.4	61.6	-	-	-	-
30000 TO 59999 POUNDS.	3	100.0	-	46.1	53.9	-	-	-	-
60000 TO 89999 POUNDS.	1	100.0	21.2	78.8	-	-	-	-	-
90000 POUNDS AND OVER.	-	100.0	-	-	-	-	-	-	-
100 TO 199 MILES........	28	100.0	.4	73.7	25.2	.4	-	.2	.1
UNDER 1000 POUNDS.....	2	100.0	-	81.9	11.4	4.2	.1	1.4	1.0
1000 TO 9999 POUNDS...	11	100.0	.9	75.7	23.2	-	-	.1	.1
10000 TO 29999 POUNDS.	7	100.0	-	70.6	29.4	-	-	-	-
30000 TO 59999 POUNDS.	6	100.0	-	67.6	32.4	-	-	-	-
60000 TO 89999 POUNDS.	-	100.0	-	100.0	-	-	-	-	-
90000 POUNDS AND OVER.	-	100.0	-	-	-	-	-	-	-

See footnotes at end of table 4.

TABLE 4. **TCC GROUP 369**—Percent Distribution of Distance Shipped and Weight of Shipment, by Means of Transport: 1972—Continued

Distance shipped and weight of shipment[2] [3]	Number	Percent distribution by means of transport							
		All means of transport	Rail	Motor carrier	Private truck	Air	Water	Other	Unknown
TON-MILES OF SHIPMENTS	(millions of ton-miles)								
200 TO 299 MILES........	52	100.0	5.3	72.9	21.1	.2	-	.3	.2
UNDER 1000 POUNDS.....	4	100.0	.5	88.8	5.7	1.7	-	3.2	.2
1000 TO 9999 POUNDS...	19	100.0	.4	85.1	14.4	.2	-	-	-
10000 TO 29999 POUNDS.	10	100.0	.3	58.9	39.8	-	-	-	1.0
30000 TO 59999 POUNDS.	16	100.0	10.3	64.8	24.9	-	-	-	-
60000 TO 89999 POUNDS.	2	100.0	38.9	61.1	-	-	-	-	-
90000 POUNDS AND OVER.	-	100.0	100.0	-	-	-	-	-	-
300 TO 499 MILES........	97	100.0	11.2	60.8	27.2	.5	-	.2	.1
UNDER 1000 POUNDS.....	7	100.0	.2	83.6	8.8	4.8	-	2.4	.2
1000 TO 9999 POUNDS...	31	100.0	1.9	73.4	24.1	.3	-	-	.4
10000 TO 29999 POUNDS.	20	100.0	2.2	62.4	35.4	-	-	-	-
30000 TO 59999 POUNDS.	34	100.0	20.7	47.8	31.5	-	-	-	-
60000 TO 89999 POUNDS.	1	100.0	94.9	5.1	-	-	-	-	-
90000 POUNDS AND OVER.	-	100.0	100.0	-	-	-	-	-	-
500 TO 999 MILES........	194	100.0	14.4	76.3	7.1	1.4	-	.6	.2
UNDER 1000 POUNDS.....	24	100.0	.4	83.6	3.7	6.1	-	4.5	1.7
1000 TO 9999 POUNDS...	61	100.0	1.5	88.8	7.7	1.8	-	.2	-
10000 TO 29999 POUNDS.	33	100.0	2.8	88.5	8.7	-	-	-	-
30000 TO 59999 POUNDS.	63	100.0	28.0	63.7	8.3	-	-	-	-
60000 TO 89999 POUNDS.	6	100.0	58.0	42.0	-	-	-	-	-
90000 POUNDS AND OVER.	4	100.0	100.0	-	-	-	-	-	-
1000 TO 1499 MILES......	60	100.0	6.6	71.0	19.0	2.6	-	.7	.1
UNDER 1000 POUNDS.....	12	100.0	1.3	82.4	2.1	11.2	-	2.5	.4
1000 TO 9999 POUNDS...	15	100.0	11.4	85.9	1.2	.8	-	.7	-
10000 TO 29999 POUNDS.	3	100.0	-	56.5	43.5	-	-	-	-
30000 TO 59999 POUNDS.	19	100.0	7.0	45.0	47.9	-	-	-	-
60000 TO 89999 POUNDS.	-	100.0	100.0	-	-	-	-	-	-
90000 POUNDS AND OVER.	8	100.0	-	100.0	-	-	-	-	-
1500 MILES OR OVER......	154	100.0	25.1	57.0	4.3	2.3	7.6	1.1	2.6
UNDER 1000 POUNDS.....	26	100.0	3.1	74.9	3.3	12.6	.7	5.3	.1
1000 TO 9999 POUNDS...	34	100.0	1.6	88.7	4.8	.6	3.5	.9	-
10000 TO 29999 POUNDS.	47	100.0	25.9	34.8	8.8	-	21.9	-	8.6
30000 TO 59999 POUNDS.	39	100.0	45.7	54.3	-	-	-	-	-
60000 TO 89999 POUNDS.	7	100.0	100.0	-	-	-	-	-	-
90000 POUNDS AND OVER.	-	100.0	-	-	-	-	-	-	-

Note: Detail may not add to total due to rounding. The introductory table shows the estimates of sampling variability for tons; sampling variability for ton-miles has not been estimated. See the map in the Introduction for the States comprising the geographic divisions of the United States.

Shipments excluded from the survey are those moving by pipeline (primarily petroleum products from refineries), parcel post shipments, and commodities moved by own power (motorized vehicles, aircraft, etc.) or towed (prefabricated buildings, etc.). Local shipments (commodities shipped less than 25 miles from the plant) and shipments within the same city are also excluded. Shipments to Alaska and Hawaii from the 48 conterminous States and the District of Columbia are included; however, no data were obtained for shipments originating in Alaska and Hawaii.

- Represents zero or rounds to zero.   (D) Withheld to avoid disclosing figures for individual companies.

[1]Production of this commodity is concentrated in the geographic divisions shown; figures and distributions for geographic divisions not shown are included in the total.

[2]Distances of shipments to foreign destinations are calculated only to the U.S. port of exit.

[3]Includes only shipments represented by bills of lading and invoices. Summary records which did not show individual weights of shipments are not included.

Transportation Equipment

CONTENTS

[Page numbers listed here omit the State prefix number that appears as part of the number for each page]

TABLES (The tables listed below are shown for each of the Transportation Commodity Classification groups in this report)

Comparisons of Tons and Ton-Miles of Shipments for Geographic Divisions of Origin and for Sampling Variability: 1972 and 1967

1. Percent Distribution of Geographic Division of Origin and Distance Shipped, by Means of Transport: 1972

2. Percent Distribution of Geographic Division of Origin and Means of Transport, by Geographic Division of Destination: 1972

3. Percent Distribution of Geographic Division of Destination and Means of Transport, by Geographic Division of Origin: 1972

4. Percent Distribution of Distance Shipped and Weight of Shipment, by Means of Transport: 1972

TCC 371. Motor Vehicles and Equipment

Comparisons of Tons and Ton-Miles of Shipments for
Geographic Divisions of Origin and for Sampling Variability: 1972 and 1967

Geographic division of origin	Estimates				Relative sampling variability in tons (percent)	
	1972		1967		1972	1967
	Tons (thousands)	Ton-miles (millions)	Tons (thousands)	Ton-miles (millions)	1972	1967
U.S. total	38,948	30,990	31,312	14,310	1.6	3.2
New England	(D)	(D)	217	54	(*)	(*)
Middle Atlantic	6,692	2,417	2,486	830	4.5	(*)
East North Central	33,919	19,931	22,143	10,471	2.2	(*)
West North Central	7,449	4,771	2,307	1,212	3.6	(*)
South Atlantic	3,593	1,487	1,928	574	5.5	(*)
East South Central	1,058	561	647	307	25.7	(*)
West South Central	(D)	(D)	307	97	(*)	(*)
Mountain	(D)	(D)	—	—	(*)	—
Pacific	(D)	(D)	1,277	765	(*)	(*)

— Represents or rounds to zero.   (D) Withheld to avoid disclosing figures for individual companies.   (*) Data not published.

TABLE 1. **TCC GROUP 371**—Percent Distribution of Geographic Division of Origin and Distance Shipped, by Means of Transport: 1972

Geographic division of origin[1] and distance shipped[2]	Number	Percent distribution by means of transport							
		All means of transport	Rail	Motor carrier	Private truck	Air	Water	Other	Unknown
TONS OF SHIPMENTS	(thousands of tons)								
U.S. TOTAL..........	38 948	100.0	57.3	38.7	3.4	.1	.1	.2	.1
MIDDLE ATLANTIC.........	6 692	100.0	38.7	59.7	1.3	.1	-	.1	.1
UNDER 100 MILES.......	1 737	100.0	3.9	93.6	2.3	-	-	.1	.2
100 TO 199 MILES......	1 524	100.0	4.2	94.6	1.2	-	-	-	-
200 TO 299 MILES......	1 203	100.0	57.1	42.2	.6	-	-	.1	-
300 TO 499 MILES......	615	100.0	47.8	49.6	1.9	.3	-	.1	.3
500 TO 999 MILES......	1 043	100.0	89.3	9.6	.9	-	-	-	.1
1000 TO 1499 MILES....	416	100.0	97.4	2.1	.4	-	-	-	-
1500 MILES OR OVER....	151	100.0	94.1	4.2	.1	.7	-	.1	.7
EAST NORTH CENTRAL......	33 919	100.0	60.4	34.7	4.4	.1	-	.2	.2
UNDER 100 MILES.......	4 936	100.0	23.2	60.4	16.1	-	-	.1	.1
100 TO 199 MILES......	3 617	100.0	22.8	70.5	6.5	-	-	.1	.1
200 TO 299 MILES......	4 902	100.0	34.1	61.9	3.4	.2	-	.2	.1
300 TO 499 MILES......	6 219	100.0	65.2	32.8	1.1	.2	.1	.2	.3
500 TO 999 MILES......	8 458	100.0	87.6	9.8	2.2	.2	-	.1	.1
1000 TO 1499 MILES....	2 062	100.0	94.0	3.9	1.0	-	-	.3	.7
1500 MILES OR OVER....	3 723	100.0	92.1	6.4	.7	.2	-	.2	.5
WEST NORTH CENTRAL......	7 449	100.0	77.0	21.8	.8	.1	-	.4	-
UNDER 100 MILES.......	146	100.0	1.2	95.1	2.6	-	-	1.1	-
100 TO 199 MILES......	204	100.0	-	95.3	3.1	-	-	1.6	-
200 TO 299 MILES......	722	100.0	20.7	76.1	2.0	-	-	1.2	-
300 TO 499 MILES......	2 086	100.0	75.6	23.1	.8	-	-	.4	-
500 TO 999 MILES......	2 764	100.0	91.1	8.2	.5	.1	-	.1	-
1000 TO 1499 MILES....	1 308	100.0	98.3	1.0	.4	-	-	.2	-
1500 MILES OR OVER....	217	100.0	91.5	7.5	-	-	-	.8	.1
SOUTH ATLANTIC..........	3 593	100.0	42.0	53.8	4.0	.1	.1	.1	-
UNDER 100 MILES.......	432	100.0	2.2	87.9	9.9	-	-	-	-
100 TO 199 MILES......	711	100.0	.9	88.1	11.0	-	-	.1	-
200 TO 299 MILES......	572	100.0	23.4	75.9	.5	-	-	.2	-
300 TO 499 MILES......	949	100.0	56.6	41.9	1.3	-	-	.2	-
500 TO 999 MILES......	747	100.0	86.5	12.4	.4	.5	-	.2	-
1000 TO 1499 MILES....	36	100.0	93.0	.6	6.4	-	-	-	-
1500 MILES OR OVER....	142	100.0	98.3	-	.2	-	1.5	-	-
EAST SOUTH CENTRAL......	1 058	100.0	28.9	64.0	5.5	.1	-	1.2	.2
UNDER 100 MILES.......	82	100.0	-	96.9	3.1	-	-	.1	-
100 TO 199 MILES......	180	100.0	-	95.3	3.6	-	-	.9	.2
200 TO 299 MILES......	122	100.0	4.1	92.6	1.2	-	-	1.7	.4
300 TO 499 MILES......	287	100.0	43.0	52.1	3.3	.1	-	1.3	.2
500 TO 999 MILES......	269	100.0	49.8	37.0	10.9	.1	-	2.0	.4
1000 TO 1499 MILES....	23	100.0	41.8	20.2	38.0	-	-	-	-
1500 MILES OR OVER....	91	100.0	36.7	62.5	.4	.4	-	-	-
TON-MILES OF SHIPMENTS	(millions of ton-miles)								
U.S. TOTAL..........	30 990	100.0	80.1	17.7	1.5	.1	.2	.2	.2
MIDDLE ATLANTIC.........	2 417	100.0	72.9	25.9	.8	.1	-	.1	.2
UNDER 100 MILES.......	79	100.0	4.4	92.4	2.8	-	-	.1	.2
100 TO 199 MILES......	230	100.0	4.1	94.8	1.1	-	-	-	-
200 TO 299 MILES......	300	100.0	60.2	39.2	.6	-	-	.1	-
300 TO 499 MILES......	241	100.0	50.2	47.4	1.7	.3	-	.1	.3
500 TO 999 MILES......	765	100.0	88.9	10.0	.8	-	-	-	.1
1000 TO 1499 MILES....	460	100.0	97.3	2.2	.4	-	-	.1	-
1500 MILES OR OVER....	340	100.0	93.5	4.8	.1	.7	-	.1	.7
EAST NORTH CENTRAL......	19 931	100.0	81.8	15.8	1.6	.1	-	.2	.3
UNDER 100 MILES.......	241	100.0	23.5	66.0	10.3	-	-	.1	-
100 TO 199 MILES......	538	100.0	23.8	70.2	5.8	-	-	.1	.1
200 TO 299 MILES......	1 196	100.0	34.3	61.3	3.8	.2	-	.2	.1
300 TO 499 MILES......	2 568	100.0	67.5	30.6	1.1	.1	.1	.2	.3
500 TO 999 MILES......	5 720	100.0	88.0	9.4	2.3	.2	-	.1	.1
1000 TO 1499 MILES....	2 399	100.0	94.1	3.9	1.0	-	-	.3	.6
1500 MILES OR OVER....	7 265	100.0	92.1	6.4	.6	.2	-	.2	.5
WEST NORTH CENTRAL......	4 771	100.0	87.7	11.2	.6	.1	.2	.2	-
UNDER 100 MILES.......	6	100.0	2.1	94.6	1.8	-	-	1.5	-
100 TO 199 MILES......	30	100.0	-	95.5	3.0	-	-	1.5	-
200 TO 299 MILES......	181	100.0	21.5	75.1	2.0	-	-	1.3	-
300 TO 499 MILES......	833	100.0	76.6	22.0	.9	-	-	.4	-
500 TO 999 MILES......	1 804	100.0	91.8	7.4	.6	.1	-	.1	-
1000 TO 1499 MILES....	1 550	100.0	98.4	1.0	.4	-	-	.2	-
1500 MILES OR OVER....	364	100.0	89.0	8.8	-	-	2.0	.1	-
SOUTH ATLANTIC..........	1 487	100.0	68.6	29.2	1.6	.2	.3	.1	-
UNDER 100 MILES.......	22	100.0	1.3	90.0	8.7	-	-	-	-
100 TO 199 MILES......	105	100.0	.9	88.1	10.9	-	-	.1	-
200 TO 299 MILES......	145	100.0	25.3	74.1	.4	-	-	.1	-
300 TO 499 MILES......	377	100.0	58.9	39.7	1.3	-	-	.1	-
500 TO 999 MILES......	513	100.0	86.8	12.1	.4	.5	-	.2	-
1000 TO 1499 MILES....	41	100.0	93.0	.8	6.2	-	-	-	-
1500 MILES OR OVER....	281	100.0	98.1	-	.2	-	1.8	-	-

See footnotes at end of table 4.

TABLE 1. **TCC GROUP 371**—Percent Distribution of Geographic Division of Origin and Distance Shipped, by Means of Transport: 1972—Continued

Geographic division of origin[1] and distance shipped[2]	Number	Percent distribution by means of transport							
		All means of transport	Rail	Motor carrier	Private truck	Air	Water	Other	Unknown
TON-MILES OF SHIPMENTS	(millions of ton-miles)								
EAST SOUTH CENTRAL......	561	100.0	38.6	53.2	6.8	.2	-	1.0	.2
UNDER 100 MILES........	5	100.0	-	97.2	2.7	-	-	-	-
100 TO 199 MILES......	30	100.0	-	95.9	3.2	-	-	.7	.3
200 TO 299 MILES......	30	100.0	4.7	92.0	1.2	-	-	1.6	.5
300 TO 499 MILES......	111	100.0	44.2	50.8	3.3	.1	-	1.3	.2
500 TO 999 MILES......	180	100.0	48.6	36.2	12.8	.1	-	1.9	.4
1000 TO 1499 MILES....	28	100.0	48.6	18.4	33.0	-	-	-	-
1500 MILES OR OVER....	175	100.0	36.7	62.5	.3	.4	-	-	-

See footnotes at end of table 4.

TABLE 2. **TCC GROUP 371**—Percent Distribution of Geographic Division of Origin and Means of Transport, by Geographic Division of Destination: 1972

Geographic division of origin[1] and means of transport	Number	Percent distribution by division of destination									
		U.S. total	New England	Middle Atlantic	East North Central	West North Central	South Atlantic	East South Central	West South Central	Mountain	Pacific
TONS OF SHIPMENTS	(thousands of tons)										
U.S. TOTAL..............	38 948	100.0	4.3	13.8	28.2	9.4	15.1	5.2	10.2	3.7	10.0
RAIL.................	31 914	100.0	3.4	9.9	16.2	11.4	18.9	5.2	15.9	5.9	13.2
MOTOR CARRIER........	21 561	100.0	6.1	20.0	42.8	7.0	9.9	5.3	2.4	.6	5.9
PRIVATE TRUCK........	1 914	100.0	.6	8.7	64.8	3.7	10.4	3.7	4.2	.7	3.1
AIR..................	60	100.0	6.1	7.6	31.8	14.5	23.1	1.4	1.8	.2	13.6
WATER................	30	100.0	-	6.3	19.7	-	12.4	-	-	-	61.6
OTHER................	109	100.0	3.5	14.6	29.4	14.2	14.4	3.6	7.3	6.5	6.6
UNKNOWN..............	83	100.0	-	7.7	17.1	25.4	2.6	-	23.1	.4	23.7
MIDDLE ATLANTIC.........	6 692	100.0	15.1	38.1	13.3	2.4	25.3	2.3	1.3	.3	2.0
RAIL.................	2 592	100.0	.8	11.7	26.3	5.5	42.0	5.4	2.7	.6	4.9
MOTOR CARRIER........	3 997	100.0	24.6	54.7	4.7	.4	14.8	.2	.4	-	.1
PRIVATE TRUCK........	87	100.0	2.0	64.3	20.2	.8	10.4	2.0	.1	.2	-
AIR..................	3	100.0	.7	.4	55.7	4.8	5.8	.9	.9	-	30.8
WATER................	-	100.0	-	-	-	-	-	-	-	-	-
OTHER................	4	100.0	1.1	39.4	13.2	5.4	28.6	2.7	4.4	.7	4.3
UNKNOWN..............	6	100.0	-	42.9	28.0	-	14.5	-	-	-	14.5
EAST NORTH CENTRAL......	33 919	100.0	2.7	11.2	37.4	10.8	12.4	4.4	8.5	2.6	10.0
RAIL.................	20 476	100.0	3.8	11.7	17.1	13.9	16.8	4.3	13.1	4.0	15.2
MOTOR CARRIER........	11 759	100.0	1.0	11.6	67.6	6.1	5.6	4.6	1.2	.4	1.9
PRIVATE TRUCK........	1 500	100.0	.4	2.2	79.2	2.9	5.7	3.5	4.1	.5	1.6
AIR..................	45	100.0	.3	9.5	29.3	17.1	27.8	.7	1.9	.2	13.2
WATER................	11	100.0	-	16.5	51.4	-	32.1	-	-	-	-
OTHER................	55	100.0	2.9	18.3	33.1	7.5	12.1	3.8	8.2	6.5	7.8
UNKNOWN..............	70	100.0	-	4.3	15.0	29.7	.8	-	25.0	-	25.2
WEST NORTH CENTRAL......	7 449	100.0	3.1	4.7	18.7	15.9	7.9	7.2	25.8	9.8	6.9
RAIL.................	5 732	100.0	4.0	5.7	13.6	7.9	9.8	6.7	31.5	12.4	8.6
MOTOR CARRIER........	1 622	100.0	.2	1.0	35.7	43.7	1.4	9.2	6.9	.8	1.1
PRIVATE TRUCK........	62	100.0	2.5	9.1	38.9	27.1	6.0	4.4	4.1	6.5	1.5
AIR..................	4	100.0	-	1.6	64.0	2.3	8.7	6.8	4.0	-	12.6
WATER................	1	100.0	-	-	-	-	-	-	-	-	100.0
OTHER................	26	100.0	4.2	.7	42.9	34.5	.2	-	6.7	9.6	1.2
UNKNOWN..............	-	100.0	-	-	21.4	-	-	-	-	-	78.6
SOUTH ATLANTIC..........	3 593	100.0	3.3	19.4	9.4	2.0	43.9	10.7	6.9	.7	3.7
RAIL.................	1 507	100.0	1.5	5.7	9.6	4.3	47.8	7.0	13.8	1.7	8.6
MOTOR CARRIER........	1 932	100.0	4.7	28.8	9.9	.3	40.0	14.3	2.0	-	-
PRIVATE TRUCK........	142	100.0	.6	38.1	.2	1.4	57.0	2.2	.2	.2	-
AIR..................	4	100.0	88.3	-	11.2	.1	.3	.2	-	-	.2
WATER................	2	100.0	-	-	-	-	.3	-	-	-	99.7
OTHER................	4	100.0	3.5	10.1	12.7	.1	56.2	13.5	3.7	.1	.1
UNKNOWN..............	-	100.0	-	-	-	-	-	-	-	-	-
EAST SOUTH CENTRAL......	1 058	100.0	1.2	13.1	27.4	4.5	14.4	19.0	10.5	1.7	8.2
RAIL.................	306	100.0	-	20.3	2.0	1.8	21.9	15.6	24.0	3.3	10.9
MOTOR CARRIER........	677	100.0	1.7	8.1	41.0	5.8	9.1	21.2	4.3	1.1	7.7
PRIVATE TRUCK........	58	100.0	.2	30.3	5.7	2.8	32.8	15.0	12.2	.5	.5
AIR..................	-	100.0	-	6.2	39.5	.6	2.8	-	1.2	-	49.7
WATER................	-	100.0	-	-	-	-	-	-	-	-	-
OTHER................	12	100.0	5.4	26.7	9.9	12.8	31.4	7.7	6.1	-	-
UNKNOWN..............	2	100.0	-	16.5	62.2	.4	20.7	-	.2	-	-

See footnotes at end of table 4.

TABLE 2. **TCC GROUP 371—Percent Distribution of Geographic Division of Origin and Means of Transport, by Geographic Division of Destination: 1972**—Continued

Geographic division of origin[1] and means of transport	Number	Percent distribution by division of destination									
		U.S. total	New England	Middle Atlantic	East North Central	West North Central	South Atlantic	East South Central	West South Central	Mountain	Pacific
TON-MILES OF SHIPMENTS	(millions of ton-miles)										
U.S. TOTAL..............	30 990	100.0	3.6	8.1	10.2	8.5	16.0	4.2	14.4	7.0	28.1
RAIL..................	24 817	100.0	3.3	6.5	5.5	8.2	16.9	3.8	16.6	8.1	31.2
MOTOR CARRIER.........	5 480	100.0	5.1	15.2	29.9	9.6	12.1	6.0	5.0	2.4	14.6
PRIVATE TRUCK.........	464	100.0	1.8	11.8	26.9	6.5	19.0	6.6	12.7	2.7	12.1
AIR...................	41	100.0	5.2	6.7	14.7	10.1	19.9	1.1	2.5	.4	39.4
WATER.................	53	100.0	-	2.2	3.9	-	2.5	-	-	-	91.4
OTHER.................	57	100.0	5.6	11.4	12.4	10.7	11.6	1.9	11.8	15.6	18.9
UNKNOWN...............	75	100.0	-	2.9	4.5	13.5	2.0	-	25.2	.2	51.7
MIDDLE ATLANTIC.........	2 417	100.0	7.0	11.1	13.1	5.2	40.3	4.8	4.3	1.4	12.7
RAIL..................	1 761	100.0	.4	4.2	13.5	6.3	46.4	6.3	4.9	1.8	16.2
MOTOR CARRIER.........	627	100.0	25.8	30.0	11.5	2.4	24.3	.8	2.6	.2	2.4
PRIVATE TRUCK.........	19	100.0	2.8	28.0	36.5	3.1	20.9	6.2	.3	1.8	.4
AIR...................	3	100.0	.2	.1	23.5	3.8	·3.8	.6	1.2	-	66.8
WATER.................	-	100.0	-	-	-	-	-	-	-	-	-
OTHER.................	1	100.0	.8	12.7	11.9	11.9	10.9	4.4	15.7	3.4	28.3
UNKNOWN...............	4	100.0	-	4.4	18.2	-	22.3	-	-	-	55.0
EAST NORTH CENTRAL......	19 931	100.0	2.8	8.2	9.5	9.3	13.0	3.5	14.0	6.1	33.6
RAIL..................	16 312	100.0	2.9	6.9	3.7	9.2	13.6	3.0	15.9	7.0	37.8
MOTOR CARRIER.........	3 154	100.0	2.3	15.3	37.5	9.9	9.4	6.0	4.0	2.0	13.5
PRIVATE TRUCK.........	328	100.0	1.4	4.6	30.6	6.0	17.4	7.7	15.9	2.4	13.8
AIR...................	28	100.0	.3	8.3	10.4	11.5	22.8	.4	3.2	.5	42.7
WATER.................	4	100.0	-	25.2	45.6	-	29.2	-	-	-	-
OTHER.................	33	100.0	3.0	10.2	7.5	7.5	9.9	1.9	14.6	17.9	27.5
UNKNOWN...............	68	100.0	-	2.3	3.1	15.0	.2	-	25.9	-	53.4
WEST NORTH CENTRAL......	4 771	100.0	6.0	7.3	12.0	8.5	11.7	5.2	20.8	12.2	16.1
RAIL..................	4 184	100.0	6.6	7.9	8.5	5.6	12.9	4.7	22.7	13.6	17.4
MOTOR CARRIER.........	536	100.0	.7	2.9	37.5	31.0	2.8	9.1	7.5	2.1	6.2
PRIVATE TRUCK.........	29	100.0	6.2	18.9	32.4	9.7	11.7	3.4	4.5	8.8	4.4
AIR...................	2	100.0	-	2.3	51.3	1.5	12.2	4.6	2.7	-	25.4
WATER.................	7	100.0	-	-	-	-	-	-	-	-	100.0
OTHER.................	10	100.0	10.8	1.3	32.1	20.8	.5	-	8.2	21.6	4.6
UNKNOWN...............	-	100.0	-	-	8.2	-	-	-	-	-	91.8
SOUTH ATLANTIC.........	1 487	100.0	2.5	9.1	10.6	2.9	36.9	6.6	11.2	2.3	17.9
RAIL..................	1 020	100.0	.9	4.3	7.2	3.5	37.2	4.2	13.8	3.4	25.6
MOTOR CARRIER.........	433	100.0	5.8	18.7	19.4	1.2	36.7	12.4	5.9	-	-
PRIVATE TRUCK.........	23	100.0	1.9	41.4	.9	9.5	39.7	3.7	1.2	1.8	.1
AIR...................	2	100.0	86.8	-	12.2	.2	-	.2	-	-	.6
WATER.................	4	100.0	-	-	-	-	.1	-	-	-	99.9
OTHER.................	1	100.0	7.8	17.8	19.1	.2	39.4	9.8	4.9	.3	.7
UNKNOWN...............	-	100.0	-	-	-	-	-	-	-	-	-
EAST SOUTH CENTRAL......	561	100.0	1.7	14.9	13.4	3.6	12.9	7.0	12.3	4.5	29.8
RAIL..................	216	100.0	-	15.2	1.6	1.5	16.4	8.2	21.0	6.4	29.7
MOTOR CARRIER.........	298	100.0	2.9	10.1	23.1	5.2	7.4	6.7	6.8	3.7	34.0
PRIVATE TRUCK.........	38	100.0	.3	46.3	4.3	2.3	34.0	3.6	6.9	.8	1.5
AIR...................	-	100.0	-	3.8	15.4	.3	2.0	-	.6	-	77.9
WATER.................	-	100.0	-	-	-	-	-	-	-	-	-
OTHER.................	5	100.0	10.0	38.0	7.7	11.8	21.9	2.5	8.1	-	-
UNKNOWN...............	1	100.0	-	35.0	35.2	.5	28.9	-	.3	-	.1

See footnotes at end of table 4.

TABLE 3. **TCC GROUP 371**—Percent Distribution of Geographic Division of Destination and Means of Transport, by Geographic Division of Origin: 1972

Geographic division of destination and means of transport	Number	Percent distribution by division of origin[1]									
		U.S. total	New England	Middle Atlantic	East North Central	West North Central	South Atlantic	East South Central	West South Central	Mountain	Pacific
TONS OF SHIPMENTS	(thousands of tons)										
U.S. TOTAL.............	38 948	100.0	(D)	12.0	60.9	13.4	6.5	1.9	(D)	(D)	(D)
RAIL................	31 914	100.0	(D)	8.1	64.2	18.0	4.7	1.0	(D)	(D)	(D)
MOTOR CARRIER........	21 561	100.0	(D)	18.5	54.5	7.5	9.0	3.1	(D)	(D)	(D)
PRIVATE TRUCK........	1 914	100.0	(D)	4.6	78.4	3.2	7.4	3.1	(D)	(D)	(D)
AIR.................	60	100.0	(D)	5.8	75.5	7.1	6.6	1.3	(D)	(D)	(D)
WATER...............	30	100.0	(D)	-	38.3	5.7	6.9	-	(D)	(D)	(D)
OTHER...............	109	100.0	(D)	3.9	50.1	24.3	4.5	11.6	(D)	(D)	(D)
UNKNOWN.............	83	100.0	(D)	8.4	85.2	-	-	3.1	(D)	(D)	(D)
NEW ENGLAND............	2 396	100.0	(D)	42.1	37.8	9.8	4.9	.5	(D)	(D)	(D)
RAIL................	1 073	100.0	(D)	2.0	73.2	21.3	2.1	-	(D)	(D)	(D)
MOTOR CARRIER........	1 305	100.0	(D)	75.5	8.7	.3	6.9	.9	(D)	(D)	(D)
PRIVATE TRUCK........	11	100.0	(D)	16.0	55.4	13.7	8.1	1.0	(D)	(D)	(D)
AIR.................	3	100.0	(D)	.6	3.4	-	96.0	-	(D)	(D)	(D)
WATER...............	-	100.0	(D)	-	-	-	-	-	(D)	(D)	(D)
OTHER...............	3	100.0	(D)	1.2	41.7	29.1	4.6	17.7	(D)	(D)	(D)
UNKNOWN.............	-	100.0	(D)	-	100.0	-	-	-	(D)	(D)	(D)
MIDDLE ATLANTIC........	7 685	100.0	(D)	33.2	49.6	4.5	9.1	1.8	(D)	(D)	(D)
RAIL................	3 173	100.0	(D)	9.6	75.4	10.3	2.7	2.0	(D)	(D)	(D)
MOTOR CARRIER........	4 315	100.0	(D)	50.6	31.7	.4	12.9	1.3	(D)	(D)	(D)
PRIVATE TRUCK........	167	100.0	(D)	33.6	19.5	3.4	32.4	10.6	(D)	(D)	(D)
AIR.................	4	100.0	(D)	.3	94.3	1.5	-	1.1	(D)	(D)	(D)
WATER...............	1	100.0	(D)	-	100.0	-	-	-	(D)	(D)	(D)
OTHER...............	16	100.0	(D)	10.4	62.7	1.2	3.1	21.2	(D)	(D)	(D)
UNKNOWN.............	6	100.0	(D)	46.7	46.8	-	-	6.5	(D)	(D)	(D)
EAST NORTH CENTRAL......	15 722	100.0	(D)	5.7	80.7	8.9	2.1	1.8	(D)	(D)	(D)
RAIL................	5 185	100.0	(D)	13.1	67.5	15.0	2.8	.1	(D)	(D)	(D)
MOTOR CARRIER........	9 223	100.0	(D)	2.0	86.2	6.3	2.1	3.0	(D)	(D)	(D)
PRIVATE TRUCK........	1 241	100.0	(D)	1.4	95.7	1.9	-	.3	(D)	(D)	(D)
AIR.................	19	100.0	(D)	10.1	69.6	14.3	2.3	1.6	(D)	(D)	(D)
WATER...............	6	100.0	(D)	-	100.0	-	-	-	(D)	(D)	(D)
OTHER...............	32	100.0	(D)	1.7	56.5	35.4	2.0	3.9	(D)	(D)	(D)
UNKNOWN.............	14	100.0	(D)	13.8	74.8	.1	-	11.2	(D)	(D)	(D)
WEST NORTH CENTRAL......	5 252	100.0	(D)	3.0	69.5	22.6	1.4	.9	(D)	(D)	(D)
RAIL................	3 625	100.0	(D)	3.9	78.7	12.4	1.8	.2	(D)	(D)	(D)
MOTOR CARRIER........	1 510	100.0	(D)	1.1	47.8	46.9	.4	2.6	(D)	(D)	(D)
PRIVATE TRUCK........	71	100.0	(D)	1.0	60.7	23.7	2.9	2.3	(D)	(D)	(D)
AIR.................	8	100.0	(D)	1.9	89.2	1.2	.1	.1	(D)	(D)	(D)
WATER...............	-	100.0	(D)	-	-	-	-	-	(D)	(D)	(D)
OTHER...............	15	100.0	(D)	1.5	26.5	59.1	-	10.5	(D)	(D)	(D)
UNKNOWN.............	21	100.0	(D)	-	100.0	-	-	-	(D)	(D)	(D)
SOUTH ATLANTIC.........	8 413	100.0	(D)	20.1	50.1	7.0	18.8	1.8	(D)	(D)	(D)
RAIL................	6 041	100.0	(D)	18.0	57.1	9.3	11.9	1.1	(D)	(D)	(D)
MOTOR CARRIER........	2 136	100.0	(D)	27.7	30.7	1.1	36.2	2.9	(D)	(D)	(D)
PRIVATE TRUCK........	198	100.0	(D)	4.5	42.6	1.9	40.7	9.7	(D)	(D)	(D)
AIR.................	13	100.0	(D)	1.5	90.7	2.7	-	.2	(D)	(D)	(D)
WATER...............	3	100.0	(D)	-	99.5	-	.2	-	(D)	(D)	(D)
OTHER...............	15	100.0	(D)	7.7	41.9	.3	17.7	25.2	(D)	(D)	(D)
UNKNOWN.............	2	100.0	(D)	47.4	28.0	-	-	24.6	(D)	(D)	(D)
EAST SOUTH CENTRAL......	2 874	100.0	(D)	5.3	51.8	18.7	13.4	7.0	(D)	(D)	(D)
RAIL................	1 649	100.0	(D)	8.6	53.8	23.3	6.4	2.9	(D)	(D)	(D)
MOTOR CARRIER........	1 149	100.0	(D)	.9	47.4	13.0	24.0	12.5	(D)	(D)	(D)
PRIVATE TRUCK........	70	100.0	(D)	2.5	75.1	3.8	4.4	12.5	(D)	(D)	(D)
AIR.................	-	100.0	(D)	3.8	39.6	35.2	1.0	-	(D)	(D)	(D)
WATER...............	-	100.0	(D)	-	-	-	-	-	(D)	(D)	(D)
OTHER...............	3	100.0	(D)	2.9	53.1	-	17.2	25.0	(D)	(D)	(D)
UNKNOWN.............	-	100.0	(D)	-	-	-	-	-	(D)	(D)	(D)
WEST SOUTH CENTRAL......	5 693	100.0	(D)	1.5	50.9	33.7	4.4	1.9	(D)	(D)	(D)
RAIL................	5 072	100.0	(D)	1.4	52.7	35.6	4.1	1.5	(D)	(D)	(D)
MOTOR CARRIER........	511	100.0	(D)	3.1	27.6	21.8	7.6	5.7	(D)	(D)	(D)
PRIVATE TRUCK........	81	100.0	(D)	.1	76.2	3.1	.3	8.8	(D)	(D)	(D)
AIR.................	1	100.0	(D)	2.9	79.3	15.4	-	.9	(D)	(D)	(D)
WATER...............	-	100.0	(D)	-	-	-	-	-	(D)	(D)	(D)
OTHER...............	8	100.0	(D)	2.3	56.2	22.3	2.3	9.7	(D)	(D)	(D)
UNKNOWN.............	19	100.0	(D)	-	92.1	-	-	-	(D)	(D)	(D)
MOUNTAIN...............	2 046	100.0	(D)	.9	42.4	35.7	1.2	.9	(D)	(D)	(D)
RAIL................	1 886	100.0	(D)	.9	43.3	37.7	1.3	.5	(D)	(D)	(D)
MOTOR CARRIER........	139	100.0	(D)	.5	30.3	9.7	-	5.5	(D)	(D)	(D)
PRIVATE TRUCK........	13	100.0	(D)	1.4	51.2	30.4	1.9	2.4	(D)	(D)	(D)
AIR.................	-	100.0	(D)	-	99.8	-	-	.1	(D)	(D)	(D)
WATER...............	-	100.0	(D)	-	-	-	-	-	(D)	(D)	(D)
OTHER...............	7	100.0	(D)	.4	50.1	36.0	-	-	(D)	(D)	(D)
UNKNOWN.............	-	100.0	(D)	-	.6	-	-	-	(D)	(D)	(D)
PACIFIC................	5 588	100.0	(D)	2.4	60.7	9.2	2.4	1.5	(D)	(D)	(D)
RAIL................	4 205	100.0	(D)	3.0	74.2	11.7	3.1	.8	(D)	(D)	(D)
MOTOR CARRIER........	1 268	100.0	(D)	.4	17.1	1.4	-	4.1	(D)	(D)	(D)
PRIVATE TRUCK........	60	100.0	(D)	.1	40.0	1.6	-	.5	(D)	(D)	(D)
AIR.................	8	100.0	(D)	13.1	73.5	6.6	.1	4.8	(D)	(D)	(D)
WATER...............	18	100.0	(D)	-	-	9.3	11.2	-	(D)	(D)	(D)
OTHER...............	7	100.0	(D)	2.5	58.9	4.4	.1	-	(D)	(D)	(D)
UNKNOWN.............	19	100.0	(D)	5.2	90.4	.1	-	-	(D)	(D)	(D)

See footnotes at end of table 4.

TABLE 3. TCC GROUP 371—Percent Distribution of Geographic Division of Destination and Means of Transport, by Geographic Division of Origin: 1972—Continued

Geographic division of destination and means of transport	Number	Percent distribution by division of origin[1]									
		U.S. total	New England	Middle Atlantic	East North Central	West North Central	South Atlantic	East South Central	West South Central	Mountain	Pacific
TON-MILES OF SHIPMENTS	(millions of ton-miles)										
U.S. TOTAL	30 990	100.0	(D)	7.8	64.3	15.4	4.8	1.8	(D)	(D)	(D)
RAIL	24 817	100.0	(D)	7.1	65.7	16.9	4.1	.9	(D)	(D)	(D)
MOTOR CARRIER	5 480	100.0	(D)	11.4	57.6	9.8	7.9	5.5	(D)	(D)	(D)
PRIVATE TRUCK	464	100.0	(D)	4.1	70.7	6.3	5.2	8.3	(D)	(D)	(D)
AIR	41	100.0	(D)	8.7	69.1	7.0	5.8	2.3	(D)	(D)	(D)
WATER	53	100.0	(D)	-	8.6	13.5	9.3	-	(D)	(D)	(D)
OTHER	57	100.0	(D)	2.7	59.1	19.0	3.3	9.6	(D)	(D)	(D)
UNKNOWN	75	100.0	(D)	5.9	90.4	.1	-	1.6	(D)	(D)	(D)
NEW ENGLAND	1 105	100.0	(D)	15.4	49.9	25.8	3.3	.9	(D)	(D)	(D)
RAIL	809	100.0	(D)	.9	58.5	34.3	1.1	-	(D)	(D)	(D)
MOTOR CARRIER	281	100.0	(D)	57.5	25.7	1.4	8.9	3.1	(D)	(D)	(D)
PRIVATE TRUCK	8	100.0	(D)	6.5	56.3	22.1	5.5	1.5	(D)	(D)	(D)
AIR	2	100.0	(D)	.4	3.3	-	96.2	-	(D)	(D)	(D)
WATER	-	100.0	(D)	-	-	-	-	-	(D)	(D)	(D)
OTHER	3	100.0	(D)	.4	31.6	36.8	4.6	17.3	(D)	(D)	(D)
UNKNOWN	-	100.0	(D)	-	100.0	-	-	-	(D)	(D)	(D)
MIDDLE ATLANTIC	2 508	100.0	(D)	10.7	65.1	14.0	5.4	3.3	(D)	(D)	(D)
RAIL	1 608	100.0	(D)	4.6	70.0	20.5	2.7	2.0	(D)	(D)	(D)
MOTOR CARRIER	832	100.0	(D)	22.6	58.0	1.9	9.7	3.6	(D)	(D)	(D)
PRIVATE TRUCK	54	100.0	(D)	9.8	27.5	10.1	18.0	32.3	(D)	(D)	(D)
AIR	2	100.0	(D)	.1	84.6	2.4	-	1.3	(D)	(D)	(D)
WATER	1	100.0	(D)	-	100.0	-	-	-	(D)	(D)	(D)
OTHER	6	100.0	(D)	3.0	52.9	2.2	5.2	32.1	(D)	(D)	(D)
UNKNOWN	2	100.0	(D)	9.0	72.3	-	-	18.7	(D)	(D)	(D)
EAST NORTH CENTRAL	3 146	100.0	(D)	10.1	60.2	18.2	5.0	2.4	(D)	(D)	(D)
RAIL	1 365	100.0	(D)	17.4	44.0	26.1	5.4	.3	(D)	(D)	(D)
MOTOR CARRIER	1 637	100.0	(D)	4.4	72.3	12.3	5.1	4.2	(D)	(D)	(D)
PRIVATE TRUCK	124	100.0	(D)	5.6	80.6	7.6	.2	1.3	(D)	(D)	(D)
AIR	6	100.0	(D)	13.9	48.8	24.5	4.8	2.4	(D)	(D)	(D)
WATER	2	100.0	(D)	-	100.0	-	-	-	(D)	(D)	(D)
OTHER	7	100.0	(D)	2.6	35.6	49.1	5.1	6.0	(D)	(D)	(D)
UNKNOWN	3	100.0	(D)	24.1	63.1	.1	-	12.3	(D)	(D)	(D)
WEST NORTH CENTRAL	2 620	100.0	(D)	4.8	70.7	15.5	1.7	.8	(D)	(D)	(D)
RAIL	2 041	100.0	(D)	5.4	73.7	11.6	1.7	.2	(D)	(D)	(D)
MOTOR CARRIER	527	100.0	(D)	2.8	59.3	31.5	1.0	2.9	(D)	(D)	(D)
PRIVATE TRUCK	30	100.0	(D)	2.0	65.4	9.5	7.6	3.0	(D)	(D)	(D)
AIR	4	100.0	(D)	3.3	78.8	1.1	.1	.1	(D)	(D)	(D)
WATER	-	100.0	(D)	-	-	-	-	-	(D)	(D)	(D)
OTHER	6	100.0	(D)	3.0	41.4	36.9	.1	10.6	(D)	(D)	(D)
UNKNOWN	10	100.0	(D)	-	99.9	-	-	.1	(D)	(D)	(D)
SOUTH ATLANTIC	4 953	100.0	(D)	19.7	52.3	11.3	11.1	1.5	(D)	(D)	(D)
RAIL	4 183	100.0	(D)	19.5	53.2	12.9	9.1	.8	(D)	(D)	(D)
MOTOR CARRIER	664	100.0	(D)	23.0	44.5	2.3	23.9	3.4	(D)	(D)	(D)
PRIVATE TRUCK	88	100.0	(D)	4.5	64.8	3.9	10.7	14.7	(D)	(D)	(D)
AIR	8	100.0	(D)	1.7	79.2	4.3	-	.2	(D)	(D)	(D)
WATER	1	100.0	(D)	-	98.6	-	.2	-	(D)	(D)	(D)
OTHER	6	100.0	(D)	2.6	50.7	.9	11.3	18.2	(D)	(D)	(D)
UNKNOWN	1	100.0	(D)	67.3	9.7	-	-	23.0	(D)	(D)	(D)
EAST SOUTH CENTRAL	1 301	100.0	(D)	9.0	54.1	19.1	7.5	3.0	(D)	(D)	(D)
RAIL	938	100.0	(D)	11.8	52.0	21.1	4.6	1.9	(D)	(D)	(D)
MOTOR CARRIER	331	100.0	(D)	1.5	57.3	14.8	16.2	6.1	(D)	(D)	(D)
PRIVATE TRUCK	30	100.0	(D)	3.9	83.3	3.3	2.9	4.6	(D)	(D)	(D)
AIR	-	100.0	(D)	4.9	26.5	29.6	.9	-	(D)	(D)	(D)
WATER	-	100.0	(D)	-	-	-	-	-	(D)	(D)	(D)
OTHER	1	100.0	(D)	6.3	59.8	-	17.3	12.8	(D)	(D)	(D)
UNKNOWN	-	100.0	(D)	-	-	-	-	-	(D)	(D)	(D)
WEST SOUTH CENTRAL	4 473	100.0	(D)	2.3	62.5	22.2	3.7	1.5	(D)	(D)	(D)
RAIL	4 115	100.0	(D)	2.1	63.0	23.1	3.4	1.1	(D)	(D)	(D)
MOTOR CARRIER	271	100.0	(D)	6.1	46.9	14.8	9.5	7.4	(D)	(D)	(D)
PRIVATE TRUCK	59	100.0	(D)	.1	88.5	2.2	.5	4.5	(D)	(D)	(D)
AIR	1	100.0	(D)	4.0	85.9	7.4	-	.5	(D)	(D)	(D)
WATER	-	100.0	(D)	-	-	-	-	-	(D)	(D)	(D)
OTHER	6	100.0	(D)	3.6	72.8	13.3	1.4	6.6	(D)	(D)	(D)
UNKNOWN	18	100.0	(D)	-	93.0	-	-	-	(D)	(D)	(D)
MOUNTAIN	2 160	100.0	(D)	1.6	56.2	27.0	1.6	1.2	(D)	(D)	(D)
RAIL	2 007	100.0	(D)	1.6	56.6	28.3	1.7	.7	(D)	(D)	(D)
MOTOR CARRIER	131	100.0	(D)	.8	47.4	8.7	-	8.4	(D)	(D)	(D)
PRIVATE TRUCK	12	100.0	(D)	2.7	64.4	20.9	3.4	2.4	(D)	(D)	(D)
AIR	-	100.0	(D)	-	99.9	-	-	.1	(D)	(D)	(D)
WATER	-	100.0	(D)	-	-	-	-	-	(D)	(D)	(D)
OTHER	8	100.0	(D)	.6	67.8	26.3	.1	-	(D)	(D)	(D)
UNKNOWN	-	100.0	(D)	-	1.0	-	-	-	(D)	(D)	(D)
PACIFIC	8 720	100.0	(D)	3.5	76.7	8.8	3.1	1.9	(D)	(D)	(D)
RAIL	7 747	100.0	(D)	3.7	79.5	9.4	3.4	.8	(D)	(D)	(D)
MOTOR CARRIER	801	100.0	(D)	1.8	53.2	4.2	-	12.7	(D)	(D)	(D)
PRIVATE TRUCK	56	100.0	(D)	.1	81.1	2.3	-	1.0	(D)	(D)	(D)
AIR	16	100.0	(D)	14.8	75.0	4.5	.1	4.5	(D)	(D)	(D)
WATER	48	100.0	(D)	-	-	14.7	10.1	-	(D)	(D)	(D)
OTHER	10	100.0	(D)	4.1	86.1	4.7	.1	-	(D)	(D)	(D)
UNKNOWN	38	100.0	(D)	6.3	93.5	.1	-	-	(D)	(D)	(D)

See footnotes at end of table 4.

TABLE 4. TCC GROUP 371—Percent Distribution of Distance Shipped and Weight of Shipment, by Means of Transport: 1972

Distance shipped and weight of shipment[2][3]	Number	Percent distribution by means of transport							
		All means of transport	Rail	Motor carrier	Private truck	Air	Water	Other	Unknown
TONS OF SHIPMENTS	(thousands of tons)								
U.S. TOTAL..........	22 926	100.0	60.9	34.8	3.8	.1	.1	.3	.1
UNDER 100 MILES.........	5 380	100.0	17.7	71.2	10.7	-	-	.2	.1
UNDER 1000 POUNDS.....	36	100.0	.2	63.4	29.8	.6	-	5.2	.8
1000 TO 9999 POUNDS...	1 282	100.0	3.3	89.6	6.5	.1	-	.4	.1
10000 TO 29999 POUNDS.	2 194	100.0	5.0	85.6	9.3	-	-	.1	.1
30000 TO 59999 POUNDS.	1 022	100.0	13.7	62.8	23.2	-	-	.1	.2
60000 TO 89999 POUNDS.	329	100.0	57.6	29.2	13.1	-	-	-	-
90000 POUNDS AND OVER.	515	100.0	91.5	8.5	-	-	-	-	-
100 TO 199 MILES........	4 468	100.0	18.1	74.0	7.5	-	-	.2	.1
UNDER 1000 POUNDS.....	39	100.0	.1	82.0	12.4	2.1	-	3.2	.2
1000 TO 9999 POUNDS...	1 141	100.0	3.6	91.6	4.4	-	-	.4	-
10000 TO 29999 POUNDS.	2 091	100.0	4.5	89.2	6.0	-	-	.2	.1
30000 TO 59999 POUNDS.	695	100.0	26.9	50.9	22.3	-	-	-	-
60000 TO 89999 POUNDS.	170	100.0	91.3	7.7	1.0	-	-	-	-
90000 POUNDS AND OVER.	330	100.0	100.0	-	-	-	-	-	-
200 TO 299 MILES........	5 064	100.0	40.8	54.7	3.8	-	-	.5	.1
UNDER 1000 POUNDS.....	35	100.0	.2	90.4	3.4	2.9	-	2.8	.2
1000 TO 9999 POUNDS...	1 350	100.0	6.4	90.5	2.5	-	.1	.3	-
10000 TO 29999 POUNDS.	1 422	100.0	19.9	70.8	7.9	-	-	1.2	.3
30000 TO 59999 POUNDS.	1 050	100.0	50.3	45.3	4.3	-	-	-	.1
60000 TO 89999 POUNDS.	518	100.0	99.3	.7	-	-	-	-	-
90000 POUNDS AND OVER.	686	100.0	95.5	4.5	-	-	-	-	-
300 TO 499 MILES........	7 056	100.0	63.0	34.8	1.6	.1	.1	.4	.1
UNDER 1000 POUNDS.....	51	100.0	.8	86.4	1.7	8.4	-	2.6	.1
1000 TO 9999 POUNDS...	2 172	100.0	39.1	58.7	1.5	.1	.2	.3	-
10000 TO 29999 POUNDS.	1 063	100.0	22.3	72.1	3.5	-	.4	1.7	-
30000 TO 59999 POUNDS.	2 272	100.0	82.5	15.6	1.6	-	-	.1	.1
60000 TO 89999 POUNDS.	678	100.0	99.2	.8	-	-	-	-	-
90000 POUNDS AND OVER.	816	100.0	98.7	.7	.6	-	-	-	-
500 TO 999 MILES........	10 285	100.0	86.5	10.7	2.4	.2	-	.2	.1
UNDER 1000 POUNDS.....	105	100.0	.5	92.1	1.1	3.9	-	2.4	-
1000 TO 9999 POUNDS...	2 353	100.0	77.8	20.9	1.0	.2	-	.1	.1
10000 TO 29999 POUNDS.	725	100.0	46.2	35.1	16.7	-	-	1.4	.5
30000 TO 59999 POUNDS.	3 487	100.0	90.4	6.3	2.9	.2	.1	.1	-
60000 TO 89999 POUNDS.	2 412	100.0	100.0	-	-	-	-	-	-
90000 POUNDS AND OVER.	1 201	100.0	97.4	2.6	-	-	-	-	-
1000 TO 1499 MILES......	3 502	100.0	96.2	2.4	1.1	-	-	.3	-
UNDER 1000 POUNDS.....	17	100.0	-	90.1	.7	3.2	.1	5.9	-
1000 TO 9999 POUNDS...	528	100.0	90.8	7.3	1.0	.1	-	.9	-
10000 TO 29999 POUNDS.	167	100.0	70.3	12.1	15.3	-	-	2.3	-
30000 TO 59999 POUNDS.	1 574	100.0	99.2	.4	.5	-	-	-	-
60000 TO 89999 POUNDS.	1 129	100.0	99.8	.2	-	-	-	-	-
90000 POUNDS AND OVER.	85	100.0	100.0	-	-	-	-	-	-
1500 MILES OR OVER......	3 895	100.0	92.6	6.0	.5	.2	.5	.1	-
UNDER 1000 POUNDS.....	24	100.0	3.9	81.6	.3	13.0	-	1.1	-
1000 TO 9999 POUNDS...	819	100.0	83.2	14.0	.1	.2	2.0	.3	.1
10000 TO 29999 POUNDS.	183	100.0	61.7	31.1	4.9	.5	.2	1.6	-
30000 TO 59999 POUNDS.	412	100.0	87.7	9.3	2.0	.5	.5	-	-
60000 TO 89999 POUNDS.	2 115	100.0	99.9	.1	-	-	-	-	-
90000 POUNDS AND OVER.	338	100.0	99.5	.5	-	-	-	-	-
TON-MILES OF SHIPMENTS	(millions of ton-miles)								
U.S. TOTAL..........	23 712	100.0	82.6	15.0	1.7	.1	.2	.2	-
UNDER 100 MILES.........	276	100.0	17.9	75.0	6.7	-	-	.1	.1
UNDER 1000 POUNDS.....	1	100.0	.3	75.1	19.2	.6	-	4.1	.7
1000 TO 9999 POUNDS...	67	100.0	1.7	93.5	4.3	.1	-	.3	.1
10000 TO 29999 POUNDS.	105	100.0	4.7	88.9	6.2	-	-	.1	.1
30000 TO 59999 POUNDS.	55	100.0	12.9	72.0	14.8	-	-	-	.3
60000 TO 89999 POUNDS.	15	100.0	63.1	33.1	3.8	-	-	-	-
90000 POUNDS AND OVER.	29	100.0	88.3	11.7	-	-	-	-	-
100 TO 199 MILES........	674	100.0	18.3	74.6	6.8	-	-	.2	.1
UNDER 1000 POUNDS.....	5	100.0	.1	82.5	11.5	2.5	-	3.3	.2
1000 TO 9999 POUNDS...	168	100.0	3.9	91.3	4.4	-	-	.3	-
10000 TO 29999 POUNDS.	317	100.0	4.4	89.8	5.5	-	-	.2	.2
30000 TO 59999 POUNDS.	104	100.0	27.2	53.6	19.1	-	-	-	-
60000 TO 89999 POUNDS.	25	100.0	91.1	7.6	1.3	-	-	-	-
90000 POUNDS AND OVER.	51	100.0	100.0	-	-	-	-	-	-

See footnotes at end of table 4.

TABLE 4. TCC GROUP 371—Percent Distribution of Distance Shipped and Weight of Shipment, by Means of Transport: 1972—Continued

Distance shipped and weight of shipment[2] [3]	Number	Percent distribution by means of transport							
		All means of transport	Rail	Motor carrier	Private truck	Air	Water	Other	Unknown
TON-MILES OF SHIPMENTS	(millions of ton-miles)								
200 TO 299 MILES	1 261	100.0	41.8	53.4	4.1	-	-	.5	.1
UNDER 1000 POUNDS	8	100.0	.2	90.6	3.0	3.0	-	2.8	.3
1000 TO 9999 POUNDS	333	100.0	6.9	90.1	2.5	-	.2	.3	-
10000 TO 29999 POUNDS	349	100.0	20.7	68.9	8.8	-	-	1.3	.3
30000 TO 59999 POUNDS	267	100.0	52.2	43.2	4.5	-	-	-	.1
60000 TO 89999 POUNDS	129	100.0	99.4	.6	-	-	-	-	-
90000 POUNDS AND OVER	171	100.0	95.5	4.5	-	-	-	-	-
300 TO 499 MILES	2 837	100.0	65.2	32.6	1.6	.1	.1	.4	.1
UNDER 1000 POUNDS	20	100.0	.8	86.6	1.8	8.2	-	2.6	.1
1000 TO 9999 POUNDS	864	100.0	42.2	55.7	1.4	.1	.2	.3	-
10000 TO 29999 POUNDS	412	100.0	24.9	69.3	3.7	-	.3	1.7	-
30000 TO 59999 POUNDS	913	100.0	83.3	14.8	1.6	-	-	.1	.1
60000 TO 89999 POUNDS	295	100.0	99.3	.7	-	-	-	-	-
90000 POUNDS AND OVER	331	100.0	98.8	.6	.6	-	-	-	-
500 TO 999 MILES	6 985	100.0	87.0	10.1	2.5	.1	-	.2	.1
UNDER 1000 POUNDS	74	100.0	.4	92.5	1.0	3.4	-	2.7	-
1000 TO 9999 POUNDS	1 633	100.0	79.4	19.3	1.0	.1	-	.1	.1
10000 TO 29999 POUNDS	485	100.0	46.9	33.1	18.1	-	-	1.4	.4
30000 TO 59999 POUNDS	2 344	100.0	90.7	6.0	3.0	.2	-	.1	-
60000 TO 89999 POUNDS	1 709	100.0	100.0	-	-	-	-	-	-
90000 POUNDS AND OVER	738	100.0	97.2	2.8	-	-	-	-	-
1000 TO 1499 MILES	4 094	100.0	96.3	2.4	1.0	-	-	.3	-
UNDER 1000 POUNDS	21	100.0	-	90.2	.6	3.1	.1	6.0	-
1000 TO 9999 POUNDS	626	100.0	90.9	7.2	.9	.1	-	.8	-
10000 TO 29999 POUNDS	186	100.0	70.0	12.5	15.2	-	-	2.3	-
30000 TO 59999 POUNDS	1 850	100.0	99.2	.4	.4	-	-	-	-
60000 TO 89999 POUNDS	1 314	100.0	99.8	.2	-	-	-	-	-
90000 POUNDS AND OVER	95	100.0	100.0	-	-	-	-	-	-
1500 MILES OR OVER	7 582	100.0	92.5	6.0	.4	.2	.6	.2	-
UNDER 1000 POUNDS	47	100.0	4.1	80.4	.3	14.1	-	1.1	-
1000 TO 9999 POUNDS	1 534	100.0	81.9	14.5	.1	.3	2.8	.3	.2
10000 TO 29999 POUNDS	374	100.0	62.6	30.4	4.4	.5	.3	1.9	-
30000 TO 59999 POUNDS	772	100.0	87.9	8.9	2.0	.5	.6	-	-
60000 TO 89999 POUNDS	4 171	100.0	99.9	.1	-	-	-	-	-
90000 POUNDS AND OVER	681	100.0	99.5	.5	-	-	-	-	-

Note: Detail may not add to total due to rounding. The introductory table shows the estimates of sampling variability for tons; sampling variability for ton-miles has not been estimated. See the map in the Introduction for the States comprising the geographic divisions of the United States.

Shipments excluded from the survey are those moving by pipeline (primarily petroleum products from refineries), parcel post shipments, and commodities moved by own power (motorized vehicles, aircraft, etc.) or towed (prefabricated buildings, etc.). Local shipments (commodities shipped less than 25 miles from the plant) and shipments within the same city are also excluded. Shipments to Alaska and Hawaii from the 48 conterminous States and the District of Columbia are included; however, no data were obtained for shipments originating in Alaska and Hawaii.

- Represents zero or rounds to zero.   (D) Withheld to avoid disclosing figures for individual companies.

[1]Production of this commodity is concentrated in the geographic divisions shown; figures and distributions for geographic divisions not shown are included in the total.

[2]Distances of shipments to foreign destinations are calculated only to the U.S. port of exit.

[3]Includes only shipments represented by bills of lading and invoices. Summary records which did not show individual weights of shipments are not included.

TCC 374. Railroad Equipment

Comparisons of Tons and Ton-Miles of Shipments for
Geographic Divisions of Origin and for Sampling Variability: 1972 and 1967

Geographic division of origin	Estimates				Relative sampling variability in tons (percent)	
	1972		1967		1972	1967
	Tons (thousands)	Ton-miles (millions)	Tons (thousands)	Ton-miles (millions)		
U.S. total	1,420	618	2,238	841	11.3	(*)
New England	(D)	(D)	(*)	(*)	(*)	(*)
Middle Atlantic	645	224	(*)	(*)	12.6	(*)
East North Central	560	248	(*)	(*)	20.6	(*)
West North Central	57	34	(*)	(*)	24.6	(*)
South Atlantic	(D)	(D)	(*)	(*)	(*)	(*)
East South Central	(D)	(D)	(*)	(*)	(*)	(*)
West South Central	(D)	(D)	(*)	(*)	(*)	(*)
Mountain	—	—	(*)	(*)	—	(*)
Pacific	(D)	(D)	(*)	(*)	(*)	(*)

— Represents or rounds to zero.   (D) Withheld to avoid disclosing figures for individual companies.   (*) Data not published.

TABLE 1. **TCC GROUP 374—Percent Distribution of Geographic Division of Origin and Distance Shipped, by Means of Transport: 1972**

Geographic division of origin[1] and distance shipped[2]	Number	Percent distribution by means of transport							
		All means of transport	Rail	Motor carrier	Private truck	Air	Water	Other	Unknown
TONS OF SHIPMENTS	(thousands of tons)								
U.S. TOTAL............	1 420	100.0	79.9	18.6	1.5	.1	-	-	-
MIDDLE ATLANTIC........	645	100.0	88.0	11.6	.3	.1	-	-	-
UNDER 100 MILES......	160	100.0	94.4	5.0	.6	-	-	-	-
100 TO 199 MILES......	141	100.0	78.2	21.2	.6	-	-	-	-
200 TO 299 MILES......	112	100.0	94.3	5.7	-	-	-	-	-
300 TO 499 MILES......	106	100.0	92.3	7.1	.4	.3	-	-	-
500 TO 999 MILES......	98	100.0	80.3	19.6	-	.1	-	-	-
1000 TO 1499 MILES....	8	100.0	69.7	30.2	-	-	-	.2	-
1500 MILES OR OVER....	18	100.0	93.1	6.8	-	.1	-	-	-
EAST NORTH CENTRAL......	560	100.0	78.1	20.7	1.0	.1	-	.1	-
UNDER 100 MILES......	192	100.0	80.6	17.3	2.1	-	-	-	-
100 TO 199 MILES......	22	100.0	77.0	22.9	.1	-	-	-	-
200 TO 299 MILES......	73	100.0	70.7	29.3	-	-	-	-	-
300 TO 499 MILES......	143	100.0	73.7	25.0	1.1	-	-	-	.1
500 TO 999 MILES......	60	100.0	86.0	12.7	-	.4	-	.8	-
1000 TO 1499 MILES....	7	100.0	47.2	52.4	-	.1	-	.3	-
1500 MILES OR OVER....	58	100.0	85.9	14.0	-	.1	-	-	-
WEST NORTH CENTRAL......	57	100.0	46.2	34.7	19.1	-	-	-	-
UNDER 100 MILES......	2	100.0	65.8	26.7	7.4	-	-	-	-
100 TO 199 MILES......	-	100.0	70.1	9.5	20.3	-	-	-	-
200 TO 299 MILES......	8	100.0	78.6	21.4	-	-	-	-	-
300 TO 499 MILES......	19	100.0	10.9	71.4	17.6	-	-	-	-
500 TO 999 MILES......	20	100.0	64.2	7.5	28.3	-	-	-	-
1000 TO 1499 MILES....	2	100.0	-	57.0	43.0	.1	-	-	-
1500 MILES OR OVER....	2	100.0	98.9	1.1	-	-	-	-	-
TON-MILES OF SHIPMENTS	(millions of ton-miles)								
U.S. TOTAL............	618	100.0	79.9	18.4	1.5	.1	-	.1	-
MIDDLE ATLANTIC........	224	100.0	87.8	12.0	.1	.1	-	-	-
UNDER 100 MILES......	8	100.0	94.9	4.9	.2	-	-	-	-
100 TO 199 MILES......	20	100.0	80.1	19.3	.7	-	-	-	-
200 TO 299 MILES......	30	100.0	94.2	5.8	-	-	-	-	-
300 TO 499 MILES......	41	100.0	93.0	6.5	.3	.2	-	-	-
500 TO 999 MILES......	72	100.0	82.7	17.2	-	.1	-	-	-
1000 TO 1499 MILES....	10	100.0	71.7	28.2	-	-	-	.1	-
1500 MILES OR OVER....	40	100.0	93.1	6.8	-	.1	-	-	-
EAST NORTH CENTRAL......	248	100.0	81.6	17.8	.3	.1	-	.2	-
UNDER 100 MILES......	4	100.0	78.0	19.5	2.6	-	-	-	-
100 TO 199 MILES......	3	100.0	77.0	22.8	.2	-	-	-	-
200 TO 299 MILES......	17	100.0	70.1	29.9	-	-	-	-	-
300 TO 499 MILES......	59	100.0	78.1	20.7	1.1	-	-	-	.2
500 TO 999 MILES......	47	100.0	87.6	11.2	-	.4	-	.7	-
1000 TO 1499 MILES....	9	100.0	44.2	55.4	-	.1	-	.3	-
1500 MILES OR OVER....	106	100.0	86.4	13.5	-	.1	-	-	-
WEST NORTH CENTRAL......	34	100.0	51.0	27.6	21.4	-	-	-	-
UNDER 100 MILES......	-	100.0	65.4	33.0	1.6	-	-	-	-
100 TO 199 MILES......	-	100.0	68.7	9.4	21.9	-	-	-	-
200 TO 299 MILES......	1	100.0	77.7	22.3	-	-	-	-	-
300 TO 499 MILES......	8	100.0	9.3	73.0	17.6	.1	-	-	-
500 TO 999 MILES......	16	100.0	67.9	5.9	26.3	-	-	-	-
1000 TO 1499 MILES....	3	100.0	-	56.7	43.3	.1	-	-	-
1500 MILES OR OVER....	3	100.0	99.0	1.0	-	-	-	-	-

See footnotes at end of table 4.

TABLE 2. **TCC GROUP 374—Percent Distribution of Geographic Division of Origin and Means of Transport, by Geographic Division of Destination: 1972**

Geographic division of origin[1] and means of transport	Number	Percent distribution by division of destination								
		U.S. total	New England	Middle Atlantic	East North Central	West North Central	South Atlantic	East South Central	West South Central	Mountain	Pacific
TONS OF SHIPMENTS	(thousands of tons)									
U.S. TOTAL.............	1 420	100.0	.1	23.3	35.1	11.5	9.4	6.2	7.5	1.0	6.0
RAIL..................	1 134	100.0	-	23.6	32.0	12.3	10.1	6.6	8.6	.7	6.2
MOTOR CARRIER.........	263	100.0	.6	21.3	48.3	8.3	6.6	5.1	2.8	1.9	5.0
PRIVATE TRUCK.........	20	100.0	-	29.5	37.9	11.0	3.9	3.1	4.1	4.8	5.7
AIR...................	-	100.0	-	54.9	5.5	10.2	5.6	-	11.4	1.7	10.7
WATER.................	-	100.0	-	-	-	-	-	-	-	-	-
OTHER.................	-	100.0	.4	51.6	11.1	.5	6.0	1.1	27.7	-	1.7
UNKNOWN...............	-	100.0	-	65.7	12.5	-	2.3	.2	17.3	-	1.9

See footnotes at end of table 4.

TABLE 2. **TCC GROUP 374—Percent Distribution of Geographic Division of Origin and Means of Transport, by Geographic Division of Destination: 1972**—Continued

Geographic division of origin[1] and means of transport	Number	Percent distribution by division of destination									
		U.S. total	New England	Middle Atlantic	East North Central	West North Central	South Atlantic	East South Central	West South Central	Mountain	Pacific
TONS OF SHIPMENTS	(thousands of tons)										
MIDDLE ATLANTIC	645	100.0	-	36.0	24.5	8.0	16.0	10.0	2.2	.9	2.4
RAIL	568	100.0	-	35.3	23.6	8.0	17.0	10.5	2.0	1.0	2.5
MOTOR CARRIER	74	100.0	.1	40.2	32.1	7.8	7.8	6.9	3.5	.3	1.4
PRIVATE TRUCK	2	100.0	-	63.0	.9	-	36.1	-	-	-	-
AIR	-	100.0	-	74.0	7.0	15.6	-	-	.1	1.3	2.0
WATER	-	100.0	-	-	-	-	-	-	-	-	-
OTHER	-	100.0	.5	34.0	19.9	.3	11.3	11.3	20.9	-	1.7
UNKNOWN	-	100.0	-	76.5	-	-	23.5	-	-	-	-
EAST NORTH CENTRAL	560	100.0	.1	10.0	48.0	18.1	2.7	2.4	7.5	1.1	10.1
RAIL	437	100.0	-	9.6	43.9	20.8	2.5	2.7	9.0	.4	11.1
MOTOR CARRIER	116	100.0	.4	9.5	63.6	8.9	3.4	1.5	2.1	3.9	6.8
PRIVATE TRUCK	5	100.0	-	43.6	56.4	-	-	-	-	-	-
AIR	-	100.0	-	40.9	1.8	5.8	8.5	-	22.1	2.3	18.6
WATER	-	100.0	-	-	-	-	-	-	-	-	-
OTHER	-	100.0	-	62.7	.5	-	1.1	-	33.8	-	2.0
UNKNOWN	-	100.0	-	81.8	14.9	-	2.9	.3	-	-	-
WEST NORTH CENTRAL	57	100.0	-	26.4	50.6	9.0	.6	.7	2.1	1.9	8.7
RAIL	26	100.0	-	50.4	33.9	6.6	-	-	.6	.6	8.5
MOTOR CARRIER	19	100.0	-	3.8	77.5	5.8	1.8	1.9	.9	.4	7.9
PRIVATE TRUCK	10	100.0	-	9.4	42.3	20.8	-	-	7.7	9.1	10.7
AIR	-	100.0	-	-	84.1	-	-	-	-	-	15.9
WATER	-	100.0	-	-	-	-	-	-	-	-	-
OTHER	-	100.0	-	-	-	-	-	-	-	-	-
UNKNOWN	-	100.0	-	-	-	-	-	-	-	-	-
TON-MILES OF SHIPMENTS	(millions of ton-miles)										
U.S. TOTAL	618	100.0	.1	12.8	16.6	14.5	6.6	5.8	15.1	3.2	25.3
RAIL	494	100.0	-	12.2	12.7	15.7	7.0	5.9	17.3	2.6	26.7
MOTOR CARRIER	113	100.0	.6	14.0	32.5	9.8	5.3	6.2	6.0	5.7	19.9
PRIVATE TRUCK	9	100.0	-	26.4	30.0	9.2	1.4	.1	7.5	8.3	17.1
AIR	-	100.0	-	35.7	2.9	10.2	5.8	-	14.3	3.2	27.8
WATER	-	100.0	-	-	-	-	-	-	-	-	-
OTHER	-	100.0	.3	47.5	6.0	.6	2.3	1.1	37.4	-	4.9
UNKNOWN	-	100.0	-	83.2	4.6	-	2.6	.3	8.7	-	.6
MIDDLE ATLANTIC	224	100.0	-	12.0	18.7	19.0	13.6	11.5	5.6	4.6	15.2
RAIL	197	100.0	-	11.3	17.2	19.5	14.5	11.6	4.8	5.0	16.0
MOTOR CARRIER	26	100.0	.1	16.5	29.4	15.3	6.5	11.2	10.8	1.4	8.9
PRIVATE TRUCK	-	100.0	-	54.7	1.2	-	44.1	-	-	-	-
AIR	-	100.0	-	49.7	5.4	25.7	-	-	.3	4.0	14.9
WATER	-	100.0	-	-	-	-	-	-	-	-	-
OTHER	-	100.0	.4	13.0	14.1	.5	6.9	14.9	42.7	-	7.5
UNKNOWN	-	100.0	-	61.7	-	-	38.3	-	-	-	-
EAST NORTH CENTRAL	248	100.0	.1	8.6	10.2	16.7	2.1	2.4	14.6	3.5	41.8
RAIL	202	100.0	-	7.9	6.3	18.8	1.9	2.5	16.9	1.3	44.3
MOTOR CARRIER	44	100.0	.7	9.9	27.9	7.6	3.1	2.0	4.0	13.4	31.4
PRIVATE TRUCK	-	100.0	-	88.7	11.3	-	-	-	-	-	-
AIR	-	100.0	-	30.7	.6	3.1	7.3	-	20.5	2.9	34.9
WATER	-	100.0	-	-	-	-	-	-	-	-	-
OTHER	-	100.0	-	54.2	-	-	.8	-	40.1	-	4.9
UNKNOWN	-	100.0	-	89.0	6.6	-	3.8	.6	-	-	-
WEST NORTH CENTRAL	34	100.0	-	37.0	32.6	3.1	.5	.5	2.4	2.4	21.6
RAIL	17	100.0	-	64.2	13.4	.3	.3	-	.3	-	21.8
MOTOR CARRIER	9	100.0	-	5.3	65.8	1.9	2.0	1.8	1.0	.6	21.6
PRIVATE TRUCK	7	100.0	-	13.1	35.4	11.3	-	-	9.1	10.2	20.9
AIR	-	100.0	-	-	64.6	-	-	-	-	-	35.4
WATER	-	100.0	-	-	-	-	-	-	-	-	-
OTHER	-	100.0	-	-	-	-	-	-	-	-	-
UNKNOWN	-	100.0	-	-	-	-	-	-	-	-	-

See footnotes at end of table 4.

TABLE 3. **TCC GROUP 374—Percent Distribution of Geographic Division of Destination and Means of Transport, by Geographic Division of Origin: 1972**

Geographic division of destination and means of transport	Number	Percent distribution by division of origin[1]									
		U.S. total	New England	Middle Atlantic	East North Central	West North Central	South Atlantic	East South Central	West South Central	Mountain	Pacific
TONS OF SHIPMENTS	(thousands of tons)										
U.S. TOTAL..............	1 420	100.0	(D)	45.5	39.4	4.0	(D)	(D)	(D)	(D)	(D)
RAIL..................	1 134	100.0	(D)	50.1	38.5	2.3	(D)	(D)	(D)	(D)	(D)
MOTOR CARRIER.........	263	100.0	(D)	28.4	44.0	7.5	(D)	(D)	(D)	(D)	(D)
PRIVATE TRUCK.........	20	100.0	(D)	10.4	27.2	53.0	(D)	(D)	(D)	(D)	(D)
AIR...................	-	100.0	(D)	47.3	48.5	1.6	(D)	(D)	(D)	(D)	(D)
WATER.................	-	100.0	(D)	-	-	-	(D)	(D)	(D)	(D)	(D)
OTHER.................	-	100.0	(D)	9.4	75.7	-	(D)	(D)	(D)	(D)	(D)
UNKNOWN...............	-	100.0	(D)	.9	72.7	-	(D)	(D)	(D)	(D)	(D)
NEW ENGLAND............	1	100.0	(D)	3.7	25.8	-	(D)	(D)	(D)	(D)	(D)
RAIL..................	-	100.0	(D)	-	-	-	(D)	(D)	(D)	(D)	(D)
MOTOR CARRIER.........	1	100.0	(D)	3.6	25.8		(D)	(D)	(D)	(D)	(D)
PRIVATE TRUCK.........	-	100.0	(D)	-	-	-	(D)	(D)	(D)	(D)	(D)
AIR...................	-	100.0	(D)	100.0	-	-	(D)	(D)	(D)	(D)	(D)
WATER.................	-	100.0	(D)	-	-	-	(D)	(D)	(D)	(D)	(D)
OTHER.................	-	100.0	(D)	12.6	-	-	(D)	(D)	(D)	(D)	(D)
UNKNOWN...............	-	100.0	(D)	-	-	-	(D)	(D)	(D)	(D)	(D)
MIDDLE ATLANTIC........	330	100.0	(D)	70.3	16.9	4.6	(D)	(D)	(D)	(D)	(D)
RAIL..................	267	100.0	(D)	75.0	15.6	5.0	(D)	(D)	(D)	(D)	(D)
MOTOR CARRIER.........	56	100.0	(D)	53.5	19.6	1.4	(D)	(D)	(D)	(D)	(D)
PRIVATE TRUCK.........	6	100.0	(D)	22.1	40.2	17.0	(D)	(D)	(D)	(D)	(D)
AIR...................	-	100.0	(D)	63.7	36.1	-	(D)	(D)	(D)	(D)	(D)
WATER.................	-	100.0	(D)	-	-	-	(D)	(D)	(D)	(D)	(D)
OTHER.................	-	100.0	(D)	6.2	92.0	-	(D)	(D)	(D)	(D)	(D)
UNKNOWN...............	-	100.0	(D)	1.0	90.5	-	(D)	(D)	(D)	(D)	(D)
EAST NORTH CENTRAL.....	498	100.0	(D)	31.8	54.0	5.8	(D)	(D)	(D)	(D)	(D)
RAIL..................	362	100.0	(D)	37.0	52.9	2.5	(D)	(D)	(D)	(D)	(D)
MOTOR CARRIER.........	127	100.0	(D)	18.9	58.0	12.1	(D)	(D)	(D)	(D)	(D)
PRIVATE TRUCK.........	7	100.0	(D)	.2	40.6	59.2	(D)	(D)	(D)	(D)	(D)
AIR...................	-	100.0	(D)	60.4	15.8	23.9	(D)	(D)	(D)	(D)	(D)
WATER.................	-	100.0	(D)	-	-	-	(D)	(D)	(D)	(D)	(D)
OTHER.................	-	100.0	(D)	17.0	3.2	-	(D)	(D)	(D)	(D)	(D)
UNKNOWN...............	-	100.0	(D)	-	86.5	-	(D)	(D)	(D)	(D)	(D)
WEST NORTH CENTRAL.....	163	100.0	(D)	31.5	61.9	3.2	(D)	(D)	(D)	(D)	(D)
RAIL..................	139	100.0	(D)	32.8	65.2	1.2	(D)	(D)	(D)	(D)	(D)
MOTOR CARRIER.........	21	100.0	(D)	26.7	47.1	5.2	(D)	(D)	(D)	(D)	(D)
PRIVATE TRUCK.........	2	100.0	(D)	-	-	100.0	(D)	(D)	(D)	(D)	(D)
AIR...................	-	100.0	(D)	72.4	27.6	-	(D)	(D)	(D)	(D)	(D)
WATER.................	-	100.0	(D)	-	-	-	(D)	(D)	(D)	(D)	(D)
OTHER.................	-	100.0	(D)	6.9	-	-	(D)	(D)	(D)	(D)	(D)
UNKNOWN...............	-	100.0	(D)	-	-	-	(D)	(D)	(D)	(D)	(D)
SOUTH ATLANTIC.........	132	100.0	(D)	77.6	11.3	.3	(D)	(D)	(D)	(D)	(D)
RAIL..................	114	100.0	(D)	84.3	9.7	-	(D)	(D)	(D)	(D)	(D)
MOTOR CARRIER.........	17	100.0	(D)	33.5	22.3	2.1	(D)	(D)	(D)	(D)	(D)
PRIVATE TRUCK.........	-	100.0	(D)	94.8	-	-	(D)	(D)	(D)	(D)	(D)
AIR...................	-	100.0	(D)	.3	73.8	-	(D)	(D)	(D)	(D)	(D)
WATER.................	-	100.0	(D)	-	-	-	(D)	(D)	(D)	(D)	(D)
OTHER.................	-	100.0	(D)	17.9	13.9	-	(D)	(D)	(D)	(D)	(D)
UNKNOWN...............	-	100.0	(D)	9.0	91.0	-	(D)	(D)	(D)	(D)	(D)
EAST SOUTH CENTRAL.....	88	100.0	(D)	73.1	15.0	.4	(D)	(D)	(D)	(D)	(D)
RAIL..................	74	100.0	(D)	79.9	15.6	-	(D)	(D)	(D)	(D)	(D)
MOTOR CARRIER.........	13	100.0	(D)	38.4	12.9	2.8	(D)	(D)	(D)	(D)	(D)
PRIVATE TRUCK.........	-	100.0	(D)	-	-	-	(D)	(D)	(D)	(D)	(D)
AIR...................	-	100.0	(D)	-	-	-	(D)	(D)	(D)	(D)	(D)
WATER.................	-	100.0	(D)	-	-	-	(D)	(D)	(D)	(D)	(D)
OTHER.................	-	100.0	(D)	93.6	-	-	(D)	(D)	(D)	(D)	(D)
UNKNOWN...............	-	100.0	(D)	-	100.0	-	(D)	(D)	(D)	(D)	(D)
WEST SOUTH CENTRAL.....	106	100.0	(D)	13.2	39.7	1.1	(D)	(D)	(D)	(D)	(D)
RAIL..................	97	100.0	(D)	11.7	40.4	.2	(D)	(D)	(D)	(D)	(D)
MOTOR CARRIER.........	7	100.0	(D)	35.4	33.9	2.5	(D)	(D)	(D)	(D)	(D)
PRIVATE TRUCK.........	-	100.0	(D)	-	-	100.0	(D)	(D)	(D)	(D)	(D)
AIR...................	-	100.0	(D)	.5	94.0	-	(D)	(D)	(D)	(D)	(D)
WATER.................	-	100.0	(D)	-	-	-	(D)	(D)	(D)	(D)	(D)
OTHER.................	-	100.0	(D)	7.1	92.4	-	(D)	(D)	(D)	(D)	(D)
UNKNOWN...............	-	100.0	(D)	-	-	-	(D)	(D)	(D)	(D)	(D)
MOUNTAIN...............	13	100.0	(D)	44.4	45.9	7.9	(D)	(D)	(D)	(D)	(D)
RAIL..................	7	100.0	(D)	76.7	22.6	-	(D)	(D)	(D)	(D)	(D)
MOTOR CARRIER.........	4	100.0	(D)	4.0	90.7	1.6	(D)	(D)	(D)	(D)	(D)
PRIVATE TRUCK.........	-	100.0	(D)	-	-	100.0	(D)	(D)	(D)	(D)	(D)
AIR...................	-	100.0	(D)	34.9	65.1	-	(D)	(D)	(D)	(D)	(D)
WATER.................	-	100.0	(D)	-	-	-	(D)	(D)	(D)	(D)	(D)
OTHER.................	-	100.0	(D)	-	-	-	(D)	(D)	(D)	(D)	(D)
UNKNOWN...............	-	100.0	(D)	-	-	-	(D)	(D)	(D)	(D)	(D)
PACIFIC................	85	100.0	(D)	17.9	66.6	5.9	(D)	(D)	(D)	(D)	(D)
RAIL..................	70	100.0	(D)	20.0	69.1	3.2	(D)	(D)	(D)	(D)	(D)
MOTOR CARRIER.........	13	100.0	(D)	8.1	59.1	11.8	(D)	(D)	(D)	(D)	(D)
PRIVATE TRUCK.........	1	100.0	(D)	-	-	99.8	(D)	(D)	(D)	(D)	(D)
AIR...................	-	100.0	(D)	8.7	84.2	2.3	(D)	(D)	(D)	(D)	(D)
WATER.................	-	100.0	(D)	-	-	-	(D)	(D)	(D)	(D)	(D)
OTHER.................	-	100.0	(D)	9.3	87.4	-	(D)	(D)	(D)	(D)	(D)
UNKNOWN...............	-	100.0	(D)	-	-	-	(D)	(D)	(D)	(D)	(D)

See footnotes at end of table 4.

TABLE 3. TCC GROUP 374—Percent Distribution of Geographic Division of Destination and Means of Transport, by Geographic Division of Origin: 1972—Continued

Geographic division of destination and means of transport	Number	Percent distribution by division of origin[1]									
		U.S. total	New England	Middle Atlantic	East North Central	West North Central	South Atlantic	East South Central	West South Central	Mountain	Pacific
TON-MILES OF SHIPMENTS	(millions of ton-miles)										
U.S. TOTAL...............	618	100.0	(D)	36.3	40.1	5.6	(D)	(D)	(D)	(D)	(D)
RAIL..................	494	100.0	(D)	39.9	41.0	3.6	(D)	(D)	(D)	(D)	(D)
MOTOR CARRIER.........	113	100.0	(D)	23.7	38.7	8.4	(D)	(D)	(D)	(D)	(D)
PRIVATE TRUCK.........	9	100.0	(D)	3.1	8.5	81.8	(D)	(D)	(D)	(D)	(D)
AIR...................	-	100.0	(D)	32.0	64.4	1.3	(D)	(D)	(D)	(D)	(D)
WATER.................	-	100.0	(D)	-	-	-	(D)	(D)	(D)	(D)	(D)
OTHER.................	-	100.0	(D)	7.0	85.5	-	(D)	(D)	(D)	(D)	(D)
UNKNOWN...............	-	100.0	(D)	.8	60.3	-	(D)	(D)	(D)	(D)	(D)
NEW ENGLAND.............	-	100.0	(D)	3.1	47.4	-	(D)	(D)	(D)	(D)	(D)
RAIL..................	-	100.0	(D)	-	-	-	(D)	(D)	(D)	(D)	(D)
MOTOR CARRIER.........	-	100.0	(D)	3.1	47.5	-	(D)	(D)	(D)	(D)	(D)
PRIVATE TRUCK.........	-	100.0	(D)	-	-	-	(D)	(D)	(D)	(D)	(D)
AIR...................	-	100.0	(D)	100.0	-	-	(D)	(D)	(D)	(D)	(D)
WATER.................	-	100.0	(D)	-	-	-	(D)	(D)	(D)	(D)	(D)
OTHER.................	-	100.0	(D)	11.6	-	-	(D)	(D)	(D)	(D)	(D)
UNKNOWN...............	-	100.0	(D)	-	-	-	(D)	(D)	(D)	(D)	(D)
MIDDLE ATLANTIC.........	79	100.0	(D)	34.2	27.1	16.2	(D)	(D)	(D)	(D)	(D)
RAIL..................	60	100.0	(D)	37.1	26.5	18.8	(D)	(D)	(D)	(D)	(D)
MOTOR CARRIER.........	15	100.0	(D)	27.9	27.4	3.2	(D)	(D)	(D)	(D)	(D)
PRIVATE TRUCK.........	2	100.0	(D)	6.4	28.5	40.6	(D)	(D)	(D)	(D)	(D)
AIR...................	-	100.0	(D)	44.5	55.4	-	(D)	(D)	(D)	(D)	(D)
WATER.................	-	100.0	(D)	-	-	-	(D)	(D)	(D)	(D)	(D)
OTHER.................	-	100.0	(D)	1.9	97.5	-	(D)	(D)	(D)	(D)	(D)
UNKNOWN...............	-	100.0	(D)	.6	64.6	-	(D)	(D)	(D)	(D)	(D)
EAST NORTH CENTRAL......	102	100.0	(D)	41.0	24.6	11.0	(D)	(D)	(D)	(D)	(D)
RAIL..................	62	100.0	(D)	54.4	20.5	3.8	(D)	(D)	(D)	(D)	(D)
MOTOR CARRIER.........	37	100.0	(D)	21.4	33.3	17.0	(D)	(D)	(D)	(D)	(D)
PRIVATE TRUCK.........	2	100.0	(D)	.1	3.2	96.7	(D)	(D)	(D)	(D)	(D)
AIR...................	-	100.0	(D)	58.8	13.0	28.2	(D)	(D)	(D)	(D)	(D)
WATER.................	-	100.0	(D)	-	-	-	(D)	(D)	(D)	(D)	(D)
OTHER.................	-	100.0	(D)	16.4	.6	-	(D)	(D)	(D)	(D)	(D)
UNKNOWN...............	-	100.0	(D)	-	85.8	-	(D)	(D)	(D)	(D)	(D)
WEST NORTH CENTRAL......	89	100.0	(D)	47.7	46.4	1.2	(D)	(D)	(D)	(D)	(D)
RAIL..................	77	100.0	(D)	49.7	49.3	.1	(D)	(D)	(D)	(D)	(D)
MOTOR CARRIER.........	11	100.0	(D)	37.1	30.0	1.6	(D)	(D)	(D)	(D)	(D)
PRIVATE TRUCK.........	-	100.0	(D)	-	-	100.0	(D)	(D)	(D)	(D)	(D)
AIR...................	-	100.0	(D)	80.4	19.6	-	(D)	(D)	(D)	(D)	(D)
WATER.................	-	100.0	(D)	-	-	-	(D)	(D)	(D)	(D)	(D)
OTHER.................	-	100.0	(D)	6.7	-	-	(D)	(D)	(D)	(D)	(D)
UNKNOWN...............	-	100.0	(D)	-	-	-	(D)	(D)	(D)	(D)	(D)
SOUTH ATLANTIC..........	40	100.0	(D)	74.5	13.0	.5	(D)	(D)	(D)	(D)	(D)
RAIL..................	34	100.0	(D)	82.3	11.2	-	(D)	(D)	(D)	(D)	(D)
MOTOR CARRIER.........	6	100.0	(D)	29.2	22.9	3.2	(D)	(D)	(D)	(D)	(D)
PRIVATE TRUCK.........	-	100.0	(D)	99.3	-	-	(D)	(D)	(D)	(D)	(D)
AIR...................	-	100.0	(D)	.2	80.7	-	(D)	(D)	(D)	(D)	(D)
WATER.................	-	100.0	(D)	-	-	-	(D)	(D)	(D)	(D)	(D)
OTHER.................	-	100.0	(D)	21.2	30.2	-	(D)	(D)	(D)	(D)	(D)
UNKNOWN...............	-	100.0	(D)	11.7	88.3	-	(D)	(D)	(D)	(D)	(D)
EAST SOUTH CENTRAL......	36	100.0	(D)	71.5	16.5	.5	(D)	(D)	(D)	(D)	(D)
RAIL..................	29	100.0	(D)	78.3	17.5	-	(D)	(D)	(D)	(D)	(D)
MOTOR CARRIER.........	7	100.0	(D)	43.0	12.5	2.4	(D)	(D)	(D)	(D)	(D)
PRIVATE TRUCK.........	-	100.0	(D)	-	-	-	(D)	(D)	(D)	(D)	(D)
AIR...................	-	100.0	(D)	-	-	-	(D)	(D)	(D)	(D)	(D)
WATER.................	-	100.0	(D)	-	-	-	(D)	(D)	(D)	(D)	(D)
OTHER.................	-	100.0	(D)	96.4	-	-	(D)	(D)	(D)	(D)	(D)
UNKNOWN...............	-	100.0	(D)	-	100.0	-	(D)	(D)	(D)	(D)	(D)
WEST SOUTH CENTRAL......	93	100.0	(D)	13.4	38.8	.9	(D)	(D)	(D)	(D)	(D)
RAIL..................	85	100.0	(D)	11.2	40.0	.1	(D)	(D)	(D)	(D)	(D)
MOTOR CARRIER.........	6	100.0	(D)	42.6	25.7	1.4	(D)	(D)	(D)	(D)	(D)
PRIVATE TRUCK.........	-	100.0	(D)	-	-	100.0	(D)	(D)	(D)	(D)	(D)
AIR...................	-	100.0	(D)	.6	92.2	-	(D)	(D)	(D)	(D)	(D)
WATER.................	-	100.0	(D)	-	-	-	(D)	(D)	(D)	(D)	(D)
OTHER.................	-	100.0	(D)	8.0	91.6	-	(D)	(D)	(D)	(D)	(D)
UNKNOWN...............	-	100.0	(D)	-	-	-	(D)	(D)	(D)	(D)	(D)
MOUNTAIN................	19	100.0	(D)	51.4	43.3	4.1	(D)	(D)	(D)	(D)	(D)
RAIL..................	12	100.0	(D)	78.1	21.6	-	(D)	(D)	(D)	(D)	(D)
MOTOR CARRIER.........	6	100.0	(D)	5.6	90.5	.9	(D)	(D)	(D)	(D)	(D)
PRIVATE TRUCK.........	-	100.0	(D)	-	-	100.0	(D)	(D)	(D)	(D)	(D)
AIR...................	-	100.0	(D)	40.1	59.9	-	(D)	(D)	(D)	(D)	(D)
WATER.................	-	100.0	(D)	-	-	-	(D)	(D)	(D)	(D)	(D)
OTHER.................	-	100.0	(D)	-	-	-	(D)	(D)	(D)	(D)	(D)
UNKNOWN...............	-	100.0	(D)	-	-	-	(D)	(D)	(D)	(D)	(D)
PACIFIC.................	156	100.0	(D)	21.8	66.3	4.8	(D)	(D)	(D)	(D)	(D)
RAIL..................	132	100.0	(D)	24.0	67.9	2.9	(D)	(D)	(D)	(D)	(D)
MOTOR CARRIER.........	22	100.0	(D)	10.6	61.2	9.1	(D)	(D)	(D)	(D)	(D)
PRIVATE TRUCK.........	1	100.0	(D)	-	-	99.8	(D)	(D)	(D)	(D)	(D)
AIR...................	-	100.0	(D)	17.1	80.7	1.6	(D)	(D)	(D)	(D)	(D)
WATER.................	-	100.0	(D)	-	-	-	(D)	(D)	(D)	(D)	(D)
OTHER.................	-	100.0	(D)	10.7	85.9	-	(D)	(D)	(D)	(D)	(D)
UNKNOWN...............	-	100.0	(D)	-	-	-	(D)	(D)	(D)	(D)	(D)

See footnotes at end of table 4.

TABLE 4. TCC GROUP 374—Percent Distribution of Distance Shipped and Weight of Shipment, by Means of Transport: 1972

Distance shipped and weight of shipment[2] [3]	Number	Percent distribution by means of transport							
		All means of transport	Rail	Motor carrier	Private truck	Air	Water	Other	Unknown
TONS OF SHIPMENTS	(thousands of tons)								
U.S. TOTAL..........	1 377	100.0	81.3	17.1	1.5	.1	-	-	-
UNDER 100 MILES.........	364	100.0	86.6	11.8	1.5	-	-	-	-
UNDER 1000 POUNDS.....	2	100.0	-	58.8	40.5	-	-	.2	.4
1000 TO 9999 POUNDS...	14	100.0	.9	79.6	19.5	-	-	-	-
10000 TO 29999 POUNDS.	17	100.0	15.6	77.7	6.7	-	-	-	-
30000 TO 59999 POUNDS.	21	100.0	55.5	41.5	3.0	-	-	-	-
60000 TO 89999 POUNDS.	40	100.0	81.9	18.1	-	-	-	-	-
90000 POUNDS AND OVER.	267	100.0	100.0	-	-	-	-	-	-
100 TO 199 MILES........	165	100.0	78.3	21.1	.6	-	-	-	-
UNDER 1000 POUNDS.....	1	100.0	.4	98.8	.3	-	-	.5	-
1000 TO 9999 POUNDS...	4	100.0	8.6	84.8	6.5	-	-	-	.2
10000 TO 29999 POUNDS.	5	100.0	58.0	42.0	-	-	-	-	-
30000 TO 59999 POUNDS.	35	100.0	20.7	77.2	2.2	-	-	-	-
60000 TO 89999 POUNDS.	31	100.0	100.0	-	-	-	-	-	-
90000 POUNDS AND OVER.	87	100.0	100.0	-	-	-	-	-	-
200 TO 299 MILES........	202	100.0	85.2	14.7	-	-	-	-	-
UNDER 1000 POUNDS.....	1	100.0	.2	96.0	2.0	.5	-	1.1	.3
1000 TO 9999 POUNDS...	4	100.0	2.8	95.4	-	-	-	-	1.9
10000 TO 29999 POUNDS.	4	100.0	59.4	40.6	-	-	-	-	-
30000 TO 59999 POUNDS.	47	100.0	55.1	44.9	-	-	-	-	-
60000 TO 89999 POUNDS.	43	100.0	98.1	1.9	-	-	-	-	-
90000 POUNDS AND OVER.	101	100.0	100.0	-	-	-	-	-	-
300 TO 499 MILES........	295	100.0	76.3	21.3	2.3	.1	-	-	.1
UNDER 1000 POUNDS.....	2	100.0	8.1	71.8	18.1	1.3	-	.7	.1
1000 TO 9999 POUNDS...	15	100.0	10.8	69.8	19.0	.4	-	-	-
10000 TO 29999 POUNDS.	19	100.0	50.8	41.4	5.8	1.0	-	-	1.1
30000 TO 59999 POUNDS.	85	100.0	48.1	49.4	2.6	-	-	-	-
60000 TO 89999 POUNDS.	21	100.0	100.0	-	-	-	-	-	-
90000 POUNDS AND OVER.	151	100.0	100.0	-	-	-	-	-	-
500 TO 999 MILES........	215	100.0	78.1	18.8	2.7	.2	-	.2	-
UNDER 1000 POUNDS.....	3	100.0	.2	85.1	.8	10.1	-	3.6	.3
1000 TO 9999 POUNDS...	13	100.0	5.6	87.9	3.7	.1	-	2.7	-
10000 TO 29999 POUNDS.	27	100.0	33.1	56.6	10.3	-	-	-	-
30000 TO 59999 POUNDS.	38	100.0	65.4	27.9	6.7	-	-	-	-
60000 TO 89999 POUNDS.	11	100.0	100.0	-	-	-	-	-	-
90000 POUNDS AND OVER.	122	100.0	100.0	-	-	-	-	-	-
1000 TO 1499 MILES......	33	100.0	56.4	39.9	3.5	-	-	.1	-
UNDER 1000 POUNDS.....	-	100.0	1.3	90.2	-	2.3	-	6.1	-
1000 TO 9999 POUNDS...	3	100.0	7.8	90.9	1.3	-	-	-	-
10000 TO 29999 POUNDS.	-	100.0	-	53.9	46.1	-	-	-	-
30000 TO 59999 POUNDS.	20	100.0	51.5	44.1	4.4	-	-	-	-
60000 TO 89999 POUNDS.	3	100.0	100.0	-	-	-	-	-	-
90000 POUNDS AND OVER.	4	100.0	100.0	-	-	-	-	-	-
1500 MILES OR OVER......	99	100.0	89.1	10.8	-	.1	-	-	-
UNDER 1000 POUNDS.....	-	100.0	-	80.3	.4	16.8	-	2.5	-
1000 TO 9999 POUNDS...	3	100.0	4.0	96.0	-	-	-	-	-
10000 TO 29999 POUNDS.	1	100.0	-	98.5	-	-	-	-	1.5
30000 TO 59999 POUNDS.	15	100.0	61.6	38.4	-	-	-	-	-
60000 TO 89999 POUNDS.	27	100.0	100.0	-	-	-	-	-	-
90000 POUNDS AND OVER.	51	100.0	100.0	-	-	-	-	-	-
TON-MILES OF SHIPMENTS	(millions of ton-miles)								
U.S. TOTAL..........	599	100.0	81.4	16.9	1.5	.1	-	.1	-
UNDER 100 MILES.........	13	100.0	89.2	9.7	1.0	-	-	-	-
UNDER 1000 POUNDS.....	-	100.0	-	59.1	40.3	-	-	.3	.3
1000 TO 9999 POUNDS...	-	100.0	1.9	79.2	18.9	-	-	-	-
10000 TO 29999 POUNDS.	-	100.0	14.3	84.7	1.0	-	-	-	-
30000 TO 59999 POUNDS.	-	100.0	66.2	33.0	.8	-	-	-	-
60000 TO 89999 POUNDS.	1	100.0	92.8	7.2	-	-	-	-	-
90000 POUNDS AND OVER.	9	100.0	100.0	-	-	-	-	-	-
100 TO 199 MILES........	24	100.0	79.9	19.4	.7	-	-	-	-
UNDER 1000 POUNDS.....	-	100.0	.4	98.9	.2	-	-	.5	-
1000 TO 9999 POUNDS...	-	100.0	7.6	85.0	7.3	-	-	-	.1
10000 TO 29999 POUNDS.	-	100.0	59.5	40.5	-	-	-	-	-
30000 TO 59999 POUNDS.	4	100.0	23.0	74.4	2.6	-	-	-	-
60000 TO 89999 POUNDS.	3	100.0	100.0	-	-	-	-	-	-
90000 POUNDS AND OVER.	13	100.0	100.0	-	-	-	-	-	-

See footnotes at end of table 4.

TABLE 4. **TCC GROUP 374—Percent Distribution of Distance Shipped and Weight of Shipment, by Means of Transport: 1972**—Continued

Distance shipped and weight of shipment[2] [3]	Number	Percent distribution by means of transport							
		All means of transport	Rail	Motor carrier	Private truck	Air	Water	Other	Unknown
TON-MILES OF SHIPMENTS	(millions of ton-miles)								
200 TO 299 MILES.........	52	100.0	85.5	14.5	-	-	-	-	-
UNDER 1000 POUNDS.....	-	100.0	.2	96.0	1.9	.4	-	1.1	.3
1000 TO 9999 POUNDS...	1	100.0	2.8	95.4	-	-	-	-	1.7
10000 TO 29999 POUNDS.	1	100.0	60.2	39.8	-	-	-	-	-
30000 TO 59999 POUNDS.	11	100.0	54.1	45.9	-	-	-	-	-
60000 TO 89999 POUNDS.	10	100.0	98.3	1.7	-	-	-	-	-
90000 POUNDS AND OVER.	26	100.0	100.0	-	-	-	-	-	-
300 TO 499 MILES........	118	100.0	78.3	19.2	2.4	.1	-	-	.1
UNDER 1000 POUNDS.....	1	100.0	8.8	72.6	16.7	1.2	-	.7	.1
1000 TO 9999 POUNDS...	5	100.0	9.2	69.4	21.0	.4	-	-	-
10000 TO 29999 POUNDS.	8	100.0	54.3	38.4	5.4	.8	-	-	1.1
30000 TO 59999 POUNDS.	32	100.0	52.0	45.2	2.9	-	-	-	-
60000 TO 89999 POUNDS.	8	100.0	100.0	-	-	-	-	-	-
90000 POUNDS AND OVER.	61	100.0	100.0	-	-	-	-	-	-
500 TO 999 MILES........	165	100.0	79.4	17.6	2.7	.2	-	.2	-
UNDER 1000 POUNDS.....	2	100.0	.1	84.8	.8	10.7	-	3.5	.2
1000 TO 9999 POUNDS...	9	100.0	4.8	87.3	4.6	.1	-	3.1	-
10000 TO 29999 POUNDS.	18	100.0	34.5	54.0	11.5	-	-	-	-
30000 TO 59999 POUNDS.	29	100.0	63.6	30.4	6.0	-	-	-	-
60000 TO 89999 POUNDS.	7	100.0	100.0	-	-	-	-	-	-
90000 POUNDS AND OVER.	97	100.0	100.0	-	-	-	-	-	-
1000 TO 1499 MILES......	39	100.0	54.9	41.1	3.9	-	-	.1	-
UNDER 1000 POUNDS.....	-	100.0	1.3	90.3	-	2.4	-	6.0	-
1000 TO 9999 POUNDS...	4	100.0	8.0	90.9	1.2	-	-	-	-
10000 TO 29999 POUNDS.	-	100.0	-	51.9	48.1	-	-	-	-
30000 TO 59999 POUNDS.	24	100.0	49.3	45.9	4.9	-	-	-	-
60000 TO 89999 POUNDS.	3	100.0	100.0	-	-	-	-	-	-
90000 POUNDS AND OVER.	5	100.0	100.0	-	-	-	-	-	-
1500 MILES OR OVER......	186	100.0	89.3	10.6	-	.1	-	-	-
UNDER 1000 POUNDS.....	-	100.0	-	79.4	.4	17.5	-	2.7	-
1000 TO 9999 POUNDS...	5	100.0	3.6	96.4	-	-	-	-	-
10000 TO 29999 POUNDS.	2	100.0	-	98.3	-	-	-	-	1.7
30000 TO 59999 POUNDS.	29	100.0	63.3	36.7	-	-	-	-	-
60000 TO 89999 POUNDS.	53	100.0	100.0	-	-	-	-	-	-
90000 POUNDS AND OVER.	93	100.0	100.0	-	-	-	-	-	-

Note: Detail may not add to total due to rounding. The introductory table shows the estimates of sampling variability for tons; sampling variability for ton-miles has not been estimated. See the map in the Introduction for the States comprising the geographic divisions of the United States.
  Shipments excluded from the survey are those moving by pipeline (primarily petroleum products from refineries), parcel post shipments, and commodities moved by own power (motorized vehicles, aircraft, etc.) or towed (prefabricated buildings, etc.). Local shipments (commodities shipped less than 25 miles from the plant) and shipments within the same city are also excluded. Shipments to Alaska and Hawaii from the 48 conterminous States and the District of Columbia are included; however, no data were obtained for shipments originating in Alaska and Hawaii.

  - Represents zero or rounds to zero.   (D) Withheld to avoid disclosing figures for individual companies.

[1]Production of this commodity is concentrated in the geographic divisions shown; figures and distributions for geographic divisions not shown are included in the total.
[2]Distances of shipments to foreign destinations are calculated only to the U.S. port of exit.
[3]Includes only shipments represented by bills of lading and invoices. Summary records which did not show individual weights of shipments are not included.

TCC 379. Miscellaneous Transportation Equipment

Comparisons of Tons and Ton-Miles of Shipments for
Geographic Divisions of Origin and for Sampling Variability: 1972 and 1967

Geographic division of origin	Estimates				Relative sampling variability in tons (percent)	
	1972		1967			
	Tons (thousands)	Ton-miles (millions)	Tons (thousands)	Ton-miles (millions)	1972	1967
U.S. total	2,666	953	1,059	507	12.0	27.0
New England	—	—	—	—	—	(*)
Middle Atlantic	79	22	141	74	37.1	(*)
East North Central	529	234	267	79	44.3	(*)
West North Central	449	156	412	278	45.6	(*)
South Atlantic	(D)	(D)	12	5	(*)	(*)
East South Central	(D)	(D)	21	6	(*)	(*)
West South Central	494	167	132	33	43.4	(*)
Mountain	(D)	(D)	22	9	(*)	(*)
Pacific	498	136	52	23	27.5	(*)

— Represents or rounds to zero.   (D) Withheld to avoid disclosing figures for individual companies.   (*) Data not published.

TABLE 1. **TCC GROUP 379**—Percent Distribution of Geographic Division of Origin and Distance Shipped, by Means of Transport: 1972

Geographic division of origin[1] and distance shipped[2]	Number	Percent distribution by means of transport							
		All means of transport	Rail	Motor carrier	Private truck	Air	Water	Other	Unknown
TONS OF SHIPMENTS	(thousands of tons)								
U.S. TOTAL	2 666	100.0	5.5	24.3	68.8	-	-	.3	1.0
MIDDLE ATLANTIC	79	100.0	18.3	30.4	20.3	-	-	-	30.9
UNDER 100 MILES	16	100.0	-	21.0	26.9	-	-	-	52.1
100 TO 199 MILES	22	100.0	6.3	24.2	28.6	-	-	-	40.9
200 TO 299 MILES	8	100.0	-	68.1	15.1	-	-	-	16.8
300 TO 499 MILES	23	100.0	43.0	24.7	10.9	-	-	-	21.4
500 TO 999 MILES	6	100.0	43.6	46.9	9.4	.1	-	-	-
1000 TO 1499 MILES	-	100.0	-	15.7	84.3	-	-	-	-
1500 MILES OR OVER	-	100.0	-	33.5	66.4	-	-	.2	-
EAST NORTH CENTRAL	529	100.0	7.5	24.0	68.3	-	-	.1	-
UNDER 100 MILES	82	100.0	2.2	49.0	48.6	-	-	.2	-
100 TO 199 MILES	95	100.0	.2	25.9	73.6	-	-	.1	.3
200 TO 299 MILES	71	100.0	9.2	34.9	55.9	-	-	.1	-
300 TO 499 MILES	121	100.0	9.1	16.9	73.9	-	-	.1	-
500 TO 999 MILES	115	100.0	5.3	12.4	82.1	.1	-	.2	-
1000 TO 1499 MILES	13	100.0	-	8.6	90.9	.2	-	.2	-
1500 MILES OR OVER	30	100.0	45.6	3.4	50.9	.1	-	.1	-
WEST NORTH CENTRAL	449	100.0	-	10.9	88.7	-	-	.3	.1
UNDER 100 MILES	52	100.0	-	9.2	90.8	-	-	.1	-
100 TO 199 MILES	150	100.0	-	13.5	86.0	-	-	.1	.4
200 TO 299 MILES	65	100.0	-	14.1	85.8	-	-	-	-
300 TO 499 MILES	89	100.0	-	11.6	88.3	-	-	-	-
500 TO 999 MILES	78	100.0	-	4.7	94.9	-	-	.4	-
1000 TO 1499 MILES	5	100.0	-	5.8	94.2	-	-	.1	-
1500 MILES OR OVER	6	100.0	-	-	87.1	-	-	12.8	-
WEST SOUTH CENTRAL	494	100.0	-	.8	99.2	-	-	-	-
UNDER 100 MILES	89	100.0	-	.1	99.9	-	-	-	-
100 TO 199 MILES	95	100.0	-	.9	99.1	-	-	-	-
200 TO 299 MILES	77	100.0	-	.7	99.3	-	-	-	-
300 TO 499 MILES	127	100.0	-	.4	99.6	-	-	-	-
500 TO 999 MILES	86	100.0	-	1.3	98.7	-	-	-	-
1000 TO 1499 MILES	16	100.0	-	3.6	96.4	-	-	-	-
1500 MILES OR OVER	1	100.0	-	22.6	77.4	-	-	-	-
PACIFIC	498	100.0	.9	40.4	57.2	-	.1	.9	.5
UNDER 100 MILES	171	100.0	-	32.0	66.8	-	-	.7	.5
100 TO 199 MILES	99	100.0	-	31.7	67.6	-	-	.7	-
200 TO 299 MILES	62	100.0	-	46.7	50.6	-	-	1.3	1.4
300 TO 499 MILES	103	100.0	-	64.6	34.3	-	-	.5	.5
500 TO 999 MILES	45	100.0	-	32.3	65.7	-	-	2.0	-
1000 TO 1499 MILES	5	100.0	-	52.6	47.2	.2	-	-	-
1500 MILES OR OVER	9	100.0	49.1	6.1	34.9	.9	4.6	4.4	-
TON-MILES OF SHIPMENTS	(millions of ton-miles)								
U.S. TOTAL	953	100.0	12.2	21.1	65.6	-	.1	.4	.5
MIDDLE ATLANTIC	22	100.0	28.4	35.3	17.2	-	-	-	19.0
UNDER 100 MILES	1	100.0	-	27.8	22.0	-	-	-	50.2
100 TO 199 MILES	3	100.0	8.2	26.0	24.1	-	-	-	41.6
200 TO 299 MILES	2	100.0	-	68.5	15.6	-	-	-	15.9
300 TO 499 MILES	9	100.0	45.6	24.3	9.2	-	-	-	21.0
500 TO 999 MILES	4	100.0	39.7	50.8	9.5	.1	-	-	-
1000 TO 1499 MILES	-	100.0	-	17.6	82.4	-	-	-	-
1500 MILES OR OVER	1	100.0	-	36.9	62.9	-	-	.2	-
EAST NORTH CENTRAL	234	100.0	15.1	14.4	70.3	.1	-	.1	-
UNDER 100 MILES	4	100.0	1.1	46.3	52.4	-	-	.2	-
100 TO 199 MILES	13	100.0	.2	25.5	73.9	-	-	.1	.3
200 TO 299 MILES	17	100.0	9.4	36.1	54.4	-	-	.1	-
300 TO 499 MILES	48	100.0	8.9	16.4	74.6	-	-	.1	-
500 TO 999 MILES	79	100.0	4.8	13.1	81.9	.1	-	.2	-
1000 TO 1499 MILES	14	100.0	-	8.5	91.0	.3	-	.2	-
1500 MILES OR OVER	55	100.0	46.4	3.4	50.0	.1	-	.1	-
WEST NORTH CENTRAL	156	100.0	-	7.6	91.4	-	-	.9	.1
UNDER 100 MILES	3	100.0	-	12.9	87.0	-	-	.1	-
100 TO 199 MILES	23	100.0	-	13.4	86.1	-	-	.1	.4
200 TO 299 MILES	15	100.0	-	13.3	86.7	-	-	-	-
300 TO 499 MILES	35	100.0	-	9.2	90.8	-	-	-	-
500 TO 999 MILES	52	100.0	-	4.7	94.9	-	-	.5	-
1000 TO 1499 MILES	7	100.0	-	5.6	94.3	-	-	.1	-
1500 MILES OR OVER	18	100.0	-	-	93.4	-	-	6.6	-
WEST SOUTH CENTRAL	167	100.0	-	2.0	98.0	-	-	-	-
UNDER 100 MILES	5	100.0	-	.1	99.9	-	-	-	-
100 TO 199 MILES	13	100.0	-	1.1	98.9	-	-	-	-
200 TO 299 MILES	19	100.0	-	.7	99.3	-	-	-	-
300 TO 499 MILES	49	100.0	-	.4	99.6	-	-	-	-
500 TO 999 MILES	55	100.0	-	1.5	98.5	-	-	-	-
1000 TO 1499 MILES	19	100.0	-	4.0	96.0	-	-	-	-
1500 MILES OR OVER	5	100.0	-	22.9	77.1	-	-	-	-

See footnotes at end of table 4.

TABLE 1. **TCC GROUP 379**—Percent Distribution of Geographic Division of Origin and Distance Shipped, by Means of Transport: 1972—Continued

Geographic division of origin[1] and distance shipped[2]	Number	Percent distribution by means of transport							
		All means of transport	Rail	Motor carrier	Private truck	Air	Water	Other	Unknown
TON-MILES OF SHIPMENTS	(millions of ton-miles)								
PACIFIC.................	136	100.0	6.8	39.7	50.7	.1	.7	1.6	.3
UNDER 100 MILES.......	7	100.0	-	37.4	61.3	-	-	1.0	.3
100 TO 199 MILES......	14	100.0	-	30.9	68.4	-	-	.7	-
200 TO 299 MILES......	15	100.0	-	49.8	47.3	-	-	1.4	1.5
300 TO 499 MILES......	38	100.0	-	65.1	33.9	-	-	.5	.5
500 TO 999 MILES......	33	100.0	-	27.4	70.7	-	-	1.9	-
1000 TO 1499 MILES....	6	100.0	-	50.0	49.7	.2	-	-	-
1500 MILES OR OVER....	19	100.0	48.1	5.9	35.5	.8	4.8	4.9	-

See footnotes at end of table 4.

TABLE 2. **TCC GROUP 379**—Percent Distribution of Geographic Division of Origin and Means of Transport, by Geographic Division of Destination: 1972

Geographic division of origin[1] and means of transport	Number	Percent distribution by division of destination									
		U.S. total	New England	Middle Atlantic	East North Central	West North Central	South Atlantic	East South Central	West South Central	Mountain	Pacific
TONS OF SHIPMENTS	(thousands of tons)										
U.S. TOTAL..............	2 666	100.0	2.0	7.0	14.0	11.3	10.4	8.3	18.8	10.2	17.9
RAIL................	147	100.0	1.5	36.3	41.1	5.2	2.4	3.0	.5	.5	9.6
MOTOR CARRIER........	647	100.0	1.7	4.6	19.6	9.4	9.6	14.3	3.7	9.1	28.0
PRIVATE TRUCK........	1 835	100.0	1.9	4.7	10.1	12.6	11.4	6.8	25.9	11.4	15.1
AIR.................	-	100.0	1.4	1.7	.4	5.3	2.0	61.0	21.2	2.1	4.9
WATER...............	-	100.0	-	-	-	-	-	-	-	-	100.0
OTHER...............	7	100.0	.6	5.9	3.7	2.8	4.5	10.2	.5	22.0	49.9
UNKNOWN.............	27	100.0	21.9	61.1	.9	2.0	5.8	-	-	3.0	5.2
MIDDLE ATLANTIC.........	79	100.0	20.8	44.3	18.8	-	12.1	2.8	.2	.1	.9
RAIL................	14	100.0	-	9.8	80.1	-	-	10.1	-	-	-
MOTOR CARRIER........	24	100.0	24.7	30.5	11.3	-	31.2	.6	.5	-	1.1
PRIVATE TRUCK........	16	100.0	27.8	59.0	3.2	-	2.8	3.9	-	.6	2.8
AIR.................	-	100.0	-	-	1.1	91.0	-	7.9	-	-	-
WATER...............	-	100.0	-	-	-	-	-	-	-	-	-
OTHER...............	-	100.0	3.4	61.1	9.3	.6	-	-	-	-	25.5
UNKNOWN.............	24	100.0	24.7	68.9	-	-	6.4	-	-	-	-
EAST NORTH CENTRAL......	529	100.0	3.6	14.6	43.4	11.6	11.8	4.0	4.0	2.1	5.0
RAIL................	39	100.0	-	18.7	6.9	19.3	9.1	7.3	1.8	1.8	35.0
MOTOR CARRIER........	127	100.0	.7	9.8	65.6	10.2	7.1	1.8	3.5	.5	.7
PRIVATE TRUCK........	361	100.0	5.0	15.8	39.5	11.2	13.8	4.4	4.4	2.6	3.2
AIR.................	-	100.0	7.7	10.0	1.9	17.7	12.2	3.5	18.6	13.1	15.3
WATER...............	-	100.0	-	-	-	-	-	-	-	-	-
OTHER...............	-	100.0	5.6	18.3	40.3	8.9	12.3	4.2	3.7	3.6	3.1
UNKNOWN.............	-	100.0	-	-	100.0	-	-	-	-	-	-
WEST NORTH CENTRAL......	449	100.0	.5	.5	3.3	40.0	2.7	.3	29.6	20.9	2.1
RAIL................	-	100.0	-	-	18.9	81.1	-	-	-	-	-
MOTOR CARRIER........	49	100.0	.5	.2	7.5	85.3	2.7	-	3.0	.6	.2
PRIVATE TRUCK........	398	100.0	.5	.5	2.8	34.5	2.7	.3	33.0	23.5	2.2
AIR.................	-	100.0	1.6	-	14.8	23.8	4.2	9.8	3.2	-	42.5
WATER...............	-	100.0	-	-	-	-	-	-	-	-	-
OTHER...............	1	100.0	.1	20.9	.6	12.3	.3	.4	.7	2.0	62.9
UNKNOWN.............	-	100.0	-	-	-	100.0	-	-	-	-	-
WEST SOUTH CENTRAL......	494	100.0	.3	2.2	5.4	10.1	.6	4.6	61.4	14.7	.7
RAIL................	-	100.0	-	-	-	-	-	-	-	-	-
MOTOR CARRIER........	4	100.0	-	4.5	8.1	9.1	12.3	12.3	33.9	4.8	15.0
PRIVATE TRUCK........	490	100.0	.3	2.2	5.4	10.1	.5	4.5	61.7	14.8	.6
AIR.................	-	100.0	-	-	-	-	-	-	-	-	-
WATER...............	-	100.0	-	-	-	-	-	-	-	-	-
OTHER...............	-	100.0	-	-	-	-	-	-	-	-	-
UNKNOWN.............	-	100.0	-	-	-	-	-	-	-	-	-
PACIFIC.................	498	100.0	-	.2	.8	.1	-	-	1.4	15.6	81.8
RAIL................	4	100.0	-	14.8	85.2	-	-	-	-	-	-
MOTOR CARRIER........	201	100.0	-	.1	-	.2	-	.1	1.6	22.4	75.6
PRIVATE TRUCK........	285	100.0	-	-	-	-	-	-	1.4	10.7	87.9
AIR.................	-	100.0	-	1.0	-	11.1	-	-	71.2	-	16.7
WATER...............	-	100.0	-	-	-	-	-	-	-	-	100.0
OTHER...............	4	100.0	-	-	-	-	-	-	-	35.2	64.7
UNKNOWN.............	2	100.0	-	-	-	-	-	-	-	36.6	63.4

See footnotes at end of table 4.

TABLE 2. **TCC GROUP 379—Percent Distribution of Geographic Division of Origin and Means of Transport, by Geographic Division of Destination: 1972**—Continued

Geographic division of origin[1] and means of transport	Number	Percent distribution by division of destination									
		U.S. total	New England	Middle Atlantic	East North Central	West North Central	South Atlantic	East South Central	West South Central	Mountain	Pacific
TON-MILES OF SHIPMENTS	(millions of ton-miles)										
U.S. TOTAL..............	953	100.0	3.9	10.6	12.9	8.9	10.6	4.7	14.6	14.1	19.6
RAIL..................	116	100.0	1.7	33.3	35.9	2.2	1.4	1.9	.4	.5	22.5
MOTOR CARRIER.........	201	100.0	4.5	8.2	18.2	9.0	10.6	6.3	6.6	11.4	25.1
PRIVATE TRUCK.........	625	100.0	3.9	6.9	7.1	10.2	12.5	4.8	20.1	17.6	17.0
AIR...................	-	100.0	2.2	2.8	.2	9.0	2.6	11.4	46.0	5.4	20.4
WATER.................	-	100.0	-	-	-	-	-	-	-	-	100.0
OTHER.................	4	100.0	.8	7.5	1.1	1.2	2.5	3.1	.6	17.3	65.8
UNKNOWN...............	4	100.0	44.9	38.3	.8	2.2	4.4	-	-	4.7	4.7
MIDDLE ATLANTIC.........	22	100.0	23.2	18.3	29.0	-	15.0	6.3	.6	.6	6.9
RAIL..................	6	100.0	-	4.5	81.7	-	-	13.8	-	-	-
MOTOR CARRIER.........	7	100.0	23.4	14.2	13.8	-	37.8	1.4	1.7	-	7.7
PRIVATE TRUCK.........	3	100.0	30.3	21.2	5.1	-	4.2	11.2	-	3.6	24.4
AIR...................	-	100.0	-	-	.8	90.8	-	8.3	-	-	-
WATER.................	-	100.0	-	-	-	-	-	-	-	-	-
OTHER.................	-	100.0	1.2	18.3	4.6	.5	-	-	-	-	75.3
UNKNOWN...............	4	100.0	51.3	43.8	-	-	4.9	-	-	-	-
EAST NORTH CENTRAL......	234	100.0	6.1	14.7	14.0	11.4	15.7	3.5	7.8	6.0	20.7
RAIL..................	35	100.0	-	8.2	.8	7.2	4.7	3.9	1.3	1.8	72.0
MOTOR CARRIER.........	33	100.0	2.2	18.1	32.5	15.6	10.6	2.5	11.2	2.4	4.8
PRIVATE TRUCK.........	164	100.0	8.2	15.4	13.0	11.5	19.1	3.6	8.5	7.7	13.0
AIR...................	-	100.0	5.4	6.9	.1	12.4	7.7	1.4	15.7	16.6	33.7
WATER.................	-	100.0	-	-	-	-	-	-	-	-	-
OTHER.................	-	100.0	9.6	21.9	13.0	8.4	15.6	4.5	6.5	9.0	11.5
UNKNOWN...............	-	100.0	-	-	100.0	-	-	-	-	-	-
WEST NORTH CENTRAL......	156	100.0	1.8	1.3	3.0	21.3	6.7	.4	22.9	28.3	14.4
RAIL..................	-	100.0	-	-	-	33.2	66.8	-	-	-	-
MOTOR CARRIER.........	11	100.0	2.3	.7	6.4	74.7	9.9	.1	3.6	1.4	.9
PRIVATE TRUCK.........	142	100.0	1.8	1.2	2.7	17.0	6.5	.4	24.8	30.8	14.8
AIR...................	-	100.0	1.7	-	7.9	6.8	3.8	8.6	2.5	-	68.6
WATER.................	-	100.0	-	-	-	-	-	-	-	-	-
OTHER.................	1	100.0	.1	14.9	.3	1.6	.2	.2	.3	.8	81.6
UNKNOWN...............	-	100.0	-	-	-	100.0	-	-	-	-	-
WEST SOUTH CENTRAL......	167	100.0	1.5	6.9	10.4	11.1	1.4	4.7	36.8	22.9	4.5
RAIL..................	-	100.0	-	-	-	-	-	-	-	-	-
MOTOR CARRIER.........	3	100.0	-	6.8	7.9	6.1	11.7	5.3	9.8	5.6	46.8
PRIVATE TRUCK.........	164	100.0	1.5	6.9	10.4	11.2	1.2	4.7	37.4	23.3	3.6
AIR...................	-	100.0	-	-	-	-	-	-	-	-	-
WATER.................	-	100.0	-	-	-	-	-	-	-	-	-
OTHER.................	-	100.0	-	-	-	-	-	-	-	-	-
UNKNOWN...............	-	100.0	-	-	-	-	-	-	-	-	-
PACIFIC.................	136	100.0	-	1.4	5.8	.5	.1	.2	6.5	23.3	62.1
RAIL..................	9	100.0	-	16.3	83.7	-	-	-	-	-	-
MOTOR CARRIER.........	53	100.0	.1	.8	.1	1.1	.2	.6	6.5	31.2	59.4
PRIVATE TRUCK.........	69	100.0	-	-	-	.2	.1	-	7.4	20.3	72.0
AIR...................	-	100.0	-	1.4	-	8.6	-	-	70.3	-	19.8
WATER.................	-	100.0	-	-	-	-	-	-	-	31.2	100.0
OTHER.................	2	100.0	-	-	-	-	-	-	.1	31.3	68.6
UNKNOWN...............	-	100.0	-	-	-	-	-	-	-	49.8	50.2

See footnotes at end of table 4.

TABLE 3. **TCC GROUP 379**—Percent Distribution of Geographic Division of Destination and Means of Transport, by Geographic Division of Origin: 1972

Geographic division of destination and means of transport	Number	Percent distribution by division of origin[1]									
		U.S. total	New England	Middle Atlantic	East North Central	West North Central	South Atlantic	East South Central	West South Central	Mountain	Pacific
TONS OF SHIPMENTS	(thousands of tons)										
U.S. TOTAL.............	2 666	100.0	(D)	3.0	19.9	16.9	(D)	(D)	18.6	(D)	18.7
RAIL.................	147	100.0	(D)	9.9	26.8	-	(D)	(D)	-	(D)	3.2
MOTOR CARRIER........	647	100.0	(D)	3.7	19.6	7.6	(D)	(D)	.6	(D)	31.1
PRIVATE TRUCK........	1 835	100.0	(D)	.9	19.7	21.7	(D)	(D)	26.7	(D)	15.5
AIR.................	-	100.0	(D)	1.0	15.9	.8	(D)	(D)	-	(D)	12.6
WATER...............	-	100.0	(D)	-	-	-	(D)	(D)	-	(D)	100.0
OTHER...............	7	100.0	(D)	.1	8.8	16.5	(D)	(D)	-	(D)	60.5
UNKNOWN.............	27	100.0	(D)	88.7	.9	2.0	(D)	(D)	-	(D)	8.2
NEW ENGLAND.............	54	100.0	(D)	30.4	35.1	4.2	(D)	(D)	3.1	(D)	-
RAIL.................	2	100.0	(D)	-	-	-	(D)	(D)	-	(D)	-
MOTOR CARRIER........	11	100.0	(D)	53.4	8.2	2.0	(D)	(D)	-	(D)	.1
PRIVATE TRUCK........	34	100.0	(D)	12.9	52.0	5.9	(D)	(D)	4.8	(D)	-
AIR.................	-	100.0	(D)	-	84.3	.9	(D)	(D)	-	(D)	-
WATER...............	-	100.0	(D)	-	-	-	(D)	(D)	-	(D)	-
OTHER...............	-	100.0	(D)	.4	84.4	2.6	(D)	(D)	-	(D)	.1
UNKNOWN.............	6	100.0	(D)	100.0	-	-	(D)	(D)	-	(D)	-
MIDDLE ATLANTIC........	187	100.0	(D)	18.7	41.1	1.2	(D)	(D)	5.8	(D)	.5
RAIL.................	53	100.0	(D)	2.7	13.8	-	(D)	(D)	-	(D)	1.3
MOTOR CARRIER........	30	100.0	(D)	24.5	41.2	.3	(D)	(D)	.6	(D)	.7
PRIVATE TRUCK........	86	100.0	(D)	11.0	66.0	2.1	(D)	(D)	12.3	(D)	-
AIR.................	-	100.0	(D)	-	92.5	-	(D)	(D)	-	(D)	7.5
WATER...............	-	100.0	(D)	-	-	-	(D)	(D)	-	(D)	-
OTHER...............	-	100.0	(D)	.8	27.4	58.8	(D)	(D)	-	(D)	-
UNKNOWN.............	16	100.0	(D)	100.0	-	-	(D)	(D)	-	(D)	-
EAST NORTH CENTRAL......	373	100.0	(D)	4.0	61.5	4.0	(D)	(D)	7.2	(D)	1.1
RAIL.................	60	100.0	(D)	19.2	4.5	-	(D)	(D)	-	(D)	6.6
MOTOR CARRIER........	126	100.0	(D)	2.2	65.8	2.9	(D)	(D)	.3	(D)	-
PRIVATE TRUCK........	185	100.0	(D)	.3	77.1	6.1	(D)	(D)	14.3	(D)	-
AIR.................	-	100.0	(D)	2.5	69.3	28.3	(D)	(D)	-	(D)	-
WATER...............	-	100.0	(D)	-	-	-	(D)	(D)	-	(D)	-
OTHER...............	-	100.0	(D)	.2	96.7	2.8	(D)	(D)	-	(D)	-
UNKNOWN.............	-	100.0	(D)	-	100.0	-	(D)	(D)	-	(D)	-
WEST NORTH CENTRAL......	301	100.0	(D)	-	20.3	59.6	(D)	(D)	16.6	(D)	.2
RAIL.................	7	100.0	(D)	-	99.8	.2	(D)	(D)	-	(D)	-
MOTOR CARRIER........	60	100.0	(D)	-	21.3	68.6	(D)	(D)	.6	(D)	.8
PRIVATE TRUCK........	232	100.0	(D)	-	17.5	59.2	(D)	(D)	21.5	(D)	-
AIR.................	-	100.0	(D)	16.8	52.9	3.8	(D)	(D)	-	(D)	26.5
WATER...............	-	100.0	(D)	-	-	-	(D)	(D)	-	(D)	-
OTHER...............	-	100.0	(D)	-	27.8	72.2	(D)	(D)	-	(D)	-
UNKNOWN.............	-	100.0	(D)	-	-	100.0	(D)	(D)	-	(D)	-
SOUTH ATLANTIC..........	276	100.0	(D)	3.5	22.6	4.4	(D)	(D)	1.0	(D)	-
RAIL.................	3	100.0	(D)	-	100.0	-	(D)	(D)	-	(D)	-
MOTOR CARRIER........	62	100.0	(D)	12.2	14.6	2.1	(D)	(D)	.8	(D)	.1
PRIVATE TRUCK........	209	100.0	(D)	.2	23.8	5.2	(D)	(D)	1.1	(D)	-
AIR.................	-	100.0	(D)	-	98.2	1.8	(D)	(D)	-	(D)	-
WATER...............	-	100.0	(D)	-	-	-	(D)	(D)	-	(D)	-
OTHER...............	-	100.0	(D)	-	23.9	.9	(D)	(D)	-	(D)	-
UNKNOWN.............	1	100.0	(D)	97.8	-	-	(D)	(D)	-	(D)	-
EAST SOUTH CENTRAL......	222	100.0	(D)	1.0	9.5	.6	(D)	(D)	10.1	(D)	.1
RAIL.................	4	100.0	(D)	33.7	66.3	-	(D)	(D)	-	(D)	-
MOTOR CARRIER........	92	100.0	(D)	.2	2.5	-	(D)	(D)	.5	(D)	.2
PRIVATE TRUCK........	124	100.0	(D)	.5	12.7	1.1	(D)	(D)	17.7	(D)	-
AIR.................	-	100.0	(D)	.1	.9	.1	(D)	(D)	-	(D)	-
WATER...............	-	100.0	(D)	-	-	-	(D)	(D)	-	(D)	-
OTHER...............	-	100.0	(D)	-	3.6	.6	(D)	(D)	-	(D)	-
UNKNOWN.............	-	100.0	(D)	-	-	-	(D)	(D)	-	(D)	-
WEST SOUTH CENTRAL......	500	100.0	(D)	-	4.2	26.5	(D)	(D)	60.7	(D)	1.4
RAIL.................	-	100.0	(D)	-	100.0	-	(D)	(D)	-	(D)	-
MOTOR CARRIER........	23	100.0	(D)	.5	18.4	6.2	(D)	(D)	5.7	(D)	13.0
PRIVATE TRUCK........	475	100.0	(D)	-	3.4	27.6	(D)	(D)	63.6	(D)	.8
AIR.................	-	100.0	(D)	-	13.9	.1	(D)	(D)	-	(D)	42.5
WATER...............	-	100.0	(D)	-	-	-	(D)	(D)	-	(D)	-
OTHER...............	-	100.0	(D)	-	72.1	24.0	(D)	(D)	-	(D)	4.0
UNKNOWN.............	-	100.0	(D)	-	-	-	(D)	(D)	-	(D)	-
MOUNTAIN................	272	100.0	(D)	-	4.0	34.5	(D)	(D)	26.7	(D)	28.6
RAIL.................	-	100.0	(D)	-	100.0	-	(D)	(D)	-	(D)	-
MOTOR CARRIER........	58	100.0	(D)	-	1.1	.5	(D)	(D)	.3	(D)	76.5
PRIVATE TRUCK........	210	100.0	(D)	-	4.5	44.6	(D)	(D)	34.5	(D)	14.5
AIR.................	-	100.0	(D)	-	100.0	-	(D)	(D)	-	(D)	-
WATER...............	-	100.0	(D)	-	-	-	(D)	(D)	-	(D)	-
OTHER...............	1	100.0	(D)	-	1.5	1.5	(D)	(D)	-	(D)	97.0
UNKNOWN.............	-	100.0	(D)	-	-	-	(D)	(D)	-	(D)	100.0
PACIFIC.................	477	100.0	(D)	.1	5.5	2.0	(D)	(D)	.7	(D)	85.3
RAIL.................	14	100.0	(D)	-	97.7	-	(D)	(D)	-	(D)	-
MOTOR CARRIER........	181	100.0	(D)	.1	.5	-	(D)	(D)	.3	(D)	83.8
PRIVATE TRUCK........	276	100.0	(D)	.2	4.2	3.2	(D)	(D)	1.0	(D)	90.7
AIR.................	-	100.0	(D)	-	49.6	7.3	(D)	(D)	-	(D)	43.1
WATER...............	-	100.0	(D)	-	-	-	(D)	(D)	-	(D)	100.0
OTHER...............	3	100.0	(D)	-	.5	20.8	(D)	(D)	-	(D)	78.5
UNKNOWN.............	1	100.0	(D)	-	-	-	(D)	(D)	-	(D)	100.0

See footnotes at end of table 4.

TABLE 3. **TCC GROUP 379**—Percent Distribution of Geographic Division of Destination and Means of Transport, by Geographic Division of Origin: 1972—Continued

Geographic division of destination and means of transport	Number	Percent distribution by division of origin[1]									
		U.S. total	New England	Middle Atlantic	East North Central	West North Central	South Atlantic	East South Central	West South Central	Mountain	Pacific
TON-MILES OF SHIPMENTS	(millions of ton-miles)										
U.S. TOTAL..............	953	100.0	(D)	2.3	24.6	16.4	(D)	(D)	17.6	(D)	14.3
RAIL...................	116	100.0	(D)	5.4	30.4	-	(D)	(D)	-	(D)	8.0
MOTOR CARRIER..........	201	100.0	(D)	3.9	16.8	5.9	(D)	(D)	1.6	(D)	26.8
PRIVATE TRUCK..........	625	100.0	(D)	.6	26.4	22.8	(D)	(D)	26.3	(D)	11.0
AIR....................	-	100.0	(D)	1.4	32.8	1.6	(D)	(D)	-	(D)	41.8
WATER..................	-	100.0	(D)	-	-	-	(D)	(D)	-	(D)	100.0
OTHER..................	4	100.0	(D)	.1	7.4	35.7	(D)	(D)	-	(D)	52.1
UNKNOWN................	4	100.0	(D)	87.5	.8	2.2	(D)	(D)	-	(D)	9.4
NEW ENGLAND............	37	100.0	(D)	13.8	38.1	7.6	(D)	(D)	6.6	(D)	.1
RAIL...................	2	100.0	(D)	-	-	-	(D)	(D)	-	(D)	-
MOTOR CARRIER..........	9	100.0	(D)	20.2	8.1	2.9	(D)	(D)	-	(D)	.5
PRIVATE TRUCK..........	24	100.0	(D)	4.8	55.8	10.7	(D)	(D)	10.1	(D)	-
AIR....................	-	100.0	(D)	-	82.8	1.3	(D)	(D)	-	(D)	-
WATER..................	-	100.0	(D)	-	-	-	(D)	(D)	-	(D)	-
OTHER..................	-	100.0	(D)	.2	87.4	4.1	(D)	(D)	-	(D)	.3
UNKNOWN................	2	100.0	(D)	100.0	-	-	(D)	(D)	-	(D)	-
MIDDLE ATLANTIC........	100	100.0	(D)	4.0	34.3	2.0	(D)	(D)	11.5	(D)	1.9
RAIL...................	38	100.0	(D)	.7	7.5	-	(D)	(D)	-	(D)	3.9
MOTOR CARRIER..........	16	100.0	(D)	6.7	36.9	.5	(D)	(D)	1.4	(D)	2.5
PRIVATE TRUCK..........	43	100.0	(D)	1.9	58.9	3.9	(D)	(D)	26.3	(D)	-
AIR....................	-	100.0	(D)	-	80.0	-	(D)	(D)	-	(D)	20.0
WATER..................	-	100.0	(D)	-	-	-	(D)	(D)	-	(D)	-
OTHER..................	-	100.0	(D)	.3	21.6	70.9	(D)	(D)	-	(D)	-
UNKNOWN................	1	100.0	(D)	100.0	-	-	(D)	(D)	-	(D)	-
EAST NORTH CENTRAL.....	122	100.0	(D)	5.2	26.6	3.8	(D)	(D)	14.1	(D)	6.4
RAIL...................	41	100.0	(D)	12.3	.7	-	(D)	(D)	-	(D)	18.6
MOTOR CARRIER..........	36	100.0	(D)	3.0	30.0	2.0	(D)	(D)	.7	(D)	.2
PRIVATE TRUCK..........	44	100.0	(D)	.4	48.2	8.7	(D)	(D)	38.6	(D)	-
AIR....................	-	100.0	(D)	7.5	12.7	79.8	(D)	(D)	-	(D)	-
WATER..................	-	100.0	(D)	-	-	-	(D)	(D)	-	(D)	-
OTHER..................	-	100.0	(D)	.5	89.6	8.4	(D)	(D)	-	(D)	-
UNKNOWN................	-	100.0	(D)	-	100.0	-	(D)	(D)	-	(D)	-
WEST NORTH CENTRAL.....	84	100.0	(D)	-	31.7	39.4	(D)	(D)	22.0	(D)	.9
RAIL...................	2	100.0	(D)	-	99.9	.1	(D)	(D)	-	(D)	-
MOTOR CARRIER..........	18	100.0	(D)	-	29.1	48.8	(D)	(D)	1.1	(D)	3.3
PRIVATE TRUCK..........	63	100.0	(D)	-	29.7	38.2	(D)	(D)	28.8	(D)	.2
AIR....................	-	100.0	(D)	13.8	45.2	1.2	(D)	(D)	-	(D)	39.8
WATER..................	-	100.0	(D)	-	-	-	(D)	(D)	-	(D)	-
OTHER..................	-	100.0	(D)	-	51.7	48.2	(D)	(D)	-	(D)	-
UNKNOWN................	-	100.0	(D)	-	-	100.0	(D)	(D)	-	(D)	-
SOUTH ATLANTIC.........	101	100.0	(D)	3.3	36.3	10.3	(D)	(D)	2.3	(D)	.2
RAIL...................	1	100.0	(D)	-	100.0	-	(D)	(D)	-	(D)	.6
MOTOR CARRIER..........	21	100.0	(D)	13.8	16.7	5.5	(D)	(D)	1.8	(D)	.6
PRIVATE TRUCK..........	78	100.0	(D)	.2	40.3	11.8	(D)	(D)	2.5	(D)	.1
AIR....................	-	100.0	(D)	-	97.7	2.3	(D)	(D)	-	(D)	-
WATER..................	-	100.0	(D)	-	-	-	(D)	(D)	-	(D)	-
OTHER..................	-	100.0	(D)	-	45.9	2.8	(D)	(D)	-	(D)	-
UNKNOWN................	-	100.0	(D)	97.3	-	-	(D)	(D)	-	(D)	-
EAST SOUTH CENTRAL.....	45	100.0	(D)	3.1	18.3	1.3	(D)	(D)	17.3	(D)	.7
RAIL...................	2	100.0	(D)	38.6	61.4	-	(D)	(D)	-	(D)	-
MOTOR CARRIER..........	12	100.0	(D)	.9	6.7	.1	(D)	(D)	1.4	(D)	2.4
PRIVATE TRUCK..........	30	100.0	(D)	1.4	20.0	1.9	(D)	(D)	25.5	(D)	-
AIR....................	-	100.0	(D)	1.0	4.1	1.2	(D)	(D)	-	(D)	-
WATER..................	-	100.0	(D)	-	-	-	(D)	(D)	-	(D)	-
OTHER..................	-	100.0	(D)	-	10.8	2.5	(D)	(D)	-	(D)	-
UNKNOWN................	-	100.0	(D)	-	-	-	(D)	(D)	-	(D)	-
WEST SOUTH CENTRAL.....	139	100.0	(D)	.1	13.1	25.6	(D)	(D)	44.3	(D)	6.3
RAIL...................	-	100.0	(D)	-	100.0	-	(D)	(D)	-	(D)	-
MOTOR CARRIER..........	13	100.0	(D)	1.0	28.4	3.2	(D)	(D)	2.4	(D)	26.4
PRIVATE TRUCK..........	125	100.0	(D)	-	11.1	28.1	(D)	(D)	49.0	(D)	4.1
AIR....................	-	100.0	(D)	-	11.2	.1	(D)	(D)	-	(D)	63.8
WATER..................	-	100.0	(D)	-	-	-	(D)	(D)	-	(D)	-
OTHER..................	-	100.0	(D)	-	75.0	17.0	(D)	(D)	-	(D)	8.0
UNKNOWN................	-	100.0	(D)	-	-	-	(D)	(D)	-	(D)	-
MOUNTAIN...............	134	100.0	(D)	.1	10.5	32.7	(D)	(D)	28.5	(D)	23.5
RAIL...................	-	100.0	(D)	-	100.0	-	(D)	(D)	-	(D)	-
MOTOR CARRIER..........	23	100.0	(D)	-	3.5	.7	(D)	(D)	.8	(D)	73.1
PRIVATE TRUCK..........	110	100.0	(D)	.1	11.5	39.9	(D)	(D)	34.8	(D)	12.7
AIR....................	-	100.0	(D)	-	100.0	-	(D)	(D)	-	(D)	-
WATER..................	-	100.0	(D)	-	-	-	(D)	(D)	-	(D)	-
OTHER..................	-	100.0	(D)	-	3.9	1.7	(D)	(D)	-	(D)	94.5
UNKNOWN................	-	100.0	(D)	-	-	-	(D)	(D)	-	(D)	100.0
PACIFIC................	186	100.0	(D)	.8	26.1	12.0	(D)	(D)	4.0	(D)	45.2
RAIL...................	26	100.0	(D)	-	97.4	-	(D)	(D)	-	(D)	-
MOTOR CARRIER..........	50	100.0	(D)	1.2	3.2	.2	(D)	(D)	3.1	(D)	63.6
PRIVATE TRUCK..........	106	100.0	(D)	.9	20.2	20.0	(D)	(D)	5.6	(D)	46.9
AIR....................	-	100.0	(D)	-	54.3	5.3	(D)	(D)	-	(D)	40.5
WATER..................	-	100.0	(D)	-	-	-	(D)	(D)	-	(D)	100.0
OTHER..................	2	100.0	(D)	.1	1.3	44.2	(D)	(D)	-	(D)	54.3
UNKNOWN................	-	100.0	(D)	-	-	-	(D)	(D)	-	(D)	100.0

See footnotes at end of table 4.

TABLE 4. TCC GROUP 379—Percent Distribution of Distance Shipped and Weight of Shipment, by Means of Transport: 1972

Distance shipped and weight of shipment[2][3]	Number	Percent distribution by means of transport							
		All means of transport	Rail	Motor carrier	Private truck	Air	Water	Other	Unknown
TONS OF SHIPMENTS	(thousands of tons)								
U.S. TOTAL..........	2 199	100.0	6.7	25.9	66.9	-	-	.3	.1
UNDER 100 MILES........	403	100.0	.5	38.4	60.5	.1	-	.3	.2
UNDER 1000 POUNDS.....	5	100.0	-	25.7	68.5	1.5	-	4.1	.2
1000 TO 9999 POUNDS...	58	100.0	-	28.3	69.7	.6	-	1.4	-
10000 TO 29999 POUNDS.	257	100.0	-	31.2	68.7	-	-	.1	-
30000 TO 59999 POUNDS.	79	100.0	-	70.9	28.0	-	-	-	1.0
60000 TO 89999 POUNDS.	-	100.0	-	-	-	-	-	-	-
90000 POUNDS AND OVER.	1	100.0	100.0	-	-	-	-	-	-
100 TO 199 MILES........	454	100.0	.4	19.3	79.9	-	-	.3	.2
UNDER 1000 POUNDS.....	3	100.0	-	43.2	48.3	-	-	7.4	1.1
1000 TO 9999 POUNDS...	65	100.0	-	12.8	86.3	-	-	.5	.4
10000 TO 29999 POUNDS.	355	100.0	-	19.3	80.3	-	-	.3	.2
30000 TO 59999 POUNDS.	28	100.0	.7	32.0	67.2	-	-	-	-
60000 TO 89999 POUNDS.	-	100.0	-	-	-	-	-	-	-
90000 POUNDS AND OVER.	1	100.0	100.0	-	-	-	-	-	-
200 TO 299 MILES........	318	100.0	2.1	27.2	70.1	-	-	.4	.3
UNDER 1000 POUNDS.....	2	100.0	.5	56.3	35.5	.1	-	6.1	1.5
1000 TO 9999 POUNDS...	47	100.0	-	26.0	74.0	-	-	-	-
10000 TO 29999 POUNDS.	218	100.0	.3	26.7	72.5	-	-	.5	-
30000 TO 59999 POUNDS.	43	100.0	3.2	32.0	62.9	-	-	-	1.9
60000 TO 89999 POUNDS.	-	100.0	100.0	-	-	-	-	-	-
90000 POUNDS AND OVER.	3	100.0	100.0	-	-	-	-	-	-
300 TO 499 MILES........	495	100.0	4.3	29.2	66.3	-	-	.2	.1
UNDER 1000 POUNDS.....	5	100.0	-	81.4	13.2	.1	-	5.3	-
1000 TO 9999 POUNDS...	89	100.0	-	42.7	57.3	-	-	-	-
10000 TO 29999 POUNDS.	282	100.0	.1	26.4	73.2	-	-	.2	.2
30000 TO 59999 POUNDS.	92	100.0	.4	28.8	70.8	-	-	-	-
60000 TO 89999 POUNDS.	4	100.0	50.4	16.4	33.2	-	-	-	-
90000 POUNDS AND OVER.	20	100.0	89.9	-	10.1	-	-	-	-
500 TO 999 MILES........	434	100.0	22.3	19.4	58.0	-	-	.3	-
UNDER 1000 POUNDS.....	5	100.0	.1	75.2	18.9	1.3	-	4.6	-
1000 TO 9999 POUNDS...	130	100.0	-	30.7	68.7	.1	-	.5	-
10000 TO 29999 POUNDS.	183	100.0	16.6	21.3	61.8	-	-	.3	-
30000 TO 59999 POUNDS.	64	100.0	23.3	1.8	74.9	-	-	-	-
60000 TO 89999 POUNDS.	47	100.0	100.0	-	-	-	-	-	-
90000 POUNDS AND OVE`.	3	100.0	100.0	-	-	-	-	-	-
1000 TO 1499 MILES......	39	100.0	-	11.4	88.4	.1	-	.1	-
UNDER 1000 POUNDS.....	1	100.0	-	71.2	22.8	2.8	-	3.1	-
1000 TO 9999 POUNDS...	19	100.0	-	11.2	88.8	-	-	-	-
10000 TO 29999 POUNDS.	12	100.0	-	12.3	87.7	-	-	-	-
30000 TO 59999 POUNDS.	6	100.0	-	-	100.0	-	-	-	-
60000 TO 89999 POUNDS.	-	100.0	-	-	-	-	-	-	-
90000 POUNDS AND OVER.	-	100.0	-	-	-	-	-	-	-
1500 MILES OR OVER......	54	100.0	34.8	14.3	48.4	.2	-	2.3	-
UNDER 1000 POUNDS.....	-	100.0	-	86.4	3.4	6.5	-	3.6	-
1000 TO 9999 POUNDS...	24	100.0	19.4	22.4	54.7	.2	-	3.2	-
10000 TO 29999 POUNDS.	14	100.0	2.3	11.8	83.0	-	-	2.9	-
30000 TO 59999 POUNDS.	1	100.0	-	-	100.0	-	-	-	-
60000 TO 89999 POUNDS.	-	100.0	100.0	-	-	-	-	-	-
90000 POUNDS AND OVER.	13	100.0	100.0	-	-	-	-	-	-
TON-MILES OF SHIPMENTS	(millions of ton-miles)								
U.S. TOTAL..........	822	100.0	14.1	21.6	63.7	-	-	.5	.1
UNDER 100 MILES........	25	100.0	.2	42.9	56.2	.2	-	.4	.1
UNDER 1000 POUNDS.....	-	100.0	-	30.5	61.5	2.6	-	5.4	.1
1000 TO 9999 POUNDS...	3	100.0	-	30.4	67.5	.9	-	1.2	-
10000 TO 29999 POUNDS.	15	100.0	-	34.8	65.1	-	-	.2	-
30000 TO 59999 POUNDS.	5	100.0	-	75.6	24.0	-	-	-	.5
60000 TO 89999 POUNDS.	-	100.0	-	-	-	-	-	-	-
90000 POUNDS AND OVER.	-	100.0	100.0	-	-	-	-	-	-
100 TO 199 MILES........	68	100.0	.5	19.0	80.0	-	-	.3	.2
UNDER 1000 POUNDS.....	-	100.0	-	42.1	49.8	-	-	7.2	.9
1000 TO 9999 POUNDS...	9	100.0	-	13.8	85.2	-	-	.5	.4
10000 TO 29999 POUNDS.	54	100.0	-	18.7	80.8	-	-	.2	.2
30000 TO 59999 POUNDS.	3	100.0	.8	34.4	64.7	-	-	-	-
60000 TO 89999 POUNDS.	-	100.0	-	-	-	-	-	-	-
90000 POUNDS AND OVER.	-	100.0	100.0	-	-	-	-	-	-

See footnotes at end of table 4.

TABLE 4. **TCC GROUP 379—Percent Distribution of Distance Shipped and Weight of Shipment, by Means of Transport: 1972**—Continued

Distance shipped and weight of shipment[2] [3]	Number	Percent distribution by means of transport							
		All means of transport	Rail	Motor carrier	Private truck	Air	Water	Other	Unknown
TON-MILES OF SHIPMENTS	(millions of ton-miles)								
200 TO 299 MILES.........	79	100.0	2.1	27.8	69.4	-	-	.4	.3
UNDER 1000 POUNDS.....	-	100.0	.5	55.5	36.2	.1	-	6.3	1.4
1000 TO 9999 POUNDS...	11	100.0	-	27.1	72.9	-	-	-	-
10000 TO 29999 POUNDS.	54	100.0	.4	27.0	72.2	-	-	.5	-
30000 TO 59999 POUNDS.	11	100.0	3.0	33.0	62.0	-	-	-	2.0
60000 TO 89999 POUNDS.	-	100.0	100.0	-	..	-	-	-	-
90000 POUNDS AND OVER.	1	100.0	100.0	-	-	-	-	-	-
300 TO 499 MILES........	191	100.0	4.5	27.7	67.6	-	-	.2	.1
UNDER 1000 POUNDS.....	1	100.0	-	81.7	12.8	.1	-	5.4	-
1000 TO 9999 POUNDS...	33	100.0	-	39.2	60.8	-	-	-	-
10000 TO 29999 POUNDS.	106	100.0	.1	25.2	74.4	-	-	.2	.2
30000 TO 59999 POUNDS.	38	100.0	.4	27.9	71.8	-	-	-	-
60000 TO 89999 POUNDS.	1	100.0	51.5	17.9	30.6	-	-	-	-
90000 POUNDS AND OVER.	7	100.0	91.9	-	8.1	-	-	-	-
500 TO 999 MILES........	298	100.0	23.4	19.6	56.6	-	-	.3	-
UNDER 1000 POUNDS.....	3	100.0	.1	75.0	19.1	1.4	-	4.4	-
1000 TO 9999 POUNDS...	91	100.0	-	30.8	68.5	.1	-	.6	-
10000 TO 29999 POUNDS.	123	100.0	18.3	21.5	59.9	-	-	.2	-
30000 TO 59999 POUNDS.	42	100.0	25.6	1.6	72.9	-	-	-	-
60000 TO 89999 POUNDS.	34	100.0	100.0	-	-	-	-	-	-
90000 POUNDS AND OVER.	1	100.0	100.0	-	-	-	-	-	-
1000 TO 1499 MILES......	45	100.0	-	11.4	88.5	.1	-	.1	-
UNDER 1000 POUNDS.....	1	100.0	-	69.1	24.8	3.0	-	3.0	-
1000 TO 9999 POUNDS...	23	100.0	-	11.0	89.0	-	-	-	-
10000 TO 29999 POUNDS.	13	100.0	-	13.1	86.9	-	-	-	-
30000 TO 59999 POUNDS.	7	100.0	-	-	100.0	-	-	-	-
60000 TO 89999 POUNDS.	-	100.0	-	-	-	-	-	-	-
90000 POUNDS AND OVER.	-	100.0	-	-	-	-	-	-	-
1500 MILES OR OVER......	113	100.0	31.2	13.1	53.5	.2	-	1.9	-
UNDER 1000 POUNDS.....	1	100.0	-	86.6	3.2	7.0	-	3.3	-
1000 TO 9999 POUNDS...	43	100.0	21.2	22.7	53.1	.2	-	2.8	-
10000 TO 29999 POUNDS.	39	100.0	1.8	9.4	86.4	-	-	2.4	-
30000 TO 59999 POUNDS.	3	100.0	-	-	100.0	-	-	-	-
60000 TO 89999 POUNDS.	-	100.0	100.0	-	-	-	-	-	-
90000 POUNDS AND OVER.	24	100.0	100.0	-	-	-	-	-	-

Note: Detail may not add to total due to rounding. The introductory table shows the estimates of sampling variability for tons; sampling variability for ton-miles has not been estimated. See the map in the Introduction for the States comprising the geographic divisions of the United States.

Shipments excluded from the survey are those moving by pipeline (primarily petroleum products from refineries), parcel post shipments, and commodities moved by own power (motorized vehicles, aircraft, etc.) or towed (prefabricated buildings, etc.). Local shipments (commodities shipped less than 25 miles from the plant) and shipments within the same city are also excluded. Shipments to Alaska and Hawaii from the 48 conterminous States and the District of Columbia are included; however, no data were obtained for shipments originating in Alaska and Hawaii.

- Represents zero or rounds to zero.   (D) Withheld to avoid disclosing figures for individual companies.

[1]Production of this commodity is concentrated in the geographic divisions shown; figures and distributions for geographic divisions not shown are included in the total.

[2]Distances of shipments to foreign destinations are calculated only to the U.S. port of exit.

[3]Includes only shipments represented by bills of lading and invoices. Summary records which did not show individual weights of shipments are not included.

Instruments, Photographic and Medical Goods, Watches and Clocks

CONTENTS

[Page numbers listed here omit the State prefix number that appears as part of the number for each page]

TABLES   (The tables listed below are shown for each of the Transportation Commodity Classification groups in this report)

Comparisons of Tons and Ton-Miles of Shipments for Geographic Divisions of Origin and for
Sampling Variability: 1972 and 1967

1. Percent Distribution of Geographic Division of Origin and Distance Shipped, by Means of
Transport: 1972

2. Percent Distribution of Geographic Division of Origin and Means of Transport, by Geographic
Division of Destination: 1972

3. Percent Distribution of Geographic Division of Destination and Means of Transport, by Geographic
Division of Origin: 1972

4. Percent Distribution of Distance Shipped and Weight of Shipment, by Means of Transport: 1972

TCC 381. Engineering, Scientific, and Laboratory Instruments

Comparisons of Tons and Ton-Miles of Shipments for
Geographic Divisions of Origin and for Sampling Variability: 1972 and 1967

Geographic division of origin	Estimates				Relative sampling variability in tons (percent)	
	1972		1967		1972	1967
	Tons (thousands)	Ton-miles (millions)	Tons (thousands)	Ton-miles (millions)		
U.S. total	67	55	76	49	25.1	(*)
New England	1	1	(*)	(*)	51.8	(*)
Middle Atlantic	23	18	(*)	(*)	34.1	(*)
East North Central	(D)	(D)	(*)	(*)	(*)	(*)
West North Central	(D)	(D)	(*)	(*)	(*)	(*)
South Atlantic	4	3	(*)	(*)	44.0	(*)
East South Central	(D)	(D)	(*)	(*)	(*)	(*)
West South Central	(D)	(D)	(*)	(*)	(*)	(*)
Mountain	(D)	(D)	(*)	(*)	(*)	(*)
Pacific	(D)	(D)	(*)	(*)	(*)	(*)

Note: One general criterion for publication of data in this series provided for a maximum relative sampling variability of 50 percent of the total tons for any origin division. In other words, data would not be published if 1 standard error exceeded 50 percent of the estimate with which it was associated; see "Reliability of Data", page VIII. However, for this commodity group the absolute standard errors are generally low and division data are published even though some of the measured relative errors exceed 50 percent.

(D) Withheld to avoid disclosing figures for individual companies.   *Data not published.

TABLE 1. TCC GROUP 381—Percent Distribution of Geographic Division of Origin and Distance Shipped, by Means of Transport: 1972

Geographic division of origin[1] and distance shipped[2]	Number	Percent distribution by means of transport							
		All means of transport	Rail	Motor carrier	Private truck	Air	Water	Other	Unknown
TONS OF SHIPMENTS	(thousands of tons)								
U.S. TOTAL	67	100.0	1.1	48.7	25.9	16.1	.9	7.0	.4
NEW ENGLAND	1	100.0	.4	42.8	4.1	13.9	-	38.7	-
UNDER 100 MILES	-	100.0	-	15.9	17.7	1.3	-	65.2	-
100 TO 199 MILES	-	100.0	-	70.5	.1	13.0	-	16.4	-
200 TO 299 MILES	-	100.0	2.9	21.8	-	10.8	-	64.4	-
300 TO 499 MILES	-	100.0	-	38.0	7.0	1.4	-	53.5	-
500 TO 999 MILES	-	100.0	1.4	65.2	-	7.9	-	25.5	-
1000 TO 1499 MILES	-	100.0	-	21.3	-	20.4	-	58.3	-
1500 MILES OR OVER	-	100.0	-	44.0	-	42.4	-	13.6	-
MIDDLE ATLANTIC	23	100.0	1.7	71.9	3.8	9.3	.9	11.8	.6
UNDER 100 MILES	7	100.0	-	66.1	11.8	.1	2.9	17.2	1.8
100 TO 199 MILES	1	100.0	-	90.4	.9	.8	-	7.9	-
200 TO 299 MILES	2	100.0	-	73.0	-	13.8	-	12.2	1.0
300 TO 499 MILES	2	100.0	15.4	41.7	.1	25.4	-	17.4	-
500 TO 999 MILES	2	100.0	-	55.2	-	27.2	-	17.5	-
1000 TO 1499 MILES	4	100.0	.1	86.9	-	8.2	-	4.8	-
1500 MILES OR OVER	3	100.0	1.1	87.5	1.1	6.9	-	3.4	-
SOUTH ATLANTIC	4	100.0	2.6	55.1	1.1	21.5	-	19.8	-
UNDER 100 MILES	-	100.0	-	78.2	4.8	.4	-	16.5	-
100 TO 199 MILES	-	100.0	-	69.2	-	5.6	-	25.2	-
200 TO 299 MILES	-	100.0	-	21.0	.9	40.8	-	37.4	-
300 TO 499 MILES	-	100.0	12.2	24.1	-	33.3	-	30.5	-
500 TO 999 MILES	1	100.0	.6	64.6	-	20.4	-	14.4	-
1000 TO 1499 MILES	-	100.0	-	34.2	-	42.7	-	23.1	-
1500 MILES OR OVER	-	100.0	-	56.4	-	31.9	-	11.7	-
TON-MILES OF SHIPMENTS	(millions of ton-miles)								
U.S. TOTAL	55	100.0	1.0	51.3	13.2	29.2	.7	4.5	.2
NEW ENGLAND	1	100.0	.4	43.4	.5	26.0	-	29.8	-
UNDER 100 MILES	-	100.0	-	16.9	15.6	.1	-	67.4	-
100 TO 199 MILES	-	100.0	-	70.8	-	13.3	-	15.9	-
200 TO 299 MILES	-	100.0	3.0	20.5	-	10.4	-	66.1	-
300 TO 499 MILES	-	100.0	-	35.5	6.4	1.4	-	56.8	-
500 TO 999 MILES	-	100.0	1.5	65.9	-	6.6	-	26.0	-
1000 TO 1499 MILES	-	100.0	-	21.3	-	21.2	-	57.5	-
1500 MILES OR OVER	-	100.0	-	43.7	-	42.6	-	13.7	-
MIDDLE ATLANTIC	18	100.0	1.1	81.6	.7	10.1	-	6.4	-
UNDER 100 MILES	-	100.0	-	76.3	7.1	.2	1.3	14.1	1.0
100 TO 199 MILES	-	100.0	-	91.7	.7	.6	-	7.1	-
200 TO 299 MILES	-	100.0	-	75.3	-	12.3	-	11.4	1.0
300 TO 499 MILES	-	100.0	12.3	42.9	.1	28.2	-	16.5	-
500 TO 999 MILES	1	100.0	-	54.8	-	28.0	-	17.2	-
1000 TO 1499 MILES	5	100.0	.1	87.9	-	7.3	-	4.7	-
1500 MILES OR OVER	8	100.0	1.0	87.8	1.1	6.7	-	3.4	-
SOUTH ATLANTIC	3	100.0	1.4	52.4	.1	31.1	-	15.0	-
UNDER 100 MILES	-	100.0	-	81.5	2.6	.3	-	15.6	-
100 TO 199 MILES	-	100.0	-	69.6	-	5.0	-	25.4	-
200 TO 299 MILES	-	100.0	-	20.5	.9	37.5	-	41.1	-
300 TO 499 MILES	-	100.0	12.0	26.2	-	31.3	-	30.5	-
500 TO 999 MILES	1	100.0	.5	64.8	-	20.9	-	13.8	-
1000 TO 1499 MILES	-	100.0	-	33.9	-	42.5	-	23.6	-
1500 MILES OR OVER	1	100.0	-	49.2	-	41.0	-	9.7	-

See footnotes at end of table 4.

TABLE 2. TCC GROUP 381—Percent Distribution of Geographic Division of Origin and Means of Transport, by Geographic Division of Destination: 1972

Geographic division of origin[1] and means of transport	Number	Percent distribution by division of destination									
		U.S. total	New England	Middle Atlantic	East North Central	West North Central	South Atlantic	East South Central	West South Central	Mountain	Pacific
TONS OF SHIPMENTS	(thousands of tons)										
U.S. TOTAL	67	100.0	5.3	31.0	14.7	3.9	13.7	3.6	8.8	3.1	16.0
RAIL	-	100.0	4.1	64.4	2.6	6.6	1.7	4.5	3.2	4.8	8.1
MOTOR CARRIER	32	100.0	4.6	29.6	10.2	3.6	12.7	3.2	14.0	4.0	18.1
PRIVATE TRUCK	17	100.0	6.9	29.5	22.4	5.9	7.7	6.1	-	2.8	18.6
AIR	10	100.0	4.1	27.9	18.1	2.3	25.0	1.0	8.5	2.1	11.1
WATER	-	100.0	-	74.2	-	-	25.8	-	-	-	-
OTHER	4	100.0	8.5	40.3	13.3	3.0	17.0	2.7	8.4	.8	6.0
UNKNOWN	-	100.0	-	69.9	7.8	-	5.3	.3	4.0	.3	12.4

See footnotes at end of table 4.

TABLE 2. TCC GROUP 381—Percent Distribution of Geographic Division of Origin and Means of Transport, by Geographic Division of Destination: 1972—Continued

Geographic division of origin[1] and means of transport	Number	Percent distribution by division of destination									
		U.S. total	New England	Middle Atlantic	East North Central	West North Central	South Atlantic	East South Central	West South Central	Mountain	Pacific
TONS OF SHIPMENTS	(thousands of tons)										
NEW ENGLAND.............	1	100.0	10.4	33.5	16.4	4.2	19.4	.5	2.8	.6	12.2
RAIL...................	-	100.0	-	20.0	-	-	80.0	-	-	-	-
MOTOR CARRIER..........	-	100.0	11.9	27.8	28.0	7.3	9.6	-	2.6	-	12.8
PRIVATE TRUCK..........	-	100.0	87.8	12.2	-	-	-	-	-	-	-
AIR...................	-	100.0	1.9	16.2	11.3	.6	20.7	.5	7.5	4.5	36.8
WATER.................	-	100.0	-	-	-	-	-	-	-	-	-
OTHER.................	-	100.0	3.6	48.5	7.4	2.5	31.0	1.0	1.7	-	4.3
UNKNOWN...............	-	100.0	-	-	-	-	-	-	-	-	-
MIDDLE ATLANTIC........	23	100.0	2.2	39.8	9.9	2.1	14.2	1.2	16.3	4.4	9.9
RAIL...................	-	100.0	-	88.5	.8	-	-	-	1.1	2.1	7.5
MOTOR CARRIER..........	17	100.0	1.4	37.9	8.3	2.3	11.8	1.2	19.7	5.9	11.4
PRIVATE TRUCK..........	-	100.0	1.7	89.5	-	-	4.7	-	-	-	4.2
AIR...................	2	100.0	.1	2.7	27.2	3.0	42.2	.1	13.6	1.2	9.9
WATER.................	-	100.0	-	100.0	-	-	-	-	-	-	-
OTHER.................	2	100.0	9.4	50.1	12.2	1.3	13.3	3.0	6.5	-	4.1
UNKNOWN...............	-	100.0	-	99.8	-	-	-	-	.2	-	-
SOUTH ATLANTIC.........	4	100.0	11.8	23.1	11.0	3.7	19.8	15.2	3.8	.6	11.0
RAIL...................	-	100.0	8.5	91.5	-	-	-	-	-	-	-
MOTOR CARRIER..........	2	100.0	6.1	25.8	7.5	3.1	18.6	25.4	1.4	-	12.2
PRIVATE TRUCK..........	-	100.0	-	5.9	-	-	94.1	-	-	-	-
AIR...................	1	100.0	27.3	13.1	12.9	2.2	19.8	2.9	4.2	-	17.6
WATER.................	-	100.0	-	-	-	-	-	-	-	-	-
OTHER.................	-	100.0	11.7	18.6	20.6	7.5	21.8	3.1	10.8	3.2	2.8
UNKNOWN...............	-	100.0	-	-	-	-	-	-	-	-	-
TON-MILES OF SHIPMENTS	(millions of ton-miles)										
U.S. TOTAL.............	55	100.0	5.0	22.7	10.8	3.5	14.6	3.2	14.1	6.8	19.4
RAIL...................	-	100.0	10.4	28.9	5.5	12.0	4.1	11.1	5.9	6.6	15.6
MOTOR CARRIER..........	28	100.0	4.6	12.5	5.8	3.9	10.3	3.4	21.8	9.5	28.3
PRIVATE TRUCK..........	7	100.0	11.0	33.4	19.1	5.3	9.2	7.0	-	10.3	4.7
AIR...................	16	100.0	3.0	35.9	15.5	1.7	23.8	1.0	6.7	1.3	11.1
WATER.................	-	100.0	-	62.2	-	-	37.8	-	-	-	-
OTHER.................	2	100.0	4.3	12.8	14.0	5.1	18.6	3.5	20.2	2.4	19.1
UNKNOWN...............	-	100.0	-	45.2	26.5	-	17.1	.8	9.4	.3	.6
NEW ENGLAND.............	1	100.0	1.3	7.1	15.1	5.9	22.8	.5	5.4	1.8	40.1
RAIL...................	-	100.0	-	7.6	-	-	92.4	-	-	-	-
MOTOR CARRIER..........	-	100.0	2.0	6.6	26.0	10.0	9.1	-	4.9	-	41.4
PRIVATE TRUCK..........	-	100.0	66.2	33.8	-	-	-	-	-	-	-
AIR...................	-	100.0	-	1.9	4.3	.4	14.4	.3	7.6	6.7	64.4
WATER.................	-	100.0	-	-	-	-	-	-	-	-	-
OTHER.................	-	100.0	.3	12.0	9.2	4.9	49.6	1.3	4.2	.1	18.4
UNKNOWN...............	-	100.0	-	-	-	-	-	-	-	-	-
MIDDLE ATLANTIC........	18	100.0	.5	5.4	7.3	2.5	7.7	1.4	29.4	13.5	32.2
RAIL...................	-	100.0	-	54.3	.7	-	-	-	2.3	6.7	35.9
MOTOR CARRIER..........	15	100.0	.4	4.7	4.8	2.5	5.4	1.3	32.0	16.1	32.9
PRIVATE TRUCK..........	-	100.0	1.0	20.7	-	-	1.6	-	-	-	76.8
AIR...................	1	100.0	-	.9	22.6	3.1	22.9	.1	19.4	2.5	28.6
WATER.................	-	100.0	-	100.0	-	-	-	-	-	-	-
OTHER.................	1	100.0	3.6	10.5	17.9	3.0	14.3	5.5	21.5	-	23.6
UNKNOWN...............	-	100.0	-	96.4	-	-	-	-	3.6	-	-
SOUTH ATLANTIC.........	3	100.0	7.4	7.1	7.5	4.4	8.7	18.6	5.9	1.7	38.7
RAIL...................	-	100.0	13.4	86.6	-	-	-	-	-	-	-
MOTOR CARRIER..........	1	100.0	5.6	6.6	5.2	3.5	4.7	33.7	2.3	-	38.4
PRIVATE TRUCK..........	-	100.0	-	36.5	-	-	63.5	-	-	-	-
AIR...................	1	100.0	9.4	2.8	7.9	2.2	16.9	1.9	4.9	-	54.0
WATER.................	-	100.0	-	-	-	-	-	-	-	-	-
OTHER.................	-	100.0	8.9	9.9	15.5	12.7	6.1	2.5	21.4	11.0	12.0
UNKNOWN...............	-	100.0	-	-	-	-	-	-	-	-	-

See footnotes at end of table 4.

TABLE 3. **TCC GROUP 381**—Percent Distribution of Geographic Division of Destination and Means of Transport, by Geographic Division of Origin: 1972

Geographic division of destination and means of transport	Number	Percent distribution by division of origin[1]									
	(thousands of tons)	U.S. total	New England	Middle Atlantic	East North Central	West North Central	South Atlantic	East South Central	West South Central	Mountain	Pacific
TONS OF SHIPMENTS											
U.S. TOTAL	67	100.0	1.9	35.6	(D)	(D)	7.0	(D)	(D)	(D)	(D)
RAIL	-	100.0	.8	55.5	(D)	(D)	16.5	(D)	(D)	(D)	(D)
MOTOR CARRIER	32	100.0	1.7	52.7	(D)	(D)	8.0	(D)	(D)	(D)	(D)
PRIVATE TRUCK	17	100.0	.3	5.2	(D)	(D)	.3	(D)	(D)	(D)	(D)
AIR	10	100.0	1.7	20.5	(D)	(D)	9.4	(D)	(D)	(D)	(D)
WATER	-	100.0	-	35.7	(D)	(D)	-	(D)	(D)	(D)	(D)
OTHER	4	100.0	10.6	60.2	(D)	(D)	19.9	(D)	(D)	(D)	(D)
UNKNOWN	-	100.0	-	61.5	(D)	(D)	-	(D)	(D)	(D)	(D)
NEW ENGLAND	3	100.0	3.7	14.9	(D)	(D)	15.5	(D)	(D)	(D)	(D)
RAIL	-	100.0	-	-	(D)	(D)	34.2	(D)	(D)	(D)	(D)
MOTOR CARRIER	1	100.0	4.4	16.5	(D)	(D)	10.5	(D)	(D)	(D)	(D)
PRIVATE TRUCK	1	100.0	3.9	1.3	(D)	(D)	-	(D)	(D)	(D)	(D)
AIR	-	100.0	.8	.7	(D)	(D)	63.0	(D)	(D)	(D)	(D)
WATER	-	100.0	-	-	(D)	(D)	-	(D)	(D)	(D)	(D)
OTHER	-	100.0	4.4	66.3	(D)	(D)	27.1	(D)	(D)	(D)	(D)
UNKNOWN	-	100.0	-	-	(D)	(D)	-	(D)	(D)	(D)	(D)
MIDDLE ATLANTIC	20	100.0	2.1	45.8	(D)	(D)	5.3	(D)	(D)	(D)	(D)
RAIL	-	100.0	.2	76.3	(D)	(D)	23.5	(D)	(D)	(D)	(D)
MOTOR CARRIER	9	100.0	1.6	67.5	(D)	(D)	6.9	(D)	(D)	(D)	(D)
PRIVATE TRUCK	5	100.0	.1	15.7	(D)	(D)	.1	(D)	(D)	(D)	(D)
AIR	3	100.0	1.0	2.0	(D)	(D)	4.4	(D)	(D)	(D)	(D)
WATER	-	100.0	-	48.1	(D)	(D)	-	(D)	(D)	(D)	(D)
OTHER	1	100.0	12.8	74.8	(D)	(D)	9.2	(D)	(D)	(D)	(D)
UNKNOWN	-	100.0	-	87.8	(D)	(D)	-	(D)	(D)	(D)	(D)
EAST NORTH CENTRAL	9	100.0	2.1	24.0	(D)	(D)	5.3	(D)	(D)	(D)	(D)
RAIL	-	100.0	-	17.9	(D)	(D)	-	(D)	(D)	(D)	(D)
MOTOR CARRIER	3	100.0	4.6	42.5	(D)	(D)	5.9	(D)	(D)	(D)	(D)
PRIVATE TRUCK	3	100.0	-	-	(D)	(D)	-	(D)	(D)	(D)	(D)
AIR	1	100.0	1.0	30.8	(D)	(D)	6.7	(D)	(D)	(D)	(D)
WATER	-	100.0	-	-	(D)	(D)	-	(D)	(D)	(D)	(D)
OTHER	-	100.0	5.9	55.5	(D)	(D)	30.8	(D)	(D)	(D)	(D)
UNKNOWN	-	100.0	-	-	(D)	(D)	-	(D)	(D)	(D)	(D)
WEST NORTH CENTRAL	2	100.0	2.0	18.6	(D)	(D)	6.6	(D)	(D)	(D)	(D)
RAIL	-	100.0	-	-	(D)	(D)	-	(D)	(D)	(D)	(D)
MOTOR CARRIER	1	100.0	3.4	32.9	(D)	(D)	6.8	(D)	(D)	(D)	(D)
PRIVATE TRUCK	1	100.0	-	-	(D)	(D)	-	(D)	(D)	(D)	(D)
AIR	-	100.0	.4	26.8	(D)	(D)	9.2	(D)	(D)	(D)	(D)
WATER	-	100.0	-	-	(D)	(D)	-	(D)	(D)	(D)	(D)
OTHER	-	100.0	9.0	27.1	(D)	(D)	50.2	(D)	(D)	(D)	(D)
UNKNOWN	-	100.0	-	-	(D)	(D)	-	(D)	(D)	(D)	(D)
SOUTH ATLANTIC	9	100.0	2.7	37.0	(D)	(D)	10.2	(D)	(D)	(D)	(D)
RAIL	-	100.0	35.1	-	(D)	(D)	-	(D)	(D)	(D)	(D)
MOTOR CARRIER	4	100.0	1.3	49.0	(D)	(D)	11.7	(D)	(D)	(D)	(D)
PRIVATE TRUCK	1	100.0	-	3.1	(D)	(D)	3.6	(D)	(D)	(D)	(D)
AIR	2	100.0	1.4	34.7	(D)	(D)	7.5	(D)	(D)	(D)	(D)
WATER	-	100.0	-	-	(D)	(D)	-	(D)	(D)	(D)	(D)
OTHER	-	100.0	19.3	47.1	(D)	(D)	25.4	(D)	(D)	(D)	(D)
UNKNOWN	-	100.0	-	-	(D)	(D)	-	(D)	(D)	(D)	(D)
EAST SOUTH CENTRAL	2	100.0	.3	12.2	(D)	(D)	30.1	(D)	(D)	(D)	(D)
RAIL	-	100.0	-	-	(D)	(D)	-	(D)	(D)	(D)	(D)
MOTOR CARRIER	1	100.0	-	19.3	(D)	(D)	62.8	(D)	(D)	(D)	(D)
PRIVATE TRUCK	1	100.0	-	-	(D)	(D)	-	(D)	(D)	(D)	(D)
AIR	-	100.0	.8	2.0	(D)	(D)	26.3	(D)	(D)	(D)	(D)
WATER	-	100.0	-	-	(D)	(D)	-	(D)	(D)	(D)	(D)
OTHER	-	100.0	4.1	68.5	(D)	(D)	22.8	(D)	(D)	(D)	(D)
UNKNOWN	-	100.0	-	-	(D)	(D)	-	(D)	(D)	(D)	(D)
WEST SOUTH CENTRAL	5	100.0	.6	65.8	(D)	(D)	3.0	(D)	(D)	(D)	(D)
RAIL	-	100.0	-	18.9	(D)	(D)	-	(D)	(D)	(D)	(D)
MOTOR CARRIER	4	100.0	.3	74.5	(D)	(D)	.8	(D)	(D)	(D)	(D)
PRIVATE TRUCK	-	100.0	-	-	(D)	(D)	-	(D)	(D)	(D)	(D)
AIR	-	100.0	1.5	33.0	(D)	(D)	4.7	(D)	(D)	(D)	(D)
WATER	-	100.0	-	-	(D)	(D)	-	(D)	(D)	(D)	(D)
OTHER	-	100.0	2.1	46.3	(D)	(D)	25.5	(D)	(D)	(D)	(D)
UNKNOWN	-	100.0	-	2.5	(D)	(D)	-	(D)	(D)	(D)	(D)
MOUNTAIN	2	100.0	.4	50.7	(D)	(D)	1.4	(D)	(D)	(D)	(D)
RAIL	-	100.0	-	23.8	(D)	(D)	-	(D)	(D)	(D)	(D)
MOTOR CARRIER	1	100.0	-	78.6	(D)	(D)	-	(D)	(D)	(D)	(D)
PRIVATE TRUCK	-	100.0	-	-	(D)	(D)	-	(D)	(D)	(D)	(D)
AIR	-	100.0	3.6	11.6	(D)	(D)	-	(D)	(D)	(D)	(D)
WATER	-	100.0	-	-	(D)	(D)	-	(D)	(D)	(D)	(D)
OTHER	-	100.0	.6	.5	(D)	(D)	82.8	(D)	(D)	(D)	(D)
UNKNOWN	-	100.0	-	-	(D)	(D)	-	(D)	(D)	(D)	(D)
PACIFIC	10	100.0	1.5	22.1	(D)	(D)	4.9	(D)	(D)	(D)	(D)
RAIL	-	100.0	-	51.1	(D)	(D)	-	(D)	(D)	(D)	(D)
MOTOR CARRIER	5	100.0	1.2	33.3	(D)	(D)	5.4	(D)	(D)	(D)	(D)
PRIVATE TRUCK	3	100.0	-	1.2	(D)	(D)	-	(D)	(D)	(D)	(D)
AIR	1	100.0	5.5	18.5	(D)	(D)	15.0	(D)	(D)	(D)	(D)
WATER	-	100.0	-	-	(D)	(D)	-	(D)	(D)	(D)	(D)
OTHER	-	100.0	7.5	40.5	(D)	(D)	9.1	(D)	(D)	(D)	(D)
UNKNOWN	-	100.0	-	-	(D)	(D)	-	(D)	(D)	(D)	(D)

See footnotes at end of table 4.

TABLE 3. **TCC GROUP 381—Percent Distribution of Geographic Division of Destination and Means of Transport, by Geographic Division of Origin: 1972**—Continued

Geographic division of destination and means of transport	Number	Percent distribution by division of origin[1]									
		U.S. total	New England	Middle Atlantic	East North Central	West North Central	South Atlantic	East South Central	West South Central	Mountain	Pacific
TON-MILES OF SHIPMENTS	(millions of ton-miles)										
U.S. TOTAL	55	100.0	1.8	33.5	(D)	(D)	6.0	(D)	(D)	(D)	(D)
RAIL	-	100.0	.7	38.8	(D)	(D)	9.0	(D)	(D)	(D)	(D)
MOTOR CARRIER	28	100.0	1.6	53.3	(D)	(D)	6.2	(D)	(D)	(D)	(D)
PRIVATE TRUCK	7	100.0	.1	1.7	(D)	(D)	-	(D)	(D)	(D)	(D)
AIR	16	100.0	1.6	11.6	(D)	(D)	6.4	(D)	(D)	(D)	(D)
WATER	-	100.0	-	1.3	(D)	(D)	-	(D)	(D)	(D)	(D)
OTHER	2	100.0	12.3	48.1	(D)	(D)	20.3	(D)	(D)	(D)	(D)
UNKNOWN	-	100.0	-	6.7	(D)	(D)	-	(D)	(D)	(D)	(D)
NEW ENGLAND	2	100.0	.5	3.7	(D)	(D)	9.0	(D)	(D)	(D)	(D)
RAIL	-	100.0	-	-	(D)	(D)	11.7	(D)	(D)	(D)	(D)
MOTOR CARRIER	1	100.0	.7	4.4	(D)	(D)	7.6	(D)	(D)	(D)	(D)
PRIVATE TRUCK	-	100.0	.4	.2	(D)	(D)	-	(D)	(D)	(D)	(D)
AIR	-	100.0	-	.1	(D)	(D)	20.0	(D)	(D)	(D)	(D)
WATER	-	100.0	-	-	(D)	(D)	-	(D)	(D)	(D)	(D)
OTHER	-	100.0	.8	40.6	(D)	(D)	42.1	(D)	(D)	(D)	(D)
UNKNOWN	-	100.0	-	-	(D)	(D)	-	(D)	(D)	(D)	(D)
MIDDLE ATLANTIC	12	100.0	.6	8.0	(D)	(D)	1.9	(D)	(D)	(D)	(D)
RAIL	-	100.0	.2	72.7	(D)	(D)	27.1	(D)	(D)	(D)	(D)
MOTOR CARRIER	3	100.0	.8	19.9	(D)	(D)	3.3	(D)	(D)	(D)	(D)
PRIVATE TRUCK	2	100.0	.1	1.1	(D)	(D)	-	(D)	(D)	(D)	(D)
AIR	5	100.0	.1	.3	(D)	(D)	.5	(D)	(D)	(D)	(D)
WATER	-	100.0	-	2.1	(D)	(D)	-	(D)	(D)	(D)	(D)
OTHER	-	100.0	11.5	39.6	(D)	(D)	15.6	(D)	(D)	(D)	(D)
UNKNOWN	-	100.0	-	14.3	(D)	(D)	-	(D)	(D)	(D)	(D)
EAST NORTH CENTRAL	5	100.0	2.6	22.8	(D)	(D)	4.2	(D)	(D)	(D)	(D)
RAIL	-	100.0	-	4.9	(D)	(D)	-	(D)	(D)	(D)	(D)
MOTOR CARRIER	1	100.0	7.0	43.6	(D)	(D)	5.5	(D)	(D)	(D)	(D)
PRIVATE TRUCK	1	100.0	-	-	(D)	(D)	-	(D)	(D)	(D)	(D)
AIR	2	100.0	.5	16.9	(D)	(D)	3.3	(D)	(D)	(D)	(D)
WATER	-	100.0	-	-	(D)	(D)	-	(D)	(D)	(D)	(D)
OTHER	-	100.0	8.1	61.1	(D)	(D)	22.5	(D)	(D)	(D)	(D)
UNKNOWN	-	100.0	-	-	(D)	(D)	-	(D)	(D)	(D)	(D)
WEST NORTH CENTRAL	1	100.0	3.1	23.9	(D)	(D)	7.6	(D)	(D)	(D)	(D)
RAIL	-	100.0	-	-	(D)	(D)	-	(D)	(D)	(D)	(D)
MOTOR CARRIER	1	100.0	4.0	34.0	(D)	(D)	5.6	(D)	(D)	(D)	(D)
PRIVATE TRUCK	-	100.0	-	-	(D)	(D)	-	(D)	(D)	(D)	(D)
AIR	-	100.0	.4	20.3	(D)	(D)	8.2	(D)	(D)	(D)	(D)
WATER	-	100.0	-	-	(D)	(D)	-	(D)	(D)	(D)	(D)
OTHER	-	100.0	11.8	28.8	(D)	(D)	51.2	(D)	(D)	(D)	(D)
UNKNOWN	-	100.0	-	-	(D)	(D)	-	(D)	(D)	(D)	(D)
SOUTH ATLANTIC	8	100.0	2.9	17.5	(D)	(D)	3.6	(D)	(D)	(D)	(D)
RAIL	-	100.0	16.5	-	(D)	(D)	-	(D)	(D)	(D)	(D)
MOTOR CARRIER	2	100.0	1.4	27.9	(D)	(D)	2.8	(D)	(D)	(D)	(D)
PRIVATE TRUCK	-	100.0	-	.3	(D)	(D)	.2	(D)	(D)	(D)	(D)
AIR	3	100.0	1.0	11.1	(D)	(D)	4.6	(D)	(D)	(D)	(D)
WATER	-	100.0	-	-	(D)	(D)	-	(D)	(D)	(D)	(D)
OTHER	-	100.0	32.7	36.8	(D)	(D)	6.6	(D)	(D)	(D)	(D)
UNKNOWN	-	100.0	-	-	(D)	(D)	-	(D)	(D)	(D)	(D)
EAST SOUTH CENTRAL	1	100.0	.3	14.7	(D)	(D)	35.3	(D)	(D)	(D)	(D)
RAIL	-	100.0	-	-	(D)	(D)	-	(D)	(D)	(D)	(D)
MOTOR CARRIER	-	100.0	-	20.2	(D)	(D)	62.1	(D)	(D)	(D)	(D)
PRIVATE TRUCK	-	100.0	-	-	(D)	(D)	-	(D)	(D)	(D)	(D)
AIR	-	100.0	.6	1.3	(D)	(D)	12.7	(D)	(D)	(D)	(D)
WATER	-	100.0	-	-	(D)	(D)	-	(D)	(D)	(D)	(D)
OTHER	-	100.0	4.6	75.9	(D)	(D)	14.6	(D)	(D)	(D)	(D)
UNKNOWN	-	100.0	-	-	(D)	(D)	-	(D)	(D)	(D)	(D)
WEST SOUTH CENTRAL	7	100.0	.7	69.9	(D)	(D)	2.5	(D)	(D)	(D)	(D)
RAIL	-	100.0	-	15.3	(D)	(D)	-	(D)	(D)	(D)	(D)
MOTOR CARRIER	6	100.0	.4	78.2	(D)	(D)	.6	(D)	(D)	(D)	(D)
PRIVATE TRUCK	-	100.0	-	-	(D)	(D)	-	(D)	(D)	(D)	(D)
AIR	1	100.0	1.8	33.6	(D)	(D)	4.7	(D)	(D)	(D)	(D)
WATER	-	100.0	-	-	(D)	(D)	-	(D)	(D)	(D)	(D)
OTHER	-	100.0	2.5	51.3	(D)	(D)	21.6	(D)	(D)	(D)	(D)
UNKNOWN	-	100.0	-	2.5	(D)	(D)	-	(D)	(D)	(D)	(D)
MOUNTAIN	3	100.0	.5	66.5	(D)	(D)	1.5	(D)	(D)	(D)	(D)
RAIL	-	100.0	-	39.8	(D)	(D)	-	(D)	(D)	(D)	(D)
MOTOR CARRIER	2	100.0	-	90.5	(D)	(D)	-	(D)	(D)	(D)	(D)
PRIVATE TRUCK	-	100.0	-	-	(D)	(D)	-	(D)	(D)	(D)	(D)
AIR	-	100.0	8.2	21.4	(D)	(D)	.1	(D)	(D)	(D)	(D)
WATER	-	100.0	-	-	(D)	(D)	-	(D)	(D)	(D)	(D)
OTHER	-	100.0	.7	.5	(D)	(D)	91.7	(D)	(D)	(D)	(D)
UNKNOWN	-	100.0	-	-	(D)	(D)	-	(D)	(D)	(D)	(D)
PACIFIC	10	100.0	3.8	55.7	(D)	(D)	12.1	(D)	(D)	(D)	(D)
RAIL	-	100.0	-	89.3	(D)	(D)	-	(D)	(D)	(D)	(D)
MOTOR CARRIER	8	100.0	2.3	62.0	(D)	(D)	8.4	(D)	(D)	(D)	(D)
PRIVATE TRUCK	-	100.0	-	28.3	(D)	(D)	-	(D)	(D)	(D)	(D)
AIR	1	100.0	9.5	29.9	(D)	(D)	31.4	(D)	(D)	(D)	(D)
WATER	-	100.0	-	-	(D)	(D)	-	(D)	(D)	(D)	(D)
OTHER	-	100.0	11.8	59.4	(D)	(D)	12.7	(D)	(D)	(D)	(D)
UNKNOWN	-	100.0	-	-	(D)	(D)	-	(D)	(D)	(D)	(D)

See footnotes at end of table 4.

TABLE 4. TCC GROUP 381—Percent Distribution of Distance Shipped and Weight of Shipment, by Means of Transport: 1972

Distance shipped and weight of shipment[2][3]	Number	Percent distribution by means of transport							
		All means of transport	Rail	Motor carrier	Private truck	Air	Water	Other	Unknown
TONS OF SHIPMENTS	(thousands of tons)								
U.S. TOTAL..........	51	100.0	1.0	52.1	26.7	9.9	1.1	8.9	.3
UNDER 100 MILES.........	10	100.0	-	63.6	16.6	1.0	2.0	15.6	1.2
UNDER 1000 POUNDS.....	5	100.0	-	52.6	9.7	1.7	3.9	29.8	2.4
1000 TO 9999 POUNDS...	4	100.0	-	84.9	14.9	.2	-	-	-
10000 TO 29999 POUNDS.	-	100.0	-	28.3	71.7	-	-	-	-
30000 TO 59999 POUNDS.	-	100.0	-	-	-	-	-	-	-
60000 TO 89999 POUNDS.	-	100.0	-	-	-	-	-	-	-
90000 POUNDS AND OVER.	-	100.0	-	-	-	-	-	-	-
100 TO 199 MILES........	3	100.0	-	55.7	36.3	1.5	-	6.5	-
UNDER 1000 POUNDS.....	2	100.0	-	86.0	.7	2.5	-	10.8	-
1000 TO 9999 POUNDS...	-	100.0	-	36.8	63.2	-	-	-	-
10000 TO 29999 POUNDS.	1	100.0	-	-	100.0	-	-	-	-
30000 TO 59999 POUNDS.	-	100.0	-	-	-	-	-	-	-
60000 TO 89999 POUNDS.	-	100.0	-	-	-	-	-	-	-
90000 POUNDS AND OVER.	-	100.0	-	-	-	-	-	-	-
200 TO 299 MILES........	3	100.0	-	43.6	34.9	11.3	-	10.2	-
UNDER 1000 POUNDS.....	1	100.0	-	54.0	.2	24.1	-	21.7	-
1000 TO 9999 POUNDS...	-	100.0	-	100.0	-	-	-	-	-
10000 TO 29999 POUNDS.	1	100.0	-	8.7	91.3	-	-	-	-
30000 TO 59999 POUNDS.	-	100.0	-	-	-	-	-	-	-
60000 TO 89999 POUNDS.	-	100.0	-	-	-	-	-	-	-
90000 POUNDS AND OVER.	-	100.0	-	-	-	-	-	-	-
300 TO 499 MILES........	8	100.0	5.6	23.8	48.8	12.6	-	9.1	-
UNDER 1000 POUNDS.....	3	100.0	15.1	28.9	.2	31.2	-	24.6	-
1000 TO 9999 POUNDS...	1	100.0	-	92.8	-	7.2	-	-	-
10000 TO 29999 POUNDS.	4	100.0	-	-	100.0	-	-	-	-
30000 TO 59999 POUNDS.	-	100.0	-	-	-	-	-	-	-
60000 TO 89999 POUNDS.	-	100.0	-	-	-	-	-	-	-
90000 POUNDS AND OVER.	-	100.0	-	-	-	-	-	-	-
500 TO 999 MILES........	13	100.0	.1	44.9	35.5	12.0	1.2	6.3	-
UNDER 1000 POUNDS.....	4	100.0	.2	53.0	-	27.3	-	19.3	.1
1000 TO 9999 POUNDS...	4	100.0	-	64.8	26.7	8.5	-	-	-
10000 TO 29999 POUNDS.	4	100.0	-	14.8	81.6	-	3.6	-	-
30000 TO 59999 POUNDS.	-	100.0	-	-	-	-	-	-	-
60000 TO 89999 POUNDS.	-	100.0	-	-	-	-	-	-	-
90000 POUNDS AND OVER.	-	100.0	-	-	-	-	-	-	-
1000 TO 1499 MILES......	5	100.0	.1	75.1	-	13.9	3.8	7.1	-
UNDER 1000 POUNDS.....	1	100.0	.3	41.5	-	33.5	-	24.7	-
1000 TO 9999 POUNDS...	4	100.0	-	92.0	-	6.2	1.8	-	-
10000 TO 29999 POUNDS.	-	100.0	-	-	-	-	100.0	-	-
30000 TO 59999 POUNDS.	-	100.0	-	-	-	-	-	-	-
60000 TO 89999 POUNDS.	-	100.0	-	-	-	-	-	-	-
90000 POUNDS AND OVER.	-	100.0	-	-	-	-	-	-	-
1500 MILES OR OVER......	6	100.0	.6	68.0	8.6	17.7	-	5.1	-
UNDER 1000 POUNDS.....	4	100.0	.9	68.9	.2	22.6	-	7.3	-
1000 TO 9999 POUNDS...	1	100.0	-	89.5	2.3	8.3	-	-	-
10000 TO 29999 POUNDS.	-	100.0	-	-	100.0	-	-	-	-
30000 TO 59999 POUNDS.	-	100.0	-	-	-	-	-	-	-
60000 TO 89999 POUNDS.	-	100.0	-	-	-	-	-	-	-
90000 POUNDS AND OVER.	-	100.0	-	-	-	-	-	-	-
TON-MILES OF SHIPMENTS	(millions of ton-miles)								
U.S. TOTAL..........	36	100.0	.7	60.4	16.8	14.5	1.0	6.5	-
UNDER 100 MILES.........	-	100.0	-	66.5	17.3	.5	.9	14.2	.7
UNDER 1000 POUNDS.....	-	100.0	-	54.3	8.0	1.1	2.1	32.8	1.6
1000 TO 9999 POUNDS...	-	100.0	-	91.7	8.2	-	-	-	-
10000 TO 29999 POUNDS.	-	100.0	-	15.1	84.9	-	-	-	-
30000 TO 59999 POUNDS.	-	100.0	-	-	-	-	-	-	-
60000 TO 89999 POUNDS.	-	100.0	-	-	-	-	-	-	-
90000 POUNDS AND OVER.	-	100.0	-	-	-	-	-	-	-
100 TO 199 MILES........	-	100.0	-	58.5	34.1	1.4	-	6.1	-
UNDER 1000 POUNDS.....	-	100.0	-	87.5	.5	2.2	-	9.8	-
1000 TO 9999 POUNDS...	-	100.0	-	31.3	68.7	-	-	-	-
10000 TO 29999 POUNDS.	-	100.0	-	-	100.0	-	-	-	-
30000 TO 59999 POUNDS.	-	100.0	-	-	-	-	-	-	-
60000 TO 89999 POUNDS.	-	100.0	-	-	-	-	-	-	-
90000 POUNDS AND OVER.	-	100.0	-	-	-	-	-	-	-

See footnotes at end of table 4.

TABLE 4. **TCC GROUP 381—Percent Distribution of Distance Shipped and Weight of Shipment, by Means of Transport: 1972**—Continued

Distance shipped and weight of shipment[2] [3]	Number	Percent distribution by means of transport							
		All means of transport	Rail	Motor carrier	Private truck	Air	Water	Other	Unknown
TON-MILES OF SHIPMENTS	(millions of ton-miles)								
200 TO 299 MILES........	-	100.0	-	45.6	34.0	10.3	-	10.1	-
UNDER 1000 POUNDS.....	-	100.0	-	55.7	.2	22.3	-	21.8	-
1000 TO 9999 POUNDS...	-	100.0	-	100.0	-	-	-	-	-
10000 TO 29999 POUNDS.	-	100.0	-	9.0	91.0	-	-	-	-
30000 TO 59999 POUNDS.	-	100.0	-	-	-	-	-	-	-
60000 TO 89999 POUNDS.	-	100.0	-	-	-	-	-	-	-
90000 POUNDS AND OVER.	-	100.0	-	-	-	-	-	-	-
300 TO 499 MILES........	3	100.0	4.6	23.6	50.7	12.6	-	8.5	-
UNDER 1000 POUNDS.....	1	100.0	12.9	29.7	.2	33.0	-	24.1	-
1000 TO 9999 POUNDS...	-	100.0	-	93.2	-	6.8	-	-	-
10000 TO 29999 POUNDS.	1	100.0	-	-	100.0	-	-	-	-
30000 TO 59999 POUNDS.	-	100.0	-	-	-	-	-	-	-
60000 TO 89999 POUNDS.	-	100.0	-	-	-	-	-	-	-
90000 POUNDS AND OVER.	-	100.0	-	-	-	-	-	-	-
500 TO 999 MILES........	9	100.0	.1	47.2	31.3	13.2	1.5	6.7	-
UNDER 1000 POUNDS.....	3	100.0	.2	51.2	-	28.8	-	19.7	.1
1000 TO 9999 POUNDS...	3	100.0	-	68.4	22.4	9.2	-	-	-
10000 TO 29999 POUNDS.	2	100.0	-	15.9	78.9	-	5.3	-	-
30000 TO 59999 POUNDS.	-	100.0	-	-	-	-	-	-	-
60000 TO 89999 POUNDS.	-	100.0	-	-	-	-	-	-	-
90000 POUNDS AND OVER.	-	100.0	-	-	-	-	-	-	-
1000 TO 1499 MILES......	7	100.0	.1	77.6	-	12.4	3.0	7.0	-
UNDER 1000 POUNDS.....	2	100.0	.2	42.8	-	31.4	-	25.5	-
1000 TO 9999 POUNDS...	5	100.0	-	93.2	-	5.5	1.4	-	-
10000 TO 29999 POUNDS.	-	100.0	-	-	-	-	100.0	-	-
30000 TO 59999 POUNDS.	-	100.0	-	-	-	-	-	-	-
60000 TO 89999 POUNDS.	-	100.0	-	-	-	-	-	-	-
90000 POUNDS AND OVER.	-	100.0	-	-	-	-	-	-	-
1500 MILES OR OVER......	13	100.0	.6	69.6	6.1	18.5	-	5.1	-
UNDER 1000 POUNDS.....	10	100.0	.9	69.3	.2	22.7	-	6.9	-
1000 TO 9999 POUNDS...	2	100.0	-	88.9	2.8	8.4	-	-	-
10000 TO 29999 POUNDS.	-	100.0	-	-	100.0	-	-	-	-
30000 TO 59999 POUNDS.	-	100.0	-	-	-	-	-	-	-
60000 TO 89999 POUNDS.	-	100.0	-	-	-	-	-	-	-
90000 POUNDS AND OVER.	-	100.0	-	-	-	-	-	-	-

Note: Detail may not add to total due to rounding. The introductory table shows the estimates of sampling variability for tons; sampling variability for ton-miles has not been estimated. See the map in the Introduction for the States comprising the geographic divisions of the United States.

Shipments excluded from the survey are those moving by pipeline (primarily petroleum products from refineries), parcel post shipments, and commodities moved by own power (motorized vehicles, aircraft, etc.) or towed (prefabricated buildings, etc.). Local shipments (commodities shipped less than 25 miles from the plant) and shipments within the same city are also excluded. Shipments to Alaska and Hawaii from the 48 conterminous States and the District of Columbia are included; however, no data were obtained for shipments originating in Alaska and Hawaii.

- Represents zero or rounds to zero.   (D) Withheld to avoid disclosing figures for individual companies.

[1]Production of this commodity is concentrated in the geographic divisions shown; figures and distributions for geographic divisions not shown are included in the total.
[2]Distances of shipments to foreign destinations are calculated only to the U.S. port of exit.
[3]Includes only shipments represented by bills of lading and invoices. Summary records which did not show individual weights of shipments are not included.

TCC 382. Measuring and Controlling Instruments

Comparisons of Tons and Ton-Miles of Shipments for
Geographic Divisions of Origin and for Sampling Variability: 1972 and 1967

Geographic division of origin	Estimates				Relative sampling variability in tons (percent)	
	1972		1967		1972	1967
	Tons (thousands)	Ton-miles (millions)	Tons (thousands)	Ton-miles (millions)		
U.S. total	334	234	229	144	13.6	14.8
New England	31	37	57	23	58.7	(*)
Middle Atlantic	41	31	40	28	62.3	(*)
East North Central	85	27	96	57	37.5	(*)
West North Central	(D)	(D)	15	12	(*)	(*)
South Atlantic	4	3	5	3	55.1	(*)
East South Central	(D)	(D)	5	3	(*)	(*)
West South Central	(D)	(D)	—	—	(*)	(*)
Mountain	(D)	(D)	—	—	(*)	(*)
Pacific	(D)	(D)	11	18	(*)	(*)

Note: One general criterion for publication of data in this series provided for a maximum relative sampling variability of 50 percent of the total tons for any origin division. In other words, data would not be published if 1 standard error exceeded 50 percent of the estimate with which it was associated; see "Reliability of Data", page VIII. However, for this commodity group the absolute standard errors are generally low and division data are published even though some of the measured relative errors exceed 50 percent.

— Represents or rounds to zero.   (D) Withheld to avoid disclosing figures for individual companies.   *Data not published.

TABLE 1. **TCC GROUP 382**—Percent Distribution of Geographic Division of Origin and Distance Shipped, by Means of Transport: 1972

Geographic division of origin[1] and distance shipped[2]	Number	Percent distribution by means of transport							
		All means of transport	Rail	Motor carrier	Private truck	Air	Water	Other	Unknown
TONS OF SHIPMENTS	(thousands of tons)								
U.S. TOTAL...........	334	100.0	7.4	63.4	26.2	1.5	-	1.5	-
NEW ENGLAND..............	31	100.0	30.9	66.2	-	1.0	-	1.8	-
UNDER 100 MILES.......	1	100.0	-	91.8	-	.1	-	8.1	-
100 TO 199 MILES......	8	100.0	-	99.1	-	-	-	.9	-
200 TO 299 MILES......	-	100.0	-	89.9	2.4	3.3	-	4.3	-
300 TO 499 MILES......	1	100.0	-	96.0	-	1.7	-	2.4	-
500 TO 999 MILES......	6	100.0	-	94.8	-	1.1	-	4.1	-
1000 TO 1499 MILES....	1	100.0	-	91.4	-	7.1	-	1.5	-
1500 MILES OR OVER....	11	100.0	83.8	14.9	-	.7	-	.5	-
MIDDLE ATLANTIC..........	41	100.0	-	93.7	1.6	1.0	-	3.6	-
UNDER 100 MILES.......	6	100.0	-	96.5	.1	.6	-	2.7	-
100 TO 199 MILES......	3	100.0	-	88.5	-	-	-	11.5	-
200 TO 299 MILES......	2	100.0	-	94.3	-	1.3	-	4.4	-
300 TO 499 MILES......	6	100.0	-	86.5	10.9	.5	-	2.1	-
500 TO 999 MILES......	8	100.0	-	93.8	-	.9	-	5.4	-
1000 TO 1499 MILES....	8	100.0	-	96.1	-	1.8	-	2.0	-
1500 MILES OR OVER....	5	100.0	-	97.5	-	1.5	-	.9	-
EAST NORTH CENTRAL......	85	100.0	1.2	48.3	47.4	1.2	-	1.9	-
UNDER 100 MILES.......	8	100.0	-	68.7	28.3	-	-	3.0	-
100 TO 199 MILES......	35	100.0	2.9	9.7	87.0	-	-	.4	-
200 TO 299 MILES......	9	100.0	-	64.9	32.5	.9	-	1.6	.2
300 TO 499 MILES......	16	100.0	-	71.7	25.4	1.1	-	1.8	-
500 TO 999 MILES......	11	100.0	-	92.1	-	4.0	-	3.9	.1
1000 TO 1499 MILES....	1	100.0	-	92.4	-	3.8	-	3.9	-
1500 MILES OR OVER....	2	100.0	-	76.3	.1	12.6	-	11.0	-
SOUTH ATLANTIC..........	4	100.0	-	92.5	-	2.4	-	5.0	-
UNDER 100 MILES.......	-	100.0	-	61.0	4.2	1.5	-	33.2	-
100 TO 199 MILES......	-	100.0	-	78.1	-	-	-	21.9	-
200 TO 299 MILES......	-	100.0	-	74.1	.7	-	-	25.2	-
300 TO 499 MILES......	-	100.0	-	91.1	.1	4.1	-	4.7	-
500 TO 999 MILES......	2	100.0	-	93.5	-	1.6	-	4.9	-
1000 TO 1499 MILES....	-	100.0	-	82.1	-	14.0	-	3.9	-
1500 MILES OR OVER....	-	100.0	-	97.9	-	.9	-	1.1	-
TON-MILES OF SHIPMENTS	(millions of ton-miles)								
U.S. TOTAL...........	234	100.0	17.7	64.3	13.4	3.0	-	1.6	-
NEW ENGLAND..............	37	100.0	67.3	30.7	-	1.0	-	1.0	-
UNDER 100 MILES.......	-	100.0	-	94.3	-	.1	-	5.6	-
100 TO 199 MILES......	1	100.0	-	99.2	-	-	-	.8	-
200 TO 299 MILES......	-	100.0	-	89.9	2.0	3.7	-	4.4	-
300 TO 499 MILES......	-	100.0	-	95.9	-	1.7	-	2.5	-
500 TO 999 MILES......	4	100.0	-	95.0	-	1.1	-	4.0	-
1000 TO 1499 MILES....	1	100.0	-	92.3	-	6.2	-	1.4	-
1500 MILES OR OVER....	28	100.0	87.3	11.5	-	.7	-	.5	-
MIDDLE ATLANTIC..........	31	100.0	-	95.2	.9	1.4	-	2.5	-
UNDER 100 MILES.......	-	100.0	-	95.5	.2	.5	-	3.8	-
100 TO 199 MILES......	-	100.0	-	88.2	-	-	-	11.8	-
200 TO 299 MILES......	-	100.0	-	93.9	-	1.2	-	4.9	-
300 TO 499 MILES......	2	100.0	-	85.0	12.4	.6	-	2.0	-
500 TO 999 MILES......	5	100.0	-	93.6	-	.8	-	5.6	-
1000 TO 1499 MILES....	10	100.0	-	96.2	-	1.9	-	1.9	-
1500 MILES OR OVER....	12	100.0	-	97.5	-	1.6	-	.9	-
EAST NORTH CENTRAL......	27	100.0	.6	69.4	22.5	3.6	-	3.8	-
UNDER 100 MILES.......	-	100.0	-	70.9	26.2	-	-	2.8	-
100 TO 199 MILES......	4	100.0	3.8	10.7	85.0	-	-	.5	-
200 TO 299 MILES......	2	100.0	-	66.8	30.5	.9	-	1.6	.1
300 TO 499 MILES......	6	100.0	-	71.2	26.0	1.1	-	1.8	-
500 TO 999 MILES......	8	100.0	-	92.0	-	4.1	-	3.9	.1
1000 TO 1499 MILES....	1	100.0	-	91.7	-	4.2	-	4.1	-
1500 MILES OR OVER....	4	100.0	-	75.8	.1	12.3	-	11.8	-
SOUTH ATLANTIC..........	3	100.0	-	94.0	-	2.4	-	3.6	-
UNDER 100 MILES.......	-	100.0	-	52.4	4.2	1.7	-	41.7	-
100 TO 199 MILES......	-	100.0	-	78.7	-	-	-	21.3	-
200 TO 299 MILES......	-	100.0	-	74.4	.6	-	-	24.9	-
300 TO 499 MILES......	-	100.0	-	91.2	.1	3.9	-	4.9	-
500 TO 999 MILES......	1	100.0	-	93.9	-	1.3	-	4.8	-
1000 TO 1499 MILES....	-	100.0	-	82.4	-	14.2	-	3.4	-
1500 MILES OR OVER....	1	100.0	-	97.4	-	1.5	-	1.1	-

See footnotes at end of table 4.

TABLE 2. TCC GROUP 382—Percent Distribution of Geographic Division of Origin and Means of Transport, by Geographic Division of Destination: 1972

Geographic division of origin[1] and means of transport	Number	U.S. total	New England	Middle Atlantic	East North Central	West North Central	South Atlantic	East South Central	West South Central	Mountain	Pacific
TONS OF SHIPMENTS	(thousands of tons)										
U.S. TOTAL..............	334	100.0	2.3	16.8	46.1	4.6	6.4	5.2	4.7	1.8	12.0
RAIL..................	24	100.0	–	34.7	4.1	–	2.8	–	.2	3.0	55.2
MOTOR CARRIER.........	211	100.0	3.3	20.6	33.0	6.9	8.8	6.2	7.1	2.2	12.0
PRIVATE TRUCK.........	87	100.0	–	2.4	93.0	.1	.9	3.6	–	–	.1
AIR...................	5	100.0	3.8	24.8	16.3	6.3	15.9	7.7	6.7	6.2	12.3
WATER.................	–	100.0	–	–	–	–	–	–	–	–	–
OTHER.................	5	100.0	10.3	16.3	20.4	5.1	13.4	16.0	2.7	6.9	9.0
UNKNOWN...............	–	100.0	2.8	1.3	34.7	–	16.4	–	–	–	44.8
NEW ENGLAND...........	31	100.0	4.5	30.8	12.9	2.0	9.9	1.8	3.7	2.3	32.2
RAIL..................	9	100.0	–	–	–	–	–	–	.4	1.1	98.4
MOTOR CARRIER.........	20	100.0	6.1	45.9	18.5	2.3	14.5	2.4	5.2	2.9	2.1
PRIVATE TRUCK.........	–	100.0	–	100.0	–	–	–	–	–	–	–
AIR...................	–	100.0	–	9.6	16.4	35.2	6.3	3.6	8.8	1.9	18.3
WATER.................	–	100.0	–	–	–	–	–	–	–	–	–
OTHER.................	–	100.0	23.6	13.6	24.5	5.4	12.8	7.3	3.4	1.4	8.0
UNKNOWN...............	–	100.0	–	–	–	–	–	–	–	–	–
MIDDLE ATLANTIC.......	41	100.0	3.6	28.5	20.6	14.3	6.6	4.4	9.2	3.0	9.9
RAIL..................	–	100.0	–	–	–	–	–	–	–	–	–
MOTOR CARRIER.........	39	100.0	3.1	29.4	20.9	14.7	6.0	2.9	9.7	3.2	10.2
PRIVATE TRUCK.........	–	100.0	–	1.2	–	–	–	98.8	–	–	–
AIR...................	–	100.0	.6	20.7	15.2	22.8	9.7	.5	11.0	1.8	17.7
WATER.................	–	100.0	–	–	–	–	–	–	–	–	–
OTHER.................	1	100.0	19.5	19.6	22.2	8.0	24.0	2.1	1.9	–	2.7
UNKNOWN...............	–	100.0	–	–	100.0	–	–	–	–	–	–
EAST NORTH CENTRAL....	85	100.0	2.5	9.5	64.7	4.6	4.1	6.5	4.8	.8	2.4
RAIL..................	1	100.0	–	–	100.0	–	–	–	–	–	–
MOTOR CARRIER.........	41	100.0	4.9	13.2	43.8	9.1	7.2	7.0	9.6	1.3	4.0
PRIVATE TRUCK.........	40	100.0	–	5.0	87.7	.2	.9	6.1	–	–	–
AIR...................	1	100.0	3.2	25.8	11.5	5.4	4.5	11.1	9.5	11.1	17.9
WATER.................	–	100.0	–	–	–	–	–	–	–	–	–
OTHER.................	1	100.0	3.1	24.1	33.3	3.9	10.5	3.0	4.8	2.4	15.0
UNKNOWN...............	–	100.0	–	–	66.8	–	33.2	–	–	–	–
SOUTH ATLANTIC........	4	100.0	2.3	22.3	27.8	2.9	4.5	5.0	21.6	.6	12.9
RAIL..................	–	100.0	–	–	–	–	–	–	–	–	–
MOTOR CARRIER.........	4	100.0	1.3	23.0	28.2	2.2	3.3	5.4	22.4	.6	13.7
PRIVATE TRUCK.........	–	100.0	–	16.0	18.6	–	56.1	9.3	–	–	–
AIR...................	–	100.0	10.1	1.1	55.9	.6	.8	.2	26.2	1.5	3.5
WATER.................	–	100.0	–	–	–	–	–	–	–	–	–
OTHER.................	–	100.0	18.2	19.9	8.3	17.0	27.7	.5	5.5	–	2.9
UNKNOWN...............	–	100.0	–	–	–	–	–	–	–	–	–
TON-MILES OF SHIPMENTS	(millions of ton-miles)										
U.S. TOTAL..............	234	100.0	2.1	15.1	27.2	5.0	7.9	4.8	6.5	3.2	28.3
RAIL..................	41	100.0	–	20.8	.4	–	1.7	–	.2	2.5	74.5
MOTOR CARRIER.........	150	100.0	2.9	15.9	22.0	7.4	10.3	5.6	9.7	3.9	22.2
PRIVATE TRUCK.........	31	100.0	–	2.4	92.9	.1	1.1	3.6	–	–	–
AIR...................	7	100.0	5.6	24.1	10.7	4.8	22.2	7.0	5.7	4.4	15.6
WATER.................	–	100.0	–	–	–	–	–	–	–	–	–
OTHER.................	3	100.0	4.0	9.8	10.1	5.2	10.8	33.0	4.2	3.5	19.5
UNKNOWN...............	–	100.0	16.8	5.4	29.0	–	39.1	–	–	–	9.7
NEW ENGLAND...........	37	100.0	.2	4.2	7.9	1.9	5.9	1.3	4.8	3.6	70.1
RAIL..................	24	100.0	–	–	–	–	–	–	.3	1.0	98.8
MOTOR CARRIER.........	11	100.0	.7	13.5	24.5	4.8	18.9	4.0	14.5	9.4	9.7
PRIVATE TRUCK.........	–	100.0	–	100.0	–	–	–	–	–	–	–
AIR...................	–	100.0	–	2.4	9.7	30.6	2.6	2.5	10.8	2.9	38.4
WATER.................	–	100.0	–	–	–	–	–	–	–	–	–
OTHER.................	–	100.0	2.7	3.0	25.0	7.5	11.5	8.2	7.1	4.5	30.4
UNKNOWN...............	–	100.0	–	–	–	–	–	–	–	–	–
MIDDLE ATLANTIC.......	31	100.0	.9	4.5	14.8	18.1	4.7	2.8	16.0	6.6	31.6
RAIL..................	–	100.0	–	–	–	–	–	–	–	–	–
MOTOR CARRIER.........	30	100.0	.8	4.5	14.8	18.3	4.0	1.9	16.5	6.8	32.3
PRIVATE TRUCK.........	–	100.0	–	.1	–	–	–	99.9	–	–	–
AIR...................	–	100.0	.2	2.8	7.6	25.0	7.3	.4	13.4	2.8	40.4
WATER.................	–	100.0	–	–	–	–	–	–	–	–	–
OTHER.................	–	100.0	6.2	5.6	24.9	14.5	29.2	2.5	4.5	.1	12.5
UNKNOWN...............	–	100.0	–	–	100.0	–	–	–	–	–	–
EAST NORTH CENTRAL....	27	100.0	5.7	13.4	29.9	5.8	7.0	7.9	12.9	3.0	14.4
RAIL..................	–	100.0	–	–	100.0	–	–	–	–	–	–
MOTOR CARRIER.........	19	100.0	7.8	13.5	18.3	8.0	8.6	6.7	17.6	3.3	16.3
PRIVATE TRUCK.........	6	100.0	–	11.8	72.1	.6	2.3	13.2	–	–	.1
AIR...................	1	100.0	2.8	18.2	3.3	2.8	3.8	5.4	10.1	15.9	37.7
WATER.................	–	100.0	–	–	–	–	–	–	–	–	–
OTHER.................	1	100.0	3.6	19.4	6.9	2.3	9.4	1.3	7.7	3.5	45.7
UNKNOWN...............	–	100.0	–	–	40.3	–	59.7	–	–	–	–
SOUTH ATLANTIC........	3	100.0	2.1	17.7	16.4	2.6	1.5	3.3	22.1	.9	33.4
RAIL..................	–	100.0	–	–	–	–	–	–	–	–	–
MOTOR CARRIER.........	3	100.0	1.2	18.0	16.4	2.0	1.0	3.5	22.2	.9	34.7
PRIVATE TRUCK.........	–	100.0	–	25.5	49.9	–	21.3	3.4	–	–	–
AIR...................	–	100.0	6.1	.9	32.8	.5	.2	.1	38.2	2.9	18.3
WATER.................	–	100.0	–	–	–	–	–	–	–	–	–
OTHER.................	–	100.0	22.2	18.9	6.7	19.7	13.5	.2	8.8	–	9.9
UNKNOWN...............	–	100.0	–	–	–	–	–	–	–	–	–

See footnotes at end of table 4.

TABLE 3. **TCC GROUP 382**—Percent Distribution of Geographic Division of Destination and Means of Transport, by Geographic Division of Origin: 1972

Geographic division of destination and means of transport	Number	Percent distribution by division of origin[1]									
		U.S. total	New England	Middle Atlantic	East North Central	West North Central	South Atlantic	East South Central	West South Central	Mountain	Pacific
TONS OF SHIPMENTS	(thousands of tons)										
U.S. TOTAL...............	334	100.0	9.4	12.6	25.6	(D)	1.3	(D)	(D)	(D)	(D)
RAIL..................	24	100.0	39.5	-	4.1	(D)	-	(D)	(D)	(D)	(D)
MOTOR CARRIER.........	211	100.0	9.8	18.6	19.5	(D)	1.9	(D)	(D)	(D)	(D)
PRIVATE TRUCK.........	87	100.0	-	.8	46.3	(D)	-	(D)	(D)	(D)	(D)
AIR...................	5	100.0	6.0	8.5	21.0	(D)	2.1	(D)	(D)	(D)	(D)
WATER.................	-	100.0	-	-	-	(D)	-	(D)	(D)	(D)	(D)
OTHER.................	5	100.0	11.1	29.5	30.9	(D)	4.3	(D)	(D)	(D)	(D)
UNKNOWN...............	-	100.0	-	1.7	49.4	(D)	-	(D)	(D)	(D)	(D)
NEW ENGLAND.............	7	100.0	18.3	19.9	27.5	(D)	1.3	(D)	(D)	(D)	(D)
RAIL..................	-	100.0	-	-	-	(D)	-	(D)	(D)	(D)	(D)
MOTOR CARRIER.........	6	100.0	18.2	17.6	29.2	(D)	.7	(D)	(D)	(D)	(D)
PRIVATE TRUCK.........	-	100.0	-	-	-	(D)	-	(D)	(D)	(D)	(D)
AIR...................	-	100.0	-	1.3	17.7	(D)	5.7	(D)	(D)	(D)	(D)
WATER.................	-	100.0	-	-	-	(D)	-	(D)	(D)	(D)	(D)
OTHER.................	-	100.0	25.5	55.8	9.3	(D)	7.6	(D)	(D)	(D)	(D)
UNKNOWN...............	-	100.0	-	-	-	(D)	-	(D)	(D)	(D)	(D)
MIDDLE ATLANTIC.........	56	100.0	17.2	21.2	14.5	(D)	1.8	(D)	(D)	(D)	(D)
RAIL..................	8	100.0	-	-	-	(D)	-	(D)	(D)	(D)	(D)
MOTOR CARRIER.........	43	100.0	21.9	26.5	12.5	(D)	2.2	(D)	(D)	(D)	(D)
PRIVATE TRUCK.........	2	100.0	.7	.4	98.9	(D)	-	(D)	(D)	(D)	(D)
AIR...................	1	100.0	2.3	7.1	21.9	(D)	.1	(D)	(D)	(D)	(D)
WATER.................	-	100.0	-	-	-	(D)	-	(D)	(D)	(D)	(D)
OTHER.................	-	100.0	9.3	35.5	45.5	(D)	5.3	(D)	(D)	(D)	(D)
UNKNOWN...............	-	100.0	-	-	-	(D)	-	(D)	(D)	(D)	(D)
EAST NORTH CENTRAL......	154	100.0	2.6	5.6	35.9	(D)	.8	(D)	(D)	(D)	(D)
RAIL..................	1	100.0	-	-	100.0	(D)	-	(D)	(D)	(D)	(D)
MOTOR CARRIER.........	69	100.0	5.5	11.8	25.8	(D)	1.7	(D)	(D)	(D)	(D)
PRIVATE TRUCK.........	81	100.0	-	-	43.7	(D)	-	(D)	(D)	(D)	(D)
AIR...................	-	100.0	6.0	7.9	14.8	(D)	7.3	(D)	(D)	(D)	(D)
WATER.................	-	100.0	-	-	-	(D)	-	(D)	(D)	(D)	(D)
OTHER.................	1	100.0	13.4	32.2	50.5	(D)	1.8	(D)	(D)	(D)	(D)
UNKNOWN...............	-	100.0	-	4.9	95.1	(D)	-	(D)	(D)	(D)	(D)
WEST NORTH CENTRAL......	15	100.0	4.0	39.1	25.6	(D)	.8	(D)	(D)	(D)	(D)
RAIL..................	-	100.0	-	-	-	(D)	-	(D)	(D)	(D)	(D)
MOTOR CARRIER.........	14	100.0	3.3	39.4	25.4	(D)	.6	(D)	(D)	(D)	(D)
PRIVATE TRUCK.........	-	100.0	-	-	100.0	(D)	-	(D)	(D)	(D)	(D)
AIR...................	-	100.0	33.7	31.1	18.1	(D)	.2	(D)	(D)	(D)	(D)
WATER.................	-	100.0	-	-	-	(D)	-	(D)	(D)	(D)	(D)
OTHER.................	-	100.0	11.8	46.5	23.5	(D)	14.5	(D)	(D)	(D)	(D)
UNKNOWN...............	-	100.0	-	-	-	(D)	-	(D)	(D)	(D)	(D)
SOUTH ATLANTIC..........	21	100.0	14.4	12.8	16.5	(D)	.9	(D)	(D)	(D)	(D)
RAIL..................	-	100.0	-	-	-	(D)	-	(D)	(D)	(D)	(D)
MOTOR CARRIER.........	18	100.0	16.2	12.7	15.9	(D)	.7	(D)	(D)	(D)	(D)
PRIVATE TRUCK.........	-	100.0	-	-	47.4	(D)	.2	(D)	(D)	(D)	(D)
AIR...................	-	100.0	2.4	5.2	6.0	(D)	.1	(D)	(D)	(D)	(D)
WATER.................	-	100.0	-	-	-	(D)	-	(D)	(D)	(D)	(D)
OTHER.................	-	100.0	10.7	52.8	24.2	(D)	8.9	(D)	(D)	(D)	(D)
UNKNOWN...............	-	100.0	-	-	100.0	(D)	-	(D)	(D)	(D)	(D)
EAST SOUTH CENTRAL......	17	100.0	3.2	10.5	31.9	(D)	1.3	(D)	(D)	(D)	(D)
RAIL..................	-	100.0	-	-	-	(D)	-	(D)	(D)	(D)	(D)
MOTOR CARRIER.........	13	100.0	3.9	8.6	22.2	(D)	1.7	(D)	(D)	(D)	(D)
PRIVATE TRUCK.........	3	100.0	-	21.2	78.8	(D)	-	(D)	(D)	(D)	(D)
AIR...................	-	100.0	2.8	.5	30.3	(D)	.1	(D)	(D)	(D)	(D)
WATER.................	-	100.0	-	-	-	(D)	-	(D)	(D)	(D)	(D)
OTHER.................	-	100.0	5.1	3.9	5.8	(D)	.1	(D)	(D)	(D)	(D)
UNKNOWN...............	-	100.0	-	-	-	(D)	-	(D)	(D)	(D)	(D)
WEST SOUTH CENTRAL......	15	100.0	7.5	24.8	26.3	(D)	6.1	(D)	(D)	(D)	(D)
RAIL..................	-	100.0	99.0	-	-	(D)	-	(D)	(D)	(D)	(D)
MOTOR CARRIER.........	15	100.0	7.1	25.1	26.0	(D)	6.1	(D)	(D)	(D)	(D)
PRIVATE TRUCK.........	-	100.0	-	-	-	(D)	-	(D)	(D)	(D)	(D)
AIR...................	-	100.0	7.8	13.9	29.7	(D)	8.3	(D)	(D)	(D)	(D)
WATER.................	-	100.0	-	-	-	(D)	-	(D)	(D)	(D)	(D)
OTHER.................	-	100.0	13.6	20.3	54.5	(D)	8.6	(D)	(D)	(D)	(D)
UNKNOWN...............	-	100.0	-	-	-	(D)	-	(D)	(D)	(D)	(D)
MOUNTAIN................	6	100.0	12.1	21.0	11.2	(D)	.4	(D)	(D)	(D)	(D)
RAIL..................	-	100.0	15.2	-	-	(D)	-	(D)	(D)	(D)	(D)
MOTOR CARRIER.........	4	100.0	13.1	27.2	11.2	(D)	.5	(D)	(D)	(D)	(D)
PRIVATE TRUCK.........	-	100.0	-	-	-	(D)	-	(D)	(D)	(D)	(D)
AIR...................	-	100.0	1.8	2.5	37.4	(D)	.5	(D)	(D)	(D)	(D)
WATER.................	-	100.0	-	-	-	(D)	-	(D)	(D)	(D)	(D)
OTHER.................	-	100.0	2.3	.1	10.7	(D)	-	(D)	(D)	(D)	(D)
UNKNOWN...............	-	100.0	-	-	-	(D)	-	(D)	(D)	(D)	(D)
PACIFIC.................	40	100.0	25.2	10.3	5.2	(D)	1.4	(D)	(D)	(D)	(D)
RAIL..................	13	100.0	70.4	-	-	(D)	-	(D)	(D)	(D)	(D)
MOTOR CARRIER.........	25	100.0	1.7	15.9	6.5	(D)	2.2	(D)	(D)	(D)	(D)
PRIVATE TRUCK.........	-	100.0	-	-	2.7	(D)	-	(D)	(D)	(D)	(D)
AIR...................	-	100.0	8.9	12.2	30.5	(D)	.6	(D)	(D)	(D)	(D)
WATER.................	-	100.0	-	-	-	(D)	-	(D)	(D)	(D)	(D)
OTHER.................	-	100.0	9.9	8.8	51.7	(D)	1.4	(D)	(D)	(D)	(D)
UNKNOWN...............	-	100.0	-	-	-	(D)	-	(D)	(D)	(D)	(D)

See footnotes at end of table 4.

TABLE 3. **TCC GROUP 382—Percent Distribution of Geographic Division of Destination and Means of Transport, by Geographic Division of Origin: 1972**—Continued

Geographic division of destination and means of transport	Number	Percent distribution by division of origin[1]									
		U.S. total	New England	Middle Atlantic	East North Central	West North Central	South Atlantic	East South Central	West South Central	Mountain	Pacific
TON-MILES OF SHIPMENTS	(millions of ton-miles)										
U.S. TOTAL..............	234	100.0	15.9	13.5	11.8	(D)	1.6	(D)	(D)	(D)	(D)
RAIL..................	41	100.0	60.3	-	.4	(D)	-	(D)	(D)	(D)	(D)
MOTOR CARRIER.........	150	100.0	7.6	20.0	12.8	(D)	2.3	(D)	(D)	(D)	(D)
PRIVATE TRUCK.........	31	100.0	-	.9	19.9	(D)	-	(D)	(D)	(D)	(D)
AIR...................	7	100.0	5.3	6.5	14.3	(D)	1.3	(D)	(D)	(D)	(D)
WATER.................	-	100.0	-	-	-	(D)	-	(D)	(D)	(D)	(D)
OTHER.................	3	100.0	10.1	20.5	28.0	(D)	3.5	(D)	(D)	(D)	(D)
UNKNOWN...............	-	100.0	-	2.6	65.4	(D)	-	(D)	(D)	(D)	(D)
NEW ENGLAND.............	4	100.0	1.8	6.0	31.8	(D)	1.5	(D)	(D)	(D)	(D)
RAIL..................	-	100.0	-	-	-	(D)	-	(D)	(D)	(D)	(D)
MOTOR CARRIER.........	4	100.0	1.7	5.6	34.3	(D)	.9	(D)	(D)	(D)	(D)
PRIVATE TRUCK.........	-	100.0	-	-	-	(D)	-	(D)	(D)	(D)	(D)
AIR...................	-	100.0	-	.3	7.2	(D)	1.4	(D)	(D)	(D)	(D)
WATER.................	-	100.0	-	-	-	(D)	-	(D)	(D)	(D)	(D)
OTHER.................	-	100.0	7.0	32.0	25.4	(D)	19.6	(D)	(D)	(D)	(D)
UNKNOWN...............	-	100.0	-	-	-	(D)	-	(D)	(D)	(D)	(D)
MIDDLE ATLANTIC.........	35	100.0	4.4	4.0	10.5	(D)	1.9	(D)	(D)	(D)	(D)
RAIL..................	8	100.0	-	-	-	(D)	-	(D)	(D)	(D)	(D)
MOTOR CARRIER.........	23	100.0	6.4	5.7	10.9	(D)	2.6	(D)	(D)	(D)	(D)
PRIVATE TRUCK.........	-	100.0	.4	-	99.6	(D)	-	(D)	(D)	(D)	(D)
AIR...................	1	100.0	.5	.7	10.8	(D)	-	(D)	(D)	(D)	(D)
WATER.................	-	100.0	-	-	-	(D)	-	(D)	(D)	(D)	(D)
OTHER.................	-	100.0	3.2	11.8	55.7	(D)	6.8	(D)	(D)	(D)	(D)
UNKNOWN...............	-	100.0	-	-	-	(D)	-	(D)	(D)	(D)	(D)
EAST NORTH CENTRAL......	63	100.0	4.6	7.4	13.0	(D)	1.0	(D)	(D)	(D)	(D)
RAIL..................	-	100.0	-	-	100.0	(D)	-	(D)	(D)	(D)	(D)
MOTOR CARRIER.........	33	100.0	8.4	13.4	10.6	(D)	1.7	(D)	(D)	(D)	(D)
PRIVATE TRUCK.........	29	100.0	-	-	15.5	(D)	-	(D)	(D)	(D)	(D)
AIR...................	-	100.0	4.8	4.6	4.4	(D)	3.9	(D)	(D)	(D)	(D)
WATER.................	-	100.0	-	-	-	(D)	-	(D)	(D)	(D)	(D)
OTHER.................	-	100.0	25.1	50.5	19.3	(D)	2.3	(D)	(D)	(D)	(D)
UNKNOWN...............	-	100.0	-	9.1	90.9	(D)	-	(D)	(D)	(D)	(D)
WEST NORTH CENTRAL......	11	100.0	5.9	48.9	13.8	(D)	.8	(D)	(D)	(D)	(D)
RAIL..................	-	100.0	-	-	-	(D)	-	(D)	(D)	(D)	(D)
MOTOR CARRIER.........	11	100.0	4.9	49.3	13.7	(D)	.6	(D)	(D)	(D)	(D)
PRIVATE TRUCK.........	-	100.0	-	-	100.0	(D)	-	(D)	(D)	(D)	(D)
AIR...................	-	100.0	34.1	34.0	8.4	(D)	.1	(D)	(D)	(D)	(D)
WATER.................	-	100.0	-	-	-	(D)	-	(D)	(D)	(D)	(D)
OTHER.................	-	100.0	14.8	57.3	12.6	(D)	13.4	(D)	(D)	(D)	(D)
UNKNOWN...............	-	100.0	-	-	-	(D)	-	(D)	(D)	(D)	(D)
SOUTH ATLANTIC..........	18	100.0	12.0	8.0	10.5	(D)	.3	(D)	(D)	(D)	(D)
RAIL..................	-	100.0	-	-	-	(D)	-	(D)	(D)	(D)	(D)
MOTOR CARRIER.........	15	100.0	14.0	7.9	10.7	(D)	.2	(D)	(D)	(D)	(D)
PRIVATE TRUCK.........	-	100.0	-	-	43.2	(D)	-	(D)	(D)	(D)	(D)
AIR...................	1	100.0	.6	2.1	2.4	(D)	-	(D)	(D)	(D)	(D)
WATER.................	-	100.0	-	-	-	(D)	-	(D)	(D)	(D)	(D)
OTHER.................	-	100.0	10.7	55.2	24.4	(D)	4.4	(D)	(D)	(D)	(D)
UNKNOWN...............	-	100.0	-	-	100.0	(D)	-	(D)	(D)	(D)	(D)
EAST SOUTH CENTRAL......	11	100.0	4.4	8.0	19.5	(D)	1.1	(D)	(D)	(D)	(D)
RAIL..................	-	100.0	-	-	-	(D)	-	(D)	(D)	(D)	(D)
MOTOR CARRIER.........	8	100.0	5.4	6.9	15.5	(D)	1.5	(D)	(D)	(D)	(D)
PRIVATE TRUCK.........	1	100.0	-	26.5	73.5	(D)	-	(D)	(D)	(D)	(D)
AIR...................	-	100.0	1.9	.4	11.1	(D)	-	(D)	(D)	(D)	(D)
WATER.................	-	100.0	-	-	-	(D)	-	(D)	(D)	(D)	(D)
OTHER.................	1	100.0	2.5	1.6	1.1	(D)	-	(D)	(D)	(D)	(D)
UNKNOWN...............	-	100.0	-	-	-	(D)	-	(D)	(D)	(D)	(D)
WEST SOUTH CENTRAL......	15	100.0	11.7	33.3	23.4	(D)	5.4	(D)	(D)	(D)	(D)
RAIL..................	-	100.0	99.1	-	-	(D)	-	(D)	(D)	(D)	(D)
MOTOR CARRIER.........	14	100.0	11.3	34.0	23.1	(D)	5.3	(D)	(D)	(D)	(D)
PRIVATE TRUCK.........	-	100.0	-	-	-	(D)	-	(D)	(D)	(D)	(D)
AIR...................	-	100.0	10.1	15.2	25.4	(D)	8.6	(D)	(D)	(D)	(D)
WATER.................	-	100.0	-	-	-	(D)	-	(D)	(D)	(D)	(D)
OTHER.................	-	100.0	17.0	21.9	51.1	(D)	7.3	(D)	(D)	(D)	(D)
UNKNOWN...............	-	100.0	-	-	-	(D)	-	(D)	(D)	(D)	(D)
MOUNTAIN................	7	100.0	18.1	28.1	11.1	(D)	.5	(D)	(D)	(D)	(D)
RAIL..................	1	100.0	23.9	-	-	(D)	-	(D)	(D)	(D)	(D)
MOTOR CARRIER.........	5	100.0	18.0	34.8	10.6	(D)	.5	(D)	(D)	(D)	(D)
PRIVATE TRUCK.........	-	100.0	-	-	-	(D)	-	(D)	(D)	(D)	(D)
AIR...................	-	100.0	3.5	4.2	51.9	(D)	.8	(D)	(D)	(D)	(D)
WATER.................	-	100.0	-	-	-	(D)	-	(D)	(D)	(D)	(D)
OTHER.................	-	100.0	13.2	.4	28.3	(D)	-	(D)	(D)	(D)	(D)
UNKNOWN...............	-	100.0	-	-	-	(D)	-	(D)	(D)	(D)	(D)
PACIFIC.................	66	100.0	39.4	15.1	6.0	(D)	1.9	(D)	(D)	(D)	(D)
RAIL..................	30	100.0	80.0	-	-	(D)	-	(D)	(D)	(D)	(D)
MOTOR CARRIER.........	33	100.0	3.3	29.0	9.3	(D)	3.6	(D)	(D)	(D)	(D)
PRIVATE TRUCK.........	-	100.0	-	-	42.1	(D)	-	(D)	(D)	(D)	(D)
AIR...................	1	100.0	13.0	16.7	34.5	(D)	1.5	(D)	(D)	(D)	(D)
WATER.................	-	100.0	-	-	-	(D)	-	(D)	(D)	(D)	(D)
OTHER.................	-	100.0	15.8	13.2	65.7	(D)	1.8	(D)	(D)	(D)	(D)
UNKNOWN...............	-	100.0	-	-	-	(D)	-	(D)	(D)	(D)	(D)

See footnotes at end of table 4.

TABLE 4. TCC GROUP 382—Percent Distribution of Distance Shipped and Weight of Shipment, by Means of Transport: 1972

Distance shipped and weight of shipment[2][3]	Number	Percent distribution by means of transport							
		All means of transport	Rail	Motor carrier	Private truck	Air	Water	Other	Unknown
TONS OF SHIPMENTS	(thousands of tons)								
U.S. TOTAL..........	315	100.0	7.8	61.6	27.6	1.5	-	1.5	-
UNDER 100 MILES.........	21	100.0	-	77.8	19.1	.2	-	2.8	.1
UNDER 1000 POUNDS.....	8	100.0	-	91.3	1.1	.6	-	6.9	.2
1000 TO 9999 POUNDS...	8	100.0	-	100.0	-	-	-	-	-
10000 TO 29999 POUNDS.	4	100.0	-	11.2	88.8	-	-	-	-
30000 TO 59999 POUNDS.	-	100.0	-	-	-	-	-	-	-
60000 TO 89999 POUNDS.	-	100.0	-	-	-	-	-	-	-
90000 POUNDS AND OVER.	-	100.0	-	-	-	-	-	-	-
100 TO 199 MILES........	51	100.0	2.0	37.4	59.2	.1	-	1.3	-
UNDER 1000 POUNDS.....	6	100.0	-	84.5	4.5	.4	-	10.6	-
1000 TO 9999 POUNDS...	13	100.0	-	50.4	49.4	.2	-	-	-
10000 TO 29999 POUNDS.	21	100.0	4.7	-	95.3	-	-	-	-
30000 TO 59999 POUNDS.	7	100.0	-	100.0	-	-	-	-	-
60000 TO 89999 POUNDS.	3	100.0	-	-	100.0	-	-	-	-
90000 POUNDS AND OVER.	-	100.0	-	-	-	-	-	-	-
200 TO 299 MILES........	15	100.0	-	74.7	20.6	.8	-	3.8	.1
UNDER 1000 POUNDS.....	6	100.0	-	92.3	.2	2.2	-	5.1	.3
1000 TO 9999 POUNDS...	8	100.0	-	57.8	38.9	-	-	3.4	-
10000 TO 29999 POUNDS.	1	100.0	-	100.0	-	-	-	-	-
30000 TO 59999 POUNDS.	-	100.0	-	-	-	-	-	-	-
60000 TO 89999 POUNDS.	-	100.0	-	-	-	-	-	-	-
90000 POUNDS AND OVER.	-	100.0	-	-	-	-	-	-	-
300 TO 499 MILES........	54	100.0	-	89.3	8.9	.9	-	.8	-
UNDER 1000 POUNDS.....	14	100.0	-	93.4	-	3.4	-	3.2	-
1000 TO 9999 POUNDS...	29	100.0	-	97.2	2.8	-	-	-	-
10000 TO 29999 POUNDS.	7	100.0	-	72.4	27.6	-	-	-	-
30000 TO 59999 POUNDS.	3	100.0	-	45.9	54.1	-	-	-	-
60000 TO 89999 POUNDS.	-	100.0	-	-	-	-	-	-	-
90000 POUNDS AND OVER.	-	100.0	-	-	-	-	-	-	-
500 TO 999 MILES........	91	100.0	.2	49.6	48.0	.9	-	1.3	-
UNDER 1000 POUNDS.....	23	100.0	.6	90.7	-	3.5	-	5.2	-
1000 TO 9999 POUNDS...	25	100.0	-	81.1	18.9	-	-	-	-
10000 TO 29999 POUNDS.	35	100.0	-	9.9	90.1	-	-	-	-
30000 TO 59999 POUNDS.	7	100.0	-	3.4	96.6	-	-	-	-
60000 TO 89999 POUNDS.	-	100.0	-	-	-	-	-	-	-
90000 POUNDS AND OVER.	-	100.0	-	-	-	-	-	-	-
1000 TO 1499 MILES......	34	100.0	28.0	69.0	-	2.3	-	.7	-
UNDER 1000 POUNDS.....	11	100.0	1.4	92.4	-	3.9	-	2.3	-
1000 TO 9999 POUNDS...	8	100.0	12.7	83.2	-	4.1	-	-	-
10000 TO 29999 POUNDS.	-	100.0	-	-	-	-	-	-	-
30000 TO 59999 POUNDS.	15	100.0	56.2	43.8	-	-	-	-	-
60000 TO 89999 POUNDS.	-	100.0	-	-	-	-	-	-	-
90000 POUNDS AND OVER.	-	100.0	-	-	-	-	-	-	-
1500 MILES OR OVER......	45	100.0	29.9	62.6	-	5.2	-	2.3	-
UNDER 1000 POUNDS.....	12	100.0	2.0	80.2	-	15.0	-	2.8	-
1000 TO 9999 POUNDS...	12	100.0	9.5	86.4	-	3.7	-	.4	-
10000 TO 29999 POUNDS.	3	100.0	84.3	-	-	-	-	15.7	-
30000 TO 59999 POUNDS.	16	100.0	54.3	45.7	-	-	-	-	-
60000 TO 89999 POUNDS.	-	100.0	-	-	-	-	-	-	-
90000 POUNDS AND OVER.	-	100.0	-	-	-	-	-	-	-
TON-MILES OF SHIPMENTS	(millions of ton-miles)								
U.S. TOTAL..........	221	100.0	18.7	62.6	14.0	3.1	-	1.6	-
UNDER 100 MILES.........	-	100.0	-	75.8	20.2	.2	-	3.7	.2
UNDER 1000 POUNDS.....	-	100.0	-	89.6	1.4	.3	-	8.4	.4
1000 TO 9999 POUNDS...	-	100.0	-	100.0	-	-	-	-	-
10000 TO 29999 POUNDS.	-	100.0	-	13.0	87.0	-	-	-	-
30000 TO 59999 POUNDS.	-	100.0	-	-	-	-	-	-	-
60000 TO 89999 POUNDS.	-	100.0	-	-	-	-	-	-	-
90000 POUNDS AND OVER.	-	100.0	-	-	-	-	-	-	-
100 TO 199 MILES........	7	100.0	2.3	43.2	52.8	.1	-	1.6	-
UNDER 1000 POUNDS.....	-	100.0	-	84.7	3.8	.4	-	11.1	-
1000 TO 9999 POUNDS...	1	100.0	-	55.6	44.2	.2	-	-	-
10000 TO 29999 POUNDS.	2	100.0	6.6	-	93.4	-	-	-	-
30000 TO 59999 POUNDS.	1	100.0	-	100.0	-	-	-	-	-
60000 TO 89999 POUNDS.	-	100.0	-	-	100.0	-	-	-	-
90000 POUNDS AND OVER.	-	100.0	-	-	-	-	-	-	-

See footnotes at end of table 4.

TABLE 4. TCC GROUP 382—Percent Distribution of Distance Shipped and Weight of Shipment, by Means of Transport: 1972—Continued

Distance shipped and weight of shipment[2][3]	Number	Percent distribution by means of transport							
		All means of transport	Rail	Motor carrier	Private truck	Air	Water	Other	Unknown
TON-MILES OF SHIPMENTS	(millions of ton-miles)								
200 TO 299 MILES.........	3	100.0	-	76.0	19.3	.8	-	3.7	.1
UNDER 1000 POUNDS.....	1	100.0	-	92.4	.2	2.1	-	5.1	.2
1000 TO 9999 POUNDS...	1	100.0	-	59.4	37.3	-	-	3.3	-
10000 TO 29999 POUNDS.	-	100.0	-	100.0	-	-	-	-	-
30000 TO 59999 POUNDS.	-	100.0	-	-	-	-	-	-	-
60000 TO 89999 POUNDS.	-	100.0	-	-	-	-	-	-	-
90000 POUNDS AND OVER.	-	100.0	-	-	-	-	-	-	-
300 TO 499 MILES.........	20	100.0	-	88.8	9.4	.9	-	.8	-
UNDER 1000 POUNDS.....	5	100.0	-	93.1	-	3.6	-	3.2	-
1000 TO 9999 POUNDS...	10	100.0	-	97.0	3.0	-	-	-	-
10000 TO 29999 POUNDS.	2	100.0	-	69.6	30.4	-	-	-	-
30000 TO 59999 POUNDS.	1	100.0	-	45.0	55.0	-	-	-	-
60000 TO 89999 POUNDS.	-	100.0	-	-	-	-	-	-	-
90000 POUNDS AND OVER.	-	100.0	-	-	-	-	-	-	-
500 TO 999 MILES.........	59	100.0	.2	55.9	41.5	1.0	-	1.5	-
UNDER 1000 POUNDS.....	17	100.0	.7	90.9	-	3.5	-	4.9	-
1000 TO 9999 POUNDS...	16	100.0	-	82.7	17.3	-	-	-	-
10000 TO 29999 POUNDS.	21	100.0	-	15.1	84.9	-	-	-	-
30000 TO 59999 POUNDS.	4	100.0	-	5.1	94.9	-	-	-	-
60000 TO 89999 POUNDS.	-	100.0	-	-	-	-	-	-	-
90000 POUNDS AND OVER.	-	100.0	-	-	-	-	-	-	-
1000 TO 1499 MILES......	38	100.0	26.1	70.8	-	2.3	-	.8	-
UNDER 1000 POUNDS.....	13	100.0	1.5	92.4	-	3.9	-	2.2	-
1000 TO 9999 POUNDS...	9	100.0	12.8	83.3	-	3.8	-	-	-
10000 TO 29999 POUNDS.	-	100.0	-	-	-	-	-	-	-
30000 TO 59999 POUNDS.	15	100.0	55.8	44.2	-	-	-	-	-
60000 TO 89999 POUNDS.	-	100.0	-	-	-	-	-	-	-
90000 POUNDS AND OVER.	-	100.0	-	-	-	-	-	-	-
1500 MILES OR OVER......	91	100.0	33.9	58.5	-	5.5	-	2.2	-
UNDER 1000 POUNDS.....	25	100.0	2.1	79.1	-	15.6	-	3.1	-
1000 TO 9999 POUNDS...	25	100.0	9.6	86.0	-	4.0	-	.3	-
10000 TO 29999 POUNDS.	6	100.0	82.1	-	-	-	-	17.9	-
30000 TO 59999 POUNDS.	34	100.0	66.7	33.3	-	-	-	-	-
60000 TO 89999 POUNDS.	-	100.0	-	-	-	-	-	-	-
90000 POUNDS AND OVER.	-	100.0	-	-	-	-	-	-	-

Note: Detail may not add to total due to rounding. The introductory table shows the estimates of sampling variability for tons; sampling variability for ton-miles has not been estimated. See the map in the Introduction for the States comprising the geographic divisions of the United States.

Shipments excluded from the survey are those moving by pipeline (primarily petroleum products from refineries), parcel post shipments, and commodities moved by own power (motorized vehicles, aircraft, etc.) or towed (prefabricated buildings, etc.). Local shipments (commodities shipped less than 25 miles from the plant) and shipments within the same city are also excluded. Shipments to Alaska and Hawaii from the 48 conterminous States and the District of Columbia are included; however, no data were obtained for shipments originating in Alaska and Hawaii.

- Represents zero or rounds to zero.   (D) Withheld to avoid disclosing figures for individual companies.

[1]Production of this commodity is concentrated in the geographic divisions shown; figures and distributions for geographic divisions not shown are included in the total.

[2]Distances of shipments to foreign destinations are calculated only to the U.S. port of exit.

[3]Includes only shipments represented by bills of lading and invoices. Summary records which did not show individual weights of shipments are not included.

TCC 384. Surgical, Medical, Dental Instruments and Supplies

Comparisons of Tons and Ton-Miles of Shipments for
Geographic Divisions of Origin and for Sampling Variability: 1972 and 1967

Geographic division of origin	Estimates				Relative sampling variability in tons (percent)	
	1972		1967		1972	1967
	Tons (thousands)	Ton-miles (millions)	Tons (thousands)	Ton-miles (millions)		
U.S. total	309	254	233	121	18.5	(*)
New England	(D)	(D)	(*)	(*)	(*)	(*)
Middle Atlantic	58	40	(*)	(*)	18.1	(*)
East North Central	65	48	(*)	(*)	32.6	(*)
West North Central	50	44	(*)	(*)	66.2	(*)
South Atlantic	(D)	(D)	(*)	(*)	(*)	(*)
East South Central	(D)	(D)	(*)	(*)	(*)	(*)
West South Central	(D)	(D)	(*)	(*)	(*)	(*)
Mountain	(D)	(D)	(*)	(*)	(*)	(*)
Pacific	(D)	(D)	(*)	(*)	(*)	(*)

Note: One general criterion for publication of data in this series provided for a maximum relative sampling variability of 50 percent of the total tons for any origin division. In other words, data would not be published if 1 standard error exceeded 50 percent of the estimate with which it was associated; see "Reliability of Data", page VIII. However, for this commodity group the absolute standard errors are generally low and division data are published even though some of the measured relative errors exceed 50 percent.

(D) Withheld to avoid disclosing figures for individual companies.   *Data not published.

TABLE 1. **TCC GROUP 384—Percent Distribution of Geographic Division of Origin and Distance Shipped, by Means of Transport: 1972**

Geographic division of origin[1] and distance shipped[2]	Number	Percent distribution by means of transport							
		All means of transport	Rail	Motor carrier	Private truck	Air	Water	Other	Unknown
TONS OF SHIPMENTS	(thousands of tons)								
U.S. TOTAL..........	309	100.0	17.3	69.7	8.0	1.5	.3	2.6	.6
MIDDLE ATLANTIC.........	58	100.0	4.8	83.0	4.0	2.9	-	4.0	1.2
UNDER 100 MILES.......	10	100.0	-	91.9	.1	3.8	.1	3.4	.8
100 TO 199 MILES......	8	100.0	-	94.8	.3	2.7	-	2.2	-
200 TO 299 MILES......	6	100.0	-	95.5	.8	.3	-	3.4	-
300 TO 499 MILES......	7	100.0	-	88.5	6.1	1.2	-	4.1	-
500 TO 999 MILES......	11	100.0	20.3	61.8	8.9	2.7	-	6.4	-
1000 TO 1499 MILES....	6	100.0	-	79.6	11.6	4.1	-	4.6	-
1500 MILES OR OVER....	8	100.0	5.8	78.7	-	4.7	-	3.0	7.8
EAST NORTH CENTRAL......	65	100.0	28.9	63.0	2.4	.8	-	4.1	.9
UNDER 100 MILES.......	3	100.0	-	54.1	38.9	-	-	7.1	-
100 TO 199 MILES......	5	100.0	-	92.4	.5	.1	-	7.0	-
200 TO 299 MILES......	7	100.0	.5	91.3	1.2	.1	-	6.9	-
300 TO 499 MILES......	16	100.0	.1	95.1	.2	.2	-	4.0	.4
500 TO 999 MILES......	17	100.0	56.6	35.8	.3	1.5	-	3.1	2.7
1000 TO 1499 MILES....	1	100.0	2.2	86.4	-	1.4	-	8.7	1.3
1500 MILES OR OVER....	14	100.0	64.6	32.8	-	1.3	-	1.3	-
WEST NORTH CENTRAL......	50	100.0	32.9	62.9	-	-	-	4.2	-
UNDER 100 MILES.......	-	100.0	-	67.8	-	-	-	32.2	-
100 TO 199 MILES......	2	100.0	-	99.1	-	-	-	.9	-
200 TO 299 MILES......	2	100.0	-	96.1	-	-	-	3.9	-
300 TO 499 MILES......	5	100.0	20.8	74.8	.1	-	-	4.2	-
500 TO 999 MILES......	15	100.0	20.1	73.4	-	-	-	6.5	-
1000 TO 1499 MILES....	23	100.0	52.6	44.8	-	-	-	2.6	-
1500 MILES OR OVER....	-	100.0	-	89.9	-	.1	-	10.0	-
TON-MILES OF SHIPMENTS	(millions of ton-miles)								
U.S. TOTAL..........	254	100.0	24.6	68.4	1.8	2.4	.2	2.2	.5
MIDDLE ATLANTIC.........	40	100.0	6.9	78.0	4.6	3.8	-	4.2	2.5
UNDER 100 MILES.......	-	100.0	-	90.7	-	3.2	.1	5.7	.2
100 TO 199 MILES......	1	100.0	-	94.6	.3	3.0	-	2.1	-
200 TO 299 MILES......	1	100.0	-	95.5	.7	.3	-	3.5	-
300 TO 499 MILES......	2	100.0	-	88.4	5.7	1.4	-	4.5	-
500 TO 999 MILES......	8	100.0	18.7	64.1	8.1	2.7	-	6.4	-
1000 TO 1499 MILES....	7	100.0	-	78.6	12.9	4.0	-	4.5	-
1500 MILES OR OVER....	17	100.0	6.5	79.9	-	4.9	-	3.1	5.6
EAST NORTH CENTRAL......	48	100.0	47.4	47.6	.2	1.2	-	2.9	.6
UNDER 100 MILES.......	-	100.0	-	66.4	25.5	-	-	8.1	-
100 TO 199 MILES......	-	100.0	-	92.2	.5	.2	-	7.1	-
200 TO 299 MILES......	1	100.0	.4	91.1	1.2	.1	-	7.2	-
300 TO 499 MILES......	6	100.0	.1	95.1	.2	.2	-	3.9	.4
500 TO 999 MILES......	11	100.0	57.5	35.4	.3	1.5	-	3.4	2.0
1000 TO 1499 MILES....	2	100.0	2.1	86.6	-	1.5	-	8.7	1.1
1500 MILES OR OVER....	25	100.0	63.3	33.7	-	1.5	-	1.5	-
WEST NORTH CENTRAL......	44	100.0	40.6	55.7	-	-	-	3.7	-
UNDER 100 MILES.......	-	100.0	-	91.7	-	-	-	8.3	-
100 TO 199 MILES......	-	100.0	-	98.6	-	-	-	1.4	-
200 TO 299 MILES......	-	100.0	-	96.2	-	-	-	3.8	-
300 TO 499 MILES......	2	100.0	17.3	77.9	-	-	-	4.7	-
500 TO 999 MILES......	11	100.0	23.6	69.7	.1	-	-	6.7	-
1000 TO 1499 MILES....	29	100.0	51.5	46.2	-	-	-	2.3	-
1500 MILES OR OVER....	-	100.0	-	89.8	-	.1	-	10.1	-

See footnotes at end of table 4.

TABLE 2. **TCC GROUP 384—Percent Distribution of Geographic Division of Origin and Means of Transport, by Geographic Division of Destination: 1972**

Geographic division of origin[1] and means of transport	Number	Percent distribution by division of destination									
		U.S. total	New England	Middle Atlantic	East North Central	West North Central	South Atlantic	East South Central	West South Central	Mountain	Pacific
TONS OF SHIPMENTS	(thousands of tons)										
U.S. TOTAL..............	309	100.0	4.1	26.4	19.2	5.4	11.4	5.3	12.9	1.7	13.7
RAIL...................	53	100.0	4.6	33.1	19.1	1.9	4.9	1.1	2.9	-	32.4
MOTOR CARRIER..........	216	100.0	4.1	27.4	20.3	6.7	13.6	6.9	7.8	2.2	10.9
PRIVATE TRUCK..........	24	100.0	2.4	6.3	11.6	-	2.0	.4	76.8	-	.5
AIR....................	4	100.0	3.9	24.5	13.7	7.5	19.6	2.9	6.3	5.1	16.5
WATER..................	1	100.0	-	4.2	-	-	-	-	86.8	-	9.0
OTHER..................	8	100.0	3.3	18.7	23.4	11.1	15.4	10.1	7.9	2.9	7.3
UNKNOWN................	1	100.0	5.1	26.2	2.1	-	30.9	-	34.9	.2	.5

See footnotes at end of table 4.

TABLE 2. TCC GROUP 384—Percent Distribution of Geographic Division of Origin and Means of Transport, by Geographic Division of Destination: 1972—Continued

Geographic division of origin[1] and means of transport	Number	Percent distribution by division of destination									
		U.S. total	New England	Middle Atlantic	East North Central	West North Central	South Atlantic	East South Central	West South Central	Mountain	Pacific
TONS OF SHIPMENTS	(thousands of tons)										
MIDDLE ATLANTIC	58	100.0	9.1	28.8	11.5	5.1	22.3	3.3	7.3	1.3	11.4
RAIL	2	100.0	-	-	64.0	-	19.2	-	-	-	16.8
MOTOR CARRIER	48	100.0	10.3	32.5	6.7	5.3	23.4	3.5	5.2	1.2	11.8
PRIVATE TRUCK	2	100.0	2.0	1.2	48.4	-	16.1	-	32.2	-	11.8
AIR	1	100.0	7.0	23.6	10.8	8.9	14.6	3.8	8.0	8.5	14.8
WATER	-	100.0	-	100.0	-	-	-	-	-	-	-
OTHER	2	100.0	6.7	21.5	15.7	10.6	19.9	6.9	9.0	1.4	8.4
UNKNOWN	-	100.0	-	11.6	-	-	-	-	86.6	.5	1.3
EAST NORTH CENTRAL	65	100.0	1.3	22.1	24.5	5.6	6.3	15.0	2.6	1.2	21.4
RAIL	18	100.0	-	50.5	.2	-	.2	-	1.1	-	48.0
MOTOR CARRIER	41	100.0	2.0	11.1	32.6	8.2	7.5	22.9	2.9	1.8	11.1
PRIVATE TRUCK	1	100.0	-	1.8	95.0	-	1.5	-	1.7	-	-
AIR	-	100.0	-	2.3	7.7	5.8	37.4	2.5	3.9	4.2	36.3
WATER	-	100.0	-	-	-	-	-	-	-	-	-
OTHER	2	100.0	1.2	8.9	38.4	8.8	13.6	13.3	8.8	.1	6.9
UNKNOWN	-	100.0	-	10.6	1.4	-	83.9	-	4.0	-	-
WEST NORTH CENTRAL	50	100.0	3.3	32.0	28.3	9.0	6.4	3.9	3.8	.8	12.6
RAIL	16	100.0	7.6	30.8	25.6	-	-	-	5.7	.8	36.0
MOTOR CARRIER	31	100.0	1.0	33.1	30.5	13.3	9.2	5.3	-	-	1.2
PRIVATE TRUCK	-	100.0	-	-	-	1.6	-	-	98.4	-	-
AIR	-	100.0	-	31.5	4.2	-	50.2	-	-	-	14.0
WATER	-	100.0	-	-	-	-	-	-	-	-	-
OTHER	2	100.0	2.3	24.9	16.5	14.4	14.1	12.3	5.5	8.5	1.4
UNKNOWN	-	100.0	-	-	-	-	-	-	-	-	-
TON-MILES OF SHIPMENTS	(millions of ton-miles)										
U.S. TOTAL	254	100.0	2.9	22.6	16.1	4.9	12.7	3.7	10.6	2.0	24.6
RAIL	62	100.0	4.1	29.1	15.0	1.2	2.3	.4	1.9	-	46.0
MOTOR CARRIER	173	100.0	2.5	21.0	16.8	6.2	16.6	4.9	11.7	2.6	17.7
PRIVATE TRUCK	4	100.0	.8	6.1	21.8	.2	3.3	.5	66.7	-	.7
AIR	6	100.0	2.0	27.1	10.0	6.2	14.1	2.5	6.0	5.9	26.3
WATER	-	100.0	-	1.2	-	-	-	-	47.2	5.0	51.6
OTHER	5	100.0	2.4	14.1	12.1	10.0	15.6	8.9	12.1	-	19.8
UNKNOWN	1	100.0	.2	4.7	2.3	-	19.3	-	71.4	.4	1.6
MIDDLE ATLANTIC	40	100.0	3.2	5.3	10.2	7.1	16.1	3.4	13.3	3.2	38.2
RAIL	2	100.0	-	-	44.7	-	13.9	-	-	-	41.4
MOTOR CARRIER	31	100.0	3.9	6.5	5.8	7.9	17.8	3.7	9.6	3.1	41.7
PRIVATE TRUCK	1	100.0	.6	.2	40.0	-	6.7	-	52.5	-	-
AIR	1	100.0	1.4	1.2	6.2	9.9	9.2	3.3	10.5	16.9	41.4
WATER	-	100.0	-	100.0	-	-	-	-	-	-	-
OTHER	1	100.0	-	3.6	11.3	13.5	15.5	7.5	15.1	3.8	27.5
UNKNOWN	-	100.0	2.3	.1	-	-	-	-	97.1	.6	2.2
EAST NORTH CENTRAL	48	100.0	1.2	18.8	6.1	3.2	5.2	8.1	3.1	2.1	52.4
RAIL	22	100.0	-	28.9	-	-	.2	-	-	-	70.1
MOTOR CARRIER	23	100.0	2.4	10.2	11.5	5.9	8.1	16.4	4.5	4.2	36.8
PRIVATE TRUCK	-	100.0	-	9.9	56.4	-	12.9	-	20.8	-	-
AIR	-	100.0	-	1.1	2.0	3.5	21.7	.9	3.1	4.8	62.7
WATER	-	100.0	-	-	-	-	-	-	-	.5	26.9
OTHER	1	100.0	1.4	5.0	14.1	10.1	15.9	10.4	15.8	-	.1
UNKNOWN	-	100.0	-	8.0	.9	-	83.0	-	8.0	-	-
WEST NORTH CENTRAL	44	100.0	3.9	45.4	18.4	2.0	7.4	1.7	2.9	1.1	17.2
RAIL	18	100.0	7.4	36.6	17.0	-	-	-	4.8	1.2	39.1
MOTOR CARRIER	24	100.0	1.4	52.7	20.0	3.3	12.0	2.4	-	-	2.3
PRIVATE TRUCK	-	100.0	-	-	-	.7	-	-	99.3	-	-
AIR	-	100.0	-	35.8	1.4	-	42.1	-	-	-	20.7
WATER	-	100.0	-	-	-	-	-	-	-	-	-
OTHER	1	100.0	3.3	32.2	9.2	5.0	18.7	10.9	6.4	11.6	2.7
UNKNOWN	-	100.0	-	-	-	-	-	-	-	-	-

See footnotes at end of table 4.

TABLE 3. **TCC GROUP 384**—Percent Distribution of Geographic Division of Destination and Means of Transport, by Geographic Division of Origin: 1972

Geographic division of destination and means of transport	Number (thousands of tons)	Percent distribution by division of origin[1]									
		U.S. total	New England	Middle Atlantic	East North Central	West North Central	South Atlantic	East South Central	West South Central	Mountain	Pacific
TONS OF SHIPMENTS											
U.S. TOTAL	309	100.0	(D)	18.9	21.2	16.3	(D)	(D)	(D)	(D)	(D)
RAIL	53	100.0	(D)	5.3	35.5	31.0	(D)	(D)	(D)	(D)	(D)
MOTOR CARRIER	216	100.0	(D)	22.5	19.2	14.7	(D)	(D)	(D)	(D)	(D)
PRIVATE TRUCK	24	100.0	(D)	9.4	6.5	-	(D)	(D)	(D)	(D)	(D)
AIR	4	100.0	(D)	36.9	11.4	.1	(D)	(D)	(D)	(D)	(D)
WATER	1	100.0	(D)	1.2	-	-	(D)	(D)	(D)	(D)	(D)
OTHER	8	100.0	(D)	28.8	32.8	26.2	(D)	(D)	(D)	(D)	(D)
UNKNOWN	1	100.0	(D)	39.0	30.6	-	(D)	(D)	(D)	(D)	(D)
NEW ENGLAND	12	100.0	(D)	42.7	6.7	13.1	(D)	(D)	(D)	(D)	(D)
RAIL	2	100.0	(D)	-	-	50.9	(D)	(D)	(D)	(D)	(D)
MOTOR CARRIER	8	100.0	(D)	56.4	9.1	3.7	(D)	(D)	(D)	(D)	(D)
PRIVATE TRUCK	-	100.0	(D)	7.9	-	-	(D)	(D)	(D)	(D)	(D)
AIR	-	100.0	(D)	66.0	.1	-	(D)	(D)	(D)	(D)	(D)
WATER	-	100.0	(D)	-	-	-	(D)	(D)	(D)	(D)	(D)
OTHER	-	100.0	(D)	58.4	12.1	18.3	(D)	(D)	(D)	(D)	(D)
UNKNOWN	-	100.0	(D)	-	-	-	(D)	(D)	(D)	(D)	(D)
MIDDLE ATLANTIC	81	100.0	(D)	20.6	17.8	19.7	(D)	(D)	(D)	(D)	(D)
RAIL	17	100.0	(D)	-	54.3	28.8	(D)	(D)	(D)	(D)	(D)
MOTOR CARRIER	59	100.0	(D)	26.7	7.8	17.7	(D)	(D)	(D)	(D)	(D)
PRIVATE TRUCK	1	100.0	(D)	1.9	1.9	-	(D)	(D)	(D)	(D)	(D)
AIR	1	100.0	(D)	35.5	1.1	.1	(D)	(D)	(D)	(D)	(D)
WATER	-	100.0	(D)	28.1	-	-	(D)	(D)	(D)	(D)	(D)
OTHER	1	100.0	(D)	33.1	15.7	34.9	(D)	(D)	(D)	(D)	(D)
UNKNOWN	-	100.0	(D)	17.2	12.4	-	(D)	(D)	(D)	(D)	(D)
EAST NORTH CENTRAL	59	100.0	(D)	11.3	27.1	23.9	(D)	(D)	(D)	(D)	(D)
RAIL	10	100.0	(D)	17.8	.3	41.6	(D)	(D)	(D)	(D)	(D)
MOTOR CARRIER	43	100.0	(D)	7.4	30.7	22.0	(D)	(D)	(D)	(D)	(D)
PRIVATE TRUCK	2	100.0	(D)	39.4	52.9	-	(D)	(D)	(D)	(D)	(D)
AIR	-	100.0	(D)	29.1	6.4	-	(D)	(D)	(D)	(D)	(D)
WATER	-	100.0	(D)	-	-	-	(D)	(D)	(D)	(D)	(D)
OTHER	1	100.0	(D)	19.3	53.8	18.5	(D)	(D)	(D)	(D)	(D)
UNKNOWN	-	100.0	(D)	-	21.4	-	(D)	(D)	(D)	(D)	(D)
WEST NORTH CENTRAL	16	100.0	(D)	17.9	22.0	27.0	(D)	(D)	(D)	(D)	(D)
RAIL	1	100.0	(D)	-	-	-	(D)	(D)	(D)	(D)	(D)
MOTOR CARRIER	14	100.0	(D)	18.0	23.6	29.2	(D)	(D)	(D)	(D)	(D)
PRIVATE TRUCK	-	100.0	(D)	-	-	1.0	(D)	(D)	(D)	(D)	(D)
AIR	-	100.0	(D)	43.9	8.8	-	(D)	(D)	(D)	(D)	(D)
WATER	-	100.0	(D)	-	-	-	(D)	(D)	(D)	(D)	(D)
OTHER	-	100.0	(D)	27.5	26.0	34.0	(D)	(D)	(D)	(D)	(D)
UNKNOWN	-	100.0	(D)	-	-	-	(D)	(D)	(D)	(D)	(D)
SOUTH ATLANTIC	35	100.0	(D)	37.0	11.8	9.1	(D)	(D)	(D)	(D)	(D)
RAIL	2	100.0	(D)	21.0	1.2	-	(D)	(D)	(D)	(D)	(D)
MOTOR CARRIER	29	100.0	(D)	38.8	10.5	9.9	(D)	(D)	(D)	(D)	(D)
PRIVATE TRUCK	-	100.0	(D)	76.9	4.8	-	(D)	(D)	(D)	(D)	(D)
AIR	-	100.0	(D)	27.5	21.8	.2	(D)	(D)	(D)	(D)	(D)
WATER	-	100.0	(D)	-	-	-	(D)	(D)	(D)	(D)	(D)
OTHER	1	100.0	(D)	37.4	29.0	24.1	(D)	(D)	(D)	(D)	(D)
UNKNOWN	-	100.0	(D)	-	83.2	-	(D)	(D)	(D)	(D)	(D)
EAST SOUTH CENTRAL	16	100.0	(D)	11.7	59.5	11.7	(D)	(D)	(D)	(D)	(D)
RAIL	-	100.0	(D)	-	-	-	(D)	(D)	(D)	(D)	(D)
MOTOR CARRIER	14	100.0	(D)	11.5	63.6	11.3	(D)	(D)	(D)	(D)	(D)
PRIVATE TRUCK	-	100.0	(D)	-	-	-	(D)	(D)	(D)	(D)	(D)
AIR	-	100.0	(D)	48.2	9.6	-	(D)	(D)	(D)	(D)	(D)
WATER	-	100.0	(D)	-	-	-	(D)	(D)	(D)	(D)	(D)
OTHER	-	100.0	(D)	19.6	43.3	32.1	(D)	(D)	(D)	(D)	(D)
UNKNOWN	-	100.0	(D)	-	-	-	(D)	(D)	(D)	(D)	(D)
WEST SOUTH CENTRAL	39	100.0	(D)	10.7	4.3	4.8	(D)	(D)	(D)	(D)	(D)
RAIL	1	100.0	(D)	-	13.9	-	(D)	(D)	(D)	(D)	(D)
MOTOR CARRIER	16	100.0	(D)	15.1	7.1	10.7	(D)	(D)	(D)	(D)	(D)
PRIVATE TRUCK	19	100.0	(D)	4.0	.1	-	(D)	(D)	(D)	(D)	(D)
AIR	-	100.0	(D)	46.7	7.0	-	(D)	(D)	(D)	(D)	(D)
WATER	-	100.0	(D)	-	-	-	(D)	(D)	(D)	(D)	(D)
OTHER	-	100.0	(D)	32.7	36.3	18.2	(D)	(D)	(D)	(D)	(D)
UNKNOWN	-	100.0	(D)	96.5	3.5	-	(D)	(D)	(D)	(D)	(D)
MOUNTAIN	5	100.0	(D)	14.3	14.4	8.0	(D)	(D)	(D)	(D)	(D)
RAIL	-	100.0	(D)	-	-	-	(D)	(D)	(D)	(D)	(D)
MOTOR CARRIER	4	100.0	(D)	11.9	15.3	5.0	(D)	(D)	(D)	(D)	(D)
PRIVATE TRUCK	-	100.0	(D)	-	-	-	(D)	(D)	(D)	(D)	(D)
AIR	-	100.0	(D)	61.9	9.4	-	(D)	(D)	(D)	(D)	(D)
WATER	-	100.0	(D)	-	-	-	(D)	(D)	(D)	(D)	(D)
OTHER	-	100.0	(D)	14.0	1.7	77.6	(D)	(D)	(D)	(D)	(D)
UNKNOWN	-	100.0	(D)	100.0	-	-	(D)	(D)	(D)	(D)	(D)
PACIFIC	42	100.0	(D)	15.7	33.2	15.0	(D)	(D)	(D)	(D)	(D)
RAIL	17	100.0	(D)	2.7	52.6	34.3	(D)	(D)	(D)	(D)	(D)
MOTOR CARRIER	23	100.0	(D)	24.4	19.5	1.6	(D)	(D)	(D)	(D)	(D)
PRIVATE TRUCK	-	100.0	(D)	-	-	-	(D)	(D)	(D)	(D)	(D)
AIR	-	100.0	(D)	33.0	25.0	.1	(D)	(D)	(D)	(D)	(D)
WATER	-	100.0	(D)	-	-	-	(D)	(D)	(D)	(D)	(D)
OTHER	-	100.0	(D)	33.1	31.1	5.1	(D)	(D)	(D)	(D)	(D)
UNKNOWN	-	100.0	(D)	98.3	1.7	-	(D)	(D)	(D)	(D)	(D)

See footnotes at end of table 4.

TABLE 3. TCC GROUP 384—Percent Distribution of Geographic Division of Destination and Means of Transport, by Geographic Division of Origin: 1972—Continued

Geographic division of destination and means of transport	Number	Percent distribution by division of origin[1]									
		U.S. total	New England	Middle Atlantic	East North Central	West North Central	South Atlantic	East South Central	West South Central	Mountain	Pacific
TON-MILES OF SHIPMENTS	(millions of ton-miles)										
U.S. TOTAL...............	254	100.0	(D)	15.9	19.1	17.5	(D)	(D)	(D)	(D)	(D)
RAIL...................	62	100.0	(D)	4.5	36.7	29.0	(D)	(D)	(D)	(D)	(D)
MOTOR CARRIER..........	173	100.0	(D)	18.2	13.3	14.3	(D)	(D)	(D)	(D)	(D)
PRIVATE TRUCK..........	4	100.0	(D)	41.3	2.5	-	(D)	(D)	(D)	(D)	(D)
AIR....................	6	100.0	(D)	25.5	10.1	.1	(D)	(D)	(D)	(D)	(D)
WATER..................	-	100.0	(D)	.1	-	-	(D)	(D)	(D)	(D)	(D)
OTHER..................	5	100.0	(D)	31.0	25.9	30.0	(D)	(D)	(D)	(D)	(D)
UNKNOWN................	1	100.0	(D)	71.9	20.6	-	(D)	(D)	(D)	(D)	(D)
NEW ENGLAND..............	7	100.0	(D)	18.0	8.0	23.9	(D)	(D)	(D)	(D)	(D)
RAIL...................	2	100.0	(D)	-	-	52.6	(D)	(D)	(D)	(D)	(D)
MOTOR CARRIER..........	4	100.0	(D)	27.8	12.7	7.8	(D)	(D)	(D)	(D)	(D)
PRIVATE TRUCK..........	-	100.0	(D)	30.7	-	-	(D)	(D)	(D)	(D)	(D)
AIR....................	-	100.0	(D)	17.4	.1	-	(D)	(D)	(D)	(D)	(D)
WATER..................	-	100.0	(D)	-	-	-	(D)	(D)	(D)	(D)	(D)
OTHER..................	-	100.0	(D)	30.0	14.6	40.6	(D)	(D)	(D)	(D)	(D)
UNKNOWN................	-	100.0	(D)	-	-	-	(D)	(D)	(D)	(D)	(D)
MIDDLE ATLANTIC..........	57	100.0	(D)	3.7	15.9	35.2	(D)	(D)	(D)	(D)	(D)
RAIL...................	18	100.0	(D)	-	36.5	36.4	(D)	(D)	(D)	(D)	(D)
MOTOR CARRIER..........	36	100.0	(D)	5.6	6.4	35.9	(D)	(D)	(D)	(D)	(D)
PRIVATE TRUCK..........	-	100.0	(D)	1.6	4.1	-	(D)	(D)	(D)	(D)	(D)
AIR....................	1	100.0	(D)	1.1	.4	.1	(D)	(D)	(D)	(D)	(D)
WATER..................	-	100.0	(D)	6.1	-	-	(D)	(D)	(D)	(D)	(D)
OTHER..................	-	100.0	(D)	7.9	9.1	68.9	(D)	(D)	(D)	(D)	(D)
UNKNOWN................	-	100.0	(D)	1.4	35.3	-	(D)	(D)	(D)	(D)	(D)
EAST NORTH CENTRAL......	40	100.0	(D)	10.1	7.2	20.1	(D)	(D)	(D)	(D)	(D)
RAIL...................	9	100.0	(D)	13.4	.1	32.8	(D)	(D)	(D)	(D)	(D)
MOTOR CARRIER..........	29	100.0	(D)	6.3	9.1	17.0	(D)	(D)	(D)	(D)	(D)
PRIVATE TRUCK..........	-	100.0	(D)	75.7	6.5	-	(D)	(D)	(D)	(D)	(D)
AIR....................	-	100.0	(D)	15.9	2.0	-	(D)	(D)	(D)	(D)	(D)
WATER..................	-	100.0	(D)	-	-	-	(D)	(D)	(D)	(D)	(D)
OTHER..................	-	100.0	(D)	28.9	30.2	22.8	(D)	(D)	(D)	(D)	(D)
UNKNOWN................	-	100.0	(D)	-	8.6	-	(D)	(D)	(D)	(D)	(D)
WEST NORTH CENTRAL......	12	100.0	(D)	23.3	12.4	7.2	(D)	(D)	(D)	(D)	(D)
RAIL...................	-	100.0	(D)	-	-	-	(D)	(D)	(D)	(D)	(D)
MOTOR CARRIER..........	10	100.0	(D)	23.4	12.8	7.6	(D)	(D)	(D)	(D)	(D)
PRIVATE TRUCK..........	-	100.0	(D)	-	-	.1	(D)	(D)	(D)	(D)	(D)
AIR....................	-	100.0	(D)	40.6	5.7	-	(D)	(D)	(D)	(D)	(D)
WATER..................	-	100.0	(D)	-	-	-	(D)	(D)	(D)	(D)	(D)
OTHER..................	-	100.0	(D)	41.8	26.2	15.1	(D)	(D)	(D)	(D)	(D)
UNKNOWN................	-	100.0	(D)	-	-	-	(D)	(D)	(D)	(D)	(D)
SOUTH ATLANTIC..........	32	100.0	(D)	20.2	7.7	10.1	(D)	(D)	(D)	(D)	(D)
RAIL...................	1	100.0	(D)	27.3	2.4	-	(D)	(D)	(D)	(D)	(D)
MOTOR CARRIER..........	28	100.0	(D)	19.5	6.5	10.3	(D)	(D)	(D)	(D)	(D)
PRIVATE TRUCK..........	-	100.0	(D)	84.3	9.9	-	(D)	(D)	(D)	(D)	(D)
AIR....................	-	100.0	(D)	16.7	15.6	.2	(D)	(D)	(D)	(D)	(D)
WATER..................	-	100.0	(D)	-	-	-	(D)	(D)	(D)	(D)	(D)
OTHER..................	-	100.0	(D)	30.9	26.4	36.0	(D)	(D)	(D)	(D)	(D)
UNKNOWN................	-	100.0	(D)	-	88.8	-	(D)	(D)	(D)	(D)	(D)
EAST SOUTH CENTRAL......	9	100.0	(D)	14.4	41.6	8.2	(D)	(D)	(D)	(D)	(D)
RAIL...................	-	100.0	(D)	-	-	-	(D)	(D)	(D)	(D)	(D)
MOTOR CARRIER..........	8	100.0	(D)	13.9	44.3	7.0	(D)	(D)	(D)	(D)	(D)
PRIVATE TRUCK..........	-	100.0	(D)	-	-	-	(D)	(D)	(D)	(D)	(D)
AIR....................	-	100.0	(D)	33.8	3.6	-	(D)	(D)	(D)	(D)	(D)
WATER..................	-	100.0	(D)	-	-	-	(D)	(D)	(D)	(D)	(D)
OTHER..................	-	100.0	(D)	26.1	30.3	36.6	(D)	(D)	(D)	(D)	(D)
UNKNOWN................	-	100.0	(D)	-	-	-	(D)	(D)	(D)	(D)	(D)
WEST SOUTH CENTRAL......	26	100.0	(D)	20.1	5.6	4.8	(D)	(D)	(D)	(D)	(D)
RAIL...................	1	100.0	(D)	-	15.2	-	(D)	(D)	(D)	(D)	(D)
MOTOR CARRIER..........	20	100.0	(D)	14.8	5.1	5.8	(D)	(D)	(D)	(D)	(D)
PRIVATE TRUCK..........	3	100.0	(D)	32.6	.8	-	(D)	(D)	(D)	(D)	(D)
AIR....................	-	100.0	(D)	44.6	5.2	-	(D)	(D)	(D)	(D)	(D)
WATER..................	-	100.0	(D)	-	-	-	(D)	(D)	(D)	(D)	(D)
OTHER..................	-	100.0	(D)	38.8	33.9	15.8	(D)	(D)	(D)	(D)	(D)
UNKNOWN................	-	100.0	(D)	97.7	2.3	-	(D)	(D)	(D)	(D)	(D)
MOUNTAIN................	5	100.0	(D)	25.1	19.5	9.6	(D)	(D)	(D)	(D)	(D)
RAIL...................	-	100.0	(D)	-	-	-	(D)	(D)	(D)	(D)	(D)
MOTOR CARRIER..........	4	100.0	(D)	21.4	21.5	6.7	(D)	(D)	(D)	(D)	(D)
PRIVATE TRUCK..........	-	100.0	(D)	-	-	-	(D)	(D)	(D)	(D)	(D)
AIR....................	-	100.0	(D)	73.5	8.3	-	(D)	(D)	(D)	(D)	(D)
WATER..................	-	100.0	(D)	-	-	-	(D)	(D)	(D)	(D)	(D)
OTHER..................	-	100.0	(D)	23.4	2.5	69.6	(D)	(D)	(D)	(D)	(D)
UNKNOWN................	-	100.0	(D)	100.0	-	-	(D)	(D)	(D)	(D)	(D)
PACIFIC.................	62	100.0	(D)	24.8	40.7	12.3	(D)	(D)	(D)	(D)	(D)
RAIL...................	28	100.0	(D)	4.0	56.0	24.6	(D)	(D)	(D)	(D)	(D)
MOTOR CARRIER..........	30	100.0	(D)	42.9	27.7	1.8	(D)	(D)	(D)	(D)	(D)
PRIVATE TRUCK..........	-	100.0	(D)	-	-	-	(D)	(D)	(D)	(D)	(D)
AIR....................	1	100.0	(D)	40.2	24.1	.1	(D)	(D)	(D)	(D)	(D)
WATER..................	-	100.0	(D)	-	-	-	(D)	(D)	(D)	(D)	(D)
OTHER..................	1	100.0	(D)	43.0	35.2	4.1	(D)	(D)	(D)	(D)	(D)
UNKNOWN................	-	100.0	(D)	98.6	1.4	-	(D)	(D)	(D)	(D)	(D)

See footnotes at end of table 4.

TABLE 4. TCC GROUP 384—Percent Distribution of Distance Shipped and Weight of Shipment, by Means of Transport: 1972

Distance shipped and weight of shipment[2][3]	Number	Percent distribution by means of transport							
		All means of transport	Rail	Motor carrier	Private truck	Air	Water	Other	Unknown
TONS OF SHIPMENTS	(thousands of tons)								
U.S. TOTAL..........	197	100.0	18.5	72.1	2.5	2.2	.5	3.3	.9
UNDER 100 MILES.........	18	100.0	-	85.2	8.3	2.4	.1	3.2	.8
UNDER 1000 POUNDS.....	9	100.0	-	87.8	2.2	3.0	.1	6.0	.8
1000 TO 9999 POUNDS...	5	100.0	-	95.0	.7	2.9	-	-	1.5
10000 TO 29999 POUNDS.	2	100.0	-	100.0	-	-	-	-	-
30000 TO 59999 POUNDS.	1	100.0	-	-	100.0	-	-	-	-
60000 TO 89999 POUNDS.	-	100.0	-	-	-	-	-	-	-
90000 POUNDS AND OVER.	-	100.0	-	-	-	-	-	-	-
100 TO 199 MILES........	17	100.0	-	89.3	3.6	1.4	.2	3.1	2.4
UNDER 1000 POUNDS.....	8	100.0	-	89.6	.7	2.7	.4	6.5	.1
1000 TO 9999 POUNDS...	9	100.0	-	88.9	6.3	.3	-	-	4.6
10000 TO 29999 POUNDS.	-	100.0	-	-	-	-	-	-	-
30000 TO 59999 POUNDS.	-	100.0	-	-	-	-	-	-	-
60000 TO 89999 POUNDS.	-	100.0	-	-	-	-	-	-	-
90000 POUNDS AND OVER.	-	100.0	-	-	-	-	-	-	-
200 TO 299 MILES........	18	100.0	.2	89.5	.9	.1	4.8	4.5	-
UNDER 1000 POUNDS.....	9	100.0	.4	89.9	.6	.3	-	8.9	-
1000 TO 9999 POUNDS...	8	100.0	-	88.8	1.2	-	10.1	-	-
10000 TO 29999 POUNDS.	-	100.0	-	100.0	-	-	-	-	-
30000 TO 59999 POUNDS.	-	100.0	-	-	-	-	-	-	-
60000 TO 89999 POUNDS.	-	100.0	-	-	-	-	-	-	-
90000 POUNDS AND OVER.	-	100.0	-	-	-	-	-	-	-
300 TO 499 MILES........	38	100.0	10.0	84.9	1.4	.6	-	2.9	.2
UNDER 1000 POUNDS.....	12	100.0	.1	88.1	.5	2.0	-	9.3	.1
1000 TO 9999 POUNDS...	12	100.0	-	98.8	.8	-	-	-	.5
10000 TO 29999 POUNDS.	3	100.0	57.2	32.6	10.2	-	-	-	-
30000 TO 59999 POUNDS.	8	100.0	6.9	93.1	-	-	-	-	-
60000 TO 89999 POUNDS.	1	100.0	100.0	-	-	-	-	-	-
90000 POUNDS AND OVER.	-	100.0	-	-	-	-	-	-	-
500 TO 999 MILES........	50	100.0	36.6	54.0	2.5	2.0	-	4.0	1.0
UNDER 1000 POUNDS.....	14	100.0	1.5	78.9	.2	5.4	-	13.7	.2
1000 TO 9999 POUNDS...	9	100.0	2.4	88.4	2.1	2.0	-	-	5.1
10000 TO 29999 POUNDS.	18	100.0	59.3	39.8	.9	-	-	-	-
30000 TO 59999 POUNDS.	6	100.0	93.9	-	6.1	-	-	-	-
60000 TO 89999 POUNDS.	1	100.0	69.1	-	30.9	-	-	-	-
90000 POUNDS AND OVER.	-	100.0	-	-	-	-	-	-	-
1000 TO 1499 MILES......	16	100.0	13.8	72.7	4.5	3.1	-	5.8	.1
UNDER 1000 POUNDS.....	8	100.0	.2	81.6	.1	6.2	-	11.6	.3
1000 TO 9999 POUNDS...	5	100.0	-	100.0	-	-	-	-	-
10000 TO 29999 POUNDS.	-	100.0	-	100.0	-	-	-	-	-
30000 TO 59999 POUNDS.	1	100.0	57.7	-	42.3	-	-	-	-
60000 TO 89999 POUNDS.	1	100.0	100.0	-	-	-	-	-	-
90000 POUNDS AND OVER.	-	100.0	-	-	-	-	-	-	-
1500 MILES OR OVER......	36	100.0	32.1	60.0	-	4.9	-	1.3	1.7
UNDER 1000 POUNDS.....	8	100.0	1.9	76.3	-	16.0	-	5.4	.2
1000 TO 9999 POUNDS...	12	100.0	1.1	90.3	.1	3.5	-	-	5.1
10000 TO 29999 POUNDS.	7	100.0	36.1	63.9	-	-	-	-	-
30000 TO 59999 POUNDS.	2	100.0	100.0	-	-	-	-	-	-
60000 TO 89999 POUNDS.	-	100.0	100.0	-	-	-	-	-	-
90000 POUNDS AND OVER.	5	100.0	100.0	-	-	-	-	-	-
TON-MILES OF SHIPMENTS	(millions of ton-miles)								
U.S. TOTAL..........	150	100.0	26.1	64.8	1.5	3.7	.2	2.9	.9
UNDER 100 MILES.........	-	100.0	-	88.4	5.9	2.2	-	3.2	.3
UNDER 1000 POUNDS.....	-	100.0	-	91.1	.9	2.5	.1	5.3	.2
1000 TO 9999 POUNDS...	-	100.0	-	95.5	1.4	2.5	-	-	.5
10000 TO 29999 POUNDS.	-	100.0	-	100.0	-	-	-	-	-
30000 TO 59999 POUNDS.	-	100.0	-	-	100.0	-	-	-	-
60000 TO 89999 POUNDS.	-	100.0	-	-	-	-	-	-	-
90000 POUNDS AND OVER.	-	100.0	-	-	-	-	-	-	-
100 TO 199 MILES........	2	100.0	-	90.0	3.1	1.6	.2	3.0	2.0
UNDER 1000 POUNDS.....	1	100.0	-	89.5	.6	3.1	.4	6.3	.1
1000 TO 9999 POUNDS...	1	100.0	-	90.3	5.5	.3	-	-	3.9
10000 TO 29999 POUNDS.	-	100.0	-	-	-	-	-	-	-
30000 TO 59999 POUNDS.	-	100.0	-	-	-	-	-	-	-
60000 TO 89999 POUNDS.	-	100.0	-	-	-	-	-	-	-
90000 POUNDS AND OVER.	-	100.0	-	-	-	-	-	-	-

See footnotes at end of table 4.

TABLE 4. TCC GROUP 384—Percent Distribution of Distance Shipped and Weight of Shipment, by Means of Transport: 1972—Continued

Distance shipped and weight of shipment[2] [3]	Number	Percent distribution by means of transport							
		All means of transport	Rail	Motor carrier	Private truck	Air	Water	Other	Unknown
TON-MILES OF SHIPMENTS	(millions of ton-miles)								
200 TO 299 MILES........	4	100.0	.2	89.2	.8	.1	5.1	4.6	-
UNDER 1000 POUNDS.....	2	100.0	.4	89.9	.6	.3	-	9.0	-
1000 TO 9999 POUNDS...	2	100.0	-	88.2	1.0	-	10.8	-	-
10000 TO 29999 POUNDS.	-	100.0	-	100.0	-	-	-	-	-
30000 TO 59999 POUNDS.	-	100.0	-	-	-	-	-	-	-
60000 TO 89999 POUNDS.	-	100.0	-	-	-	-	-	-	-
90000 POUNDS AND OVER.	-	100.0	-	-	-	-	-	-	-
300 TO 499 MILES........	14	100.0	10.8	84.2	1.2	.6	-	3.0	.2
UNDER 1000 POUNDS.....	4	100.0	.1	87.8	.5	2.0	-	9.4	.1
1000 TO 9999 POUNDS...	4	100.0	-	98.8	.7	-	-	-	.5
10000 TO 29999 POUNDS.	1	100.0	64.0	27.7	8.3	-	-	-	-
30000 TO 59999 POUNDS.	3	100.0	8.1	91.9	-	-	-	-	-
60000 TO 89999 POUNDS.	-	100.0	100.0	-	-	-	-	-	-
90000 POUNDS AND OVER.	-	100.0	-	-	-	-	-	-	-
500 TO 999 MILES........	35	100.0	36.1	54.3	2.5	2.1	-	4.3	.8
UNDER 1000 POUNDS.....	10	100.0	1.7	78.0	.2	5.4	-	14.4	.3
1000 TO 9999 POUNDS...	6	100.0	2.2	89.5	2.4	2.3	-	-	3.5
10000 TO 29999 POUNDS.	12	100.0	60.2	38.9	.9	-	-	-	-
30000 TO 59999 POUNDS.	4	100.0	93.9	-	6.1	-	-	-	-
60000 TO 89999 POUNDS.	1	100.0	69.1	-	30.9	-	-	-	-
90000 POUNDS AND OVER.	-	100.0	-	-	-	-	-	-	-
1000 TO 1499 MILES......	19	100.0	14.5	71.8	5.0	3.2	-	5.4	.1
UNDER 1000 POUNDS.....	9	100.0	.2	82.2	.1	6.3	-	10.9	.2
1000 TO 9999 POUNDS...	5	100.0	-	100.0	-	-	-	-	-
10000 TO 29999 POUNDS.	-	100.0	-	100.0	-	-	-	-	-
30000 TO 59999 POUNDS.	2	100.0	60.7	-	39.3	-	-	-	-
60000 TO 89999 POUNDS.	1	100.0	100.0	-	-	-	-	-	-
90000 POUNDS AND OVER.	-	100.0	-	-	-	-	-	-	-
1500 MILES OR OVER......	72	100.0	30.3	61.4	-	5.6	-	1.3	1.4
UNDER 1000 POUNDS.....	18	100.0	1.9	75.7	.1	16.8	-	5.2	.2
1000 TO 9999 POUNDS...	24	100.0	1.1	90.9	-	4.1	-	-	3.9
10000 TO 29999 POUNDS.	13	100.0	38.6	61.4	-	-	-	-	-
30000 TO 59999 POUNDS.	4	100.0	100.0	-	-	-	-	-	-
60000 TO 89999 POUNDS.	1	100.0	100.0	-	-	-	-	-	-
90000 POUNDS AND OVER.	10	100.0	100.0	-	-	-	-	-	-

Note: Detail may not add to total due to rounding. The introductory table shows the estimates of sampling variability for tons; sampling variability for ton-miles has not been estimated. See the map in the Introduction for the States comprising the geographic divisions of the United States.

Shipments excluded from the survey are those moving by pipeline (primarily petroleum products from refineries), parcel post shipments, and commodities moved by own power (motorized vehicles, aircraft, etc.) or towed (prefabricated buildings, etc.). Local shipments (commodities shipped less than 25 miles from the plant) and shipments within the same city are also excluded. Shipments to Alaska and Hawaii from the 48 conterminous States and the District of Columbia are included; however, no data were obtained for shipments originating in Alaska and Hawaii.

- Represents zero or rounds to zero.   (D) Withheld to avoid disclosing figures for individual companies.

[1] Production of this commodity is concentrated in the geographic divisions shown; figures and distributions for geographic divisions not shown are included in the total.

[2] Distances of shipments to foreign destinations are calculated only to the U.S. port of exit.

[3] Includes only shipments represented by bills of lading and invoices. Summary records which did not show individual weights of shipments are not included.

TCC 387. Watches, Clocks, Clockwork Operated Devices, and Parts

Comparisons of Tons and Ton-Miles of Shipments for
Geographic Divisions of Origin and for Sampling Variability: 1972 and 1967

Geographic division of origin	Estimates				Relative sampling variability in tons (percent)	
	1972		1967		1972	1967
	Tons (thousands)	Ton-miles (millions)	Tons (thousands)	Ton-miles (millions)		
U.S. total	88	65	61	40	26.8	(*)
New England	14	17	(*)	(*)	55.9	(*)
Middle Atlantic	19	10	(*)	(*)	69.6	(*)
East North Central	25	16	(*)	(*)	64.5	(*)
West North Central	(D)	(D)	(*)	(*)	(*)	(*)
South Atlantic	(D)	(D)	(*)	(*)	(*)	(*)
East South Central	(D)	(D)	(*)	(*)	(*)	(*)
West South Central	(D)	(D)	(*)	(*)	(*)	(*)
Mountain	—	—	(*)	(*)	—	(*)
Pacific	(D)	(D)	(*)	(*)	(*)	(*)

Note: One general criterion for publication of data in this series provided for a maximum relative sampling variability of 50 percent of the total tons for any origin division. In other words, data would not be published if 1 standard error exceeded 50 percent of the estimate with which it was associated; see "Reliability of Data", page VIII. However, for this commodity group the absolute standard errors are generally low and division data are published even though some of the measured relative errors exceed 50 percent.

— Represents or rounds to zero.   (D) Withheld to avoid disclosing figures for individual companies.   *Data not published.

TABLE 1. TCC GROUP 387—Percent Distribution of Geographic Division of Origin and Distance Shipped, by Means of Transport: 1972

Geographic division of origin[1] and distance shipped[2]	Number	Percent distribution by means of transport							
		All means of transport	Rail	Motor carrier	Private truck	Air	Water	Other	Unknown
TONS OF SHIPMENTS	(thousands of tons)								
U.S. TOTAL..........	88	100.0	9.8	73.8	5.3	1.8	-	9.1	.2
NEW ENGLAND.............	14	100.0	21.8	74.7	.1	2.5	-	.8	-
UNDER 100 MILES.......	1	100.0	-	96.4	-	.9	-	2.5	.2
100 TO 199 MILES......	1	100.0	-	96.9	-	1.4	-	1.6	.2
200 TO 299 MILES......	-	100.0	-	91.4	4.9	-	-	3.7	-
300 TO 499 MILES......	-	100.0	-	98.0	-	.2	-	1.7	.1
500 TO 999 MILES......	4	100.0	11.2	86.6	-	2.0	-	.2	-
1000 TO 1499 MILES....	1	100.0	8.6	78.5	-	12.4	-	.5	-
1500 MILES OR OVER....	4	100.0	55.5	43.0	-	1.3	-	.2	-
MIDDLE ATLANTIC.........	19	100.0	-	67.5	16.7	5.1	-	10.7	-
UNDER 100 MILES.......	3	100.0	-	87.2	5.6	-	-	7.3	-
100 TO 199 MILES......	-	100.0	-	69.1	-	.5	-	30.4	-
200 TO 299 MILES......	4	100.0	-	81.3	15.3	-	-	3.5	-
300 TO 499 MILES......	1	100.0	-	45.2	37.5	.3	-	16.9	.1
500 TO 999 MILES......	6	100.0	-	49.3	25.6	13.8	-	11.3	-
1000 TO 1499 MILES....	-	100.0	-	51.9	-	11.1	-	37.0	-
1500 MILES OR OVER....	1	100.0	-	86.0	2.4	.9	-	10.8	-
EAST NORTH CENTRAL......	25	100.0	-	82.3	5.0	.2	-	12.5	-
UNDER 100 MILES.......	1	100.0	-	73.0	10.5	-	-	16.5	-
100 TO 199 MILES......	2	100.0	-	47.1	13.3	.8	-	38.8	-
200 TO 299 MILES......	2	100.0	-	90.1	.8	-	-	9.2	-
300 TO 499 MILES......	4	100.0	-	96.7	-	.3	-	3.0	-
500 TO 999 MILES......	10	100.0	-	82.3	6.5	.1	-	11.1	-
1000 TO 1499 MILES....	-	100.0	-	73.3	-	-	-	26.7	-
1500 MILES OR OVER....	2	100.0	-	96.8	-	-	-	3.2	-
MOUNTAIN................	-	100.0	-	-	-	-	-	-	-
UNDER 100 MILES.......	-	100.0	-	-	-	-	-	-	-
100 TO 199 MILES......	-	100.0	-	-	-	-	-	-	-
200 TO 299 MILES......	-	100.0	-	-	-	-	-	-	-
300 TO 499 MILES......	-	100.0	-	-	-	-	-	-	-
500 TO 999 MILES......	-	100.0	-	-	-	-	-	-	-
1000 TO 1499 MILES....	-	100.0	-	-	-	-	-	-	-
1500 MILES OR OVER....	-	100.0	-	-	-	-	-	-	-
TON-MILES OF SHIPMENTS	(millions of ton-miles)								
U.S. TOTAL..........	65	100.0	21.7	66.7	3.6	1.9	-	6.0	.1
NEW ENGLAND.............	17	100.0	40.7	56.2	-	2.8	-	.3	-
UNDER 100 MILES.......	-	100.0	-	97.3	-	.5	-	1.9	.2
100 TO 199 MILES......	-	100.0	-	97.1	-	1.3	-	1.4	.2
200 TO 299 MILES......	-	100.0	-	91.4	4.5	-	-	4.1	-
300 TO 499 MILES......	-	100.0	-	98.0	-	.2	-	1.8	.1
500 TO 999 MILES......	3	100.0	12.6	85.4	-	1.8	-	.2	-
1000 TO 1499 MILES....	1	100.0	7.9	77.5	-	14.2	-	.4	-
1500 MILES OR OVER....	11	100.0	56.9	41.7	-	1.2	-	.2	-
MIDDLE ATLANTIC.........	10	100.0	-	66.1	14.6	6.1	-	13.2	-
UNDER 100 MILES.......	-	100.0	-	88.0	4.7	-	-	7.3	-
100 TO 199 MILES......	-	100.0	-	66.4	-	.5	-	33.1	-
200 TO 299 MILES......	1	100.0	-	82.3	14.8	-	-	2.9	-
300 TO 499 MILES......	-	100.0	-	42.6	38.9	.3	-	18.2	.1
500 TO 999 MILES......	4	100.0	-	52.9	23.3	11.9	-	11.9	-
1000 TO 1499 MILES....	-	100.0	-	49.7	-	12.3	-	37.9	-
1500 MILES OR OVER....	3	100.0	-	86.4	1.8	.9	-	11.0	-
EAST NORTH CENTRAL......	16	100.0	-	87.5	4.1	.1	-	8.3	-
UNDER 100 MILES.......	-	100.0	-	75.7	13.5	-	-	10.8	-
100 TO 199 MILES......	-	100.0	-	44.7	11.6	.9	-	42.8	-
200 TO 299 MILES......	-	100.0	-	89.6	.7	-	-	9.8	-
300 TO 499 MILES......	1	100.0	-	96.8	-	.2	-	2.9	-
500 TO 999 MILES......	7	100.0	-	83.0	7.7	.1	-	9.2	-
1000 TO 1499 MILES....	-	100.0	-	73.3	-	-	-	26.7	-
1500 MILES OR OVER....	4	100.0	-	96.8	-	-	-	3.2	-
MOUNTAIN................	-	100.0	-	-	-	-	-	-	-
UNDER 100 MILES.......	-	100.0	-	-	-	-	-	-	-
100 TO 199 MILES......	-	100.0	-	-	-	-	-	-	-
200 TO 299 MILES......	-	100.0	-	-	-	-	-	-	-
300 TO 499 MILES......	-	100.0	-	-	-	-	-	-	-
500 TO 999 MILES......	-	100.0	-	-	-	-	-	-	-
1000 TO 1499 MILES....	-	100.0	-	-	-	-	-	-	-
1500 MILES OR OVER....	-	100.0	-	-	-	-	-	-	-

See footnotes at end of table 4.

TABLE 2. TCC GROUP 387—Percent Distribution of Geographic Division of Origin and Means of Transport, by Geographic Division of Destination: 1972

Geographic division of origin[1] and means of transport	Number	Percent distribution by division of destination									
		U.S. total	New England	Middle Atlantic	East North Central	West North Central	South Atlantic	East South Central	West South Central	Mountain	Pacific
TONS OF SHIPMENTS	(thousands of tons)										
U.S. TOTAL	88	100.0	5.1	25.5	26.0	4.6	12.3	5.2	6.5	4.1	10.8
RAIL	8	100.0	-	.7	9.6	5.5	2.7	-	18.1	30.9	32.5
MOTOR CARRIER	65	100.0	6.2	32.7	23.7	5.0	10.8	6.1	4.6	1.3	9.7
PRIVATE TRUCK	4	100.0	.1	5.7	69.6	.4	14.5	6.5	2.7	.6	-
AIR	1	100.0	.8	2.8	66.3	.8	6.1	1.1	16.4	2.0	3.7
WATER	-	100.0	-	-	-	-	-	-	-	-	-
OTHER	8	100.0	5.7	10.3	29.8	3.7	33.1	3.6	9.3	.2	4.3
UNKNOWN	-	100.0	5.6	4.6	2.2	-	87.6	-	-	-	-
NEW ENGLAND	14	100.0	5.3	19.2	21.5	5.0	8.2	4.0	6.9	2.2	27.6
RAIL	3	100.0	-	-	15.1	4.0	.2	-	6.3	.7	73.7
MOTOR CARRIER	11	100.0	6.6	25.0	23.7	5.4	10.6	5.4	5.7	2.5	15.2
PRIVATE TRUCK	-	100.0	-	100.0	-	-	-	-	-	-	-
AIR	-	100.0	3.2	5.9	16.7	2.7	6.2	-	48.8	8.4	8.0
WATER	-	100.0	-	-	-	-	-	-	-	-	-
OTHER	-	100.0	35.7	28.5	11.5	3.0	9.1	2.4	7.0	-	2.7
UNKNOWN	-	100.0	-	92.5	7.5	-	-	-	-	-	-
MIDDLE ATLANTIC	19	100.0	2.9	41.1	36.9	3.1	5.1	3.4	1.2	.7	5.6
RAIL	-	100.0	-	-	-	-	-	-	-	-	-
MOTOR CARRIER	13	100.0	2.8	56.6	22.0	3.3	4.6	2.0	.5	.8	7.3
PRIVATE TRUCK	3	100.0	-	6.6	82.7	.5	-	9.3	-	.9	-
AIR	-	100.0	-	.4	88.4	-	1.9	1.5	6.7	-	1.1
WATER	-	100.0	-	-	-	-	-	-	-	-	-
OTHER	2	100.0	9.3	16.8	34.4	7.5	17.3	3.8	4.7	.5	5.8
UNKNOWN	-	100.0	-	45.9	54.1	-	-	-	-	-	-
EAST NORTH CENTRAL	25	100.0	8.8	25.6	28.1	2.3	11.7	6.0	6.1	1.1	10.3
RAIL	-	100.0	-	-	-	-	-	-	-	-	-
MOTOR CARRIER	20	100.0	10.5	29.9	23.6	2.4	7.9	7.1	5.2	1.3	12.1
PRIVATE TRUCK	1	100.0	-	-	45.8	-	54.2	-	-	-	-
AIR	-	100.0	-	.3	74.1	.3	9.5	4.0	11.8	-	-
WATER	-	100.0	-	-	-	-	-	-	-	-	-
OTHER	3	100.0	1.0	8.2	50.0	2.3	20.4	.5	14.8	.1	2.7
UNKNOWN	-	100.0	-	-	-	-	-	-	-	-	-
MOUNTAIN	-	100.0	-	-	-	-	-	-	-	-	-
RAIL	-	100.0	-	-	-	-	-	-	-	-	-
MOTOR CARRIER	-	100.0	-	-	-	-	-	-	-	-	-
PRIVATE TRUCK	-	100.0	-	-	-	-	-	-	-	-	-
AIR	-	100.0	-	-	-	-	-	-	-	-	-
WATER	-	100.0	-	-	-	-	-	-	-	-	-
OTHER	-	100.0	-	-	-	-	-	-	-	-	-
UNKNOWN	-	100.0	-	-	-	-	-	-	-	-	-
TON-MILES OF SHIPMENTS	(millions of ton-miles)										
U.S. TOTAL	65	100.0	4.2	13.5	15.8	4.9	8.8	3.4	8.6	8.0	32.8
RAIL	14	100.0	-	.2	4.2	3.7	1.3	-	12.6	26.5	51.5
MOTOR CARRIER	43	100.0	5.9	19.4	16.0	5.5	9.1	4.4	6.3	3.0	30.4
PRIVATE TRUCK	2	100.0	.1	1.8	60.2	.5	25.5	6.9	2.5	2.2	.1
AIR	1	100.0	.1	1.2	46.8	1.1	4.7	.8	29.4	5.5	10.4
WATER	-	100.0	-	-	-	-	-	-	-	-	-
OTHER	3	100.0	4.6	7.1	19.5	6.4	23.0	3.0	16.8	.7	18.9
UNKNOWN	-	100.0	12.9	1.9	3.2	-	82.0	-	-	-	-
NEW ENGLAND	17	100.0	.3	2.6	12.7	4.7	4.7	3.0	8.6	3.7	59.8
RAIL	7	100.0	-	-	5.8	2.1	.1	-	4.4	.5	87.1
MOTOR CARRIER	9	100.0	.6	4.4	17.9	6.6	8.0	5.3	9.3	5.5	42.4
PRIVATE TRUCK	-	100.0	-	100.0	-	-	-	-	-	-	-
AIR	-	100.0	.1	.7	8.0	2.3	3.9	-	55.7	14.1	15.3
WATER	-	100.0	-	-	-	-	-	-	-	-	-
OTHER	-	100.0	6.1	13.3	16.4	7.2	9.2	5.0	27.1	-	15.8
UNKNOWN	-	100.0	-	74.5	25.5	-	-	-	-	-	-
MIDDLE ATLANTIC	10	100.0	1.0	12.9	39.3	6.2	5.3	4.4	3.1	2.3	25.5
RAIL	-	100.0	-	-	-	-	-	-	-	-	-
MOTOR CARRIER	7	100.0	1.0	19.0	27.2	6.7	5.0	3.4	1.5	2.4	33.9
PRIVATE TRUCK	1	100.0	-	.5	84.9	.8	-	10.3	-	3.3	.2
AIR	-	100.0	-	.1	77.4	-	3.2	1.4	13.7	-	4.2
WATER	-	100.0	-	-	-	-	-	-	-	-	-
OTHER	1	100.0	2.6	2.2	32.1	12.7	13.9	4.1	9.4	1.4	21.5
UNKNOWN	-	100.0	-	11.8	88.2	-	-	-	-	-	-
EAST NORTH CENTRAL	16	100.0	11.2	22.6	7.1	1.5	14.1	4.3	8.1	2.2	29.0
RAIL	-	100.0	-	-	-	-	-	-	-	-	-
MOTOR CARRIER	14	100.0	12.6	24.7	5.8	1.6	9.4	4.9	6.5	2.5	32.1
PRIVATE TRUCK	-	100.0	-	-	10.1	-	89.9	-	-	-	-
AIR	-	100.0	-	.5	44.5	.4	18.6	6.9	29.0	-	-
WATER	-	100.0	-	-	-	-	-	-	-	-	-
OTHER	1	100.0	1.8	11.3	18.4	1.6	26.4	.5	28.4	.5	11.1
UNKNOWN	-	100.0	-	-	-	-	-	-	-	-	-
MOUNTAIN	-	100.0	-	-	-	-	-	-	-	-	-
RAIL	-	100.0	-	-	-	-	-	-	-	-	-
MOTOR CARRIER	-	100.0	-	-	-	-	-	-	-	-	-
PRIVATE TRUCK	-	100.0	-	-	-	-	-	-	-	-	-
AIR	-	100.0	-	-	-	-	-	-	-	-	-
WATER	-	100.0	-	-	-	-	-	-	-	-	-
OTHER	-	100.0	-	-	-	-	-	-	-	-	-
UNKNOWN	-	100.0	-	-	-	-	-	-	-	-	-

See footnotes at end of table 4.

TABLE 3. **TCC GROUP 387—Percent Distribution of Geographic Division of Destination and Means of Transport, by Geographic Division of Origin: 1972**

Geographic division of destination and means of transport	Number	Percent distribution by division of origin[1]									
		U.S. total	New England	Middle Atlantic	East North Central	West North Central	South Atlantic	East South Central	West South Central	Mountain	Pacific
TONS OF SHIPMENTS	(thousands of tons)										
U.S. TOTAL..............	88	100.0	16.6	22.2	28.3	(D)	(D)	(D)	(D)	-	(D)
RAIL................	8	100.0	36.8	-	-	(D)	(D)	(D)	(D)	-	(D)
MOTOR CARRIER.........	65	100.0	16.8	20.3	31.6	(D)	(D)	(D)	(D)	-	(D)
PRIVATE TRUCK.........	4	100.0	.5	69.5	26.6	(D)	(D)	(D)	(D)	-	(D)
AIR..................	1	100.0	24.0	64.1	3.0	(D)	(D)	(D)	(D)	-	(D)
WATER................	-	100.0	-	-	-	(D)	(D)	(D)	(D)	-	(D)
OTHER................	8	100.0	1.5	26.2	38.9	(D)	(D)	(D)	(D)	-	(D)
UNKNOWN..............	-	100.0	3.4	1.6	-	(D)	(D)	(D)	(D)	-	(D)
NEW ENGLAND............	4	100.0	17.1	12.6	48.5	(D)	(D)	(D)	(D)	-	(D)
RAIL................	-	100.0	-	-	-	(D)	(D)	(D)	(D)	-	(D)
MOTOR CARRIER.........	4	100.0	17.8	9.3	53.5	(D)	(D)	(D)	(D)	-	(D)
PRIVATE TRUCK.........	-	100.0	-	-	-	(D)	(D)	(D)	(D)	-	(D)
AIR..................	-	100.0	99.2	-	-	(D)	(D)	(D)	(D)	-	(D)
WATER................	-	100.0	-	-	-	(D)	(D)	(D)	(D)	-	(D)
OTHER................	-	100.0	9.3	42.5	6.8	(D)	(D)	(D)	(D)	-	(D)
UNKNOWN..............	-	100.0	-	-	-	(D)	(D)	(D)	(D)	-	(D)
MIDDLE ATLANTIC........	22	100.0	12.5	35.8	28.5	(D)	(D)	(D)	(D)	-	(D)
RAIL................	-	100.0	-	-	-	(D)	(D)	(D)	(D)	-	(D)
MOTOR CARRIER.........	21	100.0	12.8	35.2	28.9	(D)	(D)	(D)	(D)	-	(D)
PRIVATE TRUCK.........	-	100.0	8.1	80.3	-	(D)	(D)	(D)	(D)	-	(D)
AIR..................	-	100.0	49.4	8.2	.3	(D)	(D)	(D)	(D)	-	(D)
WATER................	-	100.0	-	-	-	(D)	(D)	(D)	(D)	-	(D)
OTHER................	-	100.0	4.1	42.6	31.0	(D)	(D)	(D)	(D)	-	(D)
UNKNOWN..............	-	100.0	68.9	15.8	-	(D)	(D)	(D)	(D)	-	(D)
EAST NORTH CENTRAL......	23	100.0	13.7	31.4	30.6	(D)	(D)	(D)	(D)	-	(D)
RAIL................	-	100.0	58.0	-	-	(D)	(D)	(D)	(D)	-	(D)
MOTOR CARRIER.........	15	100.0	16.8	18.9	31.4	(D)	(D)	(D)	(D)	-	(D)
PRIVATE TRUCK.........	3	100.0	-	82.5	17.5	(D)	(D)	(D)	(D)	-	(D)
AIR..................	1	100.0	6.0	85.4	3.4	(D)	(D)	(D)	(D)	-	(D)
WATER................	-	100.0	-	-	-	(D)	(D)	(D)	(D)	-	(D)
OTHER................	2	100.0	.6	30.2	65.2	(D)	(D)	(D)	(D)	-	(D)
UNKNOWN..............	-	100.0	11.7	38.9	-	(D)	(D)	(D)	(D)	-	(D)
WEST NORTH CENTRAL......	4	100.0	18.3	15.2	14.1	(D)	(D)	(D)	(D)	-	(D)
RAIL................	-	100.0	27.0	-	-	(D)	(D)	(D)	(D)	-	(D)
MOTOR CARRIER.........	3	100.0	18.4	13.6	15.4	(D)	(D)	(D)	(D)	-	(D)
PRIVATE TRUCK.........	-	100.0	-	100.0	-	(D)	(D)	(D)	(D)	-	(D)
AIR..................	-	100.0	77.7	-	1.2	(D)	(D)	(D)	(D)	-	(D)
WATER................	-	100.0	-	-	-	(D)	(D)	(D)	(D)	-	(D)
OTHER................	-	100.0	1.2	53.4	24.6	(D)	(D)	(D)	(D)	-	(D)
UNKNOWN..............	-	100.0	-	-	-	(D)	(D)	(D)	(D)	-	(D)
SOUTH ATLANTIC.........	10	100.0	11.1	9.2	27.1	(D)	(D)	(D)	(D)	-	(D)
RAIL................	-	100.0	2.1	-	-	(D)	(D)	(D)	(D)	-	(D)
MOTOR CARRIER.........	7	100.0	16.6	8.7	23.0	(D)	(D)	(D)	(D)	-	(D)
PRIVATE TRUCK.........	-	100.0	-	-	99.2	(D)	(D)	(D)	(D)	-	(D)
AIR..................	-	100.0	24.3	20.2	4.7	(D)	(D)	(D)	(D)	-	(D)
WATER................	-	100.0	-	-	-	(D)	(D)	(D)	(D)	-	(D)
OTHER................	2	100.0	.4	13.6	23.9	(D)	(D)	(D)	(D)	-	(D)
UNKNOWN..............	-	100.0	-	-	-	(D)	(D)	(D)	(D)	-	(D)
EAST SOUTH CENTRAL......	4	100.0	12.9	14.6	32.6	(D)	(D)	(D)	(D)	-	(D)
RAIL................	-	100.0	-	-	-	(D)	(D)	(D)	(D)	-	(D)
MOTOR CARRIER.........	3	100.0	14.8	6.7	37.2	(D)	(D)	(D)	(D)	-	(D)
PRIVATE TRUCK.........	-	100.0	-	99.9	.1	(D)	(D)	(D)	(D)	-	(D)
AIR..................	-	100.0	-	88.8	11.2	(D)	(D)	(D)	(D)	-	(D)
WATER................	-	100.0	-	-	-	(D)	(D)	(D)	(D)	-	(D)
OTHER................	-	100.0	1.0	27.7	5.2	(D)	(D)	(D)	(D)	-	(D)
UNKNOWN..............	-	100.0	-	-	-	(D)	(D)	(D)	(D)	-	(D)
WEST SOUTH CENTRAL......	5	100.0	17.9	4.1	26.9	(D)	(D)	(D)	(D)	-	(D)
RAIL................	1	100.0	12.8	-	-	(D)	(D)	(D)	(D)	-	(D)
MOTOR CARRIER.........	3	100.0	20.9	2.4	35.4	(D)	(D)	(D)	(D)	-	(D)
PRIVATE TRUCK.........	-	100.0	-	-	-	(D)	(D)	(D)	(D)	-	(D)
AIR..................	-	100.0	71.6	26.3	2.2	(D)	(D)	(D)	(D)	-	(D)
WATER................	-	100.0	-	-	-	(D)	(D)	(D)	(D)	-	(D)
OTHER................	-	100.0	1.1	13.1	61.9	(D)	(D)	(D)	(D)	-	(D)
UNKNOWN..............	-	100.0	-	-	-	(D)	(D)	(D)	(D)	-	(D)
MOUNTAIN...............	3	100.0	9.0	3.9	7.5	(D)	(D)	(D)	(D)	-	(D)
RAIL................	2	100.0	.8	-	-	(D)	(D)	(D)	(D)	-	(D)
MOTOR CARRIER.........	-	100.0	31.6	11.9	31.1	(D)	(D)	(D)	(D)	-	(D)
PRIVATE TRUCK.........	-	100.0	-	100.0	-	(D)	(D)	(D)	(D)	-	(D)
AIR..................	-	100.0	100.0	-	-	(D)	(D)	(D)	(D)	-	(D)
WATER................	-	100.0	-	-	-	(D)	(D)	(D)	(D)	-	(D)
OTHER................	-	100.0	-	70.6	29.4	(D)	(D)	(D)	(D)	-	(D)
UNKNOWN..............	-	100.0	-	-	-	(D)	(D)	(D)	(D)	-	(D)
PACIFIC................	9	100.0	42.5	11.5	27.1	(D)	(D)	(D)	(D)	-	(D)
RAIL................	2	100.0	83.6	-	-	(D)	(D)	(D)	(D)	-	(D)
MOTOR CARRIER.........	6	100.0	26.3	15.2	39.6	(D)	(D)	(D)	(D)	-	(D)
PRIVATE TRUCK.........	-	100.0	-	100.0	-	(D)	(D)	(D)	(D)	-	(D)
AIR..................	-	100.0	52.8	19.9	-	(D)	(D)	(D)	(D)	-	(D)
WATER................	-	100.0	-	-	-	(D)	(D)	(D)	(D)	-	(D)
OTHER................	-	100.0	1.0	35.6	24.3	(D)	(D)	(D)	(D)	-	(D)
UNKNOWN..............	-	100.0	-	-	-	(D)	(D)	(D)	(D)	-	(D)

See footnotes at end of table 4.

TABLE 3. **TCC GROUP 387—Percent Distribution of Geographic Division of Destination and Means of Transport, by Geographic Division of Origin: 1972**—Continued

Geographic division of destination and means of transport	Number (millions of ton-miles)	Percent distribution by division of origin[1] U.S. total	New England	Middle Atlantic	East North Central	West North Central	South Atlantic	East South Central	West South Central	Mountain	Pacific
TON-MILES OF SHIPMENTS											
U.S. TOTAL...............	65	100.0	27.0	16.5	24.8	(D)	(D)	(D)	(D)	-	(D)
RAIL.................	14	100.0	50.6	-	-	(D)	(D)	(D)	(D)	-	(D)
MOTOR CARRIER........	43	100.0	22.7	16.3	32.5	(D)	(D)	(D)	(D)	-	(D)
PRIVATE TRUCK........	2	100.0	.2	67.5	28.3	(D)	(D)	(D)	(D)	-	(D)
AIR..................	1	100.0	39.0	52.9	1.4	(D)	(D)	(D)	(D)	-	(D)
WATER................	-	100.0	-	-	-	(D)	(D)	(D)	(D)	-	(D)
OTHER................	3	100.0	1.3	36.0	34.1	(D)	(D)	(D)	(D)	-	(D)
UNKNOWN..............	-	100.0	1.2	1.1	-	(D)	(D)	(D)	(D)	-	(D)
NEW ENGLAND..............	2	100.0	2.2	3.9	65.4	(D)	(D)	(D)	(D)	-	(D)
RAIL.................	-	100.0	-	-	-	(D)	(D)	(D)	(D)	-	(D)
MOTOR CARRIER........	2	100.0	2.2	2.8	69.4	(D)	(D)	(D)	(D)	-	(D)
PRIVATE TRUCK........	-	100.0	-	-	-	(D)	(D)	(D)	(D)	-	(D)
AIR..................	-	100.0	58.4	-	-	(D)	(D)	(D)	(D)	-	(D)
WATER................	-	100.0	-	-	-	(D)	(D)	(D)	(D)	-	(D)
OTHER................	-	100.0	1.7	20.1	13.6	(D)	(D)	(D)	(D)	-	(D)
UNKNOWN..............	-	100.0	-	-	-	(D)	(D)	(D)	(D)	-	(D)
MIDDLE ATLANTIC..........	8	100.0	5.1	15.8	41.5	(D)	(D)	(D)	(D)	-	(D)
RAIL.................	-	100.0	-	-	-	(D)	(D)	(D)	(D)	-	(D)
MOTOR CARRIER........	8	100.0	5.2	16.0	41.5	(D)	(D)	(D)	(D)	-	(D)
PRIVATE TRUCK........	-	100.0	11.6	20.2	-	(D)	(D)	(D)	(D)	-	(D)
AIR..................	-	100.0	21.1	3.1	.6	(D)	(D)	(D)	(D)	-	(D)
WATER................	-	100.0	-	-	-	(D)	(D)	(D)	(D)	-	(D)
OTHER................	-	100.0	2.5	11.2	54.0	(D)	(D)	(D)	(D)	-	(D)
UNKNOWN..............	-	100.0	48.0	6.8	-	(D)	(D)	(D)	(D)	-	(D)
EAST NORTH CENTRAL......	10	100.0	21.7	41.0	11.1	(D)	(D)	(D)	(D)	-	(D)
RAIL.................	-	100.0	69.9	-	-	(D)	(D)	(D)	(D)	-	(D)
MOTOR CARRIER........	6	100.0	25.4	27.7	11.8	(D)	(D)	(D)	(D)	-	(D)
PRIVATE TRUCK........	1	100.0	-	95.2	4.8	(D)	(D)	(D)	(D)	-	(D)
AIR..................	-	100.0	6.7	87.4	1.4	(D)	(D)	(D)	(D)	-	(D)
WATER................	-	100.0	-	-	-	(D)	(D)	(D)	(D)	-	(D)
OTHER................	-	100.0	1.1	59.3	32.2	(D)	(D)	(D)	(D)	-	(D)
UNKNOWN..............	-	100.0	9.9	30.8	-	(D)	(D)	(D)	(D)	-	(D)
WEST NORTH CENTRAL......	3	100.0	25.7	20.9	7.6	(D)	(D)	(D)	(D)	-	(D)
RAIL.................	-	100.0	28.8	-	-	(D)	(D)	(D)	(D)	-	(D)
MOTOR CARRIER........	2	100.0	27.4	19.8	9.3	(D)	(D)	(D)	(D)	-	(D)
PRIVATE TRUCK........	-	100.0	-	100.0	-	(D)	(D)	(D)	(D)	-	(D)
AIR..................	-	100.0	82.6	-	.6	(D)	(D)	(D)	(D)	-	(D)
WATER................	-	100.0	-	-	-	(D)	(D)	(D)	(D)	-	(D)
OTHER................	-	100.0	1.5	71.8	8.5	(D)	(D)	(D)	(D)	-	(D)
UNKNOWN..............	-	100.0	-	-	-	(D)	(D)	(D)	(D)	-	(D)
SOUTH ATLANTIC..........	5	100.0	14.3	10.0	39.5	(D)	(D)	(D)	(D)	-	(D)
RAIL.................	-	100.0	3.1	-	-	(D)	(D)	(D)	(D)	-	(D)
MOTOR CARRIER........	3	100.0	20.1	9.0	33.5	(D)	(D)	(D)	(D)	-	(D)
PRIVATE TRUCK........	-	100.0	-	-	99.5	(D)	(D)	(D)	(D)	-	(D)
AIR..................	-	100.0	32.6	36.6	5.7	(D)	(D)	(D)	(D)	-	(D)
WATER................	-	100.0	-	-	-	(D)	(D)	(D)	(D)	-	(D)
OTHER................	-	100.0	.5	21.7	39.1	(D)	(D)	(D)	(D)	-	(D)
UNKNOWN..............	-	100.0	-	-	-	(D)	(D)	(D)	(D)	-	(D)
EAST SOUTH CENTRAL......	2	100.0	23.9	21.1	31.4	(D)	(D)	(D)	(D)	-	(D)
RAIL.................	-	100.0	-	-	-	(D)	(D)	(D)	(D)	-	(D)
MOTOR CARRIER........	1	100.0	27.4	12.4	35.7	(D)	(D)	(D)	(D)	-	(D)
PRIVATE TRUCK........	-	100.0	-	100.0	-	(D)	(D)	(D)	(D)	-	(D)
AIR..................	-	100.0	-	88.1	11.9	(D)	(D)	(D)	(D)	-	(D)
WATER................	-	100.0	-	-	-	(D)	(D)	(D)	(D)	-	(D)
OTHER................	-	100.0	2.2	49.4	6.0	(D)	(D)	(D)	(D)	-	(D)
UNKNOWN..............	-	100.0	-	-	-	(D)	(D)	(D)	(D)	-	(D)
WEST SOUTH CENTRAL......	5	100.0	27.0	5.9	23.3	(D)	(D)	(D)	(D)	-	(D)
RAIL.................	1	100.0	17.6	-	-	(D)	(D)	(D)	(D)	-	(D)
MOTOR CARRIER........	2	100.0	33.5	3.8	33.7	(D)	(D)	(D)	(D)	-	(D)
PRIVATE TRUCK........	-	100.0	-	-	-	(D)	(D)	(D)	(D)	-	(D)
AIR..................	-	100.0	73.9	24.7	1.4	(D)	(D)	(D)	(D)	-	(D)
WATER................	-	100.0	-	-	-	(D)	(D)	(D)	(D)	-	(D)
OTHER................	-	100.0	2.1	20.2	57.7	(D)	(D)	(D)	(D)	-	(D)
UNKNOWN..............	-	100.0	-	-	-	(D)	(D)	(D)	(D)	-	(D)
MOUNTAIN................	5	100.0	12.4	4.7	6.8	(D)	(D)	(D)	(D)	-	(D)
RAIL.................	3	100.0	1.0	-	-	(D)	(D)	(D)	(D)	-	(D)
MOTOR CARRIER........	1	100.0	40.9	13.0	26.5	(D)	(D)	(D)	(D)	-	(D)
PRIVATE TRUCK........	-	100.0	-	100.0	-	(D)	(D)	(D)	(D)	-	(D)
AIR..................	-	100.0	100.0	-	-	(D)	(D)	(D)	(D)	-	(D)
WATER................	-	100.0	-	-	-	(D)	(D)	(D)	(D)	-	(D)
OTHER................	-	100.0	-	76.0	24.0	(D)	(D)	(D)	(D)	-	(D)
UNKNOWN..............	-	100.0	-	-	-	(D)	(D)	(D)	(D)	-	(D)
PACIFIC.................	21	100.0	49.1	12.8	21.9	(D)	(D)	(D)	(D)	-	(D)
RAIL.................	7	100.0	85.5	-	-	(D)	(D)	(D)	(D)	-	(D)
MOTOR CARRIER........	13	100.0	31.7	18.2	34.3	(D)	(D)	(D)	(D)	-	(D)
PRIVATE TRUCK........	-	100.0	-	100.0	-	(D)	(D)	(D)	(D)	-	(D)
AIR..................	-	100.0	57.1	21.3	-	(D)	(D)	(D)	(D)	-	(D)
WATER................	-	100.0	-	-	-	(D)	(D)	(D)	(D)	-	(D)
OTHER................	-	100.0	1.1	40.9	20.0	(D)	(D)	(D)	(D)	-	(D)
UNKNOWN..............	-	100.0	-	-	-	(D)	(D)	(D)	(D)	-	(D)

See footnotes at end of table 4.

TABLE 4. TCC GROUP 387—Percent Distribution of Distance Shipped and Weight of Shipment, by Means of Transport: 1972

Distance shipped and weight of shipment[2][3]	Number	Percent distribution by means of transport							
		All means of transport	Rail	Motor carrier	Private truck	Air	Water	Other	Unknown
TONS OF SHIPMENTS	(thousands of tons)								
U.S. TOTAL	61	100.0	5.9	75.8	7.5	2.4	-	8.4	-
UNDER 100 MILES	4	100.0	-	76.8	9.7	.4	-	12.9	.1
UNDER 1000 POUNDS	2	100.0	-	73.8	7.4	.5	-	18.0	.2
1000 TO 9999 POUNDS	-	100.0	-	81.0	19.0	-	-	-	-
10000 TO 29999 POUNDS	-	100.0	-	100.0	-	-	-	-	-
30000 TO 59999 POUNDS	-	100.0	-	-	-	-	-	-	-
60000 TO 89999 POUNDS	-	100.0	-	-	-	-	-	-	-
90000 POUNDS AND OVER	-	100.0	-	-	-	-	-	-	-
100 TO 199 MILES	4	100.0	-	61.9	8.2	.9	-	29.0	-
UNDER 1000 POUNDS	3	100.0	-	50.7	10.6	1.2	-	37.5	.1
1000 TO 9999 POUNDS	1	100.0	-	100.0	-	-	-	-	-
10000 TO 29999 POUNDS	-	100.0	-	-	-	-	-	-	-
30000 TO 59999 POUNDS	-	100.0	-	-	-	-	-	-	-
60000 TO 89999 POUNDS	-	100.0	-	-	-	-	-	-	-
90000 POUNDS AND OVER	-	100.0	-	-	-	-	-	-	-
200 TO 299 MILES	5	100.0	-	77.1	15.2	.6	-	7.2	-
UNDER 1000 POUNDS	3	100.0	-	85.6	1.4	.9	-	12.0	-
1000 TO 9999 POUNDS	1	100.0	-	71.9	28.1	-	-	-	-
10000 TO 29999 POUNDS	-	100.0	-	-	100.0	-	-	-	-
30000 TO 59999 POUNDS	-	100.0	-	-	-	-	-	-	-
60000 TO 89999 POUNDS	-	100.0	-	-	-	-	-	-	-
90000 POUNDS AND OVER	-	100.0	-	-	-	-	-	-	-
300 TO 499 MILES	9	100.0	-	88.3	6.9	.4	-	4.4	-
UNDER 1000 POUNDS	6	100.0	-	92.0	1.3	.6	-	6.0	-
1000 TO 9999 POUNDS	1	100.0	-	55.5	44.5	-	-	-	-
10000 TO 29999 POUNDS	1	100.0	-	100.0	-	-	-	-	-
30000 TO 59999 POUNDS	-	100.0	-	-	-	-	-	-	-
60000 TO 89999 POUNDS	-	100.0	-	-	-	-	-	-	-
90000 POUNDS AND OVER	-	100.0	-	-	-	-	-	-	-
500 TO 999 MILES	26	100.0	3.5	76.3	9.1	4.1	-	7.1	-
UNDER 1000 POUNDS	15	100.0	1.1	80.9	1.0	4.8	-	12.1	-
1000 TO 9999 POUNDS	7	100.0	9.9	80.4	5.4	4.4	-	-	-
10000 TO 29999 POUNDS	1	100.0	-	35.9	64.1	-	-	-	-
30000 TO 59999 POUNDS	1	100.0	-	58.2	41.8	-	-	-	-
60000 TO 89999 POUNDS	-	100.0	-	-	-	-	-	-	-
90000 POUNDS AND OVER	-	100.0	-	-	-	-	-	-	-
1000 TO 1499 MILES	3	100.0	3.9	79.2	.1	6.4	-	10.5	-
UNDER 1000 POUNDS	2	100.0	3.1	80.5	.1	2.2	-	14.1	-
1000 TO 9999 POUNDS	-	100.0	5.9	75.3	-	18.8	-	-	-
10000 TO 29999 POUNDS	-	100.0	-	-	-	-	-	-	-
30000 TO 59999 POUNDS	-	100.0	-	-	-	-	-	-	-
60000 TO 89999 POUNDS	-	100.0	-	-	-	-	-	-	-
90000 POUNDS AND OVER	-	100.0	-	-	-	-	-	-	-
1500 MILES OR OVER	8	100.0	29.7	65.8	.4	1.0	-	3.2	-
UNDER 1000 POUNDS	4	100.0	1.6	89.9	-	2.0	-	6.5	-
1000 TO 9999 POUNDS	2	100.0	20.2	78.5	1.2	-	-	-	-
10000 TO 29999 POUNDS	2	100.0	100.0	-	-	-	-	-	-
30000 TO 59999 POUNDS	-	100.0	-	-	-	-	-	-	-
60000 TO 89999 POUNDS	-	100.0	-	-	-	-	-	-	-
90000 POUNDS AND OVER	-	100.0	-	-	-	-	-	-	-
TON-MILES OF SHIPMENTS	(millions of ton-miles)								
U.S. TOTAL	47	100.0	15.4	71.7	4.7	2.4	-	5.8	-
UNDER 100 MILES	-	100.0	-	82.0	8.1	.3	-	9.4	.1
UNDER 1000 POUNDS	-	100.0	-	76.9	7.7	.5	-	14.7	.2
1000 TO 9999 POUNDS	-	100.0	-	89.0	11.0	-	-	-	-
10000 TO 29999 POUNDS	-	100.0	-	100.0	-	-	-	-	-
30000 TO 59999 POUNDS	-	100.0	-	-	-	-	-	-	-
60000 TO 89999 POUNDS	-	100.0	-	-	-	-	-	-	-
90000 POUNDS AND OVER	-	100.0	-	-	-	-	-	-	-
100 TO 199 MILES	-	100.0	-	59.6	7.3	.9	-	32.1	-
UNDER 1000 POUNDS	-	100.0	-	48.1	9.4	1.2	-	41.2	.1
1000 TO 9999 POUNDS	-	100.0	-	100.0	-	-	-	-	-
10000 TO 29999 POUNDS	-	100.0	-	-	-	-	-	-	-
30000 TO 59999 POUNDS	-	100.0	-	-	-	-	-	-	-
60000 TO 89999 POUNDS	-	100.0	-	-	-	-	-	-	-
90000 POUNDS AND OVER	-	100.0	-	-	-	-	-	-	-

See footnotes at end of table 4.

TABLE 4. **TCC GROUP 387**—Percent Distribution of Distance Shipped and Weight of Shipment, by Means of Transport: 1972—Continued

Distance shipped and weight of shipment[2] [3]	Number	Percent distribution by means of transport							
		All means of transport	Rail	Motor carrier	Private truck	Air	Water	Other	Unknown
TON-MILES OF SHIPMENTS	(millions of ton-miles)								
200 TO 299 MILES.........	1	100.0	-	75.4	16.8	.5	-	7.3	-
UNDER 1000 POUNDS.....	-	100.0	-	85.2	1.5	.9	-	12.4	-
1000 TO 9999 POUNDS...	-	100.0	-	69.0	31.0	-	-	-	-
10000 TO 29999 POUNDS.	-	100.0	-	-	100.0	-	-	-	-
30000 TO 59999 POUNDS.	-	100.0	-	-	-	-	-	-	-
60000 TO 89999 POUNDS.	-	100.0	-	-	-	-	-	-	-
90000 POUNDS AND OVER.	-	100.0	-	-	-	-	-	-	-
300 TO 499 MILES.........	3	100.0	-	87.8	7.2	.4	-	4.5	-
UNDER 1000 POUNDS.....	2	100.0	-	91.9	1.4	.6	-	6.2	-
1000 TO 9999 POUNDS...	-	100.0	-	51.2	48.8	-	-	-	-
10000 TO 29999 POUNDS.	-	100.0	-	100.0	-	-	-	-	-
30000 TO 59999 POUNDS.	-	100.0	-	-	-	-	-	-	-
60000 TO 89999 POUNDS.	-	100.0	-	-	-	-	-	-	-
90000 POUNDS AND OVER.	-	100.0	-	-	-	-	-	-	-
500 TO 999 MILES.........	18	100.0	3.4	77.9	8.8	3.4	-	6.5	-
UNDER 1000 POUNDS.....	10	100.0	1.1	82.7	1.0	4.0	-	11.2	-
1000 TO 9999 POUNDS...	5	100.0	9.7	82.1	4.5	3.6	-	-	-
10000 TO 29999 POUNDS.	1	100.0	-	40.8	59.2	-	-	-	-
30000 TO 59999 POUNDS.	1	100.0	-	57.2	42.8	-	-	-	-
60000 TO 89999 POUNDS.	-	100.0	-	-	-	-	-	-	-
90000 POUNDS AND OVER.	-	100.0	-	-	-	-	-	-	-
1000 TO 1499 MILES......	4	100.0	3.7	78.5	.1	7.5	-	10.3	-
UNDER 1000 POUNDS.....	3	100.0	3.1	80.5	.1	2.3	-	14.0	-
1000 TO 9999 POUNDS...	1	100.0	5.2	72.8	-	22.0	-	-	-
10000 TO 29999 POUNDS.	-	100.0	-	-	-	-	-	-	-
30000 TO 59999 POUNDS.	-	100.0	-	-	-	-	-	-	-
60000 TO 89999 POUNDS.	-	100.0	-	-	-	-	-	-	-
90000 POUNDS AND OVER.	-	100.0	-	-	-	-	-	-	-
1500 MILES OR OVER......	19	100.0	34.8	60.8	.3	1.0	-	3.2	-
UNDER 1000 POUNDS.....	8	100.0	1.7	88.7	-	2.3	-	7.2	-
1000 TO 9999 POUNDS...	5	100.0	20.0	79.0	1.0	-	-	-	-
10000 TO 29999 POUNDS.	5	100.0	100.0	-	-	-	-	-	-
30000 TO 59999 POUNDS.	-	100.0	-	-	-	-	-	-	-
60000 TO 89999 POUNDS.	-	100.0	-	-	-	-	-	-	-
90000 POUNDS AND OVER.	-	100.0	-	-	-	-	-	-	-

Note: Detail may not add to total due to rounding. The introductory table shows the estimates of sampling variability for tons; sampling variability for ton-miles has not been estimated. See the map in the Introduction for the States comprising the geographic divisions of the United States.
    Shipments excluded from the survey are those moving by pipeline (primarily petroleum products from refineries), parcel post shipments, and commodities moved by own power (motorized vehicles, aircraft, etc.) or towed (prefabricated buildings, etc.). Local shipments (commodities shipped less than 25 miles from the plant) and shipments within the same city are also excluded. Shipments to Alaska and Hawaii from the 48 conterminous States and the District of Columbia are included; however, no data were obtained for shipments originating in Alaska and Hawaii.

    - Represents zero or rounds to zero.   (D) Withheld to avoid disclosing figures for individual companies.

[1]Production of this commodity is concentrated in the geographic divisions shown; figures and distributions for geographic divisions not shown are included in the total.

[2]Distances of shipments to foreign destinations are calculated only to the U.S. port of exit.

[3]Includes only shipments represented by bills of lading and invoices. Summary records which did not show individual weights of shipments are not included.

TCC 394. Toys, Amusement, Sporting, and Athletic Goods

Comparisons of Tons and Ton-Miles of Shipments for
Geographic Divisions of Origin and for Sampling Variability: 1972 and 1967

Geographic division of origin	Estimates				Relative sampling variability in tons (percent)	
	1972		1967		1972	1967
	Tons (thousands)	Ton-miles (millions)	Tons (thousands)	Ton-miles (millions)		
U.S. total	1,672	1,181	668	604	18.9	(*)
New England	299	280	(*)	(*)	57.1	(*)
Middle Atlantic	427	332	(*)	(*)	17.2	(*)
East North Central	491	268	(*)	(*)	42.8	(*)
West North Central	(D)	(D)	(*)	(*)	(*)	(*)
South Atlantic	(D)	(D)	(*)	(*)	(*)	(*)
East South Central	(D)	(D)	(*)	(*)	(*)	(*)
West South Central	(D)	(D) ·	(*)	(*)	(*)	(*)
Mountain	(D)	(D)	(*)	(*)	(*)	(*)
Pacific	43	60	(*)	(*)	35.0	(*)

Note: One general criterion for publication of data in this series provided for a maximum relative sampling variability of 50 percent of the total tons for any origin division. In other words, data would not be published if 1 standard error exceeded 50 percent of the estimate with which it was associated; see "Reliability of Data", page VIII. However, for this commodity group the absolute standard errors are generally low and division data are published even though some of the measured relative errors exceed 50 percent.

(D) Withheld to avoid disclosing figures for individual companies.   *Data not published.

TABLE 1. TCC GROUP 394—Percent Distribution of Geographic Division of Origin and Distance Shipped, by Means of Transport: 1972

Geographic division of origin[1] and distance shipped[2]	Number	Percent distribution by means of transport							
		All means of transport	Rail	Motor carrier	Private truck	Air	Water	Other	Unknown
TONS OF SHIPMENTS	(thousands of tons)								
U.S. TOTAL..........	1 672	100.0	24.6	55.8	16.7	.3	.9	1.3	.3
NEW ENGLAND.............	299	100.0	43.6	48.2	5.9	.1	-	2.1	.1
UNDER 100 MILES.......	28	100.0	-	67.4	28.9	.5	-	3.3	-
100 TO 199 MILES......	47	100.0	2.1	94.4	2.2	-	-	1.3	-
200 TO 299 MILES......	16	100.0	-	92.8	5.3	-	-	1.9	-
300 TO 499 MILES......	27	100.0	49.0	43.8	4.7	-	-	2.5	-
500 TO 999 MILES......	86	100.0	53.7	37.3	6.4	.1	-	2.6	-
1000 TO 1499 MILES....	33	100.0	53.4	41.8	1.9	.4	-	2.4	-
1500 MILES OR OVER....	60	100.0	86.3	11.7	.3	-	-	1.4	.3
MIDDLE ATLANTIC.........	427	100.0	28.3	59.6	10.6	.6	-	.7	.2
UNDER 100 MILES.......	83	100.0	-	60.3	39.3	-	-	.4	-
100 TO 199 MILES......	42	100.0	15.7	76.3	7.4	-	-	.6	-
200 TO 299 MILES......	30	100.0	41.1	54.6	1.5	.9	-	1.9	-
300 TO 499 MILES......	39	100.0	31.1	63.6	.3	2.4	-	2.3	.3
500 TO 999 MILES......	112	100.0	16.6	74.4	7.8	.6	-	.5	.2
1000 TO 1499 MILES....	39	100.0	28.5	70.0	-	-	-	.4	1.1
1500 MILES OR OVER....	79	100.0	75.0	23.8	-	.7	-	.3	.3
EAST NORTH CENTRAL......	491	100.0	7.2	51.6	39.4	.2	-	1.1	.6
UNDER 100 MILES.......	78	100.0	4.6	31.5	63.3	.2	-	.5	-
100 TO 199 MILES......	109	100.0	-	24.5	75.0	.3	-	.1	-
200 TO 299 MILES......	46	100.0	-	72.4	27.1	-	-	.4	.1
300 TO 499 MILES......	58	100.0	.4	57.1	41.7	.1	-	.7	-
500 TO 999 MILES......	121	100.0	3.6	70.4	20.2	.2	-	3.5	2.1
1000 TO 1499 MILES....	19	100.0	2.9	96.2	.8	-	-	.1	-
1500 MILES OR OVER....	57	100.0	46.2	52.9	.5	.1	-	.1	.2
PACIFIC.................	43	100.0	12.0	75.3	10.2	.4	1.2	.6	.3
UNDER 100 MILES.......	4	100.0	-	47.3	41.6	-	9.4	1.7	-
100 TO 199 MILES......	1	100.0	-	96.9	1.8	-	-	1.3	-
200 TO 299 MILES......	-	100.0	-	90.5	-	-	-	9.5	-
300 TO 499 MILES......	1	100.0	-	95.5	2.1	-	-	2.4	-
500 TO 999 MILES......	7	100.0	.6	97.7	1.1	.6	-	-	-
1000 TO 1499 MILES....	4	100.0	3.1	92.9	-	-	-	.6	3.3
1500 MILES OR OVER....	23	100.0	21.0	68.0	9.8	.4	.3	.4	-
TON-MILES OF SHIPMENTS	(millions of ton-miles)								
U.S. TOTAL..........	1 181	100.0	42.0	48.4	6.2	.6	1.0	1.4	.4
NEW ENGLAND.............	280	100.0	68.7	26.4	2.6	.1	-	1.9	.3
UNDER 100 MILES.......	1	100.0	-	84.3	12.4	.1	-	3.1	-
100 TO 199 MILES......	7	100.0	1.6	95.6	1.7	-	-	1.1	-
200 TO 299 MILES......	3	100.0	-	91.9	6.1	-	-	2.0	-
300 TO 499 MILES......	11	100.0	49.7	44.3	3.5	-	-	2.4	-
500 TO 999 MILES......	70	100.0	54.4	35.6	7.4	.1	-	2.5	-
1000 TO 1499 MILES....	39	100.0	54.6	40.8	2.0	.4	-	2.1	-
1500 MILES OR OVER....	144	100.0	87.2	10.4	.3	-	-	1.4	.7
MIDDLE ATLANTIC.........	332	100.0	49.0	47.3	2.1	.7	-	.5	.3
UNDER 100 MILES.......	3	100.0	-	69.6	29.7	-	-	.7	-
100 TO 199 MILES......	6	100.0	14.1	77.2	8.1	-	-	.6	-
200 TO 299 MILES......	7	100.0	43.2	52.4	1.6	1.0	-	1.8	-
300 TO 499 MILES......	16	100.0	31.2	63.1	.3	2.6	-	2.5	.3
500 TO 999 MILES......	79	100.0	16.9	75.0	6.8	.5	-	.5	.2
1000 TO 1499 MILES....	46	100.0	28.3	70.3	-	-	-	.4	1.0
1500 MILES OR OVER....	173	100.0	73.3	25.3	-	.9	-	.3	.2
EAST NORTH CENTRAL......	268	100.0	19.3	62.0	16.2	.1	-	1.6	.7
UNDER 100 MILES.......	5	100.0	2.0	33.5	64.1	.2	-	.1	-
100 TO 199 MILES......	16	100.0	-	23.8	75.7	.4	-	.1	-
200 TO 299 MILES......	11	100.0	-	72.3	27.2	-	-	.4	.1
300 TO 499 MILES......	24	100.0	.4	56.3	42.5	-	-	.7	-
500 TO 999 MILES......	80	100.0	4.3	72.2	16.3	.2	-	4.9	2.1
1000 TO 1499 MILES....	23	100.0	3.5	95.6	.8	-	-	.1	-
1500 MILES OR OVER....	105	100.0	44.7	54.4	.5	.1	-	.1	.2
PACIFIC.................	60	100.0	16.1	75.2	7.1	.5	.4	.4	.3
UNDER 100 MILES.......	-	100.0	-	52.3	32.4	-	13.3	2.0	-
100 TO 199 MILES......	-	100.0	-	96.8	1.9	-	-	1.3	-
200 TO 299 MILES......	-	100.0	-	90.4	-	-	-	9.6	-
300 TO 499 MILES......	-	100.0	-	95.3	2.6	-	-	2.2	-
500 TO 999 MILES......	5	100.0	.8	96.9	1.5	.9	-	-	-
1000 TO 1499 MILES....	4	100.0	3.2	92.6	-	-	-	.6	3.5
1500 MILES OR OVER....	49	100.0	19.3	70.9	8.4	.5	.5	.4	-

See footnotes at end of table 4.

TABLE 2. **TCC GROUP 394—Percent Distribution of Geographic Division of Origin and Means of Transport, by Geographic Division of Destination: 1972**

Geographic division of origin[1] and means of transport	Number	Percent distribution by division of destination									
		U.S. total	New England	Middle Atlantic	East North Central	West North Central	South Atlantic	East South Central	West South Central	Mountain	Pacific
TONS OF SHIPMENTS	(thousands of tons)										
U.S. TOTAL	1 672	100.0	4.7	17.6	28.5	6.3	16.8	5.5	6.3	3.0	11.4
RAIL	412	100.0	3.0	7.6	28.2	3.5	10.1	5.6	8.2	6.8	27.0
MOTOR CARRIER	933	100.0	5.9	21.9	23.5	7.0	20.2	5.2	6.3	2.2	7.8
PRIVATE TRUCK	279	100.0	3.1	15.9	48.3	8.2	15.0	6.8	1.7	.1	.9
AIR	5	100.0	2.5	19.6	38.4	1.1	5.6	1.5	.5	1.9	28.7
WATER	14	100.0	-	48.2	-	-	-	-	48.3	-	3.5
OTHER	22	100.0	10.6	11.6	20.2	7.9	35.8	3.5	3.6	1.1	5.7
UNKNOWN	4	100.0	-	58.2	.5	6.3	15.6	-	.1	4.7	14.5
NEW ENGLAND	299	100.0	10.0	27.0	14.8	4.1	15.3	6.7	4.3	2.0	15.8
RAIL	130	100.0	.8	7.9	18.9	3.5	12.6	12.6	7.9	3.0	32.7
MOTOR CARRIER	144	100.0	13.3	46.3	12.6	4.6	15.4	2.4	1.7	1.3	2.4
PRIVATE TRUCK	17	100.0	47.3	16.8	.2	3.6	31.3	-	-	-	.9
AIR	-	100.0	37.0	1.3	13.4	12.7	24.3	6.4	4.3	.4	.2
WATER	-	100.0	-	-	-	-	-	-	-	-	-
OTHER	6	100.0	21.0	12.0	22.2	6.0	24.2	2.8	.8	1.0	10.1
UNKNOWN	-	100.0	-	-	-	-	-	-	-	-	100.0
MIDDLE ATLANTIC	427	100.0	4.7	28.0	21.1	4.3	14.7	3.7	5.6	5.7	12.1
RAIL	121	100.0	4.4	7.8	12.8	6.0	10.5	5.1	6.8	16.7	30.0
MOTOR CARRIER	254	100.0	5.8	29.2	27.1	4.2	16.5	3.8	6.1	1.5	5.8
PRIVATE TRUCK	45	100.0	.3	77.9	6.1	.4	15.3	-	.4	-	-
AIR	2	100.0	-	11.7	61.6	.6	2.8	-	.4	.9	22.0
WATER	-	100.0	-	-	-	-	-	-	-	-	-
OTHER	2	100.0	1.4	16.1	43.7	4.9	15.0	6.9	4.5	.6	6.8
UNKNOWN	1	100.0	-	.7	1.1	9.4	67.8	-	.4	20.5	-
EAST NORTH CENTRAL	491	100.0	1.2	9.3	40.9	8.7	13.7	6.7	5.5	2.7	11.4
RAIL	35	100.0	2.4	.6	10.4	-	.8	-	.1	11.0	74.7
MOTOR CARRIER	253	100.0	1.8	14.6	27.4	9.7	16.1	5.7	9.5	3.6	11.6
PRIVATE TRUCK	193	100.0	-	2.8	65.4	9.1	11.8	9.4	1.3	.1	.2
AIR	-	100.0	-	21.7	69.4	-	1.5	2.9	.2	.4	3.9
WATER	-	100.0	-	-	-	-	-	-	-	-	-
OTHER	5	100.0	5.9	4.4	11.6	4.2	65.0	2.8	4.1	.8	1.4
UNKNOWN	2	100.0	-	94.2	.4	1.8	-	-	-	-	3.6
PACIFIC	43	100.0	4.4	15.3	19.6	2.4	10.4	4.4	6.6	1.4	35.5
RAIL	5	100.0	.4	-	59.4	-	35.7	-	2.7	-	1.8
MOTOR CARRIER	32	100.0	5.7	20.1	10.1	2.7	7.4	5.5	8.3	1.7	38.5
PRIVATE TRUCK	4	100.0	.1	-	47.6	-	4.3	1.1	-	1.3	45.6
AIR	-	100.0	-	44.1	.5	-	.9	22.5	-	8.8	23.1
WATER	-	100.0	-	-	-	-	-	-	-	-	-
OTHER	-	100.0	-	-	-	-	-	-	-	-	100.0
UNKNOWN	-	100.0	-	6.9	7.2	11.7	13.7	6.0	2.1	2.0	50.4
TON-MILES OF SHIPMENTS	(millions of ton-miles)										
U.S. TOTAL	1 181	100.0	3.2	8.7	16.6	5.2	14.1	4.2	8.5	6.3	33.2
RAIL	496	100.0	2.0	2.3	13.9	2.8	7.1	4.0	7.1	9.4	51.3
MOTOR CARRIER	571	100.0	4.6	13.1	17.8	6.2	17.2	4.4	9.9	4.6	22.2
PRIVATE TRUCK	73	100.0	.8	7.5	30.5	14.6	35.1	5.9	3.8	.3	1.4
AIR	6	100.0	-	13.9	14.1	.9	3.1	1.5	.5	2.0	64.1
WATER	11	100.0	-	59.6	-	-	-	-	38.3	-	2.1
OTHER	16	100.0	7.4	9.2	14.6	7.1	37.7	3.2	4.0	1.7	15.0
UNKNOWN	4	100.0	-	34.6	.2	6.1	11.6	-	.1	8.3	39.2
NEW ENGLAND	280	100.0	.7	7.0	11.8	5.2	14.0	6.7	6.9	4.1	43.6
RAIL	192	100.0	.1	2.4	9.7	2.7	7.8	7.9	8.0	4.1	57.3
MOTOR CARRIER	74	100.0	1.9	19.0	17.8	10.9	24.1	4.6	5.0	4.6	12.2
PRIVATE TRUCK	7	100.0	3.1	10.0	.2	10.8	70.3	-	-	-	5.5
AIR	-	100.0	.7	.7	15.3	21.5	44.1	7.0	8.7	1.4	.6
WATER	-	100.0	-	-	-	-	-	-	-	-	-
OTHER	5	100.0	2.0	4.4	21.7	9.7	22.2	3.6	1.6	2.6	32.2
UNKNOWN	-	100.0	-	-	-	-	-	-	-	-	100.0
MIDDLE ATLANTIC	332	100.0	1.7	3.5	14.8	5.1	11.6	3.7	9.2	12.9	37.6
RAIL	163	100.0	1.5	1.6	2.5	3.6	6.5	2.7	6.8	21.4	53.4
MOTOR CARRIER	157	100.0	2.0	4.7	26.6	6.8	15.0	4.9	12.3	4.8	22.9
PRIVATE TRUCK	6	100.0	.7	18.7	27.8	2.0	50.8	-	.4	-	-
AIR	2	100.0	-	3.0	32.7	.4	1.6	-	.4	1.7	60.1
WATER	-	100.0	-	-	-	-	-	-	-	-	-
OTHER	1	100.0	.6	3.6	29.3	7.5	13.0	7.9	8.4	2.4	27.3
UNKNOWN	1	100.0	-	-	.4	10.2	51.8	-	.6	36.9	-
EAST NORTH CENTRAL	268	100.0	1.6	9.3	10.7	6.6	15.1	3.4	9.0	5.8	38.6
RAIL	51	100.0	1.1	.2	.3	.3	.5	-	.1	7.4	90.5
MOTOR CARRIER	166	100.0	2.1	12.0	7.7	5.0	16.4	3.0	13.4	6.9	33.5
PRIVATE TRUCK	43	100.0	-	6.5	35.9	21.2	22.2	9.2	3.5	.4	1.2
AIR	-	100.0	-	40.3	28.4	-	1.7	5.9	.7	1.6	21.3
WATER	-	100.0	-	-	-	-	-	-	-	-	-
OTHER	4	100.0	6.2	3.1	1.3	2.2	76.7	1.7	4.7	.9	3.3
UNKNOWN	1	100.0	-	90.3	.2	.6	-	-	-	-	9.0
PACIFIC	60	100.0	7.9	25.5	24.7	2.3	16.4	5.4	5.9	.6	11.3
RAIL	9	100.0	.6	-	54.6	-	41.9	-	2.0	.6	.9
MOTOR CARRIER	45	100.0	10.4	33.4	13.1	2.6	11.7	6.8	7.4	.6	14.0
PRIVATE TRUCK	4	100.0	.2	-	84.9	-	9.8	1.9	-	.9	2.3
AIR	-	100.0	-	59.4	.5	-	1.2	22.2	-	4.2	12.6
WATER	-	100.0	-	-	-	-	-	-	-	-	-
OTHER	-	100.0	-	-	-	-	-	-	-	-	100.0
UNKNOWN	-	100.0	-	16.7	13.4	17.1	30.6	11.4	3.1	.7	6.9

See footnotes at end of table 4.

TABLE 3. **TCC GROUP 394**—Percent Distribution of Geographic Division of Destination and Means of Transport, by Geographic Division of Origin: 1972

Geographic division of destination and means of transport	Number	Percent distribution by division of origin[1]									
		U.S. total	New England	Middle Atlantic	East North Central	West North Central	South Atlantic	East South Central	West South Central	Mountain	Pacific
TONS OF SHIPMENTS	(thousands of tons)										
U.S. TOTAL	1 672	100.0	17.9	25.6	29.4	(D)	(D)	(D)	(D)	(D)	2.6
RAIL	412	100.0	31.7	29.4	8.6	(D)	(D)	(D)	(D)	(D)	1.3
MOTOR CARRIER	933	100.0	15.5	27.3	27.2	(D)	(D)	(D)	(D)	(D)	3.5
PRIVATE TRUCK	279	100.0	6.3	16.2	69.2	(D)	(D)	(D)	(D)	(D)	1.6
AIR	5	100.0	6.8	45.2	14.0	(D)	(D)	(D)	(D)	(D)	2.9
WATER	14	100.0	-	-	-	(D)	(D)	(D)	(D)	(D)	3.5
OTHER	22	100.0	28.5	13.0	24.2	(D)	(D)	(D)	(D)	(D)	1.2
UNKNOWN	4	100.0	4.2	23.1	61.7	(D)	(D)	(D)	(D)	(D)	3.0
NEW ENGLAND	78	100.0	38.4	25.9	7.3	(D)	(D)	(D)	(D)	(D)	2.4
RAIL	12	100.0	8.1	43.8	7.0	(D)	(D)	(D)	(D)	(D)	.2
MOTOR CARRIER	54	100.0	35.1	26.9	8.3	(D)	(D)	(D)	(D)	(D)	3.4
PRIVATE TRUCK	8	100.0	95.5	1.5	-	(D)	(D)	(D)	(D)	(D)	-
AIR	-	100.0	100.0	-	-	(D)	(D)	(D)	(D)	(D)	-
WATER	-	100.0	-	-	-	(D)	(D)	(D)	(D)	(D)	-
OTHER	2	100.0	56.2	1.7	13.3	(D)	(D)	(D)	(D)	(D)	-
UNKNOWN	-	100.0				(D)	(D)	(D)	(D)	(D)	
MIDDLE ATLANTIC	293	100.0	27.5	40.8	15.6	(D)	(D)	(D)	(D)	(D)	2.3
RAIL	31	100.0	33.0	30.0	.7	(D)	(D)	(D)	(D)	(D)	-
MOTOR CARRIER	204	100.0	32.7	36.4	18.1	(D)	(D)	(D)	(D)	(D)	3.2
PRIVATE TRUCK	44	100.0	6.7	79.5	12.4	(D)	(D)	(D)	(D)	(D)	-
AIR	1	100.0	.5	26.9	15.4	(D)	(D)	(D)	(D)	(D)	6.6
WATER	7	100.0	-	-	-	(D)	(D)	(D)	(D)	(D)	-
OTHER	2	100.0	29.5	18.1	9.1	(D)	(D)	(D)	(D)	(D)	.7
UNKNOWN	2	100.0	-	.3	99.7	(D)	(D)	(D)	(D)	(D)	-
EAST NORTH CENTRAL	477	100.0	9.3	18.8	42.1	(D)	(D)	(D)	(D)	(D)	1.8
RAIL	116	100.0	21.3	13.3	3.1	(D)	(D)	(D)	(D)	(D)	2.7
MOTOR CARRIER	219	100.0	8.3	31.5	31.7	(D)	(D)	(D)	(D)	(D)	1.5
PRIVATE TRUCK	135	100.0	-	2.0	93.6	(D)	(D)	(D)	(D)	(D)	1.6
AIR	2	100.0	2.4	72.4	25.2	(D)	(D)	(D)	(D)	(D)	-
WATER	-	100.0	-	-	-	(D)	(D)	(D)	(D)	(D)	-
OTHER	4	100.0	31.3	28.2	13.9	(D)	(D)	(D)	(D)	(D)	.4
UNKNOWN	-	100.0	-	54.4	45.6	(D)	(D)	(D)	(D)	(D)	-
WEST NORTH CENTRAL	104	100.0	11.7	17.5	40.6	(D)	(D)	(D)	(D)	(D)	1.0
RAIL	14	100.0	31.6	49.6	-	(D)	(D)	(D)	(D)	(D)	-
MOTOR CARRIER	65	100.0	10.1	16.4	37.8	(D)	(D)	(D)	(D)	(D)	1.3
PRIVATE TRUCK	23	100.0	2.8	.8	76.7	(D)	(D)	(D)	(D)	(D)	-
AIR	-	100.0	77.1	22.9	-	(D)	(D)	(D)	(D)	(D)	-
WATER	-	100.0	-	-	-	(D)	(D)	(D)	(D)	(D)	-
OTHER	1	100.0	21.8	8.1	12.9	(D)	(D)	(D)	(D)	(D)	1.8
UNKNOWN	-	100.0	-	34.5	17.8	(D)	(D)	(D)	(D)	(D)	47.7
SOUTH ATLANTIC	281	100.0	16.3	22.4	24.0	(D)	(D)	(D)	(D)	(D)	1.6
RAIL	41	100.0	39.8	30.5	.7	(D)	(D)	(D)	(D)	(D)	4.5
MOTOR CARRIER	188	100.0	11.8	22.3	21.6	(D)	(D)	(D)	(D)	(D)	1.3
PRIVATE TRUCK	42	100.0	13.2	16.6	54.5	(D)	(D)	(D)	(D)	(D)	.5
AIR	-	100.0	29.6	22.7	3.8	(D)	(D)	(D)	(D)	(D)	.5
WATER	-	100.0	-	-	-	(D)	(D)	(D)	(D)	(D)	-
OTHER	8	100.0	19.3	5.5	43.9	(D)	(D)	(D)	(D)	(D)	.5
UNKNOWN	-	100.0	-	100.0	-	(D)	(D)	(D)	(D)	(D)	-
EAST SOUTH CENTRAL	91	100.0	22.0	17.5	36.0	(D)	(D)	(D)	(D)	(D)	2.1
RAIL	23	100.0	71.1	26.7	-	(D)	(D)	(D)	(D)	(D)	-
MOTOR CARRIER	48	100.0	7.2	19.8	30.0	(D)	(D)	(D)	(D)	(D)	3.8
PRIVATE TRUCK	19	100.0	-	-	95.7	(D)	(D)	(D)	(D)	(D)	.3
AIR	-	100.0	28.9	-	27.1	(D)	(D)	(D)	(D)	(D)	43.9
WATER	-	100.0	-	-	-	(D)	(D)	(D)	(D)	(D)	-
OTHER	-	100.0	22.7	25.6	19.1	(D)	(D)	(D)	(D)	(D)	2.1
UNKNOWN	-	100.0	-	-	-	(D)	(D)	(D)	(D)	(D)	-
WEST SOUTH CENTRAL	105	100.0	12.1	22.7	25.5	(D)	(D)	(D)	(D)	(D)	2.7
RAIL	33	100.0	30.6	24.5	.1	(D)	(D)	(D)	(D)	(D)	.4
MOTOR CARRIER	58	100.0	4.1	26.3	41.1	(D)	(D)	(D)	(D)	(D)	4.6
PRIVATE TRUCK	4	100.0	-	-	51.5	(D)	(D)	(D)	(D)	(D)	-
AIR	-	100.0	58.9	34.3	6.8	(D)	(D)	(D)	(D)	(D)	-
WATER	7	100.0	-	-	-	(D)	(D)	(D)	(D)	(D)	-
OTHER	-	100.0	6.3	16.1	27.5	(D)	(D)	(D)	(D)	(D)	.7
UNKNOWN	-	100.0	-	100.0	-	(D)	(D)	(D)	(D)	(D)	-
MOUNTAIN	49	100.0	12.0	49.1	26.6	(D)	(D)	(D)	(D)	(D)	1.3
RAIL	28	100.0	14.0	71.8	13.8	(D)	(D)	(D)	(D)	(D)	-
MOTOR CARRIER	20	100.0	9.3	18.7	44.0	(D)	(D)	(D)	(D)	(D)	2.6
PRIVATE TRUCK	-	100.0	-	-	73.2	(D)	(D)	(D)	(D)	(D)	26.4
AIR	-	100.0	1.5	21.8	2.6	(D)	(D)	(D)	(D)	(D)	13.7
WATER	-	100.0	-	-	-	(D)	(D)	(D)	(D)	(D)	-
OTHER	-	100.0	24.0	7.1	15.9	(D)	(D)	(D)	(D)	(D)	2.1
UNKNOWN	-	100.0	-	100.0	-	(D)	(D)	(D)	(D)	(D)	-
PACIFIC	190	100.0	24.8	27.2	29.5	(D)	(D)	(D)	(D)	(D)	8.1
RAIL	111	100.0	38.5	32.6	23.7	(D)	(D)	(D)	(D)	(D)	.1
MOTOR CARRIER	72	100.0	4.8	20.3	40.3	(D)	(D)	(D)	(D)	(D)	17.3
PRIVATE TRUCK	2	100.0	6.3	-	12.3	(D)	(D)	(D)	(D)	(D)	81.4
AIR	1	100.0	-	34.7	1.9	(D)	(D)	(D)	(D)	(D)	2.4
WATER	-	100.0	-	-	-	(D)	(D)	(D)	(D)	(D)	100.0
OTHER	1	100.0	50.6	15.7	6.1	(D)	(D)	(D)	(D)	(D)	10.8
UNKNOWN	-	100.0	28.9	-	15.5	(D)	(D)	(D)	(D)	(D)	-

See footnotes at end of table 4.

TABLE 3. **TCC GROUP 394—Percent Distribution of Geographic Division of Destination and Means of Transport, by Geographic Division of Origin: 1972**—Continued

Geographic division of destination and means of transport	Number (millions of ton-miles)	Percent distribution by division of origin[1]									
		U.S. total	New England	Middle Atlantic	East North Central	West North Central	South Atlantic	East South Central	West South Central	Mountain	Pacific
TON-MILES OF SHIPMENTS											
U.S. TOTAL	1 181	100.0	23.7	28.1	22.7	(D)	(D)	(D)	(D)	(D)	5.1
RAIL	496	100.0	38.7	32.8	10.4	(D)	(D)	(D)	(D)	(D)	2.0
MOTOR CARRIER	571	100.0	13.0	27.5	29.1	(D)	(D)	(D)	(D)	(D)	8.0
PRIVATE TRUCK	73	100.0	10.1	9.6	59.4	(D)	(D)	(D)	(D)	(D)	5.9
AIR	6	100.0	3.7	37.5	4.3	(D)	(D)	(D)	(D)	(D)	4.3
WATER	11	100.0	-	-	-	(D)	(D)	(D)	(D)	(D)	2.1
OTHER	16	100.0	30.9	9.9	25.6	(D)	(D)	(D)	(D)	(D)	1.5
UNKNOWN	4	100.0	19.4	22.4	38.3	(D)	(D)	(D)	(D)	(D)	3.6
NEW ENGLAND	37	100.0	4.9	15.2	11.6	(D)	(D)	(D)	(D)	(D)	12.7
RAIL	9	100.0	1.3	25.2	6.0	(D)	(D)	(D)	(D)	(D)	.5
MOTOR CARRIER	26	100.0	5.3	12.3	13.5	(D)	(D)	(D)	(D)	(D)	18.1
PRIVATE TRUCK	-	100.0	37.8	7.9	-	(D)	(D)	(D)	(D)	(D)	1.7
AIR	-	100.0	100.0	-	-	(D)	(D)	(D)	(D)	(D)	-
WATER	-	100.0	-	-	-	(D)	(D)	(D)	(D)	(D)	-
OTHER	1	100.0	8.2	.9	21.4	(D)	(D)	(D)	(D)	(D)	-
UNKNOWN	-	100.0	-	-	-	(D)	(D)	(D)	(D)	(D)	-
MIDDLE ATLANTIC	103	100.0	19.1	11.1	24.1	(D)	(D)	(D)	(D)	(D)	15.0
RAIL	11	100.0	40.1	22.3	.8	(D)	(D)	(D)	(D)	(D)	-
MOTOR CARRIER	74	100.0	18.8	10.0	26.7	(D)	(D)	(D)	(D)	(D)	20.4
PRIVATE TRUCK	5	100.0	13.4	23.7	51.2	(D)	(D)	(D)	(D)	(D)	-
AIR	-	100.0	.2	8.1	12.4	(D)	(D)	(D)	(D)	(D)	18.5
WATER	7	100.0	-	-	-	(D)	(D)	(D)	(D)	(D)	-
OTHER	1	100.0	14.7	3.9	8.5	(D)	(D)	(D)	(D)	(D)	2.8
UNKNOWN	1	100.0	-	-	100.0	(D)	(D)	(D)	(D)	(D)	-
EAST NORTH CENTRAL	196	100.0	16.8	25.0	14.6	(D)	(D)	(D)	(D)	(D)	7.6
RAIL	68	100.0	27.1	6.0	.2	(D)	(D)	(D)	(D)	(D)	7.7
MOTOR CARRIER	102	100.0	12.9	40.9	12.6	(D)	(D)	(D)	(D)	(D)	5.9
PRIVATE TRUCK	22	100.0	.1	8.7	69.8	(D)	(D)	(D)	(D)	(D)	16.4
AIR	-	100.0	4.0	87.3	8.6	(D)	(D)	(D)	(D)	(D)	.1
WATER	-	100.0	-	-	-	(D)	(D)	(D)	(D)	(D)	-
OTHER	2	100.0	45.9	19.9	2.3	(D)	(D)	(D)	(D)	(D)	1.4
UNKNOWN	-	100.0	-	58.4	41.6	(D)	(D)	(D)	(D)	(D)	-
WEST NORTH CENTRAL	61	100.0	23.8	27.5	28.6	(D)	(D)	(D)	(D)	(D)	2.3
RAIL	13	100.0	37.7	41.8	-	(D)	(D)	(D)	(D)	(D)	-
MOTOR CARRIER	35	100.0	22.8	30.3	23.4	(D)	(D)	(D)	(D)	(D)	3.4
PRIVATE TRUCK	10	100.0	7.5	1.3	86.4	(D)	(D)	(D)	(D)	(D)	-
AIR	-	100.0	83.0	17.0	-	(D)	(D)	(D)	(D)	(D)	-
WATER	-	100.0	-	-	-	(D)	(D)	(D)	(D)	(D)	-
OTHER	1	100.0	41.9	10.4	8.1	(D)	(D)	(D)	(D)	(D)	3.7
UNKNOWN	-	100.0	-	37.7	3.7	(D)	(D)	(D)	(D)	(D)	58.7
SOUTH ATLANTIC	166	100.0	23.6	23.2	24.4	(D)	(D)	(D)	(D)	(D)	6.0
RAIL	35	100.0	42.3	29.8	.8	(D)	(D)	(D)	(D)	(D)	11.5
MOTOR CARRIER	98	100.0	18.2	24.1	27.8	(D)	(D)	(D)	(D)	(D)	5.4
PRIVATE TRUCK	25	100.0	20.3	13.8	37.6	(D)	(D)	(D)	(D)	(D)	1.6
AIR	-	100.0	52.4	19.5	2.3	(D)	(D)	(D)	(D)	(D)	1.7
WATER	-	100.0	-	-	-	(D)	(D)	(D)	(D)	(D)	-
OTHER	6	100.0	18.2	3.4	52.2	(D)	(D)	(D)	(D)	(D)	1.3
UNKNOWN	-	100.0	-	100.0	-	(D)	(D)	(D)	(D)	(D)	-
EAST SOUTH CENTRAL	49	100.0	37.6	24.5	18.3	(D)	(D)	(D)	(D)	(D)	6.6
RAIL	19	100.0	76.4	22.3	-	(D)	(D)	(D)	(D)	(D)	-
MOTOR CARRIER	25	100.0	13.7	30.6	20.0	(D)	(D)	(D)	(D)	(D)	12.3
PRIVATE TRUCK	4	100.0	-	-	92.1	(D)	(D)	(D)	(D)	(D)	1.9
AIR	-	100.0	17.4	-	17.3	(D)	(D)	(D)	(D)	(D)	65.3
WATER	-	100.0	-	-	-	(D)	(D)	(D)	(D)	(D)	-
OTHER	-	100.0	34.8	24.7	13.9	(D)	(D)	(D)	(D)	(D)	5.6
UNKNOWN	-	100.0	-	-	-	(D)	(D)	(D)	(D)	(D)	-
WEST SOUTH CENTRAL	100	100.0	19.2	30.6	24.0	(D)	(D)	(D)	(D)	(D)	3.6
RAIL	35	100.0	43.6	31.4	.1	(D)	(D)	(D)	(D)	(D)	.6
MOTOR CARRIER	56	100.0	6.5	34.1	39.3	(D)	(D)	(D)	(D)	(D)	5.9
PRIVATE TRUCK	2	100.0	-	-	54.2	(D)	(D)	(D)	(D)	(D)	-
AIR	-	100.0	62.1	32.0	6.0	(D)	(D)	(D)	(D)	(D)	-
WATER	4	100.0	-	-	-	(D)	(D)	(D)	(D)	(D)	1.2
OTHER	-	100.0	12.2	20.7	29.5	(D)	(D)	(D)	(D)	(D)	-
UNKNOWN	-	100.0	-	100.0	-	(D)	(D)	(D)	(D)	(D)	-
MOUNTAIN	74	100.0	15.5	57.8	20.8	(D)	(D)	(D)	(D)	(D)	.5
RAIL	46	100.0	17.0	74.6	8.2	(D)	(D)	(D)	(D)	(D)	-
MOTOR CARRIER	26	100.0	12.9	28.3	43.2	(D)	(D)	(D)	(D)	(D)	1.1
PRIVATE TRUCK	-	100.0	-	-	81.9	(D)	(D)	(D)	(D)	(D)	17.9
AIR	-	100.0	2.7	33.3	3.6	(D)	(D)	(D)	(D)	(D)	9.3
WATER	-	100.0	-	-	-	(D)	(D)	(D)	(D)	(D)	-
OTHER	-	100.0	48.8	13.9	13.4	(D)	(D)	(D)	(D)	(D)	.7
UNKNOWN	-	100.0	-	100.0	-	(D)	(D)	(D)	(D)	(D)	-
PACIFIC	392	100.0	31.2	31.9	26.4	(D)	(D)	(D)	(D)	(D)	1.8
RAIL	255	100.0	43.2	34.1	18.4	(D)	(D)	(D)	(D)	(D)	-
MOTOR CARRIER	127	100.0	7.1	28.3	43.8	(D)	(D)	(D)	(D)	(D)	5.0
PRIVATE TRUCK	1	100.0	39.7	-	50.8	(D)	(D)	(D)	(D)	(D)	9.5
AIR	4	100.0	-	35.2	1.4	(D)	(D)	(D)	(D)	(D)	.9
WATER	-	100.0	-	-	-	(D)	(D)	(D)	(D)	(D)	100.0
OTHER	2	100.0	66.2	18.0	5.5	(D)	(D)	(D)	(D)	(D)	.7
UNKNOWN	1	100.0	49.5	-	8.8	(D)	(D)	(D)	(D)	(D)	-

See footnotes at end of table 4.

TABLE 4. TCC GROUP 394—Percent Distribution of Distance Shipped and Weight of Shipment, by Means of Transport: 1972

Distance shipped and weight of shipment[2] [3]	Number	Percent distribution by means of transport							
		All means of transport	Rail	Motor carrier	Private truck	Air	Water	Other	Unknown
TONS OF SHIPMENTS	(thousands of tons)								
U.S. TOTAL	1 617	100.0	24.4	55.6	17.3	.2	.9	1.3	.2
UNDER 100 MILES	202	100.0	1.8	50.8	46.0	.1	.2	1.0	-
UNDER 1000 POUNDS	38	100.0	.2	55.2	39.0	.3	.2	5.0	-
1000 TO 9999 POUNDS	69	100.0	-	69.2	29.8	.2	.5	.3	-
10000 TO 29999 POUNDS	70	100.0	-	37.0	63.0	-	-	-	-
30000 TO 59999 POUNDS	18	100.0	-	31.5	68.5	-	-	-	-
60000 TO 89999 POUNDS	5	100.0	68.8	31.2	-	-	-	-	-
90000 POUNDS AND OVER	-	100.0	-	-	-	-	-	-	-
100 TO 199 MILES	260	100.0	3.0	60.9	35.5	.1	-	.5	-
UNDER 1000 POUNDS	23	100.0	.2	84.7	7.4	1.6	-	6.0	-
1000 TO 9999 POUNDS	73	100.0	1.4	77.9	20.7	-	-	-	-
10000 TO 29999 POUNDS	76	100.0	8.7	52.2	39.1	-	-	-	-
30000 TO 59999 POUNDS	87	100.0	-	47.8	52.2	-	-	-	-
60000 TO 89999 POUNDS	-	100.0	-	-	-	-	-	-	-
90000 POUNDS AND OVER	-	100.0	-	-	-	-	-	-	-
200 TO 299 MILES	115	100.0	11.4	75.2	12.2	-	-	1.2	-
UNDER 1000 POUNDS	20	100.0	3.0	89.4	.4	-	-	7.0	.2
1000 TO 9999 POUNDS	50	100.0	-	97.8	2.2	-	-	-	-
10000 TO 29999 POUNDS	33	100.0	36.2	57.6	6.2	-	-	-	-
30000 TO 59999 POUNDS	11	100.0	3.2	-	96.8	-	-	-	-
60000 TO 89999 POUNDS	-	100.0	-	-	-	-	-	-	-
90000 POUNDS AND OVER	-	100.0	-	-	-	-	-	-	-
300 TO 499 MILES	207	100.0	27.4	57.6	13.6	.1	-	1.3	.1
UNDER 1000 POUNDS	35	100.0	4.6	86.1	.7	.5	-	7.8	.3
1000 TO 9999 POUNDS	69	100.0	7.3	87.4	5.3	-	-	-	-
10000 TO 29999 POUNDS	67	100.0	54.0	41.9	4.1	-	-	-	-
30000 TO 59999 POUNDS	34	100.0	38.4	-	61.6	-	-	-	-
60000 TO 89999 POUNDS	-	100.0	-	-	-	-	-	-	-
90000 POUNDS AND OVER	-	100.0	-	-	-	-	-	-	-
500 TO 999 MILES	485	100.0	29.2	56.4	8.6	.1	3.0	2.1	.6
UNDER 1000 POUNDS	77	100.0	5.3	84.3	1.0	.6	-	8.7	.1
1000 TO 9999 POUNDS	127	100.0	9.2	80.3	10.2	-	-	.1	.2
10000 TO 29999 POUNDS	143	100.0	27.3	55.5	7.1	-	10.1	-	-
30000 TO 59999 POUNDS	132	100.0	65.2	16.7	13.5	-	-	2.6	1.9
60000 TO 89999 POUNDS	4	100.0	-	100.0	-	-	-	-	-
90000 POUNDS AND OVER	-	100.0	-	-	-	-	-	-	-
1000 TO 1499 MILES	126	100.0	31.3	61.1	5.6	.5	-	1.4	.2
UNDER 1000 POUNDS	31	100.0	13.4	77.5	1.2	2.0	-	5.5	.3
1000 TO 9999 POUNDS	43	100.0	20.6	77.3	1.8	-	-	-	.3
10000 TO 29999 POUNDS	45	100.0	57.9	29.1	13.0	-	-	-	-
30000 TO 59999 POUNDS	6	100.0	-	100.0	-	-	-	-	-
60000 TO 89999 POUNDS	-	100.0	-	-	-	-	-	-	-
90000 POUNDS AND OVER	-	100.0	-	-	-	-	-	-	-
1500 MILES OR OVER	219	100.0	60.3	36.7	1.3	.5	-	.8	.3
UNDER 1000 POUNDS	30	100.0	16.1	73.9	2.9	.9	.3	4.4	1.5
1000 TO 9999 POUNDS	52	100.0	43.0	50.3	3.9	1.6	-	.9	.4
10000 TO 29999 POUNDS	62	100.0	73.8	26.2	-	-	-	-	-
30000 TO 59999 POUNDS	52	100.0	93.0	7.0	-	-	-	-	-
60000 TO 89999 POUNDS	22	100.0	47.1	52.9	-	-	-	-	-
90000 POUNDS AND OVER	-	100.0	-	-	-	-	-	-	-
TON-MILES OF SHIPMENTS	(millions of ton-miles)								
U.S. TOTAL	1 120	100.0	41.1	49.1	6.5	.4	1.1	1.4	.4
UNDER 100 MILES	10	100.0	1.1	52.9	44.7	.1	.2	.9	-
UNDER 1000 POUNDS	1	100.0	.4	63.2	29.9	.7	.2	5.6	-
1000 TO 9999 POUNDS	3	100.0	-	78.5	20.8	-	.4	.2	-
10000 TO 29999 POUNDS	4	100.0	-	40.8	59.2	-	-	-	-
30000 TO 59999 POUNDS	1	100.0	-	9.6	90.4	-	-	-	-
60000 TO 89999 POUNDS	-	100.0	61.8	38.2	-	-	-	-	-
90000 POUNDS AND OVER	-	100.0	-	-	-	-	-	-	-
100 TO 199 MILES	40	100.0	2.4	63.1	33.9	.2	-	.5	-
UNDER 1000 POUNDS	3	100.0	.2	85.9	6.2	1.8	-	5.9	-
1000 TO 9999 POUNDS	11	100.0	1.1	78.8	20.1	-	-	-	-
10000 TO 29999 POUNDS	11	100.0	7.4	55.3	37.3	-	-	-	-
30000 TO 59999 POUNDS	14	100.0	-	51.7	48.3	-	-	-	-
60000 TO 89999 POUNDS	-	100.0	-	-	-	-	-	-	-
90000 POUNDS AND OVER	-	100.0	-	-	-	-	-	-	-

See footnotes at end of table 4.

TABLE 4. TCC GROUP 394—Percent Distribution of Distance Shipped and Weight of Shipment, by Means of Transport: 1972—Continued

Distance shipped and weight of shipment[2] [3]	Number	Percent distribution by means of transport							
		All means of transport	Rail	Motor carrier	Private truck	Air	Water	Other	Unknown
TON-MILES OF SHIPMENTS	(millions of ton-miles)								
200 TO 299 MILES........	28	100.0	12.2	74.2	12.4	-	-	1.2	-
UNDER 1000 POUNDS.....	5	100.0	3.3	89.1	.5	-	-	6.9	.2
1000 TO 9999 POUNDS...	12	100.0	-	97.7	2.3	-	-	-	-
10000 TO 29999 POUNDS.	8	100.0	38.4	55.6	6.0	-	-	-	-
30000 TO 59999 POUNDS.	2	100.0	3.3	-	96.7	-	-	-	-
60000 TO 89999 POUNDS.	-	100.0	-	-	-	-	-	-	-
90000 POUNDS AND OVER.	-	100.0	-	-	-	-	-	-	-
300 TO 499 MILES........	86	100.0	28.4	56.6	13.6	.1	-	1.3	.1
UNDER 1000 POUNDS.....	14	100.0	5.1	85.7	.7	.4	-	7.8	.3
1000 TO 9999 POUNDS...	28	100.0	7.9	87.3	4.8	-	-	-	-
10000 TO 29999 POUNDS.	27	100.0	54.3	41.4	4.3	-	-	-	-
30000 TO 59999 POUNDS.	15	100.0	41.8	-	58.2	-	-	-	-
60000 TO 89999 POUNDS.	-	100.0	-	-	-	-	-	-	-
90000 POUNDS AND OVER.	-	100.0	-	-	-	-	-	-	-
500 TO 999 MILES........	340	100.0	28.8	56.9	7.6	.1	3.4	2.6	.6
UNDER 1000 POUNDS.....	57	100.0	5.4	83.5	1.0	.7	-	9.3	.1
1000 TO 9999 POUNDS...	88	100.0	9.4	81.1	9.1	-	-	.1	.2
10000 TO 29999 POUNDS.	104	100.0	27.3	54.0	7.5	-	11.2	-	-
30000 TO 59999 POUNDS.	87	100.0	66.8	16.9	10.7	-	-	3.7	1.9
60000 TO 89999 POUNDS.	2	100.0	-	100.0	-	-	-	-	-
90000 POUNDS AND OVER.	-	100.0	-	-	-	-	-	-	-
1000 TO 1499 MILES......	149	100.0	32.5	60.1	5.4	.5	-	1.3	.2
UNDER 1000 POUNDS.....	37	100.0	14.3	77.2	1.1	1.9	-	5.2	.3
1000 TO 9999 POUNDS...	51	100.0	21.2	76.6	1.8	-	-	-	.3
10000 TO 29999 POUNDS.	54	100.0	59.9	27.6	12.5	-	-	-	-
30000 TO 59999 POUNDS.	6	100.0	-	100.0	-	-	-	-	-
60000 TO 89999 POUNDS.	-	100.0	-	-	-	-	-	-	-
90000 POUNDS AND OVER.	-	100.0	-	-	-	-	-	-	-
1500 MILES OR OVER......	463	100.0	61.4	35.5	1.1	.6	-	.8	.4
UNDER 1000 POUNDS.....	61	100.0	16.1	74.1	2.8	.8	.4	4.2	1.6
1000 TO 9999 POUNDS...	107	100.0	40.7	51.8	3.3	2.3	-	1.1	.9
10000 TO 29999 POUNDS.	139	100.0	75.9	24.1	-	-	-	-	-
30000 TO 59999 POUNDS.	114	100.0	93.0	7.0	-	-	-	-	-
60000 TO 89999 POUNDS.	41	100.0	46.8	53.2	-	-	-	-	-
90000 POUNDS AND OVER.	-	100.0	-	-	-	-	-	-	-

Note: Detail may not add to total due to rounding. The introductory table shows the estimates of sampling variability for tons; sampling variability for ton-miles has not been estimated. See the map in the Introduction for the States comprising the geographic divisions of the United States.

Shipments excluded from the survey are those moving by pipeline (primarily petroleum products from refineries), parcel post shipments, and commodities moved by own power (motorized vehicles, aircraft, etc.) or towed (prefabricated buildings, etc.). Local shipments (commodities shipped less than 25 miles from the plant) and shipments within the same city are also excluded. Shipments to Alaska and Hawaii from the 48 conterminous States and the District of Columbia are included; however, no data were obtained for shipments originating in Alaska and Hawaii.

- Represents zero or rounds to zero.   (D) Withheld to avoid disclosing figures for individual companies.

[1]Production of this commodity is concentrated in the geographic divisions shown; figures and distributions for geographic divisions not shown are included in the total.

[2]Distances of shipments to foreign destinations are calculated only to the U.S. port of exit.

[3]Includes only shipments represented by bills of lading and invoices. Summary records which did not show individual weights of shipments are not included.

TCC 399. Miscellaneous Manufactured Products

Comparisons of Tons and Ton-Miles of Shipments for
Geographic Divisions of Origin and for Sampling Variability: 1972 and 1967

Geographic division of origin	Estimates				Relative sampling variability in tons (percent)	
	1972		1967		1972	1967
	Tons (thousands)	Ton-miles (millions)	Tons (thousands)	Ton-miles (millions)		
U.S. total	1,768	1,146	1,026	595	18.9	(*)
New England	152	145	(*)	(*)	24.9	(*)
Middle Atlantic	419	290	(*)	(*)	12.2	(*)
East North Central	642	285	(*)	(*)	23.8	(*)
West North Central	402	347	(*)	(*)	69.1	(*)
South Atlantic	63	36	(*)	(*)	48.3	(*)
East South Central	15	6	(*)	(*)	58.5	(*)
West South Central	42	14	(*)	(*)	46.5	(*)
Mountain	—	—	(*)	(*)	58.2	(*)
Pacific	29	19	(*)	(*)	40.4	(*)

Note: One general criterion for publication of data in this series provided for a maximum relative sampling variability of 50 percent of the total tons for any origin division. In other words, data would not be published if 1 standard error exceeded 50 percent of the estimate with which it was associated; see "Reliability of Data", page VIII. However, for this commodity group the absolute standard errors are generally low and division data are published even though some of the measured relative errors exceed 50 percent.

— Represents or rounds to zero.   (D) Withheld to avoid disclosing figures for individual companies.   *Data not published.

TABLE 1. TCC GROUP 399—Percent Distribution of Geographic Division of Origin and Distance Shipped, by Means of Transport: 1972

Geographic division of origin[1] and distance shipped[2]	Number	Percent distribution by means of transport							
		All means of transport	Rail	Motor carrier	Private truck	Air	Water	Other	Unknown
TONS OF SHIPMENTS	(thousands of tons)								
U.S. TOTAL	1 768	100.0	24.9	43.5	24.3	.3	.1	5.5	1.6
NEW ENGLAND	152	100.0	25.2	59.4	3.4	.8	-	7.9	3.3
UNDER 100 MILES	9	100.0	-	48.8	39.9	-	-	5.6	5.8
100 TO 199 MILES	29	100.0	-	83.0	.1	-	-	16.6	.2
200 TO 299 MILES	6	100.0	.2	86.6	.4	-	-	12.8	-
300 TO 499 MILES	7	100.0	-	93.9	.2	.2	-	5.6	-
500 TO 999 MILES	38	100.0	25.5	54.0	-	.4	-	8.5	11.5
1000 TO 1499 MILES	32	100.0	29.5	59.9	4.0	2.5	-	4.1	.1
1500 MILES OR OVER	28	100.0	65.8	30.6	-	.8	-	2.7	-
MIDDLE ATLANTIC	419	100.0	15.3	68.6	11.2	.3	.2	3.7	.7
UNDER 100 MILES	58	100.0	-	75.7	17.5	-	.4	5.9	.6
100 TO 199 MILES	61	100.0	9.0	68.1	17.9	-	-	4.9	-
200 TO 299 MILES	64	100.0	.1	90.9	6.4	-	-	1.4	1.3
300 TO 499 MILES	45	100.0	4.9	75.6	13.8	.3	-	4.4	.9
500 TO 999 MILES	89	100.0	13.4	77.0	4.7	.5	-	4.3	-
1000 TO 1499 MILES	42	100.0	7.0	62.4	21.4	.2	1.8	4.4	2.8
1500 MILES OR OVER	56	100.0	72.6	22.2	3.7	.7	-	.8	-
EAST NORTH CENTRAL	642	100.0	17.4	46.2	26.2	.1	.1	9.3	.7
UNDER 100 MILES	83	100.0	-	40.2	56.6	-	-	2.1	1.1
100 TO 199 MILES	71	100.0	11.8	45.2	40.7	-	-	2.2	.1
200 TO 299 MILES	140	100.0	41.6	40.3	15.4	-	-	2.5	.1
300 TO 499 MILES	124	100.0	1.2	51.2	28.8	.3	-	18.0	.5
500 TO 999 MILES	190	100.0	15.5	50.4	17.4	.1	.3	14.9	1.4
1000 TO 1499 MILES	8	100.0	14.7	42.1	18.9	.6	-	23.7	-
1500 MILES OR OVER	25	100.0	50.3	45.8	.4	.4	-	1.4	1.7
WEST NORTH CENTRAL	402	100.0	47.8	5.9	44.2	.2	-	1.6	.4
UNDER 100 MILES	11	100.0	-	2.3	81.5	-	-	6.2	10.0
100 TO 199 MILES	26	100.0	-	4.8	93.9	-	-	1.2	.1
200 TO 299 MILES	11	100.0	1.0	33.5	55.7	.1	-	9.7	-
300 TO 499 MILES	29	100.0	.2	26.3	69.6	.2	-	3.7	-
500 TO 999 MILES	120	100.0	46.2	5.1	46.6	.2	-	1.8	-
1000 TO 1499 MILES	161	100.0	77.7	1.7	20.0	.2	-	.5	-
1500 MILES OR OVER	41	100.0	27.1	3.9	67.6	-	-	.9	.4
SOUTH ATLANTIC	63	100.0	52.5	33.6	11.2	.2	-	1.1	1.4
UNDER 100 MILES	9	100.0	.2	57.9	41.0	.1	-	.9	-
100 TO 199 MILES	5	100.0	-	60.3	37.8	-	-	1.9	-
200 TO 299 MILES	3	100.0	-	72.2	26.1	.5	-	1.2	-
300 TO 499 MILES	10	100.0	56.7	41.1	.1	.5	-	1.1	.5
500 TO 999 MILES	30	100.0	83.1	13.5	-	.2	-	.5	2.6
1000 TO 1499 MILES	1	100.0	69.7	28.7	-	.6	-	1.0	-
1500 MILES OR OVER	1	100.0	30.4	56.9	-	.1	-	12.7	-
EAST SOUTH CENTRAL	15	100.0	-	43.1	33.9	.1	-	9.0	13.8
UNDER 100 MILES	-	100.0	-	3.8	62.5	-	-	2.5	31.3
100 TO 199 MILES	3	100.0	-	24.2	31.2	-	-	3.8	40.8
200 TO 299 MILES	1	100.0	-	40.4	57.8	-	-	1.7	-
300 TO 499 MILES	6	100.0	-	57.1	35.0	.3	-	7.4	.2
500 TO 999 MILES	2	100.0	-	55.8	27.2	.1	-	2.4	14.5
1000 TO 1499 MILES	-	100.0	-	69.3	14.3	-	-	16.4	-
1500 MILES OR OVER	-	100.0	-	16.7	-	-	-	83.3	-
WEST SOUTH CENTRAL	42	100.0	-	63.2	16.2	.3	.1	.1	20.1
UNDER 100 MILES	14	100.0	-	53.1	1.9	-	.3	-	44.6
100 TO 199 MILES	4	100.0	-	68.3	31.7	-	-	-	-
200 TO 299 MILES	5	100.0	-	85.6	13.8	-	-	.6	-
300 TO 499 MILES	4	100.0	-	58.4	21.5	-	-	-	20.1
500 TO 999 MILES	8	100.0	-	72.8	16.4	.2	-	.1	10.6
1000 TO 1499 MILES	3	100.0	-	44.1	53.1	2.7	-	-	-
1500 MILES OR OVER	-	100.0	-	99.3	-	-	-	.7	-
MOUNTAIN	-	100.0	-	33.4	-	14.8	-	-	51.8
UNDER 100 MILES	-	100.0	-	100.0	-	-	-	-	-
100 TO 199 MILES	-	100.0	-	100.0	-	-	-	-	-
200 TO 299 MILES	-	100.0	-	-	-	-	-	-	-
300 TO 499 MILES	-	100.0	-	-	-	-	-	-	-
500 TO 999 MILES	-	100.0	-	-	-	-	-	-	-
1000 TO 1499 MILES	-	100.0	-	-	-	22.3	-	-	77.7
1500 MILES OR OVER	-	100.0	-	100.0	-	-	-	-	-
PACIFIC	29	100.0	-	50.5	38.1	1.6	-	2.0	7.7
UNDER 100 MILES	10	100.0	-	10.9	82.7	-	-	3.6	2.9
100 TO 199 MILES	4	100.0	-	20.6	30.9	-	-	.2	48.2
200 TO 299 MILES	1	100.0	-	78.4	13.5	7.5	-	.6	-
300 TO 499 MILES	2	100.0	-	85.0	9.5	.4	.4	4.7	.1
500 TO 999 MILES	1	100.0	-	58.3	37.5	1.0	-	1.2	2.0
1000 TO 1499 MILES	2	100.0	-	98.5	-	.9	-	.5	-
1500 MILES OR OVER	6	100.0	-	94.9	.2	4.4	-	.5	-

See footnotes at end of table 4.

TABLE 1. TCC GROUP 399—Percent Distribution of Geographic Division of Origin and Distance Shipped, by Means of Transport: 1972—Continued

Geographic division of origin[1] and distance shipped[2]	Number	Percent distribution by means of transport							
		All means of transport	Rail	Motor carrier	Private truck	Air	Water	Other	Unknown
TON-MILES OF SHIPMENTS	(millions of ton-miles)								
U.S. TOTAL............	1 146	100.0	40.2	34.8	19.0	.5	.1	4.5	.9
NEW ENGLAND.............	145	100.0	46.2	45.0	1.1	1.3	-	4.4	2.0
UNDER 100 MILES........	-	100.0	-	60.2	33.9	-	-	4.1	1.8
100 TO 199 MILES......	3	100.0	-	82.6	.1	-	-	17.0	.2
200 TO 299 MILES......	1	100.0	.2	87.3	.4	-	-	12.1	-
300 TO 499 MILES......	2	100.0	-	94.1	.2	.2	-	5.5	-
500 TO 999 MILES......	27	100.0	25.6	55.8	-	.5	-	8.0	10.2
1000 TO 1499 MILES....	39	100.0	31.2	58.2	3.6	2.9	-	4.0	.1
1500 MILES OR OVER....	69	100.0	68.8	28.1	-	.7	-	2.3	-
MIDDLE ATLANTIC.........	290	100.0	37.6	50.3	7.8	.5	.4	2.7	.7
UNDER 100 MILES........	3	100.0	-	75.4	19.3	-	.1	4.7	.5
100 TO 199 MILES......	9	100.0	10.6	67.4	16.9	-	-	5.1	-
200 TO 299 MILES......	16	100.0	.1	91.7	5.5	-	-	1.4	1.2
300 TO 499 MILES......	17	100.0	5.8	73.7	14.5	.3	-	4.6	1.0
500 TO 999 MILES......	65	100.0	12.4	78.5	4.1	.5	-	4.4	-
1000 TO 1499 MILES....	50	100.0	7.7	62.5	20.1	.2	2.1	4.4	3.2
1500 MILES OR OVER....	127	100.0	74.6	20.5	3.3	.7	-	.8	-
EAST NORTH CENTRAL......	285	100.0	22.5	47.2	17.9	.2	.1	11.1	1.0
UNDER 100 MILES........	4	100.0	-	41.6	55.5	-	-	2.0	.8
100 TO 199 MILES......	10	100.0	8.5	49.1	40.5	-	-	1.8	.1
200 TO 299 MILES......	35	100.0	44.9	38.1	14.2	-	-	2.6	.1
300 TO 499 MILES......	46	100.0	1.2	51.1	28.1	.3	-	18.7	.6
500 TO 999 MILES......	131	100.0	17.0	49.2	18.1	.1	.2	14.2	1.2
1000 TO 1499 MILES....	10	100.0	15.1	44.9	16.8	.6	-	22.5	-
1500 MILES OR OVER....	45	100.0	50.5	45.1	.4	.6	-	1.7	1.7
WEST NORTH CENTRAL......	347	100.0	55.7	4.3	38.7	.2	-	1.1	.1
UNDER 100 MILES........	-	100.0	-	2.1	90.1	-	-	2.1	5.7
100 TO 199 MILES......	3	100.0	-	5.8	92.6	-	-	1.5	.1
200 TO 299 MILES......	3	100.0	.9	28.4	61.1	.1	-	9.5	-
300 TO 499 MILES......	11	100.0	.2	28.3	67.3	.2	-	4.0	-
500 TO 999 MILES....	85	100.0	47.9	5.5	44.5	.3	-	1.7	-
1000 TO 1499 MILES....	177	100.0	76.0	1.8	21.5	.2	-	.5	-
1500 MILES OR OVER....	65	100.0	26.2	4.0	68.5	-	-	.9	.4
SOUTH ATLANTIC..........	36	100.0	72.2	22.3	1.9	.2	-	1.7	1.7
UNDER 100 MILES........	-	100.0	.3	64.8	33.9	.1	-	.9	-
100 TO 199 MILES......	-	100.0	-	66.4	31.1	-	-	2.5	-
200 TO 299 MILES......	-	100.0	-	70.8	27.5	.4	-	1.3	-
300 TO 499 MILES......	4	100.0	56.8	40.9	.1	.5	-	1.1	.6
500 TO 999 MILES....	25	100.0	86.2	10.9	-	.2	-	.4	2.3
1000 TO 1499 MILES....	1	100.0	70.2	27.9	-	.6	-	1.2	-
1500 MILES OR OVER....	3	100.0	33.7	52.6	-	.1	-	13.7	-
EAST SOUTH CENTRAL......	6	100.0	-	44.5	24.8	.2	-	22.8	7.8
UNDER 100 MILES........	-	100.0	-	4.9	73.5	-	-	2.3	19.3
100 TO 199 MILES......	-	100.0	-	23.8	30.0	-	-	3.5	42.7
200 TO 299 MILES......	-	100.0	-	40.5	57.7	-	-	1.8	-
300 TO 499 MILES......	2	100.0	-	58.1	34.5	.4	-	6.8	.3
500 TO 999 MILES....	1	100.0	-	58.1	25.4	.1	-	2.4	14.1
1000 TO 1499 MILES....	-	100.0	-	70.3	13.6	-	-	16.1	-
1500 MILES OR OVER....	1	100.0	-	17.2	-	-	-	82.8	-
WEST SOUTH CENTRAL......	14	100.0	-	64.7	26.6	.8	-	.1	7.7
UNDER 100 MILES........	-	100.0	-	80.3	1.9	-	.4	-	17.4
100 TO 199 MILES......	-	100.0	-	72.9	27.1	-	-	-	-
200 TO 299 MILES......	1	100.0	-	84.8	14.5	-	-	.8	-
300 TO 499 MILES......	1	100.0	-	58.7	18.3	-	-	-	23.0
500 TO 999 MILES....	5	100.0	-	71.4	18.3	.2	-	-	10.0
1000 TO 1499 MILES....	4	100.0	-	42.7	54.5	2.7	-	-	-
1500 MILES OR OVER....	-	100.0	-	99.3	-	-	-	.7	-
MOUNTAIN................	-	100.0	-	7.2	-	18.3	-	-	74.4
UNDER 100 MILES........	-	100.0	-	100.0	-	-	-	-	-
100 TO 199 MILES......	-	100.0	-	100.0	-	-	-	-	-
200 TO 299 MILES......	-	100.0	-	-	-	-	-	-	-
300 TO 499 MILES......	-	100.0	-	-	-	-	-	-	-
500 TO 999 MILES....	-	100.0	-	-	-	-	-	-	-
1000 TO 1499 MILES....	-	100.0	-	-	-	19.8	-	-	80.2
1500 MILES OR OVER....	-	100.0	-	100.0	-	-	-	-	-
PACIFIC.................	19	100.0	-	88.4	5.2	3.5	-	.9	2.0
UNDER 100 MILES........	-	100.0	-	17.2	76.5	-	-	3.9	2.4
100 TO 199 MILES......	-	100.0	-	19.8	25.3	-	-	.2	54.7
200 TO 299 MILES......	-	100.0	-	81.4	11.6	6.4	-	.5	-
300 TO 499 MILES......	-	100.0	-	85.3	9.2	.3	.4	4.7	.1
500 TO 999 MILES....	1	100.0	-	63.1	31.6	1.2	-	1.5	2.6
1000 TO 1499 MILES....	2	100.0	-	98.5	-	1.0	-	.5	-
1500 MILES OR OVER....	12	100.0	-	94.6	.1	4.7	-	.6	-

See footnotes at end of table 4.

TABLE 2. TCC GROUP 399—Percent Distribution of Geographic Division of Origin and Means of Transport, by Geographic Division of Destination: 1972

Geographic division of origin[1] and means of transport	Number	Percent distribution by division of destination									
		U.S. total	New England	Middle Atlantic	East North Central	West North Central	South Atlantic	East South Central	West South Central	Mountain	Pacific
TONS OF SHIPMENTS	(thousands of tons)										
U.S. TOTAL..............	1 768	100.0	5.2	13.5	19.5	10.0	17.1	6.1	14.0	5.0	9.5
RAIL................	439	100.0	4.0	5.5	10.6	6.0	28.1	.8	22.0	3.4	19.6
MOTOR CARRIER........	768	100.0	7.0	21.5	24.4	7.3	15.3	8.5	8.7	3.6	3.7
PRIVATE TRUCK........	429	100.0	2.0	7.7	20.3	18.4	9.1	5.3	16.3	10.1	10.8
AIR.................	4	100.0	4.2	12.7	11.0	7.1	13.6	7.7	22.1	5.5	16.0
WATER...............	1	100.0	-	46.2	-	-	-	-	53.0	-	.8
OTHER...............	96	100.0	11.0	15.1	17.8	15.0	18.1	14.4	5.1	.9	2.6
UNKNOWN.............	27	100.0	5.2	4.3	20.8	4.6	12.8	6.7	30.4	4.7	10.4
NEW ENGLAND.............	152	100.0	7.6	21.4	16.9	10.4	13.1	4.3	9.9	1.7	14.7
RAIL................	38	100.0	-	-	21.9	11.5	3.9	-	15.3	5.5	41.8
MOTOR CARRIER........	90	100.0	7.2	29.6	11.5	10.3	19.3	6.7	8.6	.3	6.5
PRIVATE TRUCK........	5	100.0	74.0	.9	-	24.9	.1	-	-	.1	-
AIR.................	1	100.0	-	1.7	7.1	6.2	5.7	-	66.0	3.2	10.2
WATER...............	-	100.0	-	-	-	-	-	-	-	-	-
OTHER...............	11	100.0	5.2	47.8	21.8	5.5	6.3	4.6	4.7	1.5	2.6
UNKNOWN.............	5	100.0	11.7	.4	84.8	.3	2.8	-	-	-	-
MIDDLE ATLANTIC.........	419	100.0	10.9	28.6	18.5	2.8	15.2	3.8	6.1	2.2	11.7
RAIL................	64	100.0	.1	8.5	19.4	.7	1.9	.8	3.0	2.7	62.8
MOTOR CARRIER........	287	100.0	13.4	31.3	19.4	3.3	17.5	4.3	6.2	2.2	2.5
PRIVATE TRUCK........	47	100.0	8.6	40.4	13.7	.9	20.7	3.6	7.8	1.9	2.5
AIR.................	1	100.0	.2	1.4	16.3	10.3	11.0	22.4	3.7	2.7	32.0
WATER...............	-	100.0	-	22.9	-	-	-	-	77.1	-	-
OTHER...............	15	100.0	17.2	27.0	17.4	7.4	14.4	7.9	5.9	.6	2.3
UNKNOWN.............	2	100.0	14.0	36.2	1.6	.2	4.8	-	28.9	14.0	.2
EAST NORTH CENTRAL......	642	100.0	3.5	11.0	32.9	10.3	18.8	11.5	6.4	2.1	3.4
RAIL................	111	100.0	6.8	8.3	10.3	2.2	51.2	.9	8.7	-	11.5
MOTOR CARRIER........	296	100.0	2.4	14.9	37.3	10.6	9.1	14.0	4.6	4.4	2.8
PRIVATE TRUCK........	168	100.0	.5	7.5	46.2	12.3	12.4	11.5	9.3	.2	.1
AIR.................	-	100.0	15.2	13.6	8.8	7.7	36.3	1.4	5.3	.1	11.6
WATER...............	-	100.0	-	100.0	-	-	-	-	-	-	-
OTHER...............	60	100.0	11.8	6.8	16.4	18.9	22.1	19.0	4.1	.4	.5
UNKNOWN.............	4	100.0	1.5	3.8	27.9	.5	51.0	5.3	1.0	-	9.0
WEST NORTH CENTRAL......	402	100.0	2.1	2.4	5.1	15.8	15.5	.6	31.2	14.0	13.2
RAIL................	192	100.0	3.6	3.8	6.6	1.0	31.1	-	39.6	5.7	8.6
MOTOR CARRIER........	23	100.0	5.2	7.0	23.1	14.6	6.2	8.6	9.3	18.8	7.2
PRIVATE TRUCK........	177	100.0	-	-	.2	31.4	-	-	25.9	23.0	19.4
AIR.................	-	100.0	7.3	50.4	6.9	6.3	9.2	-	11.2	5.0	3.7
WATER...............	-	100.0	-	-	-	-	-	-	-	-	-
OTHER...............	6	100.0	2.1	6.2	30.7	19.7	14.4	4.3	14.4	2.7	5.6
UNKNOWN.............	1	100.0	4.2	-	.1	81.3	-	-	3.7	-	10.7
SOUTH ATLANTIC..........	63	100.0	6.1	4.5	3.2	27.3	44.8	5.3	6.3	.6	1.8
RAIL................	33	100.0	9.3	6.0	4.6	51.5	12.3	6.1	8.9	-	1.4
MOTOR CARRIER........	21	100.0	1.8	3.5	2.1	.2	81.4	2.2	4.8	1.7	2.3
PRIVATE TRUCK........	7	100.0	-	-	.1	-	88.2	11.7	-	-	-
AIR.................	-	100.0	6.0	17.4	36.4	6.0	23.4	1.3	9.4	-	-
WATER...............	-	100.0	-	-	-	-	-	-	-	-	-
OTHER...............	-	100.0	10.4	13.5	2.3	8.1	29.3	5.2	2.3	2.3	26.6
UNKNOWN.............	-	100.0	37.8	-	-	8.5	53.7	-	-	-	-
EAST SOUTH CENTRAL......	15	100.0	.3	3.9	25.1	4.6	28.5	26.0	5.8	1.5	4.2
RAIL................	-	100.0	-	-	-	-	-	-	-	-	-
MOTOR CARRIER........	6	100.0	.6	7.9	28.2	2.6	30.3	20.5	7.2	.9	1.9
PRIVATE TRUCK........	5	100.0	-	.8	34.7	9.9	35.0	11.7	7.7	.3	-
AIR.................	-	100.0	-	6.7	8.0	-	85.4	-	-	-	-
WATER...............	-	100.0	-	-	-	-	-	-	-	-	-
OTHER...............	1	100.0	.6	2.8	3.9	1.2	11.9	29.9	.7	11.1	37.7
UNKNOWN.............	2	100.0	-	-	6.2	-	17.5	76.3	-	-	-
WEST SOUTH CENTRAL......	42	100.0	-	3.7	3.4	1.9	3.8	2.2	79.4	5.0	.6
RAIL................	-	100.0	-	-	-	-	-	-	-	-	-
MOTOR CARRIER........	26	100.0	-	1.5	3.0	2.5	4.2	2.6	81.3	4.4	.6
PRIVATE TRUCK........	6	100.0	-	17.2	9.3	2.3	7.0	3.3	60.9	-	-
AIR.................	-	100.0	-	.4	-	-	5.8	10.2	-	3.5	80.2
WATER...............	-	100.0	-	-	-	-	-	-	100.0	-	-
OTHER...............	-	100.0	-	1.7	-	-	-	-	92.3	-	6.0
UNKNOWN.............	8	100.0	-	-	-	-	-	-	89.0	11.0	-
MOUNTAIN................	-	100.0	2.1	-	14.8	-	51.8	-	-	22.8	8.5
RAIL................	-	100.0	-	-	-	-	-	-	-	-	-
MOTOR CARRIER........	-	100.0	6.2	-	-	-	-	-	-	68.2	25.6
PRIVATE TRUCK........	-	100.0	-	-	-	-	-	-	-	-	-
AIR.................	-	100.0	-	-	100.0	-	-	-	-	-	-
WATER...............	-	100.0	-	-	-	-	-	-	-	-	-
OTHER...............	-	100.0	-	-	-	-	-	-	-	-	-
UNKNOWN.............	-	100.0	-	-	-	-	100.0	-	-	-	-
PACIFIC.................	29	100.0	.2	3.9	7.6	3.8	4.3	2.2	7.1	10.2	60.8
RAIL................	-	100.0	100.0	-	-	-	-	-	-	-	-
MOTOR CARRIER........	15	100.0	.2	7.1	14.5	7.2	8.3	3.8	13.8	12.6	32.4
PRIVATE TRUCK........	11	100.0	-	-	-	.1	-	-	-	8.5	91.4
AIR.................	-	100.0	2.5	19.3	11.7	5.1	4.1	15.5	2.5	30.3	9.0
WATER...............	-	100.0	-	-	-	-	-	-	-	-	100.0
OTHER...............	-	100.0	.9	.9	1.8	.1	1.9	.1	1.8	9.1	83.4
UNKNOWN.............	2	100.0	-	-	-	-	-	-	-	-	100.0

See footnotes at end of table 4.

TABLE 2. TCC GROUP 399—Percent Distribution of Geographic Division of Origin and Means of Transport, by Geographic Division of Destination: 1972—Continued

Geographic division of origin[1] and means of transport	Number	Percent distribution by division of destination									
		U.S. total	New England	Middle Atlantic	East North Central	West North Central	South Atlantic	East South Central	West South Central	Mountain	Pacific
TON-MILES OF SHIPMENTS	(millions of ton-miles)										
U.S. TOTAL...............	1 146	100.0	3.4	6.3	9.7	9.2	15.1	4.1	17.9	8.0	26.5
RAIL..................	460	100.0	3.1	3.2	5.0	4.9	17.3	.4	22.5	3.3	40.3
MOTOR CARRIER.........	398	100.0	4.4	11.3	16.1	9.8	16.5	7.5	13.7	7.5	13.3
PRIVATE TRUCK.........	217	100.0	.8	3.5	6.2	15.5	6.9	3.3	17.3	20.1	26.4
AIR...................	5	100.0	3.1	11.4	6.4	5.2	7.5	6.2	25.5	4.2	30.6
WATER.................	1	100.0	-	19.9	-	-	-	-	79.4	-	.7
OTHER.................	52	100.0	9.3	5.8	13.4	18.1	18.2	15.0	9.3	2.3	8.6
UNKNOWN...............	10	100.0	4.3	2.3	27.4	1.5	21.3	3.7	16.4	10.1	13.1
NEW ENGLAND..............	145	100.0	.6	3.2	11.9	11.6	9.7	3.9	15.2	3.3	40.4
RAIL..................	67	100.0	-	-	8.8	6.8	2.1	-	12.9	5.6	63.7
MOTOR CARRIER.........	65	100.0	1.0	5.9	10.5	15.3	18.4	7.9	17.4	.8	22.8
PRIVATE TRUCK.........	1	100.0	11.1	.7	-	87.4	.2	-	-	.5	-
AIR...................	1	100.0	-	.3	3.8	4.4	3.3	-	66.2	4.9	17.1
WATER.................	-	100.0	-	-	-	-	-	-	-	-	-
OTHER.................	6	100.0	.6	13.2	27.2	11.9	8.5	8.0	13.4	5.1	12.3
UNKNOWN...............	2	100.0	.5	.1	94.2	.6	4.5	-	.1	-	-
MIDDLE ATLANTIC..........	290	100.0	3.9	5.5	13.5	3.9	12.7	4.6	11.1	5.2	39.5
RAIL..................	109	100.0	-	.9	7.1	.4	.9	.4	2.3	2.6	85.4
MOTOR CARRIER.........	146	100.0	6.7	8.6	18.5	6.2	19.0	7.4	15.1	6.7	11.8
PRIVATE TRUCK.........	22	100.0	3.7	8.9	12.4	2.0	31.9	3.5	19.2	7.4	10.9
AIR...................	1	100.0	-	.2	7.4	7.1	4.1	12.8	3.7	4.4	60.3
WATER.................	1	100.0	-	.2	-	-	-	-	99.8	-	-
OTHER.................	7	100.0	6.3	4.9	20.4	15.3	11.7	13.2	15.0	1.9	11.2
UNKNOWN...............	2	100.0	8.6	9.0	1.4	.4	1.5	-	53.2	24.9	1.0
EAST NORTH CENTRAL......	285	100.0	5.4	12.4	12.8	12.6	17.0	8.2	12.1	5.5	14.1
RAIL..................	64	100.0	8.8	9.5	2.7	1.5	27.5	.9	12.7	.1	36.2
MOTOR CARRIER.........	134	100.0	3.7	17.4	16.6	12.7	11.7	7.9	7.7	11.1	11.3
PRIVATE TRUCK.........	51	100.0	1.4	8.0	18.0	20.9	12.4	11.7	26.8	.5	.4
AIR...................	-	100.0	11.6	7.5	2.5	4.7	25.3	.7	5.5	.1	42.0
WATER.................	-	100.0	-	100.0	-	-	-	-	-	-	-
OTHER.................	31	100.0	12.9	4.4	9.1	22.6	22.1	18.9	7.0	.9	2.1
UNKNOWN...............	2	100.0	1.5	1.9	6.6	.3	55.8	4.4	1.6	-	27.9
WEST NORTH CENTRAL......	347	100.0	2.6	2.7	2.8	6.6	16.9	.4	29.2	15.0	23.8
RAIL..................	193	100.0	3.7	3.6	3.6	.6	29.1	-	42.1	4.3	12.9
MOTOR CARRIER.........	14	100.0	10.4	11.1	12.2	5.9	9.7	8.0	8.8	15.9	17.9
PRIVATE TRUCK.........	134	100.0	-	-	.1	15.5	-	-	13.4	30.7	40.3
AIR...................	-	100.0	9.6	56.5	2.7	3.7	9.6	-	6.7	5.5	5.5
WATER.................	-	100.0	-	-	-	-	-	-	-	-	-
OTHER.................	3	100.0	4.0	9.4	18.0	6.1	24.5	3.3	15.2	4.4	15.2
UNKNOWN...............	-	100.0	15.7	-	.1	13.6	-	-	9.0	-	61.7
SOUTH ATLANTIC..........	36	100.0	5.7	2.8	2.9	42.8	22.9	3.5	10.8	1.6	7.1
RAIL..................	26	100.0	6.0	2.6	2.8	58.6	11.6	3.4	11.1	-	4.0
MOTOR CARRIER.........	8	100.0	3.7	3.5	3.3	.6	54.5	1.8	12.3	6.8	13.5
PRIVATE TRUCK.........	-	100.0	-	.3	-	.3	65.7	33.9	-	-	-
AIR...................	-	100.0	6.9	12.8	37.3	9.9	12.5	1.2	19.5	-	-
WATER.................	-	100.0	-	-	-	-	-	-	-	-	-
OTHER.................	-	100.0	6.7	5.7	1.5	6.9	5.1	1.4	1.2	3.6	67.9
UNKNOWN...............	-	100.0	28.1	-	-	11.7	60.2	-	-	-	-
EAST SOUTH CENTRAL......	6	100.0	.7	5.0	21.5	4.9	21.2	12.8	9.5	4.8	19.5
RAIL..................	-	100.0	-	-	-	-	-	-	-	-	-
MOTOR CARRIER.........	3	100.0	1.4	9.8	27.8	3.6	22.2	12.0	12.3	2.3	8.5
PRIVATE TRUCK.........	1	100.0	-	1.5	35.3	12.6	28.6	5.3	15.8	.9	-
AIR...................	-	100.0	-	10.5	7.6	-	82.0	-	-	-	-
WATER.................	-	100.0	-	-	-	-	-	-	-	-	-
OTHER.................	1	100.0	.5	1.1	1.2	.8	2.3	9.0	.4	15.4	69.2
UNKNOWN...............	-	100.0	-	-	1.6	-	45.7	52.7	-	-	-
WEST SOUTH CENTRAL......	14	100.0	.2	14.3	9.1	3.6	11.2	4.3	46.0	9.4	1.9
RAIL..................	-	100.0	-	-	-	-	-	-	-	-	-
MOTOR CARRIER.........	9	100.0	.2	6.4	7.8	4.3	12.5	4.7	53.5	8.7	1.8
PRIVATE TRUCK.........	3	100.0	-	38.2	15.3	2.9	11.4	4.5	27.8	-	-
AIR...................	-	100.0	-	.4	-	-	4.8	7.2	-	3.5	84.1
WATER.................	-	100.0	-	-	-	-	-	-	100.0	-	-
OTHER.................	-	100.0	-	5.2	-	-	-	-	69.6	-	25.1
UNKNOWN...............	1	100.0	-	-	-	-	-	-	50.5	49.5	-
MOUNTAIN................	-	100.0	4.6	-	18.3	-	74.4	-	-	1.3	1.3
RAIL..................	-	100.0	-	-	-	-	-	-	-	-	-
MOTOR CARRIER.........	-	100.0	64.0	-	-	-	-	-	-	17.5	18.5
PRIVATE TRUCK.........	-	100.0	-	-	-	-	-	-	-	-	-
AIR...................	-	100.0	-	-	100.0	-	-	-	-	-	-
WATER.................	-	100.0	-	-	-	-	-	-	-	-	-
OTHER.................	-	100.0	-	-	-	-	-	-	-	-	-
UNKNOWN...............	-	100.0	-	-	-	-	100.0	-	-	-	-
PACIFIC.................	19	100.0	.7	14.2	22.1	8.3	14.2	6.1	14.8	6.9	12.6
RAIL..................	-	100.0	100.0	-	-	-	-	-	-	-	-
MOTOR CARRIER.........	17	100.0	.5	14.7	24.4	9.1	15.6	6.1	16.6	4.7	8.4
PRIVATE TRUCK.........	1	100.0	-	-	-	1.9	-	-	-	49.2	48.9
AIR...................	-	100.0	4.6	32.4	14.4	5.3	6.5	19.7	2.4	5.4	9.3
WATER.................	-	100.0	-	-	-	-	-	-	-	-	100.0
OTHER.................	-	100.0	8.5	7.5	11.5	.6	14.1	.9	7.8	12.1	37.1
UNKNOWN...............	-	100.0	-	-	-	-	-	-	-	-	100.0

See footnotes at end of table 4.

TABLE 3. TCC GROUP 399—Percent Distribution of Geographic Division of Destination and Means of Transport, by Geographic Division of Origin: 1972

Geographic division of destination and means of transport	Number	Percent distribution by division of origin[1]									
		U.S. total	New England	Middle Atlantic	East North Central	West North Central	South Atlantic	East South Central	West South Central	Mountain	Pacific
TONS OF SHIPMENTS	(thousands of tons)										
U.S. TOTAL...............	1 768	100.0	8.6	23.7	36.4	22.8	3.6	.9	2.4	-	1.7
RAIL....................	439	100.0	8.7	14.6	25.4	43.8	7.5	-	-	-	-
MOTOR CARRIER...........	768	100.0	11.8	37.5	38.6	3.1	2.8	.9	3.5	-	2.0
PRIVATE TRUCK...........	429	100.0	1.2	11.0	39.2	41.4	1.6	1.2	1.6	.1	2.7
AIR.....................	4	100.0	27.6	24.6	17.3	13.7	3.4	.5	2.4	-	10.5
WATER...................	1	100.0	-	64.4	31.5	-	-	-	3.3	-	.8
OTHER...................	96	100.0	12.4	16.2	61.9	6.7	.7	1.4	-	-	.6
UNKNOWN.................	27	100.0	18.1	10.0	17.2	5.1	3.1	7.7	30.5	-	8.3
NEW ENGLAND.............	92	100.0	12.5	49.5	24.6	9.1	4.2	.1	-	-	.1
RAIL....................	17	100.0	-	.4	42.7	39.6	17.4	-	-	-	-
MOTOR CARRIER...........	53	100.0	12.1	71.6	13.2	2.3	.7	.1	-	-	.1
PRIVATE TRUCK...........	8	100.0	44.2	46.4	9.4	-	-	-	-	-	-
AIR.....................	-	100.0	-	1.3	63.3	24.1	5.0	-	-	-	6.4
WATER...................	-	100.0	-	-	-	-	-	-	-	-	-
OTHER...................	10	100.0	5.8	25.3	66.8	1.3	.7	.1	-	-	.1
UNKNOWN.................	1	100.0	40.9	27.1	5.0	4.2	22.8	-	-	-	-
MIDDLE ATLANTIC.........	239	100.0	13.6	50.1	29.6	4.1	1.2	.3	.7	-	.5
RAIL....................	24	100.0	.1	22.7	38.5	30.4	8.3	-	-	-	-
MOTOR CARRIER...........	165	100.0	16.2	54.5	26.7	1.0	.4	.3	.2	-	.7
PRIVATE TRUCK...........	32	100.0	.1	57.9	38.3	-	-	.1	3.5	-	-
AIR.....................	-	100.0	3.6	2.7	18.5	54.3	4.7	.3	.1	-	15.9
WATER...................	-	100.0	-	31.9	68.1	-	-	-	-	-	-
OTHER...................	14	100.0	39.2	29.0	28.1	2.8	.7	.3	-	-	-
UNKNOWN.................	1	100.0	1.7	83.3	15.1	-	-	-	-	-	-
EAST NORTH CENTRAL......	344	100.0	7.5	22.6	61.2	5.9	.6	1.1	.4	-	.7
RAIL....................	46	100.0	18.0	26.8	24.8	27.2	3.3	-	-	-	-
MOTOR CARRIER...........	187	100.0	5.5	29.8	58.9	2.9	.2	1.0	.4	-	1.2
PRIVATE TRUCK...........	87	100.0	-	7.4	89.4	.4	-	2.1	.7	-	-
AIR.....................	-	100.0	17.7	36.4	13.9	8.6	11.3	.4	-	.6	11.1
WATER...................	-	100.0	-	-	-	-	-	-	-	-	-
OTHER...................	17	100.0	15.2	15.8	57.0	11.6	.1	.3	-	-	.1
UNKNOWN.................	5	100.0	73.8	.8	23.1	-	-	2.3	-	-	-
WEST NORTH CENTRAL......	177	100.0	8.9	6.6	37.3	36.0	9.7	.4	.5	-	.6
RAIL....................	26	100.0	16.7	1.7	9.3	7.5	64.8	-	-	-	-
MOTOR CARRIER...........	55	100.0	16.7	17.1	56.5	6.2	.1	.3	1.2	-	2.0
PRIVATE TRUCK...........	79	100.0	1.6	.5	26.3	70.7	-	.7	.2	-	-
AIR.....................	-	100.0	23.8	35.3	18.5	12.1	2.9	-	-	-	7.4
WATER...................	-	100.0	-	-	-	-	-	-	-	-	-
OTHER...................	14	100.0	4.6	8.0	78.1	8.8	.4	.1	-	-	-
UNKNOWN.................	1	100.0	1.2	.5	1.7	90.9	5.7	-	-	-	-
SOUTH ATLANTIC..........	302	100.0	6.6	21.1	39.9	20.6	9.4	1.5	.5	-	.4
RAIL....................	123	100.0	1.2	1.0	46.1	48.4	3.3	-	-	-	-
MOTOR CARRIER...........	117	100.0	14.8	42.7	22.8	1.2	14.7	1.7	1.0	-	1.1
PRIVATE TRUCK...........	39	100.0	-	24.9	53.3	-	15.9	4.7	1.2	-	-
AIR.....................	-	100.0	11.5	19.9	46.2	9.3	5.9	3.0	1.0	-	3.2
WATER...................	-	100.0	-	-	-	-	-	-	-	-	-
OTHER...................	17	100.0	4.3	12.8	75.4	5.3	1.2	.9	-	-	.1
UNKNOWN.................	3	100.0	4.0	3.8	68.5	-	13.0	10.4	-	.3	-
EAST SOUTH CENTRAL......	107	100.0	6.1	14.9	68.5	2.2	3.1	3.7	.9	-	.6
RAIL....................	3	100.0	-	14.4	28.2	-	57.4	-	-	-	-
MOTOR CARRIER...........	65	100.0	9.2	19.0	63.8	3.1	.7	2.1	1.1	-	.9
PRIVATE TRUCK...........	22	100.0	-	7.4	85.3	-	3.6	2.7	1.0	-	-
AIR.....................	-	100.0	-	71.9	3.2	-	.6	-	3.2	-	21.2
WATER...................	-	100.0	-	-	-	-	-	-	-	-	-
OTHER...................	13	100.0	3.9	8.9	81.9	2.0	.3	3.0	-	-	-
UNKNOWN.................	1	100.0	-	-	13.4	-	-	86.6	-	-	-
WEST SOUTH CENTRAL......	248	100.0	6.1	10.4	16.7	50.6	1.6	.4	13.5	-	.8
RAIL....................	96	100.0	6.0	2.0	10.1	78.9	3.1	-	-	-	-
MOTOR CARRIER...........	66	100.0	11.7	26.6	20.3	3.3	1.5	.7	32.6	-	3.1
PRIVATE TRUCK...........	69	100.0	-	5.2	22.3	65.9	-	.6	5.9	-	-
AIR.....................	-	100.0	82.2	4.2	4.1	6.9	1.5	-	-	-	1.2
WATER...................	-	100.0	-	93.7	-	-	-	-	6.3	-	-
OTHER...................	4	100.0	11.4	18.6	49.5	19.0	.3	.2	.8	-	.2
UNKNOWN.................	8	100.0	-	9.5	.6	.6	-	-	89.3	-	-
MOUNTAIN................	88	100.0	3.0	10.7	15.6	64.2	.4	.3	2.4	-	3.5
RAIL....................	14	100.0	14.3	11.7	.2	73.8	-	-	-	-	-
MOTOR CARRIER...........	27	100.0	1.0	22.5	47.6	16.2	1.3	.2	4.2	-	6.9
PRIVATE TRUCK...........	43	100.0	-	2.1	.7	94.9	-	-	-	-	2.2
AIR.....................	-	100.0	16.1	12.0	.2	12.5	-	-	1.5	-	57.6
WATER...................	-	100.0	-	-	-	-	-	-	-	-	-
OTHER...................	-	100.0	19.7	9.8	26.2	19.2	1.8	17.2	-	-	6.0
UNKNOWN.................	1	100.0	-	29.5	-	-	-	-	70.5	-	-
PACIFIC.................	167	100.0	13.3	29.5	13.2	31.9	.7	.4	.1	-	10.9
RAIL....................	86	100.0	18.6	46.8	14.9	19.2	.5	-	-	-	-
MOTOR CARRIER...........	28	100.0	20.5	24.8	29.0	6.0	1.7	.4	.5	-	17.1
PRIVATE TRUCK...........	46	100.0	-	2.5	.2	74.7	-	-	-	-	22.5
AIR.....................	-	100.0	17.5	49.0	12.5	3.2	-	-	12.0	-	5.9
WATER...................	-	100.0	-	-	-	-	-	-	-	-	100.0
OTHER...................	2	100.0	12.2	13.9	11.7	14.3	7.5	20.7	.1	-	19.7
UNKNOWN.................	2	100.0	-	.1	14.8	5.3	-	-	-	-	79.7

See footnotes at end of table 4.

TABLE 3. **TCC GROUP 399**—Percent Distribution of Geographic Division of Destination and Means of Transport, by Geographic Division of Origin: 1972—Continued

Geographic division of destination and means of transport	Number	Percent distribution by division of origin[1]									
		U.S. total	New England	Middle Atlantic	East North Central	West North Central	South Atlantic	East South Central	West South Central	Mountain	Pacific
TON-MILES OF SHIPMENTS	(millions of ton-miles)										
U.S. TOTAL..............	1 146	100.0	12.7	25.4	24.9	30.3	3.2	.6	1.3	-	1.7
RAIL...................	460	100.0	14.6	23.8	14.0	42.0	5.7	-	-	-	-
MOTOR CARRIER..........	398	100.0	16.4	36.7	33.7	3.7	2.0	.8	2.4	-	4.3
PRIVATE TRUCK..........	217	100.0	.7	10.5	23.5	61.9	.3	.8	1.8	-	.5
AIR....................	5	100.0	34.1	26.6	11.8	10.5	1.5	.2	2.4	.1	12.9
WATER.................	1	100.0	-	79.3	19.8	-	-	-	.2	-	.7
OTHER.................	52	100.0	12.3	15.0	60.9	7.2	1.2	3.0	-	-	.3
UNKNOWN...............	10	100.0	26.9	19.2	25.3	3.7	5.6	4.9	10.7	.1	3.6
NEW ENGLAND............	39	100.0	2.3	28.9	39.8	23.1	5.4	.1	.1	-	.3
RAIL...................	14	100.0	-	.1	39.1	49.9	10.9	-	-	-	-
MOTOR CARRIER..........	17	100.0	3.9	56.0	28.6	8.8	1.7	.2	.1	-	.5
PRIVATE TRUCK..........	1	100.0	10.4	48.8	40.8	-	-	-	-	-	-
AIR....................	-	100.0	-	.3	44.4	32.6	3.5	-	-	-	19.2
WATER.................	-	100.0	-	-	-	-	-	-	-	-	-
OTHER.................	4	100.0	.8	10.2	84.6	3.1	.9	.2	-	-	.3
UNKNOWN...............	-	100.0	3.2	38.4	8.6	13.3	36.5	-	-	-	-
MIDDLE ATLANTIC.........	71	100.0	6.5	22.5	49.3	13.0	1.4	.5	3.0	-	3.8
RAIL...................	14	100.0	-	6.7	41.4	47.3	4.6	-	-	-	-
MOTOR CARRIER..........	45	100.0	8.5	27.8	51.9	3.6	.6	.7	1.4	-	5.6
PRIVATE TRUCK..........	7	100.0	.2	26.5	53.1	-	-	.3	19.9	-	-
AIR....................	-	100.0	1.0	.5	7.8	52.1	1.7	.2	.1	-	36.7
WATER.................	-	100.0	-	.6	99.4	-	-	-	-	-	-
OTHER.................	3	100.0	27.7	12.6	45.9	11.6	1.2	.6	-	-	.4
UNKNOWN...............	-	100.0	1.6	76.6	21.8	-	-	-	-	-	-
EAST NORTH CENTRAL......	110	100.0	15.6	35.5	32.8	8.7	.9	1.3	1.2	-	3.9
RAIL...................	23	100.0	25.5	33.3	7.6	30.3	3.2	-	-	-	-
MOTOR CARRIER..........	64	100.0	10.7	42.2	34.8	2.8	.4	1.3	1.2	-	6.5
PRIVATE TRUCK..........	13	100.0	-	21.2	68.7	1.1	-	4.4	4.6	-	-
AIR....................	-	100.0	20.2	31.1	4.7	4.5	9.0	.2	-	1.0	29.2
WATER.................	-	100.0	-	-	-	-	-	-	-	-	-
OTHER.................	6	100.0	24.9	23.0	41.6	9.7	.1	.3	-	-	.3
UNKNOWN...............	2	100.0	92.6	1.0	6.1	-	-	.3	-	-	-
WEST NORTH CENTRAL......	105	100.0	16.0	10.7	34.1	22.0	14.8	.3	.5	-	1.5
RAIL...................	22	100.0	20.4	1.9	4.3	4.8	68.7	-	-	-	-
MOTOR CARRIER..........	39	100.0	25.5	23.1	43.6	2.2	.1	.3	1.1	-	4.0
PRIVATE TRUCK..........	33	100.0	4.2	1.3	31.6	61.8	-	.6	.3	-	.1
AIR....................	-	100.0	28.9	36.6	10.8	7.5	2.9	-	-	-	13.3
WATER.................	-	100.0	-	-	-	-	-	-	-	-	-
OTHER.................	9	100.0	8.1	12.7	76.2	2.4	.5	.1	-	-	-
UNKNOWN...............	-	100.0	10.8	5.5	4.9	33.9	44.8	-	.1	-	-
SOUTH ATLANTIC..........	172	100.0	8.2	21.4	28.0	34.1	4.8	.8	1.0	-	1.6
RAIL...................	79	100.0	1.8	1.2	22.2	70.9	3.8	-	-	-	-
MOTOR CARRIER..........	65	100.0	18.2	42.1	23.8	2.2	6.7	1.0	1.8	-	4.1
PRIVATE TRUCK..........	15	100.0	-	48.5	42.3	-	3.0	3.2	3.0	-	-
AIR....................	-	100.0	15.0	14.6	39.6	13.4	2.6	2.2	1.5	-	11.1
WATER.................	-	100.0	-	-	-	-	-	-	-	-	-
OTHER.................	9	100.0	5.7	9.7	73.9	9.7	.3	.4	-	-	.2
UNKNOWN...............	2	100.0	5.6	1.3	66.1	-	15.8	10.5	-	.6	-
EAST SOUTH CENTRAL......	47	100.0	12.0	28.0	48.9	2.8	2.7	1.8	1.4	-	2.5
RAIL...................	1	100.0	-	22.1	31.2	-	46.6	-	-	-	-
MOTOR CARRIER..........	29	100.0	17.3	36.5	35.4	4.0	.5	1.2	1.5	-	3.5
PRIVATE TRUCK..........	7	100.0	-	11.1	81.9	-	3.2	1.2	2.5	-	-
AIR....................	-	100.0	-	54.8	1.3	-	.3	-	2.7	-	40.9
WATER.................	-	100.0	-	-	-	-	-	-	-	-	-
OTHER.................	7	100.0	6.5	13.2	76.7	1.6	.1	1.8	-	-	-
UNKNOWN...............	-	100.0	-	-	30.3	-	-	69.7	-	-	-
WEST SOUTH CENTRAL......	204	100.0	10.8	15.8	16.8	49.6	1.9	.3	3.4	-	1.4
RAIL...................	103	100.0	8.4	2.5	7.9	78.5	2.8	-	-	-	-
MOTOR CARRIER..........	54	100.0	20.9	40.5	18.9	2.4	1.8	.7	9.5	-	5.2
PRIVATE TRUCK..........	37	100.0	-	11.7	36.4	48.2	-	.7	3.0	-	-
AIR....................	1	100.0	88.5	3.8	2.5	2.8	1.2	-	-	-	1.2
WATER.................	1	100.0	-	99.7	-	-	-	-	.3	-	-
OTHER.................	4	100.0	17.7	24.2	45.5	11.8	.2	.1	.2	-	.3
UNKNOWN...............	1	100.0	.2	62.3	2.5	2.0	-	-	33.1	-	-
MOUNTAIN...............	91	100.0	5.2	16.5	17.0	57.2	.6	.4	1.5	-	1.5
RAIL...................	15	100.0	25.1	18.8	.3	55.8	-	-	-	-	-
MOTOR CARRIER..........	29	100.0	1.8	32.9	49.9	7.9	1.9	.2	2.8	-	2.7
PRIVATE TRUCK..........	43	100.0	-	3.9	.6	94.3	-	-	-	-	1.1
AIR....................	-	100.0	39.6	27.8	.3	13.8	-	-	2.0	-	16.5
WATER.................	-	100.0	-	-	-	-	-	-	-	-	-
OTHER.................	1	100.0	26.7	12.6	23.9	13.6	1.9	19.6	-	-	1.7
UNKNOWN...............	1	100.0	-	47.4	-	-	-	-	52.6	-	-
PACIFIC................	303	100.0	19.3	37.9	13.3	27.2	.9	.4	.1	-	.8
RAIL...................	185	100.0	23.0	50.4	12.5	13.5	.6	-	-	-	-
MOTOR CARRIER..........	52	100.0	28.1	32.7	28.6	5.0	2.1	.5	.3	-	2.7
PRIVATE TRUCK..........	57	100.0	-	4.3	.3	94.5	-	-	-	-	.9
AIR....................	1	100.0	19.1	52.4	16.2	1.9	-	-	6.5	-	3.9
WATER.................	-	100.0	-	-	-	-	-	-	-	-	100.0
OTHER.................	4	100.0	17.5	19.6	15.1	12.7	9.6	23.9	.1	-	1.4
UNKNOWN...............	1	100.0	-	1.5	53.9	17.2	-	-	-	-	27.4

See footnotes at end of table 4.

TABLE 4. TCC GROUP 399—Percent Distribution of Distance Shipped and Weight of Shipment, by Means of Transport: 1972

Distance shipped and weight of shipment[2] [3]	Number	Percent distribution by means of transport							
		All means of transport	Rail	Motor carrier	Private truck	Air	Water	Other	Unknown
TONS OF SHIPMENTS	(thousands of tons)								
U.S. TOTAL.........	1 663	100.0	25.8	43.2	23.5	.3	.1	5.6	1.7
UNDER 100 MILES.........	184	100.0	-	48.2	42.7	-	.2	3.4	5.5
UNDER 1000 POUNDS.....	60	100.0	-	57.8	32.5	-	.1	9.2	.4
1000 TO 9999 POUNDS...	55	100.0	-	30.0	65.5	-	-	1.4	3.2
10000 TO 29999 POUNDS.	43	100.0	-	50.0	46.1	-	.5	-	3.4
30000 TO 59999 POUNDS.	15	100.0	-	82.3	17.7	-	-	-	-
60000 TO 89999 POUNDS.	-	100.0	-	-	-	-	-	-	-
90000 POUNDS AND OVER.	9	100.0	-	29.6	-	-	-	-	70.4
100 TO 199 MILES........	190	100.0	7.3	55.7	30.0	-	-	5.2	1.9
UNDER 1000 POUNDS.....	37	100.0	-	78.5	6.9	.1	-	14.4	.1
1000 TO 9999 POUNDS...	63	100.0	-	64.9	34.7	-	-	.2	.1
10000 TO 29999 POUNDS.	57	100.0	-	34.8	53.2	-	-	7.4	4.5
30000 TO 59999 POUNDS.	23	100.0	23.7	65.0	7.4	-	-	-	3.9
60000 TO 89999 POUNDS.	-	100.0	-	-	-	-	-	-	-
90000 POUNDS AND OVER.	8	100.0	100.0	-	-	-	-	-	-
200 TO 299 MILES........	200	100.0	29.2	53.2	14.0	.1	-	3.2	.4
UNDER 1000 POUNDS.....	33	100.0	.7	78.1	5.6	.7	-	14.9	-
1000 TO 9999 POUNDS...	51	100.0	4.0	70.6	21.9	-	-	2.5	1.0
10000 TO 29999 POUNDS.	19	100.0	-	33.6	64.9	-	-	-	1.5
30000 TO 59999 POUNDS.	41	100.0	6.1	88.8	5.2	-	-	-	-
60000 TO 89999 POUNDS.	-	100.0	-	-	-	-	-	-	-
90000 POUNDS AND OVER.	53	100.0	100.0	-	-	-	-	-	-
300 TO 499 MILES........	216	100.0	4.4	55.9	26.2	.3	-	12.2	.9
UNDER 1000 POUNDS.....	57	100.0	2.8	54.8	2.5	.8	-	38.9	.2
1000 TO 9999 POUNDS...	73	100.0	.3	68.9	29.3	.2	-	.7	.7
10000 TO 29999 POUNDS.	51	100.0	1.2	28.4	64.3	-	-	5.6	.6
30000 TO 59999 POUNDS.	27	100.0	5.3	86.5	2.9	-	-	1.9	3.3
60000 TO 89999 POUNDS.	5	100.0	95.5	-	-	-	-	-	4.5
90000 POUNDS AND OVER.	-	100.0	100.0	-	-	-	-	-	-
500 TO 999 MILES........	459	100.0	26.8	43.0	20.2	.3	.1	7.6	2.0
UNDER 1000 POUNDS.....	117	100.0	4.8	65.2	1.4	.6	-	27.9	.1
1000 TO 9999 POUNDS...	73	100.0	3.1	75.4	10.0	.6	.7	3.0	7.2
10000 TO 29999 POUNDS.	116	100.0	22.1	11.5	66.4	-	-	-	-
30000 TO 59999 POUNDS.	134	100.0	53.4	38.7	5.1	-	-	-	2.7
60000 TO 89999 POUNDS.	15	100.0	100.0	-	-	-	-	-	-
90000 POUNDS AND OVER.	2	100.0	100.0	-	-	-	-	-	-
1000 TO 1499 MILES......	252	100.0	55.8	22.2	18.3	.5	.3	2.3	.5
UNDER 1000 POUNDS.....	25	100.0	9.0	66.4	.3	1.9	-	22.2	.1
1000 TO 9999 POUNDS...	23	100.0	12.2	68.5	13.4	3.4	-	1.0	1.6
10000 TO 29999 POUNDS.	48	100.0	15.8	2.8	81.3	-	-	-	.1
30000 TO 59999 POUNDS.	40	100.0	33.5	52.9	9.8	-	1.9	-	2.0
60000 TO 89999 POUNDS.	12	100.0	100.0	-	-	-	-	-	-
90000 POUNDS AND OVER.	101	100.0	100.0	-	-	-	-	-	-
1500 MILES OR OVER......	158	100.0	52.2	25.9	19.1	.6	-	1.8	.4
UNDER 1000 POUNDS.....	19	100.0	24.5	60.0	.6	3.4	-	11.2	.2
1000 TO 9999 POUNDS...	26	100.0	26.0	69.6	1.2	1.0	-	1.4	.8
10000 TO 29999 POUNDS.	45	100.0	24.6	9.3	65.0	-	-	.4	.7
30000 TO 59999 POUNDS.	30	100.0	78.0	22.0	-	-	-	-	-
60000 TO 89999 POUNDS.	26	100.0	100.0	-	-	-	-	-	-
90000 POUNDS AND OVER.	10	100.0	100.0	-	-	-	-	-	-
TON-MILES OF SHIPMENTS	(millions of ton-miles)								
U.S. TOTAL.........	1 107	100.0	40.6	34.5	18.8	.5	.1	4.5	1.0
UNDER 100 MILES.........	10	100.0	-	51.2	43.5	-	-	2.8	2.5
UNDER 1000 POUNDS.....	3	100.0	.1	68.3	23.0	-	.1	8.0	.5
1000 TO 9999 POUNDS...	3	100.0	-	28.3	69.6	-	-	.4	1.7
10000 TO 29999 POUNDS.	2	100.0	-	48.9	48.9	-	.1	-	2.1
30000 TO 59999 POUNDS.	-	100.0	-	83.1	16.9	-	-	-	-
60000 TO 89999 POUNDS.	-	100.0	-	-	-	-	-	-	-
90000 POUNDS AND OVER.	-	100.0	-	21.5	-	-	-	-	78.5
100 TO 199 MILES........	27	100.0	6.9	58.0	27.8	-	-	5.0	2.3
UNDER 1000 POUNDS.....	5	100.0	-	79.1	6.5	.1	-	14.2	.1
1000 TO 9999 POUNDS...	9	100.0	-	67.0	32.6	-	-	.3	.1
10000 TO 29999 POUNDS.	7	100.0	-	36.9	50.3	-	-	7.2	5.7
30000 TO 59999 POUNDS.	3	100.0	26.7	60.9	7.5	-	-	-	4.8
60000 TO 89999 POUNDS.	-	100.0	-	-	-	-	-	-	-
90000 POUNDS AND OVER.	-	100.0	100.0	-	-	-	-	-	-

See footnotes at end of table 4.

TABLE 4. TCC GROUP 399—Percent Distribution of Distance Shipped and Weight of Shipment, by Means of Transport: 1972—Continued

Distance shipped and weight of shipment[2][3]	Number	Percent distribution by means of transport							
		All means of transport	Rail	Motor carrier	Private truck	Air	Water	Other	Unknown
TON-MILES OF SHIPMENTS	(millions of ton-miles)								
200 TO 299 MILES.........	51	100.0	31.2	51.8	13.4	.1	-	3.2	.4
UNDER 1000 POUNDS......	8	100.0	.7	77.6	5.4	.7	-	15.6	-
1000 TO 9999 POUNDS...	12	100.0	3.8	71.0	21.7	-	-	2.5	1.0
10000 TO 29999 POUNDS.	5	100.0	-	32.0	66.4	-	-	-	1.5
30000 TO 59999 POUNDS.	10	100.0	6.1	90.0	4.0	-	-	-	-
60000 TO 89999 POUNDS.	-	100.0	-	-	-	-	-	-	-
90000 POUNDS AND OVER.	14	100.0	100.0	-	-	-	-	-	-
300 TO 499 MILES.........	83	100.0	4.8	55.6	25.8	.3	-	12.4	1.1
UNDER 1000 POUNDS......	22	100.0	2.7	54.5	2.6	.9	-	39.2	.2
1000 TO 9999 POUNDS...	28	100.0	.4	67.1	30.9	.2	-	.6	.8
10000 TO 29999 POUNDS.	19	100.0	1.1	31.0	61.2	-	-	6.0	.6
30000 TO 59999 POUNDS.	10	100.0	6.2	84.7	2.8	-	-	2.3	4.0
60000 TO 89999 POUNDS.	2	100.0	94.8	-	-	-	-	-	5.2
90000 POUNDS AND OVER.	-	100.0	100.0	-	-	-	-	-	-
500 TO 999 MILES.........	328	100.0	28.3	42.7	19.7	.3	.1	7.1	1.8
UNDER 1000 POUNDS......	81	100.0	5.7	65.0	1.4	.6	-	27.0	.2
1000 TO 9999 POUNDS...	52	100.0	3.2	76.2	10.2	.7	.5	2.6	6.7
10000 TO 29999 POUNDS.	84	100.0	26.2	11.0	62.8	-	-	-	-
30000 TO 59999 POUNDS.	95	100.0	52.9	39.3	5.5	-	-	-	2.3
60000 TO 89999 POUNDS.	12	100.0	100.0	-	-	-	-	-	-
90000 POUNDS AND OVER.	1	100.0	100.0	-	-	-	-	-	-
1000 TO 1499 MILES......	286	100.0	53.9	23.4	18.8	.6	.4	2.4	.6
UNDER 1000 POUNDS......	30	100.0	9.3	67.1	.3	1.9	-	21.4	.1
1000 TO 9999 POUNDS...	28	100.0	13.8	66.6	12.8	4.1	-	.9	1.8
10000 TO 29999 POUNDS.	58	100.0	18.4	3.1	78.5	-	-	-	.1
30000 TO 59999 POUNDS.	47	100.0	32.8	53.9	8.8	-	2.2	-	2.3
60000 TO 89999 POUNDS.	14	100.0	100.0	-	-	-	-	-	-
90000 POUNDS AND OVER.	106	100.0	100.0	-	-	-	-	-	-
1500 MILES OR OVER......	320	100.0	56.4	25.4	15.4	.7	-	1.8	.3
UNDER 1000 POUNDS......	42	100.0	26.8	57.8	.5	3.6	-	11.0	.2
1000 TO 9999 POUNDS...	56	100.0	31.0	65.2	1.1	1.1	-	1.0	.6
10000 TO 29999 POUNDS.	81	100.0	29.6	9.6	59.5	-	-	.5	.7
30000 TO 59999 POUNDS.	59	100.0	79.1	20.9	-	-	-	-	-
60000 TO 89999 POUNDS.	57	100.0	100.0	-	-	-	-	-	-
90000 POUNDS AND OVER.	23	100.0	100.0	-	-	-	-	-	-

Note: Detail may not add to total due to rounding. The introductory table shows the estimates of sampling variability for tons; sampling variability for ton-miles has not been estimated. See the map in the Introduction for the States comprising the geographic divisions of the United States.

Shipments excluded from the survey are those moving by pipeline (primarily petroleum products from refineries), parcel post shipments, and commodities moved by own power (motorized vehicles, aircraft, etc.) or towed (prefabricated buildings, etc.). Local shipments (commodities shipped less than 25 miles from the plant) and shipments within the same city are also excluded. Shipments to Alaska and Hawaii from the 48 conterminous States and the District of Columbia are included; however, no data were obtained for shipments originating in Alaska and Hawaii.

- Represents zero or rounds to zero.

[1]Production of this commodity is concentrated in the geographic divisions shown; figures and distributions for geographic divisions not shown are included in the total.

[2]Distances of shipments to foreign destinations are calculated only to the U.S. port of exit.

[3]Includes only shipments represented by bills of lading and invoices. Summary records which did not show individual weights of shipments are not included.

Special Statistics

Printing, Publishing, and Allied Industries (Except Newspaper and Periodicals)

CONTENTS

The tables listed below are shown for the United States and each of the geographical regions:

1. Percent Distribution of Commodities Shipped by Means of Transport: 1972
2. Percent Distribution of Commodities Shipped by Distance of Shipment: 1972
3. Percent Distribution of Commodities Shipped by Domestic and Foreign Destinations: 1972

INTRODUCTION

DESCRIPTION OF THE COMMODITY TRANSPORTATION SURVEY

General

The Commodity Transportation Survey is one of the three components of the Census of Transportation, one of the Economic Censuses conducted every 5 years ending in "2" and "7". Two previous Commodity Transportation Surveys have been conducted—the first in 1963 and the second in 1967. The prime objective of this survey is to measure the transportation and geographic distribution of commodities shipped by manufacturing establishments in the United States beyond the local area. The Commodity Transportation Survey, as it now exists, consists of two independent surveys: A mail summary-data survey and a main shipper survey.

Shipper Survey

The major part of the Commodity Transportation Survey is commonly referred to as the Shipper Survey. Traffic flow data is gathered, processed, and disseminated relating to the volume of commodities shipped by means of transport, length of haul, size of shipment, and areas of origin and destination in tons and ton-miles. The data sources are bills of lading or other shipping documents pertaining to individual shipments from a sample of about 13,000 plants selected from the census of manufactures universe of manufacturing establishments with 20 employees or more. The sample design is multistaged, utilizing a stratified probability sampling to obtain approximately 13,000 plants at the first stage and a systematic random sample of 1.6 million shipping documents (100 to 200 from each sampled plant) at the second stage. Although the source of the shipping information pertaining to each individual shipment is the shipping document, the primary sampling unit (PSU) may be either a plant or the shipping document itself. The primary sampling unit is the plant for all but the "certainty plants," those with a probability of "1" or greater at the first stage. For certainty plants, the PSU is usually the shipping document (bill of lading) drawn systematically from a random start.

Mail Survey

The smaller component of the survey consists of data collection by mail on a simplified 1-page summary questionnaire. About 2,000 plants are sampled which have 10 to 19 employees, and about 1,000 plants are sampled in the Printing and Publishing Industry. In this mail survey, information relating to individual shipments is not collected. The respondent replies only to questions in terms of annual-percent-of-total-value shipped. Value is used as a unit of measure rather than tons since it was felt that the small manufacturers would not have summary data available on tons shipped. Data collected for the census year as a whole include value of product and services, major product shipped, distance shipped (six categories), type of transport used (six modes), and the geographic division of destination. Also included is the percent shipped for export to foreign countries. The sample designs used for these surveys are simple one-stage systematic random samples of plants from the respective universes.

PURPOSE AND SCOPE OF THE MAIL SURVEY

General

The printing and publishing industries were included for the first time in the 1967 Census of Transportation. Little was known previously regarding the transportation requirements of these industries, especially with respect to the volume of inter-city or "long-haul" traffic as compared with local distribution. For that reason it was decided that a mail summary questionnaire designed primarily to measure the general transportation and distribution patterns would meet the most urgent data needs, rather than the greater detail that was obtained in the main shipper survey.

Report Form and Basic Data

In early 1973, Form TC-420 (see appendix A for facsimile of form) was mailed to each printing and publishing establishment in the sample requesting data on shipments made during 1972. The value of products and services (item II) was used as an indicator of the volume of shipments. An estimate of tons shipped would have been preferable as a measure of the transportation volume, but it was believed that a large proportion of the establishments would not have been able to provide estimates of tons. However, all establishments were able to supply data based on total value figures.

The primary data items for the survey were the percentage distributions of value shipped during 1972 by distance and by means of transport (items IV and V). This information was requested in the form of percentage distributions rather than

Figure 1. Percent Distribution of Shipments of Printing, Publishing, and Allied Industries (Except Newspapers and Periodicals), by Characteristic: 1972

(Based on total value)

MEANS OF TRANSPORT

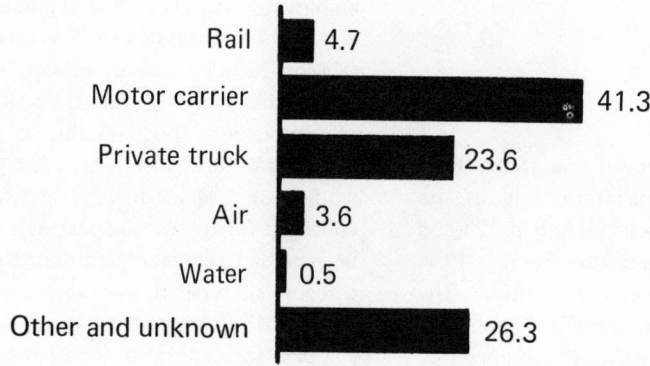

Rail	4.7
Motor carrier	41.3
Private truck	23.6
Air	3.6
Water	0.5
Other and unknown	26.3

DISTANCE OF SHIPMENT

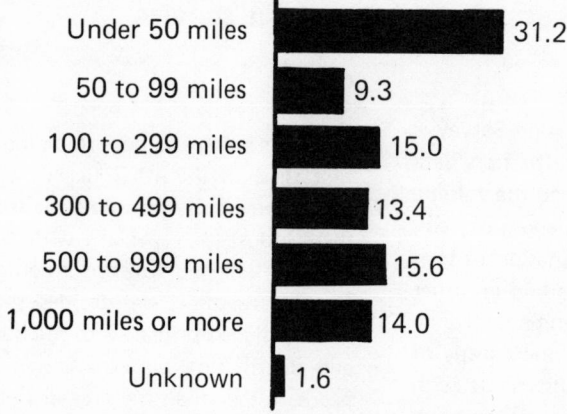

Under 50 miles	31.2
50 to 99 miles	9.3
100 to 299 miles	15.0
300 to 499 miles	13.4
500 to 999 miles	15.6
1,000 miles or more	14.0
Unknown	1.6

DOMESTIC AND FOREIGN DESTINATIONS

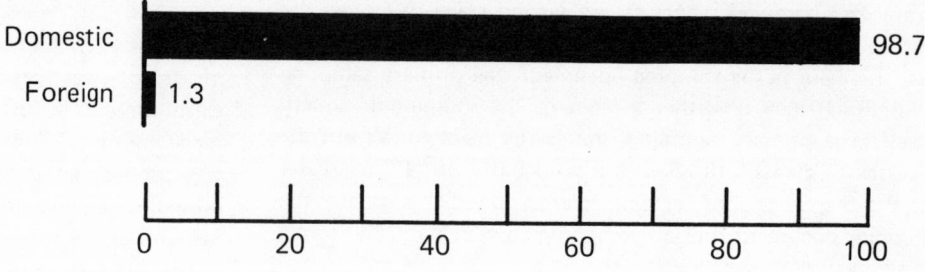

Domestic	98.7
Foreign	1.3

0   20   40   60   80   100

absolutes (tons or value) because the latter information usually is not available and is more difficult for shippers to estimate than relative distributions.

The 1972 questionnaire was basically the same as that used in 1967. Two items were added: Item III asks for the major product shipped and item VI asks U.S. area of destination by the nine census divisions. A question asked in 1967 relating to available shipping facilities was deleted.

Estimation Procedure

The method for aggregating and expanding the sample of individual reports to universe levels involved two steps. The first step was conversion of percentages into estimated value of shipments for each plant. This was done by multiplying the reported total value of products and services times the percentages reported in each category times the nonresponse adjustment factor for the industry times the plant expansion (sampling fraction which was 1 in 19). These results were finally ratio adjusted to known census of manufactures value of shipments for 1972 after allowing for Commodity Transportation Survey out-of-scope industries. The second step involved the aggregation of plant values and the computation of percentage distributions shown in the tables.

Other Related Surveys

A similar survey was taken to obtain comparable traffic-pattern data from "small plants" in all of the industries covered by the 1972 Commodity Transportation Survey.[1] Small plants were defined to be manufacturing establishments with 10 to 19 employees. Form TC-420 was used for both surveys, and recognizing the scope of each, the data for the two surveys are comparable.

In the Shipper Survey,[2] detailed data were collected based on bills of lading or other shipping documents to measure commodity flows in terms of volume (tons and ton-miles). Since the same report form (TC-420) was used for all employee size classes[3] in the printing and publishing industries, rough comparisons may be made between the percentage distributions by means of transport and by distance shown in this survey and corresponding distributions in the 3-digit

---

[1] See special report entitled "Traffic Patterns of Small Manufacturing Plants" in the Commodity Transportation Survey.

[2] The major part of the Commodity Transportation Survey is referred to as the Shipper Survey. See introduction to any Area or Commodity Series Report of the 1972 CTS for a brief description of the survey method.

[3] Except that manufacturing plants with less than 10 employees were not included in any phase of the 1972 Commodity Transportation Survey.

Commodities Series, provided allowance is made for differences created by local shipments. Three-digit commodity data relate to intercity or long-haul shipments, while printing and publishing data represent total output including products used in or near the plant.

SUMMARY OF FINDINGS

The survey estimates showed motor carrier as being the predominant means of transport used by the printing and publishing industries. About 41 percent of the total value shipped in 1972 traveled by motor carrier. The next largest handlers were in the "other" category, accounting for about 25 percent. This included services such as parcel post, air and rail express, and united parcel service. The West Region was the only area to differ from the National pattern, showing about 40 percent of the shipments moving by private truck.

The market area for the industry appeared concentrated. About 40 percent of the total volume traveled less than 100 miles. However, distribution within the mileage blocks beyond 100 miles was a relatively even 14 to 15 percent of shipments. Again the West broke the National pattern, sending over half of the originating volume less than 100 miles. Almost all shipments (99 percent) had a domestic destination.

COMPARISON WITH THE 1967 SURVEY

Generally, the 1967 and 1972 surveys were similar and produced comparable results. The 1967 data were tabulated and presented by SIC (Standard Industrial Classification); the 1972 data were collected and tabulated by major product shipped (Transportation Commodity Code, TCC). This was done to make the results more compatible with the main shipper survey of establishments with 20 employees or more and to produce commodity based statistics. The TCC and SIC are generally comparable at the 3-digit level of presentation.

The destination region of shipments was collected for the first time in 1972 in order to produce origin/destination data for the printing and publishing industries (except newspapers and periodicals). However, multidimensional matrices (such as origin/destination by means of transport) are not possible because of the summary nature of the questionnaire.

The 1972 survey showed that even though the value of the shipment increased, the distribution by means of transport and distance shipped remained near the levels reported in 1967. As with 1967, motor carrier was the primary means of transport in 1972, with about 46 and 41 percent, respectively. Use of private truck was the same, 24 percent for both survey years. The "other" handled substantial proportions of the industries shipping, accounting for about 20 percent in 1967 and about

Figure 2. Shipments of Printing, Publishing, and Allied Industries (Except Newspapers and Periodicals), by Geographic Division of Destination: 1972

(Based on total value)

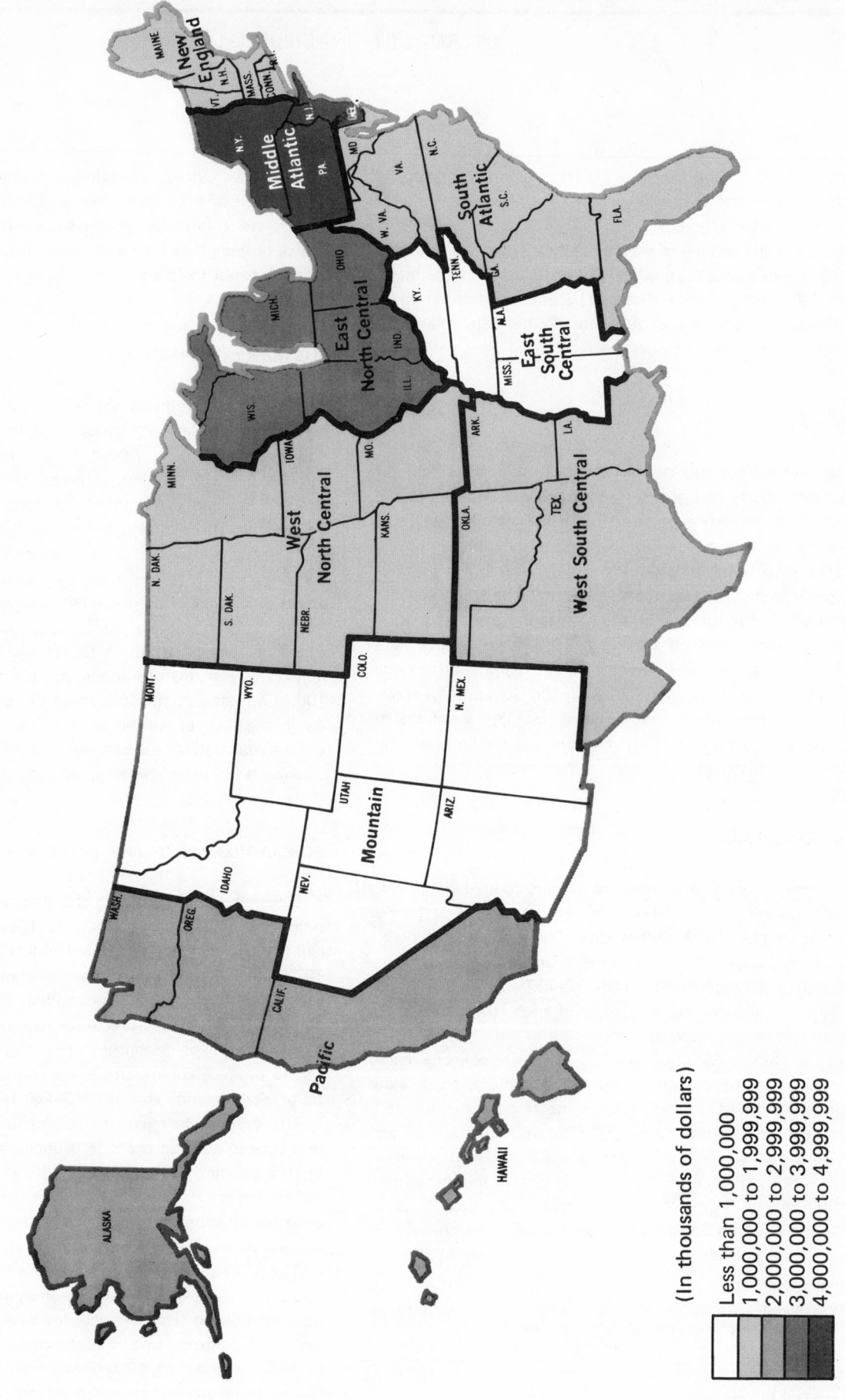

(In thousands of dollars)

Less than 1,000,000
1,000,000 to 1,999,999
2,000,000 to 2,999,999
3,000,000 to 3,999,999
4,000,000 to 4,999,999

U.S. DEPARTMENT OF COMMERCE Social and Economic Statistics Administration BUREAU OF THE CENSUS

25 percent in 1972. Rail, air, and water combined for about 9 percent of the total value shipped in 1972 and just over 10 percent in 1967.

Distribution by means of transport was relatively unchanged between 1967 and 1972 in the Northeast. The three other regions showed an increase in the use of "other" between survey years, increasing about 10 percentage points. Contrary to the National pattern, the major means of transport in the West was private truck. Between 1967 and 1972 motor carrier decreased by about 14 percent (from 47 to 33 percent).

The North Central Region in both 1967 and 1972 shipped more than 60 percent of the total value 100 miles or more. About three-fifths of all 1972 value of shipments traveled more than 100 miles. In contrast, in 1967, the West moved about 60 percent of its value of shipments less than 100 miles. In 1972, the proportion was about 54 percent. There was no change in the proportion being shipped with foreign destinations.

RELIABILITY OF THE ESTIMATES

General Description

The statistics in this report are estimates derived from a sample survey. There are two types of errors possible in an estimate based on a sample survey—sampling and nonsampling. Sampling errors occur because observations are made only on a sample, not on the entire population. Nonsampling errors can be attributed to many sources: inability to obtain information about all cases in the sample, definitional difficulties, differences in the interpretation of questions, inability or unwillingness to provide correct information on the part of respondents, mistakes in recording or coding the data obtained, and other errors of collection, response, processing, coverage, and estimation for missing data. Nonsampling errors also occur in complete censuses. The "accuracy" of a survey result is determined by the joint effects of sampling and nonsampling errors. This total error therefore is dependent upon sampling and nonsampling errors and is usually of the order of size indicated by the standard error. However, for some estimates, the total error may considerably exceed the standard errors shown.

Nonsampling Errors

Generally, the response was very good and no discernable bias in the nonresponse was detected. The overall response rate was 91 percent. Processing errors are primarily related to coding, transcription, and key punching of data. However, clerical editing and computer-edit correction programs reduce these errors to a minimum.

Most plants do not maintain book records on the percentage distribution of shipments by means of transport and distance. As a result, much of the data could possibly be based on the day-to-day experience of plant personnel. Therefore, particular care should be exercised in the interpretation of figures based on a relatively small number of cases as well as small differences between the data.

Sampling Errors

The sample estimate and an estimate of its standard error permit us to construct interval estimates with prescribed confidence that the interval includes the average result of all possible samples.

To illustrate, if all possible samples were selected, each of these were surveyed under essentially the same conditions, and an estimate and its estimated standard error were calculated from each sample, then—

(1) Approximately two-thirds of the intervals from one standard error below the estimate to one standard error above the estimate would include the average value of all possible samples. We call an interval from one standard error below the estimate to one standard error above the estimate a two-thirds confidence interval.

(2) Approximately nine-tenths of the intervals from 1.6 standard errors below the estimate to 1.6 standard errors above the estimate would include the average value of all possible samples. We call an interval from 1.6 standard errors below the estimate to 1.6 standard errors above the estimate a 90-percent confidence interval.

(3) Approximately nineteen-twentieths of the intervals from two standard errors below the estimate to two standard errors above the estimate would include the average value of all possible samples. We call an interval from two standard errors below the estimate to two standard errors above the estimate a 95-percent confidence interval.

(4) Almost all intervals from three standard errors below the sample estimate to three standard errors above the sample estimate would include the average value of all possible samples.

Thus, for a particular sample, one can say with specified confidence that the average of all possible samples is included in the constructed interval.

Use of Tables of Standard Errors

To derive estimates of standard errors that would be applicable to a wide variety of items and could be prepared at a moderate cost, a number of approximations were required. As a result, the standard errors presented provide a general order of magnitude rather than the exact standard error for any specific item. For example, table 1 of this report shows about 20.2 percent of the total value of all shipments from plants whose primary product shipped was TCC 27611 was handled by private truck. The table below shows that, for a 1972 U.S. total, column 1 should be used to calculate the standard error. Column 1 shows the standard error on an estimate of this size (20.2) to be approximately 1.8 percentage points.

Standard Errors of Estimated Percentages: 1972

(68 chances out of 100)

Percent estimated from data	Standard errors for column[1] —			
	1	2	3	4
0.5	0.2	0.5	0.1	0.4
1	.3	.8	.2	.6
5	.7	2.2	.7	1.6
10	1.1	3.7	1.4	2.9
15	1.4	5.2	2.0	4.1
20	1.8	6.7	2.6	5.3
25	2.2	8.1	3.3	6.6
35	2.9	11.1	4.6	9.0
50	3.9	15.5	6.5	12.6

Note: Estimates of standard errors were not calculated for 1967 data. However, the standard errors should approximate those of 1972 data.

[1] To calculate the standard error of an estimate for the United States and geographic regions, use the appropriate column as follows:

United States, column 1
Northeast Region, column 3
North Central Region, column 3
South Region column 2
West Region, column 4

Based on these data, the two-thirds confidence interval for this sample is from 18.4 to 22.0 percent. A conclusion that the average estimate of the percentage derived from all possible samples lies within a range computed in this way would be correct for roughly two-thirds of all possible samples. Similarly we can conclude that the average estimate of the percentage derived from all possible samples lies within the interval from 17.3 to 23.1 percent with 90-percent confidence in our conclusion, or that the average estimate of the percentage lies within the interval from 16.6 to 23.8 percent with 95-percent confidence, or that the average estimate of the percentage lies within the interval from 14.8 to 25.6 percent almost certainly.

Standard Error of a Difference— Illustration

The estimate of a certain characteristic for the Northeast is 46.5 percent and the estimate of the same characteristic for the West is 29.8 percent. Since both of these estimates are based on samples, the estimated difference of 16.7 percentage points (46.5 − 29.8 = 16.7) is also subject to sampling error. The table above shows that the estimated standard error of 46.5 percent for the Northeast is 6.5 and the estimated standard error of 29.8 for the West is 7.8 (6.6 + 9.0)/2 = 7.8) percentage points. A rough estimate of the standard error of the difference may be obtained by multiplying the larger of the two standard errors by 1.4[4]. Thus the standard error of the 16.7 percentage point difference is approximately 10.9 percentage points. Based on these data, the two-thirds confidence interval is from 5.8 to 27.6 percent, and a conclusion that the average estimate of the percentage difference, derived from all possible samples, lies within a range computed in this way would be correct for roughly two-thirds of all possible samples. Similarly, a conclusion that the average estimate of the percentage difference, derived from all possible samples, lies within the interval from -5.1 to 38.5 percent would correspond to 95-percent confidence. Therefore, at the higher confidence level we would not conclude that the percent for the Northeast is actually less than the percent for the West.

---

[4] The standard error of a difference is actually

$$\sigma_{A-B} = \sqrt{\sigma^2_A + \sigma^2_B - 2\sigma_{AB}}$$

where

σ^2_A is the variance of A, σ^2_B is the variance of B, and

σ_{AB} is the covariance of A and B.

Table A1. Selected Sample by 1967 Standard Industrial Classification

SIC Code	Classification	Total	Plant size (number of employees)		
			10 to 19	100 to 249	250 and over
	Total	1,075	496	110	469
2731	Book publishing	79	18	7	54
2732	Book printing	76	18	6	52
2741	Miscellaneous publishing	56	21	4	31
2751	Commercial printing, except lithographic	275	160	22	93
2752	Commercial printing, lithographic	314	150	35	129
2753	Engraving and plate printing	16	13	2	1
2761	Manifold business forms	56	16	9	31
2771	Greeting card publishing	29	4	1	24
2782	Blankbooks and looseleaf binders	35	10	5	20
2789	Bookbinding and related work	45	23	6	16
2791	Typesetting	55	34	9	12
2793	Photoengraving	27	18	3	6
2794	Electrotyping and stereotyping	12	11	1	—

Note: The sample includes establishments determined to be out of scope during the survey.

Table A2. Net Sample by Primary Transportation Commodity Classification

TCC Code	Classification	United States	North-east	North Central	South	West
	Total[1]	898	317	310	165	106
273	Books	118	53	39	18	8
274	Miscellaneous printed matter	487	163	174	86	60
276	Manifold business forms	73	19	22	20	12
277	Greeting cards	26	12	10	—	—
278	Blankbooks and looseleaf binders	38	14	10	—	—
279	Service industries for the printing trade[2]	102	37	35	20	10
	All other	54	19	20	21	16

Note: There is no TCC equivalent for SIC 275. Products shipped from establishments in SIC 275 are coded by the Major TCC Code of the shipment.

[1] Excludes establishments reporting but determined to be out of scope to the survey.
[2] Although these are classified as "service establishments" shipments originate including commodities such as electrotype, engravers, plates, shells, blocks, bars, and printers.

Table B. Value of Shipments of Printing, Publishing, and Allied Industries
(Millions of dollars)

SIC Code	Classification	Total	Plants with 10 employees or more	
			1972	1967
	Total[1]	18,367	16,622	11,851
2731	Book publishing	2,868	2,756	2,063
2732	Book printing	924	893	763
2741	Miscellaneous publishing	1,070	937	547
2751	Commercial printing, except lithographic	3,279	2,476	2,791
2752	Commercial printing, lithographic	5,190	4,737	2,871
2753	Engraving and plate printing	202	173	116
2754	Commercial printing, gravure.	679	705	(2)
2761	Manifold business forms	1,430	1,410	920
2771	Greeting card publishing	774	765	512
2782	Blankbooks and looseleaf binders	582	568	370
2789	Bookbinding and related work	377	342	316
2791	Typesetting	481	401	314
2793	Photoengraving	217	186	209
2794	Electrotyping and stereotyping	37	32	59
2795	Lithographic platemaking and related services	257	241	(3)

Note: Derived from data collected in the census of manufactures.

[1] Survey excludes SIC 2711 (Newspapers) and 2712 (Periodicals).
[2] SIC 2754 was included in SIC 2751.
[3] SIC 2795 was included in SIC 2752.

Table C. United States—Percent Distribution of Shipments by Means of Transport, Distance Shipped, and Domestic and Foreign Destinations: 1972 and 1967

(Based on value of shipments)

Item	1972	1967	Percent change, 1972 from 1967
Value of shipments (thousands of dollars) [1]	*16,621,800*	*11,850,587*	*(X)*
PERCENT DISTRIBUTION			
Means of Transport	100.0	100.0	(X)
Rail	4.7	6.5	−1.8
Motor carrier	41.3	45.6	−4.3
Private truck	23.6	23.8	−.2
Air	3.6	3.3	+.3
Water	.5	.5	—
Other and unknown [2]	26.3	20.3	+6.0
Distance shipped	100.0	100.0	(X)
Under 50 miles	31.2	36.9	−5.7
50 to 99 miles	9.3	9.4	−.1
100 to 299 miles	15.0	14.4	+.6
300 to 499 miles	13.4	12.7	+.7
500 to 999 miles	15.6	14.2	+1.4
1,000 miles and over	14.0	12.4	+1.6
Unknown [2]	1.6	—	(X)
Destination	100.0	100.0	(X)
Domestic	98.7	98.2	+.5
Foreign	1.3	1.8	−.5

— Represents zero.   (X) Not applicable.

[1] Totals are derived from data collected in the census of manufactures.
[2] Unknowns were not classified separately for 1967 data. Includes local shipments with interplant transfers.

Table D. Geographic Regions—Percent Distribution of Shipments by Means of Transport, Distance Shipped, and Domestic and Foreign Destinations: 1972 and 1967

(Based on value of shipments)

Item	1972	1967	Percent change, 1972 from 1967	Item	1972	1967	Percent change, 1972 from 1967
	NORTHEAST REGION				**NORTH CENTRAL REGION**		
Value of shipments (thousands of dollars)[1]	5,191,645	4,620,600	(X)	Value of shipments (thousands of dollars)[1]	6,357,051	4,589,700	(X)
PERCENT DISTRIBUTION				**PERCENT DISTRIBUTION**			
Means of transport	100.0	100.0	(X)	Means of transport	100.0	100.0	(X)
Rail	2.6	5.2	−2.6	Rail	7.1	8.9	−1.8
Motor carrier	42.4	42.7	−.3	Motor carrier	41.0	47.6	−6.6
Private truck	23.3	22.4	+.9	Private truck	19.7	19.7	—
Air	3.9	3.7	+.2	Air	3.1	3.3	−.2
Water	.8	.9	−.1	Water	.2	.1	+.1
Other and unknown[2]	26.9	25.1	+1.8	Other and unknown[2]	28.9	20.4	+8.5
Distance shipped	100.0	100.0	(X)	Distance shipped	100.0	100.0	(X)
Under 50 miles	35.4	40.5	−5.1	Under 50 miles	24.3	30.0	−5.7
50 to 99 miles	11.4	11.0	+.4	50 to 99 miles	7.6	8.0	−.4
100 to 299 miles	17.6	15.7	+1.9	100 to 299 miles	13.8	13.5	+.3
300 to 499 miles	10.7	10.0	+.7	300 to 499 miles	13.5	15.9	−2.4
500 to 999 miles	10.5	9.9	+.6	500 to 999 miles	22.4	18.8	+3.6
1,000 miles and over	12.9	12.9	—	1,000 miles and over	17.1	13.8	+3.3
Unknown[2]	1.5	—	(X)	Unknown[2]	1.4	—	(X)
Destination	100.0	100.0	(X)	Destination	100.0	100.0	(X)
Domestic	98.6	98.3	+.3	Domestic	98.6	97.7	+.9
Foreign	1.4	1.7	−.3	Foreign	1.4	2.3	−.9

See footnotes at end of table.

Table D. Geographic Regions—Percent Distribution of Shipments by Means of Transport, Distance Shipped, and Domestic and Foreign Destinations: 1972 and 1967—Continued

(Based on value of shipments)

Item	1972	1967	Percent change, 1972 from 1967	Item	1972	1967	Percent change, 1972 from 1967
	SOUTH REGION				WEST REGION		
Value of shipments (thousands of dollars)[1] . . .	3,433,770	1,608,100	(X)	Value of shipments (thousands of dollars)[1] . .	1,639,334	1,032,187	(X)
PERCENT DISTRIBUTION				PERCENT DISTRIBUTION			
Means of transport	100.0	100.0	(X)	Means of transport	100.0	100.0	(X)
Rail	5.3	6.5	−1.2	Rail	.9	2.4	−1.5
Motor carrier	44.1	46.6	−2.5	Motor carrier	33.1	47.5	−14.4
Private truck	22.4	29.8	−7.4	Private Truck	41.6	39.1	+2.5
Air	3.5	2.6	+.9	Air	4.9	2.7	+2.2
Water	.2	.1	+.1	Water	1.4	.6	+.8
Other and unknown[2] . . .	24.4	14.4	+10.0	Other and unknown[2] .	18.2	7.7	+10.5
Distance shipped	100.0	100.0	(X)	Distance shipped	100.0	100.0	(X)
Under 50 miles	30.9	36.4	−5.5	Under 50 miles	45.1	51.6	−6.5
50 to 99 miles	9.3	8.3	+1.0	50 to 99 miles	9.2	9.9	−.7
100 to 299 miles	15.0	16.5	−1.5	100 to 299 miles	11.8	9.8	+2.0
300 to 499 miles	19.0	13.8	+5.2	300 to 499 miles	9.2	9.6	−.4
500 to 999 miles	14.4	17.8	−3.4	500 to 999 miles	8.0	7.3	+.7
1,000 miles and over . . .	8.7	7.2	+1.5	1,000 miles and over . .	16.5	11.8	+4.7
Unknown[2]	2.7	—	(X)	Unknown[2]	.3	—	(X)
Destination	100.0	100.0	(X)	Destination	100.0	100.0	(X)
Domestic	99.0	98.9	+.1	Domestic	98.9	99.2	−.3
Foreign	1.0	1.1	−.1	Foreign	1.1	.8	+.3

— Represents zero.   (X) Not applicable.

[1] Totals are derived from data collected in the census of manufactures.
[2] Unknowns were not classified separately for 1967 data. Includes local shipments with interplant transfers.

Table E. Percent Distribution of Shipments From Geographic Regions, by Division of Destination: 1972

(Based on value of shipments)

Division of destination	United States	Region of origin			
		North-east	North Central	South	West
Value of shipments (thousands of dollars)[1]	*16,621,800*	*5,191,645*	*6,357,051*	*3,433,770*	*1,639,334*
PERCENT DISTRIBUTION					
Total	100.0	100.0	100.0	100.0	100.0
New England	7.2	14.8	3.8	4.7	1.1
Middle Atlantic	24.8	45.5	15.9	20.1	3.2
East North Central	18.7	9.8	35.4	9.0	2.9
West North Central	8.3	4.4	15.1	4.7	1.7
South Atlantic	11.4	8.0	7.8	27.3	2.5
East South Central	4.9	3.7	4.3	9.7	1.3
West South Central	6.9	3.7	5.8	16.0	2.4
Mountain	3.8	2.6	3.0	1.8	14.6
Pacific	12.6	6.2	7.5	4.1	70.0
Unknown	1.5	1.4	1.4	2.7	.3

[1] Totals are derived from data collected in the census of manufactures.

UNITED STATES

TABLE 1. Percent Distribution of Commodities Shipped by Means of Transport: 1972

TCC code	Commodity description	Total value[1] (thousands)	All means of transport	Rail	Motor carrier	Private truck	Air	Water	Other[2]	Un-known
	Total...	16,621,800	100.0	4.7	41.3	23.6	3.6	0.5	25.4	0.9
27111	Newspapers..	268,014	100.0	-	20.7	61.7	.1	-	3.9	13.6
27211	Periodicals..	736,533	100.0	22.8	48.4	5.1	2.5	.2	20.4	.7
27311	Books..	2,846,276	100.0	4.2	40.8	8.5	1.7	1.6	43.3	-
27411	Catalogs and directories............................	1,373,899	100.0	9.5	42.1	25.5	4.5	.1	18.4	-
27417	Labels, seals, tags, and wrappers...................	720,473	100.0	4.6	57.5	9.2	2.6	.1	26.0	-
27419	Printed matter, n.e.c................................	6,056,662	100.0	3.0	36.1	32.4	4.7	.2	22.5	1.1
27611	Manifold business forms.............................	1,786,011	100.0	4.9	62.4	20.2	1.4	.6	8.8	1.7
27711	Greeting cards......................................	936,667	100.0	4.5	51.6	4.2	2.3	.1	37.3	-
27811	Blankbooks, pads and tablets........................	502,771	100.0	2.4	18.4	11.2	.4	.6	67.1	-
27812	Looseleaf binders and devices.......................	119,770	100.0	.5	56.2	23.7	2.1	1.2	16.3	-
27911	Products of service industries for the printing trades..	1,186,543	100.0	1.0	24.5	51.1	9.4	.4	12.3	1.2
	All other[3]..	88,108	100.0	.4	70.1	4.7	4.9	1.8	18.1	-

See footnotes at bottom of page.

TABLE 2. Percent Distribution of Commodities Shipped by Distance of Shipment: 1972

TCC code	Commodity description	Total value[1] (thousands)	All dis-tances	Under 50 miles	50 to 99 miles	100 to 299 miles	300 to 499 miles	500 to 999 miles	1,000 miles and over	Un-known
	Total...	16,621,800	100.0	31.2	9.3	15.0	13.4	15.6	14.0	1.6
27111	Newspapers..	268,014	100.0	73.4	9.2	2.3	1.1	2.8	1.4	9.9
27211	Periodicals..	736,533	100.0	7.5	6.4	12.7	19.9	30.0	22.8	.7
27311	Books..	2,846,276	100.0	13.1	7.1	20.1	17.2	19.9	22.6	-
27411	Catalogs and directories............................	1,373,899	100.0	30.3	7.7	12.6	15.1	17.0	16.2	1.2
27417	Labels, seals, tags, and wrappers...................	720,473	100.0	19.3	12.0	15.5	15.4	21.3	15.6	1.0
27419	Printed matter, n.e.c................................	6,056,662	100.0	41.7	11.6	13.6	9.8	12.7	8.1	2.6
27611	Manifold business forms.............................	1,786,011	100.0	28.6	9.0	16.6	20.3	15.0	8.8	1.7
27711	Greeting cards......................................	936,667	100.0	7.6	4.0	14.5	17.0	21.3	35.1	.6
27811	Blankbooks, pads and tablets........................	502,771	100.0	37.8	13.2	19.6	9.4	8.8	11.1	-
27812	Looseleaf binders and devices.......................	119,770	100.0	38.9	4.6	24.7	9.0	8.3	14.5	-
27911	Products of service industries for the printing trades..	1,186,543	100.0	53.8	8.4	12.9	7.0	7.4	9.3	1.2
	All other[3]..	88,108	100.0	25.9	10.1	6.5	5.6	37.2	14.8	-

See footnotes at bottom of page.

TABLE 3. Percent Distribution of Commodities Shipped by Domestic and Foreign Destinations: 1972

TCC code	Commodity description	Total value[1] (thousands)	All destinations	Domestic	Foreign
	Total...	16,621,800	100.0	98.7	1.3
27111	Newspapers..	268,014	100.0	99.9	.1
27211	Periodicals..	736,533	100.0	97.8	2.2
27311	Books..	2,846,276	100.0	96.4	3.6
27411	Catalogs and directories............................	1,373,899	100.0	99.3	.7
27417	Labels, seals, tags, and wrappers...................	720,473	100.0	99.2	.8
27419	Printed matter, n.e.c................................	6,056,662	100.0	99.2	.8
27611	Manifold business forms.............................	1,786,011	100.0	99.7	.3
27711	Greeting cards......................................	936,667	100.0	98.7	1.3
27811	Blankbooks, pads and tablets........................	502,771	100.0	99.6	.4
27812	Looseleaf binders and devices.......................	119,770	100.0	98.6	1.4
27911	Products of service industries for the printing trades......	1,186,543	100.0	99.4	.6
	All other[3]..	88,108	100.0	98.2	1.8

Note: Detail may not add to totals due to rounding. The survey excludes SIC 2711 (Newspapers) and SIC 2712 (Periodicals).

- Represents zero or rounds to zero.

[1]Value of shipments derived from census of manufactures total value of shipments for 1972. [2]Includes railway and air express, United Parcel, parcel post, and other "package carriers". [3]Represents balance of commodities not shown due to disclosure.

NORTHEAST REGION

TABLE 1. Percent Distribution of Commodities Shipped by Means of Transport: 1972

TCC code	Commodity description	Total value[1] (thousands)	All means of transport	Rail	Motor carrier	Private truck	Air	Water	Other[2]	Un-known
	Total..............................	5,191,645	100.0	2.6	42.4	23.3	3.9	0.8	26.0	0.9
27111	Newspapers.........................	47,579	100.0	-	17.9	46.5	.5	-	-	35.1
27211	Periodicals........................	182,814	100.0	8.9	60.6	7.1	5.7	.3	14.6	2.9
27311	Books..............................	1,393,092	100.0	4.0	44.4	9.7	1.0	1.8	39.0	-
27411	Catalogs and directories...........	323,148	100.0	3.3	50.5	18.9	4.7	.2	22.4	-
27419	Printed matter, n.e.c..............	1,864,746	100.0	1.5	34.2	34.7	5.6	.2	23.9	-
27611	Manifold business forms............	208,792	100.0	.3	71.1	9.9	2.2	2.5	8.9	5.1
27711	Greeting cards.....................	342,919	100.0	3.0	66.8	7.7	1.1	.2	21.3	-
27811	Blankbooks, pads and tablets.......	167,357	100.0	5.3	22.8	25.8	-	1.7	44.4	-
27812	Looseleaf binders and devices......	68,430	100.0	.9	47.0	28.7	2.5	.4	20.6	-
27911	Products of service industries for the printing trades..	410,073	100.0	-	24.4	48.1	10.0	.2	13.8	3.5
	All other[3].......................	182,701	100.0	3.5	63.2	13.9	3.1	1.0	15.3	-

See footnotes at bottom of page.

TABLE 2. Percent Distribution of Commodities Shipped by Distance of Shipment: 1972

TCC code	Commodity description	Total value[1] (thousands)	All dis-tances	Under 50 miles	50 to 99 miles	100 to 299 miles	300 to 499 miles	500 to 999 miles	1,000 miles and over	Un-known
	Total..............................	5,191,645	100.0	35.4	11.4	17.6	10.7	10.5	12.9	1.5
27111	Newspapers.........................	47,579	100.0	39.6	4.1	5.7	4.4	10.0	1.0	35.1
27211	Periodicals........................	182,814	100.0	10.3	13.1	14.6	18.4	24.4	16.4	2.9
27311	Books..............................	1,393,092	100.0	18.2	10.1	25.2	14.0	13.1	19.4	-
27411	Catalogs and directories...........	323,148	100.0	42.2	11.5	13.5	12.8	9.6	10.4	-
27419	Printed matter, n.e.c..............	1,864,746	100.0	50.0	13.8	11.5	8.4	7.8	7.2	1.3
27611	Manifold business forms............	208,792	100.0	22.8	12.9	33.8	9.2	8.2	8.1	5.1
27711	Greeting cards.....................	342,919	100.0	14.9	6.2	15.1	15.3	14.1	34.4	-
27811	Blankbooks, pads and tablets.......	167,357	100.0	36.0	11.4	31.8	6.0	8.4	6.4	-
27812	Looseleaf binders and devices......	68,430	100.0	35.1	4.2	38.4	12.5	5.5	4.4	-
27911	Products of service industries for the printing trades..	410,073	100.0	58.0	6.4	10.2	4.7	8.0	9.1	3.5
	All other[3].......................	182,701	100.0	31.8	19.7	17.2	9.8	10.7	7.4	3.4

See footnotes at bottom of page.

TABLE 3. Percent Distribution of Commodities Shipped by Domestic and Foreign Destinations: 1972

TCC code	Commodity description	Total value[1] (thousands)	All destinations	Domestic	Foreign
	Total..............................	5,191,645	100.0	98.6	1.4
27111	Newspapers.........................	47,579	100.0	99.6	.4
27211	Periodicals........................	182,814	100.0	99.1	.9
27311	Books..............................	1,393,092	100.0	96.6	3.4
27411	Catalogs and directories...........	323,148	100.0	99.5	.5
27419	Printed matter, n.e.c..............	1,864,746	100.0	99.6	.4
27611	Manifold business forms............	208,792	100.0	99.0	1.0
27711	Greeting cards.....................	342,919	100.0	98.7	1.3
27811	Blankbooks, pads and tablets.......	167,357	100.0	99.1	.9
27812	Looseleaf binders and devices......	68,430	100.0	97.7	2.3
27911	Products of service industries for the printing trades.......	410,073	100.0	99.2	.8
	All other[3].......................	182,701	100.0	98.9	1.1

Note: Detail may not add to totals due to rounding. The survey excludes SIC 2711 (Newspapers) and SIC 2712 (Periodicals).

- Represents zero or rounds to zero.

[1]Value of shipments derived from census of manufactures total value of shipments for 1972.   [2]Includes railway and air express, United Parcel, parcel post, and other "package carriers".   [3]Represents balance of commodities not shown due to disclosure.

NORTH CENTRAL REGION

TABLE 1. Percent Distribution of Commodities Shipped by Means of Transport: 1972

TCC code	Commodity description	Total value[1] (thousands)	All means of transport	Rail	Motor carrier	Private truck	Air	Water	Other[2]	Un-known
	Total..	6,357,051	100.0	7.1	41.0	19.7	3.1	0.2	28.8	0.2
27211	Periodicals....................................	416,243	100.0	35.7	43.8	1.6	1.3	-	17.6	-
27311	Books..	1,022,594	100.0	4.9	35.9	5.4	1.2	.2	52.4	-
27411	Catalogs and directories......................	774,144	100.0	14.7	43.3	22.5	3.4	-	16.1	-
27417	Labels, seals, tags, and wrappers..........	232,205	100.0	1.8	52.4	5.2	4.1	-	36.5	-
27419	Printed matter, n.e.c..........................	2,337,272	100.0	4.3	38.4	27.8	3.5	.2	25.9	-
27611	Manifold business forms........................	332,990	100.0	.5	83.0	8.2	1.5	.3	6.6	-
27711	Greeting cards.................................	530,726	100.0	5.8	45.7	2.4	3.2	-	42.9	-
27811	Blankbooks, pads and tablets...................	156,742	100.0	2.2	30.9	8.3	1.2	-	57.4	-
27911	Products of service industries for the printing trades..	364,897	100.0	.1	22.1	51.1	10.5	1.2	15.1	-
	All other[3]...................................	189,166	100.0	.2	27.5	60.9	.1	-	6.1	5.3

See footnotes at bottom of page.

TABLE 2. Percent Distribution of Commodities Shipped by Distance of Shipment: 1972

TCC code	Commodity description	Total value[1] (thousands)	All dis-tances	Under 50 miles	50 to 99 miles	100 to 299 miles	300 to 499 miles	500 to 999 miles	1,000 miles and over	Un-known
	Total..	6,357,051	100.0	24.3	7.6	13.8	13.5	22.4	17.1	1.4
27211	Periodicals....................................	416,243	100.0	3.2	4.0	10.6	21.4	36.5	24.3	-
27311	Books..	1,022,594	100.0	5.0	3.9	16.9	19.1	25.9	29.3	-
27411	Catalogs and directories......................	774,144	100.0	22.0	6.5	14.3	13.3	22.7	19.2	2.1
27417	Labels, seals, tags, and wrappers.............	232,205	100.0	33.3	11.5	11.4	10.8	19.7	13.3	-
27419	Printed matter, n.e.c..........................	2,337,272	100.0	35.2	10.6	12.4	9.1	20.0	9.7	2.9
27611	Manifold business forms........................	332,990	100.0	12.6	5.0	23.4	23.1	30.2	5.6	.1
27711	Greeting cards.................................	530,726	100.0	2.4	1.2	14.4	18.7	26.8	35.6	1.0
27811	Blankbooks, pads and tablets...................	156,742	100.0	20.0	9.1	4.9	18.6	18.6	28.9	-
27911	Products of service industries for the printing trades..	364,897	100.0	54.5	13.0	17.3	5.9	5.6	3.8	-
	All other[3]...................................	189,166	100.0	66.3	8.1	2.9	2.7	13.7	6.3	-

See footnotes at bottom of page.

TABLE 3. Percent Distribution of Commodities Shipped by Domestic and Foreign Destinations: 1972

TCC code	Commodity description	Total value[1] (thousands)	All destinations	Domestic	Foreign
	Total..	6,357,051	100.0	98.7	1.3
27211	Periodicals....................................	416,243	100.0	98.8	1.2
27311	Books..	1,022,594	100.0	96.6	3.4
27411	Catalogs and directories......................	774,144	100.0	99.6	.4
27417	Labels, seals, tags, and wrappers.............	232,205	100.0	99.6	.4
27419	Printed matter, n.e.c..........................	2,337,272	100.0	98.6	1.4
27611	Manifold business forms........................	332,990	100.0	99.4	.6
27711	Greeting cards.................................	530,726	100.0	98.6	1.4
27811	Blankbooks, pads and tablets...................	156,742	100.0	99.7	.3
27911	Products of service industries for the printing trades.......	364,897	100.0	99.9	.1
	All other[3]...................................	189,166	100.0	100.0	-

Note: Detail may not add to totals due to rounding. The survey excludes SIC 2711 (Newspapers) and SIC 2712 (Periodicals).

- Represents zero or rounds to zero.

[1]Value of shipments derived from census of manufactures total value of shipments for 1972.   [2]Includes railway and air express, United Parcel, parcel post, and other "package carriers".   [3]Represents balance of commodities not shown due to disclosure.

SOUTH REGION

TABLE 1. Percent Distribution of Commodities Shipped by Means of Transport: 1972

TCC code	Commodity description	Total value[1] (thousands)	All means of transport	Rail	Motor carrier	Private truck	Air	Water	Other[2]	Un-known
	Total..	3,433,770	100.0	5.3	44.1	22.4	3.5	0.2	21.7	2.7
27111	Newspapers..	65,547	100.0	-	64.3	4.8	-	-	15.9	15.0
27211	Periodicals..	117,580	100.0	2.3	43.1	11.2	.8	1.1	41.5	-
27311	Books..	320,510	100.0	3.1	44.6	5.4	2.3	.9	43.7	-
27411	Catalogs and directories..........................	128,479	100.0	2.1	20.2	44.0	2.2	-	31.4	-
27417	Labels, seals, tags, and wrappers.....................	255,134	100.0	6.6	63.6	6.3	1.6	-	22.0	-
27419	Printed matter, n.e.c..............................	1,216,488	100.0	4.5	33.5	32.7	6.9	.2	16.5	5.6
27611	Manifold business forms............................	911,654	100.0	9.3	63.0	15.8	1.2	-	9.0	1.7
27911	Products of service industries for the printing trades..	270,847	100.0	4.4	37.7	44.9	3.3	-	9.8	-
	All other[3]..	147,532	100.0	-	4.6	.2	-	-	95.2	-

See footnotes at bottom of page.

TABLE 2. Percent Distribution of Commodities Shipped by Distance of Shipment: 1972

TCC code	Commodity description	Total value[1] (thousands)	All dis-tances	Under 50 miles	50 to 99 miles	100 to 299 miles	300 to 499 miles	500 to 999 miles	1,000 miles and over	Un-known
	Total..	3,433,770	100.0	30.9	9.3	15.0	19.0	14.5	8.7	2.7
27111	Newspapers..	65,547	100.0	56.9	14.6	4.0	1.3	3.4	4.8	15.0
27211	Periodicals..	117,580	100.0	9.7	2.8	19.0	17.5	20.2	30.9	-
27311	Books..	320,510	100.0	8.1	4.6	12.6	26.9	33.5	14.2	-
27411	Catalogs and directories..........................	128,479	100.0	19.9	4.7	8.9	45.2	10.3	11.1	-
27417	Labels, seals, tags, and wrappers.....................	255,134	100.0	3.1	1.8	18.6	24.3	33.0	19.3	-
27419	Printed matter, n.e.c..............................	1,216,488	100.0	36.7	12.5	17.7	11.8	11.5	4.3	5.6
27611	Manifold business forms............................	911,654	100.0	36.3	8.4	11.1	25.9	10.2	6.4	1.7
27911	Products of service industries for the printing trades..	270,847	100.0	35.4	8.6	16.1	13.9	11.8	14.2	-
	All other[3]..	147,532	100.0	53.3	19.0	20.9	6.4	.3	-	-

See footnotes at bottom of page.

TABLE 3. Percent Distribution of Commodities Shipped by Domestic and Foreign Destinations: 1972

TCC code	Commodity description	Total value[1] (thousands)	All destinations	Domestic	Foreign
	Total..	3,433,770	100.0	99.0	1.0
27111	Newspapers..	65,547	100.0	100.0	-
27211	Periodicals..	117,580	100.0	91.7	8.3
27311	Books..	320,510	100.0	97.7	2.3
27411	Catalogs and directories..........................	128,479	100.0	97.3	2.7
27417	Labels, seals, tags, and wrappers.....................	255,134	100.0	98.6	1.4
27419	Printed matter, n.e.c..............................	1,216,488	100.0	99.5	.5
27611	Manifold business forms............................	911,654	100.0	99.9	.1
27911	Products of service industries for the printing trades.......	270,847	100.0	99.0	1.0
	All other[3]..	147,532	100.0	100.0	-

Note: Detail may not add to totals due to rounding. The survey excludes SIC 2711 (Newspapers) and SIC 2712 (Periodicals).

- Represents zero or rounds to zero.

[1]Value of shipments derived from census of manufactures total value of shipments for 1972.   [2]Includes railway and air express, United Parcel, parcel post, and other "package carriers".   [3]Represents balance of commodities not shown due to disclosure.

WEST REGION

TABLE 1. Percent Distribution of Commodities Shipped by Means of Transport: 1972

TCC code	Commodity description	Total value[1] (thousands)	All means of transport	Rail	Motor carrier	Private truck	Air	Water	Other[2]	Un-known
	Total...	1,639,334	100.0	0.9	33.1	41.6	4.9	1.4	17.9	0.3
27311	Books...	110,081	100.0	2.3	29.8	29.8	12.5	14.2	11.4	-
27411	Catalogs and directories............................	148,127	100.0	1.7	36.2	38.9	11.8	.4	11.0	-
27419	Printed matter, n.e.c...............................	638,161	100.0	.2	38.4	41.8	2.1	.1	17.5	-
27611	Manifold business forms.............................	332,576	100.0	-	34.9	50.5	1.5	1.4	10.4	1.3
27911	Products of service industries for the printing trades..	140,726	100.0	-	5.5	72.3	16.5	-	5.8	-
	All other[3]..	269,664	100.0	2.9	32.6	20.3	2.5	.7	40.9	-

See footnotes at bottom of page.

TABLE 2. Percent Distribution of Commodities Shipped by Distance of Shipment: 1972

TCC code	Commodity description	Total value[1] (thousands)	All distances	Under 50 miles	50 to 99 miles	100 to 299 miles	300 to 499 miles	500 to 999 miles	1,000 miles and over	Un-known
	Total...	1,639,334	100.0	45.1	9.2	11.8	9.2	8.0	16.5	0.3
27311	Books...	110,081	100.0	39.1	7.8	7.6	12.3	9.1	24.1	-
27411	Catalogs and directories............................	148,127	100.0	56.8	7.8	4.6	3.8	9.2	17.7	-
27419	Printed matter, n.e.c...............................	638,161	100.0	50.4	6.5	15.9	12.2	2.9	12.1	-
27611	Manifold business forms.............................	332,576	100.0	27.1	12.0	13.8	9.3	17.3	19.3	1.3
27911	Products of service industries for the printing trades..	140,726	100.0	74.8	2.2	3.4	3.2	1.9	14.5	-
	All other[3]..	269,664	100.0	35.0	17.3	9.5	6.8	10.2	21.0	.2

See footnotes at bottom of page.

TABLE 3. Percent Distribution of Commodities Shipped by Domestic and Foreign Destinations: 1972

TCC code	Commodity description	Total value[1] (thousands)	All destinations	Domestic	Foreign
	Total...	1,639,334	100.0	98.9	1.1
27311	Books...	110,081	100.0	87.7	12.3
27411	Catalogs and directories............................	148,127	100.0	98.9	1.1
27419	Printed matter, n.e.c...............................	638,161	100.0	99.9	.1
27611	Manifold business forms.............................	332,576	100.0	99.8	.2
27911	Products of service industries for the printing trades......	140,726	100.0	99.8	.2
	All other[3]..	269,664	100.0	99.6	.4

Note: Detail may not add to totals due to rounding. The survey excludes SIC 2711 (Newspapers) and SIC 2712 (Periodicals).

- Represents zero or rounds to zero.

[1]Value of shipments derived from census of manufactures total value of shipments for 1972.   [2]Includes railway and air express, United Parcel, parcel post, and other "package carriers".   [3]Represents balance of commodities not shown due to disclosure.

Traffic Patterns of Small Manufacturing Plants

CONTENTS

The tables listed below are shown for the United States and each of the geographical regions:

1. Percent Distribution of Commodities Shipped by Means of Transport: 1972
2. Percent Distribution of Commodities Shipped by Distance of Shipment: 1972
3. Percent Distribution of Commodities Shipped by Domestic and Foreign Destinations: 1972

INTRODUCTION

DESCRIPTION OF THE COMMODITY TRANSPORTATION SURVEY

General

The Commodity Transportation Survey is one of the three components of the Census of Transportation, one of the Economic Censuses conducted every 5 years ending in "2" and "7". Two previous Commodity Transportation Surveys have been conducted—the first in 1963 and the second in 1967. The prime objective of this survey is to measure the transportation and geographic distribution of commodities[1] shipped by manufacturing establishments in the United States beyond the local area. The Commodity Transportation Survey, as it now exists, consists of two independent surveys: A mail summary-data survey and a main shipper survey.

Shipper Survey

The major part of the Commodity Transportation Survey is commonly referred to as the Shipper Survey. Traffic flow data is gathered, processed, and disseminated relating to the volume of commodities shipped by means of transport, length of haul, size of shipment, and areas of origin and destination in tons and ton-miles. The data sources are bills of lading or other shipping documents pertaining to individual shipments from a sample of about 13,000 plants selected from the census of manufactures universe of manufacturing establishments with 20 employees or more. The sample design is multistaged, utilizing a stratified probability sampling to obtain approximately 13,000 plants at the first stage and a systematic random sample of 1.6 million shipping documents (100 to 200 from each sampled plant) at the second stage. Although the source of the shipping information pertaining to each individual shipment is the shipping document, the primary sampling unit (PSU) may be either a plant or the shipping document itself. The primary sampling unit is the plant for all but the "certainty plants," those with a probability of "1" or greater at the first stage. For certainty plants, the PSU is usually the shipping document (bill of lading) drawn systematically from a random start.

Mail Survey

The smaller component of the survey consists of data collection by mail on a simplified 1-page summary question-naire. About 2,000 plants are sampled which have 10 to 19 employees, and about 1,000 plants are sampled in the Printing and Publishing Industry. In this mail survey, information relating to individual shipments is not collected. The respondent replies only to questions in terms of annual-percent-of-total-value shipped. Value is used as a unit of measure rather than tons since it was felt that the small manufacturers would not have summary data available on tons shipped. Data collected for the census year as a whole include value of product and services, major product shipped, distance shipped (six categories), type of transport used (six modes), and the geographic division of destination. Also included is the percent shipped for export to foreign countries. The sample designs used for these surveys are simple one-stage systematic random samples of plants from the respective universes.

PURPOSE AND SCOPE OF THE MAIL SURVEY

General

This report presents transportation data for a sample of manufacturing establishments with 10 to 19 employees (small plants) in the industries represented by the 1972 Commodity Transportation Survey.[2] Some comparisons also are made between the data for 1967 and the current 1972 survey years.

The "small plant" survey was introduced in 1967. Data from the 1963 Commodity Transportation Survey showed that the primary distribution of products by plants with less than 20 employees tended to be local and that this segment of the industry generated only about 4 percent of the total inter-city tons shipped by all manufacturing plants. However, these "small plants" constitute about two-thirds of the total number of establishments in the industrial universe. These findings led to the conclusion that survey costs and reporting effort for "small plants" could be reduced by using a different reporting plan without substantially reducing the usefulness of the traffic-flow data. So, in 1967, plants with 10 to 19 employees were sampled and asked to report by mail on only the general characteristics of their shipping pattern. Plants with less than 10 employees were omitted completely because they originated a small portion of the total intercity shipments.

---

[1] See appendix B for a description of changes between the 1967 and 1972 version of the Transportation Commodity Code (TCC) used for shipment commodity classifications.

[2] This included all manufacturing industries with Standard Industrial Classification Codes (SIC) of 201 through 399 except: SIC 2026—Fluid milk, SIC 2051—Bakery products, SIC 2097—Manufactured ice, SIC 2411—Primary forest products, and SIC 27—Printing, publishing, and allied industries. SIC 27 was surveyed by mail and the results published separately.

Figure 1. Percent Distribution of Shipments of Small Manufacturing Plants, by Characteristic: 1972

(Based on value of shipments)

MEANS OF TRANSPORT

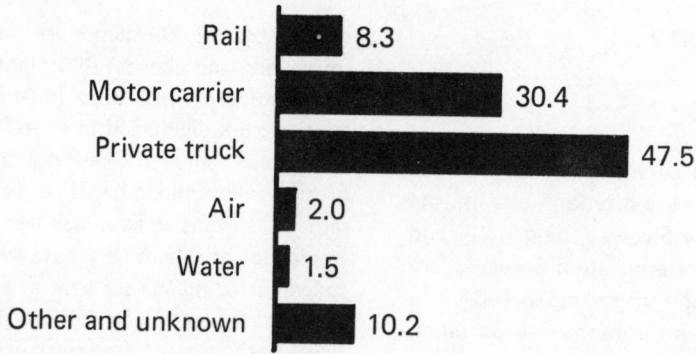

Rail	8.3
Motor carrier	30.4
Private truck	47.5
Air	2.0
Water	1.5
Other and unknown	10.2

DISTANCE OF SHIPMENT

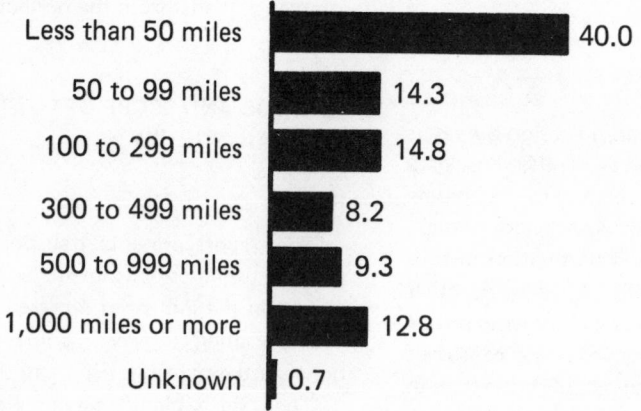

Less than 50 miles	40.0
50 to 99 miles	14.3
100 to 299 miles	14.8
300 to 499 miles	8.2
500 to 999 miles	9.3
1,000 miles or more	12.8
Unknown	0.7

DOMESTIC OR FOREIGN DESTINATIONS

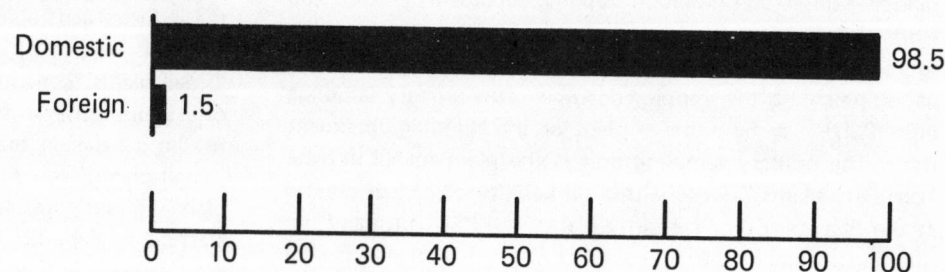

Domestic	98.5
Foreign	1.5

0 10 20 30 40 50 60 70 80 90 100

U.S. DEPARTMENT OF COMMERCE Social and Economic Statistics Administration BUREAU OF THE CENSUS

Report Form and Basic Data

In early 1973, Form TC-420 (see appendix A for facsimile of questionnaire) was mailed to each establishment in the sample requesting data on shipments made during 1972. The value of products and services (item II) was used as an indicator of the volume of shipments. An estimate of tons shipped would have been preferable as a measure of the transportation volume, but it was believed that a large proportion of the plants would not have been able to provide estimates of tons. However, all establishments were able to supply data based on total value figures.

The primary data items for the survey were the percentage distributions of value shipped during 1972 by distance and by means of transport (items IV and V). This information was requested in the form of percentage distributions rather than absolutes (tons or value) because the latter information usually is not available and is more difficult for shippers to estimate than relative distributions.

The 1972 questionnaire was basically the same as that used in 1967. Two items were added: Item III asks for the major product shipped and item VI asks U.S. area of destination by the nine geographic divisions. A question asked in 1967 relating to available shipping facilities was deleted.

Estimation Procedure

The method for aggregating and expanding the sample of individual reports to universe levels involved two steps. The first step was conversion of percentages into estimated value of shipments for each plant. This was done by multiplying the reported total value of products and services times the percentages reported in each category times the nonresponse adjustment factor for the industry times the plant expansion (sampling fraction which was 1 in 19). These results were finally ratio adjusted to known census of manufactures value of shipments for 1972 after allowing for Commodity Transportation Survey out-of-scope industries. The second step involved the aggregation of plant values and the computation of percentage distributions shown in the tables.

Other Related Surveys

A similar survey was taken to obtain comparable traffic-pattern data for the printing and publishing industry, except newspapers and periodicals.[3] The same report form was used

(TC-420), but the sample represented plants in all size classes[4] in contrast to the single size class in this survey. The data for the two surveys are comparable in all other respects.

Comparison to and use with the main shipper survey component of the Commodity Transportation Survey data of shipments from plants with 20 employees or more must be qualified by the following. The small-plant survey collects total value of shipments while the main survey presents data in tons shipped beyond the local area (generally 25 miles or more from the plant). Local shippers are thereby excluded from the main survey and included in this survey. The main survey obtains tons shipped by specific commodity (Transportation Commodity Code—TCC) while this survey attributes the entire plant's value of shipments to the principal commodity shipped.

Rough comparisons may be made between the percentage distributions by means of transportation and distance in each of the commodity groups represented by this survey with corresponding percentage distributions of tons for 3-digit commodities in the Commodity Series reports, providing allowance is made for differences created by local shipments. The 3-digit commodity data relate to intercity or long-haul shipments, while the distribution for small manufacturing plants and for printing and publishing include products used in or near the plant.

SUMMARY OF FINDINGS

About 78 percent of the total value of shipments by small plants was transported by truck with about 48 percent being handled by private truck and the remaining 30 percent by motor carrier. Railroads handled about 8 percent, air and water each about 2 percent, and other and unknown about 10 percent (unknown was less than 1 percent).

In all four geographic regions, the majority of volume was controlled by motor carrier and private truck, with private truck predominating except in the Northeast. Collectively, air and water accounted for less than 5 percent in each of the regions. However, the railroad share varied from about 1 percent in the Northeast to about 16 percent in the West.

The market area for small plants appears to be relatively small. Less than half of the total value of shipments was transported 100 miles or more from the plant. About 40 percent of the total value traveled less than 50 miles. Both of these statements are true at the national as well as regional levels.

As expected, the majority of total volume had domestic destinations. Nationally, this represented almost all (98 percent) of the total volume. Regional data show similar results.

---

[3] See report on "Printing, Publishing, and Allied Industries (Except Newspapers and Periodicals)" in the Commodity Transportation Survey.

[4] Except that manufacturing plants with less than 10 employees were not included in any phase of the Commodity Transportation Survey.

Figure 2. Shipments of Small Manufacturing Plants, by Geographic Division of Destination: 1972

(Based on value of shipments)

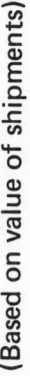

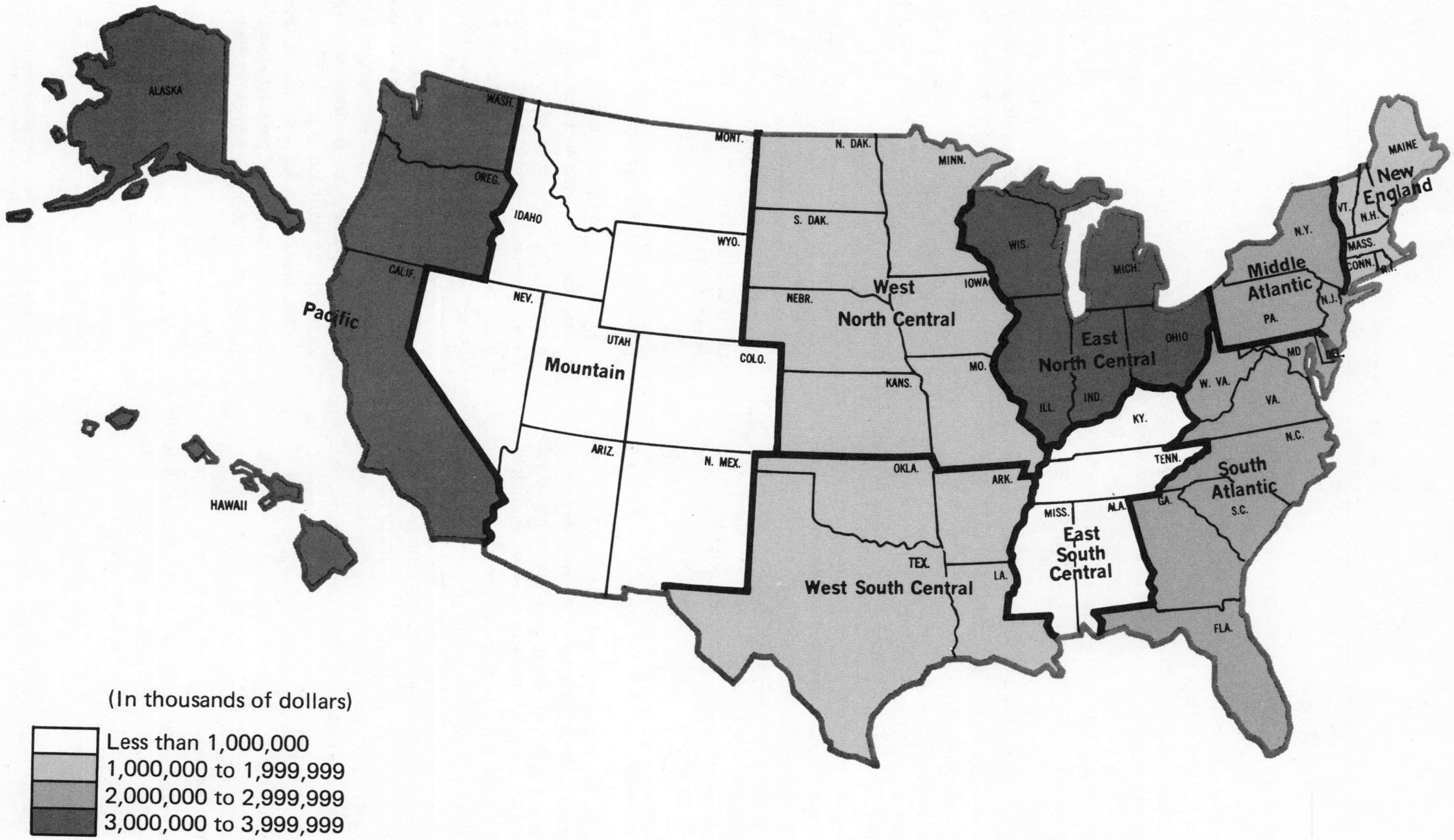

(In thousands of dollars)

Less than 1,000,000
1,000,000 to 1,999,999
2,000,000 to 2,999,999
3,000,000 to 3,999,999

U.S. DEPARTMENT OF COMMERCE Social and Economic Statistics Administration BUREAU OF THE CENSUS

COMPARISON WITH THE 1967 SURVEY[5]

Generally, the 1967 and 1972 surveys were similar and produced comparable results. However, there are several qualifications. The 1967 data were tabulated and presented by shipper group (groups of SIC's); the 1972 data were collected and tabulated by major product shipped (Transportation Commodity Code, TCC). This was done to make the results more compatible with the main shipper survey of establishments with 20 employees or more and to produce commodity based statistics. The TCC and SIC are generally comparable at the 3-digit level of presentation.

The destination region of shipments was collected for the first time in 1972 in order to produce origin/destination data for small plants. However, multidimensional matrices (such as origin/destination by means of transport) are not possible because of the summary nature of the questionnaire.

In 1967, three major industrial groups[5] were unintentionally omitted from the survey universe. These groups were included in the 1972 survey, and therefore, caution must be exercised by users wishing to make comparisons between the two surveys or with other census data. The value of shipments made by these three groups in 1972 was about 2.8 million dollars or about 14 percent of the total value shipped by all establishments in the survey.

The 1972 data showed an increase in the total value of shipments of about 62 percent over 1967[5]. Where SIC's 201, 202, and 203 are excluded from 1972 data, the increase is about 39 percent. Distribution by means of transport showed a reversal in the role of major carrier. In 1967, motor carriers handled about half of the total value shipped. Their share dropped to about 30 percent (33 percent adjusted) in 1972. Private truck, which had about 30 percent in 1967, carried almost half of the total value (48 percent) in 1972. Much of this change could be attributed to the West where motor carrier experienced a decrease from 75 percent in 1967 to 23 percent in 1972. Also in the West, the percent shipped by rail, private truck, and water more than doubled. Most noticable in the Northeast were the declines in shipment by rail and by water. Both means decreased by about 80 percent of their 1967 share. Rail shipments in the North Central Region more than doubled since 1967. The modal splits for the South remained near the levels reported in 1967.

The market areas for small plants continued to be relatively concentrated. About two-thirds of the total value of all shipments traveled less than 300 miles and more than half traveled less than 100 miles. However, the percentage that traveled less than 50 miles decreased from about 53 percent in 1967 to 40 percent in 1972.

The percent of total value with foreign destinations decreased. This can be seen in all regions except the North Central; however, a partial adjustment made to allow for the industries omitted in 1967 indicates that there may also have been a decrease in this region.

RELIABILITY OF THE ESTIMATES

General Description

The statistics in this report are estimates derived from a sample survey. There are two types of errors possible in an estimate based on a sample survey—sampling and nonsampling. Sampling errors occur because observations are made only on a sample, not on the entire population. Nonsampling errors can be attributed to many sources: inability to obtain information about all cases in the sample, definitional difficulties, differences in the interpretation of questions, inability or unwillingness to provide correct information on the part of respondents, mistakes in recording or coding the data obtained, and other errors of collection, response, processing, coverage, and estimation for missing data. Nonsampling errors also occur in complete censuses. The "accuracy" of a survey result is determined by the joint effects of sampling and nonsampling errors. This total error therefore is dependent upon sampling and nonsampling errors and is usually of the order of size indicated by the standard error. However, for some estimates, the total error may considerably exceed the standard errors shown.

Nonsampling Errors

Generally, the response was very good and no discernable bias in the nonresponse was detected. The overall response rate was 88 percent. Processing errors are primarily related to coding, transcription, and key punching of data. However, clerical editing and computer-edit correction programs reduce these errors to a minimum.

Most of the small plants do not maintain book records on the percentage distribution of shipments by means of transport and distance. As a result, much of the data could possibly be based on the day-to-day experience of plant personnel. Therefore, particular care should be exercised in the interpretation of figures based on a relatively small number of cases as well as small differences between the data.

Sampling Errors

The sample estimate and an estimate of its standard error permit us to construct interval estimates with prescribed confi-

---

[5] Three major industries were omitted from 1967 data: Meat Products (SIC 201), Dairy Products (SIC 202), and Canned and Frozen Foods (SIC 203). Since shipments from the industries were predominantly private truck, the inclusion of these industries in 1972 accounts for a portion of the shift of the total to private truck and may affect other direct comparisons. Because of tabulation and disclosure procedures, regional adjustments were not possible; however, adjustments were made at the U.S. level.

dence that the interval includes the average result of all possible samples.

To illustrate, if all possible samples were selected, each of these were surveyed under essentially the same conditions, and an estimate and its estimated standard error were calculated from each sample, then—

(1) Approximately two-thirds of the intervals from one standard error below the estimate to one standard error above the estimate would include the average value of all possible samples. We call an interval from one standard error below the estimate to one standard error above the estimate a two-thirds confidence interval.

(2) Approximately nine-tenths of the intervals from 1.6 standard errors below the estimate to 1.6 standard errors above the estimate would include the average value of all possible samples. We call an interval from 1.6 standard errors below the estimate to 1.6 standard errors above the estimate a 90-percent confidence interval.

(3) Approximately nineteen-twentieths of the intervals from two standard errors below the estimate to two standard errors above the estimate would include the average value of all possible samples. We call an interval from two standard errors below the estimate to two standard errors above the estimate a 95-percent confidence interval.

(4) Almost all intervals from three standard errors below the sample estimate to three standard errors above the sample estimate would include the average value of all possible samples.

Thus, for a particular sample, one can say with specified confidence that the average of all possible samples is included in the constructed interval.

Use of Tables of Standard Errors

To derive estimates of standard errors that would be applicable to a wide variety of items and could be prepared at a moderate cost, a number of approximations were required. As a result, the standard errors presented provide a general order of magnitude rather than the exact standard error for any specific item. For example, table 1 of this report shows about 25 percent of the total value of all shipments from plants whose primary product shipped was TCC 209 was handled by motor carriers. The table below shows that for a 1972 U.S. total, column 1 should be used to calculate the standard error. Column 1 shows the standard error on an estimate of this size (25) to be approximately 3.5 percentage points.

Standard Errors of Estimated Percentages: 1972

(68 chances out of 100)

Percent estimated from data	Standard errors for column[1]—		
	1	2	3
0.5	0.3	0.4	0.4
1 or 99	.5	.5	.6
5 or 95	1.2	1.6	1.9
10 or 90	1.8	2.7	3.4
15 or 85	2.4	3.8	4.9
20 or 80	3.0	5.0	6.4
25 or 75	3.5	6.1	7.8
35 or 65	4.6	8.3	10.7
50	6.3	11.7	15.1

Note: Estimates of standard errors were not calculated for 1967 data. However, the standard errors should approximate those of 1972 data.

[1] To calculate the standard error of an estimate for the United States and geographic regions, use the appropriate column as follows:
United States, column 1   South Region, column 2
Northeast Region, column 3   West Region, column 3
North Central Region, column 3

Based on these data, the two-thirds confidence interval for this sample is from 21.5 to 28.5 percent. A conclusion that the average estimate of the percentage derived from all possible samples lies within a range computed in this way would be correct for roughly two-thirds of all possible samples. Similarly, we can conclude that the average estimate of the percentage derived from all possible samples lies within the interval from 19.4 to 30.6 percent with 90-percent confidence in our conclusion; or that the average estimate of the percentage lies within the interval from 18.0 to 32.0 percent with 95-percent confidence; or that the average estimate of the percentage lies within the interval from 14.5 to 35.5 percent almost certainly.

Standard Error of a Difference— Illustration

The estimate of a certain characteristic for the Northeast is 34.6 percent and the estimate of the same characteristic for the South is 61.3 percent. Since both of these estimates are based on samples, the estimated difference of 26.7 percentage points (61.3 − 34.6 = 26.7) is also subject to sampling error. The table above shows that the estimated standard error of 34.6 percent for the Northeast is 10.7 and the estimated standard error of 61.3 for the South is 8.4 percentage points. A rough estimate of the standard error of the difference may be ob-

tained by multiplying the larger of the two standard errors by 1.4[6]. Thus the standard error of the 26.7 percentage point difference is approximately 15.0 percentage points. Based on these data, the two-thirds confidence interval is from 11.7 to

---

[6] The standard error of a difference is actually

$$\sigma_{A-B} = \sqrt{\sigma^2_A + \sigma^2_B - 2\sigma_{AB}}$$

where

σ^2_A is the variance of A, σ^2_B is the variance of B, and

σ_{AB} is the covariance of A and B.

41.6 percent, and a conclusion that the average estimate of the percentage difference, derived from all possible samples, lies within a range computed in this way would be correct for roughly two-thirds of all possible samples. Similarly, a conclusion that the average estimate of the percentage difference, derived from all possible samples, lies within the interval from −3.3 to 56.7 percent would correspond to 95-percent confidence. Therefore, at the higher confidence level we would not conclude that the percent for the Northeast is actually less than the percent for the South.

Table A. Number of Plants in Net Sample, by Transportation Commodity Classification, for Geographic Regions

TCC Code and description	United States	Geographic region			
		North-east	North Central	South	West
Total	1,625	542	463	318	302
20. Food and kindred products	135	28	44	33	30
22. Textile mill products	25	17	(*)	6	(*)
23. Apparel and other finished textile products, including knit	158	102	14	16	26
24. Lumber and wood products, except furniture	129	24	31	49	25
25. Furniture and fixtures	57	17	13	15	12
26. Pulp, paper, and allied products	28	13	8	(*)	(*)
28. Chemicals and allied products	85	26	21	19	19
29. Petroleum and coal products	13	(*)	(*)	(*)	(*)
30. Rubber and miscellaneous plastics products	51	17	16	8	10
31. Leather and leather products	17	11	(*)	(*)	(*)
32. Stone, clay, glass, and concrete products	128	28	44	36	20
33. Primary metal products	34	9	15	5	5
34. Fabricated metal products, except ordnance, machinery and transportation	209	59	76	38	36
35. Machinery, except electrical	301	85	123	44	49
36. Electrical machinery, equipment, and supplies	76	32	15	9	20
37. Transportation equipment	41	8	12	10	11
38. Instruments, photographic and medical goods, watches, and clocks	29	11	(*)	(*)	9
39. Miscellaneous products of manufacturing	107	51	19	18	19
All other[1]	2	4	12	12	11

*Potential disclosure in data; number of plants not tabulated.

[1] Two plants shipped a primary commodity outside the TCC 20-to-39 range although they were classified and sampled in the SIC 20-to-39 range.

Table B1. United States—Percent Distribution of Shipments by Means of Transport, Distance Shipped, and Domestic and Foreign Destinations: 1972 and 1967

(Based on value of shipments)

Item	1972[1]	1972[2]	1967[3]	Percent change, 1972 from 1967
Value of shipments (thousands of dollars)	18,156,900	15,542,300	12,089,500	(X)
MEANS OF TRANSPORT	PERCENT			
Total	100.0	100.0	100.0	(X)
Rail	8.3	8.2	5.8	+2.4
Motor carrier	30.4	33.4	50.4	−17.0
Private truck	47.5	43.0	31.5	+11.5
Air	2.0	2.4	3.0	−.6
Water	1.5	1.1	1.0	+.1
Other[4]	10.2	11.9	8.3	+3.6
DISTANCE SHIPPED				
Total	100.0	100.0	100.0	(X)
Under 50 miles	40.0	40.3	52.6	−12.3
50 to 99 miles	14.3	14.1	8.7	+5.4
100 to 299 miles	14.8	14.3	12.2	+2.1
300 to 499 miles	8.2	8.2	7.8	+.4
500 to 999 miles	9.3	8.6	9.8	−1.2
1,000 miles and over	12.8	13.8	8.9	+4.9
Unknown[5]	.7	.8	—	(X)
DESTINATION				
Total	100.0	100.0	100.0	(X)
Domestic destinations	98.5	98.9	97.1	+1.8
Foreign destionations	1.5	1.1	2.9	−1.8

Note: Detail may not add to total due to rounding. —Represents zero. (X) Not applicable.

[1] Derived by using 1972 Census of Manufactures total value of shipments.
[2] TCC's 201, 202, and 203 were excluded from these estimates to make comparable with 1967 Commodity Transportation Survey estimates.
[3] Excludes SIC 201, 202, and 203 groups.
[4] Means of transport data for "other" and "unknown" were collapsed for 1972 and mileage was imputed for 1967 data.
[5] "Unknown" were not classified separately for 1967 data.

Table B2. Geographic Regions—Percent Distribution of Shipments by Means of Transport, Distance Shipped, and Domestic and Foreign Destinations: 1972 and 1967

(Based on value of shipments)

Item	1972	1967[1]	Percent change, 1972 from 1967	Item	1972	1967[1]	Percent change, 1972 from 1967
	NORTHEAST REGION				NORTH CENTRAL REGION		
MEANS OF TRANSPORT				MEANS OF TRANSPORT			
Total	100.0	100.0	(X)	Total	100.0	100.0	(X)
Rail	1.0	5.4	−4.4	Rail	9.3	4.1	+5.2
Motor carrier	40.1	40.8	−.7	Motor carrier	29.4	36.0	−6.6
Private truck	34.6	29.6	+5.0	Private truck	49.8	51.1	−1.3
Air	3.3	2.8	+.5	Air	1.2	1.3	−.1
Water	.4	2.2	−1.8	Water	2.6	.1	+2.5
Other[2]	20.6	19.2	+1.4	Other[2]	7.7	7.4	+.3
DISTANCE SHIPPED				DISTANCE SHIPPED			
Total	100.0	100.0	(X)	Total	100.0	100.0	(X)
Under 50 miles	42.2	43.1	−.9	Under 50 miles	40.2	53.7	−13.5
50 to 99 miles	14.7	12.3	+2.4	50 to 99 miles	12.8	10.3	+2.5
100 to 299 miles	13.7	16.6	−2.9	100 to 299 miles	15.5	15.2	+.3
300 to 499 miles	6.4	8.4	−2.0	300 to 499 miles	12.6	8.0	+4.6
500 to 999 miles	8.6	9.9	−1.3	500 to 999 miles	10.0	8.4	+1.6
1,000 miles and over	13.7	9.7	+4.0	1,000 miles and over	7.5	4.4	+3.1
Unknown[3]	.7	−	(X)	Unknown[3]	1.3	−	(X)
DESTINATION				DESTINATION			
Total	100.0	100.0	(X)	Total	100.0	100.0	(X)
Domestic destination	98.4	97.1	+1.3	Domestic destination . . .	97.5	98.6	−1.1
Foreign destination	1.6	2.9	−1.3	Foreign destination	2.5	1.4	+1.1

See footnotes at end of table.

Table B2. Geographic Regions—Percent Distribution of Shipments by Means of Transport, Distance Shipped, and Domestic and Foreign Destinations: 1972 and 1967—Continued

(Based on value of shipments)

Item	1972	1967[1]	Percent change, 1972 from 1967	Item	1972	1967[1]	Percent change, 1972 from 1967
	SOUTH REGION				**WEST REGION**		
MEANS OF TRANSPORT				MEANS OF TRANSPORT			
Total	100.0	100.0	(X)	Total	100.0	100.0	(X)
Rail	6.5	10.2	−3.7	Rail	16.2	5.2	+11.0
Motor carrier	28.0	22.9	+5.1	Motor carrier	22.9	75.0	−52.1
Private truck	61.3	58.2	+3.1	Private truck	49.2	14.0	+35.2
Air	1.3	2.3	−1.0	Air	2.1	4.2	−2.1
Water	.3	1.1	−.8	Water	2.3	.3	+2.0
Other[2]	2.6	5.3	−2.7	Other[2]	7.2	1.3	+5.9
DISTANCE SHIPPED				DISTANCE SHIPPED			
Total	100.0	100.0	(X)	Total	100.0	100.0	(X)
Under 50 miles	37.3	42.4	−5.1	Under 50 miles	39.4	63.9	−24.5
50 to 99 miles	13.6	13.8	−.2	50 to 99 miles	15.6	3.0	+12.6
100 to 299 miles	20.8	16.6	+4.2	100 to 299 miles	11.1	5.5	+5.6
300 to 499 miles	7.7	13.8	−6.1	300 to 499 miles	6.2	5.0	+1.2
500 to 999 miles	16.3	7.2	+9.1	500 to 999 miles	4.6	11.3	−6.7
1,000 miles and over	4.1	6.2	−2.1	1,000 miles and over	22.7	11.3	+11.4
Unknown[3]	.2	—	(X)	Unknown[3]	.3	—	(X)
DESTINATION				DESTINATION			
Total	100.0	100.0	(X)	Total	100.0	100.0	(X)
Domestic destination	99.1	97.7	+1.4	Domestic destination	99.1	96.2	+2.9
Foreign destination	.9	2.3	−1.4	Foreign destination	.9	3.8	−2.9

Note: Detail may not add to total due to rounding.

—Represents zero.　(X) Not applicable.

[1] Estimates exclude SIC's 201, 202, and 203 for 1967.

[2] Means of transport data for other and unknown were collapsed for 1972 and mileage was imputed for 1967 data.

[3] "Unknown" were not classified separately for 1967 data.

Table C. Percent Distribution of Shipments from Geographic Regions, by Division of Destination: 1972

(Based on value of shipments)

Division of destination	United States	Region of origin			
		Northeast	North Central	South	West
Value of shipments[1] *(thousands of dollars)*	*18,156,900*	*5,089,625*	*4,729,081*	*3,374,446*	*4,963,160*
PERCENT DISTRIBUTION					
Total	100.0	100.0	100.0	100.0	100.0
New England	6.3	19.4	1.9	1.3	.6
Middle Atlantic	16.2	48.5	5.6	3.5	1.6
East North Central	19.6	6.9	52.4	7.7	9.6
West North Central	7.8	2.5	23.5	1.9	2.2
South Atlantic	13.3	8.6	5.2	49.7	1.1
East South Central	5.4	2.5	3.1	15.6	3.5
West South Central	6.1	3.0	5.0	18.1	2.3
Mountain	4.0	1.5	1.4	.8	11.4
Pacific	20.4	5.3	1.6	.6	67.1
Unknown	.9	1.7	.3	.8	.6

Note: Detail may not add to total due to rounding.

[1] Derived using 1972 Census of Manufactures total value of shipments and Commodity Transportation Survey proportions.

UNITED STATES

TABLE 1. Percent Distribution of Commodities Shipped by Means of Transport: 1972

TCC code	Commodity description	Value[1] (thousands)	All means of transport	Rail	Motor carrier	Private truck	Air	Water	Other[2]	Un-known
	United States, total...................................	18,156,900	100.0	8.3	30.4	47.5	2.0	1.5	9.6	0.6
20	Food and kindred products..............................	4,068,719	100.0	10.7	15.1	68.9	.6	3.0	1.7	–
201	Meat; fresh, chilled, frozen..............................	878,555	100.0	6.8	5.2	76.7	–	11.4	. –	–
202	Dairy products...	1,315,488	100.0	–	9.4	90.6	–	–	–	–
203	Canned and preserved fruits, vegetables, seafoods...........	407,589	100.0	43.9	39.2	15.8	.9	.1	.2	–
204	Grain mill products.....................................	661,859	100.0	27.6	29.1	43.3	–	–	.1	–
207	Confectionery and related products..........................	33,061	100.0	–	77.3	22.6	–	–	.2	–
208	Beverages and flavoring extracts..........................	567,804	100.0	.3	3.5	76.6	3.9	3.9	11.9	–
209	Miscellaneous food preparations...........................	186,034	100.0	.4	25.0	74.5	–	–	.1	–
22	Textile mill products.........................•...........	203,479	100.0	1.3	72.6	19.3	1.5	.4	5.0	–
225	Knit fabrics...	65,437	100.0	–	85.8	7.4	3.2	–	3.6	–
229	Miscellaneous textile goods..............................	103,200	100.0	.1	69.1	21.8	.9	.7	7.4	–
23	Apparel and other finished textile products, including knit.	1,724,343	100.0	1.4	37.4	15.1	7.0	.3	36.5	2.4
231	Men's, youth's, and boys' clothing.........................	363,471	100.0	.8	46.6	1.3	7.7	–	43.6	–
233	Women's, misses', children's, and infants' clothing..........	772,603	100.0	2.0	36.9	7.6	9.3	.5	41.2	2.6
237	Fur goods..	107,171	100.0	–	9.9	37.6	10.2	–	22.1	20.2
238	Miscellaneous apparel and accessories.....................	104,851	100.0	–	61.4	2.8	2.5	–	33.3	–
239	Miscellaneous fabricated textile products..................	341,477	100.0	1.3	27.1	43.8	1.9	.1	25.9	–
24	Lumber and wood products, except furniture.................	1,180,546	100.0	11.7	21.1	66.0	–	.1	.4	.8
242	Sawmill and planing mill products.........................	643,025	100.0	20.1	23.3	55.3	–	–	–	1.4
243	Millwork, plywood, and prefabricated wood products..........	189,767	100.0	3.2	15.4	80.7	.1	–	.6	–
244	Wood containers..	58,328	100.0	.2	31.3	68.5	–	–	–	–
249	Miscellaneous wood products..............................	285,934	100.0	1.1	18.1	79.3	–	.3	1.1	–
25	Furniture and fixtures..................................	325,874	100.0	1.6	23.3	73.6	–	.2	1.2	–
251	Household and office furniture............................	154,159	100.0	.6	21.0	77.7	–	–	.7	–
254	Partitions, shelving, lockers, office and store fixtures....	35,091	100.0	–	11.5	87.0	.1	–	1.4	–
259	Miscellaneous furniture and fixtures......................	127,810	100.0	3.4	30.0	64.2	–	.6	1.8	–
26	Pulp, paper, and allied products..........................	240,730	100.0	–	28.6	69.1	.1	.2	2.0	–
264	Converted paper and paperboard products, except containers..	59,023	100.0	–	52.3	40.9	.5	.7	5.6	–
265	Containers and boxes, paperboard..........................	97,845	100.0	–	14.0	85.8	–	–	.3	–
28	Chemicals and allied products.......................	1,634,805	100.0	14.9	44.4	30.7	.2	7.0	2.7	–
281	Industrial inorganic and organic chemicals................	602,682	100.0	37.3	28.2	15.5	–	18.5	.5	–
282	Plastics materials......................................	108,598	100.0	–	87.9	10.3	.4	.1	1.3	–
284	Soap and other detergents................................	145,009	100.0	.3	58.2	27.9	.4	.2	13.1	–
285	Paints, enamels, lacquers, shellacs, and allied products....	108,429	100.0	–	16.1	83.3	–	–	.7	–
287	Agricultural chemicals..................................	150,535	100.0	3.9	10.9	84.8	–	–	.4	–
289	Miscellaneous chemical products...........................	505,617	100.0	2.6	66.7	26.7	.3	.4	3.3	–
29	Petroleum and coal products..............................	191,025	100.0	–	49.9	45.0	.2	.6	4.3	–
295	Asphalt paving and roofing materials......................	80,418	100.0	–	39.7	60.3	–	–	–	–
30	Rubber and miscellaneous plastics products.................	494,478	100.0	10.7	56.6	23.9	1.1	–	7.7	–
306	Miscellaneous fabricated rubber products..................	75,882	100.0	42.3	17.5	21.1	.5	–	18.6	–
307	Miscellaneous plastics products..........................	411,460	100.0	5.1	64.8	24.0	1.3	–	5.0	–
31	Leather and leather products.............................	204,822	100.0	–	62.2	4.7	1.8	.5	30.8	–
319	Leather goods, n.e.c.....................................	21,538	100.0	.1	46.6	10.5	11.1	–	31.7	–
32	Stone, clay, glass, and concrete products.................	1,398,410	100.0	2.2	20.2	74.7	.4	.1	2.4	–
322	Glass and glassware, pressed and blown....................	51,596	100.0	1.3	37.6	55.5	3.2	.2	2.1	–
325	Structural clay products................................	44,068	100.0	2.5	54.0	43.0	.2	–	.3	–
327	Concrete, gypsum, and plaster products....................	755,427	100.0	–	11.2	88.6	.1	–	.1	–
328	Cut stone and stone products.............................	27,446	100.0	.3	60.3	39.0	–	.3	.2	–
329	Abrasives and asbestos products..........................	381,797	100.0	1.3	25.6	66.1	.7	.3	6.0	–
33	Primary metal products..................................	277,511	100.0	.1	40.5	48.7	.9	–	8.2	1.5
336	Nonferrous metal castings................................	57,429	100.0	–	9.9	75.1	1.6	–	13.5	–
339	Miscellaneous primary metal products......................	85,120	100.0	–	32.4	51.5	.8	–	10.3	5.0

See footnotes at end of table.

UNITED STATES

TABLE 1. Percent Distribution of Commodities Shipped by Means of Transport: 1972—Continued

TCC code	Commodity description	Value[1] (thousands)	All means of transport	Rail	Motor carrier	Private truck	Air	Water	Other[2]	Un-known
34	Fabricated metal products except ordnance, machinery and transportation.............................	1,834,781	100.0	3.0	42.3	46.7	1.2	0.2	5.7	0.9
342	Cutlery, hand tools and general hardware....................	111,590	100.0	5.7	47.6	18.5	3.9	.8	23.6	–
343	Plumbing fixtures and heating apparatus.....................	56,416	100.0	–	42.0	47.5	2.8	.6	7.2	–
344	Fabricated structural metal products.......................	657,597	100.0	1.5	31.7	65.1	.2	–	2.0	–
345	Bolts, nuts, screws, rivets, and washers...................	69,563	100.0	–	48.3	18.4	1.0	–	22.4	10.0
346	Metal stampings...	212,769	100.0	2.1	52.6	28.9	1.8	–	10.0	4.6
348	Miscellaneous fabricated wire products.....................	58,520	100.0	.4	72.2	12.6	.3	1.3	13.3	–
349	Miscellaneous fabricated metal products....................	618,849	100.0	1.7	48.9	44.5	1.7	.2	3.0	–
35	Machinery, except electrical..............................	1,800,618	100.0	.3	37.8	47.9	2.8	.3	10.5	.2
352	Farm machinery and equipment..............................	118,718	100.0	2.3	41.5	53.4	–	.1	2.8	–
353	Construction, mining, materials handling machinery and equipment...	120,532	100.0	.3	56.9	30.8	2.5	.5	9.0	–
354	Metalworking machinery and equipment......................	551,893	100.0	.3	27.8	54.6	2.9	.2	13.3	.9
355	Special industry machinery...............................	170,151	100.0	–	60.3	28.8	1.7	–	9.2	–
356	General industrial machinery and equipment................	128,996	100.0	–	47.8	45.4	1.4	.3	5.2	–
358	Refrigeration and service industry machines...............	44,355	100.0	–	53.5	39.3	2.3	–	5.0	–
359	Miscellaneous machinery and parts.........................	633,552	100.0	.1	33.5	52.2	3.4	.5	10.3	–
36	Electrical machinery, equipment, and supplies.............	1,126,309	100.0	35.6	26.0	16.9	5.1	.9	15.3	.3
361	Electrical transmission equipment.........................	55,780	100.0	.9	12.2	34.7	7.8	–	44.4	–
362	Electrical industrial apparatus..........................	72,948	100.0	–	50.9	7.0	22.4	14.3	5.4	–
364	Electric lighting and wiring equipment....................	70,002	100.0	6.7	44.9	29.8	1.2	.1	17.3	–
366	Communication equipment...................................	27,372	100.0	–	4.7	8.8	13.9	–	59.2	13.4
367	Electronic components and accessories.....................	110,761	100.0	–	18.7	24.7	9.2	–	47.4	–
369	Miscellaneous electrical machinery, equipment, and supplies.	279,016	100.0	1.9	47.8	20.5	7.5	.1	22.3	–
37	Transportation equipment..................................	585,101	100.0	19.4	14.6	56.4	.2	1.1	3.9	4.6
371	Motor vehicles and equipment..............................	321,087	100.0	35.3	14.3	44.5	.1	1.4	4.5	–
373	Ships and boats...	38,320	100.0	–	33.8	61.6	–	4.4	.2	–
379	Miscellaneous transportation equipment....................	200,145	100.0	–	7.2	79.2	.2	–	.1	13.4
38	Instruments, photographic, and medical goods, watches and clocks	212,462	100.0	2.0	19.3	12.4	21.0	.8	44.5	–
382	Measuring and controlling instruments.....................	47,213	100.0	–	22.7	15.8	33.3	.4	27.8	–
384	Surgical, medical, dental instruments and supplies.........	35,460	100.0	2.1	30.0	9.5	7.1	1.1	50.3	–
39	Miscellaneous products of manufacturing...................	643,972	100.0	.6	33.1	26.1	3.8	.1	35.9	.3
391	Jewelry, silverware, and plated ware......................	115,928	100.0	.5	6.2	14.9	14.3	–	64.2	–
394	Toys, amusement, sporting, and athletic goods..............	109,905	100.0	2.2	63.0	7.4	1.4	.2	25.8	–
395	Pens, pencils, other office and artists' materials..........	47,942	100.0	–	32.8	4.3	–	.8	62.1	–
396	Costume jewelry, novelties, buttons and notions............	74,330	100.0	.1	32.2	32.6	1.3	–	33.8	–
399	Miscellaneous manufactured products.......................	290,428	100.0	.3	32.4	40.0	1.9	.1	24.7	.7
---	All other miscellaneous[3]................................	1,526,269	100.0	29.9	31.5	24.3	2.3	.2	11.7	–
--	All other miscellaneous[3]................................	8,355	100.0	–	57.4	41.9	–	–	.6	–

Note: Detail may not add to total due to rounding.

- Represents zero.

[1] Value of shipments derived from census of manufactures total value of shipments for 1972.
[2] Includes railway and air express, United Parcel, parcel post, and other "package carriers."
[3] Represents balance of commodities not shown at each level of detail due to disclosures and those commodities shipped by manufacturing establishments not specifically listed.

UNITED STATES

TABLE 2. Percent Distribution of Commodities Shipped by Distance of Shipment: 1972

TCC code	Commodity description	Value[1] (thousands)	All distances	Under[2] 50 miles	50 to 99 miles	100 to 299 miles	300 to 499 miles	500 to 999 miles	1,000 miles or more	Unknown
	United States, total................................	18,156,900	100.0	40.0	14.3	14.8	8.2	9.3	12.8	0.7
20	Food and kindred products..........................	4,068,719	100.0	42.3	14.7	16.1	8.4	10.7	7.0	.9
201	Meat; fresh, chilled, frozen.......................	878,555	100.0	29.5	10.0	30.1	2.3	28.1	.1	–
202	Dairy products.....................................	1,315,488	100.0	53.5	22.2	11.2	12.2	.9	–	–
203	Canned and preserved fruits, vegetables, seafoods..........	407,589	100.0	7.6	4.9	10.4	10.5	24.3	42.3	–
204	Grain mill products................................	661,859	100.0	38.1	12.0	15.4	10.9	6.3	12.0	5.3
207	Confectionery and related products.................	33,061	100.0	19.2	25.2	16.4	16.2	15.8	7.1	–
208	Beverages and flavoring extracts...................	567,804	100.0	67.4	11.7	8.5	3.6	4.0	4.8	–
209	Miscellaneous food preparations....................	186,034	100.0	41.9	22.8	18.8	10.8	4.0	1.8	–
22	Textile mill products..............................	203,479	100.0	25.3	27.2	13.8	13.3	6.2	7.8	6.4
225	Knit fabrics.......................................	65,437	100.0	18.8	57.3	15.9	.5	5.4	2.3	–
229	Miscellaneous textile goods........................	103,200	100.0	29.8	14.5	7.4	17.2	7.2	11.5	12.5
23	Apparel and other finished textile products, including knit.	1,724,343	100.0	31.4	10.6	15.7	8.4	11.2	21.8	.9
231	Men's, youths', and boys' clothing.................	363,471	100.0	23.1	10.8	21.5	10.4	8.4	25.9	–
233	Women's, misses', children's, and infants' clothing........	772,603	100.0	24.6	10.0	16.2	9.2	14.4	25.4	.4
237	Fur goods..	107,171	100.0	63.9	.7	3.5	6.6	1.1	17.3	6.8
238	Miscellaneous apparel and accessories..............	104,851	100.0	41.8	7.9	10.9	5.9	6.6	21.9	5.1
239	Miscellaneous fabricated textile products..........	341,477	100.0	39.8	14.6	14.6	6.5	12.2	12.2	–
24	Lumber and wood products, except furniture.........	1,180,546	100.0	33.7	14.3	17.9	10.8	13.0	9.3	1.2
242	Sawmill and planing mill products..................	643,025	100.0	21.8	14.3	23.5	12.7	10.1	15.9	1.7
243	Millwork, plywood, and prefabricated wood products..........	189,767	100.0	63.6	16.4	6.7	10.8	1.7	.9	–
244	Wood containers....................................	58,328	100.0	59.6	7.9	8.7	1.9	21.9	–	–
249	Miscellaneous wood products........................	285,934	100.0	34.3	14.2	14.8	8.3	25.5	1.9	1.0
25	Furniture and fixtures.............................	325,874	100.0	48.3	13.1	22.6	6.9	7.1	2.1	–
251	Household and office furniture.....................	154,159	100.0	53.6	11.8	20.7	4.3	8.8	.8	–
254	Partitions, shelving, lockers, office and store fixtures....	35,091	100.0	72.1	8.9	7.9	1.2	9.7	.2	–
259	Miscellaneous furniture and fixtures...............	127,810	100.0	34.1	15.8	29.7	11.6	4.7	4.2	–
26	Pulp, paper, and allied products...................	240,730	100.0	70.0	14.9	5.6	5.2	5.5	1.8	–
264	Converted paper and paperboard products, except containers..	59,023	100.0	49.4	17.2	6.7	9.9	11.4	5.4	–
265	Containers and boxes, paperboard...................	97,845	100.0	76.4	14.3	7.8	1.1	.2	.1	–
28	Chemicals and allied products......................	1,634,805	100.0	33.3	23.2	17.4	7.4	7.5	11.2	–
281	Industrial inorganic and organic chemicals.........	602,682	100.0	20.4	40.4	13.2	3.8	4.1	18.2	–
282	Plastics materials.................................	108,598	100.0	42.5	9.3	38.5	2.2	2.0	5.5	–
284	Soap and other detergents..........................	145,009	100.0	35.5	11.6	15.2	14.9	11.4	11.5	–
285	Paints, enamels, lacquers, shellacs, and allied products....	108,429	100.0	83.0	7.3	5.3	1.1	2.7	.7	–
287	Agricultural chemicals.............................	150,535	100.0	43.4	25.0	27.5	2.5	.8	.7	–
289	Miscellaneous chemical products....................	505,617	100.0	33.2	12.0	18.0	13.0	14.6	9.4	–
29	Petroleum and coal products........................	191,025	100.0	61.8	14.4	8.2	4.1	4.6	6.9	–
295	Asphalt paving and roofing materials...............	80,418	100.0	77.4	15.6	7.1	–	–	–	–
30	Rubber and miscellaneous plastics products.........	494,478	100.0	26.3	23.7	6.9	17.9	9.9	14.6	.7
306	Miscellaneous fabricated rubber products...........	75,882	100.0	23.5	10.6	8.5	5.5	5.4	46.6	–
307	Miscellaneous plastics products....................	411,460	100.0	26.4	26.5	6.7	20.5	10.9	9.0	–
31	Leather and leather products.......................	204,822	100.0	23.7	23.8	7.8	7.3	14.0	23.3	–
319	Leather goods, n.e.c...............................	21,538	100.0	70.9	6.2	2.2	2.2	5.1	13.4	–
32	Stone, clay, glass, and concrete products..........	1,398,410	100.0	75.0	11.2	7.6	2.3	1.2	2.6	–
322	Glass and glassware, pressed and blown.............	51,596	100.0	43.0	6.5	10.4	4.6	17.2	18.3	–
325	Structural clay products...........................	44,068	100.0	17.8	53.4	24.3	.3	2.3	1.9	–
327	Concrete, gypsum, and plaster products.............	755,427	100.0	88.8	8.0	2.5	.5	.2	.1	–
328	Cut stone and stone products.......................	27,446	100.0	29.9	34.7	30.5	3.7	.6	.8	–
329	Abrasives and asbestos products....................	381,797	100.0	81.1	5.6	4.8	1.2	1.3	6.0	–
33	Primary metal products.............................	277,511	100.0	49.6	11.5	16.3	7.0	12.7	2.9	–
336	Nonferrous metal castings..........................	57,429	100.0	82.0	8.2	3.2	1.5	3.0	2.1	–
339	Miscellaneous primary metal products...............	85,120	100.0	25.6	15.2	15.9	7.9	30.2	5.2	–

See footnotes at end of table.

UNITED STATES

TABLE 2. Percent Distribution of Commodities Shipped by Distance of Shipment: 1972 —Continued

TCC code	Commodity description	Value[1] (thousands)	All dis-tances	Under[2] 50 miles	50 to 99 miles	100 to 299 miles	300 to 499 miles	500 to 999 miles	1,000 miles or more	Un-known
34	Fabricated metal products except ordnance, machinery and transportation..	1,834,781	100.0	42.9	15.8	17.4	5.9	8.2	9.6	0.3
342	Cutlery, hand tools and general hardware....................	111,590	100.0	25.8	7.9	20.9	16.8	13.4	15.3	-
343	Plumbing fixtures and heating apparatus.....................	56,416	100.0	26.5	6.6	38.0	20.5	6.2	2.2	-
344	Fabricated structural metal products.......................	657,597	100.0	50.1	20.8	20.4	3.9	2.5	2.3	-
345	Bolts, nuts, screws, rivets, and washers...................	69,563	100.0	31.9	9.0	19.8	7.7	9.0	12.6	10.0
346	Metal stampings..	212,769	100.0	42.4	21.6	9.5	4.7	13.4	8.3	-
348	Miscellaneous fabricated wire products.....................	58,520	100.0	42.4	17.0	10.3	3.9	22.5	3.9	-
349	Miscellaneous fabricated metal products....................	618,849	100.0	39.9	11.8	13.6	5.5	10.9	18.3	-
35	Machinery, except electrical...............................	1,800,618	100.0	45.5	10.0	15.0	13.1	7.5	9.0	-
352	Farm machinery and equipment...............................	118,718	100.0	11.5	13.9	24.2	21.4	19.2	9.9	-
353	Construction, mining, materials handling machinery and equipment..	120,532	100.0	32.5	9.4	17.2	14.4	15.7	10.8	-
354	Metalworking machinery and equipment.......................	551,893	100.0	54.2	8.5	16.5	14.5	2.3	4.1	-
355	Special industry machinery.................................	170,151	100.0	23.2	13.6	28.1	12.6	7.4	15.2	-
356	General industrial machinery and equipment.................	128,996	100.0	42.1	10.5	13.5	17.5	10.3	6.2	-
358	Refrigeration and service industry machines................	44,355	100.0	28.1	18.3	16.7	10.4	23.2	3.3	-
359	Miscellaneous machinery and parts..........................	633,552	100.0	55.9	9.2	8.6	9.7	6.5	10.2	-
36	Electrical machinery, equipment, and supplies..............	1,126,309	100.0	15.2	8.8	11.3	5.9	5.2	52.7	1.0
361	Electrical transmission equipment..........................	55,780	100.0	34.6	5.7	14.5	6.0	5.9	33.4	-
362	Electrical industrial apparatus............................	72,948	100.0	6.2	21.7	16.9	5.0	11.5	23.9	14.9
364	Electric lighting and wiring equipment.....................	70,002	100.0	25.7	16.9	21.8	9.1	14.7	11.7	-
366	Communication equipment....................................	27,372	100.0	12.7	15.9	23.3	11.5	12.2	24.3	-
367	Electronic components and accessories......................	110,761	100.0	42.0	15.1	7.6	7.8	4.5	23.1	-
369	Miscellaneous electrical machinery, equipment, and supplies.	279,016	100.0	25.9	15.2	25.0	14.6	9.8	9.5	-
37	Transportation equipment...................................	585,101	100.0	27.3	11.1	19.5	8.3	26.1	5.8	1.8
371	Motor vehicles and equipment...............................	321,087	100.0	27.2	8.1	11.0	7.5	40.3	5.9	-
373	Ships and boats..	38,320	100.0	71.8	6.1	5.6	2.7	8.0	5.8	-
379	Miscellaneous transportation equipment.....................	200,145	100.0	20.1	17.7	36.4	9.2	6.8	4.5	5.3
38	Instruments, photographic, and medical goods, watches and clocks	212,462	100.0	20.0	8.8	7.8	6.4	15.1	39.2	2.7
382	Measuring and controlling instruments......................	47,213	100.0	4.7	15.9	12.9	6.7	10.7	49.1	-
384	Surgical, medical, dental instruments and supplies.........	35,460	100.0	31.9	8.5	6.3	6.6	17.6	29.1	-
39	Miscellaneous products of manufacturing....................	643,972	100.0	34.8	14.7	12.7	9.0	11.1	16.9	.7
391	Jewelry, silverware, and plated ware.......................	115,928	100.0	26.3	6.6	9.6	7.4	7.9	39.3	2.9
394	Toys, amusement, sporting, and athletic goods..............	109,905	100.0	12.3	11.1	19.9	15.7	22.2	17.7	1.1
395	Pens, pencils, other office and artists' materials.........	47,942	100.0	42.7	6.5	14.4	6.4	10.3	19.8	-
396	Costume jewelry, novelties, buttons and notions............	74,330	100.0	45.0	11.0	12.2	5.6	16.7	9.5	-
399	Miscellaneous manufactured products........................	290,428	100.0	43.3	21.8	11.3	8.2	6.9	8.6	-
---	All other miscellaneous[3].................................	1,526,269	100.0	24.6	10.7	11.0	6.1	5.7	41.3	.6
--	All other miscellaneous[3].................................	8,355	100.0	50.5	17.8	31.7	-	-	-	-

Note: Detail may not add to total due to rounding.

- Represents zero.

[1]Value of shipments derived from census of manufactures total value of shipments for 1972.
[2]Includes local shipments.
[3]Represents balance of commodities not shown at each level of detail due to disclosures and those commodities shipped by manufacturing establishments not specifically listed.

UNITED STATES

TABLE 3. Percent Distribution of Commodities Shipped by Domestic and Foreign Destinations: 1972

TCC code	Commodity description	Value[1] (thousands)	All shipments	Domestic	Foreign
	United States, total................................	18,156,900	100.0	98.5	1.5
20	Food and kindred products.........................	4,068,719	100.0	97.2	2.8
201	Meat; fresh, chilled, frozen......................	878,555	100.0	90.2	9.8
202	Dairy products....................................	1,315,488	100.0	100.0	–
203	Canned and preserved fruits, vegetables, seafoods............	407,589	100.0	96.1	3.9
204	Grain mill products...............................	661,859	100.0	99.9	.1
207	Confectionery and related products...............	33,061	100.0	99.0	1.0
208	Beverages and flavoring extracts..................	567,804	100.0	98.1	1.9
209	Miscellaneous food preparations...................	186,034	100.0	99.6	.4
22	Textile mill products.............................	203,479	100.0	98.5	1.5
225	Knit fabrics......................................	65,437	100.0	100.0	–
229	Miscellaneous textile goods.......................	103,200	100.0	99.0	1.0
23	Apparel and other finished textile products, including knit..	1,724,343	100.0	99.2	.8
231	Men's, youths', and boys' clothing................	363,471	100.0	99.9	.1
233	Women's, misses', children's, and infants' clothing..........	772,603	100.0	99.9	.1
237	Fur goods...	107,171	100.0	99.9	.1
238	Miscellaneous apparel and accessories.............	104,851	100.0	99.5	.5
239	Miscellaneous fabricated textile products.........	341,477	100.0	96.4	3.6
24	Lumber and wood products, except furniture........	1,180,546	100.0	99.6	.4
242	Sawmill and planing mill products.................	643,025	100.0	99.6	.4
243	Millwork, plywood, and prefabricated wood products...........	189,767	100.0	100.0	–
244	Wood containers...................................	58,328	100.0	99.4	.6
249	Miscellaneous wood products.......................	285,934	100.0	99.6	.4
25	Furniture and fixtures............................	325,874	100.0	100.0	–
251	Household and office furniture....................	154,159	100.0	99.9	.1
254	Partitions, shelving, lockers, office and store fixtures.....	35,091	100.0	100.0	–
259	Miscellaneous furniture and fixtures..............	127,810	100.0	100.0	–
26	Pulp, paper, and allied products..................	240,730	100.0	99.8	.2
264	Converted paper and paperboard products, except containers...	59,023	100.0	99.4	.6
265	Containers and boxes, paperboard..................	97,845	100.0	100.0	–
28	Chemicals and allied products.....................	1,634,805	100.0	99.7	.3
281	Industrial inorganic and organic chemicals.................	602,682	100.0	99.9	.1
282	Plastics materials................................	108,598	100.0	99.9	.1
284	Soap and other detergents.........................	145,009	100.0	99.8	.2
285	Paints, enamels, lacquers, shellacs, and allied products.....	108,429	100.0	100.0	–
287	Agricultural chemicals............................	150,535	100.0	100.0	–
289	Miscellaneous chemical products...................	505,617	100.0	99.1	.9
29	Petroleum and coal products.......................	191,025	100.0	97.0	3.0
295	Asphalt paving and roofing materials..............	80,418	100.0	100.0	–
30	Rubber and miscellaneous plastics products................	494,478	100.0	99.5	.5
306	Miscellaneous fabricated rubber products..........	75,882	100.0	99.7	.3
307	Miscellaneous plastics products...................	411,460	100.0	99.4	.6
31	Leather and leather products......................	204,822	100.0	94.2	5.8
319	Leather goods, n.e.c..............................	21,538	100.0	100.0	–
32	Stone, clay, glass, and concrete products.................	1,398,410	100.0	99.7	.3
322	Glass and glassware, pressed and blown............	51,596	100.0	100.0	–
325	Structural clay products..........................	44,068	100.0	95.1	4.9
327	Concrete, gypsum, and plaster products............	755,427	100.0	100.0	–
328	Cut stone and stone products......................	27,446	100.0	99.0	1.0
329	Abrasives and asbestos products...................	381,797	100.0	99.4	.6
33	Primary metal products............................	277,511	100.0	99.6	.4
336	Nonferrous metal castings.........................	57,429	100.0	98.1	1.9
339	Miscellaneous primary metal products..............	85,120	100.0	100.0	–

See footnotes at end of table.

UNITED STATES

TABLE 3. Percent Distribution of Commodities Shipped by Domestic and Foreign Destinations: 1972 —Continued

TCC code	Commodity description	Value[1] (thousands)	All shipments	Domestic	Foreign
34	Fabricated metal products except ordnance, machinery and transportation...................................	1,834,781	100.0	99.5	0.5
342	Cutlery, hand tools and general hardware....................	111,590	100.0	99.2	.8
343	Plumbing fixtures and heating apparatus.....................	56,416	100.0	100.0	-
344	Fabricated structural metal products.......................	657,597	100.0	99.8	.2
345	Bolts, nuts, screws, rivets, and washers...................	69,563	100.0	99.8	.2
346	Metal stampings..	212,769	100.0	99.9	.1
348	Miscellaneous fabricated wire products.....................	58,520	100.0	99.6	.4
349	Miscellaneous fabricated metal products....................	618,849	100.0	99.0	1.0
35	Machinery, except electrical...............................	1,800,618	100.0	98.1	1.9
352	Farm machinery and equipment...............................	118,718	100.0	99.8	.2
353	Construction, mining, materials handling machinery and equipment...	120,532	100.0	99.6	.4
354	Metalworking machinery and equipment.......................	551,893	100.0	99.1	.9
355	Special industry machinery.................................	170,151	100.0	97.3	2.7
356	General industrial machinery and equipment.................	128,996	100.0	99.0	1.0
358	Refrigeration and service industry machines................	44,355	100.0	99.9	.1
359	Miscellaneous machinery and parts..........................	633,552	100.0	96.5	3.5
36	Electrical machinery, equipment, and supplies..............	1,126,309	100.0	97.1	2.9
361	Electrical transmission equipment..........................	55,780	100.0	99.5	.5
362	Electrical industrial apparatus............................	72,948	100.0	64.6	35.4
364	Electric lighting and wiring equipment.....................	70,002	100.0	98.5	1.5
366	Communication equipment....................................	27,372	100.0	98.7	1.3
367	Electronic components and accessories......................	110,761	100.0	99.4	.6
369	Miscellaneous electrical machinery, equipment, and supplies..	279,016	100.0	98.6	1.4
37	Transportation equipment...................................	585,101	100.0	97.7	2.3
371	Motor vehicles and equipment...............................	321,087	100.0	96.0	4.0
373	Ships and boats..	38,320	100.0	99.6	.4
379	Miscellaneous transportation equipment.....................	200,145	100.0	99.8	.2
38	Instruments, photographic, and medical goods, watches and clocks	212,462	100.0	95.9	4.1
382	Measuring and controlling instruments......................	47,213	100.0	98.4	1.6
384	Surgical, medical, dental instruments and supplies.........	35,460	100.0	92.6	7.4
39	Miscellaneous products of manufacturing....................	643,972	100.0	98.4	1.6
391	Jewelry, silverware, and plated ware.......................	115,928	100.0	95.7	4.3
394	Toys, amusement, sporting, and athletic goods..............	109,905	100.0	98.9	1.1
395	Pens, pencils, other office and artists' materials..........	47,942	100.0	99.1	.9
396	Costume jewelry, novelties, buttons and notions............	74,330	100.0	99.7	.3
399	Miscellaneous manufactured products........................	290,428	100.0	98.9	1.1
---	All other miscellaneous[2]..................................	1,526,269	100.0	98.3	1.7
--	All other miscellaneous[2]..................................	8,355	100.0	100.0	-

Note: Detail may not add to total due to rounding.

- Represents zero.

[1]Value of shipments derived from census of manufactures total value of shipments for 1972.
[2]Represents balance of commodities not shown at each level of detail due to disclosures and those commodities shipped by manufacturing establishments not specifically listed.

NORTHEAST REGION

TABLE 1. Percent Distribution of Commodities Shipped by Means of Transport: 1972

TCC code	Commodity description	Value[1] (thousands)	All means of transport	Rail	Motor carrier	Private truck	Air	Water	Other[2]	Un-known
	Northeast Region, total...............................	5,089,625	100.0	1.0	40.1	34.6	3.3	0.5	19.6	1.0
20	Food and kindred products.............................	324,838	100.0	.7	36.0	63.3	–	–	.1	–
201	Meat; fresh, chilled, frozen..........................	52,996	100.0	–	–	100.0	–	–	–	–
208	Beverages and flavoring extracts......................	66,773	100.0	–	14.8	85.0	–	–	.2	–
22	Textile mill products.................................	148,097	100.0	–	79.5	12.7	1.4	–	6.4	–
225	Knit fabrics..	62,073	100.0	–	87.8	5.1	3.4	–	3.8	–
229	Miscellaneous textile goods...........................	70,106	100.0	–	68.1	21.9	–	–	10.1	–
23	Apparel and other finished textile products, including knit.	1,333,024	100.0	1.6	38.8	14.0	7.7	.3	35.0	2.6
231	Men's, youths', and boys' clothing....................	332,675	100.0	.9	50.1	–	8.2	–	40.8	–
233	Women's, misses', children's, and infants' clothing........	606,986	100.0	2.1	38.8	7.6	10.0	.6	38.8	2.0
237	Fur goods...	91,833	100.0	–	10.4	43.9	11.4	–	10.7	23.6
238	Miscellaneous apparel and accessories.................	55,888	100.0	–	74.7	5.1	–	–	20.2	–
239	Miscellaneous fabricated textile products.............	218,173	100.0	2.1	20.6	42.8	2.1	–	32.4	–
24	Lumber and wood products, except furniture............	146,556	100.0	1.6	24.4	71.6	–	–	2.3	–
242	Sawmill and planing mill products.....................	30,928	100.0	2.9	44.6	52.5	–	–	–	–
243	Millwork, plywood, and prefabricated wood products.........	41,239	100.0	2.7	13.7	81.8	–	–	1.8	–
249	Miscellaneous wood products...........................	48,901	100.0	.8	33.3	60.4	.1	–	5.5	–
25	Furniture and fixtures................................	75,532	100.0	1.0	36.2	60.6	–	1.0	1.3	–
251	Household and office furniture........................	27,630	100.0	–	21.5	78.3	–	–	.2	–
26	Pulp, paper, and allied products......................	110,119	100.0	–	14.8	81.5	–	.3	3.4	–
265	Containers and boxes, paperboard......................	33,285	100.0	–	15.7	83.5	–	–	.8	–
28	Chemicals and allied products.........................	425,594	100.0	.1	72.8	21.2	.7	.2	5.0	–
281	Industrial inorganic and organic chemicals............	61,679	100.0	–	41.2	54.2	.4	–	4.3	–
289	Miscellaneous chemical products.......................	184,012	100.0	–	82.8	9.2	.9	.5	6.7	–
30	Rubber and miscellaneous plastics products............	117,456	100.0	2.4	60.5	14.6	.7	–	21.7	–
307	Miscellaneous plastics products.......................	90,608	100.0	3.1	70.4	11.6	10.0	–	14.0	–
31	Leather and leather products..........................	179,888	100.0	–	65.1	4.1	.7	.6	29.6	–
32	Stone, clay, glass, and concrete products.............	428,041	100.0	.3	23.4	75.1	.2	–	1.1	–
327	Concrete, gypsum, and plaster products................	119,260	100.0	–	12.6	87.4	–	–	–	–
329	Abrasives and asbestos products.......................	252,503	100.0	–	18.0	80.2	–	–	1.8	–
33	Primary metal products................................	53,366	100.0	–	30.5	43.5	1.3	–	16.7	8.0
34	Fabricated metal products except ordnance, machinery and transportation......................................	543,255	100.0	1.4	42.7	43.4	.9	.2	10.2	1.3
344	Fabricated structural metal products..................	185,377	100.0	–	20.7	75.4	.5	–	3.4	–
345	Bolts, nuts, screws, rivets, and washers..............	35,583	100.0	–	51.6	3.5	.7	–	24.8	19.5
346	Metal stampings.......................................	97,981	100.0	–	47.6	33.5	.1	–	18.8	–
349	Miscellaneous fabricated metal products...............	169,455	100.0	1.2	67.5	28.4	2.0	–	1.0	–
35	Machinery, except electrical..........................	435,233	100.0	–	38.4	40.6	3.2	.4	17.3	–
354	Metalworking machinery and equipment..................	89,871	100.0	–	21.1	48.1	7.6	.6	22.6	–
355	Special industry machinery............................	67,874	100.0	–	62.1	26.3	1.2	–	10.4	–
356	General industrial machinery and equipment............	47,912	100.0	–	85.3	6.7	2.2	.8	5.1	–
359	Miscellaneous machinery and parts.....................	179,676	100.0	.1	26.2	52.3	1.6	.4	19.4	–
36	Electrical machinery, equipment, and supplies.........	194,932	100.0	2.7	29.6	26.4	6.0	5.3	28.2	1.9
364	Electrical lighting and wiring equipment..............	45,518	100.0	10.3	37.7	32.3	1.8	.1	17.8	–
367	Electronic components and accessories.................	44,685	100.0	–	14.9	35.5	14.2	–	35.5	–
37	Transportation equipment..............................	66,152	100.0	–	7.0	74.5	.4	–	18.1	–
38	Instruments, photographic and medical goods, watches and clocks...	99,657	100.0	3.6	11.3	16.6	7.8	1.1	59.7	–
39	Miscellaneous products of manufacturing...............	326,494	100.0	.4	24.0	28.7	5.0	.2	41.1	.6
391	Jewelry, silverware, and plated ware..................	88,995	100.0	.6	2.4	14.8	17.5	–	64.6	–
394	Toys, amusement, sporting, and athletic goods.........	51,024	100.0	–	68.3	8.7	–	–	23.1	–
396	Costume jewelry, novelties, buttons and notions...........	41,650	100.0	–	7.5	43.0	.2	–	49.3	–
399	Miscellaneous manufactured products...................	115,334	100.0	.6	23.1	50.3	.7	.2	23.6	1.6
---	All other miscellaneous[3]............................	1,381,156	100.0	1.1	45.3	32.4	1.5	1.2	18.0	.6
--	All other miscellaneous[3]............................	81,459	100.0	–	56.0	32.1	.6	1.4	10.0	–

Note: Detail may not add to total due to rounding.   – Represents zero.

[1]Value of shipments derived from census of manufactures total value of shipments for 1972.

[2]Includes railway and air express, United Parcel, parcel post, and other "package carriers."

[3]Represents balance of commodities not shown at each level of detail due to disclosures and those commodities shipped by manufacturing establishments not specifically listed.

NORTHEAST REGION

TABLE 2. Percent Distribution of Commodities Shipped by Distance of Shipment: 1972

TCC code	Commodity description	Value[1] (thousands)	All dis-tances	Under[2] 50 miles	50 to 99 miles	100 to 299 miles	300 to 499 miles	500 to 999 miles	1,000 miles or more	Un-known
	Northeast Region, total..............................	5,089,625	100.0	42.3	14.7	13.7	6.4	8.6	13.7	0.7
20	Food and kindred products........................	324,838	100.0	60.6	16.1	13.0	4.4	4.1	1.9	-
201	Meat; fresh, chilled, frozen.....................	52,996	100.0	73.9	16.6	9.5	-	-	-	-
208	Beverages and flavoring extracts.................	66,773	100.0	82.4	8.2	4.3	-	.4	4.7	-
22	Textile mill products............................	148,097	100.0	30.4	35.5	15.8	4.2	5.8	8.3	-
225	Knit fabrics.....................................	62,073	100.0	17.1	59.3	16.7	.5	4.1	2.4	-
229	Miscellaneous textile goods......................	70,106	100.0	38.5	21.2	10.7	7.1	7.8	14.7	-
23	Apparel and other finished textile products, including knit.	1,333,024	100.0	32.9	11.2	16.3	7.5	9.8	21.1	1.2
231	Men's, youths', and boys' clothing...............	332,675	100.0	21.7	11.5	22.4	9.5	8.8	26.1	-
233	Women's, misses', children's, and infants' clothing........	606,986	100.0	27.0	9.9	17.5	9.1	11.9	24.1	-
237	Fur goods..	91,833	100.0	74.6	-	1.6	1.0	1.3	13.6	8.0
238	Miscellaneous apparel and accessories............	55,888	100.0	79.0	-	10.7	-	-	-	10.4
239	Miscellaneous fabricated textile products........	218,173	100.0	33.9	20.1	12.5	5.4	12.2	15.9	-
24	Lumber and wood products, except furniture.......	146,556	100.0	55.8	16.9	13.0	4.7	4.7	3.0	2.0
242	Sawmill and planing mill products................	30,928	100.0	42.1	25.0	15.3	10.4	2.0	5.4	-
243	Millwork, plywood, and prefabricated wood products..........	41,239	100.0	66.7	17.0	4.9	5.9	2.9	2.6	-
249	Miscellaneous wood products......................	48,901	100.0	48.7	14.0	16.0	1.8	10.4	3.4	5.9
25	Furniture and fixtures...........................	75,532	100.0	61.4	13.4	15.7	1.7	6.4	1.6	-
251	Household and office furniture...................	27,630	100.0	60.4	21.7	17.7	.2	-	-	-
26	Pulp, paper, and allied products.................	110,119	100.0	74.5	11.4	6.7	2.4	3.6	1.4	-
265	Containers and boxes, paperboard.................	33,285	100.0	63.6	17.7	15.4	2.5	.5	.3	-
28	Chemicals and allied products....................	425,594	100.0	34.2	12.3	16.4	8.4	16.9	11.8	-
281	Industrial inorganic and organic chemicals.................	61,679	100.0	54.3	12.1	.7	.4	21.3	11.2	-
289	Miscellaneous chemical products..................	184,012	100.0	14.4	12.4	14.9	12.8	27.4	18.1	-
30	Rubber and miscellaneous plastics products.......	117,456	100.0	36.0	14.7	10.0	9.6	12.6	14.1	3.1
307	Miscellaneous plastics products..................	90,608	100.0	36.5	16.2	8.6	10.2	12.6	15.8	-
31	Leather and leather products.....................	179,888	100.0	25.2	26.7	7.1	5.6	13.4	22.0	-
32	Stone, clay, glass, and concrete products........	428,041	100.0	85.1	8.2	4.4	.5	1.7	-	-
327	Concrete, gypsum, and plaster products...........	119,260	100.0	93.3	5.8	.8	-	-	-	-
329	Abrasives and asbestos products..................	252,503	100.0	96.3	1.4	1.7	.2	.3	-	-
33	Primary metal products...........................	53,366	100.0	42.6	11.1	28.5	8.4	5.6	3.8	-
34	Fabricated metal products except ordnance, machinery and transportation......................................	543,255	100.0	30.3	25.3	15.0	4.7	6.5	17.0	1.3
344	Fabricated structural metal products.............	185,377	100.0	29.2	44.0	16.6	2.5	2.7	5.0	-
345	Bolts, nuts, screws, rivets, and washers.........	35,583	100.0	21.5	9.8	14.7	8.8	4.6	21.1	19.5
346	Metal stampings..................................	97,981	100.0	39.9	33.0	13.2	4.1	4.1	5.8	-
349	Miscellaneous fabricated metal products..........	169,455	100.0	26.3	5.7	14.1	4.8	12.6	36.6	-
35	Machinery, except electrical.....................	435,233	100.0	41.0	10.5	16.5	10.9	11.6	9.4	-
354	Metalworking machinery and equipment.............	89,871	100.0	53.7	7.9	16.0	7.1	4.6	10.6	-
355	Special industry machinery......................	67,874	100.0	17.3	18.3	31.8	18.1	5.4	9.1	-
356	General industrial machinery and equipment.......	47,912	100.0	16.9	5.1	17.9	32.7	16.5	10.9	-
359	Miscellaneous machinery and parts................	179,676	100.0	52.1	10.3	11.3	4.1	16.3	6.0	-
36	Electrical machinery, equipment, and supplies....	194,932	100.0	30.1	13.9	20.7	8.3	8.7	18.4	-
364	Electric lighting and wiring equipment...........	45,518	100.0	20.9	17.3	28.0	10.0	12.4	11.4	-
367	Electronic components and accessories............	44,685	100.0	52.8	9.4	6.1	11.0	3.7	17.0	-
37	Transportation equipment.........................	66,152	100.0	81.3	4.0	4.3	4.9	1.2	4.3	-
38	Instruments, photographic and medical goods, watches and clocks...	99,657	100.0	25.0	9.9	8.9	6.5	8.8	35.3	5.7
39	Miscellaneous products of manufacturing..........	326,494	100.0	36.4	18.2	10.9	7.0	8.2	19.3	-
391	Jewelry, silverware, and plated ware.............	88,995	100.0	22.1	6.1	9.2	6.3	7.5	48.8	-
394	Toys, amusement, sporting, and athletic goods....	51,024	100.0	18.8	17.8	28.4	13.1	13.9	7.8	-
396	Costume jewelry, novelties, buttons and notions....	41,650	100.0	71.1	12.6	4.6	4.1	4.0	3.6	-
399	Miscellaneous manufactured products..............	115,334	100.0	44.6	32.6	7.6	5.8	5.6	3.9	-
---	All other miscellaneous[3].........................	1,381,156	100.0	43.1	15.5	14.8	6.4	8.0	11.7	.7
--	All other miscellaneous[3].........................	81,459	100.0	49.8	5.6	9.1	9.7	10.7	15.1	-

Note: Detail may not add to total due to rounding.   - Represents zero.

[1] Value of shipments derived from census of manufactures total value of shipments for 1972.
[2] Includes local shipments.
[3] Represents balance of commodities not shown at each level of detail due to disclosures and those commodities shipped by manufacturing establishments not specifically listed.

NORTHEAST REGION

TABLE 3. Percent Distribution of Commodities Shipped by Domestic and Foreign Destinations: 1972

TCC code	Commodity description	Value[1] (thousands)	All shipments	Domestic	Foreign
	Northeast Region, total..................................	5,089,625	100.0	98.4	1.6
20	Food and kindred products...........................	324,838	100.0	99.8	.2
201	Meat; fresh, chilled, frozen........................	52,996	100.0	100.0	–
208	Beverages and flavoring extracts....................	66,773	100.0	100.0	–
22	Textile mill products...............................	148,097	100.0	99.8	.2
225	Knit fabrics..	62,073	100.0	100.0	–
229	Miscellaneous textile goods.........................	70,106	100.0	99.7	.3
23	Apparel and other finished textile products, including knit..	1,333,024	100.0	99.1	.9
231	Men's, youths', and boys' clothing..........................	332,675	100.0	99.9	.1
233	Women's, misses', children's, and infants' clothing.........	606,986	100.0	100.0	–
237	Fur goods...	91,833	100.0	99.9	.1
238	Miscellaneous apparel and accessories................	55,888	100.0	100.0	–
239	Miscellaneous fabricated textile products............	218,173	100.0	94.6	5.4
24	Lumber and wood products, except furniture..................	146,556	100.0	98.5	1.5
242	Sawmill and planing mill products....................	30,928	100.0	92.9	7.2
243	Millwork, plywood, and prefabricated wood products..........	41,239	100.0	100.0	–
249	Miscellaneous wood products..........................	48,901	100.0	99.9	.1
25	Furniture and fixtures...............................	75,532	100.0	100.0	–
251	Household and office furniture.......................	27,630	100.0	100.0	–
26	Pulp, paper, and allied products.....................	110,119	100.0	99.7	.3
265	Containers and boxes, paperboard.....................	33,285	100.0	100.0	–
28	Chemicals and allied products........................	425,594	100.0	99.1	.9
281	Industrial inorganic and organic chemicals..................	61,679	100.0	99.8	.2
289	Miscellaneous chemical products......................	184,012	100.0	98.1	1.9
30	Rubber and miscellaneous plastics products..................	117,456	100.0	98.6	1.4
307	Miscellaneous plastics products......................	90,608	100.0	98.2	1.8
31	Leather and leather products.........................	179,888	100.0	94.2	5.8
32	Stone, clay, glass, and concrete products...................	428,041	100.0	99.5	.5
327	Concrete, gypsum, and plaster products...............	119,260	100.0	100.0	–
329	Abrasives and asbestos products......................	252,503	100.0	100.0	–
33	Primary metal products...............................	53,366	100.0	98.7	1.3
34	Fabricated metal products except ordnance, machinery and transportation....................................	543,255	100.0	98.8	1.2
344	Fabricated structural metal products.................	185,377	100.0	99.7	.3
345	Bolts, nuts, screws, rivets, and washers....................	35,583	100.0	100.0	–
346	Metal stampings.....................................	97,981	100.0	99.7	.3
349	Miscellaneous fabricated metal products...............	169,455	100.0	97.3	2.7
35	Machinery, except electrical.........................	435,233	100.0	96.6	3.4
354	Metalworking machinery and equipment.................	89,871	100.0	99.2	.8
355	Special industry machinery...........................	67,874	100.0	99.5	.5
356	General industrial machinery and equipment..................	47,912	100.0	97.5	2.6
359	Miscellaneous machinery and parts....................	179,676	100.0	93.6	6.4
36	Electrical machinery, equipment, and supplies..............	194,932	100.0	93.3	6.7
364	Electric lighting and wiring equipment...............	45,518	100.0	99.0	1.0
367	Electronic components and accessories................	44,685	100.0	99.9	.1
37	Transportation equipment.............................	66,152	100.0	100.0	–
38	Instruments, photographic and medical goods, watches and clocks......................................	99,657	100.0	97.1	2.9
39	Miscellaneous products of manufacturing.....................	326,494	100.0	98.1	1.9
391	Jewelry, silverware, and plated ware.................	88,995	100.0	94.4	5.6
394	Toys, amusement, sporting, and athletic goods..............	51,024	100.0	100.0	–
396	Costume jewelry, novelties, buttons and notions.............	41,650	100.0	100.0	–
399	Miscellaneous manufactured products..................	115,334	100.0	99.2	.8
---	All other miscellaneous[2]...........................	1,381,156	100.0	97.3	2.7
--	All other miscellaneous[2]...........................	81,459	100.0	93.1	6.9

Note: Detail may not add to total due to rounding.   - Represents zero.

[1]Value of shipments derived from census of manufactures total value of shipments for 1972.
[2]Represents balance of commodities not shown at each level of detail due to disclosures and those commodities shipped by manufacturing establishments not specifically listed.

NORTH CENTRAL REGION

TABLE 1. Percent Distribution of Commodities Shipped by Means of Transport: 1972

TCC code	Commodity description	Value¹ (thousands)	All means of transport	Rail	Motor carrier	Private truck	Air	Water	Other²	Unknown
	North Central Region, total............................	4,729,081	100.0	9.3	29.5	49.8	1.2	2.6	7.2	0.5
20	Food and kindred products.................................	1,449,988	100.0	21.4	18.1	46.0	1.5	8.4	4.7	-
201	Meat; fresh, chilled, frozen.............................	273,167	100.0	20.7	4.7	38.1	-	36.5	-	-
202	Dairy products..	217,125	100.0	-	26.5	73.5	-	-	-	-
204	Grain mill products.....................................	443,861	100.0	30.3	30.2	39.4	-	-	-	-
208	Beverages and flavoring extracts........................	288,429	100.0	.5	.5	60.4	7.6	7.6	23.4	-
23	Apparel and other finished textile products, including knit.	79,661	100.0	-	32.5	16.8	3.6	-	47.2	-
238	Miscellaneous apparel and accessories...................	28,183	100.0	-	42.3	1.1	2.0	.2	54.5	-
239	Miscellaneous fabricated textile products...............	24,833	100.0	-	37.2	51.2	6.3	-	5.3	-
24	Lumber and wood products, except furniture...............	286,391	100.0	27.9	17.9	50.8	.1	-	.1	3.2
242	Sawmill and planing mill products.......................	171,106	100.0	43.7	18.8	32.2	-	-	-	5.4
243	Millwork, plywood, and prefabricated wood products.........	73,863	100.0	6.1	11.6	81.7	.3	-	.3	-
249	Miscellaneous wood products.............................	38,940	100.0	1.4	27.2	71.4	-	-	-	-
25	Furniture and fixtures...................................	82,532	100.0	1.2	30.3	66.0	.1	-	2.6	-
251	Household and office furniture..........................	59,913	100.0	1.6	28.4	68.4	-	-	1.6	-
26	Pulp, paper, and allied products.........................	76,760	100.0	-	53.1	45.3	.4	-	1.2	-
28	Chemicals and allied products............................	249,617	100.0	.4	38.8	54.2	.2	.2	6.2	-
284	Soap and other detergents...............................	49,485	100.0	-	29.4	46.7	.9	-	23.0	-
289	Miscellaneous chemical products.........................	130,287	100.0	.8	62.1	33.7	.1	.3	3.0	-
30	Rubber and miscellaneous plastics products...............	121,739	100.0	12.8	38.9	44.3	.5	-	3.5	-
307	Miscellaneous plastics products.........................	106,238	100.0	14.8	40.8	41.2	.4	-	2.8	-
32	Stone, clay, glass, and concrete products................	489,751	100.0	5.1	19.1	71.7	.6	-	3.6	-
327	Concrete, gypsum, and plaster products..................	302,156	100.0	-	14.0	86.0	-	-	-	-
329	Abrasives and asbestos products.........................	51,386	100.0	-	21.7	40.7	4.6	-	32.9	-
33	Primary metal products...................................	105,995	100.0	.3	20.9	70.9	1.5	-	6.4	-
339	Miscellaneous primary metal products....................	48,709	100.0	-	29.7	69.3	-	-	1.1	-
34	Fabricated metal products except ordnance, machinery and transportation...	556,409	100.0	.9	36.7	56.4	.6	.1	3.6	1.7
342	Cutlery, hand tools and general hardware................	40,365	100.0	-	64.5	33.1	.1	-	2.4	-
344	Fabricated structural metal products...................	171,297	100.0	2.5	25.5	71.6	-	-	.5	-
345	Bolts, nuts, screws, rivets, and washers................	28,934	100.0	-	48.7	39.8	1.5	-	10.1	-
346	Metal stampings...	41,264	100.0	-	51.1	24.0	.3	-	1.2	23.5
348	Miscellaneous fabricated wire products..................	31,190	100.0	-	81.5	10.8	-	-	7.6	-
349	Miscellaneous fabricated metal products.................	197,491	100.0	.4	26.4	68.3	.5	.1	4.3	-
35	Machinery, except electrical.............................	716,825	100.0	.4	40.4	47.3	1.5	.2	9.5	.7
352	Farm machinery and equipment............................	64,142	100.0	4.3	40.5	54.6	-	.1	.5	-
353	Construction, mining, materials handling machinery and equipment..	59,574	100.0	.2	71.5	20.1	.7	-	7.5	-
354	Metalworking machinery and equipment....................	317,447	100.0	.1	36.9	45.8	2.2	.1	13.4	1.6
355	Special industry machinery.............................	54,540	100.0	-	56.5	32.0	.8	-	10.8	-
356	General industrial machinery and equipment.............	34,746	100.0	-	19.7	75.6	.1	-	4.6	-
359	Miscellaneous machinery and parts.......................	164,198	100.0	-	32.3	58.3	1.4	.6	7.4	-
36	Electrical machinery, equipment, and supplies..............	201,181	100.0	.2	61.2	15.9	3.9	-	18.7	-
369	Miscellaneous electrical machinery, equipment, and supplies.	140,268	100.0	.3	57.8	19.7	5.1	-	17.1	-
37	Transportation equipment.................................	109,225	100.0	-	43.4	54.0	.4	-	2.3	-
371	Motor vehicles and equipment............................	51,583	100.0	-	68.2	28.6	.5	-	2.7	-
379	Miscellaneous transportation equipment..................	44,814	100.0	-	1.5	98.3	-	-	.2	-
39	Miscellaneous products of manufacturing..................	118,390	100.0	.1	42.5	18.9	.5	.1	37.8	-
399	Miscellaneous manufactured products.....................	88,134	100.0	.2	46.0	21.3	.7	-	31.8	-
---	All other miscellaneous³.................................	891,423	100.0	16.0	30.8	43.3	.8	.1	9.1	-
--	All other miscellaneous³.................................	84,628	100.0	-	16.4	66.7	.9	-	16.0	-

Note: Detail may not add to total due to rounding.   - Represents zero.

¹Value of shipments derived from census of manufactures total value of shipments for 1972.
²Includes railway and air express, United Parcel, parcel post, and other "package carriers."
³Represents balance of commodities not shown at each level of detail due to disclosures and those commodities shipped by manufacturing establishments not specifically listed.

NORTH CENTRAL REGION

TABLE 2. Percent Distribution of Commodities Shipped by Distance of Shipment: 1972

TCC code	Commodity description	Value[1] (thousands)	All dis-tances	Under[2] 50 miles	50 to 99 miles	100 to 299 miles	300 to 499 miles	500 to 999 miles	1,000 miles or more	Un-known
	North Central Region, total............................	4,729,081	100.0	40.2	12.8	15.5	12.6	10.1	7.5	1.3
20	Food and kindred products...................................	1,449,988	100.0	30.5	13.5	12.6	16.4	13.6	11.1	2.4
201	Meat; fresh, chilled, frozen................................	273,167	100.0	41.6	12.6	12.8	5.4	27.5	.2	-
202	Dairy products..	217,125	100.0	11.9	22.5	11.2	53.6	.8	-	-
204	Grain mill products...	443,861	100.0	32.3	12.5	15.0	14.6	5.1	12.7	7.9
208	Beverages and flavoring extracts............................	288,429	100.0	47.0	18.3	12.4	7.1	7.7	7.6	-
23	Apparel and other finished textile products, including knit.	79,661	100.0	24.4	9.0	24.6	18.1	9.5	14.5	-
238	Miscellaneous apparel and accessories.......................	28,183	100.0	12.1	14.5	23.2	24.1	18.3	8.0	-
239	Miscellaneous fabricated textile products..................	24,833	100.0	52.1	8.5	16.1	2.1	8.5	12.7	-
24	Lumber and wood products, except furniture.................	286,391	100.0	29.5	11.8	15.4	14.0	6.3	22.0	1.2
242	Sawmill and planing mill products..........................	171,106	100.0	17.1	4.7	20.4	12.4	6.8	36.7	1.9
243	Millwork, plywood, and prefabricated wood products.........	73,863	100.0	52.3	25.2	1.0	20.9	.5	.1	-
249	Miscellaneous wood products................................	38,940	100.0	37.1	17.3	21.3	8.7	15.4	.3	-
25	Furniture and fixtures.....................................	82,532	100.0	37.5	8.0	31.8	7.8	12.8	2.1	-
251	Household and office furniture.............................	59,913	100.0	32.8	7.0	31.8	9.7	17.1	1.6	-
26	Pulp, paper, and allied products...........................	76,760	100.0	47.3	24.1	5.9	11.0	8.8	2.9	-
28	Chemicals and allied products..............................	249,617	100.0	53.2	16.9	9.0	10.4	7.6	2.9	-
284	Soap and other detergents..................................	49,485	100.0	38.2	14.6	12.4	12.2	13.3	9.3	-
289	Miscellaneous chemical products............................	130,287	100.0	49.0	13.5	11.0	15.0	9.5	2.1	-
30	Rubber and miscellaneous plastics products.................	121,739	100.0	35.6	14.6	10.1	13.7	13.6	12.5	-
307	Miscellaneous plastics products............................	106,238	100.0	32.2	12.5	10.0	15.7	15.4	14.3	-
32	Stone, clay, glass, and concrete products.................	489,751	100.0	69.3	12.9	11.8	4.6	.3	1.1	-
327	Concrete, gypsum, and plaster products.....................	302,156	100.0	90.1	6.5	2.8	.6	.1	-	-
329	Abrasives and asbestos products............................	51,386	100.0	65.6	13.4	9.7	2.4	2.4	6.6	-
33	Primary metal products.....................................	105,995	100.0	37.7	11.3	18.3	4.5	25.4	2.8	-
339	Miscellaneous primary metal products.......................	48,709	100.0	27.8	7.2	3.9	5.9	50.2	5.0	-
34	Fabricated metal products except ordnance, machinery and transportation...	556,409	100.0	48.6	12.1	21.4	6.1	8.5	3.3	-
342	Cutlery, hand tools and general hardware...................	40,365	100.0	42.8	3.6	41.0	3.8	6.8	2.0	-
344	Fabricated structural metal products......................	171,297	100.0	54.5	12.6	24.2	4.8	2.4	1.5	-
345	Bolts, nuts, screws, rivets, and washers..................	28,934	100.0	46.8	6.9	22.7	6.0	15.1	2.7	-
346	Metal stampings..	41,264	100.0	41.9	32.7	4.7	.5	19.6	.6	-
348	Miscellaneous fabricated wire products.....................	31,190	100.0	54.3	18.2	8.3	2.2	16.4	.6	-
349	Miscellaneous fabricated metal products....................	197,491	100.0	54.0	10.0	14.6	5.1	9.9	6.4	-
35	Machinery, except electrical...............................	716,825	100.0	43.7	10.3	19.1	15.2	8.4	3.4	-
352	Farm machinery and equipment...............................	64,142	100.0	3.7	3.2	19.4	25.7	35.0	13.0	-
353	Construction, mining, materials handling machinery and equipment..	59,574	100.0	25.4	4.9	21.7	17.4	26.3	4.3	-
354	Metalworking machinery and equipment.......................	317,447	100.0	46.4	9.2	19.1	20.5	2.2	2.8	-
355	Special industry machinery.................................	54,540	100.0	39.2	11.4	34.5	9.2	3.5	2.2	-
356	General industrial machinery and equipment................	34,746	100.0	56.9	17.6	12.3	4.7	8.3	.2	-
359	Miscellaneous machinery and parts..........................	164,198	100.0	62.0	13.4	12.9	5.3	4.9	1.5	-
36	Electrical machinery, equipment, and supplies..............	201,181	100.0	15.0	18.9	23.3	19.2	11.0	7.3	5.4
369	Miscellaneous electrical machinery, equipment, and supplies..	140,268	100.0	12.8	19.1	27.7	24.0	11.1	5.4	-
37	Transportation equipment...................................	109,225	100.0	9.7	5.3	19.4	17.9	23.9	14.1	9.8
371	Motor vehicles and equipment...............................	51,583	100.0	12.9	4.5	13.1	22.9	24.7	21.9	-
379	Miscellaneous transportation equipment.....................	44,814	100.0	8.3	6.8	29.4	13.0	16.8	1.9	23.9
39	Miscellaneous products of manufacturing....................	118,390	100.0	46.1	9.9	10.5	15.0	10.6	6.9	1.0
399	Miscellaneous manufactured products........................	88,134	100.0	55.7	12.1	9.7	12.3	3.7	6.5	-
---	All other miscellaneous[3].................................	891,423	100.0	31.2	14.5	17.5	9.9	13.0	12.4	1.4
--	All other miscellaneous[3].................................	84,628	100.0	63.9	17.1	9.2	2.1	4.6	3.1	-

Note: Detail may not add to total due to rounding.   - Represents zero.

[1]Value of shipments derived from census of manufactures total value of shipments for 1972.
[2]Includes local shipments.
[3]Represents balance of commodities not shown at each level of detail due to disclosures and those commodities shipped by manufacturing establishments not specifically listed.

NORTH CENTRAL REGION

TABLE 3. **Percent Distribution of Commodities Shipped by Domestic and Foreign Destinations:. 1972**

TCC code	Commodity description	Value[1] (thousands)	All shipments	Domestic	Foreign
	North Central Region, total..........................	4,729,081	100.0	97.5	2.5
20	Food and kindred products............................	1,449,988	100.0	93.3	6.8
201	Meat; fresh, chilled, frozen........................	273,167	100.0	68.4	31.6
202	Dairy products......................................	217,125	100.0	100.0	-
204	Grain mill products.................................	443,861	100.0	99.8	.2
208	Beverages and flavoring extracts....................	288,429	100.0	96.2	3.8
23	Apparel and other finished textile products, including knit..	79,661	100.0	99.0	1.0
238	Miscellaneous apparel and accessories...............	28,183	100.0	98.0	2.0
239	Miscellaneous fabricated textile products...........	24,833	100.0	98.9	1.1
24	Lumber and wood products, except furniture..........	286,391	100.0	100.0	-
242	Sawmill and planing mill products...................	171,106	100.0	100.0	-
243	Millwork, plywood, and prefabricated wood products..........	73,863	100.0	100.0	-
249	Miscellaneous wood products.........................	38,940	100.0	100.0	-
25	Furniture and fixtures..............................	82,532	100.0	99.9	.1
251	Household and office furniture......................	59,913	100.0	99.8	.2
26	Pulp, paper, and allied products....................	76,760	100.0	100.0	-
28	Chemicals and allied products.......................	249,617	100.0	99.8	.2
284	Soap and other detergents...........................	49,485	100.0	99.9	.2
289	Miscellaneous chemical products.....................	130,287	100.0	99.7	.3
30	Rubber and miscellaneous plastics products..........	121,739	100.0	99.7	.3
307	Miscellaneous plastics products.....................	106,238	100.0	99.8	.2
32	Stone, clay, glass, and concrete products..........	489,751	100.0	99.8	.2
327	Concrete, gypsum, and plaster products..............	302,156	100.0	100.0	-
329	Abrasives and asbestos products.....................	51,386	100.0	97.7	2.3
33	Primary metal products..............................	105,995	100.0	100.0	-
339	Miscellaneous primary metal products................	48,709	100.0	100.0	-
34	Fabricated metal products except ordnance, machinery and transportation..	556,409	100.0	99.8	.2
342	Cutlery, hand tools and general hardware............	40,365	100.0	100.0	-
344	Fabricated structural metal products...............	171,297	100.0	99.7	.3
345	Bolts, nuts, screws, rivets, and washers...........	28,934	100.0	99.7	.3
346	Metal stampings.....................................	41,264	100.0	99.9	.1
348	Miscellaneous fabricated wire products..............	31,190	100.0	100.0	-
349	Miscellaneous fabricated metal products.............	197,491	100.0	99.6	.4
35	Machinery, except electrical........................	716,825	100.0	99.2	.8
352	Farm machinery and equipment........................	64,142	100.0	99.7	.3
353	Construction, mining, materials handling machinery and equipment...	59,574	100.0	99.9	.1
354	Metalworking machinery and equipment................	317,447	100.0	99.0	1.0
355	Special industry machinery..........................	54,540	100.0	98.1	1.9
356	General industrial machinery and equipment..........	34,746	100.0	100.0	-
359	Miscellaneous machinery and parts...................	164,198	100.0	99.5	.5
36	Electrical machinery, equipment, and supplies...............	201,181	100.0	99.0	1.0
369	Miscellaneous electrical machinery, equipment, and supplies..	140,268	100.0	100.0	-
37	Transportation equipment............................	109,225	100.0	93.6	6.4
371	Motor vehicles and equipment........................	51,583	100.0	86.7	13.3
379	Miscellaneous transportation equipment..............	44,814	100.0	100.0	-
39	Miscellaneous products of manufacturing.............	118,390	100.0	99.9	.1
399	Miscellaneous manufactured products.................	88,134	100.0	99.9	.1
---	All other miscellaneous[2]...........................	891,423	100.0	99.4	.6
--	All other miscellaneous[2]...........................	84,628	100.0	96.8	3.2

Note: Detail may not add to total due to rounding.

- Represents zero.

[1]Value of shipments derived from census of manufactures total value of shipments for 1972.

[2]Represents balance of commodities not shown at each level of detail due to disclosures and those commodities shipped by manufacturing establishments not specifically listed.

SOUTH REGION

TABLE 1. Percent Distribution of Commodities Shipped by Means of Transport: 1972

TCC code	Commodity description	Value[1] (thousands)	All means of transport	Rail	Motor carrier	Private truck	Air	Water	Other[2]	Unknown
	South Region, total...........................	3,374,446	100.0	6.5	28.0	61.3	1.3	0.3	2.6	–
20	Food and kindred products........................	719,427	100.0	3.5	11.1	85.3	–	–	.1	–
201	Meat; fresh, chilled, frozen.....................	467,412	100.0	.7	6.7	92.7	–	–	–	–
203	Canned and preserved fruits, vegetables, seafoods...........	33,082	100.0	1.2	71.6	25.1	–	–	2.1	–
204	Grain mill products..............................	87,094	100.0	13.7	14.9	71.4	–	–	–	–
208	Beverages and flavoring extracts.................	57,385	100.0	–	–	100.0	–	–	–	–
209	Miscellaneous food preparations..................	56,593	100.0	–	10.1	89.9		–	–	–
22	Textile mill products............................	40,580	100.0	6.7	53.9	39.4	–	–	–	–
23	Apparel and other finished textile products, including knit.	113,913	100.0	–	57.3	26.3	.7	.2	15.6	–
239	Miscellaneous fabricated textile products..................	63,071	100.0	–	46.9	42.0	.1	–	10.9	–
24	Lumber and wood products, except furniture..............	499,463	100.0	7.7	22.0	70.2	–	–	.1	–
242	Sawmill and planing mill products..................	273,594	100.0	13.3	23.4	63.3	–	–	–	–
243	Millwork, plywood, and prefabricated wood products..........	46,824	100.0	–	16.5	83.5	–	–	–	–
249	Miscellaneous wood products......................	158,022	100.0	1.3	12.9	85.4	.1	–	.3	–
25	Furniture and fixtures...........................	101,481	100.0	3.6	22.1	73.6	–	–	.8	–
259	Miscellaneous furniture and fixtures.......................	61,430	100.0	5.9	23.0	69.8	–	–	1.2	–
28	Chemicals and allied products....................	314,930	100.0	4.9	35.1	58.3	–	–	1.8	–
287	Agricultural chemicals...........................	103,747	100.0	5.4	10.2	84.1	–	–	.3	–
289	Miscellaneous chemical products..................	148,306	100.0	6.6	54.3	39.0	–	–	.1	–
30	Rubber and miscellaneous plastics products..................	48,159	100.0	4.4	53.5	34.6	2.3	–	5.3	–
307	Miscellaneous plastics products..................	44,207	100.0	4.8	54.7	35.9	2.5	–	2.2	–
32	Stone, clay, glass, and concrete products..................	337,553	100.0	1.4	21.3	76.5	.2	.4	.2	–
327	Concrete, gypsum, and plaster products....................	241,697	100.0	–	10.2	89.8	–	–	–	–
33	Primary metal products...........................	60,721	100.0	–	57.6	40.9	.6	–	1.0	–
34	Fabricated metal products except ordnance, machinery and transportation............	376,743	100.0	2.4	46.5	45.7	2.4	.4	2.7	–
344	Fabricated structural metal products.....................	211,896	100.0	2.1	53.7	43.0	–	–	1.2	–
349	Miscellaneous fabricated metal products....................	80,141	100.0	.1	19.9	71.1	6.6	.9	1.3	–
35	Machinery, except electrical.....................	263,770	100.0	.2	43.8	47.7	2.1	.4	5.8	–
354	Metalworking machinery and equipment.......................	24,393	100.0	–	16.5	81.2	–	–	2.3	–
359	Miscellaneous machinery and parts..........................	121,860	100.0	.2	54.5	32.3	4.1	.9	8.1	–
36	Electrical machinery, equipment, and supplies...............	80,185	100.0	6.0	29.2	33.8	24.3	.3	6.4	–
37	Transportation equipment.........................	251,031	100.0	45.1	4.4	47.4	–	2.5	.6	–
371	Motor vehicles and equipment.....................	210,130	100.0	53.9	1.8	41.4	–	2.2	.7	–
39	Miscellaneous products of manufacturing....................	86,309	100.0	–	27.1	48.6	2.9	–	21.4	–
399	Miscellaneous manufactured products.......................	41,859	100.0	–	2.6	83.8	3.7	–	9.9	–
---	All other miscellaneous[3]........................	841,708	100.0	3.1	46.5	39.6	3.5	.5	6.8	–
--	All other miscellaneous[3]........................	80,187	100.0	–	68.2	18.8	3.8	–	9.2	–

Note: Detail may not add to total due to rounding.

– Represents zero.

[1]Value of shipments derived from census of manufactures total value of shipments for 1972.
[2]Includes railway and air express, United Parcel, parcel post, and other "package carriers."
[3]Represents balance of commodities not shown at each level of detail due to disclosures and those commodities shipped by manufacturing establishments not specifically listed.

SOUTH REGION

TABLE 2. Percent Distribution of Commodities Shipped by Distance of Shipment: 1972

TCC code	Commodity description	Value[1] (thousands)	All distances	Under[2] 50 miles	50 to 99 miles	100 to 299 miles	300 to 499 miles	500 to 999 miles	1,000 miles or more	Unknown
	South Region, total................................	3,374,446	100.0	37.3	13.6	20.8	7.7	16.3	4.1	0.2
20	Food and kindred products..................................	719,427	100.0	28.0	8.9	33.8	2.6	25.7	1.1	–
201	Meat; fresh, chilled, frozen..........................	467,412	100.0	14.6	5.6	42.0	1.1	36.8	–	–
203	Canned and preserved fruits, vegetables, seafoods..........	33,082	100.0	12.0	13.4	15.3	17.1	22.9	19.4	–
204	Grain mill products..................................	87,094	100.0	63.0	11.0	18.6	4.6	2.7	.1	–
208	Beverages and flavoring extracts..........................	57,385	100.0	94.6	5.4	–	–	–	–	–
209	Miscellaneous food preparations..........................	56,593	100.0	31.4	34.4	26.2	3.4	2.6	2.2	–
22	Textile mill products.......................................	40,580	100.0	15.7	6.9	11.2	51.4	9.4	5.4	–
23	Apparel and other finished textile products, including knit.	113,913	100.0	25.2	4.6	17.5	10.8	30.2	11.8	–
239	Miscellaneous fabricated textile products..................	63,071	100.0	39.2	2.4	24.7	12.6	17.8	3.4	–
24	Lumber and wood products, except furniture.................	499,463	100.0	30.6	21.1	16.7	8.7	19.2	2.1	1.6
242	Sawmill and planing mill products..........................	273,594	100.0	30.2	27.1	19.0	10.1	7.9	2.9	2.9
243	Millwork, plywood, and prefabricated wood products..........	46,824	100.0	69.5	10.5	16.7	2.5	.8	–	–
249	Miscellaneous wood products................................	158,022	100.0	19.9	15.9	15.1	8.9	38.8	1.4	–
25	Furniture and fixtures.....................................	101,481	100.0	28.5	17.8	29.9	13.2	7.0	3.6	–
259	Miscellaneous furniture and fixtures.......................	61,430	100.0	16.3	16.3	34.4	20.9	6.2	5.9	–
28	Chemicals and allied products..............................	314,930	100.0	39.5	15.0	28.6	7.6	5.5	3.8	–
287	Agricultural chemicals.....................................	103,747	100.0	34.0	25.4	37.1	1.6	.8	1.1	–
289	Miscellaneous chemical products............................	148,306	100.0	37.9	11.5	31.7	9.9	6.8	2.2	–
30	Rubber and miscellaneous plastics products.................	48,159	100.0	23.5	29.5	13.7	25.2	7.3	.8	–
307	Miscellaneous plastics products............................	44,207	100.0	24.7	31.2	14.1	23.0	7.0	–	–
32	Stone, clay, glass, and concrete products..................	337,553	100.0	69.1	13.1	5.9	1.6	2.1	8.2	–
327	Concrete, gypsum, and plaster products.....................	241,697	100.0	87.5	9.4	2.4	.5	.2	–	–
33	Primary metal products.....................................	60,721	100.0	42.1	16.4	15.5	13.8	8.0	4.2	–
34	Fabricated metal products except ordnance, machinery and transportation.....................................	376,743	100.0	55.5	10.1	19.4	3.9	7.2	3.9	–
344	Fabricated structural metal products......................	211,896	100.0	59.6	10.8	24.9	2.5	2.0	.1	–
349	Miscellaneous fabricated metal products....................	80,141	100.0	53.3	17.9	15.9	3.8	6.5	2.6	–
35	Machinery, except electrical...............................	263,770	100.0	38.8	16.7	15.3	19.1	4.1	6.0	–
354	Metalworking machinery and equipment.......................	24,393	100.0	53.4	9.1	30.9	6.0	.7	–	–
359	Miscellaneous machinery and parts..........................	121,860	100.0	43.3	12.1	9.1	32.0	2.1	1.4	–
36	Electrical machinery, equipment, and supplies...............	80,185	100.0	11.9	18.7	32.4	11.8	15.0	10.3	–
37	Transportation equipment...................................	251,031	100.0	21.5	8.6	13.2	5.4	47.5	3.9	–
371	Motor vehicles and equipment...............................	210,130	100.0	14.2	9.6	11.9	5.1	55.5	3.7	–
39	Miscellaneous products of manufacturing....................	86,309	100.0	32.7	16.9	15.3	10.0	17.9	7.2	–
399	Miscellaneous manufactured products........................	41,859	100.0	47.4	27.8	13.2	9.5	.9	1.3	–
---	All other miscellaneous[3]................................	841,708	100.0	33.2	13.6	16.2	10.5	15.0	11.6	–
--	All other miscellaneous[3]................................	80,187	100.0	51.9	18.3	10.3	5.5	9.3	4.8	–

Note: Detail may not add to total due to rounding.

– Represents zero.

[1]Value of shipments derived from census of manufactures total value of shipments for 1972.

[2]Includes local shipments.

[3]Represents balance of commodities not shown at each level of detail due to disclosures and those commodities shipped by manufacturing establishments not specifically listed.

SOUTH REGION

TABLE 3. Percent Distribution of Commodities Shipped by Domestic and Foreign Destinations: 1972

TCC code	Commodity description	Value[1] (thousands)	All shipments	Domestic	Foreign
	South Region, total.....................................	3,374,446	100.0	99.1	0.9
20	Food and kindred products...................................	719,427	100.0	100.0	-
201	Meat; fresh, chilled, frozen.............................	467,412	100.0	100.0	-
203	Canned and preserved fruits, vegetables, seafoods...........	33,082	100.0	100.0	-
204	Grain mill products......................................	87,094	100.0	100.0	-
208	Beverages and flavoring extracts.........................	57,385	100.0	100.0	-
209	Miscellaneous food preparations..........................	56,593	100.0	100.0	-
22	Textile mill products......................................	40,580	100.0	94.8	5.2
23	Apparel and other finished textile products, including knit..	113,913	100.0	99.4	.6
239	Miscellaneous fabricated textile products...................	63,071	100.0	99.7	.3
24	Lumber and wood products, except furniture..................	199,463	100.0	99.8	.2
242	Sawmill and planing mill products...........................	273,594	100.0	99.8	.2
243	Millwork, plywood, and prefabricated wood products..........	46,824	100.0	100.0	-
249	Miscellaneous wood products.................................	158,022	100.0	99.9	.1
25	Furniture and fixtures.....................................	101,481	100.0	100.0	-
259	Miscellaneous furniture and fixtures.......................	61,430	100.0	100.0	-
28	Chemicals and allied products..............................	314,930	100.0	100.0	-
287	Agricultural chemicals.....................................	103,747	100.0	100.0	-
289	Miscellaneous chemical products............................	148,306	100.0	100.0	-
30	Rubber and miscellaneous plastics products..................	48,159	100.0	99.0	1.1
307	Miscellaneous plastics products............................	44,207	100.0	98.9	1.1
32	Stone, clay, glass, and concrete products...................	337,553	100.0	99.7	.3
327	Concrete, gypsum, and plaster products.....................	241,697	100.0	100.0	-
33	Primary metal products.....................................	60,721	100.0	99.1	.9
34	Fabricated metal products except ordnance, machinery and transportation..	376,743	100.0	99.8	.2
344	Fabricated structural metal products........................	211,896	100.0	100.0	-
349	Miscellaneous fabricated metal products.....................	80,141	100.0	99.1	1.0
35	Machinery, except electrical...............................	263,770	100.0	99.4	.6
354	Metalworking machinery and equipment.......................	24,393	100.0	100.0	-
359	Miscellaneous machinery and parts..........................	121,860	100.0	99.1	.9
36	Electrical machinery, equipment, and supplies...............	80,185	100.0	82.5	17.5
37	Transportation equipment...................................	251,031	100.0	97.6	2.4
371	Motor vehicles and equipment...............................	210,130	100.0	97.1	2.9
39	Miscellaneous products of manufacturing....................	86,309	100.0	99.0	1.0
399	Miscellaneous manufactured products........................	41,859	100.0	98.4	1.6
---	All other miscellaneous[2].................................	841,708	100.0	99.1	.9
--	All other miscellaneous[2].................................	80,187	100.0	97.6	2.4

Note: Detail may not add to total due to rounding.

- Represents zero.

[1]Value of shipments derived from census of manufactures total value of shipments for 1972.
[2]Represents balance of commodities not shown at each level of detail due to disclosures and those commodities shipped by manufacturing establishments not specifically listed.

WEST REGION

TABLE 1. Percent Distribution of Commodities Shipped by Means of Transport: 1972

TCC code	Commodity description	Value¹ (thousands)	All means of transport	Rail	Motor carrier	Private truck	Air	Water	Other²	Un-known
	West Region, total......................................	4,963,160	100.0	16.2	22.9	49.2	2.1	2.3	6.5	0.7
20	Food and kindred products....................................	1,574,523	100.0	6.1	9.9	83.8	.2	–	–	–
201	Meat; fresh, chilled, frozen............................	84,980	100.0	–	1.6	98.4	–	–	–	–
203	Canned and preserved fruits, vegetables, seafoods..........	126,597	100.0	48.5	42.1	6.5	2.7	.2	–	–
208	Beverages and flavoring extracts...........................	155,217	100.0	–	5.5	94.4	–	–	–	–
23	Apparel and other finished textile products, including knit.	197,745	100.0	1.3	18.6	15.5	6.7	.1	54.1	3.7
233	Women's, misses', children's, and infants' clothing........	109,985	100.0	2.4	10.6	9.1	9.1	–	62.3	6.6
239	Miscellaneous fabricated textile products...................	35,400	100.0	–	24.8	47.6	.6	.7	26.3	–
24	Lumber and wood products, except furniture.................	248,136	100.0	7.0	20.9	71.6	–	.4	.1	–
242	Sawmill and planing mill products...........................	167,397	100.0	10.1	23.6	66.3	–	–	–	–
243	Millwork, plywood, and prefabricated wood products.........	27,841	100.0	1.6	26.1	71.9	–	–	.3	–
249	Miscellaneous wood products................................	40,071	100.0	–	11.3	86.2	–	2.4	.1	–
25	Furniture and fixtures.....................................	66,329	100.0	–	1.8	98.1	–	–	.2	–
28	Chemicals and allied products..............................	644,664	100.0	35.3	32.5	14.5	–	17.4	.3	–
281	Industrial inorganic and organic chemicals..................	492,248	100.0	45.7	29.3	2.4	–	22.6	–	–
289	Miscellaneous chemicals products...........................	43,013	100.0	5.2	54.1	37.8	–	1.7	1.2	–
30	Rubber and miscellaneous plastics products.................	207,123	100.0	15.6	65.4	14.7	1.4	–	2.8	–
307	Miscellaneous plastics products............................	170,407	100.0	.2	79.3	16.7	1.6	–	2.2	–
32	Stone, clay, glass, and concrete products..................	143,065	100.0	–	11.8	79.8	.4	.1	8.0	–
327	Concrete, gypsum, and plaster products.....................	92,315	100.0	–	3.2	95.8	.4	–	.6	–
33	Primary metal products.....................................	57,429	100.0	–	68.0	21.0	–	–	11.0	–
34	Fabricated metal products except ordnance, machinery and transportation.....	358,375	100.0	9.6	46.0	37.9	1.4	.1	5.1	–
344	Fabricated structural metal products.......................	89,028	100.0	1.1	14.4	83.9	.1	.1	.4	–
349	Miscellaneous fabricated metal products....................	171,761	100.0	4.5	69.9	20.7	.5	.1	4.4	–
35	Machinery, except electrical...............................	384,790	100.0	.3	28.4	57.4	5.4	.2	8.9	–
354	Metalworking machinery and equipment.......................	120,181	100.0	1.0	11.1	77.4	2.1	–	8.5	–
359	Miscellaneous machinery and parts..........................	167,819	100.0	.1	27.3	60.5	6.9	.1	5.1	–
36	Electrical machinery, equipment, and supplies..............	650,012	100.0	60.0	13.5	12.2	2.8	–	11.5	–
367	Electronic components and accessories......................	41,616	100.0	–	4.2	22.1	8.1	–	65.6	–
369	Miscellaneous electrical machinery, equipment, and supplies.	81,546	100.0	–	34.4	11.4	13.1	–	41.2	–
37	Transportation equipment...................................	158,693	100.0	–	14.0	64.6	.2	–	4.3	16.9
379	Miscellaneous transportation equipment.....................	113,104	100.0	–	8.5	67.5	.3	–	–	23.7
38	Instruments, photographic and medical goods, watches and clocks........	77,447	100.0	1.0	26.9	4.8	45.7	.7	21.0	–
39	Miscellaneous products of manufacturing....................	112,780	100.0	2.3	53.9	9.3	4.5	–	30.0	–
394	Toys, amusement, sporting, and athletic goods..............	32,633	100.0	7.4	59.7	5.3	4.7	–	22.9	–
399	Miscellaneous manufactured products........................	45,102	100.0	.2	57.5	9.2	5.9	–	27.2	–
---	All other miscellaneous³...................................	2,554,904	100.0	18.9	16.4	57.2	2.2	.1	5.2	–
--	All other miscellaneous³...................................	82,053	100.0	–	30.5	56.6	1.1	1.1	10.7	–

Note: Detail may not add to total due to rounding.

- Represents zero.

¹Value of shipments derived from census of manufactures total value of shipments for 1972.

²Includes railway and air express, United Parcel, parcel post, and other "package carriers."

³Represents balance of commodities not shown at each level of detail due to disclosures and those commodities shipped by manufacturing establishments not specifically listed.

WEST REGION

TABLE 2. Percent Distribution of Commodities Shipped by Distance of Shipment: 1972

TCC code	Commodity description	Value[1] (thousands)	All distances	Under[2] 50 miles	50 to 99 miles	100 to 299 miles	300 to 499 miles	500 to 999 miles	1,000 miles or more	Unknown
	West Region, total.....................................	4,963,160	100.0	39.4	15.6	11.1	6.3	4.6	22.7	0.3
20	Food and kindred products............................	1,574,523	100.0	55.9	18.1	11.8	4.6	2.6	7.1	–
201	Meat; fresh, chilled, frozen.........................	84,980	100.0	44.7	21.7	33.1	.5	–	–	–
203	Canned and preserved fruits, vegetables, seafoods...........	126,597	100.0	8.2	1.3	3.8	10.8	10.1	65.9	–
208	Beverages and flavoring extracts.........................	155,217	100.0	88.8	3.1	6.3	.2	.4	1.3	–
23	Apparel and other finished textile products, including knit.	197,745	100.0	27.6	10.8	6.9	9.4	10.3	35.0	–
233	Women's, misses', children's, and infants' clothing.........	109,985	100.0	19.5	12.0	9.2	9.3	14.3	35.8	–
239	Miscellaneous fabricated textile products.................	35,400	100.0	69.2	6.5	8.6	5.7	5.1	5.0	–
24	Lumber and wood products, except furniture.................	248,136	100.0	31.6	1.7	26.1	14.8	13.2	12.7	–
242	Sawmill and planing mill products.........................	167,397	100.0	9.3	1.1	35.7	17.8	18.4	17.7	–
243	Millwork, plywood, and prefabricated wood products.........	27,841	100.0	79.1	2.1	7.5	4.9	4.7	1.6	–
249	Miscellaneous wood products.............................	40,071	100.0	71.0	4.8	5.7	13.7	·1.1	3.5	–
25	Furniture and fixtures..................................	66,329	100.0	77.2	12.0	7.6	1.9	1.0	.3	–
28	Chemicals and allied products..........................	644,664	100.0	22.1	36.8	15.9	5.5	2.2	17.6	–
281	Industrial inorganic and organic chemicals.................	492,248	100.0	12.4	44.6	15.6	4.3	2.3	20.8	–
289	Miscellaneous chemical products.........................	43,013	100.0	48.9	7.2	4.6	18.4	2.1	18.9	–
30	Rubber and miscellaneous plastics products.................	207,123	100.0	15.9	32.8	1.6	23.4	6.8	19.5	–
307	Miscellaneous plastics products.........................	170,407	100.0	17.8	39.5	1.7	28.3	8.3	4.4	–
32	Stone, clay, glass, and concrete products.................	143,065	100.0	78.4	9.4	7.2	1.8	.8	2.4	–
327	Concrete, gypsum, and plaster products...................	92,315	100.0	82.1	11.8	4.1	1.0	.6	.4	–
33	Primary metal products.................................	57,429	100.0	86.2	6.9	2.0	3.3	.5	1.0	–
34	Fabricated metal products except ordnance, machinery and transportation...	358,375	100.0	39.9	13.1	12.5	9.3	11.3	14.0	–
344	Fabricated structural metal products......................	89,028	100.0	62.4	12.4	10.3	8.1	3.5	3.3	–
349	Miscellaneous fabricated metal products...................	171,761	100.0	30.8	17.0	11.0	7.5	12.4	21.2	–
35	Machinery, except electrical............................	384,790	100.0	58.5	4.2	5.7	7.5	3.4	20.8	–
354	Metalworking machinery and equipment.....................	120,181	100.0	75.3	7.0	7.1	6.1	1.0	3.5	–
359	Miscellaneous machinery and parts........................	167,819	100.0	63.1	1.7	1.2	3.9	.7	29.5	–
36	Electrical machinery, equipment, and supplies.............	650,012	100.0	11.2	2.9	2.2	.4	1.1	82.3	–
367	Electronic components and accessories....................	41,616	100.0	41.3	5.9	5.6	5.9	5.7	35.6	–
369	Miscellaneous electrical machinery, equipment, and supplies..	81,546	100.0	50.8	14.5	13.5	–	3.9	17.4	–
37	Transportation equipment................................	158,693	100.0	26.0	22.2	36.0	7.9	4.2	3.8	–
379	Miscellaneous transportation equipment....................	113,104	100.0	8.0	26.3	46.1	9.2	5.4	5.0	–
38	Instruments, photographic and medical goods, watches and clocks..	77,447	100.0	6.2	5.1	5.7	6.1	19.4	57.6	–
39	Miscellaneous products of manufacturing...................	112,780	100.0	19.9	8.0	18.2	7.9	14.8	28.3	3.0
394	Toys, amusement, sporting, and athletic goods..............	32,633	100.0	11.8	8.3	18.3	12.7	17.6	31.3	–
399	Miscellaneous manufactured products......................	45,102	100.0	12.0	7.6	21.7	5.2	22.1	31.5	–
---	All other miscellaneous[3]..............................	2,554,904	100.0	42.6	12.9	8.9	4.5	3.2	27.3	.6
--	All other miscellaneous[3]..............................	82,053	100.0	55.0	7.2	3.8	3.1	5.1	10.0	15.7

Note: Detail may not add to total due to rounding.

– Represents zero.

[1]Value of shipments derived from census of manufactures total value of shipments for 1972.

[2]Includes local shipments.

[3]Represents balance of commodities not shown at each level of detail due to disclosures and those commodities shipped by manufacturing establishments not specifically listed.

WEST REGION

TABLE 3. **Percent Distribution of Commodities Shipped by Domestic and Foreign Destinations: 1972**

TCC code	Commodity description	Value[1] (thousands)	All shipments	Domestic	Foreign
	West Region, total......................................	4,963,160	100.0	99.1	0.9
20	Food and kindred products.............................	1,574,523	100.0	99.0	1.0
201	Meat; fresh, chilled, frozen..........................	84,980	100.0	100.0	–
203	Canned and preserved fruits, vegetables, seafoods...........	126,597	100.0	87.5	12.5
208	Beverages and flavoring extracts............................	155,217	100.0	100.0	–
23	Apparel and other finished textile products, including knit..	197,745	100.0	100.0	–
233	Women's, misses', children's, and infants' clothing..........	109,985	100.0	100.0	–
239	Miscellaneous fabricated textile products...................	35,400	100.0	100.0	–
24	Lumber and wood products, except furniture..................	248,136	100.0	99.6	.4
242	Sawmill and planing mill products...........................	167,397	100.0	100.0	–
243	Millwork, plywood, and prefabricated wood products...........	27,841	100.0	100.0	–
249	Miscellaneous wood products.................................	40,071	100.0	97.6	2.4
25	Furniture and fixtures......................................	66,329	100.0	100.0	–
28	Chemicals and allied products...............................	644,664	100.0	99.8	.2
281	Industrial inorganic and organic chemicals..................	492,248	100.0	99.9	.1
289	Miscellaneous chemical products.............................	43,013	100.0	98.7	1.3
30	Rubber and miscellaneous plastics products..................	207,123	100.0	100.0	–
307	Miscellaneous plastics products.............................	170,407	100.0	100.0	–
32	Stone, clay, glass, and concrete products...................	143,065	100.0	99.8	.2
327	Concrete, gypsum, and plaster products......................	92,315	100.0	100.0	–
33	Primary metal products......................................	57,429	100.0	100.0	–
34	Fabricated metal products except ordnance, machinery and transportation...	358,375	100.0	99.8	.2
344	Fabricated structural metal products........................	89,028	100.0	100.0	–
349	Miscellaneous fabricated metal products.....................	171,761	100.0	99.8	.2
35	Machinery, except electrical................................	384,790	100.0	96.5	3.5
354	Metalworking machinery and equipment........................	120,181	100.0	99.0	1.0
359	Miscellaneous machinery and parts...........................	167,819	100.0	94.6	5.4
36	Electrical machinery, equipment, and supplies...............	650,012	100.0	99.4	.6
367	Electronic components and accessories.......................	41,616	100.0	99.7	.3
369	Miscellaneous electrical machinery, equipment, and supplies..	81,546	100.0	96.5	3.5
37	Transportation equipment....................................	158,693	100.0	99.7	.3
379	Miscellaneous transportation equipment......................	113,104	100.0	99.7	.3
38	Instruments, photographic and medical goods, watches and clocks..	77,447	100.0	97.0	3.0
39	Miscellaneous products of manufacturing.....................	112,780	100.0	97.6	2.4
394	Toys, amusement, sporting, and athletic goods...............	32,633	100.0	96.7	3.3
399	Miscellaneous manufactured products.........................	45,102	100.0	96.5	3.5
---	All other miscellaneous[2]..................................	2,554,904	100.0	99.6	.4
--	All other miscellaneous[2]..................................	82,053	100.0	97.3	2.7

Note: Detail may not add to total due to rounding.

- Represents zero.

[1]Value of shipments derived from census of manufactures total value of shipments for 1972.
[2]Represents balance of commodities not shown at each level of detail due to disclosures and those commodities shipped by manufacturing establishments not specifically listed.

Shipper Groups

CONTENTS

INTRODUCTION

DESCRIPTION OF THE COMMODITY TRANSPORTATION SURVEY

General

The Commodity Transportation Survey is one of the three components of the Census of Transportation, one of the Economic Censuses conducted every 5 years ending in "2" and "7". Two previous Commodity Transportation Surveys have been conducted—the first in 1963 and the second in 1967. The prime objective of this survey is to measure the transportation and geographic distribution of commodities shipped by manufacturing establishments in the United States beyond the local area. The Commodity Transportation Survey, as it now exists, consists of two independent surveys: A mail summary-data survey and a main shipper survey.

Mail Survey

The first and smaller component of the survey consists of data collection by mail on a simplified 1-page summary questionnaire. About 2,000 plants are sampled which have 10 to 19 employees, and about 1,000 plants are sampled in the Printing and Publishing Industry. In this mail survey, information relating to individual shipments is not collected. The respondent replies only to questions in terms of annual-percent-of-total-value shipped. Value is used as a unit of measure rather than tons since it was felt that the small manufacturers would not have summary data available on tons shipped. Data collected for the census year as a whole include value of product and services, major product shipped, distance shipped (six categories), type of transport used (six modes), and the geographic divisions of destination. Also included is the percent shipped for export to foreign countries. The sample designs used for this survey are simple one-stage systematic random samples of plants from the respective universes. These designs are described in published reports relating to these surveys and are not discussed further in this report.

Shipper Survey

The major part of the Commodity Transportation Survey is commonly referred to as the Shipper Survey. Traffic flow data is gathered, processed, and disseminated relating to the volume of commodities shipped by means of transport, length of haul, size of shipment, and areas of origin and destination in tons and ton-miles. The data sources are bills of lading or other shipping documents pertaining to individual shipments from a sample of about 13,000 plants selected from the census of manufactures universe of manufacturing establishments with 20 employees or more. The sample design is multistaged, utilizing a stratified probability sampling to obtain approximately 13,000 plants at the first stage and a systematic random sample of 1.6 million shipping documents (100 to 200 from each sampled plant) at the second stage. Although the source of the shipping information pertaining to each individual shipment is the shipping document, the primary sampling unit (PSU) may be either a plant or the shipping document itself. The primary sampling unit is the plant for all but the "certainty plants," those with a probability of "1" or greater at the first stage. For certainty plants, the PSU is usually the shipping document (bill of lading) drawn systematically from a random start.

DATA COMPARABILITY WITH PREVIOUS SURVEYS

The 1972 survey is comparable to the 1967 survey, except that SIC 2052, Cookies and Crackers, was added to the industry scope. In 1963 and 1967, all of SIC 205, Bakery Products, was out of scope as being predominately local. Further research revealed that this was not the case for a significant tonnage of prepackaged cookies and crackers (SIC 2052). Also, in 1972, greater emphasis has been placed on the publication of commodity origin-destination data.

The 1967 survey is comparable with 1963 data in most respects, except for a difference in scope. The 1967 survey presented intercity shipments (i.e., beyond the local area) of manufacturing plants with 20 employees or more. The 1963 survey presented all establishments, irrespective of size. Adjustments were not made for this difference in scope. But in general, small plants tend to use highway transportation to a greater relative extent than large plants. This would tend to raise estimated percentages for motor carrier and private truck somewhat above those that would have been shown if adjustments had been made.

SCOPE OF THE SHIPPER SURVEY

Sample of Plants

The source list.—The universe of manufacturing plants used as the first-stage sampling frame for the Commodity Transportation Survey is the mail file of the census of manufactures as of January 1, 1972. This file consists of all manufacturing plants in the Standard Industrial Classification 20 through 39 (except as noted below) with 20 employees or more. Plants with 10 to 19 employees are surveyed independently as described above. (See Mail Survey.)

Industry universe.—The sampling frame for the Shipper Survey includes the entire industrial universe of manufacturing establishments with 20 employees or more except the following exclusions for the reasons indicated.[1]

SIC 19, Ordnance and
accessories . . . . Excluded for security reasons

SIC 2026, Fluid milk . . .
SIC 2051, Bread and
other bakery products,
except cookies
and crackers . . . .
SIC 2097, Manufactured
ice . . . .
SIC 241, Primary forest
products . . . . }
Excluded because they serve local markets and the survey is intended to measure nonlocal commodity flows.

SIC 27, Printing,
publishing, and allied
industries .
Excluded because they are covered by the Mail Summary-Data Survey with the 10-to-19-employees size establishments.

SIC 2052, Cookies and Crackers, was added to the survey in 1972. All of SIC 205, Bakery Products, was out of scope for the 1963 and 1967 surveys.

Plant size.—The 1963 Commodity Transportation Survey found that the primary distributions of products by plants with less than 20 employees tended to be local and that this segment of the industry generated only about 4 percent of the total nonlocal tons shipped by all manufacturing plants. How-ever, these small plants constitute about two-thirds of the total number of establishments in the industrial universe. These findings led to the conclusion that the survey costs and reporting effort could be significantly reduced by independently sampling and surveying the 10-to-19-employees size class plants by mail on the general characteristics of their shipping patterns. Data for plants with less than 10 employees are obtained from administrative records and therefore are not included in the census of manufactures universe mail file. Consequently, they are not included in any phase of the Commodity Transportation Survey. It is also felt that the omission of plants with fewer than 10 employees allows increased emphasis on quality of data compiled from larger establishments.

Geographic scope.—Plants located in the 48 contiguous States are eligible for inclusion in the Shipper Survey. Shipments *to* Alaska and Hawaii from these 48 origin States are also identified as are the domestic movement of exports. (See "Shipments for export," below.)

Sample of Shipments

Local shipments.—Generally, the survey is designed to exclude "local shipments." Plants shipping 90 percent or more of their volume less than 25 miles are excluded from the survey. However, if shipments from the plant are to a "local" warehouse or other temporary storage or consolidation facility, the subsequent shipments from this facility are in scope to the survey if 10 percent or more of these shipments move over 25 miles. Local shipments from plants that are in scope to the survey are excluded in the sampling process at the plant or subsequently by computer edit.

Method of transport.—The following modes of transport are in scope to the survey:

Rail, including combinations such as piggyback in which the major distance was by rail (railway express is included under other);

Motor carrier, including combinations in which the major distance was by motor carrier (This includes all highway transport, except by private truck.);

Private truck, trucks operated by the shipper or the customer;

Air, including air freight and air express and combinations in which the major distance was by air;

Water, including combinations in which the major distance was by water;

---

[1]The CTS sample was drawn from the 1972 Census of Manufactures based upon the 1967 Standard Industrial Classification (SIC) code. The 1967 code classification was the most recent available at the time of sampling. Some realinements have been effected to the SIC as defined by the Office of Management and Budget in the Standard Industrial Classification Manual: 1972.

Other, including railway express, united parcel service, bus, freight forwarder when major means of transport (such as rail and air) is not known, messenger service etc.; and

Unknown, used when the principle type of transport is not shown on shipping documents and cannot be readily determined by the respondent.

Excluded from the survey are the following:

Own power or towed "shipments", including motorized vehicles, aircraft, or vessels which are sometimes moved from the manufacturer under their own power, and other commodities (such as prefabricated buildings) which are towed away;

Pipeline, primarily affecting shipments of petroleum products from refineries; and

Parcel post, shipments through the U.S. postal service.

Shipments for export.—Shipments for export are included in the survey with destination of the U.S. port of export. Distances and other characteristics of these shipments relate only to the domestic movement from the shipping plant to the U.S. port of export.

Classified shipments.—Shipments of manufactured commodities from an in-scope plant which would otherwise have been included in the survey are excluded if they are classified or relate to the movement of classified materials.

Mixed shipments.—When a bill of lading or other shipping document that contains more than one commodity line is selected, the total weight is taken and ascribed to the commodity that contributed the greatest proportion to the total weight.

SAMPLE DESIGN

As mentioned earlier (see Shipper Survey), a two-stage probability sample design was used. The first stage involved the drawing of a probability sample of about 13,000 plants from the universe. The second involved the selection of a probability sample of about 100 to 200 bills of lading or other shipping documents on file at each of the sampled plants.

The term "probability sample," as used here, means that the chance for selecting each document from the millions of such documents in the universe is known and is not equal to zero. The information from a probability sample can be ex-

panded to approximate the total that would have been obtained by a complete count, and the sampling variability can be estimated from the sample itself.

The sample design is rather complex.[2] In general, the first stage involved the classification of manufacturing plants into 85 shipper classes based upon the plant's Standard Industrial Classification (SIC). These classes were then regrouped into nine "tonnage divisions," based on the total tons shipped by each shipper class in the 1963 and 1967 surveys. Each manufacturing plant also was identified by its location and classified into two geographic strata: (1) Located in a "selected industrial State" or (2) located in any other State. The selected industrial States are those in which the major production areas are located and include the following:

California	Minnesota
Colorado	Missouri
Connecticut	New Jersey
Delaware	New York
Georgia	Ohio
Indiana	Pennsylvania
Illinois	Rhode Island
Maryland	Texas
Massachusetts	Washington
Michigan	Wisconsin

Within each of the nine tonnage divisions and two geographic strata, the probability of selecting any given plant in the universe was proportionate to the "intercity tonnage rating" of the plant. The rating for each plant was based on the intercity tons shipped by the average plant of the same shipper class and employee size group in the 1963 and 1967 surveys.

With respect to the allocation of plants within the sample, it was decided that the relative degree of precision and detail should be somewhat greater for the shipper classes in the large tonnage divisions than for those in the small tonnage divisions. An average of 205 plants per shipper class was obtained in each of the 4 largest tonnage divisions, 176 in the 5th division, and an average of 132 per shipper class in the 4 smallest tonnage divisions. It also was decided that greater precision was needed for data on traffic flows from production areas than from the balance of the country. The probability of selecting a specific plant located in a selected industrial State was set at 1.5 times the probability of selecting an otherwise comparable plant in any other State.

After selecting the plants, the next stage involved the selection of a probability sample of bills of lading or other

---

[2] A detailed technical description may be obtained from the Transportation Division, Bureau of the Census, Washington, D.C. 20233.

shipping papers at the company headquarters or individual plants. Several alternative standard plans were used, depending largely on the filing system used by the company. For example, in files organized by serial number, the procedure involved drawing every "nth" record, after taking a random-number start. In large chronological files, a two-stage design was used—a sample of dates and a sample of shipping papers within those dates. Special designs were made for recordkeeping situations that could not be sampled readily by one of the standard plans.

METHODS FOR ESTIMATING

The basic source document for obtaining size of shipment (in pounds) and origin/destination information is the sampled individual shipping paper—bill of lading, sales invoice, summary shipping record, etc.

Estimates of Tons

Estimates of total tons are shown in the first column of tables involving tons shipped. These figures represent the approximate total that would have been obtained by a complete enumeration of all shipments. These estimates are subject to sampling variability, response variations, and other non-sampling errors. The estimates of tons were made by multiplying the actual weight shown on the record for each shipment by the reciprocal of the sampling fraction for that shipment,[3] aggregating the expanded value, and converting to tons. For example, if a manufacturing establishment was selected at the rate of 1 in 5, and shipments within that plant were drawn at the rate of 1 in 20, the weight in pounds of that shipment would be multiplied by 100 (that is, 5 times 20) and divided by 2,000 for purposes of estimating total tons shipped.

Estimates of Ton-Miles

Estimates of total ton-miles are shown in the first column of tables involving ton-miles. These figures are the product of weight times distance. For example, a 10-ton shipment that moved between places that were 1,000 miles apart is equivalent to a 50-ton shipment that moved 200 miles. Both represent 10,000 ton-miles, although they differ in terms of both weight and distance.

Estimates of Distance

The distance component is calculated by a computer program known as PICADAD.[4] Distance is the straight-line miles between the plant as origin and the destination shown on the shipping paper, without allowance for circuity in actual route used by the carrier. The actual route-mile distance is somewhat longer. On the average, railroad "short-line" and highway "direct-route" distances exceed the calculated straight-line miles by about 24 percent and 21 percent, respectively.

Estimates of Size

Observations based on summary reports and other types of records generally show weights that are aggregates of several shipments. While both classes of records were used for estimating total tons, the latter was excluded from the analyses by size of shipment. Therefore, tabulations showing the distribution of shipments by weight class were estimated from shipment data that were based on bills of lading and sales invoices.

The size of shipment in this report is the weight shown on the bill of lading or sales invoice, and is not necessarily the weight actually shipped in one freight car, truck, or other vehicle. Doubtless many of the smaller shipments shown in this survey were consolidated by the shipper into carload or truck lots, while some large shipments were moved in more than one freight car or truck.

RELATIONSHIP BETWEEN SHIPPER GROUP AND STANDARD INDUSTRIAL CLASSIFICATION

Each manufacturing plant is assigned to a shipper group based on the Standard Industrial Classification (SIC) codes used to classify establishments in the census of manufactures. The initial assignment is made to the shipper class. The shipper classes are assembled to make up a broader classification, the shipper group.

The 1972 Commodity Transportation Survey, unlike the other 1972 economic surveys, is based on 1967 SIC's. The 1972 classifications were not available at the time the sample selection was accomplished. The following table shows the relationship between shipper groups and SIC's for 1972 and 1967 classifications.

[3] Adjusted for nonresponse. The response rate for the survey was above 99 percent.

[4] A program developed by the Bureau of the Census specifically for processing transportation data.

Table A. Relationship Between Shipper Groups and Standard Industrial Classification

Shipper group number and title	Standard Industrial Classification		Shipper group number and title	Standard Industrial Classification	
	1967	1972		1967	1972
1 Meat and dairy products	201, 202 except 2026, 2094	201, 202 except 2026	12 Furniture, fixtures and miscellaneous manufactured products	251, 252, 253, 254, 259, 391, 393, 394, 395, 396, 399	251, 252, 253, 254, 259, 391, 393, 394, 395, 396, 399
2 Canned and frozen foods and other food products except meat and dairy products	203, 204, 206, 209 except 2094 and 2097	203, 204, 2061, 2062, 2063, 207 except 2077, 209 except 2097	13 Stone, clay, and glass products	321, 322, 323, 324, 325, 326, 327, 328, 329	321, 322, 323, 324, 325, 326, 327, 328, 329
3 Candy, cookies and crackers, beverages, and tobacco products	2052, 2071, 2072, 2073 2082, 2083, 2084, 2085, 2086, 2087, 211, 212, 213, 214	2052, 2065, 2066, 2067, 2082, 2083, 2084, 2085, 2086, 2087, 211, 212, 213, 214,	14 Primary iron and steel products	331, 332, 339	331, 332, 339, 3462
			15 Primary nonferrous metal products	333, 334, 335, 336	333, 334, 335, 336, 3463
4 Basic textiles and leather products	221, 222, 223, 224, 2256, 226, 227, 228, 229, 311, 312, 313, 314, 315, 316, 317, 319,	221, 222, 223, 224, 2257, 2258, 226, 227, 228, 229, 311, 313, 314, 315, 316, 317, 319	16 Fabricated metal products, except metal cans and misc. fabricated metal products	342, 343, 344	342, 343, 344
			17 Metal cans and miscellaneous fabricated metal products	341, 345, 346, 347, 348, 349	341, 345, 346 except 3462, 347, 349
5 Apparel and related products	231, 232, 233, 234, 235, 236, 237, 238, 239, 225 except 2256	231, 232, 233, 234, 235, 236, 237, 238, 239, 225 except 2257 and 2258	18 Industrial machinery, except electrical	354, 355, 356, 3586	354, 355, 356, 3586
			19 Machinery, except electrical and industrial	351, 352, 353, 357, 358 except 3586, 359	351, 352, 353, 357, 358 except 3586, 359
6 Paper and allied products	261, 262, 263 264, 265, 266	261, 262, 263, 264, 265, 266	20 Communications products and parts	365, 366, 367	365, 366, 367
7 Basic chemicals, plastics materials, synthetic resins, rubber, and fibers	281, 282, 2895	281, 282, 286 except 2861, 2895	21 Electrical products and supplies	361, 362, 363, 364, 369	361, 362, 363, 364, 369
8 Drugs, paints, and other chemical products	283, 284, 285, 286, 287, 289 except 2895	283, 284, 285, 2861, 287, 289 except 2895	22 Motor vehicles and equipment	3711, 3712, 3713, 3714, 3715	3711, 3713, 3714, 3715
9 Petroleum and coal products	291, 295, 299	291, 295, 299	23 Transportation equipment, except motor vehicles	372, 373, 374, 375, 379	372, 373, 374, 375, 379
10 Rubber and plastics products	301, 302, 303, 306, 307	301, 302, 303, 304, 306, 307			
11 Lumber and wood products, except furniture	242, 243, 244 249	242, 243 except 2434, 244, 245, 249	24 Instruments, photographic equipment, watches, and clocks	381, 382, 383, 384, 385, 386, 387	381, 382, 383, 384, 385, 386, 387

RELIABILITY OF DATA

This report contains estimates derived from a sample of shipments by each of 24 shipper groups and the U.S. total. Tables show the percentage distributions for tons and ton-miles, by means of transport and distance, for plants by total employment size. Distributions have been presented for each shipper group provided (1) the estimates did not disclose the shipments of an individual company or plant, and (2) one relative standard error did not exceed 50 percent of the estimate with which it was associated.

SAMPLING VARIABILITY

General Description

The statistics presented in this report are estimates from a sample. The particular sample that was selected is one of the large number of all possible samples of the same size that could have been selected using the same sample design. Estimates derived from the different samples would differ from each other and from the results of a complete census using the same procedures. This variation among the possible estimates is called sampling variability.

For example, hypothesize that shipments for shipper group 3, Candy, Cookies and Crackers, Beverages, and Tobacco Products, were estimated to have been 45,678,000 tons during 1972 and the "sampling variability" was estimated to be about 8.9 percent. In this instance, the sampling variability was expressed in relative terms which is technically called the relative standard error. Variability may also be expressed in absolute terms (such as tons), which in this illustration was 4,065,300 tons or the equivalent of 8.9 percent of 45,678,000 tons. When expressed in absolute (rather than percentage) terms, the variability is known technically as one standard error.[5]

Interpretation of Sampling Variability

General guide.—The following general guide is given for the interpretation of sampling variability: Had all elements of the universe been canvassed, the value for a given item would be included in the range—

From 1.0 standard error below to 1.0 standard error above the estimate obtained for about two-thirds of all possible samples;

From 1.6 standard errors below to 1.6 standard errors above the estimate obtained for about 90 percent of all possible samples;

From 2.0 standard errors below to 2.0 standard errors above the estimate obtained for about 95 percent of all possible samples; and

From 3.0 standard errors below to 3.0 standard errors above the estimate obtained, almost always.

These values may be interpreted, therefore, as defining approximate confidences that the estimate shown would not differ by more than 1.0, 1.6, 2.0, or 3.0 of its standard errors, respectively, from the result for a complete census.

Illustration (variability).—For example, hypothesizing total shipments for shipper group 3, we estimated 45,678,000 tons plus or minus 4,065,300 tons. Using the probability guide above, those figures may be interpreted as follows:

1. The chances are 2 out of 3 that a complete enumeration would have shown between 41.61 and 49.75 million tons (i.e., plus or minus 1.0 standard error);

2. The chances are about 9 out of 10 that a complete enumeration would have shown between 39.18 and 52.18 million tons (i.e., plus or minus 1.6 times the standard error);

3. The chances are about 19 out of 20 that a complete enumeration would have shown between 37.55 and 53.81 million tons (i.e., plus or minus 2.0 times the standard error); and

4. There is almost no chance that a complete enumeration would have shown less than 33.48 or more than 57.88 million tons (i.e., plus or minus 3.0 times the standard error).

Illustration (relative variability).—The interpretation of relative variability corresponds to the interpretation for absolutes. Again using the same illustration, the relative variability was estimated to be 8.9 percent. The chances are about 2 out of 3 that the estimate is not more than 8.9 percent above or below the figure that would have been obtained by a complete enumeration. The chances are about 9 out of 10 that the estimate is within 14.2 percent of the actual (that is, plus or minus 1.6 times the relative standard error), and almost no chance that the estimate is more than 26.7 percent above or below the total that would have been obtained from a complete enumeration.

---

[5] In fact, from a computational standpoint, a standard error is estimated from the observed values, and the relative error is the standard error divided by the estimated total to which it applies.

Standard error of a percent.—The standard error of a percent in published percent distributions that are based upon an estimate from the survey cannot be determined directly from the relative standard errors published with the data tables. In general, the order of magnitude of the standard error of a percent depends upon the size of the percent and the size of the base from which it was derived.

Difference between two estimates.—Sometimes the question arises as to what is the sampling variability of the difference between two estimates. For example, for illustrative purposes, the total tonnage for Shipper Group 16 (Fabricated Metal Products Except Metal Cans and Miscellaneous Fabricated Metal Products) is 20.6 million tons as compared with 26.5 million tons for Shipper Group 17 (Metal Cans and Miscellaneous Fabricated Metal Products). The estimates indicate that approximately 5.9 million tons more were moved for Shipper Group 17 than for Shipper Group 16.

Was the tonnage actually larger? What is the variability of that 5.9 million ton difference? A rough, conservative estimate can be made readily on the basis of the standard errors shown for the two estimates. For example, say the relative errors are 7.5 percent for group 16 and 9.3 percent for group 17. Translating those into absolutes,[6] the standard errors are 1.5 million and 2.5 million tons for shipper groups 16 and 17, respectively. To obtain a rough estimate of the standard error of the difference, multiply the larger of the two standard errors by a factor of 1.4[7] which in this instance is 1.4 times 2.5 million tons or about 3.5 million tons. The chances are about 2 out of 3 that the difference attributable to sampling would not be more than 3.5 million tons and about 9 out of 10 that it would not be greater than 5.6 million tons (i.e., 1.6 times 3.5 million tons).

---

[6] 7.5 percent of 20,587 and 9.5 percent of 26,514.
[7] The standard error of a difference is actually

$$\sigma_{A-B} = \sqrt{\sigma^2{}_A + \sigma^2{}_B - 2\sigma_{AB}}$$

where

$\sigma^2{}_A$ is the variance of A, $\sigma^2{}_B$ is the variance of B, and

σ_{AB} is the covariance of A and B.

However, at the highest level of confidence (3 standard errors or near certainty), the difference attributable to sampling may be as high as 10.6 million tons (3 times 3.5 million tons) and, since the difference between statistics was 5.9 million tons, we cannot say with absolute confidence that a difference exists. As mentioned above, this is a rough but conservative estimate of variability of the difference between two items.

Ton-Miles

The sampling variability shown in this report relates to estimates of tons shipped. No variances were estimated for ton-miles. The sampling variability for ton-miles for any given item probably is similar to, but somewhat higher than, the sampling variability for tons on the same item.

Non-Sampling Errors

In addition to sampling variability, the data are subject to "response errors" at the second stage of sampling that may have arisen from misinterpretation of questions, failure to find and sample some files, or other similar sources of error. This type of error probably is generally minor in this survey; however no statistical measure of the impact of these errors has been made. For certain industries (specifically, refined petroleum products), this error may be substantial due to ambiguities concerning the exclusion of local shipments and pipeline shipments or the greater use of a date sample procedure which is believed to be subject to greater error than other methods employed. The sampling procedures at each plant were relatively clear, and the precise facts were transcribed directly from individual shipping documents by company personnel in most instances. In the processing of data, careful efforts were made at each step to reduce the effects of errors. Errors occurred through failure to obtain complete and consistant information, incorrect recording of information on the schedules, incorrect transcriptions, and the like. Computer edits and review were used to identify and correct large errors.

Table B. Comparisons of Tons and Ton-Miles of Shipments by Shipper Group and Sampling Variability: 1972 and 1967

Shipper group	Estimates				Relative sampling variability for tons (percent)	
	1972		1967		1972	1967
	Tons (thousands)	Ton-Miles (millions)	Tons (thousands)	Ton-Miles (millions)		
U.S. Total	1,467,766	631,058	[2]1,268,077	([3])	2.0	—
1. Meat and dairy products	42,616	17,520	38,675	15,540	3.7	9.0
2. Canned and frozen foods and other food products, except meat and dairy products	154,015	62,726	155,371	62,983	4.8	8.4
3. Candy, cookies and crackers, beverages, and tobacco products[1]	57,996	14,400	40,327	14,835	16.2	5.4
4. Basic textiles and leather products	14,209	6,678	14,495	6,268	8.0	11.2
5. Apparel and related products	5,798	3,146	4,514	2,377	12.9	12.8
6. Paper and allied products	89,410	40,553	71,677	34,966	3.9	4.4
7. Basic chemicals, plastics materials, synthetic resins, rubber, and fibers	111,853	47,821	97,619	43,662	6.5	5.4
8. Drugs, paints, and other chemical products	58,902	22,580	61,169	19,090	8.2	7.0
9. Petroleum and coal products	348,137	192,353	[2]301,120	([3])	5.9	7.0
10. Rubber and plastics products	15,877	8,142	10,057	5,307	4.9	5.2
11. Lumber and wood products, except furniture ..	79,991	44,179	61,859	46,658	5.7	9.2
12. Furniture, fixtures, and miscellaneous manufactured products	14,371	8,162	8,712	4,961	8.7	8.8
13. Stone, clay, and glass products	178,122	34,242	134,313	26,287	7.4	9.0
14. Primary iron and steel products	139,461	38,953	128,975	40,438	4.9	4.6
15. Primary nonferrous metal products	29,954	16,414	22,776	13,410	7.1	5.2
16. Fabricated metal products, except metal cans and miscellaneous fabricated metal products ..	14,870	7,317	16,668	6,098	11.3	9.6
17. Metal cans and miscellaneous fabricated metal products	23,695	8,801	18,408	6,148	4.5	6.8
18. Industrial machinery, except electrical	8,699	4,318	6,703	4,145	23.9	10.6
19. Machinery, except electrical and industrial	16,222	9,724	15,820	9,126	3.8	8.6
20. Communications products and parts	2,327	1,443	2,514	1,577	1.1	6.4
21. Electrical products and supplies	13,131	7,514	12,115	7,208	3.6	11.2
22. Motor vehicles and equipment	39,990	30,263	36,525	14,944	1.6	4.6
23. Transportation equipment, except motor vehicles	6,506	2,613	6,159	2,680	11.4	5.6
24. Instruments, photographic equipment, watches, and clocks	1,603	1,183	1,506	893	7.5	9.2

— Represents zero.

[1]SIC 205 was out of scope to the 1967 survey. However, for the 1972 survey, SIC 2052, Cookies and Crackers, was included while SIC 2051 remained out of scope to the survey.

[2]Revised from 1967 published data.

[3]Revised data not available.

Table C. Shipper Group Summary—Percent Distribution of Tons and Ton-Miles by Means of Transport: 1972

Shipper group	Number	Means of transport							
		All means of transport	Rail	Motor carrier	Private truck	Air	Water	Other	Unknown
	Thousands	Percent distribution							
Total tons	1,467,766	100.0	31.7	31.1	18.3	—	18.3	0.2	0.3
1. Meat and dairy products..................	42,616	100.0	18.8	41.7	39.1	—	.1	.1	.2
2. Canned and frozen foods and other food products, except meat and dairy products	154,015	100.0	50.7	20.3	23.0	—	5.5	—	.5
3. Candy, cookies and crackers, beverages, and tobacco products[1]	57,996	100.0	15.4	25.7	58.4	—	.2	—	.2
4. Basic textiles and leather products	14,209	100.0	9.7	61.4	27.7	0.1	—	.9	.2
5. Apparel and related products	5,798	100.0	8.5	69.4	15.6	2.0	—	4.3	.2
6. Paper and allied products	89,410	100.0	51.7	28.0	17.9	—	2.1	.1	.1
7. Basic chemicals, plastics materials, synthetic resins, rubber, and fibers	111,853	100.0	48.6	30.1	12.1	—	8.6	.4	.2
8. Drugs, paints, and other chemical products	58,902	100.0	37.8	38.6	15.7	—	7.4	.3	.2
9. Petroleum and coal products	348,137	100.0	9.7	16.0	8.4	—	65.3	.2	.3
10. Rubber and plastics products	15,877	100.0	24.4	59.1	15.2	.7	—	.3	.2
11. Lumber and wood products, except furniture ..	79,991	100.0	45.8	16.2	36.3	—	1.3	—	.3
12. Furniture, fixtures, and miscellaneous manufactured products	14,371	100.0	22.0	41.4	34.7	.3	.2	1.2	.2
13. Stone, clay, and glass products.............	178,122	100.0	21.9	47.2	23.7	—	6.4	—	.8
14. Primary iron and steel products	139,461	100.0	43.7	44.4	6.7	—	4.8	.3	.1
15. Primary nonferrous metal products	29,954	100.0	51.6	31.4	15.1	—	1.5	.2	.2
16. Fabricated metal products, except metal cans and miscellaneous fabricated metal products ..	14,870	100.0	17.3	55.3	25.1	.2	1.3	.5	.3
17. Metal cans and miscellaneous fabricated metal products	23,695	100.0	36.8	44.1	17.8	.3	.3	.4	.3
18. Industrial machinery, except electrical	8,699	100.0	19.6	59.4	18.9	.6	.1	1.2	.1
19. Machinery, except electrical and industrial	16,222	100.0	26.5	53.4	17.7	.6	.2	1.0	.5
20. Communications products and parts	2,327	100.0	13.0	64.5	12.4	6.1	—	3.4	.5
21. Electrical products and supplies	13,131	100.0	35.0	49.3	14.1	.4	—	.7	.2
22. Motor vehicles and equipment	39,990	100.0	59.3	37.3	3.0	—	—	.2	.2
23. Transportation equipment, except motor vehicles	6,506	100.0	19.5	23.9	54.8	.4	.4	.5	.5
24. Instruments, photographic equipment, watches, and clocks	1,603	100.0	20.9	63.8	10.9	2.0	.1	2.1	.2

See footnotes at end of table.

Table C. Shipper Group Summary—Percent Distribution of Tons and Ton-Miles by Means of Transport: 1972—Continued

Shipper group	Number	Means of transport							
	All means of transport	Rail	Motor carrier	Private Truck	Air	Water	Other	Unknown
	Millions	Percent distribution							
Total ton-miles.........................	631,058	100.0	42.0	20.9	6.8	0.2	29.6	0.2	0.3
1. Meat and dairy products	17,520	100.0	27.8	54.3	17.2	—	.2	.1	.3
2. Canned and frozen foods and other food products, except meat and dairy products	62,726	100.0	66.8	18.3	9.5	—	5.0	—	.4
3. Candy, cookies and crackers, beverages, and tobacco products[1]	14,400	100.0	43.1	28.8	25.8	—	1.9	—	.3
4. Basic textiles and leather products	6,678	100.0	16.3	61.0	21.0	.2	—	1.2	.4
5. Apparel and related products	3,146	100.0	13.4	67.0	9.5	4.8	.1	5.0	.2
6. Paper and allied products	40,553	100.0	73.8	18.9	5.6	—	1.3	—	.2
7. Basic chemicals, plastics materials, synthetic resins, rubber, and fibers	47,821	100.0	63.1	21.6	4.7	—	10.0	.2	.3
8. Drugs, paints, and other chemical products	22,580	100.0	44.3	32.0	8.4	.1	14.4	.4	.3
9. Petroleum and coal products	192,353	100.0	7.9	3.4	1.6	—	87.0	—	.1
10. Rubber and plastics products	8,142	100.0	32.1	56.8	9.3	1.0	.3	.3	.2
11. Lumber and wood products, except furniture ..	44,179	100.0	76.8	7.6	10.7	—	4.7	—	.2
12. Furniture, fixtures, and miscellaneous manufactured products	8,162	100.0	37.1	39.9	20.5	.8	.3	1.2	.2
13. Stone, clay, and glass products	34,242	100.0	45.3	36.6	11.3	—	6.1	—	.6
14. Primary iron and steel products	38,953	100.0	51.6	35.9	4.8	—	7.3	.2	.2
15. Primary nonferrous metal products	16,414	100.0	67.2	23.4	7.7	—	1.1	.2	.3
16. Fabricated metal products, except metal cans and miscellaneous fabricated metal products ..	7,317	100.0	23.3	60.1	13.0	.4	2.1	.6	.5
17. Metal cans and miscellaneous fabricated metal products	8,801	100.0	50.5	40.3	7.1	.6	.8	.4	.3
18. Industrial machinery, except electrical	4,318	100.0	12.3	75.7	8.9	1.2	.1	1.6	.1
19. Machinery, except electrical and industrial	9,724	100.0	37.7	49.7	8.9	1.3	.6	1.2	.5
20. Communications products and parts	1,443	100.0	18.0	59.9	5.6	12.0	.3	3.3	.9
21. Electrical products and supplies	7,514	100.0	43.2	46.0	8.4	.8	.5	1.0	.3
22. Motor vehicles and equipment	30,263	100.0	80.9	17.4	1.0	.1	.2	.2	.3
23. Transportation equipment, except motor vehicles	2,613	100.0	24.0	30.3	43.1	1.3	.3	.8	.3
24. Instruments, photographic equipment, watches, and clocks	1,183	100.0	34.4	53.9	5.7	3.6	.3	1.9	.2

— Represents zero.

[1]SIC 205 was out of scope to the 1967 survey. However, for the 1972 survey SIC 2052, Cookies and Crackers, was included while SIC 2051 remained out of scope to the survey.

Table D. Plant-Size Summary—Percent Distribution of Shipments by Means of Transport and Distance: 1972

Means of transport and distance of shipment	Tons of shipments				Ton-miles			
	All plants	Plants with—			All plants	Plants with—		
		20 to 99 employees	100 to 499 employees	500 employees and over		20 to 99 employees	100 to 499 employees	500 employees and over
TONS SHIPPED . . . . . . .THOUSANDS. .	1 467 766	282 663	555 821	646 007	(X)	(X)	(X)	(X)
TON MILES. . . . . . . .MILLIONS. .	(X)	(X)	(X)	(X)	631 058	77 257	219 393	334 408
MEANS OF TRANSPORT								
TOTAL.	100.0	100.0	100.0	100.0	100.0	100.0	100.0	100.0
RAIL	31.7	24.1	30.5	35.9	42.0	45.9	42.7	40.7
MOTOR CARRIER.	31.1	31.0	34.0	28.7	20.9	27.9	24.1	17.2
PRIVATE TRUCK.	18.3	38.2	20.5	7.7	6.8	16.5	9.0	3.2
AIR.	-	-	-	-	.2	.2	.2	.1
WATER.	18.3	6.1	14.2	27.2	29.6	8.9	23.4	38.5
OTHER.	.2	.3	.2	.3	.2	.4	.2	.1
UNKNOWN.	.3	.2	.6	.2	.3	.4	.4	.2
DISTANCE OF SHIPMENT								
TOTAL.	100.0	100.0	100.0	100.0	100.0	100.0	100.0	100.0
UNDER 100 MILES.	28.7	42.6	31.7	20.0	3.3	7.3	3.9	1.9
100 TO 199 MILES	16.6	19.3	18.5	13.9	5.7	10.2	6.8	3.9
200 TO 299 MILES	11.9	10.8	11.2	13.0	6.9	9.6	6.9	6.2
300 TO 499 MILES	13.7	12.0	12.5	15.5	12.6	16.6	12.2	11.8
500 TO 999 MILES	16.5	9.8	14.5	21.0	27.7	25.2	26.6	29.0
1000 TO 1499 MILES	8.0	3.1	6.4	11.4	23.5	13.7	19.3	28.5
1500 MILES AND OVER.	4.6	2.4	5.0	5.1	20.5	17.4	24.3	18.7

Note: Estimates of sampling variability are presented in table B to facilitate interpretation and analysis. Most data are subject to high sampling variability and should be treated as an approximate rather than a precise measurement of volume.
SIC 205 was out of scope to the 1967 survey. However, for the 1972 survey SIC 2052, cookies and crackers, was included while SIC 2051 remained out of scope to the survey.

- Represents or rounds to zero.   (X) Not applicable.

SHIPPER GROUP 1. Meat and Dairy Products.
Percent Distribution of Shipments by Means of Transport and Distance, for Plants: 1972

Means of transport and distance of shipment	Tons of shipments				Ton-miles			
	All plants	Plants with—			All plants	Plants with—		
		20 to 99 employees	100 to 499 employees	500 employees and over		20 to 99 employees	100 to 499 employees	500 employees and over
TONS SHIPPED . . . . . .THOUSANDS. .	42 616	11 286	17 338	13 990	(X)	(X)	(X)	(X)
TON MILES. . . . . MILLIONS. .	(X)	(X)	(X)	(X)	17 520	2 650	8 140	6 729
MEANS OF TRANSPORT								
TOTAL.	100.0	100.0	100.0	100.0	100.0	100.0	100.0	100.0
RAIL	18.8	20.0	15.6	21.6	27.8	27.6	25.6	30.6
MOTOR CARRIER.	41.7	39.7	41.8	43.0	54.3	48.0	55.9	54.9
PRIVATE TRUCK.	39.1	39.6	42.0	35.1	17.2	23.6	17.6	14.2
AIR.	-	-	-	-	-	-	-	-
WATER.	.1	.3	-	-	.2	.5	.2	-
OTHER.	.1	.1	.1	.1	.1	-	.1	.2
UNKNOWN.	.2	.2	.4	.1	.3	.2	.6	-
DISTANCE OF SHIPMENT								
TOTAL.	100.0	100.0	100.0	100.0	100.0	100.0	100.0	100.0
UNDER 100 MILES.	29.1	42.5	27.6	20.2	3.9	10.6	2.9	2.3
100 TO 199 MILES	16.4	22.5	15.2	13.1	6.0	14.2	4.9	4.0
200 TO 299 MILES	11.4	15.1	8.6	12.0	6.9	16.1	4.6	6.1
300 TO 499 MILES	13.3	9.2	12.8	17.3	12.8	15.6	10.7	14.3
500 TO 999 MILES	17.3	6.7	19.3	23.5	30.9	19.8	30.1	36.3
1000 TO 1499 MILES	10.0	2.9	13.0	11.8	29.4	14.6	34.1	29.5
1500 MILES AND OVER.	2.4	1.1	3.5	2.1	10.1	9.1	12.7	7.4

NOTE: Detail may not add to totals due to rounding. Shipments excluded from the survey are those moving by pipeline (primarily petroleum products from refineries), parcel post shipments, and commodities moved by own power (motorized vehicles, aircraft, etc.) or towed (prefabricated buildings, etc.). Local shipments (commodities shipped less than 25 miles from the plant) and shipments within the same city are also excluded. Shipments to Alaska and Hawaii from the 48 conterminous States and the District of Columbia are included; however, no data were obtained for shipments originating in Alaska and Hawaii. Distance of shipments to foreign destinations are calculated only to the U.S. port of exit. Estimates of sampling variability are presented in table B to facilitate interpretation and analysis. Most data are subject to high sampling variability and should be treated as an approximate rather than a precise measurement of volume.

- Represents or rounds to zero. (X) Not applicable.

SHIPPER GROUP 2. Canned and Frozen Foods and Other Food Products, Except Meat and Dairy Products
Percent Distribution of Shipments by Means of Transport and Distance, for Plants: 1972

Means of transport and distance of shipment	Tons of shipments				Ton-miles			
	All plants	Plants with—			All plants	Plants with—		
		20 to 99 employees	100 to 499 employees	500 employees and over		20 to 99 employees	100 to 499 employees	500 employees and over
TONS SHIPPED . . . . . .THOUSANDS. .	154 015	64 841	61 966	27 206	(X)	(X)	(X)	(X)
TON MILES. . . . . MILLIONS. .	(X)	(X)	(X)	(X)	62 726	21 972	25 851	14 903
MEANS OF TRANSPORT								
TOTAL.	100.0	100.0	100.0	100.0	100.0	100.0	100.0	100.0
RAIL	50.7	44.8	52.7	60.2	66.8	62.1	66.3	74.5
MOTOR CARRIER.	20.3	13.0	24.3	28.7	18.3	13.9	21.4	19.4
PRIVATE TRUCK.	23.0	29.8	22.0	9.3	9.5	11.7	10.4	4.6
AIR.	-	-	-	-	-	-	-	-
WATER.	5.5	12.0	.7	.7	5.0	11.7	1.6	1.0
OTHER.	-	-	-	-	-	-	-	-
UNKNOWN.	.5	.4	.3	1.1	.4	.6	.3	.5
DISTANCE OF SHIPMENT								
TOTAL.	100.0	100.0	100.0	100.0	100.0	100.0	100.0	100.0
UNDER 100 MILES.	24.2	30.1	22.3	14.4	3.2	4.9	2.9	1.3
100 TO 199 MILES	15.9	16.2	16.4	14.0	5.7	7.0	5.7	3.8
200 TO 299 MILES	14.1	11.5	17.4	12.8	8.4	8.2	10.0	5.8
300 TO 499 MILES	19.7	22.3	17.3	19.0	18.4	24.6	15.9	13.5
500 TO 999 MILES	16.9	13.6	16.5	25.8	28.9	27.8	27.3	33.3
1000 TO 1499 MILES	4.8	3.8	5.6	5.4	14.5	13.6	16.8	11.9
1500 MILES AND OVER.	4.4	2.5	4.6	8.6	20.8	13.8	21.3	30.4

NOTE: Detail may not add to totals due to rounding. Shipments excluded from the survey are those moving by pipeline (primarily petroleum products from refineries), parcel post shipments, and commodities moved by own power (motorized vehicles, aircraft, etc.) or towed (prefabricated buildings, etc.). Local shipments (commodities shipped less than 25 miles from the plant) and shipments within the same city are also excluded. Shipments to Alaska and Hawaii from the 48 conterminous States and the District of Columbia are included; however, no data were obtained for shipments originating in Alaska and Hawaii. Distance of shipments to foreign destinations are calculated only to the U.S. port of exit. Estimates of sampling variability are presented in table B to facilitate interpretation and analysis. Most data are subject to high sampling variability and should be treated as an approximate rather than a precise measurement of volume.

- Represents or rounds to zero. (X) Not applicable.

SHIPPER GROUP 3. Candy, Cookies and Crackers, Beverages, and Tobacco Products
Percent Distribution of Shipments by Means of Transport and Distance, for Plants: 1972

Means of transport and distance of shipment	Tons of shipments				Ton-miles			
	All plants	Plants with—			All plants	Plants with—		
		20 to 99 employees	100 to 499 employees	500 employees and over		20 to 99 employees	100 to 499 employees	500 employees and over
TONS SHIPPED . . . . . .THOUSANDS. .	57 996	22 829	19 570	15 596	(X)	(X)	(X)	(X)
TON MILES. . . . . MILLIONS. .	(X)	(X)	(X)	(X)	14 400	2 957	4 820	6 622
MEANS OF TRANSPORT								
TOTAL.	100.0	100.0	100.0	100.0	100.0	100.0	100.0	100.0
RAIL	15.4	3.7	18.5	28.7	43.1	22.9	42.8	52.4
MOTOR CARRIER.	25.7	18.8	26.7	34.5	28.8	26.0	32.0	27.8
PRIVATE TRUCK.	58.4	77.2	54.4	35.9	25.8	50.9	22.9	16.6
AIR.	-	-	.3	.6	1.9	-	2.1	2.7
WATER.	.2	-	-	-	-	-	.2	-
OTHER.	-	-	-	-	-	-	-	-
UNKNOWN.	.2	.3	.1	.3	.3	.1	.1	.5
DISTANCE OF SHIPMENT								
TOTAL.	100.0	100.0	100.0	100.0	100.0	100.0	100.0	100.0
UNDER 100 MILES.	46.6	61.6	49.6	20.9	8.3	20.8	8.6	2.6
100 TO 199 MILES	19.0	22.1	16.8	17.3	11.1	24.4	9.8	6.1
200 TO 299 MILES	11.3	9.0	10.0	16.3	10.9	15.8	9.9	9.4
300 TO 499 MILES	10.0	4.5	10.0	18.0	15.4	13.0	15.5	16.3
500 TO 999 MILES	9.2	1.7	9.3	19.8	25.7	9.4	26.5	32.4
1000 TO 1499 MILES	1.4	.3	2.0	2.2	6.9	3.2	9.8	6.4
1500 MILES AND OVER.	2.5	.8	2.3	5.4	21.7	13.5	19.9	26.8

Note: Detail may not add to totals due to rounding. Shipments excluded from the survey are those moving by pipeline (primarily petroleum products from refineries), parcel post shipments, and commodities moved by own power (motorized vehicles, aircraft, etc.) or towed (prefabricated buildings, etc.). Local shipments (commodities shipped less than 25 miles from the plant) and shipments within the same city are also excluded. Shipments to Alaska and Hawaii from the 48 conterminous States and the District of Columbia are included; however, no data were obtained for shipments originating in Alaska and Hawaii. Distance of shipments to foreign destinations are calculated only to the U.S. port of exit.
Estimates of sampling variability are presented in table B to facilitate interpretation and analysis. Most data are subject to high sampling variability and should be treated as an approximate rather than a precise measurementsof volume.
SIC 205 was out of scope to 1967 survey. However, for the 1972 survey SIC 2052, cookies and crackers, was included while SIC 2051 remained out of scope to the survey.

- Represents or rounds to zero.   (X) Not applicable.

SHIPPER GROUP 4. Basic Textiles and Leather Products
Percent Distribution of Shipments by Means of Transport and Distance, for Plants: 1972

Means of transport and distance of shipment	Tons of shipments				Ton-miles			
	All plants	Plants with—			All plants	Plants with—		
		20 to 99 employees	100 to 499 employees	500 employees and over		20 to 99 employees	100 to 499 employees	500 employees and over
TONS SHIPPED . . . . . .THOUSANDS. .	14 209	1 349	6 937	5 922	(X)	(X)	(X)	(X)
TON MILES. . . . . MILLIONS. .	(X)	(X)	(X)	(X)	6 678	576	3 265	2 836
MEANS OF TRANSPORT								
TOTAL.	100.0	100.0	100.0	100.0	100.0	100.0	100.0	100.0
RAIL	9.7	2.3	8.5	12.9	16.3	9.1	16.6	17.3
MOTOR CARRIER.	61.4	87.2	59.2	58.0	61.0	87.1	58.4	58.6
PRIVATE TRUCK.	27.7	9.3	31.0	28.0	21.0	2.2	23.2	22.3
AIR.	.1	.1	-	.2	.2	.3	.2	.3
WATER.	-	-	-	-	-	.1	-	-
OTHER.	.9	1.0	1.0	.7	1.2	1.1	1.2	1.1
UNKNOWN.	.2	.1	.2	.2	.4	.1	.4	.4
DISTANCE OF SHIPMENT								
TOTAL.	100.0	100.0	100.0	100.0	100.0	100.0	100.0	100.0
UNDER 100 MILES.	19.4	26.3	20.6	16.5	2.0	1.8	2.2	1.9
100 TO 199 MILES	13.7	15.4	11.8	15.5	4.2	5.3	3.5	4.7
200 TO 299 MILES	13.3	13.4	13.4	14.1	6.8	6.8	6.6	7.1
300 TO 499 MILES	14.1	14.7	13.1	15.1	11.8	13.6	10.9	12.4
500 TO 999 MILES	30.5	21.6	33.0	29.7	43.5	37.5	46.6	41.2
1000 TO 1499 MILES	4.1	2.7	4.6	3.7	10.0	7.6	11.2	9.2
1500 MILES AND OVER.	4.9	5.9	4.3	5.5	21.6	27.3	18.9	23.5

NOTE: Detail may not add to totals due to rounding. Shipments excluded from the survey are those moving by pipeline (primarily petroleum products from refineries), parcel post shipments, and commodities moved by own power (motorized vehicles, aircraft, etc.) or towed (prefabricated buildings, etc.). Local shipments (commodities shipped less than 25 miles from the plant) and shipments within the same city are also excluded. Shipments to Alaska and Hawaii from the 48 conterminous States and the District of Columbia are included; however, no data were obtained for shipments originating in Alaska and Hawaii. Distance of shipments to foreign destinations are calculated only to the U.S. port of exit.
Estimates of sampling variability are presented in table B to facilitate interpretation and analysis. Most data are subject to high sampling variability and should be treated as an approximate rather than a precise measurement of volume.

- Represents or rounds to zero.   (X) Not applicable.

SHIPPER GROUP 5. **Apparel and Related Products**

Percent Distribution of Shipments by Means of Transport and Distance, for Plants: 1972

Means of transport and distance of shipment	Tons of shipments				Ton-miles			
	All plants	Plants with—			All plants	Plants with—		
		20 to 99 employees	100 to 499 employees	500 employees and over		20 to 99 employees	100 to 499 employees	500 employees and over
TONS SHIPPED . . . . . . .THOUSANDS. .	5 798	772	3 351	1 674	(X)	(X)	(X)	(X)
TON MILES. . . . . MILLIONS. .	(X)	(X)	(X)	(X)	3 146	457	1 847	842
MEANS OF TRANSPORT								
TOTAL.	100.0	100.0	100.0	100.0	100.0	100.0	100.0	100.0
RAIL	8.5	11.7	3.9	16.4	13.4	26.5	9.0	15.9
MOTOR CARRIER.	69.4	72.2	69.5	67.7	67.0	59.3	69.4	65.9
PRIVATE TRUCK.	15.6	5.3	19.9	11.7	9.5	1.0	10.6	11.8
AIR.	2.0	1.9	2.1	1.9	4.8	4.0	5.8	3.0
WATER.	-	-	-	.9	.1	.4	-	-
OTHER.	4.3	8.1	4.5	2.2	5.0	8.0	5.1	3.1
UNKNOWN.	.2	.7	.1	.1	.2	.7	.1	.2
DISTANCE OF SHIPMENT								
TOTAL.	100.0	100.0	100.0	100.0	100.0	100.0	100.0	100.0
UNDER 100 MILES.	14.4	18.8	14.6	12.1	1.1	1.7	1.0	1.0
100 TO 199 MILES	12.5	13.6	9.0	19.0	3.4	3.4	2.5	5.6
200 TO 299 MILES	9.9	10.4	6.7	16.0	4.6	4.1	3.0	8.4
300 TO 499 MILES	25.0	14.1	30.9	18.3	16.7	9.2	19.5	14.7
500 TO 999 MILES	24.8	24.7	26.1	22.2	31.5	28.6	33.2	29.5
1000 TO 1499 MILES	5.3	8.3	5.0	4.6	12.1	18.1	11.2	10.9
1500 MILES AND OVER.	8.1	10.1	7.8	7.8	30.4	34.8	29.6	30.0

NOTE: Detail may not add to totals due to rounding. Shipments excluded from the survey are those moving by pipeline (primarily petroleum products from refineries), parcel post shipments, and commodities moved by own power (motorized vehicles, aircraft, etc.) or towed (prefabricated buildings, etc.). Local shipments (commodities shipped less than 25 miles from the plant) and shipments within the same city are also excluded. Shipments to Alaska and Hawaii from the 48 conterminous States and the District of Columbia are included; however, no data were obtained for shipments originating in Alaska and Hawaii. Distance of shipments to foreign destinations are calculated only to the U.S. port of exit. Estimates of sampling variability are presented in table B to facilitate interpretation and analysis. Most data are subject to high sampling variability and should be treated as an approximate rather than a precise measurement of volume.

- Represents or rounds to zero. (X) Not applicable.

SHIPPER GROUP 6. **Paper and Allied Products**

Percent Distribution of Shipments by Means of Transport and Distance, for Plants: 1972

Means of transport and distance of shipment	Tons of shipments				Ton-miles			
	All plants	Plants with—			All plants	Plants with—		
		20 to 99 employees	100 to 499 employees	500 employees and over		20 to 99 employees	100 to 499 employees	500 employees and over
TONS SHIPPED . . . . . .THOUSANDS. .	89 410	9 697	39 036	40 676	(X)	(X)	(X)	(X)
TON MILES. . . . . MILLIONS. .	(X)	(X)	(X)	(X)	40 553	2 194	15 437	22 921
MEANS OF TRANSPORT								
TOTAL.	100.0	100.0	100.0	100.0	100.0	100.0	100.0	100.0
RAIL	51.7	18.1	38.8	72.1	73.8	39.5	67.8	81.2
MOTOR CARRIER.	28.0	41.0	31.6	21.5	18.9	38.8	21.3	15.5
PRIVATE TRUCK.	17.9	40.3	26.4	4.3	5.6	19.6	9.1	1.9
AIR.	-	-	-	-	-	.1	-	-
WATER.	2.1	.3	2.8	1.9	1.3	1.9	1.3	1.2
OTHER.	.1	.2	.1	-	-	.1	.1	-
UNKNOWN.	.1	-	.2	-	.2	-	.3	.1
DISTANCE OF SHIPMENT								
TOTAL.	100.0	100.0	100.0	100.0	100.0	100.0	100.0	100.0
UNDER 100 MILES.	22.5	45.7	30.7	9.1	2.5	9.8	3.7	1.0
100 TO 199 MILES	14.9	19.8	16.7	11.9	4.8	12.9	6.1	3.2
200 TO 299 MILES	11.7	11.3	12.2	11.3	6.4	12.1	7.6	5.0
300 TO 499 MILES	15.0	9.2	14.0	17.4	13.1	15.7	14.0	12.3
500 TO 999 MILES	26.9	12.1	17.6	39.5	42.9	35.4	31.5	51.3
1000 TO 1499 MILES	5.0	.8	4.1	6.9	13.0	4.5	12.2	14.4
1500 MILES AND OVER.	3.9	1.1	4.7	3.8	17.2	9.6	24.8	12.8

NOTE: Detail may not add to totals due to rounding. Shipments excluded from the survey are those moving by pipeline (primarily petroleum products from refineries), parcel post shipments, and commodities moved by own power (motorized vehicles, aircraft, etc.) or towed (prefabricated buildings, etc.). Local shipments (commodities shipped less than 25 miles from the plant) and shipments within the same city are also excluded. Shipments to Alaska and Hawaii from the 48 conterminous States and the District of Columbia are included; however, no data were obtained for shipments originating in Alaska and Hawaii. Distance of shipments to foreign destinations are calculated only to the U.S. port of exit. Estimates of sampling variability are presented in table B to facilitate interpretation and analysis. Most data are subject to high sampling variability and should be treated as an approximate rather than a precise measurement of volume.

- Represents or rounds to zero. (X) Not applicable.

SHIPPER GROUP 7. **Basic Chemicals, Plastics Materials, Synthetic Resins, Rubber, and Fibers**

Percent Distribution of Shipments by Means of Transport and Distance, for Plants: 1972

Means of transport and distance of shipment	Tons of shipments				Ton-miles			
	All plants	Plants with—			All plants	Plants with—		
		20 to 99 employees	100 to 499 employees	500 employees and over		20 to 99 employees	100 to 499 employees	500 employees and over
TONS SHIPPED . . . . . .THOUSANDS. .	111 853	26 018	41 070	44 765	(X)	(X)	(X)	(X)
TON MILES. . . . . MILLIONS. .	(X)	(X)	(X)	(X)	47 821	7 256	17 065	23 499
MEANS OF TRANSPORT								
TOTAL.	100.0	100.0	100.0	100.0	100.0	100.0	100.0	100.0
RAIL	48.6	33.2	52.1	54.4	63.1	42.5	67.6	66.2
MOTOR CARRIER.	30.1	31.1	29.8	29.8	21.6	29.7	20.6	19.7
PRIVATE TRUCK.	12.1	27.9	9.8	5.0	4.7	12.5	4.2	2.7
AIR.	-	-	-	-	-	-	-	-
WATER.	8.6	7.7	7.9	9.7	10.0	15.1	6.9	10.8
OTHER.	.4	-	.1	.8	.2	-	.2	.3
UNKNOWN.	.2	-	.2	.2	.3	-	.4	.3
DISTANCE OF SHIPMENT								
TOTAL.	100.0	100.0	100.0	100.0	100.0	100.0	100.0	100.0
UNDER 100 MILES.	23.5	33.3	23.6	17.7	2.6	5.0	2.7	1.7
100 TO 199 MILES	16.8	21.8	16.9	13.7	5.8	11.3	6.0	3.9
200 TO 299 MILES	13.9	16.2	12.5	13.9	8.1	14.4	7.5	6.5
300 TO 499 MILES	15.7	11.3	18.7	15.6	14.2	15.2	17.3	11.6
500 TO 999 MILES	18.7	12.8	17.7	23.2	31.9	31.8	30.5	32.9
1000 TO 1499 MILES	8.3	3.7	7.4	11.8	23.9	16.0	21.7	27.9
1500 MILES AND OVER.	3.0	.9	3.2	4.2	13.6	6.3	14.2	15.3

NOTE: Detail may not add to totals due to rounding. Shipments excluded from the survey are those moving by pipeline (primarily petroleum products from refineries), parcel post shipments, and commodities moved by own power (motorized vehicles, aircraft, etc.) or towed (prefabricated buildings, etc.). Local shipments (commodities shipped less than 25 miles from the plant) and shipments within the same city are also excluded. Shipments to Alaska and Hawaii from the 48 conterminous States and the District of Columbia are included; however, no data were obtained for shipments originating in Alaska and Hawaii. Distance of shipments to foreign destinations are calculated only to the U.S. port of exit.
   Estimates of sampling variability are presented in table B to facilitate interpretation and analysis. Most data are subject to high sampling variability and should be treated as an approximate rather than a precise measurement of volume.

   - Represents or rounds to zero.   (X) Not applicable.

SHIPPER GROUP 8. **Drugs, Paints, and Other Chemical Products**

Percent Distribution of Shipments by Means of Transport and Distance, for Plants: 1972

Means of transport and distance of shipment	Tons of shipments				Ton-miles			
	All plants	Plants with—			All plants	Plants with—		
		20 to 99 employees	100 to 499 employees	500 employees and over		20 to 99 employees	100 to 499 employees	500 employees and over
TONS SHIPPED . . . . . .THOUSANDS. .	58 902	12 721	33 866	12 314	(X)	(X)	(X)	(X)
TON MILES. . . . . MILLIONS. .	(X)	(X)	(X)	(X)	22 580	3 401	13 654	5 525
MEANS OF TRANSPORT								
TOTAL.	100.0	100.0	100.0	100.0	100.0	100.0	100.0	100.0
RAIL	37.8	14.3	42.8	48.3	44.3	21.1	46.6	53.0
MOTOR CARRIER.	38.6	49.6	33.0	42.7	32.0	52.0	24.4	38.7
PRIVATE TRUCK.	15.7	34.9	11.4	7.5	8.4	23.6	6.8	3.2
AIR.	-	-	-	-	.1	.1	-	.3
WATER.	7.4	.4	12.3	1.0	14.4	1.2	21.8	4.0
OTHER.	.3	.3	.3	.4	.4	.7	.2	.7
UNKNOWN.	.2	.5	.2	-	.3	1.2	.2	-
DISTANCE OF SHIPMENT								
TOTAL.	100.0	100.0	100.0	100.0	100.0	100.0	100.0	100.0
UNDER 100 MILES.	28.8	40.6	25.2	26.4	4.1	7.0	3.4	4.0
100 TO 199 MILES	18.0	21.1	18.6	13.2	7.0	11.3	7.0	4.4
200 TO 299 MILES	10.3	9.3	10.8	9.7	6.6	8.6	6.6	5.3
300 TO 499 MILES	14.0	11.6	14.1	16.3	14.0	16.9	13.3	14.0
500 TO 999 MILES	21.4	14.8	22.4	25.5	40.9	40.9	41.2	40.1
1000 TO 1499 MILES	5.5	1.4	7.3	4.5	16.7	5.9	21.3	11.8
1500 MILES AND OVER.	2.0	1.2	1.5	4.4	10.7	9.3	7.2	20.5

NOTE: Detail may not add to totals due to rounding. Shipments excluded from the survey are those moving by pipeline (primarily petroleum products from refineries), parcel post shipments, and commodities moved by own power (motorized vehicles, aircraft, etc.) or towed (prefabricated buildings, etc.). Local shipments (commodities shipped less than 25 miles from the plant) and shipments within the same city are also excluded. Shipments to Alaska and Hawaii from the 48 conterminous States and the District of Columbia are included; however, no data were obtained for shipments originating in Alaska and Hawaii. Distance of shipments to foreign destinations are calculated only to the U.S. port of exit.
   Estimates of sampling variability are presented in table B to facilitate interpretation and analysis. Most data are subject to high sampling variability and should be treated as an approximate rather than a precise measurement of volume.

   - Represents or rounds to zero.   (X) Not applicable.

SHIPPER GROUP 9. Petroleum and Coal Products
Percent Distribution of Shipments by Means of Transport and Distance, for Plants: 1972

Means of transport and distance of shipment	Tons of shipments				Ton-miles			
	All plants	Plants with—			All plants	Plants with—		
		20 to 99 employees	100 to 499 employees	500 employees and over		20 to 99 employees	100 to 499 employees	500 employees and over
TONS SHIPPED . . . . . . .THOUSANDS. .	348 137	14 637	121 454	212 045	(X)	(X)	(X)	(X)
TON MILES. . . . . MILLIONS. .	(X)	(X)	(X)	(X)	192 353	2 522	55 246	134 584
MEANS OF TRANSPORT								
TOTAL.	100.0	100.0	100.0	100.0	100.0	100.0	100.0	100.0
RAIL	9.7	9.2	10.2	9.5	7.9	18.6	10.0	6.8
MOTOR CARRIER.	16.0	56.5	23.2	9.1	3.4	39.8	5.3	2.0
PRIVATE TRUCK.	8.4	28.6	11.2	5.4	1.6	18.8	2.2	1.0
AIR.	-	-	-	-	-	-	-	-
WATER.	65.3	5.4	54.5	75.6	87.0	22.6	82.1	90.2
OTHER.	.2	-	-	.4	-	-	-	-
UNKNOWN.	.3	.1	.9	-	.1	.2	.4	-
DISTANCE OF SHIPMENT								
TOTAL.	100.0	100.0	100.0	100.0	100.0	100.0	100.0	100.0
UNDER 100 MILES.	26.6	52.7	33.6	20.8	2.2	14.4	3.2	1.5
100 TO 199 MILES	13.9	27.0	20.4	9.4	3.7	21.6	6.7	2.1
200 TO 299 MILES	8.8	7.6	7.3	9.7	3.9	11.4	3.9	3.8
300 TO 499 MILES	9.8	4.7	6.7	12.0	7.2	10.4	6.0	7.6
500 TO 999 MILES	16.7	7.3	12.1	20.0	22.6	33.4	20.7	23.1
1000 TO 1499 MILES	18.6	.2	12.4	23.5	43.4	1.2	31.1	49.3
1500 MILES AND OVER.	5.5	.6	7.5	4.7	17.0	7.5	28.4	12.5

NOTE: Detail may not add to totals due to rounding. Shipments excluded from the survey are those moving by pipeline (primarily petroleum products from refineries), parcel post shipments, and commodities moved by own power (motorized vehicles, aircraft, etc.) or towed (prefabricated buildings, etc.). Local shipments (commodities shipped less than 25 miles from the plant) and shipments within the same city are also excluded. Shipments to Alaska and Hawaii from the 48 conterminous States and the District of Columbia are included; however, no data were obtained for shipments originating in Alaska and Hawaii. Distance of shipments to foreign destinations are calculated only to the U.S. port of exit.
Estimates of sampling variability are presented in table B to facilitate interpretation and analysis. Most data are subject to high sampling variability and should be treated as an approximate rather than a precise measurement of volume.

- Represents or rounds to zero.   (X) Not applicable.

SHIPPER GROUP 10. Rubber and Plastics Products
Percent Distribution of Shipments by Means of Transport and Distance, for Plants: 1972

Means of transport and distance of shipment	Tons of shipments				Ton-miles			
	All plants	Plants with—			All plants	Plants with—		
		20 to 99 employees	100 to 499 employees	500 employees and over		20 to 99 employees	100 to 499 employees	500 employees and over
TONS SHIPPED . . . . . . .THOUSANDS. .	15 877	2 079	5 446	8 351	(X)	(X)	(X)	(X)
TON MILES. . . . . MILLIONS. .	(X)	(X)	(X)	(X)	8 142	916	2 792	4 433
MEANS OF TRANSPORT								
TOTAL.	100.0	100.0	100.0	100.0	100.0	100.0	100.0	100.0
RAIL	24.4	13.5	11.3	35.8	32.1	19.8	20.1	42.2
MOTOR CARRIER.	59.1	59.6	68.0	53.1	56.8	57.2	67.8	49.8
PRIVATE TRUCK.	15.2	26.2	18.5	10.3	9.3	22.1	8.8	7.0
AIR.	.7	.2	1.6	.3	1.0	.5	2.4	.3
WATER.	-	.2	.1	-	.3	.3	.3	.2
OTHER.	.3	.3	.5	.2	.3	.2	.4	.2
UNKNOWN.	.2	-	.1	.3	.2	-	.3	.2
DISTANCE OF SHIPMENT								
TOTAL.	100.0	100.0	100.0	100.0	100.0	100.0	100.0	100.0
UNDER 100 MILES.	18.4	22.0	22.5	14.8	1.8	2.5	1.9	1.6
100 TO 199 MILES	13.2	14.9	12.5	13.3	3.9	5.4	3.4	3.8
200 TO 299 MILES	10.2	8.9	9.9	10.6	5.0	5.4	5.0	5.1
300 TO 499 MILES	19.4	23.4	14.9	21.3	15.0	20.2	11.6	16.0
500 TO 999 MILES	26.7	23.1	25.7	28.3	37.2	39.0	36.9	37.0
1000 TO 1499 MILES	6.5	3.8	9.5	5.1	15.0	10.4	22.2	11.4
1500 MILES AND OVER.	5.6	3.8	4.9	6.6	22.2	17.5	19.1	25.1

NOTE: Detail may not add to totals due to rounding. Shipments excluded from the survey are those moving by pipeline (primarily petroleum products from refineries), parcel post shipments, and commodities moved by own power (motorized vehicles, aircraft, etc.) or towed (prefabricated buildings, etc.). Local shipments (commodities shipped less than 25 miles from the plant) and shipments within the same city are also excluded. Shipments to Alaska and Hawaii from the 48 conterminous States and the District of Columbia are included; however, no data were obtained for shipments originating in Alaska and Hawaii. Distance of shipments to foreign destinations are calculated only to the U.S. port of exit.
Estimates of sampling variability are presented in table B to facilitate interpretation and analysis. Most data are subject to high sampling variability and should be treated as an approximate rather than a precise measurement of volume.

- Represents or rounds to zero.   (X) Not applicable.

SHIPPER GROUP 11. Lumber and Wood Products, Except Furniture
Percent Distribution of Shipments by Means of Transport and Distance, for Plants: 1972

Means of transport and distance of shipment	Tons of shipments				Ton-miles			
	All plants	Plants with—			All plants	Plants with—		
		20 to 99 employees	100 to 499 employees	500 employees and over		20 to 99 employees	100 to 499 employees	500 employees and over
TONS SHIPPED . . . . . .THOUSANDS. .	79 991	30 623	40 093	9 274	(X)	(X)	(X)	(X)
TON MILES. . . . . MILLIONS. .	(X)	(X)	(X)	(X)	44 179	12 320	22 686	9 173
MEANS OF TRANSPORT								
TOTAL.	100.0	100.0	100.0	100.0	100.0	100.0	100.0	100.0
RAIL	45.8	28.7	52.7	72.8	76.8	58.1	81.9	89.3
MOTOR CARRIER.	16.2	15.1	18.4	10.5	7.6	10.9	7.1	4.2
PRIVATE TRUCK.	36.3	54.0	27.7	15.0	10.7	19.1	9.5	2.6
AIR.	-	-	-	-	-	-	-	-
WATER.	1.3	1.9	.8	1.5	4.7	11.6	1.2	3.8
OTHER.	-	-	-	-	-	-	-	-
UNKNOWN.	.3	.3	.3	.3	.2	.3	.2	-
DISTANCE OF SHIPMENT								
TOTAL.	100.0	100.0	100.0	100.0	100.0	100.0	100.0	100.0
UNDER 100 MILES.	33.2	38.5	33.2	15.8	3.0	4.8	2.8	.9
100 TO 199 MILES	15.9	19.2	14.6	10.3	4.2	6.9	3.7	1.6
200 TO 299 MILES	7.9	9.1	7.7	5.1	3.5	5.5	3.3	1.3
300 TO 499 MILES	10.0	10.9	9.4	9.5	7.0	10.4	6.6	3.7
500 TO 999 MILES	13.3	10.4	14.8	16.8	17.2	18.3	18.5	12.2
1000 TO 1499 MILES	5.6	4.1	5.8	10.3	13.2	13.5	13.0	13.4
1500 MILES AND OVER.	14.0	7.8	14.5	32.2	52.0	40.6	52.1	66.8

NOTE: Detail may not add to totals due to rounding. Shipments excluded from the survey are those moving by pipeline (primarily petroleum products from refineries), parcel post shipments, and commodities moved by own power (motorized vehicles, aircraft, etc.) or towed (prefabricated buildings, etc.). Local shipments (commodities shipped less than 25 miles from the plant) and shipments within the same city are also excluded. Shipments to Alaska and Hawaii from the 48 conterminous States and the District of Columbia are included; however, no data were obtained for shipments originating in Alaska and Hawaii. Distance of shipments to foreign destinations are calculated only to the U.S. port of exit.
Estimates of sampling variability are presented in table B to facilitate interpretation and analysis. Most data are subject to high sampling variability and should be treated as an approximate rather than a precise measurement of volume.

- Represents or rounds to zero.   (X) Not applicable.

SHIPPER GROUP 12. Furniture, Fixtures, and Miscellaneous Manufactured Products
Percent Distribution of Shipments by Means of Transport and Distance, for Plants: 1972

Means of transport and distance of shipment	Tons of shipments				Ton-miles			
	All plants	Plants with—			All plants	Plants with—		
		20 to 99 employees	100 to 499 employees	500 employees and over		20 to 99 employees	100 to 499 employees	500 employees and over
TONS SHIPPED . . . . . .THOUSANDS. .	14 371	2 669	7 919	3 782	(X)	(X)	(X)	(X)
TON MILES. . . . . MILLIONS. .	(X)	(X)	(X)	(X)	8 162	954	4 603	2 604
MEANS OF TRANSPORT								
TOTAL.	100.0	100.0	100.0	100.0	100.0	100.0	100.0	100.0
RAIL	22.0	3.2	19.0	41.7	37.1	8.2	31.2	58.0
MOTOR CARRIER.	41.4	39.3	41.6	42.5	39.9	55.9	41.1	31.8
PRIVATE TRUCK.	34.7	53.4	37.9	14.9	20.5	29.8	24.9	9.3
AIR.	.3	.1	.4	.1	.8	.3	1.3	.2
WATER.	.2	-	.3	-	.3	.1	.5	-
OTHER.	1.2	3.7	.7	.6	1.2	5.3	.7	.5
UNKNOWN.	.2	.4	.2	.1	.2	.3	.2	.1
DISTANCE OF SHIPMENT								
TOTAL.	100.0	100.0	100.0	100.0	100.0	100.0	100.0	100.0
UNDER 100 MILES.	16.1	34.3	13.5	8.7	1.4	4.4	1.2	.7
100 TO 199 MILES	11.5	14.2	12.4	7.9	3.0	6.0	3.2	1.7
200 TO 299 MILES	11.2	11.1	12.0	9.6	4.9	7.7	5.1	3.6
300 TO 499 MILES	19.4	13.7	18.3	25.6	13.8	14.7	12.6	15.6
500 TO 999 MILES	27.0	18.9	29.0	28.6	33.0	36.6	34.8	28.4
1000 TO 1499 MILES	6.0	5.4	6.4	5.7	12.5	16.7	13.1	9.8
1500 MILES AND OVER.	8.8	2.5	8.5	13.9	31.4	13.8	30.1	40.2

NOTE: Detail may not add to totals due to rounding. Shipments excluded from the survey are those moving by pipeline (primarily petroleum products from refineries), parcel post shipments, and commodities moved by own power (motorized vehicles, aircraft, etc.) or towed (prefabricated buildings, etc.). Local shipments (commodities shipped less than 25 miles from the plant) and shipments within the same city are also excluded. Shipments to Alaska and Hawaii from the 48 conterminous States and the District of Columbia are included; however, no data were obtained for shipments originating in Alaska and Hawaii. Distance of shipments to foreign destinations are calculated only to the U.S. port of exit.
Estimates of sampling variability are presented in table B to facilitate interpretation and analysis. Most data are subject to high sampling variability and should be treated as an approximate rather than a precise measurement of volume.

- Represents or rounds to zero,   (X) Not applicable.

SHIPPER GROUP 13. **Stone, Clay, and Glass Products**

Percent Distribution of Shipments by Means of Transport and Distance, for Plants: 1972

Means of transport and distance of shipment	Tons of shipments				Ton-miles			
	All plants	Plants with—			All plants	Plants with—		
		20 to 99 employees	100 to 499 employees	500 employees and over		20 to 99 employees	100 to 499 employees	500 employees and over
TONS SHIPPED . . . . . .THOUSANDS. .	178 122	64 573	93 367	20 182	(X)	(X)	(X)	(X)
TON MILES. . . . . . . .MILLIONS. .	(X)	(X)	(X)	(X)	34 242	12 309	16 128	5 804
MEANS OF TRANSPORT								
TOTAL.	100.0	100.0	100.0	100.0	100.0	100.0	100.0	100.0
RAIL	21.9	15.9	26.1	21.4	45.3	52.7	43.5	34.8
MOTOR CARRIER.	47.2	41.8	50.8	47.8	36.6	26.7	42.0	42.5
PRIVATE TRUCK.	23.7	33.1	19.0	15.4	11.3	11.9	11.1	10.6
AIR.	-	-	-	-	-	-	-	-
WATER.	6.4	9.0	2.6	15.2	6.1	8.5	2.2	11.9
OTHER.	-	.1	-	-	-	-	-	-
UNKNOWN.	.8	-	1.4	-	.6	-	1.2	-
DISTANCE OF SHIPMENT								
TOTAL.	100.0	100.0	100.0	100.0	100.0	100.0	100.0	100.0
UNDER 100 MILES.	49.7	56.7	50.5	23.9	12.4	12.6	15.0	4.6
100 TO 199 MILES	21.3	17.2	23.8	23.1	15.7	12.8	19.2	11.9
200 TO 299 MILES	11.8	10.1	10.5	23.1	14.7	12.3	14.5	20.0
300 TO 499 MILES	9.0	6.0	9.3	17.4	17.5	11.9	19.6	23.8
500 TO 999 MILES	5.3	5.2	4.4	9.5	19.0	19.5	17.4	22.6
1000 TO 1499 MILES	2.0	4.1	.7	1.4	12.2	24.5	5.1	6.0
1500 MILES AND OVER.	.8	.7	.8	1.6	8.5	6.4	9.2	11.2

NOTE: Detail may not add to totals due to rounding. Shipments excluded from the survey are those moving by pipeline (primarily petroleum products from refineries), parcel post shipments, and commodities moved by own power (motorized vehicles, aircraft, etc.) or towed (prefabricated buildings, etc.). Local shipments (commodities shipped less than 25 miles from the plant) and shipments within the same city are also excluded. Shipments to Alaska and Hawaii from the 48 conterminous States and the District of Columbia are included; however, no data were obtained for shipments originating in Alaska and Hawaii. Distance of shipments to foreign destinations are calculated only to the U.S. port of exit. Estimates of sampling variability are presented in table B to facilitate interpretation and analysis. Most data are subject to high sampling variability and should be treated as an approximate rather than a precise measurement of volume.

- Represents or rounds to zero.   (X) Not applicable.

SHIPPER GROUP 14. **Primary Iron and Steel Products**

Percent Distribution of Shipments by Means of Transport and Distance, for Plants: 1972

Means of transport and distance of shipment	Tons of shipments				Ton-miles			
	All plants	Plants with—			All plants	Plants with—		
		20 to 99 employees	100 to 499 employees	500 employees and over		20 to 99 employees	100 to 499 employees	500 employees and over
TONS SHIPPED . . . . . .THOUSANDS. .	139 461	1 931	20 444	117 085	(X)	(X)	(X)	(X)
TON MILES. . . . . . . .MILLIONS. .	(X)	(X)	(X)	(X)	38 953	453	5 328	33 171
MEANS OF TRANSPORT								
TOTAL.	100.0	100.0	100.0	100.0	100.0	100.0	100.0	100.0
RAIL	43.7	4.3	46.8	43.8	51.6	5.2	50.3	52.5
MOTOR CARRIER.	44.4	26.4	38.4	45.7	35.9	48.0	36.2	35.7
PRIVATE TRUCK.	6.7	48.7	12.4	5.0	4.8	34.4	8.8	3.7
AIR.	-	.1	-	-	-	.7	-	-
WATER.	4.8	-	2.2	5.3	7.3	.2	3.9	8.0
OTHER.	.3	20.3	.1	-	.2	11.0	-	-
UNKNOWN.	.1	.2	.2	.1	.2	.5	.6	.1
DISTANCE OF SHIPMENT								
TOTAL.	100.0	100.0	100.0	100.0	100.0	100.0	100.0	100.0
UNDER 100 MILES.	27.2	24.1	22.0	28.1	4.5	5.4	4.2	4.5
100 TO 199 MILES	22.1	49.3	25.1	21.1	11.4	30.6	13.4	10.8
200 TO 299 MILES	19.9	9.9	28.1	18.7	17.2	10.4	26.0	15.9
300 TO 499 MILES	16.5	6.7	15.1	16.9	22.4	11.0	21.9	22.6
500 TO 999 MILES	11.2	6.9	7.3	11.9	26.8	20.9	18.4	28.2
1000 TO 1499 MILES	1.6	1.7	.7	1.7	6.5	8.0	3.0	7.0
1500 MILES AND OVER.	1.6	1.6	1.8	1.5	11.2	13.5	13.1	10.9

NOTE: Detail may not add to totals due to rounding. Shipments excluded from the survey are those moving by pipeline (primarily petroleum products from refineries), parcel post shipments, and commodities moved by own power (motorized vehicles, aircraft, etc.) or towed (prefabricated buildings, etc.). Local shipments (commodities shipped less than 25 miles from the plant) and shipments within the same city are also excluded. Shipments to Alaska and Hawaii from the 48 conterminous States and the District of Columbia are included; however, no data were obtained for shipments originating in Alaska and Hawaii. Distance of shipments to foreign destinations are calculated only to the U.S. port of exit. Estimates of sampling variability are presented in table B to facilitate interpretation and analysis. Most data are subject to high sampling variability and should be treated as an approximate rather than a precise measurement of volume.

- Represents or rounds to zero.   (X) Not applicable.

SHIPPER GROUP 15. Primary Nonferrous Metal Products
Percent Distribution of Shipments by Means of Transport and Distance, for Plants: 1972

Means of transport and distance of shipment	Tons of shipments				Ton-miles			
	All plants	Plants with—			All plants	Plants with—		
		20 to 99 employees	100 to 499 employees	500 employees and over		20 to 99 employees	100 to 499 employees	500 employees and over
TONS SHIPPED . . . . . .THOUSANDS. .	29 954	2 702	11 280	15 972	(X)	(X)	(X)	(X)
TON MILES. . . . . MILLIONS. .	(X)	(X)	(X)	(X)	16 414	1 097	6 297	9 019
MEANS OF TRANSPORT								
TOTAL.	100.0	100.0	100.0	100.0	100.0	100.0	100.0	100.0
RAIL	51.6	36.7	50.0	55.2	67.2	53.4	67.8	68.5
MOTOR CARRIER.	31.4	24.2	27.4	35.4	23.4	23.0	20.1	25.7
PRIVATE TRUCK.	15.1	37.5	20.9	7.3	7.7	20.8	10.8	4.0
AIR.	-	.3	-	-	-	.9	-	-
WATER.	1.5	-	1.3	1.8	1.1	-	.8	1.4
OTHER.	.2	.1	.3	-	.2	.2	.4	.1
UNKNOWN.	.2	1.3	.1	.2	.3	1.8	-	.3
DISTANCE OF SHIPMENT								
TOTAL.	100.0	100.0	100.0	100.0	100.0	100.0	100.0	100.0
UNDER 100 MILES.	15.1	27.4	12.9	14.7	1.4	3.6	1.2	1.2
100 TO 199 MILES	17.8	12.4	13.8	21.5	4.9	4.4	3.6	5.8
200 TO 299 MILES	9.4	5.3	8.2	11.0	4.3	3.1	3.6	5.0
300 TO 499 MILES	18.3	27.5	22.9	13.6	13.2	28.1	15.9	9.4
500 TO 999 MILES	23.8	20.5	27.8	21.5	31.4	32.7	36.4	27.7
1000 TO 1499 MILES	7.3	1.0	7.8	8.1	16.5	3.1	16.8	17.9
1500 MILES AND OVER.	8.2	5.9	6.7	9.7	28.4	25.0	22.4	33.0

NOTE: Detail may not add to totals due to rounding. Shipments excluded from the survey are those moving by pipeline (primarily petroleum products from refineries), parcel post shipments, and commodities moved by own power (motorized vehicles, aircraft, etc.) or towed (prefabricated buildings, etc.). Local shipments (commodities shipped less than 25 miles from the plant) and shipments within the same city are also excluded. Shipments to Alaska and Hawaii from the 48 conterminous States and the District of Columbia are included; however, no data were obtained for shipments originating in Alaska and Hawaii. Distance of shipments to foreign destinations are calculated only to the U.S. port of exit.
Estimates of sampling variability are presented in table B to facilitate interpretation and analysis. Most data are subject to high sampling variability and should be treated as an approximate rather than a precise measurement of volume.

- Represents or rounds to zero.   (X) Not applicable.

SHIPPER GROUP 16. Fabricated Metal Products, Except Metal Cans and Miscellaneous Fabricated Metal Products
Percent Distribution of Shipments by Means of Transport and Distance, for Plants: 1972

Means of transport and distance of shipment	Tons of shipments				Ton-miles			
	All plants	Plants with—			All plants	Plants with—		
		20 to 99 employees	100 to 499 employees	500 employees and over		20 to 99 employees	100 to 499 employees	500 employees and over
TONS SHIPPED . . . . . .THOUSANDS. .	14 870	2 405	7 723	4 741	(X)	(X)	(X)	(X)
TON MILES. . . . . MILLIONS. .	(X)	(X)	(X)	(X)	7 317	1 252	3 750	2 314
MEANS OF TRANSPORT								
TOTAL.	100.0	100.0	100.0	100.0	100.0	100.0	100.0	100.0
RAIL	17.3	.9	10.3	37.1	23.3	2.6	18.3	42.6
MOTOR CARRIER.	55.3	90.0	50.3	46.0	60.1	93.0	61.3	40.3
PRIVATE TRUCK.	25.1	8.4	38.8	11.2	13.0	3.1	19.4	8.0
AIR.	.2	.2	.2	.1	.4	.3	.5	.2
WATER.	1.3	.2	-	4.0	2.1	.7	-	6.3
OTHER.	.5	.2	.3	.8	.6	.2	.4	1.2
UNKNOWN.	.3	.2	-	.7	.5	-	-	1.3
DISTANCE OF SHIPMENT								
TOTAL.	100.0	100.0	100.0	100.0	100.0	100.0	100.0	100.0
UNDER 100 MILES.	20.0	16.9	21.7	18.9	2.3	1.7	2.7	2.0
100 TO 199 MILES	12.7	9.0	13.8	12.9	3.9	2.5	4.4	3.8
200 TO 299 MILES	11.0	12.0	9.6	12.8	5.5	5.8	4.9	6.4
300 TO 499 MILES	23.6	37.6	21.6	19.6	18.6	27.3	17.5	15.5
500 TO 999 MILES	20.3	11.5	20.5	24.6	29.5	14.1	30.6	36.0
1000 TO 1499 MILES	5.7	3.3	6.3	5.9	13.6	7.1	15.3	14.5
1500 MILES AND OVER.	6.7	9.7	6.7	5.3	26.6	41.5	24.6	21.9

NOTE: Detail may not add to totals due to rounding. Shipments excluded from the survey are those moving by pipeline (primarily petroleum products from refineries), parcel post shipments, and commodities moved by own power (motorized vehicles, aircraft, etc.) or towed (prefabricated buildings, etc.). Local shipments (commodities shipped less than 25 miles from the plant) and shipments within the same city are also excluded. Shipments to Alaska and Hawaii from the 48 conterminous States and the District of Columbia are included; however, no data were obtained for shipments originating in Alaska and Hawaii. Distance of shipments to foreign destinations are calculated only to the U.S. port of exit.
Estimates of sampling variability are presented in table B to facilitate interpretation and analysis. Most data are subject to high sampling variability and should be treated as an approximate rather than a precise measurement of volume.

- Represents or rounds to zero.   (X) Not applicable.

SHIPPER GROUP 17. **Metal Cans and Miscellaneous Fabricated Metal Products**

Percent Distribution of Shipments by Means of Transport and Distance, for Plants: 1972

Means of transport and distance of shipment	Tons of shipments				Ton-miles			
	All plants	Plants with—			All plants	Plants with—		
		20 to 99 employees	100 to 499 employees	500 employees and over		20 to 99 employees	100 to 499 employees	500 employees and over
TONS SHIPPED . . . . . .THOUSANDS. .	23 695	4 201	9 162	10 331	(X)	(X)	(X)	(X)
TON MILES. . . . . MILLIONS. .	(X)	(X)	(X)	(X)	8 801	939	3 894	3 967
MEANS OF TRANSPORT								
TOTAL.	100.0	100.0	100.0	100.0	100.0	100.0	100.0	100.0
RAIL	36.8	6.6	18.4	65.5	50.5	17.2	35.2	73.3
MOTOR CARRIER.	44.1	47.2	61.6	27.2	40.3	57.8	54.8	21.9
PRIVATE TRUCK.	17.8	44.2	18.7	6.3	7.1	20.7	7.9	3.0
AIR.	.3	.2	.2	.3	.3	.7	.5	.7
WATER.	.3	.1	.3	.3	.6	1.3	.8	.8
OTHER.	.4	.9	.6	.1	.4	1.4	.4	.2
UNKNOWN.	.3	.8	.2	.2	.3	.9	.4	-
DISTANCE OF SHIPMENT								
TOTAL.	100.0	100.0	100.0	100.0	100.0	100.0	100.0	100.0
UNDER 100 MILES.	29.4	48.0	26.8	24.2	3.5	9.1	3.0	2.6
100 TO 199 MILES	18.1	18.9	15.3	20.1	6.9	11.9	5.4	7.2
200 TO 299 MILES	12.6	11.9	12.1	13.4	8.3	12.6	7.1	8.5
300 TO 499 MILES	15.4	8.9	15.8	17.6	16.4	15.2	14.4	18.7
500 TO 999 MILES	17.2	9.5	20.4	17.4	31.2	29.7	33.7	29.1
1000 TO 1499 MILES	2.2	1.2	3.4	1.6	7.0	6.6	9.4	4.8
1500 MILES AND OVER.	5.2	1.6	6.1	5.7	26.7	14.9	27.1	29.2

NOTE: Detail may not add to totals due to rounding. Shipments excluded from the survey are those moving by pipeline (primarily petroleum products from refineries), parcel post shipments, and commodities moved by own power (motorized vehicles, aircraft, etc.) or towed (prefabricated buildings, etc.). Local shipments (commodities shipped less than 25 miles from the plant) and shipments within the same city are also excluded. Shipments to Alaska and Hawaii from the 48 conterminous States and the District of Columbia are included; however, no data were obtained for shipments originating in Alaska and Hawaii. Distance of shipments to foreign destinations are calculated only to the U.S. port of exit. Estimates of sampling variability are presented in table B to facilitate interpretation and analysis. Most data are subject to high sampling variability and should be treated as an approximate rather than a precise measurement of volume.

- Represents or rounds to zero.   (X) Not applicable.

SHIPPER GROUP 18. **Industrial Machinery, Except Electrical**

Percent Distribution of Shipments by Means of Transport and Distance, for Plants: 1972

Means of transport and distance of shipment	Tons of shipments				Ton-miles			
	All plants	Plants with—			All plants	Plants with—		
		20 to 99 employees	100 to 499 employees	500 employees and over		20 to 99 employees	100 to 499 employees	500 employees and over
TONS SHIPPED . . . . . .THOUSANDS. .	8 699	3 365	2 394	2 939	(X)	(X)	(X)	(X)
TON MILES. . . . . MILLIONS. .	(X)	(X)	(X)	(X)	4 318	1 489	1 358	1 470
MEANS OF TRANSPORT								
TOTAL.	100.0	100.0	100.0	100.0	100.0	100.0	100.0	100.0
RAIL	19.6	34.8	5.3	14.0	12.3	11.2	11.0	14.7
MOTOR CARRIER.	59.4	33.3	81.9	70.9	75.7	73.2	80.0	74.1
PRIVATE TRUCK.	18.9	31.0	9.9	12.3	8.9	14.2	5.5	6.9
AIR.	.6	.4	.9	.6	1.2	.7	1.6	1.4
WATER.	.1	-	.1	.2	.1	-	-	.2
OTHER.	1.2	.4	1.6	1.9	1.6	.5	1.5	2.7
UNKNOWN.	.1	-	.4	-	.1	-	.4	-
DISTANCE OF SHIPMENT								
TOTAL.	100.0	100.0	100.0	100.0	100.0	100.0	100.0	100.0
UNDER 100 MILES.	22.3	32.5	15.1	16.4	2.4	4.0	1.5	1.7
100 TO 199 MILES	21.6	35.0	12.1	13.9	6.7	12.8	3.1	4.0
200 TO 299 MILES	9.1	1.5	11.9	15.7	4.6	.8	5.1	7.8
300 TO 499 MILES	13.2	7.3	18.3	15.8	10.1	6.1	12.1	12.2
500 TO 999 MILES	20.2	9.4	27.7	26.4	28.4	14.1	35.0	36.8
1000 TO 1499 MILES	5.3	3.0	7.0	6.5	12.8	8.1	15.0	15.6
1500 MILES AND OVER.	8.4	11.3	8.0	5.4	35.0	54.1	28.1	21.9

NOTE: Detail may not add to totals due to rounding. Shipments excluded from the survey are those moving by pipeline (primarily petroleum products from refineries), parcel post shipments, and commodities moved by own power (motorized vehicles, aircraft, etc.) or towed (prefabricated buildings, etc.). Local shipments (commodities shipped less than 25 miles from the plant) and shipments within the same city are also excluded. Shipments to Alaska and Hawaii from the 48 conterminous States and the District of Columbia are included; however, no data were obtained for shipments originating in Alaska and Hawaii. Distance of shipments to foreign destinations are calculated only to the U.S. port of exit. Estimates of sampling variability are presented in table B to facilitate interpretation and analysis. Most data are subject to high sampling variability and should be treated as an approximate rather than a precise measurement of volume.

- Represents or rounds to zero.   (X) Not applicable.

SHIPPER GROUP 19. Machinery, Except Electrical and Industrial
Percent Distribution of Shipments by Means of Transport and Distance, for Plants: 1972

Means of transport and distance of shipment	Tons of shipments				Ton-miles			
	All plants	Plants with—			All plants	Plants with—		
		20 to 99 employees	100 to 499 employees	500 employees and over		20 to 99 employees	100 to 499 employees	500 employees and over
TONS SHIPPED . . . . . .THOUSANDS. .	16 222	1 740	4 342	10 139	(X)	(X)	(X)	(X)
TON MILES. . . . . MILLIONS. .	(X)	(X)	(X)	(X)	9 724	716	2 570	6 437
MEANS OF TRANSPORT								
TOTAL.	100.0	100.0	100.0	100.0	100.0	100.0	100.0	100.0
RAIL	26.5	2.6	11.4	37.0	37.7	5.8	17.0	49.6
MOTOR CARRIER.	53.4	51.6	61.2	50.4	49.7	68.9	64.9	41.5
PRIVATE TRUCK.	17.7	40.8	25.6	10.3	8.9	15.6	15.4	5.6
AIR.	.6	.5	.5	.7	1.3	1.3	.9	1.5
WATER.	.2	-	.2	.3	.6	.5	.7	.6
OTHER.	1.0	3.0	1.0	.7	1.2	7.2	1.0	.6
UNKNOWN.	.5	1.4	-	.6	.5	.8	-	.7
DISTANCE OF SHIPMENT								
TOTAL.	100.0	100.0	100.0	100.0	100.0	100.0	100.0	100.0
UNDER 100 MILES.	12.1	24.7	14.9	8.8	1.0	3.1	1.1	.7
100 TO 199 MILES	11.3	21.6	10.5	9.9	2.8	7.7	2.6	2.4
200 TO 299 MILES	11.3	11.7	11.9	10.9	4.7	7.0	5.1	4.3
300 TO 499 MILES	17.9	15.7	16.4	18.9	11.7	14.0	10.8	11.8
500 TO 999 MILES	30.9	15.8	29.2	34.2	36.7	26.9	35.6	38.2
1000 TO 1499 MILES	8.5	5.6	9.3	8.6	16.9	16.1	19.2	16.1
1500 MILES AND OVER.	8.0	5.0	7.7	8.6	26.1	25.2	25.5	26.5

NOTE: Detail may not add to totals due to rounding. Shipments excluded from the survey are those moving by pipeline (primarily petroleum products from refineries), parcel post shipments, and commodities moved by own power (motorized vehicles, aircraft, etc.) or towed (prefabricated buildings, etc.). Local shipments (commodities shipped less than 25 miles from the plant) and shipments within the same city are also excluded. Shipments to Alaska and Hawaii from the 48 conterminous States and the District of Columbia are included; however, no data were obtained for shipments originating in Alaska and Hawaii. Distance of shipments to foreign destinations are calculated only to the U.S. port of exit.
Estimates of sampling variability are presented in table B to facilitate interpretation and analysis. Most data are subject to high sampling variability and should be treated as an approximate rather than a precise measurement of volume.

- Represents or rounds to zero.   (X) Not applicable.

SHIPPER GROUP 20. Communications Products and Parts
Percent Distribution of Shipments by Means of Transport and Distance, for Plants: 1972

Means of transport and distance of shipment	Tons of shipments				Ton-miles			
	All plants	Plants with—			All plants	Plants with—		
		20 to 99 employees	100 to 499 employees	500 employees and over		20 to 99 employees	100 to 499 employees	500 employees and over
TONS SHIPPED . . . . . .THOUSANDS. .	2 327	165	447	1 714	(X)	(X)	(X)	(X)
TON MILES. . . . . MILLIONS. .	(X)	(X)	(X)	(X)	1 443	112	323	1 007
MEANS OF TRANSPORT								
TOTAL.	100.0	100.0	100.0	100.0	100.0	100.0	100.0	100.0
RAIL	13.0	.2	1.9	17.1	18.0	.3	2.1	25.0
MOTOR CARRIER.	64.5	58.6	67.0	64.4	59.9	65.2	70.9	55.8
PRIVATE TRUCK.	12.4	13.3	17.4	11.0	5.6	3.6	4.4	6.2
AIR.	6.1	15.0	10.2	4.2	12.0	20.3	19.0	8.9
WATER.	-	.2	-	-	.3	.7	-	.3
OTHER.	3.4	12.0	3.0	2.6	3.3	9.2	2.7	2.9
UNKNOWN.	.5	.7	.5	.5	.9	.7	.8	.9
DISTANCE OF SHIPMENT								
TOTAL.	100.0	100.0	100.0	100.0	100.0	100.0	100.0	100.0
UNDER 100 MILES.	17.4	23.5	10.3	18.7	1.2	1.2	.7	1.4
100 TO 199 MILES	12.3	10.9	21.1	10.1	2.9	2.6	3.6	2.7
200 TO 299 MILES	10.8	7.2	5.5	12.5	4.2	2.7	1.8	5.2
300 TO 499 MILES	13.1	8.4	17.5	12.4	8.5	4.8	9.5	8.6
500 TO 999 MILES	27.0	27.6	19.3	28.9	30.4	27.7	20.2	34.0
1000 TO 1499 MILES	8.8	6.2	8.5	9.1	17.8	10.9	15.1	19.4
1500 MILES AND OVER.	10.6	16.2	17.7	8.2	34.9	50.1	49.0	28.7

NOTE: Detail may not add to totals due to rounding. Shipments excluded from the survey are those moving by pipeline (primarily petroleum products from refineries), parcel post shipments, and commodities moved by own power (motorized vehicles, aircraft, etc.) or towed (prefabricated buildings, etc.). Local shipments (commodities shipped less than 25 miles from the plant) and shipments within the same city are also excluded. Shipments to Alaska and Hawaii from the 48 conterminous States and the District of Columbia are included; however, no data were obtained for shipments originating in Alaska and Hawaii. Distance of shipments to foreign destinations are calculated only to the U.S. port of exit.
Estimates of sampling variability are presented in table B to facilitate interpretation and analysis. Most data are subject to high sampling variability and should be treated as an approximate rather than a precise measurement of volume.

- Represents or rounds to zero.   (X) Not applicable.

SHIPPER GROUP 21. Electrical Products and Supplies
Percent Distribution of Shipments by Means of Transport and Distance, for Plants: 1972

Means of transport and distance of shipment	Tons of shipments				Ton-miles			
	All plants	Plants with—			All plants	Plants with—		
		20 to 99 employees	100 to 499 employees	500 employees and over		20 to 99 employees	100 to 499 employees	500 employees and over
TONS SHIPPED . . . . . . .THOUSANDS. .	13 131	409	3 272	9 449	(X)	(X)	(X)	(X)
TON MILES. . . . . MILLIONS. .	(X)	(X)	(X)	(X)	7 514	211	1 943	5 358
MEANS OF TRANSPORT								
TOTAL.	100.0	100.0	100.0	100.0	100.0	100.0	100.0	100.0
RAIL	35.0	2.4	11.7	44.5	43.2	3.0	15.5	54.8
MOTOR CARRIER.	49.3	83.5	65.1	42.4	46.0	85.1	68.1	36.4
PRIVATE TRUCK.	14.1	8.2	20.3	12.3	8.4	3.1	11.6	7.4
AIR.	.4	1.5	.9	.2	.8	3.7	1.5	.4
WATER.	-	.5	.1	-	.5	2.2	.6	.4
OTHER.	.7	3.8	1.6	.3	1.0	2.7	2.5	.4
UNKNOWN.	.2	.1	.1	.3	.3	.1	.1	.3
DISTANCE OF SHIPMENT								
TOTAL.	100.0	100.0	100.0	100.0	100.0	100.0	100.0	100.0
UNDER 100 MILES.	12.5	18.4	12.9	12.2	1.1	1.8	1.1	1.1
100 TO 199 MILES	11.5	12.9	11.7	11.4	3.1	3.6	3.0	3.1
200 TO 299 MILES	12.5	14.6	13.2	12.1	5.4	7.2	5.4	5.3
300 TO 499 MILES	22.3	21.4	19.0	23.5	15.6	14.6	12.5	16.7
500 TO 999 MILES	26.3	19.1	26.9	26.4	31.8	26.9	30.9	32.3
1000 TO 1499 MILES	7.0	5.6	7.2	7.0	14.8	12.8	14.3	15.1
1500 MILES AND OVER.	8.0	8.0	9.2	7.5	28.2	33.1	32.6	26.4

NOTE: Detail may not add to totals due to rounding. Shipments excluded from the survey are those moving by pipeline (primarily petroleum products from refineries), parcel post shipments, and commodities moved by own power (motorized vehicles, aircraft, etc.) or towed (prefabricated buildings, etc.). Local shipments (commodities shipped less than 25 miles from the plant) and shipments within the same city are also excluded. Shipments to Alaska and Hawaii from the 48 conterminous States and the District of Columbia are included; however, no data were obtained for shipments originating in Alaska and Hawaii. Distance of shipments to foreign destinations are calculated only to the U.S. port of exit. Estimates of sampling variability are presented in table B to facilitate interpretation and analysis. Most data are subject to high sampling variability and should be treated as an approximate rather than a precise measurement of volume.

- Represents or rounds to zero.   (X) Not applicable.

SHIPPER GROUP 22. Motor Vehicles and Equipment
Percent Distribution of Shipments by Means of Transport and Distance, for Plants: 1972

Means of transport and distance of shipment	Tons of shipments				Ton-miles			
	All plants	Plants with—			All plants	Plants with—		
		20 to 99 employees	100 to 499 employees	500 employees and over		20 to 99 employees	100 to 499 employees	500 employees and over
TONS SHIPPED . . . . . . .THOUSANDS. .	39 990	319	1 357	55 039	(X)	(X)	(X)	(X)
TON MILES. . . . . MILLIONS. .	(X)	(X)	(X)	(X)	30 263	100	554	29 608
MEANS OF TRANSPORT								
TOTAL.	100.0	100.0	100.0	100.0	100.0	100.0	100.0	100.0
RAIL	59.3	77.0	3.2	60.5	80.9	66.2	6.7	82.3
MOTOR CARRIER.	37.3	12.0	64.0	36.8	17.4	21.4	69.2	16.4
PRIVATE TRUCK.	3.0	10.8	29.2	2.3	1.0	12.3	20.6	.6
AIR.	-	-	.5	-	.1	-	.7	-
WATER.	-	-	-	-	.2	-	.3	.2
OTHER.	.2	-	2.7	-	.2	-	2.4	.1
UNKNOWN.	.2	-	.2	.2	.3	-	.2	.3
DISTANCE OF SHIPMENT								
TOTAL.	100.0	100.0	100.0	100.0	100.0	100.0	100.0	100.0
UNDER 100 MILES.	16.9	2.3	14.9	17.0	1.6	.4	2.1	1.6
100 TO 199 MILES	12.1	3.6	20.7	12.0	3.4	1.8	7.5	3.3
200 TO 299 MILES	13.9	79.2	17.8	13.4	6.4	67.9	11.4	6.1
300 TO 499 MILES	18.4	8.3	13.8	18.6	14.0	9.3	13.4	14.0
500 TO 999 MILES	23.6	4.6	26.2	23.6	30.1	10.1	41.5	30.0
1000 TO 1499 MILES	7.3	1.0	3.4	7.4	16.0	3.7	9.8	16.2
1500 MILES AND OVER.	7.8	1.1	3.2	8.0	28.5	6.8	14.3	28.9

NOTE: Detail may not add to totals due to rounding. Shipments excluded from the survey are those moving by pipeline (primarily petroleum products from refineries), parcel post shipments, and commodities moved by own power (motorized vehicles, aircraft, etc.) or towed (prefabricated buildings, etc.). Local shipments (commodities shipped less than 25 miles from the plant) and shipments within the same city are also excluded. Shipments to Alaska and Hawaii from the 48 conterminous States and the District of Columbia are included; however, no data were obtained for shipments originating in Alaska and Hawaii. Distance of shipments to foreign destinations are calculated only to the U.S. port of exit. Estimates of sampling variability are presented in table B to facilitate interpretation and analysis. Most data are subject to high sampling variability and should be treated as an approximate rather than a precise measurement of volume.

- Represents or rounds to zero.   (X) Not applicable.

SHIPPER GROUP 23. Transportation Equipment, Except Motor Vehicles

Percent Distribution of Shipments by Means of Transport and Distance. for Plants: 1972

Means of transport and distance of shipment	Tons of shipments				Ton-miles			
	All plants	Plants with—			All plants	Plants with—		
		20 to 99 employees	100 to 499 employees	500 employees and over		20 to 99 employees	100 to 499 employees	500 employees and over
TONS SHIPPED . . . . . . .THOUSANDS. .	6 506	1 217	3 525	1 763	(X)	(X)	(X)	(X)
TON MILES. . . . . MILLIONS. .	(X)	(X)	(X)	(X)	2 613	321	1 474	817
MEANS OF TRANSPORT								
TOTAL.	100.0	100.0	100.0	100.0	100.0	100.0	100.0	100.0
RAIL	19.5	6.8	5.6	52.0	24.0	22.5	13.1	39.1
MOTOR CARRIER.	23.9	29.8	14.5	37.0	30.3	30.9	14.5	51.4
PRIVATE TRUCK.	54.8	63.1	77.7	9.1	43.1	46.2	70.1	5.7
AIR.	.4	-	.1	1.1	1.3	.3	.3	2.8
WATER.	.4	-	.6	.3	.3	.3	.6	.1
OTHER.	.5	-	.6	.4	.8	-	.9	.7
UNKNOWN.	.5		.8	.1	.3		.5	.1
DISTANCE OF SHIPMENT								
TOTAL.	100.0	100.0	100.0	100.0	100.0	100.0	100.0	100.0
UNDER 100 MILES.	24.3	45.2	16.3	25.7	2.5	6.9	2.0	1.9
100 TO 199 MILES	16.9	21.9	17.9	12.0	5.9	12.7	6.3	3.4
200 TO 299 MILES	10.7	6.8	11.9	10.9	6.2	6.4	7.0	5.0
300 TO 499 MILES	21.4	11.9	27.2	16.8	19.3	16.6	25.3	12.0
500 TO 999 MILES	17.3	10.7	18.5	19.3	29.5	29.4	30.6	27.9
1000 TO 1499 MILES	4.0	.7	5.2	3.9	11.0	3.2	14.4	8.7
1500 MILES AND OVER.	5.4	2.9	3.0	11.3	25.7	24.8	14.4	41.1

NOTE: Detail may not add to totals due to rounding. Shipments excluded from the survey are those moving by pipeline (primarily petroleum products from refineries), parcel post shipments, and commodities moved by own power (motorized vehicles, aircraft, etc.) or towed (prefabricated buildings, etc.). Local shipments (commodities shipped less than 25 miles from the plant) and shipments within the same city are also excluded. Shipments to Alaska and Hawaii from the 48 conterminous States and the District of Columbia are included; however, no data were obtained for shipments originating in Alaska and Hawaii. Distance of shipments to foreign destinations are calculated only to the U.S. port of exit. Estimates of sampling variability are presented in table B to facilitate interpretation and analysis. Most data are subject to high sampling variability and should be treated as an approximate rather than a precise measurement of volume.

- Represents or rounds to zero.　　(X) Not applicable.

SHIPPER GROUP 24. Instruments, Photographic Equipment, Watches, and Clocks

Percent Distribution of Shipments by Means of Transport and Distance, for Plants: 1972

Means of transport and distance of shipment	Tons of shipments				Ton-miles			
	All plants	Plants with—			All plants	Plants with—		
		20 to 99 employees	100 to 499 employees	500 employees and over		20 to 99 employees	100 to 499 employees	500 employees and over
TONS SHIPPED . . . . . .THOUSANDS. .	1 603	103	452	1 047	(X)	(X)	(X)	(X)
TON MILES. . . . . MILLIONS. .	(X)	(X)	(X)	(X)	1 183	72	357	753
MEANS OF TRANSPORT								
TOTAL.	100.0	100.0	100.0	100.0	100.0	100.0	100.0	100.0
RAIL	20.9	.6	9.9	27.7	34.4	.6	20.1	44.5
MOTOR CARRIER.	63.8	86.1	68.9	59.3	53.9	86.9	68.3	43.9
PRIVATE TRUCK.	10.9	1.0	15.8	9.7	5.7	.3	5.8	6.1
AIR.	2.0	2.9	1.8	2.0	3.6	5.2	2.6	3.9
WATER.	.1	-	.1	.1	.3	-	.3	.3
OTHER.	2.1	9.3	3.1	1.0	1.9	7.0	2.6	1.1
UNKNOWN.	.2	-	.3	.2	.2	-	.3	.2
DISTANCE OF SHIPMENT								
TOTAL.	100.0	100.0	100.0	100.0	100.0	100.0	100.0	100.0
UNDER 100 MILES.	9.5	11.1	10.1	9.0	.6	.6	.6	.5
100 TO 199 MILES	11.1	7.3	16.2	9.2	2.1	1.7	2.9	1.9
200 TO 299 MILES	13.7	11.3	8.3	16.3	4.6	4.0	2.6	5.7
300 TO 499 MILES	11.4	14.6	10.5	11.4	5.8	8.3	5.0	6.0
500 TO 999 MILES	28.4	33.4	25.1	29.3	25.7	34.4	22.5	26.4
1000 TO 1499 MILES	10.5	8.9	12.9	9.7	17.3	15.1	20.2	16.1
1500 MILES AND OVER.	15.5	13.3	16.9	15.0	43.9	35.8	46.3	43.5

NOTE: Detail may not add to totals due to rounding. Shipments excluded from the survey are those moving by pipeline (primarily petroleum products from refineries), parcel post shipments, and commodities moved by own power (motorized vehicles, aircraft, etc.) or towed (prefabricated buildings, etc.). Local shipments (commodities shipped less than 25 miles from the plant) and shipments within the same city are also excluded. Shipments to Alaska and Hawaii from the 48 conterminous States and the District of Columbia are included; however, no data were obtained for shipments originating in Alaska and Hawaii. Distance of shipments to foreign destinations are calculated only to the U.S. port of exit. Estimates of sampling variability are presented in table B to facilitate interpretation and analysis. Most data are subject to high sampling variability and should be treated as an approximate rather than a precise measurement of volume.

- Represents or rounds to zero.　　(X) Not applicable.

Appendixes

APPENDIX A. Definitions of Major Terms

Average Length of Haul—Average length of haul is based on straight-line miles from plant to customer or primary redistribution point. It is a weighted average derived by dividing ton-miles by tons. "Average distance" and "average length of haul" are synonymous.

Distance—Distance is based on the straight-line miles between origin and destination cities in the United States calculated by the use of PICADAD (described below). Straight-line distances are essentially identical to "great circle" or "air" distances. The distance factor for exports is based on the miles from the plant to the port of exit, because the ton-miles figures represent transport service within this country only.

Means of Transport—Each shipping document is classified in terms of the major means of transport used to move the shipment to its destination. If more than one means was used, the transport used to cover the greatest distance was coded. If the shipment was made to a foreign destination, the type of transport used to move the shipment to the port of exit was coded. Means of transport was coded into seven categories as follows:

Air—Includes all shipments by air, such as "air freight," "air express," and the like.

Motor carrier—Includes all shipments transported by motor carriers that serve the public. If transport was indicated on the shipping documents by the words "truck," "cartage," "drayage," or "trucking," the shipment was coded as moving by motor carrier. No distinction was made between common or contract carriers. "For-hire" or commercial motor carriers are synonymous with "motor carrier" used in this report.

Private truck—Includes all shipments transported by trucks operated by the shipper or the customer. The combination of private trucks and motor carriers represents virtually the total shipments by highway.

Rail—Includes all shipments transported by railroad except railway express. If the word "piggyback" appeared on the shipping document, the shipment was coded as moving by railroad because the major distance was assumed to have been by railroad.

Water—Includes all shipments transported by ship, boat, barge, and the like between two points in the United States. Shipments destined for foreign ports were coded "water" only if the major distance to the port of exit was negotiated by water. Otherwise, the means used to transport the shipment to the port of exit was coded.

Other—Includes shipments transported by means other than those classified above, except by pipeline. "Other" would include railway express, freight forwarders, messenger service, hand carried parcels, bus delivery, etc.

Unknown—Those shipping documents that gave no indication of the type of transport used to move the shipments are classed as unknown.

PICADAD—This is a Census Bureau computer system used to automate the geographic aspects of this survey. One of its functions is to compute the straight-line mileage between the city of origin and the city of destination. A description of the system can be obtained from the Transportation Division, Bureau of the Census, Washington, D.C. 20233.

Production Areas—Production Areas represent relatively compact geographic concentrations of manufacturing activity. Twenty-five Production Areas were originally developed for this survey. Two additional areas were added in 1972 so that there are now 27. Each Production Area consists of one Standard Metropolitan Statistical Area[1] or more.

Shipment—In this report, tons and ton-miles of shipments relate to production that actually moves by some means of transportation (other than pipeline, parcel post, or under own power, or towed away) beyond the local area of the plant.

Shipper Group—An industry based classification of shippers. This classification of shippers (that is, industrial establishments) into shipper groups and shipper classes is based on the Standard Industrial Classification used to classify establishments in the Census of Manufactures. In that respect, the two surveys are comparable. However, with respect to commodities, the product codes used in the Census of Manufactures differ from the commodity codes used for transportation.

Ton-miles—The figure for ton-miles is the product of weight times distance (straight-line miles). For example, a 10-ton shipment that moved between places that were 1,000 miles apart is equivalent to a 50-ton shipment that moved 200 miles. Both represent 10,000 ton-miles although they differ in terms of both weight and distance.

Tons—The estimates of tons represent generally the shipping weight of commodities rather than net weight. Commodities in this sense represent any physical item, including scrap and waste. "Tons" and "tons originated" are synonymous.

---

[1] For definitions of SMSA's, see *Standard Metropolitan Statistical Areas,* Federal Information Processing Standards Publication, FIPS Pub. 8-2, 1972, U.S. Department of Commerce, National Bureau of Standards.

APPENDIX B. Relationships Between the 1967 and 1972 Transportation Commodity Codes (TCC) of In-Scope Commodities

Action	TCC changes—		Action	TCC changes—	
	From 1967 code	To 1972 code		From 1967 code	To 1972 code
New class	-- ---	29 913	Classes split	32 932	{ 32 924, 32 932 }
Changed numbers	20 155	20 171	. . . .do	34 919	{ 34 919, 34 997 }
. . . .do	20 156	20 172	. . . .do	35 229	{ 35 241, 35 229 }
. . . .do	20 374	20 381	. . . .do	37 912	{ 37 911, 37 912 }
. . . .do	24 331	24 391			
. . . .do	26 547	34 996			
. . . .do	30 611	30 411	Items shifted from one class to another:		
. . . .do	30 612	30 412	Canned meat baby food . . .	20 134	20 321
. . . .do	33 113	29 914	Household bleaches	28 199	28 422
. . . .do	35 991	35 921	Adhesives	28 211	28 911
. . . .do	35 992	35 922	Plastic film	28 211	30 714
Classes combined	{ 28 912, 28 998-9 }	28 998-9	Plastic sheets and rods	28 211	30 717
			Compounded resins	28 211	30 719-29
Classes split	19 299	{ 19 299, 37 691 }	Pesticides	28 422	28 799
			Calking compounds	28 513	28 911
. . . .do	20 379	{ 20 379, 20 389 }	Linoleum and tile cement . .	29 522	28 911
			Rubber cement	30 618-9	28 911
. . . .do	24 993	{ 24 993, 24 996 }	Rubber packing	30 618-9	32 932
			Plastics hose	30 712	30 412
. . . .do	25 174	{ 24 341, 25 174 }	Plastics footwear	30 719	30 212
			Leather packing	31 211	32 932
. . . .do	30 719	{ 30 212, 30 719 }	Metal packing	35 999	32 932
			Camping trailers	41 111	37 912

APPENDIX C. Facsimile of Form

FORM TC-420 (7-20-72)

U.S. DEPARTMENT OF COMMERCE
SOCIAL AND ECONOMIC STATISTICS
ADMINISTRATION
BUREAU OF THE CENSUS

1972 CENSUS OF TRANSPORTATION
COMMODITY TRANSPORTATION SURVEY

INSTRUCTIONS

If book figures are not readily available, please supply your best estimate for the plant shown in item I.

If you transfer goods from this plant to a nearby warehouse for redistribution, report shipments from the warehouse as though they were from this plant. If you ship to foreign countries, consider only the movement from plant to the port of exit when reporting percentage for mileage, type of transport, and destination.

Return this form in the preaddressed envelope within 20 days to:

Director
Bureau of the Census
Washington, D.C. 20233

NOTICE – Response to this inquiry is required by law (Title 13 U.S. Code). By the same law, your report to the Census Bureau is confidential. It may be seen only by sworn Census employees and may be used only for statistical purposes. The law also provides that copies retained in your files are immune from legal process.

Item I

Item II. VALUE OF PRODUCTS AND SERVICES

What was the value of all products shipped and services performed at this plant (including interplant transfers) during 1972? . . . . $

Item III. MAJOR PRODUCT SHIPPED

What was the major product shipped from this plant during 1972?

_____

Item IV. DISTANCE SHIPPED

What percent of the products in item II moved –

	Percent
1. less than 50 miles (including used in or near plant)?	
2. 50–99 miles?	
3. 100–299 miles?	
4. 300–499 miles?	
5. 500–999 miles?	
6. 1,000 miles or more?	
Total of above should equal. . .	100%

Item V. TYPE OF TRANSPORT

What percent of the products were shipped by:

	Percent
1. Rail	
2. Commercial (for hire) motor carrier .	
3. Your own or customer's truck.	
4. Air (including air cargo and air express)	
5. Water (including for hire and private carrier on rivers, harbors, lakes, oceans, etc.)	
6. REA, United Parcel, Parcel Post, and other "Package Carriers"	
Total of above should equal 100% of products shipped from your plant	100%

Item VI. What percent of item II was shipped to each United States destination area? *(See map for areas)* *(Use U.S. Port of Exit for exports.)*

U.S. destination area	Percent
1. New England	
2. Middle Atlantic . . .	
3. East North Central	
4. West North Central	
5. South Atlantic . . .	
6. East South Central	
7. West South Central	
8. Mountain	
9. Pacific – including Alaska and Hawaii	
Total of above should equal	100%

Item VII. What percent of item II was exported to foreign countries and U.S. territories?

Foreign and U.S. territories	

Name and title of person to contact	Telephone *(Area code and No.)*	Date

☆ U. S. GOVERNMENT PRINTING OFFICE : 1976 O - 215-600